DICTIONARY

OF AMERICAN BIOGRAPHY

The *Dictionary of American Biography* was published originally in twenty volumes. Supplementary volumes were added in 1944 and 1958. This edition of the work combines all twenty-two volumes.

The present Volume I (Abbe–Brazer) contains Volumes I and II of the original edition, but these are now denominated "Part 1" and "Part 2" of the Volume. Volumes II through XI are arranged similarly, the Second Part in each instance representing a volume of the original series. For ease in reference, although the articles follow one another in strict alphabetical order, each Second Part is preceded by a half-title page which relates that Part to its place in the original numbering of the volumes.

The Errata list at the head of Volume I contains corrections of fact and additional data which have come to the attention of the Editors from the first publication of the work up to the present. Minor typographical corrections have been made in many instances directly on the plates.

PUBLISHED UNDER THE AUSPICES OF
THE AMERICAN COUNCIL OF LEARNED SOCIETIES

The American Council of Learned Societies, organized in 1919 for the purpose of advancing the study of the humanities and of the humanistic aspects of the social sciences, is a nonprofit federation comprising forty-five national scholarly groups. The Council represents the humanities in the United States in the International Union of Academies, provides fellowships and grants-in-aid, supports research-and-planning conferences and symposia, and sponsors special projects and scholarly publications.

MEMBER ORGANIZATIONS

AMERICAN PHILOSOPHICAL SOCIETY, 1743
AMERICAN ACADEMY OF ARTS AND SCIENCES, 1780
AMERICAN ANTIQUARIAN SOCIETY, 1812
AMERICAN ORIENTAL SOCIETY, 1842
AMERICAN NUMISMATIC SOCIETY, 1858
AMERICAN PHILOLOGICAL ASSOCIATION, 1869
ARCHAEOLOGICAL INSTITUTE OF AMERICA, 1879
SOCIETY OF BIBLICAL LITERATURE, 1880
MODERN LANGUAGE ASSOCIATION OF AMERICA, 1883
AMERICAN HISTORICAL ASSOCIATION, 1884
AMERICAN ECONOMIC ASSOCIATION, 1885
AMERICAN FOLKLORE SOCIETY, 1888
AMERICAN DIALECT SOCIETY, 1889
AMERICAN PSYCHOLOGICAL ASSOCIATION, 1892
ASSOCIATION OF AMERICAN LAW SCHOOLS, 1900
AMERICAN PHILOSOPHICAL ASSOCIATION, 1901
AMERICAN ANTHROPOLOGICAL ASSOCIATION, 1902
AMERICAN POLITICAL SCIENCE ASSOCIATION, 1903
BIBLIOGRAPHICAL SOCIETY OF AMERICA, 1904
ASSOCIATION OF AMERICAN GEOGRAPHERS, 1904
HISPANIC SOCIETY OF AMERICA, 1904
AMERICAN SOCIOLOGICAL ASSOCIATION, 1905
AMERICAN SOCIETY OF INTERNATIONAL LAW, 1906
ORGANIZATION OF AMERICAN HISTORIANS, 1907
AMERICAN ACADEMY OF RELIGION, 1909
COLLEGE ART ASSOCIATION OF AMERICA, 1912
HISTORY OF SCIENCE SOCIETY, 1924
LINGUISTIC SOCIETY OF AMERICA, 1924
MEDIAEVAL ACADEMY OF AMERICA, 1925
AMERICAN MUSICOLOGICAL SOCIETY, 1934
SOCIETY OF ARCHITECTURAL HISTORIANS, 1940
ECONOMIC HISTORY ASSOCIATION, 1940
ASSOCIATION FOR ASIAN STUDIES, 1941
AMERICAN SOCIETY FOR AESTHETICS, 1942
AMERICAN ASSOCIATION FOR THE ADVANCEMENT OF SLAVIC STUDIES, 1948
METAPHYSICAL SOCIETY OF AMERICA, 1950
AMERICAN STUDIES ASSOCIATION, 1950
RENAISSANCE SOCIETY OF AMERICA, 1954
SOCIETY FOR ETHNOMUSICOLOGY, 1955
AMERICAN SOCIETY FOR LEGAL HISTORY, 1956
AMERICAN SOCIETY FOR THEATRE RESEARCH, 1956
SOCIETY FOR THE HISTORY OF TECHNOLOGY, 1958
AMERICAN COMPARATIVE LITERATURE ASSOCIATION, 1960
AMERICAN SOCIETY FOR EIGHTEENTH-CENTURY STUDIES, 1969
ASSOCIATION FOR JEWISH STUDIES, 1969

DICTIONARY

OF

American Biography

VOLUME II

BREARLY - CUSHING

Edited by

ALLEN JOHNSON

AND DUMAS MALONE

Charles Scribner's Sons *New York*

Prompted solely by a desire for public service the New York Times Company and its President, Mr. Adolph S. Ochs, have made possible the preparation of the manuscript of the Dictionary of American Biography through a subvention of more than $500,000 and with the understanding that the entire responsibility for the contents of the volumes rests with the American Council of Learned Societies.

VOLUME II, PART 1
BREARLY - CHANDLER

(VOLUME III OF THE ORIGINAL EDITION)

CROSS REFERENCES FROM THIS VOL-
UME ARE MADE TO THE VOLUME
NUMBERS OF THE ORIGINAL EDITION.

CONTRIBUTORS
VOLUME II, PART 1

ADELINE ADAMS . . . . A. A—s.
JAMES TRUSLOW ADAMS . . . . J. T. A.
ROBERT G. ALBION . . . . . . R. G. A.
EDMUND KIMBALL ALDEN . . . E. K. A.
ALBERT ALLEMANN . . . . . . A. A—n.
EDWARD ELLIS ALLEN . . . . E. E. A.
WILLIAM HENRY ALLISON . . . . W. H. A.
JAMES PARKHILL ANDREWS. . . J. P. A.
JOHN CLARK ARCHER . . . . . J. C. A.
FREDERICK WILLIAM ASHLEY . F. W. A.
BENJAMIN WISNER BACON . . . B. W. B—n.
THEODORE D. BACON . . . . . . T. D. B.
HAYES BAKER-CROTHERS . . . H. B–C.
RAY PALMER BAKER . . . . . R. P. B—r.
JAMES CURTIS BALLAGH . . . . J. C. B.
CLARIBEL RUTH BARNETT . . . C. R. B.
JOHN SPENCER BASSETT . . . . J. S. B—t.
ERNEST SUTHERLAND BATES . . . E. S. B.
WILLIAM AGUR BEARDSLEY . . . W. A. B.
CHARLES FRANCIS DORR BELDEN . C. F. D. B.
ELBERT JAY BENTON . . . . . E. J. B.
PERCY W. BIDWELL . . . . . . P. W. B.
GEORGE BLUMER . . . . G. B.
ROGER S. BOARDMAN . . . . . R. S. B.
HERBERT EUGENE BOLTON . . . H. E. B.
BEVERLEY W. BOND, JR. . . . . B. W. B—d.
MILLEDGE LOUIS BONHAM . . . M. L. B.
STEPHEN BONSAL . . . . S. B.
ARCHIBALD LEWIS BOUTON . . . A. L. B.
WITT BOWDEN . . . . W. B.
SARAH G. BOWERMAN . . . . . S. G. B.
CHARLES N. BOYD . . . . . . C. N. B.
WILLIAM KENNETH BOYD . . . W. K. B.
BENJAMIN BRAWLEY . . . . . B. B.
EDWARD BRECK . . . . E. B.
ROBERT BRIDGES . . . . R. B.
GEORGE W. BRIGGS . . . . . . G. W. B.
WALTER COCHRANE BRONSON . . W. C. B.
ROBERT PRESTON BROOKS . . . R. P. B—s.
L. PARMLY BROWN . . . . . . L. P. B.
JOHN S. BRUBACHER . . . . . J. S. B—r.
KATHLEEN BRUCE . . . . . . K. B.
GEORGE SANDS BRYAN. . . . . G. S. B.
OSCAR MACMILLAN BUCK . . . O. M. B.
DUNCAN BURNET . . . . D. B.
GUY H. BURNHAM . . . . . . G. H. B.
PIERCE BUTLER. . . . . P. B.
FRANCIS GORDON CAFFEY . . . F. G. C.
CHARLES T. CAHILL . . . . . C. T. C.
WILLIAM B. CAIRNS . . . . . . W. B. C.
JAMES MORTON CALLAHAN . . . J. M. C.

CHARLES F. CAREY . . . . . . C. F. C.
W. ELLISON CHALMERS . . . . W. E. C.
WAYLAND J. CHASE . . . . . . W. J. C—e.
RUSSELL HENRY CHITTENDEN . . R. H. C.
ALLEN L. CHURCHILL . . . . . A. L. C.
KATHERINE W. CLENDINNING . . K. W. C—g.
FREDERICK W. COBURN . . . . F. W. C.
SAMUEL GWYNN COE . . . . . S. G. C.
ESTHER COLE . . . . E. C.
ROSSETTER GLEASON COLE . . . R. G. C.
KENNETH WALLACE COLGROVE . K. W. C—e.
EDNA MARY COLMAN . . . . . E. M. C—n.
JOHN CORBETT . . . . J. C.
R. S. COTTERILL . . . . R. S. C.
ELLIS MERTON COULTER. . . . . E. M. C—r.
W. H. B. COURT . . . . W. H. B. C.
ISAAC JOSLIN COX . . . . . . I. J. C.
AVERY O. CRAVEN . . . . . . A. O. C.
NELSON ANTRIM CRAWFORD . . N. A. C.
WALTER HILL CROCKETT . . . . W. H. C.
WILLIAM JAMES CUNNINGHAM . . W. J. C—m.
MERLE E. CURTI . . . . M. E. C.
ROBERT E. CUSHMAN . . . . . R. E. C.
HARRISON CLIFFORD DALE . . . H. C. D.
TYLER DENNETT . . . . T. D.
HERMAN J. DEUTSCH . . . . . H. J. D.
CHARLES ALLEN DINSMORE . . . C. A. D.
FRANK HAIGH DIXON . . . . . F. H. D.
ELEANOR ROBINETTE DOBSON . . E. R. D.
DOROTHY ANNE DONDORE . . . D. A. D.
ELIZABETH DONNAN . . . . . . E. D.
WILLIAM HOWE DOWNES . . . . W. H. D.
STELLA DRUMM . . . . S. D.
RAYMOND SMITH DUGAN . . . R. S. D.
WILLIAM B. DUNNING . . . . . W. B. D.
LIONEL C. DUREL. . . . . . . L. C. D.
J. H. EASTERBY . . . . J. H. E—y.
LINDA ANNE EASTMAN. . . . . L. A. E.
WALTER PRICHARD EATON . . . W. P. E.
EDWIN FRANCIS EDGETT . . . . E. F. E.
JOHN H. EDMONDS . . . . . . J. H. E—s.
ARTHUR ELSON . . . . A. E.
LOGAN ESAREY . . . . L. E.
LAWRENCE BOYD EVANS . . . . L. B. E.
PAUL D. EVANS . . . . P. D. E.
HAROLD UNDERWOOD FAULKNER . H. U. F.
ALBERT BERNHARDT FAUST . . . A. B. F.
GEORGE EMORY FELLOWS . . . . G. E. F.
GUSTAVE JOSEPH FIEBEGER . . . G. J. F.
CARL RUSSELL FISH . . . . . . C. R. F.
WALTER LYNWOOD FLEMING . . . W. L. F.

Contributors

NORMAN FOERSTER	N. F.	STEPHEN LEACOCK	S. L.
BLANTON FORTSON	B. F.	JAMES MELVIN LEE	J. M. L.
HAROLD NORTH FOWLER	H. N. F.	ALEXANDER LEITCH	A. L.
L. WEBSTER FOX	L. W. F.	CHARLES LEE LEWIS	C. L. L.
JOHN H. FREDERICK	J. H. F.	THOMAS OLLIVE MABBOTT	T. O. M.
WILLIAM LITTLE FRIERSON	W. L. F—n.	SAMUEL BLACK McCORMICK	S. B. M.
CLAUDE MOORE FUESS	C. M. F.	THOMAS DENTON McCORMICK	T. D. M.
JOHN F. FULTON	J. F. F.	PHILIP B. McDONALD	P. B. M.
CHARLES BURLEIGH GALBREATH	C. B. G—h.	WILLIAM MacDONALD	W. M.
FRANCIS PENDLETON GAINES	F. P. G.	WALTER MARTIN McFARLAND	W. M. M.
CURTIS W. GARRISON	C. W. G.	ARTHUR CUSHMAN McGIFFERT	A. C. M.
KARL FREDERICK GEISER	K. F. G.	SETH SHEPARD McKAY	S. S. M.
GEORGE HARVEY GENZMER	G. H. G.	DONALD L. McMURRY	D. L. M.
W. J. GHENT	W. J. G.	BRUCE E. MAHAN	B. E. M.
CARDINAL GOODWIN	C. G.	DUMAS MALONE	D. M.
COLIN B. GOODYKOONTZ	C. B. G—z.	JAMES TRIMBLE MARSHALL, JR.	J. T. M. Jr.
ARMISTEAD CHURCHILL GORDON,		DAVID M. MATTESON	D. M. M.
JR.	A. C. G. Jr.	BRANDER MATTHEWS	B. M—s.
HARRIS PERLEY GOULD	H. P. G.	LEILA MECHLIN	L. M.
LOUIS HERBERT GRAY	L. H. G.	A. HOWARD MENEELY	A. H. M.
JEROME DAVIS GREENE	J. D. G.	NEWTON D. MERENESS	N. D. M.
LeROY R. HAFEN	L. R. H.	ROBERT LEE MERIWETHER	R. L. M—r.
WILLIAM J. HAIL	W. J. H.	JOHN CAMPBELL MERRIAM	J. C. M.
PHILIP MAY HAMER	P. M. H.	GEORGE PERKINS MERRILL	G. P. M.
TALBOT FAULKNER HAMLIN	T. F. H.	JANE LOUISE MESICK	J. L. M.
JOHN LOUIS HANEY	J. L. H.	TRUMAN MICHELSON	T. M.
THOMAS LeGRAND HARRIS	T. L. H.	BROADUS MITCHELL	B. M—l.
FRANCES B. HAWLEY	F. B. H.	MARY HEWITT MITCHELL	M. H. M.
MARSHALL DeLANCEY HAYWOOD	M. DeL. H.	CARL W. MITMAN	C. W. M.
GRACE RAYMOND HEBARD	G. R. H.	FRANK MONAGHAN	F. M—n.
BURTON JESSE HENDRICK	B. J. H.	FULMER MOOD	F. M—d.
ELLWOOD HENDRICK	E. H.	ROBERT E. MOODY	R. E. M.
VIVIAN ALLEN CHARLES HENMON	V. A. C. H.	CHARLES MOORE	C. M.
FREDERICK CHARLES HICKS	F. C. H.	MARY ATWELL MOORE	M. A. M.
HOMER CAREY HOCKETT	H. C. H.	SAMUEL ELIOT MORISON	S. E. M.
JEAN MacKINNON HOLT	J. M. H.	RICHARD B. MORRIS	R. B. M.
WALTER HOUGH	W. H.	RICHARD L. MORTON	R. L. M—n.
HAROLD HOWLAND	H. H.	KENNETH BALLARD MURDOCK	K. B. M.
EDGAR ERSKINE HUME	E. E. H.	DAVID SAVILLE MUZZEY	D. S. M.
EDWARD FRANK HUMPHREY	E. F. H.	EDWIN G. NASH	E. G. N.
ALBERT HYMA	A. H—a.	FRANK NASH	F. N.
THEODORE HENLEY JACK	T. H. J.	ALLAN NEVINS	A. N.
JOSEPH JACKSON	J. J.	ROY F. NICHOLS	R. F. N.
EDWARD HOPKINS JENKINS	E. H. J.	E. J. M. NUTTER	E. J. M. N.
ALLEN JOHNSON	A. J.	JOHN W. OLIVER	J. W. O.
EDGAR HUTCHINSON JOHNSON	E. H. J—n.	HENRY FAIRFIELD OSBORN	H. F. O.
MARIE A. KASTEN	M. A. K.	NORRIS GALPIN OSBORN	N. G. O.
LOUISE PHELPS KELLOGG	L. P. K.	MARIE BANKHEAD OWEN	M. B. O.
VERNON LYMAN KELLOGG	V. K.	FRANK L. OWSLEY	F. L. O.
RAYNER W. KELSEY	R. W. K.	FRANCIS RANDOLPH PACKARD	F. R. P.
WILLIAM WEBB KEMP	W. W. K.	LEIGH PAGE	L. P.
FRANK RICHARDSON KENT	F. R. K.	EDWIN WILLIAM PAHLOW	E. W. P.
PIERRE van RENSSELAER KEY	P. V. R. K.	THEODORE SHERMAN PALMER	T. S. P.
FISKE KIMBALL	F. K.	FRED LEWIS PATTEE	F. L. P—e.
EDGAR WALLACE KNIGHT	E. W. K.	CHARLES OSCAR PAULLIN	C. O. P.
GRANT C. KNIGHT	G. C. K.	FREDERIC LOGAN PAXSON	F. L. P—n.
H. W. HOWARD KNOTT	H. W. H. K.	C. C. PEARSON	C. C. P.
CONRAD H. LANZA	C. H. L.	THEODORE CALVIN PEASE	T. C. P.

Contributors

DONALD CULROSS PEATTIE	. . .	D. C. P.
FREDERICK TORREL PERSONS	. .	F. T. P.
A. EVERETT PETERSON	. . . .	A. E. P.
JAMES M. PHALEN	. . . . . .	J. M. P.
FRANCIS SAMUEL PHILBRICK	. . .	F. S. P.
PAUL CHRISLER PHILLIPS	. . .	P. C. P.
ULRICH BONNELL PHILLIPS	. . .	U. B. P.
WILLIAM WHATLEY PIERSON, JR.	.	W. W. P.
LEWIS FREDERICK PILCHER	. . .	L. F. P.
HENRY AUGUSTUS PILSBRY	. . .	H. A. P.
JOHN E. POMFRET	. . . . . .	J. E. P.
RICHARD LYLE POWER	. . . . .	R. L. P.
EDWARD PREBLE	. . . .	E. P.
RICHARD J. PURCELL	. . . . .	R. J. P.
MILO MILTON QUAIFE	. . . .	M. M. Q.
ARTHUR HOBSON QUINN	. . . .	A. H. Q.
CHARLES WILLIAM RAMSDELL	. .	C. W. R.
JAMES GARFIELD RANDALL	. . .	J. G. R.
P. ORMAN RAY	. . . .	P. O. R.
CHARLES DUDLEY RHODES	. . . .	C. D. R.
THOMAS COLE RICHARDS	. . .	T. C. R.
FRANKLIN LAFAYETTE RILEY	.	F. L. R.
FRANK H. RISTINE	. . . . . .	F. H. R.
JAMES ALEXANDER ROBERTSON	. .	J. A. R.
DAVID MOORE ROBINSON	. . .	D. M. R.
WILLIAM ALEXANDER ROBINSON	.	W. A. R.
FRANK EDWARD ROSS	. . . . .	F. E. R.
HENRY KALLOCH ROWE	. . . .	H. K. R.
ROBERT R. ROWE	. . . . . .	R. R. R.
GEORGE H. RYDEN	. . . . .	G. H. R.
JOSEPH SCHAFER	. . . . . .	J. S.
FRANKLIN WILLIAM SCOTT	. . .	F. W. S.
LOUIS MARTIN SEARS	. . . .	L. M. S.
THORSTEN SELLIN	. . . . . .	T. S.
MURIEL SHAVER	. . . . . .	M. S.
WILLIAM BRISTOL SHAW	. . . .	W. B. S.
CLIFTON LUCIEN SHERMAN	. .	C. L. S.
HENRY NOBLE SHERWOOD	. . .	H. N. S.
FLOYD CALVIN SHOEMAKER	. .	F. C. S—r.
WILLIAM ADAMS SLADE	. . . .	W. A. S.
WILLIAM E. SMITH	. . . . .	W. E. S.
A. I. SPANTON	. . . .	A. I. S.
THOMAS MARSHALL SPAULDING	.	T. M. S.
MARY NEWTON STANARD	. . . .	M. N. S.
HARRIS ELWOOD STARR	. . . .	H. E. S.
HENRY P. STEARNS	. . . . .	H. P. S.
WALTER RALPH STEINER	. . . .	W. R. S.
WITMER STONE	. . . .	W. S.
FREDERICK C. SWANSON	. . . . .	F. C. S—n.
EBEN SWIFT	. . . .	E. S.
JENNETTE R. TANDY	. . . .	J. R. T.
EDWIN PLATT TANNER	. . . .	E. P. T.
FRANK A. TAYLOR	. . . . . .	F. A. T.
MILTON HALSEY THOMAS	. . . .	M. H. T.
HARRISON JOHN THORNTON	. . .	H. J. T.
CHARLES FRANKLIN THWING	. . .	C. F. T.
EZRA SQUIRE TIPPLE	. . . . .	E. S. T.
R. P. TOLMAN	. . . .	R. P. T.
F. E. TOURSCHER	. . . . . .	F. E. T.
FRANCIS J. TSCHAN	. . . . .	F. J. T.
FREDERICK TUCKERMAN	. . . . .	F. T.
WILLIAM TREAT UPTON	. . . .	W. T. U—n.
ROLAND GREENE USHER	. . . .	R. G. U.
WILLIAM T. UTTER	. . . . .	W. T. U—r.
CARL VAN DOREN	. . . . . .	C. V-D.
GEORGE VAN SANTVOORD	. . .	G. V-S.
HENRY R. VIETS	. . . . . .	H. R. V.
JOHN MARTIN VINCENT	. . . .	J. M. V.
EUGENE M. VIOLETTE	. . . .	E. M. V.
FRANK HORACE VIZETELLY	. .	F. H. V.
JOHN DONALD WADE	. . . . .	J. D. W.
JAMES ELLIOTT WALMSLEY	. .	J. E. W—y.
MARJORIE F. WARNER	. . . . .	M. F. W.
W. RANDALL WATERMAN	. . . .	W. R. W.
FRANK WEITENKAMPF	. . . . .	F. W.
THOMAS JEFFERSON WERTENBAKER	T. J. W.
ALLAN WESTCOTT	. . . . . .	A. W.
ARTHUR P. WHITAKER	. . . .	A. P. W.
MELVIN JOHNSON WHITE	. . .	M. J. W.
W. L. WHITTLESEY	. . . . .	W. L. W.
ROBERT J. WICKENDEN	. . . .	R. J. W.
JAMES FIELD WILLARD	. . . .	J. F. W.
MARY WILHELMINE WILLIAMS	.	M. W. W.
H. PARKER WILLIS	. . . . . .	H. P. W.
JAMES E. WINSTON	. . . . .	J. E. W—n.
CLARK WISSLER	. . . .	C. W.
CARTER GODWIN WOODSON	. . .	C. G. W.
THOMAS WOODY	. . . .	T. W.
ERNEST HUNTER WRIGHT	. . .	E. H. W.
HELEN WRIGHT	. . . .	H. W.
WALTER L. WRIGHT, JR.	. . . .	W. L. W. Jr.
LAWRENCE COUNSELMAN WROTH	.	L. C. W.
JULIEN C. YONGE	. . . . . .	J. C. Y.
EDNA YOST	. . . .	E. Y.
FREDERIC GEORGE YOUNG	. . . .	F. G. Y.

DICTIONARY OF

AMERICAN BIOGRAPHY

Brearly — Chandler

BREARLY, DAVID (June 11, 1745–Aug. 16, 1790), jurist and statesman, was descended from a family of Yorkshire, England. His American ancestor, John B. Brearly, emigrated in 1680 and settled near Trenton, N. J. David Brearly was born at Spring Grove, the son of David and Mary (Clark) Brearly. He became a lawyer at Allentown, near Trenton. At the opening of the Revolution he was so outspoken in his Whig sentiments that he was arrested for high treason, but was freed by a mob of citizens. In the war he was appointed lieutenant-colonel of the 4th New Jersey, Nov. 28, 1776; and of the 1st New Jersey, Jan. 1, 1777. He resigned Aug. 4, 1779, but served after the war as colonel of militia. His career in civil affairs was more conspicuous. He was a member of the New Jersey constitutional convention, and on June 10, 1779 he was elected chief justice of the supreme court of the state. In this position there came before him for decision a case of considerable importance. A certain Elisha Walton had received a favorable verdict, May 24, 1779, given by a jury of six men, in accordance with a law recently passed by the legislature of the state, the case being tried before a justice of the peace in Monmouth County. The chief justice issued a writ of *certiorari*, returnable at the next session, and the case—*Holmes vs. Walton*—was argued at Trenton before Chief Justice Brearly, Nov. 11, 1779. Judge Brearly's opinion was given, probably orally, Sept. 7, 1780, in a significant statement regarding the law which had allowed a jury of six men. In the development of the right to overturn a legislative enactment by judicial decision, this opinion by Judge Brearly has been regarded as especially noteworthy. "No doubt remains that Brearly met the question of constitutionality squarely and on Sept. 7, 1780, announced the principle of judicial guardianship of the organic law against attempted or inadvertent encroachment by the ordinary law" (Austin Scott). The same commentator remarks: "From the 7th of September, 1780, this function of the judiciary, this principle of judicial power over unconstitutional legislation, has held sway in New Jersey." It was approved by the legislature; and reference to it was made by Gouverneur Morris in an address to the Pennsylvania Assembly in 1785.

Brearly was a delegate to the Federal Convention of 1787, and is thus described by Pierce: "As an Orator he has little to boast of, but as a Man he has every virtue to recommend him." He opposed proportional representation, and joint ballot in the election of president. As an adherent of the rights of the small states he seconded the motion for one vote for each state. He was a member of the "grand committee," and he seems to have been regular in attendance at the convention, for he wrote to his colleagues Dayton and Paterson, urging their presence at the sessions. He was closely associated with Paterson. "He (Paterson) here discussed the idea of erasing state boundaries, a scheme which he and his colleague Brearley, seem actually to have had in serious contemplation" (A. C. McLaughlin, *The Confederation and the Constitution*, 1905, p. 216). A further evidence of their connection is the fact that in Paterson's notes of the convention, two of the documents are in Brearly's handwriting (*American Historical Review*, IX, 312–40).

Brearly presided over the state convention which ratified the Federal Constitution. He was a presidential elector, and United States district judge from 1789 until his death. He stood high in Masonic circles, and was vice-president of the New Jersey Society of the Cincinnati. He was a delegate to the Episcopal General Convention of 1786, and was one of the compilers of the prayer-book. About 1767 he married Elizabeth Mullen of Trenton, and on Apr. 17, 1783, he married Elizabeth Higbee.

[W. H. Brearley, *Geneal. of the Brearley Family* (1886). Austin Scott in the *Am. Hist. Rev.*, IV, 457–69, describes the *Holmes* vs. *Walton* case. He summarizes his statement at the end by saying that Brearly was associated with Paterson and Livingston in supporting the New Jersey Plan, and that this plan proposed the "principle of judicial control in our legal system." A. C. McLaughlin, *Courts, Constitution, and Parties* (1912), p. 42, note, observes: "It will not do to stress the connection between *Holmes* vs. *Walton* and this section of the Constitution (the one referring to the 'law of the land'); it is possible, but we cannot say more, that the case was of influence on the minds of men like Paterson."]   E. K. A.

BREAUX, JOSEPH ARSENNE (Feb. 18, 1838–July 23, 1926), jurist, educator, was descended from an Acadian family which settled in Louisiana. He was the son of John B. Breaux and Margaret (Walsh) Breaux, was born on the family plantation in Iberville Parish, and was educated there until he prepared for college. Completing his college work at Georgetown (Ky.), young Breaux studied law in the University of Louisiana (now Tulane) and was graduated in 1859. He married Eugenia Mille, daughter of a planter, in 1861, and had established himself near the home of his boyhood when the Civil War began. He entered the service first as captain of the 13th Louisiana Infantry, but when this organization was merged with other units upon being mustered into the Confederate army, Breaux transferred to the 8th Louisiana Cavalry as a private. He continued in service, promoted to lieutenant, throughout the war. Resuming the practise of his profession at Lafayette, and a little later at New Iberia (1866), he became an important factor in rehabilitating the Parishes during the hard period of Reconstruction. Of wide acquaintance, very shrewd and conservative in business affairs, he won the confidence of the Creole population. He was chosen president of the First National Bank of New Iberia; but more important than this, he became president of the local school board, and demonstrated his ability to better the deplorable condition of the schools. At that time the only tongue known to large numbers of the country folk in Southwest Louisiana was a very imperfect French which had practically no written form. There were serious difficulties (due to mutual suspicion on the part of Creole and English, to sheer ignorance, to political jealousy) in the path of an effective system of schools. Fortunately for the state, Breaux was elected state superintendent of public schools (1888). He compiled the school laws then on the statute books, drafted a new school law, and by his influence with the Parishes where he was so well known won its enactment by the legislature; it became the basis of a sound system of public instruction.

Appointed by Gov. Nicholls as associate justice of the supreme court in 1890, Breaux served longer than any justice except Martin, becoming chief justice in 1904 and retiring in 1914. As a judge, he displayed that sense of fair dealing, that kindliness which had won him friends. His knowledge of the law was extensive and exact; but his decisions are rarely well written; indeed, Breaux never acquired ease in writing English; but he arrived at substantial justice and gave shrewd judgments. In 1901, he published a *Digest* of the decisions of the supreme court that was invaluable to the lawyer. He was fond of reading, and was a man of gentle, almost retiring disposition, although physically tall and powerful. His interest in many quiet philanthropies was shown by his gifts to the Charity Hospital of New Orleans for tubercular patients. He was chairman of the board for the State Museum, and for the Confederate Memorial Hall, and was actively interested in the history of the state. Having no direct heirs, he left the bulk of his estate in trust for the benefit of students of law in Tulane University and in Loyola University, with both of which he had long been connected.

[*Who's Who in La. and Miss.* (1918); J. S. Kendall, *Hist. of New Orleans* (1922), II, 822; obituaries, July 24, 1926, in *Times-Picayune, States*, etc.; memorial in *Phi Beta Kappa Key*, Mar. 1927; memorial address by Hon. W. Catesby Jones before the Supreme Court, Nov. 1926.]   P. B.

BRECK, GEORGE WILLIAM (Sept. 1, 1863–Nov. 22, 1920), mural painter, was born in Washington, D. C., son of John and Annie (Auer) Breck. When quite young he went to New York to take up mechanical drafting. Instruction at the Art Students' League marked the beginning of his technical studies and following this, he taught drawing and did some illustrating. Through his realization of the need for special study, he became greatly interested in the possibilities in the development of mural painting and entered the first competition for the Jacob H. Lazarus Scholarship for the Study of Mural Decoration, held under the auspices of the Metropolitan Museum of Art, New York, in 1896. Being the fortunate winner of this scholarship, he had the opportunity of attending the American Academy of Fine Arts in Rome for several years (1897–1902). Probably because of his long absence abroad, very little has been written concerning some of the most active years of the artist's life, but we may safely conclude that the ideal environment of Rome and the many opportunities for helpful and congenial personal contacts laid the foundation for his later successes. At the suggestion of Edwin A. Abbey, while in Rome he was commissioned by the University of Virginia to make a replica of Raphael's "School of Athens" for the Auditorium in Charlottesville. An important event in his life at this time was his marriage, June 10, 1903, to Katharine, daughter of Franklin H. Head of Chicago. He became a member of the New York Architectural League; New York Municipal Art Society; National Society of Mural Painters; the Century Club; the New York City Art Commission (1912–15); the American Fine Arts Society, and for three terms served the Art Students' League as president. At the St. Louis Exposition in 1904, he was awarded a silver medal. During 1904–09 he was director of the Academy of Fine Arts in Rome, but in 1910 established a studio in New York and made his home at Flushing, L. I., where his death occurred in 1920.

During his period of study as an associate member of the American Academy of Fine Arts, at Rome, Breck had an exhibition of his work in the Pratt Institute Department of Fine Arts, Brooklyn, N. Y., Oct. 10–25, 1902. This exhibit included the following: copies—"Jurisprudence," "Group from the Disputa," "Group from Messa di Bolsena," "Mt. Parnassus," "Poetry" and "The Temptation," from Raphael; "Prophet Esaias," from Michelangelo; "Sixtus IV" and two copies entitled "Angel" from Melozzo da Forli; "Fame" from Guercino; four works entitled "Muse," from Lo Spagna; original sketches—"America" and "Sketch for Mural Decoration" made in competition for the Lazarus Scholarship. Other important examples of Breck's work are: two mural paintings in the Watertown, N. Y., Flower Memorial Library, entitled "First Public Commemoration of the Declaration of Independence in Jefferson County, N. Y.," and "Conference between M. de la Barre, Governor of Canada, and the Representatives of the Five Nations" (1904); mosaics in the façade and interior of St. Paul's P. E. Church at Rome, Italy; three medallions for the library of the Hon. Whitelaw Reid, one, "Reflection," a beautiful ceiling panel, symbolic in treatment, the pose of the principal figure, a female, being of interest for its suggestion of grace, poise, and intellectual strength.

[E. H. Blashfield, *Mural Painting in America* (1913), p. 68; *Who's Who in America,* 1920–21; *Am. Art Annual,* XVII, 265, XIX, 436 ("Mural Paintings in Public Buildings in the United States"); Thieme-Becker, *Künstler-Lexikon,* IV, 561; Pratt Institute, Brooklyn, N. Y., Dept. of Fine Arts, *Exhibition of Sculpture, Sketches and Photographs of Work by Hermon A. MacNeil and Copies, Drawings and Sketches by Geo. W. Breck,* Oct. 10–25, 1902.]   J. M. H.

BRECK, JAMES LLOYD (June 27, 1818–Mar. 30, 1876), Episcopalian clergyman, born near Philadelphia, the fourth son among the fourteen children of George Breck and Catherine D. Israell. He was educated at the Rev. Dr. Muhlenberg's academy at Flushing, L. I., and at the University of Pennsylvania. From his boyhood, he showed himself to be of strong character, and was distinguished at school by his industry and perseverance if not by brilliance. At the age of sixteen he had already decided to offer himself to a life of hardship in the mission field. After graduation from the University of Pennsylvania in 1838, he entered the General Theological Seminary in New York. These were the early days of the Catholic Revival in the Episcopal Church, and in the seminary Breck came under the influence of the Rev. Dr. Whittingham, later Bishop of Maryland, who strengthened in him the High Church principles he had acquired from Dr. Muhlenberg. During Breck's stay in New York, Bishop Jackson Kemper returned there from his first missionary journey through the new territories of the Northwest, and appealed for volunteers. Breck saw here the opportunity for a life of service for which he had been waiting. For some time he had had in his mind the formation of a brotherhood of celibate clergy, thus reviving in the Episcopal Church a type of religious devotion in which little or nothing had been attempted since the dissolution of the monasteries by Henry VIII. In this desire he had the support of two other young clergymen, and in 1841 the three set off for Wisconsin. The next fall found the little society established at Nashotah, where the brethren bought land and built their first house. From this centre, Breck worked tirelessly at the three tasks he had set himself: missionary work among the settlers who were swarming into the new territories, the foundation of a theological seminary for the West, and the revival of a disciplined religious community life in the Church. Of the three, the last was probably the dearest to him at this time. It was his inflexible determination to insist on his brotherhood idea, in spite of the growing lukewarmness of his companions, which led him to leave Nashotah after eight years of successful struggle. Breck was nothing if not masterful, and realizing that the work could not develop on lines which he preferred, he resigned the presidency and went to Minnesota. He had not failed, for Nashotah Seminary still exists to propagate his uncompromising Church principles. After a brief and not too encouraging attempt to found a permanent religious order after his own heart at St. Paul, Breck turned with equal enthusiasm to convert the Indians. A man of great stature and commanding personality, capable of doing his forty miles a day on foot over the forest trails, dressed invariably in the full clerical attire of the period, never lacking clean linen in spite of the frequent squalor of his surroundings, Breck made a tremendous impression on the red men. From the outset of his career he had been convinced of the necessity of Church schools and religious education in connection with Christian missions; and during the five years he spent among the Chippewas he opened at Crow Wing and Leech Lake educational, agricultural, and missionary centers which were beginning to exercise a potent influence among the savages. He had already received the earnest commendation of the governor of the territory, when his dreams of a Christianized and civilized Indian population were destroyed by the withdrawal of all United States troops from Minnesota. The Civil War was imminent, and the white missionaries and their converts, now without protection, were in constant danger. With great reluctance, Breck sought a more settled neighborhood, and made new headquarters at Faribault. During his years with the Indians, the force of circumstances seems to have led him to abandon his cherished ideal of an order of celibate clergy living in community under a religious rule, for in 1855 he married Jane Maria Mills, one of his assistants. She died in 1862; and after two years as a widower Breck married his second wife, Sarah Styles, who survived him. In its outcome, the work at Faribault was the largest of all Breck's labors. In the nine years he spent there, he either founded or prepared the way for the cathedral, the Seabury Divinity School, which is the principal Episcopal seminary west of the Mississippi, and the splendid schools for boys and girls now existing there. After nine years, Faribault became too solidly established to tempt this "apostle of the wilderness" to remain longer. He was by nature a pioneer, and his last search for the frontier led him to California. In 1867 he settled at Benicia, not far from San Francisco. There he followed his usual plan of founding a theological seminary and schools for boys and girls; but before he had had sufficient time to establish his latest work on a substantially enduring basis, he died in 1876, prematurely worn out by his incessant toil.

[Chas. Breck, *Life and Letters of the Rev. Jas. Lloyd Breck* (1883) ; T. I. Holcombe, *An Apostle of the Wilderness* (1903) ; private papers in possession of Nashotah House ; documents in possession of the Wis. Hist. Soc.]   E.J.M.N.

BRECK, SAMUEL (July 17, 1771–Aug. 31, 1862), prominent citizen of Philadelphia, came of a Massachusetts Bay family prominent from the earliest settlement, and was born in Boston as the eldest son of Samuel Breck, a wealthy overseas merchant, and his wife Hannah, only daughter of Benjamin Andrews. The stately family mansion facing the Common was the resort of foreign visitors to Boston, many of whom had social or business connections with the elder Breck. In 1779 the father was appointed by the King of France to be fiscal agent of the French forces and young Samuel, who attended the Latin School, became a favorite with the French naval officers who frequented his home, one of whom, Admiral the Marquis de Vaudreuil, sent the lad, with his father's consent, to be further educated at the famous semi-religious and aristocratic military school at Sorèze, where he spent over four years, and whence he returned to Boston, in July 1787, with a foreign accent and a strong leaning toward the Roman Catholic religion. The latter he soon exchanged for the Episcopalian faith of his father. After a second visit to Europe in 1790, where he was the guest of the painter Copley and Sir William Pepperell in England, and of Noailles, Lafayette, and Vaudreuil in Paris, he was given the sum of $10,000 by his father, with which to "commence merchant." Young Samuel thereupon established a shipping business on Long Wharf, Boston. In 1792 however, partly on account of what was considered by the father to be "an iniquitous system of taxes," and partly because of an affection of his throat, the entire family moved to Philadelphia, where the elder Breck at once assumed a leading position in the social and public life of that city, at the time the national capital, among the honors falling to him being the federal appointment as one of the commissioners to pass on the claims connected with Article XXI of the Treaty of San Lorenzo (Spanish Spoliations) in 1797–99. The younger Samuel married on Christmas Eve, 1795, Jean Ross, daughter of a prominent merchant, and thereafter served his adopted city and state with distinction in many fields. His many historical addresses and dissertations, though of minor importance, are notable for their erudition and polish, the most important being his essay on "Continental Paper Money." He was the founder of the Society of the Sons of New England, and president or a high official of many other societies. He served four years in the Pennsylvania Senate, from 1817 to 1821, introducing, in February 1821, a bill for the emancipation of the slaves still remaining in the state. He was elected (1823) to the Eighteenth Congress, but failed of reëlection because, from a feeling of loyalty toward his old friend, John Quincy Adams, he alone of all the Pennsylvania delegation voted for that statesman for president. From the year 1800 he kept a singularly full diary which is still extant in many manuscript volumes, forming an agreeable and valuable social and political record of Philadelphia for nearly sixty years. His *Recollections,* which are of uncommon interest, together with extracts from the diaries, were published in 1877. While always a bitter opponent of slavery and an ardent churchman, Breck was fanatical on neither subject. His patriotism was proverbial. In his ninetieth year, at a patriotic meeting soon after the fall of Fort Sumter, Breck, at the close of the singing of the national anthem, sprang to his feet and called for three cheers for the United States, adding, "I was a man when they were formed, and God forbid that I should live to witness their downfall!" A year later, as he lay paralyzed on his death-bed, upon hearing cheering news from the front, his voiceless lips moved and with difficulty he raised his only sound hand and waved it feebly three times as if in triumph.

[The numerous MSS. of Breck's diaries and other, mostly unpublished, writings, are the best sources of information in regard to his career. Most of these are in possession of his collateral descendant, Miss Anna Shaw, Morristown, N. J. Among printed sources see *Recollections of Samuel Breck* (1877), ed. by H. E. Scudder; J. Francis Fisher, *Memoir of Samuel Breck* (1863); Jos. Reed Ingersoll, *Memoir of the Late Samuel Breck* (1863).]

E.B.

BRECKENRIDGE, JAMES (Mar. 7, 1763– May 13, 1833), soldier, lawyer, congressman, brother of John Breckinridge, 1760–1806 [*q.v.*], was the grandson of Alexander Breckenridge who emigrated from the north of Ireland to Virginia about 1738. His son Robert Breckenridge, a captain in the French and Indian War, married Letitia Preston and through her their children had influential political connections (M. S. Kennedy, *Seldens of Virginia and Allied Families,* 1911, I, 452–55). During the Revolution, James, the eighteen-year-old son of Robert and Letitia (Preston) Breckenridge, enlist-

ed as a private in a corps of Botetourt riflemen commanded by his relative Col. Preston and in 1781 he was an officer under Gen. Greene in North Carolina. Later he was a major-general of Virginia militia and served in the War of 1812 (Obituary, *Richmond Whig,* May 24, 1833). In the meantime he had taken the academic and law courses in the College of William and Mary, graduating in 1785 (*History of William and Mary College,* 1874, p. 98). The young patriot commenced to practise law in 1787 and soon entered public life. He was a member of the House of Delegates from Botetourt County for thirteen sessions between 1780 and 1824 (E. G. Swem and J. W. Williams, *A Register of the General Assembly of Virginia 1776–1918,* 1918, p. 351). He was a candidate for governor of Virginia against James Monroe, but was defeated. He represented his district in Congress, Mar. 22, 1809 to Mar. 3, 1817 (*A Biographical Congressional Directory,* 1903, p. 410). Breckenridge was a leader of the Federalist party in Virginia. Later, he supported, in the legislature, Jefferson's plans for the University of Virginia, was one of the commission to select a site for that institution and a member of its first Board of Visitors (W. C. Bruce, *History of the University of Virginia,* 1922, I, 210, 212, 220, 221, 236, 290, II, 44). On his ancestral estate near Fincastle, in Botetourt County, Breckenridge built a beautiful home, "Grove Hill," noted for its atmosphere of cordiality, patriotism, and culture, which made a fitting background for its master and was the joy of his descendants for more than a hundred years. There he kept in close touch with ruling spirits in state and national affairs through correspondence with such men as Jefferson, Monroe, Madison, and many other notables whose letters made "Grove Hill" a treasure house of historical data. The mistress of "Grove Hill" was Anne, daughter of Cary Selden, of Elizabeth City County, to whom Breckenridge was married at Old St. John's Church, Richmond, on New Year's Day 1791, by Rev. James Buchanan. He died at the home he had created, leaving many descendants. Portraits represent Breckenridge as a stately, reserved, soldierly-looking man, of thoughtful countenance and rather blond coloring. An editorial in the *Richmond Times-Despatch* declared that "The destruction of 'Grove Hill' by fire, on Oct. 24, [1909] was a genuine sentimental calamity. It was . . . a splendid specimen of late colonial architecture—rich in memories of bygone Virginia."

[In addition to references given above, see *Richmond Enquirer,* May 24, 1833.]

M.N.S.

BRECKINRIDGE, JOHN (Dec. 2, 1760–
Dec. 14, 1806), lawyer, statesman, of Scotch-
Irish ancestry, was a son of Robert Breckenridge (the spelling of the family name was for
the most part, changed in the next generation)
whose father came to Virginia about 1738. His
mother was Letitia, a daughter of John Preston.
Soon after his birth near the present site of
Staunton, Va., his family moved on westward
into Botetourt County where his father died in
1772, leaving a widow and seven children in exposed frontier surroundings. Though living in
as refined a home as could be found in that part of
the world, Breckinridge found conditions rough
and uncouth. Harboring a strong desire for
learning, he managed when nineteen years of age
to enter William and Mary College where he remained two years. While a student here, without
his previous knowledge he was elected by the
voters of Botetourt County to represent them in
the legislature. This was more than an attempt
of his fellow citizens to save money by desig-
nating some one as representative who happened
to be residing at the seat of government. On account of his youth he was not allowed to take his
seat. Twice more was he elected before he was
admitted. He now decided to study law, married
in 1785 Mary Hopkins Cabell, a daughter of
Col. Joseph Cabell of Buckingham County, and
immediately settled in Albemarle County.

The spell of Kentucky, which had seized so
many other Virginians, soon gripped him. Letters from two of his brothers and from many
friends who were there implored him to move
to that land of hope. He abandoned a position
in Congress to which he had just been elected
and crossed the mountains in 1792, settling near
Lexington in Fayette County and developing
an estate which he called Cabell's Dale. Here
he built an office and began the practise of law.
He was soon on the road to a comfortable fortune, being greatly busied with land suits. His
ablity as a lawyer recommended him to Gov.
Isaac Shelby who appointed him attorney-general for the state in 1795 following his defeat for
the United States Senate by Humphrey Marshall. It was while he was in this position that
the disputed gubernatorial election took place
in 1796. Called upon for an opinion by Benjamin Logan, who had received a plurality of the
electoral vote, he refused officially to give a decision, but privately upheld Logan's position.
The next year Breckinridge was elected to represent Fayette County in the lower house of
the legislature and he was successively reëlected
until 1801, being speaker the last two years. In
1801 he was elected to the United States Senate,

but resigned in 1805 to become attorney-general
of the United States, an appointment which
greatly pleased the West and strengthened President Jefferson there.

Breckinridge impressed himself upon the
country as no other representative of the West
had done up to that time. He believed that the
national government was making little effort to
open the Mississippi River, and he emphasized
this belief by accepting the presidency of the
Democratic Society of Kentucky, organized in
Lexington the year he arrived. He also looked
with favor on George Rogers Clark's plottings
with Genet in their efforts to open the navigation of the Mississippi and he promised a money
subscription in the undertaking. In 1794 he
wrote, "We have sat down with patience to
watch the Event of his [Pinckney's] negotiations & God send, thay may not show us that
we may fight or negotiate for ourselves" (Breckinridge Manuscripts, Sept. 15, 1794). His insistence on the rights of the West and his
friendship for Jefferson had their weight in the
Louisiana Purchase of 1803. Breckinridge's
fighting instincts led him to work readily with
Jefferson in promoting the Kentucky Resolutions of 1798. Jefferson wrote these celebrated
resolutions; Breckinridge changed two of them
slightly, introduced them in the Kentucky legislature, and forced their passage. The next year
he introduced a new set which he himself wrote.
He was not alone a destructive critic; he was a
constructive reformer as well. He remade the
penal code for Kentucky and eliminated all capital crimes except murder. His constructive
ability again was shown in his work in the second constitutional convention of Kentucky. The
document it produced was largely due to his
efforts. He died when only forty-six years of
age, but his widow lived many years thereafter.
There were born to them nine children.

[Various letters to and from Breckinridge are in the
Breckinridge MSS. in the Lib. of Cong. Other sources
of information relating to him are: *Ky. Gazette*, Dec.
15, 22, 1806; E. D. Warfield, *The Ky. Resolutions of
1798* (1887); Richard H. and Lewis Collins, *Hist. of
Ky.* (1874); *Biog. Encyc. of Ky.* (1877); H. Levin, ed.,
Lawyers and Lawmakers of Ky. (1897).]

E. M. C—r.

BRECKINRIDGE, JOHN (July 4, 1797–
Aug. 4, 1841), Presbyterian clergyman, controversialist, was a descendant of Scotch-Irish settlers in Virginia, a Kentuckian by birth, who
feared God but not the face of man. His father,
John [*q.v.*], attorney-general in Jefferson's cabinet at the time, died when his namesake was
but nine years old, and he was brought up at
his birthplace, Cabell's Dale, Ky., by a most

capable mother, Mary Hopkins Cabell, daughter of Col. Joseph Cabell of Buckingham County, Va., and by an older brother, his legal guardian. Before entering the College of New Jersey, where he enrolled in 1815 and from which he graduated with honors three years later, he had no thought of becoming a minister, for no one of his family was then a church member, and he had been destined for the law. It was in the face of considerable opposition from home, therefore, that having been converted from his "gay and wild career," he persisted in his determination to preach the gospel. In 1820–21 he was a tutor at Princeton and a student in the theological seminary there. On Aug. 1, 1822, he was licensed to preach by the Presbytery of New Brunswick, and during 1822–23 was chaplain of Congress. He was ordained, Sept. 10, 1823, by the Presbytery of West Lexington, Ky., and installed pastor of the McChord Church, Lexington.

His intellectual strength, eloquence, and ability as a debater quickly lifted him into prominence, but the intensity of his zeal soon wore out a none too robust body. His original intention had been to labor in a foreign field, but conditions outside his control, he states, forbade. He was afire with missionary ardor, however, an aggressive champion of the Protestant faith, and a crusader against heresy and wrong. In Presbyterian circles he stood forth as an uncompromising opponent of the New School theology, and while at Lexington he waged war against the liberalism of President Horace Holley [q.v.] of Transylvania University. Outside the pulpit, his principal medium of attack was the *Western Luminary,* which he edited, and is commonly said to have established. This latter honor, however, probably belongs to the publisher, Thomas T. Skillman (L. and R. H. Collins, *History of Kentucky,* 1874, I, 466; G. W. Ranck, *History of Lexington, Ky.,* 1872, p. 300). In 1826 Breckinridge became associated with Dr. John Glendy at the Second Presbyterian Church, Baltimore, and in 1831, secretary and general agent of the Board of Education of the Presbyterian Church. The General Assembly appointed him professor of pastoral theology in Princeton Seminary in 1836, which chair he relinquished in 1838 to become secretary and general agent of the Board of Foreign Missions. His health was failing, however, and he held the office but two years. At the time of his death, which occurred at his birthplace, he was pastor-elect of the Presbyterian church in New Orleans, and had been chosen president of Oglethorpe University, Ga.

As a controversialist Breckinridge became widely known through two series of debates with Rev. John Hughes [q.v.], later archbishop of New York. The first of these, on the question "Is the Protestant Religion the Religion of Christ?" was conducted in the columns of the *Presbyterian* and the *Catholic Herald* in 1833, and was published under the title *Controversy between Rev. Messrs. Hughes and Breckinridge, on the Subject, etc.* (1834?). The second was carried on in the Union Literary and Debating Institute, Philadelphia, in 1835–36, and was on the question: "Is the Roman Catholic Religion in Any or in All its Principles or Doctrines Inimical to Civil or Religious Liberty?" followed by the question, "Is the Presbyterian Religion . . . Inimical, etc.," published in 1836 under the title, *A Discussion of the Question, Is the Roman Catholic Religion, etc.* Both sides of these controversies were discussed frankly, ably, and at length, the discussions being enlivened with rather acrimonious personalities. The widespread report that on his death-bed he repented his opposition to the Roman Catholic Church and asked for the ministry of a priest seems to have been thoroughly disproved (see R. Davidson, *History of the Presbyterian Church,* 1847, p. 363).

Besides the above, his published works include *Ministerial Responsibility* (1828); *An Address Delivered July 15, 1835, before the Eucleian and Philomathian Societies of the University of the City of New York* (1836); and the tenth lecture in *Spruce Street Lectures on Missions* (1833). After the death of his first wife, Margaret Miller, daughter of Prof. Samuel Miller, of Princeton Theological Seminary, whom he married in January 1823, he published *A Memorial of Mrs. Margaret Breckinridge* (1839). He was married a second time in 1840 to Mary Ann Babcock of Stonington, Conn.

[Besides above-mentioned works, see W. B. Sprague, *Annals Am. Pulpit,* vol. IV (1858); *Baltimore Relig. and Lit. Mag.,* VIII, 475–80.]   H. E. S.

BRECKINRIDGE, JOHN CABELL (Jan. 15, 1821–May 17, 1875), soldier, statesman, was of Scotch-Irish descent. His grandfather John Breckinridge [q.v.] came to Kentucky in 1792 and subsequently became a United States senator and attorney-general under Jefferson. His father, Joseph Cabell Breckinridge, who had married Mary Clay Smith, became a distinguished lawyer and politician but died when only thirty-four years of age. John C. Breckinridge was his only son and was born near Lexington, Ky. He attended Centre College, a Presbyterian school in Danville, and was graduated in 1839. Shortly afterward he spent some time at the College of New Jersey. With his family background it was only natural that he should study law and this he did under the direction of Gov. Owsley. He also pursued further his work in law at Transylvania College during the year 1840–41. The Lexington bar was so well supplied with men of outstanding ability and success that Breckinridge decided that his opportunities there would be rather meager. He first went to Frankfort but soon concluded to settle in a less crowded region further west and chose Burlington, Iowa. Here he remained two years, but the spell of Kentucky was always upon him. Returning to his native state, he at first located for a short time at Georgetown, near Lexington, but becoming bolder and more self-confident, in 1845 he moved back to Lexington and began practise there, later forming a partnership with James B. Beck. He was soon in comfortable circumstances but was on the road to no great fortune. The call for troops in 1846 to invade Mexico failed to enlist either his enthusiasm or his services, he being in this respect unlike most of his fellow Kentuckians. But his ability as an orator had been noted and when in July 1847 a score of dead Kentuckians, officers and privates, killed at Buena Vista and at other battles, were brought to Frankfort for a great military funeral, where 20,000 people gathered, Breckinridge was selected to deliver the commemorative oration. Aided by the solemn splendor of the occasion, Breckinridge talked himself into the army. He was commissioned a major of the 3rd Kentucky Volunteers, whom he led into Mexico. But he was too late to reap any military glory, his chief accomplishment here being his defense of Gen. Pillow in a dispute which arose with Gen. Scott.

In 1849 Breckinridge made his first entry into politics when he ran for the legislature to represent Fayette County. He was elected. It was at this time that the campaign was on for the constitutional convention and that the slavery question was being hotly agitated. Being a Democrat he favored the convention and opposed the emancipationists. In this campaign he came into conflict with his imperious uncle, Robert Jefferson Breckinridge [q.v.], with whom he was hereafter to differ on almost every subject. In 1851 the Democrats chose him as their candidate for Congress representing the Ashland District, which had become under Clay's leadership one of the strongest Whig districts in the state. The Whigs with Gen. Leslie Combs, who stood next to Clay in popularity in the state, expected to win easily. But Breckinridge overturned the

normal 1,500 Whig majority and won by 500 votes. Now there had arisen a successor to Clay, who was to play almost as remarkable a part in Kentucky sentiment. The next year, when he delivered a funeral oration over the dead Clay, his position in the affections of the people was fixed. The next year the Whigs attempted without success to defeat Breckinridge, using this time the ex-governor, Robert P. Letcher. Although Breckinridge was characterized by a dignified bearing and serene nature, in 1854 on the floor of Congress he got himself involved in a heated altercation with Frank B. Cutting, a representative from New York, which came near resulting in a duel. Breckinridge had now definitely established his leadership both in Kentucky and in Congress, but at the end of his second term he decided to resume his law practise in order to repair his private fortune. At this time President Pierce offered him the diplomatic post at Madrid, which he refused.

His record in Congress had so favorably introduced him to the national Democracy that at the party convention in Cincinnati in 1856, when a Southern running-mate for Buchanan was needed, Breckinridge received the nomination. He took an active part in the campaign, making speeches in Indiana, Michigan, and Pennsylvania. His influence in Kentucky gave the state to the Democrats by 6,000 majority. When Buchanan became president in 1857, Breckinridge as vice-president became the presiding officer in the Senate. His four years of service were characterized by poise and justice in his decisions. When on Jan. 4, 1859, the Senate moved from its old chamber to its new quarters Breckinridge was chosen to deliver the parting address. He traced the development of the Union and made a strong plea for its preservation. The Kentucky Democrats now having found their leader decided to keep him before the country. Almost a year and a half before his term as vice-president would expire (December 1859), they elected him to the United States Senate for the term beginning Mar. 4, 1861.

When the Democratic National Convention met in Charleston Breckinridge's name was presented by Arkansas, but not being a candidate and not desiring to interfere with James Guthrie's aspirations, Breckinridge had his name withdrawn. No nomination having been made in Charleston, when the Southern faction of the disrupted convention later met in Baltimore, Breckinridge was selected for president despite the fact that he was still averse to having his name considered. He, however, accepted the nomination. He saw with many misgivings the

8

break-up of the Democratic party and he readily agreed to step aside when Jefferson Davis attempted unsuccessfully to reunite the party. After all efforts toward peace had failed he took an active part in the campaign and stoutly defended himself against the charges of being inconsistent and of holding disunion sentiments. He maintained that he had always stood for the non-intervention of Congress on the subject of slavery in the territories and that slavery could be excluded only when the territory should become a state. A determined effort was made to prove that he was a disunionist but he showed that neither by word nor act had he ever promoted such an idea. In 1859 after he had been elected to the Senate he said, "She [Kentucky] will cling to the Constitution while a shred of it remains . . ." (*Modern Eloquence,* edited by Thomas B. Reed, 1905, VII, 105), and in 1860 at Frankfort he said, "I am an American citizen, a Kentuckian, who never did an act nor cherished a thought that was not full of devotion to the Constitution and the Union" (*Kentucky Statesman,* July 20, 1860). He received 72 electoral votes in November, though he failed to carry his own state.

As the presiding officer of the Senate he appointed the committee on compromise in December 1860, and he used his influence to have the Crittenden Compromise, which came before that committee, adopted. He believed in the abstract right of secession but he was opposed to the adoption of such a course at that time. Yet he was just as thoroughly opposed to the coercion of a state, holding that the Constitution gave the national government no such power. After the inauguration of Lincoln, he returned to Kentucky and took an active part in the political maneuvers there. He stood out for any compromise that would save the Union, but after the firing on Fort Sumter, which set up the second wave of secession, he held that the Union no longer existed, and that Kentucky now had the right to take any course she should please. The logical action would be to call a sovereign convention, and from this time on as long as there was a chance of using this procedure, he worked for it. On Apr. 2 he addressed the legislature and on May 10 he was appointed a member of a small conference which it was hoped would unite the state on a single course of action. The movement failed and two weeks later Kentucky declared her neutrality, a solution which did not meet with Breckinridge's approval. Yet he acquiesced in it when it was established.

Being a member of the United States Senate he attended the special session beginning on July 4, 1861, and assuming that he was to represent his state and uphold her position which she had recently adopted, he opposed Lincoln's whole war policy, refusing to vote men or money. He defended this position by later declaring to the Kentuckians, "I would have blushed to meet you with the confession that I had purchased for you exemption from the perils of the battlefields and the shame of waging war against your Southern brethren by hiring others to do the work you shrank from performing" (*Rebellion Record,* edited by Frank Moore, III, 254). In early September Kentucky abandoned her neutrality when the armies of both sides invaded the state, embraced the Union troops and ordered the Confederates out. The military régime immediately took charge of the state, arresting hundreds of citizens on suspicion and sending them away without trial. Breckinridge fled to escape arrest, and on Oct. 2 the legislature requested him to resign from the Senate, and on Nov. 6, he was indicted for treason in the federal district court at Frankfort. On Dec. 2, 1861, the United States Senate declared him a traitor and went through the formality of expelling him although he had long been in the Confederate army.

In September he had returned to Kentucky and on the 8th of the following month from Bowling Green he issued a burning address to the people of his native state defending his position and castigating those who had sold out the state to the Federal army. In his address he resigned his position in the Senate, saying, "I exchange with proud satisfaction a term of six years in the Senate of the United States for the musket of a soldier" (*Rebellion Record,* III, 258). He helped to organize the provisional government of Kentucky (Confederate) and in November was appointed a brigadier-general under the command of Gen. A. S. Johnston at Bowling Green. In early 1862 he retreated out of Kentucky with the Confederates, taking part in the battle of Shiloh where he commanded the Reserve Corps. He was soon promoted to be a major-general and in the summer of 1862 he defended Vicksburg. He was then ordered to attack Baton Rouge which he did unsuccessfully; in August he fortified Port Hudson to block the Federal advance up the Mississippi River. He was ordered to join Bragg's invasion of Kentucky in the fall of 1862 but the order came too late for him to take part. On Bragg's return to Tennessee Breckinridge joined him and was in the thickest of the fight at Murfreesboro, commanding the 2nd Division of Hardee's corps. After the battle he covered Bragg's retreat with considerable skill. In May 1863 he was attached to Gen. Joseph E. Johnston in Mississippi and was present at the battle of Jackson. He then returned to the Army of Tennessee under Bragg and commanded a division of D. H. Hill's corps at Chickamauga and Missionary Ridge. In 1864 on the death of John H. Morgan he was ordered to southwest Virginia to assume command of the department, where he remained until Gen. Lee called him to the Shenandoah Valley. After some maneuvers in the Valley he was attached to Lee's army and at the battle of Cold Harbor commanded a division. He was with Gen. Jubal Early in the raid on the outskirts of Washington in July 1864, winning victories at Martinsburg and Monocacy. He was afterward ordered back to the department of southwest Virginia where he was located when President Davis made him secretary of war on Feb. 4, 1865. Although Breckinridge had had no military training beyond his Mexican War experiences, his innate ability as a leader of men, his ready adaptability to new circumstances, and his commanding personality made of him an able commander in the Civil War.

After Appomattox he fled southward with the Confederate cabinet, was present as an adviser to Gen. J. E. Johnston on his surrender to Gen. Sherman, and after the cabinet broke up at Washington, Ga., he made his way on horseback to the coast of Florida where he escaped to Cuba. He now embarked for Europe where he remained until 1868 when he went to Toronto, Canada. In March of the following year he was given permission by the federal government to return to Lexington, Ky. Here he was received with the greatest acclaim, and had his disabilities been removed he might have had any office within the gift of the people. He was now undoubtedly the most popular man in the state, and Grant thought it would have been well for the federal government to allow him to hold office. But he disclaimed all political ambitions and in a very retiring manner resumed his law practise. He was made vice-president of the Elizabethtown, Lexington, & Big Sandy Railroad and took a prominent part in the railroad development coming to the state at this time. He strongly favored the building of the Cincinnati Southern Railroad from Cincinnati to Chattanooga and he took a prominent part in the fight incident to the movement.

Breckinridge married Mary C. Burch of Scott County in December 1843. He died in Lexington in 1875 from the effects of a serious operation. In 1886 the state erected a statue of him in Lexington at an expense of $10,000.

[The Breckinridge MSS. in the Lib. of Cong.; *Biog.*

Sketches of Hon. John C. Breckinridge, Democratic Nominee for President, and Gen. Jos. Lane, Democratic Nominee for Vice-President (1860); *Buchanan and Breckinridge: Lives of Jas. Buchanan and John C. Breckinridge, Democratic Candidates for the Presidency and Vice-presidency of the U. S., with the Platforms of the Political Parties in the Presidential Canvass of 1856* (1856); *Famous Adventures and Prison Escapes of the Civil War* (1893); *Battles and Leaders of the Civil War* (1888); *Official Records,* see Index; *Lexington Weekly Press,* May 23, 1875; *Lexington Observer and Reporter,* Mar. 13, 1869; *Ky. Gazette,* May 19, 1875; *McClure's Mag.,* Jan. 1901; Ed. Porter Thompson, *Hist. of the Orphan Brigade* (1898); Richard H. and Lewis Collins, *Hist. of Ky.* (1874); Alexander Brown, *The Cabells and Their Kin* (1895).]

E.M.C—r.

BRECKINRIDGE, ROBERT JEFFERSON (Mar. 8, 1800–Nov. 27, 1871), lawyer, Presbyterian clergyman, college president, born at Cabell's Dale near Lexington, in Fayette County, Ky., was the son of John [*q.v.*] and Mary Hopkins (Cabell) Breckinridge. The father was one of the leaders in the state and nation, being a United States senator and an attorney-general under President Jefferson. Robert was given excellent preparation for college by the leading educators of the state and when sixteen years of age was sent to Jefferson College, where he remained for two years. He spent part of a year at Yale College and then changed to Union College at Schenectady, N. Y., where he was graduated in 1819. He then returned to Lexington to manage his mother's estate, and there studied law. In 1824 he began the practise of his profession, at a time when the Old Court and New Court struggle was hottest. He supported the former, ran for the legislature in 1825, and was victorious. He continued to represent Fayette County at Frankfort until 1828. The death of two of his children had a profound effect upon him, and a severe illness at this time left his health ever afterward impaired. He now turned to religion, joining the Presbyterian Church, and entered upon a new career. In 1831 he was sent to Cincinnati as a delegate from the West Lexington Presbytery to the General Assembly, and the next year he was licensed to preach. In 1832 he removed with his family to Princeton to better prepare himself for the ministry, but before the end of the year he accepted a call to the Second Presbyterian Church in Baltimore, succeeding his brother John, where he continued until 1845. Here he speedily developed into one of the greatest controversialists and crusaders of his times. He was chiefly responsible for the celebrated "Act and Testimony" of June 1834, which led to the division of the Presbyterian Church in 1837 into the Old School and New School. He allied himself with the former group. In 1836 he visited Europe in the interest of his health, acting at the same time as a representative of the General Assembly, and he engaged in Glasgow, Scotland, in a heated controversy over slavery. In 1845 he accepted the presidency of Jefferson College, in Pennsylvania, but after two troublous years there he resigned on account of the rigors of the climate and accepted a call to the First Presbyterian Church in Lexington, Ky. In 1847 Gov. William Owsley appointed him superintendent of public instruction, which position he held until 1851, first through reappointment by Gov. John J. Crittenden in 1848 and then by election in 1851. His labors for the public school system were monumental, increasing the school attendance in his six years of service from 20,000 to 201,000. He left the public schools to accept a professorship in the new Danville Theological Seminary, which the Presbyterians had just established, and he remained in this capacity until 1869 when old age, disease, and disputes brought about his resignation. He died two years later in Danville.

His career was characterized by fierce controversies. In Baltimore he began a bitter attack against the Catholics, so vigorously carried on as to cause his friends to fear for his life. He also strongly opposed the Universalists. In 1831 he unsuccessfully ran for the state legislature in Kentucky on the issue of opposition to slavery and to Sunday mails. He was also a tireless worker in the temperance movement. In 1849 he headed the attempt of the gradual emancipationists to control the constitutional convention of that year, but failed in his election as a delegate. While in Baltimore he opposed the attempt of Maryland to exclude free negroes. During the Civil War he put forth all of his fiery zeal in support of the Union and during the four years of the struggle he was Lincoln's chief counsellor and adviser in Kentucky. He was also the chief supporter of the military régime in the state. He organized the Lincoln support in Kentucky in 1864, headed the delegation to the Baltimore convention, and was made temporary chairman. He was uncompromising in his opposition to Southern sympathizers, even refusing to save members of his own family from Northern prisons and firing squads. He so hopelessly involved the Presbyterian Church in the political rancors of the times that the organization split in 1866. He was an untiring writer and speaker, writing many open letters, pamphlets, and books. His best known works are, *The Knowledge of God, Objectively Considered* (1858) and *The Knowledge of God, Subjectively Considered* (1859). He edited in Baltimore the *Literary*

and Religious Magazine and the *Spirit of the Nineteenth Century,* and from 1861 to 1865 in Danville the *Danville Quarterly Review.* He was married three times: first on Mar. 11, 1823, to his cousin Ann Sophronisba Preston, a daughter of Col. Francis Preston of Virginia, who died in 1844; secondly, in 1847 to Mrs. Virginia Shelby, a daughter of Col. Nathaniel Hart, who died in 1859; and thirdly, in 1868 to Margaret White, who survived him.

[Richard H. and Lewis Collins, *Hist. of Ky.* (1874); *Biog. Encyc. of Ky.* (1878); H. Levin, ed., *Lawyers and Lawmakers of Ky.* (1897); J. W. Townsend, *Kentuckians in Am. Letters* (1913), vol. I; *Lexington Dollar Weekly Press,* Jan. 6, 8, 1872.]   E. M. C—r.

BRECKINRIDGE, WILLIAM CAMPBELL PRESTON (Aug. 28, 1837–Nov. 19, 1904), lawyer, editor, congressman, was a son of Robert J. Breckinridge [*q.v.*], and Ann Sophronisba, a daughter of Gen. Francis Preston and a grand-daughter of Gen. William Campbell. He was a grandson of John Breckinridge, attorney-general under President Jefferson. He was born in Baltimore, Md., where his father was pastor of the Second Presbyterian Church. Later when his father became president of Jefferson College in Pennsylvania he attended school there, finishing his college course at Centre College, Danville, Ky., in 1855. He now studied medicine for a year, but deciding that he had a greater liking for law, pursued that subject at the Louisville Law College, was graduated in 1857, and began the practise of his profession in Lexington. When the Civil War broke out his sympathies were strongly with the Confederacy, but because his father was the outstanding leader of the Union cause in the state, he remained inactive until Gen. John H. Morgan invaded the state in July 1862. He then joined Morgan's 2nd Kentucky Cavalry in Georgetown as captain and immediately took a prominent part in the engagement at Cynthiana. In 1863 he was attached to the 9th Kentucky Cavalry as a colonel and continued with Morgan until this unit was detached when the latter made his raid north of the Ohio. He was present at the battle of Saltville, Va., and in various capacities was actively engaged throughout the war. He was a member of the body-guard that accompanied Jefferson Davis on his retreat southward, and when the band broke up he was released from further Confederate service by his distinguished kinsman, John Cabell Breckinridge. He returned to Lexington where he began again the practise of law and where in 1866 he assumed the editorship of the *Lexington Observer and Reporter.* In 1868 he gave up his newspaper work in order to enter more actively into his law practise. He was connected for a time with the Law School of Kentucky University (formerly Transylvania University). In 1869 he ran for county attorney but was defeated on account of his support of the admission of negro testimony in the courts. He was elected to the lower house of Congress in 1884 and was reëlected for four successive terms. In 1894 after a very bitter campaign he was defeated and in 1896 he again suffered defeat. At the latter time he ran on a fusion ticket in support of sound money. In January of the following year he became chief editorial writer on the *Lexington Morning Herald,* a paper managed by his son Desha, and in this capacity he developed journalistic ability of a high order. His writings were smooth and direct. As an orator, by common consent, he was unexcelled by any Kentuckian of his day, and as a lawyer his manner and argument were compelling before a jury. In physique he was manly, robust, and handsome. He was married three times: first, to Lucretia Clay, a grand-daughter of Henry Clay, who died in 1860; secondly, to Issa Desha, a grand-daughter of Gov. Joseph Desha, who died in Washington in 1892, and lastly, to Louise Wing. In his later days his fame was clouded by rumors and a court proceeding involving his family relations (Fayette Lexington, pseudonym, *The Celebrated Case of Col. W. C. P. Breckinridge and Madeline Pollard,* 1894). He died in Lexington in 1904.

[Letters and papers in the Breckinridge MSS. in the Lib. of Cong. Sketches and appreciations of his life may be found in *Lexington Leader,* Nov. 20–23, 1904; *Lexington Morning Herald,* Nov. 20–22, 1904; *Biog. Encyc. of Ky.* (1878); Richard H. and Lewis Collins, *Hist. of Ky.* (2 vols., 1874); John W. Townsend, *Kentuckians in Am. Letters* (1913), vol. I; Basil W. Duke, *Hist. of Morgan's Cavalry* (1867); R. U. Johnson and C. C. Buel, eds., *Battles and Leaders of the Civil War* (4 vols., 1887–88).]   E. M. C—r.

BREED, EBENEZER (May 12, 1766–Dec. 23, 1839), early advocate of protection of the shoe industry, was born in Lynn, Mass. He was the youngest of the eight children of Benjamin Breed and Ruth Allen and was of the fifth generation in line from Allen Bread (afterward Breed) who came to Salem, Mass., in 1629 and settled at Saugus, Mass., his portion of the plantation being known as "Breed's End," afterward a part of Lynn. Benjamin Breed is recorded as being a cordwainer and husbandman, combining, as was the custom, two vocations in order that no part of the year might be wasted. Ebenezer Breed's younger days were probably spent in connection with his father's business but letters written later in life indicate that he received more than an ordinary education. He early moved to Philadelphia and being reared in the Society of Friends was warmly received by several of the more prosperous Quakers, previously residents of Lynn. Foremost among them was Stephen Collins, a successful merchant of the period. Influenced by his early association Breed established himself as a wholesale shoe merchant. In his business he quickly encountered the oppressive economic conditions which beset the not-too-well established industries in the period of adjustment which followed the Revolutionary War. Being of a sanguine temperament, with a Quaker sense of the injustice of poverty from avoidable causes, he early seems to have formed definite ideas regarding the policy to be pursued in building the way to economic independence.

Three years of agitation culminated in a brilliant dinner-party given by Breed to the members of Congress at the Collins Mansion loaned for the purpose. The register of the Lynn Historical Society preserves this fragment of Breed's impassioned plea for the shoemaker: "Will you stand tamely by and see this infant industry swallowed up by the raging lions of Britain and Gaul? Will you see the homes of these operatives destroyed or abandoned and not hold out your strong arms to shield them as they shielded you when war bent his horrid front over our fair land? No, I trust and New England expects that by your suffrages we shall obtain the desired relief when the matter comes before your honorable body." This dinner took place between the meeting of the First Congress, Mar. 4, 1789, and the following July 4, when the first tariff act was passed, providing a duty of fifty cents per pair on boots, seven cents per pair on leather shoes, slippers, galoshes, and ten cents per pair on all shoes or slippers made of silk or stuff. Breed now visited England, where his correspondence shows that he was well received, and he is even said to have had his august moment in the presence of royalty, through his friend Sir Benjamin West. He made many business contacts of great advantage and became an importer of much of the shoe material that came from England and France. He also arranged for the coming of several workmen of unusual skill to the city of Lynn for the purpose of teaching the most advanced methods in the shoemaking art. He visited France for a brief period and is said to have had a few very miserable hours in endeavoring to escape the ravages of the Revolution then in progress.

Among the estimable ladies of Breed's circle in Philadelphia was one to whom he paid fervent court, Polly Atmore, daughter of a prominent Quaker, and before he went abroad in 1792 he had won the promise of her hand in marriage. But, on his return, Polly's father accused him of departing from the precepts of his youthful training in his contact with the wealthy classes abroad and directed that the nuptials be postponed for a year. When the year of probation expired, however, Polly was married to a Mr. Robinson and from that day Breed began to give color to the old Quaker's charge by being constantly in his cups. He gradually lost his health and finally his eyesight and the year 1800 found him back in his native town, an inmate of the poorhouse. A kindly disposed cobbler taught him the art of making shoes and he at various times worked whimsically at his trade, resentfully refusing the aid that well-meaning friends proffered. He died in Lynn and was buried at the public expense.

[F. J. Allen, *The Shoe Industry* (1922); *Vital Records of Lynn, Mass.* (1905–06); *Reg. of the Lynn Hist. Soc.*, 1911; Alonzo Lewis and J. R. Newhall, *Hist. of Lynn* (1865); *Essex Antiquarian*, Salem, Mass., Oct. 1907.]   C. T. C.

BREEN, PATRICK (d. Dec. 21, 1868), diarist of the Donner party, was born in Ireland and came to the United States in 1828. Of his early life nothing appears to be recorded. From Keokuk, Iowa, Apr. 5, 1846, with his wife Margaret and seven children, he set out for the emigrants' rendezvous at Independence, Mo., bound for California. Here he joined the party of George and Jacob Donner, which had come from Springfield, Ill., and which with several other parties left for the West early in May. On July 20, at the Little Sandy, in Wyoming, where more emigrants were found, the Donner party was separately organized and George Donner was elected captain. At Fort Bridger, which was reached five days later, decision was made to try the new Hastings cut-off around the south shore of Salt Lake. Instead, however, of reaching the lake by the known route through Weber Canyon, a roundabout course was taken through the mountains, which caused great delay. Other delays with great loss of live-stock followed, in traversing the Nevada desert, and when the party reached Truckee Lake (since called Donner Lake), snow was falling. Several attempts to proceed were frustrated by the increasing snowfall, and by the middle of November the leaders of the party realized that they were hemmed in, with small chance of rescue. Of the tragedy that followed, in which thirty-six out of a company of eighty-one perished, many of the survivors have left accounts. The narrative that

furnishes the most vivid realization of the scene, however, is the diary kept from Nov. 20 to Mar. 1 by Breen. Its bare, scant sentences record divided counsels, quarrels, the sending out of the relief-seekers in mid-December, the exhaustion of the food supply until nothing but hides were left, the increasing weakness and illness of the people, the succession of deaths, the arrival of the first rescue party and the departure of the first contingent of survivors; and it closes with the statement that in two or three days the remainder will start. All of the Breens lived throught the terrible ordeal, though the youngest was a nursing baby. After some shifting about, the family settled, in February 1848, at San Juan Bautista, in San Benito County. The children all lived to maturity, and five of them outlived their parents. The father died at the San Juan home, and six years later his wife followed him.

Breen's title to fame rests on his sole literary production, the diary—"one of the most highly prized treasures," says Bancroft, "of my Library." It is brief—so brief that it omits much the reader would wish to know. Its quality is that of stark literalness unrelieved by any note other than one of patient endurance based on a serene faith in ultimate rescue. Breen was a devout Catholic who had prayers read regularly every day, and his piety converted one of the other members of the party to his creed. He was in no way distinguished among his companions. Indeed, though the women of the party—particularly Tamsen Donner, Margaret Breen and Olvina Murphy—revealed outstanding qualities of greatness, all the men except Stanton seem to have been weak and uncertain, without foresight or any other of the capacities that should have enabled them to prevent an appalling disaster.

[C. F. McGlashan, *History of the Donner Party; A Tragedy of the Sierra* (2nd ed. 1880); Eliza P. Donner Houghton, *The Expedition of the Donner Party and Its Tragic Fate* (1911); H. H. Bancroft, *Hist. of Cal.*, vols. II, V (1885–86); *California and Californians*, ed. by Rockwell D. Hunt (1926), vol. II. The diary is given, with a brief introduction by Frederick J. Teggert, in *Acad. Pacific Coast Hist. Pubs.*, vol. I (July 1910).]   W. J. G.

BREESE, KIDDER RANDOLPH (Apr. 14, 1831–Sept. 13, 1881), naval officer, was born in Philadelphia and appointed a midshipman, from Rhode Island, Nov. 6, 1846. In February 1847 he was ordered to the *Saratoga*, commanded by Commander (afterward Admiral) Farragut and served in her on the Gulf Coast during the war with Mexico. In the spring of 1848 he joined the *St. Mary's* and then served in the *Brandywine* until December 1850. In February 1851 he joined the frigate *St. Lawrence,* and participated in that vessel's voyage to London, laden with articles for the World's Fair. From October 1851 to June 1852 he studied for examination at the Naval Academy, being promoted passed midshipman during the latter month and ordered to the *Mississippi,* flagship of Commodore M. C. Perry [*q.v.*], participating in the famous cruise to Japan. During this cruise he was temporarily attached to the *Macedonian,* which visited the northern end of Formosa to search for coal and to inquire into the captivity of Americans by savages of that island. Returning to the United States in the *Mississippi* in June 1855, in 1858 he was ordered to the *Preble,* and took part in the expedition to Paraguay, and afterward spent some time on the Mosquito Coast, being invalided home with "Isthmus fever" in September 1859. In 1860 he joined the *Portsmouth* on the African Coast, and then the *San Jacinto,* in which he remained until December 1861, the end of her extended cruise, in which 1,500 slaves were captured. During the same month he was ordered to command the third division of Admiral Porter's mortar flotilla, taking part in the opening of the Mississippi River in 1862. Promoted lieutenant commander, the promotion dating from July 16, 1862, he joined Porter's river squadron, commanding the flagship *Black Hawk,* and was present at nearly all the important operations on the Mississippi River and its tributaries. On the conclusion of the Red River expedition he was recommended for promotion. When Porter was ordered to command the North Atlantic blockading squadron in September 1864, he chose Breese as his fleet-captain. This command Breese held until the end of the Civil War. In the storming of Fort Fisher on Jan. 15, 1865, he commanded the storming party of sailors and marines. Admiral Porter in his report, after enumerating and highly praising the devices of Lieutenant Commander Breese, added, "He is a clever, gallant officer, and I strongly recommend his immediate promotion to a commander." Breese's commission followed on July 25, 1866. His duties after the Civil War included those of the assistant superintendency of the Naval Academy under Admiral Porter; those of the inspectorship of ordnance at the Washington Navy Yard; and others connected with the testing of breech-loading arms. He took command of the *Plymouth* of the European squadron on June 29, 1870; was on duty in the Bureau of Ordnance at the Navy Department in December 1872; and became commandant of midshipmen at the Naval Academy in June 1873. He was commissioned captain Aug. 9, 1874. In

1878 he commanded the *Pensacola,* flagship of the Pacific squadron, and was ordered home on sick-leave in 1880, his death occurring the following year.

[Admiral D. D. Porter, *Naval Hist. of the Civil War* (1886); *Report of the Sec. of the Navy,* 1861–65, inclusive; obituary in the *Army and Navy Journal,* XIX, 145; *Navy Register,* 1847–80.]   E. B.

BREESE, SIDNEY (July 15, 1800–June 27, 1878), jurist and politician, was endowed by birth with the prestige of an aristocratic family of New York. On the side of his mother, Catharine Livingston, he was a descendant of John Livingstone, the Scotch divine who negotiated with Charles II in 1650 at Breda, and on his father's side, a descendant of the picturesque soldier-merchant who was master of the port of New York on the eve of the American Revolution (E. E. Salisbury, *Family Memorials,* 1885, II, pp. 477, 503). His father, Arthur Breese, who received an honorary bachelor's degree from Yale College in 1789, followed in the wake of the westward migration, settled at Whitestown in 1793, later removed to Utica, and for seventeen years was clerk of the supreme court of Western New York. He built a spacious house where he entertained Lafayette and other notables who visited that part of the country.

Sidney Breese, the second son in a family of nine, prepared for college under a Presbyterian minister, Rev. Jesse Townsend. Entering Hamilton College, he transferred to Union College and graduated at the age of eighteen, third in his class. Shortly after leaving college, Sidney Breese, like his father, sought his fortune in the West and accepted the invitation of a friend of the family, Elias Kent Kane, to read law at Kaskaskia. It was in the office of the brilliant Kane that the first constitution of the State of Illinois was drafted. Breese was thus early identified with the group of leaders who played a conspicuous part in the development of this frontier state. Admitted to the bar in 1820, he lost his first case through stage-fright and came near to abandoning the profession. In 1821, he was postmaster of Kaskaskia; a year later Kane secured him the appointment of state's attorney; and four years later he received an appointment from President Adams as federal district attorney for Illinois, from which office as a victim of the spoils system, he was removed by President Jackson. This involved him in the bitter struggle in local politics between the Adams faction and the Jackson faction; and for years after he had become a Jacksonian Democrat he was hounded with the charge that once he had distributed "coffin hand-bills" depicting the tyranny of Jackson's martial law in New Orleans (Linder, *Reminiscences*, 144). To advance his political career he edited behind the name of R. K. Fleming the "scurrilous and libelous thumbpaper," the *Western Democrat*, published at Kaskaskia. In 1831 he was an unsuccessful candidate for representative to Congress with a platform in favor of complete state ownership of the public lands. Like Lincoln, Breese played a part in that grim prairie tragedy, the Black Hawk War. Enlisting as a private he was elected to a lieutenant-colonelcy of volunteers, thus furnishing the curious spectacle, in the camp of Gen. J. D. Henry, of a retiring scholar outranking such young warriors as Albert Sidney Johnston, Zachary Taylor, and Robert Anderson who later was the gallant defender of Fort Sumter. At the bar, Breese soon won recognition by his able defense of Judge Smith against impeachment charges in the state legislature (*Senate Journal, 1831–3*, App. 22). This led to his election as judge of the second circuit court in 1835; and, while sitting on this bench, he wrote the opinion in the case of *People* vs. *Field* holding that the governor had power to remove a subordinate from office (*Illinois State Register*, May 24, 1839, pp. 2–3). The reversal of this partisan decision by the supreme court led to the reprehensible action of the Democratic legislature in swamping this court by the addition of five new judgeships, to which were elected, among others, Breese and Stephen A. Douglas.

In 1838, Breese was an unsuccessful candidate for the Democratic nomination as governor. Four years later he again offered himself as a candidate, but withdrew in favor of Thomas Ford, as a result of an alleged bargain which won him the election as United States senator by the legislature in the winter of that year (T. C. Pease, *The Frontier State*, 1918, p. 283). His nomination, however, was contested in an all-night caucus of the Democratic party at Springfield by the supporters of Douglas—an incident which led to years of animosity between the two men.

Breese served one term in the Senate, 1843–49. Although handicapped by a persistent timidity, and impatient with details, he made a minor reputation for learning and scholarship and for five years held the position of chairman of the committee on public lands. With the Democrats of Illinois he took an extreme attitude on the Oregon question, demanding in several speeches a policy of "54° 40' or fight." He supported Polk's policy of annexation of Texas and the war with Mexico, and made an elaborate reply

to Calhoun's celebrated demand that the American army fall back to a defensive line (*Congressional Globe*, 30 Cong., 1 Sess., App. p. 344). Like many Democrats he opposed grants of public lands for the Cumberland Road and for other internal improvements, but he reluctantly approved of national aid for canals and railways, urging in particular Asa Whitney's project for a railway to the Pacific and the Illinois scheme for a railway parallel with the Mississippi (*Senate Document No. 466, 29* Cong., 1 Sess.). He was also interested in getting the lead mines of northern Illinois out of the hands of the government and into private ownership.

His congressional record was not sufficiently strong to save him from being replaced in 1849 by a military hero—Gen. Shields. Breese's retirement from the Senate was followed by an episode of considerable personal humiliation. He had prided himself on being the original proposer of the Illinois Central Railway; while a senator, he had introduced a bill to aid in the construction of the road in Illinois, but he lacked the ability to win votes, and he blocked the efforts of his colleague, Douglas, to carry the business through Congress. Thus, when Douglas secured the passage of the Illinois Central Bill in the first session after Breese's retirement, the latter's chagrin led him unwisely to engage in a bitter newspaper controversy with his old rival, in the course of which Douglas was able to show that the project had not originated with Breese, and furthermore, that Breese's bill in the Senate had envisaged a line simply from Cairo to Galena without touching Lake Michigan or reaching to the Gulf (*Illinois State Register*, Jan. 5 and Mar. 13, 1851).

Breese spiritedly plunged once more into local politics. In the autumn of 1850 he was elected without opposition to a seat in the Illinois House of Representatives and in the same year became speaker. For the next few years he camped on the trail of Douglas hoping to win the Democratic nomination for senator; but, with Lincoln and Trumbull as competitors in baiting the champion of "squatter sovereignty," Breese did not cut a conspicuous figure.

In 1857 came the turning point in his career. He was elected to the Illinois supreme court to fill a vacancy, being reëlected in 1861 for the full term of nine years and again in 1870. On the bench, the talents of this remarkable man, long warped by his incongruous political aspirations, blossomed into real genius. He became one of the leading jurists of America during a period when the rapid expansion of litigation witnessed the increase of the Illinois reports from the eighteenth to the eighty-ninth volume. Breese brought to the bench an independent method of thinking that sometimes shocked the conservative members of the bar but had a refreshing effect upon the lay mind. His wholesome impatience with the technicalities encumbering the law is illustrated by the case of *Maus* vs. *Worthing* (4 *Ill.* 26), a case in which Lincoln appeared as counsel and in which Breese dissented in vigorous language, holding that judicial proceedings should not be hidebound by arbitrary rules handed down from the past when the result was obviously to obstruct justice, and that judges should not surrender their own judgment to follow blindly the doctrine of *stare decisis* and become slaves to precedent. At the same time he vehemently opposed any tendency to exalt unduly the judiciary and was alert to prevent the courts as guardians of the people's rights from encroaching in their turn upon the liberties of the citizen. During his twenty-three years' service, he gave the opinion of the court in several famous cases, but in particular he attracted national attention by his ruling in one of the well-known "Granger cases," *Munn* vs. *Illinois* (69 *Ill.* 80). In this case, he upheld the validity of an act of the state legislature regulating grain elevators, and the United States Supreme Court, on appeal, sustained the Illinois decision upon every point (94 *U. S.* 113). This decision, rendered in 1876, was the beginning of a series of cases propounding the doctrine of the regulative power of the state over public service companies and all corporations in whose business public interests are involved. Coming at the beginning of the struggle for governmental regulation of big business —three decades before Roosevelt's war on the "trusts"—the case became one of the landmarks in the economic history of America.

The opinion in the case of *Munn* vs. *Ill.* was written in the seventy-sixth year of Breese's life —a tribute to the elasticity and alertness of his mental processes even in his old age. Early in his career, while a member of the circuit court, Breese told a Democratic rally in Montgomery County that it was compatible with judicial dignity for a judge to take an active part in politics, and even late in his career he saw nothing unbecoming in acting as a director of the Baltimore & Ohio Railroad while holding judicial office. His views in regard to the ethics of participating in politics were modified in time, but throughout his service on the bench, Breese maintained a broad sympathy with human affairs which was beneficial in the highest degree to his judicial duties. He was also conspicu-

ous for witty repartee on the bench. His opinions were couched in lucid language. His logic did not equal that of Marshall and his literary ability was inferior to Story's but his opinions were conspicuous for both argument and literary flavor. While still a young man, Breese undertook the task of reporting the decisions of the supreme court of Illinois down to date, with the result that *Breese's Reports,* published at Kaskaskia in 1831, cover the decisions of that court for the first eleven years. It was modestly announced by its editor as prompted by a "desire to discharge in some degree that duty which one of the sages of the law has said every man owes to his profession."

According to a colleague he was short in stature, deep-chested, careful in dress, near-sighted, and always wore spectacles. As a young man he was close-shaven with his black hair cut short; but in later years he suffered his beard to grow long and his hair to hang down over his shoulders, which gave him a venerable appearance. He had a weak voice. In social intercourse he was a combination of amiability and taciturnity, often delighting in learned conversation, frequently lapsing into superciliousness; he was vain, and at times obsessed with a desire to impress his associates with a sense of their inferiority. His vanity on more than one occasion proved his undoing. It led him to break with his benefactor, Kane, and it involved him in several unseemly controversies with the coarser-grained but more agile Douglas, in which he came off second best.

[W. D. Lewis, *Great Am. Lawyers* (1908), IV, 453–95; U. F. Linder, *Reminiscences of the Early Bench and Bar of Ill.* (1879), pp. 141–47; J. D. Caton, *Bench and Bar of Ill.* (1893), pp. 64, 201; *Proc. of the Chicago Bar in Memory of the Hon Sidney Breese* (1878); F. B. Crossley, *Courts and Lawyers of Ill.* (1916), I, 181–83. Breese's *Early Hist. of Ill. . . . until 1763,* ed. by T. Hoyne, was published in 1884, and contains an excellent memoir of Breese by Melville W. Fuller. The Breese-Douglas correspondence concerning the Illinois Central Ry. is reprinted in *Fergus Hist. Series,* no. XXIII, 63–98. His correspondence with Gov. Ninian Edwards is included in the *Edwards Papers* (1884), ed. by E. B. Washburne. Unpublished letters and papers of Breese are preserved in the Ill. State Hist. Lib. at Springfield and the Chicago Hist. Soc.]

K. W. C—e.

BRENNAN, ALFRED LAURENS (Feb. 14, 1853–June 14, 1921), illustrator, was born at Louisville, Ky., the son of John Fletcher and Evangeline (Williamson) Brennan. The father, a Canadian writer and publisher, served in the Northern army in the Civil War; the mother came of Pennsylvania Quaker stock. After the war the family removed to Cincinnati. The son was educated at private schools and Saint Dunstan's College, Prince Edward

Island, 1861–65, and by private tutors 1865–71. The father wanted him to take up printing; the son preferred art. Alfred's art studies began at the School of Design (McMicken bequest, University of Cincinnati), where he won a gold medal and an assistant-professorship in the school for one year. Later he worked with Frank Duveneck and H. F. Farny. After two years in Philadelphia he settled in New York City, about 1879. There he remained with an interval (1903–08) in Brookline, Mass., on an advertising contract, until his death. In pen-and-ink illustrations he attained an unsurpassed skill. Pennell pronounced him "the finest technician in America," and added that "there is probably no one living who has a greater knowledge of the requirements and limitations and possibilities of process." He was brilliant, with a vein of extravagant fancy, "an assiduous cultivator of whimsicality as a fine art." The flavor of his individuality pervaded all he did, even when he re-drew a photograph,—and there was much of that by artists in those days before the developed half-tone. He had a leaning toward classical subjects, illustrating, for example, a Greek play at Harvard. In the eighties and nineties, when this country possessed a remarkable school of pen-and-ink artists: Abbey, Blum, Pennell, Reinhart, Lungren, and others, Brennan was a commanding figure. There is in the work of some in this group the influence of Fortuny, and also of Rico, Vierge, and the Japanese. Harry Wilson Watrous explained this in part by the fact that Blum, Brennan, and others spent much time in the studio of Humphrey Moore, friend of Fortuny.

Brennan's assiduous courtship of the medium resulted in a large number of drawings,—7,000 or more. His illustrations, including delightful head and tail pieces, appeared in the *Century* (in the April 1903 number of which were published his pictures of the restored White House), *St. Nicholas, Life,* and other periodicals, as also in books, among which were F. Marion Crawford's *Katharine Lauderdale* (1894), Anthony Hope's *Phroso* and Charles Erskine Scott Wood's *Maia* (1918). Beside this, he designed book and magazine covers for Harper's, Scribner's, etc., painted in water-colors (exhibition, Keppel Galleries, New York, in 1891), painted portraits in oil (including one of T. L. DeVinne), and etched ("Divination in Tea Leaves" being published in the *American Art Review*). At the time of his death he was doing a series of water-colors reminiscent of his boyhood days. He also wrote magazine criticisms of pictures and books, both over his own name and over the pseudonym "Dirk Laurens." But it is by his pen-and-ink drawings that his position in American art is made secure. He had a picturesque personality, was fastidious, an eccentric dresser, a keen wit, and an expert pistol shot. On Feb. 14, 1883, he married Lucy Lee, a New Yorker, who survived him, with five children, when, after he had been ill in St. Luke's Hospital for two months, death came to him in Flatbush, Brooklyn, N. Y.

[For this sketch the printed accounts of Brennan's life have been verified or corrected by his daughter, Alfreda L. Brennan; *Am. Art Student,* Jan. 1922; *Who's Who in America,* 1906–07; obituaries in *N. Y. Times* and *Evening Post,* June 16, 1921, and the *Am. Art Annual,* vol. XVIII; critical estimates in *Am. Art Rev.,* I, 51 (article on Brennan's etchings by S. R. Koehler); Jos. Pennell, *Pen Drawing and Pen Draughtsmen* (1920), *Adventures of an Illustrator* (1925), and "A Forgotten Master," *Internat. Studio,* vol. LXXIV, pp. clxxxviii–ccii; F. Weitenkampf, *Am. Graphic Art* (1924).]

F. W.

BRENNER, VICTOR DAVID (June 12, 1871–Apr. 5, 1924), sculptor, medalist, was the son of George and Sarah (Margolis) Brenner. He was born in Shavli, Russia, a town of 5,000 inhabitants, not far from the Baltic. The officials were Russian, the cultural influences German. His grandfather was a blacksmith. His father set up the trade of metal-working at home. He also cut gravestones, snipped out silhouettes, carved in soapstone, engraved rings and brooches; in short, turned his hand to various forms of necessary and neighborly plastic art. In this environment of spontaneous artistic endeavor, Victor began to learn his craft at the age of thirteen, or earlier, his father meanwhile instructing him in history, languages, and the Talmud. Seals being then in vogue in Russia, the youth practised seal-making also. After three years, he became an itinerant journeyman in the simple arts he had followed, and later, he spent nine months working at line-engraving. In his eighteenth year he went to Riga, and there learned jewelry engraving. Indeed his whole life, until his final years, was an amazing interplay of earning and learning. On his arrival in America, he found employment as a die-cutter; and just as in a previous generation the young Saint-Gaudens had labored at his cameo-cutter's lathe by day, and studied at Cooper Union in the evening, so Brenner at about the same age was working at his craft by day, and following the Cooper Union courses at night. Later, he studied at the Art Students' League and at the National Academy of Design. In 1894 he was able to set up for himself as die-cutter for jewelry and silver, his early training in Russia serving him in good stead. He prospered, and sent for his family. Prof. Ettinger of the City College chanced to see a Beethoven badge he had made, and brought him to the attention of the American Numismatic Society. That body at once recognized Brenner's artistic ability, and aided him materially in establishing his fame as a medalist. Brenner was indefatigable, ambitious, filled with high ideals. By 1898, through strenuous endeavor, he had earned enough to go to Paris, there to spend three years in study under Roty and Charpentier, the world-famous medalists whose genius was then enhancing the possibilities of bas-relief. Brenner also studied sculpture at the Académie Julien, under Puech, Verlet, and Dubois. In 1900 he gained honorable mention at the Paris Salon, and a bronze medal at the Paris Exposition. Returning to New York with a mind enriched and broadened by study and travel, Brenner was again the practising die-cutter, badge-maker, medalist. He thereby earned yet another period of earnest work in Paris. The year 1906 found him once more in New York, resolved to become known as a sculptor and medalist in the purely artistic field. A Lincoln coin had been proposed in 1886. A few five-cent pieces were struck in nickel, but the project was dropped. About twenty years later, when Brenner, as one of our foremost medalists, was modeling the Panama Canal medal, to be awarded to Canal workers of two years' standing, and was receiving a sitting from Roosevelt, whose portrait is on the obverse, he showed the President a Lincoln plaque of his design. This was largely instrumental in the choice of Brenner as designer of the Lincoln cent, our first portrait coin (issued August 1909). The result was well liked, except for the too prominent initials, V. D. B. Over 22,000,000 of the coins were in circulation before the initials were removed from the final design; even the single letter B, when tried, seemed unduly conspicuous. Aside from his Schenley Memorial Fountain in Pittsburgh (1916), and a number of busts, his work in the round is little known, but how well he realized his ambition to be a medalist of the first rank is shown by the fact that many distinctively artistic societies, such as the National Academy of Design, the Fine Arts Federation of New York, the Art Institute of Chicago, and in particular the American Numismatic Society, sought his services. His designs for medals, plaquettes, and plaques mount into the hundreds, if both obverse and reverse are counted, as they should be. Most of these are struck in bronze or silver, a few are cast. In 1920, at the American Numismatic Society's international exhibition of work by contemporary medalists, sixty-nine pieces by Brenner were

on view, some of them doubling themselves by being shown both in obverse and in reverse. Many of these works were designed for clubs, societies, anniversaries, centennials, conferences. Others, either by portraiture or allegory or both, honored famous persons, quick or dead. The likenesses are excellent. Brenner's studies had given him command of the nude figure, used to advantage in his Sorolla medal, his University of Wisconsin plaquette, and other examples. He was happy in the draped figure also, as in his Fine Arts Federation plaque. Like most medalists, he often over-elaborated the anecdotal details demanded, and so missed sculptural simplicity. His Whistler medal escapes this snare of pictorial insistence. Its reverse, dominated by a peacock crying "Messieurs les Ennemis," is a triumph of imaginative suggestion, with a tang of satire. Indeed every work by Brenner was thoughtfully done. He gave his best, seeking always to make that best still better. He was of sensitive nervous organization, and his close application to his art no doubt shortened his life. His gentle, dark-bearded features often showed a trace of Slavic melancholy. His last years were clouded by long illness. But he was happy in his marriage, in 1913, to Ann Reed, and happy also in his membership in three artistic associations, the National Sculpture Society, the Architectural League of New York, the American Numismatic Society. His work is represented in the Paris Mint, and in the Luxembourg Museum; the Munich Glyptothek; the Vienna Numismatic Society; the Metropolitan Museum, New York; the Museum of Fine Arts, Boston; the American Numismatic Society, New York. He died at the New York Hospital.

[Archives of the Am. Numismatic Soc.; special illustrated article by Paul U. Kellogg, *Survey*, Oct. 2, 1915; obituaries in the *Numismatist*, May 1924, and *N. Y. Times*, Apr. 6, 1924. Illustrations of Brenner's work appear in the *Catalogue of the Exhibition of the Am. Numismatic Soc.*, 1920.]   A.A—s.

BRENT, MARGARET (1600–1670/71), America's first feminist, was one of the thirteen children of Richard Brent, lord of Admington and Stoke, and his wife, Elizabeth Reed, daughter of Edward Reed, lord of Tusburie and Witten, all of Gloucester, England. The Brents of Stoke traced their ancestry to Ode Brent, knight (1066), while Elizabeth Reed's family claimed descent from William the Conqueror. The abundant resources of the new world lured Margaret and her sister Mary to accompany their brothers Giles and Fulke Brent to St. Mary's, Md., in November 1638. Blood relationships or political affiliations secured to the Brent pioneers unusual favors in large land grants and high offices.

Margaret, bent upon individual independence, came to Gov. Leonard Calvert [*q.v.*], who later married her sister Anne, armed with letters from Lord Baltimore claiming for the Brent sisters portions of land as large and privileges as great as had been given the first arrivals. Having brought over five men and four maid servants, the sisters were entitled to 800 acres of land under the colonization inducements offered to women. Through their letters they received much larger grants. On Oct. 4, 1639, Margaret obtained from the Assembly a patent for 70½ acres in St. Mary's, which she called "Sister's Freehold." This was the first grant recorded at St. Mary's and Margaret was the first woman of Maryland to hold land in her own right. Later she obtained a tract of 1,000 acres and from time to time accumulated more land as she transported little groups of men and women. Forceful and fearless, she aided Gov. Calvert in suppressing the Claiborne Rebellion by assembling an armed group of volunteers to join his forces on his return from Virginia in August 1646. He proved his confidence in her ability by appointing her his executrix (Letters of Administration granted June 19, 1647). The Provincial court appointed her attorney for Lord Baltimore, that she might collect rents and take care of both estates. In this capacity she entered more law suits than any one in the colony. Because of her heavy responsibilities, she appealed to the Assembly, Jan. 21, 1648 (*Archives of Maryland*, I, 215), for voice in their counsels and two votes in their proceedings, one for herself as a landowner and the other as attorney for Lord Baltimore. Gov. Greene refused her plea. Resenting this action she followed her brother Giles Brent's example and established a new home called "Peace" in Westmoreland County, Va., in 1650. With vast property in both states, as lady of the manor she held court leets annually with feasts and frolics for her people. On Dec. 26, 1663, she made her will. The exact date of her death like that of her birth is not definitely known. Her will was admitted to probate May 19, 1671. Of queenly dignity, keen intelligence, ready sympathy, and great womanly charm, this Portia of Maryland possessed a broad vision far beyond her day.

[W. B. Chilton, "The Brent Family," runs through several volumes of the *Va. Mag. of Hist. and Biog.*, Apr. 1905–Jan. 1913. Hester Dorsey Richardson, *Sidelights on Md. Hist.* (2 vols., 1913), presents documentary proofs of Margaret Brent's business acumen. See also Mary E. W. Ramey, *Chronicles of Mistress Margaret Brent* (1915); Jas. Walter Thomas, *Chronicles of Colonial Md.* (1913) and John L. Bozman, *Hist. of Md.* (1837), vol. II.]   E. M. C—n.

BRENTANO, LORENZ (Nov. 4, 1813–Sept. 17, 1891), statesman, journalist, was the son of

Peter Paul Bartholomaeus Brentano and his wife Helene Haeger. He was born in Mannheim, Baden, received a classical education, and studied jurisprudence at the universities of Heidelberg and Freiburg. He had degrees from Heidelberg and Giessen. After beginning his career in Rastatt and Bruchsal, he practised law in Mannheim. Several times he was elected to the position of burgomaster of his native city, but was never confirmed by the government. Sent to the Chamber of Deputies in 1845, he joined the radical party of Hecker, Itzstein, and Sander, but he did not take part in the insurrection started by Hecker in 1848, nor in the uprising attempted by Struve and Blind in the following September. However, he courageously and eloquently defended the revolutionists at their trial in Freiburg. Elected to a seat in the Frankfurt Parliament, he attached himself to the liberal side and distinguished himself by his speeches against the then Prince of Prussia, and by his sarcastic refusal of the resulting challenge to a duel by Baron von Fincke. When the Revolution spread over Baden in 1849 and the Grand Duke had fled, Brentano was against his own protests placed at the head of the provisional revolutionary government. In the capacity of "Dictator of Baden" he labored for the maintenance of order, and stood for the confining of the Revolution to the territory of Baden. This was a tactical blunder, for which he was unjustly accused of treachery by Struve and the extremists of the party, who instituted legislation that compelled Brentano to take to flight. From Switzerland he addressed a justification of his acts to the people of Baden. The fugitive emigrated to the United States in 1850, where he heard that the restored reactionary government of Baden had sentenced him to imprisonment for life. He settled at first at Pottsville, Pa., editing a German weekly antislavery paper called *Der Leuchtturm*. In 1851 he bought a farm near Kalamazoo, Mich., which he cultivated zealously for about eight years, but hardly with distinguished success. In 1859 he removed to Chicago, engaged in the practise of law, but in the following year joined the staff of the *Illinois Staatszeitung*. From the proceeds of the sale of his farm in 1862 he bought a half-interest in the paper from George Schneider, who was sent by President Lincoln on an important mission to Helsingfors and northern Europe. Through skill and hard work with the aid of his partner A. C. Hesing, Brentano succeeded in making the *Illinois Staatszeitung* not only one of the most influential dailies of Chicago, but also the leading German Republican paper of the entire Northwest. In 1862 he was elected to the

Illinois state legislature and in 1868 was a presidential elector on the Grant-Colfax ticket. For five years he was president of the Chicago Board of Education.

After a general amnesty had been declared in Germany, Brentano revisited his native land in 1869, and served as United States consul at Dresden, 1872–76. After his return he was elected, in 1876, to the Forty-fifth Congress of the United States, continuing until Mar. 3, 1879. Upon his retirement he spent much time in historical and legal investigations, aiming to compare and contrast the American and European codes and methods of criminal procedure. Illustrative of this type of work was his report of the trial of Guiteau, the assassin of President Garfield. He also wrote a history of the case of *Kring* vs. *Missouri* (107 *U.S.* 221), which was republished in Leipzig. His last political activity was his support of Grover Cleveland for the presidency, which meant a separation from his long allegiance to the Republican party, and his first appearance as an independent voter. The last years of his life he was compelled to spend in retirement owing to a partial stroke of paralysis. He died in Chicago, Sept. 17, 1891. He was married to Caroline Aberle.

When compared with his associates of the revolutionary period of 1848–49, Brentano was described as lacking the magnetic personality and inspiring eloquence of Hecker and certain others of the revolutionary heroes. In speech incisive and intellectual, in action deliberate and calculating, in disposition conservative and cautious, he was the lawyer, not the inspirer of the Revolution in Baden. His greater adaptability enabled him to rise to higher positions in this country than Hecker and Struve and most others of his fellow revolutionists who came to the United States, with the exception of the younger, more brilliant Carl Schurz.

[*Deutsch-amerikanisches Conversations-Lexikon*, by Prof. Alex. J. Schem (1869–74), vol. II; *Chicago und sein Deutschtum, 1901–02* (German-American Biog. Publ. Co., Cleveland, Ohio); *In Memoriam: Lorenz Brentano* (a volume of memorial addresses and obituary articles in leading American and German American newspapers, 1891).]   A.B.F.

BRERETON, JOHN. [See BRIERTON, JOHN, fl. 1572–1619.]

BRETT, WILLIAM HOWARD (July 1, 1846–Aug. 24, 1918), librarian, was born in Braceville, Ohio, the son of Morgan Lewis Brett, a descendant of John Alden, and of Jane (Brokaw) Brett, of Virginian ancestry. His parents were members of the Trumbull Phalanx, a short-lived Fourierist community experiment. Soon after his birth the family moved to the larger

town of Warren, where William spent his boyhood. Among his early formative influences were W. N. Porter and his little bookshop, around the corner from the Brett home, to which the small boy made a short back-door cut, and where his intimate and broad acquaintance with books began. At fourteen he became librarian of the high school library, contributing this service until he left school at sixteen to earn his living. He was soon a clerk in Mr. Porter's store, to which he returned at intervals between other ventures during the next dozen years. During the Civil War he made repeated vigorous but unsuccessful attempts to enlist, finally learning to play the fife and drum in order to be enrolled as a musician in the 196th Ohio Volunteer Infantry, with which he managed to get into the actual fighting at once. Following the war he spent a year at the University of Michigan and another at Western Reserve, then located at Hudson, Ohio, but lack of funds prevented completion of his college course. In 1874 he entered the Cobb & Andrews Book Store in Cleveland as a clerk, and in the next ten years he became known as the best-informed bookman in the city. It was therefore natural and fortunate that when, in 1884, the trustees of the Cleveland Public Library were looking for a new librarian, Brett was chosen for the position he was to occupy for the next thirty-four years. He introduced modern methods, reclassified and catalogued the books, and opened up the shelves to give free access to readers. Under his direction this library developed from a small, badly organized institution into a great city-wide system, adding to the main library a net-work of branches, stations, and school libraries, and becoming notable among the libraries of the country for its splendid service. Largely instrumental in organizing the Library School of Western Reserve University in 1894, he was its dean until his death. Among his contributions to library progress was the *Cumulative Index*, which later became the *Reader's Guide to Periodical Literature,* an indispensable tool of all libraries. He was president of the American Library Association for the year 1896–97. He organized and was first president of the Ohio Library Association. In the American Library Association War Service in the World War his work was conspicuous, particularly at Newport News, where he spent some months organizing and directing an efficient dispatch office for books shipped overseas. Of medium height, compactly built, with well-formed blond head alertly held, keen eyes of vivid blue, and a ready smile, he kept always his eager, boyish enthusiasm and a winning friendliness, for his interest in people, like his interest in books, continued to grow with the years.

Struck by an automobile on Aug. 24, 1918, he died after a few unconscious hours. His wife, Alice (Allen) Brett, whom he married in 1879, five children, and six grandchildren survived him.

[The facts about William Howard Brett were gathered chiefly from himself, his family, and lifelong friends, with verification of dates from *Who's Who in America,* and other biographical dictionaries. The *Library Jour.,* Nov. 1918, devoted pages 793–807 to a sketch of his life and appreciations by fellow workers; the *Open Shelf* for Sept.–Oct. 1918, published by the Cleveland Pub. Lib., is entirely a memorial number; and all Cleveland newspapers published obituary notices following his death. His own writings were chiefly professional articles published in the Library periodicals.]   L. A. E.

BREVOORT, JAMES RENWICK (July 20, 1832–Dec. 15, 1918), painter, was born in Yonkers township, Westchester County, N. Y., son of Elias and Mary (Brown) Brevoort and notable member of a distinguished old family of this state whose ancestor, Jan Heinrich van Brevoort, emigrated from Holland and settled in New Amsterdam about 1643. His early years were spent in Williamsbridge and Fordham. He attended the local schools and later received most of his art education in the New York studio of the late Thomas S. Cummings, then vice-president of the National Academy of Design. For four years he worked in the office of his cousin James Renwick, architect of Grace Church, New York, assisting him in making drawings for St. Patrick's Cathedral. Brevoort took the full course given in the School of Design of New York University, and on June 28, 1854, received a testimonial from the University certifying that he had devoted several years to the study of architecture. In 1861 he was elected an associate of the National Academy of Design, and a National Academician in 1863. He was a member of the Academy for more than fifty-seven years. In 1872 he began landscape painting and at that time also became a professor of perspective at the school of the National Academy.

He married, first, Augusta Cuthill, who died early. On Apr. 14, 1873, he married, second, in Burlington, Ia., Marie Louise Bascom, recipient of the first medal awarded by the school of the National Academy. Brevoort enjoyed the opportunities for painting in interesting localities and visited nearly all the schools and art centers of Europe, studying the ancient and modern works of art in the galleries of the Old World. Most of his time was spent in England, Holland, and Italy. He was made a member of the Royal Academy at Urbino, the birthplace of Raphael.

His paintings of Italian scenery were very successful, especially those of the Italian lakes. Returning from abroad in 1880, he made his home in Yonkers, N. Y., building a private residence there in 1890. He became a member of the Century Association in 1882 and maintained interest in the organization until his death at his home in Yonkers in 1918. Brevoort was sympathetic and truthful in his portrayal of landscapes and achieved original treatment in his atmospheric effects. All of his work clearly indicated his idealism and fine feeling. His "Harvest Scene with a Storm Coming Up" shows considerable power and the effect of light is done with skill. Representative of Brevoort's style are: "A New England Scene"; "Morning in Early Winter"; "A Gray Day"; "Sunset on a Moor"; "Dawn"; "Spring"; "A Scene in Holland"; "Lake Como"; "The Night Wind Swept the Moorland Lea"; "Storm on an English Moor"; "May Morning at Lake Como"; "Wild November Comes at Last"; "Windy Evening on the Moor."

[H. T. Tuckerman, *Book of the Artists* (1867), p. 566; *Catalog of Collection of Paintings and Sketches and Studies of J. R. Brevoort, Sold 1873;* J. D. Champlin & C. C. Perkins, *Cyc. of Painters and Paintings* (1886), I, 204; C. E. Allison, *Hist. of Yonkers* (1896), p. 406; M. A. Hamm, *Famous Families of N. Y.* (1902), p. 42; *Who's Who in America,* 1916–17; family data.]   J. M. H.

BREWER, CHARLES (Mar. 27, 1804–Oct. 11, 1885), sea captain and merchant, was born in Boston, son of Moses, a dry-goods dealer, and Abigail (May) Brewer, both of old New England families. An ancestor, Daniel Brewer, had come from London to Roxbury, Mass., in 1632. His father died in 1813 and the widow carried on the business while Charles, the only boy in a family of five, attended various near-by private schools. Apprenticed to a merchant at the age of fourteen he acquired a knowledge of business but a loathing for the counting room. His mother, who knew his longing for adventure and hoped that the hardships of seafaring life would prove an antidote, allowed him when seventeen to go on a sixteen-months voyage to Calcutta. Undismayed, he next went on voyages to England and the East Indies. In 1823 he sailed on the ship *Paragon* for the Hawaiian Islands. There the loading of sandalwood was interrupted when the vessel was chartered by King Kamehameha II for a state funeral. Returning to Boston, Brewer was promoted to second officer for a trip to England, and during a storm fell from the main yard, bruising one leg so badly that he was permanently crippled. From 1825 to 1829 he was first officer on the brig *Chinchilla,* which used Honolulu as her base for trading cruises between Alaska, Kamchatka, and China. Early in 1829 he returned to Boston, but in October sailed as mate of the brig *Ivanhoe*, which traded between Canton, Honolulu, and Mazatlan in Mexico until 1831. He finally quit the vessel in Honolulu because of a quarrel arising out of a hint to the captain that the attempt to fill water casks on Sunday was an infraction of the laws which American missionaries had induced the Hawaiian king to make so strict that smoking and cooking on the Sabbath were crimes. He then became captain of a small schooner trading between Hawaii and the American coast from Mexico to Alaska. In 1833 he commanded the schooner *Unity,* the second American vessel to enter the Sea of Okhotsk, and later claimed credit for discovering the whale fishery there. In 1834 and 1835 he again visited Okhotsk and Petropavlovsk, and in February 1836 was taken as a partner in a prosperous Honolulu trading establishment by Henry A. Peirce [*q.v.*], who departed for Boston leaving him to manage the local business of bartering cotton goods, rum, and "yankee notions" for sandalwood, furs, and hides. When Peirce returned in 1839, Brewer in turn went to Boston, where he married Martha Turner and set sail with her for Hawaii in March 1841. He again took charge of the business in Honolulu, and when Peirce withdrew in 1843 the firm became C. Brewer & Company. Under this name it still flourishes. In Honolulu, then the Pacific emporium for whalers, fur traders, and China merchants, Brewer prospered greatly and established an enviable reputation for integrity and public spirit. In 1839, when France took umbrage at the refusal of the native king to allow Roman Catholic missionaries to land and threatened hostilities, his was the largest contribution to the fund of $20,000 raised to satisfy the demands of Commander La Place. He gave liberally to local charities, and in 1843 enabled King Kamehameha III, his intimate friend, to finance a mission to England which secured recognition of Hawaiian independence. Another benefaction was the introduction to the islands of the beautiful night-blooming cereus. In 1845 he disposed of most of his Hawaiian interests and took his family to Boston. A business trip to Honolulu in 1847–49 completed his seafaring life, but he continued in the Hawaiian and Far Eastern trade, establishing after the Civil War a company which owned a fine fleet of barks sailing to Hawaii, Manila, and Hong-Kong in the eighties. He retired in 1884 and in the following year died at his home in Jamaica Plain. A man of strong character and sharp tongue, he was at heart kindly in disposition and liberal in giving of the large fortune which he had accumulated.

[Charles Brewer, *Reminiscences* (1884); Josephine Sullivan, *Hist. of C. Brewer and Company, Ltd.* (1926).]

W. L. W. Jr.

BREWER, DAVID JOSIAH (June 20, 1837–Mar. 28, 1910), jurist, was born in Smyrna, Asia Minor. His father, Josiah Brewer, from Berkshire, Mass., was a Yale graduate who had gone to Turkey as a missionary in 1830. His mother, Emilia Field, was the daughter of a distinguished New England clergyman and the sister of Justice Stephen J. Field, David Dudley Field, and Cyrus W. Field. The Brewers returned in 1838 and settled in Wethersfield, Conn. After attending Wesleyan University for two years, young Brewer went to Yale where he graduated with honors in 1856. He then studied law for a year in the office of his uncle, David Dudley Field, spent a year at the Albany Law School where he graduated in 1858, and was promptly admitted to the New York bar. He decided to cast in his lot with the new West and in September settled in Leavenworth, Kan., his home until 1890. He embarked almost at once upon his long judicial career. In 1861 he was appointed commissioner of the federal circuit court for the district of Kansas; in 1862 he was elected judge of the probate and criminal courts of Leavenworth County; from 1865 to 1869 he was judge of the first judicial district of Kansas; from 1869 to 1870 he served as city attorney of Leavenworth. In 1870, at the age of thirty-three, he was elected to the supreme court of Kansas where he sat for fourteen years, being reëlected in 1876 and 1882. In 1884 President Arthur appointed him to the federal circuit court for the eighth circuit. He was appointed by President Harrison in 1889 as associate justice of the United States Supreme Court to succeed Justice Stanley Matthews. He remained on the court until his death. He and his uncle, Justice Field, were colleagues until 1898.

In his constitutional principles Brewer was a moderate conservative. He was a stern defender of personal liberty and property rights. As circuit judge he had refused to follow the dictum in the Granger Cases (*Munn* vs. *Illinois*, 94 *U. S.* 113) that legislative power to fix public utility rates is unlimited (*C. & N. W. Ry. Co.* vs. *Dey*, 35 *Fed.* 866), and spoke for the court in *Reagan* vs. *Farmers' Loan & Trust Co.* (154 *U. S.* 362), holding that due process of law entitles a carrier to a fair return on its investment. His strict regard for what he deemed reasonable freedom of contract led him to agree with the court in invalidating the ten hour law for bakers (*Lochner* vs. *New York*, 198 *U.S.* 45), and to dissent in cases sustaining an eight hour law for miners (*Holden* vs. *Hardy*, 169 *U.S.* 366), and an eight hour law on public work (*Atkin* vs. *Kansas*, 191 *U.S.* 207). He wrote the court's opinion, however, in *Muller* vs. *Oregon* (208 *U.S.* 412), upholding a ten hour law for women in industry. He dissented vigorously in the Chinese Exclusion cases (*Fong Yue Ting* vs. *United States*, 149 *U.S.* 698, *United States* vs. *Sing Tuck*, 194 *U.S.* 161, *United States* vs. *Ju Toy*, 198 *U.S.* 253), because of what he deemed arbitrary denial of personal rights. On the circuit bench he had held that brewers driven out of business by a prohibition act were entitled to compensation (*State* vs. *Walruff*, 26 *Fed.* 178). This doctrine was overruled in *Kidd* vs. *Pearson* (128 *U.S.* 1). He viewed with concern the drift toward federal centralization of power, and one of his ablest opinions is that in *Kansas* vs. *Colorado* (206 *U.S.* 46), in which he vigorously rejected the theory that Congress could deal with national problems by using powers not delegated by the Constitution. Of similar import is his opinion in *Keller* vs. *United States* (213 *U.S.* 138), and his dissent in the Lottery Case (188 *U.S.* 321). That he was not a strict constructionist, however, is shown by his notable opinions in *South Carolina* vs. *United States* (199 *U.S.* 437), sustaining a federal tax on the proceeds of the South Carolina liquor dispensary, in *Wilson* vs. *Shaw* (204 *U.S.* 24), upholding the right of Congress to build the Panama Canal, and particularly in the case of *In re Debs* (158 *U.S.* 564), in which the power of a federal court to issue an injunction in a labor dispute for the protection of federal interests was sustained. Justice Brewer was, in fact, an ardent defender of the use of the injunction (see his address, "Government by Injunction," *National Corporation Reporter*, XV, 848).

A life-long advocate of international peace, Brewer was able to render signal service to that cause as president of the commission created by Congress in 1895 to investigate the boundary between Venezuela and British Guiana after President Cleveland's startling message on that controversy (see *Report of the Commission, etc.*, 3 vols., 1897). With Chief Justice Fuller he served as American representative on the arbitral tribunal which in 1898 made the award which ended the dispute (see Latané, *A History of American Foreign Policy*, ch. XX. The official documents are found in Moore's *Digest of International Law*, VI, 533–83. See also a note by Charles Henry Butler, "The Services of Justices Fuller and Brewer in Questions of Inter-

national Law," *American Journal of International Law*, IV, 909). His continued interest in the cause of peace was evidenced by many speeches and papers. He attended nearly all of the Mohonk conferences (see *Mohonk Addresses*, 1910), and in 1909 addressed the New Jersey State Bar Association on "The Mission of the United States in the Cause of Peace" (*Yearbook*, 1909–10). With Charles Henry Butler he wrote the treatise on international law in the *Cyclopedia of Law and Procedure* (1906). He was a vice-president and supporter of the American Society of International Law from its foundation.

Brewer was unique among his judicial colleagues in the freedom and frequency with which he discussed problems of current interest before popular audiences. He was an orator of distinction, with a smack of the pulpit in his utterances. He was a vigorous anti-imperialist and believed the Philippines should be given independence with guaranteed neutrality (see his address, "The Spanish War, a Prophecy or an Exception," before the Liberal Club of Buffalo in 1899). He favored woman suffrage, and advocated the restriction of immigration. He spoke and wrote widely on legal topics, and on the high duties of lawyers and judges. He believed that fair criticism of the courts was wholesome. He addressed university and popular audiences on the obligations of citizenship (*American Citizenship*, the Dodge Lectures at Yale, 1902). In 1890 he accepted a lectureship on corporations in the law school of the Columbian University (now George Washington University).

Broad sympathies, keen civil interest, and splendid executive ability drew Brewer into many forms of public and social service. For five years before his death he was president of the Associated Charities in Washington (see "Justice Brewer and Organized Charity," *Survey*, XXIV, 119). Always interested in missions he served for years as vice-president of the American Missionary Association. He was a loyal member of the Congregational Church. In 1861 he married Louisa Landon of Burlington, Vt., who died in 1898, and in 1901 he married Emma Minor Mott of Washington, D.C. He was physically large and vigorous, genial in disposition, democratic in his social relations, and a famous story teller.

[There is no adequate biography or memoir. Brief sketches of a general sort are found in Henry Wilson Scott, *Distinguished Am. Lawyers*, p. 75 (sketch by Warren Watson); and in H. L. Carson, *The Supreme Court of the U.S.* (1902), II, 538. Obituaries appeared at the time of Brewer's death in numerous popular and legal periodicals. Besides the publications and addresses mentioned in the text he wrote many articles for law journals and popular magazines. These may be readily found in the standard periodical indices. In 1899 he edited with A. E. Allen and Wm. Schuyler *The World's Best Essays*, in ten volumes. His opinions as justice of the Supreme Court are found in 133–216 *U. S.* He wrote the opinion of the court in 526 cases, 70 of which involved constitutional problems. He dissented in 215 cases, in 53 of which he wrote separate opinions and of these 18 related to constitutional problems. He concurred in 38 cases, writing 8 separate concurring opinions.]   R. E. C.

BREWER, MARK SPENCER (Oct. 22, 1837–Mar. 18, 1901), congressman, was born in Addison Township, Oakland County, Mich., and died in Washington, D. C. His ancestor Peter Brewer, a native of Holland, had served in the Revolution and subsequently settled in Dutchess County, N. Y. Peter 2nd removed to Michigan Territory in 1832, and built a log cabin in the wilderness of Oakland County. His fifth son, Mark, spent nineteen years of his life on his father's farm. He studied law in the office of Gov. Wisner and began practise in Pontiac in 1864. As a member of the state Senate from 1872 to 1874, he established a reputation for hard work and good judgment that made him an available candidate for office in times of political emergency. He was elected to Congress in 1876 and in 1878. Appointed by his friend, President Garfield, as consul-general at Berlin in 1881, during four years of service Brewer made studies of the bimetallic standard, the credit and trade system, and wages and labor, in Germany, which enabled him to do effective work on the stump in the critical McKinley-Bryan campaign in 1896. In 1887 he was returned to the House of Representatives, where he served until the Democratic landslide of 1891. On the return of the Republicans to power, President McKinley appointed him a member of the Civil Service Commission, in which capacity he served from January 1898 until his death. He was drawn into the controversy over political contributions from federal office-holders that raged between Senators Chandler and Gallinger of New Hampshire, and made an elaborate report on the subject. Brewer was a man of large influence in Michigan affairs because he stood for sound policies rather than political expediency.

[*Dept. of State: Consular Reports* (1882–84), VI, 20, 184, XII, 40, 304, XIII, 43, 250; *Sixteenth Report* (1900) of the Civil Service Commission; *Mich. Biogs.* (1924); obituary in the *Washington Post*, Mar. 19, 1901.]   C. M.

BREWER, THOMAS MAYO (Nov. 21, 1814–Jan. 23, 1880), ornithologist and oölogist, son of Col. James Brewer, a Revolutionary patriot who took part in the "Boston Tea Party," was born in Boston, Mass., where he spent his entire life with the exception of some winters in Washington and a trip to Europe. He was edu-

cated at Harvard, graduating from the College in 1835 and from the Medical School in 1838. He practised his profession for a few years but realizing that writing was much more to his taste than medicine, and being always an ardent politician, he abandoned his practise and became a regular contributor to the *Boston Atlas*, a noted Whig journal, and later its editor. Subsequently he became associated with the publishing firm of Swan & Tileston (afterward Brewer & Tileston), a business in which he continued until his retirement in 1875. He was always interested in the cause of public education and was an active member of the Boston School Committee from 1844 until his death. In 1849 he married Sally R. Coffin, daughter of Stephen Coffin of Damariscotta, Me. In spite of his devotion to business for practically his entire life, he managed to maintain and develop an early interest in birds and to become one of the leading ornithologists of America, with a well established reputation abroad. He was a close personal friend of Audubon during the latter years of the great painter-naturalist's life and in the second edition of the *Birds of America* are to be found a number of acknowledgments for information furnished by young Brewer. He likewise made the acquaintance of Spencer F. Baird while the latter was still at his home in Carlisle, Pa., and a steady correspondence was kept up between them. Brewer joined the Boston Society of Natural History in 1835 at the age of twenty-one and for over forty years contributed ornithological papers and notes to the Society's *Proceedings*.

His first notable paper was a Supplement (1837) to Prof. Hitchcock's *Catalogue of the Birds of Massachusetts* to which he added forty-five species. Next in 1840 he published a small octavo edition of Wilson's *Ornithology* which for the first time brought this classic within the reach of every one who desired to possess it, and in an appendix Brewer added a synopsis of all the birds then known in North America. In 1857 appeared the first (and only) volume of his *North American Oölogy*, a quarto issued by the Smithsonian Institution as one of its Contributions to Knowledge, in which the eggs of each species were figured in colors, with a full description of the life history and distribution of the birds. Unfortunately the cost of the plates proved so great that the publication had to be discontinued, though it apparently gave Brewer more prestige than any other of his works. In 1875 he was fortunately enabled to publish the remainder of his bird biographies in connection with that now famous classic, the *History of*

North American Birds by Baird, Brewer and Ridgway. The entire biographical portion, amounting to about two-thirds of the letter-press, is by Brewer and demonstrates the breadth of his knowledge of American ornithological literature and his intimate acquaintance with the nests and eggs of our birds. His ornithological work was continued up to a short time before his death, which occurred after an illness of only a few weeks. He was stricken at the height of his ornithological career, just as he had retired from business with the idea of being free to prose-cute his studies.

By contemporary biographers Brewer is said to have been greatly esteemed socially, while his warm sympathy, loyalty to his friends, and his convictions of truth and duty, were marked traits in his character. His political experiences, perhaps, seem to have made him fond of argu-ment and he replied quickly to criticism and en-gaged in wordy controversies, that with Elliot Coues on the merits of the English sparrow be-ing carried on for a long time in the pages of the *American Naturalist*. Being essentially a closet ornithologist he was rather impatient at the younger bird students who ventured to dis-cover new facts regarding bird life not contained in the published accounts and was hence not one to encourage the development of new ornitholo-gists; among the rising generation at Cambridge William Brewster was said to have been the only one who could get along with him.

Brewer may be regarded as America's first oölogist, but in the widest sense of that term, as he considered the breeding habits and life his-tory of the birds, not merely the character and value of the egg-shells,—matters which are the chief concern of many oölogists of to-day.

[Editorial sketch of his life, *Bull. Nuttall Ornith. Club*, Apr. 1880, pp. 102–104; manuscript letters to Baird in Smithsonian Institution; personal recollec-tions furnished by Ruthven Deane.]   W. S.

BREWER, WILLIAM HENRY (Sept. 14, 1828–Nov. 2, 1910), scientist, was of Dutch and French Huguenot ancestry. His father, Henry, was a descendant of Adam Brouwer Berkhoven who came to New Amsterdam in 1642. The name Berkhoven was dropped about 1700, and Brouwer used as the family name, but later changed to Brower and after the Revolution to Brewer. William's mother, Rebecca DuBois, was a descendant of Louis DuBois who in 1660 settled in the Huguenot colony in Ulster County, N. Y. William was born in Poughkeepsie, N. Y., but his boyhoood was spent on a farm near Ithaca. At Ithaca Academy where he had his early schooling, he developed a keen interest in

plants and minerals which led to the reading of such books as he could obtain dealing with ge-ology, botany, and chemistry, and especially their applications to agriculture. Encouraged by his parents, he entered in 1848 the new school of science at Yale, now the Sheffield Scientific School, where he graduated in 1852 with the first class to obtain a degree. Under Silliman, Dana, and J. P. Norton his interest in science was greatly stimulated, and in 1855 he went abroad for further study, spending a year at Heidelberg under Bunsen in chemistry, and a year in Munich with Liebig. Botany and ge-ology also occupied his attention, and he made many excursions through Germany, Switzerland, and France botanizing and geologizing. In 1858 he married Angelina Jameson, who died in 1860, and in 1868 he married Georgiana Robinson.

Brewer was a man of great versatility, an ex-plorer in all the sciences underlying agriculture, never a specialist in the modern sense, but con-tributing much in many fields. For four years, 1860–64, he was in the wilds of California as first assistant to Josiah D. Whitney in the geo-logical survey of the state, gaining intimate knowledge of its geography, geology, and bot-any. As he wrote in his diary, during the first two years he traveled 2,067 miles on foot, 3,900 miles on mule-back, and 3,210 by other convey-ance. Nothing escaped his eyes, mountains were measured and named, valleys mapped, minerals and plants collected. Of plants he collected about 2,000 species, the basis of his work on the flora of California, published by Brewer and Sereno Watson, under the title of "Polypetalæ," in Vol-ume I of the *Geological Survey of California*. From 1864 to 1903 he held the chair of agri-culture in the Sheffield Scientific School at Yale. With his broad outlook, his wide knowledge and extended experience, combined with a personal-ity that radiated power and strength of purpose, he was able to bring to fruition many movements for the public good. Betterment of agriculture was his chief thought and to that end he was active, with his colleague S. W. Johnson, in the establishment of the first agricultural experiment station in this country, and for thrty-three years he was on the board of control of the Connecti-cut station. He made for the tenth census a careful study of the cereal production of the United States with special reference to distribu-tion of production in accordance with geograph-ical and climatic features; the relation of cereal production to the growing of live stock; distribu-tion of woodland and forest systems in the coun-try; also a brief history of American agriculture. As a member of the National Academy of Sciences he was active in the study of many questions submitted by the national government, such as the manufacture of glucose sugar from starch (1882); the sorghum sugar industry; preservation of the forest resources of the country (1896); desirability of scientific explorations of the Philippine Islands (1903). To the annual reports of the Connecticut Board of Agriculture he was a constant contributor for twenty-five years on a great variety of topics of interest to the farmer, such as the origin and constitution of soils; woods and woodlands; tree planting with reference to sanitary effects; pollution of streams; the art of stock breeding. He was a pioneer in public health work, active in the organization of a state board of health for Connecticut (president for sixteen years); of a city board of health for New Haven, and active in the early work of the American Public Health Association. He was influential in the establishment of the Yale Forest School (1900) and lectured there on forest physiography. One of his most important pieces of scientific work was an elaborate study of the development of the American trotting horse as a contribution to knowledge of the evolution of breeds, in which he plotted curves showing how fast horses will ultimately trot and when the maximum will be reached. He also carried on many experiments upon the conditions influencing the suspension of clays in river water with reference to the bearing of river deposits on delta formation.

[The above data are derived largely from diaries, letters, and family records, reinforced by knowledge gained through association extending over many years. In the *Biog. Memoirs Nat. Acad. Sci.*, vol. XII, is a detailed account of Brewer's life and work, written by Prof. R. H. Chittenden.]   R. H. C.

BREWSTER, BENJAMIN HARRIS (Oct. 13, 1816–Apr. 4, 1888), attorney-general of the United States, is best known because of his prosecution of the Star Route frauds in the Post Office Department, 1881–84. He was born in Salem County, N. J., and thought of himself as descended from William Brewster of Massachusetts Bay. His friendly biographer thought the same (Savidge, p. 15), but his name does not appear among the descendants recorded in the history of that family (Emma C. Brewster Jones, *The Brewster Genealogy, 1566–1907,* 1908). However this may be, his parents, Francis Enoch and Maria Hampton Brewster, were of old colonial stock with a tradition of education and standing that they transmitted to their son. Benjamin was a graduate of Princeton College (1834), and soon thereafter he became a leading member of the Philadelphia bar. He was ever a marked man. In infancy he was cruelly burned about his face, so that the scars gave him a wizened and drawn appearance; he called attention to this by assuming the costume of a fop of the later thirties and continuing the same dress throughout his life. Meticulous in costume, antique in appearance, with high stock and ruffles, he was a tradition from his early life; and his great abilities were advertised by his peculiarities. In 1846 he held a minor federal post, settling certain affairs of the Cherokee Indians. Originally a Democrat, he joined the Republicans and was thereafter associated in Pennsylvania politics with Simon Cameron. Through this connection he served as attorney-general of Pennsylvania in 1867 and 1868, and was repeatedly discussed in connection with political opportunities that did not arrive. He came first into national prominence when Attorney-General Wayne MacVeagh invited him in September 1881 to assume with George Bliss of New York the position of special counsel for the government in the Star Route prosecutions. When MacVeagh retired from the cabinet after the death of Garfield, President Arthur advanced Brewster to the seat thus vacated; and for the remainder of the Arthur administration the Star Route prosecutions formed the largest single duty of the attorney-general's office.

The Star Route frauds, after three years of partial concealment, burst upon the country when, in April 1881, President Garfield removed from office T. J. Brady, the second assistant postmaster-general, after receiving the reports of special investigators upon the management of western mail contracts. Involved with Brady were ex-Senator S. W. Dorsey and others who had for many years carried on an extensive traffic in these contracts. The case was of high political importance because Dorsey, as secretary of the Republican National Committee in the canvass of 1880, was widely credited with having carried the State of Indiana by the use of money. Efforts were made to frighten Garfield from the prosecutions, but in vain. After Garfield was shot, action in the matter halted until his death; immediately after which MacVeagh pressed the cases, with the approval of President Arthur, and brought Brewster into them. There was a long and futile struggle for convictions. Robert G. Ingersoll, chief counsel for the various defendants, was at the top of his power as a lawyer, and convictions could not be secured. There was no doubt however that scandalous mismanagement had crept into the Post Office Department; and that the profits of successful crime had been widely distributed among party workers. The failure to procure convictions was a burden upon Arthur's candidacy to secure renomination in 1884, and upon Brewster.

Brewster retired into private life with President Arthur in 1885, and died in Philadelphia three years later. He was twice married; in 1857 to Elizabeth von Myerbach de Reinfeldts who died in 1868, and in 1870 to Mary Walker, daughter of Robert J. Walker, who survived him. By the second marriage he had a son, born in 1872. Brewster had an oratorical gift, and was much in demand for ceremonial addresses. He cultivated in private a taste for ecclesiastical history. His fastidious social habits and his private means helped to give to the Arthur administration its reputation for social activity, in sharp contrast to that of the administrations immediately preceding 1881.

[The only formal work of value upon Brewster is Eugene C. Savidge, *Life of Benjamin Brewster, with Discourses and Addresses* (1891); but his peculiarities and abilities inspired a large amount of paragraph material in the newspapers of his day.]   F. L. P—n.

BREWSTER, FREDERICK CARROLL (May 15, 1825–Dec. 30, 1898), lawyer, jurist, was the son of Francis Enoch and Maria (Hampton) Brewster and the brother of Benjamin Harris Brewster [*q.v.*]. He was born in Philadelphia, and educated at the Old Friends Select School, and University of Pennsylvania, graduating from the latter in 1841. He then studied law in his father's office and was admitted to the Philadelphia bar in September 1844. His early prominence was due mainly to his association with three sensational criminal cases, in which he appeared for the defense, obtaining acquittals in each. In *Commonwealth* vs. *Cunningham*, very fine legal points were involved. The accused, a policeman, shot a man who was resisting arrest, and it was decided that a well-founded apprehension of bodily harm is sufficient to justify the taking of life. *Commonwealth* vs. *Lenairs*, another murder case with a plea of self-defense, was distinguished more by the local animosities sought to be imported into the trial than by its legal features, and Brewster's successful defense was at the time considered extremely brilliant. In the third case, one Kirkpatrick was accused of conspiracy to poison his brother. It excited great interest in society circles, the trial lasted four weeks and Brewster secured an acquittal in the face of strong public opinion and apparently convincing evidence. From that time forward he was recognized as a leader of the bar. In 1856 he achieved his greatest forensic triumph, appearing for W. B. Mann, in the celebrated political contest between the latter and L. Cassidy for the office of district attorney. Closely following came the fail-

ure of the Bank of Pennsylvania, and the indictment of its president, Thomas Allibone, for conspiracy to defraud the bank of $250,000. Brewster was retained for the defense and after a trial extending over three weeks obtained a verdict of "not guilty." An adherent of the Democratic party, but not prominent in political circles, he was in 1862 elected city solicitor after one of the most bitter contests in the history of Philadelphia. In this capacity he conducted some extremely important litigation. He was counsel in the Schollenberger-Brinton case, which established the constitutionality of the Legal Tender Act of 1862, and the Chestnut Street Bridge case, which established the right of the city to bridge the Schuylkill. On the expiration of his term in 1865 he was reëlected, but resigned in October 1866 in order to accept the position of judge of common pleas of the city and county of Philadelphia, which he occupied for three years. He became attorney-general of the state at the request of Gov. Geary, Oct. 23, 1869, and held this office till the latter part of 1872. On his retirement he resumed active practise in Philadelphia. His association with one *cause célèbre* occasioned a remarkable tribute. In the Mintzer case he had induced the jury to upset a will under unusual circumstances, and one reason adduced for a reversal on appeal was that so irresistible had been his eloquence that no twelve sane men in the world could have failed to be controlled by it! In December 1898 he started for Florida in search of health, but died on the train near Salisbury, N. C. In 1850 he had married Emma, daughter of W. P. C. Barton [*q.v.*].

He was the author of *Reports of Equity, Election and Other Important Cases—Principally in the Courts of the County of Philadelphia 1856–73* (4 vols., 1869–73), *A Treatise on Practice in the Courts of Pennsylvania* (2 vols., 1891), *A Treatise on Practice in the Orphans' Court* (1894) and *A Treatise on Equity Practice in Pennsylvania* (1895). He also made contributions to general literature including *Disraeli in Outline* (1890) and *From Independence Hall around the World* (1895).

[*Green Bag*, XII, 381; F. M. Eastman, *Courts and Lawyers of Pa.* (1922), II, 561; J. T. Scharf and T. Westcott, *Hist. of Phila.* (1884), I, 721; R. D. Coxe, *Legal Phila.* (1908), p. 110; obituaries in the *Phila. Inquirer, Press*, and *Public Ledger*, Dec. 31, 1898.]
                                   H. W. H. K.

BREWSTER, JAMES (Aug. 6, 1788–Nov. 22, 1866), carriage-builder, railway-promoter, and philanthropist, was born in Preston, New London County, Conn., the son of Joseph and Hannah (Tucker) Brewster. A farm lad, he had some slight schooling in his native town, and in

1804 was apprenticed to learn the wagon-maker's trade with Charles Chapman of Northampton, Mass. In 1809, on reaching his majority, he set out for New York by way of New Haven, where he took a job in a wagon-shop he had chanced to visit, and where in 1810 he opened a little shop of his own. In the same year he was married to Mary Hequembourg. From colonial days, heavy coaches had been built in this country for the town or traveling use of the well-to-do, but in 1810 the American carriage-building industry had yet to be developed. Chaises, sulkies, and one-horse wagons were the common forms of private conveyance. "Brewster wagons" soon became favorably known; and after this beginning, Brewster started in to build vehicles that in finish and general workmanship should equal those of English make. He turned out not only buggies but phaëtons, victorias, coaches, and other forms of equipage, and before long was specializing in fine construction. He is said to have sent to Charleston the first paneled carriage delivered by an American builder for Southern use. His output set the styles in a field in which he had been the pioneer. The spread of turnpikes naturally tended to increase the demand for lighter four-wheeled vehicles. In addition to his New Haven manufactory, Brewster established in New York (1827) a warehouse and a repair-shop.

He was one of a group of New Haven citizens that projected a railway between New Haven and Hartford and obtained a charter for it (May 1833). The charter empowered the company to use "the power and force of steam, of animals, or of any mechanical or other power or any combination of them." The rails originally laid for this road—the first opened in the state—were imported from England at a cost of $250,000, which sum, considerable in that stage of American railroading, Brewster personally guaranteed. For four years he was president of the new company, in whose financing he greatly aided and whose interests were his chief concern during that period. He then resigned and again (1838) became active in the carriage business. This enjoyed a steady growth; and Brewster, in the language of one biographer, "accumulated a handsome competency."

For more than fifty years he was an important factor in the welfare and progress of New Haven. He gave an orphan asylum to the town and provided for much-needed improvements in the local almshouse. At his own expense he extended the street system and widened streets already existing. He presented to Yale a mineralogical cabinet and equipped a company of Civil War volunteers. Probably his chief service was in connection with his efforts toward bettering the condition of the workmen employed in his own and other manufactories. He prohibited the use of liquor in his shop—a decided innovation at that time—and was a constant advocate of temperance. He built Franklin Hall, with an auditorium for evening addresses, and defrayed the cost of annual lecture courses there given on scientific subjects. In these and other ways he helped to attract employees of the better class to New Haven and to raise the standard of living in the community. At his death he was characterized as "one of the best citizens New Haven or any other city ever had" (*Palladium* [New Haven], Nov. 26, 1866).

[J. F. Babcock, *Address upon the Life and Character of the Late Jas. Brewster* (1867); E. C. B. Jones, *The Brewster Genealogy* (1908); E. E. Atwater (ed.), *Hist. of the City of New Haven to the Present Time* (1887). Brewster wrote an autobiography, never put into print.]

G.S.B.

BREWSTER, OSMYN (Aug. 2, 1797–July 15, 1889), printer, publisher, son of Dr. Moses Brewster and Lucy (Watts) Brewster, was born in Worthington, Mass. His formal schooling ended at fourteen when, as "a chubby fair-complexioned boy, dressed in a blue corduroy suit" (*Memorial of Uriel Crocker*, p. 30), he began his apprenticeship at the printer's trade in the shop of Samuel Armstrong on Cornhill, Boston. Seven years of apprenticeship in the "mystery" of this trade were so many years of real education for Brewster; each day's education began at six; there was an hour from seven to eight for breakfast and an hour for dinner; in summer the day ended at dark, but after Sept. 20 it continued after eight by candle-light until ten. At twenty-one, he and a fellow-apprentice, Uriel Crocker, were taken by their employer into partnership. The first stereotyped edition (1824) of Scott's *Family Bible* bears the imprint of S. T. Armstrong, and Crocker and Brewster. Brewster's work was in the bookshop with Armstrong and he carried on that part of the business after the latter's retirement from the firm in 1825 and the consequent change in the firm name to Crocker & Brewster. Books of a religious nature were the chief output so that the bookshop got the reputation of being "the great mart of religious literature for the Orthodox churches" (*New England Historical and Genealogical Register*, XLIV, 138). Worcester's edition of *Watts' Psalms and Hymns* is listed in the firm's catalogue of 1830; so great was the demand for this hymnal that at least four editions followed. Among the school texts published by the firm was Ethan Allen Andrews' *First Lessons in Latin*, and a very complete set of Latin texts by the same author. A very different kind of publication was the series of juvenile books by J. S. C. Abbott, one of the earliest titles being *The Child at Home; or, The Principles of Filial Duty*. The firm's imprint will be found on no book of doubtful character or of questionable morality.

Brewster was one of the old school of booksellers that believed the only way to make money was by hard work, careful publishing and buying, strict attention to business, and close economy. His was the only Boston publishing house which survived the financial panic of 1837. In 1848 he was elected to represent Boston in the Massachusetts House of Representatives, and on four other occasions his fellow citizens honored him thus. For one term (1853) he was a state senator, and he was a delegate from Boston to the state constitutional convention of 1853. He also served for three years (1856-58) on the Boston board of aldermen. He became the first president of the Franklin Savings Bank in 1881 and continued to serve in that capacity until 1887. Another organization which had his ardent support was the Massachusetts Charitable Mechanic Association, of which he was the treasurer for over twenty-five years. The *Annals* of that organization in 1853 was "from the press of Messrs. Crocker and Brewster" and "altogether a beautiful specimen of a book" (*New England Historical and Genealogical Register*, VIII, 92). Brewster enjoyed Crocker as a partner and as a friend (see portrait of the two arm-in-arm in *Memorial of Uriel Crocker*, p. 42) and both were blessed with good health and long lives; it was not until 1876 that they sold out to Houghton & Company. Brewster's home in the latter years of his life was at 32 Hancock St., Boston. He married Mary Jones at Boston, Jan. 15, 1824; she died, Jan. 27, 1872. They had two sons and seven daughters.

[*Memorial of Uriel Crocker* (1891), comp. by Uriel Haskell Crocker; obituary in *Publishers Weekly*, July 27, 1889; sketch of Samuel Armstrong in *Memorial Biogs. of the New Eng. Hist. and Geneal. Soc.* (1880), I, 232–36; *The Brewster Genealogy* (1908), by E. C. B. Jones.]   A. E. P.

BREWSTER, WILLIAM (1567–Apr. 10, 1644), Pilgrim father, was an Elder of the Pilgrim Church, first in importance during the Scrooby period, second in importance during the Leyden and Plymouth periods. A deposition of his at Leyden finally settles the dispute about the date of his birth and fixes it in the winter of 1566/67, probably in January. He came to Scrooby in 1571 with his father and mother; his father in 1575 became bailiff of the Manor of Scrooby, one of the exempt estates of the Arch-

bishop of York, and in 1588 was appointed postmaster by Elizabeth when Scrooby was made a post-house on the road between London and York. These positions made the father a man of great importance in the district and provided him with a considerable income. The boy was somehow prepared for the university and entered Peterhouse, Cambridge, in December 1580, where he himself later declared that he acquired his first Separatist ideas. He did not take a degree and perhaps remained at Cambridge only a few months. In the autumn of 1583 he became a member of the household of William Davison, then important in administrative and diplomatic life at the court of Elizabeth, and, becoming one of his trusted retainers, accompanied him on missions to the Netherlands in 1584 and in 1585–86. Despite the disgrace of Davison in 1587 as a result of his part in the execution of Mary Stuart and his consequent retirement from public life, Brewster remained in his service until news of his father's serious illness caused his return to Scrooby in 1589. He served as his father's deputy until the latter's death in 1590 and then was himself appointed to the positions of bailiff and postmaster, retaining both until the exodus to Holland in 1608. He married in 1591 Mary ——, by whom he had before 1620 six children. Gradually he became the protector and then the principal member of a little congregation of Puritans, gathered from Scrooby and the near-by villages. But they did not "separate" from the Established Church until the autumn of 1606 and it was not until a year later that John Robinson joined them. After some investigation of their proceedings by the High Commission at York, which certainly did not amount to persecution, they decided to leave so ungodly a land and finally succeeded in emigrating to Holland in 1608. Finding Amsterdam also uncongenial, they settled at Leyden in 1609. Here, if not earlier, Brewster became elder and teacher of the new church. To earn a living for his family, he became a printer of Puritan books, written by the leaders in England, and shipped back to them for sale and distribution at home. In 1617 the initiation of the plan for emigration to America took him and others to England where he interviewed officers of the Virginia Company and various royal officials to secure permission to colonize and a grant of land. Beyond much doubt he was the principal envoy. Returning to Leyden, he printed in 1618 or 1619 a book which gave great offense to James I. Of this the English government complained to the Dutch authorities in 1619 with such effect that Brewster felt it wiser to discontinue the press altogether and to return with his family to England where he seems to have lived unmolested until the *Mayflower* sailed in 1620. He played therefore no part in the final steps at Leyden for the emigration to America and was not present when the decision was reached, in April 1620, that the majority should remain at Leyden with Robinson their minister, while the minority should attempt the venture with Brewster himself as their leader. It also seems probable that he played no important part in organizing the company which sailed for America direct from England, being fearful of royal interference with his own emigration. He embarked on the *Mayflower* at London with his wife, two sons, and two boys "bound out" to him. At Plymouth, Brewster was the only church officer until 1629, but held services of prayer and praise only; he expounded the Scripture at length, but was forbidden by the rules to preach, baptize, or celebrate the communion. Though he was therefore never a minister in the Pilgrim sense of the word and though they "called" Smith, Roger Williams, Chauncey, and Reynor as their ministers later, he remained throughout his life the real leader of the church at Plymouth and the man chiefly responsible for its doctrines, observances, and worship. Administrative position was foreclosed to him by his position in the church but he was active in counsel and played a part second only to Bradford in all decisions, great and small. He became one of the Undertakers in 1627 who assumed the Pilgrim indebtedness. His library (*Proceedings of the Massachusetts Historical Society,* 2nd ser., III, 261–74; V, 37–85) proves him to have been well read in history, philosophy, and religious poetry and shows that he continued to buy books throughout his life. We have no idea of his personal appearance but we do know from the inventory of his property (*Mayflower Descendant,* III, 15–27) that he wore a violet colored cloth coat, black silk stockings, a ruff, and other clothing, of impeccable modesty, but less severe than the popular tradition attributes to the Pilgrims. Social life at Plymouth was undoubtedly quiet in the extreme but in it Brewster played a very important part, being, says Bradford, "of a very cherful Spirite, very sociable and pleasante amongst his friends." He died Apr. 10, 1644, at Plymouth, possessed of a house, lands, cattle, and personalty worth £107.

[The chief authority for Brewster's life to 1620 is H. M. and M. Dexter, *The England and Holland of the Pilgrims* (1905) and for the period after 1620, Wm. Bradford's *Hist. of Plymouth Plantation* (1856). See also: R. G. Usher, *The Pilgrims and Their History* (1918); J. A. Goodwin, *The Pilgrim Republic* (1888); W. H. Burgess, *The Pastor of the Pilgrims: John Robinson* (1920). In *Mayflower Notes and Queries,* IV, 56 ff., is a complete list of his children and grandchildren. In the *Mayflower Descendant,* vols. I, II, III,

etc., has been printed the "Brewster Book" kept by his descendants. The best list of his books printed at Leyden is now that in the *Mayflower Descendant,* XXIII, 97–105, with two not before identified. The known autographs are given in the same series in facsimile: XXII, 1; XXIII, 98; XXIV, 97.]   R.G.U.

BREWSTER, WILLIAM (July 5, 1851–July 11, 1919), ornithologist, was born at Wakefield, Mass., the son of John Brewster, a successful Boston banker, and of Rebecca Parker (Noyes) Brewster. Descended on both sides from old Massachusetts families he inherited all of the characteristics of a New England gentleman, and reared in the atmosphere of Cambridge, with Longfellow and other notable men of letters as family neighbors, he absorbed all of the spirit and tradition of the community. He was educated in the public schools of Cambridge and prepared for Harvard, but being never of robust health and suffering in youth from impaired sight he decided to forego a college course. With no leaning toward a business career he nevertheless in accordance with his father's wish entered his banking office at the age of nineteen but retired within a year convinced that he did not possess business talent and henceforth devoted himself entirely to ornithology, his father sympathizing fully with his decision. He was married on Feb. 9, 1878, to Caroline F. Kettell of Boston. Brewster's attention seems to have first drawn to birds at the age of ten by a neighbor, Daniel C. French, who was interested in hunting and was something of an amateur taxidermist. He willingly gave the boy and others of his associates instructions in preparing specimens with the result that at the age of fourteen Brewster had several cases of mounted birds and had begun what was eventually to become the finest collection of North American birds in existence, which is now preserved in the Museum of Comparative Zoölogy. Brewster became a skilful taxidermist and always took the greatest pains in preparing his specimens, for a bird skin to him was not only a scientific specimen but an object of beauty to be cherished and admired. Later in life he built a little museum on his home grounds in Cambridge where his collection and library were housed and where ornithologists were welcomed and meetings held. Wrapped up in New England traditions, Brewster's main interests were naturally in the local bird life and he kept detailed daily records of bird observations at Cambridge, Concord, Lake Umbagog, and other New England localities which he visited. He also collected specimens, however, in other parts of the country, visiting Illinois, West Virginia, Colorado, the Gulf of St. Lawrence, North Carolina, and Florida as well as the island of Trinidad, and employed skilful collectors to procure specimens from elsewhere. While he possessed a profound taxonomic knowledge of North American birds and published important papers in this field and while he served for years on the Committee on Classification and Nomenclature of the American Ornithologists' Union, his outstanding publications have dealt with the live bird rather than the dead one. He was one of the founders of the Nuttall Ornithological Club (1873) and of the American Ornithologists' Union (1883), becoming president of both organizations. He was active in behalf of bird and game preservation but in a broad-minded not sentimental way, was president of the Massachusetts Audubon Society, and was a member of the state Game Commission. He was in charge of the bird and mammal collections of the Boston Society of Natural History (1879–87) and of the ornithological collection of the Museum of Comparative Zoölogy from 1885 on. His most notable publications were: *Descriptions of the First Plumage in Various North American Birds* (1878–79), *Bird Migration* (1886), *Birds of the Cambridge Region of Massachusetts* (1906), *Birds of the Cape Region of Lower California* (1902), and the posthumous *Birds of the Lake Umbagog Region, Maine* (1924–25, still unfinished). His short papers and notes were numerous and covered a wide range of ornithological topics, those appearing in the *Bulletin of the Nuttall Club* and its successor the *Auk* numbering no less than 267. He also edited an edition of H. D. Minot's *Land Birds and Game Birds of New England* (1894), which contained many additional notes. Besides his Cambridge home Brewster possessed a large tract of farm land at Concord which he maintained primarily as a wild life preserve where for twenty years no gun was fired and where he studied the balance of nature and delighted in the association with birds and small mammals. Indeed to those who knew him well the name of William Brewster was as closely associated with Concord as was that of Thoreau, for whom he had a great reverence. He likewise had a camp at Lake Umbagog, Me., where he spent a number of seasons collecting data on the life histories of the birds of the region. His deep love of nature was contagious and association with him in the field was a privilege not soon to be forgotten. Probably he never realized the part he played in stimulating the ornithological activities of many others, especially young men. His influence upon the development of American Ornithology, extending, as it did, far beyond his printed papers, cannot well be measured.

[Henry W. Henshaw, sketch in the *Auk*, Jan. 1920; F. M. Chapman, sketch in *Bird Lore*, Sept.–Oct. 1919; obituary in *Boston Transcript*, July 12, 1919; *Who's Who in America*, 1918–19; personal acquaintance.]

W.S.

BRICE, CALVIN STEWART (Sept. 17, 1845–Dec. 15, 1898), railroad builder, senator, was descended on his father's side from the Bruces of Kinnaird, Scotland, and on the maternal side from the fifth Lord Livingston, who died about 1553. His father, William K. Brice, was a Presbyterian minister, a graduate of Hanover College and Princeton Theological Seminary, who came from Maryland to Ohio in 1840 and settled in the village of Denmark, Morrow County, where Calvin Stewart Brice was born. The latter's mother, whose maiden name was Elizabeth Stewart, was a native of Carroll County, Ohio, and is described as "a woman of fine education and exemplary traits of character." While his early education was obtained in the common schools, it is clear that the instruction of his parents had a decided effect upon his mental development, for at the age of thirteen he entered the preparatory department of Miami University, at Oxford, Ohio, and after only a year he was admitted to the freshman class. But his studies were interrupted by the war. On Apr. 1, 1861, though only fifteen years of age, he enlisted in the cause of the Union but was rejected on account of his youth; the following year he enlisted again and served for three months, when he returned to Oxford to complete his college course. He graduated in June 1863 and after teaching three months he recruited Company E of the 180th Ohio Volunteer Infantry, became its captain, and served until July 1865. A few days before the close of the war he was promoted to the rank of lieutenant-colonel for meritorious service. He was then just of age and took up the study of law in the University of Michigan. In the spring of 1866 he was admitted to the bar at Cincinnati. He soon gained distinction as a corporation lawyer, a training that fitted him for the part he was to play in the business and financial world, for in 1870 he gave up the active practise of law and embarked upon railroad enterprise, both as projector and manager. He first attracted notice in the business world when Gen. Ewing and other capitalists planned a railroad from Toledo to the Ohio coal fields. This brought him in contact with Allen G. Thurman, Judge Ranney, and Gov. Foster of Ohio. The plan as Brice outlined it was finally followed and he was given a free hand to carry the project to completion. In the winter of 1870–71 he went to Europe to procure a loan for the purpose of completing the line of the Lake Erie & Louisville Railroad as far as

Lima, Ohio. This road afterward became the Lake Erie & Western of which he became president in 1887. Besides his connection with this road he helped in the construction of the division of the Erie Railroad, known as the Chicago & Atlantic, and was responsible for the location in his home town of Lima of the machine shops of the Lake Erie & Western and the Dayton & Michigan railroads. His ability was now generally recognized and he entered upon many new ventures, all of which were successful. The conception, building, and profitable sale of the New York, Chicago & St. Louis Railway, commonly known as the "Nickel Plate," was in great measure due to him. He was connected with ten other railroads, between Duluth, the Atlantic, and the South, as an investor and an official; but perhaps his greatest project was a railroad in China under concessions from the imperial government to the China-American Development Company, known as "The Brice Chinese Syndicate," which had the exclusive right of way between Canton and Hankow with adjacent mining rights; but his death prevented him from completing the undertaking. The *Way Bill,* commenting upon his services, says: "In all Mr. Brice's official relations with various railroads and other corporate properties, he never accepted a dollar of salary for his services. We do not know of another man in a similar position of whom the same can be said" (*Magazine of Western History,* 1889, X, 719). In addition to his extensive railroad activities, he was a promoter and stockholder in many of the local interests of his home city of Lima; he was identified with the Chase National Bank of New York and one of the leading spirits and directors of the Southern Trust Company. Yet he had time for politics. As a Democrat he was on the electoral ticket of Tilden in 1876 and of Cleveland in 1884. In 1888 he was delegate at large from Ohio to the national Democratic convention at St. Louis where he was elected a member of the national Democratic committee and chairman of the national campaign committee for the ensuing campaign. On the death of William H. Barnum in 1889, he was unanimously elected chairman of the Democratic national committee, and in 1890 he was elected to the United States Senate, to succeed Henry B. Payne, for the term commencing Mar. 4, 1891. He soon became one of the leaders on the Democratic side, being a member of the steering committee and also a member of the Committee on Appropriations. While he took little part in public discussions in the Senate, he followed the proceedings closely, was a skilful questioner, and always commanded respect from the leaders of both parties. On retiring from the Senate he took up his residence in New York City and became prominent in financial circles; but after the advent of Bryan and free silver, he took little interest in politics. He was married in 1870 to Catherine Olivia Meily of Lima, Ohio, by whom he had four sons and two daughters.

[The files of *The Times-Democrat* of Lima, Ohio, especially the issues of Dec. 16, 19, and 20, 1898; *Cong. Record,* 52 Cong., 2 Sess.; obituaries in the *N. Y. Times, N. Y. Tribune,* and *Sun* (N. Y.), Dec. 16, 1898.]

K.F.G.

BRICKELL, ROBERT COMAN (Apr. 4, 1824–Nov. 20, 1900), jurist, of Welsh ancestry, was the eldest son of Richard Benjamin and Margaret Williamson (Coman) Brickell. He was born in Tuscumbia, Ala., at the home of his maternal great-grandfather, Dr. Prout, although his parents were making their home in Huntsville, Ala. From Huntsville they moved to Athens, Ala., where the father published and edited the *Athenian,* a weekly newspaper. Gifted as a writer and speaker he was elected to the state legislature in 1831 and again in 1833 from Limestone County where he died in 1835, leaving his widow and six children in straitened circumstances. Robert Brickell's mother was a woman of strong character, well educated, and devoted to her children in whom she inspired the greatest love and respect. After her husband's death she taught school. Her eldest son, Robert, was a delicate child and was always handicapped by a slight physique. With the exception of six weeks in school in Nashville, Tenn., he was taught only by his parents. When nineteen years of age, he was admitted to the bar after having read law in the private office of Judge Daniel Coleman in Athens. Although retiring in disposition he was such a deep student that his learning at a tender age was regarded as remarkable. In 1851 he located in Huntsville and became the junior partner in the law firm of Cabaniss & Brickell. Three years later Leroy Pope Walker became the head of the firm from which Mr. Cabaniss finally retired. There was hardly a case of any importance in north Alabama in which the powerful firm of Walker & Brickell did not take part on one side or the other in legal battles. Both were advocates of state rights and strong believers in the constitutional right of secession.

In 1873 Brickell was appointed associate justice of the supreme court of Alabama by the Republican governor, David P. Lewis, who knew him to be a profound lawyer, peculiarly fitted for that high judicial office. Brickell entered at once upon the discharge of his duties with a determination to lend every possible assistance in rectifying the chaotic condition of the courts in which partisan decisions had been made in total disregard of time-honored precedents. His decisions from the bench were numerous and able. He became chief justice of the supreme court in 1874 by the selection of his associates and in 1880 was nominated by the Democratic party and elected chief justice of the supreme court by the popular vote. Four years later he resigned his office to resume the practise of law with offices in Montgomery, New Decatur, and Huntsville. In 1894, however, he was persuaded by Gov. Thomas G. Jones, who recognized the state's great need of his service on the bench, to accept an appointment once more as a supreme court judge. Upon the expiration of his term of office he returned to Huntsville and resumed the practise of law, in partnership with his son, Robert C. Brickell, Jr. On Nov. 29, 1876, in Montgomery, Ala., he had married Mary Blassingame Glenn, a niece of the wife of Gov. Benjamin Fitzpatrick. On Nov. 20, 1900, he died following a stroke of paralysis.

He was possessed of a nervous temperament and his gestures were rapid and unstudied. He was especially impressive before a court or jury and on account of his masterly arguments and effective oratorical powers the court room was always filled when it was known that he would speak. His abilities were of especial use to the people of Alabama during the period of Reconstruction when the courts were administered by alien judges.

[P. J. Hamilton, "Robt. Coman Brickell," in *Great Am. Lawyers*, vol. VII (1909), ed. by W. D. Lewis; 127 *Ala. Reports*; *Report of the Twenty-fourth Annual Meeting, Ala. State Bar Ass.*, 1901, pp. 183–89; Thos. M. Owen, *Hist. of Ala. and Dict. of Ala. Biog.* (1921), vol. III; *Daily Picayune*, June 13, 1873; MSS. in the Ala. State Dept. of Archives and Hist.]   M.B.O.

BRIDGER, JAMES (Mar. 17, 1804–July 17, 1881), fur trader, frontiersman, scout, was the son of James Bridger, inn-keeper of Richmond, Va., and of his wife Chloe. Young Bridger removed with his parents to the vicinity of St. Louis about 1812. Orphaned at the age of thirteen, he was apprenticed to a blacksmith, but true to his pioneer inheritance, was attracted by Ashley's "want ad" in the *Missouri Republican* of Mar. 20, 1822, offering employment to a hundred "enterprising young men" to engage on a fur-trapping venture near the sources of the Missouri River. Joining the expedition, Bridger entered that portion of the West with which he was to become more intimately familiar than any of his contemporaries. During the next twenty years, either as an employee of, or a partner in,

various fur companies, he repeatedly traversed the area between the Canadian boundary and the southern line of Colorado and from the Missouri River westward to Idaho and Utah. He was the first white man, so far as is known, to visit (fall of 1824) Great Salt Lake. Noting the decline of the fur business and the growth of western emigration he established a way-station, Fort Bridger, on the Oregon trail in southwestern Wyoming, in 1843. All the notable figures in the western movement—Wyeth, Bonneville, Whitman, Parker, DeSmet, Frémont, the Donner party, Brigham Young and many others—recorded their indebtedness to him either for reliable information about the country or for hospitality at the "fort." To obtain a monopoly of the emigrant business the Mormons drove him from his holdings in 1853. Retiring for a time to a farm which he had purchased near Kansas City, he soon entered government service as a scout. He had already guided Stansbury on his Utah expedition in 1849 and on his return had led him east through the short-cut of Bridger's pass. In 1857–58 he guided Johnston's army in the Utah invasion, probably a not uncongenial assignment. In 1859–60 he accompanied the Raynolds Yellowstone expedition and in 1861 guided the Berthoud engineering party in their attempt to discover a direct route from Denver to Great Salt Lake. In 1865 and 1866 he acted as guide for the Powder River expeditions and in the latter year measured the distances on the Bozeman trail from Fort Kearny, Nebr., to Virginia City, Mont., a distance of 967 miles. In 1868 he retired from the plains and the mountains. He died at his home near Kansas City.

Bridger took three wives. The first was a Flathead woman who died, 1846, leaving three children. His second wife, a Ute, died, 1849, leaving a daughter. His third wife, a Snake woman, died in 1858. With the sole exception of a few Mormon contemporaries, every one of the scores of pioneers, army men, explorers, and sportsmen with whom he came in contact mentions his services, his intelligence, and his character in the highest terms. Tall, keen-eyed and of commanding personality, this completely illiterate frontiersman placed at the disposal of a multitude of varied western travelers his unrivaled knowledge of the country and of the Indians.

[J. C. Alter, *Jas. Bridger* (1925), which includes the whole of G. M. Dodge's *Biog. Sketch of Jas. Bridger* (1905); Grace R. Hebard and E. A. Briminstool, *The Bozeman Trail* (1922).]   H.C.D.

BRIDGERS, ROBERT RUFUS (Nov. 28, 1819–Dec. 10, 1888), Confederate congressman, manufacturer, railroad president, belonged to a family, long resident in southside Virginia, which came to Edgecombe County, N. C., about 1761 and took up land on Town Creek. There Robert Rufus was born, son of John Bridgers and Elizabeth Kettlewells Routh. Having graduated first in the state university's class of 1841, he was immediately licensed to practise law and three years later was sent to the state House of Representatives. Then he settled down at Tarboro. In 1849 he married Margaret Elizabeth Johnston. He worked at the law very hard and in later life is said to have been offered the attorney-generalship. With "decided gifts" for politics, in the 1850's he helped Henry T. Clark make Edgecombe a "stronghold of Democracy" (J. K. Turner and J. L. Bridgers, *Edgecombe County*, 1920, p. 152) and received three terms (1856–61) and the chairmanship of the judiciary committee in the state House of Representatives. Though not "fervent for secession," he advocated a state convention in frank anticipation that secession would be necessary. In the Confederate Congress (1862–65) he was regular in attendance, always a member of the committee on military affairs, and apparently disposed to support President Davis as far as his people's views would permit (*Congress of Confederate States, Journal*, V, 151, 154; VI, 71, 741). His chief interest, however, had already begun to be business. At Tarboro he had organized and developed a bank, of which he had become president in 1851. Next year he was purchasing large land-holdings out of which, with subsequent purchases, he made "Strabane," a plantation noted for high productivity. Simultaneously he was promoting a Tarboro branch of the Wilmington & Weldon Railroad with such success that the line was finished in 1860 and he became a director of the Wilmington & Weldon. During the war he revamped plants for the mining and manufacture of iron in Lincoln and adjacent counties (the "High Shoals property") which supplied the Carolinas with nails and plows and is said to have been the second largest of its kind in the Confederacy. He urged alike upon his railroad and the Confederate government a policy of large production of cotton and its exportation to meet coming financial obligations abroad. Later the Confederate government is said to have wanted him as secretary of the treasury; in the fall of 1865 the Wilmington & Weldon company—which had resumed business in August with four locomotives and nine cars—elected him president. For the next twenty-three years he labored unremittingly on what was to be the Atlantic Coast Line Railroad. Each year he was unanimously reëlected president of

the Wilmington & Weldon. For thirteen years he was also its general superintendent. For it he built four branch lines, totaling nearly two hundred miles in length. He became president also of the Columbia & Augusta, which continued his road from Wilmington. All of these lines were financed by a Baltimore firm to whom he had appealed in 1867 and for whom, as a condition of assistance, he had bought a controlling interest in Wilmington & Weldon, including the state's stock, during the Holden administration. That he escaped the odium and suspicion which attended the transactions of this firm (see complaint of Wilmington and New Hanover County through their attorneys, 1893) was perhaps due to his personal character as well as to the wisdom of his policies. Men noted that he had not taken advantage of the bankruptcy law when the failure of others overwhelmed him with debt at the time of the war. He knew intimately the lands which his roads served and their people individually. He picked territory for branch roads with remarkable shrewdness and aided businesses all along his lines. He fostered enthusiasm among his men through his policy of promotion to vacancies; in turn he rigidly insisted that they treat his patrons courteously. These were not always characteristics of railroad leaders in that day. And since he declined better positions elsewhere, men deemed him "public spirited." He died in harness, in Columbia, S. C., and was buried amid expressions of general esteem in St. James's churchyard, Wilmington.

[S. A. Ashe, *Biog. Hist. of N. C.* (1905), I, 171; Jerome Dowd, *Sketches of Prominent Living North Carolinians* (1888); *News and Observer* (Raleigh), Dec. 12, 1888; *Wilmington Weekly Star*, Dec. 14, 1888.]

C.C.P.

BRIDGES, ROBERT (d. 1656), Lynn iron manufacturer and magistrate, was a significant figure in the industrial history of America. He reached Massachusetts probably in 1641, for in that year (June 2) he took the oath and became a freeman. He was evidently a man of considerable ability, for from the date of his arrival until his death he took a prominent part in the affairs of the community. He was a member of the Ancient and Honorable Artillery Company in 1641 and became a captain in the militia. In 1644 he was chosen representative to the General Court and appointed a member of the Quarterly Court at Salem. In October 1646 he was elected speaker of the House of Representatives, and in the next year became an Assistant, in which office he continued until his death. For a long time he was the only magistrate in Lynn. An interesting episode in his career was his service as commissioner in 1646 to investigate the troubles between two French governors—the Huguenot, La Tour, and the Catholic, D'Aulnay —who were contending for the possession of Acadia and causing trouble to certain Plymouth traders in Maine. Edward Johnson bears witness to his prominence when he speaks of "the Band of Lyn led by the honored and much respected Capt. Robert Bridges, who is also a magistrate, being endued with able parts, and forward to improve them for the glory of God and his people's good" (*Wonder Working Providence,* ed. by J. Franklin Jameson, 1910, p. 231).

Although Bridges was an important figure for a few years in the administration of the Massachusetts colony, his chief interest to subsequent generations lies in his connection with the first iron works established in America. Bog iron was discovered at an early date in Massachusetts but it was not until 1642 that a serious effort was made to take advantage of the discovery. In that year Bridges took some specimens of the ore from the region of the Saugus River and went to London for the purpose of interesting capital. A company known as "The Company of Undertakers for the Iron Works" was formed and the eleven incorporators contributed £1,000 for the enterprise. Skilled workmen were brought over and the industry established, 1643, at Hammersmith (near Lynn) on the Saugus, so named after the English town from which some of the workmen came. The colonial authorities considered the establishment of these iron works a matter of great importance and aided them liberally with civil and religious immunities equal to any in the colony (Lewis and Newhall, *History of Lynn,* 1865, pp. 212 ff.). Although they continued to be operated to some extent until 1683, the iron works met with indifferent success, and apparently did not long occupy the major attention of their founder.

Bridges seems to have been a stern and unyielding Puritan. He was a member of the court which in 1651 regulated the dress of all persons whose estate did not exceed £200 and forbade dancing at weddings or other events in ordinaries. He also participated prominently in the Quaker persecution by ordering the arrest of Clarke, Crandall, and Holmes at Swampscott ("Ill News from New England," *Massachusetts Historical Society Collections,* 4 ser., II, 27 ff., 1854). Personally he was a man of tact, and his rapid rise and continued public service bear witness to his acceptability to the authorities of Massachusetts. His wife was Mary Woodcock of London (Charles H. Pope, *Pioneers of Massachusetts,* 1900, p. 68).

[Alonzo Lewis, *Hist. of Lynn Including Nahant* (1844); Chas. E. Mann, *The Three Lynn Captains, Robt. Bridges, Thos. Marshall, and Richard Walker* (1911), reprinted from vol. XIV of the *Lynn Hist. Soc. Reg.*; Nathan M. Hawkes, *Hearths and Homes of Old Lynn* (1907), pp. 149–58; J. L. Bishop, *Hist. of Am. Manufactures, from 1608 to 1860* (1864), I, 470 ff.]

H.U.F.

BRIDGES, ROBERT (Mar. 5, 1806–Feb. 20, 1882), physician and botanist, was the son of Culpepper Bridges and his wife Sarah Clifton. He was born in Philadelphia and was educated in that city until he went to Dickinson College, from which he graduated in 1824. He then became a pupil of Thomas T. Hewson in his private medical classes while studying medicine at the University of Pennsylvania, from which he received the degree of M.D. in 1828. Although Bridges did not practise medicine many years he became a fellow of the College of Physicians of Philadelphia in 1842. He served as its librarian from 1867 to 1879, and catalogued the Urinary Calculi in its Mutter Museum. He was one of the vaccine physicians of Philadelphia for some years, and during the cholera epidemic of 1832 he was appointed a district physician. The great interests of his life were botany and chemistry. In 1835 he became a member of the Academy of Natural Sciences, which he subsequently served at various times as librarian, corresponding secretary, vice-president, and finally president in 1864. In 1835 with Dr. Paul B. Goddard he presented to the Academy an Index of the genera in its Herbarium, and in 1843 he presented a new Index along with one of Menke's Herbarium, which had come into the Academy's possession. While yet a student with Hewson, Bridges had assisted Franklin Bache in teaching chemistry to Hewson's pupils and had shown much ability. In 1831 he assisted Bache in his chemical teaching in the Philadelphia College of Pharmacy, of which institution he became a trustee in 1839. In 1842 he was appointed professor of general and pharmaceutical chemistry in the College, becoming emeritus professor in 1879. From 1839 to 1846 he was assistant editor of the *American Journal of Pharmacy.* He was a member of the Committee for the Revision of the Pharmacopœia in 1840 and again in 1870. From 1846 to 1848 he was professor of chemistry in Franklin Medical College. He was a member of the Franklin Institute of Philadelphia (1836) and of the American Philosophical Society (1844). Besides many contributions to transactions and periodicals he edited the American edition of George Fownes's *Elementary Chemistry* and Thomas Graham's *Elements of Chemistry* and assisted George B. Wood in the preparation of several editions of the *United States*

Dispensary, as well as in his teaching of Materia Medica at the University of Pennsylvania. He was never married.

[J. W. Harshberger, *The Botanists of Phila.* (1899); W. S. W. Ruschenberber, in *Proc. Am. Philosophical Soc.,* XXI, 427, 1884.]   F. R. P.

BRIDGMAN, ELIJAH COLEMAN (Apr. 22, 1801–Nov. 2, 1861), missionary to the Chinese, sent out by the American Board of Commissioners for Foreign Missions in 1829, was born in Belchertown, Mass., a descendant of James Bridgman who settled in Hartford, Conn., in 1640; and son of Theodore and Lucretia (Warner) Bridgman. From boyhood, when he was attracted to missionary work through his reading of missionary periodicals, his one unwavering interest was in that field of activity. To prepare himself for it, he went to Amherst College, graduating in 1826, and then to Andover Theological Seminary. On the day he finished his studies there, Sept. 23, 1829, representatives of the American Board asked him to accept an appointment to China, a New York merchant, D. W. C. Olyphant, engaged in trade with Canton, having offered to support a missionary there for a year. It took him but three days to come to a decision. On Oct. 3, he was commissioned; on Oct. 6, at Belchertown, he was ordained; and the next week he was on his way, arriving in Canton the latter part of February 1830. Except for a brief visit to America, because of ill health in 1852, he spent the remainder of his life in China, never seeming to have any desire to leave his work. Here he died at the age of sixty, and his body lies buried in the Shanghai cemetery.

When he arrived in Canton the only Protestant worker in China was the celebrated English missionary and translator, Dr. Robert Morrison, under whose tutelage he soon acquired a good knowledge of the language. The open preaching of Christianity at that time was forbidden, and while he performed all the duties of a clergyman, his chief work was that of a pioneer organizer, educator, and translator. On the formation of the Society for the Diffusion of Useful Knowledge, in November 1834, he was chosen joint secretary with Dr. Charles Gützlaff. He was active in founding the Morrison Education Society, and with Drs. T. R. Colledge and Peter Parker [*q.v.*] called the public meeting in Canton, Feb. 21, 1838, which resulted in the organization of the Medical Missionary Society in China. He was also a member of the North China branch of the Royal Asiatic Society, and the editor of its journal. In 1832 a mission press was started, and in May of that year

he began the publication of the *Chinese Repository,* for the spread of information about China among English-speaking people. This periodical, widely read and valued, he edited until 1847, when S. Wells Williams [*q.v.*], who had long assisted him, took sole charge. In 1841 he published his *Chinese Chrestomathy,* to which Williams also contributed, a quarto of 734 pages, and the first practical manual of the Cantonese dialect prepared in China. After Hong-Kong was ceded to Great Britain, he removed to that city where he married, June 28, 1845, Eliza Jane Gillett. Later in the year he returned to Canton but in 1847 removed to Shanghai, and spent much of the remainder of his life working on translations of the Bible. His own version, in preparing which Rev. M. S. Culbertson collaborated, appeared in 1862. On various occasions he was of much assistance to the United States government. Caleb Cushing, in a letter published in the *Presbyterian,* Mar. 8, 1845, speaks of Bridgman's "indispensable service" as translator and adviser during the former's negotiations with China.

[B. N. and J. C. Bridgman, *Genealogy of the Bridgman Family* (1894); Eliza J. G. Bridgman, *Life and Labors of Elijah Coleman Bridgman* (1864); F. Wells Williams, *Life and Letters of Samuel Wells Williams* (1889); D. MacGillivray, *A Century of Protestant Missions in China* (1907); Wm. E. Strong, *The Story of the Am. Board* (1910); *Memorials of Protestant Missionaries to the Chinese* (1867).]   H. E. S.

BRIDGMAN, FREDERIC ARTHUR (Nov. 10, 1847–Jan. 13, 1927), painter, was born at Tuskegee, Ala., the son of Frederick and Lovina (Jennings) Bridgman. On the death of his father, his mother moved to the North with her children, and in view of the boy's earnest desire to become an artist, she took advantage of an opportunity to apprentice him to the American Bank-Note Company in New York, 1863, where he remained at work nearly four years. Meanwhile he studied drawing and painting in an art school in Brooklyn and experimented in painting at home out of business hours. In 1866 he went to France for the purpose of continuing his training and became a pupil of J. L. Gérôme in the École des Beaux-Arts, Paris, where he passed five years. During the early days in Paris he met with but scanty encouragement, but in 1870 two of his pictures, "Cirque en Province" and "De Quoi Parlent les Jeunes Filles," were hung in the Salon, several of his works were engraved in *Le Monde Illustré,* and he sold some of his productions to the Goupil Galleries. His summers were usually spent at Pont-Aven, Brittany, then the favorite resort of a colony of painters. It was there that he painted the spirited picture of a circus above mentioned, which was later exhibited in several American cities under the title of "An American Circus in France." In the summer of 1871 he visited England for a short time; then he traveled to the Pyrenees, where he met Fortuny and other painters, and stayed about two years. Thence he proceeded to Algeria, Egypt, and Nubia, in the winter of 1873–74, and, in company with other painters, made a voyage up the Nile as far as the second cataract. So well did he employ his time that when he returned to Paris in the spring of 1874 he brought with him three hundred sketches and studies, for the most part of landscapes and the ruins of temples, also a quantity of costumes and curiosities which were destined to be utilized in the oriental compositions to which he now devoted most of his attention. One of the most important of these was the "Interior of a Harem," which was shown in the Salon of 1875. The work by which he is best known is largely archeological, as for instance the "Funeral of a Mummy," which appeared in the Salon of 1877. Other scholarly and well-painted reconstructions of the life of antiquity are the "Procession of the Bull Apis" and the picture of an Assyrian king killing lions in the amphitheatre (Salon of 1879), works somewhat reminiscent of Gérôme, and, in the opinion of the critics of the time, exhibiting some of the master's best qualities. Continuing to reside and work in Paris, Bridgman became one of the best-known and most esteemed artists of the large American colony there. Medals came to him from the Salon and elsewhere; he prospered; and his paintings commanded a ready market in the United States, for he sent many of his best things to the American exhibitions, notably to the National Academy and the Society of American Artists. On the occasion of one of his periodical visits to his native land, in 1878, a loan exhibition of twenty-four of his pictures was held in Brooklyn, the collection being known as the Bridgman Gallery. This group contained, among other things, his "American Circus in France," "The Prayer in the Mosque," "The Fête in the Palace of Rameses," "The Pride of the Harem," "Woman of Kabzla," "View on the Upper Nile," and a self-portrait. His painting of "The Diligence" is in the Walker Gallery, Liverpool; "The Destruction of Pharaoh's Host" and two other works are in the Academy of Arts in Leningrad; and several of his pictures have been acquired by American museums. In addition to his accomplishments as a painter, he was the author of several books, a composer of music, and a proficient violinist. He published *Winters in Algeria* (1890), *L'Anarchie dans l'Art* (1898)—originally written in English but translated and published in French, an emphatic protest against what he regarded as the demoralizing tendencies of the radical modernists in painting, sculpture, architecture, music, literature, and criticism; and *L'Idole et l'Idéal* (1901). His musical compositions consist of orchestral pieces and several symphonies. On July 17, 1877 he was married in Paris to Florence Mott Baker of Boston. He died in Rouen, and was buried at Lyon-la-Forêt, a village in Normandy, about twenty miles from Rouen.

[B. N. and J. C. Bridgman, *Geneal. of the Bridgman Family* (1894); G. W. Sheldon, *Am. Painters* (1879); Samuel Isham, *Hist. of Am. Painting* (1905); *Art Jour.*, Feb. 1876; *Am. Art Rev.*, June 1881; *Artist*, XXIX, 138; *Art Amateur*, XL, 76; *Harper's*, Oct. 1881.]

W. H. D.

BRIDGMAN, HERBERT LAWRENCE (May 30, 1844–Sept. 24, 1924), newspaper publisher, explorer, was born in Amherst, Mass., the son of Richard Baxter and Mary (Nutting) Bridgman. After finishing the common schools he entered Amherst College, from which he graduated in 1866. He had done some apprentice work at journalism during his last two years in college, and he now made it his vocation. He began on the *Springfield Republican,* of which he became city editor, and he later worked for the Associated Press and on *Frank Leslie's*, the *Press,* and the *Tribune* of New York. In 1887 he became business manager of the *Brooklyn Standard Union,* a place he retained until his death. He was one of the founders of the American Newspaper Publishers Association, of which he was president for three terms, and was for one term chairman of the New York Publishers Association. He remained a journalist as well as a publisher; usually he had an unsigned editorial in the Sunday issue of his newspapers, and always he was a keen and an assiduous gatherer of news. An associate testifies that "he was a specialist on finding the elusive item in the least likely place," and that his contributions, jotted down in an atrocious hand, "probably worse than Greeley's," on any scrap of paper that chanced to be near, were a feature of the daily grist of copy. To the end he never forgot to be a reporter; and on the sea voyage from which he was not to return alive he sent to his newspaper a round dozen of long descriptive letters.

He is most widely known as an explorer and a patron of exploration, particularly of the Arctic. He became closely associated with Robert E. Peary in 1892 and thereafter was his staunch supporter. In 1894, following the discoverer's return to the Arctic the previous year, he accompanied the *Falcon* relief expedition, which provisioned Peary and brought back Mrs. Peary and their infant daughter, born in the Far North. Three years later, for a brief diversion from the Arctic field, he scaled, with Prof. Libby, the Mesa Encantada, in New Mexico. In 1899 he led the *Diana* relief expedition to the North, and on his return organized the Peary Arctic Club, which gave financial aid to the discoverer in all his subsequent work. Two years later, in the *Erik,* he again brought relief to Peary. In 1904 he turned to Africa, going to the headwaters of the Nile, penetrating to the Congo and returning by the same route—a journey narrated in his book, *The Sudan: Africa from Sea to Center,* published the following year. In 1906 and 1908 he was a delegate from various American societies to international gatherings of explorers in Europe. To the great cape at the northeast extremity of Greenland Peary gave the name of his friend, and it was to him that the discoverer sent his code message, received in Brooklyn, Sept. 6, 1909, announcing the discovery of the Pole. Immediately on receiving further information from Peary, Bridgman took a leading part in exposing the pretensions of Dr. Cook. In 1913 he was again a delegate to an international gathering of explorers in Europe and during the year made an extended tour through the Balkans. In 1915 he was made president of the department of geography of the Brooklyn Institute of Arts and Sciences, and two years later a regent of the state university. In 1923 he journeyed through the Panama Canal to California and Hawaii. A youthful octogenarian, he set out on July 2, 1924, for a vacation on the cruise of the New York State School-ship *Newport,* commanded by Capt. Felix Riesenberg. The journey carried him to England, the Belgian battlefields, Spain, and Madeira. On an early morning of the homeward voyage he was suddenly stricken with cerebral hemorrhage, from which he died. The body was brought to Brooklyn and buried, Oct. 1, with appropriate ceremonies, in Greenwood Cemetery.

Bridgman was twice married: in 1868 to Melia Newhall, who died in 1884, and in 1887, to Helen Bartlett, of New York, a writer, who survived him. He was a man of sturdy physique, with the chest and shoulders of an athlete. His familiar photograph shows a large head with a bald and somewhat peaked crown, a high forehead, keen eyes in which may well have "always lurked," as one writes, "a whimsical smile," and a flowing mustache. He was an indefatigable worker and is said never to have wasted a moment. He had amazingly wide interests and managed somehow to apportion his time so as to serve them all. "Had he lived in a period when there were greater undiscovered spaces," said the *New York Times,* "he would have been a Magellan or a Frobisher. . . . His last voyage, in company with youth, is a fit symbol of the whole life of this man who, with uncommon modesty, great geniality and an adventurous courage, illustrated to youth the best that one generation has to give to the next."

[*Who's Who in America,* 1924-25; *His Last Voyage: Herbert Lawrence Bridgman, 1844–1924* (a pamphlet compilation of tributes and of Bridgman's last letters, 1924); Helen Bartlett Bridgman, *Within My Horizon* (1920); Earl D. Babst, *In Memory of Herbert L. Bridgman* (1924); *N. Y. Times,* Sept. 27, Oct. 2 and 5, 1924. See also B. N. and J. C. Bridgman, *Genealogy of the Bridgman Family* (1894) and *Amherst Coll. Biog. Record* (1927).]

W. J. G.

BRIDGMAN, LAURA DEWEY (Dec. 21, 1829–May 24, 1889), blind, deaf, mute, was born in Hanover, N. H., the daughter of Daniel and Harmony Bridgman. A delicate child for a year and a half, at the age of two she had an attack of scarlet fever which left her with sight and hearing lost. For two years she was ill and feeble. As soon as she could walk, she began to explore the room and the house, to follow her mother and to imitate her in every way she could. She thus learned to sew and to knit. In 1837 Samuel Gridley Howe [*q.v.*] heard of Laura's case and visited her home. He found her an attractive child with a nervous organization which made for sensibility and activity, and persuaded her parents to let him undertake her education. In October of that year she became his pupil at the Perkins Institution in Boston. For a year or two Howe himself patiently taught her. The particular significance of her case lay in the fact that she was the first blind, deaf, mute in whose case systematic education had been at all successful. Because of her, others in her situation have had life made more worth while. In the fall of 1839, Laura was sent home with a teacher for the annual three weeks' vacation. The change in her was remarkable. Dr. Howe's success in teaching her the use of language so that she spoke by signs and wrote intelligently was considered such an achievement that his reports of it were translated into several languages. Dickens saw her on one of his American trips and was greatly impressed. At the age of fourteen she had completed *Colburn's Mental Arithmetic* in a little over a year. She finished the study of the continent of Africa in four lessons. At fifteen she visited a woolen factory and a grist-mill and understood and remembered much about both. Three years later she taught a deaf and practically blind child arithmetic for an hour a day. She returned to her father's home in Hanover when she was twenty-three with the understanding that it was to be her permanent home. Intense homesickness, however, for the varied life of the Institution made it advisable for her to return there to live. Here she spent the rest of her life. She had a light share in the household work and helped for an hour in the afternoon, teaching sewing in the workroom. She did perfect work and was a more severe task-mistress than the teacher who had sight. By a provision of Dr. Howe's will an income was secured to her which made her independent. Two years before her death a jubilee celebration of the fiftieth anniversary of her arrival at the Institution was held. Phillips Brooks was among the speakers. Howe had intentionally kept from her all formal religious teaching but in 1862, during a visit at home, she had been baptized in the Baptist church. In his last long report of her, Dr. Howe spoke of her unfailing good spirits, her affections and her enjoyment of life.

[Laura E. Richards, *Laura Bridgman* (1928); M. Howe and F. H. Hall, *Laura Bridgman* (1903); M. S. Lamson, *Life and Education of Laura D. Bridgman* (1878); *Letters and Journals of Samuel Gridley Howe* (1909), ed. by L. E. Richards; Helen Keller, *The Story of My Life* (1905).]   M. A. K.

BRIERTON, JOHN (fl. 1572–1619), was the author of the earliest English work dealing with New England. William Brierton of Hoxne, Suffolk, a grandson of Sir Randle Brereton of Malpas, Cheshire, was a farmer of small estate (J. B. Burke, *Genealogical and Heraldic Dictionary of the Landed Gentry of Great Britain and Ireland*, 1852; *Suffolk Green Book*, X, 200). His fourth son, Cuthbert, settled at Norwich where he prospered as a mercer, attaining in 1576 the civic honor of the shrievalty (H. Le Strange, *Norfolk Official Lists*, 1890). By his marriage to Joan Howse of the same city he had several children ("The Visitation of Norfolk," edited by Walter Rye, *Harleian Society Publications*, XXXII, 1891). John Brierton, the third son, was born in 1572. He attended Norwich Grammar School and at seventeen was admitted to Gonville and Caius College, Cambridge, as a pensioner. He took a bachelor's degree in 1592–93 and proceeded M.A. in 1596. Having taken deacon's orders a few months before, he entered the priesthood at Norwich June 24, 1598. His first charge was the curacy of Lawshall, Suffolk, a parish not far from Hessett (J. Venn, *Biographical History of Gonville and Caius College*, I, 135). Here resided the family of Bacon, cousins of Bartholomew Gosnold [*q.v.*]. With this navigator Brierton and thirty others embarked in a small vessel, the *Concord*, sailing from Fal-

mouth Mar. 26, 1602 (Brierton, *Relation*, 1602). That Brierton sailed with Gosnold has been denied (J. and J. A. Venn, *Alumni Cantabrigienses*, I, 210) but new evidence destroys the objection. Setting a western course Gosnold crossed the Atlantic and made a landfall on the southern coast of Maine. He touched at Cape Cod where with Brierton and three others he spent an afternoon on shore. The leaders of the expedition selected Elizabeth's Isle, now Cuttyhunk, as a base, and remained there about three weeks, busying themselves with trade and undertaking a hasty reconnaissance of the country. Brierton afterward wrote of the New England coast with enthusiasm. The party sailed from Cuttyhunk on June 17 and dropped anchor before Exmouth, Devon, July 23, 1602. On his return to England Brierton was requested by a friend, perhaps Gosnold or Hakluyt, to draw up an account of the voyage. This he did. On Oct. 29, 1602, a stationer of London, George Bishop, who had already brought out Hakluyt's *Principal Navigations*, and who was in 1605 to stand sponsor for Rosier's narrative of the Waymouth voyage, entered at Stationers' Hall the pamphlet published under the title of *A Briefe and True Relation of the Discouerie of the North Part of Virginia* (E. Arber, *Transcript of the Register of the Company of Stationers of London, 1554–1640*, 1875–77, III, 88; L. S. Livingstone, Facsimile Reprint of *Relation*, 1903). Brierton's pamphlet furnishes an optimistic account of the natural advantages of the region which was to become New England, and tells the story of Gosnold's voyage. Some trace of the influence of Verrazano's *Letter*, lately published by Hakluyt, can be detected in it (B. F. De Costa, *New England Historical and Genealogical Register*, XXXII, 77–78). The pamphlet was well received and a second, augmented impression was called for within the year. It is to-day a work of extreme rarity; a copy of the later issue sold in 1926 for £2,200. The writing of this short discourse is Brierton's only significant connection with American affairs. In 1604 he was again at Lawshall (J. Venn, *op. cit.*, I, 135). In 1619 he was rector of Brightwell, Suffolk, a parish but a few miles from Grundisburgh, the home of Bartholomew Gosnold. The date of his death has not been ascertained.

[References cited above. H. S. Burrage, *Early English and French Voyages* (1906) reprints the *Relation*. British Museum Add. MS.. 19,120 f. 112. Walter Rye, *Calendars of the Freemen of Norwich 1317–1603* (1888); *Index to Norfolk Pedigrees* (1896); *Norfolk Families* (1913); W. Hudson and J. C. Tingey, *Records of the City of Norwich* (1910); a sketch of Brierton by J. Westby-Gibson in the *Dict. Nat. Biog.* (1886) is out of date.]   F. M—d.

BRIGGS, CHARLES AUGUSTUS (Jan. 15, 1841–June 8, 1913), clergyman and theological professor, was born in New York City, the son of Alanson and Sarah Mead (Berrian) Briggs. His father was a business man and the son grew up in easy circumstances. He took his college course at the University of Virginia. At the outbreak of the Civil War he served for a few months with the 7th Regiment of New York. He then entered Union Theological Seminary where he remained for two years. After a brief period in business he married, in 1865, Julia Valentine Dobbs of New York and went abroad for four years of theological study in Berlin. Returning to America in 1870 he became pastor of the Presbyterian Church of Roselle, N. J., and in 1874 professor of Hebrew and the cognate languages in Union Theological Seminary. Here he at once made himself felt and under his influence the Seminary became a notable center of Old Testament study. In 1890 a professorship of Biblical theology was founded in memory of Edward Robinson and Briggs became the first incumbent of the new chair. From its foundation Union Seminary, though Presbyterian in its affiliations, had been independent of all ecclesiastical control, but in 1870 at the time of the reunion of the old and new school wings of the Presbyterian Church the General Assembly of the reunited church in an access of good feeling had been given by the Seminary the right to veto appointments to its faculty. At his induction into the new professorship Dr. Briggs, already widely suspect on account of his work in Old Testament criticism, gave an address on the authority of Holy Scripture which deeply offended many conservatives. The result was the veto of his appointment by the General Assembly and his trial for heresy by the Presbytery of New York in 1892. The presbytery acquitted him but the prosecution appealed to the General Assembly which condemned him and suspended him from the ministry. After waiting for some years he took orders in the Episcopal Church and remained a clergyman of that church until his death. In the meantime the Seminary's board of directors declining to recognize the right of the General Assembly to veto the transfer of a professor from one chair to another within the faculty, retained Briggs in his professorship and severed relations with the Assembly. The Seminary thus became again wholly independent and a few years later completely undenominational. His trial for heresy was the most dramatic event of Briggs's career. It seemed to many a futile affair, having to do only with the question whether he was sound in the faith according to the Westminster standards, but the issue was really much broader, and though the decision went against him the trial proved a liberating influence for multitudes and marked an epoch in the history of American Presbyterianism.

In spite of his reputation for radicalism Briggs was thoroughly conservative except in the field of Biblical criticism. His faith in the historic doctrines of the church was profound and unwavering. In his later years, as often happens, he even became suspicious of his younger colleagues who departed further from the traditional faith than he had done. He was particularly sensitive in these years concerning the person of Christ and the Virgin Birth. In matters of Biblical criticism however he maintained his early attitude. The eagerness and energy of his mind were shown when in 1904 at the age of sixty-three he resigned the chair of Biblical theology and turned to the teaching of symbolics and irenics. He had long been deeply interested in church unity, writing frequently upon the subject and discussing it with dignitaries of the Roman Catholic Church as well as of other churches, for he envisaged the reunion of all Christendom, not merely of Protestantism. During his later life his studies were carried on largely with this end in view and his teaching followed similar lines.

To the end of his life he was an untiring worker. A bibliography of his books and articles published two years before his death contains nearly two hundred titles. Most important of the former is probably his *Critical and Exegetical Commentary on the Book of Psalms* published in 1906–07 in two volumes. He was one of the founders and for ten years an editor of the *Presbyterian Review*. For some time he added the duties of librarian to those of professor. The great growth of the McAlpin Collection of British history and theology in the library of Union Theological Seminary was mainly due to his untiring efforts through many years. He was an associate editor of the *Hebrew Lexicon,* of which Francis Brown was editor-in-chief, and the theological articles in that lexicon are mostly from his pen. In recognition of his share in this work he was given the degree of Litt.D. by the University of Oxford. Among the greatest of his services to the cause of Biblical and theological learning are two series—the International Critical Commentary and the International Theological Library—which he planned and edited and in which he had the coöperation of leading scholars.

Briggs had an extraordinarily fertile mind, teeming with ideas on all sorts of subjects. He was a rapid worker, of highly nervous temperament, often impatient of the slower mental processes of others. He held positive opinions and his emphatic enunciation of them made him many enemies, but he had a deeply affectionate nature and was loved as well as admired by a large circle of devoted friends. He died of pneumonia at his home on the Seminary quadrangle at the age of seventy-two, after nearly forty years of service as a professor.

Among the more important of Briggs's writings in addition to his commentary on the Psalms already mentioned, are *American Presbyterianism: Its Origin and Early History* (1885), *Messianic Prophecy* (1886), *The Messiah of the Gospels* (1894), *The Messiah of the Apostles* (1895), *General Introduction to the Study of Holy Scripture* (1899), *Church Unity* (1909), *Theological Symbolics* (1914), and a *History of the Study of Theology* (2 vols., 1916), prepared for publication by Emilie Grace Briggs, his daughter.

[A bibliography of Briggs's writings by Chas. R. Gillett was printed in the volume entitled *Essays in Modern Theology and Related Subjects* (1911) issued by pupils and friends of Dr. Briggs to commemorate his seventieth birthday. For biographical material see Henry Preserved Smith, "Chas. Augustus Briggs," in the *Am. Jour. of Theol.*, Oct. 1913; S. Briggs, *The Archives of the Briggs Family* (1880); obituary in the *N. Y. Times*, June 9, 1913. Publications relating to the Briggs controversy include: C. A. Briggs, *Response to the Charges and Specifications Submitted to the Presbytery of N. Y.* (c. 1891); *The Case against Prof. Briggs* 2 vols. (1892–93); *The Defence of Prof. Briggs before the Presbytery of N. Y., Dec. 13, 14, 15, 19, and 22, 1892* (1893). The Lib. of Union Sem. has an extensive file of material on the controversy.]   A.C.M.

BRIGGS, CHARLES FREDERICK (Dec. 30, 1804–June 20, 1877), journalist, author, was born on the island of Nantucket, Mass., the son of Jonathan C. and Sally (Coffin) Barrett Briggs. He early went to sea, sailing to Europe and South America on several voyages, but soon gave up the idea of being a sailor, and engaged in mercantile pursuits in New York. In 1839 he published a novel called *The Adventures of Harry Franco: A Tale of the Great Panic*, in which he made use of his experiences gained on the sea. In several subsequent works of fiction he used as a pseudonym the name of the hero of this first work. In 1843 he wrote *The Haunted Merchant* and the next year founded the *Broadway Journal*. Edgar Allan Poe was a contributor from the first number and soon was made associate editor along with Henry G. Watson, a musical critic. Briggs, with characteristic friendliness, began by admiring Poe and defending him against criticism, but could not long remain blind to his talented associate's temperamental peculiarities and weaknesses. He retired

from the *Journal* in 1845 and in the next two years published *Working a Passage*, another reminiscence of his sailor days, and *The Trippings of Tom Pepper*. Some of his friends were annoyed to recognize themselves in the latter book and the author thereupon determined to write no more fiction. In 1853 he became one of the editors of *Putnam's Magazine*, in association with Parke Godwin and George William Curtis. After three years the magazine suspended and when it resumed ten years later Briggs was again one of its editors. In the interim he was an editor of the *New York Times* under Henry J. Raymond, and during the latter's absence in Europe was given editorial charge of the paper. He held a position also in the New York Custom House during this period. In 1870 he was made financial editor of the *Brooklyn Union* by Henry C. Bowen and acted in that capacity for three years. Benjamin F. Tracy, who then bought the paper, made Briggs editor, but the latter soon left to join the editorial staff of the *Independent*, which Bowen also owned. Briggs served there until a few hours before his death, which came suddenly at his home in Brooklyn. He left a widow and one daughter. Among other activities he was one of the three men who composed the first Board of Commissioners for Central Park, and for twenty-four years he wrote the annual preface for Trow's *New York City Directory*. His association with Poe caused the publishers of the *Encyclopedia Britannica* to have him write the sketch of the poet for that work. He was a friend of James Russell Lowell, with whom he had considerable correspondence at a time when Poe was attacking Longfellow and, less vigorously, Lowell himself on fancied grounds of plagiarism. Lowell in his *Fable for Critics*, which he presented to Briggs with the privilege of copyrighting it and enjoying the proceeds, gave a deservedly appreciative portrait of him under his pseudonym.

[Obituaries in the *Independent*, June 28, 1877, and in the *N. Y. Times, N. Y. Tribune, N. Y. Herald*, June 22, 1877.]   H.H.

BRIGGS, GEORGE NIXON (Apr. 12, 1796–Sept. 12, 1861), lawyer and statesman, was the eleventh child of Allen Briggs, a blacksmith notable in his community for his forceful character, and of Nancy Brown, who was of Huguenot descent. He was born at Adams, Mass., a town largely settled by Baptists from Rhode Island, but in 1803–05 resided at Manchester, Vt., and in 1805–13 at White Creek, N. Y. At the age of fourteen he was converted at a Baptist revival and at once began making religious appeals which were highly effective. Throughout his life much of his time was given to religious activity. He spent three years learning the hatter's trade. When asked, late in life, from what college he was graduated, he replied, "At a hatter's shop, madam." A year in a grammar school constituted the whole of his formal education. Assisted by one of his brothers he began the study of law in 1813 with Ambrose Kasson of Adams, Mass., but transferred his studies in 1814 to the office of Luther Washburn of Lanesboro, Mass. In May 1818 he married Harriet Hall, and in the following October was admitted to the bar. He first attracted attention by his defense of an Indian who was charged with murder. In 1824 he was elected town clerk of Lanesboro, and in 1826 he was appointed chairman of the commissioners of highways of Berkshire County. In 1830 he was elected to Congress, where he served from 1831 to 1843. In his youth he had been a Democrat, but in the break-up and reorganization of parties he followed Henry Clay on the protective tariff and became a Whig. In Congress he spoke infrequently, but was consistent in his opposition to the extension of slavery. His strongest speech in the House was delivered against the admission of Arkansas with a provision in its constitution forbidding the abolition of slavery without the consent of the slave-owners.

In 1843 he was the Whig candidate for governor of Massachusetts. No choice having been made by the people, he was elected by the legislature in January 1844. He was reëlected each year until 1851, when he received a plurality of the popular vote but was defeated before the legislature by George S. Boutwell. While he was governor, the Mexican War was fought. He strongly condemned it as unnecessary and unjust and believed it to have been entered upon for the purpose of extending slavery, but in spite of his disapproval, he coöperated loyally in supplying the troops which the federal government asked Massachusetts to furnish (*Address to the Legislature*, Jan. 12, 1847). He opposed the annexation of Texas, not only because it extended slavery but also because he questioned the power of Congress either to acquire foreign territory or to admit such territory to the Union. He also deprecated the mode of the annexation of Texas, and argued that annexation by a resolution of Congress was an invasion of the treaty-making power. He opposed the introduction of slavery into the territory acquired from Mexico and urged that the Massachusetts representatives in Congress should not consent to the admission of another slave-holding state. In state affairs his strongest interest was in education. He appreciated his own lack of academic training and

was a warm friend of the colleges. He supported the policies of Horace Mann and repeatedly called the attention of the legislature to the large number of children who never attended school and constantly urged it to provide greater educational facilities. In his first inaugural address, he used language which, in a slightly modified form, was given currency by Grover Cleveland. Briggs said: "Public offices are public trusts, created for the benefit of the whole people, and not for the benefit of those who may fill them." While he was governor the conviction of Professor Webster of the murder of Dr. Parkman occurred. Public sentiment strongly favored a pardon, but Gov. Briggs refused to interfere.

In 1851 he returned to the practise of law with his youngest son as a partner. In 1853 he was a member of the constitutional convention but his part was not conspicuous. In the same year he was appointed judge of the court of common pleas, the abolition of which in 1858 brought his official career to a close. On Sept. 4, 1861, he was appointed umpire in a dispute between the United States and New Granada. On the same day he received an accidental gunshot wound from which he died eight days later.

Briggs was active in the cause of temperance or total abstinence, and from 1856 to his death he was president of the American Temperance Union. He was the most prominent Baptist layman in the United States and from 1847 to his death he was president of the Baptist Missionary Union. He was a man of high character, and exceptional dignity and urbanity of manner.

[Wm. C. Richards, *Great in Goodness: A Memoir of Geo. N. Briggs, Governor of the Commonwealth of Mass. from 1844 to 1851* (1866), is written in a tone of unctuous piety and omits some of the most important phases of its subject's life. A sketch, not always accurate, by Jos. E. A. Smith, appears in *Memorial Biogs. New Eng. Hist. and Geneal. Soc.*, IV (1885), 297–328, and another by Rev. A. B. Whipple in the *Colls. Berkshire Hist. and Sci. Soc.*, II (1895), 151–81. See also Calvin Durfee, *Williams Coll. Biog. Annals* (1871) and S. Briggs, *Archives of The Briggs Family* (1880). Briggs's most important state papers are his seven inaugural addresses which are printed with the *Acts and Resolves* for the year in which they were delivered.]

L. B. E.

BRIGHAM, AMARIAH (Dec. 26, 1798–Sept. 8, 1849), physician, author, was the son of John Brigham of New Marlboro, Mass. On the death of his father when the boy was only eleven years of age, he was taken to live with an uncle, a physician, who promised to educate him as a doctor. Unfortunately his uncle died a year later so he was obliged to shift for himself and finally found a place in Albany as a clerk in a book-store, where he spent the next three years. Then he equipped himself as a doctor by study in the offices of Dr. E. C. Peet of New Marlboro and Dr. Plumb of Canaan, Conn., besides private study and a year spent in attending lectures in New York. At the end of this time, when almost twenty-one, he commenced practise in Enfield, but moved after two years to Greenfield, Mass., where he practised for seven years. At the end of this period he took a trip abroad but after some months of foreign travel returned to his practise in Greenfield. A little later inducements offered in Hartford caused him to remove thither. In 1837, growing tired of his strenuous practise, he went to New York to accept the professorship of anatomy and surgery in the College of Physicians and Surgeons, but remained only a year and a half, preferring his active life as a physician in Hartford. In 1840 he became a candidate for the office of physician and superintendent of the Retreat for the Insane in Hartford and received the position, only to relinquish it in the fall of 1842 for a similar appointment at the New York State Lunatic Asylum, where he founded the *American Journal of Insanity* in July 1844. There he remained until his death. His writings show him to have had a graceful diction. The first book he published, entitled *Remarks on the Influence of Mental Cultivation on Health* (1832), was designed to show the evil effects of beginning to cultivate children's minds too early. It was well received, reaching a third edition in this country, while Scotch editions issued in Glasgow and Edinburgh by Dr. Robert Macnish and James Simpson, Esq., had previously appeared abroad. In the same year, he also published *A Treatise on Epidemic Cholera* which contained little original matter but was published as a compendium of the existing knowledge of this disease, while in 1840 he wrote *An Inquiry Concerning the Diseases and Functions of the Brain, the Spinal Cord, and Nerves,* which soon found a ready sale and was favorably received by the profession. Some years previously he had written *Observations on the Influence of Religion on the Health of Mankind* (1835) which he hoped would have some influence in discouraging fanatical conduct inimical to the religion of Christ and injurious to the health and physical advancement of mankind. His last writing was published as a small duodecimo volume which was entitled the *Asylum Souvenir*. It consisted of aphorisms and maxims to aid in the restoration and preservation of health. He was married Jan. 23, 1833, to Susan C. Root of Greenfield.

[A good sketch of Brigham by E. K. Hunt is in *Lives of Eminent Am. Physicians and Surgeons* (1861), ed. by Sam. D. Gross, pp. 521–544. It was apparently separately printed in Utica in 1858, together with a sermon on the death of Dr. Brigham by Rev. Chauncey E. Goodrich, and a sketch of him by Chas. B. Coventry. See also *Am. Jour. Insanity,* VI, 185–192.]

W. R. S.

BRIGHAM, JOSEPH HENRY (Dec. 12, 1838–June 29, 1904), agriculturist, was born at Lodi, Ohio, the son of Winfield Scott and Mary Elizabeth (White) Brigham. When he was fourteen years old the family moved to a farm in Fulton County and there he grew to manhood and began a public career rather typical of the more successful who reached maturity in Ohio on the eve of the Civil War. When that struggle began he enlisted as a private in the 12th Ohio Volunteer Infantry, later becoming a captain in the 15th Ohio and still later a colonel in the 69th Ohio. He was married in 1863 to Edna Allman. Military prestige gave him civil leadership in the years following the war and although he returned to his farm he was seldom without some public office. Three times sheriff in his own county, he was, in 1880, elected to the state Senate and from that time to his death, through loyal service to the Republican party, he constantly held elective or appointive positions. In 1882 he was chosen a member of the state board of agriculture; in 1887 he was made a member of the board of control of the state experiment station and also of the board of trustees of the state university; in 1894 he was appointed a member of the board of managers of the Ohio penitentiary and in 1897 President McKinley called him to Washington as assistant secretary of agriculture. Consistently interested in agriculture, he always supervised his own farms and his greatest efforts in public life were for the improvement of the farmer. As state senator he was largely responsible for the establishment of the Ohio Agricultural Experiment Station; for three years he was president of the Wool Growers' and Sheep Breeders' Association; he was early active in the Patrons of Husbandry, rendering efficient service as an Institute lecturer; he served as the Worthy Master of the Ohio State Grange, and in 1889 became Worthy Master of the National Grange, an office to which he was reëlected four times. His services to the National Grange were particularly notable. His annual addresses were practical and his administration efficient. He urged the farmers to gain and keep control of the boards of the state experiment stations; he advocated rural free delivery of mails; he insisted that the state and national departments of agriculture should be kept close to the "dirt farmer" both in personnel and program. In the early 1890's when western farmers were inclined to seek relief from economic ills through union with the

Populist party, Brigham insisted on the "absolute political and religious freedom of the individual" within the order and denied the right of the group to bind the individual,—a move which probably saved the organization from dissension and ruin.

[T. C. Atkeson, *Semi-Centennial Hist. of the Patrons of Husbandry* (1916); *Semi-Centennial Hist. of the Ohio State Grange*; *Jours. of Proc. of the National Grange*; L. H. Bailey, *Cyc. Am. Agriculture* (1907–09); *Evening Star* (Washington), June 30, 1904. See also W. I. T. Brigham, *Hist. of the Brigham Family* (1907).]
       A. O. C.

BRIGHAM, MARY ANN (Dec. 6, 1829–June 29, 1889), educator, was born at Westboro, Mass., the daughter of Dexter and Mary Ann (Gould) Brigham. The first of her ancestors in this country is thought to have been Thomas Brigham who came from London to New England in 1635. She was educated at Mount Holyoke Seminary. For some years she taught a private school in her father's house in Westboro, and from 1855 to 1858 instructed at Mount Holyoke. For the next five years she was principal of Ingham University at Leroy, N. Y., and from 1863 until her death in 1889 she was associate principal with Dr. Charles E. West at Brooklyn Heights Seminary. She was chosen to be the first president of Mount Holyoke College after the change from a seminary to an institution of the standing of the other women's colleges in the East, Smith, Vassar, and Wellesley, but she was killed in a railroad wreck near New Haven two months before she was to have taken office. She was a woman of fine personality, both as a teacher and as a friend, with unusual executive ability and scholarship. She had done much to make Brooklyn Heights Seminary, where she had charge of the senior department, a notable school, and it was in recognition of these qualities that she was called to Mount Holyoke. She had been offered the presidency of Wellesley as well as professorships at Smith, Wellesley, and other colleges. Mary Brigham Cottage, one of the dormitories at Mount Holyoke, was named in her honor.

[Catalogues and files of Brooklyn Heights Sem.; letters from Frank W. Forbes of Westboro, Mass., containing information in the Westboro Lib., and from Sidney V. Lowell of Brooklyn, whose daughter was a student of Miss Brigham's; *N. Y. Tribune*, June 30, 1889; *Morning Jour. and Courier* (New Haven), July 1, 1889. See also W. I. T. Brigham, *Hist. of the Brigham Family* (1907).]
       M. A. K.

BRIGHT, EDWARD (Oct. 6, 1808–May 17, 1894), Baptist editor, was born in Kington, a market town of Herefordshire on the Welsh border of England. In his childhood his parents emigrated to America, settling in Utica, N. Y., where the senior Edward Bright carried on for a time the business of brewer and maltster, and later opened a tannery. The younger Edward was set to learn a trade, became an expert printer, and as his first business venture he joined the partnership of Bennet & Bright in a publishing enterprise. This was successful, but Bright's religious convictions led him to believe that he ought to enter the ministry of the church, and in 1839 he was licensed to preach. The following year he was ordained, and became pastor of the Bleecker Street Baptist Church, in Utica. As a Baptist he was a loyal denominationalist. He had grown to manhood during a time when the polemical disposition was indulged by champions of different phases of religious opinions, and the rapid growth of the Baptists and their distinctive practises occasioned general criticism. Bright never flinched in defense of his faith. After a brief pastorate his well-known interest in missions made him considered for an official position in the missionary society, and he was elected foreign secretary of the American Baptist Missionary Union with headquarters in Boston. Here his editorial ability had a chance to appear in the production of the serial numbers of the *Baptist Missionary Magazine*.

In 1855 he went to New York and purchased a Baptist newspaper called the *Register*. He changed its name to the *Examiner*. The paper became under his editorial supervision the organ of the Baptist churches in a section of the country which had a commanding influence, and he gave the paper a standing second to none in his own denomination. He conceived it to be his mission to help bear the responsibilities of the denomination through its various organizations. He took a special interest in the activities of the New York State Convention. He was a trustee of the University of Rochester and of Vassar College; he sat on various boards and committees; he was devoted to the missionary and educational affairs of the denomination; he made all its interests the weekly concern of his journal. Sometimes he was criticized; he did not hesitate to criticize others sharply. His forceful manner at times created antagonisms, but his heart was friendly and sympathetic. The paper for which he was responsible never hedged on public questions. The editor had his convictions, expressed them freely, and was ready to back them up if assailed. The *Examiner* won general recognition throughout the East as a thoroughly representative paper, and it absorbed several other sheets whose circulation was limited by their local character. Bright was married twice: first, to Adeline Osborn of Homer, N. Y., and second, to Anna Leslie Reid, of Rochester.

[*Proc. N. Y. Bapt. State Convention,* 1859, pp. 40–42; M. M. Bragg, *The Pioneers of Utica* (1877); Pomroy Jones, *Annals and Recollections of Oneida County* (1851); obituaries in the *N. Y. Times, N. Y. Herald, N. Y. Tribune,* May 18, 1894.]   H.K.R.

BRIGHT, JAMES WILSON (Oct. 2, 1852–Nov. 29, 1926), philologist, was born at Aaronsburg, Pa., the son of Samuel and Eve Margaret Bright. Samuel Bright died when James was very young, leaving his widow and children in rather straitened circumstances. Nevertheless, James went to college, graduating in 1877 from Lafayette, where he had studied under Prof. Francis A. March who was then, next to Child, the best Anglicist in America. His interest in philology aroused, he did graduate work at the Johns Hopkins University, where he was a Fellow in 1880–82. There he studied English, Old Saxon, and Icelandic under Cook and Wood, German and Gothic under Brandt, and Sanskrit under Lanman; and was granted the degree of Ph.D. in 1882. Immediately he was appointed assistant in German and during the year 1882–83 the English and German departments, which logically belong together, were combined, Bright giving courses in Old High German and in the German classical authors. In 1883–84 Bright went to Germany and studied three semesters under Sievers, Paul, and Ten Brink. He returned to America in the latter year, eager to establish a seminary with training such as he had himself secured in Germany. He was made Fellow by courtesy (1884–85) and substituted for Prof. Corson at Cornell during January and February 1885. From March to May he lectured at Johns Hopkins on historical English grammar, and won for himself an instructorship in English. The English department now established its independence and quickly became a center of research in English philology. Bright was one of the pioneers of graduate work in America. He gave his students a sound philological training and was a master of scientific method. He became professor in 1893 and was Caroline Donovan Professor of English Literature from 1905 to 1925, when he retired as professor emeritus. In these years in addition to his own contributions and his editorial work he trained fifty-five doctors of philosophy in English, most of whom hold important professorships to-day in all parts of America.

Bright was one of the original board of editors of *Modern Language Notes* (1886–1915), and was editor-in-chief 1916–25. He gave much of his time to shaping its ideals and to bringing the contributions to a high standard of scholarship. He was also an editor of *Hesperia,* a member of the advisory board of *Modern Philology,* a member of the editorial committee of the Modern Language Association (1904–14), and editor-in-chief of the Albion Series of Anglo-Saxon and Middle English Poetry. He was author and editor of an *Anglo-Saxon Reader,* and *Outlines of Anglo-Saxon Grammar* (1891); *Gospel of St. Luke in Anglo-Saxon* (1893); *St. Matthew in West-Saxon* (1904); *St. John in West-Saxon* (1904); *St. Mark in West-Saxon* (1905); *St. Luke in West-Saxon* (1906). He was joint author of *West-Saxon Psalms* (1907), and *Elements of English Versification* (1910). He was also a contributor of scholarly articles and reviews in the field of English to many philological journals. A member of many learned societies, he was secretary for America of the Early English Text Society and of the Chaucer Society, secretary (1893–1901) and president (1902–03) of the Modern Language Association, and a vice-president of the Simplified Spelling Society of London.

Bright will always be remembered as the founder of a new scientific era in English philology, one who established a new standard in the study of English. His publications in the field of Anglo-Saxon and of the West-Saxon Gospels are models of exact research and of severe scholarship. He was himself a hard taskmaster and a tireless worker. He lived all his life as a graduate student. He never married, though he had an attractive personality,—a man of average height and build with bright gray eyes and light brown hair and mustache. He belonged to the University Club of Baltimore but was a member of few social clubs, though he was in demand in social circles. Coming of Pennsylvania German stock he was always thrifty, serious, and studious, and managed to amass a fortune of more than $160,000 which he left to his relatives, selling most of his books to Goucher College.

[Records of Johns Hopkins Univ.; *Who's Who in America,* 1926–27; *Modern Language Notes,* XLI (1926), pp.v–vi; *Modern Philology,* XXIV (1927), pp. 351–52; *Johns Hopkins Alumni Mag.,* XV (1927), pp. 121–28. A portrait of Bright hangs in Gilman Hall, Johns Hopkins University.]   D.M.R.

BRIGHT, JESSE DAVID (Dec. 18, 1812–May 20, 1875), politician, was the son of David Graham and Rachel (Graham) Bright (A. G. Green, *Historical Sketch of the Bright Family,* 1900). He was born at the village of Norwich, Chenango County, N. Y., a New England settlement on the upper waters of the Susquehanna. With his father, two brothers, Michael G. and George M., and a sister he moved to Madison, Ind., in 1820. His rather limited education was obtained in the public schools. At the age of twenty-two he became probate judge, succeeding Joseph G. Marshall and serving from Aug. 9, 1834 to Mar. 26, 1839 (L. J. Monks, *Courts and Lawyers of Indiana*, 1916). In 1841 he succeeded Gamaliel Taylor as United States marshal of the Indiana district court but almost immediately had to give way to a Whig, Robert Hanna. When in the same year the Internal Improvement trouble disrupted the Whig party, Bright appeared as a state senator from Jefferson County, serving two sessions. From 1843 to 1845 he was lieutenant-governor; he represented the pro-slavery and Gov. Whitcomb the anti-slavery wing of the Democratic party. By careful manipulation of the state Senate he was elected United States senator Mar. 6, 1845; re-elected Jan. 11, 1851, and Feb. 4, 1857. On Mar. 1, 1861, he addressed a letter of introduction "To His Excellency Jefferson Davis, President of the Confederation of States." The bearer of the letter was arrested, and Bright was expelled from the Senate, Feb. 5, 1862, after a debate of twenty days participated in by thirty-three senators. The vote was 32 to 14 and was based perhaps as much on personal and political opposition as on the charge of treason. Bright returned home and stood for reëlection or vindication. The Assembly was Democratic but refused to support him. He therefore retired to a farm which he owned in Kentucky. Later he represented Trimble and Carroll counties in the Kentucky legislature. He owned coal mines on the Kanawha River and in 1874 moved to Baltimore where he died May 20, 1875. He was survived by his wife, Mary E. Turpin, whom he had married about 1840.

Bright was of robust figure, inclined to corpulency, clean-shaven, with large head, black hair and eyes, and wide mouth. He was a man of quick decisions and swift actions. He was a courteous, obliging friend and an implacable enemy; a companion and friend of Clay, Webster, and Breckinridge; an out-spoken enemy of Douglas, Sumner, and Seward. He was a reliable, voting senator, took care of his constituents, but rarely if ever rose to the level of statesmanship.

[W. W. Woollen, *Biog. and Hist. Sketches of Early Ind.* (1883); O. H. Smith, *Early Ind. Trials and Sketches* (1858); *Ind. House and Senate Journals; Cong. Globe; Indiana State Jour.*, esp. May 21, 1875; *Indianapolis Jour.*, May 21, 1875.]   L. E.

BRIGHT EYES (1854–May 26, 1903), an advocate of Indian rights, was an Omaha, born on the Nebraska reservation, and bore the name of Susette La Flesche. Her father, Joseph La Flesche (Iron Eye, or Inshtamaza, *c.* 1818–88), head chief of the tribe, was the son of a French trader, Joseph La Flesche, who had married an

Omaha woman about 1817. Iron Eye, who had some schooling in St. Louis, was a steadfast counselor of "the white man's way" among his people, and he warmly seconded his daughter's efforts toward an education. Susette attended the Presbyterian mission school on the reservation and through the interest of one of her instructors was sent to a private school in Elizabeth, N. J., where she qualified as a teacher. On her return she taught in a government day school on the reservation, where she is said to have exercised a stimulating influence on her pupils. In 1879, through a dramatic episode in Indian history, she came into prominence. The Poncas, a kindred tribe to the Omahas, living on a reservation in South Dakota claimed by the Sioux, had been forcibly removed by the government in 1877 and taken to the Indian Territory. In their new home they suffered greatly from privation and illness, many of them dying. Susette and her father visited them in the following year, giving them such aid as they could afford, and on returning made public an account of their sufferings which awakened much sympathy. Early in 1879 the chief of the Poncas, Machunazha, or Standing Bear, and thirty-four followers, including women and children, left the Territory and started north. After a six-hundred-mile journey, in which they underwent great suffering, they arrived among the Omahas late in March. They were at once arrested by the military, taken to Fort Omaha and ordered to be sent back. Two men on the editorial staff of the *Omaha Herald*—Thomas H. Tibbles [*q.v.*], later to become prominent as a Populist editor and a candidate for vice-president (1904), and W. L. Carpenter—immediately interested themselves in the case and enlisted the services of two leading attorneys of the state, who brought a *habeas corpus* proceeding before Judge Elmer S. Dundy, in the federal district court. The case was tried Apr. 30 and resulted in a decision giving the Poncas their freedom. Encouraged by the victory and at the same time apprehensive of reprisals on the part of the so-called "Indian ring," friends of the Indians thereupon proposed a movement to awaken the public interest. Under the management of Mr. Tibbles, Susette (who now, apparently at the suggestion of others, adopted the distinctively Indian name Inshtatheamba, or Bright Eyes), her brother Francis (later to win distinction as an ethnologist), and Standing Bear made a speaking tour of the East. They attracted great attention and doubtless contributed in no small measure to the abandonment of the policy of arbitrary removals of Indian tribes.

In 1881 Bright Eyes was married to Mr. Tibbles. Later she traveled with him to Scotland, where she made several addresses. She coöperated with her husband in his editorial and political work and was especially active as a writer. She edited, with an introduction, an anonymous narrative, *Ploughed Under, The Story of an Indian Chief,* which was published in 1881 and was widely reviewed. As a writer she was clear and cogent, and as a speaker she was forceful and eloquent, with a manner and bearing of native grace and dignity. Her later years were lived mainly at Lincoln. She died on the reservation, near Bancroft.

[Article by Alice Cunningham Fletcher in *Handbook of Am. Indians* (1907), ed. by F. W. Hodge; Zylyff (Thos. H. Tibbles), *The Ponca Chiefs: An Indian Attempt to Appeal from the Tomahawk to the Courts* (1879); incidental material in Alice Cunningham Fletcher and Francis La Flesche, *The Omaha Tribe* (27th Ann. Report of the Bureau of Ethnology, 1905–06); *Omaha World Herald,* May 28, 1903.] W. J. G.

BRIGHTLY, FREDERICK CHARLES (Aug. 26, 1812–Jan. 24, 1888), lawyer, author, was a native of Bungay, in the county of Suffolk, England, where his father, Henry A. Brightly, was a stereotyper and publisher. He was educated privately, with a view to adopting a naval career, and when quite young served as a midshipman in the East Indian trade, studying navigation in 1829 with J. W. Norie of London. In 1831 he emigrated to the United States, settled in Philadelphia, took up the study of law, and was admitted to the bar in 1839. Devoting much attention to the early history of Pennsylvania, he soon was recognized as an authority on legal questions arising from incidents of the old régime. At the same time he established a reputation for reliability, mainly through an infinite capacity for taking pains, and gradually acquired an extensive practise, chiefly of a consultative nature. In 1847 he published a practical treatise on *The Law of Costs in Pennsylvania,* which was followed by *Reports of Cases decided by the Judges of the Supreme Court of Pennsylvania in the Court of Nisi Prius at Philadelphia and in the Supreme Court, 1809–1851* (1851). His practise was now demanding the greater portion of his time, despite which he prepared a work of intrinsic merit, *The Equitable Jurisdiction of the Courts of Pennsylvania* (1855). The first volume of his *Analytical Digest of the Laws of the United States* appeared in 1858, the second volume, delayed till 1869, bringing the digest up to the latter date. The cordial reception accorded to his books now induced him to retire from practise and confine himself to the literary side of the law. From 1868 onward he compiled a

series of works, which, because of their accuracy, completeness, and lucidity of statement, commanded the confidence of the Pennsylvania bar and obtained a vogue beyond the confines of that state. First came a *Digest of the Decisions of the Federal Courts from the Organization of the Government* (1868), a second volume of which appeared in 1873, followed by *The Bankrupt Law of the United States* (1869); *Leading Cases on the Law of Elections in the United States* (1871); *The Constitution of Pennsylvania as Amended in 1874* (1874); *Digest of the Decisions of the Courts of the State of Pennsylvania, 1754–1877* (2 vols., 1877), and two later volumes bringing the work down to 1891; and *Digest of Decisions of the Courts of the State of New York from the Earliest Period to 1875* (1877), which later was brought down to the year 1884 in a subsequent volume. He also edited the eighth edition of Binn's *Justice or Magistrates Daily Companion* (1870). Another valuable contribution was his work on a well-known text, *Digest of the Laws of Pennsylvania from the Year 1700,* by John Purdon, Jr. He edited the eighth edition in 1853, the ninth edition in 1861, and the tenth edition in 1873, the digest being brought up to date in the intermediate years by annual supplements. He had maintained his interest in the early history of Pennsylvania, and assembled a very valuable library bearing upon this subject. His collection of Pennsylvania laws, colonial and republican, was the most complete in existence. They included The Second Bradford (1728) Laws of Pennsylvania, all the Franklin and Dunlap Laws, complete sets of the Pamphlet Laws, the Ordinances of Philadelphia, and a unique collection of rare legal periodicals.

In 1835 Brightly was married to Sarah Corfield, sister of William Corfield, with whom he had studied law. Shortly after his marriage he became a Catholic and was a prominent figure during the anti-Catholic riots of 1844. The latter years of his life he spent principally at Germantown, where he died.

[In 1885 Brightly published *Bibliotheca Brightliensis,* a descriptive catalogue of his library, some of the notes to which are autobiographic in character. A short obituary notice appeared in the *Am. Ann. Cyc. and Reg.,* 1888, p. 625. See also obituaries in Phila. papers, especially the *Public Ledger,* Jan. 25, 1888.] H. W. H. K.

BRILL, NATHAN EDWIN (Jan. 13, 1859–Dec. 13, 1925), physician, was born in the city of New York where he spent his entire life. He was the son of Simon Brill, a native of Lichtenfeld, Germany, and Adelheid Frankenthal, who was born in Fuerth, Germany. His early education was received in the public schools of New

York City and at the College of the City of New York where he received his A.B. degree in 1877, at the age of seventeen, and his M.A. in 1883. He graduated in medicine in 1880 from the medical department of New York University. During his last year as a medical student, and the first year after his graduation he served as an interne in Bellevue Hospital. About this time he came under the influence of the well-known neuro-anatomist, Edward A. Spitzka, under whom he accomplished at least one good piece of original work. In 1893 he was appointed attending physician to Mt. Sinai Hospital, and for the succeeding thirty years he served that institution faithfully and assiduously, taking a great personal interest in his patients and building up his professional experience, which eventually led to his recognition as one of the leading diagnosticians of his day. He was primarily a clinician, though he by no means disparaged the value of laboratory work. As Dr. Sachs remarks in his brief biography, he was of the opinion that the actual study of the patient at the bedside was of greater importance than any other procedure in practical medicine.

Throughout his life Brill was interested not only in clinical medicine but in public health as well. He also played his part in the administrative aspects of hospital work and in the work of medical institutions, notably the New York Academy of Medicine. Beginning in 1910, he published a series of articles concerning a febrile disease of infectious origin, which was of fairly frequent occurrence in New York City. His description of this condition was so clear-cut that others readily recognized it, and it very quickly became known as Brill's Disease. Subsequently, largely through the efforts of the late Dr. Gedide A. Friedman, it was shown that it was a modified form of typhus fever and that cases were not confined to New York City but had appeared in other cities along the Atlantic seaboard. Brill did valuable work in other fields, notably in connection with diseases of the blood-forming organs. He was one of the first to introduce into this country the operation of splenectomy for thrombocytopenic purpura. He was the first, with his colleague, Dr. Mandelbaum, to put on a firm footing the pathological anatomy and clinical features of the curious and rare disease first described by the French physician, Gaucher.

Brill was a large man, who gave the impression of strength and vitality. One of his biographers describes his nature as diffident, almost repellent. To the writer he always appeared as a genial, charming gentleman, who held his opinions with decided tenacity and was always

ready to fight for them. Even after he developed the first signs of the disease which ultimately destroyed him, and had had half his larynx removed, he had the courage to continue to attend medical meetings and to take part in discussions in spite of the fact that he was only able to talk in a whisper. When the growth in his larynx recurred and ultimately rendered him entirely voiceless he accepted his lot with fortitude. He was married, on June 8, 1899, to Elsa M. Josephthal, of New York.

[Bull. of the N. Y. Acad. of Medicine, ser. II, vol. II (1926), p. 42; Bernard Sachs, Seventy-Fourth Annual Report of the Mt. Sinai Hospital, 1926, p. 50; A. A. Berg, City College Alumnus, vol. XXII, 1926, p. 391; Who's Who in America, 1924–25; personal acquaintance; dates of birth and marriage from a brother, Henry S. Brill.]   G. B.

BRINCKLÉ, WILLIAM DRAPER (Feb. 9, 1798–Dec. 16, 1862), physician, pomologist, was born at St. Jones' Neck, Kent County, Del. The family of Brincklé or Brinckloe were early settlers in that region, and the first John Brinckloe was lieutenant-colonel of the Kent County militia in 1756. His descendant, John Brincklé, a country doctor, married Elizabeth Gordon, niece and adopted daughter of Cæsar Rodney, one of the signers of the Declaration of Independence, and William Draper Brincklé was their fifth child. He attended Wilmington Academy, graduated from Princeton in 1816, and in 1819 received his M.D. from the University of Pennsylvania. He began the practise of medicine in Wilmington, but in 1825 settled in Philadelphia, where he was active in the profession over thirty years. From 1827 to 1839 he was physician to the City Hospital, devoted to contagious diseases, and in 1832 was distinguished for his efficiency in an epidemic of Asiatic cholera. In 1859, failing health compelled him to resign his practise, and he died at Groveville, N. J., in 1862. Brincklé was twice married: in 1821, to Sarah T. Physick, niece of Dr. Philip Syng Physick of the University of Pennsylvania, who died in 1830; and in 1832, to Elizabeth Bispham Reeves, daughter of Benjamin Reeves of Philadelphia, who died at Groveville in 1858. Though his success in medicine, as measured by his practise, was considerable, Brincklé's claim to distinction rests chiefly on his work as a pomologist. He originated many varieties of fruits, besides introducing to public notice many others discovered in a state of nature, or valuable old varieties in danger of extinction. Owing to limitations of time and space he worked particularly on small fruits and pears, his experiments with the latter winning for him the name of the "American Van Mons." In one year he raised

254 strawberry seedlings, forty-three of which fruited and were described by him, with their parentage and characteristics, in the *Farmers' Cabinet* (XI, 53–57, 1846). He was a frequent contributor to the *Horticulturist,* founded by A. J. Downing, and he prepared the descriptions for *Hoffy's North American Pomologist,* a collection of colored plates of fruits published by Alfred Hoffy, a Philadelphia engraver, of which only Book I (1860) was ever issued. Most of the fruits originated by Brincklé have been superseded by newer varieties, but his work itself is valuable for the accuracy with which he performed his experiments and recorded his observations. In this scientific attitude toward fruit breeding, as also in adoption of the systematic nomenclature which was just beginning to replace the former haphazard methods of description, he was one of the foremost horticulturists of his day. He was one of the founders of the American Pomological Society, an active member of the Pennsylvania Horticultural Society, and honorary member of other leading pomological societies.

[Emile B. Gardette, *Biog. Memoir of Wm. Draper Brincklé* (1863); biographical notices, mostly signed by initials only, in *Gardener's Monthly,* ed. by Thos. Meehan, vol. V; Brincklé's own articles in *Farmers' Cabinet* and *Horticulturist* (1846–60); *Cyc. Am. Horticulture* (1900), ed. by L. H. Bailey, I, 180, and *Standard Cyc. Horticulture* (1915), III, 1566, give sketches by Wilhelm Miller, evidently based in part on information in *Gardener's Monthly,* 1863, but giving date of Brincklé's death incorrectly as 1863. Another briefer note, in Bailey, *Cyc. Am. Ag.* (1909), IV, 557, refers to the *Cyc. Am. Horticulture* and contains same error in date of death.]   M. F. W.

BRINKERHOFF, JACOB (Aug. 31, 1810– July 19, 1880), jurist and legislator, was the eldest son of Henry I. Brinkerhoff and Rachel Bevier, the father a member of an old Dutch family of New York, the mother of Huguenot ancestry (Roeliff and T. Van Wyck Brinkerhoff, *Family of Joris D. Brinckerhoff,* 1887, pp. 11–13, 67). Brinkerhoff was born at Niles, N. Y., and attended the public schools of his native town and the academy of Prattsburg, N. Y. He studied law for two years in a law office in Bath, N. Y. In 1836 he moved to Mansfield, Ohio, where he began the practise of law. He was twice married: to Caroline Campbell of Lodi, N. Y., and after her death, to Marion Titus of Detroit. His public life consisted of two terms as prosecutor of Richland County, two terms as a Democratic member of the House of Representatives (1843–47), and three terms in the supreme court of Ohio (1856–71). In Congress he was identified with a small group of northwestern Democrats, advocates of a low tariff, expansionists, and Free-Soilers. He proposed an amendment to the joint resolution for the annexation of Texas, providing that, "as a fundamental condition, . . . the existence of slavery shall be forever prohibited in one-half of all the annexed territory" (*Congressional Globe,* 28 Cong., 2 Sess., p. 192). This amendment failing, Brinkerhoff voted against the resolution. On the Oregon question he defended the claim of the United States to the whole territory. "We do not want war," he exclaimed, "but if we must have it, we would a great deal rather fight Great Britain than some other Powers, for we do not love her" (*Ibid.,* 29 Cong., 1 Sess., pp. 203 ff.). When President Polk asked for $2,000,000 to negotiate peace with Mexico, Brinkerhoff supported an amendment to prohibit slavery in the acquired territory. The facts in his contention of twenty years later that he was the author of the Wilmot Proviso are shrouded in some doubt. It is quite possible that he may have suggested to Wilmot in part or in entirety the particular verbal form of the proposed amendment (see Brinkerhoff's statement in Congress, Feb. 10, 1847, *Ibid.,* 29 Cong., 2 Sess., p. 377). The Proviso attached to the Two Million Bill in Wilmot's handwriting is in the Manuscript Division of the Library of Congress. Brinkerhoff's alleged original draft, the evidence for his part, has unfortunately been lost (C. B. Going, *David Wilmot,* 1924, ch. ix). Brinkerhoff again became a conspicuous opponent of slavery when the Oberlin rescue cases came before the supreme court of Ohio, 1859. The court sustained the Fugitive Slave Law, the vote of the judges being three to two. Brinkerhoff wrote a dissenting opinion, falling back upon the strict construction theory, and so denying to Congress the power to legislate upon the subject of fugitives from labor (*Ex parte Bushnell, ex parte Langston,* IX *Critchfield's Ohio State Reports,* 221– 29). Through the period of the slavery controversy Brinkerhoff passed from the ranks of the anti-slavery Democrats to the Free-Soil party and then to the Republican party. In 1872 he strongly indorsed the Liberal Republican movement (see *Chicago Tribune,* Feb. 12, 1872). Little is known of his personal traits or his private life. He had a local reputation as a public speaker of more than average ability, quick at repartee, having read much and possessing a remarkable memory (A. A. Graham, *History of Richland County,* 1880, pp. 381–82).

[In addition to references given above, see obituary in *Ohio Liberal* (Mansfield), vol. VIII, No. 14; and *The Recollections of a Life Time* (1900), by Gen. Roeliff Brinkerhoff.]   E. J. B.

BRINKERHOFF, ROELIFF (June 28, 1828– June 4, 1911), lawyer, banker, penologist, was

descended through his father, George Brinkerhoff, from Joris Brinckerhoff who came to this
country from Holland in 1638; and through his
mother, Jacomyntie Bevier, from a Huguenot
refugee who came in 1650. Roeliff, the youngest of nine children, was born on a farm by the
side of Owasco Lake, Cayuga County, N. Y.
Outdoor life in central New York, a region of
remarkable beauty, taught him many lessons and
made of a weakly child a strong healthy man and
a lover of nature as well. Eight years in the district school, a year in an academy in Auburn,
another at a more famous academy in Homer,
N. Y., completed his formal school work. For
two years he taught in district schools near his
father's farm. A cousin living in Tennessee attracted him to the South. In 1846–47, Roeliff,
then eighteen years of age, taught in a planter's
private school near Nashville. Then for two
years he was a tutor in the family of Andrew
Jackson, Jr., at the Hermitage. His work left
him ample time for reading in the library of
Gen. Jackson. More than three years in the
South were a happy experience and a liberalizing education for this particular northern boy.
In the summer of 1849 he entered the office of
an uncle in Mansfield, Ohio, for the study of
law, and three years later he was admitted to the
bar. He was soon drawn from the practise of
law into journalism as editor and then owner of
the *Mansfield Herald* (1855), and from that into
the army (1861). Senator Sherman returned to
Mansfield in the summer of 1861 to recruit two
new regiments and persuaded Brinkerhoff to accept a place in one of them, as quartermaster
with the rank of captain. He was in the quartermaster service five years, becoming brigadier-
general toward the end. During this service he
published a military manual, *The Volunteer
Quartermaster* (1865). As a newspaper editor
he had become actively interested in politics.
Though formerly a Democrat, he was drawn
into the Republican party on the slave issue.
During the war he spoke often at Union meetings. After the war he returned to civil life, law,
and politics. A traditional dislike for protective
tariffs made him a restless Republican. In the
campaign in Ohio in 1869 he raised the issue of
tariff reform. One result was a series of speeches throughout the Middle West in 1869–70 under
the auspices of the Free Trade League of New
York. He took a conspicuous part in the Liberal Republican movement of 1872, attending
the Cincinnati convention and later the New
York Conference of tariff reformers. In the following campaign Brinkerhoff was chairman of
the executive committee for the Liberal Repub-

licans of Ohio. He was at heart a Jeffersonian
and after the defeat of Republican liberalism he
returned to the Democratic party.

In 1873, with a neighbor, Mr. Harter, he established the Mansfield Savings Bank. His life
as a banker left him leisure to devote to philanthropy and penology. In 1873, he was appointed
to the Ohio Board of State Charities. He was
a regular attendant upon the meetings of the
National Conference of Charities and Corrections and frequently participated in its programs.
In 1883, he became a member of the National
Prison Association, and after the death of Ex-
President Hayes (1893), Brinkerhoff succeeded
him in the presidency. He was vice-president of
the International Prison Congress which met in
Paris in 1895. An interest in archæology and
pioneer history led him to take the initiative in
founding the Ohio Archæological and Historical
Society, of which he was president for fifteen
years.

Brinkerhoff was married on Feb. 3, 1852, to
Mary Lake Bently, by whom he had two sons
and two daughters.

[The chief source is Brinkerhoff's autobiography,
Recollections of a Lifetime (1900). This is more than
personal reminiscences; it is a valuable commentary
on men and events by a keen observer of wide acquaintance. Articles on Brinkerhoff appear in the *Ohio
Archæol. and Hist. Quart.*, IX (1900), and XX (1911).
For genealogy see *The Family of Joris Dircksen Brinckerhoff* (1887), comp. by Roeliff Brinkerhoff. There is a
good obituary in the *Mansfield Shield*, June 5, 1911.]
                                                E. J. B.

BRINTON, DANIEL GARRISON (May 13,
1837–July 31, 1899), anthropologist, was born
at Thornbury, Pa., of English Quaker descent,
the son of Lewis and Ann (Garrison) Brinton.
Prepared for college by the Rev. William E.
Moore, he entered Yale College in 1854. As an
undergraduate he soon made a mark in literary
activities, taking two prizes in English composition. The winter of 1856–57 he spent in Florida,
doubtless laying the foundation for his future
work. In 1857 he again distinguished himself in
literature at Yale, and in 1858 received the degree of A.B. He then entered the Jefferson Medical College and graduated with the degree of
M.D. in 1861. He spent a year studying at Heidelberg and Paris, and returned to West Chester,
ter, Pa., where he practised medicine. He entered the Federal army in the summer of 1862 as
acting assistant surgeon. His services soon won
recognition and he was rapidly promoted. He
was present in many of the great battles of the
Civil War, including Chancellorsville and Gettysburg. In the fall of 1863 he suffered a sunstroke, was compelled to relinquish active field-
duty, and took up hospital work. He remained

in the army till Aug. 5, 1865, when he was discharged with the brevet rank of lieutenant-colonel of volunteers, and on Sept. 28, of the same year, he married Sarah Tillson of Quincy, Ill. He returned to West Chester and resumed his medical practise, till he moved to Philadelphia, becoming assistant editor of the *Medical and Surgical Reporter* in 1867, and editor in 1874. He retired in 1887 to pursue the subjects dearest to him. His first work, *Notes on the Floridian Peninsula* (1859), foreshadowed where his true interests lay. In 1867 he resumed his publication of papers on Americana. In 1884 he became professor of ethnology and archeology in the Academy of Natural Sciences of Philadelphia, and in 1886 professor of American linguistics and archeology in the University of Pennsylvania. He never was a field worker and remained a closet anthropologist, apparently never feeling the necessity of coming into close contact with primitive peoples. On the other hand he delved into the libraries of Europe as well as of this country. It is also to be remarked that he utilized the results of field workers in his writings and spoke appreciatively of them. Possibly his lack of field work was due to his view that he had never fully recovered from the sunstroke which he suffered in the Civil War. It is true that his methods are not the methods of to-day. It is also true that some of his theses have been discarded, such as the denial of Asiatic (Mongolian) origin of American Indians and the affirmation of their derivation from Europe, the conviction that polysynthesis and nominal-incorporation were characteristic of all American Indian languages, that elaborate grammatical categories were the late fruit of the human intellect, and that the Lettic peoples in both appearance and language are a connecting link between the Slavonic and Teutonic peoples. It is also true that his translations from Aztec are inaccurate. His dismissal of the Toltecs as being largely purely legendary has not withstood the test of time. Undeniably no one to-day would defend his position that the likeness of Iroquoian and Algonquian mythology (and similarly in other cases) was due to the sameness of the human mind, and not the diffusion. On the other hand his first work, *Notes on the Floridian Peninsula* (1859) remains to this day of the highest value. His exposure of the fraudulent character of the famous (or rather infamous) Taensa grammar alone would win a place for him among scientists. His *The American Race* (1891) was the first systematic classification of the aboriginal languages of both North and South America. Though based on materials which are hardly adequate, this work shows a keen insight regarding the genetic relationships of American Indian languages and in some cases anticipated what has since been established. In this connection it may be said that he was the first to point out the relationship of Natchezan to Muskogean, though afterward he apparently was doubtful of it. His contention that Serian and Yuman are genetically related is gaining acceptance even if rigorous proof has not yet been furnished. His *Library of Aboriginal American Literature* is especially worth noting, for at that time unfortunately American aboriginal literature was presented in literary English, not in text and translation. The publication of his "Maya Chronicles" (Volume I of his *Library*) in 1882, by itself would establish his reputation. All of these (save one) were published in text and translated into a European language for the first time. These chronicles were the foundation upon which Mayan and Christian chronology have been coördinated, and must be considered a landmark in American archeology. His paper on the mound-builders (*Historical Magazine*, February 1866)—showing that they were plain American Indians, and not (as is unfortunately still fondly believed by the laity) a highly civilized mysterious race who were exterminated by the American Indians—is fundamental. The influence of his scattered writings has been very great. Summing up, we may say Brinton was one of the pioneers, and an able one, of anthropology in this country.

[*The Brinton Memorial Meeting* (1900), containing fully annotated list of Brinton's writings; obituaries by McGee and Chamberlain, in *Science*, n.s., X, 193–96, and *Jour. of Am. Folk-Lore*, XII, 215–25, respectively; brief review and appraisement of Brinton's activities in physical anthropology by A. Hrdlička in the *Am. Anthropologist*, n.s., XVI, 537–40; summary of Brinton's work by Boas in *Globus*, LXXVI, 165, 166; short notices in the *Public Ledger* (Phila.) and *Phila. Press*, Aug. 1, 1899; *Who's Who in America*, 1899; eulogy by Mrs. Helen C. DeS. A. Michael in the *Conservator*, Sept. 1899; sketch, largely autobiographical, in *Fourth Biog. Record of Class of Fifty-Eight, Yale Univ.* (1897); Anson Phelps Stokes, *Memorials of Eminent Yale Men* (1914), I, 351 ff.]   T. M.

BRINTON, JOHN HILL (May 21, 1832–Mar. 18, 1907), surgeon, was born in Philadelphia, the son of George and Margaret (Smith) Brinton. He was graduated with the degree of B.A. at the University of Pennsylvania in 1850, and received his degree of M.D. two years later at the Jefferson Medical College. After a year's post-graduate study in Paris and Vienna, in company with the late Prof. J. M. DaCosta, he returned to Philadelphia, entered upon general practise, and was made demonstrator in operative surgery in the Jefferson Medical College. A year later he was advanced to the position of lecturer on operative surgery which he held until the outbreak of the Civil War. In his *Personal Memoirs* he tells us that he was commissioned brigade surgeon on Aug. 3, 1861, his name being fourth on the list of volunteer surgeons. He served with Grant in the Tennessee and Cumberland River campaign in 1862, and was then ordered for duty in the office of the Surgeon-General in Washington. While there he helped to prepare *The Medical and Surgical History of the War of the Rebellion* (1870–88), writing the article on Gunshot Wounds, and was designated to establish an Army Medical Museum. Later he was relieved from duty in Washington and ordered to active service under Gen. Rosecrans, serving as medical director in the field in the Missouri campaign. He was later made superintendent of the hospitals in Nashville, Tenn., and medical director of the Army of the Cumberland. He resigned from the army on Feb. 11, 1865, returned to Philadelphia, and was again made lecturer on operative surgery at the Jefferson Medical College. Subsequently in 1882 he succeeded Dr. Samuel D. Gross as professor of the practise of surgery and clinical surgery at the same college and continued in this position until May 1906 when he was made an emeritus professor. He was visiting surgeon at St. Joseph Hospital from 1895 until his death, and filled the same position at the Philadelphia Hospital, 1867–82 and at the Jefferson Medical College Hospital from 1877 on. He wrote little, but his writings make us wish he had accomplished more with his pen. His *Personal Memoirs* were written for his children. He also edited John E. Erichsen's *Science and Art of Surgery* (1854) and delivered the valedictory address to the graduating class of the Army Medical School in 1896. Some years previously, in 1869, he had delivered in Philadelphia the Mütter lectures on surgical pathology, with "Gun Shot Injuries" as his subject. On Sept. 13, 1866, he married Sarah Ward, daughter of the Rev. Ferdinand DeWilton Ward of Geneseo, N. Y. "He was a broadly educated, cultivated, courteous, kindly gentleman."

[*Personal Memoirs of John H. Brinton* (1914); notice in the *Jeffersonian*, VIII, 65, 112–13, prepared by a committee of his friends and colleagues at the Jefferson Medical College; *Who's Who in America*, 1906–07; *N. Y. Medic. Jour.*, Mar. 23, 1907; *Public Ledger* (Phila.) and *Press* (Phila.), Mar. 19, 1907; names of parents from a son Dr. Ward Brinton of Phila.]

W. R. S.

BRISBANE, ALBERT (Aug. 22, 1809–May 1, 1890), social reformer, was born in Batavia, N. Y., where his father, James Brisbane, of Scotch descent, was one of the more prominent landowners. His mother, Mary (Stevens) Brisbane, was of English stock, and a student of no

little ability. From both of his parents Albert Brisbane inherited a sturdy and vigorous constitution, being, according to his father, "as withy as a rattlesnake." From his mother he got much of his early education, particularly in history and the sciences. When about fifteen years of age he was placed in a Long Island boarding-school, but soon removed to New York City where he studied under several tutors, the most important being John Monesca, whose teaching and social philosophy made a great impression. Before leaving Batavia, Brisbane tells us, he had begun to consider seriously the social destiny of man, and his contact with Monesca furthered his interest in the subject and inclined him to study the problem under the great thinkers of contemporary Europe. At the age of eighteen, therefore, he left New York for Paris where he studied for a time under Cousin, Guizot, and others. Disappointed in the French thinkers he next went to Berlin where he studied social philosophy under Hegel. Socially he found Berlin very pleasant, being welcomed into intellectual circles of a liberal character, but Hegel disappointed him for, he says, "I found in Hegel and among his disciples no idea of a higher social order than the European civilization" (Redelia Brisbane, *Albert Brisbane*, p. 96). Leaving Berlin, he next journeyed to Constantinople to study at first hand the civilization of the Turkish Empire and southeastern Europe. Returning to western Europe, he reached Paris shortly after the Revolution of 1830, convinced that the human misery he had witnessed could be alleviated only by a fundamental reconstruction of society. For a time he dallied with the reform ideas of Saint-Simon, but these he eventually rejected. A few months later, however, he read Charles Fourier's *Traité de l'Association Domestique-Agricole* (1821–22), and was much impressed. "Now for the first time," he says, "I had come across an idea which I had never met before—the idea of *dignifying* and *rendering attractive* the manual labors of mankind" (*Ibid.*, 172). Further investigation convinced him that in Fourier's theory he had "found a hypothesis which explained what I had been seeking to discover—a just and wise organization of human society" (*Ibid.*, 187). Two years of study under the personal direction of Fourier followed, during which Brisbane satisfied himself of the wisdom and validity of Fourier's theories. In 1834 he returned to the United States, but for several years poor health prevented the propagation of Fourierism, the general acceptance of which he firmly believed would result in "the social redemption of the *collective* man." In 1839, however, he organized a society and began lecturing in Philadelphia and New York, and the following year widened his appeal by publishing his *Social Destiny of Man; or, Association and Reorganization of Industry,* an exposition of Fourierism. This was followed in 1843 by *Association; or, A Concise Exposition of the Practical Part of Fourier's Social Science.* The earlier work so much interested Horace Greeley that he not only offered Brisbane the use of the *New York Tribune* but even got out with him a paper devoted wholly to Associationism, the *Future,* which ran for two months, when it was dropped for a column in the *Tribune.* In order to forward his educational campaign still more vigorously Brisbane also took over the editorship of the *Chronicle,* wrote twice a week for a radical democratic paper, the *Plebeian,* edited (1843–45) with Osborne Macdaniel, the *Phalanx,* the "organ of the doctrine of Association," and wrote occasionally for the *Dial.* Under the excitement of the new ideas some forty small and poorly financed experiments in practical associationism were started, a development for which Brisbane was quite unprepared and in which he took no part. The results were disastrous, convincing Brisbane of the unwisdom of "too hasty propaganda" (*Ibid.,* 218). Following the failure of these practical experiments in Fourierism, public interest in the subject waned, and Brisbane dropped his educational propaganda, although many years later, in 1876, he published a *General Introduction to Social Sciences,* the first part of which was devoted to an introduction to Fourier's theory of social organization, and the second part to a translation of the master's Theory of Universal Unity.

Brisbane, wrote one of his contemporaries, was "a well and highly educated man, of active and vigorous mind, with a keen and analytical vision, and a large power of generalization. With a great deal of candor, good temper, and kindliness, he exhibits a certain innocent simplicity of character, and a fervor of faith in abstract convictions, which can rarely fail to awaken in a high degree the confidence, interest and esteem of those who are brought into any intimacy of contact with him" (*Democratic Review,* XI, p. 302). As a practical reformer, however, he was not a success. Not only was the scheme he advocated Utopian in character, but Brisbane himself, modest and somewhat self-distrustful, was quite lacking in any real capacity for leadership. Intellectually, as well as historically, Albert Brisbane belongs among those Utopian socialists of his generation who sought in some new order of society a universal panacea for the evils they saw in the society about them. The later years of Brisbane's life were devoted to study and travel, and to his inventions, of which his system of transportation by means of hollow spheres in pneumatic tubes and a new system of burial became best known. He married twice, his first wife being Sarah White by whom he had three children, and his second wife Redelia Bates. He died in Richmond, Va.

[The chief source is Redelia Brisbane, *Albert Brisbane: A Mental Biography with a Character Study* (1893). With the exception of the first chapter, a character study by Mrs. Brisbane, this work is autobiographical. For a view of Brisbane at the height of his activity as a social reformer, see the *Democratic Review,* XI, 302.]

W. R. W.

BRISTED, CHARLES ASTOR (Oct. 6, 1820–Jan. 14, 1874), author, was the son of Rev. John Bristed [*q.v.*], and Magdalen, daughter of John Jacob Astor II. He was born in New York City, was prepared for college by tutors, and entered Yale College at the age of fifteen. When he was graduated, in 1839, after having gained three of the four classical prizes, he was influenced by relatives to remain at Yale for a year of graduate work; but he later expressed the opinion that the time was almost wasted, as a New England college town was a good place "to unmake a partially formed scholar." In 1840 he matriculated at Trinity College, Cambridge, England, where he was graduated in 1845 as a foundation scholar. He writes of himself in this period as being dressed "in the last Gothamite fashion" and proud of introducing sherry cobbler at Trinity College dinner parties, though shunning all student excesses. He won the University Latin Essay Prize and on receiving his B.A. degree evaded taking the oaths of allegiance to Church and State then required. After some European travel, he returned to the United States and began writing for his own pleasure, sometimes under the name of Carl Benson. Under this pseudonym he was for some years a regular contributor to the sporting journals, *Porter's Spirit of the Times* and *Wilkes's Spirit of the Times.* His chief works are: *Selections from Catullus, for School Use* (1849); *A Letter to the Hon. Horace Mann* (1850), a reply to some criticisms of Astor and Girard; *The Upper Ten Thousand: Sketches of American Society* (1852), sketches of New York society; *Five Years in an English University* (1852); "The English Language in America" (in *Cambridge Essays,* 1855); *Pieces of a Broken-Down Critic* (1858); *Now Is the Time to Settle It* (1862); *No Surrender* (1863); *The Cowards' Convention* (1864); *The Interference Theory of Government* (1867), against tariff and liquor prohibition; *Anacreontics* (1872); and *On Some Exaggerations in Com-*

parative Philology (1873). As a writer he showed a trained mind and fastidious taste, but considerable self-consciousness. His desire for accuracy caused too great detail and timidity in drawing conclusions from facts. Devotion to classical scholarship is evident in his literary criticisms and translations. He was a member of the American Philological Association and a contributor at its meetings, and was a trustee of the Astor Library from its foundation until his death. On Jan. 14, 1847, he married Laura Brevoort of New York, who died in 1860. In 1867 he married Grace Sedgwick of Lenox, Mass. He had homes in New York City, Washington, Lenox, and South Carolina, but spent most of his later years in Washington, where he was known in literary circles as a scholar and to his friends as a hospitable but not indiscriminate host.

[*The Todd Genealogy* (1867), by Richard Henry Greene; an article by Richard Grant White, Bristed's friend, in the *Galaxy*, Apr. 1874; Bristed's own book, *Five Years in an English University* (1852); long sketch, mainly autobiographical, in *A Quarter-Century Record of the Class of 1839, Yale Coll.* (1865); obituaries in the *Washington Chronicle*, Jan. 16, 1874, and the *N. Y. Tribune*, Jan. 17, 1874, and an obituary editorial in the Washington *Evening Star*, Jan. 15, 1874.]

S.G.B.

BRISTED, JOHN (Oct. 17, 1778–Feb. 23, 1855), author, Episcopal clergyman, was born at Sherborne in Dorsetshire, England, the son of a clergyman in the Anglican church. His general education was received at Winchester College. During his life he followed three different professions. He first studied medicine at Edinburgh and practised it for a short time; next he studied law under Joseph Chitty, editor of Blackstone's *Commentaries,* and was admitted to the Inner Temple; later in life he was to be a clergyman. Before leaving England he began writing and seems to have held ideas considered radical at the time, for Arthur Aikin, editor of the *Annual Review and History of Literature* (vol. II, 1804, p. 408), in commenting on Bristed's book *A Pedestrian Tour through Part of the Highlands of Scotland in 1801* (2 vols., 1804), denounced the young author, not only for borrowing parts of his book without giving credit, but also because he and his companion, traveling as American sailors, had gone about haranguing over the hardships of the poor and the excessive luxury of the rich until they had aroused the hostility of the Scots. Other early books of his were *The Adviser; or the Moral and Literary Tribunal* (4 vols., 1802); *Critical and Philosophical Essays* (1804); *The Society of Friends Examined* (1805); and *Edward and Anna* (1806), a novel. In 1806 Bristed came to New York City and there practised law, lectured, and wrote books

and magazine articles. In 1807 he was an editor of the *Monthly Register, Magazine and Review of the United States,* founded in 1805 by Stephen Cullen Carpenter at Charleston, S. C. Bristed's books of this period include *Hints on the National Bankruptcy of Britain, and on Her Resources to Maintain the Present Contest with France* (1809); *The Resources of the British Empire* (1811); *Oration on the Utility of Literary Establishments* (1814), at the opening of Eastburn's Literary Rooms, New York City; *The Resources of the United States of America* (1818); *Thoughts on the Anglican and Anglo-American Churches* (1823). On Mar. 8, 1820, he married Magdalen, widowed daughter of John Jacob Astor, who died in 1832. Their son, Charles Astor Bristed [*q.v.*] became a writer. Growing interested in theology, Bristed studied under Bishop Griswold of the Episcopal Church, at Bristol, R. I., and later under Bishop Smith of Vermont. In 1828 he returned to Bristol as Bishop Griswold's assistant at St. Michael's, and in 1829 succeeded the Bishop there as rector. He held this office until 1843, when he resigned on account of poor health, continuing to reside in Bristol until his death twelve years afterward. During his later years Bristed was a devoted churchman, giving liberally of his wealth both in private charities and in church extension in Rhode Island. He was especially interested in helping young men preparing for the ministry to carry on their studies. As a preacher, he was sincere, somewhat emotional, and oratorical. His writings show diligent and exhaustive study; interest in history, economic questions, and religion; a strong personal point of view, frequently amounting to prejudice; and a rather ornate style.

[Thos. F. Kirby, *Winchester Scholars* (1888), p. 280; E. A. and G. L. Duyckinck, *Cyc. of Am. Lit.* (1855); Richard H. Greene, *The Todd Genealogy* (1867); W. W. Spooner, ed., *Historic Families of America* (n.d.); obituaries in the *Providence* (R. I.) *Daily Post*, Feb. 27, 1855, and the *Newport* (R. I.) *Advertiser*, Feb. 28, 1855.]

S.G.B.

BRISTOL, JOHN BUNYAN (Mar. 14, 1826–Aug. 31, 1909), painter, was born in Hillsdale, N. Y., the son of Abner and Lydia Bristol. He was chiefly self-taught, although he had a few lessons at one time from Henry Ary, portrait painter of Hudson, N. Y. His early life is said to have been a struggle, but he seems to have been one who held tenaciously to a chosen profession and through courage, determination, and inherent talent eventually won success. He was elected associate of the National Academy of Design and a member of the Artists Fund Society in 1861. In 1875 he was made a full Academician. In 1862 he married a daughter of Alanson Church of Great Barrington, Mass., and after this made his home in New York. His summers were for the most part spent in New England with occasional trips to Lake George and Lake Champlain. In 1859 he visited Florida and made many sketches in the vicinity of St. Augustine. A painting entitled "Afternoon on the St. John's River" was the result of this sojourn. He was represented in the Centennial Exposition, Philadelphia, in 1876, and received a medal of honor. He also received honorable mention in the Paris Exposition, 1889, and a bronze medal, Pan-American Exposition, Buffalo, 1901. Among his best-known works are: "An Autumn Afternoon near Bolton, Lake George"; "Mansfield Mountain at Sunrise"; "The Adirondacks from Lake Champlain"; "An Afternoon in Haying Time—Berkshire County." H. T. Tuckerman speaks of him as a "modest and assiduous artist with somewhat of Kensett's repose in his best landscapes, some of which, besides accuracy in detail and true effect in generalization, exhibit a genuine sentiment which elevates their imitative truth" (*Book of the Artists*, 1867, p. 558). In 1905 he was reported by his colleague, Samuel Isham, as "still working with undimmed eye and unwearied hand." He died in New York, Aug. 31, 1909.

[Samuel Isham, *Hist. of Am. Painting* (1905); C. E. Clement and L. Hutton, *Artists of the 19th Century* (1879); *Art Jour.* XXXI, 110–11; *Columbia County at the End of the Century* (1900).]   L. M.

BRISTOW, BENJAMIN HELM

BRISTOW, BENJAMIN HELM (June 20, 1832–June 22, 1896), lawyer, statesman, was born in Elkton, Ky., the son of Francis M. and Emily E. (Helm) Bristow. His father, a leading lawyer and politician of the district, sat in Congress in 1854–55 and 1859–61, and was first a Whig and later an anti-slavery Unionist. These facts shaped Bristow's early life. After graduating from Jefferson College in Pennsylvania in 1851, he studied law in his father's office, was admitted to the bar in 1853, and for a time was his father's partner. On Nov. 21, 1854, he married Abbie S. Briscoe. In 1858 he removed to Hopkinsville, Ky., to practise law, and was there when the Civil War began. Being an ardent Unionist, Bristow aided in recruiting the 25th Kentucky Infantry, and on Sept. 20, 1861, was mustered into service as its lieutenant-colonel. After fighting at Fort Donelson and elsewhere, he was seriously wounded by the explosion of a shell at Shiloh, where his regiment was so badly cut up that it was merged with another. Upon recovering, he helped raise the 8th Kentucky Cavalry, became its lieutenant-colonel, and on

Apr. 1, 1863, was commissioned its colonel. He fought in many skirmishes, and was present when Morgan's raiders were captured at Wellsville, Ohio, in the summer of 1863. Offered a brevet as a major-general, he modestly refused it.

Bristow's war service was cut short by the need for strong Union men in Kentucky politics, where ex-Gov. John A. Wickliffe was leading an organized opposition to Lincoln's emancipation proclamation and other measures. In August 1863, without his knowledge, he was elected to the state Senate from Christian County. Realizing the emergency, Bristow somewhat reluctantly accepted and took his seat in December. He supported all Union enactments, labored for ratification of the Thirteenth Amendment, and was an active worker for Lincoln's reëlection. Resigning from the Senate in 1865, he removed to Louisville, and there was immediately appointed assistant United States attorney; the next spring (May 4, 1866) he was made United States attorney for the Kentucky district. This time he had to play a greater rôle in a more pressing emergency. Kentucky was in a state of lamentable disorder. Ku Klux Klan violence, spontaneous racial clashes, and conflicts between Unionists and former secessionists were everyday occurrences; while gross frauds were practised upon the internal revenue service. Bristow acted with characteristic energy and determination. He obtained twenty-nine convictions for various crimes under the first Federal Enforcement Act, one capital sentence for murder being especially effective in shaking the nerve of the Klan. The lives and property of colored people were rapidly made safe. Attacking the distillers of illicit whiskey, he obtained more than a hundred forfeitures of stocks of liquor (*Some Facts about . . . Bristow*, pp. 12 ff.).

The skill and courage which Bristow displayed attracted national attention, and led at once to higher federal office. Having resigned his United States attorneyship on Jan. 1, 1870, he was practising law in Louisville with John M. Harlan as partner when Congress created the post of solicitor-general. President Grant promptly appointed Bristow the first incumbent. He wrote many opinions, made arguments in several important constitutional cases before the Supreme Court, and won a reputation for mastery of federal jurisprudence. He quit office on Nov. 12, 1872, to accept a highly paid place as counsel of the Texas & Pacific Railroad, but found this step a mistake, for the labor required was administrative while his tastes were for legal work. Returning to Kentucky, he was practising law again when on July 3, 1874, President Grant appointed him secretary of the treasury. This appointment, his predecessor W. A. Richardson having been seriously compromised by contract scandals, was hailed by the press as promising a much-needed reform of the department.

With gratifying rapidity this promise was fulfilled. A drastic reorganization was carried through. The office of supervising architect, made notorious by Mullett, was abolished; the second comptroller and his leading subordinates were dismissed for inefficiency; the detective force was shaken up; and the new Secretary consolidated a number of collection districts in both the customs and internal revenue services. At the same time he argued vigorously for a resumption of specie payments. But his greatest service was in breaking up the notorious Whiskey Ring. This was a powerful and corrupt machine which had been devised by western distillers and their allies in the internal revenue service for the evasion of the whiskey tax, and despite general knowledge of its activities, it seemed impregnable. George W. Fishback, owner of the *St. Louis Democrat,* advised Bristow upon the best means of attacking the Ring in that city. The work of detection was assigned to men wholly outside the Treasury department; instructions were given them in a cipher different from the department code; and by maintaining complete secrecy, a mass of evidence upon the frauds was accumulated. Similar work was done in Chicago and Milwaukee. On May 10, 1875, all the suspected distilleries and rectifying houses in these three cities were seized, and the Ring was shattered at one blow. Books and papers were found proving individual guilt. Nearly 250 civil and criminal suits were instituted forthwith. Within a year Bristow had taken action to recover $3,150,000, had indicted 176 men, and had obtained sentences for 110.

The Ring, fighting back desperately, sought with some success to poison the mind of President Grant against Bristow. Through the attorney-general's office they were able to impede the Secretary's efforts to complete the destruction of the Ring; and by adroit manipulation they induced Grant to believe that Bristow was using his office to scheme for the Republican nomination. His resignation was virtually forced by the President, and was handed in on June 17, 1876 (*North American Review,* October 1876, p. 321). Since the beginning of the year he had been prominently mentioned for the presidency. The conference of moderate Republicans held at the Fifth Avenue Hotel in May regarded him as the best Republican candidate but refrained from an open indorsement (P. L. Haworth, *Hayes-Tilden Election,* pp. 15 ff.). Nominated at the Cincinnati convention in June by John M. Harlan, he received 113 votes on the first ballot, and on the fourth ballot, with 126 votes, stood second only to Blaine.

Bristow's resignation from the Treasury closed his official career, which had covered but fifteen years, two of them spent in military commands. In 1895 Cleveland offered him membership on the Venezuela Boundary Commission, but for personal reasons he declined. Removing from Louisville to New York in 1878, and on October 16 of that year forming the partnership of Bristow, Peet, Burnett, & Opdyke, he remained for the rest of his life one of the leaders of the Eastern bar. He argued many cases before the Supreme Court, and was noted among lawyers for his personal charm, the thoroughness and closeness of his argument, and the skill with which he confined himself to vital points. In 1879 he was elected the second president of the American Bar Association, and for many years was a vice-president of the Civil Service Reform Association. He was a member of the Metropolitan, Union, and Union League clubs. In 1896, while in apparently robust health, he was stricken with appendicitis, and died at his home, 27 West Fiftieth St., within four days.

[The best sketch is David Willcox, "Memorial of Benj. H. Bristow" in *Ann. Report, Ass. of the Bar of the City of N. Y.,* 1897. It is supplemented at some points by the anonymous pamphlet, *Some Facts about the Life and Public Services of Benj. H. Bristow* (New York, 1876). The best treatment of the Whiskey Ring is H. V. Boynton's long paper, "The Whiskey Ring," *North Am. Rev.,* CXXIII, 280–327. Paul L. Haworth's *The Hayes-Tilden Disputed Presidential Election* (1906) treats briefly the Bristow "boom" in 1876.]   A. N.

BRISTOW, GEORGE FREDERICK (Dec. 19, 1825–Dec. 13, 1898), composer, violinist, teacher, was born in Brooklyn, and spent his entire life in or near New York City. His father was an English organist, William Richard Bristow, who started the son's musical education so early that at the age of eleven he became a violinist in the orchestra of the Olympic Theatre in New York. Piano and organ lessons were given him by his father and by Henry C. Timm, and composition was later studied with G. A. MacFarren. In 1842 he became a violinist in the New York Philharmonic Society, a membership which continued for more than forty years. Bristow was married to Louise Westervelt Holden. His "Concert Overture," *Opus 3,* was played by the Philharmonic Society Nov. 14, 1847; his first symphony, in E flat, appeared in 1845 and a cantata "Eleutheria" in 1849, but the first work to attract general attention was the three-act opera "Rip Van Winkle," which was produced at Niblo's Garden in New York on Sept. 27, 1855 by the Pyne-Harrison English Opera Company, the composer conducting. It had seventeen performances in two months. The libretto, based on Washington Irving's story, was the work of Jonathan Howard Wainwright. Critics complained of the extreme length of the opera, the excessive prominence of solo as compared with concerted numbers, and an apparent monotony of style. The orchestration was praised, as was the staging.

On Mar. 1, 1856, the New York Philharmonic Society played Bristow's second symphony, in D minor, and on Mar. 26, 1859, his third symphony, in F sharp minor. The oratorio "Praise to God" was given first performance on Mar. 2, 1861, by the New York Harmonic Society, of which the composer was conductor. A second opera, "Columbus," was never completed, but the overture was played by the New York Philharmonic Society at the first concert in Steinway Hall, Fourteenth St., Nov. 17, 1866. Bristow's second oratorio, "Daniel," was first performed by the Mendelssohn Union, Dec. 30, 1867. The fourth or "Arcadian" Symphony, in E minor, was played by the New York Philharmonic on Feb. 14, 1874. Five years later Theodore Thomas conducted for the first time Bristow's music to an ode by William Oland Bourne entitled "The Great Republic." Bristow's "Jibbenainosay" overture was produced in 1889, and his symphony "Niagara" during the last year of his life.

Bristow conducted the Harmonic Society 1851–62, was a church organist, and from 1854 till his death was connected with musical work in the New York public schools. He was pianist at the concert in Tripler Hall, New York, on Feb. 20, 1852, at which Theodore Thomas made his first appearance in the United States as a boy violinist, and two Bristow songs were on that program. Bristow was a member of the orchestra which accompanied Jenny Lind at her first concerts in this country, and also played in the Jullien concerts in 1853–54. In addition to the music mentioned above he composed two string quartets, a set of six organ pieces, and a number of smaller pieces. He was one of the first outspoken champions of music by Americans, and as early as 1854 protested, with a group of fellow members of the Philharmonic, against the policy of favoring composers of other countries, particularly those of Germany. He was regarded as an able conductor, and was highly esteemed as a teacher. The record left by Bristow is that

of a serious, industrious and unassuming man who exerted a strong influence for good music during many years, and who deserves an honored place as one of the first Americans to compose music in the larger forms.

[G. H. Curtis, "Geo. Frederick Bristow," *Music*, III, 547–64; Waldemar Rieck, "When Bristow's 'Rip' was Sung at Niblo's Garden," *Musical America*, Dec. 5, 1925; G. L. Ritter, *Music in America* (1883); César Saerchinger in *Musical Quart.*, Apr. 1920; *Musical Record*, Jan. 1899.]

C. N. B.

BROADHEAD, GARLAND CARR (Oct. 30, 1827–Dec. 12, 1912), geologist and engineer, was born near Charlottesville, Va., son of Achilles and Mary Winston (Carr) Broadhead and brother of James Overton Broadhead [*q.v.*]. The father was a farmer, teacher, and surveyor, and a son of John Broadhead who had come to America as a soldier in Burgoyne's army and after the war settled in Albemarle County, Va. When the boy was nine years of age the family moved to Flint Hill, St. Charles County, Mo., twenty-five miles north of St. Louis, where he received his early education mainly in private schools or under tutors. He studied at the University of Missouri, 1850–51, showing most proficiency in mathematics, Latin, and history. He then entered the Western Military Institute at Drenum Springs, Ky., where he came under the tutelage of the geologist Richard Owen and the mathematician and engineer Bushrod R. Johnson. His first position after leaving these schools was that of surveyor on the Missouri Pacific Railroad then under construction. The year following he became assistant engineer in charge of location lines and in 1857 was made resident engineer of construction. Later he became engineer of railway construction in Kansas. During the Civil War, in 1862, Broadhead was commissioned assistant adjutant-general on the staff of Gen. J. B. Henderson, and in the same year he was appointed deputy collector of internal revenue for the 1st district of Missouri, a position which he occupied until the close of the war. Two years later he was appointed by President Johnson an assessor of internal revenue for the 5th district of Missouri and held the office until 1868 when he resigned to accept a position on the Geological Survey of Illinois. He took part in the preparation of the Missouri Mineral Exposition of Philadelphia under the direction of the Smithsonian Institution and became one of the jurors on awards in the division of mining and general geology. For several years subsequent to 1884 he served on the Missouri River Commission and on the board of managers of the Bureau of Geology and Mines of the state.

The survey work along the railway lines of

Missouri offered ample facilities for geological observation of which Broadhead was not slow to avail himself. These brought him into the favorable notice of State Geologist Swallow, who in 1857 employed him in making a geological reconnaissance along the line of the southwestern branch of the Pacific Railroad. Later in the capacity of assistant geologist Broadhead investigated the mineral resources of several counties and made six reports, which, owing to the troubled condition of the times, were not published until thirteen years later during the survey of R. Pumpelly. In 1868 Broadhead became an assistant geologist under Worthen on the staff of the Geological Survey of Illinois where he did good service. In 1871 he was called back to Missouri to become assistant on the survey under Pumpelly as already mentioned, and in turn to become its director on Pumpelly's resignation in 1873, continuing to act during the following year, after which the survey was discontinued. In 1881 he contributed a chapter on the building-stone resources of Missouri to the 10th Census Report on this subject, and later, important articles to the surveys of 1889 and 1900 under Winslow, Keyes, and others. In 1887 he was called to succeed J. G. Norwood in the chair of geology in the University of Missouri, retiring as professor emeritus ten years later, at the age of seventy. "The refrain running through all of his courses of instruction at the Missouri State University during the course of his long professorship there, and through his many public lectures, was the adjustment of man's life and efforts to his geological environment" (Keyes, p. 13). As a man he is described as "genial, courteous and considerate, with wide interests and a truly remarkable detailed knowledge of men and events" (*Ibid.*, p. 17). His best work, as judged by one of his colleagues, consisted first, in his differentiation of the coal measures of Missouri and Kansas, and second, in his establishment of the Ozarkian Series, "the great succession of Late Cambrian rocks found typically developed in Missouri and extending far and wide to the northward in the upper Mississippi valley" (*Ibid.*, p. 17). Broadhead's bibliography comprises nearly two hundred titles, many of which, however, are only brief notes. He was married twice, in 1864 to Marion Wallace Wright, and in 1890 to Victoria Regina Royall.

[C. R. Keyes, *Bull. Geol. Soc. of America*, vol. XXX (1919), containing bibliography of Broadhead's publications, pp. 20–27.]   G. P. M.

BROADHEAD, JAMES OVERTON (May 29, 1819–Aug. 7, 1898), congressman, diplomat, was born at Charlottesville, Albemarle County, Va. His mother, Mary Winston (Carr) Broadhead was of Scottish origin, her ancestors occupying large estates in Virginia. His father, Achilles Broadhead, was a native of Albemarle County. A brother, Garland Carr Broadhead [*q.v.*] later attained eminence as a geologist. Achilles Broadhead was a man of great force of character, intensely patriotic, and a soldier of the War of 1812. James Broadhead received a good classical education, acquiring his preparatory training under his uncle, Dr. Frank Carr, who kept a select school at Red Hills, Va. In 1835, at the age of sixteen years, he entered the University of Virginia, where he spent a year in diligent study, supporting himself wholly by his own effort. In 1837, his father having moved to Missouri, he found employment there as tutor in the family of Edward Bates, at the same time pursuing the study of law under that eminent jurist. In 1842 he was licensed and immediately began the practise of law in Bowling Green, Mo. He soon became interested in politics and in 1845 was sent to the state constitutional convention as a delegate from the second senatorial district. In 1847 he was the Whig candidate of Pike County for the legislature, running against Nicholas P. Minor. Although the county was normally Democratic, Broadhead reversed this condition and was elected. In 1850 he was a candidate for the state Senate and again he was triumphant. He removed to St. Louis in 1859 and formed a partnership with Fidelio C. Sharp. In the agitation preceding the Civil War he took a leading part. Although a Virginian, he held the Union above all else, and in conjunction with Frank P. Blair, Jr., and others, helped to organize the committee of safety in St. Louis for the purpose of resisting the tide of disunion. He also aided in effecting a military organization under the leadership of Gen. Lyon. He was a prominent member of the state convention in 1861 which declared a provincial government to be established favorable to the Union. On the report of the committee of which he was chairman, the offices of governor, lieutenant-governor, secretary of state, and treasurer were declared vacant. A provisional government was organized. While a member of this body Broadhead was appointed provost-marshal-general of the district, embracing Missouri, Southern Iowa, Kansas, Indian Territory, and Arkansas. The skill and power with which he discharged this duty gave additional proof of his ability.

In 1875, he was a member of the state constitutional convention and at once took his place as a leader in that able body of men. He labored incessantly for the formation of the constitution adopted that year. He was retained as special counsel for the government in the famous "Whiskey Ring" cases in St. Louis in 1876. In 1878, he was made president of the American Bar Association. He was a member of the commission which framed the "scheme and charter" of St. Louis under the constitution of 1875. In 1882 he was elected to the Forty-eighth Congress on the Democratic ticket and served with distinction on the judiciary committee of the House. President Cleveland, in 1885, appointed him special commissioner to visit France and examine the archives of the government in relation to the French Spoliation Claims which had long been pressing for an adjustment. Upon his report Congress took the first action toward making provision for payment. Soon after the completion of this duty Broadhead was appointed minister to Switzerland but he resigned in about two years. His success as legislator, counsel in shaping the course of military affairs, and as provost-marshal of a great department demonstrates his ability and versatility. Of all the lawyers in Missouri, he probably enjoyed the widest national reputation, as he was concerned not only in litigation within the state, but in many important controversies in the federal Supreme Court. He was forcible in speech, severely logical, candid, and truthful. His fine personal appearance, his open manly face, his genial and gentle manners, expressed his character. He was married on May 13, 1847 to Mary S. Dorsey, daughter of Edward W. Dorsey of Pike County, Mo.

[H. A. Conard, ed., *Encyc. of Hist. of Mo.*, I, 387–91; L. U. Reavis, *St. Louis: the Future Great City of the World* (biog. ed., 1875), pp. 721–25; *The Bench and Bar of St. Louis* (1884), pp. 8–10; *The Hist. of Pike County, Mo.* (1883), pp. 382–83; *Clinton Democrat*, Aug. 8, 1898; *St. Louis Republic*, Aug. 7, 8, 1898.]

F. C. S—r.

BROADUS, JOHN ALBERT (Jan. 24, 1827–Mar. 16, 1895), Baptist clergyman, was born in the Blue Ridge country of western Virginia, of Welsh ancestry. His father, Edmund Broadus, came from a family of preachers, and though not himself a minister was prominent in religious circles as well as in the Virginia legislature. The mother was Nancy Sims, the daughter of a farmer. Broadus had good schooling, and entered the University of Virginia after a period of teaching. During his college course he was converted in a revival and began to preach. Lack of a theological seminary of his own denomination in the South deterred him from further study, and after another period of teaching he became minister to the Baptist church at

Charlottesville, Va., at the same time teaching ancient languages in the University of Virginia as assistant instructor. A new period opened in his life when, after long hesitation, he accepted the chair of New Testament and homiletics in the theological seminary established by the Educational Convention of the Southern Baptists in 1858 at Greenville, S. C. He had had a commanding influence in shaping the curriculum for the new school, and he was one of four prominent ministers chosen to constitute the first faculty. Here he worked with James P. Boyce [*q.v.*], the president, in the closest intimacy. Almost at once the school was threatened with extinction by the entrance of the South into the Civil War. Broadus was sympathetic with the Confederacy, preached in the camps, and, when classes were suspended, made a living by preaching to country churches and acting as corresponding secretary of the Sunday-school Board for three years. During the last year of the war he was aide-de-camp to the governor. The seminary shared in the prostration of the South at the close of the war, and in 1870 Broadus went abroad for a year, partly for his health which was never robust. Upon his return he threw himself into the difficult task of resuscitating the seminary. Removal of the school to Louisville, Ky., proved an advantage, the student enrolment increased, and funds began to be available. At Louisville Broadus heightened his reputation as a scholar and teacher, and wrote much. In 1889 he succeeded Boyce as president of the institution. He published *Lectures on the History of Preaching* (1876); *Commentary on the Gospel of Matthew* (1886); *Sermons and Addresses* (1887); and a *Memoir of James Pettigru Boyce* (1893). In 1889 he delivered at Yale the Lyman Beecher lectures on preaching, which were never published. He was in his earlier life an editorial contributor to the *Religious Herald,* and later wrote frequently for the press of his denomination, and for Sunday-school publications. He was a member of the International Lesson Committee from 1878 until his death. He was trustee of the Slater fund. In his own city he spoke in churches and on the public platform, and was admired and loved as a man. He was twice married: on Nov. 13, 1850, to Maria Harrison, who died seven years later; and on Jan. 4, 1859, to Charlotte Eleanor Sinclair.

[Archibald T. Robertson, *Life and Letters of John Albert Broadus* (1901); A. Broadus, *Hist. of the Broadus Family* (1888); Geo. B. Taylor, *Va. Baptist Ministers* (4th ser. 1913); *Religious Herald*, Mar. 21, 1895; *News and Courier* (Charleston, S. C.), May 6, 8, 1875; *Louisville Commercial*, Mar. 16, 1895; *Courier-Jour.* (Louisville), Mar. 15, 16, 1895.]

H. K. R.

BROCKETT, LINUS PIERPONT (Oct. 16, 1820–Jan. 13, 1893), author, physician, descended from John Brockett, one of the founders of the New Haven Colony, was born in Canton, Conn., the son of a Baptist minister, Rev. Pierpont Brockett, and of Sarah (Sage) Brockett. He had the advantages of three educational institutions, the Connecticut Literary Institute at Suffield, Brown University, and Yale Medical School, from which he was graduated in 1843. After a brief attempt at practise, he left medicine in favor of literature. During 1844 and 1845 he was professor of physiology and anatomy in Georgetown College, Ky. He joined a publishing firm in Hartford in 1847 and continued the connection for ten years. During this time and afterward he contributed to various encyclopedias, among them *Appletons' Annual Cyclopaedia, Johnson's Universal Cyclopedia,* and two foreign encyclopedias. Because of his interest in medico-sociological subjects, in 1854 he was appointed a commissioner to investigate idiocy in Connecticut and published a report in 1856. Always a devoted Baptist, he wrote a volume of church history, *The Bogomils of Bulgaria and Bosnia* (1880), and an appreciative account of the Karen Mission in Bassein. As early as 1847 he began writing on historical subjects, a type of work which finally absorbed his whole time and interest. He published about fifty books, the majority on Civil War subjects. Some of the more important are: *A Geographical History of the State of New York* (with Joseph H. Mather, 1851), *The History and Progress of Education* (1860), *Woman: Her Rights, Wrongs, Privileges, and Responsibilities* (1862), *The Philanthropic Results of the War in America* (1863), *The Life and Times of Abraham Lincoln* (1865), *Our Great Captains* (1865), *A Complete History of the Great American Rebellion* (with E. G. Storke, 1863–65), *The Camp, the Battlefield, and the Hospital* (1866), *Woman's Work in the Civil War* (with Mary C. Vaughan, 1867), *Men of Our Day* (1868), *Grant and Colfax* (1868), *Epidemic and Contagious Diseases* (1873), *Our Western Empire* (1881). He edited *Our Country's Wealth and Influence* (1882), and was editor and chief writer of *Descriptive America* (1884–85). Brockett sometimes used the pseudonym "Capt. Powers Hazelton." In 1846 he married Lucy Maria Thacher of Jordan, N. Y. In 1860 he and his wife and their one child removed to Brooklyn. Here he became editor at different times of the *Brooklyn Monthly* and the *Brooklyn Advance.* He was considered, in editorial offices, in his church, and in social relations, a pleasant, kindly, rather serious man.

From his appearance he might have passed for a clergyman or a college professor. He had a roundish face, with an expression of great serenity, a high, bald forehead, a straight, classical nose, bright eyes which needed spectacles much of his life, a thin-lipped mouth uncovered by a mustache, a tuft chin-beard, and long hair curling about his ears. Intensely patriotic, a strong supporter of the Union, and an enthusiastic admirer of the great men of the Civil War period, he made his histories very eulogistic. He had respect for adequate and reliable sources but in the interpretation of events he placed more emphasis on individuals than on social forces. He esteemed integrity of character, religious principle, loyalty to country, above everything else, but, after these, placed a high value on material success. His style of writing is clear, straightforward, substantial. There is little humor, but much use is made of anecdote, especially to illustrate character. He died at his home on Steuben St., Brooklyn, and his funeral was held at Emanuel Baptist Church.

[Biographical sketch in *The Descendants of John Brockett, one of the Original Founders of the New Haven Colony* (1905), comp. by Edward J. Brockett; obituaries in the *Brooklyn Eagle, N. Y. Tribune, Evening Post* (N.Y.), Jan. 14, 1893.]   S. G. B.

BROCKMEYER, HENRY C. [See BROKMEYER, HENRY C., 1828–1906.]

BROCKWAY, ZEBULON REED (Apr. 28, 1827–Oct. 21, 1920), penologist, was born at Lyme, Conn., the son of Zebulon and Caroline Brockway, both descendants of an old New England family. At twenty-one, equipped with an elementary education and a few years of business experience, he took what proved a decisive step in his life; he became a clerk in the Wethersfield prison. Promotion followed promotion. In 1851 he went to the Albany (N. Y.) County Penitentiary as Amos Pilsbury's deputy; in 1853 he was made superintendent of the Albany Municipal and County Almshouse and in 1854 head of the new Monroe County Penitentiary at Rochester. In 1861 he went to Detroit as superintendent of the new House of Correction, a position he held until 1872, when circumstances forced his resignation. Three years in business life lent credence to the judgment pronounced on him as a boy, "That lad will never become forehanded for he has not the money-getting instinct." He again came into his own when in 1876 he accepted the superintendency of the Elmira State Reformatory for men, which he directed for twenty-five years.

In 1894 his management of the reformatory was investigated by the State Board of Charities which recommended that he be dismissed. The investigation was apparently partisan in character, however, and Gov. Flower, acting upon the report of a special commission appointed by him refused to deprive Brockway of his post (*Documents of the Assembly of the State of New York*, 1894, No. 89; *Nineteenth Yearbook of the Elmira State Reformatory*, 1893–94). In 1900 he retired from public service to devote himself to charitable and educational work, but in 1905 he was induced to run for mayor of Elmira. He served in that capacity for two years with the same deep sense of duty and uncompromising honesty which characterized his whole life. At the conferences of the National (later the American) Prison Association his fine, white-bearded countenance and patriarchal figure were frequently seen, and his opinions were eagerly sought on all important questions. In 1897–98 he served as president of the Association and in 1910 he was honorary president of the International Prison Congress, meeting in Washington. Married on Apr. 13, 1853, to Jane Woodhouse of Wethersfield, he survived his wife by nine years.

While not the innovator of the "indeterminate sentence" he was the first to put it into our statutes. All punishment had for him but one aim, the protection of society against crime. This he thought could best be secured by reforming the criminal, if possible, or by confining the incorrigible indefinitely. If reformation alone was to be the key to liberty, the fixed sentence had to give way to an absolutely indeterminate sentence and the execution of this sentence had to be entrusted to the administrative authorities of all institutions within a given jurisdiction. He presented his ideas to the National Congress on Penitentiary and Reformatory Discipline (Cincinnati, 1870) in a remarkable paper entitled "The Ideal of a True Prison System for a State" (*Transactions*, pp. 33–65). In the "three years law," drafted by him and passed by Michigan in 1869, he had incorporated some of his ideas (*Acts of the Legislature of the State of Michigan*, 1869, no. 145); they received a more complete expression in the organic law of the Elmira Reformatory, which he drafted and saw accepted by the New York legislature, in 1877 (*Laws of the State of N. Y.*, 1877, ch. 173). His original demand for a sentence without minimum and maximum was modified by the legislature, which adopted an indeterminate sentence without a minimum but with the maximum as already defined by the penal laws of the state.

Brockway early experimented with evangelistic forms and methods of reformation, but, with wider experience he lost faith in them. Greatly influenced by continental criminological thought, he gradually embraced a deterministic philosophy of conduct which became the basis for his work at Elmira. There, physical, manual, and military training, together with ethical and esthetic instruction, were the instruments he used in his task of "socializing the anti-social." Reformatory prison treatment—and to him there was no other kind—meant "education of the whole man, his capacity, his habits and tastes, by a rational procedure, whose central motive and law of development are found" in what he elsewhere calls "the ennobling influences of established industrial efficiency" ("The American Reformatory Prison System," in C. R. Henderson, *post*, I, 88–107).

[Brockway's autobiography, *Fifty Years of Prison Service*, was published in 1912 by the Russell Sage Foundation, New York City. For an evaluation of his work see F. H. Wines, "Historical Introduction," pp. 3–38 of "Prison Reform," in vol. I of *Correction and Prevention* (1910), ed. by C. R. Henderson; the minute spread upon the records of the Nat. Prison Ass. (*Proc.*, 1900, pp. 333–34) on the occasion of Brockway's retirement from Elmira; Frank L. Christian's necrology, *Proc. Am. Prison Ass.*, 1921, pp. 121–23; and Crystal Eastman's "A Non-Partisan Mayor" in *Charities and The Commons*, XIX, 953–54, Nov. 2, 1907. There was a brief obituary in the *N. Y. Times*, Oct. 22, 1920. Genealogical data may be found in F. E. Brockway, *The Brockway Family* (1890).]   T. S.

BRODERICK, DAVID COLBRETH (Feb. 4, 1820–Sept. 16, 1859), forty-niner, politician, was born in Washington, D. C. He was of Irish stock, and his father, a stone-mason for a time employed on the national Capitol, was doubtless an immigrant. Of the mother, whose maiden name was Copway, little is recorded except that she was idolized by her son. The boy had little schooling. Before he was fourteen the family moved to New York. About 1837 the father died, and the boy began his struggle for a living for himself, his mother, and his younger brother. Industrious, ambitious, belligerent, of strong physique and able to give a good account of himself in a street brawl, he literally fought his way to the front. By the time he was twenty he was a member of an engine company (of which later he became foreman) and was active in ward politics as an adherent of Tammany Hall. His mother dying and his brother being accidentally killed, he was left without kin. His struggles had molded his character; he was "stubborn, positive, unrelenting and unforgiving," self-centered also, and determined upon his advancement to the utmost of his powers. He owned a saloon, which seems to have netted a good profit, and he became politically prominent. He was a member of the city charter convention of 1846, over which he several times presided, and in the same year he was the unsuccessful Tammany nominee for Congress in the 5th district.

In the spring of 1849 he determined to go to California. Closing his saloon, emptying his casks in the street, and vowing that he would never again "sell or drink liquor, smoke a cigar or play a card," he took passage by way of Panama, and in June arrived in San Francisco. Here he found old friends ready to back him alike in business and politics. He formed a partnership with an assayer for the coining of gold "slugs" of four-dollar and eight-dollar values in metal, which passed readily, because of the scarcity of coin, for five dollars and ten dollars. The business, though highly profitable, was sold some months later, and Broderick turned his attention to the still more profitable enterprise of trading in shore-front lots. From the time he landed he was in politics. In August he was chosen a delegate to the constitutional convention, and in January of the following year was elected to fill a vacancy in the Senate. On the succession of Lieutenant-Governor McDougal to the governorship, in January 1851, Broderick was elected president of the Senate. Though his private life was exemplary, in politics he was unscrupulous. An adept in Tammany methods, he soon became a political boss; and it is said of him that from 1851 (when he was reëlected to the Senate) to 1854 he was "the Democratic party of California." He now determined upon a seat in the United States Senate, and set about to compass the defeat of William M. Gwin, whose term would expire on Mar. 4, 1855. The attempt served for the time only to divide the party and to deadlock the legislature, but on Jan. 10, 1857, he won the election by 79 votes out of 111. At the same time, through a bargain made with his rival, Gwin, he brought about the latter's reëlection and obtained the promise of a monopoly of the Federal patronage for the state.

President Buchanan refused to recognize the bargain, and Gwin, in spite of his promise, continued to distribute the patronage. Broderick turned on both men with bitter resentment. At what time he first developed sentiments hostile to the slave power and to political corruption cannot be said. But he now vehemently attacked the administration, both for its policy in Kansas and for its alleged venality, and he carried the war into his own state, where pro-slavery feeling was for the time dominant and aggressive. His attitude brought him into national prominence, but made him a marked man at home. Both he and his friends felt that he was now regarded as a menace and that means would be taken to get rid of him. A remark made by him

on June 27, 1859, concerning Chief Justice David S. Terry, one of the leaders of the pro-slavery element, brought a challenge from Terry, who resigned his judgeship, and Broderick accepted. They met on the early morning of Sept. 13. The pistol furnished Broderick was so "light on the trigger" that it was prematurely discharged by the act of raising his arm. Terry's bullet struck Broderick in the breast, and he fell mortally wounded. Conveyed to a near-by farmhouse, he lingered for three days. On his deathbed he said: "They have killed me because I was opposed to the extension of slavery and a corrupt administration." The dead body was conveyed to the city, where on Sept. 18 funeral services were held at which Col. Edward D. Baker [q.v.] delivered an eloquent and impressive eulogy. On Feb. 13, 1860, memorial services were held by both houses of Congress. Broderick was buried at the foot of Lone Mountain.

He is pictured by Lynch as a large man, robust, and of great strength, with steel-blue eyes, a large mouth filled with strong white teeth, a ruddy brown beard, and a plentiful shock of "slightly dark" hair. His face, says Lynch, was not attractive. His character has been variously portrayed; Bancroft says that it has been "distorted into something abnormal by both his enemies and his friends." The identification of the man shot down by Terry with the ward-heeler of 1850 is no easy task. He had become a student and a man of thought, an advocate of many measures of broad social significance. He read not only the historians and the statesmen, but the poets, and his favorite bard was Shelley. By whatever circumstances he had been led to a hatred of the slave power and a heightened devotion to the Union, the change was one which in a measure transformed him. Though martyrdom invested him with a glamour beyond his meed, he had given substantial promise of a great and useful career.

[Jeremiah Lynch, *A Senator of the Fifties* (1911); John W. Dwinelle, *A Funeral Oration upon David C. Broderick*, including memorial addresses delivered in Congress, Feb. 13, 1860 (pamphlet, 1860); Jas. O'Meara, *Broderick and Gwin* (1881); H. H. Bancroft, *Hist. of Cal.* (1888); Theodore H. Hittell, *Hist. of Cal.* (1897); Hermann Schussler, *The Locality of the Broderick-Terry Duel* (pamphlet, 1916).]　　　W.J.G.

BRODHEAD, DANIEL (Sept. 17, 1736–Nov. 15, 1809), Revolutionary soldier, son of Daniel Brodhead II and Hester (Wyngart) Brodhead, was probably born in Albany, N. Y., where his father was a merchant. In 1737 the family removed to Brodhead Manor in Bucks County (now Monroe County), Pa. Here Daniel III grew up in the wild surroundings of the frontier. His father was an extensive landowner and justice of the peace for Bucks County, who died on July 22, 1755. Some months later, on Dec. 11, the Indians made a fierce but unsuccessful attack upon the family home. In 1773 Daniel III moved to Reading, where he became deputy surveyor-general. At the beginning of the Revolution he was chosen delegate to the Pennsylvania Convention, and raised a company of riflemen to join Washington. After the battle of Long Island, he was commissioned lieutenant-colonel of the 4th Pennsylvania and was made colonel of the 8th Pennsylvania in March 1777. After passing the winter at Valley Forge, the regiment was sent, in March 1778, to Pittsburgh, where Gen. Lachlan McIntosh was in command. McIntosh was recalled in April 1779 and Col. Brodhead was appointed commandant in his place. It was at first designed that he should coöperate with Gen. Sullivan in invading the Iroquois country, but the commander-in-chief thought the distances too great for effective action; Brodhead, however, with 600 men made a swift march up the Allegheny, and in thirty-three days terrorized and subdued the Indians of that region (see his report in the *Olden Time,* edited by Neville B. Craig, II, 308–11).

Brodhead was successful in his negotiations with the Delawares, who gave him the name Machingwe Keesuch, "Great Moon." He made a treaty of alliance with them, which, for a time, kept the frontier from invasion. The Delawares finally went on the war-path, however, and Brodhead in the spring of 1781 raided their territory. This expedition is thought to have been undertaken to avoid coöperation with Gen. George Rogers Clark, who was planning an expedition against Detroit. Brodhead also had a serious dispute with Col. John Gibson, and a number of army officers and inhabitants of Pittsburgh asked for his removal. He was tried by court martial and acquitted, but Washington felt obliged to remove him from command. After the close of the war he was brevetted brigadier-general and retired to his home at Milford, Pike County, Pa. He had military ability, but was a martinet in discipline; he was inordinately ambitious and jealous of other officers; and he did not neglect to further his private interests even while commandant. He was not, however, discredited in Pennsylvania, served as its surveyor general, and died respected by his community, which in 1872 raised a monument to him. He was twice married: first, to Elizabeth Dupui; second, to Rebecca, widow of Gen. Mifflin.

[Brodhead papers in Wis. Hist. Lib. are largely published in Louise Phelps Kellogg, *Frontier Advance on the Upper Ohio* (1916) and *Frontier Retreat on the Upper Ohio* (1917). His services are noted in several frontier histories, especially Jos. Doddridge, *Notes on the Settlement and Indian Wars* (Williams ed. 1876); A. S. Withers, *Chronicles of Border Warfare* (Thwaites ed. 1895); C. W. Butterfield, *Hist. of the Girtys* (Cincinnati, 1890); Wills De Hass, *Hist. of the Early Settlements and Indian Wars of Western Va.* (1851); E. W. Hassler, *Old Westmoreland* (1900).]   L. P. K.

BRODHEAD, JOHN ROMEYN (Jan. 2, 1814–May 6, 1873), historian, was a descendant of Jan Jansen Bleecker who came in 1658 to New Netherland to help build up the Dutch power in America, and of Capt. Daniel Brodhead who came six years later, with the English expedition to help destroy it. The son of the Rev. Dr. Jacob and Elizabeth (Bleecker) Brodhead, he was born in Philadelphia and lived there until 1826, when his father was called to a pastorate in his old home, New York. He was educated at Albany Academy and Rutgers College, graduating with honors from the latter institution at seventeen. He then read law in the office of Hugh Maxwell and was admitted to the bar in 1835, only to abandon it after two years to accompany his invalid father to a country home at Saugerties, N. Y. Two years later he went to serve under his relative, Harmanus Bleecker, as attaché to the legation at The Hague. Here he developed a strong interest in the Dutch contribution to the early history of New York, if indeed he did not have this interest when he accepted the position, for he might well have known of the action of the New York legislature (May 2, 1839), authorizing the appointment of an agent to procure from the archives of Europe materials to fill the gaps in the state archives. In any case, after a year at the legation, he resigned and sought the new post, to which Gov. Seward appointed him in 1841. Brodhead spent the next four years in the archives of Holland, France, and England, and in spite of meager appropriations, which necessitated the most rigorous economies, he returned with eighty volumes of manuscript copies of documents. "The ship in which he came back," wrote Bancroft, "was more richly freighted with new materials for American history than any that ever crossed the Atlantic" (*Scribner's Monthly,* XIII, 461). This precious cargo was edited by E. B. O'Callaghan and B. Fernow and published by the State, as *Documents Relating to the Colonial History of the State of New York,* Albany, 1856–86. Brodhead's report was published in 1845 (*Senate Document No. 47,* 1845). After three more enjoyable and stimulating years in the diplomatic service (1846–49), as secretary of legation in London under Bancroft, Brodhead settled down to write his *History of the State of New York.* The first volume (1609–64) was published in 1853. In the same year, he was appointed naval officer of the port of New York, which was one reason why his second volume (1664–91) did not appear until 1871. A third volume (1691–1789) was begun but never completed. In 1856 Brodhead married Eugenia Bloodgood and bought a home in New York. He was an active member of the New York Historical Society and the St. Nicolas Society, a trustee of the Astor Library (1867–71), and a loyal alumnus of Rutgers College, where, with his father, he founded the Brodhead Prize for proficiency in the classics. In politics, he was a Democrat. He died on May 6, 1873, and was buried in Trinity Cemetery. "He was somewhat above average height, graceful in form and attractive in manner. His countenance was mobile and expressive. His general disposition, combined with his position and character, won for him troops of friends, and his stores of incident and anecdote, as well as his general culture, made him welcome wherever he was known" (*Scribner's Monthly*, XIII, 462). His reputation as an historian rests chiefly on his *History of the State of New York*, which remains the standard work for the period covered. He was a thorough, accurate, and conscientious scholar, trained in the classics, in law and diplomacy, and broadened by wide and intimate contact with men and things in two of the courts of Europe. If his descent from both conqueror and conquered did not assure an unpartisan spirit as completely as he thought it would do (see Preface, vol. II), his too favorable treatment of the Dutch burghers may have been caused by a reaction, more intense than he realized, against the ludicrous impression given of them in Irving's *Knickerbocker's History of New York*.

[The fullest account of Brodhead (with portrait) appeared in *Scribner's Mo.*, XIII, 459–63. There was a lengthy obituary in the *N. Y. Tribune*, May 7, 1873. Brief mention of him is made in Justin Winsor, *Narr. and Crit. Hist.* (1884–89), III, IV. Several of his letters (1840–42) are printed in H. L. P. Rice, *Harmanus Bleecker, an Albany Dutchman* (1924). His addresses before the New York Historical Society on its fortieth anniversary (1844) and on the two hundredth anniversary of the conquest of New Netherland (1864), as well as others of his papers appear in the publications of the society. He contributed to *Papers Concerning the Boundary between N. Y. and N. J.* (H. B. Dawson, ed., Yonkers, 1866).]

E.W.P.

BROKMEYER, HENRY C. (Aug. 12, 1828–July 26, 1906), philosopher, was born near Minden, Prussia, the son of Frederick William Brockmeyer (for spelling see below), a Jewish business man of moderate wealth. On his mother's side he was related to Prince Bismarck. He was educated in the common schools of the neighborhood until the age of sixteen, when, rebellious against Prussian militarism, he took passage for New York in an emigrant ship, arriving with twenty-five cents in his pocket and three words of English in his vocabulary. He worked first as a bootblack, then as a currier, and later added tanning and shoemaking to his accomplishments. Living with great frugality, he saved enough on his wages of one dollar a day to start west, traveling, mainly on foot, through Ohio and Indiana, and finally bringing up at Memphis, Tenn. There for two years he conducted a combined tanning, currying, and shoemaking establishment; through employing the cheap labor of broken-down negroes he is said to have been able to manufacture a pair of shoes for six and a quarter cents. Giving up this profitable business for the sake of further education, in 1850 he entered the preparatory department of Georgetown College, Ky. Threatened with dismissal after two years, owing to theological controversy with the president, he returned to the more liberal East and at Brown University, for another two years, engaged in joyous disputation with President Wayland. In 1854 he went west for the second time and located in an abandoned cabin in the woods of Warren County, Mo. For two years he lived the life of a recluse, devoting himself to the study of philosophy. When at last partially reconciled to the ways of civilization, chiefly through the influence of Hegel, he moved in to St. Louis and worked as an iron-molder, while still consecrating his evenings to study (see *A Mechanic's Diary*, by Brokmeyer, 1910). Having accidentally made the acquaintance of William Torrey Harris [*q.v.*], he undertook to instruct him and a group of friends in German philosophy but soon purchased a tract of eighty acres in Warren County, built himself a small cabin, and resumed his solitary life. This was effectively broken in 1858 when he was prostrated by an attack of bilious fever, and, being utterly helpless, would probably have died had he not been discovered by Harris, who brought him to St. Louis and had him properly cared for. As soon as his health was recovered, Brokmeyer resumed his philosophy class whose members pensioned him to the extent of food and lodging while he made a literal translation of Hegel's monumental *Larger Logic* which he completed within a year.

In the summer of 1861 he signalized his acceptance of society by marriage to Elizabeth Robertson, "an estimable lady" of St. Louis. During the Civil War he served in the militia and organized a regiment, for which effort he was rewarded by being arrested and thrown into prison on a charge of disloyalty fomented by personal enemies. Speedily released, he was six weeks later elected as a "War Democrat" to the legislature (1862–64) where he was prominent in opposing all measures looking toward the disfranchisement of Southern sympathizers. In 1866 he was elected to the Board of Aldermen of St. Louis. His first wife having died in 1864, he was married in January 1867 to Julia Kienlen of St. Louis. He had several children whom he ruled with a rod of iron. In 1870 he was elected to the state Senate, his followers buying him a new suit of clothes for the occasion, and in 1875 as a member of the constitutional convention he took a leading part in shaping the state's constitution. In the latter year he was also lieutenant-governor and in 1876–77 was acting governor during the illness of Gov. Phelps. Meanwhile he was far from neglecting his major interest, philosophy. In January 1866 he and his protégé Harris had organized the St. Louis Philosophical Society, of which Brokmeyer was elected president. With his intense, fiery, poetic personality, Brokmeyer became the oracle of a remarkable group composed of Harris, Denton J. Snider, Thomas Davidson, George H. Howison, Adolph Kroeger, J. Gabriel Woerner, and others who for more than a decade spread the glad tidings of German idealism throughout the Middle West and influenced to no inconsiderable degree the development of its culture. The "St. Louis Movement," initiated by Brokmeyer, differed from its predecessor at Concord in being based upon Hegel rather than Kant and in emphasizing society rather than the individual. Its weakness lay in its Hegelian idealization of the actual and in its alliance with the material prosperity of its center. Brokmeyer shared to the full in the current illusions as to the future greatness of St. Louis, "the Athens of America," and rejoiced with the others in the Chicago fire of 1871, pointing out that this rival city, an incarnation of the negative principle, had now negated itself. After 1880 the movement declined, and Brokmeyer declined with it, becoming an attorney for the Gould railroads. His last public appearance was as elector-at-large on the Cleveland ticket in 1884 when he received the largest popular vote ever cast in Missouri up to that time.

With his philosophical followers scattered, unable to get his highly Teutonized translation of the *Larger Logic* published (which he completely revised in 1892), he spent his later years in half-melancholy sorties into the farther West on long hunting and fishing expeditions or in search of health. On these trips, he was accustomed to cut down numerous mahogany and rosewood saplings which he shipped back to St. Louis, where at his leisure he whittled out beautifully polished walking-sticks for his friends; the chips

he frugally utilized for equally æsthetic toothpicks, carefully cut in three different sizes and bottled with elaborately carved corks. He also always made his own shells and fishing tackle. The Creek Indians, in admiration of his hunting ability, officially bestowed upon him the title of "Great White Father," and offered him his choice of the fairest maidens of the tribe—an offer which his Hegelianism compelled him regretfully to decline.

The personality of Brokmeyer was never adequately expressed in his own incoherent writings, which included, among others: *A Foggy Night at Newport* (a poetic drama privately printed in 1860), "The Errand Boy," and "Letters on Faust" (*Journal of Speculative Philosophy*, I, 178–87), the latter characterized by Woodbridge Riley as "neither philosophy nor literature." The manuscript of his *magnum opus,* the first English translation of Hegel's *Larger Logic,* now rests, still unpublished, in the Missouri Historical Society. His published writings mostly appeared under the name "Brockmeyer," as he had a philosophic scorn for the minutiæ of spelling, and spelled his name with or without the "c" and with "i" or "y," according as the mood took him, although the shorter form tended on the whole to predominate. Snider gives the following description of his physical appearance: "He had the quick, almost wild, eye of the hunter; his body was very compactly and stoutly knit without a flabby spot of flesh in it—tall, arrowy and lithe. His face was unshaven, though sparse of beard, which seemed rather furzy on the cheeks but somewhat denser on chin and upper lip. But the most prominent feature was an enormous nose, somewhat hooked, which had the power of flattening and bulging, of curling and curveting and crooking in a variety of ways expressive of what was going on within him. . . . The whole physical man rayed forth at every point two main qualities: agility and strength" (*A Writer of Books,* 1910, p. 303).

[Sketch in L. U. Reavis, *Saint Louis, the Future Great City of the World* (1875), pp. 336–42; *The Early St. Louis Movement* (1921); Denton J. Snider, *The St. Louis Movement* (1920); Woodbridge Riley, *Am. Thought* (1915); *Mo. Hist. Rev.,* I, 149; *St. Louis Republic,* July 27, 1906; J. H. Muirhead, "How Hegel Came to America," *Philosophical Rev.,* May 1928; information as to specific facts from Brokmeyer's son, Mr. Eugene C. Brokmeyer of Washington, D. C.]

E. S. B.

BROMFIELD, JOHN (Apr. 11, 1779–Dec. 9, 1849), philanthropist and merchant, born in Newburyport, Mass., was the son of John and Ann (Roberts) Bromfield. His father was a descendant of a family of merchants, of whom the first came to Boston from England in 1675. His mother had enjoyed all the advantages of an English university which her father had attended, and she in turn instructed her children. Her daughter relates that before the age of eight John could recite long passages from Pope's poetry and a great quantity of other verse and prose. The boy showed such studious habits and such an aptitude for languages and various subjects at Dummer Academy in Byfield and at other schools that, in 1792, his father, then living in Charlestown, wished to send him to Harvard. This could be possible, however, only through financial help from two aunts, and as the boy had an extraordinarily independent nature he refused to go under these conditions. He insisted on becoming an apprentice in some mercantile house and until he was almost twenty-one years old was in the service successively of two Charlestown firms. The failure of the second firm brought him long months of unemployment. In despair he had decided to learn the trade of a carpenter, but suddenly found an opening in Boston which made this unnecessary. As he had shown unusual industry and judgment as well as an agreeable manner during his years of apprenticeship, he was employed from 1800 to 1813 as a trusted agent for Boston firms and individuals in various parts of the world. Under the unfavorable conditions of the Napoleonic wars, his trips were on the whole financial failures, as letters to his family from Liverpool, London, and Rotterdam show.

In 1809 he was sent to China with a large sum of money, and the successful year spent there gave him a small capital as well as a knowledge of the East which made possible later enterprises of his own. In 1813, after another ruinous trip to Europe, he decided it would be prudent to remain in Boston. The China trade and careful investments of his profits gave him sufficient wealth to provide his mother and sister with many comforts and luxuries and to give quietly to individuals whom he knew to be in need. At his death he left an estate of $200,000. He never married. In more or less wretched health, he saw very little of people and lived with books, making frequent trips to see his family, which, after his mother's death in 1828, consisted of his sister and her husband. An extreme reserve, which increased as he grew older, was a further cause of his rather solitary life. The literary interests which were his main recreation had made him familiar with the needs of the Boston Athenæum, and toward the end of his life he made it a gift of $25,000, at first with the condition that his name should not be made known. He finally allowed himself to be overruled on

this point, however, by his friends, among whom was Josiah Quincy. His will showed that he had left to the Massachusetts General Hospital and the McLean Asylum in equal shares $40,000, and to the Massachusetts Eye and Ear Infirmary, the Boston Female Asylum, the Asylum for Indigent Boys, the Farm School at Thompson's Island, the Asylum for the Blind, the Seaman's Aid Society and his native town of Newburyport, each $10,000.

[Ann Bromfield Tracy, *Reminiscences of John Bromfield* (1852); Josiah Quincy, *Memoir of John Bromfield* (1850).]   M. A. K.

BROMLEY, ISAAC HILL (Mar. 6, 1833– Aug. 11, 1898), journalist, familiarly known to the intimates of his day and generation as "Brom" and to newspaper men as "I. H. B.," was one of nine children who crowded the house of their parents—Isaac and Mary (Hill)—at Norwich, Conn. As their names suggest, these parents were God-fearing people who lived ardently in the flaming light of the gospel, in awe and reverence, after the manner and spirit of the times. What might otherwise have imparted to their house an atmosphere of severity in social relations was softened by the innate whimsicality of the mother and the amiability and practical sense of the father. The literature of the family, though gradually increasing, and more or less reluctantly becoming liberal, assigned the place of honor to the Scriptures and *Fox's Book of Martyrs*. From both parents Bromley inherited a profound but undemonstrative religious faith. It was from his mother that he received the keen sense of humor which made him a writer and lecturer of fascinating quality—a picturesque figure in print, on the platform, at the banquet table, and in social intercourse. He inherited but little of the practical temperament of his father. Life was too joyous for that, the battle too strong an appeal to his sense of humor, the material reward too elusive. On Dec. 25, 1855, he married Adelaide Emma Roath whose parents were respectively Jabez and Clarissa, names also strongly suggestive of early nineteenth century social and hereditary influences. Isaac and Adelaide had only one child, another Isaac.

Bromley entered Yale College in August 1849, becoming a member of the notable class of 1853. His college course was interrupted in the sophomore year but, in 1868, the degree of B.A. was conferred upon him and he was enrolled with his class. Thereafter he was numbered among its most distinguished members. He studied law in the office of the Hon. L. F. B. Foster of Norwich, a leader at the bar from whom he imbibed a keen relish for human problems, later to convert it into a newspaper asset. He was admitted to the bar in 1854 but study of Blackstone only whetted his appetite for the wider fields of exploration and adventure which newspaper work seemed to promise him. He sought further preparation for what became his life-work in the post of assistant clerk of the Connecticut House of Representatives, to which he was called in 1856. The year following he became clerk of the House and, in 1858, clerk of the Senate. His first serious newspaper work was undertaken in November 1858 when he began the publication of the Norwich *Bulletin,* a daily whose columns he enlivened with his wit and satire. In August 1862 he enlisted in the 18th Connecticut Volunteers and was commissioned captain. After a varied and useful, but not spectacular service, he resigned, in 1864. A year later he resumed the editorship of the *Bulletin.* In 1866 he served a term in the Connecticut General Assembly and, in 1868, removed to Hartford and became the editor of the *Evening Post,* with which he remained until 1872. Between these periods of change, he visited the Far West and, as he expressed it, "subsequently fooled twenty or thirty small Connecticut towns with a lecture on the subject." Other trips, promoted by a restless desire to see the world and "get the hang of it," preceded his connection with the *New York Tribune,* which began in 1873 and continued ten years. In June 1882, he was appointed by President Arthur as a government director of the Union Pacific Railroad. There followed a series of brief editorial engagements with the *Commercial Advertiser* and the *Evening Telegram* of New York and the *Post-Express* of Rochester. Then, in 1884, he became assistant to the president of the Union Pacific Railroad. He held that office until 1889. In October 1891 he resumed his editorial connection with the *New York Tribune.* He remained in its service until a few months before his death, which occurred at Norwich.

Bromley's fame rested upon his skill and charm as a newspaper correspondent and editorial writer. Through the force of his originality and genius for estimating men and events at their true value, he brought to the editorial page of the *Tribune* a sparkle and thrust which earned him a reputation for influence and power equal to any attributed to the editor-proprietors of his day. His was the proverbial Yankee wit of New England. He was a handsome man, with clear-cut features, and black eyes which blazed with fire under provocation and melted in tenderness when the gentler emotions were touched. He was at ease with all men, in high

or in humble walks of life, for he was essentially a man's man. He drew his friends from whatever environment he found himself in and left them quivering with a sense of warm refreshment. "I like the human family" was a familiar confession of his. He was at home with actors and artists; with big and little political chiefs of all tribes; with editors and cub reporters. Bromley was a partisan in his outlook on life but his work was performed during a period in the history of the country when impressions were real and convictions were passions; when partisanship was a masculine virtue.

[The chief sources are Norris G. Osborn, *Isaac H. Bromley* (1920); Jos. Bucklin Bishop, *Notes and Anecdotes of Many Years* (1925); autobiog. sketch in *Yale Coll., Class of 1853* (1883); obituary in *N. Y. Tribune,* Aug. 12, 1898. Five scrap-books of articles from Bromley's pen are in the Yale Univ. Lib. In E. C. Stedman's *Am. Anthology* (1900), there is an exquisite portrayal of "I. H. B." by Wm. Winter.]   N. G. O.

BRONDEL, JOHN BAPTIST (Feb. 23, 1842–Nov. 3, 1903), Catholic missionary and first bishop of Helena, Mont., was the son of Charles Joseph Brondel, a successful chair manufacturer of Bruges in Belgium. Finishing the elementary school conducted by the Xaverian Brothers, he attended the local College of St. Louis (1851–61). On graduation he dedicated his life to the American missions and enrolled in the American College at Louvain as a protégé of Bishop Blanchet of Nesqually, Washington Territory. Ordained (1864) at Mechlin by Cardinal Sterckx, he set forth via Panama for Puget Sound. For ten years he served the scattered white colonists and fur-men, half-breed traders, and Indians from missions at Walla Walla and at Steilacoom on the Sound. At Olympia and Tacoma he erected the first churches. Among the Indians, he was especially successful, even among the distant Chinooks of Alaska. His selection as third bishop of Vancouver (1879) was a merited honor, but one which did not transform the humble missionary.

Four years later, he was further burdened with the administration of the vicariate of Montana, and in 1884 he was transferred to the diocese of Helena as its first bishop. The Jesuits, who had been in the field since the arrival of De Smet, assigned their church in Helena to the Bishop who was welcomed in the name of the Catholics by Hon. Thomas Carter, later a powerful Republican senator. Thereafter, the life of Brondel became the history of his diocese. Regarded as a father by the Crows, Nez Percés, Flatheads, and Blackfeet tribesmen of whom there were 10,000 in Montana, he served the government faithfully on peace missions. Before the end of his life most of the Indians were Catholics and provided with chapels and ten schools. On visitations by stage coach and horse, the Bishop averaged 9,000 miles per year, which quite astounded his French correspondents. His diocese grew during his régime from thirteen to fifty-three priests serving sixty-five churches and a hundred chapels. An orphan asylum, nine parochial schools, an industrial school, a home for the aged, eight hospitals, St. Vincent's Academy in Helena, an Ursuline academy in Miles City, and a Good Shepherd home in Helena gave further evidences of Brondel's administrative activities. As the mines were commercially developed and as railroads replaced trails, the Catholic population of his diocese grew to 50,000.

[L. B. Palladino, *Indian and White in the Northwest* (1893) with introduction by Bishop Brondel whose manuscript diary and letters were used by the author; P. Ronan, *Hist. Sketch of the Flathead Indian Nation* (1890); K. Hughes, *Father Lacombe, the Black-Robed Voyageur* (1911); J. Van Der Heyden, *The Louvain American College* (1909); *Cath. Encyc.*; Kennedy's *Cath. Dir.* (1904); *Cath. News* (N. Y.), Nov. 1903; *Helena Independent*, Nov. 3, 1903.]   R. J. P.

BRONSON, HENRY (Jan. 30, 1804–Nov. 26, 1893), physician, historian, was fifth in descent from John Brownson or Bronson, who was supposed to have settled in Hartford with Thomas Hooker in 1632. He was born in Waterbury, Conn., and was the second son of Judge Bennet Bronson and Anna (Smith) Bronson. His two brothers had graduated from Yale but had died early in their careers, so his father, denying him a college training, had destined him to become a farmer. This plan did not coincide with Henry's wishes, however, and at seventeen or eighteen years of age he was allowed to follow his inclinations and prepare for the medical profession. In 1827 he was graduated with the degree of M.D. at Yale, and shortly thereafter settled in West Springfield, Mass., where he married in 1831 Sarah Miles Lathrop, daughter of the Hon. Samuel Lathrop, a former congressman. A few years later greater opportunities came to him on moving to Albany where he practised in association with Dr. Alden March, his former preceptor. Here he soon was much occupied with a constantly increasing and demanding practise, developing at the same time considerable ability in writing newspaper articles on medical topics. When a cholera epidemic came to Montreal and threatened Albany, he was sent by the mayor and several prominent men to Montreal to study this disease. His letters home upon this malady show him to have been a close observer and form interesting reading even to-day. Not long after his return home he removed to Waterbury, where he practised with success until broken health

necessitated a trip abroad. Upon his return he was elected in 1842 to fill the chair of materia medica and therapeutics at the Yale Medical School, and in 1845 removed his residence to New Haven. This chair he filled, with the exception of a single year, until 1860 when he retired to devote himself largely to historical research and economic study. In 1860 he was chosen president of the New Haven County Bank, and served on the city board of education during 1865–66. He also acted as president of the State Medical Society in 1869 and read, besides his presidential address, several papers which included sketches of the society's history, and short lives of its prominent members. In these papers he gained a reputation as an impartial historian. He also prepared three extended and important studies for the New Haven Colony Historical Society on the history of paper currency in Connecticut, early government in Connecticut, and the early history of medicine in New Haven County. In 1858 he published his valuable *History of Waterbury,* a model of accurate and painstaking research. The inheritance which he had received from his father he increased by wise investments so that he was not dependent upon his profession and on moving to New Haven, relinquished his general practise. Of his fortune he gave liberally, Yale receiving between 1873 and 1890 about $80,000 to establish a professorship of comparative anatomy; the New Haven Hospital $10,000, and the Waterbury Hospital $5,000. After 1870, when he was operated upon for a stone in the bladder, he never enjoyed good health. In 1891 he was severely injured in a runaway accident and died two years later, of cystitis and renal disease, in his ninetieth year.

[Jos. Anderson, *The Town and City of Waterbury, Conn.* (1896), III, 855–57; *Obit. Record Grads. Yale Univ.*, 1894, pp. 253–54; *Trans. Conn. Medic. Soc.*, 1894, pp. 229–30; Memoir by Dr. Stephen G. Hubbard in *Papers of the New Haven Colony Hist. Soc.*, VI (1900), 3–99; and *Representative Citizens of Conn.* (1916), pp. 499–501.]   W. R. S.

BRONSON, WALTER COCHRANE (Aug. 17, 1862–June 2, 1928), educator, anthologist, and editor, for thirty-five years professor of English literature in Brown University, was born in Roxbury, Mass., the son of Benjamin Franklin and Anne Hasseltine (Chaplin) Bronson. Both his father and grandfather, Asa C. Bronson, were Baptist ministers. He prepared for college at the Putnam, Conn., high school, but poor health prevented him from entering college until he was twenty-one years old. He graduated from Brown with high honors in 1887, and spent the following year in the Harvard Divinity School. Interest in literature caused him to abandon his youthful intention of entering the ministry, however, and from 1888 to 1890 he did graduate work at Cornell University. After a brief period as professor at De Pauw University (1890–92) he returned to Brown as associate professor of English literature, becoming full professor in 1905, and later head of the department. On Aug. 17, 1905, he married Elsie Marion Straffin. At the age of sixty-five he voluntarily retired that he might have freedom for study and writing, but the following year death came to him while he was engaged in research work at Oxford, England.

He was a shy, modest man, happy among his books, but not lacking in practical wisdom, and endowed with a shrewd knowledge of human nature, a keen sense of humor, and a kindly, optimistic spirit, which made him a valued counselor, and an attractive personality in the lecture room. He never fell into academic ruts, was as appreciative of the new as of the ancient, and as he grew older his power increased rather than abated. His latest students were the most emphatic in praise of his stimulating force. By nature he was a poet, and his Class Day poem, "Modern Monks," a plea for a broad intellectual life, had an excellence unusual in such productions. His creative tendencies were restrained, however, by an acute critical sense, a liking for research, and his genius for teaching. He held it finer to teach great literature than to produce a middling sort. As a result his contributions to the field of literature were chiefly confined to the stimulation which he gave his pupils, and to admirable historical and editorial work. His *Poems of William Collins* (1898), prepared with meticulous care, is a definitive edition of that author's writings, and his *A Short History of American Literature* (1900) has both accurate and discriminating information, and literary atmosphere. The worth of his *English Essays* (1905), *English Poems* (1907–10), *American Poems* (1912), and *American Prose* (1916) is attested by their wide use. He was also the author of a *History of Brown University* (1914), and was a valued adviser and contributor to the *Dictionary of American Biography*.

[*Providence Jour.*, June 3, 1928; H. R. Palmer, "Walter Cochrane Bronson—In Memoriam," *Brown Alumni Mo.*, July 1928; *Who's Who in America*, 1926–27.]
                                                    H. E. S.

BROOKE, FRANCIS TALIAFERRO (Aug. 27, 1763–Mar. 3, 1851), soldier and jurist, son of Richard and Elizabeth (Taliaferro) Brooke, was a native of Smithfield, near Fredericksburg,

Va. His grandfather accompanied Gov. Spotswood in the famous pioneer journey to the Blue Ridge. His father had other sons more or less prominent, one of them, Robert, a governor of Virginia. Francis Brooke was well educated, and at the unusually early age of sixteen he enlisted in the Revolutionary army. As a lieutenant he served under Lafayette and more directly under Harrison, and in his *Narrative* he describes conditions in his state at the time of Cornwallis's campaign in 1781 and Tarleton's raid into the interior. He was sent with his company under the general command of Col. Febiger to the south, and he passed the last months of the war with Gen. Greene, and at Savannah. After the peace he studied law with his brother Robert, and became a district attorney. He also entered political life, and was in the House of Delegates 1794–95, and later in the state Senate. While serving as speaker of the Senate in 1804 he was elected judge of the general court, and henceforth his career was on the bench. In 1811 he was elected judge of the supreme court of appeals, and served with that body for the rest of his life, during six years (1824–30) being its president (*Virginia Reports 2, Randolph's Reports to 2 Leigh's Reports*). In military affairs he was a vice-president of the Cincinnati, and in the state militia he was appointed major in 1796, lieutenant-colonel in 1800, and brigadier-general in 1802. He was married twice: first, in October 1791 to Mary Randolph Spotswood (a niece of George Washington) who died in 1803; second, in 1804 to Mary Champe Carter, who died in 1846. Near the close of his life Brooke wrote for members of his family his *Narrative*. It is a full and rather naive account, especially detailed for the earlier years. Besides domestic and personal matters, the memoir has some historical value. Brooke records his acquaintance with Greene, Gates, Jefferson, Monroe, and others, and particularly with Washington. The two were neighbors, were quite intimate from Brooke's boyhood, and the *Narrative* gives a fairly close view of the President when off—as well as when on—"dress parade."

[F. T. Brooke, *Narrative of My Life for My Family* (privately printed, 1849), an excessively rare work, reprinted as "Family Narrative" in *Mag. of Hist.*, Extra No. 74, 1921; St. George T. Brooke, "The Brooke Family of Va." in *Va. Mag. of Hist. and Biog.*, Jan. 1902 to Oct. 1912; *Works of Henry Clay* (1855–57), containing many letters from Clay to Brooke.]
                                                    E. K. A.

BROOKE, JOHN MERCER (Dec. 18, 1826–Dec. 14, 1906), naval officer and scientist, was born in the Brooke Cantonment near Tampa, Fla., the son of Brevet Major-General George

Mercer Brooke, U. S. A., of Virginia, and Lucy (Thomas) Brooke of Duxbury, Mass., who died when her son was only nine years old. Becoming a midshipman in the United States Navy, Mar. 3, 1841, young Brooke saw service first on the *Delaware,* under Commander David Glasgow Farragut, in Brazilian waters. After a cruise to the Pacific round the Horn in the sloop of war *Cyane,* he entered the Naval Academy, recently established at Annapolis, in 1845, where he was graduated two years later. His next important duty was with the hydrographic party of the Coast Survey under Lieut. Samuel P. Lee, 1849–50; and with Maury at the Naval Observatory in Washington, 1851–53, where he invented a deep-sea sounding apparatus by which specimens from the ocean were first brought to light and the topography of its bottom accurately mapped. For this contribution to science, he received in 1860 from the King of Prussia the gold medal of science from the Academy of Berlin. In 1854, Brooke was attached to the *Vincennes* of the North Pacific and Bering Straits Surveying and Exploring Expedition, commanded by Commodore Cadwalader Ringgold (succeeded by Commodore John Rodgers), and given the duty of determining astronomically the geographical position of primary points and of measuring with the chronometer differences of longitude. Returning to Washington, he was there engaged with Commodore Rodgers, until May 24, 1858, in preparing the charts and records of the expedition for publication. Meanwhile having been promoted to lieutenant Sept. 15, 1855, he was assigned to the duty of surveying a route from California to China, in 1858, and accordingly, in the schooner *Fenimore Cooper,* he made deep-sea soundings and important surveys of several islands in the Pacific and of a considerable part of the east coast of Japan. A cyclone, which wrecked his ship at Giddo, Japan, while he was in conference with the American minister at Yedo, interrupted this work, and forced him to wait at Yokohama, until Feb. 10, 1860, for passage home for himself and his crew on the *Powhatan,* flagship of the Asiatic Squadron. Meanwhile he established cordial relations with the Japanese authorities, and at their request took passage on the Japanese corvette *Candinmarroo* to assist her captain in navigating his ship. This vessel, conveying the first Japanese minister to the United States, sailed in company with the *Powhatan,* but after a stormy passage arrived in San Francisco thirteen days in advance of the American ship. For this service the Japanese offered Brooke a large purse, which he declined. At the outbreak of the

Civil War, he resigned Apr. 20, 1861, and going to Richmond, joined the Virginia state navy and soon afterward entered the navy of the Confederate States, becoming a commander Sept. 13, 1862. Early in June 1861, his plan for reconstructing the U. S. S. *Merrimac* into an ironclad by making use of the "submerged ends principle" was approved by Secretary of the Navy Mallory, for which patent number 100 was granted Brooke by the Confederate government, July 29, 1862, to counteract an attempt to deprive him of this honor. He also prepared, in the Tredegar Iron Works in Richmond, the armor and guns for this ship, renamed the C. S. S. *Virginia.* From March 1863 to the close of the war he was chief of the Bureau of Ordnance and Hydrography. The "Brooke" gun, which he invented, was the most powerful one produced by the Confederates. It was a rifle, made of cast-iron but strengthened by wrought-iron hoops or jackets; it was also unique in the utilization for the first time of what is called the "air space" to diminish the initial tension of the gases. At the close of the war, Brooke became professor of physics and astronomy in the Virginia Military Institute, where a few years later Maury also became a professor. In 1899 he retired from active duty, and seven years later died at his home in Lexington very near the age of eighty. Maury-Brooke Hall at Virginia Military Institute is a memorial to the two distinguished naval officers and scientists. Brooke was twice married, his first wife being Elizabeth Selden Garnett of Norfolk, and the second, Kate Corbin of Mossneck, Va. In appearance, Brooke was slender and active, and had the fair complexion of his New England mother; in later life he wore a full beard. As a member of the Episcopal Church, he had sincere religious convictions but was simple and unpretending in his piety. He was characterized particularly by having high ideals, great determination of purpose, inflexible loyalty to his friends, an intolerance of sham and pretense, and a peculiar fitness for research work of a scientific nature.

[The principal sources of information about Brooke are his letters and papers in the hands of his daughter, Mrs. H. P. Willis, New Brighton, N. Y.; *In Memoriam,* from the minutes of the Academic Board of the Virginia Military Institute, Dec. 31, 1906; John M. Brooke, "The Plan and Construction of the Merrimac," in *Battles and Leaders of the Civil War* (1887–88), I, 715; John M. Brooke, "The Virginia, or Merrimac: her Real Projector" in *Southern Hist. Soc. Papers,* XIX, 3–34; *Official Records (Navy)*; and the *Navy Register,* 1842–61.]   C. L. L.

BROOKE, JOHN RUTTER (July 21, 1838–Sept. 5, 1926), Union soldier, was born in Montgomery County, Pa., the son of William and Martha (Rutter) Brooke. His first American ancestor came from Yorkshire in 1698. He was educated at Freeland Seminary (in whose buildings Ursinus College was afterward organized) and in West Chester, Pa. Responding to the call for three months' service, at the outbreak of the Civil War, he was mustered in, Apr. 20, 1861, as captain in the 4th Pennsylvania Infantry. This was the regiment which won notoriety by claiming its discharge just before the battle of Bull Run. In spite of the personal appeals of the Secretary of War (Cameron), it marched back from Centreville on the morning of the battle, while the rest of the army moved forward into action. Brooke was mustered out on July 26, 1861, but not sharing the regiment's antipathy to fighting he still sought service, and was again mustered in, Nov. 7, 1861, as colonel of the new 53rd Pennsylvania Infantry, and with it joined the Army of the Potomac. He commanded his regiment in the Peninsular campaign, a brigade at Antietam, and his regiment once more at Fredericksburg. He was finally assigned to the command of a brigade of the 2nd Corps in December 1862, though without promotion. This he commanded at Chancellorsville and Gettysburg. In the latter battle, the 2nd Corps arrived on the field early in the morning of the second day, and was posted near the center of the Union line. When the Confederate attack was made upon the salient held by the 3rd Corps (Sickles), Caldwell's division, to which Brooke's brigade belonged, was sent to its assistance, and took part in the desperate fighting around the wheatfield. Brooke was wounded,—"severely bruised" was his own expression for it,—but continued in command. "Of the merit of Col. Brooke, commanding 4th Brigade, too much can scarcely be said," wrote Gen. Caldwell in his report. "His services on this as well as many other fields have fairly earned him promotion" (*Official Records*, ser. I, vol. XXVII, pt. 1, pp. 380–81). Through the winter of 1863–64 Brooke was in command of the veteran camp at Harrisburg, returning to the army before it took the field for the spring campaign. He sustained and enhanced his reputation for hard fighting, at last receiving appointment as brigadier-general of volunteers, May 12, 1864, the commission itself reciting that it was conferred "for distinguished services during the recent battles of the Old Wilderness and Spottsylvania Court House, Va." In the great assault at Cold Harbor, June 3, he was severely wounded, and was carried from the field insensible. He could not return to duty until September, and being still unfit for field ser-

vice, was then employed on boards and courts until March 1865, when he took command of a division of the Army of the Shenandoah. He resigned from the army on Feb. 1, 1866, but returned to service on being appointed, July 28, 1866, lieutenant-colonel of the 37th Infantry, in the regular army. He was promoted to colonel, Mar. 20, 1879, to brigadier-general, Apr. 6, 1888, and to major-general, May 22, 1897. At the beginning of the war with Spain he was assigned to the command of the 1st Corps, and put in charge of the camp at Chickamauga Park, Ga., where his own corps, and also the 3rd (Wade's) were stationed. As the responsible commander, he incurred some of the blame for the deplorable sanitary conditions in that camp. Late in July he was sent with part of his troops to participate in the campaign in Porto Rico. Landing at Arroyo, July 31, he advanced to Guayama where he had a slight skirmish, Aug. 5, and then to Cayey. He was preparing to attack the Spaniards at this place,—the guns were laid and awaiting the order to fire,—when notice reached him that the armistice had been concluded. After the Spanish evacuation he was military governor of Porto Rico for a few months, and of Cuba for a year, returning to the United States to take command of the Department of the East. He was twice married: first, Dec. 24, 1863, to Louisa Roberts, who died in 1867, and second, Sept. 19, 1877, to Mary L. Stearns, of Concord, N. H. He died in Philadelphia.

[F. B. Heitman, *Hist. Reg.* (1903), I, 248; *Official Records (Army)*, 1 ser. XI (pt. 1), XIX (pt. 1), XXI, XXV, XXVII (pt. 1), XXIX (pt. 1), XXXVI (pts. 1, 2, 3); "Report of the Commission to Investigate the Conduct of the War Dept. in the War with Spain," *Sen. Doc. No. 221*, 56 Cong., 2 Sess., VI, 3064–3106, giving Brooke's testimony on conditions at Chickamauga Park; *Harper's Pictorial Hist. of the War with Spain* (1899), II, 393–406; obituary in *Phila. Inquirer*, Sept. 6, 1926.]   T. M. S.

BROOKER, CHARLES FREDERICK (Mar. 4, 1847–Dec. 20, 1926), manufacturer and financier, was descended in the sixth generation from John Brooker, shipwright, who settled in Guilford, Conn., about 1695. He was born in Litchfield, Conn., the son of Martin Cook and Sarah Maria (Seymour) Brooker. One of six children, and the only living son, his early years were divided between work on his father's farm and attendance at the Litchfield and Torrington district schools. His business career commenced at the early age of twelve as clerk in the general store at Torrington and was followed by similar work in Waterbury. His manufacturing career started in 1864 when at the age of seventeen he was employed by Lyman

W. Coe, who the year before had acquired the Wolcottville Brass Company of Wolcottville (later Torrington). Under the guiding hand of Coe, a mid-century leader in the Connecticut brass industry, Brooker's capacity as a salesman and executive developed rapidly; he eventually became secretary of the Coe Brass Manufacturing Company and upon the death of Lyman W. Coe in 1893 succeeded the latter as president.

Brooker was identified with the development of the brass industry of Connecticut for sixty-two years and during most of that period in a prominent capacity. As business organizer, his most important work was the formation of the American Brass Company in 1899, a holding company into which were originally amalgamated four of the leading brass manufacturing units of the Naugatuck Valley. Thirteen years later under his supervision the subsidiary companies were dissolved and the American Brass Company became an operating company. In 1921 the Anaconda Copper Mining Company, the largest producer of copper and zinc in the world, desiring to ally itself more closely with what was then the greatest fabricating interest in the business, approached Brooker with a plan for consolidation. His approval and the ratification by the stockholders resulted in the purchase of the stock of the American Brass Company by the Anaconda Copper Mining Company. Brooker as president of the American Brass Company (1900–20) and later as chairman of the board of directors was the chief figure in these reorganizations. After the consolidation Brooker became a director of the Anaconda Company and of its most important subsidiaries. His business interests, however, extended beyond the metal industries. He was at one time president of the Ansonia National Bank and a director of banks in Torrington, New Haven, Boston, Chicago, and New York. He was also for many years a director of the New York, New Haven & Hartford Railroad Company and of several of its subsidiaries. It was at that time that Brooker's influence was exerted to secure the double-tracking and other transportation improvements necessary for the industrial future of the Naugatuck Valley.

Brooker's interest in politics was life-long, and his influence in Connecticut politics was important. He was elected to the Connecticut House of Representatives in 1875 and to the Senate in 1893 on the Republican ticket, but he preferred to act in an advisory capacity rather than through elective office. He was for many years a member of the Republican state central committee, a member of the Republican national committee (1900–16) and of the executive committee of the latter organization (1904–08). He represented Connecticut as a delegate at large at the Republican National Conventions of 1900, 1904, 1908, 1912, and 1920. Although a personal friend of Roosevelt he maintained in 1912 his allegiance to the conservative wing of the party.

Tactful in his dealings, and of an approachable disposition, Brooker was a man with a wide circle of friends and numerous club memberships. Comparatively late in life (1894) he married Julia E. Clarke Farrel of Ansonia, who died in 1917. Interested in philanthropy, he founded the Maria Seymour Brooker Memorial at Torrington and the "Julia" day nursery at Ansonia, the former in memory of his mother and the latter of his wife. He was especially interested in the Gaylord Farm Sanitorium, maintained by the New Haven County Anti-Tuberculosis Association, of which he was president. His will contained bequests of over $500,000 to various educational and philanthropic enterprises. Active in business until within a few months of the end, he died at Daytona, Fla., where he had spent his last winter in search of health.

[The records of the Am. Brass Co. supply the chief sources for Brooker's career. A scrap-book of newspaper and other clippings relating to him are preserved in the office of the president at Waterbury. The *Ansonia Sentinel, Torrington Register, Waterbury Democrat*, of Dec. 20, 1926, contain obituary notices. See also *Metal Industry*, Jan. 1927, p. 23. The *Waterbury Republican* for Jan. 12, and the *Torrington Register* for Jan. 25, 1927, contain long reports of a memorial address delivered by John A. Coe, his successor as president of the Am. Brass Co. There are brief references to his work in Wm. G. Lathrop, *The Brass Industry in the U. S.* (1926), pp. 118–21, 156.]   H.U.F.

BROOKS, ALFRED HULSE (July 18, 1871– Nov. 22, 1924), geologist and geographer, was born in Ann Arbor, Mich. His father was Thomas Benton Brooks [*q.v.*], who in company with Raphael Pumpelly made the first systematic investigations of the copper regions of Lake Superior and northern Michigan. His mother's maiden name was Hannah Hulse. When a child of but six months he was taken with his parents to Germany where they remained until he was five years of age. Returning to America, they settled at Newburgh, N. Y., where he received his elementary education in the public schools and from private tutors. After several years of residence in Decatur County, Ga., late in 1889 the Brooks family again went to Germany, remaining until 1891 when Alfred returned and entered Harvard University. He was a hard student, and it is stated by his biographer that throughout his college course he "knew definitely what he wanted and went after it with unremitting enthusiasm." Owing to ill health he was obliged to abandon his studies in 1893 and went to Roseland, Ga., where the family had settled on their return from their second trip abroad. His health soon permitting, he began in connection with A. F. Foerste a geological study of the local Tertiary deposits and in the fall of the same year returned to Harvard and graduated with his class in 1894, with the degree of B.S.

In June 1894 he became a member of a corps of United States geologists working under the immediate direction of C. W. Hayes in the Southern Appalachian regions. In company with numerous Americans, he attended the Geological Congress of 1897 in Russia, but instead of returning directly home, passed a few months of study at the Sorbonne in Paris, devoting his attention principally to petrography and geology under La Croix, Fouqué, Bertrand, and De Launay. While here he was offered once more a position on the United States Geological Survey which he promptly accepted and was assigned in 1898 to field work in Alaska. In 1902, after serving the intervening seasons under various parties, he was placed in entire charge of the geologic work of the territory, and to this he devoted his energies until his death, interrupted only by his army service during the World War.

Brooks was a man of unusual breadth, clearness of vision, and of prompt action. He was not merely a geologist. Far-seeing, he early realized the possibilities of engineering information as applied to modern methods of warfare and in May 1915 submitted to the director of the United States Geological Survey a memorandum suggesting the establishment by the War Department of a roster of the engineers and others in the government service whose special qualifications might be of value were they known to be available. Not content with mere suggestion, Brooks with his customary habit of following up his convictions with action promptly enlisted, in May 1916, in a citizens' training camp at Fort Oglethorpe, Ga., and in December 1916 made application for a commission in the Engineer Officers' Reserve Corps which resulted in his appointment as a captain and his sailing with the American Expeditionary Forces for France on Aug. 15, 1917. He was subsequently appointed Chief Geologist, A. E. F. Little can be said here of his accomplishments, other than to quote from a personal letter from Gen. Pershing accompanying his promotion to the rank of lieutenant-colonel when he left the service. "Your work," wrote Pershing, "was of a constructive character in a field new to military service, and the results of your efforts were becoming manifest to all."

As another has expressed it: he "for the first time 'sold' geology to the military establishment through the sheer force of having delivered useful service." Returning from France, he resumed his position at the head of the Alaskan division and died in the harness Nov. 22, 1924.

Brooks's interests were broad. At first his inclinations were toward topographic work and while this naturally threw him into companionship with geologists it is probable that the real turning-point in his life was due to the influence at Harvard of the magnetic N. S. Shaler [q.v.] and the students with whom he associated. That he should have also become a geographer, under like influences and training, followed almost as a matter of course. Brooks was a likeable, companionable man and thoroughly loyal to his calling and to his friends. His merits were recognized both by the Survey and by other organizations. In 1912 on the retirement of C. W. Hayes from the position of chief geologist of the Survey, the position was offered Brooks, who however, wisely as it proved, refused it, preferring the Alaskan field. He served on the Alaskan Railroad Commission in 1912–13 and his work here in connection with his monograph on Mt. McKinley in 1911 brought him in 1913 the Daly medal from the American Geographical Society and the same year the Malte-Brun medal from the Société de Géographie de Paris. This same year he was designated one of the delegates to the twelfth International Geologic Congress at Toronto. He was made a member of the Department of Commerce party on its trip to Alaska and Japan and was a delegate to the second Pan-Pacific Scientific Congress to Australia.

His publications though numerous and voluminous were necessarily not monographic, though his compilation in 1906 of over 300 pages on the *Geography and Geology of Alaska* is to this day the most complete treatise on the subject extant. In 1914–16 and in 1919–23 he prepared annually for publication detailed statements of the Alaskan mineral industry. Other important publications were his *Geologic Features of Alaskan Metalliferous Lodes* (1911); *The Future of Gold Placer Mining in Alaska* (1915); *Antimony Deposits in Alaska* (1916); *The Future of Alaska's Mining* (1920). As an interesting characteristic of the man it is told of him that in the preparation of his reports he dictated very little but wrote voluminously in a large and not very legible hand. His thoughts often outran his ability to transcribe them and words and sentences were left incomplete. The most singular feature was, however, that he never went over these first drafts, correcting and completing them, but practically disregarded them as having seemingly served merely to formulate his ideas, and wrote an entirely new article, sometimes re-writing several times but leaving all minor corrections, such as spelling and punctuation, to his secretary.

Personally Brooks was of medium height, rather stoutly built with an unusually large head, and with sandy hair and beard. He was married Feb. 23, 1903, to Mabel Baker of Washington, D. C., by whom he had two children.

[Philip S. Smith, *Bull. Geol. Soc. of America,* XXXVII (1926), containing full bibliography.]

G. P. M.

BROOKS, BYRON ALDEN (Dec. 12, 1845–Sept. 28, 1911), teacher, inventor, was born at Theresa, Jefferson County, N. Y., the son of Thompson and Hannah (Parrish) Brooks. Thompson Brooks was the miller of Theresa, and his grist-mill was the environment in which Byron developed his interest in mechanics. As a boy he devised and applied several successful improvements in the mill machinery and further indicated his interest in his eager study of mathematics, in which science he was far enough advanced to teach at the Antwerp (N.Y.) Academy, when at his father's death in 1861 he had to contribute to the support of the family. In 1866 he entered Wesleyan University at Middletown, Conn., where he supported himself by tutoring. Though he lost a year through illness, he completed his work in time to graduate with his class in 1871. From 1871 to 1872 he taught at Dobbs Ferry, N. Y., where he was principal of the Union Free School. From there he went to New York City where he was assistant editor of the *National Quarterly Review* (1873) and a teacher and principal in the public schools. As a writer and educator he became interested in the possibilities of the typewriter and as one having some mechanical skill, he studied the machine and attempted improvements. For his first successful improvement he received Patent No. 202,923, Apr. 30, 1878, the feature of which is the location of both a capital and a small letter on the same striking lever and the shifting of the paper roller by a key to bring either the large or small letter into printing position. He sold this patent for $7,000 to the Remingtons who immediately incorporated the improvement in their next model, the Remington No. 2, the first machine to write other than capital letters and the one from which the universal use of the typewriter dates. Following this success, Brooks devoted considerable time to typewriter inventions and obtained more than thirty patents, none of which approached the first in importance. In fact, only

one equally important improvement remained to be made, namely, the provision for visible writing, and though Brooks sought to incorporate this feature in a machine which he manufactured and sold as the Brooks Typewriter, he succeeded in making visible only two lines of printing at a time and for lack of any other outstanding features the machine was discontinued. In 1900 the Brooks Typewriter Company was sold to the Union Typewriter Company, which Brooks served as patent expert to the time of his death. He also attempted improvements in type-casting and composing machines and was president of the Bandotype Company, formed to promote his inventions in this field. At the time of his death in Brooklyn, N. Y., he was also working on a printing telegraph. Brooks married Sarah Davis of Middletown, Conn., in 1872, and after her death married, in 1906, Ella J. Ball of Brooklyn, N. Y. Brooks wrote *King Saul: A Tragedy* (1876); *Those Children and Their Teachers* (1882); *Phil Vernon and His Schoolmasters* (1885); and *Earth Revisited* (1893).

[C. V. Oden, *Evolution of the Typewriter* (1917); E. W. Byrn, *The Progress of Invention in the Nineteenth Century* (1900); Records of the Wesleyan Univ. Alumni Council; Patent Office Records; correspondence with members of family; obituary in *N. Y. Herald,* Sept. 30, and *N. Y. Times,* Sept. 29, 1911, and *Typewriter Topics,* Nov. 1911.]

F. A. T.

BROOKS, CHARLES (Oct. 30, 1795–July 7 1872), Unitarian educationist, clergyman, was born in Medford, Mass., the son of Jonathan and Elizabeth (Albree) Brooks. He fitted for college under Dr. Luther Stearns who was both teacher and physician. In 1812 he entered Harvard and graduated in 1816. Remaining for graduate work in theology he took his M.A. degree in 1819, delivering the valedictory address in Latin. The next year he became pastor of the Third Congregational Church (Unitarian) at Hingham, Mass., and remained there till 1839. In 1821 he published a *Family Prayer Book* of which eighteen editions appeared. In 1833–34 he visited Europe where he became impressed with the superior excellence of the Prussian schools and resolved to bring about improvement in the schools of Massachusetts. Soon after his return he began, in 1835, through printed articles and addresses to carry his message to the people of his state. Starting with a Thanksgiving Day address in Hingham, he spoke to large audiences in many of the chief towns, describing the needs of the schools of the state, dwelling much upon the theme "As is the teacher, so is the school," and urging that the state establish schools for the training of teachers. At the next session of the legislature he made two addresses to the members. It was at this session, subsequently, that the act was passed establishing the first real state board of education in the United States. At the request of its secretary, Horace Mann, Brooks began what proved to be a carriage journey of more than 2,000 miles back and forth through the state as he addressed the people of town after town. In this way he won to his cause the constituents of the members of the legislature who in 1838 voted the sum needed for the first state normal schools. To still further promote the normal-school movement he addressed the legislatures of New Hampshire, Vermont, Maine, and New Jersey, and bodies of citizens in Rhode Island and Pennsylvania. In 1839 having accepted the professorship of natural history in the University of the City of New York and resigned from his pastorate at Hingham, he went again to Europe where he spent four years in scientific study. On his return to this country because of failing sight he relinquished his professorship and retired to private life. Besides the *Family Prayer Book,* the most important of his published works were *Remarks on Europe, Relating to Education, Peace and Labor, and Their Reference to the United States* (1846), *Elements of Ornithology* (1847), and *History of the Town of Medford, Middlesex County, Mass.* (1855). He was married in 1827 to Cecilia Williams who died in 1837 leaving a son and daughter. In 1839 he was married to Mrs. Charlotte Ann (Haven) Lord. Slender in stature, Brooks was of attractive presence and winning personality. The closing years of his life were spent in Medford where he died.

[Memoir by Solomon Lincoln in *Proc. Mass. Hist. Soc.,* XVIII, 174; John Albree, *Chas. Brooks and His Work for Normal Schools* (1907); Henry Barnard's *Am. Jour. Educ.,* I, 587.]   W.J.C—e.

BROOKS, CHARLES TIMOTHY (June 20, 1813–June 14, 1883), Unitarian clergyman, poet, translator, was born in Salem, Mass., a descendant in the eighth generation of Henry Brooks, who came to Woburn, Mass., some time before 1649, and the son of Timothy Brooks. His mother was Mary King (Mason) Brooks. He prepared for college at the Salem Latin Grammar School, and entered Harvard at the age of fifteen, graduating in 1832. The next three years he spent in the Harvard Divinity School from which he graduated with honors. After supplying several churches for brief periods he was called to the Unitarian Congregational Church, Newport, R. I., beginning work there Jan. 1, 1837, although he was not ordained until June 14. Here he served as pastor until November 1871, and at Newport he made his home till his

death twelve years later. On Oct. 18, 1837, he married Harriet Lyman Hazard, daughter of Benjamin Hazard of Newport. His health was never robust and he suffered long from a throat affection, because of which he spent the winters of 1842 and 1851 in Mobile, Ala., where he took charge of the Unitarian Church. On account of his health he also spent almost a year (1853–54) in India. From October 1865 to September 1866 he was in Europe where he made the acquaintance of many eminent literary people.

Brooks was modest, peace-loving, somewhat disinclined to engage in practical affairs, fond of nature, a delightful companion, with a keen sense of humor, and power of lively repartee. His main interest was always in literature, and he gave as much time as possible to writing. Even in preparatory school he became noted for his proficiency in languages, and at Harvard he studied them eagerly, especially German. Accordingly, while he wrote on literary and theological subjects for periodicals, and produced some excellent verse, drolleries, and children's books, he became best known through his translations from the German. His first considerable work of this kind was his translation of Schiller's *William Tell* (1837). The following year he published *German Lyrics,* which constituted vol. XIV of Ripley's Specimens of Foreign Literature. In 1842 appeared his *German Lyric Poetry,* to which Longfellow and others contributed; in 1846, Schiller's *Homage of the Arts;* in 1853 another edition of *German Lyrics;* in 1856, the first part of *Faust* in the original meters and in rhyme, with notes; in 1862, Jean Paul Richter's *Titan,* and in 1864, his *Hesperus.* He also published translations of Leopold Schefer's *Layman's Breviary* (1867) and *World's Priest* (1873), and several of Auerbach's novels. The most notable work of his later days was his English version of Friedrich Rückert's great poem *The Wisdom of the Brahmin,* the first six books of which appeared in 1882, the other two being in manuscript at the time of his death. His original writings include *Aquidneck . . . with Other Commemorative Pieces* (1848), *Songs of Field and Flood* (1853), and *The Old Stone Mill Controversy* (1851).

[W. P. Andrews, *Poems, Original and Translated by Chas. T. Brooks with a Memoir by Chas. W. Wendte* (1885). This contains a full bibliography of Brooks's works. See also *Essex Inst. Hist. Colls.,* vol. XX (1883), vol. XXI (1884).]   H.E.S.

BROOKS, ELBRIDGE STREETER (Apr. 14, 1846–Jan. 7, 1902), author, was born at Lowell, Mass., the son of Elbridge Gerry Brooks, a Universalist minister and anti-slavery man, and

Martha (Monroe) Brooks. During the boyhood of his son, the elder Brooks served churches in Bath, Me., Lynn, Mass., and New York City, and at the public schools of Lynn and New York the boy received his preliminary education. In 1861 he entered the Free Academy, afterward the College of the City of New York, where he remained only until the middle of his junior year. His lifelong connection with publishing houses began at this time with a clerkship with D. Appleton & Company. In 1873 he was with Ford & Company and Sheldon & Company; in 1876 he became head of the English educational and subscription department of E. Steiger & Company; and in 1879 he joined the staff of the *Publishers' Weekly*. He was from 1883 to 1885 literary editor and dramatic critic on the *Brooklyn Daily Times*. In 1884 he became associate editor of *St. Nicholas Magazine* and in 1887 removed to Somerville, Mass., to become an editor for D. Lothrop & Company. His relations with this firm were suspended for a short time between 1892 and 1895, during financial troubles and reorganization, but thereafter continued until his death. In 1891–93 he was editor of *Wide Awake*. In 1870 he married Hannah-Melissa Debaun of New York. One of his two daughters, Geraldine, became a writer.

Brooks began writing works for young people in 1880 and altogether published over forty books of this kind, some of the most popular of which are: *Story of the American Indian* (1887), *Story of the American Sailor* (1888), *Story of the American Soldier* (1889), *True Story of Christopher Columbus* (1892), *Century Book for Young Americans* (1894), issued under the auspices of the Sons of the American Revolution, *True Story of George Washington* (1895), *Boy Life of Napoleon* (1895), *True Story of Abraham Lincoln* (1896), *Century Book of Famous Americans* (1896), issued under the auspices of the Daughters of the American Revolution, *True Story of U. S. Grant* (1897), *True Story of the United States* (1897), *True Story of Benjamin Franklin* (1898), *True Story of Lafayette* (1899). The popularity of his books among young people has continued almost unabated and, although experts in juvenile literature criticize them as "machine-made," they still find them so decidedly interesting that they grudgingly approve them. Until a short time before his death at Somerville, Brooks was to be seen regularly at his office, a man of intellectual appearance, with large head, aquiline nose, deep, keen, spectacled eyes, white hair, and full white beard.

[*Who's Who in America*, 1901–02; *The Origin and Hist. of the Name of Brooks, with Biographies of All the Most Noted Persons of that Name—the Crescent Family Record* (1905); obituaries in the *Boston Transcript*, Jan. 7, 1902, and *Boston Herald*, Jan. 8, 1902.]   S. G. B.

BROOKS, ERASTUS (Jan. 31, 1815–Nov. 25, 1886), journalist, politician, was the son of James and Elizabeth (Folsom) Brooks. His father, while of English birth, had spent most of his life in the United States and had become so thoroughly an American that he commanded the cruiser *Yankee* against his native country in the War of 1812. Erastus was a posthumous son, born in Portland, Me. At the age of eight he was working in a grocery store in Boston for his board and clothes and studying in an evening school. He was later apprenticed to a compositor. While still very young he entered Brown University and supported himself entirely by working at the case in a printing office. He did not graduate but left college to start a paper called the *Yankee* in Wiscasset, Me. He soon went to Haverhill, Mass., and taught school under a school board of which the poet Whittier was a member. But the smell of printer's ink was in his nostrils and before long he was editor and proprietor of the *Haverhill Gazette*. An experience as reporter on the *Portland Advertiser* followed, and in his twentieth year he went to Washington where he wrote correspondence for a group of papers composed of the *New York Daily Advertiser,* the *Boston Transcript,* the *Portland Advertiser,* the *Baltimore American,* the *St. Louis Republican,* and the *New York Express.* Five years later we find him back in Portland, editing the *Advertiser* during the Harrison presidential campaign. At its close he was selected to carry Maine's electoral vote to Washington and remained there a year or two. In 1843 he made a tour from Queenstown to Moscow, writing for his group of papers vivid articles which were widely appreciated. On the return voyage the steamer was wrecked off Sandy Hook and Brooks was one of the few survivors. He then joined his brother James [*q.v.*] in the editorial management of the *New York Express,* subsequently assuming the entire control. His editorial career of thirty-four years was marked by exceptional enterprise and originality. During an epidemic of cholera in the city he got out the paper almost single-handed, acting as reporter and compositor as well as editor, and setting news stories and editorials at the case without first committing them to paper. His enterprise and inventiveness were exemplified in two journalistic "beats." In those days the state election news went first to Thurlow Weed's newspaper in Albany. Brooks took compositors with him to the capital, secured the election results from

Weed, turned a stateroom on the Albany boat into a composing-room, and reached New York with the type all set and ready for the press. The other "beat" was made by telegraph. The inaugural message of Gov. Silas Wright was telegraphed to the *Express* and when the famous pony express established by James Gordon Bennett, who scorned to use the telegraph in preference to it, reached Westchester County with a copy of the message on the way to the *Herald* office, it was met by Brooks's messengers with copies of the *Express* containing the document in print. Brooks took an active part in the controversy over the exemption of Catholic church property from taxation, debating vigorously with Archbishop Hughes the point that, since the property was held in the name of the bishops, it should be taxed like other personal holdings of realty. He was consequently elected, in 1853, to the state Senate on the American or Know-Nothing ticket, and continued to discuss the subject there. In 1856 he was nominated for governor by the same party but was defeated. The same year he was a member of the convention of the party which nominated Fillmore for president and in 1860 of the convention of the Constitutional Union party which named Bell and Everett. He served in the New York state constitutional convention of 1866–67, being made chairman of the committee on charities, and on the constitutional commission of 1872–73. In 1877 the *Express* passed into new ownership and Brooks retired to devote himself to politics and public affairs. He was elected five times from Richmond County to the New York Assembly where he served as a member of the important committees on ways and means, cities, and rules. He was active in many public and philanthropic bodies, was one of the founders of the Associated Press, and was for a time its manager. He was married to Margaret Dawes, daughter of Chief Justice Cranch of the circuit court of the District of Columbia. He died at his home on Staten Island.

[*Biography of the Hon. Erastus Brooks* (privately printed, Boston, 1882); *Am. Ann. Cyc.,* 1886; obituaries in the *N. Y. Mail and Express* and the *N. Y. Times,* Nov. 26, 1886.]   H. H.

BROOKS, GEORGE WASHINGTON (Mar. 16, 1821–Jan. 6, 1882), judge, was born at Elizabeth City, N. C., the son of William C. and Catherine (Davis) Brooks, widow of Capt. Hugh Knox. His ancestors, English in origin, migrated from Virginia to North Carolina (Albemarle), late in the seventeenth century. His schooling was obtained at Belvidere Academy in Perquimans County, a Quaker school of some reputation. Later, under difficulties, he studied

law, and was licensed to practise in the county courts in 1844 and in the superior courts in 1846. His industry in his chosen profession soon providing him with an adequate income, he married Margaret Costin, June 20, 1850, and by her had three sons and two daughters. A Whig in politics, he represented his county in the House of Commons in 1852, and by voting with the insurgent element in the Democratic party had a share in preventing the election of a United States senator at that session. By 1861 he had become a considerable owner of lands and slaves, but he believed that slavery was doomed, and throughout the Civil War he was confident that the Federal cause would prevail. In the convention of 1865–66 he again represented his county and spoke bitterly of the trials and tribulations endured by a Southern Union man during the war. His open allegiance to the Union caused President Johnson to appoint him United States judge of the district of North Carolina, in August 1865; the nomination was duly confirmed by the Senate, Jan. 22, 1866. His conduct of this office until his death was marked by industry and sound judgment. One incident in his judicial career must be noticed. In the summer of 1870 North Carolina was, and had been for two years, in the throes of reconstruction:—on the one side corruption so brazen as to amount to rapine; on the other, midnight rovers, ministers of "wild justice," intimidating by their weird symbols and disguises, and flogging here or, if need be, hanging there. The governor, Holden, declared two counties in a state of insurrection, suspended the writ of *habeas corpus,* sent troops and had many prominent citizens arrested, and proposed to try them in a military court constituted by himself. The supreme court of the state was appealed to, but its writ was treated with contempt (64 *N. C.,* 820). The recently adopted Fourteenth Amendment (July 28, 1868) and the Habeas Corpus Act of Feb. 5, 1867 (14 *Statutes at Large, U. S.,* 385) were invoked before Judge Brooks with success, for he issued the writ and as, after notice, no evidence was produced against them, the prisoners were discharged in August 1870, the first instance in which the Amendment was invoked in defense of the personal liberty of a white man. A sound lawyer, Brooks was, as a judge, noted for patience, benevolence, and moral courage.

[John H. Wheeler, *Reminiscences and Memoirs of N. C.* (1884), pp. 365–68; J. G. de R. Hamilton, *Reconstruction in N. C.* (1914), pp. 131, 525 ff.; Samuel Ashe, *Hist. of N. C.,* II (1925), 1108.]   F. N.

BROOKS, JAMES (Nov. 10, 1810–Apr. 30, 1873), journalist, was born in Portland, Me., the son of James and Elizabeth (Folsom) Brooks and the brother of Erastus Brooks [*q.v.*]. His father, of English nativity but a loyal American citizen, was lost while commanding a privateer during the War of 1812. The family was left in poverty. James, after attending a public school in Portland, was bound out to a storekeeper of Lewiston. Fortunately his employer was impressed by the lad's ability, released him from the apprenticeship, and assisted him in gaining an education. He first entered an academy at Monmouth, Me., and was graduated from Waterville College (now Colby University) in 1831 (Waterville College Records). Supporting himself by school-teaching in Portland, he began to study law in the office of John Neal, and was inspired by Neal to write for the *Portland Advertiser*. By the time he was admitted to the Maine bar the *Advertiser* offered him $500 a year, and he took up journalism.

In a period when new enterprise was rapidly being infused into the newspaper world Brooks made a brilliant reputation as a correspondent. His political letters from Washington were copied all over the Union, and James Gordon Bennett was one of the journalists who gained useful lessons from them. Equally good were his letters from the South, and especially those from the Creek, Cherokee, and Choctaw districts at the time the two latter tribes were being forced to remove. Maine seemed too small for his talents, and entrance to the legislature in 1835, followed by an unsuccessful candidacy on the Whig ticket for Congress, failed to hold him there. Returning from a European tour late in 1835, he settled in New York, obtained Whig backing, and on June 20, 1836, began publication of the *New York Express*, first as a morning newspaper only, and later with an evening edition as well. Its fortunes were precarious. Brooks later declared that for many years he had labored sixteen hours daily to supply it with letters, editorials, shipping news, and other matter. But as a commercial rather than a political organ, though it called itself "decidedly Whig," it became firmly established by 1840 (*New York Express*, Apr. 29, 1873: historical review on occasion of removal to a new building).

Until his death Brooks combined editorial labors with political activity, and twice changed his party. He volunteered as a campaign speaker in 1840 for William Henry Harrison, one result being his marriage in that year to a relative of Harrison, Mrs. Mary L. (Cunningham) Randolph of Virginia. After service in the New York legislature, he was carried to Congress in Zachary Taylor's sweep of 1848, serving two terms as a Whig. He supported Clay's compromise mea-

sures of 1850, and a temporary identification with the Native American party in 1854 bridged over his conversion to Democracy as the slavery struggle grew warmer. He wished at all costs to avoid civil war, his newspaper representing the conservatism of the New York commercial community in this regard. For this reason he supported Buchanan in 1856 and Douglas in 1860; and in the spring of 1861 he argued so vigorously for letting the Southern states "depart in peace" that the office of the *Express* was threatened with mob violence. During the Civil War he was a Democrat of the copperhead type, and was identified with Tilden, August Belmont, and other wealthy men in supporting the Society for the Diffusion of Political Knowledge. The *Express* was characterized by the *Evening Post* in 1863 as a journal "which has called repeatedly upon the mob to oust the regular government at Washington, and upon the army to proclaim McClellan its chief at all hazards."

Brooks was elected from New York City to the Thirty-ninth Congress in 1864; he claimed election again in 1866, but was unseated in favor of William E. Dodge; and thereafter biennially until his death he was reëlected. His position on the Democratic side was one of influence, for he was an aggressive and able debater. Twice his party supported him for speaker, and he served on the Ways and Means and other important committees. His opponents correctly characterized him as "pugnacious" and untiring (T. C. Smith, *James Abram Garfield*, 1925, I, 362). In the stormy years after the war he opposed the impeachment of President Johnson, argued for a conciliatory and rapid process of Southern reconstruction, and hotly denounced the carpet-bag governments. He was prominent also in the demand for tariff reduction and revenue reform. His downfall as a result of the Crédit Mobilier scandal, therefore, attracted wide attention. President Johnson had appointed him a government director of the Union Pacific Railroad on Oct. 1, 1867. In the following December he demanded of the Crédit Mobilier officials a large amount of stock, and after much negotiation was assigned 100 shares at par, $10,000, though the market value was then about $20,000. Further demands from him led to a highly irregular issue of 50 more shares in his name. The House investigating committee in 1873 found him guilty of accepting a bribe for the use of his official influence, and recommended his expulsion; he was, however, let off with a vote of censure. His defense, which rested chiefly on the assertion that the shares in question had really been bought by his son-in-law, C. H. Neilson, has not convinced hi?

torical students (cf. James Ford Rhodes, *History of the United States,* vol. VII, 1906, p. 11).

Distress over this affair shortened Brooks's life; he had made a tour of the world in 1872, had contracted a fever in India, and now succumbed, maintaining to the end that he had been made a scapegoat because he was a Democrat. He had been given the satisfaction of an unprecedented majority in his district in 1872, while he retained to the last a host of personal friends. He was of fine presence, well-read, a cultivated linguist, suave and courteous, and held a high place in both Washington and New York society.

[See *Am. Annual Cyc.* (1873), p. 81, for a succinct sketch. The pamphlet *Crédit Mobilier: Speeches of Hon. Daniel W. Voorhees, etc.* (Washington, 1873) contains Brooks's own defense. The pamphlet *Biography of the Hon. Erastus Brooks* (Boston, 1882) contains incidental material. Brooks presents his travel impressions in *Seven Months Run, Up, and Down, and Around the World* (1872). Articles in the *N. Y. Express,* Apr. 29–30, and May 1, 1873, throw light on his career. Many of his speeches were reprinted in pamphlet form; *e.g., Not Reconstruction but Destruction* (1867). Cf. J. B. Crawford, *The Crédit Mobilier of America* (Boston, 1880) and the Poland Committee Report (*House Reports,* 42 Cong., 3 Sess., nos. 77, 78).]
A.N.

BROOKS, JAMES GORDON (Sept. 3, 1801–Feb. 20, 1841), editor, poet, often confused with James Brooks [*q.v.*], was probably born at Red Hook, N. Y., though some authorities give Claverack as his birthplace. His father was David Brooks, an officer of the Revolution, afterward a member of Congress. J. G. Brooks was graduated from Union College in 1818. He studied law at Poughkeepsie but his interest was soon turned in other directions and he never applied for admission to the bar. As early as 1817 he had begun to publish verse and prose in periodicals and in 1819 he adopted the pen name "Florio," by which he long succeeded in concealing his identity as an author from even his friends. In 1823 he went to New York, where for two years he was literary editor of the *Minerva,* which called itself a "literary, entertaining, and scientific journal." The *Minerva* was combined with the *Literary Gazette,* which had a brief existence and was then absorbed by the *American Athenæum.* Brooks continued with these journals until 1827, when he became an editor of the *Morning Courier,* an influential Democratic paper, strong in its support of Andrew Jackson. In 1829 it was merged with the *Enquirer* and later became the *Courier and Enquirer.* Brooks remained with the paper until 1830. At one time previous to 1830 he was also an editor of the *New York Daily Sentinel.* His verse was published in the journals with which he was connected and in the *Commercial Advertiser.* In 1828 he married Mary Elizabeth Aiken of Poughkeepsie, who, under the name of "Norma," was a contributor of verse to periodicals. In 1829 they collected their poems in a volume, *The Rivals of Este, and Other Poems.* The title poem, by Mary Brooks, is a melodramatic narrative of medieval Italian intrigue, in stilted verse. Of her other poems, "Hebrew Melodies," verse renderings of selections from the Psalms and the Prophets, are the best. The longest poem by James Gordon Brooks is "Genius," the Phi Beta Kappa anniversary poem delivered at Yale, Sept. 12, 1826. It is a eulogy of intellect, in stately but uninspired verse. His minor poems are of better quality, especially "Greece," an ode full of feeling for liberty, and "The Last Song," his farewell verse. His poems, better than his wife's, are reflective in tone, conventional in rhyme and meter. After the publication of this volume he wrote little verse. Though his poems were fairly popular in his time, his chief distinction is as a journalist. In 1830 Mr. and Mrs. Brooks removed to Winchester, Va., where he was editor of the *Republican.* In 1838 they returned to New York State and settled in Albany. There he was for about a year editor of the *Albany Advertiser* but got into trouble with the Van Rensselaers, who owned the paper, and resigned, after a fight, in 1839. He was then for a short time an editor of the *New Era* in New York. He died at the old Franklin House in Albany.

[Frederic Hudson, *Journalism in the U. S., from 1690 to 1872* (1873), pp. 280, 346, 425, 517; Rufus Wilmot Griswold, *The Poets and Poetry of America* (1874), p. 278; *Centennial Cat. of Union Coll.* (1895); *Record of the Officers and Alumni of Union Coll. 1797–1884* (1884); *Phi Beta Kappa Cat.* (1923); *Albany Daily Argus,* Feb. 22, 1841; *Troy Daily Whig,* Feb. 22, 1841.]
S. G. B.

BROOKS, JOHN (1752–Mar. 1, 1825), Revolutionary soldier, the son of Caleb Brooks, farmer, and Ruth (Albree), was born in a part of Medford, Mass., now within the boundaries of Winchester, and baptized May 4, 1752 (*Vital Records of Medford,* 1907, p. 31). Dr. Simon Tufts, the local physician, took a liking to the boy, and received him as a medical apprentice in his family in 1766. Graduating, as it were, from Dr. Tufts' college in 1773, John Brooks began to practise medicine in the near-by town of Reading, and (1774) there married Lucy Smith. Interested from boyhood in drilling, he joined the Minute Men, and as captain of the Reading company hastened to Concord on Apr. 19, 1775, joined the fight at Meriam's Corner, and pursued the British in their retreat (W. H. Sumner, *History of East Boston,* 1858, pp. 355–56). Shortly after, he received a majority from the State, and played an important part in the battle of Bunker Hill. He was appointed, on Jan. 1, 1776, to the same rank in the Continental Army and served with constant zeal and energy throughout the war. After taking part in the battles of Long Island and White Plains, he was promoted lieutenant-colonel in the 8th Massachusetts line regiment, which he commanded and gallantly led in the taking of Breyman's fort on Bemis's Heights, Oct. 7, 1777 (*Proceedings of the Massachusetts Historical Society*, III, 273–75). On Mar. 24, 1778, Washington offered him a position on the inspector-general's staff, which he filled with great satisfaction to Baron Steuben, although at times detached for active service with the army in the field. When stationed at Newburgh, in the winter of 1782–83, he was appointed by the discontented officers one of a committee of three to present their claims to Congress. He had already gone on a similar mission to the Massachusetts legislature, for the officers of the state. He brought back to camp the committee's account of their discouraging reception; but his exact relation to the "Newburgh Addresses" remains obscure, on account of the later efforts of every one involved to clear himself and blame others. Brooks was accused of being a member of a conspiracy, and of afterward informing upon it to Washington (L. C. Hatch, *Administration of the American Revolutionary Army*, 1904, pp. 167–70); on the other hand he is represented as having stood by Washington from the first (Charles Brooks, *History of Medford*, p. 138; F. Kapp, *Life of Frederick William von Steuben*, 1859, p. 534). One may infer from his long letter of 1823 in the Pickering Manuscripts that he was not in the secret, and thought the enterprise both reprehensible and desperate. After receiving his honorable discharge (June 12, 1783), Brooks took over the medical practise of Dr. Tufts at Medford, and became a highly successful physician, "the grace and ornament of the profession." Dignified though democratic, interested in people and helpful in their troubles, a useful townsman and faithful member of the First Church (changing with it from Calvinism to Unitarianism), Brooks appeared the ideal republican soldier and citizen, the sort of man every one loved, and delighted to honor. He was president of numerous organizations such as the Cincinnati, the Massachusetts Medical Society and Bible Society, and the Bunker Hill Monument Association. Gov. Bowdoin in 1786 appointed him major-general over the militia of Middlesex, with which he marched to Worcester during the Shays rebellion (*Massachusetts Historical Society Collections*, 7 ser. VI, 133–34). President Washington made him

federal marshal for the Massachusetts district in 1791, and brigadier-general, U. S. A., in 1792 (resigned 1796). President Adams nominated him to a major-generalcy in the provisional army during the difficulties with France. Harvard College adopted him as a Master of Arts in 1787, made him honorary M.D. in 1810, Overseer in 1815, and LL.D. in 1817. From 1788, when he became a silent but active member of the Massachusetts Ratifying Convention, Brooks was a staunch Federalist, but never belonged to the inner circle of leaders. He had already twice (1785–86) been elected to the House, and in 1791 was chosen a state senator for Middlesex County whose Jeffersonian Republicanism lost him further opportunities of the same sort. Like the rest of his party, he strongly disapproved the War of 1812; and said so publicly, when declining a nomination to Congress (Washburn Manuscripts, 55). As adjutant-general of the Commonwealth and of the Council (1812–16) he greatly improved the efficiency of the state militia, the right to control which he considered "one of the most essential attributes of state sovereignty." This quotation, and other matters in his correspondence with Timothy Pickering [*q.v.*], with whom he served on a special commission for the defense of the seacoast in 1814, show that he approved the Hartford Convention, and other measures of his state in 1814, taking the same view of the situation as H. G. Otis [*q.v.*]. Both his sons, however, served in the war. In 1816, when Gov. Strong declined to stand again for governor, Brooks was nominated by the Federalists, and elected, although opposed by Gen. Henry Dearborn [*q.v.*], who had served at the front. He was six times reëlected, 1817–22, by substantial majorities over Republican candidates. Brooks's administrations were known as the "Indian Summer of Federalism" in Massachusetts, and his cordial reception to President Monroe in 1817 inaugurated the "Era of Good Feeling" (*Columbian Centinel*, July 12, 1817). He was a competent governor in a period which his popularity and good manners helped to make a placid one. He sympathized with the maritime rather than the manufacturing interests of Massachusetts, and regretted, while he did not attempt to oppose, the separation of Maine. In 1823, when he refused to stand again, the Republican candidate was elected; and the Federalist party, after dominating Massachusetts for a generation, ceased to exist. Brooks died at his home in Medford, Mar. 1, 1825.

[Memoirs by Chas. Brooks in *Hist. of Medford* (1855) and *New Eng. Hist. and Geneal. Reg.*, XIX, 193–200;

by W. H. Sumner, *Ibid.*, XIII, 102–07 and *Proc. Mass. Hist. Soc.*, III, 271–77; by Rev. A. Bigelow, in *Christian Examiner*, II, 103–17 (1825). See also Knox, Keith, Pickering, and Washburn MSS. in Mass. Hist. Soc.]

S. E. M.

BROOKS, MARIA GOWEN (c. 1794–Nov. 11, 1845), poet, called "Maria del Occidente," was born at Medford, Mass., of Welsh extraction. Her paternal grandfather lost money during the Revolution and moved from Cambridge to Medford. Her father, William Gowen, a goldsmith and a man of cultivation, and the friend of Harvard professors, who perhaps encouraged the child in her reading by the age of nine of Shakespeare, Milton's *Comus,* and Southey's *Madoc,* was further reduced in wealth before his death in 1809. Her mother was Eleanor (Cutter) Gowen. Maria was cared for by John Brooks, a merchant of Boston, who had previously married her older sister Lucretia. He was a widower of nearly fifty, with two sons, but he married Maria Aug. 26, 1810, when she was fourteen or fifteen. She bore him two sons, Horace and Edgar, but although he was not unkind, the marriage was not a happy one. Since there was no understanding of the girl on Mr. Brooks's part, he won her respect, not her love. Mr. Brooks lost money invested in privateers during the War of 1812, and retired to Portland. There Maria, who is described as "a very handsome lady, winning manners, purest blonde complexion, blue eyes, abundant pale gold hair, who sang very sweetly," devoted herself to her sons and step-sons. She also composed a poem which was never published, and fell violently in love with a young Canadian officer, whom she had met but once. Of this passion she gave for the time no sign, but she handled with great delicacy another ardent gentleman's unwelcome attentions, rebuking the lover but retaining the friend. In 1819 the General Court allowed her to change her baptismal name of Abigail, and on July 31 she was baptized Mary Abigail Brooks in King's Chapel. Later she always called herself Maria Gowen Brooks. Her life in the narrow and provincial town was unhappy, but her books were her solace, and in 1820 she published at Boston a small volume, *Judith, Esther, and Other Poems, by a Lover of the Fine Arts.*

In 1823 Mr. Brooks died, and on Oct. 20, Maria sailed for Cuba, to live on the coffee plantation of a brother, William Cutter Gowen. There she was urged to marry a neighboring planter, but declined, and soon visited other relatives in Canada. During her visit she again met the British officer, whose initials were E. W. R. A., and who figures as "Ethelwald" in her novel *Idomen.* She became engaged to him, but in some way they were estranged, and Maria twice attempted suicide by drinking laudanum, at the same time praying that she might be spared if it was God's will. She was restored to health through the ministrations of a friend, and returned to Cuba where she inherited considerable property. At Boston in 1825 she published the first canto of *Zóphiël,* a poem on the love of a fallen angel for a mortal, based on a story in the apocryphal Book of Tobit. About 1826 she began a correspondence with Southey. In Cuba, on the Cafétal San Patricio, near Matanzas, in a little Grecian temple erected for her, dressed all in white, and with a passion flower in her hair, she continued work on *Zóphiël,* which was completed in 1829. She proceeded with her son Horace to Hanover, N. H., where he studied with one of the Dartmouth professors, preparatory to entering West Point. His appointment was delayed. Mrs. Brooks visited Europe with a brother. In Paris she met Washington Irving, and through him Lafayette, who finally procured the appointment of Horace Brooks. In 1831 she stayed for a few weeks at Keswick, where she saw much of Southey who undertook to supervise the publication in London of *Zóphiël* which she signed with the pen name "Maria del Occidente." She became in a sense the American member of the group of Lake poets. *Zóphiël* appeared in 1833 after her return to America; the first American edition consisted of the English sheets with a cancel title; a second American edition appeared at Boston in 1834. The poem had little sale but won, especially by the "Song" beginning "Day in melting purple dying," and the allegory of Marriage, the admiration of John Quincy Adams, Southey, and Lamb. Four letters to Southey, 1833–40, tell much of Maria's life during this period. Her son graduated from West Point in 1835. She completed her prose tale *Idomen,* a curiously involved but beautifully frank account of her unhappy love affair, and published it serially, beginning Feb. 17, 1838, in the Boston *Saturday Evening Gazette,* to which she contributed some minor poems, 1838–40. Her son Edgar and a stepson fell ill and died in Cuba before she could reach them, and to their memory she wrote several odes, and the (touchingly simple) song beginning "My fair haired boy." Meanwhile Mrs. Brooks resided with her son Horace on Governor's Island; and corresponded with Halleck (1842) and E. P. Whipple (1843) about *Idomen,* which the Harpers rejected as "too elevated to sell," but which she published privately in New York in 1843. R. W. Griswold, who praised Maria in the *Southern Literary Messenger,* in

1839, spoke of her as the foremost American poetess in his *Poets and Poetry of America* (1842), endeavored vainly to bring out an edition of her *Works,* and inserted some of her poems in *Graham's Magazine.* In May 1843 she wrote Ticknor about Southey's letters to her; in December she returned to Cuba. On Sept. 3, 1844, she sent a poem to W. B. Force, editor of the Washington *Army and Navy Chronicle.* In 1845 she and her stepson fell ill of a tropical fever. Both died—Mrs. Brooks on November 11, 1845—and were buried beneath a white marble cross at Limonal, near Matanzas. Her poetry had the faults of its time but its three or four best passages have imagination, and exalted passion.

[The chief published sources are Southey's *The Doctor* (1834 f.), chapter LIV; Griswold's articles mentioned above, and those by him in *Graham's Mag., Aug.* 1848, and in the *Female Poets of America,* 1849—the two latter accompanied by engraved portraits; the introduction to Zadel Barnes Gustafson's edition of *Zóphiël* (1879); Caroline E. Swift's "Maria del Occidente" in *Medford Hist. Reg.* (Oct. 1899), pp. 1-11, 150–66; Ruth S. Granniss's *An American Friend of Southey* (N. Y., privately printed 1913); Thos. Ollive Mabbott, "Maria del Occidente," *Am. Collector,* Aug. 1926. There are manuscripts of Mrs. Brooks's letters and poems in the Boston Pub. Lib., Yale, and the Lib. of Cong., and there is a collection of her books and manuscripts formed by Beverly Chew and and now in the possession of T. O. Mabbott.]   T. O. M.

BROOKS, MARY ELIZABETH AIKEN. [See Brooks, James Gordon, 1801–1841.]

BROOKS, NOAH (Oct. 24, 1830–Aug. 16, 1903), journalist, author, was born in Castine, Me., the son of Barker Brooks, a master shipbuilder, and Margaret (Perkins) Brooks. His earliest American ancestor on his father's side, William Brooks, of the County of Kent in England, was a passenger on the ship *Blessing,* landing at Scituate, Mass., in 1635. The Perkinses were also an old Massachusetts family. He attended the public schools of Castine until he was eighteen, when he went to Boston to study landscape painting. He soon discovered, however, that the pen fitted his hand better than the brush and began to write. By the time he was twenty-one he was contributing short sketches, essays, and humorous stories to magazines and weekly newspapers and was serving on the staff of a Boston daily, the *Atlas.* When he was twenty-five his writing career was interrupted for a few years. He went to Illinois and entered into a business partnership with an intimate friend, John G. Brooks. The business failed and Noah Brooks moved to Kansas, for a brief stay during which he took an active part in the free state movement, and then on to California with a company of emigrants who crossed the plains with ox teams. Coming to rest in Marysville, Cal., he joined with Benjamin P. Avery [*q.v.*], afterward United States minister to China, in publishing the *Daily Appeal.* In addition to his editorial work Brooks steadily contributed to the *Overland Monthly,* then edited by Bret Harte. A friendship developed between the two men which persisted after Brooks left California. This removal took place in 1862, when he sold out his interest in the newspaper and went East to become Washington correspondent of the *Sacramento Union.* In Washington an acquaintance with Abraham Lincoln, begun in Illinois and continued during the period of the Lincoln-Douglas debates, was renewed at the instance of the President. Brooks became a frequent visitor at the White House and an intimate friend of the Lincoln family. He accompanied the President on trips to the front and after the Baltimore convention which nominated Lincoln and Johnson went to the White House at Lincoln's request to give him an eye-witness's picture of the convention's progress. If it had not been for a severe cold which kept him at home Brooks would have been a guest in the presidential box on the fatal night in Ford's Theatre. Shortly before this the President had invited Brooks to become his private secretary in place of John G. Nicolay, who was to go as consul to Paris, but Lincoln's death came before the change could be effected. Brooks was appointed by President Johnson naval officer in the custom house at San Francisco but was removed at the end of a year and a half for refusal to comply with certain of the administration's political requirements. In 1866 he became managing editor of the *Alta California* in San Francisco. A red-headed youngster setting type for the paper timidly submitted an article to the managing editor which greatly astonished Brooks by the brilliancy of its style. He encouraged the youth's impulse to write and must have felt his efforts to that end repaid some years later when *Progress and Poverty* appeared with the name of the red-haired compositor, Henry George, on the title-page. In 1871 Brooks went to New York and joined the staff of the *New York Tribune.* After five years there he became an editor of the *New York Times* and eight years later was made the editor of the *Newark Daily Advertiser.* In 1892 he retired from journalism. The remaining years of his life were uneventful, except for a tour of Egypt, Turkey, and the Holy Land in 1894 and 1895, and were largely spent at his country home in Castine, which he named "The Ark." He was a jovial companion and a good story-teller, one of the founders of the

Authors Club of New York, and a member of the Century Club, the Lotus Club, and the New England Society. Belonging to the Congregational Church, he took an active part in church affairs and charitable undertakings. He was married in 1856 to Caroline, daughter of Oliver Fellows, of Salem, Mass. His wife and an infant child died just as the Civil War was beginning. Brooks himself died in Pasadena, Cal., where he had gone in the hope of restoring his health.

His published works include *The Boy Emigrants* (1876, 1903), based on the experiences of his first journey to California; *The Fairport Nine* (1880, 1903); *Our Baseball Club* (1884); *The Boy Settlers* (1891, 1906); *American Statesmen* (1893, 1904); *Tales of the Maine Coast* (1894); *Abraham Lincoln and the Downfall of American Slavery* (1894); *How the Republic is Governed* (1895); *Washington in Lincoln's Time* (1896); *Short Studies in American Party Politics* (1896); *The Story of Marco Polo* (1896); *The Mediterranean Trip* (1896); *History of the United States* (1896); *Henry Knox, a Soldier of the Revolution* (1900); *Abraham Lincoln; His Youth and Early Manhood* (1901).

[Biog. sketch by Frederick F. Evans in the *Lamp*, Sept. 1903; obituaries in the *N. Y. Herald, N. Y. Tribune, N. Y. Times*, Aug. 18, 1903.]   H. H.

BROOKS, PETER CHARDON (Jan. 11, 1767–Jan. 1, 1849), merchant, was born at North Yarmouth, Me., where his father, Rev. Edward Brooks (Harvard College, 1757), was minister of the First Parish. Peter's mother was Abigail Brown, daughter of the minister of Haverhill, Mass. His ancestors were among the earliest settlers of Watertown, Mass. His own branch of the family belonged in Medford, whither the Rev. Edward Brooks returned in 1769, when his theology proved too liberal for his down-East parish. The father's death in 1781 left the family almost destitute; and Peter was apprenticed to a merchant in Boston, but on attaining his majority, in 1789 set up as an insurance broker at the Bunch of Grapes tavern. In underwriting vessels, and in his adventures of money in the East Indian trade, Brooks was so uniformly successful that he was able to retire in 1803 with a considerable fortune. He married in 1792 Nancy, daughter of Nathaniel Gorham [*q.v.*]; she bore to him thirteen children. In 1805 he built a mansion house at Medford on the ancestral farm, which he made a model farm. Finding time rather heavy on his hands, he returned to business in 1806 as president of the New England Marine Insurance Company, but retired again after a few years. The Federalists

in 1806 insisted on sending Brooks to the state Senate, an honor which both pleased and worried him, for, as he wrote his brother, "I have not learning enough to make any figure in this way." He was annually reëlected to the state Senate until 1814; to the Council, 1817–19, when his second cousin, John Brooks [*q.v.*], was governor; to the constitutional convention of 1820; and alternately to the House and Senate, 1819–23. He is not associated with any measure excepting a committee report of 1821 denouncing lotteries, which is said to have procured legislation against them. Peter C. Brooks did not speculate, or invest largely in manufactures or railroads or western land, but kept turning his money over in loans and mortgages for which, if we may believe his biographers, he never took over six per cent interest; yet at the time of his death (in Boston, January 1, 1849), he was reputed the wealthiest man in New England. His property was put to good use in various philanthropic enterprises, and in promoting the political ambition of his sons-in-law, Edward Everett and Charles Francis Adams [*qq.v.*].

[Edward Everett, "Peter C. Brooks," in Freeman Hunt, *Lives of Am. Merchants* (1858), I, 133–83; Brooks MSS. in Mass. Hist. Soc., containing his letters to his brother Cotton, a merchant at Haverhill, Mass., and Portland, Me.; Jos. T. Buckingham, *Personal Memoirs* (1852), II, 181–85.]   S. E. M.

BROOKS, PHILLIPS (Dec. 13, 1835–Jan. 23, 1893), Episcopal bishop, was fortunate in his name, which, balanced and virile, clearly indicated the two streams of hereditary influence that shaped his life. The Phillips family had been conspicuous in the religious and educational interests of Massachusetts from 1630, when Rev. George Phillips came from England with Winthrop and settled in Watertown, Mass. His son, Samuel, was pastor in Rowley, Mass., for forty-five years. The next in line, also named Samuel, broke the clerical succession and became a goldsmith, but had a minister's daughter, Mary Emerson, for his wife; and their son, Samuel [*q.v.*], was minister of the South Church, Andover, Mass., for sixty-two years. The latter's three sons, Samuel, John [*q.v.*], and William [*q.v.*], turned to secular pursuits, acquired wealth, and used it for philanthropic and educational purposes. John founded Phillips Exeter Academy, and Samuel's son, Judge Samuel Phillips [*q.v.*], having enlisted the coöperation of his father and two uncles, founded the Phillips Andover Academy. The Judge's wife, Phœbe Foxcroft, brought into the family wealth, social grace, and intellectual life of a high order, her great stature and large dark eyes reappearing in Phillips Brooks. Carrying out her husband's wishes, she, with her son John, established the Andover Theological Seminary. This John was the father of Mary A. Phillips, the mother of Phillips Brooks.

In the Brooks family there was less conspicuous idealism and other-worldliness. The founder of the line in this country was Thomas Brooke, who was a freeman of Watertown in 1636 and must have sat under the ministrations of the Rev. George Phillips. The only minister in this descent was the Rev. Edward Brooks whose liberal tendencies led him to give up his parish, and whose wife was a direct descendant of the Rev. John Cotton [q.v.]. Their two sons were Cotton Brown Brooks and Peter Chardon Brooks [q.v.]. The elder became a merchant in Portland, Me., the younger, a prominent Unitarian layman in Boston, at his death considered to be the richest man in the city. When William Gray Brooks, son of Cotton Brown Brooks, came, at the age of nineteen, to Boston to establish himself in business, he met, at the house of his uncle Peter, his aunt's niece, Mary Ann Phillips, whom he married in 1833. Of this union Phillips Brooks was born, the second of six sons, four of whom entered the ministry.

From each parent he inherited superior virtues in balanced proportion. His mother had all the staunch spiritual passion of the Phillips blood. She was richly endowed with an intense and powerful emotional nature, which revealed itself in a glowing idealism, and the reformer's zeal for the establishment of righteousness. Yet her ethical earnestness and unquestioning faith were blended with an ardent mother love which lavished itself without stint upon her children. This fervor of spirituality was tempered and directed in her son by the more humanitarian qualities of the Brooks lineage. From his father, a substantial business man, accurate and methodical, and keenly observant of the ways of men, he inherited executive ability, fondness for art and literature, a sense of present values, and a disinclination to interfere with the personal rights of others. The son was like his father also in his fortunate habit of writing down, constantly and at length, the thoughts which grew out of his reading and observations.

He was baptized in the First Church of Boston, but when he was four years of age the family identified itself with St. Paul's Episcopal Church. After studying in the Latin School, he was admitted to Harvard in 1851, when not quite sixteen, yet even then he stood six feet, three and one-half inches and weighed 161 pounds. In college he excelled in the languages, and ranked high in logic and philosophy. Much of his time was given to general reading. He showed no sign of being an orator but wrote excellent papers for the societies of which he was a member, and graduated the thirteenth in a class of sixty-six. Intending to give his life to teaching, he secured a position in the Boston Latin School. Over the thirty-five young barbarians of nearly his own age assigned to his charge, he could not maintain discipline and in six months he resigned, deeply chagrined to have failed in his home town, and in his first work. His notebooks of this time are remarkable for their lack of introspection or spiritual struggle. They reveal a mind serene, chiefly concerned with discerning the richness of life and its significance for faith, and naturally inclined to generate and proclaim moral ideas. Almost invariably he wrote as if addressing an audience. One reading these random thoughts sees how impossible it was that he should be anything but a preacher. Yet he hesitated, then suddenly, after the term commenced, went to study in the seminary at Alexandria, Va.

It is indicative of the creative vigor of his mind that he took with him a number of notebooks, which he divided into two equal parts, one for facts and thoughts which he found in his reading, the other for his own reflections. So imperative was the need of self-expression that he filled the latter first, and then overflowed into the former. These meditations reveal the uncommon maturity of his mind and the ripened perfection of his style. For him the seminary years were not a period of distressing intellectual and spiritual unsettlement. There is no record of a prolonged struggle with religious doubts, or of a battle with self to renounce the world, its values, and its ambitions. Neither theological systems nor the findings of the critics interested him overmuch. Life, its varied experiences, its amazing possibilities, alone concerned him. From the first he seems to have had three convictions, unclouded and abiding: God, personal, living, in all and over all; man by nature the child of God and capable of a life abounding in blessedness; Christ the revelation of what God is and man may be. These were to him luminous certainties, the sure intuitions of spiritual genius. His problem was not the attainment of a rational faith, but how to convey to men an understanding of the liberty, the joy, the abounding life one may find in the spirit and by the power of Christ. That this was to be his message Phillips Brooks discovered in his second year in the Seminary and the succeeding years only deepened its glory and significance to his own mind and increased his marvelous power of enforcing it.

An observation written in his note-book when he had just turned twenty-one reveals that unlike most young men he was not inclined to disregard the ways of his fathers and to break new paths. "We shall pretty generally find," he remarks, "that it is with theories as with country roads, they may take us a little out of our way, but if they reach our point at last, it will be the easier and altogether the shortest way to keep by them, gaining in the smoothness and pleasantness which the road builders have made ready for us, much more than we lose by not taking a straight line across rough new fields." All his life Brooks not only kept in the middle of the road, he walked in the old roads. His eye was not for the horizon, but for values, for the unfamiliar beauty of familiar things. He was an interpreter, not a pioneer.

Ordained a deacon at Alexandria, Va., July 1, 1859, he began his ministry in the Church of the Advent, Philadelphia, the following month. Immediately his impressive personality and uncommon eloquence attracted attention. Crowds came to hear him. In January 1862 he became rector of Holy Trinity in the same city. Distinguished success attended his ministry. He was a leader not only in spiritual things, but in the stress of Civil War attained local prominence by his unwavering loyalty to Lincoln and the Union cause. When the body of the martyred President was lying in state in Independence Hall, Brooks preached a sermon of such insight and power on the "Character, Life and Death of Mr. Lincoln" that it attracted wide attention. In July of that same year, 1865, he came again into prominence in a most unique manner. Harvard College appointed a commemoration day in honor of her sons who had died in the war, and Phillips Brooks was invited to make the prayer. What is usually a function became an event. "It was the most impressive utterance," said President Eliot, "of a proud and happy day. Even Lowell's Commemoration Ode did not, at the moment, so touch the heart of his hearers. This one spontaneous and intimate expression of Brooks' noble spirit convinced all Harvard men that a young prophet had risen up in Israel." Another who was present said: "One would rather have been able to pray that prayer than to lead an army or conduct a State." It was no formal prayer written in majestic liturgical sentences; the flowing piety of nine generations of praying men broke forth that day in marvelous utterance.

In the summer of 1865 Brooks went abroad for a year of travel. On his return he was called to become the head of the new Episcopal Theological School in Cambridge. The invitation tempted him but was finally declined. In the meantime his influence was extending its range and deepening its impression, yet the permanent contribution to the spiritual wealth of America which belongs to the Philadelphia pastorate is the carol, "O Little Town of Bethlehem," written for his Sunday-school and sung for the first time at Christmas 1868 to music composed by Mr. Redner. Of a rich poetic nature Brooks easily wrote verse, as his note-books testify, but in this sweet carol he expressed the Christmas feeling with a simple beauty that will be held by his Church in perpetual possession.

Being a son of Boston, his increasing fame attracted the attention of his native city and Trinity Church, the stronghold of Episcopalianism, called him in August 1868 to become its rector. At first he declined, but Trinity, after waiting nearly a year, renewed the call so urgently that Brooks accepted and began his memorable ministry in Boston, Oct. 31, 1869. Trinity Church edifice then stood on Summer St. near Washington, a dignified and impressive structure built of granite in Gothic style. In 1872 the great Boston fire destroyed this church, and the noble building in Copley Square was erected and consecrated on Feb. 9, 1877. The architect, H. H. Richardson, and the decorator, John La Farge, combined their signal artistic abilities to make it an outstanding architectural achievement and a fit tabernacle for the ministry of its great preacher.

Immediately upon coming to Boston Phillips Brooks aroused public interest in his person and message. While Trinity Church was building he preached in Huntington Hall to audiences which packed at both services that large auditorium. Now from the pulpit of his centrally located and magnificent church he commanded the attention of Boston and attracted the notice of religious minds everywhere. The conditions of the spiritual life of his city and of his generation were especially favorable to his peculiar genius. Boston was the capital of Puritanism, and Puritanism was always prone to emphasize the intellectual aspects of Christianity to the exclusion of the æsthetic and emotional elements. Its excessive dogmatism had resulted in the cold intellectualism of Unitarianism. The Episcopalians occupied a mediating position though their ecclesiastical exclusiveness was a limitation. They had not been involved in ancient theological conflicts. Their forms of worship were not uncongenial to an increasing number of people of social aspirations in a city of growing prosperity; they had tradition, they had wealth, but no preacher of preëminent abilities. Accordingly, when this radiant spiritual athlete, having the fervent piety and profound convictions of the most religious, combined with all the intellectual freedom and breadth of tolerance which was the boast of the liberals, stepped into the very center of the arena and preached the eternal verities of religion in undogmatic form and with contagious enthusiasm people flocked to hear him.

Neither in thought nor method was he a pioneer. He was sensitive to the finest spiritual currents of the times. Coleridge, Tennyson, Maurice, Robertson, Bushnell, all had ministered to his thought and enkindled his spirit. In face of the questionings aroused by an awakened scientific spirit, he did not try to reconcile religion and science, or combat a materialistic philosophy with argument. His method of meeting mental doubts he suggests in an essay on the "Pulpit and Modern Scepticism" (*Essays and Addresses*): "It seems to me as if, were I a layman in the days when some doctrine had got loose as it were into the wind and was being blown across the Common and up and down the streets, I should go to church on Sunday, not wanting my minister to give me an oracular answer to all the questions that had been started about it which I should not believe if he did give it, but hoping that out of his sermon I might refresh my knowledge of Christ, get Him, His nature, His work, His desire for me once more clear before me, and go out more ready to see this disputed truth of the moment in His light and as an utterance of Him. . . ."

During January and February of 1877 he delivered his valuable *Lectures on Preaching* before the Yale Divinity School. These addresses unveil as do no other writings of the great preacher his own personal experiences, and his noble conception of the joy and purpose of the Christian minister. Their predominant idea is that "Preaching is the communication of truth by man to men. It has two essential elements, truth and personality. . . . Preaching is the bringing of truth through personality." Therefore the preacher must apprehend and live the truth he enunciates; he must love and reverence men. His description of religion as "the life of man in gratitude and obedience and gradually developing likeness to God" is classic in completeness and suggestiveness. In this year Harvard College conferred on him the degree of S.T.D. and in 1878 was published his first volume of sermons. In February of 1879 he delivered in Philadelphia the Bohlen Lectures on "The Influence of Jesus." His fame having spread to England he was invited by Dean Stanley to preach in Westminster Abbey on July 4, 1880, and the following Sunday at the expressed wish of the Queen he preached before Her Majesty in the Royal Chapel at Windsor, this being the first instance of this distinction coming to an American. The next year he was invited to be the preacher to Harvard University and professor of Christian ethics. To this call he gave long and earnest consideration, as he was strongly inclined to accept the opportunity there offered to influence the students. Reluctantly he declined it. Harvard then abolished the office of preacher and adopted the plan of having a group of ministers selected from different denominations officiate successively for short periods. Oxford gave Brooks the degree of D.D. in 1885, and Columbia in 1887. He declined election as assistant bishop of Pennsylvania in 1886. In October of the same year the General Convention entertained a resolution to change the name of the church from Protestant Episcopal to "The American Church," or "The Church of the United States." Against this he protested vigorously on the ground that the denomination was not large enough to make such a pretentious claim, and that the assumption of such a name doomed the Episcopal Church to become the church of those who accepted the theory of an apostolical succession conferring certain exclusive privileges. The resolution was lost in the convention, but Brooks was apprehensive that the attempt might be renewed and preached a sermon in his own pulpit against the proposition in which he declared that if the change was made he "did not see how he or any, who did not believe in apostolical succession could remain in the Episcopal Church." This sermon had an important influence in this country and in England.

In the Lenten season of 1890 he conducted a memorable series of services at the noon hour in Trinity Church, New York, addressing crowded audiences of the business men of Wall St., who recognized in him a great man, having full knowledge of the world in which he lived, speaking to them in no conventional way of the deepest satisfactions of life.

In the earlier part of his ministry Phillips Brooks was little interested in the machinery of denominational administration. Conventions he disliked and their discussions seemed to him for the most part trivial; bishops he held in good-humored toleration. But his friend, Bishop Potter of New York, affirms that in his later years Brooks experienced a fundamental change of mind regarding the episcopate. "He came to see that what he had reckoned a calling of dry routine might be transformed . . . into a ministry of noblest opportunities and most potential service." Therefore, when at the death of Bishop Paddock there was a spontaneous movement on the part of the churches of the diocese for his election to the vacant bishopric, he was not only willing, but anxious to accept it. The election occurred Apr. 29, 1891, and he was chosen on the first ballot by a large majority of the clergy and a larger majority of the laity of the diocesan convention. Immediately strong opposition was aroused among the narrower elements of the church throughout the nation. He was accused of doctrinal unsoundness and of ecclesiastical latitudinarianism. For some ten weeks the issue was in doubt, and it was not until July 10 that the presiding bishop announced that the election was confirmed by a majority of the bishops. These misrepresentations of his teachings and of his churchmanship he endured in dignified silence. The consecration took place in Trinity Church, Oct. 14, 1891. Many had feared, and some had hoped, that one who was so conspicuously of the prophetic spirit would hold the canons of his church in slight regard, and would treat the red tape of administrative office with disdain. Quite the contrary. During the fifteen months of his incumbency he scrupulously obeyed the laws of the church and faithfully enforced them, yet his chief service was the unusual spiritual inspiration which his presence brought to the churches committed to his charge. Then on Jan. 23, 1893, after a short illness, when he had just passed his fifty-seventh birthday, he died, and the news fell upon the city and multitudes beyond as a crushing public calamity. A great tower of spiritual light had been extinguished. More impressive than the funeral services in Trinity Church were the thousands of reverent men and women gathered in Copley Square whose sense of personal bereavement was expressed in prayer and hymns. The city of Boston held a memorial service in his honor, sermons of commemoration were preached everywhere in this country and in England. Ninety-five thousand dollars came spontaneously from the people for a bronze statue. This was afterward executed by Saint-Gaudens and stands near Trinity Church. The Phillips Brooks House was established at Harvard, dedicated to Piety, Charity, and Hospitality, and a memorial window has been placed in St. Margaret's, Westminster.

Phillips Brooks's supreme contribution to this country was himself. A great bishop, a greater preacher, he was greatest as a superbly molded and an harmoniously developed man, glowing with human sympathy and spiritual light. He is the "only one I ever knew," writes his intimate friend, Dr. Weir Mitchell, "who seemed to me entirely great." Physically he was majestic, standing six feet four inches, weighing in his prime three hundred pounds, broad shouldered, well proportioned, with a perfectly smooth, open face lighted by luminous brown eyes. "He was the most beautiful man I ever saw," said Justice Harlan of the United States Supreme Court. "I sat opposite to him once at dinner, and could not take my eyes off him." His dress was unconventional, his manner simple without the slightest suggestion of ecclesiastical *hauteur*; little children instinctively loved him, and to all he gave the impression of sincere and radiant goodness. He enjoyed his religion; he had abundant humor and "the deep wisdom of fine fooling," yet wrong awoke in him the blazing wrath of a strong man. Success made him humble, and his steady prosperity increased his eagerness to give of himself unsparingly.

Extreme rapidity of utterance characterized his public speech. Stenographers reckoned that he spoke 213 words a minute. This was due to the excessive energy of his emotions. He kindled in the presence of an audience, his tremendous vitality energized his whole being so that when he attempted to retard his speech all his mental processes slowed down and self-consciousness confused him. "He spoke to his audience as a man might speak to a friend, pouring forth with swift, yet quiet and seldom impassioned earnestness the thoughts and feelings of a singularly pure and lofty spirit. The listeners never thought of style or manner, but only of the substance of the thoughts. . . . In this blending of perfect simplicity of treatment with singular fertility and elevation of thought, no other among the famous preachers of the generation that is now vanishing approached him. . . ." (James Bryce, *The Westminster Gazette*, Feb. 6, 1893).

Because he kept voluminous journals, and had a wide correspondence, Brooks left a wealth of material for his literary executor. This was put at the disposal of Prof. A. V. G. Allen who published in two large volumes what must always be the standard biography of the great preacher (*Life and Letters of Phillips Brooks*, 1900). Its chief defects are the mass of unimportant letters embodied, the tone of excessive laudation, and a lack of humor on the part of the author which led him to treat as of solemn moment experiences common to all.

Brooks's principal writings were his *Yale Lectures on Preaching* (1877), *The Influence of Jesus* (1879), *Essays and Addresses* (1892);

and volumes of sermons entitled: *Sermons* (1878), *The Candle of the Lord* (1881), *Sermons Preached in English Churches* (1883), *Twenty Sermons* (1886), *The Light of the World* (1890), *New Starts in Life* (1896), *The Law of Growth* (1902).

[There is a *Memorial Sermon* (1893) by his brother, Rev. Arthur Brooks; *Phillips Brooks* (1903), a study by Bishop Wm. Lawrence; an analysis of Brooks as a preacher in *Representative Modern Preachers* (1904), by Prof. L. O. Brastow, and a singularly interesting contrast in *Huxley and Phillips Brooks* (1903), by W. Newton Clarke. There are sections devoted to Brooks in the memoirs of contemporaries such as *My Education and Religion* (1925) by G. A. Gordon, *Memories of a Happy Life* (1926) by Bishop Wm. Lawrence, *Men I Have Known* (1897) by Dean F. W. Farrar, *Reminiscences of Bishops and Archbishops* (1906) by Bishop Henry C. Potter.]   C. A. D.

BROOKS, PRESTON SMITH (Aug. 6, 1819–Jan. 27, 1857), South Carolina congressman, was the eldest son of Whitfield Brooks and Mary P. Carroll, and was born on the Brooks plantation at Edgefield, S. C. He was educated at the South Carolina College, graduating in 1839, and practised law for a short time after his graduation. During the Mexican War he served as the captain of the Ninety-six Company of the Palmetto Regiment, and was known as an admirable drill officer and an inflexible disciplinarian. He was married twice, in 1841 to Caroline H. Means, and after her death, in 1843, to her cousin, Martha C. Means.

Brooks had served two years in the South Carolina legislature, previous to his war service, but after the disbanding of his regiment he engaged in his chosen work of agriculture, until 1852 when he was elected to the Thirty-third Congress. He served through this and the succeeding Congress, speaking rarely but remembered for two or three speeches of unusual oratorical ability. On May 20, 1856, Senator Charles Sumner of Massachusetts, during the discussion of the Kansas-Nebraska bill, delivered a coarse and violent speech in the Senate, denouncing by name Brooks's uncle, Senator A. P. Butler of South Carolina, who was at the time absent from the Senate. Two days later Brooks, who claimed to have waited for an apology from Senator Sumner and to have searched for him on the streets, found him seated at his desk in the Senate room, after the adjournment of the Senate, struck him over the head repeatedly with a gutta percha cane, which was broken by the blows, and left him apparently insensible on the floor. Senator Sumner is said never to have recovered fully from his injuries. A special investigating committee of the House reported in favor of the expulsion of Brooks, but the report (*House Report No. 182,* 34 Cong., 1 Sess.) on a strictly party

vote failed of the necessary two-thirds majority. Brooks, however, resigned after a speech in his own justification, and was unanimously reëlected by his constituents.

The Brooks-Sumner episode created intense excitement, most of which was partisan, the North fiercely denouncing Brooks, while Southern states and communities passed resolutions approving his conduct, and presented him with a number of gold-headed canes and at least one gold-handled cowhide. A month after the assault Brooks was charged in a speech by Anson Burlingame [*q.v.*], representative from Massachusetts, with cowardice and lack of fair play. Brooks challenged Burlingame to a duel; the latter accepted but named as the place the Canadian side of Niagara Falls, which it was difficult, if not impossible, for Brooks to reach with safety. Brooks said Burlingame might as well have named Boston Common and refused to go. His refusal was of course capitalized in the North as revealing lack of courage. He lived less than a year after this event, dying at Brown's Hotel, Washington, Jan. 27, 1857. He was striking in appearance, six feet in height, said to be the handsomest man in the House, of a winning presence, and, except when under the influence of a hasty temper, gentle and gracious in manner. He is said to have suffered in the last months of his life from the fear that his attack on Sumner had hurt the section he was trying to defend.

[There is a large scrap-book of articles, mostly laudatory, concerning Brooks, in the possession of his granddaughter, Mrs. Lucile A. Rion of Greenville, S. C. This includes newspaper sketches of his life. Of easily accessible references, see speeches in House and Senate, Jan. 29, 1857, *Cong. Globe,* 34 Cong., 3 Sess.; Edward L. Pierce, *Memoir and Letters of Chas. Sumner,* vol. III (1893); John Bigelow, *Retrospection of an Active Life* (1909–13); Jas. E. Campbell, "Sumner, Brooks, Burlingame, or the Last of the Great Challenges," in *Ohio Arch. and Hist. Soc. Pubs.,* XXXIV (1925), 435–73.]   J. E. W—y.

BROOKS, RICHARD EDWIN (Oct. 28, 1865–May 2, 1919), sculptor, was born at Braintree, Mass. His father, John Brooks, a spinner by trade, was a native of England; his mother, Julia (Arnold) Brooks, was born in Scotland. The fact that Richard Brooks grew up in the vicinity of the granite quarries of Quincy doubtless had to do with his choice of profession. He is said to have begun to model and carve when a mere boy. He early obtained employment in the workshop of a terra-cotta company, and later established a business of his own, doing many kinds of commercial sculpture, but always endeavoring to improve himself. He studied for a time in Boston under T. H. Bartlett. His first important order was for a bust of Gov. Russell, and the result was so satisfactory that the young sculptor was encouraged to go to Paris and devote himself to study. There his masters were Aubé and Injalbert. His first Salon subject was "Chant de la Vague,"—a graceful nude female figure presumably seated on the shore of the sea —for which he received honorable mention in 1895. His next important exhibit was the statue of Col. Thomas Cass which now stands in the public gardens in Boston, as fine a statue of a quiet, soldierly figure as any which an American sculptor has yet produced. For this figure Brooks was honored with a gold medal at the Paris Exposition in 1900, and in 1901 at Buffalo he received a gold medal for an exhibit comprising the statue of Col. Cass, two portrait busts, a number of medals and two interesting examples of applied art,—a curious candlestick and a necklace. Among his later awards was a silver medal for medals, Panama-Pacific Exposition, San Francisco, 1915.

Brooks lived a great part of his professional life in Paris. In 1911, shortly after the Metropolitan Museum acquired two of his bronzes, "The Bather" and "The Song of the Wave," he came to this country to superintend the erection of his statue of Gen. Hood in Baltimore. At that time he planned to establish a studio in Washington, partly no doubt because his colleagues, Paul Bartlett, the son of his old master, and Frank D. Millet, the well-known mural painter, had studios there. He returned to Paris in the winter of 1911–12 to complete certain commissions. These occupied him so long that it was January 1914 before he opened his studio in Washington. He had some years earlier executed statues of John Hanson and Charles Carroll for Statuary Hall in the United States Capitol, had lately completed statues of William H. Seward and Ex-Gov. John H. McGraw for Seattle, and had received a commission for a statue of Col. Wadsworth of colonial fame for Hartford, Conn. The Wadsworth statue was executed in the studio of Robert Hinckley, portrait painter, on Massachusetts Ave. Among Brooks's other well-known works are statues of John Haynes and Roger Ludlow of Connecticut for the façade of the Connecticut State Capitol at Hartford. In 1915 he executed for the Corcoran School of Art in Washington a bronze portrait tablet of the late E. F. Andrews, first principal of the school. This work was interrupted by the sculptor's illness and his temporary absence in Bermuda. It was unveiled on May 27, 1917, in the vestibule of the school. In an exhibition held by the Society of Washington Artists in the Corcoran Gallery of Art he showed a spirited figure of a boxer and two reclining figures purposed as architectural ornament. In a previous exhibition held under the same auspices he exhibited two frames of portrait medals. As a portrait medalist, Brooks excelled, having caught from the French the lightness of touch and subtlety of expression which mark their work in this field. Brooks was a member of the National Sculpture Society and National Institute of Arts and Letters. He was a man of medium height, rather slight build, great refinement of feature, and alertness of expression. He was found ill in his studio by one of his models and died suddenly after being taken to the hospital.

[Lorado Taft, *Hist. of Am. Sculpture* (rev. ed. 1924); *Am. Art Annual*, vol. XVI (1919); obituary in *Boston Transcript*, May 3, 1919; files of the Washington *Star*; Vital Records of Braintree, Mass.]   L. M.

BROOKS, THOMAS BENTON (June 19, 1836–Nov. 22, 1900), geologist and mining engineer, was born at Monroe, N. Y., the son of John Brooks and Sarah Ketchum Brooks, his wife. His early training was limited to instruction at home, the district public schools, two years (1856–58) at the Union College School of Engineering, and in 1858–59 a single course of lectures under J. P. Lesley at the University of Pennsylvania. He had, however, the happy faculty of learning from observation, and sufficiently mastered the use of the newly introduced plane table, while serving as an axman with the topographic branch of the Geological Survey of New Jersey, to supersede his immediate superior. This was when he was but seventeen years of age, and prior to his Union College training. While in college he made surveys in the mountain regions west of the Hudson and later worked with a Coast Survey party in the region of the Gulf of Mexico. With the outbreak of the Civil War, Brooks enlisted as a private, being then twenty-five years of age, and was mustered into service as first lieutenant, Company A, New York Volunteer Engineers, in September 1861, serving until the fall of 1864 and resigning only at the earnest request of his parents after the death of his brother in the trenches before Petersburg. He won recognition for conspicuous bravery during the sieges of Forts Pulaski and Wagner and at the time of his resignation had risen to the rank of colonel by brevet.

After his retirement from the army he served a year on the Geological Survey of New Jersey under Dr. G. H. Cook and in 1865 became vice-president and general manager of the Iron Cliff mine, near Negaunee in the Marquette District of Michigan. Here he began the geological work upon which his reputation is mainly based. In 1869 he was employed, in recognition of his authority on the iron bearing formations, to take charge of the economic division of the state geological survey of the Upper Peninsula under Alexander Winchell. The difficulties encountered in this work are to-day little comprehended, except by those who have likewise worked in the region. The country was—at that time—heavily wooded and swampy. Outcrops were poor and often entirely lacking; prospect holes were few, and fewer yet were mines. There were no maps other than the very defective and often misleading ones furnished by the Land Office. The geological structure was exceedingly complicated owing to repeated folding of the rocks. Nevertheless, by his pertinacity and originality Brooks succeeded in producing a work of value from a scientific standpoint as well as of the greatest use to the prospector and to those who came after him—a work indeed concerning which it has been said that it was only superseded after twenty years of study by an able corps of geologists with a hundredfold better facilities.

For use in his work Brooks designed the dial compass and adapted the dip needle to the purposes of the prospector. Determined to carry through his undertaking to a successful conclusion, notwithstanding the meagerness of the appropriation, he worked without salary and exhausted his vitality to an extent from which he never fully recovered. Broken in health he went abroad and finished writing his report in 1873 while residing in London and Dresden. This report was written with the intention of making it a manual of information as complete as possible, relating to the finding, extracting, transporting, and smelting of the iron ores of the Lake Superior region. With this in view he presented first, an historical sketch of the discovery and development of the iron mines; second, the geology of the Upper Peninsula, including the lithology; third, the geology of the Marquette iron region; fourth, the geology of the Menominee iron region; fifth, the Lake Gogebic and Montreal River iron ridge; sixth, a chapter on exploration and prospecting for ore; and seventh, the magnetism of rocks and the use of the magnetic needle in exploring, concluding with chapters on the methods and cost of mining specular and magnetic ores and their chemical composition.

In 1876 he returned to the United States to reside for a winter at Monroe, thence moving to a suburb of Newburgh, N. Y., where he lived the life of a country gentleman. In 1883, in company with a friend and business associate, Raphael Pumpelly [q.v.], he purchased some eight and one-half square miles of land in Decatur County, Ga., where the two families for several years lived a truly ideal communistic life. In 1889 the Brooks family went once more abroad to obtain for his children the advantage of German educational facilities of which Brooks had a very high opinion. He was twice married, first to Hannah Hulse, who died in 1883 and by whom he had five children, one of whom, Alfred Hulse Brooks [q.v.], won distinction as a geologist, and second, in 1887, to Martha Giesler, a Prussian by birth.

[Full bibliography of Brooks's publications in *Bull. 746, U. S. Geol. Survey*; biographical sketch in D. N. Freeland, *Chronicles of Monroe in the Olden Time* (1898); memorial by Bailey Willis, *Science*, n.s., XIII (1901); G. P. Merrill, *Contributions to a Hist. of State Geol. and Natural Hist. Surveys* (1920), being Bull. 109 of the U. S. Nat. Museum.]   G.P.M.

BROOKS, WILLIAM KEITH (Mar. 25, 1848–Nov. 12, 1908), zoölogist, was the second of four brothers, sons of Oliver Allen and Ellenora (Kingsley) Brooks. His ancestry goes back to Thomas Brooke, who was a freeman of Watertown, Mass., in 1636 and later settled in Concord. On the maternal side Brooks was descended from John Kingsley, who came to Dorchester, Mass., about 1638, from England. He was born in Cleveland, Ohio, to which place his father had removed from Burlington, Vt., in 1835, and became one of the early merchants of that city. He grew up in a large, comfortable, old-time home on Euclid Ave., attending the public schools, where he was a quick pupil, and living the normal boy life of that time in the Middle West. A congenital defect of the heart prevented his joining in athletic sports. The assiduous study of several books on natural history—*Thompson's History of Vermont, Wood's Natural History*— and association with the sons of the geologist, Prof. J. S. Newberry, then a neighbor, showed the bent of his mind at this time. His country walks were collecting trips. He learned to stuff birds, became interested in aquaria, and established a sort of museum in the barn. His first microscope was made for him by Charles F. Brush, afterward well known for inventions in electric lighting. While in public school Brooks had private tuition in Greek; ever after, that language had a charm for him second only to the natural sciences. In 1866 he entered Hobart College where, as he wrote years after, "I learned to study, and I hope, to profit by, but not blindly follow, the writings of that great thinker on the principles of science, George Berkeley." Two years later he transferred to the junior class of Williams College, where he was graduated in 1870.

Having no taste for business life, Brooks decided to teach, and for the following two years was a master at DeVeaux College, Niagara

Falls. In 1873 he entered the Harvard graduate school, where he came for a brief time under the influence of Louis Agassiz. At Harvard it is said that his life was studious and generally solitary save for the companionship of a great St. Bernard dog, "Tige," who always walked with him when he went abroad, and who occupied most of his bed at night.

He spent the summer of 1873 at Agassiz's seaside laboratory at Penekese, and after that a part, at least, of every summer at the shore. In 1875 he was at A. Agassiz's laboratory at Newport. In 1878 he founded the Chesapeake Zoölogical Laboratory, which he directed for many years. Subsequently he worked at the United States Fish Commission laboratories at Woods Hole, Mass., and at Beaufort, N. C., and in 1905 and 1906 at the marine laboratory of the Carnegie Institution at Tortugas, Fla.

During 1875 and 1876 Brooks was an assistant in the museum of the Boston Society of Natural History; but museum work did not attract him, and on the founding of Johns Hopkins University in 1876 he applied for one of their fellowships, and was appointed associate in biology. In 1883 he was made associate professor of morphology, in 1889 professor of morphology, and in 1894 head of the biological department. As a teacher he was noted for the vividness and picturesqueness of his lectures and for his ability to stimulate his students to individual investigation.

Brooks was the author of about a hundred papers, fourteen relating to oysters, their embryology and conservation, seventeen to tunicates, twenty-six dealing with molluscan structure and embryology. Other important papers relate to the Crustacea; the significance of their larval stages in phylogeny being lucidly discussed. The life history of the Hydromedusæ was dealt with in one of his most beautiful and satisfactory papers. His principal books are *The Law of Heredity* (1883), and *The Foundations of Zoölogy* (1899). Of the latter David Starr Jordan wrote: "It belongs to literature as well as to science; it belongs to philosophy as much as to either, for it is full of fundamental wisdom about realities which alone is worthy of the name of science." His essay on "The Origin of the Oldest Fossils and the Discovery of the Bottom of the Ocean" (*Journal of Geology*, July–August 1894) offered a highly original solution of one of the great problems of zoölogy and paleontology. His only text-book was an excellent *Handbook of Invertebrate Zoölogy* (1882).

In personal appearance Brooks was short and stout, with straight brown hair and heavy dark-brown mustache. He was rather thoughtless about dress, deliberate in movement and speech, undemonstrative in manner. "If he had no answer ready when a question was asked he usually gave no answer until he was ready—it might be several days later—when he would answer as naturally as if the question had been asked only a moment before." He enjoyed a good joke. "In spite of quiet reserve, he was usually a very companionable man, and his company was sought and prized by his friends." In 1878 he married Amelia Katharine Schultz, a woman of charming personality. They lived at the beautiful estate "Brightside," on the shore of Lake Roland, seven miles from Baltimore.

[Edwin G. Conklin, "Biog. Memoir of Wm. Keith Brooks," *Nat. Acad. Sci. Biog. Memoirs*, vol. VII (1910); Edward G. Spaulding, "Prof. Brooks's Philosophy," *Pop. Sci. Mo.*, Feb. 1911.]   H. A. P.

BROOKS, WILLIAM ROBERT (June 11, 1844–May 3, 1921), astronomer, was born at Maidstone, England, the son of Rev. William and Caroline (Wickings) Brooks. The family came to America in 1857 and settled in Darien, N. Y. William was educated in the English and American public and private schools. A prolonged trip to Australia and back at the age of seven and eight, and his voyage to America at thirteen, probably started his interest in astronomy. He made his first telescope when he was fourteen years old, just in time to get a view of Donati's great comet of 1858. His first astronomical lecture was delivered in his father's church at the age of seventeen. He became much interested in the development of photography and was one of the pioneers in its application to celestial observation. He was for a time employed at the Shepherd Iron Works in Buffalo and there gained practical experience as a mechanician and draftsman which was of great value to him in constructing his astronomical instruments. In 1868 he married Mary E. Smith and in 1870 moved to Phelps, N. Y., and established himself as the village photographer. During his leisure hours Brooks applied himself to the construction of his telescopes. With the third one he discovered his first comet in 1881; the fourth, a reflector of nine inches aperture, was the chief instrument of the "Red House Observatory," a primitive structure in the apple orchard. With this instrument he discovered ten more comets. Encouraged by his success he now, regardless of his small income, devoted all his time to astronomy. A studious and thorough worker, he was calm of temperament and a well-liked citizen. His interesting presentation and his generous wit brought him much in demand as a lecturer. In 1888 he moved to Geneva, N. Y., where he was given charge of the William Smith Observatory. At Geneva he discovered sixteen more comets, bringing his total up to twenty-seven, only one less than the record number by Pons. He became professor of astronomy at Hobart College in 1900. His cometary discoveries brought him many prizes and medals.

["A Comet Finder," *Century Mag.*, XLVII, 838; "Photographing by Venus Light," *ibid.*, LXII, 529; obituaries in the *Monthly Notices of the Royal Astronomical Soc.*, LXXXII, 246, Geneva (N.Y.) *Daily Times*, May 4, 1921; letter from Anna C. Brooks, daughter of William Robert Brooks.]   R.S.D.

BROOKS, WILLIAM THOMAS HARBAUGH (Jan. 28, 1821–July 19, 1870), Union soldier, was born at New Lisbon, Ohio. In an environment and at a period when attainment of a higher education was difficult, young Brooks eagerly accepted appointment, July 1, 1837, as a cadet at the United States Military Academy. Not a brilliant student, but with work marked by industry and thoroughness, he was graduated in the year 1841, Number 41 in a class which had been reduced by elimination from 113 original cadets to 52 successful graduates. His first assignment was to the 3rd Infantry, and his first field service after joining his regiment was against hostile Seminole Indians in Florida, 1842–43. This was followed, up to the beginning of the war with Mexico, by arduous duty at various isolated frontier posts. In 1846 he joined Gen. Taylor's army, and took part in the battles of Palo Alto (May 8), and of Resaca de la Palma (May 9), receiving his first lieutenancy Sept. 21 of the same year. Thereafter, he participated in nearly all the important battles and engagements of the war—Monterey, Vera Cruz, Cerro Gordo, Ocalaca, Contreras, Churubusco, and the final capture of the City of Mexico. He was brevetted a captain, Sept. 23, 1846, for gallant and meritorious services at Monterey; and on the same date brevetted a major for similar distinguished services at Contreras and Churubusco. At Contreras, working under the direct supervision of that distinguished soldier, Capt. Robert E. Lee, Brooks had made a particularly hazardous and difficult night reconnaissance of a ravine which served as the approach to the enemy's position, when the successful assault was made by Scott's army the following day. For a time thereafter, he served as acting adjutant-general for Gen. Twigg's division, a duty of marked responsibility for so young an officer; and later, from Aug. 19, 1848, until Nov. 10, 1851, when he received his captaincy in the regular army, Brooks served as Gen. Twigg's aide-de-camp. There followed a long period of difficult field service in New Mexico and Texas, which included almost continuous scouting against hostile Indians, and one skirmish with the warlike Navajos in New Mexico, Oct. 10, 1858. During this prolonged period of exposure to danger and to the rigors of climatic extremes, Brooks's ill health required several sick-leaves.

With the outbreak of the Civil War, Brooks was well prepared, except as to impaired physical condition, for promotion to high command, so that his advancement, Sept. 28, 1861, from captain in the regular army to brigadier-general of volunteers, followed naturally and logically. He took part with distinction, in McClellan's Peninsular campaign, being engaged in the siege of Yorktown (Apr. 5–May 4, 1862), the skirmish of Lee's Mills (Apr. 16), the action at Golden's Farm (June 28), and in the battles of Savage Station (June 29) and of Glendale (June 30, 1862). Meanwhile, Mar. 12, 1862, he had become a major in the regular service. In the Maryland campaign of the Army of the Potomac, which followed, Brooks was engaged in the action at Crampton Pass (Sept. 14), the battle of Antietam (Sept. 17), and in the march to Falmouth, Va., during which he commanded his division, from Oct. 22, 1862. In the subsequent Rappahannock campaign, he commanded his division from December 1862 to May 1863; commanded the Department of Monongahela, June 1863 to April 1864; commanded a division of the 18th Corps, Army of the James, April to June, and a division of the 10th Corps, June to July 1864. As division commander, Brooks participated in the battles around Richmond, including Cold Harbor and the siege of Petersburg. But he had been wounded in the battle of Savage Station, and again at Antietam, so that just as victory was about to crown with success the final campaigns of the Union Army, his health broke down completely, and he was forced to resign from the service, June 14, 1864. After a period of rest and recuperation, he moved to Huntsville, Ala., where he engaged in farming until his death, July 19, 1870. His premature end at the age of forty-nine years was mourned not alone by a large circle of army friends and acquaintants, but by his more recent Southern neighbors, who, at a time when the status of former Union officers was strained, loved Brooks for his amiable disposition, simplicity of character, and sound common sense.

[G. W. Cullum, *Biog. Reg.* (3rd ed., 1891); sketch by Gen. Z. B. Tower in *Annual Reunion, Ass. Grads. U.S. Mil. Acad.*, 1871; Justin Smith, *The War with Mexico* (1919); C. M. Wilcox, *Hist. of the Mexican War* (1892); *Battles and Leaders of the Civil War* (1887–88).]   C.D.R.

BROPHY, TRUMAN WILLIAM (Apr. 12, 1848–Feb. 4, 1928), oral surgeon, was born at Goodings Grove, Ill., the son of William Brophy and Amelia (Cleveland) Brophy. He received his academic education at Elgin Academy, Elgin, Ill., 1863–65 and at Dyrenforth's College, 1867–69; and his professional training from the Pennsylvania College of Dental Surgery, where he graduated with the degree of D.D.S., in 1872. In 1880 he graduated from Rush Medical College with the degree of M.D. Early in his career he became interested in the surgery of the mouth. This determination of his life's work was made through an interesting incident. While visiting surgical clinics in the leading cities of the eastern states, he attended in New York a clinical demonstration to medical students given by Dr. Lewis Sayre, the distinguished orthopedic surgeon. Dr. Sayre presented a case of extreme cleft palate and double harelip in an infant two weeks old, a condition which, should the child survive, meant a repulsive and life-long deformity. The mother, in obvious poverty, had brought her baby to the great surgeon, hoping that it might be cured. Dr. Sayre took the child in his hands and explained the details and extent of the deformity—calling attention to the wide cleft between the maxillary bones. By grasping the child's face he could press the flexible bones nearly to contact, saying that if only it were possible to carry the bones to actual contact, with freshened edges, and to immobilize them, and so to effect a union, "we could go far toward correcting the most conspicuous deformity known to mankind." He then stated to his audience the fact that such an operation had never been performed—"we have no way of doing it." The child was returned to the pale-faced and disappointed mother with the conclusive though kindly word that surgery could do nothing in that sad case.

Brophy was deeply stirred by the pathos of the incident and at the same time fired with enthusiasm to devise a way to overcome a surgical difficulty so intricate and so important. As it turned out, his long professional career was devoted to this problem of reconstruction whereby from the vestiges of natural parts were produced, in so far as possible, a hard palate of normal breadth, a flexible soft palate, and a well-shaped lip and nose. After much study and experimentation, he hit upon a plan to immobilize the maxillæ, when brought into contact, by means of lead plates secured by silver wire, and this kind of splint was first used by him on a human subject in 1886. When the union of the bones was established, the cleft lip was united, and later the edges of the soft palate were brought together. This procedure, with minor improvements, has become the accepted method the world over for the treatment of a deformity which had been considered hopeless of correction except by mechanical appliances. During a period of over forty years Brophy performed this operation throughout the United States and in foreign countries, and the relief of human suffering due to him is beyond calculation.

He was distinguished not only as an oral surgeon but also as an educator and writer. He was dean of the Chicago College of Dental Surgery for forty years. He took an active and prominent part in the work of local and national and international dental and medical associations, during the same period, and was a constant writer in the field of oral and facial surgery. An exhaustive book of reference, *Oral Surgery*, was brought out by him in 1915; also *Cleft Lip and Palate*, in 1923. He was married twice: on May 8, 1873, to Emma Jean Mason, who died in 1899; and on Mar. 31, 1908, to Mrs. E. W. Strawbridge.

[Sketch in the *Dental Cosmos*, Apr. 1928; bibliography in *Index to Dental Periodical Lit.*, 1886–1927.]

W. B. D.

BROSS, WILLIAM (Nov. 4, 1813–Jan. 27, 1890), journalist, was the eldest son of Deacon Moses Bross of Sussex County, N. J. When he was a child of nine his family moved to Milford, Pa., where they lived until he was grown. Deacon Bross went into the lumber business when work was started on the Delaware & Hudson Canal, and William was his father's assistant. In 1832 he began his studies at Milford Academy and in 1834 he entered Williams College. He was an earnest student and in 1838 was graduated with honors. Shortly after, in 1839, he married the only daughter of Dr. John T. Jansen of Goshen, N. Y. He secured a position as principal of Ridgebury Academy where he taught 1838–43. He then taught in Chester Academy for five years. In 1848 he moved to Chicago as a partner in the bookselling firm of Griggs, Bross & Company, remaining in this business a year and a half, after which the firm was dissolved. After this, in connection with the Rev. J. A. Wight, he started (1849) the *Prairie Herald*, a religious newspaper which continued for about two years with only moderate success. In 1852 Bross joined with John L. Scripps in starting a paper called the *Democratic Press*. The paper was rather conservative and especially marked for its commercial and financial features. When the Republican party was formed in 1854, the political course of the paper was changed, Bross became an ardent Republican, and his strong advocacy of the doctrines of the new party led him to speak in their behalf. He soon became known as a strong and effective speaker as well as a comprehensive writer. Into this paper Bross introduced the feature of publishing a review of Chicago's business at the beginning of each year. The paper also served as an outlet for his deep enthusiasm for the future prospects of Chicago and the Northwest. Most of his predictions for the former became statistical facts. During the panic of 1857 the *Democratic Press* united with the *Tribune* under the name of the *Press Tribune*. Two years later the first half of the name was dropped and the paper remained the *Tribune*. Bross was a personal friend of Abraham Lincoln, and the *Tribune* very early advocated Lincoln's nomination for president of the United States. In 1864 Bross was elected lieutenant-governor of Illinois. During his term of office he was influential in repealing the so-called Black Laws of Illinois. Immediately after the Chicago fire in 1871, he began working for the rebuilding of the city. He brought considerable aid from other cities through personal contacts which he had made. Bross seemed deeply concerned with religious and moral welfare and often spoke before various religious groups. He was an energetic, resolute man of medium height, robust frame, and square features, and was known as a toiler. Both his speaking and writing were effective because of the frank determination behind each effort that he made. In 1876 he wrote a brief *History of Chicago* dealing chiefly with the commercial progress of the city and its physical advantages. During a vacation near his old home in 1887, he wrote a biographical sketch, *Tom Quick,* which contained an old legend of the Deleware. His death occurred in Chicago.

[*Biog. Sketches of the Leading Men of Chicago* (1868); *Biog. Encyc. Ill.* (1875); *Hist. Encyc. Ill.* (1897); obituaries in *Chicago-Herald,* and *Inter-Ocean,* Jan. 28, 1890, and esp. *Chicago Tribune,* Jan. 28–31, 1890. A paper read before the Chicago Hist. Soc., Jan. 20, 1880, entitled *Chicago and the Sources of Her Past and Future Growth,* and his *Hist. of Chicago* show Bross's interest and knowledge of social and economic tendencies. His religious views are evident from the address before Williams College Alumni, entitled *America as a Field for the Exertions of the Christian Scholar* (1866).]   M. S.

BROUGH, JOHN (Sept. 17, 1811–Aug. 29, 1865), governor of Ohio, was the son of John Brough, a Londoner who came to Ohio in 1806, and in December 1810, by license of the court, opened a tavern "under the court house" in Marietta. In this two-story log building, the first "temple of Justice" in the Northwest Territory, John Brough, eldest of five, was born. The mother, Jane Garnet, died in October 1821, the father a year later. A pioneer editor gave the boy a home and taught him to set type. Printing offices were to be his college, for even in his few terms in Ohio University at Athens (of which he was later a trustee, 1840–43) he supported himself by typesetting. Before he was twenty, he started in Marietta a Democratic paper, the *Western Republican,* sold it in 1833, bought the *Ohio Eagle* in Lancaster, Ohio, and made it a pathway into politics. The Ohio Senate chose him as its clerk for two terms, 1835–37. At twenty-six he was a member of the House and as chairman of the committee on banking and currency, he aided materially in the state's recovery from the panic of 1837. The legislature electing him auditor of state for six years, 1839–45, he reorganized the state system of accounts, corrected many abuses, added to the tax list a million acres of untaxed lands, raised the state's credit from 67 to par,—and made many enemies. Upon the Whig victory of 1844 Brough returned to journalism. He bought the *Cincinnati Advertiser,* changed its name to *Cincinnati Enquirer,* and became its editor. At the same time he practised law. He also entered actively into state politics. Well-informed in public affairs, clear-thinking, self-possessed, clever in argument, favored with a massive frame and a powerful voice, he was deemed the best Democratic speaker in Ohio. From 1848 to 1863 his energies were wholly given to railroads, as president, successively, of the Madison & Indianapolis Railroad, the Bellefontaine Line, and the Indianapolis, Pittsburgh & Cleveland Railroad. He made Madison, Ind., his home, then Indianapolis, and finally Cleveland.

At the outbreak of the Civil War, refusing to follow his party into opposition, he greatly aided the government in the transport of troops and supplies. As the war progressed Ohio was rent with discord. Secret organizations to resist the draft spread fear among the loyal. There was grave peril that the election would be carried by the disaffected, sore over conscription and angered by the arrest of their magnetic leader Vallandigham. In June 1863 before a great meeting at Marietta, his boyhood home, Brough spoke so movingly in support of the Union that within a week he was nominated by the Republicans for governor. The fierce campaign brought out a record poll; Vallandigham's vote surpassed that of all his Democratic predecessors, but Brough's unprecedented majority of 100,099 remained unequaled for forty years.

Inaugurated Jan. 11, 1864, the new governor's great energies were first directed to securing increased taxes for the support of the soldiers' families. The number of welfare agencies near the armies was next increased. The hospitals were brought under inspection. A seniority system of promotions in the army displaced advancement based on favoritism, popular sentiment, and political influence. Acrimonious disputes with officers whose powers were diminished by the new policy arose at once. The governor remained firm in the face of disrespect and open hostility. Large numbers of veteran soldiers whose services were needed in the field were engaged in duties that recruits could well perform—manning fortifications, guarding supply depots, military prisons, and long lines of communications. At a conference of the governors in Washington, Brough led a movement to raise fresh troops to serve for one hundred days, without bounty, in fortifications or wherever needed. The President accepted the offer and Brough telegraphed home a call for 30,000 men. Within sixteen days 34,000 were organized, equipped, and sent forward, releasing an equal number of veterans for Grant's army. He continued to have the confidence of Lincoln and Stanton, grateful for his instant response to calls for support; but powerful enemies within and without the army finally combined to defeat him for a renomination. His last days were embittered but he was not to be moved from any chosen course. He wrote to a friend (February 1865): "I have no fear of any assaults that may be made upon my public acts. . . . They may be marked by errors but not by weakness or dishonesty. And so time and truth will prove them." He still had hosts of friends who overlooked offensive manners and incorrect personal habits in their admiration for his great executive ability, his incorruptible honesty, his zeal, energy, and devotion to the public service. But although he believed he could be renominated and elected, he issued an address "to the people of Ohio" on June 15, 1865, withdrawing as a candidate, "owing the people of the state too much to embarrass their future action for the gratification of [his] own ambition" and doubting whether his health would sustain him through a vigorous campaign. That fear was too soon realized. He did not live to complete his term of office. A sprained ankle compelled the use of a cane and his great weight injured the hand on which he leaned. Gangrene in both foot and hand ended his life after two months of intense suffering. His ashes rest in Woodland Cemetery in Cleveland.

Brough married: first, Achsa Pruden in 1832. She died in 1838, leaving a son and a daughter.

He married second, Caroline A. Nelson in 1843, who bore him two sons and two daughters. She survived him by twenty-five years.

[*Ohio Archæol. and Hist. Quart.*, XIII, 40–70; corrected in some details by vol. XVII, 105–11. Much valuable material about his administration as governor appears in Whitelaw Reid, *Ohio in the War* (1867), I, 166–71, 182–237, 1022–26; and in E. O. Randall and D. F. Ryan, *Hist. of Ohio* (5 vols. 1912). A sympathetic appraisal of him appeared in the *Cincinnati Commercial*, Aug. 30, 1865.]   F. W. A.

BROUGHAM, JOHN (May 9, 1810–June 7, 1880), actor, playwright, was born in Dublin, of Irish and French ancestry. He studied at Trinity College and the Peter Street Hospital, but, when he was twenty, family adversity cut short his medical career, and he went to London and drifted into the theatre, in July 1830. In 1831 he was a member of Mme. Vestris's company at the Olympic, following her to Covent Garden, where, so he always affirmed, he supplied Dion Boucicault [*q.v.*] with the idea of *London Assurance*. In 1840 he managed the London Lyceum, and wrote several plays for its repertoire. He began his American career as Felix O'Callaghan in *His Last Legs* at the Park Theatre, New York, Oct. 4, 1842 (*New York Daily Express*, Oct. 4, 1842), and thereafter was chiefly identified with the United States. He joined Burton's company as an actor and playwright at the famous Chambers Street Theatre, New York, and while there wrote many plays and burlesques, including a dramatization of *Dombey and Son* in which Burton played Captain Cuttle. For this he received, he later declared, only $250. In 1850 he opened Brougham's Lyceum, on the corner of Broadway and Broome St., New York, but lost on the venture because the public thought the theatre walls unsafe after an adjoining building was torn down. He then revived *King John* at the Bowery, and later joined Wallack's company, meanwhile continuing prolific as a playwright. For Wallack, he made, among other works, a dramatization of *Bleak House*, and wrote perhaps his most famous burlesque, *Pocahontas*. That Indian maiden had already served as the heroine of more than one romantic play, and Brougham had lively fun with them all, though his burlesque is marred for us to-day by its incessant stream of puns. He presently rejoined Burton, and wrote another famous burlesque, *Columbus*, one of his most interesting plays, not without a touch of dignity and pathos amid its fun. In 1860 he went to England and acted there for five years, and also made for Charles Fechter an English version of *The Duke's Motto*, for which he declared he was rewarded with a box of cigars,

He returned to America in 1865 and never went abroad again. On Jan. 25, 1869 he opened Brougham's Theatre on West Twenty-fourth St., New York, with *Better Late Than Never* and *The Dramatic Review for 1868,* a forerunner of the reviews of the twentieth century (See *New York Herald,* Jan. 25, 26, 1869). But the owner of the theatre, the notorious Jim Fisk, Jr., was dissatisfied with the box office returns, or pretended to be, and took the house away from him. This was his last effort at management. On Jan. 17, 1878, after he had become distressingly poor, a testimonial benefit was held for him at the Academy of Music, and yielded the sum of $10,000 which was settled on him as an annuity. He died on June 7, 1880. Brougham was first married to Emma Williams, an English actress and beauty, from whom he soon separated. His second wife was Annette Nelson (Mrs. Hodges), daughter of an English naval officer, but herself an actress. She died in 1870. He wrote, during his fifty years on the stage, about seventy-five dramatic pieces and played a great variety of parts. His best work as author was probably his broadly comic and burlesque writing, and his best work as actor was his impersonation of comic characters (especially Irish) who were also gentlemen. His burlesques had a contemporary freshness, and his acting a genial ease, which foreshadowed more modern methods. He himself was gay, full of contagious animal spirits, kindly, generous to a fault, unfailingly courteous, and something of a scholar. His witty curtain speeches were famous, and socially he was extremely popular, being a handsome man of medium height and sturdy stature, with a sparkling discourse, a ready wit, and charming manners. In all business matters he was a trusting child, however, and his later life was clouded by his financial distresses resulting from this temperamental carelessness.

[*Life, Stories, and Poems of John Brougham* (1881), ed. by Wm. Winter; *Appleton's Annual Cyc.,* 1880; Wm. Winter, *Other Days* (1908), and *The Wallet of Time* (1913); *N. Y. Times, N. Y. Tribune,* June 8, 1880.]
W. P. E.

BROWARD, NAPOLEON BONAPARTE (Apr. 19, 1857–Oct. 1, 1910), governor of Florida, is notable for his filibustering expeditions in aid of the Cuban revolutionists, and for his promotion of the drainage of the Everglades. Some of his ancestors were residents of Spanish Florida; his father, also Napoleon Bonaparte Broward, who married Mary Parsons, was a farmer of Duval County. There the son was born and lived until the fighting of the Civil War forced a removal to Hamilton County. An or-

phan at twelve, the future governor worked on the old farm near Jacksonville and attended a country school for several winters. While still a boy he was employed as deck-hand on a steamboat, and on reaching manhood went to Cape Cod and followed the sea for two years. Returning to the St. John's River he was owner and captain of a steamboat until his appointment as sheriff of Duval County in 1889, to which office he was elected in 1892 and again in 1896. But the water never ceased to call him and meanwhile he had built and operated the steamer *Three Friends,* in 1896 commanding her on several filibustering expeditions, successfully landing men and munitions on the coast of Cuba. In 1900 he served in the Florida House of Representatives, and was appointed a member of the state board of health.

A growing interest in the state's welfare and her future led him to the question of the drainage of the Everglades, and with this as a platform and aided by the fame of his Cuban expeditions he was elected governor of Florida in 1904. The project of drainage had been discussed for fifty years and a foundation for the work had been laid by the former administration, but Broward from the stump developed for it a wide popular support of which it was in need. During his term of office (1905–09) dredging was begun (October 1906) and 13.22 miles of canal were completed (see message [on drainage] to the legislature, May 3, 1905). On his recommendation, the legislature created a Board of Control for all state institutions of higher education; these schools were consolidated, and the University of Florida and the Florida Female College (later Florida State College for Women) were established. Other recommendations, at least partly carried out, were greater state aid for common schools, taxation of franchises, primary election legislation, and a resolution proposing an amendment to the constitution to create a board of drainage commissioners. Broward also proposed and strongly advocated state life insurance, and a resolution memorializing Congress to segregate the entire negro race in the United States under a government of its own (see biennial messages to the legislature, Apr. 4, 1905; and Apr. 2, 1907). In the primary election of 1910 Broward was nominated as Democratic candidate for United States senator (virtually equivalent to election), but died before the vote was taken. He was survived by his wife, Annie Douglas, and nine children.

[In addition to his messages to the Fla. legislature (to be found in the *Journals* of both houses) see Caroline M. Brevard, *A Hist. of Fla.,* vol. II (1925); *Fla. Ed. Makers of America* (1911), IV, 17–23; *Certain*

Live Public Questions, An Open Letter of Gov. Bro-ward (Tallahassee, 1907); and an obituary in the *Times-Union*, Jacksonville, Fla., Oct. 2, 1910, as well as obituaries in other Fla. newspapers.]   J. C. Y.

BROWER, JACOB VRADENBERG (Jan. 21, 1844–June 1, 1905), explorer, archeologist, was born at York, Mich., and at thirteen years of age moved with his parents, Abraham Duryea and Mary R. Brower, to Minnesota. Here he continued his common school education. The young man saw service in the volunteer army and navy, and at a later period held various state and federal appointments. Much remaining to be done to complete the knowledge of the region of the sources of the Mississippi, in 1889 Brower undertook exploration about Lake Itasca. During this work he discovered traces of ancient habitations, which impelled him to devote his energies to archeology, especially of the rich fields of Minnesota and Kansas. As Itasca State Park Commissioner (1891–95) for which office he was particularly fitted on account of his explorations of the region, he continued to note sites of archeological interest. Continuing his geographic studies, in 1896 he traced the sources of the Missouri River. In this period he rediscovered Quivira, the legendary locality in central and eastern Kansas reached by the Coronado expedition in 1541. Always exploring with an indefatigable energy, he located the surprising number of 1,125 ancient aboriginal mounds at Mille Lac, Minn., evidently a populous ancient Indian center. In the prolific field of Minnesota archeology no one has done more than Brower. In one decade he contributed 100,000 specimens to the State Historical Society at St. Paul. Not only did he collect, but he made it a rule to publish promptly. That he found means to publish, and most voluminously, indicates an enviable situation rarely accorded to scientific men. As an example of his perseverance, after a fire which destroyed the notes of years of research, he calmly began the work anew. Necessarily most of his contributions were confined to the essential preliminary investigations which science demands as a groundwork. Other more original contributions resulted from excavations in graves, mounds, and village sites. While not having the training required by present day archeologists, Brower accomplished much by self-education and in following the lead of Henry R. Schoolcraft. Of his published writings the most important are, *Prehistoric Man at the Headwater Basin of the Mississippi* (1895); *Quivira* (1898); *Harahey* (1899); *Mille Lac* (1900); *Kathio* (1901); and *Kakabikansing* (1902). His historical and geographical works include *The Mississippi River*

and *Its Source* (1893); *The Missouri River and Its Utmost Source* (1896); *Minnesota: Discovery of Its Area, 1540–1665* (1903); *Kansas: Monumental Perpetuation of Its Earliest History 1541–1896* (1903); *Itasca State Park, an Illustrated History* (1904); and many shorter articles. These works were published mainly at his own expense, and at the height of his productive period he issued usually one volume a year. In appearance Brower was like the ideal pathfinder, over six feet, quite erect and slender, but muscular, and capable of feats of endurance. He was unmarried.

[*Who's Who in America*, 1903–05, *Am. Anthropologist*, n.s. VII, 362; obituary in the *Daily Pioneer Press* (St. Paul), June 2, 1905.]   W. H.

BROWERE, JOHN HENRI ISAAC (Nov. 18, 1792–Sept. 10, 1834), sculptor, made a unique and valuable contribution to American culture in a series of life masks of great Americans. The son of Jacob Browere and Ann Catherine Gendon, he was born in 1792, at 55 Warren St., New York. He was of Dutch descent, and was one of the many claimants to heirship from Anneke Jans, through Adam Brouwer, who came from Holland to settle in Long Island in 1642. The man's name was really Berkhoven, but the name of his business of brewer clung to him and to his descendants. Young Browere entered Columbia, but was not graduated. At nineteen, he married Eliza Derrick of London, England. He studied art with Archibald Robertson, who had come to America from Scotland in 1791 with a commission from the Earl of Buchan to paint for his gallery at Aberdeen a portrait of Washington, and who later with his brother Alexander opened the Columbian Academy in Liberty St., New York, where for thirty years they taught drawing and painting. Browere's brother, captain of a trading vessel to Italy, took Browere abroad, and for nearly two years the young man traveled afoot in Italy, Austria, Greece, Switzerland, France, and England, "studying art, especially sculpture." On his return to New York, he made a bust of Alexander Hamilton, from a miniature by Robertson. Experimenting to produce life masks by means of a molding material superior to that in general use, he at length perfected a composition and a process now unknown, and in 1825, his bust of Lafayette brought him fame. His ambition was to create a portrait gallery of great characters, to be interpreted, he hoped, in bronze. That hope was not realized. "Pecuniary emolument," he wrote to Madison, "has never been my aim." And later, "I have expended $12,087 in the procuration of the specimens

I now have." Included among "specimens" bequeathed to his family were busts of John Adams, John Quincy Adams, Charles Francis Adams, Jefferson, Madison, and Van Buren; Charles Carroll of Carrollton, De Witt Clinton; Generals Philip Van Cortlandt, Alexander Macomb, Jacob Brown; Commodore David Porter, who declared the mask to be "a perfect facsimile of my person, owing to the peculiar neatness and dexterity which guide his scientific operation"; Secretary of the Navy Samuel Southard, Secretary of the Treasury Richard Rush, Justice Barbour, Henry Clay; Drs. Mitchill, Mott, and Hosack; Edwin Forrest and Tom Hilson, actors; Thomas Emmet, Col. Stone, Maj. Noah; that historic trio, Paulding, Williams, and Van Wart; Gilbert Stuart, and other famous men. Dolly Madison at fifty-three was the only woman whose face was handed down by Browere.

The times were not ripe for his plan of permanency in bronze. Abandoning his scheme because of lack of support, and because of what he called "the jealous enmity" of his fellow artists, Browere at one time considered giving some of his works to the South American republics, to incite them to a wider freedom. A versatile individualist, of active mind, he not only wrote verses, but painted pictures, and profitably exhibited them; yet to his wrath he was kept out of the National Academy of Design. A feud with Trumbull was later patched up. Browere made both friends and foes. When the press attacked him for rumored ill treatment of the aged Jefferson under the "process," he retorted that his method was infinitely milder than the usual course, and obtained from Jefferson a satisfactory indorsement.

He died in 1834, after a few hours' illness of cholera, "at his house opposite the old milestone in the Bowery," and was buried in the Carmine Street churchyard. On his deathbed, he directed that the heads of some of his most important works should be sawed off, and packed away for forty years. This was not done. Some of the busts were shown at the Centennial of 1876, but it is doubtful whether their value as records was then appreciated. He left a wife and eight children. His second child, Alburtis (1814–87) became a painter of considerable note. A small water-color made by him of his father shows an energetic manly profile, with upstanding hair, stock, and coat collar. Alburtis knew Browere's process but, like his father, did not divulge the secret. He is said to have added to many of the life masks the draperies which perhaps enhanced them as busts, but which in no way contributed to their paramount virtue, historic authenticity.

[The chief authority on Browere is Chas. Henry Hart, who published in 1898 a well-illustrated book, *Browere's Life Masks of Great Americans*. Hart had previously written an article on these life masks, published in *McClure's Mag.*, IX, 1053–61. Further information is given in letters of famous Americans, notably Jefferson, Madison, John Adams, and others whose masks were made by Browere.]   A. A—s.

BROWN, AARON VENABLE (Aug. 15, 1795–Mar. 8, 1859), congressman, governor of Tennessee, was the sixth child of Rev. Aaron Brown, a Methodist minister, and his second wife, Elizabeth Melton. He was born in Brunswick County, Va., where his father was one of the seven justices from 1800 to 1813. With the exception of his very early training, the younger Brown received all of his education in the state of North Carolina. He was sent when very young to Westrayville Academy in Nash County where he received instruction from John Bobbitt, one of the best teachers and scholars of that time. After spending two years at this place he entered the University of North Carolina in 1812. He was graduated in 1814, valedictorian of his class, showing ability as an orator, even at this early date. While he was still in school his family moved to Giles County, Tenn., nine miles south of Pulaski. After graduation, young Brown also moved to Tennessee, began the study of law with Judge Trimble in Nashville and after two years was admitted to the bar. He practised for a time in Nashville, then took over the law business of Alfred M. Harris in Pulaski, and later formed a partnership with James K. Polk of Maury County which lasted until Polk's public life called him out of the state. Together, they built up a very large practise and also became close personal friends.

In 1821, Brown was elected to the Senate of Tennessee from Lincoln and Giles counties and served until 1827 with the exception of 1825. Again in 1831 he was elected to represent Giles County in the lower house of the state legislature. He exerted all his efforts to have the number of capital crimes reduced, and presented to the legislature a scholarly and philosophical dissertation in defense of his position (*Speeches*, pp. 376, 557 ff.). In 1839 he was elected to Congress over E. J. Shields, a prominent Whig who had served in the two preceding Congresses, and in 1841 and 1843 he was reëlected. He served on the committee which formulated the tariff bill of 1842 and spoke against the bill on the ground that it violated the spirit of the compromise tariff law of 1833 (*Congressional Globe*, 27 Cong., 2 Sess. App., 482). He championed in his speeches the whole Democratic program of the "reoccupation of Oregon" and the "reannexation of Texas," and made a speech against receiving, referring or reporting abolition petitions (*Ibid.*, 28 Cong., 1 Sess., 128).

In 1845, Brown decided to retire from public life and was on his way home from Washington when he received word that he had been nominated for governor of Tennessee by the Democrats. He accepted with reluctance. His opponent was Ephraim H. Foster, a popular Whig. During the campaign Brown made some of his most famous speeches and showed marked ability as an orator. He was elected by a majority of 1,600. An important school program was inaugurated during his administration: a number of male and female academies, including a medical college at Memphis, were established and the Tennessee Deaf and Dumb School at Knoxville was incorporated. The East Tennessee & Virginia Railroad (now the Southern) was granted a charter in 1847. (*Acts of Tennessee 1845–46.*) Brown was governor during the time of the Mexican War and the call for 2,800 soldiers was answered by no less than 30,000 volunteers though only four regiments were accepted. In 1847 he was defeated for reëlection by Neill S. Brown. Aaron Brown was a member of the Nashville convention of 1850 and was author of the Tennessee Platform. He opposed the compromise pending in Congress at this time though he finally acquiesced—but on the other hand, he opposed disunion as a remedy, offering in its stead sectional retaliation by refusing to trade with the North. He was a member of the Democratic convention in 1852 and was chairman of the committee which reported the Baltimore platform on which Pierce was elected. In the Cincinnati convention of 1856, he received 29 votes for the vice-presidency. His last official office was that of postmaster-general in Buchanan's cabinet, in which position he showed a great deal of administrative ability, establishing a much shorter mail route to California by way of the isthmus of Tehuantepec, another route overland from Memphis to St. Louis and San Francisco, and a third across the continent by way of Salt Lake (*Congressional Globe*, 35 Cong., 1 Sess., App., 19–28, 2 Sess., App., 21–26). He was for many years a leader in the Democratic party and his approbation and support were sought in all important measures.

He was first married to Sarah Burruss of Giles County who died leaving four children. In 1845, he was married to Mrs. Cynthia (Pillow) Saunders and had one child, a son.

[*Nashville Republican Banner*, Mar. 9, 1859; Public Papers of Aaron V. Brown in Tenn. State Archives;

A. V. Brown, *Speeches, Congressional and Political, and Other Writings* (1854); *Jour. of the Senate of Tenn.*, 1821, '22, '23, '26; *Jour. of the House of Tenn.*, 1831; *Acts of Tenn.*, 1845–46; *Cong. Globe*, 26, 27, 28, 35 Congresses; John Livingston, *Portraits of Eminent Americans Now Living*, vol. I (1853); Family Records furnished by Old Glory Chapter of D. A. R. in Tenn. State Lib. Many encyclopedias give Brown's middle name as Vail, but he himself made the statement that his name was Venable and not Vail, *Speeches*, p. 507.]

F.L.O.

BROWN, ADDISON (Feb. 21, 1830–Apr. 9, 1913), jurist, author, came of Puritan stock, his father, Addison Brown, tracing his descent from the earliest settlers in Massachusetts, and his mother, Catharine Babson (Griffin) Brown, having among her ancestors Rev. John Rogers, president of Harvard in 1682, and Thomas Dudley, second governor of Massachusetts. He was born at West Newbury, Mass. His early education having been obtained privately at Bradford, Mass., he entered Amherst College in 1848, but proceeded to Harvard in 1849, where he graduated in 1852, being placed second in his class, which included Joseph H. Choate. The following year he entered the Harvard Law School, graduated LL.B. in 1854, and was admitted to the New York bar in 1855. He practised law in New York City for twenty-six years, acquiring a good connection, though he was never identified with any outstanding litigation. He was appointed United States district judge for the southern district of New York by President Garfield June 2, 1881, during a recess of the Senate, and the appointment was repeated by President Arthur the same year. Remaining on the bench for over twenty years, he acquired a high reputation as a judge in the particular class of cases which chiefly came before him, *i.e.*, those involving bankruptcy and admiralty law, and in professional circles was considered as perhaps the finest admiralty lawyer who ever occupied the position. Most of his opinions are reported in 8–115 *Federal Reporter*. The outstanding incident of his judicial career was his refusal in 1895 to issue an extradition order in the case of Charles A. Dana, whom it was sought to have removed from New York to Washington for trial on a charge of libeling the United States government. Prompted by failing health he retired from the bench Sept. 3, 1901. In 1902 he prepared and published *Index Digest of Decisions of Hon. Addison Brown, U. S. District Judge for the Southern District of N. Y., 1881–1901.* Thenceforward he lived a somewhat retired life till his death, which occurred in New York City.

Throughout his life he was deeply interested in scientific investigation, and an address delivered by him in 1891 before the New York Scientific Alliance on "The Need of Endowments for Scientific Research and Publication" was published by the Smithsonian Institution. He was an enthusiastic student of botany, on which subject he was widely recognized as an authority. One of the founders of the New York Botanical Garden, he drafted the act of the New York legislature passed in 1891, under which it was established, became one of its scientific directors, and was its president for two years. He also was an extensive contributor to the botanical collections of Harvard University. In collaboration with Nathaniel L. Britton he wrote *Illustrated Flora of the Northern United States, Canada and the British Possessions* (3 vols., 1896–98), a work of a very elaborate character, containing over 4,000 illustrations embracing every recognized species, a revision of which he had just completed at the time of his death. He also wrote *The Elgin Botanical Garden, Its Later History and Relation to Columbia College, the New Hampshire Grants and the Treaty with Vermont in 1790* (1908), which appeared as a Bulletin of the New York Botanical Garden. Another subject to which he devoted much study was astronomy, and his observations on the corona of the solar eclipse of 1878 were published through the Smithsonian Institution. He was married twice: in 1856 to Mary C. Barrett, who died in 1887, and in 1893 to Helen Carpenter Gaskin.

[G. W. Edes, *Annals of the Harvard Class of 1852* (1922); *Proc. of the Bar in Memory of Hon. Addison Brown . . . June 3, 1913* (1913). An appreciation of his judicial career appeared in *Case and Comment*, n.s., IV, 125, and the obituary notice in the *N. Y. Times*, Apr. 10, 1913, is comprehensive and sympathetic.]

H.W.H.K.

BROWN, ALBERT GALLATIN (May 31, 1813–June 12, 1880), congressman, governor of Mississippi, was born in Chester District, S. C. In 1823 his father, Joseph Brown, a poor but ambitious farmer, braved the dangers and hardships of a long, overland journey through a savage-infested wilderness to establish a new home for his wife and two sons in southern Mississippi. They settled a few miles south of Jackson, the new capital of the state, in what is now Copiah County. Albert Gallatin Brown, the second son, was given such meager school advantages as a frontier settlement afforded, though much of his early life was devoted to farm work. These experiences gave him a life-long sympathy for the farming class and a genuine interest in the welfare of all other laborers. At the age of sixteen he entered Mississippi College, at Clinton, which was a few miles from his home. His college career was limited to three years in that institu-

tion and six months in Jefferson College, at Washington, the old territorial capital of Mississippi. Because of financial limitations he was unable to complete his education at Yale or Princeton, as he desired. His six months of military training at Jefferson College resulted in his election to the office of colonel of the militia of Copiah County, at the age of nineteen, and in his promotion a year later to the rank of brigadier-general. Meantime, he was studying law in the office of E. G. Peyton, at Gallatin, the county seat of Copiah County. Within a year he passed a creditable examination before the supreme court of the state and was admitted to the bar before he reached his majority, the court having failed to ask his age. In the autumn of 1833 he entered upon the practise of law in partnership with his law preceptor. Two years later he gave up a lucrative practise to enter politics, and was elected to the state legislature. Although his father had been a Federalist of the old school, the son was a most ardent Jacksonian Democrat. As chairman of a committee to consider the recommendation of Gov. Lynch in favor of the National Bank, Brown made an adverse report (*Speeches*, pp. 19–26), which with his speeches on the subject put him in the forefront of his party in the state. In his absence, 750 of the 900 voters of his county in 1838 signed a paper demanding that he should either support a candidate for the United States Senate who was favorable to the Bank, or resign. He promptly resigned and announced his candidacy for reëlection to fill the vacancy. After a spirited campaign he was triumphantly returned to his vacant seat. Shortly thereafter he was unanimously nominated for Congress on the Democratic ticket. At that time the Bank issue absorbed the attention of the voters of Mississippi, the Whigs having swept the state in the preceding election. As congressmen were then elected on a general state ticket, Brown and his colleague, Jacob Thompson, canvassed the entire state; they were elected by a large majority. Young Brown took his seat in Congress in December 1839, and entered into active participation in the debates, as a champion of the Independent Treasury and other Democratic measures. The most important of his early speeches in Congress was delivered Apr. 17, 1840, in defense of Van Buren's administration (*Ibid.*, pp. 27–47). After the adjournment of Congress in 1840 he made a vigorous but unsuccessful canvass of Mississippi in behalf of Van Buren, who had been renominated for president on the Democratic ticket. Brown's first wife, Elizabeth Frances Taliaferro of Virginia, having died in October 1835, about five months after their marriage, he was married a second time, Jan. 12, 1841, to Roberta E. Young of Alexandria, Va. At the end of his term in Congress (1841) he declined a renomination; but he was induced to run for circuit judge, and defeated the former incumbent by a vote of almost three to one. Two years later he resigned this office to accept the Democratic nomination for governor. His platform declared that the "Union Bank Bonds" had been issued in violation of the state constitution and should be repudiated. The opposing candidates were the nominee of the Whig party and a distinguished ex-senator, who had been nominated by "the independent bond-paying Democrats" of the state. After a heated campaign Brown was elected by a large majority over the combined votes of his two opponents. This election settled the fate of the Union Bank Bonds. In his inaugural address Brown made a strong plea for the establishment of a free school system and for a liberal support of higher education in the state (*Ibid.*, pp. 55–66). His plan for the common schools was not followed by the legislature, and the system which was created proved ineffective, but better results followed his efforts to establish a state university. At the end of his second term as governor he returned to the lower house of Congress, taking his seat in the latter part of January 1848, two months after the beginning of the session. In his last legislative message (Jan. 3, 1848) he recommended the establishment of a state normal school, a school for the blind, and a lunatic asylum, and he urged again, as he had repeatedly urged before, the payment in full of the "Planters Bank Bonds" (*Ibid.*, pp. 92–105). Feb. 10, 1848, he made a bold defense in Congress of the policies of President Polk, and especially of the Mexican War (*Ibid.*, pp. 105–19). From this time until 1854, Brown was an active participant in the sectional debates in the House of Representatives, and from 1854 until the secession of his state he was in the forefront of the more serious controversies in the Senate. He opposed the Wilmot Proviso, the compromise measures of 1850, Know-Nothingism, and the Topeka constitution. He was a man of striking personality, with a handsome and animated face, an open and pleasing countenance, dark curly hair and beard, an expressive mouth, kindly eyes, and a well-proportioned forehead. His manner was courteous and void of ostentation or vanity. His early speeches, though somewhat ornate, were convincing and persuasive; later his speeches were more direct and bold, even to the point of audacity. Reuben Davis, who knew Brown well, says: "He was the best-balanced man I ever

knew. . . . In politics, he had strategy without corruption, and handled all his opponents with skill, but never descended to intrigue" (*Recollections,* pp. 164–5). In 1860 many Democratic papers advocated Brown's nomination for the presidency. In a conference of senators and congressmen from Mississippi, held at Jackson Nov. 22, 1860, at the request of Gov. Pettus to advise with him in reference to secession, Jefferson Davis, Brown, and L. Q. C. Lamar voted against a resolution to call a convention for the purpose of seceding "by separate State action"; the other three congressmen and the Governor voted in favor of the resolution, and the vote was then made unanimous (Mayes, *Lucius Q. C. Lamar,* pp. 86–7).

After secession Brown organized the "Brown Rebels" of which he became captain. He served with this company in the 18th Mississippi Regiment in Virginia, until his election to the Confederate Senate from Mississippi. He served in that body from Feb. 18, 1862, to Mar. 18, 1865. In the Reconstruction period he advised the people of his state "to meet Congress on its own platform and shake hands." As this policy was very unpopular, he never ran for public office after the war, but spent his last days quietly at his home near Terry, Hinds County, Miss., in his old age declaring his disgust with politics. He died June 12, 1880, and was buried in Greenwood Cemetery, Jackson. His two sons, Robert Y. Brown and Joseph Albert Brown, became lawyers, but following their father's advice, neither of them ever entered politics.

[Principal sources of information are the newspapers of Miss., 1835–80, and the *Cong. Globe,* 26, and 30–36 Cong., inclusive. M. W. Cluskey, *Speeches, Messages and Other Writings of the Hon. Albert G. Brown* (1859), contains a biographical sketch, from the *Democratic Rev.* of 1849, with additions by the editor of the volume to cover the period from 1849 to 1859. This book contains seventy-two documents, which are invaluable to students of the political history of the ante bellum period. See also *Biog. and Hist. Memoirs of Miss.* (1891); Jas. D. Lynch, *Bench and Bar of Miss.* (1881); Dunbar Rowland, *Official and Statistical Reg. of Miss.* (1908) and *Mississippi* (1907); *Miss. Hist. Soc. Pubs.,* vols. I–XIV (1898–1914); Edward Mayes, *Lucius Q. C. Lamar* (1896); Reuben Davis, *Recollections of Miss. and Mississippians* (1889).]   F. L. R.

BROWN, ALEXANDER (Nov. 17, 1764–Apr. 3, 1834), banker, one of America's first millionaires, landed in Baltimore, Md., in 1800, seeking his fortune. The son of William and Margaretta (Davison) Brown, born at Ballymena, County Antrim, Ireland, he had been keeper of a small but successful linen store in Belfast. While no precise reason is known for his coming to America, it is altogether likely that the rampant lawlessness in Ireland and the precarious ness of all existence there in the late eighteenth century dictated his decision. He brought with him his wife, Grace Davison, and his oldest son, William, then sixteen years old, leaving his other three sons, George, John, and James, in England. He also brought with him a stock of Irish linens and the date of his business start in America is fixed by the appearance Dec. 20, 1800, of an advertisement in the *Federal Gazette and Baltimore Daily Advertiser,* announcing that these linens, three dozen "very nice mahogany hair bottom chairs" and four eight day clocks would be "sold very low." From this modest start as an importer of Irish linen, the swiftness with which the Alexander Brown house expanded, the way in which it developed into one of the greatest business and banking firms in the country, the scope of its affairs and the extent of its influence, constitute one of the commercial romances of American history. During all his life Brown made Baltimore his home and business headquarters and from there directed the banking, the trading and importing operations, the movement of his ships, and the world-wide commercial activities he had begun in the new republic and which his sons were helping him to carry on. One by one he took his sons into partnership and sent them out to establish branches. William, the eldest, went to Liverpool in 1809 and started the firm later known as Brown, Shipley & Company. John A. Brown [*q.v.*] went to Philadelphia and organized what later became the firm of Brown Brothers & Company, while James [1791–1877, *q.v.*] entered the field in New York, establishing Brown Brothers & Company there. The modest linen import business Alexander Brown had begun in 1800 grew into an export business as well. First he had undertaken the exporting of cotton to Great Britain, then tobacco. From this as a natural and indispensable adjunct, an international banking business developed. Family and business connections and acquaintanceships in England put the Baltimore firm in an exceptionally advantageous position to handle matters of this sort—a better position, in fact, than almost any other firm of American merchants then occupied. The change in Alexander Brown's business from that of mercantile house to that of a merchant banking house, was inevitable and rapid. Continuing to expand, he became a ship-owner, for his extensive importations and exportations made it profitable for him to buy and build ships.

It was through his foresight, intuition, and courage in the handling of these ships and their cargoes at a time in the world's history when ocean travel was slow and hazardous, not only from wind and weather but from privateers and war-vessels, that Alexander Brown achieved his greatest business triumphs and most of his international reputation as a trader and banker. His alertness and carefulness kept his firm and its branches on an even keel during the War of 1812, and in the years following the war. Many of the oldest and strongest banking and mercantile houses in the country failed during those years. Brown suffered losses but not great ones, and about 1824 his firm began a period of swift growth. From then until the founder died its record of prosperity in America and England was virtually unbroken. The scope of its trading extended far beyond the early fields of linen, tobacco and cotton, and included everything merchantable from champagne to indigo. Yet Alexander Brown was cautious about scattering his strength and frequently had to curb the ambitions of his sons to go into other lines of business such as insurance. His reputation, and that of his firm everywhere, for soundness and integrity seems to have been based on a principle he often repeated in his correspondence with his son William, "It is essential for us in all our dealings not only to be fair but never to have the appearance of unfairness."

Brown was identified with every progressive development and civic movement in Baltimore in its early days, helping to incorporate the Maryland Institute of Art, to establish a municipal water-works, to erect the nation's first monument to George Washington, and so on. He and his son, George Brown [1787–1859, *q.v.*], were among the founders of the Baltimore & Ohio Railroad, were, in fact, more responsible than any others for the idea of building the road. When in the last year of his life the Bank of Maryland failed suddenly, and disaster threatened the entire community, a group of merchants and bankers called upon Brown for his advice. He assured them calmly but emphatically, "No firm inherently solvent will be allowed to fail," thus pledging himself to save the business men of Baltimore.

His death on Apr. 3, 1834, at the age of seventy was called by newspapers, in Liverpool and London as well as in this country, the passing of one of the foremost mercantile figures in America. His wealth was estimated at about $2,000,-000,—a great sum in those days. The firm he established, Alexander Brown & Sons, now the oldest banking house in the United States, still exists in Baltimore as one of the most highly respected institutions of its kind in the country. The branches established by the sons, severed now from the parent bank, are to-day directed by their descendants and known throughout the world.

[Old letter books and ledgers dating back to 1800 and now in the vaults of the firm of Alexander Brown & Sons, in Baltimore, form the chief sources of information; many of these were written by Alexander Brown himself. Much of the story is told in the privately printed volume, *A Hundred Years of Merchant Banking* (1909), issued by the late John Crosby Brown of N. Y.; *Experiences of a Century* (1919), issued by Brown Bros. & Co. of Phila., and *The Story of Alexander Brown & Sons* (1925), by F. R. Kent. See also Mary E. Brown, *Alexander Brown and His Descendants* (privately printed, 1917) and a sketch of Sir Wm. Brown in *Dict. Nat. Biog.*, III, 37.]   F.R.K.

BROWN, ALEXANDER (Sept. 5, 1843–Aug. 25, 1906), historian, was born at Glenmore, Nelson County, Va. He was the son of Robert Lawrence Brown and Sarah Cabell (Callaway) Brown. He studied under Horace W. Jones, noted as a molder of the minds and characters of boys, and in his library acquired his taste for history. In 1860 he matriculated at Lynchburg College. The outbreak of the Civil War interrupted his education, and at the age of seventeen he enlisted in the Confederate army. In December 1864 the explosion of a powder-boat, near Fort Fisher, N. C., rendered him almost totally deaf. For several years after the war he was a salesman in Washington, D. C., but his deafness unfitted him for business, and he returned to Nelson County, where he engaged in farming. He led a retired life, devoting every spare moment to historical research. His interest centered in the first two decades of Virginia history, and he spared no effort in searching out original evidence on that period. Year after year he labored patiently, writing to librarians and historians, securing experts to search the archives and copy manuscripts, and practising rigid economy to meet the costs. He married Caroline Augusta Cabell on Dec. 27, 1873. His wife died in 1876, and on Apr. 28, 1886, he married Sarah Randolph Cabell.

His first work, *New Views of Early Virginia History*, appeared in 1886. There followed, in 1890, *The Genesis of the United States*, a collection of documents, many never before published, relating to the founding of the British Empire in America. *The Cabells and Their Kin* appeared in 1895, *The First Republic in America* and *The History of Our Earliest History* in 1898, and *English Politics in Early Virginia History* in 1901.

Brown contended that the history of early Virginia had been falsified by the Court party in England, to discredit the liberal group in the London Company. This was done by suppressing the Company's records, and licensing Captain John Smith's "incorrect, unjust, and ungenerous" works. Brown devoted himself to correcting this age-old injustice and to vindicating the true heroes of the founding of Virginia--Sir Edwin Sandys and those who labored with him to set up liberal institutions. He forced historians to reconstruct their views on the early history of Virginia. Although some of his conclusions have not been fully accepted, his place as the leading authority in his field is established.

[*Encyc. Va. Biog.*, ed. by L. G. Tyler, III (1915), 256–57; *Who's Who in America*, 1906–07. Many facts relating to Brown's life and work appear in the prefaces of *The Genesis of the United States* and *The First Republic in America*.]   T.J.W.

BROWN, ALEXANDER EPHRAIM (May 14, 1852–Apr. 26, 1911), inventor and manufacturer, was the son of Fayette Brown [*q.v.*] and his wife Cornelia Curtis. The father had a noteworthy part in Cleveland's industrial development as a banker, iron manufacturer, and owner of a fleet of ore boats. Alexander E. Brown was one of five children. He received his early education in the Cleveland public schools, completing the course at the old Central High School. In the autumn of 1869 he entered the Brooklyn Polytechnic Institute, Brooklyn, N. Y., graduating in an engineering course in June 1872. Immediately after graduation he joined the United States Geological Survey, and for six months was engaged in the exploration of the Yellowstone region. During the ensuing two years he was employed as chief engineer for the Massillon Iron Bridge Company of Massillon, Ohio, and from 1875 to 1878 was employed as an engineer in construction work and in superintending iron mines in the Lake Superior iron region. During part of 1878 and 1879 he was in Cleveland, connected as a mechanical engineer with the Brush Electric Company, then known as the Telegraph Supply Company, a corporation developing the inventions of the founder, Charles F. Brush.

During the year 1879 Alexander Brown made his most important invention, that of the Brown hoisting and conveying machine for handling coal and iron ore at the lake ports. In the following year patents were obtained, and the first Brown hoisting and conveying machine was set up on the ore docks in Cleveland. The Brown Hoisting Machinery Company was organized to manufacture such machinery, with Brown's father as president and himself as vice-president and general manager. In 1910, upon the death of his father he became president, a position which he held until his own death. As a result of Brown's achievement, the construction of lake boats for transportation of bulky materials was revolutionized. Before his time the largest lake boats did not exceed 1,200 tons capacity. He made the operation of such small craft unprofitable; lake boats of 8,000, 10,000, and even 12,000 tons came into use. It became possible to unload a 12,000-ton ore vessel in as many hours as it formerly took days to unload a 500-ton boat.

Brown was identified with many professional and social organizations. He was an engineer and inventor of great ability and versatility. Nearly fourscore patents in various fields are on record in Washington. On Nov. 14, 1877, he was married to Carrie M. Barnett, the daughter of Gen. James Barnett. Their son, Alexander C. Brown, succeeded his father as president of the Brown Hoisting Machinery Company.

[Elroy M. Avery, *Hist. of Cleveland* (1918), III, 533–34; *Who's Who in America*, 1910–11; the Reports of the Cleveland Board of Trade; an article by Alexander C. Brown in *Trade Winds*, a Cleveland publication, Apr. 1925; obituaries in the *Cleveland Plain Dealer* and *Cleveland Leader*, Apr. 27, 1911.]   E. J. B.

BROWN, ANTOINETTE. [See Blackwell, Antoinette Louisa Brown, 1825–1921.]

BROWN, BEDFORD (1792–Dec. 6, 1870), senator, was the son of Jethro B. and Lucy (Williamson) Brown of Caswell County, N. C. Both parents were of good English stock, the Williamsons being socially prominent. As the representative of the large and politically-minded planters who dominated Caswell, young Brown, after two years at the state university, was sent to the lower house for four years (1815–18, 1823) and then to the Senate (1828–29). Having fought successfully for Jackson electors in 1824 and 1828, in 1829 he was chosen speaker by the Senate; and when President Jackson transferred United States Senator Branch to his cabinet, Brown essayed to back Thomas Ruffin for the unexpired term. "In the scrambling," however, Brown was elected—by mistake, apparently, in the casting of one vote. In the federal Senate his importance consisted chiefly in his support, whole-hearted and vigorous, of the Jackson and Van Buren administrations, particularly as to nullification and fiscal policy. Though never of the Jacksonian inner circle, he was trusted by its members; and it was as an administration candidate that he participated in the legislative elections of 1834 and secured a full term. His retirement from the Senate was melodramatic. A Whig legislature having sent him resolutions condemning Jacksonian policies and referring to "party servility," he announced in the Senate that he "desired his public course should be tested by the popular will of his State," and so would resign after the coming legislative elections (Jan. 14, 1839; *Congressional Globe*, 25 Cong., 3 Sess., p. 117). The legislature, how-

ever, being won by the Whigs, accepted his resignation (1840); and when two years later he sought reëlection from a Democratic legislature, the Calhoun wing of his party blocked him despite his own presence in the Senate and the efforts of his powerful friends outside the state. Disgusted, he moved to Missouri about 1844, but by 1852 had returned and begun anew the game of national politics. State rights within the Union was now his leading principle. In the Democratic national convention of 1856 he favored Buchanan and in that of 1860, Dickenson, on a platform guaranteeing the rights of the Southern States through constitutional amendment (Brown, *Remarks . . . in the Senate of North Carolina, on Dec. 19, 1860*). Back again in the state Senate (1858–63), he led the fight against secession in 1860. His speech of Dec. 19, which was reprinted and circulated, berated alike abolitionists and advocates of a "Southern 'higher law,'" and urged a policy of terms within the Union. Failing in this, in the secession convention and at first in the Senate he advocated a "most vigorous prosecution of the war"; but by the summer of 1863 this mood had passed. The war over, his old Unionist attitude caused Governors Vance and Worth to enlist him—unsuccessfully—as a mediator in Washington. He served in the constitutional convention of 1865. He was elected to Congress in 1865 and to the constitutional convention of 1867, but was denied a seat in each. Though he supported Holden for governor, his county was ravaged by the Reconstructionists and he himself when he sought amelioration from President Grant met curt rebuff.

Brown owned a large plantation in Caswell and lived there, on the aristocratic "Locust Hill." Tall, spare, smooth-shaven, firm of carriage, he cultivated the arts of dress and deportment. His intellectual equipment was mediocre. A deep, husky voice and a slow, labored style made him an unusually poor speaker; but a protruding lower jaw and a habit of clinching his teeth gave him an appearance of resoluteness and, when he was angry, of dangerous fierceness. Some laughed at his pompousness, but none questioned his individual courage. President Jackson was his personal friend and, perhaps, his model. The great Jackson leaders, though they flattered him, really liked him; and he treasured their letters. He was married to Mary L. Glenn, and their son, Bedford Brown (1825–1897), became a noted physician (see Kelly and Burrage, *American Medical Biographies*, 1920, p. 148).

[There is no biography of Bedford Brown. See David Schenck, *Personal Sketches* (1885); *Biog. Hist. of N.*

C., vol. I (1905), ed. by S. A. Ashe; J. G. de Roulhac Hamilton, *Party Politics in N. C. 1835–1860* (1916); *The Correspondence of Jonathan Worth* (1909), and *The Papers of Thos. Ruffin* (1918–20), ed. by J. G. de R. Hamilton; *The Papers of Archibald D. Murphy* (1914), ed. by Wm. H. Hoyt. Brown's correspondence was published in the *Trinity Coll. Hist. Soc. Papers* (1906–07).] C. C. P.

BROWN, BENJAMIN GRATZ (May 28, 1826–Dec. 13, 1885), senator, governor of Missouri, was born at Lexington, Ky., the son of Mason and Judith (Bledsoe) Brown. His father, Mason Brown, was a jurist of some note who served as judge of a Kentucky circuit court and, from 1856 to 1859, as secretary of state. His grandfather, John Brown, was the first United States senator from Kentucky. The Browns were related to the Prestons, Breckenridges, Blairs, Bentons, and other well-known Kentucky families.

Brown entered Transylvania University but withdrew in 1845 and entered Yale University, where he was graduated in 1847. He then studied law in Louisville, was admitted to the Kentucky bar, and, in 1849, moved to St. Louis. The same year he took the stump in support of Thomas H. Benton's attack upon the "Jackson Resolutions" adopted by the Missouri legislature that year. He again came actively to the support of Benton in the Atchison-Benton senatorial contest of 1852–53. Appreciating the importance of the large German vote in St. Louis, he early cultivated its support; and, largely as a result, he was elected, and reëlected, to the lower branch of the state legislature between 1852 and 1859. For upward of two decades the St. Louis Germans constituted the principal element in his political following. In the Missouri legislature of 1857, Brown took an especially prominent part. A joint resolution was introduced declaring emancipation of the slaves to be impracticable, and that any movement in that direction was "inexpedient, impolitic, unwise, and unjust." In reply to this, Brown, at some personal risk, it is said, made an able and forceful anti-slavery speech in which he advocated and prophesied the abolition of slavery in Missouri on economic grounds—more out of regard to the interest of poor white laborers than as an act of humanity to the slaves. This incident has been regarded by some as the beginning of the Free-Soil movement in Missouri (*Speech of Hon. B. Gratz Brown of St. Louis on the Subject of Gradual Emancipation in Missouri, Feb. 12, 1857*, Pamphlet, 1857). Brown's speech apparently made him the Free-Soil Democratic candidate for governor the same year. He failed of election by the narrow margin of about 500 votes. Between 1854 and 1859, most of Brown's energies were absorbed in newspaper editorial work for the *Missouri Democrat*—a paper of strong Free-Soil, and, later, Republican, principles. In its columns, Brown persistently assailed the institution of slavery in Missouri and advocated emancipation. In 1856 he fought a duel with Thomas C. Reynolds over differences growing out of editorials relating to the Know-Nothing movement in St. Louis. Brown was shot near the knee, and limped during the rest of his life.

In the formation of the Republican party in Missouri in 1860 Brown took an active part and was a delegate-at-large to the Chicago convention which nominated Lincoln. At the opening of the Civil War, he became colonel of the 4th Regiment of Missouri (three months) Volunteers, and energetically coöperated with Gen. Lyon and Frank P. Blair, Jr.. in circumventing the Missouri secessionists.

In the state election of 1862 the abolition of slavery was the outstanding issue, especially in the eastern part of the state. Brown led the radicals, who insisted upon immediate emancipation, in opposition to the gradual emancipationists led by his cousin, Frank P. Blair, Jr. Although the policy of the latter was indorsed two years later by the state convention which adopted an ordinance for the gradual extinction of slavery, Brown's faction won a majority of the seats in both branches of the next legislature, and nominated him for the United States Senate. After a prolonged contest, Brown was elected on the thirty-second ballot (1863) for the unexpired term of W. P. Johnson, who had been expelled as a secessionist. He took the oath of office Dec. 14, 1863, and served until Mar. 4, 1867. In 1864, he was one of the signers of the call for the Cleveland convention of radicals who opposed the renomination of Lincoln and nominated Frémont and Cochrane.

While in the Senate, Brown served upon the committees on military affairs, Indian affairs, Pacific railroad, printing, public buildings and grounds, and also as chairman of the committee on contingent expenses. Although frequently taking part in Senate debates, he made only one extended speech. This was in support of an amendment to a bill to promote enlistments in the army, confirming and making of full effect as law the President's emancipation proclamation, and adding a section declaring the immediate abolition of slavery in all states and territories of the United States, as a war measure (Mar. 8, 1864. *Congressional Globe*, 38 Cong., 1 Sess.. pt. II, pp. 984–90). His next longest speech was in opposition to the proposed reading and writing tests for voting in the District of Columbia and in advocacy of woman suffrage for the District. "I stand," he declared, "for universal suffrage, and as a matter of fundamental principle do not recognize the right of society to limit it on any ground of race, color, or sex . . . I recognize the right of franchise as being intrinsically a natural right . . ." (Dec. 12, 1866. *Congressional Globe*, 39 Cong., 2 Sess., pt. I, p. 76). He also spoke, or introduced resolutions, in favor of the eight-hour day for government employees, approving retaliation for rebel mistreatment of Northern prisoners of war, advocating government construction, ownership, and operation of telegraph lines, and urging the establishment of the merit system in the civil service. His speeches are noteworthy for their obvious sincerity and absence of buncombe, their dignified simplicity of diction, and unusual directness and incisiveness.

Before the end of his senatorial career, Brown became prominently identified with the so-called Liberal movement in Missouri for the repeal of the drastic test-oaths prescribed in the Missouri constitution of 1865 and aimed at sympathizers with the Confederate cause. Later, this Liberal movement, which came to embody a reaction against the radical Republican reconstruction policy and in favor of amnesty for former rebels and reconciliation between the sections, culminated in the nomination of Brown for governor, in 1870, and his triumphant election by a majority of more than 40,000. At the same election, constitutional amendments were approved repealing the obnoxious test-oaths.

In his messages as governor (1871–73), Brown recommended constitutional amendments reorganizing the courts, including the grand jury system, and the better regulation of railroads through the creation of a board of railroad commissioners. The bankruptcy of a number of railroads whose bonds had been guaranteed by the state embarrassed his administration, and resulted in a loss to the state of approximately $25,000,000.

The success of the Liberal movement in Missouri encouraged liberals and reformers in other states and led directly to the launching of the Liberal Republican party in 1872 in opposition to the renomination of President Grant and in favor of tariff and civil service reform and abandonment of radical Republican reconstruction policies. Brown's prominence naturally led to serious consideration of his availability as the presidential candidate of this independent movement; and at the Cincinnati convention of the Liberal Republicans, in May 1872, he stood

fourth on the first ballot for the presidential nomination, receiving ninety-five votes. Suspecting that his delegates were being enticed away by the friends of Charles Francis Adams, Brown unexpectedly appeared in Cincinnati, obtained permission to address the convention, and in his speech astonished the delegates by warmly urging the nomination of Horace Greeley. On the sixth ballot Greeley was nominated, and, later, Brown himself received the vice-presidential nomination. Afterward, Carl Schurz and others charged that the ticket was the result of a deliberate bargain between the friends of Greeley and Brown (F. Bancroft, *Speeches, Correspondence, and Political Papers of Carl Schurz*, 1907–08, II, 362–63). Brown's nomination, however, seems to have been of little or no help to the Liberal Republican campaign, although he participated actively in the canvass. In August he attended a class banquet at Yale, became intoxicated, and made a speech in bad taste, criticizing things eastern (E. D. Ross, *The Liberal Republican Movement*, 1919, p. 156). Following this campaign, Brown gave up active participation in politics and devoted himself to the practise of law, making a specialty of railway cases. By 1876 he had virtually gone over to the Democratic party. He attended that party's national convention, where "loud calls for Gratz Brown brought that gentleman to the rostrum, accompanied by a round of applause" (*Official Report of the Proceedings*, p. 91). In his brief response, he expressed sympathy with Democratic demands for reform and the belief that former Liberals would warmly support those demands. Brown's death in 1885 was the direct result of overwork, following close upon a serious illness, in completing a report as referee in an important railroad case pending in the federal court at St. Louis. In person, Brown is described as of medium height, of very slender figure, and "immediately noticeable for his wealth of red hair and beard."

[A disparaging sketch by a political opponent in 1872, pointing out Brown's weaknesses, appears in E. Chamberlin, *The Struggle of '72* (1872), pp. 540–47. A more favorable, and generally more satisfactory sketch is printed in W. B. Davis and D. S. Durrie, *An Illus. Hist. of Mo.* (1876), pp. 482–83. Other Missouri histories contain scattered references to Brown's opposition to secession, advocacy of emancipation in Missouri, and administration as governor, especially, W. F. Switzler, *Illus. Hist. of Mo.* (1879); and *The Province and States* (1904), ed. by W. A. Goodspeed, vol. IV. The Brown-Reynolds duel is described in some detail in W. B. Stevens, *St. Louis—the Fourth City, 1764–1911* (1911), I, 377–85; *Mo. Hist. Rev.*, XIX, 423–26. Brown's senatorial speeches appear in the *Cong. Globe* for the 38th and 39th Congresses. For his political campaign speeches one must consult contemporary newspaper files. Interesting light on Brown's appearance at the Cincinnati convention is shed by H. Watterson, "The Humor and Tragedy of the Greeley

Campaign," *Century,* LXXXV, 27–45. His connection with the earlier stages of the Liberal Movement may best be traced in T. S. Barclay, "The Liberal Republican Movement in Mo.," *Mo. Hist. Rev.,* vol. XX.]

P. O. R.

BROWN, CHARLES BROCKDEN (Jan. 17, 1771–Feb. 22, 1810), novelist, journalist, the first person in the United States to make authorship his principal profession, was descended from James Brown, a Quaker who came to America before William Penn. Charles Brockden Brown was the son of Elijah Brown, a merchant of Philadelphia, and his wife, Mary Armitt. Born into a family in good standing and in fair circumstances, he had at the outset such advantages as the time and place could offer him, except the advantage of robust health. Whether because his being frail made him studious or his being studious made him frail, at least he was both frail and studious. At home and in the school of Robert Proud [*q.v.*] which Brown attended between the ages of eleven and sixteen, the boy gave himself up to violent reading in miscellaneous directions, and thereby got, in an ambitious, uncritical society, an early reputation for scholarship which then or later was never quite justified by the facts. Nor was he eager merely to read. While still at school he produced versions of parts of the Bible and of Ossian, and planned three epics on the grandiose themes of Columbus, Pizarro, and Cortez—thus showing himself to be a contemporary of Joel Barlow [*q.v.*] and a forerunner of Irving and Prescott. Brown's earliest published work was a series of papers called "The Rhapsodist," contributed to the *Columbian Magazine* (Philadelphia, August–November, 1789), and devoted to glorifying the romantic revolutionary soul.

Romance and revolution, however, did not constitute a career in the Philadelphia of the early republic. Brown was accordingly in 1787 apprenticed to Alexander Wilcocks, a Philadelphia lawyer. The law, in the words of Brown's first biographer, "to a mind so ardent in the pursuit of information, opened a wide and inexhaustible field for indulgence. It is withal, in this country, one of the roads to opulence, and the most certain path to political importance and fame" (William Dunlap, *The Life of Charles Brockden Brown,* 1815, I, 15). What was perhaps more attractive, the law was generally thought of as a calling so close to literature that both might naturally be followed by the same man. Brown, along with his legal studies, still found time to speculate and debate, particularly at the meetings of the Belles Lettres Club which he and eight of his friends established for the improvement of their minds during the hours

not claimed by the law. Had he been, as his family hoped and expected, only an amateur in literature, Brown might have ridden his two horses at once. But he had in him too many of the instincts of a professional writer, and in 1793 gave up the law altogether, against the advice of his parents and his elder brothers who presumably saw themselves obliged to support him in his adventure.

Authorship had hitherto occupied the major attention of few Americans and had provided a livelihood for none. Brown, taking so precarious a step, must have seemed to sentence himself to be either a dilettante or a vagabond. He did not become a vagabond. Instead, he only drifted back and forth between Philadelphia and New York, possibly for a time a teacher in his native town, but primarily reading and forming designs for masterpieces. What drew him to New York was less the chances which that town gave him for a literary career than the presence there of Elihu Hubbard Smith [*q.v.*] whom Brown had encountered as a medical student in Philadelphia and who in New York was somehow contriving to write verse and prose as well as heal the sick. At Smith's house in Pine Street Brown met, along with others, Samuel Latham Mitchill [*q.v.*], James Kent [*q.v.*] and William Dunlap [*q.v.*], men of promise who belonged to the Friendly Society, a club which for Brown filled the place of the Belles Lettres Club in Philadelphia. His first visit to New York he apparently made in 1793, another certainly in 1795. From 1798 to 1801 he lived there almost continuously. Without much question the Friendly Society furnished the most stimulating companionship of Brown's life. New York did for him what Philadelphia could not do.

Politically inclined to the party of Jefferson, Brown had by 1795 already come to accept most of the radical doctrines current in the United States, but he owed his special impetus to William Godwin, in whose *Caleb Williams* (1794) he saw "transcendant merits." Before undertaking a novel, however, the young philosopher wrote a treatise in dialogue on the rights of women. A part of the work was published in New York early in 1798, with the title *Alcuin: A Dialogue,* and with a note by Elihu Hubbard Smith; the remainder first appeared in the Dunlap *Life* five years after Brown had died. Because the original *Alcuin* is extremely rare, and has never been reprinted, most comments upon the treatise have gone on the assumption that the portion available in the *Life* is the same as that in the separate book. This accident of bibliography has had few serious results, for *Alcuin* had no appreciable influence at the time and is not now important, though the curious will find in it various enlightened, if unexciting and undramatic, arguments for the equality of the sexes and the freedom of divorce (David Lee Clark, *Brockden Brown and the Rights of Women,* University of Texas Bulletin, No. 2212, Mar. 22, 1922).

The admirer of *Caleb Williams,* not content with argument, next proceeded to fiction. Toward the end of 1797 Brown wrote a romance presumably to be identified as the "Sky-Walk" which he announced in a letter to the *Weekly Magazine* (Philadelphia) of Mar. 17, 1798, but of which the manuscript was lost before it could be published. Whatever his practise may have been, Brown's theory of fiction was impressive. "The value of such works," he told the readers of the *Weekly Magazine,* "lies without doubt in their moral tendency. . . . The world is governed, not by the simpleton, but by the men of soaring passions and intellectual energy. By the display of such only can we hope to enchain the attention and ravish the souls of those who study and reflect." At the same time, Brown did not mean to write for geniuses alone. He held that the same novel which could stir thinkers by its ideas might capture ordinary people with its plot—or, in his own less simple words, that "a contexture of facts capable of suspending the faculties of every soul in curiosity, may be joined with depth of views into human nature and all the subtleties of reasoning."

With the principles of his art thus thought out and with his model chosen, Brown now plunged into the two fecund, nervous years which saw the composition of all his noteworthy books. *Arthur Mervyn,* begun in Philadelphia before the summer of 1798, was completed in New York, and was published in two parts in 1799 and 1800. *Wieland* appeared in 1798, and *Ormond* and *Edgar Huntly* in 1799; only the less interesting *Clara Howard* and *Jane Talbot* have so late a date as 1801. Writing at such speed, Brown had little opportunity to grow in experience or to vary his materials. His novels all bear the marks of haste, immaturity, and Godwin.

Brown's indebtedness to Godwin is to be found chiefly in a fondness for the central situation of *Caleb Williams:* an innocent and more or less helpless youth in the grasp of a patron turned enemy. *Arthur Mervyn,* to take the clearest example, brings a young man from the country to Philadelphia, makes him blunder into the secret of a murder, and subjects him to crafty persecutions from the murderer. In *Ormond* by a variation of the formula the victim is a wo-

man, Constantia Dudley, pursued by the philosophical villain Ormond until she is obliged to kill him in self-defense. Constantia was a favorite heroine of Shelley, to whom she seemed a perfect type of virtue harassed by evil men. But Brown's victims do not suffer the gradual, increasing agony of Godwin's, for the reason that Brown could not construct a plot as Godwin could. The disciple had neither the steady art nor the weighty conviction of the master. Furthermore, American life, loose-knit and easy-going, afforded in Brown's decade an inadequate setting for a story of social persecution.

The method which Brown derived from Godwin is less notable than the material which he took, at first hand, from native conditions. In 1793 he had fled with his family to the country to escape the epidemic of yellow fever which then visited Philadelphia; five years later, just after his arrival in New York, he had gone through a similar invasion of the plague which caused the death of his friend Smith. His letters show how deeply he was moved by the only personal contact he ever had with such affairs of danger and terror as he ordinarily wrote about. Composing *Ormond* almost before the later epidemic had passed, Brown transferred his impressions from the New York of 1798 to the Philadelphia of 1793, as he did in *Arthur Mervyn,* perhaps for some gain in perspective; but in both he wrote with his eye on the fact as nowhere else in his books. With unsparing, not to say sickening, veracity, he represented the physical horrors of the plague, and he was even more veracious in his account of the mental and spiritual horrors which accompanied it. Less successful than his handling of the plague was his handling of the frontier in *Edgar Huntly.* American novelists, he said in his preface, ought no longer to make use of "puerile superstition and exploded manners, Gothic castles and chimeras. . . . The incidents of Indian hostility, and the perils of the Western wilderness, are far more suitable." So far as his knowledge and his prepossessions went, Brown succeeded in this experiment. But he knew little of the frontier and little of the Indians. He merely used a new setting for actions not strikingly unlike those in his Godwinian plots. Huntly is not a frontiersman; he is a sleep-walker, whose adventures might almost be his dreams. Of the Indians, the visible ones are none of them so memorable as the old woman called Queen Mab, who, never appearing in person, stands as a symbol of the vanquished race. Always what interested Brown was the tormented states of mind which he studied in his characters.

This clearly appears in his most compact, most reflective, and most powerful novel, *Wieland*. Its plot was founded upon the deeds of an actual religious fanatic of Tomhannock, New York, who in a mad vision had heard himself commanded to destroy all his idols, and had murdered his wife and children with ferocious brutality (Carl Van Doren, "Early American Realism," *Nation*, Nov. 12, 1914). With this theme Brown involved the story of a trouble-breeding ventriloquist, in order to make the mysterious voices credible. As ventriloquism itself was mysterious in 1798, the solution of the plot probably did not then seem so trivial as it now seems. And Brown did not rely too much upon his trivial solution. He saw, perhaps better than he understood, that the essential mystery in Carwin was not his ventriloquism, but the driving spirit of malice which forced him to meddle in other people's lives without really intending to do harm. Moreover, the murderer, though stung into activity by the voices which he hears, would of course not have acted but for the depths of frenzy already sleeping in his nature. For Brown, who after all was only twenty-seven when he wrote *Wieland*, such cases of speculative pathology were more real, or at least more arousing, than any of the customary aspects of behavior which he might have chosen to represent.

Maturity did not turn the novelist to another reality in fiction, for after this short burst Brown wrote no more novels. (For a detailed account of his other imaginative writings produced in the same period see Carl Van Doren, "Minor Tales of Brockden Brown 1798–1800," *Nation*, Jan. 14, 1915.) Possibly he had exhausted his creative vein. At any rate, he had modified his schemes for freedom. His novels earned him little money. *The Monthly Magazine and American Review* (New York), founded by the Friendly Society and edited chiefly by Brown from its hopeful beginnings in April 1799, came to a gloomy end in December 1800. The next year he went back to Philadelphia, as if to signalize the return of a prodigal, and became a partner with two of his brothers in a mercantile house. At first it prospered, but losses at sea, due both to storms and to the French and British navies, brought this firm near bankruptcy in 1804 and forced it to dissolve in 1806. From 1807 till his death Brown traded independently on a small scale. Though a busy journalist, he could not by his pen alone support the wife, Elizabeth Linn of New York, whom he had married in November 1804, and the four children born to them.

His writings during this latter period were almost wholly hack work. He edited and wrote for the *Literary Magazine and American Register* (1803–07), which a Philadelphia publisher had asked him to undertake, and the *American Register or General Repository of History, Politics, and Science* (1807–11). In addition he translated Volney's *Tableau* under the title *A View of the Soil and Climate of the United States* (1804), wrote three pamphlets on political matters, and planned *A System of General Geography* which never got beyond the prospectus (1809?). Writing, for Brown, was more than a career; it was an itch. "This employment," he told a friend, "was just as necessary to my mind as sustenance to my frame. It was synonymous with a vital function. . . . Had I been exiled to Kamschatka, I must have written as a mental necessity, and in it I have still found my highest enjoyment" (John Bernard, *Retrospections of America 1797–1811*, 1887, p. 254). The sole evidence that his imagination still worked in him is the story that he wrote two acts of a tragedy for John Bernard, and, told that the play would not act, burned the manuscript and kept the ashes in a snuff-box (*Ibid.*, pp. 254–55). Romance had been only a chapter in Brown's life, and it belonged primarily to New York. The later Philadelphia chapter was plain prose.

Brown's place in literary history is not altogether due to the fact that he was the first American who tried to live by his pen or even that he was the first American novelist who won an international hearing. He continues to be occasionally read for his intrinsic merits—for the somber intensity which, given a chance with any but superficial readers, outweighs his shambling structure and his verbose, stilted language. Like Poe and Hawthorne, whom he in several respects anticipates, Brown had a personal acquaintance with the dark moods which he enlarged and projected in his novels. He had an eager intellectual curiosity which gives his work, even at its most naïve, a certain air of range and significance. It is now useless to debate whether, in more favorable circumstances, he might have done more and better work. Writers must be judged by the books they write, not by the books they might have written. Nevertheless, it is difficult not to feel that a community both more critical and more responsive than the United States was at the end of the eighteenth century might have enabled Brown to husband and direct his powers to greater advantage. As it was, he first squandered his strength and then failed to regain it. Authorship was a profession which, as matters stood, he had to pay an extravagant price to enter.

[The original source of information concerning Brown is *The Life of Chas. Brockden Brown* (2 vols., 1815), which was begun by Paul Allen and completed by Brown's friend, Wm. Dunlap, whose name alone appears on the title-page. An abridged version of the work was issued in London in one volume as *Memoirs of Chas. Brockden Brown* (1822). Dunlap was extremely inaccurate, but he has been followed by most later writers on the subject. A critical biography, however, has been prepared by David Lee Clark and is now awaiting publication. A printed abstract of this work, made in 1923, may be consulted in the Lib. of Columbia Univ. See also *The Cambridge Hist. of Am. Lit.* (vol. I, 1917, pp. 287–92 and pp. 527–29) for the most precise recent account of Brown's life and an extended bibliography of the writings by and about him.]
C. V–D.

BROWN, CHARLES RUFUS (Feb. 22, 1849– Feb. 1, 1914), Baptist clergyman, educator, was the son of Rev. Samuel Emmons and Elvira (Small) Brown. Born in East Kingston, N. H., in a Baptist manse, he was reared conscientiously in an evangelical home. In his teens he was a student at Phillips Exeter Academy. Attracted to the sea, near which he lived for a time, he was admitted to the Naval Academy at Annapolis. His training gave him qualities of precision and discipline that served him well as an instructor in later years, but in 1874 he abandoned a naval career for a professional life in the ministry. In order to prepare himself for this he attended Newton Theological Institution (1874–75) and Harvard College, graduating from the latter in 1877, and he then pursued theological studies at Newton and Union seminaries, and at Berlin and Leipzig universities in Europe. In 1881 he entered upon the active ministry as pastor of the Baptist church at Franklin Falls, N. H.

His training had fitted him for service as an educator, and after two years he was elected associate professor of Biblical interpretation of the Old Testament at Newton Theological Institution. Three years later he became full professor. For thirty years he directed his department and inspired his pupils with a sense of the values of the Old Testament. The study of Hebrew was never a drudgery in his classes. He was painstaking and accurate himself, and demanded a mastery of the lesson from others, but he had such an appreciation of shades of thought and fineness of expression and worked with such enthusiasm as to kindle interest even in a dull subject. In addition to his work at Newton, he lectured at the University of Chicago in a summer quarter, and was acting professor in Boston University for a term of seven months. He edited the Bible Union Sunday-school Lessons at various times. In 1910–11 he served as director of the American School of Oriental Research at Jerusalem. He never lost his interest in preaching, and during part of one year he was acting pastor of the Main Street Baptist Church in Worcester.

As a scholar he was happiest in his exegetical studies of the Old Testament, and the fruit of his learning appeared in his *Commentary on Jeremiah,* published in 1907, but he was familiar with the languages cognate to Hebrew and prepared *An Aramaic Method,* which was published in 1884. As a man he was outspoken in his assertion of his opinions, honest and courageous by nature, and demanding no more from another than he would give himself. He was conscientiously industrious, setting high standards of workmanship and careful of the smallest details. In 1884 he had married Clarissa L. Dodge. He died at Stoneham, Mass., after months of failing health.

[*Watchman-Examiner,* Feb. 5, 1914; *Who's Who in America,* 1912–13; *Harvard College Class of 1877, 7th Report* (1917); *Boston Transcript,* Feb. 2, 1914.]
H. K. R.

BROWN, CHARLOTTE EMERSON (Apr. 21, 1838–Feb. 5, 1895), club-woman, organizer, was born at Andover, Mass. Her father, Ralph Emerson, clergyman and professor of ecclesiastical history and pastoral theology in Andover Theological Seminary, came of a long ancestry of New England clergymen and educators and was a relative of Ralph Waldo Emerson. Her mother was Eliza Rockwell of Colebrook, Conn. Charlotte was graduated from Abbot Academy at Andover. She early showed an aptitude for languages and could read, write, and speak French before she was twelve. After her school days she mastered several other languages by private study and learned Greek from her brother Joseph Emerson, professor at Beloit College. She spent a year in Montreal, teaching Latin, French, and mathematics, with Hannah Lyman, later first woman principal of Vassar College. Her education was continued by several years of travel and study of music and languages abroad. The Emerson family, having left Andover and having lived for five years in Newburyport, Mass., removed to Rockford, Ill. Charlotte Emerson, eager for further knowledge, took a commercial course of six weeks in Chicago and then became private secretary to her brother Ralph, a Rockford manufacturer. At Rockford she began her work as a club organizer, founding a musical club, the Euterpe, and a French club, as well as the Rockford Conservatory of Music. She also taught modern languages in Rockford Seminary. She married, July 27, 1880, the Rev. William B. Brown, pastor of the First Congregational Church of Newark, N. J. They went abroad for three years, where Mrs. Brown continued the studies which were her absorbing interest in life. On their return they settled in

East Orange, N. J., where she was very soon elected president of the Woman's Club. At about this time the club Sorosis took the lead in a movement for club federation, and Mrs. Brown was one of the committee of seven which formed the General Federation of Women's Clubs and in 1890 she became its first president. Under her leadership the federation membership increased in two years from fifty to 120 clubs, representing twenty-nine states and numbering 20,000 women. The organization of the Fortnightly Club of East Orange was also her work. After her marriage she became much interested in the foreign missions of the Congregational Church and traveled, spoke, wrote, and planned work for the Woman's Board of Missions. She wrote much on different club activities for newspapers and magazines and at the time of her death had gathered material for a projected history of the woman's club movement. She was a person of unusual memory, unlimited enthusiasm, great energy and power of concentration—both as a student and as a business woman. Her efficiency never made her dictatorial, but her tact, consideration for the opinions of others, and coöperativeness caused her to be generally liked. In appearance she was large and impressive, with a full round face, large serious eyes, and an expression indicating poise and placidity. Her death occurred at East Orange and delegations from women's clubs all over the East attended her funeral.

[Benj. K. Emerson, *The Ipswich Emersons* (1900); *American Women*, vol. I (1897), ed. by Frances E. Willard and Mary A. Livermore; obituaries in the *N. Y. Tribune* and *N. Y. Times*, Feb. 6, 1895.]

S.G.B.

BROWN, DAVID PAUL (Sept. 28, 1795–July 11, 1872), lawyer, orator, and dramatist, was the only child of well-born, well-educated, and wealthy parents. His father, Paul Brown, was descended from Quaker ancestors who came from England with Lord Berkeley and settled in New Jersey. In 1790 Paul Brown removed from Berkeley, N. J., to Philadelphia, where he married Rhoda Thackara of Salem, N. J., and where in 1795 their son David Paul was born. David was taught by his mother till he was eight and he owed to her his unusual discrimination in speech. Later he was trained by tutors and attended the best local schools. His parents brought him up in an atmosphere of wealth, and encouraged him to spend money freely and intelligently. After the death of his mother in 1810 he was sent to the home of the Rev. Dr. Daggett, a Massachusetts clergyman, who directed the youth's education until 1812. Although David favored the profession of law, he then took up medicine to please his father and became a pupil of the famous Philadelphian, Dr. Benjamin Rush. Six months later (1813) Dr. Rush died; David was then permitted to transfer his studies to law, with an equally famous lawyer, William Rawle, as his preceptor. He read zealously, attended the courts, and enjoyed the society of such leaders at the bar as Lewis, Tilghman, Ingersoll, Dallas, and Binney. His father died in 1815, leaving him a comfortable fortune. In September 1816, just as he attained his majority, Brown was admitted to the Philadelphia bar and soon afterward to the bar of the supreme court of Pennsylvania, the district and circuit courts, and the Supreme Court of the United States.

His reputation as a public speaker quickly vied with his professional fame. At twenty-four he addressed a notable audience at the celebration of Washington's birthday. Five years later (1824) he delivered the address of welcome to Lafayette. During the same year he won distinction for his brilliant and successful defense of Judge Robert Porter, who had been impeached before the Senate of Pennsylvania. On Dec. 24, 1826, he married Emmeline Catharine Handy. Meanwhile he continued to be honored with invitations to deliver his florid eulogiums whenever a notable occasion suggested a speaker of unusual oratorical repute.

In spite of his growing practise and the numerous demands on his time, he found opportunity to write reviews of current books and likewise to try his hand at poems and plays. His casual poetry, which appeared in the Philadelphia *Sunday Despatch* and elsewhere, is largely negligible. His efforts as a dramatist, however, are more significant. Within two weeks, and principally while riding on horseback to a fashionable suburban spa, he composed a tragedy in verse entitled *Sertorius; or, The Roman Patriot*, which was produced Dec. 14, 1830, at the Chestnut Street Theatre, Philadelphia, with Junius Brutus Booth in the title rôle. *Sertorius* is a somewhat vapid imitation of Shakespeare's *Julius Cæsar* and Addison's *Cato*, but its sonorous lines were so well delivered by the famous actor that it was presented nine times. It was revived at the Arch Street Theatre, Philadelphia, on Feb. 6, 1832, and figured thereafter in the repertoire of the elder Booth. A romantic comedy, *The Prophet of St. Paul's*, also written in 1830, received a wretched belated performance at the Walnut Street Theatre, Philadelphia, on Mar. 20, 1837, and succumbed after the third performance. It dealt with the popular love-story of Princess Mary and Charles Brandon, Duke of Suffolk. Less significant plays were

The Trial, a tragedy, and a farce called *Love and Honor, or, The Generous Soldier.*

Brown was not concerned over the failure of his dramatic efforts, as they represented mere diversions in the life of a busy lawyer. His skill in cross-examination resulted in his being retained in almost every important criminal case in the Philadelphia courts. Though his practise was lucrative, it did not result in the accumulation of a fortune. He lived on a most lavish scale in accord with his father's theory that a prosperous man should spend his income freely to avoid the evils of indolence. He thought sufficiently well of himself to publish his reminiscences in two large volumes (1856) under the title *The Forum; or, Forty Years Full Practice at the Philadelphia Bar.*

Brown was a man of medium height, compactly built, with a high broad forehead, flashing dark eyes, a large mouth, and a voice of great compass. Friends testified to his amiable disposition, his urbanity of manner, and his other social graces. In court he was preëminently histrionic and perhaps too fond of the orotund phraseology that characterized the old-school lawyer. In 1873 his son, Robert Eden Brown, edited *The Forensic Speeches of David Paul Brown, Selected from Important Trials and Embracing a Period of Forty Years.* Brown regularly declined to consider public office and rarely practised in any courts outside of Pennsylvania.

[In addition to *The Forum* and *The Forensic Speeches* above mentioned, see *Phila. North American and U. S. Gazette,* July 12, 1872, and *Phila. Public Ledger,* July 15, 1872. For an account of the performances of *Sertorius* and *The Prophet of St. Pauls,* see Charles Durang, "The Phila. Stage" (in *Phila. Sunday Dispatch*), ser. III (beginning July 8, 1860), chs. IV, XLVIII, respectively. These plays were printed in Phila., the first in 1830, the second in 1836. See also the reprint of *Sertorius* in M. J. Moses, *Representative Plays by Am. Dramatists,* II (1925), 185–252, which is preceded by a critical note on Brown. A. H. Quinn, *A Hist. of the Am. Drama from the Beginning to the Civil War* (1923), 249–50, cites passing references to Brown in Rees, Wemyss, Wood, and other commentators. For portraits of Brown, see J. T. Scharf and T. Westcott, *Hist. of Phila.* (1884), II, 1549, and *Am. Hist. Reg.* (1896), III, 622.]
         J.L.H.

BROWN, EBENEZER (1795–Jan. 3, 1889), Methodist clergyman, first manufacturer of detachable collars, was born in Massachusetts, probably at Chesterfield. He entered the Methodist ministry in 1818, being received on trial in that year by the New York Conference and appointed to Stowe (Vt.), in the Champlain District, and in the next year sent to Suffolk, in the New York District. In the same year upon the advice of Bishop McKendree, Brown was selected by Bishop George "to preach to the French inhabitants of the South" (J. M. Reid, *Missions*

and *Missionary Society of the Methodist Episcopal Church,* 1879, I, 80). Brown, who for some time had devoted himself to a study of French in preparation for this work, found upon his arrival in New Orleans that the French people had "no ready ear for the Gospel" and he devoted himself to the ministry of a small group of English-speaking Methodists in that city. Brown's mission to the French, although a failure, marked the first missionary enterprise of American Methodism, and Brown, himself, was the first missionary sent out by the Methodist Board. Returning North in 1821 he served pastorates in Middlebury, Vt. (1821), in Hartford, Conn. (1822), and in New York City 1823 and 1824 (*Minutes of the Annual Conferences of the Methodist Episcopal Church for the Years 1773–1828,* 1840). Although a gifted and successful minister, he retired from the active work at the early age of thirty, because of continued ill health.

Shortly after his retirement Brown engaged, about 1827, in the business of a dry-goods merchant at 285 River St., Troy. Just about this time Hannah Lord Montague (1794–1878), daughter of William Lord, a Revolutionary officer, and wife of Orlando Montague, conceived the idea of saving laundry work by cutting off the collars from her husband's shirts. The commercial possibilities of a detachable collar appealed to Brown and in 1829 he "bargained with a number of women to make, wash and iron them, and to accept such goods as were sold by him in payment for their labor. The collars in assorted sizes were placed in paper-boxes, sixteen or more inches in length, and sold to customers and dealers patronizing him" (Weise, p. 174). These first "string collars," as they were known, were worn with the old-fashioned stock tie, and tied around the neck with a string attached to each end of the collar. Brown continued the manufacture until his removal to New York in 1834, when the production was taken up on a larger scale by the firm of Orlando Montague & Austin Granger. Upon his removal to New York, Brown organized the firm of E. Brown & Company which carried on a commission business for many years. His last residence after his retirement was the home of his daughter in Baltimore, where he died in his ninety-fourth year. He was buried at Woodlawn Cemetery, Philadelphia.

[In addition to works cited above consult obituary in the *Christian Advocate* (N. Y.), Jan. 24, 1889; *Seventieth Ann. Report of the Missionary Soc. of the M. E. Ch.* (1888), p. 15; Arthur J. Weise, *Troy's One Hundred Years 1789–1889* (1891), pp. 174 ff.; Geo. B. Anderson, *Landmarks of Rensselaer County, N.Y.* (1897), pp. 275–76 and article by Theodore Sweedy in *N. Y. Times Mag.,* Oct. 31, 1926, p. 2.]
         H.U.F.

BROWN, ETHAN ALLEN (July 4, 1766–
Feb. 24, 1852), politician, was born at Darien,
Conn., the son of Roger Brown, a considerable
land-owner. He received private instruction in
the classics, but his subsequent education for the
law was delayed by financial embarrassments
due to the Revolution. Business ventures proving profitable, however, in 1797 he entered the
law office of Alexander Hamilton, and was finally
admitted to practise in 1802 (*A Portrait and Biographical Record of Portage and of Summit
Counties, Ohio*, 1898, pp. 136–37). A trip
through western Pennsylvania, then down the
Ohio and the Mississippi to New Orleans, with
a subsequent voyage to Europe to dispose of
flour for which the local market was not advantageous, proved to be the turning-point of
Brown's career. Returning to the West, he purchased a tract of land at what is now Rising Sun,
Ind., and in 1804 established a law practise at
Cincinnati. Professional progress was rapid,
and in 1810 he was appointed by the legislature
to a judgeship of the supreme court of Ohio.
This he resigned in December 1818, having previously been elected governor by a vote of 30,194
as against 8,075 for James Dunlap, also a Democrat (William A. Taylor, *Ohio in Congress*,
1900, pp. 50–51).

Two problems confronted Brown as governor.
The first was the active opposition in the state to
the rechartered Bank of the United States. This
struggle, in which the Governor was actively interested, culminated in virtual nullification when,
in total defiance of the decision of the United
States Supreme Court in *McCulloch* vs. *Maryland,* the State of Ohio forcibly taxed the branch
banks at Cincinnati and Chillicothe (Daniel J.
Ryan, "Nullification in Ohio" in the *Ohio Archæological and Historical Quarterly*, II, 413–
22. See also *Senate Document No. 72*, 16 Cong.,
2 Sess.). The second problem was indicated
in the message to the legislature, Jan. 8, 1819,
wherein the Governor asserted that "Roads and
canals are veins and arteries to the body politic
that diffuse supplies, health, vigor and animation
to the whole system, nor is this idea of their extensive use and beneficial influence new" (Emi-
lius O. Randall and Daniel J. Ryan, *History of
Ohio*, 1912, III, 341). The canals were dug, and
Brown became to Ohio what De Witt Clinton
was to New York.

Reëlected governor in 1820 by a vote of 34,836,
as against 9,426 for Jeremiah Morrow, and 4,348
for William Henry Harrison, Brown resigned in
1822, in order to fill the unexpired senatorial
term of William A. Trimble, deceased. His previous activity in canals now obtained for Brown

the chairmanship of the Committee on Roads and
Canals. He favored particularly the Cumberland Road as helpful alike to Ohio and the nation.
He was friendly, also, to a "grand connection of
the whole coast of the Atlantic by internal navigation," and cited Gallatin's report on a chain
of canals as "sufficient to immortalize his memory" (*Register of the Debates in Congress*, 18
Cong., 2 Sess., Feb. 24, 1825).

Succeeded in the Senate by William Henry
Harrison, Brown held from 1825 to 1830 the congenial post of canal commissioner in Ohio (*The
Democratic Party of the State of Ohio*, 1913, ed.
by Thomas E. Powell and others, I, 54). In
1830 he was named by President Jackson United
States minister to Brazil, remaining there four
years, a conscientious representative of his government during a troubled time in Brazilian
history. The slave trade and American claims
against Brazil were the mission's chief concern.
On Brown's return he was for one year commissioner of the General Land Office at Washington,
a position for which he was well fitted by integrity and experience. Retiring from public life in
1836 at the age of seventy, Brown resided among
his kindred at Rising Sun. Sixteen years later
his sudden death at Indianapolis, where he was
acting as vice-president at a political convention,
called forth the eulogy that his many virtues "reflected honor on offices which are supposed to
confer honor on their incumbents" (John S. C.
Abbott, *The History of the State of Ohio from
the Discovery of the Great Valley to the Present
Time*, 1875, p. 737).

[In addition to authorities cited above, see State Dept.
Despatches, vols. VIII, IX, Brazil, nos. 1–68, with
seven unnumbered, in the Archives of the State Dept.,
Washington, D. C.]   L. M. S.

BROWN, FAYETTE (Dec. 17, 1823–Jan. 20,
1910), banker, inventor, manufacturer, was the
son of Ephraim and Mary (Huntington) Brown.
In 1814 Ephraim Brown, originally of Westmoreland, N. H., joined with a friend and purchased a township in the Connecticut Western
Reserve, now known as North Bloomfield, Trumbull County, Ohio, and the following year he
moved west and settled there with his wife and
several children and became a leader in that
transplanted New England community. There
Fayette was born, the youngest of nine children,
and was brought up in that characteristic atmosphere of thrift and honesty. His elementary education was that afforded by the public schools of
Gambier, Ohio, after which he attended Jefferson College in Pennsylvania. When eighteen
years old, however, he left home and entered the
dry-goods store of an elder brother in Pittsburgh
where he remained until 1851, becoming a mem-

ber of the firm in 1845. Just prior to the termination of the store partnership Brown had formed a partnership with a friend, George Mygatt, to engage in the banking business, and in 1851 he went to Cleveland, Ohio, to join Mygatt, remaining there for the succeeding ten years. At the outbreak of the Civil War in 1861 he accepted an appointment as paymaster in the Union army. After serving for over a year he resigned with the rank of major. Upon his return to Cleveland he became general agent and manager of the Jackson Iron Company, manufacturers of iron and steel. He continued here for the next twenty-five years, building up a reputation as one of the most competent iron manufacturers of his time. During this period he secured four patents, two for hoisting apparatus in connection with the charging of blast furnaces, and two for improvements in blast furnace design. These were issued in 1884 and 1885. It was during this time, too, that Brown became interested in Great Lakes shipping and built up a large fleet of lake steamers, particularly for the transportation of iron ore. In fact, he was the first to bring iron ore by boat from the Lake Superior district to Cleveland. When the Brown Hoisting Machinery Company was organized in 1880 to develop the inventions of his son, Alexander Ephraim [q.v.], Brown assumed the presidency and continued in this capacity until his death. For the first seven years he also continued as general manager of the Jackson Iron Company but relinquished this office in 1887. In later years Brown served also as president of the Union Steel Screw Company, the National Chemical Company, and the G. C. Kuhlman Car Company, respectively, and was also a member of his younger son's firm, H. H. Brown & Company, dealers in iron ore, as well as chairman of the board of directors of the Stewart Iron Company of Sharon, Pa. On July 15, 1847, Brown married Cornelia C. Curtis of Pittsburgh, who died several years before he did. They were survived, however, by their four children, two sons and two daughters.

[*Who's Who in America*, 1910–11; letters from Harvey H. Brown & Co., Cleveland; Patent Office Records; *Cleveland Plain Dealer*, Jan. 21, 1910.]   C. W. M.

BROWN, FRANCIS (Jan. 11, 1784–July 27, 1820), college president, son of Benjamin and Prudence (Kelly) Brown, was born at Chester, N. H. His father was a country merchant of limited means, but thanks to his stepmother, who seems to have had a better appreciation of the boy's possibilities, he secured a good education, attending Atkinson Academy and graduating from Dartmouth College in 1805. After a

year's experience as a private tutor he received an appointment as tutor at Dartmouth. He remained at the college for three years, studying theology in addition to carrying on his teaching duties. On Jan. 11, 1810, he began his pastorate at North Yarmouth, Me., where he remained for the next five years. Here, on Feb. 4, 1811, he married Elizabeth, daughter of Rev. Tristram Gilman of the same town. Soon after ordination he declined the offer of a professorship in languages at Dartmouth, but his continued interest in educational matters is apparent in his service as overseer (1810–14) and trustee (1814–15) of Bowdoin College and in his close friendship with President Appleton of that institution. His pastorate at North Yarmouth was successful but without special incident. By training and association Brown naturally belonged among the conservative and orthodox Congregationalist clergy. Like most members of that body he combined devout Calvinism in theology with fervent Federalism in politics. His faith in the former is set forth in two bulky and controversial pamphlets in defense of Calvin and Calvinism which he published at Portland in 1815 (*Calvin and Calvinism* and *Reply to Rev. Martin Ruter's Letter relating to Calvin and Calvinism*). His political views are to be found in a published sermon (July 23, 1812) on the occasion of the declaration of war against Great Britain, in which he denounced the Madison administration for its subservience to France, "Babylon the great, the mother of harlots and abominations of the earth."

In the meantime there was developing in New Hampshire, its genesis in an obscure parochial quarrel, the controversy which resulted in the "Dartmouth College case." On Aug. 26, 1815, the trustees removed President Wheelock and offered the position to Francis Brown who assumed the duties of president a month later. The local quarrel, because of the religious and political affiliations of the participants, rapidly assumed state-wide importance with legislative intervention as a natural result. Until Chief Justice Marshall handed down the final decision in February 1819 (*The Trustees of Dartmouth College* vs. *Woodward*, 4 *Wheaton*, 518), the life of the college hung in the balance. With its charter virtually annulled by the Act of June 27, 1816, with a new institution, "Dartmouth University," functioning under the sanction of the state, with funds unavailable because of litigation, with the student body depleted, and confronted with public hostility and internal dissension, there was need of the highest qualities of leadership. President Brown proved equal to the occasion. The college work went on in spite of severe handicaps. He conducted classes, raised money, defended the cause before the public, advised with counsel, and by the dignity and tact displayed toward opponents, kept the controversy from degenerating into either a brawl or a comedy as might easily have happened under less competent guidance. His correspondence shows that he had a clear perception of the constitutional and political issues involved, and their bearing on the future of chartered institutions throughout the country. That his services were appreciated elsewhere is seen by the fact that Hamilton and Williams honored him with the degree of D.D.

His health broke under the strain of constant work and anxiety and he did not live to take part in the rehabilitation which followed the victory of 1819, a task for which he would have been admirably qualified. After a vain effort to recover his health in the milder climate of the South he returned to Hanover in June 1820, his death occurring a few weeks later. Brown's portrait, now in the possession of the college, is chiefly expressive of the gentle and scholarly character of the youthful teacher and clergyman but the artist has also caught something of the shrewdness, courage, and determination of the Federalist leader and executive, ready to fight to the death against what he regarded as Democratic encroachment on private rights.

Brown's son, Samuel Gilman Brown [*q.v.*], was for many years a professor at Dartmouth and later president of Hamilton College; his grandson, Francis Brown [*q.v.*], became president of Union Seminary.

[Henry Wood, *Sketch of the Life of President Brown* (1834), first published in *Am. Quart. Reg.*, Nov. 1834; John K. Lord, *Hist. of Dartmouth Coll., 1815-1909* (1913); Benj. Chase, *Hist. of Old Chester* (1869); manuscript letters and miscellany in Dartmouth Coll. archives.]   W. A. R.

BROWN, FRANCIS (Dec. 26, 1849–Oct. 15, 1916), theological professor, and president of Union Seminary, was born in Hanover, N. H., the son of Sarah (Van Vechten) and Samuel Gilman Brown [*q.v.*]. He graduated from Dartmouth in the class of 1870 and after teaching for four years entered Union Theological Seminary, graduating there in 1877. Awarded a traveling fellowship he spent the next two years in study in Berlin. He was the favorite pupil and most devoted disciple of Dr. Charles A. Briggs [*q.v.*] and he followed him in making the Old Testament his special subject of study. In 1879 he married Louise Reiss of Berlin and returned to America to become instructor and later associate professor of Biblical philology in Union

Seminary. In 1890 when Dr. Briggs was transferred to the chair of Biblical theology Brown succeeded him as professor of Hebrew and the cognate languages, a position he held until his death. For some years he taught in the Seminary not only Hebrew and Greek but also Aramaic and Assyrian. In Berlin he had studied Assyrian—which was then beginning to attract the attention of Old Testament scholars—under Eberhard Schrader and he was the first person in America to give instruction in the language. In 1885 he published a little book on *Assyriology, its Use and Abuse,* declaring that "The root of the misuse of Assyriology in Bible study" was "an ill-directed and excessive Apologetics." In 1907 he gave a course of public lectures at the Seminary (the Ely Lectures) on the relations of Israel with Babylonia and Assyria, but unfortunately the lectures were never published. In 1884 he issued with President Roswell D. Hitchcock the first American edition of the newly discovered *Teaching of the Twelve Apostles,* republished the following year in an enlarged form and with extensive notes for which he was chiefly responsible, as he was also for the translation. In 1907–08 he served as director of the American School of Oriental Study and Research at Jerusalem.

From the beginning Brown displayed those qualities as a scholar which were to make him eminent—untiring diligence, painstaking accuracy, absolute fairness, maturity of judgment, careful weighing of evidence, caution in drawing and stating conclusions. He was not a rapid worker like his teacher Dr. Briggs, and he was not given to venturesome hypotheses, but his scholarship was solid and sound. As a teacher his influence was invigorating and wholesome and he had the unqualified respect of his students. No one could come under him without having his ideals of scholarship heightened and his conscience as a scholar quickened.

The lasting monument of his scholarship is the great *Hebrew and English Lexicon of the Old Testament,* completed in 1906, of which he was the editor-in-chief and to which he devoted more than twenty years. During all those years it consumed the major part of his time and attention and kept him from publishing many other works which he had planned. It was in recognition of his work on the lexicon that he was given the honorary degree of Litt.D. by the University of Oxford.

While primarily a scholar, he became interested in ecclesiastical affairs as a result of the controversy over Dr. Briggs. Throughout the struggle he was Briggs's right hand man and supported him loyally, and after the latter left the Presbyterian Church Brown became a recognized leader of the liberal Presbyterian group. He was a man of strong convictions, but with all the firmness which these gave him he was yet considerate of the opinions of others and was always slow to express dissent. It was quite in accord with his general spirit and attitude that he interested himself in the cause of church unity. In company with Dr. Briggs he worked actively in its behalf for a number of years.

In 1908 upon the death of Charles Cuthbert Hall he succeeded him as president of Union Seminary and though he retained his professorship and continued his teaching, his days of productive scholarship were over. His great-grandfather, John H. Mason, had been president of Dickinson College, his grandfather, Francis Brown [q.v.], of Dartmouth, and his father of Hamilton, so that he came of presidential stock. He himself was called to the presidency of Dartmouth but declined, preferring to remain at Union. His administration there was notable. In 1910 the Seminary moved to its new site on Morningside Heights opposite Columbia University, and the affiliation between the two institutions became even closer than it had been. Under him the endowment of the Seminary was greatly increased and both the faculty and student body were enlarged by more than a half.

Brown had a massive frame and great personal dignity. Many thought him unapproachable and it is true that he was not a man of easy intimacies. It was often difficult to get beyond the barrier of his reserve, but no one ever had a kinder heart or readier sympathy. He was a tower of strength yet extraordinarily gentle, full of generosity and quick to help where help was needed.

[Memorial Service in Honour of the Rev. Francis Brown (1917); Henry Preserved Smith, "Francis Brown—An Appreciation" in the Am. Jour. of Semitic Languages and Literatures, Jan. 1917; G. L. Prentiss, The Union Theol. Sem. . . . Another Decade of its Hist. (1899); obituary in N. Y. Times, Oct. 16, 1916.]

A. C. M.

BROWN, FREDERIC TILDEN (Oct. 7, 1853–May 7, 1910), surgeon, the son of David Tilden Brown the alienist by his wife, Cornelia Wells Clapp, was born in New York City. From his father Frederic inherited a bold and enterprising nature. He was graduated from Harvard College in the class of 1877. During his early years he rowed on several victorious crews and was believed to have strained his heart in his efforts. He received his M.D. from the College of Physicians and Surgeons in New York

in 1880 and became house surgeon in the same year at Mt. Sinai Hospital, New York. He became associated shortly afterward with the Bellevue Hospital (attending surgeon) and subsequently with the Presbyterian, Nassau, and Mineola Hospitals as consulting surgeon. He was later made professor of genito-urinary diseases at the University and Bellevue Hospital Medical College, and as teacher and lecturer enjoyed great popularity.

Brown's most important professional contributions lay in the introduction of delicate instruments for use in genito-urinary surgery. His improvements in the lamp-bearing cystoscope made possible better visual definition than had any earlier instrument (Annals of Surgery, XXXV, 642–43). He also made a special study of infections of the urinary tract ("A Case of Cystitis, Pyelonephritis, and Pyonephrosis due to Colon-Bacillus Infection," etc., Journal of Cutaneous and Genito-Urinary Diseases, XIII, 133–42). In addition to his numerous papers in his special field one finds that he reported two cases of amputation at the hip-joint by a new method (Annals of Surgery, XXIII, 153–62); indeed he prided himself upon being a general surgeon as well as a specialist. Through his exceptional operative skill as well as through invention of instruments of precision, Brown "became one of the conspicuous landmarks in his specialty" (Kelly). He was a tremendous worker and throughout his active career was an exponent of vigorous exercise. His avocations were shooting, natural history, and art.

He married in 1884 Mrs. Mary Crosby (Renwick) Strong and there were two children, a boy and a girl. A nervous breakdown which was the direct result of over-work led him to go to Bethel, Me., for his health in the spring of 1910. He died there by his own hand on May 7, 1910.

[Several short notices of Brown's death appeared in the N. Y. medical journals but no obituaries were published. The above material is taken chiefly from H. A. Kelly's account in H. A. Kelly and W. L. Burrage, Am. Medic. Biogs. (1920). See also Harvard Coll. Class of 1877, Report No. 5 (1897) for an autobiographical sketch, and Report No. 7 (1917) for a memorial. Paul M. Pilcher, Practical Cystoscopy (1915) gives descriptions and diagrams of Brown's instruments.]

J. F. F.

BROWN, GEORGE (Apr. 17, 1787–Aug. 26, 1859), pioneer railroad promoter, was born in Ballymena, County Antrim, Ireland, the second son of Grace (Davison) and Alexander Brown [q.v.]. With his brothers, James and John A. Brown [qq.v.], he followed his father to Baltimore in 1802, and in time became a member of the firm of Alexander Brown & Sons. On Feb. 12, 1827, twenty-five leading citizens of

Baltimore called together by George Brown met at his house in Baltimore to consider the best means of restoring to the city trade which had been diverted by the introduction of steam navigation and the opening up of the Erie and other canals in the West. At this meeting the plan of the Baltimore & Ohio Railroad, the first passenger steam railroad in the United States, was conceived. Stock subscription books were opened on Mar. 20, 1827, and 41,781 shares of stock almost immediately subscribed. George Brown was made treasurer of the Baltimore & Ohio Railroad Company and, with his father, virtually supervised the construction of the road, which was begun on July 4, 1828. In 1831–32 he stimulated Ross Winans [q.v.] to design and construct the first eight-wheel car, the forerunner of the modern railway car, to supersede the modified stage coaches then in use. George Brown held the position of treasurer, declining to accept any compensation, until 1834, when Alexander Brown died, and George, as the ranking member of the firm in this country, was required to undertake the heavy responsibility of directing the banking affairs of the Browns. To do this he had to give up all outside interests.

Of all the lessons George Brown had learned from his pioneer father, the one he had learned most thoroughly was the lesson of conservatism. Under his guidance, therefore, the Brown firms curtailed rather than expanded their activities. The intrepid pioneers of the profitable but hazardous field of international mercantile banking began to withdraw from the business of shipping and trading, and to devote themselves more exclusively to banking. The independent fortunes of the Browns had been made by the elder Brown's shrewd piloting past the rocks of early nineteenth-century trade, and it was a big job merely to conserve those fortunes. This the sons, advised by George, elected to do to the exclusion of most other activities, and they did it successfully.

George Brown was a leader in every important civic movement in Baltimore in his time, and gave liberally of his money to worthy institutions. He was the first president of the first systematized charitable organization in Baltimore, and among his especial interests outside of business were the House of Refuge and the Peabody Institute of Baltimore. A marble shaft erected to his memory commemorates his tireless and unselfish work for the House of Refuge. Brown Memorial Presbyterian Church erected by his widow, Isabella (McLanahan) Brown, whom he had married in 1818, is another of his city's monuments to him.

[Wm. P. Smith, *A Hist. and Description of the B. & O. R. R.* (1853); Edward Hungerford, *The Story of the B. & O. R. R. 1827–1927* (1928); John C. Brown, *A Hundred Years of Merchant Banking* (priv. printed, 1909); Frank R. Kent, *The Story of Alexander Brown and Sons* (1925); Mary E. Brown, *Alexander Brown and his Descendants* (priv. printed, 1917); obituary in the *Sun* (Baltimore), Aug. 27, 1859.]   F. R. K.

BROWN, GEORGE (Oct. 11, 1823–May 6, 1892), physician, educator of the feeble-minded, was descended from Thomas and Bridget Brown who settled in Concord, Mass., in 1638. He was the son of Ephraim Brown, a man of unusual mechanical gifts, and of Sarah (King) Brown, and was born at Wilton, N. H. After attending Phillips Academy, Andover, Mass., and the University of Vermont, he began the study of medicine with Dr. Norman Smith of Groton, Mass., matriculated at Jefferson Medical College, Philadelphia, and took his medical degree in 1850 from the University of the City of New York. In this year he went to Barre, Mass., to practise there and immediately became interested in the Elm Hill School, a small private institution for feeble-minded children, the first of its kind in America, established two years before by Dr. Hervey B. Wilbur. On Nov. 28, 1850, he married Catherine Wood who also became a devoted worker in this school. In the summer of 1851, Dr. Wilbur left to take charge of the New York State Institute for Feeble-minded at Albany, and Brown decided to take over the superintendency of the Elm Hill School and make it his life-work. He threw himself into the problem with a scientific skill which was completely modern, and a spirit as fine as any his profession has ever produced. The institution consisted at this time of an ordinary house with space for fifteen children. These ranged in age from five to thirteen years. The types varied from simply retarded mental development to the purely idiotic. At this early period there were twenty acres of land for playgrounds, walks and gardens. Various simple games were taught, one hour before school was devoted to gymnasium work, the older boys were instructed in the management of horses and cattle, the smaller ones in the care of poultry, rabbits, and squirrels. They used tools and learned ordinary trades. Under Brown's supervision the institution grew to have several buildings, and an estate of 250 acres of land, and became the largest private institution of its kind in the United States. Its purpose, as expressed in an early report, was, "to solve the great problem, whether the idiot could be developed to take rank in the scale of our common humanity, and be fitted not only for useful employments but for general observation, comparison, and judgment." Brown was an active participant in the development of Barre. He was one of the founders of the library association, and twice a member of the school board. A founder also of the Glen Valley Association, he was its president until his death. For years he was a leading member of and liberal contributor to the Congregational Church. Originally a Whig, he joined the Republican party when it was formed. After his death his son, Dr. George A. Brown, succeeded to the superintendency of the Elm Hill School.

[*Elm Hill Private School for Feeble-Minded Youth, Barre, Mass., Report*, 1853; *Gen. Alumni Cat. N. Y. Univ. 1833–1907, Medic. Alumni* (1908); *Gen. Cat. of the Univ. of Vt.* (1901); A. A. Livermore and Sewall Putnam, *Hist. of the Town of Wilton, Hillsborough County, N. H.* (1888); *Biog. Rev. . . . of Worcester County, Mass.* (1899), pp. 78–81.] M.A.K.

BROWN, GEORGE PLINY (Nov. 10, 1836–Feb. 1, 1910), educator, was born in Lenox township, Ashtabula County, Ohio. His father was William P. Brown and his mother was Rachel (Piper) Brown. He was educated in the common schools of Lenox township and at the Grand River Institute, Austinburg, Ohio, a small preparatory school established on a sound basis in 1831. Ill health prevented him from completing a college course. Beginning his career as an educator at the age of sixteen when he taught a rural school in Cherry Valley Township, Ohio, he advanced steadily in his chosen profession. In 1854 he taught in a small academy of Geauga County, and from 1855 to 1860 he was principal of the school at Waynesville. It was in 1860 that he went to Indiana to fill the position of superintendent of schools at Richmond. There he remained until 1865 when he became the head of the New Albany, Ind., schools. The next year saw him back in Richmond holding his former position. He resigned after two years.

Brown had been studying law during his leisure for a number of years, and thinking he would like the legal profession, he established himself as a lawyer· He practised law until 1871. That year, his first love, the school, took him to Indianapolis. After two years as principal of the Indianapolis High School, he was promoted to the superintendence of the system. It was as superintendent of the Indianapolis public schools that Brown received recognition which placed him as an educational leader of the state. His articles and editorials in the *Indiana School Journal* of which he was associate editor for a time (vols. XX, XXI, XXII) reveal his conception of the public school as an institution. He firmly believed and emphatically contended that "the school is a spiritual and not a material entity" (*Indiana School Journal*, February 1876). At the end of the school year in 1878 Brown ac-

cepted a position with D. Appleton & Company, publishers, intending to forsake the teaching profession. During the summer of 1879, however, he was elected president of the Indiana State Normal School at Terre Haute. In this position he became nationally known as an educator of vision. James H. Smart, a former superintendent of public instruction in Indiana, and a contemporary of Brown, expressed a widely accepted estimate of the latter when he said, "He has proven himself to be one of the ablest educators in the West." Brown resigned as president of the Indiana State Normal School in 1886 and moved to Bloomington, Ill. In 1888 he purchased the *Illinois School Journal* which was published there, changed its title to *Public School Journal* and later to *School and Home Education*, and devoted the rest of his life to it as editor. Brown was tall, well formed, of remarkably fine address, ready in decision and prompt in action, a gentleman of heart and intellect whom both teachers and children respected. He died at Bloomington survived by his wife, Mary Seymour Brown, whom he had married in 1855, and four sons.

[Files of the *Ill. School Jour.* and its successors, and of the *Ind. School Jour.*; John W. Cook, *Educ. Hist. of Ill.* (1912); Jas. H. Smart, *The Ind. Schools and the Men Who Have Worked in Them* (1876); obituary in the *Daily Pantagraph* (Bloomington, Ill.), Feb. 2, 1910.] H.N.S.

BROWN, GEORGE WILLIAM (Oct. 13, 1812–Sept. 5, 1890), lawyer, judge, was the eldest son of George John and Esther (Allison) Brown. Baltimore, Md., his birthplace, and the fitting environment of his eventful life, had been selected in 1783 by his grandfather, Dr. George Brown, a physician, as the most promising home for the American branch of an old Irish family (*The Sun*, Baltimore, Sept. 8, 1890). George William Brown entered Dartmouth at the age of sixteen, and, later, Rutgers, where he graduated in 1831 with the highest honors. After a short preparation in Baltimore, he was admitted to the practise of law, and, in 1839, formed a partnership with Frederick W. Brune, Jr., whose sister he later married. Four years earlier he had actively identified himself with the forces for orderly government when he joined the body of citizens organized under Gen. Samuel Smith to suppress the riots attending the failure of the Bank of Maryland (*Johns Hopkins University Circulars*, vol. X, no. 83, p. 8). This incident was typical of his life. Throughout his career he was a fearless independent in the interests of an orderly democratic government. The energies of such a man were constantly called to action during that chaotic decade in American politics preceding the Civil War, when the Know-Nothing party fixed its hold on Baltimore and maintained it by the methods of mob rule. This hold was not broken until November 1859 when Brown was elected mayor by a large majority on an independent platform. (L. F. Schmeckebier, *History of the Know-Nothing Party in Maryland*, 1899, pp. 41–42, 112–113). His feelings during the Civil War can be taken as representing the feelings of the state, and they are well presented in his *Baltimore and the 19th of April, 1861, a Study of the War* (1887). "The problem of slavery" he says, "was to me a Gordian knot which I knew not how to untie, and which I dared not attempt to cut with the sword" (p. 115). Though opposed to slavery he thought the eventual decay of the system and the arts of persuasion would certainly, in time, bring the states of the Confederacy back to the Union. His brave action in protecting against a mob the 6th Massachusetts Regiment when it marched through Baltimore on Apr. 19, 1860, and his burning of the bridges north of the city to prevent worse bloodshed, are matters of common historical record. On Sept. 11, 1861, Secretary of War Cameron issued an order to prevent the passage of any secession act by the Maryland legislature even at the cost of arresting all the members. Acting ostensibly under this order, Gen. Dix, on Sept. 12, included Brown with those arrested and the latter spent fifteen months in imprisonment.

Brown's long legal career culminated in 1872 with his appointment as judge of the supreme bench of Baltimore, which position he held until 1888. His published addresses, though they show no keen penetration or great original thinking, mark Brown as a liberal who was constantly thinking and acting for the good of society. They are scholarly and worth reading. His usefulness as a public man is apparent from the many positions which he held at the time of his death. He was one of the founders of the University of Maryland and a trustee, one of the original trustees of Johns Hopkins University, a trustee of the Peabody Institute, of Saint Johns College, of Enoch Pratt Library, and of other institutions which need not be noted.

[See *Johns Hopkins Univ. Circulars*, vol. X, no. 83, pp. 6–8; the *Sun* (Baltimore), Sept. 8, 1890; F. A. Richardson and W. A. Bennett, *Baltimore, Past and Present* (1871), pp. 199–206; J. T. Scharf, *Hist. of Md.*, vol. III (1879). Brown's Addresses are deposited in the Peabody Lib., Baltimore. See also *Official Records (Army)*, ser. 1, esp. vols. II. and V.]   C. W. G.

BROWN, GOOLD (Mar. 7, 1791–Mar. 31, 1857), grammarian, was born in Providence, R. I., the son of Smith and Lydia (Gould) Brown. (His mother's name is given here in the spelling of the Providence records.) His parents were Quakers. His father, a school-teacher and essayist, began to instruct him in Greek and Latin at an age when even children with quick minds are only learning to read their mother tongue; but after making a brilliant record in the Friends School Brown was compelled to forego a college education and to aid in supporting the family. He is said to have engaged first in "mercantile pursuits" and to have found the work thoroughly repugnant to him. He next taught a district school near Providence and in 1811 was appointed to a position in the Nine Partners Boarding School at Mechanic, Dutchess County, N. Y. Two years later he became a teacher in John Griscom's school in New York. Finally he opened an academy of his own and conducted it for about twenty years. He published the *Child's First Book* (1822); *Institutes of English Grammar* (1823); *First Lines of English Grammar, Being a Brief Abstract of the Author's Larger Work* (1823); *Key to the Exercises for Writing Contained in the Institutes of English Grammar* (1825); and a *Catechism of English Grammar; with Parsing Exercises* (1827). Although his text-books never enjoyed the enormous vogue of Lindley Murray's or Samuel Kirkham's, the *Institutes* and the *First Lines* sold well from the beginning and gained steadily in popular esteem. Twice revised by later hands, they were still in use in 1929 in many Catholic parochial schools and in some of the public schools of New York City. Of English grammars only William Cobbett's has enjoyed so long a life. Brown seems to have been active, though not especially prominent, among New York Friends: in the autumn of 1830, as a member of a joint committee of the New York and Philadelphia Yearly Meetings, he approved a circular urging the support of a proposed school (Haverford School) that in time became Haverford College. In 1835–36 his name appears for the last time in the New York *City Directory*, his residence then being 374 Pearl St.; but whether he moved immediately to Lynn, Mass., where he spent his last years, is uncertain. Possessed of a sufficient income, he was free to devote himself to his favorite subject. He studied grammar after his own fashion with religious fervor and in 1851 published that leviathan of school books, the *Grammar of English Grammars*, an awe-inspiring octavo of over 1,100 pages. Like all grammarians, he professed to base his work on actual usage; in fact, however, he disdained the spoken language altogether and gave his approval only to such constructions as met his rigid notions of logic and propriety. One of the features of the book was the hundreds of examples of "false syntax" culled from the works of rival grammarians. Brown had a real gift for defining terms and for discriminating usage, but the merits of his book are buried under a heap of pedantic rubbish. As a scientific student of the English language he has no standing whatever, but over the methods of teaching grammar and over the content of later American text-books he has exercised a strong and not entirely happy influence. The *Grammar of English Grammars* went into its tenth edition in 1880; in 1929 a sound copy was still worth ten dollars in antiquarian book stores. Brown finished reading the proof sheets of the second edition just three weeks before he died in his home on South Common St. in Lynn. His wife and two adopted daughters survived him. In conventional phrases but with probable truth the local newspaper spoke of the many nameless acts of kindness and of love that had endeared him to his fellow townsmen.

[*Alphabetical Index of the Births, Marriages, and Deaths Recorded in Providence 1636–1850* (1879); *Longworth's Am. Almanac, N. Y. Reg. and City Dir.* (1816–36); *Hist. of Haverford Coll. for the First Sixty Years* (1892), p. 67; *Bull. of Friends' Hist. Soc. of Phila.,* vol. X, no. 1 (1920), p. 14; *Bay State* (Lynn, Mass.), Apr. 2, 1857; R. L. Lyman, *English Grammar in Am. Schools before 1850* (Dept. of the Interior, Bureau of Educ., *Bull.,* 1921, no. 12; pub. also by Univ. of Chicago Libraries, 1922).]   G.H.G.

BROWN, HENRY BILLINGS (Mar. 2, 1836–Sept. 4, 1913), jurist, was born at South Lee, Berkshire County, Mass. His parents, Billings and Mary (Tyler) Brown, were well-to-do, his father being a prosperous merchant and manufacturer, and he received an excellent private education after which he entered Yale University, graduating there in 1856. He then spent a year in Europe, traveling and studying, and on his return entered a law office in Ellington, Conn. He also attended the Law Schools at Yale and Harvard, but did not complete his course at either. In December 1859 he went to Detroit, Mich., continued his legal studies there, and was admitted to the Wayne County bar in July 1860. Commencing practise in Detroit, he was early in 1861 appointed deputy United States marshal. The port of Detroit was at that time one of the most active on the Great Lakes, and much of the litigation there concerned commercial and maritime matters, to which he specially devoted himself. Two years later he became assistant United States attorney for the eastern district of Michigan which included the city of Detroit. He held this position till May 1868, and in July of that year was appointed a circuit judge for the county of Wayne to fill a vacancy. He remained on the bench only till his successor was elected, when he resumed private practise in Detroit. He became recognized as the leading authority on admiralty law in the Lakes region, and was constantly retained in important shipping cases. In March 1875 he was appointed by President Grant United States judge for the eastern district of Michigan, a position which he was peculiarly fitted to fill, inasmuch as a large proportion of the suits which came before him were maritime. In 1876 he compiled and published *Reports of Admiralty and Revenue Cases, Argued and Determined in the Circuit and District Courts of the United States for the Western Lake and River Districts,* embracing the cases between 1859 and 1875. This was the first volume of an intended series, but no more were published. In court he was dignified almost to austerity, and displayed remarkable readiness in grasping and deciding any point of law which was raised before him. In the conduct of the proceedings he was expeditious, at the same time displaying great patience in examining the merits of every case. Having served on the district court bench for fifteen years with great distinction, he was appointed by President Harrison an associate justice of the Supreme Court of the United States, Dec. 29, 1890. In this larger sphere his legal attainments found full scope, and during his tenure of office he was one of the dominant figures of the Court. Its volume of work was at that time very heavy, the calendar being four years in arrears, and the circuit court of appeals not having been created. His opinions in extradition appeals were always accorded the greatest respect, and he was regarded as the highest authority in the country in points of admiralty law. His outstanding opinion, however, was that in which he expressed his dissent from the majority of the Court in their decision that sections 27–37 of the Income Tax Act of 1894 were unconstitutional (*Pollock* vs. *Farmers Loan & Trust Company,* 158 U. S., 601 at p. 686). He was a majority member of the Court before whom the "Insular Cases" were argued, including *Downes* vs. *Bidwell* (182 U. S., 244). This latter case decided that the island of Porto Rico is not a part of the United States within that provision of the Constitution which declares that all duties, imports, and excises shall be uniform throughout the United States. Though concurring in the decision, Brown's process of reasoning was fundamentally at variance with that of his colleagues, his opinion being that no territory is part of the United States, and that the constitutional rights which the constitutional limitations create do not belong to the citizens of any territory, whether incorporated or not, until by Act of Congress they have been extended to them

(*Ibid.,* p. 247). These propositions have been the subject of severe criticism.

In 1890 he experienced an attack of neuritis and lost the sight of one eye, being threatened for a time with total blindness. Though his vision subsequently improved, he was thereafter compelled to rely in a large measure upon assistance in his judicial work. He resigned from the bench May 28, 1906, on attaining the age of seventy, and lived thenceforth in comparative retirement at Bronxville, N. Y. He was twice married: in 1864 to Caroline Pitts of Detroit, and in 1904 to Mrs. Josephine E. Tyler of Crosswicks, N. J., widow of Lieut. F. H. Tyler, U. S. N. In private life he was somewhat reserved and inclined to formality. "Whether afoot or on horseback he was almost painfully neat in his appearance."

Though a fine classical scholar and great reader, his sole contributions to general literature were a paper on *Judicial Independence,* read before the American Bar Association at Chicago, May 28, 1889, and subsequently published; *A Biographical Sketch of Samuel Tyler* (1909); and an address on Woman Suffrage to the Ladies Congressional Club, Washington (1910).

[Chas. A. Kent, *Memoir of Henry Billings Brown* (1915), contains autobiographical material. An excellent appreciation of his career from the legal standpoint, by Chas. H. Butler, appeared in the *Green Bag,* XVIII, 321. See also *Case and Comment,* II, 79; *Am. Law Rev.,* XXV, 99 and XL, 548; *Green Bag,* I, 207, and III, 91; and the *N. Y. Times,* Sept. 5, 1913.]

H. W. H. K.

BROWN, HENRY CORDIS (Nov. 18, 1820– Mar. 6, 1906), capitalist, was the son of Polly (Newkirk) Brown and Samuel Brown, a New Englander who fought in the battle of Bunker Hill and late in life moved to Ohio. Henry was born near St. Clairsville, Belmont County. The mother died when the boy was two years old; the father five years later. Bound out to work on a farm until he was sixteen, the boy had meager opportunities for an education; such as he had were in the local district school and at Brook's Academy in St. Clairsville. He learned the carpenter's trade and followed it in Wheeling, Va., and after 1844, in St. Louis. In 1852 he yielded to the lure of the West and set out on a journey that took him to the Pacific Coast and around South America. He drove an ox-team to California, but not finding a satisfactory opening went on to Oregon and Washington. For eight months he was interested in a saw-mill on Bellingham Bay. He returned to California and for three years worked as contractor and builder in San Francisco. His restless spirit carried him next to Peru, but after nine months he took passage on a ship bound for the eastern coast of the United States. In May 1858 he was back in St. Louis. After a few months he went to Sioux City, Iowa, and there joined the Decatur (Nebr.) Town Company. He built a hotel in the new town of Decatur but that venture soon proved a failure. After a few months in St. Joseph, Mo., he again turned his face to the Far West. He arrived in Denver in June 1860, realized the possibilities of this straggling frontier town, and settled there. He followed his trade and invested his money in real estate. The basis of his fortune was laid when he secured by preëmption 160 acres of land on the outskirts of Denver. Within that tract are now located the State Capitol—on a beautiful site donated by Brown for that purpose in 1867—and some of the best business and residence lots in Denver. By 1870 he was one of the wealthiest men in Colorado, and was in position to take an active part in the various business enterprises of a growing city. From 1870 to 1875 he was the owner of the *Denver Tribune;* he was active in the organization of the Denver Pacific Railway, the Denver Tramway Company, and the Bank of Denver. The climax of his business career was reached in the construction in 1889 of the Brown Palace Hotel, which soon became and remains one of the most famous hostelries of the West. Large financial obligations incurred in the building of a hotel that cost more than a million dollars, and the panic of 1893 that followed soon after its completion, seriously impaired Brown's financial power. He was land poor, and became involved in litigation that lasted until his death in San Diego, Cal., in 1906. He was three times married: in 1841 to Anna L. Inskepp at St. Clairsville, Ohio; in 1858 to Jane C. Thompson at Decatur, Nebr.; late in life to Helen Mathews in Denver. He devoted his life to business, but there was something of the dreamer and the poet in his nature; he had a vision of a beautiful city at the gateway to the Rockies, and did much to make that vision a reality.

[J. C. Smiley, *Semi-Centennial Hist. of the State of Colo.* (1913), II, 160–65; obituaries in the *Denver Republican, Rocky Mt. News,* and *Denver Post,* for Mar. 7, 1906.]

C. B. G.—z.

BROWN, HENRY KIRKE (Feb. 24, 1814– July 10, 1886), sculptor, was a descendant of Charles Brown, one of the early settlers of Connecticut, and the son of Elijah Brown and Rhoda (Childs) Brown. He was born and brought up on a farm in Leyden, Mass., and received an academic education. Arriving on the New England scene a little after the Concord philosophers, he outlived Emerson, and with a year or two more would have outlived the venerable Alcott also. He himself was accounted a philosopher, in his own vein. When he was about fourteen years old, his artistic imagination was stirred by an itinerant artist who made silhouettes. The boy practised this art by himself until he gained confidence, and then, without seeking paternal consent, started for Albany, paying his way by cutting silhouettes. When almost in sight of the city he was overtaken by his father, with whom he returned to the family fold. One of the neighbors was a blind old man named Parker, who had something of a library. Young Henry, made welcome to its shelves, read Swedenborg aloud to his host, who would sometimes stop him to explain the text. Parker's head was of noble type, and inspired the imaginative lad to attempt a portrait in color. On a canvas prepared from sheeting, with brushes made of hair from the head of an ox, and with colors obtained from a house painter, Henry Brown made a creditable portrait. His parents, recognizing the inevitable, declared that if he must be an artist he should be a good one, and apprenticed him in 1832 to Chester Harding, then the leading portrait painter in Boston. The youth worked diligently, making many friends. In 1836, he went to Cincinnati, planning to establish himself there as a portrait painter. But in Cincinnati he modeled his first head in clay. It was called the best portrait ever modeled in that city, and he became so fascinated with this new mode of plastic endeavor that he turned from paint to clay, choosing definitely a sculptor's career. For him as for previous aspirants, beyond the sea lay Italy. To reach that goal he must earn the necessary money. Fortunately he had the pioneer's gift of a versatile hand, and through Christopher Armes, then state engineer for Illinois, he found work as a surveyor on the state railroads. In this service his target-boy was fifteen-year-old George Fuller, destined to win fame as a painter. Fuller became Brown's pupil in art, and a life-long friendship was begun. Brown's earnings enabled him to study in Cincinnati, where for a brief period he and Shobal Vail Clevenger pursued their chosen art together, each assisting the other, student-fashion, and both profiting by the criticism of a German modeler. In that city, in 1837, the year when Hiram Powers sailed for Italy, Brown produced his first bust in marble, an ideal female head. Returning to the East, he spent a winter in Boston. Among influential New Englanders who gave him encouragement and assistance was Judge James Udall of Hartford, Windsor County, Vt., in whose home the young sculptor was always welcome. In 1839 he married the Judge's daughter, Lydia Louise Udall, and for the next three years the couple re-

sided in Troy and in Albany, Brown meanwhile devoting himself with the utmost diligence to sculpture, until in 1842 he was at last enabled through the help of sympathetic friends to go to Italy. Among many portrait busts made by him during his stay in Albany and its neighborhood are those of Erastus Corning, Silas Dutcher, Eliphalet Nott, William B. Sprague. He is said to have produced at this time no less than forty busts, as well as several figures. Doubtless many of these works showed facility rather than felicity, and seemed "topographical" rather than "artistic," but all in all, they must have proved to Brown's sponsors his ardent determination as well as his considerable manual skill.

His wife accompanied him to Rome, where they made their home. Under Italian skies, the young man's industry was unabated. During his four years' stay, surrounded as he was by classic masterpieces and their imitators, he busily produced for the culture of his countrymen the customary marble statuettes and reliefs. Among his works of this period are his "David," "Rebecca," "Adonis"; also the "Ruth" and the "Boy and Dog" belonging to the New York Historical Society. The work last cited has its "real chain," a prized sculptural adjunct of that day. But Brown was not by nature the typical pseudo-classicist. He was not content with what was then called "the spiritual quality of the pure white marble." He longed to make some more robust expression of his plentiful ideas. Later in his career, he preceded his pupil, John Quincy Adams Ward, in denying the value or necessity of a lengthy sojourn in Italy. On his return to his own country in 1846, he set up a studio in New York City. His first enterprise was characteristic. Breaking away from "real chains" and the like, he produced a bronze group of native inspiration, an "Indian and Panther." "That Mr. Brown installed a miniature foundry in his studio," writes Taft in his *History of American Sculpture*, "and successfully carried into the ultimate metal many small works, speaks volumes for his courage and his ingenuity. It is Mr. Ward's recollection, however, that on account of its size, the group of the 'Indian and Panther' was cast outside, by a Frenchman, but that the finishing was done in the studio." Besides the "Indian and Panther," there was an "Aboriginal Hunter." Even when established in his New York studio, and later in his Brooklyn studio (1850), Brown sometimes refreshed his mind by visits and studies among the Indians, as has often since been done by sculptors weary of academic subject-matter, and interested in primitive man or in animal form. And in animal form, Brown was both interested and competent. His sculpture in this branch compelled the interest of others. In 1851, his election to full membership in the National Academy of Design showed the regard in which his work was held by his fellow-artists; both painters and sculptors appreciated his fine draftsmanship. Among his commissions at this time were a large bas-relief for the Church of the Annunciation in New York City, and many portrait busts of famous men, including those of his warm personal friends, Dr. Willard Parker and William Cullen Bryant.

The commission for what proved to be Brown's highest achievement, the equestrian statue of Washington, had been projected by Greenough, who had planned to execute it in collaboration with Brown, but who later withdrew, leaving the field to his friend (Tuckerman, *Book of the Artists*). The funds for payment came chiefly from a group of New York business men and art patrons, who were to subscribe $500 each. There were delays, changes in contract, withdrawals of contributors. In February 1853, two months after Greenough's death, Brown began the Union Square group. On July 4, 1856, it was unveiled, meeting with applause from artists, critics, and laymen. A still larger appreciation was accorded in after years. In 1856, naturally enough, most Americans knew little about those two equestrian masterpieces of the Italian Renaissance, Donatello's "Gattamelata" in Padua, Verrocchio's "Colleoni" in Venice. Had the writers of Brown's day been familiar with those groups, they would have noted that the American's work is founded on the same principles of art that sustain the two others. It achieves nobility through poise rather than pose, through unity of action in horse and rider, through an adequate feeling for drama, through a wise interpretation of heroic human character, and through an unemphatic, harmonious modeling of form. The very absence of purple passages in the group gives it longer life. Washington is shown in an attitude of native majesty, his arm uplifted in the act of recalling his troops. Simplicity rules both the bronze and its pedestal. A replica of this work has been erected at West Point, in beautiful surroundings.

Brown produced three equestrian statues, the second less good than the first, the third less good than the second. Yet the second, a group cast from cannon captured in the Mexican War, and portraying Gen. Winfield Scott, soldier in three wars, has much to admire in its adequate composition and its fine four-square dignity of man and horse. Unveiled in Washington in 1874, it is perhaps the most generally popular of all Brown's sculptures. His third equestrian monument, erected in the same city three years afterward, in long-delayed pursuance of a vote of the Continental Congress thus to honor Gen. Nathanael Greene, falls far short of the artist's attainment in 1856. Its conscientious modeling does not inspire emotion, and its overdone naturalism in the type and action of the horse and in the pose of the rider lets it down into the purlieus of the commonplace,—a commonplace just touched with eccentricity. In 1858 the state of South Carolina commissioned Brown to make a large pedimental group for the new state house in Columbia (Tuckerman, *Book of the Artists*). A colossal central figure of "South Carolina" was to be flanked by "Justice" and "Liberty"; the industries were to be celebrated by sculptured forms of workers in rice and cotton fields. The "South Carolina" was far advanced when the Civil War put a stop to the whole work. When Sherman's soldiers passed through Columbia in 1865, they destroyed this figure, because they regarded it as a typical statue of Secession. Brown made a host of friends in the South; in vain they urged him to cast in his lot with theirs. Stanch to the Union, he was an officer in the United States Sanitary Commission. During 1859 and 1860, he served on an art commission appointed by Buchanan, and submitted a report designed to spread correct ideas on art among senators and congressmen. From 1861 until his death in 1886, he lived and worked in Newburgh, N. Y. Here he executed four figures destined for Statuary Hall, in the Capitol at Washington,—Gen. Nathanael Greene, marble (1869), Gov. George Clinton, bronze (1873), Brigadier-General Philip Kearny, bronze (1875), and Richard Stockton, marble (1886). From the Newburgh studio came other works, including the equestrian groups, Scott and Greene, already mentioned; an "Angel of the Resurrection," Greenwood Cemetery (1877); and the bronze statue of Lincoln, erected in Union Square in 1868, by popular subscription under the auspices of the Union League Club.

Brown's influence on his pupils was valuable and enduring. At one time they had the privilege of an evening drawing-class, in which master and students worked together from the living model; his kindness in such matters was long remembered. Ward, his most famous apprentice, spoke often of his goodness, and described him as a tall, bearded, fine-looking man, of genially philosophic speech. Among his later assistants was his nephew, Henry K. Bush-Brown.

A lover and knower of horses, a student of the processes of bronze casting, he was the first American to disclose the possibilities of dignity and power in the monumental bronze equestrian statue. His talent was frequently defeated by its own versatility. Moreover, that very quality of unemphatic balance which had helped to make his equestrian statue of Washington a work of high rank led him at times into a commonplace pedestrian interpretation of great themes. He was the first of our sculptors to make any serious attempt to shake off the "real chains" of the contemporary Italianate pseudo-classicism, but he came too early to profit by the vigorous new naturalism taught in the French schools.

[Lorado Taft, *Hist. of Am. Sculpture* (1903) ; Henry T. Tuckerman, *Book of the Artists* (1867) ; Monograph by Jas. Lee, *The Equestrian Statue of Washington in Union Square* (1864) ; C. E. Clement and L. Hutton, *Artists of the Nineteenth Century* (1879) ; S. G. W. Benjamin, *Art in America* (1879) ; A. G. Radcliffe, *Schools and Masters of Sculpture* (1902) ; Chas. H. Caffin, *Am. Masters of Sculpture* (1903) ; Adeline Adams, *John Quincy Adams Ward, an Appreciation* (National Sculpture Society, 1912). Fremont Rider's *Washington* (1922) gives information as to Brown's sculpture in that city, and Charles Edwin Fairman's *Art and Artists of the Capitol of the United States of America* (1927) includes a sketch of Brown, with mention of his chief works.]   A. A—s.

BROWN, ISAAC VAN ARSDALE (Nov. 4, 1784–Apr. 19, 1861), Presbyterian clergyman, founder of Lawrenceville School, was born at Pluckemin, Somerset County, N. J. The son of Abraham R. and Margaret Brown, he was of Huguenot descent. He took his degree at Princeton in 1802, and was tutor there during the year 1805–06. In the meantime he had studied theology under Dr. John Woodhull of Freehold, N. J., and was licensed and ordained by the New Brunswick Presbytery in 1807. He was given the pastorate of the church at Lawrenceville, known until 1816 as Maidenhead. He married in 1807 Mary Wright Houston of Philadelphia. Three years later he established Lawrenceville Classical and Commercial School, first called the Maidenhead Academy. He was its principal until 1833. For eleven years he continued as pastor of the church in Lawrenceville and during the remainder of the period of his residence here was carried on the minutes of the Presbyterian Church as minister of that denomination. In 1842 he moved to Mount Holly, N. J., where he was instrumental in organizing a Presbyterian church. He also preached occasionally at Plattsburg, N. J., and organized a church there. Various records report him as living at Trenton, Somerville, Bordentown and New Brunswick, N. J., for the remaining years of his life, in all of which places he preached at various times. He was one of the founders of the American Colonization Society and also one of the original members of the American Bible Society. It was

said of him that he was a man of "rare talents and learning, enterprising and public spirited, a warm friend, a liberal and zealous supporter and defender of what he felt was the right." He was a trustee of Princeton College from 1816 and of Princeton Seminary from 1822 until his death. Lafayette College conferred the degree of D.D. on him in 1858. After he left Lawrenceville he devoted some time to literary work, and published a *Historical Vindication of the Abrogation of the Plan of Union by the Presbyterian Church* (1855) ; and *Slavery Irreconcilable with Christianity and Sound Reason; or, An Anti-Slavery Agreement* (1858; republished in 1860 under the name of *White Diamonds Better than "Black Diamonds"; Slave States Impoverished by Slave Labor*). A *Sermon on the Work of the Holy Spirit* delivered before the Synod of New Jersey had been published in 1837. The *Memories of Robert Finley* (1819) were written during the period of his pastorate and the early years of the School in Lawrenceville. Finley, who seems to have been much the same type of man, interested in the same movements, made a great appeal to Brown, who says of the book in the preface that "the memorial . . . is an act not less of justice than of kindness to ourselves."

[*Princeton Gen. Cat., 1746–1905* (1908) ; E. M. Woodward and J. F. Hageman, *Hist. of Burlington and Mercer Counties, N. J.* (1883) ; F. B. Lee, *Geneal. and Personal Memorial of Mercer County* (1907) ; *Encyc. of the Presbyt. Ch. in the U. S. A.* (1884), ed. by Alfred Nevin ; *Minutes of the Gen. Assembly of the Presbyt. Ch. in the U. S. A.,* 1809–1861. A letter from R. J. Mulford, Princeton, N. J., gives Jan. 14, 1782, as the date of Brown's birth, quoting his great-great-grand-daughter who gives as her authority "a pencilled note and a newspaper clipping found in my Father's desk" which agrees with the date "sent to the Sons of the American Revolution by some member of the family." The tombstone and the Trenton Vital Statistics give his age as 77 in 1861.]   M. A. K.

BROWN, JACOB JENNINGS (May 9, 1775– Feb. 24, 1828), soldier, was born in Bucks County, Pa., the son of Samuel Brown and his wife, Abi White. His ancestors were among the earliest settlers in the colony, and Quakers all. His father, originally a prosperous farmer, was ruined by the failure of commercial ventures, and at the age of eighteen the son found himself thrown on the world to earn his own living. He taught school in New Jersey for some three years, and then spent two years in surveying near Cincinnati. Returning east in 1798 he again taught for a few months in New York City, also writing political articles for the newspapers. His stay in New York was short, however, for his residence in Ohio had impressed him with the possibilities of enterprise in a new country. By 1799 he had arranged the purchase of several thousand acres of wilderness on the shore of Lake Ontario, and to this place he removed, founding the village of Brownville, near Watertown. Successful in farming and land operations, he soon found himself in comfortable circumstances. In 1802 he married Pamelia Williams. In 1809 he received the command of a militia regiment. His military knowledge at this time was practically nil, but his energy made amends for many deficiencies. In 1811 he was appointed brigadier-general of militia. At the outbreak of the War of 1812, he was put in command of a section of the frontier, and was present at a skirmish at Ogdensburg. During the winter and spring, Chauncey, the American naval commander, made strenuous preparations to gain control of Lake Ontario, to frustrate which the British moved against Sackett's Harbor, the American base. Called upon to take charge of the defense, Brown found a force of 400 regulars and 500 militia to meet the attack, which was made on May 29, 1813. The British force was slightly inferior in numbers, but superior in quality, being mostly regulars. With thoughts, perhaps, of Guilford and Cowpens, Brown placed his militia in front, expecting them to break but to inflict some damage first. They scattered unexpectedly early, but the British then found themselves facing the unshaken regulars of the second line, who checked the advance with heavy loss. Meanwhile Brown in person rallied part of the militia and harassed the enemy's flank, until the British withdrew to their ships. The successful defense of this important post caused Brown's appointment, on July 19, 1813, as a brigadier-general in the army. He participated in the miserable fiasco of Gen. Wilkinson's expedition directed against Montreal in November, but his own reputation was unimpaired. On Jan. 24, 1814, he was appointed major-general, and assumed command in western New York, with two able brigadiers, Scott and Ripley, under him. "The major-general, though full of zeal and vigor, was not a technical soldier: that is, knew little of organization, tactics, police, etc." (Winfield Scott, *Memoirs*, 1864, I, 118). But he was a natural leader of men and a determined fighter, while Scott, who possessed all the technical knowledge which Brown lacked, was placed in immediate charge of the training of the troops, —still raw and undisciplined, though regulars in name. The American plan of campaign contemplated an advance of Brown's army across the Niagara River and around the end of Lake Ontario against York (Toronto), to be made in conjunction with Chauncey's flotilla. The crossing was made on the night of July 2–3, and Fort

Erie, at the southern end of the river, surrendered at once. Moving northward on the Canadian side, toward the Chippewa River, Scott's brigade was attacked, late in the afternoon of July 4, by a somewhat superior force, and a sharp battle ensued. The remainder of the American army was brought up, but before it was seriously engaged Scott delivered an attack which drove the British from the field. Advancing north toward Lake Ontario, Brown discovered that Chauncey had not left Sackett's Harbor, and that no naval coöperation could be expected. There was now no hope of a successful issue to the campaign. Brown remained on Canadian soil, however, and on July 25 fought the fierce battle of Niagara, or Lundy's Lane. Again Scott's brigade first made contact with the enemy, but this time the other regular brigade (Ripley's) and the militia were in line early in the fight. The British position was carried by assault, and their guns taken, but it was found impossible to carry them off. Brown himself was severely wounded. Though able to claim a tactical victory, the Americans could not continue the campaign, and the next day fell back to Fort Erie. To this day, though the contending forces numbered less than three thousand men each, Niagara is one of the famous battles of our army. During this same summer the militia at Bladensburg dissolved into thin air after a loss of one-half of one per cent, while the regulars, led by Brown and disciplined by Scott, sustained at Lundy's Lane a loss of one-third their number, with organization and morale unimpaired. The British assaulted Fort Erie on Aug. 15, and were repulsed with great loss, while the defenders suffered little. Siege operations continued for a month, and then, on Sept. 17, Brown made a sortie, disabling guns and inflicting other destruction which compelled the British to raise the siege. This ended the campaign, and so far as the northern border was concerned, the war also. Of Brown's operations Admiral Mahan says: "Barring the single episode of the battle of New Orleans, his career on the Niagara peninsula is the one operation of the land war of 1812 upon which thoughtful and understanding Americans of the following generation could look back with satisfaction" (*Sea-Power in its Relations to the War of 1812*, 1905, II, 317–18). In 1815 Brown became the senior officer in service, and in 1821 was regularly assigned to the command of the United States Army, which he retained until his death.

[Brief accounts of Brown are in John S. Jenkins, *Generals of the Last War with Gt. Brit.* (1849), pp. 13–60, and Chas. J. Peterson, *Mil. Heroes of the War of 1812* (1848), pp. 141–58. See also W. H. H. Davis,

"Five Bucks County Generals," and Elizabeth Wager-Smith, "Jacob Jennings Brown, the 'Fighting Quaker' of Bucks County," in *A Collection of Papers read before the Bucks County Hist. Soc.*, vol. III (1909). For Brown's military career, consult the standard works on the War of 1812. A. T. Mahan's work cited above has an exceptionally clear account of the land campaigns. B. J. Lossing, *Pictorial Field Book of the War of 1812* (1869) is full of detail. See also Henry Adams, *Hist. of the U. S.* (1891), vols. VII, VIII. For detailed study, Ernest A. Cruikshank, *Doc. Hist. of the Campaigns on the Niagara Frontier* (1896).]   T. M. S.

BROWN, JAMES (Sept. 11, 1766–Apr. 7, 1835), senator, diplomat, was born near Staunton, Va., the son of John and Margaret (Preston) Brown and brother of John [1757–1837, *q.v.*], Samuel [*q.v.*], and Preston W. Brown. He attended an academy at Lexington, Va., which later developed into Washington College (now Washington and Lee University), and available evidence seems to warrant the conclusion that he attended and graduated from William and Mary College. He later studied law, was admitted to the bar, and began practise in Kentucky. In 1789 he settled in Lexington, Ky., and two years later commanded a company of Lexington riflemen in a war against the Northwest Indians. While living at Lexington he married a Miss Hart, sister of Mrs. Henry Clay and daughter of Col. Thomas Hart. With the formation of a state government and the admission of Kentucky to the Union, in 1792, he became secretary of state under Gov. Shelby, which necessitated his removal to Frankfort, the capital. Soon after the purchase of Louisiana, Brown settled in New Orleans, and during his residence in the Southwest accumulated a comfortable fortune in the practise of his profession. He was appointed secretary of the Territory of Orleans, Oct. 1, 1804, and subsequently became district attorney. The Legislative Council of the Territory at its first session passed an act, approved Apr. 19, 1805, for the establishment of a university, and James Brown was named one of its regents. This institution did not materialize. In 1806 he and Moreau Lislet were appointed a commission to prepare a civil code for the use of the Territory. Their work, entitled, *A Digest of the Civil Laws Now in Force in the Territory of Orleans with Alterations and Amendments Adapted to the Present System of Government*, published in both English and French, was adopted in 1808, and became known as the code of that year. It required amendment after a few years, and was replaced by the Livingston code. Brown was a member of the convention which framed the first constitution of Louisiana, in 1812, and the next year was elected to the United States Senate to fill a vacancy caused by the resignation of J. N. Detrehan. He served from

Feb. 5, 1813, to Mar. 3, 1817. He was defeated for reëlection, but with the death of his successor, W. C. C. Claiborne, he was again elected to the United States Senate, and served from Dec. 6, 1819, until his resignation, Dec. 10, 1823, to accept an appointment from President Monroe as minister to France. Here he succeeded Albert Gallatin, and remained through the remainder of Monroe's second term and through the administration of John Quincy Adams. He died of apoplexy at Philadelphia. John Quincy Adams described him as "a man of large fortune, respectable talents, handsome person, polished manners, and elegant deportment."

[Chief sources are the *Annals of Cong.*, and the *Memoirs of John Quincy Adams* (12 vols., 1874–77), ed. by C. F. Adams. The *Official Letter Books of W. C. C. Claiborne, 1801–16* (6 vols., 1917), ed. by Dunbar Rowland, have been found useful, and the alumni records of Washington and Lee Univ. have supplied a few facts. See also *The Works of Henry Clay* (6 vols., 1855–57), ed. by Calvin Colton; F. X. Martin, *Hist. of La.* (1882); A. Fortier, *Hist. of La.* (4 vols., 1904); C. Gayarré, *Hist. of La.* (3rd ed., 4 vols., 1885); R. H. and L. Collins, *Hist. of Ky.* (1874), vol. II; and G. W. Ranck, *Hist. of Lexington, Ky.* (1872). Obituary notices are published in *Niles' Weekly Reg.*, Apr. 11, 1835, and in the *Bee* (New Orleans), Apr. 28, 1835.]
M. J. W.

BROWN, JAMES (Feb. 4, 1791–Nov. 1, 1877), banker, was the youngest of the four sons of Alexander Brown [*q.v.*] and Grace (Davison) Brown. He came to America in 1802, with his brothers George and John [*qq.v.*] "They landed on a hot Sunday morning in July, dressed in thick woolen Irish suits and heavy plaid stockings and they created quite a sensation among the good people of Baltimore, quietly wending their way to church. Thither their mother took them, with a heart thankful for their safe arrival, after she had borrowed from her neighbors thinner clothing better suited to the American climate" (John Crosby Brown, *A Hundred Years of Merchant Banking*, 1909, p. 9).

Like his brothers, James Brown became a member of the firm of Alexander Brown & Sons. In 1825 Alexander Brown began to feel that the time had come to establish a branch in New York. This was the year the Erie Canal was opened for service. James Brown was sent up to begin business under the firm name of Brown Brothers & Company. The Boston branch grew out of the New York branch, and was given the same name. James Brown made his firm one of the most influential houses in the country. Its business, like the business of the other Brown firms in London, Philadelphia, Boston, and Baltimore, grew to such proportions that eventually it became wise to break the ties and let it stand alone. Inheriting his father's rare business ability, as, indeed, had his brothers, he guided the New York house through many financial crises, notably those of 1837 and 1857, and the critical period of the Civil War. James Brown was the most influential member of the family during that struggle, and spent much of his time in Europe during 1861, in close touch with the American minister in Paris, W. L. Dayton. His many letters on the subject of the war, not only to his elder brother, William, but to the other partners on both sides of the ocean, helped the Brown firms to ride the storm safely.

He was a member of the chamber of commerce of New York State in 1827, and was active in its affairs until his death a half century later. He was one of the earliest trustees of the New York Life Insurance Company; was trustee for the Bank for Savings, and was connected with several railroad companies. Like his brothers, interested in local philanthropies, he was one of the founders of the Association for Improving the Condition of the Poor; among the founders of the Presbyterian Hospital; president of the board of trustees of the New York Orthopedic Dispensary and Hospital; and, from its beginning, a trustee of Union College. He was made a director of Union Theological Seminary, and many churches were beneficiaries of his liberal contributions to religious work. He was married twice: in 1817 to Louisa Kirkland Benedict, and in 1831 to Eliza Maria Coe. At his death the mayor of New York ordered all flags on public buildings to be placed at half-mast.

[Old letter books preserved in the vaults of Alexander Brown & Sons in Baltimore, pamphlets and booklets issued by the Brown houses; Mary E. Brown, *Alexander Brown and his Descendants* (1917); Frank R. Kent, *The Story of Alexander Brown and Sons* (1925).]   F. R. K.

BROWN, JAMES (May 19, 1800–Mar. 10, 1855), publisher, bookseller, was born at Acton, Mass., the eleventh of thirteen children of Capt. Joseph Brown, a Revolutionary veteran. The mother, Abigail Putnam, a second wife, was a woman of excellent understanding who encouraged this willing son to make good use of such schooling and books as a country town afforded. In 1815 he became a servant of Levi Hedge, professor at Harvard College, who gave him some instruction and directed his avid reading. It was a natural step when in 1818 he entered the employment of William Hilliard, publisher and bookseller at Cambridge. After several upward movements, in 1837 Brown formed a copartnership with Charles C. Little, which later became Little, Brown & Company. They dealt in standard books, especially law and importations.

Among their publications were works by Bancroft, Bowditch, Child, Dana, Greenleaf, Lieber, Parkman, Prescott, Sparks, Story, the *United States Digest* and *United States Statutes at Large*, the collected works of John Adams and Webster, a law review, and reprints of famous English authors. Brown's special charge was the importations. He went abroad five times (1842–53) to make personal selections, becoming acquainted with John Murray, Pickering, Rodd, the Didots, Tauchnitz, and other great publishers and booksellers. The catalogues of the firm show the high quality of his choosing. That of 1846 states that the "editions are generally those best fitted for Libraries, printed in large types and substantially bound—avoiding in these respects, the extremes of cheapness and extravagance." There were imprints as early as 1657, and specially-bound books are also listed "in morocco by Hayday." The 1854 catalogue gives 826 titles in foreign languages. This activity established Brown not only as a tradesman, but as a bibliophile; his store became the gathering place of those who made the Boston of that period a literary center. In the collecting of his own large private library his tastes were catholic, but his greatest interest was in Burnsiana and ornithology. He was a patron of the Boston Athenæum, and the Natural History Society, a member of the Agricultural Society, and he bequeathed $5,000 to the Harvard College Library.

Brown was twice married: first in May 1825, to Mary Anne Perry, who died in October 1844, and then to Mary Derby Hobbs in April 1846. His business brought him wealth, and in his later years he developed a country estate at Watertown, where he dispensed "becoming hospitality." Brown is described as of "vigorous tread, erect bearing and ample presence," dignified, of perfect good temper, cheery, fond, when young, of practical jokes, and "remarkable for his insatiable love of knowledge."

[See G. S. Hillard, *A Memoir of Jas. Brown* (1856); Edwin M. Bacon, sketch in *Bookman*, V, 373. The catalogues of Little, Brown & Co., are the best source on his business career.]   D. M. M.

BROWN, JAMES SALISBURY (Dec. 23, 1802–Dec. 29, 1879), inventor, manufacturer, was the only son of Sylvanus [*q.v.*] and Ruth (Salisbury) Brown, of Pawtucket, R. I. His youth was spent in an industrious home environment, as evidenced by the fact that when he was fifteen he had not only finished the school curriculum but also had partially completed his apprenticeship of pattern-making under the instruction of his father. This he accomplished in spite of the fact that he had the use of but one eye, the other having been almost totally destroyed in an accident when he was six years old. In 1817 Brown began work at his trade in the cotton-machinery manufactory of David Wilkinson at Pawtucket and remained there for two years, leaving to go to work in the plant of Pitcher & Gay, another firm of cotton-machinery manufacturers. Within a year, when eighteen, he patented an improvement for the slide rest invented by his father, which permitted the height of the tool to be adjusted while the lathe was in motion. Four years later upon the retirement of Gay from the firm, Brown was taken into partnership and as Pitcher & Brown they continued in business until 1842 when Pitcher retired and Brown continued alone until his son was old enough to join him. Pitcher & Brown had a successful and constantly growing business which did not, however, prevent Brown from pursuing his inventive bent. Thus in 1830 he devised another useful tool—a cutter for cutting bevel gears. Its feature was that it required no change of the head stock to make the proper taper in going once around the wheel. Again in 1838 he patented a specialized drilling machine, and in 1842 devised a number of improvements on the Blanchard lathe for turning irregular forms. Shortly after gaining control of the business in 1842, Brown planned and built an entirely new establishment, the first unit of which, the foundry, was completed in 1847. Two years later the main machine shop was erected, being 400 by 60 feet in size, and in 1859 a pattern house was added. To man the plant fully required three hundred men and it was recognized in 1860 as one of the largest and most complete establishments of its kind in the United States. An interesting fact in connection with the construction of his mill and indicative of Brown's thoroughness is that, not finding the proper quality of bricks suited to his purpose, he bought an island in the Pawtucket River having a fine bed of clay, erected a plant, and made his own bricks. The two outstanding contributions which Brown made to the textile industry were his adaptation to American practise of the Sharpe and Roberts self-acting mule, originally imported from England in 1840, and his improvements of the American long-flyer roving machine, both cotton-manufacturing machines. To supply the demand for these taxed to the limit the capacity of his new plant, and, in fact, after he had devised and patented his speeder in January 1857, and it went into production, he was compelled to abandon for a time the building of mules. Practically all of the tools used in the construction of these machines

were devised by Brown and many were in use years after his death. Thus he changed the planing machine for fluting rolls, increasing its capacity four-fold, and patented a grinding machine for the making of spindles. Upon the outbreak of the Civil War Brown turned his whole plant over to the manufacture of guns and gun-making machinery, using particularly to turn gun barrels his improved lathe, originally designed for the turning of rolls for cotton machinery. His later inventions included a machine for grinding file blanks, a tempering furnace for files, and finally an improved spinning mule, patented on Mar. 7, 1876. About five years before his death Brown became nearly blind, but otherwise enjoyed to the very end the most robust health. His business relations were of the best, and he had the reputation of making every sacrifice to produce the best tools and machines. In 1829 Brown was married to Sarah Phillips Gridley. By her he had two daughters and one son, James, who inherited and carried on the Brown Machine Works.

[J. Leander Bishop, *Hist. of Am. Manufactures from 1608 to 1860*, vol. III (1866) ; J. W. Roe, *Eng. and Am. Tool Builders* (1916, new ed. 1926) ; R. M. Bayles, *Hist. of Providence County, R.I.* (1891), vol. II ; Robt. Grieve, *An Illustrated Hist. of Pawtucket, Central Falls and Vicinity* (1897) ; Massena Goodrich, *Hist. Sketch of the Town of Pawtucket, R. I.* (1876).]

C. W. M.

BROWN, JOHN (Jan. 27, 1736–Sept. 20, 1803), son of James and Hope (Power) Brown, was the third of the four brothers (Nicholas [*q.v.*], Joseph [*q.v.*], John, and Moses [*q.v.*]) who formed the mercantile house of Nicholas Brown & Company of Providence. About the year 1770, John, who has been described as "a man of magnificent projects and extraordinary enterprises," withdrew from the firm headed by the more conservative Nicholas and set up business on his own account. His service to the American cause in the Revolution was begun spectacularly enough by his leadership in 1772 of the party that boarded and burned the British armed schooner *Gaspee* as she lay aground in Narragansett Bay. A reward of £1,000 was offered for proof of the identity of the leader of the expedition, and John Brown was arrested on suspicion. He was released from imprisonment and saved from the more unpleasant consequences of his action by the influence of Moses Brown, who, though the youngest of the brothers, seems to have been their helper in all times of serious trouble. Afterward John Brown and his brother Nicholas served the cause by supplying the continental troops with clothing and munitions of war. The records of their dealings with a secret committee of the Continental

Congress show that their ships and their foreign connections were put to good service in the American cause. He was interested in the development of the "Furnace Hope" and during the Revolution made it the chief business of the furnace to manufacture cannon for the army and navy. In his public life, John Brown seems to have supported the American contentions from the beginning. He was active in the Assembly of his state in opposition to the Stamp Act, in support of the non-importation proceedings in 1769 and 1775, and in all crises throughout the Revolutionary period that called for determination and ability. His vigorous efforts in behalf of the adoption of the Constitution were instrumental in bringing Rhode Island into accord with the other federated states. He was elected to Congress twice, in 1784 and 1785, but failed to put in an appearance at either session. He served one term in Congress, however, from 1799 to 1801. In 1787 the firm of Brown & Francis, composed of John Brown and his son-in-law John Francis (husband of Abby Brown), sent out the first Providence vessel to engage in the East India and China trade, only three or four years after this trade had been begun by a shipmaster of Salem, Mass. In December of that year the *General Washington* cleared for the East, carrying a cargo valued at $26,348, composed of anchors, cordage, sail cloth, cannon, bar iron, sheet copper, steel, spars, liquors, cheese, and spermaceti candles. A year and a half later she returned to Providence, loaded with tea, silks, china, cotton goods, lacquered ware, and cloves to the amount of $99,848. This was the auspicious beginning of a trade that continued to bring fortune to Rhode Island for more than half a century.

With his brothers, John Brown was forward in the movement to bring Rhode Island College to Providence from its first location at Warren. It was his hand that laid in 1770 the cornerstone of the first building, the present University Hall of Brown University, and his care as treasurer of the institution during twenty uneasy years helped to establish it on an enduring financial basis. The house he built on Power St. in 1787, probably designed by his brother Joseph, was said in 1800 to be the finest residence in New England, and it remains to-day one of the most strikingly beautiful examples of eighteenth-century architecture in the country. Modern historians have not always approved the character and actions of John Brown. When Congress provided for the building of two ships of war in Rhode Island, he was named one of the committee to oversee the work. It is said that in

this capacity he permitted work on the vessels to be held up so that his own privateersmen might earlier be fitted for the sea, and that in other particulars he allowed self-interest to guide his actions to a degree disapproved of by his fellow-townsmen. There seems to be evidence that he rode the wave of patriotic fervor to his own advantage, but even those who criticize specific actions concede him a life of courageous and vigorous commercial activity which brought wealth and prestige to his community. He was the Elizabethan merchant-adventurer type in a new setting. Of his appearance, it is on record that he was a man of such "large physical proportions" as to take up a whole chaise seat ordinarily occupied by two persons. He married, Nov. 27, 1760, Sarah, daughter of Daniel and Dorcas (Harris) Smith, by whom he had six children.

[For bibliography see list following the sketch of Nicholas Brown (1729–91), and also *State of R. I. and Providence Plantations at the End of the Century: A Hist.* (1902), ed. by Edward Field; Wm. B. Weeden, "Early Oriental Commerce in Providence," *Proc. Mass. Hist. Soc.*, Dec. 1907.]   L. C. W.

BROWN, JOHN (Oct. 19, 1744–Oct. 19, 1780), Revolutionary soldier, was born in Haverhill and grew up in Sandisfield, Mass., where his parents, Daniel and Mehitabel (Sanford) Brown, settled about 1752. He graduated from Yale in 1771, studied law in Providence with his brother-in-law, Oliver Arnold, and in December 1772 was admitted to the bar in Tryon County, N. Y. (Archibald M. Howe, *Col. John Brown of Pittsfield*, 1908, p. 2). He began to practise in Johnstown, N. Y., where he is said to have held the post of king's attorney, but in 1773 removed to Pittsfield, Mass. Here he served on the town's Committee of Correspondence (appointed June 30, 1774), and on the committee which drafted the non-intercourse resolutions adopted by the Berkshire convention at Stockbridge on July 6, 1774. After the suppression of the county courts he was a member of the board of arbitrators appointed to settle civil disputes, and he represented his town in the Provincial Congress from October 1774 to February 1775. In the latter month he volunteered to go to Montreal as agent for the Boston Committee of Correspondence, and set out, charged with the double task of discovering Canadian sentiment toward the revolutionary cause, and of "establishing a reliable channel of correspondence" with the sympathetic element. On Mar. 29, his mission accomplished, he reported to Adams and Warren from Montreal. In crossing the New Hampshire Grants he had been impressed by the strategic importance of Fort Ticonderoga, which, he wrote, "must be seized as soon as possible, should hostilities be committed by the king's troops"; he added that the people of the New Hampshire Grants were ready for "the job" (letter to Adams and Warren, published in L. E. Chittenden, *The Capture of Ticonderoga*, 1872, App.). On May 10, Brown and a little group of Pittsfield men were present with the Connecticut forces when Ticonderoga was taken, and Brown was detailed to carry the news to the Continental Congress (see *Pennsylvania Packet*, May 22, 1775).

He was commissioned major in Easton's regiment on July 6, 1775, and from July 24 to Aug. 10 scouted into Canada, reporting to Schuyler at Crown Point and by letter to Gov. Trumbull of Connecticut (*American Archives*, 4 ser., III, 135). In command for a time of the flotilla on Lake Champlain and discovering that the enemy were preparing gunboats, he counseled immediate advance, volunteering to lead (*Ibid.*, p. 468), and on Sept. 15 commanded the detachment of 134 men which initiated the invasion of Canada. The next week, away from headquarters enlisting recruits, he encountered Ethan Allen on the same business, at Longueuil. Brown had 200 men, Allen had eighty, so they decided to capture Montreal. The attack failed and Allen was taken prisoner (*A Narrative of Col. Ethan Allen's Captivity*, 1807, pp. 28 ff.). On the night of Oct. 19 Brown and James Livingston [*q.v.*], in command of fifty New Englanders and 300 Canadian boatmen, floated guns on bateaux down the rapids of the Sorel (Richelieu), and surprised and captured Fort Chambly with six tons of the powder which the Continentals sorely needed. After the fall of St. Johns (Nov. 3), Brown and Easton started down the Sorel, driving before them Allen Maclean and his irregulars. At the mouth of the stream they stopped to complete fortifications begun by Maclean and there on Nov. 19 by audacity as much as by force they intimidated the British fleet coming down the river from Montreal, and caused it to surrender (see *The Journal of Charles Carroll of Carrollton During His Visit to Canada in 1776*, 1876, p. 97). Before Quebec, in December, Brown was involved in a bit of insubordination due to distrust of Benedict Arnold, but was won back to duty by Montgomery (*American Archives*, 4 ser., IV, 464). After the latter's death Brown claimed a promotion which Arnold refused, charging Brown with plundering the baggage of the officers captured at Sorel (*Ibid.*, p. 907). The quarrel thus precipitated lasted for months, during which, his attempts to obtain a court of inquiry repeatedly thwarted, Brown began to make

charges against the character and conduct of Arnold (*Ibid.*, 5 ser., II, 143) and finally resigned his commission in February 1777. (He had been commissioned lieutenant-colonel in Elmore's Connecticut Regiment on July 29, 1776). Returning to Pittsfield, he published there on Apr. 12 a handbill appealing to the public and vigorously attacking his enemy. (There seems, however, to be little evidence to support the story told by W. L. Stone in his *Life of Joseph Brant*, 1838, II, 116 ff., that in 1776–77 Brown published an attack on Arnold predicting Arnold's treason.)

Elected colonel of the middle regiment of Berkshire militia, Brown was called into the field at the time of Burgoyne's advance in the autumn of 1777. Leading a picked detachment of light troops from Pawlet (Oct. 13–18), he captured Fort George, destroyed the British stores there, and, surprising the enemy's outworks along the Lake, took 293 prisoners but was without sufficient strength to take Ticonderoga. Returning to Pittsfield, he resumed his law practise, in 1778 was elected to the General Court, and in February 1779 was commissioned judge of the county court of common pleas. In the summer of 1780 he entered the field once more, with the Massachusetts levies summoned to oppose Brant and Sir John Johnson in the Mohawk Valley. On the morning of Oct. 19, leaving Fort Paris with 300 men to join Gen. Van Rensselaer, he was drawn into an ambuscade near Stone Arabia, N. Y., and killed. Some time after his death, his widow, Huldah Kilbourne, married Jared Ingersoll of Pittsfield.

[F. B. Dexter, *Biog. Sketches Grads. Yale Coll.*, vol. III (1903) lists other sources and mentions literary and legendary references to Brown. J. E. A. Smith, *Hist. of Pittsfield (Berkshire County), Mass.*, vol. I (1869) follows most of his career and gives the best account of the quarrel with Arnold. Justin H. Smith, *Our Struggle for the Fourteenth Colony* (1907) covers the Canadian episodes. The two last-named works contain footnote references to sources, for which see also *Am. Arch.*, 4 and 5 ser., and *The Jours. of Each Provincial Cong. of Mass. . . . with the Proc. of the County Conventions, etc.* (1838). Brown's mother's name is given on p. 237, vol. II, of "Pittsfield Families," MS. in possession of New Eng. Hist. and Geneal. Soc.]

E. R. D.

BROWN, JOHN (Sept. 12, 1757–Aug. 28, 1837), senator, Kentucky legislator, came of distinguished ancestry. His father, having the same name, was for almost half a century a Presbyterian minister in Rockbridge County, Va., and his mother, Margaret, was a daughter of John Preston, a connection which related him to the Clays and Breckinridges. He was born in Staunton, Va., one of four brothers (John, James [1766–1835, *q.v.*], Samuel [*q.v.*], and Preston

W.). He entered Princeton College and being there when the Americans retreated through New Jersey, he joined Washington's forces and later became one of the Rockbridge soldiers under Lafayette. After his military career he continued his education at William and Mary College and then studied law under the supervision of Thomas Jefferson. In 1782 he moved to Kentucky, and settled first at Danville, the political center at that time, but soon removed to Frankfort where he lived thereafter. He readily adapted himself to the Western country and soon became its most outstanding supporter and spokesman. He promoted the material growth of Frankfort and was responsible for securing the machinery for the Kentucky Manufacturing Society which was organized in Danville in 1789 for the manufacture of cotton goods.

He was one of the principal leaders in Kentucky's tortuous course toward statehood, assuming at times an attitude toward the Union which brought against him charges of plotting with the Spaniards for the independence of Kentucky. In 1787 he had conversations with Don Gardoqui, the Spanish minister, which led him to advocate the immediate separation of Kentucky from Virginia and the nation, for the purpose of taking advantage of Spain's offer of the free navigation of the Mississippi River. He represented Kentucky in the Virginia legislature in 1787, and as a means of pacifying Kentucky that body appointed him a representative in the Confederation Congress. He returned to Kentucky in 1788 and was immediately elected a delegate to the Kentucky constitutional convention of that year. Soon afterward he was elected one of Kentucky's delegates to the Virginia convention called to consider the new Federal Constitution, where he voted against its ratification. In 1789 upon the establishment of the new government, he represented the Kentucky district of Virginia in Congress and was reëlected for a second term, but on the entry of Kentucky into the Union as a state in 1792 he became a United States senator and continued in that position until 1805. In 1803–04 he was president *pro tempore* of the Senate. When Aaron Burr came west on his mysterious journeys he stayed in the home of Brown at Frankfort. Though he was thus friendly with Burr, Brown was a constant supporter of Jefferson and had stood for his election to the presidency in 1800–01. He was widely acquainted and was on intimate terms of friendship with the first five presidents of the United States, though he never accepted proffered favors from any of them. In 1799 he married Margaretta, a daughter of John Mason of New York who was Lafay-

ette's chaplain in the Revolution, and the same year he built in Frankfort "Liberty Hall," his residence, from plans drawn by Jefferson.

[See *Lawyers and Lawmakers of Ky.* (1897), ed. by H. Levin, and R. H. and L. Collins, *Hist. of Ky.* (1874), I, II. Various papers relating to Brown's public career may be found in Innes MSS. in the Lib. of Cong. For his Spanish dealings the following are valuable: Wm. Littell, *Political Transactions in and Concerning Ky. from the First Settlement Thereof, until It Became an Independent State, in June 1792* (1806, repr. 1926 as Filson Club Pub. no. 31); T. M. Green, *Spanish Conspiracy: A Review of Early Spanish Movements in the South-West* (1891), a hostile account; J. M. Brown, *Political Beginnings of Ky.* (1889), a friendly account; and Humphrey Marshall, *Hist. of Ky.* (1824), I, II.]   E. M. C—r.

BROWN, JOHN (May 9, 1800–Dec. 2, 1859), "Old Brown of Osawatomie," is now chiefly remembered for his raid on Harper's Ferry. He was born at Torrington, Conn., the son of Owen and Ruth (Mills) Brown. His biographers have pointed out with much satisfaction that he came of the best New England stock, with only slight dilution of the strain from a Dutch ancestor on the maternal side. They have passed over lightly much more significant facts of inheritance. John Brown's mother, who died when he was only eight years old, was insane for a number of years before her death and died insane, as had her mother before her. A sister of Ruth Mills had also died insane, while three sons of her brother Gideon Mills became insane and were confined in asylums (affidavit of Gideon Mills). Two sons of another brother were also adjudged insane. Owen Brown plied various trades in the Connecticut villages in which he sojourned. By his own admission he was "very quick on the moove." One of these moves took him to Hudson, Ohio, where John passed his boyhood. Owen Brown was twice married and became the father of sixteen children. He was a man of much piety, an abolitionist, and an agent of the underground railroad.

John's schooling was scanty, and reading formed the principal part of his early education. As he himself said, school always meant to him, even in later life, confinement and restraint. More to his liking was the free life of the wilderness. He delighted in the long journeys with droves of beef cattle with which he was sent to supply troops in the War of 1812. Later he worked at the tanner's trade, acting as his father's foreman (letter to Henry L. Stearns, July 15, 1857, in F. B. Sanborn's *Life and Letters of John Brown*, ch. I). In 1820 he married Dianthe Lusk, who in the twelve years of her married life bore him seven children. She, like her husband's mother, suffered from mental aberration in her later years and died in 1831. Two of her sons were of unsound mind. Within a year John Brown married Mary Anne Day, a girl of sixteen, of robust physique, who in twenty-one years bore him thirteen more children.

In 1825 Brown moved to Richmond, Pa., where he cleared the land of timber and set up a tannery. This was the first of ten migrations before his adventures in Kansas, in the course of which he established and sold tanneries, dabbled unsuccessfully in land speculation, and incurred debts. Then he turned shepherd, buying Saxon sheep on credit. One sum advanced by the New England Woolen Company he seems—apparently without any dishonest intent—to have diverted to his own use, but he was treated with leniency by his creditors after he had declared himself a bankrupt. He earnestly hoped that "Devine Providence" would enable him to make full amends—but it never did. His family also changed its abode frequently as he changed his pursuits; but he was often absent for long stretches of time. The story of his business career is a tale of repeated failures, complicated by law-suits which aggrieved parties instituted to recover money loaned on notes or to secure damages for non-fulfilment of contracts. Many of these were decided against the defendant, proving clearly enough his utter incapacity for business. His last business venture was a partnership with one Simon Perkins to raise sheep and to establish a brokerage for wool-growers. Brown went to Springfield, Mass., and opened an office, but failure soon overtook this enterprise. Prolonged litigation followed; and one suit involving $60,000 for breach of contract was settled out of court by Brown's counsel (O. G. Villard, *John Brown*, p. 66). As his various ventures came to naught and his inability to earn a livelihood for his numerous progeny became manifest, he began to take more thought about the affairs of others, particularly about those who were or who had been in bondage. He determined to settle with his family in a newly-founded community of negroes at North Elba, N. Y., on lands donated by Gerrit Smith. His purpose was "to aid them by precept and example," avers his latest biographer without any intentional humor. Within two years, however, he had again moved, to Akron, Ohio, followed by his family.

Brown was well over fifty years of age before the idea of freeing the slaves by force dominated his mind. He had always been an abolitionist; he had made his barn at Richmond a station on the underground railroad; he had formed a League of Gileadites among the negroes in Springfield, to help them protect themselves and

fugitive slaves. Now he began to have visions of a servile insurrection—the establishment of a stronghold somewhere in the mountains whence fugitive slaves and their white friends could sally forth and terrorize slaveholders (*Ibid.*, pp. 53–56). These visions were never very clear or very coherent, and they were overcast by events in Kansas where protagonists of slavery and free-soilers from the North were contending passionately for possession of the territorial government and where a condition bordering on civil war was soon to exist. In the spring of 1855, five of his sons went to Kansas to help win the territory for freedom and incidentally to take up lands for themselves. In May John Brown, Jr., sent a Macedonian cry to his father for arms to fight the battle for free soil (*Ibid.*, pp. 83–84). Brown then transferred what was left of his family to North Elba again, and in August set out for Kansas in a one-horse wagon filled with guns and ammunition. Ostensibly he was to join the colony on the Osawatomie as surveyor. At once, however, he became their leader and captain of the local militia company. As such he commanded it in the bloodless Wakarusa War, whose indecisive outcome left him ill at ease. The ensuing disorders, particularly the sack of Lawrence in May 1856 by the pro-slavery forces, preyed upon his mind. The cause of free-soil took on the aspect of a crusade. Members of his company met and resolved that acts of retaliation were necessary "to cause a restraining fear" (*Ibid.*, p. 152). A list of victims was made out and on May 23, Capt. John Brown with a party of six, four of whom were his sons, set out for the Potawatomi country to discharge their bloody mission. During the night of May 24 they fell upon their five hapless victims without warning and hacked them to pieces with their sabers. Probably Brown killed no one with his own hand, but he assumed full responsibility for the massacre, asserting as he was wont to do that he was but an instrument in the hands of God. From this time on the name of "Old Osawatomie Brown" became a terror to pro-slavery settlers. Eventually, however, he and his men were beaten and dispersed, while in revenge Osawatomie was sacked and burned. In this guerrilla warfare, Frederick, one of the sons whose mind had become unbalanced, was killed.

Old acquaintances who saw Brown after his return from Kansas, in the autumn of 1856, commented on the change in his appearance and manner. With his gray hair and bent figure he looked like an old man. His inability to talk about anything except slavery, and that always with abnormal intensity, left many with the impression that he had become a monomaniac (affidavits). One keen observer, who did not know Brown's family history, detected "a little touch of insanity about his glittering gray-blue eyes" (*Letters and Recollections of John Murray Forbes,* 1899, I, 179). Upon less keen observers in Massachusetts—less keen perhaps, because more preoccupied with the struggle for Kansas —he made a happier impression. Emerson spoke of him as "a pure idealist of artless goodness." It is charitable to suppose that the Concord philosopher was at this time ignorant of the murders on the Potawatomi; but another ardent resident of Concord, Frank B. Sanborn, could hardly have been so ignorant, nor his friends, G. L. Stearns, T. W. Higginson, Theodore Parker, and S. G. Howe, who were members of the Massachusetts State Kansas Committee and who gave Brown some supplies and arms, a little money, and many assurances of moral support in the fight for freedom in Kansas. When Brown returned to Kansas in the late autumn of 1857, he found both parties disposed to have recourse to ballots instead of bullets, and therefore had no opportunity to employ his peculiar methods of persuasion. He now began to recruit a body of men for a new enterprise. He proposed to transfer his offensive against slavery to a new front. In the following spring, at an extraordinary convention of his followers and negroes at Chatham in Canada, he divulged his plans for the liberation of slaves in the Southern states. He and his band were to establish a base in the mountains of Maryland and Virginia, to which slaves and free negroes would resort, and there—beating off all attacking forces whether state or federal—were to form a free state under a constitution. A provisional constitution was then adopted by the convention and Brown elected commander-in-chief (Villard, pp. 331–36).

Brown's funds were now exhausted and he turned again to Gerrit Smith and to his Massachusetts friends. That they were aware of the wide reach of his new plans cannot now be doubted; yet they encouraged him with promises of financial support in what was essentially a treasonable conspiracy. For the immediate present, however, they counseled delay; and in the early summer of 1858 Brown returned to Kansas to resume operations under the name of Shubel Morgan. His chief exploit was a descent upon some plantations across the border in Missouri, in the course of which one planter was killed while defending his property and some eleven slaves were liberated. In the eyes of the government he was now no better than a dangerous outlaw. The president of the United States and the governor of Missouri offered rewards for his arrest; but Brown and his men, appropriating horses, wagons, and whatever served their purpose, eluded pursuit and finally succeeded in reaching Canada with the liberated slaves. Even this exploit did not cost Brown the confidence of his supporters. He made public speeches at Cleveland and at Rochester, and no one attempted to arrest him. Gerrit Smith declared him "most truly a Christian" and headed a subscription list with a pledge of $400. From the Massachusetts group Brown received $3,800, "with a clear knowledge of the use to which it would be put" (Sanborn, p. 523).

In the early summer of 1859, Brown fixed upon Harper's Ferry as the base of his operations in Virginia and rented a farm about five miles distant where he could collect his arms and his band of followers. By midsummer his little army of twenty-one men had rendezvoused secretly at Kennedy Farm; but it was not until the night of Oct. 16 that the commander-in-chief gave the order to proceed to the Ferry. Even after all these weeks of preparation he seems to have had no coherent plan of attack. That he should have fixed upon this quiet town of mechanics, many of whom came from the North, as the place for an assault upon slavery, is inexplicable on any rational grounds. Neither it nor its environs contained many slaves; and it is one of the tragic ironies of the affair that the first man killed should have been a respectable free negro who was discharging his duty as baggage-master at the railroad station. When morning dawned, Brown and his men were in possession of the United States armory and the bridges leading to the Ferry, had made many inhabitants prisoners, among them one slaveholder from a plantation five miles away, and had persuaded a few slaves to join them; but there Brown's initiative failed. For some unexplained reason he did not make off to the mountains as he might easily have done. Meantime the news of the raid spread through the country-side. By mid-day local militia companies from Charlestown had arrived on the scene and had closed Brown's only way of escape. Desultory firing followed, with some casualties on both sides, while Brown with the remnant of his forces, the slaves, and some of his prisoners were shut up in the engine-house of the armory. During the following night a company of United States marines arrived under the command of Col. Robert E. Lee; and at dawn, upon Brown's refusal to surrender, carried the building by assault. Brown fought with amazing coolness and courage over the body of his dying son but was finally overpowered with four of his men. Seven had already been taken prisoner and ten had either been killed or mortally wounded, including two of Brown's sons. Brown himself was wounded but not seriously. Next morning he was taken to Charlestown and lodged in the jail. One week later he was indicted for "treason to the Commonwealth, conspiring with slaves to commit treason and murder." His trial was conducted with expedition but with exemplary fairness and decorum. It ended inevitably in the sentence of death; and on Dec. 2, John Brown was hanged.

From the moment of his capture to his execution Brown conducted himself with a fortitude and dignity that commanded the respect of his captors and judges. To all questions regarding his motives he had only one answer: he had desired to free the slaves—he believed himself an instrument in the hands of Providence to this end. When confronted with the bloody consequences of his acts and with the designs he had entertained to incite a slave insurrection, he would recognize no inconsistency. It was this obsession regarding his mission and his unaccountableness to anybody but his Maker that created doubts as to his sanity. Before his execution seventeen affidavits from neighbors and relatives who believed Brown to be insane were sent to Gov. Wise, but he decided for some reason not to follow his first inclination and have an alienist examine Brown. These remarkable affidavits with their unimpeachable testimony as to Brown's family history and his own erratic behavior constitute prima facie evidence which no modern court of law could ignore.

It is significant of the passions aroused by the Harper's Ferry raid that Brown was hailed both as a noble martyr in a great cause and as a common assassin. Probably Abraham Lincoln anticipated the final verdict of history when he said in his Cooper Union speech (Feb. 27, 1860): "That affair, in its philosophy, corresponds with the many attempts, related in history, at the assassination of kings and emperors. An enthusiast broods over the oppression of a people till he fancies himself commissioned by Heaven to liberate them. He ventures the attempt, which ends in little else than his own execution. Orsini's attempt on Louis Napoleon, and John Brown's attempt at Harper's Ferry were in their philosophy precisely the same."

[The first biography of John Brown was written by James Redpath: *The Public Life of Capt. John Brown,* published in 1860 with a preface dated Dec. 25, 1859. It is valuable only as reflecting the contemporary opinion of Brown's partisans. Equally partisan but valuable for its letters, documents, and personal recollections is F. B. Sanborn's *The Life and Letters of John Brown* (1885). The references in the text are to the fourth edition (1910). Richard J. Hinton in his *John Brown and His Men* (1894) also holds a brief for his hero. Of the later biographies O. G. Villard's *John Brown* (1910) is by far the best and most extensive. It contains much new material on the earlier career of Brown, drawn from widely scattered sources. Considering the undisguised admiration of the author for Brown as "a great and lasting figure in American History," he has written with commendable fairness. The question of Brown's insanity, however, he dismisses too readily. A valuable bibliography of the literature concerning John Brown is appended to the book. The affidavits relating to Brown's alleged insanity are in the possession of Mr. Edwin Tatham of New York, who has permitted the writer to examine them.]   A.J.

BROWN, JOHN A. (May 21, 1788–Dec. 31, 1872), banker, was the third son of Grace (Davison) Brown and Alexander Brown [*q.v.*]. He was born in Ireland, received his elementary schooling there, and in 1802 with his brothers, George and James [*qq.v.*], followed his father to America. Receiving his business training from his father, in time he became a member of the firm of Alexander Brown & Sons, merchant bankers of Baltimore. In 1818 he went to Philadelphia to establish the first American branch of the house. In October of that year the following advertisement appeared in the *Union, United States Gazette,* and *True American* of Philadelphia: "John A. Brown & Company take this opportunity of informing those who have been in the habit of purchasing the linens imported by Alexander Brown & Sons of Baltimore, that the above firm is a branch of that concern and that both houses will import a constant supply of Cheap Linens." The name was changed later to Brown & Bowen and finally to Brown Brothers & Company, but the firm has continued to do business from its foundation to the present day.

John was the most conservative of the four sons of Alexander Brown, yet he had good judgment, shrewd knowledge of men, and alertness in seizing opportunities for the use of capital, and his wise investments at a time when American railroads were first developing enabled him to amass an ample fortune which he used in furthering leading philanthropic enterprises in Philadelphia. He retired from the Philadelphia firm after the panic of 1837 had impaired his health, but continued his philanthropies, which concerned church work mainly. He organized and contributed to the erection of a building for Calvary Presbyterian Church, Philadelphia, and became interested in the work of the New School branch of the Presbyterian Church. Through his influence and assistance and that of his friend and neighbor, Matthias W. Baldwin, that branch of the church became the owner of the Presbyterian House on Chestnut St. He was also a member of and contributor to the American

Sunday School Union, and a short time before his death, made a gift of $300,000 to the Presbyterian Hospital.

The middle "A" in John Brown's name really stood for nothing at all. He adopted it as an initial in order to avoid confusion with another John Brown whose mail frequently had become mixed with his while he lived in Baltimore. His first wife, Isabella Patrick of Ballymena, whom he had married in 1813, died in 1820, and in 1823 he married Grace Brown, a daughter of Dr. George Brown of Baltimore.

[The chief sources of information are the letters, papers, and privately printed biographies of the Brown family, in the vaults and offices of Alexander Brown & Sons, Baltimore; see also J. C. Brown, *A Hundred Years of Merchant Banking* (1909) and Mary E. Brown, *Alexander Brown and his Descendants, 1764–1916* (1917).]

F. R. K.

BROWN, JOHN APPLETON (July 12, 1844–Jan. 18, 1902), landscape painter, was the son of George Frederick Handel and Asenath Lyons (Page) Brown, who were living in West Newbury, Mass., at the time of their son's birth. Early developing a taste for art, Brown studied as a youth with a certain Mr. Porter then well known as a portrait painter. At the age of twenty-one he came to Boston to open his first studio in 1865. Two years later he sailed for Paris for further study under Émile Lambinet, returning to Newburyport to marry Agnes Bartlet, daughter of Edmund and Louisa S. Bartlet of that city. His wife also was an artist, though less widely known than her husband. Brown was ever a mild, lovable man, his temperament showing in the gentle treatment of nature in his paintings. Though he spent some months in England in the early eighties, working with Edwin Abbey and Parsons, and painting in Italy and along the Riviera, most of his work was done in his native New England. The marsh lands and orchards, the scenes of his childhood in his own state of Massachusetts, he immortalized on canvas. Neither realistic nor detailed in his work he portrayed forcibly and directly his subject, realistic outline merging into vagueness. When he painted the sea he caught its cold, grey color, even the weight, density, and mass of the water being preserved and emphasized in his tints. "He had the felicity to utter the right word with just the right accent, never forcing the note. He made us think not of the painter, but of the thing painted" (William Howe Downes in *American Magazine of Art*, August 1923). Brown painted nocturnal scenes; marine pieces; flower gardens; cattle pieces; and architectural compositions; but it is as a painter of apple orchards that he is best

known. He was never fatigued, blasé, or disillusioned in a world of trees, blossoms, grass, flowers, running water, and blue skies. Among his better-known paintings are "Springtime" painted in 1899; "Summer" and "A View at Dives Calvades, France," which were accepted by the Paris Salon in 1875; and "November" exhibited in the Boston Museum of Fine Arts. His work was never impulsive or impassionate, but of an even quiet, having a definite note of serene cheerfulness, typical of the artist's own nature. Though his work shows the influence of Corot he was imitative of none, developing the rural scene into a symbolic reflection typically American in its unquenchable optimism, hopefulness and buoyancy. For many years Mr. and Mrs. Brown lived in the famous Quincy mansion in Boston, returning to Newburyport for their summers, where most of Brown's painting was done directly from nature. Brown never grew old; to his joyous spirit each spring appeared entirely new. He died in New York City.

[C. E. Clement and L. Hutton, *Artists of the Nineteenth Century* (1879); John Currier, *Hist. of Newburyport, Mass.* (1909); *Atlantic Mo.*, Dec. 1877; *Art Jour.* (London), XXXI, 74. Although *Who's Who in America*, 1899, gives the date of Brown's birth as July 24, the *Vital Records of West Newbury, Mass.* (1918), give July 12.]

J. T. M., Jr.

BROWN, JOHN CALVIN (Jan. 6, 1827–Aug. 17, 1889), governor of Tennessee, was born in Giles County, Tenn., and died at Red Boiling Springs, Tenn. His parents, Duncan Brown and Margaret Smith Brown, both of Scotch-Irish descent, were strict Presbyterians and belonged to the small-farmer class of western North Carolina. His grandfather, Angus Brown, had emigrated from Scotland and had fought in the American Revolution under Francis Marion. An older brother, Neill S. Brown [*q.v.*], was governor of Tennessee in 1847–49. John Calvin Brown was known by his contemporaries as one of the best-educated men of his section. He attended the country schools and later Jackson College at Columbia, Tenn., where he was graduated in 1846. It is said that he spoke both Latin and French. He studied law with his brother Neill, was admitted to the bar in Pulaski in 1848, and soon had a good practise in Giles County and in the surrounding counties. Though a Whig, like his older brother, and a follower of John Bell, Brown was never a candidate for office before 1860 when he was an elector on the Bell and Everett ticket and made a vigorous canvass in opposition to secession and Republicanism, occupying, like nearly all Whigs, a middle ground between the extreme Democrats and the Republicans.

His health becoming impaired by too much hard work, he decided to travel and made a tour of North America, England, the Continent, Palestine, and Egypt, returning just before the Civil War began. At the beginning of the war, though he had been opposed to secession, Brown enlisted in the Confederate service as a private, was soon made captain, and on May 16, 1861, became colonel of the 3rd Tennessee Infantry. Captured at Fort Donelson, he was for a time imprisoned in Fort Warren, Boston Harbor, but was exchanged in August 1862. He was then made a brigadier-general and in 1864 a major-general. His command was engaged in the Kentucky and Tennessee campaigns under Bragg, and in the Georgia and later Tennessee campaigns under Johnston and Hood. He was wounded in the battle of Perryville, had a horse killed under him at Missionary Ridge, and while leading a charge in the battle of Franklin was again seriously wounded. For a time he was disfranchised under the Brownlow régime in Tennessee, but his Whig antecedents gave him influence with the moderate Unionists and his war record aided him with those Democrats who were permitted to vote. In 1869 he was elected to the state legislature, and in 1870 was made president of the state constitutional convention where he exerted a strong influence in the making of a new constitution for Tennessee. Largely on account of his work in the constitutional convention Brown was elected governor of Tennessee on the Democratic ticket in 1870 and was reëlected in 1872. His task was to reduce to order the economic and political chaos following war and reconstruction. He secured the payment of the floating debt of $3,000,000, and reduced the bonded debt, but had to leave unsolved the problem of what bonded debts were legal and what were fraudulent. While governor he sponsored a constructive railroad policy and secured legislation authorizing the consolidation of the smaller lines. Among other constructive measures of his administration were the reorganization of the state prisons, the revision of the system of Chancery courts, the establishment of a state system of public schools, a better apportionment of the state into congressional and legislative districts.

His stand on the state debt brought him defeat in 1875 when he was a candidate for the United States Senate against Andrew Johnson. He then returned for a short time to his law practise, but soon entered the railroad business in which he remained until his death. Immediately after the close of the war he had become interested in some of the short lines in Middle Tennessee and was president of the Nashville Railway. This experience and the railroad legislation framed by him when governor caused him to be made vice-president of the Texas & Pacific Railway in 1876, in charge of the construction, the politics, and the legal interests of the road in Washington, D. C., and in Texas. He built the road east to New Orleans and west to the Rio Grande. One of his chief opponents in railway policy was C. P. Huntington. When Jay Gould acquired the Texas & Pacific in 1880, Brown was retained in charge, and in 1881 he was made general solicitor of the half-dozen Gould roads west of the Mississippi. He was made receiver of the Texas & Pacific in 1885, and three years later president; he practically rebuilt the road. A few months before his death in 1889, he returned to Tennessee as president of the Tennessee Coal, Iron & Railroad Company. He was married twice: first to Ann Pointer of Pulaski, who died leaving no children; and second to Elizabeth Childress of Murfreesboro, by whom he had four children.

Brown was a moderate in his political views, and frank and outspoken on all public questions, but he was not a successful politician. He made a good business governor and gave the state a constructive administration. He was a man of strong and attractive personality. As a lawyer his arguments were notable for ability, learning, and eloquence. His claim to remembrance rests upon his military career and upon his constructive work as governor of Tennessee and as a western railroad builder.

[*Hist. of Nashville, Tenn.* (1890), ed. by John Wooldridge; J. W. Caldwell, *Sketches of the Bench and Bar of Tenn.* (1898); *Tenn., the Volunteer State 1769–1923* (1923), ed. by John T. Moore; *Jour. of the Proc. of the Convention of Delegates, etc.* (1870); *Official Records* (1880–1902); obituary in the *Daily American* (Nashville), Aug. 18, 1889.]
W. L. F.

BROWN, JOHN CARTER (Aug. 28, 1797– June 10, 1874), book collector, was the youngest son of Nicholas [*q.v.*] and Ann (Carter) Brown, and the grandson of John Carter, the second printer of Providence. After learning the details of the family business, he was sent to the Ohio country to select land for purchase, and though he met with experiences distasteful to his youthful fastidiousness, he acquired an interest in the section that led him later to interest himself in its problems and to contribute gifts of money to its struggling societies and institutions. His tastes were for travel and the amenities of life rather than for the restraints of business, and though he never lost touch with the large responsibilities he had inherited, he gave his greatest care to the correct enjoyment of his fortune and to the collection of books. In the beginning as a collector of the type common enough in the first half of the century, he brought together a library of works printed at the Aldine presses, a series of the magnificently printed polyglot Bibles, a few fine editions of the classics, and some notable sets of extra-illustrated books. He possessed an inherited and a trained appreciation of relative cultural values united to the zeal of a real collector. He was not satisfied long with his gentleman-collector's library, and sometime in the early 1840's he found his interest turning toward early books on America. He came into touch with the bookseller Obadiah Rich, and later with Henry Stevens, a young Yale graduate in process of becoming a great London bookseller. In the course of the early dealings with Stevens, Brown arrived at a comprehensive conception of what the scope of his collection was to be; that is, that he was to buy for it printed books dealing with the Western Hemisphere from the Discovery to the year 1801. With this field marked out he set about an intensive cultivation, remarkable in its results. Though James Lenox [q.v.], his summer neighbor at Newport and great rival in the collection of American books, excelled him in the pursuit of the rare and elusive variant editions of familiar treasures, yet Brown's training and association led him to give to his American collection a comprehensiveness not attained by the other. These two collectors and their London agent, Henry Stevens of Vermont, created in the purchase and sale of Americana a new branch of the antiquarian book business. The collection was famous among scholars before 1865, when the first volume of a catalogue, compiled under the direction of John Russell Bartlett [q.v.], was printed. This was completed in 1871, in four volumes, describing 5,600 titles of books printed before the year 1800, which relate in some way to the Americas. When Brown died his collection numbered about 7,500 volumes, many of them of very great rarity, and the whole forming a well-rounded collection as useful to the scholar as to the bibliographer and bookman.

Brown made substantial gifts in continuation of his inherited obligations, but he drew out of active connection with some of those which had come to rely perhaps unduly upon his support, transferring his special attention to the Butler Hospital, of which his father was in a measure the founder, and to the Rhode Island Hospital, to which he gave largely in his lifetime. His gifts to Brown University in the form of books, land, and buildings, including a new building for the University Library, equalled in amount the benefactions of his father for whom the institution had been named. He was chosen a trustee of the University in 1828 and from then until his death he maintained an effective interest in its affairs. He served one term in the state legislature as representative from Newport. On June 23, 1859, he married Sophia Augusta, daughter of the Hon. Patrick Brown, member of the Council and associate justice of the General Court of the Bahama Islands. His widow transferred the title of the John Carter Brown collection to her elder son, John Nicholas Brown (1861–1900), by the terms of whose will it passed to trustees who deeded it to Brown University, with an endowment fund of $500,000, and $150,000 to erect a special building for it on the campus.

[Henry Stevens, *Recollections of Mr. James Lenox of N. Y. and the Formation of his Library* (London, 1886) contains much information about the formation of Brown's collection, which is supplemented by the correspondence and bills preserved at the library. These were used in G. P. Winship's *The John Carter Brown Library, a History* (1914). See also sketches in the *Providence Jour.*, June 11, 24, 1874.]   L. C. W.

BROWN, JOHN GEORGE (Nov. 11, 1831–Feb. 8, 1913), genre painter, was the son of Ann and John Brown, the latter a poor lawyer of Durham, England. As a boy he knew little of home life, being apprenticed at an early age to a glass-cutter in Newcastle-on-Tyne. There he remained an apprentice seven years, earning the sum of six dollars a week. Half of this amount was sent to his mother and the other half was used to live on; he received no financial aid from his father. The lad early developed a taste for art, doing a portrait of his mother and sister when he was nine years old. While learning the glass-cutting industry, he studied in his spare time with the well-known English artist Scott Lowdes. After leaving Newcastle-on-Tyne he continued the study of art in Scotland under William D. Scott. In 1853, when he was twenty-two years of age, he went to London and there supported himself by drawing and by the painting of portraits. One night he chanced to hear Henry Russell, then a well-known music hall singer, sing of the immigrants that came to the States. The youth was so impressed with the vivid pictures of American life as painted by the singer's words, that he came almost immediately to America, supporting himself in Brooklyn, N. Y., by his trade of glass-cutting. His employer was a benevolent old gentleman by the name of William Owen. Sketches made for stained glass work and decorations so impressed Mr. Owen with Brown's artistic ability that he enabled him to study in New York with Thomas Cummings.

In 1856 Brown married Mary Owen, the eldest daughter of William Owen. After her death he married her younger sister, Emma A. Owen, in 1871. His natural sympathy and kindness for all children was definitely demonstrated in the love he bore his own family of seven.

Opening a studio in the Old Studio Building of New York City in 1860, he started painting street urchins, and in the beginning received for his pictures from five to thirty dollars apiece. A painting of a small boy called "His First Cigar," first brought Brown's work into national consideration, this painting selling for $150 and being exhibited in the Academy of Design of New York in 1860. Another painting, "Curling in Central Park," caused him to be made an Academician. Nine years later he was made president of the National Academy. Although never high art, his paintings of American town and country types were always true to nature and are an invaluable addition to the history of his generation. His work was essentially American, cleverly executed, and intensely realistic. To quote his own words, "I do not paint poor boys solely because the public likes them and pays me for them, but because I love the boys myself, for I was once a poor lad." He died at the age of eighty-two, a wealthy man, his paintings in the latter part of his life having yielded him an annual income of from forty to fifty thousand dollars, which he had invested to a large extent in New York real estate.

[C. E. Clement and L. Hutton, *Artists of the Nineteenth Century* (1879); G. W. Sheldon, *Am. Painters* (1881); *Mag. of Art*, Apr. 1882; *Am. Art News*, Jan. 6, 1906, and Feb. 15, 1913; *N. Y. Herald*, Feb. 9, 1913; Notes of Philip Gilbert Hamerton on "American Exhibition of Paintings" in Paris Exhibition of 1878.]

J. T. M., Jr.

BROWN, JOHN MIFFLIN (Sept. 8, 1817–Mar. 16, 1893), bishop of the African Methodist Episcopal Church, was a mulatto born at what is now called Odessa, Del. There he spent the first ten years of his life. He then moved to Wilmington, Del., where he lived with a Quaker family. These Friends gave him religious instruction at home and sent him to a private school. He had the opportunity for further instruction under a Catholic priest, but declined it for the reason that he desired to adhere to the principles of the Methodist Church. He next found friends in Philadelphia, where he lived in the home of Dr. Emerson and Henry Chester, who continued his education. For a number of years he attended the St. Thomas Protestant Episcopal Church, but in 1836 united with the Bethel African Methodist Episcopal Church. There he attended an evening school and began his preparation for the minis-

try. He made several efforts to obtain advanced training, but had his first such opportunity when he entered the Wesleyan Academy at Wilbraham, Mass. He studied there from 1838 to 1840, when he had to leave on account of poor health. After recovery, he studied further at Oberlin, but did not complete a course. Much better educated than most of his fellows, however, he began a private school in Detroit in 1844. At the same time he was engaged in religious work, for he had charge of a church in that city the following three years. He next served as a pastor in Columbus from 1844 to 1847. From this position he was called to the most significant work with which he had ever been connected. He was chosen the principal of Union Seminary, organized as a result of a vote of the African Methodist Episcopal Conference in 1844. This is often referred to as the original Wilberforce University. It was started in the African Methodist Episcopal Chapel in Columbus; but, being unsuccessful, it was soon moved twelve miles from the city and established on a farm of 120 acres. This was the first national educational effort of the African Methodist Episcopal Church. Being in need of educated ministers, the conference established this institution on the manual labor plan by which poor students could work at some useful occupation to earn what they learned. Brown started the school with three students and left it with 100. Eventually Union Seminary was merged with the actual Wilberforce University founded by the Methodists in 1856 at Tawawa Springs, near Xenia.

Prior to this time, however, Brown had resumed his work in the church. In 1853 he had married Mary Louise Lewis of Louisville, who bore him eleven children. He became a pastor in New Orleans and served at various other places in the South. In 1864 he was chosen editor of the *Christian Recorder*, the organ of the African Methodist Episcopal Church, which still exists as the oldest negro newspaper in the United States. Brown did not remain in this position long. During the same year he was made director of the rapidly expanding missionary work of the church, which required systematization and stimulus. He continued in this capacity for four years. In 1868, the unusual growth of the church after the emancipation of the freedmen necessitated his advancement to the highest post in the denomination, and he was ordained bishop. In this position he toiled successfully for twenty-five years, contributing to the urgent needs of belated people who now had their first opportunity for intellectual and spiritual uplift. To him belongs the credit for establishing Payne

Institute, now Allen University, at Columbia, S. C.; and for founding Paul Quinn College at Waco, Tex. He died at his home in Washington, D. C.

[Sketches of Brown appear in Wm. J. Simmons, *Men of Mark* (1887) and in the *A. M. E. Ch. Rev.*, July 1893; for additional facts see Daniel A. Payne, *Recollections of Seventy Years* (1888); and B. T. Tanner, *Outline of Our Hist. and Govt. for African Meth. Churches.*]   C.G.W.

BROWN, JOHN NEWTON (June 29, 1803– May 14, 1868), Baptist clergyman, was the son of Charles and Hester (Darrow) Brown. His early home was in New London, Conn., where he was born. He graduated from Madison College (now Colgate) in 1823, standing at the head of his class. The next year he was ordained to the Baptist ministry at Buffalo, N. Y., and he preached there for a year before going to New England for his principal pastorates. In 1827 he was settled at Malden, Mass., and two years later went to Exeter, N. H., for a ministry of nearly ten years. During that time he compiled a single-volume religious encyclopedia, *Fessenden and Company's Encyclopedia of Religious Knowledge* (1837). It has been superseded by later and larger works, but for a time it was used widely. In 1838 Brown's scholarly attainments brought him the appointment of professor of theology and church history in the Academical and Theological Institution of New Hampton, in central New Hampshire, where he remained for seven years. In 1845 ill health sent Brown south, and he became pastor at Lexington, Va., for four years. At the end of that time he was made editorial secretary of the American Baptist Publication Society, and also editor of their journals, the *Christian Chronicle* and *National Baptist*. A number of books notable in their time were published under his direction, including the works of the English Baptists, Bunyan and Fuller, and Fleetwood's *Life of Our Lord and Saviour, Jesus Christ* (1866). Brown was himself the author of *Emily and Other Poems* (1840), and he translated the medieval hymn *Dies Irae*. His most permanent work was the preparation of the *New Hampshire Confession of Faith* in 1833. Nearly a century earlier the Philadelphia Association of Baptist churches had adopted a confession based on a seventeenth-century confession of English Baptists, which itself was adapted from the famous Westminster Confession of the English Presbyterians. This was strongly Calvinistic in character, and, while it suited most of the American Baptist churches, it was not entirely satisfactory as an expression of Baptist theology, especially where the Baptists were in contact with the Freewill Baptists of northern New England. Brown was appointed one of a committee to draw up a briefer statement which would be more moderately Calvinistic. This was accepted by the New Hampshire convention as a satisfactory declaration, and came into general use in the North by a denomination that has had little liking for creeds. Brown's part in the work appears to have been most constructive, and his name remains associated with its history. Never very robust in body or in spirit, he was inclined to mysticism in his religion. The New Hampshire Confession has been characterized as "like the mild Dr. Brown."

[Wm. Cathcart, *Bapt. Encyc.* (1881); L. C. Barnes and others, *Pioneers of Light* (1924), p. 301; Wm. Hurlin and others, *The Baptists in New Hampshire* (1902); *The First Half Century of Madison Univ. 1819–69* (1872); obituaries in the *Press* and *Pub. Ledger* of Phila., May 18, 1868; Conn. Vital Records, State Lib., Hartford.]   H.K.R.

BROWN, JOHN PORTER (Aug. 17, 1814– Apr. 28, 1872), diplomat, Orientalist, was born at Chillicothe, Ohio, the son of an obscure tanner and of Mary (Porter) Brown, daughter of David Porter, a captain in the American navy during the Revolution. Navy Department records do not confirm the statement of Admiral David D. Porter that Brown was in 1829 an acting midshipman in the navy. In 1832 he joined his uncle, Commodore David Porter, minister-resident at Constantinople, where he began the study of Turkish and Arabic. He became assistant dragoman of the legation the following year and was then successively commissioned consul (1835), dragoman (1836), consul-general (1857), and secretary of legation (1858). He was nine times chargé d'affaires *ad interim*. In 1850 he helped to secure the first Turkish mission to the United States, by suggesting to the Grand Vizier, Reshid Pasha, the advisability of sending an agent to inspect American military and naval establishments, Brown having in mind the eventual displacement by Americans of the British in the service of the Sultan. Without credentials, Amin Bey was brought to the United States in the U. S. S. *Erie*, received by the president and cabinet, entertained by Secretary Webster at Marshfield, and with his suite, accompanied by Brown, toured the United States as the guest of the nation. The mission was featured by the widely copied denunciation of Brown that characterized Amin Bey as an impostor (*New York Morning Express*, Dec. 2, 1850). Characteristically Brown attempted to secure the appropriation of entertainment money by Congress through his friend Lewis Cass, without consulting the Department of State. This independence and audacity was even more strikingly exemplified in the Koszta affair. A certain Martin Koszta, a Hungarian refugee and an adherent of Kossuth's insurrection against Austria, came to the United States in 1851 and in the following year declared his intention of becoming an American citizen, in the New York court of common pleas. After a residence of nearly two years he went to Turkey, where he traveled by means of *tezkerehs* (Turkish passports) procured by the American consul in Smyrna and by Brown in Constantinople. He was seized at Smyrna by order of the Austrian consul and imprisoned on the Austrian brig *Hussar*. Although not subject to Brown's instructions, Capt. Ingraham of the United States sloop of war *St. Louis* appealed to the chargé for counsel. Brown advised him to demand Koszta's surrender, and if it were not complied with, to *"take him out of the vessel"* (sic). Ingraham served his ultimatum on the Austrian commander at eight o'clock on the morning of July 2, 1853, and demanded a reply by four o'clock in the afternoon, in the meantime clearing the decks and preparing to fight it out in Smyrna harbor. The Austrian consul-general prevented bloodshed only by delivering Koszta in chains into the custody of the French consul-general. After months of negotiation he was released and returned to the United States. The action of Brown and Ingraham, while high-handed and of questionable legality, was fully upheld by the United States Government. Although admitting that Koszta was not an American citizen, President Pierce declared that he was "clothed with the nationality of the United States" (*Congressional Globe*, 33 Cong., 1 Sess., p. 8).

Brown attained a considerable reputation as an Orientalist among his contemporaries. His translations of the Turkish version of al-Tabari's "Conquest of Persia by the Arabs," Muhammad Misri's "On the Tesavuf, or Spiritual Life of the Soffees" (*Journal of the American Oriental Society*, vols. I, II and VIII), and of Patriarch Constantine's Greek guidebook to Constantinople and its environs (*Ancient and Modern Constantinople*, London, 1868), while interesting, are now of little value. His best translation was Ahmad bin Hamdan Suahili's "Wonders of Remarkable Incidents and Rareties of Anecdotes," a seventeenth-century Turkish collection of Arabic and Persian fairy tales, published under the title of *Turkish Evening Entertainments* (1850). *The Dervishes, or Oriental Spiritualism* (London, 1868; new edition, edited by H. A. Rose, London, 1927) is a fairly accurate account based on first hand knowledge.

After forty years of official life in the Orient Brown died at Constantinople of heart disease, so poor that his widow, Mrs. Mary A. P. Brown, was able to return home only through the generosity of the Sultan.

[*Senate Ex. Doc. No. 43*, 31 Cong., 1 Sess.; *House Ex. Doc. No. 78*, 32 Cong., 1 Sess.; *Senate Ex. Doc. No. 40* and *No. 53* and *House Ex. Doc. No. 1* and *No. 91*, 33 Cong., 1 Sess.; *House Ex. Doc. No. 82*, 34 Cong., 3 Sess.; *Senate Ex. Doc. No. 54*, 35 Cong., 1 Sess.; *House Ex. Doc. No. 63*, 35 Cong., 2 Sess.; *Senate Ex. Doc. No. 1*, 37 Cong., 2 Sess.; *House Ex. Doc. No. 1*, 38 Cong., 2 Sess.; *House Ex. Doc. No. 1*, 42 Cong., 3 Sess.; *Senate Report No. 357*, 33 Cong., 1 Sess.; *Senate Report No. 359*, 34 Cong., 3 Sess.; *Senate Report No. 135*, 36 Cong., 1 Sess.; *House Report No. 40*, 42 Cong., 3 Sess.; *Cong. Globe*, 31 Cong., 1 Sess., pp. 1872–73, 1930; *Ibid.*, 33 Cong., 1 Sess., p. 313; Francis Dainese, *The Hist. of Mr. Seward's Pet in Egypt* (1867); *Daily National Intelligencer* (Washington, D. C.), Sept. 23, 1850; *Boston Courier*, Nov. 5–7, 1850; *Scioto Gazette* (Chillicothe, Ohio), Nov. 26–27, 1850, May 1, 1872; *Daily Commercial* (Cincinnati), Dec. 16, 1850; *The Levant Times* and *The Levant Herald* (both Constantinople), Apr. 30, May 1, 1872; manuscript letters and records in the Dept. of State, Washington, D. C.]

L.H.G.
F.E.R.

BROWN, JOHN YOUNG (June 28, 1835– Jan. 11, 1904), congressman, governor of Kentucky, was the son of Thomas Dudley and Elizabeth (Young) Brown and was born in Elizabethtown, Hardin County, Ky. His father was a man of some note, serving in the state legislature five terms and being a member of the constitutional convention of 1849–50. Thus, his son at an early age heard much speaking and oratory and developed a strong desire to excel in this art. He entered Centre College when sixteen years of age and according to his classmate, W. C. P. Breckinridge, was the outstanding member of his class. He was graduated in 1855 and immediately began the study of law in Elizabethtown where he commenced practise the following year. His interest in politics led him to attack the Know-Nothings with such vigor as to draw threats on his life from that group. In 1859 while attending the Democratic convention at Bardstown he was nominated for Congress despite his protestations of being a year too young. Nevertheless, he entered vigorously into the campaign and was elected, though he was not allowed to take his seat until the meeting of the short session by which time he had reached the constitutional age.

In 1860 he was a supporter of Douglas and a presidential elector, entering into a joint campaign with W. C. P. Breckinridge, who was supporting his kinsman, John C. Breckinridge. About this time (September 1860) he married Rebecca, a daughter of Archibald Dixon, a former United States senator and a conservative Union man. Brown's sympathies for the Union were so alienated during the Civil War by the régime of the Federal army in Kentucky and his support of the war became so infinitesimally small that when in 1867 he was elected to Congress from the 2nd district he was not allowed to take his seat. In 1872 he was elected again by a vote of 10,888 to 457 for his Republican opponent and served for the next four years, refusing to run thereafter. In 1875 he made a withering speech against Benjamin F. Butler, for which he was censured by the House. A subsequent Congress expunged the resolution of censure.

Brown now resumed his law practise in Henderson, whither he had moved about the time of the outbreak of the Civil War, and apparently retired from politics. But his desire to be governor was too strong. In 1891 he sought and secured the nomination, over the protests of the Farmers' Alliance delegates. He won by a majority of 28,000 votes over his Republican opponent and entered in December upon a four-year term characterized by many veto messages brought forth by loose legislation incident to putting into effect the new constitution of 1890. On the expiration of his term, he began again the practise of law in Louisville, but the following year (1896) he ran for Congress and was defeated. In 1899 his hostility to Goebel, the Democratic nominee for governor, led him to run on an independent Democratic ticket. He received 14,000 votes and greatly contributed to the disputed election which resulted in Goebel's assassination. Later he acted as attorney for the defense of Caleb Powers, who was charged with the crime.

[H. Levin, ed., *Lawyers and Lawmakers of Ky.* (1897); Richard H. and Lewis Collins, *Hist. of Ky.* (1874), vol. I; *Lexington Morning Herald*, Jan. 12, 1904; *Courier-Jour.* (Louisville, Ky.), Jan. 12, 1904.]
E.M.C—r.

BROWN, JOSEPH (Dec. 3/14, 1733–Dec. 3, 1785), manufacturer interested in scientific investigation, son of James and Hope (Power) Brown, was the second of the "Four Brothers," of whom Nicholas, John, and Moses [qq.v.] were the others. Following the precedent of the elder brother, Nicholas, he entered the paternal store which, in the next generation, was to become a mercantile establishment of international standing. He remained in business with his three brothers, trading as Nicholas Brown & Company, only until he had acquired a competency. His interest in physical science was stronger than his mercantile instinct, and soon after the middle of the century he was living in Providence the life of an investigator and student, while the brothers continued their successful careers in commerce. It was perhaps because of

his interest in physical science that he was given charge at its beginning of the iron manufactory controlled by the firm, the "Furnace Hope" at Scituate, R. I. His influence on the conduct of this industry did not cease when he withdrew from the firm, for he remained until his death a partner in the venture and its technical adviser in important undertakings. His interest in physics led him in the direction of electrical experimentation, while his study of mechanics bore fruit in the mastery of the practical problems of house building and architecture. He was associated with James Sumner in the building of the beautiful First Baptist Church of Providence, constructed after a design by James Gibbs. It is said that he was the architect of his own residence on South Main St. in Providence, of the notably fine Power St. house of his brother John, of the Market House, all of which are still standing, and of other buildings that have helped to give Providence a peculiarly distinguished architectural character. In public life, Brown served for several years in the Rhode Island Assembly, but it is probable that he is best remembered for his scientific interests, and locally at least for his connection with the observation of the Transit of Venus made in Providence under Benjamin West on June 3, 1769, an astronomical experiment that has given the name Transit St. to one of the thoroughfares of that city. West's pamphlet, published in Providence in 1769 by John Carter, recorded this early American astronomical observation and his paper on the subject in the *Transactions of the American Philosophical Society*, I, gave the event wider importance. In 1769 Brown became a trustee of Rhode Island College, which was brought to Providence chiefly through the enterprise of himself and his brother Nicholas. In 1770 this institution conferred upon him the honorary degree of Master of Arts, and in 1784 invited him to fill its chair of natural philosophy. One-half of his first subscription to the college in 1769 had been allocated by the donor to the purchase of "philosophical apparatus." Brown was married on Sept. 30, 1759, to Elizabeth Power.

[*The Chad Browne Memorial* (1888) comp. by Abby Isabel Brown Bulkley; Gertrude S. Kimball, *Providence in Colonial Times* (1912); Benjamin West, *An Account of the Observation of Venus upon the Sun* (1769).]
L.C.W.

BROWN, JOSEPH EMERSON (Apr. 15, 1821–Nov. 30, 1894), lawyer, statesman, was of Scotch-Irish descent. His father, Mackey Brown, and his mother, Sally Rice, were of Virginian ancestry. He was born in Pickens District, S. C., but during his early boyhood his parents removed to Union County in the mountainous country of northern Georgia. This section of the state was in the remote interior, without railroads or good schools and far from the plantation areas, which were the centers of the aristocracy, wealth, and political power of Georgia. Until near manhood Brown led the life of a day laborer on the farm, acquiring meanwhile the rudiments of an education in the neighborhood rural schools. In his nineteenth year he left home and attended an excellent school in Anderson District, S. C. After two or three years there he returned and settled at Canton, in northern Georgia. There he had charge of the town academy (1844), and read law. After being admitted to the bar (1845) he entered the Yale Law School (October 1845) and was graduated the following year. He returned to Canton and settled down as a practitioner. He was a Democrat in politics, and a member of the Baptist Church. In 1847 he was married to Elizabeth Grisham, the daughter of a Baptist preacher. Two years later his political career was begun with his election to the state Senate. Close application to the business of the state quickly brought him recognition as a man of force. He was made a Pierce elector in 1852 and in 1855 was elected judge of the Blue Ridge circuit—a position he was holding when he received the Democratic nomination for governor in the convention of 1857. Brown was a compromise candidate, his nomination coming as a result of a deadlock involving five strong and well-known politicians. He defeated the Know-Nothing candidate, Benjamin H. Hill, in the subsequent election, and was reëlected in 1859, 1861, and 1863, and thus became Georgia's war governor.

Brown's predecessors in office had been for many years men of distinguished family—wealthy, well educated, and experienced in political life; Brown, on the contrary, was unknown and untried. The legislature was full of men who considered themselves his superiors in statecraft. Under the circumstances it was expected that he would be guided by the recognized leaders and not be disposed to press his own opinions. The politicians were mistaken. He was frequently in conflict with the legislature and freely exercised the veto power. He opposed measures looking to the relief of banks from the penalties provided by law for the suspension of specie payments (this was the most important political issue in his first term); he vetoed measures seeking by legislative enactment to pardon criminals; in vigorous messages he advocated the establishment of free schools and the endowment of the state university, then struggling for its existence.

One of his most noteworthy accomplishments was the reform in the administration of the state-owned Western & Atlantic Railroad. Under Brown's administration the net profits from the operation of the road were increased four-fold. An ardent state rights and pro-slavery man, Brown correctly read the signs of the time, and, in anticipation of war, carried through important reforms in the militia system. He held that Congress had no right to restrict slavery in the Territories and advocated secession as the only remedy for northern aggressions. But throughout the Civil War Brown, while complying with all demands for troops, was in conflict with the Confederate government. The trouble arose from the fact that he was almost fanatical in his adherence to the doctrine of state sovereignty, while the exigencies of war forced President Davis to move in the direction of centralization of government. Whenever Brown considered that the acts of Davis or of the Confederate Congress transcended the powers granted by the Confederate constitution, he protested vigorously. Thus the state government and the Confederate authorities quarrelled over Davis's accepting state troops without reference to Brown's authority, and over the appointment of officers to command Georgia troops in the Confederate army, Davis maintaining that military efficiency demanded that all officers be named by himself, Brown that the constitution conferred on enlisted men the power to elect their own company officers—the President's right to appoint field and staff officers not being contested. Brown opposed the practise of allowing substitutes after conscription had commenced; he disputed both the wisdom and constitutionality of the conscription law and at times obstructed its operation; he protested against the seizure of property without compensation by agents of the Confederacy; he opposed the suspension of *habeas corpus*.

On Lee's surrender in 1865 Brown was paroled by Gen. Wilson, but shortly thereafter his parole was ignored. He was taken to Washington and imprisoned for a short while. Pardoned by President Johnson, he returned to Georgia and, finding the state controlled by military authorities, resigned the governorship (June 1865). It will be recalled that the Johnsonian reconstruction was carried out by the President at a time when Congress was not in session. When Congress met in December 1865 it refused to seat Southern representatives and Senators elected under the Johnson plan, declared the President's course illegal, and required the Southern states to adopt the Fourteenth Amendment as a condition of readmission to the Union. This amendment guaranteed civil rights to the negro, disfranchised the Confederate leaders, and placed before the Southern states the alternatives of enfranchising the negroes or of having their congressional representation proportionately reduced. At this stage of affairs the Southern leaders were confronted with a momentous decision. Should they advocate acceptance of the amendment, thus conferring on their former slaves full political rights, but thereby escaping the evils of bayonet rule, or should they follow their natural inclinations and refuse to yield? In Georgia the old line leaders were practically unanimous in their opposition to the congressional program. Brown stood almost alone in counselling compliance with the will of Congress. The state, he held, was helpless to resist. Opposition would serve only to inflame the Republican leaders, to prolong military control, and to delay the restoration of normal conditions. This attitude brought down on the ex-governor's head the bitter hatred of his former associates and friends. He was denounced by the conservatives and the press as a renegade to every principle that a Southern man should hold dear.

Abandoning the Democratic party and affiliating with the Republicans, Brown assisted in putting through the Congressional Reconstruction measures. A new state constitution was drafted by the convention of 1868; the negroes were enfranchised; and in the subsequent election, Rufus B. Bullock, a Republican, became governor. The legislature elected at the same time was dominated by Republican carpet-baggers, negroes, and a number of native white Republicans. Before this legislature Brown became a candidate for the United States Senate and was defeated, this being the only defeat he ever suffered in a campaign. Shortly thereafter (1868) Gov. Bullock appointed him chief justice of the supreme court of Georgia. Bullock's administration became involved in charges of corruption, and as the election of a new legislature in 1870 had resulted in returning a majority hostile to him, the Governor fled from the state. At a special election in 1871 a Conservative Democrat, James M. Smith, was elected governor and normal political conditions were restored. At this juncture Brown withdrew from his Republican affiliations, reëntered the Democratic party, and assisted in the Smith campaign.

Meanwhile, in 1870, he had resigned from the court to accept the presidency of the Western & Atlantic Company, a corporation organized to take over on lease the state-owned railroad. Benjamin H. Hill and Alexander H. Stephens were also members of this company. Brown developed remarkable business ability, made a great success of the road, entered the coal and iron mining industries, invested largely in Atlanta real estate, and became a wealthy man. In 1880 Gen. John B. Gordon, United States senator, suddenly resigned within three weeks of the end of a session. Gov. Colquitt appointed Brown to fill the unexpired term. Immediately all the old fires of hatred were rekindled. When Colquitt came up for reëlection the opposition to him centered on his appointment of Brown to the Senate. Brown threw himself into the campaign, assisted in the reëlection of Colquitt, and offered himself for reëlection to the Senate before the new legislature. He was successful (1880), was twice reëlected, and served until Mar. 3, 1891.

As to the wisdom of Brown's conduct during the Reconstruction period there would seem to be little argument, but even now, a half century after the event, the older people of the state strongly question his motives. A recent historian of the Reconstruction era, while refraining from adverse criticism, points out that "He was first in secession, first in reconstruction and very nearly first in the restoration of Democratic home rule. Consequently he came up on top at every revolution of the wheel of destiny" (Thompson, p. 223). The impression is left by this statement that his conduct was distinctly opportunist, but the ultimate verdict of history will probably be otherwise.

[Herbert Fielder, *A Sketch of the Life and Times and Speeches of Joseph E. Brown* (1883) is the only comprehensive biography. Fielder was Brown's contemporary and life-long friend. The inclusion of copious extracts from Brown's messages and other official papers adds greatly to the value of his work. An appendix contains most of Brown's speeches in the Senate. *Confederate Records of the State of Georgia* (1909-10), vols. I–III, give in full Brown's messages to the legislature, and other papers. R. P. Brooks, "Conscription in the Confederate States," *Military Historian and Economist*, vol. I, no. 4, and A. B. Moore, *Conscription and Conflict in the Confederacy* (1924) discuss Brown's relations with the Confederate authorities. C. M. Thompson, *Reconstruction in Ga.* (1915) is a detailed critical study of the Reconstruction period.]

R. P. B—s.

BROWN, JOSEPH ROGERS (Jan. 26, 1810–July 23, 1876), inventor, manufacturer, was the eldest son of David and Patience (Rogers) Brown. He was born in Warren, R. I., where his father was modestly established as a manufacturer and dealer in clocks, watches, jewelry, and particularly silverware. Brown, as a youth, obtained the limited education which the district school afforded and at the same time, after school and during summer vacations, assisted his father in the conduct of the manufactory. When barely seventeen years old he left home to learn the general machinist's trade in Valley Falls, R. I. Within three months he was entrusted with the making of the finest and most important parts of cotton machinery. After a second short term with another manufacturer, in 1829 he joined his father who was then established at Pawtucket, R. I., in the manufacture of tower clocks. The construction and installation of clocks in churches of towns both in Rhode Island and Massachusetts kept Brown busy for the next two years, but, upon reaching his majority, he went into business for himself in Pawtucket, manufacturing lathes and small tools for machinists. After conducting this business in a modest way for two years he rejoined his father in Providence as partner, to engage in the manufacture of watches, clocks, and surveying and mathematical instruments. For eight years father and son continued in their chosen profession and when the elder Brown retired in 1841 the son continued alone for twelve years. The highest degree of mechanical accuracy and perfection seems to have been their goal, as evidenced by the tower clocks built by them and still in use. This same incentive led the younger Brown early in his career to design a linear dividing engine which he finally perfected and built in 1850. It was, so far as is known, the first automatic machine for graduating rules in the United States and is, together with two more built in 1854 and 1859, in use to-day, meeting all modern requirements for accuracy. Following the graduating machine, Brown brought out in 1851 the vernier caliper reading to thousandths of an inch, applied the vernier to protractors in 1852, and introduced the micrometer caliper in 1867. By 1853 Brown's business had grown to the point of employing fourteen persons, and it was then that Lucian Sharpe was taken into partnership and the firm became J. R. Brown & Sharpe. Fifteen years later they incorporated under the name of Brown & Sharpe Manufacturing Company. In 1855 Brown invented a precision gear cutter to make clock gears and to supply his jobbing customers with gears. The machine was capable not only of producing accurate gears but also of drilling index plates and doing circular graduating. Several of them were built and sold and one is still preserved for its historic significance. The introduction of these several precision tools and their acceptance both in this country and abroad, coupled with a contract in 1861 to make Wilcox & Gibbs sewing machines, marked a turning point in Brown's life in that he stopped making clocks and gave his whole time and thought to his manufacturing interests and the development of machine tools. The Civil War proved a stimulus to this development because of ordnance requirements. Thus Brown in 1861 designed and built a turret screw machine for a company manufacturing muskets. He also invented and built during this and the following year a universal milling machine which embodied such important advantages in all types of manufacturing that the demand taxed to the limit the facilities of his plant. Ten machines were sold in 1862 and seventeen were made for as many gun factories during the remaining three years of the war. By 1870 twenty machines had been distributed abroad into twelve different countries. For this invention Brown received Patent No. 46,621 on Feb. 21, 1865, and so far as is known, it was always respected. Brown's greatest achievement, probably, was the invention of the universal grinding machine, Patent No. 187,770, Feb. 27, 1877, issued after his death. In this he introduced an entirely new conception of manufacturing procedure in that articles could be hardened first and then ground with the utmost accuracy and the least waste. This is the universal practise to-day in all modern manufacturing and tool plants. It was the result of over ten years' constant thought and experimenting, beginning about the time he started making sewing machines and ending just before his death. It was also during this most productive period in Brown's career, namely, 1860 to 1870, that he invented the formed gear cutter which could be sharpened on its face without changing its form. This improvement on earlier gear cutters had a marked influence in the general adoption by manufacturers of the involute form for cut gearing as well as for the use of diametral pitch. Brown had always the respect and love of his employees. He had a contagious enthusiasm about his inventions which was shared by all of his associates and his whole-souled affection for each new mechanism was most genuine. His death was very unexpected, occurring at Isles of Shoals, N. H., while he was taking a short vacation.

In 1837 Brown was married to Caroline B. Niles, who died in 1851; in 1852 he was married to Jane Frances Mowray, who with one daughter survived him.

[J. W. Roe, *Eng. and Am. Tool Builders* (1916); Van Slyke, *Representatives of New England* (Boston, 1879); *Sci. Am.*, 1855; *Representative Men and Old Families of R. I.* (1908); *Machinery*, July 1910; *Am. Machinist*, Jan. 5, 1911; Patent Office Records.]

C. W. M.

BROWN, MATHER (Oct. 7, 1761–May 25, 1831), portrait painter, was a son of Gawen Brown, clock-maker, and Elizabeth (Byles) Brown, a daughter of Rev. Mather Byles of Boston [*q.v.*]. He was descended on his mother's side from Cotton Mather, Increase Mather, and John Cotton. His mother dying in his infancy, the boy was brought up by his aunts, the Misses Mary and Catharine Byles, for whom he had a life-long affection. He had lessons in painting from his Aunt Mary, an amateur, and from Gilbert Stuart, of whom he wrote, Aug. 22, 1817, "I wish to know particularly how Mr. Stewart goes on. He was the first person who learnt me to draw at about 12 years of age at Boston." In 1777 he painted miniatures and sold wine in a trip extending through Worcester and Springfield to Peekskill, whence he wrote to his aunts, "The Yankeys are going to Philadelphia; I believe I shall follow them." He returned, however, to Boston and with money earned from his miniatures he went in 1780 to Paris, carrying letters of introduction from Byles to Benjamin Franklin and Copley, the latter already in London. In 1781 Brown became a pupil of West, making good progress and influential friends. He wrote, in 1783: "I have exhibited four Pictures at the Exhibition (Royal Academy). The King and Queen were to see it yesterday. . . . I spent three weeks at Windsor where I often hunted with the King, and I have a bow from him."

Brown rented (1784) a house, 20 Cavendish Square, and set up as portrait painter. He was styled, perhaps originally self-styled, "Historical Painter to His Majesty and the Duke of York." Among his portraits of members of the royal family was the very fine full length of the Prince of Wales, later George IV, now at Buckingham Palace. His most important American portraits are of this period, as of Presidents John Adams and Thomas Jefferson; of Charles Bulfinch, Sir William Pepperell, and Thomas Paine. In 1784 he designed two historical pieces for a new church in the Strand. His "Marquis Cornwallis Receiving as Hostages the Sons of Tippo Sahib" was exhibited, admired, and engraved. He was among those invited to contribute paintings for the Boydell Shakespeare Gallery.

Despite a large practise Brown found his fashionable establishment too expensive. He wrote in 1801: "Every possible exertion which human Industry could do, I have done; and I have adopted the greatest Prudence in my Affairs, and yet have scarcely been able to live." He never married. He failed to inherit, as he had expected to do, a considerable fortune from his father in Boston. In 1809, his lease having expired, he gave up his London studio. He painted for thirteen years at Manchester, Liverpool, and other provincial towns whence he wrote letters vividly descriptive of depressed conditions in the Napo-

leonic era. At the age of fifty he painted, to send home to his aunts, the excellent self-portrait formerly owned by Frederick L. Gay and now in the possession of the American Antiquarian Society, Worcester, Mass. From July 20, 1824, Brown's letters were again dated from London, 23 Newman St., where, living upon a small annuity, he continued to paint industriously and to exhibit regularly at the Royal Academy. He was much interested in politics and in the Church of England. He was taken suddenly ill while visiting an art exhibition, dying soon afterward, May 25, 1831. He was buried at St. John's Wood, Marylebone.

Mather Brown is well represented in the royal collections, in the National Portrait Gallery, London, and in several American collections. Interest in Brown as painter and person has notably revived in the present century, and the sterling qualities of his art are now better appreciated than at any time since his death. Those familiar with his unpublished correspondence resent the imputation of "imbecility," into which he has been said to have fallen in old age. His later letters reveal a disappointed but not embittered man of keen mentality, always industrious, courteous, and intensely interested in professional, political, and religious affairs.

[Letter-books of Mary and Catharine Byles (transcripts in Mass. Hist. Soc. Lib. of originals at Halifax, N. S.); F. W. Coburn, "Mather Brown," *Art in America*, Aug. 1923; Wm. Dunlap, *Hist of the Rise and Progress of the Arts of Design in the U. S.*, ed. by Frank W. Bayley and Chas. E. Goodspeed (1918).]

F. W. C.

BROWN, MORRIS (Feb. 12, 1770–May 9, 1849), bishop of the African Methodist Episcopal Church, was born in that unusual circle commonly referred to as the "free people of color" in Charleston, S. C. Whereas negroes in other parts of the state were handicapped by various restrictions looking toward rigid slave control, this particular group in the largest city of the state had such close relations with the aristocratic whites with the most of whom they were connected by ties of blood, that they were, legally or actually, exempted from such restrictions. As these free people of color were always permitted to maintain schools and churches for their uplift, Morris Brown acquired what was considered a good education for that day. Early converted in the African Methodist Episcopal Church, and being free, too, he secured a license to preach as soon as he professed religion. He was ordained deacon in 1817 and elder the next year, became a traveling minister, and exercised much influence in and around Charleston. In his work as a preacher, however, he soon faced obstacles. Although free himself he could not forget those of his race who were enslaved. He did for their uplift all that the custom of the times permitted a freeman to do for the oppressed, and occasionally he went beyond the limit set by law and public opinion. He was once imprisoned for manifesting too much sympathy for slaves. His career as a preacher in Charleston was abruptly brought to a close when the Denmark Vesey Insurrection broke out there in 1822. This plan to liberate the slaves of South Carolina by killing off the whites remaining in the city, while the majority of the aristocrats were away at summer resorts, so startled the authorities that almost any negro of influence among his people was suspected of being implicated in the plot. An investigation showed that in the freedom of the African Methodist Episcopal Church, which was an organization conducted independently of the whites, there was offered an opportunity for fomenting such plots as that of this projected uprising; although, in spite of the connection of some members with it, there was no evidence that the church had officially instigated this plot. Coming under the ban, however, and subjected to unusual persecution, suspected free negroes had to take measures for saving their lives. Morris Brown escaped, and finally reached Philadelphia in 1823. There he was not exactly a stranger, having been north before to attend conferences of the church and having made a favorable impression upon his co-workers. He quickly took rank as a leader in every movement of concern to negroes. In the decline of Bishop Allen, who was then becoming incapacitated for the strenuous services which had characterized the first years of his life, Brown rose to the actual leadership of his church. Recognizing his services, the African Methodist Episcopal Conference of 1828 elevated him to the episcopate. Upon him, therefore, fell the important task of carrying forward the expansion of this church. He had to travel in various parts of the country where the body which he represented was unknown and was not welcomed. Despite these handicaps, however, he prosecuted the work with great success, and attained such control that when he became the sole bishop of the church, after the death of Bishop Allen in 1831, the denomination suffered no diminution of interest or loss of prestige. Under Brown the influence of the church was extended to states which had not hitherto been touched, and fields already invaded were evangelized more intensively. To administer the affairs of his ever-growing constituency, it was necessary to associate with him Bishop Edward Waters in 1836.

[R. R. Wright, Jr., *Centennial Encyc. of the A. M. E. Ch.* (1916), pp. 47–48; Daniel A. Payne, *Recollections of Seventy Years* (1888), pp. 64, 73–74, 76–77, 80; A. W. Wayman, *Cyc. of African Methodism* (1882), pp. 2–3. For date of birth see obituary by Bishop Daniel A. Payne in the *Pub. Ledger* (Phila.), May 12, 1849.]
C. G. W.

BROWN, MOSES (Sept. 12/23, 1738–Sept. 7, 1836), manufacturer and philanthropist, was born in Providence, R. I., the youngest of the four distinguished sons of James and Hope (Power) Brown, the others being Nicholas, John, and Joseph [*qq.v.*]. James Brown died in 1739, leaving his boys to be brought up by their mother, a woman "of rare force of mind and character." At thirteen, Moses left school and went to live with his uncle, Obadiah Brown, part of whose fortune he inherited. In 1763 he was admitted to the firm of Nicholas Brown & Company, established by his brothers, but retired in 1773. In 1764 he married his cousin, Anna Brown, by whom he had three children,— Sarah, Obadiah [*q.v.*], and a daughter who did not survive infancy. Mrs. Brown's death in 1773 was a crushing blow to her husband, temporarily turning his mind away from worldly matters. A year later he became a Quaker, freed his slaves, and helped to start the Rhode Island Abolition Society. After the Revolutionary War, he was one of the first in this country to become interested in cotton manufacturing and in 1789 he purchased a carding machine, which he set up under the management of his son-in-law, William Almy, and a young relative, Smith Brown, the firm name being Brown & Almy. Having made some experiments with a jenney and spinning frame which operated by hand, in the manner of Arkwright's famous invention, Moses Brown induced Samuel Slater [*q.v.*], one of Arkwright's men, to come to America, writing him (Dec. 12, 1789), "Come and work our machines, and have the credit as well as advantage of perfecting the first water mill in America." Slater evaded the stringent British laws and came to Rhode Island, where, under Brown's patronage, he built from memory, without plans or drawings, a frame of twenty-four spindles and put it into sucessful operation. The venture was prosperous from the beginning, and added to Brown's already large estate. Although he was troubled with attacks of vertigo, Brown was able, by living quietly, to keep his health, and all his senses were alert up to the time of his death near the close of his ninety-eighth year. In 1779 he married Mary Olney, who died in 1798, and a year later he took a third wife, Phœbe Lockwood, who died in 1808.

In 1770 Moses Brown took the leading step toward moving Rhode Island College (founded at Warren, R. I., in 1764) to Providence, where it was later, because of the benefactions of his family, renamed Brown University; and in 1771 he gave $1,000 to its endowment. In 1780 when subscriptions were solicited for a Friends' School, he contributed £115 and, when it was opened at Portsmouth, R. I., in 1784 under Isaac Lawton as principal, he became its treasurer. Owing to lack of funds, the school was discontinued four years later, but it was reopened in 1819 in Providence, its property having accumulated in Brown's hands to $9,300. Brown provided regularly for the school from that time on, and gave it in his will the sum of $15,000, with some land and his library. It is to-day known as the Moses Brown School.

Brown was a member of the Rhode Island General Assembly from 1764 to 1771, and was the founder of many societies, including the Providence Athenæum Library, the Rhode Island Bible Society, and the Rhode Island Peace Society. His punctuality in business became proverbial. Although he was retiring by nature, he had many interests and left behind him an enormous private correspondence. He was a man of sound judgment, unblemished integrity, and liberal spirit.

[The best and fullest account of Brown's career is a sketch read, Oct. 18, 1892, before the R. I. Hist. Soc. by Augustine Jones, principal of the Friends' School, and later printed under the title *Moses Brown; His Life and Services.* See also J. N. Arnold, *Vital Record of R. I.,* vol. II (1892), pt. I, p. 214, and obituary in *Mfrs. and Farmers Jour.* (Providence), Sept. 7, 1836.]
C. M. F.

BROWN, MOSES (Oct. 2, 1742–Feb. 9, 1827), merchant, philanthropist, was the youngest of thirteen children of Joseph, Jr., and Abigail (Pearson) Brown, of Newbury, Mass. As a mere boy he was apprenticed to a chaise-maker, and, on reaching manhood, started in business himself as a carriage manufacturer. Eventually he turned to commerce, developing a large foreign and domestic trade, especially in sugar and molasses with the West Indies. He increased his investments until he was the owner of several wharves, warehouses, and distilleries, as well as of extensive real estate in Newburyport and vicinity. In 1772 Brown married Mary Hall, of Newburyport, who died, without issue, in 1778. Eight years later he took a second wife, Mary White of Haverhill, who had a large amount of property. She died, Aug. 11, 1821. When Brown died, in Newburyport, he was survived by one daughter, Mrs. William B. Bannister, and no one of his direct descendants is living to-day.

At the time in the early nineteenth century when a project for a Calvinistic theological institution in New England was being discussed as a means of counteracting the strongly Unitarian influence of Harvard College, Moses Brown, encouraged by his wife and persuaded by his pastor, Dr. Samuel Spring, gave, in 1808, $10,000 to the "Associate Foundation" of Andover Theological Seminary, the other donors being William Bartlet of Newburyport, and John Norris of Salem. When the Seminary was opened, Brown contributed $1,000 to start a library, and in 1819, after a period of prosperity in mercantile affairs, turned over an additional sum of $25,000 to establish a professorship of ecclesiastical history. In 1843, Brown's granddaughter, Sarah (Bannister) Hale, who had inherited much of his property, completed the family benefactions to the Seminary by providing a dwelling house on Andover Hill for the Brown professor. In his will Moses Brown left to the inhabitants of Newburyport the sum of $6,000, to be kept at interest until it reached $15,000, when the capital was to be used "as a fund for the use and support of a grammar school in said town forever."

Moses Brown was a thin wiry person, of vigorous constitution and energetic manner. Through force of character and the rectitude of his life he won the respect of his neighbors and associates. A methodical and progressive business man, he organized many enterprises and kept alert and active to the end of his career. Through the years of his financial success he remembered his own less prosperous young manhood and never refused aid to those who had not been so fortunate as he. He gave cheerfully and liberally to all deserving causes; indeed he was described by a fellow townsman as "always engaged in doing good." He was equally remarkable for his modesty, and he never told others of his charities. It was said of him at his funeral, "He pursued business as though the gains therefrom were not for his use alone, and he distributed them as a trust for the good of others."

[John J. Currier, *Ould Newbury: Hist. & Biog. Sketches* (1896); Leonard Woods, *Hist. of Andover Theol. Seminary* (1884).]
C. M. F.

BROWN, NEILL SMITH (Apr. 18, 1810– Jan. 30, 1886), lawyer, politician, was born near Pulaski, Giles County, Tenn., and died in Nashville, Tenn. His grandfather, Angus Brown, came from Scotland to America in time to fight under Francis Marion in the American Revolution. His parents, Duncan Brown and Margaret (Smith) Brown, emigrated from Robertson County, N. C., to Tennessee, in 1809. The Browns in America were small farmers and strict Presbyterians. Neill S. Brown began work on a arm at the age of seven years and with his small savings managed to attend school now and then, but before his seventeenth year he had learned little more than reading and writing. He was then able to spend two sessions at the Manual Labor Academy in Maury County. Securing funds for further education by teaching school, he next studied law with Chancellor Bramlett, was admitted to the bar in 1834, and began the practise of law in Pulaski. A year later he moved to Texas, opening a law office in Matagordo, but, disappointed, soon returned to Tennessee, and is next heard of when he enlisted in Robert Armstrong's brigade of Tennessee troops for service against the Seminoles in Florida.

Joining the anti-Jackson movement, which was led by those in the state whom Jackson had discomfited in politics, Brown was nominated elector on the Whig presidential ticket in 1836, and in 1837 was elected to the state legislature, where he was the youngest member. Defeated for Congress in 1843 by Aaron V. Brown, Democrat, in the so-called "Brown" race, he was elected governor over the same competitor in 1847, the youngest governor of the state up to that time. Again defeated by a Democrat in 1849, he was sent as minister to Russia in 1850. After three years he returned to the state legislature as speaker of the House. The Whig party of the state was now disintegrating, as its old anti-Jackson leaders disappeared, and Brown, though taking no active part in politics after 1856, allied himself with the Democrats. Though opposed to secession, he took office in 1861 under the state government of Tennessee as a member of the military and financial board. When the Union forces captured Nashville in 1862, he was imprisoned for a time by Andrew Johnson, the military governor. During the remainder of the conflict he was neutral in action but with Southern sympathies.

Brown was "one of the most amiable characters and brightest minds in Tennessee history," but failed of opportunity to round out his public career on account of the decline of the Whig party after he reached the age of forty. His administration as governor was not notable and his best work, which extended throughout his life, was his unvarying and constructive support of the public schools before and after the Civil War. He aided in securing grants from the Peabody fund, upon which Peabody College was later established. He was a successful lawyer for fifty years except for the frequent diversions into politics which he made in early life. His fame and influence were due in large part to effective oratory. He said of himself: "I had a native ambition to rise from obscurity and to make myself useful in the world, to shine and be distinguished. . . . My poverty pushed me on. I started life on nothing, was as poor as any man in Tennessee who ever became at all known." His last public service was as delegate to the Tennessee constitutional convention of 1870, of which his younger brother, John Calvin Brown [q.v.], was president. Brown married in 1839 Mary Ann Trimble, daughter of Judge James Trimble of Nashville, who was a man of position and influence and opposed to secession. There were eight children.

[John Allison, *Notable Men of Tenn.* (1905); J. T. Moore, *Tennessee, The Volunteer State* (1923); W. W. Clayton, *Hist. of Davidson County, Tenn.* (1880); H. S. Foote, *Bench and Bar of the South and Southwest* (1876); Joshua W. Caldwell, *Sketches of the Bench and Bar of Tenn.* (1898); W. S. Speer, *Sketches of Prominent Tennesseeans* (1888); obituary in the *Daily American* (Nashville), Jan. 31, 1886; executive and legislative docs. in the State Capitol.]   W. L. F.

BROWN, NICHOLAS (July 28, 1729 o.s.– May 29, 1791), merchant, was the son of James and Hope (Power) Brown and the eldest of the four brothers (Nicholas, Joseph [q.v.], John [q.v.], and Moses [q.v.]) who became in the closing years of the eighteenth century the leading merchants and citizens of Rhode Island. James Brown and his brother Obadiah had established a general store in Providence, and in 1739 controlled the movements of eight vessels in the West India trade. In that year James Brown died. The business was carried on by Obadiah, at first alone, and then, as they grew up, with four of the sons of James as assistants and partners under the firm name Obadiah Brown & Company. At the death of the uncle in 1762, the four brothers continued the business as Nicholas Brown & Company. The firm attained international standing during the years between 1762 and the Revolution. Its ventures were extended from the West Indies to London, Marseilles, Nantes, Copenhagen, and Hamburg, while at home its members were active in the development of local manufactures. It is credited with having brought about the change in the spermaceti candle business from the household to the factory stage of development by the gathering of all who had been previously working at the manufacture in their homes into a building erected for the purpose on the outskirts of Providence. When the increase in the business there and in Newport brought about a scarcity of head matter and spermaceti oil, a competitive struggle for this choice product of the whale ensued between the Brown interests and the wealthy Jewish manufacturers of Newport. Useless competition was avoided by the formation in 1761 of a "union" or United Company of spermaceti-candle manufacturers of Providence and New-port, with associates in Boston and Philadelphia. In 1763 the combination was renewed and the Browns were the leading members of the organization. The agreements fixed the price of purchase, provided for preventing the establishment of new manufactories, and designated and limited the dealers in oil to be patronized by the associates. These documents are said to record the earliest monopolistic combination made in America. The effort on the part of the brothers in or soon after 1764 to establish an iron manufactory in Rhode Island to utilize the ore dug from the pits at Cranston resulted in the buildings of the "Furnace Hope" at Scituate, where until the last decade of the century a successful industry was carried on by the firm and certain associates. Pig iron and articles for their trading cargoes were made at the furnace, and in the Revolution cannon of all sizes up to eighteen pounders were cast for the Congress. The firm was interested in distilling; and in the French Wars and later, Nicholas and John Brown were large shareholders in various successful privateering ventures. Though the Newport merchants who were their contemporaries were successful in the Guinea trade, yet the interest of Nicholas Brown & Company in the "triangular voyage" seems to have been only occasional in its character. During the non-importation proceedings in 1769 Nicholas Brown was prominently engaged in the American interest; in the Revolution he served a secret committee of Congress by using his ships and foreign connections for the importation of clothing and munitions for the soldiers; in the struggle in Rhode Island over the Constitution he exercised a strong influence in favor of adoption. In 1767 it was the personal contributions and the guarantee of the pledges of their fellow citizens by Nicholas and his brother Joseph that determined Providence as the location of Rhode Island College, afterward, because of the benefactions of a later member of the family, to be known as Brown University. It was under the oversight of the firm that the first college building, now University Hall, was erected on a piece of ground formerly a Brown family possession. Nicholas was a prominent benefactor, too, of the Baptist Society of Providence.

He married first, on May 2, 1762, Rhoda Jenckes, who died Dec. 16, 1783, survived by two of their ten children, Nicholas [q.v.] and Hope, who married Thomas Poynton Ives. Brown maried second, on Sept. 9, 1785, Avis Binney. He died May 29, 1791. His tombstone records the otherwise forgotten fact that "His stature was large; his personal appearance manly and noble."

[*The Chad Browne Memorial* (1888), comp. by Abby Isabel Brown Bulkley; Reuben A. Guild, *Hist. of Brown Univ.* (1867); Gertrude S. Kimball, *Providence in Colonial Times* (1912); Wm. R. Staples, *Annals of the Town of Providence* (1843); "Commerce of R. I., 1726–1800," in *Colls. Mass. Hist. Soc.*, ser. 7, vols. IX, X (1914–15); Irving B. Richman, *Rhode Island* (1905); Wm. B. Weeden, *Early R. I.* (1910).]   L. C. W.

BROWN, NICHOLAS (Apr. 4, 1769–Sept. 27, 1841), merchant, philanthropist, was the son of the preceding Nicholas Brown and his wife, Rhoda Jenckes. After graduating in 1786 from Rhode Island College, which afterward assumed his name, he went into his father's counting house, and three years later when he became of age the firm was reorganized with the father and son and George Benson as Brown & Benson. In 1792, after the death of the elder Nicholas Brown, the latter's son-in-law, Thomas Poynton Ives, was admitted into the firm, and his name added to that of the partners. Four years later, when Benson withdrew, the younger men, trading as Brown & Ives, the name under which part of the family interests are still managed, set out upon a career notable in the history of American commercial activity. The earlier energies of the firm were devoted at first to the development of the East India and China trade, just then becoming an important element in American commercial life. Seven years after John Brown, uncle of Nicholas, had inaugurated in 1787 a trade between East India and Providence by sending the *General Washington* with a cargo to India, the firm of Brown, Benson & Ives built the *John Jay* and launched her in the eastern trade. Thereafter until the sale of their last ship, the *Hanover*, in 1838, many vessels, the *Ann and Hope*, the *Rising Sun*, and others, kept the name of Brown & Ives constantly on the distant seas, and this in spite of depredation by English and French, of embargo by our own government, and of shipwreck, and a failing trade. With the foresight and caution that characterized his father and himself, Nicholas Brown waited until the manufacturing of cotton had been well established by his uncle Moses Brown [q.v.] before his firm bought in 1804 its first water rights on the Blackstone River. When the Embargo of 1812 put a temporary check on shipping, the firm was found well established in the cotton manufactory and in control of a large part of the Blackstone River water power. With the formation of the Lonsdale Company in the thirties, the character of the firm's business had definitely changed to its present interest. With a similar caution, and a like reward, Brown &

Ives did not at once follow John Brown in his purchase, late in the eighteenth century, of lands in western New York, but ten years afterward they invested a part of their surplus in large tracts on the Ohio. In the years following the Civil War the Ohio farm-land holdings of the successors of the firm attained great value as urban properties in growing middle-western cities.

The relations of Nicholas Brown with the University which bears his name were not simply those of a wealthy benefactor to a chosen object of charity, for family pride and personal affection engaged his interest. He was educated in the building erected for the old Rhode Island College by the efforts of his father and his uncles; he was a trustee by the year 1791, and treasurer from 1796 until 1825. In 1804 he gave $5,000 for the endowment of a professorship of oratory and belles lettres, a gift that resulted in the change of the college's name to Brown University as a recognition of the beneficence of himself and of other members of his family. In 1823 he erected as a gift from him and his nephews, Hope College, named after his sister, Hope (Brown) Ives, and in 1834 he built Manning Hall. Gifts to the library and the laboratories and to other building funds brought his benefactions to the college to the amount of $160,000. Great in amount for those days, his gifts came furthermore at a time in the life of the college that determined its future as an important American educational institution. Nicholas Brown was for many years a member of the Rhode Island General Assembly. He was one of the founders of the Providence Athenæum, and a generous contributor to the Baptist Society and to other local charities. The $30,000 left in his will for the care of the insane resulted in the building and maintenance of the Butler Hospital for the Insane, in the management of which his descendants have continuously had an active part. In him was found in special degree the mingling of shrewd business sense, respect for things of the mind and spirit, and sense of responsibility to his community that have always characterized this family of merchants and philanthropists. President Wayland said of him that his success "testified that boldness of enterprise may be harmoniously united with vigorous and deliberate judgment." In the same *Discourse,* Wayland observes: "In his ample brow and well-developed forehead, you could not but observe the marks of a vigorous and expansive intellect; while his mouth indicated a spirit tenderly alive to human suffering, and habitually occupied in the contemplation

of deeds of compassion." Brown married twice: first on Nov. 3, 1791, Ann, daughter of John Carter, long the leading printer of Providence; and second, Mary Bowen Stelle on July 22, 1801. The younger of the two sons by the first wife was John Carter Brown [*q.v.*]

[Francis Wayland, *A Discourse in Commemoration of the Life and Character of the Hon. Nicholas Brown* (1841); Abby Isabel Brown Bulkley, *The Chad Browne Memorial* (1888); obituary in the *Providence Journal,* Oct, 4, 1841.]　　　　　　　　　L. C. W.

BROWN, OBADIAH (July 15, 1771–Oct. 15, 1822), merchant and philanthropist, was born in Providence, R. I., the only son of Moses Brown [*q.v.*] and Anna (Brown) Brown. He was sent by his father, who had become a Quaker in 1774, to the Friends' Yearly Meeting School at Portsmouth, R. I., in 1787, but this institution closed in October 1788, because of lack of funds, after four years of existence. Obadiah had almost no other formal schooling, but went directly into business.

About this time his father formed a firm, consisting of William Almy (Moses Brown's son-in-law), together with Slater and Smith Brown, whose place was taken in 1792 by Obadiah Brown. This company, known later as Brown & Almy, produced the first pure cotton goods made in the United States, all the previous warps having been linen. The Brown mills, located at Pawtucket, were immediately prosperous, and the Embargo Act of 1808 furnished an additional stimulus to manufacturing, whereby Obadiah Brown and his partners accumulated a considerable fortune. In 1798, Brown married Dorcas Hadwen, daughter of John and Elizabeth Hadwen, of Newport.

When, early in the nineteenth century, it was proposed to reëstablish the Friends' Yearly Meeting School, the Brown family took up the project. In 1814 Moses Brown offered a suitable tract of land, located in Providence, and when, in 1815, subscriptions were solicited, Obadiah Brown contributed $2,000 for construction, $500 for furnishings, and $1,000 annually for five years toward the school's maintenance. Obadiah Brown and William Almy took the contract for erecting the main hall, and the former drove every day in his chaise to superintend the laborers. In 1817, when the available funds were exhausted, he and Almy agreed to provide half of the additional $7,500 required, on condition that other Friends supply the remainder. The stipulation was met, and the building was completed. After the school was formally opened in 1819, Obadiah and his wife, Dorcas, regularly attended meeting there, and it became his custom to present each scholar at graduation with a book as a token of his personal regard. Although his father was actually treasurer of the school, Obadiah watched over its affairs with a zealous care as a valuable member of the school committee. When he died in 1822, after a brief illness, he left to the school the sum of $100,000, the largest single bequest made to any institution of learning in the United States up to that time, and also a fine library of books and maps. The will, signed in 1814, was drawn up in his father's handwriting. The school thus founded has grown and prospered, and in 1904 was renamed the Moses Brown School. The original building, since much enlarged, still stands as the central feature of the campus.

Personally Brown was gracious and urbane, with an unostentatious and conciliating manner. When decisions were made, he was firm in standing by them, but he instinctively tried to avoid disputes. He was a patient and industrious man, with much public spirit and a genius for wise philanthropy.

[See *Moses Brown: a Sketch by Augustine Jones, Read before the R. I. Hist. Soc., Oct. 18, 1892*; R. W. Kelsey, *Centennial Hist. of the Moses Brown School, 1819–1919* (1919). There are interesting manuscript letters of Obadiah Brown in possession of the R. I. Hist. Soc. For date of birth see J. N. Arnold, *Vital Record of R. I.*, vol. II (1892), pt. I, p. 214.] C.M.F.

BROWN, OLYMPIA (Jan. 5, 1835–Oct. 23, 1926), feminist, was born in a log cabin at Prairie Ronde, Mich. Her parents, Asa B. and Lephia Brown, were New Englanders, having moved to Michigan from Plymouth, Mass. In later life, Miss Brown stated that from early childhood she remembered her mother taking the unpopular view of public questions and it was from her that she received her first ideas of equal rights for men and women. Olympia desired to attend the University of Michigan, but it would not admit women. She therefore entered Antioch College, at Yellow Springs, Ohio, from which she received a degree of bachelor of arts in 1860. While there she decided that the ministry held golden opportunities for women, so she enrolled in the Theological School of St. Lawrence University, at Canton, N. Y. She was graduated in 1863 and ordained to the ministry of the Universalist Church in the same year, the first woman in America to be ordained to the ministry of a regularly constituted ecclesiastical body. She served pastorates at Weymouth, Mass., 1864, Bridgeport, Conn., 1869, and subsequently at Racine, Mukwonago, Neenah, and Columbus, Wis. In 1866 she met Susan B. Anthony at an Equal Rights meeting in New York City and from a passive believer in woman's rights, became an ardent advocate. The following year, when a Republican legislature in Kansas submitted to

the vote of the people of that state a proposition to amend the state constitution by striking out the word "male," suffrage leaders selected her to campaign for the cause in Kansas. It was the first time that the men of any state had been asked to vote on such a measure. So thorough was the campaign that, notwithstanding the fact that the Republican party, which had fathered the amendment, refused to aid in its support and even sent out circulars opposing it, the election showed one-third of the votes in its favor. When the campaign was over Miss Brown returned to preaching in New England, but continued actively interested in woman suffrage and all matters affecting women workers and the homes of the nation. In April 1873 she married John Henry Willis, a printer and newspaper-man. By agreement with her husband she retained her maiden name and in all her public work was known as the Rev. Olympia Brown. She became president of the Wisconsin Woman's Suffrage Association in 1887 and continued as such for thirty years. When her husband died in 1893, she became manager of his daily and weekly newspaper and job printing office in Racine, Wis. For many years she traveled from state to state lecturing and campaigning for woman suffrage until at last equal suffrage was made nation-wide by the Federal Constitution. In 1914 she decided to make Baltimore her home and live with her daughter, Gwendolen B. Willis. In the presidential campaign of 1924, she was an ardent supporter of Robert M. La Follette. In 1925, at the age of ninety, she accompanied her daughter on a trip to France and Italy. When she died in Baltimore, an editorial in the Baltimore *Sun* said of her, "Perhaps no phase of her life better exemplified her vitality and intellectual independence than the mental discomfort she succeeded in arousing, between her eightieth and ninetieth birthdays, among conservatively-minded Baltimoreans." She published a book in 1911, entitled *Acquaintances, Old and New, Among Reformers*, which is her own account of her life and activities with many references to her contemporaries. She also published a memorial sketch of Clara B. Colby, in 1917, called *Democratic Ideals*.

[A biography of Olympia Brown is found in the *Hist. of Woman Suffrage*, by Elizabeth Cady Stanton, Matilda Gage, and Susan B. Anthony, vol. III (1886); see also *Who's Who in America*, 1914–15; *Equal Rights*, Oct. 30, 1926; the *Sun* (Baltimore), Oct. 24, 25, 1926.]
M.S.

BROWN, PHŒBE HINSDALE (May 1, 1783–Aug. 10, 1861), an early American hymn writer, though of New England ancestry, was born in Canaan, N. Y., the seventh and youngest child of George and Phœbe (Allen) Hinsdale. It is commonly stated that when two years old she was left an orphan, but the sketch of her life in the *Hinsdale Genealogy* (1906), based on an autobiography then in the hands of her grand-daughter, gives the date of her father's death as Mar. 20, 1784, and that of her mother as Apr. 17, 1791. She was early taken in charge by a pious grandmother, Mrs. Allen, who gave her religious instruction, and before she was nine, it is said, she had read the Bible through three times. From her ninth till her eighteenth year she lived with her married sister, Chloe Noyes. The latter's husband proved a hard taskmaster, and Phœbe was deprived of instruction, forbidden books, and made to work like a slave. Later she got a few months' schooling, and on June 1, 1805, at Canaan, N. Y., she married Timothy Hill Brown, a carpenter and painter. They removed to Connecticut where they lived at East Windsor for eight years, then at Ellington for five. From 1818 until Mr. Brown's death in 1853, their home was at Monson, Mass. Both became members of the Congregational Church. Four children were born to them, one of them, Samuel Robbins Brown [q.v.], destined to become a well-known educator and missionary. Mrs. Brown's life was one of comparative poverty and some hardship. Her deep religious devotion found expression in simple but sincere verse. At Ellington she was accustomed at each day's close to make her escape from household cares and repair to a quiet spot for meditation. Unkind interpretations of this habit led her to write "Apology for My Twilight Rambles Addressed to a Lady." From this was taken one of her best known hymns, still sung in the churches, "I Love to Steal Awhile Away." It appeared with three others by her in Nettleton's *Village Hymns* (1824). In 1853 it was incorporated in the *Leeds Hymn Book*, and thus came into use in England. Two additional hymns from her pen were published in Hastings's *Spiritual Songs* (1831). Others appeared in *Mother's Hymn Book* (1834), Linsley and Davis, *Select Hymns* (1836), and *Parish Hymns* (1843). Some of these have had wide use in this country and abroad. Two now forgotten prose works were also written by her and published in 1836; *The Tree and Its Fruits*, a collection of little homilies, directed against intemperance, gambling, and infidelity; and *The Village School*, describing the religious instruction given by a teacher, and its effects.

[Herbert C. Andrews, *Hinsdale Genealogy, Descendants of Robt. Hinsdale* (1906) ; Sam. W. Duffield, *English Hymns* (1886) ; John Julian, *A Dict. of Hymnology* (1891); Wm. E. Griffis, *A Maker of the New Orient, Samuel Robbins Brown* (1902).]   H. E. S.

BROWN, SAMUEL (Jan. 30, 1769–Jan. 12 1830), physician, was born in a rural section of what is now Rockbridge County, Va., to Rev. John Brown, Presbyterian minister, and Margaret Preston. His education began in the grammar school which his father conducted in addition to his pastoral duties. Later, he attended a seminary conducted by Rev. James Waddell in Louisa County, Va., followed by two years at Dickinson College at Carlisle, Pa., where he graduated in 1789 with the degree of bachelor of arts. He began the study of medicine with his brother-in-law, Dr. Humphrey, at Staunton, Va., later becoming a private pupil of Dr. Rush in Philadelphia. After two years at the University of Edinburgh and a short time at the University of Aberdeen he obtained his degree of doctor of medicine from the latter institution. Returning to America, he began the practise of medicine at Bladensburg, Md., but in 1797 he left to join his brother James [q.v.], who was practising law in Lexington, Ky. He gave up his practise here to follow his brother again, this time to New Orleans, in 1806. In 1809 he married Catherine Percy of Natchez, Miss., and went to live upon a plantation near that city, relinquishing the practise of his profession. The death of his wife a few years later caused him to give up his Natchez home and to establish himself upon a plantation adjacent to that of his brother-in-law, Col. Thomas Percy, near Huntsville, Ala. Here he lived until 1819, devoting himself to the education of his two surviving children. Brown had long had in mind the idea of starting a medical school in his section of the country, and in 1819 he entered into an agreement with Dr. Daniel Drake for the establishment of such a school at Cincinnati. While Drake was obtaining the charter for the Ohio school, however, the trustees of Transylvania University at Lexington offered Brown the chair of theory and practise of medicine in the medical school recently organized there. He accepted this position and held it until 1825 when he resigned and retired to his former home in Alabama. His remaining years were spent largely in travel in America and Europe. He suffered a stroke of apoplexy in 1826 and died from a succeeding stroke at the home of his brother-in-law near Huntsville.

Brown was a man of attractive personality and of unusual scholarship for his time. His portrait shows a round, full, smoothly shaven face, suggesting boundless benevolence. His personality made him a popular practitioner wherever he located. He was, however, a dilettante in medicine as in his other interests. Though he introduced vaccination for smallpox at Lexington as early as 1802, its interest for him lay in its novelty. His lectures were rambling discourses full of interesting even though unrelated facts. He was averse to continued effort and incapable of pursuing any inquiry to its conclusion. His medical writings were sketchy case reports and his few contributions to scientific journals were mere notices of striking or curious phenomena, such as his paper on "Nitre Caves of Kentucky" in the first volume of *Bruce's Journal*. The Kappa Lambda Society of Hippocrates, a society of medical men pledged to professional ideals, was founded by him, and under its auspices, the *North American Medical and Surgical Journal* was started in Philadelphia in 1825. Two treatises often credited to him, *An Inaugural Dissertation on the Bilious Malignant Fever* (1797). and *A Treatise on the Nature, Origin and Progress of the Yellow Fever* (1800), were really written by Dr. Samuel Brown of Boston (1769–1805).

[The sketch of Brown by R. La Roche in Samuel D. Gross, *Lives of Eminent Am. Physicians and Surgeons* (1861), is the undiscriminating eulogy of a warm personal friend. The obituary in the *Western Jour. Medic. and Phys. Sci.*, vol. III (Cincinnati, 1830), and "Dr. Samuel Brown as an Author" by L. P. Yarnell in the *Western Jour. of Medicine and Surgery*, vol. II (Louisville, 1854), give a better idea of Brown's qualities and defects. In the *Ky. Medic. Jour.*, vol. XV (1917) there is a brief sketch of Brown's career.]   J.M.P.

BROWN, SAMUEL GILMAN (Jan. 4, 1813–Nov. 4, 1885), college president, was a descendant on both sides of Calvinist stock, distinguished in the ministerial and educational life of New England. His father was Francis Brown [1784–1820, *q.v.*], Congregational pastor at North Yarmouth, Me., at the time of the son's birth, and later the third president of Dartmouth College. His mother, Elizabeth Gilman, was a woman trained in the sturdiest Puritan traditions. To her, on the untimely death of her husband, fell the bringing up of the seven-year-old boy, the only surviving child.

Brown's boyhood and youth were passed in Hanover, N. H. Here he attended Dartmouth College, graduating in 1831 at the age of eighteen. For the following two years he taught in the high school of Ellington, Conn., and then entered Andover Theological Seminary, acting at the same time as principal of the local Abbot Academy. Following his graduation from Andover in 1837, he devoted two years to travel in Europe and the East. On his return in 1840 he was called to the faculty of Dartmouth, where he taught for twenty-seven consecutive years, occupying successively the chairs of oratory and belles lettres and of intellectual philosophy and political economy. His broad and cultivated taste found expression in many articles and reviews contributed to periodicals, chiefly on literary and biographical topics. His most ambitious undertaking, an edition of *The Works of Rufus Choate, with a Memoir of His Life* (2 vols., 1862), was favorably received (*North American Review*, XCVI, 194–220; *Atlantic Monthly*, XI, 139–142) and remains the standard work on the subject. The *Memoir*, with some additions, was reprinted separately in 1870. Brown married, in February 1846, Mrs. Sarah (Van Vechten) Savage of Schenectady, N. Y. To them were born seven children. In 1867 Brown accepted the invitation to become president of Hamilton College and to fill the related chair of Christian evidences on its faculty. The new president brought scholarly rather than executive gifts to his office, and a winning rather than forceful personality. His conservative administration of fourteen years was unmarked by significant change of educational policy or important development within the college. He relinquished the office in 1881, feeling that the needs of the institution, then in serious financial straits, called for executive qualities which he did not possess. For a few years following his resignation he gave occasional instruction in mental and moral philosophy, first at Dartmouth (1882–83) and then at Bowdoin (1883–85). He died suddenly, in his seventy-third year, at Utica, N. Y., his home since quitting Hamilton, leaving his eldest son Francis [1849–1916, *q.v.*] to carry into the third generation the distinguished ministerial and educational heritage of the family.

Brown's most impressive work was done in the pulpit and on the platform. While he never held a pastorate, he was ordained to the Congregational ministry in 1852, and throughout his career was much in demand as a preacher. As a lecturer, he appeared before the Lowell Institute of Boston in 1859, and was frequently chosen for commemorative orations and for addresses on important occasions. Almost a score of these discourses, separately published, testify to the breadth of his interests and to his command of a graceful and felicitous style. In his well-rounded humanism, gracious and unassuming personality, and high religious purpose, he was representative of the best traditions in American educational life of his time.

[*Memorial of Samuel Gilman Brown* (1886) contains portrait, biographical sketch, memorial addresses, obituary notices, bibliography of publications, etc. See also Arthur Gilman, *The Gilman Family* (1869), and J. K. Lord, *Hist. of Dartmouth Coll. 1815–1909* (1913).]
                                                          F.H.R.

BROWN, SAMUEL ROBBINS (June 16, 1810–June 20, 1880), missionary, educator, was born in East Windsor, Conn., the son of Timothy Hill and Phœbe (Hinsdale) Brown [*q.v.*]. Due in no small part to the religious faith and missionary zeal of his parents, though, he states, they never suggested the course to him, he had from childhood but one plan for the future, namely, "to get a liberal education, to study for the sacred ministry, and then to be a missionary to some heathen people." His preliminary education was received at Monson Academy, Monson, Mass., where after 1818 the Browns resided. His father's income as a carpenter and painter was too meager to afford Samuel a college education, but he succeeded in graduating from Yale in 1832, having supported himself by sawing wood, instructing fellow students in music, and ringing the college bell. For more than three years he taught in the New York Institute for the Deaf and Dumb. An attack of pneumonia led him to go South in 1835, and for two years he studied at Columbia Theological Seminary, Columbia, S. C., and later at Union Seminary, New York. He was accepted by the American Board for appointment to China, but seized an immediate opportunity to go there as a teacher for the Morrison Educational Society. On Oct. 10, 1838, he married Elizabeth, daughter of Rev. Shubael Bartlett of East Windsor, Conn.; on Oct. 14, he was ordained by the Third Presbytery of New York; and on Oct. 17, he began a one hundred and twenty-five days' voyage to Macao.

His life embraced two distinct and influential missionary careers: one in China (1839–47); and one in Japan (1859–79). In both countries he was a pioneer in secular education combined with religious instruction. The school he established for the Morrison Society, and conducted, first at Macao, then at Hong Kong, was the parent of its kind. When forced to return in 1847, owing to his wife's ill health, he brought with him three of his students. Their coming marks the beginning of Chinese education in America. One of them, Yung Wing, was the first Chinese graduate of Yale, and through his influence the Chinese government later sent more than a hundred boys to this country.

In Japan, where he went in 1859 as one of the first three members of the Dutch Reformed Mission, he occupied himself largely with teaching, first at Kanagawa, then at Yokohama. Scores of his students became prominent in the Empire. He was a founder and president of the Asiatic Society of Japan and was also (1874–79) chairman of the committee which translated the New Testament into Japanese, his own contributions being translations of Acts, Philippians, Philemon, and Revelation. He prepared the Canton

Colloquial portion for James Legge's Lexilogus, and also published *Colloquial Japanese* (1863); *Prendergast's Mastery System Adapted to the Japanese* (1875); a translation, published in the *Journal of the North-China Branch of the Royal Asiatic Society* (n.s., vols. II, III, 1865–66), of Arai Hakuseki's *Sei Yo Ki-Bun;* biographies of Yung Wing, Wong Shin, and Wong Fun, in Japanese, intended to stimulate young men in Japan to become benefactors of their country— and a number of articles in the *Chinese Repository.* Ill health compelled him to return to America in 1879, and he died at Monson the following year.

In the interim between his Chinese and his Japanese missions, he contributed to the educational progress of his own country. From 1848 to 1851 he conducted a school in Rome, N. Y., and while pastor of the Reformed Dutch Church, Owasco Outlet, N. Y. (1851–59), he was one of the most active of the founders and directors of Elmira College.

[Wm. E. Griffis, *A Maker of the New Orient* (1902); Edward T. Corwin, *A Manual of the Reformed Church in America* (1902); Evarts B. Greene, *A New Englander in Japan, Daniel Crosby Greene* (1927); Yung Wing, *My Life in China and America* (1909); *Biog. Memoranda Respecting . . . Members of the Class of 1832 in Yale Coll.* (1880), ed. by E. E. Salisbury; *Obit. Record Grads. Yale Coll.,* 2nd ser., 1870–1880.]

H. E. S.

BROWN, SIMON (Nov. 29, 1802–Feb. 26, 1873), agricultural editor, was born in Newburyport, Mass., the son of Nathaniel and Mary (Sleeper) Brown. In 1811 Nathaniel Brown's property was destroyed by fire and he was reduced from comparative wealth to poverty. He moved with his family to a farm near Chester, N. H. It was necessary for the children to help their father on the farm; at the early age of nine Simon received his first training in practical agriculture, and soon developed a keen interest in the work. He attended the common schools for a few weeks each year and for the rest of the year devoted his entire time to farming. While residing on his father's farm he attended Pembroke Academy, at Pembroke, N. H., for six months. This was the extent of his education. In 1818 he entered a printing-office in Concord, N. H., as an apprentice. He worked in this shop for several years and then spent a year traveling in the South studying southern agriculture and observing the relations existing between master and slaves. When he returned in 1826 he settled in Hingham, Mass., and commenced the publication of a newspaper called the *Hingham Gazette.* He was married in 1828 to Ann Caroline French of Chester, N. H. A year afterward he sold his interest in the Hingham paper and returned to Chester where he opened a printing-office and published the *New Hampshire Law Reports.* In 1830 in company with his brother-in-law, B. B. French, he purchased a printing-office and a newspaper called the *New Hampshire Spectator,* in Newport. He remained in Newport for the next five years, then moved to Concord, Mass., and established himself as a book and job-printer. In 1838 he received an appointment in the office of the clerk of the House of Representatives at Washington. Within a short time he was appointed librarian to the House and he kept this position until 1848. He had at last saved enough money to realize a life-long dream, which was to live on a farm of his own. He purchased a small, almost worthless place near Concord, Mass., and went there to live for the rest of his days. While working relentlessly to make the farm successful he found time to publish a paper in Concord called the *Concord Freeman,* for one year. In 1858 he became editor of the *New England Farmer,* an agricultural newspaper published in Boston. At various intervals he wrote articles for other periodicals and government agricultural reports. For several years he served on the Massachusetts State Board of Agriculture. In 1855 he was elected lieutenant-governor of Massachusetts. He was a modest, affable man seeking success in the thing which interested him most, agriculture. At the time of his death, which occurred at his home, his farm was known to be very valuable, and many farms in the neighborhood had been materially improved through suggestions made by him.

[*Memoirs of Members of the Social Circle in Concord,* 3 ser. (1907); *New Eng. Farmer,* Mar. 8, 1873.]

M. S.

BROWN, SOLYMAN (Nov. 17, 1790–Feb. 13, 1876), poet, teacher, clergyman, dentist, and one of the founders of dentistry as an organized profession, was born in Litchfield, Conn., a son of Nathaniel and Thankful (Woodruff) Brown. Educated with a view to the ministry in the Morris Academy at Litchfield and Yale College, he graduated from the latter in 1812 and received its A.M. in 1817. In 1813, after a year of special preparatory study, he was licensed as a Congregational minister for four years, and occupied several pulpits in northern Connecticut during that period. A renewal of his license was refused through the opposition of the Rev. Lyman Beecher [*q.v.*], who held that two years of special study were necessary for a minister. During the controversy that followed, Brown published *An Address to the People of Litchfield County* (1818); *Second Address ...* (1818); and

Servile Spirits and Spiritual Masters (1820); all three containing biographical data. In 1818 he also published *An Essay on American Poetry* (a long poem), together with *Miscellaneous Pieces* (most of which had appeared originally in the *New Haven Herald*). Failing to obtain a renewal of his license, he removed in 1820 to New York City, where he was engaged as a classical instructor in several fashionable private schools for the next twelve years. In 1822 he embraced Swedenborgianism, and preached in the New Jerusalem Church in New York for many years. During his school-teaching period he published *The Birth of Washington; a Poem* (1822); *A Comparative View of the Systems of Pestalozzi and Lancaster* (1825), and *Sermons* (Swedenborgian, 1829).

His later career was largely influenced by his close friendship with an eminent dentist of New York City, Eleazar Parmly [*q.v.*]. They lived together for six years, until Parmly married (1828), and in 1832 and 1833 were again together in Parmly's house, where Brown studied dentistry and wrote his best known work, *Dentologia* (1833). It is the only dental didactic poem in English, a real literary curiosity, which was favorably received by reviewers, and has been quoted frequently by dental writers. It was reprinted five times; it "had a great influence in elevating dentistry as a profession," and the author has been called "The Poet Laureate of the Dental Profession" (B. K. Thorpe, "Solyman Brown," in C. R. E. Koch's *History of Dental Surgery,* 1909, vol. II). Brown left the Parmly house, and practised dentistry with Samuel Avery in 1834, in which year (Dec. 23) he married Elizabeth, a daughter of Amos Butler, editor and proprietor of the *Mercantile Advertiser* of New York. During the previous two years a dozen of his poems appeared in the *New York Mirror,* the earliest being signed "Mynalos," an anagram of Solyman. In the *Mirror* for 1834 he published *The Hermit of the Baikal,* a long prose poem; and in the same year he and Parmly were the prime movers in the organization of the world's first dental association, the Society of Surgeon Dentists of the City and State of New York (L. Parmly Brown, "New Light on Dental History," in the *Dental Cosmos,* August 1920). In 1837 he received his brother, Augustus Woodruff Brown, as student-assistant, and they were associated in dentistry till 1844. To this brother Solyman Brown dedicated his *Dental Hygeia: a Poem* (1838), and about the same time he wrote a novel of the American Revolution, "Elizabeth of Litchfield," published posthumously in the *Litchfield Enquirer* (1917–18), with an Introduction containing the only published account of his early life, by his grandson, L. Parmly Brown.

Among Solyman Brown's numerous contributions to dental literature, ten articles and various editorials appeared in Volumes I and II (1839–42) of the world's first dental periodical, the *American Journal of Dental Science,* of which he was one of the promoters and editors; while his *Treatise on Mechanical Dentistry,* one of the first practical works on the subject, ran serially through Volumes II and III of the same journal and was reprinted in 1843 with J. B. Savier's translation of F. Maury's *L'Art du Dentiste.* In 1840 he published *Llewellen's Dog; a Ballad,* and in the same year he was one of the organizers of the first national dental association, the American Society of Dental Surgeons, from which as a member he received one of the original degrees of Doctor of Dental Surgery. His essay on *The Importance of Regulating the Teeth of Children* (1841) was the earliest treatise on orthodontia published in America, and on the title page the author first appears with his M.D. (honorary). In 1842 he received the honorary D.D.S. of the Baltimore College of Dental Surgery, and published his *Cholera King, and Other Poems.*

In 1844 Brown was preacher, teacher, and dentist in a short-lived Fourieristic "phalanx" at Leraysville, Pa. He practised dentistry and preached in the Swedenborgian churches at Ithaca and Danby, N. Y., from 1846 to 1850; and then returned to New York City, where he opened a dental supply depot and published his *Semi-Annual Dental Expositor* (1852–54). He was one of a group that conducted the New York Teeth Manufacturing Company from 1854 to 1860, and at the time of the World's Fair in the Crystal Palace, 1853, he edited and published the *Citizens' and Strangers' Pictorial and Business Directory for the City of New York.* His *Union of Extremes: a Discourse on Liberty and Slavery* followed about 1858.

Returning to Danby in 1862, he served as a Swedenborgian minister till 1870, when he retired. He died in his eighty-sixth year at the home of a married daughter in Dodge Center, Minn., and was buried with Masonic honors, having been a Mason some sixty years. He was survived by his wife and six of their eight children, one of whom, E. Parmly Brown (1844–1916), was a prominent dentist of New York for nearly fifty years.

Solyman Brown was a typical tall New Englander. A forceful public speaker, with marked mechanical ability and literary talent, he did much for the elevation of dentistry; but his pre-dominant interests were always religious, and he was seldom without a pulpit. Poetry was his chief hobby; he made frequent contributions of verses to newspapers and periodicals, and has a section in C. W. Everest's *Poets of Connecticut* (1843), with a biographical sketch. He also had talent as a sculptor and painter in oil, his bust and portrait of Eleazar Parmly being his best-known art works.

[See sources of information cited above; also F. B. Dexter, *Biog. Sketches of Grads. of Yale Coll.,* vol. VI (1912); Jas. A. Taylor, *Hist. of Dentistry* (1922); *New Jerusalem Messenger,* Mar. 1, 1876; *New Ch. Messenger,* Mar. 10, 1909 and Apr. 11, 1917.]   L. P. B.

BROWN, SYLVANUS (May 24, 1747 O.S.–July 30, 1824), inventor and millwright, was born at Valley Falls, R. I., the first son of Philip and Priscilla (Carpenter) Brown and a descendant in the sixth generation of John Browne [*q.v.*], of Plymouth Colony. Philip Brown mined ore and coal and manufactured iron at the blast furnace which had been operated by the family since its erection very early in the history of Rhode Island. At Philip's death the furnace was discontinued, and Sylvanus, then ten years old, was placed in the care of an uncle, a millwright, whose trade he learned and followed until he reached twenty-one, when he engaged in business for himself. At the outbreak of the Revolution he enlisted in the Navy and served as master-at-arms on the *Alfred,* flagship of Esek Hopkins, first commodore of the Colonial navy. At the end of his naval service he was engaged at Providence by the State of Rhode Island to stock rifles made by the State, and afterward, by the governor of New Brunswick to superintend the construction and erection of the machinery for several grist and sawmills at St. John, N. B. After the completion of this commission, followed by a short trip to Europe, Brown returned to Pawtucket where he established his machine shop and rapidly earned a reputation as a clever millwright. In 1790 Samuel Slater [*q.v.*], the English millwright, was engaged by William Almy and Smith Brown of Pawtucket to construct replicas of the Arkwright series of spinning machines. Sylvanus Brown was selected to assist Slater, and Brown's shop was used for the work. Brown agreed to work for one dollar a day and furnished bond not to divulge any of the secrets of construction. Slater then, from memory, traced on timbers the outlines of the machine members which Brown cut out and assembled. Within the year the machines were completed and in successful operation in the Almy & Brown mill, the first instance of practical spinning by power in the United States. Slater for this work is now known as the "father of American textile manufactures," while most of the recognition of Sylvanus Brown is merely incidental in stories and accounts extolling Slater. It is a fact, however, that the skill of Brown was a large factor in the success of the machines, and many records credit him with finding and correcting the faults in the card teeth, a weak spot which gave Slater much trouble and nearly caused him to give up the undertaking. Of great importance to the growth of the industry of Brown's development of the tools and machinery necessary to manufacture textile machinery rapidly and cheaply enough to supply the mills. In this connection he constructed and used a slide-crest lathe for turning straight rolls of uniform size some three years prior to the invention of the slide-rest by Maudslay who is generally credited with this achievement. Brown also built a practical machine for fluting the rolls mechanically and rapidly. From 1796 to 1801 he superintended furnaces at Scituate, R. I., for John Brown, manufacturer of cannon, returning then to Pawtucket where he continued his millwright business until his death. He was married to Ruth Salisbury of Westport, Mass. James Salisbury Brown [q.v.] was his only son.

[J. N. Arnold, *Vital Record of R. I.*, vol. III, pt. 5, p. 86; *Representative Men and Old Families of R. I.* (1908); Wm. R. Bagnall, *Samuel Slater and the Early Development of the Cotton Manufactures in the U. S.* (1890); R. M. Bayles, *Hist. of Providence County, R. I.* (1891); *Cotton Centennial 1790–1890* (1890); Jos. W. Roe, *Eng. and Am. Tool Builders* (1916).]

F. A. T.

BROWN, WILLIAM (1752–Jan. 11, 1792), physician, belonged to a Maryland family strikingly devoted to medicine. His grandfather, Gustavus Brown of "Rich Hills," Charles County, his uncle, Gustavus Richard Brown of Port Tobacco, his brother, Gustavus Brown of St. Mary's County, and his own son, Gustavus Alexander Brown, were all medical men. A child of Richard and Helen (Bailey) Brown, he was born in Haddingtonshire, Scotland, where his father was studying for the ministry. His early education was obtained in King and Queen Parish, St. Mary's County, Md., and his academic and medical education in the University of Edinburgh where he received his M.D. degree in 1770. After graduation he returned to America and settled in Alexandria, Va., where he soon established a reputation as a physician. He was a man of culture and was well acquainted with the American leaders of the day, particularly with Washington, Jefferson, and Madison. On the outbreak of the Revolutionary War he was appointed surgeon to the 2nd Virginia Regiment (Col. Woodford). After serving with this regiment about a year he was appointed by Congress, on the recommendation of Dr. Hugh Mercer, to succeed Dr. Benjamin Rush as surgeon-general to the middle department of the Revolutionary army. In February 1778, he was promoted to the office of physician-general to superintend the practise of physic in the army hospital of the middle department. This position he held until July 21, 1780, when he resigned and returned to practise in Alexandria. The physicians who served in the Virginia regiments during the Revolutionary War were entitled by a law of the state not only to their pay but also to a land bounty, provided they served for a period of three years. As Brown resigned after serving with a Virginia regiment for only a year he forfeited his rights, but the esteem in which he was held was so high that in a special act passed on Oct. 21, 1782 he was given not only his back pay but also his land bounty.

While he was serving in the Revolutionary army, in 1778, Brown brought out the first pharmacopeia ever published in the United States, a pamphlet of thirty-two pages, written entirely in Latin. This pharmacopeia was designed to serve the military hospitals and was based on the Edinburgh Pharmacopeia of that day, modified to suit the exigencies of the times, since the pressure of war made certain standard supplies unobtainable. Brown's career as a general practitioner both before and after the Revolutionary War amply demonstrated his efficiency and popularity. He was chairman of the trustees of Alexandria Academy, a position which he accepted at the direct request of George Washington. His tombstone, now in the churchyard of the Old Pohick Church, near Alexandria, Va., sets forth his patience, diligence, and skill as a physician, and his benevolence and integrity as a man. He was married to his cousin, Catherine Scott, of Kalorama, near Washington, D. C., by whom he is said to have had a large family.

[J. M. Toner, *The Medical Men of the Revolution* (1876); W. W. Hening, *Statutes at Large of Va.* (1823), XI, 106; *The First Century of the Phila. Coll. of Pharmacy, 1821–1921*, ed. by Jos. W. England (1922); Bessie Wilmarth Gahn, in *Jour. Am. Pharmaceutical Ass.*, vol. XVI, no. 11 (1927); F. B. Heitman, *Hist. Reg. of the Officers of the Continental Army* (new ed., 1914).]

G. B.

BROWN, WILLIAM CARLOS (July 29, 1853–Dec. 6, 1924), railroad executive, was born in Norway, Herkimer County, N. Y., a son of Charles E. Brown, a Baptist clergyman, and Frances (Lyon) Brown. With but a limited education in the public schools of Iowa he began his railroad career at the age of sixteen as track laborer on the Chicago, Milwaukee & St. Paul

Railroad. His work included the physical handling of wood for locomotives and he soon transferred to train service as a locomotive fireman. While thus employed he taught himself telegraphy and became an operator. From 1872 to 1875 he was train dispatcher on the Illinois Central Railroad, returning in the latter year for a few months to the Chicago, Milwaukee & St. Paul in the same capacity. He was married, on June 3, 1874, to Mary Ella Hewitt, at Lime Springs, Iowa. His long and successful service with the Chicago, Burlington & Quincy Railroad began in 1876 when he became train dispatcher. His progress was steady: chief train dispatcher in 1880, trainmaster in 1881, assistant superintendent in 1884, superintendent in 1887, general manager of parts of the system in 1890, and general manager of the entire system in 1896. During that period the mileage and business of the Burlington increased rapidly.

His work with the Burlington system had come under the observation of W. H. Newman, president of the Lake Shore & Michigan Southern Railroad. When the latter road passed to the control of the New York Central & Hudson River Railroad, of which Newman was made president, he induced Brown to leave the Burlington and take charge of the Lake Shore as vice-president and general manager. A year later Brown was transferred to New York as senior vice-president of the New York Central System, a newly-created position. Newman gradually turned over more and more of his responsibilities to Brown and when Newman retired from the presidency, in 1909, Brown succeeded him. When responsibilities began to weigh too heavily, Brown transferred a part of the burden to Alfred H. Smith, who had followed him from the Lake Shore to the New York Central, and finally, sensitive over the affliction of growing deafness, he resigned from the presidency on Jan. 1, 1914. With his retirement from railroad service, he gave up nearly all business activities and led a quiet life, part of the time in Iowa, where he had farming interests, and during his last years, in Pasadena, Cal., where he died.

With comparatively little school training in youth, Brown later gave evidence of consistent and continuous self-education in economics, finance, and government. While general manager of the Burlington he studied grammar with his secretary. By extensive reading, he broadened his view-point, and he was well informed on the current literature in his own and bordering subjects. Although his practical training up to the time he moved to New York had been in the technique of operation, he began a program for improving the relations between the New York Central and the public, issuing a series of addresses and pamphlets, evidencing a broad grasp of economics. These were published in a bound volume of over 200 pages, which also included an effective document called "The Freight Rate Primer." At that time the railroads were endeavoring to convince the Interstate Commerce Commission that an increase in freight rates was justified by the growing costs of operation, —and the public attitude toward railroads was unfriendly. Brown had to combat not only the nation-wide lack of confidence in railroad management but also certain adverse traditions attaching specifically to the New York Central. To the work of creating an attitude of friendly understanding, he gave himself energetically, and by his forward-looking policy of publicity, —a painstaking effort to broadcast in simple terms the fundamental economic facts concerning the interdependence of railroads and their patrons—he achieved a measure of success. At the same time, he met the heavy demands upon him for executive guidance in the expansion of the company's facilities and business. During his period of service with the New York Central its revenues and traffic doubled in volume, and engineering works of large proportions were successfully carried on. Among them were the reconstruction of the Grand Central Terminal in New York City and the electrification of the lines in and near that city.

Personally Brown was courteous and modest. A moderate disciplinarian, he was kind-hearted and considerate. He displayed a keen interest in the work of the Railroad Y. M. C. A. Toward labor unions he was not as uncompromising as many of his contemporaries, although he was not lacking in firmness when, as a superintendent, he did more than his part in keeping the Burlington road open during the great strike of 1888. He had strong organizing ability and the faculty of harmonizing departmental differences. His qualities were thus summarized by an editorial writer for the *Railway Age Gazette*: studious, clear-headed, possessed of retentive memory, able to learn new things quickly, an accurate judge of men and subjects.

[*Who's Who in America*, 1914–15; obituaries in *Ry. Age* and *Ry. Rev.*, Dec. 13, 1924; *N. Y. Times* and *Sioux City* (Iowa) *Jour.*, Dec. 9, 1924; other sketches in railroad journals (1900–24); correspondence with business associates, and personal recollections.]

W. J. C—m.

BROWN, WILLIAM GARROTT (Apr. 24, 1868–Oct. 19, 1913), author, was the son of Wilson Richard and Mary Cogdale (Parish) Brown.

Chiefly of English strain, his ancestors were of Virginia and North Carolina, with a Connecticut branch. His family settled in Alabama in 1832–33. Brown was born at Marion, Ala., and remained there until 1889. After good preparatory schooling, he graduated from Howard College in 1886. He devoted the next year to reading, with occasional contributions to the *Montgomery Advertiser,* after which followed two years of teaching. He then entered Harvard, where he spent thirteen years: three, as student, receiving the degrees of A.B., 1891, and A.M., 1892; nine, as assistant in the college library; one, as lecturer in American history. Increase of deafness, an affliction from youth, prevented an academic career, and he turned exclusively to writing. His principal books appeared between 1902 and 1905. During that period he traveled much in the South, although Cambridge remained his permanent residence. In 1905 he moved to New York, the immediate purpose being to study material about Gen. Grant, whose biography he had engaged to prepare. Finding he had tuberculosis, from 1906 to 1913 he fought a losing battle for health (see "Some Confessions of a 'T. B.,'" *Atlantic Monthly,* CXIII, 747), during a part of which period he wrote editorials for *Harper's Weekly,* working in bed for two and a half years. He died in New Canaan, Conn.

His best books are *Andrew Jackson* (1900), *The Lower South in American History* (1902), *Stephen Arnold Douglas* (1902), *The Foe of Compromise and Other Essays* (1903), and *A Continental Congressman; Oliver Ellsworth* (1905). Posthumously some papers on political topics were gathered from periodicals into *The New Politics and Other Essays* (1914). His *Lower South* is a picture of the Cotton States from 1820 to 1860. He called it "thin and fragmentary"; yet if he had written nothing else, that alone should perpetuate his memory. His most impressive essay, *Foe of Compromise,* expresses what perhaps stood uppermost in his character: willingness to fight on despite certainty of defeat. In *Jackson* and *Douglas* he illustrated how, without confusing detail, a political figure can be made to live again in the imagination. His *Ellsworth,* by telling clearly Ellsworth's part in establishing the government, rescued the third Chief Justice for the average reader from unmerited obscurity. His lesser writings include: *History of Alabama* (1900); *Golf* (1902); *A Gentleman of the South* (1903) and numerous magazine articles.

Born during the poverty of Reconstruction, Brown credited his opportunity to two brothers who, as he stated, "stood aside to let me pass." Though away from Alabama over half his life, he carried to the end the mark of his own section. In person he was tall, angular, spare, with high forehead and the orator's long lips. With a genius for friendship, he was chivalric, eager for truth, painstaking for facts, scholarly, and lucid of statement. On a worthy theme he wrote with compelling eloquence and always with distinction. While his passion was history, it is a question whether "man of letters," "essayist," or "historian" more nearly describes him. James Bryce said, "Mr. Brown's mind was singularly fair, penetrating and judicious. He was an admirable critic, seeing clearly and deep; and to his capacity for a discriminative appreciation there was joined a remarkable gift of fine expression. In point of style and diction, he seemed to me to stand in the front rank of the men of his generation, and he would doubtless, had his life been prolonged, have been an ornament to American literature."

[For estimates see *Nation,* XCVII, 389; *Outlook,* CV, 461; *Harvard Alumni Bull.,* XVI, 88; *Harvard Grads. Mag.,* XXII, 255; *South Atlantic Quart.,* XIII, 69, XVI, 97; *Hist. of Ala. and Dict. of Ala. Biog.,* III, 237.]

F.G.C.

BROWN, WILLIAM HENRY (Feb. 29, 1836–June 25, 1910), civil engineer, was born in Little Britain Township, Lancaster County, Pa. His parents, Levi K., and Hannah C. (Moore) Brown, were Quakers and people of limited means. William was sent to the district public school and later to the Central High School in Philadelphia, but was unable to go to college. He was determined, however, to become a civil engineer. As a boy he had collected sticks to make axe handles, selling them to procure money to buy books on engineering. Eventually he saved enough money to purchase the most primitive of surveyor's instruments, a Jacob's staff, and he taught himself surveying by practising on the neighbors' farms with their deeds to guide him. On Oct. 15, 1863, he married Sarah A. Rimmel in Pittsburgh.

At the close of the Civil War, in which Brown had rendered effective work of an engineering nature for the Union forces, he entered the employ of the Pennsylvania Railroad Company to which he gave over forty years of continuous service (1864–1906). For the last twenty-five years of that time he was chief engineer. His work included everything that pertains to the construction of a railroad—the building of great stations, tunnels, bridges, railroad shops and yards, piers and docks. He believed that the most important operation he ever undertook was the construction of the Broad Street Terminal and Station in Philadelphia. He was especially proud of the construction of the train-shed there with sixteen tracks under one roof which was supported by twenty trusses set in pairs nine feet apart. It was almost twice the size of any train-shed in existence at the time of its construction. No railroad chief engineer of his time had as much money at his disposal as Brown had as chief engineer for the Pennsylvania Railroad Company, especially after A. J. Cassatt [q.v.] became president of the company in 1899. Brown was a great believer in stone bridges, and wherever it was possible built them to take the place of steel ones. Among the important bridges he constructed is the one across the Susquehanna River five miles west of Harrisburg—one of the longest bridges in the United States, and at the time of its construction the largest stone-arched bridge in the world. Some of the other operations of which Brown had charge were: improvements of the Company's terminals in Jersey City; rebuilding the Jersey City Station four times and the Jersey City Elevator; a bridge across the Hackensack River; the elevated road through Newark, New Brunswick, and Elizabeth; the Delaware River Bridge and Railroad, the grade-crossing tunnels at the Zoological Gardens, the piers and docks on the Delaware River front, and the Forty-first St. and Grand Avenue bridges, in Philadelphia, and a practically new line all the way from that city to Harrisburg. He erected two new stations at Harrisburg and built the tunnel through the Alleghany Mountains at Gallitzen, Pa. His services during the Johnstown Flood should not be forgotten. At the risk of his own life he personally took charge of the work that opened up the railroad to bring relief to the sufferers.

Brown's death, due to heart failure, occurred at Belfast, Ireland, where he was visiting with Mrs. Brown. His home, for many years, had been in Philadelphia. He was a member of the Historical Society of Pennsylvania and of the Pennsylvania Society of Sons of the Revolution.

[*Engineering News Record*, vol. LIII, no. 9; *Engineering News*, vol. LXIV, no. 2; *Railroad Gazette*, vol. XL, no. 9, vol. XLIX, no. 1.]   E. Y.

BROWN, WILLIAM HUGHEY (Jan. 15, 1815–Oct. 12, 1875), coal operator, was born in North Huntington Township, Westmoreland County, Pa., the son of James and Sarah Brown. His education was limited to the usual courses taught in the common schools of that day. By turns, he was employed as a laborer on the old Portage Canal, worked on a farm in the summer, and dug coal in the winter. While working as a

coal digger, the idea occurred to him that many people would rather buy their coal than come to the mines and dig it. So he bought a horse and wagon and began to peddle coal. In a short time, he had a number of other men with teams hauling coal for him. Next (1845–56) he began to float coal down the Monongahela River, and sold it in Pittsburgh. His profits soon enabled him to buy a coal mine of his own; two years later, he formed a partnership with the owners of the Kensington Iron Works in Pittsburgh. The firm, under Brown's direction, began mining and operating in coal at the Nine-Mile Run on the Monongahela. They furnished coal to passenger boats and steamboats. Also, they established a few coke ovens at the mines.

In 1858 Brown attempted an experiment that places him among America's business pioneers, that of towing coal by steamers down the Ohio River. Prior to this, coal had been floated down in barges, a class of large keel-boats. But the expenses absorbed all the profits. Brown conceived the plan of towing a number of flatboats with steamers. He collected twelve boats, loaded some 230,000 bushels of coal on board, attached the steamer *Grampus* on one side and the *General Larimer* on the other, and started them down the river in charge of his son Samuel S. Brown. The venture succeeded beyond all expectation. There was now no limit to the future coal industry of the Pittsburgh district. In the same year Brown entered the firm of Reis, Brown & Berger, and bought a large rolling-mill at New Castle, Pa. On this occasion he is said to have given his personal check for $100,-000 in order to complete the deal,—ample evidence of the wealth he had accumulated.

At the outbreak of the Civil War, Brown secured contracts for supplying coal to the fleet of the Federal forces at Cairo, Memphis, and Vicksburg. During this period he also shipped coal to St. Louis for the gas works of that city. These were years of great activity and responsibility; also of great risks and personal danger. Many times he barely escaped capture by regular armed forces and also by guerrilla bands, but so far as is known, he never lost a single cargo of coal. At the time of his death in 1875, he had fifteen steamboats in operation on the Ohio River. In his obituary notices he was described as "a mental and physical giant," but he broke down from overwork. He retired from active business in 1873, suffered a paralytic stroke, and died in the Kirkbride Asylum, Philadelphia. On Sept. 3, 1840, he had married Mary Smith, daughter of Samuel and Elizabeth Smith of Minersville, Pa.

[Brief sketches of Brown are found in *Hist. of Allegheny County, Pa.* (1889) ; and in the *Century Cyc. of Hist. and Biog.* (1910), vol II ; obituary notices in the Pittsburgh newspapers of Oct. 13, 14, 1875, relate several incidents of interest.]   J. W. O.

BROWN, WILLIAM WELLS (*c.* 1816–Nov. 6, 1884), negro reformer, historian, was born in Lexington, Ky. The year is variously given as 1814, 1815, and 1816. His mother was a slave, his father is said to have been one George Higgins, a white slaveholder. When a youth Brown was taken to St. Louis and was hired out on a steamboat. He was next employed in the print-shop of Elijah P. Lovejoy, then editor of the *St. Louis Times*. Working in this capacity, Brown got his start in education; but he was hired out on a steamboat again at the close of the next year. In 1834 he escaped into Ohio, intending to cross Lake Erie into Canada. On the way he was sheltered by a Quaker, Wells Brown, whose name he assumed in addition to the name William which he had borne as a slave. He now took up steamboating on Lake Erie and obtained the position of steward in which he was able to help many a fugitive to freedom. In the year of his escape he married a free colored woman by whom he had two daughters. Profiting by school instruction and some help from friends, he acquired considerable knowledge of the fundamentals. In the North he soon learned to speak the English language so fluently that he could easily present the claims of the negro for freedom. During 1843–49 he was variously employed as a lecturer of the Western New York Anti-Slavery Society, and the Massachusetts Anti-Slavery Society. He was also interested in temperance, woman's suffrage, and prison reform, and was associated with the most ardent abolitionists like William Lloyd Garrison and Wendell Phillips. In 1849 he visited England and represented the American Peace Society at the Peace Congress in Paris. Highly recommended by the American Anti-Slavery Society as an apostle of freedom, he was welcomed by famous Europeans such as Victor Hugo, James Haughton, George Thompson, and Richard Cobden. He remained abroad until the autumn of 1854. During these years of his activity as a reformer Brown found time also to study medicine. Like many of the physicians of his time, he did not undergo formal training in this field. He attended lectures in medical science and obtained privately other knowledge requisite to service as a practitioner. But although he knew sufficient medicine to be useful in the profession, the urgent need for fighting the battles of the negro kept him in the work of reform. Brown's reputation rests largely on his ability as an historian. His writings covered various fields. The first to appear was his *Narrative of William W. Brown, a Fugitive Slave* (1847). His next important book was *Three Years in Europe* (1852). In 1853 he published *Clotel, or the President's Daughter, a Narrative of Slave Life in the United States*. He next wrote a drama entitled *The Dough Face*, which was well received and was followed by another play, *The Escape or A Leap for Freedom*. In 1863 he published his first history entitled, *The Black Man, His Antecedents, His Genius, and His Achievements*, including an autobiographical memoir, which ran through ten editions in three years. *The Negro in the American Rebellion, His Heroism and His Fidelity* (1867) also made a favorable impression and supplied the need for an account of the part played by the negroes in the Civil War. The last work of importance which he wrote was *The Rising Son: or, the Antecedents and the Advancement of the Colored Race* (1874). In this treatise he undertook to trace the history of the negro from Africa to America. The abolitionists gave the author unstinted praise and widely circulated his books in this country and Europe. Although, like most historians of his day, he did not approach his subject scientifically, he passed for many years as the outstanding authority on the negro. At the time of his death his home was in Chelsea, Mass.

[In addition to Brown's autobiographical writings, see Josephine Brown, *The Biog. of an Am. Bondman, by His Daughter* (1856) ; memoir by Wm. Farmer in *Three Years in Europe* (1852) ; memoir by Alonzo D. Moore in *The Rising Son* (1874) ; W. J. Simmons, *Men of Mark* (1887), pp. 447–50 ; C. G. Woodson, *The Negro in Our History* (4th ed., 1927), pp. 266–69 ; obituary in the *Boston Transcript*, Nov. 8, 1884.]   C. G. W.

BROWNE, BENJAMIN FREDERICK (July 14, 1793–Nov. 23, 1873), druggist, author, was born in Salem, Mass., the son of Benjamin and Elizabeth (Andrew) Browne, and was baptized in the East Church that same day by the Rev. William Bentley [*q.v.*]. On his father's side he was a descendant in the seventh generation of John Browne, who joined the First Church in Salem in 1637, and on his mother's side of the Rev. Francis Higginson, the first minister of the First Church. He entered the shop of E. S. Lang, an apothecary, Aug. 3, 1807, and completed a five years' apprenticeship just as the outbreak of war with England destroyed the commerce of the port and made it impossible for Browne to find gainful employment on land. Though short of stature and delicate of health, he shipped in September 1812 as surgeon's assistant on the privateer *Alfred*. The cruise began auspiciously with the capture of two brigs laden with cotton, sugar, and dye stuffs, but thereafter the captain was inexplicably timid and ended the venture suddenly at Portsmouth, N. H., Jan. 7, 1813. Browne next enlisted on the privateer *Frolic*. This schooner, with her wedge-shaped bottom and reedy masts, was a freak of marine architecture and behaved so alarmingly in the first white squall that the crew returned their bounty money and the captain put back to port. Rebuilt, the *Frolic* set forth again, with Browne acting as captain's clerk, purser, and sergeant of marines. On Jan. 25, 1814, after a plucky attempt to escape, she was captured by the English man-of-war *Heron* and the crew carried as prisoners to Barbados. In August of the same year Browne, with the other enlisted men, was shipped to England and marched across the hills from Plymouth to Dartmoor, where he was incarcerated until May 1, 1815. The scanty fare and other hardships of the prison so told on his health that at the time of his discharge he weighed only ninety-four pounds. He returned to Salem and to fifty-eight years of humdrum. On Jan. 1, 1823, he set up a drug store of his own. On Jan. 23, 1825, he married Sally Bott. He was representative to the General Court in 1831, state senator in 1843, postmaster of Salem 1845–49. For fifty years he attended the Independent Congregational Church in Barton Square. On Jan. 1, 1860, he retired from business, but until stricken with paralysis three months before his death he returned daily to the store to occupy his old chair, watch his erstwhile partner compound prescriptions, and exchange gossip with droppers-in. Sometime in middle life, however, he wrote out the story of his three years of sailing, fighting, and imprisonment. As the "Papers of an Old Dartmoor Prisoner, Edited by Nathaniel Hawthorne," these reminiscences appeared serially in the *United States Magazine and Democratic Review* during 1846. The author had the faculty of presenting just those details about which a reader will be curious, and he wrote with admirable sureness, vigor, and humor. "A careful comparison of the original manuscript with the printed copy shows that the narrative owes nothing whatever to the accomplishments of the editor except some slight use of the pruning knife" (Memoir, p. 88). With the addition from Hawthorne's manuscript copy of some chapters on life in Barbados, the account was republished in 1926 as *The Yarn of a Yankee Privateer*. The publishers did not know the name of the author and offered a reward of $500 for his identification.

["Memoir of Benj. Frederick Browne" in *Essex Inst. Hist. Colls.*, XIII, 81–88; *N. Y. Times*, Mar. 6, 20, 1927.]
G. H. G.

BROWNE, CHARLES FARRAR (Apr. 26, 1834–Mar. 6, 1867), humorist, better known under his pen-name of "Artemus Ward," was the son of Levi and Caroline (Farrar) Brown. The Browns (Charles himself added an "e" to the name) were a pioneer New England family. The father of Artemus was a substantial citizen of Waterford, Me., a civil engineer of sorts, at one time a member of the state legislature. "Charley" was born on a farm just outside of Waterford but his family during his infancy moved into the town itself and occupied the house still shown as "Artemus Ward's home." When the boy was thirteen his father died, and Charley Brown, following in the wake of an elder brother, Cyrus, went to work to learn the printer's trade under a Mr. John Rix of the *Weekly Democrat* in Lancaster, N. H. A year later he got a place with the *Norway Advertiser*, edited by his brother. On this and various other local journals young Browne set type, wrote news items, and learned the general work of a country newspaper. He presently found his way to Boston where he spent three years in the printing trade. His first genuine literary production was published in the (Boston) *Carpet Bag*, Apr. 17, 1852, under the title, "The Surrender of Cornwallis." From Boston, Charley Browne, now a lanky sandy-haired youth of a queer and melancholy countenance, following the fashion of his day and his trade, wandered westward. He worked in Cincinnati, Toledo, and various places of the rising "West." "I didn't know," he said, "but what I might get as far as China." But his errant steps took him instead to Cleveland, Ohio.

It was at Cleveland that young Browne made his real start in the world. He secured a post on the *Plain Dealer* (at ten dollars a week) which gave him his first opportunity to develop his peculiar vein of comic humor. Here he appears as "Artemus Ward,"—a name selected for fancy's sake from certain old records of land surveyed by a bygone member of his family (Seitz, *post*, p. 25). In the pages of the *Plain Dealer* he created (beginning Feb. 3, 1858) the quaint fiction of a traveling showman who signs himself "Artemus Ward," or "A. Ward" and who is anxious to exhibit wax works, tame bears, and a kangaroo, and is apparently approaching nearer and nearer to the city. The wax works are said to include "figgers of G. Washington, Gen. Taylor, John Bunyan, Capt. Kidd and Dr. Webster in the act of killing Dr. Parkman, besides several miscellanyus moral wax statoots of celebrated piruts & murderers &c ekalled by few and exceld by none." This whimsical idea led to the publication of a series of Artemus Ward letters and became the basis of Browne's literary work. Henceforth, as his reputation grew, he was known to the world only as Artemus Ward.

While still at Cleveland, Artemus had already become a contributor to *Vanity Fair,* a newly established illustrated journal of New York, intended to rival the London *Punch.* This connection led him to leave Cleveland for New York (1859), the process of migration itself involving several weeks of wandering. On the staff of *Vanity Fair* at No. 100 Nassau St., Artemus received regular employment at twenty dollars a week and to this paper he contributed some of the most brilliant of his "goaks" and sketches and burlesque romances. These were presently (1862) gathered into a little volume with the title *Artemus Ward: His Book.* A sale of 40,000 copies indicated its immediate popularity. Meantime the idea of being in some sort "a showman" had made a real as well as imaginative appeal to the young man. On a vacation trip to the westward he fell in with E. R. Hingston, the well-known manager of entertainments, then conducting a tour, and arranged with him that he would some day "manage" Artemus as a "moral lecturer." On his return to New York, Ward gathered together from his writings a collection of random material which he strung together as a lecture, under the title "The Babes in the Wood." It was delivered first at New London, Conn. (Nov. 26, 1861), was pronounced by the local press a "decided success," and was repeated in various New England towns including Boston. "Mr. Browne," said the *Boston Post,* "is a young man of some twenty-eight years, with a pleasant genial face, a keen, humorous eye, and a countenance suggestive of close powers of observation, and a fresh, live intellect." Finally the lecture on "The Babes in the Wood" was given in Clinton Hall, New York, on Dec. 23, 1861. Bad weather prevented a large attendance, but in the month following Artemus "spoke his piece" in various cities (including his adopted Cleveland) with huge success. It was characteristic of him that this lecture on "The Babes in the Wood" concerned neither babes nor woods. At the end of it he was wont to add in a sort of reverie of afterthought: "I suppose that you want to hear something about the children in the wood. They were good children, they were unfortunate and, as far as I have been able to ascertain, entirely respectable."

It was a lecture trip to Washington which led to the imaginary personal contact between Artemus Ward and Abraham Lincoln, as described in the sketch, "Artemus Ward in Washington."

In reality they never met. But Lincoln knew and admired Artemus Ward's work and it is a matter of history that at the cabinet meeting of Sept. 22, 1862, the President read aloud Ward's "High Handed Outrage in Utica," laughed heartily over it amid the anxious silence of his advisers, and then, with a sigh, opened and read the draft of the Emancipation Proclamation. The circumstance recalls the fact that Artemus Ward's comic and humorous work was carried on during the stress and struggle of the Civil War. His sympathies were all with the Union; he is said to have given many thousand dollars to the cause. Many of his "pieces" ("Interview with President Lincoln," "The Show is Confiscated," etc.) reflect this attitude, in his own humane way; and his admiration for the President was early and abiding.

Ward's restless nature sought a farther field. A San Francisco theatre manager had telegraphed to him "What will you take for forty nights in California?" and Artemus had wired back, "Brandy and water." The project was fulfilled in the spirit if not to the letter. Under the management of Hingston, Artemus sailed from New York for Panama, Oct. 3, 1863, and on Nov. 1 reached San Francisco. The Pacific tour which followed was from the start a wild and hilarious success. The receipts for "The Babes in the Wood" lecture in San Francisco ran in a single night to $1,465. Ward lectured all through California and Nevada, in cities, in mining camps, in theatres, churches, and billiard saloons, and everywhere with triumphal success and with fatal conviviality. He met all the rising literary stars of the Pacific Coast including, as the most intimate friendship of all, a gaunt young newspaper man of Virginia City, Nev., then known only as Sam Clemens.

The tour was carried on as far as Salt Lake City and Denver. In the former place, Artemus met the Mormons who became for the future his favorite topic of discourse.

On his return from the West, Ward again took the lecture platform in New York (1864), in the eastern states, and in Canada. The principal subject was now "Artemus Ward among the Mormons," and the lecture was illustrated after the fashion of the day by a panorama, itself presently reduced by the comic genius of Artemus to a sort of caricature. The "program" covering four pages was a masterpiece of comic art. In June 1866 Ward sailed for England. The reception awarded to him in London was the crowning triumph of his brief life. The Savage Club became his headquarters. His contributions to *Punch* excited the laughter of all England, while the delivery of his "Mormon" lecture in the Egyptian Hall was an overwhelming success of which the tradition still lingers. But the end was near. His audiences were laughing at a dying man, whose assumed accents of melancholy reflected only too truly the approaching decline. Stricken with consumption Artemus was compelled after six weeks of lecturing to abandon his work and died at Southampton Mar. 6, 1867.

The humor of Artemus Ward on the platform depended in large part on his peculiar personality, on his whimsical assumptions of distress and ignorance, on his sudden flashes of apparent interest, fading rapidly again into despair, not to be reproduced in mere words. In his writings the comic effect is connected on the surface with the use of queer spelling, verbal quips, and puns, long passed out of use and distasteful to the reader of to-day. Had this been all, Artemus Ward would long since have been forgotten. But beneath the comic superficiality of his written work, as behind the "mask of melancholy" of the comic lecture, there was always the fuller, deeper meaning of the true humorist, based on reality, on the contrasts, the incongruities, and the shortcomings of life itself.

[Artemus Ward's works include sketches, etc., in the *Carpet Bag* (Boston), 1852–53, in the Cleveland *Plain Dealer* (1858–59), in *Vanity Fair* (N. Y., 1860–62); *Artemus Ward: His Book* (first ed., N. Y., 1862); *Artemus Ward: His Travels* (first ed., N. Y., 1865); contributions to *Punch* (London), Sept., Nov., 1866. Of the many critical works and notices mention may be made of "Artemus Ward" in A. S. Nock, *On Doing the Right Thing* (1928), and D. C. Seitz's *Artemus Ward* (1919) as admirable as it is complete, and containing an exhaustive bibliography.]   S.L.

BROWNE, DANIEL JAY (b. Dec. 4, 1804), agricultural and scientific writer, was born in Fremont, N. H., the son of Isaac and Mary Browne. He was bred and educated a practical farmer. It is not known what schools he attended except that he took some courses at Harvard University. He began his literary career at the age of twenty-six by publishing a monthly journal called *The Naturalist*. When only twenty-eight he published two books, *Sylva Americana* and *Etymological Encyclopaedia of Technical Words and Phrases Used in the Arts and Sciences*. The years 1833–35 he spent mostly in foreign travel in the West Indies, Cuba, Canary Islands, Spain, France, Sicily, Madeira, Cape Verde Islands and South America, being part of the time on the United States ships *Vandalia* and *Erie*. During 1836–42 he was engaged in various engineering projects in New York State and Cuba. For the next few years his time was largely devoted to his literary work. He served at this time as the first corresponding secretary of the American Agricultural Association and as a member of the Board of Agriculture of the American Institute in New York. From 1845 to 1851 he was employed in the agricultural warehouse of R. L. Allen & Company, New York, and assisted in the editing of their paper, the *American Agriculturalist*. During this period he also published four books, *Trees of America* (1846), *American Bird Fancier* (1850), *American Poultry Yard* (1850), and *American Muck Book* (1851).

In 1852 he was appointed to a position in the United States Census Office where he was chiefly occupied with agricultural statistics. In June 1853 he was appointed as Agricultural Clerk in the United States Patent Office. He edited the agricultural reports of that office for 1854 to 1859 and prepared numerous articles. In 1854 and 1855 he was sent to Europe by the Patent Office to obtain information on agricultural subjects and to make arrangements for procuring seeds and cuttings, probably the first instances of the use of government funds for such purposes. Browne may therefore be regarded as the first official United States agricultural explorer. During his later years in the Patent Office his activities, particularly in the distribution of seeds, were the subject of much controversy and criticism in the agricultural press. The complaints reached the Agricultural Committee of the House of Representatives, which instituted an investigation. The results were published in the *Washington Union* for June 8, 1858, and reprinted as a separate pamphlet entitled *Vindication of the Agricultural Division of the Patent Office*. (This pamphlet contains practically the only available biographical information regarding Browne.) The Committee, at the end of its investigation, stated that it believed Browne to be "fully qualified for the important duties committed to him." Nevertheless the criticism of his administration and of the seed distribution continued, and later resulted in the appointment by the Secretary of the Interior of an "Advisory Board of Agriculture of the Patent Office," of which Marshall P. Wilder was chairman. The Board approved the general plan of operations of the Patent Office but Browne's appointment was terminated on Oct. 10, 1859, due probably to the criticism which was leveled against him. On May 1, 1861, he was appointed by the Patent Office to visit Europe to investigate the cultivation and manufacture of flax. The results of his investigations are given as the leading article in the *Patent Office Report for 1861* (pp. 21–83). This is the last contribution from his pen which has been found. Whatever errors he may have committed, the fair-minded critics of his day seemed to believe that he was sincerely and earnestly devoted to the advancement of the agricultural interests of the country. Much of the most bitter criticism against him emanated from persons connected with the seed business and naturally opposed to government seed distribution. Other critics were those opposed to any national agricultural department. Browne's literary productions were mostly compilations but nevertheless useful in their day, particularly the agricultural books, each of which ran through two or more editions.

[For tne adverse and favorable criticism of Browne in the agricultural press, see *Am. Agriculturist*, XVII, 40, 72, 104, 198–99, 230–31 (1858); XVIII, 103, 104, 326 (1859); *Am. Farmers' Mag.*, XI, 151–53, 182, 467–73 (1858); *Cultivator*, VII, 66, 67, 76 (1859); IX, 226 (1861). For summary of transactions of Advisory Bd. of Agric. of the Patent Office, see Washington *States and Union*, Jan. 4–12, 1859. and the *Patent Office Report for 1858*, pp. iv–v.]   C.R.B.

BROWNE, FRANCIS FISHER (Dec. 1, 1843–May 11, 1913), editor, was of direct Puritan descent. He was born at South Halifax, Vt., the son of William Goldsmith Browne and Eunice (Fisher) Browne. He inherited the love of personal freedom and the literary tendency which dominated his life. Early in his childhood the family moved to western Massachusetts where the boy went to school and learned the printing trade in his father's newspaper office at Chicopee. In 1862 he enlisted and served one year with the 46th Massachusetts Regiment. After leaving the army he went to Rochester, N. Y., to work in a law office, later deciding to enroll in the law department of the University of Michigan. He soon abandoned the law course and returned to Rochester to follow his printing trade. In 1867 he married Susan Seaman Brooks. To this union nine children were born. Soon after his marriage he moved to Chicago with the definite intention of following literary pursuits. He found an opening with the *Western Monthly*, a newly established periodical, gradually gained control of the magazine, and at the end of two years, rechristened it the *Lakeside Monthly*. He enlisted the best writers of the West and for the next six years slaved to produce a creditable and distinguished magazine. Just as the *Monthly* was practically self-sustaining Browne suffered a complete physical breakdown and retired for a few years, and the *Monthly* went out of existence. While searching for health, Browne wrote special editorials for some of the leading Chicago newspapers and for a time acted as literary editor of the *Alliance*, then an influential weekly journal, but his mind was preoccupied with plans for a new periodical. In 1880 under the imprint of Jansen, McClurg & Company, Browne's magazine appeared, named *The Dial*. It was a monthly review and index of current literature. His task was a difficult one,—especially in a city such as Chicago, which was concerned almost entirely with commercial interests, but he succeeded in establishing the foremost American journal of literary criticism of that time and the only one of its class which has survived. For several years he contributed a large portion of the writing in the *Dial*, and still edited the magazine at the time of his death which occurred in Santa Barbara, Cal. It was courage and persistency which enabled him to succeed, for he battled against poverty, ill health, and many personal disasters. Along with his literary interests he possessed a marked analytical insight which enabled him to realize the essential truth of a situation or problem, because of which he invariably found himself with the minority. He was not blinded by the sophistries with which American newspapers sought to justify the war with Spain, and he protested from the first against the United States policy in the Philippines. Scarcely one of his judgments on the political events of his time has not since been verified. A student of Burns, Byron, Wordsworth, Arnold, and Tennyson, it is said that he was able to recite by heart almost all of Tennyson's poems and a great quantity of the work of the other poets. He has been likened to Arnold in his habits of thought. During the years that he edited the *Dial* he compiled and edited several anthologies among which are *Golden Poems by British and American Authors* (1881); *The Golden Treasury of Poetry and Prose* (1883); *Bugle Echoes* (1886); and seven volumes of *Laurel Crowned Verse* (1891–92). He was also the author of a small volume called *Volunteer Grain* (1895), a collection of poems none of which are distinguished. Probably his best work was *The Everyday Life of Abraham Lincoln*, published in 1886. It deals with the human-interest side of Lincoln, the material for which was collected from some five hundred persons who were living at that time and had personally known him.

[*Who's Who in America*, 1912–13; *Dial*, May 1, June 1, 16, 1913; *Book Buyer*, May 1900; *Bookman*, May 1900; *Public* (Chicago), May 30, 1913; *Rev. of Revs.* (N. Y.), July 1913.]   M.S.

BROWNE, IRVING (Sept. 14, 1835–Feb. 6, 1899), legal writer, was born at Marshall, Oneida County, N. Y., the son of two persons of strongly contrasting personality, Lewis C. Browne, a Universalist clergyman of austere character, and his wife, Harriet Hand, a lady of attractive personality and social charm. He was educated in the common schools at Nashua, N. H., and Norwich, Conn., leaving at the age of fourteen in order to learn the printing trade. In his leisure he studied telegraphy and was employed for a time in a telegraph office at Boston. In 1853 he went to Hudson, N. Y., and there commenced the study of law, which he continued in New York City, finally entering the Law School at Albany, where he graduated in 1857. He was admitted to the bar the same year and commenced practise at Troy, N. Y., joining the firm of M. R. & I. Townsend. There he remained for twenty-one years, first as office manager and then as counsel for his firm, which conducted a wide and diversified business. He early evinced the possession of unusual gifts of lucid statement and his arguments in the appellate courts were considered models (Kirchwey, *post*). From his youth he had always been a student of literature and in 1876 he published a book of slight sketches termed *Humorous Phases of the Law,* followed two years later by *Short Studies of Great Lawyers.* In 1878 he retired from the firm, intending to practise alone, but on the death in 1879 of J. J. Thompson, the founder and editor of the *Albany Law Journal,* he was offered and accepted the position of editor, and took up his residence in Albany. He had read widely, and being endowed with great determination, facility of expression and capacity for incessant work, he quickly brought the *Albany Law Journal* to a foremost place among the legal periodicals of the day. He was a prolific contributor to its pages, giving to its contents a lightness of touch which made it eminently readable. In 1880 he published *National Bank Cases, Federal and State Courts, 1878-80.* This was followed by *Judicial Interpretation of Common Words and Phrases* (1883) and *Index-Digest of New York Court of Appeals Reports Volumes 1-95, Keyes, Abbott and Transcript Appeals, 1847-84* (1884), the latter being found of great utility by the profession. His text-books, *Elements of the Law of Domestic Relations and of Employer and Employed* (1883) and *Elements of Criminal Law: Principles, Pleading and Procedure* (1892) met with a cordial reception. Concurrently with the preparation of these books, and his editorial work, he was engaged in completing *American Reports: Decisions, Courts of Last Resort of the Several States,* volumes 28 to 60 of which were edited by him, the last volume appearing in 1888. He was continuously at work, contributing largely each week to the *Journal* and also to other periodicals. In 1893 he resigned his editorial position and removed to Buffalo, but did not resume practise. He had, while at Albany, for eleven years been professor of criminal law and the law of domestic relations

at the Law School there, and he now joined the faculty of the Buffalo Law School, delivering also special courses of legal lectures at Cornell and Boston. In 1896 he was appointed librarian of the supreme court at Buffalo. His subsequent contributions to legal literature included *Admissibility of Parol Evidence in Respect of Written Instruments* (1893); *Elements of the American Law of Sales of Personal Property* (1894); *Short Studies in Evidence* (1897); and *Elements of the Law of Bailments and Common Carriers* (1902). In addition he edited and annotated an edition of the *New York Reports,* volumes 16-100, and assumed editorial charge of the American edition of the English *Ruling Cases,* a work which was uncompleted at his death. Despite the volume of his output it is doubtful if he contributed anything of permanent value to the store of legal literature, and his annotations were never profound, though the clarity of his style caused him to be widely read. His causeries were always delightful. Apart from his legal writing, he was an attractive essayist, with a vein of real humor appealing to a wide audience. His published works in addition to the legal volumes before-mentioned were an English translation of Racine's *Les Plaideurs* (1871); *Our Best Society* (1876), a parlor comedy; *Iconoclasm and Whitewash* (1885); *Rhyminiscenses of Travel* (1891), in verse; *In the Track of the Bookworm* (1897); and *The House of the Heart* (1897), verse. He married, first, in 1858, Delia, daughter of Richard F. Clark of Hudson, N. Y., and, second, in 1894, Lizzie B. Ferris, daughter of Frederick Buell of Buffalo, N. Y.

[Biographical sketch by Geo. W. Kirchwey, in *Albany Law Jour.,* Feb. 18, 1899, p. 212; a more critical article in *Am. Law Rev.;* XXXIII, 271. See also *Green Bag,* Dec. 1889, Apr. 1890, Aug. 1897; *Chicago Legal News,* May 2, 1896, Feb. 18, 1899; obituary in *Buffalo Morning Express,* Feb. 7, 1899. *A Cat. of the Lib. of Irving Browne* (1878) contains an introduction and notes valuable as an indication of Browne's wide literary interests.]

H. W. H. K.

BROWNE, JOHN (d. Apr. 10, 1662), Plymouth Colony magistrate, brought his family to America about 1634. He was led to settle in Plymouth Colony by a pleasant acquaintance formed years before with John Robinson's congregation at Leyden (Nathaniel Morton, *New-England's Memoriall,* 1669). Browne was a man of gentle birth, as "Mr." prefixed to his name in the colony records indicates. Chosen one of the Governor's Assistants in January 1635/36, he was reëlected annually (with the exception of the year 1646) for nineteen years, was a member of the Council of War in 1642, 1646, and 1653, and a Commissioner of the United Colonies of New England from 1644 to 1656. Removing from Plymouth to Cohannet, he was a proprietor when that settlement was incorporated as the town of Taunton in 1639. He had the respect and confidence of the Indians and was frequently the Colony's agent in dealings with them. In 1641 he and Edward Winslow [q.v.] were appointed to purchase from Massasoit the land comprising the present towns of Seekonk, Rehoboth, East Providence, and Pawtucket. Two years later he was an incorporator of Rehoboth. Going to Providence in 1645, on behalf of Plymouth Colony he opposed putting into effect Roger Williams's charter. He then proceeded to Shawomet where the outcast Samuel Gorton and his followers had settled, and forbade some twenty families from Massachusetts Bay to interfere with Gorton, claiming that the land belonged to Plymouth. Again in 1651 by setting Plymouth Colony's claim to jurisdiction in opposition to that of Massachusetts Bay he created a deadlock, the result of which was that Gorton retained his land. In October 1645, pursuant to a vote of a Rehoboth town meeting, Browne advanced money to purchase from the Wampanoags a tract known as Wannamoiset, lying between the Pawtucket River and Narragansett Bay. Here he settled permanently. One of the well-to-do among the colonists, he was characterized by a sturdy liberalism already exhibited in his championing of Gorton. He opposed the persecution of the Quakers and favored religious toleration, in 1655 pledging his estate to cover possible deficiencies in voluntary contributions so that Rehoboth need not be subjected to taxation for church support. In 1656 he went to England to take charge of the estate of his friend Sir Henry Vane, returning some four years later to his Wannamoiset home, where he died in 1662. His wife, Dorothy, died in 1674/75, aged about ninety. Browne had descendants through two sons and a daughter, the latter married to Thomas Willett, first English mayor of New York City.

[Wm. Bradford, *Hist. of Plymouth Plantation* (Mass. Hist. Soc. ed., 1912); *Winthrop's Journal*, ed by Jas. K. Hosmer (1908), II, 228–29, 261; Samuel Gorton, "Simplicities Defence against Seven-Headed Policy" with notes by Wm. R. Staples, *R. I. Hist. Soc. Colls.*, II (1835), 167 f., 249; Adelos Gorton, *The Life and Times of Samuel Gorton* (1907), pp. 18, 62, 64, 69; *New Eng. Hist. and Geneal. Reg.*, XXXVI, 368; *Mass. House Report No. 801*, Jan. 1915. The best account of Browne is by John A. Goodwin, in *The Pilgrim Republic* (1888), pp. 517–21. Many of the references to Browne in the *Records of the Colony of New Plymouth* and other publications have been compiled by Geo. Tilden Browne in *John Browne, Gentleman, of Plymouth* (privately printed, 1919).]   E. R. D.

BROWNE, JOHN ROSS (Feb. 11, 1821–Dec. 8, 1875), traveler and author, was born in Dublin and came to the United States with his parents, Thomas Egerton and Elana Buck Browne, in 1832 or 1833. He was the third of four children. The family settled in Louisville, Ky., and there John Ross spent the next half dozen years. The advantages of college training were denied him, but the direction of intelligent parents and his own easy acquisition of knowledge gave him a fund of information which he used to practical advantage. He wrote easily and was clever at caricaturing people and things about him. Both of these talents were cultivated from his early boyhood. At the age of eighteen he determined to travel. In order to secure funds necessary to gratify his desire, he deemed it wise to prepare himself for work in which competition was limited. With this in mind he studied shorthand. In November 1841 he went to Washington and had no difficulty in securing a position as reporter in the United States Senate. This lasted until the summer of 1842. He saved little money during the interval, but he accumulated quantities of contempt for the "big men" in Congress. Leaving Washington on July 5, he went to New Bedford, Mass., and shipped as a common sailor on a whaling vessel. The next quarter of a century was spent very largely in travel. He told a son years later that on one of his trips he had covered a hundred thousand miles. Observations made during these wanderings, and presented usually in a humorous vein, are found in *Etchings of a Whaling Cruise, with Notes of a Sojourn on the Island of Zanzibar* (1846); *Yusef; or, The Journey of the Frangi: A Crusade in the East* (1853); *Crusoe's Island: A Ramble in the Footsteps of Alexander Selkirk; With Sketches of Adventures in California and Washoe* (1864); *An American Family in Germany* (1866); *The Land of Thor* (1867); and *Adventures in the Apache Country: A Tour through Arizona and Sonora* (1869). He published numerous sketches in *Harper's Magazine*, many of which were later assembled in book form. (For a complete list see the Index to *Harper's New Monthly Magazine*, vols. I–XL.) Pen drawings of his own frequently accompanied his narratives. There are several reports that came from his pen while he was engaged in the government service, among which *Resources of the Pacific Slope* (1869) has been one of the most widely used. He was the official reporter for the convention that drew up California's first state constitution in 1849, and received $10,000 for his services. In 1868 he was appointed minister to China, but soon after arriving there expressed opinions which were contrary to the ideas of the Government as embodied in the Burlingame Treaty, and was recalled. In 1870 he settled in Oakland, Cal., a place he had called "home" since 1855, and entered the real estate business with offices in San Francisco. He was engaged in this at the time of his death. Browne had married, in 1844, Lucy Anna Mitchell, daughter of Dr. Spencer Cochrane Mitchell of Washington. Eight of his ten children reached maturity. Browne had a keen sense of humor, was versatile, modest, good-natured, cordial, and generous.

[A short sketch was published in *Harper's Weekly*, Feb. 22, 1868, later copied in the *Daily Alta California*, Mar. 21, 1868; *San Francisco Chronicle*, Feb. 13, 1881; H. H. Bancroft, *Hist. of Cal.*, VI (1888), 286, note 65. Obituaries in the *Oakland Daily Evening Tribune* and in the San Francisco *Evening Bulletin* for Dec. 8, 1875; in the *San Francisco Chronicle* and the *Sacramento Daily Record-Union* for Dec. 9, 1875; and in *Daily Alta California* for Dec. 9 and 12, 1875; additional information from Ross E. Browne, of Oakland, Cal.]

            C. G.

BROWNE, JUNIUS HENRI (Oct. 14, 1833– Apr. 2, 1902), journalist, was born in Seneca Falls, N. Y. His boyhood was spent in Cincinnati, where he received his education at St. Xavier College. At sixteen he went into his father's banking house but two years later left it for journalism. He served on several papers in Cincinnati and when the Civil War broke out became a war correspondent for the *New York Tribune*. For two years he followed the campaigns in the Southwest, witnessing several battles and the activities of the Union gunboat flotilla on the Mississippi. On May 3, 1863, with two other journalists, he accompanied an expedition which tried to run the Vicksburg batteries. The boat was sunk, and the journalists were captured by the Confederates. One of them, Richard T. Colburn of the New York *World*, was promptly paroled but Browne and his *Tribune* colleague, Albert D. Richardson, were not so fortunate. Apparently because of their connection with that paper and their presumed abolitionist convictions they were kept in prison with no prospect of release before the end of the war. Lieutenant-Colonel William H. Ludlow, agent for the exchange of prisoners, sought repeatedly, under special instructions from President Lincoln and Secretary Stanton, to obtain their liberation, but in vain (*Official Records,* Army). During a year and a half they were passed from prison to prison in Vicksburg, Jackson, Atlanta, Richmond—where they were incarcerated both in the famous Libby Prison and in Castle Thunder—and Salisbury. Their privations and sufferings in these institutions are told by Browne in his book, *Four Years in Secessia* (1865) with complete naïveté and the quiet assumption that adherence to the Con-

federate cause was in itself enough to turn ordinary human beings into creatures addicted to injustice, cruelty, and bad faith. Browne and Richardson finally escaped from Salisbury with three companions and traveled four hundred miles through the enemy's country. They suffered greatly from cold, hunger, and fatigue but with aid received from negroes, bushwackers, and Union sympathizers they succeeded in reaching the Union lines at Knoxville. After the war Browne was connected with the editorial staffs of the *New York Times* and the *Tribune* and acted as correspondent for many other newspapers throughout the country. He contributed to a number of magazines and wrote several books, including *The Great Metropolis; a Mirror of New York* (1869), *Sights and Sensations in Europe* (1871), and a series of small volumes on the French Revolution. He died in New York City.

[Obituaries in the *N. Y. Tribune* and *N. Y. Evening Post,* for Apr. 3, 1902.]

            H. H.

BROWNE, THOMAS (d. Aug. 3, 1825), was one of the most noted Tory partisan commanders in the South, during the Revolutionary War. The date and place of his birth are unknown, but he is described as a young man residing in Augusta, Ga., at the beginning of the war. He early declared his opposition to the Revolution, and ridiculed the Continental Congress in toasts given at dinner. Following this action he fled from the town, but was brought back; he was tarred, feathered, and carried for several miles in a cart, but refused to retract. Vengeance for this treatment was henceforth a controlling motive with him. He began raiding in 1776, and took part in an attack on Fort McIntosh in the southeastern part of the state in 1777. His importance began with his organization in Florida in 1778 of a regiment called the King's Rangers; of this regiment he was lieutenant-colonel, and he was soon notorious for his raids in Georgia. In the following year he was defeated in two engagements near Waynesboro by an inferior force led by Col. Twiggs, Col. Benjamin Few, and Col. William Few. He was present at the successful defense of Savannah. In 1780 he occupied Augusta, a strategic point on the Savannah River, banished the Whigs, and sequestrated their property. Here he was repeatedly attacked by Col. Clarke in September of that year. Browne, whose force comprised Florida Rangers, Creeks, and Cherokees, showed bravery, skill, and determination in the defense. He was wounded, and nearly on the point of surrender, when the siege was raised by the arrival of British forces under Col. Cruger. This period of irregular partisan warfare in the South abounded in atrocities, and Browne had an unenviable preëminence in this respect. After the successful defense of Augusta, some of his prisoners were hanged in his presence, and others were given to the Indians to be tortured to death. In 1781 he repulsed a night attack by Col. Harden, and soon afterward he was again besieged in Augusta by Pickens and Lee. By the use of a tower of logs which commanded his defenses, they compelled his surrender with about 300 men, June 5, 1781. So intense was the hatred felt toward Browne that he was especially guarded from avenging Whigs on his journey to the coast. That he was treated as a prisoner of war and exchanged was probably due to the British threat of hanging six Whig captives. After his release he was colonel of Queen's Rangers of South Carolina and superintendent of Indian Affairs in the South. His last conflict was on May 21–22, 1782; in an attempted sortie from Savannah he was defeated in a night attack by Wayne, who charged with the bayonet. Browne's rangers were dispersed in Florida and elsewhere, his estates in South Carolina and Georgia were confiscated, and he went to the Bahamas. From there in 1786 he wrote a criticism of Ramsay's history of the war which had severely condemned his cruelty (George White, *Historical Collections of Georgia,* 3rd ed., 1855, pp. 614–19). He received a grant in the island of St. Vincent in 1809, and died there in 1825. According to Charles C. Jones, *History of Georgia,* he was convicted of forgery in London in 1812 (doubted, with good reasons, by Sabine in his *Loyalists*). Browne undoubtedly had the qualities of bravery and good discipline, but he was revengeful and cruel. One biographer says, "Of all the human characters developed during this abnormal period . . . none can be named more notorious than Thomas Brown."

[Hugh McCall, *Hist. of Ga.* (1811–16); Chas. C. Jones, *Hist. of Ga.* (1883); Wm. B. Stevens, *Hist. of Ga.* (1847); Lorenzo Sabine, *Biog. Sketches of the Loyalists of the Am. Revolution* (1864); David Ramsay, *Hist. of the Revolution of S. C. from a British Province to an Independent State* (1785) and *Hist. of the Am. Revolution* (1793); Chas. Shephard, *Hist. Acct. of the Island of St. Vincent* (1831); obituary note in *Gentleman's Mag.,* Oct. 1825, p. 382.]   E. K. A.

BROWNE, WILLIAM (Mar. 5, 1737–Feb. 13, 1802), Loyalist, judge of the superior court of Massachusetts, governor of Bermuda, was born in Salem. His father, Samuel Browne, a graduate of Harvard in the class of 1727, was a member of a mercantile family, "the most respectable that has ever lived in the town of Salem, holding places of the highest trust in town, county, and State, and possessing great riches"

(*The Diary of William Pynchon,* 1890, p. 94n). His mother, Catherine Winthrop, daughter of John and Ann (Dudley) Winthrop, was descended from four colonial governors. William was brought up presumably by his mother and his step-father, for Samuel Browne died in 1742 and two years later his widow married Col. Epes Sargent, himself the founder of a distinguished family. William graduated from Harvard in 1755, valedictorian of his class (*The Holyoke Diaries,* 1911, p. 14) and third in order of social position. He studied law, but abandoned practise to attend to the increase of his already considerable estate.

In 1762 he was elected to the Assembly, and two years later was appointed collector of the port of Salem. At this time he was in sympathy with those who resented the imposition of taxes by Parliament, and his leniency in enforcing the odious Sugar Act caused his dismissal from the collectorship in the winter of 1766–67 (Joseph B. Felt, *Annals of Salem,* 1849, II, 262 f.). Later, however, his inherent love of order made him unwilling to offer resistance to established authority, and in 1768 when the Massachusetts legislature received instructions from England to rescind its resolutions expressing protest against the Townshend Acts, Browne voted with the minority of seventeen in favor of rescinding. This action lost him his seat at the succeeding general election. In 1770 he became judge of the court of common pleas of Essex County, and in 1771 was commissioned by Gov. Hutchinson colonel of the Essex militia. In May 1774 Gov. Gage nominated him as judge of the superior court; the nomination met with opposition and was not confirmed until June. In August he was one of those appointed to the Governor's Council by writ of *mandamus,* a proceeding bitterly resented by the more radical colonials. Of the thirty-six appointees only ten, Browne among them, took the required oath. He was approached on Sept. 9 by a committee of the patriot convention then meeting at Ipswich who asked him to resign both of the offices he held under the Crown. This he declined to do, stating that "neither persuasions can allure me, nor shall menaces compel me to do anything derogatory to the character of a councillor of his majesty's province of the Massachusetts Bay" (*Journals of Each Provincial Congress of Massachusetts, etc.,* 1838, p. 618). On Oct. 4 the officers of his militia regiment resigned their commissions, refusing to serve under him, and within the month he left Salem. He went to Boston, where he remained until March 1776, when the British forces under Lord Howe evacuated the city, then went to England by way of Halifax, bearing Howe's dispatches to the home government and reaching London about the first of May (*The Journal and Letters of Samuel Curwen*, 4th ed., 1864, p. 58). Here he resided for the next five years, continuing to draw £200 per annum as judge of the superior court of Massachusetts Bay. His name was included in the Banishment Act passed by the Massachusetts legislature in 1778, and in 1779, by the Conspiracy Act, his property was declared forfeit.

Early in 1781, possibly through the influence of Benjamin Thompson (later Count Rumford), whom as a youth Browne had befriended (*Pynchon*, p. 94n), he was appointed governor of Bermuda, entering upon his new office in January 1782. Because of his own colonial birth and experience he understood the view-point of the island colonials as none of his home-born predecessors had been able to do, and won favor by his first speech to the legislature. He opened the whale-fishery, which for years had been restricted by high gubernatorial license, encouraged cotton culture, and promoted ship building. At his coming the public finances had been in bad condition; he reorganized them and left them flourishing. In 1788 he returned to England, his departure sincerely regretted (William Frith Williams, *An Historical and Statistical Account of the Bermudas*, 1848, pp. 97-101). For the rest of his life he made his home in Percy St., Westminster. His wife, Ruth Wanton, daughter of Gov. Joseph Wanton of Rhode Island, died on May 13, 1799 (*Gentleman's Magazine*, May 1799), and he survived her less than three years.

Browne was characterized by his classmate, John Adams, as "a solid, judicious character." Adams continued, "They made him a judge of the superior court and that society made of him a refugee. A Tory I verily believe he never was" (*Works of John Adams*, 1856, X, 195-96). He retained the esteem of his Salem neighbors throughout his life, and was cordially welcomed when he paid them a visit in 1784 while governor of Bermuda.

[In addition to sources cited see *The Diary of Wm. Bentley*, II (1907), 425; *The Diaries of Benj. Lynde and of Benj. Lynde, Jr.* (1880), esp. p. 145; *Essex Inst. Hist. Colls.*, XLIII, 290 ff.; Emory Washburn, *Sketches of the Judicial Hist. of Mass.* (1840); John Russell Bartlett, *Hist. of the Wanton Family of Newport, R. I.* (1878), esp. p. 78; *New Eng. Hist. and Geneal. Reg.*, V, 49, 51; obituary note in *Gentleman's Mag.* (London), Mar. 1802, p. 275. Ezra D. Hines, "Browne Hill and Some History Connected with It," in *Essex Inst. Hist. Colls.*, vol. XXXII (1896), presents an incomplete account and Dean Dudley, *Hist. of the Dudley Family* (1886-94), pp. 682, 1035, 1057, is inaccurate in some details.]
E. R. D.

BROWNE, WILLIAM HAND (Dec. 31, 1828–Dec. 13, 1912), author, educator, was born in a house on Paca St., Baltimore. His father,

William Browne, descendant of an old family on the Eastern Shore of Maryland, had moved to Baltimore and was a member of a firm of commission merchants, trading largely with the West Indies. His mother, Patience Hand, had come to Baltimore in 1794 with her father, Moses Hand, an artist of commendable ability as a painter of landscapes and portraits, who upon settling in Baltimore continued the pursuit of his profession. William Hand Browne obtained all of his education in Baltimore, first in the private school of T. P. Carter, later in a local college no longer existing, and finally in the University of Maryland, where he received the degree of M.D. in 1850. The practise of medicine, however, was distasteful to him, and he never entered upon it. For the next ten years he was associated with his cousin, T. J. Hand, in the commission business. When this firm was dissolved in 1861 Browne's literary career began with the publication in the *South*, a Baltimore daily, of a translation from the German of a story entitled "The Armourer," which owing to the state of the public mind attracted wide attention. This was followed by a period of travel and observation in the South. In June 1863, Browne married Mary Catherine Owings, daughter of Dr. Thomas Owings of Baltimore, and removed his residence to Baltimore County. After the close of the Civil War he came into prominence, in the work of restoring the cultural conditions of the South, through his connection with various literary periodicals. In January 1867 he joined with Alfred Taylor Bledsoe in founding the *Southern Review*, and remained as editor for two years, after which he became co-editor with Lawrence Turnbull of the *New Eclectic Magazine*, later called the *Southern Magazine*, with which he remained till 1875. During part of this time he was also editor of the *Statesman*, a weekly paper devoted to politics, literature, and art, started in 1868, but lasting only a year and a half. He was also joint editor of text-books on English literature and the history of Maryland, and of a concise English dictionary. With Richard Malcolm Johnston he brought out a *Life of Alexander H. Stephens* in 1878. In 1879 he became librarian of the Johns Hopkins University and remained with that institution in various capacities until the time of his death as professor emeritus of English literature. During this academic period Browne rendered important services to the history of Maryland. In 1882 an act of the General Assembly placed the provincial records in the charge of the Maryland Historical Society with provision for publication. Browne was chosen editor and carried out his task with expert knowledge and meticulous care. At the close of his life he had brought out thirty-two of the large quarto volumes of these *Archives of Maryland*. Further historical contributions included volumes on *Maryland: the History of a Palatinate* (Commonwealth Series, 1884); and *George Calvert and Cecilius Calvert, Barons Baltimore of Baltimore* (1890). Browne also edited the first two parts of the "Calvert Papers" (*Maryland Historical Society Fund Publications*, vols. XXVIII and XXXIV, 1889–94) and the *Writings of Severn Teakle Wallis* (1896). Upon the establishment by the Historical Society of the quarterly *Maryland Historical Magazine* he was made editor and became responsible for the first five volumes (1906–10).

Browne's activities as a teacher began after he had passed his fiftieth year. Of medium height, of vigorous frame, but slightly stooping in carriage, his twinkling eyes set in a full bearded face, his careful enunciation and moderated tones were marked with the playful humor of the cultivated gentleman. His broad scope of information and his artistic skill made him a recourse for colleagues in difficulty about almost any subject from bibliography or cryptograms to heraldry and music, and to every one his office door was hospitably open. The wide range of his learning in classical as well as modern literature made deep impression upon serious students, although his lectures were too much like polished essays to attract the indifferent. His devotion to Scottish poetry as a theme of instruction resulted in the publication of *Selections from the Early Scottish Poets* (1896), and *The Taill of Rauf Coilyear* (1903). His literary monuments, however, are to be found in the field of American colonial history.

[Biographical sketch by J. W. Bright, with tributes by other writers, in *Johns Hopkins Univ. Circulars*, 1913, No. 2, under the title "In Memoriam, William Hand Browne, 1828–1912."]   J.M.V.

BROWNELL, HENRY HOWARD (Feb. 6, 1820–Oct. 31, 1872), poet, was born in Providence, R. I. His father was Dr. Pardon Brownell, a physician, brother of Bishop Thomas Church Brownell [*q.v.*]; his mother, Lucia de Wolf. In 1862 he published in the Hartford (Conn.) *Evening Press* a rhymed version of Farragut's "General Orders" which brought him to the commander's attention; and that the author's desire to witness a naval battle might be gratified, Farragut secured his appointment as master mate in the navy, from which position he was advanced to ensign with special duties on the *Hartford* as the commander's secretary. He was in the battle of Mobile Bay and several other en-

gagements, and wrote, almost in the smoke of them, a number of descriptive poems of great vividness and force. In 1864 he published *Lyrics of a Day, or Newspaper-Poetry by a Volunteer in the U. S. Service*. He was one of the most popular of the war poets. Oliver Wendell Holmes dubbed him "Our Battle Laureate" (*Atlantic Monthly*, May 1865). After the war he accompanied Admiral Farragut on his European tour. again acting as ensign and secretary.

His naval service was the one great episode in a comparatively short life. He came of seafaring ancestors, loved the sea, and a spirit of adventure was in him; yet he was of modest, retiring disposition, preëminently a scholar. Holmes called him one of the "most highly endowed persons" he had ever met, and Thomas Bailey Aldrich, in two poems bearing Brownell's name, pays high tribute to his worth as a man and poet (*Ibid.*, May 1873, April 1888). He lived a quiet bachelor's life in East Hartford, Conn., to which place his family had moved when he was a child. Summers he found recreation sailing his cat-boat on Narragansett Bay. He had graduated from Washington (now Trinity) College, Hartford, in 1841, and had taught in Mobile, Ala., for a period, but returning to Hartford, had been admitted to the bar in 1844. He soon turned from practise to literary work, in which he was associated with his brother. In 1851 he published *The People's Book of Ancient and Modern History*, and in 1853 *The Discoverers, Pioneers, and Settlers of North and South America*. As early as 1847 he had published *Poems,* and in 1855 appeared *Ephemerson,* so called from a poem it contains dealing with conditions leading up to the Crimean War. His career ended in his fifty-second year after he had bravely endured a lingering death from cancer of the face.

Considered as a whole, his poems are often tediously long, frequently imitative, and sometimes crude in form. His war poems, however, have high merit. Accuracy of observation is recorded in vivid descriptions, the language of which is vigorous and sometimes racy, while through them all burn passionate loyalty and invincible faith in the Union cause. A selection from these, entitled *Lines of Battle*, by M. A. De Wolfe Howe was published in 1912, and has an informing introduction.

[In addition to references above see Richard Burton, *Literary Likings* (1898); *Cambridge Hist. of Am. Lit.* (1918), II, 277–78; *Atlantic Mo.*, C, 588–93; Ferris Greenslet, *Thos. Bailey Aldrich* (1908), 156–57; C. E. Norton, *Letters of James Russell Lowell*, II, 350–51; *Hartford Courant*, Nov. 9, 1872.]   H.E.S.

BROWNELL, THOMAS CHURCH (Oct. 19, 1779–Jan. 13, 1865), Episcopal bishop, college president, was descended from Thomas, son of Sir Thomas Brownell, who came from England about 1650 and made his home in Little Compton, R. I.; and he was the son of Sylvester and Nancy (Church) Brownell, who lived in Westport, Mass. Here Thomas Church Brownell was born. His early training was that of a farmer's boy, and his education was that of the district school. When he was about eighteen years old, on the advice of the village pastor, with whom he had studied for a time, he went to Bristol Academy in Taunton to prepare for admission to the College of Rhode Island, now Brown University. He entered that institution in the fall of 1800. He remained there only two years, however, for when the then president, the Rev. Dr. Maxcy, accepted the presidency of Union College, Brownell followed him to Union, where he graduated with high honors in the class of 1804. On Apr. 5, 1805, he became tutor in the Latin and Greek languages in Union College and two years later was made professor of belles lettres and moral philosophy and, again after two years, professor of chemistry and mineralogy. The latter was a new department at Union, and Brownell was given a year's leave of absence in Europe to study similar departments there. His marriage in August 1811 to Charlotte Dickinson of Lansingburg, N. Y., an ardent Episcopalian, changed the course of his life. For some time he had been interested in theological matters. He had investigated the doctrines of Calvinism professed by his family, but had been unable to accept them, even in the "mitigated form" presented by the Rev. Eliphalet Potter, whose guidance he had sought. Further study had convinced him of the historical and scriptural grounds of Episcopacy. Now, under his wife's influence, he became an Episcopalian and began the study of theology with the ministry in view. On Apr. 11, 1816, he was ordained deacon by Bishop Hobart in Trinity Church, New York City, and on Aug. 4 of that year was advanced to the priesthood by the same bishop. On June 11, 1818, he was nominated by the rector of Trinity Church, New York, as an assistant minister, and was working in that capacity when the Diocese of Connecticut unanimously elected him to be the successor of Bishop Jarvis. He was consecrated bishop in Trinity Church, New Haven, Oct. 27, 1819. His advancement was remarkable, for it was only three years and a half since he had been made a deacon.

The first year of his episcopate Brownell lived in Hartford, serving as rector of Christ Church in addition to performing his duties as bishop.

The General Theological Seminary, at first located in New York City, was in 1820 removed to New Haven, and Brownell took up his residence there to be in close touch with the Seminary. But in less than two years it went back to New York, and the Bishop again made his home in Hartford. Connecticut Episcopalians had long had it in mind to establish in Connecticut a college of their own. They had vainly tried to enlarge the charter of the Episcopal Academy of Connecticut, so that it might confer degrees. With the adoption of the new state constitution in 1818, and the consequent loosening of the grip of the Congregational standing order, their chance had come, and a charter was granted in 1823 to Washington, now Trinity, College. It was located in Hartford, and Brownell became its first president. He was essentially an educator, and he threw himself heart and soul into the task of placing the newly organized college upon a firm foundation. The diocese, however, soon felt that his whole time and energy should be given to his episcopal duties, and in 1831 he relinquished the presidency, though he continued to hold the office of chancellor. In 1829, in response to the request of the Missionary Society, he made an extensive tour through the states of Kentucky, Mississippi, Louisiana, and Alabama, and again in the winter and spring of 1834–35 he visited this region, and as a result of his journeys an impetus was given to the Episcopal Church throughout the entire section. He compiled a Commentary on the Book of Common Prayer, which in its day was highly regarded. He also compiled other works of a religious character, and many of his addresses and charges to his convention were printed in pamphlet form. On the death of Bishop Philander Chase in 1852, Brownell became the presiding bishop by right of seniority. For the ten years immediately preceding his death his physical condition was such that he could do but little work, and his life slowly and wearily dragged to its end. He died in Hartford and was buried there.

[Brownell's autobiography, printed in E. E. Beardsley, *Hist. of the Episc. Ch. in Conn.*, vol. II (1868); *Calendar*, Jan. 1865; *Ch. Rev.*, July 1865; various memorial sermons and addresses; information from a grand-daughter, Mrs. Thomas Brownell Chapman.]
W. A. B.

BROWNELL, WILLIAM CRARY (Aug. 30, 1851–July 22, 1928), critic, was descended on both sides from early New England settlers. His father, Isaac Wilbour Brownell, a commission merchant in New York City, was born at Westport, Mass., on the border of Rhode Island; his mother, Lucia Emilie (Brown) Brownell, was born near-by in the town of Little Compton,

R. I. His maternal grandmother belonged to another branch of the Brownell family which included Bishop Thomas Church Brownell [*q.v.*], author of a commentary on the Prayer Book, and his nephew Henry Howard Brownell [*q.v.*], a Civil War poet. Thus the future critic's New England inheritance was flavored with Episcopalianism and a tradition of literary achievement. He was born in New York City, but when he was five years old the family moved to Buffalo and there remained for another five years. An only child, he first attended a dame's school, and then Miss Gardner's school for larger children, where Platt Rogers Spencer [*q.v.*], inventor of the Spencerian penmanship, was visiting writing master and doubtless helped to develop the habits of precision later so notable in his pupil. From this period also dated Brownell's love of France, first inspired by his drawing teacher, M. Liard. Always an absorbed reader, during these early years he was especially devoted to the stories of the Old Testament, his familiarity with which is attested by the unusual number of Biblical quotations in his works. Precociously interested in politics and religion, he was already at the age of ten a confirmed Democrat, an Abolitionist, and an Episcopalian.

On the death of his mother Brownell was taken to live with her parents at Adamsville, R. I., where he attended a country school for two years, after which he went to Mr. Fay's boarding-school in Newport until the age of sixteen when he entered Amherst College. After his graduation in 1871, he became a reporter on the New York *World,* and at the age of twenty-one was made city editor. Journalism was then still a literary art; the *World's* staff included such writers as Manton Marble, Montgomery Schuyler, Andrew Carpenter Wheeler, and David Goodman Croly [*qq.v.*]. Brownell's life, always mainly constituted by his friendships for men and books, became unusually rich in intellectual contacts. At this time he began to frequent the art studios of Homer Martin, Thomas Eakins, John La Farge, Olin Warner, and John Quincy Adams Ward [*qq.v.*]. From 1879 to 1881 he was on the staff of the *Nation,* where again he was associated with a brilliant group, headed by Edward Lawrence Godkin [*q.v.*]. Married in January 1878 to Virginia Shields Swinburne, daughter of Daniel T. Swinburne of Newport, Brownell sailed with his wife in October 1881 for a three years' residence abroad, mainly in Paris. He and his wife returned to America in August 1884 and then lived for nearly two years in Philadelphia, where he was employed on the staff of the *Philadelphia Press.* In January 1888

he became editor and literary adviser in the firm of Charles Scribner's Sons, a position which he was to retain until his death more than forty years later. His first wife died in 1911, and in January 1921 he married Gertrude Hall, poet and translator of Verlaine and Rostand.

During the long years with Scribner's, Brownell's rich humanity lifted the editorial work far above the level of routine. He was uncompromising in his standards, but his critical severity was tempered by kindness and quiet geniality. "In spite of the great dignity of Mr. Brownell's bearing and expression, which might have made people stand in awe of him, he was in human touch with all the employees in the building. . . . He was truly, instinctively democratic,—one who knew that the largest elements in men are shared by all of them—that distinctions of intellect and education are comparatively trifling ones" (Robert Bridges, *A Companionable Colleague,* pamphlet, 1929).

Above financial need and devoid of zeal for fame, writing carefully and unhurriedly, Brownell brought out, at comparatively long intervals, a series of critical volumes notable for their polished Latinized style and serious content. His work, even when it dealt with foreign themes, was fundamentally a criticism of American culture as expressed in manners, art, and letters. Thus his first volume *French Traits* (1889), bearing as a sub-title, "An Essay in Comparative Criticism," elaborates a series of antitheses between Gallic idealization of reason and honor, Gallic respect for institutions, Gallic social instinct, and American idealization of emotion and duty, American distrust of institutions, American individualism. As a study of racial characteristics the book ranks with Emerson's *English Traits.* Finding the central evil of American life in its excessive individualism, self-condemned by the astonishing number of eccentrics, fanatics, and ill-mannered bores which it has bred, Brownell was still well aware of the value of the individual creative energy released by the romantic ideal, and in his criticism here as always he strove for sanity and the mean. The same orientation governed his second work, *French Art* (1892) which, probably more than any other critical writing, brought to America due recognition of the value of modern French painting and sculpture. At the same time it revealed certain limitations in the critic's sympathies. Brownell shared his generation's antipathy to England: this prevented his acknowledging the influence of Constable and Turner on French painting; he also shared, though in slighter measure, his generation's antipathy to radical experiment or self-expression, and thus, although he accepted Rodin enthusiastically because of his poetic quality, he entirely missed Daumier, Renoir, and Cézanne. After *Newport* (1896), a charming descriptive sketch of the city of his youth, Brownell's next three works, *Victorian Prose Masters* (1901), *American Prose Masters* (1909), and *Criticism* (1914) embodied a defense and exemplification of judicial criticism. Every work of art being the concrete expression of a personality, the task of criticism, according to Brownell, is the interpretation and evaluation of this personality according to the norms of beauty or "reason expressed in form." The application of this criterion led in *Victorian Prose Masters* to eulogistic judgments of Thackeray and Arnold, a cool appraisal of George Eliot and Meredith, and derogatory estimates of Carlyle and Ruskin; in *American Prose Masters* it resulted in a glorification of Emerson, a rehabilitation of Cooper, a much qualified respect for Hawthorne and Lowell, an absolute refusal to accept Poe as a great writer, and a rather puzzled attitude toward Henry James. The basis for the evaluation in each case was a ruthless analysis of the author's content and manner, conducted with such thoroughness as to give an appearance of objective finality to Brownell's conclusions even in this dangerously subjective field. In *Standards* (1917) he pointed out the contemporary decline of public taste and of literary style, due, he thought, to the disintegrating individualism and sensationalism of the day; in *The Genius of Style* (1924) he enlarged upon the same theme, contrasting the ideal of disciplined inspiration consciously directed toward impersonal ends with the current surrender to personal impulse, egotism, and anarchy. Finally, in what he knew was to be his last book, *Democratic Distinction in America* (1927), he made his peace with the world in a reiteration of faith in the organic spirit of society as competent in the long run to curb individual extravagance and levity.

Brownell was the last of the Victorians. Brought up in a period of expanding industry, he never questioned the virtues of industrialism and had less than his usual patience with its radical critics, such as Carlyle and Ruskin; hence its inevitable but less desirable social consequences seemed to him merely wilful and to be overcome by a simple change of heart. He had little of the philosopher's skepticism; indeed, he considered "a smattering of philosophy" sufficient for the critic; for this reason he never examined the ethical presuppositions upon which his theoretical universe was constructed. Thus he quite

failed to understand the naturalistic basis of the passionate revolt whose echoes disturbed his later years. On the other hand, if he was unable, fundamentally, to justify the Victorian attitude theoretically, he illustrated it in his practise most attractively. The quiet self-respect and reticence of his style were in themselves a rebuke to contemporary vulgarity; his devotion to high, even though often vaguely defined ideals, gave the cast of nobility to his work; his instinct for the avoidance of extremes, accompanied by a gracious worldly wisdom and a kind of enlightened common sense, lent weight to his judgments. He may be regarded as a connecting link between the Sainte-Beuve–Arnold tradition and the New Humanism of Irving Babbitt, Paul Elmer More, and Stuart Sherman: but he was too well disciplined to share the later school's excessive praise of discipline. While neither the most profound nor learned of American critics he was, perhaps, the sanest.

[*Amherst College Biog. Record* (1927), p. 307; *N. Y. Times, N. Y. Herald-Tribune*, July 23, 1928; *Who's Who in America*, 1928–29; information as to specific facts from Mrs. Gertrude Hall Brownell, N. Y. City.]
E. S. B.

BROWNING, JOHN MOSES (Jan. 21, 1855– Nov. 26, 1926), inventor, was born in Ogden, Utah, of Mormon parentage, son of Jonathan Browning, a gunsmith, and Elizabeth Caroline (Clark). From childhood Browning displayed a remarkable talent for invention. At the age of thirteen he made his first gun of scrap iron in his father's gunshop. In 1879 he secured his first patent for a breech-loading single-shot rifle. He, with his brother Mathew, made about 600 of these rifles, one of which was brought to the attention of the Winchester Repeating Arms Company who were so impressed with the simple and effective design of the arm that they paid the brothers large royalties to allow the Winchester Company to produce this rifle, which is still being made by them. Browning's association with the Winchester Company led him into the field of repeating rifles and shotguns. He designed many types of sporting firearms, such as the Remington Auto-loading shotguns and rifles; the Winchester repeating shotguns; single-shot and repeating rifles; the Stevens rifles; and the Colt automatic pistols. The repeating rifle was patented in 1884; the box magazine in 1895; and numerous other patents were secured on rapid-fire guns. From all of these Browning drew large royalties. With his brother, he organized the J. M. & M. S. Browning Company, and the Browning Brothers Company, branching out from gun-making to banking and stock-raising, until their estates, at the time of his death, were rated in many millions.

In 1890 a machine gun of Browning design, but known as the Colt, was adopted by the United States Army. The first machine gun turned out by Browning was made famous during the Spanish-American conflict through its effective work in both land and naval engagements around Santiago. It became known as the "Peacemaker." Browning produced in 1896 the automatic pistol, later improved and used by the United States Army in the World War. The manufacturing rights for this weapon were obtained by the Colt Patent Firearms Manufacturing Company of Hartford, Conn.

In May 1917, when the secretary of war ordered a Machine Gun Board to test all machine guns and automatic rifles submitted to it, Browning submitted through the Colt Company two guns, one, the heavy water-cooled machine gun, and the other the light Browning automatic rifle, demonstrating these guns himself. They proved to be superior to anything else tested or known, and were so declared by the Board. The Browning Machine Gun, Model of 1917, the Browning Automatic Rifle, Model of 1918, and the Automatic Pistol, Model of 1911, were supplied to the United States Army in large numbers. The Browning Aircraft Machine Gun, which is the Browning heavy type machine gun modified for use in aircraft, has a rate of fire of 1150–1250 shots per minute and can be used with a synchronizer to fire through propeller blades, being fired from a special aircraft mounting. One of Browning's machine guns, adopted by the United States Army in 1918, at its official trial fired 39,500 rounds before a breakage developed.

Browning's inventions never lacked a market. From the time he manufactured his first gun until the World War made him more widely known, he received flattering offers for his ideas and inventions almost as soon as they had taken definite shape on the work bench. No design of Browning's ever proved a failure, nor was any arm produced by him ever discontinued. At the time of his death he was working on an "over and under" double-barrelled shotgun. He always avoided publicity and his name was used in one establishment only, the Fabrique National at Liège, Belgium, and only on his last machine gun and automatic rifle. He was made a Chevalier of the Order of Leopold and was decorated by King Albert of Belgium on the occasion of the completion of the millionth automatic pistol at Liège. His longest and last association in this country was with the officials of the Colt Patent Firearms Company, with whom he worked for many years. He was considered one of the greatest inventors of small arms in history and was foremost in the field of automatic weapons. He was a man of sterling character, a cheerful companion, modest, quiet, and unassuming. He died suddenly of heart disease at Herstals, near Liège, Belgium, where he had gone on a mission to Belgium's national armament factory, in which he was interested. When his remains were brought to this country they were received with military honors and forwarded to his home at Ogden, Utah. He was married in 1879 to Rachel D. Child.

[*Who's Who in America*, 1926–27; Patent Office Records; *Army Ordnance*, vol. VII; *New Internat. Year Book*, 1926; *Salt Lake Tribune*, Nov. 27, 1926.]

C. F. C.

BROWNING, ORVILLE HICKMAN (Feb. 10, 1806–Aug. 10, 1881), lawyer, politician, was born in Harrison County, Ky., the son of Micaijah Browning and Sally Brown. He attended Augusta College, but financial reverses in his family compelled him to leave before receiving his degree. He studied law at Cynthiana, Ky., and in 1831 settled in Quincy, the county seat of Adams County, Ill. Here he soon engaged in politics, and was elected state senator as a Whig in 1836. He gained momentary unpopularity by refusing to support the internal improvement scheme espoused by Abraham Lincoln which almost wrecked the state financially. In 1842 he was elected to the lower house in the General Assembly and in 1843 he contested the seat in Congress with Stephen A. Douglas. The district had been formed by a Democratic legislature with the express intention of giving Douglas a seat but Browning ran him so strenuous a race that both men broke down physically on the eve of Douglas's election. In 1850 and 1852 Browning was again defeated. Like many conservative Illinois Whigs, he was slow to cast in his lot with the Republican party. In the state convention of 1856, he drafted the platform, helping to give it the conservative slant that would attract the old Whigs to the new party. It is quite possible that Browning felt some jealousy at the rapid rise of his old associate, Abraham Lincoln, although the two had been most intimate friends for many years. He was suspected, probably not without reason, of lukewarmness in the cause of Lincoln's presidential aspirations. As a member of the state delegation to the Republican Convention of 1860, however, Browning took a prominent part in winning over other delegates to accept Lincoln as a second choice. His own choice for the nomination was Judge Edward Bates of Missouri and he had endeavored in the earlier part of 1860 to line up the state of Illinois for him.

Lincoln showed Browning in advance the copy of his inaugural address and Browning suggested some important changes, regarding the new president's attitude toward federal property in the South, which Lincoln incorporated. On the death of Stephen A. Douglas, Browning was appointed by Gov. Yates to fill the unexpired term. This brought him to Washington for the special session of 1861 and the regular session of 1861–62. In the Senate, for a while, he was the spokesman of Lincoln's Border State policy but gradually as Lincoln moved on in the direction of emancipation, he and Browning drifted apart. Browning took his political life in his hand by opposing the second Confiscation Act and made no secret of the fact that he regarded the Emancipation Proclamation as a calamity. His backward attitude in the election of 1862 was partly responsible for the election of a Democratic legislature in Illinois, which in turn promptly elected William A. Richardson senator in his room.

In the course of 1863 Browning returned to Washington to establish what was ostensibly a law partnership with Thomas Ewing, ex-Senator Cowan, and Britton Hill. Actually, Ewing and Browning traded on their influence with the leaders of the Republican party in securing special favors for contractors. Browning renewed his old intimacy with Lincoln and in connection with James W. Singleton, an old Illinois Whig who had become something of a copperhead, planned to secure special permission to bring Confederate produce through the Federal lines with huge profits to himself and his associates. The collapse of the Confederacy prevented him from reaping his profits.

As Browning was the advocate of the old Border State policy, he naturally turned with disgust from the radical reconstruction policy that followed the assassination of Lincoln. Accordingly, he became a supporter of Andrew Johnson. In May 1866 he was installed as Johnson's adviser on the Illinois patronage. He took an active part in the Philadelphia Convention and on Sept. 1, 1866, became secretary of the interior in Johnson's cabinet. For a few months he also held the office of attorney-general. He had for some time foreseen the impeachment of Johnson and stood loyally by the President during his struggle. Along with Johnson, he left office on Mar. 4, 1869. On his return to Illinois he was elected on the Democratic ticket to the state constitutional convention of 1869–70. His influence was mainly responsible for the adoption of the principle of minority representation. It is interest-ing to note that he had willingly pledged himself to oppose the principle of negro suffrage.

Browning and his partner, Nehemiah Bushnell, had been engaged in a steadily expanding legal business since the fifties. Both men took a warm interest in the railroad development, Browning becoming one of the special attorneys for the Chicago, Burlington & Quincy. He argued before the Supreme Court the case of *Chicago, Burlington & Quincy* vs. *Iowa* which was one of the leading Granger cases. He was consistently a lawyer defending vested interests against the principles of government regulation. In person, he was tall, well-built, of stately carriage, bald in later years, and with a ruddy complexion. He had the suave and formal manners of a Kentucky gentleman of the old school and wore ruffled shirts to the end of his life. He was married, in 1836, to Eliza Caldwell.

[Browning's diary, written intermittently from 1850 to 1881, is being published in the *Ill. State Hist. Lib. Colls.* Aside from this, the obituary in *Proc. Ill. State Bar Ass.*, 1882, is the best life of Browning available. There is also an obituary in the *Chi. Daily Tribune*, Aug. 12, 1881.]   T.C.P.

BROWNLEE, WILLIAM CRAIG (1784–Feb. 10, 1860), Presbyterian clergyman, was the fifth child of James Brownlee, a farmer of Lanarkshire, Scotland, and his wife Margaret Craig. He graduated and took his M.A. with honors at the University of Glasgow, studied theology under Rev. Dr. Bruce and was licensed by the Presbytery of Sterling in 1808. He came to America at about this time and became pastor of the Associate Church, Mount Pleasant, Pa. From 1813 to 1816, he was pastor of the Associate Scotch Church, Philadelphia. From 1816 to 1819, he had charge of the Queen's College (Rutgers) Academy, New Brunswick, N. J. From 1819 to 1825 he was pastor of the Presbyterian Church, Basking Ridge, N. J., and principal of a classical academy there. In 1825 he became a professor of languages at Rutgers, and on June 18, 1826 he was installed associate pastor of the Collegiate Church, New York City, his particular charge being the Middle Church on Lafayette Place. On Sept. 23, 1843, while in Newburgh to fulfil a lecture engagement, he was stricken down with paralysis which incapacitated him for all further work. He lived however till Feb. 10, 1860. He received the degree of D.D. by unanimous vote of the Senate of Glasgow University, Dec. 6, 1824, in recognition of his *Inquiry into the Principles of the Quakers* (1824).

Brownlee was an orthodox Calvinist. His sermons were doctrinal and scriptural and were characterized by a clear, finished, extemporaneous style, with much use of the imagination. He was an eloquent preacher with a strong Scotch brogue. He was one of the earliest of the Protestant clergy of America to take a firm anti-Catholic stand and he at times incurred personal danger therefrom. He was also an uncompromising foe of Unitarianism and Universalism. All his convictions were strong and he held them with an unswerving tenacity inherited from generations of Covenanter ancestry. His scholarship was exact and his learning extensive. From 1826 to 1830 he edited the *Magazine of the Reformed Dutch Church of America,* writing many of its articles himself. He was the author of several anti-Catholic works, such as *Letters in the Roman Catholic Controversy* (1834), *Popery an Enemy to Civil and Religious Liberty* (1836), *The Doctrinal Decrees and Canons of the Council of Trent* (1836), *Romanism in the Light of Prophecy and History; its Final Downfall and Triumph of the Church of Christ* (1854) ; a number of general religious and theological subjects; and is credited with a novel, *The Whigs of Scotland; a Romance.*

There is a very impressive portrait of Brownlee in gown and bands, at the Collegiate Church of St. Nicholas, Fifth Ave., N. Y. He had a fresh, open countenance and a kindly expression. In 1807, he married at Kilsyth, Scotland, Maria McDougall who lived till September 1849.

[Shortly after Brownlee's death, a volume was issued entitled *Memorial of the Rev. Dr. Brownlee,* which contains much biographical material. Corwin's *Manual of the Reformed Ch. in America* (4th ed. 1902) contains a good article, with a complete list of Brownlee's publications. Another sketch is found in the *Collegiate Ch. Year Book, 1896.*]   F.T.P.

BROWNLOW, WILLIAM GANNAWAY (Aug. 29, 1805–Apr. 29, 1877), governor of Tennessee, was born in Wythe County, Va. His parents, Joseph A. Brownlow and Catharine (Gannaway) Brownlow, were among the many Virginians who migrated to eastern Tennessee in the early nineteenth century and developed in that somewhat isolated region a community distinct in culture and opinion. Some five years after the birth of their son they settled near Knoxville. Joseph Brownlow died in 1816, and the death of his wife three months later left the boy to grow up in the care of his mother's relatives. He had little schooling, but, while learning the carpenter's trade, studied the common branches and acquired a fair education, especially in English literature and the Bible, and subsequently prepared for the Methodist ministry, which he entered in 1826. For ten years he served as an itinerant preacher, but his intense interest in public questions, and a natural gift of pungent speech soon led him into political as well as religious controversy. In his speeches and in a pamphlet defending his political activity, he avowed beliefs and displayed a fearlessness that were to make him a national figure thirty years later. This pamphlet, a controversy with a Calvinistic preacher named Posey (October 1832), contained his first published utterance on the slavery question. He said that he expected to see the day when slavery, not the tariff, would shake the government to its foundations, and that when such a day came he, though no opponent of slavery, would stand by the government. He became in 1838 the editor of the *Tennessee Whig* (Elizabethton), and the following year, of the *Jonesboro Whig and Independent* which he edited until 1849. In that year he entered upon his editorship of the *Knoxville Whig,* which under his hand was soon the most influential paper in eastern Tennessee and before the Civil War had a circulation larger than that of any other political paper in the state. He was a candidate against Andrew Johnson for nomination to Congress in 1843 and in 1850 was one of several commissioners appointed by President Fillmore to carry out the improvement of the Missouri River for which Congress had made provision. He had always been a "Federal Whig" of the Washington and Hamilton type," always a "national" man, an unconditional advocate of the preservation of the Union. On Nov. 17, 1860, he declared editorially that Lincoln, though elected by a sectional vote, "is chosen president, and whether with or without the consent and participation of the South, will be and ought to be inaugurated on the 4th of March, 1861." His was the last house in Knoxville over which the Union flag was displayed, and the *Whig* was the last Union paper in the South. Until it was suppressed (Oct. 24, 1861) every issue contained arguments and appeals to the Union men of the South and defiance of and contempt for the leaders of secession. In the last issue Brownlow declared that he would rather be imprisoned than "recognize the hand of God in the work of breaking up the American Government." After he had refused allegiance to the Confederate government his arrest was imminent and on Nov. 5, 1861 (*Congressional Record,* 42 Cong., 2 Sess., pp. 1038–40), he fled to the mountains on the North Carolina border. His press and types were destroyed. He was found by Confederate scouts, returned to Knoxville, and notified that he would be given a passport beyond the Confederate lines into Kentucky. But on Dec. 6 he was arrested and placed in jail under suspicion of having had a hand in the state-wide burning of railway bridges on Nov. 6, and charged with treason because of his final editorial in the *Whig*. He suffered from typhoid during his imprisonment and after a month was allowed to go to his home, where he was kept under guard for nearly eight weeks. On order of Judah P. Benjamin, Confederate secretary of war, he was sent inside the Federal lines on Mar. 3, 1862. Going at once to Ohio, he spent some time regaining his health and writing his *Sketches of the Rise, Progress, and Decline of Secession; With a Narrative of Personal Adventure Among the Rebels* (1862), after which he made an extensive lecture tour through the North where he was shown distinguished attention by public officials and large audiences. His ideas in regard to slavery changed and he supported President Lincoln's emancipation policy (*Cincinnati Gazette*, Apr. 30, 1877).

Returning to eastern Tennessee with Burnside's army in the fall of 1863, he again became a leader among the Unionists of that section, was among those who called a nominating convention for May 30,—preliminary to restoring civil government in the state,—and was a member of the Union central committee until elected governor by acclamation in 1865. His first message gave a remarkably comprehensive view of conditions and needs in the state, and outlined closely the course afterward followed by legislation. He was determined to disfranchise all who had fought against the United States, and asked the legislature for a military force to make such a measure effective. The Ku Klux Klan became a dangerous power after the franchise law had been made more severe, and when the protection of federal troops was denied, Brownlow gathered 1,600 state guards and proclaimed martial law in nine counties. He was afflicted with palsy and unable to make an active campaign for reëlection, but was returned by a large majority. Before the close of his second term he was elected to the United States Senate to succeed David T. Patterson, and took office on Mar. 4, 1869. His career in the Senate was not distinguished. He usually acted with the Republicans, and for a while spoke often and vigorously in debate. His health was failing, however, and although he attended regularly until toward the end of his term, he became unable to speak, and several addresses, mainly defenses against attack, were read by the clerk. The last bill introduced by him was for the purchase of a site for Fisk University. At the end of his term, he returned to Knoxville, bought control of the *Whig*, which he had sold in 1869, and edited it with something of his old-time vigor until a short time before his death.

Brownlow was of robust figure, six feet in height, and weighed 175 pounds. He had, he said, as strong a voice as any man in east Tennessee. When not in controversy he was a peaceful and charming man, but his fearless and ruthless honesty in expressing his opinions made him always a storm center. Besides the book already mentioned, he wrote *Helps to the Study of Presbyterianism* (1834); *A Political Register, Setting forth the Principles of the Whig and Locofoco Parties in the United States, with the Life and Public Services of Henry Clay* (1844); *Americanism Contrasted with Foreignism, Romanism, and Bogus Democracy* (1856); *The Great Iron Wheel Examined, and an Exhibition of Elder [J. R.] Graves, its Builder* (1856). He was married to Eliza, daughter of James S. and Susan Dabney (Everet) O'Brien.

[The chief sources are the works mentioned above, especially *Sketches of the Rise . . . of Secession.* See also *Parson Brownlow and the Unionists of East Tenn.: with a Sketch of His Life* (1862); *Portrait and Biog. of Parson Brownlow, the Tenn. Patriot, Together with His Last Editorial in the Knoxville Whig; Also His Recent Speeches, Rehearsing His Experience with Secession and His Prison Life* (1862); Jas. Walter Fertig, *The Secession and Reconstruction of Tenn.* (1898); J. T. Moore and A. P. Foster, *Tenn. the Volunteer State* (1923); O. P. Temple, *Notable Men of Tenn.* (1912); John R. Neal, *Disunion and Restoration in Tenn.* (1899). W. F. G. Shanks compared Brownlow and Andrew Johnson in *Putnam's Mag.,* April 1869, pp. 428 ff. Obituaries were published in the *Public Ledger* (Memphis, Tenn.), May 1, 1877, and in the *Evening Post* (N. Y.), *N. Y. Tribune,* and *N. Y. Times,* the *Cincinnati Gazette,* and other papers of Apr. 30, 1877.]

F. W. S.

BROWNSON, ORESTES AUGUSTUS (Sept. 16, 1803–Apr. 17, 1876), author, was born at Stockbridge, Vt., of an old Connecticut family. The death of his father, Sylvester Augustus Brownson, left the widow, Relief Metcalf, in straitened circumstances, and after six years of unsuccessful struggle against poverty she was obliged to leave to charitable neighbors the care of her two youngest children, Orestes Augustus and Daphne Augusta (twins). Brought up on a small farm, the boy grew into a stalwart youth over six feet tall with no education save that supplied by omnivorous reading largely of a religious character. In 1822 he joined the Presbyterian Church but, repelled by its doctrines of election and reprobation, he left it after two years to become a Universalist, and on June 15, 1826, was ordained as a Universalist minister. He was married on June 19, 1827, to Sally, daughter of John Healy of Elbridge, N. Y. During the next few years he preached in various churches in Vermont, New Hampshire, and northern New York, and in 1829 became editor of the *Gospel Advocate,* published in Auburn, N Y. The expression of his increasingly liberal views in regard to the inspiration of the Scriptures, the divinity of Jesus, and the future life offended his fellow-Universalists and he gradually withdrew from their communion and became a kind of ministerial free lance, preaching and writing as opportunity permitted. For a time he associated with Robert Dale Owen and Fanny Wright in their socialistic schemes, acted as corresponding editor of the *Free Enquirer,* and helped to organize the short-lived Workingmen's Party. Always identified in sympathy with the laboring classes, he nevertheless hoped to ameliorate their condition by moral suasion rather than by political action, and at length drifted back into the Church, this time as a Unitarian, serving parishes at Walpole, N. H. (1832–34) and at Canton, Mass. (1834–36). In 1836 he organized his own church among the laboring men of Boston, calling it the Society for Christian Union and Progress, and during the same year published his first book, *New Views of Christianity, Society and the Church,* in which he condemned both Catholicism and Protestantism, and celebrated the "Church of the Future." Eloquent and irascible, Brownson had now become a force both on the platform and in the press. In January 1838 he established the *Boston Quarterly Review,* an influential Democratic organ which in July 1840 made itself notorious by attacking, in the interest of the common man, organized Christianity, the inheritance of wealth, and the existing penal code. In 1840, also, he published *Charles Elwood; or, the Infidel Converted,* a semi-autobiographical romance, in which the infidel hero is converted, through Cousin's philosophy, to a rather tepid unitarianism. Two years later *The Mediatorial Life of Jesus* showed that the position of the author had shifted to a virtual trinitarianism. In 1842 the *Boston Quarterly Review* was merged with the *Democratic Review* of New York to which Brownson contributed a series of articles on "Synthetic Philosophy" and on "The Origin and Constitution of Government" (revised and republished in 1865 as *The American Republic; its Constitution, Tendencies and Destiny*). Brownson's hostility to the extreme political theories of popular sovereignty offended his constituents so that he soon severed his connection with the *Democratic Review* and in January 1844 resumed the publication of his own journal in Boston with its named changed to *Brownson's Quarterly Review.* During these years he had become closely associated with Channing, Thoreau, Bancroft, George Ripley (with whose Brook Farm experiment he sympathized to the extent of sending his son Orestes

to join the community), and J. C. Calhoun (whom he supported for the presidency in 1844). He was still so much identified, in men's minds, with New England liberalism that his conversion to Catholicism in October 1844 came with much of the same shock that the conversion of Newman was to bring just a year later. Less subtle and profound than Newman, Brownson reached the same goal by much the same path, acceptance of the divine mediatorial power of Jesus seeming to both to involve necessarily the acceptance of the divine mediatorial power of the church. As with Newman, though less startlingly so, Brownson's conversion involved a sacrifice of worldly prosperity. It cost the *Review* a large number of its New England supporters and almost all its Southern constituency. He continued to publish it, however, until January 1865, when it was suspended until October 1872. Meanwhile he changed his residence in 1855 to New York City and again in 1857 to Elizabeth, N. J. A polemicist by nature, he chiefly devoted his pen, after his conversion, to an uncompromising assertion of the claims of the Catholic Church and to trenchant attacks upon her enemies. In *The Spirit-Rapper; an Autobiography* (1854), really a fantastic romance, he traced the spiritualistic phenomena of the day to Satanic influence. In his more important *The Convert; or, Leaves from my Experience* (1857) he gave a valuable, if inevitably partisan, account of his own religious development. He died on Apr. 17, 1876, in Detroit, Mich., whither he had removed in the previous year. His complete works were published in twenty volumes (1882–87), ably edited by his son, Henry F. Brownson.

[The standard biography is *Orestes A. Brownson's Early Life, Middle Life, Latter Life* (3 vols., 1898–1900), by Henry F. Brownson, who also has a sketch of his father in the *Cath. Encyc.* An interesting dissertation on *The Critical Principles of Orestes A. Brownson,* by Virgil G. Michel (Cath. Univ., Washington, 1918), contains a full list of important magazine articles on the man and his work.]   E. S. B.

BRUCE, ARCHIBALD (February 1777–Feb. 22, 1818), physician, mineralogist, was born in New York City. His father, William Bruce, a native of Dumfries, Scotland, was a medical officer in the British Army stationed in New York, where he married Judith (Bayard) Van Rensselaer, a widow, and where their son was born. William Bruce was later transferred to Barbados where he died of yellow fever. The young Archibald was left in New York with his mother, who sent him to Halifax to the care of Dr. William Almon, a friend of his father. He remained there but a short time when, returning to New York, he was placed in a private school conducted by Peter Wilson at Flatbush, Long

Island. Thence he proceeded to Columbia College. For reasons of his own, his father had been strongly opposed to the idea that his son should follow him in the study and practise of medicine and the boy's mother and her friends had been charged with carrying out the father's wishes. Even while a student of the school of arts, however, the young man was attending the medical lectures of Dr. Nicholas Romayne, a popular instructor of the time. Later he attended the private medical school of Dr. David Hosack and pursued the several courses of instruction given by the Medical Faculty of Columbia College. After his graduation with the A.B. degree in 1797, he went to Europe and in 1800 he was given the degree of M.D. from the University of Edinburgh. His thesis on that occasion was entitled *De variola vaccina*. While taking medical instruction from Dr. Hosack in New York, he had learned to share the latter's interest in mineralogy. Therefore, after finishing at Edinburgh, he went to the Continent where during two years spent in France, Switzerland, and Italy he pursued the study of minerals and the assembling of a mineralogical collection. Returning to England, he was married in London, and in the summer of 1803 he returned to New York to take up the practise of medicine. With Dr. Romayne and others, he organized the state and county medical societies and in 1807 secured a charter for the College of Physicians and Surgeons of the State of New York. He was given the chair of materia medica and mineralogy in the new faculty, the first professorship of these branches created in America. A reorganization of the school in 1811 deprived him of his professorship and the post of registrar. Again associated with Romayne and others, he organized a new medical faculty where again he lectured on materia medica and mineralogy, but the new organization was soon disbanded. He was at one time (1812–18) connected with the faculty of Queens (now Rutgers) College. In 1810 he established the *American Mineralogical Journal,* the first purely scientific journal in America. It completed but one volume.

It is probably as a mineralogist that Bruce will be longest remembered. His name is given to the metal brucite, a native magnesium hydroxide, which he discovered in New Jersey. He also discovered the deposits of zinc oxide in Sussex County, N. J., and published a paper *On the Ores of Titanium Occurring Within the United States.* There is no record of any medical writing other than the inaugural thesis. The biographer of his day credits him with "conciliating social habits and disposition" together with "dig-

nity of character and urbanity of manner." His portrait shows a round, full, smooth-shaven face with bovine eyes. His appearance was that of one who enjoyed his food and drink. He died from apoplexy, at the age of forty-one, in his native city.

[In the *Am. Jour. of Sci.,* vol. I, 1819, there is a biographical sketch with portrait, which is apparently the basis for all subsequent biographies. See also the *Gen. Catalogue* of Columbia Univ.]   J.M.P.

BRUCE, BLANCHE K. (Mar. 1, 1841–Mar. 17, 1898), negro senator, was born in Farmville, Prince Edward County, Va. At an early age he moved to Missouri. For two years he attended Oberlin College where he pursued a special course in the fundamentals. He then in 1868 started life as a planter at Floreyville, Miss., and accumulated considerable property. For a while he engaged in teaching and at the same time he entered politics. By judgment, tact, and executive ability, he easily made himself a leader of a large constituency which rewarded him with many political honors. He served the state Senate of Mississippi as sergeant-at-arms in 1870, secured the appointment of assessor of Bolivar County in 1871, became its sheriff in 1872, and the same year obtained a seat in the Board of Levee Commissioners of the Mississippi. To give him the opportunity to crown these efforts with a service for the whole country, his constituents elected him to the United States Senate in 1874. On June 24, 1878, he was married to Josephine B. Wilson of Cleveland. He served creditably in the Senate for six years from 1875 to 1881. Although he spent much time and energy in the debates on election frauds, Southern disorders, and civil rights, he was equal to the occasion in dealing with other important problems. He fearlessly opposed the Chinese exclusion policy, he forcefully combated our selfish attitude toward the Indians, and he worked for the removal of the disabilities of men who had opposed the emancipation of the race to which he belonged. He showed statesmanlike foresight, too, in his advocacy of the improvement of the navigation of the Mississippi. He not only labored to prevent the periodical inundation of that stream, but endeavored so to improve the waterway as to furnish increased facilities for interstate and foreign commence. Deprived of further political preferment as the result of the overthrow of the Reconstruction governments in the South, he settled in Washington. At the expiration of his term in the Senate, President Garfield made him Register of the Treasury, a position which he held for four years. In 1889, President Harrison appointed him Recorder of

Deeds in the District of Columbia when the position meant much more than it does to-day. President McKinley called him back to the office of Register of the Treasury in 1895. He served in this capacity until his death.

[*Jour. of Negro History*, vol. VII (1922); *Biog. Dir. of the Am. Cong.* (1928); W. J. Simmons, *Men of Mark* (1887); *Evening Star* (Washington, D. C.), Mar. 17, 1898.]

C. G. W.

BRUCE, GEORGE (June 26, 1781–July 5, 1866), typefounder, was born in the outskirts of Edinburgh, Scotland. He was the son of a tanner, and was educated in the public schools. Before he was fifteen he gained the consent of his family to join his older brother, David, in Philadelphia, Pa. There he became an apprentice in book-binding, but, chafing under the direction of a tyrannical and exacting master, he apprenticed himself to Thomas Dobson, a Philadelphia printer by whom David was also employed. The destruction of the Dobson plant by fire in 1798 and the prevalence of a fever in Philadelphia, led the brothers to leave the city. Traveling by foot, George was stricken with the yellow fever at Amboy, N. J., and was nursed by David. For a time both worked in a printing office at Albany, N. Y., but the firm there failed, and they followed the Post Road on foot to New York City. George was employed in various offices until 1803, when he was made foreman on the *Daily Advertiser,* to which he had contributed articles, and in the same year he became the printer and publisher of that newspaper for the proprietor, David being associated with him in this venture. In 1806 the brothers opened a book-printing office at the corner of Pearl St. and Coffee House Slip, and in the same year brought out an edition of Lavoisier's *Chemistry* on their own account, doing all the work with their own hands, with borrowed type and press. Their industry and zeal soon brought them abundant commissions, and, in 1809, when they removed to Sloat Lane, near Hanover Square, they were running a veritable battery of presses. In 1812, David brought from England the secret of stereotyping, but their attempt to introduce the process here encountered many difficulties which it required all of their ingenuity to surmount. The type of that day was cast with so low a beveled shoulder that it was not suitable for stereotyping, since it interfered with the moulding and weakened the plate. The brothers found it necessary, therefore, to cast their own type. At the same time they added several important improvements to the English process. Their first stereotyped works were school editions of the New Testament in bourgeois, and the Bible in nonpareil, about 1814–15, and they subse-

quently stereotyped the earlier issues of the American Bible Society, and a series of Latin classics. In 1816 they sold their printing business and bought a building in Eldridge St. for their foundry, and two years later they erected their own foundry in Chambers St. George gave his attention not alone to the typemaking end but to the enlargement and development of the business. The partnership was dissolved in 1822. Soon thereafter, George relinquished stereotyping to give his whole attention to type-founding. He introduced valuable improvements into the business, cutting his own punches, making constantly new and tasteful designs, and graduating the size of the body of the type so as to give it a proper relative proportion to the size of the letter. In connection with his nephew he invented the only type-casting machine that has stood the test of experience, and which is still in general use. His scripts early became famous among printers, and he was the first to take advantage of the Act of Congress of 1842 protecting designs. At the age of nearly fourscore he cut punches for a primer script. He was for several terms president of the Mechanics Institute of New York and of the New York Typefounders' Association; an officer in the General Society of Mechanics and Tradesmen and in the Apprentices' Library; a patron of the New York Typographical Society and of the Printers' Library, and a member of the New York Historical Society and of the St. Andrew's Society. His death called forth memorials from the various printing industries in New York. Bruce was twice married: on Jan. 1, 1803 to Margaret Watson of Schenectady, who died of yellow fever in October of that year, and in 1811 to Catherine Wolfe.

[The life and work of Bruce are mentioned in a variety of papers of the old Printers' Lib., now a part of the collection of the N. Y. Pub. Lib. The "Horace Greeley Papers" also contain occasional reference to him and to his relations with the editor of the *Tribune.* Obituaries were published in the *N. Y. Evening Post,* July 7, 1866, and *N. Y. Tribune,* July 10, 1866, the latter being the Typographical Soc. memoir. See also sketch in Wm. N. MacBean, *Biog. Reg. of the St. Andrew's Soc. of the State of N. Y.,* vol. I (1922), p. 383.]

R. R. R.

BRUCE, ROBERT (Feb. 20, 1778–June 14, 1846), Presbyterian clergyman, educator, believed to have been a descendant of King Robert Bruce, was born in the parish of Scone, Perthshire, Scotland. He studied theology for five years in Associate Hall under A. Bruce, and was licensed to preach in 1806 by the Presbytery of Perth Associate Church. Adventurous, filled with missionary zeal, he declined the preferment awaiting him in his native country, and committed himself to the crude life of new America.

Two years in Pennsylvania and the Carolinas, preaching to congregations as opportunity offered, brought him definitely to the decision to make the frontier village of Pittsburgh his future home. On Dec. 14, 1808 he was ordained and became pastor of the Associate Church in Pittsburgh (and at Peter's Creek also, relinquishing this charge in 1813). For thirty-eight years he was pastor of this church, now the First United Presbyterian, until his death. As early as 1810 he was prominent enough to be moderator of the Synod. He became a strong preacher, an influential presbyter, a leader in his denomination, and one of Pittsburgh's most distinguished citizens. Of gentle voice and gracious manner he was a man of intense convictions and fearless conscience. In 1818 bitter controversy arose in his congregation over giving out two lines instead of one in the service of praise; and in 1822 charges were laid against him of too great liberality in respect to other communions. In 1829 he published a volume of discourses on Christian doctrine and practise (J. B. Scouller, *Manual U. P. Church,* 1887, pp. 249–50; *Glasgow's Manual,* 1903, pp. 60–61). Meanwhile the Pittsburgh Academy, chartered in 1787, was in 1819 rechartered as the Western University of Pennsylvania. A new curriculum and a new faculty were necessary. Bruce was elected principal and his associates in the faculty were John Black of Glasgow University, a Covenanter, Joseph McElroy of Jefferson College, Associate Reformed, Elisha P. Swift of Williams College, Presbyterian, and Charles B. Maguire, educated in Belgium, Roman Catholic, all scholarly men and destined to eminence in years to follow. This faculty was installed with picturesque and brilliant ceremony in the First Presbyterian Church May 10, 1822. Except for one year Bruce held his office of principal until 1843. Under his guidance the Western University took high rank and sent out many graduates later distinguished in church and state. After Bruce resigned as principal of the University in 1843 he was instrumental in establishing Duquesne College which was chartered in February 1844. That year it had seventy-two students, graduating a class of six young men (Isaac Harris, *Business Directory of Pittsburgh,* 1844, p. 71). While the life of this college was brief it did excellent educational service particularly in the vicissitudes of the University after the fire of 1845. Its alumni were later made alumni of the University. The portrait of Bruce in the possession of the University of Pittsburgh reveals a dignified personality, benign, refined, forceful; a fine face, a noble head, crowned with abundant white hair.

His son, David D. Bruce, who died in 1907, became one of the eminent lawyers of Pittsburgh.

[Wm. J. Reid, *Hist. of the First United Presbyt. Ch., Pittsburgh 1801–1901* (n.d.) ; *125th Anniversary Univ. of Pittsburgh* (1912), pp. 112–115 ; minutes Session First United Presbyt. Ch., Pittsburgh.]   S.B.M.

BRÜHL, GUSTAV (May 31, 1826–Feb. 16, 1903), physician, author, was born in the village of Herdorf, Rhenish Prussia. His father, owner of mines and smelting works, was able to provide for him a classical education at the gymnasia of Siegen, Münster-Eifel, and Trier. Following upon this, Gustav studied medicine, philosophy, and history at the universities of Munich, Halle, and Berlin. The so-called "emigration fever" of the revolutionary period of 1848–49 and the overcrowded condition of the medical profession at home induced the young man to lend a willing ear to the alluring letters of his uncle John Gerlach Brühl, who had settled in Missouri. Gustav came to the United States in 1848, and was on his way to Missouri, when a period of low water on the Ohio compelled him to stop over in Cincinnati. There a relative on the maternal side persuaded him to tarry longer, and a very successful beginning as a medical practitioner soon encouraged him to settle down and cast in his lot with the thriving city of Cincinnati. For several years he was practising physician at St. Mary's Hospital, and also lectured on diseases of the throat and laryngoscopy in Miami Medical College, Cincinnati. He wrote scientific articles for medical journals, and was an active participant in the numerous scientific, educational, historical, and philosophical societies that sprung up about him. He was one of the founders of the Peter Claver Society for the education of negro children, and a member of the board of examiners of the public schools. Subsequently he became a member of the council of the newly organized University of Cincinnati. As a public-spirited citizen of untiring energy he advocated reforms in education and politics. He stood for Tilden in 1876 and was one of the presidential electors in that memorable conflict. He was nominated by the Democratic party for the position of state treasurer, but was not elected, though he won the distinction of running ahead of his ticket.

In spite of his public service and heavy professional duties, Brühl found time for an avocation. This was the study of American archæology. For this he made extensive trips to Mexico, Central and South America, as well as the far western sections of the United States, and embodied the results of his studies in lectures and books. The following publications, written in German, are noteworthy: *Die Culturvölker Alt-Amerikas* (Benziger Brothers, New York, Cincinnati, St. Louis, 1875–87); *Aztlan-Chicomoztoc. Eine ethnologische Studie* (same publishers, 1879); *Zwischen Alaska und Feuerland. Bilder aus der Neuen Welt* (A. Ascher & Company, Berlin, 1896). The last is a popular work descriptive of the natural wonders of the Far West, in Arizona, New Mexico, California, Wyoming, and Alaska, giving special attention to the American Indian in his home, and passing on to a portrayal of the land of the Montezumas and the Incas and of conditions then existing in the South American republics.

Intimately connected with his archæological and ethnographical studies were Brühl's writings in German verse. He was a passionate lover of nature in her grand moods, and these he photographed in such lyrics as: *"Auf dem Corcovado," "Im Thale von Jucay," "Am See von Atitlan," "In den Anden";* or he would embody some Indian legend in heroic or elegiac stanzas, as: *"Die Heldin des Amazon," "Winona (eine Dakota Sage)," "Tupac-Amaru."* Still more numerous were his poetical dedications to the German pioneers in American colonial history, such as: *"Pilgerzug der Mährischen Brüder," "Das Feuerschiff," "Die Frau des Pioneers," "Regina"* (the child kidnapped by Indians identified by her mother's singing a German hymn), *"Vinum, linum textrinum"* (the motto of the Germantown settlers), *"Leisler," "Christian Schell," "Capt. Hiester," "Steuben," "De Kalb," "Herckheimer,"* etc. All of these lyrics and ballads first appeared in the volumes of the Cincinnati monthly *Der Deutsche Pionier*, 1869–87, published to record the history of German pioneers in the United States. Of this journal Brühl was editor during 1869–70, after which he continued to contribute over the signature *Kara Giorg* (a Serbian pen-name, meaning Black George). A collection of his poems was published in Cincinnati under the title *Poesien des Urwalds* in 1871, and a second volume was prepared about 1878. There appeared also: *Charlotte: Eine Episode aus der Colonialgeschichte Louisianas* (Cincinnati, 1883). A photograph of the author reveals a massive frame and large features radiating virility, intelligence, and energy. A long, shaggy beard and the professional man's spectacles cannot altogether conceal gentler aspects of expression. Brühl was married to Margarete Reis, by whom he had two sons and one daughter.

[*Der deutsche Pionier: Erinnerungen aus dem Pionier-Leben der Deutschen in Amerika* (1869–87); *Deutsch-amerikanisches Conversations-Lexicon*, by Prof. Alex. J. Schem (1869–74), vol. II; *Cincinnati, Sonst und Jetzt*, by Armin Tenner (1878); *Deutsch in Amerika*, by Dr G. A. Zimmermann (1892).]   A.B.F.

BRULÉ, ÉTIENNE (*c.* 1592–1632), French explorer, was born in Champigny and came in 1608, when a mere lad, with Champlain to New France. He took part in the building of the "habitation" at Quebec, escaped the scurvy, which destroyed so many of its colonists, and in 1610 at Champlain's suggestion went to the wilderness with the Algonquin chief Iroquet. The next year he came back, clad like a native, speaking the Indian language, equipped with a superior knowledge of woodcraft. As an interpreter, therefore, he was useful to Champlain and as an explorer he described the hinterland of Canada. In 1612 he went with the Huron tribesmen to their home on Georgian Bay. He would seem thus to have been the first white man to see any of the Great Lakes. He accompanied Champlain in his voyage of 1615 to Huronia and was sent by him on a perilous mission to the Andastes, dwelling on the headwaters of the Susquehanna River. Later in the same year he explored that stream to its outlet, and probably coasted Chesapeake Bay to the ocean. These explorations he related to Champlain in 1618, describing also his capture and torture by the Iroquois, and his rescue by a seemingly miraculous storm.

Champlain sent him back to the Hurons, where he lived thereafter, and where he received a salary of one hundred pistoles per year for his services to the fur trade company. He explored widely, but the extent of his voyages is uncertain. There is evidence to show that he visited Lake Superior in 1622 and saw its copper mines: he was also in the Neutrals country in 1624, and probably saw Lake Erie. In that case, he traversed first of any European four of the five Great Lakes—Huron, Ontario, Superior, and Erie.

Coming with the Indians to Tadoussac in 1629 Brulé sold his services to the English invaders, for which act of treason Champlain bitterly reproached him. During the English occupation (1629–32) he lived among the Hurons, where his life was so dissipated and licentious that the Bear clan of that tribe killed him in a quarrel and ate his remains. Champlain refused, on his return in 1633, to take vengeance for Brulé's murder, declaring that because of his treason he was no longer a Frenchman.

Brulé was one of that class of wanderers who, while brave and adventurous, became among savages more savage than the aborigines. His life was scandalous, and his only title to remembrance rests on his early discoveries in interior North America.

[The sources for Brulé's career are Samuel de Champlain's *Voyages*, of which there are many editions; see W. L. Grant, *Voyages of Samuel de Champlain* (1907). Gabriel Sagard-Theodat, *Le Grand Voyage du Pays des Hurons* (Paris, 1632) and *Histoire du Canada* (Paris,

1636), reprinted in 1865 and 1866, give the reports concerning the exploration of Lake Superior. Brulé's death is noted in *Jesuit Relations* (Thwaites edition, 1896–1902), Index. Modern works are Consul W. Butterfield, *Hist. of Brulé's Discoveries and Explorations, 1610–26* (1898); Benjamin Sulte, "Étienne Brulé," in *Proc. and Trans. of the Canada Royal Soc.,* 1907, sec. I, 97–126; Louise P. Kellogg, *The French Régime in Wisconsin and the Northwest* (1925).]   L.P.K.

BRUMBY, RICHARD TRAPIER (Aug. 4, 1804–Oct. 6, 1875), educator, son of Thomas and Susannah (Greening) Brumby, of English and Swiss ancestry, was born in Sumter District, S. C. When he was six years old his father died, leaving a large family with barely more than a scant livelihood. Young Brumby's education was begun in a small "academy" about four and a half miles from his home, a distance which he walked daily. From there in January 1821 he went to the classical school of the Rev. John Marshall at Statesville, N. C., paying for his passage on this "pedestrian tour of thirteen days" by assisting the wagon driver whom he accompanied. He continued his studies at Statesville and later Lincolnton, N. C., until October 1822, when he entered the junior class of the South Carolina College. By supplementing his slender resources with money earned through teaching school during vacation, he managed to meet the expenses of the course, and was graduated with first honors in the class of 1824. While tutoring in the family of Richard Singleton, he read law under the direction of Stephen D. Miller, later governor of South Carolina, and William C. Preston, from whom he probably derived the ardent state's rights views which he entertained throughout the rest of his life. With Preston he entered into partnership at the time of his admission to the bar (December 1825), but in 1827 he was forced to withdraw from this connection on account of ill health induced by his excessive labors. After a year's sojourn in the western country, with his health temporarily restored, he recommenced the practise of law at Lincolnton, N. C. There he married Mary Isabelle Brevard (Apr. 22, 1828), daughter of Capt. Alexander Brevard, veteran of the Revolutionary War. From Lincolnton Brumby removed in 1831 to Montgomery, Ala., and subsequently to Tuscaloosa where he edited the *Expositor,* a newspaper established to advance the cause of Nullification. On Aug. 12, 1834, though apparently without special qualifications for the position, he was elected to the chair of chemistry, mineralogy, and geology in the University of Alabama; and here he found occupation both agreeable to his tastes and, as it proved, well adapted to his talents. He had soon added physiology, conchology, and agricultural chemistry to the curriculum of his department, and in 1838 he prepared the first sys-

tematic report of the mineral resources of Alabama (published in *Barnard's Almanac,* 1839; an abstract in W. B. Jones, "Index to the Mineral Resources of Alabama," *Geological Survey of Alabama,* Bulletin No. 28, 1926). In January 1849 he resigned in order to accept a professorship in his alma mater, where Preston, his former law partner, had been made president. He filled this position until July 1855, when his health again failed and he took up his residence at Marietta, Ga., the home of his brother Arnoldus. He does not appear to have returned to active life. During the Civil War he converted practically all of his property into Confederate bonds and sent his five sons into the Southern army.

[The best account of Brumby's life up to the time of his retirement from teaching is contained in the *Hist. of the S. C. Coll.* (1859, rev. ed. 1874), by Dr. Maximilian La Borde, one of his colleagues. The sketch of him in the *Hist. of Ala. and Dict. of Ala. Biog.* (1921), vol. III, by Thos. M. Owen, is based upon this but introduces new material.]   J.H.E—y.

BRUMIDI, CONSTANTINO (July 26, 1805–Feb. 19, 1880), painter, was born in Rome, his father a Greek and his mother an Italian. As a young boy, he showed great talent for drawing and became a pupil of the Academy of Fine Arts. When thirteen years old, he was admitted to the Academia di San Lucca, studying painting under Baron Camuccini and modeling under Canova and Thorwaldsen. During the pontificate of Pius IX, he was commissioned with three other Roman artists to restore the Raphael frescoes in the Loggia of the Vatican. He also painted the Pope's portrait for the Vatican Gallery, for which he received a gold medal. He was made a captain of the papal guards, and in 1848 when Rossi was assassinated and the Pope fled to Gaeta, Brumidi was ordered to turn the guns of his command upon the people. This he refused to do, with the result that he was arrested and thrown into prison, where he remained fourteen months. When the Pope was restored to power, he had the artist released and advised him to leave Italy forever. He decided upon America as the haven of his exile and arrived in New York in 1852. He at once received recognition and painted an altar piece, "The Crucifixion," for St. Stephen's Church. Later he went to Mexico where he painted "The Holy Trinity" in the Cathedral at Mexico City. Upon his return, he secured his naturalization papers in Washington, and there became inspired by the possibilities of the Capitol as adapted to fresco. At his first meeting with Capt. Meigs, superintendent of the Capitol, who was apparently interested in examples of Roman grandeur, Brumidi's services were accepted. His first work was the decoration of the Agricultural Committee room, where he selected as his subject "Cincinnatus at the Plough." This was painted in 1855, being the first example of fresco in America. His work in the Capitol, from then on, extended over thirty years. In the corridors, Washington at Valley Forge, the battle of Lexington, the death of Gen. Wooster, the storming of Stony Point, and the Boston Massacre, were all graphically portrayed. In the committee rooms, Brumidi painted symbolic figures, typifying History, Geography, Arts and Sciences, Mechanics, Commerce and War; also portraits of Robert Fulton, Franklin, Morse, and John Fitch. When he began his work he received only $8 a day; later Jefferson Davis had this increased to $10. The decoration of the Rotunda was his great ambition. He knew that the tremendous height and width of the vaulted room would lend themselves to mural decoration, and at every spare moment he worked on the cartoons for the decoration of the canopy and the frieze. The frieze was done in imitation of sculpture, in alto-relievo. The belt upon which the frieze is painted is one hundred feet from the floor. When Brumidi began his work on the frieze he was over seventy years old, but he planned and rigged the scaffolding, a sliding affair, and every day the striking figure of the old man, his hair and beard snow white, might be seen being hoisted by a system of pulleys to what he called his "shop." He worked from ten in the morning until three in the afternoon, and his descent from the lofty height was an event of the day to the visitors, who watched anxiously the slowly moving ropes until his cage was safely landed. He was three years on this work and received $30,000, the only decoration for which he was paid a lump sum. In January 1880 he was taken ill, as the result of a partial fall, and never recovered. The decoration was left unfinished. Brumidi painted many portraits of distinguished men and was painting a portrait of Clay at the time of his death, but he was essentially a decorative artist, knowing well the technical side of his craft: how to draw and paint large figures in distemper on curved plaster surfaces. Many years after his death, original studies of some of his ceiling frescoes were discovered; also paintings which were acquired by distant relatives. Brumidi was twice married before leaving Italy, and late in life he married a Washington woman, said to be a great beauty, Lola V. Germon. He left one son, who also became an artist.

[Chas. E. Fairman, "Art and Artists of the Capitol of the U. S. A.," *Senate Doc., No. 95,* 69 Cong., 1 Sess., and "Works of Art in the U. S. Capitol Bldg.," *Senate Doc., No. 169,* 63 Cong., 1 Sess.; *Fine Arts Jour.,* Aug. 1910; *Jour. Am. Institute of Architects,* Sept. 1914; *Washington Post,* Feb. 20, 1880; Phila. *Evening Telegraph,* Feb. 19, 20, 1880; Washington *Sunday Star,* Apr. 15, 1928.]   H. W.

BRUNNER, ARNOLD WILLIAM (Sept. 25, 1857–Feb. 12, 1925), architect and city planner, son of William Brunner and Isabella Solomon, was born in New York City. He received his education in the New York public schools, in the schools of Manchester, England (where the family was resident for a while in connection with the elder Brunner's business), and then again in the New York City public schools. In 1877 he entered the earliest-developed academic school of architecture in the United States, that of the Massachusetts Institute of Technology, then under the brilliant leadership of William R. Ware [*q.v.*], where he graduated in 1879. He then entered the office of George B. Post in New York City, remaining there for five years; the next three, 1883–85, were spent in extensive travelling in Europe, sketching and studying intensively. Soon after his return to New York, he formed a partnership with Thomas Tryon, under the name of Brunner & Tryon. It was this partnership which, in 1888, designed the studio of Daniel Chester French on Eleventh St., and in 1890, Temple Bethel, at Fifth Ave. and Seventy-sixth St. In 1898, shortly after the partnership of Brunner & Tryon had been dissolved, Brunner won the competition for the Mt. Sinai Hospital; in 1901 the competition for the Federal Building of Cleveland; and in 1910, the competition for a proposed building for the Department of State in Washington, unfortunately never constructed. The winning of these competitions in which the best of the profession participated, gave Brunner a nation-wide fame. Outside of New York the two chief centers of his activity were Harrisburg, Pa., and Cleveland, Ohio. At Harrisburg, in his conduct of the work under his charge, the Capitol Park State Office Buildings, the Plaza between them, and the first design for the Memorial Bridge (not constructed), he set a high standard of honesty and professional idealism, even refusing a salary that would have brought his total receipts up to an amount greater than the usual fee. In recognition of his important work in connection with the Cleveland Civic Centre, he was appointed in 1902 a member of the Board of Supervision of Public Buildings and Grounds, of which he became chairman in 1912. He was also member of the city planning commissions of Baltimore, Denver, and Rochester, and was appointed to the National Council of Fine Arts by President Roosevelt. In 1913 and 1914 he was architect for the improvement of the water front of the City of Albany, creating out of what had been a dreary chaos, a beautiful composition of river walls, piers, and parked open spaces.

In 1923 Mayor John Hylan of New York City,

seeking for someone to put into concrete form his ideas of an art center in Central Park, just north of Fifty-ninth St., appointed Brunner as his architect for this, and a monumental scheme was developed and published. There was an immediate storm of public protest at the proposed use of park land for great buildings, and the scheme was accordingly abandoned. At the time of his death, Brunner was working on another of those great inclusive schemes so dear to him, a layout for Denison University, Granville, Ohio.

Brunner's art was preëminently large in conception, monumental, often severe. His sense of monumental planning was complete; he always attempted to gain an almost rugged simplicity of general idea. In style, his taste was toward an ever-increasing Roman classicism, for he never returned to the brilliant originality of his first great achievement, the square domed Temple Bethel, whose detail is somewhat reminiscent of the modified Romanesque of Richardson. Although the Mt. Sinai and Columbia buildings are somewhat French in their Renaissance feeling, it was in such purely classic work as that at Harrisburg and Cleveland that Brunner's personality found most complete expression; the square masses at Cleveland with their heavy rusticated basements and ranked orders above being peculiarly characteristic in their almost stark strength. In his work for Denison University, however, there is greater lightness and delicacy; Georgian influence is noticeable.

Brunner was the author, in collaboration with Thomas Tryon, of *Interior Decoration* (1887); in collaboration with Charles Downing Lay, landscape architect, of *Studies for Albany* (1914), prepared at the request of the Mayor of Albany; and in collaboration with Frederick Law Olmstead and Bion J. Arnold, of the *City Plan for Rochester* (1911). He was married in 1906, to Emma B. Kaufman of San Francisco. He was for many years a member of the American Institute of Architects, and president of its New York chapter, 1909–10, and of the Architectural League, 1903–04. He was made a member of the National Institute of Arts and Letters in 1913, and was its treasurer, 1914–25. He was also a member of the National Sculpture Society, and of the Fine Arts Federation of New York, vice-president of the American Civic Association; associate of the National Academy of Design, 1910, and member, 1916; member of the New York Board of Education, 1902, and of the New York Fine Arts Commission, 1908–10.

[R. I. Aitken and others, *Arnold W. Brunner and His Work* (1926), with many illustrations of his work, and a reproduction of an excellent portrait by Irving R. Wiles; *Who's Who in America*, 1922–23; *N. Y. Times*, Feb. 15, 1925; *Arch. Record*, LVII, 461; *Am. Mag. of Art*, XVI, 253; *Am. Architect*, CXXVII, 167; *Architect*, IV, 33; *Arch. Forum*, XLII, 49; *Architecture*, LI, 124.]
                                                T.F.H.

BRUNTON, DAVID WILLIAM (June 11, 1849–Dec. 20, 1927), mining engineer, inventor, was born at Ayr, Ontario, son of James and Agnes (Dickie) Brunton, both of whom had come from Scotland, where the families are historically known along the border. After attending public school, he went to Toronto at the age of twenty-one and worked as an apprentice under J. C. Bailey, a prominent civil engineer. Three years later he came to the United States, and in 1874–75 he took courses in geology and chemistry at the University of Michigan. Going then to Colorado, he held a variety of jobs for different companies and assisted James Douglas, the Guggenheims, and other pioneers to develop mines and treat the complex ores in the new metal-mining districts then being opened. With F. M. Taylor, in 1880, he built the first custom-mill at Leadville, where he also became manager of the largest mine in the district, the Colonel Sellers. In 1888 he was made manager of a group of mines at Aspen, and distinguished himself by driving under Smuggler Mountain the difficult Cowenhoven tunnel, two and one-half miles long, for draining and opening the principal Aspen mines. Brunton's account of this achievement, for the (British) Institution of Civil Engineers, published in their *Proceedings* for 1898, won him the Telford Premium. The Cowenhoven initiated him in what became his greatest specialty, driving long tunnels. At Aspen he also designed an early electric hoist which was for many years the largest in the world. Later he was associated in the driving of the Roosevelt tunnel at Cripple Creek, where the new Leyner water-feed hammer-drill attracted attention. While continuing his Colorado engagements, he was retained through the 1890's by the Anaconda interests of Butte, Mont., as consulting engineer in litigation over mining rights and the geology of the apex law. He made visits to Butte to testify and to organize the technical part of the suits, becoming also technical adviser in general to Marcus Daly and H. H. Rogers. When this work increased, he secured Horace V. Winchell as chief geologist for the Anaconda company, and a staff was developed which greatly influenced American mining by applying geology systematically to mining. This technique is described in the *Transactions of the American Institute of Mining Engineers* for July 1905. Brunton opened an office in Denver with F. M. Taylor, and the firm of Taylor & Brunton became noted for skilful and reliable sampling of ores such as smelters buy and mix;

for this important work, special machinery had to be designed and plants erected at strategic centers, and a reputation for integrity was essential. Brunton had invented a mechanical sampler as early as 1884. These developments in sampling were described by him in the *Transactions of the American Institute of Mining Engineers* for 1896.

The Brunton pocket-transit for engineers, patented in 1904, became popular all over the world because of its simplicity and lightness; during the World War military variations of it were adopted by the United States army and thousands of the instruments were used in France. Brunton was chairman of the War Committee of Technical Societies and an active member of other governmental boards to develop inventions to be used in the war. Other inventions of his own include a mine pump, a velocipede tunnel-car, a car coupling, improvements in revolving ore-roasters and in leaching ores, and a system of round-timber framing for mines. In 1922 he was made chairman of the board of consulting engineers for the Moffat railroad tunnel in the Rockies. In 1909–10 he was president of the American Institute of Mining Engineers and in 1927 he received the first Saunders gold medal, given by the Institute for "achievement in mining." Besides many technical papers, he was author of *Safety and Efficiency in Mine Tunneling* and *Modern Tunneling*, both published in 1914. Though he lived in Denver, he traveled extensively and made examinations of mines in all parts of the world for the Exploration Syndicate of London. He was later called upon to advise on mining methods by many companies, including the Rio Tinto in Spain. He was married on Feb. 11, 1885, to Katherine, daughter of John C. Kemble, a merchant of Stone Ridge, Ulster County, N. Y., and they had four children.

[*Mining and Scientific Press*, May 28, 1921; *Engineering and Mining Jour.*, Feb. 18, 1928; *Rocky Mt. News*, Dec. 21, 1927; *Who's Who in America*, 1926–27; *Who's Who in Engineering*, 1922–23; *Who's Who in Science*, 1912–14; *Am. Men of Science* (1927).]

P. B. M.

BRUSH, GEORGE JARVIS (Dec. 15, 1831– Feb. 6, 1912), mineralogist and executive, son of Jarvis Brush and his wife, Sarah (Keeler) Brush, was born in Brooklyn, N. Y., being the seventh in line of descent from Thomas Brush who settled in Southold, Long Island, in 1653, and who is believed to have been the first of the family in America. At the time of his son's birth, Jarvis Brush was in business as a commission and importing merchant, but in 1835 he retired and moved to Danbury, Conn., where the boy George began his education in private schools. In 1841

the family returned to Brooklyn, but five years later, when he was fifteen years of age, the boy was sent to the private school of Theodore S. Gold at West Cornwall, Conn. Aside from being an admirable teacher, Gold was an enthusiast in mineralogy and other of the natural sciences. It was undoubtedly while here that the boy got his first insight into the studies that were to occupy his future life. Not long after his return from school, however, he took a position with a mercantile house where he remained some two years, only occasionally indulging in mineralogical excursions. Ill health forced him to give up this position, and he decided to try farming. With this in view, he went to New Haven in 1848 to attend lectures in practical chemistry and agriculture under J. P. Norton and Benjamin Silliman. In October 1850 he left New Haven for Louisville, Ky., to become an assistant to Benjamin Silliman, Jr., who was instructor in chemistry and toxicology in the medical department of the University of Louisville. This position he held until the spring of 1852, though in the meantime making a trip to Europe in company with the elder Silliman. Notwithstanding these absences from New Haven he was able to pass the necessary examinations and graduate, as a member of the first class, from what was later to become the strong and flourishing Sheffield Scientific School.

The college year of 1852–53 was passed as an assistant in chemistry in the University of Virginia where he was associated with the well-known mineral chemist, J. Lawrence Smith, and with him made a series of mineralogical studies, the results of which were published in 1853–55, under the caption of "A Reëxamination of American Minerals," in the *American Journal of Science*. Becoming convinced of the need of further studies, after spending the summer of 1853 as an assistant in the department of mineralogy in the Crystal Palace at the International Exposition in New York, he went to Germany, passing the years 1853–55 with Liebig, von Kobell and Pettenkofer, and going later to the celebrated mining school at Freiberg, Saxony. On his return to America in 1855, he was elected professor of metallurgy in the Sheffield Scientific School. To fit himself for his new duties he went once more abroad, studied at the Royal School of Mines in London, and visited the principal mines and smelting works of both Great Britain and the Continent, finally entering upon his duties in New Haven, in January 1857. In 1864 he was married to Harriet Silliman Trumbull. In the same year his professorial position was broadened to include mineralogy. Later it was limited to mineralogy only. In 1872 he was made director of the Sheffield Scientific School, holding that position until 1898, when he resigned, though continuing to act as secretary and treasurer of the Sheffield Trustees until 1900, when he was elected president of the board. It is stated by his biographer and collaborator, Prof. E. S. Dana, that Brush's labors in connection with the development of the Sheffield Scientific School showed him to possess the faculty of "quick, sure judgement, firmness of resolution and great energy." In all of his work there he was remarkably successful, as he was also in the management of the affairs of the Peabody Museum of which he was a trustee. For many years he was a director in the Jackson Iron Company of the Lake Superior district and in the New York, New Haven & Hartford Railroad Company. He was elected a member of the National Academy of Sciences in 1868; an honorary member of the Mineralogical Society of England, a foreign member of the Geological Societies of London and Edinburgh, and of the Royal Bavarian Academy of Sciences of Munich.

Brush was an associate editor of the *American Journal of Science* and also an important contributor to J. D. Dana's *System of Mineralogy*. His *Manual of Determinative Mineralogy* (1874) was for many years (and its revised edition still is) the standard work on the subject. He developed a wonderfully keen eye for recognition of the essential features of mineral species and in the course of his career built up a collection, numbering some 15,000 specimens, unexcelled at that time in the number of type specimens and in value for scientific study. This collection, since widely known as the Brush Collection, he, in 1904, presented to the Sheffield Scientific School together with an endowment of $10,000, the income of which was to be utilized in its increase and maintenance.

He was of medium height, stocky build, and ruddy complexion, with long mustache, according to the fashion of those days. He is stated to have been of a very kindly disposition, although in his earlier days he could occasionally show a sharp temper. It is told of him that when matters were unusually irritating he would go into the room behind his office in the old Scientific School building, and, pulling out a drawer in which he kept his collection, spend some time looking over his specimens. This would serve to comfort and quiet him: the "minerals would not talk back," and he would shortly recover his normal temper. He was an entertaining talker, with a good sense of humor.

[Sketch by E. S. Dana, in *Memoirs of the Nat. Acad. of Sci.*, XVII, 105–12, containing full bibliography of Brush's publications.]   G. P. M.

BRUTÉ DE RÉMUR, SIMON WILLIAM GABRIEL (Mar. 20, 1779–June 26, 1839), theologian and first Catholic bishop of Vincennes, was born in Rennes, France, where his father, Simon Gabriel Bruté, was superintendent of the royal domains in Brittany and his mother, Jeanne Renée le Saulnier, managed a former husband's printing establishment. The elder Bruté died in 1787 leaving an entangled estate, due to loans and back rentals, which the mother straightened out with business skill, paying off all debts and caring for her family. Simon attended the local school until the Revolution closed its doors. Then he was taught by private tutors, stressing the classics, literature, and mathematics in preparation for the Polytechnical School. During the Terror, the boy worked for two years as a typesetter in his mother's shop. In his home there was dread but a high degree of courage. A private chapel was maintained; hunted priests were given an asylum; Simon disguised as baker's boy attended trials and visited prisons carrying the host to the dying and running messages for condemned priests and royalists. Mere suspicion of these activities would have meant the death penalty. When the red danger passed, he commenced the study of medicine in Rennes and later went to Paris where he was graduated (1803) from the Medical School with the highest prize in a contending class of 1,100. Bruté's reaction from the radicalism and materialism of faculty and fellow students was so sharp that he turned from a promising medical career to enter the Seminary of St. Sulpice.

In the seminary, Bruté became as profound a student of theology and scripture as he had been of science. On ordination (1808), he declined an assistant chaplaincy to Napoleon and joined the Sulpicians. It was as a professor in their College of Rennes, that he met Bishop Flaget of Bardstown, Ky., in search of missionary priests for America. Bruté listened to the appeal and on approval of his superior sailed for the States with Flaget. For two years he taught in St. Mary's Seminary, Baltimore, when he was called by President Dubois to St. Mary's College, Emittsburg, as a teacher of moral philosophy, science, and Scripture. He soon won renown for scholarship and self-sacrificing goodness. Despite his humility, he was soon regarded as an oracle by the American hierarchy. In 1815, he returned to France but friends in high places could not induce him to remain. He brought back several priests and seminarians and his library of 5,000 volumes which was unusually rich in medical, philosophical, and scientific books. He was now appointed rector of the Baltimore seminary where he also bore his burden of teaching. His health failing, he was transferred to Emittsburg (1818) where he taught for sixteen years, improving the school and serving as spiritual director of the neighboring Sisters of Charity. When St. Mary's became a secular institution (1826), he still continued on its faculty until he was named first bishop of Vincennes at the suggestion of Bishops Flaget and Chabrat.

Bruté was alarmed at the appointment, for he had the Sulpician aversion to a mitre and no money for the westward trip. His friends collected a purse of $200, and he journeyed to St. Louis where he was consecrated by Bishop Flaget in the new cathedral. Vincennes was an outpost with 25,000 Catholics, largely illiterate French and half-breeds, scattered over an area of 6,000 square miles. There were only three priests and a few small log chapels. Bruté was an organizer and a business man. A physician in a land of "doubtful doctors," he could cure physical as well as spiritual ills. Soon Vincennes became the site of the bare brick Cathedral of St. Francis Xavier, a seminary, a college, a convent, an orphan asylum, and a Catholic cemetery, though the last institution met local opposition. On his visits to Rome and France, Bruté enlisted a number of priests for his diocese and obtained financial aid from the Leopoldine Association and the Society for the Propagation of the Faith. With the coming of Irish and Bavarian immigrants, the diocese grew in population, and the bishop and his score of priests saw no idleness as mission chapels were widely separated and travel was arduous. Bruté succumbed to consumption brought on by exposure on long stage-coach journeys (1837).

[J. R. Bayley, *Memoirs of the Rt. Rev. Simon Wm. Gabriel Bruté* (1876) ; *Vie de Mgr. Bruté de Rémur* (Rennes, 1887) ; Rev. John McCaffrey, *Funeral Discourse* (1839) ; H. J. Alerding, *Hist. of the Cath. Ch. in the Diocese of Vincennes* (1883) ; R. H. Clarke, *Lives of the Deceased Bishops of the Cath. Ch. in the U. S.* (1872), II, 1-43 ; C. G. Herberman, *The Sulpicians in the U. S.* (1916) ; J. G. Shea, *Hist. of the Cath. Ch. in the U. S.* (1886-90) ; T. O'Gorman, *Hist. of the Roman Cath. Ch. in the U. S.* (1895) ; C. I. White, *Life of Mrs. Eliza A. Seton* (1853) ; P. Guilday, *Life and Times of John England* (1927) ; J. R. G. Hassard, *Life of the Most Rev. John Hughes* (1866) ; *Cath. Encyc.* ; J. O'K. Murray, *Lives of Catholic Heroes and Heroines of America* (1880).]   R.J.P.

BRYAN, GEORGE (Aug. 11, 1731–Jan. 27, 1791), jurist, politician, was born in Dublin, Ireland, the son of Samuel Bryan, a merchant, and his wife, Sarah Dennis. He came to America in 1752, settling in Philadelphia and entering a partnership with one James Wallace in the importing business. In 1755 the partnership was dissolved and Bryan continued in business alone; two years later, on Apr. 21, 1757, he married Elizabeth, daughter of Samuel Smith. As a Presbyterian he early became associated with the Scotch-Irish Presbyterians of Philadelphia, who were a distinct political faction, and gradually rose to prominence in their ranks. He was fined five pounds, in 1758, for refusing to serve as constable (*Passages from the Remembrancer of Christopher Marshall*, 1839, App., p. v) but in 1762 he accepted office as member of a commission to apply receipts from tonnage dues to the improvement of Philadelphia harbor. In 1764, Bryan and Thomas Willing were elected by the conservative party to represent Philadelphia in the Assembly. They defeated Benjamin Franklin and Joseph Galloway, the leaders of the party desirous of substituting Royal for Proprietary government, although the Anti-Proprietary forces carried the rest of the provinces. In the same year Gov. John Penn reorganized the judiciary, appointing new judges from among the conservatives, and Bryan was made judge of the orphans' court and the court of common pleas. He continued at the same time to serve in the Assembly, and in 1765 was a member of the committee which drafted instructions for Pennsylvania's delegates to the Stamp Act Congress to meet in New York on Oct. 1 of that year. On Sept. 11, Bryan, Dickinson, and John Morton were chosen as delegates to the congress. During their absence in New York the Philadelphia elections took place, Franklin's party won, and Bryan was defeated. He returned from the congress, signed the non-importation agreements, and resumed his judicial service. He was recommissioned judge in 1770 and again in 1772, by which time he had retired from a failing business. He was appointed naval officer of the port of Philadelphia in 1776. After the adoption in that year of the new Pennsylvania constitution, with a share in the framing of which—though not a member of the convention—he had been credited (Alexander Graydon, *Memoirs of a Life, etc.*, 1811, p. 266), he was elected to the Supreme Executive Council and by it chosen vice-president. In this capacity he served from Mar. 5, 1777 until Oct. 11, 1779, acting as president between the death of Wharton and the election of Joseph Reed (May 23–Dec. 1, 1778). In 1779 he was a member of a commission to settle the boundary dispute with Virginia.

Elected to the Assembly on Oct. 12, 1779, he was given the chairmanship of several committees on special bills, notably those which framed the "Divesting Act," transferring title in the proprietary estates to the Commonwealth of Pennsylvania, the act revoking the charter of the College of Philadelphia and vesting its property in a new institution, the University of the State of

Pennsylvania, and the act for the gradual abolition of slavery. The authorship of the last-named law is usually attributed to Bryan as his major claim to remembrance. He was commissioned a judge of the supreme court of Pennsylvania on Apr. 3, 1780, and held the office until his death. For some years he acted as trustee of the University of the State of Pennsylvania. In 1784 he was elected to the septennial Council of Censors. A stout (state) constitutionalist, he opposed every tendency toward nationalism, even attacking the Bank of North America. When the Federal Constitution was submitted to the states in 1787 he fought it earnestly, and after its ratification by Pennsylvania was a member of the Harrisburg convention of irreconcilables which met Sept. 3, 1788 to urge a revision of the Constitution by a new federal convention. But resistance, however stubborn, was of no avail against the inevitable; the old order passed, and Bryan outlived it only a little time, dying in 1791, two years after the inauguration of the federal government and five months after the adoption of a new state constitution by Pennsylvania.

[The Hist. Soc. of Pa. has five boxes of Bryan MSS., and the Lib. of Cong. has several of his letters to Justice Atlee and a "memorandum of events" of the years 1758–64 entered in the back of an almanac. There are letters to and from Bryan in Wm. B. Reed, *Life and Correspondence of Joseph Reed* (1847), and official communications in the *Pa. Archives*. Burton Alva Konkle, *Geo. Bryan and the Constitution of Pa.* (1922) contains previously unpublished biographical material but overestimates Bryan's importance. An obituary in *Dunlap's Am. Daily Advertiser*, Jan. 31, 1791, was copied by other Phila. papers.]

E. R. D.

BRYAN, MARY EDWARDS (May 17, 1842–June 15, 1913), journalist, author, the daughter of Maj. John D. and Louisa Critchfield (Houghton) Edwards, was born near Tallahassee, Fla. The family later moved to Thomasville, Ga., and Mary received her education at the Fletcher Institute at Thomasville. While yet in school, at the age of fifteen she married I. E. Bryan, a wealthy Louisianian. Her first experience in the literary field was as literary editor of the *Literary Crusader* at Atlanta, Ga., in 1862. For a time she was a regular correspondent of *Southern Field and Fireside*. In 1866 she became editor of the *Natchitoches* (La.), *Tri-Weekly*. She was associate editor of the *Sunny South* from 1874 to 1884. To these papers she contributed sketches, poems, stories, and, not infrequently, political articles. In 1880 she published her novel called *Manch,* which is a shortening of the Indian proper name "Comanche." The next year she published *Wild Work,* a novel dealing with the reign of the carpet-baggers and the Ku Klux Klan in the South. Eight other novels and three volumes of verse followed in due time. She wrote all her

books at night. *His Legal Wife,* her favorite novel, is said to have been written in a week and a half (*Atlanta Constitution,* June 17, 1913). Her stories were very sensational, invariably reaching many dramatic climaxes. In spite of being produced according to a general formula, they covered a wide variety of settings, including the Western frontier, the South, and New York City. Invariably they brought out the moral lessons which would appeal to the undiscriminating readers of popular novels. Several of her books ran through a number of editions. She went to New York in 1885 to superintend the publication of her novels and was engaged as assistant editor of the *New York Fashion Bazaar* and the *Fireside Companion.* In 1887 she edited *Munroe's Star Recitations for Parlor, School, and Exhibition.* G. Munroe was for some time her principal publisher. She was also one of the early writers for Street & Smith. In 1895 she returned to Georgia to work on the *Sunny South* which subsequently merged into *Uncle Remus' Magazine.* In the latter she conducted a popular page entitled "Open House" in which she made editorial comments on current issues and in turn published individual letters sent to the paper. She was also an editor of the *Half Hour Magazine.* At the time of her death she was writing for the *Golden Age,* a magazine published in Atlanta.

[*Who's Who in America,* 1912–13; *Atlanta Constitution,* June 15, 17, 1913; Mary T. Tardy, *The Living Female Writers of the South* (1872); *Men and Women of America* (1910).]

M. S.

BRYAN, THOMAS BARBOUR (Dec. 22, 1828–Jan. 25, 1906), lawyer, was born in Alexandria, Va., and died in Washington, D. C. His parents, Daniel and Mary Barbour Bryan were both representatives of Virginia families accustomed to public leadership. At the age of twelve he delivered a sermon before a large congregation; at seventeen he did his part toward the war in Mexico by giving of his oratory as an aid to recruiting; at twenty-one he published a grammar for the use of Germans desiring to learn English; at twenty-two, he married Jane Byrd Page, the daughter of an army chaplain. He attended a Southern school, and in 1849 was graduated in law at Harvard. He practised law in Cincinnati from 1849 till 1853, when he removed to Chicago, partly to find a more lucrative practise and partly to avail himself of financial opportunities in real estate. Both of these objectives were realized. He became a leading "office-counsellor," and in business his enterprises ranged from the promotion of auditoriums to cemeteries. A brisk, energetic little man, capable in affairs, he had the reputation of being widely erudite in languages and literature. He wrote poems and epigrams, adapted fables, translated sermons to read aloud in his private chapel, entertained sumptuously, and spoke brightly at many banquets. Chicago twice refused to elect him mayor, but otherwise accepted him without reservation, overlooking the "old-Virginian haughtiness" which, cropping out at times, it was complained, made him not altogether agreeable. During the 1860's he was ardently pro-Union. He devoted his resources liberally to the Northern cause, and, indorsing the view that the Southern leaders were "arch traitors, alone responsible for the war" (Bryan, *Stephen A. Douglas,* p. 1), made frequent speeches to enhearten troops. At the conclusion of hostilities he went with his family for an extended residence in Europe, in order to rest himself, but before leaving, as newly elected president of the Old Soldiers' Home, he purchased and gave to his wounded veterans the original copy of the Emancipation Proclamation. In 1875–78 he was a commissioner of the District of Columbia, but it was in the years 1889–93 that he was most generally known. He was among the first to suggest bringing the World's Fair to Chicago, and in January 1890, he presented before a committee of the Senate in Washington the claims of his city as the fittest place for the projected celebration. His speech is generally regarded as having governed the committee in its decision. As vice-president of the great Fair, he was tireless and effective, going twice to Europe as its advocate and interpreter. He had two children, several palatial residences, and countless close friends.

[T. B. Bryan, *Englische Sprachlehre* (1849); *Stephen A. Douglas on the Cause and Effect of the Rebellion* (1863); *Arguments in support of the Application of Chicago for the Location of the World's Exposition* (1890); anonymous, *Biog. Sketches of the Leading Men of Chicago* (1868); *Biog. Dict. of Chicago* (1892); C. Dean, *World's Fair City* (1892); *Who's Who in America,* 1906–07; *Harvard Univ. Quinquennial Cat. 1636–1915* (1915); Washington *Evening Star,* Jan. 26, 1906.]   J. D. W.

BRYAN, WILLIAM JENNINGS (Mar. 19, 1860–July 26, 1925), political leader, was born in Salem, Ill., the son of Silas Lilliard and Mariah Elizabeth (Jennings) Bryan. The elder Bryan was of Virginia farmer stock, a Democrat, and in 1872 an unsuccessful candidate for Congress. He was an ardent believer in education, and sent William Jennings to Jacksonville to stay at the Academy and College for six years. Bryan graduated from Illinois College in 1881, and for the next two years read law at the Union College of Law in Chicago. Here he came to know Lyman Trumbull, a political friend of his father, and spent much of his time reading law

in Trumbull's office. In college and law school he took a prominent part in school debates but little part in athletics, though he excelled in broad jumping. He was industrious and obedient to discipline, but he was not noted for originality of thought. His college orations have an easy direct manner of statement, though the thought in them is commonplace.

From 1883 to 1887 he practised law in Jacksonville, Ill. He opened his office on July 4, influenced, as he says, by a certain hankering for important dates (*Memoirs,* 62). In the beginning he saw very severe days, but by virtue of his economy he ended the year with as much success as a young lawyer without influential friends had a right to expect. In 1884 he was doing well enough to venture on matrimony. The bride was Mary Baird, daughter of a merchant in a near-by town. She was a woman of unusual mind. After her marriage she read law under her husband's instruction, and in 1888 was admitted to the bar in Nebraska. In the autumn of 1887 Bryan moved to Lincoln, Nebr., where he had to begin again at the bottom. He understood the law of small-town courts; he had much of that resourcefulness which enables a lawyer to win such cases; he had a ready and convincing manner with a jury; and he had much of that fair and generous conduct that brings to a young lawyer the good will and assistance of the older lawyers. Yet he had not attained a position at the bar which pointed to a great career when he was drawn into politics and gave up his practise. The ease with which he threw over the law indicates that he was not deeply interested in it, and, if not interested, he could hardly have been deeply versed in its principles.

In 1890 he became a Democratic candidate for Congress. The district was normally Republican, but he carried it by 6,713 majority. In 1892 he was reëlected but the state had been redistricted and his majority was only 140. In 1894 he announced his candidacy for the United States Senate, and made speeches with the hope that his friends would carry the legislature. The effort was unsuccessful; and so, without office, he had to find a way of making a living. He turned to journalism and became editor-in-chief of the *Omaha World-Herald* at a fair salary. By this time he had developed a vogue as a lecturer and was employed in that capacity by the Chautauquas. He kept in close touch with public questions, and when the monetary problem came to the fore he was in much demand as an advocate of the free coinage of silver. During his four years in Congress Bryan had lived simply and quietly at 131 B St., S. E. He did not try to go into society and there is not much reason to think that he came into close contact with the leaders of his party. His father had been a friend of William M. Springer of Illinois, however, and by that means he got a position on the Ways and Means Committee, of which Springer was chairman. It was an unusual beginning for a new member. The Ways and Means Committee was at that time a committee of special importance, for the tariff was the livest political question before the country. But there is nothing to show that Bryan took special interest in the tariff. He made some effective speeches on the floor, but they were more notable for fluency of expression than for grasp of the subject. He identified himself with the silver men in Congress; voted against the repeal of the silver-purchase law of 1890; and made a brilliant speech in which he used violent language against President Cleveland for demanding its unconditional repeal. The silver men now set out to control the next Democratic national convention in 1896, and conducted in 1894 and 1895 a vigorous campaign with that end in view. They sent speakers into all parts of the country in which there was a considerable amount of silver sentiment, winning the support of the voters and laying plans for electing silver men to the next national convention. Into this movement Bryan threw himself with enthusiasm. He was the most popular of the speakers and probably the most energetic. When the convention met in Chicago in 1896 the free-silver men were in control. They used their power without sympathy for their opponents. The New York leaders, who for many years had controlled the party, were brusquely thrown aside and a new alignment, composed of Western and Southern men was set up. In discussing the platform, Bryan made his notable "Cross of Gold" speech, in which he narrated the history of the silver movement, declaring that silver Democrats had gone from victory to victory and were now assembled "not to discuss, not to debate, but to enter upon the judgment already rendered by the plain people." "Having behind us the producing masses of this nation and the world, supported by the commercial interests, the laboring interests, and the toilers everywhere, we will answer their demand for a gold standard by saying to them: You shall not press down upon the brow of labor this crown of thorns, you shall not crucify mankind upon a cross of gold" (Bryan, *First Battle*, 199). This speech swept the silver ranks like fire and won him the presidential nomination on the fifth ballot, despite the fact that he was only thirty-six years of age (*Chicago Daily Tribune*, July 10, 1896).

Bryan was honestly in favor of the free coinage of silver. His speech of acceptance, delivered in Madison Square Garden, read to the large audience, and perhaps well revised under the inspection of other Democrats, has the ring of sincerity. His enemies called him a demagogue and a deceiver. They made fun of his youth, of his oratory, and of his slips of speech. Dignified Eastern newspapers abused him in terms falling little short of Billingsgate. In all this torrent of abuse, Bryan, two years earlier only an inconspicuous newspaper editor in a rural state, carried himself with composure. His speeches, though based on an economic fallacy, were clear and easily understood by his auditors. His magnificent voice was a perfect medium of expression. He went everywhere, spoke to hundreds of audiences, and carried home his ideas to the country as no other candidate had done since the days of Henry Clay. While his opponent remained snugly at his home and uttered truthful platitudes to trainloads of excursionists which an over-rich campaign committee sent to his front door, Bryan, fighting brilliantly in behalf of error, traveled 18,000 miles, kept his poise, always was on the aggressive, and never broke down physically or mentally. It was a remarkable achievement. The campaign was also a social and sectional struggle. Bryan told his hearers that it was a conflict between Wall Street and the great "toiling masses," between the rich men and the poor men. His defeat in this campaign, however, was on the silver issue, not on the class issue. At the time little attention was paid to the two-fold nature of Bryan's position. Probably he himself was not greatly conscious of it. He looked on himself as a crusader for silver.

The outcome of this extraordinary campaign was a popular majority for McKinley over Bryan of about 600,000 in a total vote of 13,600,000. The electoral vote stood 271 to 176. Bryan's defeat was hailed by his enemies as the end of his public career. Had he stood solely on the money question, the prediction would probably have been realized. But the basis of his fight, the people *vs.* the power of wealth, was more permanent. To all who wished to free the party from the domination of the New York group, itself in close association with the so-called money power, Bryan was still the leader. The alliance between the South and West was a salient fact in his career. Then the Spanish-American War intervened. In 1898 he was made a colonel by the governor of Nebraska and raised a regiment for service in the war with Spain, but did not serve outside the United States. He resigned the day the treaty with Spain was signed, after serving five months. The only military glory that he won was the title of colonel.

As the year 1900 approached he was seen to be as strongly entrenched in party affection as in 1896. The organization of 1896 was now in control and it was thoroughly committed to Bryan. A move started by his Eastern opponents to drop the silver plank from the platform failed because he refused to be the candidate on that basis. At the same time he was willing to consider "expansion" and not silver the "paramount issue," and on that basis made the campaign against McKinley. He had used his influence with Democratic senators to get the treaty with Spain ratified, and defended that action on the ground that the people wanted the war ended, that other nations would oppose a Philippine Republic and that it would be easier to accept the Philippines and then urge the United States to make them independent. It was not a convincing argument. Bryan's opponents charged that he got the treaty accepted in 1899 so that he could make a campaign in 1900 out of anti-expansion. He miscalculated the feeling of the country. Flushed with victory, the voters looked on the Philippines as its fruits and felt no hesitation in taking them for national dependencies. The election showed that Bryan was less popular in 1900 than in 1896, and he received only 155 of the 447 electoral votes, whereas he had had 176 four years before. His strength was confined to the South and the states of Idaho, Colorado, Montana, Nevada.

In 1903 Bryan became involved in a lawsuit known as the Bennett Will Case. In that year Mr. Philo S. Bennett, of New Haven, died, leaving $80,000 at Bryan's disposal: $30,000 for charity and $50,000 for himself if he wanted it—otherwise he was to give it also to charity. This will had been written at Lincoln, Nebr., by Bryan, on a visit of the testator to his home. It was contested on the ground of being imperfectly drawn. Bryan then decided not to accept the $50,000 for himself but insisted on his right to administer the fund. The decision was entirely in his favor, and the money was distributed for charitable purposes. This incident caused much comment at the time, although there were few who believed that Bryan had acted dishonestly. He was a man of personal integrity and by this time he had materially improved his financial position by lecturing. Moreover, he frequently lectured for nothing. On Jan. 23, 1901, appeared the first issue of the *Commoner,* a weekly newspaper in which Bryan sought to carry on his fight against the influence of wealth in politics. It started with 17,000 advance subscribers, and was suc-

cessful from the first. It was widely quoted by the local Bryan papers, thus keeping the ideas of the editor before the country. It was also bitterly denounced by his opponents, who continued to consider him a demagogue who set the poor against the rich. Bryan wrote its leading articles until he entered Wilson's cabinet in 1913. The paper was thereafter conducted merely as a monthly.

As the election of 1904 approached the anti-Bryan Democrats began to take courage. Roosevelt was unpopular with the "business men" of the East, and it was hoped that they would aid the election of a conservative Democrat if Roosevelt, as was expected, got the Republican nomination. The Eastern Democrats believed, therefore, that they had a chance of success, provided they had a "safe and sane" candidate. After much consideration they united on Judge Alton B. Parker of New York, who was conservative enough for the business men of the East and whose character and legal ability were of the highest order. The party was to be rescued from the wild leaders of the past eight years, Bryan was to be thrown over, and the ship *Democracy* was to return to her old tack. To the Bryan men it soon became evident that their position in the party was at stake, and they decided to fight to retain it. They could not present a Bryan man who would make a better candidate than Bryan himself, but they could exert themselves to control the nominating convention and keep it out of the hands of their enemies. In this spirit they chose delegates to the convention of 1904. At that convention the extreme Bryan men were in the minority, and Parker was nominated as a "compromise candidate." Senator David B. Hill of New York directed the convention, and Bryan found the platform already made when he arrived in St. Louis, and the candidate picked out. He fought until the platform was changed. William Randolph Hearst had the support of the extreme radicals, but Bryan, in one of his best speeches, seconded the nomination of Senator Cockrell of Missouri, although he says in his *Memoirs* (1925) that ex-Governor Pattison of Pennsylvania would have been a more acceptable candidate. The Parker men offered a platform in which were expressions that the Bryan men thought offensive, among them a gold plank. Through a long night session of the platform committee Bryan got one plank after another modified, until he could say at last, "I kept out of the platform everything to which I objected." When it was known that a platform was adopted which the Bryan men no longer opposed, there was a feeling of relief and the convention proceeded to nominate Parker on the first ballot. The sense of security was suddenly disrupted by the receipt of Parker's famous telegram, announcing himself in favor of a gold standard.

The prolonged contest had left Bryan ill and he was sent to bed by an attending physician who warned him of pneumonia. On hearing of Parker's telegram he rose instantly and a few minutes later stalked down the aisle of the convention hall, to assume the leadership of the fight. His face was pale, his brow was wet with perspiration, but his mouth was clinched and his eye gleamed. Gasping for breath, he climbed to the platform and took part in the discussion. He made motion after motion trying to get an expression of free-silver opinion into the records. They were voted down, his friends standing by him bravely, but the men of expediency voting for the indorsement of Parker and the action that had been taken. Bryan left the convention with the full conviction that he had been beaten but with his friends in the party more strongly bound to him than ever before. A month's rest restored his health, and he took active part in the campaign, though he could not put much heart into his advocacy of the man whom he had denounced as a man of "the money power." The election showed the effects. Parker received only 140 electoral votes while Roosevelt had 336. Parker lost every Northern and Western and one Southern state, and it was a more overwhelming defeat than Bryan ever sustained. The defeat of Parker, "safe and sane" candidate, proved that the Democratic party could not win with a conservative at its head. Bryan quickly regained control of the party organization in the nominating convention of 1908 he was named presidential candidate on the first ballot. If Bryan's policies were to be followed Bryan was undoubtedly the strongest candidate. But the country was under the Roosevelt spell, and Taft, Roosevelt's selection to carry out the Roosevelt policies, was elected. Bryan did better than Parker in 1904, but he received only 162 of the 483 electoral votes. "Three times and out," exclaimed the country in baseball language. Bryan knew it. In his home in Nebraska he continued to appeal to the country in the *Commoner* and through his lectures, and he did not give up his grasp on the Democratic organization; but he realized that he would never be president.

When the next presidential election came around the Republicans were hopelessly split. The party found that it could no longer exist with the most conservative and the most radical of the large political groups within its fold. The

two wings were divided, and there was good opportunity for the Democrats to win, for they were ordinarily less radical than the Roosevelt wing and less conservative than the Taft wing. In the party, however, the old division reappeared. The New York conservatives, directed by Charles F. Murphy, Tammany leader, supported Gov. Judson Harmon of Ohio, who had been a conservative Democrat in 1896. There were several other candidates who had been recommended in the primaries as progressives, among whom were Gov. Woodrow Wilson of New Jersey, and Champ Clark of Missouri, speaker of the House of Representatives. The New York group was in a strong position in the convention. The national committee put forward Judge Alton B. Parker for temporary chairman. Bryan took this step as a challenge, and endeavored to unite the progressive delegates on John W. Kern of Indiana, but Kern insisted upon nominating Bryan himself as chairman. Thus the convention had to choose between Parker and Bryan, and it named Parker. In this contest many of the Clark men voted for Parker, while most of the Wilson men supported Bryan. Bryan's defeat was heralded by the Eastern papers as conclusive. Yet Bryan was offered the chairmanship of the platform committee and also the permanent chairmanship; but he refused both posts, declaring that he would not be responsible for what the convention did until it took some step to show that it was not controlled by the reactionaries (*Baltimore American*, June 26, 1910). He served as a member of the committee on resolutions, however, and was not seriously opposed. The platform reported was a series of planks chiefly taken from the three preceding Democratic platforms.

In order to draw the attention of the country to the situation in the convention, Bryan opened an attack on August Belmont of New York and Thomas F. Ryan of Virginia. He offered two resolutions, one regretting their appearance in the convention, and the other demanding their withdrawal (*Memoirs*, p. 174). This action was truly described as "a bombshell." The air was full of protests; Bryan was denounced as a marplot. Yet the first resolution passed by a vote of 899 to 196. As the vote was about to be taken on the second resolution Bryan withdrew it. In defending his belligerent course Bryan told the delegates that there was not one of them who did not know that "an effort was being made to sell the Democratic party to the predatory interests of the country." He received showers of approving telegrams, and he succeeded in calling the attention of the country to the fight going on in the convention between the conservative and progressive forces. When the balloting began, New York led the Harmon forces, which amounted to 148 votes on the first trial. Clark had 440½ and Wilson had 324, while other candidates had 173½. Altogether 1,085 votes were cast, and 725 were necessary for the nomination. On the tenth ballot New York did what had been expected, transferred her 90 votes from Harmon to Clark. The uproar that followed brought Bryan into the convention hall. He had been using his personal influence for Wilson, although his delegation had been instructed for Clark as long as there was hope of a nomination. On the fourteenth ballot Bryan announced that he no longer felt himself bound by his instructions. Clark, he said, was supported by Nebraska with the understanding that he was a progressive, but his support by New York showed that he did not deserve that designation. He said that he, Bryan, would not vote for any man whose selection depended on the vote of New York. The result was to check any further defection to Clark, and for many ballots the situation remained the same, Clark having about 550 votes, and Wilson about 400. Clark issued a statement repudiating the charge that he was or would be under the control of Wall St., and pronouncing Bryan's accusations "false and infamous." To this Bryan replied in a circular letter disclaiming personal feelings against Clark, but asserting that the same forces that had ruled at the Republican convention were seeking to control at Baltimore. On the twenty-fifth ballot Wilson led Clark, gaining slowly as delegates came under the influence of a strong back-fire of opinion from the country. On the forty-sixth ballot he was nominated. The Illinois delegation had broken away from Murphy's grasp on the forty-third ballot and precipitated the victory. In this remarkable contest Bryan perhaps reached the summit of his career. In courage and honesty, in the wise mastery of a political convention, he has not been surpassed in our political history. It was something like irony that he fought better when fighting for another than when fighting for himself. During the severest hours of the crisis his friends came to urge that he would allow them to put his own name into nomination. It was a time when many a man's judgment was distorted by excitement, but Bryan's judgment remained true, though in the realm of ideas it had so often gone astray. Had he yielded, the glory of his fight would have faded.

Wilson's election carried Bryan into the State Department where he served from Mar. 4, 1913, to June 9, 1915. The appointment was not popular, for nothing in his training prepared him to direct our foreign policy. He knew nothing about international law, which, however, might have been said of some of his predecessors in the office. More important still, his range of thought was narrow. He had been to Europe and once around the world, but he had not shown that it broadened his concept of policies. On the other hand, his appointment had deep political significance. He was head of the strongest faction in the Democratic party and he had been responsible for the nomination of Wilson. It was natural to give him his choice of offices, and it was natural for him to choose the best. In itself Wilson's action was politically wise. Bryan made it even better. He served Wilson faithfully and used his large political influence to carry administration measures through Congress, a principal instance being his aid in framing and passing the bill for the Federal Reserve Bank. The program of reform that made the first seventeen months of President Wilson's administration remarkable was carried through Congress largely through Bryan's influence. A selfish man could have exacted his price for such efforts. Bryan asked for nothing and took no credit for what he did. Persons in the State Department were impressed with his honest desire to understand foreign affairs, and, as the months passed, with his increasing grasp on policies and the justness of his views about them. The Mexican policy of the administration was approved by him thoroughly; he was in complete accord with the decision not to continue government support to the Six-Power Loan to China; and he gave aggressive aid to those who opposed "dollar diplomacy" in Latin-American countries. In April 1913 the President sent Bryan to California to do what he could to dissuade the legislature of that state from passing a bill prohibiting the holding of land by aliens—the point of the bill being directed against the Japanese. No one expected him to do much, but what could be done was done, and it was largely due to Bryan's good nature that a somewhat less offensive bill was substituted and passed.

His long and steady devotion to peace was more personal, and it expressed itself in the negotiation of arbitration treaties with nations situated in all parts of the world. He considered these treaties the most notable thing in his service at the head of the State Department. His plan for international arbitration was formulated in his own mind as early as 1905 (*Commoner*, Feb. 17, 24, 1905), and he had advocated it on several occasions before becoming secretary of state. He took his appointment to that office as an opportunity to give his plan practical application. Soon after he took office he laid it before the Conference of the Diplomatic Corps in Washington. Its distinctive feature was the creation of a Commission of Five by the two nations accepting it, one member chosen by each country from its own citizens, one member chosen by each country from the other country, and the fifth member chosen by the other four. When diplomacy failed to settle a dispute this Commission was to function and to reach a decision within a year during which time neither side should begin hostilities. But at the end of that time either party was to take such action as it chose. The strength of the plan was in the hope that no states would begin war if they had to wait a year while investigation was in progress. Bryan prudently submitted his plan to the Senate Committee on Foreign Relations and got its approval. He then took it up with the nations separately and found no opposition. Thirty states signed such treaties with the United States, but the Senate refused to sign with Panama or the Dominican Republic (*Treaties for the Advancement of Peace, negotiated by William Jennings Bryan,* 1920).

In the crisis of 1914 the Bryan treaties proved ineffective. Germany had not accepted the Bryan arbitration treaty when the war began, but she did so immediately afterward. The United States Senate, however, had not acted on the matter when the *Lusitania* was sunk, May 7, 1915. Bryan thought that Germany should be given the benefit of the doubt and that a commission should be set up to investigate the quarrel, with the assurance that it would have a year to come to a decision; but the President and the cabinet were against using Bryan's treaties. The Secretary had also convinced himself that it was against the spirit of neutrality, international law to the contrary notwithstanding, to allow neutral ships to carry ammunition to a belligerent. Rather than dispatch the second *Lusitania* note which President Wilson had drafted he resigned his post, to take effect the day the note was sent, June 9. Bryan's resignation was made necessary by the very nature of his views. He was a pacifist at heart, and in the struggle then going on had a fixed idea that the United States by preserving strict neutrality would be in a position to make peace between the other nations and thus in some hazy way tremendously enhance her own glory and happiness.

Of all the causes which he led this plea for peace during the World War was the most futile. The people were too much excited to heed him

—all but a few pacifists. Moreover, the warmth with which the pro-Germans received his plea but added to his unpopularity. He was dubbed pacifist and pro-German, and little short of disloyal. This impression of pro-Germanism was increased by a report circulated soon after he retired from the State Department that the careless manner in which Germany took Wilson's first *Lusitania* note, if not his second, was due to verbal assurance given by Bryan to Dumba, Austrian ambassador, that the strong tone of the note was merely intended for home consumption. Bryan denied the charge and produced notes of his conversation with Dumba, in which no such sentiment appeared. Dumba testified to the correctness of the notes and said that his report had been "misinterpreted" in Europe. The responsibility for this "misinterpretation" has never been fixed. Bryan was, however, loyal to Wilson, and out of the cabinet he refused to criticize him. He supported him in 1916, speaking chiefly in the West and Southwest, and when the country entered the war he offered his services in any capacity desired. But he was not the man for war.

Bryan's last fight in politics was in the Democratic national convention in New York, 1924. He was a supporter of William G. McAdoo, around whom rallied the men who held the old progressive doctrines and who represented most of the "dry" sentiment in the party. The faction next strongest was that of Gov. Smith of New York. The convention was very turbulent, due to the fact that a vast number of Smith's followers gained admission and howled down the speakers who displeased them. This element vented its wrath against Bryan, interrupting his speaking and filling the air with insulting epithets. When he began a sentence, saying, "This is probably the last convention of my party to which I shall be a delegate," some of them began to applaud. Bryan's good humor came to his aid and he shouted back, "Don't applaud. I may change my mind." It was, in fact, his last convention. He was not broken in health, but his frame, his nerves, and his energies were worn out.

J. S. B—t.

[Since Prof. Bassett had not given his article a final revision before his death, the editor has added the following paragraphs.]

For thirty years Bryan had been probably the most popular lecturer on Chautauqua platforms. "Each year," wrote Mrs. Bryan (*Memoirs,* p. 286), "when he returned from his tours he had not only spoken to, but had listened to, the mind of America." It was this insight into the minds of his auditors that made him seem a leader when he was often only a follower. He could think their thoughts, divine their aspirations, and give simple and cogent expression to their half-formed convictions. It was thus that he became the champion of many causes which he did not originate. The public came to think of him as a champion of national prohibition; but as late as 1908 he was arguing in favor of local county option in the control of the liquor traffic in Nebraska (*Memoirs,* p. 290). He had been a total abstainer since boyhood and he had always deplored intemperance; but he was only slowly converted to the notion of making men temperate by a national prohibitory law. An incident while he was secretary of state gave newspaper men their chance to make him appear ridiculous as champion of this new cause. Before taking office he had asked President Wilson "whether he would regard the exclusion of intoxicating liquors from our table as an insurmountable objection to my assuming the duties of the office." He was assured that he might follow his own wishes, whereupon followed the farewell luncheon for Ambassador Bryce when thirsty diplomats were given the alternative of drinking water or grape juice. "Not that we thought of drawing a contrast between wine and grape juice," explains Bryan in his *Memoirs,* "but because the glasses for plain and mineral water looked a little lonesome."

Bryan had joined the Presbyterian church as a boy and had always maintained his connection with it. After 1900, when there was no certainty of being a candidate again, he felt "no longer justified in avoiding religious activity" (*Memoirs,* p. 451). He became an elder in the church at Lincoln and began to accept more and more invitations to address religious gatherings. He was troubled by the sceptical attitude of young men, never having himself experienced any doubts regarding Christian dogmas and creeds. To meet these frequent calls for addresses, he prepared his lectures on "The Prince of Peace" and "The Value of an Ideal." Holding firmly with childlike faith to a literal interpretation of the Bible, as he grew older he became more and more hostile to the teachings of biological science which he had never had the inclination to study. Theories of evolution seemed to him to contradict flatly the straightforward words of Genesis and to cheapen the significance of man's earthly career.

In 1924 he drafted the text of a resolution passed by the legislature of Florida which declared it improper and subversive of the best interests of the people of the state for any public teacher "to teach as true Darwinism or any other hypothesis that links man in blood relationship to any other form of life." He was interested also in a bill under consideration by the legislature of Tennessee, which declared it unlawful for any public teacher "to teach the theory which denies the story of the divine creation of man as taught in the Bible, and to teach instead that man has descended from a lower order of animals." His lecture "Is the Bible True?" was circulated in pamphlet form among the members of the legislature and was believed to have aided the supporters of the bill in securing the necessary votes for its passage (*Memoirs,* p. 481). When, then, a teacher in Dayton, Tenn., was indicted for violation of this statute and Bryan was invited to join the prosecuting attorneys, he accepted the call as a summons to battle. In the course of the trial Bryan was summoned as a witness and subjected to a relentless cross-examination by Clarence Darrow, one of the counsel for the defense. So far as Bryan was concerned, the trial only revealed the naïveté of his religious faith and his want of familiarity with the trend of biological science. Five days after the conclusion of the trial, he was found dead in his bed, having passed away quietly in his sleep.

[*The Memoirs of Wm. Jennings Bryan* (1925) were begun by himself and finished by Mrs. Bryan after his death, with the aid of his correspondence and her own diary. The value of the book lies in its unconscious revelation of personal habits and modes of thought. Bryan had already published three books bearing on his political career: *The First Battle: A Story of the Campaign of 1896* (1896); *The Second Battle or The New Declaration of Independence 1776–1900: An Account of the Struggle of 1900* (1900); and *A Tale of Two Conventions* (1912), containing his account as special correspondent of the national conventions of 1912. *Speeches of Wm. Jennings Bryan Revised and Arranged by Himself,* with a biographical introduction by Mary Baird Bryan, had appeared in two volumes in 1909. Several biographies have been written, all by ardent admirers: H. E. Newbranch, *Wm. Jennings Bryan* (1900); A. L. Gale and G. W. Kline, *Bryan the Man* (1908); G. F. and J. O. Herrick, *The Life of Wm. Jennings Bryan* (1925). More discriminating appraisals are those by C. E. Merriam, in *Four Am. Party Leaders* (1926) and Albert Shaw in the *Rev. of Revs.* (N. Y.), Sept. 1925. The latest biography, *Bryan* (1929), by M. R. Werner is a readable account of his career but adds little that is new.]   A. J.

BRYANT, GRIDLEY (Aug. 26, 1789–June 13, 1867), inventor, civil engineer, was born at Scituate, Mass., the son of Zina and Eunice (Wade) Bryant. His father dying poor, the boy reeceived only a meager common school education. He early displayed a mechanical bent, and, at fifteen, was apprenticed by his mother to a Boston contractor. By 1808 he was in complete charge of his employer's affairs and two years later himself became a contractor. On Dec. 3, 1815, he married Maria Winship Fox, of Boston, by whom he had ten children. He was for a time a contractor for the United States Government and in 1823 built the branch of the United States Bank in Boston, at which time he invented the portable derrick that afterward came into general use. In 1825 he suggested to the Bunker Hill Monument Association that a railroad be built for the transportation of granite over the rough country from the Quincy quarry to the Neponsit River, a little less than three miles. Bryant and his associates, chief among whom was Thomas H. Perkins, received a charter from the Massachusetts General Court, Mar. 4, 1826, which incorporated them as the Granite Railway Company, although the enterprise was popularly known as the Quincy Railroad. Work was begun Apr. 1, 1826, Bryant acting as engineer. Wooden rails, six inches thick and twelve inches in height, were laid on stone sleepers, which were placed eight feet apart. The rails were covered with iron plates, four inches wide and one-fourth of an inch thick. At crossings stone rails were used. Bryant then built four-wheeled trucks, each with a projecting platform, two trucks being joined to form an eight-wheeled car, and erected a switch and a turntable. These inventions he never patented. He had, as he later declared, "abandoned [them] to the public." Others improved the inventions and they became standard railroad equipment. The road was completed at a cost of $50,000 and was opened Oct. 7, 1826, by a train of horse-drawn cars (*Boston Daily Advertiser*, Oct. 9, 1826). It was one of the pioneer American railroads, but it was not, as is alleged, the first railroad in the United States, although it was probably the first American railroad to cover wooden rails with iron plates.

Bryant's later years, devoted to the care of the Quincy quarry and the Granite Railway Company, were featured by the eight-wheeled car controversy. In 1859 he declared that, "Every railroad in the country is now using my eight-wheeled car, and I have never received one cent for the invention" (Stuart, *post*, pp. 120–21). Ross Winans [*q.v.*] adapted the eight-wheeled car to high-speed freight and passenger transportation, and for his adaptation he received a patent in 1834. Sometime after the renewal of the patent in 1848 Winans began suit against the railroads for violation of patent rights. Litigation continued for years, during which Bryant assisted the railroads, whose chief defense consisted of the Bryant car used on the Quincy Railroad. In 1858 the Supreme Court of the United States refused to sustain the Winans patent on the ground that it was too broad (21 *Howard*,

88). Bryant never received the promised financial settlement from the railroads and he died poor at Scituate at the age of seventy-eight.

[Percy Bryant, "Descendants of John Briant, Sen., of Scituate, Mass.," *New Eng. Hist. and Geneal. Reg.*, Jan. 1894; Henry T. Bailey, "An Architect of the Old School," *New Eng. Mag.*, Nov. 1901; *Laws of the Commonwealth of Mass.*, 1826, ch. CLXXXIII; "Internal Improvements," by Agricola, in the *National Aegis* (Worcester, Mass.), Nov. 29, Dec. 6, 1826; Wm. H. Brown, *The Hist. of the First Locomotives in America* (1871); Chas. B. Stuart, *Lives and Works of Civil and Military Engineers of America* (1871); Angus Sinclair, *Development of the Locomotive Engine* (1907); Seymour Dunbar, *A Hist. of Travel in America* (1915).]
F.E.R.

BRYANT, JOHN HOWARD (July 22, 1807–Jan. 14, 1902), Illinois pioneer, the youngest child of Dr. Peter and Sarah (Snell) Bryant and brother of William Cullen Bryant [*q.v.*], was born at Cummington, Mass. In the spring of 1831 he went to Jacksonville, Ill., clerked there for a year, and then squatted on land just south of Princeton. There he lived for seventy years while the untenanted prairie became a populous farming country. His brothers, Austin, Arthur, and Cyrus, settled in the same neighborhood. On June 7, 1833, he married Harriet Elizabeth Wiswall, who had come with her parents from Norton, Mass., to Jacksonville. In 1835, when the land he occupied was thrown on the market, he entered a half section, to which he later added tracts of 160 and 80 acres. Like his friend Lincoln he was large, powerful, and of great endurance, able in the course of a day to split a hundred rails, labor sixteen hours about the farm, or ride seventy-five miles across country on horseback. In temper and interests he was of much the same stuff as his brother, William Cullen, to whom he was devoted. Although farming was his chief occupation, he built roads and bridges, manufactured brick for a time, and edited a local newspaper. He was probably the most useful citizen in his community. He was instrumental in getting Bureau County organized and in erecting at Princeton the first township high school in Illinois, took an active part in the Illinois State Agricultural Society, was recorder of deeds, chairman of the county board of supervisors, census taker of the county in 1840, member of the legislature in 1842 and in 1858, and collector of internal revenue for the fifth Illinois district 1862–66. In politics he began as a Democrat, and became in turn a member of the Liberty party, a Free-Soiler, a Republican, a Liberal Republican in 1872, and a Democrat. He prided himself on having been a member of the Republican conventions at Pittsburgh in 1856 and at Chicago in 1860. He gave hearty support to Owen Lovejoy [*q.v.*], and, as a maintainer of the "Underground Railroad," lodged as many as fifteen fugitive negroes under his roof at one time in 1854. Though his education had been scanty and irregular, he had a cultivated mind and was fond of writing verse, publishing *Poems* in 1855 and *Life and Poems* in 1894. In his preference for simple stanza forms, a diction tinctured with eighteenth-century classicism, and themes drawn from nature, he resembles his greater brother.

[*Who's Who in America*, 1901–02; H. C. Bradsby, ed., *Hist. of Bureau County, Ill.* (Chicago, 1885); *Current Lit.*, Apr. 1902, pp. 488–89; P. Godwin, *Life of William Cullen Bryant* (1883); J. A. Boutelle, "Stephen Bryant and His Descendants," in *New Eng. Hist. and Geneal. Reg.*, July 1870. Examples of his poems are to be found in the later editions of Rufus Griswold's *Poets and Poetry of America* (1842).]　　　G.H.G.

BRYANT, JOSEPH DECATUR (Mar. 12, 1845–Apr. 7, 1914), surgeon and medical educator, the only child of Alonzo Ambrose Bryant, by his wife, Harriet Adkins, was born in East Troy, Walworth County, Wis. His ancestors on both sides were English, his mother being of the family of Adkins who took part in the Crusades. His father was one of twelve children, none of whom died before the age of seventy. Joseph was brought up on a farm and received his early education at the public school in his native town, and was later sent to Norwich Academy (New York). He began the study of medicine under Dr. George Avery of New York and received his degree in 1868 from the Bellevue Hospital Medical College. He served as a surgical interne at Bellevue Hospital during 1869–71. His success was immediate and outstanding. He became visiting and consulting surgeon to the Bellevue, St. Vincent's, and other hospitals in New York City. In 1884 he increased his reputation by the publication of his successful two-volume *Manual of Operative Surgery*, which passed through four editions, the last appearing in 1905. He became a friend and the private surgeon of Grover Cleveland, and during Cleveland's presidency performed an heroic operation upon him for a malignant growth (sarcoma) of the left upper jaw in which almost all bony structures were removed except the floor of the orbit. The major part of the operation, which proved life-saving, occurred on July 1, 1893, on Commodore E. C. Benedict's yacht, the *Oneida*, which at the time lay at anchor in New York harbor. The public was not informed of the operation until 1917, after the death of both the President and the surgeon. It was described by W. W. Keen in a paper entitled "The surgical operations on President Cleveland in 1893" which appeared in the *Saturday Evening Post*, Sept. 22, 1917. Many of Bryant's students have testified to his

gifts and deep enthusiasm for teaching (see J. A. A. Sutcliffe, *Indianapolis Medical Journal*, XVII, 248). He made his ward rounds attractive and his lectures were always anticipated with much pleasure by his students. It was also his custom during the six winter months to hold an evening "quiz" class in surgery, as he termed it, for those who were preparing for graduation. On these occasions he often surprised his students by his complete familiarity not only with his immediate subject but with the fundamental sciences of physiology, biological chemistry and anatomy. As a leader in public health, he served for six years in the New York Health Department and became at various times both City and State Commissioner of Health. He championed crusades against pulmonary tuberculosis, secured systematic enforcement of the tenement laws against overcrowding, and acted energetically when New York was threatened with an epidemic of cholera (1892). Political pressure was brought to bear upon him at the time of the cholera epidemic because his quarantine measures threatened commercial activities. He was unmoved, however, and within a short time had the epidemic completely under control.

As a writer Bryan was always lucid and painstaking, but apart from his text-books his surgical contributions were few. The most noteworthy were his paper on "The Treatment of penetrating gun-shot wounds of the cranium" (*New York Medical Journal*, May 5, 1888), and "The relation between the gross anatomy of the appendix and appendicitis" (*Medical News*, Mar. 3, 1894). He also rendered important service to surgery by becoming the senior editor (with A. H. Buck [*q.v.*]) of the *American Practice of Surgery* which appeared in eight volumes between 1906 and 1911. He was an indefatigable worker, painstaking and conservative as a surgeon, a keen observer and a remarkable diagnostician. He studied his patients with exceptional care and was noted for his generosity to the poor. In 1874 he married Annette Amelia, daughter of Samuel Crum. They had one child, Florence, who married Frederick Augustus de Peyster. For many years Bryant was the victim of diabetes but he continued his professional activities until a few days before his death.

[The obituaries and appreciations of Bryant are numerous and are listed in the *Index Cat. of the Surgeon-General's Lib.*, 3 ser. Those in the *N. Y. State Jour. of Medicine*, 1914, XIV, 229–30, the *N. Y. Times*, Apr. 8, 1914, and the *Indianapolis Medic. Jour.*, 1914, XVII, 248–51 (by J. A. A. Sutcliffe) are the most adequate. The N. Y. Acad. of Medicine possesses a scrap-book of newspaper-cuttings, photographs, and other documents relating to Bryant's operation upon Cleveland, compiled by Dr. Kasson C. Gibson, the dentist who devised the rubber jaw for the President.]　　　J.F.F.

BRYANT, WILLIAM CULLEN (Nov. 3, 1794–June 12, 1878), poet, editor, was descended from Stephen Bryant, who settled in the Plymouth colony in 1632 and became a town officer of Duxbury, Mass. For several generations the Bryants were farmers, but the poet's grandfather, Philip Bryant, and his father, Peter Bryant, were physicians. The latter settled at Cummington, in western Massachusetts, married Sarah Snell, who traced her ancestry back to the *Mayflower,* and carried on a laborious and ill-paid practise. He was a skilful surgeon, who had been trained under the French refugee, Leprilète; he had traveled widely as a surgeon in a merchant vessel; he had musical taste, playing much on the violin; and he was a lover of poetry, possessing a well-stocked library and writing light verse in both Latin and English. His strength was such that he could easily lift a barrel of cider over a cartwheel. The poet's mother was tall, strong, known for her common sense and stern moral qualities, and with certain literary habits; she kept a diary in which she concisely noted the occurrences in the neighborhood. Bryant's health in early childhood was delicate, his head seemed excessively large, and he was of a painfully nervous temperament, but by a stern regimen, including daily cold baths, his father made him a sturdy boy. The mother took pride in his precocity, teaching him the alphabet at sixteen months. The future poet was fortunate in his natural surroundings. His birthplace was a farmhouse surrounded with apple-trees, standing amid fields which sloped steeply down to the north fork of the Westfield River. In his fifth year the family removed to a place of still greater attractiveness, the homestead of his maternal grandfather, Ebenezer Snell, also of Cummington. The boy delighted in the brooks, the river, the rocky hillsides, and the deep forests, as yet only partly invaded by settlement, and enjoyed nutting, gathering spearmint, fishing, and other outdoor pastimes. He was fortunate also in the fact that his father's political interests—Dr. Bryant represented Cummington first in the lower and later the upper branch of the legislature—kept the door of the farmhouse partly open upon the wider world of Boston.

Measured in years of formal tuition, Bryant's education was limited. The district schools gave him a training in reading, writing, arithmetic, geography, and the Westminster Catechism. At the age of twelve, his parents having decided that he deserved a college education, he was sent to live with the Rev. Thomas Snell, an uncle in North Brookfield, to learn Latin, and the following year was transferred to the care of the Rev.

Moses Hallock to acquire Greek. Both were men of great dignity, elevated moral standards, and austere influence. In the eight months with his uncle, Bryant showed a remarkably acquisitive mind, reading Virgil, the select orations of Cicero, and the colloquies of Corderius, while after two months with the Rev. Mr. Hallock "I knew the Greek New Testament from end to end almost as if it had been English" (Godwin, *Bryant,* I, 33). Meanwhile poetical ambitions had awakened in the boy. He owed much to his early and ingrained familiarity with the Scriptures, and when he was ten or eleven his grandfather Snell gave him the whole book of Job to turn into verse. A more important incentive came from his father's library, a collection ultimately numbering about 700 volumes. "In the long winter evenings and stormy winter days," Bryant wrote later, "I read with my elder brother. . . . I remember well the delight with which we welcomed the translation of the *Iliad* by Pope when it was brought into the house. I had met with passages from it before, and thought them the finest verses ever written" (*Ibid.,* I, 24). In childhood he often prayed "that I might receive the gift of poetic genius, and write verses that might endure" (*Ibid.,* I, 26). Before he was in his teens he had scribbled on many subjects, with the encouragement and also the sharp criticism of his father. Taken to Williamstown in September 1810, Bryant passed an easy examination for entrance to the sophomore class of Williams College. The institution was small and poverty-stricken, with a faculty of four who taught a meager curriculum for ill-prepared country lads. Bryant's chief amusements were woodland rambles, participation in the meetings of the Philotechnian literary society, and a course of miscellaneous reading, in which he profited particularly by his study of the Greek poets. Classmates remembered him later as modest, unobtrusive, studious, inclined to choose sober and bookish friends, and competent but not brilliant in the classroom. But his college career was brief. Withdrawing from Williams to prepare himself to enter the junior class at Yale, he worked at his books all summer (1811), only to have his father declare that his means were insufficient for the step.

Already Bryant had appeared, in a way which he later regretted, in print. In 1808, catching the indignant spirit of the Federalists about him, he had written a satire called "The Embargo," which in five hundred lines or more assailed President Jefferson as unpatriotic, a cowardly truckler to the French, an eccentric dabbler in science, and a man of low personal morals. Dr. Bryant unwisely carried this production up to Boston and had it published under the title of *The Embargo: or Sketches of the Times, a Satire; by a Youth of Thirteen.* It sold well, was praised by some reviewers, and attracted so much attention that in 1809 Dr. Bryant had it republished with several other pieces taken from the Hampshire *Gazette,* and placed his son's name on the title-page. Not a line of the volume was ever included by Bryant in his later writings, and he spoke of the pamphlet with testy disgust as "stuff." But it proved the precursor of a really great poem. The autumn after he left Williamstown witnessed the composition of the first form of "Thanatopsis," a work written under several clearly traceable influences. His father had brought home the melancholy poetry of Henry Kirke White, and Bryant, hanging over it eagerly, read also Blair's *Grave,* and Bishop Porteus's poem upon *Death.* Simultaneously he was captivated by the fine blank verse of Cowper's *Task.* Under these circumstances—imbued with the mortuary meditations of Blair and Kirke White, watching the onset of the dark Berkshire winter, and supplied by Cowper with a superior and fascinating metrical form—he began the poem which was to make him famous; a great Puritan dirge, the first fine poetic expression of the stern New England mind. But after completing the poem he was content to stuff it into a corner of his desk. It was necessary for him to turn seriously to a career, and guided largely by his father, he determined to study for the bar. In December 1811 he entered the office of a Mr. Howe of Worthington, four or five miles distant, and there remained until June 1814, an unhappy period. He had no liking for legal study, and was troubled by the fear that his sensitive nature was unfitted for the controversies of the law courts. Meanwhile he made the acquaintance, momentous for his future work, of Wordsworth's *Lyrical Ballads.* For the first time he understood the true character of the impulses which had caused him to pray to be a poet, and realized that they were inextricably bound up with his intense love of natural beauty. As yet, however, he was still groping for an authentic poetic expression. An unfortunate and obscure love affair was reflected in conventional verse, much of it callow in thought and hackneyed in imagery. In the late spring of 1814 he transferred his legal studies to the office of William Baylies in Bridgewater, and there completed them, passing his preliminary examination for the bar in August. These were the years of the second war with England, which awakened no enthusiasm in Bryant. His letters attack the conflict vehemently, and show that he, like other New England Federalists, was thinking seriously of the possibility of secession from the Union and of conflict with the Southern States.

Bryant was fully admitted to the bar in August 1815. While the young lawyer would have liked to embark upon practise in Boston, his purse was too thin to support him in a large city, and he somewhat hastily decided to hang out his sign in Plainfield, a village seven miles from his Cummington home. In December 1815 he walked over to make some preliminary inquiries. While striding along the highway he saw in the afterglow of sunset, flooding the western sky with gold and opal, a solitary bird winging along the horizon; his mind was filled with the beauty of the scene, and at his lodgings that night he wrote the finest of his lyrics, "To a Waterfowl." This also went into his drawer. After eight months in Plainfield, he found a larger opening in Great Barrington, in partnership with a young established lawyer whose practise was worth $1,200 a year. Bryant's experience as a lawyer in Great Barrington endured till the beginning of 1825. There were then three grades of lawyers in the state, entitled respectively to plead in the lower courts, to manage cases in the supreme court, and to argue before the supreme court bench; and Bryant by the fall of 1819 had been admitted to the third category. His name appears four or five times in the supreme court reports, indicating a practise larger than that of most young lawyers. But he found the contentious life of the bar uncongenial, while the frequent miscarriages of justice offended him. Tradition ascribes his final decision to relinquish practise to a decision of the state supreme court in 1824 reversing upon a flimsy technical quibble a judgment for $500 which Bryant had obtained for a plaintiff in a libel suit. But the basic reason was financial. On June 11, 1821, Bryant married Frances Fairchild, daughter of a neighboring farmer—the beginning of a union of singular harmony and devotion; and shortly afterward a daughter was born. As head of a family he required a larger income, and fortunately his pen enabled him to find it.

His fame as a poet dates from the almost accidental publication of "Thanatopsis" in the *North American Review* in 1817. One of the editors, Willard Phillips, had told Dr. Bryant that he wished William Cullen to contribute; Dr. Bryant found in his son's desk the manuscript of "Thanatopsis," "To a Waterfowl," and a briefer piece; and Phillips excitedly carried them at once to his Cambridge associates. "Ah, Phillips, you have been imposed upon," said R. H. Dana; "no one on this side of the Atlantic is capable of writing such verses." When in September the first abbreviated version of "Thanatopsis" was published, its effect was somewhat blunted by four weak stanzas on death which were accidentally prefaced to it; but thereafter Bryant's position in the narrow American literary world was secure. He contributed several other poems and three prose essays, one on American poetry, to the *Review*. Four years later, in 1821, he was invited to read the Phi Beta Kappa poem at the Harvard Commencement to a distinguished audience, and wrote "The Ages," one of his longest productions, which contains many fine passages but is deplorably uneven. His Boston acquaintances prevailed upon him to publish it and some of his other verse, and the result was a pamphlet of forty-four pages, containing twelve pieces in all (*Poems:* Cambridge, 1821). Besides the final version of "Thanatopsis," to which he had added a stately exordium and conclusion, it contained three lyrics of unmistakable genius—"Green River," "To a Waterfowl," and "The Yellow Violet"; and it was warmly praised not merely by American reviewers, but by *Blackwood's*.

Among the fruits of this literary success were a visit to New York (1824) at the invitation of Henry Sedgwick of Stockbridge, and an engagement to furnish an average of one hundred lines a month to the *United States Literary Gazette* of Boston for $200 a year. This ushered in a period of unexampled productivity in Bryant's career, for in about eighteen months (1824–25) he wrote between twenty and thirty poems for the *Gazette*, including some of his finest work—"Rizpah," "An Indian at the Burial Place of his Fathers," "Monument Mountain," "Autumn Woods," and the "Forest Hymn." By 1825 he had clearly emerged as America's one great poet. The result was an invitation (January 1825) to assume the co-editorship with Henry J. Anderson of the monthly called the *New York Review and Athenæum Magazine,* at $1,000 a year. Bryant accepted, left his wife and baby in Great Barrington, and for a little more than a year was exclusively employed upon a magazine of precarious and declining fortunes. He made the acquaintance of the literary circle of New York—Halleck, S. F. B. Morse, Verplanck, Chancellor Kent, and others; he wrote for the *Review* a few fine poems, notably "The Death of the Flowers," as well as much hack work. But he was increasingly worried by poverty and had obtained a license to practise law in the city courts when he was rescued by an offer from the *Evening Post*. Its editor, William Coleman [*q.v.*], had been injured in an accident, and Bryant stepped in (June 1826) as assistant.

For the next three years Bryant was sub-editor of the *Evening Post,* and upon the death of Coleman in July 1829 he assumed the editorial chair which he was to hold for almost a half-century. He quickly acquired a one-eighth share in the journal, which in 1830 became one-fourth, and in 1833 one-third. From the standpoint of material gain the step was fortunate. For the first time it lifted Bryant above financial anxiety, giving him an annual income during the first four years of between $3,300 and $4,000, sums then counted large in New York. He became at one step a public figure of prominence and influence, for the *Evening Post,* founded under the auspices of Alexander Hamilton, had long been one of the country's leading newspapers. But as a poet he unquestionably suffered by the new demands upon his time. Of the whole quantity of verse which he wrote during his long life, about one-third had been composed before 1829. During 1830 he wrote but thirty lines, during 1831 but sixty, and in 1833 apparently none at all. Newspaper staffs were small, and for the first fifteen years of his control Bryant had but one permanent editorial assistant. He wrote editorials, clipped exchanges, reviewed books, and sometimes gathered news. Usually he was at his desk soon after seven in the morning and remained till nearly five. This confining labor irked him, he cared little at the outset for journalism as a career, bracketing it with the law as "a wrangling profession," and his letters show that at first he meant to escape from it to find "leisure for literary occupations that I love better." Meanwhile he gave the *Evening Post* increased strength as a Jacksonian and free trade organ, enlarged its news, and improved its format. But he relied more and more heavily upon his able, aggressive, and highly radical assistant, William Leggett, and after 1830 spent much time out of the office. He enjoyed excursions to the Catskills, Berkshires, and Alleghanies; in 1832 he made a journey to Illinois, where the prairies delighted him, and where he is said to have met Abraham Lincoln; and in 1833 he went on a Canadian tour. In June 1834 he sailed for Europe with his wife and children, intending to leave the *Post* forever and live upon his one-third share. He was absent during the whole of 1835 and was spending the winter of 1835–36 in Heidelberg when news reached him that Leggett was dangerously ill and the *Evening Post* in financial difficulties. He arrived in New York in March 1836, to find the journal without an editor, its business manager just dead, and its circulation, advertising revenue, and influence disastrously injured by the ill-temper and lack of judgment with which Leggett had asserted a Locofoco Democracy, attacked monopoly and inflation, and harried the Whigs. It was necessary to plunge in and labor with unwearying assiduity to rescue the paper. Leggett's connection with it was severed, and Bryant became half-owner. During 1837 and 1838 he worked again from dawn until dark, alarming his wife by his neglect of his health. As editor he had been taught a sharp lesson, and for three decades thereafter his primary allegiance—at times his sole allegiance—was to the *Evening Post*.

By 1840 he had become one of the leading Democratic editors of the nation, and had begun to take advanced ground against slavery. He supported Jackson and Van Buren, demanded a low tariff, opposed the use of public money for internal improvements, and advocated a complete separation between government and banking. He vigorously championed the workingman against judges who held that labor unions were a conspiracy to obstruct trade. When J. Q. Adams defended the right of petition against Calhoun and the South, the *Evening Post* stood with him; it opposed the annexation of Texas; and it assailed Van Buren for pledging himself to maintain slavery in the District of Columbia. Bryant was able in 1840 to wage a whole-hearted campaign against Harrison, and four years later still kept the *Evening Post* on the Democratic side, though in his revulsion against Polk and the annexation of Texas he considered bolting the ticket. His chief aid during these years was Parke Godwin [*q.v.*], later his son-in-law, who assisted in a steady expansion of the news features. To the editorial page Bryant gave dignity and moderation; in vivacity, cleverness, and force it was not equal to the *Tribune* or *Springfield Republican,* but in occasional bursts of noble eloquence it was far superior, and his stately, elevated style was a model for American journalism.

In 1832 he had brought out a collection called *Poems* containing eighty-nine pieces in all; the most notable additions to his previous work being "To the Fringed Gentian" and "The Song of Marion's Men." It was a slender sheaf to represent the entire production of a man who had written "Thanatopsis" twenty-one years earlier, but the *North American Review* rightly pronounced it "the best volume of American verse that has ever appeared." So marked was the American success of his work that Bryant sent a copy to Irving, who was then abroad, asking him to find an English publisher. The English edition came out (London, 1832), with a dedication to Samuel Rogers and an introduction by Irving which made in too unqualified terms the generally valid claim that "the descriptive writings of Mr. Bryant are essentially American"— a claim which some reviewers at once challenged. Irving also slightly displeased Bryant by altering a line of "The Song of Marion's Men" from "The British foeman trembles" to "The foeman trembles in his camp." The English reception of the poems was friendly, and John Wilson wrote an extended and for the most part eulogistic review for *Blackwood's.* This same year Bryant edited a prose collection called *Tales of the Glauber Spa* which was published anonymously, and which contained several stories, creditable but by no means distinguished, from his own pen. This line of endeavor, a fruit of his contacts with Robert Sands and others, he wisely abandoned.

After the first heavy labor of restoring the *Evening Post* was accomplished Bryant resumed his pen, and the half-dozen years following 1838 evinced a partial renewal of his poetic energy. He wrote some fifteen poems in this period, and the fresh material enabled him to issue *The Fountain, and Other Poems* (1842) and *The White-Footed Doe, and Other Poems* (1844), the former containing fourteen pieces, and the latter ten. A prefatory remark in the first volume shows that he had in contemplation a long reflective and descriptive poem somewhat resembling Wordsworth's *Excursion* and Cowper's *Task;* for he says that some of the poems are presented "merely as parts of a longer one planned by the author, which may possibly be finished hereafter." His friend R. H. Dana, Sr., had for years been insistently urging him to compose an extended poem; but it is probable that Bryant found when he attempted it that he did not have a sufficiently fertile and broad imagination, and that his art lacked flexibility and variety. The real value of the project was in furnishing him a much-needed incentive to write the brief lyrics which he hoped to fit into a larger scheme. The reason usually assigned for the slenderness of his output, his preoccupation with the conduct of the *Evening Post,* has partial, but only partial, validity. After the early forties he was free to take long vacations from the office, and did take them. The journal prospered, its annual average dividends during the forties being almost $10,000, while in the fifties it rapidly became a veritable gold-mine. From beginning to end of his life the poet-editor lived with a simplicity that was in some respects almost Spartan. But Bryant's growing wealth enabled him to buy in 1843 an old farmhouse and forty acres of land at Roslyn, Long Island, on the shores of an inlet of the Sound. Here, following the outdoor pursuits he always loved, he was able to spend week-ends and even whole weeks together in summer and fall. He delighted to work in his garden, to take long walks, to swim, and to botanize. He collected a large library, in which he spent much time. He could continue, moreover, those extensive travels which he loved, and which he partially described in correspondence to the *Evening Post* collected under the title of *Letters of a Traveller* (1850)—a wide tour of the South, four trips in close succession to Europe, and a jaunt to Cuba. Had it been only leisure and peace that were lacking, Bryant might have written as much in these years as Longfellow; and his keen professional interest in current events might, had he possessed a different temperament, have inspired his pen as passing history inspired Whittier's.

Yet despite increased leisure and frequent absences, Bryant devoted much hard labor to the *Evening Post* and after 1848 gave it a leading place in the national discussion of the slavery question. It broke sharply with the Democratic party in 1848, supporting the Free-Soil candidacy of Van Buren against Zachary Taylor with such ardor as to be the most efficient advocate of the new party. Two years later it opposed Clay's compromise bill, urging the free states not to give up a single principle. In 1852 it reluctantly indorsed the Democratic nominee, Franklin Pierce, but the following year its utterances against slavery were so radical that the Richmond *Enquirer* called it "abolitionist in fact." Bryant's disgust with the subserviency of Pierce to the South, and his resentment at the Kansas-Nebraska bill, made him quickly and completely dissever the *Post* from the Democratic party. In 1856 he enthusiastically allied the paper with the new Republican organization, while his assistant editor, John Bigelow [*q.v.*], was one of the men instrumental in bringing Frémont forward as its candidate. In the four heated years which ensued Bryant made the *Evening Post* one of the most vigorous of the "Black Republican" organs. He encouraged the despatch of settlers and rifles to Kansas, denounced the Dred Scott decision as an unallowable perversion of the Constitution, and called John Brown a martyr and hero. When Lincoln made his Cooper Union speech in 1860, Bryant introduced him, and the poet-editor was heartily glad to see him defeat Seward for the nomination. After secession began, Bryant never wavered in denouncing all plans for compromise, and in demanding that rebellion be put down by the sword. Many of his editorial utterances for these years display a grandeur of style, and a force and eloquence not to be matched elsewhere in the press of the period, and they produced an effect out of all proportion to the slender circulation of the *Evening Post*.

Throughout the Civil War Bryant belonged to the radical faction which demanded greater energy in its prosecution and assailed Lincoln for his moderation and his reluctance to emancipate the slaves. He was indignant at the modification of Frémont's proclamation. The *Evening Post* repeatedly urged the President to act, and pointed out that Antietam furnished a favorable opportunity. In his criticism of many administration policies Bryant was in close contact with Salmon P. Chase, whose appointment to a cabinet position he had urged upon Lincoln; but the editor objected warmly to some of Chase's own fiscal policies, notably the inflation of the currency by the issue of treasury notes as legal tender. For a time in 1864 the *Evening Post* hesitated to advocate the renomination of Lincoln, but in midsummer Bryant fell into line, and thereafter his praise of the Chief Executive lacked nothing in fervor. After the close of the war he broke from his former radical associates upon the issue of reconstruction in the South, the *Evening Post* maintaining an unflinching advocacy of President Johnson's mild policy, and attacking the harsh measures of Congress. Bryant regretted the impeachment of Johnson, and rejoiced when the Senate failed to convict him. After Grant's inauguration his active interest in the management of the *Evening Post* materially relaxed. The death of Mrs. Bryant on July 27, 1865, had been a heavy blow. In 1866 he tried to escape from his depression of mind by beginning a translation of the whole of Homer, completed in 1871, and showing a fine mastery of blank verse; and in 1866–67 he made a dispirited tour, his sixth and last, of Europe. He had been everywhere regarded for many years as the first citizen of New York, and he was unweariedly at the service of all good causes. In civic, social, and charitable movements his name took precedence of all others. But he was never in any sense popular; austere, chill, precise, and dignified, his demeanor made familiarity impossible, and even in small gatherings he was not a clubbable man. Though he was a polished and impressive orator, and spoke often, his immense influence as a public leader was almost wholly an indirect influence; he reached the minds of those who in turn could reach the masses. His volume of original writing in this period was not large, but it maintained the even merit which had usually marked his production since the appearance of "Thanatopsis." In 1876 he harked back to the subject of mortality in the noble poem "The Flood of Years," and followed it by his retrospective meditation, "A Lifetime," the last of all his works. To the end of his life, always athletic and active, he continued to give several hours daily when in town to the *Evening Post,* walking to and from his home. He was estranged from the Grant Administration by its blunders, its tariff policy, its course at the South, and its low moral tone, and he regarded the Liberal Republican movement with guarded approbation. Had the Liberal Republican convention in 1872 nominated Charles Francis Adams he might have supported him, but he regarded Greeley's candidacy as preposterous. Four years later, associates urged him to side with Tilden (an old personal friend) against Hayes, but he kept the *Evening Post* Republican. He labored as usual in the office on the day (Apr. 29, 1878) when he delivered an oration under a hot sun at the unveiling of the Mazzini statue in Central Park. Returning after the ceremonies to the home of James Grant Wilson, he fell on the steps, sustained a concussion of the brain, and shortly lapsed from partial consciousness into coma. His death in June was followed by a funeral in All Souls' Unitarian Church and burial in Roslyn Cemetery.

Bryant holds a double place in American history. He brought to his editorial chair some qualities which no editor of his time possessed in equal degree. In culture and scholarship he surpassed Raymond, Bowles, and Greeley, while in dignity and adherence to moral principle he was far in advance of Bennett and Dana. Few men of his time did half so much to lift journalism from a vulgar calling to a place of high honor and national influence. The literary correctness of the *Evening Post,* controlled by Bryant's fastidious taste—his *index expurgatorius* is still quoted— was famous. But, preoccupied with the great aims of his editorial page, he lacked the faculty of Bowles and Greeley for creating a broad newspaper which would appeal by enterprise in newsgathering and by special features to a great popular audience. He was responsible for few innovations in journalism, and they were not of high importance. His journalistic vein had something of the narrowness which marked his poetic genius, and though the *Post's* editorials, political news, literary articles, and foreign correspondence were of the highest merit, they were for the few and not the many. As a poet he holds a position in American letters akin to that of Wordsworth in English. He is our great poet of nature, with which more than one hundred of his total of about one hundred and sixty poems deal. He had certain clear limitations: he lacked warmth of emotion, and especially human emotion, while his imagination was restricted in range, and he

seldom revealed intellectual profundity. But he possessed a sensitively artistic perception of what was lovely in nature, and a capacity for its imaginative interpretation, which are not equaled by any other American writer. It is not nature in general, but the untouched nature of the New World, and of New England in particular, which his verse pictures with definiteness and accuracy. With this descriptive power are joined an elemental piety, a pervading sense of the transiency of all earthly things, and a meditative philosophy which, while melancholy, is also peaceful and consoling; qualities which give to much of his work a religious depth, and make his poetry as cool and restful as the deep forests he loved. His range was not wide nor high, but within that range he wrought with a classical love of restraint, purity, and objectivity, chiseling his work as out of marble; and he produced a small body of poetry which may be called imperishable.

[The standard life is Parke Godwin's *A Biography of Wm. Cullen Bryant, with Extracts from His Private Correspondence* (1883), in two large volumes. Godwin also edited Bryant's *Poetical Works* and *Complete Prose Writings* (1883, 1884). The latter includes a selection of articles from the *Evening Post,* but the paper's editorial pages contain additional material of value which has never been collected. Godwin also made a selection from Bryant's travel writings, but these are found more fully in Bryant's own *Letters of a Traveller* (1850), dealing with his European, Western, and Southern wanderings. John Bigelow's brief volume in the American Men of Letters series, *Wm. Cullen Bryant* (1890), reflects the author's intimacy with the poet, as does also Jas. Grant Wilson's *Bryant and His Friends* (1886). The aim of Wm. Aspenwall Bradley's *Bryant* (1905) in the English Men of Letters series is critical rather than biographical. A note by Carl Van Doren on the origin of "Thanatopsis" may be found in the *Nation,* CI, 432–33. Some light is thrown upon Bryant's work as editor by Geo. Cary Eggleston, *Recollections of a Varied Life* (1910), and by Allan Nevins, *The Evening Post: A Century of Journalism* (1922), while a sharply critical sidelight is furnished by a manuscript volume of memoirs by J. Ranken Towse, in the possession of the *Evening Post.* The best brief critical studies are by E. C. Stedman in *Poets of America* (1885), and Wm. Ellery Leonard in the *Cambridge Hist. of Am. Lit.* (1917), I, 260 ff. The last-named volume contains a full bibliography.]   A.N.

BRYCE, LLOYD STEPHENS (Sept. 20, 1851–Apr. 2, 1917), politician, author, was born at Flushing, L. I., the son of Joseph Smith Bryce and Elyzabeth (Stephens) Bryce. His father, whose name was originally Joseph Brice Smith, graduated from West Point in 1829, was assistant professor of mathematics at the Academy for the next two years, became a successful lawyer in New York, reëntered the army at the outbreak of the Civil War, was stationed most of the time in or near Washington, and rose to the rank of brevet major of volunteers. His mother was a sister of John Lloyd Stephens [*q.v.*]. Bryce spent his boyhood at Georgetown, D. C., the home of the Smith family. He received his schooling there from the Jesuits of Georgetown College and in New York from Charles Anthon [*q.v.*]. In 1867 he traveled in Europe and copied pictures in the Louvre. He was matriculated at Christ Church, Oxford, on Jan. 28, 1870, and graduated in 1874. Well educated and well connected, more than comfortable financially, a member of the best clubs and the best society, Bryce interested himself in a number of things, always acquitted himself well, but did not persist with anything long enough to attain eminence. Home again in New York he studied law but never practised. He entered politics as a Democrat, and in 1886 Gov. Hill appointed him paymaster-general of the state with the rank of brigadier-general. That autumn he ran for Congress from the seventh district on an anti-single-tax platform and was elected. Discovering in Washington that the single tax was not imminent, he devoted himself during the Fiftieth Congress to the improvement of New York harbor and to the copyright laws, in which he had recently acquired a personal interest. In 1887 had appeared his first novel, *Paradise*. The next year he was defeated for reëlection. Subsequently he published *The Romance of an Alter Ego* (1889), which was reissued as *An Extraordinary Experience* (1891); *Friends in Exile* (1893); and *Lady Blanche's Salon* (1899). His novels were amusing but have no claim to remembrance. He also wrote shorter fiction, magazine articles, and reviews. In 1889 his friend Allen Thorndike Rice [*q.v.*] died suddenly and left him a controlling interest in the *North American Review*. Bryce hastened home from Europe, assumed the editorship with the issue for September 1889, bought the other interests in the magazine, and conducted it until 1896. In his editorial policy he followed the lines laid down by Rice, secured able and eminent contributors, and showed a canny regard for timeliness. On President Taft's appointment Bryce served as United States minister to the Netherlands and Luxembourg from August 1911 till September 1913. He was a delegate to the Opium Conference of 1913, was an honorary vice-president of a Conference on Bills of Exchange, and furthered the building of the Peace Palace at The Hague. His wife was Edith Cooper, daughter of Mayor Edward Cooper of New York and grand-daughter of Peter Cooper.

[*Who's Who in America*, 1916–17; *Who's Who in N. Y. C.*, 1904; *Rev. of Revs.* (N. Y.), May 1891; J. Foster, ed., *Alumni Oxonienses, 1715–1886*, vol. I (1887); G. W. Cullum, *Biog. Reg.* (3rd ed., 1891), I, 424–25; *Biog. Cong. Dir. 1774–1911* (1913); *N. Y. Times*, Apr. 3, 1917; information from Peter Cooper Bryce, Esq. (son).]   G. H. G.

BUCHANAN, FRANKLIN (Sept. 17, 1800–May 11, 1874), naval officer, was born at "Auchentorlie," Baltimore, the eighth of eleven children. His father was Dr. George Buchanan, son of a distinguished Scotch physician who came to Maryland in 1723; his mother, Laetitia McKean, was the daughter of the Pennsylvania "Signer" Thomas McKean, who was of Scotch-Irish descent. Young Buchanan, becoming a midshipman Jan. 28, 1815, served first on the *Java*, Commodore Oliver Hazard Perry. After five years on various ships, chiefly in the Mediterranean, he made, with the permission of the Navy Department, a fifteen months' voyage to China as mate on a merchant vessel. He then spent six strenuous years in the West India Squadron, suppressing piracy in the Caribbean. Meanwhile, becoming a lieutenant Jan. 13, 1825, Buchanan in July following, delivered at Rio de Janeiro the frigate *Baltimore*, to the Emperor of Brazil. After another Mediterranean cruise in the *Constellation*, he went in 1833 as first lieutenant on the ship of the line *Delaware* which carried the United States minister Edward Livingston to France, and among other officers was invited to dine with King Louis Philippe. He was afterward ordered to shore duty, during which he tested guns at the Philadelphia Navy Yard and then commanded the receiving ship at Baltimore. This service was followed by a cruise in the Pacific, April 1839–June 1840, in the frigate *Constitution* and the sloop *Falmouth*. Promoted to commander Sept. 8, 1841, he was early the next year placed in command of the steam frigate *Mississippi*; but after a few months he was transferred to the sloop *Vincennes*, which he commanded for nearly two years. While cruising in this ship in search of pirates and slave-traders, he assisted two British merchantmen in peril in Galveston Harbor, for which service he received the official thanks of Great Britain. On Aug. 14, 1845, having submitted, in obedience to Secretary of the Navy Bancroft, a plan for organizing the new Naval School at Annapolis, he was appointed its first superintendent, which position he filled, from the formal opening of the School, Oct. 10, 1845, until his detachment, Mar. 2, 1847, after "renewed" application for active service in the Mexican War. Buchanan initiated the high standards of discipline and efficiency for which the Naval Academy is famous; Bancroft commended his "precision and sound judgment" and his "wise adaptation of simple and moderate means to a great and noble end" (*Annual Report*, Dec. 1, 1845). Throughout the Mexican War Buchanan commanded the sloop

Germantown, which coöperated in the operations against Tuxpan, Apr. 18, and Tabasco, June 16, 1847. In 1852, after some years of shore duty chiefly at Baltimore, he took command of the steam frigate *Susquehanna,* the flagship of Perry's squadron in the expedition to Japan. When on July 14, 1853, the President's letter was presented with due ceremony to representatives of the Emperor at Uraga, Buchanan was the first officer to set foot on Japanese soil. On his return home, he became a member of the Board of Officers to Promote Efficiency of the Navy, and was afterward made commander of the Washington Navy Yard, meanwhile becoming captain Sept. 14, 1855. Under the impression that Maryland would secede from the Union, he resigned from the navy Apr. 22, 1861; but soon thereafter becoming convinced that there would be a reconciliation between the North and the South, he wrote to the Navy Department requesting to withdraw his resignation. On May 14, 1861, however, he was "dismissed" from the service. Going to Richmond soon afterward, he joined the Confederate States Navy, with the rank of captain, Sept. 5, 1861. He was chief of the Bureau of Orders and Detail until Feb. 24, 1862, when he was placed in command of the Chesapeake Bay Squadron, with his flag on the reconstructed U. S. S. *Merrimac,* renamed the C. S. S. *Virginia.* On Mar. 8, he surprised the Union squadron in Hampton Roads, and destroyed the frigate *Congress,* of which his brother McKean was purser, the sloop of war *Cumberland,* and three small steamers. Having been seriously wounded, however, in the left thigh by a Minié ball from the shore batteries during the engagement, he was prevented from commanding his ironclad in the *Monitor-Merrimac* battle of the following day. He was "promoted for gallant and meritorious conduct" (*Official Records,* 1 ser., VII, 62) to admiral, Aug. 26, 1862, thus becoming the ranking officer, and was then made commander of the naval forces at Mobile. In the battle of Mobile Bay, Aug. 5, 1864, he commanded the Confederate squadron, his flagship being the ram *Tennessee.* His smaller vessels having been captured or driven to cover, "Old Buck" made a heroic attack single-handed against Farragut's entire squadron. In the furious engagement, the *Tennessee's* rudder chain jammed, she became unmanageable, and other injuries forced her to surrender. Her commander, seriously wounded again, remained a prisoner of war until exchanged in February 1865. Returning to his home, "The Rest," Talbot County, Md., he became president of the Maryland Agricultural College, September 1868–June 1869. After about

a year in Mobile where he was secretary of the Alabama Branch of the Life Insurance Company of America, he returned again to his Maryland home where he died May 11, 1874. He was buried in the cemetery of the Lloyd family at Wye House, four miles distant from "The Rest." In appearance Buchanan was slightly below middle stature, but he was compactly built and had great physical strength, being in his prime the third strongest man in the navy, according to his brother McKean. He moved with grace and had an affable, courteous bearing; while his magnetism and great personal courage gave him a remarkable influence over men. He was married at Annapolis on Feb. 19, 1835, to Ann Catharine, daughter of Gov. Edward Lloyd of Wye House.

[See *Official Records* (*Navy*); the *Navy Register,* 1821–62; letter-books, ships' journals, etc., in U. S. Naval Acad. Lib.; other manuscript letters and papers access to which may be had through Franklin Buchanan Owen, Cleveland, Ohio, and Wm. W. Gordon, Savannah, Ga. Information is to be found also in Roberdeau Buchanan, *McKean Genealogy* (Lancaster, Pa., 1890); *Battles and Leaders of the Civil War,* vols. I, IV, and "Narrative of the Expedition of an American Squadron to the China Seas and Japan, 1852–1854, under the command of Commodore M. C. Perry, U. S. Navy," in *House Ex. Doc. No. 97,* 33 Cong., 2 Sess. An obituary appeared in the *New Eng. Hist. and Geneal. Reg.,* XXVIII, 364.]
C. L. L.

BUCHANAN, JAMES (Apr. 23, 1791–June 1, 1868), fifteenth president of the United States, was born near Mercersburg, Pa. His ancestors —Buchanans, Russels, Speers, and Pattersons— were all North-Ireland Scottish Presbyterians who emigrated to south-central Pennsylvania. His father, James Buchanan, who came to America in 1783, was a successful, hard-headed storekeeper, who wisely invested in farm lands. His mother, Elizabeth Speer, was a hard-working frontier wife, with a taste for good reading. James had a good classical preparation at a school in Mercersburg, and in the fall of 1807 entered the junior class of Dickinson College, of which his memories were not complimentary. In 1809 he graduated. There followed three years of diligent reading for the bar at Lancaster, and admission to the bar in 1812. His rise in his profession was so rapid that within three years his income was $11,297. This legal success was founded on Buchanan's knowledge of the law, and also upon his capacity for oratorical presentation, which had been developed in the society debates then so prominent a feature of college life, and which he had assiduously cultivated by the habit of speech-making when walking. His debating power soon made him an available figure for politics. Politics also appealed to him because of the close personal associations that it made possible. His nature was adapted to friendships, and those which he made were lasting and satisfying to him.

In 1814 he entered the Pennsylvania House of Representatives as a Federalist of the middle-states type. He had opposed the declaration of war with England but he believed it his duty to support the administration when once war began; and he enrolled as a volunteer in a company of dragoons. On July 4, 1815, he delivered an oration before a branch of the Federalist Washingtonian Society of Lancaster, in which the phraseology used by President Monroe in his famous message of 1823 was almost anticipated by the words: "We are separated from the nations of Europe by an immense ocean. We are still more disconnected with them by a different form of government, and by the enjoyment of true liberty. Why, then, should we injure ourselves by taking part in the ambitious contests of foreign despots and kings?" (*Works*, I, 9). In 1815 he was reëlected and exerted himself to protect the banks by delaying the return to specie payment. It was his intention to retire from politics at the close of this term, but there fell upon him a calamity, from which he never fully recovered. He was engaged to be married. Some mischief-makers spread tales, which caused the young lady to break the engagement. It seems to have been a trivial lovers' quarrel, which he fully expected to heal. Before this happened, however, the young lady died. This irremediable sorrow put away all thought of marriage, and he turned for consolation to the associations of politics. In 1820 he was elected to Congress, and his devotion to his political duties is indicated by his dwindling professional income. Buchanan, however, was never poor. His savings were judiciously invested, and his fortune grew to the comfortable sum of three hundred thousand dollars. He was elected as a Federalist, but his positions were those of a moderate, and he had friends on both sides of the house.

As the election of 1824 approached it was plain that the Federalist party was dead; what would become of its members was a problem which excited much discussion. Ultimately the majority, because of a general similarity of views, became Whigs. Buchanan was of the smaller number who went the other way. But it was not long before the relations which he formed with Gen. Jackson and his following were temporarily imperiled. In December 1824 Buchanan had an interview with Jackson in which he mentioned a conversation which he had had with a friend of Clay. In 1827 Jackson stated that Buchanan had come to him with a proposal from the friends of Clay for a political bargain. This put Buchanan

in a very awkward position, for the statement was important and untrue, while Jackson's sensitiveness to personal differences was well known. Buchanan both denied the statement, and maintained his relations with Jackson—no small achievement. During the Adams administration he was active in opposition to the administration and in particular disapproved the Panama mission. In the course of a debate on the latter subject he made his first public statement on slavery, to the effect that it was a moral and political evil, that it was irremediable, and that he recognized his duty to help the Southern whites in case of a servile insurrection. In 1828 he played a prominent part in the Jackson campaign. It may have been as a reward for his party services that his brother, George W. Buchanan, was appointed district attorney while he, himself, became chairman of the committee on judiciary, in which position he enhanced his reputation for solid legal attainment and sound judgment, although he failed to bring about the success of an impeachment brought against Judge Peck in 1831. On the positive side he saved the appellate jurisdiction of the United States Supreme Court based on writs of error.

Having served ten years in the House of Representatives, Buchanan once more determined to retire from politics and to resume his law practise. He was now, however, a well-known political figure in the dominant party. He was even mentioned for the vice-presidency, and he was finally offered the ministry to Russia. In June 1831 he accepted the latter, and by the next June he was in St. Petersburg. The mission was not important, but it gave his mind a slant toward international affairs, and he achieved some small successes and a considerable popularity. His successes were sufficient to cause him to be mentioned in 1833 as a successor to Edward Livingston in the secretaryship of state. On his return to the United States, he was elected to the Senate, from Pennsylvania, first for an unfinished term, and then in 1837 for a full one, and again in 1843. Here he took his stand as an administration man, a full-fledged Democrat, and came to be relied upon as one of the chief supporters of the measures of Jackson and Van Buren. In 1839 he was offered by Van Buren the position of attorney-general, but he preferred to remain in the Senate.

The slavery question had now begun to divide parties, and to test the quality of every man aiming at a national career. Buchanan stood the test well so far as consistency was concerned. He shared the Pennsylvania opinion against slavery in the abstract; he fully recognized the constitutional defenses of slavery and the duty of the national government to protect slavery where it existed: he expressed strongly his sympathy with the Southern whites, in their fear of the harmful effects of agitation upon the negroes and the peril which it might bring to Southern homes; he denounced the abolitionists as dangerous fanatics; but at the same time, as a constitutionalist, he defended the right of petition, and besought the Southerners not to create the impression "that the sacred right of petition and the cause of the abolitionists must rise or must fall together." He joined with the Southerners, however, in supporting a bill which made it unlawful for postmasters to distribute any material touching slavery, where the circulation of such material was forbidden by state laws.

Under the Tyler administration Buchanan continued to be one of the leaders and spokesmen of his party. As the election of 1844 approached he was mentioned for the presidency as "Pennsylvania's favorite candidate." He wrote friends on the Pennsylvania delegation in the Democratic convention at Baltimore that his support was pledged to Van Buren, but that should the latter's nomination become impossible, he would be willing to have his name used. The choice of the convention was neither Van Buren nor Buchanan but James K. Polk of Tennessee, whose nomination was considered by many an affront to better-known men such as Buchanan. The latter, however, bore himself with dignity, accepted the inevitable, and gave Polk his support, writing privately that Polk had "greatly improved, since he had been a member of congress." He exerted himself in the campaign particularly to prevent the anti-tariff views of the Southern Democrats from being so expressed as to alarm the protectionist Democrats of Pennsylvania, for he considered the outcome in the Keystone State very doubtful.

When, then, the Pennsylvania electors cast their votes for Polk, and recommended Buchanan as secretary of state, the President-elect could hardly ignore his claims. He offered him the position, but at the same time sought to exact from him a promise that if he should become a candidate for the presidency or vice-presidency, he would retire from the cabinet (Curtis, I, 548). Buchanan replied that he could not promise not to become a candidate in 1848, but that he would not agitate the question, and if he were presented as a candidate by a state or national convention, he would retire from the cabinet. Actually he served the full term of four years. During this term he greatly enhanced his reputation and provided himself for the first time with a definite program, though his chief policies and methods were those directed by the President. He was fortunate in many of his diplomatic agents, though whether this was his own work or that of Polk it is difficult to say. What he did contribute was laborious study of the history of cases, careful writing of dispatches, and a certain oratorical appeal to patriotism. These notes were read by the public; and made him a popular figure. His habitual tact, discretion, and moderation were generally recognized. The Texan situation was the chief interest of the new administration, and was one of unusual complexity. Congress had voted to annex Texas, but Texas had not yet accepted annexation. Great Britain and France were anxious to prevent acceptance. Mexico refused to recognize the independence of Texas, and hoped that the Oregon question might involve the United States and Great Britain in difficulties which would enable her to insist strongly on her position. The speedy settlement of the Oregon question was, therefore, earnestly desired by President Polk and his advisers. Buchanan's contribution was a powerful statement of the American claim to the whole of Oregon, with a refusal of arbitration, while he kept the road open to negotiation.

To Mexico Buchanan sent a note which Webster regarded as "mild and conciliatory," but which held firmly that the annexation of Texas must be considered as an accomplished fact. His confidence was not misplaced. In July 1845 a Texas convention accepted annexation. The administration now started two lines of action in dealing with Mexico. One was the occupation of Texan territory by United States troops; this occupation including certain regions claimed by both Mexico and Texas. The second was the sending of a minister to Mexico in the person of John Slidell of Louisiana, a close friend of Buchanan. He was instructed to refuse negotiation on the Texan boundary, since the United States supported the claims of Texas in their entirety. He was to insist on certain claims of United States citizens against Mexico which had been violently pressed by President Jackson in a message of 1837. These had been accepted by Mexico, but had remained unpaid. Slidell was to demand payment, but to accept as payment the territory between Texas and the Pacific, to the acquisition of which many in the United States had long looked forward, and which Polk had determined to secure during his presidency. The instructions were Buchanan's; and his was the skilful delay of negotiations until a revolutionary change in Mexico gave a new chance of settlement. The negotiation was the work of Slidell.

It resulted in an *impasse* which President Polk considered, when the dispatches reached Washington in April 1846, as justifying a war message to Congress. It so happened that this diplomatic crisis practically coincided with a military skirmish on the Texan border. The two incidents were combined in Polk's message to Congress which declared that war existed by act of Mexico. In the midst of these events Buchanan concluded a treaty with the British ambassador which put an end to the Oregon question by a sensible compromise of territorial claims. In the negotiation of the treaty of peace which ended the Mexican War, the President played a larger part than his secretary of state.

It was the Secretary of State, however, who shaped the policy of the administration in many other matters of international importance. It seems that it was by Buchanan's advice that President Polk in his first message made a vigorous restatement of the Monroe Doctrine, which was intended to discourage suspected British designs in California. He was largely responsible, too, for Polk's second statement on the Monroe Doctrine, in his annual message of 1848. He was keenly interested in all Central American affairs. On his advice President Polk recommended in a message of Apr. 29, 1848, that Congress take action to prevent the acquisition of Yucatan by Great Britain. Buchanan was so much disturbed at the foothold which Great Britain had already acquired in Nicaragua by a protectorate over the Mosquito Indians that in June 1848 he sent a chargé, Mr. Hise, to Guatemala, instructed to promote the reformation of the Central American Confederation, and to oppose the designs of the British. Peculiarly his own policy, however, was his attempt to secure the island of Cuba. The ultimate annexation of this island had long been in the minds of American statesmen, but it had been held that this was an affair of the future, and that in the meantime Spanish rule should be supported. Buchanan believed that the hour had now struck, and he made a proposal to Spain for its purchase for $120,000,000. The offer was refused, but Buchanan to the end of his career continued to insist upon this program.

On retiring from office in 1849, Buchanan gave up his house in Lancaster and bought a country estate near-by, called Wheatland. His domestic interest was centered in his orphan niece, Harriet Lane, of whose upbringing he took entire charge. Her charm brought about him the most exclusive society of the day. In his retirement a vigorous campaign was pressed to give him the presidential nomination of 1852, the three other leading candidates being Lewis Cass, William L. Marcy, and Stephen A. Douglas, but on the forty-ninth ballot a much less prominent man, Franklin Pierce of New Hampshire, was nominated. If Buchanan was disappointed, he successfully disguised his feelings and gave Pierce his cordial support. His speech at Greensburgh, Pa., in October, in which he traversed the career of the Whig candidate, Gen. Winfield Scott, was generally regarded as a campaign document of the first importance. That he would receive some important post in the new Democratic administration was a foregone conclusion. Disappointed he must have been, however, when the post offered was the ministry to Great Britain, instead of the state department which was given his rival and intimate, William L. Marcy. Buchanan accepted with the understanding that he should be allowed to conduct a general negotiation in London, whereby he hoped to combine a reciprocity treaty, an agreement on the fisheries, and a check to British influence in Central America, which he considered to have been too liberally recognized by the Whigs in the Clayton-Bulwer Treaty of 1850. Marcy, however, kept the first two matters in his own hands at Washington, and without these for trafficking Buchanan was unable to accomplish anything on the third during his two years in London.

His mission, however, was very agreeable. It began with a curious episode. Secretary Marcy had issued a circular to the effect that our ministers abroad should appear only in the "simple dress of an American citizen" in place of the uniform previously prescribed, unless such rule would seriously interfere with the conduct of their business. Buchanan, rather amused, determined to adhere to the rule, perhaps in order to prevent his friend Marcy from reaping Democratic laurels at home, and for a time it seemed that he might be excluded from court functions. In the end he was accepted as he chose to appear in "frock-dress" with the addition of a plain dress sword, and seems to have gained by the episode. At least he was popular in society, and when Miss Lane visited him, the mission became one of the most generally popular the United States has had in England. The most interesting episode of his stay occurred when Secretary Marcy requested Pierre Soulé, minister at Madrid, to consult with the United States ministers at Paris and London, John Y. Mason and Buchanan, on the Cuban question. The three met first at Ostend and then at Aix-la-Chapelle in October 1854, and drew up a document which became known as the "Ostend Manifesto" (*House Ex. Doc. No. 93*, 33 Cong., 2 Sess.). It included an historical discussion of the Cuban problem, and set forth the danger of European interference, particularly with reference to the possible emancipation of slaves. It recommended that an offer be made to Spain for the purchase of the island. What made it remarkable was its discussion of what should take place if Spain refused. "We should . . . be recreant to our duty . . . should we permit Cuba to be Africanized and become a second St. Domingo, with all its attendant horrors to the white race, and suffer the flames to extend to our neighboring shores, seriously to endanger or actually to consume the fair fabric of our Union. We fear that the course and current of events are rapidly tending towards such a catastrophe." "Self preservation is the first law of nature, with States as with individuals. . . . We must, in any event, preserve our own conscious rectitude and our own self-respect." Should Cuba become necessary to our safety, then "by every law, human and divine, we shall be justified in wresting it from Spain if we possess the power."

Buchanan was, therefore, more than ever a presidential possibility when he returned in April 1856, having made these appeals to Southern and to Democratic feeling. By his absence, moreover, he had escaped the domestic conflicts over the Kansas-Nebraska bill. He was again presented for the presidency by the Pennsylvania Democracy, with the strong support of his close friends, Schell of the "Hard" New York Democracy and Slidell of Louisiana, and with that of his old party associates in Virginia. Most of his support, however, came from the North. He led from the first ballot, and on the seventeenth was unanimously nominated, John C. Breckinridge of Kentucky being chosen as candidate for vice-president. The platform contained a statement of the finality of the compromise of 1850, and an indorsement of the principle of non-interference by Congress with slavery in the territories. Buchanan did little speaking during the campaign, and when he did speak he was most emphatic in his denunciation of the abolitionists. He failed of a popular majority vote, receiving 1,800,000 to 1,300,000 for Frémont, the Republican candidate, and about 900,000 for Fillmore, on the American and Whig tickets. Of the electoral votes he received 174 to 114 for Frémont, and 8 for Fillmore. He carried Pennsylvania, New Jersey, Indiana, Illinois, California, and all the slaveholding states except Maryland.

Buchanan's inaugural address was emphatic in its statement of his conversion to the principle of strict construction. Nevertheless, he recommended, for military purposes, the construction of a national railroad to the Pacific. He stood for economy, for the payment of the public debt, but for a small increase in the navy. Most important was his statement that the question of slavery in the territories was one for judicial decision, and he referred to the Dred Scott Case, then pending, of the progress of which he had somewhat irregularly informed himself (*Works*, X, 106–08), as destined to give a solution to which all good citizens would cheerfully submit. His individual opinion he stated to be that popular sovereignty, or local control, began with the formation of a state constitution. He reiterated his well-known belief that a president should not be reëlected. On taking office he made an appeal to democratic sentiment by enunciating the principle of rotation in office, which meant that although succeeding a Democratic president, he would re-man the civil service. The selection of his cabinet was directed by another principle, which he maintained with reference to all important appointments; that of giving, as far as possible, equal representation to slave and non-slaveholding states—"the sacred balance." Lewis Cass became secretary of state, and the other most important appointments were those of Howell Cobb, the Georgia Unionist, as secretary of the treasury, of John B. Floyd of Virginia as secretary of war, and of the Pennsylvania lawyer, his personal friend, Jeremiah S. Black, as attorney-general. With Miss Lane as mistress of the White House, the administration was one of the most successful, socially, in our history. Its height was marked by the visit in 1860, of the Prince of Wales. The tone of Washington society at the time was set by a group of brilliant women from the South, such as Mrs. Roger Pryor of Virginia, Mrs. Chesnut of South Carolina, and Mrs. Clay of Alabama. The Gwins, formerly of Mississippi and now of California, entertained lavishly. One of the closest intimates at the White House was Senator Jefferson Davis of Mississippi.

It was Buchanan's intention that his administration should be chiefly characterized by a vigorous foreign policy. In this he had some success, which seems to have been due for the most part to his own careful and minute attention. He was instrumental in the conclusion of arrangements between Great Britain and Nicaragua and Honduras, which, in his opinion, neutralized some of the dangerous features of the Clayton-Bulwer Treaty, and he checked the activity of the British fleet in searching vessels suspected of being engaged in the slave trade in American waters. He secured reparation from Paraguay for the firing on the *Water Witch*, a United States naval vessel, surveying La Plata. He made an advantageous treaty with China, and cemented our relations in the Far East by his reception of embassies from Japan and Siam. His main purpose, however, the annexation of Cuba, was blocked by the impossibility of securing from Congress the appropriation necessary to initiate negotiation. The same was true of his policy with regard to Mexico. Whether he looked to acquisition of Mexican territory is uncertain. It is certain, however, that his avowed purpose was to prevent European intervention by aiding the Liberal party of Juarez to establish order. In 1859 he had negotiated a treaty of "Transit and Commerce" and a convention "to maintain order and security in the territory of the Republic of Mexico and the United States," the main point of which was the payment of $2,000,000 by the United States to Mexico, with which it was hoped that Juarez would be enabled to establish himself. These were not ratified. The most dramatic diplomatic episode was the checking of a filibustering expedition to Nicaragua of the well-known William Walker, by Commodore Paulding under direction of Isaac Toucey, the secretary of the navy. This vigor in dealing with such irregular activities of Americans was new. It was supported by conservative Southern opinion, but it did little to convince the North that Buchanan was not striving to expand the United States to the south for the benefit of the slave states (William O. Scroggs, *Filibusters and Financiers*, 1916, pp. 333–67).

On the subjects of finance and the tariff Buchanan did not assume leadership, presenting them as subjects which belonged to Congress. This left the executive direction to Howell Cobb, the secretary of the treasury, at whose suggestion a tariff bill was passed in 1857. However this act may be judged from an economic point of view, it was one of the worst political blunders ever committed in the United States, uniting as it did the influence of the South and New England, an alliance of no political potentiality, and alienating from the Democrats the protectionist interests of the President's own Pennsylvania and of the Northwest, and thus giving the Republicans an opportunity of which they took immediate advantage. In the financial crisis of 1857, the President was stopped by his accepted principles from taking any policy except that of protecting the government. The credit even of the government did not recover during his administration. The attempt of the opposition to convict the President of maladministration by means of the "Covode Investigation" failed to re-

veal any condition of unusual laxity in the administration.

The main subject of discussion, however, was the territories. In Utah the President firmly but peacefully established the authority of the United States government by a military expedition. So far as the status of slavery in Kansas and Nebraska was concerned, Buchanan accepted the Dred Scott decision as final. In administration he showed apparent wisdom and strength. To the territory of Kansas, where something very like civil war prevailed between the Free-State party and the Slave-State party, he sent Robert J. Walker, one of the ablest men at his disposal, whose conduct now receives the general approval of historians. It was not, however, a situation calling for wise administration only, but for Congressional action. When the Lecompton convention in January 1858 presented its request for statehood under the pro-slavery constitution which it had drawn up, the President at once presented it to Congress with his recommendation. He argued that it was republican in form, that opportunity had been given for a popular vote on the all-important question of slavery, that acceptance would banish the question of slavery from Congress, and that once admitted as a state the people of Kansas could decide as they saw fit. This stand at once brought about a break between the two factions of the Democratic party. It identified the administration with the Southern wing, and caused the revolt of the supporters of Stephen A. Douglas. Both factions still claimed to be in good party standing, but from now on the full powers of the administration, including that of the patronage, were thrown against Douglas. In the campaign of 1860, the sole public part taken by Buchanan was a speech delivered at the White House, on July 9, 1860, beginning "I have ever been the friend of regular nominations. I have never struck a political ticket in my life," and giving a vigorous support to John C. Breckinridge as Democrat candidate.

The election of Lincoln in November 1860 brought Buchanan to the most critical portion of his career. In October Gen. Scott had advised the President that the result of the election might well be an attempted dissolution of the Union, and that certain preparatory steps be taken, such as the adequate garrisoning of the Southern ports. This advice Buchanan refused to consider. By the end of November it was obvious that secession, at least in South Carolina, would soon follow. The President prepared his message with care, taking legal advice from his attorney-general. Black. It contained a strong denial of the right of secession, but a confession of helplessness in dealing with actual secession, since the federal officers in South Carolina through whom the national executive could enforce the law had resigned. Aside from the collection of the customs and the defense of the property of the United States in South Carolina, the Executive had no authority to act. Congress alone had the power to decide whether the present laws could or could not be amended so as to carry out the objects of the Constitution. The President violently attacked the abolitionists and recommended the repeal of the personal-liberty laws by the Northern states. He also urged an "explanatory amendment" of the Constitution giving express recognition of the right of property in slaves in the states where it existed or might exist, declaring it the duty of the national government to protect this right in the territories, and giving a like recognition of the right to recover fugitive slaves.

In the meantime he exerted his personal influence to keep the peace. He sent Caleb Cushing to Gov. Pickens of South Carolina "to state to you the reasons which exist to prevent, or to delay, the action of the state" (Curtis, *Buchanan,* p. 368). On Dec. 8 he met the South Carolina members of Congress, the result of the conference being an understanding on their part that no violence should be used by the government or people of South Carolina until "an offer has been made through an accredited representative to negotiate for an amiable arrangement of all matters between the State and the Federal Government." Buchanan subsequently declared that he had refused to pledge himself, but on Dec. 15 again refused the advice of Gen. Scott that the forts in Charleston harbor be reinforced. On Dec. 20, 1860 the South Carolina convention voted secession. On Dec. 22 three commissioners were appointed to go to Washington. On Dec. 25 Maj. Anderson, in charge of the United States forces at Charleston, removed his troops from the indefensible Fort Moultrie to the defensible Fort Sumter. This was immediately taken by the South Carolina commissioners to be a change in the *status quo* to the maintenance of which they considered the President committed.

In the meantime Buchanan's administration had begun to fall to pieces. On Dec. 12, 1860, Secretary Cass resigned on the ground that the Charleston forts should be reinforced. Already on Dec. 2, Secretary Cobb had resigned because of the President's denial of the right of secession. Black was immediately appointed secretary of state, his place as attorney-general being taken on Dec. 19 by another Pennsylvania Democrat, Edwin M. Stanton. This changed the balance among the President's advisers during the critical days of Dec. 26 to 31, days in which by the evidence of such observers as Stanton the President lived through an agony of indecision. On Dec. 31 Buchanan replied to the South Carolina commissioners in a letter conciliatory in character, but sustaining the action of Maj. Anderson. Meantime on Dec. 29 the Secretary of War, John B. Floyd of Virginia, resigned, it was said, as a result of financial irregularities. On Jan. 8, 1861, Jacob Thompson of Mississippi, Secretary of the Interior, and on Jan. 11, Philip F. Thomas of Maryland, who had succeeded Howell Cobb as secretary of the treasury, resigned. These resignations were followed by appointments of John A. Dix of New York, as secretary of the treasury, of Joseph Holt of Kentucky, as secretary of war, and Horatio King of Maine, as postmaster-general.

The policy of the administration now changed. The *Star of the West* was sent to Charleston with reinforcements for Fort Sumter. On Jan. 9 it was fired upon by the South Carolina batteries. This resulted in an interchange of notes between Maj. Anderson, who threatened to use his guns on all vessels in and out of Charleston, and Gov. Pickens, who demanded the surrender of Fort Sumter. The matter was referred to Washington. The administration stated its intention to hold Fort Sumter and reinforce it if necessary, but also its intention to keep the peace until "the question shall have been settled by competent authority." In the case of Fort Pickens at Pensacola an agreement was authorized that it should not be reinforced, if not attacked. Meantime the President sponsored bills for a popular referendum on certain proposed amendments to the Constitution, to give the President power to call the militia under certain circumstances, and to provide for the collection of duties at Charleston. None of these bills were passed. Further executive acts were confined to the bringing to Washington of a small force to insure the tranquillity of Lincoln's inauguration. Buchanan took his part in the inauguration, and on Mar. 9 left for Wheatland (J. F. Rhodes, *History of the United States,* chs. XIII and XIV).

Buchanan continued to reside at Wheatland until his death. On Mar. 18, 1861, he wrote John A. Dix, "There is a general desire for peace," but on Apr. 19, 1861, he wrote, "The present administration had no alternative but accept the war instigated by South Carolina or the Southern Confederacy. The North will sustain the administration almost to a man; and it

Buchanan

ought to be sustained at all hazards." He supported the administration throughout the war as a Union Democrat. Much of his time he devoted to the preparation of a careful defense of his administration.

Buchanan's career has been viewed almost entirely from the point of view of the last months of his administration. The estimates of his conduct at this time have been colored by the fact that it was pleasing to neither the North nor the South. This came from his sharing in part the views of both, but neither completely. He hated the Abolitionists whom he regarded as the chief cause of dissension; he liked the Southerners personally; he became a strict constructionist; and he favored a laissez-faire policy for the national government. His chief public policy was expansion, which, under the circumstances, meant expansion southward. His administration was undoubtedly strongly influenced by Southern interests. He trusted men who, to some degree at least, were working for the South, and he left the government less prepared for a vigorous enforcement of the laws than he could have done had he exercised a stricter administrative control. The Southern leaders, however, failed to perceive that his devotion to the preservation of the Union was the strongest of his convictions, and were bitterly disappointed when they found that, his effort to content the South having failed, he reverted to the other side. The Northern criticism, that by vigor he might have prevented secession and the formation of the Southern Confederacy, is quite unjustified. The United States did not possess the military force to accomplish such a result. Unlike Lincoln, he failed to find the legal authority to meet secession, but action by Buchanan would probably only have begun the war earlier. There is nothing in his conduct, at the time, however, which indicates political wisdom. He was primarily a constitutional lawyer, confident that the mechanics of law, as established in the United States by the divine voice of the people, was sufficient to solve all problems, and his most distinct emotion was irritation with those who failed to consider legal solutions all-sufficient. He was fitted neither by nature nor by self-training to "ride the whirlwind and command the storm," to which test he was put by an unkind fate.

[Numerous Buchanan MSS. are in the Lib. of Cong., and letters from him are frequent in the papers of many of the men of his time. *The Works of Jas. Buchanan* (1908–11), ed. by J. B. Moore in twelve volumes, contains many public papers and speeches, as well as private correspondence. G. T. Curtis, *Life of Jas. Buchanan* (1883) is a substantial biography, containing many papers by and to Buchanan; it is distinct-

Buchanan

ly a defense. J. F. Rhodes, *Hist. of the U. S.* (1900) vols. II and III, is the most complete historical account yet written of Buchanan's administration. Buchanan's own book, *Mr. Buchanan's Administration on the Eve of the Rebellion* (1866), is an unusually careful document. Extracts from the diary of William L. Marcy, *Am. Hist. Rev.*, XXIV, 641–53, are of some importance. R. G. Horton, *Life and Public Services of Jas. Buchanan* (1856) and C. Jerome, *Life of Jas. Buchanan* (1856) are campaign biographies. Horatio King, *Turning on the Light* (1895) contains letters.]   C. R. F.

BUCHANAN, JOHN (1772–Nov. 6, 1844), Maryland jurist, was born in Prince Georges County, the son of Thomas Buchanan, an English emigrant who settled in Maryland about 1760 and married Mary Cook, a daughter of William and Eliza (Tilghman) Cook. Death having claimed both parents while he was yet a child, he was sent to Charlotte Hall Academy in St. Marys County, and later to the office of Judge Robert White of Winchester, Va., to study law. He remained there but a short time when he found an opportunity to complete his studies with John Thompson Mason of Hagerstown, Md. He served in the lower house of the state legislature, 1797–99, and in 1806 received the appointment as chief judge of the fifth judicial district, by virtue of which he became an associate justice of the Maryland court of appeals. On Oct. 4, 1808 he was married to Sophia, daughter of Judge Eli Williams. Upon the resignation of Judge J. T. Chase he became chief justice of the appellate court, July 27, 1824. He served in that capacity in every session of the court until his death, except for a brief period in 1837 when he was sent to England as one of the commissioners on the part of Maryland to negotiate the sale in London of $8,000,000 of state-secured railroad and canal stocks. The commissioners failed in England (message of Gov. T. W. Veazey, *Maryland Senate Journal*, December Session, 1837), but they did succeed in getting the Chesapeake & Ohio Canal Company and the Baltimore & Ohio Railroad Company to agree, conditionally, to take $6,000,000 of the state stock before they set out for Europe—an arrangement that resulted in heavy losses to both companies (*Maryland Senate Journal*, "Document O," December Session, 1837).

Buchanan has been called one of Maryland's greatest jurists. His diction was polished and unlabored; he was not given to copious citations of authorities; he sought his decisions in an analysis of the social and economic factors which produced the cause rather than in a compilation of obsolete legal precedents. Among his important decisions were those in the cases of *Chesapeake & Ohio Canal Company* vs. *Baltimore & Ohio Railroad Company* (4 *Gill and Johnson*), argued by Daniel Webster and Reverdy Johnson, determining the railroad's privileges conferred by its charter (*Acts of 1826*, ch. 123); and *Calvert* vs. *Davis* (5 *Gill and Johnson*), a leading case in Maryland on testamentary capacity.

[See Wm. McSherry, "The Former Chief Justices of the Court of Appeals of Md." in *Md. State Bar Ass. Report*, 1904; T. J. C. Williams, *Hist. of Washington County, Md.*, vol. I (1906); A. W. P. Buchanan, *The Buchanan Book* (1911); *Laws of the General Assembly State of Md.*, 1836–38; *Baltimore Clipper*, Nov. 8, 1844; *Green Bag*, VI, 229; *Torchlight and Public Advertiser* (Hagerstown, Md.) Nov. 7, 1844. Buchanan's decisions are found in 7 *Harris and Johnson*; 1–2 *Harris and Gill*; 1–12 *Gill and Johnson*; 1–3 *Gill*.]

T. D. M.

BUCHANAN, JOSEPH (Aug. 24, 1785–Sept. 29, 1829), philosopher, educator, inventor, was born in Washington County, Va., the son of Andrew and Joanna Buchanan. His boyhood, spent in Tennessee, was marked by unusual hardships, poverty, and illness. Despite the scantiest opportunities for education, in 1804 he entered Transylvania University. Proficiency in mathematics and critical skepticism of mere authority compensated for his rusticity and diffidence. His empiricism early led him to experiment with devices for improving mills and for producing a color symphony from glasses of different chemical composition—"the music of light," as he called it. Putting aside these experiments without perfecting them, he began the study of medicine, and in 1807, while at Port Gibson, Miss., wrote a volume on fever. He took this with him to Philadelphia, but although Dr. Benjamin Rush is said to have spoken highly of the manuscript, Buchanan was too poor to publish it, or to remain for the medical lectures in Philadelphia. Hence, in 1808, he returned by foot to Lexington, Ky., determined to devote himself to the medical department of Transylvania University, which had only a nominal existence. He was appointed by the trustees as professor of the institutes of medicine, and, in his twenty-fourth year, began the preparation of a course of introductory lectures for medical students. These lectures were published as the *Philosophy of Human Nature* (Richmond, Ky., 1812). For his emphasis on matter rather than on mind and his attempt to construct a materialistic monism he has been called "the earliest native physiological psychologist" (Woodbridge Riley, *American Philosophy: The Early Schools*, 1907, p. 395). He appears later to have modified his views by postulating the spiritualization of matter, although he did not abandon his fundamental monism.

A true pioneer, Buchanan left to others the development of the medical school and went to Philadelphia to study the Pestalozzian system of education, in order to introduce it into Kentucky. While teaching and popularizing this method he prepared *A Practical Grammar of the English Language* (Lexington, 1826). Educational work could no more hold his undivided attention than medicine or philosophy, however, and after studying law, he delivered a course of lectures to a private law class, and entered the field of journalism. After association with the Lexington *Reporter*, the Frankfort *Palladium*, and the *Western Spy and Literary Gazette*, he edited at Louisville, from 1826 till his death, the *Focus*. Although this journal was rather a literary and scientific than a controversial organ, it opposed Jackson and supported Clay (William Henry Perrin, *The Pioneer Press of Kentucky*, 1888, p. 72). Buchanan's early interest in invention continued, and in 1821–22 he constructed a spiral boiler which, because of its superior lightness and efficiency, he hoped might be applied to aerial navigation. In 1824–25 he applied his engine, which seems to have been a prototype of the exploding tubular boiler, to a wagon, with sufficient success, apparently, to astonish "a throng of spectators" in Louisville.

He was married to Nancy Rodes Garth and inculcated in their son, Joseph Rodes Buchanan [*q.v.*], many of his own interests. An admirer remembers the father for his "slender form, massive head, and thoughtful, intellectual face" (Dr. Robert Peter, *The History of the Medical Department of Transylvania University*, 1905, p. 14). His manners were simple and amiable, and his spirit, though ardent and enthusiastic, was critical. Doubtless his great and varied mental powers were dissipated by desultory labors, and by his inability to concentrate on a single task. Essentially an intellectual pioneer working in an environment which encouraged versatility rather than specialization and profundity, he contributed substantially to the development of culture in the Ohio River Valley.

[In addition to references given above, see sketch of Buchanan by his son in Lewis Collins, *Hist. Sketches of Ky.* (1847), pp. 559–60, and compare Lewis and R. H. Collins, *Hist. of Ky.* (1874), II, 218.] M. E. C.

BUCHANAN, JOSEPH RAY (Dec. 6, 1851–Sept. 13, 1924), labor agitator, was born in Hannibal, Mo., the son of Robert Sylvester and Mary Ellen (Holt) Buchanan. After leaving the public schools he was for a time variously employed. About 1876 he obtained work on a Hannibal newspaper, where he learned typesetting. Two years later he went to Denver, where he set type on a daily newspaper, later becoming its managing editor. With a partner he started a printing office, but he soon gave it up and went to prospecting, from which he turned again to typesetting, this time on a newspaper in Leadville, Colo. On Dec. 16, 1879, he was married to Lucy A. Clise. The entrance of the first railway into Leadville, in the summer of 1880 brought to the town hundreds of men in search of work, glutting the labor market. The mine-owners thereupon ordered a reduction of wages, and a strike followed. The contest was carried on with great bitterness, and the leaders of the striking miners were fiercely assailed. Buchanan had made his first acquaintance with the labor movement in Denver, where he had joined the Typographical Union. He had become an ardent trade-unionist and soon became prominent in the strike. A vigilance committee ordered him to leave town; he resisted the order for a time, but on his friends' advice obeyed, and in the spring of 1881 returned to Denver, where he resumed work as a typesetter. In 1882 he was the Denver representative at the convention of the International Typographical Union, and in December, with Samuel H. Laverty as partner, he started a weekly newspaper, the *Labor Enquirer*. In the brief but successful strike of the Union Pacific shopmen against a wage reduction in May 1884, he acted as adviser, as also, about the same time, in the strike of the Colorado coal miners. He was further active in the strike of the shopmen on the Gould lines and later on the Denver & Rio Grande Railroad in the spring of 1885. In the growing conflict between the Knights of Labor and the American Federation of Labor he essayed the futile rôle of peacemaker. He had joined the former organization in 1882 and two years later had been elected to its general board. In 1886 he was a delegate to its convention in Richmond, where, against his protests, action was taken which brought on an open warfare between the two bodies and caused the ruin of the Knights of Labor. His newspaper had been a financial failure from the start and had been maintained only by great personal sacrifice. In 1887 he turned it over to others and moved to Chicago. Here he was active in the unsuccessful effort to obtain a commutation of the sentences of the men convicted of the Haymarket bomb-throwing. In 1888 he moved to New York, subsequently making his home in Montclair, N. J. For many years he was the labor editor of the plate service furnished by the American Press Association. Twice an unsuccessful candidate for Congress in the Montclair district, he each time made an active campaign. From 1904 to 1915 he was the labor editor of the *New York Evening Journal*, and from February 1918 to July 1921 a member of the conciliation council of the Department of Labor. His last years were inactive. He died at his home in Montclair.

In labor politics Buchanan was an opportunist. His policy of "seeking the line of least resistance" carried him into and out of many radical and reform organizations. A Socialist in principle, he belonged for a time to the Socialist Labor party, but he did not join the newer organization, the Socialist party. He was one of the organizers of the People's (Populist) party, which held its first convention in Omaha in 1892, and he served on its national committee in 1892, 1896, and 1900. He was also a member of Hearst's Independence League, and in his Denver years had been a member of the International Workmen's Association. To the end he was a devoted trade-unionist. He was an eloquent and forceful speaker. Tall, somewhat slender, with a shock of unruly hair that even in his middle years had become white, and bearing himself with a native grace of manner, he was an impressive figure on the platform. His personality was attractive, his character was honest, and in the fierce conflicts that from time to time divided the labor and radical movements he retained the esteem even of those who strongly opposed him.

[*Who's Who in America*, 1924–25; *The Story of a Labor Agitator* (an autobiography, 1903); recollections of the writer, based on an acquaintance of thirty-nine years.]   W. J. G.

BUCHANAN, JOSEPH RODES (Dec. 11, 1814–Dec. 26, 1899), erratic physician and writer, was born in Frankfort, Ky., of a Virginia family which had early moved to Kentucky. He was the son of Joseph Buchanan [*q.v.*] and Nancy Rodes (Garth) Buchanan. From his father, an intellectual jack-of-all-trades, philosopher, educator, physician, and journalist, he seems to have inherited an unstable disposition and a brilliant mind which the eager parent over-stimulated in childhood. An infant prodigy, the boy was versed in geometry and astronomy at the age of six, then took up sociology, and at the age of twelve began to study law. After the death of his father in 1829, he supported himself for a time first as a printer, then as a school-teacher. Becoming interested in phrenology and cerebral physiology, he entered the Medical School of the University of Louisville where he graduated in 1842. While still in college he laid the foundations for two new so-called sciences which he later elaborated, "psychometry" and "sarcognomy," the former demonstrating the excitability of cerebral tissue by the aura of another person, the latter dealing with the sympathetic relations between other parts of the body and the indwelling soul. The trained psychometer, he held, could diagnose any disease at sight of the patient or even by letter, while the sarcognomist could heal all diseases by making dispersive passes over the body, particularly if the patient sat with his feet in a tub of water. Buchanan lectured upon his alleged discoveries with great success throughout both the North and the South, and established a periodical, *The Journal of Man,* in which for many years he promulgated his extraordinary views. On Mar. 25, 1846, he joined the faculty of the Eclectic Medical Institute of Cincinnati, and during the next decade his truculent disposition made him a prominent figure in the turbulent history of that institution. Forced out in 1856, he at first started a rival institution, the Eclectic College of Medicine, but, soon disagreeing with his colleagues, he removed to Louisville, and in 1863 unsuccessfully ran for Congress as the Peace party candidate. Later he removed to Syracuse, N. Y., and manufactured salt. In 1867 he became professor of physiology in the Eclectic Medical College of New York City, where he remained until 1881 when he established his own college of therapeutics in Boston. On account of his health he removed in 1892 to Kansas City, Mo., and in 1893 to San José, Cal., where he resided until his death. He was married three times: in 1841 to Anne Rowan of Louisville; in 1881 to Mrs. Cornelia H. Decker, a clairvoyant of New York City; in 1894 to Elizabeth S. Worthington of Denver. His highly original medical theories, which may have influenced the later career of the notorious Albert Abrams [*q.v.*] were set forth in a series of volumes of which the most important were *Therapeutic Sarcognomy* (1884) and *Manual of Psychometry* (1885). His last production was a two-volume semi-spiritualistic work entitled *Primitive Christianity* (1897–98), including lives of the Apostles which he said had been dictated to him by the Apostles themselves. He was a man who loved humanity in general, who hated his neighbors, and who throughout his long life remained peculiarly gifted with self-confidence, expressed in his erect carriage, lifted head, and smile of infinite condescension.

[Harvey Wickes Felter, *Hist. of the Eclectic Medic. Institute* (1902), containing sketch and numerous references; less full accounts in *Allibone's Dict. of Authors, Supp.* (1891) and in Kelly and Burrage, *Am. Medic. Biogs.* (1920).]

                             E. S. B.

BUCHANAN, ROBERT CHRISTIE (Mar. 1, 1811–Nov. 29, 1878), Union soldier, was born in Baltimore, Md. His paternal ancestry dated back to Dr. George Buchanan, an immigrant from Scotland to Maryland as early as the year 1698, whose son, Andrew Buchanan, was a brigadier-general of the Maryland militia during the American Revolution. The father of Robert Christie Buchanan was Andrew Buchanan of Baltimore; his mother was Carolina Virginia Marylanda Johnson, daughter of Joshua Johnson, Esq., and sister of Mrs. John Quincy Adams (Roberdeau Buchanan, *Genealogy of the McKean Family of Pennsylvania,* 1890). When but fifteen years of age, young Buchanan received appointment to the United States Military Academy from the District of Columbia,—his legal guardian at the time being Mr. Nathaniel Frye, Jr. He graduated Number 31 in a class of forty-two members, and on July 1, 1830, received his commission as second lieutenant, 4th Infantry. Upon graduation, he participated in the Black Hawk War of 1832, and commanded the gunboats in the engagement of Bad Axe River. He served as adjutant of his regiment from 1835 to 1838,—having been promoted first lieutenant, Mar. 16, 1836, and captain, Nov. 1, 1838. In 1837–38 he took part in the arduous campaign against the Seminole Indians.

Buchanan entered the war with Mexico as a captain in the 4th Infantry, Ulysses S. Grant being a lieutenant in the same organization. He went through the campaigns of both Generals Taylor and Scott, and was brevetted major, May 9, 1846, for gallant and distinguished services at Palo Alto and at Resaca de la Palma; and lieutenant-colonel Sept. 8, 1847, for gallant and meritorious services at the taking of Molino del Rey, where it is said Buchanan forced the doors of the stronghold with his own hands (J. C. Ropes, *The Army under Pope,* 1881, p. 140). Shortly after the war with Mexico he married Miss Winder, a grand-daughter of Gov. Lloyd of Maryland. He received his majority in the regular army, Feb. 3, 1855, his lieutenant-colonelcy Sept. 9, 1861, and during the decade preceding the Civil War, was associated in the old 4th Infantry, with such distinguished officers as Grant, Sheridan, Judah, Crook, Alvord, and D. A. Russell.

At the outbreak of the Civil War, Buchanan's regiment formed part of the defense of Washington; and from November 1861 to March 1862 during McClellan's Peninsular Campaign he commanded with distinction a brigade in Gen. Sykes's famous "Regular Division." On June 27, 1862, he was brevetted colonel for services at Gaines's Mill, and was brevetted brigadier-general, Mar. 13, 1865, for similar distinguished service at Malvern Hill, where his brigade drove a portion of the enemy from the field and captured a flag. In the much discussed withdrawal of McClellan's army to Harrison's Landing, following the battles before Richmond, Buchanan had the difficult responsibility of covering much of the movement with his brigade. And of the Second Battle of Bull Run, which followed, Gen. John Pope has said: "Porter's Corps . . . was pushed to the support of our left, where it rendered distinguished service, especially the brigade of regulars under Colonel (then Lieutenant-Colonel) Buchanan" (*Battles and Leaders of the Civil War*, II, 487, and *The Army under Pope*, p. 142). Buchanan was made a brigadier-general of volunteers, Nov. 29, 1862, and commanded his brigade in the bloody battle of Antietam, and in front of the famous "stone wall" at Fredericksburg, where his command suffered serious casualties. His commission as brigadier-general having expired, Mar. 4, 1863, he was placed in command of the defenses of Fort Delaware, and attained his colonelcy in the regular army, Feb. 8, 1864. On Mar. 13, 1865, as the war was about to end, he received the brevet of major-general for his distinguished services in the battles of Second Bull Run (Manassas) and Fredericksburg.

Late in the year 1865, Buchanan was a member of an important military commission, investigating complaints by the government of Prussia regarding enlistments, and in the year 1867 was a member of the Iowa Claims Commission. In 1868, after serving for a short period as an assistant commissioner in the Freedman's Bureau, he was placed in command of the important Department of Louisiana, where the work of reconstruction and the problems attendant upon the readmission of Louisiana to the Union were beset with many difficulties. On Apr. 16 and 17, 1868, the state voted for state officers, as well as for a constitution which would permit of entrance into the Union; and while the election passed off quietly, many controversies subsequently followed and much ill-feeling resulted. Acting under instructions from Gen. Grant, Buchanan installed into office the newly elected Gov. H. C. Warmoth, and Lieut.-Gov. Oscar J. Dunn (a negro), and later, upon the ratification by Louisiana of the Fourteenth Amendment, Buchanan declared military law no longer existent in the state (J. R. Ficklen, *History of Reconstruction in Louisiana*, 1910, pp. 199–204, and *Appleton's Annual Cyclopedia*, vol. VIII, 1878, p. 431). Buchanan commanded Fort Porter, New York, during 1869–70, was retired from active service, Dec. 31, 1870, and died in Washington, D. C., Nov. 29, 1878. He was affectionately known to Civil War soldiers as "Old Buck," and his brigade of regular soldiers proved always a dependable reserve in many of the earlier battles of

the war. That such was the case was largely due to his wide experience, fine attainments, and high sense of duty and of discipline.

[In addition to references given above, see F. B. Heitman, *Hist. Reg.* (1914); Justin H. Smith, *The War with Mexico* (1919); C. M. Wilcox, *Hist. of the Mexican War* (1892); *Battles and Leaders of the Civil War* (1887–88), vols. II, III.]

C.D.R.

BUCHANAN, THOMAS (Dec. 24, 1744–Nov. 10, 1815), merchant, descended from a line of prosperous Scotch merchants, was born at Glasgow, the son of George and Jean (Lowden) Buchanan. His father was a man of liberal education and young Thomas studied at the University of Glasgow in addition to acquiring experience in his father's counting-house. In 1763 he went to New York where he soon entered into partnership with his father's cousin Walter, who was already established in business there. This firm of W. & T. Buchanan owned several ships and their extensive trade with the British ports gave them a place among the foremost New York commercial houses. Thomas Buchanan married Almy, the daughter of Jacob Townsend of Oyster Bay, on Mar. 17, 1766. He signed the original non-importation agreement in 1766 and was elected a member of the Chamber of Commerce at its second meeting in 1768. Two years later, he was active in the attempt to restore normal trade (*Post Boy*, July 23, 1770). There seems to be no authority for the frequently repeated statement that Buchanan, who had dissolved the partnership with his cousin in 1772, was the consignee of the New York tea ship *Nancy* in 1773 (Francis S. Drake, *Tea Leaves*, 1884, p. 305). In 1775, he was a member of the local Committee of One Hundred (Carl L. Becker, *The History of Political Parties in the Province of New York, 1760–1776*, 1909, p. 198), but a year later he signed the Loyalist address to Howe. During the war, he continued active business, maintaining a fairly neutral stand, for his own Loyalist position was counterbalanced by the activity of his wife's family on the other side. He served as vice-president of the Chamber of Commerce from 1780 to 1783 when he was elected president. He prudently declined to serve, for the Chamber was soon reorganized with "patriot" officers who had been absent from the city during the British occupation. His property escaped confiscation and his Tory stand did not prevent him from carrying on an extensive foreign trade, principally with Scotland and Jamaica, for more than thirty years after the Revolution. His son George was later taken into partnership. Like many American firms, the Buchanans suffered from the suspension of trade during the embargo and the War of 1812. In 1815, the year of his death, Thomas

Buchanan's estate was valued at $50,000 (*Valentine's Manual*, 1864, p. 756). He had a residence and counting-house on Wall St. and a country seat on the East River near Hell Gate. He was a member of the First Presbyterian Church and the St. Andrew's Society, and a director of the United Insurance Company. He is described as of middle height, slender in youth but quite corpulent later, with sandy hair, light-blue eyes, and a florid complexion. He died at his home on Wall St. Nov. 10, 1815, not Sept. 10, as has been frequently stated (*Commercial Advertiser*, Nov. 11, 1815).

[Short biographical sketches appear in John Austin Stevens, *Colonial Records of the Chamber of Commerce of the State of N. Y., 1768–84* (1867), pp. 125–28; Wm. M. MacBean, *Biog. Reg. of the St. Andrew's Soc. of the State of N. Y.* (1922), I, 96; and A. W. Buchanan, *The Buchanan Book* (1911), p. 457. These incorporate some of the half-dozen errors found in the scattered remarks concerning Buchanan in Jos. A. Scoville, *The Old Merchants of N. Y.* (1863–66). The extent of Buchanan's trade may be judged by the advertisements of his firm which appeared regularly in the N. Y. newspapers of the period. A few of his business letters are preserved by the N. Y. Hist. Soc.]

R.G.A.

BUCHANAN, WILLIAM INSCO (Sept. 10, 1852–Oct. 16, 1909), business man, amusement-manager, diplomat, was descended from a Scotch family which had been settled in Virginia since the second half of the eighteenth century. His grandfather, Col. George Buchanan, in 1806 moved to Miami County, Ohio, where, near the town of Covington, William Insco Buchanan was born, the son of George Preston and Mary Elizabeth (Gibson) Buchanan. Left an orphan before he was nine years old, William received his only schooling from the country schools. Before he was thirty he had learned the trade of edge-tool making, had nibbled at politics (he was engrossing clerk of the Indiana legislature, 1874–75), and had been for half a dozen years a commercial traveler. He was married on Apr. 16, 1878, to Lulu Williams of Dayton, Ohio. In 1882 he settled in Sioux City, Iowa, and there, after a venture in wholesale trade as a jobber of crockery, he opened a theatre. In this enterprise, and in promoting the four "corn-palaces" of that city (1887–90), of which he was the moving spirit— serving as manager of the last and most elaborate —he revealed rare talents as an amusement-manager and executive, which led to his appointment as the Democratic member of the Iowa commission to the World's Columbian Exposition held in Chicago in 1893. In this he was chief of the department of agriculture (1890–93) and organizer of the departments of live stock and forestry (1891), and was remarkably successful. In these varied callings he found opportunity to exercise the social sense and judgment of men that were essential factors in his achievements in the diplomatic service which filled the rest of his life.

Buchanan's diplomatic career began with his appointment by President Cleveland in 1894 as envoy extraordinary and minister plenipotentiary to the Argentine Republic. One evidence of his felicitous discharge of his duties in this post, which he held for six years, was his designation by Chile and Argentina as umpire of a commission appointed by those countries to settle their extreme northern boundary line in the desert of Atacama. After an interim of one year's service as director-general of the Pan-American Exposition held in Buffalo in 1901, Buchanan represented his country, successively, as one of the delegates to the Second International Conference of American States (at Mexico City, October 1901); as its first envoy extraordinary and minister plenipotentiary accredited, first on special mission (Dec. 12, 1903) and then on regular appointment, to Panama (Dec. 17, 1903–05); as chairman of its delegation to the Third International Conference of American States (at Rio de Janeiro, July 1906); as one of its commissioners to the second Peace Conference at The Hague (June–October, 1907); as its representative in attendance upon the Central American Peace Conference held in Washington in 1907 (November–December); as high commissioner at the installation of the Central American Court of Justice at Cartago, Costa Rica (May 25, 1908); as high commissioner charged with the renewal of diplomatic relations with Venezuela (Dec. 21, 1908–09) after the overthrow of President Cipriano Castro; and as agent of the United States in the prospective arbitration before the international court of arbitration at The Hague of the only claim against Venezuela that he had failed to settle diplomatically. He was also a member of a Pan-American committee appointed by Secretary of State Elihu Root in 1907 to stimulate Pan-American comity, and was appointed chairman (Feb. 21, 1908) of another Pan-American committee charged with the preparation of the Fourth International Conference of American States. His discharge of his diplomatic duties was unvaryingly felicitous, as the mere list of his appointments indicates. He gained tariff concessions for United States commodities, settled old claims, consummated long-pending negotiations. Particularly notable were his services at the Central American Peace Conference and in settlement of our distempered relations with Venezuela. He was extremely well informed on Latin-American affairs, and seemed to possess an intuitive understanding of Latin-Americans. Upon his retirement from the Argentine post

Buchanan became the representative of the New York Life Insurance Company in the adjustment of differences arising between it and foreign governments, particularly those of South America, and remained in the Company's service until his death. About 1902 he also joined the Westinghouse interests, serving from 1903 to 1905 as managing director of the British Westinghouse Company and an officer of the French Westinghouse Company, and through life continuing otherwise to serve the parent American company. In these very important business duties his success was as uniform as in his governmental service. In both he showed a broad and liberal spirit, "basing his claims upon justice and pressing them with courtesy and with proper regard for the rights and customs of the people with whom he dealt" (resolutions of the New York Life Insurance Company, Oct. 20, 1909) ; and in both fields his country reaped the legitimate fruits of a sound diplomacy, an increase of commercial intercourse and a better international understanding.

[See A. W. P. Buchanan, *The Buchanan Book* (1911), and the *Buffalo Morning Express,* the *Evening Star* (Washington, D. C.), the *N. Y. Tribune,* the *Chicago Daily Tribune,* the *Sioux City Jour.,* all of Oct. 18, 1909 ; *Hist. of the Counties of Woodbury and Plymouth, Iowa* (1890–91), pp. 92, 746 ; *Who's Who in America,* 1908–09. Buchanan's diplomatic career can be traced through the *Monthly Bulletin of the International Bureau of the American Republics* and in the Department of State's lists of its diplomatic representatives. The year of his birth, sometimes given as 1853, was really 1852 according to Buchanan's daughter.]
F.S.P.

BUCHER, JOHN CONRAD (June 10, 1730–Aug. 15, 1780), German Reformed clergyman, soldier, was born at Neunkirch, Switzerland, six miles west of Schaffhausen, the third of the six children of Hans Jacob and Anna Dorothea (Burgauer) Bucher. He was sixth in descent from Claus Bucher of Lindau, who became a citizen of Schaffhausen in the first half of the sixteenth century. His father was made *landvogt* of Neunkirch in 1745. Bucher studied at the gymnasium in Schaffhausen, at St. Gall, and at the University of Marburg, where he matriculated July 14, 1752. While a student he paid several visits to some friends stationed at Namur as officers of Swiss troops, and these visits are thought to have awakened in him a desire for military experience. He was last in Marburg, according to his album book, in April 1755. The circumstances under which he came, shortly after, to Pennsylvania are unknown. According to John Christian Stahlschmidt's *Pilgerreise zu Wasser und zu Land* (Nuremberg, 1799, p. 287) Bucher was an officer of Dutch troops that were sent to America to serve as mercenaries under Braddock ; and the date of his landing at Philadelphia is sometimes given as Nov. 1, 1755 ; but

the first authenticated fact about his American career is that on Apr. 11, 1758, he was commissioned ensign in the 1st Battalion of the Pennsylvania Regiment. He took part in the expedition against Fort Duquesne in that year and was stationed over winter at Carlisle. During the next two winters he commanded the garrison at Carlisle. He was commissioned lieutenant of the 2nd Battalion Apr. 19, 1760, participated in the War of Pontiac's Conspiracy, and was commissioned adjutant July 12 and captain July 31, 1764. He was a trusted and capable officer. When the war ended next spring he resigned.

Meanwhile, on Feb. 26, 1760, he was married at Carlisle to Mary Magdalena, daughter of John George Hoke (Hans Georg Hauk). She and four of their six children survived him. While still in the militia Bucher began to preach ; his earliest sermon notes and records of ministerial acts date from March 1763. In 1766 the Coetus of Pennsylvania, in applying to the Classis of Amsterdam for authority to ordain him, described Bucher as one "made willing by the Lord to serve these people, who devotes himself with all diligence to learn the truth and to expound it to others, and is also content to share the poverty of his hearers" (*Minutes,* p. 244). The Classis authorized his ordination in a letter of June 20, 1767. Until 1768 he served congregations at Carlisle, Middletown, Hummelstown, and Falling Spring (Chambersburg). From time to time he made missionary trips westward to Bedford near Fort Cumberland, Redstone (Brownsville), Big Crossings of the Yiogheny, and Fort Pitt, riding hundreds of miles through the forest and over rugged mountains. He was the first minister to preach in German beyond the Alleghanies. After 1770, however, he seldom crossed the Susquehanna. Making Lebanon his headquarters, he ministered to about eleven scattered little congregations, including Quittapahilla, Manheim, Weisseichenland, Hummelstown, and Lancaster. In 1775 he was secretary of the Coetus. At the outbreak of the Revolution he was a chaplain in the "German Regiment" under Baron von Arnt, but ill health caused him to resign Aug. 1, 1777. A backwoods missionary, he kept up his scholarship ; several hundred sermon outlines, with citations from Latin, Greek, and Hebrew, have been preserved among his papers. He died at Annville of a heart attack during the festivities attendant on a wedding. His body was carried to Lebanon for burial.

[H. Harbaugh, *The Fathers of the Ger. Ref. Ch.,* vol. II (1857) ; T. C. Porter, "The Bucher Album" in *Proc. and Addresses Pa. Ger. Soc.,* V, 133–40 (1895) ; G. B. Ayres, "Rev. Capt. J. C. Bucher" in W. H. Egle's *Notes and Queries Hist. and Geneal.,* II, 411–16 (1895) ; W. H. Agle, *Pa. Genealogies* (1886 ; 2nd ed., 1896) ;

Pa. Archives, 5 ser., vols. I and VII; A. Stapleton, "Rev. John Conrad Bucher" in the Pa. German, IV, 291–308 (1903); Minutes and Letters of the Coetus of the Ger. Ref. Congregations in Pa. 1747–92 (1903): F. B. Heitman, Hist. Reg. of Officers of the Continental Army (new ed., 1914); an unpublished article on Bucher by Prof. Wm. J. Hinke of Auburn Theological Seminary, who has also given his personal assistance in the preparation of this article.]   G. H. G.

BUCHTEL, JOHN RICHARDS (Jan. 18, 1820–May 23, 1892), business man, philanthropist, son of John and Catharine (Richards) Buchtel, was born in Green Township, then in Stark County, now a part of Summit County, Ohio. His boyhood was spent in hard work on his father's farm. Educational advantages were meager. In his later teens he sold clocks and bought and sold horses, but these ventures proved unprofitable and he returned to farming. In 1844 he married Elizabeth Davidson. In 1854 he became a salesman for Ball, Aultman & Company of Canton, Ohio, manufacturers of mowers and reapers. He was largely instrumental in persuading the firm to build an Akron branch ten years later, and became the first president of the Buckeye Company, as the Akron branch was popularly known. In 1877, with other capitalists, he undertook the development of the mineral resources of the Hocking Valley. The extent of this project may be guessed from the fact that in 1880 alone the company paid the Hocking Valley Railroad a million dollars for freight charges. For several years Buchtel had the active management of this enterprise, and its remarkable success was due largely to his energy and wisdom. He was keenly interested in civic affairs, and gave generously of time and money to whatever he believed was for the public good. In 1872 he was a presidential elector; in 1874, candidate for secretary of state on the Prohibition ticket; and for several years a trustee of the State Agricultural College.

In 1887, while in the Hocking Valley, he was stricken with paralysis, and was never again able to take an active part in business. Buchtel's greatest monument is Buchtel College (now the University of Akron). While tolerant of all religious faiths, he was an ardent Universalist, and when in 1870, the Universalists of Ohio undertook to found a college, his gift of $31,000 brought the college to Akron. Thenceforward he and Mrs. Buchtel, being childless, lavished upon the new college their affection and generosity. By 1882 their gifts had reached $138,828 and eventually nearly half a million. Buchtel was one of the incorporators of the college, and was president of the Board of Trustees until his death. His leading characteristics were energy, sincerity, bluntness of manner with sympathy and kindness of heart.

[Samuel Lane, Fifty Years and Over of Akron and Summit County (1892); A. I. Spanton, ed., Fifty Years of Buchtel, 1870–1920 (1922).]   A. I. S.

BUCK, ALBERT HENRY (Oct. 20, 1842–Nov. 16, 1922), otologist and medical historian, was one of five children of Gurdon Buck [q.v.], surgeon of New York, by his wife, Henriette Elisabeth Wolff of Geneva, Switzerland. He received a part of his early education near his mother's native haunts in Switzerland and there laid the foundation of the linguistic powers for which he became subsequently distinguished. He was graduated from Yale in 1864 and obtained his M.D. from the College of Physicians and Surgeons of Columbia in 1867. After an internship in the New York Hospital he spent several years in Germany and Austria studying the physiology and diseases of the ear. He was married in 1871 to Laura S. Abbott, daughter of John S. C. Abbott [q.v.]. In 1872 he was made aural surgeon at the New York Eye and Ear Infirmary, with which institution he remained associated until his death. From 1888 to 1904 he held the post of clinical professor of diseases of the ear in the College of Physicians and Surgeons of Columbia University. Throughout his life he was a prolific writer and made numerous contributions to otological journals. One of his early literary accomplishments was the editing of the American edition of H. W. Ziemssen's Cyclopædia of the Practice of Medicine in fifteen volumes, published between 1874 and 1880; a second edition appeared in 1890. In association with Joseph Decatur Bryant [q.v.], he edited the American Practice of Surgery in eight volumes, published between 1906 and 1911. Smaller works were his editions of Salomon Stricker's Manual of Histology (1872) and of the two-volume Treatise on Hygiene and Public Health (1879). His most important contribution was his Diagnosis and Treatment of Ear Diseases (1880), which passed through three editions. This last work represented the results of his own observation and study and was for many years the vade-mecum of students and otologists. Buck's studies on the physiology of the ear were also important. His first published paper (1870) was entitled "An Essay on the Mechanism of the Ossicles of the Ear," and three years later he edited the New York edition of Helmholtz's classic work bearing the same title.

After Buck resigned his professorship in 1904 he gradually withdrew from private practise, and about 1910 began an intensive study of the history of medicine. His first contribution in this field, The Growth of Medicine from the Earliest Times to about 1800 was published in 1917 under the auspices of the Williams Memorial Publication Fund of Yale University. The book is admittedly a compilation chiefly from secondary sources, but Buck's gift for writing and his energetic style made the volume attractive and stimulating. His second historical work, *The Dawn of Modern Medicine*, was published in 1920 and was intended as a sequel to the first. For it the sources were thoroughly studied and advantage was taken of the rich collection of early nineteenth century medical works in the library of Transylvania College at Lexington, Ky. The chapters on Bichat and Laennec are particularly attractive.

[See A. H. Buck, *The Bucks of Wethersfield, Conn.* (1909); *Hist. of the Class of 1864, Yale Coll.* (1895); obituary by R. Lewis and E. B. Dench in the *N. Y. Medical Jour.*, CXVII, 48. Extensive lists of Buck's papers are given in the *Index Cat. of the Surgeon-General's Library*, 1, 2, 3 ser.] J.F.F.

BUCK, DANIEL (Nov. 9, 1753–Aug. 16, 1816), lawyer, legislator, was the second son of Thomas and Jane Buck. He was born in Hebron, Conn., and while young emigrated to Thetford, Vt., which was largely settled by emigrants from Hebron. During the American Revolution, he lost an arm in the battle of Bennington. In 1784 or 1785 he removed to Norwich, Vt., where he was one of the first settlers. He studied law and was the first lawyer to open an office in Norwich. In 1791 he represented Norwich in the convention called to determine whether Vermont would ratify or reject the United States Constitution. The chief opposition came from a group of Windsor County towns and Buck was its leader and spokesman, but he finally voted for immediate union with the new nation. That his opposition to statehood did not prejudice Vermonters against him is shown by his election as speaker of the Assembly in 1793 and 1794. He served one term in Congress as a Federalist (1795–97), making the journey to the seat of government on horseback with his fellow townsmen accompanying him to the border of the neighboring town. He made one of the ablest speeches delivered in defense of the position of the Washington administration on the Jay Treaty, opposing the attempt to compel the executive department to deliver to Congress its instructions to the American envoy (*Annals of Congress*, 4 Cong., 1 Sess., pp. 430–35, 703–17), but he was defeated for reëlection. He served as a member of the Council of Censors (1792), as attorney-general of the state (1794), and as state's attorney of Windsor County (1802–03). In 1806 he was again in the legislature and was active in establishing a state bank. He was married on Sept. 22, 1786 to Content Ashley of Norwich by whom he had eleven children. The eldest son, Daniel A. A. Buck, became a member of Congress.

[M. E. Goddard and H. V. Partridge, *Hist. of Norwich, Vt.* (1905); Leonard Deming, *Cat. of the Principal Officers of Vt.* (1851); *Biog. Cong. Dir.* (1903); W. H. Crockett, *Vt., the Green Mt. State* (1921), vols. II, III.] W.H.C.

BUCK, DUDLEY (Mar. 10, 1839–Oct. 6, 1909), composer, organist, was born in Hartford, Conn., the son of Dudley and Martha Church (Adams) Buck, and grandson of Daniel Buck, also of Hartford. His earliest American ancestor was Emanuel Buck, who, soon after his arrival at Plymouth Colony from England, became one of the original settlers of Wethersfield, Conn., in 1647. There is no evidence of musical ability in any of his immediate ancestors. His mother, however, had a deep love of poetry and it was her custom to read aloud her favorite poems to her son during his early years. Young Dudley had been destined for a business career by his father, who was a prominent shipping merchant and owner of a line of steamships plying between Hartford and New York City. But he early displayed an unusual aptitude for music, and, although he was self-taught until he was sixteen years old, he finally obtained, with some difficulty, the consent of his parents to prepare himself for a professional career in music,—a procedure directly athwart the New England prejudices of the time. In 1855 he took his first piano lessons of W. J. Babcock of Hartford, and at the same time entered Trinity College, where he remained three years. He applied himself to his music with such ardor and revealed such unmistakable talent that his father sent him to Europe in 1858 for extended study,—eighteen months (1858–59) at the Leipzig Conservatory with Hauptmann and Richter (harmony and composition), Plaidy and Moscheles (piano), and J. Rietz (orchestration); later at Dresden with Rietz and Johann Schneider (organ); and one year (1861–62) in Paris. On his return to Hartford in 1862 he was appointed organist of the North Congregational Church. He was married on Oct. 3, 1865, to Mary Elizabeth van Wagener of Burlington, N. J., and in 1869, heeding the call of the West, he went to Chicago to become organist at St. James's Episcopal Church. After the great fire of Oct. 9, 1871, which destroyed his home with valuable library and manuscripts, he removed to Boston (1872) as organist of St. Paul's Church and, soon after, of Music Hall, the highest honor a Boston musician of that period could attain. In 1875 he was official organist of the Cincinnati May Festival and on his return to Boston accepted the invitation of Theodore Thomas to be assistant conductor of his orchestral concerts at Central Park Garden in New York. He removed his family to Brooklyn and began his long musical career there as organist in various churches, while from 1877 to 1903 he was conductor of the Apollo Club (male chorus). In 1903 he resigned all positions and retired to private life, dividing his "playtime," as he called it, between travel and composition. His death occurred at Orange, N. J.

Buck was one of the first American composers to possess musicianship of genuine solidity, with respect both to technical equipment and creative ability. American organ-music practically begins with him. As a concert-organist of imposing ability, his extensive tours during the first fifteen years of his public life helped greatly to uplift standards of organ-playing and organ-music, both of which were in dire need of improvement. He was the first American composer to gain wide recognition in this field. His best organ works include two Sonatas (in E-flat and G-minor), Concert Variations on "The Star Spangled Banner," and several shorter pieces (as "At Evening"); also a valuable handbook, *Illustrations in Choir Accompaniment, with Hints on Registration*. His first published compositions were written to supply the needs of his own choir in Hartford. When his first *Motet Collection* appeared in 1864 (a second book followed later), it met with immediate success, which led him to give increasing attention, as composer, to church-music. Indeed, his influence in this field was probably stronger and more lasting than in any other to which he contributed, for the needs of American Protestant church-music could not be met, as could those of choral societies and organists, by mere importation of foreign-made music. His many excellent anthems, solos, hymns, *Te Deums*, etc. (there are about 140 of these),— fluent, attractive, well-constructed, and many of them of real depth and fervor—offered a refreshing contrast to the insipid and trivial music in general use in American churches of this period and produced a marked improvement in public taste. His versatility led him to write also in the large forms: *Serápis* (1895), text by himself, an unperformed grand opera on an Egyptian subject; *Deseret* (1880), a comic opera on a Mormon theme; "In Springtime," a symphony; "Marmion," a symphonic overture (first performed by the Thomas Orchestra, 1881); some chamber music, etc. By far the most important of his large works, however, are his concert cantatas. Of these, five are for male chorus and twelve for mixed chorus. Of the former group the best probably are "The Nun of Nidaros" and "Paul Revere's Ride." Of the latter group especial mention must be made of "The Centennial Meditation of Columbia," written for the Centennial Exposition and performed at Philadelphia,

May 10, 1876, under Theodore Thomas's direction by a chorus of 1,000 and an orchestra of 200, by which Buck's reputation as a composer was firmly established; "The Golden Legend," which won the prize offered by the Cincinnati May Festival Association for the best work by an American and was first performed at the Festival in 1880; "The Light of Asia," his largest and most pretentious choral work (first English performance at St. James's Hall, London, Mar. 19, 1889); and "The Christian Year," a series of five effective cantatas for the important church festivals. Mention must be made of his wide influence as a teacher, for he was the direct source of inspiration to a large number of pupils. In disposition he was genial and warm-hearted; and he combined tact and practical wisdom in dealing with his public.

[A. H. Buck, *The Bucks of Wethersfield, Conn.* (1909); *Grove's Dict. of Music and Musicians* (Am. Supp., revised ed., 1928), pp. 146–47; *Baker's Biog. Dict. of Musicians* (3rd ed., 1919); Rossetter Cole, *Choral and Ch. Music* (1916), pp. 218–20, 498; R. Hughes and A. Elson, *Am. Composers* (1914), pp. 165–74; G. P. Upton, *The Standard Cantatas* (1888), pp. 101–22; Louis C. Elson, *The Hist. of Am. Music* (1904), pp. 230–32.]   R.G.C.

BUCK, GURDON (May 4, 1807–Mar. 6, 1877), surgeon, was the son of a New York merchant bearing the same name, by his cousin, Susannah Manwaring, who, like her husband, was a grandchild of Gov. Gurdon Saltonstall of Connecticut. Buck received his preliminary education at the Nelson Classical School where he prepared for higher studies, but instead of going to college he yielded to his father's wishes and became a clerk in the house of G. & D. Buck. Soon developing an interest in medicine, however, he left his position and entered the office of Dr. Thomas Cock, under whom he completed his medical studies. In 1830 he obtained his M.D. from the College of Physicians and Surgeons at New York. After eighteen months in the New York Hospital (1832) he had the advantage of two years' study in the hospitals of Paris, Berlin, and Vienna. On a second trip to Europe in 1836 he married (July 27), Henriette Elizabeth Wolff of Geneva, Switzerland. When he finally settled in New York (1837) he became visiting surgeon to the New York Hospital, and later to St. Luke's (1846) and to the Presbyterian Hospital (1872); in addition he was associated from 1852 to 1862 with the New York Eye and Ear Infirmary.

Buck was one of the great American surgeons of the pre-Lister era. A scholarly anatomist and a bold operator, he was at the same time rapid, skilful, and humane. He studied his cases with a diligence that was rare in those early days, and especially praiseworthy was the attention which he bestowed upon post-operative treatment. He kept careful case histories and his surgical publications always reflected his painstaking methods. His chief contributions relate to his methods of managing fractures and to plastic surgery. His advocacy of treatment of fractures of the thigh by means of weights and pulleys received prompt recognition in other parts of the world. The device which he introduced is still used and is known as "Buck's extension." His methods were well described in a pamphlet published in 1867 entitled *Description of an Improved Extension Apparatus for the Treatment of Fracture of the Thigh*. As early as 1842 Buck had performed a successful excision of the olecranon process of the elbow joint (*American Journal of Medical Science*, April 1843, pp. 297–301). He was also a pioneer in plastic surgery of the face, and the year before his death he published *Contributions to Reparative Surgery* (1876), an admirable monograph describing his own experience in this field. It was excellently illustrated from photographs of his cases and attracted wide attention, being translated into three foreign languages. A complete bibliography of his numerous contributions to medical and surgical journals is given in the *Transactions of the Medical Society of the State of New York* for 1877, pp. 370–74. His son, Albert H. Buck [*q.v.*] was a physician.

[A. H. Buck, *The Bucks of Wethersfield* (1909); F. A. Castle, obituary in the *Trans. Med. Soc. of the State of N. Y.* (1877), pp. 367–70; *Medic. Record*, Mar. 10, 1877, p. 158; Buck's introduction to his *Reparative Surgery* (1876).]   J.F.F.

BUCK, LEFFERT LEFFERTS (Feb. 5, 1837–July 17, 1909), civil engineer, was born at Canton, N. Y., the third son of Lemuel and Elizabeth (Baldridge) Buck. He inherited the courage and dexterity as well as the gaunt frame and swarthy countenance of his New England ancestors who had participated in every conflict that had arisen since Emanuel Buck settled at Wethersfield, Conn., in 1647 (Cornelius B. Harvey, *Origin, History and Genealogy of the Buck Family*, 1889, pp. 25-28). He had spent nearly five years in a machine shop and two years at St. Lawrence University, before he left college to enlist in the Union army. When he was discharged as captain with the rank of brevet major, he selected engineering as the field for which he was best adapted by temperament and training and entered Rensselaer Polytechnic Institute, from which he received the degree of civil engineer in 1868. After an apprenticeship in the Croton Aqueduct department of New York City, he secured his first retainer in South America. During two years in which he was engaged on the Oroya Railroad, in Peru, he erected the original Verrugas Viaduct, in its day the highest and, possibly, the most remarkable bridge in the world. In 1875 he constructed several bridges on the Chimbote & Huarez Railroad. Seven years later he designed a number of bridges in Mexico; and, in 1890, he built the second Verrugas Viaduct, of the cantilever type. From 1890 to 1908 he represented Peru and Ecuador upon the International Railway Commission. On his return from his first trip, he spent two years in the shops of the Toledo & Wabash Railroad; and, in 1880–81, he served as resident engineer of the Central Railroad of New Jersey, for which he constructed the Lake Hopatcong Division. Except for this interruption, he devoted himself almost exclusively to the design and construction of bridges. As early as 1873 he supervised the manufacture of material for the Louisiana Railroad Bridge. In 1883 he built several bridges for the Northern Pacific Railroad. Between 1886 and 1888 he designed for it those across the White River, the Yakima River, and the Columbia River. For the Great Northern Railroad he drew plans for the Nooksack Drawbridge (1892).

Like many civil engineers of the nineteenth century, Buck was a wanderer. Although he was associated with George McNulty during 1883–88, he did not establish himself in independent practise until 1902. In the same year he married Myra Rebecca Gould of Paducah, Ky. Wide as was the range of his work, he is remembered primarily for his achievements at Niagara Falls and New York. His connection with the Falls began in 1877, when he repaired the cables in the Railway Suspension Bridge. Three years later he replaced the wooden superstructure; and, in 1886, he substituted iron towers for the stone towers. This feat, which, as in previous alterations, he accomplished without interrupting traffic, has been described as "the most difficult, delicate, and daring piece of bridgework ever undertaken" (*Transactions of the Society of Civil Engineers*, LXXIII, 495). Again, in 1896, he erected, without interrupting traffic, the present spandrel-braced arch. In Rochester, N. Y., where he had constructed the Platt Street Bridge, he had also constructed the Driving Park Avenue Bridge of the three-hinged type; and it was through a study of the vibrations of this bridge that he eliminated the central hinge at the Falls. There he rebuilt the Niagara and Clifton Suspension Bridge in 1888–89 and, in 1896–87, replaced it by the longest steel arch span in the world, once more maintaining traffic without material interruption. He was also consulting engineer for the Lewiston and Queenston Suspension

Bridge (1899). In New York, although he promoted the development of the metropolitan tunnels, his name is linked more closely with the bridges of the district. As one of a committee of three, he recommended that the New York and Brooklyn Suspension Bridge be opened to surface and elevated trains (*Report of the Board of Experts*, Feb. 8, 1897). His chief monument, however, is the Williamsburg Bridge, which is distinguished for its vast reach and massive symmetry. Although he is known as one of the great bridge-builders of his time, his career must be considered in connection with the history and influence of Rensselaer Polytechnic Institute; for, from the beginning, he drew constantly upon its graduates for aid in design, manufacture, and supervision. He received the Norman Medal in 1881 and the Telford Premium in 1901.

[The most detailed accounts of Buck's career are those in Henry B. Nason's *Biog. Record Officers and Grads. Rensselaer Polytechnic Inst.* (1887) and Wm. R. Cutter's *Geneal. and Family Hist. of Northern N. Y.* (1910). C. D. Christie's *Notes on the Central and Southern Railways of Peru* (1917) touches his life in South America. The memoir by Richard S. Buck in the *Trans. Am. Soc. Civil Engineers*, LXXIII, 493–97, is a personal impression stressing his military services and his achievements at Niagara Falls and New York. His work at the Gorge is treated in his *Report on the Renewal of the Niagara Suspension Bridge* (1880) and in his papers in the *Trans. Am. Soc. Civil Engineers*, X, 195–224, and the *Minutes of the Proc. of the Inst. of Civil Engineers*, CXLIV, 69–94. Several points are amplified in the *Engineering News*, Dec. 10, 1887, and in Richard S. Buck's study of the Niagara railway arch in the *Trans. Am. Soc. Civil Engineers*, XL, 125–50. Buck's most important work in New York is described in the *Engineering Record*, Dec. 19, 1903, and in Edward Hungerford's *The Williamsburg Bridge* (1893). In Ray Palmer Baker's *A Chapter in Am. Education* (1924), Buck's accomplishments are related to the tradition of bridge-building at Rensselaer Polytechnic Institute. Among obituaries are a pamphlet published by the Loyal Legion of the United States, Sept. 10, 1909, and an appreciation by Albert Shaw in the *Rev. of Revs.* (N. Y.), XL, 175–76.]   R. P. B—r.

BUCK, PHILO MELVIN (May 15, 1846–Sept. 8, 1924), Methodist missionary, was born in Corning, N. Y., the son of Ethal Curry Buck and Mariam (Underwood) Buck. His parents moved West and finally settled in Kansas, where their son's educational opportunities were meager and most of his early reading was necessarily self-directed. When he was seventeen he began to preach and two years later he joined the Kansas Conference of the Methodist Episcopal Church. In 1868 he married Angie M. Tibbott who died the next year. Having volunteered for foreign mission service, he was sent to India in 1870. In 1872, in India, he was married to Caroline Louisa MacMillan of Gettysburg, Pa. His earliest appointment in India was at Shahjahanpur where he remained from 1871 to 1876. During 1876–78 he studied in Drew Theological Seminary, Madi-

son, N. J., graduating in the latter year. He returned to India and was successively stationed at Kumaun (1879–84), Cawnpore (1885), and Mussourie (1889–92), where he was principal of Philander Smith Institute. But it was as superintendent of the Meerut District (1893–1914) that he first had full scope for his exceptional qualities as a missionary. He traveled continually over the district, using a bicycle for the most part, everywhere making friends with persons of every caste and religion. As his work prospered, he acquired property, secured funds, and trained Indian men and women to meet his needs. Under his leadership a great movement toward Christianity, known as the "Mass Movement," began. The new converts were from the lowest, "untouchable" groups, Tanners and Sweepers, and utterly illiterate. The training of a large number of pastors and teachers to care for them became necessary. Buck's workers were drawn, mostly, from the "untouchable" groups. Since no literature was available for use in the training of these workers, he began to write books. His first catechism was prepared for the quarterly conferences in his own district and for his summer schools. Then to meet the growing needs of his workers he prepared books to serve all classes from beginners to members of annual conferences. His district became an example for other superintendents and his books had a very wide use. For nearly a quarter of a century, he conducted a department in the *Kaukab-i-Hind*, a religious weekly published in Roman Urdu at Lucknow. Through the columns of this paper he became the teacher of preachers throughout the Urdu-speaking areas of India. The usefulness of his literary work, as well as of his preaching, was due, in no small measure, to a remarkable and idiomatic use of Urdu, and, late in life, of Hindi. Of his numerous works the most important was *Christianity in Doctrine and in Experience* (1914), which first appeared in Urdu and was translated into Hindi, Marathi, Gujurati, Chinese, Korean, and even Spanish—for use in Latin America.

[J. M. Reed, *Missions and Missionary Soc. of the M. E. Ch.* (3 vols., 1895–96); *Who's Who in America*, 1924–25; files of the minutes of the North India Conference, of the North-West India Conference and of the Central Conference of Southern Asia; also files of the *Kaukab-i-Hind* and of the *Indian Witness*.]   G. W. B.

BUCKALEW, CHARLES ROLLIN (Dec. 28, 1821–May 19, 1899), senator, was descended from a branch of the Buccleugh family which emigrated from Scotland to France in the sixteenth century and later, during the Huguenot persecutions, emigrated to America. By 1775 one branch of the family, changing its name to

Buckalew, had pioneered to Muncy, Pa. In 1808, one John McKinney Buckalew acquired a large tract of land in Columbia County, where he married Martha Funston, by whom he became the father of Charles Rollin Buckalew. The latter's academic education was mainly at Harford Academy, Harford, Pa. His early career included school-teaching, selling goods in a local store, and the study of law in a local attorney's office. His wife, Permelia Stevens Wadsworth, was a member of a Connecticut family notable in colonial history. Entering politics at the age of twenty-four, by the traditional route of the local prosecuting attorney's office, he rapidly assumed local political leadership and within five years was elected as Democratic state senator. This position he retained from 1850 to 1858, supporting such policies as the reform of the penal code and the relinquishment by the state of its transportation facilities to private corporations. In 1854 he served as one of the United States commissioners to ratify a treaty with Paraguay. His position as a lawyer and as a party leader was recognized by his appointment in 1857 by Gov. Packer as a member of a commission to revise the penal code of the state. This position, as well as the chairmanship of the state Democratic committee, and his office as state senator, he resigned in 1858 to accept appointment by President Buchanan as minister to Ecuador (letter to Buchanan, June 29, 1858). After his return in 1861, his leadership in his party was recognized by his election in 1863 as United States senator. His career in the Senate, though dignified and creditable, was not distinguished. His position was a most difficult one, due in part to the turbulent character of national politics, when Democrats generally were subjected to the harshest criticism; and in part to the fact that his party in Pennsylvania was in a measure out of sympathy with the national party, especially on tariff questions. Furthermore, his modesty, moderation, and disinclination to depend on the arts of political maneuvering, qualities admirable no doubt in themselves, unfitted him for effective participation in the troubled course of events. He opposed the extreme war powers of the Government, the Freedman's Bureau, the impeachment of President Johnson, and other distinctively Republican policies. He advocated, alike for the nation and the state, a system of proportional representation (see his speeches in Congress on the subject and his book, *Proportional Representation*, 1872), and he was influential in minor matters of a non-controversial nature, as in much-needed improvements in Congressional buildings (*Congressional Globe*, 1863–69).

Upon the expiration of Buckalew's term as federal senator, Pennsylvania was under Republican control. He returned to the state Senate, where his chief activity was as chairman of the committee on constitutional reform. In 1872 he was the unsuccessful Democratic candidate for governor. He was also a delegate to the convention which rewrote the state constitution in 1872–73, and although an outstanding member of the convention, was unable to secure the inclusion of provisions which he particularly favored. A modified form of his view of minority representation was, however, included in the constitution (see his *Examination of the Constitution of Pennsylvania*, 1883). His later career was marked by his return to national politics as Congressman in 1887. After the expiration of his second term as Congressman in 1891, he spent the remainder of his life in retirement at his home in Bloomsburg, Columbia County.

[Buckalew's work in the state legislature may be studied in the *Journal* of the state Senate, the *Legislative Journal*, and the *Daily Legislative Record*. For his career in the federal Congress, see *Cong. Globe* and *Cong. Record*. There are brief estimates in the memoirs of such men as J. G. Blaine and G. W. Julian. For his work in the state constitutional convention, see the *Debates* (9 vols.) and the *Journals* (2 vols.) of the convention; and A. D. Harlan, *Pa. Constitutional Convention* (1873). Some of his letters are preserved in the manuscript collections of the Pa. Hist. Soc.]   W. B.

BUCKHOUT, ISAAC CRAIG (Nov. 7, 1830– Sept. 27, 1874), civil engineer, descended from an old Knickerbocker family and the son of Jacob and Charlotte Eveline (De Val) Buckhout, was born in Eastchester, N. Y., on the old Gouverneur Morris estate of which his father was manager. As a boy he was of a studious nature and was considered to be somewhat of a mathematical genius. Early in life he decided to become a civil engineer and by hard work got enough money together to take an engineering course under a Prof. Davies. When he was seventeen he began the practical experience which was to lead him into engineering prominence in spite of his short life. He was fortunate in the tutelage through which he laid the foundations of his profession. In 1848, when he first entered the employ of the Harlem Railroad as a rodman, he worked under Allan Campbell, a civil engineer who later became president of the railroad. Shortly afterward he engaged in surveying at Paterson, N. J., where his chief was Col. J. W. Allen. In a short while Buckhout rose to the position of engineer and superintendent of the waterworks at Paterson but he gave this up to return to New York as city surveyor. In 1853, however, he returned to the employ of the Harlem Railroad and it was in railroad work that he achieved outstanding prominence in his day. His earlier work included the construction of an aqueduct over the Harlem flats and of a bridge over the Harlem River. But he will chiefly be remembered for the old Grand Central Depot, which he designed, and the "Fourth Avenue Improvement," the name given at the time to a new line to run from the Harlem River to Forty-second St., New York City. A board of four engineers was appointed by the state legislature when the charter for this "Improvement" was granted, and Isaac Buckhout was put in charge of the work. He resigned his position as superintendent of the New York and Harlem Railroad in order to give his time completely as engineer in charge of the new work. It was his literal devotion to duty here that caused his untimely death. Standing day after day in the marshland that is now New York's exclusive East Sixties, he contracted acute rheumatism and typhoid fever which resulted in his death at his home in White Plains.

Buckhout also drew up plans for an underground railroad to run from Grand Central Depot to City Hall, and for another underground road in Brooklyn. He had been appointed a member of the Committee on Rapid Transit shortly before his death. He was an engineer whose advice was sought not only because of his innate practical ability and the indefatigable care which he took with details but also because of the qualities of manhood which made him a warm personal friend and inspired trust and confidence in those with whom he came in contact. In personal appearance he so much resembled Henry Ward Beecher that he was often mistaken for him.

[The files of the Am. Soc. of Civil Engineers, especially their *Proceedings,* vol. I; *Railroad Gazette,* Oct. 3, 1874; *Sun* (N.Y.) and *N. Y. Tribune,* Sept. 29, 1874.]

E.Y.

BUCKINGHAM, JOSEPH TINKER (Dec. 21, 1779–Apr. 11, 1861), editor, was born in Windham, Conn., the son of Nehemiah Tinker—whom he believed to be a descendant of the Thomas Tinker who came over in the Mayflower—and of Mary (Huntington) Tinker. The family name of his maternal grandmother was Buckingham, and he records that "By request of a relative and intimate friend of my mother's, I was baptized by the name of Joseph Buckingham." (In 1804, for reasons concerning which his usually frank and detailed *Memoirs* are reticent, he secured a legal change of name to Joseph Tinker Buckingham). When he was little more than three years old, his father died, leaving a wife and ten children in indigent circumstances. After various vicissitudes the fam-

ily was broken up, and Joseph was bound out to a farmer until he was sixteen. His schooling was very slight and desultory. After leaving the farm he served an apprenticeship to the printer's trade in Walpole, N. H., Greenfield, Mass., Northampton, and Boston. During one summer he traveled with a theatrical troupe, and at a later time he taught school for a year and a half; but during most of his active career he was printer, publisher, and editor. He carried on the *Polyanthos,* a monthly, 1806–07 and 1812–14; the *Ordeal,* a Federalist weekly, 1809; the *New England Galaxy* (for a time the *New England Galaxy and Masonic Magazine*), a non-political weekly, 1817–28; the *Boston Courier,* a daily founded to advocate protectionist principles in 1824; and the *New England Magazine,* an ambitious and not discreditable attempt to give Boston a literary monthly, 1831–34. The last-named periodical was established in part to give an opportunity to the proprietor's son, a young man of promise who performed many of the editorial duties for the first two years, but who died at the age of twenty-three. Buckingham continued as editor of the *Boston Daily Courier* until 1848. At that time he felt himself unable to support Gen. Taylor, the Whig nominee for the presidency, and rather than inflict on his financial backers the loss that would follow if the paper repudiated the Whig ticket he withdrew from the editorship. For the rest of his life he is said to have been an occasional contributor to various journals, and he wrote and compiled *Specimens of Newspaper Literature, with Personal Memoirs, Anecdotes, and Reminiscences* (1850) and *Personal Memoirs and Recollections of Editorial Life* (1852).

As an editor Buckingham had qualities that led his eulogists to describe him as "a terrible opponent," and "the most independent editor of his time." He not only engaged other editors in ferocious word-combats, which was the custom of his age and often led to no serious break in personal friendship, but he often became involved in troubles with others who resented his outspoken comments. The first of these difficulties that he records came in the days of the *Polyanthos,* when Mr. Poe, father of Edgar Allan Poe, called to chastise him for his strictures on Mrs. Poe as an actress. He was later the defendant in several libel suits, and he had quarrels with many who did not wish to resort either to personal violence or to the law. It was no doubt partly because of his fearless aggressiveness that none of his publications was highly successful financially; and he seems to have felt keenly the lack of a substantial reward for his labors. With all his readiness to open an attack on anything that he regarded as false he was never seriously accused of intellectual dishonesty, and he was usually on the side of reforms that time has approved. Both he and his periodicals commanded the respect and support of New Englanders of importance. Mrs. Rowson, William Austin, Edward Everett, and others of equal note in their day wrote for the *Galaxy*. The list of contributors to the *New England Magazine* included Frothingham, Edward Everett, Story, Hildreth, Longfellow, Holmes, and many more. The columns of the *Boston Courier* were open to contributors and correspondents of all opinions; and prominent New Englanders, particularly those of liberal views, often took advantage of the liberty extended them. It was in the *Courier* that Lowell printed "The Present Crisis" and the first series of the "Biglow Papers," and it was to "Mister Buckinum," personally, that the letters of Hosea Biglow which introduced some of the numbers were addressed.

Buckingham was for seven years a representative and for four years a senator in the Massachusetts legislature. For the earlier terms he was elected as a Whig, but after his refusal to support Taylor in 1848 he was nominated by the Free Soil and the Democratic parties as a union candidate for state senator. In the address issued at this time he denied that he had changed his views, and characteristically exclaimed: *Left the Whig party! . . . the party left me.*"

[The chief sources of information regarding Buckingham's early life and active career are the *Memoirs* mentioned above, which all subsequent sketches seem to have followed. Obituary notices and tributes appeared in the *Boston Transcript*, Apr. 11, 1861 (reprinted, *Living Age*, LXIX, 447), and the *Boston Courier*, Apr. 12, 1861. Interesting bits of self-revelation are found in many of his published editorials and addresses to his readers. He touched the life of his time in many ways, and anecdotes and personal estimates are found in the biographies, letters, and personal memoirs of other New Englanders.]   W. B. C.

BUCKINGHAM, WILLIAM ALFRED (May 28, 1804–Feb. 5, 1875), governor of Connecticut, senator, was born in Lebanon, New London County, Conn., the son of Samuel and Joanna (Matson) Buckingham. He attended the local schools and afterward the Bacon Academy in Colchester. Until he was twenty, he worked on the home farm. Then he clerked in a Norwich dry-goods shop; was employed for a brief time in a wholesale establishment in New York; and finally in 1826 opened at Norwich a dry-goods store of his own. In 1830 he also took up the manufacture of ingrain carpet, then much in vogue. In the same year he was married to Eliza Ripley. Both the dry-goods business and carpet-weaving he relinquished in 1848 to help organize the Hayward Rubber Company. Its plant for the making of India-rubber goods was situated in Colchester and he became its treasurer. Twice—in 1849–50 and again in 1856–57—he served as mayor of Norwich. In 1858 he was elected governor on the ticket of the newly-formed Republican party. Reëlected seven consecutive times, he was in office eight years, the longest period of service of any Connecticut governor since the days of Oliver Wolcott (1817–27).

In 1860 his opponent was Thomas H. Seymour, sometimes called "the Democratic war-horse," who had been governor in 1850–53. The contest was watched with peculiar interest, particularly in the South. Buckingham won by the close margin of 541 votes. Abraham Lincoln, already known to the East through his Cooper Union speech of Feb. 27, 1860, visited Connecticut in March of that year and met the man who was to be one of the relatively small group of distinguished "war governors," and who was to render him much the same kind of support that Trumbull had given Washington. Of Buckingham it has been said, "The military and civil history of Connecticut during the war of 1861–65, is almost wholly the story of his administration" (*Representative Men of Connecticut*, 1894, p. 6). On Jan. 17, 1861, Buckingham issued to the state militia a proclamation of warning, advising readiness for "any exigency." Nevertheless when the President on Apr. 15 summoned to arms 75,000 three months militia, so far from ready were the Connecticut forces that the State could not furnish even the one regiment fixed as her quota. Buckingham on his own responsibility had already ordered equipments for 5,000 men; and although without due authority, he now called for a regiment of volunteers. In May the General Assembly met, ratified what Buckingham had done, and voted $2,000,000 for military purposes. Connecticut's first regiment did not arrive in Washington until May 13, but it arrived fully prepared for active duty. Two more regiments followed. Though he did not resort to the draft, Buckingham eventually furnished during the period of the war no less than 54,882 volunteers—this at a time when the population numbered but 461,000 and the voters only about 80,000. The governor's concern for the welfare of Connecticut troops was unfailing. Both the national administration and the citizens of his state had particular confidence in his ability and spirit.

After two years of private life, he was elected (1868) to the United States Senate, to serve from Mar. 4, 1869. There, respected for his personal qualities, he was also valued for his services—especially as a conscientious and hardworking member of the committees on commerce and on Indian affairs (chairman). He died shortly before his term would have expired. His associate John J. Ingalls said of him, "While the powers of his intellect were upon a high plane, yet were I called upon to define the impression that remains strongest with me, I should say it was that of incomparable rectitude and dignity" (*Memorial Addresses . . . Delivered in the Senate and House of Representatives*). Buckingham was a corporate member of the American Board of Commissioners for Foreign Missions and the moderator of the first National Council of the Congregational Churches (1865); and he became president of the American Temperance Union. He was among the founders of Norwich Free Academy (1856) and the benefactors of the Yale Divinity School. In him strong convictions and a high ideal of public service were united to a winning temperament and an old-school dignity and courtesy. On June 18, 1884, a badly-placed bronze statue of him, modeled by Olin L. Warner, was unveiled in the battle-flag vestibule of the capitol at Hartford.

[S. G. Buckingham (a brother), *The Life of Wm. A. Buckingham* (Springfield, Mass., 1894); F. W. Chapman, *The Buckingham Family* (Hartford, 1872); W. A. Croffut and J. M. Morris, *The Military and Civil Hist. of Connecticut during the War of 1861–65* (1868); Alexander Johnston, *Connecticut* (1887); F. C. Norton, *The Governors of Connecticut* (1905); I. N. Tarbox, *Sketch of Wm. Alfred Buckingham* (1876), reprinted from the *Cong. Quarterly* for April 1876. The date of Buckingham's death is sometimes given as Feb. 3, but this is erroneous.]   G. S. B.

BUCKLAND, CYRUS (Aug. 10, 1799–Feb. 26, 1891), inventor, was born at East Hartford (now Manchester), Conn., the youngest in the family of eleven children belonging to George and Elizabeth Buckland. His youth was that of the farmer's son of the period: his time was spent in attending school a few months each year and in helping with the farm work. An older brother was practising his trade of wheelwright in the neighborhood, and in helping him Cyrus gained considerable mechanical knowledge and experience by the time he came of age. When twenty-two he left home and went to Monson, Mass., where he obtained employment in a cotton-machinery manufacturing plant. This kind of work apparently appealed to him for he continued in it for the next seven years both in Monson and in Chicopee Falls, Mass. A slump in the cotton business in 1828 necessitated his finding work elsewhere and he entered the Government Armory at Springfield, Mass., as a pattern maker. He continued here for twenty-nine years until poor health compelled him to give up all active work. During the first ten years of his service Buckland rose to the position of proof-master and inspector of barrels but as early as 1833 a note appears on the pay-roll opposite his name as "making patterns for new machines." The system of interchangeability of parts was being especially applied in firearms manufacture during this period and afforded many opportunities to Buckland to apply his inventive powers and mechanical skill. In 1843 he was instrumental in the manufacture of an eccentric bit and auger used in cutting the lock, guard plate, side plate, breech plate, rod spring, and barrels to gunstocks. He perfected a change in the form of the cone for percussion muskets in 1847, and devised the machines and tools to alter flintlock muskets to percussion on Dr. Edward Maynard's plan in 1848. In 1846 Buckland made improvements in Blanchard's system of making gun-stocks which resulted in doubling the previous production and in a fourfold gain in output over hand-made stocks. This increase was effected by building thirteen machines each one of which had a special function to perform in the process which transformed the lumber as it came from the mills into gunstocks, completed save for final rubbing. In 1854 Buckland devised the machines to manufacture a lock and chamber breech for altering rifles to the Maynard percussion type. In no single instance up to this time had he applied for a patent on any of the improvements which he had made, and private manufacturers of firearms both in the United States and other countries availed themselves of his devices. When, therefore, he was called upon in 1855 to design a rifling machine to cut a groove of a regularly decreasing depth from the breech to the muzzle, he decided, upon designing such a machine, to patent it, and so notified the secretary of war. This was his only patent and it was a year after his retirement in 1857 that Congress, on the recommendation of the secretary of war, J. B. Floyd, paid Buckland $10,000 for the government rights to his invention. He relinquished his duties in the armory in November 1857, as inspector of arms and master machinist, but continued to reside in Springfield until his death thirty-four years later. He was married at Monson on May 18, 1824, to Mary A. Locke, and the two lived to observe their sixty-sixth wedding anniversary, surviving their three children and leaving two grandchildren.

[Sources of information on Cyrus Buckland are original correspondence and reports of the U. S. War Dept., and the *Springfield Daily Republican*, Feb. 27, 1891.]   C. W. M.

BUCKLAND, RALPH POMEROY (Jan. 20, 1812–May 27, 1892), lawyer, soldier, was the grandson of Stephen Buckland, of East Hartford, Conn., a Revolutionary artillery captain who died on a British prison ship, and the son of Ralph and Anna (Kent) Buckland. He was born in Ravenna, Ohio, whither his parents had recently moved from Massachusetts, and where his father died not long afterward. His mother marying again, Ralph Pomeroy, as the eldest of a numerous family, was, while quite young, thrown partly upon his own resources, living much of the time with an uncle, helping upon the farm, and acquiring the rudiments of an education in the country school. At the age of eighteen he descended the Ohio and Mississippi Rivers with a boatload of western produce. Finding employment at New Orleans, he remained there for three years; then, returning to Ohio, he attended Kenyon College for a year, afterward reading law under attorneys at Middlebury and Canfield until admitted to the bar in 1837. Beginning practise at Fremont almost penniless, he prospered, married Charlotte Boughton, who traced descent from William Bradford, won the confidence of his neighbors, and held a succession of local offices. In 1848 he went as delegate to the Whig national convention which nominated Gen. Taylor for the presidency. During the Free-Soil controversies he was carried from his old party moorings into the incipient Republican organization. In 1855 he was elected to the state Senate, serving for two terms. He organized the 72nd Ohio Volunteer Infantry in the autumn of 1861, was mustered into the United States service early in 1862, and was soon assigned to the command of the fourth brigade of Sherman's division. This brigade was the only unit of its size in Sherman's army that retained its organization during the hard fighting at Pittsburg Landing and Shiloh, and by many critics is credited with preventing a complete disaster to the Union forces. Buckland was especially commended by Sherman in his report on these engagements (*Official Records*, Army, 1 ser. X, pt. I, 266–69). He continued field service till January 1864 when he was placed in command of the District of Memphis. In August 1866 he was commissioned brevet major-general, United States Volunteers, for meritorious service. Meantime his friends at home had elected him to Congress, and in January 1865, he had resigned from the army preparatory to taking his seat. After two consecutive terms he resumed his law practise at Fremont, but continued to participate in public affairs. In 1870 he became president of the Ohio Soldiers' and Sailors' Orphans Home, at Xenia; in 1876 he was a delegate to the Republican national convention which nominated Hayes; and from 1878 to 1881 he held the post of government director of the Union Pacific Railroad. In early manhood he was slender and somewhat dyspeptic, but systematic out-of-door exercise resulted in robust health in middle life. Although a semi-invalid during his last few years, he continued active to the day of his death, going to his home from his office only two or three hours before his demise. Rutherford B. Hayes, a law partner from 1846 to 1849, thought that Buckland's appearance was "against him" (Charles R. Williams, *Diary and Letters of R. B. Hayes*, I, 191); but a post-war portrait gives no such impression. On the morning following Buckland's death Hayes entered in his diary this estimate: "a strong and conspicuous figure for more than forty years, at the bar, as a citizen, as a public man, and especially as a soldier. His traits . . . were honesty, amazing industry, tenacity of purpose, and perseverance, and a courage, physical and moral, unsurpassed" (*Ibid.*, V, 86–87).

[There are biographical sketches of Buckland in *The Biog. Cyc. of the State of Ohio*, vol. I (1883–91); Geo. I. Reed, *Bench and Bar of Ohio* (1897); and Basil Meek, ed., *Twentieth Century Hist. of Sandusky County, Ohio* (1909). Buckland's military career may be traced in the *Official Records* (Army), and is briefly summarized in Whitelaw Reid, *Ohio in the War* (1868). Many allusions to him are to be found in C. R. Williams, ed., *Diary and Letters of R. B. Hayes* (1922–26).]
H. C. H.

BUCKLER, THOMAS HEPBURN (Jan. 4, 1812–Apr. 20, 1901), physician, son of William Buckler, a merchant who emigrated from Warminster, England, in 1783, and his wife, Anne Thomas Hepburn, was born at "Evergreen," near Baltimore, Md. He was educated at St. Mary's College (Baltimore) and in 1835 obtained from the University of Maryland his degree of M.D., for which he presented a thesis on Animal Heat. After spending a short time in the office of his brother, Dr. John Buckler, who had a large practise in Baltimore, he left in 1836 for Europe on a sailing vessel, and spent six months in the clinics of Paris where he studied under Louis, Chomel, and Ricord. After his return to Baltimore he became physician to the City and County Almshouse for some years. During the period from 1850 to 1855 his practise rapidly increased; he attended Chief Justice Taney and President Buchanan, and was consulted by Gen. R. E. Lee (*Recollections and Letters of Gen. Robert E. Lee*, 1904, pp. 412, 419–20). His sympathies during the Civil War were with the South and at the close of the conflict, partly as a result of the outcome, he moved to Paris where he remained from 1866 to 1890 practising under license from the French Government. His medical writings, which are fully listed by Quinan, were bold and original. He was an early advocate of laparotomy for intestinal obstruction (*American Journal of the Medical Sciences*, Jan. 1869), recommended the use of ammonium phosphate for the treatment of rheumatism (*Ibid.*, Jan. 1846) and wrote extensively on the pathology of uterine affections (*Boston Medical and Surgical Journal*, Jan. 15, 22, Sept. 16, Oct. 28, 1880). His most important contribution, however, was to the study of cholera and other epidemic infections. In 1851 he wrote *A History of Epidemic Cholera, as it appeared at the Baltimore City and County Almshouse, in the Summer of 1849, with Some Remarks on the Medical Topography and Diseases of this Region.* "If the history of epidemic cholera," he said, "as it first appeared throughout the country in 1832 be compared with the invasion of 1849, it will be remarked, as one of the most striking facts connected with this disease, that it returned to every place which it had visited during the first epidemic, unless, during the interval, the locality had undergone some marked change or entire renovation." From this he argued that sanitary improvement of the districts which had been revisited was urgently needed. He proposed the filling of the "basin" or inner harbor of Baltimore with the earth from "Federal Hill," and was of opinion that the waters of the Gunpowder River should be used to supply the city, a suggestion not carried out until 1875 (see W. T. Howard, Jr., *Public Health Administration . . . in Baltimore*, 1924, pp. 128, 132). In 1853 he also published a useful monograph *On the Etiology, Pathology and Treatment of Fibrobronchitis and Rheumatic Pneumonia.* Owing to his trust in *vis medicatrix Naturæ*, Buckler preferred to the use of drugs, whenever possible, diet, exercise, baths, mineral water (especially at the Virginia "Healing Springs"), and residence in sea or mountain air. He was thus in the fifties among the first to treat tuberculosis by no other means than life in the open air, rest, and nourishment (especially with cod-liver oil). Drugs he believed in only for some specific purpose. Personally independent and somewhat eccentric, he was much sought after on account of his wide reading, charm of manner, and brilliant conversational powers. He was twice married: in 1861 to Anne, daughter of the Rev. Richard Fuller, who died within a year; and on Nov. 21, 1865, to Eliza, daughter of John Ridgely, and widow of John Campbell White, who died in 1894.

[*Baltimore News*, Apr. 22, 1901; W. T. Howard, in *Trans. Medic. and Chir. Fac. Md.*, 1903, pp. 46–40; J. R. Quinan, *Medic. Annals of Baltimore*, 1884, pp. 71–72; E. F. Cordell, *Medic. Annals of Md.*, 1903, pp. 338–39; personal information.]   J.F.F.

BUCKLEY, JAMES MONROE (Dec. 16, 1836–Feb. 8, 1920), Methodist clergyman, was born in Rahway, N. J., the son of the Rev. John Buckley. The latter, a native of Lancashire, England, emigrated to this country in 1827, became a Methodist preacher, married Abbie Lonsdale Monroe, and soon died of consumption, as had both his parents, leaving behind James, not yet six, and another son still younger. The boys were brought up in the home of their grandfather, Judge Monroe, at Mount Holly, N. J., their mother helping to support them by teaching. James early displayed a restless energy, quickness of mind, varied interests, ability as a public speaker, and skill in debate, but also a tendency to the family malady. Because of his slender means and poor health, his schooling was limited to several years of preparatory work at Pennington Seminary, and a year in Wesleyan University where he enrolled in 1856. So effective a speaker had he become by this time, however, that he went about stumping for Frémont in the presidential campaign of that year. After having taught several schools, and supplied a Wesleyan Methodist church at Exeter, N. H., in 1859 he was admitted to the New Hampshire Conference of the Methodist Episcopal Church, and was immediately appointed to the church at Dover, one of the largest in the state. His advancement was rapid and his reputation steadily increased. After pastorates in Manchester, N. H., Detroit, Stamford, Conn., and Brooklyn, in 1880 the General Conference elected him editor of the *Christian Advocate*, which office he held for thirty-two years, during which time the paper became one of the best-known religious journals in the country.

He was married three times: first, on Aug. 2, 1864, to Eliza A. Burns of Detroit; second, on Apr. 22, 1874, to Mrs. Sarah Isabella (French) Staples, a widow of Detroit; and, third, on Aug. 23, 1886, to Adelaide Shackford Hill of Dover, N. H. He was small of stature and slight of frame, but had a massive head, almost entirely bald. Dark, thin whiskers and mustache covered his face. His eyes were round, dark, and steady. When a young man the doctors told him his days were numbered, but by keeping much in the open air and by taking long walks and breathing exercises, he held the disease in check. Requirements of health, calls for lectures, and an acquisitive mind, made him a traveler, and he visited almost every place of interest in the United States, Canada, and Europe, and parts of Asia and Africa. Though but twenty-seven when he first went abroad, in 1863, his patriotic addresses had made him known to national leaders, and he carried letters from Horace Greeley, Charles Sumner and others to members of the British Parliament, certifying his fitness to explain the Constitution with reference to the Civil War. Many accounts of his travels appeared in his own and other periodicals, and he published *The Midnight Sun, the Tsar, and the Nihilist* (1886) and *Travels in Three Continents* (1895). His meager schooling was no handicap. Possessing a virile and versatile mind, a retentive memory, and the ability to read with great rapidity, he acquired knowledge of extraordinary extent and variety. A resourceful, logical debater, well informed on everything pertaining to Methodism, he was a power in ecclesiastical councils, being a member of eleven General Conferences, and of the Ecumenical Conferences at London (1881), Washington (1891), and Toronto (1911). Although a conservative and opposed to many changes that were finally effected, he left a decided impress upon the laws and institutions of his church. In addition to the works mentioned, his principal publications include *Christians and the Theater* (1875) in which he holds that, "No habit which does not imply a positive renunciation of morality is more pernicious than that of theater going"; *Oats or Wild Oats?* (1885), containing much sane discussion of the problems of young men; *Faith Healing, Christian Science, and Kindred Phenomena* (1892); *A History of Methodists in the United States* (1896), being vol. V in the American Church History Series; *The Fundamentals and Their Contrasts* (1906); *The Wrong and Peril of Woman's Suffrage* (1909); *Theory and Practice of Foreign Missions* (1911); *Constitutional and Parliamentary History of the Methodist Episcopal Church* (1912).

[Geo. P. Mains, *Jas. Monroe Buckley* (1917); *Who's Who in America*, 1918–19; *N. Y. Times*, Feb. 9, 1920; *Christian Advocate*, Feb. 19, 1920; *Outlook*, Feb. 18, 1920.]   H. E. S.

BUCKLEY, SAMUEL BOTSFORD (May 9, 1809–Feb. 18, 1883), botanist, field naturalist, was born at Torrey, in Yates County, N. Y. He graduated from Wesleyan University, Middletown, Conn., in the class of 1836, studied medicine at the College of Physicians and Surgeons in New York, 1842–43, and received the degree of Ph.D. from Waco University, Tex., in 1872. After leaving college he taught for a time in Illinois and Alabama and for two years was principal of the Allenton Academy in Wilcox County in the latter state. In 1842 he visited various parts of Alabama, collecting plants, and secured a skeleton of a zeuglodon seventy feet in length. He also made collections in the mountains of Tennessee, North Carolina, and South Carolina, where he obtained twenty-four new species of plants and a new genus which bears his name. In 1843 he went to Florida to collect plants and shells. The following twelve years were passed on the homestead farm, and then for a time in 1855 and 1856 he was employed in a bookstore at Yellow Springs, Ohio. The summer of 1858 was spent in the mountains of North Carolina and Tennessee in the determination of the elevation of some of the higher peaks in the southern Alleghanies, and in the following years he traveled through the South collecting material for a Supplement to Michaux and Nuttall's *Sylva*.

In 1860–61 he was assistant geologist and naturalist on the Texas Geological Survey and began his labors in the state which became the scene of his activities during his later years. With the outbreak of the Civil War he returned North and from 1862 to 1865 occupied the position of chief examiner in the Statistical Department of the United States Sanitary Commission. After the close of the War Buckley returned to Texas and succeeded in securing appointment as state geologist, but the work of the Survey was terminated in 1867. Upon the organization of the Second Geological Survey of Texas he again received appointment as state geologist from 1874 to 1877 during which time he issued two reports.

After his retirement from office he devoted his time largely to literary work. In 1871–72 he was agricultural and scientific editor of the *State Gazette* in Austin, and for some years he was engaged in preparing a work on the geology and natural history of Texas. He also prepared several articles in 1881 for the *Library of Universal Knowledge*. His more important papers included his description of the skeleton of zeuglodon and of his new plants, several entomological contributions, and the account of his work in determining elevations in the mountains of North Carolina and Tennessee. Apparently the narrative of his botanical trips and his natural history of Texas were never published. His field work in the South is commemorated in the names of the black-backed rock squirrel of Texas (*Citellus variegatus buckleyi*) and the peculiar parasitic shrub *Buckleya,* and in "Buckley's Peak," one of the highest elevations in the Great Smoky Mountains in Tennessee. He was married three times: (1) in

1852 to Charlotte Sullivan of Naples, N. Y., who died in 1854; (2) in 1855 to Sarah Porter of Naples who died in 1858; and (3) in 1864 to Libbie Myers of Elbridge, N. Y. His death occurred in Austin, Tex.

[Geo. P. Merrill, *First One Hundred Years of Am. Geology* (1924), pp. 401–02; sketch by S. H. Wright in *Bull. of the Torrey Bot. Club*, XI, 46; *Am. Jour. of Sci.*, 3 ser., XXIX, pp. 171–72; *Bull. 109, U. S. Nat. Museum*, pp. 474–80; *Alumni Record of Wesleyan Univ.*, 1883, containing a chronology, p. 10, and a bibliography, pp. 547–49.]   T. S. P.

BUCKMINSTER, JOSEPH STEVENS (May 26, 1784–June 9, 1812), Unitarian clergyman, author, descended in the seventh generation from Thomas Buckminster of Scituate and Brookline who came to America about 1640, was the son of the Rev. Joseph Buckminster and his wife Sarah Stevens, daughter of the Rev. Benjamin Stevens of Kittery Point, N. H. He was born in Portsmouth, N. H., during his father's pastorate of the North Church in that city. Educated largely at home by his father, he went to Phillips Exeter Academy at eleven, finished his preparation in a year, and in 1797 entered the sophomore class of Harvard College, where he took his first degree in 1800 at the age of sixteen. During the next two years, which he spent as an instructor at Exeter, he suffered the first of a series of epileptic attacks, which foreshadowed an early death. In 1803 he returned to live as a tutor in the family of his relative Theodore Lyman of Boston and Waltham, where his duties left him ample time to continue his reading, both in general literature and in theology, to which he now turned. With several generations of devoted service to the church behind him, Buckminster's choice of the ministry as his profession was natural, and his association at this time with Dr. James Freeman, minister of King's Chapel in Boston, influenced his decision to break away from his orthodox inheritance and join the Unitarian movement, then well under way, although no break had yet occurred in the Congregational ranks. After a year of further study, he preached his first sermon as a candidate for the ministry, in the spring of 1804, at York, Me., and shortly afterward was called to the pulpit of the Brattle Street Church in Boston, where he was ordained and installed, Jan. 30, 1805. His defection from the orthodox creed had bitterly disappointed his father, but the latter nevertheless consented to preach the ordination sermon (published in Boston, 1805), a composition of unusual tenderness and pathos. After a brilliant year in Brattle Street, Buckminster's health failed, and he went to Europe in the spring of 1806, remaining over

a year. He traveled part of the time with his friend Rev. Samuel Cooper Thacher, preached occasionally in Great Britain, and, having familiarized himself with British and Continental scholarship, brought home a library of some three thousand volumes, unique in New England at that time for its size, rarity, and scholarly character. The introduction of Biblical scholarship into this country must be credited in large measure to the efforts of Buckminster after his return (letter of Edward Everett, his successor at Brattle Street, in W. B. Sprague, *Annals of the American Pulpit*, VIII, 1865, 400; H. B. Adams, *Life and Writings of Jared Sparks*, I, 104). His preaching was also an innovation, combining the results of his critical studies and a deep interest in human affairs with enthusiasm and a freshness of point of view which drew to him eager support and great popularity. Although his pastoral duties were exacting, Buckminster by no means confined his efforts to his congregation. He secured the publication of, and saw through the press, the American edition of Griesbach's Greek Testament (2 vols., 1809), and he delivered the Phi Beta Kappa oration at Harvard in 1809 (*Monthly Anthology*, Sept. 1809, VII, 145–58). He was a member during its entire existence of the Anthology Club of Boston, a small group of literary men who met weekly to dine and discuss original contributions, which were later published in the *Monthly Anthology*. From this circle grew the Boston Athenæum, of which Buckminster was a founder, in 1807. When the Dexter Lectureship on Biblical Criticism was established at Harvard in 1811, Buckminster was given the first appointment, but he had scarcely begun his preparation for these duties when death came to him in a severe epileptic attack at the parsonage on Court Street, Boston, in the twenty-eighth year of his age. Two identical Stuart portraits of Buckminster, painted about 1810, show a fine and unusually intelligent face, but betray a lack of physical strength (L. Park, *Gilbert Stuart*, I, 184–86; III, 78). His stature was somewhat below the medium, a defect amply compensated by his grace and dignity of carriage.

[Mrs. Eliza Buckminster Lee, *Memoirs of Rev. Jos. Buckminster, D.D., and of his son Rev. Jos. Stevens Buckminster* (1849); Wm. B. Sprague, *Annals of the Am. Pulpit, VIII* (1865), pp. 384–406; Jas. Savage, *Mass. Hist. Soc. Colls.*, 2 ser., II, 271–74; Andrews Norton, *General Repository*, Oct. 1812, II, 306–14, and Rev. Samuel Cooper Thacher's memoir, prefixed (pp. xi–lxii) to the first collection of Buckminster's sermons (1814). Buckminster's only separate publications in his lifetime were funeral sermons on Gov. Jas. Sullivan and Rev. Wm. Emerson, and a hymn book edited for his congregation, the earliest collection of Unitarian character published in this country, which was the subject of considerable controversy (cf. *The Panoplist and Missionary Mag.*, Sept. and Nov., 1808, n.s. I, 170–77, 275–82). Two volumes of collected works by and about Buckminster were published in Boston by Jas. Munroe & Co. in 1839. *The Jour. of the Anthology Soc.* (1910) records Buckminster's activities in the society, and identifies his contributions to the magazine. He also contributed articles, reviews, and translations to the *Literary Review* and the *General Repository*. A catalogue of his library was printed previous to its sale at auction in August 1812. For Buckminster's part in the development of American Unitarianism, see H. C. Goddard, *Studies in New Eng. Transcendentalism* (Columbia doctoral dissertation, 1908), p. 27.]   M. H. T.

BUCKNELL, WILLIAM (Apr. 1, 1811–Mar. 5, 1890), business man, philanthropist, was born near Marcus Hook, Delaware County, Pa., the son of William and Sarah (Walker) Bucknell. His father, one of the pioneer settlers of Delaware County, had been a Lincolnshire farmer and carpenter. The boy's education consisted only of a short period in a country school. He then learned the trade of a wood carver and as he had been taught thrift at home was soon able, with some small savings, to start a business of his own. Even as early as this, through the teachings of his father, he set aside a tenth of his earnings for philanthropic and religious purposes. At twenty-five he married Harriet Ashton. Soon after, he found speculation in real estate more profitable than following a trade. By purchase of outlying land, by building, and by taking contracts for constructing gas and waterworks in various cities and accepting stock as payment, he made a fortune. Later in his life he was a broker in Philadelphia and dealt in securities and improvement of real estate. He was a large owner in railroads, various coal and iron mines, and other property. He was not desirous of political office nor was he a member of clubs, but he took a great interest in his church and in religious and educational philanthropies. His many gifts included over $140,000 to the University of Lewisburg, renamed in 1887 Bucknell University, and over $525,000 to missions and churches of the Baptist denomination. His ability to carry out his policy of giving away one-tenth of his fortune developed as that fortune grew until toward the end of his life his gifts averaged $1,000 a week. At his death he had given a total of a million dollars for public purposes. A man of strong likes and dislikes and independent in all his activities, he showed these characteristics by withdrawing from connection with the University of Lewisburg although his name was continued on the list of trustees until 1863, because he disapproved of the financial management. When David Jayne Hill was elected president of the college in 1879 he reënlisted

Bucknell's interest on a thoroughly businesslike basis. Bucknell became chairman of the board of trustees and remained so until his death. He had married in 1839 Margaret Crozer, and at her decease Emma Ward.

[H. Hall, *America's Successful Men of Affairs* (1896), vol. II; J. H. Harris, *Thirty Years as President of Bucknell, with Baccalaureate and Other Addresses* (1926); *Appletons' Annual Cyc.* (1890); Phila. *Press*, Mar. 7, 1890.]   M. A. K.

BUCKNER, SIMON BOLIVAR (Apr. 1, 1823–Jan. 8, 1914), Confederate soldier, was born of English ancestry near Munfordville in Hart County, Ky., the son of Aylett Hartswell Buckner and Elizabeth Ann (Morehead) Buckner. His father was a farmer and iron manufacturer, who had taken part in the second war with Great Britain and who was present at the battle of the Thames. Simon received whatever education Hart County could afford and when seventeen years old he was appointed to West Point Military Academy. Four years later (in 1844) he finished the course there in a class not conspicuous for subsequent greatness and was immediately made brevet second lieutenant of the 2nd Regiment of Infantry and stationed at Sackets Harbor, N. Y. The next year he was appointed assistant professor of ethics at West Point but in 1846 on the outbreak of the war with Mexico he was released at his own request to enter active service. He was now attached to the 6th Infantry as second lieutenant where he served as regimental quartermaster from August until December 1847. At first he was attached to Gen. Taylor's army and was with him at Saltillo. He was then joined to Gen. Scott's command and was actively engaged at the siege and capture of Vera Cruz. He was in almost every engagement from the sea to Mexico City, and for bravery at Churubusco he was brevetted first lieutenant and for gallantry at Molino del Rey he was promoted to the rank of captain. Before leaving Mexico he visited the volcano of Popocatepetl and wrote an account of his trip which was published in *Putnam's Magazine* (April 1853).

He returned to West Point in August 1848 as assistant professor in infantry tactics and filled this position until January 1850 when he was ordered to New York harbor. He remained here only a few months before going to Fort Snelling in Minnesota Territory. In September 1851 he was moved to Fort Atkinson on the Upper Arkansas River. Here he came in contact with the wild life of the Indians for a year, after which he was ordered back to New York where he served as captain in the subsistence department.

Seeing no great future in the army and no private fortune whatever, he resigned in 1855 to enter business, engaging in work which led him to short residences in Nashville, Tenn., and in Chicago. At the latter place he was made superintendent in charge of the construction of the Chicago customs house, and while here he laid in city real estate the beginnings of a small fortune. When the difficulties with Brigham Young and his Mormons arose in Utah, Buckner was made colonel in a regiment of Illinois volunteers, who were, however, never called into service. In 1858 he removed to Louisville.

Buckner had shown good business sense and had accumulated a considerable amount of wealth, but he could never quite forget his love and regard for military affairs. As the dangers of a civil war approached he showed no disposition to take part in politics and in the sectional debate as did many others; he chose rather to express his energies in the way of military preparedness for Kentucky. In 1860 he drew up an elaborate militia bill which the legislature adopted in March of that year. By its provisions all able-bodied men between eighteen and forty-five years of age were made to constitute what was termed the enrolled militia, from whom should be selected the active militia or state guards. The legislature at the time made him inspector-general with the rank of major-general. He now feverishly set to work to develop a well-trained and well-armed force which he hoped might play an important part in any war that might come. With funds that he secured from private sources he held an encampment in the summer of 1860 near Louisville, which was made to assume much the purpose of an officers' training camp. By the beginning of 1861 he had developed a well-organized army of sixty-one companies. For the purpose of further arming the state, he advocated the expenditure of $3,500,000, but by this time the interplay of the various forces of party desires and ambitions led many Kentuckians to fear for the outcome if the state guards were enlarged and armed under the command of Buckner. The result was that most of the money spent for military purposes by the state during the summer of 1861 went to another force called the home guards, over whom Buckner had no control.

Out of the initial confusion came the state's neutrality doctrine which was fully adopted by May 24, 1861. In the meantime Gov. Beriah Magoffin, hoping to avert war, attempted to set up a League of Neutrality among the border states, North and South in the Mississippi Valley, and sent Buckner to the states of Missouri and Tennessee to secure their adherence. Buckner succeeded in his mission, but the league was never organized because of the attitude of the states north of the Ohio River. Kentucky alone having declared her neutrality, Buckner in June entered into negotiations with Gen. George B. McClellan, who commanded Federal troops north of the Ohio, and secured an agreement wherein the latter promised to respect Kentucky's position. On June 24, carrying out the pact agreed upon, Buckner sent six companies of troops to Columbus, on the Mississippi River, to relieve the danger of invasion by the Confederates; but a little later when Federal forces from Cairo invaded Kentucky and when Buckner called on McClellan to act, he refused. This ended the agreement and strongly inclined Buckner toward the Confederates. During the summer of 1861 Gov. Magoffin sent Buckner to Washington to secure Lincoln's adherence to Kentucky's neutrality. Accompanied by John J. Crittenden he saw the President but received a cautious and equivocal answer, though the President offered him a commission as brigadier-general in the Federal army. Still bent on maintaining Kentucky's neutrality Buckner declined the offer.

By July the Union leadership in Kentucky had become so strong and had so hampered the military power that Buckner resigned his command, and in September visited Richmond, the capital of the Confederacy, where he was offered a commission in the Confederate army. This, too, he declined. On his return he heard at Nashville of Gen. Leonidas Polk's invasion of Kentucky and seizure of Columbus. He considered it a great political blunder and sought without avail to have the Confederates withdraw. When the state legislature officially abandoned neutrality, he issued an address in which he bitterly denounced that body for betraying the state. He forthwith joined the Confederates, receiving a commission as brigadier-general. His control over the state guards and his popularity with them had been so complete that many had already left to join the Confederates and now most of those remaining departed to join their comrades. Bitterly disappointed, the Union leaders declared Buckner a traitor and in November the Federal army seized his estate in Hart County.

On joining the Confederates Buckner was attached to Gen. Albert Sidney Johnston's command and stationed at Bowling Green. On the retreat of the Confederates out of Kentucky he was ordered with eight regiments in February 1862 to go to the rescue of Fort Donelson. After Gen. Grant's forces had surrounded the fort Buckner sought to cut his way through the Federal lines, but did not succeed, owing to the failure of Generals Floyd and Pillow to coöperate.

When capture seemed inevitable, Floyd and Pillow escaped and left Buckner in command. Soon thereafter the latter was forced to surrender unconditionally to Grant. He was taken as a prisoner first to Camp Morton in Indianapolis, and soon afterward to Fort Warren in Boston harbor where he was kept in solitary confinement until his exchange in the following August (1862). While Buckner was in prison, Garret Davis, a United States senator from Kentucky, sought unsuccessfully to have him turned over to the civil authorities to be tried for treason. After Buckner's return to the Confederacy he was promoted to be a major-general and was assigned to Gen. Bragg's army in Chattanooga. He took part in Bragg's invasion of Kentucky in the fall of 1862, commanding the 3rd division of infantry under Gen. Hardee. For a time he was detached at Lexington for recruiting service but took his regular command again in time to be present at the battle of Perryville on Oct. 8. In December he was sent by President Davis to build the defenses of Mobile and after four months' work he succeeded in creating a strongly fortified city. In the summer of 1863 he was placed in command of east Tennessee and in September of that year he joined Bragg in northern Georgia. In the battle of Chickamauga which followed he commanded a corps of the left wing. The next year he was put in command of the Department of Louisiana and was made a lieutenant-general. Little fighting took place there, and after Lee's surrender at Appomattox Buckner and General Sterling Price negotiated terms of capitulation with Gen. Canby for the trans-Mississippi armies.

Being denied by the terms of surrender the right to return to Kentucky, Buckner settled in New Orleans where he engaged in newspaper work and in insurance business. In 1866 he became the head of an insurance company. By 1868 the Confederate element in Kentucky had become so completely dominant that Buckner thought it would be to his advantage to return. He received wide applause and immediately became editor of the Louisville *Courier,* a newspaper which during the war had been driven out of the state by the Federal régime. For a number of years Buckner was busied with efforts to regain various properties which had been confiscated. When he had joined the Confederates in 1861 he had deeded some valuable property in the heart of Chicago to a brother-in-law who joined the Federal army, and who before his death willed it back to Buckner. After a long-drawn-out litigation Buckner succeeded in recovering the property, which he sold for $500,000. As a

record of service in the Confederate army was now a great political advantage in Kentucky he received the Democratic nomination for governor in 1887 and was elected by a large majority. His four years' term as governor was creditable but not brilliant. In 1891 he was elected a delegate to the constitutional convention and was instrumental in making the Kentucky constitution of that year. He then returned to his estate, "Glen Lily," near Munfordville, where he carried on farming operations, often engaging in manual labor himself. He visited Louisville frequently and was a familiar figure at the historic Galt House, where he might often be seen in the lobby smoking his corn-cob pipe. In 1896 when the Democrats embraced free silver he bolted the party and was himself nominated for the vice-presidency on a national Democratic ticket headed by John M. Palmer, another native-born Kentuckian. Buckner was active in the campaign and so completely was the Democratic party split in Kentucky that McKinley received the state vote, the first time the Republicans ever received the electoral vote of the state. Buckner died near Munfordville in 1914, the last of the lieutenant-generals of the Confederacy, and was buried in the Frankfort Cemetery.

He was married twice: first in May 1850 to Mary Kingsbury, who died soon after the Civil War, and then in 1885 to Delia H. Claiborne of Richmond, Va. Tall and manly in appearance, he was friendly and considerate to the most lowly, and was always unassuming in whatever position he occupied. He maintained a life-long friendship with Gen. Grant, which began at West Point and was not broken even when he surrendered to Grant at Fort Donelson; he was one of those who offered to come to Grant's assistance in his financial difficulties, and he acted as a pall-bearer at Grant's funeral.

[For Buckner's military career as well as a sketch of his earlier career see E. P. Thompson, *Hist. of the First Ky. Brigade* (1886); *Hist. of the Orphan Brigade* (1898); Jos. Cross, *Papers from the Portfolio of an Army Chaplain;* and E. M. Coulter, *Civil War and Readjustment in Ky.* (1926). The *Official Records* (Army), contain his official military dispatches, and the documents relating to his governorship are in the state library in Frankfort. Obituaries containing appreciations of his life may be found in Louisville *Courier-Journal, Lexington Leader, Lexington Herald,* and *N. Y. Times,* for Jan. 9, 1914.]　　　　　　　　　　E. M. C—r.

BUDD, JOSEPH LANCASTER (July 3, 1835–Dec. 20, 1904), pioneer in horticulture, was born near Peekskill, N. Y. His early life was spent on the farm and he was prepared to take a college course. This plan, however, he was obliged to abandon. In 1857 he moved to Rockport, Ill., where he spent two years in teaching. Then, first at Wheaton, Ill., and soon after at

Shellsburg, Ia., he entered on a successful career as a nurseryman, orchardist, and instructor in horticulture. He was made secretary of the Iowa Horticultural Society and for twenty-one years prepared its annual reports. In 1876 he became professor of horticulture and forestry in the Iowa Agricultural College. Old-world methods and foreign text-books were of subordinate value for the American climate and agricultural conditions. For the great Northwestern states a very different horticultural practise had to be developed. Budd became the leader in this work and one from whom many in this field received their first training and enthusiasm. Following a journey to Russia in 1882, he imported into the Northwest from that country hardier varieties of fruit trees to withstand the severe winters. This work proved to be of the greatest value to the Northwestern states. In Dakota and Manitoba practically the only varieties of apples grown are of Budd's introduction, and hundreds of orchards and groves in the colder parts of the Northwest bear testimony to his great service. His work extended successful fruit-growing much further north than had ever before been possible. Assisted by N. E. Hansen he published in 1902–03 a *Manual of American Horticulture* in two volumes. He was a man of sterling integrity, buoyant nature, considerable literary ability, and great enthusiasm and energy. In 1869, his health broken by his strenuous life, he resigned his active professorship, remaining emeritus professor. He was married on Jan. 26, 1861, to Sarah M. Breed. He died at Phœnix, Ariz.

[*Proc. Iowa Park and Forestry Ass.*, Dec. 1904, p. 116; L. H. Bailey, ed., *Cyc. of Am. Ag.*, vol. IV (1909); Clarence Ray Aurner, *Hist. of Ed. in Iowa*, vol. IV (1916); B. F. Gue, *Hist. of Iowa*, vol. IV (1903).]
E. H. J.

BUEHLER, HUBER GRAY (Dec. 3, 1864–June 20, 1924), educator, was of German descent through his father, David A. Buehler, lawyer, journalist, and president of Pennsylvania College, while through his mother, Fanny Guyon, he traced his ancestry back to the French Huguenot settlers of Staten Island. From both sides came a strong religious heritage which led him to enter the ministry of the Lutheran Church (1889). He was born in Gettysburg, Pa., and except for two years spent in teaching at St. James' College, Maryland (1883–85), he lived in his native town until his twenty-eighth year. Gettysburg provided him an education in its Preparatory School (1877–79), in the Pennsylvania College (1879–83), which granted him its B.A. in 1883 and its M.A. in 1886, and finally in its Lutheran Theological Seminary (1885–89). It offered him also experience in teaching and administration (1887–92) as professor of Latin and Greek in the College and as principal of the Preparatory School.

Meantime in 1891 he received an invitation from Edward G. Coy to join the faculty of the newly-founded Hotchkiss School for boys at Lakeville, Conn. His acceptance ended his connection with Gettysburg except for his return to marry Roberta Wolf in 1892 and for occasional visits with his family. At the formal opening of Hotchkiss in October 1892 he began his new duties as master in English. Of medium height, rather slender build, and somewhat diffident manner, he did not reveal his real power to the casual observer. But his students soon recognized in him a precision and orderliness of thought and an ability to present facts clearly which brought him a wide reputation with the publication of three little books that grew out of his teaching—*Practical Exercises in English* (1895), *A Modern English Grammar* (1900), and, in collaboration with Caroline W. Hotchkiss, *Modern English Lessons* (1903). These qualities were turned to new uses when, after Coy's death, he was appointed headmaster of Hotchkiss (1904) after a year as acting headmaster. His genius for organization brought new vigor and efficiency to the school, whether directed toward enlarging the buildings, beautifying the grounds, or building up a strong teaching staff and attracting able students. His achievement was recognized by election to the presidency of the Headmasters' Association (1914–15). Thoughtful always of the atmosphere of dignity he believed should characterize a great school, he had a handsome study built in the headmaster's house commanding a splendid view of lake and mountains, and arranged carefully every detail of the entertainment of guests and the formal ceremonial of school life. With his enthusiastic support, plans were laid out for the eventual replacement of the old buildings by others at once more beautiful and permanent. As the years passed, his whitening hair and the gradual filling out of his figure made him more and more impressive in appearance, and his natural shyness became overlaid with a certain formality of manner that led his boys to call him "the King," though it failed to conceal from them the essential kindliness, simplicity, and genuine humor of the man. A fine portrait in the school library records his appearance during these years. After nearly twenty years of service as headmaster, he was warned by a series of heart attacks that he needed rest. Arrangements were made for a year's leave of absence during 1924–25, but death intervened less than a week after the school commencement.

[Material about Buehler's parentage, his father's connection with Pennsylvania College, and his own life there as a student is to be found in the *Pennsylvania College Book* (1882). For his life at Hotchkiss much material is available scattered through the weekly *Hotchkiss Record* and the *Mischianza*, the school annual. The issues of the latter during his headmastership contain a brief biographical sketch listing his various accomplishments, with dates for each. The *Hotchkiss Alumni Bulletin* issued a Memorial number in August 1924 with eulogies and estimates of his services to the school. MSS. in the possession of Mrs. Buehler, and the records of the school and college at Gettysburg and those of Hotchkiss contain further material about him.]   G. V–S.

BUEL, JESSE (Jan. 4, 1778–Oct. 6, 1839), agriculturist, the youngest of the fourteen children of Elias Buel, farmer and Revolutionary major, was born in Coventry, Conn. In 1790 the family moved to Rutland, Vt., where two years later Jesse was apprenticed to a printer. Learning the trade in four years instead of the customary seven, he worked for a year as a journeyman printer, and then successively, with various partners, started three weekly newspapers in Troy and Poughkeepsie. In the meantime, in 1801, he married Susan Pierce of Troy. In 1803, Buel's accumulations were wiped out by business losses. Undiscouraged, however, he immediately founded the *Kingston Plebeian,* which he ran for ten years, serving also for a time as judge of the Ulster county court. In 1813 he moved from Kingston to Albany, where he founded his fifth weekly newspaper, the *Argus.* He published the *Argus* for seven years, during the last six of which he was also printer to the State. He had already begun to be interested in farm problems, and devoted space in his paper to agricultural articles. In 1821, having achieved a competence, he disposed of his publishing interests and began the agricultural efforts that were to make him widely known both in the United States and abroad. He bought for $30 an acre a tract of eighty-five acres lying in the "Sandy Barrens," west of Albany. Unhampered by the prejudices of the traditional farmer, Buel applied scientific practises to his own farm—drainage, deep plowing, destruction of weeds, maintenance of livestock, application of manure and plowing under of green crops for fertilizer, and crop rotation instead of the customary naked-fallow system. As a result, his farm became a show place and by 1839, eighteen years after he had purchased it, was yielding returns on a valuation of more than $200 an acre (Preface to *The Farmer's Companion,* 1893). From his entrance into farming, he devoted tireless energy to the improvement of agriculture and rural life. In 1822 he became recording secretary to the State Board of Agriculture, and two of the three volumes issued by that body in its six years of existence

were apparently edited by him (*Memoirs of the Board of Agriculture of the State of New York,* vol. II, 1823; vol. III, 1826). In 1823 he was elected from Albany County to the New York Assembly. Immediately this unassuming, quietly dressed, smooth-faced printer-farmer became the leading spokesman for agriculture. He was a member of the committee on agriculture, and offered a resolution looking to the establishment of a state agricultural school (*New York Assembly Journal,* 1823, p. 796). For the next thirteen years, in and out of the legislature, he advocated this educational enterprise, and, finally, under pressure of a state agricultural convention, in 1836, over which he presided, the legislature acted. The money, however, was to be raised by public subscription rather than by legislative appropriation, and efforts by Buel and others to enlist support were discouraging. In the meantime, under the auspices of the State Agricultural Society, Buel had in 1834 established the *Cultivator,* one of the first popular agricultural journals. Although a number of other farm periodicals were being published, their subscription prices ranged from $2 to $4 a year, while the *Cultivator* charged but fifty cents. Notwithstanding this fact, the magazine was markedly superior to other farm journals of the time. In it Buel emphasized not only scientific farm practises but also the need for professional schools of agriculture and for agricultural instruction in the district schools. In 1836, running as a Whig, Buel was defeated for the governorship of New York by William L. Marcy, but he made no mention of his candidacy or any other party matter in his magazine. His interest in education led to his appointment as a regent of the University of the State of New York. The Massachusetts Board of Education urged him to prepare a book for school and rural libraries, which he did under the title of *The Farmer's Companion.* First published in 1839, this book went through at least six editions. A two-volume work, *The Farmer's Instructor,* made up chiefly of reprints from the *Cultivator,* was issued in the same year. Buel also edited an edition of *A Treatise in Agriculture,* by John Armstrong. He had planned still another book, to deal with grain crops, gardening, and similar topics, but his unexpected death at Danbury, Conn., intervened (see Note to *The Farmer's Companion,* 2nd edition, p. 4). Buel is properly considered by Bidwell and Falconer "to typify the movement for agricultural improvement in the East from 1820 to 1840" (*History of Agriculture in the Northern United States, 1620–1860,* 1925). This simple, self-educated man not only exerted powerful influence on the rural thought of his own time, but laid out an educational program which was in large measure adopted in the late nineteenth and early twentieth centuries.

[Authoritative information as to Buel's views and agricultural activities is obtainable from his books and from the files of the *Cultivator*, 1834–39. Two speeches, *Address Before the Berkshire Ag. Soc.* (1837), and *Address Delivered Before the Ag. and Hort. Soc. of New Haven County, Conn.* (1839) are also of interest. *A Eulogy on the Life and Character of the Late Judge Jesse Buel* (1840), delivered by Amos Dean before the N. Y. State Ag. Soc. embodies a biographical sketch. This is reprinted in the 6th edition of *The Farmer's Companion*, pp. vii–xxiv. The *Cultivator* for November 1839 contains a brief obituary.]   N. A. C.

BUELL, ABEL (Feb. 1, 1741/42–Mar. 10, 1822), silversmith, typefounder, and engraver, the son of John Buell of Killingworth, Conn., served his apprenticeship with the silversmith Ebenezer Chittenden and about the year 1762 set up on his own account in his native town of Killingworth. Almost his first action was to employ his craftsman's skill in raising a series of five-shilling Connecticut notes to the more comfortable denomination of five pounds. For this error in judgment and conduct he was tried at Norwich in March 1764 and sentenced to branding, imprisonment, and confiscation of property. Released from prison by the Assembly some months later, "from a compassionate regard and pity on his youthful follies," Buell succeeded in gaining a restoration of civic rights by the construction of a lapidary machine of his own invention for the cutting and polishing of crystals and precious stones. He next applied his ingenious mind to learning the art of typefounding. In May 1769, Edes & Gill of Boston printed the proof of an advertisement set in types of Buell's design and casting. A copy of this "first Proof struck by American Types" as Gale described it remains to-day in the Yale University Library, the first crude specimen sheet of an English-American typefounder. In October 1769, as the answer to a printed petition set in another font of his own making, Buell was granted a subsidy of £100 by the Connecticut Assembly to aid him in the establishment of a type foundry in New Haven, but he took no further steps toward the immediate realization of this enterprise. About the year 1770, he began to exercise his clever fingers in the art of copperplate engraving. In 1773 or 1774 he engraved the Chart of Saybrook Bar drawn from surveys made by Abner Parker to render the entrance to the Connecticut River easier of navigation. In March 1784 he achieved his chief work as engraver in the publication of a large wall map of the territories of the United States according to the Peace of 1783. Crude in some respects and soon outmoded, this map of 41 x 46 inches yet has distinction in that it was the first map of the new political division to be compiled and engraved by one of its citizens. It was probably while employed as an engraver on the Bernard Romans charts of the Florida coast that Buell fell in debt to James Rivington, the New York printer of the Romans maps, and it was probably, too, this work that gave rise to the tradition that Buell surveyed for Romans the Pensacola section of the Florida coast. It is not certain that Buell was ever in Florida or that he came in contact with Romans until the surveys for the charts were completed and the eccentric engineer had come to New York to arrange for their publication. The debt to Rivington and the unreturned £100 he had received from the Connecticut Assembly forced Buell to abscond from New Haven and to remain outside the Connecticut jurisdiction from 1775 until 1778. He was enabled to return through the loyalty and industry of his wife Aletta, who kept his silversmith establishment, "At the Sign of the Coffee Pot," in operation during the period of his absence and ultimately discharged his indebtedness to the government. The claim of the "inhuman varlet" Rivington, as Aletta called him, lapsed because the printer had joined the British and could no longer prosecute in the Connecticut courts.

At last in 1781 Buell began to supply type in quantity to the Greens of New Haven and New London. Meanwhile typefounding had become an established industry in Germantown, Pa., and thus, though Buell was the initiator of the art in English America, he had forfeited the distinction of being the first to put it on a practical commercial basis. Until the end of the century he remained in New Haven busily employed as a man of affairs. He operated a line of packet boats, helped develop a marble quarry, conducted a regular vendue, owned or had an owner's interest in two privateersmen, fashioned silver and jewelry, cast type, practised the art of engraving, made plans, drawings and models for all sorts of engineering work, invented a machine for planting corn, exhibited a negro in the process of turning white, and in many directions turned his hand to things interesting and useful to his community but rarely profitable to himself. In 1785 he invented a machine for coining money and formed a company that made copper coins under the supervision of the state for the ensuing two or three years. In 1789 he went to England to learn cotton manufacturing and in 1793 is found for a short time at "the cotton manufactory near New York." Two years later he built at New Haven a cotton mill which drew a prophecy of success from President Stiles, but like most of his projects this seems to have failed soon after its beginning operations. In 1799 he removed to Hartford and began his life anew as silversmith, armorer, and engraver of printers' ornaments. About 1805 he is found as a silversmith in Stockbridge, Mass., where under the influence of the religious revival of 1813 he abjured the doctrines of Thomas Paine, which he had previously held, and threw himself into the practise of Christianity with the fervor that characterized all his actions. He died in the Alms House in New Haven at the age of eighty-one years, described in the newspaper notice of his death as "an ingenious mechanic." He was married first in 1762 to Mary (Parker); second, probably in 1771, to Aletta Devoe; third in 1779, to Mrs. Rebecca (Parkman) Townsend; fourth, to Sarah ——, who died in 1803.

[Lawrence C. Wroth, *Abel Buell of Conn., Silver-smith, Type Founder and Engraver* (1926); E. G. Jones, *Stockbridge, Past and Present* (1854); J. W. Barber, *Conn. Hist. Colls.* (1836).]   L. C. W.

BUELL, DON CARLOS (Mar. 23, 1818–Nov. 19, 1898), Union soldier, descended from William Buell, a Welshman who settled in Windsor, Conn., about 1639, was born near Marietta, Ohio, the son of Salmon D. and Eliza (Buell) Buell. When he was five years old his father died, and the boy was taken to his uncle, George P. Buell of Lawrenceburg, Ind., where he remained—barring five years passed with his step-father in Marietta—until 1837 (M. R. Martin, *History of Marietta and Washington County, Ohio,* 1902, pp. 697 ff.). In the latter year he was appointed cadet at West Point, and four years later he graduated as second lieutenant, 3rd Infantry. He participated in the Seminole War. In 1846 he joined Taylor's army in Texas. Promoted first lieutenant, he was brevetted captain for gallant and meritorious conduct at Monterey on Sept. 23, 1846. Transferred to Scott's army, he was again brevetted in the following year for gallant conduct at the battles of Contreras and Churubusco. After the Mexican War he became an adjutant-general, and at the commencement of the Civil War was a lieutenant-colonel in the Adjutant-General's Department.

He was appointed brigadier-general United States Volunteers, on May 17, 1861, and aided in organizing the Army of the Potomac. Selected by Gen. McClellan to organize and train the Federal forces in Kentucky, he arrived at Louisville early in November, assuming command of the Army of the Ohio. The mission assigned this army was to invade and liberate east Tennessee, largely Union in sentiment. Buell foresaw the difficulties of moving from Louisville toward Knoxville, in a country lacking roads and railroads, especially in view of the presence of large Confederate forces then at Bowling Green, and on Nov. 27, profiting by the suggestion of an engineering officer, he recommended to McClellan an advance by the Cumberland and Tennessee Rivers toward Nashville, as auxiliary to the desired advance toward east Tennessee. Both McClellan and President Lincoln strongly disapproved of this plan, but Buell stuck to his recommendation, and urged the abandonment of the East Tennessee project. On Feb. 6, 1862, he was authorized to march on Bowling Green, in support of an advance under Grant up the Cumberland and Tennessee Rivers.

With 50,000 men, Buell started out. Due to Grant's victories at Forts Henry and Donelson, he met no opposition, and reached Nashville on Feb. 24. On Mar. 11, President Lincoln placed Buell under the orders of Gen. Halleck, and the latter ordered him to advance on Savannah, twenty-two miles north of Corinth on the Tennessee River. Nothing being said about haste, Buell marched very leisurely. As late as Apr. 4, he was advised by Grant that there was no need to hurry. By good luck, the leading division of Buell's army arrived on the Tennessee River on Apr. 6, the first day of the Confederate attack at Shiloh. Ferried across the river, this division by its presence restored the sinking fortunes of the Federal troops. During that night two more divisions came up and crossed the river. On Apr. 7, Buell attacked the Confederates. He had fresh troops and superior numbers, and forced the enemy back until they abandoned the field. No effort was made to pursue them.

Buell had been promoted on Mar. 21 to be a major-general, United States Volunteers. He accompanied Halleck's army to Corinth, but on June 10 was detached with four divisions, and ordered to proceed to Chattanooga following the railroad to that place. He was directed to repair this railroad as he advanced, an order which caused the failure of his expedition. The work was interrupted by raiding parties, and constant repairing so delayed Buell that he never arrived at his destination. On July 28, Morgan's cavalry completely stopped his advance by destroying railroad communications, and on Aug. 6 Buell knew that Bragg's Confederate army had reached Chattanooga. Buell then concentrated his forces near Murfreesboro, Tenn. On Sept. 2, Buell learned that the Confederate general, Kirby

Smith, advancing by Cumberland Gap, had defeated the Federal forces at Richmond, Ky. Knowing also that Bragg had started north from Chattanooga, he suspected that the latter was en route to join Kirby Smith. Buell therefore decided to leave a small force to cover Nashville, and to march at once with the greater part of his forces into Kentucky. Arriving at Bowling Green on Sept. 14, he found Bragg ahead of him at Glasgow, and between him and his base at Louisville. He decided not to attack on a field chosen by his antagonist, and soon Bragg moved away and left the road to Louisville open. Buell arrived at that city on Sept. 25.

On Oct. 1, Buell marched out to seek battle, and on Oct. 8, three divisions of his army found Bragg's forces at Perryville. A severe battle was fought, with indecisive results. Bragg however withdrew, leaving the battlefield in Buell's possession. The latter followed slowly for four days, when he discontinued the pursuit. Disappointed in the escape of Bragg's army, the Federal government relieved Buell on Oct. 24, and on Oct. 30, he surrendered the command of his army to Rosecrans. The army did not regret the change. It was the general opinion that Bragg should have been forced to a decisive battle, and relentlessly pursued thereafter. Buell's explanation that his failure to pursue was due to his inability to live off the country has been questioned, as Bragg subsisted his army in that way, and the Federal forces were better supplied than the Confederates. A military commission was convened in November 1862 to investigate Buell's conduct. On Apr. 15, 1863, the commission reported the facts without recommendation. The government, however, after keeping him for a year in waiting orders, discharged Buell as a major-general of volunteers, and he thereupon immediately resigned his regular commission on June 1, 1864. Grant later recommended his restoration to duty, but no action was taken. After the war Buell settled in Kentucky and engaged in mining; for a time he was a pension agent. He died at Rockport, Ky.

Buell was an excellent organizer and disciplinarian. He utterly disregarded politics. A friend of McClellan, to whom he owed his first important assignment, he was charged with being opposed to the administration. His reserved and studious character emphasized this belief, and led to the difficulties of the Kentucky campaign not being rightly estimated. His campaigns showed no military genius, but they were as good as those of other generals in the West. The early departure of Buell from military life prevented the development of what might have been a good

general. Grant evidently thought so, and he was probably correct. Buell was of medium stature, wore a full beard, and had a stern, determined appearance. His wife was Margaret (Hunter) Mason of Mobile (*Courier-Journal*, Louisville, Sept. 4, Nov. 20, 1898).

[*Official Records (Army)*, 1 ser., X, XVI, XX, XXIII; Jas. B. Fry, *Operations of the Army under Buell . . . and the "Buell Commission"* (1884); J. C. Ropes, *The Story of the Civil War* (1894–1913); *Battles and Leaders of the Civil War* (1887–88); *Thirtieth Annual Reunion Ass. Grads. Mil. Acad.* (1899), pp. 105–18; Jas. B. Hudnut, *Commanders of the Army of the Cumberland* (1884).]
           C. H. L.

BUFFALO BILL. [See CODY, WILLIAM FREDERICK, 1846–1917.]

BUFFUM, ARNOLD (Dec. 13, 1782–Mar. 13, 1859), Quaker, anti-slavery lecturer, was the grandson of Joseph Buffum, of the second or third generation of his family in America, who moved from Massachusetts to Smithfield, R. I., in 1715. There Arnold, second son among eight children of William and Lydia (Arnold) Buffum, was born. William Buffum was a farmer and merchant, a Quaker, and a member of the Providence Society for Promoting the Abolition of Slavery. Fugitive slaves sheltered in his household enlisted his son's sympathies for anti-slavery. Without extensive education, Arnold became a hatter; but having an inventive mind, he conceived and patented various mechanical contrivances. Until he was fifty he was but partially successful at his trade, residing now at Smithfield or Providence, now in Massachusetts or Connecticut. Between 1825 and 1831 business led him twice to Europe, where he met Thomas Clarkson, Amelia Opie, and Lafayette. Returning, he established in Fall River certain "infant schools," based on some foreign educational theory.

As president of the New England Anti-Slavery Society from its organization in January 1832, Buffum was commissioned as its lecturing agent, thereafter devoting what time he could to forwarding emancipation. This meant personal danger and sacrifice of friends and business interests, but his moral courage, eloquence, and telling appeals for the negro's freedom made a deep impression. He was one of the founders of the American Anti-Slavery Society in Philadelphia in 1833. Thither he moved about 1834, establishing himself in the hatting industry. In 1840–41 he aroused serious reflection, ripening into anti-slavery sentiment, throughout Ohio and Indiana by lecturing and by editing at New Garden (now Fountain City), Ind., the *Protectionist*. Rejecting Garrison's and Phillips's radical principles, Buffum, by voice and vote, supported successively the Liberty, Free-Soil, and Republican parties. He also exerted himself in behalf of temperance.

Buffum married (1803) Rebecca Gould, from near Newport, R. I. His daughter, Elizabeth (Buffum) Chace [q.v.], became a Garrisonian anti-slavery worker, his younger son, Edward Gould Buffum, Paris correspondent of the *New York Herald*. Muhlenberg, Arnold Buffum's fellow passenger on a European trip (1843), thus describes him: "An Old Hickory Abolitionist . . . a tall, gray-headed, gold-spectacled patriarch . . . a very sharp old fellow [who] has all his facts ready, . . . abuses his country outrageously" as being pro-slavery, but still a "genuine democratic American." Buffum was of religious nature, and had high literary tastes. In 1854 he entered the Raritan Bay Union, Perth Amboy, N. J., where he died.

[Lillie B. C. Wyman and Arthur C. Wyman, *Elizabeth Buffum Chace* (1914); W. P. and F. J. Garrison, *Wm. Lloyd Garrison* (1889); Anne Ayres, *The Life and Work of Wm. A. Muhlenberg* (1880); information from Mrs. L. B. C. Wyman, Buffum's grand-daughter.]

R.S.B.

BUFORD, ABRAHAM (July 31, 1749–June 30, 1833), Revolutionary soldier, was descended from Richard Beauford who emigrated from England about 1635 and some years later received grants of land along the Rappahannock River. He was born in Culpeper County, Va., the son of John and Judith Beauford. In the first year of the Revolution he raised a company of minutemen from his county, and had a share in the operations which resulted in the expulsion of the royal governor, Lord Dunmore. He served throughout the war, in the earlier years with the army in the North, and later under Morgan. He was commissioned major of the 14th Virginia Nov. 13, 1776, lieutenant-colonel 5th Virginia Apr. 1, 1777, and colonel May 15, 1778, taking command of the 11th Virginia Sept. 14, 1778, and of the 3rd Virginia Feb. 12, 1781. Early in 1780 the condition of affairs at Charleston became precarious. Buford enlisted recruits for its relief, marched southward, and had reached a point on the Santee River when he learned that the city had capitulated. He was ordered by Gen. Huger to return to North Carolina, removing or destroying the military stores. His little army numbered about 300 to 400 men. To intercept him, Lord Cornwallis dispatched 270 men under Col. Tarleton, and by forced marches this famous cavalry commander overtook Buford at the Waxhaws, a locality nine miles from Lancaster, near the state boundary. A parley ensued; the events following are a matter of controversy. American historians have usually charged Tarleton with treachery. His own account is: "A report

among the cavalry that they had lost their commanding officer (when his horse was shot) stimulated the soldiers to a vindictive asperity not easily restrained" (Tarleton, quoted in H. B. Carrington, *Battles of the American Revolution*, 1876, p. 498). John Marshall gives the common American view: Tarleton "demanded a surrender on the terms which had been granted to the garrison of Charleston. This was refused. While the flags were passing, Tarleton continued to make his depositions for the assault, and the instant the truce was over, his cavalry made a furious charge on the Americans, who had received no orders to engage, and who seem to have been uncertain whether to defend themselves or not. In this state of dismay and confusion, some fired on the assailants, while others threw down their arms and begged for quarter. None was given" (*Life of Washington*, 1884–87, I, 337). The Americans lost 113 killed, and about 200 prisoners, of whom about 150 were badly wounded. All the stores were captured, and Buford with a remnant of his force was saved only by rapid flight. "Tarleton's Quarter" became proverbial; "Buford" was the countersign of the day of the frontiersmen who a few months later stormed King's Mountain (Theodore Roosevelt, *The Winning of the West*, 1889–96, II, 272). Tarleton himself defended his course, as we have seen, and Cornwallis in a dispatch to Clinton recommended him for especial favor. But the contemporary English historian, Stedman, observed, "The virtue of humanity was totally forgot."

After the war, Buford received warrants for land grants, and bought the claims of his brother. In October 1788 he was married to Martha, daughter of Judge Samuel and Mary (McClung) McDowell. Migrating to Kentucky, he became a deputy surveyor, and located his grants in the Blue Grass region and elsewhere. He settled near Georgetown in Scott County, where he possessed a fine estate, entertained many persons of prominence, and died.

[M. B. Buford, *Hist. and Genealogy of the Buford Family* (1903), revised and enlarged by G. W. Buford and M. B. Minter (1924); T. M. Green, *Historic Families of Ky.* (1889).]

E.K.A.

BUFORD, ABRAHAM (Jan. 18, 1820–June 9, 1884), Confederate soldier, stock-raiser, belonged to a family which was originally of French origin and which later held large estates in England and Scotland. The first American Bufords settled in Virginia, descendants later migrating to Woodford County, Ky., where William B. Buford, formerly of Culpeper County, Va., became noted as a breeder of blooded horses and cattle. Abraham Buford, the son of William B. and Frances Walker (Kirtley) Buford, was born in Woodford County. He received his earlier education under Verpyle Payne, a teacher of some note, and at Centre College; and was graduated from the Military Academy at West Point in 1841, with such men as D. C. Buell, Z. B. Tower, H. G. Wright, A. P. Howe, and Thomas J. Rodman. Upon graduation, young Buford was assigned to the First Dragoons, and saw immediate service in Kansas and Iowa, then part of the frontier. Promoted to a first lieutenancy in 1846, he participated in the war with Mexico, and was brevetted captain for gallant and meritorious services in the battle of Buena Vista. From the years 1848 to 1851 he was stationed in New Mexico; and, after being promoted to captain in 1853, was assigned to duty the year following at the cavalry school for practise at Carlisle. His resignation from the army followed, Oct. 22, 1854, and he retired to his stock farm, Bosque Bonita, near Versailles, Ky., where for some years he specialized in the breeding of thoroughbred horses and short-horn cattle. With the outbreak of the Civil War, he was appointed in 1862 a brigadier-general in the Confederate army. His command of Kentucky troops covered the retreat of Gen. Bragg to Knoxville, Tenn., and thereafter he commanded a brigade of Loring's division until the spring of the year 1864. He was then assigned to a cavalry brigade of Gen. Forrest's command, consisting of the 3rd, 7th, and 8th Kentucky Cavalry, and participated with this noted leader in numerous engagements and raids. He was severely wounded at Lindville, Dec. 24, 1864, and was unable to resume active command until the spring of 1865. After the war, he returned to his stock farm, which became a great social-center in the Blue-Grass region, where he became one of the best known turfmen in Kentucky. He acquired ownership of the celebrated horses, Crossland, Nellie Gray, Selena, Inquirer, Hollywood, Marion, and Versailles, and delighted in lavish entertaining of noted sportsmen from all over the country. Himself a man of marked force of character and mentality, with magnificent physique, he took a deep interest in politics; and although originally strongly espousing state rights and having reluctantly yielded to secession, he subsequently used his best efforts for a united country. In the year 1845, he had married Amanda Harris of New York, from which union he had one son William, who died in 1872. With the loss of this son, and the loss of his wife afterward, came severe financial reverses also, resulting in the eventual loss of his home. Crushed by grief and advancing years, Buford ended his life by his own hand at Danville, Ind.

[M. B. Buford, *Hist. and Geneal. of the Buford Family in America* (1903); J. M. Armstrong, *Biog. Encyc. of Ky.* (1878); *Official Records (Army)*; *Army Register of the U. S. for One Hundred Years (1779–1879)*; *15th Ann. Report, Ass. Grads. U. S. Mil. Acad.* (1884); Louisville *Courier-Journal*, June 10, 1884. Although certain authorities give Buford the name "Abram," he matriculated at West Point as "Abraham," and this is confirmed by the President of the Woodford Sun Co., Versailles, Ky. (letter of Feb. 10, 1927), who furthermore confirms the date of Buford's death as June 9, 1884, and not 1864, as mistakenly given in certain biographies.]   C. D. R.

BUFORD, JOHN (Mar. 4, 1826–Dec. 16, 1863), Union soldier, was eighth in descent from Richard Beauford, who came from England in 1635, at the age of eighteen, and settled in Lancaster County, Va. Members of the family became extensive landowners, devoted themselves to horse raising and the cultivation of tobacco, and furnished many soldiers in the early Indian wars and in the Revolution. A change was made in the spelling of the name as a result of the troubles with the mother country. John was the son of John and Anne (Bannister) Watson Buford, widow of John Watson. He was born in Woodford County, Ky., was appointed to the West Point Military Academy from Illinois, and graduated in 1848, standing sixteenth in a class of thirty-eight members. On May 9, 1854 he married Martha McDonald Duke. After a year as brevet second lieutenant he was promoted to second lieutenant in the 2nd Dragoons, and to first lieutenant on July 9, 1853. He saw frontier service in Texas, New Mexico, and Kansas and was appointed regimental quartermaster in 1855 at the time when the Sioux expedition was organized to punish the Indians who had massacred Lieut. Grattan's party. In the winter campaign which followed, ending with the defeat of Little Thunder's band, near Ash Hollow, Nebr., on Sept. 3, he won the approval of Col. Philip St. George Cooke, the commanding officer. The expedition was broken up in July 1856, and the troops hastened to a new field of action in the Kansas troubles of that year. Just then the danger point shifted to the difficulties with the Mormons in Utah. The 2nd Dragoons were recalled in haste from duty in Kansas, on three or four days' notice, and ordered to make a march of 1,100 miles in the dead of winter through an uninhabited wilderness, under the conditions of war. During this march the quartermaster was the hardest-worked man in the command, and Col. Cooke reported Buford as a "most efficient officer." Next came the troublous times of 1861. The regiment marched overland for sixty days to Fort Leavenworth, and made its camp in Washington in October 1861. More than a year after the war began, Gen. Pope came to Washington to take a high command. He was surprised to find Buford there in an unimportant position, and at once asked for his advancement. Buford was accordingly promoted brigadier-general on July 7, 1862. Two days later he took command of the reserve brigade of cavalry and within less than ten days was in action at Madison Court House. Pope's movement had been delayed too long and Lee's Manassas Campaign had begun. Finding the enemy on his front, flank, and rear, Buford extricated his command and retreated toward Sperryville. When Jackson appeared in Pope's rear on Aug. 28, McDowell sent Buford beyond Thoroughfare Gap for observation. Buford captured fifty of Jackson's stragglers, struck the head of Longstreet's column, delayed him for several hours, and counted seventeen regiments of infantry, five hundred cavalry, and a battery of artillery. He then made his report, retreated, and acted as rear guard for Ricketts's Division. When Pope's army retreated to Centerville on the 30th, Buford's brigade covered the withdrawal across Bull Run at Lewis Ford, on the extreme left. The pursuing cavalry attacked, and Buford was so severely wounded that he was at first reported to be dead. The Confederate commander claimed a victory.

Buford was disabled by his wound and on sick-leave until Sept. 10, 1862, when he was announced as chief of cavalry of the Army of the Potomac. The position had only nominal importance on the staff of the commanding general. Buford seems to have still been suffering from his wound, as he served in this minor capacity under Mc-Clellan and Burnside at the battles of South Mountain, Antietam, and Fredericksburg. When Gen. Hooker in February 1863 consolidated the cavalry into an army corps, Buford resumed command of the reserve brigade, and rendered effective service both in Stoneman's raid toward Richmond and in covering the retreat of Hooker's army after Chancellorsville. When Lee began his second invasion of the North, well covered by Stuart's cavalry on his right, the efforts of the Federal cavalry to penetrate the screen brought on daily combats and considerable actions at Aldie Gap, Upperville, Middleburg, and Ashby's Gap. Buford, now in command of a division, crossed the Potomac on June 27, reached Gettysburg on June 30, and drove back the advance of Hill's corps which was approaching from Cashtown. On July 1 the Confederate advance on the Cashtown road was opposed by a single brigade of Buford's cavalry, dismounted at about one man to a yard of front, with one battery against two of the enemy. Hill was delayed for about two hours, at the end of which

time Buford was relieved by the arrival of Reynolds's corps. Later in the afternoon the cavalry was withdrawn to Seminary Ridge where it was opposed to McGowan's South Carolina brigade. Meanwhile Buford's other brigade was doing equally good work on the other roads which entered Gettysburg further to the north and east; it reported the advance of Ewell's corps, and held its ground until relieved by Howard's corps. On July 3 Buford was sent to Westminster ostensibly to guard the trains but more probably to relieve the fears of Washington concerning an enemy raid. His absence from the battlefield gave Longstreet the opportunity to surprise and defeat Sickles's corps on the 3rd. From Westminster Buford was sent to Williamsport on the Potomac to capture Lee's retreating trains, but when he arrived on July 6 he found the Confederates there, with cavalry, infantry, and artillery, trains parked and intrenched. Cavalry actions were fought at Westminster, Boonsboro, Beaver Creek, and Funkstown. When the opposing armies got back into Virginia a season of maneuvering began and lasted for months. Buford's division was heavily engaged at Manassas Gap, Chester Gap, Morton's Ford, and Rixeyville. Toward the latter part of November, Buford received leave of absence owing to failing health. He went for treatment to Washington where he died on Dec. 16. His commission as major-general was put in his hands just before his death. He was buried at West Point.

[*Official Records* (*Army*); G. W. Cullum, *Biog. Reg.* (3rd ed., 1891); J. C. Ropes, *The Army under Pope* (1881) and *The Story of the Civil War* (1894–1913); *Battles and Leaders of the Civil War* (1887–88); obituary in the Washington *Evening Star*, Dec. 17, 1863; M. B. Buford, *Genealogy of the Buford Family in America* (1903).]   E. S.

BUFORD, NAPOLEON BONAPARTE (Jan. 13, 1807–Mar. 28, 1883), Union soldier, half-brother of John Buford [*q.v.*], was born on a plantation in Woodford County, Ky., the second child of John Buford by his first wife, Nancy Hickman. He was a grandson of Simeon Buford, who migrated from Virginia to Kentucky in 1790 and settled in what was to become Woodford County. Napoleon Buford graduated sixth in his class in the United States Military Academy, July 1, 1827, and was commissioned a lieutenant of artillery. He attended the artillery school at Fortress Monroe, Va., 1827–28; was on topographical duty along the Kentucky River and at the Rock Island and Des Moines Rapids of the Mississippi, 1828–29; was in garrison at Fort Sullivan, Me., 1830–31 and 1832–34; studied on leave of absence at the Harvard University Law School during 1831; was assistant professor of natural and experimental philosophy at West Point 1834–35; and resigned from the Army, Dec. 31, 1835. For the next seven years he was in the service of his native state as engineer in charge of the Licking River improvement. He then followed his family to Rock Island, Ill., where he was successively a merchant, iron founder, railroad promoter, and banker. In 1850 he was a member and secretary of the board of visitors of the Military Academy. The outbreak of the Civil War ruined him financially, for his bank had invested heavily in the bonds of Southern states. Making over his entire property to his creditors, he helped raise the 27th Illinois Volunteers, was commissioned its colonel, Aug. 10, 1861, and was presently in action.

At Belmont, Mo., Nov. 7, 1861, the 27th Illinois was left behind in the retreat and might easily have fallen into the hands of the enemy; Buford, with a cool head and accurate information about the terrain, took his men down a byroad to the river and got them aboard a gunboat without mishap. In a subsequent parley over the exchange of prisoners he met his classmate, Leonidas Polk [q.v.], who wrote of him to Mrs. Polk: "He is as good a fellow as ever lived, and most devotedly my friend; a true Christian, a true soldier, and a gentleman, every inch of him." Buford took part in the demonstration on Columbus, Ky., Feb. 23, 1862, and was in command of the town, Mar. 4–14, after its evacuation by the Confederates. He was in the siege of Island No. 10 Mar. 14–Apr. 7, and commanded the garrison after its capitulation. During the siege he took a small detachment and fell on Union City, Tenn., early in the morning of Mar. 31, taking the town by surprise and capturing a number of prisoners, one hundred horses, and a quantity of munitions and stores. For this exploit he was promoted to brigadier-general of volunteers, Apr. 15, 1862. He participated in the expedition to Fort Pillow, Tenn., Apr. 10–20, and served in the Mississippi campaign of the following summer. During the pursuit after the second day's fighting at Corinth, Miss., Oct. 4, 1862, he suffered a sunstroke. While recuperating he was sent to Washington on court-martial duty and was a member of the court that convicted Gen. Fitz-John Porter [q.v.]. On his return to the West he was in command of Cairo, Ill., Mar.–Sept., 1863, and of the District of East Arkansas, with headquarters at Helena, Sept. 12, 1863–Mar. 9, 1865. There he did his most notable work. He coped successfully with smugglers, guerrilla parties, and lessees of plantations (some of whom, he declared, were as bad as the enemy), organized a freedmen's department of 5,000 men,

established an orphan asylum and an industrial school for liberated slaves, and prosecuted dishonesty among his own subordinates. In spite of an inadequate force of men and much illness, he gave an excellent account of himself. The state of his health finally compelled him to ask for a change of duties. He was relieved of his command by an order of Mar. 6, 1865, was brevetted major-general of volunteers, Mar. 13, "for gallant and meritorious service during the Rebellion," and was on leave of absence from Mar. 9 until Aug. 24, 1865, when he was mustered out of the volunteer service.

He was superintendent of the Federal Union Mining Company in Colorado June 1–Dec. 1, 1866, special United States commissioner of Indian affairs, Feb. 7–Sept. 1, 1867, and special United States commissioner to inspect the completed Union Pacific Railroad, Sept. 1, 1867–Mar. 10, 1869. The latter years of his life were spent in Chicago, where he was one of the founders of the Chicago Society of the Sons of Virginia and was a social favorite. He was twice married: first, to Sarah Childs of Cazenovia, N. Y.; and second, to Mrs. Mary Anne (Greenwood) Pierce. He died in Chicago and was buried at Rock Island.

[*Official Records*, ser. I, II, III; G. W. Cullum, *Biog. Reg.*, I, 389–90 (3rd ed., 1891); T. M. Eddy, *The Patriotism of Ill.*, II, 53–57 (1866); *Battles and Leaders of the Civil War* (1884–88); W. M. Polk, *Leonidas Polk, Bishop and General* (1893); M. B. Buford, *Geneal. of the Buford Family in America* (San Francisco, 1903; rev. ed. by G. W. Buford and M. B. Minter, LaBelle, Mo., 1924); *Biog. Encyc. of Ill.* (1875); *Quinquennial Cat. Harv. Univ. Law School 1817–1924* (1925); *Chicago Daily Inter-Ocean*, Mar. 29, 31, 1883.]
G. H. G.

BULFINCH, CHARLES (Aug. 8, 1763–Apr. 4, 1844), architect, public official, was descended from Adino Bulfinch, a sail maker, who was surveyor of highways in Boston in 1706. The son of Thomas Bulfinch and his wife Susan Apthorp, Charles came of a wealthy and cultivated Boston family. He graduated at Harvard in 1781, and early cultivated a taste for architecture which was greatly stimulated during a tour of England and the Continent in 1785–87. He saw the monuments of Paris under the suggestions of Jefferson, whose classical tendency influenced his young compatriot, and he then followed Jefferson's route through Southern France and Northern Italy, pressing on to Florence and Rome. On his return to Boston his talents were soon laid under contribution by friends, to whom he gave gratuitous advice in architecture. He was married on Nov. 20, 1788 to Hannah Apthorp, by whom he had eleven children, one of them Thomas Bulfinch [q.v.], the author. March and April following his marriage were passed b

Bulfinch in a visit to Philadelphia and New York. The observations of this tour were quite as influential in forming his style as were those of foreign travel. His first design, submitted in November 1787, soon after his return from abroad, had been for a new State House, but this project remained for a time in abeyance. In 1788 the old Hollis Street Church was built from his plans, and was followed by designs for churches at Taunton and Pittsfield. The Beacon monument of 1789, a Doric column sixty feet high, testified to his classical interests, as did the triumphal arch erected the same year for Washington's reception in Boston. The State House at Hartford, begun in 1792 from his plans, was on the most ambitious scale yet attempted in New England. He was one of the projectors of the Boston Theatre and gave the design for the fine building erected in 1793 (burned, and rebuilt by him, 1798). His public work of this first period was crowned by the building of the Massachusetts State House on Beacon Hill, with its portico and the famous dome, later gilded, which served Oliver Wendell Holmes as "the hub of the universe." Although the Capitol at Washington, which inaugurated the prevailing domed type of American governmental buildings, had been begun on a still larger scale in 1793, it remained long unfinished, so that the Boston State House was at its completion in 1800 the most conspicuous public building in the United States. In the same period Bulfinch inaugurated likewise a reformation of the domestic architecture of New England, where he introduced the delicate detail of the Adam style. His first houses, from 1792, were those for Joseph Coolidge, and, more important, the one for Joseph Barrell in Charlestown. This had an oval parlor projecting on the garden side in the manner of the design adopted the same year for the president's house at Washington. Above was a semicircular portico with tall columns. In these houses curved staircases were adopted for the first time in New England. The scheme of the Barrell house was soon followed in the famous mansion of Elias Hasket Derby in Salem (design by Bulfinch, modified and executed by Samuel McIntire). Bulfinch's public services had led to his election in 1791, at the age of twenty-seven, to the board of selectmen of the town of Boston, on which he was to serve, with one interval, for twenty-six years. Here he was active on committees which for the first time lighted the streets of the town in 1792, admitted children of both sexes to the public schools, and attempted to secure the adoption of a form of city government.

Events meanwhile brought about a tragic change in Bulfinch's situation in life. In 1793, following models seen in England, he had projected for the first time in America a row of houses of coherent design, the Tontine or Franklin Crescent, which still gives the line to Franklin St. in Boston. It consisted of sixteen houses with an arch in the center, over which were rooms assigned to the Boston Library Society and the Massachusetts Historical Society. The houses at the ends and others opposite were adorned with tall pilasters. Enthusiastic for the success of the project, Bulfinch took over the shares of less sanguine backers. In 1795 he declined his reëlection as a selectman to devote himself to the State House and to his own affairs, but in the financial depression of that year he became so deeply involved that in January 1796 he was adjudged bankrupt and the large monetary rewards were later reaped by others. His talents in architecture, hitherto so generously exercised for others by the amateur and gentleman of fortune, now became the basis of a professional practise by which he gradually reëstablished a modest livelihood. In these years he built the first of three houses for Harrison Gray Otis which is still standing on Cambridge St., the Morton house in Roxbury, a court house at Dedham, and other buildings. In 1799 he was reelected to the board of selectmen of which he now acted as chairman until his departure for Washington in 1817. This service was unpaid, though when a police system was created Bulfinch was also appointed superintendent of police at a salary of $600. The years of his chairmanship were those of the great development of old Boston, the form of which is due in large degree to Bulfinch in his dual capacity of official and architect. The neglected Common was turned into a park and fronted on three sides with fine buildings of uniform character: Park St., 1803–04; Colonnade Row on Tremont St., 1809–11; and Beacon St., from about 1800. Bulfinch also laid out on regular plans the lands on Boston Neck, those in South Boston (1804), and those on the site of the Mill Pond (1808). He designed India Wharf with its admirable warehouses, and also designed for the town the fine almshouse, two school-houses, the enlargement of Faneuil Hall (1805), the Boylston Market (afterward Public Library), and the Court House (later City Hall, demolished 1862). During this period his architectural practise included a number of public buildings elsewhere in Massachusetts, the State Prison at Charlestown, the Massachusetts General Hospital (1817–20), several banks, as well as many churches and private houses. Of the churches the most notable were the Cathedral of the Holy Cross (1803) and the New South Church (1814), both in Boston, and Christ Church in Lancaster (1816–17). Following in general the schemes of Wren's churches in London, Bulfinch gave great attention to the varieties of the type, which are illustrated in a series of his manuscript drawings.

In December 1817, on the resignation of Latrobe, the architect of the Capitol in Washington, President Monroe offered the post to Bulfinch, who removed with his family to Washington and remained in charge until the building was finished in 1830. Essentially he was called on to complete the wings and construct the central part according to the lines already established by the earlier architects, Hallet, Thornton, and Latrobe. His principal contribution was the detailed form of the western front. His mildness of temper enabled him to avoid the controversies which had enmeshed Latrobe, on whom had fallen the burden of establishing professional standards, and led Bulfinch to compromise in certain matters such as the excessive height of the central and lateral domes. Meanwhile he had found time to design the Unitarian Church in Washington (demolished in 1900), the state capitol at Augusta, Me. (1828–31), and several institutional buildings. After his return to Boston at the age of sixty-seven he lived in retirement, with occasional visits elsewhere, until his death in 1844.

Bulfinch exercised a wide influence on the architecture of New England, where his version of the Adam style became characteristic of the early republican period. His earliest and most gifted follower was Samuel McIntire of Salem who remodeled his style after seeing the Barrell and Derby designs. Alexander Parris similarly followed Bulfinch's style in his houses in Portland. Asher Benjamin made its forms widely accessible through his early publications, and it remained dominant in New England until the advent of the Greek revival about 1820.

[C. A. Place, *Chas. Bulfinch, Architect and Citizen* (1925) assembles the material on Bulfinch's life, for which the principal source is the *Life and Letters* (1896) by his grand-daughter Ellen S. Bulfinch. Additional detail on various phases of his work may be gleaned from Thos. A. Fox, "A Brief Hist. of the Boston State House" in the *Am. Architect*, XLVIII, 127; C. A. Place, "From Meeting House to Church in New England" in *Old-Time New Eng.*, vols. XIII, XIV, and "The New South Church," *Ibid.*, vol. XI; Fiske Kimball, *Domestic Architecture . . . of the Early Republic* (1922), and "The Derby Mansion" in *Essex Inst. Hist. Colls.*, LX, 273; Glenn Brown, *Hist. of the U. S. Capitol* (1900–03); and *The Documentary Hist. of the U. S. Capitol* (1904). Bulfinch's library and a number of his manuscript drawings are preserved by the architectural department of the Mass. Inst. of Technology, other drawings by the Essex Inst., Salem.]   F. K.

BULFINCH, THOMAS (July 15, 1796–May 27, 1867), author, was one of the eleven children of Charles Bulfinch [*q.v.*] and Hannah Apthorp, and was born at Newton, Mass. His education was obtained at the Boston Latin School, Phillips Exeter Academy, and Harvard University, where he was graduated in 1814, having W. H. Prescott as a classmate. After graduation he taught for a year in the Boston Latin School and was then for a short time an assistant in the store of his elder brother. In 1818 he accompanied his family to Washington, D. C., where his father had been appointed architect of the Capitol, and was in business there for six years. In 1825 he returned to Boston and attempted various business enterprises, without success. In 1837 he received a clerkship in the Merchants' Bank of Boston, which he held until his death. He seems to have lacked initiative in the world of affairs and to have been content with the small position which insured him a livelihood and left him considerable leisure, which he devoted to study and writing. Natural history interested him and he was for six years secretary of the Boston Society of Natural History. He cared little for politics and hated controversy but supported William Lloyd Garrison in the anti-slavery movement. Literature was his chief interest and a number of books resulted from his hours of study: *Hebrew Lyrical History* (1853), *The Age of Fable* (1855), *The Age of Chivalry* (1858), *The Boy Inventor* (1860), *Legends of Charlemagne* (1863), *Poetry of the Age of Fable* (1863), *Shakespeare Adapted for Reading Classes* (1865), and *Oregon and Eldorado* (1866). The *Boy Inventor* is a memoir of his brilliant pupil Matthew Edwards who died early. *Oregon and Eldorado* was suggested by his father's connection, as an organizer, with a sea expedition to the Northwest coast, which had much to do with the discovery of the Columbia River. Bulfinch's best-known work is *The Age of Fable*. It is a successful attempt to make mythology interesting, has gone through several editions, and is still widely used as a reference book by students. Greek and Roman mythology receive the most attention but chapters are devoted to Scandinavian, Celtic, and the various Oriental mythologies. *The Age of Chivalry* is a similar but less successful attempt to popularize the Arthurian and early Welsh legends. At the time of his death Bulfinch was at work on *Heroes and Sages of Greece and Rome*. He always remained a bachelor and lived with his parents, to whom he was devoted. His short experience in teaching had interested him in boys and he was helpful to them on many later occasions. His was a gentle, modest personality. The excitement which his material life lacked he supplied by his mental absorption in the deeds of heroes and adventurers. He died in Boston and his funeral was held in King's Chapel.

[The chief source of information is an appendix to a sermon preached by the Rev. Andrew Preston Peabody at King's Chapel, Boston, the Sunday following the decease of Bulfinch, and published under the title *Voices of the Dead* (1867). This appendix gives the facts of Bulfinch's life, taken from the class-book of his Harvard class, of which he was secretary; a genealogy of the direct descendants of Adino Bulfinch; and an appreciation of Thos. Bulfinch by Mr. Peabody. *Memorials of the Dead in Boston; Containing Exact Transcripts of Inscriptions on the Sepulchral Monuments in the King's Chapel Burial Ground* (1853), by Thos. Bridgman, contains chapters on the Bulfinch and Apthorp families. Obituaries were published in the *Boston Commonwealth*, June 1, 1867, and the *Boston Daily Advertiser*, May 28, 1867.]   S. G. B.

BULKELEY, MORGAN GARDNER (Dec. 26, 1837–Nov. 6, 1922), governor of Connecticut, senator, was born in East Haddam, Conn., the son of Judge Eliphalet Adams Bulkeley (1803–1872) and Lydia S. (Morgan) Bulkeley. His ancestry went back to Peter Bulkeley [q.v.], the first pastor of the church at Concord, Mass., and included the Rev. Gershom Bulkeley (1636–1713), clergyman, physician, magistrate and publicist. Judge Bulkeley moved to Hartford when Morgan was nine years old. President of the Aetna Life Insurance Company, judge of the police court, commissioner of the school fund, and a founder of the Republican party in Connecticut as well as its first speaker of the House, Judge Bulkeley was a man of considerable moment. At the age of fifteen Morgan left the Hartford Public High School to take a job as errand boy in an uncle's store in Brooklyn, N. Y. There he became in turn confidential clerk and partner. His work was interrupted by the Civil War. He enlisted with the 13th New York Regiment and was with Gen. McClellan in the Peninsular campaign. Later he was to be commander of the Grand Army of the Republic in Connecticut and war memories were always to color his political views. On the death of his father in 1872 he returned to Hartford. There he helped to found the United States Bank and was its first president. In 1879 he became the third president of the Aetna Life Insurance Company and continued as such until his death. Under his management the Aetna became one of America's soundest financial institutions; its assets rose from twenty-five million dollars to over two hundred million dollars and the number of employees increased from twenty-nine to fifteen hundred. Bulkeley was responsible for the establishment of two subsidiary companies, the Aetna Casualty and Surety Company, and the Automobile In-

surance Company of Hartford, and was also instrumental in merging the Aetna National and the Hartford National banks, as well as the Charter Oak and the Phœnix National banks. He was a trustee and director in many corporations; his financial interests covered a wide field.

He early entered politics. In Brooklyn he served on the Republican general committee for Kings County. In Hartford, starting as councilman, he passed from alderman to president of the court of common council. Elected mayor in 1880, he served for four terms, 1880–88, and then was nominated on the Republican ticket for governor. Luzon B. Morris, the Democratic candidate received 75,074 votes to Bulkeley's 73,569, but five thousand scattering votes made it so that neither candidate had a "majority of all the votes cast," as was required by the constitution. The Republican legislature accordingly seated Bulkeley. The next election, that of 1890, was the first to be held under a new secret-ballot law, and it proved to be much more complicated than that of 1888. Morris, Democrat, received 82,787 votes to 76,745 for Merwin, Republican. There were, however, enough scattering votes to prevent a clear majority, providing all the ballots cast were counted. But in the counting, Morris sympathizers had thrown out certain "specked" ballots though the defects were purely mechanical. The two branches of the legislature were of opposite political faiths and could not agree on what should be done. The Democratic Senate held that the "specked" ballots were illegal and that Morris was accordingly clearly elected; consequently they refused to concur with the Republican House in a legislative election. There resulted a deadlock and Gov. Bulkeley held over. A Democratic comptroller, Staub, had, however, been unquestionably elected and was seated. As custodian of the capitol he tried to recognize Morris as his superior. Locking the governor's office he detailed special officers to keep Bulkeley out. The Governor, thereupon, called a superior force and sending for a crowbar pried his way into office. A decision by the supreme court upheld him but a legislative deadlock continued throughout his term; no laws, appointments, or appropriations were made. For two years the state was financed from the private funds of Bulkeley and the Aetna.

Elected governor in 1892, Morris had all the acts and accounts of his predecessor validated, and a constitutional amendment instituted plurality elections, but the larger question of Connecticut's system of representation smoldered till the legislative session of 1901. At that time it was possible for twenty per cent of the voters of

Connecticut to elect a clear majority of both branches of the legislature. Gov. George P. McLean called attention to this fact and when remedial legislation was blocked a movement for a constitutional convention was inaugurated. This movement Ex-Governor Bulkeley vigorously opposed. He debated the matter before the legislative committee with James G. Batterson, president of the Travelers Insurance Company. (See *The Debate on Constitutional Amendments, Session 1901,* by James G. Batterson and Morgan Gardner Bulkeley.) He was defeated, the question went to the voters, and the convention was authorized. There Bulkeley decided to kill the proposed revision with kindness. A final resolution of the convention (No. 253) discloses his hand: "Whereas, Ex-Governor Morgan G. Bulkeley and the Honorable Delegate Lewis Sperry have correctly revised . . . the original Constitution of 1818, . . . be it Resolved by this honorable body that we extend to them our thanks." The proposed constitution was submitted to the people and, as Bulkeley had anticipated, was overwhelmingly defeated.

During 1905–11 Bulkeley was United States senator and was often out of sympathy with President Roosevelt. He joined Senator Foraker in fighting the President's order which summarily discharged—in dishonor—a whole battalion of colored troops of the 24th Infantry, because some of its individual members had been charged with "shooting up" the town of Brownsville, Tex. He also opposed Roosevelt on the Philippine tariff issue. He strenuously objected to placing the tobacco growers of Connecticut in competition with the labor standards of the Filipino and when the President sent for him on this matter he frankly informed the President that he was in Washington to represent the interests of the Commonwealth of Connecticut. Roosevelt's "New Nationalism" ran squarely counter to all of Bulkeley's principles. Perhaps no other matter so vitally affected the Senator as did insurance. Insurance affairs came to a head in 1905. Roosevelt's nationalistic idea was immediately in evidence and there was much talk of federal regulation. Bulkeley was extremely active and the idea did not get very far in the Senate. The question was referred to the Judiciary Committee and on June 25, 1906, that body reported that it was unanimously of the opinion "that the Congress is without authority under the Constitution to supervise and regulate the business of marine, fire, and life insurance, except in the District of Columbia, the Territories, and the insular possessions of the United States."

Greatly interested in sports, Bulkeley was con-

nected with the National Trotting Association for thirty years. He organized numerous baseball teams and was president of the National League when it was founded in 1876. He was also an antiquarian and collector. He arranged for the restoration of the Nathan Hale School-House in East Haddam and led the movement of private citizens for the preservation of the Bulfinch Old State House in Hartford. He was married to Fannie Briggs Houghton in 1885.

[*Hartford Courant,* Nov. 7, 1922; *Hartford Times,* Nov. 7, 1922; *Hartford Telegram,* July 2, 1888; *The Aetna-Izer,* vol. VII, no. 13, special issue, Dec. 1922; *Life Insurance Sales Training Course for Aetna-Izers* (Hartford, 1925), Bk. II, sections on "The Early Development of Life Insurance in Conn." and "Hist. of the Aetna Life Insurance Co."; *Commemorative Biog. Records of Hartford City* (2 vols., 1901); F. C. Norton, *Governors of Conn.* (1895); F. W. Chapman, *The Bulkeley Family* (1875); J. H. Trumbull, *Memorial Hist. of Hartford County, Conn., 1633–1884* (1886).]

E. F. H.

BULKELEY, PETER (Jan. 31, 1582/3–Mar. 9, 1658/9), Puritan clergyman, son of Edward and Olyff (Irby) Bulkeley, was born at Odell in Bedfordshire, England, and died in Concord, Mass. Both his parents were of distinguished ancestry. His father, a man of independent means, was a Church of England clergyman somewhat touched with dissent. At about sixteen, Peter entered St. John's College, Cambridge, where he remained for a long time as student (M.A., 1608) and fellow, acquiring an education to be approved of later by Cotton Mather as "Learned, . . . Genteel, and which was the top of all, very Pious" (*Magnalia,* 1702, Bk. III, p. 96). In January 1619/20, upon the death of his father, he succeeded to a considerable fortune and to his father's position as rector of Odell. He was married twice. His first wife, Jane Allen, after giving birth to twelve children, died in 1626. "A thundering preacher and a judicious divine" (Daniel Neal, *The History of the Puritans,* 1754, p. 585), he was clear in his disapproval of ritualism and of men with long hair, but not so clear that his recalcitrance could not be overlooked by ecclesiastical superiors who were themselves often of his view-point. But on the accession of Laud to the archbishopric, recognizing the divergence between himself and those in control of the Church, Bulkeley determined in 1634 or 1635 to emigrate to Massachusetts. His second wife, Grace Chetwode, whom he had but recently married, and his many children and servants came with him in 1636. After a short residence in Cambridge, he went up "further into the Woods" (Mather, *Magnalia,* Bk. III, p. 96) and established a new town, with a church of which he was officially made "teacher." He was from that time head of the theocracy of Concord, diligently and with substantial results, so far as one can judge, furthering the interests of his followers in both this world and the next. His chief participation in affairs away from Concord was in 1637, when, with Thomas Hooker, he served as moderator of a church council held in Cambridge, to determine among other things, whether for salvation one should look more confidently to grace or to works. Himself a partisan of works, he denounced Anne Hutchinson as a "Jezabell whom the Devill sent over thither to poison these American Churches with her depths of Satan" (*New England Historical and Genealogical Register,* XXXI, 157). His *Gospel Covenant,* made up of a number of his sermons, was published in London in 1646, and again in 1651—"one of those massive, exhaustive, ponderous treatises, into which the Puritan theologians put their enormous Biblical learning, their acumen, their industry, the fervor, pathos, and consecration of their lives" (M. C. Tyler, *History of American Literature during the Colonial Time,* 1897, I, 217).

[Additional references: *New Eng. Hist. and Geneal. Reg.,* vol. X; F. W. Chapman, *Bulkeley Family* (1875); J. W. Bailey, *Paternal Pedigree* (1907).]   J. D. W.

BULKLEY, JOHN WILLIAMS (Nov. 3, 1802–June 19, 1888), educator, was descended from the Rev. Peter Bulkeley [*q.v.*], an emigrant from Bedfordshire, England, in 1636 and one of the early settlers of Concord, Mass. One branch of the family spread into Connecticut, in which state, at Fairfield, John Bulkley was born. It was his father's intention that his son on leaving the common school should take up an occupation of a mechanical nature. Intellectual pursuits appealing more to the youth, however, he betook himself to Clinton, N. Y., where he entered upon a study of the classics and mathematics with a view to entering Hamilton College in an advanced class. Although intending to enter the ministry on graduation, he was forced to make a temporary digression in favor of a sea voyage to restore his health which had become impaired during his studies. In 1825, after his return, he took up "school keeping" but only as a temporary expedient. He found the work so congenial, however, that he made a permanent profession of it. After teaching for six years in his home town, he was called to Troy, N. Y., where as teacher and principal he was so successful that his services were sought by numerous academies and public schools. In 1838 he accepted a position in a new public school in Albany, N. Y. Williamsburg secured his services in 1850 and when Williamsburg, Bushwick, and Brooklyn united into a single municipality, he was chosen

as the first superintendent of schools. It was Bulkley's fortune to spend his most productive years during the period commonly known as the American "common school revival," a period during which education was becoming popularized and a professional consciousness was being developed among teachers. His early reports as superintendent of schools in Brooklyn were definite attempts to stimulate his board of education and his community to espouse the cause of educational improvement. He early advocated teacher training and Pestalozzian object teaching. His chief contribution, however, lay in his activities in organizing teachers' associations. While he was still in Troy, he aided in the organization of the Troy Teachers' Society, one of the first in the state. He assisted in projecting the convention at Syracuse in 1845 which launched a New York state teachers' association, the first of its kind in the country. As the first president of the association and as president again in 1851 he continued his leadership of the convention. He was one of the eleven original founders of the National Teachers' Association, now the National Education Association. He served this great organization as its first secretary and fourth president. In 1873 he was made assistant superintendent of schools. This unusual demotion seems to have been made because of his advanced age and in lieu of dismissing so old and tried a public servant. In 1885 he declined reëlection for the triennial period on account of failing health, and three years later he died at the age of eighty-six.

[The principal sources of biographical material are Henry Barnard's *Am. Jour. of Ed.,* XIV, 28, XV, 349; and the *N. E. A. Jour. of Proc. and Addresses,* 1888, p. 677. An obituary appeared in the *N. Y. Times,* June 21, 1888. Bulkley's reports to the Brooklyn Board of Education also are of interest for the period 1855–73. The *Brooklyn Daily Eagle,* July 9, 1873 contains an account of his election as assistant superintendent.]

J. S. B—r.

BULKLEY, LUCIUS DUNCAN (Jan. 12, 1845–July 20, 1928), physician, was born in New York City, the son of Henry D. and Juliana (Barnes) Bulkley. His father was a prominent general practitioner with a special interest in skin diseases, and his own career was largely a continuation of his father's dermatological activity. Having graduated in arts at Yale in 1866 and in medicine from the College of Physicians and Surgeons in 1869, he studied dermatology in Europe under such masters as Von Hebra and Neumann of Vienna, and Hardy of Paris, and in 1872 settled in his native city with the aim of limiting his practise to dermatology. On May 28, 1872, he was married to Katherine La Rue Mellick. His father was now dead, but aided by the professional support of the latter's friends, he soon laid the foundations of a large and select practise. In the conviction, however, that a practise cannot be self-perpetuating but requires incessant publicity to thrive, he plunged into many professional activities beginning with a translation of Isidor Neumann's *Lehrbuch der Hautkrankheiten* (1872), which he had begun while in Vienna. With others he organized the clinical activity of the Demilt Dispensary into a teaching force and thus laid the foundation for systematic post-graduate teaching which culminated in the New York Post-Graduate Medical School and the New York Polyclinic. He founded (1874) and for eight years edited the *Archives of Dermatology* and was throughout his career a contributor to medical journal literature, and published many text-books. He took an active part in the work of the then new local and national dermatological societies, but as his aggressiveness made enemies he failed in two of his aims,— the presidency of the American Dermatological Association and the chair of dermatology in his alma mater. He became, however, professor of dermatology in the Post-Graduate Medical School and Hospital, was from 1887 to 1900 chairman of the section on dermatology of the American Medical Association, and in 1897 was president of the American Academy of Medicine. Beginning in 1877, he gave free courses of instruction in dermatology at the New York Hospital, later transferred to the New York Skin and Cancer Hospital which he founded in 1882. He traveled much in the interest of his special work, attending many congresses both in this country and Europe and studying exotic diseases in their habitat, and he accumulated an unrivaled collection of books, pamphlets, plates, models, etc., pertaining to his special work. On retiring from dermatological activity he astonished the profession by coming out for the non-surgical treatment of cancer, at first with reservations but eventually limiting it to diet, hygiene, and drugs. He published books and journal articles on his attitude, established a free clinic, and founded a special society and a quarterly journal, *Cancer*. The reaction of the profession was on the whole very unfavorable, his motives were impugned, and he was forced to sever some of his society and hospital affiliations. But his motives were certainly not mercenary, for he was worth a large fortune and his crusade cost him thousands of dollars. He had an instinctive horror of the knife (never forgetting the death of his father from incision of a carbuncle, now regarded as bad surgery) ; he was a religious mystic who believed that his life had often been spared for some

special end which might well have been the conquest of cancer ; he loved controversy, especially when on the weak side ; and he needed an outlet for his energies, old as he then was. His mentality was highly extroverted and he was unequal to reflection and self-criticism; but, while he often blundered, he usually won his case by sheer energy and persistence. He did not abandon his work until blinded by double cataract and did not long survive his enforced rest. *Eczema* (1882, 3rd edition, 1901) ; *Acne* (1885) ; *Manual of Diseases of the Skin* (1882, 6th edition, 1912) ; *Syphilis in the Innocent* (1894), the Alvarenga Prize Essay ; are the best-known of his writings, but he published a number of smaller works on dermatology and several volumes on the medical treatment of cancer which were not convincing to the profession: *Cancer, its Cause and Treatment* (2 vols., 1915–17) ; *Cancer and Its Non-Surgical Treatment* (1921; a second edition in press at the time of his death) ; and *Cancer of the Breast* (1924).

[*N. Y. Times* and *N. Y. Herald-Tribune*, July 21, 1928 ; *Archives of Dermatology and Syphilology*, Nov. 1928 ; *Jour. of the Am. Medic. Ass.*, July 28, 1928 ; Herman Goodman, "A Pioneer of Am. Dermatology," *Medic. Life*, Aug. 1928 ; *Who's Who in America*, 1924–25 ; personal information.]   E. P.

BULL, EPHRAIM WALES (Mar. 4, 1806– Sept. 26, 1895), horticulturist, was born in Boston, Mass., the son of Epaphras Bull of Bullsville, N. Y., and Esther Wales of Dorchester, Mass. He was a studious child, winning the Franklin medal for scholarship in the Boston public schools at the age of eleven, but was also given to strenuous physical work in his father's vineyard. Though from the first interested in grape raising, he was when a boy apprenticed to Louis Lauriat, a Boston chemist, to learn the trade of goldbeating, and this, until his reputation as a horticulturist was established many years later, was his profession. While practising it, he raised grapes in his garden on Fayette Street in Boston, and later on a more extensive scale at Concord, Mass. He worked chiefly with native stock, rather than the European wine grape, and was led to the use of sexual propagation by reading the classic treatise of Van Mons on raising pears from seed. At that time the "Isabella" was the earliest-ripened grape in the country ; yet early as it was it did not always escape an early frost. Having discovered an extraordinarily early-ripening specimen of *Vitis labrusca*, the northern fox grape, Bull planted the grapes whole, and nursed the seedlings for six years. On Sept. 10, 1849, he picked the first fruit of these seedlings. For five years more he cared for the vines, reproducing them by cuttings, and continuing to replant the seeds. He obtained an astonishing number of variations by this method, even white grapes appearing from black parents. It is not certain just when Bull realized the superiority of one of the new strains that was to become the famous "Concord." He exhibited it on Sept. 3, 1853, at Massachusetts Horticultural Hall. Through a mishap the specimens almost failed to be noted by the judges; when brought to light, however, the new variety proved to be earlier than the "Isabella," extremely hardy, prolific, and phenomenally heavy, handsome, fragrant and juicy; it was both a good table grape and a wine grape. Bull sold this new grape at five dollars a vine, and the first year obtained $3,200 net income, but when nurseries bought the stock and propagated it for sale, he received almost no further income from the "Concord." For this reason he hated commercial grape culture, and died embittered. He produced also the white "Esther," the "Rockwood," the "Iona," and the "August Rose." He is said to have raised 22,000 seedlings, and to have saved only twenty-one as worthy of preservation. A member of the Massachusetts House of Representatives in 1855, he was chairman of the committee on agriculture, and the ensuing year occupied the same position in the Massachusetts Senate. From 1856 to 1858 he was a member of the Massachusetts State Board of Agriculture. Personally he was eccentric, and a lover of homely philosophy. His intimates included Louis Agassiz and Nathaniel Hawthorne. He was married on Sept. 10, 1826, to Mary Elden Walker of Dorchester, Mass.

[Sketch by Wm. Barrett in *Memoirs of Members of the Social Circle in Concord*, 4th ser. (1909); *Am. Breeder's Mag.*, I, 238–42; *The Story of Concord told by Concord Writers* (1906), ed. by Josephine Latham Swayne, pp. 157–58.]   D. C. P.

BULL, WILLIAM (1683–Mar. 21, 1755), lieutenant-governor of South Carolina, was the son of Stephen Bull, a man prominent in the first settlement of South Carolina and a deputy of Lord Ashley, a proprietor. Stephen was a member of the Council and engaged extensively in the Indian trade. His son, William, followed his father's example in both politics and trade. He was a member of the Commons House, 1706–19. During the Tuscarora and Yemassee wars he served as a captain of the militia. He was appointed Lord Proprietor's Deputy in 1719; and when the proprietary government was overthrown in the same year by the people with the connivance of the Crown, he was loyal to the proprietors. Despite his support of the defeated faction he was so prominent that he was made a member of the Council in 1721 under the new government and

served in that capacity until 1737. Also in 1721 he was chosen one of the three commissioners to manage the colony's lucrative Indian trade (*South Carolina Statutes*, III, 141–46), and his knowledge of colonial conditions led to his selection in 1733 as adviser to Oglethorpe in locating his first settlement in Georgia. Savannah was chosen, and Bull furnished laborers who worked for a month in building the new town. When Lieut.-Gov. Broughton died in 1737 Bull as senior member of the Council became acting governor and in 1738 lieutenant-governor, an office which he held until his death. His active administration lasted from 1737 until the arrival of Gov. Glen in 1743. From 1740 to 1742 his son, William Bull II [*q.v.*], was speaker of the House, and the laws of the province were authenticated by the signatures of father and son during this period. Bull's administration was notable for three constitutional advances. The governor was excluded from the Council's legislative sessions; the House secured control of money bills; and it obtained the right of electing a treasurer without the consent of the governor and Council. The colony was ready for these changes, but they were perhaps more easily obtained under a native-born governor who could readily understand the temper of the people. During Bull's administration the colony was menaced by war with Spain and by servile insurrection. In the handling of both situations he showed resource and decision. He persuaded the Assembly to vote 600 men and £120,000 paper money to aid Oglethorpe in an attack on St. Augustine, which failed because of Oglethorpe's incompetence. Bull himself sounded the alarm of the slave outbreak. On his way to Charleston he saw the negroes plundering, murdering, and compelling others to join the insurrection. Avoiding them, he hastened to his destination, gave the alarm, raised the militia, and succeeded in ending the revolt before it gained great headway. In addition to Ashley Hall and other property which he inherited from his father he obtained large grants in the province and settled on the Sheldon estate, adding materially to the family fortune. He was married to Mary, daughter of Richard Quintyne, who died on Mar. 19, 1738/39.

[A short sketch of Bull is in the *S. C. Hist. and Geneal. Mag.*, Jan. 1900. Some information regarding his public career may be found in Edward McCrady, *S. C. under the Proprietary Govt., 1670–1719* (1897), and *Hist. of S. C. under the Royal Govt., 1719–76* (1899). Source material is contained in the Commons House Jours.; the Council Jours.; the Pub. Records, and the *S. C. Hist. Soc. Colls.* (1858).]   H. B-C.

BULL, WILLIAM (Sept. 24, 1710–July 4, 1791), colonial governor of South Carolina, the second son of Lieut.-Gov. William Bull [*q.v.*], and of Mary (Quintyne) Bull, was born at Ashley Hall, South Carolina. He studied medicine at Leyden and was the first native-born American to receive the degree of Doctor of Medicine. After his return to South Carolina he did not practise his profession but devoted himself to agriculture and politics. His own ability, combined with the advantages of wealth and social position, made him important in the colony. He was a member of the Commons House in 1736–49, and was speaker, 1740–42 and 1744–49. In the war with Spain he was captain of one of the South Carolina companies. In 1748 he was appointed to the Council and served with distinction until he became lieutenant-governor in 1759. While in this position, he acted five times as governor, 1760–61, 1764–66, 1768, 1769–71, 1773–75, a total of eight years. In his relations with the Indians he showed moderation, but when forced to action against them he was energetic and determined. He was sent as commissioner to an Indian conference at Albany, in 1752, where peace was concluded between the Catawbas of South Carolina and the Iroquois of New York, allies of the English but at war with each other. He tried to avert the Cherokee war in 1759, counseling patience and further conferences with the Indians. His advice was not taken by Gov. Lyttleton, and for more than two years South Carolina was embroiled in Indian warfare. Once Bull took part in an active campaign, and after he had replaced Lyttleton as acting governor in 1760, he secured British and colonial aid, and finally in 1761 subdued the Indians. While Bull was primarily concerned with politics he was also interested in education. He contributed £150 to the College of Philadelphia (forerunner of the University of Pennsylvania) and in 1770 recommended that the colony establish public schools and a college for higher education, thus foreshadowing a public school system. His plan for free schools was lost because the colony was becoming absorbed in opposition to England. Bull's last four administrations as acting governor occurred during the critical period, 1764–75, and his tact and ability were tried to the utmost. Born and reared in the colony, he had a true understanding of colonial prejudices, but he was loyal to the British government and vainly endeavored to stem the growing revolutionary sentiment. At the time of the Stamp Act, he had the stamps landed at Fort Johnson at Charleston and prevented a clash with the mob in its first attempt to destroy the paper. When the tea ships arrived at Charleston, he acted with his usual dispatch and, before a hostile populace expected the move, he ordered the Collector to seize the tea and store it. In the summer of 1774 despite his efforts South Carolina advanced rapidly toward colonial union. Delegates were appointed by the people of Charleston to the First Continental Congress. A sympathetic House would have confirmed this action had not Bull kept it prorogued. Finally a meeting was contrived for an early hour in the morning, and, before the governor could order the House prorogued, the Charleston election was ratified, and £1,500 were appropriated for the delegates' expenses. By the summer of 1774 practically all power had passed out of the Governor's hands into those of the Provincial Congress, and when Bull was replaced by Lord William Campbell in 1775, his public career closed and royal authority ended in South Carolina. Bull retained the love and respect of the people, and his extensive estates were exempted from the act confiscating the property of royalists. He left the colony with the British troops in 1782 and spent the remaining nine years of his life in London. He had married on Aug. 17, 1746, Hannah, daughter of Othneal Beale.

[An outline of Bull's life is in the *S. C. Hist. and Geneal. Mag.*, vol. I. E. McCrady's *Hist. of S. C. under the Royal Government* (1899) and W. R. Smith's *S. C. as a Royal Province* (1903) give an account of his public career as identified with the colony's history in the period before the Revolution.]   H. B–C.

BULL, WILLIAM TILLINGHAST (May 18, 1849–Feb. 22, 1909), surgeon, the son of Henry B. Bull by his wife, Henrietta Melville, was born in Newport, R. I. The Bulls were descended from Henry Bull, one of the founders of the Roger Williams settlement at Newport (Aquidneck), who later was twice made governor of the colony. William was graduated from Harvard College in 1869 and in 1872 received the degree of M.D. from the College of Physicians and Surgeons of the City of New York. Following his internship at the Bellevue Hospital he studied for two years in the leading clinics of Vienna, Berlin, Paris, and London and then returned to New York City where he passed the rest of his life engaged in an active surgical practise. At various times he was associated with the New York Dispensary (1875–77), the Chambers Street Hospital (1877–78), the New York Hospital (1883), St. Luke's Hospital (1880–83), the Hospital for the Ruptured and Crippled, the Woman's and the Roosevelt hospitals. In these several positions he was active as teacher, consultant, and surgeon. From 1889 to 1904 he was professor of surgery at the College of Physicians and Surgeons.

Bull specialized upon the surgery of the abdomen, and his important contributions concern procedures which he studied and later advocated for treatment of gunshot wounds of the abdomen, for hernia, and for cancer of the breast. It is related that during his service at the Chambers Street Hospital a woman died following an abdominal bullet wound. At the autopsy Bull became convinced that through prompt laparotomy with suture of the damaged intestines such cases might be saved. A few months later (Nov. 2, 1884) a man was brought in with a similar wound and was promptly operated upon with complete success even though the intestines had to be sutured in seven places. Since then Bull's procedure for such emergencies has been adopted by all surgeons. With William B. Coley he published "Observations on the Mechanical and Operative Treatment of Hernia at the Hospital for Ruptured and Crippled" (*Annals of Surgery,* May 1893), in which he pointed out the inadequacy of the methods then employed and suggested improvements. With Coley also he wrote the sections on hernia in F. S. Dennis's *System of Surgery* (1896) and in the *International Textbook of Surgery* (1900). In 1894 he published a noteworthy paper on "Cases of Cancer of the Breast treated by Radical Operation, with a Report of 118 Cases" (*Medical Record,* N. Y., Aug. 18, 1894) which was the most valuable contribution by an American surgeon up to that time. With W. Martin he edited the translation of Bergmann, Bruns, and Mikulicz's *System of Practical Surgery* in five volumes which appeared in 1904. Early in 1908 he developed cancer of the neck, and as surgery and X-ray proved of no avail, he succumbed, February 22, 1909. He was married on May 30, 1893, to Mary, widow of James G. Blaine, Jr., and daughter of Col. Richard Nevins of Ohio.

Bull, like A. T. Cabot [*q.v.*], was deeply impressed by the early papers of Lister, with the result that he became one of the first in America to adopt antisepsis, and the large measure of success which immediately came to him on his return from Europe was undoubtedly due to this fact. He had in addition remarkable technical skill, great acumen in diagnosis, and a broad understanding of human problems. He is said to have been the first American who devoted himself entirely to surgery from the beginning of his practise. His avocations were music and art.

[There are numerous obituaries, but that by his co-worker, W. B. Coley, in the *Trans. Am. Surgic. Ass.,* 1909, XXVII, pp. 29–30, is the most complete and authentic; see also *N. Y. Times,* Feb. 23, 1909, and obituaries listed in the *Index Cat. of the Surgeon-General's Lib.,* 3 ser.]

J.F.F.

BULLARD, HENRY ADAMS (Sept. 9, 1788–Apr. 17, 1851), jurist, was born at Pepperell, Mass., the son of John and Elizabeth (Adams) Bullard. His father was a Congregational clergyman, his mother a member of the distinguished Adams family. He was sent to Harvard University where he took his A.B. degree in 1807. The Harvard alumni records also show that the degree of M.A. was conferred upon him in 1836. After graduating from the university he studied law, first in Boston and later in Philadelphia, and, at the same time, indulged a fondness for the modern languages by studying French, Spanish, German, and Italian, all four of which he is said to have been able to read and to speak with fluency. Soon after completing his legal studies, but before practising, he enlisted with Toledo, a Mexican revolutionary general who was in Philadelphia gathering recruits for an expedition into Mexico, then strongly affected by the liberation movement taking place in Latin-America. Toledo was so impressed by the young man, especially by his ability to speak Spanish, that he made him his secretary and aide-de-camp. They departed for the West, spent the winter of 1812–13 in Nashville, Tenn., and in the spring made their way to the frontier town of Natchitoches, La. From here they entered Spanish territory where, on Aug. 13, 1813, their force was defeated and scattered by Spanish troops in an engagement near San Antonio, Tex. Bullard, and a few companions, after great hardships and dangers, managed to return to Natchitoches, where he decided, since he was friendless and destitute, to remain and open a law office. His ability to speak French and Spanish soon enabled him to form acquaintances with members of the leading families, most of whom were of French or Spanish origin; his education and culture, his handsome face, his musical voice, and his kindly sympathy created a favorable impression; he made himself familiar with the Napoleonic Code and with the Louisiana code of 1808; his practise increased and he prospered. On Oct. 24, 1816, he married at Natchitoches Sarah Maria Kaiser, a native of Lexington, Ky. Between 1822 and 1830 he twice served as state district judge. In 1830 he was elected, on the Whig ticket, to represent the Western District of Louisiana in the Twenty-second Congress. Reëlected to the Twenty-third Congress, he served until 1834, when he was appointed a judge of the supreme court of Louisiana. With the exception of a few months in 1839, when he was secretary of state of Louisiana, he remained upon the state supreme bench until 1846, when the judiciary was remodeled under a new constitution and the old bench replaced by a new. With Judge Curry he undertook to make a digest of the laws of the state, but only one volume was published because they knew that the constitutional convention, which was about to assemble, would necessarily change or abrogate many of the important laws. From 1847 to 1850 Bullard was professor of civil law in the University of Louisiana (now Tulane University). In 1850 he was elected to the state House of Representatives, but had served only a short time when he was elected to the Thirty-first Congress, as a Whig, to fill a vacancy in the 2nd Louisiana Congressional District caused by the resignation of Charles M. Conrad, appointed secretary of state in the cabinet of President Fillmore. Bullard was probably the founder of the Louisiana Historical Society in 1836, and was its first president. It fell into decay, was revived in the summer of 1846, and Judge Martin, the historian, was made president. The next year the society was incorporated. When Judge Martin died in December 1846, Bullard was again chosen president, and continued in that office until the time of his death. He was also a corresponding member of the Massachusetts Historical Society. He died in New Orleans, and is buried in the Girod Street Cemetery.

[B. F. French, *Hist. Colls. of La.*, pt. II (1851), pp. 5–8, including resolutions passed by the members of the New Orleans bar at the time of Bullard's death; *De Bow's Rev. of the Southern and Western States*, vol. XII (n.s., vol. V), pp. 50–56; New Orleans *Daily Picayune*, Apr. 22, 1851; inscription upon the tombstone in the Girod Street cemetery; Harvard University alumni records; records of Tulane University; information from Mr. Arthur Lastrapes, great-grandson, and Mrs. Robert Strother Moore and Mrs. O. W. McNeese, great-grand-daughters of Bullard.]   M. J. W.

BULLARD, WILLIAM HANNUM GRUBB (Dec. 6, 1866–Nov. 24, 1927), naval officer, the son of Orson Flagg and Rebecca Ann (Huston) Bullard, was born in Media, Pa., and graduated from the United States Naval Academy in 1886. He became ensign July 1, 1888; lieutenant, junior grade, Sept. 5, 1896; lieutenant Mar. 3, 1899; lieutenant commander Jan. 1, 1905; commander Feb. 1, 1909; captain July 1, 1912; rear admiral (temporary rank) July 1, 1918; and permanent rear admiral Oct. 20, 1919. Throughout the service he was known for his accomplishments, his poise of mind, and his invariable courtesy. In the Spanish-American War he served on the U. S. S. *Columbia*, and in 1905–06 and 1906–07 on the U. S. S. *Maine*, the first year as navigator and then as executive officer. During the following four years he was on duty at the Naval Academy, where he reorganized the department of electrical engineering, in which subject he was considered an expert. His *Naval Electricians' Test and Hand Book*, published in 1904, proved so useful that it has been reissued in several editions. In 1911 and 1912 he was commandant of the naval station at San Fran-

cisco, and from 1912 to 1916 superintendent of the naval radio service. He commanded the battleship *Arkansas*, 1916–18, his ship forming part of the American division of the British Grand Fleet in the World War. Later he commanded the American forces in the Eastern Mediterranean, and became a member of the Inter-Allied Commission to put into effect the naval terms of the armistice with Austria-Hungary, effecting, with notable tact and forbearance, the surrender of the Austro-Hungarian fleet. In January and August 1919, he was a member of the Inter-Allied conference on radio, and from 1919 to 1921 served as director of communications in the Navy Department. He commanded the Yangtze Patrol Force, U. S. Asiatic Fleet, in 1921–22, and retired Sept. 30, 1922.

Bullard has, with some show of justice, been called "the father of American radio," and there can be no doubt that his extraordinary knowledge of this subject, added to his firm stand for his country's rights, preserved to the United States her prestige in this field. The decisive turning point of his activities came in 1919, when, by his persistence and the convincing presentation of his views, he prevented the sale to foreign interests of the patent rights in the Alexanderson alternator. At the same time he counseled the formation of an independent company which developed into the Radio Corporation of America, the foremost body of the kind in the world. At his death he was chairman of the Federal Radio Commission. He was married to Beirne Saunders of Baltimore on Oct. 30, 1889, and had one son, a naval officer.

[*Who's Who in America*, 1926–27; Navy Registers, 1887–1927; "Admiral Bullard," by Capt. Edwin T. Pollock, *Army and Navy Reg.*, Dec. 24, 1927; "Admiral Wm. H. G. Bullard," in the *Outlook*, Dec. 7, 1927.]   E. B.

BULLITT, ALEXANDER SCOTT (1762–Apr. 13, 1816), lieutenant-governor of Kentucky, the son of Cuthbert and Helen (Scott) Bullitt, was of Huguenot descent, the first of the line in America having come from France in 1685 and settled at Port Tobacco, Md. The family later moved to Dumfries, Va., where Alexander Scott Bullitt was born. His father was a judge of the supreme court of Virginia and an uncle, Capt. Thomas Bullitt, was one of the first explorers of Kentucky. Alexander Scott Bullitt was educated for law and in 1783 was elected to the Virginia House of Delegates. During the same year, however, he was induced by the lure of frontier life to move to Kentucky where he settled on Bull Skin Creek in Shelby County. Being too much exposed to the Indians there, he removed in two years to Jefferson County and settled about eight miles from Louisville on an estate which he named "Oxmoor" from Tristram Shandy (T. W. Bullitt, *post*, p. 16).

Bullitt was one of the outstanding men of Kentucky from the beginning. In 1786 he was appointed county-lieutenant of Jefferson County and the next year was made a trustee of Louisville (*History of the Ohio Falls Cities and their Counties*, 1882, I, 200). He entered state politics in 1788 as a member of the convention to secure statehood and in 1792 became a member of the convention which drafted the first constitution (B. H. Young, *History and Texts of the Three Constitutions of Kentucky*, 1890, p. 31). One of the electors for selecting the governor under the first constitution, he was also chosen as one of the first state senators. He remained in the Senate by successive reëlections until 1800 and throughout this period was its speaker (Lewis and R. H. Collins, *History of Kentucky*, 1874, II, 357). In 1799 he was president of the convention which drafted the second constitution for Kentucky, and the next year he was elected lieutenant-governor, in which capacity he continued to preside over the Senate. At the expiration of his term he was again elected to the Senate in 1804 where he remained until 1808, at which time he retired to private life. His long service in the Senate was without brilliance or special incident. The undoubtedly great influence he exerted was due to his reputation for probity and integrity. He was greatly honored by his contemporaries and Bullitt County was named for him. He was twice married: first, in October 1785 to Priscilla Christian, daughter of Col. William Christian, one of the best known of early Kentuckians; second, after her death, to Mary (Churchill) Prather, a widow.

[Thos. Walker Bullitt's *My Life at Oxmoor* (Louisville, 1911) is a book of reminiscences by A. S. Bullitt's grandson. Much the same ground is covered by E. H. Ellwanger, "Oxmoor—Its Builder and Its Historian" in the *Reg. of the Ky. State Hist. Soc.*, Jan. 1919. Kathleen Jennings, *Louisville's First Families* (1920) supplies some collateral facts. See also H. E. Hayden, *Va. Genealogies* (1891). The *Jours. of the Ky. Senate* give glimpses of Bullitt as a presiding officer.]
					R. S. C.

BULLITT, HENRY MASSIE (Feb. 28, 1817–Feb. 5, 1880), physician and teacher of medicine, of Huguenot descent, a son of Cuthbert Bullitt and his wife Harriet Willit, was born in Shelby County, Ky. At the age of seventeen he began the study of medicine in the office of Dr. Coleman Rogers, Sr., of Louisville, subsequently entering the University of Pennsylvania, where he graduated with distinction in 1838. He thereupon returned to Louisville and practised his profession until 1845 when he went to Europe for further study. A year later he returned to America to accept a professorship at the St. Louis Medical College where he lectured on the practise of medicine during the academic years 1846–47 and 1847–48. In 1849 he became professor of materia medica at Transylvania University at Lexington, Ky., the medical department of which institution (founded 1819) was the best known as well as the oldest school in the Ohio Valley. In the following year he founded the Kentucky School of Medicine at Louisville. He gave his attention to the new school until 1866 when he was called to the chair of the principles and practise of medicine at the University of Louisville. In the next spring he became, in addition, professor of physiology. In 1868 he established the Louisville Medical College, remaining connected therewith until his death, which occurred in that city following a long and painful illness borne with brave cheerfulness. He was married first on May 26, 1841, to Julia Anderson of Louisville, who died on Jan. 16, 1853, leaving seven children, but two of whom survived childhood. His second wife was Mrs. Sarah Crow Paradise whom he married on Sept. 14, 1854. Of the second marriage there were a son and five daughters.

Bullitt is best known as a teacher, though he labored under the handicap of extreme deafness which necessarily limited his teaching in his last years. He was successively professor in no less than five medical schools, of two of which he was a founder. As these two have since his death become a part of the University of Louisville, he may properly be considered one of the fathers of that institution. His best-known contributions to medical literature are: "The Art of Observing in Medicine," *St. Louis Medical Journal*, 1847; "On the Pathology of Inflammation," "Medical Organization and Reform," and other articles in the *Transylvania Journal of Medicine*. He was associate editor of both of these journals as well as of the *Louisville Medical Record* which he helped to found. Perhaps his best-known paper was a reply (published in the *Medical Examiner*, Philadelphia, 1844) to Dr. Charles Caldwell, who had claimed that to understand Southern and Western diseases, a physician must have been trained in the South or West. This paper is an excellent example of the controversial medical writing of the period, and in it Bullitt held his own against Caldwell then firmly established as the dean of medical teachers west of the Alleghanies.

[See sketch of Bullitt's life by his colleague Dr. Jas. Morrison Bodine of Louisville in Burrage and Kelly, *Am. Medic. Biogs.* (1920). Bullitt's editorials and articles in the journals of which he was editor throw light on his life, character, and attainments.]

E. E. H.

BULLOCH, ARCHIBALD (1729/30–February 1777), first president of the Provincial Congress of Georgia, was born at Charleston, S. C., the son of a Scotch clergyman and planter, James Bulloch, and his wife, Jean Stobo. After the family had moved to a plantation on the Savannah River, Georgia (*c.* 1750), he studied law and was admitted to practise. He remained both lawyer and planter until his removal to Savannah in the early seventies. On Oct. 9, 1764, he was married to Mary de Veaux, daughter of Judge James de Veaux of Shaftesbury, Ga. Elected to the Commons House in 1768, he served continuously until 1773, when he declined the seat to which he had been chosen. He was a member of the committee that corresponded with Benjamin Franklin, the colonial agent in London, and in April 1772 he was chosen speaker—an empty honor when Acting-Governor James Habersham dissolved the Assembly immediately after his election. Consequently Bulloch allied himself more firmly with the irreconcilable colonial party and his name was one of four signed to the first call, June 14, 1774, for an assemblage of patriots in Savannah. From July 4, 1775, until his death Bulloch was president of the Provincial Congress, was a delegate in occasional attendance in the Continental Congress, and in April 1776, on the flight of Sir James Wright the royal governor, he was made "President and Commander-in-chief of Georgia."

In official life Bulloch disclosed something of the energy and vivid conception of patriotic duty that characterized his descendant Theodore Roosevelt. His personal popularity and vigorous espousal of the cause of liberty made him influential in molding public opinion in the early years of the war. In his efforts to defeat the enemy he was not to be limited to his numerous civil offices: he led the party of militia and Creek Indians that destroyed the British and Tory base on Tybee Island, Mar. 25, 1776; and, in case the sins of Georgians should have been responsible for the late military reverses suffered by the colonies, he issued a proclamation against swearing in the streets of Savannah, "especially on the Sabbath," and set aside a day of prayer "to implore his divine goodness to restore our Adversaries to reason and Justice, and thereby to relieve the United States from the distresses of an Unnatural War" (*Revolutionary Records,*

State of Ga., I, 1908, p. 304). An ordinance of the council of safety, Feb. 22, 1777, recognized an established fact when it conferred upon him "the whole executive power of government." The gesture came too late, for he died before the end of the month.

[A. D. Candler, ed., *Rev. Records, State of Ga.* (1908) and *Colonial Records, State of Ga.* (1904–16); J. G. B. Bulloch, *Biog. Sketch of Hon. Archibald Bulloch,* n.d.; W. F. Northen, *Men of Mark of Georgia,* vol. I (1907); L. L. Knight, *Georgia's Landmarks, Memorials and Legends,* vol. II (1914), p. 642.]

T. D. M.

BULLOCH, JAMES DUNWODY (June 25, 1823–Jan. 7, 1901), naval officer, Confederate agent, was descended from a distinguished Georgia family of Scotch-Irish and Huguenot extraction. His great-grandfather, Archibald Bulloch [*q.v.*], held many important positions under the colonial government, and his father, Maj. James Stephens Bulloch was a member of the company under whose auspices the *Savannah* made her famous voyage across the Atlantic from Savannah to Liverpool. His mother, Hester Amarinthia, was a daughter of Senator John Elliott and his wife Esther. His half-sister, Martha Bulloch, was married in 1853 to Theodore Roosevelt, Sr., and was the mother of President Roosevelt. James Dunwody Bulloch was born near Savannah, Ga. His later home was "Bulloch Hall" at Roswell near Atlanta. In 1839 he became a midshipman in the United States navy. He served first on board the *United States* and later on board the United States sailing sloop of war *Decatur,* on the Brazil station, first under command of Henry W. Ogden and later under command of David G. Farragut. In 1842 he was transferred to the battle-ship *Delaware,* cruising in the Mediterranean. After a brief attendance at the navy school at Philadelphia in 1844–45 he returned to active service, on the Pacific coast. In 1849–51 he served in the coast survey. He succeeded Lieut. (later Admiral) D. D. Porter in command of the *Georgia,* the first subsidized mail steamer to California, and subsequently he commanded various vessels in the Gulf mail service. He was one of a small number of lieutenants of the United States navy who were detailed by the government to enter the mail service to enlarge the school for experience in steam navigation. Later, influenced by the demand of the growing packet and mail service for commanders and by the slowness of promotion in the navy, he retired and entered private mail service, becoming identified with the shipping enterprises of New York. Immediately after the opening of the Civil War, he accepted from Secretary Mal-

257

lory the foreign mission as agent of the Confederate navy, especially to buy or build naval vessels in England. Arriving at Liverpool in June he promptly began operations, aided by the generous confidence of Fraser, Trenholm & Company. Under his instructions were dispatched and equipped all Confederate cruising ships except the *Georgia*. After laying the keel of the *Oreto* (the later *Florida*) and arranging for the construction of *No. 290* (the later *Alabama*) he returned to the Confederacy on the blockade-runner *Fingal* sailing via Nassau and carrying much-needed supplies to Savannah. In February 1862 he returned to Liverpool on a steamer blockade-runner of Fraser, Trenholm & Company, sailing from Wilmington. Soon thereafter he dispatched the cruiser *Florida* and later another cruiser the *Alabama* to seize United States merchant vessels. All these operations he claimed were justified under English law and the rules of war. In March 1863, following the manifest intention of the British ministry to enforce the Foreign Enlistment Act more strictly, he went to Paris, having received intimations that French authorities would not interfere with the departure of Confederate vessels built in French ports.

After the War he decided to establish his residence at Liverpool, partly because he belonged to a class which was excluded from pardon under the post-bellum amnesty proclamations, and partly influenced by friendships formed in England. At Liverpool he entered the mercantile (cotton) business. He was regarded as an accomplished scholar with a thorough knowledge of maritime and international law. He had a distinguished personality, magnetic courtly manners, and was courteous and kind. In 1881–83 he wrote the history of his secret service in Europe during the Civil War. He was, however, very reserved in talking of himself and his achievements. He was married twice: on Nov. 19, 1851, at Richmond, to Elizabeth Euphemia Caskie who died at Mobile, Jan. 23, 1854; and in January 1857 to Mrs. Harriott Cross Foster, a daughter of Brigadier-General Osborne Cross of Maryland.

[Jos. Gaston B. Bulloch: *A Hist. and Geneal. of the Families of Bulloch and Stobo* (1911); Jas. D. Bulloch, *The Secret Service of the Confed. States in Europe* (2 vols., 1884); J. M. Callahan, *Diplomatic Hist. of the Southern Confederacy* (1901); Clement A. Evans, *Confed. Mil. Hist.*, vol. I (1899); *Official Records* (Navy), 2 ser., II, III; newspaper clippings lent by Martha Louise Bulloch of Liverpool.]   J.M.C.

BULLOCK, RUFUS BROWN (Mar. 28, 1834–Apr. 27, 1907), Reconstruction governor of Georgia, the son of Volckert Veeder Bullock and his wife Jane Eliza Brown, was born in Bethlehem, N. Y. After securing a high school education, he became interested in telegraphy, in which art he became an expert. He developed executive talent and for several years was employed in supervising the building of telegraph lines between New York and the South. The year 1859 found him located at Augusta, Ga., as the representative of the Adams Express Company. He organized the express business in the South and became an official of the Southern Express Company. On the outbreak of the Civil War he offered his services as a telegraph expert to the Confederacy and was used in the establishment of telegraph and railroad lines on interior points. At the close of the War he had reached the rank of lieutenant-colonel and was paroled at Appomattox as acting assistant quartermaster-general. He then returned to Augusta, resumed his connection with the express business, organized a bank, and became (1867) president of the Macon & Augusta Railroad.

Bullock's entrance into politics was as a Republican member of the constitutional convention of 1868. Congress had overthrown the state government set up by President Johnson, had reestablished military control, and had required as the condition of readmission the adoption of the Fourteenth Amendment, already rejected by the Johnson government. Congress ordered the adoption of a new state constitution, and, by disfranchising the responsible native white element and empowering the negro to vote for members of the convention and to sit in it, assured the election of a convention which would carry into effect the will of Congress. To this convention Bullock, who heartily favored the Congressional plan of reconstruction, was elected. Being a man of considerable ability, large, handsome, pleasant-mannered and popular, he at once became the leader of the carpet-bag and negro element of the convention. Under his leadership the constitutional convention was turned into a party nominating convention and he was nominated as the Republican candidate for governor in the election shortly to be held. The reviving Democratic party nominated Gen. John B. Gordon, but was defeated in the November 1868 election.

As governor from 1868 to the fall of 1871 Bullock was charged by the contemporary Democratic newspapers and other partisan opponents with every known form of political rascality,— with almost wrecking the state-owned Western & Atlantic Railroad by placing its control in the hands of incompetent and venal carpet-baggers (it piled up a debt of three-quarters of a million dollars during Bullock's administration instead of yielding a steady net revenue to the state as it had done during the previous administration);

with seeking to prolong military control for personal and party ends; with the sale of pardons; with purchasing the influence of the press by wasteful publications of public documents; with allowing the state penitentiary to be plundered; with gross corruption in the payment of subsidies to railroads; with selling state bonds and appropriating the proceeds; with general extravagance and corruption in every department of his administration. Two years of misrule were enough for the state, and in 1870 the conservatives returned an overwhelming majority to the legislature. The Governor saw that his rule was over; fearing criminal indictment, he resigned, on Oct. 23, and fled from the state. On the restoration of Democratic control the legislature appointed a committee to investigate his official conduct. The report, covering 166 pages, pronounced Bullock guilty of various charges of corruption and mismanagement. Bullock undertook to defend himself in October 1872, in an *Address to the People of Georgia.* The historian of the Reconstruction period (C. M. Thompson, *Reconstruction in Georgia,* 1915) says of the defense that it "fails to bring conviction that he disproved a single charge of the investigating committee." Bullock eluded efforts to capture him until 1876, when he was arrested, brought back to Georgia, tried on an indictment charging embezzlement of public funds, and acquitted for lack of evidence. At a much later period he again published a defense, this time in the *Independent,* Mar. 19, 1903. It is wholly unconvincing. The truth appears to be that Bullock and his crew "instituted a carnival of public spoliation" (U. B. Phillips, *Life of Robert Toombs,* 1913, p. 262). Through the device of issuing state bonds (later repudiated) to subsidize railroad corporations, they poured public money into their own pockets. During the fight over the matter of repudiating these bonds, Henry Clews & Co. of New York, who acted as Bullock's financial agents, published a card in the *Atlanta Constitution* in which they admitted that the proceeds of the bonds were misapplied and that the state had failed to receive value for them, but urged that they be not repudiated, as this would hurt the credit of the state.

After his acquittal by the jury, Bullock remained in Atlanta and rehabilitated himself, at least in the contemporary business world. He became president of the Atlanta Cotton Mills, president of the Chamber of Commerce, vice-president of the Piedmont Exposition, and a director of the Union Pacific Railroad. He was married to Marie Salisbury of Pawtucket, R. I., and was a vestryman in St. Philip's Church.

[A definitive history of the Reconstruction period in Georgia has been written by C. Mildred Thompson, now professor of history in Vassar College: *Reconstruction in Georgia* (1915). The most interesting contemporary account of the period is to be found in I. W. Avery, *Hist. of Georgia, 1850–81* (1881). Avery was editor of the *Atlanta Constitution* from 1869 to 1874 and was thus in a position to keep a close watch over events. A condensed account of the Reconstruction period is in R. P. Brooks, *Hist. of Georgia* (1913), chapters XXIII, XXIV. The *Atlanta Constitution* of Apr. 28, 1907, contains a long and highly flattering account of Bullock's career.]
R. P. B—s.

BULLOCK, WILLIAM A. (1813–Apr. 12, 1867), inventor, manufacturer, was born in Greenville, N. Y., of parents of whom nothing is known. At the age of eight he was an orphan. An elder brother in Catskill gave him a place in which to live and put him to work immediately to learn the trade of iron founder and machinist. Bullock seems to have shown great aptitude in these crafts, becoming expert even before completing his apprenticeship. At the same time he taught himself pattern-making and devoted his leisure time to the study of all books on mechanics that he could secure. When twenty-three years old he left his brother's home and started a machine shop of his own in Prattsville, N. Y. Besides the varied work that he could pick up he devised several mechanical contrivances amongst which was a shingle-cutting machine. Armed with this, perfected during the two years in Prattsville, Bullock went to Savannah, Ga., to engage in shingle manufacture. This venture was not successful, however, and in a short time he returned North, this time to New York City where he set up shop and made hay and cotton presses of his own design and also artificial legs. He gave up this business in 1849 and began a patent agency and shop in Philadelphia. The only products known from this shop were three of his own invention,—a grain drill, a seed planter, and a lath-cutting machine, for which he received patents between 1850 and 1854. In connection with his agency Bullock started printing a daily newspaper, *The Banner of the Union,* which he continued from 1849 to 1853. This experience turned his attention to printing-machinery and the balance of his life was devoted to improving the press. He worked simultaneously on three ideas,—a mechanical paper feed, a more rapid cutting method, and the printing of both sides of the paper. By the time he was satisfied with his improvements and undertook the manufacture of a single press embodying all of them, fifteen more years had passed. During this time he was at work in Philadelphia, then in New York, and finally after 1859 in Pittsburgh where the presses were made under U. S. Patent 38,200, issued Apr. 14, 1863. The Bullock Press, when eventually marketed in 1865, revolutionized the art of press building. It was the first to print from a continuous roll of paper, to print both sides of the sheet, and to cut it either before or after printing. The speed of printing, too, was phenomenal. For the next two years Bullock devoted himself to the manufacture and installation of presses for which there was a great demand and, as might be expected of a mechanical genius, he was constantly working on improvements which were to be added as they were perfected. One of these installations was for the Philadelphia *Public Ledger,* and just as the last test on the press was being made Bullock's foot was caught in the driving belt and so badly crushed that he died nine days after the accident at the age of fifty-three years. It is said that he had imparted many of his ideas for improvements to one of his faithful employees and that after Bullock's death these ideas were brought to perfection and incorporated in the later presses. According to report, Bullock was married and had a daughter living in Pittsburgh, but no definite information can be found concerning his surviving family.

[J. Ringwalt, ed., *Encyc. of Printing* (1871) ; W. W. Pasko, ed., *Am. Dict. of Printing and Bookmaking* (1894) ; *Public Ledger* (Phila.), Apr. 3–16, 1867 ; U.S. Patent Office Records.]   C. W. M.

BUMSTEAD, FREEMAN JOSIAH (Apr. 21, 1826–Nov. 28, 1879), surgeon, perhaps the first reputable practitioner in America to limit himself to the specialty of venereal diseases and hold a professorship of the same, was born in Boston, the son of Josiah Freeman Bumstead and Lucy Douglas Willis. His father, engaged in mercantile business, was also an author of school text-books and a member of the department of education of Boston; his brother Horace Bumstead [*q.v.*] was a prominent educator and college president; his mother was a sister of N. P. Willis and "Fanny Fern." Bumstead was educated in the Chauncey Hall School, English High, and Latin Schools of his native city, and entered Williams College in 1843, graduating in the arts in 1847. Although his father was prosperous, the son resolved to pay his own way and taught school in Roxbury while attending lectures and dissections at the Tremont Medical School. He entered Harvard Medical School in 1849 but interrupted his course to visit Europe, as surgeon on a sailing vessel, to study disease in the London and Paris hospitals. On his return he served as house surgeon in the Massachusetts General Hospital and received the degree of M.D. from Harvard in 1851. He then made a second voyage to Europe where he sojourned for a year, set-

tling on his return in New York City as a general practitioner. His first appointment (1853), which he held for two years, was as surgeon to the Northern Dispensary. In the meantime he seems to have begun to specialize on the eye and ear and in 1857 obtained the appointment of surgeon to the New York Eye and Ear Infirmary, resigning in 1862. His first public connection with venereal diseases goes back to 1853, in which year he published a translation from the French of Philippe Ricord's translation and amplification of John Hunter's *Treatise on the Venereal Diseases,* which went through a second edition in 1859. He had also been appointed surgeon to the venereal wards of Charity Hospital. About 1860 he decided to limit his practise to venereal including male genito-urinary diseases and in 1861 appeared his classical *Pathology and Treatment of Venereal Diseases,* which received the honor of an Italian translation and went through new editions in 1864, 1870, and 1879, the last in collaboration with R. W. Taylor. He served as professor of venereal diseases in the College of Physicians and Surgeons from 1867 to 1871 when, owing to overwork, he was obliged to resign and spend two years abroad. He traveled extensively, visiting the principal schools and hospitals of Great Britain and the Continent, and thus did much to strengthen his European reputation. In 1868 he had added to his reputation at home by bringing out an English edition of A. F. A. Cullerier's *Précis iconographique des maladies vénériennes.* From 1871 until his untimely death eight years later we hear but little from him. He was a tremendous worker, often sitting up all night, but this was offset in a measure by his long summer vacations which were devoted to the study of botany and ornithology. He made a complete collection of the bird life of Massachusetts which he presented to the Natural History Society of Boston. A duplicate collection remained in his possession, and his skill in taxidermy and mounting made these exhibits works of art. His collection of plants and flowers, of equal value, was presented to his alma mater, Williams College. In 1861 he married Mary Josephine White of Boston. He was a man of the highest character and integrity. His relatively early death must be charged chiefly to overwork. He lived barely long enough to see the fourth edition of his book through the press.

[G. A. Peters, *In Memory of Freeman J. Bumstead* (1880) ; *Medic. Record,* XVI, 551, Dec. 6, 1879 ; *N. Y. Medic. Jour.,* XXXI, 110, Jan. 1880.]   E. P.

BUMSTEAD, HENRY ANDREWS (Mar. 12, 1870–Dec. 31, 1920), teacher, physicist, was born in the small town of Pekin, Ill., close to

Peoria. His father was Samuel Josiah Bumstead, a physician of local prominence, and his mother, Sarah Ellen Seiwell. His elementary education was obtained in the high school of the neighboring city of Decatur, from which he went to Johns Hopkins in 1887 with the intention of preparing himself to follow his father's profession. There he came under the influence of Rowland, who so stimulated the interest which he had already shown in physics that he decided to specialize in that subject. In 1893 he went to New Haven as instructor in the Sheffield Scientific School and received his doctor's degree in physics from Yale in 1897. The year before, he had married Luetta Ullrich of Decatur, Ill., who survived him. In 1900 his success as a teacher was recognized by promotion to an assistant professorship. In spite of his heavy teaching schedule he always found time for research. Among his earlier investigations were: a theoretical discussion of the reflection of electric waves at the free end of a parallel wire system (*American Journal of Science*, November 1902, p. 359), and two papers with L. P. Wheeler on radioactive gases in surface water (*Ibid.*, October 1903, p. 328, and February 1904, p. 97). With R. G. Van Name he edited the *Scientific Papers of J. Willard Gibbs* in 1906.

The first Silliman lectures at Yale were given by J. J. Thomson in 1903. Bumstead was greatly interested in the investigations in progress at the Cavendish Laboratory and decided to spend the year 1904–05 at Cambridge in research. His experiments there (*London, Edinburgh and Dublin Philosophical Magazine*, February 1906, p. 292) led to the surprising conclusion that the heat developed by the absorption of X-rays in lead is double that produced in zinc, which seemed explicable only on the ground that the rays effected a disintegration of the lead atoms through which they passed, liberating energy which was then converted into heat. Unfortunately later work by Angerer and by Bumstead himself (*Ibid.*, April 1908, p. 432) failed to confirm the earlier result, which was shown to be due to faulty heat insulation of the metals under investigation. On his return to New Haven, Bumstead succeeded A. W. Wright as professor of physics in Yale College and director of the Sloane Laboratory. These positions, with occasional leaves of absence, he held until his death from heart failure at the age of fifty.

Since the preparation of the critical survey of electro-magnetic theories which had constituted his doctor's thesis, Bumstead had maintained a keen interest in theoretical physics. In 1908 he published a critical comparison of the scientific view-points of Einstein and Lorenz (*American Journal of Science*, November 1908, p. 493) in which he made an attempt to extend Einstein's methods to gravitational problems. He is best remembered, however, for the experimental investigations of the properties of delta rays emitted by metals under the influence of alpha rays which he began in 1911 and continued with some interruptions during the remainder of his life (*Ibid.*, December 1911, p. 403, October 1912, p. 309, August 1913, p. 91). The later of these researches (*Physical Review*, December 1916, p. 715) showed that fast-moving electrons are produced when alpha rays collide with gaseous molecules.

During the early stages of the World War Bumstead was a member of the national committee appointed to examine the merits of proposed anti-submarine devices. Early in 1918 he went to London as scientific attaché of the American Embassy. While there his tact and wide acquaintance among men of science enhanced his services as a clearing house for scientific information of military value. On his return to New Haven a few months after the Armistice he took an active part in the reorganization of the University then in progress. Before the end of the academic year he was called to succeed James Rowland Angell, president-elect of Yale, as chairman of the National Research Council. For many years a fellow of the American Physical Society, he had been an editor of its official publication, the *Physical Review*, and president of the Society. As retiring vice-president of the American Association for the Advancement of Science he delivered the annual address at the meeting in Pittsburgh in December 1917 on "Present Tendencies in Theoretical Physics" (*Science*, Jan. 18, 1918, p. 51). In 1913 he was elected a member of the National Academy of Sciences.

[Obituaries in the *Yale Daily News*, Jan. 4, 1921 and *Science*, Jan. 28, 1921, and sketches of Bumstead's life in the *Am. Jour. of Sci.*, June 1921, p. 469, and *Yale Alumni Weekly*, Mar. 18, 1921.]   L. P.

BUMSTEAD, HORACE (Sept. 29, 1841–Oct. 14, 1919), Congregational minister, educator, was the son of Josiah Freeman Bumstead, a Boston merchant, author of a series of text-books, and for many years before the Civil War superintendent of a negro Sunday-school. Nathaniel Willis, his maternal grandfather, was founder, publisher, and editor of the *Boston Recorder*, said to be the earliest of religious periodicals, and of the *Youth's Companion*. His mother, Lucy Douglas (Willis) Bumstead was sister to the poet Nathaniel Parker Willis. Bumstead was prepared for college at the Boston Latin School, and in 1863 was graduated with honor from Yale College. He then entered a training school for officers and, after passing an examination before a military board at Washington, was commissioned major of the 43rd Massachusetts Regiment of colored troops. His military service extended from April 1864 to December 1865. Although only twenty-three years old and with scant preparation for such responsibility, he was during most of the time in command of the entire regiment and had active service around Petersburg and Richmond. In the fall of 1866 he entered Andover Theological Seminary and completed the course there in 1870. For fourteen months he traveled and studied in Europe, spending the greater part of two semesters at the University of Tübingen. In January 1872 he married Anna M. Hoit, daughter of Albert G. Hoit, portrait painter. He was ordained a Congregational minister and for three years was pastor of a church in Minneapolis. A classmate in Yale, Edmund Asa Ware, was president of Atlanta University, recently organized for the higher education of negro youth. After accepting an invitation to join in this work, Bumstead moved to Atlanta in October 1875 and became an instructor in natural science. He continued in this department till 1880, was professor of Latin from 1880 to 1896, acting president 1886–87, and president from 1888 to 1907 when he retired and was given a pension by the Carnegie Foundation. He was a man of dignity, courtesy, and of high devotion to the educational work for which he considered himself "almost foreordained." While he believed in industrial education for negro youth he maintained that the leaders and teachers of the race should have opportunity for the broadest culture and to this conviction Atlanta University became committed. Bumstead and Atlanta University are in this respect to be contrasted with Booker T. Washington and Tuskegee Institute. As president Bumstead spent much of his time in the North raising funds (about $30,000 yearly) with which to carry on the work of the institution.

[*The Hist. of the Class of 1863, Yale Coll.* (1905), pp. 47–56, contains a sketch of Horace Bumstead written by himself. The account in the *Nat. Cyc. of Am. Biog.*, V, 381, was written by his wife. The *Atlanta University Bull.* of July 1917 contains an address by Bumstead in commemoration of the semi-centennial of the charter of Atlanta University. The January 1920 number of the same bulletin gives extracts from letters, articles, and addresses called forth by his death.]

E. H. J—n.

BUNCE, OLIVER BELL (Feb. 8, 1828–May 15, 1890), author, publisher, was born in New York City, of English stock. After attending Rand's Academy he became while still young a clerk in the stationery firm of Jansen & Bell, of which his uncle was a partner. He read avidly in his leisure hours and developed a competent literary style, his first play *The Morning of Life* being produced at the Bowery Theatre, Aug. 30, 1848, while he was still selling foolscap and blank books over the counter. The play is no longer extant, but A. H. Quinn infers from the cast of characters that it was a rural comedy. Bunce wrote three other plays: *Marco Bozzaris,* also lost, a dramatization of recent Greek history, produced at the Bowery Theatre, June 10, 1850, with J. W. Wallack, Jr., in the hero's part; *Fate, or the Prophet* (1856), a romantic tragedy in verse, which Wallack is also said to have produced, although Quinn has found no record of its production; and *Love in '76,* one of the best of the Revolutionary comedies, produced at Laura Keene's Theatre, Feb. 28, 1857, with Miss Keene in the part of Rose Elsworth. His theatrical work bringing him nothing more tangible than a certain name as a man of letters, Bunce turned to publishing, starting out for himself at the age of twenty-five years under the name of Bunce & Brother. The firm had little capital and lasted only a few years. He then became manager of the publishing house of James C. Gregory. His two conspicuous achievements at this time were a notable edition of Cooper's novels with illustrations on steel and wood by F. O. C. Darley and the discovery, now become commonplace, that highly embellished editions of favorite poems will enjoy a brisk sale at Christmas time. He began this sort of enterprise with a volume called *In the Woods with Bryant, Longfellow, and Halleck,* with illustrations by John A. How. After a short period with Harper & Brothers he became literary manager of D. Appleton & Company, with whom he remained for the rest of his life. He edited *Appleton's Journal* and had much to do with the policy of the house. He took a keen interest in his authors, often sending one a four-page letter, criticizing his manuscript unmercifully for three pages and accepting it on the fourth. Similar treatment, kindly meant but sometimes frightening, was meted out orally to writers who called at the office. His Sunday evening suppers were a happy institution among many New York literary men. His most ambitious undertaking for the Appletons was *Picturesque America* (1872–74), two handsome volumes, sumptuously illustrated, which were sold in parts by the old subscription method. The work was nominally under the editorship of William Cullen Bryant, but the conception and execution were really Bunce's. It cost a fortune to produce, but was an enormous success, and was followed by *Picturesque Europe* (1875–79) and *Picturesque Palestine* (1881–84). In all 600,000 sets of these works were sold. *Don't* (1884), a little book on etiquette and grammar, was in its way equally successful. His own books were: *The Romance of the Revolution* (1852); *A Bachelor's Story* (1859); *Life before Him* (1860); *Bensley* (1863); *The Opinions and Disputations of Bachelor Bluff* (1881); *My House, an Ideal* (1885); and *The Adventures of Timias Terrystone* (1885). He also compiled an anthology, *Fair Words about Fair Women* (1884). The last twenty years of his life were a brave battle with tuberculosis. He died, as he claimed that he wished to, in harness, working in his office till a week before the end, and taking manuscripts home with him to read for his employers on his deathbed. He was survived by a wife and four children.

[Obituaries in *Publisher's Weekly*, XXXVII, 649–50, *Critic*, XVI, 262, *N. Y. Times* and *Tribune*, May 16, 1890; A. H. Quinn, *Hist. of the Am. Drama* (1923); J. C. Derby, *Fifty Years among Authors, Books, and Publishers* (1884), pp. 158, 184, 600–01; S. G. W. Benjamin, *Life and Adventures of a Freelance* (1914), pp. 303–04. *Love in '76* is accessible in M. J. Moses, *Representative Plays by Am. Dramatists*, III (1920).]

G.H.G.

BUNCE, WILLIAM GEDNEY (Sept. 19, 1840–Nov. 5, 1916), painter, was born in Hartford, Conn., the son of James M. and Elizabeth Chester Bunce. Before entering seriously into art studies he enlisted during the Civil War in the 1st Connecticut Cavalry. Here he served two years, retiring from the Union army upon receiving a wound in one of his legs, which caused him to limp during the remainder of his life. His early art education was obtained at the Cooper Union School of New York and from the artist William Hart of that city, with whom he continued to study until he sailed for Europe in 1867 to become an artist resident of Paris. His studio there joined that of the famous sculptor Saint-Gaudens, who became his intimate friend and materially influenced the work of the young artist (*American Art News*, Nov. 11, 1916). Later he studied art technique under Achenbach in Munich, taking still further studies with the well-known marine painter P. J. Hays in Antwerp. A painting by Ziem led Bunce to go to Venice to live, study, and paint. Here he did his greatest amount of work. When asked to whom he owed most of his training, he replied, "Titian is my master." He worked in oil, water-color, and pastel, using oil most extensively. His early work was done with a brush, but later he developed a method entirely his own, gaining delightful color effects by the use of finger and scraping

knife, several of his most striking works being done in this manner. He was of the impressionistic school though never an extremist. Painting with a total disregard for minute detail in his desire to produce effects, he emphasized the sentiment of a scene rather than the photographic reproduction. Placing the emotional emphasis of his work in the color compositions rather than in the design, he caused nature, which he loved so well to paint, to awaken the artistic appreciation that the artist himself must have felt. His greatest subjects were nearly all Venetian. Attracted to Venice by its moist atmosphere, he made of Venice a dream city, being little influenced by its architecture, but preserving its poetry and its spirit. This is clearly demonstrated in such paintings as "Venice" (in the Montclair, N. J., Art Museum) and "On the Lagoon" (in the Rhode Island School of Design, Providence, R. I.). "Though unified in subject, the work of Bunce is always varied in expression, his skies, clouds, and water being never the same. His work shows exquisite aerial perspective and his use of life is ever varied and always charming" (Charles D. Warner in *Century Magazine*, August 1900). A few of his more important paintings are "Morning View in Venice" and "Early Morning," both of which are now in the Metropolitan Museum of Art in New York City; "Sunset, San Giorgio, Venice," in the National Gallery, Washington, D. C., and "A Venice Night" awarded the Paris Salon prize in 1870. One of his paintings, a Venetian landscape, was ordered by Queen Victoria and now hangs in Osborne House. He never married, but made his home with one of his sisters, Mrs. Archibald A. Welsh. In 1916 as the result of an automobile accident he died in a hospital in Hartford. The popularity of his work was in a great measure due to the interest of Stanford White, the American architect, and Daniel Cottier, the art dealer.

[C. E. Clement and L. Hutton, *Artists of the Nineteenth Century*, vol. I (1879); *Am. Mag. of Art*, Jan. 1917; *Century Mag.*, Aug. 1900; *Am. Art News*, Nov. 11, 1916; *Art in America*, Feb. 1926; Mantle Fielding, *Dict. of Am. Painters, Sculptors and Engravers* (1926).]

J.T.M.Jr.

BUNDY, JONAS MILLS (Apr. 17, 1835–Sept. 8, 1891), journalist, was born at Colebrook, N. H., and while still young went with his parents to Beloit, Wis. After graduating from Beloit College in 1853 he studied law at the Harvard Law School and in the office of United States Senator Matthew H. Carpenter. He did not pursue the practise of the law, however, but became a reporter on the Milwaukee *Daily Wisconsin*. He created for the paper a new department of market reports. Later he joined the staff of the

Milwaukee Sentinel. During the Civil War he joined the Federal army and in the early part of 1865 was appointed major of the 3rd Regiment United States Volunteer Infantry. At the close of the war, going to New York, he secured the position of dramatic, musical, and literary critic on the *Evening Post* under William Cullen Bryant. Three years later he joined in founding the *New York Evening Mail* and became its editor-in-chief. In 1879 the *Mail* passed into the ownership of Cyrus W. Field, who two years later bought the *New York Evening Express,* in order to obtain an Associated Press franchise, and consolidated it with the *Mail* under the title of the *Mail and Express.* He continued Bundy as editor-in-chief as did Elliott F. Shepard, who bought the paper in 1887. In 1871, when the "Executive Committee of Citizens and Taxpayers for the Financial Reform of the City and County of New York," popularly known as the "Committee of Seventy," was organized to fight the Tweed Ring, Bundy was made chairman of the Committee on Address. The "Appeal to the People of the State of New York" adopted by the Committee of Seventy was prepared under his leadership. Although the youngest member of the Committee, he proved to be one of its real working members. In 1880 he was selected by James A. Garfield to write his campaign biography and went to Mentor, Ohio, the candidate's home, where he completed the task in six weeks. He was a consistent Republican in politics and his advice was sought by many of the party's leaders, including three presidents, Grant, Garfield and Arthur. He was recognized by those about him as a valuable associate, a loyal and devoted friend, and a stout antagonist in matters of public concern. In July 1891 he went to Europe for a vacation and died suddenly in Paris.

[Obituaries appeared in the *Weekly Mail and Express,* Sept. 16, 1891; *Evening Post* (N. Y.) and *Evening Wisconsin* (Milwaukee), Sept. 9, 1891; *Milwaukee Sentinel,* Sept. 10, 1891.]   H. H.

BUNNER, HENRY CUYLER (Aug. 3, 1855–May 11, 1896), author, the son of Rudolph and Ruth (Tuckerman) Bunner, was born in Oswego, N. Y. His father belonged to an old New York family; his mother was of New England stock, being a sister of Henry T. Tuckerman; and it was in the ample library of this uncle that Bunner browsed in his boyhood and acquired his intimate acquaintance with English literature. He went to school in New York; he was prepared for Columbia College; but—like that earlier New Yorker, Washington Irving—he had to forego the advantages of college. After a brief stay in an office, he became a newspaper man,

contributing to a short-lived weekly, the *Arcadian,* and soon joining the staff of *Puck,* the earliest American comic weekly to establish itself. In 1886 he was married to Alice Learned. He remained with *Puck* until his death, and into its columns he poured a profusion of prose and verse, jokes, parodies, lyrics of all sorts, brief stories, character-sketches, and editorials. He often suggested the cartoons; and he was responsible (in 1884) for what is perhaps the most famous of all American cartoons,—that of Blaine as the Tattooed Man. His editorials were directed to the intelligence of his readers; they were effective because they were always simple, sincere, straight-forward, and because they were never aggressive, domineering, or abusive. To him his work as a journalist was as important as his work as a man of letters; and he gave to his newspaper articles the polish which characterized his more ambitious and less ephemeral efforts.

Although he never weakened in his allegiance to *Puck,* Bunner began early to contribute poems and stories to the magazines. His first volume of poems, *Airs from Arcady and Elsewhere,* appeared in 1884; it was followed in 1892 by a second collection, *Rowen;* and after his death these two volumes (enriched by later lyrics and by half-a-dozen "Ballads of the Town") were issued as *The Poems of H. C. Bunner* (1896). He had the lyric gift; his blithe and cheerful verse sang itself into the memory; and few of those who have once read "The Way to Arcady" are likely to have forgotten its lilting lyric quality, its grace, and its charm. But he was seen at his best in a department of poetry in which the literature of our language is more abundant than the literature of any other tongue and which has in English no exact name, for to call it *vers de société* is both inadequate and unsatisfactory, since it is not mere society verse. Perhaps the best name for it is that which Cowper gave it—"familiar verse." Bunner's work in this form has had the good fortune to please both the critical and the uncritical. It has the finish, the flavor of scholarship which the cultivated recognize and relish; and it has also the freshness, the spontaneity, the heartiness, and above all the human sympathy without which no poetry has ever won a welcome outside the narrow circle of the dilettants. Many of his more comic lyrics Bunner regarded as too broadly and boldly humorous to deserve inclusion in either of the volumes of verse by which he wished to be judged as a poet. He was a facile and fecund parodist; but in his collected poems he reprinted only one evidence of his mastery of this difficult art—

"Home, Sweet Home" as it might have been written by Pope and Goldsmith, Horace and Austin Dobson, Swinburne, Bret Harte, and Walt Whitman—in which he recaptured the essential spirit of these various bards as skilfully as he echoed their external mannerisms. He had profited by his intimacy with these poets and with many others; but in his own lyrics he was himself with a pungent individuality of his own.

Beginning as a journalist Bunner was also a story-teller, adventuring successfully in both fields of prose fiction, the short-story and the novel. His prose was the prose of a poet in that it was pure and pellucid. As a teller of tales he had rich invention and adroit construction. He was a devoted student of the craft of story-telling, analyzing the processes of the masters of fiction, especially Boccaccio and Hawthorne and Maupassant. He worked with ease within the rigid limits of the short-story where selection and compression are of the essence of the contract. His two novels, *The Midge* (1886) and *The Story of a New York House* (1887) might almost be called short-stories writ large; and his delightfully fantastic tale of varied adventure, *The Runaway Browns* (1892) has for its sub-title "a story of small stories." *In Partnership: Studies in Story-telling* (1884) contained two stories written by Bunner in collaboration with Brander Matthews and three other tales by each of the two partners. Other volumes for which Bunner was solely responsible were *Short Sixes* (1890), "stories to be read while the candle burns"; *Zadoc Pine* (1891); *More Short Sixes* (1894); and *Made in France* (1893), in which he retold half a score of Maupassant's stories, frankly readjusting their incidents to American life and character,—an experiment as daring as it was successful. No anthology of the American short-story is likely to appear which shall fail to include at least one example of Bunner's mastery in this form. And it will matter little whether the chosen specimen shall be "Love in Old Cloathes" or "Zadoc Pine" or "As One Having Authority."

It remains only to be noted that while Bunner sat at the feet of many European masters of prose and of verse, spying out the secrets of their art, he was himself intensely an American and specifically a New Yorker. His subjects were almost always chosen from the life of his own country—and most of them from the life of his own city. He was one of the first American writers of fiction to find a fertile field in the sprawling metropolis so multiplex in its aspects and so tumultuous in its manifestations; and here he was truly a pioneer, driving a furrow of his own in soil scarcely scratched before he tilled it.

[Brander Matthews, "H. C. Bunner" in *The Hist. Novel and Other Essays* (1901); "The Uncollected Poems of H. C. Bunner" in *The Recreations of an Anthologist* (1904); sketch in *Scribner's Mag.*, Sept. 1896; Benj. W. Wells in *Sewanee Rev.*, Jan. 1897; H. G. Paine in *Critic*, May 23, 1896; Laurence Hutton in *Bookman*, July 1896.]
                        B. M—s.

BURBANK, LUTHER (Mar. 7, 1849–Apr. 11, 1926), plant breeder and originator of many new cultivated varieties of fruits, flowers, vegetables, grains and grasses, was born in Lancaster, Worcester County, Mass. His ancestry was chiefly English, with some Scotch and a dash of both French and Dutch. He was the thirteenth child of Samuel Walton Burbank, a farmer, a maker of brick and pottery, and a level-headed business man. Luther's mother, Olive Ross of Sterling, Mass., was the third wife of Samuel, and Luther was the third of her five children. Although Burbank's New England ancestors included no men or women of illustrious names they were an eminently respectable lot of whom he has been able to say: "All my ancestors and all my relatives on both sides, as far as known, without exception have been industrious, happy, prosperous, respected, self-supporting citizens in their several communities. Not one of them, either on the Burbank or the Ross side, has been deaf, blind, imbecile, insane, incompetent, intemperate, or addicted to the use of drugs or liquor" (Beeson, pp. 17–18). In a word, Luther Burbank's was a sound heredity; although one looks at the records of his ancestors in vain for an indication of the precise source from which he might have derived by particular inheritance his absorbing, almost passionate, love of plants; unless, perhaps, that indication lies in a statement by his sister, Emma Burbank Beeson: "Olive, the mother of Luther Burbank . . . was especially fond of nature even as a little child. She used to bring into the house so many wild flowers, bright-colored leaves and pretty stones that the busy mother would be compelled to sweep these treasures from chairs and floor, much to the sorrow of the little girl. She loved the robin, bluebird and wren, their plumage as well as their notes of joy, and her first effort with pencil was to sketch the birds that flew about the door" (*Ibid.*, pp. 31–32). But this sounds rather more like a trait of artistry than one of close study, which was Burbank's special possession. Burbank had, however, not a little of the artistic temperament in his make-up. He had much imagination—as have most of the greater scientific men—and he was extremely sensitive. He would burst into tears when some one praised him too strongly to his face, and, also, when some one said something too unkind to him. This very sensitiveness, a sensitiveness to plant behavior as well as to human behavior, was important in that group of traits which enabled him to succeed so unusually as a plant breeder.

Burbank's early environment was not unfavorable to the development of his love and study of plant life. To be sure, it included almost nothing in the way of formal education and nothing at all of a scientific education, in the usual acceptation of that phrase. Of schooling he had only that which he obtained from a simple New England district school until he was fifteen, and then what he got from four winters in Lancaster Academy, which seems to have been, however, a rather unusually well-conducted academy, with special lecturers of some eminence brought from various places to take part in its "forum." One of these, who made "a deep and lasting impression upon Luther's life," according to his sister, was a certain Prof. Gunning, a German, who gave a series of lectures on astronomy, physical geography, geology, mineralogy, paleontology, and still other scientific subjects.

There was a good public library in Lancaster, and Burbank made use of it. In a letter written in January 1909, he made the following interesting statements: "When I was about nineteen, in 1868, probably the turning point of my career in fixing my life work in the production of new species and varieties of plant life was fixed by the reading of Darwin's *Variation of Animals and Plants under Domestication* which I obtained from the library at Lancaster, Mass., my old home. Well do I remember reading that work of Darwin's—that the whole world seemed placed on a new foundation. It was without question the most inspiring book I had ever read, and I had read very widely from one of the best libraries in the state on similar scientific subjects. I think it is impossible for most people to realize the thrills of joy I had in reading this most wonderful work. At once, as soon as I was able, I purchased other books written by Charles Darwin, and today I have still one to read, which probably influenced the general public more than all the rest of his writings—*Origin of Species*. I have been so busy producing living forms from the thought inspired by Master Darwin's conclusions that I have never, to the present date, had time to read his *Origin of Species*. However, I imagine I could write the *Origin of Species* myself from what I have read of his other works. The second book which I purchased of Darwin's was *Cross and Self-Fertilization in the Vegetable Kingdom*" (*Ibid.*, pp. 74-75).

But outside of district school, academy, and books, young Burbank obtained a special educa-

tion very much to the point in connection with his later career. This special education came from his opportunities and experiences as a boy on the New England farm. Here he gained knowledge at first hand of the life of plants. This knowledge together with his innate love of plants led him, two or three years after his father's death in 1868, deliberately to take up the business or profession of market gardening. With a little money obtained from his father's estate, and by the help of a mortgage, he purchased, when he was just twenty-one years old, a tract of seventeen acres of land in or adjoining the small town of Lunenburg where the Burbank family then lived. Original and practical in his methods, Burbank made a modest success of his gardening from the very outset, bringing vegetables of special quality into the neighboring city of Fitchburg earlier than other gardeners were able to bring inferior ones there. It was in this garden, too, that he produced his first "new creation," the Burbank potato, and thus began the lifework that made him famous.

The fact that Burbank's three elder brothers, George (in 1854), David (in 1859), and Alfred (in 1870), had all gone to California and were living there,—added to the fact that he and a certain Mary had a falling out—probably accounts more for Luther's removal from Massachusetts to California than any reasoning on his part with regard to the relative advantages of the two regions as locations for a market gardener and plant breeder. Whatever the reason, however, he continued his gardening at Lunenburg for but four years, and in the summer of 1875, sold his land, paid his mortgage, and bought a ticket for California. The $140 which this ticket cost was, according to the sister's account, taken from the $150 he had been paid by J. J. H. Gregory, the seedsman of Marblehead, for the total rights in the Burbank potato. Gregory, however, generously allowed him to retain ten potatoes of the new variety with which to get a start in California. These ten potatoes constituted most of his capital to support the new venture.

The trip West was made in October 1875 and took nine days and nights with Burbank sleeping in a day coach and living on the contents of the large lunch basket packed by his tearful mother and sister. His daily letters to the Massachusetts home during the course of the journey are of much interest. They reveal a mind eagerly open to new impressions and eyes quick and happy to see the beauties of mountains, plains, and desert. Once arrived at Santa Rosa, which was the Californian town that had been decided on in Massachusetts as goal of the journey, the enthusiastic newcomer burst into a dithyramb: "I firmly believe from what I have seen," he wrote, "that it is the chosen spot of all this earth as far as Nature is concerned. . . . The climate is perfect—all must like it. The air is so sweet that it is a pleasure to drink it in. The sunshine is pure and soft; the mountains which gird the valley are lovely. The valley is covered with majestic oaks placed as no human hand could arrange them for beauty. I cannot describe it! I almost have to cry for joy when I look upon the lovely valley from the hillsides" (*Ibid.*, p. 93).

In this paradise Burbank settled down in a little nursery garden with greenhouse which was soon to become famous the world over, and in which, with certain added acres near another town a few miles away, he was to carry on uninterruptedly his experimental and creative work for fifty years. This work was on the grand scale. It involved experimentation with thousands of kinds of plants, and the experimental rearing of hundreds of thousands of plant individuals. It was not conducted to prove or test any particular scientific theories or to make scientific discoveries, but it had for its sole aim the production of more and better varieties of cultivated plants. "I shall be contented if because of me there shall be better fruits and fairer flowers," he said. By the very nature of his experimenting he inevitably accumulated masses of data of scientific value, if he had cared to preserve them. But he did not. Almost all of his delicate work was done by himself, and, never strong and always overworked, he simply had no time or energy left to assemble and preserve these data. He kept for as long as he needed them the records necessary to be before him during the course of a given experiment, but when the experiment was concluded and the "new creation" established, the records were, in most cases, destroyed. Tangible results in the way of new varieties produced and taking their place in agriculture and horticulture were what he sought. Scientific results in the way of contributions to the knowledge of such subjects as variation, heredity, selection, hybridization, acquired character, and mutations were not his goal. One notable effort, to be sure, was made to collect and preserve some of the scientific data that sprang to light during his long observing and experimenting. In 1905 the Carnegie Institution of Washington made an arrangement with him by which he was to receive $10,000 a year for ten years, partly as salary and partly for expenses, with the understanding that the Institution was interested in collating such scientific data as might become available during the course of Burbank's work. To effect this, Dr. George

H. Shull, a scientific botanist, and member of the Carnegie Institution's staff, was sent to Santa Rosa to devote himself, with Burbank's coöperation, to this work of collation. The arrangement, however, was not, on the whole, a successful one, and was terminated by mutual agreement at the end of five years.

Before reference is made to any of the many new plant varieties produced by Burbank, it may be well to attempt to analyze, in general terms at least, the various processes which, either singly, or in combinations of two or three, or all together, were used by him in his work. These processes, or means, may be roughly classified.

First, there was the importation from foreign countries, through many correspondents, of a host of various kinds of plants, some of economic value in their native land and some not, any of which grown under different conditions might prove especially vigorous or prolific or hardy, or show other desirable changes or new qualities. Among these importations were often special kinds particularly sought for by Burbank to use in his multiple hybridizations; kinds which were closely related to American native or already cultivated races and which, despite many worthless characteristics, might possess one or more valuable ones needed to be added to a race already useful in order to make it more useful. Such an addition makes a new race.

Second, the production of variations, abundant and extreme, by various methods, as (a) the growing under new and, usually, more favorable environment (food supply, water, temperature, light, space, etc.) of various wild or cultivated forms; and (b) by hybridizations between forms closely related, between others less closely related and, finally, between those as dissimilar as may be (not producing sterility), this hybridizing being often immensely complicated by multiplying crosses, *i.e.*, the offspring from one cross being immediately crossed with a third form, and so on. These hybridizations were made sometimes with very little reference to the actual useful or non-useful characteristics of the crossed parents, but with the primary intention of producing an unsettling or instability in the heredity; of causing, as Burbank sometimes said, "perturbation" in the plants, so as to get just as wide and as large variation as possible. Other crosses were made, of course, in the deliberate attempt to blend, mix, to add together, two desirable characteristics, each possessed by only one of the crossed forms. Some crosses were made in the attempt to extinguish an undesirable characteristic.

Third, there was always, immediately following the unusual production of variations, the recognition of desirable modifications and the intelligent and effective selection of them, *i.e.*, the saving of those plants to produce seed or cuttings which showed the desirable variations, and the discarding of all the others. In Burbank's gardens the few tenderly cared for little potted plants or carefully grafted seedlings represented the surviving fittest, and the great bonfires of scores of thousands of uprooted others, the unfit, in this close mimicry of Darwin and Spencer's struggle and survival in nature.

It was precisely in this double process of the recognition and selection of desirable variations that Burbank's special genius came into particular play. Right there he brought something to bear on his work that few, if any, other men have been able to do in similar degree. This was his extraordinary keenness of perception, his delicacy of recognition of desirable variations in their (usually) small and to most men imperceptible beginnings. Was it a fragrance that was sought? To Burbank in a bed of hundreds of seedlings scores of the odors of the plant kingdom were arising and mingling from the fresh green leaves, but each from a certain single seedling or perhaps from a similar pair or trio. To the visitor until the master prover pointed out two or three of the more dominant single odors, the impression on the olfactories was simply (or confusedly) that of one soft elusive fragrance of fresh green leaves. Similarly Burbank was a master at seeing, and a master at feeling. And besides he had his own unique knowledge of correlations. Did this plum seedling with its score of leaves on its thin stem have those leaves infinitesimally plumper, smoother, or stronger, or with more even margins and stronger petiole or what not else, than any other among a thousand similar childish trees? Then it was saved, for it would bear a larger, or a sweeter, or a firmer sort of plum, or more plums than the others. So to the bonfires with the others and to the company of the elect with this "fittest" one. It was this extraordinary knowledge of correlations in plant characters, developed through many years of testing and perfecting that was perhaps the most important single new thing which Burbank brought to his work. He had enormous industry, utter concentration and single-mindedness, deftness in manipulation, and fertility in practical resource. So have other plant breeders. But in his special perception of variability in its forming, his keen recognition of its possibilities of outcome, and in his scientific knowledge of correlations Burbank had a special advantage over his fellow-workers.

But let us follow our saved plum seedling. Have we now to wait the six or seven years before a plum tree comes into bearing to know by actual seeing and testing what new sort of plum we have? No; and here again was one of Burbank's contributions (not wholly original to be sure, but original in the extent and perfection of its development) to the scientific aspects of plant-breeding. This saved seedling and other similar saved ones (for from the examination of 20,000 seedlings, say, Burbank would find a few tens or even scores in which he had faith of reward) would be taken from their plots and grafted on to the sturdy branches of some full-grown vigorous plum tree, so that in the next season or second next our seedling-stem would bear its flowers and fruits. Here are years saved. Twenty, forty, sixty, different seedlings grafted on to one strong tree (in a particular instance Burbank had 600 plum grafts on a single tree!) ; and each seedling-stem certain to bear its own kind of leaf and flower and fruit. (It has long been known that the scion is not modified radically by the stock nor the stock by the scion, although grafting sometimes increases or otherwise modifies the vigor of growth and the extent of the root system of the stock.) If now the fruit from our variant seedling is sufficiently desirable; if it produces earlier or later, sweeter or larger, firmer or more abundant, plums, we have a new race of plums, a "new creation" to add to the catalogue of results. For by simply subdividing the wood of the new branch, *i.e.*, making new grafts from it, the new plum can be perpetuated and increased at will.

Although Burbank's experimental and creative work ranged over a long list of plant kinds his most intensive and long persisting work was done with plums, berries, and lilies. He originated no less than two score new varieties of plums and prunes, some of which are among the best known and most successful kinds now grown. Most of these new plum and prune varieties are the result of multiple crossings in which Japanese plums played an important part. Hundreds of thousands of seedlings, the results of these crossings, were grown and carefully worked over in the forty years of plum experimentation. Next in extent, probably, to Burbank's work with plums and prunes was his long and successful experimentation with berries. This ran through about thirty-five years, involved the use of over fifty different species of *Rubus,* and resulted in the origination and commercial introduction of ten or more new varieties mostly obtained through various hybridizations of dewberries, blackberries, and raspberries.

An interesting feature of Burbank's brief account, in his *New Creations* catalogue of 1894, of the berry experimentation, is a reproduction of a photograph showing "a sample pile of brush 12 ft. wide, 14 ft. high, and 22 ft. long, containing 65,000 two and three-year-old seedling berry bushes (40,000 blackberry x raspberry hybrids and 25,000 Shaffer x Gregg hybrids) all dug up with their crop of ripening berries. . . . Of the 40,000 blackberry x raspberry hybrids of this kind 'Phenomenal' is the only one now in existence. From the other 25,000 hybrids, two dozen bushes were reserved for further trial."

Burbank's work with lilies came to culmination after sixteen years of steady experimentation in which he used more than half a hundred varieties in his hybridizings and produced a brilliant array of new forms. His love of his work and the satisfaction and thrill he found in it are well revealed in a brief paragraph in the account of the work with the lilies written for his *New Creations* catalogue for 1893. "Can my thoughts be imagined," he said, "when, after so many years of patient care and labor, as walking among them on a dewy morning I look upon these new forms of beauty on which other eyes have never gazed? Here a plant six feet high with yellow flowers, beside it one only six inches high with dark red flowers, and further on one of pale straw or snowy white, or with curious dots and shadings; some deliciously fragrant, others faintly so; some with upright, others with nodding flowers; some with dark green, woolly leaves in whorls, or with polished, light green, lance-like scattered leaves."

Among Burbank's other better-known new flowers are numerous roses, several callas, including a fragrant variety, several poppies and clematises, the two giant Shasta and Alaska daisies, several Nicotianas, and a wax myrtle. The famous Shasta daisy—one of Burbank's special prides—is the result of a multiple crossing between an American and a European species of field daisy and then between these hybrids and a Japanese form. The fragrant calla, known as "Fragrance," is descended from a single individual found by Burbank while critically examining a block of "Little Gem" calla seedlings. He was surprised to note a fragrance resembling that of violets or water lilies, and found that it came from a single individual. This little seedling was removed and tenderly taken care of. No further selecting was done; this single plant was the immediate ancestor of the fragrant new race. The blue Shirley poppy was obtained solely by long selection from the crimson field poppy of Europe, but the Fire poppy, a brilliant flame-

colored new variety is the result of hybridizing a butter-colored species and a pure white species in the ancestry of which there was red of a shade much less bright than that characteristic of the new race.

Burbank's new fruits, besides his numerous new plums and prunes, make a list too long to be recorded here. They include notable varieties of apples, peaches, quinces, and nectarines, and certain interesting although not profitable crosses of the peach and almond and of the almond and plum.

Of new vegetables Burbank introduced, besides the Burbank and several other new potatoes, new forms of tomatoes, sweet and field corn, squashes, asparagus, peas, etc. One of his most extensive and interesting experiments was that extending through sixteen years and resulting in the production of a series of luxuriantly growing spineless cactus useful for feeding cattle in arid regions. In this work selection was first made from three hardy northern cactus forms. These selected plants were then crossed with three southern forms, one from Southern California, one from Central America, and one from Spain. On the whole pure selection proved to be more efficacious than hybridization in getting the desired results in this cactus work. The cross-bred forms tended constantly to revert to the ancestral spiny condition.

Burbank's home life during the fifty years in which he lived and worked in California was extremely simple. In 1877, only two years after he had removed from Massachusetts to California, his mother and sister joined him in Santa Rosa. The mother was then sixty-four years old but with hair still black and eyes still wide open to the beauties of nature. She died in the Santa Rosa home in 1909, at the age of ninety-six. Burbank was twice married but there were no children; and he loved children. "I love sunshine, the blue sky, trees, flowers, mountains, green meadows, sunny brooks, the ocean when its waves softly ripple along the sandy beach or when pounding the rocky cliffs with its thunder and roar, the birds of the field, waterfalls, the rainbow, the dawn, the noonday and the evening sunset—but children above them all" (*Ibid.*, p. 93).

Many will ask if Burbank did not make a great deal of money from his plant creations. The answer is, he did not and, in fact, could not. He could get a fairly good price from the nurseryman for his single sale of the new plum or berry or flower, and the nurseryman could sell the offspring or the grafts from the new plant for a season or two—and then the control was gone.

Reproduction and distribution of the new thing were now possible to any of the buyers. So Burbank made no money beyond that needed for a comfortable simple living. But that was all he cared to make. Various attempts by friendly, or self-interested business men to make his work reap larger financial returns all resulted only in troubles for him, and were put aside. He found his reward in his work and in its results. "Becoming tired with the years, he now rests beneath the Cedar of Lebanon by the vine-covered cottage."

[The printed records of Burbank's life and work, and of the many and various new plant varieties produced by him are to be found in newspapers, magazines, and books. They vary a great deal as regards authenticity. Burbank suffered both in reputation and spirit because of the unauthentic and absurdly exaggerated character of certain newspaper and even magazine accounts of him and his work. So intent were some of the writers of these accounts on making a wizard out of Burbank that they led some persons to believe him a faker. In addition, in the very last months of his life he expressed certain opinions about religious dogmas and creeds that brought down on him the displeasure of many theologians of the fundamentalist type. The bitterness of these attacks both surprised and pained him. Among the books about his life and work may be mentioned *The Early Life and Letters of Luther Burbank* (1927), by his sister, Emma Burbank Beeson; W. S. Harwood, *New Creations in Plant Life* (1905); H. de Vries, *Comments on the Experiments of Nilson and Burbank* (1907); David Starr Jordan and Vernon Kellogg, *The Scientific Aspects of Luther Burbank's Work* (1909); H. S. Williams, *Luther Burbank, His Life and Work* (1915); Luther Burbank and Wilbur Hall, *Harvest of the Years* (1927). Written under Burbank's immediate direction are twelve beautifully illustrated volumes entitled *Luther Burbank, His Methods and Discoveries and Their Practical Application* (1914-15); and another set of eight volumes, entitled, *How Plants are Trained to Work for Man* (1921). Of peculiar interest is Burbank's brief series of descriptive catalogues entitled, *New Creations* (1893-1901).]   V. L. K.

BURBRIDGE, STEPHEN GANO (Aug. 19, 1831–Dec. 2, 1894), Union soldier, was the grandson of Capt. George Burbridge (a Revolutionary soldier who settled in Kentucky during her early history), and the son of Capt. Robert Burbridge (a soldier in the War of 1812) and his wife, Eliza Ann Barnes of Mississippi (*History of Bourbon, Scott, Harrison, and Nicholas Counties*, 1882, edited by W. H. Perrin). He was born in Scott County, Ky., attended Georgetown College and Kentucky Military Institute, and then studied law, but did not practise. When the Civil War began he was a farmer in Logan County. Entering the Union Army as colonel of the 26th Kentucky Infantry, a regiment he himself had raised, he served with the Army of the Ohio at the battle of Shiloh. He was appointed brigadier-general of volunteers, June 9, 1862, and commanded a brigade of the 13th Corps at the taking of Arkansas Post and in the Vicksburg campaign. On Feb. 15, 1864,

he was assigned temporarily to the command of the District of Kentucky, with extensive civil as well as military powers. The post was one of extreme difficulty, for Kentucky was a border state; its people were divided in sentiment, and its territory was constantly subject to raids from the east and south. On the whole, his military operations were successful, forwarding the Union cause and reflecting credit upon himself. He defeated and dispersed Gen. John Morgan's forces in June 1864, thus turning into disaster a raid which had been highly successful in the beginning. An advance into southwestern Virginia in October, for the purpose of destroying the salt works and lead mines which were of vital importance to the Confederacy, failed to accomplish its purpose; but a second attempt, in December, made in conjunction with Generals Stoneman and Gillem, was more fortunate. As civil official, however, Burbridge was shortsighted and injudicious, making no attempt to conciliate the disaffected, and actually antagonizing the moderate Union men by his severe and seemingly arbitrary measures. He sought to control the election of 1864 by the free use of the military, making numerous arrests (it was charged) of persons whose only offense was that they had opposed Lincoln. He involved himself in what the people of the state regarded as a deliberate swindle when by orders issued Oct. 28, 1864, and later, he practically forced the farmers to sell their hogs only to the Federal agents and at a price considerably lower than that offered in the Cincinnati markets. The injustice of the action was recognized by Lincoln and upon instruction from the War Department Burbridge revoked his orders (Nov. 27, 1864). He suppressed the "Home Guards" and disbanded the state troops raised to resist guerrillas, but the policy which won him the ardent hatred of the majority of the people of his state was the system of reprisals inaugurated as a means of suppressing guerrilla warfare—a system so rigorous that he was accused of the "murder" of many citizens (Basil Duke, *Reminiscences*, 1911, p. 478). Complaints of Burbridge's policies were made by the civil governor, Thomas E. Bramlette [*q.v.*], and others, to Lincoln and to Grant—the latter as early as November 1864 earnestly advocated his removal—but at first his ruthless punishment of guerrillas was approved at Washington and for a time Stanton seems to have hesitated to yield to the Bramlette party in effecting his removal. In December 1864, however, the Assistant Inspector General reported that though "his administration has been mainly a good one," nevertheless "the substitution of a man stronger in capacity and character would be an advantage." He was relieved from his command in January 1865, and resigned from the army in December. He was ostracized for the rest of his life. In 1867 he wrote that he was not "able to live in safety or do business in Kentucky"; and again, "my services to my country have caused me to be exiled from my home, and made my wife and children wanderers." He applied for appointment as marshal of the District of Columbia, and later as commissioner of internal revenue, but without success. He died in Brooklyn, N. Y., where he had resided for some time, and only one of the Louisville papers contained a notice of his death. He was married twice: first, to Lizzie Goff; second, to Sara R. Burbridge, who survived him.

[See Lewis and R. H. Collins, *Hist. of Ky.* (1874), vol. I; E. M. Coulter, *The Civil War and Readjustment in Ky.* (1926); F. B. Heitman, *Hist. Reg.* (1890); *Official Records* (Army), ser. I, vols. XVI (pt. 2), XVII (pt. 1), XXIV (pts. 1, 2), XXVI (pt. 1), XXXII (pts. 2, 3); XXXVIII (pt. 5), XXXIX (pts. 1, 2, 3), XLV (pts. 1, 2), XLIX (pt. 1), LII (pt. 1); ser. II, vol. VII; ser. III, vol. IV. In response to attacks made upon him in the *Cincinnati Commercial* and the Louisville *Courier-Journal*, Burbridge published a defense of his conduct as commander of the district of Ky., *Louisville Commercial*, Feb. 5, 1882.]   T. M. S.

BURCHARD, SAMUEL DICKINSON (Sept. 6, 1812–Sept. 25, 1891), Presbyterian clergyman, was born in Steuben, Oneida County, N. Y., the son of Jabez and Lucina Burchard. The first Burchard in America was Thomas, who came over in the ship *True Love* in 1635. Jabez Burchard served in the Revolutionary War in the so-called Hampshire regiment of Massachusetts under Capt. David Barton. After the Revolution he married the captain's daughter and the two families made the long trek to Western New York and settled in Oneida County. Jabez Burchard bought the land for his farm from Baron Steuben, general in the Continental army, to whom a large grant of land had been made by the State of New York. On this farm Samuel was born. After receiving a common-school education, he taught school himself for a time but when he was eighteen moved to Kentucky where he entered Centre College. In 1832 during an epidemic of cholera in Kentucky he was the only student who did not leave the college. He was indefatigable in nursing the sick and became known as "the student nurse of Danville." On his graduation in 1836 he became a lecturer, attracting large audiences to hear him speak on abolition and temperance. He received his license to preach the same year from the Transylvania Presbytery, but did not accept a call to a pastorate until three years later. Then he became the pastor of the Houston Street Presbyterian Church in New York City, a position which he held for forty years. In 1846 a new church building was erected in Thirteenth St., which was destroyed by fire nine years later. It was rebuilt and Burchard continued to preach in it until 1879. His second and last pastorate was of the Murray Hill Presbyterian Church, where he served six years, becoming pastor emeritus in 1885. In 1866 he was made chancellor of Ingham University and continued in this position for eight years, making semi-annual visits to the institution. Later he accepted the presidency of Rutgers Female Academy.

The most dramatic event of Burchard's life had far-reaching consequences. It came in the closing days of the bitterly fought presidential campaign between Grover Cleveland and James G. Blaine. On Oct. 29, 1884, Burchard was the spokesman—selected at the last moment in the absence of the Rev. Dr. McArthur, the designated leader—of a body of several hundred clergymen of all denominations who called upon Blaine at the Fifth Avenue Hotel in New York to assure him of their support. Burchard's address to the candidate contained these words: "We expect to vote for you next Tuesday. We have higher expectations, which are that you will be the President of the United States and that you will do honor to your name and to the high office you will occupy. We are Republicans and don't propose to leave our party and identify ourselves with the party whose antecedents are rum, Romanism, and rebellion. We are loyal to our flag. We are loyal to you." Blaine either did not take in the words "rum, Romanism, and rebellion" or did not realize the danger involved in them, for he made no comment. But the Democrats did not treat them so carelessly. They were seized upon as campaign material, printed on leaflets which were spread broadcast, and displayed on flaring posters. It was inevitable in the crowded closing hours of a hard-fought campaign that the words should be attributed to Blaine himself, and there were plenty of his opponents to accuse him of being an announced and bitter anti-Catholic. There is good reason to believe that in New York State sufficient votes were alienated by the phrase to turn the election to Cleveland. The Democratic plurality in the state was only 1,047 so that a change of less than six hundred votes would have reversed the result. New York's electoral vote decided the election. Burchard suffered much annoyance and recrimination after the election but he made no apology for his words, declaring that if he had been an instrument in the hands of Providence against his own will he was content to abide by the consequences. He died at Saratoga, N. Y.

[Obituaries in the N. Y. papers of Sept. 26, 1891; accounts of the "Rum, Romanism, and Rebellion" incident in *Life and Public Services of Hon. Jas. G. Blaine* (1893) by Henry Davenport Northrop, in *An American Statesman, the Works and Words of Jas. G. Blaine* (1892) by Willis Fletcher Johnson, and in the life by Edward Stanwood (1908) in the American Statesmen Series.]   H. H.

BURDEN, HENRY (Apr. 22, 1791–Jan. 19, 1871), ironmaster, inventor, was born in Dunblane, Stirlingshire, Scotland, the son of Peter and Elizabeth (Abercrombie) Burden. As a youth, while working for his father, a small farmer, he is said to have given evidence of marked inventive talent. He attended the local school of William Hawley, a mathematician, and afterward studied mathematics, drawing, and engineering at the University of Edinburgh. In 1819, bearing letters from the American minister at London to Stephen Van Rensselaer and Senators Benton and Calhoun, he came to America. At Van Rensselaer's suggestion he went to Albany, where he found work in making agricultural implements in the establishment of Townsend & Corning. He invented an improved plow, which took the first premium at three county fairs, and a cultivator which is said to have been the first to be put into practical operation on this side of the Atlantic. On Jan. 27, 1821, he was married in Montreal to Helen McOuat, whom he had known in Scotland. The next year he moved to Troy to become the superintendent of a small and ill-equipped plant, the Troy Iron and Nail Factory, and by his executive ability and his inventive skill he gradually transformed it into one of the largest iron factories in the country. In 1825 he received a patent for a machine for making wrought iron spikes. An improvement was added to the machine in 1834, and another in 1836 (patented in 1840), by which it was altered to make the hook-headed spike, which soon came into general use in track-laying on all American railways. The patent was bitterly contested in litigation lasting for twenty years between Burden and the Albany Iron Works, but in the end Burden won a complete victory. The most widely known of his inventions was the horseshoe machine, first patented in 1835, and successively improved in 1843, 1857, and 1862, which produced virtually all the horseshoes used by the Federal armies in the Civil War. In 1840 Burden patented the "rotary concentric squeezer," for rolling puddled iron into cylindrical bars, a machine declared by the commissioner of patents to be the most important invention in the manufacture of iron which had been reported to the patent office. From the beginning of Burden's connection with the Troy Iron and Nail Factory, and as rapidly as his means would permit, he bought its stock, so that by 1835 he owned half of it and by 1848 was sole owner. He thereupon established the partnership of H. Burden & Sons, which continued till his death. He had early shown a deep interest in steam navigation, and in 1825 had made suggestions to the Troy Steamboat Association that later were largely adopted in the building of the *Hendrick Hudson,* which in 1845 made the trip from New York to Albany in seven and a half hours. One of the innovations credited to Burden is the placing of sleeping berths on the upper decks. In 1833 he built for the Hudson traffic a passenger and freight boat of two cigar-shaped hulks, with a thirty foot paddle-wheel in the center. It was lost, however, in an accident the following year. He was an advocate of larger and faster boats for the Atlantic trade, and in 1846 was instrumental in the formation by Glasgow capitalists of Burden's Atlantic Steam Ferry Company, of which nothing came. His later years were passed in the general supervision of his immense and ever-growing establishment. He died of heart disease in his suburban home of Woodside, and the body was interred in the family vault in the Albany Rural Cemetery. Burden is described as a tall and well-made man, with a large head, prominent though regular features, a wide and high forehead, deep-set eyes, and a mouth which betokened a kindly and cheerful disposition. As an inventor his rank is high; and he had the good fortune, rare among inventors, to reap the rewards of his creations, by reason of his ownership of a factory. In his closing years he was doubtless Troy's most prominent citizen; and his death evoked from all classes a chorus of exceptional tributes.

[Margaret Burden Proudfit, *Henry Burden; His Life, and a Hist. of His Inventions* (1904); *A Memorial of Mrs. Henry Burden* (N. Y., 1860).]   W. J. G.

BURDETTE, ROBERT JONES (July 30, 1844–Nov. 19, 1914), humorist, Baptist clergyman, the son of Frederick Edwin and Sophia Eberhart (Jones) Burdette, was born in Greensboro, Pa., of Welsh and French Huguenot ancestry. In later life he turned to literary account the sentimental memories of a boyhood spent in the villages of Cumminsville, Ohio, and Peoria, Ill. In 1862 he enlisted with the 47th Illinois Regiment from Peoria. His first battle was fought before Vicksburg in May 1863. Returning to Illinois in 1866, he taught district school near Peoria for a few months, was a United States railway mail clerk, and then went to New York to study French, German, and art at Cooper Institute. While there he embarked (1869) for Cuba on the blockade runner *Lillian* and was wounded while landing a consignment of arms for the Cuban insurgents. He went West in 1869 to work on the *Peoria Daily Transcript*. His first interview was with Horace Greeley. In 1871 he assisted in founding the Peoria *Review*. Upon its collapse in 1874 he joined the staff of the *Burlington Daily Hawk-Eye*. His "Hawkeyetems of Roaming Robert, the Hawkeye man," were for many years a biweekly feature of the *Hawk-Eye* and earned for it a national circulation.

Gradually Burdette became absorbed in the work of a platform lecturer, though he kept always his newspaper connections. His first lecture (Keokuk, Iowa, December 1876), "The Rise and Fall of the Moustache," was afterward delivered nearly five thousand times and in almost every state of the union. He had many close friends among his lyceum associates, notably Henry Ward Beecher, H. W. Shaw (Josh Billings), Bill Nye, Mark Twain, Robert Ingersoll, Sol Smith Russell, and James Whitcomb Riley. In 1883 he removed to Ardmore, Pa. From this headquarters he continued to arrange lecture tours, and to contribute to his regular column on the *Brooklyn Daily Eagle* verse parodies, and skits on Master Bilderback, Mr. Dresseldorf, the rooster who expected to die "necks tweak," and other homely creatures of his fancy.

In 1888, while living at the "Robin's Nest" at Bryn Mawr, Burdette was licensed to preach in Baptist pulpits. His "one-day" pastorates while on lecture tours, were scattered from Maine to Texas. Upon his removal to California in 1898 he was for some months supply pastor of the First Presbyterian Church of Pasadena. In 1903 he became the first pastor of the Temple Baptist Church of Los Angeles. Under his pastorate the roll increased from a charter membership of two hundred and eighty-five to a church of one thousand and sixty-nine, with an average attendance of three thousand at the two Sunday services. In six years the Sunday-school was enlarged from one hundred and seventy-five to nearly a thousand pupils. Burdette's later life was given to his church work, occasional addresses, contributions to newspapers, and the editing of various manuscripts and addresses for book publication. A spinal injury, incurred through a fall in 1909, brought on a lingering semi-invalidism, and finally death. He was married twice: on Mar. 4, 1870 to Carrie S. Garrett, and on Mar. 25, 1899 to Mrs. Clara (Bradley) Wheeler-Baker.

"The physician of the merry heart," as Burdette was often called, embodied his philosophy in several volumes of humorous sketches: *The Rise and Fall of the Moustache and Other Hawkeyetems* (1877); *Hawk-Eyes* (1879); *Schoon-*

ers *that Pass in the Dark* (1894); *Chimes from a Jester's Bells* (1897); *Old Time and Young Tom* (1912). Of the verse parodies scattered among his prose contributions, *Smiles Yoked with Sighs* was collected and published in 1900, and *The Silver Trumpets* was assembled in 1912 from poems first printed in the *Temple Herald*. Several of his later sermons were circulated in pamphlet form. He contributed a *Life of William Penn* (1882) to Henry Holt's series of the Lives of American Worthies, and supervised the California edition of *American Biography and Genealogy* (2 vols.). In his last year he saw the publication of *The Drums of the 47th* (1914) an account of his Civil War experiences which had appeared serially in the *Sunday School Times*.

[The standard biography is *Robt. J. Burdette, His Message* (1922), by his wife, Clara B. Burdette.]

J. R. T.

BURDICK, FRANCIS MARION (Aug. 1, 1845–June 3, 1920), legal writer, son of Albert G. and Eunetia Yale (Wheeler) Burdick, was a descendant of Robert Burdick, a freeman of Newport, R. I. in 1655 and one-time member of the Assembly. He was born at De Ruyter, N. Y., where his father was a farmer, and his early education was obtained at De Ruyter Institute and Cazenovia Seminary, whence he proceeded to Hamilton College, where he graduated in 1869. He then for a short time became a classical teacher at Whitestown Seminary (New York) and in 1870 joined the editorial staff of the Utica *Herald*. Later in that year he returned to Hamilton to study law under Prof. Theodore Dwight, was graduated LL.B., and was admitted to the bar in 1872. He commenced practise in Utica and soon acquired a substantial connection, identifying himself with all matters of civic interest. In 1882 he was elected mayor on a reform platform. His inclinations had always been academic, and, in that year the Maynard Knox Professorship of Law and History at Hamilton becoming vacant, he accepted an invitation to occupy the chair. In this position he was an unqualified success, thorough scholarship being united in him with an innate capacity for imparting knowledge and attracting students. In 1887 on the establishment of a college of law in connection with Cornell University he was appointed one of its first professors. "He was an important factor in establishing the new school on a firm basis," and while there "began to make use of original sources as the basis of class room instruction, a method which has come to be somewhat inaccurately and quite incompletely described as the 'case system'" (Harlan F. Stone). Four years later the trustees of Columbia University reorganized its law school, and appointed him Theodore Dwight Professor of Law. This position he occupied for twenty-five years, in the course of which he lectured on a number of subjects. His lectures, prepared with meticulous care, systematic in arrangement and development, admirably illustrated, and delivered with unusual lucidity and simplicity of exposition, invariably drew large, appreciative audiences. His attention was particularly directed to torts, sales, and partnership, and for the elucidation of these special topics he prepared a number of text-books and collections of cases. His first book, *Cases on Torts*, was published in 1891. *The Law of Sales of Personal Property* and a companion volume of *Selected Cases on the Law of Sales of Personal Property* appeared in 1897. They were followed by *Selected Cases on the Law of Partnership including Limited Partnerships* (1898), *The Law of Partnership* (1899), and *The Law of Torts* (1905). Designed for class study, in connection with the curriculum, these works were welcomed by the profession and student body alike and passed through a number of editions. In 1907 Burdick was appointed one of the commissioners on uniform laws. In this capacity he took a leading part in drafting the uniform laws which were indorsed by the commission, recommended for adoption, and subsequently enacted in the various states. He resigned his professorship in 1916, being appointed emeritus professor, and lived in comparative retirement till his death, which occurred at De Ruyter. He was married, on June 8, 1875, to Sarah Underhill, daughter of Gustavus A. Kellogg of Utica.

In addition to the works already mentioned, Burdick wrote *The Essentials of Business Law* (1902) and *The Uniform Sales Act of 1908, with Annotations* (1908). He contributed the articles "Law and Jurisprudence" to the *American Year Book* for 1910, 1911, 1913, and 1915. As a trustee of the *Columbia Law Review* he took a lively interest in its progress, regularly contributing book reviews of a general character in addition to articles of legal interest. He also wrote largely for other periodicals on matters of law, history, and jurisprudence.

[The "Memorial" in *Ass. of the Bar of the City of N. Y., Yearbook* 1921, p. 159, by Judge Harlan F. Stone of the U. S. Supreme Court, at that time dean of the Columbia Law School, and the same author's article in *Columbia Law Rev.*, Nov. 1920, contain an authoritative summary of Burdick's career and a competent appraisal of his academic achievements. The latter article also gives a complete bibliography, listing all Burdick's contributions to periodicals, prepared by Prof. F. C. Hicks, See also *Case and Comment*, Sept. 1916; *Green Bag*, Nov. 1889.]   H. W. H. K.

BURGESS, ALEXANDER (Oct. 31, 1819– Oct. 8, 1901), Episcopal bishop, was descended from Thomas Burgess, who came from England about 1630, and ultimately established himself in Sandwich, Mass. One of Thomas's descendants, who also bore the name Thomas, made his home in Providence, R. I., and in 1803 married Mary Mackie of Scotch descent, whose home was in Wareham, Mass. These were the parents of Alexander Burgess, who was born in Providence.

Following in the footsteps of his father, Alexander prepared himself for admission to Brown University, and graduated in the class of 1838. He then went to the General Theological Seminary, New York, to fit himself for the Episcopal ministry, graduating from that institution in 1841. He was ordained deacon Nov. 3, 1842, by the Rt. Rev. Alexander Viets Griswold, bishop of what was then known as the Eastern Diocese, which included all of New England except Connecticut, and was advanced to the priesthood, Nov. 1, 1843, by the Rt. Rev. John P. K. Henshaw, bishop of Rhode Island, that part of the Eastern Diocese having within the year elected its own bishop. On Dec. 11, 1842, Burgess took charge of St. Stephen's Church, East Haddam, Conn., remaining there about a year, when he was called to the rectorship of St. Mark's Church, Augusta, Me. After serving over ten years in this charge he completed a rectorship of nearly thirteen years in St. Luke's Church, Portland. From there he went to be rector of St. John's Church, Brooklyn, L. I., but remained only three years, when he assumed the rectorship of Christ Church, Springfield, Mass. In whatever diocese he served he was chosen for positions of importance and responsibility. In the dioceses of Maine, Long Island, and Massachusetts he was almost continuously from 1845 to 1877 a member of their respective standing committees. He was elected as a deputy to eight general conventions from the Diocese of Maine, and to three from the Diocese of Massachusetts. At the last convention in which he served as a deputy, that of 1877, he was made the president of the House of Deputies. Before this convention there came an application from the Diocese of Illinois asking that two additional dioceses might be set up within the limits of the State of Illinois. This application was granted, and one of these dioceses became the Diocese of Quincy. At a special convention held Feb. 26, 1878, Burgess was elected bishop on the forty-fourth ballot, and on May 15, 1878, in Christ Church, Springfield, Mass., was consecrated the first Bishop of Quincy.

It was a difficult field to which Bishop Burgess had been called, and the work was pioneer work.

He was an Eastern man by birth and education, and all his ministry hitherto had been in the East. But he adapted himself to the new conditions, and by his strong scriptural preaching, by his faithful and sympathetic labors, and by his broad-mindedness, he started the new diocese well on its way. He was especially skilled in the canon law of the Church, and an able parliamentarian. Though possessed of rich intellectual gifts, yet in his busy life as pastor and bishop he found little time for literary work. In 1869 he published a Memoir of his brother, George Burgess [*q.v.*], the Bishop of Maine, which, however, was more a compilation of the impressions of others than an original production. Bishop Burgess was twice married: in September 1845 to Mary Williams Selden, who died Apr. 22, 1856; and on June 1, 1858, to Maria Annette Howard, daughter of the Hon. Joseph Howard of Portland, Me., who died Jan. 4, 1899. He died in St. Albans, Vt., and was buried there.

[H. G. Batterson, *A Sketch Book of the Am. Episcopate* (1878); Wm. Stevens Perry, *The Episcopate of America* (1895); E. Burgess, *Burgess Genealogy* (1865); *Jour. of Convention, Diocese of Quincy*, 1902; information from Bishop Burgess's daughter, Miss Caroline Howard Burgess.]

W. A. B.

BURGESS, EDWARD (June 30, 1848–July 12, 1891), yacht designer, entomologist, was born in West Sandwich, Mass., the son of Benjamin F. and Cordelia (Ellis) Burgess. His father was a wealthy Boston merchant in the West Indian trade. After a preparatory course in a private Latin school the son in 1866 entered Harvard, from which he graduated in 1871, with the degree of A.B. He left college with two well-developed hobbies, entomology and boating. His attachment to the former prompted him to accept the secretaryship of the Natural History Society of Boston in 1872, and his attachment to the latter led him, during his travels in Europe, to make some study of yacht building. Through his father's failure in business in 1879 he was left without means. He returned to Harvard as an instructor of entomology in the Bussey Institution and remained there four years. At the request of the United States Entomological Commission, he and Charles S. Minot contributed a paper "On the Anatomy of Aletio" (published as Chapter V of *House Miscellaneous Documents, No. 39*, 48 Cong., 2 Sess.). Other scientific papers were published by him in *Science* and in the *Proceedings of the Boston Society of Natural History*. In the fall of 1883 he and his younger brother Sidney started in business as yacht designers under the firm name of Burgess Brothers. There were few orders, and Sidney, discouraged, left the firm and went abroad. A revival of English

interest in the contest for the *America's* Cup brought about a challenge for another race, which was accepted by a syndicate of Boston yachtsmen headed by J. Malcolm Forbes, and Burgess was chosen to design the American contender. The undertaking was one before which he might well have faltered, for his previous experiments in designing could help him little in the planning of a vessel such as the one now demanded. "He had nothing to guide him—no yacht from which to obtain any data," writes McVey. Nevertheless he resolutely set to work and in the end produced the *Puritan*, which in the race of 1885 defeated the English cutter, the *Genesta*. The victory brought him instant fame and a favorable turn in fortune. In the next year he designed the *Mayflower*, which outsailed the English *Galatea*, and in 1887 the *Volunteer* which defeated the English *Thistle*. His services were now in great demand among wealthy yachtsmen. In the short period of his professional career he designed over two hundred vessels. In 1887 he was appointed a member of the United States Naval Board to award prizes for the designs of cruisers and battle-ships, and in 1888 permanent chairman of the board of life-saving appliances of the United States Life-Saving Service. He died of typhoid fever in his home in Boston.

Burgess was married to Caroline L. Sullivant, of Columbus, Ohio, who with two sons survived him. He was a man of cultivation and refinement, in manner quiet and reserved and in speech reticent. His tastes were intellectual and artistic, and his home, largely designed by himself, is said to have been a characteristic expression of his personality. Among his intimate friends his studied reserve was doffed; he was capable of jesting and could play the boy; and it is recorded of him that he signalized every victory by turning a double somersault on the deck of his vessel. As a naval architect he is celebrated less for being an originator than for being an effective combiner. His genius, writes one of his eulogists, lay in his remarkable powers of observation and selection; though he did not discover any new element of speed, as did some of the others of his time, he still excelled his rivals in uniting known elements of speed as they had never before been combined.

[*Burgess Genealogy* (1865); *Eleventh Report of the Class of 1871 of Harvard College* (1921); A. G. McVey, "Edward Burgess and His Work," *New Eng. Mag.*, Sept. 1891; Samuel H. Scudder, "The Services of Edward Burgess to Natural Science," in *Proc. Boston Soc. Natural Hist.*, vol. XXV, containing bibliography of Burgess's writings; Thos. W. Lawson, *The Lawson Hist. of the America's Cup* (1902); H. L. Stone, *The "America's" Cup Races* (1914); Edward Burgess, "Yachts and Yachting" in *Am. and Eng. Yachts* (1887); obituaries in the *Boston Daily Advertiser*, the *Boston Herald*, and *N. Y. Times*, July 13, 1891.]

W. J. G.

BURGESS, GEORGE (Oct. 31, 1809–Apr. 23, 1866), Episcopal bishop, was born in Providence, R. I., the second son of Thomas and Mary Mackie Burgess, and an older brother of Bishop Alexander Burgess [q.v.]. As a young lad he was exceptionally studious, and possessed a remarkable power of concentration, so that he was ready for college before he was twelve years old. But his father was averse to his entering so young, and kept him back for a year. In 1822, he entered Brown University, and after a brilliant academic career graduated with high honors in the class of 1826. His father was a lawyer of prominence in Providence, and young Burgess after his graduation studied law in his office and completed his preparation, though he never applied to be admitted to the bar. His family were Congregationalists, and in that faith had been his early training. But his study and reading led him into the Episcopal Church, and even while he was working in his father's law office he began to experience a drawing toward the ministry. From 1829 to 1831 he served as tutor at Brown, at the same time studying theology under the guidance of his rector, the Rev. Dr. Nathan B. Crocker. The three years following he spent abroad attending lectures at the Universities of Berlin, Bonn, and Göttingen, and in traveling. Upon his return he was ordained deacon in Grace Church, Providence, by Bishop Alexander Viets Griswold, and was advanced to the priesthood, Nov. 2, 1834, in Christ Church, Hartford, Conn., by Bishop Thomas Church Brownell. He was immediately made rector of Christ Church, Hartford. Under his wise administration the parish grew, and his work there was congenial. But he was destined for promotion. Maine, which had been a diocese since 1820, had continued under the bishop of the Eastern Diocese, that is, of all New England except Connecticut. But the time had now come when Maine desired its own bishop, and so at a special convention held in Portland, Oct. 4, 1847, Burgess was unanimously elected to that office. He was consecrated in Christ Church, Hartford, Oct. 31, 1847. When he went to Maine he made his home in Gardiner, assuming the rectorship of the church there, which position he held until his death, performing his duties as rector in conjunction with and in addition to his duties as bishop, such doubling of duties being necessary because of the inadequacy of the support available for the episcopate. His diocese was weak, but by his steadfast devotion and saintly life, by his unwearying energy and convincing preaching, he had the satisfaction of seeing it develop and increase in influence under his guidance.

Bishop Burgess possessed a well-informed mind, and the ability to give clear expression to his thoughts. As a result he wrote much, in spite of the demands which his work as bishop made upon him. There was a poetic strain in his nature, and *The Poems of the Rt. Rev. George Burgess* (1868), published after his death, constituted, perhaps, his chief literary production. He translated the Book of Psalms into verse (1840), wrote *Pages from the Ecclesiastical History of New England between 1740 and 1840* (1847), and *The Last Enemy, Conquering and Conquered* (1850), and in addition published numerous sermons and addresses in pamphlet form. Trouble with his throat began to show itself, and early in 1865 the suggestion was made to him that he visit Hayti and look over the missionary work there. Toward the end of the year he undertook the journey, with the double purpose of seeking benefit to his health and studying the conditions of the mission stations at Hayti. It was on this journey that he died on board ship as he was going from Port au Prince to the port whence he was intending to sail for home. His body was taken to Gardiner, Me., and buried in the churchyard there. He was married on Oct. 26, 1846, to Sophia, daughter of Leonard Kip.

[Alexander Burgess, *Memoir of the Rt. Rev. Geo. Burgess* (1869); *Am. Quart. Ch. Rev. and Ecclesiastical Reg.*, July 1867; Calvin R. Batchelder, *A Hist. of the Eastern Diocese* (1876).]   W. A. B.

BURGESS, NEIL (June 29, 1851?–Feb. 19, 1910), actor, was born in Boston, his mother's name being Ellen A. Lunt. He was educated in the public schools of Cambridge, and, after a brief time in business, made his professional beginning, at the age of nineteen, with Spaulding's Bell Ringers, and in the vaudeville theatres. One evening in Providence, while he was stage manager with a company on tour playing *The Quiet Family*, the actress who had been impersonating Mrs. Barnaby Bibbs was unable to appear, and Burgess took her place, for that performance only, as he thought. Although he disliked his task, he found favor with the audience, and his destiny was thereby settled. After that his entire life on the stage was spent in grotesque impersonations in which he burlesqued rather than interpreted the eccentric personalities of elderly women. For his effects, and for the laughter across the footlights, he relied largely upon extravagances of feminine costume. He starred first in 1879 in *Vim, or, a Visit to Puffy Farm*. Interspersed with his experiences in this play were appearances, beginning in 1879, in *Widow Bedott, or, a Hunt for a Husband*, a dramatization of *The Widow Bedott Papers*. But his most popular part was Abigail Prue, and his most popular play *The County Fair*, written by Charles Barnard, and produced in Burlington, N. J., Oct. 6, 1888, and at Proctor's Fifth Avenue Theatre, New York, Mar. 5, 1889, after which it was acted more than five thousand times during the ensuing seasons. In it was utilized the treadmill device for a horse race later used effectively and with great spectacular effect in the chariot race in *Ben Hur*. In San Francisco, Sept. 7, 1880, Burgess had married a member of his company, Mary E. Stoddart, a niece of James H. Stoddart, the actor. She accompanied him on his tours through many seasons, and died in 1905, leaving one son. When not on the road they made their home at Atlantic Highlands, N. J., during the years of Burgess's prosperity. As a reward for his stage success, he acquired considerable wealth, but lost the greater part of it through injudicious investments and unprofitable theatrical ventures. He was essentially a single character performer, doing his one specialty with an individual ingenuity that brought him, for a considerable period, unbounded popularity. He attempted a tour of England with *The County Fair* in 1897, but the English public failed to understand and appreciate his peculiar type of humor. During his last years on the stage he gave a condensed version of *The County Fair* in vaudeville.

[A. D. Storms, *The Players Blue Book* (1901); J. B. Clapp and E. F. Edgett, *Players of the Present* (1899–1901); *Boston Morning Jour.*, Apr. 2, 1892, Feb. 13, 1893; *Providence Daily Jour.*, Feb. 16, 1903; *Illustrated American*, Jan. 14, 1893; *Boston Evening Transcript*, Feb. 19, 1910; *N. Y. Dramatic Mirror, N. Y. Dramatic News, N. Y. Clipper*, Feb. 26, 1910. The year of birth was either 1851 (Storms and the *Transcript*) or 1846 (*Mirror, News, Clipper*).]   E. F. E.

BURGEVINE, HENRY ANDREA (1836–June 26, 1865), adventurer, was the second of four children born to Gen. Andrea and Julia (Gillette) Burgevine. His father had been one of Napoleon's officers who, subsequent to the Peninsular campaign, served with the king of Spain, and was granted an extensive tract of land in Florida on which he spent many years surveying and vainly trying to secure recognition of the claim. His headquarters were at New Bern, N. C., in the French colony there. For a few months in 1836 he was a professor of modern languages at Chapel Hill, and possibly Henry was born there. The latter was educated in the public schools, but when still young went forth to adventure. After some service in the Crimea he wandered about and eventually appeared on the China coast. When, in 1860, Frederick Townsend Ward [*q.v.*] was recruiting a foreign company to recapture Sungkiang from the Taiping rebels he enrolled Burgevine as an officer. The young

leader showed dash and gallantry in a fruitless attack on Tsingpu, leading a charge after Ward was wounded. In the "Ever Victorious Army" which emerged from this nondescript company, Burgevine was third in command. Ward's untimely death in September 1862 precipitated a British-American rivalry for the command of the army which now numbered about 4,000. Li Hung Chang, Governor of Kiangsu, despite misgivings regarding Burgevine's character and aims, awarded him the post, deferring to the representations of the American minister, Anson Burlingame [*q.v.*], whom the British authorities eventually supported. The governor soon had cause to rue his compliance. Early in November, the Taiping forces in full strength challenged their besiegers outside Nanking. The imperialist cause stood in dire peril. His superior requested Li Hung Chang to send Gen. Ch'en to the rescue, but, owing to complications, Burgevine was offered instead,—an offer reluctantly accepted. To the governor's intense chagrin Burgevine, advancing various excuses, failed to move until at last the danger disappeared. Insult was added to injury when, early in January, December payments being overdue, Burgevine quelled an incipient mutiny in Sungkiang by promising to make payments within a limited time and proceeded to fulfil the promise by leading an armed guard to the home of the paymaster in Shanghai, there to seize forty thousand *taels*, wounding an official slightly in the mêlée. Li Hung Chang was fairly beside himself with anger, and would have executed the offender but for the latter's extraterritorial status. Dismissal and refusal to reinstate naturally followed, although Burgevine went to Peking and secured powerful support, including that of Burlingame.

Undaunted by his failure, Burgevine enrolled a hundred or more kindred spirits whom he led to join the insurgents in Soochow. Becoming dissatisfied there, he made overtures in October to come over with his entire following to Charles George Gordon, now in command of the "Ever Victorious Army." Li Hung Chang made no objections, but warned Gordon not to trust the man. Most of the company actually changed sides during a battle, but Burgevine himself was too closely watched. Gordon thereupon negotiated for his release,—the rebels apparently happy to be rid of him—and he was delivered to the United States consul at Shanghai, charged with treason. Eventually he was released on promising to leave China permanently. There was general relief at his departure. Nevertheless, shortly before the fall of Nanking, he was again in China attempting to join the insurgents, but was hindered by imperialist vigilance. In May 1865 he appeared in Fukien on his way to join the last unconquered Taiping chief. Being recognized by a foreign military instructor attached to the imperialists, he was arrested, together with a British companion. Once more Li Hung Chang sought to secure his execution, chafing at treaty restrictions that precluded direct action. He did not show undue grief when news came that the small boat conveying the prisoners had capsized, drowning them both. Shanghai foreigners suspected foul play, but it could not be proved and is improbable.

[Burlingame's reports to the State Dept. in *Foreign Relations of the U. S., 1863–66*; files of the *North China Herald*; Gen. Edward Forester, "Personal Recollections of the Tai-Ping Rebellion" in the *Cosmopolitan*, Oct., Nov., Dec., 1896; Gerald Browne, "Last Months of the Taeping War," *Harper's*, 1866; Wm. J. Hail, *Tseng Kuo-Fan and the Taiping Rebellion* (1927).]
W.J.H.

BURGIS, WILLIAM (fl. 1718–1731), artist and engraver, came from London to New York about 1718, and published by subscription "A South Prospect of ye Flourishing City of New York," sending it to London to be engraved by John Harris. Having been successful in New York, he went to Boston and, with his associates, William Price and Thomas Selby, ran a series of advertisements in James Franklin's *New England Courant* from Oct. 8, 1722, to Jan. 6, 1723/24, which resulted in the publishing, by subscription, of "A South East View of the Great Town of Boston," also engraved in London by John Harris, which gives the first known portrayal of a two-masted schooner in a view originating in America. One of his said associates, Thomas Selby, Senior Warden of King's Chapel, and keeper of the Crown Coffee House, where Burgis resided, died rather suddenly, and his widow, Mehitable, who had inherited £659-10-4 from him, and had an estate of her own besides, married William Burgis on Oct. 1, 1728. From that time on he is variously referred to in the records as draftsman, painter, innholder, taverner, and gentleman, until Feb. 11, 1730/31, when he was defaulted in a civil suit, having apparently left town. This is confirmed by his wife's unsuccessful petition to the Governor's Council on July 20, 1736, for a divorce, on grounds that he had got what he could of her estate into his hands, about five years since, had left her, and "has never returned into the Province again . . . and that whether he be living or dead she knows not, and no further trace has as yet been found of him." Besides the two works mentioned above (only one copy of the first state of each being known) he is associated with the following engraved works as delineator, engraver or publisher: "A

Prospect of the Colledges in Cambridge in New England," issued July 14, 1726, just too late for commencement (only one copy known, in the Massachusetts Historical Society, Boston); "A Draught of the Meeting-House of the Old (First) Church in Boston with the New Spire & Gallery," issued June 5, 1727 (no copy known); "Plan of Boston in New England," issued about July 3, 1729 (only three copies known, one in possession of R. T. H. Halsey of New York, another belonging to the estate of the late Dr. John Collins Warren of Boston, and the third in the Library of Congress); "Boston Light," issued Aug. 11, 1729, engraved in "mezzotinto," possibly the second plate so done in America and the only known work that carries Burgis's name as engraver (only one copy known, in possession of the United States Light House Board, Washington, D. C.); "View of the New Dutch Church (New York), founded A. D. 1727 and finished A. D. 1731" issued between July 31, 1731, and Aug. 1, 1732 (only one copy known, lately in possession of William Loring Andrews of New York).

[The principal sources of information are the *Boston News-Letter*, 1718–32; *Boston Gazette*, 1719–32; *New Eng. Courant*, 1721–26; *New Eng. Weekly Jour.*, 1727–32; *Reports of the Record Commissioners of the City of Boston* (1876–1909); Suffolk Court Files and Records, MS., 1718–32, Court House, Boston; John H. Edmonds, "The Burgis-Price View of Boston" in *Mass. Colonial Soc. Pubs.*, vol. XI (1910), and "The Burgis Views of N. Y. and Boston," in *Proc. Bostonian Soc.*, 1915.]
J. H. E—s.

BURK, FREDERIC LISTER (Sept. 1, 1862– June 12, 1924), educator, was born in Blenheim, Ontario, Canada, of an American father, Erastus, and an English mother, Matilda Turner. At the age of seven he was brought to California, the family settling in the town of Coloma, El Dorado County, a spot made famous by the discovery of gold there in 1848. Graduating from the Sacramento City High School, Burk entered the University of California and was graduated with the degree B.L. in 1883. When Stanford University opened in 1891, he became one of the first candidates for the M.A. degree which was conferred upon him in 1892. In the immediate years following, he was successively teacher in a country school and in a military academy, and then became a writer of feature articles for various San Francisco journals. The latter experience colored his whole career, giving him access to the press and also a sense of news values.

As a writer he became interested in psychology, and in 1896 he went to study under G. Stanley Hall at Clark University, where he received the Ph.D. degree in 1898. During the same year he was married to Caroline Frear (B.S., Wellesley, M.A., Stanford). In the following year he became president of the State Normal School at San Francisco. This office made him automatically a member of the California State Board of Education in which capacity he served until the Board's reorganization in 1911. In his normal school for a number of years everything was subordinated to psychology. Later, becoming disappointed in the results obtained, he threw out psychology, not to take it up again until tests and measurements came to his attention.

Burk became a challenger of accepted opinion in educational matters. He held that no subject should be put into the curriculum unless a case could be made out for it. First, let the subject prove its educational value, then add it to the course of study. His greatest contribution to educational progress was his theory of motivated individual instruction. Pioneering in that field, he held to his course in spite of criticism and indifference. As a public speaker he was unusual. Full of wit and sudden turns of thought, he depended on the intellectual force he could put back of his ideas rather than on persuasion. From the standpoint of inspiration he was a notable leader—especially in the loyalties he developed. There can be no doubt that his inspiring of a small group of men and women, including Carleton Washburne of Winnetka and Willard Beatty of Bronxville, will perpetuate his name and methods into the years ahead. He was the author of *From Fundamental to Accessory in the Development of the Nervous System and of Movements* (1898), his doctoral dissertation; *A Study of the Kindergarten Problem in the Public Kindergartens of Santa Barbara, Calif., for the Year 1898–99* (1899), in collaboration with his wife; *A Simplified Course of Study in Grammar* (1912); *In Re Everychild, A Minor vs. Lockstep Schooling* (1915).

[*Who's Who in America*, 1924–25; *Bulls. of the San Francisco State Normal School;* articles in the *Sierra Ed. News* and the *Western Jour. of Ed.* (both published in San Francisco); personal acquaintance; interviews with members of the family.]

W. W. K.

BURK, JOHN DALY (*c.* 1775–Apr. 11, 1808), dramatist, was born in Ireland and came to America in 1796, evidently a political refugee. He had, he said, been a student at Trinity College, Dublin, and was reputed to have attempted the rescue of a condemned political prisoner and then himself escaped the country in woman's clothes, supplied by a Miss Daly, whose name he added to his own in gratitude. He settled first in Boston, where, on Oct. 6, 1796, he started a newspaper, the *Polar Star and Boston Daily Advertiser*. This venture lasted only six months.

From Boston he went to New York and attempted the publication of another paper, the *Time Piece*. This also failed. He then went to Petersburg, Va., where he finally settled. Here, on April 11, 1808, he was killed in a duel with a Frenchman named Coquebert. Burk's hot temper was probably the cause of the quarrel (*Some Materials to Serve for a Brief Memoir of John Daly Burk,* by Charles Campbell, Albany, 1868).

Burk was the author of *A History of the Late War in Ireland* (Philadelphia, 1799), "An Historical Essay on the Character and Antiquity of Irish Songs" (*Richmond Enquirer*, May 27, 1808), and a four-volume *History of Virginia* (vol. I, 1804; vols. II, III, 1805; vol. IV, completed by others, 1816). It was as a playwright, however, that he chiefly figured in American letters. He was among the earliest to put an American battle scene on the stage, in *Bunker Hill, or the Death of General Warren,* produced first at the Haymarket Theatre, Boston, Feb. 17, 1797, and at the John Street Theatre, New York, the following September. Burk apparently earned $2,000 from the Boston engagement, a very considerable sum for a playwright in those days, and the play remained popular on such holidays as the Fourth of July for almost fifty years. A full and interesting description of how the battle scene was staged will be found in a letter from Burk to the manager of the New York theatre (Brander Matthews's introduction to the reprint of the play, Dunlap Society, New York, 1891). The play was full of inflated rhetoric and bombastic blank verse, to-day highly ludicrous. One character refers to nightingales singing in Boston. President Adams saw the play in New York, and said to the manager, "My friend Gen. Warren was a scholar and a gentleman, but your author has made him a bully and a blackguard." Of course Burk had no intention of doing this, and to tastes less fastidious than Adams's it did not seem that he had done so. The public of the day at any rate forgave the inflated rhetoric (if they did not enjoy it!) for the sake of the battle scene. In 1798, at the Park Theatre, New York, Burk's *Female Patriotism, or the Death of Joan d'Arc* was produced. Professor Quinn (*A History of the American Drama from the Beginning to the Civil War*, 1923, pp. 117–18) calls this play one of the best of all our early American dramas. Joan, he says, is a human character and the verse rises to a respectable level of eloquence. Other plays by Burk were *The Death of General Montgomery in Storming the City of Quebec* (1797); *Bethlem Gabor, Lord of Transylvania, or the Man-hating Palatine* (published in 1807, in Petersburg, Va., where it had been acted by Burk and other amateurs, as well as by the professional company at Richmond) ; *The Innkeeper of Abbeville;* and (attributed to Burk by some writers) a lost play called *Which Do You Like Best, the Poor Man or the Lord?* Burk had an undoubted love for freedom and this was reflected in his plays, however crude. He also appealed to the patriotic emotions of the day, and by making a stage pageant out of national history helped our infant drama to identify itself with the national life.

[In addition to the sources cited above, see Oscar Wegelin, *Early Am. Plays* (1900) ; Wm. W. Clapp, Jr., *A Record of the Boston Stage* (1853) ; Wm. Dunlap, manuscript journals in the N. Y. Hist. Soc.]

W. P. E.

BURKE, ÆDANUS (1743–Mar. 30, 1802), congressman, jurist, was born in Galway, Ireland, and was the grandson of an officer under James II in the Irish uprising of 1689–90. A letter of Dec. 2, 1769, shows him at that time hard at work studying law in Stafford County, Va. (*State Records of North Carolina,* XV, 676–78). In February 1778 he resigned a lieutenant's commission in the 2nd South Carolina Continental Regiment (*Year Book, City of Charleston,* 1893, p. 209), and a month later was appointed one of the associate judges of the state. In his charge to the grand jury of Ninety Six District in May, he set forth the democratic basis of the new state government, and rejoiced in the abolition of the "unnatural distinctions of nobleman and commons." On the fall of Charleston two years later the courts were suspended not to be opened until 1783 (D. J. McCord, *Statutes of South Carolina,* VII, 206), and the judge again took the field, this time as captain of the militia. He was representative in the legislature in 1781 and 1782, and from 1784 to 1789. The leading issue in South Carolina during the years immediately following the Revolution was the treatment of the Loyalists. Burke always voted for leniency. In 1783 he published an admirably written pamphlet, *An Address to the Freemen of South Carolina,* in which he appealed for amnesty on grounds of humanity, public policy, and legal principle. He flayed John Rutledge as the originator of the confiscation policy. In another pamphlet of the same year he gave full vent to his distrust of the forms of nobility. His *Considerations on the Order of the Cincinnati* (1783) had a wide circulation in the United States, and was translated by Mirabeau into French under his name. English and German translations of this then appeared. In the South Carolina convention for ratifying the Federal Constitution Burke appeared as a representative of a back-country district, and voted against adoption. He declared that the eligibil-

ity of the President to succeed himself was dangerous to the liberties of the people, and moved an amendment to prohibit it. He was elected to the First Congress and there continued his fight for the qualification of the general powers of the government, to keep, he said, "our liberties from being fooled away." He opposed the excise tax and the establishment of the United States Bank. But the assumption of state debts he vigorously urged, as a measure of justice, both because the debts were incurred in the common cause, and because South Carolina, deprived by the Constitution of her import duties, would become bankrupt without it. Likewise he spoke and voted with the majority on paying the Continental obligations at par, basing his argument on public policy. He was a firm proponent of slavery. He did not return to Congress, and devoted the rest of his life to his judicial duties. In 1785 an act of the legislature appointed him, with Justices Grimké and Pendleton, on a commission to revise and digest the South Carolina law. The digest was reported in 1789. It was not adopted as a whole, but it had an influence on the Constitution of 1790, and portions were enacted as separate statutes (Thomas Cooper, *Statutes of South Carolina,* I, 435). In December 1799 Burke was elected chancellor of the court of equity. He never married, but lived in comfortable quarters in Charleston. He was first and foremost the judge, his solid legal learning and careful reasoning determining his conduct in all important matters. He was, next, the ardent democrat. But neither principle nor policy obscured his courage, his Irish wit, or his irascible temper.

[Jos. Johnson, *Traditions of the Am. Rev.* (1851) ; J. B. O'Neall, *Bench and Bar of S. C.* (1859) ; *S. C. Hist. and Gen. Mag.,* XIII, 146, XXVII, 45–48 ; *Am. Hist. Ass. Report,* 1896, I, 885–87.]   R. L. M—r.

BURKE, CHARLES ST. THOMAS (Mar. 27, 1822–Nov. 10, 1854), actor, dramatist, was the son of Thomas Burke, an actor of some repute, and Cornelia Frances Thomas, a capable actress of French ancestry who, after the death of her first husband, became the wife of the second Joseph Jefferson and the mother of the third and most celebrated actor of that name. Burke's career on the stage began in infancy, his early childhood experiences in the theatre culminating in his appearance at the National Theatre, New York, on Sept. 3, 1836, as the Prince of Wales to the Richard III of Junius Brutus Booth. Later in the same season he was seen as Prince John in *Henry IV* with James H. Hackett as Falstaff, and as Irus in Talfourd's tragedy *Ion* with George Jones. At this time he began the singing of comic songs in a manner that gained him an added popularity throughout his career. Toward the end of 1837, Mr. and Mrs. Jefferson, accompanied by their family, began journeys through the west and south which gave Burke intimate acquaintance with the life and hardships of the wandering actor. His aunt, Elizabeth Jefferson, says of him during this period that "he grew up to be one of the best actors we ever had," that "as a boy he was full of promise," and that "a more talented and kind-hearted man never lived." He returned to the east in 1847, and the rest of his short life was passed mainly in the theatres of New York and Philadelphia, notably in association with William E. Burton. Joseph Jefferson refers to them as "these two great artists," and in the course of his *Autobiography* mentions Burke again and again in the most affectionate terms. Burke acted many of the favorite heroes of comedy, including Paul Pry in John Poole's comedy, Dickory in *The Spectre Bridegroom*, Ichabod Crane, Solon Shingle, Touchstone, Sir Andrew Aguecheek, Bob Acres, Caleb Plummer, and Rip Van Winkle. He made his own version of the Washington Irving story, and portions of it were later utilized by Joseph Jefferson, who at one time acted Seth the innkeeper to his half-brother's Rip. The famous line, "Are we so soon forgot when we are gone?" is Burke's. He was twice married, first to Margaret Murcoyne of Philadelphia, and upon her death to Mrs. Sutherland, who survived him. A stepdaughter, Ione Sutherland, took his name, and had a brief career on the stage as Ione Burke. He had many of the appealing physical and mental attributes of the comedian. His figure was slender, graceful, and lithe, and his features though plain were notably expressive. He was a typical example of the born actor to whom the stage is a world of reality as well as of illusion, and the results of whose work come from intuition rather than from study. William Winter says that his "art concealed every vestige of effort." He died in New York in his thirty-third year, almost at the outset of what might have been a great career.

[T. A. Brown, *Hist. of the N. Y. Stage* (1903); J. N. Ireland, *Record of the N. Y. Stage* (1866–67); Wm. Winter, *The Jeffersons* (1881); Jos. Jefferson, *Autobiography* (1890); the *Era* (London), Dec. 2, 1899; *Lippincott's Mag.*, July 1879.]   E. F. E.

BURKE, JOHN G. [See BOURKE, JOHN GREGORY, 1846–1896.]

BURKE, STEVENSON (Nov. 26, 1826–Apr. 24, 1904), lawyer, railroad promoter, was the son of two Scotch-Irish immigrants from the North of Ireland, David and Isabella Burke, who in 1825 landed at New York and proceeded to a farm near Ogdensburg in Lawrence County, N. Y. Nine years later they moved to North Ridgeville, Ohio. Stevenson was the oldest of four children. For several years he attended the local school for a short time in the winter and worked on his father's farm in the summer. He also went to private schools at Ridgeville Center and Elyria. At the age of seventeen he began teaching in the district schools. In 1846 he entered Ohio Wesleyan University, but soon left to take up the study of law. He was admitted to the bar on Aug. 11, 1848. From 1848 to 1862 he practised law at Elyria. In 1861 he was elected common pleas judge, an office he held until 1869. He then moved to Cleveland to resume the practise of law in a larger field. He had a conspicuous part in the Oberlin-Wellington slave rescue case, but more representative of his practise, which was usually concerned with corporation law, particularly after his removal to Cleveland, were the Utah silver mine cases (the "Nez Percés" and the "Old Telegraph" mining companies) involving title to the properties; the Butzman and Mueller case testing the constitutionality of the Scott liquor license law of Ohio; and the series of cases connected with the foreclosure of mortgages on the Indianapolis & St. Louis Railway. For many years Burke was the general counsel of the Cleveland, Columbus, Cincinnati & St. Louis Railway and also for the Cleveland & Mahoning Valley Railway Company (Erie). From the practise of law he easily turned to the actual management of railway affairs. One of his early ventures in the railroad world was the consolidation of three lines into one company, the Columbus, Hocking Valley & Toledo Railway (about 1881). He was led into this merger in order to care for his coal properties in the Hocking Valley. In 1882 he negotiated the purchase of the New York, Chicago & St. Louis Railway ("Nickel Plate") for William H. Vanderbilt. In 1880 he became president of the Cleveland & Mahoning Valley Railway Company. After the organization of the Columbus, Hocking Valley & Toledo Railway, he was actively connected with its financial management. The "Big Four" Railway had his services as director, as chairman of the financial and executive committee, as vice-president, and later as president. Extensive as were his interests in the railroad world, however, Burke found time and energy to enter into other forms of business, among them iron manufacture, and coal and nickel mining. In his later years he gradually withdrew from active business management, although he remained president of the

Cleveland & Mahoning Valley Railway until the time of his death. In two fields, as a corporation lawyer and as an organizer and owner of railroads, he was distinguished among men of the Middle West. He was always interested in current affairs and was unusually well-read on a wide range of subjects, including art, education, finance, and government. A patron of the Western Reserve Historical Society, he was also the leading spirit in the foundation of the Cleveland School of Art, president of its board of trustees, and one of its foremost benefactors. He was married twice: on Apr. 26, 1849, to Parthenia Poppleton of Bellville, Ohio, who died on Apr. 7, 1878; and on June 22, 1882, to Mrs. Ella M. Southworth of Clinton, N. Y.

[Manuscript biography in the Western Reserve Hist. Soc.; sketch in the *Mag. of Western Hist.*, 1885–86, III, 296–306, by a local historian, J. H. Kennedy; another in the *Bench and Bar of Ohio* (1897), II, 360–66; articles including a resolution of the Cleveland Bar Association of Apr. 26, 1904, with estimates of character, as given by various members; *Cleveland Plain Dealer*, Apr. 25, 26, 1904; *Cleveland Leader*, Apr. 25, 27, 1904.]   E. J. B.

BURKE, THOMAS (*c.* 1747–Dec. 2, 1783), governor of North Carolina in the period of the Revolution, also a member of the Continental Congress, was born in County Galway, Ireland, of Norman-French descent. He was the son of Ulick Burke and his wife Letitia Ould. He attended one of the universities, probably Dublin, and after a family quarrel emigrated to America, settling first in Accomac County, Va., later in Norfolk. In Virginia he began the practise of medicine which he soon relinquished for law. In 1771 he removed to North Carolina and located in Orange County, about two miles north of Hillsboro, calling his estate "Tyaquin," the name of the Burke family seat in Ireland. He was licensed to practise law in the superior court of Orange in 1772 and soon became active in the political affairs of the county and of North Carolina.

In Virginia Burke had written and spoken against the Stamp Act and in North Carolina he represented Orange County in all of the provincial congresses save the first. In the third congress which met at Hillsboro in August 1775 he was very active, being a member of the committee which framed the test oath and also of the committees to prepare an address to the people, to conciliate the disaffected, and to provide ways and means. In the next congress, which met at Halifax in April 1776, he was a member of thirteen committees. Of these the most important was that on Usurpations and Grievances, which on Apr. 12 reported a resolution, unanimously adopted, empowering the delegates of

North Carolina in the Continental Congress to concur with the delegates from the other colonies in declaring independence—a measure which gave North Carolina a distinct priority in the movement for separation from Great Britain. Of barely less importance was the committee to report a frame of government for North Carolina. The committee, and also the congress, was divided into two groups, conservatives and radicals. Burke belonged to the latter group, advocating sovereignty of the people, annual elections, the separation of the organs of the government, the separation of church and state, and ratification by the people. Division of opinion was so strong that no decision could be reached, and the problem of constitutional principles was referred to the next congress, called to meet at Halifax in November 1776. The ensuing election was warmly contested; Burke and other candidates of like political creed in Orange County were defeated, but the congress, when it assembled, unseated the delegates chosen and ordered a new election in which Burke was successful. He then took his seat on Dec. 16, 1776. The constitution which was adopted was a compromise, but it embodied the principles of sovereignty of the people, separation of powers, separation of church and state, and annual elections. According to tradition the final draft of the Constitution and also of the bill of rights was the work of Burke, Richard Caswell [*q.v.*], and Thomas Jones. Burke's prominence in these political agitations resulted in his election to the Continental Congress by the Halifax Convention in December 1776. He appeared in Congress the following February and continued to represent North Carolina until June 1781, with the exception of the period from April to August 1778. He had no sympathy with the secrecy of the proceedings in Congress and was very critical whenever the military power seemed to infringe on civil rights. He was a severe critic of the Articles of Confederation while that document was in process of formation and after it was completed, and he was responsible for the final form of Article II of the Articles, which guaranteed to each state the powers not specifically delegated to Congress.

In the spring of 1778 Burke gave a practical demonstration of his conception of state sovereignty. A certain group in Congress hostile to Washington secured the adoption of instructions which interfered with a cartel which he was negotiating. Washington wrote Congress asking for a modification of the instruction and intimated that his sensibilities were wounded. The reply of Congress, as drafted by a committee, contained language which Burke did not approve, and, after a prolonged debate on the night of Apr. 10, seeing that his presence was necessary to make a quorum, he left the hall. Congress then summoned him to return. Believing that the message was from an individual, Burke refused. The next day when Congress attempted to discipline him, Burke declared that such action was an unwarranted exercise of power and that in his official actions he was responsible to the State of North Carolina. He therefore left Philadelphia, laid his case before the North Carolina Assembly, was exonerated and reëlected. This incident probably saved his political career, for in April 1778 he had been defeated for reëlection because he had favored the appointment of a Pennsylvania military officer as brigadier over North Carolina troops; but the issues of the instruction to Washington and responsibility to the State brought about his return to Congress in August.

In October 1779, Burke was officially thanked by the Assembly for his services in Congress. In the summer of 1780 he was in Hillsboro and he soon assumed a leadership in state affairs. The Continental Army, under command of Gen. Horatio Gates, was in the neighborhood. Complaint and dissatisfaction were aroused by the arbitrary seizure of supplies for military purposes. Burke became the spokesman of the people, declaring that the policies of the military warranted resistance. He entered into correspondence with Gates and the President of Congress and soon secured a satisfactory revision of policy. In June 1781 he was elected governor of North Carolina. It was a time of utmost demoralization because of the British invasion. Troops and supplies had to be mobilized quickly. Burke undertook the direction of this task with such vigor that he came into conflict with the board of war, to which state military administration had been entrusted in 1780; the outcome was the establishment of his authority as supreme executive. He was so active in rallying the people and in assembling soldiers and supplies that British and Tory leaders decided that he must be captured, and this was accomplished by a Tory raid on Hillsboro on Sept. 12, 1781. He was taken first to Wilmington, N. C., where he was held as prisoner of state, then to Sullivan's Island in the harbor of Charleston, S. C., where he was placed in close confinement. In November he was paroled to James Island. There he was treated with consideration and respect, but in a few weeks refugees were also admitted to the island and the resulting disorder became so great that Burke believed his life was

in danger. He therefore asked for a parole to the American lines; the reply was that he was held as a hostage to secure the life of David Fanning, notorious Tory leader. Acting on the theory that the British had violated the terms of parole and that he was thereby released from its obligation, he managed to escape and took refuge at the headquarters of Gen. Greene. On Greene's advice he notified Gen. Leslie, British commander at Charleston, of his escape, and offered to secure an exchange or to return within the British lines if the terms of parole would be guaranteed. Receiving no reply, he returned to North Carolina and resumed his official duties, but refused to be considered for reëlection in the spring of 1782. So ended his public career. He died at "Tyaquin" the next year, being survived by his wife, Mary Freeman, whom he had married in 1770, and by a daughter Mary. Burke County, N. C., created in 1777, was named for him.

[Marshall D. Haywood, sketch in *Biog. Hist. of N. C.*, vol. II (1905); J. G. de R. Hamilton, sketch in *N. C. Booklet* (Oct. 1906); *Colonial and State Records of N. C.* (vols. X–XXII); "Letters of Members of the Continental Cong." being *Carnegie Inst. of Washington Pubs.*, *No. 229* (1921); and the *Jours. of the Continental Cong.* (L. C. ed. 1904–22).]   W. K. B.

BURKE, THOMAS (Dec. 22, 1849–Dec. 4, 1925), lawyer, was born in Clinton County, N. Y., the son of James Burke, an Irish immigrant, and his wife, Bridget Delia Ryan. He obtained a smattering of education at the Clinton public school, but in 1862 his mother died and the family removed to Iowa, where for the following four years he worked on a farm and in a store, earning money which enabled him to attend school intermittently. In 1866 he went to Michigan, and, pursuing the same method, saved sufficient to defray a year's attendance at Ypsilanti Academy, where he graduated in 1870. He then entered the law department of the University of Michigan, teaching school in vacations. In 1872 he studied in a law office at Marshall, Mich., and in 1873 was admitted to the Michigan bar, being immediately afterward elected city attorney. Business conditions, however, were not promising, and he borrowed money to travel to the Pacific Coast, arriving in Seattle, Wash., May 3, 1875. There he opened a law office, and for the remainder of his life—a period of fifty years— his career was synonymous with the history of the city. He was married in 1876 to Caroline E., daughter of J. J. McGilvra of Seattle. In the same year he was elected probate judge of King County, and, being reëlected, served till 1880 but declined a third term. A strong Democrat, he was the party nominee for delegate to Congress in 1880 and 1882, but was unable to overcome the Republican majority. He was prominent as a successful advocate, but gradually withdrew from court work, confining his professional work to consultations and associating himself more with business enterprise. When the anti-Chinese troubles arose in 1886 he defended the Chinese at the risk of his life, narrowly escaping being lynched by an excited mob. In 1888 he temporarily accepted the appointment of chief justice of the supreme court of Washington Territory in order to relieve a critical situation which had arisen owing to the sudden deaths of two successive occupants of that position, but retained office only until April 1889. He organized the Seattle & Walla Walla Railway and the Seattle, Lake Shore & Eastern Railway to connect with the Union Pacific and the Canadian Pacific railroads, the accomplishment of which in 1892 gave Seattle the transportation facilities she needed. In 1893 when J. J. Hill was planning to extend the St. Paul, Minneapolis & Manitoba Railway to the Pacific Coast as the Great Northern Railroad, Burke was retained as general western counsel to the company. He became the intimate friend and adviser of Hill, and it was mainly due to his efforts that Seattle was made the Pacific terminus of the new trans-continental line. He conducted for the Great Northern Railroad all the negotiations relative to the acquisition of real estate, the tunnel under Seattle, and the right of way through the state. He also actively interested himself in stimulating trade between Seattle and China and Japan, paying several visits to those countries and acting as counsel for the Nippon Yusen Kaisha Steamship Company. In politics he refused to follow Bryan in 1896, was active in campaigning throughout the state on behalf of McKinley, and shortly afterward joined the Republican party. In 1907 he withdrew from practise. He was one of the originators of the Alaska-Yukon Exposition and went in 1908 as commissioner on its behalf to Japan and China. The following year he was offered by President Taft the position of minister to China but declined. He was a candidate for the Senate at the ensuing election, but suffered defeat in the general Republican débâcle. In 1910 he was appointed a trustee of the Carnegie Endowment for International Peace. He died Dec. 4, 1925, in New York City. Burke was a sound lawyer, but his professional success was largely due to his great business ability and foresight. His services to the city of Seattle were fundamental, and he was recognized as preëminently her foremost citizen. Small of stature, unassuming and genial in company, he had great force of character and an infinite capacity for hard work, which, joined to a natural felicity of speech and intense earnestness, made him a dominating figure in public affairs.

[The chief source of information is *Thos. Burke 1849–1925*, (1926), comp. and ed. by Chas. T. Conover. See also "Judge Thos. Burke" by S. B. L. Penrose in *Whitman Coll. Quart.*, June 1926, and *Sketches of Washingtonians* (1907), p. 125.]   H. W. H. K.

BURLEIGH, CHARLES CALISTUS (Nov. 3, 1810–June 13, 1878), abolitionist, was a son of Rinaldo and Lydia (Bradford) Burleigh, and a member of a family of reformers. Born in Plainfield, Conn., he received his schooling at Plainfield Academy, and while continuing to help with the work of his father's farm, began the study of law. But early in 1833 an attack on the Connecticut "Black Law" which he had published in the *Genius of Temperance* attracted the attention of the Rev. Samuel J. May [*q.v.*], through whose instrumentality he became editor of Arthur Tappan's new paper the *Unionist,* published at Brooklyn, Conn., in defense of Prudence Crandall [*q.v.*] and her negro school. Burleigh—later assisted by his brother, William Henry [*q.v.*],—edited the *Unionist* for some two years during which he won a reputation for fearless and forceful writing. He had continued his study of law, and in January 1835 was admitted to the bar, but again the Rev. S. J. May and the call of reform intervened, and Burleigh turned his back on a professional career to become agent and lecturer for the Middlesex Anti-Slavery Society. In the same year he was in the company of William Lloyd Garrison when the latter was mobbed in Boston, wrote the account of the mob published in the *Liberator* (Oct. 24, 1835), and helped conduct that journal during Garrison's absence from the city. His name appeared frequently in the *Liberator* thereafter, and his long thin figure, "flowing beard and ringlets and eccentric costume" (Garrison, III, 298) became familiar on lecture platforms throughout the northeastern states. In 1838 he was a witness of another mob when Pennsylvania Hall in Philadelphia was burned. At this time and for some years he was editor of the *Pennsylvania Freeman,* after 1844 the regular organ of the Eastern Pennsylvania Anti-Slavery Society. As a member of the business committee of the American Anti-Slavery Society he introduced at the meeting in 1840 a resolution stating that the constitution of the society should not be interpreted as requiring members either to exercise or refuse to exercise their political votes; this resolution led to the repudiation by the society of both Harrison and Van Buren as candidates for the presidency. In 1859 Burleigh succeeded Sydney H. Gay as corresponding secretary of the American Anti-Slavery Society, and in that capacity prepared its twenty-seventh annual report, published under the title, *The Anti-Slavery History of the John Brown Year* (1861). He also prepared the introduction to *Reception of George Thompson in Great Britain* (1836); and an appendix to *Discussion on American Slavery between George Thompson, Esq., and Rev. Robert J. Breckinridge* (1836); and was the author of *Slavery and the North* (Anti-Slavery Tracts, No. 10, 1855); and an address, extracts from which appeared in *No Slave-Hunting in the Old Bay State* (Anti-Slavery Tracts, new series, No. 13, 1859).

Burleigh's zeal in the anti-slavery cause led him indirectly into another crusade. Twice jailed in West Chester, Pa., for selling anti-slavery literature on Sunday, he plunged into Anti-Sabbatarianism, joining with others in a call for a convention, held in New York in March 1848, at which he was prominent among the speakers. He also dabbled from time to time in other reforms: opposed capital punishment in a pamphlet, *Thoughts on the Death Penalty* (1845) and on the platform in Philadelphia (*A Defence of Capital Punishment by Elder Frederick Plummer in a Discussion of Six Evenings with Charles Burleigh*, 1846); and supported woman suffrage, notably by his speeches in the conventions at Cleveland and New York in 1853 and at the first annual meeting of the American Equal Rights Association at New York in May 1867 (Susan B. Anthony and others, *History of Woman Suffrage*, 1881–82, I, 148, 549, II, 194). He later followed his brother William Henry into the field of temperance reform (*Centennial Temperance Volume*, 1877, p. 83).

Burleigh's personal appearance, his eccentricity of dress and manner, were against him, in the opinion of Samuel J. May, who nevertheless reckoned Burleigh among his ablest associates, characterizing him as "a single-minded, purehearted, conscientious, self-sacrificing man," who often "delighted and astonished his hearers by the brilliancy of his rhetoric and the surpassing beauty of his imagery" (May, p. 66). The son of William Lloyd Garrison said that as a close debater Burleigh "was easily first of all the abolition orators" (Garrison, IV, 319). During his later years he made his home at Northampton, Mass., where he died in 1878 from injuries received in a railroad accident at Florence, Mass. On Oct. 24, 1842, he had married Gertrude Kimber of Chester County, Pa., who bore him three children.

[Chas. Burleigh, *Genealogy of the Burley or Burleigh Family of America* (1880); Ellen D. Larned,

Hist. of Windham County, Conn., vol. II (1880), p. 497; Samuel J. May, *Some Recollections of Our Antislavery Conflict* (1869); W. P. and F. J. Garrison, *Wm. Lloyd Garrison* (1885–89); J. T. Scharf and T. Westcott, *Hist. of Phila.* (1884), III, 2015; files of the *Liberator* (Boston); obituary in *Boston Transcript*, June 14, 1878.]　　　　　　　　　　　　　　　E. R. D.

BURLEIGH, GEORGE SHEPARD (Mar. 26, 1821–July 20, 1903), poet, reformer, was born at Plainfield, Conn., the youngest child of Rinaldo and Lydia (Bradford) Burleigh. His father, a graduate of Yale College, had been principal of the local academy, but became blind from excessive study, and had to betake himself to a farm. Owing to the straitened circumstances of the family, none of the children received much of an education, but they were all influenced by various aspects of Transcendentalism—religious, educational, philanthropic, ethical—then permeating New England culture, and the home became a veritable seed-bed of reformers, five of the six brothers—Charles Calistus, William Henry [*qq.v.*], Lucian, Cyrus, and George Shepard—attaining some note in the anti-slavery or other causes. The father himself was one of the early abolitionists and sympathized with his fellow townsman, Prudence Crandall [*q.v.*], in her brave attempt (1832–34) to provide school facilities for negro children. George received a common school education and until well on in life was engaged in farming. He also wrote verses and went about the country lecturing on the slavery question. In 1846 he published an *Elegiac Poem on the Death of Nathaniel Peabody Rogers*, an abolitionist so devoted to personal liberty that he objected to having a presiding officer at anti-slavery gatherings and quarreled irreconcilably with William Lloyd Garrison. The poem, both in thought and phrasing, owes much to *Lycidas* and *Adonais*. The year 1846–47 Burleigh spent at Hartford as editor of the *Charter Oak*, an abolitionist paper. On one of his lecture trips he met Ruth Burgess of Little Compton, R. I., whose father was one of the helpers on the "Underground Railroad." He married her Mar. 17, 1849. In that year he published at Philadelphia *The Maniac and Other Poems*. The title poem has some interest as an attempt at Wordsworthian narrative, but in general Burleigh has little claim on posterity as a poet. He shows a preference for elaborate stanza forms and sententious or ornate, not to say turgid, language; much too frequently he hides his fundamental image behind a mass of opaque metaphor. As a tribute to John C. Frémont, then Republican candidate for president, he issued in 1856, without his name, *Signal Fires on the Trail of the Pathfinder*, a poetical campaign tract, more dashing—as befitted its subject—than his other work. He also contributed verse to magazines and in 1874 published privately a translation of Victor Hugo's *Légende des Siècles*. He made his home for about fifty years at Sakonnet Point, R. I., spending the winters latterly with his son in Providence.

[*Who's Who in America*, 1903–05 ; *Providence Jour.*, July 22, 24, 1903 ; Chas. Burleigh, *Geneal. of the Burley or Burleigh Family of America* (1880).]

G. H. G.

BURLEIGH, WILLIAM HENRY (Feb. 2, 1812–Mar. 18, 1871), journalist, reformer, was the fourth of the six sons of Rinaldo Burleigh, a Yale graduate and a classical teacher until failing sight forced him to retire, and his wife Lydia Bradford, a descendant of Gov. William Bradford. He was born at Woodstock, Conn., but spent most of his boyhood on his father's farm at Plainfield, Conn., where he early became a sharer in the family responsibilities, which meant hard work and few recreations. His education was received at the district school and the Plainfield Academy, of which his father was in charge until William was eleven. Winter schooling and summer work alternated for a number of years. He was apprenticed to a dyer, then to a printer, in order that he might quickly become self-supporting. In 1830 he became a journeyman on the *Stonington Phenix*, where he was soon setting up articles of his own composition. In 1832 he was printer and contributor to the *Schenectady* (New York) *Cabinet* and in 1833 assisted his brother, Charles Calistus Burleigh [*q.v.*], in editing the *Unionist*, Brooklyn, Conn., a paper founded to support Prudence Crandall's colored school in which William Burleigh also taught for a time. He was married to Harriet Adelia Frink of Stonington, Conn., by whom he had seven children. He early felt interest in reform causes, especially anti-slavery, temperance, peace, and woman suffrage, and in 1836 began lecturing for the American Anti-Slavery Society. At about the same time he was editor of the *Literary Journal*, Schenectady, but left that in 1837 to become editor of the *Christian Witness* and afterward the *Temperance Banner*, in Pittsburgh. In 1843 he went to Hartford at the invitation of the Connecticut Anti-Slavery Society, to take charge of its organ, the *Christian Freeman*, afterward the *Charter Oak*. In 1849 he was employed by the New York State Temperance Society, with headquarters at Albany and Syracuse, as corresponding secretary, lecturer, and editor of the *Prohibitionist*. He remained in this position until 1855, when he was appointed harbor master of the port of New York and went to live in Brooklyn.

Later he was made a port warden, but in 1870 was displaced for a Democrat. His first wife died in 1864 and in 1865 he married Mrs. Celia Burr of Troy, a teacher, prominent in woman suffrage work, and afterward a Unitarian minister. Burleigh's fiery tilts against the evils of his day often made life hard for himself and his family. He denounced the Mexican War, as waged in the interest of the slave power, and for this and on other occasions narrowly escaped mob violence. Yet he really disliked controversy and preferred purely literary work. Poetry was the form he chose for personal literary expression, apart from editorial and lecture composition. A volume of *Poems* was published in 1841 and enlarged editions appeared in 1845 and 1850. After his death his wife collected these poems in a new edition (1871). His poetry is not without beauty and vigor and shows his longing for the quiet, studious life which, because of his goading conscience, he was never able to enjoy. This conscience also dictated a certain amount of propaganda verse, such as *The Rum Fiend and Other Poems* (1871). His picture, taken shortly before his death, shows a worn, kindly face, with high cheek bones, unusually alert dark eyes, heavy, drooping, white mustache, and white hair worn long and brushed straight back. He was brought up by his parents a strict Presbyterian but later became a Unitarian. He died in Brooklyn, N. Y., as a result of what were called epileptic attacks, and his funeral was held at the Second Unitarian Church, where Samuel Longfellow had preached and where John White Chadwick was then pastor. His old friend John G. Whittier visited him shortly before his death.

[The chief source of information about Burleigh is the memoir by his wife Celia Burleigh, which forms the preface to his collected *Poems* (1871). A long obituary appeared in the *N. Y. Tribune*, Mar. 20, 1871, and an obituary notice in the *N. Y. Times*, Mar. 19, 1871. See also Chas. Burleigh, *The Genealogy of the Burley or Burleigh Family of America* (1880), p. 141.]

S. G. B.

BURLESON, EDWARD (Dec. 15, 1798–Dec. 26, 1851), soldier, frontier leader, was born in Buncombe County, N. C. He was descended from Aaron Burleson, who emigrated from England to North Carolina in 1726. His father was James Burleson who had married Elizabeth Shipman. James Burleson moved to Tennessee about 1812 and commanded a company of Tennessee volunteers under Andrew Jackson in the Creek War in Alabama. Young Edward accompanied him and seems to have acquired a taste for military life. At the age of seventen he married Sarah Owen of Madison County, Ala. In 1816 he moved to Howard County, Mo., and became a captain and then a colonel of militia. He moved back to Tennessee in 1823 where he again became a militia colonel. In 1830 he visited Texas, and the next year he moved his family there and settled on the Colorado River about eleven miles below the town of Bastrop. This was on the extreme frontier and subject to frequent incursions of hostile Indians. Burleson, who was a natural leader, took the principal part in repelling the raids, and in December 1832 he was made lieutenant-colonel of his municipality. When the revolution broke out, he joined the Texans who besieged the Mexican general, Cos, in San Antonio; and when Stephen F. Austin resigned the command of the besieging army, Burleson was elected by the men to succeed him, Nov. 24, 1835. San Antonio was stormed and Cos surrendered on Dec. 10. Soon afterward Burleson returned to his farm, but the news of Santa Anna's approach the next spring again brought him into the field. He was made colonel of a regiment that was organized at Gonzales and commanded it, under Gen. Sam Houston, in the retreat which ended in the victory of San Jacinto and the capture of Santa Anna. Burleson played a conspicuous part in that battle and afterward commanded the forces that followed the Mexican divisions under Filisola to the Rio Grande. In 1836 he was elected to the first Senate of the Republic of Texas. In 1838 he discovered, from papers captured from Mexican raiders in the vicinity of Austin, that the Mexicans and the Cherokee Indians, with other tribes, were planning a hostile combination against the Texans. In January 1839 he was made colonel of a regiment of regulars and commanded them in the Cherokee War the following summer until the Cherokees were expelled from Texas. In the same year he took part in the fight on Brushy Creek with the Comanches, and in 1840 he was in command in the great fight at Plum Creek with the same fierce tribe. He resigned his commission in the army and in 1841 he was elected vice-president of the Republic over Memucan Hunt. Burleson presided over the Senate with great dignity and fairness and won the respect of all parties. In 1844 he was a candidate for the presidency, but was defeated. He supported the movement for annexation to the United States, and when war broke out with Mexico he went with the troops raised in Texas to the support of Gen. Zachary Taylor. He was at the battle of Monterey as aide to Gen. J. P. Henderson. After he returned, he removed from his old home to the site of the present town of San Marcos. He was elected to the state Senate and died in Austin while in attendance upon that body. Though he had but little formal education, he was a man of unusual gifts, and these, with his unaffected simplicity, dignity, honesty, and fearlessness, had made him one of the loved figures of Texas.

[There is a good sketch of Burleson's life in the *Texas Almanac for 1859*, pp. 197–204. Other material may be found in the *Papers of Mirabeau Buonaparte Lamar* (1921–24); John Henry Brown, *Hist. of Texas* (1892–93); J. W. Wilbarger, *Indian Depredations in Texas* (1889); *Jour. of the Senate of the Republic of Texas* and *Jour.* of the 3rd and 4th Leg.; Memorial Proc. of the Senate and House of the 4th Leg., Dec. 26, 27, 1851 (published in *Texas State Gazette*, Jan. 3, 1852); and *A Brief Hist. of the Burleson Family* (1889). There is much also in various early Texas newspapers, especially the *Telegraph and Texas Register* of Houston.]

C. W. R.

BURLESON, RUFUS CLARENCE (Aug. 7, 1823–May 14, 1901), Baptist clergyman, educator, was descended from Aaron Burleson, who emigrated from England to North Carolina about 1726. His father, Jonathan Burleson, was a native of Kentucky and commanded a volunteer company in the Creek War. His mother, Elizabeth (Byrd) Burleson, also a native of Kentucky, was descended from the Byrd family of Virginia. Jonathan Burleson and his wife settled in Morgan County, northern Alabama, in 1813, where Rufus, their sixth child, was born. He attended the local schools and academies, and spent one year in a college at Nashville. Then his health became impaired by over-zealous study and he returned to his father's farm. In the meantime he had been ordained as a Baptist preacher. After teaching for two or three years in Mississippi, he began preaching and took part vigorously in the theological controversies of the period. In January 1846 he entered the Western Baptist Theological Seminary at Covington, Ky., where he graduated in June 1847. He had determined to go to Texas and received an appointment to that field from the mission board of his church. Soon afterward he was elected pastor of the Baptist church in Houston. He arrived there early in January 1848, and remained for more than three years. In June 1851 he was elected to the presidency of Baylor University, then a small school at Independence, Tex., which had been founded by the "Baptist Education Society" in 1845. The task of building a college in a new country whose people were generally poor was one of extreme difficulty. There were only two small buildings at the college in 1851 and only fifty-two students. The salaries of the faculty were very small and had not been paid in full. Burleson set himself to his task with energy and enthusiasm. Through the arduous labors of himself and the agents more buildings were erected, more equipment and more money for salaries were procured, standards were raised, and a competent law faculty added. But a controversy arose in the school and church between Burleson and the head of the "female department," which was virtually a separate institution, and in 1861 Burleson resigned. The entire faculty and the senior class of the "male department" went with him to Waco where they took over a school which they renamed Waco University. It was feebly supported by the Waco Baptist association and struggled on through the Civil War. From 1861 Burleson's career was identified with that of the school in Waco. At Baylor he had been opposed to coeducation but now he came to favor it, and it was established at Waco in 1865. Waco and Baylor remained rival institutions until 1886. During this period Waco grew steadily in size and importance, for it was in a section of the state which was increasing rapidly in population and wealth. After 1868 it received the official support of the Baptist General Association of Texas, which covered the greater part of northern Texas. Meanwhile Baylor had declined in attendance, as Independence was not on a railroad. About 1870 a movement for the consolidation of the two schools began, but their partisans could not agree and nothing was done until 1886, when the older institution was moved from Independence to Waco; the old name, Baylor, was given to the consolidated school; and Burleson was made president. He remained in that position until 1897, despite some controversies with the trustees, when he was retired as president emeritus on full salary. At this time Baylor was the largest of the denominational colleges in Texas. Burleson was a man of high ideals, devoted to the promotion of education and of his church. He was of a kindly disposition and a playful humor; but he was noted also for a naïve egotism and great tenacity of opinion, traits which sometimes involved him in unprofitable controversy. He was married in 1853 to Georgia Jenkins of Independence.

[The most complete account of Burleson, rather fulsome and badly arranged, is *The Life and Writings of Rufus C. Burleson* (1901) containing a biography by Harry Haynes, comp. and pub. by Mrs. Georgia J. Burleson. There is a useful sketch in the *Quarterly of the Tex. State Hist. Ass.*, V, 49. Other material may be found in J. M. Carroll, *A Hist. of Tex. Baptists* (1923); Frederick Eby, *The Development of Ed. in Tex.* (1925); J. J. Lane, *Hist. of Ed. in Tex.* (1903); and *A Brief Hist. of the Burleson Family* (1889).]   C. W. R.

BURLIN, NATALIE CURTIS (Apr. 26, 1875–Oct. 23, 1921), student of Indian and negro music, was born in New York City, the daughter of Edward and Augusta Lawler (Stacey) Curtis and niece of George William Curtis. She first studied in the National Conservatory of Music,

New York, with Arthur Friedheim; later, in Europe, with Busoni at Berlin, Giraudet in Paris, Wolf in Bonn, and Julius Kniese at the "Wagner-Schule" in Baireuth. On returning to America it was evidently her purpose to continue her career as pianist, but while visiting her brother in Arizona she became so much interested in the Indians of that region and in their music that she visited many different encampments, taking down their songs by word of mouth. From that time on, her great interest lay in this sort of research. The first tangible result of these studies came in the form of *The Indians' Book* (1907), a collection of two hundred songs gathered from eighteen different tribes of North American Indians, mostly those of the Southwest, the Plains and the Pueblo tribes.

As indicative of her deep and genuine interest in her subject and her ability to communicate this interest to others, it may be noted that when she began her studies the Indians were not allowed to sing their native songs in the government schools and that her earnest appeal to Theodore Roosevelt, then president, had the effect not only of revoking this rule, but also of giving the Indians every encouragement in the performance of their own music. The publication of *The Indians' Book* aroused so much enthusiasm that an urgent request came that she should do for the negro music what she had so successfully accomplished for the Indian. This request resulted in her making at Hampton Institute a thorough study of negro songs. In 1918–19 she published four volumes of *Hampton Series Negro Folk-Songs* for male quartet, retaining the instinctive harmonization of the singers themselves with no retouching on her part. This artistic restraint naturally gives to these volumes great historical value. Percy Grainger, in the *New York Times*, Apr. 14, 1918, said: "When I peruse these her strangely perfect and satisfying recordings of these superb American negro part songs, I cannot refrain from exclaiming: How lucky she to have found such noble material, and it such an inspired transcriber!" Mrs. Burlin,—she had been married in 1917 to Paul Burlin, painter, of New York—obtained the material for her last published book, *Songs and Tales from the Dark Continent* (1920) from two native-born African students at Hampton Institute who gave her freely of the songs and stories of their native land. In 1921 she died as the result of an automobile accident in Paris. In addition to the works noted above she published, *Songs of Ancient America* (1905), *Songs from a Child's Garden of Verses by Robert Louis Stevenson* (Wa-Wan Press), and various other songs and choruses. A new edition of *The Indians' Book*, with added material and new drawings made by Indians especially for the purpose, was issued in 1923.

[A. Eaglefield Hull, *Dict. of Modern Music and Musicians* (1924); *Outlook*, Nov. 23, 1921; Preface to *The Indians' Book* (edition of 1923).] W. T. U—n.

BURLINGAME, ANSON (Nov. 14, 1820–Feb. 23, 1870), congressman, diplomat, the son of Joel Burlingame, a Methodist exhorter and lay preacher, and his wife, Freelove (Angell) Burlingame, was born at New Berlin, Chenango County, N. Y. As a small child he went with his parents to Seneca County, Ohio, and thence ten years later to Detroit. His early education was in the common schools and his undergraduate days were concluded in the Detroit branch of the then very young University of Michigan. Although in his later years he displayed an urbanity not usually bred in frontier life there was also in him a marked freedom and directness of manner characteristic of the environment in which he was reared. At the age of twenty-three he came eastward to the Harvard Law School and then settled in Massachusetts where he became a junior law partner in Boston with George P. Briggs, son of Ex-Governor George Nixon Briggs. On June 3, 1847, he married Jane Cornelia Livermore, a daughter of Isaac Livermore of Cambridge.

Burlingame's gift of oratory together with his exceptional personal charm led him quickly into politics where he found ample opportunities in the tumultuous fifties. He was elected to the Massachusetts Senate in 1852 and in the following year was a member of the Massachusetts constitutional convention. In 1855 he was elected to Congress where he served three terms, being defeated in 1860 by William Appleton. A Free-Soiler and one of the organizers of the Republican party in Massachusetts, he was also an outspoken admirer of Kossuth and was at one time associated with the Know-Nothing party. Few records remain of his Congressional career. His speeches were unwritten and the reports in the *Congressional Globe* are fragmentary. He usually voted with his New England colleagues, he was a faithful representative of his constituents, and he was quickly responsive to appeals of justice and humanity. As the result of a stinging speech in castigation of Preston Brooks [*q.v.*], the assailant of Sumner, he was challenged to a duel by Brooks. Burlingame formally accepted, but named as the place the Canadian side of Niagara Falls, which was difficult for Brooks to reach with safety. Brooks declined to go and the duel was averted. Burlingame's ostensible acceptance gained him great popularity in the North. (For the fullest and most recent account of this affair, see James E. Campbell, "Sumner, Brooks, Burlingame, or the Last of the Great Challenges," *Ohio Archæological and Historical Quarterly*, XXXIV, 1925, 435–73; for an earlier account, more favorable to Burlingame, see John Bigelow, *Retrospection of an Active Life*, I, 1909, 165–70.)

In the campaign of 1860 Burlingame did yeoman service for the Republican party and was rewarded by the appointment of minister to Vienna. Because of his previous sympathy for Kossuth and for Sardinian independence he was unacceptable to the Austrian court and his appointment was changed to Peking, a capital in which his former constituents maintained a lively interest because of the large share of Massachusetts in the China trade. Although by the treaties of 1858 the powers had at last attained the right of resident diplomatic representation in Peking, they had overreached themselves in China in more than one important respect. The imperial government was by no means able to carry out all of the provisions of the treaties because of the semi-autonomous character of the local governments. The treaty-port merchants, long held back from direct participation in the interior trade were both jubilant at the recent chastisement administered to China and truculent in claiming their new treaty rights. The situation was ominous when Burlingame arrived. Further military conflicts with the provinces seemed very possible and there was even the prospect that either by conquest or penetration the European nations would assert and seek to maintain full sovereign rights at least in the treaty-ports where they had been granted the right of residence and trade. While even the prospect of a partition of China presented itself to the American Government, practically all naval forces had to be withdrawn from the Far East because of the Civil War. Burlingame had to meet his problem single-handed.

With a sagacity singularly in contrast with the temerity of some of his other foreign policies at the outbreak of the war, Secretary Seward had instructed Burlingame to coöperate closely with the powers in China. Almost immediately, Burlingame assumed the leadership among the diplomatic representatives in Peking, although they were all far more experienced than he, and coöperation under his direction involved the agreement among the ministers to withstand the pressure of the treaty-port merchants and to assume toward the imperial government a tolerant attitude. This policy in turn gave to Burlingame great influence among the Chinese officials who sought his advice on a variety of problems such as the Lay-Osborn flotilla fiasco, the appointment of Robert Hart to the Foreign Inspectorate of Maritime Customs, and the suppression of the Taiping Rebellion. To Burlingame much credit is due for thwarting the early efforts of the foreign merchants to set up in the treaty-ports government wholly independent of the imperial authority. He developed a great admiration for and confidence in the Chinese and during a visit to the United States in 1865–66 he sought by speeches and personal conference to spread his enthusiasm and confidence among American mercantile houses. He also sought to promote the practise, which became common in later years, of placing American technical advisers in the employ of the Chinese Government. One may sum up the policy of Burlingame in China in the words of Raphael Pumpelly, who for a time was the guest of the American Legation in Peking and subsequently engaged in some surveys of the Chinese mineral resources, as a policy "based upon justness and freed from prejudice of race."

Among other projects which Burlingame urged upon China was the sending of diplomatic representatives to the western powers, an innovation which Japan had already adopted with some success in 1860. Very likely because of Burlingame's suggestion, Seward, on Dec. 15, 1865, instructed him to urge such a course upon China. The idea seems to have met also with the approval of Robert Hart and it came about very naturally, when Burlingame let it be known in Peking in November 1867 that he was about to resign as minister, that the Chinese Government offered him the post as the head of an official delegation with two Chinese colleagues to visit the western powers, both to observe western civilization and also to plead with the governments not to press their demands for a revision of the treaties of 1858.

Burlingame set out promptly, visiting first the United States, then Europe. While the so-called Burlingame Mission met with unqualified hostility in China and was relatively barren of results on the Continent it fully accomplished its purpose in America and measurably succeeded in England. On July 28, 1868, Burlingame had signed with Secretary Seward a convention supplementary to the American treaty of 1858, which convention pledged the American Government to respect Chinese sovereignty and stated that the Chinese emperor by granting foreigners certain rights of trade and residence in China had "by no means relinquished his right of eminent domain or dominion." It contained other provisions which were also mere amplifications of

rights granted ten years before. There was added also a bilateral immigration clause, designed to promote the importation of Chinese laborers to the Pacific Coast, particularly for work on the construction of the Union Pacific Railroad which had been experiencing labor difficulties. This article subsequently proved to be most ill-advised and was a fundamental cause of friction which brought the two governments twenty-five or more years later to a prolonged state of diplomatic non-intercourse. It may be questioned whether the treaty itself did not in the end do more harm than good but the immediate effect was beneficial to China and to Chinese-American relations. Supported by the most emphatic approval of the American Government, Burlingame visited London, arriving just on the eve of the inauguration of the first Gladstone ministry. From Lord Clarendon he secured not a treaty but a declaration that China was "entitled to count upon the forbearance of foreign nations," and this was followed by an instruction from London to Peking which clearly revealed that the new government in London was not disposed to support the extravagant demands of the foreign merchants in China for the revision of the treaties. After London, Burlingame visited Paris, Berlin, and other European capitals, reaching St. Petersburg in February 1870, where he was stricken with pneumonia and died on the twenty-third of that month. His diplomatic career may fairly be described as brilliant. With the exception of the bilateral immigration clause in the treaty of 1868, for which Seward was at least as much responsible as Burlingame, few Americans in the Far East have served their own country so beneficially and certainly none has given to China a more sincere friendship.

[The most extensive bibliography with reference to Burlingame is to be found in *Anson Burlingame and the First Chinese Mission to Foreign Powers* (1912) by Frederick Wells Williams. While less a biography than an interpretation of Burlingame's services with respect to China, it is appreciative and yet judicial in purpose. The contemporary estimates of Burlingame vary with the nationality of the writers. For the British point of view see Alexander Michie, *The Englishman in China* (1900); J. Barr Robertson, "Our Policy in China," *Westminster Rev.*, Jan. 1870; *Blackwood's Edinburgh Mag.*, Feb. 1869. J. Von Gumpach, in his *The Burlingame Mission; a Political Disclosure* (1872), seeks to demonstrate from documentary sources that the Burlingame Mission greatly exceeded its powers and misrepresented many important facts. Of a very much more favorable character are the appreciations of Burlingame by Jas. G. Blaine, *Atlantic Mo.*, Nov. 1870; W. A. P. Martin, *A Cycle of Cathay* (1896); Raphael Pumpelly, *Across America and Asia* (1870), and *My Reminiscences* (1918).]　　　　T. D.

BURLINGAME, EDWARD LIVERMORE (May 30, 1848–Nov. 15, 1922), editor, was the son of Anson Burlingame [*q.v.*], and Jane (Livermore) Burlingame. The surroundings and contacts of his formative years were Boston and Cambridge. His father was an eminent congressman from Massachusetts, and his mother belonged to an old Cambridge family. With such a parentage it was natural for Edward to go to Harvard where he entered the class that was graduated in 1869. President Lincoln had appointed Anson Burlingame minister to China in 1861, and his son left Harvard College in the first year of his course to become his father's secretary in China. Later, when Anson Burlingame was made Ambassador Extraordinary of China to negotiate treaties with the United States and European powers, Edward followed him in that most interesting pilgrimage, and, though still a very young man, found abundant opportunity to study in Paris, Heidelberg, Berlin, and St. Petersburg. At Heidelberg he received the degree of Ph.D. in 1869. His father's position opened to him the doors of many people eminent in literature, art, and statesmanship. This cosmopolitan training, of which he made the most by reason of his fluent knowledge of French and German, gave his natural aptitude for letters just the right nourishment for an ambitious youth. The European sojourn was abruptly ended by the sudden death of his father in 1870 while negotiating a treaty with Russia. Soon afterward, the son came home and began his long literary and editorial career. He was on the *New York Tribune* in 1871 and there formed a life-long friendship with John Hay. In the same year he was married to Ella Frances Badger. For four years, 1872–76, he was associated in the making of the *American Cyclopedia*.

In 1879 he became one of the literary advisers of the publishing house of Charles Scribner's Sons, and for the rest of his life was associated with it. When Charles Scribner, the son of the founder of the house, formulated a plan for *Scribner's Magazine* in 1886, Burlingame became the editor from the first number (January 1887) until his resignation in 1914. As an editor, his aim was "a magazine of good literature in the widest sense." During the many years of his editorship, he formed lasting literary friendships with Stevenson, Meredith, Barrie, Page, Hopkinson Smith, Brander Matthews, Edith Wharton, Robert Grant, F. J. Stimson, Bunner, E. S. Martin, Henry van Dyke, and many others. He was keen in discernment of new talent and a discriminating and severe critic of the output of new and old writers. His wide knowledge of international affairs and acquaintance with celebrated people gave his editorial judgment authority and unusual foresight. He had a particular *flair* for

what was of permanent interest in letters, and his acquaintance with several literatures made him impatient of the casual and unimportant. He edited *Current Discussion; a Collection from the Chief English Essays on Questions of the Time* (2 vols., 1878), *Stories by American Authors* (10 vols., 1884–85), and *Stories from Scribner's* compiled after the magazine had been running for many years. In 1875 he published *Art Life and Theories of Richard Wagner, Selected from his Writings and Translated by Edward L. Burlingame,* one of the earliest books on Wagner to be published in this country.

[Robt. Grant, "Edward Livermore Burlingame," *Harvard Grads. Mag.,* Mar. 1923; *Boston Evening Transcript,* Nov. 17, 1922; *N. Y. Times,* Nov. 17, 1922; *Scribner's Mag.,* Jan. 1923.]   R. B.

BURNAM, JOHN MILLER (Apr. 9, 1864–Nov. 21, 1921), educator, was born at Irvine, near Richmond, Ky., the son of Edmund Hall Burnam, a Baptist minister, and Margaret Shackelford (Miller) Burnam. His mother died when he was about two years old, and he was brought up by a kind stepmother. Until he was thirteen he received most of his education from his father. In 1877 he entered Central University, then at Richmond, Ky., and in 1878 Washington University, St. Louis, where he remained until 1880, when, at the age of sixteen, he entered Yale College. Here he was distinguished for regular attendance at classes, diligence, and ability. He received the degree of A.B. with honors in 1884. Remaining at Yale University as a graduate student in Sanskrit and Latin, he gained the degree of Ph.D. in 1886. Then followed nearly three years of study in Europe. He was professor of Latin and French in Georgetown (Kentucky) College, 1889–91, and assistant professor of Latin in the University of Missouri, 1891–99. After a year in Europe he became, in 1900, professor of Latin at the University of Cincinnati in the College of Liberal Arts, a position which was later changed to that of research professor of Latin and Romance palæography in the Graduate School. He was devoted to pure scholarship, and when he was relieved from the duty of teaching undergraduates he looked forward joyously to a future rich in scholarly achievement. He spent many summers in Europe working in libraries containing important manuscripts. His knowledge of Latin was profound, he possessed unusually perfect command of French, Spanish, and Italian, and read with ease all the languages of Europe, including Russian; but his chief interest was in palæography. His published writings include, in addition to numerous contributions to periodicals, monographs on *The Paris Prudentius* (1900), *The So-Called Placidus Scholia of Statius* (1902), *Glossemata de Prudentio* (1905), *Technologia Lucensis* (1919). His greatest work, *Palæographia Iberica,* was written in French and was to consist of eighteen parts. The first part appeared in 1912, the second in 1920, the third, completed by Prof. Rodney Potter Robinson, in 1925. The graduate students found him an inspiring teacher whose scholarship combined love for his chosen work, the authority which resulted from years of training and research, the independence of a vigorous and original mind, and the modesty of a sincere and gentle nature. He had no love of ostentation and no yearning for wide popularity, but his friends regarded him with deep and lasting affection. He was never married. On Aug. 26, 1921, while on a vacation in California, he received a paralytic stroke from which he suffered until his death, which occurred nearly three months later at Pomona, Cal.

[*Who's Who in America,* 1922–23; *Classical Journal,* Feb. 1922; Leonard M. Daggett, *A Hist. of the Class of Eighty-four, Yale Coll.* (1914); *Regular Baptist,* Dec. 1922; *Yale Univ. Obit. Record* (1922).]

       H. N. F.

BURNAP, GEORGE WASHINGTON (Nov. 30, 1802–Sept. 8, 1859), Unitarian clergyman, writer, a lineal descendant of Isaac Burnap, one of the founders of Reading, Mass., was born in Merrimac, N. H., where his father, Jacob, was for almost fifty years pastor of the Congregational Church. He was the youngest of thirteen children. His mother, Elizabeth Brooks, sister of Gov. John Brooks [*q.v.*] of Massachusetts, died when he was seven years old, and he was brought up under the supervision of a sister. The size of the family and the meagerness of his father's salary put difficulties in the way of the boy's schooling, but with the help of relatives he secured sufficient education at Groton Academy and an academy at Thetford, Vt., to enable him to enter Harvard as a sophomore in 1821. Though the state of his finances compelled him to teach more or less during his course, he graduated in 1824, and then spent three years at the Harvard Divinity School. A careful study of the whole Bible pursued while in college had made him a Unitarian, and immediately upon his graduation from the divinity school he was called to the pastorate of the First Independent Church of Baltimore, Md., as successor to Jared Sparks. Here he was ordained, Apr. 23, 1828. On July 18, 1831, he married Nancy, daughter of Amos Williams, who had married his cousin, Nancy Williams.

Until the end of his life, thirty-two years later,

Burnap was the pastor of the Baltimore church. Although performing his professional duties acceptably and taking active part in public enterprises, he was preëminently a student, and gave much of his time to writing and lecturing. The fact that Unitarianism was widely misunderstood and misrepresented, rather than zest for controversy, he states, made him an aggressive exponent and vindicator of its doctrines. More than twenty-five thousand copies of his books were sold during his lifetime. He was of the conservative wing of his church, basing his arguments upon a none too critical acceptance of the authority of the Scriptures, and betraying a rather limited intellectual range. His *Lectures on the Doctrines of Christianity in Controversy between Unitarians and Other Denominations of Christians,* published in 1835, was followed by *Lectures on the History of Christianity* (1842); *Expository Lectures on the Principal Passages of the Scriptures which Relate to the Doctrine of the Trinity* (1845); *Discourses on the Rectitude of Human Nature* (1850); *Popular Objections to Unitarian Christianity Considered and Answered* (1848); *Christianity, Its Essence and Evidence* (1855). Two works of a different character which had a large circulation were *Lectures to Young Men* (1840) and *Lectures on the Sphere and Duties of Women* (1841). He was a regent of the University of Maryland, one of the original trustees of the Peabody Institute, and a founder of the Maryland Historical Society. Among his other writings are *A Life of Leonard Calvert,* Sparks's Library of American Biography, 2nd series, vol. IX (1846) and a *Memoir of Henry Augustus Ingalls* (1846).

[*Memorial Biographies of the New Eng. Hist. and Geneal. Soc.,* vol. III (1883), which lists thirty separate publications by Burnap; *Mo. Religious Mag.,* XXII, 313; Jos. Palmer, *Necrology of Alumni of Harvard Coll.* (1864); S. A. Eliot, ed., *Heralds of a Liberal Faith,* vol. III (1910).]

       H. E. S.

BURNET, DAVID GOUVERNEUR (Apr. 4, 1788–Dec. 5, 1870), Texas politician, was born at Newark, N. J., the son of William Burnet [*q.v.*], and Gertrude (Gouverneur) Burnet. His parents died when he was very young and he was reared by his elder brothers and given a good education. One of these brothers, Jacob Burnet [*q.v.*], became a justice of the supreme court of Ohio and United States senator from that state. Another became mayor of Cincinnati. When seventeen years old David became a clerk in a counting-house in New York; but the firm soon failed. In 1806 he joined, as a lieutenant, Francisco de Miranda's expedition to Venezuela to free that country from Spain. The expedition failed and Burnet barely escaped with his life.

But he joined Miranda again in the abortive attempt of 1808. On his return Burnet went to his brothers in Ohio. In 1817 he purchased a mercantile business in Natchitoches, La.; but having developed tuberculosis, he sold his business and went to live among the Comanche Indians on the upper Colorado River in Texas. Then, his health being completely restored, he returned to Ohio. His visit to Texas resulted in a series of articles for the Cincinnati papers descriptive of the region he had seen. He studied and practised law for a time, but drifted back to Louisiana and Texas. In the summer of 1826, bearing letters from Henry Clay and Stephen F. Austin, he went to Saltillo and obtained from the Mexican government an empresario's contract to settle three hundred families near Nacogdoches. But the enterprise proved beyond his means and he sold the contract to a firm in New York. In 1831 he married a Miss Estis of New York and, returning to Texas, settled on the San Jacinto River. In 1833 he was a member of a convention at San Felipe, the capital of Austin's colony, which was called to petition the central authorities of Mexico for the separation of Texas and Coahuila. Burnet drew the petition, which was rejected in Mexico. In 1834 he was appointed judge of the municipality of San Felipe de Austin. The Texas Revolution was brewing. On Aug. 8, 1835, Burnet drew a set of very able and conservative resolutions for the San Jacinto community in which the rights of the citizens of Texas were firmly declared but desire for separation from Mexico was denied. Later in the same year he was a member of the General Consultation at Washington on the Brazos, which was called to protest against the measures of Santa Anna; and he was made a member of the committee of vigilance and safety. Hostilities had begun at Gonzales and San Antonio, and Burnet was gradually won over to the cause of independence. In the spring of 1836 he was a member of the convention at Washington which issued the Texas Declaration of Independence. Two weeks later he was elected by the convention president *ad interim* of the infant Republic of Texas. Burnet's administration, which lasted only until the following October, was as troubled as it was short. Santa Anna's forces had destroyed the Texan garrison at the Alamo and all the other small commands in the west except the little army under Gen. Sam Houston, and Houston was in retreat. As the Mexicans swept nearer, panic seized the people and a stampede began toward the Sabine. Deeming Washington unsafe, Burnet moved the seat of government to Harrisburg, near the present

city of Houston; later he removed again to Galveston Island, and after the battle of San Jacinto, to Velasco. About all his government could attempt in the meanwhile was to allay the fears of the people, increase the army, and procure supplies. Burnet was not conspicuously successful in these efforts. The people paid little attention to his assurances; recruits came in slowly; and the agents in New Orleans whom Burnet appointed to forward supplies failed miserably. After San Jacinto, fresh troubles arose over the disposition to be made of the captive dictator, Santa Anna, and the command of the Texan army. The government was too weak to enforce its will upon the undisciplined spirits who came in from the United States. Burnet also became involved in a quarrel with Houston. In September Houston was chosen president; and on Oct. 22 Burnet resigned his office. He retired to his farm, but two years later he was elected vice-president. During part of the administration of Lamar he acted as secretary of state, and later as president because of Lamar's illness and absence from the Republic. In 1841 Burnet ran for the presidency against Houston, but was defeated. The campaign had been marked by rancorous personalities which developed in Burnet a hatred of Houston that never abated. From this time on Burnet was only intermittently interested in politics. He lived on his farm, which he cultivated with his own hands, and struggled unsuccessfully against poverty. During 1846 and 1847 he served as secretary of state under the first governor, J. P. Henderson. He had lost all his children except one; and his wife died in 1858 leaving him disconsolate. He opposed secession, but his only son was killed in battle at Mobile in 1865. In 1866 he was elected by the first Reconstruction legislature to the United States Senate, but was not allowed to take his seat. In 1868 he was a delegate to the national Democratic convention in New York and was a presidential elector. This was his last contact with public affairs. During the final years of his life he was too feeble to work his farm and lived with friends in Galveston, where he died. That Burnet was a man of ability his public papers show, but he evidently was not a successful administrator. He was of unyielding temper, quick to resent offense, and prone to controversy: while his inflexible honesty and high sense of self-respect made it impossible for him to cultivate the arts of popularity.

[A. M. Hobby, *The Life and Times of David G. Burnet,* is a pamphlet published shortly after Burnet's death. Hobby also wrote a sketch for the *Texas Almanac* for 1873. Considerable material may be found in F. W. Johnson and E. C. Barker, *A Hist. of Texas and Texans*, vol. I (1916); John Henry Brown, *Hist. of Texas*; Chas. A. Gulick, ed., *The Papers of Mirabeau Buonaparte Lamar* (1921–24); E. C. Barker, ed., *The Austin Papers* (1924); D. G. Burnet, *Review of the Life of Gen. Sam Houston*, pamphlet (1852); and various early Texas newspapers, especially the *Telegraph and Texas Register* (Houston). The most complete study of Burnet's administration is an unpublished M.A. thesis by Sallie E. Sloan, "The Presidential Administration of David G. Burnet" in the Lib. of the Univ. of Texas.]   C.W.R.

BURNET, JACOB (Feb. 22, 1770–May 10, 1853), lawyer, senator, was a son of William Burnet [*q.v.*], and of Mary Camp, daughter of Nathaniel Camp. He was born in Newark, N. J., graduated at Nassau Hall in 1791, and studied law. In 1796 he settled in Cincinnati, where in 1800 he married Rebecca Wallace of Kentucky. When he first came to the Old Northwest, there were only a few scattered settlements along the watercourses. In the work of building modern commonwealths there, young Burnet was to play a leading part, as he was able and practical, with exceptionally fine judgment. Although he disliked public office, the record of his service is a long one, beginning in 1799 when he was appointed a member of the Legislative Council in the newly organized territorial government. For this office he was eminently qualified by his legal training and also by many professional trips throughout the territory. Soon he was called upon to help straighten out the legal tangle left over from the régime of the judges, and he drew up a number of laws that were to become of basic importance in the Ohio code. In his next public office, as a member of the state legislature, 1812–16, he gave important aid to the Federal government during the Western campaigns.

As president of the Cincinnati branch of the second National Bank, he keenly appreciated the distress caused by the sale of public lands on credit under the Act of 1800. Many settlers were hopelessly in debt to the government and were threatened with the loss of their lands with all improvements. This situation Burnet clearly explained in a memorial to Congress, copies of which he sent to influential men throughout the Western country. By this means public opinion was aroused, and strong pressure was brought to bear upon Congress. The sequel was the Land Act of 1820 which followed essentially the plan of relief proposed by Burnet, and really prevented a catastrophe in the Western settlements. Appointed judge of the supreme court of Ohio in 1821, he resigned in 1828, and almost immediately was chosen to fill the vacancy in the United States Senate, caused by the resignation of William Henry Harrison. Burnet

served until the end of the Twenty-first Congress, interesting himself especially in measures that concerned the West. Of utmost importance to Ohio was an extensive grant of public lands to aid the Miami Canal from Dayton to the Maumee. Unfortunately the act as first passed imposed impossible conditions, but by persistent efforts Burnet secured such favorable terms that the construction of the canal became possible. Equally important was his work to secure permission for the erection, by the State of Ohio, of toll-gates along the National Road. Although a maintenance fund was an obvious necessity, the proposed grant of this authority threatened to arouse an extended debate upon the general subject of Internal Improvements. By arguments that skilfully avoided controversies, Burnet secured the necessary act, and saved the National Road in Ohio (Register of Debates in Congress, 21 Cong., 2 Sess., pp. 287–92). In the Hayne-Webster Debate, he took only a very minor part, but it has been asserted, upon plausible grounds, that his notes on Hayne's speech on the first day formed the basis for a part of Webster's reply. In 1831 the legislature of Kentucky elected Burnet to be one of the commissioners to settle certain territorial disputes with Virginia. His last notable public act was the speech at the Harrisburg Convention in 1839 which nominated his friend, William Henry Harrison, for the presidency.

In an active professional life Burnet found time for a leading part in the intellectual and social movements of Cincinnati, serving as president of the local Astronomical Society, the Colonization Society, the Cincinnati College, and the Medical College of Ohio. These intellectual interests received notable recognition when he was elected a corresponding member of the French Academy of Science upon the nomination of Lafayette. In politics, Burnet took special pride in calling himself a Federalist, considering this the party of Washington and the one that was loyal to the Federal Union. This political conservatism was characteristic. Disdaining half-way measures he never hesitated to express his opinions in no uncertain terms. His very appearance was indicative of the tenacity of his views. Tall and dignified, he retained the style and manners of an older generation, wearing a queue long after it had been generally discarded. In 1847 he published his *Notes on the Northwestern Territory*, a work that is essentially autobiographical, and is still one of the most important historical sources for the period of transition in Ohio from a territorial government to statehood.

[*Cincinnati Daily Commercial*, May 11, 1853; G. A. Worth, *Recollections of Cincinnati, 1817–21* (1851), p. 61; *Hist. of Cincinnati and Hamilton County, Ohio* (1894), pp. 165–67; C. T. Greve, *Centennial Hist. of Cincinnati* (1904), vol. I, *passim*.]   B. W. B—d.

BURNET, WILLIAM (March 1688–Sept. 7, 1729), colonial governor, who was born at The Hague during his father's temporary residence there, was the son of Gilbert Burnet, the celebrated Bishop of Salisbury, and his second wife, Mary Scott. The Bishop was not only a man of intellectual distinction himself but had a wide acquaintance among men both of mind and action so that the atmosphere of the home into which the young William was born was one to stimulate his own abilities and ambition. He was, however, by no means a model student, and, although he entered Trinity College, Cambridge, at thirteen, he was soon removed for "idleness and disobedience." He then received private instruction from tutors and was subsequently called to the bar. About May 1712 he made an imprudent love-match with a daughter of Dean Stanhope, his wife dying within three years from a broken heart, it was said, due to a previous attachment.

Burnet was a man of ability who had his own way to make in the world. Fortunately, he was the godson of King William and Queen Mary and had numerous friends in high places. On Apr. 19, 1720, he was appointed governor of New York and New Jersey. He promptly sailed from England on July 10 and arrived at New York on Sept. 16. Both at this post and at his subsequent one in Massachusetts, his record was an honorable one.

New York, owing to its geographical position with relation to the French in Canada by way of Lake Champlain, and to the Indian fur trade routes to the westward through the Mohawk Valley, was the key colony in regard to the entire colonial Indian policy. Burnet at once sensed the importance of the Indian problem. The English were able to import the goods used in the Indian trade to purchase furs at much lower prices than could the French at Montreal, and this should have given them a great advantage in dealing with the savages. But although the New Yorkers held a powerful weapon in their hands in the cheapness of their trading goods, this was blunted to a great extent by the fact that there were important merchants who found it more profitable and easier to sell their goods to the French than to trade them with the Indians. Burnet realized that by this French trade the English were handing their strongest weapon to their enemies. It was his endeavor to prevent this and to rectify the Indian policy of the English which furnished the main-spring of his policy as governor. In his first year he secured the passage of a law prohibiting the Canadian trade and subsequently established a trading post at Tirondequot where goods were sold to the savages at half the price at which the French sold them. His Indian policy was not without mistakes in detail but was wise and far-sighted in principle. He at once, of course, came into conflict with powerful mercantile forces which cared more for their private gain than for the public benefit. His struggle with certain mercantile groups and with the Assembly became increasingly bitter. He made enemies of such powerful families as the Philipses and De Lanceys, and his action in setting up a court of chancery was roundly denounced by the Assembly in 1727. The English government transferred him to Massachusetts and he left for Boston soon after the arrival of his successor on Apr. 15, 1728.

The few months which were left to him before death were marked by the culmination of the contest between the Massachusetts Assembly and governor over the salary question. The argument took constitutional ground and both sides stated their positions, which were irreconcilable, with greater clearness and fulness than at any other point in the interminable wrangle (see E. B. Greene, *The Provincial Governor in the English Colonies of North America*, 1898, pp. 171 ff.). Burnet's stand was honorable throughout and in no way dictated by avarice, from which vice he was entirely free. Worn out by the work of his office, he died Sept. 7, 1729. While governor of New York, he had married Anna Maria (Mary) Van Horne, daughter of Abraham Van Horne and Mary Prevoost of that city.

Burnet was distinctly above the average of colonial governors. He was able, cultivated, charitable, just, genuinely solicitous to promote the welfare of the provinces he governed and not unwilling to make personal sacrifices for their good. His struggles with the Assemblies were always for principles and not for personal advantage.

[Some facts as to Burnet's early life may be found in *A Life of Gilbert Burnet* (1907), by T. E. S. Clarke and H. C. Foxcroft. His will and some other documents were printed by Wm. Nelson in *Original Papers Relating to Wm. Burnet* (1897). For his career in N. Y. and N. J. much material may be found in the *N. J. Archives*, 1 ser., IV, V, VI, and in *Docs. Relating to the Colonial Hist. of N. Y.* as stated in the index volume. Wm. Smith, *Hist. of N. Y.* (London, 1757) may also be consulted. For Mass. see Thos. Hutchinson, *Hist. of Mass. Bay* (London, 1828), vol. III; *A Collection of the Proc. of the Great and General Court of His Majesty's Province of the Mass. Bay* (1729); Greene's *Provincial Governor* as cited above, and the general histories.]   J. T. A.

BURNET, WILLIAM (Dec. 2, 1730 o.s.–Oct. 7, 1791), member of the Continental Congress, surgeon-general, was the son of Dr. Ichabod and Hannah Burnet, both natives of Scotland. He was born at Lyon's Farms, a hamlet between Elizabethtown and Newark, and was brought up in a home in which the father was one who took the popular side in the political controversies of the time. Educated at the College of New Jersey under the presidency of the Rev. Aaron Burr, he was a member of its second class, 1749, which was graduated before the College was removed to Princeton. Thereafter he studied medicine under a Dr. Staats of New York and then established himself in Newark where he lived and practised, except for the interruption due to the Revolution, until his death. At the outbreak of hostilities, although an extensive and lucrative practise had made him a man of means, he took an active part with those organizing opposition to royal authority. In May 1775 he became chairman of the committee of public safety for Newark and a little later chairman of the Essex County committee of safety, both committees laboring to keep the powerful Loyalist element under control. In June 1776 by direction of Washington he took measures for securing the person of Gov. William Franklin, who, after having given his parole, had issued a proclamation reconvening the defunct Loyalist legislature. Meanwhile in March 1776, at the call of Lord Stirling, Burnet collected and dispatched several military companies in aid of the defense of New York, his eldest son, Dr. William, Jr., going as surgeon attached to these companies. In addition Burnet was shortly made presiding judge of the Essex County courts, having as an early duty the sentencing of Loyalist neighbors and friends for furnishing aid to the enemy. The exercise of dictatorial and judicial powers did not interfere with the establishment, in 1775, on his own responsibility and largely at his own expense, of a military hospital located at Newark, to which he and his son gave personal supervision. In the winter of 1776–77 New Jersey sent him to the Continental Congress, which shortly after elected him physician and surgeon-general of the Eastern District. In 1780 he was again a member of the Continental Congress. As one result of his connection with Washington's headquarters there was formed between him, his sons, and the young Lafayette a lasting attachment, of which a memento in the brace of pistols worn by the Marquis at the Yorktown surrender is still in the possession of descendants. Since he was the chief suppressor of Loyalist activities in eastern New Jersey his property was the object of especial attack during times of British successes. Among other losses his medical library, spoken of as one of the most extensive in the colonies, was carried off. Following the cessation of hostilities he returned to an extensive practise in Newark, being described as a skilful and successful physician, and engaging also in agricultural pursuits. He was shortly after appointed presiding judge of the court of common pleas as well as chosen president of the New Jersey Medical Society, of which years before he had been one of the founders. On taking the chair at a meeting in Princeton he revived the custom of delivering the inaugural address in Latin. He died suddenly at the age of sixty-one. He was married twice: first, in 1754 to Mary, daughter of Nathaniel Camp, by whom he had eleven children; second, to Gertrude, daughter of Nicholas Gouverneur and widow of Anthony Rutgers by whom he had three children.

[Jos. P. Bradley, *Biog. Sketch of Wm. Burnet, M. D.* (n.d.); Jacob Burnet, *Notes on the Early Settlement of the Northwestern Territory* (1847); Samuel W. Fisher, *The Unfolding of God's Providence* (1853); Stephen Wickes, *Hist. of Medicine in N. J.* (1879); C. T. Greve, *Centennial Hist. of Cincinnati*, vol. I (1904); Gen. Wm. Fitzpatrick, "Letters" in *N. Y. Times*, Nov. 7, 1926; J. H. Clark, *Medical Men of N. J. in Essex District 1666–1866* (1867); *N. J. Provincial Cong. Jours. for 1775–76*; *Jours. of the Continental Cong.* (L. C. ed. 1904–22, 25 vols.); *Colls. N.J.Hist. Soc.*, vol. VI, suppl. (1866); *Geneal. and Memorial Hist. of the State of N. J.* (1910); John Livingston, *Portraits and Memoirs of Eminent Americans* (1854), p. 153.]
         D. B.

BURNETT, CHARLES HENRY (May 28, 1842–Jan. 30, 1902), otologist, son of Eli Seal Burnett and Hannah Kennedy Mustin Burnett, was born in Philadelphia and received his preliminary education in that city. He graduated from Yale College in 1864 and from the Medical Department of the University of Pennsylvania in 1867. After serving as resident physician in the Episcopal Hospital of Philadelphia, he went abroad, spending ten months in post-graduate work. Returning to Philadelphia he practised for a year. In the course of his studies abroad he had become much interested in diseases of the ear, and in 1870 he gave up his practise and went to Vienna to pursue his otological studies under Politzer and to Berlin where he worked with Virchow and Helmholtz. He continued his friendship with these scientists in later life. It was in Helmholtz's laboratory in 1871 that Burnett conducted his very valuable investigations into the condition of the membrane of the round window during the movements of the auditory ossicles and upon the results of changes in intralabyrinthine pressure. These were published in the *Archives of Ophthalmology and Otology* in 1872. On his findings Burnett based the operation which he subsequently devised and performed in many cases for the relief of progressive deafness in chronic catarrhal otitis media, consisting in the performance of tympanotomy and removal of the incus. Burnett later advocated the same procedure for the relief of vertigo in chronic catarrhal otitis media. In 1872 he entered into practise once more, now devoting his energies solely to diseases of the ear. On June 18, 1874, he was married to Anna L. Davis. In spite of the exacting claims of a very large practise, throughout his life he was able to devote much time to laboratory research and became known as one of the foremost investigators into the physiology of hearing. He was for many years professor of otology in the Philadelphia Polyclinic and served on the staff of several hospitals. Most of his operative work was done in the Presbyterian Hospital.

Burnett was of frail physique and suffered much from ill health. He was an indefatigable worker and must often have overtaxed himself with the combined labors of his practise and his scientific work. In addition to his very frequent contributions to periodical medical literature he edited the department of progress of otology in the *American Journal of Medical Sciences*. In 1877 he published *The Ear; Its Anatomy, Physiology, and Diseases* and in 1879 *Hearing, and How to Keep It*. In 1893 he edited a *System of Diseases of the Ear, Nose and Throat*. He also contributed the sections on otology in Keating's *Cyclopedia of the Diseases of Children* (1888–89) and in the *American Textbook of Surgery* (1892) and the *American Year-book of Medicine and Surgery*. In 1901 in conjunction with Dr. E. Fletcher Ingalls of Chicago, and Dr. James E. Newcomb of New York, he edited a *Textbook of Diseases of the Ear, Nose and Throat*. On Jan. 15, 1902, he attended the meeting of the Section of Otology and Laryngology of the College of Physicians of Philadelphia and participated in the discussion of the papers read on that occasion. A few days later he developed pneumonia and died on Jan. 30, at his home in Bryn Mawr. He was a fellow of the College of Physicians of Philadelphia, a member of many other medical societies, and at one time president of the American Otological Society.

[Chas. G. Rockwood, *Hist. of the Class of 1864, Yale Coll.* (1895) and *Supplement* (1907); *Trans. of the Lehigh Valley Medic. Ass.* (1902); F. R. Packard, memoir in *Trans. of the College of Physicians of Phila.*, ser. 3, vol. XXV (1903), containing complete bibliography of Burnett's writings.]   F. R. P.

BURNETT, FRANCES ELIZA HODGSON (Nov. 24, 1849–Oct. 29, 1924), author, born at Cheetham Hill, Manchester, England, and reared until her sixteenth year in her native city, was thoroughly English even to the end of her life. Her father, Edwin Hodgson, a small shopkeeper, had died at thirty-eight, leaving the mother, Eliza Boond Hodgson, with a family of four small children and with inadequate means of support. Heroically she attempted to carry on the small shop, but with steadily decreasing income until soon the family was forced to move into the tenement district of Islington Square. Here amid the mill population with their broad dialect and their narrow horizon Frances Hodgson spent her formative years. She was a highly imaginative child, living in a world of her own creation, dramatizing always her environment and her experiences into fairy creations, and all her life long she kept vividly alive this childhood accomplishment. The Civil War, which stopped the supply of cotton, closing the mills and bringing disaster and want to the city of Manchester, brought ruin to the mother's business and the prospect of starvation to the family. A brother of the mother, William Boond, had early migrated to America, settling at Knoxville, Tenn., where he had succeeded as the proprietor of a general store, and, following his advice, the family in the spring of 1865 set sail on the steamer *Moravian* for the new world, settling finally near Knoxville. Life in the new environment seems to have made small impression upon the sensitive girl. Though she lived for more than eight years in the Tennessee mountain region, there is no trace of the fact in her later writings. She was dwelling in a world of her own. At seventeen she was writing stories, and to obtain the money required for paper and for postage to editors she was gathering and selling wild grapes. *Godey's Lady's Book* was the first to publish her work, then came *Peterson's*, and in 1872 *Scribner's Monthly*, with her story in broadest Lancashire dialect "Surly Tim's Trouble." All of this early work was essentially English in tone, language, and setting, so English indeed that it was often viewed by editors with suspicion. In 1873 she was married to Dr. Swan Moses Burnett [*q.v.*], who in 1875 took her to Europe, where for the next two years he studied diseases of the eye and throat in England and France. Returning, he settled in Washington, D. C., where he became widely known as a specialist in ophthalmic and aural surgery.

Two years later came Mrs. Burnett's first literary success, the publication in *Scribner's Monthly* (August 1876–May 1877) of her Lancashire story "That Lass o' Lowrie's," issued as a volume in 1877. Wide-spread popularity was immediate. In England a first edition of 30,000 was quickly exhausted and in America the sale was vastly greater, edition following edition. Following it came a rapid series of fictions, first a republication of earlier work, then a succession of novels keyed to the popular demand,—*Haworth's* (1879), *Louisiana* (1880), *A Fair Barbarian* (1880), *Through One Administration* (1883), and her second sensational success *Little Lord Fauntleroy*, issued as a book in 1886. Quickly the latter became a best-seller despite a loud chorus of humorous comment and sarcastic criticism. Fauntleroy, a study of Mrs. Burnett's own son, undoubtedly was made too perfect. As he is represented, he is an insufferable mollycoddle, and even a prig. Chiefly is he made up of wardrobe and manners. The story was at once dramatized, and largely through the genius of Elsie Leslie, who took the title rôle, it became the dramatic success of the season. Other plays from Mrs. Burnett's pen followed, all of them successful: *Esmeralda* (October 1881) in collaboration with William Gillette; *The First Gentleman of Europe* (January 1897) produced by Daniel Frohman; and *The Lady of Quality* (1896), perhaps Mrs. Burnett's best dramatic effort. Her pen was busy to the last: the titles of her novels mount up to forty or more. Perhaps the most significant of her later stories are *Sara Crewe* (1888), *The Pretty Sister of José* (1889), *Little Saint Elizabeth* (1890), *In Connection with the De Willoughby Claim* (1899), *The Shuttle* (1907), *T. Tembarom* (1913). Much of her later life she spent in England. She was divorced from her first husband in 1898, and two years later was married to Stephen Townesend, an English physician and litterateur, a man many years her junior. For a time she made her home at Maytham Hall, in Kent, his residence, but, soon leaving him, spent the rest of her life near Plandome Park on Long Island. Her novels had all the characteristics of mid-nineteenth-century feminine fiction; over-emotionalism, sentiment even to sentimentality, ultra-romanticism; but her sense of the dramatic and her power to throw into her narratives something of the vividness of her own personality begot sympathy and interest in her readers. To her own generation she seemed advanced in realism and in daring, especially in her first novel which introduced coarse characters and scenes from the mill areas of Lancashire with all the dialogue in broadest dialect, yet over even this novel she threw thickly an atmosphere of the romantic. Unquestionably she was at her best in her stories for juveniles, work that has been termed "fairy tales of real life." It is her juveniles like *Little Lord Faunt-*

leroy, Sara Crewe, and *Little Saint Elizabeth,* that will keep her name alive in future years.

[Mrs. Burnett's autobiographic study, *The One I Knew Best of All, A Memory of the Mind of a Child* (1893), brings her life with minuteness up to her eighteenth year. Her biography entitled "Dearest," by her son Vivian Burnett, the Little Lord Fauntleroy of the novel and the play, was published in *McCall's Mag.,* May–Sept. 1927, and in book form, with additions, under the title *The Romantick Lady* (1927). The titles of two biographical articles, one in the *Bookman,* Feb. 1925, "Frances Hodgson Burnett: 'Romantic Lady,'" and one in the *Outlook,* Nov. 12, 1924, "A Portrayer of Lovable Children" sufficiently characterize her and her work.]   F. L. P—e.

BURNETT, HENRY LAWRENCE (Dec. 26, 1838–Jan. 4, 1916), Union soldier, lawyer, was born in Youngstown, Ohio, the son of Henry and Nancy (Jones) Burnett, and a descendant of William Burnet, colonial governor of New York, 1720–28. At fifteen, determined upon getting an education, he stole away from home, equipped with a bundle of clothing, forty-six dollars, and copies of *Thaddeus of Warsaw* and *The Lady of Lyons,* and walked about one hundred miles to Chester Academy. Admitted to the school, he remained for two or three years, when he entered the Ohio State National Law School, from which he graduated with the degree of LL.B. in 1859. In the same year he began the practise of law at Warren. On the outbreak of the Civil War he became active in support of the Union. At one of these meetings he was challenged by a man in the audience with the question, "Why don't you enlist?" "I will," he promptly replied. He at once volunteered in Company C of the 2nd Ohio Cavalry, of which he was chosen captain on Aug. 23. With his regiment he was sent to Missouri and saw service in the actions at Carthage, Fort Wayne, and Gibson, later taking part in the campaigns in southern Kentucky. In the fall of 1863, with the rank of major, he was appointed judge-advocate of the Department of the Ohio. A year later at Gov. Morton's request, he was sent to Indiana to prosecute members of the Knights of the Golden Circle and later took part in the cases growing out of the Chicago conspiracy to liberate the Confederate prisoners at Camp Douglas. In these trials he obtained seven convictions. He was also prominent in the trial of L. P. Milligan for treason before a military commission. He was brevetted a colonel of volunteers Mar. 8, 1865, and in the omnibus promotions of Mar. 13 was brevetted a brigadier-general. In the prosecution of the assassins of Lincoln he served under Judge-Advocate Joseph Holt [*q.v.*] with Gen. John A. Bingham [*q.v.*] as a special assistant, and seems to have borne a major part in the preparation of the evidence. After the trials he moved to Cincinnati, where he practised law with Judge T. W. Bartley until 1869, and then with Ex-Governor J. D. Cox and John F. Follett until 1872. He then moved to New York, where at various times he was in partnership with E. W. Stoughton, with B. H. Bristow, William Peet, and W. S. Opdyke, and with Judge James Emott. He was for a time counsel for the Erie railroad, and was engaged in many noted cases, including the litigation over the Emma mine, in which he acted as attorney for the English bondholders. Probably his greatest case was that of the Rutland Railroad Company against John B. Page: in the closing argument he spoke for sixteen hours with a "consummate ability" that stamped him "the peer of the greatest advocate of the age" (D. McAdam and others, *Bench and Bar of New York*, 1899, II, 64). He was an organization Republican, a participant in the party councils, and was on especially close terms with McKinley who used to call him "Lightning Eyes Burnett." In January 1898 McKinley appointed him federal district attorney for the southern district of New York, and on the completion of his four-year term he was reappointed by Roosevelt.

Burnett was married three times. His last wife was Agnes Suffern Tailer, of a prominent New York family, who survived him. In his later years he spent much of his time at his country home, Hillside Farm, Goshen, N. Y., where he kept a large stable of harness horses which he drove on the track of the Goshen Driving Club. In the middle of November 1915, while at the farm, he was taken ill with pneumonia. Despite his serious condition he insisted on being taken by train to his city home, where, two months later, he died.

[Burnett's article, "Assassination of President Lincoln and the Trial of the Assassins," in *Hist. of the Ohio Soc. of N. Y.* (1906); David Miller DeWitt, *The Assassination of Abraham Lincoln* (1909); *The Conspiracy Trial* (3 vols., 1865-66), ed. by Benj. Perley Poore; *Official Records* (Army); *Who's Who in America*, 1912-13; obituaries in the *N. Y. Times* and *N. Y. Tribune*, Jan. 5, 1916.]   W.J.G.

BURNETT, JOSEPH (Nov. 11, 1820–Aug. 11, 1894), philanthropist, manufacturing chemist, the son of Charles and Keziah (Pond) Burnett, was born in Southborough, Mass., and educated in the district schools there. The name Burnett appears among those of the pioneer citizens of the town. John Burnett was the founder of the family in New England. At fifteen Joseph went to the English and Latin School in Worcester, but never attended college. The study of medicine, which, however, he never practised, gave him the title of Doctor. At seventeen he established with Theodore Metcalf a perfumery

and extract manufacturing business,—one of the earliest in America—from which he made a fortune. In 1854 he sold his interest and started a firm of his own, Joseph Burnett & Company, manufacturing chemists. This firm became so successful that its products are now known the world over. Burnett was also a pioneer in the raising of high-bred stock in New England and started in 1847 the well-known "Deerfoot Farm" at Southborough. He married in 1847 Josephine Cutter, the daughter of Edward and Ruth Cutter of Boston, by whom he had eleven children. He was devoted to Southborough and until he was fifty-five years old and business took him to Boston, he spent every winter there. He showed his love for the town in benefactions of every kind. As early as 1860 he built a small stone church, the first Episcopal church in Southborough. Services had been held ten years before in the schoolhouse at Southville with ten or twelve people present. After a decade of only occasional services at Southborough, St. Mark's Parish was organized and received help from other places for a year or two. Burnett then gave the parish a lot in the center of the township on the condition that the church to be built here was to be free to all with no distinction as to wealth, color, race, or station. The cost of building it was paid by Burnett. His religious interests were an unusually large factor in his life and led later to the founding of St. Mark's School. He had sent his oldest son, Edward, to St. Paul's, the first church school in New England. This had been founded in 1855, and ten years later was so successful that it had a long waiting list. When he was entering another son, Harry, the head master, Dr. Coit, suggested to him that as he had four sons it might be a good thing to start a church school in Massachusetts. The great success of St. Paul's probably encouraged Burnett in carrying out the suggestion. In 1865 the school was started. Its founder gave it the benefits of his wide business experience, his time, and his wealth, and spared no pains to make it in every way successful. Until his death, as a result of an accident in 1894, he was treasurer of the corporation and his son then succeeded him. One of his greatest gifts, according to historians of the school, was the example set by his own life of Christian reverence, unselfishness, and modesty. He "was at the school *every afternoon* the first year" wrote one boy of the class of 1871, "and not only took an intense interest in the school itself as a whole, but also in each boy, in fact, he looked after the younger boys as if he were their father, and perhaps more than some of their fathers ever had." Records of the meetings of the Board of Trustees show the constant growth of the school and its founder's interest. Burnett found opportunity also to give his services in various other channels of usefulness during his life. He was member of the school board of Southborough, vestryman of St. John's Church, Framingham, of St. Paul's, Hopkinton, and was one of the original incorporators of the Church of the Advent in Boston. Gov. Alexander H. Rice appointed him prison commissioner and he became chairman of that body when it was entrusted with the erection of a reformatory for women at Sherborn. He was the first road commissioner appointed by the town, and to him it largely owes its excellent roads and beautiful trees.

[Obituary in *Boston Evening Transcript*, Aug. 13, 1894; A. E. Benson, *Hist. of St. Mark's School* (1925).]
M.A.K.

BURNETT, PETER HARDEMAN (Nov. 15, 1807–May 17, 1895), Oregon and California pioneer, was born in Nashville, Tenn., the eldest son of George and Dorothy (Hardeman) Burnet. When about nineteen he added the second *t* to the surname to make it "more complete and emphatic," and his brothers followed his example. Burnett's father, a carpenter and farmer, came of a humble family, while the mother's family was distinguished. When the boy was about four his parents moved to a farm, and in the fall of 1817 to Howard County, Mo. Nine years later the youth returned to Tennessee, where for a time he was clerk in a hotel at $100 a year, and, afterward, at double the wages, clerk in a store. On Aug. 20, 1828, he married Harriet W. Rogers. In the following spring he bought out his employer, but after three years of unsuccessful storekeeping gave up and went back to the Missouri frontier, settling at Liberty. Though he had received little schooling, he had read widely and had made some progress in the study of law; and in the spring of 1839, after becoming heavily in debt through the failure of several efforts in business, he turned to the law for a livelihood. In the following winter he was appointed prosecuting attorney for the Liberty district. Two years later, deeply concerned over the continued illness of his wife and hopeless of earning enough money in Missouri to pay his debts, he decided to move to Oregon. Consulting his creditors and receiving their approval, he set out with his family on the historic migration of 875 men, women, and children that left the vicinity of Independence, Mo., May 22, 1843. On June 1 he was elected captain of the expedition, but a week later resigned. Reaching Whitman's Mission on Oct. 14, he went on to Fort Van-

couver, subsequently taking up a farm near the mouth of the Willamette and later another farm near the present town of Hillsboro, Ore.

He at once became prominent in the affairs of the new colony. He was chosen one of the nine members of the legislative committee of Oregon in 1844, in 1845 judge of the supreme court, and on the preliminary establishment of a territorial government in 1848 was elected to the legislature. In August of the last-named year, on the passage by Congress of the territorial organization bill, he was appointed by President Polk one of the territory's supreme court justices—an honor of which he was not to learn for many months. In September, leading a company of 150 men, he started for the California goldfields, arriving at the Yuba mines on Nov. 5. Six weeks later he left the mines to become the attorney and general agent of John A. Sutter, Jr. In July 1849 he left the employ of Sutter and on Aug. 13 was appointed by Gen. Bennet Riley judge of the superior tribunal of California. In the movement for statehood that year he took an active part, and in the election of Nov. 13, which ratified the constitution, was chosen governor by a vote almost equal to the combined vote of the four other contestants. The government thus set up in December of that year was legitimized by the admission of California, Sept. 9, 1850, but by the time the news arrived Burnett had tired of his post and on Jan. 9, 1851, he resigned. For several years thereafter he practised law. In the beginning of 1857 he was appointed to fill a vacancy in the supreme court of the state, serving until October 1858. During his early years in California he succeeded in paying off the indebtedness incurred in Missouri. From San José, which he had made his home since about 1854, he moved to San Francisco in 1863 and with Sam Brannan and Joseph W. Winans founded the Pacific Bank, of which he was made president. In 1880 he retired from business and the same year brought out his *Recollections and Opinions of an Old Pioneer*. He died of old age in his San Francisco home.

Hittell describes Burnett as tall and spare, but strong and rugged, and adds that he was of a cheerful disposition, with a fondness for reminiscences and anecdotes. Bancroft rates him as a man of no particular force, but with an ability to accommodate himself to circumstances and to make friends and avoid making enemies. Though his life was crowned by no great or noble achievement, continues Bancroft, it was marked by not a single conspicuous error. Gray, in his *History of Oregon* (1870), makes some strictures upon Burnett as lacking in candor and disinterestedness, but the censure seems captious and prompted by personal dislike. Certainly the man revealed in the *Recollections,* a book written with almost childish *naïveté,* has the virtues of straightforwardness and strict integrity.

[Theodore H. Hittell, *Hist. of Cal.* (1885–97) ; H. H. Bancroft, *Hist. of Cal.,* vol. VI (1888) ; *San Francisco Chronicle,* May 15, 18, 1895.]   W.J.G.

BURNETT, SWAN MOSES (Mar. 16, 1847–Jan. 18, 1906), physician, was born in New Market, Jefferson County, Tenn., the son of Dr. John M. and Lydia (Peck) Burnett. His medical education was begun in the Miami Medical College, Cincinnati, Ohio, which he attended in 1866–67, and was continued at the Bellevue Hospital Medical College in New York City during 1869–70, from which institution he received his degree in medicine. He first located in Knoxville, Tenn., where he was a general practitioner from 1870 to 1875. In 1873 he married Frances E. Hodgson, who subsequently became well-known as the author of *Little Lord Fauntleroy.* In 1875, tiring of the demands made upon him by general practise, Burnett left Knoxville and went abroad, spending the major portion of two years in London and Paris preparing himself in ophthalmology and otology, in which he specialized upon his return to America in 1876. He now located in Washington, D. C., with which city the rest of his professional activities were connected. In 1878 he was appointed lecturer in ophthalmology and otology, and in 1883, clinical professor in these subjects in the Medical School of Georgetown University, attaining full professorship in 1889. He was likewise connected with the teaching staff of the Washington Postgraduate Medical School. He was a member of the staff of the Dispensary & Emergency Hospital, and of the Children's, Providence, and Episcopal Eye, Ear & Throat Hospitals. With Dr. Louis Marple, Dr. James E. Morgan, and others he founded the Emergency Hospital in 1881, and established the Lionel Laboratory as a memorial to a son who died in childhood. He was a skilful operator and a teacher of no mean ability. At the time of his death he possessed the largest individually owned medical library in Washington. He contributed several books to medical literature, including a translation of E. Landolt's *Manual of Examination of the Eyes* (1879) ; *A Theoretical and Practical Treatise on Astigmatism* (1887) ; *The Principles of Refraction in the Human Eye, based on the Laws of Conjugate Foci* (1904) ; *Study of Refraction from a New Viewpoint* (1905) ; the section on "Diseases of the Conjunctiva and Sclera," in W. F. Norris and C. A. Oliver, *System of Ophthalmology* (1898) ; the sec-

tion on "Diseases of the Cornea and Sclera" in De Schweinitz and Randall, *American Textbook of Diseases of the Eye, Ear, Nose and Throat* (1899). Burnett was also associated with Dr. John S. Billings in the production of the *National Medical Dictionary* (1889). He devised an ophthalmoscope with a rack for holding the correcting lenses of the observer while making an examination. The large ophthalmic field among the colored population of Washington afforded him countless opportunities for making original observations among these people, and his minor writings contain diagnostic and therapeutic points concerning the negro that heretofore had not been recorded. He also wrote extensively on his hobby, Japanese art, for the *International Studio,* the *Craftsman,* and the *Connoisseur.* The first Mrs. Burnett obtained a divorce from him in 1898, and in March 1904 he married Margaret Brady of Washington.

[Sketch by H. V. Würdemann, in *Ophthalmic Record,* Feb. 1906 (repr. in *Ophthalmology,* Apr. 1906) ; *Ophthalmic Year Book,* 1907 ; Casey A. Wood, ed., *Am. Encyc. and Dict. of Ophthalmology,* vol. II (1913) ; *Index Cat. of Lib. of Surgeon-Gen.* ; *Washington Post,* Jan. 19, 1906 ; *Who's Who in America,* 1906–07.]   L.W.F.

BURNHAM, CLARA LOUISE ROOT (May 26, 1854–June 20, 1927), author, descendant of two families of musical ability through several generations, was the daughter of George F. Root, composer, and Mary O. Woodman, musician. George F. Root was descended from a Puritan settler of Connecticut in 1640. Clara Louise was born in Newton, Mass., and passed her early childhood there and in North Reading, Mass. When she was nine, the family removed to Chicago which was thereafter her home. There she attended public and private schools and studied music, which she intended to make her profession. Before she was twenty, she married Walter Burnham, a lawyer. Soon after her marriage she began to write, under the influence of a brother, who said she should make a good fiction writer because she had a vivid imagination, not too much hampered by truth, and playfully locked her in a room with pad and pencils, telling her to stay until she had produced a story. Her first efforts, novelettes, were rejected, with the advice to give up writing. Her first accepted work was a poem, published in *Wide Awake,* and her first published novel *No Gentlemen* (1881). She wrote easily and fluently and produced many novels, stories, and poems, besides librettos for her father's cantatas. Her stories and poems were frequently contributed to *Wide Awake, St. Nicholas,* and the *Youth's Companion.* Her novels include: *A Sane Lunatic*

(1882); *Dearly Bought* (1884); *Next Door* (1886); *Young Maids and Old* (1889); *The Mistress of Beech Knoll* (1890); *Miss Bagg's Secretary* (1892); *Dr. Latimer* (1893); *Sweet Clover* (1894); *The Wise Woman* (1895); *Miss Archer Archer* (1897); *Miss Pritchard's Wedding Trip* (1901); *The Right Princess* (1902); *Jewel* (1903); *Jewel's Story Book* (1904); *The Opened Shutters* (1906); *The Leaven of Love* (1908); *Clever Betsy* (1910); *The Inner Flame* (1912); *The Right Track* (1914); *A Great Love* (1915); *Instead of the Thorn* (1916); *Hearts' Haven* (1918); *In Apple-Blossom Time* (1919); *The Key-Note* (1921); *The Queen of Farrandale* (1923); *The Lavarons* (1925).

Through ill health, Mrs. Burnham became interested in Christian Science as early as 1902 and her later novels have a strong Christian Science flavor, which sometimes suggests propaganda. In *A View of Christian Science* (1912) she explains how her own early antagonism was changed to adherence and says: "One after another of the conditions which hampered my life slipped away." In appearance she was tall, slender, and blonde, with expressive blue eyes. She enjoyed people and had many social contacts; her vivacity and conversational gift made her generally popular. Her fiction is not notable, but shows a certain cleverness in plot situations, realistic characterization and dialogue, and a simple, unaffected style. It is of a type known as perfectly "safe" for young people. Shortly before her death Mrs. Burnham returned from a visit to Hollywood, Cal., where she sold the motion picture rights of *The Lavarons*. She died at her summer home, "The Mooring," Bailey Island, Casco Bay, Me.

[*Root Genealogical Records 1600–1870* (1870), by Jas. Pierce Root; a biographical sketch by Lydia Avery Coonley in the *Writer*, Sept. 1895, p. 133; *Who's Who in America*, 1926–27; obituaries in the *N.Y. Times*, *Boston Transcript*, and *Boston Herald*, all June 22, 1927.]

S.G.B.

BURNHAM, DANIEL HUDSON (Sept. 4, 1846–June 1, 1912), architect, was born at Henderson, N. Y., a small town near Lake Ontario, in a substantial stone house still shown as a memorial of him. The Burnham family in America began in Ipswich, Mass., in 1635, and there continued for a century and a quarter, undertaking the duties and enjoying those honors in church, town, and colony which were a part of life in a Puritan community. Then two John Burnhams, father and son, made their way first to Connecticut and next to the inchoate state of Vermont, with whose beginnings both were conspicuously identified. In 1785 the younger John established himself at Middletown, Vt., and in a valley still

known as Burnham's Hollow built a forge and foundry, and mills of various kinds, including a distillery. In 1811, a freshet having swept away the labor of years, Nathan, the eldest son of the family, removed to the New York frontier, where speculation in lands was rife. In 1832 Nathan's son Edwin married Elizabeth Keith Weeks, of Pilgrim ancestry on both sides of her family. The daughter of a Swedenborgian minister, she was deeply imbued with the poetic qualities of that religion and imparted them to her seven children, of whom Daniel Hudson was the sixth.

In 1855, Edwin Burnham removed his family to the fast growing city of Chicago, where he established himself as a wholesale merchant in drugs. Daniel was destined by his parents for the ministry, and after a year or more in the Chicago High School he was sent to the New Church School of the Worcesters at Waltham, Mass., to be fitted for Harvard. He had a marked propensity for drawing but no aptitude for study; and his tutor, Tilly B. Hayward of Bridgewater, was unable to get him into Harvard, and he failed also to pass the Yale examinations. Both universities afterward bestowed upon him honorary degrees.

Returning to Chicago he tried business, but a mercantile life did not interest him. So he was placed in an architect's office, whence he was lured by the prospect of finding gold in Nevada. After a sorry experience in that field he again returned to Chicago and settled down to his life work in architecture. In 1872, at the age of twenty-six, he entered the office of Carter, Drake & Wight. Among his fellow draftsmen with that prosperous firm was John Wellborn Root, of Vermont antecedents and Southern birth. The two became first friends, then partners in an office of their own. After months that seemed years of struggle, success came with a commission to build a house for the influential manager of the Chicago Stock Yards, John B. Sherman, whose daughter, Margaret, Burnham married before the house was completed. The devastation caused by the Chicago fire of 1871, and the subsequent rebuilding, gave to the young firm opportunities they were not slow to seize. Burnham's facility with his tongue and with pencil sketches engaged the interest of clients; and Root's early education in England (whither he was taken in one of his father's blockade-runners) and his architectural training in the New York office of James Renwick made a combination of talents that quickly won success. Root was versatile, romantic, and inventive; Burnham was practical and business-like, he had a keen appreciation of the points that make an office-building a paying enterprise, and his clients were not led into heavier expenditures than they had planned to make.

The term "sky-scraper" is said to have been first applied to Burnham & Root's Montauk Building, ten stories in height, the first distinctly tall building in Chicago. Its commercial success made it the forerunner of tall fire-proof buildings throughout the United States. Here for the first time the iron floor-beams were encased in fire-clay tiles, in order to overcome the defects caused by the bending and giving way of exposed iron beams when subjected to fire. This general form of protection, afterward highly developed by the firm, proved to be successful even in the combined earthquake and fire in San Francisco.

The Chicago firm of Holabird & Roche was one of the first to erect a building having a complete riveted steel frame above the foundations. Burnham & Root saw that this construction was good and immediately adopted it for all their tall buildings. In 1890 they built the Masonic Temple at the northeast corner of State and Randolph Sts.—in its day famous as "the tallest building in the world," and famous also for its beauty of design according to the standards of that era, an achievement that gave Root fame among architects. In 1902, Burnham's Flatiron Building, New York's first sky-scraper, broke the record for "the tallest building in the world." It was a nine years' wonder. Meanwhile Burnham's theory that above all architecture should express the uses to which a building is to be put found expression in his Monadnock Building, austere, but abounding in such subtleties of proportion as to make it a work of art. During their partnership from 1873 to 1891, Burnham & Root erected, in cities from Detroit to San Francisco, buildings that cost upwards of forty million dollars—a record unprecedented in those days.

Congress having decreed that the celebration of the four-hundredth anniversary of the discovery of America should center in Chicago, the State of Illinois, on Apr. 9, 1890, licensed the corporation known as the World's Columbian Exposition, of which Lyman J. Gage (afterward secretary of the treasury) became the president. Due to the insistence of James W. Ellsworth, Frederick Law Olmsted was entrusted with the selection of site and the design of the land and water features. He was ably assisted by his partner, Henry Sargent Codman, a young man of rare discernment and taste in matters of adapting landscape to buildings.

After the usual delays, in October 1890 the construction force was organized, with F. L. Olmsted & Company, consulting landscape archi-

tects; A. Gottlieb, consulting engineer; J. W. Root, consulting architect; D. H. Burnham, chief of construction, with autocratic powers. By December a tentative scheme of canals, lagoons, and islands had been worked out by Olmsted, Codman, Root, and Burnham in coöperation. Jackson Park, then a sandy waste, was selected as the location, and improvements were designed to fit the area ultimately for use as a park. Supplementary buildings were to be erected on the lake front near the center of Chicago. Then five outside and five local firms of architects were selected to design the principal buildings: Richard M. Hunt, McKim, Mead & White, and George B. Post of New York; Peabody & Stearns of Boston; Van Brunt & Howe of Kansas City; and Burling & Whitehouse, Jenney & Mundie, Henry Ives Cobb, S. S. Beman, and Adler & Sullivan of Chicago. It was no small achievement on Burnham's part to secure the promise of effective and interested coöperation on the part of the reluctant eastern architects, unacquainted as they were with the energy, resources, and spirit of Chicago.

During the first meeting of the architects, in January 1891, Root died suddenly, leaving on Burnham's shoulders the responsibility of securing and maintaining the team-work necessary to accomplish the opening of the Fair by 1893, an achievement seemingly impossible. At a meeting in New York the eastern architects determined that the buildings surrounding the Court of Honor should be classical in design, with a uniform cornice line; and this scheme was adopted in spite of the fact that up to this time no building of classical design had been erected in Chicago. In the East Richardson had died in 1886, leaving Trinity Church in Boston as the supreme enduring product of his genius. Because the style he adopted fitted the temperament of the times, it was eagerly seized upon; but by 1890 round arches and great wall spaces were found lacking in respect of providing light and air. Also, in the hands of men of small artistic sense, the revived Romanesque became lawless and altogether lacking in those elements of strength and bigness which expressed Richardson the artist. Richardson's death left Richard M. Hunt the undisputed leader among American architects. Hunt was made chairman of the board of architects for the Fair. Both Hunt and Richardson had been trained at the École des Beaux Arts; but Hunt had brought from France a respect for authority and tradition, which had been strengthened by work on the buildings connecting the Louvre with the Tuileries and by employment under Walter on the extension of the United States Capitol. In his own practise, however, he inclined to the French style expressed in their chateaux, and his greatest remaining monument is at Biltmore, N. C. It is commonly said that, had John Root lived, his authority, versatility, and strong predilection for the romantic in architecture would have given an altogether different and picturesque character to the general appearance of the Chicago Fair. Possibly and probably this is so, in a measure. It is to be considered, however, that the domination of the classic motives for the Court of Honor had been decided upon while Root was living, with his and Burnham's assent. Moreover, the minds of both men were attuned to the new architectural notes which had already been struck in the east, notably by McKim, Mead & White in plans based on classical precedents, for the Boston Public Library, accepted in 1887,— a building to face Richardson's masterpiece across Copley Square.

To Burnham, left without professional support, the sense of orderliness and the largeness of the conception involved in a series of related public buildings strongly appealed. Denied the advantages of European training or even travel, Burnham instinctively was drawn to the big conception representing power, dominating vast spaces, and withal arranged as one organism. Moreover, he was then and to the end of his life an assiduous student of architecture, ever seeking to supply those early deficiencies against which his practise brought him. Never for a moment did he abdicate the architectural throne. Trained and brilliant draftsmen came and went, but every design bore his individual stamp both in conception and in execution. His own mind meeting the mind of his clients solved the fundamental problems. His was the vision; he made others see it.

It was at this critical time in the development of the plans for the World's Fair that Burnham met Charles F. McKim. Between the two men a friendship gradually grew up, not without sharp conflicts and misunderstandings. This friendship kept them together in public service and in ideals for the future, and will keep their names associated both in the plans for the development of the national capital and in the school for the training of artists known as the American Academy in Rome. Burnham's tremendous energy, his grasp of details, and his ability to handle clients on the one hand, and on the other to build up the organization for carrying out great undertakings, obscured during his lifetime the purely artistic side of his character; and yet his power to dream dreams, and to make

others see with him, was the direct cause of his success. To him the Chicago Fair far transcended the mere bringing together of displays of American prowess in manufactures, invention, and production, important as was that side of the undertaking. In the project he realized the opportunity to express to the world the capacity of this country in architecture, in sculpture, in painting, each art contributing its full share to bring a unified result. Happily the time was ripe for such a combination. During the decade and a half since the Philadelphia Exposition which marked the first century of our life as a nation, the sense of permanence, of wealth and power, of appreciation of national heroes—explorers, founders and preservers—had developed a body of artists the like of which this country had never before known. It was Burnham's opportunity to call together this band and to bring them into one united service to secure one unified result.

In the associations created and fostered during the two years of the construction period, Burnham found his greatest pleasure. His large and generous nature led him to give full credit to those who under his leadership and his management found opportunity to express each his own individuality. Nor were they unappreciative. At a dinner given to Burnham in New York, Mar. 25, 1893, on the eve of the opening of the Chicago Fair, their appreciation found full expression. The event, arranged "in recognition of the great benefit to architecture, sculpture and painting that had resulted from Mr. Burnham's connection with the World's Columbian Exposition," was participated in by artists, men of letters, leaders in business and at the bar, from all parts of the country.

The immediate results of the success of the Chicago Fair were honorary degrees bestowed on Burnham at the following commencement by Harvard and Yale; election as president of the American Institute of Architects; and membership in the Century Club of New York, where he ever after, among congenial companions, made headquarters when in the metropolis.

The winding up of the World's Fair at the end of 1893 left Burnham with a practise broken by the loss of his partner and two years of interrupted work, a debt of some $20,000 incurred by becoming involved in the venture of a friend, and the reputation of being the best-known architect in America. He called into partnership with himself three of his associates at the Fair: Ernest R. Graham, the assistant chief of construction; E. C. Shankland, the chief engineer; and Charles Atwood, a designer of unusual taste and refinement, whose achievements in the Peristyle and the Art Gallery were the more conspicuous of many successes. His arrangements with his partners made him dominant in the office; also he was left free to do public work, and to engage in underwriting the finances of large buildings, then becoming a profitable form of enterprise. The work done by the firm assumed colossal proportions—in New York, Boston, Pittsburgh, San Francisco, Washington, and many another city besides Chicago. Living much on trains and in clubs and hotels, Burnham nevertheless found opportunity to indulge his propensity for the quiet home life in the midst of a growing family of children, who regarded him as their best friend.

In the spring of 1901, the United States Senate Committee on the District of Columbia, by virtue of a resolution offered by Senator James McMillan of Michigan, was directed to report a plan for the development of the national capital, with authority to employ experts. The chairmanship of the commission of experts was offered to Burnham; and Charles McKim, Augustus Saint-Gaudens, and Frederick Law Olmsted, Jr., were selected as the other members. At the first meeting Burnham insisted that studies be made of those European capitals which had furnished precedents for the original plan of Washington, drawn by the French engineer Pierre Charles L'Enfant in 1792, under the direction of President Washington and approved by him. The Senate Park Commission became convinced that, first, the L'Enfant plan should be taken as the basis of their work; and, secondly, that that plan was inspired by the plans made for Versailles and Paris by the architects of Louis XIV, and especially by André Le Nôtre, greatest of landscape architects. While the Commission was visiting European cities, studies of the topography of the District of Columbia were in progress. On Jan. 15, 1902, Senator McMillan reported the completed plan to the Senate, with illustrative models, drawings, and photographs. This report was the beginning of the city-planning movement in the United States.

The essential features of the Le Nôtre design were long, tree-lined vistas, stretching even to the horizon and adorned with fountains and basins; and also focal points with radiating avenues. These features L'Enfant brought to Washington from Versailles, then the capital city of his native country. It was the aim of the Burnham Commission to restore the unity of the Mall, which had been cut into sections; to revert to the main axis of the original central composition, by drawing a new axis from the dome of the Capitol through the Washington Monument and prolonging it to the bank of the Potomac, where a location was created for the Lincoln Memorial. Thus both historical and artistic considerations would be subserved. The obstacle to the Mall restoration was the fact that railroad tracks divided the area, and the removal of them was fundamental to success.

Fortunately, even before the Park Commission was created, Burnham had been commissioned by the Pennsylvania Railroad to design their new Washington station. While in London, Burnham secured the consent of President Cassatt to withdraw the tracks from the Mall and to build a station in an entirely new location. The present Union Station was the result. This station and the adjoining Post Office Building were planned to be subordinate to the Capitol, while still under the domination of that structure. In this subordination, no less than in the monumental character of the group, Burnham achieved a result which marks his sense of proportion and his desire for team-work, to use his favorite phrase.

Burnham thus became the recognized leader and authority in the new field of city-planning. His services were sought by Cleveland and San Francisco, for both of which cities his ideas of orderliness, dignity, and beauty found expression in the plans for civic development. Unfortunately, in neither case were his plans carried out without serious modification. In 1904 the secretary of war, William H. Taft, asked Burnham to undertake a plan for Manila, and one for a summer capital in the hills at Baguio. In this work he was assisted by Peirce Anderson of his office. In Manila the French idea of turning outgrown fortifications into boulevards was successfully carried out. On Burnham's return, the execution of both plans was placed in the hands of William E. Parsons, who interpreted them in buildings, parks, and driveways in accordance with the Burnham spirit and climatic and topographical requirements.

In 1906, all conditions were favorable to carrying out ideas long cherished in Burnham's mind for creating a plan to make Chicago the finest commercial city in the world—a city in which people should labor and live under the most perfect conditions. For the production of this plan the men of the city met in council week after week for three years. Building a workshop on the roof of the Railway Exchange, his own business building of seventeen stories, Burnham had spread before his far vision the great expanse of land and water and sky, and the city of Chicago at his feet. With the aid of

Edward H. Bennett and a band of assistants, and
with the strong and steady support of the Commercial Club, he made the Plan of Chicago, and
in 1909 presented it to the public in compelling
fashion. After the inevitable pause for explanation and mental expansion to allow the people to
rise to an appreciation of so stupendous an
undertaking, the City of Chicago took up with
enthusiasm the Burnham conception. They
taught the plan to the children in the public
schools. They appointed and financed an influential committee to carry it out. By taxation
and bond issues voted by the people, they purchased thousands of acres for an outer park
system, cut broad thoroughfares through blight-
ed districts, filled in miles of parkways along the
lake front, built recreation piers out into the
lake, adorned the parks and created playgrounds.
The leadership, unfaltering, enthusiastic, inspiring, was Burnham's; and his, too, was the
conception, and the faith that a great plan adequately recorded would so take hold on the
imagination of men that they would find the
means to carry it out.

On June 15, 1910, President Taft appointed
Burnham chairman of the National Commission
of Fine Arts, an organization then created by
Congress to give advice to the president, to the
executive officers, and to committees of Congress,
on matters of art for which appropriations are
made from the federal treasury. The creation of
a body of precedents and the overcoming of
prejudice against the exercise of authority in
matters of taste, even though such authority is
disguised as advice,—such were the intangible
problems which the commission successfully met
under Burnham's wise and tactful guidance.
One of its first duties was to advise the Lincoln
Memorial Commission (of which President
Taft was chairman) as to the location for that
monument. The fact that a site had been fixed
in the Burnham Report (as it is frequently
called) did not preclude Burnham from giving
serious consideration to other proposed sites,
only to find that logic and history combined to
determine the location on the main axis, where
the Memorial now stands with such appropriate-
ness that long controversy now seems incon-
ceivable. No less important was the choice of
architect. For a decade the tentative plans
made by Charles McKim and presented in the
Burnham Report had been before the public, and
had come to be tacitly accepted as fulfilling the
requirements of intrinsic impressiveness and
harmony with the Capitol and the Washington
Monument, with which structures it was to stand
in relationship. In his own mind Burnham had

selected Henry Bacon as the man peculiarly fitted by habit of thought and technical training to
design the Lincoln Memorial. This conviction
was formed from experience gained at the
World's Fair, where Bacon acted as the interpreter and executive in carrying out the designs
of McKim, Mead & White in the construction of
their monumental buildings. Time has justified
the choice of Bacon by the Commission of Fine
Arts.

In Burnham's thought and speech, standards
of taste in this country had their origin in the
association of architects, landscape architects,
sculptors, and mural painters which produced
the Chicago Fair. He realized that these men
based their work firmly on precedents drawn
from the great work done in the past. To provide for the adequate training of American artists for future tasks of even greater importance,
due to the increase in wealth and taste, seemed
to him a matter of the first consequence. Therefore he joined heartily with McKim, Hunt,
Saint-Gaudens, French, La Farge, Blashfield,
and the other artists who organized, immediately after the World's Fair of 1893, the American School of Architecture in Rome, which
broadened into the American Academy in Rome.
So keen was his interest, and so steady were his
money contributions to this enterprise during its
early years of uncertainty and struggle, that he
has come to be recognized as a founder second
only to McKim in this work of training successors to carry on the tradition of patriotic service.

For his public work in Washington, San
Francisco, the Philippines, and Chicago, Burnham would accept no compensation. He declined
to place himself in the position of working for
and under a client, when that client was the
public. He felt it requisite to the success of his
studies and the presentation of them to be absolutely free from the always unsatisfactory necessity of compromise. He would make the finest
design his mind could conceive, and would present it in the most adequate and convincing manner possible. He required freedom, and he took
to himself the text selected by President Eliot
for the Water Gate at the World's Fair: "Ye
shall know the truth, and the truth shall make
you free."

To the very end he was a keen student. His
visits to Europe, which came to be annual, were
periods snatched from a busy life and devoted
to the enjoyment of family intercourse and to the
training of himself and his sons. It was on one
such visit in 1912 that the infirmities which had
been gathering for several years overcame him
at Heidelberg, where he died suddenly on June

1. He was buried on an island in Graceland Cemetery, Chicago. His continuing monument is the Burnham Architectural Library at the Chicago Art Institute.

[D. H. Burnham and F. D. Millet, *World's Columbian Exposition* (1894) uncompleted; "The Improvement of the Park System of the District of Columbia," ed. by Chas. Moore, *Senate Report No. 166, 57 Cong., 1 Sess.* (1902); *Report on a Plan for San Francisco* (1905), by D. H. Burnham assisted by Edward H. Bennett, ed. by Edward F. O'Day; *The Group Plan of the Public Buildings of the City of Cleveland* (2nd ed. 1907), . . . by D. H. Burnham, John M. Carrère, Arnold W. Brunner; *Plan of Chicago* (1909), by D. H. Burnham and Edward H. Bennett, ed. by Chas. Moore; *Daniel H. Burnham, Architect, Planner of Cities* (2 vols., 1921), by Chas. Moore.]   C. M.

BURNHAM, SHERBURNE WESLEY

(Dec. 12, 1838–Mar. 11, 1921), astronomer, son of Roswell O. and Marinda (Foote) Burnham, was born at Thetford, Vt., where, too, his graduation from the Academy marked the end of his schooling. During the Civil War he was stationed with the Federal army in New Orleans as shorthand reporter. He had practised shorthand by himself and had gone to New York in 1857 or 1858. After the war he went to Chicago and acted as official court reporter for more than twenty years, winning, at the same time, with his tireless energy, a world-wide reputation as an astronomer. His days were fully occupied in taking down the court reports and writing them out in long hand; at night, he carried out a full program of observing. In 1868 he was married to Mary Cleland. Twenty years later he went to the Lick Observatory as a member of the staff and remained there until 1892, when he returned to Chicago, serving from then until 1902 as clerk of the United States circuit court. From 1897 to 1902 he acted as receiver for the Northern Pacific Railway. From 1897 until his retirement in 1914, he was senior astronomer at the Yerkes Observatory.

Burnham's first interest in astronomy seems to have been aroused by reading Barritt's *Geography of the Heavens,* purchased in New Orleans. He soon began to trace out the constellations pictured in the book. A small, cheap telescope, which he purchased, was soon exchanged for a better one. In 1869 he ordered from Alvan Clark & Sons a six-inch telescope which was to be the best that they could make, especially in respect to its defining power, for by this time his interest had become focused on the observation of double stars. He brought to this work an exceptionally keen eye, a tireless industry, and boundless enthusiasm. His discoveries with the six-inch telescope number over four hundred double stars, some of them difficult objects with much larger telescopes. The six-inch had no driving clock, but this difficulty he overcame by a contrivance of his own. He had no micrometer, but he soon secured the sympathetic interest of the Polish astronomer, Baron Dembowski, who devoted much of his time to measuring the new Burnham stars. Burnham dedicated the "General Catalogue" of his own double stars (*Publications of the Yerkes Observatory,* Volume I) to this staunch friend.

The major part of his astronomical library, at this time, consisted of a copy of Webb's *Celestial Objects for Common Telescopes.* The literature of double stars was scattered through periodicals and observatory publications, few of which were easily accessible to him. The need of a single catalogue was very insistent. In the interests of his own work he felt compelled to make manuscript copies from various libraries, some of them at a considerable distance, of all the material bearing on the subject. This material, brought together in a manuscript catalogue, contained the data on every known double star within 121° of the north pole, and enabled Burnham quickly to discriminate between known and new double stars. This catalogue passed into a second and a third edition, and finally appeared as *A General Catalogue of Double Stars,* published in 1906 by the Carnegie Institution of Washington. The manuscript edition was continued and kept up to date with all published observations. It is now being carried forward by Prof. Aitken. The preparation of this catalogue constantly suggested the necessity of re-observation of many stars, and Burnham's observations at the forty-inch Yerkes telescope, from 1900 to 1906, were mainly devoted to supplying this need. His later observations were chiefly the measurement of double stars with reference to faint stars in their vicinity, with a view to the eventual knowledge of their proper motions.

His work on double stars was begun at a time when it was generally supposed that the Struves and the Herschels had left no more double stars to be found. Burnham's keen eye detected many double stars with a separation of only a small fraction of a second of arc, and other close pairs in which the difference in brightness of the two components made the discovery extremely difficult. His keen insight kept his attention on these pairs as having a large probability of orbital motion. An occasional measurement was sufficient for the more widely separated pairs. His observations, which were of the highest accuracy, were made with great rapidity. He is said to have measured as many as one hundred double stars, with the forty-inch telescope, in a single night.

After he resigned his position as court clerk he

still preferred to live in Chicago and travel out to the Yerkes Observatory for the two nights a week, Saturday and Sunday, during which the forty-inch was entirely reserved for his use. The round trip involved a distance of about 160 miles on the railroad and a three-mile walk. In winter he often had to break his own path through the snow between the railroad station and the Observatory. He is described by Prof. Barnard as a man of slight, wiry build, tough as iron, with not an ounce of surplus flesh. Among his greatest pleasures was a tramp in the rough country about Mt. Hamilton, or a bicycle ride near the Yerkes Observatory. His camera always went with him and his photographs were almost always works of art. His professional associates had a high opinion of him as an astronomer; he had many friends among the judges and lawyers with whom he came in contact in his daily life, and other friends who knew him only during his wanderings and recreations.

[The very intimate story told by E. E. Barnard (*Pop. Astronomy*, June–July 1921) is of especial interest. The history of Burnham's early life is related by John Frazer in the *Century Mag.*, June 1889. See also *Astrophysical Jour.*, July 1921; *Observatory*, XLIV, 154–58, 163–64; *Pubs. of the Astronomical Soc. of the Pacific*, 1921, pp. 85–90; *Astronomische Nachrichten*, CCXIII, 141–44; *Monthly Notices of the Royal Astronomical Soc.*, Feb. 1922; *Populär Astronomisk Tideskrift*, 1921, pp. 178–80; *Science*, Apr. 22, 1921; *Pubs. of the Yerkes Observatory*, vol. I (1900), intro.; *A Gen. Cat. of Double Stars, Carnegie Inst. of Washington, Pub. No. 5* (1906), intro.]   R.S.D.

BURNS, ANTHONY (May 31, 1834–July 27, 1862), fugitive slave, was born in Stafford County, Va. It is said, but without certainty, that his father, who died when the child was very young, had been a freeman and had come from the North. Certainly the boy from the beginning showed unusual independence and character. At six, in return for little services he did them, he learned the alphabet from white children with whom he was thrown in contact. He was converted while a youth to the Baptist faith and two years later became a "slave preacher." As a young man he was sent to take a position in Richmond, for which his master was to be paid. A transfer of positions left him free to escape, and in February 1854 he fled from Richmond on a vessel on which he had a friend. On May 24, he was arrested in Boston on the charge of theft. The excitement in Boston during the following week was said to have been without parallel since the days of the Revolution. The abolitionists and the woman suffragists were holding anniversary conventions at the time but people poured in also from neighboring suburbs. A mass meeting two days after the arrest was addressed by Wendell Phillips and Theodore Parker. An attack was made on the Court House, in which one of the deputy marshals was killed. President Pierce and the Mayor of Boston brought together military forces to prevent a second attack. Burns was defended by R. H. Dana and others, but without success. He had been immediately identified by his master. To prevent his release, he was taken down State St. between armed troops. The Grand Jury was charged by Judge B. R. Curtis to indict Parker, Wendell Phillips, and Higginson for their Faneuil Hall talks on "obstructing the process of the United States," but the indictments were quashed on technical grounds. The cost to the United States of sending this one fugitive back to Virginia was $100,000. A sum of money had been raised to purchase Burns's freedom but this was not possible at the time. A few months later he fell into the hands of a friendly master, who sold him to individuals in Boston interested in setting him free. He attended the preparatory department of Oberlin College, 1855–56, and is supposed to have attended Fremont Academy, 1856–57. From 1857 to 1862, through the generosity of a Boston woman, he was able to study at Oberlin College. For a short time in 1860 he was in charge of a colored Baptist church in Indianapolis, but was forced to leave. Later he went to Canada, and became pastor of the Zion Baptist Church at St. Catherines, where he died.

[*Boston Slave Riot and Trial of Anthony Burns* (1854); C. E. Stevens, *Anthony Burns, A Hist.* (1856); M. G. McDougall, *Fugitive Slaves* (1891); Wm. Lloyd Garrison, *The Story of His Life, Told by His Children* (1885–89); the *Liberator*, June, July 1854, Aug. 22, 1862; Fred Landon, "Anthony Burns in Canada," in *Ontario Hist. Soc. Papers and Records*, vol. XXII (1925).]   M.A.K.

BURNS, OTWAY (1775?–Oct. 25, 1850), privateer, shipbuilder, legislator, born in Onslow County, N. C., near the present village of Swannsboro, was the son of Otway Burns whose father, Francis, came to North Carolina from Glasgow in 1734. He early went to sea and at the outbreak of the War of 1812 was in command of a merchantman plying between New Bern, N. C., and Portland, Me. Learning of the declaration of war he sold his vessel in New York and for eight thousand dollars bought the *Levere*, a Baltimore clipper noted for her speed. He took her to New Bern where books of subscription were opened to equip her as a privateer. She was renamed the *Snap-Dragon* and carried six guns and a crew of a hundred. For three years Burns was a terror to the enemy. He preyed on British commerce from Greenland to Brazil. The command of a privateer gave him every opportunity to display his reckless courage and skilful seamanship. His daring exploits were many: he dashed into the midst of armed convoys to seize his prey; he pounced on British commerce under the guns of Halifax. He attacked British men-of-war; at St. Thomas he escaped from five of them; at other times capture semed so inevitable that the crew packed their baggage for the long journey to England and to Dartmoor. There are no estimates of the total damage he did to British shipping, but in a single cruise of about three months in 1813 he captured or destroyed commerce of over two and a half millions (*North Carolina University Magazine*, April 1856, p. 131). The profits of these ventures were enormous; they would have been greater but for his miserable set of prize masters who allowed many of the most valuable prizes to be retaken. The British government offered a prize of $50,000 for his capture, dead or alive. In June 1814 through a skilful stratagem the *Leopard* captured the *Snap-Dragon* but Burns was not in command; rheumatism had kept him in port.

After the war he returned to shipbuilding. In 1820 he built the *Prometheus*, the first steamer that plied the waters of Cape Fear, three years later the *Warrior*, and in 1831 the brig *Henry*. Elected to the General Assembly in 1821 he represented Carteret County, in the Commons or in the Senate, until 1835. His career as a legislator was independent and enlightened. In the historic Eastern and Western controversy Burns played an important part, acting with a sense of justice unintelligible to the narrow interests of his constituency. His vote in the Senate in January 1835 carried the measure calling the Constitutional Convention, and ended his political career. Reckless extravagance and heavy investments in the Dismal Swamp Canal dissipated his large fortune and in 1835 his friend, Andrew Jackson, appointed him keeper of the Brant Island Shoal Light. He settled in the village of Portsmouth and there sank into his anecdotage. He was fond of his brilliant naval uniform and cocked hat, he liked good whiskey, and he liked a good fight, whether on the water-front or in the legislature. The figure of this picturesque patriot early became wrapped in legends from which his biographers have not wholly disengaged themselves. He was married three times: first, to a Miss Grant; second, in 1814, to Jane Hall of Beaufort, N. C.; and, third, in 1842, to Jane Smith of Smyrna, N. C.

[*N. C. Univ. Mag.*, IV (1855), 407–13, 461–67; V (1856), 126–31, 205–08; *Capt. Otway Burns* (1905), ed. by W. F. Burns; S. A. Ashe, *Biog. Hist. of N. C.*, I (1905), 200–02; John H. Wheeler's *Reminiscences* (1884), pp. 102–03; Edgar Stanton Maclay, "The Exploits of Otway Burns, Privateersman and Statesman," in *U. S. Naval Inst. Proc.*, May–June, 1916; private information.]   F. M—n.

BURNSIDE, AMBROSE EVERETT (May 23, 1824–Sept. 13, 1881), Union soldier, was born at Liberty, Ind., the son of Edghill and Pamelia (Brown) Burnside. His great-grandfather, Robert Burnside, came from Scotland to South Carolina about 1750; some of the later generations settled in Kentucky but his branch went to Indiana. Until the age of eighteen he was educated in the seminary at Liberty whose principal was a ripe scholar and born teacher, where he received an education that prepared him well for college work. At this time, however, his father was unable to give him further assistance as he was in moderate circumstances with a large family. Young Burnside was therefore apprenticed to a tailor and a year later with a partner opened a shop in Liberty. Shortly thereafter his father became a member of the state Senate of Indiana and through friends secured for his son an appointment to the United States Military Academy, which he entered July 1, 1843, and from which he graduated four years later, entering the army as a lieutenant of artillery. He joined his battery in Mexico but was too late to see much active service. On Apr. 27, 1852, he was married to Mary Richmond Bishop of Providence, R. I. Before he resigned his commission in October 1853 he had served on the frontier and in garrison.

While in the army he invented a breech-loading rifle and he resigned to engage in its manufacture. His last post was Fort Adams, R. I., and at Bristol, R. I., he formed a company to manufacture his new arm. He had counted on the support of the government in his new venture, but in this he was disappointed, and in 1857 he was obliged to turn over his works to his creditors and begin life anew. During these years, however, due to his pleasing personality, genial manners, and the interest he showed in local military organizations, he made many friends, was appointed major-general of the state militia, and was nominated for Congress on the Democratic ticket. Gen. McClellan, who was then connected with the Illinois Central Railroad, secured for him a position in its land department, and he was later made treasurer of the company.

In April 1861, at the request of the governor, he organized the 1st Rhode Island Regiment and became its colonel; it was among the first regiments to reach Washington. The promptness with which Burnside had responded to the call, his imposing person, pleasing manners, and the fine condition of his regiment made for him a strong friend in President Lincoln who often visited his camp. In the Bull Run campaign he commanded the brigade which opened that battle. On Aug. 6, 1861, he was commissioned brigadier-general of volunteers, and that autumn was engaged in organizing at Annapolis, Md., a division of New England troops for coastal operations. In January 1862 this force, with a fleet under the command of Flag Officer Goldsborough, sailed from Hampton Roads to Hatteras Inlet on the coast of North Carolina to secure a base of operations and destroy a small Confederate fleet in Albemarle and Pamlico Sounds. The expedition was eminently successful. Roanoke Island, which had been fortified to prevent entrance into Albemarle Sound, was captured in February with 2,600 prisoners and thirty-two guns. In March the Confederates were driven from their lines covering New Bern and that town occupied. Beaufort was next seized and Fort Macon, a permanent fortress on the coast, was besieged and taken in April. In the meantime the Confederate fleet was captured and destroyed by the naval vessels. This completed the program of the expedition. Although one of the minor operations of the war, it excited great interest at the time. Burnside was commissioned major-general on Mar. 18, and received a sword from Rhode Island and the thanks of the legislatures of Massachusetts and Ohio.

In July it was decided to withdraw some troops from both North and South Carolina and send them under Burnside to reinforce the Army of the Potomac. At this time he was offered the command of that army and declined. When it was decided to withdraw the army from the vicinity of Richmond, Burnside's troops were sent to Pope, but as Burnside ranked Pope they went under the command of Reno. Before the opening of the Antietam campaign Burnside was again offered the command of the Army of the Potomac but again declined.

In the Antietam campaign he was assigned to the command of the right wing, consisting of the 1st Corps under Hooker and his own 9th Corps. His command was in advance and was charged with the attack on the Confederate position on South Mountain where Lee planned to check the advance of the main Union column. This position was carried by the 1st and 9th Corps on Sept. 14, 1862, and the Confederates retired across Antietam Creek. In the advance from South Mountain, Hooker's corps was temporarily detached from Burnside's command and at Antietam was engaged on the extreme right while the 9th Corps was on the extreme left. Burnside accompanied the latter but refused to assume command as he still considered himself the commander of a unit composed of two corps. This militated against proper preparation for the

coming battle. The 9th Corps reached its position in the line on the night of Sept. 15, and the following day should have been employed in making a careful reconnaissance of the creek in its front and in the preparation of a plan of attack. This was not done as Burnside did not consider himself in command, the corps staff was absent attending the funeral of Gen. Reno, killed on the preceding day, and the senior division commander remained with his division as he considered Burnside the commander of the corps. McClellan visited Burnside in person that day and assigned the duties to the various divisions, but he relied on Burnside to make the necessary reconnaissances. The consequence was that on the 17th, the day of the battle, much time was lost in attacking the strongest position of the enemy's defense at the Burnside bridge, which might easily have been turned by crossing the stream at a lightly guarded ford a mile below. After the stream was crossed, about 1.00 P. M., the 9th Corps made a spirited attack, but it was too late to have the influence on the course of the battle that McClellan had expected.

After the Confederate Army recrossed the Potomac there was a period of inaction during which the two armies were reorganized and reequipped. Toward the end of October the Army of the Potomac crossed the river and advanced on Warrenton, Va. En route, Burnside received the President's order assigning him to the command of the Army. It was a responsibility which he did not seek, for which he felt himself incompetent, but which he now felt it his duty to accept. When McClellan left the Army on Nov. 10 the situation was as follows: the main body of the Army of the Potomac was in the vicinity of Warrenton with a cavalry screen some ten miles in advance; one corps and part of another were guarding the Potomac against operations from the Shenandoah Valley; the two Confederate corps were widely separated, Longstreet at Culpeper and Jackson in the Shenandoah Valley near Winchester with one division in the mountain pass on the road connecting the two towns. Burnside was not long in deciding on his plan of operations and on Nov. 9 sent it to Gen. Halleck for the consideration of the President. It was to march the army to Fredericksburg where supplies were to meet him, cross the river on pontoon bridges, and make a rapid march on Richmond. It was not the plan the President desired; he wanted Burnside to pursue the Confederate army. On Nov. 12 he sent Halleck to Burnside to confer with him. Burnside adhered to his plan and gave practically the same reasons that induced Grant to move on a parallel line from

Culpeper in 1864. On the Fredericksburg-Richmond line it would be easier to supply the army, the lines of supply would be more easily protected, and it was a shorter line. Had the Army of the Potomac been equipped with mobile bridge trains as in 1864, the first phase of the operation, the concentration south of the Rappahannock at Fredericksburg, would have been effected without difficulty, but unfortunately in 1862 the Army was not equipped with such trains. The bridge equipment of the Army was in charge of an engineer brigade with a depot in Washington, and at this time the available boats were in the two bridges over which the army had crossed the Potomac below Harper's Ferry. Burnside knew that McClellan had issued an order on Nov. 6 to have these bridges dismantled and the material taken to Washington where a mobile train was to be organized. On this order he based his plan, but he did not know that the order was delayed in transmission and was not delivered until Nov. 12.

On Nov. 14 Burnside received the following message from Halleck: "The President has just assented to your plan. He thinks it will succeed if you move rapidly, otherwise not." Burnside immediately gave the order to start the movement on the following day, and at the same time had inquiries made of the commander of the engineer brigade as to the status of the ponton train. On Nov. 15 he learned that the last of the boats would reach Washington that day but that it would be several days before the train could start.

Burnside was now confronted with the choice of adhering to his original plan and waiting for the pontons or of crossing the river above Fredericksburg by fords as Halleck had recommended to him. On Nov. 17 Sumner's grand division of two corps reached the north bank of the Rappahannock and finding no pontons but the river above still fordable, requested permission to cross over, but Burnside would not consent. Hooker's grand division arrived shortly after, and on Nov. 19 he informed the Secretary of War that the fords were available and also requested permission to cross. Lee was early informed of the movement, and as the Union troops did not cross the river, Longstreet was started for Fredericksburg on Nov. 18, and several days before the pontons arrived, he was in possession of the heights of Fredericksburg. Toward the end of the month Jackson joined him and the armies faced each other across the river.

From this situation there resulted the battle of Fredericksburg in which the Army of the Potomac crossed the river under the protection of its artillery, and on Dec. 13 made a frontal attack on the Confederates in their well-chosen position, and was repulsed with heavy loss. On Dec. 15 the Army was withdrawn across the river. To silence the rumors that he had been directed from Washington to make this attack, Burnside on Dec. 17 in a manly letter to Halleck assumed the entire responsibility: "The fact that I decided to move from Warrenton on this line, rather against the opinion of the President, Secretary of War, and yourself, and that you left the whole movement in my hands, without giving me orders, makes me responsible."

In the latter part of the month Burnside decided to make an attempt to cross the river at the fords above Fredericksburg, but in a letter to the President said that none of his grand division commanders approved his plan. In his discouragement he wrote, "It is my belief that I ought to retire to private life." After an interview with the President he wrote him that he had decided to carry out the plan, and inclosed the resignation of his commission to relieve the President of embarrassment should he not approve. The President approved the plan and wrote that he could not yet see any advantage in a change of commanders of the army and in any case would not accept his resignation. The movement was begun in the latter part of January but had to be abandoned because of unfavorable weather. Burnside was opposed in his plans by Gen. Hooker and others. He decided that he must have a clear field if he retained the command so he prepared General Order No. 8, Jan. 23, 1863, in which he dismissed from the United States Army Gen. Hooker, Gen. Brooks and Gen. Newton, while two other major-generals, two brigadier-generals and a lieutenant-colonel were relieved from their duties and ordered to report to the adjutant-general at Washington. Burnside went to Washington and asked Lincoln either to sanction the order or to relieve him of the command. Lincoln relieved him and gave the command to Gen. Hooker. Order No. 8 was never officially issued (*Official Records (Army)*, 1 ser., XXI, 998).

In March 1863 Burnside was assigned to the command of the Department of the Ohio which included the states of Ohio, Indiana, Illinois, Michigan, and Kentucky. It was Lincoln's great desire to send military protection to the loyal inhabitants of East Tennessee and he now proposed to reinforce the troops in Kentucky by the 9th Corps so that Burnside could advance on Knoxville when Rosecrans moved on Chattanooga. On taking command of his department, Burnside learned that military operations had been greatly hampered by disloyal persons within the lines who gave information and aid to the enemy. To break up these practises he issued his General Order No. 38 in which after giving a list of the acts considered treasonable, he said, "The habit of declaring sympathies for the enemy will no longer be tolerated in this department. Persons committing such offenses will be at once arrested with a view to being tried as above stated or sent beyond our lines into the lines of their friends." The most noted case that came under this order was that of Clement L. Vallandigham who had been a member of Congress from Ohio from May 1858 to March 1863 and had made himself conspicuous in that body by his attacks on the government from the beginning of the war. On May 1, 1863, at Mount Vernon, Ohio, he made a speech in which he characterized Lincoln as a tyrant and reminded his hearers that "resistance to tyrants is obedience to God." This speech the loyalty of Burnside for the President could not tolerate: Vallandigham was promptly arrested and when his appeal to the United States courts for a writ of *habeas corpus* was denied, he was tried by a military commission for "declaring disloyal sentiments and opinions with the object and purpose of weakening the power of the government in its efforts to suppress unlawful rebellion." The commission found him guilty and sentenced him to be imprisoned until the close of the war, but the sentence was commuted by the President who directed that Vallandigham be sent to Gen. Rosecrans to be passed through the lines to the Confederate Army in his front. Under this same General Order No. 38, on June 1, 1863, by Order No. 84, Burnside suppressed the *Chicago Times* and forbade the circulation of the *New York World* in his department. By the President's direction this Order No. 84 was soon revoked.

The advance into East Tennessee was delayed by various causes until the middle of August when Rosecrans maneuvered Bragg out of Chattanooga and Burnside advanced on Knoxville, which he entered on Sept. 2; at Cumberland Gap on Sept. 9 he received the surrender of the main Confederate force left in East Tennessee. On the following day he was informed by Rosecrans that Bragg was in full retreat, and he immediately wrote the President that as the rebellion seemed pretty well checked he would like to resign his commission. The President, however, did not think it advisable to permit his resignation at that time.

After the battle of Chickamauga, Sept. 19–20, Bragg invested Chattanooga, held by Rosecrans, and early in November when Union reinforce-

ments had reached there and Bragg gave up hope of capturing it, he decided to send Longstreet's veteran corps of the Army of Northern Virginia reinforced by a large body of cavalry to capture Burnside. Such a movement had been expected by the latter and he called up all his available forces from Kentucky and fortified Knoxville to withstand a siege. When Longstreet made his appearance in his front about the middle of November, Burnside had the option of abandoning the Tennessee Valley or of retreating to Knoxville. He decided on the latter as he would thus, by drawing Longstreet so far north that he would be unable to return to take part in the battle, assist Gen. Grant who was preparing to attack Bragg as soon as sufficient troops had arrived. Burnside withdrew his troops to Knoxville in what Longstreet called a very cleverly conducted retreat, and there awaited the assault. The position was so strong that for ten days Longstreet could not make up his mind where to attack. In the meantime Grant had defeated Bragg in the battle of Chattanooga, Nov. 24–25, and the latter was retreating. Immediately after the battle Sherman was directed to march to the relief of Knoxville and was en route when Longstreet made his assault on Nov. 29 and was repulsed. On Dec. 4, on the approach of Sherman, Longstreet raised the siege and moved eastward. Shortly thereafter Burnside turned over his command to his successor who had been appointed Nov. 16 but was unable to reach Knoxville until after the siege.

In preparation for the operations of 1864 it was decided to bring the 9th Corps back to the East and recruit it to full strength. This was work which it was felt could be best done by Burnside, and in January he was assigned to its command and the corps was reorganized at Annapolis, Md. It now consisted of four divisions, one of which was composed wholly of colored troops. The 9th Corps reinforced the Army of the Potomac as an independent unit under the command of Grant, and as such took part in the battles of the Wilderness and Spottsylvania. After the latter battle, as Burnside consented to serve under his junior, Gen. Meade, it was made a corps of the Army of the Potomac and as such took part in the battle of Cold Harbor and in the operations leading up to the investment of Petersburg. While Burnside was intrenched before Petersburg a mine was driven under the Confederate works in his front, and Grant determined to take advantage of the favorable opportunity to make a strong assault on the enemy's position. The 9th Corps was to take the lead and to be supported by the corps on either side. The task assigned to the 9th Corps was one requiring fresh troops and able leadership. Unfortunately, with the exception of the colored division which had not hitherto been engaged, the corps had no fresh troops, and the commander of the division selected by lot to lead the attack proved hopelessly inefficient. Burnside wanted to employ the colored division to lead but was overruled. The mine was blown up early on the morning of July 30 and produced a crater 150 feet long, 60 wide, and 25 deep, the Confederates abandoning the trenches for a considerable distance on either side. The leading division of the 9th Corps, which was to seize a ridge some 500 yards beyond the crater, got no farther than the crater itself and before other troops arrived the Confederates had recovered from their surprise. The result was that the 9th Corps lost 4,000 in killed, wounded, and prisoners. Meade held Burnside largely responsible and asked Grant for a court martial for him, which the latter refused. Meade then ordered a court of inquiry, which blamed Burnside for the failure. Shortly thereafter Burnside left the army on leave and was not recalled. Toward the close of the war he resigned his commission.

In the years following his active service in the war, because of his experience as a leader and his reputation for integrity, Burnside was elected to important positions in railroad and other corporations. In 1864 he became a director of the Illinois Central Railroad Company; in 1865, president of the Cincinnati & Martinsville Railroad Company; in 1866, president of the Rhode Island Locomotive Works; in 1867, president of the Indianapolis & Vincennes Railroad Company and director of the Narragansett Steamship Company. Although he held some of these offices for years, he was nevertheless elected governor of Rhode Island in 1866 and was reëlected in 1867 and 1868. In 1870 he was abroad on business connected with one of his corporations and while there became a voluntary and trusted medium of communication in the interests of conciliation between the French and Germans then at war. In 1874 he was elected United States senator from Rhode Island and served as such from March 1875 until his death which occurred at Bristol, R. I., Sept. 13, 1881.

[B. P. Poore, *The Life and Public Services of Ambrose E. Burnside* (1882); Augustus Woodbury, *Maj.-Gen. Ambrose E. Burnside and the Ninth Army Corps* (1867); G. W. Cullum, *Biog. Reg.* (3rd ed., 1891); *Personal Memoirs of U. S. Grant* (1885–86); Jas. Longstreet, *From Manassas to Appomattox* (1896); *Battles and Leaders of the Civil War* (1887–88); *Senate Report No. 108*, 37 Cong., 3 Sess. and *Senate Report No. 142*, 38 Cong., 2 Sess. (covering congressional investigations of the battles of Fredericksburg and Petersburg).]   G. J. F.

BURR, AARON (Jan. 4, 1715/16–Sept. 24, 1757), Presbyterian clergyman, college president, son of Daniel and Elizabeth Burr, was the descendant of a family distinguished in the early history of the American colonies and the father of a son who was to be even more famous in their later history—Col. Aaron Burr [q.v.]. His great-grandfather, Jehu Burr, had come from England with Winthrop's fleet in 1630 and had assisted William Pynchon in the founding of Springfield, Mass., settling eventually in Fairfield, Conn. His grandfather, Jehu the younger, had been one of the Proprietors under the Fairfield Patent of 1685, a deputy to the General Court, a lieutenant in the Fairfield train-band, and a member of the Standing Council. His father was, at the time of Aaron's birth, a wealthy landholder in Fairfield. From his earliest childhood Aaron displayed an extraordinary quickness of intellect and a strong inclination for learning. He was graduated from Yale College with highest honors at the age of nineteen, and, being particularly proficient in Latin and Greek, won a Berkeley scholarship for advanced work in the classics. During this period of graduate study he underwent a marked religious experience which turned him to theological study, and in 1736 he was licensed to preach. After short pastorates at Greenfield, Mass., and at Hanover, N. J., he was called on Dec. 21, 1736, to the First Church of Newark, N. J. Here he engaged in extensive religious revivals and started his career as educator, very early in his pastorate gathering in his parsonage a class of eight or ten pupils for the study of English and the classical languages. Soon he became identified with a movement to establish a college in the Middle Colonies to rank with Harvard and Yale in New England and William and Mary in Virginia, and he was named one of the seven trustees of the College of New Jersey (later Princeton University) in its first charter which passed the seal of the Province on Oct. 22, 1746. The college was opened May 1747, at Elizabethtown (now Elizabeth), N. J., in the parsonage of Jonathan Dickinson, its first president. Less than six months later Dickinson died, and Burr became acting president. He was formally elected the second president of the college on Nov. 9, 1748, and the college was moved to his parsonage in Newark.

Burr paused in his labors long enough to marry, on June 29, 1752, Esther Edwards, daughter of Jonathan Edwards [q.v.]. He was thirty-six at the time of his marriage, his bride only twenty-one. Meantime he had made of the College of New Jersey a reality. He drew up its first entrance requirements, its first course of study, its first code of rules for internal government; he created its first treasury and supervised the erection of its first building in the Borough of Princeton where the college was to find a more adequate and permanent home. On the completion of Nassau Hall in the autumn of 1756, he and seventy students moved to Princeton. Here he set himself to the task of organizing the college life under its new and improved conditions. But the new building required funds for upkeep and money was needed for the instruction of a growing student body, so Burr was obliged to make frequent trips through the Colonies in an effort to interest the wealthy in his college. Returning from an arduous journey through New England in August of 1757, he learned that Gov. Belcher, his close friend and ally, and patron and benefactor of the college, had died. He spent nearly the whole of a night preparing a funeral sermon and the next morning, nearly delirious with fever, traveled to Elizabeth where he presided at the Governor's funeral. Less than a month later, on Sept. 24, 1757, he died and was buried in the Princeton Cemetery.

[There are biographical sketches in Wm. A. Packard, *The Princeton Book* (1879) and Chas. Burr Todd, *A Gen. Hist. of the Burr Family* (4th ed., 1902). Other sources are: F. B. Dexter, *Biog. Sketches Grads. Yale Coll.,* ser. I (1885); John Frelinghuysen Hageman, *Hist. of Princeton and its Institutions* (1879); John De Witt, "Hist. Sketch of Princeton Univ." in the *Memorial Book of the Sesquicentennial Celebration of the Founding of the Coll. of N. J. and of the Ceremonies Inaugurating Princeton Univ.* (1898); Varnum Lansing Collins, *Princeton* (1914); and Caleb Smith, *Diligence in the Work of God, and Activity During Life, A Sermon Occasioned by the Much-Lamented Death of the Rev. Mr. Aaron Burr* (1758).]   A. L.

BURR, AARON (Feb. 6, 1756–Sept. 14, 1836), Revolutionary soldier, lawyer, United States senator, and third vice-president of the United States, came of an ancestry remarkable as well for its ecclesiastical eminence as for its intellectual vigor. His father was Aaron Burr [*q.v.*], scholar, theologian, and second president of the College of New Jersey; his mother was Esther Edwards, daughter of Jonathan Edwards [*q.v.*], the greatest of the New England divines. Burr and his sister Sarah, or "Sally," were born at Newark, N. J., where for some years the elder Burr had acted as pastor of the First Presbyterian Church. Shortly after the birth of his son, however, he moved to Princeton, where he died in September 1757. After the death of Burr's mother and of her parents within a few months, a maternal uncle, Timothy Edwards, became guardian of the children, essaying to rear them in the family tradition. Tapping Reeve, who subsequently became judge of the supreme court

of Connecticut, and a famous preceptor in law, served for a time as their tutor and later married Sally Burr (Davis, *post,* I, 25, 26).

From all accounts Burr was an attractive boy, fair of face, sprightly and merry, but not readily submissive to the discipline of his austere uncle. There was always in him a certain independence and audacity of spirit that carried him over or around artificial barriers. Yet he could apply himself to the task that engaged his interest. He prepared for college as a matter of course, ambition here coinciding with the wishes of his family; and he entered the sophomore class of the College of New Jersey at the age of thirteen. Tradition has it that he was a brilliant student but dissipated. Brilliant he was in whatever enlisted his interest, but Parton doubts that he was guilty of serious dereliction in these early years, arguing that part of his dissipation in college was "merely a dissipation of mind in multifarious reading." Be this as it may, Burr graduated with distinction at the age of sixteen. He is described as a youth of winning presence, rather short in stature but graceful in manner, who made friends easily among both sexes. A fondness for adventure and intrigue, however, gave a certain instability to his character, and a degree of waywardness to his life. He hesitated for a time over the choice of a career. During his college course a revival that had stirred many of his mates had awakened his curiosity and led him to consult the president of the college. That conservative mentor, John Witherspoon [*q.v.*], expressed disbelief in revivals, and thus reassured, Burr did not yield to the zealous expostulations of his fellows. Some months later, however, motivated by curiosity fully as much as by a pious desire to follow in the footsteps of his fathers, he entered upon the study of theology. But his curiosity was too much for his teacher, and in 1774 he left theology for law.

Less than a year later, the clash at Lexington summoned him to arms. After a few weeks with the motley host that beleaguered Boston, he joined the expedition against Quebec. On the difficult march thither, in the unsuccessful attack on the city (during which he is credited with an attempt to rescue the body of the commander, Montgomery), and during the gloomy winter that followed, he showed marked soldierly qualities. In the spring of 1776, having served Arnold as staff officer with the rank of captain, he was sent to New York. Here he served with the rank of major in the official household of Gen. Washington, but Burr's want of regard for military decorum, and perhaps occasional impertinence, antagonized his chief, and the intimacy of a few weeks led only to mutual dislike and distrust. Transferred to the staff of Gen. Putnam, Burr gave a good account of himself in the battle of Long Island and in the evacuation of New York—and had time to indulge in one of his numerous amatory intrigues. In July 1777 he was appointed lieutenant-colonel in the Continental line and assigned to a regiment stationed in Orange County, N. Y., and as its virtual commander established a commendable reputation for discipline and daring.

Throughout his life Burr displayed an unfortunate tendency to follow impulses which were prompted by personal likes or dislikes, as, for example, at Valley Forge where he narrowly missed inclusion in the notorious "Conway Cabal," and again at Monmouth where he suffered a repulse —a misfortune that led him to sympathize openly with Gen. Charles Lee. Following Monmouth, he spent the winter on patrol duty with his regiment in Westchester County, N. Y., where he maintained his reputation for vigilance and discipline. The hardships of this service, plus the exertions of the previous summer's campaign, eventually forced him to resign from the army in March 1779 (*Ibid.*, I, ch. V–XI).

He desired to enter upon professional training at once, but ill health forced a long wait. In the fall of 1780 he took up the study of law at Raritan, N. J., with William Paterson, an older friend of college days, but later transferred to an office in Haverstraw, N. Y. By means of this transfer and through the favor of Judge Robert Yates, of the state supreme court, he hastened his training and early in 1782 was licensed as attorney and counselor-at-law. In preparing for a profession Burr, as usual, had preferred to follow his own bent and was not averse to short cuts (Parton, *post*, 130–34).

In July 1782, he married Mrs. Theodosia (Bartow) Prevost, some ten years his senior, the widow of a former British officer. Though possessed of little fortune and of no great beauty, she was a woman of charm and intellectual vigor, and despite the disparity in their ages, her invalidism, and his exacting temperament, their twelve years of married life were apparently stimulating to both. Burr has been charged with more than one intrigue before his marriage and with many more after his wife's death, but he seems to have been true to her, if not as passionately devoted to her as she was to him, and he was an affectionate and zealous parent to their one daughter, Théodosia [*q.v.*]. His circle of stimulating regard included his stepsons, Frederick and Bartow Prevost, and numerous pro-

tégés, who, like his daughter, were always his devoted admirers.

In the fall of 1783 Burr moved to New York. Here he soon shared with Alexander Hamilton the pick of legal practise and for six years stuck closely to the law. In pleading he was noted for clarity and conciseness of utterance. He never ranted nor lost his temper, but as a contemporary noted, "He is more remarkable for dexterity than sound judgment or logic." Burr's practise brought him a substantial income which he tried to increase by extensive speculations. Generosity as well as self-indulgence made an incurable spendthrift of him. His carelessness in money matters was often a cause of grief to clients as well as to friends.

Burr's attempts to enter politics during his early residence in New York were uniformly unsuccessful. His professional rival, Hamilton, was the leader of one group, and Gov. George Clinton, who headed the opposing forces, at first made no bid for his support. But in September 1789 Clinton made him his attorney-general. From that office, after participating in a questionable deal in state lands, he was transferred, in 1791, to the United States Senate. He owed his elevation to his own finesse in fusing the Clinton and Livingston factions in opposition to the financial plans of Hamilton. The coalition defeated the latter's father-in-law, Gen. Philip Schuyler, and thereby gained for Burr Hamilton's persistent enmity.

During his term as senator (1791–97) Burr was twice mentioned for the governorship and in 1797 received thirty electoral votes for president. He took his membership seriously, applied himself to routine tasks, did nothing unseemly, and accomplished nothing of great repute. He attracted public attention and gained some worthwhile friends, including Gallatin and Jackson, but was not really accepted by either of the major party groups then being formed. He was defeated for reëlection to the Senate but in April 1797 was elected to the state Assembly. Here he introduced a measure to choose presidential electors by separate districts and was influential in the passage of a bill to aid the Holland Land Company in which he himself had a financial interest (Paul D. Evans, *The Holland Land Company*, 1924, pp. 180, 212–13). These measures, coupled with efforts in obtaining a charter for the Manhattan Company, a banking corporation disguised as a water company, led to his defeat in April 1799.

For some years past Burr had been gathering about himself a band of enthusiastic young helpers, who by letter urged their leader's claims to high office and directed operations at "Mart-ling's Long Room," where met St. Tammany's Society. Burr did not openly affiliate with the mechanics and small householders who largely made up this organization but through hench-men kept informed of their activities and around them built up his political machine. With this, he proposed to make himself a power in local politics and force Jefferson and his associates to recognize his leadership. He first secured his election to the state assembly from Orange County and then in New York City brought about the selection of a strong legislative ticket headed by Clinton, Brockholst Livingston, and his own friend, Gen. Horatio Gates. With this coalition ticket and using the "Martling Men" as a nucleus, he definitely listed and organized the voters of the city and in April 1800 roundly defeated Hamilton. The city returned a Republi-can delegation which gave that party control of the legislature by a narrow majority, and thus assured it the entire vote of New York in the electoral college. Then through a clever by-play, Burr procured his own indorsement for vice-president (*American Historical Review,* VIII, 512) and later journeyed to Philadelphia and secured from the Republican members of Con-gress a pledge to support him equally with Jefferson.

Owing to this agreement Burr tied with Jef-ferson for the presidency, each receiving seven-ty-three votes. The Federalists, who controlled a slight majority in the House of Representa-tives, determined to vote for him rather than Jefferson. Burr at once disclaimed competition for the office and his letter to that effect was published (Davis, II, 75). He also wrote a vig-orous disclaimer to one of the Virginia group (Burr to John Taylor, Dec. 18, 1800, manuscript in the Pennsylvania Historical Society). Later he kept quiet, in part, perhaps, because he learned that his local party associates were pre-paring to repudiate him and that Jefferson fa-vored them rather than himself in the prospec-tive division of patronage (P. L. Ford, ed., *Writings of Thomas Jefferson,* VIII, 102). He issued no more disclaimers, but apparently re-pelled all direct attempts of the Federalists to bargain with him. "Had Burr done anything for himself," wrote one of them in the midst of the balloting to break the tie, "he would long ere this have been president" (Davis, II, 113), and that, too, we may add, despite the bitter secret opposition of Hamilton. But he did nothing and on the thirty-sixth ballot the Federalists permit-ted the election of his rival. The share of patron-age accorded to him was not wholly satisfactory

but he helped in the reëlection of Gov. Clinton and presided over the convention that in 1801 amended the state constitution. He alienated both Republicans and Federalists by his vote when the Senate was evenly divided over the Judiciary Act and further antagonized the Re-publicans by taking part in the Federalist cele-bration of Washington's birthday. He was also attacked for suppressing a lengthy scurrilous pamphlet against the administration of John Adams. From this the editors who directed it passed to the more serious charge that Burr had intrigued with the Federalists to supplant Jeffer-son. Then followed two years of unstinted news-paper abuse. A pamphlet by Van Ness in re-joinder gave the presidential group a pretext for finding another running mate. Accordingly, at the party caucus on Feb. 25, 1804 George Clinton replaced Burr on the Republican ticket.

Burr's friends in the New York legislature had already nominated him on Feb. 18 for the governorship. In this contest there was some prospect of receiving Federalist aid through those New England leaders who were looking forward to a Northern confederacy. Burr re-fused to commit himself to their disunion schemes, but in spite of his attitude and Hamilton's re-newed opposition, the rank and file of the Fed-eralists voted for him and helped him carry the city and some outlying counties. Nevertheless, the regular Republican candidate, Morgan Lewis, supported by the Clinton and Livingston factions and countenanced by Jefferson and Hamilton, defeated him by a heavy majority.

Following this contest came the fatal duel with Hamilton. For fifteen years in contests for the Senate, the presidency, and the governorship the latter had filled his private correspondence with invective against Burr's public and private char-acter. Their personal relations during all this time had generally been friendly. Now Burr re-garded himself for the third time as the pecu-liar victim of Hamilton's malevolence. "These things," he significantly stated in the correspon-dence that preceded the fatal encounter, "must have an end." In the course of the campaign there had been published three compromising letters in which Hamilton was represented as stating publicly that Burr was a "dangerous man and one who ought not to be trusted with the reins of government." This ill-considered re-mark ended with reference to a "still more des-picable opinion which Gen. Hamilton had ex-pressed of Mr. Burr" (Wandell and Minnege-rode, I, 274). These statements provoked Burr's challenge. They must be interpreted in connec-tion with Hamilton's long-continued secret abuse, which the other had certainly not repaid in kind. The correspondence that preceded the duel favors Burr. His demands were peremptory, and Hamilton's replies were evasive. As the latter was unwilling to repudiate his previous harsh judgments, he reluctantly accepted the challenge (Davis, II, ch. XXI). In addition to settling past grievances, however, Burr may have wished to forestall further unwelcome rivalry, either in a possible Northern confederacy or on the Southwestern border. The latter was the more probable field, for both Burr and Hamilton cherished the ambition to lead an army thither in an effort to free the Spanish colonies. Viewed in this light the duel with Hamilton may be regarded as the opening move in the "Conspiracy," as well as the lurid finale to Burr's local political career. The meeting itself took place on the morning of July 11, 1804, at Weehawken, N. J., a circumstance that permitted two states to bring indictments against the survivor. Each man fired a single shot; Hamilton fell mortally wounded and died the next day. Burr fled, first to Philadelphia and thence southward, while his enemies took revenge on his heavily encumbered property and reputation.

Burr's journey was not an aimless one. Both before and after the duel he had conferred with Gen. James Wilkinson [q.v.], a friend of long standing who had just come northward from New Orleans. The two had evidently agreed upon a plan of action in case war should break out with Spain. As a preliminary step Burr was to visit East Florida; but much to the relief of his prospective hosts, a series of destructive tempests prevented him from reaching his destination (East Florida Papers, Casa Yrujo to Enrique White, Aug. 12; Burr to White, Sept. 22, 1804). Apparently he saw enough to convince him that the way to Mexico did not lie in that direction. Before leaving Philadelphia he had requested the British minister, Anthony Merry, to aid financially and otherwise in bringing about the separation of the Western states from the Union. This proposal was distinctly treasonable, but Burr probably never seriously intended to carry it out. Wilkinson may have told him how successfully he had used the lure of separatism with the Spaniards and had suggested that Burr approach Merry with a similar proposal. Merry readily listened to the project, which was broached to him through an intermediary, but his superiors refused to countenance it (H. Adams, II, 395).

At the next session of Congress, 1804–05, it fell to Burr's lot to preside over the impeachment of Justice Samuel Chase of the Supreme Court. Because Jefferson was anxious to have the latter removed, the administration leaders showed the retiring vice-president unusual attention and gave two of his family connections and his friend Wilkinson lucrative territorial appointments (Beveridge, *Marshall*, II, 182). Nevertheless Burr conducted the trial "with the dignity and impartiality of an archangel, but with the rigor of a devil," and at the end his most bitter critics commended his rulings and also gave him a general vote of appreciation for the "impartiality, dignity and ability with which he had presided over their deliberations" (Plumer, 312; Adams, *Memoirs*, I, 365; *Annals of Congress*, 8 Cong., 2 Sess., col. 72). This vote followed his valedictory address to the Senate on Mar. 2, a remarkable address that moved some of the senators to tears.

During this winter in Washington, Wilkinson and Burr frequently conferred over maps of the Floridas, Louisiana, and adjacent regions. Their purpose may be inferred from a letter of John Adair to the former, which ends thus: "Mexico glitters in our Eyes—the word is all we wait for" (Julius W. Pratt, *Expansionists of 1812*, 1925, p. 62). Burr accordingly planned to journey westward with Wilkinson when the other went to take over his new post in St. Louis. But other projects besides the invasion of Mexico occupied Burr's attention. There was the possibility of being returned to Congress from one of the western districts, or of obtaining a territorial appointment. Moreover he and a number of his friends were concerned in a dubious project to construct a canal around the falls of the Ohio. Inspired by these various possibilities Burr left Washington in the middle of March 1805 on his westward journey. His first stop was at Philadelphia, where he brought his separatist project once more to Merry's attention, reinforced it with reference to discontent among the French Creoles of Louisiana, and definitely asked for a half million loan and the use of a British fleet at the mouth of the Mississippi. Merry could only transmit these proposals to his government.

In this westward journey Burr touched all the important river towns of the Mississippi Valley from Pittsburgh to New Orleans and coursed over the connecting trails. He everywhere received marked public attentions while his movements continually provoked surmise and inquiry. In the Creole capital his faith in the invasion of Mexico was confirmed by the so-called "Mexican Association"—a loose aggregation of persons that vaguely planned to make that country independent. Press reports spoke of his appointment as governor of Orleans in place of W. C. C. Claiborne and mentioned other projects of pecuniary or political character. But if his journey had any purpose aside from putting himself in touch with those who would be helpful in case of war with Spain, it was apparently a failure. He had aroused in many quarters an unfortunate suspicion as to his own motives and loyalty, which the Spanish minister, Casa Yrujo, fully cognizant of his proposals to Merry, took care to disseminate widely.

Burr passed the following winter and spring in the East. He tried to interest Jefferson in giving him a diplomatic appointment but the President told him that the country had lost confidence in him. Then he sought to persuade either the British or the Spanish minister, or both, to finance his inchoate western plans. When Merry could report no response from his superiors, the conspirators—for Ex-Senator Jonathan Dayton [q.v.] of New Jersey was now actively associated with Burr—approached Casa Yrujo for ready funds and future pensions. The attempt to persuade Spain to finance an expedition that might be aimed at her own colonies came to nothing (McCaleb, ch. III).

Early in 1806 Burr asked a dissatisfied and idle friend, Commodore Thomas Truxtun [q.v.], to command a phantom naval contingent. Truxtun later testified that Burr's statements to him were wholly concerned with Mexico, but when he learned that the government was not immediately behind the undertaking he refused to entertain Burr's offer (Pickering Papers, January and February 1807). Far different was the testimony of William Eaton [q.v.], an adventurer then also unemployed, who had both a claim and a grudge against the administration. He later testified—when assured that his claim would be paid—that Burr mentioned in addition to the above invasion, a hare-brained plot to seize the president and cabinet and establish himself as dictator in Washington, or, failing in this, to loot bank and arsenal, seize vessels in the navy yard, and sail for New Orleans, where the independence of the West was to be proclaimed. Burr occasionally gave evidence of mental aberration, but uttered nothing like this drivel.

Unable to get money elsewhere, Burr next approached his friends and family connections. His plan was to take over a part interest in the Bastrop grant, lying on the Washita River, and convey thither young men who might serve as settlers in peace and soldiers in war. To this plan his supporters in New York, his son-in-law, and friends in Kentucky ultimately contributed the modest sums with which he contracted for

the building of boats, the gathering of provisions, and for making the first payment on the contract.

Burr and his associates had hoped that the administration would be forced into a war with Spain. When instead it resorted to diplomacy under the "Two Million Act"—an appropriation for the purchase of the Floridas—and when the death of the younger Pitt early in 1806 removed all hope of aid from England, they fell back upon the prospect of hostilities being provoked along the border. Dayton tried to stimulate Wilkinson to precipitate a clash, by warning him that he was to be supplanted in the army, and Burr sent a longer cipher letter to the same effect (Adams, III, 252–55; McCaleb, 73–75).

In the first week in August 1806, Burr again started westward. The simultaneous advance of the Spaniards east of the Sabine seemed to promise a belated chance to realize his dream of conquest, but rumors of the last twelve months had done their work and suspicion everywhere greeted him. Alarming reports of his movements began to rain in on Washington. Harman Blennerhassett [q.v.], a wealthy expatriated Irishman living near Marietta, helped Burr finance the Bastrop speculation, provided for gathering and transporting settlers thither, and also contributed to a local paper a series of articles which frankly discussed the probability of a separation of the Western states from the Union. The cause now became publicly associated with Western separatism and on this basis Burr was twice arraigned before a federal grand jury in Kentucky. Thanks in part to his own frank bearing, he was triumphantly cleared on both occasions. Nevertheless the reiterated charges were now working out their natural result. Jefferson and his advisers were finally convinced that something serious was afoot and late in October had sent an observer on Burr's trail; and on Nov. 27, after receiving alarming communications from Wilkinson, who had made a border settlement with the Spaniards and was preparing to betray Burr, the President issued a proclamation, announcing that a group was illegally plotting an expedition against Spain and warning all citizens not to participate.

Following the two arraignments in Kentucky, Burr went to Nashville and then late in December to the mouth of the Cumberland, where his followers joined him. Hostile manifestations had driven these presumptive settlers from the rendezvous at Blennerhassett Island. With the opening of the new year Burr with his modest array of nine boats and some sixty men recruited at the various stopping points, was on the Mississippi, totally ignorant of the hostile reception that his whilom friend and confederate Wilkinson was preparing for him. That general was now in New Orleans, intriguing to apprehend Burr and his Washita colonists and to send the former eastward as a tangible exhibit of his charges. Burr first learned of this meditated treachery, when on Jan. 10, 1807, he reached the settlements in Mississippi Territory. He immediately submitted to the authorities, was indicted before another federal jury, and was again triumphantly acquitted. This fiasco added to Burr's popularity, but the judge refused to release him from bond. Burr suspected with only too much truth, that Wilkinson was planning to kidnap him and bring him before a pretended court martial, and, after vain attempts to change the court decision, he fled toward Mobile. When within a few miles of the border, he was detected, apprehended, and within a few days was being escorted back to the region he had shortly before renounced forever.

On Mar. 30, 1807, Burr was brought before Chief Justice Marshall in the United States Circuit Court of the district of Virginia for a preliminary examination. After three days of discussion by counsel and deliberation by the court, he was held for a misdemeanor in organizing an expedition against Spanish territory. The question of treason was left for a grand jury to determine, and it proved difficult to select that tribunal. The panel finally obtained consisted of fourteen Republicans and two Federalists headed by John Randolph as foreman. The trial formally began on May 22, 1807. Burr was present with an array of distinguished counsel, and was faced by others, able but distinctly inferior to his own. The audience was generally hostile to the prisoner. The rulings of the court and the influence of the President—unseen but distinctly felt through his constant communication with the district attorney—determined that the proceedings should take on a political character. These were delayed at first by the absence of Wilkinson. Finally, after the General reached Richmond and gave his testimony—upon which he himself narrowly escaped indictment—the grand jury established a charge of treason against Burr. This was based largely upon a mistaken interpretation of Marshall's previous ruling in the hearing of J. Erich Bollman and Samuel Swartwout [*qq.v.*], Burr's luckless messengers to Wilkinson, who by falling into the General's hands had experienced something of the treatment he had reserved for Burr. The outcome of the trial depended largely upon the article of the Constitution defining treason. Marshall ruled

that "levying war" as there mentioned could only be established by an overt act in which the accused actually participated. The assemblage on Blennerhassett's Island was selected to meet this requirement. It was definitely shown that Burr was not present, nor near enough to affect actual proceedings. The theory of "constructive treason" which would have made him "contributory" to that assemblage and equally guilty with those who were present, was rejected. Hence it was impossible to establish the "overt act" necessary to convict. This failure meant the exclusion of much testimony as to collateral events, which, indeed, was mostly hearsay. The jury, on Sept. 1, basing its decision on the "evidence submitted," acquitted Burr and his associates of treason. Jefferson urged the district attorney to press the charge of misdeameanor against him but upon this charge also the jury decided in his favor. Burr and Blennerhassett, however, were remanded to trial in the district court of Ohio, but the prisoners did not appear within the state nor did the government press the suit further.

Late in October 1807 Burr was free but no less a fugitive. In Baltimore a mob hanged him in effigy along with Blennerhassett, Marshall, and Luther Martin, his chief defender, while he and the faithful Swartwout fled to Philadelphia, where numerous creditors besieged him. In June 1808 he sailed for England, still hopefully pursuing his plan to revolutionize Mexico. In England he became acquainted with many of the leaders of thought and letters—notable among them Jeremy Bentham and William Godwin—but failed, through the interference of the American minister and consuls, to gain official support, and was later ordered to leave, perhaps on the request of the Spanish *junta,* then allied with England (Parton, p. 535).

He spent several months in Sweden, Denmark, and Germany, and in February 1810 went to Paris, hoping to lay before Napoleon his projects for freeing the Spanish colonies and Louisiana and inciting war between the United States and England which should result in the acquisition of Canada by France. In March he presented to the Ministry of Relations Extérieures, through an affable young deputy, M. Roux, several memoranda embodying his schemes. In one of the wildest of these (Archives Nationales, no. 37, *post*) he stated that the people of the United States were discontented with their form of government, but the majority would oppose a change. However, he continued, there is "a third party, superior in talent and in energy; they desire something grand and stable, something which in giving occupation to active spirits will assure the tranquillity of reasonable men. This party has a recognized head; they ask only to follow him and obey him." This head was Burr himself, who, as the ministry evidently inferred (Archives Nationales, no. 36, *post*) "inclines toward monarchy" and was ready to use the 40,-000 sailors that he had represented as idle on account of the embargo, "to overthrow the republican government. The declaration of war against the English would follow this change." Another proposal according to an anonymous report (Dec. 10, 1811, Madison Papers, New York Public Library), was to bring about a reconciliation between England and France, and to use their combined forces against the United States. These proposals reached the chief of the foreign office who forwarded them to the Emperor with the comment that Mr. Burr apparently could initiate nothing except in Florida or Louisiana and that "he could not be employed without giving great offense to the United States" (Archives Nationales, no. 106, *post*). Burr, continuing to call upon M. Roux and trying to obtain the interest of other officials, was constantly met by the statement that there was no reply from the Emperor, and after four or five months he abandoned his effort to be heard. His attention now was given to getting a passport so that he might return to the United States and to Theodosia, but for one whole year his requests were persistently refused, by the French officials and by the American consul and chargé d'affaires. He fell into dire poverty—even pawning one after another the books and "pretty things" he had bought for Theodosia and his grandson—but his buoyant spirit remained unchecked, hopefully considering various expedients to gain ready cash or possibly a fortune. In July 1811 he was at last granted his passport, but the French ship on which he sailed was captured and taken to England, he was detained there, and it was not until\May 1812 that he reached the United States.

He had little difficulty in reëstablishing his legal practise in New York, but before he had been at home two months he received news of the death of his grandson. In December of the same year Theodosia, sailing from Charleston harbor, was lost at sea. For more than a score of years he survived these crushing blows. During the greater part of this period he had a good law practise, but never abandoned his ingrained amatory habits or his carelessness in money matters. He also kept his interest in the Spanish colonies but when asked to take part in their struggle for independence, was unable to accept (Davis, II, 442–45). In July 1833, when he was

seventy-seven, he married the widow of Stephen Jumel [*q.v.*], some twenty years his junior. After four months of domestic wrangling over finances, for Burr threatened to run through her substantial property, his wife brought suit for divorce in July 1834. The decree confirming her request bore the date of his death. The latter occurred at Port Richmond, Staten Island, on Sept. 14, 1836 (Wandell and Minnegerode, II, 323–40). To the bitter experiences of his later years as to the ephemeral successes of his earlier life he had presented the same unruffled serenity that had so often disarmed opponents and captivated followers. Shortly before his death he had again protested that he had never designed the separation of the West from the Union.

[The most important printed sources for Burr are Matthew L. Davis, *Memoirs of Aaron Burr* (2 vols., 1836–37) and *The Private Jour. of Aaron Burr During His Residence of Four Years in Europe* (2 vols., 1838, repr. 1903, from the MS. in library of Wm. K. Bixby of St. Louis, Mo.). The printed works of many of Burr's contemporaries are important, especially those of Jefferson (Ford, ed.), Hamilton, and King. For the trial consult "Reports of the Trials of Col. Aaron Burr," reported by David Robertson (2 vols., 1808); *Annals of Cong.*, 9 Cong., 2 Sess., 1008–19, and 10 Cong., 1 Sess., 385–778; and *Am. State Papers Misc.* (1834), I, 468–645. Jas. Wilkinson, *Memoirs of My Own Times* (1816) is necessary but unreliable. For events in Mississippi and Orleans territories the most significant source is Dunbar Rowland (ed.), *Letter Books of Wm. C. C. Claiborne*, vols. I–III (1916). For nearly a score of years contemporary newspapers contained frequent references to Burr's political career, some items of which under the names of Jas. Cheetham and W. P. Van Ness appeared also in pamphlet form. Casual but important references to Burr occur in E. S. Brown (ed.), *Wm. Plumer's Memorandum* (1923), and in C. F. Adams (ed.), *Memoirs of John Quincy Adams*, vol. I (1874). The manuscript sources are also valuable. Of chief importance are the Papers of Jefferson, Madison, and Monroe, in the Lib. of Cong., and the Papers of Harry Innes, vol. XVIII, Papers in Relation to Burr's Conspiracy, and the East Florida Papers, in the same repository. The Papers of Jas. Wilkinson in the Chicago Hist. Soc., the Durrett Papers in the Univ. of Chicago, the Pickering Papers in the Mass. Hist. Soc., and the collections of the Miss. Dept. of Archives and Hist., and of the La. Hist. Soc. are also worthy of attention. For material in Spanish the Bexar Archives in the Univ. of Texas and the general archives in Mexico City, Madrid, and Seville are especially important. Some MSS. relating to Burr were discovered by Dr. Waldo G. Leland in the Archives Nationales: AF iv, 1681 A, Nos. 36–40 and Nos. 106, 107, 110, 114, 115. Among the earlier biographies Jas. Parton, *The Life and Times of Aaron Burr* (1858) is a sympathetic account. The most recent life, S. H. Wandell and Meade Minnegerode, *Aaron Burr* (1925), is a sprightly narrative that is often too favorable to its subject. It is, however, based on much patient and long continued investigation by the first-named author. Isaac Jenkinson, *Aaron Burr, His Personal and Political Relations with Thos. Jefferson and Alex. Hamilton* (1902) is likewise an overly favorable interpretation of some disputed phases of his career. W. F. McCaleb, *The Aaron Burr Conspiracy* (1903) and Henry Adams, *Hist. of the U.S.*, vols. II and III (1889–90), present opposing views of the conspiracy, of which that of the former is the more substantial and convincing. A. J. Beveridge, *The Life of John Marshall* (1916–19), vol. III, ch. VI–IX is the best account of the trial at Richmond. Edward Channing, *Hist. of the U. S.*, vol. IV (1917), is excellent for bibliographic references and John B. McMaster, *Hist. of the People of the U. S.* (1891), vol. III, presents an unfavorable summary of the events of the conspiracy.]

I. J. C.

BURR, ALFRED EDMUND (Mar. 27, 1815–Jan. 8, 1900), editor, was descended from Benjamin Burr, who came to the shores of the Connecticut river from Newtown, Mass., with the earliest settlers in 1636. Alfred's mother, before her marriage Lucretia Olcott, was also a descendant of the first settlers in Connecticut. The eighth of fourteen children of James Burr, Alfred at the age of twelve began to earn his own living at the printer's trade in the office of the *Hartford Courant*. At the age of twenty he was foreman of the composing room and at twenty-four he rejected an offer to become part owner of the paper because it was conditional on his joining the Whig party and attending the Congregational church. Thus early he showed the independence in opinion evident throughout his life of nearly eighty-five years. Accordingly, in 1839 he turned his attention to the *Hartford Weekly Times* established in 1817. The *Weekly Times* had fought for religious toleration under John M. Niles (United States senator 1835–39 and 1842–48, and postmaster-general under President Van Buren). On Jan. 1, 1839, Judge Henry A. Mitchell accepted Burr's offer to buy a half interest in the paper on advice of Gideon Welles, a frequent contributor from 1824 until he became a member of President Lincoln's cabinet. On Jan. 1, 1841, Burr became sole owner, and on Mar. 2 the first issue of the *Daily Times* appeared. From the start Burr took a lively interest in national issues and this led to many antagonisms in the sharp political controversies that raged prior to and during the Civil War. He believed that the war might have been avoided by a spirit of conciliation and adherence to the Constitution. He made the *Daily Times* a steadfast democratic newspaper and vigorously opposed the movement to repeal the Missouri Compromise. His influence in Connecticut was shown by the result of the election in 1860, when 16,493 Democrats voted for Breckinridge whom he had supported, 17,374 for Stephen A. Douglas and 3,291 for Bell. In other New England states the vote for Breckinridge was proportionally much smaller. He did not swerve from his course of opposing the conflict and, in 1864, 42,285 Connecticut voters supported the policy advocated by the *Daily Times* or 48.61 per cent of the total vote. No one at that time or later questioned his motives as other than pure and patriotic. Another example of his independence was afforded in the three campaigns of William Jennings Bryan for the presidency, opposed in each case by the *Daily Times*, which re-

pudiated free silver heresies and stood for sound money. Burr's only elective office was as representative in the Connecticut legislature, two terms, in 1853 and 1866. He stood high in the state and national councils of the Democratic party, however, and was repeatedly a delegate to national conventions. For many years no Democratic platform was adopted in Connecticut which was not wholly or in part prepared by him. He was a pioneer in shaping the Democratic party's tariff-reform policy so that due allowance should be made for the difference between the wages of American and foreign labor. He refused a seat in President Cleveland's cabinet. His leadership in local affairs was indicated by his choice as chairman of the commission that built the state capitol, and by his influence in pushing park projects and in enlarging Hartford's water supply and school facilities. In appearance he was tall and spare, and he often walked from his home to the office carrying his editorial copy in his tall silk hat. In April 1841 he married Sarah A. Booth. His son, Willie Olcott Burr, succeeded his father as editor of the *Daily Times*. The service of the father was sixty-one years, that of the son sixty years, a total given to the *Hartford Daily Times* by both of 121 years, a record probably unequaled in newspapers of the United States.

[Wm. F. Moore, ed., *Representative Men of Conn.* (1894), pp. 30–32; N. G. Osborn, *Men of Mark in Conn.,* I (1906), 265; A. E. Burr, *Founder of the Hartford Daily Times* (1900); *Hartford Daily Times,* Jan. 8, 1900.]

C. L. S.

BURR, ENOCH FITCH (Oct. 21, 1818–May 8, 1907), Congregational minister, the son of Zalmon and Mary (Hanford) Burr, and descended from Jonathan Edwards, was born at Greens Farms, near Westport, Conn. He prepared for college at the local academy and at Wilton, Conn., under Dr. Hawley Olmstead, entering the same class at Yale with Zalmon B., his older brother. He graduated with the distinction of "class orator" in 1839 and continued for a year in the Divinity School, then led by Nathaniel W. Taylor [*q.v.*]. Two further years were spent at the college in scientific study, but failing health kept him for the next three at home. On his mother's death he returned to New Haven and devoted nearly four years to higher mathematics and physical astronomy, his studies resulting in an application of calculus to the theory of Neptune entitled *Results of Analytical Researches in the Neptunian Theory of Uranus* (1848).

Renewed religious interest interrupted the scientific career thus auspiciously begun. Burr had been licensed to preach in 1842. On Oct. 3, 1850, he was ordained pastor of the village church of

Hamburg, Conn., part of the ancient town of Lyme. Ten months later he married Harriet A., daughter of Peter Lord of Lyme. Save for a year of travel abroad in 1855, accompanied by his wife and brother Zalmon, Hamburg remained Burr's home for life.

But his energies sought wider outlet. A theological essay, *Christ the Revealer of God* (1854), was followed (1857–62) by a series of tracts and sermons, and finally, after an interval of five years, by a volume destined to give him wider reputation. *Ecce Coelum, or Parish Astronomy* (1867) met so well the popular demand for science in the service of apologetics as to pass through sixteen or more editions. It also led to his appointment at Amherst from 1868 to 1874 as lecturer on The Scientific Evidences of Religion, with further invitations to lecture in New York and Boston, and at Yale and Williams. Two volumes, *Pater Mundi* (1870) and *The Doctrine of Evolution* (1873), contain these lectures, and show, together with two successors of similar type, *Celestial Empires* (1885) and *Universal Beliefs* (1887), the reaction of New England orthodoxy to the inroads of science. Three later volumes of sermons, *Ad Fidem* (1871), *Toward the Strait Gate* (1875), *In the Vineyard* (1876); a book of verse, *Thy Voyage* (1875); and two biblico-historical novels, *Dio, the Athenian* (1880) and *Aleph the Chaldean* (1891) may be mentioned.

Literary pursuits so absorbing could scarcely fail to remove the spare, austere, and often Quixotic minister from his farmer parishioners. Among his conservative ministerial associates Dr. Burr loomed up as the scientific champion of the ancient faith. To his flock also he seemed a great man, but increasingly removed from common life. Nevertheless, when, after fifty-six years of service, the aged pastor resigned his charge the church declined to accept his resignation, continuing him as pastor until his death.

[*Quarter-Century Record of the Class of 1839, Yale Coll.* (1865); *Obit. Record Grads. Yale Univ.* (1907), pp. 669 ff.; *Who's Who in America*, 1906–07; *Hartford Courant*, May 9, 1907.] B. W. B—n.

BURR, THEODOSIA (June 21, 1783–January 1813), daughter of Aaron Burr, was born in Albany, but passed most of her girlhood in New York City. Her education, under the careful direction of her father, included mental discipline such as did not fall to the lot of many girls of her generation. "If I could foresee," Aaron Burr wrote once to his wife, "that Theo would become a mere fashionable woman, with all the attendant frivolity and vacuity of mind, adorned with whatever grace and allurement, I would earnestly pray

God to take her forthwith hence. But I yet hope by her to convince the world what neither sex appears to believe—that women have souls" (Pidgin, 165). So, in addition to the customary French, music, and dancing, Theodosia began early to apply her mind to arithmetic, Latin, Greek, and English composition—the last in the form of letters to her father which were promptly returned with detailed criticisms. After the death of her mother, when Theodosia was eleven, her father gave his personal attention to her social education, instructing her—and few other teachers were so competent—in the arts and artifices of getting on with people. At fourteen she was beginning to be hostess for him at Richmond Hill. The story is told that in 1797, while Burr was away, at his request she entertained Joseph Brant, chief of the Six Nations, giving a dinner in his honor to which she invited, among other guests, Dr. Hosack, Dr. Bard, and the Bishop of New York (W. L. Stone, *Life of Joseph Brant*, 1838, II, 455–56). At sixteen she was one of the belles of New York society, but without "the attendant vacuity of mind." The following year (Feb. 2, 1801) she was married to Joseph Alston [*q.v.*], and became prominent in South Carolina social circles. This step some of her friends thought to be a political move on the part of her father, and bewailed her "sacrifice" to "affluence and influential connections" (Maria Nicholson to Mrs. Gallatin, Henry Adams, *Life of Albert Gallatin*, 1879, pp. 244–45). But her letters show that Theodosia was attached to her husband, and the birth of their son in 1802 gave her a new interest so overwhelming that the comments of friends mattered naught. The next few years were broken by trips to Saratoga and Ballston Spa in the effort to restore Theodosia's health—very delicate since the birth of the boy—and by visits to her father in New York. In the summer of 1806, she took Aaron Burr Alston and went with Burr to Blennerhassett's Island in the Ohio, where she completely captivated both the proprietor and his wife. She was joined by Alston in October, some weeks later returning with him to South Carolina. Burr was arrested the following spring, and during his trial Theodosia was with him in Richmond, sharing his anxiety, her graciousness and charm exerting a potent influence in his favor (Blennerhassett's journal, W. H. Safford, *Blennerhassett Papers*, 1861, p. 469). In June 1808 Burr took passage for Europe, under an assumed name. Theodosia, also under an assumed name, went north to bid him farewell. The night before he embarked she met him for the last time, and received his papers and final instructions.

During the four years of his exile she was his agent in America, raising money—whenever she could—and sending it to him, and transmitting messages. On her own initiative she wrote to Gallatin and to Mrs. Madison, in an attempt to smooth the way for his return. But when in July 1812 Burr was once again established in New York, Theodosia was unable to go to him immediately. She had been in feeble health, and the death of her son of fever, on June 30, had nearly prostrated her. It was not until December that she was ready to undertake the voyage. Gov. Alston's public duties prevented his accompanying her, so she was escorted by "a gentleman with some medical knowledge" whom her father sent down from New York. On Dec. 30, 1812, they embarked on the *Patriot,* and sailed out of Georgetown Harbor, but the *Patriot* never reached port. Whether, as seems most probable, it foundered in the terrific storm which struck the Carolina coast early in January, or whether, as some legends have it, the *Patriot* was captured by pirates and the passengers forced to walk the plank, or was driven ashore by the storm to be the prey of the notorious Carolina "bankers," is a question which has never been settled.

The mystery attending her fate has so enveloped Theodosia that in the many forms in which her story has been told she has usually appeared as the shadowy heroine of romance rather than as the vital young woman one sees in her letters. She is most interesting in her relations with that erratic father, to whom, through all the vicissitudes of his career, she was passionately devoted. She was his confidante, whom he did not try to deceive. But she seems to have been blind to his frailties. When he was in the deepest disgrace,—already an exile from home, he had been asked to leave England,—she wrote to him: "You appear to me so superior, so elevated above other men; I contemplate you with such strange mixture of humility, admiration, reverence, love and pride, that very little superstition would be necessary to make me worship you as a superior being. . . . I had rather not live than not be the daughter of such a man" (Parton, II, 188).

[Biographies of Aaron Burr, especially Jas. Parton, *Life and Times of Aaron Burr* (enl. ed., 1885) and S. H. Wandell and Meade Minnigerode, *Aaron Burr* (1925) contain material on Theodosia. Perhaps the most comprehensive recent sketch is that by Meade Minnigerode, "Theodosia Burr, Prodigy, An Informal Biography," in the *Sat. Eve. Post,* Sept. 6, 1924. Chas. Felton Pidgin, *Theodosia* (1907) is useful chiefly as a compilation of documents. See also Virginia T. Peacock, *Famous Am. Belles of the Nineteenth Century* (1901) ; and Gamaliel Bradford, *Wives* (1925). The most commonly reproduced portrait is from a miniature by Vanderlyn, but the previously unpublished portraits, contained in Wandell and Minnigerode, of the child by Stuart and of the young matron by Vanderlyn, accord more fully with the tradition of striking beauty, aristocratic features, and remarkable dark eyes. There are photostat copies of some of Theodosia's letters in the Lib. of Cong.]

E. R. D.

BURRAGE, HENRY SWEETSER (Jan. 7, 1837–Mar. 9, 1926), editor, historian, was descended in the seventh generation from John Burridge of Norfolkshire, who was imprisoned for refusing to pay ship money demanded by Charles I. and who migrated by 1637 to Charlestown, Mass. He was also seventh in descent from Maj. Simon Willard, the founder of Concord. His father, Jonathan Burrage, a varnish manufacturer, married Mary T. Upton. Henry was born at Fitchburg and prepared for college at Pierce Academy in Middleton, being graduated from Brown University in 1861. He was admitted to Phi Beta Kappa, while his literary ability was recognized in his election as class poet. After one year at Newton Theological Institution, he enlisted as a private in the 36th Massachusetts Volunteer Infantry and rose to the rank of major. Wounded in the shoulder at Cold Harbor, he was captured at Petersburg soon after his return from the necessary furlough and spent some time in Libby Prison. At the close of the war he resumed his theological studies at Newton, being graduated in 1867. The year 1868–69 he spent at the University of Halle, living in the home of Prof. Tholuck, enjoying associations which he ever cherished. His first and only pastorate was at the Baptist Church in Waterville, Me., 1869–73. He then became editor of *Zion's Advocate,* residing in Portland for the thirty-two years he held this position. Although this paper was most specifically devoted to the Baptist interests in Maine and factors of local circulation remained economic necessities, in its broad appeal and with its high literary and spiritual standards, it ranked among the best of the provincial religious journals. Although Burrage had no assistant in his editorial task, he kept in constant touch with the religious movements and workers in all parts of the state, making more vital his editorials which maintained a high degree of scholarship. While positive in his convictions, he did not display the dogmatic and disputative temper which marred much contemporary religious journalism. His avocational interests and services were many and valuable. He was recording secretary of numerous organizations, including the American Baptist Missionary Union, which brought him into close touch with foreign mission affairs. His educational judgment was sought as trustee of Colby College, 1881–1906, of Newton Theological Institution, 1881–1906, and of Brown University, 1889–1901, and as Fellow of Brown from 1901. He kept in close touch with the interests of the Civil War veterans, serving as recorder of the Maine Commandery, Loyal Legion, 1889–1912, and as chaplain of the National Soldiers' Home at Togus, 1905–12. His historical work may be considered avocational until his appointment as state historian of Maine in 1907, but for sixty years his pen turned frequently to historical themes and he greatly stimulated the development of the Maine Historical Society. A large part of his published works deal with the history of Maine and with that of the Baptists. Of the more extensive works may be mentioned: *The Act of Baptism in the History of the Christian Church* (1879); *History of the Anabaptists of Switzerland* (1882); *Baptist Hymn Writers and Their Hymns* (1888); *History of the Baptists in New England* (1894); *History of the Baptists of Maine* (1904); *The Beginnings of Colonial Maine, 1602–1658* (1914); *Maine in the Northeastern Boundary Controversy* (1919); *Maine Historical Memorials* (1922). As state historian, he examined and arranged the correspondence of the governors of Maine during the Civil War.

He was married twice: first, in 1873 to Caroline Champlin, who died in 1875; and, second, in 1881, to Ernestine Maie Giddings.

[Private papers at Burrage's late home, Kennebunkport, Me.; *Who's Who in America*, 1924–25; *Portland Press Herald*, Mar. 10, 1926.]   W.H.A.

BURRALL, WILLIAM PORTER (Sept. 18, 1806–Mar. 3, 1874), lawyer and railroad executive, was born at Canaan, Conn., the son of the Hon. William M. Burrall by his wife Abigail Porter Stoddard of Salisbury, Conn. He was educated in the public schools and by private tutors and entered Yale College, graduating in the class of 1826. Immediately upon graduation he began the study of law with his father. After one year he entered the office of the Hon. Samuel Church (afterward chief justice of the State of Connecticut) in Salisbury, subsequently attended a course of lectures at the Litchfield Law School, and was admitted to the bar of Litchfield County in April 1829. In May 1831 he was married to Harriet Holley. He practised law in Canaan, Conn., until October 1839 at which time he was elected president of the Housatonic Railroad Company which was just being organized. He held this office until his resignation due to press of other business in 1854, during which time he lived in Bridgeport, Conn. In 1856 he was made vice-president of the Hartford and New Haven Railroad Company then being constructed and held the position until 1867 when he was elected president, which office he occupied until

the road was consolidated with the New York, New Haven and Hartford Railroad Company in 1872. At this time he was made vice-president of the consolidated corporation which position he held until his death. He was also connected with the Illinois Central Company having been elected treasurer in 1852 and president in 1853, and holding this office until 1855 when he resigned but continued in the service of the company as advisory counsel until 1857. In 1859 he made his permanent home in Salisbury, Conn., and took an active part in local politics, representing that town in the General Assembly in 1861. He died from apoplexy in Hartford, Conn.

Burrall was considered one of the ablest railroad executives of his time, particularly in the legal phases. As a negotiator of railroad contracts he was most successful and his services were of very great value in consolidations. Under his management the Hartford and New Haven Railroad Company was known as one of the best paying roads in the country. In manner he was quiet and reserved, a practical business man, admirably fitted for an executive position requiring coolness, forethought, and decision.

[*Yale Univ., Class of 1826 Biog. Sketches* (1866); *Obit. Record of Grads. of Yale Coll.* (1874); obituaries in the *N. Y. Herald, N. Y. Times*, and *Hartford Courant*, Mar. 4, 1874.]   J.H.F.

BURRELL, DAVID JAMES (Aug. 1, 1844–Dec. 5, 1926), clergyman, pastor of Presbyterian and Reformed Dutch churches, was born in Mount Pleasant, Pa., the son of David and Elizabeth (Felgar) Burrell. His great-grandfather, John Burrell, a descendant of French Huguenots who had been driven out of Alsace by the revocation of the Edict of Nantes, had emigrated from County Armagh, Ireland, in the middle of the eighteenth century, and had settled in Westmoreland County, Pa. His mother was the daughter of Ludwig and Catharine (Dunn) Felgar, the latter having been born on the ocean while her parents were coming to America from the north of Ireland. Having prepared for college in the high school, Freeport, Ill., to which place his family had moved, and later at Phillips Academy, Andover, he graduated from Yale in 1867; and from Union Theological Seminary in 1870. After a brief period of mission work in New York (1870–71) he went to Chicago and took charge of the Peoria Street Chapel of the Third Presbyterian Church. On Oct. 18, 1871, he married Clara DeForest, daughter of George F. and Caroline (Sergeant) DeForest of Freeport, Ill. His ordination occurred on Apr. 9, 1872. The chapel he served became the Westminster Presbyterian Church, and of this he was pastor until 1876. From 1876 to 1887 he was pastor of the Second Church, Dubuque, Iowa, and from 1887 to 1891 of the Westminster Church, Minneapolis. These churches had remarkable growth under his ministry. In 1891 he accepted a call to the Marble Collegiate Church, Reformed Dutch, of New York, with which he remained connected till his death.

From his college days he was noted for proficiency in rhetoric and for oratorical ability. His sermons grounded in the old-fashioned evangelical theology, which he championed, were well-planned, direct, fervent, copiously illustrated, and effectively delivered. For several years, beginning in 1903, he was acting professor of homiletics in the Princeton Theological Seminary. He also served as associate editor of *The Presbyterian*, Philadelphia, and *The Christian Herald*. From 1909 to 1913 he was president of the World's Council of the Reformed and Presbyterian Churches. He was active in behalf of temperance and Sunday observance, being long a manager of the American Sabbath Union, later the Lord's Day Alliance of the United States, and one of the seven incorporators of the Anti-Saloon League of New York. Of the latter he was a director (1905–24), and president (1921–23). He was also a director of the Anti-Saloon League of America. His publications were numerous. They are mostly books of a religious nature, popular rather than scholarly, and of passing value. Among them are: *The Religions of the World* (1888); *The Early Church: Studies in the Acts of the Apostles* (1897), in collaboration with his brother, Rev. Joseph Dunn Burrell; *Christ and Progress* (1903); *The Verities of Jesus* (1903); *Teachings of Jesus Concerning the Scriptures* (1904); *The Evolution of a Christian* (1906); *The Sermon, Its Construction and Delivery* (1913); *The Apostles' Creed* (1915); *Why I Believe the Bible* (1917); *Paul's Campaigns* (1918); *Paul's Companions* (1921); *Paul's Letters* (1921).

[*Gen. Cat. of Union Theol. Sem.* (1919); *Who's Who in America*, 1926–27; *Yale Univ. Obit. Record*, 1926–27, which lists forty-two of his publications; *N. Y. Herald-Tribune*, *N. Y. Times*, *N. Y. Evening Post*, Dec. 6, 1926; *Presbyterian*, Dec. 16, 23, 1926; David De Forest Burrell, *David James Burrell* (1929).] H.E.S.

BURRILL, ALEXANDER MANSFIELD (June 19, 1807–Feb. 7, 1869), lawyer, author, was a member of the well-known Burrill family of Lynn. George Burrill, probably of Boston, England, was one of the proprietors of Lynn, Mass., in 1638 and his descendants were very prominent in the early colonial days. Sixth in the direct line from him was Ebenezer Burrill, a prosperous business man, who married Phebe,

daughter of Capt. James Cahoone of Newport, R. I., and moved to New York City in 1802 where their son, Alexander Mansfield Burrill, was born. His early education was received at the hands of private tutors, and he entered Columbia College in 1820, graduating in 1824 with the highest honors. He then took up the study of law under Chancellor Kent, and was admitted to the New York bar in 1828. He commenced the practise of his profession in New York City, but did not achieve any measure of success. His temperament was not such as to fit him for litigation, and he had a natural aversion to the sharp contests inevitable in court work. In consequence he withdrew from active practise in order to devote himself to legal authorship. His first publication was *Practice of the Supreme Court of the State of New York in Personal Actions* (2 vols., 1840). The reception accorded to it by the profession was so favorable that a second edition was quickly called for. It was followed by a *New Law Dictionary and Glossary* in two parts (1850–51), a work of a very high standard, which at once took its place as perhaps the best book of its kind so far produced. *Law and Practice of Voluntary Assignments for the Benefit of Creditors* followed in 1853, and was equally well received. His last work, *The Nature, Principles and Rules of Circumstantial Evidence, Especially That of the Presumptive Kind, in Criminal Cases* (1856) deals with a difficult and very technical branch of the law, in a scientific spirit alien to previous treatises on the subject. All his books were distinguished for their graceful style and a scholarly precision and finish which earned the unstinted commendation of the judiciary. In addition their accuracy of statement and definition was fully recognized at the time by the profession at large. He also assisted in the preparation of *Worcester's Dictionary*.

Refined in his nature and tastes, he made his immediate circle of intimates, in the main, from men of similar scholarly attainments and interests. Endowed with keen intellectual perception and high ideals he had no inclination for the public life of the day. With the members of the bar his reputation was of the highest and he enjoyed universal respect.

[Ellen Mudge Burrill, *The Burrill Family of Lynn* (1907), containing full details of ancestry; Paul C. Burrill, *Burrill Lineage* (1910); brief obituary in the *Am. Law Times*, II, 77.] H. W. H. K.

BURRILL, JAMES (Apr. 25, 1772–Dec. 25, 1820) lawyer, Rhode Island politician, and senator, was born in Providence, the son of James and Elizabeth (Rawson) Burrill. He prepared for college in the school of William Wilkinson, at that time a celebrated classical and mathematical teacher in Providence. After graduating from Rhode Island College (now Brown University) in 1788, he began the study of law in the office of Theodore Foster, a Providence lawyer of extensive practise. Wher Foster, elected to the Senate in May 1790, relinquished his law practise, Burrill went into the office of David Howell, a prominent Rhode Island politician, where he remained until he was admitted to the bar in September 1791. He then began the practise of law in Providence. In the summer of 1795 he served as secretary of protest against a new apportionment of state taxes that had been ordered by the General Assembly, and in August 1797 served on the committee of three that welcomed President John Adams to the town of Providence. In the following month (Oct. 8, 1797) he married Sally Arnold. Although little more than a youth Burrill now became attorney-general of Rhode Island, which post he held from October 1797 to May 1813. During the next seven years he served as trustee of Brown University. In politics he was a Federalist. On June 7, 1813, he was elected to the General Assembly, and in May 1814, was chosen speaker of the House, which office he held until he resigned from the House in October 1816. At the May session of the latter year he was elected chief justice of the supreme judicial court of Rhode Island. A contemporary, writing in after years, speaks of Burrill at this time as the acknowledged head of the Rhode Island bar (Henry L. Bowen, *Memoir of Tristam Burges,* 1835, p. 38). On June 21, 1816, the General Assembly, in grand committee, unanimously elected Burrill to the Senate. He declined to serve, on the ground that there was some doubt as to the constitutionality of his election (*Rhode Island Acts and Resolves,* Feb. Sess., 1817, p. 5). The General Assembly, however, unanimously confirmed his election Feb. 19, 1817, and Burrill represented his state in the Senate from December 1817 until his death, during which time he came to be recognized as one of the leading orators in that body. The *Annals of Congress* and the *Senate Journal* testify to his activity. He served on the committees on commerce and manufactures and on the judiciary. His first important effort was on Nov. 26, 1818, when he unsuccessfully attempted to obtain an increase in the salaries of the chief justice and the associate justices of the Supreme Court of the United States (*Annals of Congress,* 15 Cong., 2 Sess., col. 27). The most important questions before the Senate were those of the admission of Maine and Missouri to the Union. Although a member of the committee that reported

the resolution, Burrill vigorously opposed the bill in two important speeches. In the first, Jan. 13, 1820, he opposed binding the two questions together and urged that each be considered separately on its merits (*Ibid.,* 16 Cong., 1 Sess., col. 94–97). The second speech, delivered Dec. 7, 1820, was an attempt to prevent the passage of the resolution. He urged that Section 26, Article 3, of the Missouri constitution, which made it the duty of the Missouri legislature to prevent free negroes and mulattoes from settling in Missouri, was ". . . entirely repugnant to the Constitution of the United States . . ." on the ground that it distinguished between classes of citizens (*Ibid.,* 16 Cong., 2 Sess., col. 45–50). The resolution passed the Senate Dec. 12, 1820. Burrill died in Washington and was given a memorable funeral in the Senate chamber (*Daily National Intelligencer,* Washington, D. C., Dec. 27, 28, 1820).

[Wm. R. Staples, *Annals of the Town of Providence, from its First Settlement, to the Organization of the City Govt., in June 1832* (1843); Wm. G. Goddard, "Biog. Notices of Early Grads. at Brown Univ.," *Am. Quart. Reg.,* May 1839, p. 360; *Biog. Cong. Dir.* (1928); *R. I. Am. and General Advertiser,* Jan. 2, 5, 9, 1821.]
F. E. R.

BURRILL, THOMAS JONATHAN (Apr. 25, 1839–Apr. 14, 1916), botanist, horticulturist, was of Irish and Scotch descent, the son of John and Mary (Francis) Burrill. He was born on a farm near Pittsfield, Mass., and while still a child went to work in a cotton-mill. When he was nine his family moved to Stephenson County, in northwestern Illinois, where in the time that was not occupied at school or in farm chores the little boy was busy at the loom. His education was in log school-houses until he went to high school in Freeport at nineteen, whence shyness and consciousness of his country clothes and manners drove him home. He returned to school, however, at Rockford, working at chores to earn his board, and in 1862 he entered the State Normal School where the museum of the State Natural History Society was located. In his attachment to natural history he gravitated to the museum, where he made the acquaintance of B. D. Walsh the entomologist and George Vasey the botanist. These men guided his studies in the natural sciences. He graduated from the Illinois State Normal School in 1865, and in 1865–68 was superintendent of schools in Urbana. On July 22, 1868, he was married to Sarah H. Alexander of Seneca Falls, N. Y. In the same year he became assistant professor of natural history in the University of Illinois, and in the following year he conducted with his students a natural history survey and collecting trip from Cairo to

Chicago, in other words from the southern extremity of the state and its austral life zones to the northern end where it borders Lake Michigan. The next year he began contributing articles to the Illinois Horticultural Society's publications, and continued to write with vigor and precision on subjects horticultural, botanical, and pathological up to 1915, some eighty-two articles in all, practically every one of which has an integral place of importance in its subject. He was for nearly fifty years the moving spirit in the Illinois Horticultural Society and in the Agricultural School of the University of Illinois; beside this he threw himself into administrative duties, was long the vice-president of the University (acting president 1891–94 and again in 1902), and held, when he died, the presidency of the Society of American Bacteriologists.

He was among the first of the modern microscopists. One of his publications was on the rusts and mildews of Illinois, part of a survey of the cryptogamic flora of his state which was never completed. In 1877 he announced his suspicion that the terrific epidemic of "fire blight" of pears then sweeping the Middle West was caused by bacteria, which had previously been supposed to cause disease only in animals. His views were cautiously regarded in America and received with scorn in Europe, but by 1880 his intensive microscopical investigations and his inoculations of healthy pears with the virus of fireblight, causing the appearance of fire-blight symptoms, had gone far toward proving his contention, though he still offered his views with orthodox modesty and tentativeness. His prediction that many mysterious diseases, such as the mosaic blights, would prove to be bacterial, has been fully justified, so that he may be said to have been the pioneer American in perhaps the most economically important branch of botany in the last fifty years, that of the bacterial diseases of plants. His pathological investigations were extended constantly and included such important crop diseases as ear rot of corn, potato scab, blackberry rust, peach yellows, and, especially, bitter rot of apples. When the first news of the appearance of this last disease in Illinois reached him he sat up all night preparing a circular for farmers on methods of combating it, rushed it through the printing, and had it distributed in a few hours. In the meantime he had telegraphed warnings to every corner of the state. His last work was an attempt to domesticate or cultivate the beneficial wild bacteria of the soil. He was not what is known as an inspiring teacher, if personal magnetism and eloquence make a teacher inspiring, for his manner was deliberate, even

somewhat rustic, but he had those qualities of the sterling scientist which most appeal to the modern laboratory student. In 1876 Northwestern University conferred the degree of A.M. upon him, and in 1893 the degree of LL.D. The latter degree was given him also by his own university in 1912, and he had previously (1881) received a Ph.D. from the old University of Chicago. His private life was marked by uprightness, kindness, and sincerity. It has been said of him that he acknowledged but one God, never loved but one woman, and had but one ideal in his work, the spirit of true science.

[The "Memorial Address" by E. Davenport, *Trans. Ill. State Hort. Soc.*, n.s., L, 67–97, with bibliography, is decidedly the fullest and most valuable; it draws liberally upon some reminiscences by S. A. Forbes, *Alumni Quart. of the Univ. of Ill.*, July 1916. Other notices are Wm. Trelease in *Bot. Gaz.*, LXII, 153–54, and J. Barrett in *Phytopathology*, VIII, 1–4. See also "Scientific Writings of T. J. Burrill" in *Trans. Ind. State Hort. Soc.*, n.s., LI, 195–201, and Erwin F. Smith's estimate of his work in the historical introduction to his *Bacterial Diseases of Plants* (1920). For list of administrative positions held by Burrill see *Who's Who in America*, 1916–17.]   D. C. P.

BURRINGTON, GEORGE (*c.* 1680–February 1759), colonial governor of North Carolina, belonged to a family of good standing in the county of Devon, and was probably born in that shire. One member of his family is accredited by English historians as being the first gentleman of consequence to join the standard of William of Orange when that prince invaded England in 1688 (Sir James Mackintosh, *History of the Revolution in England in 1688*, 1834, ch. XV). The favor in which his family was held by the House of Hanover gained for Burrington a captain's commission in the British army before he was sent to America as governor of North Carolina. In 1732 he proudly declared: "I have served the crown in every reign since the Abdication of King James, & always was allowed to behave as became a Man of Honour, and the Family whose name I bear; their Services at the Revolution and during the life of King William of glorious memory I hope are not yet in Oblivion" (*Colonial Records of North Carolina*, III, 375). At a session of the Royal Council on Feb. 26, 1723, King George the First gave his approval to the appointment by the Lords Proprietors of Burrington, as governor of North Carolina. The latter took the oath of office at Edenton, the colonial capital, on Jan. 15, 1724. His first administration was of short duration, ending, after about a year and a half, when he was superseded by Sir Richard Everard, Baronet, who took the oath of office on July 17, 1725. Burrington had attempted to assault Chief Justice Christopher Gale, and, when that gentleman barricaded his house, had threatened to burn it or blow it up with gunpowder. Gale thereupon went to England to prefer charges, substantiated by the written statements of seven members of the Provincial Council, and Burrington was displaced in consequence. When his successor arrived, Burrington challenged the newcomer to single combat, and denounced him as a "calf's head," "noodle," and "ape, no more fit to be governor than a hog in the woods or Sancho Panza." For this outbreak he was indicted, but left Edenton before the case was tried, and it was later nolle-prossed. Notwithstanding his violent conduct, he had many strong friends in the colonial assembly. At the end of his first administration, and after Everard had qualified, the assembly in an address referred to "the great happiness which this Province lately enjoy'd" under Burrington, and referred to "his Carryage & behaviour being very Affable & courteous, his Justice very Exemplary & his care and Industry to promote . . . the welfare of this Province being very Eminent and Conspicuous" (*Ibid.*, II, 577–78).

After North Carolina became a royal province in 1729, governors were appointed by the king. One of King George's secretaries of state was the Duke of Newcastle. Some bond of friendship existed between Newcastle and Burrington in consequence of which Burrington was again appointed governor of North Carolina in 1731. In this second administration he rendered services of the greatest value to the colony. He laid out roads and built bridges, making personal inspections from time to time to see that they were kept in proper repair. He pushed to completion a highway from New Bern to the settlements further south; and another, of still greater length, running from the Virginia boundary to the banks of the Cape Fear River, was undertaken at his instance. He was largely instrumental in developing the Cape Fear section of North Carolina. Three different times he went on expeditions for the purpose of taking the soundings of the inlets, bars, and rivers of the province. He discovered and made known the channels of the Cape Fear River and Beaufort or Topsail inlets, theretofore unused and unknown. Often he made journeys on foot through dense forests and dangerous morasses, accompanied by only one man, finally arriving at some frontier settlement with the clothing almost entirely torn from his body. Once he lived on a single biscuit for three days. On these journeys he often carried considerable sums of money for distribution among the poorer families to relieve the hardships incident to their new location. Hugh

Williamson truly says of him: "He is not charged, nor was he chargeable, with fraud or corruption; for he despised rogues, whether they were small or great" (*History of North Carolina*, 1812, II, 14). He spent his private fortune in carrying on his work in North Carolina, never receiving a penny of salary, though he had the King's order for its payment. Nor was he reimbursed for his large personal expenditures in the interest of public works. He himself declared that the only reward he ever received was a vote of thanks from the colonial assembly. He was finally relieved from office at his own request in 1734. After his return to England he was the author of at least two works: *Seasonable Considerations on the Expendiency of a War with France* (1743) and *An Answer to Dr. William Brakenridge's Letter Concerning the Number of Inhabitants within the London Bills of Mortality* (1757). In February 1759 he was mysteriously murdered in the Bird Cage Walk, St. James's Park, London, and his body thrown in the Canal (*London Evening Post*, Feb. 24–27, 1759).

[The chief sources of information about Burrington are in the *Colonial Records of North Carolina*, especially those cited in the monograph *Gov. Geo. Burrington* (1896) by M. DeL. Haywood.]   M. DeL. H.

BURRITT, ELIHU (Dec. 8, 1810–Mar. 6, 1879), "The Learned Blacksmith," reformer, linguist, was born in New Britain, Conn. Named after his father, an eccentric shoemaker and farmer, he also derived from him an enthusiasm for impracticable ventures. From his mother, Elizabeth Hinsdale, who bore nine other children, he learned self-denial and whole-hearted devotion to the ideal of service. If, as a child, he tried to persuade her to borrow fewer sermons and more histories from the meager church library, he nevertheless made her deep religious feelings his own. Neither the district school nor a term at his brother's boarding-school satisfied his appetite for knowledge, and hence he imagined and solved quaint problems of mental arithmetic and learned Greek verbs while blowing the bellows at the smithy where he was an apprentice. At the age of twenty-seven he made in his Journal this entry, a typical one: "June 19, Sixty lines of Hebrew; thirty pages of French; ten pages of Cuvier's Theory of the Earth; eight lines of Syriac; ten lines of Danish; ten ditto Bohemian; nine ditto of Polish; fifteen names of stars; ten hours' forging." Overwork undermined the health of this narrow-chested, stouthanded youth, and for his entire life he paid the price in acute suffering. Awkward as he was, and in spite of excessive shyness, his clear blue eyes, his broad, sloping forehead, and his fine mouth compelled sympathy. With scarce a dollar in his pocket he set out from his native village in the year 1837 seeking work and a chance to further his self-education. Worcester, Mass., offered both. His attainments in all the European and several Asiatic languages reached the ear of Gov. Edward Everett, who referred to them in an address and offered him the advantages of Harvard, which Burritt refused. Although chagrined at such undesired publicity, he did, however, bring himself to accept lecture invitations.

While preparing a lecture on "the anatomy of the earth," he was so struck by the unity and interdependency of its parts that he ended by writing a plea for international peace. Into that cause, which had just lost its chief apostle by the death of William Ladd in 1841, Burritt now threw himself heart and soul. With the help of a business partner he founded at Worcester, in 1844, a weekly newspaper, the *Christian Citizen*. This truly international pacifist publication dragged Burritt deeply into debt before, in 1851, he was forced to abandon it.

During the Oregon crisis, when Burritt was also editing the *Advocate of Peace and Universal Brotherhood,* he besieged Congress with peace propaganda and cooperated with Friends in Manchester, England, in a picturesque exchange of "Friendly Addresses" between British and American cities, merchants, ministers, and laborers. According to Burritt eight hundred newspapers printed these "Friendly Addresses" (*Advocate of Peace and Universal Brotherhood,* February 1846, p. 56). He himself carried the "Friendly Address" from Edinburgh, with its impressive list of signatures, to Washington, where Calhoun and other senators expressed much interest in this "popular handshaking" across the Atlantic (Burritt, Manuscript Journal, Mar. 31, 1851).

This cooperation with British friends of peace led Burritt to cross the Atlantic in June 1846, and during that autumn he formed there the League of Universal Brotherhood. By 1850 this "world peace society" had, through his efforts, twenty thousand British and as many American signatures to its pledge of complete abstinence from all war. It sponsored a "Friendly Address" movement between British and French cities when war seemed imminent in 1852, Burritt personally delivering the friendly interchange of opinion to appropriate municipal officials in France. He also induced the League to sponsor "The Olive Leaf Mission," through which peace propaganda was inserted in forty influential Continental newspapers. This work was financed by woman Leaguers whom Burritt organized into sewing circles. Between 1850 and 1856 he estimated that the *Olive Leaves* reached monthly one million European readers.

Almost single-handed this enthusiast organized in 1848 the Brussels Peace Congress, which inaugurated the series held in the following years at Paris, Frankfort, London, Manchester, and Edinburgh. Burritt's Journals exhibit incredible activity which included traveling widely in Germany to enlist delegates and soliciting and gaining the cooperation of Victor Hugo, Lamartine, and distinguished French economists and philanthropists. To bring the American peace movement into this truly international peace organization, Burritt in 1850 organized eighteen state peace conventions, with the result that forty Americans attended the Frankfort Congress that year. These peace congresses won increasing attention from the European and British press, and Burritt's name was celebrated in popular periodicals like those of Douglas Jerrold, Charles Dickens, and Thomas Chambers, and ridiculed in *Blackwood's* and the influential London *Times.* At each Congress Burritt ably pled for such a Congress and Court of Nations as William Ladd had advocated.

The Crimean War interrupted this European peace work, and Burritt devoted more time to the related scheme of cheap international postage, and to plans for preventing civil war in his own country. Urging by pen and lecture the utilization of the public domain for compensated emancipation, he also organized a convention to stimulate interest in this plan, and during one winter traveled 10,000 miles from Maine to Iowa in its behalf.

Burritt, who had identified himself with the thoroughgoing anti-war group, opposed the Civil War on pacifist grounds, but he was appointed by Lincoln in 1863 as consular agent at Birmingham. In several volumes he described industrial and rural England with insight, vigor, and charm. From 1870 until his death in 1879 he lived in New Britain, devoting himself to the improvement of a few stony acres of land, to writing, and to teaching languages. He never married, but his entire life was rich in friendships.

Almost uniquely in the America of his generation, Burritt was capable of thinking in international terms. Deprecating sectarianism, he found solace in Quaker meetings and the Anglican ritual as well as in his own Congregationalism. His sympathies with free trade and labor were intelligent and realistic. Only two years after the publication of the *Communist Mani-*

festo (1848) he was advocating, in *Olive Leaves* printed in the German press, a strike of the workers of the world against war as the only alternative to a Congress and Court of Nations. In his numerous writings in behalf of peace he used statistical evidence skilfully, though his chief appeal was to the brotherhood of man. This maker of horseshoes and a Sanscrit grammar endured the most irksome poverty and physical suffering in order to devote himself to the greatest value he found in life, "the capacity and space of labouring for humanity."

[The chief sources of information about Elihu Burritt are his manuscript Journals, 28 vols. (1837–60) in the Lib. of the Inst. of New Britain, Conn., and his newspaper, the *Christian Citizen*, Worcester, Mass. (1844–51), a complete file of which is in the Am. Antiquarian Soc. A small portion of the Journals was included in the uncritical compilation of Chas. Northend, *Elihu Burritt: a Memorial Volume containing a Sketch of His Life and Labors* (1879). Of Burritt's sixteen published volumes the most characteristic are, *Sparks from the Anvil* (1846); *Thoughts of Things at Home and Abroad, with a Memoir by Mary Howitt* (1854); *Lectures and Speeches* (1866); *Walk from London to John O'Groat's* (1864); and *Ten Minute Talks* (1873).]   M. E. C.

BURROUGHS, JOHN (Apr. 3, 1837–Mar. 29, 1921), author, was descended from early seventeenth century settlers in New England. Ephraim Burroughs, his great-grandfather, born in 1740, removed to a farm in Delaware County, N. Y., and Eden, son of Ephraim, in 1795 settled near the village of Beaver Dam (later called Roxbury). Among the children of Eden was Chauncey A. Burroughs, farmer, the father of John Burroughs. The latter's maternal grandfather, Edmund Kelly, of Irish descent, born in Dutchess County, N. Y., in 1767, was with Washington at Valley Forge; his maternal grandmother, Lovina Liscom, was a practical housewife. Among their children was Amy Kelly, the mother of John Burroughs; like the father, she was an Old-School Baptist. In his own view Burroughs derived from his paternal ancestry his love of peace and solitude and his intellectual impetus, and from his maternal, his love of nature and introspective habit and idealism. The seventh of ten children, he was born on a farm near Roxbury. Among his brothers, "homebodies, rather timid, non-aggressive men . . . the kind of men that are so often crowded to the wall" (as he described them), he felt himself closest to Hiram, "who was curious about strange lands, but who lost heart and hope as soon as he got beyond the sight of his native hills" (*Life and Letters*, I, 17). It is impossible to exaggerate Burroughs's own love of his native hills, the lower pastoral ranges of the Catskills, where he lived and wrote during most of his long life. He early took delight in exploring the fields and woods and

especially in watching the birds, the passenger pigeons that came in armies, or the beautiful wood-warblers whose names he did not know.

After some schooling in the neighborhood, he went to teach, as a youth of seventeen, at Tongore, in Ulster County, and saved enough money to study for a time in the Ashland Collegiate Institute in Greene County; then returned to teach at Tongore. About this time he began writing essays, Johnsonian in style. In 1856 he studied at Cooperstown Seminary, where his literary enthusiasms included Wordsworth, Saint-Pierre's *Studies of Nature,* and especially Emerson, whom he read "in a sort of ecstacy. I got him in my blood, and he colored my whole intellectual outlook" (*Ibid.,* I, 41). For six months he taught school near Polo, Ill. On Sept 12, 1857, when but twenty years old, he married Ursula North, whom he had come to know at Tongore, "A self-complacent, thrifty, and forceful young woman, thirteen months his senior" (*Ibid.,* I, 44), whom he informed, a week after the wedding, "If I live, I shall be an author. My life will be one of study" (*Ibid.,* I, 80). It was nearly two years before a teaching post at East Orange, N. J., enabled them to set up housekeeping. At the age of twenty-three he wrote an essay, "Expression," so Emersonian in thought and manner that Lowell, before printing it in the *Atlantic Monthly* (Nov. 1860), looked through Emerson's writings for it. Unsigned, it went into *Poole's Index* as Emerson's work. His self-reliance thus challenged, Burroughs now began to write for the *New York Leader* a series of nature essays entitled "From the Back Country." The necessity of securing a livelihood, however, kept him at his task of teaching, except when he abandoned it for the study of medicine, and that in turn, on one occasion, to write "Waiting," a poem first published in *Knickerbocker's,* March 1863, and frequently reprinted in later years. In the spring of 1863 he began to take a livelier interest in the study of wild flowers, owing partly to the influence of a friend, a botanist named Eddy; and by summer he was so enthusiastic over the study of birds that he said he could think or talk of nothing else—such was the effect of his chancing upon Audubon's book in the library at West Point. Breaking away from his home country in October 1863, he went to Washington, where for nearly ten years he was to sit at a desk in the Currency Bureau of the Treasury Department. In Washington he formed the most important friendship of his life, and wrote his first books. The friendship was with Walt Whitman, in whose poetry he had become interested at least two years before their meeting in the autumn of 1863, when Burroughs was twenty-six and Whitman forty-four. They had walks and talks together, and oyster-eating orgies, and sometimes Burroughs accompanied Whitman in his hospital rounds. "I loved him," said Burroughs, "as I never loved any man. We were companionable without talking. I owe more to him than to any other man in the world. He brooded me; he gave me things to think of; he taught me generosity, breadth, and an all-embracing charity" (*Ibid.*, I, 113). His complete acceptance of Whitman found expression in his first published book, *Notes on Walt Whitman as Poet and Person* (1867), to which Whitman contributed the title, some of the chapter-titles, a large part of the notes in the second edition (1871), passages of the text itself, and much detailed revision: "I have no doubt," Burroughs conceded in 1920, "that half the book is his" (*Ibid.*, I, 129).

Meantime, in the spring of 1865, he published the first of his *Atlantic* essays on nature, "With the Birds," which became the initial chapter of his first book on nature. It was followed by "In the Hemlocks" and other essays. The rebound from his clerical work, from the iron door of the Treasury vault, was sending Burroughs back to the fields and woods of his boyhood. His love of his Northern home country, his fresh poetic feeling for the beauty and eager life of birds, united with an accuracy of observation superior to that of Thoreau, and a gift for expression neither too homespun nor too cultivated, resulted in writing that he probably never excelled in all his subsequent career as an author. As early as 1866, however, he informed Benton, "I think I have had my say about the birds, for the present, at least. Sometimes I may make a book of these, and other articles, but am in no hurry" (*Ibid.*, I, 118). He was in no hurry chiefly because Whitman as poet and person was absorbing his energies; it was five years before the book on the birds, *Wake-Robin* (1871), so named by Whitman, actually appeared. It was favorably received, William Dean Howells, for example, writing, "The dusk and cool and quiet of the forest seem to wrap the reader . . . It is sort of summer vacation to turn its pages. It is written with a grace which continually subordinates itself to the material" (*Atlantic Monthly*, August 1871). In the same year Burroughs was sent by the Treasury Department to England, where he incidentally gained the matter of four essays published in *Winter Sunshine* (1875). Reviewing this book in the *Nation* (Jan. 27, 1876), Henry James described the author as "a sort of reduced, but also more humourous, more available, and more sociable Thoreau" and conceded his possession of "a style sometimes indeed idiomatic and unfinished to a fault, but capable of remarkable felicity and vividness." Burroughs was now safely launched upon his literary career; a third nature book soon followed, *Birds and Poets* (1877), and for the rest of his long life he published at the average rate of one book every two years.

Upon leaving Washington in 1873, Burroughs returned to his native mountain country, with which he became associated as intimately as Wordsworth with the English Lakes. He purchased a farm and built a house, which he named "Riverby," near Esopus, on the west shore of the Hudson about eighty miles from New York, and there cultivated fruit-trees, berries, and grapes. In 1895 he built, in the hills about a mile from his river home, a secluded bar-covered cabin which he called "Slabsides." The summers following 1908 he was accustomed to spend at a farmhouse, "Woodchuck Lodge," on the old home farm near Roxbury, using the hay-barn as his literary workshop. In these several retreats he read and wrote, observed wild life, and welcomed friends and admirers; in his last years, indeed, when he was regarded not only as a naturalist but also as a sage and prophet, all manner of persons made the pilgrimage to "Slabsides," and many of them reported their experience in magazines and newspapers. Through innumerable photographs, his erect, substantial figure, steady eyes, long rustic beard, and pervasive air of repose, formed an image familiar to readers throughout the country, an image that blended easily with a background of woods and pastures and long sloping hills. Despite his attachment to his home region, however, Burroughs traveled extensively—in the Western and Southern states, to Jamaica and Bermuda, to Hawaii, in Canada, in the Maine woods, in Europe (*Fresh Fields*, 1885). He cruised with the Harriman Expedition to Alaska (*Far and Near*, 1904). He camped in the Yosemite with John Muir, and in the Yellowstone with President Roosevelt (*Camping and Tramping with Roosevelt*, 1907). He was associated with Roosevelt also in a campaign against the "Nature Fakers,"—writers who colored and embroidered the facts of natural history —a campaign opened by his *Atlantic* paper, "Real and Sham Natural History" (1903) and brought to a climax by the President four years later in an interview given to *Everybody's Magazine*. Among the friends of his last years were Thomas Edison and Henry Ford. Honorary degrees were conferred upon him by Yale (1910), Colgate (1911), and the University of Georgia (1915).

The interval between the departure of Burroughs from the Capital in 1873 and his death in 1921 was almost a half century, a period in which his outward life pursued an even tenor, while his inner life, recorded in his books, was undergoing significant changes. The title of his 1877 volume, *Birds and Poets,* is symbolical; he had had his say about the birds, and had reached the end of his most poetic epoch. His next epoch, which may be said to begin with *Locusts and Wild Honey* in 1879 and to close with *Leaf and Tendril* in 1908, was one in which his main passion was "Straight Seeing and Straight Thinking," that is, deliberate, faithful observation accompanied by reasonable inference, as opposed to the careless use of the senses and the hasty guessing that characterize most people in their contact with nature. His poetic feeling for nature was less, his scientific study of fact greater, both in his reading and in his saunterings afield. Yet he did not adopt the method of science; he wanted the facts in so far as he could secure them without method, by the simple expedient of random and affectionate observation. When Maeterlinck called Fabre "the insects' Homer," Burroughs pointed out that he was really the insects' Sherlock Holmes; and he himself was assuredly a Sherlock Holmes, the most proficient detective of nature in American literature.

Gradually, however, Burroughs drifted into what may be designated as another period in his literary history, a period of lively enthusiasm for science that accompanied, rather than supplanted, his detective observation. More and more he was reading books of science; in 1883, for instance, *The Origin of Species* and *The Descent of Man,* and in 1887 the work of John Fiske. The next year he asked Benton, "Can you still read the great poets? I cannot. I have not looked in Shakespeare for years, and do not care to . . . I read Wordsworth a little, and Tennyson, but expect by and by I shall read none of the old poets" (*Ibid.,* I, 294). Though not wholly inconsistent in enjoying field observation and scorning laboratories and museums, he made himself a little absurd by celebrating the results of modern science while deploring the methods necessarily employed in the attainment of those results. Earnestly did he welcome the results offered by geology and biology, including the "cosmic chill," because he believed exact objective knowledge to be better than the shifting subjectivity of the poets and the "pretty little anthropomorphic views of things" that religion proposes. His writings in this period express the same time spirit that actuated John Fiske, who by 1885 had substantially secured American recognition of the Darwinian theory of life; though it was not until

1900, when he published *The Light of Day,* that Burroughs fully and enthusiastically set forth his indorsement of the results of Victorian science. The light of day is reason, which demolished the authority of revealed religion and establishes the only true interpretation of the universe. Seeking truth, science is, indeed, profoundly religious: "Think you the man of science does not also find God? that Huxley and Darwin and Tyndall do not find God, though they may hesitate to use that name? Whoever finds truth finds God, does he not? whoever loves truth loves God?" Literature and religion, in the old sense, are passing away, but science is probably only "in the heat of its forenoon work." Great will be its high noon!

But when, a dozen years later, it seemed to Burroughs that science had reached the meridian, his glad faith in reason had departed and he had come to a fresh period in his inner history. "In the Noon of Science," an essay in *The Summit of the Years* (1914), while conceding the achievements of natural science, is in the main a criticism of science on the ground that the civilization it creates is "like an engine running without a headlight": it may draw us to our destruction. The salvation of society depends upon "vision," or "intuitive perception of the great fundamental truths of the inner spiritual world," and for this we must look not to those who are intent upon explaining life in terms of physics and chemistry but to "the great teachers and prophets, poets and mystics." To one of these, Walt Whitman, he had long been devoted, without, however, being able to reconcile the spiritual *aplomb* of *Leaves of Grass* with the rational certitude of the successors of Darwin and Huxley. In his mature book on his friend, *Whitman, A Study* (1896), Burroughs had asserted that Whitman "does not have to stretch himself at all to match in the human and emotional realm the stupendous discoveries and deductions of science." To match science by emotionally absorbing the whole of nature is not, of course, to enter into the point of view of science and proceed to spiritual conquest from that point of view. In Bergson, however, whom Burroughs began reading in 1911, it seemed that modern thought had its most acceptable leader, a man at once scientist, philosopher, poet, and a prophet of the soul, proving at last that such words as "soul" and "spirit" stand "for real truths." Where Whitman only felt, Bergson demonstrated the immanence of spirit in nature and so enabled us to enter joyously into the fellowship of creation. The exhilarating influence of this new master dominates *Time and Change* (1912), *The Summit of the Years* (1913),

The Breath of Life (1915), and *Under the Apple-Trees* (1916).

Under the apple-trees in the years of the World War, Burroughs brooded less upon Bergson and the fellowship of creation, and more upon Germany and the fellowship of destruction. "The gods of science," whom he had always sought loyally to serve, were, he thought, with Germany; "the gods of the moral law," whom he had comparatively neglected, with the Allies. He now ranged his mind and heart with the latter, believing that "our blended inheritance from Greece and Judea and the meditative Orient" faced the prospect of extinction; although he had never largely availed himself of this humanistic and religious inheritance, in the hour of crisis it seemed to him of supreme importance. He was frankly savage in his hatred of the Germans on the ground that they were savage. "When told [1918] that if the war lasted much longer, he could qualify as one of Whitman's 'race of savage old men,' he admitted it was so; that the war poisoned his blood and allowed to come to the surface feelings that had seldom found expression through all his life" (*Ibid.*, II, 208, 267).

Between 1919 and 1922 came his last four books, in which he sought, with an increasing melancholy, to make the best of a dubious universe. "I am trying again," he confessed, "to read Bergson's *Creative Evolution,* with poor success. . . . Bergson's work now seems to me a mixture of two things that won't mix—metaphysics and natural science." Faced anew with the necessity of choosing between a philosophy of intuition and scientific reason, Burroughs showed the fundamental bent of his mind by remarking that if the heart often knows what the head does not, it is because the intellect tells it so. "The animals live by instinct, and we live largely in our emotions, but it is reason that has placed man at the head of the animal kingdom." By reason he means essentially the reason of science, which knows nothing of the gods of the moral law but insists that, "Hedge or qualify as we will, man is a part of Nature. . . . Can there be anything in the universe that is not of the Universe? Can we make two or three out of the one?" Finally, in "Facing the Mystery," the last essay in his last book, Burroughs with admirable integrity recants the greatest emotional enthusiasm of his life, his devotion to Whitman, poet of immortality, and accepts the prospect of personal extinction. At the time of his death, and, indeed, for the last four decades of his life, Burroughs may plausibly be said to have had "more of a personal following, more contacts with his readers, both through correspondence and in person, than any

other American author has had, and, probably, more than any other author of modern times" (*Ibid.*, I, 247). The Sage of "Slabsides" was a national figure, picturesque in his simplicity of life, exact and sympathetic in his observation of nature, friendly alike to the voice of science and of essential religion; he was poet, detective, and priest of nature, and the greatest of these, in the public mind, was the priest, the wise man who in a time of decaying creeds expounded a way of life that could free men from Mammon, frivolity, and insincerity and render them content to accept the universe with all its beauty, wonder, and apparent evil. He continued the work of the three authors of the nineteenth century whom he most admired,—Carlyle, Emerson, and Whitman— bringing to his spiritual quest a far more scientific frame of mind than any one of them had possessed, but also, it must be admitted, a far smaller moral and spiritual endowment and an inferior order of literary talent. In the decades beginning with 1870, when American literature was feeling the scientific impulse, the desire to be faithful to locality, to the facts of human life, and to the phenomena of nature, Burroughs served his time by showing how blunt the eyes and ears of writers generally are, and thus he played a part in the rise of that latter-day movement in our literature known as realism. Passing beyond the bounds of literature, his influence extended to a popular impulse of the epoch,—"nature study," both within and without the schools. He was an inspiration to immense numbers of people who with more or less seriousness pursued the study of birds and flowers in the field, and of geology and biology in the library. If the scientists were unable to think of him as one of themselves, he assuredly served their ends by stimulating popular interest in the facts of nature.

Time will doubtless adjudge Burroughs most significant, however, not as a sage or observer of nature, but as a writer by whom the American "nature essay" was definitely established as a literary *genre*. This form of expression emerged, in the American romantic movement, by means of the Transcendental emotional interest in nature and the scientific interest manifested by naturalists and travelers. Both interests were marked in Thoreau. Thoreau was followed by Lowell, Wilson Flagg, T. W. Higginson, and many others, but it was Burroughs who employed the form with the greatest frequency and most thoroughly exploited its capacities. His debt to Thoreau was probably much greater than he was willing to acknowledge, and he may have been under obligations to other predecessors; but to him belongs what measure of credit may attach to bringing the nature essay into widespread vogue (a vogue declining since the World War) and of contributing to American literature a long series of essays marked by delicate feeling, fine observation, honest thought, and a style simple and natural without affront to the traditions of English prose.

[There is much autobiography in the writings of John Burroughs, with which should be included the "Autobiographical Sketches" in Clara Barrus's *Our Friend, John Burroughs* (1914) and the first 132 pages of the volume entitled *My Boyhood* (1922). To the latter, Julian Burroughs contributed a concluding chapter entitled "My Father." Clara Barrus has written, in addition to the book named above, *John Burroughs, Boy and Man* (1920), and the official biography in two volumes, *The Life and Letters of John Burroughs* (1925), and has edited *The Heart of Burroughs' Journals* (1928). Associated with Burroughs for the last twenty years of his life, she faithfully accumulated an immense amount of material, "heavily taxing," as she conceded, her "powers of selection"; believing her subject "worthy of immortal regard," she made her work a Boswellian record. Clifton Johnson, after many interviews, published a readable and generally accurate work, *John Burroughs Talks: His Reminiscences and Comments* (1922). Accounts of others' interviews, in magazines and newspapers, are innumerable. The correspondence of *John Burroughs and Ludella Peck* (1925) covers the years 1892–1912. There is much matter relating to Burroughs in Horace Traubel's *With Walt Whitman in Camden* (3 vols., 1906–14). Of works of scholarship and criticism, two may be mentioned: Norman Foerster's *Nature in Am. Lit.* (1923), ch. IX, and Philip M. Hicks's dissertation on *The Development of the Natural Hist. Essay in Am. Lit.* (1924), ch. VI.]   N. F.

BURROUGHS, JOHN CURTIS (Dec. 2, 1817–Apr. 21, 1892), Baptist clergyman, educator, was born in Stamford, Delaware County, N. Y. He entered Yale at twenty-two, graduated three years later (1842), and was married to Elvira S. Fields of New Haven the following year. He was a divinity student at Hamilton Literary and Theological Institution until 1846. After a year as a Baptist clergyman in the little town of Waterford, N. Y., and five years in a pulpit in West Troy, he left New York state for the rapidly growing city of Chicago (1852), to become pastor of the First Baptist church. It was here that his career of distinction in education took definite form. The community itself was swiftly changing and expanding, and Burroughs took active interest in its educational problems. Three years after his arrival, he was offered the presidency of Shurtleff College, which he declined. But in the following year he gave up his pastorate to engage in the movement which resulted, largely through his own tireless industry, in the establishment of the (old) University of Chicago. Stephen A. Douglas had given impetus to the undertaking in 1855 by his gift of a ten-acre tract. Burroughs was elected the first president of the University in 1857 and remained in this position until 1873. For the next four years he was its

chancellor. Financial difficulties forced the institution to close its doors in 1886, and the buildings were torn down. Burroughs, who lived in the immediate neighborhood, never thereafter allowed himself to look at the spot where they had stood. He served on the Chicago Board of Education, with special supervision over the high schools, from 1880 to 1883, when he was made assistant superintendent of schools, a position he held until his death.

[T. W. Goodspeed, *A Hist. of the Univ. of Chicago* (1916); *Obit. Record Grads. Yale Univ.*, 1890–1900; *Colgate Univ., Gen. Cat., 1819–1919*; *Univ. of Chicago, Annual Register*, 1925–26; *Chicago Tribune*, Apr. 22, 1892.]   M.A.K.

BURROWES, EDWARD THOMAS (July 25, 1852–Mar. 19, 1918), manufacturer and inventor, was born at Sherbrooke, Canada, the son of Ambrose and Jane (Hall) Burrowes. He removed with his parents shortly before his fifteenth birthday to Portland, Me., which became his residence until his death. After working several years with Hayes & Douglas, dealers in crockery, he entered in 1873 the Maine Wesleyan Seminary at Kent's Hill. Upon graduation he matriculated at Wesleyan University in 1876, but left during his freshman year. While at seminary and college he had supported himself through his own efforts, chiefly by the manufacture of screens. After leaving school he turned naturally to the production of screens and through intense industry and business capacity built up the largest screen factory in the world. He was a man of considerable inventive capacity as well as a business executive. His first patent, that of a window screen, was taken out in 1878, and between that date and 1919 over forty patents were either secured by him or assigned to him. These patents fall into four main divisions: (1) window screens; (2) spring actuated curtains and shades; (3) automobile accessories; (4) folding tables, particularly card and billiard tables. Burrowes built up a large manufacturing business in curtains and shades and is credited with inventing the first curtains used in passenger cars, and of manufacturing ninety per cent of those used (1918) in railroad and street cars. These were manufactured by the Curtain Supply Company of Chicago of which he was president. The E. T. Burrowes Company of Portland produced not only screens but billiard and pool tables, folding card tables, and folding chairs.

Outside of his business affairs Burrowes was noted for his sustained interest in charitable and educational projects, especially those connected with the Methodist Episcopal Church. His grandfather had been a class leader under

Wesley, and he, himself, was an active member of the Chestnut Street Church of Portland. He practically built a church in the Italian section of that city, was a trustee of the Maine Wesleyan Seminary at Kent's Hill, and of Boston University (1901–18). He is described as "quiet in manner, reticent in conversation, genial and pleasant to his intimate friends. His qualities best shone in his home life and among his business associates" (Minutes of the Board of Trustees of Boston University, Apr. 11, 1918). He was married on Oct. 4, 1880, to Frances E. Norcross of Portland.

[*Zion's Herald*, Mar. 27, 1918; *Bostonia*, Mar. 1918; *Daily Eastern Argus* (Portland), Mar. 20, 1918; *Who's Who in America*, 1918–19.]   H.U.F.

BURROWES, THOMAS HENRY (Nov. 16, 1805–Feb. 25, 1871), politician, educator, was born at Strasburg, Pa., the son of Thomas Bredin Burrowes, an Irish immigrant, and Anne (Smith) Burrowes. His education was more noteworthy for its varied sources than for any great profundity: private tutors, Trinity College, Dublin, a Quebec classical school, and Yale College, are supposed to have assisted in the project that Amos Ellmaker, a Lancaster lawyer, completed when Thomas Henry was admitted to the bar in 1829.

Burrowes was a politician by choice and an educator by accident. He was elected to the lower house of the Pennsylvania legislature in 1831 and 1832, where, as a member of the Whig minority, he distinguished himself only by acquiring influence in his state party such that he could give valuable aid in the election of Joseph Ritner as governor in 1835, and secure for himself an appointment as secretary of the commonwealth, to which were attached the duties of state superintendent of schools. Burrowes, Thaddeus Stevens [*q.v.*], and Theophilus Fenn became the "Kitchen Cabinet" of the Ritner administration, and under their leadership every public and private measure was shaped to serve political ends. So well satisfied was the triumvirate with their administration that as the days of office-holding waned they became more and more loath to surrender their scepters to the incoming Porter régime. The Anti-Masonic Whig party, of which Burrowes was state chairman, was defeated by alleged frauds at the Philadelphia polls. Instead of submitting the evidence of fraud to the legislature, the secretary, in a proclamation dated Oct. 15, 1838, called on "the good people" of the state to "treat the election of the 9th instant as if we had not been defeated" (*Pennsylvanian*, Dec. 8, 1838)—an invitation to revolution that precipitated the bloodless Buckshot War. In an attempt to seat the defeated Anti-Masonic Whigs of Philadelphia in the House of Representatives Ritner called in the state militia and appealed to President Van Buren for aid, while the tainted but victorious Democrats brought a mob of thugs from their constituency to aid them in the organization of the legislature. The militia, recruited largely from the City of Brotherly Love, refused to assist the defeated governor; the President of the United States was not interested; and the threatening mob was in possession of the senate galleries, so Burrowes left office through a window in the rear of the senate chamber to take up the more peaceful pursuit of agriculture. The charge of treason, although seriously considered, was never pressed.

Paradoxically, a man, totally ignorant of the requirements of a state educational system, and who had voted against the free school measure, was destined to play a leading rôle in the establishment of Pennsylvania's public schools. Burrowes, during the Ritner administration, revised the school law of 1834 and organized the free school system of the state, the most distinctly creditable feature of the régime. Although he insisted in his *Report* of Feb. 19, 1837, that only the "elements of a good business education—reading, writing, and arithmetic" should be taught in the common schools, and that any individual who had not learned his "three R's" before he reached the age of fifteen could not learn them afterward, he became and remained the oracle of the Pennsylvania educational crusade until his death. He gave advice on almost every important school measure brought before the legislature after 1836, founded the *Pennsylvania School Journal* in 1852 and edited it for eighteen years, served as state superintendent of schools, 1860–63, organized the Soldiers' Orphans' Schools after the Civil War, and died as president of Pennsylvania Agricultural College. None of Burrowes's projects were cut from whole cloth, for his strength was in his sagacious sifting of practical ideas from the mass of suggestions proffered by his contemporaries. Hence he could set the public school system in motion during 1835–38, but in 1860, when the system had passed the formative stage, he was unable to contribute further to the growth of his creation.

He was married on Apr. 6, 1837, to Salome Jane Carpenter, by whom he had fifteen children.

[Burrowes, the politician, appears in W. H. Egle, "The Buckshot War," *Pa. Mag. Hist. and Biog.*, July 1899, pp. 137–56, and in the files of the *Nat. Gazette and Lit. Reg.*, and the *Pennsylvanian* (both Phila.) for the period Oct. to Dec. 1838; the educator is discussed in *Pa. Sch. Jour.*, Apr. 1871, pp, 281–85, and in J. P. Wickersham, *Hist. of Educ. in Pa.* (1886), pp. 346–53.]
                T.D.M.

BURROWS, JULIUS CÆSAR (Jan. 9, 1837–Nov. 16, 1915), senator, son of William and Marie Burrows, was born in Northeast, Erie County, Pa. As a boy of seven years he heard Daniel Webster speak and the impression made by the great orator mastered the youthful auditor. Later, when the Burrows family removed to Ashtabula County, Ohio, Burrows came under the influence of Benjamin F. Wade and Joshua R. Giddings, whose children attended the school he taught. In 1859, he secured the principalship of a female seminary at Richland, Mich. In 1861 he was admitted to the bar, formed a partnership with A. A. Knappen, an able and successful lawyer, and began practise in Kalamazoo, which city ever after was his home. He came into local prominence by his stump speeches in the first Lincoln campaign, and Gov. Blair commissioned him a captain in the 17th Michigan Infantry, a position given primarily for recruiting ability. On Aug. 22, 1862, the regiment left for the front, on Sept. 4 it took part in the bloody battle of South Mountain, and three days later it fought at Antietam. The arduous and disastrous battles at Fredericksburg sapped Burrows's strength, and when the 17th was sent to the western army he was transferred to staff duty. After three more engagements, his failing health and the value of his services on the stump led to his resignation. He became the law partner of Henry F. Severens, afterward United States district judge. He spoke in the second Lincoln campaign, when, to use his own phrase, "Sheridan's guns were knocking every plank out of the Chicago platform." In 1865–67 he was prosecuting attorney for Kalamazoo County. Entering the national House of Representatives in 1873, he found the Republican party broken by dissensions and by the Crédit Mobilier scandals. He ranged himself with the reform element in the earliest efforts to subject the railroads to government control. Having been trained from youth in the camp of the abolitionists, and having fought to preserve the Union, he naturally worked in Congress with those who believed in securing civil rights to the negro by federal bayonets if necessary. Defeated for the nomination in 1874, he was reëlected to Congress in 1878, and continuously thereafter (except to the 48th Congress, 1883–85) until elected to the Senate in 1894. In the House he was an influential member of the small group (including Thomas B. Reed, William McKinley, and Joseph G. Cannon) that dominated the Republican side. With eloquence he supported party policies when in the majority; and with all the resources of an alert and trained parliamentarian he obstructed or defeated the aims of the Democrats when that

party was in control. As a member of the Committee on Ways and Means he had an active share in arranging tariff schedules. On the stump he attained such a reputation as a vote-winning speaker that wherever the political battle raged most fiercely, from Maine to California, he was called to defend or to expound Republican policies. His honorable military service took the sting out of his advocacy of the Harrison "Force Bill." He marched with his party through the wilderness of silver coinage and came to victory for "sound money" in the McKinley campaign of 1896. If he was not a leader, he was an effective supporter of leaders.

When he was elected to the Senate in 1894, his work in the House was permitted to count in the matter of committee assignments. As chairman of the Committee on Privileges and Elections, he established a precedent by causing the Senate to exclude Senator Matthew S. Quay, who had been appointed by the governor of Pennsylvania to fill the vacancy caused by the failure of the state legislature to elect. While able constitutional lawyers, like George F. Hoar, took issue with Burrows (maintaining that a state should not be suffered to go without full representation in the Senate) the arguments of the latter prevailed, and the case was decided against seating Senator Quay, in spite of his political prestige. In both House and Senate Burrows worked to make effective the laws against polygamous marriages in Utah. After three years' investigation of the case of Senator Reed Smoot, Burrows reported from the Committee on Privileges and Elections a resolution unseating that senator; but the Senate voted otherwise. The decision, however, was influenced largely by the belief that polygamy had ceased to be practised among the Mormons. Also the personality and manifest ability of Senator Smoot had much to do with the vote in his favor. Burrows attained the height of senatorial ambition by being assigned a place on the Committee on Finance, a position to which his House service on Ways and Means gave him claims over those of Senator Thomas A. Platt of New York, who was Burrows's senior in senatorial service. The Finance Committee, under the able leadership of Nelson A. Aldrich, was considering the methods of changing the financial system so as to avert money panics by broadening the basis of note circulation. The Vreeland-Aldrich Act of 1908 was a preliminary step. That act created the Monetary Commission, of which body Burrows became an active member. The Commission made a study of the general subject of the currency, and the years of investigation and discussion prepared the way for the present Federal Reserve Act. When Burrows came up for reëlection in 1910, the younger element of the party had been brought into prominence by the intensity of the first McKinley campaign against the free coinage of silver. Michigan had enacted a law whereby the people might indicate to the legislature their preference for senators. Burrows announced his adherence to this method. Defeated by Charles E. Townsend he retired from the Senate Mar. 3, 1911; but as a member of the Monetary Commission he served until the submission of the Commission report, Jan. 9, 1912. After a public life covering half a century, he spent his remaining years in retirement at Kalamazoo. His career may be summed up in Joseph G. Cannon's laconic phrase: "You always found Burrows nearest the load."

Burrows was married twice: on Jan. 29, 1856 to Jennie S. Hibbard of Harpersfield, Ohio; and on Dec. 25, 1867, to Frances S. Peck of Richmond, Mich.

[Wm. Dana Orcutt, *Burrows of Mich. and the Republican Party* (1917); *Who's Who in America*, 1914–15; *Detroit Jour.*, Nov. 17, 1915.]   C.M.

BURROWS, WILLIAM (Oct. 6, 1785–Sept. 5, 1813), naval officer, was born at Kinderton, near Philadelphia. His father was Lieut.-Col. W. W. Burrows, first commandant of the United States Marine Corps, after its reorganization as such in 1798 (Richard S. Collum, *History of the United States Marines,* 1890), who afforded his son an excellent education, both in the classics and in modern languages. William was warranted a midshipman in November 1799 and joined the 24-gun ship *Portsmouth* in the following January, under the gallant though eccentric Capt. Daniel McNeill. After a cruise to France, during which two French privateers were captured, he obtained a furlough of several months, for the purpose of perfecting himself in navigation and the French language. In 1803, as acting lieutenant, he joined the *Constitution,* serving in her throughout the Tripolitan war. In 1808 he commanded a gunboat in the Delaware flotilla, engaged in enforcing the embargo law. In 1809 he was transferred to the *President,* Capt. Bainbridge, and then to the *Hornet,* Capt. Hunt, as first lieutenant, in which vessel he gave proof, during a violent gale, of intrepidity and sound seamanship.

Discovering that he was outranked by certain of his former juniors, Burrows sent in his resignation, which, however, was not accepted by Secretary Hamilton, who instead offered the young officer a furlough of nearly a year. This was accepted and spent in a voyage to India and China as officer of a merchant ship, the *Thomas Pen-*

rose, which on the return voyage was captured by a British ship and taken into Barbados. Paroled shortly afterward, Burrows returned home and was given command of the sloop-of-war *Enterprise,* 16 guns. Sailing from Portsmouth on Sept. 5, 1813, he fell in the next day with the British brig *Boxer* of about equal strength, which, with colors nailed to the mast, fired several shots in challenge and closed with the American ship. A sharp action of some forty-five minutes at close quarters ensued, in which Burrows gave proof of great gallantry and tactical resourcefulness. At 4 p. m. the fire of the *Boxer,* which had been repeatedly raked and had lost her main-topmast, ceased, and the vessel was surrendered. Burrows, who had been wounded but had remained on deck to direct the fight, was later mortally wounded by a canister shot, and lived only long enough to receive the surrender of the British ship, whose brave commander, Capt. Blythe, had been cut in two by a cannon ball. The *Enterprise* and her capture were brought into Portland, Me., where the two commanders were buried side by side. As this was the first American naval success since the loss of the *Chesapeake,* it was hailed with delight, and Congress passed a resolution of praise and regret, and presented a gold medal to Burrows's next of kin. He died unmarried.

[J. Fenimore Cooper, *Hist. of the Navy of the U. S.* (1839); John Howard Brown, *Am. Naval Heroes* (1899); *Analectic Mag.,* II, 396–403; *Port Folio,* 3 ser., III, 114–26.]   E.B.

BURSON, WILLIAM WORTH (Sept. 22, 1832–Apr. 10, 1913), inventor, manufacturer, was born on his father's farm near Utica, Venango County, Pa., the son of Samuel and Mary (Henry) Burson. When he was nine years old his parents migrated in stages to McDonough County, Ill., and a year later settled in Fulton County where young Burson passed most of his boyhood and early manhood, sharing the experiences of pioneer life which included a limited education. This he augmented later when, with his own savings, he entered Lombard University, Galesburg, Ill., graduating with the first class in 1856. Reared to the occupation of farming and early developing considerable mechanical ingenuity, Burson became much interested in the improvement of farm machinery, his first work in this field being the designing of a self-rake reaper in 1858. He then turned to grain binders and on June 26, 1860, received a patent for a twine binder. This was attached to his self-rake reaper and operated by hand. Twine, however, was not easily obtained, and Burson adapted his machine to use wire. On Feb. 26, 1861, he obtained a patent on this improvement and that year twenty-five binders were made and used in the harvests from Vandalia, Ill., as far north as Red Wing, Minn. The following year fifty more were made, one of which was entered in the great reaper trial at Dixon, Ill., and proved a decided sensation. Emerson & Company of Rockford, Ill., manufacturers of the Manny reaper, immediately contracted to build 1,100 binders for Burson who in 1863 moved with his family from Yates City, Knox County, Ill., to Rockford. In the course of building these machines he devised and patented two improvements, Mar. 3 and Aug. 11, 1863, respectively. Prejudice against wire binders, however, developed, and their cost at war prices operated against them; while the machines were eventually sold, a profitable market could not be established and their manufacture was discontinued. Burson then returned to twine binders, patenting certain improvements in 1864–65 which resulted in a practical machine. The following year he began experimenting with automatic knitting machinery and in the succeeding twelve years devised and patented a number of machines for the manufacture of knit goods and hose. On Apr. 23, 1870, the first hose were knit on his machine in Rockford, and in 1872, with the perfection of his parallel row machine, Rockford's great knitting industry was definitely launched. In 1878 Burson withdrew from the knitting business to devote his whole time to invention, and in the succeeding thirteen years made many improvements in knitting and grain harvesting machinery, totalling about fifty patents. In 1892 he organized the Burson Manufacturing Company for the manufacture of knitting machinery and accepted the vice-presidency of the Burson Knitting Company, manufacturer of knit goods. He married Emily S. Wilson of New Jersey, Oct. 5, 1856, who with three children survived him at the time of his death in Rockford.

[R. L. Ardrey, *Am. Ag. Implements* (1894); Newton Bateman, *Hist. Encyc. of Ill.* (1916), vol. II; *Hist. of Winnebago County, Ill.* (1877); Chas. A. Church, *Past and Present of the City of Rockford and Winnebago County, Ill.* (1905); *Textile World*, May 19, 1913; *Am. Inventor*, Aug. 1, 1901; Patent Office Records.]
C. W. M.

BURT, JOHN (Apr. 18, 1814–Aug. 16, 1886), inventor, capitalist, was the eldest of the five sons born to William Austin and Phebe (Coles) Burt, at that time residents of Wales, Erie County, N. Y. The first ten years of his life were spent in the rather settled community in which his father was justice of the peace, school inspector, postmaster, land surveyor, and builder of saw and grist-mills, but in 1824 the elder Burt took his little family to Michigan, settling in the township of Washington, Macomb County. In this virgin territory John shared the characteristic life of all pioneers, helping in the hard labor of clearing land; attending school spasmodically; and, in addition, receiving from his father instruction in surveying, mill construction, and engineering. He developed an aptitude along mechanical lines and from the age of sixteen assisted his father in his millwright work. When he came of age he acquired a farm of his own near his father's and for five years thereafter cleared and developed it. In 1840, however, when his father was deputized by the federal government to survey the upper peninsula of Michigan in conjunction with the Geological Survey then in progress, John and his four brothers were taken along as assistants. A year later, on May 18, 1841, John was appointed a deputy surveyor and in this capacity continued in the work for the next ten years. While his father made the original iron discovery in this area, John, in 1848, subdivided the Jackson Mine District and discovered amongst other deposits, the Republic and Humboldt Mines. He gradually became thoroughly familiar with the whole area and its iron ores. When the survey was completed in 1851, after receiving an opinion from the United States attorney-general that iron ore lands did not come under the head of mineral lands, he purchased 15,000 acres, which later formed part of the lands of the Lake Superior Iron Company. After being unsuccessful in interesting any other men in purchasing shares in his acquisition, he returned to the Carp River, where the city of Marquette is now located, and built a dam and a saw-mill, preparatory to the erection of a forge for the manufacture of iron blooms. Shortly thereafter, with the cooperation of Heman B. Ely of Cleveland, he began the construction of a railroad from Marquette to Lake Superior, which was completed in 1857. Meanwhile, foreseeing the need of a ship canal around the Sault Ste. Marie rapids, Burt, aided by his father and friends, induced Congress to aid his state in building such a canal. On its completion in 1855 he was made the first superintendent. With the resolve to devote his life to the industrial development of the upper peninsula, Burt spent his time in organizing companies, building additional railroads,—looking toward a complete transportation system for the whole peninsula—engaging in extensive lumbering activities, and organizing ore mining companies and steel works. In each of these enterprises he served actively as an officer or director. In addition, he found time to devise a number of improvements for the manufacture of pig and wrought iron, involving methods of effecting carbonization, for which he obtained patents in 1869. Again, as early as 1867, when the ship canal needed to be enlarged, he devised and patented a type of canal lock which was incorporated in the enlarged structure completed in 1881. Finally, in the seventies and early eighties, Burt obtained patents for purifying blast furnace gases; for a ventilating system; and for a by-product charcoal burning process. Burt also for four years (1885–89) published the first newspaper in Marquette, known as the *Marquette Mining Journal*. He was little interested in public life but did serve as Republican elector-at-large in 1868, delivering in Washington the Michigan vote for President Grant. At the time of his death he was president of the Lake Superior & Peninsula Iron Companies and the Burt Freestone Company. He was married on Dec. 3, 1835 to Julia A. Calkins, who with two sons and a daughter survived him at the time of his death in Detroit where he made his home for many years.

[Henry M. Burt, *Early Days in New Eng. Life and Times of Henry Burt of Springfield, and Some of his Descendants* (1893); Silas Farmer, *Hist. of Detroit and Mich.* (1889), vol. II; La Verne W. Spring, *Non-Technical Chats on Iron and Steel* (1917); *Detroit Free Press*, Aug. 17, 1886; Patent Office Records; U. S. Nat. Mus. Records.]   C. W. M.

BURT, MARY ELIZABETH (June 11, 1850–Oct. 17, 1918), educator, author, was the daughter of Roswell and Rotalana Burt. She was born at Lake Geneva, Wis., and received her earliest education in the public schools there. She then went to Anna Moody's Academy and for one year to Oberlin College. Unable to continue her college course, she completed its equivalent with private teachers. In the year 1870–71 she began her teaching career at the River Falls (Wisconsin) Normal School and for twenty-two years thereafter was a teacher in the Chicago public schools, three years of that time in the Cook County Normal School. She was also for three years a member of the Chicago Board of Education. In 1893 she went to New York, taught for a time in a private school, and became the editor of the Scribner School Reading Series. She had already had considerable experience in the editing of school texts and brought to this work a knowledge of the needs and tastes of children, as well as a firm belief in the value of the best literature as a means of character education. She wrote several books of literary criticism, *Browning's Women* (1887), *Literary Landmarks* (1889), *The World's Literature* (1890), but most of her literary work was editing, and she wrote in the introduction to one of her texts: "There

is more religion in *editing* one *good* book that shall carry forth and hand down the torch of life, than in *writing* a dozen of indifferent merit." Her more important texts are a school edition of John Burroughs's *Birds and Bees* (1888), *Seed Thoughts for the Growing Life from Robert Browning* (1885), *The Story of the German Iliad* (1892), *The Eugene Field Book* (with M. B. Cable) (1898), *The Cable Story Book* (with L. L. Cable) (1899), *The Lanier Book* (1904), *Poems Every Child Should Know* (1904), and *Prose Every Child Should Know* (1908). The last two volumes show excellent selection, adapted to the memorizing of good literature by children, and are widely used in schools. Miss Burt's *Bird Song Phonetic Charts* (1913) have value in nature study. She wrote articles and lectured on educational subjects at various times, before the National Education Association, the Illinois State Teachers' Association, and in 1911 before the College for the Training of Teachers in Cambridge, England. In educational practise she believed in the Socratic and Froebelian methods, in manual training, and in psychological methods of teaching reading. She was active in the contest for equal pay for primary teachers and favored woman suffrage, but found little time for organization work. Her personality was a very earnest one, with all its enthusiasms devoted to children, whom she loved and understood well. During the last few years of her life she was something of an invalid and lived in retirement at her home, Englewood Cliffs, Coytesville, N. J., where she died.

[*Who's Who in America*, 1916–17; *The Woman's Who's Who of America*, 1914–15; *N. Y. Tribune*, Oct. 20, 1918; information from Miss Burt's brother, Dr. J. C. Burt, of Lake Geneva, Wis.]   S. G. B.

BURT, WILLIAM AUSTIN (June 13, 1792–Aug. 18, 1858), inventor, surveyor, was the son of Alvin and Wealthy (Austin) Burt, and of the seventh generation descended from Richard Burt who settled in Taunton, Mass., about 1634. He was born in Petersham, Mass., on his father's farm. When he was ten years old his family moved to Freehold, N. Y., and within a year again moved to Broadalbin, N. Y. Burt was able to attend school from the time he learned his alphabet until he was nine years of age and for three weeks when he was fourteen. This was the extent of his schooling. Circumstances compelled him to assist his father and at an early age his mechanical skill was well developed. In writing of his early youth, "Judge Burt," as he came to be known in later life, stated that his mother had instructed him early in "piety and virtue" and that his whole life had been influenced by her teachings. He was always a student but had small means for acquiring information through books or from individuals. Access to a book on navigation, however, when he was about sixteen years of age, had a marked influence on him and seemingly led him into his loved occupation of surveying. (It is interesting to note, in this connection, that his ancestor, Richard Burt, in 1658, was appointed "Surveyor of Highways.") A continuous home study, whenever possible, of astronomy, mathematics, navigation, and mechanics, using whatever books he could secure, coupled with a natural mechanical skill which he religiously cultivated, brought him recognition and enabled him to earn a living by the time he was seventeen, in the neighborhood of his father's home in Erie County, N. Y., not far from Buffalo. When he was twenty-one he married Phœbe Cole and settled in Wales, about twenty miles from Buffalo. During the succeeding ten years he practised the trade of millwright, and also served as justice of the peace, postmaster, and county surveyor. A desire to know the West caused him to undertake a journey alone in 1817 from his home to Pittsburgh and St. Louis, and then north through Illinois and Indiana to Detroit and back to Buffalo. A second trip in 1822, this time to Michigan Territory, resulted in his purchasing a tract of land in Macomb County, not far from Detroit, and in 1824 he moved his family there. For a time he engaged in his usual occupation and took contracts for the construction of saw and grist-mills. It was during this time that he conceived the idea of a writing machine. This he perfected and called "The Typographer," receiving United States Patent No. 259 on July 23, 1829. This invention is recognized to-day as the ancestor of the typewriter. In 1831 he was elected surveyor of Macomb County, and also served as district surveyor through appointment by the governor. In 1833 he was appointed an associate judge of the circuit court, being at the same time postmaster of Mt. Vernon, and was selected by the General Land Office in Washington as United States deputy surveyor, in which latter capacity he continued to serve till within three years of his death. While executing a surveying contract in the vicinity of Milwaukee, Wis., in 1834, he encountered difficulties due to magnetic attraction, which made the surveyor's compass needle unreliable. This difficulty suggested to him the need of a solar device and with his knowledge and skill he eventually constructed an instrument which he named the "solar compass," for which he received letters patent of the United States in 1836. This instrument, which de-termines the true meridian by a single observa-tion, the sun being on the observer's meridian, was adopted by the United States Government for use in surveying the public domains and has been so used to the present time. In his capacity of deputy surveyor Burt ran the course of the fifth principal meridian in Iowa, and with the assistance of his five sons, all of whom he trained to be surveyors and who successively became deputy surveyors, he surveyed the upper peninsula of Michigan between 1840 and 1847. At the same time a geological survey was in progress and, upon the sudden death of the geologist Douglass Houghton [q.v.], Burt took over his notes, completed the work, and prepared the report (*Senate Executive Document No. 1*, 31 Cong., 1 Sess., Pt. III). In the course of this survey Burt made the first discovery of iron ore in Marquette County, Mich., on Sept. 19, 1844. This survey demonstrated the great value of the solar compass, without which it could not have been completed with any degree of accuracy. Franklin Institute in 1840 awarded Burt the Scott medal and twenty dollars in gold for the invention of the solar compass. His lifetime interest in navigation caused him, on a return voyage from England in 1851, to take passage on a sailing vessel especially to observe the accuracy of the course laid by the ship's compass. As a result of these observations Burt began working on his third invention, that of the equatorial sextant (Patent No. 16,002 granted on Nov. 4, 1856; Burt's description of invention in *Senate Executive Document, No. 53, 34* Cong., 3 Sess.). He was elected as one of two members of the Territorial Legislative Council of Michigan for 1826–27; was a member of the House of Representatives in the state legislature of 1853; and served as chairman of the Committee on Internal Improvements. In this connection he is recognized as one of the prime movers for the construction of what is now known as the Sault Ste. Marie Canal. He wrote *Key to the Solar Compass and Surveyor's Companion*, first published in 1855, with a second edition in 1858.

[Henry M. Burt, *Early Days in New Eng. Life and Times of Henry Burt of Springfield and Some of his Descendants* (1893); Horace E. Burt, *Wm. Austin Burt* (1920); John Burt, *Hist. of the Solar Compass invented by Wm. A. Burt* (1878); *Mich. Pioneer and Hist. Soc. Colls.*, vols. V, XXVIII, XXXVIII; Silas Farmer, *Hist. of Detroit and Mich.* (1889); Records of the General Land Office; Records of the United States Patent Office.]   C. W. M.

BURTON, ASA (Aug. 25, 1752–May 1, 1836), Congregational clergyman, was the son of Jacob and Rachel Burton and was born in Stonington, Conn. When he was sixteen years of age, the family removed to Norwich, Vt., where he spent a number of years in severe pioneer labor. He prepared himself for Dartmouth in eight months, entered college on his twenty-first birthday, and graduated in 1777. He studied divinity with the Rev. Levi Hart of Preston, Conn., and was ordained in January 1779 at Thetford, Vt., where he became pastor for life. From very unpromising beginnings he built up a strong church and lifted the life of the entire region. Though rigid in his doctrinal and moral standards, he received nearly five hundred members into the church. Through his monthly conferences with the youth of the town, he became a pioneer in young people's work. Although a believer in evangelism he opposed the Methodists and kept out of Thetford all denominations but his own.

Burton was best known as a teacher of theology. The number of candidates for the ministry which he trained wholly or in part, is variously estimated at from sixty to a hundred. He was a great promoter of education and was a founder of Thetford Academy and of Kimball Union Academy at Meriden, N. H. He was also a founder and trustee of the University of Vermont and a member of the corporation of Middlebury College. In 1804 he received the degree of D.D. from Middlebury, but declined its presidency in 1809. He was honored with many prominent offices by the churches of Vermont. Beginning in January 1809, he edited for several years the *Adviser; or Vermont Evangelical Magazine*. In addition to about twenty sermons, he published one book, *Essays on Some of the first Principles of Metaphysics, Ethicks and Theology* (1824). In it he sets forth his "taste" scheme of theology which holds that regeneration consists in the impartation to the disposition of a new relish or "taste" for good, in opposition to the "exercise scheme" of Nathaniel Emmons (Williston Walker, *A History of the Congregational Churches in the United States*, 1894, p. 303). In this work also, he foreshadows many things in the modern psychologies. In a sermon on *The Works of God* (1811) he seems to anticipate the theory of evolution, and he predicted a foreign missionary society twelve years before the American Board, and a theological seminary ten years before the founding of Andover (E. A. Park, *Memoir of Nathaniel Emmons*, 1861, p. 176).

Burton's only known portrait, copies of which were once found in many Thetford homes, is reproduced in the *American Quarterly Register* for May 1838. It represents a rugged face with a pronounced aquiline nose, but was not considered a good likeness. He lived a laborious and self-sacrificing life. He was not sociably in-

clined and was not a wide reader except in theology and metaphysics. He was a preacher of marked originality, and was a clear and able reasoner rather than an orator. He was married three times: in 1778 to Mercy Burton, his half-cousin, who died in 1800; in 1801 to Polly Child of Thetford, who died in 1806; in 1809 to Mrs. Rhoda (Braman) White of Randolph, Mass., who died in 1818.

[Burton left a brief autobiography in MS. This is the basis of a rather full biographical article by Rev. Thos. Adams, in the *Am. Quart. Reg.* for May 1838. Other sketches are found in Wm. B. Sprague, *Annals Am. Pulpit*, II (1857), and in A. M. Hemenway, *Vt. Hist. Gazeteer*, II (1871). There is also an excellent survey of his life and work in "Churches and Ministers of Vt., 1762–1830," by P. H. White and A. W. Weld, which exists in MS. in the Congreg. Lib. in Boston. The writer is also indebted to the Rev. Wm. Slade of Thetford, Vt., who has contributed much valuable information.]   F. T. P.

BURTON, ERNEST DE WITT (Feb. 4, 1856–May 26, 1925), college president, the son of the Rev. Nathan Smith Burton and his wife Sarah J. Fairfield, came of distinguished Virginia and Vermont ancestry. He was born in Granville, Ohio, and was educated at Griswold College, Davenport, Ia., and at Denison University, Granville, Ohio, where he graduated in 1876. In Denison, he had as teachers, E. Benjamin Andrews [*q.v.*] and W. A. Stevens [*q.v.*] a future colleague. After brief teaching at Kalamazoo, Mich., and serving in executive places in high schools in Xenia, Ohio, and in Norwood, a suburb of Cincinnati, he entered Rochester Theological Seminary (Baptist) in 1879. Graduating in 1882, he was in the following year ordained to the Baptist ministry, married to Frances Mary Townson of Rochester, N. Y., and elected professor of New Testament Greek in Newton (Mass.) Theological Seminary, the historic seminary of the Baptist Church. Promoted presently to the full chair, he remained until 1892 when he was elected by the University of Chicago as head of its department of New Testament and Early Christian Literature. This department was coördinate with the department of Oriental Languages and Literatures, of which President Harper was the head. In this chair, Burton continued till chosen president of the University, July 12, 1923 (after a service of six months as acting president). As president he served until his death. For thirty-three years he was an officer of the University.

To his professorships in both Newton and Chicago, Burton brought qualities intellectual, ethical, religious, personal, of the highest order. He was learned in classical and in New Testament Greek. While serving as professor in Chicago, he edited the *Biblical World* and the *Amer-*

ican Journal of Theology, and wrote numerous books on New Testament questions, including his widely studied *Harmony of the Gospels* (1894) in collaboration with W. A. Stevens. He served as director of the university libraries. He was chairman, also, of the China Educational Commission of 1921–22 to inquire into the whole educational condition in China in its broadest relationships.

To his presidency, Burton brought the qualities and elements embodied in his professorship, and more. He was gifted with imagination and vision. His personality represented leadership without autocracy and with real affection for his associates. His power of work, like that of his two predecessors, Harper and Judson, was tireless. The results of less than two years of his presidency were great and apparently enduring. A reorganization of various departments was made, especially of the Medical School to which Rush Medical School was joined. A new medical center was established. A great building plan, including graduate and undergraduate halls, was adopted. The endowments were largely increased,—to fifty-four millions,—and the standards of scholarship were advanced.

[Thos. Wakefield Goodspeed, *Ernest DeWitt Burton* (1926); Harold R. Willoughby, ed., *Christianity in the Modern World, Papers and Addresses by Ernest De Witt Burton* (1926), containing full bibliography; *Univ. Record* (Chicago), July 1925; *Christian Century,* June 4, 1925.]   C. F. T.

BURTON, FREDERICK RUSSELL (Feb. 23, 1861–Sept. 30, 1909), composer, student of Indian music, was born at Jonesville, Mich., the son of a Universalist clergyman, the Rev. William S. Burton. His mother was Sarah Evelyn (Mason) Burton. He was fitted for college at West Newton English and Classical School and graduated from Harvard in 1882, *summa cum laude,* receiving at the same time the highest honors in music, which he had studied throughout his college course with John Knowles Paine. He had always felt a deep, personal interest in Longfellow's poem *Hiawatha,* which he regarded as one of the world's real epics. Indeed, it is a tradition in his family that he had read the poem when but seven years old and pronounced it good! This poem he set to music while at college and it was sung by the Glee Club in 1882. About the same time he published a number of songs: *Sea-Weed, The Engineer, My Cigarette, Kitty Bahn.* After graduation he taught music until January 1883 when he became a reporter on the *Boston Globe,* being made night city editor in 1884. He went to Troy, N. Y., in June 1884 to write editorials for the *Daily Telegram* and was made city editor soon after his arrival.

In the following September he went to Fall River, Mass., as editor of the *Fall River Daily Herald,* but remained there only one month when he secured city editorship of the *Boston Post.* Later he was on the staff of the New York *Sun* under Dana and he also at one time did considerable journalistic work in London, England. In 1885 he married Winifred Baxter, who died in 1892. In 1895 he married Susan M. Carr. In 1896 he organized the Yonkers Choral Society which in 1898 performed his cantata *Hiawatha.* Its chief interest lay in the fact that he had tried to reproduce in its music the Indian mood of the text; and to this end he had made use of a true Indian melody, jotted down by Henry E. Krehbiel when heard at some tribal dance. This was undoubtedly one of the earliest instances of the use of an authentic Indian melody in legitimate music. In 1900 Burton published a second cantata, *The Legend of Sleepy Hollow;* in 1901 an *Inauguration Ode* (for the inauguration of President McKinley); in 1904 a *Carnegie Library Dedication Ode.*

By far his most important work, however, was to come in the logical development of his interest in and knowledge of Indian music. This he obtained at first hand, both in Canada and the United States, by spending long periods in intimate association with the Indians, particularly the Ojibways, who lived round about Lakes Huron and Superior. This intensive study resulted in the publication in 1903 of *Songs of the Ojibway Indians,* later amplified and developed into *American Primitive Music,* which has been generally accepted as "one of the most important contributions to the literature of American folk music" (*Art of Music,* IV, 347). This work was posthumously published in 1909. An interesting opportunity for Burton to make constructive use of his authoritative knowledge of Indian music came in the summer of 1902 when he was asked to supervise the music in the production of the Indian play of *Hiawatha* which had already been given annually for some time at Desbarats, Ontario, on the shore of Lake Huron. (This play is not to be confused with Burton's cantata of the same name.) He threw himself with enthusiasm into the task, writing certain incidental music himself, based upon Indian *motifs,* while he helped the Indians in their choice of original material. So successful was the result that, with the permission of the Canadian government, the group of Indian players accompanied Burton to England, where the play was presented at Earl's Court, London.

Burton also published the following narratives: *The Mission of Poubalov* (1897); *Shift-*

ing Sands (1898); *A Seven Days' Mystery* (1900); *The Song and the Singer* (1902); *Her Wedding Interlude* (1902); *Strongheart* (1908); and *Redcloud of the Lakes* (1909). He died suddenly on Sept. 30, 1909, at his summer home on Lake Hopatcong, N. J.

[Grove's *Dict. of Music* (*Am. Supp.*, 1920); *Class of 1882, Harvard Coll., 6th Report of the Sec.* (1907); N. Y. *Sun*, Oct. 2, 1909, quoted in *Musical Courier*, Oct. 6, 1909; Wm. E. Brigham, in the *Boston Evening Transcript*, Nov. 27, 1925; Hughes and Elson, *Am. Composers* (new rev. ed., 1914); Eugene E. Simpson, *America's Position in Music* (1920).] W. T. U—n.

BURTON, HUTCHINS GORDON (*c.* 1774–Apr. 21, 1836), governor of North Carolina, was the son of John and Mary (Gordon) Burton. There is a conflict of opinion as to his birthplace, with statements that he was a native of Virginia and on the other hand that he was born in Granville County, N. C. It is certain that while he was still a youth his parents died and that he was reared and educated in the household of his uncle, Robert Burton, of Mecklenburg County, N. C. He attended the University of North Carolina as a student, 1795–98, was trained in the law, and achieved an early success in his profession, becoming ultimately a leader of the state bar. There is evidence that his genial personality and social gifts made him a general favorite. His marriage to Sarah, a daughter of Willie Jones, a man distinguished in politics and society, contributed to his success. His political career began with his election to the House of Commons in 1809. For six years (1810–16), by election of the General Assembly, he served as attorney-general of the state, resigning to reënter the Commons in 1817. From 1819 to 1824, he was a representative in Congress. His service was inconspicuous; he remained silent through most of the proceedings; his speeches on vaccination and the bank were modestly apologetic. His participation in the work of the committees on the judiciary and on military affairs, however, appears to have been more active. In 1824, he resigned to become governor, being elected by the Assembly. Twice reëlected, he served from December 1824 to December 1827. His administrations were uneventful. Perhaps the most colorful happening was the visit and reception of Gen. Lafayette in 1825. Burton's messages were concerned, in the main, with the advocacy of internal improvements,—development of resources, deepening of watercourses, and construction of roads —and with educational reform. (His three messages on education appear in C. L. Coon, *The Beginnings of Public Education in North Carolina*, 1908, I, 263–64, 294–95, 362–64.) He also

interested himself in an effort to modify the criminal code. One act, passed in 1827, authorized the directors of the Literary Fund to sell a lottery for $50,000, $25,000 of which was to aid Archibald D. Murphey in the preparation and publication of a history of the state. This measure was one of several attempts to raise funds by means of a lottery. Some notice was taken of a resolution of the legislature of Ohio looking toward gradual emancipation of slaves and their colonization. Although leaving the matter to the Assembly for disposal, Burton commented on it, calling Ohio's attention to the eleventh commandment: "Let every one attend to his own concerns."

Burton was not a Jackson man; so although he was nominated at the end of John Quincy Adams's term to be territorial governor of Arkansas, this nomination was not confirmed by the next administration. His remaining years were spent in retirement.

[A short sketch of Burton by Marshall DeLancey Haywood appears in S. A. Ashe, ed., *Biog. Hist. of N. C.*, IV (1906), 68 ff. A brief, but authoritative review of his administration as governor may be found in S. A. Ashe, *Hist. of N. C.*, II (1925), 295–312. His speeches in Congress are reported in *Annals of Cong.* (16 Cong., 2 Sess., and 17 Cong., 1 Sess.). His official correspondence may be consulted in his manuscript Letter-Book and Correspondence (2 vols.), N. C. Hist. Commission.] W. W. P.

BURTON, MARION LE ROY (Aug. 30, 1874–Feb. 18, 1925), Congregational clergyman, college president, was born in Brooklyn, Iowa. He was the son of Ira John Henry Burton and Jane Adeliza (Simmons) Burton. After spending a part of his boyhood in Minneapolis, he entered Carleton College (Minnesota) where he graduated in 1900. On June 14, 1900 he was married to Nina Leona Moses of Northfield, Minn. His public life was divided into three parts, unequal in importance as well as in length. Its first third was occupied in teaching in the Academy of Carleton College (1899–1900), in the principalship of Windom Institute, Minnesota (1900–03), and in an assistant professorship of theology at Yale (1907–08). At the Yale School of Divinity he had studied, and received the degree of B.D., *summa cum laude,* in 1906 and of Ph.D., in 1907. The second part of his career, and briefest, lay in the pastorate of the Church of the Pilgrims, Brooklyn, N. Y. (1908–09), a pulpit occupied for fifty years by the eloquent Richard Salter Storrs [*q.v.*]. The third and most important part covered three university presidencies. The first, preceded by a visit to European universities, in special preparation for his administration, was at Smith College (1910–17); the second was at the University of Minnesota (1917–20) ; the third was at the University of Michigan (1920–25). Burton possessed unique ability in the raising of funds and in influencing legislatures. He secured a one million dollar endowment for Smith, ten millions for the University of Minnesota, and fourteen millions for the University of Michigan. He was endowed with a gift of flowing and persuasive speech before either a political or a popular audience, making the nominating speech for Calvin Coolidge at Cleveland in 1924. He published *The Problem of Evil; a Criticism of the Augustinian Point of View* (1909) ; and *Our Intellectual Attitude in an Age of Criticism* (1913). His educational policy was twofold, to build up the physical side of the institution and also to raise its intellectual standards. To his service as administrator, he gave great qualities of personal character—enthusiasm, friendliness, vigor—both intellectual and physical, a just union of humility and of self-respect, optimism, and a distinct charm of manner.

[*Ann. Report of the President of Smith Coll.*, 1910–17 ; *Univ. of Minn., President's Report*, 1917–20 ; *Univ. of Mich., President's Report*, 1920–25 ; *Detroit Free Press* and *N. Y. Times*, Feb. 19, 1925 ; *Mich. Alumnus*, Feb. 26, 1925 ; *Yale Univ. Obit. Record*, 1925.]

C. F. T.

BURTON, NATHANIEL JUDSON (Dec. 17, 1824–Oct. 13, 1887), Congregational clergyman, came of old Connecticut stock, his family having settled in that state in the seventeenth century, and was born in Trumbull, Conn., the son of the Rev. Henry and Betsy (Porter) Burton. As a boy he shared the fortunes of an itinerant Methodist preacher, and in one of his lectures ("Parish Inconveniences," *Yale Lectures*, p. 152) he speaks of the period as one when "my clothes were not as expensive as I would have liked, and my spending money was limited, and when my father had offers from well-to-do childless women to adopt me for their own." He prepared for college at Wilbraham Academy, a Methodist school in Wilbraham, Mass., and graduated from Wesleyan University in 1850. After a year of teaching in Newark, N. J., he entered the Yale Divinity School, from which he graduated in 1854. On July 20, 1853, he was ordained and made pastor of the Second Congregational Church of Fairhaven, Conn., now Pilgrim Church, New Haven. The same year, Sept. 14, he married Rachel, daughter of Rev. Henry and Rachel (Pine) Chase of New York. In October 1857 he became pastor of the Fourth Congregational Church, Hartford, Conn., and in March 1870 succeeded Horace Bushnell as pastor of Park Church, Hartford, where he remained until his death.

During his thirty years' residence in Hartford,

he became known as one of the leading preachers of New England. He resembled Bushnell in his originality of thought and his poetic imagination. He was a man of broad culture, fine social qualities, practical common sense, and engaging humor, and was intimate with members of the literary and clerical coterie of Hartford, which included Charles Dudley Warner, Mark Twain, and Joseph Twichell. In 1884 he delivered the Lyman Beecher Lectures at Yale, and in the two following years was a special lecturer at the Yale Divinity School. From 1882 until his death he was a member of the Yale Corporation. He never said or did anything in order to attract attention, was careless with respect to perpetuating his influence, and was strongly disinclined to publish. Letters on his travels in Europe were printed in the *Hartford Evening Post* in 1868 and 1869. Extracts from these, his lectures at Yale, and some of his sermons and addresses were published by his son, Richard E. Burton, under the title, *Yale Lectures on Preaching, and Other Writings by Nathaniel J. Burton, D.D.* in 1888. His lectures were republished in 1925 with the title *In Pulpit and Parish*. They are written in an attractive literary style, and their content, the result both of keen thought and of long experience, is of permanent value.

[*Congreg. Year-book* (1888) ; *Hartford Courant*, Oct. 14, 18, 1887 ; Timothy Dwight, *Memories of Yale Life and Men* (1903).]

H. E. S.

BURTON, WARREN (Nov. 23, 1800–June 6, 1866), Unitarian and Swedenborgian clergyman, the son of Jonathan and Persis (Warren) Burton, was born at Wilton, N. H. While still young, he lost his mother, whose memory he later celebrated in the character of Mary Smith, in *The District School as it Was*. His early home training was in the circle of his grandparents, and with no additional schooling, he prepared, by private study and with the occasional help of a minister, to enter Harvard (1817), whence he graduated with distinction in 1821. After an apprenticeship in school-keeping, he entered the theological school at Cambridge, studied three years, was ordained, and settled at East Cambridge in 1828. The same year he married Sarah Flint ; and, in 1845, his second wife, Mary Merritt of Salem, Mass. After a year's ministry at East Cambridge, he withdrew to engage in various reforms, by speaking and writing, preaching only occasionally. Later, he was minister at South Hingham, 1833–35 ; at Waltham, 1835–37 ; and at Boston, irregularly, 1844–48. He rendered public ministerial service as chaplain in Worcester prison, 1849 ; in the state Senate, 1852 ; at the constitutional convention, 1853 ; and in the House of Representatives, 1853 and 1860. Though at first in the Unitarian ministry, in later life he became a Swedenborgian. With the movements of his day, such as transcendentalism, phrenology, Pestalozzianism, he identified himself closely. From 1841 to 1844, he was associated with the Brook Farm experiment. In education he saw the chief means of effecting the reforms ardently desired in society. One or another of these contemporary interests runs throughout his books; it was to improve society in general, the home and the school in particular, that most of his lectures, books, and periodical articles were prepared. His chief works in the order of their appearance were: *My Religious Experience at my Native Home* (1829); *Cheering Views of Man and Providence* (1832); *The District School as it Was* (1833), which was republished in New York and London; *Essay on the Divine Agency in the Material Universe* (1834); *Uncle Sam's Recommendations of Phrenology to His Millions of Friends in the United States* (1842); *The Scenery-Shower or Word-Paintings of the Beautiful, Picturesque, and the Grand in Nature* (1844); *Helps to Education in the Homes of Our Country* (1863); and *The Culture of the Observing Faculties in the Family and the School* (1855). As representative of his shorter essays may be named: "A Supplication," a plea for pure English, "A Traveller's Story for the Perusal of Parents," and "Emulation, as a Motive to Study," which was delivered before the American Institute of Instruction, in 1834.

The influence of Burton was widespread, due to popularity as a lyceum lecturer, and the circulation of his major works, *The District School as it Was* and *Helps to Education*. The former, by its charm, attracted many to a knowledge of their schools, who would not have read a formal treatise; the latter, by its practical suggestions could not fail to open to parents a new view of their responsibilities and opportunities. Burton was an early promoter of the parent-teacher association idea, being convinced that "all the improvements in schools and modes of teaching" amounted to little, as long as home education was comparatively neglected. To remedy this defect, he advocated that "during the more leisure season of the year, meetings of parents, teachers, and others, should be held, from week to week, for the discussion of questions appertaining to family discipline, to the relation of the home to the school, and to education generally."

[*Salem Reg.*, June 11, 1866; *Salem Observer*, June 9, 1866; *Boston Evening Transcript*, June 7, 1866, Mar. 20, 1897; *Barnard's Am. Jour. of Ed.*, II, 333–36, XVI, 430; Abiel A. Livermore and Sewall Putnam, *Hist. of the Town of Wilton, N. H.* (1888).]   T.W.

BURTON, WILLIAM (Oct. 16, 1789–Aug. 5, 1866), physician, governor of Delaware, was the son of John Burton, farmer in Sussex County, Del., and of Mary (Vaughan) Burton. After receiving an elementary training he studied medicine in the office of Dr. Sudler in Milford, Del., and at the University of Pennsylvania, where he graduated with the degree of M.D. After beginning his profession in Lewes, Del., he soon removed to Milford, where he built up a good practise, living on a farm near the town. Here he delighted in dispensing a gracious hospitality and enjoyed a wide circle of friends. He was married twice, his first wife being Mrs. Eliza Wolcott, daughter of William Sorden of Kent County, his second, Ann C. Hill, daughter of Robert and Rhoda (Davis) Hill. Active in state politics, first as a Whig, he was elected sheriff of Kent County in 1830. In 1848, like so many other Whigs, he joined the Democratic party, and in 1854 was nominated for the office of governor of the state, but was defeated by the candidate of the Know-Nothing party, Peter F. Causey. Nominated again for the governorship in 1858 he defeated the candidate of the People's party and was inaugurated on Jan. 18, 1859. A Democratic legislature was likewise elected. Burton served his state the full constitutional term of four years, retiring in January 1863 in favor of William Cannon, the candidate of the Union party.

Although Delaware was a slave state and the Breckinridge Democrats had carried it in 1860, the state administration proved loyal to the Union, while at the same time it endeavored to conciliate those elements of the population who were strongly opposed to the war. Delaware's answer to Mississippi's invitation to join the Southern Confederacy was an "unqualified disapproval." On the other hand, Delaware sent five delegates to the Peace Convention in the following month of February, and a large peace meeting was permitted to assemble in Dover in June of the same year. When Lincoln called upon Delaware for its first quota of troops in April, however, Burton complied immediately by issuing a proclamation calling for volunteers (there being no state militia to order into the Federal service), and by his subsequent measures acted in harmony with the Federal authorities except on occasions when he felt that the Federal power was encroaching too much upon the rights of Delaware, *e.g.*, when making what he, and the Democrats in general, regarded as illegal arrests. The so-called invasion of the state by Federal troops at the general election in November 1862 and the consequent victory of the Lincoln candidate for governor brought forth from Burton in his last message to the legislature in January 1863 severe strictures upon the methods of the Union party.

[J. T. Scharf, *Hist. of Del.* (1888), I, 328 ff.; Henry C. Conrad, *Hist. of the State of Del.* (1908), I, 194 ff., III, 843; Records of Executive Acts for years 1859 ff., in the Governor's office, Dover; *Official Records,* 1, 3, 4 ser.; Senate Jours., Nos. XIX, XX, XXI and House Jours. Nos. XIX, XX, XXI for the years 1859 to 1863 inclusive, in the State Lib., Dover.]   G.H.R.

BURTON, WILLIAM EVANS (Sept. 24, 1804–Feb. 10, 1860), actor, author, was the son of a London printer, William George Burton, who was the author of a work entitled *Researches . . . Illustrative of the Sacred Scriptures, etc.* (2 vols., 1805). This title suggests why the son was sent to St. Paul's School, and destined for the Church. His father died, however, when young Burton was eighteen, and the boy had to leave school to run the printing business. Like many other young men of the period, he took part in amateur plays, and in 1825 joined a professional company in the provinces. After six years of this training, in which he developed a natural aptitude for comedy, he appeared in 1831 at the London Pavilion, as Wormwood in *The Lottery Ticket.* The following year he succeeded Liston as comedian at the Haymarket, when the latter left that company in a huff. But presently Liston decided to come back, so Burton was once more out of steady employment, and readily consented, in 1834, to accept an offer from America. As early as Apr. 10, 1823, he had married an actress but apparently was divorced from her, as on July 18, 1834, he was married to Caroline Glessing of London (T. A. Brown, *History of the New York Stage,* vol. I, 1903, pp. 358–59). On Sept. 3, 1834, he appeared as Wormwood, and as Dr. Ollapod in *The Poor Gentleman,* at the Arch Street Theatre, Philadelphia, then one of the leading playhouses of the country. He remained four years in Philadelphia, playing such parts as Goldfinch in *The Road to Ruin,* Sir Peter Teazle, Dogberry, and Bob Acres. Meanwhile he also wrote numerous magazine sketches later collected in a volume called *Waggeries and Vagaries* (1848). He also started the *Gentleman's Magazine* (1837–40) a monthly publication, of which Edgar Allan Poe was editor during the last year, but the two men did not get on together. Meanwhile Burton visited other cities as a traveling star, acting first in New York in October 1837, at the National Theatre, for the benefit of Samuel Woodworth, author of "The Old Oaken Bucket." In 1841 he essayed management in New York, but the theatre burned down and he returned to Philadelphia, managing not only two theatres there but the Front Street Theatre in Baltimore and a theatre in Washington. He also acted constantly himself. Evidently a man of tireless energy, on July 10, 1848, he again entered the New York field, opening a small, intimate house on Chambers St., rechristened Burton's Theatre, which soon became and remained for eight years, the most popular playhouse in New York, if not in America. It was regarded with much the same affection that Manhattan later bestowed on the intimate little Weber and Fields Music Hall. It was a theatre where more or less serious plays, including the classics, alternated with hilarious broad comedy, or even burlesque, where the company was composed of a happy family of excellent players, and where the audience was always sure of a well-produced entertainment and a good time. It was a school for actors, for in the company during its eight years were Henry Placide, John Brougham, Lester Wallack, Lawrence Barrett, George Holland, Charles Fisher, and many more who later became leaders on the stage. Here were acted stage versions of *Dombey and Son* and *David Copperfield,* with Burton as Cap'n Cuttle and Micawber (two or his most famous parts), here Shakespeare was carefully revived with Burton as Falstaff, Bottom, Sir Toby, and even Caliban, and here he made the town roar as Sleek and Toodle. In his company was Miss Jane Hill, wife of James Hilson, stage-doorkeeper; after April 1853 she appeared under the name of Mrs. Burton (Brown, *op. cit.,* p. 342; Ireland, *Records of the New York Stage,* 1867, II, 235). In 1856 Burton moved to a larger house uptown, but the intimacy was gone in the new surroundings, and the venture failed in two years. He then toured the country with much success. At Mechanics Hall, Hamilton, Canada, in December 1859, he made his last appearance, returning to New York exhausted, and dying of heart disease on Feb. 10, 1860. He was a born comedian, with a broad, genial face which could assume any expression, and a joyous, hearty nature which always infected an audience with good humor. Everybody loved him. He was also a painstaking, intelligent impersonator, in spite of the somewhat broadly exaggerated style of acting he had learned from Liston, and he had a high ideal of ensemble playing and careful stage direction. His New York company set a standard of all-round excellence which materially affected the American theatre for good. Having a large income, Burton collected a very considerable library, especially of Shakespeariana, which was housed in his residence on Hudson St., New York, and he enjoyed the reputation of a scholar and gentleman, thus helping to stabilize the actor's profession in this country. His three daughters are mentioned pleasantly by Jefferson in his *Autobiography*. Besides the literary work mentioned above, Burton was the author of two domestic farces, *Ellen Wareham* (1833) and *The Toodles*; an adaptation of R. J. Raymond's *The Farmer's Daughter of the Severn Side*; *The Court Fool*; and *Burton's Comic Songster* (1837). He contributed a series of papers called "The Actor's Alloquy" to the *Knickerbocker Magazine* and edited *The Literary Souvenir* (1838–40) and *The Cyclopædia of Wit and Humor* (1858).

[In addition to sources cited above see W. L. Keese, *Wm. E. Burton, Actor, Author and Manager* (1885), and "Wm. E. Burton," *Dunlap Soc. Pub. No. 14* (1891); and *Actors and Actresses of Gt. Britain and the U. S.*, vol. III (1886), ed. by Brander Matthews and Lawrence Hutton.]   W.P.E.

BUSH, GEORGE (June 12, 1796–Sept. 19, 1859), Presbyterian clergyman, later a Swedenborgian, prominent in his day as a scholar, writer, and controversialist, was born in Norwich, Vt., where his grandfather, Timothy, immigrating from Connecticut, had settled. He was the son of John and Abigail (Marvin) Bush. The former, a graduate of Dartmouth, had studied law but never practised. George Bush graduated from Dartmouth in 1818, studied theology and served as tutor at Princeton, preached for a time in Morristown, N. J., and in 1824 went as a home missionary pastor to Indiana. Here he was ordained by the Salem Presbytery, Mar. 5, 1825, and installed pastor of the church in Indianapolis. The same year he married a daughter of Hon. Lewis Condict of Morristown, who died Nov. 9, 1827. A statement which he made in the pulpit to the effect that there was not a shadow of Scriptural authority for the Presbyterian form of church government caused a controversy with his session, which in 1828 brought about a termination of the pastoral relationship. From 1831 to 1847 he was professor of Hebrew language and literature in New York University, also serving, 1836–37, as instructor in sacred literature at Union Theological Seminary. In 1845 he associated himself with the Church of the New Jerusalem, and for the remainder of his life, as a writer, lecturer, and preacher, promulgated the doctrines of Swedenborg. Although opposed to all ecclesiastical rites he consented to be re-ordained to the New Church ministry privately in August 1848.

His knowledge was encyclopedic. As a boy his sole interest had been in books. Put into a printing office that he might not injure his health by too much study, he was tolerated there but a short time because he would become so interested in reading the manuscripts that he forgot to set the type. Before his second marriage, Jan. 4, 1849, to Mary W. Fisher, he had a study in the third story of a building on Nassau St., described as a "perfect den of learning," where barricaded with books he might be found at almost any time of day or night. Even those who were not able to accept the theological conclusions of his later days, professed great admiration for his scholarship. A modest, kindly man, he made no display of learning, but without regard for personal interests, stubbornly contended for what he believed to be the truth. His first important publication was *The Life of Mohammed* (1830), constituting Volume X in Harper's Family Library. This was followed in 1832 by *A Treatise on the Millennium*. In 1835 he published *A Grammar of the Hebrew Language*, a second edition of which appeared in 1838. Between 1840 and 1858 he issued a number of commentaries on books of the Old Testament. A work of his which was widely read and created much controversy was *Anastasis: or, the Doctrine of the Resurrection of the Body, Rationally and Scripturally Considered* (1844) in which he opposed the doctrine of the physical construction of the body in the future life. In 1846 he published *Statement of Reasons for Embracing the Doctrines and Disclosures of Emanuel Swedenborg*, and the same year edited *The Memorabilia of Swedenborg*. Another work which occasioned discussion was his *Mesmer and Swedenborg* (1847), in which he attempted to show that what is involved in mesmerism tends to support Swedenborg's teachings. His most radical treatise perhaps was his *Priesthood and Clergy Unknown to Christianity, or The Church a Community of Co-equal Brethren* (1857). Besides these more important works he published many others, including pamphlets, letters and compilations. He also issued from June 1842 to May 1843, the *Hierophant*, a monthly journal of sacred symbols and prophecy, and beginning in 1848 edited for a number of years the *New Church Repository and Monthly Review*.

[*Gen. Cat. Dartmouth Coll.* (1900); *Gen. Cat. Princeton Univ.* (1908); *Princeton Theolog. Sch. Biog. Cat.* (1909); W. M. Fernald, *Memoir and Reminiscences of the Late Prof. Geo. Bush* (1860); H. A. Edson, *Contributions to the Early Hist. of the Presbyt. Ch. in Indiana* (1898); R. W. Griswold, *Prose Writers of America* (1847).]   H.E.S.

BUSHNELL, ASA SMITH (Sept. 16, 1834–Jan. 15, 1904), governor of Ohio, was reputed to be the descendant of Francis Bushnell of Surrey, who came to New Haven in 1639 as one of the original signers of the plantation covenant. He was born at Rome, N. Y., where his father, Daniel Bushnell, taught school. His mother, Harriet (Smith) Bushnell, was a woman, according to the son, of "great energy," whose "house was a model," whose "life was a benediction," and whose "presence was always an inspiration." When the boy was eleven years old the family removed to Cincinnati; but six years later, after a limited attendance at school, he went to Springfield where for several years he struggled as clerk and bookkeeper. In 1857 he married Ellen Ludlow, and the outbreak of the Civil War found him engaged in the drug business in partnership with his father-in-law. This he left for service as captain of Company E of the 162nd Ohio Volunteer Infantry, which was assigned in 1864 to guard and picket duty in the Shenandoah Valley. After the war Bushnell's fortunes rose rapidly. Becoming a partner in 1867 in a concern in which he had formerly been an employee, he promoted its incorporation as the Warder, Bushnell & Glessner Company, becoming its president in 1886. This corporation was engaged in the manufacture of harvesting machinery; but other banking and public service enterprises also enlisted Bushnell's attention, and he speedily acquired both wealth and reputation as a keen and progressive man of affairs.

Although in politics from 1885 to 1900, a political career seems always to have been a secondary matter with him. His first venture in this sphere was as Joseph B. Foraker's manager in his successful gubernatorial campaign of 1885. He served for four years as quartermaster-general under Gov. Foraker, but resisted the importunities of his friends, in the years that followed, to become a candidate for elective office. In 1895, however, he was nominated for governor as a result of the factional strife within the Republican party in Ohio. The Foraker forces gained control of the state convention in that year and signalized their victory by nominating Bushnell. He was elected by a plurality of 92,622, the largest that had been received by an Ohio governor since John Brough's war-time defeat of Clement L. Vallandigham. In 1897 the candidacy of Senator Marcus A. Hanna to succeed himself became the issue of the state legislative campaign, and Bushnell, reëlected governor, was believed to have sought to frustrate Hanna's plan. Whether or not the ill-feeling engendered by this episode influenced Bushnell's career is a question; at any rate, he virtually abandoned politics when his term expired. Notwithstanding the Hanna incident, his administrations were less notable for political maneuvering than for efficient handling of the state's business, for which his experience fitted him well. The management of the finances was improved to such a degree that many thousands of dollars were saved; and the merit system in the civil service, which he advocated, was introduced so far as he could do it without legislation to support him. His energy as governor is well illustrated by the fact that, in the Spanish-American War, the Ohio troops were mobilized and placed in the field before those of any other state. On Jan. 11, 1904, he was stricken with apoplexy while attending the inauguration of Gov. Herrick, and died in a Columbus hospital four days later.

[A sketch of Bushnell, written in 1882, while he was president of the Springfield City Council, is given in *The Biog. Cyc. . . . of the State of Ohio*, vol. I (1883). A recent study is that in G. F. Wright, *Representative Citizens of Ohio* (1918). B. F. Prince, ed., *A Standard Hist. of Springfield and Clark County, Ohio* (1922), contains an appreciation, and numerous notes on Bushnell's part in Springfield's industrial development. An obituary by the Rev. J. W. Atwood appeared in the *Ohio Archæol. and Hist. Quart.*, Apr. 1904, and a "Sketch and Genealogy," by Geo. W. Knight, was published in the *Old Northwest Geneal. Quart.*, July 1904. The Hanna-Foraker factional contest and Bushnell's relation to it is told from the two points of view, respectively, by H. D. Croly, *Marcus Alonzo Hanna* (1912), and J. B. Foraker, *Notes of a Busy Life* (1916).]
H.C.H.

BUSHNELL, DAVID (*c.* 1742–1824), inventor, a descendant of Francis Bushnell, an Englishman, who in 1639 joined the New Haven Colony and subsequently helped to found Guilford, Conn., was born on his father's farm in Saybrook, Conn. The home was located in an extremely secluded portion of the township and here young Bushnell grew up, helping his father with the farm duties, devoting his leisure moments to reading, and shunning all society. When he was twenty-seven his father died, and, as his mother had died some years before, the farm descended to David and his brother. David immediately sold his inheritance, moved into town, and began to prepare for college, securing as tutor, the Rev. John Devotion, pastor of the local Congregational church. Two years later Bushnell entered Yale, and completed the four-year course in 1775. On one occasion as a result, presumably, of a discussion with members of the faculty, he demonstrated, in a small way, the fact that gunpowder could be exploded under water. This is thought to have suggested to him the idea of a submarine mine or torpedo. Apparently he gave much time and attention to this during his college years, for in 1775 he completed at Saybrook a man-propelled submarine boat on the outside shell of which was attached a wooden magazine containing gunpowder and a clock mechanism for igniting it at any particular time. The boat, built entirely of heavy oak beams, had the shape of a top. In fact, its exterior appearance was said to resemble a structure which would result from joining together the upper shells of two turtles and weighting the whole so that the tail end pointed downward and the head skyward. For this reason it was called "Bushnell's Turtle." The vessel was equipped with a vertical and horizontal screw propeller and rudder, operated by hand from the interior; a water gauge to indicate the boat's depth; a compass for direction, lighted up with phosphorus; a foot-operated valve in the keel to admit water for descending; and two hand-operated pumps to eject the water for ascending. The magazine, or torpedo, was located above the rudder and was connected by a line with a wooden screw, turned from within, which could be driven into a ship's hull. A further arrangement was contrived so that as the submarine moved away the clockwork in the mechanism was set in motion, having been previously set to ignite the charge at a certain time, the maximum being twelve hours. Bushnell successfully demonstrated his idea to the governor and Council of Safety of Connecticut who approved of his plan and suggested that he proceed with further experiment if necessary, with the expectation of a proper public reward. During 1776–77 Bushnell attempted to blow up British ships but was never successful, owing entirely to his inability to obtain a skilled operator, he personally being too frail. Attempts were made in Boston Harbor; off Governor's Island, N. Y.; and in the Delaware River above Philadelphia. After the failure at Philadelphia, in December 1777, Bushnell gave up further attempts amidst general popular ridicule, although to-day he is recognized as the father of the submarine. His inability to prove the merits of his invention in actual warfare, however, did not entirely discredit him, for when Gen. Washington in 1779 organized companies of sappers and miners, Bushnell was made a captain-lieutenant. He was promoted to captain in 1781, and was stationed at West Point in command of the Corps of Engineers on June 4, 1783. In November of that year he was mustered out of service, receiving the commutation of five-years' pay in lieu of one-half pay for life. During the following ten or twelve years it is believed that he went to France. In 1795, however, he appeared in Columbia County, Ga., as a school teacher, under the name of Dr. Bush. He lived with a fellow soldier, Abraham Baldwin [*q.v.*] who was the only person who knew his real identity, and through him Bushnell became head of a private school. Several years later he settled in Warrenton, Ga., and began the practise of medicine which he continued until his death at the age of eighty-four. As far as is known he never married.

[F. B. Dexter, *Biog. Sketches of the Grads. of Yale Coll.*, vol. III (1903); Henry Howe, *Memoirs of the Most Eminent Am. Mechanics* (1844); D. Bushnell, "General Principles and Construction of a Submarine Vessel," in *Trans. Am. Phil. Soc.*, vol. IV (1799), No. 37; *Beginning of Modern Submarine Warfare*, arranged by Lieut.-Col. Henry L. Abbot (1881); contemporary account of submarine (1775) in *Conn. Hist. Soc. Colls.*, vol. II (1870); contemporary account of attempts to destroy British vessels in *Am. Jour. of Sci.*, Apr. 1820; Geo. White, *Hist. Colls. of Ga.* (3rd ed., 1855), pp. 406–09.]
C. W. M.

BUSHNELL, GEORGE ENSIGN (Sept. 10, 1853–July 19, 1924), tuberculosis specialist of the United States army, born in Worcester, Mass., a descendant of Francis Bushnell, a Connecticut pioneer, was the son of the Rev. George Bushnell by his wife, Mary Elizabeth Blake. He attended Beloit College for one year, entered Yale as a sophomore, and graduated in 1876 in the class with President Hadley. As undergraduates these two young men distinguished themselves by their linguistic attainments and were the only two undergraduates of the class to study Sanskrit. In 1880 Bushnell received his M.D from the Yale Medical School. Pulmonary symptoms developed a few months later while he was serving as an interne in the German Hospital, New York City, but he regarded them lightly, and in February 1881 was made first lieutenant and assistant surgeon in the United States army. During the next few years he received a series of appointments of various army posts in the middle west and obtained a wide experience. At the time of the Spanish-American War he worked in the surgeon-general's office, but the strain provoked a recrudescence of his pulmonary symptoms and he passed a six-months' sick leave under the care of Dr. Charles L. Minor at Asheville, N. C. Later he was cared for by C. E. Edson of Denver, and from these two physicians he learned the value of rest in the treatment of pulmonary tuberculosis. From 1904 until 1917 Bushnell was commanding officer of the army tuberculosis hospital at Fort Bayard, N. Mex. There he had extensive experience and an unusual measure of success in treating the disease. He made the surroundings of the patients extremely attractive but maintained vigorous discipline for which he became widely known. His views concerning tuberculosis were at the time new and in part original. He maintained that in adults active tuberculosis was caused by infection from within. He minimized the value of the tuberculin test as a diagnostic measure and was a strong advocate of moderate eating and drinking for those afflicted. He attempted to introduce the Carton diet, but his judgment on this point proved less sound than in his other measures. During his years at Fort

Bayard, he kept abreast of medical literature, reading widely in all the foreign journals, and he even conducted classes in medical German for his officers. His greatest services were rendered during the World War. He introduced measures for rapid examination of large numbers of men and did much to quell the popular alarm concerning the high incidence of tuberculosis in the army. He established a school of diagnosis to train officers in the rapid detection of tuberculosis, and at the end of a year had turned out 450 examiners. The local tuberculosis boards during the war examined 3,288,699 men, of whom 23,991, or 0.73 per cent, were rejected. Bushnell's activity at this time was so strenuous that by the end of 1918 his health had again broken and he was forced to turn his work over to others. As soon as he had regained his strength he began to write his well-known book, *A Study in the Epidemiology of Tuberculosis,* which was published in 1920, and immediately this was completed he began another, *Physical Diagnosis of Diseases of the Chest,* in conjunction with Dr. Joseph H. Pratt of Boston, which did not appear until 1925, after Bushnell's death. In 1922–23 he was professor of military science and tactics in the Harvard Medical School. He spent his last years on his farm at Bedford, Mass., but was taken suddenly ill in California whither he had gone for his health, and finally succumbed to pulmonary tuberculosis, at the age of seventy, after a life-long fight. He was married twice: on Aug. 22, 1881, to Adra Vergilia Holmes, who died in 1896; and on Dec. 24, 1902 to Ethel Maitland Barnard.

[An excellent estimate of Bushnell by "E. H. B." in the *Am. Rev. of Tuberculosis,* June 1925, pp. 275–91; *Military Surgeon,* Sept. 1924; *Yale Univ. Obit. Rec. of Grads.* (1925); additional information from Dr. Jos. H. Pratt.]   J.F.F.

BUSHNELL, HORACE (Apr. 14, 1802–Feb. 17, 1876), Congregational minister, theologian, descended from Francis Bushnell, one of the founders of Guilford, Conn., in 1639, was the grandson of Abraham and Molly (Ensign) Bushnell. His grandmother was a woman of forceful character. Unable to torture her religious experience into the Calvinistic system held by the Congregational churches of New England of that day she heard with gladness a Methodist preacher and joined that denomination. Her grandson saw her but twice in his childhood, yet her vivid personality made so deep an impression on him that in after years he wrote: "Somehow she has been always with me, felt as a silent subtly-operative presence for good." Her son, Ensign, married Dotha Bishop, and the first of their six children was Horace, who was born

in Bantam, Conn. When he was three years old the family moved to a farm in New Preston some fourteen miles away; here the boy grew up. The father was a sagacious, industrious, cheerful man who gave his children of his best; yet it was to the uncommon character and ability of his mother that Bushnell felt he owed the greatest debt. "She was the only person I have known," he wrote, "in the close intimacy of years who never did an inconsiderate, imprudent, or any way excessive thing that required to be afterwards mended. In this attribute of discretion she rose even to a kind of sublimity. I never knew her to give advice that was not justified by results. Such wisdom, as I look upon it, marks a truly great character." She interested herself in her children's studies, trained them in correct habits, refused to be broken by drudgery, and kept the atmosphere of the home genially religious. Bushnell's sensitive spirit was also moulded by the unusual beauty of the neighboring country, a locality notable for its rounded hills, its frequent lakes, its extended and pleasant views. The love of nature and respect for her laws were early awakened within him and profoundly influenced the thought of his maturer years.

He attended the schools of the town, united with the Congregational church when he was nineteen, and worked on the farm under no eight-hour law, "but holding fast the astronomic ordinance in a service of from thirteen to fourteen hours." Clad in homespun, he entered Yale College in 1823 when he was twenty-one years of age. Here he worked hard and achieved both athletic and intellectual eminence in his class. Graduating in 1827, he taught school for a few months in Norwich, Conn., and for ten months served on the editorial staff of the New York *Journal of Commerce.* He next studied for the bar at the Law School in New Haven, having given up, on account of religious doubts, his earlier intention of entering the ministry. Accepting an appointment as tutor in Yale College, he still continued his law studies, passed his examinations, and was ready for admission to the bar when his course of life was suddenly changed. In the winter of 1831 a revival of spiritual interest developed in the college. Bushnell for a while stood aloof, but feeling his responsibility for the students who looked to him for guidance, he changed his attitude, silenced his doubts by religious activities, and in the following autumn entered the Divinity School at Yale. Here he came into the invigorating atmosphere of Nathaniel W. Taylor, the champion of the "new divinity," whose independent and courageous spirit he admired, but from whose methods and conclusions he reacted sharply. Taylor was a vigorous dialectician, promulgating and defending a theological system by formal logic. Bushnell's intuitive, imaginative mind was ill at ease in the iron cage of Calvinism, even when interpreted by the ablest thinker of its broadest school: so he turned to Coleridge, whose *Aids to Reflection,* deeply pondered at this time, opened to him "a whole other world somewhere overhead, a range of realities in a higher tier." In old age he affirmed that to this book he owed more than to any other save the Bible.

On May 22, 1833 he was ordained pastor of the North Church of Hartford, Conn., and on Sept. 13, 1833 he wedded Mary Apthorp of New Haven, a descendant of John Davenport. Bushnell entered the ministry at a time when the Old and New School of New England theologians were in fierce debate, but he sided with neither, having little sympathy with their spirit and none with their dialectical methods of reaching the truth. In a sermon preached on the twentieth anniversary of his ordination, he thus describes his position and purpose: "I was just then passing into a vein of comprehensiveness, questioning whether all parties were not in reality standing for some one side or article of truth . . . accordingly my preaching never was to overthrow one school and set up another, neither was it to find a position of neutrality midway between them, but as far as theology is concerned, it was to comprehend, if possible, the truth contended for in both." From the first his thought was mature and his language had the "beauty and high solemnity" which characterized all his later writings. His sermon on "Every Man's Life a Plan of God," delivered in those early years, was later ranked by a writer in the *New York Tribune* as one of the three most notable of modern times, the other two being Canon Mozley's "Reversal of Human Judgments" and Phillips Brooks's "Gold and the Calf."

In 1840 Bushnell declined a call to be president of Middlebury (Vt.) College. In July 1845, broken in health, he sailed for a year's sojourn in Europe. On his return he published *Christian Nurture* (1847). Two years later there came to him a mystical experience which profoundly influenced his after life and thought. It was a spiritual birthday, such as came to Augustine and Luther and Wesley—a vision of truth whose light lingered permanently on his soul and whose power gave him perfect freedom. His daughter thus describes the event: "On an early morning in February his wife awoke to hear that the light they had waited for, more than they that watch

for the morning, had risen indeed. She asked, 'What have you seen?' He replied, 'The Gospel.' It came to him at last, after all his thought and study, not as something reasoned out, but as an inspiration—a revelation from the mind of God himself." Referring to it in his closing years, he remarked: "I seemed to pass a boundary . . . from . . . partial seeings, glimpses and doubts, into a clearer knowledge of God and into his inspirations, which I have never wholly lost. The change was into faith—a sense of the freeness of God and the ease of approach to him." Made a new man in the joy and power of his vision, he naturally incorporated its meaning in a book, issued from the press within a year, entitled *God in Christ* (1849). But his glorious intuition was uncongenial to the rigid orthodoxy of the day, and from New Haven, Bangor, Princeton there came immediately severe reviews. Repeated efforts were made by the conservative ministers of the state to bring the author to trial for heresy, but the fellowship of the Congregational churches was organized for conference and fraternal helpfulness, not for dogmatic overlordship of faith, and the common sense of the ministers of the General Association forbade them putting restraint upon a mind that was so evidently rooted in the essentials of religion. Bushnell answered his critics and redefined his position in a new publication, *Christ in Theology* (1851).

Unfortunately the invalidism which was to afflict Bushnell's subsequent life now made its appearance. What had been at first a minister's sore throat took a deeper hold until increasing bronchial trouble compelled Bushnell to seek a milder climate and 1856 found him in California. This new country greatly stimulated those more mundane faculties which had lain dormant during his theological controversies. Being a man of robust common sense with the talents of an engineer, he took keen interest in the problems of this developing region. He predicted a railroad across the continent, studied all feasible entrances into San Francisco, and selected the one ultimately adopted. Interesting himself in the establishment of a college in this state whose greatness he foresaw, he examined seven proposed sites and finally designated Berkeley as having the proper requirements of situation, soil, and water supply. Here the college was founded which afterward became the University of California. He was offered the presidency of the young institution but declined. Returning to Hartford, he gathered up the fruits of twenty-five years of his ministry in a volume of *Sermons for the New Life* (1858). Despairing of regaining his health, he resigned his pastorate in April

1861. Yet to such an extent did his vigorous mind triumph over his growing weakness that nearly half of his published works were issued after his retirement from active service. *Christian Nurture* came from the press in its final form in 1861; *Work and Play*, a volume of essays and addresses, in 1864; and in the same year another book of sermons, *Christ and his Salvation*. In 1866 was given to the world the most permanently significant of his works, *The Vicarious Sacrifice*, in which is set forth at length his conception of the atoning work of Christ, now commonly known as the "moral influence" theory of the Atonement. This was followed in 1868 by a collection of essays entitled, *Moral Uses of Dark Things* which reveal Bushnell's breadth of culture and his mastery of literary form. In 1869 he declared against woman's suffrage in a small treatise whose central thought is shown in its title, *Women's Suffrage; The Reform against Nature,* and in 1872 he issued a final volume of sermons bearing the title, *Sermons on Living Subjects.* He continued his discussion of the Atonement, somewhat modifying his previous restatement of that doctrine, in *Forgiveness and Law* (1874). Although his health was rapidly failing, he projected a new book to be called "The Inspirations." "I do not expect," he said, "to live the labor through. I undertake it, in fact, to get a *sense of being* from it." On the morning of Feb. 17, 1876, he died, in his seventy-fourth year. Two days before his death he received news from the Common Council of Hartford that the park in which the capitol now stands had been named Bushnell Park in his honor. After his death a group of his essays and addresses were published under the title *Building Eras in Religion* (1881), and in the same year a uniform edition of his works was issued. In 1903 *Nature and the Supernatural, Sermons for the New Life, Work and Play* were reissued; also a volume of sermons and selections under the title *The Spirit in Man.*

In national questions Bushnell adhered to his principle of seeing the truth on both sides. He strenuously opposed the fugitive slave law, yet he was not an abolitionist. His faith in Lincoln was pronounced from the first for he believed that wisdom dwelt in a mind so simply honest, and this confidence he maintained during the dark days which followed. At the Commemorative Celebration held in honor of the men of Yale who died in the Civil War he was chosen to deliver the oration, which he entitled "Our Obligation to the Dead" (1865). In this oration his forward-looking spirit saw a nobler future coming out of the tragic sacrifices of the war. He predicted a new birth of literature such as had followed the wars of Elizabeth and Anne and Napoleon. "Henceforth," he said, "we are not going to write English but American. We have gotten our position, we are now to have our own civilization, think our own thoughts, rhyme our own measures . . . make our own canons of criticism. . . . In place of politicians we are going to have, at least, some statesmen; for we have gotten the pitch of a grand, new, Abrahamic statesmanship, unsophisticated, honest and real. . . . We seem, as it were, in a day, to be set in loftier ranges of thought, by this huge flood-tide that has lifted our nationality." The scope of Bushnell's public interests may best be shown by naming some of his contributions to the discussions of his day: *The True Wealth and Weal of Nations* (1837); *Barbarism the First Danger* (1847), a paper which had immense influence in founding Christian colleges in the West; *Common Schools* (1853); and *Popular Government by Divine Right* (1864). On his return from Italy, in 1846, having been profoundly impressed by the evidences of misgovernment in the Papal States, he wrote a *Letter to His Holiness, Pope Gregory XVI,* recounting the iniquities he had seen and urging reform both ecclesiastical and political. The letter was written and published in England; was translated into Italian and widely circulated, was placed on the *Index Expurgatorius* and specified by proclamation as one of the seditious publications to be suppressed by the police. *The Age of Homespun* (1851), one of the finest pieces of historical writing produced by Bushnell, is a vivid picture of early New England life when strong men enjoyed religion and enlarged their minds by profound metaphysical discussions.

He was not a popular preacher, but his was one of the most original and deeply penetrating minds which ever uttered itself from the pulpit in America. He reasoned, not with his intellect merely, but with his whole nature, and his solid thought moved steadily forward with a mastery of energetic words, a majesty of statement, a glow of spiritual passion which have given his sermons what appears to be a permanent place in the literature of the Church. George Adam Smith rightly classified him when he stated that as Spenser was the poet's poet, so Bushnell was the preachers' preacher; "his sermons are on the shelves of every manse in Scotland." Essentially a poet with a mystic's high vision he spoke with all the fervor and authority of a seer, yet a seer of profound and practical realities.

His daughter thus describes his personal appearance in his prime: "The spare sinewy figure, tense yet easy in its motions; the face, then smoothly shaven, showing delicate outlines about the cordial, sweet-tempered mouth; the high, broad forehead, straight to the line where it was swept by the careless hair, just streaked with gray; the kindling gray eyes, deep-set under beetling eyebrows; and, above all, the abrupt yet kindly manner, indicating in its unaffected simplicity a fund of conscious power."

It now remains to state the distinctive character of the service Bushnell rendered to his times and to the future. In New England Jonathan Edwards had reshaped the Calvinistic system of theological thought with such astonishing ability and urged it with such impressive fervor that it became the intellectual and spiritual home of the leading religious thinkers of the country. Yet they were not quite comfortable in it. It limited them in too many places. Hopkins, Bellamy, Emmons, Taylor, Hodge each changed a little this marvelously constructed house. They shared its grandeur and they were involved in its tragic error—a conception of human nature which ran athwart the best instincts of the heart. Disagreeing in many respects, they were at one in their method. Theology to them was essentially an intellectual system and was to be established by processes of exact logical deduction. Defining words with utmost care, they fashioned their statements of doctrine with meticulous precision. All being dialecticians, they differed violently and ranged themselves into distinct schools of thought. Now into this group of dialectical rationalists came a poet, a mystic, who apprehended truth by intuition, who gave the instincts of the heart full hearing, and whose appeal was to life rather than to logic. The theologians did not understand him for he belonged to a different order. What was still more puzzling, he used language in a manner quite incomprehensible to them. Interested in metaphysical speculation they endeavored to employ words as precise instruments to express nicest distinctions in thought. Bushnell denied that this was possible, and so cut under the very foundations of their work. He used language, not as the logicians, but as the common people and the poets have always done, as suggestive of truth, as a symbol of thought. This theory of the limitation of speech he early adopted and set forth with great care in his introductory chapter on language in the volume *God in Christ,* and in a more popular form in the essay, "Our Gospel a Gift to the Imagination." Spiritual things, he contended, cannot be precisely expressed in formal statements. Words are suggestive of religious truth but cannot be definitive. The gospel yields its secrets to the disciplined imagination—the eye of the soul—rather than to severe intellectual processes. Such use of language, of course, discredited all theological attempts at exact system building.

At four points he broke decidedly with the prevailing theological views and became the pioneer of a new order. First, he protested against the common view of the relation of children to the church. The Puritan churches were depending for their growth largely on revivals, and revivals aimed at the conversion of adults. In their scheme of thought there was no place for children which was satisfactory to the mind and heart. The criticism is well taken that they reversed the gospel precept so that it read, "Except ye become as grown men and be converted, ye shall not enter into the kingdom of heaven." Over this perversion of nature and Christianity Bushnell brooded for ten years before he attacked the prevalent system in his book *Christian Nurture.* Its main thesis is that "the child is to grow up a Christian, and never know himself as being otherwise." This little volume turned the attention of the churches toward the training of the young, gave them a clearly defined doctrine of Christian growth, and suggested a working method in the religious training of children.

Of less permanent importance, but of real service to his day, was the relief he brought to orthodox Christians in respect to the doctrine of the Trinity. The audacious speculations of the theologians regarding the triune nature of God had issued in a conception which was practically tritheistic and caused much intellectual bewilderment. In this as in all things, Bushnell appealed to life. We experience, he argued, the one God under three different expressions. But that these three aspects of the divine revelation represented eternal distinctions in the Godhead, he refused to affirm, for here was a mystery which the human mind could not penetrate.

The third point at which he broke from the accepted opinion of his day was in his interpretation of the meaning of the cross. He repudiated both the penal and the governmental theories of the Atonement then in vogue, and affirmed that God's holy love was not satisfied until it was so revealed and brought to men in Christ that the love and power of sin in them is conquered and they are united in living spiritual union with God. This explanation is known in theology as "the moral influence theory" and has been widely approved because it shows that the atoning work of Christ falls under a law of self-sacrifice which is of universal validity.

A final service he rendered by recalling men

from the fatal dualism into which their philosophy had led them. According to Calvinism, human nature and nature itself were involved in the fall of Adam, humanity was alienated from God and was fast moving toward the fires of everlasting burning. This monstrous view of nature had caused theologians to draw a sharp line between nature and the supernatural, it divided further reason and revelation, the sacred and the profane. It was not original with New England, or even with Calvinistic theology, it was equally pronounced in the thought of medieval Catholicism. Already Bushnell had reacted against this perverted conception in his *Christian Nurture,* and he attacked it more explicitly in his volume entitled *Nature and the Supernatural as Together Constituting the One System of God.* This exaltation of nature his biographer, Dr. Theodore T. Munger, finds to be the key to Bushnell's thinking. "Bushnell," he writes, "outrunning his day, conceived of God as immanent in his works—the soul and life of them. Their laws were his laws. Therefore if one would know how God feels and thinks and acts, one must go to nature, and to humanity as its culmination. God is the spiritual reality of which nature is the manifestation." This book brought great help to the younger men in the ministry of that day on the vexing question of miracles. The prevalent notion was that a miracle implied the suspension of natural law. Bushnell affirmed that a miracle is not a violation of law, but is under law, the law of the supernatural which works through the order of nature.

His place in the history of religious thought may be stated as follows. He was the exponent on this side of the Atlantic of that spiritual movement in theology which was represented in Germany by Schleiermacher and in England by Coleridge. Like them he revolted against the dry rationalism of the times and endeavored to restate the truths of religion in terms of human experience. Like them he would give the emotions and intuitions their due recognition. Like them he saw nature and humanity filled with the divine presence and expressive of its purpose. Many were feeling the inspiration of this liberalizing movement, but Bushnell was the first notable theologian in New England to apprehend the full meaning to religion of that conception of nature which was finding such memorable utterance in the literature of the century, especially in Wordsworth, and to translate the doctrines of the church in harmony with the laws of life. His contemporaries in England embodying the same tendency were Maurice and Robertson, in America his essential message reached

the people through the more widely acclaimed ministries of Beecher and Brooks. Emerson was, indeed, a more conspicuous herald of this enfranchising movement which was sweeping through Europe and was disturbing our shores; and he had his own audience and his own peculiar work. Bushnell's appeal was to the more conservative religious mind of the churches, first of New England and then of the country. He brought to the interpretation of the supreme doctrines of Christianity a sense of the divine in nature, of life as the superlative test of truth, of the heart as a means of spiritual knowledge, of language as suggestive, not precise, in the realm of the spirit; thus his coming marked the end of that school of thought which began with Edwards and is known as the New England Theology; it ushered in new habits of thinking and new methods of expression.

[The chief sources of information are an excellent biography, *Life and Letters of Horace Bushnell* (1880, 1903), prepared by his daughter, Mary Bushnell Cheney, with the help of others. Very valuable is Dr. T. T. Munger's analysis of Bushnell's genius and work in *Horace Bushnell, Preacher and Theologian* (1899), and also his essay, "The Secret of Horace Bushnell," in *Essays for the Day* (1904). In 1902 the General Association of Connecticut held a meeting in Bushnell's honor in Hartford, and the addresses were published in a pamphlet entitled *Bushnell Centenary* (1902). *My Four Religious Teachers* (1903), by H. C. Trumbull; "Horace Bushnell and Albrecht Ritschl," by G. B. Stevens in *Am. Jour. Theol.,* Jan. 1902; "Horace Bushnell and His Work for Theology," by C. F. Dole in *The New World,* Dec. 1899, are valuable. See also Frank Hugh Foster, *A Genetic Hist. of the New Eng. Theology* (1907), *passim.* A list of Bushnell's published articles, the replies they evoked, references to him in books and periodicals including the year 1903, was assembled by Henry B. Learned, *Bibliography of the Writings of Horace Bushnell* (n.d.); it takes slight account, however, of Bushnell's pamphlets and books published in Great Britain, and only of editions involving some alteration of the text.]
                                        C. A. D.

BUSSEY, CYRUS (Oct. 5, 1833–Mar. 2, 1915), Union soldier, was born at Hubbard, Trumbull County, Ohio, the son of Amos Bussey, a Methodist minister, and his wife Hannah Tylee. Four years later the family moved to Indiana. Cyrus went to work in a dry-goods store at the age of fourteen, and at sixteen started a small business for himself at Dupont, Ind. He was married to Ellen Kiser of Rockford, Ind., on May 15, 1855. In the same year he removed to Bloomfield, Ia., continuing in business and entering politics. He was elected to the Iowa Senate in 1858, as a Democrat, and in 1860 was a delegate to the Democratic national convention which met at Charleston and Baltimore and nominated Stephen A. Douglas for the presidency. Early in 1861 the governor of Iowa appointed him as one of his aides in charge of the defense of the state. Invading Missouri with a force of Iowa militia,

Bussey dispersed a body of secessionists in a skirmish at Athens, and assisted in saving Missouri to the Union. Appointed colonel of the 3rd Iowa Cavalry, he was mustered into the volunteer service of the United States on Sept. 5, 1861. At the battle of Pea Ridge, where his regiment was first engaged with the enemy, he was in charge of a small force of cavalry, with three guns, in addition to his own men. He commanded a brigade of cavalry in the Army of the Tennessee (Grant) during the Vicksburg campaign of 1863. He was appointed brigadier-general of volunteers, Jan. 5, 1864, and commanded a brigade and division, employed in minor operations and on garrison duty in the southwest, until his muster out, Aug. 24, 1865, with the brevet rank of major-general of volunteers. After the war he resumed business as a commission merchant, first in St. Louis and later in New Orleans. He was president of the chamber of commerce of the latter city for six years, and was chairman of a committee which secured the appropriation for the construction of the Eads jetties to improve navigation at the mouth of the Mississippi River. In 1881 he removed his business to New York. The war having made him a Republican in politics, he was elected a delegate to the national convention of that party in 1868 and again in 1884. President Harrison appointed him assistant secretary of the interior in 1889, and he held that office until 1893, his administration being marked by a lavish policy in the award of pensions. He then established a law office in the city of Washington, where he spent the remainder of his life. He was buried in Arlington National Cemetery.

[*Who's Who in America*, 1914–15; *Annals of Iowa*, 3rd ser., vol. V (1901–03), pp. 81–92, and vol. XII (1915), pp. 153–54; *Official Records*, ser. I, vols. III, VIII, XXIV (pts. 2, 3), XLI (pts. 2, 3), XLVIII (pts. 1, 2); F. B. Heitman, *Hist. Reg.* (1903), I, 268.]

T. M. S.

BUTLER, ANDREW PICKENS (Nov. 18, 1796–May 25, 1857), lawyer, senator, was the fifth child of William Butler [*q.v.*], the Revolutionary soldier, and his wife Behethland Foote Moore, who when seventeen years old had made a celebrated midnight ride of warning to the Continental troops, through which she first met her future husband. Andrew attended Moses Waddell's academy in Abbeville District—the training school of Calhoun, McDuffie, and other men famous in state history—and then entered South Carolina College, graduating in 1817. Two years later he was admitted to the bar. After a brief residence in Columbia he moved to Edgefield and soon built up a wide practise in the courts of the state. In 1824 he was elected to the legislature where he became recognized as a leader of the

Calhoun faction and a champion of nullification. From 1829 until the end of his legislative term, he was a trustee of South Carolina College. After a brief service as circuit judge in 1833, he was advanced in the same year to the bench of the court of appeals where he remained for thirteen years. Judicial responsibilities were not particularly congenial to him and he welcomed an opportunity, in December 1846, to go to the Senate as successor to McDuffie, who had resigned. He was reëlected in 1848 and again in 1854, both times without opposition.

Partly because of Calhoun's influence, the younger senator early assumed a place of measurable prominence; in 1849, for example, he was elected by the Senate chairman of the Judiciary Committee, defeating Seward and Chase. Standing necessarily somewhat in the shadow of his conspicuous colleague, Butler was vigorous in the debates and active in routine work. He devoted himself faithfully to the interests of his slaveholding constituency, opposing the admission of California, supporting the fugitive-slave law, and reaching the climax of his senatorial career in the forensic battle over Kansas. His speech on this topic in part drew forth Sumner's address on May 19, 1856, in which the Massachusetts senator attacked Butler in a vituperative manner. Three days later, while Sumner was seated at his desk in the Senate chamber, Preston Brooks [*q.v.*], congressman from South Carolina and nephew of Butler, beat him over the head with his cane until he was insensible. The following year, Butler, who had been in weak health for some time, died at his Edgefield home, "Stonelands."

Within the councils of his own state, Butler was more temperate than many of his contemporaries. He represented in the main the up-country point of view as opposed to the more radical attitude of the coastal leaders. In the early fifties he resolutely opposed the secession agitation, and argued strongly against any form of separate state action. He was known for his wit, sometimes caustic, and for his qualities of good comradeship. Gov. Perry, who was in the opposing political camp, thought him too impatient and sarcastic for highest judicial excellence and reported his speaking as rather dull; but even Perry freely conceded to him force of intellect and character. Butler was impressive in personal appearance, tall, clean-shaven, with a mass of fine hair on a large head. His domestic life was sad. His first wife, Susan Anne Simkins, lived after marriage only a few months, and his second wife, Harriet Hayne, died in 1834 after two years of marriage. Through the long period of his loneliness, Butler's mother kept his house until her death in 1851. By his second wife he had one child, Nancy, who married Johnson Hagood, a general of the Confederate army.

[Sketches of Butler are in John Belton O'Neal, *The Bench and Bar of S. C.* (1859), in B. F. Perry, *Reminiscences of Public Men* (1883), and in U. R. Brook, *S. C. Bench and Bar* (1908). Many of his speeches in the Senate are in the *Cong. Globe* for the decade of his tenure. Records of the Butler family are in "The Butlers of S. C.," in *S. C. Hist. and Geneal. Mag.*, Oct. 1903.]
F.P.G.

BUTLER, BENJAMIN FRANKLIN (Dec. 14, 1795–Nov. 8, 1858), lawyer, politician, was descended from Jonathan Butler, who settled at Saybrook, Conn., in 1724. Jonathan's grandson Medad migrated from Branford, Conn., to Kinderhook Landing (Stuyvesant) in Columbia County, N. Y. Here he married Hannah Tylee in 1794, and here their eldest son, Benjamin, was born the next year. After completing the scanty education offered by the district school, he studied law and was admitted to the bar in 1817. For four years thereafter he was a partner at Albany in the office of Martin Van Buren, for whom he retained a life-long admiration and affection. The year after his admission to the bar he married Harriet Allen, whose parents (the mother a Quaker related to Benjamin Franklin) had moved from Nantucket, Mass., to Hudson, N. Y., about the same time that his own father had left Branford. As Butler rose in his profession, honors and duties came to him rapidly. He was district attorney of Albany County from 1821 to 1824, and the next year was associated with John Duer and John C. Spencer in the important commission for the revision of the statutes of the State of New York. From 1827 to 1833 he was a member of the state legislature, which would have elected him to the United States Senate had he given his consent. At the same time he declined an appointment by Gov. Marcy to the supreme court of the state. He did, however, yield to the urgent invitation of his former law partner, Van Buren, now vice-president of the United States, to enter President Jackson's cabinet as attorney-general in the autumn of 1833,—perhaps on Van Buren's assurance that his acceptance would not interfere with his continued practise in the courts of New York and Albany, the former of which cities might be reached in fifteen hours and the latter in a day and a night from Washington, "next season, when the railroad is completed." Butler held the office of attorney-general for five years, and added to its duties the secretaryship of war in the closing months of Jackson's administration (October 1836–March 1837) when Lewis Cass retired from the cabinet to become minister to France. He might have

had his pick of cabinet posts under Van Buren, but the practise of law appealed more strongly to him than political office. Nor could President Polk persuade him seven years later to reënter the cabinet as secretary of war. He did, however, accept both Van Buren's and Polk's appointments as United States attorney for the southern district of New York (1838–41, 1845–48), a position which was less incompatible with his professional duties. The last ten years of his life (1848–58) he devoted entirely to the law, withdrawing more and more from general practise to the management of a small group of corporation cases involving very large sums of money. His rank among the leaders of the New York bar was firmly established. Chancellor Kent spoke of him as "this remarkable lawyer whose memoranda the student finds in all his books." Butler's interest in the law as a science led him to organize the department of law in the University of the City of New York in 1838 and to serve for several years as its leading professor. In politics he was a staunch Jacksonian Democrat. He headed the electoral college of New York which cast its vote for Polk in 1845. As the contest over slavery grew more heated, however, he began to waver. He supported his old chief, Van Buren, who ran on the Free-Soil ticket in 1848, but he returned to the Democratic fold in 1852 to vote for Pierce and the finality of the compromise acts of 1850. The Kansas-Nebraska Act of 1854, however, drove him out of the Democratic ranks. With thousands of other Anti-Nebraska Democrats he joined the new Republican party, and he cast his last presidential ballot for Frémont in 1856. He appeared at a mass meeting in City Hall Park, New York, on May 13, 1854, to denounce the repeal of the Missouri Compromise. But he did not live to see the Republican victory in 1860 and the civil strife which followed. In the summer of 1858 he went to Europe to recuperate from his heavy labors and died at Paris of Bright's disease. His body was brought back to New York and buried from the Mercer Street Presbyterian Church, of which he had been a devoted member, although he would never accept any office in the church, because there were articles in the Westminster Confession of Faith to which he could not subscribe. Aside from his legal opinions and arguments, the work in collaboration with Duer and Spencer in the revision of the statutes of New York, and the convention (approved by Act of Congress in June 1834) by which he and five associated commissioners settled the controversy of fifty years' standing over the boundary line between New York and New Jersey, Butler left but a scanty literary legacy. His grasp of history and power of lucid exposition, however, are amply shown in his "Outline of the Constitutional History of New York" (1847), an address on the occasion of the forty-third anniversary of the founding of the New York Historical Society, tracing the changes in government in New York from the days of the Dutch rule down to the adoption of the Constitution of 1846 (published in the *Collections of the New York Historical Society, 2* ser., II, 1848, 9–75).

[Wm. Allen Butler (B. F. Butler's son), *A Retrospect of Forty Years, 1825–1865*, ed. by Harriet Allen Butler (1911); *Procs. and Addresses on the Occasion of the Death of Benj. Franklin Butler*, a memorial privately printed for the family (1889); Wm. Lyon Mackenzie, *The Lives and Opinions of Benj. Franklin Butler . . . and Jesse Hoyt* (1845); L. B. Proctor, *Bench and Bar of N. Y.* (1870).]   D. S. M.

BUTLER, BENJAMIN FRANKLIN (Nov. 5, 1818–Jan. 11, 1893), Union soldier, congressman, governor of Massachusetts, was born at Deerfield, N. H. His family was largely of Scotch-Irish stock, settled on the New England frontier before the Revolution. His father, John, was captain of dragoons under Jackson at New Orleans, traded in the West Indies, and held a privateer's commission from Bolivar. His mother was Charlotte Ellison, of the Londonderry (N. H.) Cilleys, or Seelyes. After Capt. Butler's death she ultimately settled, in 1828, at Lowell, Mass., running one of the famous factory boarding houses there.

Benjamin was sent to Waterbury (now Colby) College in Maine to continue the family Baptist Calvinism; but he rejected Calvinism altogether. He graduated in 1838, and returned to Lowell where he taught school and studied law. He was admitted to the bar in 1840 and began a successful practise which continued until his death. At first he was chiefly occupied with criminal cases in which he built up a reputation for remarkable quickness of wit, resourcefulness, and mastery of all the defensive devices of the law. His practise gradually extended so that he maintained offices in both Boston and Lowell. He was shrewd in investment, and in spite of rather lavish expenditures built up a fortune. On May 16, 1844, he married Sarah Hildreth, an actress. Their daughter Blanche married Adelbert Ames, who during the period of Reconstruction was senator from Mississippi, and governor of that state. After the Civil War, Butler maintained residences at Lowell, Washington, and on the New England coast. He was interested in yachting, and at one time owned the famous cup-winner *America.*

Butler early entered politics, as a Democrat, being elected to the Massachusetts House of Representatives in 1853, and the Senate in 1859. He was an effective public speaker. His method, which seems to have been instinctive with him, was to draw attack upon himself, and then confute his assailants. He made friends of labor and of the Roman Catholic element in his home district, whose support he always retained. In the legislature he stood for a ten-hour day, and for compensation for the burning of the Ursuline Convent. He took great pains to be in the intimate councils of his party, but was seldom trusted by the party leaders. His talent for biting epigrams, and his picturesque controversies made him one of the most widely known men in politics from 1860 till his death. In the national Democratic convention of 1860 he advocated a renewal of the Cincinnati platform, opposed Douglas, and voted to nominate Jefferson Davis. With Caleb Cushing and other seceders from the adjourned Baltimore meeting he joined in putting forward Breckinridge and Lane. It was characteristic of him that in thus supporting the Southern candidate, he advanced as his reason for leaving the Douglas convention the fact that the reopening of the slave-trade had there been discussed. As was the case with so many Northern supporters of Breckinridge, Butler was a strong Andrew Jackson Unionist. He had always been interested in military affairs, and to the confusion of the Republican majority in Massachusetts had been elected brigadier-general of militia. At the news of the firing on Fort Sumter he was promptly and dramatically ready, with men and money, and left Boston for Washington with his regiment on Apr. 17, 1861.

Thereupon began one of the most astounding careers of the war. Butler was, until Grant took control, as much a news item as any man except Lincoln. He did many things so clever as to be almost brilliant. He moved in a continual atmosphere of controversy which gradually widened from local quarrels with Gov. Andrew of Massachusetts until it included most of the governments of the world; in which controversies he was sometimes right. He expected the war to advance his political fortunes and the financial fortunes of his family and friends. His belief in the Union and in his own ability were both strong and sincere. He had hopes of the Unionist presidential nomination in 1864. A thorn in the side of those in authority, his position as a Democrat fighting for the Union and his prominence in the public eye, made it impossible to ignore or effectively to discipline him.

At the beginning of the war, his relief of blockaded Washington by landing at Annapolis with the 8th Massachusetts, and by repairing the railroad from that point, was splendidly accomplished. Probably because of his Southern connections, he was chosen to occupy Baltimore, which he did on May 13, 1861, peacefully, with but 900 troops. On May 16 he was nominated major-general of volunteers. His next command was at Fortress Monroe. Here he admirably administered the extraordinary provisions necessary for increased numbers. The problem of how to deal with slaves fleeing from Confederate owners to the Union lines he solved by declaring these slaves contraband; and the term "Contraband" clung to them throughout the war. He undertook a military expedition which ended disastrously in the battle of Big Bethel. On Aug. 8, 1861, he was replaced by the venerable Gen. Wool. He was then given command of the military forces in a joint military and naval attack on the forts at Hatteras Inlet, and took possession of them on Aug. 27 and 28. He then returned to Massachusetts with authority to enlist troops; which led to a conflict with the state authorities. His plan was to use his independent command to reduce the peninsula of eastern Virginia, but he was attached instead to the expedition against New Orleans, again commanding the land forces. On May 1, 1862, he entered the city, which lay under the guns of the fleet. He was assigned the difficult task of the military government of this hostile population.

Butler's administration of New Orleans is the most controversial portion of his career. It is at least evident that he preserved the peace and effectively governed the city, improving sanitation, and doing other useful things. It is equally evident that his conduct of affairs was high-handed. Ignoring the United States government, he assumed full financial control, collecting taxes, and expending monies. He hung William Mumford for hauling down the United States flag. He seized $800,000 in bullion belonging to Southern owners, which had been left in charge of the French consul; thereby bringing upon the United States government protests from practically all the governments of Europe. A portion of the bullion was not turned over to the United States government until the whole country had become excited over its fate. Still more sensational was his Order No. 28. It certainly was true that the women of New Orleans had rendered themselves unpleasant to the occupying troops. To meet this situation Butler ordered that . . . "When any female shall, by word, or gesture, or movement, insult or show contempt for any officer or soldier of the United States, she shall be regarded and held liable to be treated as a woman of the town plying her avocation." To the international storm of indignation which

this aroused, it could only be replied that no violence was intended. In addition to these overt acts, there hangs about Butler's administration a cloud of suspicion of financial irregularity, popularly characterized in the tradition that he stole the spoons from the house he occupied. That corruption was rampant there can be no doubt. It seems that his brother was implicated. In so far as Gen. Butler is concerned the historian must be content to recognize that if he were guilty, he was certainly too clever to leave proofs behind; a cleverness somewhat unfortunate for him, if he were indeed not guilty. On Dec. 16, 1862, he was removed.

In 1863 he was given command of the districts of eastern Virginia and North Carolina, and was put in command of the Army of the James, consisting of two corps. In this position Grant, the next year, used him as commissioner for the exchange of prisoners, perhaps hoping (it being contrary to Grant's policy to exchange) that the Confederate commander would refuse to recognize him, as President Davis had issued a proclamation declaring that his conduct at New Orleans had placed him outside the rules of war. Butler, however, conducted some exchanges, and forced the Confederacy to recognize the military status of the United States negro troops. He encouraged trade in his districts, almost violating the orders of the government. Having made an independent advance, this resulted in the bottling of his army at Bermuda Hundred, where they remained blocked by a greatly inferior number of Confederates. In November 1864 he was sent to New York to preserve order during the election, riots being anticipated. His adroitness and his popularity with the Democrats prevented all disorders; if any were indeed brewing. On Jan. 7, 1865, he was ordered by Grant to return to Lowell.

He had by this time become identified with the Radical element among the Republicans. In the elections of 1866 he was elected to Congress, as a Republican, serving until 1875. He lived at Washington lavishly, the Radicals were the dominant element, and he became prominent among them. In the management of the Johnson impeachment for the House of Representatives he was, owing to the feebleness of Thaddeus Stevens, the most impressive figure. After Stevens's death in 1868 he seems to have aspired to succeed him as Radical chief, taking a drastic stand on all questions of reconstruction as they came up during the Grant administration. At this stage, his influence with Grant seems to have been strong. In the Democratic wave of 1875 he lost his seat.

In the meantime he had been having difficulties with the ruling element in the Republican party in his own state. He was hardly more hated in Louisiana than by the conservative elements of both parties in Massachusetts, because of his radical proposals, his unconventionality, and their questioning of his honesty. This hostility he took as a challenge, and determined to become governor of the Bay State. In 1871 he ran for the Republican nomination for governor, and was defeated. In 1872 he ran again, and was again defeated. After his defeat for Congress in 1875 he actively took up the cause of the Greenbacks, which indeed he had supported from the beginning. In 1878 he was again elected to Congress, as an independent Greenbacker. In the same year he ran for the governorship, with the support of the Greenbackers and a portion of the Democrats. Defeated, he ran again in 1879, as Democratic candidate, but there was a split in the party, and again he was defeated. In 1880 he attended the national Democratic convention and supported Gen. Hancock, who received the nomination. In 1882 he at length succeeded in obtaining the undivided support of the Democratic party of his state, and had the advantage of the general reaction against the Republicans. His persistency, also, appealed to many, who felt that he was unduly attacked and should have a chance. He was elected, alone of his ticket, by a majority of 14,000. His position gave him no power, as in Massachusetts no executive steps could be taken without the assent of the council, which was controlled, as were both Houses of the legislature, by his opponents. He attacked the administration of the charitable institutions of the state, especially the Tewkesbury State Almshouse; but the investigation which he instigated led to no results. He characteristically attended with full military escort the Commencement at Harvard, after that institution had decided to break its tradition and not award a degree to the governor of the commonwealth. His drastic Thanksgiving proclamation created a scandal, until he pointed out that it was copied complete from that of Christopher Gore in 1810, with the addition of an admonition to the clergy to abstain from political discussion. In 1883 he was defeated for reëlection. In 1884 he was an avowed candidate for the presidency. He was nominated on May 14, by a new party called Anti-Monopoly, demanding national control of interstate commerce and the eight-hour day. On May 28 he was nominated by the National [Greenback] party. He was a delegate to the Democratic convention, where he sought to control the platform and secure the nomination; but was de-

feated. In the election he received 175,370 votes, scattered in all but nine states, and most numerous in Michigan, where he received 42,243. This was his last political activity. He died at Washington, Jan. 11, 1893.

[Butler's autobiography, *Butler's Book*, 2 vols. (1892), is entertaining and valuable as a reflection of the man. *The Private and Official Correspondence of Gen. Benj. F. Butler, during the Period of the Civil War*, 5 vols. (1917), is a fascinating collection of all varieties of material, but not complete with respect to any. His speeches and public letters outside of Congress have not been collected, and exist scattered in newspapers and pamphlets. He is constantly referred to in the letters and reminiscences of the men of his time. There is no standard life. Among the sketches are: Blanche B. Ames, *The Butler Ancestry of Gen. Benj. Franklin Butler* (1895); Jas. Parton, *Gen. Butler in New Orleans* (1864); Edward Pierrepont, *Review of Defence of Gen. Butler Before the House of Representatives, in Relation to the New Orleans Gold* (1865); *Life and Public Services of Maj.-Gen. Butler* (1864); J. F. McLaughlin, *The American Cyclops, the Hero of New Orleans, and the Spoiler of Silver Spoons, Dubbed LL.D. by Pasquino* (1868); M. M. Pomeroy, *Life and Public Services of Benj. F. Butler* (1879); T. A. Bland, *Life of Benj. F. Butler* (1879); *Record of Benj. F. Butler Compiled from the Original Sources* (1883). For Butler's military career see also the *Official Records* (Army).]   C.R.F.

BUTLER, CHARLES (Jan. 15, 1802–Dec. 13, 1897), lawyer, philanthropist, the son of Medad and Hannah (Tylee) Butler and brother of Benjamin Franklin Butler [*q.v.*], was born at Kinderhook Landing (now Stuyvesant), Columbia County, N. Y. In June 1819 he became a clerk, at a salary of $100 a year, in the office of Martin Van Buren at Albany, and later studied at Kinderhook and Albany in the offices of Judge James Vanderpoel and of Benjamin Franklin Butler, who had renewed a partnership with Van Buren. In 1822 he was made deputy clerk of the state Senate, an appointment which gave him the opportunity to become acquainted with many of the leading men in New York politics. He was admitted to the bar in 1824, and, after practising for a few months at Lyons, moved to Geneva to become a partner of Judge Bowen Whiting, a state senator and the district attorney of Ontario County. On Oct. 10, 1825, Butler married Eliza A. Ogden of Walton, N. Y., niece of his uncle William Butler's wife. At Geneva he took an active part in the establishment of Hobart College, and, in the long absences of his partner at Albany, he not only conducted a large part of the law business of the firm but also acted as assistant district attorney of the county. It was in this latter capacity that he prosecuted the kidnappers of William Morgan the Free Mason, in 1826–27, a case which attracted nation-wide attention and deeply stirred the political waters of the country.

In 1833 Butler made a journey to the West, "attended with great privations, fatigue, exposure, and difficulty," which had an important influence on his subsequent activities and laid the basis for his large personal fortune. He bought real estate both at Toledo and at Chicago, and later acquired large interests in the Michigan Southern, the Rock Island, and the Chicago & Northwestern railroads. "There is to-day," says his biographer F. H. Stoddard, "scarcely a railroad leading to or from Chicago, east, west, north, or south, with which he did not have important association and to which he did not render efficient service, so that his acts are written in lines of steel all over the west." In 1834 he moved to New York, where he resided for the remaining sixty-three years of his life. Always interested in the development of the West, as agent of the New York Life Insurance & Trust Company he loaned the farmers of western New York large sums of money for the development of the lands to which the opening of the Erie Canal in 1825 had given enhanced prospective values, and for the conversion of their leaseholds from the large land-grant companies into estates in fee simple. Meanwhile his extensive real estate interests in Chicago were looked after by his brother-in-law, William B. Ogden, who became the first mayor of Chicago upon its incorporation into a city in 1837. When several of the Western states threatened to repudiate their bonds (Mississippi actually did so) during the hard times which followed the over-confident extension of canal and railroad construction in the early thirties, Butler performed a service which won him lasting gratitude both in this country and abroad. As agent for the domestic and foreign holders of the bonds of Michigan and Indiana, he spent weeks in Detroit (spring of 1843) and Indianapolis (winter of 1845–46) laboring to convince the legislators and governors of their responsibility for preserving the plighted faith of their states, in the face of public sentiment, "shared by 99 persons in 100," that there was "no obligation resting on them to recognize or pay any of the bonds." In the end Butler succeeded in getting the bills passed and signed for the preservation of the public credit in both of the states. The letters written to his wife from Detroit and Indianapolis, often at midnight, after fifteen hours of work with wabbling legislators and obstinate officials, furnish an interesting combination of childlike trust in Providence and shrewd political manipulation.

Butler's services in the promotion of education were constant and conspicuous for a period of more than threescore years. He was one of the twenty-four "Founders" of the Union Theological Seminary in 1836, a member of its first board

of directors, and president of the board from 1870 to his death in 1897. Until his ninety-third year he was constant in his attendance at the meetings of the board and distributed the diplomas to the graduating class of the Seminary. In 1836 he became a member of the Council of the University of the City of New York, on which he served for more than half a century. He was a man of singular charm and sterling character, unheralded in his large charities, fond of books and works of art, simple and sincere in his religion. He made frequent trips abroad and numbered among his friends some of the most eminent men of England and the Continent. J. A. Froude, Goldwin Smith, Charles Kingsley, and Matthew Arnold were among the guests who enjoyed the unostentatious hospitality of his house in Fourteenth St., and his beautiful country estate at Fox Meadows in Westchester County.

[Francis H. Stoddard, *The Life and Letters of Chas. Butler* (1903); Geo. L. Prentiss, "A Sketch of the Life and Public Services of Chas. Butler," being pt. V of *The Union Seminary in the City of N. Y.* (1899); *Letter of Chas. Butler, Esq., to the Legislature of Indiana and Other Docs. in Relation to the Public Debt* (1845).]

D. S. M.

BUTLER, EZRA (Sept. 24, 1763–July 12, 1838), congressman, governor of Vermont, was the fifth of seven children born to Asaph and Jane (McAllister) Butler in the town of Lancaster, Mass. When he was a child of seven years the family emigrated to West Windsor, Vt. The mother died and the lad was bound out to service. He had only six months' schooling, and in his youth was a hunter and trapper. For six months he was a soldier in the American Revolution. He settled in Weathersfield, Vt., and with a brother removed to Waterbury, Vt., when there was only one family in the new township. He married Tryphena Diggins of Weathersfield, built a log cabin, and later erected the first frame house in Waterbury. Active in organizing the town, he was elected its first town clerk. He served as town representative from 1794 to 1807 with the exception of the years 1798 and 1805. Ordained to the Baptist ministry in 1801, in his subsequent political activity he continued his church duties when he was not absent from home. He was an active Republican in politics, was elected a member of Congress in 1812, and entered that body in 1813 with Daniel Webster. He delivered a speech in opposition to Webster's resolution calling for information from the President concerning Napoleon's revocation of decrees against American shipping. Elected governor in 1826, he was reëlected in 1827, declining to be again a candidate. While governor he was active in curbing the lottery and in promoting a more liberal system of education. He was a presidential elector in 1804, 1820, 1828, and 1832. In the last-named year, Vermont was the only state to cast its electoral vote for the candidates of the Anti-Masonic party. Butler also served on committees to locate the first state house, the state arsenal, and the state prison. His public career included service on the bench, as a member of the governor's council, the council of censors, and the constitutional convention of 1822. He was a trustee of the University of Vermont (1810–16). In personal appearance he was slightly stooping, and had a dark and sallow complexion and penetrating black eyes. He is numbered among the influential governors of the state during the first half of the nineteenth century.

[*Hist. of Waterbury, Vt.* (1915), compiled by Theo. G. Lewis; sketch by Rev. C. C. Parker in A. M. Hemenway's *Vt. Hist. Gazetteer*, IV (1882), 816; W. H. Crockett, *Vt. the Green Mt. State* (1921), vols. II, III.]
W. H. C.

BUTLER, HOWARD CROSBY (Mar. 7, 1872–Aug. 13?, 1922), archeologist, son of Edward Marchant and Helen Belden (Crosby) Butler, was born at Croton Falls, N. Y. His mother, a woman of great talent, devoted to music and literature, taught him his Latin and exercised a lifelong influence upon his development. Early letters reveal his love of farm life, of flowers and trees, of gentle hills and meadows. The whole course of his education was singularly fortunate. Aided by private tutors at the Lyons Collegiate Institute and the Berkeley School, New York, he entered the class of 1892 at Princeton University as a sophomore. His moderate scholarship in sophomore and junior years gave slight promise of the coming powers of his senior and graduate years. His studies lay in history, Greek and Latin languages, ancient and modern art; starting with a thorough grounding in classical history and English literature, he gained a command of French and Italian and, subsequently, a working knowledge of Arabic, Turkish, and modern Greek which served him well throughout his extensive exploration in the Near East. In art and architecture he came under the genial influence of Prof. Allen Marquand, founder of the Princeton departments of art and architecture. He had a prominent share in reviving the original drama at Princeton through the now well-known Triangle Club, himself playing the part of Bianca in John Kendrick Bangs's *Katharine* and of Portia in *The Hon. Julius Cæsar*, by Post Wheeler and Booth Tarkington. Throughout his life the plays of Shakespeare were his favorite reading, next to the daily reading of his Bible. Having received the degrees of A.B. (1892) and A.M. (1893) from Princeton, he then pursued post-

graduate studies in the Columbia School of Architecture, became lecturer on architecture at Princeton (1895–97), and was Fellow in Archeology at the American Schools of Classical Studies in Rome and Athens (1897–98). In 1899–1900 he organized an archeological expedition to the deserts of north-central Syria. The next year he returned to Princeton where he became professor of art and archeology (1901–22), first master in residence of the Graduate College (1905–22) and director of the School of Archæology (1920–22). He published *Scotland's Ruined Abbeys* (1899) and *The Story of Athens* (1902) and was contributing editor of *Art and Archeology* (1906–22). His major work, however, was in connection with two later expeditions to Syria (1904–05, 1909). It was the sterling integrity, as well as the consummate skill, of Butler's work there which led to the highest distinction ever offered to an American and Christian explorer by a Mohammedan government, namely, the unsolicited invitation to enter and take command of the excavation of Sardis. The Turks knew they could trust Butler; they knew that he was absolutely honorable. The difficulties of Sardis exploration had seemed insurmountable to others; the great period of civilization and culture of Asia Minor, just older than the Syrian and extending back to the Lydian and beyond, was buried fathoms deep. These deeply buried ruins were entered under Butler's leadership between 1910 and 1922. His splendid Syrian and Sardis monographs were published as *Archæology and Other Arts* (1903) and *Sardis* (1922). He died in the American Hospital at Neuilly, France on either Aug. 13, 1922 (Collins), Aug. 14 (*New York Herald*, Aug. 16), or Aug 15 (*New York Times*, Aug. 16, and *Who's Who in America*, 1924–25). His remains were brought back to Croton Falls, N. Y., to be interred beside the quiet country church of his boyhood. He was unmarried.

[The chief sources of information are the tribute by Henry Fairfield Osborn, *Impressions of Great Naturalists* (1924), pp. 206–12, and *Howard Crosby Butler, 1872–1922* (1923), a memorial volume from the Princeton Press which contains a biography by V. Lansing Collins, pp. 3–41, tributes by President Hibben, Edward Robinson, and others, and a complete bibliography of Butler's writings by H. S. Leach (reprinted separately as *A Bibliography of Howard Crosby Butler*, 1924).]
H. F. O.

BUTLER, JOHN (1728–May 1796), Loyalist, soldier, Indian agent, was born in New London, Conn., the son of Capt. Walter and Deborah Butler. In 1742 his father moved his family to the Mohawk Valley, where he had been for many years commandant at Fort Hunter and at Oswego. Commissioned captain, John served under

Sir William Johnson in the expedition against Crown Point (1755), under Abercromby at Ticonderoga, under Bradstreet at the capture of Fort Frontenac, and in 1759 accompanied Johnson as second in command of the Indian auxiliaries in the campaign against Fort Niagara, becoming leader of the Indian allies during the siege when Johnson took over the command-in-chief. In the conduct of Indian affairs he was a trusted agent of Sir William Johnson. With the outbreak of Revolution he and his son Walter [q.v.], together with Guy Johnson and Col. Daniel Claus, fled to Canada. Stationed at Niagara by Guy Johnson as deputy Indian commissioner, Butler was instructed by Sir Guy Carleton to preserve the good will of the Indians and to keep them neutral. In the spring of 1777, acting under orders from Carleton, he collected as many Indians as possible and joined St. Leger in his unavailing march down the Mohawk Valley, during which Claus, Sir John Johnson, and Butler issued an appeal to the Loyalists of Tryon County. After the battle of Oriskany he obtained permission from the Governor-General to recruit a battalion of rangers to serve with the Indians, which he should command with the rank of major. This body of troops, known as Butler's Rangers, he recruited from the refugee Loyalists at Niagara, and in the spring and summer of 1778 he undertook his famous invasion of the Wyoming Valley in Pennsylvania, aided by a detachment of the King's Royal Regiment of New York (Sir John Johnson's Loyalist regiment) and a large number of Indians led by the Seneca chief Old King (Sayenqueraghta). Two forts were captured easily and Butler sent a summons to Forty Fort. The Continental forces, led by Lieut.-Col. Zebulon Butler [q.v.], determined to leave the fort and attack the invaders, which unwise decision the British commander reported "pleased the Indians highly, who observed they should be on an equal footing with them in the woods." In the battle of July 3, 1778 the Indians made a flank attack and the Continentals, outnumbered, fled to Forty Fort, which capitulated on July 4. Maj. Butler attempted to restrain his dusky allies, but failing, there followed a number of atrocities, which historians with imagination have depicted as a general massacre, rendered immortal by Thomas Campbell in his famous poem *Gertrude of Wyoming* (London, 1809). The caustic strictures on Butler by the historians of Wyoming, on the ground of inhumanity, seem to be wholly unjustified. With the invasion of the Iroquois country by Maj.-Gen. John Sullivan [q.v.] in 1779, Butler opposed him with his Rangers and a number of Indians led by the famous Mohawk chief, Joseph Brant (Thayendanegea), but was defeated in the battle of Newtown (Elmira), Aug. 29, 1779. Commissioned lieutenant-colonel, Butler joined Sir John Johnson in his raid upon the Mohawk and Schoharie valleys (1780). His wife Catherine and the younger children, held as hostages at Albany, were exchanged for Cherry Valley captives by his son Walter and joined him at Niagara. Attainted by the New York Assembly and his property confiscated, Butler received a grant of land and a pension from the British government at the close of the war and served as His Majesty's commissioner of Indian affairs at Niagara and as a member of the land board for the district of Nassau. He is described as being short and fat but very active. He died at Niagara, respected as an honorable and faithful servant of his King, and was buried on May 15, 1796.

[*Ontario Hist. Soc. Papers and Records*, vols. III (1901), XXIII (1926); *Report of the Bureau of Archives for the Province of Ontario*, 1904–05; *Docs. Relative to the Colonial Hist. of . . . N. Y.* (1850–61); *House Doc. No. 203, 25 Cong., 3 Sess.*; *The Papers of Sir Wm. Johnson* (1921 . . .); *Buffalo Hist. Soc. Pubs.*, vols. I (1879), IV (1895); *Jour. of the Mil. Exped. of Maj.-Gen. John Sullivan* (1887); *Orderly Book of Sir John Johnson* (1882); "Diary of Joshua Hempstead of New London, Conn.," *Colls. of the New London County Hist. Soc.*, I (1901), 401; *Mich. Pioneer and Hist. Soc. Colls.*, XIX (1892); E. A. Cruikshank, *The Story of Butler's Rangers*, etc. (1893); J. Carnochan, *Hist. of Niagara* (1914); Wm. Kirby, *Annals of Niagara* (2nd ed., 1927); F. M. Caulkins, *Hist. of New London, Conn.* (1852); Wm. W. Campbell, *Annals of Tryon County* (1831); Wm. L. Stone, *Life of Jos. Brant-Thayendanegea* (1838); Chas. Miner, *Hist. of Wyoming* (1845); Wm. M. Reid, *The Story of Old Fort Johnson* (1906); Butler's report of the battle of Wyoming to Lieut.-Col. Mason Bolton, dated July 8, 1778, printed in Geo. Peck, *Wyoming* (1858) and in *Proc. and Colls. of the Wyoming Hist. and Geol. Soc.*, vol. XVI (1918).]   F. E. R.

BUTLER, JOHN WESLEY (Oct. 13, 1851–Mar. 17, 1918), Methodist missionary, was born in Shelburn Falls, Mass., the son of Julia (Lewis) Butler and William Butler, founder of the missions of the Methodist Episcopal Church in India (1856) and Mexico (1873). On his father's departure for India, he was put in a boarding school at Wilton, Conn. Rejoining his father on the latter's return (1865), he had two years in the Chelsea (Mass.) High School and a year in the Boston Latin School, and graduated from the Passaic (N. J.) Collegiate Institute (1871). His delicate health making a college course inadvisable he went to the Boston University School of Theology for three years of study (1871–74). While a student in theology he held small pastorates in the city of Boston. He was ordained at the age of twenty-two, and appointed to Mexico for missionary service, arriving May 9, 1874. He reported to his father who was superintendent of the mission. For almost forty-four years he held his residence continuously in Mexico City, and was at death one of the best known and most influential men in the capital, for he was not an ardent denominational ecclesiastic, but a broad-souled and eager lover of men. As pastor and "preacher in charge" (1874-88); as publishing agent (1886-90, 1898); as overseer of schools and acting-president of the Mexico Methodist Institute (1895-97) and of the Mexico Methodist Theological School (1897); as editor of *El Abogado Cristiano* and other religious publications (1892-1907); as presiding elder or district superintendent (Mexico or Central District, 1889-1918 with exception of the year 1891 when he was in charge of the Hidalgo District); as president of the Mexico Annual Conference (1911); as treasurer and attorney for the Mission; and as author of books, pamphlets, and articles on Mexico he rendered long and notable service. In addition, he was delegate to two Ecumenical Conferences (1901, 1911), and to eight successive quadrennial General Conferences of the Methodist Episcopal Church (1888-1916). He represented his church at the Congress on Christian Work in Latin America (Panama, 1916). His principal books are *Sketches of Mexico* (1894), *Mexico Coming into Light* (1906), and *The History of the Methodist Episcopal Church in Mexico* (issued on the very day of his death in 1918). He wrote the article "Christianity in Mexico" for the *New Encyclopædia Americana* (1907). He was married on Aug. 13, 1878 to Sara A. Aston, who also became a writer on Mexican themes.

The work of the Methodist Episcopal Church in Mexico stands as his enduring monument. He lived to see some 30,000 communicants and adherents and 5,000 children in schools. He aided the beginnings of interdenominational co-operation; the Union Hymn Book and Union Theological Seminary. Greater than these, however, was the regard of Mexicans for this humble Protestant missionary. He had the interests of Mexico at heart and Mexicans knew it. He enjoyed personal and friendly relations with every president from Lerdo de Tejada on. No Mexican ever harmed him in his frequent travels. Many Roman Catholic priests were among his acquaintances. He kept outside of national politics. In Mexico he pleaded for popular education, and in America for a free hand for Mexico in her own internal affairs.

[*Annual Reports of the Mexico Annual Conference of the M. E. Ch.* (1885-1919); *Reports of the Board of Foreign Missions of the M. E. Ch.* (1874-1918); C. Butler, *Wm. Butler, the Founder of Two Missions of* the *M. E. Ch.* (1902); files of *Mexico*, especially Apr. 1918; article by C. Butler in *Missionary Rev. of the World*, June 1918.]   O. M. B.

BUTLER, MATTHEW CALBRAITH (Mar. 8, 1836-Apr. 14, 1909), Confederate soldier, senator, was the son of Dr. William Butler, naval surgeon, and Jane (Perry) Butler, sister of Commodores Oliver Hazard and Matthew Calbraith Perry. He was born in Greenville, S. C., the eleventh of sixteen children. He attended the male academy in Greenville and then in 1848 went with his father to Fort Gibson, where Dr. Butler, who had previously served a term in Congress, took up his work as agent to the Cherokees. On the death of his father in 1850, young Butler returned to live with his uncle, Senator A. P. Butler [*q.v.*], and his grandmother, Behethland Butler, at Edgefield. After more study at a local academy, he entered South Carolina College in 1856 as a junior but did not remain through his senior year. He was admitted to the bar in 1857, having studied law with his uncle, and the following year married Maria, daughter of Gov. F. W. Pickens. Having returned to Edgefield, he was elected in 1860 to the legislature but resigned at the coming of war in order to become captain of the Edgefield company of cavalry, which formed part of the Hampton Legion. Six of his brothers also bore arms for the South. After the first battle of Manassas, in which Butler had a part, he was made major. After Williamsburg he was commended for bravery; and in August 1862 he was named colonel of the 2nd South Carolina Regiment. He lost his right foot at the battle of Brandy Station. In September of this year, 1863, he was promoted to be brigadier-general when only twenty-seven years old. He saw much fighting around Richmond, his most important engagement being the clash at Trevilian Station. In September 1864 he was advanced to the rank of major-general. The close of the war found him in South Carolina where he had come in the spring of 1865 to oppose Sherman's progress.

Financially ruined by the war, Butler returned to the practise of law in Edgefield. In 1865 he was chosen for the legislature; and from this time he was throughout the period of Reconstruction a prominent figure in the political life of the state. Feeling at first that the best hope lay in a fusion of the honest elements, white and colored, he was a member of the Union Reform Convention of 1870, to which he submitted the platform and from which he received the nomination for lieutenant-governor. He waged a vigorous but fruitless campaign. For the next year or two, he was active in behalf of the tax-payers who were seeking improvement of fiscal conditions. He was a member of the convention of May 1871 and was one of a committee which waited upon President Grant. Finally convinced that the only resource was in Democratic control of the state, he renounced his allegiance to any fusion party and became one of the most energetic promoters of the "straightout" movement. When the convention met in August 1876 he nominated Wade Hampton for governor. Meantime, he had been connected with several race riots, one in Edgefield where the residence on his own plantation had been burned, and one, far more notable, at Hamburg, where he had gone to represent the whites in civil action against a company of negro militia. When questioned later by a senatorial committee, he insisted that his connection with the Hamburg disturbance had been merely that of an attorney. Foremost among the campaigners in behalf of the Hampton ticket, in December 1876, he was elected to the Senate without opposition, by the Democratic legislature. It seemed an empty compliment, since the Republican legislature, sitting in competition, declared D. T. Corbin, conspicuous in the prosecution of Ku Klux cases, duly elected. The contest between Butler and Corbin hung fire for a year until Butler was sworn in, Nov. 30, 1877. Well-authenticated historical gossip attributes Butler's triumph to the secret influence of Senator James Donald Cameron of Pennsylvania who was thus paying a debt of gratitude for a kindness rendered by A. P. Butler, years before, to Simon Cameron. Butler served three terms in the Senate. He secured many improvements for his state, notably public buildings and enlargement of the Charleston harbor. Instinctively friendly and wholly free from inflammatory rhetoric, he did much to conciliate more stubborn Northern sentiment concerning the South. In 1894 he went down in defeat before Ben Tillman. This political reaction was partly a kind of agrarian revolt and partly an expression of the temper of a new generation of voters, which, coming into power twenty-five years after the Civil War, no longer reverenced the heroes of that conflict and sought new leaders. After his retirement, Butler practised law in Washington until the Spanish-American War, when he was appointed by McKinley major-general of volunteers. Later he served as a member of the commission for the Spanish evacuation of Cuba. Then he returned to Washington. In 1903 he was elected vice-president of the Southern History Association. In the next year he undertook new business ventures as president of the Hidalgo Placer Mining

and Milling Company of Mexico. In 1906 he married Mrs. Nannie Whitman of New York, his first wife having been dead for several years. The second Mrs. Butler was a descendant of Pierre Robert, first pastor of the Carolina Huguenots. Butler's death occurred in Washington but his body was brought to the old home place in Edgefield for burial.

In war Butler was a striking figure. Handsome, graceful, cool, he personally led his soldiers to battle, with only a silver-mounted riding whip in his hand. Solicitous of the welfare of his men, he was regarded by them with affection. In peace he manifested uncommon gifts for political success. He possessed a remarkable memory for names and faces; he was affable in manner; he adapted himself easily to almost any social group.

[For records of Butler's military service see U. R. Brooks, *Butler and His Cavalry in the War of Secession* (1909), Ellison Capers's account in *Confed. Mil. Hist.*, vol. V (1899), and E. L. Wells, *Hampton and His Cavalry in '64* (1899); for sympathetic narratives of his career during Reconstruction days see John S. Reynolds, *Reconstruction in S. C.* (1905), and H. T. Thompson, *Ousting the Carpet-Bagger* (1927); for brief biographical sketches see J. C. Hemphill, *Men of Mark in S. C.*, vol. III (1909), J. C. Garlington, *Men of the Time* (1902), and B. F. Perry, *Reminiscences of Public Men* (1889); for senatorial investigation and for Butler's career in this body, see *Cong. Record* for the years involved. Full obituaries were published in the papers Apr. 15, 1909, notably the Charleston *News and Courier*, the Columbia *State*, and the Greenville *News*.]
F. P. G.

BUTLER, PIERCE (July 11, 1744–Feb. 15, 1822), senator, was born in County Carlow, Ireland, the third son of Sir Richard Butler, Baronet, Member of Parliament for County Carlow 1729–61, and of Henrietta (Percy) Butler (*Burke's Peerage*). He became major of H. M. 29th Regiment, but on Jan. 10, 1771 married Mary, the daughter of Thomas Middleton, of Prince William's Parish, in South Carolina, and there made his home thenceforward. In 1773 he resigned his commission and devoted himself to planting and politics. In 1779 he was adjutant-general of the state (Edward McCrady, *The History of South Carolina in the Revolution, 1775–80*, 1901, p. 366). From 1778 to 1782 and from 1784 to 1789 he was a representative in the state legislature. His failure to act with the planter-merchant group in state politics may have been due to the enmity of Christopher Gadsden (*State Gazette*, Sept. 9, 1784), to his political ambition, or to his independent, impulsive nature. Whatever his motives, this wealthy, somewhat dictatorial aristocrat championed the inadequately-led democracy of the back country, and pushed its enterprises for the reform of representation, removal of the state capital, and revaluation of property. In 1786 he was elected by the legislature to commissions to fix the boundaries of the state. On Mar. 6, 1787, he was elected delegate to the Congress of the Confederation, and two days later to the Federal Convention. There his proposals were for a strong central government, with property as part of the basis for representation. He was author of the fugitive slave clause. He returned to South Carolina in time to defend the Constitution in the Assembly, but did not sit in the ratifying convention. He was elected to the United States Senate as a Federalist in 1789, and was reëlected in 1792, but refused to observe party lines. During the first session he voted for the funding bill and the assumption of state debts, but opposed the tariff and judiciary bills. He later opposed the Jay treaty. In October 1796 he resigned and repaired to his state, apparently intending to become candidate for governor (*American Historical Review,* July 1909). At the time of the election, however, though the Federalist Harper said that he was still strong in the back country and had "no inconsiderable support" in the tidewater, he refused to allow his name to be used (*City Gazette,* Dec. 10, 1796). But in 1802 he was elected to fill an unexpired term in the Senate. He denounced the Twelfth Amendment, and charged that the Republican party was abusing its powers as the Federalists had done. In January 1806 he resigned. He died in Philadelphia in 1822.

[Sketch of Butler in Jos. Johnson, *Traditions and Reminiscences, Chiefly of the Am. Rev. in the South* (1851); *Biog. Cong. Dir.* (1903); *Franklin Gazette* (Phila.), Feb. 16, 1822; C. Jervey, *Inscriptions on the Tablets and Gravestones in St. Michael's Church and Churchyard, Charleston, S. C.* (1906); *S. C. Hist. and Geneal. Mag.,* Jan. 1900; Assembly Jours.; *Annals of Cong.*; Max Farrand, ed., *The Records of the Federal Convention of 1787* (1911).]   R. L. M—r.

BUTLER, PIERCE MASON (Apr. 11, 1798– Aug. 20, 1847), governor of South Carolina, was born at Mount Willing in Edgefield District, the sixth child of William Butler [*q.v.*], a Revolutionary soldier, and his wife, Behethland Foote Moore. Like his older brother, Andrew Pickens Butler [*q.v.*], Pierce was trained at Moses Waddell's academy in Abbeville. Evincing ambition for a military career, he was, through Calhoun's influence, appointed in 1818 lieutenant in the United States army. By 1825 he was a captain. Much of his service was at Fort Gibson, where he met his future wife, Miranda Julia Duval of Maryland who was visiting her brother, Edward, agent to the Cherokees. Shortly after his marriage, Butler resigned from the army in 1829 and settled in Columbia. In civil life again, he chose banking as his field and became in a few

years president of the state bank of South Carolina. He had more than passing interest in public affairs, however, and manifested particular enthusiasm for nullification, signing the ordinance of November 1832. Particularly active in behalf of education, he was elected a trustee of South Carolina College in 1833.

When the excitement of the Seminole War was at its height, he accepted a commission as lieutenant-colonel of Godwyn's South Carolina regiment. Returning to Columbia, he was elected governor in 1836, though, true to his declared conviction that the office should seek the man, he made no campaign. Earnestly seeking to give a practical and helpful administration, he endeavored to eliminate the residual bitterness from the long discussion of tariff and nullification and to initiate beneficial measures. He had a vision —rare in the ante-bellum South—of a public school system for the whole state, and appointed a commission headed by Stephen Elliott to make surveys and recommendations. He threw his influence in favor of the proposed Louisville, Cincinnati & Charleston Railway, believing that better commercial and political relations between the South and West would follow. Shortly after he left office in 1838, he was named agent to the Cherokees and returned to Fort Gibson where he remained until ill health prompted his resignation in 1846. According to a tribute published in an Indian journal (Tahlequah *Advocate,* Sept. 30, 1847) he was just with and showed sympathy for the Cherokees. At the outbreak of the Mexican War he was called to be colonel of the Palmetto Regiment. He was killed at Churubusco while leading this regiment in the face of what Gen. James Shields, writing to Gov. Johnson (Sept. 2, 1847), called "one of the most terrific fires to which soldiers were ever subjected." Wounded in the early stages of the conflict, Butler had continued to advance until a musket ball through the head caused instantaneous death. His body was brought back to Edgefield. Many tributes in verse were written at the time of his death, one of them being by the youthful Paul Hamilton Hayne.

Tall and distinguished in personal appearance, Butler was by temperament more of a military officer than a politician. He was marked, however, by broad social interests and at the time of his death was a member of many fraternal organizations in his state. Shields bears witness to the Carolinian's popularity in the brigade to which he was attached.

[A brief sketch of Butler is in "The Butlers of S. C." by T. D. Jervey in *S. C. Hist. and Geneal. Mag.,* Oct. 1903. A brief summary of his administration is in Yates Snowden, *Hist. of S. C.,* vol. II (1920). The fullest collection of material is a file of newspaper clippings, drawn largely from the Charleston *Mercury* and *Courier*, now in the possession of Mrs. Elizabeth Butler Carson of Greenville, a niece of P. M. Butler.]

F. P. G.

BUTLER, RICHARD (Apr. 1, 1743–Nov. 4, 1791), Revolutionary soldier, Indian agent, was born in the parish of St. Bridget's, Dublin, Ireland, the son of Thomas and Eleanor (Parker) Butler. His father later came to America and settled in Lancaster, Pa. Richard served as an ensign with the Bouquet expedition of 1764, after which he and his brother William ventured a partnership as Indian traders at Chillicothe, Ohio, and at Pittsburgh. Richard married Mary (or Maria) Smith and had numerous descendants. During the dispute between Pennsylvania and Virginia he raised a company of men to resist the authority of the Virginia commandant sent to Pittsburgh by Lord Dunmore. In 1775 he became an Indian agent but in the following year entered into active military service as major and in 1777 became lieutenant-colonel of Morgan's Rifles. He took part in the battle of Saratoga, commanded Wayne's left column at the storming of Stony Point and later aided Wayne in quelling the mutiny of the Pennsylvania line. After Yorktown he went with Wayne to Georgia and was brevetted brigadier-general (1783). Appointed Indian commissioner by Congress, he negotiated, together with Oliver Wolcott and Arthur Lee, an important treaty with the Iroquis confederacy defining their western boundary (Oct. 22, 1784). In the following year, Butler, Lee, and George Rogers Clark negotiated a boundary treaty with the Wyandot, Delaware, Chippewa, and Ottawa nations (Jan. 21, 1785). The most striking feature of Butler's career as an Indian agent was the negotiation of the famous treaty with the Shawnees (Jan. 31, 1786). With Clark and Samuel H. Parsons as fellow commissioners he met the Shawnees at the mouth of the Great Miami, and so overawed them that they signed a treaty ceding a great area of land to the United States and yielding hostages. In response to an inquiry from Congress, Butler and Parsons reported, June 19, 1786, that the western tribes were distinctly hostile and were encouraged in their continued depredations by the British (Papers of the Continental Congress, No. 56, pp. 283–85, in the Library of Congress). On Aug. 14, 1786, Congress elected Butler superintendent of Indian affairs for the Northern District. He served as state senator, as judge of the court of common pleas, and as president of the court of inquiry *re* Gen. Josiah Harmar [*q.v.*]. In 1791 he was appointed second in command, with the rank of

major-general, of the army under Gen. Arthur St. Clair [*q.v.*] sent into the Ohio country to avenge the ill-fated Harmar expedition. In reply to the protests of army officers against Butler's appointment, President Washington wrote to Col. William Darke, Aug. 9, 1791, admitting that because of illness Butler wasn't what he should be but appealing to Darke's loyalty to suuport him (Jared Sparks, *The Writings of George Washington*, X, 183). Nowhere is Butler's military incompetence better exemplified than in his change of St. Clair's order of march while he was in command during St. Clair's absence, Butler's order of march requiring that a forty-foot road be cut. The expedition finally reached the Indian country north of the Ohio River and was attacked by the Indians on Nov. 4, 1791. Butler, commanding the right wing, fought bravely, but was mortally wounded and carried to the middle of the camp, where he was soon joined by his wounded brother, Maj. Thomas Butler. St. Clair ordering a retreat, Capt. Edward Butler came to remove his brothers. As he could save only one, Gen. Butler urged him to take his brother Thomas. Edward Butler did so, writing to his brother Percival in Kentucky that, "We left the worthiest of brothers . . . in the hands of the savages . . . nearly dead."

[*Jours. of Cong.*, May 16, 1776, June 3, 1785, Apr. 17 and Aug. 14, 1786; *Minutes of the Supreme Exec. Council of Pa.*; *Pa. Archives*; *Am. State Papers, Military Affairs*, vol. I and *Indian Affairs*, vol. I (both 1832); *Mil. Jour. of Maj. Ebenezer Denny* (1859); *Diary of Col. Winthrop Sargent . . . during the Campaign of 1791* (1851); *Olden Time*, Mar.–Dec. 1847; *Hist. Reg.* (Harrisburg), Jan. 1883; *Pa. Mag. of Hist. and Biog.*, Apr. 1883; Jas. A. James, *Life of Geo. Rogers Clark* (1928); Wm. H. Smith, *The St. Clair Papers* (1882); Chas. J. Stillé, *Maj.-Gen. Anthony Wayne and the Pa. Line in the Continental Army* (1893); Chas. S. Hall, *Life and Letters of Samuel Holden Parsons* (1905); Wm. D. Butler and others, *The Butler Family in America* (1909).]

F. E. R.

BUTLER, SIMEON (Mar. 25, 1770?–Nov. 7, 1847), publisher, was probably the oldest son of Josiah and Martha (Ranney) Butler, and was probably born at Wethersfield, Conn. He migrated about 1790 from Hartford to Northampton, Mass., where he had been preceded by two cousins, William and Daniel Butler, both of whom were already prominent in that town, the former having established in 1786 the *Hampshire Gazette* for the purpose of opposing the malcontents of the Shays Rebellion, while the latter for many years (1817–49) operated the paper-mill built by his brother, William, in 1795. Immediately upon his arrival Simeon established himself as a bookbinder and bookseller. For a short time (1793) he was in partnership with William Butler, but after 1794 seems to have conducted the business alone. The bookselling speedily became subordinated to publishing and binding, and the shop of Simeon Butler became famous not only as the first, but for a half century the most important publishing house in western Massachusetts. According to William Allen, his fellow townsman and contemporary, "he published the first volume of the Massachusetts Reports and two or three hundred thousand other volumes of valuable books" (Allen's *American Biographical Dictionary,* 3rd ed., 1857, pp. 177–78). Although his interests were chiefly centered upon publishing books, for a time he manufactured paper in partnership with his brother, Asa, in Suffield, Conn., and, it is believed, produced the first American letter paper used in the United States Senate. In 1800 he was appointed postmaster of Northampton, an office which he held for six years. He was a man of force of character and distinct individuality, the autocrat of his household and of his business. Endowed with great business capacity he amassed a considerable fortune for his day. Shortly after his arrival in Northampton he married in 1795 Mary Hunt (1774–1829), a member of a prominent local family, by whom he had ten children; after her death he married Charlotte McNeill of New York (1833). His book-shop, to-day operated under the firm name of Bridgman & Lyman, is still doing business on the same spot, one of the two or three oldest bookstores in the country.

[The *New Eng. Hist. and Geneal. Reg.,* Jan. 1862, contains items concerning the Wethersfield Butlers, and the Judd MSS. in the Forbes Lib. of Northampton contain the local genealogical records. The *Centennial Hampshire Gazette* (1886) contains some information. An unsigned article by Clifford H. Lyman in the *Hampshire Gazette* of Jan. 22, 1927, gives a short history of the business founded by Simeon Butler, and *Theodore Bliss, Publisher and Bookseller* (Norwalk, Ohio, 1911), tells of the life of an apprentice in the store during the days of Simeon's son, J. H. Butler. The Forbes Lib. contains an oil portrait of Simeon Butler, and books containing his imprint.]   H. U. F.

BUTLER, THOMAS BELDEN (Aug. 22, 1806–June 8, 1873), jurist, was born in Wethersfield, Conn., the son of Frederick and Mary (Belden) Butler. His elementary schooling completed, he decided to study medicine. For two years he attended the Yale Medical School, graduating in 1828. He afterward settled in Norwalk, Conn. (then a town of less than 4,000 inhabitants), where he was married (Mar. 14, 1831) to Mary Phillip Crosby and where he practised for a number of years. In 1835 he determined to forsake medicine and essay the law. He thereupon studied in the office of Judge Clark Bissell [*q.v.*] of Norwalk, who later was to become a professor in the Yale Law School; and in

1837 he was admitted to the Fairfield County bar and began practise in Norwalk. Thaddeus Betts, Orrin S. Terry, and Josiah M. Carter were successively his partners. For him, as for many another in those days, the law was a stepping-stone to a career in politics. In his case the career began in 1849 with an election as representative in the United States Congress, where he served one term. His later political services were in the General Assembly of his state. No less than five times he was chosen from Norwalk to the state House of Representatives; and in 1848, 1852, and 1853 he was a member of the state Senate. It was not, however, in the legislature, but in the judiciary that he was to become best known. In 1855 he was appointed by the General Assembly to the bench of the superior court and in 1861 to that of the supreme court of errors. Upon the death of Joel Hinman of Waterbury, chief justice of the supreme court, he was selected to fill the vacancy thus created; and he was chief justice for the remainder of his life. Butler found a hobby in examining weather phenomena. After years of research, he published *The Philosophy of the Weather, And a Guide to Its Changes* (1856). In 1870 he reissued this compendium of weather-wisdom in a revised and enlarged form as *A Concise, Analytical, and Logical Development of the Atmospheric System* (Norwalk) and *A Concise Analytical and Logical Development of the Atmospheric System as God Made It* (Hartford). These copious works have now only a historical interest. *The Slave Question,* a speech delivered by Butler in the House of Representatives on Mar. 12, 1850—five days after Webster's great Senate speech on the Constitution and the Union,—was officially printed (Washington, 1850). He was esteemed for his good mind in matters judicial; and as a "natural philosopher" he possessed considerable native ability. He likewise had a Yankee fondness for mechanics, and is said to have obtained patents on several of his inventions.

[S. W. Adams and H. R. Stiles, *The Hist. of Ancient Wethersfield, Conn.* (1904); C. M. Selleck, *Norwalk* (Norwalk, 1896); D. Loomis and J. G. Calhoun, *The Judicial and Civil Hist. of Conn.* (1895); *Obit. Record Grads. Yale Coll.* (1873); *Hartford Courant,* June 10, 1873.]   G. S. B.

BUTLER, WALTER N. (d. Oct. 30, 1781), Loyalist, soldier, was born near Johnstown, N. Y., the son of Lieut.-Col. John Butler [*q.v.*] by his wife Catherine. He studied law at Albany but with the outbreak of the Revolution he joined his father and the other Loyalist leaders of the Mohawk Valley in flight to Canada. Accompanying St. Leger on his march down the valley in 1777, Ensign Butler was active in exhorting the

Loyalists to rise. Soon after his father, Col. Daniel Claus, and Sir John Johnson had issued a proclamation to the inhabitants of Tryon County, he was captured while attending a nocturnal conference at the house of a Loyalist. He was ordered court-martialed by Arnold and was condemned as a spy, but, upon the intercession of Continental officers whom he had known while a law student in Albany, he was reprieved and imprisoned in that town. When he became ill, his friends prevailed upon Gen. Lafayette to place him under guard in the home of a family with secret Loyalist sympathies, from which he escaped by eluding a conveniently inebriated sentinel. Governor-General Sir Frederick Haldimand approving the plan, Capt. Butler, commanding his father's Loyalist troops (Butler's Rangers) and accompanied by a number of Indians led by the famous Mohawk chief Joseph Brant (Thayendanegea), made an attack on Cherry Valley, Nov. 11, 1778, in which he is generally alleged to have shown great cruelty, suffering his Indian allies to commit many atrocities. To Gen. Schuyler he declared that "I have done everything in my power to restrain the fury of the Indians from hurting women and children, or killing the prisoners who fell into our hands," and he wrote to Gen. James Clinton that "the inhabitants killed at Cherry Valley do not lay [sic] at my door—my conscience acquits me." His mother and the younger children, held as hostages at Albany, he exchanged for Cherry Valley captives (1779). In October 1781 he accompanied Major Ross in a raid on the Mohawk Valley, with regular troops, Rangers, and Indians. Repulsed by Col. Marinus Willett, the British forces retreated, Butler commanding the detachment covering the retreat. They had succeeded in crossing West Canada Creek when the fog that hung over the stream lifted and Butler was shot from the opposite bank by the pursuing Continental scouts.

Historians of the Revolution have invariably depicted Butler as a fiend incarnate because of the Cherry Valley massacre. It is quite possible that he may not have been able to prevent it (like his father in his attack on Wyoming Valley), but it is also true that he was a sterner man than John Butler, and is described as morose, vindictive, and governed by strong passions.

[Jas. F. Kenney, "Walter Butler's Journal . . ." in the *Canadian Hist. Rev.*, Dec. 1920 ; Wm. W. Campbell, *Annals of Tryon County* (1831) ; Wm. L. Stone, *Life of Jos. Brant-Thayendanegea* (1838) ; *Docs. Relative to the Colonial Hist. of . . . N. Y.*, VIII (1857), 721 ; Wm. M. Willett, *A Narrative of the Military Actions of Col. Marinus Willett* (1831) ; J. R. Sims, *The Frontiersmen of N. Y.* (1882–83) ; Lorenzo Sabine, *The Am. Loyalists* (1847) ; Butler's report of the attack on Cherry

Valley to Lieutenant-Colonel Mason Bolton, dated Nov. 17, 1778, printed in part in Ernest A. Cruikshank, *The Story of Butler's Rangers and the Settlement of Niagara,* published in 1893 by the Lundy's Lane Hist. Soc.]
                                                        F.E.R.

BUTLER, WILLIAM (Dec. 17, 1759–Sept. 23, 1821), Revolutionary soldier, congressman, was the son of James Butler of Prince William County, Va., who with his wife Mary Simpson and eight children moved to Ninety Six District, S. C., about 1772. James Butler served in several campaigns of the first half of the Revolution, but in 1781 he and his second son, James, were killed at Cloud's Creek by "Bloody Bill" Cuningham, the notorious Loyalist leader. William Butler, the eldest son, was in the battle of Stono, and several other actions of 1779 and 1780. He was lieutenant of militia before he was of age (*Accounts Audited,* State Archives). In November 1781 he was appointed captain in the militia under Gen. Pickens, but was usually on detached service. His most noted exploit was the surprise and dispersing of Cuningham's force, in May 1782. He appears to have been elected to the state House of Representatives in 1786. In 1788 he opposed the calling of the convention to ratify the Federal Constitution, and in that convention voted against ratification. In the legislature he consistently opposed leniency to the Loyalists, and in this as in other important matters accurately reflected the dominant sentiment of the back country. In 1791 he was elected sheriff of Ninety Six District, and held the office for many years. In 1794 he was made brigadier-general of militia, and later became major-general. In 1796 he was candidate for Congress against R. G. Harper, the Federalist lawyer, but was defeated by a vote of more than two to one. In 1800 Harper did not run (*City Gazette,* Oct. 31, 1800), and Butler gained the seat which he held until 1813. In Congress he seems never to have debated but to have attended faithfully. He voted against the anti-slavery motions, but supported proposals for the removal of judges on address of both houses of Congress, and for removal of senators on address of legislatures. He steadily supported the embargo. In 1810 he was chairman of the committee which investigated the charges against Gen. Wilkinson. He is described as a tall, handsome man, and a lover of fine horses. His home was in Edgefield County. On June 3, 1784, he married Behethland Foote Moore and they had eight children: James, George, William, Frank M., Andrew P. [*q.v.*], Pierce M. [*q.v.*], Emmala, and Leontine, several of whom were distinguished in the later history of the state.

[See esp. *The Memoirs of Gen. Wm. Butler* (1885), based largely on a manuscript by A. P. Butler. In Joseph Johnson, *Traditions and Reminiscences Chiefly of the American Revolution in the South* (1851) and in Alexander Garden, *Anecdotes of the Revolutionary War in America* (1822), there are brief sketches. T. D. Jervey in *S. C. Hist. and Geneal. Mag.*, Oct. 1903, 296–311, gives a genealogy of the family. Butler's public career may be followed in the journals of the bodies in which he sat. There was a trader James Butler among the Cherokees,—*e.g.*, *S. C. Council Jour.*, Mar. 29, 1748, *S. C. Gazette*, Nov. 29, 1760,—but he was not the James Butler of this sketch.]   R.L.M—r.

BUTLER, WILLIAM (Jan. 30, 1818–Aug. 18, 1899), Methodist missionary, was born in Dublin of English parentage. Orphaned soon after birth he was reared by a great-grandmother who instilled into him permanent religious ideals which were realized through Methodist channels. In young manhood he became a Methodist and entered the Hardwick Street Mission Seminary (Wesleyan) of Dublin to prepare for the ministry. Upon graduation he was given a charge in Lisburn and later went to a Donegal circuit. Eager for further training he went over to Didsbury College, Manchester, England, but returned to Ireland after finishing the course, bringing a Manchester lady as his wife. In 1850 he and Mrs. Butler and their three sons crossed to America, which was to be thenceforth the land of their citizenship. On May 5, 1851, he was admitted to the New York East Conference. He served churches in Williamsburg, Shelburne Falls, and Westfield. His first wife died suddenly at Westfield, and on Nov. 23, 1854, he was married in Portland, Me., to Clementina Rowe of Wexford, England, whom he had met in her father's house, and who came at his persuasion by letter to be his bride. On Oct. 10, 1856, while pastor of a church in Lynn, Mass., he accepted a call to the superintendency of the proposed India Mission of his Church. With his wife and two of his sons he sailed on Apr. 9 to "lay broad and deep foundations for Methodism in India." After five weeks of enquiry he decided to open the Mission in Oudh and Rohilkhand (the Northwest Provinces). He could find no quarters in Lucknow, the capital of Oudh, and therefore moved on to Bareilly in the next province. Hardly had he settled at his task when the Mutiny broke out, compelling him to flee for his life. After the Mutiny he resumed work in Bareilly and also began work in Lucknow. At Bareilly the first official meeting of the Mission was held on Aug. 20, 1858. The foundation of the Mission was a girls' orphanage, established in Bareilly, and a boys' orphanage, in Lucknow. In time, but under other hands, there developed in the former place a theological seminary and in the latter two standard colleges.

In 1864 Butler fell ill in Calcutta and was obliged to leave India for home, after trying in vain to recuperate by a voyage to Burmah. On arrival in America he was given a charge in Chelsea, Mass. Thence he removed to Dorchester Street Church, Boston, from which he retired to take the secretaryship of the American and Foreign Christian Union (organized for work in Papal lands), and to make his headquarters in New York City, while living in Passaic, N. J. He took time in his new post to write his useful volume, *The Land of the Veda* (1872).

When the Methodist Church decided upon a mission in Mexico, Butler, at the age of fifty-five, was given the superintendency. He sailed for Vera Cruz on Feb. 4, 1873, and proceeded to Mexico City, where he soon found quarters for the new work. The evangelical message and the open Bible proved welcome to many. Butler also established a Union Church, and acted for a time as its pastor; and took steps toward the founding of a Mission Press. In 1879, however, lung trouble developed and he was forced to return home.

After serving for a time the Freedman's Aid Society, he took a pastorate at Melrose, Mass., from which he was invited to visit India again. Accordingly, he sailed from New York in May 1883, bound for India by way of Great Britain and the Suez Canal. He included in his India itinerary all the points at which the Mission was operating and was cordially greeted everywhere. He returned home in 1885, including a trip through the Holy Land on the way.

In 1887 he made another journey to Mexico, this time by rail, and spent the winter there. On his return he gave himself to the "Million and a Quarter for Missions" campaign of his Church. But failure of health caused him shortly to retire to Newton Center, Mass., where increasing invalidism held him for eight years. His end came in the Missionary Rest Home, Old Orchard, Me. He willed the proceeds of his insurance to the seminary and to the Press in Mexico City. In addition to his *Land of the Veda* he wrote the article on "Methodist Missions" in *Newcomb's Encyclopædia*; *From Boston to Bareilly and Back* (1885); and *Mexico in Transition* (4th ed., 1892).

[*Wm. Butler, the Founder of Two Missions of the M. E. Church* (1902), by his daughter, Clementina Butler; *Official Minutes, New Eng. Conf. of the M. E. Ch.* (1900).]   J.C.A.

BUTLER, WILLIAM ALLEN (Feb. 20, 1825–Sept. 9, 1902), lawyer, author, son of Benjamin Franklin Butler, 1795–1858 [*q.v.*], and Harriet (Allen) Butler, was born at Albany, N. Y. He was eight years old when the family moved to Washington on his father's acceptance of the attorney-generalship in President Jackson's cabinet. The journey from Albany to Washington took four days of travel by water, rail, and stagecoach. From January to June 1834, young "Allen" went to a select school kept by Silas Hill at Georgetown, where the staggering bill presented to his father for the six months' tuition, books and supplies, and fuel came to $25.56. The next year he was sent to school at Hudson, N. Y., and in the winter of 1837 he studied at the Grammar School of the University of the City of New York. It was only natural that he should go to the University, near which the family lived after his father's retirement from the cabinet and Washington, and with which both his father and his uncle Charles were intimately associated. He graduated in the class of 1843, studied law in his father's office, and was admitted to the bar in July 1846. His practise became extensive and varied, including important cases in bankruptcy, insurance, partnerships, contracts, and patents, and he was a sound authority on admiralty law. His interest in this branch of the profession was undoubtedly due in large measure to his marriage on Mar. 21, 1850, to Mary Russell Marshall, daughter of Capt. Charles H. Marshall, agent and part owner of the famous Black Ball line of Liverpool packets. Capt. Marshall was a member of the Board of Pilot Commissioners, a voluntary association formed by the Chamber of Commerce and the Marine Underwriters of New York. When the legislature of the state passed an act (1853) legalizing this voluntary association, the statute was attacked as conflicting with the mode of appointment prescribed in the state constitution and with the powers of Congress to control interstate and foreign commerce, as enumerated in the Federal Constitution. Butler successfully defended the constitutionality of the act of 1853 (and incidentally confirmed his father-in-law's position) in the case of *Sturgis* vs. *Spofford* (45 *N. Y.* 446). In the case of *People* vs. *Vanderbilt* (26 *N. Y.* 287) he performed a lasting service to the general shipping interests of New York by preventing the monopoly of the piers in the North River by private steamship lines. Three gifts were combined in Butler's mentality to make his legal arguments unusually effective: a faculty of memory which enabled him to repeat poems or addresses almost verbatim after a lapse of several years; a power of analysis which moved Chief Justice Waite of the Supreme Court to speak of his argument in the case of *Hoyt* vs. *Sprague* (103 *U. S.* 613) as "the most lucid statement of complicated facts that I have

ever heard"; and a keen sense of humor which never failed to relieve a dull case or refresh a jaded jury. Though he never held any political office, Butler found time in the midst of his busy practise for many activities that testified to his strong spirit of public service. He was closely identified with the University of the City of New York for nearly sixty years from his graduation to his death, lecturing at times on admiralty law in the new department of law created by his father's efforts, serving as a member of the Council from 1862 on, and as its president after the death of his uncle Charles Butler [*q.v.*] in 1897. He was a member of the board of trustees of the New York Public Library, was president of the American Bar Association in 1885 and of the Bar Association of New York in 1886 and 1887, and was one of the speakers, with Grover Cleveland, Chief Justice Fuller, and Justice Field, at the celebration at the Metropolitan Opera House, New York, in 1890, of the hundredth anniversary of the organization of the Supreme Court of the United States. When he moved to Yonkers in 1865, he immediately became one of the leading citizens of the town, helping to improve the school system, contributing to the establishment of hospitals, and making possible the organization of the Women's Institute. As a staunch Republican and Presbyterian (though, like his father, he never consented to hold office in the church), he was active in the political and religious life of the town, until the increasing blindness of his last years confined him to his home at "Round Oak." Somewhat to his chagrin, he believed that his "chief, if not only, claim to public recognition was the writing of a few pages of society verse." Gifted with a nimble wit and a faculty for rhyming which reminds one often of Lowell's, he wrote a number of satirical poems (*Two Millions*, 1858, "The Sexton and the Thermometer" in the *Literary World*, Mar. 24, 1849, *Dobbs, his Ferry*, 1875, etc.), one of which, *Nothing to Wear; an Episode of City Life* (1857), has become an American classic. William Dean Howells said of him, in a notice of the 1899 edition of his poems, "But for the professional devotion of this able lawyer, we might have counted in him the cleverest of our society poets." Butler's attempts at novel writing (*Domesticus; a Tale of the Imperial City*, 1886, and *Mrs. Limber's Raffle; or, a Church Fair and its Victims*, 1876) were less successful. He was the author also of *Martin Van Buren, Lawyer, Statesman and Man* (1862); *Memorial of Charles H. Marshall* (1867); *Lawyer and Client: their Relation, Rights, and Duties* (1871); *Evert Augustus Duyckinck* (1879); *Samuel J. Tilden*

(1886) ; *The Revision of the Statutes of the State of New York and the Revisers* (1889) ; *Oberammergau* (1891). It has been said of him that, while there were greater lawyers and greater literary men than Butler, perhaps "no man of his time, either in England or America, held an equally high rank, both as lawyer and a literary man."

[Wm. Allen Butler, *A Retrospect of Forty Years, 1825–65* (1911), ed. by Harriet Allen Butler, with appendices containing the Memorial Addresses of Geo. C. Holt, John E. Parsons, and Alton B. Parker ; also a sketch of Butler's legal career by Geo. C. Hoyt in *Annual Report, Ass. of the Bar of the City of N. Y.*, 1904.]

D. S. M.

BUTLER, WILLIAM ORLANDO (Apr. 19, 1791–Aug. 6, 1880), soldier, lawyer, congressman, vice-presidential candidate, was of Irish descent, the second of four brothers, all destined to become men of note, and a son of Percival Butler, who with three brothers played a prominent part in the Revolution and won the attention of Washington and Lafayette. Percival Butler moved to Kentucky in 1784, and marrying Mildred Hawkins, a sister-in-law of Col. John Todd, a victim of the battle of the Blue Licks, settled in Jessamine County, where William O. Butler was born. In 1796 he removed to the mouth of the Kentucky River and established there the famous Butler estate. William O. Butler attended Transylvania University where he graduated in 1812. He immediately began the study of law in Lexington under the celebrated Robert Wickliffe, but on the declaration of war against Great Britain in June he volunteered as a private. He well maintained the traditional military glory of the Butler family, for it was his war record that gave him his greatest claim to remembrance. He was attached to Winchester's army and was sent to the relief of Fort Wayne. He took part in the battle at the River Raisin, Jan. 18 and 22, 1813. At the second engagement he was wounded and captured but escaped the massacre that was meted out to many of his comrades. He was taken to Fort Niagara and after many sufferings and hardships was exchanged. Making his way back to Kentucky, he won a commission as a captain, and raised a company which he led under Andrew Jackson against Pensacola. He took part in the battle of New Orleans, leading the attack on Pakenham on the night of Dec. 23, 1814, thereby making it possible to throw up the defenses at Chaumette. He also took a prominent part in the battle on Jan. 8. His bravery and resourcefulness won him the unstinted praise of Jackson, a brevet majorship, and in 1816 a position on Jackson's staff, succeeding his brother Thomas B. Butler. He came eloquently to the defense of Jackson in his conflict with the New Orleans authorities following the battle.

Butler showed unmistakable military genius and he greatly disappointed Jackson when he resigned from the army in 1817 to finish the study of law. He chose to practise his profession in Carrollton (Port William), his father's home, and soon became one of the most prominent and best-liked Democrats in the state. On the declaration of war against Mexico in 1846 he was appointed by President Polk major-general of volunteers and assigned to Gen. Taylor's command. He took an important part in the campaign, being second in command at Monterey, where, in the street fighting, he was wounded in the leg. After spending some time at home recuperating, he joined Gen. Scott in 1848 and was present at the capture of Mexico City. Shortly before the treaty of peace was made he succeeded Gen. Scott in command of the army in Mexico. For his bravery at Monterey he was voted a sword by Congress and also by Kentucky. On returning home he gave up the practise of law to engage in farming.

Butler's military record from the beginning gave him outstanding political opportunities. In 1817 and 1818 he represented Gallatin County in the legislature and in 1839 took his seat in Congress, being reëlected for the following term. He refused to stand for a third term. With a successful congressional career back of him, he was drafted by the Democrats as their candidate for governor in 1844. Although the state was almost impregnably Whig at this time he reduced the majority against him to less than 5,000. In 1848 when both parties were capitalizing war records the Democrats nominated him for vice-president to run with Lewis Cass. In addition to his military record, as a Southern slaveholder he gave strength to the ticket. In 1851 the Kentucky Democrats attempted without success to elect him to the United States Senate, and in the following year, encouraged by his friends, he developed ambitions for the presidency. In 1855 President Pierce offered him the governorship of Nebraska but he declined it.

Butler, though a slaveholder, was opposed to the extension of slavery and in 1861 stood staunchly for the maintenance of the Union. He was one of Kentucky's delegates to the Washington Peace Congress in February of that year. He was a Union Democrat during the Civil War, too old to serve in the army. He had some literary ability and often wrote poetry, published in the state press. A book of his poems was published called, *The Boatman's Horn and Other Poems*. He was tall, dignified, and refined, not a brilliant orator but an able speaker. He died in Carrollton.

[Short sketches may be found in R. H. and L. Collins, *Hist. of Ky.* (1874), vols. I, II. More extensive accounts are Francis P. Blair, Jr., "Biog. Sketch of Gen. W. O. Butler," *Graham's Mag.*, Jan. 1848; and *Life of Gen. Lewis Cass: Comprising an Account of His Military Service in the North-West During the War with Gt. Brit., His Diplomatic Career and Civil Hist. To Which Is Appended a Sketch of the Public and Private Hist. of Maj.-Gen. W. O. Butler, of the Volunteer Service of the U. S.* (1848). For Butler family see J. A. Murray, "The Butlers of the Cumberland Valley" in *Hist. Reg.* (Harrisburg), Jan. 1883; T. M. Green, *Hist. Families of Ky.* (1889); *Pa. Mag. of Hist. and Biog.*, Apr. 1883.]   E. M. C—r.

BUTLER, ZEBULON (Jan. 23, 1731–July 28, 1795), soldier, was born at Ipswich, Mass., the son of John and Hannah (Perkins) Butler and the grandson of Lieut. William Butler of Ipswich. His youth was spent in Lyme, Conn., where his parents settled in 1736 and where he is usually alleged to have been born. Here he engaged in the West India trade, owning one or more sloops. In the French and Indian War he saw service as ensign (1757), lieutenant and quartermaster (1759), and captain (1760). Ordered to Cuba in 1762, he was shipwrecked during the voyage but arrived in time to participate in the latter part of the siege of Havana. Returning to civilian life at the close of the war he led a band of Connecticut settlers to the Wyoming Valley (now Luzerne County, Pa.), where they settled along the Susquehanna (1769) on land claimed by Connecticut by virtue of her charter and through purchase from the Indians. In the ensuing Pennamite Wars between Connecticut and Pennsylvania, Butler acted as leader of the Connecticut settlers, serving as director of the Susquehanna Company and representing Wyoming in the Connecticut Assembly (1774–76). In July 1771 he laid siege to Fort Wyoming, garrisoned by Pennsylvania troops, forced its capitulation, and later repulsed Col. Plunkett's invasion of the valley in a battle at the Nanticoke Gap (1775). With the outbreak of the Revolution he was commissioned colonel of the Connecticut militia. He later became lieutenant-colonel (1776) and colonel (1778) of the Continental line. In March 1778 invasion of the valley became imminent, and Butler, acting on behalf of the "Town of Westmoreland," appealed to the Board of War for its protection, the Wyoming regiments then being with the Continental army. Before aid arrived, the valley was invaded by the New York Loyalist leader, Maj. John Butler [*q.v.*], with an army consisting of Rangers, a detachment of Sir John Johnson's loyalist regiment (the King's Royal Regiment of New York), and several hundred Indians led by the Seneca chief Old King

(Sayenqueraghta). Lieutenant-Colonel Zebulon Butler, home on leave, on assuming command of the Continental forces, found himself at the head of barely sixty regulars and about 300 militia consisting largely of "the undisciplined, the youthful, and the aged." He wished to await reinforcements but was overruled by his council of war, and it was decided to leave Forty Fort and seek battle, an unfortunate decision that made victory for the invaders almost a certainty. Outnumbered, and the Indians making a flank attack, the Continental forces fled to the fort (July 3, 1778), which capitulated on the following day, Butler fleeing to prevent capture. While there were many atrocities committed, there was not the wholesale massacre so vividly described by Thomas Campbell in *Gertrude of Wyoming* (London, 1809). After the departure of the invaders Butler returned to Wyoming as commandant, where he remained during the Sullivan expedition of 1779 against the Iroquois confederacy. The expedition detached by Gen. Sullivan, Sept. 20, 1779, to destroy the Indian villages east of Cayuga Lake, frequently credited to Col. Butler, was commanded by Lieutenant-Colonel William Butler of the 4th Pennsylvania regiment. On Dec. 29, 1780, Butler was recalled from Wyoming by Washington at the request of Congress to prevent any recurrence of friction between Connecticut and Pennsylvania, and he was then stationed at West Point, retiring from the army at the close of the Revolution. He was married three times: first, on Dec. 23, 1760, to Anna Lord, who died in 1773; second, in August 1775 to Lydia Johnson, who died on June 26, 1781; third, in November 1781 to Phebe Haight. He died at Wilkesbarre at the age of sixty-four leaving children by each of his three wives.

[*House Doc. No. 203*, 25 Cong., 3 Sess.; *Minutes of the Provincial Council of Pa.*; *Pa. Archives*; *Jour. of the Military Exped. of Maj.-Gen. John Sullivan* (1887); *Proc. and Colls. of the Wyoming Hist. and Geol. Soc.*, vols. II to XVI *passim*; *Buffalo Hist. Soc. Pubs.*, vols. I (1879), IV (1896); *Vital Records of Ipswich, Mass.* (1910); Geo. A. Perkins, *The Family of John Perkins of Ipswich, Mass.* (1889); H. E. Hayden, *The Massacre of Wyoming* (1895) and *Geneal. and Family Hist. of the Wyoming and Lackawanna Valleys, Pa.* (1906); Thos. J. Rogers, *A New Am. Biog. Dict.* (3rd ed., Easton, Pa., 1824); Wm. L. Stone, *Life of Jos. Brant-Thayendanegea* (1838); Chas. Miner, *Hist. of Wyoming* (1845); Geo. Peck, *Wyoming* (1858); O. J. Harvey, *A Hist. of Wilkes-Barre, Luzerne County, Pa.* (1909); *Conn. Mag.*, Mar.–Apr. 1900; Butler's report of the battle of Wyoming to the Board of War, dated July 10, 1778, printed in John Marshall, *Life of Geo. Washington* (2nd ed., 1832, I, 281).]   F. E. R.

BUTTERFIELD, DANIEL (Oct. 31, 1831–July 17, 1901), Union soldier, the third son of John [*q.v.*] and Malinda Harriet (Baker) Butterfield, was born in Utica, N. Y. He inherited from his father, a genius for organization, an indomitable will, and a natural ability for promoting large enterprises. After preparatory work in private schools and the Utica Academy, he entered Union College, where he made a fair scholastic record and from which he graduated in 1849 at the age of eighteen, with the degree of Bachelor of Arts. He then studied law, but finding himself too young for admittance to the bar, traveled extensively through the South, and incidentally became convinced of the certainty of conflict between the states over slavery. Soon after, he established himself in New York City as superintendent of the eastern division of the American Express Company. Having in mind, however, the inevitability of civil war, he entered the New York militia as a captain in the 71st Regiment, and after rising through intermediate grades, became colonel of the 12th Regiment, an organization in which he had a peculiar interest during his entire life. On Apr. 14, 1861, Fort Sumter was evacuated, and official records show that within two days, Butterfield was appointed first sergeant of the *Clay Guards,* a battalion of three hundred prominent citizens of Washington, hastily recruited to defend the city from expected attack. Butterfield's 12th New York Regiment was mustered into the Federal service on May 2, 1861, and on May 24 crossed the historic Long Bridge, the first Union regiment to enter Virginia. The regiment was soon ordered to reinforce Gen. Patterson's command at Martinsburg, W. Va., and participated in many early operations in that vicinity, with Butterfield temporarily in command of a brigade of New York regiments. The coming of army reorganization brought to him appointment as a brigadier-general of volunteers, Sept. 7, 1861, and assignment to command of the 3rd Brigade, 1st Division (Morrell), 5th Army Corps (Fitz-John Porter).

As a brigade commander, Butterfield participated most creditably in McClellan's Peninsular campaign, and was wounded at the battle of Gaines's Mill, June 21, 1862. Thirty years later, Congress awarded Butterfield a medal of honor for distinguished gallantry on this occasion, the citation reading, "where he seized the colors of the 83rd Pennsylvania Infantry Volunteers at a critical moment, and under galling fire of the enemy led the command." His brigade covered the important withdrawal of the Army of the Potomac to Harrison's Landing, when it changed base to join Pope, and at the end of October, Butterfield assumed command of Morrell's division, succeeding by virtue of seniority to command of the 5th Army Corps, Nov. 16, 1862. On Nov. 29, he received his appointment as

major-general, and on Dec. 13, commanded the 5th Corps in the Central Grand Division at the battle of Fredericksburg. On Dec. 16, his corps covered Burnside's withdrawal.

When Gen. Hooker succeeded Burnside in command of the Army of the Potomac, Jan. 26, 1863, Butterfield became Hooker's chief of staff, and served as such during the battle of Chancellorsville. At about this time he devised a system of corps badges, which gained immediate popularity with officers and men. He remained as chief of staff of the army after assumption of command by Gen. Meade, and was severely wounded at the battle of Gettysburg, July 3, 1863, by the Confederate shell fire which preceded Pickett's charge. Following this decisive battle, both Gen. Meade and Gen. Butterfield were parties to a controversy which lasted long after the Civil War as to Meade's real intentions on the critical morning of July 2, 1863,— Meade contending that a preparatory order covering the withdrawal of the Army of the Potomac from the field of Gettysburg was merely tentative and precautionary; while Butterfield and certain other generals regarded the order as positive and mandatory on Meade's part to surrender the field without further battle (*Battles and Leaders of the Civil War,* III, 243–97, 410–11).

The following October, Butterfield joined the Army of the Cumberland as Hooker's chief of staff, in time to act as such at the battle of Lookout Mountain. In Sherman's march to the sea he commanded the 3rd Division, 20th Army Corps, under Generals Thomas and Hooker, and was engaged at Buzzard's Roost, at Resaca (where his troops captured the first guns lost by Johnston in the Atlanta campaign), at Dallas, New Hope Church, and at Lost and Kenesaw Mountains. Before the Atlanta campaign ended, he was seriously stricken with fever and was never able to rejoin his old command. When convalescent, he was ordered on special duty at Vicksburg, and later went to New York City, where on Aug. 24, 1865, he was mustered out of the volunteer service, but was retained as superintendent of the general recruiting service, by virtue of his appointment, July 1, 1863, as colonel of the 5th Infantry, Regular Army. On Mar. 13, 1865, he was honored with brevet appointment as brigadier-general, United States Army, for gallant and meritorious services during the war; and on the same date with the brevet of major-general, United States Army, for similar services in the field during the war.

In January 1866, at the suggestion of Alexander T. Stewart of New York, Butterfield became the prime mover in raising a testimonial fund amounting to $105,000 from patriotic citizens of New York, which was presented to Gen. Grant, Feb. 15, 1866.

On Mar. 14, 1870, Butterfield's resignation from the army was accepted, that he might become assistant United States treasurer at New York City, under President Grant. Various considerations induced Butterfield's resignation from the military service, chief among which was the death of his father and the constant attention required in the administration of a large estate. After retirement to private life, Butterfield became associated with many important business enterprises, and exhibited the same tireless energy and sound judgment in these affairs which had marked his army career. He constructed a railroad in the republic of Guatemala; was president of the Albany & Troy Steamboat Company; and was financially interested in the Apartment Hotel Company, the Butterfield Real Estate Company, and the National Bank of Cold Spring, N. Y. He was also owner of the Brooklyn Annex steamships, connecting with the Pennsylvania Railroad, and was a director of the Mechanics & Traders Bank of New York. In 1870, he visited Europe, where he made an exhaustive study of the London and Paris post-office systems, the subject of a report to the Postmaster-General of the United States. On June 4, 1877, he lost his wife to whom he was married on Feb. 12, 1857; and on Sept. 21, 1886, he was married in London, to Mrs. Julia Lorillard (Safford) James, of New York City and Cold Spring. On two subsequent trips to Europe, he visited Russia with a view to securing concessions to build a Siberian railroad, in which his efforts were unsuccessful. During these visits, he received many social attentions and honors from the Emperor of Russia. At the Washington Centennial Celebration in New York City, in May 1889, he acted as grand marshal of the parade, where over 100,000 men passed in review. In the year 1892, he established a course of thirty lectures at Union College, on popular topics of the day. He was during this period of his career at one time or another, president of the Society of the Army of the Potomac, member of the Grand Army of the Republic, and chancellor of the New York Commandery of the Loyal Legion. On July 2, 1893, at Gettysburg, he acted as grand marshal of the dedication exercises of the New York State Memorial Monument, attended by over 10,000 veterans. As a testimonial to his war service, he was, at various times, made the recipient of a sword of superb workmanship, set with emeralds; a 5th Corps

Badge, set with diamonds; and badges of the 20th Corps and of the Army of the Potomac, set with precious stones,—all presented by former comrades of the Civil War. In politics, he was a Republican, and in 1892, rather against his will, consented to become a candidate for Congress, but was defeated. He was actively interested in military preparedness, and in 1900 framed legislation for submission to Congress which contemplated uniform organization and training for the militia of the country, and for the organization of army reserves. In this connection Gov. Roosevelt appointed him a delegate to a conference called by the Governor of Florida, to consider plans for the rapid mobilization of troops in time of war.

Early in April 1901, Butterfield suffered a stroke of paralysis, and two months later was taken from his home in New York City to "Cragside," his country residence at Cold Spring. Here he passed away, in the seventieth year of his age. By special authority of the War Department, the interment took place at West Point, where his remains received the major-general's salute of thirteen guns and where the escort of honor included his old regiment, the 12th New York. Over his grave a magnificent white marble monument has been erected, thirty-five feet in height, consisting in the main of sixteen slender columns upon which rests an ornate superstructure. Butterfield died, honored and mourned by a host of friends in both military and civil life.

[A very complete account of Butterfield's life and services is to be found in Julia Lorillard Butterfield, *A Biog. Memorial of Gen. Daniel Butterfield* (1904). See also *Battles and Leaders of the Civil War* (vols. II, III, IV), and the *Official Records* (Army).]

C. D. R.

BUTTERFIELD, JOHN (Nov. 18, 1801–Nov. 14, 1869), expressman, financier, was descended from Benjamin Butterfield, who brought his family to the Bay Colony in 1638. His grandfather saw service in the American Revolution, while others of his kinsmen participated in the French and Indian War. His father, Daniel Butterfield, was a native of Berne, near Albany, N. Y., and here it was that John Butterfield was born. Brief periods of attendance at the primitive schools in the Helderberg provided his meager formal training, while the broader education of his practical career was begun as a stage driver. He rose from the driver's seat to a share in the proprietorship and soon most of the stage lines of western New York were under his control. He became interested in packet-boats on the canal, steamboats on Lake Ontario, and plank roads in the region; he originated the street railway of Utica and aided in the promotion of railroads. With Wells, Livingston, and others he established the New York, Albany & Buffalo Telegraph Company. He was not the originator of the express business but was one of the first to see the possibilities of such service. In 1849 he formed the express company of Butterfield, Wasson & Company. The year following there was effected at his suggestion a consolidation of his firm and two others to create the American Express Company. When in 1857 Congress provided for the establishment of the first great transcontinental stage line Butterfield and his associates were awarded the contract at $600,000 per year. It was to be the longest stage-coach line in America, extending from St. Louis via El Paso, Tucson, and Los Angeles to San Francisco. The route was nearly 2,800 miles long and coaches were to be run semiweekly each way on a twenty-five day schedule. As president of the Overland Mail Company Butterfield displayed his executive ability in planning and establishing this service. Upon arrival of the pioneer eastbound stage at St. Louis he telegraphed the good news to Washington and President Buchanan replied: "I cordially congratulate you upon the result. It is a glorious triumph for civilization and the Union." This overland service was maintained with outstanding success. In Utica, his home city, Butterfield continued to be an important factor. He was director of the Utica City National Bank, was builder of the Butterfield House and the Butterfield Block, and was interested in land investments and development. He was elected mayor of the city in 1865. His portrait reveals a man of regular features and rather handsome appearance, with aggressive ability and determination written on his face. He was married to Malinda Harriet Baker in February 1822, and to them were born nine children; of these, their third son, Daniel [q.v.], was a general in the Union army in the Civil War. In 1867 he was stricken by paralysis, from the effects of which he lingered until Nov. 14, 1869. His wife survived him, living until Aug. 20, 1883.

[Julia Lorillard Butterfield's *A Biog. Memorial of Gen. Daniel Butterfield* (1904) is devoted primarily to the son of John Butterfield but presents considerable data upon the father. Mention of Butterfield's express service is found in *Harper's Mag.*, August 1875, and a fuller treatment in LeRoy R. Hafen's *The Overland Mail* (1926). For ancestry see Geo. A. Gordon's "The Butterfields of Middlesex" in *New Eng. Hist. and Geneal. Reg.*, Jan. 1890.]   L. R. H.

BUTTERICK, EBENEZER (May 29, 1826– Mar. 31, 1903), inventor of standardized paper patterns for clothes, was the seventh child of Francis and Ruhamah (Buss) Butterick. His father was a carpenter in the small town of Sterling, Mass. There Ebenezer was born and became a tailor and shirt-maker. About 1859, either he or his wife Ellen conceived the idea of a set of graded shirt patterns, by which it would be possible to reproduce these garments in unlimited quantities. Experiments on such patterns were continued for several years, until, on June 16, 1863, the first patterns, cut from stiff paper, were placed on the market. The cheapness and practical utility of these patterns made them instantly successful, and the demand for them was so widespread that Butterick removed, later in 1863, to the larger town of Fitchburg, where there were better facilities for manufacture and distribution. At the suggestion of his wife that mothers would welcome patterns from which to make clothes for their children, he added to his shirt patterns a graded set of patterns for boys' suits. At this time, Giuseppe Garibaldi was an international hero, and these first juvenile patterns were for "Garibaldi" suits, modeled after the uniform worn by him and his men. These garments, picturesque, and easily made at home from these simple patterns, became immensely popular throughout the country. The demand for his patterns so increased that Butterick removed his factory from his home to a disused academy in Fitchburg. The desirability of a metropolitan office became evident, and in 1864 quarters were opened at 192 Broadway, New York City. The patterns, now made from tissue paper, were chiefly for children's suits, and especially for the "Garibaldi." Butterick sold his patterns largely through agents, and one of these, J. W. Wilder, reported a demand for similar patterns for women's garments. The suggestion was at once adopted, and with this step the business expanded to enormous proportions. In 1867, Wilder and A. W. Pollard were associated with Butterick as E. Butterick & Company, and two years later the factory was removed from Fitchburg to Brooklyn. Wilder, an aggressive and imaginative business genius, became the active and controlling member of the firm. One of his inspirations was a magazine with fashion reports to stimulate the sale of the patterns, and the *Metropolitan* established in 1869. This later became the *Delineator*. In 1871 the company sold 6,000,000 patterns, and by 1876 branches had been placed in London, Paris, Berlin, and Vienna. The business was reorganized in 1881, and was renamed The Butterick Publishing Company, Ltd., with J. W. Wilder as president, and Ebenezer Butterick as secretary. Butterick held this position until 1894, when he retired from active participation in the business. It may be noted that Butterick's priority as inventor of paper patterns has been disputed and that the credit has also been given to Mrs. John Ellis, of Manchester, England. Investigation has shown, however, that Mrs. Ellis made her first patterns in 1866, and that they were for her own use only. Butterick patterns, whether first conceived by Ebenezer, or by Ellen, his wife, were undoubtedly the first to be practically and commercially utilized.

[Data for the life of Ebenezer Butterick have been obtained from the files of The Butterick Company, and from the recollections of G. W. Wilder, now president of that company. Obituaries were pub. in the *Brooklyn Times, Brooklyn Eagle, N. Y. Evening Post,* and *N. Y. Times,* all for Apr. 1, 1903.]   A. L. C.

BUTTERWORTH, BENJAMIN (Oct. 22, 1837–Jan. 16, 1898), lawyer, politician, came of Quaker stock on both sides. His grandfather, Benjamin Butterworth, a planter of Campbell County, Va., and a member of the Society of Friends, in 1812 migrated to Ohio, taking up a homestead in Warren County. His father, William Butterworth, a school-teacher and farmer, married Elizabeth, daughter of Nathan Linton of Clinton County, also a member of the Society of Friends, and Benjamin was born in Hamilton township, Warren County. He received an excellent preparatory schooling, completing his education at Lebanon Academy and Ohio University (Athens). He then studied law at Cincinnati, graduating from the Cincinnati Law School and being admitted to the bar in 1861. Serving during the war in an Ohio regiment he later commenced practise at Lebanon and quickly obtained an extensive clientele, owing to his attractive personality and powers of speech. In 1870 he was appointed United States district attorney for Southern Ohio but shortly resigned in order to resume practise. From 1873 to 1875 as a Republican he represented the district of Butler and Warren Counties in the state Senate. In 1875 he moved to Cincinnati, which city offered a wider scope for legal talent, and he rapidly acquired a prominent position at the bar. At the call of party, however, he practically sacrificed his professional career and reëntered politics, being elected in 1878 to the 46th Congress as Republican representative for the 1st District of Ohio. Reëlected in 1880, he retained his seat until 1882, when he was defeated. Returning to practise, he was retained by the attorney-general of the United States as special counsel in the South Carolina election cases and also acted as commissioner to investigate certain phases of the Northern Pacific Railway. President Arthur had desired to appoint him post-

master-general but the exigencies of local politics would not permit, and he accepted, June 1883, the commissionership of patents, a position where his legal ability found adequate scope. He resigned, however, Mar. 23, 1885, having been elected as representative from his old district to the 49th Congress. Reëlected in 1886 and 1888, he ranked among the party leaders in the House, though noted for the independent standpoint from which he was wont to view questions of the day. In 1890, he retired from Congress and opened a law office in Washington. In 1892 President Harrison appointed him president of the commission to the European governments in the interests of the Columbian Exposition, and the fine foreign exhibits at Chicago were in great measure due to his labors. He was a close personal friend of President McKinley and in April 1897 at the latter's request, he again became commissioner of patents. He died at Thomasville, Ga. He married, Nov. 2, 1863, Mary E., daughter of Jacob Seiler of Harrisburg, Pa. "During the last quarter of a century [1875–1900] no more picturesque and charming personality occupied the position of Representative from Ohio than Benjamin Butterworth" (F. Starek, *post*). Broad-minded, tolerant and genial, he was popular with all members, irrespective of politics.

[Butterworth's ancestry is traced in *Hist. of Warren County, Ohio* (1882), p. 939. A contemporary review of his earlier career appeared in *Biog. Cyc. and Portrait Gallery of the State of Ohio,* III (1884), 661. There are sketches of his life in *Appleton's Annual Cyc. and Register,* 1898, p. 528, and in W. A. Taylor, *Ohio in Cong. from 1803 to 1901* (1900), p. 264. See also article by F. Starek in O. O. Stealey, *Twenty Years in the Press Gallery* (1906), p. 288, and obituaries in *Cincinnati Times-Star, Cincinnati Enquirer, Cincinnati Commerical Tribune, Washington Post* and *Evening Star,* Washington, D. C., Jan. 17, 1898.]
                                                H. W. H. K.

BUTTERWORTH, HEZEKIAH (Dec. 22, 1839–Sept. 5, 1905), journalist, author, was born at Warren, R. I., of a substantial New England family whose ancestor had emigrated from England to Massachusetts before the middle of the seventeenth century. His father, Gardiner M. Butterworth, was a "good-natured, Bible-reading farmer," while from his mother, Susan (Ritchie) Butterworth, he inherited a poetic temperament. We are told that Hezekiah was different from the five other children of the family, a nervous, timid, superstitious boy, with a love for ghost stories. He never lost his keen interest in the traditions of the locality in which he was brought up. As a child, he was prevented by poor health from any extended schooling. He intended to go to Brown University after graduation from the high school at Warren, but never got beyond studying under the direction of one of the Brown professors. He evinced quite early a taste for journalism, writing for a local paper and contributing to periodicals. Having attracted the attention of the owner and editor of the *Youth's Companion* through a series of articles on self-education, he came into prominence through his connection with that periodical,—a connection which was maintained for almost a quarter-century (1870–94). It is said that during 1877–87, when his influence was the strongest, the circulation of the *Youth's Companion* increased from 140,000 to 400,000. Authorities differ in regard to the amount of foreign travel in which he was engaged throughout his life. It is certain that he went to Europe at least once and took one voyage to South America, but his travels were perhaps never so extensive as his seventeen volumes of *Zig Zag Journeys* to various parts of the world would indicate. He was known especially as a juvenile and patriotic writer, and while the literary value of his works may be questioned, there is no doubt of their wholesome moral influence. In his journal in 1885 he wrote: "Resolved, it is my purpose to give my whole heart and thought to my work with the pen and to write only that which will tend to make my readers better in heart and life and richer in spiritual knowledge." Most of his writings and his lectures took on a moral or religious tone, and he became especially known for his interest in church music. His book *The Story of the Hymns* received in 1875 the George Wood Gold Medal awarded to the book of the year which had exerted the best influence. He was also a popular religious lecturer the character of whose lectures is indicated by two of his favorite topics, "Men Who Overcame Obstacles to Spiritual Success" and "The Religious Experiences of Famous Men."

Much of his work was characterized by an exaggerated sentimentality. In literature his critical standards were affected by his kindliness and ready sympathy; he was, as a personal friend has said, "very hospitable to poets, good and bad." Prolific in output, he lacked the ability to criticize himself. He was very charitable, both with his money and with his interest, and the honesty and geniality which were expressed in his "transparently good" face won him the sincere affection of hosts of friends, especially among the poor. He never married, and there is very little reference to love and marriage in his books. The "touch of medieval asceticism" which his friends noted in him became very marked in his later years.

[Very little has been written about Hezekiah Butterworth although he was for many years a familiar figure to hosts of Americans. Most of the information in the above sketch came by word of mouth from his former associates on the *Youth's Companion*, such as C. A. Stephens and M. A. DeWolfe Howe. Ralph Davol in the *New England Mag.* of Jan. 1906 shortly after Butterworth's death wrote an appreciation of his work and personality and M. B. Thrasher reproduces in the *National Mag.*, X, 530, a personal interview with him. There is a tribute in an article by Nixon Waterman in the *Boston Evening Transcript*, Sept. 6, 1905. For bibliography of his writings see *Who's Who in America*, 1903–05.]   J. L. M.

BUTTRICK, WALLACE (Oct. 23, 1853–May 27, 1926), Baptist clergyman, educator, was born in Potsdam, N. Y. His father, Charles Henry Buttrick (1823–77), was a direct descendant of William Buttrick who came from Kingston-on-Thames in 1640 and settled at Concord, Mass. His mother, Polly Dodge Warren (1828–1919), was descended from Richard Warren who came over in the *Mayflower* in 1620. Buttrick attended Ogdensburg Academy and the Potsdam Normal School between 1868 and 1872. On Dec. 1, 1875, he married Isabella Allen of Saginaw, Mich. Early possessed of a desire to enter the ministry, his hopes were deferred by the necessity of earning a livelihood, and for a time he was employed as a clerk in the railway mail service. Subsequently he entered the Rochester Theological Seminary and was graduated there in 1883. The same year he became pastor of the First Baptist Church of New Haven, Conn., where he served until 1889. He then accepted a call to a pastorate in St. Paul, Minn., and after three years there became pastor of a Baptist church at Albany, N. Y. Ten years later he was invited to become secretary and executive officer of the General Education Board which had just been established by Mr. John D. Rockefeller for the promotion of education in the United States. While money had been provided by Mr. Rockefeller for the administrative needs of the new organization, no endowment funds had then been received, the policy of the Board and its founder being to make first of all a thorough survey of the educational needs of the country with a view to discovering the strategic points to which the efforts of the Board could be most wisely directed, and the methods by which private funds could best be used, so as to stimulate the efforts and the self-reliance of each community. To the study of this great problem Buttrick devoted himself with wisdom, tact, and assiduity. Although he neither possessed nor claimed to possess the formal qualifications of an educational expert, his firm grasp of the essential purposes of education, his abundant common sense, and a remarkable understanding of human nature, equipped him admirably to take a fresh view of the educational field and to discover the points at which reinforcement was needed. While the work of the Board, soon supported by generous endowment, covered many aspects of education, its main efforts were exerted in two directions: first, to promote the better endowment of those colleges in different parts of the country which, by reason of their location, by the evidences of vitality already manifested, and by their possession of constituencies capable of carrying the main burden of future support, gave promise of permanent usefulness; the second point to which the Board directed its attention was the general condition of education in the Southern states. While the needs of higher education in this section were not overlooked, the improvement and extension of primary and secondary schools were recognized as of more urgent importance. Economic development was the indispensable means of providing the resources necessary for education. Accordingly, Buttrick's efforts turned in the direction of popular education to increase the productivity of the land through the demonstration on a wide scale of improved agricultural methods. Fortunately, a beginning had been made by Dr. Seaman A. Knapp of the Department of Agriculture. In cooperation with that Department, farm demonstration was extended and maintained for many years under the guidance of the General Education Board. The merit of this work, however, was that while it entailed a moderate expense in the employment of agricultural experts and demonstrators, the chief contribution was that of guidance and stimulus. With land, equipment, and labor furnished by the farmers themselves, the expense incurred by the Board was insignificant as compared with returns in increased productivity of the land. While these efforts were under way, the Board, through its agents, was studying the problem of secondary education in the South so that, with gradually increasing resources, improvements in the number and quality of schools could be financed by the Southern communities themselves. Buttrick lived to see these improvements largely realized. The special problems of negro education, as well as those which the negroes shared with the whites, also largely engaged his attention, and he contributed much to their solution, exhibiting a tact, sympathy, and understanding which won the confidence of both races. In his later years he turned his attention to the needs of education for the professions, especially in medicine; and his Board assumed large responsibilities in this field for the expenditure of the sums placed at its disposal by Mr. Rockefeller. In 1914 he assumed the direction of the China

Medical Board of the Rockefeller Foundation in addition to his activities as executive officer of the General Education Board. He spent some weeks of the year 1917 in Great Britain, meeting leaders of public opinion, addressing large popular gatherings on the subject of American participation in the war, and interpreting to the British public the sentiments and aims by which that participation was inspired. In 1917 he was made president of the General Education Board and held that office until 1923 when he became chairman. He was also a trustee of the Rockefeller Foundation and a member of the International Health Board, the China Medical Board, the Peking Union Medical College, and the International Education Board. To the discharge of these responsibilities he brought great wisdom, a passionate devotion to his work, an ever-present sense of humor, geniality, and a kindliness that found spontaneous expression in his close personal relations with men of every station and calling. He died in Baltimore on May 27, 1926.

[*Who's Who in America,* 1903–05; *Gen. Ed. Board: an Account of its Activities,* 1902–14 (1915); *Annual Report of the Gen. Ed. Board,* 1925–26; *N. Y. Times,* May 28, 1926.]   J.D.G.

BUTTS, ISAAC (Jan. 11, 1816–Nov. 20, 1874), newspaper editor, the son of Nicholas and Elizabeth (De Witt) Butts, was born in Dutchess County, N. Y. When twelve years old he went with his parents to Irondequoit, Monroe County, N. Y. The death of the father within four years left the management of the farm to the six children, of whom Isaac was the second in age. There was no opportunity for any formal education beyond what was offered by the district school. In spite of handicaps, young Butts made steady progress. Before he was thirty he had become the owner of the *Daily Advertiser,* published in the neighboring city of Rochester and said to be the oldest daily paper west of Albany. At a time when personal journalism in New York State was in the ascendant, with Greeley, Bryant, and Bennett setting the pace in the metropolis, Butts quickly found his place as a writer of political editorials. Rochester already had a newspaper-reading public of more than ordinary discrimination. Butts developed a pungent, terse, editorial style that won readers in a day when the editor's opinions on public questions received attention and respect in proportion to his independence of judgment and the forcefulness with which he gave it expression. Butts measured up to both criteria in an exceptional way. He was a Democrat and his advocacy of the Wilmot Proviso led to his taking an advanced position in the party on the slavery question. In 1848 he was among the Democratic editors of New York who went over to the "Barnburner" wing of the party and came out for the Van Buren ticket. The triumph of the "Hunkers," or conservative Democrats, in that election caused his retirement, for a brief season, from editorial responsibilities, but he was soon back in harness. In 1852, after the election of President Pierce, Butts became one of the owners of the Rochester *Daily Union* and continued as the political editor of that journal for twelve years (the *Advertiser* having in 1857 been consolidated with the *Union*). He was a leading exponent of the Douglas, or Squatter Sovereignty, idea and upheld the Missouri Compromise. He consistently opposed the Lincoln administration in its conduct of the Civil War and his final withdrawal from journalism in 1864 has been attributed to his conviction that the war was wholly wrong and that nothing but evil could result from it, so far as the nation was concerned. He was a life-long enemy of protective tariffs for home industry. A treatise on free trade that he had written in the last year of his life was published after his death (*Protection and Free Trade*, 1875). He had become independently rich through the success of the Western Union Telegraph Company, in which he was interested at an early stage of its development. In 1844 he was married to Mary Smyles, who with two sons and three daughters survived him.

[Rochester *Evening Express*, Nov. 20, 1874; Wm. F. Peck, *Semi-Centennial Hist. of Rochester* (1884); the *World* (N. Y.), Nov. 22, 1874.]   W. B. S.

BUTTZ, HENRY ANSON (Apr. 18, 1835–Oct. 6, 1920), Methodist clergyman, educator, was born at Middle Smithfield, Pa. He attended the village school there and at fifteen taught a district school. Then there followed alternate periods of attending school and teaching, until 1858, when he was graduated from Princeton University. His theological studies were pursued in the Theological Seminary of the Reformed Church at New Brunswick, N. J. His ecclesiastical affiliations were with the Newark Conference of the Methodist Episcopal Church, in which he served as pastor of several churches during the ten years of his public ministry, before being called to the work of the newly opened Drew Theological Seminary in Madison, N. J., to which he gave a most fruitful half-century of distinguished service. He was adjunct professor of Greek and Hebrew 1868–70; professor of Greek and New Testament Exegesis 1871–1918; president of the faculty 1880–1912, and president emeritus 1912–20. While primarily not an administrator, his tastes and training being along other lines, his presidency was a notable one, for

when he resigned in 1912 every new building on the campus, six in all, had been secured by him, and practically the entire endowment had been built up through his efforts. Nearly three thousand students of almost every nationality had come under his influence. It was said of him that he *was* Drew Theological Seminary. In this he lived and moved and had his being. No other opportunity appealed to him. He declined an election to the editorship of the *Methodist Review*. He was indifferent to a possible election to the bishopric of the Church. Essentially a teacher, a scholarly, ardent, interpretative teacher of the Greek New Testament, he was himself an example of the interest he sought to awaken in others. Various works were edited by him: *Epistle to the Romans in Greek* (1876); *The New Life Dawning* (1873), by B. H. Nadal; and *The Student's Commentary—The Book of Psalms* (1896), by Dr. James Strong. He was a member of various societies such as the American Exegetical Society and the American Philological Association, and of several ecclesiastical organizations, but his voice was seldom heard in debate. Never dogmatic, even though a man of strong convictions, he was urbane without obsequiousness, gentle without effeminacy, and, when necessary, firm without harshness. He was married, on Apr. 11, 1860, to Emily Hoagland.

[*Henry Anson Buttz, His Book: Lectures, Essays, Sermons, Exegetical Notes* (2 vols.), ed. by Chas. Fremont Sitterly (1922); the *Methodist Rev.*, Mar.–Apr. 1921; E. S. Tipple, *Drew Theol. Sem. 1867–1917* (1917); *Minutes of the Newark Conference of the M. E. Ch.* (1921).]   E. S. T.

BYFORD, WILLIAM HEATH (Mar. 20, 1817–May 21, 1890), gynecologist, descended from a family of Suffolk, England, was the eldest child of Henry T. and Hannah Byford. He was born in the village of Eaton, Ohio, where his father worked as a mechanic. In 1821 the family moved to the Falls of the Ohio River, now New Albany, Ind., and later moved to Hindostan, in the same state, where the father died when William was nine years old. With but three or four years of elementary schooling, William was forced to give up his studies and help his mother in the support of the family. When he was twelve years old, the family went to live with Mrs. Byford's father on a farm near Palestine, Ill., and two years later William began an apprenticeship with a tailor in that village. Later he went to Vincennes, Ind., to finish learning his trade. While serving his apprenticeship, he was acquiring an education. By diligent study, he mastered the structure of his native tongue and gained a useful knowledge of Latin, Greek, and French. With an eye to a medical career, he also studied physiology, chemistry, and natural history, and, during the last year of his apprenticeship, associated himself with Dr. Joseph Maddox of Vincennes. At the age of twenty-one he was able to pass the required examination, and began practise in Owensville, Ind. In 1840 he moved to Mt. Vernon, Ind., where he associated himself with Dr. Hezekiah Holland, whose daughter he afterward married. He remained at Mt. Vernon until 1850, during which time he pursued a course at the Ohio Medical College and, in 1845, obtained his medical degree. In 1850 he was appointed to the chair of anatomy at the Evansville Medical College and in 1852 was transferred to the chair of theory and practise of medicine. In 1857 he was called to the professorship of obstetrics and diseases of women and children in Rush Medical College in Chicago. Two years later he was transferred to a similar chair in the newly organized Chicago Medical College of which he was one of the founders. In 1879, Rush Medical College created especially for him a chair of gynecology, which he held until his death. In 1870, he was active in the organization of the Woman's Medical College of Chicago.

As a pioneer in gynecology and a medical teacher for nearly forty years, Byford made a deep impression upon the profession of his time. Good judgment combined with patient industry and singleness of purpose gave him leadership. His name is associated with many important innovations in gynecological practise, some of which have subsequently given way to improved methods while others remain as permanent contributions. He will be longest remembered, however, as a systematic writer on the subjects of obstetrics and gynecology. His most ambitious work was his *Treatise on the Theory and Practice of Obstetrics* (1870) ; others were: *A Treatise on the Chronic Inflammation and Displacements of the Impregnated Uterus* (1864) ; *The Practice of Medicine and Surgery applied to the Diseases and Accidents Incident to Women* (1865), widely used as a text-book; *The Philosophy of Domestic Life* (1869). In these works he also was a pioneer advocate of medical and nursing education for women. Deeply religious and of abstemious habits, he cared little for ordinary diversions and had practically no interests beyond his family life and his professional work. Physically of short and vigorous body, he had a triangular face with high and broad forehead, abundant wavy hair, full beard, and deep-set kindly eyes, with a suggestion of Butler's:

> "Grave synod men that were revered
> For solid face and depth of beard."

He continued his active practise to the end. Having retired in his usual health on the night of May 20, 1890, in the early hours of the next morning he succumbed to an attack of angina pectoris. He was married twice : on Oct. 3, 1840, at Mt. Vernon, Ind., to Mary Ann Holland, who died in 1864 ; and, in 1873, to Lina Flersheim.

[*Am. Jour. of Obstetrics*, June 1890 ; *Trans. Am. Gynecological Soc.*, 1890, vol. XV ; *Trans. Ill. State Medic. Soc.*, 1891 ; *North Am. Practitioner*, 1890, vol. II ; *Album of Fellows, Am. Gynecological Soc.*, 1918 ; Kelly and Burrage, *Am. Medic. Biog.* (1920).]

            J.M.P.

BYINGTON, CYRUS (Mar. 11, 1793–Dec. 31, 1868), missionary to the Choctaw Indians, one of nine children of Capt. Asahel and Lucy (Peck) Byington, was born at Stockbridge, Mass. His father was a tanner and farmer, industrious and respected, but, the family being in humble circumstances, the future missionary to the Choctaws necessarily received a limited early education. Grown to be a sturdy lad, his career began when Joseph Woodbridge received him into his family and taught him Latin and Greek, a most important aid in his life-work. Apparently law was prescribed by Mr. Woodbridge as a profession for his protégé, and in fact Byington became a lawyer and practised for a few years in his native town and at Sheffield, Mass. The profession of law seemingly would have satisfied him but for the fact that he became, as he said, "a subject of divine grace," and was turned toward the ministry. Entering the Andover Theological Seminary he graduated in 1819, received ordination as a minister of the gospel, and was licensed to preach. Intent upon missionary work and hoping to go to the Armenians of Turkey, he bided his time till an opportunity should offer. Meanwhile he continued to preach in various churches in Massachusetts. At this time (1820) recruits to the number of twenty or twenty-five persons set out from Hampshire County, Mass., under the direction of the American Board, for the Choctaw Indian nation then in Mississippi. With them went Byington, who was placed in charge of the party. They proceeded by land to Pittsburgh, by flatboats down the Ohio and Mississippi to the mouth of the Yalobusha River, and by another land journey of 200 miles to their destination. Byington soon began the preparation of a Choctaw grammar and dictionary. Without the help of modern philological science, he had to take up the subject *de novo*. Assiduously he labored at the grammar and at the time of his death, nearly fifty years later, was making the seventh revision. The dictionary, representing a work of magnitude which he never concluded to his satisfaction, was of good use to him in translating into Choctaw several books of both the Old and New Testament, and in preparing Choctaw almanacs and a Choctaw definer. His grammar was published posthumously, edited by Daniel G. Brinton, in *Proceedings of the American Philosophical Society,* 1871, XII, 317–67, and his dictionary, edited by J. R. Swanton and H. S. Halbert, in *Bulletin 46, Bureau of American Ethnology* (1915). Byington's work is highly regarded by philologists. His portrait shows an alert and enthusiastic face, with clear, piercing eyes and tender mouth. Garbed in a long black coat with broad lapels, a soft collar, and flowing tie, he typified the clergyman of more than a hundred years ago.

[E. F. Jones, *Stockbridge, Past and Present; or, Records of an Old Mission Station* (1854); H. B. Cushman, *Hist. of the Choctaw, Chickasaw, and Natchez Indians* (1899); *Annual Report Am. Bd. of Commissioners for Foreign Missions,* 1821–59; *Gen. Cat. Theol. Sem., Andover, Mass.,* 1909.]   W.H.

BYLES, MATHER (Mar. 15, 1706/7–July 5, 1788), Congregational clergyman, was the son of Josiah or Josias Byles, a saddler, who came from England late in the seventeenth century and joined the Second Church of Boston in 1696, and of his wife Elizabeth, widow of William Greenough and daughter of Increase Mather. Josiah Byles died in 1708, and Mather Byles was brought up by his mother, aided by her father and by his uncle, Cotton Mather. Probably he attended the Boston Latin School; certainly in 1725 he took his A.B. at Harvard. His life-long friend, Benjamin Franklin, said that in college Byles "distinguished himself by a close application to his studies" (Manuscript Letter in the Massachusetts Historical Society). Probably in part because of his grandfather's expressed wish (H. E. Mather, *Lineage of Rev. Richard Mather,* 1890, p. 67), he prepared himself for the ministry, taking his A.M. in 1728. In 1732 he was ordained minister of the Hollis Street Congregational Church, founded in that year, and continued in office there until the Revolution ended his active career. He associated with the prosperous aristocrats of Boston, with whom he allied himself by marriage, and was a Tory at heart, although he did not air his politics in the pulpit. When the British occupied Boston he stayed in town while the ardent patriots fled. His own church was used by the troops. For a time he preached at the First Church (Manuscript Letter of his daughter, Oct. 4, 1783, in New England Historic Genealogical Society), and throughout the siege he maintained friendships with the "invaders." After the British evacuation, the patriots in his congregation preferred charges, and, at a meeting which he held to be illegal, dismissed him

from his pulpit. This was followed by a court trial resulting in a sentence of banishment which was not enforced, though for a time he was imprisoned in his own house. For the rest of his life he lived quietly with his two daughters. The generosity of friends, old and new, saved him from want. In 1783 he had a paralytic shock; five years later he died. He was married in 1733 to Mrs. Anna Gale, whose uncle, Gov. Jonathan Belcher, had been a benefactor of the Hollis Street Church. She died in 1744, and Byles married in 1747 Rebecca Tailer, daughter of William Tailer, an erstwhile lieutenant-governor of Massachusetts. By his first wife he had six children, but only the eldest, a boy, outlived him. By his second wife he had one son who died in infancy and two daughters who survived.

In his own day Byles enjoyed fame as preacher, writer, and scholar. In 1765 the University of Aberdeen gave him the degree of S.T.D. He inherited a large part of the great library accumulated by Increase and Cotton Mather, and formed a curious collection of oddities, scientific and otherwise. His interest in literature developed early, and he wrote admiring letters to several English writers, Pope, Watts, and Thomson among them, and rejoiced at receiving answers from the first two. In the *New England Weekly Journal* and elsewhere he printed much verse, markedly imitative of his English literary idols, and some conventional prose essays. After 1744, when he bade "adieu to the airy Muse" (*Poems on Several Occasions,* Preface), his publications were largely theological.

Most of his best poetry is in his *Poems on Several Occasions* (1744) or in *The Conflagration Applied to that Grand Period or Catastrophe of Our World, When the Face of Nature is to be Changed by a Deluge of Fire, As Formerly it was by That of Water. The God of Tempest and Earthquake* (1755). The most interesting of his other publications are *A Discourse on the Present Vileness of the Body, and its Future Glorious Change by Christ. To which is added, A Sermon on the Nature and Importance of Conversion* (1732); *Affection on Things Above* (1740); *The Glories of the Lord of Hosts, and the Fortitude of the Religious Hero* (1740); and *The Flourish of the Annual Spring* (1741).

To-day Byles seems undistinguished as a scholar and writer, though his verse is as fluent as that of any of his American contemporaries. Nor does he stand out as a theologian. He remained orthodox in his Calvinism, with neither the narrowness nor the ardor of his Puritan forebears. As a preacher his popularity was aided by his large stature and imposing presence, and by the fact that he often lived up to his belief that good sermons demanded "lively Descriptions, a clear Method, and pathetick Language." It is as an incorrigible punster and amateur of repartee that he is most marked among divines of his period. Few of his *mots* are intrinsically excellent, but in New England they won him celebrity—and sometimes censure (*Massachusetts Historical Society Collections*, 1891, 6 ser., IV, 122). They are fairly represented by his remark, on seeing the British soldiers enter Boston, that at last the colonists' wrongs were "red (d) ressed," or by his calling a sentry, set to guard him, his "Observe-a-Tory."

Historically Byles has interest as a man reared in the old Puritan tradition who became not only a divine but a jester, liked good society and light verse as well as sound theology, and seemed more akin to the worldly English parsons of his time than to the colonial Puritans. He never formally deserted Congregationalism, but his Loyalist sympathies and taste for the society of the wealthy, associated him with Episcopalians. The logical development of some of his tendencies appears in his children. His son, Mather, Jr., entered the Anglican ministry. His two daughters lived in Boston well into the nineteenth century, loyal to English government and the English Church, and, like their father, perhaps, more concerned with polite society in this world than with aspirations toward sainthood in the next.

[The Massachusetts Historical Society has many manuscripts, originals and copies, bearing on Byles and his family. The New England Historic Genealogical Society has copies of letters written by Byles and his daughters. There is a brief biography in Sprague, *Annals Am. Pulpit* (1857), I, 376–82, and another in E. A. Duyckinck, *Cyc. of Am. Lit.* (1855), I, 116–20. Some of Byles's witticisms are in Wm. Tudor, *Life of Jas. Otis* (1823), and in L. M. Sargent, *Dealings with the Dead* (1856). A. W. H. Eaton in *The Famous Mather Byles* (1914) makes use of this and other material, and the notes give references to further sources of information. Dr. Eaton includes a brief bibliography of Byles's chief publications. From this should be omitted *Divine Power and Anger Displayed in Earthquakes* (1755), which was written by Mather Byles, Jr., according to his sister's memorandum, a copy of which is in the Mass. Hist. Soc. The same authority ascribes to the elder Byles *A Present for Children* (No. 9246 in Chas. Evans, *Am. Bibliography* 1903–25), which is not included in Dr. Eaton's list. The portraits of Byles are discussed by John H. Edmonds in his "Account of the Mather-Byles Portraits" in *Proc. Am. Antiquarian Soc.*, XXXIII, 285–90. J. H. Tuttle, "The Libraries of the Mathers" in *Idem*, XX, 269–356, gives data on books owned by Byles.]   K. B. M.

BYNUM, WILLIAM PRESTON (June 16, 1820–Dec. 30, 1909), jurist, was born in Stokes County, N. C., whither his grandfather Gray Bynum had moved from Virginia prior to the Revolution. William's father, Hampton Bynum, was a large landowner in the county and married Mary Colman, daughter of Col. John Martin.

His early education was received at home, but he subsequently proceeded to Davidson College where he graduated with distinction in 1843. He then studied law with Chief Justice Pearson and was admitted to the bar in 1844. He commenced practise at Rutherfordton, but removed to Lincoln County when he married Ann Eliza, daughter of Bartlett Shipp and sister of Judge W. M. Shipp of the supreme court of North Carolina. He practised at Lincolnton up to the outbreak of the Civil War, and acquired an extensive legal connection. Politically a Whig, he strongly opposed the movement for secession, both on the platform and in the press. When Lincoln called for volunteers to coerce the South, however, he threw in his lot with his state, and in 1861 was appointed lieutenant-colonel of the 2nd North Carolina Regiment by Gov. Ellis. For two years he was on active service, participating in the battles in the neighborhood of Richmond and in the first battle of Fredericksburg. In 1863 he was appointed by the North Carolina legislature solicitor for the 6th judicial district of the state, and retired from the army in order to take up his duties. He occupied this position for eleven years, resigning on his appointment to the supreme court in 1873. He was a delegate from Lincoln County to the state constitutional convention which assembled at Charlotte in October 1865 and held an adjourned session in May 1866. Its proceedings were important, involving radical changes in the constitution, and Bynum took an active part in the discussions, serving on the Committee on Amendments to the Constitution not otherwise referred and the Committee on Acts of the Convention, the Legislature and the Courts since 1861 (see *Journal of the Convention of the State of North Carolina*, 1865). In 1866 he was elected state senator for Lincoln, Gaston, and Catawba Counties, but served only one term. He was appointed by Gov. Caldrock an associate justice of the supreme court of North Carolina, on Nov. 20, 1873, and remained on the bench till the expiration of his term on Jan. 6, 1879. Possessed of a strong individuality, clear intellect, and keen analytical powers, he was an excellent judge. His legal knowledge was exact and extensive, and his impartiality unassailable. Though strongly urged to accept nomination for another term, he declined, and resumed law practise in Charlotte, to which city he had removed. As he was financially independent, he thereafter did not concern himself much with either professional work or public affairs. He declined the Republican nomination for chief justice, and on several occasions refused to consider nomination for governor of the state. He died at Charlotte.

[An excellent contemporary review of Bynum's career appeared in Jerome Dowd, *Sketches of Prominent Living North Carolinians* (1888). See also S. A. Ashe, *Hist. of N. C.*, II (1925), 1151; the *Green Bag*, Dec. 1892; *Charlotte Daily Observer*, Dec. 31, 1909.]

H. W. H. K.

BYRD, WILLIAM (1652–Dec. 4, 1704), planter, merchant, Indian trader, was the oldest son of John Byrd, a London goldsmith of moderate means, and Grace, daughter of Capt. Thomas Stegg. He came to Virginia when young, where he at once became a person of influence as the heir of his uncle, Thomas Stegg. Under Stegg's will, which was proved May 15, 1671, he acquired lands on both sides of the James at the present site of Richmond. In 1673 he married Mary, daughter of Warham Horsmanden, a Royalist refugee. Ambitious, possessing great business ability, rich, well connected both by blood and by marriage, his advancement was rapid. In 1675, when twenty-three years old, he was called Capt. Byrd. In 1676 he courted ruin by accompanying Bacon the Rebel on his southern Indian expedition but later made his peace with Gov. Berkeley. He was a member of the House of Burgesses from 1677 to 1682, and on Jan. 11, 1683, entered the Council of State, "the House of Lords of Virginia." Five years later he assumed the post of auditor-general of Virginia. In 1691 he moved his residence to Westover, which was nearer Jamestown and better suited for the home of a wealthy planter than the frontier estate at the Falls. In 1703 he became president of the Council. He died Dec. 4, 1704.

Byrd was one of the most prominent members of that small group of seventeenth-century Virginians who grew wealthy by planting tobacco and trading. Their success depended largely upon their ability to secure slave labor, and Byrd imported large numbers of negroes, some for his own use, some for sale to his neighbors. "If you sent the *Pinke* to Barbadoes on our account, I would have by her 506 negroes," he wrote to Perry and Lane, in 1684 (*Virginia Magazine of History and Biography*, July 1916, p. 232). For his tobacco, hundreds of hogsheads of which he shipped to England, he received all manner of manufactured articles—cloth, hats, iron work, brandy, wire, guns, hoes, powder, chairs, tables, shoes, brushes, horse collars, files, and above all else indentured servants. "If you could send me six, eight, or ten servants (men or lusty boys) . . . they would much assist in purchasing some of our best crops," he wrote his factor (*Virginia Historical Register*, Apr. 1848, p. 63). From Barbados he imported slaves, rum, sugar, molasses and ginger; and sent in return corn, flour, and pipe staves.

He was also deeply engaged in the fur trade. His estate at the Falls was at the head of the 400-mile trail southwest to the Catawba, and along it he sent his rough wood rangers with pack-horses carrying cloth, guns, powder, kettles, knives, and beads, in exchange for deer skins, and beaver and raccoon furs. It was a dangerous business, for in 1684 five traders were killed by the Indians, and in 1686 two more lost their lives. So great was Byrd's knowledge of Indian affairs, that he was often selected to represent the colony in treating with the natives. In 1685 he went to Albany, accompanied by several Virginia Indians, where he signed a treaty with the Iroquois. As the commander of the Henrico County militia, upon him fell the duty of protecting the upper James from Indian raids. Not satisfied with these multiform activities, Byrd was part owner of several merchantmen, and speculated extensively in land. Tobacco planter, merchant, fur trader, slave dealer, importer, speculator, public official, colonel of militia, he typified the spirit of the seventeenth-century Virginia aristocracy.

[There is an excellent biographical sketch in *The Writings of Col. William Byrd* (1901), by the editor, J. S. Bassett. The most important source of information is Byrd's "Letter Book," in the possession of the Va. Hist. Soc., Richmond, Va. Some of these letters are published in the *Va. Hist. Reg.*, Apr., July 1848, Apr., Oct. 1849, others in the *Va. Mag. of Hist. and Biog.*, June 1916 to Jan. 1920. Valuable material is found also in the *Jours. of the House of Burgesses of Va.* (1905–15), *Exec. Jours. of the Council of Va.*, vol. I (1925), *Legislative Jours. of the Council of Colonial Va.* (1918–19), and in the Correspondence of the Board of Trade, in the Public Record Office, London.]

T. J. W.

BYRD, WILLIAM (Mar. 28, 1674–Aug. 26, 1744), planter, author, colonial official, was the son of William Byrd [*q.v.*], and Mary, daughter of Warham Horsmanden. As a frontier plantation, peopled chiefly with negroes, was no place to educate a boy, he was early entrusted to relatives in England. In 1684 he was at school under Christopher Glassock. Six years later he visited Holland, and in 1692 was pursuing his studies at the Middle Temple. Later in the same year he returned to Virginia. Heir to a large estate, well educated, socially charming, enjoying the friendship of prominent men both in England and Virginia, Byrd at once assumed an important position in the colony. The very year of his return he was elected to the House of Burgesses. In 1697 he was back in England, defending Sir Edmund Andros against charges of hostility to the Anglican Church in Virginia. The next year we find him acting as agent for the colony. Upon the death of his father he returned to Virginia. In 1706 he married Lucy, daughter of Gen. Daniel Parke. The same year he was made receiver-general, but did not enter the Council of State until Sept. 12, 1709. The early years of his official career were full of strife. In 1710 Alexander Spotswood came to Virginia as lieutenant-governor. Energetic, forceful, stubborn, Spotswood soon found himself embroiled with the group of wealthy planters whose power centered in the Council. He tried to put an end to the monopolizing of vast tracts of land by enforcing the collection of quit-rents. And then, while Byrd, Ludwell, Carter, Blair, and the others were still angrily resisting this measure, Spotswood delivered a blow at their judicial power. For decades the Council had served as the supreme court in Virginia. Spotswood now announced his intention of setting up a court of oyer and terminer, and of appointing to it others than members of the Council. The Council replied by preferring charges against Spotswood, which Byrd, who was once more in England, pressed before the Board of Trade. It was a serious menace to liberty, he pointed out, for a governor to "take upon him by his own absolute will . . . to appoint judges, who without appeal are to determine concerning not only the lives and liberties, but also concerning the whole estates" of the colonists. Spotswood maintained that his action was necessary if the king's prerogative was to be preserved. The power of the governor had been "reduced to a desperate gasp," he wrote, and unless the Council were curbed, "the haughtiness of a Carter, the hypocrisy of a Blair . . . the malice of a Byrd," would henceforth rule the colony. In 1718 Spotswood attempted unsuccessfully to have Byrd removed from the Council. Byrd returned to Virginia in 1720 with orders to both sides to reconcile their differences, and Spotswood's removal soon after left the Council with powers undiminished.

Byrd's later years were spent in peace, at his beautiful home, which he had erected at Westover, Va. "A library, a garden, a grove, and a purling stream are the innocent scenes that divert our leisure," he wrote. Despite the elegance of his life, he was more than once so oppressed with debt that he had to sell land and negroes to satisfy his creditors. In 1728 he served as one of the commissioners to run the dividing line between Virginia and North Carolina, and in 1736 he surveyed the bounds of the Northern Neck. An extensive landowner on the frontiers, he was deeply interested in western expansion. Decades before the French established themselves on the Ohio, Byrd pointed out the danger from that source. "They may build forts to command the passes," he wrote, "to secure their own traffic and settlements westward

. . . (and) to invade the British colonies from thence" (*Virginia Magazine of History and Biography*, January 1902, p. 226). Byrd was author of "The History of the Dividing Line," "A Journey to the Land of Eden," and the "Progress to the Mines," all of which were first published as *The Westover Manuscripts* in 1841. These works, as well as his private letters, show a grace, wit, and sprightliness unique among the colonists.

Byrd's portrait reveals a well-built man, elegantly attired, with prominent nose, firm mouth, broad forehead, and rather haughty demeanor. He was a Fellow of the Royal Society, and was a warm friend of Charles Boyle, Earl of Orrery. His first wife died in 1716, and later he married Maria, daughter of Thomas Taylor of Kensington. In 1743 he became president of the Council. He died Aug. 26, 1744, and was buried in the garden at Westover. As William Byrd I possessed to a superlative degree the business acumen of the wealthy seventeenth-century Virginians, so William Byrd II typified the grace, charm, the culture, and also the rather lax business methods of the Virginians of the eighteenth century.

[There is an excellent biography by the editor, J. S. Bassett, in *The Writings of Col. Wm. Byrd* (1901). The most important primary sources are: *Correspondence of the Board of Trade,* Public Record Office, London; Spotswood's "Official Letters," in *Colls. of the Va. Hist. Soc.,* n.s., vols. I, II; "Letters of Wm. Byrd II," *Va. Mag. of Hist. and Biog.,* Oct. 1901, Jan. 1902.]

T.J.W.

BYRNE, ANDREW (Dec. 5, 1802–June 10, 1862), Roman Catholic bishop, a pioneer in the establishment of Catholicism in the United States, was born of pious parents in Navan, County Meath, Ireland. He early determined to enter the priesthood, and began his preparation in the Diocesan Seminary of his native town. While a student there he volunteered to come to America with Bishop John England [*q.v.*] who had just been consecrated to the See of Charleston, S. C. He continued his studies under the tutelage of the bishop and was by him ordained, Nov. 11, 1827. The Charleston diocese of this time included North Carolina, South Carolina, and Georgia, and for nearly ten years he ably assisted his superior in the latter's notable administration, serving at various arduous posts, making frequent long and fatiguing journeys, and enduring all the privations of missionary life, until, his health somewhat impaired, he was made pastor of St. Mary's Church, Charleston. For several years he was the bishop's vicar-general, and accompanied him as theologian to the Second Provincial Council at Baltimore. In 1836 he removed to New York where he served as assistant at the Cathedral, and pastor of St. James, of the Church of the Nativity, and finally of St. Andrew's, the fruit of his own zeal and energy. In 1841 Bishop John Hughes [q.v.] sent him to Ireland to secure a community of Christian Brothers for New York, a mission which was unsuccessful because of the great demand at that time for the service of these Brothers. While here he became keenly interested in the agitation for the repeal of the union between Great Britain and Ireland, and upon his return publicly advocated it, and became a member of an organization formed in its interests.

His unselfish devotion, administrative ability, and missionary experience, led to his being appointed in 1844 first bishop of the diocese of Little Rock, comprising Arkansas and the Indian Territory, and he was consecrated on Mar. 10, by Bishop Hughes. Here he renewed his earlier strenuous journeyings and labors. He twice visited Ireland to procure priests, nuns, and educators, securing among others a colony of Sisters of Mercy from Dublin who established St. Mary's Academy at Little Rock, a parent institution. He was active also in promoting Catholic immigration to the Southwest. He attended the Sixth Provincial Council at Baltimore in 1846, and the First Provincial Council of New Orleans in 1856. His health gradually failed, and he died in the midst of his labors at the comparatively early age of sixty, leaving important projects unfinished.

[Richard H. Clarke, *Lives of the Deceased Bishops of the Cath. Ch. in the U. S.*, vol. II (1872) ; John G. Shea, *The Cath. Churches of N. Y. City* (1878), and *A Hist. of the Cath. Ch. within the Limits of the U. S.*, vol. IV (1892), which contains portrait ; *Cath. Encyc.*, vol. III (1913).]   H. E. S.

BYRNE, DONN. [See DONN-BYRNE, BRIAN OSWALD, 1889–1928.]

BYRNE, JOHN (Oct. 13, 1825–Oct. 1, 1902), physician, pioneer in electric surgery, was born in the small town of Kilkeel, County Down, Ireland. He was the son of Stephen Byrne, a successful merchant, and his wife Elizabeth Sloane. As a boy he received a classical education, partly under the tutorship of William Craig, a Moravian minister and classical and mathematical scholar. At seventeen he began the study of medicine at the Royal Institute at Belfast under the guidance of Dr. Daniel Murray, a prominent practitioner of that city. He continued his medical studies in Dublin, Glasgow, and finally Edinburgh, where he received his medical degree in 1846. His graduation being contemporaneous with one of the periods of famine and pestilence which scourged Ireland in the nineteenth century, he received an appointment as medical of-

ficer to a fever hospital in his native town and at once showed his mettle. His knowledge of hospital routine and the more advanced sanitary methods of the day, his energy, and his executive ability resulted in a remarkable lowering of the mortality in the institution under his care. In 1848 he left Ireland for the United States and settled in Brooklyn, N. Y., where he spent the remainder of his life. Five years later, feeling perhaps that an American degree would help him, he graduated from the New York Medical College. In 1857 he was prominent in bringing about the merger between the German General Dispensary and the Long Island College Hospital. Later he was appointed a member of the executive board and he was for many years clinical professor of uterine surgery. He was also surgeon-in-chief to St. Mary's Hospital from 1858 to the year of his death.

Byrne was always a student of physics and it was therefore natural that he should become interested in the application of this subject to surgery. His chief claim to distinction lies in his ingenious adaptation of the electric cautery-knife to the surgery of malignant disease of the uterus. His early researches were published in *Clinical Notes on the Electric Cautery in Uterine Surgery* (1872), in which he described in detail the instrument he had devised and the technique of its use. In 1889 he published in the *Transactions of the American Gynecological Society* a report covering twenty years' experience in the treatment of uterine cancer by the cautery-knife. This paper showed that his mortality rates were low and his final results good ; in fact, better results were probably obtained by him than by any other method of treatment in the hands of other surgeons at that time.

Byrne's success was due to a sound general and medical education, an energetic disposition, an inquiring mind, and a capacity for hard work and attention to detail. His associate, Dr. MacEvett, describes him as of medium height, rather portly in build, with a florid complexion and prematurely gray hair and mustache ; the stocky type so often associated with great physical energy and staying power. While his expression was serious he had a fund of kindliness and good nature, the saving grace of humor, and the gift of the raconteur. He exemplified the value of training and interest in the sciences underlying medicine at a time when the importance of such training was not fully appreciated in this country. His death occurred at Montreux, Switzerland.

[*N. Y. Jour. of Gynecology and Obstetrics*, Jan. 1892, p. 42 ; Jas. J. Walsh, *Hist. of Medicine in N. Y.* (1919) ; Wm. B. Atkinson, *Physicians and Surgeons of the U. S.* (1878) ; *Trans. Am. Gynecological Soc.*,

1903, vol. XXVIII; *Album of Fellows, Am. Gynecological Soc.* (1918); obituary in *Brooklyn Eagle,* Oct. 2, 1902.]
                                                    G.B.

BYRNES, THOMAS (1842–May 7, 1910), police executive, was born in Ireland and brought as an infant by his parents, James and Rose (Smith) Byrnes, to New York. He had the most meager education. When the Civil War came on he had learned the trade of gas-fitter and was at work in New York City. He enlisted with Ellsworth's Zouaves in 1861 and served two years with that unit. In 1863 he was taken on the New York police force as patrolman, became a roundsman five years later, and a captain in 1870. He gained widespread reputation in 1878 by running down the gang of Manhattan Savings Bank robbers. Two years later, as inspector in charge of the Detective Bureau, he reorganized that branch of the police service, established a Wall Street office, and practically ended the depredations of thieves in that part of the city. As Inspector Byrnes he quickly won national distinction. He increased the detective force from twenty-eight to forty men and soon caused it to be known as the most efficient body of its size and kind in the world. In four years it made 3,300 arrests. Byrnes brought about the conviction of many criminals,—in some cases when the evidence of guilt was far from complete. What became known as the application of "the third degree" in dealing with criminals has been ascribed to him. He acted on the theory that it is not remorse, but mental strain, that leads the hardened criminal to confess his misdeeds. The practise he adopted in procuring confessions involved far more than sheer brutality. Indeed in many cases no physical pain accompanied the process,—not that Byrnes had any scruples against employing bodily torture, but he frequently thought other methods more effective. He was himself a man of powerful imagination. He would reconstruct in his own mind the scene and incidents of a crime and so vividly reproduce them in conversation with the suspect that the average mentality could not withstand the shock. Jacob A. Riis, who as police reporter for the New York *Sun* knew Byrnes well, declared that he was "a great actor" and hence a great detective. All agreed that he was a man of unusual intellectual force. He was thought by his contemporaries to have the common failings imputed to the police of his day. Riis called him an unscrupulous autocrat, a "big policeman," a veritable giant in his time. In 1894 Byrnes testified before the Lexow Committee investigating the New York police that he had made $350,000 through Wall Street "tips" from Jay Gould and other important operators who were among his friends. No personal misdemeanor on his part was disclosed,—and that at a time when graft in high places was characteristic of the police department. Byrnes had stated repeatedly that he was not a member of any political organization. In 1892 he had been made superintendent and three years later became chief of police, retiring in the same month on the reorganization attending the disclosures of the Lexow Committee. Julian Hawthorne, who knew Byrnes intimately, described his personal appearance at the height of his career in these words: "He is a handsome man, large and powerful in every sense of the word. His head is well shaped, with a compact forehead, strong nose, and resolute mouth and chin, shaded with a heavy moustache. His figure is erect, his step light, his bearing alert and easy. His eyes are his most remarkable feature. They are set rather close together in his head, increasing the concentration of his gaze. They have in moments of earnestness an extraordinary gaze. His voice is melodious and agreeable, but he often seems to speak between his teeth, and when aroused his utterance acquires an impressive energy." He was the author of *Professional Criminals of America* (1886). At his death he was survived by his wife Ophelia and five daughters.

[*N. Y. Times, Tribune,* and *Sun,* of May 8, 1910; Jacob A. Riis, *The Making of an American* (1901).]
                                                    W.B.S.

CABELL, JAMES LAWRENCE (Aug. 26, 1813–Aug. 13, 1889), physician, educator, was born in Nelson County, Va., the sixth and youngest child of George and Susanna (Wyatt) Cabell. His father was a physician. The founder of the family was James's great-grandfather, William Cabell, who was born in Wiltshire and is said to have been a surgeon in the Royal Navy. He settled in Virginia about 1724, acquired extensive holdings in land, and practised medicine with success until his death in 1774. James Lawrence Cabell entered the University of Virginia in 1829 and graduated M.A. in 1833. He received the degree of M.D. the next year from the University of Maryland. He continued his studies in the Baltimore Almshouse and in one or more Philadelphia hospitals and went to Paris for further instruction and observation in 1836. While in France he was appointed professor of anatomy, surgery, and physiology in the University of Virginia. To call a man to an important academic post at the outset instead of toward the close of his career has never been customary in the United States, and since Cabell was in addition the nephew of Joseph Carrington

Cabell [*q.v.*] he entered on his duties in the autumn of 1837 amid much unfriendly gossip about "nepotism." But he was undeniably a gentleman and a scholar, and he soon proved to be also an able physician and a distinguished teacher. He gained the respect of the entire University and exercised as great an influence as anyone over the intellectual life of the community. In 1846–47 he was chairman of the faculty. In 1849 a separate chair of anatomy was established, but Cabell continued to teach surgery and physiology until a few months before his death. He kept abreast of his subjects, contributed occasionally to medical periodicals, and was one of the early leaders of the public health movement. During the Civil War he was chief surgeon of the Confederate hospitals in Charlottesville. He was president of the Medical Society of Virginia in 1876 and of the National Board of Health, 1879–84; he also served for one year as president of the American Public Health Association. A man of broad culture, he was almost as well versed in philosophy and pure science as in medicine. At times he seems to have felt that he ought not to confine himself to the teaching of medicine, and in 1846 he was a candidate to succeed George Tucker [*q.v.*] as professor of moral philosophy. He wrote little: his one book, *The Testimony of Modern Science to the Unity of Mankind* (N. Y., 1858; 2nd ed., 1859) attempts to show, from such evidence as was at hand, that the different races of mankind descend from a common ancestor. The essay is especially interesting as an indication of the state of scientific thought in the South just before the appearance of Darwin's *Origin of Species.* The fact that the author was deeply concerned for the truth of the Biblical account of Creation and that he was addressing readers who were fain to regard the negro as a species quite separate from their own makes the book now seem a little quaint but does not disguise its solid merits. Cabell was married on Feb. 5, 1839, to Margaret Gibbons, who died in 1874. They had no children. Cabell died at the home of his friend, Maj. Edward B. Smith, in Albemarle County.

[Alex. Brown, *The Cabells and Their Kin* (1895); P. A. Bruce, *Hist. of the Univ. of Va. 1819–1919* (1920–22); R. M. Slaughter, article in Kelly and Burrage, *Am. Medic. Biogs.* (1920).]   G. H. G.

CABELL, JOSEPH CARRINGTON (Dec. 28, 1778–Feb. 5, 1856), principal coadjutor of Thomas Jefferson in founding the University of Virginia, was born in Amherst (now Nelson) County, in Virginia, to which colony his grandfather, Dr. William Cabell, had emigrated from England in the early eighteenth century. He was the son of Col. Nicholas and Hannah (Carrington) Cabell, both of them of stock socially and politically distinguished in the colony, and was the brother of William H. Cabell [*q.v.*]. After graduating from William and Mary College (1798) and studying law, he resided abroad for more than three years, during which he attended lectures under famous scholars and sojourned at a half-dozen leading universities. He won the friendship of Robert Fulton and Washington Allston, traveled with Washington Irving, and enjoyed the acquaintance of Cuvier, Pestalozzi, Volney, Kosciusko, and William Godwin. On Jan. 1, 1807, he married Mary Walker Carter, of Lancaster, Va., granddaughter of Sir Peyton Skipwith, but had no issue. The next year he returned to Amherst County, entered politics, and was elected to the House of Delegates, where he served two terms and was instrumental in establishing the important Literary Fund. From 1810 to 1829 he was a member of the Virginia Senate, in which body he espoused ardently the cause of state betterment, advocating especially local government, popular education, and internal improvements; from 1831 to 1835 he again served in the House of Delegates, reëntering that branch that he might further the interests of the James River and Kanawha Canal. His labors in behalf of a great state university, helping first to secure legislative sanction therefor and subsequently to obtain financial appropriations toward its construction, have led the institution's historians to designate him as Jefferson's right hand man; nor did he promote merely the material needs of the University, but for thirty-seven years, as visitor and as rector, he helped to shape its destiny. At the same time he used his powers to extend to both sexes general opportunities for modern primary and secondary instruction; won the title of "the De Witt Clinton of Virginia" for his services as pioneer and president of the James River & Kanawha Canal Company; and, himself a progressive and large-scale plantation owner, supported before the Assembly all bills to improve agricultural conditions in the state. Although he held no office of national importance, he won more than sectional recognition for his conspicuous talents, his persuasive oratory, his sense of integrity and justice, his dignity, amenity, conscientiousness, and honor. His personal and political creed is epitomized by his own comment: "I think the greatest service a man can render is to speak the truth and to show that is his only object." He was peculiarly and emphatically "the Virginia statesman," for without thought of self he dedicated deliberately his entire life to his commonwealth, declining the diplomatic posts which Jefferson tendered him, refusing to stand for the governorship or the federal congress though repeatedly solicited, and rejecting cabinet seats probably under Madison and certainly under Monroe.

[The best account of Cabell is that in P. A. Bruce, *Hist. of the Univ. of Va.* (1920), I, 145–57, with innumerable references to him elsewhere in that work. N. F. Cabell, *Early Hist. of the Univ. of Va. as Contained in the Letters of Thos. Jefferson and Jos. C. Cabell* (1856) contains a ten-page sketch in addition to the voluminous correspondence that passed between Cabell and Jefferson. J. S. Patton, *Jefferson, Cabell, and the Univ. of Va.* (1906) and D. M. R. Culbreth, *The Univ. of Va.* (1908) cover more briefly the same ground. For Cabell's ancestry see Alexander Brown, *The Cabells and Their Kin* (1895). There is frequent mention of Cabell in *De Bow's Rev.*, the *Southern Lit. Messenger*, the correspondence of William Wirt, and the various biographies of Jefferson. His letters and manuscripts are in the possession of the Univ. of Va. Lib.]   A. C. G., Jr.

CABELL, NATHANIEL FRANCIS (July 23, 1807–Sept. 1, 1891), author, was most fortunate in his ancestry. His father, Nicholas Cabell, Jr., was a grandson of Dr. William Cabell of England, the emigrant ancestor of a distinguished family of Virginia, and his mother, Margaret Read (Venable) Cabell came from some of the most prominent families of southside Virginia. His father died when Nathaniel was an infant, and his mother reared him amid Presbyterian surroundings. He attended a Presbyterian college, Hampden Sidney, where he graduated in 1825. His great interest in religion in after life was probably due to the atmosphere in which he was reared. In 1827 he received his degree of bachelor of laws from Harvard College. During the next four years, he was located in Prince Edward County, but in 1832 returned to "Warminster," Nelson County, the place of his birth. A few years later he removed to the "Liberty Hall" estate, which he had inherited. The wide range of his interests may be seen in his voluminous writings, especially in the fields of religion, genealogy, and the history of agriculture. Largely through the influence of Richard K. Cralle of Lynchburg, friend and biographer of John C. Calhoun, he became a follower of Emanuel Swedenborg, being baptized into the New Church in 1842. During this period (1840–42) he had written in the *New Jerusalem Magazine* a number of articles, "Excerpts, or Readings with My Pencil," etc. He also contributed to the *New Churchman*. Among his numerous religious writings may be mentioned an article on the New Christian Church in Israel D. Rupp's *An Original History of the Religious Denominations at Present Existing in the United States* (1844); *Reply to Rev. Dr*

Pond's "Swedenborgianism Reviewed" (1848); *A Letter on the Trinal Order for the Ministry of the New Church* (1848, 1857); *The Progress of Literature during the Preceding Century When Viewed from a Religious Standpoint* (only the introductory chapter published, 1868); and papers on the theology of Paul, published under the title "Horæ Paulinæ" in the *New Jerusalem Messenger*, 1873–74. In the meanwhile he was writing in other fields. He edited the *Early History of the University of Virginia as Contained in the Letters of Thomas Jefferson and Joseph C. Cabell* (1856); rearranged and edited in part "The Lee Papers" portions of which reappeared in seventeen numbers of the *Southern Literary Messenger*, 1858–60; and contributed to the *Memoirs of Professor George Bush* (1860). He contributed a number of essays on agriculture and on the history of agriculture in Virginia to the *Farmers' Register* and other magazines. It was his purpose to write a history of agriculture in Virginia. For that purpose he made a valuable collection of manuscripts on the subject. This material annotated by Cabell may now be found in the Virginia State Library. From 1832 until his death he collected much material relating to genealogy and prepared manuscript family memoirs, Cabelliana, Carringtoniana, etc. He was married twice: on Sept. 14, 1831 to Anne Blaws Cocke, and, after her death in 1862, to Mary M. Keller of Baltimore. The last few years of his life were spent in Bedford City at the home of his daughter, Mrs. R. Kenna Campbell. He was buried in the Cabell cemetery at "Liberty Hall."

[Alexander Brown, Cabell's friend and neighbor has the best account, in *The Cabells and their Kin* (1895), pp. 601–05. See also Earl G. Swem, "A List of MSS. Relating to the Hist. of Ag. in Va., Collected by N. F. Cabell and Now in the Va. State Lib." (*Va. State Lib. Bull.*, Jan. 1913), and "An Analysis of Ruffin's Farmer's Reg." (*Ibid.*, July–Oct. 1918).]   R. L. M—n.

CABELL, SAMUEL JORDAN (Dec. 15, 1756–Aug. 4, 1818), Revolutionary soldier, congressman, born in Amherst County, Va., was the son of Col. William Cabell [*q.v.*] and Margaret Jordan, his wife. The former was a prominent Virginian, a member of the Revolutionary Committee of Safety in the colony. At the outbreak of the Revolutionary War, S. J. Cabell left the College of William and Mary to assume command as captain of a company of expert riflemen of Amherst County. Upon his arrival at Williamsburg in March 1776, his company was assigned as light infantry to the 6th Virginia Regiment, in Gen. Andrew Lewis's brigade, and during the same year it was sent to join Gen. Washington in New Jersey. Washington placed t in Gen. Morgan's body of expert riflemen, which he sent to aid Gen. Gates at Saratoga. For his skill and bravery in this campaign, Cabell (not yet twenty-one years old) was commissioned major. He then rejoined Washington's army, was at Valley Forge, and in Washington's campaigns of 1778 and 1779. In the latter year he was made lieutenant-colonel and was dispatched to Gen. Lincoln at Charleston. Here he was made prisoner in May 1780 and remained in prison fourteen months, until paroled. He was married in 1781 to Sally Syme, daughter of Col. John Syme of Hanover County, a half-brother of Patrick Henry. He was, in 1784, county lieutenant of Amherst County, and represented that county in the Virginia legislature of 1785–86, and in several subsequent sessions. He and his father were elected, almost unanimously, to the Convention of 1788. They both followed Patrick Henry in opposing the adoption of the Constitution. In 1795 S. J. Cabell was elected to the federal House of Representatives. He retained his seat until he retired from active politics in 1803. He was an ardent Republican, "an impetuous follower of Jefferson." So active was he in opposition to Federalist policies that the grand jury of the United States district court, in session at Richmond, acting under the spell of Judge Iredell's fiery charge to the jury, brought in the following presentment: "We . . . present as a real evil, the circular letters of several members of the late Congress and particularly those with the signature of Samuel J. Cabell, endeavoring, at a time of real public danger, to disseminate unfounded calumnies against the happy government of the United States. . . ." The Virginia legislature, prompted doubtless by Jefferson, responded with a vigorous protest, a prelude to Madison's famous Resolutions of 1798. (For the protest see *Journal of the House of Delegates,* 1797–98, pp. 64–65.) When Nelson County was created out of Amherst, Cabell, who had served as justice in the latter, became one of the first justices in the former. The last thirty-three years of his life were spent at his home, "Soldier's Joy," in Nelson County. Cabell was one of the original members of the Virginia Society of the Cincinnati. He was impulsive, kind-hearted, hospitable, and fluent in speech.

[Alexander Brown, *The Cabells and Their Kin* (1895) is the best source. Brown had access to numerous Cabell manuscripts, including Col. William Cabell's Diary. See also F. B. Heitman, *Hist. Reg.* (1893) and widely scattered items in the *Va. Mag. of Hist. and Biog.*]   R. L. M—n.

CABELL, WILLIAM (Mar. 13, 1729/30–Mar. 23, 1798), Revolutionary patriot, known as Col.

William, Senior, of Union Hill, Amherst County, was the son of William and Elizabeth (Burks) Cabell. The elder William Cabell, of Bugley near Warminster, in Wiltshire, England, was of ancient lineage and trained in surgery. Migrating to Virginia, he married in 1726 and by 1741 had carried settlements fifty miles westward. As pioneer, Indian fighter, surveyor, deputy sheriff, justice of the peace, vestryman, coroner, trader, planter, and surgeon with a private hospital on the fringe of the forest, from which he dispensed physic, and wooden legs made by his artisans, until he died in 1774, he hastened Virginia's westward growth. This tall, lithe, black-eyed man, audacious in action, liberal in thought, scientific in method, having by 1753 accumulated 26,000 picked acres, tossed his surveyor's mantle to his eldest son, who like his father speedily became a constructive leader of men.

Tradition but no evidence makes the younger William Cabell a student in William and Mary. A vestryman at the age of twenty-one, second sheriff two years later, and settled on 2,700 acres granted him by the Crown in 1753, by 1761 he was first presiding magistrate, first lieutenant, first surveyor and first coroner for Amherst County, vestryman, church warden, and burgess. He held stock in the Hardware River Iron Company and in the James River Canal Company. No evidence shows that as burgess he supported Patrick Henry's Resolutions of May 1765. When the Stamp Act was repealed he hoped for reconciliation. But in May 1769, when rebel burgesses drew up Articles of Association in Raleigh Tavern, Williamsburg, Cabell signed them. A delegate to all Virginia's revolutionary conventions, he stoutly supported the patriot measures, was elected member of the Committee of Safety, when Gov. Dunmore fled the Colony, and was reëlected upon its revision in January 1776. Meanwhile he was chairman of the Amherst County Committee. Owing no debt to English merchants, he risked all for the Revolution. A member of the famous committee which prepared a Declaration of Rights and a form of government for Virginia, he served also on the Committee of Propositions and Grievances. He was first state senator for his district (Buckingham, Albemarle, and Amherst Counties), retiring in 1781 because of Virginia's rule of rotation. Elected delegate immediately thereafter, he served in the House (1781–83, 1787–88) and was a member of the celebrated Virginian Convention in 1788 where he voted against ratification of the Federal Constitution. Probably his last political service was to cast an electoral vote for Washington for first president under the Constitution.

He now retired after some thirty years in public life, but remained a trustee of Hampden Sidney College until his death. He succumbed in 1798, leaving 30,000 acres, many slaves and other property, all free from debt. His wife, Margaret Jordan Cabell (married, 1756), four sons, and three daughters survived him. Six feet high, corpulent, with capacious forehead, he was of superior brain, strikingly liberal in mind and pocket, of ceaseless energy and infinite capacity for work. Of equal caliber perhaps with his nationally significant contemporaries in a great American era, Fate designed him to be primarily a builder of Virginia.

[Alexander Brown, *The Cabells and Their Kin* (1895); *Jours. of the House of Burgesses of Va.* (1905–15); *Jour. of the Senate, 1776–81*; *Jour. of the House of Delegates, 1781–88*; the Cabell papers preserved in the Va. State Lib. in Richmond.]   K. B.

CABELL, WILLIAM H. (Dec. 16, 1772–Jan. 12, 1853), governor of Virginia, was a grandson of Dr. William Cabell, who came to Virginia in the early eighteenth century. The son of Col. Nicholas and Hannah (Carrington) Cabell and brother of Joseph Carrington Cabell [*q.v.*], he was born at "Boston Hill" near Cartersville, Cumberland County, Va. He attended Hampden Sidney College, 1785–89, and then entered the College of William and Mary, from which he received his law degree in 1793. In the fall of that year he moved to Richmond, and was licensed to practise law in the following year. On Apr. 9, 1795, he married his cousin Elizabeth, daughter of Col. William Cabell [*q.v.*] of "Union Hill." He lived for several years in her home, and since there were two other William Cabells there he added the initial "H" to his name. His political career began in 1796, when he was elected to the legislature from Amherst County. He was reëlected four times, and was also presidential elector in 1800 and in 1804. He voted for Madison's famous Virginia Resolutions of 1798. In December 1805 the legislature elected him governor of the state. After reëlecting him twice—the maximum number of times under the constitution of Virginia—the legislature appointed him judge of the general court, a position which he held until appointed by Gov. Monroe member of the court of appeals in April 1811. He was also placed on the governor's council that year. Under the new constitution of 1830, he was reappointed to the court of appeals, and was made president of that body in 1842, in which position he continued until he retired in 1851. He was an advocate of public schools and was deeply interested in higher education. From 1809 to 1830 he was one of the trustees of Hampden Sidney College. He was a member of the board of commissioners appointed by the Virginia Assembly in 1818 to select a site for the University of Virginia and to give a plan for its organization. On Nov. 5, 1801, Elizabeth Cabell, his wife, died, and four years later (Mar. 11, 1805) he maried Agnes S. B. Gamble, daughter of Col. Robert Gamble of Richmond. He had a beautiful summer home overlooking the James River at Montevideo, in Buckingham County, but in 1822 he sold this estate and thenceforward made Richmond his home. He was buried in Shockoe Cemetery in that city. He was vigorous in mind and in body, respected and trusted as a public officer, and loved for his genial spirit.

[Alexander Brown, *The Cabells and their Kin* (1895) contains a sketch of Cabell, including a brief autobiographical account. There is a good sketch in R. A. Brock, a reliable historian, *Virginia and Virginians* (1888), pp. 98–103. Cabell's official papers are in the Va. State Lib. in Richmond. For his messages as governor see *Jour. of House of Delegates*, 1805–08. Note also court records, 1808–51.]   R. L. M—n.

CABELL, WILLIAM LEWIS (Jan. 1, 1827–Feb. 22, 1911), Confederate soldier, lawyer, a descendant of Dr. William Cabell who came to Virginia in the early part of the eighteenth century (see sketch of William Cabell, 1730–98), was born in Danville, Va., the son of Benjamin W. S. and his wife Sarah Epes (Doswell) Cabell. His father was a veteran of the War of 1812, member of the Virginia Assembly, member of the constitutional convention of 1829–30, and a newspaper editor. William graduated from West Point Military Academy in 1850, entered the United States army, and by 1858 had attained the rank of captain. In July 1856 he was married to Harriet A. Rector. He served in Gen. Harney's Utah campaign, and continued in the West until he resigned his commission in 1861. He was commissioned as major in the Confederate army. President Davis sent him to Richmond to organize the commissary and ordnance departments. He was next transferred to Manassas as chief quartermaster on Gen. Beauregard's staff and later served on the staff of J. E. Johnston. He aided Generals Johnston and Beauregard to devise the first Confederate battle flag (W. L. Cabell in *Southern Historical Society Papers*, XXXI, 68–70). In January 1862 he reported to Gen. Albert Sidney Johnston, as chief quartermaster (*List of Staff Officers of the Confederate States Army*, Government Printing Office, Washington, 1891, p. 26). He was placed in the Trans-Mississippi department under Gen. Van Dorn. His excellent record gained for him promotion to the rank of brigadier-general in command of all the troops on White River. After the battle of Elk Horn (March 1862) he successfully transferred the entire Trans-Mississippi army to the east bank within a week. In the battles which followed he distinguished himself for his bravery in attack. He was wounded while leading his men at Corinth and at Hatchers Ridge in October 1862. As a result he was rendered incapable of command in the field. While still disabled, however, he was ordered to inspect the staff department of the Trans-Mississippi army. When he again reported for active duty in February 1863 he was placed in command of all the forces in northwest Arkansas. Here he organized one of the largest and most efficient cavalry brigades west of the Mississippi. This brigade took part in many engagements during 1863 and 1864. While on a raid in Missouri under Gen. Price, Cabell was captured on Oct. 24, 1864. Upon his release from prison on Aug. 28, 1865, he went to Fort Smith, Ark., studied law, and was admitted to the bar. In December 1872 he moved to Dallas, Tex., and in 1874, 1875, 1876, and 1882 was elected mayor of that city. He was a delegate to to the Democratic national conventions of 1876, 1884, and 1892. During Cleveland's first administration he served as United States marshal. He was vice-president and general manager of the Texas Trunk Railway (later the Texas & New Orleans Railway). In 1890 the United Confederate Veterans elected him commander of the Trans-Mississippi department, a position which he held until elected honorary commander-in-chief of the Confederate Veterans.

[Alexander Brown, *The Cabells and Their Kin* (1895); *Who's Who in America,* 1903–05; *Official Records (Army),* 1, 2 ser.; obituaries in the *Confederate Veteran,* Apr. 1911, and *Dallas Morning News,* Feb. 23, 1911.]   R.L.M—n.

CABET, ÉTIENNE (Jan. 1, 1788–Nov. 8, 1856), communist, reformer, was the fourth and youngest son of a cooper of Dijon, France. In childhood he was strongly impressed by echoes of the great revolution. Unable because of his frail body and his nearsightedness to follow the paternal occupation, he was given a thorough education. At fifteen, he became a lycée instructor under Jacotot. He began the study of medicine in the university, but soon turned to law, where he was influenced by the liberal Proudhon of the Dijon faculty. In 1810 he was licensed and in 1812 took the doctor's degree in law (Jules Prudhommeaux, *Icarie et son Fondateur,* pp. 5–7). For pleading the cause of patriots he was denied access to the courts of his native village for a year. Obtaining a secretaryship in Paris, he identified himself with the Carbonari and other secret societies. He took part in the July Revolution. In 1831, Louis Philippe, in conciliating the proletarian and intellectualist factions, appointed him procureur-général in Corsica. Due to his anti-administration activities, he was soon recalled. Elected to the Chamber of Deputies in July, he joined the extreme radicals. In 1833, he established *Le Populaire* which he used as an organ of the workingmen's cause. Two articles of January 1834 gave a pretext for convicting him as a traitor. In preference to two years in prison, he spent five years in exile in London. There he married Delphine Lesage, who had joined him after the birth of their daughter, Celine. His wife, like himself, was of plebeian origin and a native of Dijon (*Ibid.,* p. 98, n. 3).

Encouraged by his contact with Robert Owen, Cabet wrote the interesting Utopian romance, *Voyage et Aventures de Lord William Carisdall en Icarie,* which he published on his return to France in 1839 (republished in 1840 as *Voyage en Icarie*). Its circulation was tremendous, and adherents of the Icarian doctrine were reported to be 400,000 by 1847. During the years 1843 to 1847, Cabet's annual *Almanach Icarien, astronomique, scientifique, pratique, industriel, statistique,* his *Histoire populaire de la révolution française de 1789 à 1830* (1839–40), and his *Le vrai christianisme suivant Jésus-Christ* (1846) all found a large audience. An article describing the projected community in America appeared in May 1847. Finding several hundred ready for the venture, Cabet, after consulting Owen, contracted for a million acres on the Red River in Texas. The advance guard of sixty-nine persons discovered after a long journey through the wilderness that the land was in half-section tracts widely scattered. Cabet had trusted too utterly the land company's representative. Discouraged, the men retreated to New Orleans, where they met Cabet with the main body of five hundred. Hearing of the abandonment of the community at Nauvoo, Ill., by the Mormons, the Icarians in 1849 leased the land and houses there, and for six years enjoyed a rapid increase in fortune and numbers. In 1852, Cabet went to Paris to vindicate himself of the charges of fraud brought by those who had turned back at New Orleans. In 1854, he became an American citizen. Icaria had its own printing-press and library and operated a mill and a distillery. Freedom of religion was allowed. Cabet was annually reëlected president, but in 1856, dissensions arose involving the Paris office in charge of Madame Cabet. When the civil authorities intervened and confirmed three newly-elected directors of the opposing party, Cabet with 180 followers withdrew to St. Louis. Within the week he died from a stroke of apoplexy and was buried at St. Louis. Chief of the colonies of Icaria were those of Cheltenham, near St. Louis; Corning, Iowa (the successor of Nauvoo), dissolved in 1884; and Cloverdale, Cal., which survived until 1895.

[The best short sketches of Cabet are found in Morris Hillquit, *Hist. of Socialism in the U. S.* (1903), Albert Shaw, *Icaria* (1884), and Adolph Hepner, *Die Ikarier in Nordamerika* (1886). More extensive biographies are those of H. Carle and J. P. Beluze, *Biographie de Étienne Cabet* (1861–62); Felix Bonnaud, *Étienne Cabet et son œuvre* (1900); and Jules Prudhommeaux, *Icarie et son fondateur, Étienne Cabet* (1907), the last being the most complete and up-to-date.]

E.C.

CABLE, GEORGE WASHINGTON (Oct. 12, 1844–Jan. 31, 1925), author, was an unusual blending of diverse elements. His father, George W., was from an old slaveholding family of Virginia, his mother, Rebecca Boardman, was a native of New England, a Puritan of the straitest sect. They met in Indiana and were married there in 1834. Three years later, attracted by a business opening, they removed to New Orleans where was born the future novelist. The hard times of 1837 all but destroyed the family fortunes, but the father struggled on with his business until 1859, when, after a second business reverse, he died, leaving the boy of fourteen head of the family which included several children. For several years the boy was his mother's chief support, finding employment as he could. He was small for his years and physically frail. When in 1863 the family was sent outside the Union lines for refusing to take the "Yankee" oath of allegiance, his sisters had no difficulty in obtaining permission for their "little brother" to accompany them. Immediately, however, he enlisted in the 4th Mississippi Cavalry and with them he served to the end of the war. Despite the headlong activities of a trooper with the enemy never far away, he found time to pursue with intensity self-imposed studies in mathematics, Latin, and the Bible. His troop was in several engagements in one of which he was severely wounded. The war over, he found employment immediately on the state survey of the levees along the Atchafalaya River, but contracting malarial fever, he was for two years almost totally incapacitated for labor.

It was during this period that he began to write, his first product being a weekly miscellany in the New Orleans *Picayune* under the heading "Drop Shot." The success of the column led to its being made a daily feature of the paper, and in 1869 its author was added to the staff as a reporter. His journalistic career, however, was short. Refusing to report theatrical performances, he was summarily dropped. Employment more congenial came quickly in the firm of A. C. Black & Company, cotton factors, who employed him as an accountant and correspondence clerk. Seemingly he was settled now for life. On Dec. 7, 1869, he was married to Louise S. Bartlett of New Orleans, he established a home in the city, and in due time found himself the head of a family of seven children. But the ambition for culture and scholarship which had driven him to study in his army days still kept him restless. He had been denied school and college: he would educate himself. He arose at four in the morning and pored over his books: he wasted not a moment. He made himself master of French and then began to delve among the old records in the city archives, fascinated by the strange true romance that he found in them. At first he had no thought of literary production, but at length he began to put the old records into narratives of his own. "It seemed a pity," he explained in later years, "to let them go to waste." Publication of these narratives and then literary fame came to him seemingly by accident. Edward King, who had been sent by *Scribner's Monthly* in 1872 on a tour of the Southern States for the series of papers later issued with the title *The Great South* (1875), came across the busy young delver, examined his papers, and induced him to send some of them to J. G. Holland, editor of the monthly. The result was a glowing letter from R. W. Gilder, a member of the staff, and the publication in the magazine in October 1873 of the short story " 'Sieur George." During the following three years five others were published, and then in 1879 came the volume *Old Creole Days*, containing the six stories and also "Posson Jone" which had appeared in *Appleton's*. The recognition of the work as an American classic in its field was instant and unanimous. Its success, too, came at the moment when the death of Cable's employer and the dissolution of the firm threw him out of employment. He turned at once to authorship as a profession. A year later, after it had run serially in *Scribner's*, he published *The Grandissimes* (1884), an ambitious historical romance, following it with "Madame Delphine," which has been incorporated in later editions of *Old Creole Days*; *The Creoles of Louisiana* (1884); *Dr. Sevier* (1885); *Bonaventure* (1888); and *Strange True Stories of Louisiana* (1889).

His life now became one of intense activity in many fields. He was a zealous advocate with pen and voice of changed election laws, of reform in prison administration, of abolition of the contract labor system, and of justice for the negro. His outspoken views, especially in the series of papers later collected under the title *The Silent South* (1885), aroused the resentment of his native region against him. It was not this alone, however, that caused him to remove his residence to the North: he would be nearer his work and his literary market. After 1885 Northampton, Mass., became his residence and the radiating center of a remarkable series of reading tours into all parts of the nation. Reading from his own works became for a time his profession. He made tours with Mark Twain; for some years his yearly journeyings averaged more than ten thousand miles. At Northampton he started the Home-Culture Clubs, now the Northampton People's Institute, and to the project he gave for years generously of his time and his enthusiasm (see an account of the Clubs by Cable in the *World's Work,* October 1906). No sketch of his life can omit to mention his work as a philanthropist, a reformer, a religious leader, a Bible-class teacher. The titles of some of his later books show the range of his interests: *The Negro Question* (1888); *The Southern Struggle for Pure Government* (1890); *The Busy Man's Bible and How to Teach It* (1893); *John March, Southerner* (1894); and *The Amateur Garden* (1914).

In later years he applied himself again to the writing of romance, producing some eight volumes: *Strong Hearts* (1899); *The Cavalier* (1901); *Bylow Hill* (1902); *Kincaid's Battery* (1908); *Posson Jone and Père Raphael* (1909); *Gideon's Band* (1914); *The Flower of the Chapdelaines* (1918); and *Lovers of Louisiana* (1918); but, save in rare flashes, the old charm and power are not in them. His hand had lost its cunning, the intensity of his first enthusiasms had evaporated. More and more it is evident that his ultimate literary fame will depend upon a few of his earlier romantic creations. There is a vivacity, a Gallic brilliance, an exotic atmosphere about these creations that make them stand alone among American works of fiction. Coming as they did at the moment that new literary forces were gathering for the new literary period following the Civil War, they were widely influential. With Bret Harte he was one of the causes of the so-called "local color episode" in American fiction. Not without criticism did he gain his place, however. His representation of the Creole was sharply challenged by the South; it was charged that he drew his characters from the lower grade of the Creole population and left the inference that there was no higher grade. It was to correct Cable's picture and to represent the Creole in what she, herself educated in a Creole school, believed to be the true light, that

Grace King in later days wrote her tales of New Orleans life.

[*Geo. W. Cable, his Life and Letters* (1928), by his daughter, Lucy L. Cable Bikle; "The Literary Career of Cable," by E. F. Harkins, in *Famous Authors* (1906); "Geo. W. Cable in Northampton, Mass.," by F. W. Halsey in *Am. Authors and their Homes* (1901).]

F. L. P—e.

CABOT, ARTHUR TRACY (Jan. 25, 1852–Nov. 4, 1912), surgeon, was the third son of Samuel Cabot, surgeon to the Massachusetts General Hospital, by his wife, Hannah Jackson. The traits of the Cabot family, ardently conscientious, scrupulous almost to a fault in their dealings with men, and possessed of an extraordinary sense of personal responsibility to their immediate community, were sublimated in the personality of Arthur Tracy. He entered Harvard College in 1869 and received his A.B. degree from that institution in 1872, having done good work without special distinction. He received his M.D. from the Harvard Medical School in 1876 and entered immediately upon a surgical internship at the Massachusetts General Hospital, at which institution he had previously served as house pupil. In August 1877 he went abroad to study surgical pathology and arrived in London in time to hear Lister's inaugural address (October 1877) at King's College ("On the Nature of Fermentation"), this being Lister's first public appearance in London after leaving Scotland. Soon after this lecture, Cabot became an ardent protagonist of the antiseptic system, and on returning to Boston a few months later he did much to spread the gospel of "Listerism" among his surgical contemporaries. For several years after his return, he occupied himself in building up a general practise in medicine and surgery, in order to approach surgery in its broadest aspects. At the end of ten years he found it necessary to confine himself entirely to surgery. On Aug. 16, 1882, he was married to Susan Shattuck, daughter of George O. Shattuck. From 1886 until 1902 he was visiting surgeon at the Massachusetts General Hospital. H. J. Bigelow [*q.v.*], recognizing the ability of the young surgeon, gradually turned over to him his extensive clinic, and Cabot became in a very short time the leading genito-urinary surgeon of New England. He always prided himself, however, on having been a general surgeon.

Cabot's career of public service began with his instructorship in oral pathology and surgery (1878–80) at the Harvard Medical School; subsequently he was appointed clinical instructor in genito-urinary surgery (1885–96). In 1896 he was elected a Fellow of the University, a position of responsibility demanding much time. Throughout his life he was active in campaigns against tuberculosis and in promoting the cause of public health. His last published work, which appeared in the *Atlantic Monthly* for November 1912, was a plea for the employment of energetic measures in the prophylaxis and treatment of juvenile tuberculosis. In 1907 the governor of Massachusetts appointed him trustee (subsequently he became chairman) of the State Hospital for Consumptives, into the work of which he threw himself with whole-hearted enthusiasm.

Cabot's medical writings were extensive. Between 1886 and 1896 he published in the *Boston Medical and Surgical Journal* a series of eighteen contributions on various aspects of genito-urinary surgery. They were issued in four groups (1886, 1887, 1893, and 1896). In 1891 there appeared from his pen a series of seven papers on abdominal surgery in the same journal. He also published a paper on spina bifida and cephalocele (*Annals of Surgery*, Aug. 1892), and he contributed to W. W. Keen's *Surgery; its Principles and Practice*, vol. IV (1908), the section on stone in the bladder.

[Obituaries in the *Boston Medic. and Surgic. Jour.*, Nov. 28, 1912, 784–86; *Ibid.*, Mar. 20, 1913, 409–15 (H. P. Walcott and others); *Ibid.*, Aug. 28, 1919, 302–04; and in the *British Medic. Jour.*, 1912, pt. II, p. 1775; more extensive memoirs in the *Proc. Am. Acad. of Arts and Sci.*, 1918, III, 793–98 (F. C. Shattuck) and in the *Harvard Grads. Mag.*, Mar. 1913; personal information from Mrs. Arthur Tracy Cabot.]

J.F.F.

CABOT, EDWARD CLARKE (Apr. 17, 1818–Jan. 5, 1901), architect, was born in Boston, the third of the eleven children of Samuel Cabot and Eliza Perkins, daughter of Thomas Handasyd Perkins, a well-known merchant. Cabot's father, too, was a merchant in Boston, largely interested in the China and East India trade. A somewhat delicate child, Cabot was educated at private schools in Boston and Brookline, spent his early summers at Nahant, and had no university training. At the age of seventeen he went to Illinois, where, in partnership with George Curzon, he engaged in sheep raising. This venture, in which Cabot's father had invested some $12,000, ended disastrously and Cabot returned to the East in 1841. Then for more than four years he had a sheep farm at Windsor, Vt. In 1845 the Boston Athenæum invited designs for a new building, and, from his farm, Cabot submitted a sketch which was accepted with the proviso that he associate himself with George M. Dexter, a civil engineer, as supervisor. Cabot stayed some time in Dexter's office and later opened his own office in Boston. In 1849–58 and

1862–65 he was associated with his brother, James Elliot Cabot, and in 1875 he entered into partnership with Frank W. Chandler, under the firm name of Cabot & Chandler. When, a few years later, Chandler became professor of architecture at the Massachusetts Institute of Technology, two members of the office force were made partners and the firm name was changed to Cabot, Everett & Meade. During the Civil War, Cabot served for less than a year as lieutenant-colonel of the 44th Massachusetts Infantry. His architectural practise consisted largely of country houses of the more informal type, in the picturesque style then in vogue, to which he gave great charm by the restraint and exquisiteness of his taste. His two largest commissions were the Boston Theatre (1852–53), and the hospital of Johns Hopkins University, finally opened in 1889, which was done in association with Chandler. Before working on the Boston Theatre, Cabot spent a year abroad and made an intensive study of La Scala in Milan in preparation for his Boston work. After his retirement in 1888, he devoted the major portion of his time to painting and became an accomplished water-colorist, exhibiting frequently in Boston. He was twice married: first, at Salem, Mass., July 7, 1842, to Martha Eunice Robinson (died Brookline, Mass., Nov. 28, 1871), by whom he had five children; second, at Melrose, Mass., Oct. 13, 1873, to Louisa Winslow Sewall (died Brookline, Mass., Aug. 10, 1907), by whom he had three children. He lived all his life in Boston and its suburbs, building for himself two houses in Brookline, and spending his later summers at Nonquitt.

Cabot's work was distinguished by its delicacy, its restraint, and its schooled originality. The Boston Athenæum is in a fine Italian Renaissance, an extraordinary style for that date, 1845; and still more extraordinary is the beauty with which it was carried out, as it was the work of one till then a mere amateur. But Cabot's influence upon architecture in America was less through his own work than through his personality. His position as president of the Boston Society of Architects was an expression of the general esteem and affection in which he was held, and through it he came in contact with every important architect in Boston for thirty years. He was, says an editorial in the *American Architect and Building News* (Jan. 12, 1901), "a model of kind and gentle dignity."

[There is a tribute by Chas. A. Cummings in *Am. Architect and Bldg. News*, LXXI, 45, and an obituary in the *Am. Art Annual*, IV, 137. L. Vernon Briggs. *Hist. and Genealogy of the Cabot Family* (2 vols., 1927), pp. 686–93, gives an extended notice of some of the more intimate details of Cabot's life.]

T.F.H.

CABOT, GEORGE (Jan. 16, 1752–Apr. 18, 1823), merchant, senator, was the son of Joseph Cabot, whose father, John, emigrated from the Channel Islands to Salem, Mass., in 1700. Joseph, a successful merchant, married Elizabeth Higginson. George, the seventh of their eleven children, was born in Salem. In the autumn of 1766, he entered Harvard College, and was "placed" seventeenth in a class of forty-two. He took part in the "rebellion of 1766" against bad butter in commons, and was freshman member of a committee elected by the students to deal with the authorities (*Publications of the Colonial Society of Massachusetts*, X, 54–57). He withdrew from college on Mar. 19, 1768, just in time to escape public admonition for "his great Neglect of his Exercises" and "idle Behavior" (MS. Faculty Records). His elder brothers John and Andrew Cabot of Beverly, who were carrying on their father's rum, fish, and iron trade with the Southern colonies and Spain, promptly sent him to sea as cabin-boy under a strict disciplinarian. On his eighteenth birthday he was already skipper of his brothers' schooner *Sally*, taking a load of salt codfish from Beverly to Bilbao. The following year, for a salary of £3 a month and primage, he commanded their new schooner *Premium*, exchanged at the James River a cargo of rum and cider for wheat, which he delivered to his brothers' correspondents at Bilbao, and returned with a cargo of silk handkerchiefs.

In 1774 he was married to his double first-cousin, Elizabeth Higginson, "prudent, energetic, and commanding," who so far overcame his "invincible indolence of disposition" that he acquired one-sixth of the family distillery, and was entrusted with some of their best ships. About 1777 he gave up active seafaring, and was taken into his brothers' firm, which during the war owned at least forty privateers and letter-of-marque ships. Their armed merchantmen continued to trade with Spain, making their headquarters at Bilbao, where all the prizes taken by the firm's vessels were sold, and the proceeds deposited with Gardoqui & Sons. By this means the Cabots, unlike most privateering firms, kept their gains until peace was concluded. In 1784, two of their ships first carried the American flag to St. Petersburg. In the same year George Cabot became director of the Massachusetts Bank, the earliest in the state. He was the leading promoter of two important corporate enterprises of 1788, the Essex bridge and the Beverly cotton manufactory (James S. Davis, *Essays in the Earlier History of American Corporations*, vol. II). In 1785 he formed a partnership with his brother-in-law Joseph Lee which was so successful that within ten years he retired from the mercantile and shipping business with a "reasonable and sufficient fortune."

In 1778 Cabot began taking an active part in politics with the group of Essex County merchants and lawyers who became the nucleus of the Federalist party. As a member of the Concord convention of 1779 on the high cost of living, he argued in vain against price-fixing. As delegate to the adjourned session of the state constitutional convention in 1780 he served on the committee, which so juggled the returns that every clause appeared to have the requisite majority (*Proceedings of the Massachusetts Historical Society*, L, 397). For a few months in 1783 he was state senator for Essex County. Both temperament and interest made him an ardent advocate of a strong federal government. He did not attend the Annapolis Convention to which he was elected, but in the Massachusetts ratifying convention of 1788, while condescending to pose as "one of the people," he acted in close concert with the Federalist leaders. In 1789 he entertained President Washington at Beverly, and in June 1791 was chosen United States senator from Massachusetts.

Of commanding stature and dignified presence, yet easy and gracious in manner, with a good conversational style though an indifferent public speaker, and well informed on all business matters, Senator Cabot was well fitted for useful work in a small house, with closed sessions. He became a trusted follower and adviser of Alexander Hamilton, and, until the end of 1793, a director of the United States Bank. He framed the Act of 1792 granting bounties for codfishing. During the session of 1793–94 he was chairman of the committee on appropriations. He was one of the New England senators who supported Hamilton in urging the Jay mission to England, the results of which he accepted as satisfactory. For the same reason as Hamilton, Cabot abhorred the French Revolution, and wished to maintain peace with England at any price. One of his last acts in the Senate, in 1796, was to strike out the phrase "that magnanimous nation" from a resolution returning thanks to the French Republic for a flag presented by it to the United States. As late as 1807 he favored an offensive-defensive alliance with Great Britain.

Upon retiring from mercantile business, Cabot had sold his house in Beverly and purchased a farm in Brookline, near Boston. Weary of politics at the age of forty-four, he resigned his seat in the Senate (May 1796), retired to private life, and two years later refused an appointment by President Adams as the first secretary of the navy. In 1803, having sold his Brookline estate and moved to 3 Park St., Boston, Cabot became president of the Boston branch of the United States Bank, a director of the Suffolk Insurance Company, and (about 1809) president of the Boston Marine Insurance Company. His real position in Boston was that of Federalist sage. "George Cabot," wrote John C. Hamilton, "was one of those rare men, who, without ambition, without effort, almost without the consciousness of admitted superiority, control, and become the oracles of communities" (*History of the Republic*, 1859, III, 411). Rather than economic power or political wire-pulling, his constant interchange of ideas with other members of the "Essex Junto" explains the hold which that group had on Massachusetts politics and political thought. Socially, the solidarity of those plain, energetic Essex County families of Cabot, Lowell, Lee, Higginson, and Jackson, who moved to Boston after the Revolution, was equally significant. For over a generation they remained a compact social group, frequently intermarrying, and helping one another in business, to such good purpose that eventually they were regarded as typical Boston aristocrats.

After the election of Jefferson, whom he considered an "anarchist," Cabot revelled in pessimism. His very indolence became a virtue when opposed to the secessionist zeal of Timothy Pickering, and led him thrice to intervene in politics in order to exert a moderating and unionist influence: as state councillor during the Embargo, as member of a Federalist corresponding committee to nominate a Clinton for the presidency in 1808 and 1812 (Samuel E. Morison, *H. G. Otis*, 1913, I, 305, 318), and as member of the Hartford Convention in 1814. "Dragged in like a conscript to the duty of a delegate," he was chosen president, where his cool wisdom seconded the cautious leadership of H. G. Otis [*q.v.*], in preventing radical action (C. R. King, *Rufus King*, 1894–1900, V, 476). That was his last public service. In 1821 he was attacked by a disease of the gall-bladder, from which he died on Apr. 18, 1823.

[*Life and Letters of Geo. Cabot* (1877) by Henry Cabot Lodge [*q.v.*], his great-grandson, is the standard authority, but is almost exclusively confined to Cabot's political career and correspondence. The letter of Feb. 14, 1804 to Pickering on pp. 341–44 (also in Henry Adams, *Documents Relating to New Eng. Federalism*, 1877, pp. 346–49), is a succinct expression of Cabot's political views. Additional letters are in Geo. Gibbs, *Memoirs of the Administrations of Washington and John Adams* (1846); in the Pickering MSS., Mass. Hist. Soc. (Calendared in *Mass. Hist. Soc. Colls.*, 6 ser., VIII); the Pa. Hist. Soc.; the Ridgway Library, Phila.; and the Lib. of Cong. His privateering ventures

are described by O. T. Howe in "Beverly Privateers in the Am. Revolution," *Mass. Colonial Soc. Pubs.*, XXIV, 318–435, and his early voyages are treated by L. V. Briggs, *Hist. and Geneal. of the Cabot Family* (1927), I, 119–62. Abundant material on these subjects is in the Dane and Lee-Cabot MSS. (Mass. Hist. Soc.), the Essex Institute, Salem, and the Beverly Hist. Soc.]

S. E. M.

CABRILLO, JUAN RODRIGUEZ (d. Jan. 3, 1543), explorer, was a Portuguese by birth, and a skilled mariner. He went to Mexico in 1520 with Narvaez, took part with Cortés in the capture of Mexico City, joined Orozco's expedition to Oaxaca, and assisted in the conquest of Guatemala. Balboa's discovery of the South Sea in 1513 had set in motion a series of voyages up the Pacific coast of North America. From Panama sailors ran the Central-American shore-line. Cortés founded Zacatula on the western coast of Mexico, and another series of explorations began. In 1533 Lower California was discovered. Interest in the north was stimulated by Cabeza de Vaca's journey across the continent (1528–36), and in 1539 Ulloa, sent out by Cortés, rounded the Peninsula of California. Next year Pedro de Alvarado sailed from Guatemala with a fleet designed for northwestern explorations, with Cabrillo as *almirante*. Alvarado landed on the west coast of Mexico, and there met his death. Viceroy Mendoza now took charge of the vessels and sent Cabrillo with two of them to continue northward explorations. The expedition comprised the flagship *San Salvador* and the fragata *Victoria*. Bartolomé Ferrelo, or Ferrer, a native of the Levant, went as chief pilot, and there was a chaplain on board. The start was made on June 27, 1542, from Navidad, on the western coast of Mexico. Cabrillo reached the southern extremity of the Peninsula on July 3, Magdalena Bay on July 19, and Cerros Island on Aug. 5. On Aug. 22 he anchored and took possession of Port San Quintín. On Sept. 28 he discovered San Diego Bay, naming it San Miguel. Proceeding up the coast, he discovered Santa Catalina Island, San Pedro Bay, Santa Monica Bay, and Santa Bárbara Channel. Here, at San Miguel Island, he fell and broke his leg. Continuing north, nevertheless, he discovered the Santa Lucía Mountains and Point Reyes. Being driven out to sea he neared the shore again, turned south, missed the Golden Gate, discovered Monterey Bay, and returned to San Miguel Island, where he died from illness caused by his fall while previously on the island. The command of the expedition now fell to Ferrelo. From Cabrillo's northern limit he continued up the coast to latitude 44°, according to his observations, which Davidson corrects to 42½°, placing the limit of the voyage near the mouth of the Rogue River, Ore. Wagner concludes that Ferrelo did not get above 42°. On Apr. 14, 1543, the expedition reached Navidad, whence it had sailed the previous June.

[The source of most of what is known of the Cabrillo expedition is the diary commonly, but erroneously, attributed to Juan Paez. This was published in Spanish in 1857 by Buckingham Smith in his *Colección de Varios Documentos para la Historia de la Florida y Tierras Adyacentes* (London), pp. 173–89. Another Spanish version was printed in 1870 by Joaquín Pacheco and Francisco de Cárdenas, in their *Colección de Documentos Inéditos* (Madrid), XIV, 165–91. English translations have been published: (1) by Richard Stuart Evans, in Geo. M. Wheeler, *Report upon U. S. Geographical Surveys West of the One Hundredth Meridian* (1879), VII, 293–314; (2) by Geo. Davidson, in "Report of the Superintendent of the U. S. Geodetic Survey," being *House Ex. Doc. No. 40, 49* Cong., 2 Sess., pp. 160–241; (3) by Herbert E. Bolton, in *Spanish Exploration in the Southwest* (1916, 1925), pp. 3–29; (4) by Henry R. Wagner, in *Cal. Hist. Soc. Quart.*, vol. VII, no. 1 (Mar. 1929). Mr. Wagner has made a thorough study of the itinerary, reaching conclusions considerably at variance with earlier opinions.]   H. E. B.

CADILLAC, ANTOINE DE LA MOTHE, Sieur (*c.* 1656–Oct. 18, 1730), founder of Detroit, governor of Louisiana, was born in Gascony, son of a minor nobleman, Jean de la Mothe, who owned the seigneury of Cadillac. His mother was Jeanne de Malenfant; and although in his marriage contract of 1687 Antoine declared himself about twenty-six, he was in fact some years older. Like lads of his ancestry he early entered the army, first as cadet, then as lieutenant (1677) in the regiment of Clairembault. In 1683 he came to America and had a home at Port Royal (now Annapolis); after his marriage at Quebec in 1687 to Marie Thérèse Guyon, he lived for a brief time on his grant in what is now Maine, including the island of Mount Desert. In 1689 he visited France, and during his absence his Port Royal place was sacked and burned by the British (1691). He obtained a recommendation to Count de Frontenac, who greatly favored him, and whose anti-Jesuit principles he embraced. In 1694 Frontenac gave Cadillac, whom he calls "a worthy man, good officer, keen witted," the command of the post at Mackinac, the most important position in the western country. Cadillac himself was not pleased with his position; he complained of the climate, the food, and the savages; later he became reconciled and declared his post the healthiest place in the world (memoir in Margry, V, 75–132; translation in *Wisconsin Historical Collections*, XVI, 350–63).

In 1697 the posts in the West were abandoned by order of the crown; Cadillac returned to Canada, and in 1699 went to France, where he laid before the ministry his plan for a post on Detroit River, which would protect the western fur trade from the English. His rank at this time was captain in the troops of the Marine (that is, of the colonies), and he obtained a grant of Detroit and the title of lieutenant of the King. In 1701 he set forth with many colonists to found Detroit; he was also head of a company which had the trade monopoly. Recollet missionaries were part of his colony, and he planned to attract the western tribesmen to the region of Detroit, and to place them under the care of these missionaries. The Jesuits, especially those at Mackinac, bitterly opposed the removal of their neophytes and other Indians. This and other high-handed procedure brought about Cadillac a swarm of enemies. In 1704 he was arrested, tried at Quebec, and acquitted, when he returned in triumph to Detroit. His enthusiasm for his new colony was so great and his communications to the minister in France so diffuse, that the latter rallied him upon his anticipations, writing in 1706, "I am glad to be assured that Detroit will become the Paris of New France" (*Report on Canadian Archives,* 1899, Supplement, p. 391).

Cadillac brought his wife and family to Detroit, and planned to make this place his lifelong home; but in 1711 he was recalled, and appointed to the governorship of the new colony of Louisiana, which was granted in 1712 to a company founded by Antoine Crozat. Cadillac reached Louisiana with his family in 1713 and again expressed in his reports his dissatisfaction with his appointment. He treated the Louisianians haughtily and incurred the ill will of the former governor, Bienville, and his Canadian relatives. During his three years in Louisiana, Cadillac sought every means to enrich himself, and in 1715 made a trip to Illinois in search of silver mines reported to exist there. He was much disappointed at finding only lead.

In 1716 Cadillac, of whose complaints Crozat had tired, was recalled, and is thought to have suffered a short imprisonment in the Bastille, whence he was released in February 1717. Thenceforward he made his home in his native province and died there at Castle Sarrazin. His heirs made several attempts to realize on Cadillac's American grants. Finally in 1787 his granddaughter, Madame Gregoire, visited America, introduced by Lafayette. In a burst of generosity the Massachusetts Assembly confirmed her title to that part of Mount Desert and the neighboring mainland yet unsold, after which she and her family lived there for several years.

Cadillac's name is yet potent in Detroit, where buildings and monuments have been christened in his honor. He seems to have been a typical

Gascon, alternately buoyant and depressed, of inordinate pride and much self-esteem, but withal able and clever. Had he been permitted to remain at Detroit and carry out his plans for that colony, he might have succeeded, although his enmities were stronger than his friendships. He had a wide vision of the French situation in the West, and brilliant plans for expanding French power; but he was covetous and grasping, unable to lend himself unselfishly to broad enterprises. In Louisiana his rule was a failure, by which his last years were embittered.

[The sources for Cadillac's life are scattered. C. M. Burton collected his papers and published them in *Mich. Pioneer and Hist. Colls.*, vol. XXXIII. Several of his reports or memoirs are in Pierre Margry, *Découvertes et établissements des français dans l'Amérique septentrionale* (Paris, 1876–86),vol. V, and E. B. O'Callaghan, *N. Y. Colonial Docs.*, vol. IX. In *Maine Hist. Soc. Colls.*, 1859, pp. 273–89 and 1902, p. 89 are his grants in that state. B. F. French, *Hist. Colls. of La.*, pt. III (1851), gives a contemporary report on his governorship. For a modern work there is *Antoine de la Mothe Cadillac and Detroit before the Conspiracy of Pontiac: a Bibliography* (Detroit Pub. Lib., 1912). C. M. Burton has written several pamphlets on the life of Cadillac; see also *Mich. Pioneer and Hist. Colls.*, XXIV, 303. Chas. Gayarré's account of Cadillac in Louisiana in his *Hist. of Louisiana* (4th ed., New Orleans, 1903), I, 175–89 is incorrect and prejudiced.]   L. P. K.

CADWALADER, JOHN (January 1742–Feb. 10, 1786), Revolutionary soldier, was born in Philadelphia, the son of Dr. Thomas Cadwalader [*q.v.*] and Hannah (Lambert) Cadwalader. He was educated at the College and Academy of Philadelphia (now University of Pennsylvania) but apparently never graduated. Prior to the Revolution he engaged in business with his brother, Lambert Cadwalader [*q.v.*], under the firm name of John & Lambert Cadwalader. A man of considerable wealth and position, he espoused the popular side in the struggle with Great Britain. He was a member of the Philadelphia Committee of Safety, and was captain of a city troop known as the Silk-Stocking Company. He became colonel of a Philadelphia battalion, and was appointed brigadier-general of Pennsylvania militia, Dec. 25, 1776. To his later regret, he twice declined the offer by Congress of a brigadier-generalship in the Continental army.

Cadwalader came into notice in the Trenton campaign. Washington's plan contemplated crossing the Delaware by three columns quite widely separated, his own, Ewing's, and Cadwalader's. The latter could not carry out his part of the program on account of ice, though he exerted himself, and transferred part of the infantry. Two days later with about 1,800 men he crossed from Bristol to Burlington, marching thence to Bordentown, in time to be present at the battle of Princeton. As Sir William Howe's invasion approached Philadelphia, Cadwalader, at Washington's request, organized the militia on the eastern shore of Maryland. He fought at Brandywine and Germantown, engaged in the irregular warfare of the following season near Philadelphia, and was active in the Monmouth campaign. The winter of 1777–78 was that of the Conway cabal. Cadwalader was a strong supporter of Washington in this attempt to undermine the authority of the Commander-in-Chief, and he challenged Gen. Conway to a duel. The encounter took place near Philadelphia, and Conway fell, severely—and as he at first believed, mortally—wounded. Conway's confession to Washington, his disappearance from the scene, and the collapse of the "cabal" followed. After this year, Cadwalader had no prominent part in affairs, though he served in the legislature of Maryland. He was married twice: first, in October 1768 to Elizabeth Lloyd; second, on Jan. 30, 1779, to Williamina Bond. He died in 1786 and is buried at Shrewsbury Church, Kent County, Md.

Cadwalader was a man of "polished manners." He was regarded as a good disciplinarian, and the esteem in which he was held by Washington is shown by two letters, one written from Valley Forge, and the other sent at the time of Arnold's treason. Cadwalader wrote *A Reply to General Joseph Reed's Remarks on a Late Publication in the Independent Gazetteer* (1783), which was part of a controversy dealing with events in the time of the Trenton campaign, Reed having thought that Cadwalader was the author of the so-called "Brutus letter," in 1782, containing innuendos.

[Jared Sparks, *The Writings of Geo. Washington* (1834–37); Thos. J. Rogers, *A New Am. Biog. Dict.* (3rd ed., Easton, Pa., 1824); Chas. P. Keith, *The Provincial Councillors of Pa.* (1883); Wm. S. Stryker, *The Battles of Trenton and Princeton* (1898); "Selections from the Military Papers of Gen. John Cadwalader," *Pa. Mag. of Hist. and Biog.*, Apr. 1908.]
E. K. A.

CADWALADER, JOHN (Apr. 1, 1805–Jan. 26, 1879), jurist, was descended from John Cadwalader, who came from Pembroke, Wales, toward the close of the seventeenth century, settled in Philadelphia, and died there in 1734. Thomas Cadwalader, of the third generation from John, was a lawyer in Philadelphia and later acted as land agent for the Penns and other owners of extensive interests in Pennsylvania. He married Mary, daughter of Col. Clement Biddle, Washington's friend, and their son John was born at Philadelphia. John was educated at the University of Pennsylvania, graduating in 1821, and then entered the law office of Horace Binney, at the same time assisting his father in the management of the Penn estates. He was admitted to the bar Sept. 30, 1825, while still a minor, and commenced practise in Philadelphia. His father was able to influence much important business and John very quickly acquired a large practise, particularly in matters involving the law of real property, in which he became recognized as an expert. In this connection he prepared a history of the title of William Penn's family to their large estates in America (*Pennsylvania Magazine of History and Biography,* April 1899, p. 60). In 1830 he was retained as counsel by the Bank of the United States, and acted as such throughout the extensive and prolonged litigation arising out of its failure. He became vice-provost of the Law Academy of Philadelphia in 1833, continuing as such for twenty years. As an advocate he had early acquired a prominent position through his thorough preparation and exhaustive study of his briefs, and this trait, combined with a forceful style and remarkably wide knowledge of law in general, gave him a professional prestige second to none. Among the many important cases in which he appeared were the "Cloth Cases" in 1839—perhaps the most important proceedings ever instituted by the revenue department—in which he was specially retained by the attorney-general in behalf of the United States. Another was the Girard Will case, where he was associated with Daniel Webster. During the riots of 1844 he raised and commanded a company of city militia. His interests were wide, and he was an active supporter of all schemes which had for their object the improvement of conditions in Philadelphia. He was leader of the movement advocating the consolidation of the city with the surrounding incorporated districts into one municipal corporation, which was carried into effect in 1854. Always a strong constitutional Democrat, he was in 1854 nominated for the office of city solicitor, but was defeated. In the same year, however, he was elected congressional representative for the fifth district by a narrow majority after a bitter contest, and took a leading part in the deliberations of the House during his term but did not seek reëlection. He was appointed by President Buchanan judge of the United States district court for the eastern district of Pennsylvania, Apr. 24, 1858, and retained this position till his death. His tenure of office coincided with the Civil War and Reconstruction periods, and many difficult questions incident thereto came before him for adjudication. One of the most important services rendered by him as a judge was his pioneer exposition of the provisions of the Bankruptcy Act of

1867. Coming to the bench with a wide experience acquired at the bar, and equipped with a knowledge of law in respect of which he "had no contemporary superior," his opinions on difficult or novel points were brilliant, though he had a tendency to over-elaboration. In matters involving no new principles, however, he frequently delivered extempore judgments, a practise which had been seldom adopted in the United States courts up to that time. Counsel frequently found it difficult to present an argument before him owing to his habit of constantly intervening, but this failing was attributed to his innate fairness and scrupulous anxiety to render absolute justice. "In admiralty proceedings he availed himself of the expert assistance of a retired shipmaster, nautical nomenclature being to him an absolutely sealed book, altogether beyond his ability to master" (R. D. Coxe, *Legal Philadelphia,* 1908, p. 82). He died in Philadelphia, Jan. 26, 1879. He was twice married: (1) in 1825 to Mary, daughter of Horace Binney, who died in 1831; (2) in 1833 to Henrietta Maria, daughter of Charles Nicoll Bancker of Philadelphia. In 1907 appeared *Cadwalader's Cases* (2 vols.), comprising his judicial opinions on questions of prize and belligerency arising during the Civil War, together with decisions in admiralty, in equity and at common law, between 1858 and 1879. This work, prepared by his son, included an introductory sketch of the judge's life, and reproduced the proceedings in the circuit court and at the meeting of the Philadelphia Bar on the occasion of his death.

[Sketches of the careers of Cadwalader and his immediate ancestors will be found in Chas. P. Keith, *The Provincial Councillors of Pa.* (1883), pp. 370–96. See also Robt. C. Moon, *The Morris Family of Phila.* (1890), I, p. 198; J. T. Scharf and T. Westcott, *Hist. of Phila.* (1884), II, 1538; F. M. Eastman, *Courts and Lawyers of Pa.* (1922), II, 387; *N. J. Law Jour.,* II, 61; *Legal Intelligencer,* Jan. 31, 1879, p. 46.]   H. W. H. K.

CADWALADER, LAMBERT (1743–Sept. 13, 1823), Revolutionary soldier, was a native of Trenton, and was descended from Welsh and Quaker ancestry, being the son of Dr. Thomas Cadwalader [*q.v.*] and Hannah (Lambert) Cadwalader. He was well educated, studying at the College and Academy of Philadelphia (now the University of Pennsylvania). Prior to the Revolution he engaged in business with his brother, John Cadwalader [1742–1786, *q.v.*], under the name John & Lambert Cadwalader. When the conflict with England began, he was actively patriotic. He signed the non-importation agreement in 1765, was a member of the Committee of Correspondence, of the Provincial Convention of 1775, and of the state constitutional convention of 1776. Like his brother, he was captain of an aristocratic company in Philadelphia, the Greens. He was appointed lieutenant-colonel, 3rd Pennsylvania Battalion, Jan. 4, 1776, and colonel, 4th Pennsylvania, later in the year. He was one of the commanders in the disastrous battle of Fort Washington. After performing his part well in the fighting, he was taken prisoner, Nov. 16, 1776, but was released, and resigned from the army in 1779. He held no further command in the war, but was a delegate to the Continental Congress, 1784–87, and a member of Congress in the lower house, 1789–91, and 1793–95. He was not marked as a debater, but was an efficient worker. In the Continental Congress he was a member of the Grand Committee which received the report of the Annapolis Convention. In 1793 he was married to Mary, daughter of Archibald McCall of Philadelphia. He owned a large estate at Greenwood, near Trenton, where he died in 1823.

[Wm. Henry Rawle, *Col. Lambert Cadwalader* (privately printed, 1878), also in *Pa. Mag. of Hist. and Biog.*, Oct. 1886; Chas. P. Keith, *The Provincial Councillors of Pa.* (1883).]   E. K. A.

CADWALADER, THOMAS (1707 or 1708–Nov. 14, 1799), physician, of Philadelphia, was the son of John Cadwalader and his wife Martha Jones, daughter of Edward Jones and Mary Wynne. He was educated at the Friends' Public School, now known as the Penn Charter School. He was then apprenticed to his uncle Dr. Evan Jones. When he was nineteen or twenty, his father sent him abroad to complete his medical education. He is said to have spent a year studying under Cheselden and to have attended courses at the University of Rheims. Returning to Philadelphia, he soon acquired a large practise and distinguished himself by his activity in public affairs. He was associated with Benjamin Franklin in founding the Philadelphia Library in 1731. In 1730 or 1731, according to Dr. Caspar Wistar, he made dissections and demonstrations for the instruction of the elder Dr. Shippen and some others who had not been abroad. At about the same time he is noted as employing inoculation against smallpox. In 1738 he married Hannah, daughter of Thomas Lambert, Jr., a wealthy man who owned a great tract of land on and near where the city of Trenton, N. J., now flourishes. Cadwalader then left Philadelphia to live on his father-in-law's estate, but although he was elected to several minor political offices in New Jersey, he maintained a residence in Passyunk Township in Philadelphia, in which he passed part of each year. He undoubtedly also practised his profession in New Jersey as he was physician to Gov. Belcher, and had at least one pupil. In 1750 he resigned his office of burgess

in Trenton, presenting to the town £500 to found a public library, and again took up his permanent residence in Philadelphia. In 1751 he subscribed toward the founding of the Pennsylvania Hospital and was asked by the board of managers, along with Drs. Graeme, Moore, and Redman, "to assist in consultations on extraordinary cases," in which capacity he continued to give his services until 1779, when he resigned. In 1751 he was elected a trustee of the Academy of Philadelphia (later the College of Philadelphia, and now the University of Pennsylvania). He was very active in the affairs of the American Philosophical Society, being at one time vice-president. He was also prominent in civic and colonial affairs. He was a member of the Common Council of Philadelphia from 1751 to 1774, and of the Provincial Council from 1755 until that body was dissolved at the outbreak of the Revolution. From an early date he rendered himself obnoxious to the Government by the patriotic zeal which he manifested in colonial matters. After Braddock's defeat he was one of twenty citizens who offered to pay £500 each for purposes of defense against the French and Indians, the Governor having refused to allow the Assembly the right to impose a tax for this purpose. In 1765 he affixed his signature to the "Non-Importation Articles" and that year was a prominent participant in a great meeting in the State House yard to protest against the Stamp Act. Although there is no record of his having held any military position during the Revolution there is evidence that he from time to time performed certain duties requested of him by the American authorities. Thus in 1776 he was asked to examine into the health of Gen. Prescott of the British army, then a prisoner of war in Philadelphia, and to report on the sanitary conditions of the jail. Prescott seems to have appreciated his services on this occasion, for, some time later, after his own release, he secured the release of Cadwalader's son Lambert [*q.v.*], who had been taken prisoner by the British. He is also said to have helped Dr. John Morgan in his work as director-general of the American military hospitals.

Cadwalader's only contribution to medical literature was *An Essay on the West-India Dry-Gripes; with the Method of Preventing and Curing that Cruel Distemper; to Which Is Added an Extraordinary Case in Physick. Philadelphia. Printed and sold by B. Franklin, M. DCC. XLV.* The "Dry-Gripes" was the name given to a very frequent complaint in Cadwalader's day, due to the prevalent custom of drinking punch made with Jamaica rum. It was a form of lead-poisoning due to the lead pipes which were used in distilling the rum. The most usual form of treatment consisted in the administration of mercury and drastic purgatives. Cadwalader recommended instead the use of mild cathartics and opium. The "Extraordinary Case" was one of osteomalacia, or as it was then called "mollities osseum." Cadwalader performed an autopsy on the body in 1742, which may be regarded as one of the earliest recorded autopsies in this country. Courteous and kind, he enjoyed the esteem and affection of his fellow-townsmen. Of him it might be said, as Dr. Johnson wrote of the great physician Richard Mead, "No man lived more in the broad sunshine of life." He died while visiting his son Lambert, in Trenton, and was buried in that city.

[Sketch by Chas. W. Dulles, in *Pa. Mag. of Hist. and Biog.*, July 1903; Geo. W. Norris, *The Early Hist. of Medicine in Phila.* (1886); John F. Watson, *Annals of Phila.* (1830); Jas. Thacher, *Am. Med. Biogs.* (1828); T. G. Morton, *Hist. of the Pa. Hospital* (1895).]

F.R.P.

CADY, DANIEL (Apr. 29, 1773–Oct. 31, 1859), jurist, was descended from Nicholas Cady, who, coming probably from Suffolk, England, settled at Watertown, Mass., in 1630. Fourth in the direct line from Nicholas, Eleazer Cady, a Connecticut farmer, married Tryphena, daughter of John Beebe of Kent, Conn. They moved to Columbia County, N. Y., and their son Daniel was born at Chatham (Canaan) in that county. He was educated at the public schools and worked on his father's farm. Later he was apprenticed to a shoemaker, but in 1791 through an accident at the bench lost the sight of one eye. He thereupon became a school-teacher, at the same time studying law at Canaan, and in 1794 entered an Albany law office. He was admitted as an attorney in 1795, "having worn a pair of boots of his own manufacture at the time of his examination" (W. Raymond, *post*). He commenced practise at Florida, Montgomery County, but at the end of a year removed to Johnstown, the county seat, being admitted as a counsellor in 1798. A Federalist in politics, he was elected to the state legislature in 1808, being reëlected in 1809, 1811, 1812, and 1813. For one term, Mar. 4, 1815, to Mar. 3, 1817, he was representative in Congress for Montgomery County, but did not make any mark in the political field, and thereafter devoted his attention to his law practise. In his early years at the bar he had become favorably known as an advocate, and in 1812 had distinguished himself in the trial of Solomon Southwick for attempting to bribe the speaker of the New York Assembly to vote for the incorporation of the Bank of North America, appearing for the defense in association with Aaron Burr and pro-

curing an acquittal. Later on he came to the front as an "ejectment lawyer." He specialized in equity and real property law with its accompanying technicalities and ancient learning, and, practising in a neighborhood where titles were always involved and frequently litigated, acquired a large and lucrative business. Among his clients were the heirs of Sir William Johnson, who were contemplating action against the Government in regard to the confiscation of their ancestor's extensive estate.

Cady's remarkable knowledge of all the intricacies of the most difficult branch of the law was in great measure due to his method of study. "He had no patience with the digest-mongers and book-manufacturers of the day," but invariably went to the fountainhead, reading *Coke upon Littleton, Fearne on Contingent Remainders,* and *Shepard's Touchstone.* Always interested in agricultural problems, he invested largely in wild land contiguous to Johnstown, and expended much time and money in experiments in reclamation and cultivation. In 1847, when seventy-four years old, he was elected an associate judge of the supreme court of New York, as organized under the state constitution of 1846, there being at that date no age limit on officeholders. In 1849 he was reëlected for a term of eight years, and retained his seat on the bench till Dec. 31, 1854, when he resigned, owing to his hearing having become seriously impaired. As a judge he was capable, dignified, and conscientiously painstaking, but had little scope for exhibiting his peculiar learning. Despite his age, his intellectual vigor remained undiminished, and he enjoyed to a remarkable degree the confidence and esteem of the community. "He was more than once retained, after his judicial career was finished, merely to look virtuous; to say nothing and to do nothing but to nod assent to all his associate might say, and wag a vigorous dissent from all the opposition might utter" (Irving Browne, *post*). Somewhat paradoxically he had inherited a strain of Puritan narrowness, and in his everyday contacts was "secretive and taciturn to an extraordinary degree"(Franklin Ellis, *post*). He died at Johnstown, Oct. 31, 1859, having shortly prior thereto become totally blind. He was married on July 8, 1801, to Margaret, daughter of Col. James Livingston, and their daughter Elizabeth later became, as Mrs. Elizabeth Cady Stanton [*q.v.*], the champion of women's rights.

[Details of Cady's ancestry appear in Orrin Peer Allen, *Descendants of Nicholas Cady of Watertown, Mass., 1645–1910* (1910), which also contains an outline of his life at p. 173. The *Green Bag,* June 1890, has a short character sketch by Irving Browne. Other biographical notices will be found in Alden Chester, *Courts and Lawyers of N. Y.* (1925), pp. 1043, 1126; Franklin Ellis, *Hist. of Columbia County, N. Y.* (1878), p. 104; Wm. Raymond, *Biog. Sketches of the Distinguished Men of Columbia County* (1851), p. 44; Peyton Farrell Miller, *A Group of Great Lawyers of Columbia County, N. Y.* (1904), p. 126; the *Green Bag*, Mar. 1897; 18 *Barbour*, p. 659.]   H. W. H. K.

CADY, SARAH LOUISE ENSIGN (Sept. 13, 1829–Nov. 8, 1912), educator, was the daughter of Salmon and Melinda (Cobb) Ensign. Her father was a coachmaker of Northampton, Mass. Family tradition told of a coach built by him for President Pierce, which, beautifully ornamented, lined with tufted gold brocade, was drawn by horses to Philadelphia, rousing great admiration along the way. The family moved to Westfield, where at seventeen Sarah was graduated from the Normal School. Then followed the practical training of teaching in district schools, under customary conditions of pupils older than the teacher, belief in using the rod when necessary, and adventures of "boarding round,"—all excellent means of developing personality. On Oct. 10, 1850, Sarah was married to Henry Stearns Cady, a merchant in Springfield, a second cousin, descended like herself from Samuel Cobb, physician, who came from England in 1630. Left on her husband's death (1863) with only a small life insurance to support three little children, she naturally returned to teaching, and opened a school in Westfield. After two years she was invited to teach in Maplewood Hall (Pittsfield), a large boarding-school for young women, and later became associate principal. In 1870 she established her own school, West End Institute, in New Haven, Conn., attended during twenty-nine years of existence by several hundred pupils. Mrs. Cady's sincere interest and enthusiasm for her profession, and belief in the serious education of girls, made this more than the usual finishing school of the day. It earned a standing which enabled its pupils to enter colleges without examination. The first pupil to enter Vassar from Connecticut was fitted here in the early seventies; no other school in the state gave the necessary instruction. Mrs. Cady was a born teacher and disciplinarian, thorough in her methods, generous in the number and quality of her teachers. They were college graduates, native teachers in foreign languages, special lecturers and instructors. The school also had one of the earliest kindergartens. About 1891 the school moved to a building on the famous Hillhouse Ave. belonging to Yale University, which (1899) refused to renew the lease. The difficulty, at her age, of finding another suitable location, and of moving the establishment, caused Mrs. Cady reluctantly to close the school after graduating the largest class in its history. She spent the rest of her life in New York City with a daughter. Naturally active and a leader, she became a member of various clubs,—Sorosis, Clio, and others— was prominent in the Broadway Tabernacle, and served on executive boards and committees of the Y. W. C. A., W. C. T. U., and so forth.

In appearance stately and handsome, with beautiful coloring, she had unusual talent in reading and elocution. In 1920, as a jubilee gift and memorial to her, the Alumnæ Association established at Connecticut College an annual prize for reading and public speaking.

[School records and information supplied by Mrs. Cady's daughter, Mrs. Charles A. Terry; O. P. Allen, *Descendants of Nicholas Cady of Watertown, Mass., 1645–1910* (1910).]   M. H. M.

CAFFERY, DONELSON (Sept. 10, 1835– Dec. 30, 1906), senator, was born on his father's sugar plantation near Franklin, St. Mary's Parish, La. He was of Scotch-Irish descent. His father was Donelson Caffery, a native of middle Tennessee, who came to Louisiana as a young man in 1811. His mother was Lydia (Murphy) Caffery, who when a child came with her father, John Murphy, from Edenton, N. C., to St. Mary's Parish. Donelson Caffery attended a private school at Franklin and St. Mary's College in Baltimore. He then studied law in the office of Joseph W. Walker at Franklin and at the old Louisiana University in New Orleans. After completing his course, however, he engaged in sugar planting on Bayou Cypremont, bordering on the Gulf of Mexico. Though he did not favor secession, when Louisiana seceded from the Union, he left his business in the hands of his overseer and joined the Crescent Rifles in New Orleans in January 1862. Shortly afterward he was transferred to the 13th Louisiana Regiment and under that command fought in the two days' battle of Shiloh. Later he became a lieutenant and was detailed to the staff of Brigadier-General W. W. Walker, on which he continued until the close of the war.

After the war he engaged in the practise of law at Franklin, and in sugar planting. He was active in the movement to rid the state of carpet-baggers, and with several others was indicted for attempting to drive out J. Hale Sypher, a Republican official. In the trial at New Orleans, his masterly speech before the jury is said to have obtained the verdict of acquittal for himself and the others. In 1869 he was married to Bethia Richardson, daughter of Francis D. Richardson, a prominent sugar planter of Jeanerette, La. Ten years later he was elected to the Louisiana state constitutional convention. The main question before that body concerned the debt that had been incurred by the state during the Reconstruction period. The convention was inclined to repudiate the debt, but Caffery's activity, both on the floor and in personal contact with the members, contributed much toward getting it ratified. In 1892 he was elected to the state Senate and later in the same year he was appointed to the United States Senate to succeed Randall L. Gibson who had died. Two years later he was reëlected and served until the expiration of his term in 1901. As senator he opposed both free silver and the war with Spain. He was particularly active in the formation of the National or "Gold" Democratic party in 1896 after the nomination of Bryan by the Democrats at Chicago on the free silver platform. He was permanent chairman of the convention at Indianapolis that nominated Palmer and Buckner for president and vice-president. In 1900 he was nominated for president by the convention of the National Party, composed chiefly of "Gold" Democrats and Anti-Imperialists, but declined the nomination. On retiring from the Senate he returned to his home in Franklin and resumed the practise of law and the cultivation of his sugar plantation in St. Mary's Parish. Contrary to current reports, he was a man of only ordinary means throughout his entire life. He died while on a visit to New Orleans and was buried at Franklin. He was survived by his wife and eight of their nine children.

Caffery was a man of medium height, rather stockily built, with a flowing beard and large features. The dominant trait of his character was his independence of thought and action. He had strong convictions and obeyed his sense of justice even when it ran counter to his own interests. Though he was himself a sugar planter, he opposed the sugar bounty and so alienated one of the most powerful industrial interests in his own state. His private life was one of great purity and unselfishness.

[There is a brief sketch in Alcée Fortier, *Louisiana* (1914), I, 145–46; New Orleans newspapers (*Daily Picayune* and *Times-Democrat*) for Dec. 31, 1906, contain more or less lengthy but not altogether reliable obituaries.]   E.M.V.

CAFFIN, CHARLES HENRY (June 4, 1854– Jan. 14, 1918), author, was born at Sittingbourne, Kent, England, the son of Rev. Charles Smart and Harriet C. Caffin. He graduated in 1876 from Magdalen College, Oxford, with a splendid background of culture and a finely developed æsthetic sense. The years following his college career were occupied with teaching and theatrical work. The training gained in these pursuits quickened his powers of observation and descrip-

tion. In 1888 he married Caroline Scurfield and in 1892 came to the United States, where he was engaged in the decoration department of the Chicago Exposition. In 1897 he settled in New York and entered upon his profession as an art critic for *Harper's Weekly,* the New York *Evening Post,* the New York *Sun* (1901–04), the *International Studio,* and the *New York American.* His press articles, characterized by ease of style and much individuality, attracted wide attention. In 1897 was published the volume, *Handbook of the New Library of Congress, compiled by Herbert Small; with Essays on the Architecture, Sculpture and Painting by Charles Caffin.* In 1901, Caffin's first of a long series of books, popular in style, was issued under the title of *Photography as a Fine Art.* It was followed by : *American Masters of Painting* (1902) ; *American Masters of Sculpture* (1903) ; *How to Study Pictures by Means of a Series of Comparisons of Paintings and Painters* (1905) ; *The Story of American Painting* (1907) ; *A Child's Guide to Pictures* (1908) ; *The Appreciation of the Drama* (1908) ; *The Art of Dwight W. Tryon* (1909) ; *The Story of Dutch Painting* (1909) ; *The Story of Spanish Painting* (1910) ; *A Guide to Pictures for Beginners and Students* (1910) ; *The Story of French Painting* (1911) ; *Francisco Goya Lucientes* (1912) ; *Art for Life's Sake* (1913) ; *How to Study the Modern Painters* (1914) ; *How to Study the Old Masters* (1914) ; *The A. B. C. Guide to Pictures* (1914) ; *How to Study Architecture* (1917). This long list of works, written in addition to Caffin's onerous editorial duties, exercised a wide-spread influence. They were suggestive and stimulating to the layman and did much to elicit interest in the various fields of art. The essay, *Art for Life's Sake,* describes Caffin's philosophy. "Art is not confined . . . to painting, or sculpture, or architecture, or music, but is, in its highest and broadest sense, organization—susceptible of application to, or expression through, every kind of human activity, high or humble, practical or idealistic" (*International Studio,* February 1918).

[*Am. Art Annual,* vol. XV (1918) ; the *Evening Post* (N.Y.), Jan. 14, 1918 ; *Who's Who in America,* 1916–17.]   L.F.P.

CAIN, RICHARD HARVEY (Apr. 12, 1825– Jan. 18, 1887), negro clergyman and politician, was born of free parents in Greenbrier County, Va., and remained there throughout his boyhood. His parents then moved to Ohio, first to Portsmouth and later to Cincinnati. There he had some opportunity to ground himself in the common school branches. Like so many enterprising negroes of that day, he entered upon the steamboat service on the Ohio River. This was a much more lucrative employment at that time than years later because, prior to the development of the railroad and Pullman service, the sort of travel preferred by the rich and aristocratic was by way of steamboat. Cain began the serious work of his life after he was converted in 1841. Upon moving to Hannibal, Mo., in 1844, he was licensed to preach by the Rev. William Jackson of the Methodist Episcopal Church. Returning to Cincinnati soon after, and dissatisfied with the conditions then obtaining in the Methodist Episcopal Church, he joined the African Methodist Episcopal Church. He was then assigned a church at Muscatine, Iowa, and was ordained deacon by Bishop W. P. Quinn in 1859, but, feeling the need of more learning, he temporarily abandoned the work to study for a year at Wilberforce University. In 1861 he was transferred to the New York Conference to serve four years in Brooklyn. He was ordained elder by Bishop Payne in Washington in 1862. Three years later he was sent to the South Carolina Conference where he had the opportunity to extend the influence of his church and to take the initiative in the reconstruction of the religious work among the freedmen in that state. In this field, he was not only a minister, but rendered valuable service also in the publication of a newspaper entitled the *Missionary Record*.

Being in South Carolina at the time when the enfranchised negroes together with their white friends controlled the politics of the state, Cain was quickly sought to represent them in politics. He was a member of the constitutional convention of 1868 which revised the fundamental law along liberal lines. He next served two years as state senator from the Charleston district. In 1872 he was elected to represent South Carolina in the Forty-third Congress. He was elected also to the Forty-fifth Congress. As a member of that body, he not only manifested interest in those measures which peculiarly concerned the freedmen, but took an active part in all matters pertaining to the general welfare of the country. To eliminate fraud from South Carolina, he joined with others in the organization of the Honest Government League. To keep the federal government out of the mire of corruption, he spoke and wrote fearlessly in behalf of clean politics. In spite of the vituperation and recrimination with which the atmosphere was charged in the conflict of the Reconstructionists and their opponents, he was generally referred to, even by his enemies, as an upright and honest man who deserved the good will of all citizens.

Upon the elimination of the negro from poli-

tics, Cain devoted himself altogether to the work of the church. He was elected bishop in 1880 and was assigned to the Louisiana and Texas diocese. There he had not only the religious work to direct but that of education, as it centered in Paul Quinn College of which he became president. Throughout his career, he made the impression of a man of clear vision, good judgment, strong resolution, and firm convictions.

[Wm. J. Simmons, *Men of Mark* (1887), pp. 866–71; A. A. Taylor, *The Negro in S. C. During the Reconstruction* (1924), *passim*; *Jour. of Negro Hist.*, Apr. 1922, July, Oct. 1924; *A.M.E.Ch.Rev.*, Apr. 1887; L. G. Tyler, *Encyc. of Va. Biog.* (1915), vol. III.]

C.G.W.

CAINES, GEORGE (1771–July 10, 1825), lawyer, author, was a prominent figure in New York legal circles for over thirty years, but no details of his parentage or the place or exact date of his birth have survived. He was practising as a counsellor-at-law in New York City when in 1802 he published anonymously the first volume of *An Enquiry into the Law Merchant of the United States; or, Lex Mercatoria Americana on Several Heads of Commercial Importance*. Marvin (*post*, p. 189) says that other volumes of this work were intended but the indifferent reception accorded to it induced Caines to abandon his project. Up to this time all legal reports in the United States had been private ventures with no official sanction, but in 1804 the New York legislature provided for the appointment by the state supreme court of a reporter of its decisions and Caines received the appointment, being thus the first official reporter on this continent. In this capacity he issued *New York Term Reports of Cases Argued and Determined in the Supreme Court of that State*, in three volumes covering the period May 1803–Nov. 1805 (1804–06), of which a second edition appeared with corrections and additions in 1813–14. These reports were distinguished by brevity and accuracy, and for long enjoyed a high reputation with both bench and bar, but subsequent statutory amendments have deprived them of much of their utility. At the same time he was engaged upon a compilation of *Cases Argued and Determined in the Court for the Trial of Impeachments and Correction of Errors in the State of New York*, two volumes (1805–07), commonly cited as *Caines' Cases in Error*. This work, embracing cases from the court of errors from 1801 to 1805 inclusive and supreme court cases from 1796, contains much important matter, displays much ability, and is esteemed authoritative. Caines also edited a second edition (1808) of William Coleman's *Reports of Cases of Practice Determined in the Supreme Court of Judicature of the State of New York*

1794 to 1800, adding cases up to November 1805, which is generally cited as *Coleman and Caines' Cases,* a later edition appearing in 1883. He was in addition the author of a practical manual, *Summary of the Practice in the Supreme Court of the State of New York* (1808) and *Practical Forms of the Supreme Court [of New York] Taken from Tidd's Appendix* (1808). He retained the position of official reporter for less than three years and after the publication of the two last mentioned works, devoted himself to his practise in New York City, ultimately achieving a prominent position at the New York bar. In 1816 he was counsel for the plaintiff in a suit for assault and battery under unique circumstances, his client complaining that when a passenger on the British ship *Thomas* he had, on the high seas off the Newfoundland Banks, been subjected against his will to ignominious treatment at the hands of Father Neptune and his acolytes impersonated by members of the crew. The trial took place in the Marine Court of New York City and the jury returned a verdict in favor of the plaintiff for $46.00 (*Duffie* vs. *Matthewson et al., 2 American State Trials,* ed. J. D. Lawson, 1914, p. 901). Caines retired from practise in 1825 and shortly afterward died suddenly at Catskill, N. Y., when on his way to take up his residence at Windham.

[D. McAdam *et al.,* ed., *Hist. of the Bench and Bar of N. Y.,* vol. I (1897); B. V. Abbott and A. Abbott, *Digest of N. Y. Statutes and Reports* (1860), I, xiv, xv; J. G. Marvin, *Legal Bibliography* (1847), p. 169; Chas. Warren, *Hist. of the Am. Bar* (1911), p. 331; *N. Y. Spectator,* July 15, 1825.]   H. W. H. K.

CALDWELL, ALEXANDER (Mar. 1, 1830–May 19, 1917), Kansas politician, business man, was born at Drake's Ferry, Huntingdon County, Pa. He was the son of Jane Matilda (Drake) Caldwell and James Caldwell, who came to America as a child with his parents from County Donegal, Ireland. As a boy Alexander had only very limited advantages but secured a common school education and became a clerk in a store. When the Mexican War broke out he enlisted at the age of seventeen in a company of volunteers of which his father was captain. He took part in all of the principal battles fought by Gen. Scott's army. His father was killed in a skirmish just outside the City of Mexico, Sept. 13, 1847. At the close of the war Alexander became a successful banking official at Columbia, Pa. While living there he married Pace A. Heise, a member of a prominent family of Columbia. In the spring of 1861 he came to Leavenworth, Kan., where he took contracts for transporting military supplies to the army posts west of the Missouri River. His business soon became very large. Five thousand men were employed; an equal number of wagons and many thousand oxen were used. With the coming of railroads in the West, the business of carrying freight in wagons declined and was discontinued by Caldwell in 1870. He now became interested in railway construction and secured the contract for building the Missouri Pacific from Kansas City to Leavenworth. A few years later he extended this line to Atchison, Kan., and became its president until it was sold. His next venture was the organization of the Kansas Central Railroad Company which constructed a line between Leavenworth and Miltonvale, Kan., a distance of one hundred and seventy miles.

In the winter of 1870–71 Caldwell was chosen United States senator for the term beginning Mar. 4, 1871. Serious charges were afterward made as to the methods used to secure his election. The Kansas legislature appointed a joint committee of investigation. On Feb. 24, 1872, a unanimous report was presented in which it was alleged that bribery had been freely used to obtain votes for him (Report of Joint Legislative Committee, *Annals of Kansas,* pp. 570 ff.). On May 11, 1872, the Senate adopted a resolution to investigate his election (*Congressional Globe,* 42 Cong., 2 Sess., pp. 3316–17). This committee later reported unfavorably and offered a resolution that Caldwell was "not duly elected to a seat in the Senate of the United States." They added however that he "was as much sinned against as sinning," owing to the fact that he "was a novice in politics." His defense was that he had done nothing in violation of any laws either state or Federal in securing his election. A long debate ensued (*Congressional Record,* 43 Cong., Special Session of the Senate, pp. 30 ff.). Before any vote was taken on the committee's resolution it was officially announced that Caldwell had resigned. This closed the incident (*Ibid.,* p. 164). His next business venture was the organization of the Kansas Manufacturing Company which made yearly about seven thousand wagons and gave employment to hundreds of men. He was also head of the Idaho & Oregon Land Improvement Company for locating towns and constructing irrigation ditches in the new country made available for settlement by the completion of the Union Pacific Railroad. In 1897 he bought a large block of stock in the First National Bank of Leavenworth and became its president. Under his able and efficient management it soon became one of the largest and most prosperous banks in Kansas. His death occurred just as America was entering the World War and attracted little attention.

[*Who's Who in America*, 1916–17; *Kansas State Hist. Soc. Colls.*, vol. XII (1912); Daniel W. Wilder, *Annals of Kansas* (1875); Frank W. Blackmar, *Kansas, a Cyc. of State Hist.* (1912), vol. I; *Portrait and Biog. Record of Leavenworth, Douglas, and Franklin Counties, Kan.* (1899); *Leavenworth Times*, May 20, 1917.]
T. L. H.

CALDWELL, CHARLES (May 14, 1772–July 9, 1853), physician, was the son of Lieut. Charles Caldwell and —— Murray, both of the Presbyterian gentry of County Tyrone, Ulster, who emigrated in 1752 to Newark, Del., and a few years later to Caswell County, N. C. Here the younger Charles Caldwell was born. He received the educational basis for his subsequent training from private tutors and the primitive schools of the state. For several years he taught school to acquire funds for his professional education. He had been designed for the pulpit but after brief study abandoned this career for that of medicine, beginning his medical training in 1791 in the office of Dr. Harris of Salisbury, N. C. In the following year he entered the Medical Department of the University of Pennsylvania where, under Rush, Wistar, Shippen, Barton, Khun, and others he completed his education. Shortly thereafter he obtained a commission as surgeon and served in the bloodless "Whiskey Insurrection" in western Pennsylvania (1794). Thereafter he declined a permanent army commission. Immediately after obtaining his M.D. (1796) he began the practise of medicine in Philadelphia. At first he had been Rush's favorite pupil; later they were estranged; but ultimately they became friends again and after Rush's death Caldwell wrote a sketch of his life for *Delaplaine's Repository* (1813). Due chiefly to the opposition of Rush he never became professor in the Medical Department of the University of Pennsylvania, though made professor in the faculty of physical sciences. He declined invitations to take part in the formation of three medical schools in New York, Baltimore, and Philadelphia respectively. In 1812 he edited the *Port Folio* of Philadelphia. His correspondence with many prominent officers made his record of the events of the War of 1812 prompt and interesting. In 1819 he accepted an invitation to become a founder of the Medical Department of Transylvania University at Lexington, Ky., and professor of the institutes of medicine and clinical practise. With $10,000 contributed by the state he purchased in Europe (1821) books for the Transylvania library, the first collection in the West. After eighteen years of successful work in Lexington, he concluded that industrial Louisville was a more logical city for a great medical center. He became the first professor at the Louisville Medical Institute (now University of Louisville) founded in 1837, and continued in this capacity until 1849 when he retired on account of advanced age. He was married, first, in 1799 to Eliza, daughter of Thomas Leaming of Philadelphia, and second, to Mrs. Barton, *née* Warner, of Kentucky. He succeeded in his purpose of being "the first introducer of true medical science into the Mississippi Valley." His literary work extended over more than sixty years during which time he wrote more than two hundred books and papers. He was strong in his belief in the power of nature to preserve health and cure disease as opposed to Rush's doctrine of "turning nature out of doors." Sound in the light of our present knowledge in many of his opinions, he nevertheless advocated phrenology, mesmerism, the theory of spontaneous generation, and the like.

[The chief source is the caustic *Autobiography of Chas. Caldwell* (1855) which has been called "the choicest repository of medical scandal in existence." An appendix to that volume lists Caldwell's many publications. Biographies are found in the *Western Jour. of Medicine and Surgery* (1853) and in a notice by B. H. Coates in *Proc. Am. Philos. Soc.*, vol. VI (1859).]
E. E. H.

CALDWELL, CHARLES HENRY BROMEDGE (June 11, 1823–Nov. 30, 1877), naval officer, son of Charles H. and Susan (Blagge) Caldwell, was born at Hingham, Mass. He entered the navy as midshipman on Feb. 27, 1838, and was promoted to lieutenant on Sept. 4, 1852. On Oct. 11, 1858, while on duty in the *Vandalia*, he commanded a detachment from that vessel, defeated a force of cannibal savages at Wega in the Fiji Islands, and burned their town. In 1862 he commanded the gunboat *Itasca* of the West Gulf blockading squadron under Admiral Farragut, and took part in the bombardment of Forts Jackson and St. Philip. On Apr. 20, 1862, Lieut. Caldwell in the *Itasca* and Lieut. Peirce Crosby in the *Pinola*, under Capt. H. H. Bell, were detailed on a night expedition to break a chain which extended from shore to shore below the forts. The movement was detected by the defenders of Fort Jackson, and its fire concentrated on the two vessels, without however preventing the parting of the cable, which left a passageway open on the left bank of the river. On Apr. 24 came the long-prepared execution of the plan to pass the forts, the entire success of which led to the speedy reduction of these important defenses and the capture of New Orleans. During the running fight, the *Itasca*, crippled by a shot which wrecked her boiler, was one of the three vessels of the fleet unable to get by the forts. Caldwell was obliged to drop down the river, out of action, and run his ship, which bore the scars of fourteen shots, ashore. He took part in the action at Grand Gulf on June 9, 1862. His promotion to commander followed, dating from July 16, 1862, during the autumn of which year he received command of the *Essex* and of the mortar flotilla in the Mississippi squadron, participating in the operations at Port Hudson during the spring of 1863. He was then transferred to the command of the *Glaucus* of the North Atlantic blockading squadron, 1863–64, and of the *R. R. Cuyler* of the same squadron until 1865. He was commissioned captain Dec. 12, 1867, was chief-of-staff of the North Atlantic Fleet in 1870, and was promoted commodore June 14, 1874.

[David D. Porter, *Naval Hist. of the Civil War* (1886) ; *Official Records* (*Navy*), 1 ser. XVIII; *Hist. of the Town of Hingham, Mass.* (1893), II, 117; *Report of the Secretary of the Navy*, 1862–65, inclusive; Navy Registers, 1824–1877.] **E. B.**

CALDWELL, DAVID (Mar. 22, 1725–Aug. 25, 1824), Presbyterian clergyman, the son of Andrew Caldwell, a Scotchman who emigrated to America and married Ann Stewart in 1718, was born in Lancaster County, Pa. A farmer's son, David followed the occupation of a carpenter in his early life. After graduation at the College of New Jersey (now Princeton)—where he was a friend of Benjamin Rush—in 1761, he studied for the Presbyterian ministry. He was licensed by the New Brunswick (N. J.) Presbytery in 1763, and ordained at Trenton in 1765. In 1766 he married Rachel Craighead. Becoming a missionary in North Carolina, he was installed pastor of the two churches at Buffalo and Alamance in that province in 1768. Thenceforth for half a century he was foremost in the community. He was a man of varied activities, owning a farm, conducting a classical school which had a high reputation, practising medicine, and reaching eminence as a preacher and as a leader in public affairs. In 1771 the agitation of the North Carolina Regulators reached its climax in civil war near his home. In an attempt to thwart hostilities, he negotiated both with Gov. Tryon and with the Regulators but was unable to prevent the battle of Alamance. He was prominent in the Revolution, being a member of the state constitutional convention in 1776. A few years later Cornwallis offered a reward of £200 for his capture, and he was obliged to remain in hiding for a while. His home was situated near the battlefield of Guilford Court House, and in that campaign his house was plundered by the enemy, and his library and papers were destroyed. After the battle (Mar. 15, 1781), he aided in caring for the sick and wounded. He was a member of the state convention which met to consider the new Federal Constitution, and like many other delegates he was opposed to ratification. One of the features in the proposed instrument of government to which he objected was the absence of a religious test. Soon after, he declined the presidency of the University of North Carolina on account of his age. He lived, however, many years longer, conducting his school, supporting the War of 1812, and preaching until 1820. He died in North Carolina, having very nearly rounded a century.

[E. W. Caruthers, *A Sketch of the Life and Character of the Rev. David Caldwell* (1842) ; Wm. H. Foote, *Sketches of N. C.* (1846) ; S. A. Ashe, *Biog. Hist. of N. C.*, vol. I (1905) ; Alex. Harris, *A Biog. Hist. of Lancaster County* (1872).] **E. K. A.**

CALDWELL, EUGENE WILSON (Dec. 3, 1870–June 20, 1918), Roentgenologist, born in Savannah, Mo., was the son of W. W. and Camilla (Kellogg) Caldwell. In his early boyhood, his parents moved to Kansas, in which state he grew up. After attending the public school, he studied electrical engineering at the University of Kansas. During his university studies he assisted Prof. Lucien O. Blake in his experiments on submarine telephony and gained the high praise of his teacher for his ingenuity. After his graduation as an electrical engineer in 1892 he went to New York and entered the service of the New York Telephone Company. In 1898 he had occasion to buy a second-hand Roentgen apparatus. He took such an intense interest in the new branch of sciences, foreseeing its great value for medicine and surgery, that he entered the University and Bellevue Hospital Medical College to study medicine, obtaining the degree of M.D. in 1905. In the meantime he had been appointed director of the Edward N. Gibbs Memorial X-Ray Laboratory which post he held until 1908.

He became one of the foremost Roentgenologists of the country. His inventive genius enabled him to make many valuable improvements on the Roentgen apparatus, among which may be mentioned an electrical interrupter, a new induction coil, an X-ray generator with valve tube rectification, a moving grid for the elimination of secondary radiation in Roentgenography, and various types of X-ray tubes. His work also on the Roentgen examination of the nasal accessory sinuses is of permanent value. In collaboration with Wm. A. Pusey he published *The Practical Application of the Roentgen Rays in Therapeutics and Diagnosis* (1903). During the World War he was commissioned major in the Medical Corps. He died a martyr to science. So intense was his application to the X-ray work that he contracted serious injuries which led to his death in 1918.

He was a member of the New York Academy

of Medicine; of the College of Physicians and Surgeons, Columbia University; of the Roentgen Ray Society of London; of the German Roentgen Society; and of a number of other scientific societies. He was married in 1913 to Elizabeth Perkins.

[*Am. Jour. of Roentgenology*, Dec. 1918, V, 575; *Am. Jour. of Electrotherapeutics and Radiology*, June 1918; *N. Y. Medic. Jour.*, June 29, 1918; *Jour. of the Am. Medic. Ass.*, June 29, 1918; *Who's Who in America*, 1916–17.]   A. A.—n.

CALDWELL, HENRY CLAY (Sept. 4, 1832–Feb. 15, 1915), jurist, was the son of Van and Susan M. Caldwell of Marshall County, Va., where he was born. His father, a well-known frontier character, moved in 1836 to Davis County on the Des Moines River, at that time part of Wisconsin Territory, and Henry passed his youth there, attending the common schools, where he obtained all the education he ever received. He then entered the law office of Wright & Knapp at Keosauqua, Van Buren County, Iowa, and, on his admission to the Iowa bar in 1852 in his twentieth year, became a partner in the firm. In 1856 he was elected prosecuting attorney for Van Buren County. On Mar. 25, 1857, he was married to Harriet Benton. A year later he became a member of the state legislature, acting as chairman of its judiciary committee during two sessions. In 1860 he was a delegate from Iowa to the Republican convention at Chicago which nominated Lincoln for the presidency. On the outbreak of the Civil War he enlisted in the 3rd Iowa Cavalry, was commissioned major, and subsequently became colonel of his regiment, participating in much heavy fighting in the Mississippi Valley. In June 1864, while yet on active service, he was appointed by President Lincoln United States district judge for the District of Arkansas. The situation at that time in the district was a difficult one, the judicial machinery being disorganized and the population sullen and impoverished. In addition, as an aftermath of the war, the volume of litigation was great, most of the cases involving novel and intricate problems, requiring extreme delicacy of treatment. The people of Arkansas viewed Caldwell at first with suspicion, if not aversion, as a Northern soldier and intruder. Displaying, however, great firmness and courage, and resolutely resisting political pressure, he administered justice with scrupulous impartiality, and by his tact, common sense, and expedition gradually obtained the respect and confidence of the populace. It was said of him that "during the six years that the carpet-bag régime lasted he was the greatest protection that the people of the state had," and it was through his

influence that a subsequent attempt in Congress to reimpose repressive conditions was frustrated. He remained district judge for twenty-five years, and was appointed circuit judge for the eighth Federal district in 1890 by President Harrison. He accepted the new position with reluctance as the district extended from Arkansas north to Minnesota and westward to Wyoming, but the creation of the United States circuit court of appeals ultimately enabled him as presiding judge to concentrate his work in St. Louis. In 1896 his name was prominently mentioned in connection with the Republican nomination for president. Four years later he dissociated himself from the party on its stand in relation to the gold standard, but firmly declined an offer of the nomination for vice-president in conjunction with W. J. Bryan. He resigned from the bench in 1903, retiring into private life, and in 1906 went to California where he passed his last days, dying in Los Angeles. His judicial career was distinguished by practical common sense and sturdy independence. He was identified with numerous important reforms in the Arkansas laws, including the introduction of code pleading, the amendment of the "Anaconda mortgage" law, and the state regulation of the liquor traffic. Standing six feet four inches in height, he had a massive head with a broad forehead and a flowing beard. In manner genial, sympathetic, and eminently approachable, he held strong opinions on most subjects and never hesitated to express them in clear, pungent language. His scrupulous honesty of mind and conduct was exemplified in his declining the appointment of chief justice of the United States Supreme Court, offered him by President Cleveland, assigning as a reason his lack of the necessary qualities of training and legal equipment.

[The article "Henry Clay Caldwell" by Edward H. Stiles in *Annals of Iowa*, 3 ser., VIII, 241, contains an excellent summary of Caldwell's judicial activities and the main incidents of his career. See also *Am. Law Rev.*, XXIV, 299, XXX, 282; *Case and Comment*, IV, 133, XXII, 87; and Fay Hempstead, *Hist. Rev. of Ark.* (1911).]   H. W. H. K.

CALDWELL, JAMES (Apr. 1734–Nov. 24, 1781), was a militant clergyman during the Revolutionary War. The family, traditionally of Huguenot origin, had emigrated from Scotland to Ireland, and thence to America, and James Caldwell, son of settler John Caldwell, was born in Charlotte County, Va. He graduated at Princeton in 1759, and was ordained by the presbytery of New Brunswick, N. J., in 1761. He was settled as pastor of the First Presbyterian Church at Elizabethtown (now Elizabeth), N. J.; his congregation included men of unusual prominence, Gov. Livingston, Col. Francis Barber, Boudinot, Dayton, and others. On Mar. 14, 1763 he was married to Hannah Ogden.

Caldwell belonged to the "muscular type" of Christianity. He was an eloquent preacher, and during the war was very active in his patriotism. In 1776 he was appointed chaplain of Dayton's New Jersey brigade, and for a time was assistant commissary-general, with headquarters at Chatham. Rewards were offered, so it is stated, for his capture, and he often went armed. His church was used as a hospital during the war, but on Jan. 25, 1780 it was burned by a refugee. Caldwell's family, meanwhile, on account of exposure to attack had moved to the neighboring village of Connecticut Farms (Union), where on June 7, 1780 Mrs. Caldwell was killed by a random bullet during Knyphausen's invasion. Two weeks later the battle of Springfield took place (June 23) in which Caldwell—often known as the "Soldier Parson"—according to an often repeated story, urged his men to use the hymn-books in the neighboring church as extemporized wadding, exhorting them, "Now put Watts into them, boys." The following year, at Elizabethtown Point, he was shot and killed by an American sentry. The two men were in dispute over a package which Caldwell carried, and various charges were made regarding the sentinel's conduct; he was eventually tried and executed for murder. A monument to the memory of Mr. and Mrs. Caldwell was erected at Elizabeth. Another, in front of the church at Springfield, commemorates the battle and Caldwell's part therein.

[Nicholas Murray, *Notes, Hist. and Biog., Concerning Elizabethtown* (1844), and "A Memoir of the Rev. Jas. Caldwell," *Proc. of the N. J. Hist. Soc.*, 1848–49; E. Kempshall, *Caldwell and the Revolution* (1880); Wm. B. Sprague, *Annals of the Am. Pulpit*, vol. III (1858); *Inscriptions on Tombstones . . . of the First Presbyt. Ch. . . . at Elizabeth, N. J.* (1892); Jas. F. Folsom, "Manuscript Light on Chaplain Jas. Caldwell's Death," *Proc. of the N. J. Hist. Soc.*, Jan. 1916.]

E. K. A.

CALDWELL, JOSEPH (Apr. 21, 1773–Jan. 27, 1835), mathematician, college president, the youngest of the three children of Joseph Caldwell and Rachel (Harker) Caldwell, was born in Lamington, N. J., two days after his father's death. The family, in somewhat straitened financial circumstances, moved to Princeton when Joseph was eleven years old. There he entered the grammar school which had the personal attention of Dr. John Witherspoon, for several years the distinguished head of the College of New Jersey (Princeton). His early education was interrupted by the removal of the family to Newark and later still to Elizabethtown (now Elizabeth). But in 1787, when Joseph was four-

teen years old, he reëntered the grammar school at Princeton and a few months later entered the college from which he was graduated in the class of 1791 at the age of nineteen. For a short time he taught in a school for young children and later was assistant in an academy. In 1795 he was made a tutor in mathematics in Princeton, and in 1796 he was called to the professorship of mathematics in the University of North Carolina which had opened its doors in 1795. In 1804 he was elected president. In 1812 he retired from the presidency to resume the chair of mathematics in order to devote more time to study and teaching. In 1817 he was induced to resume the chief office of the institution and in that position he continued during the remainder of his life.

In the spring and summer of 1824 he went to Europe to secure philosophical and scientific apparatus and books for the University library. In 1830 he erected, out of his personal funds, for which he was reimbursed by the University trustees a few days before his death, a building in which use could be made of the telescope and other astronomical instruments which he had brought from Europe. This was the first observatory established in connection with any educational institution in the United States. Caldwell's European experience also aroused his imagination and interest on the subject of internal improvements. His very advanced and practical views, which were set out in a series of articles (1828), over the pen name of "Carlton," in which he urged the state to provide transportation facilities, gained for him the name of the "father of internal improvements" in North Carolina.

He was an early and conspicuous advocate of the cause of common schools. In 1832, three years before his death, he published a series of eleven *Letters on Popular Education Addressed to the People of North Carolina*. In these writings he described the backward educational condition of the state which he charged to the "fatal delusion" that taxation was "contrary to the genius of republican government." He criticized the state for its failure to provide schools and suggested plans for public elementary, secondary, and higher education, provisions for the training of teachers, and other features of a modern school system.

He was married twice: in 1804 to Susan Rowan of Fayetteville, who died three years later; and in 1809 to Mrs. Helen (Hogg) Hooper of Hillsboro, the widow of William Hooper, son of one of the signers of the Declaration of Independence. He was an effective teacher and a scientist of wide and disciplined knowledge. In 1813 he served North Carolina as scientific expert in running the boundary line between North Carolina and South Carolina. He was a man of deeply religious nature, had been licensed to preach by the Presbytery of New Brunswick while he was at Princeton, and was an effective if not eloquent preacher. Dignified and often stern in manner, he was described as "strong of arm and swift of foot," capable of inspiring respect and confidence and, in the disorderly, fear. A spirited and militant controversialist, utterly fearless, and a keen analyst, he was often driven into bitter partisan controversies by attacks upon himself or upon the University for alleged aristocratic views or tendencies. A monument to his memory was erected on the campus of the University of North Carolina in 1858.

[See *The Autobiography and Biography of Rev. Jos. Caldwell* (1860); Walker Anderson, *Oration on the Life and Character of the Rev. Jos. Caldwell* (1835); Kemp P. Battle, *Hist. of the Univ. of N. C.* (2 vols., 1907, 1912); Hope Summerell Chamberlain, *Old Days in Chapel Hill* (1926); *Univ. of N. C. Record*, Apr. 1900; *N. C. Univ. Mag.*, May 1844, Mar. 1860; F. P. Venable, "A College President of a Hundred Years Ago," in *Univ. of N. C. Record*, Apr. 1911; C. A. Smith, "Presbyterians in Educational Work in N. C. since 1813," in *Union Seminary Rev.*, Dec. 1913, Jan. 1914. Caldwell's *Letters on Popular Education* were reprinted in Chas. L. Coon, *The Beginnings of Public Education in N. C.*, vol. II (1908), and are treated briefly by Edgar W. Knight in *Public School Education in N. C.* (1916). Some of his sermons were printed in Colin McIver, *The Southern Preacher* (1824). His *Compendious System of Elementary Geometry* was published in 1822. The manuscript of his *A New System of Geometry* (1806) is in the Univ. of N. C. Lib.]
E. W. K.

CALEF, ROBERT (1648–Apr. 13, 1719), Boston merchant, writer and disputant on the subject of witchcraft, was probably born in England. By 1688 he was settled as a cloth merchant in Boston where he came into prominence in 1693 by accusing Cotton Mather of attempting to stir up a Boston witchcraft delusion in the wake of the Salem tragedy. Calef obtained a copy of "Another Brand Pluckt out of the Burning," Cotton Mather's manuscript account of his efforts to exorcise Margaret Rule, and circulated his own observations concerning the seance, containing unsavory insinuations as to Mather's, and his father's, motives and methods. Cotton Mather caused Calef to be arrested for libel, but dropped the case after receiving a temperate but ambiguous explanation. Calef incorporated "Another Brand," with the correspondence, in a book called *More Wonders of the Invisible World*, which he completed in 1697, but was unable to induce any Boston printer to publish. It was printed in London, in 1700, and caused a great sensation in Boston, for it not only at-

tacked the Mathers, but included a well-documented and devastating account of the Salem trials of 1692. A committee of Cotton Mather's congregation replied in a pamphlet, *Some Few Remarks upon a Scandalous Book* (1701). Increase Mather caused a copy of *More Wonders* to be burned in the Harvard yard.

The controversy between the partisans of Calef and of the Mathers has never ceased. William F. Poole, for instance, declares that Calef was only stirring the ashes of a dead fire, with the purpose of maligning the Boston clergy (*Memorial History of Boston*, 1882, II, 165 ff.), whilst Charles W. Upham asserts, "Calef's book . . . drove the Devil out of the preaching, the literature, and the popular sentiment of the world" (*Salem Witchcraft and Cotton Mather*, 1869, p. 83). The truth no doubt lies between these extremes. That *More Wonders* was a direct and powerful condemnation of the seventeenth century view of witchcraft, written in terms to arouse the most intellectually inert, there can be no doubt. That Cotton Mather failed to reply is significant.

Calef was not a rationalist. He rested his arguments on the Bible, and admitted "That there are Witches . . . but what this witchcraft is, or wherein it does consist, seems to be the whole difficulty." Yet this common basis of thought with his contemporaries made his book the more powerful. One may, however, admit that *More Wonders* occupies an important place in the literature of witchcraft, without sharing Calef's opinion of his opponents. Their counter charges that his motives were political, and that he was assisted in writing the book, have never been substantiated. There is no reason to question his declared motive of discrediting the doctrines that produced the Salem tragedy; and he succeeded, completely.

A persistent belief that *More Wonders* is the work of Robert Calef, Jr. (1676?–1722?) was effectually refuted by George Lincoln Burr. This younger Calef, who generally signed himself Calfe, was one of eight children. The father in later life held several town offices in Boston and Roxbury, where he died on Apr. 13, 1719. The son held several petty offices in Boston.

[*More Wonders*. There are six editions after the first (of which there were two impressions), the best being contained in S. G. Drake, *Annals of the Witchcraft* (3 vols., 1866), and in G. L. Burr, *Narratives of the Witchcraft Cases* (1914), which includes a critical discussion of the question of authorship. See also W. S. Harris, "Robert Calef," *Granite Mo.*, May 1907.] R. L. P.

CALHOUN, JOHN (Oct. 14, 1806–Oct. 13, 1859), politician, was best known for his friendship with Lincoln and his reputed complicity in election abuses in early Kansas. He has sometimes been confused with the John Calhoun (1808–59) who founded the *Chicago Democrat*. Born in Boston, the son of Andrew and Martha (Chamberlin) Calhoun, he studied law in New York state, and settled in 1830 at Springfield, Ill. On Dec. 29, 1831, he was married to Sarah Cutter of Sangamon County, by whom he had nine children. He served in the Black Hawk war and became surveyor of Sangamon County. Being attracted to Lincoln, he assisted him in the study of surveying and made him his deputy, thus forming a friendship which, in spite of Calhoun's prominence as a Douglas Democrat, persisted through life. He was elected to the Illinois legislature in 1838; was made clerk of the Illinois House of Representatives (1839–40 and 1840–41); engaged in the business of constructing a railroad from Jacksonville to Springfield; served as clerk of the circuit court of Sangamon County; and was thrice chosen mayor of Springfield. In contests for Congress, for the state Senate, and for the Democratic gubernatorial nomination, he was unsuccessful. At a state fair at Springfield in October 1854 he joined in a debate in which Lincoln and Douglas were also participants; and Lincoln always had a high regard for his ability as a stump speaker. Through the influence of Douglas, Calhoun was appointed in 1854 by President Pierce as surveyor general of Kansas and Nebraska. He attended the constitutional convention of 1857 at Lecompton as delegate, and was made president of that body. At first he led the fight to have the Lecompton Constitution submitted to the people; but, failing in this, he acquiesced in the program by which the vote of Dec. 21, 1857, was so taken as virtually to deny the ballot to free-state men, and his report of this vote, transmitted to Buchanan, produced a crisis in the Kansas situation. When in 1858 the legislature, then in free-state hands, ordered an investigation concerning alleged frauds in the December election, Calhoun left for Missouri, and his clerk, L. A. McLean, asserted that he had taken the election returns with him. A melodramatic scene followed when a sheriff found the coveted papers where McLean had concealed them, in a candle box buried under a woodpile near the surveyor's office in Lecompton. So intense was the popular indignation that McLean fled, and President Buchanan accommodated Calhoun by removing his office to Nebraska City, as he could not have returned to Kansas. Much of the odium for the Lecompton Constitution was visited upon Calhoun; and he was censured by Gov. Walker when testifying before a committee of Congress. In a vindication by his brother, A. H. Calhoun

(manuscript, cited in *Transactions of the Kansas State Historical Society,* VIII, 1–2) the blame for the candle-box episode is placed upon McLean; and Calhoun is represented as a conservative who opposed the design of the Southern element to fasten slavery upon Kansas in the face of a preponderant free-state sentiment. Calhoun died at St. Joseph, Mo., Oct. 13, 1859, much broken in spirit.

[See G. A. Crawford, "The Candle-Box under the Wood-Pile," *Trans. Kan. Hist. Soc.*, X, 196–204; John Carroll Power, *Hist. of the Early Settlers of Sangamon County, Ill.* (1876), a somewhat inaccurate volume; "The Covode Investigation," *House Report No. 648, 36 Cong.*, 1 Sess.; A. J. Beveridge, *Abraham Lincoln, 1809–58* (1928); Paul M. Angle, "The Minor Collection: A Criticism," *Atlantic Mo.* 143:516–25 (Apr. 1929). In the article by Mr. Angle certain supposed Lincoln documents published in the *Atlantic Mo.* (1928–29), including alleged letters from Lincoln to Calhoun, are shown to be forgeries; and "Sally Calhoun" (supposed daughter of John), who is represented as one of the links in the transmittal of the reputed Lincoln material to posterity, is proved never to have existed.]   J. G. R.

CALHOUN, JOHN CALDWELL (Mar. 18, 1782–Mar. 31, 1850), was secretary of war, vice-president, senator, secretary of state, and political philosopher. Three Scotch-Irish brothers Colquhoun, Colhoun or Calhoun, in the unstable spelling of the time, entered Pennsylvania about 1733, and moved southward by stages. By 1746 one of them, James, was dwelling with Catherine his wife, four sons and a daughter in Bath County on the Virginia frontier. Driven thence by the Indian disorders after Braddock's defeat, this family and some of its kinsfolk founded the "Calhoun settlement" in the South Carolina uplands near the Savannah River. James appears to have died in peace, but Catherine was killed by a party of Cherokees in 1760 at a spot which her youngest son Patrick marked with a slab. The four sons clung to their steadings through foul times and fair, supporting the American cause against Great Britain and attaining considerable repute. Patrick in particular was for many years a member of the South Carolina legislature. As a pronounced individualist in political philosophy, he opposed the ratification of the Federal Constitution. Having lost a first wife without surviving issue, he married Martha Caldwell and by her had a daughter and four sons, of whom the youngest but one was named for an uncle whom Tories had murdered, John Caldwell.

After a normal childhood in a family prosperous enough to possess a score or two of slaves when slaves were few in that primitive region, the youth went in his fourteenth year to become a pupil of his brother-in-law, the talented Moses Waddel, in Columbia County, Ga. But Mrs. Waddel's death soon caused the academy to suspend, and young Calhoun returned home, where his father's death in the same year, 1796, cast some of the burdens of the farm upon him. Here he continued at work and at play till the turn of the century. Then an elder brother, who was in business at Charleston, prompted him to prepare for a profession. John returned for a time to Waddel's academy, then entered the junior class at Yale College, graduated in 1804, studied law in Tapping Reeve's school at Litchfield, Conn., and in Henry W. DeSaussure's office at Charleston, was admitted to the bar in 1807, and opened an office at Abbeville near his native home. Though quickly acquiring a substantial practise, he found the pursuit uncongenial and resolved to abandon it as soon as opportunity should permit. This came within a few years through his marriage and his entrance into public life.

John Ewing Calhoun, cousin of Patrick, had attained wealth and distinction in the South Carolina lowlands, partly through his marriage to Floride Bouneau, who inherited from her Huguenot family a plantation on Cooper River. After her husband's death in 1802, the widow continued a practise, fairly common among grandees of the "rice coast," of spending the summers at Newport and the winters at Charleston or on the plantation. John C. Calhoun became a protégé of hers and an intimate of her household. Friendship with her daughter Floride, who was ten years his junior, ripened into love which led to a happy marriage in January 1811. His bride brought him a modest fortune, which, because of his objection to the lowland custom of marriage settlements, was put under his control. This property when added to his own patrimony and savings made Calhoun financially independent, though the increase of his family (nine children all told) kept a degree of frugality expedient. Calhoun enlarged his landholdings and in 1825 established a commodious plantation homestead in his native district. Named "Fort Hill" from its having been a fortified spot in days of Indian warfare, the dwelling still stands on what is now the campus of Clemson College.

Calhoun's interest in public affairs doubtless began at his father's knee, and his Republicanism was intensified by his encounters with Federalists during his years at New Haven and Litchfield. His own political career began in 1807 with a speech at a public meeting in Abbeville denouncing British aggressions upon American maritime rights. In the next year he was elected to the South Carolina legislature, in time to share in the revision of representation to give numerical preponderance in the lower house to the uplands of the state while the control of the Senate was left with the lowlands. This device

of "concurrent majorities" or mutual checks was one which he was eventually to propose for the relief of sectional apprehensions in the United States. But at the time of his election to Congress in 1810, and for long thereafter, his federal program had quite another direction.

Calhoun's service in national halls began with the convening of the Twelfth Congress which the "war hawks" were to make famous. Regardless of consequences in Europe and impatient of opposition from New England, these young men were resolute for war with Britain. Clay as speaker made the most effective use of the copious talent available in committee assignments, and Calhoun soon became acting chairman of the committee on foreign affairs. After months of labor to gain a favorable majority in the House, he presented on June 3, 1812, a report in ringing phrase recommending a declaration of war. Since James Monroe's authorship of this (*American Historical Review*, XIII, 309, 310) was kept secret, the episode spread Calhoun's fame afar.

As long as the war continued he wrought constantly to raise troops, to provide funds, to speed the service of supply, to improve the currency, to regulate commerce, to do everything in short which he thought conducive to military success. Disasters to American arms made him double his legislative efforts to wring victory from defeat. He was in the thick of every important debate, laboring to overcome the obstructionism of Randolph and Webster alike but occasionally separating himself from the bulk of his customary associates to find other allies wherever he might. A. J. Dallas called him, in happy phrase, "the young Hercules who carried the war on his shoulders."

Calhoun was sufficiently a supporter of the administration to indorse the treaty of Ghent; but its inconclusive character as concerned the issues which had provoked the war gave him an expectation that the peace would prove but a truce and left him with a continued zeal for promoting American strength. In a speech of Jan. 31, 1816, he advocated as the first consideration an effective navy, including steam frigates, and in the second place a standing army of adequate size; and as further preparation for emergency "great permanent roads," "a certain encouragement" to manufactures, and a system of internal taxation which would not be subject like customs duties to collapse by a war-time shrinkage of maritime trade (*Works*, II, 135–53). In the further course of the session he spoke for a national bank and again for internal improvements and protective tariff, deprecating sectional spirit and "refined arguments on the constitution" (*Works*, II, 101,

192), and asserting his own preference for "that erectness of mind which in all cases is disposed to embrace what is in itself just and wise." There can be no doubt that in this period Calhoun's early Republicanism in so far as it connoted allegiance to state rights was in eclipse. The word "nation" was often on his lips, and his conscious aim was to enhance national unity which he identified with national power.

Calhoun was at this time described as "the most elegant speaker that sits in the House. . . . His gestures are easy and graceful, his manner forcible, and language elegant; but above all, he confines himself closely to the subject, which he always understands, and enlightens everyone within hearing; having said all that a statesman should say, he is done" (letter of J. C. Jewett, in *William and Mary Quarterly*, XVII, 143). His talent for public speaking seems to have been acquired by systematic effort. A later critic, remarking the sharp contrast between his talking and speaking tones, said that Calhoun "had so carefully cultivated his naturally poor voice as to make his utterance clear, full, and distinct in speaking and while not at all musical it yet fell pleasantly on the ear" (H. S. Fulkerson, *Random Recollections of Early Days in Mississippi*, 1885, p. 63).

But his power in debate did not incline Calhoun to remain always in legislative halls. Before the end of his third term in Congress he accepted appointment as secretary of war in Monroe's cabinet. His conspicuous concern with military affairs made him an obvious choice for this post; and during the seven and a half years of his tenure he discharged its functions with marked capacity, improving the organization of the army in general and establishing in particular the useful bureaux of the surgeon-general, commissary-general, and quartermaster-general.

In the cabinet Crawford and Calhoun were in habitual disagreement, but Adams and he were for some years in close accord. As late as the fall of 1821 Adams wrote in his diary: "Calhoun is a man of fair and candid mind, of honorable principles, of clear and quick understanding, of cool self-possession, of enlarged philosophical views, and of ardent patriotism. He is above all sectional and factious prejudices, more than any other statesman of this Union with whom I have ever acted" (Adams, *Memoirs*, V, 361). But with the Federalist party dead and Monroe reëlected for a final term in the presidency there now began a free-for-all race for the succession. Crawford was the candidate of the reviving state-rights school now styled Radicals; Adams and Clay, Lowndes and Calhoun became rivals for

the leadership of the nationalists; while Jackson turned from military to civilian campaigning as the candidate of those who were more interested in popular power than with details of policy. The homes of these candidates lay in an arc reaching from Massachusetts through Kentucky and Tennessee to Georgia and South Carolina. The choice among them must needs lie with the states of the middle seaboard. Lowndes's death left Calhoun the favorite son of his state; Pennsylvania for a while gave promise of support because of his advocacy of tariff protection, and he had hopes also of New York and some lesser states. But the nominating convention in Pennsylvania gave its indorsement to Jackson for the first office and to Calhoun for the second. Thereupon Calhoun lowered his ambition for the time being and was elected vice-president in 1824 by a large majority. For the presidency Jackson had a plurality in the electoral college, but Clay's influence gave Adams the victory at the hands of the House of Representatives. Adams's appointment of Clay as secretary of state in sequel to this gave Jackson a mighty grudge, spurred Randolph to seek new epithets, and caused Calhoun to remark that it created a most dangerous precedent which the people would presumably reprove at the next election (*Correspondence*, p. 231).

In presiding over the Senate Calhoun was meticulous, attending assiduously but confining his participation within the positive specifications of the Constitution. His abstinence from interrupting Randolph's vituperations of Adams and Clay, except when a senator raised a point of order, involved him in a newspaper controversy in which the president himself was his putative opponent. Another episode of some salience arose from a journalist's charge that Calhoun while secretary of war had participated in the profits of a fortification contract. Calhoun asked the House of Representatives to investigate the matter as a "grand inquest of the nation," and he discontinued his attendance upon the Senate until a House committee had cleared him. Conspicuously cherishing his repute, he was shaping his course for the White House, though the Adams-Jackson battle clearly postponed the goal for him for another quadrennium. For the time being he chose the Jackson alliance and was elected in 1828 on the Jackson ticket for a second term as vice-president. His hope now was to succeed to the presidency after a single term of Jackson.

But the next four years brought events great and small which impinged heavily upon Calhoun's career and upon the course of American history. Jackson's predilection for Van Buren whom he put at the head of the cabinet was itself ominous; and Eaton's appointment as secretary of war, followed by his indiscreet marriage and Mrs. Calhoun's exclusion of his wife from social recognition, brought a strain between the President and Vice-President. Close upon this came Crawford's betrayal of the fact that in Monroe's cabinet in 1818 Calhoun had censured the capture of Spanish posts by Jackson during his campaign against the Seminoles. Jackson's egotistic sense of outrage now produced a breach which Calhoun found irreparable.

Meanwhile developments in South Carolina, which for some years had followed an ominous course, were producing a national crisis. Successive measures in Congress enhancing and proposing further enhancement of protection to favored industries caused increasingly stringent opposition, coming as they did in a decade of declining cotton prices. By the middle of the twenties this opposition movement was spreading widely in the South and was becoming linked with a denial of the constitutional power of Congress in the premises. Calhoun was an object of censure in anti-tariff publications because of his formerly conspicuous and still unrecanted protectionism. He confronted a grave dilemma. If he held his course South Carolina would repudiate him, and if he changed it he would lose his following in Pennsylvania. But his personal fortunes, whether as a cotton planter or a presidential aspirant, were of smaller concern than the national prospect. Early in 1827 he defeated the Woollens Bill by his casting vote in the Senate; and before the end of the year he was deprecating the project of a higher-tariff convention as tending to place the great geographical interests in hostile array, to promote political plundering, and eventually "to make two of one nation." He was now finding it "a great defect of our system; that the separate geographical interests are not sufficiently guarded." But these reflections were expressed only in a confidential letter (*Correspondence*, pp. 250, 251). At the beginning of the next year he joined in a jockeying project to divide the eastern and western groups of protectionists to the defeat of both; but the plan was thwarted by Van Buren and the result was the "tariff of abominations" (*Works*, III, 48–51).

During the congressional recess of 1828, which Calhoun spent as usual at his plantation home, he painstakingly informed himself of the South Carolina situation. He was already acquainted with the legislature's resolutions of 1825 and 1827 denying the constitutionality of protective tariffs and with the turbulent writings of Thomas Cooper, R. J. Turnbull, and sundry others. Reaching now the conviction that without mitigation

of grievances desperate recourses were in train, he complied with a request of W. C. Preston and wrote a report for a committee of the legislature. The result, modified by the committee, was the "South Carolina Exposition" (*Works*, VI, 1–57), embodying the doctrine which was to become famous as nullification. After asserting the unconstitutionality of the protective tariff and maintaining the power of a state within its own area to estop the enforcement of an unconstitutional act, the document concluded by recommending that decisive steps be deferred in the hope that reflection by the people and Congress might bring abandonment of the obnoxious policy. The legislature ordered the report printed in a large edition, and it adopted resolutions asking the sister states to express their sentiments in the premises. The Exposition was a warning of what might be done should the protectionist program be pursued. Its promulgation did not commit the state to a course of action; and in particular it committed Calhoun to nothing, for he kept his authorship confidential until the middle of 1831.

Having thus devised a plan for use in a contingency, Calhoun sought in various ways to prevent the contingency from coming. For a while he pinned his faith to Jackson; then he nursed a project for a complete intersectional accord. The West, by a constitutional amendment, was to be given a great public-land fund for internal improvements; the South was to procure a reduction of the tariff in the main to a revenue basis; but the North was to be placated by sundry special tariff concessions (*American Historical Review*, VI, 741–45, conversation reported by J. H. Hammond). But events proceeded otherwise. The systematically protective tariff of 1832 was enacted by Congress and approved by Jackson in July, whereupon Calhoun hastened home to guide proceedings there.

In August he published his famous letter to Gov. Hamilton (*Works*, VI, 144–93), containing the final embodiment of nullification doctrine. This is a superb piece of rigorous reasoning. Premising the possession of sovereignty by the people and the trustee character of all governments, and asserting that in the American federal system the central and state governments alike are mere organs of popular power, it argued, on the basis of the records of the Federal Convention, that "with us *the people* mean *the people of the several states*," whose delegates and conventions framed and ratified the Constitution creating the general government as their common agent. The ratification by any state bound all its citizens to obey the Constitution although some of them might individually have opposed it. The purpose of any constitution is at once to empower and to restrain the government; and if the general government should exceed its powers against the will of the people of a state it is within their legitimate power, by means of a convention though not by act of the legislature, to declare the congressional act null and to require the state government to prohibit enforcement within the limits of the state. "It is the constitution that annuls an unconstitutional act. Such an act is itself void and of no effect." Any court may proclaim such nullity, but the people of a state retain a similar power which no federal agency may override. Indeed, the general government in all its branches must acquiesce in such declaration of nullity, so far as enforcement within the state is concerned; or, as an escape, it may apply to the states to obtain a grant of the disputed power in the form of an amendment to the Constitution. But if the amendment should fail of ratification, "no alternative would remain for the general government but a compromise or its permanent abandonment." Nullification would give no ground for clash of arms; it would be "a conflict of moral, and not physical force," a trial before courts and juries. The rights of nullification and secession inhere in the sovereign states; but the two programs are poles apart in their purposes and effects. The object of secession is to withdraw a member from the Union; while the object of nullification is to confine the general government within its prescribed limits of power in order to perpetuate the Union on an equable basis. Nullification may indeed be followed by secession in case a proposed amendment should be ratified by the sister states to such effect as to defeat the object of the Union so far as the nullifying member is concerned. The power of nullification, it is true, tends to weaken the general government; but the power of amendment is an adequate offset. The two powers establish a system of mutual checks, in effect a system of government requiring agreement by concurrent majorities in critical issues, and as such it is in the line which genuinely free institutions have followed ever since the Tribunate in ancient Rome. Such a system, which inheres in the Federal Constitution as thus interpreted, maintains "the ascendency of the constitution-making authority over the law-making—the concurring over the absolute majority." It maintains a power, essential for liberty and the general welfare, "to compel the parts of society to be just to one another by compelling them to consult the interest of one another."

Affairs now marched rapidly. A legislature was elected in South Carolina with an over-whelming majority favorable to nullification; this was called into special session and in turn it ordered the election of delegates to a convention of the state; the convention adopted an ordinance nullifying the tariff acts of 1828 and 1832; and the legislature thereupon enacted sundry laws to make the ordinance effective. Thus by the beginning of December 1832 the schedule was complete, though by its own terms the ordinance was not to take effect until the first day of February following.

December brought a battle of proclamations between President Jackson and the governor of South Carolina, and a mustering of military forces. But these things had somewhat of a sham character, for the concrete issue was the tariff, which could only be handled by Congress. In the Senate R. Y. Hayne had proved not letter-perfect in the nullification doctrine, and he was now shifted to the governor's chair to make room for Calhoun who resigned the vice-presidency and appeared on the floor of the Senate at the turn of the year. Jackson soon sent a message to Congress asking to be empowered in case of need to use armed force to execute the laws. A bill introduced in response, commonly known as the Force Bill, brought Calhoun into debate with Webster in which he opposed argument to eloquence with better effect than Hayne had done two years before. Meanwhile Calhoun joined hands with Clay in support of a tariff bill to reduce duties by degrees and put the customs on a revenue basis at the end of a decade. This bill, which repealed the tariff act of 1832, was passed and became law on the same day as the Force Bill.

In South Carolina an informal meeting of the leading nullifiers had postponed the effectuation of the ordinance, and Gov. Hayne had called a second meeting of the convention for Mar. 11, 1833. Calhoun hastened to Columbia to persuade the members to accept the compromise tariff as a settlement of the essential issue. B. W. Leigh as commissioner from Virginia to South Carolina aided these efforts; and the convention repealed the ordinance nullifying the tariff but adopted another nullifying the Force Bill. Thus every one saved his face. The result of the contretemps as a whole was in South Carolina the virtual destruction of Calhoun's opponents and an eclipse of his own lieutenants; in the United States an alignment of new parties with Calhoun holding himself and South Carolina somewhat aloof from both.

For some years the advocates of Clay's "American system" had maintained a rudimentary organization as National Republicans to oppose the administration. And now state-rights adherents in many Southern states reacted so strongly against Jackson's proclamation and the Force Bill that they were disposed to embrace an alliance against the President. Hence the coalition in the middle thirties to form the Whig party opposing the Democratic. It was under this régime that the final phase of Calhoun's career took form. In sequel to the recent clash he retained his repugnance toward Jackson and his favorites. At the same time he distrusted Clay and held Webster in low esteem except for oratory, and he was not disposed to make a "choice of evils" (*Correspondence*, p. 330). He revived his presidential ambitions ere long and acted as an auxiliary of the Whigs. But no sooner was Jackson succeeded in the White House by the mild-mannered Van Buren than Calhoun began to shift to the Democratic side. In the Senate he was constantly attentive to the public business; and whatever were his views upon banking, public lands, or foreign relations, he voiced them in a manner which proved his concern with sound government for the whole country. The growth of his prestige gave him a following in all parts of the South and rehabilitated him in many Northern quarters. But the rise of the abolition agitation made impossible for him any return to nationalistic paths.

In the premises of negro slavery the South was more conspicuously marked as a distinct community with a minority status than in regard to the tariff; and the menace of a hostile domination was reckoned to involve not mere shrinkage of income but destruction of capital and a precipitation of social chaos. Organization and strategy were widely demanded in Southern defense, and Calhoun came to be regarded as the main source of plans, arguments, and inspiration. His devices were manifold: to suppress agitation, to praise the slaveholding system; to promote Southern prosperity and expansion; to procure a Western alliance; to frame a fresh plan of government by concurrent majorities; to form a Southern bloc; to warn the North of the dangers of Southern desperation; to appeal for Northern magnanimity as indispensable for the saving of the Union. A devoted lieutenant, Dixon H. Lewis of Alabama, wrote in 1840: "Calhoun is now my principal associate, and he is too intellectual, too industrious, too intent in the struggle of politics to suit me except as an occasional companion. There is no relaxation in him. On the contrary, when I seek relaxation in him, he screws me only the higher in some sort of excitement" (Hunt, *Calhoun*, p. 228).

Was the conflict irrepressible? Calhoun feared it might prove so, but he hoped and labored unceasingly to find means for its avoidance. If he turned again and again to formulæ, that was the ingrained bent of his mind. He could never consent to mere "muddling through."

Reluctantly he faced the slavery issue. In 1815 he had expressed shame at the record of South Carolina in having caused the Constitution to forbid for twenty years any congressional prohibition of the foreign slave trade (*Works*, II, 133). In 1820 the stringency of debate on the Missouri question caused him to remark that he could "scarcely conceive of a cause of sufficient power to divide this Union, unless a belief in the slaveholding states, that it is the intention of the other states gradually to undermine their property in their slaves and that a disunion is the only means to avert the evil. Should so dangerous a mode of believing once take root, no one can calculate the consequences" (Hunt, *Calhoun*, p. 54). In the next year he expressed relief at the prospect "that a question which has so deeply agitated this country will be settled forever" (*Correspondence*, p. 181). But Garrison's work revived his apprehensions and set his feet upon their final path. At the close of his debate with Webster in February 1833, he said that slavery might give the South greater reason than the tariff to cherish state-rights.

Within the next two years the increase of anti-slavery activities and a turbulent counter-agitation in the South determined him to meet the issue "on the frontier"; and he became the most thoroughgoing advocate of the exclusion of incendiary publications from the mails and of anti-slavery petitions from Congress. His own devices in these premises were too technical to procure much indorsement, though the essential purposes were attained for the time being by other means. There was virtually no Southern dissent from his declaration in 1836 that abolition "strikes directly and fatally, not only at our prosperity, but our existence as a people. . . . The door must be closed against all interference on the part of the general government in any form, whether in the District of Columbia, or in the states or territories. The highest grounds are the safest" (*Niles' Weekly Register*, L, 432).

By the next year he had followed Governors Miller and McDuffie of South Carolina and the Rev. James Smylie of Mississippi toward asserting that slavery was a positive good: "Our fate, as a people, is bound up in the question. If we yield we will be extirpated; but if we successfully resist, we will be the greatest and most flourishing people of modern time. It is the best substratum of population in the world; and one on which great and flourishing Commonwealths may be most easily and safely reared" (*Corre-*

spondence, p. 369; see also *Works*, III, 179, 180). And by 1838 he was even contemplating a separation of the Union, though resolved still to labor for less drastic programs (*Correspondence*, p. 391).

The issue, ramifying endlessly, involved the mathematics of equilibrium in the Senate, the admission of new states, the organization of territories as prospective states, and the cherishing of sectional prestige for the sake of morale. In premises which he considered unessential Calhoun deprecated controversy. Thus he suppressed a movement in South Carolina to nullify the tariff of 1842; and on sundry other matters he was conciliatory in this period when his hopes were high for the presidency through a Democratic nomination. But in the main, and upon every issue which he thought vital, he was disposed to force the fighting, to lead a campaign of aggressive defense of "Southern rights."

He had spoken in favor of the annexation of Texas immediately after the battle of San Jacinto in 1836. But his assertions from the outset that the slaveholding states had a special interest in the question operated rather to delay than to speed the achievement. At length A. P. Upshur, secretary of state under Tyler, negotiated a treaty; and upon Upshur's death a maneuver by H. A. Wise carried Calhoun into that office to complete the proceedings. In the department Calhoun found a note from Mr. Pakenham communicating a dispatch from Lord Aberdeen to the effect that the British government desired to see slavery abolished in Texas and throughout the world, but that it had no purpose to disturb the domestic tranquillity of the slaveholding states of the Union. Calhoun seized the occasion to write and publish a reply to Pakenham saying that abolition in Texas would necessarily impinge upon the domestic security of the states adjacent, and proceeding to praise negro slavery in terms even stronger than he had previously used (*Works*, II, 333–339). This again was bad strategy. The treaty was defeated in the Senate by anti-slavery votes; and only after months of further delay was annexation accomplished by joint resolution of Congress.

Where Calhoun sat in cabinet, there was the head of the table. In this Tyler acquiesced; but Polk, wishing to be chief of his own administration, did not invite Calhoun to continue in office. Most of the year 1845 was accordingly spent by the latter in private life, though not without participation in public projects. He had long desired to see a system of railroads linking the West with the South, preferably a connection from Charleston across Georgia as against Hayne's plan of piercing the Blue Ridge in a line to Cincinnati. As a culmination of similar meetings, a large railroad and waterway convention was held at Memphis in November which Calhoun was persuaded to attend as a delegate from South Carolina. After a journey signalized by thronged public entertainment at every stopping-place, he was chosen to preside over the sessions. The address he delivered urged his railroad program and in addition argued that Congress had constitutional power to improve the navigation of the Mississippi because the Father of Waters, washing the shores of many states, was virtually an inland sea. The splitting of a logical hair seemed expedient in behalf of the desired alliance of sections.

This interlude was abbreviated by a summons once more into the public service. With war clouds lowering on two horizons, Calhoun was urgently needed in the national councils. D. F. Huger willingly resigned his seat in the Senate, and the legislature elected Calhoun unanimously to fill the vacancy. Arrived in Washington, his positions on the Oregon and Texas boundary questions proved much alike, for he advocated conciliation toward both Great Britain and Mexico. The Oregon issue resulted as he wished; but to his dismay and against his vehement opposition, the war with Mexico was precipitated.

Wilmot's proposal to prohibit slavery in all areas to be acquired by this war set Calhoun to spinning his last fine theory and involved him in the most desperate of his struggles. Aware as he was that the region was unsuited to plantation industry and slave labor (*The Diary of James K. Polk*, 1910, II, 283–84), he took the Proviso to be a gratuitous affront to the South, an index of aggressive disposition by Northern Democrats, and a culminating ground of Southern apprehension. To make state sovereignty applicable he framed a new series of syllogisms: that all territories were an estate owned by the states in common, to be administered by the central government only as a trustee for them; that any citizen of any state had full right to emigrate to any territory, carrying with him whatever property he possessed in his own state, and was entitled to Federal protection in the enjoyment of that property in his new home until the community should itself become a state. Therefore, whether his migration be to California, New Mexico, or Oregon, no slaveholder could be debarred from the transport and continued use of his slaves (*Works*, IV, 344–49). In short, notwithstanding the precedents of the ordinance of 1787 and the Missouri Compromise act, which he now considered erroneous, Congress was estopped from restricting the spread of slaveholding. He was perhaps willing to be outvoted in the organization of Oregon if he could carry his point as concerned the more southerly regions; but a sense that this hope was forlorn drove him to two devices which he had held somewhat in reserve. For permanent purposes he sped his pen to complete his treatises on government in general and the Federal Constitution in particular; and to meet the present exigency he strove to rouse and organize the South with a view to its issue of an ultimatum.

His treatises, destined to have only a posthumous publication, embodied his final philosophy. In the "Disquisition on Government" (*Works*, I, 1–107) he declares that society is essential to mankind, and government necessary to preserve and perfect society by curbing individual selfishness. But government itself must be held in check by constitutions in order that public agents may be prevented from abusing their power whether by self-aggrandizement or by promoting majority interests through the spoliation of minorities. The problem here, he said, is extremely difficult. No plan devised abstractly can suffice, but a satisfactory system can arise only as the product of an intelligent community seeking in the light of experience to meet its own conscious needs. On the one hand authority must be adequate to meet external emergencies by summoning the whole strength of the community. In domestic affairs, on the other hand, apparatus must be available by which minorities may compel majorities to compromise issues between them. That the two requirements are not mutually exclusive is shown by the common success of the jury system in forcing unanimous verdicts and by the long duration of the Polish Kingdom despite the possession of a veto by every member of its Diet. Far better designed, however, and therefore more lasting, were the constitutions of ancient Rome and modern England embodying less extreme examples of automatic check upon authority. The elements of aristocracy and monarchy embodied in them were wholesome in correcting the tendency of numerical majorities to tyrannize; but such elements are not indispensable, for a democracy may combine equity with efficiency if it avoid the "great and dangerous error" of considering all people equally entitled to liberty and if at the same time it maintain government by concurrent majorities and avoid the demagogic tendency and the despotic proclivities inherent in control by mere numbers.

In the "Discourse on the Constitution and Government of the United States" these lessons are given specific application, but in a tone of argument rather than of exposition. With elaborate citation of eighteenth-century records he contends that the American system is in no sense national, but purely federal. The people of the several states ordained alike their separate state governments and the general government. "Deriving their respective powers . . . from the same source, . . . the two governments, State and Federal, must, of necessity be equal in their respective spheres" (*Works*, I, 167). Sovereignty, which is indivisible, remains in the people of the several states; but the exercise of "the powers of sovereignty" may be distributed and have actually been divided between the two agencies. To make it efficient the central government was clothed with the attribute of deciding, in the first instance, on the extent of its powers (*Works*, I, 168); but the people of any state may challenge any assumption of undelegated authority in order to preserve the equilibrium of the complex system. The sectionalizing of interests or policies in the Union has made it imperative upon the South as the minority to oppose the concentration of despotic force. Calhoun's contentions of 1832, though he repeats them, now seem to him inefficacious in view of the progress of unconstitutional centralization in the interim. He, therefore, concludes that the domestic tranquillity of the South can be secured and the Union perpetuated only by a new device. To this end he advocates an amendment to the Constitution to replace the single president by a dual executive, each of the two chief magistrates to be chosen by one of the great sections of the country, and the assent of both to be requisite for the validation of acts of Congress (*Works*, I, 392–95).

These writings had influence upon political thought and projects not only at home but in the German Confederation (C. E. Merriam in *Studies in Southern History and Politics*, 1914, p. 336). The North in one case and Prussia in the other were quite unconvinced; but Lord Acton echoed Calhoun by saying that liberty can only be safeguarded by a multiplicity of checks— and the conversion of the British Empire into a "commonwealth of nations" has given practical embodiment to the precepts of decentralization.

But the current crisis could not be solved by a dissertation even if it had been ready for the press. Convinced as he was that the existing political parties were so constituted that the control of both must lie in the North and be used for Southern injury, Calhoun summoned a meeting, in January 1849, of the Southern senators and congressmen to consider an address which he had written for their adoption. This reviewed the history of the slavery issue, foretold disaster from the continuance of the existing scheme of politics, and called for unity in holding Southern rights paramount over party allegiance. The prophecy in this document was amazingly corroborated within two decades; abolition by a dominant North against Southern resistance; hatred between the whites of the two sections; enfranchisement of the negroes and a party union between them and the North to hold the Southern whites in subjection; a carnival of profligacy and a bottomless degradation (*Works*, VI, 310–11). But most of the members attending were unconvinced, and a mere minority signed the address for issue to their constituents. Calhoun next turned to local committees and newspaper agitation to procure a call from some commonwealth for a convention of the slaveholding states, and was rejoiced when Mississippi responded and the convention was scheduled to meet at Nashville (*Correspondence*, pp. 765–79).

Before the end of the year an irregular convention in California applied for statehood with a constitution excluding slavery. This met Calhoun's trenchant opposition on the grounds that the proceedings had not been authorized by an enabling act, and that their validation would at once and forever destroy the Senate equilibrium. Nearing the allotted span of three score and ten, his life was drawing to a close in baffled zeal and unrelaxed strain. His tall frame emaciated by half a decade of intermittent illness, his voice failing but his piercing eyes undimmed, he tottered from his lodgings to the Senate chamber day by day to save the Union if it might be saved upon a basis of comity and to preach Southern resistance to the point of independence if that should prove essential for social security.

The California demand, which put his territorial theorizing to scorn, was clearly not to be denied nor long delayed in its granting. A crisis was at hand, and the South, or its lower half at least, was at length girding its loins. Demonstrations became too vigorous to be longer disregarded. Clay framed the celebrated Omnibus Bill to settle the many pending issues on a give-and-take basis. Calhoun approved the purpose but criticized the text as failing to provide adequate guarantees for the South. To express these views he wrote his last formal speech, which was read to the Senate on Mar. 4, 1850, by Senator Mason while its author sat voiceless in his chair. A few days later he expressed praise of Webster's great speech of Mar. 7, but still thought it "difficult to see how two peoples so different and hostile can exist together in one common Union" (*Correspondence*, p. 784). At the end of this, his last letter, he wrote: "Kiss the children for their grandfather"; but virtually his last spoken words were "The South, the poor South." Fading out of life, he died at the end of the month. His body was carried in state to Charleston and interred with an outpouring praise and lamentation, for he was first in the hearts of his Carolina countrymen. His course was run, but his work was to have a mighty sequel.

[To promote his presidential prospects, there was published in 1843 a volume of Calhoun's *Speeches*, including sundry public papers; and simultaneously a *Life of John C. Calhoun*. The latter, unusually substantial for a campaign biography, was currently attributed to R. M. T. Hunter, but latterly Calhoun himself has been proved to have been its principal author (*Am. Hist. Review*, XIII, 310–13). Just after Calhoun's death R. K. Crallé edited his *Works* (1851–55), including the "Disquisition on Government" and the unfinished "Discourse on the Constitution" in the first volume, the speeches in the next three, and reports and public papers in the fifth and sixth. In 1857 was published *The Carolina Tribute to Calhoun*, J. P. Thomas, ed., containing the record of obsequies along with the text of many eulogies; and in 1888 *A Hist. of the Calhoun Monument* at Charleston, S. C. with its chief item the notable commemorative address by L. Q. C. Lamar. Biographies have been written by John S. Jenkins (1851), a perfunctory product; Hermann von Holst (1882), censorious and homiletic; Gustavus M. Pinckney (1903), eulogistic; Gaillard Hunt (1908), discriminatingly sympathetic; and William M. Meigs (2 volumes, 1917), elaborate and painstaking. A stout volume of Calhoun's correspondence, J. F. Jameson ed., has been published in the *Annual Report of the Am. Hist. Ass. for the Year 1899*, vol. II, being *House Doc. No. 733*, 56 Cong., 1 Sess.; and a supplementary volume, to consist mainly of letters to Calhoun, is now awaiting publication by the same agency.]   U. B. P.

CALHOUN, WILLIAM BARRON (Dec. 29, 1795–Nov. 8, 1865), lawyer, politician and educator, was the eldest child of Martha (Chamberlain) and Andrew Calhoun, a Scotch merchant of Boston. After a thorough preparation by William Wells of Harvard, he entered Yale College, where he graduated in 1814. Private study of law, carried on at Concord, N. H., and at Springfield with George Bliss, prepared him for admission to the bar in 1818, and the beginning of his practise at Springfield in 1822. In the latter he was not particularly happy or successful. It has been truthfully said that he was "an erudite writer" but not "a great orator"; that he "was lacking in the qualities that shine in a court of law." Bowles insisted that he needed "some pepper injected into his veins." In truth, Calhoun was more interested in economic, social, and political affairs than in his personal fame or prosperity. Though early concerned with problems of public welfare, and honored by numerous offices, he appears to have attended to the former "with the spirit of a philosopher," rather than with the usual self-interest of politicians, and to have made little or no effort to secure the latter. From 1825 to 1835, he was a member of the state legislature, serving as speaker of the House (1828–33) save for one year. In 1834, he was elected to Congress on the Whig ticket and served acceptably till 1843, declining further reëlection because of tubercular and catarrhal trouble. Other offices followed, however, in rapid succession. He was presidential elector for Clay (1844), was elected state senator (1846)—in which position he served as presiding officer—and was secretary of the commonwealth from 1848 to 1851. From 1853 to 1855 he served as bank commissioner; in 1859, he was made mayor of Springfield; and, two years later, was again sent to the legislature. Throughout his mature life he was an interested and effective promoter of public education. As member of the legislature, he presented the report of the select committee on a "Seminary for the instruction of school teachers" (1827), as also the memorial of James G. Carter on the same subject. In reporting a bill to provide for such an institution he made a strong plea: "In what more suitable and rational way can the government interpose than in providing the means for furnishing the schools with competent instructors . . . and in encouraging the establishment of seminaries, whose object shall be to teach the art of communicating knowledge?" (*House Report No. 10, 1827*, p. 5). Calhoun was chairman of the convention which founded the American Institute of Instruction in 1830, served as vice-president, and later, for many years, as president. From 1829 till his death he was a trustee of Amherst and, in 1850, was a lecturer there on political economy. In 1854 he edited the *Connecticut Valley Farmer*. A religious steadfastness, dignified self-respect, and purity of mind marked both his public and private life. He was married, on May 11, 1837, to Margaret Howard Kingsbury. Among his writings which are scattered here and there, a patriotic *Address Delivered in Springfield* (1825), *Addresses at the Dedication of the New Cabinet and Observatory of Amherst College* (1848), an examination into the condition of banks in Massachusetts (1849), and the articles and editorials in the *Springfield Republican* are fair samples. They indicate not a brilliant writer but a careful, logical, exact one.

[Frederick J. Kingsbury, *Genealogy of the Descendants of Henry Kingsbury* (1905) ; F. B. Dexter, *Biog. Sketches Grads. Yale Coll.*, vol. VI (1912) ; Chas. W.

Chapin, *Sketches of the Old Inhabitants . . . of Old Springfield* (1893) ; Mason A. Green, *Hist. of Springfield* (1888).]   T. W.

CALHOUN, WILLIAM JAMES (Oct. 5, 1848–Sept. 19, 1916), diplomat, was born in Pittsburgh, Pa., the son of Robert and Sarah (Knox) Calhoun. He was educated at the Union Seminary, Poland, Ohio. His family having removed to Danville, Ill., he was admitted to the bar in that town and practised law there from 1875 to 1898 when he removed to Chicago. While acting as western counsel for the Baltimore & Ohio Railroad, he was the legal opponent of Elbert Gary, later to become head of the United States Steel Corporation. The friendship that was one of the results of this forensic battle had a widening influence upon Calhoun's career, and it was upon Gary's suggestion that in 1897 Calhoun was sent on a special mission by President McKinley to the war-racked island of Cuba to study conditions and to report on the manner in which, under Captain-General Weyler's decree, the civilian population of the war zones was being herded into insanitary reconcentration camps. His reports, which substantiated the inhumanity of the conditions prevailing, reconciled the President to intervention. Shortly after his return from Cuba, early in 1898, Calhoun was appointed by McKinley a member of the United States Interstate Commerce Commission. Here he served acceptably for two years. In 1900 he resigned to return to Chicago and the active practise of law.

In 1905 he was sent to Venezuela as confidential agent of President Roosevelt at a time when the Caribbean republic was in the throes of a revolution which by some was thought to indicate European inspiration and financial support. In 1909 he was appointed by President Taft Envoy Extraordinary and Minister Plenipotentiary to China where he served for four years. Throughout this period of political transition and travail in China, Calhoun was successful in maintaining the traditional American attitude of non-intervention, at the same time demonstrating on many critical occasions a helpful understanding of the long-accumulating problems with which the unprepared Chinese people were confronted.

Calhoun was a graceful speaker as well as a trained, industrious lawyer. He led several reform movements within the Republican party of Illinois and it has been said that the positions of responsibility which he held were due rather to the opposition than to the indorsement of the regular party machine of his state. He was married twice: first, on Dec. 26, 1875, to Alice D.

Harmon, who died in 1898; second, in 1904, to Lucy Monroe of Chicago.

[*Who's Who in America,* 1914–15; obituaries in *Chicago Herald* and *Chicago Daily Tribune,* Sept. 20, 1916; information from Judge John Barton Payne.]

S. B.

CALIFORNIA JOE (May 8, 1829–Oct. 29, 1876), frontiersman, scout, was born near Stanford, Ky. His real name was Moses Embree Milner. In 1849 he journeyed overland to California, later going to the Oregon country and working at various occupations. He came into general notice during the Civil War as a member of Berdan's Sharpshooters. After the war he drifted to the plains, serving in the Indian campaigns, and was with the 7th Cavalry, near Fort Dodge, in October 1868, when Custer reassumed command. His odd appearance, engaging personality, and shrewd comments on Indian warfare attracted the General, who appointed him chief of scouts; but he lost the honor within a few hours by getting uproariously drunk. As an ordinary scout he took part in the Washita expedition, and after the battle of Nov. 27 was chosen by Custer to carry the news to Sheridan. Declining any escort but that of his partner, Jack Corbin, he traversed on muleback the hundred miles of snowbound, hostile country to Camp Supply in eighteen hours. "An invaluable guide and Indian fighter," wrote Sheridan in recording the incident, "whenever the clause of the statute prohibiting liquors in the Indian country happened to be in full force."

In 1875 he guided Col. Dodge's escort to Prof. Jenney's Black Hills expedition, and after his discharge at Fort Laramie returned to the Hills as a prospector. From Deadwood, in July 1876, when news came of Custer's death, he went to Camp Robinson and joined the 5th Cavalry as a guide, serving throughout the campaign and returning with the troops in October. Two days before the time set for his departure with Mackenzie's winter expedition, a civilian, Tom Newcomb, who bore him a grudge, shot him in the back, killing him instantly.

California Joe came into enduring fame through the writings of Custer and his wife. He was more than six feet tall, well proportioned, with lustrous black eyes and dark brown hair, mustache and beard, which he wore long. His face, as far as it was revealed from its hirsute framing, was, according to Custer, "full of intelligence and pleasant to look upon." His dress was conspicuous for its oddity and slouchiness. His mount was usually a mule. He smoked a pipe almost incessantly and usually chewed at the same time, though with an art that permitted neither habit to interfere with his conversation. Though reticent about his personal history, on other matters he was garrulous, especially when well liquored; and his stories, told in a jargon of frontier, gambling, and Indian terms and plentifully adorned with fiction, were listened to with delight. He was brave, self-reliant, and faithful. His skill as a scout, trailer, and marksman is attested by all under whom he served. As a "character" of the frontier he occupies a unique place.

[See "California Joe," *Harper's Weekly,* Aug. 2, 1862; G. A. Custer, *My Life on the Plains* (1874); E. B. Custer, *Following the Guidon* (1890); E. L. Sabin, "California Joe, Good Old Scout," *Frontier Stories,* Apr. 1927; De B. R. Keim, *Sheridan's Troopers on the Border* (1885); Harry Young, *Hard Knocks* (1915); G. W. Stokes, *Deadwood Gold* (1926); J. Brown and A. M. Willard, *The Black Hills Trails* (1924). The scout is several times mentioned in the second volume of Sheridan's *Memoirs,* as well as in various writings that appeared under the name of W. F. Cody, and is made the hero of a number of fantastic adventures in J. W. Buel's *Heroes of the Plains* (1883).]

W. J. G.

CALKINS, NORMAN ALLISON (Sept. 9, 1822–Dec. 22, 1895), educator, author, descended from a Plymouth settler of 1640, was the son of Elisha Deming Calkins and Abigail (Lockwood) Calkins, pioneer settlers of Gainesville, N. Y., where he was born. The family had moved to this community from Connecticut with that general westward expansion of New England population which occurred in the first part of the nineteenth century. The New England school tradition seems to have been carried to Gainesville, for young Calkins not only attended the common schools of the district but also spent several terms at a classical academy. At the early age of eighteen he began teaching during the winter terms in Castile, N. Y., returning to his own studies during the summer and vacation terms. Later he went back to Gainesville where he became principal of the Central School. He was elected county superintendent during the school year 1845–46 but resigned the position in the fall of the latter year to go to New York City to become editor of the *Student.* The monthly issues of this magazine were intended not only as a family miscellany but also as a school reader, for Calkins had a conviction that reading in the schools could be much improved by the frequent introduction of fresh reading matter. The magazine was well received and provided him with an income on which to marry Mary Hoosier in 1854. So successful did the *Student* prove that it encouraged competition in a similar publication called the *Schoolmate* with which it later consolidated under the title of *Student and Schoolmate.* At this juncture, however, Calkins vacated the editorial chair, as he was getting ready for the publication of his most outstanding book. Always interested in new and better methods of teaching, he had studied Robert Owen's experiment at New Harmony, Ind., and thus early became acquainted with Pestalozzian principles of object teaching. These he set forth in 1861 in a volume entitled *Primary Object Lessons for a Graduated Course of Development* which ultimately went through at least forty editions and was translated into several foreign languages. Distinction quickly followed in his election as assistant superintendent of schools in New York City in charge of the primary grades. Reëlection followed reëlection to this post to the year of his death. He further popularized the new educational theory and greatly added to his prestige as lecturer in the methods and principles of education at the Saturday classes held for teachers in New York City for approximately twenty years. Further books followed from his pen, all based on Pestalozzian principles: *Teaching Color* (1877); *Manual of Object-Teaching* (1882); *First Reading, from Blackboard to Books* (1883); *How to Teach Phonics* (1889). He served the National Education Association as president of the department of elementary schools, as president of the department of superintendents, as treasurer, and finally in 1886 as president.

[Obituaries in the *N. Y. Times*, Dec. 23, and *N. Y. Tribune*, Dec. 24, 1895; memorial published in the *N. E. A. Jour. of Proc. and Addresses*, 1896.]
J. S. B—r.

CALKINS, PHINEAS WOLCOTT (June 10, 1831–Dec. 31, 1924), clergyman, was descended from Hugh Calkins, who came from Wales to Gloucester, Mass., in 1640. His parents were James and Sarah Newton (Trowbridge) Calkins. His birthplace was Painted Post, now Corning, N. Y., and his father was the first white child born at Painted Post. Born on a farm, as a boy Calkins was a mechanical genius and throughout his life his avocation consisted in all kinds of mechanical pursuits in which he was an adept. Before entering college he taught for several years in order to pay his expenses. He graduated as valedictorian in the class of 1856 at Yale. Continuing his studies at Union Theological Seminary, 1859–60, and at the University of Halle, Germany, 1860–62, and traveling meantime in Europe, he was ordained to the Congregational ministry, Oct. 22, 1862. After his student days he dropped his first name, Phineas. He was associate pastor of Center (Congregational) Church, Hartford, Conn., 1862–64; pastor of Calvary (Presbyterian) Church, Philadelphia,

1864–66; pastor of the North Presbyterian Church, Buffalo, N. Y., 1866–80; pastor of Eliot (Congregational) Church, Newton, Mass., 1880–95; supplied Clyde Congregational Church, Kansas City, Mo., 1896–98; was pastor of Montvale (Congregational) Church, Woburn, Mass., 1898–1907 and pastor emeritus of the same church until his death. In 1886 he was acting pastor of the American Chapel in Paris and preached frequently in England between 1890 and 1902. On his various visits to Europe he acted as correspondent for the *New York Observer* and *Boston Transcript*. To the periodical press he was a frequent contributor, chiefly on religious subjects. He was author of a sketch of Matthias W. Baldwin published in *Memorial of Matthias W. Baldwin* (1867), and of the following books: *Keystones of Faith* (1888), *Essays* (1890), *Parables for Our Times* (1901). Nearly to the end of his ninety-three years he was characterized by great physical and intellectual vigor. The mathematical mind which made him a prize winner at Yale was of great value in working out all the details of personal and parish administration. His originality of exposition and expression were a feature of his preaching. He was married, on June 6, 1860, in Worcester, Mass., to Charlotte Grosvenor Whiton.

[*Congreg. Year Book*, 1924; *Congregationalist*, CX, 93; *Who's Who in America*, 1924–25; *Reports of the Class of 1856, Yale College*; *Obit. Record Yale Grads.*, 1924–25; personal information from Calkins's son, Dr. Raymond Calkins.]
T. C. R.

CALKINS, WOLCOTT. [See CALKINS, PHINEAS WOLCOTT, 1831–1924.]

CALL, RICHARD KEITH (1791–Sept. 14, 1862), governor of Florida, was born in Prince George County, Va., the third of four children. His father, William Call, fought in the Revolution, and his uncle, Richard Keith Call, friend and aide to Washington, was a charter member of the Order of the Cincinnati. His father died while Richard was a mere lad, and his mother (Helen Mead Walker) soon afterward moved to Kentucky. As in most pioneer families, the Call children had little actual schooling, but after their mother's death (August 1810), Richard attended an academy in Montgomery County, Tenn. This he left in 1813 to join an expedition against the Creeks; and later in the same year volunteered under Jackson. In January 1814, although his whole company mutinied and went home, Call (third lieutenant) served in the ranks until the end of the campaign. This incident and his courage were the basis for Jackson's deep attachment to him. Shortly afterward Call joined the regular army with the rank of lieutenant. For gallantry in Jackson's operations about Pensacola and in the battle of New Orleans he was soon promoted to captain and later became a member of Jackson's staff. He fought in Jackson's campaigns of 1818 and 1820; negotiated with Gov. José Masot at Pensacola in the former year; and in 1821 arranged with Gov. José Callava for the transfer of West Florida. In 1821 he resigned his commission to practise law in Pensacola, but in 1823 he was appointed brigadier-general of militia. The same year, while a member of the municipal board of Pensacola and of the first territorial council, he was appointed delegate to Congress, succeeding Gen. Joseph M. Hernandez. Before going to Washington (1824), he married Mary Letitia Kirkham (died 1836) of Nashville. Returning to the territory in 1825 (his successor in Congress being Joseph M. White, who also defeated him as delegate in 1832), Call removed to Tallahassee, and besides his town house acquired a large plantation on Lake Jackson. In 1829 Jackson sent him to Havana to obtain the documents relating to land grants, surveys, and claims taken thither by the Spaniards in 1821. After his return to the United States he was frequently consulted about these matters and in one case, argued before the Supreme Court, was associated with William Wirt. In 1832–34, he built the third railroad in the United States—the Tallahassee-St. Marks—and as a feeder to it founded the town of Port Leon. He was active in the Indian troubles during the period 1826–42. In 1836 (while governor during his first term, 1836–39), the War Department, at his request, authorized him to conduct a summer campaign; but notwithstanding the soundness of Call's plan and the care exercised by him, the campaign was not a complete success, and Call was superseded in the command. Heatedly, Call accused the War Department of injustice and discrimination; which caused Van Buren, in 1839, notwithstanding that Call had been reappointed governor for three years more, to rescind the appointment. Call retaliated by turning Whig: and after the Harrison-Tyler victory was reappointed governor (1841–44). During his terms the most important issues, aside from the Indian hostilities, were those of the banks and statehood. When the banks failed and Florida repudiated the "faith bonds" issued by the territory, Call was greatly disturbed. He declared for statehood in 1837, but this was not obtained until 1845, although the St. Joseph convention (1838–39) drafted a state constitution. His defeat by a small margin in the first state election caused him to withdraw from active politics. In the Baltimore convention of 1856, he re-

fused nomination for the vice-presidency, and himself nominated Donelson. Being an ardent unionist, though a slaveholder, he attempted unsuccessfully to save Florida from secession; but stood with his state, offered his services to the Confederacy, and was grieved because his military experience was not availed of. He was a man of great integrity and sincerity and was highly regarded as a lawyer and orator. He was somewhat obstinate, loved his friends and hated his enemies with true Jackson fervor, and did not hesitate to challenge when he considered his honor impugned.

[The best printed biography of Call is that by his grand-daughter, Caroline Mays Brevard, in the *Fla. Hist. Soc. Quart.*, July, Oct. 1908. This is based in part upon an uncompleted autobiography in manuscript among the Call papers in Tallahassee. These papers have also many letters and documents of prime importance. The Lib. of Cong. has considerable Jackson-Call correspondence; and the archives of the State Dept., the records pertaining to the mission to Cuba. The *Am. State Papers, Military Affairs*, vols. VI and VII, publish many of the letters and documents relating to Call's campaigns against the Indians. See also C. M. Brevard, *A Hist. of Fla.* (2 vols. 1924–25), ed. by J. A. Robertson.]
J.A.R.

CALLAWAY, SAMUEL RODGER (Dec. 24, 1850–June 1, 1904), railroad executive, was born in Toronto, Ont., the son of Frederick William Callaway of Wiltshire, England, and Margaret (Rodger) Callaway of Crieff, Scotland. The fact that he began railroad work at the early age of thirteen, as an apprentice in the auditor's office of the Grand Trunk, indicates that his formal education was meager. His father, who was a dry-goods merchant, had lost his life and everything he owned in the Toronto fire of 1863. After six years' training in detail, young Callaway became chief clerk to the superintendent of the Great Western, a position which he held from 1869 to 1871. From the latter year to 1874 he was private secretary to the general manager of the same company; and then he became superintendent of the Detroit, Grand Haven & Milwaukee. On June 7, 1875, he was married at Hamilton, Ontario, to Elizabeth Ecclestone. In 1878 he was appointed superintendent of the Detroit, Saginaw & Bay City and in 1881 became general manager of the Chicago & Grand Trunk. These properties, with the exception of the Detroit, Saginaw & Bay City, were affiliated with or were controlled by the Grand Trunk System. In 1884 Callaway accepted the vice-presidency and general managership of the Union Pacific. After three years in this position, he was asked to take charge of the Toledo, St. Louis & Kansas City during the trying period between 1887 and 1895. The company was reorganized and the railroad practically rebuilt under his direction, first as president and then as receiver. Callaway's work attracted the attention of the Vanderbilt interests and in 1895 he became president of the New York, Chicago & St. Louis. About that time he was offered the presidency of the Grand Trunk System, but declined it because he feared that he would not be given a free hand by the English directors. In 1897 he was elected president of the Lake Shore & Michigan Southern and one year later (Apr. 20, 1898) he was selected by William K. Vanderbilt to succeed Chauncey M. Depew when the latter retired from the presidency of the New York Central & Hudson River to become chairman of the board of directors. After three years in the presidency of the New York Central, Callaway was sought as the president of a new company formed to take over the locomotive construction plants at Schenectady, N. Y., Paterson, N. J., Dunkirk, N. Y., Providence, R. I., Manchester, N. H., Pittsburgh, Pa., and Richmond, Va., with other smaller properties. These were all merged into the American Locomotive Company, an undertaking of magnitude in that early period of large industrial combines. The merger, when first discussed, did not inspire the public confidence that was necessary to insure its initial success, and the promoters thought that if Callaway were made the chief executive his prestige would be a valuable asset. Although Callaway's chief interest was in railroads, the financial inducements were so attractive that he could not resist. He had always been on a salary, his investments had not been wisely chosen, and his personal fortune was small. He was elected president of the new company in May 1901. While he never was as happy in that position as he had been in railroad service, he found interesting problems of coördination and wide latitude for the exercise of his ability as an organizer. The success of the American Locomotive Company in later years was due in substantial part to the leadership of Callaway during the period of unification and the formulation of policies of finance, production and sales. Unfortunately he did not live to see the permanency of the structure to which he contributed so much in the formative period, as he died on June 1, 1904.

In the earlier years of his railroad service Callaway displayed unusual capacity for detail as well as broad qualities of leadership. As he progressed to positions of greater responsibility he did not, as so many do who rise from the ranks, carry with him this burden of detail. Instead, he adopted a policy of developing the initiative and resourcefulness of subordinates by insisting that they assume responsibilities, subject only to broad executive supervision and the test of accomplishment. From the time he first became

a railroad president, Callaway would not load himself with departmental minutiæ. He discouraged letter writing, would not sign a letter consisting of more than one page, and would never allow papers to remain on his deck. Instead, he encouraged accomplishment through team work and conference, and granted an exceptional measure of departmental autonomy. These characteristics were frequently criticized at the time as extreme. He would often be wholly out of touch with his office for several days at a time and subordinates were sometimes required to take action in matters which Callaway personally should have directed. One feature of his administration should be noted specifically. He believed that adequate publicity of corporate accounts was one of the best methods of dispelling public suspicion of large combinations of capital. The completeness and frankness of the early annual reports of the American Locomotive Company attracted favorable public attention at the time.

[The foregoing based in the main on correspondence with business associates; other data gleaned from biographical notes in *N. Y. State's Prominent and Progressive Men* (1900), *Railroad Gazette* and *Railway Age,* and an article in *Cassier's Mag.*, Apr. 1902.]

W. J. C—m.

CALLENDER, GUY STEVENS (Nov. 9, 1865–Aug. 8, 1915), economist and historian, was the ninth of ten children of Robert Foster and Lois (Winslow) Callender, both emigrants from New England to the Western Reserve. As a boy on his father's farm in Hartsgrove, Ohio, he showed the active mind, intellectual curiosity, retentive memory, and fondness for argument which characterized his later life and work. "He devoured the contents of all the books he could get hold of, especially history. He was always ready for discussion with his friends or his elders. In an argument he was outspoken, without regard for the feelings of his opponent." The human qualities which later endeared him to his small circle of intimate friends were also evident. His teaching career began at the age of fifteen in the district schools of Ashtabula County. By the savings of several winters of teaching, supplemented by summer earnings, he paid for a college preparatory course at New Lyme Institute. At the age of twenty-one he was ready for Oberlin College. "With the money earned in haying and harvesting he bought himself a suit of clothes, and with $40 in his pocket he said goodbye to his family. When asked how he expected to get through, he replied with tears in his eyes that he didn't know, but he was going just the same."

With the same pluck and ability which had characterized his earlier struggle he put himself through Oberlin, graduating in 1891. For a year his choice of a career was undecided, and he spent the time traveling through the Middle West in the interests of a publishing house. But his thirst for knowledge proved still unsatisfied and in 1892 he entered the senior class of Harvard College, where he remained as undergraduate, graduate student, and finally as instructor in economics until 1900. "He was an outstanding man among our graduate students of his time," writes Professor Taussig. "His high intellectual quality, and the independence and originality of his work, impressed us from the start." In 1900 he was called to Bowdoin College as professor of political economy, but remained there only until 1903 when he accepted a professorship in the Sheffield Scientific School of Yale University which he held until his death. On June 14, 1904, he was married to Harriet Rice in Cambridge, Mass. Just at the beginning of his work he had a complete nervous breakdown from which he never entirely recovered. The daily grind of drilling large classes of undergraduates and the administrative work accompanying the teaching deprived him of the time and energy which he longed to devote to historical research. *Selections from the Economic History of the United States 1765–1860* (1909) was practically his only published work, but it was enough to establish him as the leading authority in his field. Always intolerant of loose thinking and of verbosity, he compressed into the masterly introductory essays which he prefixed to each chapter his entire theory of the progress of the United States from the beginnings of colonization until the Civil War. In his view economic history should not be a chronological recital of events of industrial and commercial importance, but an explanation by the principles of economic science of the economic and social development of communities. He insisted that the economic historian must not shirk the vital task of interpretation of his facts ("The Position of American Economic History," *American Historical Review*, XIX, 80–97). He himself was master of a surprisingly wide range of facts from which he drew conclusions which have illumined the colonial and early national periods of United States history. His analysis of the part played by economic factors in the adoption of the Federal Constitution and his discussion of the economic basis of slavery in the South were two of his outstanding contributions.

[The material for this sketch has been taken from letters from Prof. Callender's family and friends and from a biographical article written by Dr. C. W. Mixter in the *Yale Alumni Weekly* of Oct. 1, 1915.]

P. W. B.

CALLENDER, JAMES THOMSON (1758– July 17, 1803), political writer, was born in Scotland in 1758, acquired by some means a fair classical education, and became in 1792 a messenger at arms and writer in Edinburgh. There his propensity for intemperate political discussion expressed itself in a pamphlet, *The Political Progress of Britain* (Part I), which he termed an impartial history of the abuses of government, but which led to his indictment for sedition in January 1793. Ofttimes called in court, he did not appear and was pronounced a fugitive and outlaw. He found temporary safety, if not peace, in America. Here he was regarded by Jefferson and other lovers of liberty as a man of genius suffering under persecution. Until the spring of 1796 he was a reporter of congressional debates for the Philadelphia *Gazette*. In 1797 appeared his *American Annual Register*, a discursive partisan work. In his *History of the United States for 1796*, his genius as a scandal-monger first became conspicuous. Here he uncovered to public gaze the intimate affairs of Hamilton and forced that statesman to bare his personal shame in the Reynolds affair to vindicate his official honor. In 1798, frightened by the Sedition Law, he fled Philadelphia and took refuge in Virginia. In 1799 he went to Richmond and attached himself to Meriwether Jones of the *Examiner*, who utilized his dangerous talents in connection with that Republican paper. Here, under the secretive patronage of Jefferson, he published in 1800 his most notorious pamphlet, *The Prospect Before Us* (vol. I), which, despite certain palpable hits was more characterized by abuse than valid criticism of Federalist leaders. For remarks about President John Adams in this work, he was tried under the Sedition Law in May and June, fined $200, and sentenced to nine months' imprisonment. No sufferer under this unwise law deserved less sympathy than Callender, but the political aspects of the case gained him strong support from his party, and the bullying tactics of Justice Chase in the trial aroused a storm of indignation in behalf of the eminent Virginia lawyers of the defense and their client. From prison, Callender hurled against the administration two fiery pamphlets, on both of which Jefferson advanced him money. Following the inauguration of his benefactor in 1801, Callender was pardoned and was singled out by the remission of his fine. Irritated, however, because of delay in the receipt of the money, he was already talking of the ingratitude of the President, who appears rather to have been excessively gullible and long-suffering. Having broken with his old employer, Jones, whom he later attacked, Callender became asso-

425

ciated, in February 1802, with Henry Pace in the publication of the Richmond *Recorder*. Now increasingly critical of an administration which had failed to reward him with an appointment, he was openly charged with apostasy. By the autumn of 1802, he was turning the artillery of slander full on his most illustrious patron. Accusing Jefferson of dishonesty, cowardice, and gross personal immorality, he gave currency to most of the scandals which have been associated with the private life of the third President, and, despite the extravagance of the charges, left on him, as he had left on Hamilton, a stain which can never be entirely effaced.

Callender was married and had at least four children, whose needs served at times to stimulate his reckless pen. His wife apparently died before him, and his children were supported during his last years at least by Thomas Leiper of Philadelphia. Toward the end of his life, Callender was destitute, in part because of mistreatment by his partner. Shunned by his former associates, constantly intoxicated, he several times threatened suicide. He was drowned in three feet of water in the James River, July 17, 1803. The coroner's jury pronounced his death accidental, following intoxication.

[The best account of Callender is contained in Worthington C. Ford's *Thos. Jefferson and Jas. Thomson Callender* (1897), where the correspondence between the two men is published. For his indictment in Edinburgh, see T. B. and T. J. Howell, *State Trials* (1817), XXIII, 79–84. For Hamilton's reply to his charges, see Lodge's edition of Hamilton's *Works* (1886), VI, 449–81. For Callender's trial in 1800, see Francis Wharton, *State Trials* (1849), pp. 688–721. For an editorial on his death, see Richmond *Examiner*, July 27, 1803.]

D.M.

CALLENDER, JOHN (1706–Jan. 26, 1748), Baptist clergyman, the son of John Callender, was born in Boston, where his grandfather, the Rev. Ellis Callender, was pastor of the First Baptist Church from 1708 to 1726. At the age of thirteen he entered Harvard College. There he shared in the income derived from benefactions of Thomas Hollis, a London Baptist, who had endowed two chairs and supplied scholarship funds. In the year of his graduation from college he joined the Baptist church in Boston, and a few years later was licensed to preach. He soon was invited to preach for the church at Swansea, the oldest church of the denomination in Massachusetts, and he remained there until 1730. Upon leaving Swansea he married Elizabeth Hardin of that town, by whom he had three sons and three daughters. The next year he was ordained to the regular ministry and became pastor of the Baptist church at Newport, R. I., the second church of that faith in the United States. There he remained until his death.

Callender was a man of pleasing appearance, with fair complexion and a kindly, serious expression. His brilliant blue eyes and high forehead indicated keenness of intelligence. His character was irreproachable, and he had many friends both in and outside of the church. He was highly esteemed in the community, and was a member of a select literary and philosophical society in Newport, having been suggested for membership, it is thought, by Bishop Berkeley, the English philosopher, who resided for a time at Newport. He made an important contribution to Rhode Island history in his *Historical Discourse on the Civil and Religious Affairs of the Colony of Rhode Island and Providence Plantations* (1739). He was also the author of several published sermons. His interest in history led him to collect historical material relating to the colonial history of churches of his own faith, which proved a valuable source of information for Isaac Backus when he wrote his history of the Baptists in New England about sixty years later. Callender was honored among Baptists, even though he declared himself in favor of admitting non-Baptists to the communion table, an act of generosity not often practised. After a long illness he died in 1748 in the forty-second year of his age, and was buried at Newport. The epitaph on his tomb credited him with being "distinguished as a shining and very burning light by a true and faithful ministry."

[Memoir by Romeo Elton in *R. I. Hist. Soc. Colls.*, IV (1888), 9–25.]

H.K.R.

CALVERLEY, CHARLES (Nov. 1, 1833– Feb. 25, 1914), sculptor, of English parentage, was born in Albany, N. Y., where he received his education. He became a marble-cutter and while he was engaged at this trade his ability was noticed by Erastus D. Palmer, the sculptor, who took him as an assistant. He remained with Palmer about fourteen years. At some time in the later sixties he went to New York and opened a studio of his own. In 1872 he was elected an associate member of the National Academy and in 1875 a full academician. "The Little Companions" and "Little Ida" (a medallion) seem to have been comparatively early works. He became known as a maker of busts and particularly of portrait medallions. He did, however, make larger statues on occasion; such are the statue of Robert Burns in Washington Park, Albany, and the bronze figure of "Meditation" on the Boulware Lot in the Albany Rural Cemetery. The latter was one of his last works. He was represented at the Centennial Exposition of 1876 by a bas-relief of Peter Cooper and a large bronze bust of John Brown (1873), the latter of which now belongs to the Union League Club. Among his large busts in bronze are those of Horace Greeley (1876) and Elias Howe (1884), both in Greenwood Cemetery. At the exhibition of the National Sculpture Society in 1895 he showed a portrait bust of himself. He also did busts of Lincoln, Charles Loring Elliott, and the Rev. John MacLean, a former president of Princeton. A bust of Burns by him is in the Metropolitan Museum. Examples of his medallions are preserved in the Historical and Art Society of Albany. He is likewise said to have done some remarkable cameo cutting.

In his busts and medallions Calverley showed fine workmanship and skill in portraiture. Taft calls him "a craftsman of sterling worth," and says: "Mr. Calverley's permanent reputation will rest largely upon his medallions, which, in their precision and firmness of construction, are among the admirable products of the art. A forceful characterization of aged Louis Menand is especially noteworthy."

Calverley lived to an advanced age and in later life photographs show him to have been a man of venerable appearance with mustache and long flowing beard. For the last few years of his life he lived with his daughter, Mrs. Francis Byrne-Ivy, and died at her house in Essex Fells, N. J. He was apparently in good health to within a few days of his death which was caused by acute bronchitis.

[C. E. Clement and L. Hutton, *Artists of the Nineteenth Century* (3rd ed., 1885) ; Lorado Taft, *Hist. of Am. Sculpture* (rev. ed., 1925) ; *Albany Evening Jour.*, Feb. 26, 1914 ; *N. Y. Times,* Feb. 27, 1914.]

E.G.N.

CALVERT, CHARLES (Aug. 27, 1637–Feb. 21, 1715), third Lord Baltimore, second proprietor of the province of Maryland, was the only son of Cecilius Calvert, second Lord Baltimore, and of his wife, Anne Arundell, daughter of Lord Arundell of Wardour. He was commissioned governor of Maryland, Sept. 14, 1661, and served in that capacity until the death of his father, Nov. 30, 1675, when he succeeded to the proprietorship of the province. His task both as governor and as proprietor was beset with many difficulties. He was a Catholic. Protestants in the colony outnumbered Catholics by at least ten to one and the fabrication of a rumor of a "Popish Plot" became a formidable weapon. The ranks of the malcontents were strengthened with recruits from those who had come to the colony as convicts or as indentured servants. The Susquehanna Indians were hostile, and the spirit of Bacon's rebellion in Virginia was contagious. A boundary dispute with William Penn required Calvert's presence in England where his troubles culminated in the Protestant Revolution of 1688 and the hostile attitude of King William toward proprietary charters. Calvert was energetic in his efforts to cope with these difficulties but his efforts were directed, with an irritable temper, chiefly toward the suppression of opposition. He was lacking in the range of vision and personal magnetism so essential to success. In 1670, following a stormy experience with the Assembly the preceding year, suffrage was restricted to such freemen as had a freehold of at least fifty acres or a visible estate of forty pounds sterling, and at the same time there was commenced the practise of summoning to the Assembly only one-half of the delegates who had been elected. Calvert was accused of abusing the privilege of appointing sheriffs to control elections. In 1672 he brought about the election of Thomas Notley, a stalwart supporter, as speaker, and wrote his father that he was resolved to keep him there. Occasionally, when the delegates to the Assembly were stubborn, he called them before him in the council chamber and prevailed upon them to yield. He vetoed acts of the Assembly several years after they had been passed.

Calvert was married four times. By his second wife, Jane, daughter of Vincent Lowe and widow of Henry Sewall, he had five children, and these were married with a view to making the government more and more a family affair. It was successfully administered during a brief visit of Calvert to England in 1676, but it passed to incompetent guardians not long after his departure in 1684 to defend his charter and his territorial jurisdiction from the attacks of William Penn. It was overthrown in 1689 by a Protestant association led by the blasphemous John Coode [*q.v.*], and in 1692 a royal government was established. Until his death, however, Calvert contended successfully against encroachments on his territorial rights.

[The chief sources of information are the *Archives of Md.* and *The Calvert Papers* (1889). For reviews of Calvert's administration of the government see C. C. Hall, *The Lords Baltimore and the Md. Palatinate* (1902), and N. D. Mereness, *Md. as a Proprietary Province* (1901). For family history see John Bailey Calvert Nicklin, "The Calvert Family" in *Md. Hist. Mag.*, vol. XVI (1921).]

N. D. M.

CALVERT, CHARLES BENEDICT (Aug. 23, 1808–May 12, 1864), congressman, was the grandson of Benedict Calvert, earlier known as Benedict Swingate. The latter, of uncertain maternity, was the son of Charles, fifth Lord Baltimore. Benedict's son George Calvert, removed from Mt. Airy to Riverdale, Md., occupying there a large estate which still remains in the family. He married Rosalie Eugenia Stier, of

Belgian parentage (John B. Calvert Nicklin, "The Calvert Family" in *Maryland Historical Magazine*, XVI, 313–16), who became the mother of George Henry Calvert [*q.v.*] and Charles Benedict Calvert. The large Riverdale farm probably induced Charles to study the problems of agriculture, for his whole life was devoted to furthering its development. After attending school in Philadelphia he entered the University of Virginia, graduating in 1827. On June 6, 1839 he married Charlotte Augusta Norris. The Journal of the legislature of Maryland records his appearance at the sessions of 1838, 1843, and 1844, but of his activities therein there is no mention. The project to establish the Maryland Agricultural College must have taken much of his time for he is commonly regarded as the one through whose efforts the college was established. It was finally located on 428 acres of his land which he sold the corporation for $10,000, remaining its creditor. In addition he loaned it over $2,000 cash (*Report of the Trustees of the Maryland Agricultural College to the Legislature of Maryland*, January session, 1864, pp. 13–14). Shortly after the outbreak of the Civil War he appears as a representative in the Thirty-seventh Congress. His ardent unionism was tempered strongly by an inherent sense of justice. At one time he advocated a direct tax on all property, personal and real, saying it would be "not half as odious as this rebellion," and at another time proposed to reimburse loyal owners of escaped slaves at the rate of $1,000 for each fugitive (*Congressional Globe*, 37 Cong., 1 Sess., pp. 212, 272–73; 2 Sess., pp. 1549, 3215).

As a promoter of the Department of Agriculture Calvert's efforts were directed mainly outside of Congress. In 1852 the United States Agricultural Society was organized, which, during the brief eight years of its existence, had a marked influence in congressional circles. At every meeting we find Calvert waging a persistent, determined fight for a department of agriculture. "When a cabinet minister represents agriculture," he said, "the farmer will be appreciated by the government, and proper steps will be taken to advance his noble calling by all means possible; but until such a platform is formed and such a representative takes his seat in the Cabinet, the hope the farmer cherishes that the government will regard agriculture as its chief bulwark and cherish its advance accordingly, is fallacious" (*Journal of the United States Agricultural Society*, 1856, p. 67). The society's influence was concentrated on Calvert's favorite project, and in 1853 it adopted his resolution memorializing Congress to establish a de-

partment of agriculture. When he entered Congress, Calvert was assigned to the Committee on Agriculture, which had under consideration a bill for the establishment of a department. This was reported favorably Jan. 7, 1862, but the House amended it over his protest by changing the word "Department" to "Bureau," in which form it became a law. Although a Department was not established until 1889 the Act of 1862 is generally regarded as the organic law (Henry Barrett Learned, *The President's Cabinet*, 315, 323 ff.; *Congressional Globe*, 37 Cong., 2 Sess., pp. 855–56). Calvert's untimely death at his home, Riverdale, Md., probably deprived the farmers of many interesting ideas on the development of agriculture.

[Chas. Lanman, *Biog. Annals of the Civil Govt. of the U. S.* (1887); *Country Gentleman*, XXIII, May 19, 1864, p. 321; *Jour. of the U. S. Agr. Soc.*, 1852–59 (see references in Learned, *ante*, pp. 321 ff.); personal information.]   C. W. G.

CALVERT, GEORGE (*c.* 1580–Apr. 15, 1632), first Lord Baltimore, projector of the province of Maryland, belonged to a family whose name occurs in the records of Yorkshire, England, as early as 1366. Its unbroken record begins about two centuries later with the marriage of Leonard Calvert, a country gentleman, and Grace Crossland, a lady of gentle birth in the same neighborhood. George, their eldest, if not their only son, was born at Kipling, in the chapelry of Bolton, in 1580 or very close to that year. At the age of fourteen he entered Trinity College, Oxford, where he became proficient in Latin, obtaining his bachelor's degree in 1597 and the honorary degree of Master of Arts in 1605. In 1604–05 he was married to Anne, daughter of George Mynne of Hertingfordbury, Hertfordshire. Shortly after receiving the first degree he traveled on the continent and became familiar with the French, Spanish, and Italian languages. In 1606 he became private secretary to Sir Robert Cecil, principal secretary of state and until his death, in 1612, controller of the policy of King James. Under Cecil's influence Calvert enjoyed rapid advancement and won the confidence of the King. He was made clerk of the crown of assize and peace in County Clare, Ireland, in 1606. He was returned a member of Parliament for Bossiney, in Cornwall, in 1609; was sent on a special mission to France in 1610; and assisted the King in a theological dispute witht Vorstius, a Dutch theologian. He was appointed a clerk of the Privy Council in 1613, and served on a commission to inquire into religious grievances in Ireland. He was knighted in 1617; and in 1619 the King, in opposition to the wishes of the Duke of Buckingham, appointed him a principal secretary of state to serve as a colleague of the less active Sir Robert Naunton. In this office, which made him a member of the Privy Council, Calvert faithfully discharged important diplomatic functions and was a staunch defender in Parliament of the unpopular policy and measures of King James, particularly the negotiations for a marriage alliance with Catholic Spain. Those negotiations failed, and Calvert, in 1624, lost the seat in Parliament which he had held for Yorkshire since 1621. He was immediately returned as one of the members for the University of Oxford, but in the face of pending measures for the persecution of Catholics he announced his conversion to that faith and tendered his resignation of the secretaryship. In accepting the resignation, in January 1625, the King retained him as a member of the Privy Council and created him Baron of Baltimore in the Kingdom of Ireland.

Calvert's interest in American colonization is first disclosed by his membership in the Virginia Company from 1609 to 1620 and by his admission as one of the council of the New England Company in 1622. In 1620 King James granted him an increased duty on silk and the same year he acquired by purchase a portion of the peninsula of Avalon, the southeastern section of Newfoundland. In December 1622 he received from the King a grant of the whole country of Newfoundland. By a re-grant, in March 1623, the territory was restricted to the peninsula of Avalon, and this, by a royal charter, dated Apr. 7 of the same year, was erected into the province of Avalon, modeled after the county palatine of Durham, a great crown fief, the powers of whose lord were regal in kind and inferior only in degree to those of the king. A small colony was established at Ferryland in 1620. There was some building and planting but the colony did not prosper. Lord Baltimore made it a short visit in the summer of 1627 and returned to it in 1628 with his second wife, Joan, and all, except Cecilius, of the children by his first wife. After an engagement with three French ships in the summer of 1628, Lord Baltimore appealed to the King for special protection. In August 1629, he complained of the severity of the weather from October to May, stated that his house had been a hospital all winter, and prayed for a grant of land in the warmer climate of Virginia. Before the King's unfavorable reply had been received he departed for Jamestown where Lady Baltimore had gone in the autumn of 1628. Objecting to Papists, the Virginians treated him harshly and hastened his departure for England by tendering him the oaths of supremacy

and allegiance. Yielding to his appeal, King Charles, in February 1632, granted him the territory extending southward from the James River to the Roanoke and westward to the mountains, as the province of Carolina. Bitter opposition by members of the late Virginia Company resulted in the substitution of the territory between the 40th degree of north latitude and the Potomac River extending westward from the ocean to the longitude of the first source of the river, as the province of Maryland. Lord Baltimore died, Apr. 15, 1632, before the charter, copied from that of Avalon, had passed the great seal, but, bearing date of June 20, of the same year, it was issued to his eldest son, Cecilius.

A portrait of Calvert by Daniel Mytens exhibits an oval face, a mustache and pointed beard, large straight nose, melancholy eyes, and marks of refinement. Although not brilliant, he was an industrious and reliable public servant, zealously intent upon the welfare of England; and in the charter of Maryland he laid the foundation for one of the most successful governments in the American colonies.

[The most important primary source is the *Calendar of* (British) *State Papers*, colonial and domestic series. B. C. Steiner, "The First Lord Baltimore and His Colonial Projects" in the *Ann. Report, Am. Hist. Ass.* for 1905, contains a long list of authorities. Consult also C. C. Hall, *The Lords Baltimore and the Md. Palatinate* (1902); the sketch in H. F. Powell, *Tercentenary Hist. of Md.* (1925); and Anthony Wood, *Athenæ Oxonienses* (1721). For family history see J. B. C. Nicklin, "The Calvert Family" in *Md. Hist. Mag.*, vol. XVI (1921).]

N. D. M.

CALVERT, GEORGE HENRY (June 2, 1803–May 24, 1889), poet, essayist, was the eldest son of George Calvert, and was born on his father's estate, Riverdale, near Bladensburg, Md. His great-grandfather was the fifth Lord Baltimore, and his mother was Rosalie Eugenia Stier, daughter of a Belgian emigré who had settled temporarily in Maryland. He completed his education at Harvard (1819–23), and at eighteen was described by his father as "a very clever fellow . . . a little spoiled by the ladies as he is thought by them very handsome" (*Ancestry of Rosalie Morris Johnson*, 1905, II, 48). In the summer of 1823 he sailed for England, under the care of Stratford Canning, the British Minister at Washington; visited at his uncle's chateau seven miles from Antwerp; and then settled in Göttingen—one of the earliest American students there—for fifteen months' work in history and philosophy. During the summer of 1825 he visited Weimar, saw the aged Goethe, and was welcomed in the society of the Weimar court. The next winter he was in Edinburgh, and during the following year he saw much of the best social life of Antwerp and Paris. Two years after his return from abroad he was married, on Mar. 8, 1829, to Elizabeth, daughter of Dr. James Steuart of Baltimore. For some years, until Aug. 18, 1836, he was an editor of the *Baltimore American*. Upon the marriage and establishment in charge of the family estate of his younger brother, Charles Benedict Calvert [*q.v.*], he again went abroad, 1840–43, spending three days with Wordsworth, Aug. 1–3, 1840, and later sojourning in Germany and Italy. On his return he established his home in Newport, R. I., where, aside from travel, he spent his remaining years. For some time he was chairman of the Newport School Committee, and he was Democratic mayor of Newport, 1853–54. He was once more abroad in 1851–52. One who remembers him in old age describes him as living with his wife a retired life in his Newport home, "a rambling conglomeration of architecture in a setting of somber fir trees." He was "of great courtesy and dignity of manner, interested in spiritualism, tall, dark, gaunt, stooped, steeped in introspection, universally respected and beloved."

Calvert's verse includes many lyric and narrative poems in a diluted Tennysonian strain, such as *Cabiro, a Poem* (1840), *Anyta and Other Poems* (1866), *Ellen, a Poem for the Times* (1867), *Life, Death, and Other Poems* (1882); two comedies laid in Renaissance Italy (*Comedies*, 1856), and the historical closet dramas in respectable blank verse: *Count Julian, a Tragedy* (1840); *Arnold and André* (1864); *Mirabeau* (1873); *Maid of Orleans* (1873); *Brangomar* (1883), a tragedy of Napoleon. In the seventies he published the critical, or in his phrase "biographic æsthetic" studies, *Goethe, His Life and Works* (1872), *Wordsworth* (1878), *Shakespeare* (1879), *Coleridge, Shelley and Goethe* (1880). From time to time throughout his life he delivered public addresses on political, literary, and artistic themes, several of which were put in print. His mild interest in the theories of the French socialists Fourier and Godin appears in his *Introduction to Social Science* (1856). "Essentially a feeble and commonplace writer of poetry, although his prose compositions have a certain degree of merit"—this verdict of Poe on Calvert, though written in 1841 (*A Chapter on Autography*) when Calvert had produced little, will apply without great modification to all his thirty-odd slender volumes of narrative and dramatic verse, travel, criticism, and translation. The prose works, as Poe says, are the better, and of these perhaps the best worth reopening to-day are his essay on manners, *The Gentleman* (1863), which went to three editions, his *First Years in Europe* (1866), and his second

volume of *Scenes and Thoughts in Europe* (vol. I, 1845, vol. II, 1852), which gives an interesting account of the temper of Germany after 1848 and of France under Louis Napoleon. These works reveal the author in his most significant aspect, as a middle-states gentleman of distinguished family and independent means, a devoted American, who gave his life to literature and the translation of old-world culture to the new.

[See E. A. and G. L. Duyckinck, *Cyc. of Am. Lit.* (1855), vol. II, and *A Bibliography of the Works of Geo. Henry Calvert* (1900), by H. B. Tompkins, with biographical sketch and portrait, published by the Redwood Library, Newport, to which Calvert gave his books. Four letters written to John P. Kennedy in 1861–62, one of them expressing his sympathy with the North in the Civil War, are in the Kennedy MSS., Peabody Inst., Baltimore.]
A. W.

CALVERT, LEONARD (1606–June 9, 1647), colonial governor, was the second son of George Calvert [*q.v.*], first Lord Baltimore and of his wife, Anne Mynne. His elder brother, Cecilius (1605–75), was the second Lord Baltimore and the first proprietor of the province of Maryland. As the presence of Cecilius was needed in England to defend his charter from repeated attacks of enemies he never visited the province, as he had planned to do, but entrusted the exercise of his authority there to Leonard who served under a commission as governor. The record of Leonard's early life is obscure. He went with his father to Newfoundland in 1628, at about the age of twenty-one, returned to England with some French prizes, and petitioned the king for letters of marque. With two vessels, the *Ark* and the *Dove,* carrying about three hundred colonists, he sailed from England, Nov. 22, 1633, and landed at St. Clements (now Blackistone) Island, in Maryland, Mar. 25, 1634. Here he immediately took "solemn possession of the Country for our Saviour and for our Sovereign Lord the King of England." The following month, after some days of exploration and friendly intercourse with the Indians, he established the seat of government at St. Mary's, in St. Mary's County. Up to this time he was directed by instructions of Nov. 15, 1633, covering chiefly early proceedings and addressed to himself as governor and to two commissioners who were to assist him. He was particularly enjoined to give no offense to the Protestant members of the colony and to cultivate friendly relations with Virginia. By the first extant commission to him as governor, dated Apr. 15, 1637, he was made commander-in-chief of armed forces by land and sea; was made chief magistrate with large power of appointment; was authorized to call, prorogue, and dissolve the legislative Assembly;

was made chancellor and chief justice with full power to hear and determine all criminal and civil cases not involving life, member, or freehold, and to grant pardons. He was authorized to grant patents for lands and appoint places for ports of entry, fairs, and markets. Instructions for the discharge of these functions were occasionally issued by the proprietor, who also appointed a council to advise him.

Calvert gave early attention to the promotion and regulation of trade with the Indians, and in the summer of 1634 he sent the *Dove* with a cargo of corn to Boston to trade for fish and other commodities. He called the first Assembly of freemen to meet at St. Mary's in February, 1634/35, and the laws which it passed he sent to the proprietor for approval. The proprietor rejected them and sent others for the assent of the second Assembly. In January 1637/38 all members of that body, except Calvert and the secretary of the province, voted against them. To a suggestion that some laws be agreed upon until the proprietor had again been heard from, the governor replied that the Assembly had no power to do this. But he yielded to a proposition that he govern during this period according to the laws of England, or, if necessary, by martial law. Forty-two bills were subsequently passed. The governor signed them and wrote the proprietor, "I am persuaded they will appear unto you to provide both for your honor and profit as much as those you sent us did." The proprietor yielded, and the right of initiative in legislation passed to the Assembly. It was the first important step in the transition to popular government in Maryland. In February 1637/38, Calvert, at the head of a small force, reduced to submission a trading post on Kent Island which had been established there in 1631 by William Claiborne. In April 1643 he sailed for England to confer with his brother. Shortly after his return, in September 1644, Claiborne and Richard Ingle incited an insurrection of Protestants against Catholics. St. Mary's was seized and the governor took refuge in Virginia. Two years later he returned with a force of Virginians and Marylanders, recovered possession, and restored order. He died June 9, 1647, leaving two children: William and Anne, whose mother, Anne (Brent), had died some time before. He made his sister-in-law, Margaret Brent [*q.v.*], his executrix. Calvert was industrious and faithful to his brother's interest but was lacking in tact and personal magnetism. He governed by force rather than by leadership.

[The chief primary sources are the *Archives of Md.,* vols. I, III, and the *Calvert Papers* (1889). The best secondary sources are B. C. Steiner, *Beginnings of Md.*

(1903) and W. H. Browne, *Md., the Hist. of a Palatinate* (1884). For family history see J. B. C. Nicklin, "The Calvert Family," *Md. Hist. Mag.,* vol. XVI (1921).]

N. D. M.

CALVIN, SAMUEL (Feb. 2, 1840–Apr. 17, 1911), geologist, was born of Scottish parents, Thomas and Elizabeth Calvin, in Wigtonshire, Scotland, where he lived until eleven years of age. The family was one of only moderate means, and his early schooling limited. Among his school associates was James Wilson, who in after years became secretary of agriculture in the United States.

When Samuel was eleven years old the family emigrated to the United States, living for three years near Saratoga in New York State and then moving on to the open prairie lands of Buchanan County, Iowa. The country was then largely a wilderness scantily peopled by a few hardy pioneers, and, owing to a lack of qualified teachers, educational facilities were few and poor. At the age of sixteen, Calvin was himself called upon to teach in the local district school, but is stated to have been also an expert carpenter and cabinet-maker. In 1861 or 1862 he entered Lenox College, in the town of Hopkinton. Later he became an instructor there. Lenox College was one of the many small denominational colleges so abundant throughout the middle west, with scanty endowment, poor equipment, and affording opportunities for only the simplest and most fundamental training. There Calvin remained until 1864 when, in company with others of the faculty and student body, he enlisted. Before he was called into serious service, the war came to an end and Calvin returned to Lenox and labored under the discouraging conditions incidental to building up a nearly wrecked institution.

In 1867 and 1868 he served as county superintendent of Delaware County, and from 1869 to 1873 was principal of one of the Dubuque schools. While at Lenox he found among other members of the faculty Thomas H. Macbride, a botanist, to whom he became warmly attached and with whom he made frequent excursions and collecting trips. In the course of this work he came in contact with Dr. C. A. White, then state geologist and later professor of geology at the State University. When Dr. White resigned to accept a call from an eastern college, Calvin in 1874 succeeded him as professor of natural history at the University and when the state survey was reorganized in 1892, became state geologist as well. It was with this organization that his name first became known to the country at large. This, it may be well to note, was the third attempt at a geological survey on the part of the state, and Calvin continued at its head until 1904, when he resigned, to be appointed again in 1906, serving until his death in 1911.

Calvin's scientific training, as is evident, was largely self-acquired. When he entered upon his work as teacher, the geology of the upper Mississippi region was known only in the most general way and it is perhaps fortunate that he began with no preconceived notions. "He found his inspiration in a deep love and enthusiastic appreciation of nature and he brought to his work a critically keen judgment and an uncompromising allegiance to simple truth which made for thoroughness and accuracy" (Shimek, *post,* p. 5). Calvin's individual research, quite aside from his teaching and executive duties, was largely paleontological and stratigraphic. It is stated that he considered his discovery and proper interpretation of an interglacial mammalian fauna in the state as his most important contribution to science. In the course of his work, he described and named some thirty species of invertebrate fossils, and in turn had eleven species and varieties named after him by others. He was one of the founders of the *American Geologist* in 1888, and its editor-in-chief until 1894; a member of the Geological Society of America (president 1908); of the Paleontological Society of America; the American Association for the Advancement of Science; and other scientific societies. In 1870 he was married to Louise Jackson by whom he had two children, a son and a daughter.

[H. Foster Bain, *Jour. of Geology,* XIX (1911), 385–91, whose statement that the family home was south of Manchester, *i.e.,* in Delaware County, is an error; B. Shimek, *Bull. Geol. Soc. of America,* vol. XXIII, 1912; full bibliography of Calvin's publications in Nickles, *Bull. 746, U. S. Geol. Survey.*]   G. P. M.

CAMBRELENG, CHURCHILL CALDOM (1786–Apr. 30, 1862), congressman, diplomat, was born in Washington, Beaufort County, N. C. Of his family and childhood little is known except that one brother became a New York attorney, another a naval officer, and Cambreleng himself a student in New Bern, N. C. He went to New York in 1802 and achieved success in commerce, at one time being associated with J. J. Astor, traveling extensively in America and abroad for the firm. At other times he was head of the firms of Cambreleng & Chrystie and Cambreleng & Pearson. He was one of the first directors for the Farmers Fire Insurance & Loan Company. He married a Miss Glover but had no children. From 1821 to 1839 he was a member of Congress, being the House administration leader for Jackson and Van Buren. His most important committee assignments were the

chairmanships of the committees on Ways and Means, on Commerce and on Foreign Affairs. He took a prominent part in the debates, his remarks being characterized by clarity and common sense. Considered an unscrupulous henchman of Jackson and Van Buren by their enemies, he was described by one of them—William Lyon Mackenzie, the Canadian rebel—as "very short made and very stout—no great orator but well acquainted with business and politics." Van Buren, on the other hand, called Cambreleng "as honest as the steelyard and as direct in the pursuit of his purpose as a shot from a culverin." Cambreleng approved Jackson's course toward the Bank of the United States and opposed the tariffs of 1824 and 1828. He favored a vigorous assertion of American claims to Oregon and a firm attitude toward France concerning the treaty of 1831, but opposed sending delegates to the Panama Congress. While traveling in Europe he was appointed minister to Russia by Van Buren and served from May 1840 to July 1841. His interest in public affairs persisted after his return. He represented Suffolk County in the constitutional convention of 1846. As chairman of the Committee on Currency and Banking he gave a masterly exposition of the nature and necessity of a sound currency. It is significant that he was frequently bracketed with such leaders as John A. Dix, Preston King, William Cullen Bryant, and Samuel J. Tilden. The "Hunkers" having secured control of the state Democratic convention in 1847, the "Barnburners" withdrew and held one of their own, presided over by Cambreleng. He took a prominent part in the convention at Utica in 1848 which nominated Van Buren for president and paved the way for the national Free-Soil convention at Buffalo. Cambreleng's published works include: his report as the chairman of the Committee on Commerce and Navigation (1830), which passed through several editions and was republished in London; *An Examination of the New Tariff Proposed by the Honorable Henry Baldwin* (1821); *A Defence of Direct Taxes and of Protective Duties for the Encouragement of Manufactures* (1822); *Eulogy Pronounced in the City of New York, July 17, 1826* (on John Adams and Jefferson); *Speech on the Proposition . . . to Amend the Constitution . . . Respecting the Election of President and Vice-President* (1826); *Speech . . . on the Bill Regulating the Deposit of Public Money* (1835). Neither the violent demagogue his enemies thought, nor the paragon his friends esteemed him, Cambreleng was an industrious, astute politician. His successful mercantile career contributed much to his success in politics. He died at his home at West Neck, Long Island, Apr. 30, 1862.

[Many Cambreleng letters are in the Van Buren Papers in the Library of Congress, a few in the libraries at Albany and N. Y., some in Wm. Lyon Mackenzie's *Lives and Opinions of Benj. Franklin Butler and Jesse Hoyt* (1845) and *The Life and Times of Martin Van Buren* (1846). Other sources are: the N. Y. and Washington newspapers of the period; "The Autobiography of Martin Van Buren," being *House Doc. No. 819*, 66 Cong., 2 Sess.; the *Documents* and *Journals* of the N. Y. Constitutional Convention of 1846; the *Annals of Cong.*; the *Reg. of Debates*; and the *Cong. Globe*. Scattered items may be found in De Alva S. Alexander, *Polit. Hist. of N. Y.* (1906); Chas. E. Fitch, *Memorial Encyc. of the State of N. Y.* (1916); Wm. T. Bonner, *N. Y.—the World Metropolis* (1924); Jas. Schouler, *Hist. of the U. S. Under the Constitution* (1880–91); and the biographies and writings of Bryant, Jackson, Polk, Tilden, and Van Buren.]   M. L. B.

CAMDEN, JOHNSON NEWLON (Mar. 6, 1828–Apr. 25, 1908), business man, senator, of Maryland descent, was the eldest of the eight children of John Scribner Camden and Nancy (Newlon) Camden. He was born at the Collins Settlement, Va. Early in 1838 he moved with his father to the neighboring Braxton County, where as a boy he obtained a thorough knowledge of woodcraft and some insight into mineral resources. His basic training for business was obtained from a brief experience as assistant to the county clerk at Weston (1842–43), two years of study at the Northwestern Academy at Clarksburg (1843–45), a year of service as deputy-clerk of the circuit court of Braxton County (1845–46), and a period of study as a cadet at the United States Military Academy at West Point (1846–48). Resigning from West Point to study law, he was admitted to the bar in 1851 and for a time held the local office of state attorney, first in Braxton County, then in Nicholas County; but, influenced by his interest in surveying and in large tracts of wild lands, he soon abandoned law for the purchase of leases for wild lands with which he combined for a time (1853–58) an assistant's position in the Exchange Bank at Weston. In 1858 he married Anna Thompson, a daughter of Judge George W. and Elizabeth (Steenrod) Thompson of Wheeling. Later he applied his business genius to the development of oil production beginning with exciting pioneer work at Burning Springs on the Little Kanawha in Wirt County in 1860 and forming a partnership with the Rathbone Brothers during the Civil War. In 1869 he sold his Little Kanawha interests and at Parkersburg entered the oil refining business which soon resulted in association with the recently organized Standard Oil Company. In the latter he became a director and was especially in charge of the prosperous Camden Consolidated Oil Company at Parkersburg and later consolidated the refin-

eries of Baltimore under a single management of which he became president. In connection with his plans for wild land development he completed a branch railroad from Clarksburg to Weston in 1879 and extended it southward to the Elk and Gauley rivers in 1889–90, merging the various branches into the West Virginia & Pittsburgh of which he became president and which in 1890 was leased to the Baltimore & Ohio Company. Meantime in 1882 he was a leader in the organization of the Ohio River Railroad which was completed from Wheeling to Parkersburg in 1884 and to Huntington in 1888.

Camden was active in movements for repeal of the state constitutional disfranchisement of Confederates. In 1868 and again in 1872 he was the Conservative-Democrat candidate for governor but was defeated. He declined to be a candidate for the nomination in 1870. In 1868, 1872, and 1876 he was a delegate to the Democratic national conventions. For the United States Senate he was strongly supported in the contest of 1874, was unanimously nominated by the Democratic caucus in 1880, and was elected by the legislature in 1881. He was the caucus nominee of 1887 for reëlection and, although defeated by the defection of twelve Democrat members of the legislature who opposed his political methods, he named his successor. With the intention of retiring from politics he declined the offer of the nomination for governor. In January 1893 he was again elected to the United States Senate to complete the unexpired term of Senator John A. Kenna (deceased) and served until Mar. 4, 1895, when he was succeeded by Senator Stephen B. Elkins.

[J. M. Callahan, *Hist. of W. Va. Old and New* (1923); Geo. W. Atkinson and Alvaro F. Gibbons, *Prominent Men of W. Va.* (1890); *Biog. Directory Am. Cong.* (1928); *Daily State Jour.* (Parkersburg, W. Va.), Apr. 27, 1908.]   J. M. C.

CAMERON, ANDREW CARR (Sept. 28, 1834–May 28, 1890), labor leader and publisher, the son of a Scotch printer, lived for the first seventeen years of his life in Berwick-on-Tweed, England. After a short but rigorous elementary education, he was placed in his father's shop, where he worked until the family emigrated to America and settled in a small village near Chicago. Within a few months the father was able to find an opening for young Cameron on a Chicago paper, at that time called the *Courant*, later merged into *Young America*, and afterward into the *Chicago Times*. With the latter reorganization, it became the official organ of Stephen A. Douglas. While working on this paper Cameron joined and became a prominent member of the Typographical Union. A printers' strike in 1864 led to the establishment of the *Workingman's Advocate,* and Cameron left the *Times* to become its editor. Two years later he took complete control. This weekly paper was the official organ of the Chicago Trades Assembly, and later of the National Labor Union. By forceful and clear editorials, Cameron extended his influence throughout the labor movement of the country, and became the greatest labor editor of his time. In editing the "paper devoted exclusively to the interests of the producing classes" his work was characterized, as an associate described it, "by all the 'vim' and independent characteristics of a Scotch Covenanter who hated tyranny and oppression from whatever source." Cameron's activities were by no means confined to his desk through this period, for during the first six years of his editorship he took part in all the leading labor deliberations, was four years president of the Chicago Trades Assembly, and was also president of the Grand Eight Hour League, and of the Illinois State Labor Association. The labor movement of the middle West during this period believed strongly in the value of independent political action and the editorial columns of the *Advocate* continually expressed this view. Cameron was one of the organizers of the National Labor Union, which had throughout its brief existence as its cardinal tenet the formation of a labor party. For six consecutive years he was chairman of the Platform Committee of the National Labor Union, and was secretary of the conference called by it which nominated Judge Davis for president of the United States. With the unemployment that came with the first attempts at deflation in 1867 and 1868, Cameron and a number of other leaders within the National Labor Union began to stress the greenback theory of "plentiful money." Independent political action, with the issues of the eight-hour day through legislative action, monetary and land reform, and coöperation were the doctrines that he continually dwelt on in the *Workingman's Advocate* and which he impressed upon the National Labor Union. As a part of his program he also emphasized the very limited possibilities of the strike. Though the *Advocate* continued publication until 1880 and was widely read, Cameron's influence began to decline from about 1870. Many workers were losing faith in the power of political action, and inclining toward a more strictly economic organization. New leaders were being heard who urged the economic value of unionism and advocated the use of the strike where necessary. Though Cameron never lost faith in his own beliefs, he was fair enough to give the new leaders a hearing and encourage-

ment through the columns of the *Advocate.* By 1875 the drift away from political action was very marked, and the National Labor Union held its last convention, with Cameron and a few more of the old leaders as the only delegates in attendance. Though he was unable to see in the tendency away from political action any reason for giving up his own beliefs, he never became bitter at the new leaders or the changed emphasis. He continued to urge political action leading to monetary reform for it would, he believed, "do more to dignify labor, secure to the laborer an equitable distribution of this world's goods than all trade unions" (*Workingman's Advocate,* Jan. 25, 1873). After sixteen years as publisher of the *Advocate,* he discontinued the paper, and became editor of the *Inland Printer,* the leading technical journal for the trade in the United States at that time. He had in no way lost his sympathy and enthusiasm for the welfare of the producing classes, but the movement had passed to other issues, issues for which Cameron had not the same zeal. After eight years he purchased the *Artist Printer,* which he edited until his death.

[See the brief biography in the *Western British American,* Mar. 19, 1888. Most of the material from the pages of the *Workingman's Advocate,* including the yearly proceedings of the National Labor Union, has been collected in John R. Commons and others, *Documentary Hist. of Am. Industrial Soc.,* vol. IX (1910), containing the significant "Address to Workingmen" prepared by Cameron for the National Labor Union. The place of Cameron in the labor movement of the period is outlined in John R. Commons and others, *Hist. of Labour in the U. S.* (1918), vol. II.]   W.E.C.

CAMERON, ARCHIBALD (*c.* 1771–Dec. 4, 1836), Presbyterian minister, was the youngest of six children born to John and Jannet (McDonald) Cameron of Ken Loch in Lochaber, Scotland. In 1773–74 the family emigrated to America and located near Redstone, on the Monongahela River in western Virginia, whence the family moved, in 1781, to Kentucky and eventually settled on a farm near Bardstown in Nelson County. The parents died soon after their arrival in Kentucky, and Angus Cameron—a strange anomaly among frontiersmen, in that he was quite at home with Greek and Latin texts— directed the early training of his younger brother, Archibald. After spending about a year at Transylvania Seminary, Lexington, Archibald finished his literary course under the guidance of James Priestley of Bardstown, and then studied theology with David Rice of Danville. Licensed to preach in 1795 and ordained the following year, he began a ministry of forty years' duration which left its imprint on Presbyterianism in Kentucky, though his labors were confined to the counties of Nelson, Shelby, and Jefferson.

Freed from "worldly cares and avocations" by an emolument, which, in 1806, amounted to $217.75 if all the subscriptions were paid, Cameron rode about the country, often swimming his horse across the Salt River, to organize new churches and to encourage the struggling congregations already established. He combated with an unbending orthodoxy the schisms which threatened to destroy the Presbyterianism his Calvinistic inheritance and training had led him to support. With New Light, Shakerism, Socinianism, and even with the "absurdities of Methodism" which he deemed "more pernicious, owing to their prevalence, than the Papist errors," he contended in church assembly and in pamphlet. He was a member of the commission appointed by the Kentucky Synod of 1804 to inquire into the Cumberland controversy. He was prominent in the state synods from the first, in 1802, until his death, and usually served on the judiciary committees so that he came to be recognized by his contemporaries as the greatest judicial theologian of Presbyterianism in Kentucky. His published works, including such titles as *The Faithful Steward* (1806), *A Defense of the Doctrines of Grace* (1816), *A Reply to Some Questions on Divine Predestination* (1822) and *An Exposure of Falsehood and Folly* (1829), were brochures, controversial in nature, opposing certain doctrines such as that of "abstracted atonement," which were fashionable in some sections of the Presbyterian church. Cameron was a tireless student, blunt and reserved in manner, and careless in dress, but possessed of a native eloquence and keen powers of satire that made him a much feared adversary. He never married.

[Manuscript copy of papers in the possession of relatives, furnished to J. H. Logan as material for a biography of Archibald Cameron, now in possession of the Presbyt. Hist. Soc. Lib., Phila.; Wm. B. Sprague, *Annals Am. Pulpit*, IV (1858), pp. 168–72; Robt. Davidson, *Hist. of the Presbyt. Ch. in the State of Ky.* (1847), pp. 120–21; the *Presbyterian*, Dec. 24, 1836.]

T. D. M.

CAMERON, JAMES DONALD (May 14, 1833–Aug. 30, 1918), railroad president, secretary of war, senator, the son of Simon Cameron [*q.v.*], and Margaret (Brua) Cameron, was born at Middletown, Pa. After graduating from Princeton in 1852, he returned to his native town to begin a business career. His father had established the Bank of Middletown, had organized and developed the Northern Central Railroad, and had interested himself in numerous other projects. Young Cameron, therefore, found ample opportunities awaiting him. He began his apprenticeship as a clerk in the bank, but was soon promoted to cashier and subsequently became president. Other family properties came under his management early because of the elder Cameron's increasing absorption in state and national politics. During the Civil War the son was active in forwarding Union troops over the "Cameron Road," and from 1863 to 1874 he was president of the company. It is said that he personally made the railroad arrangements to get Lincoln to Washington in 1861 when there were rumors of plots against the President. He seems to have had much of his father's ability, energy, and shrewdness, and to have been typical of the men of affairs who were beginning to dominate the life of the nation. But it was not as a business man that he earned a nation-wide reputation: it was as an audacious politician. Here also his father had paved the way for him, but once in the rough and tumble of politics, Don Cameron was well able to stand alone. In his father's notable struggle against Gov. Andrew G. Curtin for the senatorship in 1867, the son successfully directed the maneuvers in the legislature from start to finish. The Governor's defeat gave the Camerons undisputed domination of the politics of the state. The father also acquired great influence with President Grant and when a vacancy occurred in the War Office in 1876 he succeeded in having his son appointed as secretary of war. Don Cameron's incumbency was brief (May 22, 1876–Mar. 3, 1877), but his energetic handling of departmental business amply demonstrated his competence. He was not averse to using his office, however, to serve political ends. When Hayes's chances of winning the electoral votes of Florida and Louisiana in 1877 were doubtful, Cameron placed Federal troops at the disposal of Republican politicians in these states. For this service and for the notable assistance that he had rendered Hayes in the Republican nominating convention, the elder Cameron and other Pennsylvania Republicans demanded that the Secretary be continued in the War Department under the new administration. Hayes refused; he disapproved of the political methods of the Camerons and wanted an entirely new cabinet. Senator Cameron then decided to surrender his own place to his son as a consolation prize. The subservient Pennsylvania legislature readily acquiesced and elected Don Cameron for the remaining two years of his father's term. A more striking example of entrenched political power could hardly be found. At the same time Don also took over the active management of the state political machine which his father had built up and with the aid of lieutenants like Matthew

Quay ran it skilfully and defiantly as long as he remained in public life. It enabled him to be returned to the Senate in 1879, 1885, and 1891. Election to the chairmanship of the Republican national committee in 1879 for a time widened his influence in national politics. He promptly turned it to Grant's advantage, joining with Conkling of New York and Logan of Illinois in a strenuous campaign to have the war hero nominated for a third term. Shrewd plans were laid to control the convention of 1880, but their strategy was discovered and defeated. Although successful as a politician, Cameron never employed the arts commonly used by public men to popularize themselves with the people. He despised all such methods. He was a judicious, reticent, unemotional man. His speeches were few and brief, but direct and forceful. Like his father he worked in ante-rooms, committees, and caucuses to attain his ends. On the whole his twenty years in the Senate were undistinguished. He made politics, not statesmanship, his principal public business. At a time when the public treasury was being drained for pensions, relief measures, and the like, he was in the forefront of those serving private causes. In national legislation he generally stood with his party, but on occasion, as in the case of the "Force Bill" of 1890, showed admirable and courageous independence. And, unlike his father, he would not bend or yield to public sentiment. He was especially earnest in his support of a high tariff and other measures favorable to the rapidly expanding business interests. In 1883 he went so far as to vote against a protective tariff because its iron duty seemed too low. Yet for some unknown reason he supported free silver as "honest money, the money of the people" (*Congressional Record,* 53 Cong., 1 Sess., p. 2930), and on Oct. 30, 1893, he voted against the repeal of the Sherman Silver Purchase Law. At the end of his third full term, 1897, possibly foreseeing defeat, he retired voluntarily from the Senate and spent the rest of his life in the management of his private affairs and in the quiet enjoyment of his Lancaster farm and his houseboat on the Southern coast. Thoroughly honest in personal matters, he was held in high regard by his friends. He was married twice. His first wife, Mary McCormick, died in 1874. Four years later he married Elizabeth Sherman, niece of John and William T. Sherman.

[There is little in print about Cameron. The most extensive account is in Alexander K. McClure, *Old Time Notes of Pa.* (1905). McClure was a political opponent, but seems to write fairly. References to particular incidents in Cameron's career are to be found in Jas. F. Rhodes, *Hist. of the U. S.,* vol. VIII (1919); E. P. Oberholtzer, *Hist. of the U. S. Since the Civil War,* vol. III (1926); Jas. G. Blaine, *Twenty Years of Congress* (1884–93); G. F. Hoar, *Autobiog. of Seventy Years* (1903); Chas. R. Williams, *Life of Rutherford B. Hayes* (1914). Obituaries in the *N. Y. Times, N. Y. Tribune,* Phila. *Public Ledger,* and *Phila. Press,* Aug. 31, 1918, give brief but useful sketches of Cameron's life.]   A.H.M.

CAMERON, ROBERT ALEXANDER (Feb. 22, 1828–Mar. 15, 1894), Union soldier, land colonizer, was born in Brooklyn, N. Y. About the time he was fourteen years old his parents moved to Valparaiso, Ind. After finishing at the public schools he entered the Indiana Medical College, from which he graduated in 1849, later attending Rush Medical College in Chicago. In 1857 he bought the *Valparaiso Republican,* which he conducted for several years. He was a delegate to the Republican national convention, where he voted for the nomination of Lincoln, and in the fall of the year he was elected to the lower house of the legislature. On the news of the firing on Fort Sumter he began at once to organize a company of three-months' men. Two days later he telegraphed Gov. Morton that his company was ready, and on Apr. 23 he was mustered in as a captain of the 9th Indiana Volunteers. His first service was in the West Virginia campaign under McClellan. In July he reënlisted, and on the 29th was commissioned a lieutenant-colonel and transferred to the 19th Indiana. On Feb. 3, 1862, he was transferred to the 34th Indiana, of which he was made colonel on June 15. He served at Island No. 10, New Madrid, and at the capture of Memphis. For gallant conduct during the siege of Vicksburg he was recommended by Grant, with five other colonels, for promotion, and on Aug. 11, 1863, was commissioned a brigadier-general. He commanded one of the two divisions (the third) of the 13th Corps that took part in the Red River expedition in the fore part of 1864, and on the wounding of Ransom, at Sabine Cross Roads, Apr. 8, assumed command of the corps. With the defeat and return of the army to the Mississippi and the transfer of the corps to Grant in Virginia, he was placed in command of the Lafourche district of the Department of the Gulf, with headquarters at Thibodaux, La., where he remained till the close of the war. In the omnibus promotions dated Mar. 13, 1865, he was brevetted a major-general.

He resigned from the army June 22 and went to New York. Here he formed the acquaintance of Nathan C. Meeker [*q.v.*], agricultural editor of the *Tribune,* and became greatly interested in the movement for planting farm colonies in the West. On the organization, in Cooper Union, Dec. 23, 1869, of the Union Colony, he was made vice-president, and in the following year, with Meeker and A. C. Fisk, went to Colorado and selected the site now occupied by Greeley. He took a leading part in the founding of the colony, and at the first election, May 1871, was chosen one of the town trustees and subsequently was made president. Three months later, however, he resigned, to take the superintendency of the Fountain Colony, which established Colorado Springs. At the end of the year he returned to Greeley, but in the spring of 1873 took part in the founding of Fort Collins, a venture that proved personally disastrous. After an attempt to recoup his fortunes in San Francisco, he returned to Colorado and settled in Denver. For several years he was inspector of mail service in that city, a post in which he is credited with doing efficient work. In 1885 he was appointed warden of the penitentiary at Canon City, but a change in the state administration two years later caused him to lose the place before he had time to introduce the reforms he had planned. In 1888 he was engaged as immigration agent of the Fort Worth & Denver City Railway. In the outskirts of Canon City he developed a fruit farm and continued to reside there until his death.

Cameron married a daughter of J. B. Flower, one of the founders of Greeley Colony and at one time his partner. He was a large man, somewhat above six feet in height and weighing more than 200 pounds. The Denver *News,* on his death, said of him that "as a citizen" none "was more highly esteemed." Boyd, one of the Union colonists, though acknowledging that he had a certain kind of ability, speaks of him as one who "was fertile in expedients," who was "a man of policy rather than a devotee of principle" and finds fault with him for taking for himself and his partner Flower the best location in Greeley.

[F. B. Heitman, *Hist. Reg.* (1903) ; *Battles and Leaders of the Civil War,* IV (1888) ; John Formby, *The Am. Civil War* (1910) ; Jerome C. Smiley and others, *Semi-Centennial Hist. of the State of Colo.* (1913) ; Jas. F. Willard, *The Union Colony at Greeley, Colo.* (1918) ; David Boyd, *Greeley and the Union Colony of Colo.* (1890) ; obituaries in *The News* and *The Republican* of Denver, Mar. 16, 1894.]   W. J. G.

CAMERON, SIMON (Mar. 8, 1799–June 26, 1889), senator, secretary of war, diplomat, was born in Lancaster County, Pa., of Scotch and German ancestry, the son of Charles and Martha (Pfoutz) Cameron. Reverses and misfortunes in his father's family cast him upon the world early and he was obliged to apprentice himself for a time in a printing business in Harrisburg. In January 1821, at the solicitation of Samuel D. Ingham, he went to Doylestown, Pa., where he edited the *Bucks County Messenger,* soon merged with the *Doylestown Democrat* as the *Bucks County Democrat.* On the decease of this paper at the close of the year 1821, he returned to

Harrisburg for a short time as partner of Charles Mowry in the management of the *Pennsylvania Intelligencer,* but during 1822 he went to Washington to study national political movements, obtained work in the printing house of Gales & Seaton who printed the congressional debates, and spent his spare time in the houses of Congress and in making useful friends,—among them Monroe and Calhoun. About 1824 he returned to Harrisburg, bought the *Republican,* and was soon exercising considerable influence in state and national politics. He was then, as later, a staunch advocate of the protective tariff. The remunerative position of state printer was given him and in 1826 he was made adjutant-general of the state. Newspaper editing did not hold him long. As soon as his position was established and his purse sufficient, he left the press and entered pursuits which promised greater financial gain. It was the era of internal improvements, and the ambitious young Cameron was quick to see money-making possibilities. He became a contractor for the construction of canals and began a network of railroads in Pennsylvania which he later united into the Northern Central Railroad. In 1832 he set up the Bank of Middletown with himself as cashier, and soon afterward entered the iron business. Subsequently he also engaged in insurance and became interested in other projects. Notwithstanding the diversity of these undertakings Cameron managed them with skill and success and amassed a fortune. At no time, however, did he lose his interest in state and national politics. It was partly through his efforts that the state legislature in 1830 was induced to head a movement for Jackson's renomination, and two years later he aided materially in having Van Buren nominated for vice-president in place of Calhoun. It was also largely through Cameron's maneuvering that James Buchanan was sent to the Senate in 1833 just at the time when he despaired of political opportunities and was seriously considering a return to the practise of law. Prior to 1838 Cameron had held no public office except the position of adjutant-general of Pennsylvania, but in that year he received an appointment as commissioner to settle certain claims of the Winnebago Indians, a place he acquired with Buchanan's assistance. Considerable scandal arose from his activities because of his adjusting the claims by the payment of notes on his own bank, an arrangement which enriched himself and earned for him the derisive sobriquet, "The Great Winnebago Chief." Following this episode, Cameron's political influence decreased for a time, but actually his career as a great politician was only beginning. In 1845 by a coalition of Whigs, Native Americans, and Protectionist Democrats he won the Senate seat vacated by Buchanan who resigned to enter Polk's cabinet. Buchanan was irritated at Cameron's defeat of the regular party candidate, George Woodward, a free-trader, and the two men parted political company. Alexander K. McClure, an old political foe, has written that from 1845 until Cameron's death nearly a half-century later, "There is not an important complete chapter of political history in the State that can be written with the omission of his defeats or triumphs, and even after his death until the present time [1905] no important chapter of political history can be fully written without recognizing his successors and assigns in politics as leading or controlling factors" (*Old Time Notes of Pennsylvania*, 1905, I, 98). Still, the victory of 1845 did not crown Cameron as the political czar of his state. He had won by fusion methods and incurred bitter Democratic opposition. In 1849 he was unable to command Democratic support and failed to effect a strong enough coalition in the legislature to win a reëlection. His first term in the Senate is of interest principally because in 1846 he made the one important speech of his career. It was in opposition to the Walker revenue tariff. Another attempt in 1855 to return to the Senate with Know-Nothing support also resulted in failure. Cameron then decided to cast his lot with the new Republican party and in 1856 actively supported Frémont for President. The following year Republican backing and three Democratic votes, obtained by bargaining, enabled him to return to the Senate. There he became an implacable foe of President Buchanan. Cameron's political somersaulting was now at an end; he remained a Republican for the rest of his life and gave much of his time and energy to the building up of a smooth-running party machine in Pennsylvania. In the management and control of it he was unequalled. His leadership was sometimes challenged; he suffered subsequent defeats; but no one ever dislodged him from control of the organization. In 1860 it helped him to make a presentable showing in the Republican national convention as a candidate for president. He could not be nominated, but his henchmen traded Pennsylvania votes for Lincoln in exchange for a cabinet post for Cameron. After much hesitation Lincoln abided by the bargain his managers had made without his consent. Cameron resigned his seat in the Senate and became secretary of war. The choice proved a most unfortunate one. Although Cameron was an able business executive, political considerations too often governed his judg-

ments and his actions in departmental administration. He dispensed civil and military offices and army contracts in a notorious fashion; corruption became rampant. Although it does not appear that he enriched himself, there were many who did profit shamefully. Complaints against his management and his favoritism poured into Washington almost daily and demands for his removal were persistent. In an effort to retrieve popular support he began to advocate the freeing and arming of slaves, policies which were rapidly gaining public favor, but which were not then acceptable to the President. So embarrassing did the Secretary's presence become that Lincoln in January 1862 appointed him minister to Russia to be rid of him. Three months later the House of Representatives censured his conduct in the handling of contracts. Cameron had no intention of remaining long in Russia, however, and was back in the United States in time to try for the Senate again in 1863. He failed of election, but in 1867, after a struggle of unexampled desperation, was successful. For ten years thereafter the Senator reigned supreme in Pennsylvania, and in 1873 returned to the Senate without a contest. He also became a power in Grant's administration, controlled the patronage of his state, and in 1876 succeeded in having his son, James Donald Cameron [*q.v.*], appointed secretary of war. When President Hayes in 1877 refused to continue the son in that office, Cameron resigned his own place in the Senate upon receiving assurances from the subservient Pennsylvania legislature that it would elect his son as his successor. With this bold stroke the Senator closed his remarkable political career. At the same time he handed over to his son the control of the state machine. No politician of his generation understood the science of politics better than Simon Cameron; none enjoyed greater power. He studied and understood individuals who could be of service to him; he knew the precise value of men and could marshal them when occasion arose. His methods were often circuitous, the means employed were often questionable, but the end in view was always clear. Cameron was of broad intellectual force, if not of fine learning; he could employ his faculties to the utmost and meet each new problem in an eminently practical way. He could be patient and conservative, or keen and aggressive, as the situation demanded. Tradition and precedent bore lightly upon him and were promptly brushed aside when new conditions and necessities arose. He lived in a time when men firmly believed that "to the victor belongs the spoils," and to this doctrine he gladly subscribed.

By patronage he built up a political despotism in Pennsylvania; with it he rewarded his friends and punished his foes. It was commonly said that he never forgot a friend or an enemy. In his senatorial career there was little that was statesmanlike or brilliant. He had no aptitude for Websterian oratory or flights of verbal fancy. He said little in public that was vital, but did much in private that was practical, far-seeing, and astute. His business in the Senate, as elsewhere, was politics, and he governed his conduct accordingly. In appearance he was tall and slim, with a "marked Scotch face," keen gray eyes, a high broad forehead crowned with a luxuriant crop of hair. His manners and speech were kindly and gentle, and his genial, democratic manner won many people to him. He prided himself on possessing the doggedness and determination of his German forebears and the aggressiveness of the "Scotch rebels." His fighting qualities were great. Time dealt lightly with him and at the end of his half-century of political activity and struggle, he was hale and hearty as ever. For twelve years after leaving the Senate he enjoyed freedom from the cares and perplexities of political life on his farm at Donegal Springs, and saw his son three times elected to the place he had surrendered to him. In his ninety-first year, rich in honors and fortune, he passed away. His wife Margaret Brua died several years before, leaving five children.

[The Coryell and Buchanan papers in the Pa. Hist. Soc. contain a number of Cameron letters relating to his earlier years. Some others written in later life are to be found in the Lib. of Cong., in the manuscript collections of his political contemporaries. The files of the War Dept. and the *Official Records* contain most of his war correspondence, and the "Report of the Committee on Contracts" (*House Report No. 2,* 37 Cong., 2 Sess.) reveals much regarding his deficiencies as secretary of war. The most useful accounts of his life are in Alexander K. McClure, *Old Time Notes of Pa.* (1905) and *Abraham Lincoln and Men of War Time* (1892). These are critical, but not unfriendly. Standard histories and the biographies of public men of Cameron's time also are helpful. Additional information is to be found in A. H. Meneely, *The War Dept., 1861* (1928); Ellis and Evans, *Hist. of Lancaster County, Pa.* (1883); *N. Y. Times,* Mar. 13, 14, 1877, June 3, 1878, June 27, 1889; *Pittsburgh Dispatch,* June 27, 1889; *Harrisburg Daily Patriot,* June 27, 1889; *Phila. Press,* Mar. 13, 14, 15, 1877, Jan. 20, June 27, 1889.]
A. H. M.

CAMERON, WILLIAM EVELYN (Nov. 29, 1842–Jan. 25, 1927), newspaper editor, governor of Virginia, son of Walker Anderson Cameron and Elizabeth Byrd Walker, was born in Petersburg, Va., of aristocratic and distinguished descent from the Scottish chieftain Ewan Lochiel. After attending local schools and a North Carolina military academy, he entered Washington University, St. Louis, but soon left college for a clerkship on a Mississippi steamboat. He was in St. Louis again, preparing for a cadetship at West Point, when the Civil War broke out, and he acted as drillmaster for the Missouri troops until captured at Fort Jackson by the Federals. Escaping the same night, he made his way home and enlisted in the 12th Virginia Regiment; fought in all the battles of Lee's army (except Sharpsburg) from Seven Pines onward; was severely wounded at second Manassas; and when he surrendered at Appomattox had risen from private to assistant adjutant-general.

Returning to Petersburg, he commenced his professional career as local editor of a daily newspaper founded by Anthony Keiley, and when Gen. Canby suppressed this for "disloyalty," obtained a similar position on the *Index.* In 1866 he was made editor of the newly-established *Norfolk Virginian.* The next year he bought the Petersburg *Index,* and waged active and effectual warfare in behalf of the conservative political policies which resulted in the election of Gilbert Carlton Walker as governor and in the state's release from carpet-bag rule. In the heat of this campaign he became involved in a duel with Judge Robert W. Hughes, and was badly wounded. In 1872 he sold the *Index,* and, with Baker P. Lee, acquired control of the *Richmond Enquirer.* He married, Oct. 1, 1868, Louisa Clara Egerton, of St. Paul.

After serving three years as mayor of Petersburg, in 1879 he allied himself with the "anti-Bourbon" forces, who, advocating a readjustment of the state debt, were read out of the Democratic party. Unshaken by this ostracism, he battled for his convictions through the columns of the *Richmond Whig;* served as a Hancock elector on his faction's presidential ticket; and in 1881, nominated for governor by the Readjuster convention, was victorious over John W. Daniel, the regular Democratic candidate. His administration, 1882–86, saw the execution of the Readjuster platform, which, although involving repudiation of the state debt and abuse of patronage, provided much progressive economic and social legislation designed to benefit the masses and to break the power of the privileged. At the end of his term of office Cameron engaged in the practise of law at Petersburg, for which profession he had qualified ten years earlier, and won recognition as a capable constitutional lawyer. During 1892–94 he was in Chicago as an official of the Columbian Exposition, served on its Jury of Awards of Liberal Arts, and was appointed historian of the enterprise. In 1901 he represented Petersburg in the Vir-

439

ginia Constitutional Convention, was chairman of the committee on the executive department, a member of the committees on the judiciary and on final revision, and participated in all of the proceedings of the Assembly. He moved to Norfolk in 1908 and edited the *Norfolk Virginian* until 1915, when he became editor-in-chief of the *Virginian-Pilot,* a position which he held until failing health compelled his retirement in 1919.

Impetuous, eager, courageous, and independent, his forceful personality combined with his talents to make him a leader of local political thought in his day, and although the majority of Virginians did not always agree with him,—especially in his general indorsement of Mahone policies or his treatment of the race problem— they never questioned his patriotism or his sincerity of purpose. He was equally eloquent with tongue and pen: a brilliant and uncommonly powerful editorial writer, a cultured, polished stylist, a convincing speaker, and a master of debate. Among his publications were: *History of the World's Columbian Exposition* (1893); *The Life and Character of Robert E. Lee* (1901); sketches of Tyler, Wise, and other prominent Virginians; and a number of fugitive lyrics, at least one of which, "In the Twilight," achieved a deserved and lasting popularity.

[L. G. Tyler, *Men of Mark in Va.* (1906), I, 108–11; *Who's Who in America,* 1918–19; C. C. Pearson, *The Readjuster Movement in Va.* (1917); Richmond *Times-Dispatch,* Jan. 26, 27, 1927; Norfolk *Virginian-Pilot,* Jan. 26, 27, 1927; R. L. Morton, *Hist. of Va.* (1924), vol. III.]   A.C.G., Jr.

CAMM, JOHN (1718–1778), Anglican clergyman, president of the College of William and Mary, was the son of Thomas Camm of Hornsea, Yorkshire, England. After attending school at Beverley, in Yorkshire, he entered Trinity College, Cambridge, at the age of twenty. Soon after receiving his bachelor's degree, he emigrated to Virginia. In 1745 he was appointed minister of Newport Parish, Isle of Wight County. Four years later, the young minister was appointed professor of divinity in the College of William and Mary, to be associated with that institution for twenty-eight years. He was at the same time appointed minister of the neighboring York-Hampton parish. Camm was in sympathy a Tory, an ardent champion of the Crown and of the clergy. In December 1755, the Virginia Assembly, because of a shortage of tobacco, the common medium of exchange, enacted a law enabling the inhabitants to pay their debts in money at the rate of 16 s. 8 d. a hundred pounds, the equivalent of two pence a pound. The act, known as the Two Penny Act, did not

carry the usual suspending clause for the King's pleasure. Although it was general in its application, only the clergymen protested. Their salaries had been placed by law at 1,600 pounds of tobacco. They felt that the law was not just. Commissary Dawson, John Camm, and three other professors in the College of William and Mary protested vigorously against its passage. Meanwhile, Dawson was made president of the College. Camm and his three confederates now tried in vain to have the Commissary call a convocation of the clergy to oppose the act. When he refused to grant their request, they severely criticized him and called the clergy to meet. But the clergy, finding the price of tobacco not above the normal, remained passive. Ill feeling between president and faculty, however, resulted in the resignation of one of the latter and the expulsion of three others, one of whom was Camm. In 1758, another Two Penny Act was passed, to continue in operation twelve months. The clergy now met in convocation at the college, drew up an appeal to the King to veto the act, and chose Camm to present it at Court. He was successful in having the objectionable acts of 1755 and of 1758 disallowed by the King in Council in August 1759. His attorney in Virginia, with the encouragement of his parishioners, immediately brought suit for his salary. There was great excitement in Virginia when news came of the King's action. Upon his return from England, Camm found himself the center of attack and the leader of the clergy in their fight against the Two Penny Act. He engaged in a war of pamphlets with Col. Richard Bland and Col. Landon Carter. His articles were forceful, clear, and well written. It was this quarrel which brought to public notice Patrick Henry. Camm's own case was finally appealed to the Privy Council, but was thrown out on a technicality. He did succeed, however, in securing his reinstatement, by the Privy Council, to his former position in the college. He drew another storm about himself in 1771, in advocating the establishment of a bishopric in Virginia,—a very unpopular movement, which failed. In that year he was appointed president of the College of William and Mary, rector of Bruton Parish, commissary of the Bishop of London, and member of the Governor's Council. Although his fellow Tories deserted him at the outbreak of the Revolution, Camm held his position in the college until removed in the spring of 1777. He had opposed the separation from England. Dr. Arthur Lee said that he was "the center of all the disaffection in the Colony" (*William and Mary Quarterly,* I, 69–73). On one occasion the Governor exclaimed that the Visitors of the College allowed President Camm to lead them around by the nose. In 1769, when fifty-one years old, Camm married the youthful Betsy Hansford, a descendant of one of the rebel lieutenants. There is a charming family tradition of their courtship, a story which might well rank with that of John Alden and Priscilla (see *William and Mary Quarterly*, XIX, 29; and John Fiske, *Old Virginia and Her Neighbors*, 1897, II, 127).

[See Lyon G. Tyler in *Wm. and Mary College Hist. Quart.*, I, 69–73; XIX, 28–30. Other references in that Quarterly are: III, 65; I, 237, a sprightly letter to a friend in England; the manuscript minutes of the William and Mary College faculty in volumes I, II, III, IV, V, XIII, XIV, XV; an interesting account of the part played by Camm in the Two Penny Act controversy, XX, 10 ff. Other accounts of the Two Penny Act controversy may be had in *Va. Mag. of Hist. and Biog.*, X, 350–56; Wm. Wirt Henry, *Patrick Henry, Life, Correspondence, and Speeches* (1891), I, 28–48; Chas. Campbell, *Hist. of Va.* (1860), 507–18; Bishop Wm. Meade, *Old Churches and Families of Va.* (1857), I, 216–25; H. J. Eckenrode, *Separation of Church and State in Va.* (1910); Wm. Stevens Perry, *Papers Relating to the Hist. of the Church in Va., A. D., 1650–1776* (1870).]   R. L. M—n.

CAMMERHOFF, JOHN CHRISTOPHER FREDERICK (July 28, 1721–Apr. 28, 1751), Moravian missionary, was born at Hillersleben, near Magdeburg, Germany, of religious parents who dedicated him, even before his birth, to the ministry. He was first instructed at home by private tutors, then attended the celebrated Protestant school of Kloster Bergen, and in 1738 entered the University of Jena where he came under Moravian influence in the persons of John Nitschmann and Count C. R. Zinzendorf. Upon graduation, out of deference to his parents' wishes, he accepted a position as tutor at Kloster Bergen, but he was increasingly repelled by the formality of Lutheranism and in 1743, with two fellow-teachers, Schumann and Zurmucklen, he sought admission into the Moravian Brotherhood and received an appointment in the Theological Seminary at Marienborn in Wetteravia. He found the religious views prevalent in that region entirely congenial, sharing to the full in the extreme emotionalism, the mystic emphasis upon the Passion, the delight in fantastic symbolism, and the conviction of being in a state of special grace which were characteristic of the Wetteravian group. He once more came under the direct influence of Zinzendorf, and after two years was made his amanuensis. At the early age of twenty-five, he was appointed assistant to Bishop A. G. Spangenberg [*q.v.*] in Pennsylvania. He was immediately married, on July 23, 1746, to Anna von Pahlen, a Livonian baroness; was consecrated bishop in London

two months later; and arrived in America toward the end of the year.

Spangenberg distrusted the emotional fervor of his young assistant but felt powerless to prevent his introduction of Wetteravian methods, as he soon perceived that Cammerhoff was acting under secret instructions from their mutual superiors in Germany. The influence of the younger man rapidly increased. He maintained an extensive correspondence with Zinzendorf and other officials of the Church—his letters sometimes running to more than one hundred closely written pages, preached widely among the settlers of Pennsylvania and New York, and made extensive missionary journeys among the Indians. The supposedly stolid aborigines were quick to respond to Cammerhoff's child-like enthusiasm, and he came to enjoy their confidence to a marked degree, being formally adopted into the Turtle tribe of the Oneida nation, on Apr. 15, 1748, under the name of Gallichwio, or "Good Message." His longest journey was to the Grand Council of the Iroquis Confederacy at Onondaga, N. Y., in 1750, in which accompanied by David Zeisberger, he covered 1,600 miles in three months, being exposed, in addition to the customary perils of the wilderness, to the dangers of four nights in an Indian village where all the males were crazed with drink. His health was broken by the hardships of this journey, and he died in the ensuing spring, at the age of twenty-nine. With his death the Wetteravian influence in this country came to an end.

[See *Trans. Moravian Hist. Soc.*, vols. II (1886), III (1888), V (1899); also Geo. H. Loskiel, *Hist. of the Mission of the United Brethren among the Indians of North America* (London, 1794), pt. II, ch. 9. Cammerhoff's diary of his journey to Onondaga may be found in *Moravian Jours. Relating to Central N. Y., 1745–66* (Onondaga Hist. Ass., Syracuse, N. Y., 1916). There are voluminous Cammerhoff MSS. in the Bethlehem Archives at Bethlehem, Pa., many of them unfortunately defaced by some later hand which expunged the extravagant Wetteravian phraseology.]   E. S. B.

CAMP, DAVID NELSON (Oct. 13, 1820–Oct. 19, 1916), educator, was born in Durham, Conn. His father was Elah Camp, a descendant of settlers who came from Essex County, England, in 1630; his mother, Orit (Lee) Camp, was a descendant of Theophilus Eaton, governor of the New Haven colony. Life on the farm laid hard work and many responsibilities on young Camp's shoulders. His mother, "a devout Christian woman," brought him up "in the Fear of the Lord" and taught him to read; but the Bible, Scott's *Commentaries*, psalm books, "a few religious books," some school texts, and occasional newspapers constituted the range of his early reading. Beyond the home, his education was continued in the district school, the private school of Mrs. Goodwin, Durham Academy, Hartford Grammar School, Meriden Academy, and the temporary normal school instituted by Barnard at Hartford in 1839. His own ill health, and that of his father, hindered regular preparatory schooling and frustrated his plans for college. Nevertheless, with the aid of special masters, he studied Latin, bookkeeping, surveying, higher mathematics, poetry, history, natural, moral, and intellectual philosophy, astronomy, German and French. At eighteen, he first taught at North Guilford for thirty-nine dollars a quarter, with the privilege (and necessity) of "boarding 'round." Other successful schools at Cromwell, Branford, and Meriden brought his work to the attention of Henry Barnard [*q.v.*]. In 1844 he was married to Sarah Adaline Howd. He began institute work in 1845, was made secretary of the State Teachers' Association in 1847, was called to a professorship in the State Normal School in 1849, and was made the associate principal in 1855. On Philbrick's resignation, in 1857, Camp became commissioner of common schools and principal of the Normal School. He resigned (1866) on account of ill health. While abroad he accepted a professorship in St. John's College, Annapolis, but resigned to become an assistant to Barnard (1867) in the United States Bureau of Education. He soon, however, retired from Washington and conducted the New Britain (Conn.) Seminary till he discontinued active school work.

Besides his teaching and administrative duties, Camp was editor of the *Connecticut Common School Journal* and the *American Year Book,* and was the author of a *History of New Britain, Farmington, and Berlin* (1889). For schools, he prepared the small *Globe Manual* (1864), *Manual of Illustrative Teaching* (1865), four different *Geographies,* with *Outline Maps,* and revised Mitchell's *Outline Maps* and the *Government Instructor.* His later life was given over to church, business, and municipal affairs. In New Britain he was councilman (1871), alderman for three years, and mayor 1887–89. He was elected to the legislature in 1889, being chairman of the Committee on Education. His educational labors and his text-books made him one of the influential educators in Connecticut in the nineteenth century.

[The most complete single source of information is Camp's *Recollections of a Long and Active Life* (1917); other sources are his widely scattered addresses, published in proceedings of various educational associations, editorials, and periodical articles, the records of his administration at Hartford, printed reports of the New Britain School Society, and the books of which he was author or editor.]   T. W.

CAMP, HIRAM (Apr. 9, 1811–July 8, 1893), clock-maker, philanthropist, was the son of Deacon Samuel Camp, a farmer of Plymouth, Conn., and of his wife Jeannette Jerome, a sister of the clock-maker, Chauncey Jerome. His grandfather, Samuel Camp, was a Revolutionary soldier who saw service at Crown Point, Ticonderoga, and on Staten Island. Hiram passed his boyhood on the farm, with slender schooling during those months when he might best be spared from farm labors. He entered the Jerome shops at Bristol in 1829 and continued in business there with his uncle for twenty-four years. During just this period metal works and machine production were being introduced into the clock industry, with their accompanying lessening of the cost of production. Chauncey Jerome and Hiram Camp were largely instrumental in effecting this change. By 1837 the Jerome works had perfected a small brass-works clock that could be sold for $6.00, the price later being reduced to seventy-five cents. A branch of the Jerome works was opened in New Haven in 1843, and when the Bristol shops burned in 1845 the whole establishment was moved to that city. Camp supervised the erection of the New Haven plant. In 1851 he went into business for himself, manufacturing clock movements, and in 1853 he organized the New Haven Clock Company (of which he was president), a joint stock company capitalized at $20,000 for the purpose of making cases. The Jerome company failed in 1855, and the New Haven Clock Company purchased its entire business. With the elimination of the Jerome competition the New Haven Clock Company soon became the world's greatest clock manufacturing organization. It reached out for world markets; it improved its clock-making machinery; it developed sound financial policies; it perfected the mass-production of cheap standardized time pieces, such as the nickel alarm clock and the pioneer "dollar watch"; it diversified production so as to cover all markets with a complete line of goods: metronomes, jewelers' regulators, electro-mechanical movements, telegraph devices, miniature clocks, and high-grade movements with periodized and ornate cases in granites and different kinds of woods. Camp continued as president of the company until 1892 and was a trustee until his death.

He found time for numerous avocations. He served his city as selectman, councilman, and chief engineer of the fire department. As a Republican he represented his district in the Connecticut legislature of 1859 and held a place on its Finance Committee. But his chief interest, aside from his regular labor, was in his church.

He memorized his daily text and he exhibited a veritable passion for evangelization; he went from house to house with his Bible in his hand, he organized Sunday-schools, he supported city and frontier missions, he built a church next door to his own home, and he subscribed liberally to charities and religious education. With the evangelist D. C. Moody [q.v.], he established the Mount Hermon Boys' School and the North-field Seminary for Young Ladies. He served as trustee for these institutions and at various times donated approximately $100,000 to their support. Interest in Christian morality drew him to the Prohibition movement. He contributed to its campaign chest and he took the stump in its behalf. Finally he even accepted nomination as its candidate for governor in 1888. He was married twice: to Elvira Rockwell Skinner, and, after her death, to Lucy Davis.

[*The Daily Morning Jour. and Courier* (New Haven), July 10, 12, 1893; *New Haven Evening Reg.*, July 11, 1893; Geo. B. Chandler, "Industrial History," section on "Clocks and Watches" in *Hist. of Connecticut*, ed. by Norris G. Osborn (1925), vol. IV; *Chauncey Je-rome, Hist. of the Am. Clock Business for the Past Sixty Years and Life of Chauncey Jerome* (1860); *Hist. of the City of New Haven*, ed. by Edward E. At-water (1887), pp. 580–81; Francis Atwater, *Hist. of the Town of Plymouth, Conn.* (1895), pp. 234–35; *In-dustrial Advantages of New Haven* (1889), p. 134; *Commerce, Manufactures and Resources of the City of New Haven and Environs* (1882), p. 101.] E.F.H.

CAMP, JOHN LAFAYETTE (Feb. 20, 1828–July 16, 1891), Confederate officer and Texas political leader, was born on a farm near Bir-mingham, Ala. He was the son of John Lafay-ette Camp and Elizabeth (Brown) Camp. He was graduated from the University of Tennes-see in 1848 and moved to Texas the next year, locating at Gilmer, in Upshur County. There he taught school and practised law, soon taking his place as the leading attorney of that section of east Texas. He was married in 1851 to Mary Ann Ward, daughter of Dr. William Ward, well-known east Texas physician. During the next ten years he established an enviable reputa-tion as a lawyer and was a prosperous cotton planter. When the Civil War broke out he left his wife and five children to enlist in the Con-federate army. He was at first captain of an Upshur County company, but was soon elected colonel of the 14th Texas Cavalry. His regiment served in the Missouri campaign, also in Loui-siana and Arkansas. He distinguished himself at Murfreesboro, and participated in the battles at Richmond, Cumberland Gap, and Chickamauga. His last battle was at Altoona, Ga. He was twice wounded and twice captured and was imprisoned for many months. In 1866 he was elected by the first Texas district to serve in the national Con-gress, but was not permitted to take his seat. He was a delegate to the Texas constitutional convention of 1866, where he advocated mea-sures which, following the Presidential plan of reconstruction, would have restored Texas to her former place in the Union. As a delegate to the national Democratic convention in 1872 he advocated coöperation with the Liberal Repub-licans. In 1874 he entered the state Senate, where he was an administration leader. He ad-vocated the more rapid settlement of the frontier portion of the state through the encouragement of railroad building by donation of state lands, and led the campaign for a new constitution. Before the legislature had decided to favor a convention, a joint committee of Senator Camp and two representatives prepared a constitution, adoption of which was proposed as amendments, and which was admitted by all to be superior to the existing constitution (S. S. McKay, *Making the Texas Constitution of 1876*, 1924, p. 57).

In 1878 Camp was appointed by Gov. Hubbard to be judge of the district court sitting at Jef-ferson, Marshall, Palestine, and Tyler. In 1884 he accepted an appointment from President Cleveland as registrar of the land office of Ari-zona, hoping the change of climate would im-prove his health; but, this not resulting, he re-signed after two years of service. He then moved to San Antonio, where he died in 1891. Camp County, Texas, created in April 1874, was named for him.

[*Official Records* (Army); *Tex. Almanac*, 1867; J. H. Brown, *Hist. of Tex.* (2 vols., 1893); J. J. Lane, *Hist. of Education in Tex.* (1903); *Jour. of the Sen-ate of Tex.*, 1874; Z. T. Fulmore, *Hist. and Geography of Tex. as Told in County Names* (Austin, 1915); W. C. Raines, *Yearbook of Tex.* (Austin, 1901); Dudley G. Wooten, *A Comprehensive Hist. of Tex.* (2 vols., Dallas, 1898).] S. S. M.

CAMP, JOHN LAFAYETTE (Sept. 23, 1855–Aug. 10, 1918), Texas judge and federal district attorney, was the son of John Lafayette Camp [q.v.], and Mary Ann (Ward) Camp. He was born at Gilmer, Upshur County, Tex., and was educated at Gilmer Academy, Texas Military In-stitute, and Trinity University. In 1881 he mar-ried Lamartine Felder, daughter of Dr. J. L. Felder, a well-known physician of Leesburg, Tex. He served a term in the state Senate, 1887–91 and then moved to San Antonio, where he prac-tised law for six years. In 1897 he was appoint-ed, by Gov. Culberson, judge of the forty-fifth district court, and he served for more than sev-enteen years, his work being so acceptable that he was usually reëlected without opposition. During his tenure he tried a great many notable cases and had to his credit a larger percentage of sustained decisions than any other district judge in Texas has ever had. In 1912 he was instrumental in preserving the Alamo, shrine of Texas liberty, as it stands to-day. A state law of 1905 had given the "care and custody" of the Alamo property to the Daughters of the Republic. But at the suggestion of Gov. Colquitt in 1912 the legislature appropriated $5,000 to "improve" the Alamo. When the work of dismantling began, and it became known that the governor planned to make the Alamo grounds into a state park, the Daughters of the Republic appealed to Camp. A temporary and then a permanent injunction halted the work of dismantling the building. Camp held that the act of 1912 did not repeal that of 1905, that the superintendent of public buildings and grounds was given the direction of expenditure but not the power to dismantle the property, and that the Alamo was still in charge of the Daughters of the Republic of Texas. The Governor appealed to the higher courts; but the Alamo still stands.

Camp was appointed, by President Wilson, United States district attorney for the western district of Texas, which takes in the border. The position is an important one at any time; it was particularly so during Camp's incumbency. He secured the evidence which led to the arrest of Victoriano Huerta, former president of Mexico, on June 27, 1915, at Newman, N. Mex., charged with violating the United States neutrality laws in organizing a prospective military expedition against Mexico. Huerta was released under bond, but, when additional evidence was secured by Camp, he was rearrested on July 3 and was kept under guard at Fort Bliss until his death six months later. On the retirement of Judge Maxey from the bench of the western district of Texas, Camp had the unanimous indorsement of the eighteen Texas congressmen, the two United States senators from Texas, and the attorney-general for the position of federal judge. But President Wilson had decided that no man who had reached the age of sixty should be appointed as federal judge, and Camp was a few months over that age. He accepted a second appointment as federal district attorney, and filled that office creditably during the war.

[Sketch of Camp's services in J. H. Cole, *The Federal Courts of the Southern States* (Ann Arbor, 1928); *San Antonio Light*, Aug. 11, 1818; private information.]
          S.S.M.

CAMP, WALTER CHAUNCEY (Apr. 7, 1859–Mar. 14, 1925), promoter of American football, was born in New Britain, Conn., and died in his room at a New York hotel, following a football conference, his sudden death, seemingly, an anti-climax to a career devoted to the interests

of health and longevity. He came of old English stock. His father, Leverett L. Camp, was a schoolmaster, and from him he probably acquired his sense of discipline; while from his mother, Ellen Cornwell, a gentle soul, he derived that patience and poise which contributed greatly to his success as a leader. He prepared for college at the Hopkins Grammar School, New Haven, and graduated from Yale in the class of 1880. For two years he attended the Yale Medical School, where he gained a knowledge of anatomy and physiology which he was later to employ in his training of youth. During his student days he engaged enthusiastically in all outdoor sports, but specialized in football which he played for six years. Upon leaving the medical school he took a subordinate position with the Manhattan Watch Company, N. Y., and in 1883 became connected with the New York office of the New Haven Clock Company, a firm with which he was associated for the remainder of his life. On June 30, 1888, he married Alice Graham Sumner.

His business connections brought him to New Haven to live in 1888, and he soon became general athletic director and head advisory football coach at Yale. While a student, as a representative of the college at a rules conference, he had suggested modifications which revolutionized the game. The "scrimmage" was substituted for the "scrum" (the ball being put into play by one side instead of being left to a free-for-all scramble), the number of players was reduced from fifteen to eleven, and the key position of quarterback was created. His influence on the game, thus early begun, now continued for nearly thirty years. He is credited with the suggestions which led to the "fourth down rule" with the accompanying "gridiron" pattern of the field, and for the permission of tackling below the waist. Team play was his great objective, and his strategic ability contributed much to the development of its technique. An even greater contribution came from his love of clean sportsmanship which directly and indirectly he instilled into players on college fields and in school yards. He created a literature of the game in books, magazines, and newspapers, some of his publications being: *Football: How to Coach a Team* (1886); *American Football* (1891); *Walter Camp's Book of College Sports* (1893); *The Substitute* (1908); *Jack Hall at Yale* (1909). In 1889 he began his custom of selecting an "All-America Team," membership on which was considered the highest football honor,—a remarkable testimonial to public confidence in Camp's knowledge of the game and his impartial sportsmanship.

In 1917, after the United States entered the World War, Camp became a national figure in a new capacity. Realizing that to endure the war strain those at home must be kept physically fit, in connection with Dr. W. G. Anderson, Director of the Yale University Gymnasium, he organized the leading citizens of New Haven into the Senior Corps for daily physical exercises. Soon he was called to Washington where by similar exercises he undertook to keep members of the cabinet and of Congress in good condition. He thus attracted the attention of the Secretary of the Navy, Josephus Daniels, who made him chairman of the Athletic Department, United States Commission on Training Camp Activities, for the physical care and development of naval officers and men. Out of these experiences came the famous "Daily Dozen" exercises. Originally the idea of Dr. Anderson who formulated three exercises for the daily use of his classes, Camp expanded them into the "Dozen," and his name and gift for publicity gave them countrywide popularity. A memorial erected at the Yale Bowl, financed by his admirers in many colleges and schools, bears testimony to the respect and affection in which he was held.

[H. W. H. Powel, *Walter Camp, the Father of Am. Football* (1926); Parke H. Davis, *Football* (1911); Wm. G. Daggett, *A Hist. of the Class of Eighty, Yale College, 1876–1910* (1910); Grantland Rice, article in *Collier's*, May 9, 1925; *Yale Alumni Weekly*, Mar. 20, 1925; *Yale Univ. Obit. Rec. of Grads.*, 1925; Spalding's *Official Foot Ball Guide for 1926*.]   N.G.O.

CAMPANIUS, JOHN (Aug. 15, 1601–Sept. 17, 1683), Lutheran clergyman, missionary among the Delaware Indians, was born in Stockholm, the son of Jonas Peter Campanius, parish clerk of St. Clara's, was educated at the Stockholm gymnasium and the University of Upsala, and was ordained on July 19, 1633. The next year he accompanied a Swedish mission to Russia and on his return became schoolmaster at Norrtälje and later chaplain and preceptor of the Stockholm Orphans' Home. When Lieutenant-Colonel John Printz was appointed governor of the colony on the Delaware, Admiral Claes Flemming, one of the King's counsellors of state, suggested that Campanius go with him as chaplain of the settlers. Printz and his company left Stockholm on Aug. 16, 1642, touched at Antigua on Dec. 20—where they remained till Jan. 3, were entertained by the English governor, and were loaded with a gift of oranges and lemons— and dropped anchor at Fort Christina (now Wilmington, Del.), Feb. 15, 1643. Campanius took his family with him. His account of the six months' voyage is incorporated in the work on New Sweden by his grandson, Thomas Campa-

nius, "Holmiensis." During his sojourn of six years in America he ministered faithfully to his scattered congregation of German and Swedish colonists, indentured servants, and transported criminals. He also attempted to Christianize the Indians. The work began awkwardly, for when the Indians first came to the services they were amazed that one man should stand alone and talk so long while the rest listened in silence, and they suspected a trap. He gained their affection, however, learned their language, and was so successful in teaching them "that those people who were wandering in darkness were able to see the light." He translated Luther's *Shorter Catechism* into the Delaware language, but his version was not printed until 1696, when Charles XI brought it out at Stockholm at his own expense and sent 500 copies to America. *Lutheri Catechismus Öfwersatt på American-Virginiske Språket* made a duodecimo volume of 160 pages, the catechism being given in both Swedish and Delaware, with a glossary filling twenty-eight pages. Campanius's labors among the Indians, which antedated by a few years those of John Eliot at Roxbury, Mass., were eminently Christian and provided a foundation for the later work of William Penn. Besides studying the Indian folkways and language, in which as a pious seventeenth century scholar he found significant affinities with Hebrew, Campanius made careful meteorological observations twice a day for several years and farmed a tract of land at the settlement of Upland. In 1646 he built a church at Tinicum (Tennakong), nine miles southwest of Philadelphia. With his family he returned to Sweden in 1648. The legend was current in the time of Acrelius that Campanius had traveled up into the interior among the Red Men and had made his way by land to Sweden. Home again, he became pastor in 1649 of the congregations at Frosthült and Hernevi, a charge that he served until his death. Johan Danielson Svedberg described him justly as a man *ob indefessum semper amorem Dei propagandi studium summopere laudandum.*

[W. J. Mann, B. M. Schmucker, W. Germann, eds., *Nachrichten von den vereinigten Deutschen Evangelische-Lutherischen Gemeinden in Nord-America*, Erster Band (Allentown, Pa., 1886); A. L. Gräbner, *Geschichte der Lutherischen Kirche in America* (St. Louis, 1892); T. E. Schmauk, *Hist. of the Luth. Ch. in Pa.* (1903); Amandus Johnson, *The Swedish Settlements on the Delaware* (1911); Thomas Campanius Holm (sic), *Description of the Province of New Sweden Now Called by the English Pennsylvania in America*, transl. from the Swedish with notes by Peter S. Du Ponceau (1834); Israel Acrelius, *Hist. of New Sweden*, transl. from the Swedish with an introduction and notes by W. M. Reynolds (1874); Otto Norberg, *Svenska Kyrkans Mission vid Delaware i Nord-Amerika* (Stockholm, 1893); J. D. Svedberg, *Dissertatio Gradualis de Svionum in America Colonia* (Upsala, 1709).]   G.H.G.

CAMPAU, JOSEPH (Feb. 25, 1769–July 23, 1863), trader, belonged to a family line which has been numerous and prominent in Detroit since the time of Cadillac. His father was Jacques Campau, a native of Detroit, and his mother was Catherine Menard, a native of Montreal. He was the sixth of a family of twelve children born to his parents in the years 1762–81. In early manhood he entered upon a trading career at Detroit, in which he achieved a large measure of success. His trade was chiefly with the Indians, and in addition to his Detroit store he established outposts at numerous places—at Saginaw, St. Clair, near Mount Clemens, and elsewhere. Aside from his mercantile business, he displayed a life-long interest in real estate, and the profits he made in trade were persistently invested in Detroit property which he improved and leased but seldom willingly sold. About the year 1837 he retired from active business, and devoted the remainder of his long life to looking after his investments. The growth of Detroit made these increasingly valuable, and he is reputed to have been Michigan's first millionaire. At the time of his death he was supposed to be the largest landholder in Detroit and the wealthiest citizen of Michigan.

Business interests aside, Campau was long a man of prominence in Detroit, holding at different times many public offices. He served as trustee of the town, treasurer, overseer of the poor, assessor, and appraiser. He was appointed ensign in the local militia by Winthrop Sargent upon the American occupation of Detroit in 1796, and he subsequently achieved the title of major. Prior to the fire which destroyed Detroit in 1805 Campau owned and occupied a house on Ste. Anne St. After the fire he rebuilt on the same site (south side of Jefferson Ave. between Shelby and Griswold Sts.); here he lived until his death, and the house was a conspicuous feature of Jefferson Ave. for many years thereafter. On May 12, 1808, he married Adelaide Dequindre, member of one of Detroit's old French families. They lived together over half a century, and had a family of twelve children, all but two of whom lived to maturity. A sister of Campau married Thomas Williams, early Detroit merchant and magistrate. Their son, Gen. John R. Williams, was Detroit's first elective mayor and for half a century one of her leading citizens. In early life he was partner, for a time, of Campau. In 1823 Williams was defeated by Father Gabriel Richard for election as delegate to Congress. The bitterness engendered by the electoral contest (in which both contestants appealed for the ballots of the French-Catholic electors) prob-

ably materially influenced Campau in a long-continued conflict with the church authorities over the ownership of the so-called Church Farm property, a dispute which vexed the courts for a full generation after all the original contestants had passed away. In 1831 Williams was again a candidate for the delegacy and he and Campau were two of eleven associates who provided funds for establishing the *Democratic Free Press and Michigan Intelligencer,* to serve as the political organ of their party. This paper is regarded as the ancestor of the present-day *Free Press* of Detroit.

Campau was a capable business man of conservative tendencies. His character was marked by numerous eccentricities, which afforded subject matter for local gossip. Although a Catholic, he early became a Mason, and after his estrangement from the church he was fond of abusing that organization.

[Father Christian Denissen, "Detroit Genealogies" (MS. in Burton Hist. Coll.); *Barnabas Campau and his Descendants,* compiled by C. M. Burton (Detroit, 1916); C. M. Burton, *City of Detroit, Mich., 1701–1922* (1922); *Detroit Free Press,* July 25, 1863; an article by Robert B. Ross, "Detroit in 1837: Reminiscences of Joseph and Daniel J. Campau," in the Detroit *Sunday News-Tribune,* Nov. 4, 1894.]   M. M. Q.

CAMPBELL, ALEXANDER (Sept. 12, 1788–Mar. 4, 1866), one of the founders of the Disciples of Christ, was born in County Antrim, Ireland, the son of Thomas Campbell [*q.v.*], and Jane (Corneigle) Campbell. His mother's family was of French Huguenot origin, but several of its members had settled in Ireland before his birth. His father was of a Scotch family that had long resided in Ireland. Alexander derived his features from his mother, his love of preaching and teaching from his father. He obtained his earlier education in school and at home with his father, but he was so fond of sport that he found it irksome to study. His physical frame was strengthened by farm work. As he grew older his mind became active, his memory developed remarkably, and he became fond of religious literature and philosophy. His parents scrupulously attended to his religious and moral education, and he grew up sturdy, active, and conscientious.

In order to increase his income and provide further opportunity for education to his children Thomas Campbell moved his family to the town of Rich Hill when Alexander was sixteen years old, and established an academy of which he was the principal, with Alexander as his assistant. Success followed. Alexander became thoughtful about his personal religion and joined the church. Afterward he gave much study to theology and church history in anticipation of becoming a minister. The Campbells held friendly association with John Walker, an Independent minister in the same town, who later had a part in the origin of the Plymouth Brethren. Alexander was impressed with his ideas, and contrasted his independency with the arbitrary discipline of the Presbyterian ecclesiastical system. He was influenced also by the Haldanes, prominent Independents of Scotland. Upon the departure of his father to America because of impaired health, the son carried on the school. At the father's request the whole family presently undertook to emigrate to Pennsylvania, where Thomas Campbell had located as a minister, but they were delayed by smallpox and shipwreck so that Alexander studied at the University of Glasgow for a year. The family went to America in 1809. Alexander's studies and friendships and the experiences of his father, who had had unpleasant relations with the Seceders in America, made both men inclined to independency in religion. At that time in America the spirit of religious intolerance was keen and pugnacious, and the Campbells were driven presently to a new movement. This crystallized in the organization of the Christian Association of Washington (Pennsylvania) in 1809. The organization was really a local independent church, but it was not a part of the purpose of the Campbells to establish a new denomination, though it was hoped that their principles would spread and produce other associations. To this reform of religion Alexander Campbell resolved to devote himself wholly. He was well adapted by courage, energy, conviction, fine public presence, and eloquence, to become the leader of such an independent enterprise. To prepare himself more thoroughly he set apart certain hours of the day for study, devoting himself daily to the Bible and the classical languages. He became convinced that manners and morals, especially of young people, needed reform, and he wrote articles on that subject for the press. His first sermon was preached in a grove in 1810 and made a successful impression. Within a year he had preached more than a hundred times. After the organization of a full-fledged church of Disciples at Brush Run, Pa., Alexander was licensed to preach. At that time he believed in the independence and congregational government of every local church and in the toleration of infant baptism.

Disappointed by lack of growth in the number of adherents and dreading the perpetuation of a new sect, Thomas Campbell sought affiliation of the Association with the regular Presbyterians, but they declined. After Alexander in 1811 married a Presbyterian wife, Margaret Brown, and became a father, he examined into the subject of infant baptism, a matter of perennial debate between Baptists and other denominations. He decided against it, and, believing that he had never been properly baptized, he with his wife was immersed by a Baptist minister. His father and mother followed his example. This act alienated some persons in their church. It was plain that strictness in baptism might be biblical, but that it was not likely to further the purpose of Christian union.

Alexander became pastor of the Brush Run church when his father moved to Ohio. He read much, and also engaged in farming. As a neighbor he was liked. By nature he was genial, hospitable, and exceptionally interesting as a conversationalist. The Brush Run church became a member of the Redstone Baptist Association of churches, but Campbell was not acceptable to the Baptists as a preacher, because he was not rigid enough in his Calvinism, and because he magnified the differences between them. He came to believe in baptism as necessary for the remission of sins and the appropriation of God's promise of forgiveness, while the Baptists considered the new life complete before baptism. With the hope of extending his own opinions he established Buffalo Seminary in Bethany, Virginia, for the education of young folk and especially for the training of preachers. These he boarded in his own home. This was discontinued after a few years, though the first part of his purpose was highly successful. He went about preaching where he was welcome, and debating with his opponents whenever he had the opportunity. He was a skilful debater on different subjects, and he did not hesitate to meet all comers. One of his most interesting debates was on religious skepticism with Richard Owen, the English Utopian. These debates were open to the public who attended in large numbers, and they added to the growing reputation of Campbell. He was sanguine of the success of his principles, but he made the mistake of thinking that the simple language of the Bible would explain itself and serve to unite all who honestly accepted its teachings. Denominationalism was rampant, especially in the newer sections of the country, and lines were sharply drawn.

Believing in the power of the press, Alexander Campbell started the *Christian Baptist* in 1823, and built up a successful periodical, through which he disseminated his opinions. The paper was printed at home and its success encouraged him to continue the printing business uninterruptedly for forty years. In his paper he attacked missions, Sunday-schools, and sectarian societies as then conducted, carrying the war vigorously into the enemies' camp, and censuring the clergy in particular. This attitude aroused the Redstone Association to oust the Campbellites. Forecasting this action, Campbell himself withdrew with some of his followers and organized a new church which was admitted into the Mahoning Association. After 1826 the Baptist associations adopted the practise of cutting off churches of Disciples so that they became a separate denomination. On his part Campbell opposed the Baptist method of preaching, their four circuits for one rural minister, their extreme doctrinal emphasis, and their requirement of particular religious experience.

Campbell had a mastery of the English Bible and he believed a better translation was desirable. This he undertook in 1826, and his translation was published the next spring. Years later he became an active supporter of the American Bible Union, which was organized to further Baptist opinions on the proper rendition of the Greek word to baptize. In 1828 he published a volume of one hundred and twenty-five hymns, rejecting those that did not have a biblical basis. From 1830 his interest in the second coming of Christ led him to publish the *Millennial Harbinger* instead of the *Christian Baptist*. His publishing interests in a small community were so large that the Federal government established a post office for him and made him postmaster, an office which he held for thirty years.

Campbell's interests broadened as he began to travel more. His acquaintance extended rapidly. He was a delegate to a political convention called to revise the constitution of the state of Virginia. In 1835 he was relieved of a part of his editorial work that he might have more freedom to respond to numerous calls that came to him for public addresses. He traveled frequently into Kentucky, where he had many friends, and was a welcome speaker in Lexington, the center of culture of the state. He went into the states south of Virginia where he knew many people and had some followers. He visited the North, even during the Civil War. At one time he might have been pastor of a Baptist church in one of the Northern cities, but he knew that he could not withhold his peculiar views of truth, and he did not wish to cause division.

Campbell's dislike for creeds and confessions of faith found response in a group similar to the Disciples of Christ,—which was the name preferred by Campbell for his movement—the Christians, a company recruited from three different sources. One of them was Methodist. In 1793 the Republican Methodists had seceded from the Methodist Episcopal church, because of objection to episcopacy. They were fathered by James O'Kelley, who emphasized a creedless gospel. A second source was Baptist. Abner Jones in Ver-

mont led away several churches in New Hampshire and Vermont on the same basis. A third source was Presbyterian. Barton W. Stone was its leader. These three groups combined as the Christian Connection, and were commonly known as Christians. The differences between Disciples and Christians were chiefly in the matter of emphasis. The Disciples stressed the Bible, the Christians the idea of unity. The Christians were more evangelistic, appealed to all kinds of people, and gained rapidly in numbers, which the Disciples had not done. The differences were not sufficient to keep them apart when they agreed on their special principles of fidelity to the simple Word. Local churches combined voluntarily, then the union became general in Kentucky, Tennessee, and Ohio, but the two denominations still exist independently. Campbell was enthusiastically in favor of the combination of forces. He rejoiced also over the spread of his principles to Canada and Great Britain. In 1847 he sailed abroad, preached and lectured in the leading cities, and visited Paris. Later he went to Canada.

In 1840 he started Bethany College in his own west Virginian village and became its president. Much time was required to raise an endowment and he traveled for that purpose, but he gave as much of himself as possible to teaching. He instructed classes in the Bible, in intellectual and moral philosophy, in political economy. He opposed secret societies, but he was tolerant of slavery. The relation of master and servant seemed to him to be no sin, although he thought slavery inexpedient in modern civilization. This saved his denomination from the division that certain denominations suffered. In later life his mind became impaired, but he lived to old age with the satisfaction of knowing that the opinions for which he had contended were gaining adherents steadily. Besides his pocket Testament translation he was the author of *The Christian System* (1839); *Memoirs of Elder Thomas Campbell* (1861); a revised translation of the book of Acts for the American Bible Union; and much fugitive literature.

[Robt. Richardson, *Memoirs of Alexander Campbell* (1870); B. B. Tyler, *Hist. of the Disciples of Christ* (Am. Ch. Hist. Ser., vol. XII, 1894).]   H. K. R.

CAMPBELL, ALLAN (Oct. 11, 1815–Mar. 18, 1894), civil engineer, was the fourth son of Archibald and Margaret (Adams) Campbell. His father was a native of Scotland who came to this country in 1798 and was for many years deputy secretary of the State of New York. Born in Albany, N. Y., Allan was educated at the Albany Academy. In 1832 he joined John Randall, a distinguished engineer of that time and chief engincer of the Ithaca & Oswego Railroad, one of the first railroads in the United States. He served for several years as engineer in the construction of the earliest railways in the state of Georgia and it was while there that he met and married in 1843 Julia Farlie Cooper, daughter of Thomas Cooper, the tragedian. Subsequently, while chief engineer of the extension of the Harlem Railroad, Campbell received an offer from the Government of Chile to go to that country to construct railroads. He accepted this offer and left in 1850 to start the survey and construction of the Copiapo to Caldera route. Twice he crossed the Andes to Argentina, making reconnaissance of a route to connect the oceans. While in Buenos Aires he was on intimate terms and had most friendly relations with the then president of Argentina. Upon his return to this country in 1856 he again became chief engineer of the extension of the Harlem road and subsequently president, an office which he held until superseded by Cornelius Vanderbilt, who had purchased a controlling interest in the line. Later, as president of the Consolidation Coal Company, Campbell brought that concern out of financial difficulties into dividend-paying fields, a most noteworthy accomplishment. During the Civil War he was employed on the harbor defenses of New York City.

Much interested in civic affairs, he was appointed commissioner of public works in 1876 by Mayor Wickham of New York. He resigned in 1880 to accept the comptrollership of the city, an appointment by Mayor Cooper. He was also appointed in the same year, by act of legislature, one of the assessment commissioners of the State of New York. His work in all of these offices was characterized by strict integrity, industry, and conscientious application to his duties. In 1882 he was prominently mentioned as a candidate for the governorship of New York, and in the same year was nominated as a non-partisan candidate for the mayoralty of New York City. He was, however, defeated for the latter office. His defeat was laid to organized machine politics to which he was bitterly opposed. He was an honorary member of the American Society of Civil Engineers, a member of the New York Historical Society, the St. Andrews Society, the Century Club, and for many years a vestryman of Trinity Church, succeeding John Jacob Astor as warden in that organization.

[*Proc. Am. Soc. of Civil Engineers*, vol. XX; *Engineering News*, Mar. 22, 1894; *N. Y. Times*, Mar. 20, 1894; *Sun* (N. Y.), Mar. 19, 1894.]　K. W. C—g.

CAMPBELL, ANDREW (June 14, 1821– Apr. 13, 1890), inventor, manufacturer, was born near Trenton, N. J., the son of a farmer of very moderate means. As soon as he was physically able Andrew helped with the farm work and attended the country schools both at his birthplace and at Matawan, Monmouth County, N. J., whither his parents moved when he was eight years old. When he was thirteen, his father died, leaving a large family unprovided for, and Andrew immediately sought employment. He disliked farming and apprenticed himself to a carriage-maker, but before completing his apprenticeship he left home and went to Trenton to work for three months in a brush-maker's shop. Here he perfected his first invention, namely, a special vise for holding brushes. At the age of fifteen he left Trenton and headed westward, working his way gradually, and arriving eventually in Alton, Ill. Here he worked for a carriage-builder until he was twenty-one, during which time he devised and constructed a number of labor-saving machines as well as carriages and omnibuses. From Alton, Campbell went to St. Louis where he engaged in his two old trades, brush-making and carriage-building, and had his first experience with printing presses when engaged periodically to make repairs on the presses of the *St. Louis Republican*. During the following ten years he was variously engaged as a machine-merchant, bridge-builder, and farmer in Columbia, Mo., Paducah, Ky., and other towns of the Middle West. The announcement of a prize of $1,000, offered by George Bruce of New York City for a printing press to print 500 copies an hour, caused Campbell to turn his attention to the problem, and in 1853 he proceeded to New York with his design, only to find that the time limit for submitting plans had expired. He obtained employment almost immediately, however, with A. B. Taylor & Company, large manufacturers of printing presses, and as foreman, devised many novel improvements including paper-feed mechanisms, special presses with table distribution for illustrated magazines such as *Harper's* and *Frank Leslie's*, as well as automatic presses. At this time, too, Campbell conceived the idea of a special press for country newspapers, and, when convinced that a market was available, he left Taylor & Company in 1858, spent three years in experimental work, and with his new patented machine began business for himself. The Campbell Country Press proved very popular, and in 1866 Campbell erected a plant in Brooklyn where he not only constructed the Country Press but devised many others. Thus in 1867 the two-revolution picture press was developed, and in 1868 a large press for fine illustrations. A special press designed by Campbell in his factory permitted the printing of 120 almanacs a minute. On it 7,000,000 impressions were taken from one form without perceptible damage. Campbell also made the first press that printed, inserted, pasted, folded, and cut in one continuous operation. He retired from active business in 1880 and died of heart disease ten years later, leaving his widow whom he had married in Columbia, Mo., in 1848, and four children.

[*Am. Dict. of Printing and Bookmaking* (1894); *Am. Encyc. of Printing* (1871); *Am. Bookmaker,* May 1890; *N. Y. Times,* Apr. 15, 1890.]   C. W. M.

CAMPBELL, BARTLEY (Aug. 12, 1843– July 30, 1888), playwright, journalist, theatrical manager, was the son of Bartley and Mary (Eckles) Campbell, both of whom came to America from Ireland in 1840. He was born in Pittsburgh, Pa., where he was educated in private schools and for a brief period studied law. His newspaper career began on the Pittsburgh *Post,* and before he left that city he had become editor and part proprietor of the Pittsburgh *Leader.* In 1869 he founded and edited the *Southern Monthly Magazine* at New Orleans. When he began playwriting in 1871, he definitely retired from journalism, as his standards forbade him to continue as a dramatic critic while he was producing plays. After a sensational drama *Through Fire* (1871) and a social comedy *Peril; or, Love at Long Branch* (1872), he became associated with R. M. Hooley in Chicago, in the development of Hooley's Theatre, which became the chief rival to McVicker's Theatre as the home of legitimate drama. Campbell directed the plays, many of which were his own. His *Fate* (1872–73), a domestic drama, which opened the house, was played in London at the Gaiety Theatre in 1884. Among his other dramas were *Risks, or Insure Your Life* (1873), *The Virginian* (1873), and *On the Rhine* (1875), a play of the Franco-Prussian war of 1870. Campbell took his company to San Francisco in 1875, appearing at Maguire's Opera House, and anticipating in his *Bulls and Bears* (June 7, 1875), an adaptation of Gustav von Moser's *Ultimo,* Augustin Daly's version of the same play, which arrived on July 19. During this summer season Campbell met Bret Harte and Mark Twain, became a member of the Bohemian Club, and received the inspiration for his best play. In 1876 he produced *The Virginian* at St. James's Theatre in London, and while there wrote *A Heroine in Rags* (1876) and *How Women Love* (1877). The latter, a play laid in and near San Francisco, was later rewritten as *The Vigilantes; or, The Heart of the Sierras.* After a verse tragedy, *Clio* (1878), laid in Italy in the twelfth century, and revived in 1885 on a large scale at Niblo's Garden, with music by Operti, Campbell wrote his most significant play, *My Partner,* produced at

the Union Square Theatre, New York, Sept. 16, 1879. It celebrates, with sincerity and skill, the friendship which, in the frontier days in California, often sprang up between two men associated in hardships and in success. The scene in which Joe Saunders pleads for reconciliation with his murdered partner, who is apparently sitting with the divided gold beside him, is one of the most powerful in American drama. *My Partner* held the stage for many years, was performed at the Olympic Theatre, London, Apr. 10, 1884, and was played for about fifty nights at the Residenz-Theater in Berlin, beginning Sept. 15, 1884, Campbell attending the rehearsals. While *My Partner* was a great success, Campbell received a royalty of only ten dollars a performance, so he determined to produce his own plays. *The Galley Slave* (Chestnut Street Theatre, Philadelphia, Sept. 29, 1879) was a vigorous melodrama, with a European scene, which ran for eighty-three nights at the Wilhelm-Theater in Berlin in 1881. *Fairfax* (Park Theatre, Boston, Dec. 8, 1879), a romantic play of the South, has some effective character drawing. It was written for Lester Wallack, but, when a disagreement with him arose, Campbell walked out of the theatre with the play. More melodramatic was *The White Slave* (Haverley's Theatre, New York, Apr. 3, 1882) which contains the lines, "Rags are royal raiment when worn for virtue's sake," deliberately planted by Campbell for his melodramatic effect. *Siberia* (California Theatre, San Francisco, Nov. 26, 1882) portrays the terrors of exile for the Russian patriots of that day and each of its six acts possesses a telling climax. In *Separation* (Union Square Theatre, New York, Jan. 28, 1884) Campbell's theme was the puritanic prejudice against the theatre. In his last play, *Paquita,* produced at his own theatre on Fourteenth St., New York, Aug. 31, 1885, he laid the scene in the Southwest and built up a play upon a situation in which a surgeon is called upon to save the life of the lover of his wife.

Campbell was tall, with a dignified bearing and with the aspect of a scholar. He shares the honor with Augustin Daly and Bronson Howard, of establishing in America the profession of the playwright upon a firm basis. Foreign recognition came to him to an unusual degree, but his reputation has suffered from the fact that, except for one unimportant play, *Little Sunshine* (n.d., first performed in 1873), his dramas have not been published. In ten years he made and lost a large fortune, and in the effort to write, direct, and produce plays his mental powers broke down. In November 1886, he was committed to the State Hospital for the Insane at Middletown, N. Y., where he died.

[Personal information from Mr. Robt. C. Campbell, son of Bartley Campbell; G. E. M[ontgomery], *The Theatre*, I (1886), 348–49; T. Allston Brown, *A Hist. of the N. Y. Stage*, esp. II, 491–92; for the plays: A. H. Quinn, *A Hist. of the Am. Drama from the Civil War to the Present Day*, I, 118–24.]   A. H. Q.

CAMPBELL, CHARLES (May 1, 1807–July 11, 1876), historian, editor, antiquarian, was born in Petersburg, Va., the son of a local bookseller, John Wilson Campbell. When he was a mere child of six years, his father published a *History of Virginia to 1781*, which no doubt in later years had an influence in shaping the career of the son. Like many Virginians of his day, Charles Campbell went to Princeton to be educated, and, graduating from the college there in 1825, he began life as a school-teacher. In 1842 he started a classical school in Petersburg and in 1855 became the principal of Anderson Academy, a position retained until about 1870. Campbell was an industrious collector of historical manuscripts and documents and earned a reputation in scholarly circles as an antiquary. Much of his material was loaned to the well-known Bishop William Meade of Virginia, who made free use of it in his two volumes on *Old Churches and Families of Virginia* (1857). Meade published a letter from Essex to Southampton lent by Campbell with the acknowledgment that it was "furnished me by another true son of Virginia, Mr. Charles Campbell of Petersburg" (Meade, I, 130–31). As early as 1837 Campbell became a regular contributor to *The Southern Literary Messenger* (B. B. Minor, *The Southern Literary Messenger*, p. 68); and he continued this coöperation for many years both as a contributor and as one of the conductors of the Editor's Table under Minor's editorship of the periodical. In 1845, he urged, together with Minor, upon the legislature of Virginia the securing of the Colonial Records of Virginia, and in the January number of 1847 Minor announced the publication by the *Messenger* of Charles Campbell's history of Virginia. Upon this work, *An Introduction to the History of the Colony and Ancient Dominion of Virginia* (Richmond, 1847; a new and improved edition Philadelphia, 1860) rests Campbell's chief reputation as one of the best and most extensive of the writers on state history. He was the author also of a *Genealogy of the Spotswood Family* (1868), and was the editor-author of *Some Materials for a Memoir of John Daly Burk* (1868) in a manner that showed his cordial regard for past and present historians of Virginia. As an editor likewise he published the *Bland Pa-*

pers (1840–43); a reprint, with Introduction, of R. Beverley's *The History of Virginia* (1855); and the *Orderly Book of Gen. Andrew Lewis* (Richmond, 1860). He was also a contributor to the *Virginia Historical Register*.

[Beyond a brief sketch in the *South in the Building of the Nation*, XI, 169, copied from other unsatisfactory sketches, the sources of information are Campbell's own writings and those mentioned in the body of this article.]
                                                              J. C. B.

CAMPBELL, FRANCIS JOSEPH (Oct. 9, 1832–June 30, 1914), educator of the blind, was born in Winchester, Tenn., the son of Melinda and James Campbell. His father was a farmer. When about four years old Francis lost his eyesight. At the age of twelve, he was sent to the institution for the blind at Nashville. There, in spite of being told that he had no ear for music, he made himself so good a musician that he became at sixteen a music teacher. Marrying Mary F. Bond, in Massachusetts, whither he went in 1856 for collegiate study, he finally settled at Perkins Institution, Boston, where, as head of its music department for eleven years, he tested his ideas in the vocational training and placing of chosen pupils, an experience which he was to utilize in an epochal way in England. He next studied music in the conservatories of Leipzig and Berlin. By 1871, through the labors of Dr. T. R. Armitage, a blind gentleman of wealth and position in England, the way was opened for a national training school for blind youth. Armitage assured Campbell, then visiting London, that while graduates of the Paris school were succeeding in music, only about one per cent of the British blind was doing so through teaching, performing, or tuning (T. R. Armitage, *Education and Employment of the Blind*, 1886, p. 54). Thereupon, these two, having obtained the patronage of the nobility and £3,000 in money, established at Upper Norwood in 1872 the Royal Normal College and Academy of Music for the Blind. Campbell, aided by teachers from Perkins Institution and by London professors, even improved upon his Boston successes. Basing everything on a careful preparation for the vocation to be followed, with thorough mental and physical training as a groundwork, he carefully placed his graduates in positions and followed them up, eventually finding between eighty and ninety per cent of them self-sustaining. Through these achievements, unprecedented elsewhere, the college was kept in the public eye, gaining ever more assistance for its work, the greatest being the Gardner scholarship fund, which made a selection of pupils possible. Within a few years the new policy of training the blind to earn their own living and to render them independent, self-reliant citizens had become dominant. His first wife having died, Campbell married Sophia Faulkner, an American trained teacher who as lady principal of the college brought her husband seeing eyes and understanding, patience, and invaluable assistance. Small in body, he possessed tremendous energy and daring. In 1880, after climbing Mont Blanc, he became a Fellow of the Royal Geographical Society. In 1909 he was knighted by King Edward VII in recognition of his services on behalf of the blind.

[John Bernard Mannix, *Heroes of the Darkness* (1911), pp. 61–101; Wm. J. Stead in *Rev. of Revs.* (London), V, 18; *Outlook for the Blind,* July 1909, Oct. 1912, July 1913, Oct. 1914.]   E. E. A.

CAMPBELL, GEORGE WASHINGTON (Feb. 8, 1769–Feb. 17, 1848), senator, secretary of the treasury, diplomat, was born in the parish of Tongue in the shire of Sutherland, Scotland. His parents were a Scotch physician, Dr. Archibald Campbell, and Elizabeth (Mackay) Campbell, widow of Duncan Matheson. Christened George, according to tradition he himself added Washington to his name later. In 1772 his family came to Mecklenburg County, N. C., where, after his father's death, Campbell was thrown early in life upon his own resources. Working on his mother's farm and teaching school, he prepared himself for Princeton College. He entered the junior class, completed the work of two years in one, and graduated with high honors in the class of 1794. He then studied law and soon moved to Knoxville, Tenn., where he quickly took first rank among his colleagues of the bar. Public office, however, attracted him and in 1803 he entered the lower house of Congress. Here he served three successive terms, supported the Jeffersonian administration, quarreled with the vitriolic John Randolph who characterized him as "that Prince of Prigs and Puppies" (Henry Adams, *John Randolph,* p. 210), secured the chairmanship of the Committee of Ways and Means that Randolph had held, and fought a duel with B. Gardenier who had charged that the House of Representatives was controlled by French influence. Declining reëlection, he moved his residence to Nashville, served briefly as a member of Tennessee's supreme court of errors and appeals, and in 1811 as an advocate of war with Great Britain was elected to the United States Senate. In the following year he married Harriet Stoddert, daughter of Benjamin Stoddert. In 1814 he was appointed secretary of the treasury. His brief and ineffective administration of this office brought no improvement in the badly disorganized finances of the government, and in September of that year, on the plea

of impaired health but contrary to President Madison's desire, he resigned. His health improving, he returned to the Senate, served as chairman of the Committee of Finance, supported the chartering of the Second Bank of the United States, and again, in 1818, resigned, this time in order that he might accept appointment as minister to Russia. His two years at St. Petersburg were far from happy ones, however. There was no business of importance for him to conduct; within one week three of his four children died of typhus fever; and he gratefully accepted the President's permission to resign. He did not again hold public office except to serve as one of the commissioners of the United States to carry into effect the claims convention signed with France in 1831. He had long been a personal friend of Andrew Jackson, and, despite his service as one of the directors of the Nashville branch of the Bank of the United States, he continued a member of Jackson's party. Deliberate in forming his opinions and tenacious in holding to them, frankly conscious of his own abilities which he estimated highly, unwilling or unable to compete with the politicians of the new day of triumphant Jacksonian democracy, he devoted the remainder of his life to his private affairs. Before his death he was judged one of the wealthy men of his community.

[The family Bible, containing a record of Campbell's birth, and a considerable number of his papers are in the possession of his family. Occasional letters may be found in the Manuscript Division of the Lib. of Cong. Biographical sketches are in Joshua W. Caldwell, *Sketches of the Bench and Bar of Tenn.* (1898); and in *Proc. of the Nashville Bar, in Relation to the Death of Hon. G. W. Campbell* (1848), reprinted in 27 *Tenn. Reports,* xxi.]   P. M. H.

CAMPBELL, GEORGE WASHINGTON (Jan. 12, 1817–July 15, 1898), horticulturist, was born at Cherry Valley, Cortland County, N. Y., the son of David Campbell; his ancestry was Scotch. When he was four or five years old, his father moved to Sandusky, Ohio. He went to school for a time at Westfield, N. Y., and was trained for newspaper work in which he engaged with his father at Sandusky for a time. In 1849 he moved to Delaware, Ohio, and with a partner engaged in mercantile business until 1856 when this was discontinued. Having been for many years keenly interested in fruit growing, he now turned his whole attention to horticulture. From the first in his commercial work in horticulture he specialized in grapes. It was at Delaware, and during the early period of his specialization, that the Delaware grape, so named in recognition of its place of re-discovery (not of origin), began to attract attention. Campbell propagated it extensively and became largely instrumental in the wide dissemination which it received. Early in his commercial work with grapes he erected greenhouses to provide improved facilities for rooting the cuttings. The glass for these houses he imported from Europe.

It must have been during this same period that he undertook the grape-breeding activities which later brought him into prominence. His first experiments were with seedlings and crosses of the native sorts. The results, however, were disappointing. He then turned to hybridizing the native varieties and the most healthy of the foreign sorts. His ideals were very high. They were described in a paper on the "perfect grape" which he read before the meeting of the Ohio State Horticultural Society in 1891. This was the season before his seedling grape, later to be named Campbell Early, produced its first fruit. Of all the thousands of seedling grapes he had grown and fruited, this one, he was convinced, approached most nearly the ideal for which he was striving. At the present time it is by far the most valuable of all the varieties which he originated.

For many years prior to his death, he was the leading writer and speaker in the North on grape-growing and breeding, and his work had a decided influence on the trend of viticulture. He also gained some note as a potato breeder, though none of his potato introductions are now important. In 1878 he was appointed by President Hayes as commissioner to the Universal and International Exposition at Paris. He sailed for Paris on Apr. 13 and remained in France during that season. While there he wrote a series of articles on his observations which were published in the *Ohio Farmer*. His comments on the ravages of the grape phylloxera, then devastating the vineyards of France, were particularly informing. During the last years of his life, he devoted much of his time to experimenting in plant propagation, especially with soft wood grafting and the determination of the compatibility of varieties and species.

He was married, on Aug. 29, 1846, to Elizabeth Little. They lived to celebrate their golden wedding.

[*Ann. Reports Ohio State Hort. Soc.; Trans. Mass. Hort. Soc.,* 1898; *Jour. Columbus (Ohio) Hort. Soc.,* 1898; unpublished MS. by Campbell concerning his grape-breeding; personal letters.]   H. P. G.

CAMPBELL, HENRY FRASER (Feb. 10, 1824–Dec. 15, 1891), physician, the son of James C. Campbell of Ireland and his wife, Mary R. Eve, an American, was born in Augusta, Ga. He received an academic education, supplemented by a classical course under a private tutor, and entered the Medical College (now University) of Georgia where he received his M.D. in 1842. In the same year he established himself in Augusta, where two years later on June 17, 1844, he married Sarah Bosworth, daughter of Amory Sibley. Until the outbreak of the Civil War he practised his profession in Augusta. He was commissioned surgeon in the Confederate army, 1861, and served as a member of the Army Board of Medical Examiners and as medical director of the General Military Hospital at Richmond, Va. He prepared parts of the *Confederate Manual of Military Surgery* (1863). He occupied various teaching positions at the Medical College of Georgia, as professor of comparative and microscopical anatomy (1854–57), professor of anatomy (1857–66), and from 1868 to the end of his life, professor of orthopedic surgery and gynecology. During this period he was clinical lecturer in the several hospitals of Augusta. Except for the years of the Civil War, his only lengthy absence from the city of his birth was from 1866 to 1868 when he was successively professor of anatomy and professor of surgery at the New Orleans School of Medicine. He is best known for his original studies on the nature of the autonomic nervous system. In 1850 he read an "Essay on the Influence of Dentition in Producing Disease" (*Minutes of the Medical Society of Augusta,* May 2, 1850). In 1851 he published "Law Governing the Distribution of Striped and Unstriped Muscular Fibre" (*Southern Medical and Surgical Journal,* VII, 139–42). Later came articles on excito-secretory action, on reflex vasomotor action as a basis of certain diseases, on the nervous system in febrile diseases, etc. In 1857 he was awarded the prize of one hundred dollars at the tenth annual meeting of the American Medical Association for his investigation of the excito-secretory system. His work on the sympathetic nerves in reflex phenomena was much discussed and on Mar. 2, 1857, he laid claim to priority over Claude Bernard, the famous French physiologist. Dr. Marshal Hall, F.R.S., of London, adjudicated the claim and found that "the idea and designation of excito-secretory action belonged to Dr. Campbell but his details are limited to pathology and observation. The elaborate experimental demonstration of reflex excito-secretory action is the result of the experimental labours of M. Claude Bernard."

Campbell was not only an able surgeon and physiologist but was also a pioneer in preventive medicine. His observations on the abortive treatment of gonorrhea (1845), epidemic dengue fever (1851), the nature of typhoidal fever (1853), unusual forms of dysentery (1851), registration and sanitation (1875), the railroad transmission of disease germs (1876), quarantine in relation to yellow fever germs (1879) and the non-contagiousness of that disease (1880), all reflect a clear logical mind and conceptions of the nature of communicable disease well in advance of his time. His unusual powers of observation were never better demonstrated than in his presentation of his ideas on the transmission of yellow fever before the American Public Health Association's seventh annual meeting (1880), when he vigorously defended his assertion of the portability of atmospheric germs and the non-contagiousness of the disease. From 1857 to 1861, in conjunction with his brother, Dr. Robert Campbell, he was editor of the *Southern Medical and Surgical Journal,* published at Augusta. He was president of the Georgia Medical Association (1871), correspondent of the Academy of Natural Sciences of Philadelphia (1858), corresponding member of the Imperial Academy of Medicine of St. Petersburg (1860), a founder of the American Gynecological Society (1876), and member of the Georgia Board of Health (1875). He was elected vice-president (1858) and finally president of the American Medical Association and presided at its meeting in New Orleans in 1885.

[Sketches in the *Trans. Southern Surgic. and Gynec. Ass.,* XV, 429 ; *Southern Practitioner,* XIV, 89 ; Campbell's numerous papers in his own journal, the *Southern Medic. and Surgic. Jour.,* extending over many years, and his articles read before the Am. Medic. Ass. and the Am. Pub. Health Ass., and published in their official organs ; bibliography in the Index catalogue of the Surgeon-General's Lib., 1, 2 ser.]   E. E. H.

CAMPBELL, JAMES (Sept. 1, 1812–Jan. 27, 1893), postmaster-general, was born in Southwark, Pa. (now part of Philadelphia), the son of Anthony Campbell, a prosperous storekeeper, and of Catharine McGarvey, his wife, both Irish and Catholic in race and religion. His boyhood was one well-disciplined, at home, by the church, and under the schoolmasters of Southwark, John and Geraldus Stockdale, pedagogues and disciplinarians of the old school. All his early environment conspired to produce a steady-going, bookish young fellow who made a regular and industrious law student in the office of Edward D. Ingraham. In this office he applied himself, as was his habit, varying his study with such recreation as might be found in the Philadelphia Library, the Athenæum, or the debating society. He was admitted to the bar on Sept. 14, 1833. His advance was not easy; after three years of practise, he recorded in his diary, "Mind much agitated; singular that I cannot compose myself more when I am to address the

court." These were the years of the bitter anti-Catholic feeling that dominated the local partizanship of that day. Though he was not a strict religionist, Campbell was loyal to his church and became the best-known leader of the Catholic Democrats of Philadelphia. He became school commissioner in 1840 and his influential position is demonstrated by the fact that Gov. Porter appointed him to the court of common pleas in 1842 before he was thirty. He was on the bench ten years and was often called upon to bear the insults which Catholics suffered in the troublous forties. Politically he was arrayed with the Tyler forces for their brief day and then became a Buchanan man. In 1851 he was nominated for supreme court justice to strengthen the rest of the Democratic ticket among his adherents. The balance of the ticket was elected but anti-Catholic prejudice defeated Campbell. The next year Gov. Bigler appointed him attorney-general. In 1852 Campbell marshalled his forces in favor of Pierce during a campaign in which the latter was accused of anti-Catholic prejudice. As a result of this valuable service and upon the recommendations of the state chairman and of Buchanan, Pierce appointed him postmaster-general. In 1853, when Campbell undertook his new task, he was described as a fat jolly man who tended strictly to business. His ambition was to promote the efficiency of his department. He instituted new methods; he attempted to get better rates and more efficient service from the railroad and steamship companies carrying mail; he vainly strove to have the franking privilege abolished. Upon his recommendation the registry system was established. He sought more favorable postage rates with foreign nations, and his success with Bremen laid the foundation for cheaper foreign postages, although Great Britain would not yield during Campbell's term. He was an energetic and hard-working cabinet member, but he was not outstanding in the administration, and, as a Catholic, during the Know-Nothing furor of 1854–55, he probably contributed to the administration's unpopularity.

In 1857 he returned from Washington with his career behind him; Buchanan gave his confidence only to those unconnected with the Pierce administration. A few months after Campbell returned, his wife, Emilie S. Chapron whom he had married Oct. 28, 1845, died, leaving him two sons. Thenceforth, with the exception of once during the Civil War, when he was nearly elected to the United States Senate as a war Democrat, he spent his life with his law practise and as a trustee and director of various charities and institutions, among which were Girard College and Jefferson Medical College. He passed these last thirty-five years in the quiet, steady, almost monotonous mode of life devoted to duty and usefulness, which seemed best to fit his nature.

[Campbell's annual reports as postmaster-general are found in the *Senate Ex. Docs.*, 33 Cong., 34 Cong. The Pa. Hist. Soc. has a few of his letters, mostly in the Buchanan MSS., and scattering items are found in the Pierce papers in the Lib. of Cong. Campbell's son, John M. Campbell, prepared a biographical sketch which was published by the Am. Cath. Hist. Soc. in vol. V (1894) of their *Records*.]   R.F.N.

CAMPBELL, JAMES HEPBURN (Feb. 8, 1820–Apr. 12, 1895), congressman, was born in Williamsport, Pa. He was the son of Francis C. Campbell, a lawyer, and was the grandson of the Rev. John Campbell, an Episcopal clergyman. His mother was Jane Hepburn, a daughter of James Hepburn of Northumberland County, Pa., not the daughter of Judge William Hepburn, as is sometimes stated. (See John F. Meginness, *Genealogy and History of the Hepburn Family of Susquehanna Valley*, 1894.) He was admitted to the bar in 1841, having graduated from the law department of Dickinson College at Carlisle. He then located at Pottsville, Pa., where he built up a large legal practise and soon became active in politics. In 1840 he was a representative to the Young Men's Ratification Convention held at Baltimore after the nomination of William Henry Harrison. Four years later he represented his district in the national Whig convention when Henry Clay received the nomination for president. In 1845, although residing in a district largely Democratic, he was elected a Whig member of the Thirty-fourth Congress. He supported N. B. Banks for speaker, taking an active part in the protracted contest over his election. In 1856 he was defeated as a Republican by W. L. Dewart, the Democratic nominee, but two years later was returned to Congress by a vote of 7,153 as against 4,860 for this same opponent. In 1860 he was again elected. He represented his state on the Committee of Thirty-Three to which Lincoln's first inaugural address was referred, but his most important work was as chairman of the special committee on the Pacific railroad. Largely due to his energetic and adroit leadership the bill granting federal aid for the Pacific railroad by the middle route was passed in the House on May 6, 1862 (*Congressional Globe*, 37 Cong., 2 Sess., p. 1971). He was an ardent champion of protection to industry in the form of a tariff and spoke several times in favor of the Morrill Act of 1861. He supported the Legal Tender Act of 1862 and the conscription bill.

In April 1861 he left his home to aid in the defense of the national capital, and, after passing safely through the Baltimore mobs on Apr. 19, enlisted as a private in Maj. Cassius M. Clay's battalion. The following month he was elected major of the 25th Regular Pennsylvania Volunteers for three months' service. During the invasion of Pennsylvania by Gen. Lee in 1863 he aided Gen. Nagle in the recruiting of a regiment of 1,100 men and became lieutenant-colonel in command of the 39th Pennsylvania Volunteers. After he was mustered out of service, Secretary of State Seward tendered him the appointment of judge of the court for the suppression of the African slave trade, provided for by the treaty of 1862 with Great Britain. This post required residence in Capetown, Africa, and Campbell declined it. In 1864 President Lincoln appointed him United States minister to Sweden and Norway, where he resided three years. On his return he resumed his law practise in Philadelphia, later leaving the law for agricultural pursuits at his country place, Aeola, near Wayne, where he died. He was married in 1843 to Juliet H. Lewis, daughter of Chief Justice Ellis Lewis of Pennsylvania.

[*A Biog. Album of Prominent Pennsylvanians*, vol. I (1888); *Biog. Encyc. of Pa.* (1874), p. 372; *Phila. Inquirer*, Apr. 13, 1895; *Phila. Press*, Apr. 12, 1895.]   F.C.S—n.

CAMPBELL, JAMES VALENTINE (Feb. 25, 1823–Mar. 26, 1890), jurist, son of Henry Munroe Campbell, and Lois (Bushnell) Campbell, both of New England stock, was born in Buffalo, N. Y., where his father was a man of considerable prominence. In the year 1826 the family moved to Detroit, Mich. His father was affiliated with the Episcopal Church, wherefore the son was sent to the Episcopal preparatory school at Flushing, L. I. From this school he went to St. Paul's College, also located in Flushing. He graduated in 1841, and returned to Detroit, where he studied law in the office of Douglass & Walker. In 1844 he began to practise law as the partner of his two instructors. On Nov. 18, 1849, he was married to Cornelia Hotchkiss. When in the year 1858 the supreme court of Michigan was established, Campbell became one of the first three justices; and he was continuously reëlected till his death. He was, in fact, a judge and lawyer of national reputation. His opinions are recorded in seventy volumes of the *Michigan Reports*. They have left their impress not only on the jurisprudence of Michigan, but on that of the whole country. For more than half a century the state and federal judiciary and the writers of texts have cited his decisions as high authority. He was in almost all respects a non-partisan judge (see in particular his opinion in the case of *Twitchell* vs. *Blodgett*, 12 *Mich.*

127). In 1859 he was appointed professor of law in the newly-created Department of Law of the University of Michigan. Seven years later the University conferred upon him its first degree of Doctor of Laws. When he finally resigned his professorship in 1885, his loss was deeply felt by both colleagues and student body. Not only was he highly respected for his keen mind, his unflagging industry, and his sense of justice; but he also endeared himself to his friends and associates because of his sweet disposition.

In 1845 he edited Walker's *Chancery Reports,* and in 1876 he published the *Outlines of the Political History of Michigan,* a valuable contribution to American history. He also published, among others, the following addresses and papers: *The Dangers of Church Centralization* (1856) ;*Moravians in Michigan* (1858) ; *Some Remarks on the Polity of the Protestant Episcopal Church in the United States* (1865) ; *Our City Schools* (1869) ; *Does the Law Deal Unfairly with Questions of Insanity?* (1870) ; *Of the Taking of Private Property for Purposes of Utility* (1871) ; *Some Hints on Defects in the Jury System* (1876) ; *Law Abridgement* (1879) ; *Materials of Jurisprudence* (1880). On Oct. 3, 1859, at the opening of the Law Department in the University of Michigan, he delivered an address *On the Study of Law,* which was published in the same year by the University.

[*Exercises of the Supreme Court of Mich. at the Opening of the Apr. Term, 1890, in Memory of Jas. Valentine Campbell* (Lansing, 1890 ; also in 81 *Mich. Reports*) ; G. I. Reed, *Bench and Bar of Mich.* (1897), pp. 20, 236–38; R. B. Ross and G. B. Catlin, *Landmarks of Wayne County and Detroit* (1898), pp. 659–62 ; B. A. Hinsdale, *Hist. of the Univ. of Mich.* (1906), p. 233.]   A. H—a.

CAMPBELL, JOHN. [See LOUDOUN, JOHN CAMPBELL, FOURTH EARL OF, 1705–1782.]

CAMPBELL, JOHN (1653–Mar. 4, 1727/8), journalist, was a Scot, who emigrated to Boston before 1698 and probably before 1695. In 1702 he became postmaster at Boston under Neale's monopoly, with the "approbation" of Gov. Dudley. The General Court subsidized the post-office at first and in 1703 Campbell was freed from various civic duties during his employment. The subsidy was suspended in 1706. The archives contain a series of petitions by Campbell for its continuance as compensation for taking "due care of forwarding the public letters" and for the printing of the *Weekly Intelligencer.* The post-office was the center of information and Campbell utilized his position to write news-letters for regular patrons, which he franked through the mail (*Proceedings of the Massachusetts Historical Society,* IX, 485). From this developed his printed *Boston News-*

Letter, beginning Apr. 24, 1704. This weekly half-sheet was the first established newspaper in America, though not the first attempt. "Published by authority," the paper was careful to keep on the good side of that authority, but was not entirely immune from official censure (*Calendar of State Papers, Colonial Series, America and West Indies, 1706–08,* 231). It set the precedent of being concerned chiefly with foreign news. The paper was dull; the publisher wrote little himself and that awkwardly, and complained of meager returns, since in 1711 he could not "vend two hundred and fifty copies at one impression." He was not without business enterprise, however; for instance, during 1719 he made half the issues whole sheets in order to catch up on the foreign news, being thirteen months behind, whereby "in a little time all will become New that us'd formerly to seem Old"; and on Jan. 4, 1720, he announced that "such as have a Mind to pleasure their Friends with it per Post may have it every Monday a whole Sheet, one half with the News, the other half good Paper to write their Letter on (which will fully Obviate that insinuation of People's being prevented having it that live remote from hence) by only paying single Postage for both the News and their Letter every Post." He was no longer postmaster at this time, for he had lost the position in 1718. With the last issue of 1722 he turned the control of the *News-Letter* over to Bartholomew Green, who had printed it during most of the preceding years. During the latter part of his life Campbell was a justice of the peace and a man of considerable position. He was twice, possibly thrice, married. His last wife was Mary Pemberton (*née* Clarke) who took Herbert Lloyd as her third husband and published *Meditations on Divine Subjects* (1745).

[The local records and state archives contain various items on Campbell. Some of those on the post-office are in *Mass. Hist. Soc. Colls.,* 3 ser., VII, 60–84. Samuel Sewell gives some information in his Diary, *Mass. Hist. Soc. Colls.,* 5 ser., V–VII. Isaiah Thomas, *Hist. of Printing in America* (2d. ed., 2 vols., 1874), II, 12–28, is the chief source on Campbell's newspaper. For the controversy over earlier newspaper attempts, see *Mass. Colonial Soc. Pubs.,* X, 310.]   D. M. M.

CAMPBELL, JOHN ARCHIBALD (June 24, 1811–Mar. 12, 1889), lawyer, associate justice of the Supreme Court of the United States and assistant secretary of war for the Southern Confederacy, was born at Washington, in Wilkes County, Ga. Like so many of the inhabitants of the lower South, he was almost entirely of Scottish and Scotch-Irish blood. His paternal great-grandfather came to North Carolina from Scotland in the migration of Highlanders that followed the disaster at Culloden and the harsh enactments of the British Parliament. The grandfather whose full name he bore was an officer in the Continental Army upon the personal staff of Gen. Greene, and after the war a judge of the North Carolina court of Admiralty. His father, Duncan Green Campbell, moved to Georgia in 1808 and there married Mary Williamson, the daughter of Lieut.-Col. Micajah Williamson,—Revolutionary leader—and Sarah (Gilliam) Williamson. Sarah Williamson had been one of the most remarkable women of her period in Georgia. With great enterprise and courage she successfully managed a plantation and a large number of negro slaves, during the absence of her husband at the front, in spite of the depredations of the enemy who at times overran her property.

Campbell entered Franklin College (University of Georgia) when he was eleven years old and upon his graduation with first honor at fourteen was made a cadet at the United States Military Academy by John C. Calhoun, his father's friend, who was then secretary of war. His father died while nominee for governor of Georgia with every prospect of success, a year before John was to receive his commission. The unsatisfactory condition of his father's estate made it necessary for John to abandon a military career and come home. There he prepared for the bar under the tutelage of his uncle John W. Campbell, and Gov. Clarke, and was admitted to practise at eighteen, together with his fellow townsman Robert Toombs [q.v.], by virtue of a special act of the Georgia legislature. Within a year he moved to Alabama where he lived—first in Montgomery, then in Mobile—until his elevation to the bench. While there he married Anna Esther Goldthwaite, the sister of Henry and George Goldthwaite.

As a member of the bar of Alabama, Campbell rose rapidly. He twice declined an associate justiceship of the state supreme court, the first appointment having been tendered him when he was only twenty-four years of age. He was an indefatigable student, had an unusual memory, and his knowledge of the principles of both the civil and common law was extensive. The best known case in which he appeared during this period was that of *Gaines* vs. *Relf* (12 *Howard*, 472), where his argument in the circuit court on behalf of a pathetic woman who was to devote practically her entire life toward establishing her legitimacy, elicited high praise. The litigation was protracted for nearly half a century. Seven times, in one phase or another, was it appealed to the Supreme Court of the United States, but it was finally disposed of by the same process of reasoning pursued by Campbell in his argument in the circuit court. (For a history of this

cause célèbre see J. Carroll Payne, "A Celebrated Case, the Myra Clark Gaines Litigation," in *Report of the Fourteenth Annual Session of the Georgia Bar Association*, 1897.) Although his law practise was large, Campbell took an active interest in public affairs. He served with distinction for two terms in the Alabama legislature, and was a delegate to the Nashville Convention of June 1850, where he prepared the greater portion of the resolutions adopted. They were temperate and conciliatory, in striking contrast to the impassioned *Address* issued by the convention from the pen of Robert Barnwell Rhett (see Farrar Newberry, "The Nashville Convention and Southern Sentiment of 1850," *South Atlantic Quarterly*, XI, 259).

At forty Campbell had a national reputation as a lawyer and in March 1853, before he was forty-two, he was appointed an associate justice of the United States Supreme Court by President Pierce. His selection was made at the request of the justices of the Court and appears from articles in the press of the period to have given universal satisfaction. His judicial opinions indicate an unwillingness to further extend the liberal interpretation of the Constitution which prevailed under the chief-justiceship of Marshall, and also disclose a profound hostility toward monopolies. Having been nurtured and schooled in the Jeffersonian policies of strict construction and being familiar, as a student of history, with the tendency of courts to amplify and enlarge their jurisdictions, he was quick to sense judicial infringement upon the reserved powers of the states, and frequently found himself in disagreement with the majority of his colleagues on constitutional questions. On other points he was usually in agreement with the majority, and therefore could not be called, in the general acceptance of the term, a "dissenting judge."

Although he impressed the leading jurists of his time as possessing great ability and "supreme integrity of nature and intellect," he was in no sense a popular man and in the performance of duty often ran counter to public opinion. He was denounced in certain quarters of the South because while sitting as circuit judge in New Orleans he urged the grand jury to indict William Walker and other prominent and popular leaders of filibustering expeditions to Latin America, as violators of the neutrality laws. And he came in for his share of the torrent of abolitionist abuse heaped upon the majority of the court for their celebrated Dred Scott decision. Campbell, in an elaborate concurring opinion, supported the majority in holding that a negro was not a citizen of the United States, and that the Missouri Com-

457

promise, which undertook to prohibit slavery in the territories north of the thirty-sixth parallel, was without constitutional authority and void (19 *Howard*, 493). At the time when this case was decided he held no slaves. Upon his appointment to the Supreme Court he had emancipated all he owned and thereafter employed as servants only free persons of color. Although he was bitterly attacked by the extreme abolitionists, he was generally regarded as a "moderate," and in the crisis in the Democratic party in 1860 he was looked upon by more than one conservative leader as an ideal compromise candidate for the Presidency. He had no political aspirations, however, and gave no encouragement to the movement.

When, after the election of Lincoln, the lower South was aflame with the fires of secession, he openly and persistently opposed it. While he had a sympathetic understanding of the Southern point of view and believed that a failure to accord the slave states their constitutional rights within the Union legally entitled them to withdraw, he nevertheless thought secession unnecessary, believed it would prove calamitous, and held to the view that the differences between the sections could be adjusted by compromise. Nor did he cease his efforts to close the breach after the cotton states had formed a provisional government and despatched commissioners to Washington to negotiate a treaty. He was informed by his associate, Justice Nelson, that Secretary of State Seward (who apparently desired to bring about a reconciliation) was depressed by the insistence of the Confederate commissioners that they be officially recognized, since at the moment President Lincoln and the rest of the cabinet were not inclined to receive them. Campbell tendered his services as an intermediary and was assured by Seward that, if the commissioners would not press their demand for recognition, Fort Sumter, then occupied by Federal troops, would be evacuated in "five days." Campbell communicated this to the commissioners and they so advised their Government. Thus was begun that strange course of conduct by Seward concerning which much has been written. In brief, by repeated promises to Campbell that Sumter would be evacuated he held the commissioners dangling in Washington until an expedition was despatched to Charleston for the fort's replenishment. It is probable that Seward believed the fortress would be given up (Nathaniel W. Stephenson, *Lincoln and the Union*, 1921, p. 107). But whatever his motives or beliefs, he placed Campbell in an untenable position and refused to exculpate him from the charge of treachery (H. G. Connor, *post*, pp. 133 ff.). Campbell's memoranda of the conferences with Seward, made soon after the event, have every indication of accuracy and show that Campbell's conduct was above reproach (J. F. Rhodes, *post*, III, pp. 338 ff.). He forfeited for a time, however, the confidence of the Confederates, who believed that he had connived with the Federal Administration in a policy of duplicity.

There can be no question of the sincerity of Campbell's devotion to his native section, and after he had failed in his efforts to save the Southern people from what he believed to be inevitable catastrophe, he resigned his judicial position and joined fortunes with them. He took no part in the struggle until October 1862, when, the hostility toward him having abated, he was urged by the Confederate secretary of war to become an assistant secretary with the special duty of administering the conscription law. He accepted and, although the work was distasteful to him, held the position until the Confederacy collapsed (see "Papers of Hon. John A. Campbell 1861–65," in *Southern Historical Society Papers*, October 1917, pp. 3–81).

In January 1865, President Davis named him, together with Vice-President Stephens and R. M. T. Hunter, on the peace commission which met with President Lincoln and Secretary Seward at Hampton Roads. Although Lincoln's terms were unsatisfactory, Campbell believed they could be made the basis for further negotiations; Davis thought otherwise, and the conference came to nothing.

When the Confederate capital was evacuated, Campbell made a last attempt to lighten the burdens of his people. At some physical danger to himself he remained in Richmond and was able to secure an interview with President Lincoln. It resulted in an order permitting the Virginia legislature to convene to consider Lincoln's terms of reconstruction (see Campbell's own account in his *Recollections of the Evacuation of Richmond, Apr. 2nd, 1865* (1880), and *Reminiscences and Documents Relating to the Civil War During the Year 1865* (1887)). Within a few days Lee surrendered and Lincoln withdrew his sanction of the meeting in a telegram to Gen. Weitzel (Federal commander) in which he said that Campbell had misconstrued the terms under which the plan was to be carried out. The next day Lincoln was assassinated. As a result of the passion following that tragedy Campbell was arrested on the absurd charge of having misrepresented to Weitzel Lincoln's purpose in assembling the legislature—absurd, because Weitzel had participated in both of the conferences Campbell held with Lincoln and had heard everything Lincoln said. After being confined for about four months at Fort Pulaski, Campbell was released by President Johnson at the instance of his former colleagues, Justice Nelson of New York and Justice Curtis of Massachusetts.

All of Campbell's property, which consisted mainly of holdings in Mobile, had been destroyed during the war, and upon his release from prison he was faced with the necessity, at fifty-four, of beginning life anew. He went to New Orleans and soon acquired a large and lucrative law practise. He appeared in many cases of great importance in the United States Supreme Court. Among these were the famous Slaughterhouse Cases (16 *Wallace*, 36), where he again took up the cudgels against monopolies, but now, in the exigencies of the time, he was seeking the aid of the Federal power to relieve a community from the oppressive act of a state. The carpet-bag government of Louisiana had in 1869 chartered a corporation upon which it conferred for twenty-five years the exclusive right to maintain within the city and parish of New Orleans, and two adjoining parishes, all butcher-shops, slaughter-pens, stock-yards, and stables. Some thirteen hundred persons were legislated out of business. Judge Campbell attacked the statute as creating a monopoly and as being in violation of the recently adopted Fourteenth and Fifteenth Amendments to the Constitution. It was a case of first impression, as the war amendments had not before been up for judicial interpretation. Campbell's argument was elaborate and forceful, and supported by a wealth of authority, historical and judicial; but he lost his case. By a divided bench—five to four—it was held that the amendments were passed only to secure the freedom of the negro from the oppressions of those who had formerly exercised dominion over him, and would not be extended to protect rights already given to citizens by the states.

Another case in which he appeared, this time successfully, was that of *Jackson* vs. *Ludeling* (21 *Wallace*, 616), in which he prevented the consummation of what was characterized by the court as "a great wrong, perpetrated by the agency of legal forms." So too, in the case of *New York and New Hampshire* vs. *Louisiana* (108 *United States*, 76), where his argument was described by Chief Justice Waite as the greatest he had ever heard in a court of justice, he successfully defeated the collection of bonds issued by a corrupt government under "a condition bordering on anarchy," and where, as he said, "the holders knew there was no coercive power to enforce their payment."

Nearly all of Campbell's opinions as a judge, as well as his arguments at the bar, show that he had a thorough knowledge of the historical aspects of the questions involved. He had perhaps the finest private law library, in all languages, in America, and when retained in an important case he would retire to his books and lead the life of a recluse until he had completed its preparation. When he died at the age of seventy-seven he had for the second time in his life come to be recognized as one of the leading lawyers in America. He has frequently been described as austere. In fact, his large, erect frame, natural dignity, and strong, prominent features did produce a rugged aspect. But though his manners to the world were formal, to his family and intimates he was tender and considerate, and his sympathy for the unfortunate was profound. The faith of an old negro woman whose freedom he had bought and who when she was dying admonished those about her to put their "faith in God and Mr. Campbell," was no doubt shared by many beneficiaries of his charity.

[*John Archibald Campbell* (1920), by H. G. Connor, is, on the whole, excellent. It cites convincing evidence to support Campbell's memoranda and letters relating to his conferences with Seward, while the treatment of Campbell's work as a jurist leaves little to be desired. For an apparently impartial interpretation of the Sumter incident, see Jas. Ford Rhodes, *Hist. of the U. S. from the Compromise of 1850* (1893), III, 336–40; for a Northern version, see Jas. Schouler, *Hist. of the U. S. A. Under the Constitution* (1880–91), VI, 14 ff.; for a Southern view, see A. H. Stephens, *A Constitutional View of the War Between the States* (1868–70), II, 347 ff. Campbell's judicial opinions are to be found in 15–24 *Howard* (56–65 *U. S.*). An appraisal of his work as judge and advocate by leaders of the American bar may be found in 130 *U. S.*, App. VII.]   B. F.

CAMPBELL, JOHN WILSON (Feb. 23, 1782–Sept. 24, 1833), congressman, jurist, was born in Augusta County, Va., near Miller's Iron Works. His parents, William and Elizabeth (Wilson) Campbell, had come to that settlement from near Londonderry, Ireland. When he was a lad of eight or nine they moved, together with their large family, to Bourbon County, Ky. Young Campbell was not suited to the hard life on a pioneer farm, for he was not robust, and besides, he desired an education. This his parents could not afford to give him, although they had the Scotch-Presbyterian respect for learning. He grew discontented and ran away to Cincinnati, where he apprenticed himself to a carpenter. His parents prevailed on him to return home, and he was sent to a school conducted by the Rev. J. P. Campbell. His parents shortly moved to Ohio, where he was able to pay for his own schooling either by working at clearing the timberlands or by teaching school. After studying law at Morgantown, Va., with his uncle Thomas Wilson, he was admitted to the bar in 1808, and set up an office in West Union, Adams County, Ohio. Here he was shortly made prosecuting attorney and succeeded in building up a lucrative practise. In 1811 he was married to Eleanor Doak, daughter of Col. Robert Doak of Augusta County, Va. He had a short period of service in the War of 1812 (*The "Old Northwest" Genealogical Quarterly*, X, 45). In 1813 and again in 1815 he was sent by his county to the state legislature. In 1814, United States Senator Thomas Worthington resigned to become governor of Ohio, and Campbell was nominated, along with ten others, to fill the vacancy. The fact that he stood third highest in the balloting is an indication of the place he was coming to have in state politics. In 1816 he was elected to Congress by a large majority. He represented his district in five consecutive sessions (1817–27). Judging from the records, he was not an active debater. He spoke vigorously, however, against the Panama Mission, an administration measure, on Apr. 20, 1826 (*Register of Debates*, 19 Cong., 1 Sess., col. 2413 ff.). Although he was a Jackson man, he was not an intense partizan by nature, and his speeches indicate the equanimity of his disposition. In 1828 he was nominated by the state convention of the Jackson party for the governorship (*The "Old Northwest" Genealogical Quarterly*, IX, 230) but was defeated. It seems probable that he was a reluctant candidate. On the accession of Jackson to the presidency, Campbell was appointed United States district judge. In order to be near his work, he moved his residence from his farm in Brown County to Columbus, in 1831. He seems to have been well qualified both by education and disposition for his new position, but he did not live to make his mark as a judge, for he was among the victims of the cholera epidemic which decimated Ohio in 1833.

[*Biog. Sketches; with other Literary Remains of the Late John W. Campbell . . . Compiled by his Widow* (1838), containing a laudatory, but accurate sketch of his life; *Hist. Sketches of the Campbell, Pilcher and Kindred Families* (1911); obituaries in the *Cincinnati Daily Gazette*, Sept. 28, 1833, and other contemporary newspapers.]   W. T. U—r.

CAMPBELL, JOSIAH A. PATTERSON (Mar. 2, 1830–Jan. 10, 1917), jurist, was of Scotch and Irish descent, the son of the Rev. Robert B. Campbell, a Presbyterian minister, and of his wife, Mary Patterson. He was born in the Waxhaw settlement, Abbeville district, S. C., and was educated at Camden Academy and Davison College, N. C. Upon leaving college he joined his father's family in Madison County, Miss., where they had settled in 1845. He

then read law, and at the age of seventeen was admitted to the bar at Kosciusko, Miss. He there practised his profession until 1865, except during the war period. At the age of twenty-one he was elected to the legislature on the Democratic ticket. As the practise of law was more congenial to him than politics, he retired from public office at the expiration of his legislative term. In 1859 he was again elected to the legislature, and became speaker of the House. When his state seceded from the Union in 1861, he was chosen one of the seven delegates from Mississippi to the Confederate constitutional convention at Montgomery and thus became a member of the Provisional Congress of the Confederacy. In March 1862 he entered the Confederate army, and was chosen captain of Company K, which became part of the 40th Regiment, and when that regiment was organized at Meridian, Miss., he was made lieutenant-colonel. He commanded his regiment in the battles of Iuka and Corinth, being wounded in the latter engagement. He rejoined his command at Grenada and went with it to Vicksburg, where he received notice from the secretary of war that he had been assigned to the military court of Gen. Polk's corps, with the rank of colonel. He served in this capacity until the end of the war. He was then elected circuit judge of his district, to fill an unexpired term, and was reëlected in 1866 for the full term. But his inability to take the test oath required by the federal government forced him to retire from the bench in 1870. He was elected professor of law at the University of Mississippi, but declined this position and opened a law office at Canton, Miss. A short time later he formed a partnership with Judge S. S. Calhoun in the same town, and this relationship lasted until Campbell received an appointment to the supreme bench of the state. Meantime, at the request of Gov. Alcorn, he served on a commission which prepared the Code of 1871. When the Democratic party resumed control of the state government in 1876, Gov. Stone appointed Campbell to the supreme bench for a term of nine years. He was then reappointed by Gov. Lowry for a second term, which gave him a tenure of eighteen years during a third of which time he was chief justice. At the request of the state legislature he also prepared the Code of 1880, which was almost wholly in force for more than a generation. Responding to a request of the legislature of Mississippi, he delivered before that body (1890) a memorial address on the "Life and Character of Jefferson Davis." In this address he said: "I have never blamed a

Northern man for supporting *his* country, . . . and before the bar of justice and fairness, I demand the same recognition for myself and countrymen in supporting *ours* . . . This is our native earth, and rights to which we are born were in jeopardy." At the time of his death, Campbell was the sole survivor of the forty-nine signers of the Confederate constitution. He was a man of imposing appearance, with a courtly bearing that befitted the high judicial position which he filled with dignity and honor. He was about six feet two in height, with erect carriage, a sonorous voice, expressive blue eyes, a high forehead, and an intellectual, bearded face. He was married, May 23, 1850, to Eugenia E., daughter of Rev. W. W. and Nancy (Dotson) Nash, of Kosciusko, Miss.

[Sketches of Campbell will be found in *Biog. and Hist. Memoirs of Miss.* (1891), I, 495–98; *Miss. Hist. Soc. Pubs.*, IV (1901), 493, footnote; Dunbar Rowland, *Mississippi* (1907), I, 349–50; *Times-Picayune* (New Orleans) and *Commercial Appeal* (Memphis), Jan. 11, 1917. His judicial decisions will be found in *Miss. Reports* from 1876 to 1894. See also his "Planters and Union Bank Bonds" in *Miss. Hist. Soc. Pubs.*, IV, 493–97 and his *Address on the Life and Character of Jefferson Davis* (pamphlet published by authority of the legislature of Miss., Jackson, Miss., (1890).]

F. L. R.

CAMPBELL, LEWIS DAVIS (Aug. 9, 1811–Nov. 26, 1882), editor, congressman, diplomat, of Highland Scotch stock, the son of Samuel and Mary (Small) Campbell, was born at Franklin, Warren County, Ohio. After serving an apprenticeship of three years (1828–31) on the *Cincinnati Gazette,* he took over the *Hamilton Intelligencer,* which heartily championed the cause of Henry Clay and the Whig party. While engaged with this weekly paper, he found time to study law and in 1835 was admitted to the bar. His practise and reputation as a lawyer grew rapidly. His marriage to Jane H. Reily, daughter of John Reily, a prominent Ohio pioneer, added to his influence. In 1848 he was elected to Congress as a Whig, and for four consecutive sessions he was reëlected. In 1858 he and C. L. Vallandigham fought for the support of the Miami Valley. Each claimed the victory, but the seat was awarded to Vallandigham by the House of Representatives. The high point of Campbell's career in Congress was his chairmanship of the Committee of Ways and Means in the Thirty-fourth Congress. In the great debates over slavery he displayed considerable force as a speaker, particularly in his opposition to the repeal of the Missouri Compromise. On the outbreak of the Civil War he served for a time as colonel of the 69th Regiment of Ohio volunteers, but ill health compelled him to leave the service. Although not in Congress, he opposed the Congressional program of reconstruction. He was a delegate at the Philadelphia Union convention and at the Soldiers Convention at Cleveland in 1866. President Johnson appointed him minister to Mexico at a time when Secretary of State Seward was trying to compel Napoleon III to recall his troops, by diplomatic rather than military pressure. The dogged resistance of the republicans of Mexico, led by Juarez, had won the admiration of the people of the United States. Although Campbell was appointed minister in May 1866, it was not until November that he departed on his mission to the Juarez government, located somewhere in northern Mexico. To make his mission more significant diplomatically, Gen. W. T. Sherman accompanied him. They found the coast towns still in the hands of Maximilian and failed to get in touch with Juarez. Campbell for the time being set up his "Legation" at New Orleans. Gideon Welles, secretary of the navy, wrote in his diary, "The Minister, with his thumb in his mouth, stood off, went up the coast, where Sherman left him. The whole business turns out a *faux pas,* a miserable, bungling piece of business" (*Diary of Gideon Welles,* 1911, II, 649). The refusal of Maximilian to leave Mexico following the withdrawal of the French forces had by this time become the chief difficulty in the Mexican situation. Seward repeatedly ordered Campbell to depart for his post of duty with the Juarez government, but Campbell, who found his duties irksome, pleaded ill health and private business as reasons for delaying. Seward practically forced his resignation, June 15, 1867. Campbell now found himself so thoroughly out of accord with the Republican party's program, both political and economic, that he withdrew his allegiance and in 1870 ran for Congress and was elected on the Democratic ticket. In 1872 he actively supported Greeley for the presidency. He was a member and vice-president of the third Ohio constitutional convention which met in 1873. The document framed by that body did not meet with his approval and he aided the forces which accomplished its rejection. In his last years he frequently spoke and wrote in behalf of various movements for economic and political reform.

[Full sketches of Campbell were published in the *Cincinnati Commercial,* Nov. 27, 1882, and in the *Cincinnati Enquirer* of the same date. Jas. McBride, *Pioneer Biogs., Sketches of the Lives of Some of the Early Settlers of Butler County, Ohio* (1869), has a number of references to Campbell. See also *Ohio Archœol. and Hist. Quart.,* Jan., Oct. 1925. The fullest account of the Mexican episode is in Ellis P. Oberholtzer, *A Hist. of the U. S. Since the Civil War,* vol. I (1917). This author has made use of the Johnson Papers. Campbell's official correspondence as minister is to be found in

House Ex. Doc. No. 1 and No. 76, 39 Cong., 2 Sess.; House Ex. Doc. No. 30, 40 Cong., 1 Sess.; House Ex. Doc. No. 1, 40 Cong., 2 Sess., vol. I. J. M. Callahan's article "Evolution of Seward's Mexican Policy," West Va. Univ. Studies, vols. IV–VI, is useful.]

W. T. U—r.

CAMPBELL, PRINCE LUCIEN (Oct. 6, 1861–Aug. 14, 1925), college president, was of Scotch and Irish descent, the son of Thomas Franklin and Jane Eliza (Campbell) Campbell. He was born in Newmarket, Mo., but the family removed in 1869 to Monmouth, Ore., where his father became president of Christian College. There Prince Campbell graduated in 1879. He taught, reported for the *Kansas City Star,* and attended Harvard, graduating in 1886. On Sept. 12, 1887, he was married to Eugenia J. Zieber of Forest Grove, Ore. From 1886 to 1889 he was teacher of ancient languages and pedagogy in the State Normal School at Monmouth, successor to Christian College. Thereafter, to 1902, he was president of that institution. In 1902 he became president of the University of Oregon. On Aug. 20, 1908, his first wife having died in February 1891, he was married to Susan A. Church of San Francisco. The educational problems which he was called upon to meet as president of the University of Oregon were, at the outset, similar to those encountered by such institutions generally. Among these were the insignificant financial resources and limited student patronage. Campbell, during the previous four or five years, as a trusted adviser of legislative committees, had aided in establishing the public high-school system, and in the rapid multiplication of high schools he found the best assurance of student support for the university. Candidates soon began applying for admission in more generous numbers. Eventually the legislature was induced to enlarge the university's grant. But at this point the president encountered the newly adopted "Initiative and Referendum" amendment to the state constitution. This, under the existing conditions, revolutionized the history of public support for liberal higher education. No American educator had ever been called upon to present the case for higher education to the entire electorate. That is what Campbell was obliged to do, not once, but repeatedly, ultimately gaining the assured support of the people themselves. In this work, whose result was to render more secure every state-supported university in America, Campbell's inspiring personality was a major asset. Combined with rare practical judgment, organizing ability, and a positive genius for maintaining the morale of his forces, he had an abiding faith in the necessity of liberal culture for a democ-racy and great enthusiasm in presenting the argument to the voters. He was a man of splendid physique, five feet nine in stature and weighing 180 pounds, with handsome florid countenance, glowing dark eyes, black hair and mustache. He was fond of society, a noted raconteur, a gay, charming companion, a lover of his kind.

[Jos. Schafer, *Prince Lucien Campbell* (Eugene, 1926); private MSS.; newspaper clippings; Univ. of Ore. Regents Reports, 1902–26.]   J. S.

CAMPBELL, ROBERT (March 1804–Oct. 16, 1879), fur trapper, capitalist, was born of Scotch parents in Aughlane, County Tyrone, Ireland. Nothing is known of his youth. He came to America probably in 1824, and he seems to have gone at once to St. Louis. On Oct. 30, 1825, suffering from lung trouble and advised to try the mountains for a cure, he set out with Ashley's second overland expedition. His health improved and he engaged actively in trapping, soon becoming a leader and commanding various parties organized by Ashley's successors. In close association with Fitzpatrick, Smith, Bridger, the Sublettes and other noted trappers, his operations during the first seven years covered nearly the whole of the northern region. In the battle with the Blackfeet in Pierre's Hole, July 18, 1832, made famous by Irving and others, he bore a conspicuously gallant part, incidentally saving the life of his companion, W. L. Sublette. On Dec. 20 he became a partner with Sublette in an effort to contest the hold of the American Fur Company on the upper Missouri, but at the end of the following year, after a succession of disasters, the partners decided to confine themselves to the mountain trade.

In the fall of 1835 Campbell retired from the mountains and made his home in St. Louis. The firm of Sublette & Campbell, after maintaining for seven or eight years the only serious opposition encountered during that time by the American Fur Company, was dissolved on Jan. 12, 1842. Campbell engaged in extensive real estate dealings, established a large dry-goods store, and at a later time became the proprietor of the Southern Hotel and the president of both the Bank of the State of Missouri and the Merchants' National Bank. All his affairs prospered, and he amassed great wealth. Though never a candidate for office, he took an active part in public affairs. In 1846, as a member of Gov. Edwards's staff, with the rank of colonel, he distinguished himself by his indefatigable efforts toward equipping and drilling the mounted volunteers for the Mexican War. In 1851, by appointment of President Fillmore, he was one of the commissioners in the great Indian conference held near Fort Laramie, and in 1869, by appointment of President Grant, he again served as an Indian commissioner. To the end he maintained a lively interest in the scenes wherein he had spent his young manhood, and in 1868 he paid a final visit to the region, giving a reception at Fort Laramie to his old friends and acquaintances. In his later years he suffered greatly from a bronchial affection. In the summer of 1879 he journeyed to Saratoga and the Atlantic seashore, but returned in September hopeless of relief. He died at his St. Louis home.

Campbell was married, probably in Philadelphia, to Virginia Kyle, of Raleigh, N. C., who with three children survived him. He was, for many years before his death, one of the most influential and widely known business men and capitalists of the West. He was a generous man, and his benefactions, though secret, are believed to have been many and large. Though he was somewhat distant and difficult of approach, his friendships were strong and enduring. He was greatly attached to Bridger, befriending him in various ways and undertaking the care of his children—one of whom, Virginia, lived for two years in his home. He was honest, and in an era wherein the fierce competition of rivals prompted the basest accusations against one another, his reputation seems to have escaped reproach.

[Mention of Campbell is more or less frequent in the journals and letters of the fur-trapping period and in such works as Washington Irving, *The Adventures of Capt. Bonneville* (1837), Chas. G. Coutant, *Hist. of Wyoming* (1899), E. L. Sabin, *Kit Carson Days* (1914), and J. C. Alter, *Jas. Bridger* (1925). Biographical sketches are given in H. M. Chittenden, *The Am. Fur Trade of the Far West* (1902), and J. T. Scharf, *Hist. of St. Louis City and County* (1883). There are obituaries in the *St. Louis Globe-Democrat* and the *Mo. Republican* (St. Louis), Oct. 17, 1879).]   W. J. G.

CAMPBELL, THOMAS (Feb. 1, 1763–Jan. 4, 1854), one of the founders of the Disciples of Christ, was the son of Alexander Campbell. A handsome young Irishman of Scotch descent, he was religiously minded, and, after graduating from the University of Glasgow, became a minister of the Secession Church, which was a branch of the Scottish kirk that had broken away from the parent stock of Presbyterianism. The tendency to independency was strong in the seceding body, and controversy divided it. Campbell tried to bring about a reunion, and went as a delegate to the Scotch synod in an effort to make peace. This was unsuccessful, and a later attempt to free the Irish churches from Scotch control was unavailing. The experience made Campbell an enemy of sectarianism. Ill health compelled a sea voyage in 1807, and he sailed to America, hoping to find there a task to his liking. In western Pennsylvania he discovered friends and an opportunity to preach, and he sent for his family to join him. His liking for Christian unity made him invite persons of various religious professions to join in the Lord's Supper, but his Presbyterian synod censured him, thus causing him to withdraw from the Presbyterian Church. With his son Alexander Campbell [*q.v.*] he formed the Christian Association of Washington (Pa.), out of which came later a fully organized independent church, with a declaration of principles written by Thomas Campbell. Before long it was apparent that a new denomination might grow out of the experiment. That was not the wish of the Campbells and it seemed best to join the Baptists with whom they were sympathetic on the subject of baptism. But the union did not work well, the connection was broken, and the Campbellites formed a merger with the Christians, a similar group that had been organized by Barton W. Stone. The Campbellites preferred to call themselves Disciples.

Thomas Campbell was a popular preacher, sometimes lengthy in discourse, but enlivening his subject with homely illustrations. He was never strongly rooted in one locality. In 1813 he removed from Pennsylvania to a farm in Ohio, where he started a seminary. Two years later he moved to Pittsburgh with another school as his medium of usefulness. Tiring of this after another two years, he made a home at Burlington, Vt., among the Baptists, and tried to show them how to make their emotional preaching more intellectual. Meanwhile he taught school for a living. His family was happy in these surroundings and the school was prospering when Campbell became displeased with the attitude of the community toward negroes, and he peremptorily summoned his family to return to the neighborhood of their old home in Pennsylvania. There he assisted his son Alexander in the conduct of a school near by. In his later life he itinerated as a preacher, until, becoming blind, he retired from active service. He lived to the age of ninety, dying peacefully at Bethany, W. Va.

[The chief source is *The Memoir of Elder Thos. Campbell* (1861) by his son Alexander Campbell. See also Robt. Richardson, *Memoirs of Alexander Campbell* (1868–70), *passim*.]   H. K. R.

CAMPBELL, THOMAS JOSEPH (Apr. 29, 1848–Dec. 14, 1925), Jesuit priest, was born on Manhattan Island and educated at the College of St. Francis Xavier, New York City, where he was graduated in 1866. The following year after further studies in philosophy he received the degree of M.A. In the summer of 1867 he entered the Society of Jesus at Sault-au-Recollet, Canada, and in 1870 was assigned to teach the freshman class at St. John's College, Fordham (now Fordham University). From 1873 to 1876 he studied philosophy and science at Woodstock College, Maryland. After two more years of teaching at St. Francis Xavier's, he went to Louvain, Belgium, where he devoted himself to theological branches for four years, being ordained priest in 1880.

In 1885 he was appointed president of St. John's College, Fordham, and three years later provincial of the Maryland-New York Province of the Society of Jesus. This office he held until 1893, when he became vice-rector of St. Francis Xavier's for ten months. Two years were spent in missionary preaching in the eastern states, after which he was appointed a second time president of St. John's College, Fordham. In August 1900 he joined the staff of the Apostleship of Prayer in New York, as preacher, writer, and editor. Master of a clear, attractive English style, he contributed many impressive articles to the *Messenger of the Sacred Heart* and to the *Pilgrim of Our Lady of Martyrs,* the organ of the Shrine erected at Auriesville, N. Y. His interest in the mission work of New France resulted in the publication in the pages of the *Messenger* of many biographical sketches of the missionaries. These were published later on in book-form under the title *Pioneer Priests of North America* (3 vols., 1908–11). Two further volumes were devoted to *Pioneer Laymen of North America* (1915).

Two years were spent by Father Campbell in Montreal as English preacher in the Jesuit church and as research worker in the Jesuit archives, after which in 1910 he was chosen editor of the weekly Catholic review, *America,* published by the Jesuit Fathers in New York. He conducted the review with vigor and success for four years, writing especially on historical, educational, and social subjects. During this time he translated and published *The Names of God and Meditative Summaries of the Divine Perfections* (1912), by Father Leonard Lessius, S. J. After a sojourn of two more years in Canada, he again returned to New York and among other occupations lectured on American history in the Graduate School of Fordham University. Under the title *Various Discourses* (1917) he gathered into a volume the outstanding sermons and addresses of his life. In 1921 he published *The Jesuits, 1534–1921, A History of the Society of Jesus from its Foundation to the Present Time.* It was the first attempt at a full, but popular, historical account in English, written by a member of the Society. During the latter years of his life he translated the Psalms into verse, as well as the hymns of the Roman Breviary, compiled a series of sketches of distinguished members of the Society of Jesus, and prepared a sketch of the Archdiocese of New York. The last work from his pen was a revision of his monograph on Blessed Isaac Jogues and his companion martyrs, published posthumously under the title *The Martyrs of the Mohawk* (Apostleship of Prayer, 1926). After a life of labor and merit Father Campbell retired to the Jesuit Rest House at Monroe, N. Y., where he died on Dec. 14, 1925.

[The main sources for the biography of Father Campbell are the private archives, catalogues and publications of the Md.–N.Y. Province of the Society of Jesus. A brief notice will be found in *Who's Who in America,* 1912–13. Obituaries appeared in the *N.Y. Times,* Dec. 15, 1925; *America,* Dec. 26, 1925; *Cath. Hist. Rev.,* Apr. 1926.]   J. C.

CAMPBELL, Lord WILLIAM (d. Sept. 5, 1778), colonial governor of South Carolina, was the fourth son of the fourth Duke of Argyll and the Honorable Mary Bellenden, daughter of Lord Bellenden and maid of honor to Caroline, Princess of Wales. His father had a long honorable career in public service, as an officer of the army in the Continental wars of George II and in the Rebellion of 1745, as a member of Parliament, as one of the sixteen representatives of the Scotch peerage, and as a member of the Privy Council. William Campbell entered the navy and rose rapidly to the rank of captain in 1762. Two years later he was elected to the House of Commons to represent the Shire of Argyll but resigned in 1766 when appointed governor of Nova Scotia. His governorship was marked by no notable events and was broken by three visits, one to London and two to Boston, making him absent from his station almost two years. He was evidently dissatisfied in Halifax, for he petitioned twice to be transferred, once in 1771 and again in 1773. His plea was granted in 1773 when he became governor of South Carolina, where already he had private interests, for in 1763 he had visited the colony while commanding the British ship *Nightingale,* and had (Apr. 7, 1763) married Sarah, daughter of Ralph Izard, a wealthy and influential South Carolinian. Gov. Campbell arrived at Charleston, June 17, 1775, to an ominously quiet reception, for on the preceding day the Council of Safety, appointed by the Provincial Congress, had held its first meeting. The Governor was placed in an anomalous position from the outset. His wife's relatives were all patriots. The residence he intended to occupy was unready, and he accepted perforce the hospitality of Miles Brewton, a cousin by marriage and a member of the Council of Safety. With his powers usurped by this body and in the midst of disturbed and threatening conditions, the Governor summoned an Assembly, which, uncoöperative and hostile, accomplished little. In a further effort to hold the colony loyal, he turned to the frontier, where Tory support was strongest. He carried on secret negotiations for aid not only with the frontiersmen but also with the Indians. These transactions were discovered, and only the intervention of the moderates prevented the radicals from seizing him. His term of office was destined to be short, for when word was received that the British were on their way to Charleston the patriots occupied Fort Johnson, and the Governor, dissolving his Assembly, fled to the British ship *Tamar*. The Council of Safety invited him to return, but he declined, and when the royal fleet attacked Charleston, he was in the affray as a volunteer in His Majesty's service, commanding a lower gun-deck. In the British defeat he was wounded and returned to England, dying at Southampton.

[Sir Robt. Douglas, *The Peerage of Scotland* (rev. ed., 1813); Jos. Foster, *Members of Parliament, Scotland* (2nd ed., 1882); Beamish Murdock, *Hist. of Nova Scotia* (3 vols., 1867); Edward McCrady, *Hist. of S. C. in the Revolution* (1901); *S. C. Hist. and Geneal. Mag.*, vols. I, II, VII.]   H.B-C.

CAMPBELL, WILLIAM (1745–Aug. 22, 1781), Revolutionary soldier, was born in Augusta County, Va. His branch of the famous Campbell family came from Argyll, Scotland, by way of northern Ireland and Pennsylvania. His father was Charles Campbell, his mother's surname was Buchanan. He settled in the valley of the Holston River at Aspenvale (near Abingdon), Va., and married Elizabeth, sister of Patrick Henry. He was a "typical pioneer"; very tall, of great strength and endurance, fair of complexion, grim toward his enemies, and a hater of Tories. He soon rose to prominence; as captain of militia he was active in intermittent border warfare against the Cherokees, and he held office as justice of Fincastle County. Like so many other frontiersmen, he participated in Dunmore's War against the Indians in 1774. In January 1775 he with others signed an address from the people of Fincastle County to the Continental Congress, protesting their loyalty to the Crown but declaring their willingness to fight for their "constitutional rights" (*American Archives*, 4 ser., I, 1165). Campbell led a company to join Patrick Henry's regiment at the capital, Williamsburg, and aided in the expulsion of the royal governor, Lord Dunmore. Resigning in Oc-

tober 1776, he resumed his activities on the frontier; he had a share in the irregular warfare, and was boundary commissioner between Virginia and the Cherokees; in the Virginia militia he held the rank of colonel 1777–80. He was also a justice in Washington County, and a delegate to the Virginia legislature. The great event in his life came near the close of the war. By the autumn of 1780 the prospect for independence seemed almost hopeless in the South. The Americans had lost Charleston, the battle of Camden, and their hold upon South Carolina and Georgia. Ferguson, the ablest of the Loyalist commanders, was operating in the Carolinas, encouraging the Tories and terrorizing the Whigs. To defeat him, there collected a small army of backwoodsmen, the "rear-guard of the Revolution." One of their leaders, Shelby, urged Campbell to join them. At first he declined, giving as a reason the necessity of defending Virginia against invasion by Cornwallis. Finally accepting, he marched with 400 men of Washington County to the rendezvous at Sycamore Shoals (on the upper Watauga). When the army reached Cowpens, nearly in touch with Ferguson, it numbered about 1,800 men under various commanders, Shelby, Sevier, Campbell, and others. The officers being of equal rank, Campbell was elected officer of the day to execute the decisions of the council of officers. About 900 men were picked, and the march began on a rainy night toward Ferguson's position. This was on the knob of a ridge called King's Mountain. Ferguson's ground, which he held with about 1,100 men, was supposed by him to be impregnable. During the battle (Oct. 7, 1780), Campbell is said to have been in the thick of the fight, leading his men. His part in the exploit was recognized by Cornwallis with a threat of death—in the case of capture. At the battle of Guilford, Mar. 15, 1781, Campbell brought only a few Virginians to the aid of Gen. Greene, since the Cherokees were on the frontier; with his riflemen he fought under the immediate command of Gen. Henry Lee, and he claimed later that Lee withheld his support. He received the thanks of Congress for his services, and from his state legislature a vote of thanks together with a horse and a sword. He was elected again to the legislature, was appointed brigadier-general of militia, and began the final campaign under Lafayette at Jamestown, but died shortly after at Rocky Mills, Hanover County, Va. Thirty years later Shelby and Sevier questioned Campbell's share in the victory of King's Mountain, alleging that he remained in the rear; but the charge was never proved.

[L. C. Draper, *King's Mt. and Its Heroes* (1881); Wm. H. Foote, *Sketches of Va.* (2nd ser., 1885); H. Lee, *Memoirs of the War in the Southern Dept. of the*

U. S. (1812) ; Wm. Johnson, *Sketches of the Life and Correspondence of Nathanael Greene* (1822) ; Jas. Ferguson, *Two Scottish Soldiers* (Aberdeen, 1888) ; *Southern Lit. Messenger*, Sept. 1845 ; *Am. Rev.*, Dec. 1848 ; *Mag. of Western Hist.*, Jan. 1887 ; *Southern Meth. Rev.*, July, Sept. 1887 ; Isaac Shelby, *Battle of King's Mt., To the Public* (1823) ; F. Moore, *Diary of the Am. Revolution* (1860).]　　　　　　　E. K. A.

CAMPBELL, WILLIAM BOWEN (Feb. 1, 1807–Aug. 19, 1867), congressman, governor of Tennessee, the first child of David and Catherine (Bowen) Campbell, was born on his father's farm in Sumner County, Tenn., within a few miles of Nashville. He studied law under the direction of his cousin, Gov. David Campbell of Abingdon, Va., attended the lectures of Henry St. George Tucker, and began the practise of his profession at Carthage, Tenn. Here in 1835 he married Frances Owen. In his family there was a tradition of courageous military service. Paternal and maternal ancestors had distinguished themselves in colonial wars and in the American Revolution. In 1836 Campbell volunteered for the Seminole War and fought with gallantry as a captain of a company in a regiment commanded by Col. William Trousdale. In the following year he defeated Trousdale in a campaign for the lower house of Congress, despite the fact that the latter had the support of Ex-President Jackson. Campbell now became a member of the newly formed Whig party which for almost twenty years was to be the dominant party in his state. After six years in Congress he voluntarily retired to private life. He was called from retirement by the Mexican War, when he was elected to command the 1st Regiment of Tennessee Volunteers. At Monterey, at Vera Cruz, and at Cerro Gordo, he and his men of the "Bloody First" fought with a courage and success that made him a popular hero. In 1851 he was the gubernatorial candidate of the Whigs, and again William Trousdale was his Democratic opponent. Trousdale's chief issue was condemnation of the compromise measures of 1850. Campbell championed them and denounced resistance to the laws of the United States. The Whig papers carried as their campaign slogan Campbell's cry at Monterey, "Boys, Follow Me!" and Campbell was elected. He was the last Whig governor of Tennessee. At the end of his term he voluntarily retired again to private life, made his home in Lebanon, and became president of the Bank of Middle Tennessee. The final phase of his life began with the fateful presidential campaign of 1860. He gave his support to John Bell, the Union candidate; he strenuously opposed the secession of Tennessee; and when that act had been accomplished and even John Bell had given allegiance to the Confederacy, he remained the most distinguished of those few in Middle Tennessee who still remained loyal to the Union. From the Confederate authorities he refused offers of high military command. For a brief period he accepted a brigadier-generalship in the Union army. As a "conservative unionist" he worked for the return of Tennessee to the Union. In 1865 he was elected to the lower house of Congress, and when finally seated he gave his support to the conservative policies of President Johnson, but his health had long been failing and he soon died. He was a man of courage and unquestioned integrity, who commanded the respect of those who knew him.

[Campbell's papers are in the possession of members of his family in Nashville. Some of these, relating his experiences in the Mexican War, have been edited by St. George L. Sioussat and printed in the *Tenn. Hist. Mag.*, I, 129–67. A campaign biography (anon.), *Sketch of the Life and Public Services of Gen. Wm. B. Campbell, of Tenn.*, 16 pp., was published in 1851. His genealogy, his portrait, and a sketch of his life by his son, Lemuel R. Campbell, may be found in Margaret Campbell Pilcher, *Hist. Sketches of the Campbell, Pilcher and Kindred Families* (1911). A lengthy obituary appeared in the (Nashville) *Union and Dispatch*, Aug. 29, 1867.]　　　　　　　P. M. H.

CAMPBELL, WILLIAM HENRY (Sept. 14, 1808–Dec. 7, 1890), clergyman, college president, was born in Baltimore, the youngest of the ten children of William and Ann (Ditchfield) Campbell. His father had emigrated to America from Ayrshire and was a thriving merchant and an elder of the Associate Reformed Church. His mother, who was of English extraction, died when William was three weeks old, and he was brought up by his sisters. He attended a small school kept by an able teacher but unfortunate man, the Rev. John Gibson, and then went to Dickinson College (1824–28) where he formed scholarly tastes and habits under the guidance of the celebrated Alexander McClelland. His course in the Princeton Theological Seminary was cut short in 1829 by the bankruptcy of his father, who had indorsed the notes of his friends. Through the offices of his brother-in-law, the Rev. Thomas M. Strong, under whom he continued his theological studies, Campbell secured a position as assistant teacher in Erasmus Hall at Flatbush, Long Island, and was licensed to preach by the Second Presbytery of New York in 1831. In the same year he married Katherine Elsie Schoonmaker, of Flatbush, who was to be his companion for almost fifty-five years. He was co-pastor with the Rev. Andrew Yates at Chittenango, N. Y., 1831–33, giving up his charge because chronic bronchitis had temporarily incapacitated him for preaching; was principal of Erasmus Hall 1833–39; pastor at East New York 1839–41, at the same time keeping a school because his parishioners could not pay him a living wage; pastor of the Third Reformed Church in Albany 1841–48; and principal of the Albany Academy 1848–51. With twenty years of varied experience as preacher and teacher behind him, he succeeded his old master, Dr. McClelland, as professor of Oriental literature in the New Brunswick Seminary and of belles-lettres in Rutgers College, 1851–63. A man of consecrated personal life, a conservative but by no means narrow-minded theologian, and a methodical, rigorous, enthusiastic teacher, he made a lasting impression on successive generations of theological students. He required all his students to study Chaldee, instructed some of them also in Syriac, and with one faithful pupil attacked Arabic. To maintain the decorum of his office, he gave up chewing and smoking, which had solaced him for years, but the reek of his friends' tobacco pipes was always grateful to his nostrils. He instigated the movement that brought about the separation of the Seminary from Rutgers College, and in 1863 was elected president of the College. Rutgers was at that time suffering severely from the depression caused by the Civil War and its supporters were beginning to lose heart, but Campbell took hold of the new work with his customary vigor and courage. Under his administration the College grew in endowments, buildings, and students. In 1864 the State of New Jersey established at Rutgers the State College for Agriculture and the Mechanic Arts, which was to exert a constantly growing influence on the College as a whole. Increasing age and failing eyesight compelled Campbell to resign in June 1881, but he retained the presidency for another year, when a successor was found. The trustees of the College then made him professor of moral philosophy, a position without teaching duties that allowed them to show their esteem for him by paying him a salary out of their own pockets. Retirement, however, did not mean inactivity; his last years were given to establishing the Suydam Street Church in New Brunswick, in which his son followed him as pastor in 1889.

[*A Memorial of the Rev. Wm. Henry Campbell, D.D., LL.D., Late President of Rutgers College* (printed for the College, 1894); *Biog. Notices Officers and Grads. Rutgers Coll. Deceased during the Academical Year Ending in June 1891* (1891); E. T. Corwin, *A Manual of the Reformed Church in America* (4th ed., 1902); *Acts and Proc. of the 85th Regular Sess. of the Gen. Synod of the Reformed Ch. in America* (1891).]

G. H. G.

CAMPBELL, WILLIAM W. (June 10, 1806– Sept. 7, 1881), jurist, historian, congressman, was born in Cherry Valley, Otsego County, N. Y., to which place his grandfather, Samuel Campbell, had come with his parents from Londonderry, N. H., in 1742. Col. Samuel Campbell served under Gen. Nicholas Herkimer [*q.v.*] at Oriskany, and his wife, Jane, and seven-year-old son, James S., were captured at the time of the Cherry Valley massacre but later exchanged for the wife and children of Col. John Butler [*q.v.*]. James S. Campbell married Sarah Elderkin, and William W. Campbell was their son. He was graduated from Union College in 1827, and among his classmates were Preston King and Rufus W. Peckham (L. B. Proctor, *The Bench and Bar of New York*, 1870, p. 34). He took up the study of law under Chancellor Kent and began practise in New York City in 1831. His legal career was not spectacular. His service to the profession was to be in the capacity of jurist rather than of attorney. In 1841 he was appointed master in chancery, and afterward commissioner in bankruptcy, and, from 1849 until 1855, he was a justice of the superior court of New York City. His most distinguished work was done while he was justice of the state supreme court for the 6th judicial district, a post which he occupied from 1857 until 1865. During his early occupancy of the supreme court bench, he was very much under the influence of Justice Ransom Balcom, who generally wrote the opinions for the court. In 1863 Campbell became the presiding justice, and his influence among his colleagues became more apparent. He placed himself on record as opposed to the acceptance of the testimony under oath of atheists or disbelievers in a personal god, and thus helped shape the law of evidence in the state along conservative lines (*Stanbro* vs. *Hopkins*, 28 *Barbour*, 265, at p. 272). On the other hand, he took a liberal position in interpreting the married women's property acts (*White* vs. *Wagner*, 32 *Barbour*, 250).

Campbell was one of the most active members of the Native American party, and, as its nominee, he was elected to Congress, and served from 1845 until 1847. During his term of office, he addressed the House frequently on the subject of the Native American principles. Adopting as his slogan, "Americans should rule America," he made vigorous efforts to restrict the voting privileges of naturalized citizens at a time when the great Irish emigration was at its flood-tide. In his well-known speech of Jan. 27, 1846, in which he favored a compromise on the Oregon claim (*Congressional Globe*, 29 Cong., 1 Sess., p. 260; App., pp. 157–59), he attacked the proposal to give political preference to naturalized citizens. "I value too highly my American birthright to barter it for political preferment; I would not sell it for a mess of pottage," he declared. He successfully advocated restricting the right of suffrage in the Territory of Oregon to citizens of the United States, excluding those who had merely declared their intention to become citizens (*Ibid.*, p. 1204). In his public addresses he seemed unable to grasp the distinction between national and state citizenship.

Campbell made a number of historical contributions. In 1831 he published his *Annals of Tryon County; or, the Border Warfare of New-York During the Revolution*, a colorful narrative, the sources of which are chiefly regional anecdotes. Because of his researches in the field of Indian history, he staunchly favored fair treatment for the Indians (*Congressional Globe*, 29 Cong., 1 Sess., p. 409). In *The Life and Writings of De Witt Clinton* (1849), he points out the intimate personal and political association of his father and grandfather with the careers of George and De Witt Clinton. The volume comprises a brief notice of the Clintons and a selected number of Clinton's public addresses, and his Private Canal Journal for 1810. In 1813 Campbell published *An Historical Sketch of Robin Hood and Captain Kidd*, the inspiration for which was a trip a few years previously to the Yorkshire district in England. The author in his defense of the character of Kidd gave a lucid analysis of the documentary material, an analysis vindicated by modern critical scholarship.

Campbell was married twice: first on Aug. 13, 1833, to Maria Starkweather of Cooperstown, N. Y., and after her death in 1853, to Catherine, daughter of Jacob Livingston of Cherry Valley.

[*Political Reg. and Cong. Dir. 1776–1878* (1878), comp. by B. P. Poore; *Albany Jour.*, Sept. 8, 1881; C. L. Starkweather, *A Brief Geneal. Hist. of Robert Starkweather, etc.* (1904); S. T. Livermore, *A Condensed Hist. of Cooperstown* (1862); address by Campbell in *The Centennial Celebration at Cherry Valley . . . July 4th, 1840* (1840).]   R. B. M.

CANAGA, ALFRED BRUCE (Nov. 2, 1850–Dec. 24, 1906), naval engineer, the son of Elias Green Canaga and Jane (McClintock) Canaga, was born in Scio, Ohio. He was educated in the public schools of Scio (1856–68), at Scio College (1868–72), and at the United States Naval Academy (1872–74). In 1881 he was married to Ermina Carr. He was promoted through the various grades in Engineer Corps to chief engineer in 1895 and became lieutenant commander in March 1899, when the amalgamation of Line and Engineer Corps was consummated. An able, progressive, and efficient designer, he was a loyal assistant to his chief, Admiral Melville, in carrying out the latter's administrative policies.

He designed the machinery of the battleships *Alabama, Illinois, Kentucky, Maine* (second), *Missouri, Ohio,* and *Wisconsin;* of the single turret monitors *Cheyenne* (*Wyoming*), *Ozark* (*Arkansas*), *Tallahassee* (*Florida*), *Tonopah* (*Nevada*); of the armored cruisers *Maryland, West Virginia, Pennsylvania, South Dakota, Colorado, Washington.* He was on duty at the Navy Department during the war with Spain and could not be spared for service at the front. Prior to his duty as chief designer he had made a cruise in the *Chicago,* which had the most remarkable machinery of modern times, beam-engines, driving screw propellers, and cylindrical boilers of large diameter, externally fired with return tubes. Before the end of the cruise it was necessary to treat the boilers like race-horses and blanket them after a run to prevent too rapid cooling. The design of this machinery was due to the civilian engineer member of the Naval Advisory Board and was opposed by the naval engineer member, who was not supported by his naval colleagues. Owing to his imperturbable good nature, Canaga, known to all his friends as "Pop Canaga," was universally popular in the navy. He was short and stout, and died suddenly of a stroke while on duty at the Boston Navy Yard in charge of the Engineering Department.

[*Army and Navy Reg.*, Dec. 29, 1906; *Army and Navy Jour.*, Dec. 29, 1906; *Boston Transcript*, Dec. 26, 1906; *Jour. Am. Soc. Naval Engineers*, Feb. 1907.]
W. M. M.

CANBY, EDWARD RICHARD SPRIGG (Aug. 1817–Apr. 11, 1873), Union soldier, was born in Kentucky. His father, Israel T. Canby, was later Democratic candidate for governor of Indiana, to which state the family had removed. Canby was appointed from Indiana to a cadetship at West Point in 1835, graduated there in 1839, and was commissioned second lieutenant in the 2nd Infantry. He served in the Florida War and on routine duties for some years, was promoted first lieutenant in 1846, and in 1847 was appointed an assistant adjutant-general with the rank of captain. In that capacity he accompanied Riley's brigade of Gen. Scott's army in Mexico, was present at the siege of Vera Cruz, the battles of Cerro Gordo, Contreras, and Churubusco, and the taking of the City of Mexico, and was twice brevetted for gallantry. He was employed on duties pertaining to his department, at first in San Francisco and later in Washington, until 1855, when he returned to the line by appointment as major of the 10th Infantry. He then served with his regiment at various stations on the frontier, the outbreak of the Civil War finding him in garrison at Fort Defiance, N. M. He was appointed colonel of the 19th Infantry, May 14, 1861, and assigned to the command of the Department of New Mexico. The district under his charge was an almost uninhabited region, remote from the principal theatre of the war, and the operations conducted there were little noticed at the time and are now almost forgotten. Yet they had, or might have had, a great influence upon the result of the war. When Gen. Sibley led a Confederate expedition from Texas into New Mexico, his government had larger plans than the mere occupation of that territory. California was the goal which Sibley hoped to reach. Its population was scanty, and included a considerable number of secession sympathizers. Once occupied, its reconquest by Union troops would have been a difficult matter, and meanwhile the Confederate government could have drawn from it an ample supply of the gold that it so badly needed. Canby's force was small, and was largely made up of unreliable local volunteers. He fought and lost a battle at Valverde, Jan. 21, 1862, and thereafter avoided combat, using hunger, thirst, and heat as his weapons, as he drew Sibley away from his supplies. The invasion ended in complete disaster, and Sibley's demoralized command had lost half its strength before it reached Texas again. Canby was appointed brigadier-general of volunteers, Mar. 31, 1862, and ordered east. For a year and a half he was on duty as assistant adjutant-general in Washington, except for a period of four months in 1863, following the draft riots, when he was in command of the city of New York, suppressing disorder and executing the draft. He was appointed major-general of volunteers, May 7, 1864, and assigned to the command of the Military Division of West Mississippi, embracing the Gulf States and the Southwest. As all available troops had been withdrawn to strengthen Grant's and Sherman's armies, there were no large operations in his district during 1864. He was severely wounded by guerrillas in November. Soon after his recovery he managed to assemble sufficient force for a serious campaign against Mobile. The forts covering it were successively taken, by siege or assault, and the city was entered on Apr. 12, 1865. On May 4 and May 26, Canby received the surrender of the armies of Taylor and Kirby Smith, the last two Confederate armies remaining in the field. For five years following the war he was moved from place to place in the South, being sent anywhere that the administration encountered serious difficulties. "Wherever he went," says Gen. Cullum, "order good feeling, and tranquillity

followed his footsteps." He had been appointed a brigadier-general in the regular army, July 28, 1866, and was mustered out of the volunteer service, Sept. 1, 1866. In 1870 he was assigned to command on the Pacific coast. Always a friend to the Indian, he undertook a mission to the Modocs in northern California, endeavoring to arrange a peaceable settlement of the difficulties with the government, but was treacherously murdered by the Indian envoys during his conference with them. He was tall and soldierly in appearance, kind and courteous in manner, utterly devoid of selfish ambition. His superiors and subordinates knew him as a great commander; he was too modest and reserved to win the popular recognition that he merited.

[G. W. Cullum, *Biog. Reg.* (1891), II, 18–24; *Battles and Leaders of the Civil War* (1884), vols. II and IV; *Official Records*, IV, IX, XXVII, pt. 1, XXXIV, pts. 1, 3, 4, XXXIX, pts. 1, 2, 3, XLIX, pts. 1, 2; H. C. Wood, "The Assassination of Gen. Canby," in *Jour. of the Military Service Institution*, IX (1888), 395–98.]
T. M. S.

CANDEE, LEVERETT (June 1, 1795–Nov. 27, 1863), pioneer rubber manufacturer, was born at Oxford, Conn., the son of Job and Sarah (Benham) Candee. His father was a veteran of the Revolution, and later a captain of militia and a member of the Connecticut legislature. After a scanty education in the district school, Candee went to New Haven at the age of fifteen where he soon obtained employment with Capt. Gad Peck, then a prominent merchant in foreign trade. His next position was with Root & Atwater, dealers in dry-goods, the beginning of twenty-five years' connection with the dry-goods business. With two fellow clerks, James E. P. Dean and William Cutler, he organized the firm of Candee, Dean & Cutler which took over the business of their employers. Retiring from the firm in 1833, Candee removed to New York, where for two years he was partner in a firm of jobbers and commission merchants in dry-goods. He returned to New Haven in 1835 and entered into a partnership with Timothy Lester and Abraham Murdock in a general merchandise and commission business. Upon the dissolution of this firm Candee was interested for several years in the manufacture of book paper at Westville, Conn. This enterprise, carried on under the firm name of Candee, Page & Lester, and, after retirement of John G. Page in 1840, under the name of Candee & Lester, was unsuccessful. Its failure in 1842 wiped out the fortune accumulated by Candee over a period of twenty-five years.

Undaunted by failure, Candee turned immediately to the manufacture of elastic suspenders.

His interest aroused in rubber, he attempted in the same year (1842) to manufacture rubber shoes. Charles Goodyear, who had just discovered the process of vulcanization, offered him a license to use the process, the license to be confirmed and extended upon a grant of a patent. Backed financially by Henry and Lucius Hotchkiss of New Haven, Candee commenced the manufacture of rubber shoes at Hamden, Conn., being the "first person in the world to manufacture rubber over-shoes under the Goodyear Patent" (Edward E. Atwater, *History of the City of New Haven to the Present*, 1887, p. 591). These first over-shoes were exceedingly crude and the early years of their manufacture were largely taken up with improving the product and building a market. By the late forties the firm was solidly established, and a new impetus to its prosperity was given in 1852 by court decisions which upheld the validity of the Goodyear patents, a famous case in which Daniel Webster appeared for Goodyear. In 1852 the firm was organized as Candee & Company, with a capital of $200,000, and four partners,—the Hotchkiss brothers, Timothy Lester, and Candee himself. Candee from the start had been the actual manager and continued, with the exception of one year, as president of the concern. He retired shortly before his death in 1863. He married Jane Caroline Tomlinson and left one son.

[The best sketch is in *Representative New Eng. Manufacturers* (1879), pp. 152–58, with engraving. See also C. C. Baldwin, *The Candee Genealogy* (1882), pp. 30–31, 66.]   H. U. F.

CANDLER, ALLEN DANIEL (Nov. 4, 1834–Oct. 26, 1910), congressman, governor of Georgia, was born near Pigeon Roost gold mine, Lumpkin County, Ga. His father was Daniel Gill Candler; his mother's maiden name was Nancy Caroline Matthews. He was descended from William Candler, of English and Irish blood, who moved from North Carolina to Georgia and became a colonel in the Revolutionary War. In 1859 he was graduated from Mercer University and for two years taught school at Jonesboro, Ga. Enlisting as a private in 1861, as colonel of the 4th Georgia Reserves he surrendered in 1865 with Gen. Johnston's army. He participated in the battles of Bridgeport, Richmond (Ky.), Baker's Creek (Miss.), Missionary Ridge, Resaca, Kenesaw Mountain, where he was wounded, and Jonesboro, where the bursting of a shell caused the loss of an eye. He was also in the conflicts about Vicksburg and Atlanta. In January 1865 he married Eugenia Williams. After the war he returned to Jonesboro having, as he said, "one wife, one

baby, one dollar, and one eye." After teaching for five years (at Monroe, Jonesboro, and Griffin) he moved in 1870 to Gainesville where he became saw-miller and contractor, erecting some of the main buildings of the town, and constructing its street railway and a portion of the Gainesville, Jefferson & Southern Railroad. Of this road he was president from 1879 to 1892.

Beginning in 1872 Candler served five years as member of the House of Representatives of the state legislature and in 1879 was elected to the state Senate. In 1882, after an exciting contest, he defeated, for congressman of the ninth district, the eloquent Emory Speer who had been elected for two terms as an independent Democrat. Candler served four consecutive terms in Congress and then voluntarily retired. For one term he was chairman of the Committee on Education. In 1894 he became secretary of state for Georgia and served till 1898 when he was elected governor. In this office he continued two terms (four years). As governor he urged economy in appropriations, recommended compulsory local taxation for education, biennial instead of annual sessions of the legislature, child labor legislation, support of a home for Confederate soldiers, a bond issue for the prompter pay of teachers' salaries, exemption of college endowments from taxation, and the publication of the state's historical records. His successor, Gov. Terrell, appointed him to compile the Colonial, Revolutionary, and Confederate records of the state, and he continued at this task until his death. Thirty-six volumes edited by him have been published. While a member of Congress he made a study of his own family history and had printed for private circulation *The Candler Family from 1650 to 1890*, of which a revised edition was later published with the title *Col. William Candler of Georgia, His Ancestry and Progeny* (1902). In 1914 a newly-formed county was named in his honor.

He was short in stature, somewhat rugged in appearance, rather free and vigorous in the expression of his convictions, and effective as a "stump speaker." Early in his career he became known as the "one-eyed plow-boy of Pigeon Roost."

[*Men of Mark in Georgia* (1908), IV, 29–32; *Memoirs of Georgia* (1895), I, 1018–20; personal information derived from associates and relatives.]
E. H. J—n.

CANDLER, ASA GRIGGS (Dec. 30, 1851–Mar. 12, 1929), manufacturer, philanthropist, son of Samuel Charles and Martha (Beall) Candler, was born on a farm near Villa Rica, in Carroll County, Ga. His father was a country merchant and farmer of ability. The family consisted of eleven children, and, of the seven boys, at least four rose to prominence in public life. One of Asa's brothers (Warren A.), became a bishop in the Methodist Episcopal Church, South, another (John S.), served on the Georgia supreme court, and a third (Milton A.), held a seat in the federal congress. Candler's early years were spent on the farm. He had good educational opportunities for the times and was prepared, in several academies, for admission to the junior class in the state university, but never entered. Early in life he developed a desire to become a physician, spent some time studying medicine under private tuition, and while so engaged became a trained pharmacist. His ambition to practise medicine was never realized, but his knowledge of drugs led ultimately to his success in the business world. In 1873 he went to Atlanta and secured a position with a druggist, George J. Howard. He soon exhibited the business acumen for which he later became noted, developed a prosperous drug business, and was ready to seize his first great opportunity. In 1887 he bought the formula for Coca Cola from a business partner, improved the process, and about 1890, sold his wholesale drug business to devote his entire attention to the new venture. Under his direction, the Coca-Cola Company developed rapidly into one of the most prosperous business enterprises in the South. In 1909, the federal government, acting upon a report of the secretary of agriculture and under the provisions of the Food and Drugs Act, filed a libel praying the condemnation and forfeiture of a quantity of Coca Cola. The case was carried through the lower federal courts to the Supreme Court and remanded for trial in the federal court for the eastern district of Tennessee. Conflicting testimony was presented alleging and denying that the amount of caffeine contained in Coca Cola was deleterious to health. The company, however, without admitting the charges stated that it had made modifications in the process of manufacture. Judgment of forfeiture was then entered (1917) against the company and it was ordered to pay the costs of court (Supplement to notices of judgment under the Food and Drugs Act, No. 6117, *Service and Regulatory Announcements* published by the Bureau of Chemistry). Candler sold the business in 1919 for $25,000,000.

With rapidly increasing wealth at his disposal, Candler was among the first to see the great future in Atlanta real estate, a field of activity which he had entered in a small way almost upon his arrival in the city. He undoubtedly possessed in high degree the Midas-touch, but from the very beginning of his career he exhibited philanthropic interests. Almost single-handed he prevented a disastrous real-estate panic in Atlanta in 1907, buying great quantities of real estate to prevent a slump and in many cases turning later profits over to original holders. One of the most conspicuous of his altruistic services was in the early years of the World War. Cotton, the staple crop of the South, had declined far below the cost of production, growers were faced with ruin, and the "buy a bale" movement had proved ineffective. Candler suddenly came forward with an offer, widely circulated throughout the cotton region, to lend six cents a pound on all cotton stored in warehouses to an amount up to $30,000,000; and when this sum had been rapidly exhausted, he borrowed additional funds and continued to lend. To aid the plan he constructed a warehouse covering forty acres. In a relatively short time he had in large measure allayed the panic, and as the war went on and the demand for cotton increased the producers were enabled to market their stores at a fair price. Instances of similar character were frequent in his career. In a crisis in the affairs of the city government, he was drafted into service as mayor of Atlanta, 1917–18, aided in the reorganization of municipal administration, untangled financial difficulties, and frequently advanced from his private resources funds to accomplish needed public improvements, for which the city was not then able to pay. Throughout his life he was deeply attached to the Methodist church and a large part of his interest and of his wealth was devoted to that institution. He was instrumental in the construction of a down-town institutional church plant and of a hospital under church control. Long interested in Emory College, a small denominational institution, located near Atlanta, he made possible, by an initial gift of $1,000,000, its removal to Atlanta and its expansion into Emory University. All told, his gifts to that university amounted to $7,000,000. Always particularly concerned in medical education, he constructed on the campus of the university, adjoining its medical school, a teaching hospital at a cost of nearly $2,000,000. He was married on Jan. 15, 1878, to Lucy Elizabeth Howard, daughter of the druggist who gave him his first job in Atlanta and later became his business partner. In 1923, after the death of his first wife, he married Mrs. Mary L. Reagin.

[Wm. J. Northen, ed., *Men of Mark in Ga.*, vol. IV (1908); files of the *Atlanta Constitution, Atlanta Jour., Atlanta Georgian and American*; additional information from Bishop W. A. Candler, A. G. Candler's brother.]   T. H. J.

CANFIELD, JAMES HULME (Mar. 18, 1847–Mar. 29, 1909), educator, librarian, born in Delaware, Ohio, was the son of the Rev. Eli Hawley Canfield, of Vermont stock, and of Martha Hulme, a native of New Jersey. His boyhood and youth, except for an interval with relatives in Vermont after his mother's death, were spent in New York and Brooklyn, his father having become rector of Christ Church in the latter city. He attended the Polytechnic Institute in Brooklyn, where he knew Seth Low as a schoolmate, and he had a distinguished career at Williams College where he was graduated in 1868. Though destined by his father for the law, he took employment after graduation with an Iowa company engaged in building a branch of the Chicago, Milwaukee & St. Paul Railroad, and in two years acquired a vigorous and valuable experience of affairs. He then entered a law office in Jackson, Mich., and after admission to the bar in 1872 set up in practise at St. Joseph in that state. In 1873 he married Flavia Camp, who became the mother of Dorothy Canfield Fisher, the novelist.

In addition to his legal practise at St. Joseph, Canfield showed a sturdy interest in civic affairs and especially in educational policies. His work in this connection soon convinced him that he was better fitted for the chair than for the bar, and led to his cordial acceptance of a professorship in the University of Kansas in 1877. His chair was a wide one, extending over the fields of English language and literature, history, political science, and even other subjects; and in the fourteen years of his tenure he greatly enlarged his interests and abilities. He was soon known as a brilliant speaker and a facile writer in the interest of political reform in general and of a free-trade policy in particular. As an apostle of free trade in a protectionist stronghold he encountered several attempts to expel him from his professorship; but his suave though fearless persistence in uttering his views won him such a reputation for tact, courage, and vision, that, after serving as secretary of the National Education Association for three years from 1886, and very ably as its president in the year following, he was chosen in 1891 as chancellor of the University of Nebraska. During four years in this office he aided vigorously in the phenomenal development of the standards and the resources of the institution, and in the spread of education throughout the state. In the face of heavy odds, he had placed the institution on a firm financial and administrative basis and had won the admiration and affection of the great body of his colleagues and students when he was

called, in 1895, to the presidency of Ohio State University. His four years' tenure here closed when, at the invitation of Seth Low, he accepted the position of librarian at Columbia University, where he remained until his death. Aside from the library administration, he served the University on numerous occasions as a public representative, particularly in an educational mission to France and England (1907), and was in extraordinary demand as a speaker for a great variety of occasions. He was a staunch churchman and a member of many learned societies. His presence was one of unusual vitality; thick-set and swarthy, with remarkably fine eyes, he was said to bear a striking resemblance to Stephen A. Douglas; but he had also a large fund of sympathy and humor.

His interests were scarcely those of a minute scholar, but rather of an able and amiable administrator and public servant who brought great power of thought and speech to whatever problem claimed his attention. In his well-nigh innumerable reports and addresses to civic, religious, educational, and political audiences he gave form to a mass of material the vast body of which, by his special request, was withheld from the press. Nevertheless his bibliography contains scores of articles on a wide variety of topics in learned and popular periodicals. Among his longer publications are: *Taxation, a Plain Talk for Plain People* (1883), a *History of Kansas* (1884), *Local Government in Kansas* (1889), and *The College Student and his Problems* (1902).

[Calvin Thomas, "Jas. Hulme Canfield," in the *Columbia University Quart.*, June 1909; Nicholas Murray Butler, "In Memoriam," in the *Proc. of the N. E. A.*, 1909; appreciation by Arthur E. Bostwick, *Lib. Jour.*, Apr. 1909.]   E. H. W.

CANFIELD, RICHARD A. (June 17, 1855–Dec. 11, 1914), familiarly known as "Dick" Canfield to the vast sporting public who played for high stakes in his gambling houses, art connoisseur, manufacturer, and Wall Street operator, was born in New Bedford, Mass., where his ashes now lie interred. He was the son of William and Julia (Aiken) Canfield, was of Scotch Presbyterian stock, and was married, on Aug. 31, 1882, to Genevieve Wren Martin of Pawtucket, R. I. His passion for gambling, acquired during the days of his young manhood when he clerked in summer resort hotels, led to the opening of a gambling house in Providence, R. I., which was successful for five or six years before the authorities came down on him. He served a brief sentence in Cranston jail before entering upon his spectacular career in New York in the middle eighties. After success at a house on Twenty-sixth St., he acquired the famous place at 5 Eas

Forty-fourth St., next door to the then new Delmonico's. This brown stone house, entered by the elect through great bronze doors put in by Canfield, extravagantly furnished, and fitted out with valuable and beautiful ancient potteries and paintings, became the center of New York gambling gentry. In the early nineties Canfield bought the old Saratoga Club which became the Monte Carlo of America. For a while he operated a house in Newport. In 1902 District Attorney William Travers Jerome with a squad of policemen literally smashed their way into the palatial home next to Delmonico's. Canfield contested the case for two years, and it was not until Jerome obtained the passage of special legislation to compel witnesses to testify, that he yielded, prompted by a desire to lessen the difficulties of his patrons, paid the ridiculous fine of $1,000, and closed his house. He devoted his time for the next five years to the Saratoga Club adding a great park that cost in the neighborhood of $25,000 a year to maintain; but public disapproval grew, and in 1907 this place, too, was closed. The business interests of the latter years of Canfield's life were glassware and bottle-manufacturing plants at Brooklyn, N. Y., and Morgantown, W. Va. For years he was active on Wall Street, working alone, and acquiring the reputation of being one of the biggest operators on the Street. He was also an art connoisseur whose collections attracted admiring attention wherever exhibited. A man of culture and refinement, he cultivated well an innate good taste. He had a collection of ancient vases, bas-reliefs, and pottery; of rare Sheraton and Hepplewhite furniture; and his collection of Whistler oils, water-colors, pastels, and drawings, was regarded as one of the largest and best in America. This Whistler collection he sold to the Knoedler Galleries in 1914 for $300,000. His estate at the time of his death was estimated at more than $1,000,000.

[See Alexander Gardiner, "A Tintype of the Flash Age," *Saturday Evening Post*, Nov. 21, Dec. 1, 8, 15, 1928, and Jan. 5, 1929. Canfield's collection of "Rare Sheraton and Hepplewhite" is the subject of an article in *House Beautiful*, June 1916. There are numerous references to him in E. R. and J. Pennell, *The Whistler Journal* (1921), with portrait, painted by Whistler, opposite p. 234. A catalogue of his Whistler collection is to be found in the N. Y. Pub. Lib.] E.Y.

CANNON, CHARLES JAMES (Nov. 4, 1800–Nov. 9, 1860), author, was born in New York City, the son of an Irishman from whom he inherited facile sentiment, deep melancholy, a religious nature, and a love of melodramatic romance. Presumably his education was scant, since he earned his livelihood as a clerk. A portrait, frontispiece to *The Oath of Office* (1854),

reveals fine features and alert and quietly humorous eyes and mouth. Able to give to creative writing only the leisure hours of a work-a-day life, Cannon was conscious of the incompleteness of his training, and, although writing primarily for his own gratification, was sensitive to adverse critical opinion. His verse, much of which first appeared in minor periodicals of the day, was freely revised before publication in collected form. *Facts, Feelings, and Fancies,* his first book, appeared in 1835, a collection of poems and tales, the latter for the most part melodramatic and harrowing. One of them in a different vein, "Evert van Schaick," he left unfinished as too obviously an imitation of Fitz-Greene Halleck's "Fanny." *The Poet's Quest and Other Poems* followed in 1841. In addition to the title poem, the volume contains forty short poems, most of which were occasioned by the death of friends or acquaintances. Cannon is, in general, occupied with the sad retrospect of memory or the weary burden of life. In barely half a dozen poems do we find either a lighter or a more exalted strain. In 1843 a less somber collection, *The Crowning Hour and other Poems,* dealt chiefly, in the shorter poems, with religious themes. "The Crowning Hour" is a poetic version of Columbus's discovery of land; and "Love," the other long poem of the volume, details a happy poet's quest, as a concession to the critics who had complained of the "Byronic moodiness" of the previous volume. In 1855, *Ravellings from the Web of Life,* over the pseudonym of "Grandfather Greenway," was published, comprising six tales told by the members of a family group. A contemporary critic in *Brownson's Quarterly* found these tales more poetic than Cannon's poetry, saying that they displayed "nice observation, deep feeling, happy descriptive powers and now and then something of the witchery of romance." *The Oath of Office,* a tragedy of unrelieved intensity, was produced at the Bowery Theatre on Mar. 18, 1850, and was published in 1854. In characterization and power of feeling, this tragedy, the scene of which is laid in Ireland in the fifteenth century, is the best of Cannon's work. Its production, however, seems to have brought its author disappointment and bitterness, and he abandoned hope of staging his additional plays, contenting himself with their collection in two publications, *Poems, Dramatic and Miscellaneous* (1851) and *Dramas* (1857). The tragedies possess cumulative horror, rather than true dramatic quality, and have insufficient characterization or local color. Cannon was even less successful in his one comedy, "Better Late than Never" (*Dramas*), than in his tragedies. His verse, though touched with simple faith and feeling, has little originality of thought and imagery; yet it possesses an agreeable ease which enables it to rank with most transitory periodical verse. In addition to the volumes named above, Cannon's work included: *Mora Carmodi; or, Woman's Influence, A Tale* (1844); *Scenes and Characters from the Comedy of Life,* by the author of "Harry Layden" (1847); and, of uncertain date, *Father Felix, a Catholic Story,* and *Tighe Lifford,* a drama. By implication from the title of the 1847 publication, there should likewise be *Harry Layden.* Cannon is believed also to have compiled a *Practical English Spelling Book* (1852) and a series of readers.

[Prefaces and forewords to his various publications are practically the only sources of information regarding Cannon's life and work. See, however, the article reviewing *Ravellings from the Web of Life*; *Poems, Dramatic and Miscellaneous*; and *Dramas,* in *Brownson's Quarterly,* Oct. 1857.]   A. L. B.

CANNON, GEORGE QUAYLE (Jan. 11, 1827–Apr. 12, 1901), Apostle in the Church of Latter-day Saints, was born in Liverpool, England, the eldest child of George and Ann Quayle Cannon. His ancestors, sea-faring people, for several centuries were residents of the Isle of Man. He was thirteen years old when he and his parents were converted to Mormonism. In 1842 with other members of his family he migrated to Nauvoo, Ill. In 1847 with other Mormons he went to Salt Lake Valley. He had learned and practised the printer's trade while in Nauvoo, and his abilities in this line led to his assignment to editorial work on various periodicals. In 1855 he was sent on a mission to California, where from 1856 for two years he edited and published the *Western Standard,* a weekly. As this was during the period of the "Vigilantes," exciting experiences were common. He was called back to Utah in 1858, when there was apprehension of an attack by the United States army. There was a general migration south from Salt Lake City, and Cannon was appointed by Brigham Young to take the press and printing materials of the *Deseret News* to Fillmore, where for several months he continued the publication of the paper. In 1866 he began the publication of the *Juvenile Instructor.* During the remainder of his life he devoted much of his time and energy to this "Illustrated Monthly Magazine, Designed Expressly for the Education and Elevation of the Young." In 1867 he also took charge of the *Deseret News,* then issued semi-weekly, and immediately changed it into a daily. His connection with this paper continued for several years, and later, in 1877, he was again in charge of it for a time. Cannon was for three years private secretary

to Brigham Young. He had experience in the territorial legislature, as member of the Council, and in other political positions. In 1862, while in England, he was elected senator of the proposed State of Deseret and was called back temporarily to labor in Washington with his colleague, Senator Hooper, for the admission of the state to the Union. Their efforts proved unavailing. In August of 1872, Cannon was elected delegate to Congress. It was said at the time that Brigham Young favored his election because he was an apostle and a polygamist (Cannon's first wife was Elizabeth Hoagland; he had also four others). An attempt was made by a man (Maxwell) who had been an opposing candidate, to prevent Cannon from being sworn in as a delegate (O. F. Whitney, *History of Utah,* 1904, II, 731). Prominent members of Congress of both parties, however, supported Cannon, and he was duly sworn in. He served as a delegate for ten years, being reëlected four successive times. The operation of the Edmunds law in 1882 caused his retirement by a vote of the House 123 to 79. From 1884 onward there were many prosecutions of prominent Mormons. Some of them avoided prosecution for a time by voluntary exile. Cannon was advised by Taylor, the president of the Church, to leave the city. He was, however, arrested and brought back and placed under $45,000 bonds. At the advice again of President Taylor, he failed to appear for trial, and forfeited his bonds. Later, an act of Congress was passed to reimburse him, he having previously settled in full with his sureties (Andrew Jensen, *Latterday Saint Biographical Encyclopedia,* 1901, I, 50). On Sept. 17, 1888, he appeared in court and surrendered. He was fined and imprisoned about five months. Several years of legal conflict of this nature were ended by a Manifesto issued by the president of the Mormon Church on Sept. 24, 1890, which advised Latter-day Saints to "refrain from contracting any marriage forbidden by the law of the land." At a general conference of the Church in the following month, Cannon was foremost in addressing the congregation in approval of the Manifesto. He was sent to California on a mission for the Church in 1849. Here he worked in the gold mines. In 1850, with several others, he was sent to the Sandwich Islands. His associates had intended to preach to the white inhabitants, but finding the opportunities limited, wished to return. Cannon insisted upon continuing their mission to the natives. He translated Mormon books into the Hawaiian language, and in three and a half years nearly four thousand persons were baptized (M. F. Cowley, *Prophets and Patriarchs,* p. 154). While he was on a church mission in the Eastern states in 1859 he was chosen to fill a vacancy in the Council of Apostles. In 1860 he was sent to England for four years to preside over the European mission, to have charge of emigration, and to edit the *Millennial Star* at Liverpool. He founded a publishing firm; helped to organize the Utah Central Railroad; served as a director of the Union Pacific; and acted as president or director of various corporations. After the death of Brigham Young no man in Utah wielded with all classes so great an influence as Cannon. He was one of the executors of the will of Brigham Young. He was first counselor consecutively to three of the immediate successors of Brigham Young in the presidency of the Mormon Church. In the autumn of 1900 he went to Hawaii as the honored guest at the Jubilee Anniversary of the opening of his mission fifty years before. The queen and her people united in demonstrations of honor and affection (Whitney, IV, 663).

[Sources in addition to the works mentioned above: E. W. Tullidge, *Hist. of Salt Lake City* (1886) and *Life of Brigham Young* (1876); personal information from sons and other relatives and acquaintances of Cannon.]   G. E. F.

CANNON, HARRIET STARR (May 7, 1823–Apr. 5, 1896), one of the founders and the first Mother Superior of the Sisterhood of St. Mary, was born in Charleston, S. C., the daughter of William and Sally (Hinman) Cannon, and a descendant of French Huguenot refugees who came to the colony of New Netherlands about 1632. Both of her parents dying of yellow fever when she was little more than a year old, she and a sister were reared by an aunt in Bridgeport, Conn. Left practically alone in the world by the death of her sister in 1855, she determined to devote herself to a life of religious service, and on Feb. 6, 1856, was received as a candidate for the Sisterhood of the Holy Communion, the first Episcopal Sisterhood in this country, formed under the auspices of Dr. William A. Muhlenberg. On Feb. 2, 1857, she was received into full membership and for the next seven years worked in the parish of the Church of the Holy Communion and in St. Luke's Hospital. Finding that this Sisterhood did not meet her ideal of the religious life, she with several others withdrew. In 1863 they accepted an invitation to take charge of the House of Mercy, a reformatory for fallen women. The following year they added to their duties the charge of the Sheltering Arms, an institution for friendless children, and in 1867 that of St. Barnabas' House for homeless women and children. In the meantime, Feb. 2, 1865, five women, including Sister Harriet, were received by Bishop Horatio Potter in St. Michael's Church

as the first members of a society "for the performance of all spiritual and corporal works of mercy that Christians can perform, and for the quest of a higher life in perfect consecration of body, soul, and spirit to our Lord," the Sisterhood of St. Mary, incorporated in May 1865. Sister Harriet was elected Mother Superior, which office she held until her death. At first the order was persecuted as "Romanist" and the sisters forced out of St. Barnabas' House and the Sheltering Arms, but under Mother Harriet's long and wise direction it grew in favor and its work expanded. It started St. Mary's School, founded St. Mary's Hospital for Children, and assisted in the work of other institutions. Southern branches were established at Memphis and Sewanee, Tenn., and Western branches at Kenosha, Wis., and Chicago, Ill. Extensive property, later known as St. Gabriel's, was purchased at Peekskill-on-the-Hudson in 1872, which became the home of the Mother Superior and the seat of training and educational and philanthropic activity. Here Mother Harriet died on Easter Sunday, 1896.

[Morgan Dix, *Harriet Starr Cannon* (1896); Geo. F. Seymour, "Mother Harriet of the Sisterhood of St. Mary," *Church Eclectic*, June 1896; Henry C. Potter, *Sisterhoods and Deaconesses* (1873).]   H. E. S.

CANNON, JAMES GRAHAM (July 26, 1858–July 5, 1916), banker, was the son of Ann Eliza (White) Cannon and George B. Cannon, a local business man of the small town of Delhi, N. Y. In 1872 his parents moved to New York City, where he graduated from Packard's Business College in 1875. He then obtained a position as a messenger in the Fifth Avenue Bank, soon transferred to the Fourth National Bank, and steadily advanced through the different grades until he became vice-president in 1890, a post which he retained for twenty years. He became president on Aug. 9, 1910, remaining in that position until the Fourth National was amalgamated in 1914 with the Mechanics & Metals National Bank.

Cannon's earliest service to the financial community, outside of the performance of his duty as a faithful and exceptionally efficient administrative officer of his own institution, was rendered in connection with the study of commercial credit. During the decade or two after he became vice-president of the Fourth National Bank credit study and analysis in American banking institutions was at a low ebb. The profession of accountancy then hardly existed in the United States, and it was not until the early nineties that credit departments began to be established even by metropolitan banks. During these formative years of the American credit system, Cannon rendered valuable service through speeches, addresses, and articles designed to enforce the necessity of sound credit analysis as a basis for careful banking.

It was not, however, in connection with credit study and analysis that he became most widely known. In the course of his work as an operating officer he had become impressed with the importance of the clearing-house system. In due time his studies of clearings were elaborated into a volume entitled *Clearing-houses, their History, Methods and Administration* (1908) which passed through various editions and became, for its time, the standard work of reference on clearing-house practise. Cannon was one of the earliest proponents of a plan to make use of the clearing-house associations of the country as institutions for the issuance of an elastic currency on a semi-emergency basis when required by the needs of trade. He advocated this view before the so-called (Pujo) Money Trust Committee of the House of Representatives in 1912–13, and both his testimony and his earlier writings furnished material for use in connection with the framing of the Federal Reserve Act.

In addition to becoming president and one of the chief factors in the National Association of Credit Men and chairman of the committee on finance and currency of the New York State Chamber of Commerce, Cannon also played an important part as a director or trustee in various commercial and financial institutions. He rendered extensive service to educational and charitable institutions and was also prominent in church work (Congregational), besides having an active share in the work of the Young Men's Christian Association. Married during his comparatively early youth to Charlotte B. Bradley, he was survived by her and by a son and two daughters. Of a somewhat stern, rather uncompromising appearance, Cannon well represented outwardly the traditional ideal of the New York banker, but associates found him an unusually kindly and well disposed chief. His career, closely bound up with a single institution, was terminated at the time when the bank was consolidated with the Mechanics & Metals, a combination brought about against Cannon's wishes and presenting a situation in which he refused to participate. His death at the comparatively early age of fifty-eight was by some regarded as having been hastened through disappointment. His writings represent the same qualities of accuracy, system, and attention to detail without great brilliancy or ingenuity, which were characteristic of their author. Both in his early work as a "credit

man," his later career as a leader in the scientific credit movement, and in his activity as an exponent of correct clearing-house practise, these were, however, precisely the traits that were of immediate practical value.

[The major facts in Cannon's life must be gathered from current newspapers and magazines or from the numerous associates with whom he worked in the various institutions and boards of directors of which he was an officer or member. See *N. Y. Times,* July 6, 1916; *Financier,* July 8, 1916; *Commercial and Financial Chronicle,* July 8, 1916; *Financial Age,* July 8, 1916; *Chamber of Commerce of the State of N. Y., Bull.,* Sept. 1916; *Who's Who in America,* 1916–17.]

H. P. W.

CANNON, JOSEPH GURNEY (May 7, 1836–Nov. 12, 1926), congressman, was born at New Garden, Guilford County, N. C. His father, Dr. Horace Franklin Cannon, who was drowned in 1851, was one of the founders of Guilford College, North Carolina; his mother, Gulielma Hollingsworth, traced her descent from George Fox. His grandfather, Samuel Cannon, of Huguenot descent, was a native of Ireland, migrating thence to New England and from there to North Carolina. While Joseph was still a child, the family removed to a new Quaker settlement at what is now Annapolis, Ind., where the boy became a clerk in a country store. He studied law under John P. Usher [*q.v.*], spent six months at the Cincinnati Law School, and in 1858 began practise at Shelbyville, Ill., removing soon after to Tuscola and later to Danville, where he made his home for the rest of his life. In January 1862 he was married to Mary P. Reed of Canfield, Ohio. From 1861 to 1868 he was state's attorney for the 27th judicial district. While holding this office he quietly disposed of a charge of theft that had been lodged, as he believed for political purposes, against Lincoln's stepmother. Defeated as a Republican candidate for Congress in 1870, he was elected to the Forty-third Congress (1873–75), and held his seat until the end of the Fifty-first Congress (1889–91). His uncouth manners and racy speech earned for him at once the popular appellation of "the Hayseed Member from Illinois," a title subsequently replaced by that of "Uncle Joe." At the beginning of his congressional term he was assigned by Speaker James G. Blaine [*q.v.*] to the Committee on Post Offices and Post Roads, and was there made chairman of a subcommittee on the revision of the postal laws. His unprogressive attitude was shown in 1875, when he opposed the resumption of specie payment, and in 1882, when he spoke and voted against an appropriation putting into effect the Civil Service Act. In 1885 he was a member of the Holman Committee which investigated conditions on the Indian reservations. From the Forty-eighth to the Fiftieth Congress, inclusive (1883–89), during the speakership of John G. Carlisle [q.v.], he and Thomas B. Reed [q.v.] were the minority members of the Committee on Rules. At the opening of the Fifty-first Congress (1889–91) he was an unsuccessful candidate for speaker, but Reed, who was elected, made him his "lieutenant in parliamentary procedure" (Busbey, *post*, p. 167), and he took an important part in the discussions which led, on Jan. 29, 1890, to Reed's action in counting a quorum. A coarse speech in the House in August 1890, which won him temporarily the name of "foul-mouthed Joe," contributed to his defeat in the Democratic wave which swept over the country in that year, but he was elected to the Fifty-third Congress (1893–95) and sat in the House until the close of the Sixty-second Congress (Mar. 3, 1913). From the Fifty-fifth to the Fifty-seventh Congress, inclusive (1897–1903), he was chairman of the Committee on Appropriations, as he had been in the Fifty-first Congress. In March 1898, at President McKinley's request, he put through a bill, without consulting his committee, appropriating $50,000,000 for national defense (*Ibid.*, pp. 186–92). An offer of appointment as a member of the peace commission after the war with Spain, however, was declined. At the opening of the Fifty-eighth Congress (1903–05) he was elected speaker, and began the arbitrary and partisan control of procedure which became known as "Cannonism." Signs of revolt appeared by 1907, when members who resented his domination were debarred from desirable committee places. At the opening of the first session of the Sixty-first Congress (March–August 1909), under the leadership of Champ Clark [q.v.], an unsuccessful attempt was made to break his power, but it was not until March 1910, at the second session, that a combination of Democrats and insurgent Republicans carried a resolution enlarging the Committee on Rules, providing for the election of the committee by the House, and excluding the speaker from membership. A motion to declare the speakership vacant, however, failed, and Cannon retained the office until the end of the Congress (Mar. 3, 1911). His overthrow did not greatly affect his personal popularity in the House. He does not seem ever to have regretted his course, and he later insisted that his policy was substantially the same as that of some of the ablest of his predecessors and the one which other speakers would be obliged to follow. For a speech in opposition to an injunction bill, in 1906, he was attacked by

Samuel Gompers [q.v.], and in 1908 was the target of President Roosevelt's sharp criticism of Congress for its refusal to remove certain limitations on the use of appropriations for the secret service. In 1904, while speaker, he was made permanent chairman of the Republican national convention at Chicago, and in the convention of 1908, at the same place, received 58 votes for president on the first ballot, all but eleven of the votes being from Illinois. He was defeated for reëlection to the Sixty-third Congress (1913–15), but regained his seat in the Sixty-fourth Congress (1915–17) when the Democrats and Progressives met with reverses, and continued a member of the House until the close of the Sixty-seventh Congress (Mar. 3, 1923), when he retired. His attitude toward President Wilson was one of distrust, and the League of Nations evoked his ridicule and scorn. The Commemoration by the House of his eightieth birthday (May 6, 1916) seems a remarkable testimonial of personal regard when one recalls his extreme reactionism, the heated attacks upon his conduct as speaker, and his failure to connect his name with any important piece of constructive legislation during his extraordinarily long period of membership in the House.

[The principal authority for Cannon's life, aside from the *Jour. of the House of Representatives* and the *Cong. Record*, is L. W. Busbey, *Uncle Joe Cannon* (1927), a book of rambling, but on the whole good-humored, reminiscence. The author, whose work was prepared for publication after his death by his wife, Katherine G. Busbey, was for twenty years Cannon's secretary. Champ Clark, *My Quarter Century of Am. Politics* (1920), gives a judicious account of the speakership controversy. A pungent view of Cannon as a politician is presented by Wm. Hard, "Uncle Joe Cannon," in *Collier's*, May 23, 30, 1908. J. Hampton Moore, *With Speaker Cannon through the Tropics* (1907), is a popular record of a voyage to the West Indies, Venezuela, and Panama, and of Cannon's observations on American policy. See also obituary in the *N. Y. Times*, Nov. 13, 1926.]   W. M.

CANNON, NEWTON (May 22, 1781–Sept. 16, 1841), congressman, governor of Tennessee, was the son of Letitia (Thompson) Cannon and Minos Cannon, a Revolutionary soldier. Born in Guilford County, N. C., he came with his parents about 1790 to the frontier settlement of Cumberland. His education was limited. He learned the saddler's trade; he was a clerk, a merchant, a surveyor; and in time he became a wealthy planter in Williamson County. He was twice married: on Aug. 26, 1813 to Leah Pryor Perkins who died three years later, and on Aug. 27, 1818 to Rachel Starnes Wellborn. He was the father of eleven children. In 1811 and 1812 he was a member of the Tennessee Senate. In 1813 he served briefly in the Creek war as colonel of a regiment of mounted volunteers. Earlier in that year he had been overwhelmingly defeated by Felix Grundy for a seat in the United States Congress. In the following year, however, when Grundy resigned his seat, Cannon was chosen to fill it and this position he retained, except for one term, until 1823. Four years later he was a candidate for governor of Tennessee and announced as the major planks of his platform the development of a general system of public education, the improving of roads, the building of canals, and the promotion of river navigation. The politicians were opposed to him; he did not have the personal appeal of his chief opponent, Sam Houston; and he was defeated. In the state's constitutional convention of 1834, he served as chairman of the committee of the whole and took an active and influential part in its proceedings. In 1835 his opportunity came. A split in the hitherto solid ranks of the Democratic party in Tennessee was threatening; although Cannon had been a friend of the United States Bank and the politicians of the Jackson-Van Buren faction showed him no favors, the supporters of Hugh Lawson White for the presidency (the future Whigs) brought him out as their candidate for governor in opposition to William Carroll who announced his support of Van Buren. In an exciting campaign, in which the question of the presidency received more attention than questions of state policy, Cannon was elected and became the first Whig governor of Tennessee. Two years later he defeated Robert Armstrong for the office, but in 1839 the Democrats, determined to redeem the state for their party, induced James K. Polk to become their candidate. The two men undertook a joint canvass of the state, but Cannon was no match for Polk, whose ability as a stump speaker and powers of ridicule compelled the slower, less magnetic Cannon to refuse to continue to speak from the same platform. Though John Bell came to his support, Cannon was defeated and his public career was ended.

[Family Bible and manuscript sketch by his daughter, Mrs. Rebecca L. C. Bostick, now owned by Mrs. Harry W. Evans of Nashville; Eugene I. McCormac, *Jas. K. Polk* (1922); Jas. Phelan, *Hist. of Tennessee* (1888); letters in the Polk Papers, Lib. of Cong.; local newspapers and state documents; obituaries in *Nashville Whig*, Sept. 17, 1841 and *Niles' Reg.*, Oct. 9, 1841.]

P. M. H.

CANNON, WILLIAM (Mar. 15, 1809–Mar. 1, 1865), governor of Delaware, the son of Josiah and Nancy (Bowlin) Cannon, was born near Bridgeville, Sussex County, Del. He received only an elementary education before he entered the mercantile business in Bridgeville. He acquired considerable wealth for his day, be-

ing an extensive landowner and fruit grower in Sussex County, where he married Margaret N. B. Laws. A Democrat by inheritance, he early in life became identified with politics, and was elected a member of the House of Representatives for two successive terms in 1844 and 1846, and state treasurer in 1851. Ten years later he was appointed one of the five members of Delaware's delegation to the Peace Convention, but when civil war seemed inevitable he pronounced himself decidedly in favor of the Union. It was his strongly loyal proclivities that led the Union party to nominate him, notwithstanding his previous affiliations with the Democrats, as their candidate for governor in 1862, and, although a Democratic majority was elected to the legislature, Cannon defeated his opponent in November of that year, and was inaugurated in the following January. Nathaniel B. Smithers was appointed secretary of state, and it is quite probable that the very able messages, proclamations, and other state papers issued over the Governor's name were as much the product of his subordinate as of the Governor himself. Cannon's inaugural address attracted considerable attention throughout the North as he announced that vigorous measures would be undertaken by his administration to support the federal government. His record as governor bore out his promises despite the fact that he experienced difficulties at times with the legislature. Immediately after the organization of that body it took cognizance of the charges made by Cannon's predecessor (Burton) in his last message, that the Union party had won the governorship by intimidating the Democrats with Federal troops sent into the state by the Lincoln administration for the purpose of assuring the election of a Lincoln candidate. A joint committee controlled by the Democrats held an investigation, and in a long report singled out William Cannon, Nathaniel B. Smithers, and George P. Fisher as mainly responsible for the presence of the troops at the polls. When later the legislature passed an act to prevent "illegal arrests" in the state by Federal authorities, Cannon sent a special message on Mar. 3, 1863, informing that body that it was with regret that he felt "compelled to decline co-operation with a co-ordinate branch of the Government." This message was followed on Mar. 11 by a proclamation in which the Governor stated among other things that the provisions of the above-mentioned law were "calculated to lessen the estimation in which her [Delaware's] people were held, as faithful to the government of the United States." Cannon held office just two years and two months, death overtaking him as the Civil War was nearing its close.

[J. T. Scharf, *Hist. of Del.* (1888), I, 348 ff.; Henry C. Conrad, *Hist. of the State of Del.* (1908), I, 207 ff., III, 843 ff.; Records of Executive Acts for years 1863 ff., in Governor's Office, Dover; *Jour. of the Senate of the State of Del.*, 1863–65; *Jour. of the House of Representatives of the State of Del.*, 1863–65; *Report of the Committee of the General Assembly of the State of Del. Together with the Jour. of the Committee and the Testimony Taken Before them in Regard to the Interference by the U. S. Troops with the General Election, etc., Nov. 4, 1862* (Dover, 1863).]   G. H. R.

CANONCHET (d. April 1676), Narragansett chief, known also as Nanuntenoo, was the son of Miantanomo [*q.v.*], and "was chief sachem of all the Narragansetts" (Hubbard, *post*, p. 67). During the early months of King Philip's War, the settlers prevailed upon the Narragansetts to remain loyal, and, by a treaty signed July 15, 1675, Canonchet and the other sachems agreed to deliver to the English such of the hostile Indians as should fall into their hands, and to take an active part in the conflict. Since the advantage of the war first rested largely with King Philip, the Narragansetts were reluctant to join the English, although the treaty was renewed at Boston, Oct. 18, 1675, at which time Canonchet was presented with a "silver-lac'd coat." Violation of the covenant, by the sheltering of the women and children of the Wampanoags, caused the New England Confederation to send a powerful expedition against the Narragansett fort near South Kingston, R. I. Here the "Great Swamp Fight" of Dec. 19, 1675 resulted in the destruction of nearly one thousand Narragansetts with their camp and winter foodsupply. The survivors, probably led by Canonchet, on Mar. 26, 1676 lured Capt. Michael Pierce into an ambush at the Patuxet River (near Providence, R. I.) and killed him and about forty of his men. Canonchet realized that the English policy of destroying the Indians' corn was likely to starve his people, and, "foreseeing so many hundreds could not well subsist without planting," decided to raise corn in the abandoned English fields on the Connecticut River. Venturing to Seaconk (near Bristol, R. I.) with a few warriors early in April to obtain seed, he unexpectedly encountered Capt. George Denison of Stonington with over one hundred soldiers and Indian allies. Canonchet tried to escape across a stream, but, slipping on a stone, fell and wet his gun, rendering it useless. Although a man "of goodly stature, and great courage of mind, as well as strength of body," he surrendered without resistance to Robert Stanton, to whom he is reported to have said, "You much child, no understand matters of war; let your brother or your chief come, him I will an-swer." Offered his life on the condition that he make peace, the sachem proudly refused, and, when blamed for his part in the conflict, replied that "others were as forward for the war as himself, and that he desired to hear no more thereof." When informed that he was to be executed, he said that "he liked it well, that he should die before his heart was soft, or had spoken anything unworthy of himself." Capt. Denison then took Canonchet to Stonington, where he was shot and beheaded by the Pequots and Mohicans, who sent the head to the Council at Hartford "as a token of their love and fidelity." Canonchet's death was a severe blow to King Philip, since it deprived him of his ablest ally at the time of his greatest need, and, by leaving the Narragansetts without good leadership, shortened the course of the war.

[The contemporary source for Canonchet's life is Wm. Hubbard, *A Narrative of the Troubles with the Indians in New Eng.* (1677), republished, ed. by S. G. Drake, as *Hist. of the Indian Wars in New Eng.* (1865). S. G. Drake, *Book of the Indians* (1841) contains a biography.]   H. P. S.

CANONGE, LOUIS PLACIDE (June 29, 1822–Jan. 22, 1893), journalist, dramatist, was a representative Louisiana Creole, born in New Orleans of French ancestry. His father was J. F. Canonge of Santo Domingo, who had married a widow, Amelie (Mercier) Amelung of New Orleans. Intense rivalry then existed between the French and American elements of the population of Louisiana, and the parents of Canonge in order to assure to their son a position of leadership in the struggle sent him to study in France where both his parents had been educated. He attended the Collège Louis-le-Grand in Paris while the Romantic movement headed by Hugo was at its height. The exuberance of the period produced a lasting impression on the young Louisianian who returned home in 1838, his heart aglow with liberalism. The field of journalism offered the best means for the expression of his overflowing ideas. He began as a contributor to *L'Abeille*, and throughout his life he wrote for that noted French daily as well as for the numerous French journals and reviews that flourished for short intervals in Louisiana. He also took a keen interest in church publications, being editor-in-chief of *Le Propagateur Catholique*. For *La Presse*, the noted Parisian daily, he contributed a series of essays under the title of *Institutions américaines*. Politics, law, literature, and art occupied his attention in equal measure as a newspaper writer, but he showed a marked preference for theatrical criticism, being editor of *La Lorgnette*. His interest in the theatre was not limited to literary studies: tradition credits him with capacity as an an actor; and he wrote many plays: *Le maudit passeport* (1840), a vaudeville; *Gaston de St-Elme* (1840), a tragedy; *L'Ambassadeur d'Autriche* (1850); *Un grand d'Espagne*; *Le Comte de Monte-Cristo*; *Histoire sous Charles-Quint*; *France et Espagne; ou la Louisiane en 1768 et 1769* (1850); *Le Comte de Carmagnola* (1856); *Qui perd gagne*, a one-act comedy (1849) dedicated to the author of *Les Nuits*. The majority of these plays were acted in New Orleans; the last three were also published in New Orleans; and *Le Comte de Carmagnola* enjoyed a Parisian production. Canonge was also interested in the musical play, for he is reputed to have written three librettos, only one of which, *Louise de Lorraine,* is known specifically; he composed songs intensely patriotic, one of which, "La Louisiane," is preserved in the Howard Memorial Library. Canonge also served as manager of theatrical troupes, selecting one in Paris for the old Orleans Theatre immediately before the Civil War and after that struggle managing the French Opera for two seasons. In these ventures he enjoyed social and artistic, if not financial, success. Canonge took an active part in civic life. He practised law for several years. An ardent devotee of the Lost Cause he translated into French *Nojoque* (1867) written by H. R. Helper, preserving all the bitterness of the attack against the North but omitting all unpleasant allusions to his Church. He served his people as their representative at the state capital, as superintendent of education, and as professor of French at the State University. The French government decorated him twice for his labors in the field of French letters. He married Hélène Halphern who died in 1889.

Canonge's chief claim to fame resides in his journalistic work of the *feuilletoniste* type. He excelled in short articles written on the spur of the moment on all the varied topics that interested a French-speaking community fond of French literature, culture, and art. As a dramatist his work belongs solely to the French Romantic School which he imitated closely; lovers of *Les trois mousquetaires* of Dumas would find delight in his *Comte de Carmagnola,* a drama of intrigue in five acts and ten tableaux. A typical Creole he reflected the life of his times in New Orleans; a tireless energy and ready versatility characterized him as a man and as a writer.

[Three local articles of a biographical nature are extant: one in the *Daily Picayune,* Mar. 2, 1890; another, by C. P. Dimitry, in the *Times-Democrat,* Jan. 22, 1893; a recent one, by G. Wm. Nott, in the *Times-Picayune,* Feb. 6, 1927. John Kendall gives the dates of Canonge's theatrical ventures in his *Hist. of New Orleans* (1922). Alcée Fortier has contributed two short sketches as well as the plots of Canonge's most important plays in *Louisiana Studies* (1894) and in the *Lib. of Southern Lit.,* vol. II (1909). Grace King has preserved the story of the Canonge family in her *Creole Families of New Orleans* (1921). A pen picture of Canonge is to be found in *The Living Writers of the South* (1869) by J. W. Davidson.]   L. C. D.

CANONICUS (*c.* 1565–1647), Narragansett chief, ruled his powerful tribe in conjunction with his nephew Miantanomo [*q.v.*]. He was about fifty-five when the Pilgrims landed at Plymouth and he sent his well-known war challenge to them. In spite of this inauspicious beginning, he became and remained a friend to the whites. In 1633 a John Oldham was murdered by Pequots and two boys kidnapped. Canonicus and Miantanomo were found innocent, although other Narragansett sachems were implicated. The Massachusetts government then sent a punitive expedition against the Pequots, under Endicott, who behaved with great cruelty. The Pequots tried to induce Canonicus to join them in a war against the English, and Massachusetts to secure peace had to employ the good offices of the banished Roger Williams, who had obtained the grant of Rhode Island from Canonicus and always had great influence with him. In 1635 Williams was able to settle the bloody war which had been raging between the Narragansetts and the Wampanoags. The next year, Miantanomo and two sons of Canonicus went to Boston and made a new peace treaty with Massachusetts. In 1638 the tri-partite agreement between Connecticut, the Pequots, and the Narragansetts was signed, stipulating that the tribes would not war on each other without the consent of the whites.

The friendship of Canonicus was to be sorely tried. As a result of a quarrel started by the Mohegan sachem Uncas, Miantanomo received permission from the English to revenge himself, was taken prisoner by his enemy through treachery, and, when he gave himself up to the English for protection, was turned over by them to Uncas to be killed. This dastardly treatment of his nephew was naturally greatly resented by Canonicus, who treated the emissaries sent by Massachusetts, to prevent a war between the tribes, with scant courtesy. Shortly before, Canonicus and others had ceded their lands, at the instigation of some of the "Gortonites," to "the protection, care and government" of the king, and Canonicus told the Massachusetts government that the Indians were their fellow subjects and that if there were any dispute between them, it should be settled by King Charles. In spite of provocative treatment, Canonicus could well say, as he did to Williams, that he had never suffered any wrong to be done to the English and never would. Throughout his twenty-five years of relations with the whites, his record is much better than theirs, excepting that of Williams. His eldest son, Mriksah or Meika, succeeded him as sachem.

[There is a short account of Canonicus in F. W. Hodge, *Handbook of Am. Indians* (1910), and a longer one in S. G. Drake, *Book of the Indians* (1845), pp. 53–57. Otherwise his life must be patched together from scattered references in the contemporary colonial records, and the contemporary historical accounts of the colonies.]   J. T. A.

CAPEN, ELMER HEWITT (Apr. 5, 1838–Mar. 22, 1905), college president, was born in Stoughton, Norfolk County, Mass. He was educated at Pierce Academy, at the Green Mountain Institute in Woodstock, Vt., and at Tufts College, a Universalist institution, where he took his B.A. degree in 1860. While still an undergraduate he was elected to the Massachusetts legislature as a representative from his native town. He studied law, was admitted to the bar in 1864, and practised for a short time at Stoughton. Desiring, however, to enter the ministry, he studied for that purpose with the Rev. A. St. John Chambré. He preached in 1864 and was ordained the next year. His first church, where he remained until 1869, was the Independent Christian Church in Gloucester, Mass. After a year's pastorate in St. Paul, Minn., which followed the Gloucester period, he went to Providence, R. I., to the First Universalist Church, where he remained until he was asked to accept the presidency of Tufts College in 1875. He had married Letitia H. Mussey of New London, Conn. After her death he married in 1877 Mary L. Edwards, of Brookline, Mass. As president of Tufts he showed administrative ability, a capacity for work, and an ability to meet all types of conditions. He was at the head of the department of political science in which he gave four courses, and he preached regularly in the college chapel. He was also called upon frequently to speak at social, religious, educational, and political meetings. He was one of the men responsible for establishing Dean Academy, and was the first secretary of the trustees. From 1875 on he was also a trustee of the Universalist General Convention. Other important positions which he held were as chairman of the state board of education, chairman of the board of visitors of the Salem Normal School, and president of the New England Commission on Admission Examinations. He showed his interest in extra-academic matters in holding the presidency of the Citizens' Law and Order League during its entire existence and in serving in 1888 as delegate to the Republican national convention. He was a man of progressive

ideas and throughout his presidency was thoroughly in sympathy with student interests and activities. For the Universalist section of the Columbian Congress he contributed an article on the Atonement. He was the author of *Occasional Addresses* (1902), the liturgical portions of *The Gloria Patri Revised* (1903), and of *The College and the Higher Life* (1905).

[*Tufts Coll. Reg. of Officers of Instruction and Govt. and Dir. of Grads.* (1912); A. B. Start and others, *Hist. of Tufts Coll.* (1896).]   M. A. K.

CAPEN, NAHUM (Apr. 1, 1804–Jan. 8, 1886), miscellaneous writer and postmaster of Boston, the son of Andrew Capen (1757–1846) by his wife, Hannah Richards, was born at Canton, Mass. He was descended from Bernard Capen (1562–1638) who came to this country in 1630 from Dorset, England. Nahum received the ordinary Latin school education of the day and at an early age showed evidence of precocity. He read widely in the classical authors, especially Plutarch, and at nineteen he rewrote *Plutarch's Lives* for popular consumption (not published). He was also attracted to the study of the sciences, and when eighteen became enamoured of Benjamin Franklin and set out to read everything that he had written. At this time he began to study medicine under his older brother Robert, but ill health caused him to abandon this calling. In 1825 he entered the publishing house of March, Capen & Long as partner and there found ample opportunity for indulgence of his literary tastes. Soon afterward he became an aggressive protagonist of the copyright laws, making appeals to Congress and writing letters on the subject to Daniel Webster and to Henry Clay. He wrote papers on Free Trade as early as 1823, and in 1827 he published anonymously on the same subject several articles which were republished in the South. On Oct. 14, 1830 he was married to Elizabeth Ann, daughter of William and Sarah (Rand) More. During the visit of Spurzheim to the United States in 1832 Capen became the confidant and adviser of the distinguished visitor, later writing his life, and publishing his works (1833). After the death of Spurzheim, Capen organized the Boston Phrenological Society and became its secretary. The history of the early deliberations of this group was later described by Capen in a separate volume, *Reminiscences of Dr. Spurzheim and George Combe* (1881). In 1835–36 Capen spent a year abroad, where he visited hospitals, schools, asylums, and institutions for blind, deaf, dumb, and delinquent. On returning to America he did much to further the cause of popular education and was largely instrumental in securing the establishment of the State Board of Education of Massachusetts. In June 1857 he was appointed by President Buchanan postmaster of Boston, a position which he held until 1861. He is said to have been the first postmaster in the country to introduce street letter-boxes and to work out a free delivery system (*Boston Transcript*, Jan. 9, 1886). His first book, *The Republic of the United States of America, its Duties to Itself . . . Embracing also a Review of the Late War between the United States and Mexico*, published anonymously in 1848, was dedicated to President James Buchanan. It is a semi-historical, semi-political work in praise of Buchanan's political activities. *The History of Democracy in the United States* was published in four parts in 1851–52, but was later withdrawn from sale, as the author contemplated a larger work, *The History of Democracy: or Political Progress, Historically Illustrated, from the Earliest to the Latest Periods*, only one volume of which was ever published (1874). This was a creditable and scholarly work of 677 pages, though marred by numerous dogmatic statements which reflect the limitations of the writer's early education.

[Edmund Burke, "Nahum Capen," *U. S. Democratic Rev.*, May 1858, pp. 397–412, portr.; *Genealogical and Personal Memoirs relating to the Families of the State of Mass.*, ed. by W. R. Cutter (1910), IV, 2157–58; J. F. Fulton, "Early Phrenological Societies and their Journals," *Boston Medic. and Surgic. Jour.*, 1927, CXCVI, 398 ff.; obituary in *Boston Transcript*, Jan. 9, 1886.]   J.F.F.

CAPEN, SAMUEL BILLINGS (Dec. 12, 1842–Jan. 29, 1914), merchant, active in church and civic affairs, the second son of Samuel Childs Capen and his wife, Anne Billings, was born in Boston, the family home since the landing of Bernard and Jane Capen, May 30, 1630. His academic training ended with his graduation from the Boston English High School in 1858. Shortly after this he went into the carpet business of Wentworth & Bright, later Torrey, Bright & Capen. Here, a partner from 1864, he remained in active business until 1909. He was married, on Dec. 8, 1869, to Helen M. Warren.

Early interested in Sunday-school work, first in the Old Colony Mission School, then in the Central Congregational Church of Jamaica Plain, to which place he had moved shortly after his marriage, he, in 1882, became president of the Congregational Sunday-school and Publishing Society, at a time when its future seemed most problematic. To this office he brought the rare combination of unselfish devotion and great business sagacity which distinguished him throughout life. Between 1882 and his resignation in

1899, under the guidance of a board of directors reorganized to include business men as well as churchmen, the capital of the society increased from $35,127 to $125,490, most of this increase coming from the profits of its own operations. In 1899 Capen became the president of the American Board of Commissioners for Foreign Missions, a position which he administered with the same competence and high endeavor which he had brought to the earlier work. To stabilize the finances of the board and to interest the business man in what he considered the all-important duty of the Christian Church, were the tasks he set himself. His eagerness to accomplish the latter purpose brought forth from him the commercial argument for missions, that "trade follows the missionary," an argument the use of which called down upon him sharp criticism.

A new field of activity was opened to him when, at a stormy time in the history of the Boston public schools, he was elected to the Boston School Committee, on which he served from 1888 to 1893, the last year as president of the committee. During his term, more businesslike methods of administration were introduced, a building programme, long delayed, was inaugurated, the curriculum was overhauled, a "parental school" for incorrigibles was established, and manual training was given a secure place in the school system. In 1900 higher education enlisted his services. He became a member of the board of trustees of Wellesley College, of which body he was a judicious and enthusiastic president from 1905 till his death.

Among Capen's other active interests may be mentioned his work for the Municipal League, local and national, for the Indian Association, for temperance reform, and for world peace. In politics he was a conservative. His address to the Boston Ministers' Meeting in 1896 did service as a campaign document (Hawkins, *post*, p. 102; *The National Crisis of 1896*, Boston, Business Men's Sound Money League). His published work, aside from fugitive contributions to religious papers, consists of various addresses, the best known of which is probably *Foreign Missions and World Peace* (Boston, 1912, World Peace Foundation, Pamphlet series, No. 7, pt. 3). In September 1913, he sailed for the Orient, as president of the American Board and representative of the World Peace Foundation. After some active weeks in India and Ceylon, he died of pneumonia in Shanghai.

[The most substantial source is Chauncy J. Hawkins, *Samuel Billings Capen: His Life and Work* (1914). Excellent sketches were published in the *Boston Transcript*, Jan. 30, 1914, the *Missionary Herald*, March 1914, and the *Congregationalist*, Feb. 5, 1914.] E. D.

CAPERS, ELLISON (Oct. 14, 1837–Apr. 22, 1908), Confederate soldier, Episcopal bishop, was born in Charleston, S. C. His mother was Susan (McGill) Capers, adopted daughter of the widow of Gen. Peter Horry. His father was William Capers [q.v.]. With the exception of two years in Oxford, Ga., Ellison spent his childhood and youth in Charleston where he attended the two private schools and the high school. He received additional training in the Conference School, Cokesbury, and in Anderson Academy. In 1854 he entered the South Carolina Military Academy and after his graduation early in 1857 remained for that year as instructor in mathematics. During 1858 he served as principal of the preparatory department at Mt. Zion College, Winnsboro, but returned to his old school in January 1859 as assistant professor of mathematics. The next month he married Charlotte Palmer of Cherry Grove Plantation.

At the outbreak of the Civil War Capers was elected major of a volunteer regiment which took part in the bombardment of Fort Sumter. This organization gave way to a permanent unit, the 24th South Carolina Infantry, of which Capers was lieutenant-colonel. After two years of fighting in the Carolinas, the most sanguinary at the battles on James Island, the regiment was ordered to go with Johnston, in May 1863, to the relief of Vicksburg. From this time until the surrender at Bentonville, Capers was in the midst of hard campaigning and much terrific fighting. He was wounded at Jackson, Miss., in May 1863, at Chickamauga in September of the same year, and at Franklin in November 1864. He was made general, succeeding Gist in command of the brigade.

A few weeks after his return to Anderson in May 1865, Capers was chosen secretary of state for South Carolina under Gov. Orr. Moved partly by the deepening experiences of war-time, he now entered the ministry, electing not the Methodist church of his father but the Episcopal church of more remote ancestors. His first charge, which he took in 1866, was Christ Church, Greenville. The following year he resigned his political position. In 1875 he went to Selma, Ala., but returned the following year to the same Greenville parish. In 1886 he was elected bishop of the Easton, Md., diocese but declined. In 1887 he was called to Trinity Church, Columbia; on July 20, 1893, he was consecrated assistant bishop of South Carolina; and in 1904 he was elected chancellor of the University of the South at Sewanee, Tenn. His death, which followed a stroke of paralysis, occurred at his home in Columbia.

Devoted as a churchman in his activities and interests, Bishop Capers went beyond narrowly interpreted ecclesiastical duty. He was chaplain-general of the Confederate Veterans; he was an energetic member of the Southern Historical Association; he contributed to periodicals many reminiscent sketches and book reviews; and he edited Volume V, the South Carolina volume, of *Confederate Military History* (1899). He championed higher education as a function of both church and state and he protested in many official charges against the growth of lawlessness and crime. Most pleasant of his achievements, perhaps, was his contribution, made by personal contacts and by frequent addresses, to the return of good feeling between the once-divided sections of the Union.

[Records of the Capers family are in *S. C. Hist. and Geneal. Mag.*, Oct. 1901. A brief biographical sketch is in the volume of *Confed. Mil. Hist.* referred to above. Walter B. Capers, *"The Soldier-Bishop"* (1912), is the standard biography.]   F. P. G.

CAPERS, WILLIAM (Jan. 26, 1790–Jan. 29, 1855), Methodist bishop, was born on his father's plantation at Bull-Head Swamp in St. Thomas' Parish, about twenty miles from Charleston, S. C., the son of William and Mary (Singeltary) Capers. One of the molding forces in his life was his father, a strong character, a captain under Gen. Marion in the Revolution, and, for the most part, a convinced Methodist. The family was of Huguenot ancestry. In 1805 Capers entered the sophomore class of South Carolina College, injured his health by protracted study in an effort to make up for his desultory preparation, and on Dr. Maxcy's advice withdrew and entered the college again in 1807. But his mind was agitated by thoughts of religion; and, troubled in spirit, he left the college in 1808, intending to study law. During the summer he underwent a series of religious experiences, and before the end of November, somewhat to his own surprise and misgiving, he found himself a licensed Methodist preacher accompanying the Rev. William Gassaway on his circuit. In December 1810 he was admitted into full connection with the South Carolina Conference and was ordained deacon; two years later he was ordained elder. He married Anna White of Georgetown District, Jan. 13, 1813. She died in childbirth Dec. 30, 1815, and on Oct. 31, 1816, he married Susan McGill of Kershaw District. Besides serving various circuits Capers was at one time or another located at Wilmington, N. C.; Georgetown, Charleston, and Columbia, S. C.; Milledgeville, Oxford, and Savannah, Ga. Several of these charges he filled more than once. He became the most popular preacher of his denomination in the South and was a power in the General Conferences of the Church. He was superintendent of the missions to the Creek Indians along the Chattahoochee in Georgia and Alabama 1821–25, visited England in 1828 as an official representative of the American Methodist Church to that of Great Britain, and began in 1829 the work of which he was proudest,—his missions among the plantation negroes of the South Carolina littoral. For this work, difficult and perhaps even dangerous, he was peculiarly fitted by his sympathy and understanding, and he managed it with success. He was secretary of the Southern Missionary Department of the Church 1840–44. In the slavery controversy that finally split the Methodist Church into two general bodies in 1844, he was a dignified, good-tempered exponent of the Southern point of view. On May 14, 1846, he was consecrated a bishop of the Methodist Church South. In all he made eight episcopal visitations, his territory extending from Virginia to Texas across half a continent. He died of heart disease near Anderson Court House, S. C., while returning from a visit to Florida. With ample opportunity to make money, he died a poor man. No scholar and of no conspicuous ability as an administrator, he was nevertheless one of the leaders of the second generation of Southern Methodism by sheer strength and goodness of character.

[W. M. Wightman, *Life of Wm. Capers, Including an Autobiography* (1858); W. B. Sprague, ed., *Annals of the Am. Pulpit*, vol. VII (1861), inaccurate in some details; J. M. Buckley, *A Hist. of Methodists in the U. S.* (1896); J. D. Wade, *Augustus Baldwin Longstreet* (1924), valuable for social background.]

G. H. G.

CAPRON, HORACE (Aug. 31, 1804–Feb. 22, 1885), agriculturist, was born in Attleboro, Mass. He was fifth in descent from Banfield Capron, who came to Massachusetts from England about 1674. His father, Dr. Seth Capron, served with distinction during the Revolutionary War. His mother, Eunice (Mann) Capron, was a daughter of Dr. Bezaleel Mann of Attleboro. In 1806 his family moved to Whitesboro, Oneida County, and in 1823 to Walden, Orange County, N. Y. He received an academic education intended as preparatory for West Point. Failing to receive an appointment, he drifted into cotton manufacturing in which his father and older brother were extensively engaged. In 1829 he was called to Warren, Baltimore County, Md., as superintendent of the cotton factory of James Buchanan & Company. In 1834 the governor of Maryland commissioned him colonel of the 32nd Regiment of Maryland militia, for his services in ending the labor riots which took place in the neighborhood during the construction of the Baltimore & Ohio railroad. He married, June 5, 1834, Louisa

V. Snowden, daughter of Nicholas Snowden of Laurel. In 1836 he erected and became superintendent of a cotton factory in Laurel which later employed several hundred operatives and which under his management acquired a reputation as a model factory (*American Farmer*, 1845, pp. 36–37). Through his marriage he came into possession of a large tract of the Snowden estate and began farming on an extensive scale, applying scientific principles to his operations. He became widely known as a progressive farmer and took an active part in national, state, and local agricultural societies. In 1849 his wife died. This loss was followed by business reverses. Desiring to leave Laurel, he requested and received from President Fillmore, in the spring of 1852, an appointment as special agent over certain tribes of Indians in Texas, which appointment he held through 1853. In 1854 he married Margaret Baker of New York and moved to Illinois where he continued farming on an extensive scale, especially as a breeder of Devon cattle. In 1863 he was commissioned lieutenant-colonel of the 14th Illinois Cavalry, serving with distinction during the remainder of the war. He was commissioned brevet brigadier-general of volunteers in 1865 and brigadier-general in 1866. After the war he returned to his farm in Illinois. On Nov. 29, 1867, he was appointed United States commissioner of agriculture, to succeed Isaac Newton, deceased. He took charge, on Dec. 4, 1867, as second commissioner and served with ability and credit. He resigned on June 27, 1871, to accept an appointment by the Japanese Government as commissioner and chief adviser to the Kaitakushi Department in the development and settlement of the island of Yesso, now Hokkaido. By his introduction of American methods, implements, live stock, and produce he revolutionized the farming of that country.

In 1875 he returned to the United States and until his death resided in Washington. He was a public-spirited man of outstanding character, high ideals, great personal courage, and of courtly, distinguished bearing. His most important writings were *Reports and Official Letters to the Kaitakushi* (Tokyo, 1875); articles in various publications of the United States Department of Agriculture, including his annual reports as commissioner for 1868–71; and a series of articles entitled "On the Renovation of Worn-Out Soils" in the *American Farmer*, 1847.

[The principal sources of biographical information are Capron's unpublished memoirs in three volumes, in possession of his grandson, Horace M. Capron, Evanston, Ill. (Copies of two of the volumes, made by permission, are also in the U. S. Dept. of Ag. Lib.). See also F. A. Holden, *Genealogy of the Descendants of Banfield Capron* (1859); Merritt Starr, "Gen. Horace Capron" in *Ill. State Hist. Soc. Jour.*, XVIII, 259–349; Louisa Kirwin Capron Thiers, "An American Adviser to the Japanese Government," in *Jour. of Am. Hist.*, VII, 1415–25; C. H. Greathouse, *Hist. Sketch of the U. S. Dept. of Ag.* (1898), pp. 12–13; *Am. Influence upon the Ag. of Hokkaido, Japan* (1915, Tohoku Imperial Univ., Sapporo, Japan).]   C. R. B.

CAPTAIN JACK (1837?–Oct. 3, 1873), a sub-chief of the Modocs, was the leader of the hostiles in the Modoc War of 1872–73. His Indian name was Kintpuash or Kientpoos, "having the water brash"; the "captain" in the name given him by the whites was due to his fondness for brass buttons and other military ornaments. He had some hereditary claims on the chieftainship, held by Sconchin, and for a number of years was regarded by a considerable following as their real chief. An attempt to compel him and his followers to return to the Klamath reservation, from which they had escaped, resulted in a fight, Nov. 29, 1872, in which both sides suffered severe losses. The Indians, in two bands, fled to the lava beds, an almost impregnable natural fortress south of Tule Lake, in California, one of the bands killing eighteen settlers on the way. Other Indians joined them, until Jack had a force of about eighty warriors. On Jan. 17, 1873, a command of about 400 men attempted to storm the Modoc stronghold, but after an all-day battle in which probably no Indian was hit, was compelled to withdraw, with a loss of nine killed and thirty wounded. Gen. E. R. S. Canby [*q.v.*], commander of the military district, in an effort to prevent further hostilities, opened negotiations with Jack, but in a conference on Apr. 11 the commissioners were treacherously attacked, and Canby and the Rev. Eleazer Thomas were killed and A. B. Meacham was desperately wounded. Col. Jefferson C. Davis assumed command, more than a thousand soldiers, volunteers and Indian scouts were assembled, and a vigorous campaign was begun. Gradually the Indians were driven from the lava beds. Dissensions arose, the force broke up into small bands, and on May 22 sixty-five of the hostiles surrendered, several of them joining the troops in pursuit of the Indians still at large. On June 1 Jack and two other warriors, with their women and children, were captured, and the war ended. Six Indians implicated in the murder of the commissioners were tried by court martial (July 5–9), for violation of the rules of war. Three Modocs largely responsible for the trouble testified for the government and received immunity. The six defendants were found guilty and sentenced to be hanged. President Grant commuted to life imprisonment the sentences of two of them (one of whom was subsequently released), but Jack, Sconchin John (a younger brother of Chief Sconchin), Black Jim, and Bos-

ton Charley were hanged at Fort Klamath Oct. 3. Jack was not distinguished in appearance, according to Bancroft; he was below medium stature, weighing about 145 pounds, with small hands and feet, thin arms, a round face, a low, square forehead, and black, sharp, watchful eyes. He was not above profiting, according to the same authority, by the prostitution of the women of his band, and at the trial he showed a disposition to be shifty and untruthful. Others have portrayed him in a better light, and a few have lauded him for his personal, no less than his military, qualities.

[Jas. Mooney, "Kintpuash," *Handbook of Am. Indians* (1907); A. S. Gatschet, "The Klamath Indians," *Contributions to North Am. Ethnology*, vol. II, pt. I (1890); H. H. Bancroft, *Hist. of Ore.*, vol. II (1888); J. P. Dunn, Jr., *Massacres of the Mountains* (1886); *Report Bd. of Indian Commissioners for 1873* (1874); Cyrus Townsend Brady, *Northwestern Fights and Fighters* (1907); Jeff C. Riddle, *The Indian Hist. of the Modoc War* (1914).]   W. J. G.

CARBUTT, JOHN (Dec. 2, 1832–July 26, 1905), pioneer in photographic methods, was born in Sheffield, England, and emigrated to the United States in 1853, when he immediately became interested in photography. After a fruitful experience as official photographer of the Canadian Pacific Railway during the building of the road, he established himself in Chicago, and began experiments with gelatine as applied to the production of the photographic plate. "His contributions to this art industry began as early as 1868, when he successfully used gelatine in place of collodio-albumen in the preparation of dry plates in his photographic practise" (*Journal of the Franklin Institute*, CLX, 461). Dry plates were known and used before Carbutt made them, but the Taupenot plate,—a collodio-albumen process, which was invented in 1856—had a tendency to blister, and needed to receive its final preparation and development within a week or ten days. Carbutt, by the use of gelatine, abolished many of these defects and made a practical dry plate that need not be developed for months after it was made. Becoming interested in the gelatine intaglio printing process, known then as the Woodburytype method, Carbutt went to Philadelphia in 1871, where he established himself, working the process which he had radically modified to meet the exigencies arising from the American climatic conditions. The advent of the less complicated photo-collotype process, having immeasurably greater commercial possibilities than the other method, Carbutt abandoned this enterprise, and, in 1879, turned his attention to the manufacture of gelatine dry plates, thus placing on the market the first American product of the kind. At the same time he succeeded in standardizing the size of the photographic lantern-slide, which still remains 3¼ by 4½ inches, or what was known as the quarter-plate size. His success with dry plates soon brought a train of manufacturers in his wake, but his preeminence in the production of lantern-slide plates never was menaced. Always investigating and experimenting in the photographic field, Carbutt made notable contributions to the development of chromophotographic processes, having introduced the ortho-chromatic plate which for the first time permitted of photography with the correct color values. Through devising accurate color filters, he appreciably speeded the development of all color photography, including that of the processes of color engraving and printing. He was the first president of the Photographic Association of America. He died in Philadelphia.

[See Louis E. Levy and Samuel Sartain, a paper on Carbutt in the *Jour. of the Franklin Institute*, Dec. 1905; John Nicol, "The Late John Carbutt," *American Amateur Photographer*, Sept. 1905; *Wilson's Photographic Mag.*, Oct. 1905; *The Photographic Times*, Sept. 1905; Phila. *Public Ledger*, July 28, 1905.]   J. J.

CÁRDENAS, GARCÍA LÓPÉZ de (fl. 1540), was the discoverer of the Grand Canyon of the Colorado. The Cárdenas family, of high nobility, proceeded from the royal house of Vizcaya. The main branch of the family were lords of the Villa de Cárdenas, dukes of Maqueda, and marquises of Elche. García Lópéz de Cárdenas was an early settler in Mexico and played a prominent part in the Coronado expedition to New Mexico (1540–42). When the army left Compostela he was one of its six captains. As a reward for bravery he succeeded to Samaniego's position as *maestre de campo* of the expedition, and was chosen to accompany Coronado with the advance guard to Cíbola (Zuñi). The natives there resisted, and a battle ensued at Hawikuh in which Cárdenas and Alvarado saved Coronado's life. From Cíbola Coronado sent Pedro de Tovar to visit the Moqui pueblos of northeastern Arizona. While there Tovar heard of the Colorado River, and Cárdenas was dispatched from Cíbola with about a dozen companions "to go to see this river." Guides were obtained at the Moqui towns. Traveling thence west about twenty days, Cárdenas reached the Grand Canyon at a place where the river banks "seemed to be more than three or four leagues above the stream which flowed between them ... They spent three days on this bank looking for a passage down to the river, which looked from above as if the water was six feet across, although the Indians said it was half a league wide. It was impossible to descend, for after these three days Captain Melgosa and one Juan Galeras and another companion, who were

the three lightest and most agile men, made an attempt to go down at the least difficult place, and went down until those who were above were unable to keep sight of them. They returned about four o'clock in the afternoon, not having succeeded in reaching the bottom . . . Those who staid above had estimated that some huge rocks on the sides of the cliffs seemed to be about as tall as a man, but those who went down swore that when they reached these rocks they were bigger than the great tower of Seville" (Winship, p. 489). From Zuñi, Alvarado went ahead to Ácoma, Tiguex (on the Rio Grande), and the Buffalo Plains. Cárdenas followed him to prepare winter quarters at Tiguex for the main army, which was coming behind. In the course of the winter the natives at Tiguex rose in revolt, and Cárdenas played a leading part in subduing them. In the spring of 1541 he accompanied Coronado on his journey eastward in search of Quivira (Kansas). While crossing the Buffalo Plains his horse fell and his arm was broken. Soon after the return to New Mexico, a letter arrived telling Cárdenas of the death of his brother in Spain, and summoning him thither to receive the family inheritance. Bearing dispatches, with a few companions he set out for Mexico, but finding the Sonora Indians in revolt hastened back to rejoin Coronado. Coronado himself now soon returned to Mexico and Cárdenas with him. From there Cárdenas apparently went to Spain.

[The Cárdenas family are given large space in Alberto and Arturo García Carraffa's *Dicciónario Heráldico y Genealógico de Appellidos Españoles y Americanos*, XXI, 108–69 (Madrid, 1925). The sources of information regarding Cárdenas's discovery of the Grand Canyon and his part in the Coronado expedition are the same as those cited under the article on Francisco Vásquez Coronado, *q.v.* See especially G. P. Winship, "The Coronado Expedition, 1540–1542," in the *Fourteenth Annual Report of the Bureau of Ethnology* (1896), pt. I, pp. 319–613.]   H. E. B.

CARDOZO, JACOB NEWTON (June 17, 1786–Aug. 30, 1873), editor, economist, was born in Savannah, Ga., but his father, who had been a Revolutionary soldier, moved to Charleston, S. C. in 1796. After an ordinary education, Jacob was put to mechanical and mercantile pursuits, but interested himself in authorship, and in 1817 became acting editor of the *Southern Patriot*. Six years later he bought the paper and continued as proprietor and editor until 1845. Though he made the *Southern Patriot* a free trade organ, he used it to bolster commercial restriction in one notable instance. In 1818 and 1822 Congress retaliated against prohibitions of American trade with the British West Indies. In the latter year Baltimore and Norfolk remonstrated against the measures of Congress; Charleston merchants, suffering under the stoppage of trade, became excited and meant to lead the Southern ports in a memorial. Cardozo threw the weight of his paper against the movement, believing that the commerce with the West Indies would sooner be opened by America's showing Great Britain her resentment of the Orders in Council. He persuaded an adjourned meeting to his view, and later received assurances from Washington that the failure of the threatened interference had saved the effectiveness of the government's policy. Cardozo was one of the revivers in 1823 of the old Charleston Chamber of Commerce, and in 1827 or 1828 he was asked by this body to draw up a memorial against the "Bill of Abominations." This is said to have been the first petition from the South on behalf of free trade, and was the beginning of the Nullification movement. Cardozo took no part in Nullification, but continued to preach free trade as a principle. In 1826 he published, in Charleston, *Notes on Political Economy.* He had prepared the manuscript for his private use, but published it in an effort to counteract the teachings of John McVickar's *Outlines of Political Economy* (1825). Cardozo's work is an attempted refutation of cardinal points in the system of David Ricardo, whose disciple Mc-Vickar was. It contains inklings of doctrine first clearly expressed by Daniel Raymond and later developed by the American National School, of which Henry C. Carey [*q.v.*] was the leading figure. Cardozo showed that the conditions of American economic life suggested theories opposed to those of English classical writers, finding in this country a naturalness of development rather than a long history of mistaken measures of government. He did not deny the Ricardian rent theory on the absolute grounds perceived by Carey, but quarreled with parts of the doctrine. He was alive to the principle of increasing returns in industry, and believed that at least inventiveness would counteract the tendency toward decreasing returns in agriculture. The Malthusian account of population seemed to Cardozo untenable. In 1845 he sold the *Southern Patriot* and founded the *Evening News.* Two years later he disposed of his interest in the *Evening News* but continued as commercial editor until 1861, when he left Charleston for Savannah. During the Civil War he filled editorial positions in Mobile and Atlanta. In 1863 he published *A Plan of Financial Relief Addressed to the Legislature of Georgia and Confederate States Congress.* From the close of the war until the year before his death, when his eyesight failed, he wrote for the Savannah *Morning*

News. He paid a brief visit to Charleston just before his death, which occurred in Savannah.

[See Charleston *News and Courier*, Sept. 2, 3, 1873; W. L. King, *Newspaper Press of Charleston, S. C.* (1872), p. 80, and B. A. Elzas, *The Jews of S. C.* (1903), pp. 176–79. Cardozo's *Reminiscences of Charleston* (1866) contains much autobiographical matter.]

B. M—l.

CAREY, HENRY CHARLES (Dec. 15, 1793–Oct. 13, 1879), economist, publisher, was born in Philadelphia, the eldest son of Mathew Carey [*q.v.*], an Irish political refugee who, in his voluminous and spirited writings, made himself the chief advocate of protection for American manufactures. The father, after the habit of James Mill with John Stuart Mill, used to take the boy by the hand in walks through the city, impressing economic lessons upon him. The son in his ninth year attended in New York the first literary fair, and did business on his own account in a small stock of books that had been given him, attracting attention by his precociousness. Two years later he took charge for six weeks of his father's branch store in Baltimore, and on Jan. 1, 1817 he became a partner in the business and later head of the firm of Carey, Lea & Carey, which became a leading American publishing house. Lacking formal schooling, he nevertheless read widely in deciding which manuscripts and books should be issued by his firm. In this way he formed an acquaintance, though necessarily a superficial one, with many fields of learning, and this showed itself in the facility with which later he ransacked almost every department of knowledge for illustrations of his special doctrines. He became the American publisher for Thomas Carlyle, Washington Irving, and Sir Walter Scott, and, before the period of international copyright, he insisted upon making adequate payment to foreign authors. His wife, who died early, was a sister of C. R. Leslie, the painter. He was forty-two years old before he turned attention to the economic writing in which he earned his reputation. In 1835 he published his *Essay on the Rate of Wages,* and withdrew from business to devote himself exclusively to political economy. The *Essay,* which was called forth by Senior's *Lecture on Wages,* was marked by contradictory tendencies. Carey gave his assent to *laissez-faire* as a guiding principle, and accepted the efficacy of the wage-fund doctrine, but at the same time he declared that natural laws are working toward a universal harmony of interests; he denied the Ricardian principle of rent to the extent of asserting the belief that capital and invention will compensate for the infertility of poorer soils; he differed with Malthus by claiming that food increases faster than population and that distress is a consequence of human ineptitude rather than of an economic nemesis that constantly threatens mankind; he defined wealth in terms of well-being, and conceived of happiness as best promoted by attention to the nation as the unit of economic activity. In all of these latter particulars he struck the note of buoyancy and optimism which was afterward to distinguish his work from the dour forebodings of the English classical school. The following year he prepared a manuscript, "The Harmony of Nature," which, after printing, he refrained from publishing because it did not completely satisfy him. Nothing cast down, he immediately went to work on his *Principles of Political Economy,* which appeared in three volumes in 1837–38–40. This work shows his doctrinal evolution. While not denying Ricardo's implicit assumption that the best lands are those first occupied, he made the fundamental departure of declaring that land derives its value from the capital expended upon it, and thus that rent does not differ from interest. Also, he believed that progress in the "mutual fertilization" of labor and capital implies a decrease in the present labor value of all previously existing capital, necessarily involving both a relative and an absolute increase in the share of the joint product of labor and capital going to the worker, while assigning to capital a return that grows at a less rate than wages. Thus his peculiar theory of distribution, which held to a progressive diffusion of wealth among the poorest classes of society, was taking form. In another particular he foreshadowed one of his later advocacies. The panic of 1837 was confirming the administration's distrust of a paper and especially a bank-note currency, but in the midst of the banks' disgrace, Carey pointed out the virtue in a medium of exchange so readily adaptable to commercial requirements. The *Principles* enjoyed a vogue in Europe, being translated into Swedish and Italian. Carey and his friends believed that Bastiat drew from this work the inspiration for his *Harmonies Économiques* (1850), though the French economist contended that Carey's writings had not done more than confirm his own opinions. Neither his father's advocacy of protection nor the languishing prosperity which came in the wake of the tariff of 1833 shook Carey's faith in *laissez-faire.* Perhaps the ruin of a paper manufacture in New Jersey in which he had invested heavily between 1837 and 1840 helped to set his judgment against free trade, but this loss could not have had an immediate effect, for he believed that

the tariff of 1842, imposing higher duties, would make matters still worse. William Elder, declaring he quoted Carey, is authority for the statement that his conversion to protectionism came like a flash in 1844. However this may be, in 1845 in his pamphlet on *Commercial Associations in France and England* and in louder tones in his *Past, Present and Future* (1848) he announced himself the foe of the free-trade system. This was in the very moment of the exaltation of free trade in the abolition of the corn laws in England, and in the reduction of duties to a revenue basis in this country in the Walker tariff of 1846. But Carey was not deterred; rather he gathered ardor as he proceeded in his campaign for protection. He became a regular contributor to Greeley's *New York Tribune* in 1849, writing editorials as well as signed articles, and in this way continued his championing of protection until 1857, when Greeley, believing the fight was lost, supported the tariff of that year, which lowered rates on imports still further. Carey from this period forward was an intense nationalist, and opposed the cosmopolitanism of the day, particularly as impressed upon the world by England's free-trade example. In all of his writings, he was, for a number of reasons, intensely anti-British. One cannot escape the conviction that he must have been profoundly influenced by Friedrich List's *National System of Political Economy,* which appeared in 1841. In the *Past, Present and Future* he gave definitive statement to his opposition to the Ricardian theory of rent, maintaining that the order of occupation has been from poorer to better soils, and that the progress of associated labor and capital must always bring increasing rather than diminishing returns to effort. His next work, the *Harmony of Interests: Manufacturing and Commercial* (1851) further celebrated his protectionism. Particularly he developed the principle, sufficiently evident in his father's writings, that propinquity of manufactures and agriculture would render economic effort vastly more effective, lending force to that power of association which was ever his rallying cry. The centralizing tendency of England's mastership in manufactures and finance, which tended to reduce other countries to mere provinces supplying the world's workshop with raw materials, must be overcome, he declared, by the erection of protective barriers about the young industries of every nation. Ultimately, he held, a free interchange of surplus products between fully developed countries would be possible. The American tariff of 1861 commenced a reaction against unrestricted commerce in which Carey's apostleship and authority were internationally recognized. Familiarity with his works, which were translated into seven European languages and Japanese, brought him a flood of grateful correspondence from all over the world. His *Slave Trade, Domestic and Foreign* (1853) prescribed manufactures for the South; his *Letters to the President* (1858) lamented the disastrous effects of the low tariff of the year before. In 1858–59 he published the three volumes of *The Principles of Social Science,* a congeries of his doctrines, stressing the analogy between natural and social science. This marked the end of his pioneering thought. His *Unity of Law* (1872) was the only book to appear afterward, though the steady flow of pamphlets, reiterating his tenets, continued. In this same year he held his only public office, that of delegate to the state constitutional convention. He presented a striking appearance; handsome in his younger days, his face retained to the last a singular alertness and sensitiveness. The vehemence of his writings was belied by the pervasive kindliness of his personal manner. His home in Philadelphia was for years the gathering place of disciples and visitors to the city, these "Carey Vespers," as they were affectionately called, forming almost the only American counterpart to the salons of the French Physiocrats. In his robust optimism he interpreted the rapid expansion of the economic life of this country in his long span of eighty-six years. He was the leader of the only group that can be said to constitute an American school of political economy; among his followers were Stephen Colwell, Condy Raguet, E. Peshine Smith, Henry C. Baird, William Elder, Robert Ellis Thompson, Edward Atkinson, and, in a later period, Simon N. Patten. Among European disciples, Dühring, Schulze-Delitzsch, and Ferrera are the best known. Judgment of to-day, while pronouncing him uncritical in his parade of illustrations from history, and frequently fanciful in the ardor of his pursuit, cheerfully acknowledges him as not only an original thinker of power, but as the leader of the opposition to the pessimism of the classical school and also to the socialist group which took rise from the Ricardian counsel of despair.

[The main facts of Carey's life are given by Wm. Elder, *Memoir of Henry C. Carey* (1880); Henry Carey Baird, "Henry Chas. Carey," in *Am. Bookseller,* XVII, 102–06 and "Carey and Two of his Recent Critics," in *Proc. Am. Philosophical Soc.,* vol. XXIX (1891); Robt. E. Thompson, "Henry Chas. Carey," in *Penn Mo.,* X (1879), 816–34; Chas. H. Levermore, "Henry C. Carey and his Social System," in the *Political Science Quart.,* V, 553–82 which gives a condensed summary and criticism of Carey's economic writings.]   B. M—l.

CAREY, JOSEPH MAULL (Jan. 19, 1845–Feb. 5, 1924), senator, governor of Wyoming, was born at Milton, Del., the son of Robert Hood and Susan (Davis) Carey. He attended Union College and the law school of the University of Pennsylvania, and was admitted to the bar in 1867. He practised law in Pennsylvania for two years and then was appointed by President Grant first United States attorney in the newly-created territory of Wyoming, with which he was thenceforth identified, serving on the bench of the supreme court from 1872 to 1876 and thrice as delegate of the territory in Congress. In 1890 he introduced the bill providing for the admission of Wyoming as a state, and he defended ardently and successfully the clause in the constitution which conferred the suffrage on women. He had, indeed, been a consistent supporter of equal suffrage, which had been granted by the territorial legislature by act of 1869. He was chosen first United States senator from Wyoming in 1890, serving one term. During this single term, however, he secured the passage of an act (Aug. 8, 1894) which authorized the secretary of the interior to patent lands to states containing desert areas, provided they would cause such lands to be reclaimed and irrigated. The terms of this act, commonly known as the Carey Act, were accepted by Wyoming in the following year, and large areas were patented to companies.

Although most of his constituents favored the free coinage of silver, Carey supported President Cleveland in securing the repeal of the silver-purchase act of 1890, sacrificing thereby his chances of reëlection. During President Roosevelt's administration he became a Progressive Republican, and he again paid dearly for his independence, failing to obtain the nomination of the Republicans for governor in 1910. He was then nominated by the Democrats and elected. He became a promoter, with Sir Horace Plunkett, of a development company which by extensive irrigation projects at Wheatland threw open large areas to cultivation. In this undertaking he had in mind not merely financial profit but a great Wyoming with agriculture as its corner-stone. He married in 1877 Louise David of Cheyenne. The elder of their two sons, Robert D. Carey, served also as governor of Wyoming.

[*Wyo. State Tribune and Cheyenne State Leader,* Feb. 7, 8, 1924; *Progressive Men of State of Wyo.* (1903), pp. 27–29; family records; personal information.]   G. R. H.

CAREY, MATHEW (Jan. 28, 1760–Sept. 16, 1839), publisher, economist, was born in Dublin, Ireland, the son of Christopher Carey, who was at one time in the British navy and was subsequently a contractor for the army, through which means he achieved an independence. The boy was dropped by his nurse when a year old, and was lame the rest of his life. Probably as a consequence of his deformity, he was shy and apparently backward as a schoolboy. He had only the rudiments of formal education, but read much and developed a remarkable aptitude for languages; particularly, he used Latin with familiarity in all his writings. From childhood he wanted to be a printer and bookseller; his father not approving his choice of a trade, compelled the boy to find his own master, one McDaniel, with whom he served part of an apprenticeship. A threatened encounter between fellow apprentices gave occasion for Carey's first essay, an argument against duelling, published in the *Hibernian Journal* when the author was seventeen. In 1779, incensed by the wrongs of the Irish Catholics, he published, anonymously, a pamphlet in their defense. The tract was instanced in the Lords and Commons as proof of the treasonable views of the Catholics, and a conservative group of Catholics offered £40 for the author's apprehension. Carey's family sent him to Paris, where a priest introduced him to Benjamin Franklin. He worked for some months at a little printing-office which Franklin had set up at Passy. Lafayette called on him to discover the strength of revolutionary sentiment in Ireland. Returning to Dublin in a year, Carey conducted the *Freeman's Journal*, and in 1783, when he was nearly twenty-four, his father set him up as proprietor of a new paper, the *Volunteer's Journal*, the object of which was to defend Ireland, economically and politically, against the encroachments of England. The journal's career, Carey said, "was enthusiastic and violent." Its columns were used to get up a demonstration against the Duke of Rutland, the lord-lieutenant, at Daly's Theatre, and Carey was a leader in the crowd that rushed out after the lord-lieutenant's party, groaning them through the streets and up to the gates of Dublin Castle, where a few Scotch horse dispersed the taunters. The paper was only a year old when the owner was arrested for an attack on the House of Commons and the Premier and was committed for a short time to Newgate. After his release, a new prosecution threatening, he took ship for America, Sept. 7, 1784, escaping detection by dressing as a woman. Landing at Philadelphia with twelve guineas only, and no friends, he was delighted to receive a summons from Lafayette to call on the General at his lodgings. The next day, Lafayette, with no so-

licitation on the part of the young Irish immigrant, sent him a present of $400, which he refused to receive back despite Carey's protest. The debt was repaid in 1824, however, when Lafayette returned to America in broken fortune. Carey issued the first number of his *Pennsylvania Herald,* Jan. 25, 1785; the paper, which supported the conservative party in state politics, had a good circulation, mainly owing to Carey's detailed reports of sessions of the House of Assembly, which were a novelty in American journalism. He was drawn into a bitter controversy with Col. Oswald, editor of the *Independent Gazetteer*, which resulted, January 1786, in a duel in which Oswald was not injured, but Carey was badly wounded in the thigh and did not recover from the hurt for more than a year. Following the duel, Carey characteristically published his wish for reconciliation with his antagonist, which lost him the friendship of some of his supporters. With five partners, in October 1786, Carey began the publication of the *Columbian Magazine,* but soon released himself to publish the *American Museum,* a journal made up of clippings. Despite great financial worry at this time, he married, in 1791, Bridget Flahavan, the daughter of a respectable, but poor, Philadelphian. (See Joseph Willcox, *Historical Sketches of Some of the Pioneer Catholics of Philadelphia.* No place or date.) They had nine children, of whom three died young. Relinquishing the *Museum,* which never paid, despite its excellence, Carey borrowed money and set up as a publisher and bookseller; he was frequently anxious because of his heavy speculations in this business, but at length prospered conspicuously. He volunteered, with his friend Stephen Girard and others, to serve on the committee of health during the yellow fever epidemic of 1793, and described the horrors of the pestilence in a vivid pamphlet which went through numerous editions. Early in the nineties he formed the Hibernian Society for the relief of Irish immigrants, and in 1796 joined in launching the first Sunday-school society in America. A few years later, in spite of his attempts at avoidance, he became engaged in a violent controversy with William Cobbett, who was then a bookseller in Philadelphia. In 1802 he was elected a director of the Bank of Pennsylvania. In 1810 he was one of the few Republicans in Philadelphia who worked for the renewal of the charter of the Bank of the United States. The second war with England having made a serious rift between the Federalist and Republican parties, Carey published his *Olive Branch* in 1814 to bring them together. In 1819, after much labor, he published his *Vindiciae Hibernicae,* to clear the Irish of the charge of promoting the massacre of 1641. American manufactures, which had sprung up during the war, had been seriously impaired by the flood of English goods which followed the peace and Carey took a leading part in forwarding a protective policy for this country. He was a charter member of the Philadelphia Society for the Promotion of National Industry, most of the addresses of which came from his pen. These are recognized as the classic American argument in favor of the protective system, and for them Carey will be chiefly remembered in economic authorship. He did more than any one else, if we except Hamilton, to found the American nationalist school of economic thought, his son, Henry C. Carey [*q.v.*], being his most distinguished follower. His tracts and books, running to thousands of pages, cover many subjects. He was an unceasing advocate of universal education and tirelessly insisted on the importance of internal improvements. His style was clear, vigorous, and often eloquent. He took a joy in vituperation. He was a pious Catholic, and generous in his giving to charity. His funeral was the most largely attended of any in Philadelphia to that time with the exception of that of Stephen Girard.

[Carey published *Autobiographical Sketches* (Phila., 1829; only one volume issued). The *New Eng. Mag.,* vols. V–VII, contains a very full autobiography. See also E. L. Bradsher, *Mathew Carey, Editor, Author, and Publisher* (1912); *Niles' Weekly Reg.,* Sept. 21, 1839; *Am. Bookseller,* Feb. 1, 1885; E. F. J. Maier, "Mathew Carey, Publicist and Politician," *Records of the Am. Cath. Hist. Soc.,* XXXIX, 71–154; and for samples of his work, Mathew Carey, *Miscellaneous Essays* (1830).]   B. M—l.

CARLETON, HENRY (*c.* 1785–Mar. 28, 1863), jurist, author, was born in Virginia. His name was originally Henry Carleton Cox. He attended the University of Georgia for two years and then entered Yale, where he graduated in 1806. After a residence in Mississippi, he came to New Orleans in 1814. In the campaign connected with the defense of the city against the British, he served as a lieutenant of infantry under Jackson. For a while he seems to have taught school until advised by a friend to seek a field of endeavor more congenial to his talents. Having read law in the office of Edward Livingston, the great jurist, he became a worthy and successful lawyer at a time when the bar of New Orleans was adorned by an array of eminent names. He was appointed United States district attorney in 1832, serving in this capacity until 1837. His position was a difficult one, for it was during this period that the re-

lations between this country and Mexico were of a critical nature, due to the fact that New Orleans was the center of the despatch of volunteers and munitions in aid of the struggling Texans. In view of the sympathy felt by the citizens of New Orleans for those in revolt against the rule of Santa Anna, Carleton found it practically impossible to enforce the law of Apr. 20, 1818 intended to prevent violations of neutrality. On Oct. 21, 1835 he wrote the secretary of state of the difficulties encountered by him in striving to bring within the scope of the law those going to Texas with arms in their hands (*House Executive Document, No. 74,* 25 Cong., 2 Sess.; *Statutes at Large,* III, 447–50). In December 1835 a number of business men and insurance agents requested Carleton to prevent the sailing of the *Brutus,* then fitting out as a man-of-war. Witnesses were accordingly examined by Carleton, though he failed completely to make out a case. In March 1836 he instituted proceedings against a prominent citizen, William Christy, for aiding Gen. José Antonio Mexía, who was fitting out a filibustering expedition against Mexico. But here again no evidence was forthcoming to sustain the charge. On Apr. 1, 1837 Carleton became associate justice of the supreme court of Louisiana in place of Judge George Mathews, serving with distinction in this capacity until Feb. 1, 1839, when he resigned on account of ill health. For a while he traveled in Europe, then settled in Philadelphia, where he became interested in speculations of a metaphysical and philosophical nature. The fruit of these studies appeared in his *Liberty and Necessity* (1857) and *Essay on the Will* (1863). Another volume entitled *Eight Days in England* is also ascribed to him. As a writer, however, his reputation rests on his translation in collaboration with Louis Moreau Lislet of *Las Siete Partidas,* the principal Spanish code long enforced in Louisiana. An act of the state legislature of Mar. 3, 1819 authorized this task at the expense of the state. The two volumes of the edition of 1820 contain all that portion of the work which was considered as having force in Louisiana. The translation was accepted in 1820 by the legislature on the recommendation of a committee, composed of Pierre Derbigny, Mazureau, and Livingston, appointed for the purpose of examining it. The legislature ordered the translation to be circulated "as a substantial contribution toward an understanding of the laws of Spain" (*Louisiana Historical Quarterly,* IV, 35). The translators wrote in the Introduction: "The particular care and attention the translators have bestowed, in order to render their work as perfect as possible, will, they hope, secure to them the praise of having faithfully discharged the honorable task imposed upon them by the legislature." Carleton was married on May 29, 1815, to Aglaé D'Avezac de Castera, a younger sister of Auguste D'Avezac [*q.v.*], and of Louise D'Avezac, the brilliant second wife of Edward Livingston (*Louisiana Historical Quarterly,* V, 352). A daughter, Aglaé Marie Carleton, was the mother of Carleton Hunt (1836–1921), referred to by some as the "Nestor of the Louisiana bar." After the death of his first wife Carleton married Mrs. Maria (Vanderburgh) Wiltbank, who survived him.

[A very inadequate sketch of Carleton was published by Judge Edward S. Whitaker in his *Sketches of Life and Character in La.* (1847). A brief memoir is printed in *La. Reports,* vol. CXXX (1913). See also sketch by Carleton Hunt in F. B. Dexter, *Biog. Sketches Grads. Yale Coll.,* vol. VI (1912).]   J. E. W—n.

CARLETON, HENRY GUY (June 21, 1856–Dec. 10, 1910), playwright, was born at Fort Union, N. Mex., and died in Atlantic City, N. J. His father was James Henry Carleton, a general, and his mother Sophie Garland Wolfe. He studied civil and mining engineering at Santa Clara College, San Francisco, 1865–70, and from 1873 to 1876 was a cavalry officer in the army. In 1876 he came to New Orleans to write for the *Times,* of that city, and he also opened newspaper connections in Chicago and New York. He remained enough of a soldier to become an officer of militia and to take part in the riots of 1877 incident to the final suppression of the reconstruction government in Louisiana. In 1881, he wrote a blank verse tragedy, *Memnon,* its scene laid in ancient Egypt. From the age of fifteen when he wrote a play called *The Age of Gold,* he had been intensely interested in the drama, and in 1882, encouraged by *Memnon,* he went to New York in order to be near the theatres. Play followed play rapidly, the number mounting at last to more than sixteen. Whether because he confined himself largely to themes of gloom, or for other reasons, this work was not often the means of his acquiring money. He moved to Boston, and was living there, ill and in something like poverty, when in 1892, at the suggestion of Nat Goodwin, he wrote *The Gilded Fool.* This play, a tragi-comedy of the conventional type, served Goodwin admirably for a long time. Two years later, appeared *Butterflies,* through which John Drew and Maude Adams first attained wide popularity. In spite of these and other successes and of frequent work for the magazines and newspapers, Carleton's finances were usually at low ebb. He endeavored to relieve this condition by turning to

account some of his early training as an engineer, and from 1899 to 1903 he invented and patented thirty-four electrical and chemical devices. None of these proved very remunerative. He was delightful company. When prosperous, he joined yacht clubs and gave himself to a consideration of his colonial ancestry in both Virginia and Massachusetts, but even when not prosperous he retained his inveterate humor and his disposition to tease every one with whom he had contact. Once when congratulated on his military medals, he explained that he had to thank for them the fact that he had always been a grievous stammerer. As a young man he was in charge of some troops who were surprised by hostile Indians. He was terrified, but the proper order of retreat could not be coaxed to his lips. The consequence was rout for the Indians, and medals for the routers. Such raillery characterized him even in the long period of ill health which preceded his death.

[N. C. Goodwin, *Nat Goodwin's Book* (1914); *New Internat. Year Book,* 1910; *Who's Who in America,* 1910–11.]   J. D. W.

CARLETON, WILL (Oct. 21, 1845–Dec. 18, 1912), poet, originally named William McKendree Carleton (he dropped his middle name and became Will Carleton in 1873), was born on a farm two miles east of Hudson, Mich. His father, John Hancock Carleton, a direct descendant of Edward Carleton whose name appears in the records of Rowley, Mass., in 1638, was a pioneer-farmer, industrious, religious; his mother, Celestia E. (Smith) Carleton, was a sweet-tempered woman who sang ballads while rocking her children to sleep. Will was born and grew up a delicate dreamy boy, more inclined to deliver orations to the cows than to follow the plow. He attended the country schools of the neighborhood, and graduated from Hillsdale College in 1869. Then he became editor of the *Hillsdale Standard* and the *Detroit Weekly Tribune.* In 1871, reporting a divorce case, he was inspired to write "Betsy and I are Out," which was copied throughout the country. In quick succession *Harper's Weekly* featured "Out of the Old House, Nancy," "Over the Hill to the Poor House," "Gone with a Handsomer Man." These attracted wide attention, so that *Farm Ballads,* published by Harpers in 1873, within eighteen months attained a circulation of forty thousand copies. This was followed by *Farm Legends* (1875), *Young Folks' Centennial Rhymes* (1876), *Farm Festivals* (1881). In 1878 Carleton went to Boston to live, and out of the new environment came *City Ballads* (1885), *City Legends* (1889), *City Festivals* (1892). In 1882 he was married to Adora

Niles Goodell and moved to Brooklyn, N. Y., where he resided until his death. In 1894 he founded a magazine called *Every Where*. Partly from this he gleaned in 1895–96 *Rhymes of Our Planet* and *The Old Infant and Similar Stories*. In 1902 he published the *Song of Two Centuries*. He was one of the first poets of the country to give public readings from his own writings, a venture which yielded him a large income. The secret of his poetical success lay in his ability to utter in simple language the homely sentiments of the plain people. His best-known production, "Over the Hill to the Poor House," had a pathetically human note which set in vibration a sympathetic chord in the hearts of a great multitude. Superintendents of poor houses reported to him that their inmates were decreasing in numbers because children were withdrawing their parents from these institutions, shamed into filial duty by this ballad. His imagination was not wide in its range, neither did it glow in magic words or memorable sentences; he was not an artist in poetic form, but his emotions were wholesome, and he voiced without undue sentimentality the humor and pathos in the experiences of the common people. Nature plays little part in his poems; it is the heart that predominates. He sympathized with the life of the humble and interpreted their feelings without exploiting their peculiarities.

[A. Elwood Corning has written an excellent biographical study, entitled *Will Carleton* (1917). In the *Mich. Hist. Colls.*, vol. XXXIX, appears an appreciation by Byron A. Finney, together with a full bibliography, which, however, lists two works not written by Carleton—*Geraldine: a Romance in Verse* (1881), by Alonzo Hopkins, *My Wife and I Quarrelled* (1877), by Mrs. Emerson-French. The error was first pointed out by Mr. Finney himself, who is now engaged on a definitive life of Carleton.]   C. A. D.

CARLILE, JOHN SNYDER (Dec. 16, 1817–Oct. 24, 1878), lawyer, senator, West Virginia Unionist, was born in Winchester, Va. His family was Scotch-Irish, and long settled in the Shenandoah Valley. From his widowed mother, John received the early training in books and morals which the Valley Scotch believed in. At fourteen he became a store clerk. Developing rapidly, he three years later entered business on his own account, but only to find himself soon overwhelmed with debts,—debts which he later felt in honor bound to pay. Thanks to private study, however, he was able to begin life anew in 1840 as a lawyer in the little town of Beverly. Moving soon to the larger Clarksburg, he eventually fought his way to prominence, though not to preëminence, among the lawyers of the Kanawha section. Political life, however, was his great field. A "bold and forceful speaker," of attractive personality, and blessed by the gods of western politics with early poverty, his progress was rapid. He was successively senator (1847–51), member of the constitutional convention of 1850, and congressman (1855–57),—being a member in 1856 of the House Committee of Accounts. Though he obtained in none of these positions more than local distinction and met defeat as the Know-Nothing candidate for Congress in 1857, he at all times represented faithfully the dominating pro-Union sentiments of his constituents. Accordingly they sent him to the secession convention of 1861. Here his extreme views and aggressive conduct made him the target of the *Richmond Enquirer* and put him in imminent danger of mob violence. Returning home hastily and determined to create a new state and to keep that state in the Union, he worked to secure a convention at Wheeling, notably by drafting the Address of May 22, 1861, to the people of western Virginia. When his proposal that this convention as a sovereign body create a new state was defeated as premature, he accepted the chairmanship of the convention's central committee and contributed to its campaign against ratification of the secession ordinance a widely distributed pamphlet that made no mention of a new state. A little later he embodied his ideas as to the legality of secession and the sovereignty of his people in a "Declaration of the People of Virginia," which was adopted by the second Wheeling convention, June 17, 1861. A new state government, though not a new state, having been created on the basis of Carlile's argument, he was sent by it to the United States Senate. Already the House had received him as a member, from July 4 to July 13. Now the Senate welcomed him, put him on the Committee on Public Lands and the Committee on Territories; and the chairman of the latter committee, because of Carlile's "lucid mind," soon entrusted him with entire management of a bill to create the new state of West Virginia. His great ambition now within his grasp, sense and fortune suddenly failed him. For although in the August convention of his state he had favored a West Virginia which was to be limited (for the present) to enthusiastic western counties, he now included in the bill counties of the Shenandoah Valley, which were loyal to the old state, thereby endangering the whole project. Perhaps he hoped thus to defeat the emancipation provisions of the bill, relying on aid from the border state men whom he afterward joined in opposing confiscation and military draft. Instead he was swept aside. Denounced by the home legislature, he was never again elected to office. When President Grant, mindful of Carlile's loyalty, nominated him as ambassador to Sweden, senatorial leaders refused confirmation. He died at Clarksburg.

[A brief sketch by Carlile's son in Wm. P. Willey, *An Inside View of the Formation of the State of W. Va.* (1901); Jas. C. McGregor, *The Disruption of Va.* (1922); *Bench and Bar of W. Va.* (1919), ed. by G. W. Atkinson; *W. Va. Hist. and Govt. told by Contemporaries* (1928), ed. by I. G. Boughter and J. W. Pence.]
C. C. P.

CARLISLE, JAMES MANDEVILLE (May 22, 1814–May 19, 1877), lawyer, was the only son of Christopher Carlisle, a resident of Alexandria near Washington, D. C., and his wife, Anne Mandeville. In 1825 the family moved to Washington, D. C., where James attended the Catholic Seminary, completing his education at Partridge's military school. Of a studious disposition, he became a fine classical scholar, and showed a special aptitude for the French and Spanish languages. He studied law at Baltimore and Washington, giving lessons in modern languages in order to defray his expenses, and was admitted to the bar of the Supreme Court at Washington in 1837. Opening an office in Washington, he quickly secured a promising connection, his familiarity with French and Spanish inducing retainers in cases involving early land titles in Florida and Louisiana. In 1849 he obtained wide publicity as junior counsel to Horace Mann in the defense of Daniel Drayton and Edward Sayres who were tried for larceny in transporting and assisting slaves to escape. He was frequently consulted by the legations of the various Central and South American republics, and in 1852 was retained as standing legal adviser to the British legation. In 1862 he appeared as counsel for Costa Rica before the joint commission at Washington respecting the claims of United States citizens arising out of the occupation of Nicaragua by troops of Costa Rica. On the reorganization of the supreme court of the District of Columbia in 1863 he refused to take the new oath in that court, and thereafter confined his practise to the Supreme Court of the United States and the Court of Claims, where, however, for the next ten years he held a larger number of briefs than any other practitioner. In 1864 he was retained as counsel for Colombia before the commission of that year to consider the undecided claims against New Granada arising, *inter alia,* from the Panama Riots of 1856. In 1871 he was counsel for Spain before the mixed commission under the agreement of Feb. 12, 1871, and in the same year was retained as counsel for the British government before the mixed claims commission under Article 12 of the Treaty of Washington, acting throughout the proceedings which lasted two years. He had for some years suffered from paralysis of the optic nerve, and after 1866 he could never read a printed book, but continued his professional work, relying largely on his phenomenal memory. He died at Washington. A remarkably sound and versatile lawyer, of quick perception, with an intuitive grasp of vital points, he was at his best in international cases involving complicated issues, where his mastery of detail, wonderful memory, and dialectical skill had full sway. Personally he was a man of much dignity and charm. He is spoken of as "an advanced boulevardier . . . immaculately attired, given to dropping in at foreign legations and chatting on familiar terms with the titled and great" (Noel and Downing, *post*).

[*Eminent and Representative Men of Va. and the District of Columbia of the 19th century* (1893); F. R. Noel and M. B. Downing, *Court House of the District of Columbia* (1919); H. W. Crew, *Centennial Hist. of Washington* (1902).]
H. W. H. K.

CARLISLE, JOHN GRIFFIN (Sept. 5, 1835–July 31, 1910), lieutenant-governor of Kentucky, congressman and senator, secretary of the treasury, was born in Campbell (now Kenton) County, of humble parentage. He was the son of L. H. and Mary A. (Reynolds) Carlisle. His early life was spent on a rocky, begrudging farm, which gave him little opportunity for an education. But having unusual ambition for a boy in his situation, he took advantage of every opportunity, and succeeded in getting all the schooling his neighborhood had to offer. Over a period of five years, beginning when he was only fifteen years old, he taught school whenever his labors on the farm permitted. He then moved to Covington where he might have greater opportunities of advancement and began the study of law under the direction of William B. Kinkhead and John W. Stephenson, who later became governor of the state. In January 1857 he married Mary Jane, daughter of John A. Goodson of Covington. He was admitted to the bar in 1858 and for a time was in partnership with Kinkhead. His first speech before a jury won him a respectful hearing and a considerable reputation. Within a short time he had developed as large a practise as could be found in Covington. He was elected in 1859 to the Kentucky legislature and was reëlected for a second term. He took a conservative course in the great sectional dispute, living too near the Ohio River to be a secessionist and yet by nature too conservative to favor coercion. He was a member of the House Committee on Federal Relations which reported the neutrality resolutions of May 16, 1861. Indeed neutrality seemed to express best Carlisle's position throughout the war, for he did not feel called upon to fight on either side. As the Federal military régime gripped Kentucky tighter, almost superseding the civil government, he joined the party of protest and helped to promote its organization at Louisville in June 1864, its position being that, "the revocation of all unconstitutional edicts and pretended laws, an immediate armistice, a national convention for the adjustment of our difficulties, are the only measures for saving our nation from unlimited calamity and ruin" (*Lexington Observer and Reporter*, July 2, 1864). Yet he refused to serve as an elector on the McClellan ticket. In August 1865 he ran for the state Senate and was defeated, as the military authorities took almost complete charge of the election throughout the state. But when the legislature met it refused to seat seven representatives and four senators, Carlisle's opponent being among the latter, and ordered new elections. Carlisle ran again and was elected, being reëlected in 1869. While in the legislature he took a decided stand in favor of granting to the Cincinnati Southern Railway a right-of-way through Kentucky and when in 1871 the Democratic convention nominated Preston H. Leslie, an opponent of the road, for the governorship, Carlisle was nominated for the lieutenant-governorship in order to please central Kentucky which favored the road. He now resigned his senatorship and was elected lieutenant-governor in August. After an intensely bitter fight, over the third attempt of the road to secure a right-of-way, the vote in the Senate stood 19 to 19. Carlisle, now presiding over that body by virtue of being lieutenant-governor, broke the tie in favor of the road. He entered upon his national career in 1877 when he took his seat in the lower house of Congress, where he soon became the recognized leader of the Democrats. He was elected speaker in 1883 and was reëlected for the next two Congresses. To-day he is generally considered to have been one of the few great speakers of the House. His knowledge of parliamentary law and of the rules of the House was unquestioned. In an age when extreme partisanship prevailed, he was scrupulously impartial. Representative Hiscock of New York, a Republican, said at the time, "He is one of the strongest of Democrats, and I am one of the strongest of Republicans; yet . . . my imagination is not strong enough to conceive of his making an unfair ruling or doing an unfair thing against the party opposed to him in this House" (A. D. White, *Autobiography*, 1905, II, 126).

As a member of the House he was the outstanding tariff reformer, and although in theory a free-trader, he stood in reality for a tariff for revenue only. As a member of the Committee on Ways and Means he played an active part in formulating the various Democratic bills, and in 1888 he with Roger Q. Mills fought the hardest for the Mills Bill. According to Champ Clark (*My Quarter Century of American Politics*, 1920, I, 236), the tariff reform movement was due more to him than to any other man. He was also greatly interested in restoring American shipping to the seas. On May 26, 1890 he resigned his seat to accept an appointment to the Senate to fill out the unexpired term of James B. Beck, who had died. On Feb. 4, 1893, he resigned from the Senate to accept under President Cleveland the post of secretary of the treasury, which position he held to the end of Cleveland's term. At a time when most politicians considered themselves financial experts, Carlisle made a close study of the money question and well realized the intricacies of it. As secretary of the treasury he showed courage and ability, but due to the extreme difficulties of the situation he added little to his reputation. He worked in harmony with the President, who said of him, "We are just right for each other. He knows all I ought to know" (R. M. McElroy, *Grover Cleveland, the Man and the Statesman*, II, 6). The new administration was immediately confronted by a panic and a fast-disappearing gold reserve. Carlisle's announcement on Apr. 15, 1893 that no more gold certificates would be issued caused a flurry which was aggravated by the further explanation that gold would be paid for treasury notes only so long as it was "lawfully available." Soon Cleveland clarified the matter by announcing that he would use every power to preserve the parity between gold and silver. Thereafter no one misunderstood the intentions of the treasury department. To maintain the gold reserve Carlisle resorted to various bond issues, authority for which he took from the old resumption act of 1875. In embracing the "sound money" position, he stirred up bitter hostility within his party. He was charged with having deserted his earlier principles, and Champ Clark later declared that Carlisle had given the best free silver arguments ever formulated and had likewise put forth the best reasons for the gold standard. In his famous silver argument, Carlisle stood against the free coinage of either metal, but favored the unlimited coinage of both. He later stated that he would rather be right than consistent.

He had bright presidential prospects in 1892, and was rejected for Cleveland only because the latter, it was thought, would receive a greater independent vote. As the campaign of 1896 approached Carlisle was considered the inevitable "sound money" candidate, but because of the failure of Cleveland to state that he would not be a candidate, Carlisle became hesitant and lost the support of many who were urging him to become an active candidate. In the campaign he came out boldly for the gold standard and supported the Palmer and Buckner "National Democratic" ticket. He made a series of speeches in Kentucky, where the hostility of the silver Democrats became so bitter against him that he was almost mobbed in his home town of Covington. Never before in Kentucky had a leader, excepting Clay and John C. Breckinridge, been more beloved, yet no one was more detested than Carlisle after 1896. The next year, feeling that the verdict of banishment from Kentucky had been pronounced, he began the practise of law in New York City. He took no further part in politics, though he opposed Imperialism and accepted a vice-presidency in the Anti-Imperialist League. He was not a great orator, but he had a gift of keen analysis and lucid statement; and no one excelled him in direct and convincing exposition of economic and financial questions.

[A short sketch of the life of Carlisle appears in *Who's Who in America*, 1910–11. Facts concerning his career in Kentucky are noted in R. H. and L. Collins, *Hist. of Ky.* (1874), vols. I, II, and in E. M. Coulter, *The Cincinnati Southern Railroad and the Struggle for Southern Commerce, 1865–72* (1922); the Louisville *Courier-Jour.*, Aug. 1, 2, 3, 1910. Short obituaries and appreciations are in *N. Y. Times*, Aug. 1, 1910; *Nation*, Aug. 4, 1910, and *Outlook*, Aug. 13, 1910.]
E. M. C—r.

CARLL, JOHN FRANKLIN (May 7, 1828–Mar. 13, 1904), civil engineer, geologist, was born in Bushwick (now Brooklyn), L. I., the son of John and Margaret (Walters) Carll. He was educated at Union Hall Academy in Flushing, L. I. At eighteen, when he had finished his schooling, he joined his father in farming and was so occupied for about three years. He then entered the publishing field in association with his brother-in-law, E. O. Crowell, and assisted in the editing and printing of the *Daily Eagle* in Newark, N. J. Four years later he disposed of his interests in that newspaper and returned to Flushing where for ten years he was engaged in the practise of civil engineering and surveying. In October 1864 he moved to Pleasantville, Pa., and became identified with work in the development of the oil fields of that state. While so occupied, he invented the static-pressure sand pump, a removable pump chamber, and adjustable sleeves for piston rods. In 1874 Prof. J. P. Lesley, chief of the Second Geological Survey of Pennsylvania, appointed Carll as one of the as-

sistant geologists, in charge of the petroleum and natural-gas surveys. The seven reports which he compiled on this work have, from their publication to the present time, been considered by oil men as standard authorities. They are models of conscientious investigation and scientific description. Carll was the first geologist to comprehend the structure of the oil regions of Pennsylvania and to furnish in his reports a reliable exposition of their essential features. These reports cover the geology of the oil regions of Warren, Venango, Clarion, and Butler counties of Pennsylvania; they also include surveys of Garland and Panama conglomerates in Warren and Crawford counties in Pennsylvania and in Chautauqua County of New York. In them Carll described oil-well rigs and tools and discussed both the pre-glacial and post-glacial drainage of Erie County, Pa. He also gave an excellent comparison of the geology of northeastern Ohio, northwestern Pennsylvania, and western New York. It is hardly too much to say that the geology of petroleum was virtually created by Carll and his service to the science in sweeping away many popular fallacies was invaluable. For eight years he exerted an influence upon the more thoughtful part of the population of the oil regions, an influence so unpretentious, steady, and consistent as almost to elude observation, but so real and fundamental as to illustrate admirably the true function of a geological survey. Carll continued with the Survey until 1885 when he resigned to enter private practise as a consulting geologist. He was married twice: in 1853 to Hannah A. Burtis of South Oyster Bay, L. I., who died in September 1859, and in 1868 to Martha Tappan of Newark, N. J., who died in 1903. At the time of his death in 1904, in Waldron, Ark., Carll was on his way south for the benefit of his health.

[The Mar. 14, 1904 issue of the *Daily Derrick* (Oil City, Pa.), now the *Oil City Derrick*; Prof. J. P. Lesley's letter of transmittal with Carll's reports to Gov. Pattison of Pa., pub. in *Geological Report on Warren County* by J. F. Carll (1883); *Who's Who in America*, 1903–05; information as to certain facts from S. E. Carll (great-nephew of J. F. Carll), 42 Idaho St., Passaic, N. J.]
K. W. C—g.

CARMACK, EDWARD WARD (Nov. 5, 1858–Nov. 9, 1908), prohibitionist, the son of F. M. and Catherine Carmack, was a native of Sumner County, Tenn. His father, a minister of the Christian or Campbellite Church, who lived near Castalian Springs, died when his son was a small boy, leaving the family entirely without means. Edward worked on farms and at a brick yard, helping to support the family. At county schools he secured some training, and friends later aided him to attend the famous Webb School at Culleoka, Tenn. He then read law at home and in a lawyer's office, and, after a short law practise in Columbia, he entered the state legislature in 1884. He next became editor of the *Columbia Herald,* and later of the *Nashville American* (1888). In April 1890 he was married to Elizabeth Cobey Dunnington of Columbia, Tenn. In 1892 he became editor of the *Memphis Commercial Appeal.* Throughout his editorial career he fought for good government and for the prohibition of the liquor traffic. He became known as an able editor who excelled in the use of ridicule and invective. In 1897 he was elected to Congress and served two terms, after which he was elected United States senator. In 1906 he contested the governorship of Tennessee with M. R. Patterson, Carmack standing for state-wide prohibition. Defeated he again became editor of the *Nashville American* and carried the prohibition fight to the Democratic state convention, in which many of his adherents were unseated. He then planned to carry the contest to the state legislature in 1908. The struggle was bitter and it was clear that a majority would support Carmack's views. Gov. Patterson strongly opposed the prohibition policy. Bitter animosities were aroused and before the legislature met Carmack was killed on the street in Nashville by Duncan B. Cooper and his son Robin, both supporters of Gov. Patterson's policies. They were sentenced to twenty years' imprisonment but Patterson immediately pardoned the older man, and his son, granted a new trial, was not further prosecuted. The legislature, however, two months later, passed over the governor's veto the state-wide prohibition law for which Carmack had struggled.

In political campaigns and in Congress Carmack was known as a popular orator and ready debater. His manner and style were those of John Randolph but Carmack possessed greater versatility. His course in public affairs always commanded enthusiastic followers and developed bitter enemies. What he decided was right he supported with all the vigor at his command and what he thought was wrong he condemned with vitriolic ridicule and wit. Few men cared to meet him in debate. He was a good writer, a brilliant speaker, a great editor of the old-fashioned type, and during his brief and restless career one of the most influential men the state of Tennessee has produced. Only four monuments have been erected on the grounds of the state capitol in Nashville: to Andrew Jackson, James K. Polk, Sam Davis, and Edward Ward Carmack.

[W. T. Hale and D. L. Merritt, *A Hist. of Tenn. and Tennesseans* (1913); J. G. Cisco, *Historic Sumner County, Tenn.* (1909); pamphlets and newspaper files in the State Library of Tennessee.]   W. L. F.

CARMICHAEL, WILLIAM (d. Feb. 9, 1795), diplomat, was born in Queen Annes County, Md. His father was also William Carmichael, who had come to the eastern shore of Maryland as a Scotch immigrant, and there married a Miss Brooke, niece of the second wife of Richard Bennett, son of a former governor of Virginia, and one of the wealthiest landed proprietors of Maryland. This fortunate inheritance enabled William Carmichael to complete his education at Edinburgh, and to tour the British Isles. He was in London, leading a gay life, in 1775, when word came of the beginning of revolution in America. He resolved to return to America and was entrusted with dispatches by Arthur Lee, then the agent in London for some of the Colonies, but on reaching Paris, he was detained there by illness until the arrival of Silas Deane. He offered his services to Deane, and served as a secretary of the Commission (Deane, Franklin and Arthur Lee), in their efforts to enlist the aid of France for the Colonies. He was individually responsible for the coming of Lafayette to America (*Stevens' Facsimiles,* vol. III, no. 248). In October 1776 he was sent to Berlin to propose treaty relations with Frederick the Great but found that old monarch too cautious to risk the enmity of England (*Ibid.,* vol. XV, no. 1453). After rendering useful service in France, Carmichael sailed from Nantes for America, February 1778, bearing important dispatches to the Continental Congress.

He served as a member of the Continental Congress in 1778–79, and then became secretary to John Jay, chosen as minister plenipotentiary to secure a treaty with Spain. The Jay commission reached Cadiz, Jan. 22, 1780, and Carmichael was sent ahead to Madrid to ascertain whether the commission would be received or not. The answer was favorable, and for more than two years they sought a treaty with Spain, but without success, as Spain refused to allow America the navigation of the Mississippi to its mouth. When Jay left for Paris in June 1782 he left Carmichael as acting chargé d'affaires, to transact routine matters while the negotiations for a treaty were transferred to Paris. Carmichael continued at Madrid or at other residences of the Court of Spain, and was formally received by the king and royal family on Aug. 23, 1783, an honor not usually accorded to any below the rank of minister (Carmichael MSS.; Library of Congress, Carmichael to Livingston, Aug. 30, 1783). His commission as chargé was dated Apr. 20, 1790. With his health much impaired, Carmichael's letters to Jefferson, Secretary of State, became infrequent, and in January 1791 he asked to be relieved and allowed to return to America. This request Jefferson refused, and, in March 1792, a new commission, in which Carmichael was joined by William Short, was appointed by President Washington to secure a treaty with Spain. On the arrival of Short, negotiations began Mar. 23, 1793, and were continued without success until June 5, 1794, when Carmichael was recalled and Short named as his successor. Before Carmichael could arrange his affairs and take formal leave of the Court, winter set in and compelled a delay until the next spring. In February 1795 he was confined to his bed by an illness felt for years past which resulted in his death, Feb. 9, 1795. He was buried in a lot adjoining the Roman Catholic Cemetery in Madrid.

His chief public service was rendered during his fourteen years in Spain, when both the reputation and credit of the nation were very bad. Under such conditions he gained the close friendship of the Spanish foreign minister, Florida Blanca, a genuine statesman, and through him secured the aid of Spain in obtaining the release of American captives in Morocco and a favorable treaty with Morocco. He was ignored by his own government, unpaid for years, and compelled to use his personal resources to keep up appearances. Every American who had occasion to visit Madrid while Carmichael was in active service testified to his good standing and influence at the Spanish Court (Jefferson MSS.; Jefferson to Madison, Jan. 30, 1787).

William Carmichael was twice married. As a youth he wed a Miss Stirling, daughter of an Episcopal rector in Queen Annes County, Md. He was a widower with no children when he went to Spain, and there married Antonia Reynon. His widow, with one daughter, Alphonsa, came to America to live near Chestertown, Md. The estate of Carmichael was so impaired by his long public service that his family was on the verge of poverty, and only some belated generosity on the part of Congress in paying the claims advanced by Mrs. Carmichael kept her from actual suffering.

[The chief source of information is The Papers of the Continental Congress, Letters of W. Carmichael in the Lib. of Cong., Manuscripts Division. See also Francis Wharton, ed., *The Revolutionary Diplomatic Correspondence* (6 vols., 1889) ; Jared Sparks, ed., *The Diplomatic Correspondence of the Am. Rev.* (12 vols., 1829–30) ; S. F. Bemis, ed., *The Am. Secretaries of State and Their Diplomacy*, vol. I (1927) ; Samuel G. Coe, *The Mission of Wm. Carmichael to Spain* (1928).]
S.G.C.

CARNAHAN, JAMES (Nov. 15, 1775–Mar. 3, 1859), college president, was born in Cumberland County, Pa., where his ancestors had settled early in the eighteenth century. His father, for a time an officer in the state militia during the Revolution, met an untimely death in 1788.

James, after some years of study at the academy of Canonsburg, was admitted in 1798 to the junior class of the College of New Jersey (now Princeton) whence two years later he was graduated with highest honors. For more than a score of years he divided his time between preaching and teaching. In 1801–03 he was a tutor in the College of New Jersey; in 1804 he was licensed to preach by the Presbytery of New Brunswick; in 1806–12 he served the united congregation of Utica and Whitesboro (N. Y.). Resigning on account of ill health, he spent eleven years in conducting a classical academy at Georgetown, D. C. He became well known throughout the Presbyterian communion as a man of sound judgment and unflagging diligence. In May 1823 he was elected to the presidency of the College of New Jersey. For six years he had to contend with an evil heritage, as the institution was in the midst of a period of decline. Standards were low; discipline was lax; and divided counsels rent the administration. Frequent resignations from the faculty continued to undermine the reputation of the college. In 1828 the lowest ebb was reached; the enrolment had dropped from 120 to 70. The president was keenly discouraged and thought of recommending the closing of the institution. But at this juncture a young professor, John Maclean, possessed of tremendous energy and resource, put his shoulder to the wheel. Henceforth "the administration of Dr. Carnahan . . . until his resignation in 1853 was a collegiate administration in which two colleagues labored as one man" (J. DeWitt, *post*, p. 647). Maclean advised an immediate strengthening of the faculty. The adoption of this policy inaugurated an era of prosperity. Men of the stamp of Albert Dod, Joseph Henry, and John Torrey enhanced the reputation of the college. When Carnahan retired in 1854 there were 250 students enrolled. New chairs were endowed; many scholarships were established; East and West Colleges and Clio and Whig Halls were erected. A law school flourished (for a short time), and ambitious plans for a medical school were afoot. From the time of his retirement until his death Carnahan served as a trustee of the college and as president of the board of trustees of the Theological Seminary. His wife, Mary (Van Dyke) Carnahan, died five years before him in 1854.

[See John Maclean, *Hist. of the Coll. of N. J.* (1877) ; V. L. Collins, *Princeton* (1914) ; J. DeWitt, *Princeton College* (1897) ; J. F. Hageman, *Hist. of Princeton* (1879) ; and J. W. Wilson, *An Hist. Sketch of the College of N. J.* (1859). Carnahan's writings, largely addresses and sermons, are listed in Maclean, II, 405–06. A complete collection is in the Princeton Univ. Lib.]
J.E.P.

CARNEGIE, ANDREW (Nov. 25, 1835–Aug. 11, 1919), manufacturer, publicist, and "distributor" of wealth "for the improvement of mankind,"—the word "philanthropist" he scornfully rejected—was born at Dunfermline, Scotland, the son of William Carnegie, a handloom weaver, and Margaret Morrison, the daughter of Thomas Morrison, a tanner and shoemaker. These progenitors would indicate a humble origin, but Carnegie himself regarded his family inheritance as a rich one. Though Carnegie's father lacked the imaginative resourcefulness and impatient energy that made his son so conspicuous a leader in many fields, he had the political sense, the eagerness for social progress, and the love of books that had for generations distinguished the damask trade. In Dunfermline to-day, William Carnegie is remembered, above all, as "an awfu' man to read." He was moreover an active political figure in his region, and an advanced radical,—an organizer of anti-Corn Law processions and a Chartist leader. On Carnegie's maternal side these tendencies were even more marked. His grandfather, Thomas Morrison, was one of the most irrepressible agitators of Scotland. He was the friend and correspondent of William Cobbett, and himself a contributor to Cobbett's *Register*. There was not a step intended to promote human progress or to advance liberty, enlightenment and toleration,—a reformed Commons, a democratic ballot, new factory laws, Catholic emancipation, freedom of trade, the destruction of hereditary privilege, the abolition of kings and armies— that Thomas Morrison did not advocate on the public platform,—and advocate with great native eloquence, and a wealth of argument that was the product of a lifetime spent in self-education. A collection of his newspaper letters still exists in which he vigorously assails the legislative shortcomings of Lord Dalmeny, at that time (1835) the representative of Stirling Burghs in Parliament—the same Lord Dalmeny whose son, Lord Rosebery, the Prime Minister, afterward became one of Andrew Carnegie's best friends. The elder Morrison likewise enjoys a certain fame as a pioneer in technical education; an article once widely circulated was his contribution to Cobbett's *Register* (Dec. 21, 1833) on "'Heddekashun' and 'Handication,'" containing ideas of which his grandson afterward became an enthusiastic exponent.

The romantic strain acquired from his father found abundant nourishment in the surroundings of Carnegie's childhood. Dunfermline itself, as a great national shrine, is hardly second to Edinburgh. Here Scottish history began with King Malcolm Canmore, the successor of Macbeth on the Scottish throne, and his pious Queen Margaret. Dunfermline Abbey—the Westminster of Scotland—is the burial place of twenty Scottish royalties, including many kings and queens; and there lie the bones of King Robert the Bruce, only a few hundred yards from the humble Carnegie cottage, on the corner of Moodie St. and Priory Lane. The Abbey ruins; the nearby Stuart Palace in which Charles I was born; Loch Leven, with its memories of Mary Stuart, eight miles away; the Firth of Forth and the Pentland Hills, which Carnegie could see from the hill on which his birthplace stood—in all this historic country there was plenty to stimulate a sensitive child. Andrew's family and relatives exercised the liveliest effect upon his sentimental nature. His uncle, George Lauder, was his principal instructor. This uncle kept a grocery shop in the High St., the back room of which formed the favorite congregating place of Carnegie and his cousin, George. Here the older man, a gentle, dreamy soul, a lover of flowers, of music, of poetry, and of Scottish history, filled Andrew's mind with stories of Bruce, Wallace, Rob Roy, and other Celtic heroes. Above all, he implanted a love of Burns, teaching the boy to learn pages by heart, with the result that Carnegie, up to his last days, had the words of the national bard constantly on his lips. To "Uncle" Lauder, Burns meant more than mere romance, for to him, as always to Carnegie, the poet was one of the greatest preachers of democracy. Next to Scotland and Burns, Lauder's interest was the United States; the fervid admiration which Carnegie always evinced for American institutions was thus part of his childhood training. The influence that shaped his political opinion was another uncle, his mother's brother, "Bailie" Morrison. This reformer, like his father, Cobbett's friend, was a political firebrand; in his speeches the Royal Family and the House of Lords were always severely attacked; the Established Church, both of England and Scotland, aroused his most incendiary periods; and such time as he could spare from his trade of shoemaker, he spent in advocating the establishment of an English republic in place of the existing monarchy, and in promoting the interests of the workingmen. Once the Bailie was arrested for his part in the "labor cessation" of 1842; and the glimpse of his uncle behind prison bars, which Andrew obtained at the age of seven, likewise had its effect in arousing an antagonism to privileged institutions. "As a child," said Carnegie, "I could have slain king, duke, or lord, and considered their death a service to the state."

The poverty of the Carnegie family during Andrew's childhood was extreme. The factory system was invading the linen industry, and the day of the individual handloom weaver, who performed his daily task on the ground floor of his own cottage, assisted by wife and children, was passing. Andrew Carnegie vividly remembered the night when his father, after a day's unavailing search for a web, came home a picture of despair, and said, "Well, Andra, I canna get nae mair work." It marked the beginning of hard times in the Carnegie cottage. The mother, always the dominant partner, sought to repair the family fortunes by keeping a "sweetie shop" and binding shoes,—little Andrew sitting at her side threading the needles. The children's upbringing, however, was not neglected. Primary instruction was the natural right of every child born in the country of John Knox, and Andrew obtained this, and even a few scraps of Latin, at a Lancasterian school. But the mother's ambition for her two sons,—the second was Thomas M., eight years Andrew's junior,—was little less than a passion. She saw no future for them in Scotland. Her two sisters and one brother had already settled in the new world; and this became Margaret Carnegie's goal. The passage money proved a serious problem; friends of Margaret's childhood, however, lent her twenty pounds, the household effects were sold, and in May 1848 the four Carnegies sailed from the Broomielaw in Glasgow on the American ex-whaler *Wiscasset.* After a six weeks' voyage they reached New York, proceeded up the Hudson River and the Erie Canal to Lake Erie, and thence, by lake and canal, to Allegheny, Pa. Here they joined a little Scottish colony including the aunts and uncles already settled there; William Carnegie obtained modest employment in a cotton factory; Andrew was installed in the same building as bobbin boy at $1.20 a week; and little Tom was put to school.

The diminutive white-haired Scottish boy was quickly transformed into an American. At the age of sixteen Andrew began writing letters to friends in Scotland, comparing American life and institutions with those of Great Britain, much to the disadvantage of the latter country. At the same age, he also contributed letters to the newspapers, notably to the *New York Tribune,* on the great questions of the day, especially slavery,—a habit that became a lifelong one. His natural love of reading received a new impetus from the kindly action of Col. James Anderson, who opened his personal library of 400 volumes to working boys, delivering books to them each Saturday night. Carnegie became the most persistent borrower, and the recollection of the great benefits derived from Col. Anderson largely explains his own library gifts in after years. Indeed, a failure to emphasize Andrew Carnegie's interest in reading, as well as his absorption in politics, history, and certain phases of science and speculative thinking, would make the portrait most incomplete. The years he spent struggling up from poverty were devoted also to the development of his mind. He was a "self-made" man in a more comprehensive sense than the term usually implies, for he was self-made mentally as well as economically. His alertness and determination to succeed soon brought him opportunities. He spent a year or more as bobbin boy and engine tender, the latter the only occupation in which he was ever really unhappy, but his chance came when—he was now fourteen and small for his age—he obtained a job as messenger in the Pittsburgh telegraph office. The pay, $2.50 a week, seemed a fortune. To this experience he traced his great love of Shakespeare: he was frequently sent to deliver messages to the theatre, and usually contrived to make his appearance at night, after the curtain had gone up,—his plea to be permitted to remain being invariably granted by the manager. Most of the time Carnegie was not delivering messages he utilized by listening to the telegraph instrument as the words came over the wire. In those days telegraph operators did not take "by sound"; there was an elaborate instrument that transcribed the letters on a long tape. Andrew soon learned to distinguish the letters by sound, thus becoming one of the first two or three telegraphers in the country so gifted. His employers, discovering his skill, promoted him to an operator's key. "I have got past delivering messages," he wrote his cousin in Scotland (he was now sixteen) "and have got to operating. I am to have four dollars a week now and a good prospect of soon getting more." One of the influential Pittsburghers whom Carnegie met most frequently in the telegraph office was Thomas A. Scott, then beginning his brilliant career with the Pennsylvania Railroad. Presently the astonished Andrew found himself installed in Scott's office as private secretary and personal telegrapher. The salary was $35 a month; "I couldn't imagine," Carnegie used to say, recalling the episode, "what I could ever do with so much money!" He remained with the Pennsylvania twelve years (1853–65), advancing from position to position until he finally succeeded Scott as superintendent of the Pittsburgh Division. Probably Carnegie's greatest achievement as a railroad man was the introduction of Pullman sleeping cars; he acquired a one-eighth interest in the Woodruff Company, the original holder of the Pullman patents. This investment, which was profitable, represented the first considerable sum that Andrew Carnegie had ever earned. His most exciting experience came when he accompanied Mr. Scott to Washington on the outbreak of the Civil War. Scott was made assistant secretary of war in charge of military transportation, and Carnegie became his right-hand man. The first brigade of troops to reach Washington was transported by Carnegie, the doughty Scotsman taking his place on the engine of the first military train into the Federal capital. Soon afterward he superintended the transportation of the defeated Federal forces after the battle of Bull Run, personally loading train after train with the wounded. He organized the telegraph department that rendered such efficient service in the next four years (see Homer D. Bates, *Lincoln in the Telegraph Office,* 1907). His work in the field resulted in a slight sunstroke that made it necessary, for the rest of his life, to spend the summer in cool climates.

The American iron industry received a great impetus from the Civil War. Until that event, American iron had cut no figure in world trade. But the sudden demand for war materials, railway supplies and the like, brought fortunes to the previously struggling iron masters of Pittsburgh. In a small way Carnegie had joined one or two enterprises of the kind; in 1865, however, he resigned from the Pennsylvania Railroad, to devote all of his energies to the new field. Yet his first important venture, the Keystone Bridge Company, represented a continuation of his railroad work; his experience had taught him the inadequacy of wooden bridges for railroads and the usefulness of iron. His acquaintance with railroad men proved a great asset to his company; it was largely owing to Carnegie's infinite ability as a salesman that the success of the Keystone Bridge Company, as well as his other enterprises, was due. Carnegie was now thirty years old; whatever faults his enemies—and he had his share of them—may impute to him, on one point the judgment is unanimous: he was a man of vast personal charm. Far better read than most business men, and far better traveled, with a keen sense of humor, an unrivaled gift for anecdote, a great talent for good-natured controversy and raillery, and at times a genuine literary tang in expression, he soon became in all industrial centers a familiar dinner table companion. These personal qualities paid dividends in orders that poured into his mill. Yet at first his Keystone Bridge Company seemed merely one of several interests that engaged Carnegie's attention. It was not until 1873 that he concentrated on steel. He had made a small fortune in oil and taken several trips to Europe selling railroad securities, dealing chiefly with the London firm of Junius S. Morgan & Company. The last of these was as late as 1872, his commission on this transaction amounting to $150,000. Carnegie operations in bond selling, oil dealing, bridge building and the like were so dashing and so successful that conservative Pittsburgh business men regarded him somewhat doubtfully; what was really courage they looked upon as recklessness, and what was foresight, in their more prosaic minds was regarded as mere gambling. Carnegie's European tours, then and afterward, had results of great consequence. He came into close touch with British steel makers,—then the world's leaders; he obtained a close acquaintance with the Bessemer process, and he formed a friendship with Sir Henry Bessemer, which was maintained until the latter's death. By 1873, therefore, Carnegie was prepared to stake all his possessions, at this time considerable, on what was then a new American industry,—to begin his famous policy, as he himself described it, of "putting all his eggs in one basket, and then watching the basket." Americans did not realize it at the time, but, when Carnegie made this decision, the industrial supremacy of the United States was born. Carnegie himself was thirty-eight years old; significantly, in the same year (1873) that the J. Edgar Thomson Steel Mills were started, he made his first public gift—that of free baths for his native town of Dunfermline, Scotland. In Scottish phrase, Andrew Carnegie was "gathering gear."

Carnegie's business life for the next three decades is, in its larger outlines, the industrial history of the United States for the same period. In 1873 the relative positions of Great Britain and the United States in steel strikingly resembled their present positions in shipping,—England seemed to hold first place by a kind of natural right. Yet our conquest of the steel trade was achieved in a little more than sixteen years. By 1889 the production of America had passed that of Great Britain. In the succeeding forty years this nation increased its steel manufactures at such a rate that even the greatest industrial nations of Europe lagged far behind. More than one cause necessarily explains such a triumph. The great bodies of ore in the Lake Superior regions are an asset that no other country can duplicate. The Carnegie company ultimately purchased or leased the most valuable of these fields. Doubtless tariff favors proved helpful in the early days, though the time soon came when they were no longer needed. Carnegie always described himself as a protectionist of the John

Stuart Mill variety,—the tariff was justified in developing an "infant industry" but was a wicked device when used merely to swell the profits of an established business. Long before he retired (1901) he advocated the removal of duties on steel. Railroad rebates had little to do with the growth of Pittsburgh steel, though at times the Carnegie company received concessions; Carnegie's business life was largely one long battle against his old employer, the Pennsylvania Railroad, which, having a monopoly of Pittsburgh traffic, for years discriminated against that city in favor of Chicago, Cleveland, and other competitive points. The presence of the great Connellsville coke area (developed in the seventies and eighties by the genius of Henry Clay Frick [*q.v.*], who joined the Carnegie forces in 1882, becoming chairman of Carnegie Brothers, Limited, in 1889, and thus chief executive of the organization), likewise had much to do with the Carnegie triumph. Andrew Carnegie himself, in analyzing the history of his own progress, estimated one element as far more important than all the rest. The world might deprive him of his ores, his coal, his railroads, his steamship lines, his steel mills, his machinery, and, provided one thing only were left, he could guarantee to repeat his success. The one indispensable possession was his organization. The American conquest of steel was, above everything else, a personal achievement. What made Andrew Carnegie first among steel masters was the fact that he was a supreme judge of men, which is only another way of saying that he was a supreme organizer. He once suggested this as his epitaph: "Here lies the man who was able to surround himself with men far cleverer than himself." Among these forceful associates Carnegie would have placed in the first class the famous Capt. "Bill" Jones, who as a maker of steel and commander of men, as well as an inventor of new processes, has probably never had an equal; his own brother, Thomas M. Carnegie, whose early death (in 1886) at the age of forty-three has somewhat obscured his contribution, though in business ability he was entirely worthy of the name he bore; Henry Clay Frick, whose quarrel with his old associates, a sensational episode in steel history, never diminished Carnegie's admiration for his genius as an industrialist; and Charles M. Schwab. There were many more of exceptional talent.

Thus, Carnegie's steel campaign, though Napoleonic in its rapidity and the completeness of its victory, was a case of Napoleon and his marshals. He built up his organization by adhering strictly to democratic principles. His company was put together with the idea of developing talent in the rank and file. Many who ended as heads of great departments and as millionaires, started in the Carnegie works as laborers. Schwab himself began as stake driver at a dollar a day. The Carnegie company, until a few months preceding its absorption in the United States Steel, was never a corporation; not a share of its stock was publicly sold; it was a limited partnership, every dollar being held by men who were active working associates. If a member died or withdrew from the company, his stock was purchased for the treasury at book value; similarly, at any time, owners representing three-fourths of the stock could call in any shares on the same terms, thus forcing the unsuccessful partner to retire. Carnegie himself always held a majority interest; the rest was distributed among a large number of partners,—at the end, about forty. Every man acquired an interest solely on his record. If his work warranted it, he was allotted a small quota, which was increased as his value increased. He was not forced to pay for it in cash, the dividends being set aside for that purpose. The eagerness to obtain such an interest became the incentive that urged every worker to his most heroic efforts, and probably explains, more than any one circumstance, the amazing efficiency of the organization. And Andrew Carnegie, at the head, gave, for thirty years, an illustration of superb generalship. His success was the result of his optimism, enthusiasm, and courage. He was not a gambler; the speculative side of Wall Street he detested; he never bought a share of stock on margin in his life, yet he did make one gamble of titanic proportions,—and won. He wagered everything he possessed on the economic future of the United States. He was probably the most daring man in American industry; his insistence on the most up-to-date machines, his readiness to discard costly equipment as soon as something better appeared, is a tradition in the steel trade. When business was most depressed and steel was apparently facing ruin, that was always the time Carnegie took for action. It was in these periods of depression that he made immense outlays improving his plants. His competitors spent money on buildings and equipment when times were flush, but Carnegie selected hard times for two reasons: first, he could build his extensions at extremely low prices; secondly, he had unbounded faith in the United States and knew that prosperity would return. And when prosperity emerged, he proposed to be ready to supply any demand. His less far-sighted competitors, when business revived, had run-down organizations, and could not meet the requirements of the trade. They would start at once making improvements, but in good times they could do this only at high prices; Carnegie, on the other hand, was not only ready for the rush, but could sell cheaply, for his facilities had cost him so little. Thus, the era from 1893 to 1897 was one of great industrial depression and most steel factories ran to seed. This was precisely the time that Carnegie took for developing his works. When prosperity came with a flood tide, he had the whole steel industry at his mercy. The price at which he made rails, steel, and other products, meant vast profits for himself and absolute ruin for his competitors. In 1900 the profits of the Carnegie Company were $40,000,000, of which Carnegie's share was about $25,000,000.

The steel business, important as it was to Carnegie's career, seems almost to have been merely an avocation. Carnegie's early ambition inclined to journalism and authorship, and his ideas on the uses of wealth were also no improvisation of his mature years. Among his papers is a memorandum, written in 1868, before his career as a steel maker had begun: "Thirty-three," he wrote, "and an income of $50,000 per annum! . . . Beyond this never earn,—make no effort to increase fortune, but spend the surplus each year for benevolent purposes. Cast aside business for ever, except for others. Settle in Oxford and get a thorough education, making the acquaintance of literary men—this will take three years' active work—pay especial attention to speaking in public. Settle then in London and purchase a controlling interest in some newspaper or live review and give the general management of it attention, taking a part in public matters, especially those connected with education and improvement of the poorer classes. Man must have an idol—the amassing of wealth is one of the worst species of idolatry—no idol more debasing than the worship of money. Whatever I engage in I must push inordinately; therefore should I be careful to choose that life which will be the most elevating in its character. To continue much longer overwhelmed by business cares and with most of my thoughts wholly upon the way to make more money in the shortest time, must degrade me beyond hope of permanent recovery. I will resign business at thirty-five, but during the ensuing two years I wish to spend the afternoons in receiving instruction and in reading systematically."

Certain items in this program the young man did not carry out: he did not cease money making,—at least until more than thirty years afterward; he did not spend three years in Oxford;

and he did not settle permanently in London. The spirit of this memorandum, however, was precisely the spirit of Carnegie's life. He made many friends in the literary and political world. Among them were Matthew Arnold, who came to the United States in 1883 as Carnegie's guest; Sir Edwin Arnold, who gave him as a keepsake the original manuscript of "The Light of Asia"; Herbert Spencer, "the man to whom I owe most," Carnegie said; William E. Gladstone, John Morley, Lord Rosebery, Joseph Chamberlain, Sir William Vernon Harcourt, Frederic Harrison, James Bryce, William T. Stead, John Burns, and Lloyd George; while in the United States his correspondents and acquaintances included practically all the American presidents, statesmen, and writers of his time, with chief emphasis upon James G. Blaine, Theodore Roosevelt, Richard Watson Gilder, Mark Twain, Elihu Root, and Andrew D. White. The *Adventures of a Phaeton* of his friend William Black, inspired Carnegie's famous coaching trip through England and Scotland in 1881, including a triumphal entry into his birthplace, Dunfermline, where his mother, aged seventy, laid the foundation of the first Carnegie Library,—a summer experience recorded in Carnegie's book, *An American Four-in-Hand in Britain* (1883). Carnegie, though actively in business, now became a frequent contributor to serious magazines, especially the *Nineteenth Century,* under the editorship of James Knowles, and the *North American Review,* in its most influential period, under Lloyd Bryce. In 1886 he startled both America and Great Britain with his volume *Triumphant Democracy.* The book was a statistical pæan; its purpose was to exhibit the vast superiority of Republican institutions over Monarchical, and specifically of the American system over the British. The red cover displayed a representation of a royal crown, printed bottom end up, of a broken scepter and an inverted pyramid,—the latter a thrust at what Carnegie regarded as the topsy-turvy monarchical principle. The volume not only contained a glowing account of American progress, but several extremely harsh hits at the British Royal Family,— a fact that caused some scandal in England. The book first opened the eyes of Americans themselves to their rapid economic progress, and more than 40,000 copies were sold in a brief time. Carnegie's strictures on the British aristocracy implied no hostility to the British people; indeed, he loved England and Scotland with all the intensity of his nature, and one of the great purposes of his life was to do a part in making closer the bonds uniting the English-speaking nations. But he believed that the best way he could show his devotion to Britain was to assist in the reform of its political and social institutions. With this ambitious plan in mind, he purchased, in the early eighties, a string of newspapers in England, which rigorously advocated the abolition of the monarchy and the establishment of the British Republic. These manifestations never alienated Carnegie's English friendships. He was a welcome guest of Gladstone at Hawarden Castle, and to him Gladstone turned when his friend, Lord Acton, faced the possibility of losing his great library. Carnegie advanced $50,000 to prevent foreclosure, leaving the library in Acton's possession for life, and, after the great scholar's death, giving it to John Morley, who passed it on to its permanent resting place in Cambridge University. Long before this transaction John Morley had become Carnegie's closest friend. The two men corresponded for nearly forty years, from 1883 to 1919; the profound scholar and accomplished stylist discovered in the self-educated iron-master and natural philosopher the most personally congenial of his associates. In his letters Morley frequently refers to "my friends, of whom I place you and Mrs. Carnegie at the top of the list."

Carnegie caused a great stir in June 1889 when his article, "Wealth," appeared in the *North American Review.* Gladstone at once requested its republication in England, and it presently appeared in William T. Stead's *Pall Mall Gazette,* under the amended caption by which it will always be known, "The Gospel of Wealth." Gladstone was so interested that he contributed an article to the *Nineteenth Century,* and soon all the newspapers, magazines, and reviews in Europe and America were discussing Carnegie's ideas. The conception of the responsibility of rich men which Carnegie set forth was then new. The point that caught the imagination of mankind was Carnegie's central one: that the life story of a rich man should fall into two periods,—the first, that of acquiring wealth, the second, that of distributing it. The popular mind misconstrued one sentence as meaning that a "man who dies rich dies disgraced," but Carnegie never phrased the matter quite so pungently. He insisted that the first duty of every man was to provide a competence for his family. This competence, of course, should bear some relation to the manner of existence his wife and children had observed in his own lifetime. The rich man who really "died disgraced" was the one who died leaving great sums which he might himself have administered for the public good. Carnegie accepted on the whole the estab-

lished economic and political system; he was then, and so remained to his death, a disbeliever in socialism. Yet he recognized that the accumulation of enormous sums in the hands of industrial leaders was a result of capitalism that held great possibilities of evil. So far as these leaders stimulated industry and performed their part in unloosing natural and human energies for the growth of society, they were a valuable national asset, indeed, Carnegie believed, they were indispensable. But their reward, if used for their own selfish purposes, far exceeded the value of their services. Carnegie granted that the people as a whole had created the fortunes concentrated in individual hands; what the community had piled up should be returned to it. The millionaire who properly recognized his own position was merely a "trustee"; he held his surplus wealth for the benefit of his fellows. After discussing the subject in all its aspects, Carnegie concluded that the rich man should himself administer his surplus wealth in his own lifetime for the public good; the accumulator of great possessions was *prima facie* an exceptional person, and it became his duty to use the talents which had made his fortune by distributing it for "the improvement of mankind."

Carnegie was fifty-four years old when he promulgated his gospel; his fortune, in 1889, though amounting to many millions, was a small one compared with the great size it ultimately reached. In the decade from 1890 to 1900 it increased at flood tide. Yet the annual accretions did not represent his main interest. It was no secret, several years before his retirement, that he wished to sell. Certain misunderstood events, such as the Homestead strike of 1892, and personal difficulties which began to develop inside the organization, finally culminating in the break with Henry C. Frick, perhaps accentuated this desire; the main reason, however, was the same as that which had inspired the above-quoted memorandum of 1868,—a desire to use his wealth for public purposes, to cultivate his friendships, and to develop his own soul. Carnegie was a man of the deepest domestic affections. As a boy he had dreamed of becoming rich, so that his mother might dress in silks and ride in her own carriage; and the devotion he lavished on her is one of the great traditions of Pittsburgh. He remained a bachelor during his mother's lifetime; soon after her death, however, he married (1887) a lady who had been a close friend for several years,—Louise Whitfield, of New York. In his married life Carnegie was fortunate; his wife made not only an ideal companion and an accomplished hostess, but she sympathized with all his plans for distributing his wealth and assisted him in executing them. For ten years succeeding their marriage, Mr. and Mrs. Carnegie spent six months of almost every year at Cluny Castle, Kingussie, Inverness-shire, Scotland; in 1898 they acquired a large tract, eventually amounting to nearly 40,000 acres, on Dornoch Firth, Sutherlandshire, and there built Skibo Castle, which remained their favorite residence until the World War.

After one or two abortive negotiations to dispose of his business, Carnegie finally sold the Carnegie Company to the newly-formed United States Steel Corporation, in January 1901. His remark to J. P. Morgan, after signing the papers of sale, really expressed the feeling of many years. "Well, Pierpont," he said, "I am now handing the burden over to you." For his share Carnegie received $250,000,000 in five per cent fifty-year gold bonds. His first act after his retirement was to give the employees of the Carnegie Company $5,000,000 in the form of a pension and benefit fund.

Carnegie lived for nearly twenty years after abdicating his position in the industrial world, and devoted most of his time to putting into practise his own gospel of wealth. Had he merely placed his fortune at interest, subtracting the comparatively modest amount needed for personal expenses, it would have made him the first American billionaire practically in his own lifetime. But, as fortunes are estimated to-day, Carnegie died a man of moderate wealth. His benefactions amounted to $350,000,000,—for he gave away not only his annual income of something more than $12,500,000, but most of the principal as well. Of this sum, $62,000,000 was allotted to the British Empire and $288,000,000 to the United States, for Carnegie, in the main, confined his benefactions to the English-speaking nations. His largest gifts were $125,000,000 to the Carnegie Corporation of New York (this same body also became his residuary legatee), $60,000,000 to public library buildings, $20,-000,000 to colleges (usually the smaller ones), $6,000,000 to church organs, $29,000,000 to the Carnegie Foundation for the Advancement of Teaching, $22,000,000 to the Carnegie Institute of Pittsburgh, $22,000,000 to the Carnegie Institution of Washington, $10,000,000 to Hero Funds, $10,000,000 to the Endowment for International Peace, $10,000,000 to the Scottish Universities Trust, $10,000,000 to the United Kingdom Trust, and $3,750,000 to the Dunfermline Trust. These gifts fairly picture Carnegie's conception of the best ways to improve the status of the common man. They represent all his personal tastes,—

his love of books, art, music, and nature—and the reforms which he regarded as most essential to human progress,—scientific research, education both literary and technical, and, above all, the abolition of war. The expenditure the public most associates with Carnegie's name is that for public libraries. Carnegie himself frequently said that his favorite benefaction was the Hero Fund,—among other reasons, because "it came up my ain back"; but probably deep in his own mind his library gifts took precedence over all others in importance. There was only one genuine remedy, he believed, for the ills that beset the human race, and that was enlightenment. "Let there be light" was the motto that, in the early days, he insisted on placing in all his library buildings. As to the greatest endowment of all, the Carnegie Corporation, that was merely Andrew Carnegie in permanently organized form; it was established to carry on, after Carnegie's death, the work to which he had given personal attention in his own lifetime.

Many honors came to Carnegie. He received the Freedom of fifty-four cities, was granted honorary degrees from many institutions of learning, and was elected Lord Rector of the Universities of St. Andrews and Aberdeen. In 1908 King Edward, through Lord Morley, asked Carnegie if he would accept an "honor" at his hands. This clearly indicated a title. Carnegie declined: in becoming the world's second richest man, he had not surrendered his democratic principles; besides, such a distinction would mean the abandonment of his American citizenship, which he regarded as a priceless possession. All his active days Carnegie advocated world peace and arbitration; in his final years, especially as he saw the great conflagration approaching, this became his absorbing interest. Besides his peace endowments, he built the Peace Palace at The Hague, made a visit to Kaiser William II in 1907, and corresponded with that potentate on the same subject. How deeply world peace entered into Carnegie's being became painfully apparent on the outbreak of war in August 1914. Up to that time, though nearly eighty years old, he retained his activity of mind and body. He was never the same man afterward. He approved Great Britain's declaration of war, and strongly indorsed American participation in 1917. But he rapidly became a very old man, and died, at his summer home, "Shadowbrook," Mass., on Aug. 11, 1919, in his eighty-fourth year. He was survived by his wife and one daughter, Margaret Carnegie (Mrs. Roswell Miller). He was buried in Sleepy Hollow on the Hudson.

[There is as yet no adequate biography of Andrew Carnegie, though his personal papers are of great extent and value. The best account of his life is his own *Autobiography* published (and edited by John C. Van Dyke) in 1920. It is racy in style, full of character, and extremely entertaining, though most incomplete as a record of Carnegie's life,—which it was never intended to be. Wm. T. Stead's *Mr. Carnegie's Conundrum: £40,000,000: What shall I do with it?* (1900) has considerable biographical material. Bernard Alderson's *Andrew Carnegie* (1902) is a popular sketch. *The Inside Hist. of the Carnegie Steel Company* by Jas. Howard Bridge (1903) has little value as history because all too obvious purpose is to "muckrake" the great steel magnate. Herbert Casson's *The Romance of Steel* (1907) is sprightly, informative, and accurate. *A Carnegie Anthology* (1915) privately printed, by Margaret Barclay Wilson, is a most valuable compendium of Carnegie's opinions and philosophy. There are hundreds of articles on Carnegie in the magazines and newspapers of all countries, and scores of books and biographies contain passages concerning him. Carnegie's own bibliography, consisting of books, magazine articles and speeches, is a long one. His most important books are: *Round the World* (1881); *An American Four-in-Hand in Britain* (1883); *Triumphant Democracy* (1886, revised 1893); *The Gospel of Wealth* (collected essays, 1901); *The Empire of Business* (1902); *James Watt* (1905); and *Problems of To-day* (1908). *A Book of Carnegie Libraries*, by Thos. Wesley Koch (1917) is a complete history of its subject, and *A Manual of the Public Benefactions of Andrew Carnegie* (1919), published by the Carnegie Endowment for International Peace, is a statistical study, with much historical matter, of the practical outcome of Carnegie's "Gospel."]

B. J. H.

CARNEY, THOMAS (Aug. 20, 1824–July 28, 1888), governor of Kansas, the son of James and Sarah Carney, was born on a small farm in Delaware County, Ohio. When Thomas was four years old, his father died, and the boy remained with his mother to help support the family until he was nineteen. Having secured a common-school education, he took a position with a wholesale house in Cincinnati, of which in June 1852 he became a partner. He was married in 1851 to Rebecca Ann Canaday of Kenton, Ohio. Carney, Swift & Company soon became one of the most prosperous and best-known mercantile firms in the Middle West. Several years of strenuous effort here impaired his health. Desiring to recuperate and to find a new location he purchased a farm in Illinois and engaged temporarily in the live-stock business. In 1858 or 1859 he removed to Leavenworth, Kan., where he and Thomas Stevens established a wholesale house which soon did a large business. Later he became the sole proprietor of two successful wholesale houses in St. Louis. He was elected a member of the Kansas legislature in 1861. His ability and service soon brought him into favorable notice. In September 1862 he received the Republican nomination for governor and a few weeks later was elected by a majority of 4,627 votes over W. R. Wagstaff, his opponent. He then arranged to withdraw his attention from business and to give his en-

tire time and energy to the duties of his office.

An able executive was badly needed. The state's credit was poor and its treasury empty. There were dangers incident to civil war. Guerrilla bands from Missouri threatened the state on the eastern side and hostile Indians menaced its western settlements. Under the leadership of the new governor the legislature voted a bond issue sufficient to provide for the needs of the state. Being a rich man, Carney personally endorsed the bonds and guaranteed the payment of both principal and interest when due. They were then readily sold at a satisfactory price. A military patrol was organized for the eastern counties of the state and paid from the Governor's private funds until Federal troops for guard duty were available. It was after this change was made that the Quantrill's guerrillas slipped across the border, sacked the town of Lawrence on July 21, 1863, and murdered not less than one hundred and fifty unarmed men.

During Carney's administration the state's penal, philanthropic, and higher educational institutions were established. In February 1864 he was elected United States senator for the term beginning Mar. 4, 1865. As this election was held in advance of the usual time and its legality doubtful he never claimed the seat. In the fall of 1864 he called out the entire militia of the state, 12,622 in number, to resist Gen. Price who had invaded Missouri and eastern Kansas. In January 1865 Carney retired to private life with an excellent record as a public official. His remaining years were uneventful.

[*Kansas Annual Reg.* (1864); D. W. Wilder, *Annals of Kansas* (1875–86); Wm. G. Cutler, ed., *Hist. of Kansas* (1883); Frank W. Blackmar, ed., *A Cyc. of Kansas Hist.* (1912); *Kansas Hist. Colls.*, vols. VIII (1904), XI (1910), XII (1912); *Portrait and Biog. Rec. of Leavenworth, Douglas and Franklin Counties, Kan.* (1899); *Leavenworth Evening Standard*, July 28, 1888; *Topeka Daily Capital*, July 29, 1888; the Carney family records.]

T. L. H.

CARNOCHAN, JOHN MURRAY (July 4, 1817–Oct. 28, 1887), surgeon, was born in Savannah, Ga. He was the son of John Carnochan, a wealthy Scotch merchant and planter, and of Harriet Frances Putnam, a collateral descendant of Gen. Israel Putnam [*q.v.*]. On account of delicate health he was raised in Scotland, in the Carnochan homestead (Gate House, Fleet, Kirkcudbright, Galloway) and in Edinburgh, where he graduated from the high school and University (1834) and began the study of medicine. Summoned home, he completed his medical studies in New York, registering as a pupil with Valentine Mott [*q.v.*], who was to speak of him later as "his most distinguished pupil." It was at this period that he made a remarkable minute dissection of the human foot. Having received the degree of M.D. from the College of Physicians and Surgeons, New York, in 1836, he at once returned to Europe for post-graduate study, spending six full years in the Paris hospitals, walking the hospital wards with the leading local surgeons, including such men as Lisfranc, Velpeau, and Civiale. He then removed to London where he studied surgery under Sir Astley Cooper and Sir Benjamin Brodie and was offered a partnership by the surgeon Liston. He did not return to America until 1847, when he located in New York as a general practitioner. In 1851 he received the appointment of surgeon-in-chief of the new State Emigrant Hospital at Ward's Island, then the largest in the country, while from 1851 to 1862 he was professor of surgery at the New York Medical College. Beginning in 1851 he performed and published an account of a brilliant series of operations which gave him an international reputation, and in 1858 he published his first series of *Contributions to Operative Surgery and Surgical Pathology*. Among his surgical pioneer efforts were: the cure of an apparently incurable case of elephantiasis Arabum by ligation of the femoral artery; the removal of the entire lower jaw for post-typhoid necrosis; the exsection of the entire ulna with preservation of the arm functions; and the exsection of the entire superior maxillary nerve for the radical cure of neuralgia (which he performed five times). It was said of him that he had performed every capital operation, this including five cases of successful amputation at the hip joint. He had a successful record as an ovariotomist and was a pioneer in operating for congenital dislocation of the hip, on which subject he published a large monograph, *Etiology, Pathology and Treatment of Congenital Dislocation of the Head of the Femur* (1850). Among his interesting case reports was one on survival for eleven days with a bullet in the heart, the patient having been the notorious "Bill" Poole. During 1870–71, he reappeared in public life as health officer of the port. A consultation with a colleague who had been accused of flirting with homeopathic remedies led to a breach with the medical profession, terminated by Carnochan's resignation from the New York County Medical Society. From that period his chief interest was in the New York Medico-Legal Society. Continuing to publish his *Contributions to Operative Surgery*, he issued a series in 1877–78 and was at work on another volume when stricken with apoplexy. His last monograph, *Cerebral Localization in Relation to*

Insanity, appeared in 1884. Upon his death he was highly eulogized as a surgeon and man by the Medico-Legal Society. His wife, Estelle Morris, a lineal descendant of Lewis Morris [*q.v.*], was an accomplished artist who illustrated his papers.

[S. W. Francis, "Biographical Sketches of Distinguished Living N. Y. Surgeons," *Medic. and Surgic. Reporter*, XI, 383, June 18, 1864; Clark Bell and others in *Medico-Legal Jour.*, 1887–88, V, 346.]

E. P.

CARONDELET, FRANCISCO LUIS HECTOR, Baron de (c. 1748–Aug. 10, 1807), governor of Louisiana and West Florida, was born at Noyelles, Flanders. He belonged to a distinguished Burgundian family, originally from Poligny and Dole, which had played an important part in the political and artistic life of Burgundy in the fifteenth and sixteenth centuries ("Mémoire sur L'Abbaye de Montbenoit et sur les Carondelet" in *Mémoires de L'Académie de Besançon*, 1865–67). He was the son of Juan Luis Nicolas de Carondelet, Baron de Carondelet y de Noyelles, Viscount hereditary of Langle, Lord of Hernue, Hayne-Saint-Pierre, la Hestre and Briâtre, and of Rosa Plunkett of Dunsany (daughter of Edward Plunkett, Baron Dunsany in the Irish peerage, and of Maria de Alen). He himself married into an influential Spanish family, for his brother-in-law, Luis de las Casas, was captain-general of Cuba and of Louisiana and the Floridas during Carondelet's administration in Louisiana. The Baron was a man of energy, moderately enlightened, conscientious, tenacious, and brave. He devoted himself to public works, built a canal that gave New Orleans an outlet to the Gulf by way of Lake Pontchartrain, reformed the police and instituted a street lighting system in the capital, strove to ameliorate the condition of the slaves, risked his career to protect the commerce of Louisiana against the unwise policy of the Spanish Court, and labored incessantly to repel the rising tide of American frontiersmen and to extend Spain's dominion over the whole of the Mississippi Valley. Despite his family connections and personal merit, his administration was most unfortunate for Spain, for the province, and for Carondelet himself. His task was one of extreme difficulty, and he was not fitted for it by either temperament or training. The pressure of the American frontiersmen and their government, the schemes of Genêt, G. R. Clark, and William Blount, the restiveness of the French Creoles, the menace of a servile insurrection, the vagaries of powerful Indian tribes and their British traders, the incompetent meddling of a distant court—in these were problems to tax a master mind; and Carondelet was a man of quite ordinary mentality. He came to his border province, from the governorship of San Salvador in Guatemala, utterly ignorant of the English language and of local conditions. He was slow to learn, loath to take the advice of his better informed subordinates, and unable to discriminate between the false and the true, the fantastic and the probable, in the many wild rumors that came to his ears from all quarters of America and Europe.

Accompanied by his wife and daughter, he arrived at New Orleans in the twenty-ninth year of his service of the king, and on Dec. 30, 1791, he took over the government and intendancy of Louisiana and West Florida. One of the first problems that received his attention was that of Indian relations. He succeeded in capturing the interloper, W. A. Bowles, in persuading Alexander McGillivray to renounce his connection with the United States, in promoting the interests of the Anglo-Spanish fur traders, Panton, Leslie & Company, among the Southern Indians, in forming a defensive alliance with the four Southern tribes (October 1793), and in instigating the Indians to attack the American frontiersmen. He revived the separatist intrigue with James Wilkinson and other American frontiersmen, built a fleet of gunboats on the Mississippi, and extended Spain's military frontier by establishing additional posts within the territory in dispute with the United States. He made land grants to the victims of Gallipolis and to the Baron de Bastrop, and otherwise sought to stimulate the growth of Louisiana. His very successes, however, only embarrassed his government, for they were a heavy tax on the disordered finances of Spain, and offended the United States at a critical moment. His domestic policy was equally unfortunate. Arbitrary arrests alienated the Creoles, and lax enforcement of the commercial restrictions led to his removal from the intendancy in October 1793. After the treaty of San Lorenzo was signed (1795), he had some influence in delaying its execution, and continued the Kentucky intrigue with unabated vigor. On Aug. 5, 1797, he closed his term of office as governor of Louisiana, having been named president of the Royal Audiencia and governor general of Quito. On June 20, 1798, he was ordered to take possession of this post, and on Feb. 20, 1799, he reported that he had done so. He was granted release from the position on May 11, 1807, but died on Aug. 10, 1807, while still discharging his duties. He was buried in the vault of St. Peter of the Cathedral Church of the city of Quito (according to documents now in the private archives of the Duke of Bailen).

[A. P. Whitaker, *Spanish-American Frontier* (1927); "Spain and the Cherokee Indians, 1783–98," *N. C. Hist. Rev.*, IV, 252; Jane M. Berry, "The Indian Policy of Spain in the Southwest, 1783–95," *Miss. Valley Hist. Rev.*, III, 462; Manuel Serrano y Sanz, *El Brigadier Jaime Wilkinson . . .* (Madrid, 1915); *España y los Indios Cherokis y Chactas . . .* (Seville, 1916); Chas. Gayarré, *Hist. of La.* (1903), vol. III; F. X. Martin, *Hist. of La.* (1882); Alcée Fortier, *Hist. of La.* (1904), vol. II; *Am. Hist. Rev.*, II, 475–505; information from José Ma. Ots, director técnico de estudios del Instituto Hispano-Cubano.]   A.P.W.

CARPENTER, CYRUS CLAY (Nov. 24, 1829–May 29, 1898), governor of Iowa, was born of pioneer stock at Harford, Susquehanna County, Pa. His parents were Asahel and Amanda M. (Thayer) Carpenter. As a boy he worked on the farm and acquired the rudiments of an education by attending the neighborhood school in the winter. In order to prepare himself to teach he enrolled in the academy at Harford. At eighteen he began teaching school, and for the next four years divided his time between teaching and attending the academy. He chose Iowa as his future home because "he liked the looks of it on the map." On his way he stopped for two years in Licking County, Ohio, where he taught school and worked on a farm in the summer. With his meager savings he again set out for the West, arriving at Fort Dodge in the summer of 1854 without funds, but endowed with robust health, a good education for that day, and ambition to become a leader. At Fort Dodge he became the first school-teacher of the community. He also engaged in the task of surveying land, and was chosen county surveyor in 1856. In the midst of these various duties he studied law and in due time was admitted to the bar. In the early spring of 1857 he joined the relief expedition from Fort Dodge to the scene of the Spirit Lake Massacre. He never forgot the hardships suffered on this journey through deep drifts of snow and the bitter cold of northwestern Iowa. Later in 1857 he was elected to a seat in the Iowa General Assembly. At the outbreak of the Civil War he enlisted as a private, but soon received a commission as captain, serving in turn on the staff of W. S. Rosecrans, Grenville M. Dodge, and John A. Logan. With the rank of lieutenant-colonel, he was commissary of subsistence in Sherman's army on the march to the sea. At the close of the war, he was mustered out with the rank of colonel by brevet. His dependability and good judgment had enabled him to perform his laborious duties in a faithful and efficient manner that won the commendation of his superior officers. In 1864 he married Susan C. Burkholder of Fort Dodge. Both were lovers of good literature and their home was "rich with the atmosphere of books." In 1866 Carpenter was elected register of the land office by the Republicans of Iowa. He spent two terms in this capacity, and then became the candidate of his party for governor. He was elected to this office in 1871, and reëlected in 1873. His administration was during a period of adjustment, years of industrial and social transition. State control of the railroads was a paramount issue. The Governor's attitude in this controversy was clearly indicated by his oft-quoted phrase, "the exorbitant railway rate is the skeleton in the Iowa corn crib." The so-called "Granger Law" regulating railroads in Iowa was passed during his administration. Carpenter also took a firm stand in favor of adequate support for state institutions. At the close of his second term as governor he was appointed second comptroller of the Treasury of the United States, and served in that capacity nearly two years. In 1878 he accepted a position on the newly-created railroad commission in Iowa, but soon resigned in order to run for Congress. Twice elected to the House of Representatives, he occupied a seat in that body from 1879 to 1883. Perhaps his most distinguished service in Congress was his successful support of the measure to create a Department of Agriculture (*Congressional Record*, 47 Cong., 1 Sess., XIII, pp. 3719–23). In 1884 he was again elected to the General Assembly of Iowa where his age and experience made him much respected. In his later years he served as postmaster of Fort Dodge.

[Sen. J. P. Dolliver, "Ex-Gov. Cyrus C. Carpenter," in the *Midland Mo.*, X, 75–81; Benj. F. Gue, *Hist. of Iowa from the Earliest Times to the Beginning of the Twentieth Century* (1903), IV, 42; numerous references in the *Official Records* (Army); Carpenter's own account of the Spirit Lake expedition and sketches of Civil War days in the *Annals of Iowa*, 3 ser., III, 481–91; his official utterances as governor of Iowa in *The Messages and Proclamations of the Governors of Iowa*, ed. by Benj. F. Shambaugh, IV (1903), 3–279; his speeches in the Forty-sixth and the Forty-seventh Congress in the *Cong. Record*, vols. IX to XIV (see Index).] B. E. M.

CARPENTER, EDMUND JANES (Oct. 16, 1845–Feb. 21, 1924), journalist and author, found in his New England background and ancestry absorbing interests to which he gave expression in several of his printed books. On his father's side, he was descended from William Carpenter who came to Weymouth, Mass., in 1638, in the ship *Bevis*. On his mother's side he was descended from Jonathan Walcott, who was in Salem at least as early as 1662. He, himself, was born in North Attleboro, Mass., the son of George Moulton Carpenter, a minister, and, after his removal to Providence, R. I., about 1855, a presiding elder of the Methodist Episcopal Church, who, in 1843, married Sarah Lewis Walcott. They had two sons. The elder, also named George Moulton, was graduated from Brown University in 1864,

practised law, became a justice of the Supreme Court of Rhode Island, and afterward a federal judge. Edmund Janes was graduated from Brown in 1866, and received the degree of Litt.D. from that institution in 1905. After graduation, he tried his hand at several kinds of business, and finally found work to his liking, writing for the *Providence Journal.* Afterward, he worked successively on the *New Haven Palladium,* and on three Boston papers, the *Globe, Advertiser,* and *Transcript.* At the time of his death he had been writing for the last-named paper for twenty years. In 1873, he was married to Lydia Etta Snow of Providence, by whom he had six children. He died in Milton, Mass., which had been his home for many years.

Carpenter had a versatile mind and a facile pen. He was the author of short stories and occasional poems; contributed to magazines for young people, such as *Wide Awake* and *St. Nicholas,* and also to other magazines; made translations; wrote book reviews, editorials, and a number of books. His earliest book, *A Woman of Shawmut* (1891), published originally in serial form in the *New England Magazine,* was a romance, gracefully told, of colonial times; was based in part upon historical fact; and was the first fruit of Carpenter's interest in the story of the Massachusetts Bay and Plymouth settlements. The book was dedicated to William Dean Howells, to whom, in a dedicatory letter, Carpenter made acknowledgments for suggestion as well as for encouragement. Next, he aided William Kent in preparing the latter's *Memoirs and Letters of James Kent* (1898). With the acquisition of the Hawaiian Islands, Carpenter wrote *America in Hawaii* (1899), a compact and useful historical statement of the relations between the islands and the United States which led to annexation. *The American Advance* (1903) is a similar statement of the territorial expansion of the United States. A different interest is revealed in his *Hellenic Tales* (1906), stories for boys and girls, published also the same year under the title *Long Ago in Greece.* In later works Carpenter returned to his studies of New England colonial history. His *Roger Williams* (1909), based on original sources, presented in fluent style a well tempered rather than controversial account. Following this study came *The Pilgrims and Their Monument* (1918), the latter inscribed "To the memory of my far-away kinswoman, Alice Carpenter, wife of Governor Bradford."

[*Boston Transcript*, Feb. 21, 1924; Arthur S. Walcott, *The Walcott Book* (1925); Amos B. Carpenter, *A Geneal. Hist. of the Rehoboth Branch of the Carpenter Family in America* (1898); *Hist. Cat. Brown Univ.* (1914).] W. A. S.

CARPENTER, FRANCIS BICKNELL

(Aug. 6, 1830–May 23, 1900), portrait painter, was born at Homer, N. Y., the son of a farmer, Asaph A. Carpenter. As a boy he sketched pictures on smooth pieces of board and leaves torn from old account books. Later he watched an itinerant painter at work and attempted to imitate him with the crude materials that a moneyless country boy might find about the farm,—lampblack used for marking sheep, old dried lumps of Venetian red, worn carriage painters' brushes. Finally his father allowed him to spend five months at Syracuse with an artist named Sanford Thayer. With only so much training, Carpenter, now sixteen years old, set up a studio in his native village. His first big fee was ten dollars for illustrating a book on sheep husbandry by Henry Stephens Randall [q.v.], who, delighted with the pictures of the sheep, immediately ordered his own portrait. Thus encouraged, Carpenter sent examples of his work to competitions in New York, was successful, and in 1851 moved to the metropolis. The next year he married Augusta H. Prentiss, by whom he had a son and a daughter, and was made an associate of the Academy of Design. A full-length portrait of President Fillmore established his reputation, and for a number of years he enjoyed a large measure of popularity, the list of his sitters including many notable men of letters, divines, and statesmen, among them four presidents of the United States. A gentle, meditative man, with long, straight black hair and delicate features, he readily won the regard of his patrons. His exalted patriotism and generous humanitarian sympathies are expressed in a memorable historical painting of Lincoln reading the first draft of the Emancipation Proclamation to his cabinet, which now hangs in the Capitol at Washington. For painting this picture he was accorded unusual facilities. From February to July 1864, he was "turned loose"—as Lincoln put it—in the White House, setting up his huge canvas in the East Room and living on friendly terms with the President and his fractious cabinet. A second product of this association was his *Six Months at the White House* (1866), which in a subsequent edition was misnamed *The Inner Life of Abraham Lincoln* (1867). The book has an artless charm as well as the value of direct testimony. Carpenter's later career was comparatively uneventful. As a friend of Theodore Tilton, he was sucked into the vortex of the Beecher-Tilton scandal and thrown out again, disheveled and humiliated. For the last few years of his life he suffered from dropsy. He died in New York, May 23, 1900.

[*Who's Who in America*, 1899–1900; F. B. Perkins, *The Picture and the Men* (1867); *N. Y. Herald*, May 24, 1900; C. F. Marshall, *The True History of the Brooklyn Scandal* (1874); J. E. P. Doyle, *Plymouth Church and Its Pastor* (1874); J. C. Derby, *Fifty Years among Authors, Books, and Publishers* (1884).]   G. H. G.

CARPENTER, FRANK GEORGE

(May 8 1855–June 18, 1924), journalist, traveler, author, the son of George F. and Jennette Carpenter, was born at Mansfield, Ohio. He received the degrees of A.B. and A.M. from the University of Wooster, Ohio, in 1877 and 1880. In 1879 he became legislative correspondent at Columbus of the *Cleveland Leader*. His health was so frail that when he married Joanna D. Condict, of Mansfield, in 1883, she was told by a friend that he would not live a year. In Washington, where he went as correspondent for the *Cleveland Leader*, he was at first obliged to spend much time in bed, but by dictating letters to his wife he was able to do his work. In 1888, accompanied by his wife and a new machine called a "caligraph," he started around the world, having formed his own syndicate by arranging with fifteen newspapers to publish his weekly foreign travel letters. So began the travels which extended over thirty-six years, took Carpenter to nearly every part of the world, and resulted in hundreds of syndicate articles and many books. A small son and daughter prevented Mrs. Carpenter from going on later trips as his secretary, but she was his business manager at home, collecting and filing geographical clippings, having his letters typed and sent out, and handling the finances of his syndicate. On some trips his daughter Frances traveled with him as secretary. The articles and the geographical readers and volumes of travel which grew out of them were intended, he said, "for ordinary people like myself . . . and for boys and girls." His public has always appreciated his writing. Numerous adults have found entertainment and geographical education in the Carpenter letters and there are few school children who do not know and love the Carpenter *Readers*, with their simple language, anecdotes, and interesting descriptions. Carpenter's method was to take the children on an imaginary tour and to point out in each country what would interest and instruct them. His *Readers* include: *Asia* (1897); *North America* (1898); *South America* (1899); *Europe* (1902); *Australia, Our Colonies, and Other Islands of the Sea* (1904); *Africa* (1905). The series of *Readers on Commerce and Industry* includes: *How the World is Fed* (1907); *How the World is Clothed* (1908); and *How the World is Housed* (1911). Though possessing successively several comfortable homes in

Washington, Carpenter's favorite home, after 1896, was on a mountain top in the Blue Ridge, Virginia. The mountain, entirely owned and named Joannasberg after Mrs. Carpenter, was crowned by a rambling stone house, with a smaller stone house for library and workshop. There worked, with careful consideration for rest periods, a small, wiry man, never weighing over 115 pounds, with sandy hair, homely features, and blue eyes twinkling through gold-rimmed eyeglasses. After Mrs. Carpenter's death in 1920, Carpenter lived at the Cosmos Club in Washington. In 1918 he gave up his syndicate in order to revise his *Readers,* but in 1921 he formed a new syndicate and began writing a series of *World Travels* (20 vols., published). For this purpose he started on fresh journeys. Attacks of illness failed to discourage him; his last overtook him at Nanking, China.

[*Who's Who in America,* 1922–23; *Washington Evening Star,* June 18, 1924; *Washington Post,* June 18, 1924; a series of three articles written by his daughter, Mrs. Frances Carpenter Huntington, of Washington, D. C., for the Carpenter syndicate newspapers (*Boston Globe, Dallas News, Boisé Capital News, Columbia State, Detroit News, Peoria Star, Raleigh News and Observer*), Mar. 1, 8, 15, 1925; additional information furnished by Mrs. Huntington.]   S. G. B.

CARPENTER, FRANKLIN REUBEN (Nov. 5, 1848–Apr. 1, 1910), mining engineer, was descended from a Sussex family which came to America with William Penn. He was born in Parkersburg, W. Va. His father, John Woodward Carpenter, died when Franklin was less than four years old. His mother, Sarah Rebecca (Taylor) Carpenter became a teacher at the Broaddus Seminary at Clarksburg and later was postmistress there, but she was financially unable to give her son the education he craved. At sixteen he was apprenticed to a jeweler and watchmaker but continued his studies under Dr. Late, the village physician, until he secured a teacher's certificate and was thus enabled to earn a better salary. He saved enough money to take a course in civil engineering at Rector's College in Pruntytown, W. Va. In December 1874 he was married to Annette Howe of Athens, Ohio. In 1878 he opened an engineering office in Georgetown, Colo., where he had been principal of the schools. Some of his work for the next few years included the first survey of the "loop" above Georgetown, and the location of the Loveland Pass Tunnel. In 1886 he went to the Black Hills, attracted by the tin deposits. The following year he became dean of the Territorial (Dakota) School of Mines from which position he resigned two years later. From that time on, his life was devoted to mining engineering. At Deadwood he erected the Deadwood and Delaware Smelter and developed a new mode of operation in semipyritic smelting. In 1900 health conditions in his family necessitated his moving from the Black Hills. He went to Denver where he maintained a consulting mining engineering practise for the rest of his life. In 1904 he successfully turned his attention to the electrostatic concentration of the ores of the Nonesuch Copper Mine at Lake Superior. His last important work was the application of the Longmaid-Henderson process to the treatment of Sudbury copper ores, in which he showed that copper could be rendered soluble while the nickel remained insoluble, and a raw material for making nickel steel in the open-hearth furnace could be made by smelting the residual iron oxide for nickel-bearing pig iron. He contributed a score or more of valuable papers to the technical press, including "Ore-Deposits of the Black Hills of Dakota" and "Pyritic Smelting in the Black Hills" (published in the *Transactions of the American Institute of Mining and Metallurgical Engineers,* XVII, 570–98, XXX, 764–77). While in South Dakota he wrote a book on the geology of the Black Hills. He held a number of patents, largely on processes for treating metals.

[See brief notice in *Engineering News,* LXIII, 448, and the biographical sketch prepared by H. O. Hofman of Boston, in *Trans. Am. Inst. of Mining and Metallurgical Engineers,* vol. XLI.]   E. Y.

CARPENTER, GEORGE RICE (Oct. 25, 1863–Apr. 8, 1909), educator, author, was of old New England ancestry, the son of Charles Carroll Carpenter and Feronia N. (Rice) Carpenter. He was born at the Eskimo River Mission Station, on the Labrador coast, where his parents were engaged in pioneer missionary service. After preparation at Phillips Academy, Andover, he entered Harvard with the class of 1886, and on graduation gained the Rogers Fellowship, which took him abroad for two years of further study, chiefly at Paris and Berlin. On his return he became an instructor in English at Harvard (1888–90), then assistant professor at the Massachusetts Institute of Technology (till 1893), whence he was called to the chair of rhetoric at Columbia University, where he remained until death. At Columbia he showed the remarkable gifts of vision and direction which soon made him one of the natural builders of a rapidly expanding university coping with large and new problems; in various executive and advisory offices, and as leader or participant in nearly every forward movement of the institution, he exerted an influence that will long be felt in its policy. But he overspent his strength in work which, however ably done, was not of his first choice, and died on the threshold of far greater usefulness and power.

His publications were of two main kinds. He wrote and edited a large number of text-books concerned mainly with rhetoric and literary history; and if such books can scarcely win a lasting fame, the unusually high standard they set both to teachers and to publishers should not go unrecorded. More than any of his friends, he regretted that such labors, added to heavy administrative burdens, left too little time for that other work of research and criticism which was always the interest of his heart. Yet from the brilliant *Episode of the Donna Pietosa* (1888), which won him the prize of the Dante Society and a reputation among Dantists here and abroad, through a considerable body of critical writing which includes an excellent sketch of Longfellow (1901), in the Beacon Biographies, to the distinguished treatment of Whittier (1903), in the American Men of Letters Series, and of Whitman (1909), in the English Men of Letters Series, his output was varied and uniformly thoughtful. But even if he had been able to devote a lifetime to thought and writing, it would still have been the man, rather than the author or thinker, whom his friends would have desired to commemorate for his union of clarity and mysticism, of power and simplicity and very manly winsomeness.

[Articles by Wm. T. Brewster in the *Columbia Univ. Quart.*, June 1909 (with portrait), and by Jefferson B. Fletcher in the *Annual Report of the Dante Society*, Boston, 1909, pp. 7–9. A complete bibliography by H. R. Steeves is in the *Columbia Univ. Quart.*, Sept. 1909.]

E. H. W.

CARPENTER, MATTHEW HALE (Dec. 22, 1824–Feb. 24, 1881), lawyer, senator, the son of Ira and Esther Ann (Luce) Carpenter, was born in Moretown, Vt. His baptismal name was "Merritt Hammond," but not liking it, he later changed it to "Matthew Hale." His father was a man of little formal education, but of considerable influence in his community. Frail in body and precocious in mind, young Carpenter did not develop the interests usual with American youth, and he showed early two traits that ever remained with him, a cordial dislike for manual work and a great avidity for books. At fourteen he made his home with Paul Dillingham, a lawyer of Waterbury, Vt., later prominent in politics. At eighteen he entered West Point, but, chafing under military discipline, resigned and resumed his legal studies, first with Dillingham and later with Rufus Choate at Boston. Instead of remaining with either of his masters, however, he migrated to Wisconsin and settled at Beloit in June 1848. Caroline Dillingham,

youngest daughter of his benefactor, became his wife in 1855. As an ardent Democrat of the Douglas stripe he participated in the presidential campaigns of 1848, 1852, and 1856, but he did not himself accept political preferment. In the middle fifties he took up residence in Milwaukee and became for a short time the partner of E. G. Ryan, later chief justice of the Wisconsin supreme court. When the Civil War issues drew men into public controversy, Carpenter urged the election of Douglas so that secession on the part of the South would not be precipitated, something he considered inevitable if Lincoln were elected. He did not, however, believe that Republican success justified secession; that step he considered treason. Physical defects alone prevented him from taking the field. By speeches and public letters he urged vigorous prosecution of the war against the Confederates, and in 1862, in answer to the famous Ryan address—the Democratic platform of that year which arraigned Lincoln's war measures—Carpenter wrote a communication in defense of the government.

In the rôle of legal advocate Carpenter helped to shape the Reconstruction policy of the North. In the Garland case he represented an ex-Confederate, pardoned by President Johnson, who tried to establish his right to practise in United States courts; and in the case of William H. McCardle, a Mississippi editor sentenced by a military tribunal, he pleaded the cause of the United States government. This latter case involved the constitutionality of the military governments in the South as established by the Reconstruction measures of Congress. Though acting in the capacity of attorney in the interest of his clients, his arguments in both instances were in conformity with his views on Reconstruction; namely, that once rebel citizens and rebel states were restored to their position in the Union, they were entitled to full equality with other citizens and other states, but until that restoration had been effected, Congress, the omnipotent political body, had broad discretionary powers as to the method to be used in achieving that end.

Political recognition did not come to Carpenter until 1869, in which year the Republican legislature of Wisconsin sent him to the Senate. There he identified himself, for the most part, with the Radical supporters of President Grant. In one of his greatest public speeches, that at Janesville, June 26, 1873, he courageously but unwisely discussed the two most dangerous issues of the day, the "Salary Grab" and the Crédit Mobilier. He had voted for the salary increase and this mistake was not offset by his vote for its repeal the following year. Besides he had a reputation for indiscreet personal conduct and had won the enmity of the railroads by securing unfavorable decisions from the courts and by advocating federal control of interstate commerce. These obstacles proved insurmountable when he was a candidate for reëlection in 1875; even his friend, Boss E. W. Keyes, could not rally to him the united support of the party. In one of the most bitter and exciting senatorial contests in the history of the state, Carpenter was defeated by a coalition of Democrats and dissenting Republicans, most of whom were followers of the Senator's rival, the former governor, C. C. Washburn. Upon leaving the Senate, Carpenter established an office in Washington and became the attorney in two cases of nation-wide significance. He represented Secretary of War Belknap in his impeachment trial, and a little later Samuel Tilden before the electoral commission. These two unpopular causes did him no permanent harm, for when Senator Howe's third term expired in 1879, Carpenter, who had rehabilitated his political fortunes, was victor in a triangular contest between himself, the incumbent, and Boss Keyes. His second term in the Senate was cut short by his death.

[Frank A. Flower, *Life of Matthew Hale Carpenter, A View of the Honors and Achievements That in the Am. Republic are Traits of Well Directed Ambition and Persistent Industry* (Madison, 1883); Alexander MacDonald Thomson, *A Political Hist. of Wis.* (2nd ed., 1902), pp. 163–207, 308–09; John B. Cassoday, "Matthew Hale Carpenter," in *Report of the Proc. of the Meeting of the State Bar Ass. Mar. 13, 14, 1906* (Madison, 1907), pp. 155–93; "Memorial .Addresses on the Life and Character of Matthew H. Carpenter" in *Cong. Record*, 47 Cong., 1 Sess.; *Proc. of the Bench and Bar of the Supreme Court of the U. S. in Memoriam, Matthew H. Carpenter* (1881); "Death of Matthew Hale Carpenter" in 52 *Wis. Reports*, 23–36.]   H.J.D.

CARPENTER, STEPHEN CULLEN (died c. 1820), journalist, was of Irish birth, but "led by a truant disposition into the world" (*Monthly Register, Magazine and Review of the United States,* preface to Volume II, 1806). He is reputed to have been a Parliamentary reporter for the trial of Warren Hastings (Allibone, *Dictionary of British and American Authors,* 1863). This tradition is lent color by the fact that in 1804 he reported a murder trial in Charleston (*Report of the Trial of Richard Dennis for the Murder of James Shaw on Aug. 20, 1804, by S. C. Carpenter,* 1805) and by the further fact as evidenced by his editorial writing that he had an intimate knowledge of contemporary English politics. He came to Charleston not later than 1802 (see *People's Friend* for Apr. 10, 1807). In 1803 he established there in partnership with Loring Andrews the Charleston *Courier,* which

was strongly federalist in tone. He undertook in addition to this the editing of a literary and historical review, the *Monthly Register, Magazine and Review of the United States.* In this he published his history of the American Revolution, and articles, strongly Whig in viewpoint, on the history and state of English politics. He had brought out only a few numbers of this magazine, before he removed with it to New York in 1806. There with the assistance of Elias Hicks he took over the *Daily Advertiser* which he issued from Sept. 1, 1806 to Aug. 3, 1807 as the *People's Friend.* He contributed articles and editorials intended to prove that in the United States of his day "the Forms of a free and the Ends of an Arbitrary Government are not incompatible." He was almost exclusively concerned with national politics, and grew more and more bitter in his opposition to the French, and more determined to save the country "from the colossal power and dark intrigues of Bonaparte." This national partisanship probably cost him his editorship, and in August 1807 the paper was taken over by its former proprietor, Samuel Bayard (*Daily Advertiser,* Aug. 4, 1807). Carpenter then moved to Philadelphia and published there a magazine devoted to the drama under the title, the *Mirror of Taste and Dramatic Censor.* Four volumes appeared in a year and then the magazine disappeared. In 1809 he published a prejudiced life of Jefferson which was embedded in a violently anti-French history of the United States, *Memoirs of Jefferson, Containing a Concise History of the United States, from the Acknowledgement of their Independence, with a View of the Rise and Progress of French Influence and French Principles in that Country.* In 1815 he brought out *Select American Speeches, Forensic and Parliamentary, with Prefatory Remarks; a Sequel to Dr. Chapman's Select Speeches.* He is thought to have spent his latter years in the government employ at Washington, and to have died there about 1820.

[Most of the brief notices dealing with Carpenter are inaccurate. Allibone, *Dict. of Brit. and Am. Authors,* is responsible for crediting him with the authorship of *An Overland Journey to India* under the pseudonym of "Donald Campbell." The *Dict. of Nat. Biog.* (English) attributes it to an authentic Donald Campbell. Most of the information concerning his life is to be found in scattered statements in the *People's Friend* and in the *Monthly Reg. Mag. and Rev. of the U. S.*]   M.A.M.

CARPENTER, STEPHEN HASKINS (Aug. 7, 1831–Dec. 7, 1878), educator, son of Calvin G. Carpenter, was born at Little Falls, Herkimer County, N. Y. His early education was obtained at his own home and at Munro Academy, Elbridge, N. Y. In 1848 he entered Madison University, Hamilton, N. Y., where he spent his first two college years, transferring to the University of Rochester, from which he was graduated in 1852. Coming at once to Wisconsin, he was appointed tutor in succession to Obadiah Milton Conover, holding the position for two years. During the four succeeding years he was editor and one of the publishers of the *Daily Patriot,* and later of the *Western Fireside,* whereupon he became assistant state superintendent of public instruction in Wisconsin, which position he held from 1858 to 1860. He had been married in 1856 to Frances Curtis of Madison. In 1860 he was appointed professor of ancient languages in St. Paul's College, Palmyra, Mo., holding this position until the Civil War compelled the closing of the institution. Returning to Wisconsin, he was engaged in various enterprises, serving as city clerk of Madison, 1864–68, and clerk of the board of education, 1865–72. In 1868 he was appointed professor of rhetoric and English literature in the University of Wisconsin in succession to Daniel Read who had been elected president of the University. The title of the professorship was changed in 1874 to logic and English literature. In 1875 Carpenter was elected to the presidency of the University of Kansas, but declined the appointment. His premature death occurred at Geneva, N. Y., of diphtheria which had already proved fatal to his brother and a nephew, a few days before.

The versatility of Carpenter's interests is shown in his continued participation in civil affairs, in a volume of educational addresses, a collection of "Songs for the Sabbath School," a volume of twelve lectures on Christian evidences, translations from the French, papers on logic and metaphysics in the *Transactions of the Wisconsin Academy of Sciences, Arts, and Letters,* and in his contributions in the field of Anglo-Saxon and early English languages, on which, in addition to his great power as a teacher, rest his claims to remembrance. In 1872 he published *English of the Fourteenth Century,* a critical study of the English of Chaucer. In 1875 he issued a text-book, *An Introduction to the Study of the Anglo-Saxon Language,* which was widely used. His *History of the University of Wisconsin from 1849–76,* published in 1876, tells the story of the University from its founding, in 1850, through the reörganizations of 1858 and 1866. His last publication, *Elements of English Analysis* (1877), was widely used as a grammar text.

[R. B. Anderson, "Prof. Stephen Haskins Carpenter" in *Robinson's Epitome of Lit.* (1878), p. 189; C. W. Butterfield, "Univ. of Wis., Sketches Historical and Biographical," *Wis. State Jour.,* Feb. 22, 1879; R. G. Thwaites, *Univ. of Wis., Its Hist. and Alumni* (Madison, 1900); obituary in the *Wis. State Jour.,* Dec. 7, 1878, reprinted as a memorial in the *Trans. Wis. Acad. of Sci., Arts, and Letters,* IV, 318–20.] V. A. C. H.

CARR, BENJAMIN (1769–May 24, 1831), musical composer, was born and brought up in England. He was taught by the most excellent church musicians, and became known as soloist in The Antient Concerts, a London enterprise. In 1793 he emigrated, settling in Philadelphia. There he established the city's first music store, known as The Musical Repository. A branch in New York, with the same name, was sold a few years later. As composer, Carr soon became well known and deservedly popular. Some of his shorter pieces are in a manuscript collection of his, now in the New York Public Library. He was successful in many fields, orchestral as well as vocal and instrumental. His music is said to have a pleasing softness of line. His "Federal Overture" was widely known, and was given on several occasions beside that of the Norfolk concert of Oct. 7, 1796, managed by Graupner. His published works include: *Masses, Vespers, and Litanies* (1805), *Lessons in Vocal Music* (1811), *A Collection of Chants* (1816), and *The Chorister* (1820). Most ambitious among his compositions was the opera *The Archers,* produced in New York on Apr. 18, 1796, repeated there twice, and given twice in Boston. The libretto, by William Dunlap, treated the episode of William Tell; but it was weakened by the anachronism of introducing Winkelried's later sacrifice, and made trivial by the introduction of comic characters, such as the amazonian Rodolpha and the adventurous Conrad. Some effective monologues and striking contrasts gave the composer scope, but the words made the lyrics tame, and gave little chance for dramatic power in the music, though Dunlap praised the score. Only two numbers are now extant, a graceful solo entitled, "Why, huntress, why?" which deplores Rodolpha's courting of danger, and a dainty rondo from the overture. The work has been called (though wrongly) the first American opera. In 1794 Carr appeared in Arne's opera *Love in a Village,* and after that became prominent as a concert soloist, chiefly in Philadelphia. As organist he was at one time the incumbent of St. Joseph's Church, where Lafayette, Rochambeau, and other French officers attended service. Carr conducted at many concerts, often in conjunction with others, as was the fashion at that time. Soon after 1800 he edited a musical journal, and published some theoretical treatises. In 1816 he organized a practise society; and when this began to languish, he infused new vigor into it by changing it, in 1820, into the Musical Fund Society, designed to aid indigent musicians. With him on the committee were Cross (his pupil), Hupfield, and Patterson. For some years the directors' meetings were held at Carr's home, 7 Powell St. The opening concert, on Apr. 24, 1821, included a glee, "Awake, Æolian Lyre," by Danby, with "orchestra accompaniments" by Carr. Another number was Beethoven's "Grand Sinfonia in C." Carr was one of the conductors of *The Creation,* given in 1822. Other society activities included an anonymous appearance of Malibran, in 1827. The society's later historian wrote, "Above all, the personality of Benjamin Carr stands out as one who, of all the early musicians of Philadelphia, wrought most vigorously to introduce the best, chiefly in the oratorio and in the church." One may praise his concert series also, as he included works of Handel, Haydn, Pleyel, Stamitz, Linley, etc. The society erected a monument to him in St. Peter's Church. His epitaph calls him "A distinguished professor of music . . . charitable without ostentation, faithful and true in his friendships."

[Oscar G. Sonneck, *Early Concert Life in America* (Leipzig, 1907), *Early Opera in America* (N. Y., 1915), and "Early Am. Opera" in *Sammelbände der Internat. Musikgesellschaft,* VI, 428–95; Henry Simpson, *Lives of Eminent Philadelphians* (1859), pp. 186–87; "Cath. Choirs and Choir Music in Phila.," in *Am. Cath. Hist. Soc. Records,* II, 115–26; Louis Childs Madeira, *Annals of Music in Phila.* (1896).]   A.E.

CARR, DABNEY (Apr. 27, 1773–Jan. 8, 1837), jurist, was a descendant of Thomas Carr (1678–1737) of "Bear Castle," one of the first justices of Caroline County, Va., sheriff of King William County, and representative from the latter county in the House of Burgesses. Thomas Carr's son, Dabney Carr the elder, married Martha, sister of Thomas Jefferson, and their son was Dabney Carr the younger. The latter attended Hampden Sidney College, and later studied law. In 1800 he married his first cousin, Elizabeth Carr. He was closely associated in his early legal career with James Barbour [*q.v.*], William Wirt [*q.v.*], and others of like caliber. He and Wirt corresponded frequently and intimately for fully thirty-seven years. In 1807, the two friends planned to raise a legion in Virginia, should war come with Great Britain. But they took up the pen instead, and Carr was one of the contributors to Wirt's *Old Bachelor.* So good was Carr's style that Wirt advised him to take seriously to authorship. In 1811, Carr was appointed circuit judge by the Governor and Council, but when his nomination came before the Assembly, the next year, his opponents were able to defeat the confirmation of the appointment, in spite of the fact that Carr had acquitted himself creditably in the position. A new chancery district, with the seat of justice at Winchester, was created immediately, and Carr was made its chancellor. This necessitated his moving to Winchester. In 1824 he succeeded Judge Fleming in the state supreme court of appeals. Here he served with distinction until his death. He was well-read, cultured, possessed of humor and kindness of heart. In his profession he was industrious, punctual, learned, and upright.

[*Va. Mag. of Hist. and Biog.,* II, 221–28, III, 214–17, V, 441; John P. Kennedy, *Memoirs of the Life of Wm. Wirt* (2 vols., 1850); *Richmond Whig,* Jan. 10, 1837; *Southern Lit. Messenger,* IV, 65–70.]   R. L. M—n.

CARR, DABNEY SMITH (Mar. 5, 1802–Mar. 24, 1854), journalist, diplomat, was born in Albemarle County, Va., son of Peter and Hester (Smith) Carr, and nephew of Dabney Carr [*q.v.*]. His grandfather, Dabney Carr the elder, was a rival of Patrick Henry in patriotic oratory and married Martha, sister of Thomas Jefferson, while his father, a lawyer of great ability, was for a time Jefferson's private secretary but retired from public life to live in lordly elegance on his estate, "Carr's Brook." Young Dabney's career began in the counting house of his uncle, Gen. Samuel Smith, head of the firm of Smith & Buchanan, famous Baltimore merchants; but his ability as a writer and strong interest in politics led him in 1827 to found a newspaper, the *Baltimore Republican and Commercial Advertiser.* His violently partisan support of Andrew Jackson during the presidential campaign of 1828 was considered largely responsible for a sweeping victory in Maryland. For this service he was rewarded by appointment as naval officer for the port of Baltimore. To make a place for him Jackson had to remove the oldest son of Commodore Joshua Barney. This raised such a storm of criticism that for a time it was doubtful whether the Senate would consent to the President's nomination. Confirmed by a majority of one vote, Carr sold his newspaper on Apr. 16, 1829, and took up his new work. For fourteen years he held the position and became popular with local merchants through his unfailing honesty and courtesy. In 1843 President Tyler appointed him to succeed Commodore David Porter as United States minister to Turkey. There he gave six years of unostentatious but efficient service, which merited the praise of merchants, missionaries, and the Ottoman Government. Broken in health, he returned to America in 1850 and was long occupied in attempting to obtain compensation from Congress for a special mission to Syria. His wife was a daughter of Gov. W. C. Nicholas of Virginia. He died at Charlottesville, Va., and was buried at Monticello. As a political writer his style was vigorous to the point of bellicosity, though in private life he was a polished and genial gentleman.

[E. I. Carr, *The Carr Family Records* (Rockton, Ill., 1894) ; E. Woods, *Albemarle County in Va.* (Charlottesville, Va., 1901) ; J. T. Scharf, *Chronicles of Baltimore* (1874) ; *Biog. Cyc. of Md. and District of Columbia* (1882) ; *Va. Mag. of Hist. and Biog.*, II, 224 ; obituaries in *Baltimore Republican and Argus*, Mar. 28, 1854, and *Richmond* (Va.) *Enquirer*, Apr. 3, 1854.]

W.L.W.,Jr.

CARR, ELIAS (Feb. 25, 1839–July 22, 1900), governor of North Carolina, was born on the extensive and fertile "Bracebridge Farm," near Tarboro in Edgecombe County. His parents, Jonas Johnston Carr and Elizabeth Jane (Hilliard) Carr, traced their lineage back through Revolutionary fighters to Virginia emigrants who received land patents direct from the Lords Proprietors. His education was gained at the Oaks School in Orange County, the University of North Carolina, and the University of Virginia. In 1859 he married Eleanor Kearney of Warren County. Having purchased his brother's share of "Bracebridge Farm," he settled down, after the manner of his father, to its serious and intelligent cultivation. For nearly thirty years he lived the life of a country gentleman of wealth and education, entertaining his friends, raising his six children, serving his county as commissioner and his state in minor non-political ways. Then came the agrarian movement of the eighties. Disturbed by the distress of his poorer neighbors, in 1886 Carr went as state delegate to the Farmers' Convention in St. Paul and next year became president of the Farmers' Convention that met in Raleigh to foster agricultural education. When the Farmers' Alliance had been organized throughout the state, he was made its president. The year previous (1890), Alliance men had gone into the primaries of both parties and won the legislature to their program of better school facilities, especially for farmers, and regulation of railroads through a commission. Both of these movements Carr undoubtedly approved and assisted. Extreme measures such as were embodied in the St. Louis platform, however, he repudiated. Especially did he oppose the formation of a third party, fearing, it seems, that this would result in a return of negro rule, as did indeed happen a little later. In the state Democratic convention of 1892 he was nominated for governor as a compromise between the extremists of the Alliance and its opponents. This proved good party strategy, for his popularity and moderation held the party together and secured his election over a divided opposition. As governor (January 1893–January 1897) Carr suggested wholesome legislation and attended conscientiously to the state's business. "An efficient common school system," he told the legislature, "is the only hope of our people for an intelligent, thrifty laboring population upon our farms." Of roads he said, "the present system is a failure and the roads a disgrace to civilization." Unlike most of his class he was willing that taxes on realty be increased for such purposes—by constitutional amendment if necessary—though he thought, correctly enough, that intangibles should first be reached. Eschewing the exercise of political influence, he gave personal and businesslike attention to the state's institutions, especially the prison and convict farms. He supported the new railroad commission but he did not make war on railroads. Indeed his long-term lease of the state-owned North Carolina Railroad to the Southern System is now condemned by the state's historians as shortsighted policy. From the viewpoint of to-day his antagonism of the Cleveland administration seems unwise and unfortunate ; but in this he fairly represented his people. Altogether his public career exemplified the least selfish and most constructive phases of the agrarian movement. At the same time (1893–97), he was serving as first president of the North Carolina Sons of the American Revolution, of which he was a charter member. Always hospitable and jovial, he spent his remaining years pleasantly at "Bracebridge."

[There is a biographical sketch by Marshall De Lancey Haywood in the *Biog. Hist. of N. C.* (1917), VIII, 91–97 ; a eulogistic estimate in the *Raleigh Morning Post*, Aug. 30, 1900, by Capt. W. W. Carraway ; and an obituary in the Raleigh *News-Observer*, July 24, 1900. The farmers' movement is treated by J. G. de R. Hamilton, *N. C. Since 1860* (1919), and S. A. Ashe, *Hist. of N. C.* (1908).]

C.C.P.

CARR, EUGENE ASA (Mar. 20, 1830–Dec. 2, 1910), soldier, son of Clark Murwin and Delia Ann (Torrey) Carr, was born at Concord, Erie County, N. Y. Entering the United States Military Academy in 1846, he graduated in 1850, was commissioned in the Mounted Riflemen (now the 3rd Cavalry), and was sent to the Cavalry School for Practise at Carlisle, Pa., for what the present-day army would call an incubator course. For the next ten years his service was chiefly on the frontier, and included several skirmishes with Indians, in one of which (near Limpia, Tex., Oct. 10, 1854) he was severely injured by an arrow, the first of his many wounds. Upon the organization of several new regiments in 1855, he was appointed a first lieutenant in the 1st (now 4th) Cavalry, and was promoted to a captaincy in 1858. At the beginning of the Civil War he was in garrison at Fort Washita, in the Indian Territory. Sent to join Lyon's command in Missouri, he distinguished himself at the battle of Wilson's Creek, and was appointed colonel of the 3rd Illinois Cavalry a few days later. He was soon in command of a brigade and then, at the battle of Pea Ridge, of a division. Here he was three times wounded, but refused to leave the field and had his wounds bandaged as he sat on his horse. The Medal of Honor was later awarded to him for distinguished gallantry in this action. He was appointed brigadier-general of volunteers, Mar. 7, 1862. His promotion to the grade of major in the regular army followed a few months later, but this commission of course remained in abeyance so long as he held higher volunteer rank. In 1863 he commanded a division in the Vicksburg campaign, and after the surrender of the city returned to Arkansas, where he was engaged in minor operations until he joined Gen. Canby early in 1865 for the campaign which resulted in the capture of Mobile. He was mustered out of the volunteer service, Jan. 15, 1866, with the brevet rank of major-general, served for a time in North Carolina and at Washington, and then returned to the frontier. He had gained his first experience with hostile Indians before the Civil War; now began a long series of campaigns which made him, according to Gen. C. D. Rhodes, "perhaps the most famous and experienced Indian fighter of the quarter of a century following the Civil War." From 1868 until the final campaign of Pine Ridge in 1890–91, he served almost continuously in the Indian country with the 5th and 6th Cavalry, fought against Cheyenne, Sioux, and Apache, and received the thanks of the legislatures of Nebraska, Colorado, and New Mexico for bringing peace within their borders. He was promoted to lieutenant-colonel, Jan. 7, 1873, and to colonel, Apr. 29, 1879. He was appointed brigadier-general, July 19, 1892, but his active service was nearly at an end, for he was placed on the retired list, Feb. 15, 1893. Though spending the rest of his life in the East, he was a member of the Historical Society of Kansas, a state whose history he had largely helped to make. Gen. Rhodes calls him a "superb horseman" and "a born cavalry leader," and quotes Frederic Remington as saying that "Gen. Carr would rather be a colonel of cavalry than Czar of Russia." The Indians called him the War Eagle. His wife, whom he married in 1865, was Mary P. Maguire of St. Louis. He died in Washington and was buried at West Point.

[G. W. Cullum, *Biog. Reg.* (3rd ed., 1891), II, 419–21; *Bull. Ass. Grads. U. S. Mil. Acad.*, 1911, pp. 99–106; *Official Records*, ser. 1, vols. III, VIII, XIII, XXII (pts. 1, 2), XXIV (pts. 1, 2, 3), XXX (pts. 2, 3, 4), XXXIV (pts. 1, 2, 3, 4), XLI (pts. 1, 2, 3, 4), XLVIII (pt. 1), XLIX (pts. 1, 2).]   T.M.S.

CARR, JOSEPH BRADFORD (Aug. 16, 1828–Feb. 24, 1895), politician, soldier, was born in Albany, N. Y., the son of William and Ann Carr, who had come to this country from Ireland in 1824. He engaged in the tobacco business at an early age and continued in it until the outbreak of the Civil War. He was then a colonel of militia, having entered that service in 1849 and risen rapidly. On May 14, 1861, he was mustered into the service of the United States as colonel of the 2nd New York Infantry and sent to Ft. Monroe, Va. Of the experiences of the green troops there, and of the action at Big Bethel (June 10),—dignified at the time by the name of battle,—he later wrote in *Battles and Leaders of the Civil War*, II, 144–52. He soon succeeded by seniority to the command of the brigade, which belonged to the 2nd Division of the 3rd Corps, and led it in the Peninsular Campaign and at the second battle of Bull Run. On Sept. 7, 1862, he was appointed brigadier-general of volunteers, by a recess commission under which he served until Mar. 4, 1863, when the adjournment of the Senate without confirmation of his nomination terminated the appointment. He was promptly reappointed, however, Mar. 30, 1863, and in due time this nomination was confirmed. He continued to command a brigade, except for a short time when the death of Gen. Barry, killed at Chancellorsville, put him in charge of the division. The 3rd Corps (Sickles) was the one which occupied the salient in the center of the Union line and bore the brunt of the Confederate attack on the second day of the battle of Gettysburg. The division commander (Humphreys), in his report of the battle, refers to Carr's "cool courage, determination and skillful handling of troops." On Oct. 4, 1863, Carr was assigned to the command of the 3rd Division, 4th Corps. In the following spring he joined Butler's Army of the James, which was to move against Richmond from the southeast while the Army of the Potomac advanced from the north. He commanded a division of colored troops in the operations around Petersburg, and for some time was in charge of the defenses on the York and James rivers. After being mustered out of service, Aug. 24, 1865, he took up manufacturing in Troy. In 1867 he was appointed major-general of militia, and held that position for the rest of his life. For many years he was active in political life, being elected secretary of state in New York in 1879, 1881, and 1883. He was the Republican candidate for lieutenant-governor in 1885, but failed of election. He died in Troy.

[F. B. Heitman, *Hist. Reg.* (1903), I, 285; *Official Records*, ser. I, vols. XI (pt. 2), XII (pt. 2), XXI,

XXV (pts. 1, 2), XXVII (pt. 1), XXIX (pts. 1, 2), XL (pts. 1, 3), XLII (pts. 2, 3) ; C. E. Fitch, *Memorial Encyc. of Biog. of N. Y.* (1916), III, 15–18).]

T. M. S.

CARR, MATTHEW. [See CARR, THOMAS MATTHEW, 1750–1820.]

CARR, THOMAS MATTHEW (1750–Sept. 29, 1820), Austin Friar, was born probably in Galway, Ireland. He joined the Augustinians in Dublin and studied theology in Toulouse. After ordination to the priesthood he lived some years in the Dublin Friary. In 1795 he was chosen by his brethren to establish a house of the Friars in the United States. Some Friars from the Irish Province were engaged on the missions in Newfoundland, the Friars from Spain had been in Mexico since 1533; they had missions also in South America and the Philippines; but there was no house of the Order in the newly-formed United States. Early in the spring of 1796 Carr came to America bearing letters from Archbishop Troy of Dublin to Bishop Carroll. The first charge assigned by the latter was at St. Mary's in Philadelphia with residence at Old St. Joseph's. Carr remained at St. Mary's directing the work of mission stations in Wilmington, New Castle, Trenton, Burlington, South Jersey, and the counties of Southeastern Pennsylvania until the rectory at St. Augustine's was completed in 1802. In the meantime Bishop Carroll had given him powers of vicar general. The work of organizing St. Augustine's was begun in June 1796, and the corner-stone of the church was laid in September of the same year. Among the contributors was George Washington, who gave fifty dollars for the new church. In 1811 Carr opened a school known as St. Augustine's Academy, for the teaching of languages and the higher branches. This school was closed in June 1815 owing probably to the pressure of work on the missions. Carr prepared the memorial address commemorating the life and work of Washington, which was delivered in St. Mary's, Philadelphia, Feb. 22, 1800. He died at St. Augustine's, Philadelphia, Sept. 29, 1820.

[F. X. McGowan, *Hist. Sketch of St. Augustine's Ch., Phila.* (1896) ; T. C. Middleton, *Hist. Sketch of Villanova College* (1893) ; *Records of the Am. Cath. Hist. Soc.*, vols. I, II, VII, X, XIII, XVI, XVII, XVIII, XIX, XXI, XXII, XXXI; unpub. letters, registers, and records of St. Augustine's Ch., Phila.]

F. E. T.

CARRÈRE, JOHN MERVEN (Nov. 9, 1858–Mar. 1, 1911), architect, was born in Rio de Janeiro. His father, John M. Carrère, of distinguished French descent, was a coffee merchant of Baltimore. His mother, Anna Louisa Maxwell, was of a Scotch family, long resident in Baltimore, where she had been educated in a convent. John Merven Carrère, after spending his early years in Rio de Janeiro, went, at fourteen, to Switzerland to study at the Institute Breitenstein at Grenchen. His vacations were spent with his paternal grandmother at Dieppe where his architectural propensities showed themselves in the careful drawings which he made of the old house in which they lived. Entering the École des Beaux Arts at Paris, where he studied especially under Victor Robert, Charles Laisne, and Léon Ginain, the last famous for his Neo-Grèc work, he received his Diplôme in 1882. He then went to New York and in 1883 entered the office of McKim, Mead & White. Here he renewed an acquaintance, formed in Paris, with Thomas Hastings, with whom he eventually entered into partnership. Their first important commission was for Henry M. Flagler's Ponce de Leon Hotel (1887). This was followed by the Alcazar Hotel (1888) and two churches: Grace Methodist Church (1887) and the memorial Presbyterian church (1890), all of this work, in St. Augustine, Fla., in a modified Spanish Renaissance style of great brilliance. From this beginning the work of the firm known as Carrère & Hastings grew rapidly and embraced all types of buildings. The Central Congregational Church in Providence, R. I. (1891), shows the Spanish influence of their Florida work but their other buildings were more and more inspired by the French Renaissance, which was always Carrère's favorite style. This appears particularly in the Hotel Laurel-in-the-Pines, Lakewood, N. J. (1891) with many resemblances to Fontainebleau, and in the detail of their New York business buildings, especially the rich caryatid entrance of the Mail and Express Building (1891) and the charming doorway of the Life building (1893). Their other important early works were: the Benedict estate at Greenwich, Conn. (1891) ; the R. H. Townsend house, Washington, D. C. (1893) ; and the Jefferson Hotel, Richmond, Va. (1893). "Bellefontaine," for Giraud Foster at Lenox, Mass. (1897) ; the house for Mrs. Richard Gambrill at Newport, R. I. (1898) ; and "Blairsden," the Blair estate at Peapack, N. J. (1898) all show with what imaginative skill French Renaissance inspiration was applied by them to the buildings and gardens of great American country houses.

In 1901, Carrère was chief architect and chairman of the board of architects in charge of gardens, grounds, and decorations, for the Pan-American Exposition at Buffalo, and Carrère & Hastings were the architects of the memorial bridge and designed all of the gardens and smaller decorative features. From this time on their work embraced a greater and greater proportion of monumental buildings. Among these were the Richmond Borough Hall, New York City (1903–07); the McKinley monument in Buffalo (1903); the St. George ferry terminal, Staten Island, N. Y. (1904); the great agricultural building at the St. Louis Exposition (1904); the approaches and architectural work, including a great triumphal arch, of the Manhattan Bridge, New York City (1905); the Traders Bank, Toronto, Canada (1905); and the Royal Bank of Canada, Montreal (1906). Their work, however, was not limited to buildings of this kind, for the same period embraced "Whitehall," the Flagler house at Palm Beach, Fla. (1901); the elaborate house of Murry Guggenheim, Elberon, N. J. (1903), awarded the A. I. A. gold medal; the First Church of Christ Scientist, New York City (1898); Carnegie Institution, Washington, D. C. (1906); Goldwin Smith Hall at Cornell University (1903); and Woolsey Hall and Memorial Hall at Yale (1906).

The greatest achievements of the firm of Carrère & Hastings were the Senate and House Office buildings (respectively 1905 and 1906) in Washington, D. C.; the New Theatre (later called the Century Theatre), New York City (1906–09); and the New York Public Library, Carrère's favorite work, won in a competition in 1897, but after long delays completed only in 1911. Carrère had always been vitally interested in city-planning matters and in the development of Washington, so that the commission for the design of the Senate Office Building, which his firm won in competition, was particularly congenial to him. This building, with its mate, the House Office Building, was designed to form an adequate frame for the open space in front of the Capitol. Although the site necessitated an irregularly shaped plan, Carrère succeeded in embodying in these buildings a feeling of great dignity and utter simplicity and, by keeping the fronts restrained in detail, and more austere than was customary in his work, in making them give an added sense of climax to the colonnades of the Capitol. In 1903 Carrère & Hastings had received the commission to reconstruct the interior of the Empire Theatre, New York City, which they had made into an auditorium of lavish yet intimate charm. This success was followed by their masterly design for the New Theatre. This attempt to give New York a quasi-municipal theatre produced a building unique in America, occupying a whole block front, which, like the Paris Opéra, was supposed to combine the gaiety of a theatre with monu-

mentality almost official. The scheme adopted accomplished this with perfect success, and the interior of the theatre proper, with its rich proscenium arch, its coffered ceiling, and lavishly ornamented, sweeping, curved walls, is an outstanding example of its type. The New York Public Library was designed in a modernized classic style of strong French inspiration. Its plan was studied to combine simplicity and efficiency of administration with great richness and beauty of interior effect, and the exterior was devised to grow inevitably from the interior arrangement and to express frankly the functions and positions of the main interior elements. The success with which the entire building achieves these ends and the dignity of its carefully studied approach make it one of the best expressions in America of those ideals of logic in design for which the École des Beaux Arts was then particularly famous. Not only did the architects have charge of the building itself but they also designed all of its furniture and the Bryant monument (except the statue) which forms the central feature of the rear. The beauty of the detail in all of the subsidiary work is characteristic.

The last important commission which Carrère & Hastings had prior to Carrère's death was the City Hall of Portland, Me., designed by them and executed in association with Calvin Stevens of Portland. This is remarkable because of its treatment of a general composition, colonial in type, with details of French Renaissance character, and it is said that Carrère's last drawing was a study for the ship weather-vane of this building.

Carrère's interests outside of the office were extremely wide. He was an enthusiastic member of Trinity Chapel, New York. He was a tireless worker in the American Institute of Architects and its New York chapter, of which he was twice president. He was on the city plan commissions of Grand Rapids, Mich. (1909); Hartford, Conn. (1911); and Cleveland, Ohio. His interest in architectural education is shown by the fact that he helped found, and was twice president of, the Society of Beaux Arts Architects, and was a trustee of the American Academy at Rome. He was also instrumental in founding the Fine Arts Federation of New York City, and the Municipal Art Commission of New York. He succeeded D. H. Burnham [q.v.] in directing the activity of the American Institute of Architects in connection with the plan of Washington and as a result was offered but declined the post of supervising architect of the Treasury Department. Francis S. Swayles, in the

London Architectural Review (XXIX, 283), said that he was "almost the first in America to preach and practise professional ethics," and he was the author of the code of competitions which was adopted, slightly modified, by the American Institute of Architects. He published *City Improvement from the Artistic Standpoint* (1908); *Preliminary Report of the City Plan for Grand Rapids, Mich.* (1909), with Arnold Brunner; and *Plan of the City of Hartford* (1912). Carrère was made a Fellow of the American Institute of Architects in 1891 and elected as an Academician of the National Academy of Design in 1910. He was married on June 5, 1886, to Marian Sidonia Dell, of Houston, Tex., and San Francisco, Cal., who died Feb. 8, 1920. For many years he lived on Staten Island but during the latter part of his life in New York City itself. His country house, Red Oaks, White Plains, N. Y., designed by himself, was the home of which he was most fond. He was characterized by great generosity, and uncompromising integrity. Impulsive, on occasions fiery, he was, nevertheless, exceedingly popular with all types of people and had a great capacity for winning and holding the affection and confidence of others. Of medium height, with a very dark complexion inherited from his mother's family, and with a small beard, his appearance was almost that of a French aristocrat. Injured in an automobile accident, Feb. 12, 1911, he died at the Presbyterian Hospital, New York, on Mar. 1.

[Memorial notice by Thos. Hastings in the *N. Y. Architect*, V, 65–72; appreciations by W. R. Mead, Walter Cook, and others in *Brickbuilder*, XX, 41; a full and enlightening appreciation by Francis S. Swayles in the *London Architectural Rev.*, XXIX, 283–93; *Architectural Record*, XXVII, 1–120, fully illustrated and with a list of works; *Am. Art Annual*, IX, 308–09; *Am. Art News*, IX, 4; *Quart. Bull. of the Am. Inst. of Architects*, XI, 271, 296–99; *London Builder*, C, 358–60; *Am. Architect*, XCIX, 96, 129, 131; *N. Y. Tribune*, Mar. 2, 1911; *Who's Who in America*, 1910–11; information as to certain facts from Carrère's daughter, Anna M. Carrère.]   T. F. H.

CARRICK, SAMUEL (July 17, 1760–Aug. 17, 1809), Presbyterian clergyman, college president, was born in York (later Adams) County, Pa., a region from which came many of the men and women among whom he was to spend his life on the Virginia and Tennessee frontiers. At an early age he moved to the Shenandoah Valley, and here, under the instruction of William Graham who was laying the foundation for what later became Washington and Lee University, he prepared himself for the Presbyterian ministry. In 1782 he was licensed to preach, and in the following year he was installed as pastor of Rocky Spring and Wahab meeting-house in Virginia.

From the occasional references to him in the records of his church, it appears that within a few years Carrick began to go to the Tennessee frontier in something of the character of a traveling missionary. At the apex of the wedge of settlement that was being pushed rapidly down the valley of the Holston River, he gathered together such casual congregations as he could find, and with the forest as his church building, with a fallen tree or an Indian mound as his pulpit, he preached to them the gospel. By the year 1791 he had organized Lebanon Church and had made his home near the junction of the Holston and French Broad rivers. Soon he organized the first church in the near-by newly-founded Knoxville, where he continued as pastor for the remainder of his life. In September 1793, his first wife, Elizabeth Moore, whom he had married in Virginia, died, and in January of the following year he married Annis McClellen. Like many other frontier preachers, he was not only a minister of the gospel but an educator. In 1793 he opened at his home a "Seminary" where instruction was offered in Latin, Greek, English, geography, logic, natural and moral philosophy, astronomy, and rhetoric. In the following year the territorial legislature chartered Blount College, a non-denominational, co-educational college, named in honor of the governor, William Blount, and Carrick was made its president. A few years later, when this institution, that was to become in time the University of Tennessee, was transformed into East Tennessee College, he continued as its president. He was a much-needed man of culture in a pioneer community, a gentleman of commanding appearance, of great urbanity, and, as described in a brief notice of his death, "a worthy, pious man" (*Wilson's Knoxville Gazette*, Aug. 19, 1809).

[A brief sketch by R. B. McMullen is in Wm. B. Sprague, *Annals Am. Pulpit*, vol. III (1858), and a briefer one is in Wm. Henry Foote, *Sketches of Va.* (2nd ed., 1856). The little that is known about Carrick's administration as president of Blount College can be found in Moses White, *Early Hist. of the Univ. of Tenn.* (1879). See also *Knoxville Gazette*, esp. Dec. 1, 1792, Jan. 30, and Apr. 10, 1794.]   P. M. H.

CARRINGTON, HENRY BEEBEE (Mar. 2, 1824–Oct. 26, 1912), lawyer, author, the son of Miles M. and Mary (Beebee) Carrington, was born at Wallingford, Conn. His grandfather, James Carrington, was a partner of Eli Whitney from 1800 to 1825, superintendent of the manufacture of arms for the United States at Whitneyville, Conn., and inspector of work at the arsenals of Springfield and Harper's Ferry. His maternal grandfather and great-grandfather were graduates of Yale College. In his twelfth year he commenced classical studies under Rev. Epaphras Goodman and Dr. Erasmus D. Hudson. Owing to a chance address by John Brown he became an ardent abolitionist. From his early youth military affairs interested him, and, had his constitution been more rugged, he doubtless would have entered West Point. He entered Yale College in the fall of 1840, and after a temporary absence because of ill health, was graduated with the class of 1845. For a year and a half after graduation he taught in Irving Institute at Tarrytown, N. Y., where he was encouraged by Washington Irving to pursue a line of research which afterward led him to write his *Battles of the American Revolution*. Later he became a professor in the New Haven Collegiate Institute, at the same time pursuing a course of study in the Yale Law School.

In 1848 he moved to Columbus, Ohio, and entered upon the practise of the law, first with Hon. Aaron F. Perry and afterward for nine years with Hon. William Dennison, subsequently governor of Ohio. In his twelve years of law practise in Columbus he was attorney for manufacturing, banking, and railroad corporations. He was locally prominent in the organizing of the Republican party, serving with Rufus P. Spalding and other eminent leaders on the committee on resolutions in the convention of July 13, 1854, which denounced the Kansas-Nebraska policy of the national administration (Joseph Patterson Smith, *History of the Republican Party in Ohio*, 1898). He was the personal friend and supporter of Gov. Salmon P. Chase, and in 1857, at the earnest request of the latter, accepted a position on his staff to take charge of the reorganization of the militia of the state. This work was so well done that it led to Carrington's appointment as adjutant-general, a position which he held under Chase and his successor, Gov. Dennison. When President Lincoln issued his first call for troops, before the United States volunteers could be organized and mustered, nine regiments of Ohio militia were hurried across the Ohio River to save West Virginia for the Union. For this service Carrington received the thanks of the Secretary of War and of Generals Scott and Wool. Shortly afterward he was commissioned colonel of the 18th United States Infantry and placed in command of the regular army camp near Columbus, while still acting as adjutant-general of Ohio. Upon the request of Gov. Oliver P. Morton of Indiana, he was ordered to that state to organize its levies for the service. In 1862 he was promoted to the rank of brigadier-general. He was especially active in organizing and forwarding troops to the field. From In-

diana alone he superintended the recruiting of more than one hundred thousand men. Under his direction the Sons of Liberty and other disloyal orders were exposed. His course in the trial of these conspirators was bitterly denounced by the opponents of the Lincoln administration, but it was sustained by the army and by the loyal sentiment of the country. The cases were ultimately carried to the Supreme Court of the United States, where a majority of the judges held that the military court of Carrington had been illegal because held in a state that was not in rebellion (Whitelaw Reid, *Ohio in the War*, 1893). When he was mustered out of the service as brigadier-general of volunteers, Carrington rejoined his regiment in the Army of the Cumberland; was president of the commission that tried the guerrillas at Louisville in 1865, and later in the fall of the same year was ordered to the Indian service in Nebraska; built Fort Phil Kearny in the Rocky Mountain district; participated in the Red Cloud War; in 1867 established friendly relations with Spotted Tail and other Indian chiefs; was granted a year's leave of absence because of a severe wound received in the line of duty; protected the Union Pacific Railroad from Indian interruption; in 1869 was detailed as professor of military science at Wabash College (Indiana); in 1889 negotiated a treaty with the Flathead Indians of Montana and two years later moved Indians to Joco reservation, western Montana. He was a frequent contributor to periodicals and published several books, of which the following are the more important: *American Classics* (1849); *Russia Among the Nations* (1851); *Hints to Soldiers Taking the Field* (1862); *Mineral Resources of Indiana; Crisis Thoughts* (1878); *Battles of the American Revolution* (1876); *Battle Maps and Charts of the American Revolution* (1881); *The Six Nations* (1892); *Washington, the Soldier* (1898). *Ab-sa-ra-ka, Home of the Crows; or the Experience of an Officer's Wife on the Plains* (1868) was written by Carrington's first wife and in subsequent editions enlarged by Carrington himself. He was twice married: first, to Margaret Irvin Sullivant, daughter of Joseph Sullivant of Columbus, Ohio; and, second, on Apr. 3, 1871, to Fannie, widow of Col. G. W. Grummond, and daughter of Robert Courtney.

[The chief source is *Record of the Class of 1845 of Yale College, Complete to 1881*. The sketch of Carrington in this publication is autobiographical and with the exception of a few mistakes in dates, is authentic. Briefer sketches appear in *The Biog. Cyc. and Portrait Gallery, with Hist. Sketch of Ohio* (1887), IV, 1043–45, and in the *Genealogy and Family Memorial* (1874), by Jos. Sullivant.]   C. B. G—h.

CARRINGTON, PAUL (Mar. 16, 1733–June 23, 1818), jurist, was the son of George Carrington, a wealthy and influential planter of Cumberland County, Va., and of his wife, Anne Mayo—both of English descent. When he was about seventeen years old he went to that part of Lunenburg County later organized as Charlotte County, to study law with Clement Read, county clerk and a man of wealth, culture, and influence. He lived in his instructor's home, and eventually married his daughter, Margaret. His training must have been effective, for he began the practise of law when twenty-one years old, and was very successful. Fortunate family connections and his own ability brought many appointments his way. He was king's attorney of the counties of Bedford, Mecklenburg, Botetourt, and Lunenburg; was major of the Lunenburg militia; and when a portion of Lunenburg County was separated therefrom and organized as Charlotte County in 1765, was chosen as one of its representatives in the Colonial General Assembly, a position which he retained throughout the life of that body. He was also county lieutenant and presiding justice of Charlotte County. In spite of these numerous positions under the crown, he was ever loyal to the Colony. He was a member of the Mercantile Association of 1770, was chairman of the Revolutionary Committee of Charlotte County, and took an active part in each of the several Revolutionary conventions of Virginia from 1774 to 1776, inclusive, which played a large part in uniting the colonies, and in inaugurating the movement for independence. In the Virginia convention of 1776 he was a member of the committee which reported the Declaration of Rights and the Virginia Constitution of 1776. He voted for the resolutions instructing Virginia's delegates in Congress to propose independence. He was a member of the Committee of Safety (both the first and second groups) which was the revolutionary executive body in Virginia until the formation of the state government in July 1776. After representing Charlotte in the state Senate during the first two years of its existence, he began his long career on the bench as a member of the general court (created in 1779). In 1780 he was made chief justice of that body. When the new court of appeals was created in 1789, Carrington was made one of the five judges, and was continued in that position until his resignation in 1807. At that time he retired to private life after having held public office without intermission for forty-two years. The last years of his life were spent at "Mulberry Hill" on the Staunton River.

He was vigorous in body, "over six feet in height, with prominent features, bright blue eyes, and sandy hair" (Grigsby, *post*). In his sixtieth year he had married Priscilla Sims, his first wife having died in 1766. He remained active and erect until within a year of his death, which occurred at the age of eighty-five.

[See Alexander Brown, *The Cabells and Their Kin* (1895), and Hugh Blair Grigsby, *The Va. Convention of 1776* (1855). Brown had access to the manuscript material relating to the Carrington family in the possession of N. F. Cabell; Grigsby resided in the neighborhood of "Mulberry Hill," knew Carrington's children, and had access to many of the family records. Carrington's will and other documents relating to him may be found in the Charlotte County records, at Charlotte C. H., Va. Sketches of him and of his family are in Wm. Henry Foote, *Sketches of Va., Hist. and Biog.* (2nd ed., 1856), and in Bishop Wm. Meade, *Old Churches, Ministers, and Families of Va.* (1861).]

R. L. M—n.

CARROLL, CHARLES (Sept. 19, 1737–Nov. 14, 1832), Revolutionary leader, signer of the Declaration of Independence, and United States senator from Maryland, is said by his biographers to have been descended from the "old Irish princely family of the Carrolls of Ely O'Carroll, Kings County, Ireland." He was born at Annapolis, the son of Charles Carroll of Annapolis and Elizabeth (Brooke) Carroll. His early education was almost entirely in the hands of the Society of Jesus, at first in the school on Bohemia Manor in Maryland, then for six years following 1748 in the Collège de St. Omer in French Flanders. After finishing at Rheims and at the Collège de Louis le Grand in Paris, he spent the years 1753 to 1757 at Bourges and Paris, whence he went to London for the beginning of a residence of several years during which he continued the studies in civil law begun in France, though not with the intention of making professional use of his acquirements. At the age of twenty-eight, he returned to Maryland, prepared to take up the development of the ten-thousand-acre tract in Frederick County located at the mouth of the Monocacy and known as Carrollton Manor, which his father made over to him at this time. He took no part in the politics of the next few years, but lived the life of a gentleman of property, debarred from political activity by his legal disability as a Roman Catholic. On June 5, 1768, he married his cousin, Mary Darnall. In the Assembly of 1770 the question of regulating officers' fees and the stipends of the clergy of the Established Church reached such a point of bitterness between the two houses that Gov. Eden prorogued the session and issued a proclamation reaffirming the old table of fees which the lower house had been trying to reform. The bitterness aroused by this action came to a head two years later when the

Maryland Gazette, on Jan. 7, 1773, published a letter in defense of the government signed "Antilon," a pseudonym which it was generally understood concealed the identity of Daniel Dulany [*q.v.*]. This letter, in the form of a dialogue in which the arguments of "First Citizen" against the government's position were overcome by Dulany speaking as "Second Citizen," gave Carroll his opportunity. Dramatically enough he stepped into the clothes of the straw man Dulany had knocked down and under the signature of "First Citizen" reopened the argument. The controversy was carried on in the *Maryland Gazette* until July 1, 1773, and when it was over Carroll had become indeed something like the First Citizen of the province. He was active in the non-importation proceedings of 1774, and this year and the next saw him successively a member of the local Annapolis Committee of Correspondence, of the first Maryland Convention, of the provincial Committee of Correspondence, and of the Committee of Safety. In February 1776, the Continental Congress appointed a commission to visit Canada "to promote or form a union" between Canada and the colonies, naming as its members, Benjamin Franklin, Samuel Chase, and Charles Carroll. Though Carroll was not a member of Congress at this time, his standing among American Catholics and his knowledge of French fitted him peculiarly for the mission. The story of that abortive attempt, foredoomed to failure, is found in Carroll's journal of the mission. As a delegate to the Maryland Convention of 1776, he was instrumental in bringing about the passage of the resolution of separation from England that put the province into line with the other colonies on this absorbing question of the hour. Elected a delegate to the Continental Congress on July 4, Carroll went almost immediately to Philadelphia, voted for the engrossment of the Declaration of Independence on July 19 and put his name to the instrument on Aug. 2. The romantic story that he added "of Carrollton" to his name on this occasion for the first time in response to the suggestion that King George would probably hang one of the other Charles Carrolls by mistake is without foundation. He had assumed this designation first on his return to Maryland in 1765, and had used it ever since as his invariable signature to distinguish him from his father and cousins of the same name. From this time on Carroll took a prominent part in the Assembly of his state and in the Continental Congress. He was intimately concerned in the drawing up of the Maryland Constitution, and he opposed the confiscation of British property and other measures that seemed to him as tyrannical as those

from which the country was endeavoring to escape. He served in Congress from 1776 to 1778 and was appointed to the Board of War and to other important committees. In 1787 he was elected to the Constitutional Convention, but did not accept the election, though when the question of adoption was before the Maryland Senate, he allied himself with the party for adoption and remained a Federalist for the rest of his days. He represented Maryland as senator in the first federal Congress, 1789, and continued in this capacity until his resignation in 1792. His political career ended when he left the Maryland Senate in 1800 and devoted himself to the development of an estate that counted between seventy and eighty thousand acres of land in Maryland, Pennsylvania, and New York. In common with his party as a whole, he was opposed to the War of 1812, and, when the office of the *Federal Republican* of Baltimore was sacked by a mob, he contemplated moving from the state. He was a member of the Potomac Company, with its dream of a water route to Ohio and the West, and of its successor, the Chesapeake & Ohio Canal Company, organized in 1823. He was on the first board of directors of the Baltimore & Ohio Railroad and laid its corner-stone on the 4th of July 1828. His property increased with the years and when he died on Nov. 14, 1832, he was envied by many as the wealthiest citizen of the United States and revered by every one as the last surviving signer of the Declaration of Independence.

[Kate Mason Rowland, *The Life of Chas. Carroll of Carrollton, 1737–1832* (2 vols. 1898), in which are reprinted as appendices to vol. I, "Letters of the First Citizen," and the Canada "Jour. of Chas. Carroll of Carrollton," and as appendices to vol. II his will and the genealogy of the family.]   L.C.W.

CARROLL, DANIEL (July 22, 1730–May 7, 1796), was commissioner of the District of Columbia. Among the immigrant Carrolls of the sixteenth century were two descendants of a common ancestor, one of whom, Charles Carroll, established the line which was to find its greatest representative in Charles Carroll of Carrollton, and the other, Kean Carroll, was the father of Daniel Carroll of Upper Marlboro. The latter, unlike other members of the family, entered business, but, although this was considered demeaning, his character and natural presence must have inspired great respect, for about 1727 he married a provincial belle of Woodyard, Md., Eleanor Darnall (*Records of the Columbia Historical Society, Washington, D. C.,* XXI, 16–18). He had two sons who distinguished themselves; John Carroll [*q.v.*], and Daniel Carroll. In 1742 Daniel was sent for his education to Flanders where he remained for six years. After his return he married Elizabeth Carroll of Duddington, probably a first cousin of Charles Carroll of Carrollton (*American Catholic Historical Researches,* XII, 53; Peter K. Guilday, *Life and Times of John Carroll,* 1922, I, 3n.). Of his activities between the years 1753 and 1781 very little has been recorded. Upon the death of his father he probably fell heir to a large share of a considerable estate for he is spoken of much later as "a man of large fortune and influence in his state" (*Documents Illustrative of the Formation of the Union of the American States,* selected and arranged by Charles C. Tansill, 1927, p. 104). In 1781 he was elected a delegate to the Continental Congress, signing the Articles of Confederation on Mar. 1 of that year, and from that time until his death he was an active participant in the leading events. On May 26, 1787, he was appointed a delegate to the Constitutional Convention. In company with all the great property-holders of that assembly he worked for a strongly centralized government. Opposing the payment of members of Congress by the states he declared, "The dependence of both Houses on the State Legislatures would be compleat. . . . The new government in this form is nothing more than a second edition of Congress in two volumes, instead of one, and perhaps with very few amendments" (*Ibid.,* p. 544). During the struggle for ratification he wrote a judicious and persuasive letter to the *Maryland Journal* in answer to a letter written by Samuel Chase who had advised his countrymen to delay ratification (P. L. Ford, editor, *Essays on the Constitution of the United States,* 1892, pp. 325–36). Carroll was elected senator from Maryland to the First Congress of the United States and voted for the assumption bill and the bill to locate the District of Columbia on the banks of the Potomac. His residence at what is now Forest Glen, Md., near the District, and his friendship with Washington probably induced the latter on Jan. 22, 1791, to name him one of the three commissioners to survey and limit a part of the territory of the ten-mile square. The fact that he was an uncle of Daniel Carroll of Duddington who owned considerable property in the area affected, and that he himself owned tracts near-by may have been partly responsible for the embarrassing complications which finally resulted in the resignation of L'Enfant. Carroll served as commissioner until May 1795 when his age and feeble health caused him to resign. He died at his home at Rock Creek either May 6 or 7, 1796 (see deposition of his sister published in *Records of the Columbia Historical Society, Washington, D. C.,* XXI, 17 and *Federal Gazette,* May 14, 1796).

[See Thos. F. Meehan, "Daniel Carroll," article in the *Cath. Encyc.* (1913), which, however, contains numerous errors; also, W. B. Bryan, *A Hist. of the National Capital* (1914), I, 120–22, 255. Carroll's letters to Madison on the struggle for ratification in Maryland are in the Madison Papers, Lib. of Cong.; see a summary of them in *Am. Hist. Rev.,* vol. V. There is information in "D. C. Letters and Papers, Site and Bldg. for Fed. City, Letters," vol. I, in MSS. Div., Lib. of Cong.]

C.W.G.

CARROLL, HOWARD (Sept. 17, 1854–Dec. 30, 1916), author, business man, like Benjamin Franklin preferred even in his later years to be known as a journalist. In addition to these activities he was inspector-general of all New York State troops during the Spanish-American War. This interest in military affairs he doubtless derived from his father, Brigadier-General Howard Carroll, who at the outbreak of the Civil War raised a regiment in New York City and after a short but brilliant military career was killed at Antietam. The son received his early education at Albany, the city of his birth, and in New York City, but went abroad for college training at Hanover, Göttingen, and Geneva. Upon his return to the United States in 1874 he joined the reportorial staff of the *New York Times,* a paper which he later served as correspondent first at Albany and then at Washington. In 1877 he reported the yellow fever epidemic in the South for that newspaper and gathered material for his book, *A Mississippi Incident.* While on the *New York Times* he wrote several plays, of which the most important was *The American Countess* (1884),—a comedy that had a record run of two hundred nights in New York City. In 1883 he published *Twelve Americans: Their Lives and Times,* a volume which he affectionately dedicated to George Jones of the *New York Times.* His newspaper work in Washington brought him into contact with President Arthur, who offered him the position of private secretary and also the post of minister to Belgium, both of which he declined. Always active in Republican politics, a delegate to three national conventions, he ran for office only once. A candidate in 1882 for congressman-at-large for New York State, he ran 64,000 votes ahead of his ticket but was defeated by his Democratic opponent, Gen. Henry W. Slocum. A member of numerous clubs, he was possibly proudest of the honor of being president of the New York Times Association. Twice he was on the military staff of New York governors with a rank of brigadier-general, first with Gov. Morton and then with Gov. Black. To public interests in New York City where he spent his later life he gave liberally of his time. His greatest service to the city was as president of the New York Tercentenary Commission. For his liberality in entertaining German officers during the Hudson-Fulton celebration he was decorated by the German emperor with the Order of the Red Eagle of the first class. In 1888 he married Caroline Starin, whose father John H. was a member of Congress from New York City.

[The most detailed biographical sketch may be found in the obituary in the *N. Y. Times*, Dec. 31, 1916; see also *Who's Who in America*, 1916–17.]　　J.M.L.

CARROLL, JAMES (June 5, 1854–Sept. 16, 1907), bacteriologist, pathologist, investigator of yellow fever, was born in Woolwich, England, to James and Harriet Chiverton Carroll. His early education was received at Albion House Academy, Woolwich. At the age of fifteen, he emigrated to Canada and in 1874, at the age of twenty, he enlisted in the United States Army as a private of infantry. After nine years' service in the infantry, he was transferred to the Medical Department as a hospital steward. In this position he served from 1883 to 1898, during which period he studied medicine at the University of the City of New York (1886–87) and at the University of Maryland in Baltimore (1889–91), where he received his M.D. degree. The new science of bacteriology with its promise of future developments in medicine, attracted his attention and during the two winters following his graduation, he took the courses in bacteriology and pathology recently opened at Johns Hopkins University. In 1895, while still a hospital steward, he was assigned to the Army Medical Museum in Washington as assistant to the curator, Maj. Walter Reed [*q.v.*]. Upon the outbreak of the Spanish-American War in 1898, he was appointed acting assistant surgeon. His study of the fever patients in the Army camps was largely instrumental in showing that the prevailing disease was not malaria but typhoid fever. In 1899, Reed and Carroll disproved the claim of Sanarelli that the *Bacillus icteroides* was the causative agent of yellow fever. In the following year, Surgeon-General Sternberg created the so-called Yellow Fever Commission for the study of that disease in Cuba. Its members were Reed, Carroll, Jesse W. Lazear, and Aristide Agramonte. Although Reed's was the planning and organizing mind in this investigation, Carroll must be credited with much of the detailed work. It was here that his skill as a technician and his capacity for infinite pains is best shown. Reed was early convinced that the theory of mosquito transmission advanced some years before by Dr. Carlos Finlay offered the most promising line of investigation. This called for human subjects for inoculation and the Commission was naturally loath to adopt such experimentation in this highly fatal disease.

While Reed was absent in the United States, Carroll caused an infected mosquito to be applied to his arm by Lazear. Three days later, he developed a severe case of yellow fever, which nearly cost him his life. During the course of this illness, he suffered an acute dilatation of the heart, which was the beginning of the permanent lesion which caused his death seven years later. Controlled experiments upon nearly thirty subjects followed, happily without any fatal result.

Carroll's interest in yellow fever did not cease with his participation in the discovery of the method of transmission. In 1901 he returned to Cuba to make a study of the blood of patients. Perhaps his greatest individual contribution was the demonstration of the fact that the virus of yellow fever is ultra-microscopic. Either alone or in collaboration, he contributed twenty-seven articles to medical periodicals, practically all of them relating to yellow fever. His earlier contributions were written largely in collaboration with Walter Reed, with whose name that of Carroll is inseparably associated. From 1895 until Reed's death in 1902 Carroll was Reed's principal assistant. During this period he was demonstrator of bacteriology and pathology in the Medical Department of Columbian University in Washington and for a time was professor of bacteriology and pathology in the Veterinary Department of the same institution. Upon the death of Walter Reed, Carroll succeeded him in the chairs of bacteriology and pathology at Columbian University and the Army Medical School. In recognition of his contribution to the yellow fever investigation, the regulation assigning an age limit for commissions in the Army was waived and he was appointed lieutenant in the Medical Corps in October 1902. In 1907 he was given the commission of major by a special act of Congress. In the same year two universities (Maryland and Nebraska) conferred upon him the honorary degree of LL.D. Quiet, mild-mannered, soft-spoken, he was tall, with an angularity that defied all his years of army life to give him a military bearing. He had a fine high forehead, a large prominent nose and mild eyes looking out always through thick lenses. He was married in 1888 to Jennie M. G. Lucas of Cleveland, Ohio, who together with seven children survived him.

[In the *Bull. of the Johns Hopkins Hospital*, vol. XIX (1908) is contained a series of papers on Carroll by prominent men of his acquaintance. The *Mil. Surgeon*, vol. XXII (1908) contains a concise biographical sketch with portrait. The chapter on the Yellow Fever Commission in John C. Hemmeter's *Master Minds in Medicine* (1927) is largely in relation to Carroll and has a portrait and bibliography. There is also a biographical sketch by Caroline W. Latimer in Kelly and Burrage, *Am. Medic. Biogs.* (1920). Much that has been written concerning Carroll's career is colored by the feeling that the government never adequately rewarded him for his part in the yellow fever investigations.]

J.M.P.

CARROLL, JOHN (Jan. 8, 1735–Dec. 3, 1815), first Roman Catholic bishop in the United States and first archbishop of Baltimore, was the fourth of seven children born to Daniel Carroll, a merchant and landholder of Upper Marlboro, Md., and his wife, Eleanor Darnall, an heiress who traced descent to the Calverts and the English founders of the colony. Jacky Carroll, as the child was known, received his elementary training at home probably from his mother who had been schooled in France at a time when most colonial women were untutored. At the age of twelve years, he was enrolled in the short-lived local Jesuit school at Bohemia Manor. The following year along with his cousin Charles Carroll [q.v.], he was sent to St. Omer's in France, one of the best-known English refugee colleges for the Catholic gentry's sons and for British youth destined to the domestic missions of the Society of Jesus. This was quite usual for well-to-do Catholic manorial families in Maryland where the penal laws precluded the possibility of higher education for their children. Hence the Carrolls found a number of young Marylanders among their fellow students.

At the conclusion of his classical course, John entered the rigorous Jesuit novitiate at Watten (1753), not far from St. Omer's, where he passed two years in study and prayerful meditation. Here again he was associated with English and Maryland youth preparing for the Jesuit missions in the British North American plantations. Thence, he was advanced to the scholasticate at Liège where he pursued the languages and philosophical subjects for three years, before being assigned, as a teacher of boys, at St. Omer's (1758). In 1762 along with the other masters and their pupils he left for Bruges, having learned that St. Omer's was about to be seized by the French government and turned over to English seculars in preparation for the royal edict suppressing the Society of Jesus (1764).

Taking his final vows as a Jesuit, Carroll renounced all claims to a share in his late father's estate in favor of his brothers and sisters and returned to Liège, where he was ordained in 1767 or according to some authorities in 1769. At all events, he was given a leave of absence from teaching to tour Europe in 1771 as a tutor and companion of Lord Stourton's son. His manuscript journal is too fragmentary and circumspect to be interesting, although he traveled widely and met persons of rank in state and church in Germany, France, Italy, and Rome.

He had hardly returned to Liège when Pope Clement XIV, according to current expectation, suppressed the Society (Aug. 16, 1773). Like most Jesuits, Carroll was hurt and resentful but obedient. With a few Jesuits and students, he soon went to England where the penal laws were dying through non-enforcement, and as secretary of a committee drafted futile remonstrances to the Austrian government concerning property losses at Bruges. As tutor and chaplain for Lord Arundell at Wardour Castle, he lived a year in scholarly leisure, but he had no desire to continue permanently in this honorable capacity. Almost forty years old, he was anxious to visit his aged and widowed mother whom he had not seen since his departure for St. Omer's. Furthermore, he sensed the impending Revolution from the tenor of his Maryland correspondence and the tenseness of English official opinion which he gauged with unusual perspicacity. Not long after Charles Carroll had written the "Letters of the First Citizen" in answer to the loyalist arguments of the renowned Maryland lawyer, Daniel Dulany [q.v.], Father John Carroll arrived in America. Stopping with his mother at Rock Creek, Md., he lived privately, saying mass in the manorial chapel and attending to the religious needs of the surrounding country. Though an ardent patriot, he took no active part in the Revolution, save in the spring of 1776 when he was invited by Congress to accompany the American commissioners (Franklin, Chase, and Charles Carroll) to Canada. He was quite aware of the hopeless character of the mission. As an ex-Jesuit, he was not warmly welcomed by Bishop Briand of Quebec who was decidedly pro-British in tone. Carroll was, however, of service to the emissaries, and Franklin wrote (May 27, 1776) thanking him for the solicitous care which he had bestowed upon him during his illness. He was soon back in his Rock Creek retreat.

Annoyed by the chaotic condition of the Catholic Church which the Revolution had severed from any control by the vicar-apostolic of London and also annoyed by the listless character of the ex-Jesuit priests, Carroll wrote a "Plan of Reorganization" in which he pilloried the ex-Jesuits for their idleness when the possibilities of successful work were so great. The following year the arch-priest, John Lewis, called a convocation at Whitemarsh near Annapolis, which named a committee including Fathers Lewis and Carroll and three others, which petitioned Rome to recognize Lewis as superior with some essential episcopal powers (1783). Soon afterward Carroll and a few others drafted another and more respectful petition that they be allowed to select their own head. In 1784, Carroll was chosen to answer a *Letter to the Roman Catholics of the City of Worcester, England,* published in that year by his old associate, the Rev. Charles H. Wharton [*q.v.*], an ex-Jesuit who had returned to his native land as an Episcopalian minister in Burlington, N. J. Carroll's reply, *An Address to the Roman Catholics of the United States of America* (Annapolis, 1784) was highly esteemed and well received as a brilliant controversial article on a high plane.

In 1784–85 he was named prefect-apostolic by Pope Pius VI who apparently regarded Father Lewis as too old for the arduous task of organizing the infant church. Franklin in Paris heartily approved of the choice of his old friend. In the meantime there was some intriguing in French political and ecclesiastical circles to have the church in America placed under a French vicar-apostolic responsible to the papal nuncio in Paris with priests trained in a seminary in France established for that purpose. Knowledge of these schemes seems to have hurried the advancement of Carroll who was named bishop on Nov. 14, 1789, in accordance with the wishes of a convocation of clergy at Whitemarsh, and was consecrated on Aug. 15, 1790, in the Weld family chapel at Lulworth Castle by Bishop Charles Walmesley, O. S. B.

Even ere this, Carroll had been intensely active in church affairs : laying the corner-stone of St. Peter's, Barclay St., in New York City; settling difficulties in Boston; struggling against trusteeism; composing the Irish-German racial situation in Philadelphia; arranging with the bishop of Quebec about the trans-Alleghany jurisdiction; answering in a cogent document an attack on Catholicism by "Liberal" in the *Gazette of the United States* (1789) by pointing to the Revolutionary services of Catholics; carrying on an extended correspondence with English Catholic leaders in quest of financial aid; and making fatiguing visitations over great distances for the 30,000 members of his widely scattered communion. In 1789, he joined with Charles and Daniel Carroll, Thomas Fitzsimons of Philadelphia, and Dominick Lynch, a New York merchant, in drafting a felicitous *Address* to Washington on the part of the Roman Catholics, which the newly-elected President answered with equal felicity. Ten years later he was to deliver one of the finest patriotic addresses on the death of Washington (Feb. 22, 1800).

In 1791 Bishop Carroll presided over his first synod, which considered ecclesiastical regulations, administration, and education. With education he was especially concerned. In 1789 he

had established a college at Georgetown in Maryland in order that Catholic boys should no longer be compelled to go abroad for training or matriculate at the non-sectarian University of Pennsylvania which alone among American schools welcomed them. It was with relief that he saw Georgetown open in 1791 with Dr. Robert Plunkett, an English priest, as rector. Later when the Society of Jesus was revived he confided Georgetown to its care. With enthusiasm, he accepted the offer of Dr. Francis C. Nagot and his Sulpician brethren, who faced persecution in revolutionary France, to labor in America and establish a diocesan seminary (St. Mary's, Baltimore) for the training of native priests. This he urgently desired, as he dreaded and successfully combated foreign influences in the American church whether French, English, or Irish. When the Sulpicians were about to return to France after the Concordat, he begged them to remain, and, supported by Pius VII, he won the consent of their superior general in Paris. Carroll had learned to depend upon them as his most efficient aides on frontier missions or as seminary professors. In 1803, members of this community, at his desire, founded St. Mary's College for boys in Baltimore, which continued for fifty years (superseded by Loyola), and Mount St. Mary's College, Emmitsburg (1808), which has long since been assigned to secular priests. The bishop was not narrowly attracted to any particular order. He felt that there was work for all. In 1790, he welcomed the Belgian Carmelite nuns; in 1799, he gave his patronage to the Visitation Academy in Washington, the first institution of its kind in America; he received the Trappists in Baltimore and aided in the establishment of their famous monastery in Kentucky; to the Augustinians under Father Matthew Carr he assigned a parish in Philadelphia; he ardently supported the Dominicans who were engaged in the Kentucky missions; he was associated in the establishment of Mother Seton's Sisters of Charity and their College of St. Joseph at Emmitsburg (1808–09); and he sought to have a Franciscan province erected in the United States.

In 1795, the bishop commenced to collect for a cathedral, but as money came in slowly a customary lottery was tried. Not until 1806 was the corner-stone laid and not until six years after his death was the church completed. It was held by all travelers to be the finest church in the States. Growth was slow, yet, in 1808, Baltimore was made an archdiocese subdivided into the four new dioceses of Boston, New York, Philadelphia, and Bardstown, Ky. The Archbishop, however, advised concerning the affairs of all these dioceses, whose bishops he virtually nominated, and gave much thought to Louisiana, whose ecclesiastical affairs were unsettled until his administrator apostolic, Louis Dubourg [*q.v.*], was named bishop in 1815. While Archbishop Carroll had little sympathy with the anti-British group in Congress prior to 1812, he loyally supported Madison's administration during the war and ordered a *Te Deum* in his churches on the failure of the English bombardment of Baltimore, which he witnessed and vividly described in a letter to Father Plowden, an English priest. He was growing old and his work had been arduous. He was not without critics. The Irish suspected him of English sympathies; the French and Germans of being pro-Irish; the Jesuits were never altogether sure of him, yet other communities thought of him as pro-Jesuit; ardent Republicans regarded him as an aristocrat and a Federalist. Yet, he was unperturbed; he steered a straight course. He was a thorough gentleman, a good scholar, an able preacher, and a worthy bishop without any obtrusive piety in speech or correspondence. He built well and on his death left the Catholic Church in a promising condition, freed of foreign influences and well entrenched in the hearts of his people.

[Peter K. Guilday, *Life and Times of John Carroll* (1922), based on printed and archival materials and provided with a full bibliography; J. G. Shea, *Life and Times of the Most Rev. John Carroll* (1888); R. H. Clarke, *Lives of the Deceased Bishops of the Cath. Ch. in the U. S.* (1872); Daniel Brent, *Biog. Sketch of the Most Rev. John Carroll, First Archbishop of Baltimore* (1843), which appeared on Carroll's death; Thos. O'Gorman, *Hist. of the Roman Cath. Ch. in the U. S.* (1895); *Cath. Encyc.* (1913); C. H. Wharton, *Concise View of Principal Points of Controversy between Protestant and Roman Churches* (containing his 1784 address, Carroll's and his reply); Arthur O'Leary, *Review of the Important Controversy between Dr. Carroll and the Rev. Messers Wharton and Hawkins* (London, 1786).]   R. J. P.

CARROLL, JOHN LEE (Sept. 30, 1830–Feb. 27, 1911), governor of Maryland, was a great-grandson of Charles Carroll of Carrollton and his grandfather and father were also named Charles. His mother was Mary Digges Lee, grand-daughter of Thomas Sim Lee, twice governor of Maryland. John Lee Carroll was born on the Homewood estate, near Baltimore, now a part of the Johns Hopkins University campus, but was reared at the ancestral Doughoregan Manor, near Ellicott City, Md. His general education was secured from private tutors, and Roman Catholic schools of the District of Columbia and Maryland, and his legal training in the Harvard Law School and a law office in Baltimore. In 1851 he was admitted to the bar, and,

after an extensive visit to Europe, he began practise in Baltimore in 1854. Two years later he married Anita Phelps, daughter of a rich New York merchant. (She died in 1873, and in 1877 he married Mary Carter Thompson of Staunton, Va.)

He moved to New York in 1859 with the object of practising law there; but, because of his father's failing health and his own Southern sympathies in the slavery controversy, he returned to Maryland in two or three years, and took charge of Doughoregan Manor, which, a short time after their father's death, he bought from his brother Charles, and made his country home.

He was early interested in politics, and allied with the Democrats, who, in 1868, elected him state senator. In 1872 he was reëlected, and two years later, made president of the Senate. In 1875, after bitter opposition on the score of his being a Roman Catholic, he was elected governor of Maryland, a position which he filled with energy, courage, and, on the whole, interest in the common good. Especially along agricultural and commercial lines his policy was progressive. This was a time of great economic depression and resulting labor disturbances, and in July 1877, Gov. Carroll was confronted by a strike of Baltimore & Ohio Railroad employees in protest against a ten per cent reduction of wages. When substitutes were put in, the strikers became violent and began to destroy property in Cumberland. Carroll, therefore, announced that he would send state troops to the town, and when destructive rioting began in Baltimore he telegraphed President Hayes for federal troops. These came, and order was restored by July 23, after nearly a week of rioting and the loss of a number of lives; but deep bitterness survived in some labor quarters toward the Governor. After his term as state executive, Carroll refused all further political office, and spent most of his remaining years at Doughoregan, where, as "lord of the manor," he dispensed hospitality to all comers. He died at his winter home in Washington.

[The chief sources are the *Md. Senate Jour.*, 1868–74, *Md. Public Documents*, 1876–80, and the sketch, evidently based upon data furnished by Carroll himself, appearing in *The Biog. Cyc. of Representative Men of Md. and the D. C.* (1879). Heinrich Ewald Buchholz's biography of Carroll in his *Governors of Maryland* (1908) is founded almost completely upon the last-named. An obituary appears in the *Baltimore Sun* for Feb. 28, 1911.]   M. W. W.

CARROLL, SAMUEL SPRIGG (Sept. 21, 1832–Jan. 28, 1893), Union soldier, was born in Washington, D. C., a descendant of that distinguished Maryland family of whom Charles Carroll of Carrollton is the best-known member. His father, William Thomas Carroll, was for many years clerk of the Supreme Court. He was appointed a cadet at West Point in 1852 and graduated in 1856, among his classmates being Fitzhugh Lee. Commissioned in the 10th Infantry, he served on the frontier until 1860, when he returned to West Point as quartermaster of the Military Academy. He was not released for duty in the field until November 1861. Meanwhile he had been promoted to first lieutenant, Apr. 25, and to captain, Nov. 1. He was then sent to West Virginia, on Dec. 15 was appointed colonel of the 8th Ohio Infantry, and joined his regiment at Romney. He took part in the campaigns in the Shenandoah Valley and northern Virginia in the spring and summer of 1862, including the engagements at Kernstown, Port Republic, and Cedar Mountain. During part of this time he was with his regiment, but from May 24 he commanded a brigade in Shields's division, until he was wounded, Aug. 14, in a skirmish on the Rapidan. Rejoining the army in September, upon his recovery, he commanded a brigade of the 3rd Corps at Fredericksburg. He was relieved from this in April 1863, at his own request, and placed in command of a brigade of the 2nd Corps, which he led at Chancellorsville and Gettysburg. He took part in the Bristoe Station and Mine Run operations in the autumn of 1863, and in the early part of the campaign of 1864. He was wounded at the battle of the Wilderness, May 5, while commanding his brigade, but continued on duty until May 13, when he was disabled by a severe wound in the fighting around Spottsylvania, while temporarily in charge of the division. He was appointed brigadier-general of volunteers, May 12. It was December before he was again fit for duty. For a few weeks he served as a member of a court martial, and then was assigned to command in West Virginia. During the last days of the war he commanded a division in the Army of the Shenandoah. Mustered out of the volunteer service, Jan. 15, 1866, he reverted to his regular army rank of captain, but on Jan. 22, 1867, was appointed lieutenant-colonel of the 21st Infantry. His further service was short, however, for disability resulting from his wounds caused him to be placed on the retired list, June 9, 1869, the rank of major-general being given to him at the same time. He made his home in Washington, and died near that city in Montgomery County, Md. He was buried in Oak Hill Cemetery.

[G. W. Cullum, *Biog. Reg.* (3rd ed., 1891), II, 670–71; *Bull. Ass. Grads. Mil. Acad.*, 1893, pp. 102–04; *Official Records*, ser. 1, vols. XII (pts. 1, 2), XXI, XXV (pt. 1), XXVII (pt. 1), XXIX (pt. 1), XXXIII, XXXVI (pt. 1), XLVI (pts. 1, 2, 3).]   T. M S.

CARROLL, WILLIAM (Mar. 3, 1788–Mar. 22, 1844), governor of Tennessee, was born on a farm near Pittsburgh, Pa., the son of Thomas and Mary Montgomery Carroll. Thomas Carroll, a Revolutionary soldier, had moved from Maryland to Pennsylvania where he and Albert Gallatin were joint owners of a nail factory. William's early education, apparently, was meager, but he had ability, perseverance, and ambition, and such of his papers as are in existence show that he possessed an unusual clarity and vigor of thought and expression. In Pittsburgh he was a merchant, and after moving to Nashville, Tenn., about 1810, he continued for some years in the mercantile business. In Tennessee he quickly became the friend of Andrew Jackson. About 1813 he married Cecelia Bradford. During the Creek War he served with the rank of colonel, fought with great bravery against the Indians, was wounded slightly at the battle of Horse Shoe Bend, and received warm praise from Jackson. Later in 1814 when the latter was appointed major-general in the United States army, Carroll was elected to succeed him as major-general of the Tennessee militia. When the British threatened to invade Louisiana, Carroll raised a force of volunteers, transported them down the Cumberland, the Ohio, and the Mississippi, and arrived in time to give Jackson invaluable aid in repulsing the British in the battle of New Orleans.

For the next few years Carroll devoted himself to his business, but suffered severe financial losses during the depression of 1819. In 1821 he entered political life as a candidate for the office of governor. The campaign was an exciting one. His opponent, Edward Ward, was a man of wealth and superior education, and Carroll was represented as the people's candidate. He was elected by a large majority, and in 1823 and 1825 he was reëlected without opposition. The state constitution prohibited a fourth consecutive term, but in 1829, 1831, and 1833, Carroll was again elected governor without opposition. In the history of Tennessee, the twelve years of his administrations stand out as among the most notable of the period before the Civil War. Possessed of the confidence and support of the masses of the voters, he had an unusually strong influence in the legislature. He opposed successfully the popular demand for legislative interference between debtor and creditor and recommended personal economy as the remedy for the ills of the debtors. He urged a resumption of specie payments, sound banking laws, and the repeal of the act which prohibited the establishment of a branch of the United States

Bank in Tennessee. He recommended a reformation of the judicial system, the abolishment of the whipping post and the pillory, the building of a penitentiary, the development of a system of internal improvements, and the establishment of a system of public instruction for all of the children of the state. The last year of his administration saw the adoption by the state of a new and more democratic constitution, an action that was thoroughly in accord with the spirit of his administrations. Under this new constitution in 1835, he sought election to a seventh term as governor. The state was now divided into two bitter political factions, the supporters of Van Buren's candidacy for the presidency and the champions of Hugh Lawson White for that office. Carroll gave his support to the Jackson-Van Buren faction and his defeat by Newton Cannon foreshadowed the future domination of the state by the Whig party. Carroll now desired but failed to secure appointment as minister to Mexico. Yet he continued until his death an active supporter of the Democratic party in Tennessee.

[There is a brief and inadequate discussion of Carroll's career by Emma Carroll Tucker in *Am. Hist. Mag.* (Nashville), VII, 388–96. His official papers in the Tennessee archives are of slight value. A number of letters by him or about him are in the Jackson Papers, the Van Buren Papers, and the Polk Papers in the Lib. of Cong. Some have been published in J. S. Bassett (ed.), *Correspondence of Andrew Jackson* (1926). Much of the information about Carroll's public life can be secured only from newspapers and legislative journals. Information regarding his parentage has been supplied by his grand-daughter, Mrs. R. H. Vance.]
P. M. H.

CARRYL, GUY WETMORE (Mar. 4, 1873– Apr. 1, 1904), author, was born in New York City, the son of Charles Edward and Mary (Wetmore) Carryl. His father, a railroad director and member of the New York Stock Exchange, was himself the author of several volumes of fiction. The younger Carryl attended the Cutler School and Columbia College, from which he graduated in 1895. While in college he wrote plays for amateur performance and was noted for his handsome looks, good manners, literary facility, wit, and zestful enjoyment of life. A youthful epigram—"It takes two to make one seduction"—has been remembered because it scandalized his teacher, Harry Thurston Peck [*q.v.*]. He got his start in journalism as early as 1893 with a memorably vivid description in the *New York Times* of Edwin Booth's last hours. Upon his graduation he joined the staff of *Munsey's Magazine,* was promoted to managing editor, and in 1896 went to Paris as representative of Harper & Brothers. He remained in Paris until 1902, writing for *Life, Outing,*

Munsey's, and *Collier's,* and learning intimately the ways of the foreign colony in the city. On his return to the United States he made his home at Swampscott, Mass. Early in 1904 his bungalow burned. Carryl contracted rheumatic grip from exposure while fighting the fire, blood poisoning set in, and he died in the Roosevelt Hospital, New York City, in his thirty-second year. The literary career thus abruptly terminated seemed to his contemporaries to be of unusual promise. It began properly in 1898 with *Fables for the Frivolous (with Apologies to La Fontaine),* a volume of graceful light verse dedicated to his father. The tripping lines and genial, mildly cynical humor, aided by Peter Newell's illustrations, were well received; and its author followed it with two volumes in similar vein, *Mother Goose for Grown-Ups* (1900) and *Grimm Tales Made Gay* (1902). Time has not completely faded the humor of these verses. In 1903 Carryl turned to fiction with *The Lieutenant-Governor,* his most substantial book. It is temperately realistic and satirical, and the description and dialogue, as in his other fiction, are manipulated deftly. *Zut and Other Parisians* (1903) is a collection of short stories. Paris is also the background of *The Transgression of Andrew Vane* (1904), a story of blackmail with an incredible dénouement, well enough written to attract critical attention when it was published. After his death two more volumes appeared: *Far from the Maddening Girls* (1904), a rather slight novel, and *The Garden of Years* (1904), which contains his serious verse. The title poem is autobiographical.

[*Who's Who in America,* 1903–05; obituaries in *N. Y. Post,* Apr. 1, and *N. Y. Times,* Apr. 2, 1904; E. C. Stedman, "To the Reader" in *The Garden of Years.*]
G. H. G.

CARSON, CHRISTOPHER (Dec. 24, 1809– May 23, 1868), commonly known as Kit Carson, trapper, guide, Indian agent, soldier, was born in Madison County, Ky. His paternal grandfather, William, was an immigrant, probably from Scotland, who in 1761 received a land grant in Iredell County, N. C. His father, Lindsay (born about 1755), served in the Revolution and after the death of his first wife (1793) moved to Kentucky, where, in 1797, he married Rebecca Robinson. Of their ten children, Kit was the fifth. In the spring of 1811 the family moved to the Boone's Lick district of Missouri, a region for several years thereafter harassed by Indian forays. In September 1818, the father, while burning timber, was killed by a falling limb. Kit had no schooling and remained illiterate until the last five or six years of his life.

In 1825 his mother apprenticed him to a saddler in the near-by town of Franklin, but about the first of September, 1826, he ran away and joined a Santa Fé expedition as "cavvy boy." In the Southwest, after several shifts of occupation, he was engaged by Ewing Young as one of his party that left Taos in August 1829, crossed the Mohave Desert to California, and, after trapping the San Joaquin and other streams, returned to its starting place in April 1831.

This expedition was Carson's high school, from which he came out a certified trapper and Indian fighter. In the fall of 1831 he joined Thomas Fitzpatrick [*q.v.*], in a trapping venture to the North, and in the spring of 1833, after wintering at Robidou's Fort Uintah, reached the trapper's encampment at the present Pocatello, just in time to join in a fight with the Blackfeet, in which he received his only serious wound. For the next eight years, interrupted by returns to his adopted home town of Taos and by buffalo hunts to supply meat for Bent's Fort, he trapped in these regions, sometimes with Bridger's and Fitzpatrick's men but oftener with parties of his own, and many of the heroic incidents of the Carson epic date from this period. About 1836 he married, in Indian fashion, an Arapaho girl whom he called Alice, by whom he had a daughter, Adaline. In the spring of 1842, after the death of Alice, he took his five-year-old daughter to his old home in Missouri, where he placed her with relatives and provided for her education. Returning from St. Louis, he took passage on a steamboat, and on board he met Lieut. John Charles Frémont. This chance meeting opened to him a new career.

He served as guide to Frémont's first expedition (June 10–Oct. 10, 1842), and on the publication of the Pathfinder's report was brought into immediate and country-wide fame. Returning to Taos, he married, Feb. 6, 1843, Maria Josefa Jaramillo, a sister of the wife of Charles Bent. On Frémont's second expedition (1843–44) he shared the honors as guide with Thomas Fitzpatrick, while on the third, wh:ch left Bent's Fort, Aug. 26, 1845, his function at the start seems to have been undesignated. In the California conquest he bore an active and daring part until after the capture of Los Angeles, when he was appointed "lieutenant on special service" and ordered East with dispatches. Meeting Kearny's column, Oct. 6, 1846, near Socorro, N. Mex., he was compelled, against his wish, to return as guide. He fought in the battle of San Pasqual, Dec. 6, and on the third night after the disaster, with Lieut. Edward Fitzgerald Beale and a Delaware Indian, accomplished the desperate feat of crawling through the Californians' lines to bring succor from San Diego. He was in the battles of Jan. 8–9, 1847, for the recovery of Los Angeles, and in March, accompanied by Beale, again started East with dispatches. He reached Washington in June, to find himself a popular hero and to be appointed by President Polk (June 9) a lieutenant in the Mounted Riflemen. He was back in Los Angeles in October, and in the spring of 1848 was again sent East. A companion on the journey was Lieut. George Douglas Brewerton, who in an article in *Harper's Magazine* for August 1853 gave one of the most intimate and engaging portrayals of Carson that we have. At Santa Fé Carson learned that a majority of the Senate, eager to humiliate "the Benton-Frémont clique," had rejected his appointment (Jan. 28). From Washington he returned to Taos as a private citizen.

Various activities, including Indian fighting and an attempt to run a farm, engaged him during the next four years. In the summer of 1853 he drove a flock of 6,500 sheep to Sacramento, netting a good profit from its sale. Returning in December, he learned that he had been appointed a United States Indian agent. His charges were chiefly two tribes of Utes (after the first year or two exclusively so), and during his more than seven years in this post, with home and office in Taos, he rendered excellent service. He was still illiterate; though in the early sixties his contact with army officers was to prove a stimulus enabling him to solve the mysteries of reading and writing, he could at this time merely write (doubtless imitatively) his name and title, and had to delegate to others the preparation of his official reports. It was during this period, presumably the winter of 1857–58, that he dictated to the army surgeon, Lieut.-Col. De Witt C. Peters, and his wife a brief autobiography. The surgeon's expansion of this material, dressed in a somewhat grandiloquent style, into a book, could hardly have been satisfactory to the modest hero, who remarked, on hearing some of the pages read to him, that "Peters laid it on a leetle too thick."

At the outbreak of the Civil War he resigned his place as Indian agent and aided in organizing the 1st New Mexican Volunteer Infantry, of which he was commissioned lieutenant-colonel July 25, 1861, and colonel, Sept. 20. He took part in the battle of Valverde, Feb. 21, 1862, and in successful campaigns against the Mescalero Apaches and the Navajos, in the latter campaign finally breaking the war spirit of a tribe that for two hundred years had been a terror to the settlements. In the fall of 1864 he was sent against the Kiowas and Comanches. At Adobe Walls, in northwestern Texas, Nov. 25, 1864, with about 400 men and two pieces of artillery, he vigorously attacked a force of Indians variously estimated at from 3,000 to 5,000, but after a day's hard fighting was compelled to withdraw. This was his last battle.

In the general promotions dated Mar. 13, 1865, he was brevetted a brigadier-general of volunteers "for gallantry in the battle of Valverde and for distinguished services in New Mexico." In the summer of 1866 he took command of Fort Garland, in western Colorado, where he was visited by Gen. W. T. Sherman and Gen. James F. Rusling. A year later, owing to ill health, he resigned and on Nov. 22 was mustered out. An injury suffered on a hunting trip in the fall of 1860, when his horse fell on him, had resulted in the growth of a tumor pressing on the trachea. In the spring of 1868 he moved his family to Boggsville, a new town near the present La Junta, Colo. Though ill and in great pain, he accepted a call to Washington to take part in a conference with a deputation of Utes. On this journey he visited New York and Boston in the vain hope of getting medical relief. Returning, he reached Boggsville about the first week in April. On the 23rd his wife died. His health continued to fail, and on May 14 he was moved to Fort Lyon, where, though tenderly cared for, he died two weeks later.

Carson is said to have been about five feet eight inches tall. To Mrs. Frémont he seemed "very short and unmistakably bandy-legged, long-bodied and short-limbed." He weighed a mean of about 145 pounds. The color of his eyes, about which the testimony is amusingly discrepant, was probably gray-blue, and his hair was thin and light or sandy. He was ordinarily a man of few words, and there is agreement that his voice was "as soft and gentle as a woman's." In all things he was temperate, and though a confirmed smoker was abstemious of liquor. He has a unique place in history, and a fitting characterization is difficult. "He was not a great man," says Sabin, "nor a brilliant man," but "a great character." Certain it is that this plain, modest, and unlettered man had native qualities which to those who knew him equaled, if they did not transcend, the best they found in other men. To Brewerton he was "one of Dame Nature's gentlemen—a sort of article which she gets up occasionally, but nowhere in better style than among the backwoods of America." "With me Carson and truth are one," wrote Frémont. "His integrity is simply perfect," said Sherman to Rusling at Fort Garland, and Rusling adds:

"As simple as a child, but brave as a lion, he soon took our hearts by storm and grew upon our regard all the while we were with him." Beale, who seems unable to mention his dead comrade without a surge of emotion, apostrophizes him in 1870 as "Dear old Kit. . . . O wise of counsel, strong of frame, brave of heart and gentle of nature!" and says that Tasso "would have placed him by the side of Godfrey and made him the companion of Tancred and Rinaldo."

[De Witt C. Peters in *The Life and Adventures of Kit Carson, the Nestor of the Rocky Mts.* (1858), is the authority for much of the Carson history, and the other early biographers made copious drafts upon his material, without especial concern to look further. In *Kit Carson Days* (1914), Edwin L. Sabin made careful and effective use of all the documentary material then available and further added greatly to the knowledge of Carson, as well as of his environment, by correspondence and interviews with persons who had known him. Other material has since been found, most important of which is the MS. of the autobiography dictated to Peters and his wife. A part of this MS., with critical notes by Chas. L. Camp, was published in the *Cal. Hist. Soc. Quart.*, Oct. 1922, and all of it in a booklet, *Kit Carson's Own Story of His Life* (1926), ed. by Blanche C. Grant. An impressionistic biography, *Kit Carson, the Happy Warrior of the Old West*, by Stanley Vestal, appeared in 1928.]   W. J. G.

CARSON, JOSEPH (Apr. 19, 1808–Dec. 30, 1876), physician, the son of Joseph and Elizabeth (Lawrence) Carson, was born in Philadelphia. He was educated in private schools in that city and graduated from the collegiate department of the University of Pennsylvania in 1826. After working for a short time in a wholesale drug house he became a private pupil of Dr. Thomas T. Hewson while pursuing the medical course at the University of Pennsylvania, from which he received his M.D. in 1830. After graduation he was elected resident physician to the Philadelphia Almshouse. He then went to the East Indies as surgeon in the ship *Georgiana* and on his return to Philadelphia in 1832 began practise. Although he acquired a very large clientele, especially in obstetrics, he also carried on the study of botany throughout his life. In 1835 he became a member of the Academy of Natural Sciences of Philadelphia and for over forty years was most active in its affairs, making communications, serving on committees, and holding various offices. In 1836 he was chosen professor of materia medica in the Philadelphia College of Pharmacy and some years later he also taught in the Medical Institute of Philadelphia. From 1850 until 1876 he was professor of materia medica and pharmacy in the University of Pennsylvania. In 1849 he was elected one of the physicians to the Lying-in-Department of the Pennsylvania Hospital, having as his colleague the distinguished Hugh L. Hodge. Both of these men served the Hospital until the department was finally closed in 1854 in consequence of recurrent outbreaks of puerperal fever. For some years Carson edited the *American Journal of Pharmacy*. He brought out two editions of Pereira's *Materia Medica* with notes. In 1847 he published *Illustrations of Medical Botany*, for which he had himself drawn and colored many of the plates. Carson was very active in the decennial conventions for the revision of the Pharmacopœia. He was a fellow of the College of Physicians of Philadelphia, and a member of the American Philosophical Society, which he served as curator for seventeen years. In 1869 he published his invaluable *History of the Medical Department of the University of Pennsylvania*. He was married twice: in 1841 to Mary Goddard who died without issue in the following year; and in 1848 to Sarah Hollingsworth by whom he had four children.

[Jas. Darrach, "Memoir of Jos. Carson," in *Trans. of the Coll. of Physicians of Phila.*, XI, 45–67; John W. Harshberger, *The Botanists of Phila. and Their Work* (1899), containing a very complete bibliography of Carson's contributions to scientific literature; Thos. G. Morton, *Hist. of the Pa. Hospital* (1895).]

F.R.P.

CARTER, ELIAS (May 30, 1781–Mar. 23, 1864), architect, was born in Ward, Mass., the son of Timothy and Sarah (Walker) Carter. His father and his uncle Benjamin were partners in a building business in Worcester and the neighborhood, and although his father was killed by a fall when the boy was only three years old, and the widow, with her six children, moved to Greenwich, Mass., and remarried, it is certain that the tradition of building and designing remained strong in the family. Carter "certainly had the book which had been his father's guide, Battey Langley's *Treasury of Designs*" (Forbes, *post*, p. 59). Soon after building a church in Brimfield, Mass., in 1805, he settled in that town for a time, and while living there built a hotel and several houses, some still standing. But he was, in these early years, much on the move; his wife told a grand-daughter they had lived in forty different places. He was, at one time, probably before 1805, in the South, which may account for the Southern influence apparent in the high porticos he loved. Already, in the Wyles and Hitchcock houses in Brimfield, this element appears, with columns two stories high combined with a balcony. In Templeton, Mass., he built a church in 1811, and probably the Artemus Lee house, very likely from his own designs, though it is hard to trace the exact steps by which he developed from builder into architect. In 1815 from plans by the famous Ithiel Town, he

built the church in Thompson, Conn., and in 1818 that at Killingly, Conn. A church at Mendon, Mass. (1820), was built from designs by himself, and the pastor of the church at Milford, Mass., about the same date, speaks of him as "a skilful and faithful architect and amiable and pious man."

From 1828 till the time of his death Carter lived chiefly in Worcester, Mass. His known work there includes: the second Unitarian Church (1828); the Daniel Waldo house (1830), which excited much comment for the richness of its woodwork; the Waldo store, known as the "Granite Row"; the Insane Hospital (1832); houses for Alfred Dwight Foster (c. 1835), Judge Kinnicut (1835), Gov. Levi Lincoln (1836), S. M. Burnside (1836), the Burt (Smith) house, the Salisbury house, the Mason Moore and Leland houses on Main St., and the Union Church, Front St. (1836–37). Outside of Worcester he designed the Leicester Academy (1832), the Morton house in Taunton, Mass., and the Insane Asylum, Concord, N. H. (1842). His last known work is a house in Monson, Mass. (1859). He must have been a man of civic interests for he was an unsuccessful candidate for delegate to the General Court in 1834, and served on town committees in 1834 and 1837. He was married on May 25, 1807, to Eudocia Lyon who died July 23, 1869.

His importance as an architect is due to the fact that he was brought up and did his earliest work under strong "late colonial" influences, which colored his later Greek Revival work, and gave it a restraint and a harmony with its American use all too lacking in other work of the time. He was somewhat influenced by Asher Benjamin, but his work is usually more restrained, as he restricts himself, with few exceptions, to the Ionic and Doric orders. His churches were the typical white steepled churches of New England; it was the Worcester houses, in their dignity, their simple directness, and a certain monumental scale, which show best the skill and originality with which he adapted Greek detail to New England use.

[The best account of Carter is that by Harriet Merrifield Forbes, in *Old-Time New Eng.* (the Bulletin of the Soc. for the Preservation of New Eng. Antiquities), XI, 58–71. See also C. M. Hyde, *Hist. Celebration of the Town of Brimfield* (1879). A few of Carter's plans are in the possession of the Am. Antiquarian Soc. at Worcester, Mass.]

T.F.H.

CARTER, FRANKLIN (Sept. 30, 1837–Nov. 22, 1919), college president, was born in Waterbury, Conn., the son of Preserve Wood Carter, a farmer, and Ruth Wells (Holmes) Carter. At Phillips Academy, Andover, where he graduated in 1855, he was valedictorian of his class. He entered Yale with the class of 1859, but a hemorrhage at the close of his sophomore year obliged him to leave college and devote himself to restoring his shattered health. In the autumn of 1860 he joined the junior class at Williams College, taking his degree in 1862. In 1863 he married Sarah Leavenworth Kingsbury of Waterbury, with whom he spent many months traveling and studying in Europe, returning in 1865 to Williams as professor of Latin and French. Resigning in 1872, he went abroad for another year in preparation for a new position as professor of German at Yale, where he taught for the next seven years.

In 1880, upon the retirement of President Paul A. Chadbourne, Carter was called to Williams as the sixth president of that institution, being formally inaugurated on July 6, 1881. With him began the period of what Prof. Leverett Wilson Spring rightly styles "the new Williams." During the twenty years of his administration he secured funds for the college to the amount of more than a million dollars. Furthermore, eight new buildings were erected, and improvements were carried out in many of the older structures. He appointed and maintained a scholarly faculty, doubling the number of instructors and adding to the staff several remarkably brilliant men. He modernized the curriculum by announcing elective courses, first for seniors and then for juniors and sophomores also, and by dropping Greek from the list of subjects required for admission; and he adopted the honor system for examinations. While he was president, the undergraduate body increased in numbers by 68 per cent. Although he was temperamentally an aristocrat, he insisted that Williams should be democratic,—not a "refuge for rich men's sons." A thorough and cultivated scholar, Carter especially emphasized the intellectual side of college life. In 1892 Williams observed its centennial with appropriate exercises, and Carter presided over a large gathering of the alumni at Williamstown.

His health had never been rugged, and in 1901 he felt constrained to resign, being relieved from duty on Sept. 1. After that date he continued to reside in Williamstown, occasionally giving a series of "interesting and thought-provoking lectures" on "Theism," for seniors only, but going for the summer to the Adirondacks and for the winter to Florida. His wife died in 1905, leaving four children, and three years later he married Mrs. Elizabeth Sabin Leake, widow of a retired banker. He was a trustee of Phillips Academy (1891–1902) and president of Clarke School for the Deaf (1896–1919). He served as presidential elector (1896), as member of the Massachusetts Board of Education (1896–1900), as president of the Massachusetts Home Missionary Society (1896–1901), and as president of the Modern Language Association (1881–86). He published *The Life of Mark Hopkins* (1892), and an edition of Goethe's *Iphigenie auf Tauris* (1879), as well as numerous articles in scholarly periodicals; but he was not a fluent or a productive writer. He died of pneumonia, Nov. 22, 1919, at Williamstown. A bronze memorial tablet was placed in the Williams College Chapel in 1924 by his daughter, Mrs. Paul C. Ransom.

Carter was tall and slender, with flowing side whiskers. Somewhat stately in his manner, he gave the impression of being reserved if not a trifle austere, but he was actually a person of warm emotions and generous purposes. Although he was quiet and unaggressive, he was a capable executive, getting the most out of his faculty by letting them put their own theories into practise. His religious views were evangelical almost to the verge of fanaticism, and his finest and most enduring influence was exerted through his chapel prayers. In judging undergraduates, he was frequently deceived, discerning piety often where it did not and could not exist. His chronic ill health, accentuated by some domestic afflictions, cast a shadow over the middle years of his life, but in his old age he mellowed, grew more genial and sociable, and was transformed into "the Sage of Williamstown."

[*Springfield Republican*, Nov. 23, 1919; *Who's Who in America*, 1918–19; *Boston Herald*, Nov. 23, 1919; *Williams College Obit. Record*, 1919, pp. 21–30; L. W. Spring, *Hist. of Williams College* (1917); personal information from the Rev. Carroll Perry of Ipswich, Mass.]   C.M.F.

CARTER, HENRY ALPHEUS PEIRCE (Aug. 7, 1837–Nov. 1, 1891), merchant, diplomat, born in Honolulu, H. I., the son of Joseph Oliver and Hannah Trufant (Lord) Carter, was descended from Thomas Carter, a graduate of Cambridge University who came from Hertfordshire, England, to Charlestown, Mass., in 1635. His father, a shipmaster and trader from Charlestown, settled in Honolulu about 1828. In 1840 he left Henry in Boston to be educated, but disastrous speculations forced him nine years later to recall to Hawaii the boy of twelve. The latter immediately went to work, by 1851 was clerk in the local post-office, and the next year was in California working in a Stockton grocery. In 1854 he was employed by the largest Honolulu mercantile firm, C. Brewer & Company, who soon recognized his remarkable business sagacity and took him into partnership when he was twenty-five. He was among the first to realize that whaling, the great business of the islands during the fifties, was on the decline, and accordingly developed a close connection with the growing sugar industry, furnishing the plantations with supplies and capital and marketing their product. In spite of financial difficulties accompanying the Civil War, he brought the company safely through and made large profits on private ventures of his own. Until his death he retained a large and profitable interest in the firm.

Carter early took a prominent place in the civic life of Honolulu, where he enjoyed a reputation as an orator, which he gained during the Civil War by speeches made whenever a Northern victory was celebrated. On Feb. 27, 1862, he married Sybil Augusta, daughter of Gerrit P. Judd, a missionary physician who was the first Hawaiian foreign minister, and thenceforth he took a great interest in governmental affairs, giving himself by extensive study an education in diplomacy. Competent associates allowed him to relieve the pressure of business activity by tours through the United States and Europe in 1866 and 1871. The sugar industry, now producing heavily, was in critical condition for lack of a profitable market. As a solution for this difficulty Carter supported a policy of tariff reciprocity with the United States, and as early as 1872 foresaw annexation as the final outcome. Having attracted official attention by his eloquent advocacy of reciprocity, he was appointed a privy counsellor in September 1874, and less than a month later was sent to Washington with Judge Elisha H. Allen to negotiate such a treaty as he had often advocated. Two years of labor resulted in the treaty of 1876, which put sugar on the free list of imports to the United States and led to a "boom" in the industry. But England, France, and Germany protested that their "most favored nation" treaties were violated by the privileges given America. Viewing the mollification of these governments as an unfinished part of his earlier negotiation, Carter willingly went to Europe as King Kalakaua's special envoy for that purpose. The British made little difficulty and the French left their decision dependent on that of Germany. At Berlin Carter found Bismarck in an aggressive mood, demanding all the privileges accorded the United States. By a skilful combination of straightforward honesty, daring, and urbanity the chancellor was made a friend, and a treaty was signed whereby the special interest of Hawaii in the large and convenient markets of the United States was recognized and less favorable terms were accepted by Germany. Returning to Honolulu in 1879, Carter plunged into business, only to be called again into government

service the following year as minister of the interior, a post which he held for almost two years. In 1882 he went to Lisbon and negotiated a treaty which greatly facilitated the immigration of Portuguese peasants to relieve the acute labor shortage which had developed with the rapid growth of sugar production. From 1883 until his death he served as Hawaiian minister to the United States, where his remarkable knowledge of diplomacy and men was constantly used to repel the attacks of American sugar producers and other interests opposed to the reciprocity treaty. In 1887 he secured an extension of the treaty for seven years, though it cost Hawaii the grant to the United States of Pearl Harbor as a naval station. On his return from a vacation in Europe he died in a New York hotel. Carter's standing as a popular and skilful diplomat was equaled by his reputation as an able and far-sighted financier, while his personal charm made famous the hospitality of his Washington home.

[Geo. F. Nellist, ed., *Story of Hawaii and Its Builders* (Honolulu, 1925); Josephine Sullivan, *Hist. of C. Brewer & Company, Ltd.* (1926); W. D. Alexander, *Hist. of the Later Years of the Hawaiian Monarchy* (Honolulu, 1896).]

W.L.W., Jr.

CARTER, HENRY ROSE (Aug. 25, 1852–Sept. 14, 1925), sanitarian and epidemiologist, was born at Clifton plantation in Caroline County, Va. The first Carters of Virginia had come from Hertfordshire, England, in 1649. They were lords of the manor of Garston in the old country and became landowners and people of consequence in the new. From the highlands of Scotland came to Virginia the family of Rose. Hill Carter of Mine Hill married Mary Rose and of the union was born the first Henry Rose Carter, who married Emma Coleman. To them was born the younger Henry Rose Carter. After a preliminary education obtained at home and in the local schools of his community, young Carter was sent to the University of Virginia, where he pursued a scientific course, with special attention to mathematics. Here he was graduated in 1873 as a civil engineer. An injury, at the time regarded a permanent disability, turned him from an engineering career and toward the study of medicine. After three years of teaching, one as assistant in applied mathematics at the University of Virginia, he entered the University of Maryland and graduated in medicine in 1879. He entered the Marine Hospital Service in May of the same year. Shortly after his assignment to Cairo, Ill., in the fall of 1879 began his contact with yellow fever, which was to occupy much of his official career. The next few years, however, were devoted to clinical medicine. His assignment to the Gulf Quarantine Station at Ship Island in 1888 brought him into contact with the problems of maritime quarantine and particularly that of yellow fever exclusion. By systematic observation he satisfied himself of the efficiency of sulphur fumigation and provisionally fixed the incubation period of yellow fever at not to exceed six days. From these observations he introduced the principle that detention of ship personnel should be for seven days following fumigation. He found maritime quarantine procedure a haphazard system without central control and subject to no uniform regulations. He was largely instrumental in causing the transfer of quarantine stations from municipal or State control to that of the Government and in causing the formulation of uniform regulations based upon rational grounds.

When in 1893, and again in 1897–98, yellow fever gained a foothold in the Southern States, Carter was the Government's representative to coöperate with the State authorities in fighting the disease. From his observations in these epidemics, he definitely fixed the incubation period of yellow fever in man at not more than six days, confirming the provisional conclusion which he had drawn from his quarantine experience. In May 1900 he published *A Note on the Interval between Infecting and Secondary Cases of Yellow Fever,* calling attention to the "extrinsic incubation" of the disease, which accounted for the discrepancy between the incubation period and the observed time elapsing between original and secondary cases. This discrepancy (ten to seventeen days) was declared necessary for "infection of the environment" or, as was later shown, for the development of the yellow fever virus in the mosquito. The publication of this article was coincident with the order for convening the so-called Army Yellow Fever Commission for research upon the disease in Cuba. In its first report, the Commission credits the observations of Carter, together with those of Carlos Finlay on yellow fever and those of Ross and the Italian workers on malaria, with having materially influenced the decision to undertake investigation of mosquito transmission. Following the proof of this mode of transmission by Reed and his colleagues, Carter took up the presentation of the epidemiology of the disease from the new viewpoint. His papers on yellow fever, though neither numerous nor long, are classical.

Following the Spanish-American War, Carter organized the quarantine service for the new government of Cuba. In 1904 he went to Panama, where, after organizing the quarantine service of the Canal Commission, he became director of hospitals, which position he held for four years. In recognition of his distinguished work in sanitation, he was commissioned assistant surgeon-general of the Public Health Service in 1915. In the field of malariology, he also was a commanding figure. In 1913 he conducted with conspicuous success the first campaign for the control of malaria attempted in the United States, and, from that time until his retirement from active duty in the Public Health Service in 1919, he was constantly engaged in directing studies and supervising control of malaria in the Southern States. The last ten years of his life were closely identified with the yellow fever campaign of the International Health Board. He served on its special councils and in 1920, while observing an epidemic in Peru was asked by the Peruvian Government to act as its sanitary adviser. Because of his three decades of acquaintance with yellow fever and his position as leading authority on the subject, he was asked by the International Health Board to prepare a *History of Yellow Fever,* which was well on toward completion when he died in Washington of angina pectoris, after a protracted illness.

Carter was of medium height with a slight figure. He was of delicate constitution all his life and suffered frequent illnesses. He was, however, not only able to continue his activities, but he spared himself no inconveniences or physical hardship in the pursuit of his work. He was sociable and companionable, with a mind of Celtic complexity in which love of nature and the arts combined with dependability and devotion to duty. His portrait shows a thoroughly human personality, a relatively large head, a full face with a drooping *fer à cheval* mustache. He was married in 1880 at Cairo, Ill., to Laura Eugenia Hook, a resident of that place.

[A sketchy autobiography taken from the files of the Public Health Service appears in the *Va. Medical Mo.,* vol. LIII, 1926. The *Am. Jour. of Tropical Medicine,* vol. V, 1925, contains a biographical sketch with portrait. Much of the material for the present article was obtained from family sources, and from manuscripts of Dr. Wade H. Frost of Baltimore, still unpublished.]

J.M.P.

CARTER, JAMES COOLIDGE (Oct. 14, 1827–Feb. 14, 1905), lawyer, was born in Lancaster, Mass., the son of Solomon and Elizabeth (White) Carter. He attended Derby Academy, Hingham, Mass., and in 1846 entered Harvard College where he won the Bowdoin Prize, was a member of the Hasty Pudding Club, and graduated in 1850, fourth in his class. Before entering the Dane Law School at Harvard, in September 1851, he spent a year in New York City as a private tutor, and law student. Having removed to New York City, he was admitted to the New York bar in 1853, and began practise as managing clerk for the firm of Davies & Scudder of which he became a member in 1854 on the retirement of Judge Davies. He was associated with this firm, with various changes in personnel, for fifty-two years. The keynote of his career was devotion to his profession. There was no divided allegiance, even on the personal side, for he never married. His cases, and defense of the common law, made up his whole life, except in a few instances which had direct relation to the law. His ability early attracted the attention of Charles O'Conor who sought him as associate in many cases. Among the most prominent of these were the Jumel Will Case, and the Tweed Ring Cases. Out of the latter litigation grew Carter's interest in municipal reform. In 1875, at the appointment of Gov. Tilden, he served as a member of a commission of twelve to devise a plan of government for the cities of New York State. A founder of the National Municipal League, he was its president for nine years. He was counsel in many important cases in New York State, including the Singer, Tilden, Hamersley and Fayerweather will cases. In the last decade of his active practise, he was engaged chiefly in arguing cases involving constitutional questions before the United States Supreme Court. Perhaps the most noted of these was the Income Tax Case, argued in 1895, in which he brilliantly but unsuccessfully supported the constitutionality of the act.

In the court room, Carter was a striking advocate. He was of medium height, strongly built, with a rugged countenance in which "sternness, sadness and benevolence struggled for ascendancy," and he had a magnificent head described as leonine. His voice was deep, rich, and powerful. He possessed a copious vocabulary and displayed fine skill in its use. He was earnest, but used few gestures, and while not wanting in a sense of humor, was more given to irony. He was combative, aggressive, and forceful. He had the unusual habit, said Joseph H. Choate, "when he embarked in a cause, of first convincing himself of its justice, before he undertook to convince court, or jury or adversary." He formed his theory of a case, and retained it to the end through each appeal. "Nothing is finally decided," he used to say, "until it is decided right." He was almost too thoroughly in earnest in contentious argument, giving sometimes the appearance of hostility toward his adversary. Being called into critical cases where a forlorn hope had to be led, he lost in the long run as many cases as he won. His power of application was phenomenal, and his aim was absolute perfection and completeness in preparation. As a young man he twice went beyond his physical strength, so that for a year

or two he had to retire from practise. Thenceforward he gave systematic attention to his health, providing for repose, sport, and exercise. His brother lawyers recognized his position of leadership by electing him president of the American Bar Association (1894–95), and president, five times, of the Association of the Bar of the City of New York, of which he was a founder. In 1890 he was a member of the New York State Commission appointed to suggest amendments to the judiciary article of the state constitution. The high point in his career as an advocate was reached when he appeared as one of counsel for the United States before the Behring Sea Fur-Seal Tribunal of Arbitration which met in Paris in February 1893. His opening argument for the United States lasted seven days.

Among lawyers, Carter's name will always be a byword because of the fight which he led against codification. When the Civil Code of substantive law drawn up by David Dudley Field had been twice adopted by a New York legislature, and twice vetoed by a governor, and when further efforts were being made to effect its passage, Carter as a member of a Committee of the Association of the Bar of the City of New York, prepared a paper entitled *The Proposed Codification of Our Common Law* (1883), which was printed and widely distributed. This began a spirited controversy with Field which lasted until the final defeat of the Code. Carter believed that Field's plan to reduce to statutory form the entire body of law governing private transactions of men was fundamentally unsound, impossible of accomplishment, and even if possible undesirable. The foundation of his argument was a series of propositions: "That human transactions, especially private transactions, can be governed only by the principles of justice; that these have an absolute existence, and cannot be made by human enactment; that they are wrapped up with the transactions which they regulate, and are discovered by subjecting those transactions to examination; that the law is consequently a science depending upon the observation of facts, and not a contrivance to be established by legislation, that being a method directly antagonistic to science." That Carter's interest was not merely controversial, but philosophical and scientific, was shown by two further studies, "The Provinces of the Written and the Unwritten Law" (*Report of Virginia State Bar Association*, 1889), and "The Ideal and the Actual in the Law" (*Report of American Bar Association*, 1890). After his retirement from active practise, he devoted a portion of his leisure to the preparation of a fuller statement of his views, which was to have been read as a series of lectures before the Harvard Law School in the spring of 1905. After his death in New York City on Feb. 14 of that year, they were published by his executors under the title *Law: Its Origin, Growth and Function* (1907).

[Geo. A. Miller, "Jas. Coolidge Carter" in W. D. Lewis, ed., *Great Am. Lawyers*, VIII (1909), pp. 1–41; Jos. H. Choate, memorial in the *Report of the Ass. of the Bar of the City of N. Y.* (1906), pp. 120–37.]
F.C.H.

CARTER, JAMES GORDON (Sept. 7, 1795–July 21, 1849), educational reformer, was the son of Capt. James Carter of Leominster, Mass., and of Betsy (Hale) Carter. As his family was poor, young Carter secured the rudiments of learning in winter schools, which relieved the tedium of long, hard summers on the New England farm. At seventeen, he resolved to make his independent way through Groton Academy and Harvard College, which he did by teaching district and singing schools and lecturing on the history of Masonry. He graduated from Harvard, with honors (1820), and entered at once upon a career, as teacher, legislator, and author of textbooks, which placed him in the forefront of the memorable common school revival of Massachusetts. He astonished and satisfied, in turn, both the committee and pupils by his instruction and discipline of a school at Cohasset, proving himself a worthy descendant of Thomas Carter who "was apt to teach." His next venture, for which many Harvard students held him in grateful remembrance, was a private school at Lancaster, for those having difficulty with college work. He taught there till 1830. He early caught the vision of education as a science. In the views of Warren Colburn [*q.v.*], on the teaching of arithmetic, he found a practical application of the Pestalozzian principle that pupils should discover truth inductively, rather than memorize the instructions of books or teachers. The adoption of this principle he constantly urged in public addresses and published articles. He himself endeavored chiefly to apply the inductive method to geography. Assuming that "we need to know most of the places which are nearest us," he prepared and published, with William H. Brooks, illustrated geographies of Essex, Middlesex, and Worcester counties (1830), leading up to a knowledge of the larger unit, the state, afforded by geographies of Massachusetts (1830) and New Hampshire (1831). Though a step in the right direction, not much more can be said for these texts.

In 1821, Carter began his efforts in behalf of public education. His papers, which appeared in the *Boston Transcript,* were collected in a pamphlet, *Letters to the Hon. William Prescott on the Free Schools of New England, with Remarks on the Principles of Instruction* (1824). They both constituted an attack on the decadent state of education and contained suggestions for improvement. More specific proposals, first appearing in the *Boston Patriot* under the name of "Franklin," were published in a pamphlet, *Essays upon Popular Education with an Outline of an Institution for the Education of Teachers* (1826). The *Essays* were widely and favorably discussed and were reviewed in the *Literary Gazette* and the *North American Review.* In a memorial to the legislature (1827) Carter sought a practical realization of the normal school idea. A favorable report on the project, and a bill to subsidize it, were vigorously presented by W. B. Calhoun [*q.v.*], but failed in the Senate by one vote. In 1830 Carter helped to found the American Institute of Instruction, of which he was an influential member and, for some time, an officer. Being elected to the legislature, he served in the House (1835–38), then in the Senate, playing an important rôle as chairman of the committee on education. Among the more notable measures reported were those securing aid to the American Institute; "an act to provide for the better instruction of youth, employed in manufacturing establishments"; one securing one-half the surplus revenue for training common-school teachers; and another for the creation of a board of education and appointment of a state secretary of public schools (1837). Many held Carter to be the best qualified person to receive the newly created secretary's post. His disappointment over not obtaining it was probably a factor in the decline of his active participation in education. He was, however, the first member appointed to the board of education. Besides being legislator and reformer, Carter was also something of a journalist, serving as editor of the *Literary Gazette,* the *United States Gazette* (1824) and *New York Review* (1826). But his permanent reputation as an educator, which would have been augmented had he given his attention to education as completely in later as in earlier life, rests on his contribution to the growth of common schools (elementary and secondary), and his influence in favor of a rational method of teaching and the establishment of normal schools. He was married in 1827 to Anne M. Packard. He died of fever while in Chicago, July 21, 1849.

[An excellent sketch appears in Henry Barnard, *Memoirs of Teachers, Educators, and Promoters and Benefactors of Education* (1859), repub. from the *Am. Jour. of Education.* Accounts also appear in David Wilder, *Hist. of Leominster* (1853), Abijah P. Marvin, *Hist. of Lancaster* (1879), and Paul Monroe, ed., *Cyc. of Education* (1925).]
T.W.

CARTER, JESSE BENEDICT (June 16, 1872–July 20, 1917), classical scholar, was born in New York City of Scotch descent, the son of a publisher, Peter Carter, and of his wife Mary Louise Benedict. Books and studies formed a natural part of the daily life of the home in which he was brought up. In 1899 he entered New York University, but after one year went to Princeton, where he was graduated at the head of his class in 1893. In college his brilliancy and mental power caused him to surpass his classmates in all studies, and he was also an assiduous reader, especially in the fields of modern letters and the fine arts. After his graduation he studied for two years at the universities of Leipzig, Berlin, and Göttingen, for the most part in the field of the classics. He was instructor in Latin at Princeton for two years, 1895–97, when he returned to Germany, where he obtained, in 1898, the degree of Ph.D. at Halle. He was assistant professor of Latin at Princeton, 1898–1902, and in 1900 was lecturer on Roman religion in the summer school of the University of Wisconsin. On Jan. 22, 1902, he married Kate Benedict Freeman of New York. In the same year he was promoted to the rank of professor, a position which he held until 1907, though from 1904 to 1907 he was on leave of absence from Princeton and served as annual professor in the American School of Classical Studies in Rome. In 1907 he was chosen director of the School, and when, in 1911, it became a part of the American Academy in Rome, he remained as director of the Classical School of the Academy. In 1913 he was chosen director of the Academy. In the same year Princeton University conferred upon him the degree of L.H.D.

As director of the American Academy in Rome Carter displayed great executive and administrative ability. The Academy had recently been enlarged in scope and now included the School of Classical Studies as well as the School of Fine Arts. It was the director's task to further and guide the intellectual and material growth of the institution. During Carter's directorship the Academy was settled in permanent and admirable buildings, and its position as an important institution became generally recognized. The Director's own importance as a scholar also received wide recognition. He was invited to deliver the Lowell Lectures in Boston, and in 1916 he delivered, by invitation of the French Minister of Public Instruction, a course of lectures at the Sorbonne and at other French universities on "The Growth of Humanism in the United States." During the World War, Carter and other officers of the Academy were

actively engaged in the work of Italian war relief, and it was in recognition of his services in this work, as well as of his scholarship, that King Victor Emmanuel III conferred upon him in 1917 the rank of Commendator della Corona d'Italia. He died at Cervignano, Italy, from heart trouble aggravated by exposure to the heat, as he was on his way to the Italian front with a commission sent by the American Red Cross.

In person Carter was of medium height and rather rotund in face and figure. His exuberant vitality showed itself in mannerisms which were not always pleasing to Americans, but which added to his influence with the Italians among whom his later years were passed. He liked to be well dressed in the latest style. He was of a jovial and convivial disposition and enjoyed the good things of life whether of material or intellectual nature. His published writings treat for the most part topics in his chosen field, Roman religion. He was a regular collaborator in Roscher's *Ausführliches Lexikon der griechischen und römischen Mythologie* and in Hastings's *Encyclopædia of Religion and Ethics* and contributed to various periodicals. His separate publications were: *De Deorum Cognominibus* (1898), *The Roman Elegiac Poets* (1900), *Epitheta Deorum* (1902), *Virgil's Aeneid* (1903), *The Religion of Numa* (1906), *The Religious Life of Ancient Rome* (1911), and a translation of Huelsen's *Roman Forum* (1906). He was an able, even brilliant scholar, and in his presentation he succeeded in combining the salient features of his subject in an exceptionally vivid and striking manner.

[*Who's Who in America*, 1916–17; *Annual Rep. of the Am. Acad. in Rome*, 1916–17, pp. 31–33, 41–42; *Am. Jour. of Archæology*, XXI, 340; *N. Y. Times*, July 23, Aug. 6, 1917.]   H. N. F.

CARTER, JOHN (1737–1781), pioneer, was born in Virginia, where about 1758 he married Elizabeth Taylor. It is believed that he was a kinsman of Robert (or "King") Carter [*q.v.*], but the precise relationship has not been determined. Emigrating from Virginia about 1770, he was one of the first settlers in western North Carolina (now Tennessee) and in the Watauga community in the region of the Watauga River. By reason of his eminence he became the most prominent member of the community which included such distinguished pioneers as John Sevier and Charles and James Robertson. He formed a partnership with William Parker, in the establishment of a store, the chief enterprise of the growing colony. This store was robbed by Indians, who were forced to make reparation by granting the owners an extensive tract of land comprising the whole of Carter's Valley. In 1772 the Watauga pioneers organized the first government west of the Alleghanies and adopted a written constitution, sometimes said to be the first in America, entitled "Articles of the Watauga Association." Under this government, legislative and executive functions were vested in a board of thirteen commissioners, of which Carter was chairman. He was also chairman of the judicial body, the Watauga court.

In 1776 the inhabitants of "Washington District," which comprised what is now northeast Tennessee, petitioned the North Carolina Provincial Council to be annexed to North Carolina. The petition was granted, and the district chose Carter as one of the members of the North Carolina Provincial Congress of 1776. This congress made him a colonel of the district, in which capacity he was active throughout the Revolution in defending the frontier against the Indians. A public magazine of military stores was established at his house. In 1777, and again in 1781, he represented Washington District in the North Carolina Senate, serving on a committee for the protection of the frontier. He was a partner of Gen. John Sevier and Col. Richard Henderson in land speculations, and he served as public entry-taker, a position of great responsibility in a growing frontier settlement. At his death he was one of the largest landholders west of the Alleghany Mountains. He had one son, Landon Carter [*q.v.*]. Many of his descendants have filled important offices under the Tennessee or the Federal government.

[David W. Carter, *Carter of Tenn.* (Chattanooga, 1927), pp. 9–10; J. G. M. Ramsay, *Annals of Tenn.* (1853, repr. 1926); *N. C. Records*, vols. X–XII, XVII, XXIV.]   C. O. P.

CARTER, JOHN (July 21, 1745–Aug. 19, 1814), printer, editor, put behind his newspaper, the *Providence Gazette,* the resources of a strong personality, and conducted it for nearly half a century with a vigor which made it an influence in Rhode Island affairs, and an institution respected beyond state limits. He was the youngest of the five children of John and Elizabeth (Spriggs) Carter; was born in Philadelphia a few months after the death of his father, who was killed in a naval battle of the war of 1745; and learned the printing-trade of Benjamin Franklin and David Hall, whom he served as an apprentice (Isaiah Thomas, *History of Printing,* 1810, I, 430). At the age of twenty-two, he came to Providence, and became associated with Sarah Goddard in the publication of the *Providence Gazette.* The next year the business came into his possession; from that time until ill health

caused his retirement shortly before his death in 1814, he was the sole editor, and, during the same period, excepting for five or six years (Nov. 1793–May 1799), when William Wilkinson was a partner, was the sole proprietor. During the Revolutionary War, he was a member of the Committee of Correspondence. From July 1772 to June 1792 he was postmaster of Providence; a commission dated Sept. 25, 1775, was signed by Benjamin Franklin.

Carter's chief claim to remembrance rests on his work at his printing shop "at the sign of Shakespear's Head." Here, for many years, much of the local printing and publishing was done, and, for a period, all of it. Here, too, the *Gazette* was printed, with the typographical correctness which was Carter's pride, and which distinguished all of his craftsmanship (William R. Staples, *Annals of the Town of Providence,* 1843, pp. 544–45). The *Gazette* supported the Revolutionary cause; it opposed the paper-money party; it is said to have opposed the adoption of the Constitution (Edward Field, editor, *State of Rhode Island and Providence Plantations at the End of the Century,* 1902, II, 574). As the time approached of Rhode Island's final action, a paragraph in the issue of Mar. 20, 1790, was made to conclude with the words: "In short, the State is as free as an Individual in a State of Nature, and there is *no more* Reason for an Adoption of the New Constitution, than there is for such Individual to enter into a State of Government." The words in italics (so printed in the original) may hide a subtlety and imply that the writer held *some* reason to exist of a contrary tenor. In the obituary notice of Carter in the Gazette of Aug. 20, 1814, the statement is made that he "was zealous in his endeavors to induce the people of this state to adopt the Present Constitution." The opposition of the paper in 1812 to the declaration of war is unequivocal (Field, I, 297). Carter's valedictory was printed in the issue of Feb. 14, 1814. The *Providence Gazette,* he said, "since the dawn of our glorious revolution, has unceasingly disseminated the orthodox political principles of the Washington school." Miss Gertrude S. Kimball speaks of him as "the admirable and sagacious John Carter," and says that he was "possessed of that choleric and generous-hearted temperament that so frequently characterizes the Irish-American" (*Providence in Colonial Times,* 1912, pp. 318–19). He was married on May 14, 1769, to Amey Crawford, by whom he had twelve children. His name was continued in that of his great-grandson, John Carter Brown, the founder of the John Carter Brown Library at Brown University.

[A sketch of John Carter, by his great-great-grandson, John Carter Brown Woods, is printed in *R. I. Hist. Soc. Colls.*, Oct. 1918. Dates in the history of the *Providence Gazette,* and information regarding the location of files, will be found in "Bibliography of Am. Newspapers, 1690–1820, pt. 15, R. I.," by C. S. Brigham in *Proc. Am. Antiq. Soc.*, Apr. 1924. A list of Carter imprints to 1800 will be found in *R. I. Imprints, 1720–1800* (R. I. Hist. Soc., 1915).]   W. A. S.

CARTER, LANDON (Jan. 29, 1760–June 5, 1800), pioneer and public official, the only son of John [*q.v.*] and Elizabeth (Taylor) Carter, was born in Virginia and emigrated with his father to the region of the Watauga River in what is now northeast Tennessee, when he was about ten years old. He was sent to school at Liberty Hall (now Davidson College), Mecklenburg County, N. C., and was more adequately equipped for a public career than many of his Tennessee contemporaries. The last years of the Revolution found him old enough for responsible military duties. In 1780 he served as a captain in John Sevier's expedition against the Cherokees and he participated in the battle of Boyd's Creek, one of the best fought engagements of the war on the frontier. In the same year he was with Charles Robertson's command in South Carolina. In 1781–82 he fought in that state under Gen. Sevier and also under Gen. Francis Marion. On his march homeward his company was ambushed by the Indians. In 1788 the North Carolina legislature appointed him a major of horse and in 1790 Gov. Blount of the Southwest Territory made him lieutenant-colonel commandant of the militia of the Washington District. In the Indian campaign of 1792–93 he served as colonel.

In 1784 and again in 1789 Carter represented Washington County in the North Carolina House of Commons. The movement to erect what is now northeast Tennessee into the independent state of Franklin was cordially supported by Carter. He was secretary of the Jonesborough Convention of 1784 which forwarded the movement, and on the organization of Franklin he served as speaker of the first Senate and member of the first Council of State and later as secretary of state and state entry-taker. Under the government of the Southwest Territory, which was organized in 1790, he was treasurer of Washington District, one of the three districts into which the territory was divided. In 1796 he represented Washington County in the convention that adopted a constitution for the new state of Tennessee. The first legislature of the new state elected him treasurer for the two districts of Washington and Hamilton. The same legislature created Carter County which it named for him. The county seat, Elizabethton,

was named for his wife, Elizabeth Maclin, whom he married in 1784.

Carter added largely to the extensive land holdings that he inherited from his father. He received ten thousand acres from the state of North Carolina as a reimbursement for the expenses incurred by his father in connection with Col. Richard Henderson's purchase of lands from the Cherokees. Throughout his life he manifested an interest in education, serving as a trustee and incorporator of Martin Academy (later Washington College) and as trustee of Greeneville College, both located in northeast Tennessee.

[D. W. Carter, *Carter of Tenn.* (Chattanooga, 1927), pp. 10–12; S. C. Williams, *Hist. of the Lost State of Franklin* (1924), pp. 292–94; *N. C. Records,* vols. XVII–XXII, XXIV.]   C. O. P.

CARTER, ROBERT (1663–Aug. 4, 1732), colonial official, landholder, well-known as "King Carter," was the son of John and Sarah (Ludlow) Carter. He was born in Lancaster County, Va., at his father's country seat, Corotoman, situated near the Rappahannock River not far from the Chesapeake Bay. It appears that the ancestral home was in Buckinghamshire, England, and that John, the emigrant, was a distressed royalist who sought refuge in Virginia about 1649. Before his death in 1669 he had accumulated considerable wealth and had become prominent in the politics of the colony.

All that is known about Robert's education is derived from the wills of his father and elder brother. The father's will provided that a "man or youth servant" that had been brought up in a Latin school should be purchased for the son, then six years old, to teach him "his books either in English or Latin." The elder brother out of a considerable library left Robert all his law and Latin books. At the age of twenty-eight, Robert entered the colonial Assembly as a burgess from Lancaster County, in which office he served during the years 1691–92 and 1695–99. Becoming one of the most prominent members of the Assembly, he was chosen speaker in 1696 and again in 1699. In the latter year he was advanced to the Council and was also made colonial treasurer, an office that he filled for six years. That he served as treasurer while a councillor is evidence of the high esteem in which he was held, for the treasurership by right belonged to a burgess. In the council from 1699 until his death in 1732, he was for the last six years its president. After the death of Gov. Drysdale in 1726, he was for a few months acting governor of Virginia.

During the first third of the eighteenth century Carter was the most eminent resident of the

Northern Neck (the peninsula bounded by the Chesapeake Bay and the Potomac and Rappahannock rivers) and one of its chief landowners. Among the local offices that he held were those of colonel and commander-in-chief of Lancaster County, the same for Northumberland County, and naval officer for the Rappahannock River District. In 1702 he became agent for the Fairfaxes, proprietors of the Northern Neck, and he served his opulent employers in this capacity for upwards of twenty years (1702–11 and 1722–32). This was a strategic position for the acquisition of a fortune and Carter made the most of it. At his death he was one of the wealthiest of colonials, leaving more than three hundred thousand acres of land, one thousand slaves, and ten thousand pounds. Fairfax Harrison has characterized him as a "man of tremendous energy, shrewd business habits, dominant personality, and accustomed to success in whatever he undertook" (post, I, 197). Possibly because of the great power that he exercised, or possibly, as an enemy said, because of his excessive pride and ambition, he received the sobriquet "King Carter" or "King Robin." That so powerful a man had his enemies and doubtless his faults cannot be denied. As an antidote to the lofty eulogy composed by his parson and engraved upon his tombstone is the following verse scribbled thereon in chalk by a less friendly hand:

> "Here lies Robin, but not Robin Hood,
> Here lies Robin that never was good,
> Here lies Robin that God has forsaken,
> Here lies Robin the Devil has taken."

Carter was a friend and benefactor of William and Mary College, serving it as rector, trustee, and member of the board of visitors. Building at his own expense Christ Church, Lancaster County, still standing, he reserved, in addition to a large pew for his immediate family, one-fourth of the building for the use of his tenants and servants. The tombstones of the "King" and his wives in the churchyard were described in 1838 by Bishop Meade as probably the largest, richest, and heaviest in the United States. His first wife was Judith (Armistead) Carter (died 1699), his second, Elizabeth (Landon) Carter (died 1710), of the family of Landon, Herefordshire, England. The children of these unions married into the first families of the colony, and, as a result of a fortunate blending of superior strains, Carter had an unusual number of distinguished descendants—two presidents of the United States, six governors of Virginia, Gen. Robert E. Lee, and many others.

[The best account of the Carters is found in T. A. Glenn, *Some Colonial Mansions* (1898), pp. 217–60. A genealogy of the family was published by W. A. Stan-

ard in *The Critic* (Richmond), June 18, 24, 25, 1888. Fairfax Harrison, *Landmarks of Old Prince William* (1924), is excellent for Carter's career as a landowner and agent for the Fairfaxes. Frequent references to Carter are found in the *Jours. of the Va. House of Burgesses and Council*; Bishop Wm. Meade, *Old Churches, Ministers, and Families of Va.* (1857); *Wm. and Mary College Quart. Hist. Mag.*, and the *Va. Mag. of Hist. and Biog.* (especially vols. V–VIII).] C. O. P.

CARTER, ROBERT (Feb. 5, 1819–Feb. 15, 1879), editor, author, was born in Albany, N. Y., of Irish parentage. His formal education, which was rather fragmentary, was acquired in the common schools and in the Jesuit College of Chambly in Canada. At fifteen he was appointed an assistant to his guardian, who was state librarian, but he resigned in 1838 in order to take up journalism, some of his poems and sketches having already appeared in the Albany papers. "He had known extreme poverty, and used to tell the story of his mother and himself walking the streets of a city in central New York and spending their last half-dollar on a copy of Spenser's Faerie Queene, instead of a dinner" (T. W. Higginson, *Old Cambridge*, 1899, p. 47). In 1841, having become a Swedenborgian, he moved to Boston in order to prepare some religious pamphlets and there met James Russell Lowell, with whom he joined, in 1843, in editing the *Pioneer*, a literary monthly, which was abandoned after three issues, chiefly because of Lowell's poor health.

Carter was not the kind of man to settle down to any one occupation over a period of years. He edited several manuals of knowledge, acted as chief clerk in the Cambridge post-office during 1845, was employed as literary adviser to various publishing houses, and became private secretary to William H. Prescott, the historian. In 1846 he was married to Ann Augusta Gray, a writer of books for children, "who brought him as a dowry two eagles,—formidable pets,— whose butcher's bills made great inroads on his pay" (*Ibid.*, p. 48). An important phase of his career opened in 1848, when he identified himself with the Free-Soil party and shortly afterward was made the editor, with John G. Palfrey, of the Boston *Commonwealth*, the chief organ of the Free-Soilers. As secretary of the Free-Soil State Committee, he called a convention in Worcester, July 20, 1854, where the delegates, being too numerous for any hall in that city, held their sessions in the open air. A brief platform drafted by Carter was adopted, together with the name "Republican" suggested by him; and a committee of six, headed by John A. Andrew, was named to organize the new party in the state.

In 1855 Carter edited the Boston *Telegraph;*

in 1856 he took charge of the Boston *Atlas;* and during 1857–59 he was Washington correspondent for Greeley's *New York Tribune*. From 1859 until 1863 he assisted George Ripley and Charles A. Dana in editing the first edition of *The American Cyclopedia*. Then, after a few months in government service, he moved to Rochester, N. Y., as editor of the *Democrat,* remaining there for five years. In 1864 he was married to his second wife, Susan Nichols, an author of handbooks on art and a contributor to periodicals. Rossiter Johnson, one of his assistants on the *Democrat*, was much impressed by his marvelous memory for men and events. The old restlessness again seized him, however, and he became editor of *Appleton's Journal* (1870–73), resigning to take part in the revision of *The American Cyclopedia*, to which he contributed noteworthy articles on "Jefferson Davis" and "The Confederate States of America." In 1874 impaired health obliged him to give up writing, and he took several trips to Europe during the next three years. He died in Cambridge, Mass., Feb. 15, 1879, worn out by his ceaseless activity.

He wrote several novels, including *The Armenian's Daughter* and *The Great Tower of Tarudant* (published first in Poe's *Broadway Journal*), and a breezy book, *A Summer Cruise on the Coast of New England* (1864), which ran through several editions. One of his best-known achievements was a series of vigorous essays written for the Boston *Atlas* in reply to the attacks of Francis Bowen [*q.v.*], on the Hungarian revolutionists; these articles later appeared in a volume called *The Hungarian Controversy* (1852). In 1852 also, with Kossuth's sanction, Carter edited a book called *Kossuth in New England*. He was the friend of nearly all the literary men of his generation in the United States, and he left at his death some incomplete reminiscences, which, however, have never been published. He was an industrious writer, who read everything and combined an encyclopedic knowledge with a tenacious memory. It is said that, when the news of the assassination of President Lincoln reached him at Rochester, he sat down at his editor's desk and, without consulting a single reference, prepared a long article on "Notorious Regicides in History."

[See Introduction by Rossiter Johnson to Carter's *A Summer Cruise* (new ed., 1888); scattered items in Horace E. Scudder, *Jas. Russell Lowell: A Biography* (1901); obituary in *Boston Transcript*, Feb. 17, 1879.]

C. M. F.

CARTER, SAMUEL POWHATAN (Aug. 6, 1819–May 26, 1891), naval and army officer, grandson of Landon Carter [*q.v.*], and great-grandson of John Carter [*q.v.*], was the oldest of the three children of Alfred Moore Carter (1784–1850) and his second wife, Evalina B. Parry. Born at Elizabethton, Tenn., he was educated at Washington College in that state, a Presbyterian institution, and at Princeton, which he entered as a sophomore in 1837. On Feb. 14, 1840, he was appointed midshipman in the navy, making his first cruise, 1840–43, on the sloop *Dale,* of the Pacific squadron. After serving on the steamer *Michigan,* stationed on the Great Lakes, and the frigate *Potomac* of the home squadron, he late in 1845 was ordered to the Naval Academy at Annapolis where he graduated with the class of 1846. On July 11 of that year he was promoted passed midshipman. His first duty in this rank was on board the ship of the line *Ohio,* from which vessel he witnessed the fall of Vera Cruz. After periods of service at the Naval Observatory and on board the frigate *St. Lawrence* of the Mediterranean squadron, he was ordered in 1850 to the Naval Academy as assistant professor of mathematics, where he remained until 1853. He was promoted master in 1854, and lieutenant in 1855. While attached to the steam frigate *San Jacinto* of the East India squadron, he participated in the attack on the Barrier Forts, Canton River, China, in 1856. From 1857 to 1860 he was assistant to the executive officer of the Naval Academy. The outbreak of the Civil War found him serving on board the steam sloop *Seminole* of the Brazil squadron.

A letter written by Carter while on the Brazil station declaring his purpose to adhere to the Union in the event of war was widely published in his home state and led Andrew Johnson and other influential residents of east Tennessee to request his services in prosecuting the war in that quarter. Early in July 1861 he was detailed from the navy to "special duty at the War Department" and was ordered to proceed to east Tennessee for the purpose of organizing and drilling Unionist volunteers. In less than a month he had organized one full regiment and part of another,—the first Unionist troops from Tennessee. A month later he was placed in command of a Tennessee brigade and in May 1862 he was made a brigadier-general of the volunteer army. Until the close of 1862 he commanded brigades; and from that time until mustered out of service, divisions. In 1862 he commanded the first important cavalry raid made by the Unionists, in which he defeated the Confederates at Holston, Carter's Station, and Jonesville, and destroyed much valuable property. This raid brought relief to Rosecrans then hard pressed at Murfreesboro and infused new life into the Unionist cavalry. Carter received the thanks of Gen. Halleck and was recommended for promotion to the rank of major-general. At the battle of Kinston, N. C., in March 1865, he commanded the left wing of the Unionist army; and later that year, the 23rd Army Corps and the District of Goldsboro. On Mar. 13, 1865, he received the brevet of major-general of volunteers and on January 19, 1866, was honorably mustered out of service.

While serving in the army Carter in 1863 was promoted lieutenant-commander in the navy, and in 1865 commander. On his return to the navy in 1866 he was made commander of the steamer *Monocacy* of the Asiatic squadron, in which capacity he served for three years. From 1870, in which year he received his captaincy, to 1873 he was commandant of midshipmen at Annapolis. He next saw active service for two years as commander of the steamship *Alaska* on the European station. His last important duty before his retirement in 1881 was as a member of the Light-House Board, 1877–80. In 1878 he was made a commodore and in 1882 he was advanced to the grade of rear-admiral on the retired list.

Carter's career is unique. He is the only American officer who was both a rear-admiral and a major-general. He was tall, handsome and dignified, graceful in carriage, and very affable. A fellow officer described him as a "soldierly Christian" of sincere piety and undoubted courage. He married Carrie Potts, a member of the Pennsylvania family of that name. He is buried in Oak Hill Cemetery, Washington, D. C.

[Record of Officers, Bureau of Navigation, 1840–82; *Official Records* (Army), 1 ser., XX, XXX, XLVII; and *House Report No. 1858*, 48 Cong., 1 Sess.; G. C. Kniffin, "A Sailor on Horseback" in *D. C. Mil. Order of the Loyal Legion, War Papers, No. 19*; "A Sketch of the Mil. Services of Sam. P. Carter . . . 1861–65" (MS.), deposited with the Naval Hist. Foundation; sketch in the *Baltimore Weekly American*, May 20, 1882.]

C. O. P.

CARTER, THOMAS HENRY (Oct. 30, 1854– Sept. 17, 1911), senator, was born on a farm in Scioto County, Ohio. His parents, Edward C. and Margaret (Byrnes) Carter were of pure Irish blood. In 1865 they moved to central Illinois. In 1878 Thomas left his father's home and began the study of law at Burlington, Iowa. He earned his expenses by selling a book, *The Footprints of Time, a Complete Analysis of Our System of Government*. In 1882 he moved to Helena, Mont., and with Montana he was identified for the remainder of his life. He was married on Jan. 27, 1886, to Ellen L. Galen of Helena. In his early years in Montana he gave himself entirely to the practise of law, entering into part-

nership with John B. Clayberg in a firm which maintained a preeminent position for many years. In 1888 the Republican party nominated him as its candidate for territorial delegate to Congress. The territory had generally been Democratic, but this year due to a fight between Democratic leaders Carter was elected by a majority of more than 5,000 votes. The following year Montana was admitted as a state and Carter was elected its first representative in Congress. There he showed a disposition to urge free silver and was an advocate of more liberal legislation for homesteaders. In spite of his Western view-point, and of the fact that he came from a new state he gained influence rapidly. In the Democratic landslide of 1890 he was defeated for reëlection, and President Harrison gave him an appointment as commissioner of the general land office. This appointment was received with pleasure in the West where the land laws had been enforced by men with Eastern views. Carter at once satisfied the complaints of Western farmers, miners, and timbermen by a policy of liberal interpretation of the law. In 1892, four years after he had entered politics, he was selected by Harrison as chairman of the Republican national committee to manage the President's campaign for reëlection. Three years later he was elected to the United States Senate by the legislature of Montana. Upon the expiration of his term he retired to make way for a Democrat but was elected again in 1905.

Carter's chief work was as United States senator. Although a staunch Republican he strongly opposed the policy of Eastern manufacturers who desired a high tariff on finished goods and a low tariff on raw materials. Montana was a producer of wool, hides, lead, and lumber, and he advocated protection for these. His support of the Dingley Tariff and of the Payne-Aldrich Tariff was given only after protection for the raw materials of the West was included. He also forced the issue of bimetallism against the growing influence of the gold wing under Hanna, and, although he refused to bolt the St. Louis convention, after the Republican triumph in 1896 he waged a fight for international bimetallism. While McKinley was still president, Carter supported the bill for a ship subsidy and coupled it with a demand for national reclamation. He also took a leading part in many measures not of a partisan nature. He helped draft the forest reserve law of 1897 and throughout his twelve years in the Senate was an active participant in all sorts of legislation regarding the national forests. He was opposed to a policy of extensive conservation, vigorously attacking Cleveland's withdrawal of 21,000,000 acres of the public domain for forest reserve, and fighting Roosevelt's policy of conservation as primarily beneficial to the large lumber companies. In great measure he represented the older Western sentiment favorable to getting the public domain as rapidly as possible into private hands. He introduced a number of bills for the improvement of Yellowstone Park and was largely responsible for the establishment of Glacier National Park. For many years he was an advocate of postal savings banks and drafted the measure that finally became a law. He declared that this act was his greatest contribution to good government. He earnestly advocated a constitutional amendment giving Congress authority to enact a uniform marriage and divorce law. He was greatly interested in giving Alaska an adequate territorial government, and helped draft the code that went into operation in 1911. He opposed all attacks on the Civil Service Law and brought about many extensions of its regulations. Shrewd, cautious, but courageous, he was a man of great power, although his ability to obtain something for Montana and the West in all types of legislation, and the way in which he strove to reconcile opposing principles laid him open to charges of insincerity.

[There is a laudatory sketch of Carter in *Progressive Men of Mont.* (1904), and a long, eulogistic obituary in the *Helena Daily Independent*, Sept. 18, 1911. His sister, Mrs. Julia Lang, has a collection of material regarding him. His work in Congress may be followed through the *Cong. Record*, 51, 54, 56, 59, 61 Cong., vols. XXI, XXVIII, XXXIV, XL, XLVI.]   P.C.P.

CARTER, WILLIAM SAMUEL (Aug. 11, 1859–Mar. 15, 1923), trade-union official, was born in Austin, Tex., the son of Samuel Miles and Margaret Frances (Oliphant) Carter. As a youth he was studious; though most of his time until his twenty-first year was spent as a cowboy, he employed his leisure in reading, and he was enabled to get some primary schooling in Williamson County and two years of instruction in the Agricultural and Mechanical College of Texas. His introduction to railroading, with which he was to be connected for many years, occurred in 1879, when he was put in charge of a wooden tramway for hauling lumber and thus became "superintendent of seven mules, a few drivers and seven miles of track." In the same year he got a job as a fireman on an old wood-burning locomotive on what is now a part of the Gulf, Colorado & Santa Fé Railway. Except for an intermission of three years he worked successively as a baggageman, fireman, and engineer on various railroads until September 1894. In October he became editor of the *Brotherhood*

of Locomotive Firemen and Enginemen's Magazine, a place he retained until Jan. 1, 1904, when he became general secretary and treasurer of the Brotherhood. Five years later he became its president.

He attracted general attention in 1913 by refusing to call a strike that had been voted by his union after prolonged negotiations and by appealing to the government and public for support on the ground that the railway managers were trying to embarrass President Wilson in the furtherance of the executive's industrial policy. As a sequence of his action negotiations were reopened, and a revised wage scale was adopted. In February 1918, he was appointed director of the Division of Labor of the United States Railway Administration, an office he held until Mar. 15, 1920, continuing during the time as the nominal head of his union and afterward resuming active service. On June 30, 1922, he retired from the presidency and was made manager of the newly-created research department of the Brotherhood. He moved from Cleveland, which had been his home for many years, to Washington, where he began the organization of his department. Some months later his health failed. On Feb. 24, 1923, he was taken for treatment to the Church Home and Infirmary, at Baltimore, where three weeks later he died. His funeral, largely attended by trade-union and government officials, was held in Washington.

Carter was twice married: on Dec. 26, 1880, to Evelyn Gorsuch of Austin, who died June 22, 1892, and on Nov. 27, 1902, to Julia I. Cross of Peoria, Ill., who survived him. He was a man of high character, and, in his special field, of exceptional abilities. As the editor of the journal of his union, though without previous experience, he developed a marked capacity, bringing it to a high state of excellence, and winning for it a general recognition. As general secretary and treasurer he was an innovator of many improvements in the technique of union management, while as president, during a period in which the most important wage movements in the history of the Brotherhood took place, he showed a skill, tact, and patience in negotiations which usually brought success. His service in the government's railway administration has been highly praised by his colleagues. He had the confidence of the rank and file of his union to an extent few labor leaders have attained, and it seems not to have been disturbed by the high regard he won from the employers with whom he dealt. He was democratic and unassuming in manner, generous in disposition, and, though often in controversy, is said to have 'borne no resentments.

[*Who's Who in America*, 1922–23 ; *Brotherhood of Locomotive Firemen and Enginemen's Mag.*, Apr. 1923 ; *N. Y. Times*, Mar. 16, 1923.]   W.J.G.

CARTERET, PHILIP (1639–1682), first governor of New Jersey, was the son of an attorney-general of the Island of Jersey, and fourth cousin to Sir George Carteret, prominent at the Restoration Court. After the gift of New Jersey by James, Duke of York, to John Lord Berkeley and Sir George Carteret in 1664, Philip Carteret was commissioned by them as governor. Sailing in the ship, *Philip*, with a party recruited in part in the Channel Islands, he landed in August 1665, at what is now Elizabethport. On disputed authority he is said to have given to the settlement the name of Elizabethtown in honor of the wife of Sir George. It is a tradition also that Carteret went ashore carrying a hoe to symbolize his fellowship with the planters. The youthful governor faced a task of great difficulty. Though the Dutch, already established at Bergen and elsewhere, readily accepted his authority, groups of New England settlers, who had received from Col. Nicolls at New York permission to enter the country, were not eager to submit. Accustomed to the free New England ideas of settlement and land tenure they disliked the plan of the Lords Proprietors to draw large sums from quit-rents paid in perpetuity by the colonists. On Carteret's landing he found the land already occupied by the pioneers of such a group. Though no direct collision took place between Carteret and the "Associates," out of the conflict of claims later arose the famous "Elizabethtown Controversy" which long distracted the politics of New Jersey. Carteret instituted government under the "Concessions and Agreements" of the Proprietors, and in 1668 summoned the first session of the legislature of New Jersey. But when the first payment of quit-rent came due his authority was defied. The insurgents rather illogically chose as their leader Capt. James Carteret, son of Sir George, whom they elected "President of the Country." Philip Carteret at length received aid from the Lords Proprietors and the rebellion collapsed. But directly afterward occurred the Dutch reconquest of New Netherland which included New Jersey. After the Treaty of Westminster, Philip Carteret became governor of East Jersey, for the original province had been divided between Sir George Carteret and the Quaker assigns of Berkeley. East Jersey included the northern and eastern portion looking to the Hudson. This province Philip Carteret administered with some success. But the right of East Jersey to collect customs was questioned by Sir Edmund Andros of New York, and after the death of Sir George Carteret in 1680 Andros endeavored to suppress the entire jurisdiction. After resisting successfully for some time, Philip Carteret was finally seized by a force from New York, was harshly treated and was put upon trial for usurping authority. Though declared innocent, he was compelled to desist from exercising power. Meanwhile, however, the diplomacy of William Penn and his associates had virtually forced the Duke of York to surrender his claims to New Jersey, and the authority of Philip Carteret in East Jersey was reestablished. In 1682, he gave up the office to Thomas Rudyard, and died soon after. Of his personality and appearance we have no direct account. But throughout his tempestuous career as governor, he displayed firmness, tact, and stalwart fidelity to his trust. His wife was the thrice married daughter of Richard Smith of Long Island.

[The chief source of printed information on Carteret is vol. I of the *N. J. Archives*. His relations to the land question are shown in the rare *Elizabethtown Bill in Chancery* and the still rarer *Answer to the Elizabethtown Bill in Chancery*. A brief sketch of Carteret appears in the second edition of Wm. A. Whitehead, *East Jersey under the Proprietary Govt.* (2nd ed., 1875), p. 106. See also Samuel Smith, *Hist. of the Colony of Novo-Caesaria, or N. J.* (1877) ; Willis F. Johnson, "The Story of the Carterets" in *Proc. N. J. Hist. Soc.*, 4 Ser., IX, 328–33 ; *Ibid.*, 2 Ser., I, 31.]   E.P.T.

CARTWRIGHT, PETER (Sept. 1, 1785–Sept. 25, 1872), Methodist clergyman, was born in Amherst County, Va. His father, Justinian Cartwright, a Revolutionary soldier, "was quite a poor man and not so much a bad as a good-for-nothing kind of man" (Mrs. Susannah Johnson, *Recollections of the Rev. John Johnson*, Nashville, 1869, p. 32). He married a widow Wilcox, a devout Methodist but a termagant. Among her numerous children beside Peter, one son, Edmund, became a local Methodist preacher, another, John, was hanged for murder, while a daughter, Polly, led a life of debauchery. About the year 1790 Justinian moved with his family into the wilds of Kentucky and ultimately located, in 1793, in Logan County on the extreme southern edge of the state in a section known as Rogue's Harbor from the number of escaped convicts and desperadoes who congregated there. Although the more respectable settlers eventually organized into a band called the Regulators and after several pitched battles drove out the Rogues, life in this region continued turbulent and unrestrained. Here Peter grew up, a tall and lusty youth, devoted to horse-racing, card-playing, and dancing. He was almost totally without education save for the religious instruction received from his mother which made a deep impression upon his ardently emotional nature. In his sixteenth year he fell into a conviction of sin soon followed by conversion at a camp meeting and by admission into the Methodist Church. In the service of that robust communion he was thenceforth able to express the energy which had formerly gone into more purely pagan activities. Almost immediately after his own conversion he began to convert the lads of the neighborhood with such success that in the next year (1802) he was given an exhorter's license. A little later his family moved into Lewiston County where for a time Peter attended Brown's Academy, but doctrinal disputes with the teacher and the other pupils soon interrupted his schooling and he returned to the more congenial work of exhortation. In October 1803 when a little over eighteen he became a traveling preacher. His early itineraries successively included the Red River Circuit in Kentucky, the Waynesville Circuit which covered a part of Tennessee, the Salt River and Shelbyville Circuit which extended into Indiana, and the Scioto Circuit in Ohio. Through all this wide territory, "the Kentucky Boy," as Peter was called, became a well-known and popular figure. His self-reliance, his readiness with tongue and fist, his quick sense of humor, all made him dear to the hearts of the frontier. As presiding elder he had the noted William M'Kendree [q.v.], who instructed him in English grammar and laid out for him a course of study and reading which the young disciple faithfully pursued with much profit. In 1806 Peter was ordained a deacon by Bishop Francis Asbury [q.v.], and two years later, at the age of twenty-three, he was ordained an elder. On Aug. 18, 1808, he was married to Frances Gaines, a girl of nineteen, because, as he wrote, "After mature deliberation and prayer ... I thought it was my duty to marry." He continued his work as a circuit-rider mainly in Kentucky and Tennessee until 1824 when, actuated largely by hatred of slavery, he had himself transferred to the Sangamon Circuit in Illinois, with which state he was thenceforth identified.

For almost another fifty years "the Kentucky Boy," now known as "Uncle Peter," remained a leader in the religious activities of the West. His personality was almost perfectly adapted to the demands of frontier life. Early inured to physical hardship and to poverty, delighting in herculean labors, ruggedly honest and shrewdly humorous, indifferent to refinement of thought or manners, he made his Methodism a joyous battlefield against the devil and rival sects. Baptist, Presbyterian, and Shaker he overwhelmed with torrents of abuse, ridicule, and scorn. Sin (consisting in unbelief, drinking, gambling, or the wearing of ruffles) and salvation (consisting of conversion to the Church) gave him a dual theme which he manipulated with telling force. This simple ethical code, this narrow and intense religion, above all this thunderous fighting spirit literally swept his hearers off their feet, and at his camp-meetings hundreds were felled to the ground beneath his eloquence and lay prostrate until brought to the mourners' seats, whence he led them singing and shouting into the courts of heaven. If, as not infrequently happened, intruders attempted to break up his meetings, he was quick to meet force with force and seems to have been uniformly victorious in these physical encounters. There was a point of emotional excess, however, at which Cartwright's common sense revolted. For the nervous disorders which too often accompanied his meetings,—"the jerks," "the runnings and barkings," the trances and prolonged illnesses—he assumed no responsibility, regarding them as due to the wiles of the devil, who thus sought to discredit his work. So he continued on his way, a mighty figure among the Methodists of Illinois. He was for forty-five years a presiding elder, attended forty-six meetings of the Illinois Conference, and was twelve times elected to the General Conference. He was twice a member of the Illinois legislature. The one defeat of his career came in 1846 when he ran for the United States Congress against Abraham Lincoln, attempting in vain to make the issue turn upon Lincoln's alleged "infidelism." This political campaign Cartwright forgot to mention in his noted *Autobiography,* published in 1857, a work naively self-glorifying, and unsatisfactory as a record of his life, but written with great verve, revealing the author's extraordinary ability as a raconteur. His later work, *Fifty Years as a Presiding Elder* (1871), edited by the Rev. W. S. Hooper, is considerably less interesting but contains Cartwright's celebrated letter to the devil (a polemic against Calvinism). With advancing years, although he contributed liberally to Methodist colleges and publishing houses, Cartwright found some difficulty in adapting himself to the more intellectual interests of the newer Methodism. He deplored the passing of the good old days and earnestly prayed that "camp-meetings, class-meetings, prayer-meetings, and love-feasts" might "eternally" continue. Hale and hearty he himself remained: his magnificent body, supporting a massive head, with beady black eyes and disheveled hair, hardly knew a day's ill health until extreme old age. From the time of his coming to Illinois he made his home at Pleasant Hills, where in the intervals of religious duty he farmed, and, also, reared a numerous progeny. He lived to welcome nine children, fifty grandchildren, thirty-seven great-grandchildren, and seven great-great-grandchildren.

[In addition to the works mentioned above see *Minutes of the Annual Conferences of the M. E. Ch. for the Year 1873*, pp. 115–17; Abel Stevens, *A Compendious Hist. of Am. Methodism* (1868), pp. 482–86; M. H. Chamberlin, "Rev. Peter Cartwright, D.D.," in *Trans. of the Ill. State Hist. Soc.*, 1902, pp. 47–56.] E.S.B.

CARUS, PAUL (July 18, 1852–Feb. 11, 1919), philosopher, the son of Dr. Gustav and Laura (Krueger) Carus, was born at Ilsenburg, Germany, of a family of distinguished scholars. His father, then pastor at Ilsenburg, later became First Superintendent General of the Church of Eastern and Western Prussia. Carus received a good education in mathematics and the classics at the *gymnasia* of Posen and Stettin, and afterward studied at the universities of Greifswald, Strassburg, and Tübingen where he received the degree of Ph.D. in 1876. He then became a teacher in the military academy at Dresden, but his liberal views soon brought him into opposition to the authorities, and he eventually resigned. In the early eighties he went to England and later came to America. Of stocky physique and massive head, black-bearded, intense, and voluble, with a generous spirit and extraordinarily broad interests, he was already an arresting personality. He had by now worked through a devastating period of religious skepticism into what was to remain his life-long philosophy. This consisted in a thorough-going monism of mind and matter, based on community of form and on the identity of the laws of nature and the laws of mind. Philosophy, he believed, could be reduced to a science as objective as any of the other sciences. The philosopher's brain, he wrote, "should work with the regularity of a machine." While thus opposed in principle to all subjectivism, he believed that the religious aspirations of mankind could be satisfied with a scientific conception of God as the impersonal world-order, and a historical conception of immortality as the survival of one's influence. To the working out in detail of this philosophy Carus zealously devoted the rest of his long life. His auctorial energy was stupendous, his bibliography embracing more than 1,000 titles, of which over fifty were of monographs in book form. In 1887 the Chicago zinc-manufacturer, Edward C. Hegeler, founded the *Open Court* as a journal devoted to the establishment of religion and ethics on a scientific basis. Carus contributed several articles and was then appointed editor. The magazine, first as a weekly, then as a monthly, flourished under his capable management. He threw open its columns to contributors, regardless of their previous prestige, and, with

equal zest, entered into controversy with nobodies and with philosophers of established reputation. The interest of an idea, rather than its author, attracted him. His ties with Hegeler were drawn closer by his marriage on Mar. 29, 1888, to Hegeler's daughter, Mary. In 1890 Hegeler established the *Monist* as a quarterly to take care of the more technical contributions to the *Open Court*, and Carus became editor of the new magazine also. Soon the reprinting of valuable articles led to the development of the Open Court Publishing Company which, under Carus's direction, gradually enlarged its scope to include the republication at popular prices of philosophical classics, and the publication of new philosophical works and notable scientific treatises, such as those of Boole and Dedekind in mathematics, Binet and Ribot in psychology, and Mach in physics.

Carus exercised a wide popular influence on behalf of a more rational attitude toward religion and ethics than had hitherto been prevalent in America. His direct influence on American philosophy was curiously slight. In part this may be explained by the fact that philosophy, to its own loss, still tended to be the exclusive property of the universities, which looked upon any one outside their fold as an interloper and were particularly scandalized by Carus's editorial independence, but in part, also, it was due to Carus's insistent rationalism which was entirely out of harmony with the pragmatic tendencies of the time. Essentially forthright and impatient of doubt, he underrated the epistemological difficulties of his realistic position, and, in his constant endeavor toward a synthesis, sometimes strove to unify really irreconcilable doctrines. The religious tone of his writings failed to reconcile idealists to his naturalism but sufficed to alienate his fellow naturalists. Nevertheless his philosophy was well founded on his theory of forms, and it must be considered as one of the most constructive philosophical achievements in nineteenth-century America. Among his many books, probably the most important are: *Fundamental Problems* (1889); *The Soul of Man* (1891); *The Gospel of Buddha* (1894), a compilation of Buddhist scriptures, which was widely translated and was adopted in Buddhist schools in Ceylon and Japan; *De Rerum Natura*, a philosophical poem written originally in German but translated into English by Charles Alva Lane (1895) and published in its German form in the *Open Court*, September 1919; *Buddhism and Its Christian Critics* (1897); *Kant and Spencer: a Study of the Fallacies of Agnosticism* (1899); *The History of the Devil* (1900); *The Surd of Meta-*

physics (1903); *Friedrich Schiller* (1905); *Chinese Thought* (1907); *The Foundations of Mathematics* (1908); *God: an Enquiry and a Solution* (1908); *The Pleroma* (1909); *Truth on Trial* (1911), a critique of pragmatism; *Goethe, with Special Consideration of His Philosophy* (1915). Carus also translated Kant's *Prolegomena to Any Future Metaphysic* (1902) and *The Canon of Reason and Virtue ... Being Lao-Tze's Tao Teh King* (1913). His *Philosophy as a Science* (1909) gives a synopsis of his writings to that date, and *The Point of View* (1927), edited by Catherine Cook, is a volume of well-chosen selections.

[Articles by Paul Brauns, Julius Goebel, Philip E. B. Jourdain, and Lydia G. Robinson in the *Open Court*, Sept. 1919, and by Wm. Ellery Leonard in the *Dial*, May 3, 1919; an obituary note by J. R. Kantor in the *Jour. of Philosophy, Psychology and Scientific Methods*, Apr. 10, 1919.]   E. S. B.

CARUSO, ENRICO (Feb. 25, 1873–Aug. 2, 1921), grand opera tenor, was born in Naples of peasant stock, the eighteenth son (and the first to survive infancy) of Marcellino and Anna (Baldini) Caruso. Marcellino Caruso was a rather unsuccessful mechanic, overly fond of wine, who took little interest in his son's education. Anna Caruso, however, although she died when her boy was eleven, had ambitions for the child; she labored to correct the slack Neapolitan dialect which he heard in the streets by teaching him "la lingua Toscana en bocca Romana" and she cultivated his naturally strong taste for neatness and precision in every undertaking. While he was still in the kindergarten, Errico,—the name by which he was christened and known until well into his maturity—was sent to an evening school kept by Father Giuseppe Bronzetti for training boy singers in church choirs. This school the child continued to attend for some eight years, his clear contralto voice eventually raising him to the position of chief soloist. His native talent for drawing was also carefully developed by Giuseppe Spasiano, the teacher of penmanship. When he was fourteen, Carusiello, as he was affectionately called, made his first appearance on any stage, as a comedian in a church play, "I briganti nel giardino di don Raffaele." Meanwhile, from the age of ten the boy had been put to work as a mechanic. At sixteen he had progressed to be accountant and receiving clerk in the factory of Francesco Meuricoffre where he remained for the next four years. But he took eager advantage of his scanty leisure to continue his music, earning a few much needed extra *lire* by singing at cafés, public baths, and church festivals. He also studied under Guglielmo Vergine, who recognized his talent sufficiently to make a

shrewd bargain that he should receive twenty-five per cent of Caruso's earnings for *five years of actual singing,* a contract which, since it would cover practically a lifetime, even the guileless Caruso later contested, finally compromising on terms sufficiently liberal to gratify his grasping master. Vergine, however much of a Shylock, proved to be a good teacher; under his instruction Caruso learned not to force his somewhat thin tenor voice, and at the same time was encouraged, at the age of twenty, definitely to seek an operatic career.

The next five years were devoted by Caruso to a slowly victorious struggle against obscurity, poverty, professional jealousy, and his own limitations. Always best in the *mezza voce,* and often in these early years accused of being a baritone, it was not until the end of this period that he really mastered his high notes. His acting, pronounced "awful" at first, he was never able to make more than passable. He often faced the boos and hisses with which the art-loving Italians were wont to greet a false note or absurd gesture, and through his simplicity and sincerity he was an easy victim of cabals. He made his début on Nov. 16, 1894, at the Teatro Nuovo, Naples, in the première of an unsuccessful opera, *L'Amico Francesco* by one Mario Morelli. A brief season at the Cimarosa in Caserta was followed by his appearance, owing to the illness of the regular tenor, in *Faust* at the Teatro Bellini, Naples, which led to a renewed engagement in the fall. During the next two years he did not get beyond Naples and its circle of influence (Caserta, Salerno, and several towns in Sicily), but by the autumn of 1897 he had reached northern Italy (Fiume, Milan, Genoa, Trent, Leghorn), and on Nov. 17, 1898, his gradually expanding reputation suddenly became international through his widely reported performance in the world première of *Fedora* at the Teatro Lirico, Milan. During the trying period before success, Caruso owed most to the teaching of Vincenzo Lombardi for a few months in 1896 and to the friendship of the prima donna Ada Giochetti, with whom in 1898 he formed a liaison destined to endure for eleven happy years and to give him two dearly loved sons, Rodolfo and Enrico.

Following his triumph in *Fedora,* Caruso was overwhelmed with offers. In the winter of 1898–99 he went to St. Petersburg, singing Rhadames in *Aïda* for the first time; in the spring he paid the first of many visits to Buenos Aires; in the fall he appeared at the Teatro Costanzi in Rome; in the ensuing winter he conquered the critical audience of La Scala in Milan, opening with Puccini's *La Bohême,* and taking part in the world première of *Le Maschere* and the noted revival of *Elisir d'amore.* Regarding his voice as a gift which he delighted to share with others, he went to Naples in 1901 in high hopes to please his native city, but Naples, ever critical of her own offspring, received him coldly,—so coldly that he swore never to visit the town again except "to eat a plate of spaghetti." The disappointment was soon alleviated, however, by renewed triumphs: at Monte Carlo, February 1902; London, May–July 1902; Lisbon, February–March 1903; Buenos Aires, July 1903; Rio de Janeiro, August 1903. And on Nov. 21, 1903, in *Rigoletto,* Caruso opened his first season at the Metropolitan Opera House, New York,—the goal of every opera singer's desire.

Caruso's task at the Metropolitan was not an easy one. He followed the aristocratic and intellectual Jean de Reszke, and he was neither aristocratic nor intellectual. His round, genial, plebeian face, and stocky figure inclined to strut when kingly dignity or romantic grace were called for, might easily have prejudiced the audience against him; but after a few performances the marvelous beauty of his "golden" voice, its lyric passion, its range and power, had already begun to cast a spell over the Metropolitan which was never broken. The memory of the more theatrical De Reszke paled before the far richer voice and natural even if ungainly manner of his successor. Henceforth until his death, although welcomed regularly in Europe and South America, Caruso remained especially the idol of the Metropolitan.

Extraordinarily conscientious toward both his audiences and his art, at least in all that concerned its musical side, Caruso sang on every occasion as if it were the crowning event of his career. He developed a dramatic vocal technique unequalled in variety and scope. His repertoire included no less than forty-three operas (complete list in Key, *post,* p. 396). Probably his greatest successes were in tragedy, yet he was by nature a comedian. Every week an amusing and admirably drawn cartoon from his pen appeared in *La Follia.* His fellow actors were likely to be disconcerted in some serious scene through having an egg or other awkward object surreptitiously thrust in their hands or through discovering that a needed prop had been diverted to some absurd use by the ingenious Caruso. To the end he remained the incorrigible boy, ingenuously vain, impetuously kind, quickly elated or depressed. He enjoyed the pleasures of food and drink; he smoked cigarettes incessantly and with impunity; he spent his money lavishly on mul-

titudinous garments, on collections of stamps and coins, on bronzes, enamels, pottery, tapestry, watches, and furniture, on a large estate near Florence embracing forty-seven farms. But he bestowed his wealth on others in as princely a manner as on himself. Unspoiled by success, he showed the same courtesy to kings and beggars. The tales of his generosity are legion. Besides the $70 worth of tickets to which his contract at the Metropolitan entitled him for each of his own performances, he usually gave away from $300 to $400 worth of tickets to his friends. Napoleonic in loyalty to his family and early acquaintances, he included more than a hundred in his list of pensioners; twenty-one of his relatives were at one time housed in his Florentine villa. During the World War he gave $5,000,-000 to the Italian Red Cross and raised $21,000,-000 for the Allied armies by his concerts.

On Aug. 20, 1918 he was married to Dorothy Benjamin, daughter of Park Benjamin [*q.v.*], who, convinced that the marriage would be unhappy, did his best to make it so, refusing to see his daughter afterward because she had married a "public singer." Luckily the father's prophecy of evil remained unfulfilled. The autumn of 1919 was especially joyous to Caruso for two things: his appearance as Eleazar in *La Juive* on Nov. 22,—universally considered the high point of his career; and the birth of his daughter Gloria on Dec. 18. During the ensuing year he became moody and melancholy through continued ill health but scrupulously fulfilled his contracts to sing, until, on Dec. 11, 1920, after going through a whole act of *Elisir d'amore* with a broken blood-vessel in his throat, he was obliged to close the performance. The next week he appeared thrice, as usual, but on Christmas Eve he sang for the last time. On Christmas Day he was attacked with pleurisy which developed into pneumonia; for weeks he hung between life and death, with the whole world anxiously watching the bulletins; apparently recovered, he insisted upon going in the early summer back to his beloved Italy where he suffered a relapse and died, in Naples, on Aug. 2, 1921, from an abscess of the lungs.

[*Enrico Caruso* (1922) by P. V. R. Key is a detailed biography prepared in part with Caruso's assistance. The date of birth is, however, given incorrectly; the correct date will be found in Caruso's handwriting in Emil Ledner, *Erinnerungen an Caruso* (Leipzig, 1922), facing p. 30. *Wings of Song* (1928) by Dorothy Caruso and Torrance Goddard gives an intimate and yet remarkably objective account of the singer's later life. References on Caruso's art are J. H. Wagenmann, *Enrico Caruso und das Problem der Stimmbildung* (Altenburg, 1911); Henry C. Lahee, *Grand Opera Singers of Today* (1912); Arturo Lancellotti, in *Musica D'Oggi,* V, 350–55.]   E. S. B.

CARUTHERS, WILLIAM ALEXANDER

(c. 1800–Aug. 29, 1846), author, was born in Virginia and died in Marietta, Ga. The only record of his youth is that he attended Washington College (now Washington and Lee University) in 1819–20 and that during that time he witnessed a much heralded ascent of the Natural Bridge, an event of some importance as the basis of an article he later wrote for the *Knickerbocker Magazine*. Sixteen years after leaving college he was still characterizing himself as a "Virginian," but it is probable that he was already a citizen of Savannah, a city which he thought of as "outstripping Philadelphia and New York, and controlled by a class of men as much like our real old-fashioned Virginia gentlemen as can well be imagined." *The Kentuckian in New York,* which he published in 1834, is a romance set forth in a series of letters between two Virginia students, one visiting in New York, the other, in Georgia and the Carolinas. In an epilogue, the Kentuckian himself is frankly apologized for as a humorous character introduced only for the sake of popularity; the writer's true interest lay elsewhere, specifically in an historical romance, *The Cavaliers of Virginia,* which he had already nearly completed. This book, published in 1837, describes with considerable accuracy the circumstances of Bacon's Rebellion. Like all its author's work, it touches at times on humor and aphorism, but remains on the whole too voluble and stilted to be of lasting interest. *The Knights of the Horseshoe, a Traditionary Tale of the Cocked Hat Gentry in the Old Dominion* (1845) deals with the rule of Gov. Spottswood. At some unknown date Caruthers became a physician. He is referred to in a Savannah newspaper of his time as being highly respected in his profession, and in 1842 he attacked a current vogue of mesmerism. He read widely and learned much, and he maintained always, even in the troubled realm of sectional disputes, an outlook which was to a degree clear and impartial. He was universally esteemed for his kindliness and his elegance of manner. His death occurred in North Georgia, where he had gone with a son, in hope of finding relief from protracted ill health.

[W. A. Caruthers, "Climbing the Natural Bridge," *Knickerbocker Mag.*, July 1838; "Sturmer, a Tale of Mesmerism," *Magnolia* (Jan. 1842); *Lecture Delivered before Ga. Hist Soc.* (1843); *Savannah Daily Georgian* and *Savannah Daily Republican*, Sept 2, 1846; *Washington Coll. Reg. Alumni* (1858); C. Holliday, "Wm. Alexander Caruthers" in E. A. Alderman and J. C. Harris, *Lib. Southern Lit.* (1907), vol. II; J. G. Johnson, *Southern Fiction Prior to 1860* (1909).]

J. D. W.

CARVER, JOHN

(c. 1576–Apr. 5, 1621), one of the *Mayflower* Pilgrims, was the first governor of Plymouth. There is no Pilgrim whose services are better attested than his and no man of significance about whose life so few details are known. Born probably about 1576 in Nottinghamshire or Derbyshire, he spent his early life in business, moving to London in the last years of Elizabeth's reign, where he acquired in trade what for those days was a considerable fortune. Emigrating to Holland in 1609, independently of the Scrooby group, he joined the Pilgrims at Leyden probably in 1610–11. His high character, his stern piety, his maturity (most of the congregation being young men) gave him place at once among the leaders; his fortune, which he managed somehow to transfer from England, made him able to finance the congregation in part at least and explains perhaps the purchase of the Great House in which John Robinson, the pastor, lived and in which the congregation worshipped. As deacon, he ranked third among the officers of the church, following Robinson and William Brewster.

When the project for emigration to America was formed, Carver and Robert Cushman were sent to England in September 1617 as agents to secure permission from the Virginia Company to settle upon their territory. This mission failed, and Carver seems not to have been one of those who finally secured a grant of land on the Hudson River. He was, however, in all probability the one who persuaded a group of merchants, perhaps former friends of his, to finance the venture and the one responsible for the agreement, later called the Common Stock, under which the Pilgrims at last sailed for the New World. He was certainly the organizer of the London contingent, collecting the group which sailed direct from England, including Miles Standish and John Alden; he hired the *Mayflower;* and he sailed on her on July 15, 1620, from London, to meet the *Speedwell* with the Leyden contingent at Southampton. His wife sailed with him, and he brought also,—an attestation of his means—six servants, all "bound out" to him. One of these, John Howland, promptly proved his worth and remained for five decades among the most prominent of the Pilgrims.

On the voyage, Carver was certainly the mainstay of the group, and, when the decision was reached to settle in New England instead of on the Hudson where their charter granted them land, he was elected governor for one year of the new political society organized by the Pilgrim Compact, signed on Nov. 11, 1620. He commanded the two boat expeditions to spy out the land and was perhaps the first to step on shore at Plymouth on Dec. 11. During the winter, throughout the "sickness" in which so many died, he was active in all duties, including nursing the sick. Aside from his treaty with Massasoit in March 1621, we have no idea of his governmental activities or policies. On Mar. 23, he was reëlected governor. Weakened, however, by his own severe illness in the winter, and by excessive toil for the colony at manual labor, he died on Apr. 5, 1621, while working in the fields, overcome, they thought, by sunstroke. Of his appearance we have no inkling. His chair and sword are among the few relics of undoubted authenticity.

[The chief authority is Wm. Bradford's *Hist. of Plimouth Plantation* (ed. by Worthington C. Ford, 1912). See also E. Arber, *Pilgrim Fathers* (1897); O. S. Davis, *John Robinson* (1903); W. H. Burgess, *John Robinson* (1920); H. M. and M. Dexter, *England and Holland of the Pilgrims* (1905); R. G. Usher, *The Pilgrims and their Hist.* (1918).]   R.G.U.

CARVER, JONATHAN (Apr. 13, 1710–Jan. 31, 1780), traveler, son of David and Hannah (Dyer) Carver, was born in Weymouth, Mass. When he was eight years of age, his father moved to Canterbury, Conn., where after a prosperous career he died in 1727. Jonathan was left in care of a maternal uncle, and had as good an education as the colony afforded; it is claimed, but not proven, that he studied medicine. At Canterbury he married, Oct. 10, 1746, Abigail Robbins; thence he enlisted as sergeant and was at the siege of Fort William Henry in 1757, where he was wounded. He became lieutenant in 1759, and captain the next year in a Massachusetts regiment, having removed to Montague in that state, where in 1759 he was selectman. Gen. Gage testified to his military ability and good character. At the instance of Maj. Robert Rogers, then commandant at Mackinac, Carver set out on his travels in 1766. He went west by the route of the Great Lakes, crossed to the Mississippi by the Green Bay–Fox–Wisconsin route, ascended the great river and entered the St. Peter's (now the Minnesota). He reached Lake Superior by the Chippewa and St. Croix rivers, and finally returned in the autumn of 1767 to Mackinac, whence in the next spring he made his way back to Boston. Disappointed in the hope of publishing his volume of travels, he sailed on Feb. 22, 1769, for England, where he engaged in literary work during the rest of his life. In 1774 he married Mrs. Mary Harris in London, notwithstanding the fact that his American wife was still living. The first edition of his *Travels* appeared in 1778;

the second part was a compilation on Indian manners and customs, from other authors who were not cited, and so gave rise to the charge of plagiarism. The manuscript of Carver's *Travels* exists in the British Museum; it differs materially from the published account, which shows the hand of some literary hack in preparing it for publication. In 1779 Carver lent his name to a *New Universal Geography;* he also published a treatise on tobacco raising. Notwithstanding these publications and a payment of his accounts by the government, he died in great penury, and was buried in paupers' ground, whence his English wife had him removed by the charity of admirers. He left one daughter by his wife in England, and several children of his American marriage. The 1781 edition of his *Travels* contained a biography, portrait, and account of Carver's Indian grant, which he never claimed in his lifetime. On the strength of this grant, supposed to have been made in a cave near St. Paul, a number of speculators attempted to claim lands in Wisconsin and Minnesota.

[Carver's *Travels in Interior Parts of America* was a very popular book, and ran through many editions and translations; see John Thos. Lee, "A Bibliography of Carver's Travels" in *Proc. Wis. Hist. Soc.*, 1909, pp. 143–83; "Additional Data," by same author, *Ibid.*, 1912, pp. 87–123. E. G. Bourne, "The Travels of Jonathan Carver," in *Am. Hist. Rev.*, XI, 287–302, called attention to his plagiarism, and discredited his biography. He has been rehabilitated by Lee (as above) and by Wm. Browning, "Early Hist. of Jonathan Carver," in *Wis. Mag. of Hist.*, III, 291–305. See also M. M. Quaife, "Carver and the Carver Grant," in *Miss. Valley Hist. Rev.*, VII, 3–25; L. P. Kellogg, "Mission of Jonathan Carver," in *Wis. Mag. of Hist.*, XII, 127–45.]   L.P.K.

CARY, ALICE (Apr. 26, 1820–Feb. 12, 1871), poet, was descended from John Cary, who in 1630 taught the first Latin class in America, in Plymouth, Mass. A lineal descendant, in the sixth generation, from John, was Robert Cary, a pioneer farmer, who lived on a bit of land eight miles north of Cincinnati; a man of poetic temperament which the hardships of life had left undeveloped. His wife, Elizabeth Jessup, was a superior woman whose eagerness for culture was not quenched by the toil of bringing up a family of nine children; of these Alice was the fourth. The primitive conditions of her early life afforded few opportunities for intellectual development, yet these she improved so zealously that when she was eighteen years of age a poem from her pen appeared in a Cincinnati paper. In 1849, she, together with her sister Phœbe [*q.v.*], four years her junior, issued a volume entitled *Poems of Alice and Phœbe Cary.* The next year the two made a journey to New York and New England, which was especially significant to them because of a visit they paid to Whittier, which he commemorated in his poem "The Singer." The favorable reception given the collected poems and a disappointment in love moved Alice Cary to make her home in New York City in 1850, and later to send for Phœbe and a younger sister. Literary work was not then liberally paid, but the sisters lived economically, kept out of debt, and Alice worked so unremittingly and successfully that by 1856 she was well established and drew about her a brilliant circle of friends. To the home on Twentieth St. for the next fifteen years came on Sunday evenings a group, congenial and distinguished, of men and women of literary tastes. The social charm of the two sisters more than their reputation as poets was the chief attraction. Alice seemed to her friends greater and sweeter than any song she ever sang. Full of unselfish interest in individuals, she was an intelligent and eager champion of the great causes making for human advancement. Although of a self-effacing disposition, she reluctantly consented to become the first president of the first woman's club (now the Sorosis) in America. The breadth of her religious sympathies attached her to the Universalist Church and she accepted most of its doctrines. Despite the fact that she was an invalid during her later years, she worked unremittingly. This toil, partly necessary for maintaining the household and partly the conscientious effort to waste no moment of talent, injured to some extent the quality of her poetry. Widely read during her lifetime, her poems are too diffuse, too tinged with sadness, too didactic for the taste of to-day; but there is in them a genuine poetic feeling, a sincere love and interpretation of nature which is attractive. Her prose works, especially *Clovernook Papers* (1852), had a large sale in this country and in Great Britain; a second series was issued in 1853. In 1855 *Clovernook Children* proved popular with young people. Her other publications were *Hager, a Story of Today* (1852), *Lyra and Other Poems* (1852), *Married, not Mated* (1856), *Pictures of Country Life* (1859), *Ballads, Lyrics and Hymns* (1866), *Snow-Berries* (1867), *The Bishop's Son* (1867), *The Lover's Diary* (1868). She was at work on *The Born Thrall* at the time of her death which occurred in New York, Feb. 12, 1871.

[*Poetical Works of Alice and Phœbe Cary: with a Memorial of their Lives by Mary Clemmer* (1876); see also references under Phœbe Cary.]   C. A. D.

CARY, ANNIE LOUISE (Oct. 22, 1842–Apr. 3, 1921), singer, was born in Wayne, Me., a daughter of Dr. Howard Nelson Cary and of his wife, Maria Stockbridge, a descendant of Elder Brewster of *Mayflower* fame. As a young woman (1864) she began her music studies with J. Q. Wetherbee and Lyman Wheeler, in Boston. Two years later she went to Milan and prepared for an operatic career with Giovanni Corsi, and it was only fifteen months later that she made her début in Copenhagen. The Scandinavian peninsula kept the young star on the platforms of its theatres for two seasons, Miss Cary leaving only during her vacations which were devoted to study at Baden-Baden with Mme. Viardot-Garcia. A winter of study in Paris with Maurice Strakosch and Bottesini followed an appearance at Brussels, and in August 1870, Miss Cary returned to her country. After her first appearance in America as a member of Christine Nilsson's Concert Company in New York City on Sept. 19, 1870, there was in the next morning's *Sun,* the report that next to Mme. Nilsson's, Miss Cary's appearance attracted the most interest: "She has an admirable voice, full, deep, round and mellow—a voice like that of Adelaide Phillips, a great deal of that peculiarly sweet and touching quality which seems to belong more or less to all American girls who have any voice at all. She has been trained in an excellent school and is likely to prove a credit to her country." From that time until her retirement in 1882, she was one of the most celebrated of opera and concert contraltos, equally popular at the opera houses of London, St. Petersburg, and New York. Her retirement at the age of forty was simultaneous with her marriage to Charles Monson Raymond. During her short public career she attained a distinction well described by W. J. Henderson in the *New York Herald* (Apr. 10, 1921) just a week after her death: "Her repertoire included all the principal contralto parts of the day. Her voice was of rich dramatic timbre. It is pretty safe to say in the case of Miss Cary that she was the foremost contralto who trod the lyric stage within the memory of living opera-goers. No other has quite equalled her in the splendor of her tone, her command of the grand style and her heroic delivery of tragic music." Her most successful rôles were those of Siebel in *Faust,* Amneris in *Aïda,* and Martha and Pantalis in the first American performance of Boito's *Mefistofele* which antedated those of Paris and London by more than two years. After her retirement, she sang occasionally in the choir of the West Presbyterian Church in New York City. She died on Apr. 3, 1921, in her seventy-ninth year.

[H. E. Krehbiel in *Grove's Dict. of Music and Musicians* (3rd ed., 1927); Mary H. Flint in *N. Y. Times,* Apr. 10, 1921.]   P. V. R. K.

CARY, ARCHIBALD (1721–1787), planter, industrialist, Revolutionary statesman, son of Henry and Anne (Edwards) Cary, came from a typical great family of eighteenth-century Virginia. Before 1667, Miles Cary the immigrant, whose ancestors since 1546 had been prosperous merchants and high municipal officers in Bristol, England, was flourishing in Virginia. There the Carys maintained their mercantile position while they also became great planters, public officials, and aristocrats. Archibald's father, landholder and high sheriff, was the contracting builder of court-houses and churches. He built also the chapel and the president's house at William and Mary, and on the James River in Chesterfield County erected Ampthill House and a flour mill. Beyond the fall line in Henrico, afterward Goochland and Cumberland Counties, he acquired 12,000 acres, on part of which in 1742 he seated Archibald lately educated at William and Mary.

Here from 1747 to 1750, young Archibald served as justice of the peace, burgess, and vestryman. Then, his father having died, he removed to Ampthill, where he extended Henry Cary's manufacturing projects. He established a ropery, built a furnace and foundry, but after a decade ceased to manufacture iron. From his more successful flour mill he later supplied the War Board. Contemporaneously, he took an interest in experimental stock breeding, imported pure-bred cattle, and fostered road and bridge building. From 1756 he represented Chesterfield County in the Assembly, and in 1762 became chairman of the Public Claims Committee. Though of the committee which protested against Grenville's proposed Stamp Tax, he voted against Patrick Henry's flaming resolutions in 1765. He became, nevertheless, ardently revolutionary, signed the Associations of 1769, 1770, 1774, was on the Committee of Correspondence of 1773, sat in all the Virginian Revolutionary conventions, and as chairman of the Committee of the Whole read to the convention Virginia's Resolution of Independence.

In 1781 his mills were destroyed by a British force under Benedict Arnold. Six years afterward he died, speaker of the Virginia Senate and lord of 14,172 acres and 266 slaves, but financially in difficulties. Notably a lavish patriot, to whom the State in 1781 owed £58,000 in depreciated currency, he like other Virginians paid his British debts,—at least £10,000—in depreciated Virginian currency. When magistrate he prosecuted Virginian Baptists. Futilely he strove to forestall disestablishment and in the Convention of 1785 helped organize the incorporated

Episcopal Church. Bright-eyed, compact, and muscular, he was masterful, and was bitingly dubbed by a contemporary "Old Bruiser," but a British prisoner found him courteous, genial, and hospitable, and Washington, eleven years younger, affectionately called him "Archy." At twenty-three, he married Mary Randolph, granddaughter of the famous Turkey Island couple; through his mother, he was cousin to his fellow patriot, Benjamin Harrison; and his children's marriages additionally linked him with leading Virginian families.

[Fairfax Harrison, *The Virginia Carys* (1919); *William and Mary College Quart.*, 2 ser., V, 167–68, VI, 122–28; H. B. Grigsby, *The Virginia Convention of 1776* (1855), pp. 90–93; *Jours.* of the Va. House of Burgesses, Revolutionary Conventions, and Senate 1748–87. Cary's personal papers and correspondence were destroyed.]   K. B.

CARY, EDWARD (June 5, 1840–May 23, 1917), editor, son of Joseph and Lydia (Chase) Cary of Quaker stock, was born in Albany, N. Y. He grew up in his native city, where his elementary schooling was obtained. Having completed his junior year at Union College, Schenectady, N. Y., he returned to Albany to continue his studies at the Law School there. He soon began writing editorials for a paper called the *Statesman,* and after about a year decided on journalism as his life-work and went to Brooklyn, N. Y., to take the editorship of the daily *Union.* The editorials which he wrote for that newspaper soon began to attract the notice of other editors and publishers. Cary was at first a Republican, and a defender of the Lincoln administration, but after the Civil War he found himself less and less in sympathy with the tenets of the party in power. In 1871, George Jones, proprietor of the *New York Times,* was seeking an editorial writer. Cary at thirty-one, with eight years of newspaper writing behind him, was selected by Jones as the man to take the place. The opportunity appealed to the young man. The *Times* was in its fight with the Tweed ring and in national politics was assuming an independent attitude. Cary took the chair, which he was not to relinquish until his death after forty-six years of exacting but fruitful toil. Shortly after beginning work on the *Times,* he made a positive stand in opposition to free silver coinage. This he consistently maintained for more than a quarter of a century,—until the question was removed from the sphere of practical politics. Later he held an equally definite course on the subject of tariff reduction. In civil service reform he was one of the pioneers, not only warmly supporting the movement with his pen, but taking a personal part in the leadership, with George William Curtis, Carl Schurz, Dorman B. Eaton, and others. His advocacy in the *Times* of Grover Cleveland's candidacy was a factor of no slight importance in the national election of 1884. In both of Cleveland's terms as president the *Times* gave him able and hearty support.

By the time Cary came to the *Times* desk the old manner of editorial polemics had about run its course in New York. Editors were no longer calling one another scoundrels and liars,—in cold type. Cary was gifted in a style of writing that was suited to the new demands. Partisan pleas and vituperation were alike distasteful to him. He excelled in the calm, clear, and succinct statement of economic facts and principles, without embroidery. His audience may not have been large (in the early years), but it was influential to the degree that brains count for power in the long run. The *Times* editorials were widely quoted by other newspapers. According to estimates made by his colleagues, Cary's contributions to the editorial page averaged 6,000 words each week for the entire period of his service, reaching a total of more than 14,000,000 words,—the equivalent of two substantial volumes a year for the forty-six years. A remarkably large percentage of this output was of more than ephemeral interest; indeed much of it, in economic and political discussions, was of permanent value. In 1894 he contributed *George William Curtis* to the American Men of Letters series. Cary had been married in 1864 to Elisabeth Luther, of Albany. His daughter, Elisabeth Luther Cary, was for many years editor of the art department of the New York *Times*.

[*N. Y. Times, N. Y. Herald,* May 24, 1917; *Hist. of the Class of 1863 of Union College* (n.d.).]

W. B. S.

CARY, LOTT (1780?–Nov. 10, 1828), negro Baptist missionary, was born a slave in Charles City County, Va. In 1804 he went to Richmond, secured work in a tobacco warehouse, and for some years led a riotous life. In 1807 he was greatly impressed by a sermon based on the third chapter of John, and from this time forth his life showed the effect of a genuine conversion. Meanwhile his efforts to fit himself for service gave evidence of remarkable force of personality, and he was helped by his massive and erect figure. He learned to read, was given unusual authority in his work, and from time to time received special remuneration. About 1813, his first wife having died, he purchased his freedom and that of his two children for $850; and he received license to preach from the First

Baptist Church of Richmond, which in 1815 had 1,200 negro members in its congregation. Inspired by the sermons of Luther Rice, Cary in 1815 helped to organize the Richmond African Baptist Missionary Society, which after five years had $700 in the treasury. Meanwhile he married again. He himself determined to go to Africa; and on May 1, 1819, he was received for service by the Baptist Board of Foreign Missions. Before leaving, with Collin Teague and a few other associates he organized what was to be the first Baptist church in Liberia, himself being pastor. On Jan. 23, 1821, in the brig *Nautilus,* he sailed from Norfolk in company with twenty-eight colonists and their children, the expedition being in charge of two representatives of the American Colonization Society. With this organization circumstances forced Cary to cooperate; but he never fully subscribed to its policies. Having arrived at Freetown after a voyage of forty-four days, no other provision having been made for them, the colonists were accepted by the government agent as laborers and mechanics. In December the arrival of new agents of the Colonization Society led to further negotiation for land and to the real founding of Liberia; and early in 1822 Cary and others went to Cape Montserado. Between the ravages of the fever and the hostility of the natives the outlook was far from promising; but Cary was with those colonists who determined to stay. He extended his labors, and after three years he had more than sixty members in his church. In the closing months of 1823 he was prominent in opposing the authority of Jehudi Ashmun [*q.v.*], who had brought out a company of colonists and had taken charge of the colony; but the high character of Ashmun eventually won his cooperation. In 1826 he was viceagent of the colony. On Nov. 8, 1828, while he was assisting in the defense of the colony against the Deys, the overturning of a candle led to a powder explosion, and he was fatally injured along with several other persons. He died two days later.

[Miles Mark Fisher, "Lott Cary, the Colonizing Missionary," in *Jour. of Negro Hist.,* VII, 380 ff.; Jas. B. Taylor, *The Biography of Elder Lott Cary* (1837); sketch from "a Richmond paper" of the year 1825, with other material, in *Biog. Sketches and Interesting Anecdotes of Persons of Colour,* comp. by A. Mott (enlarged ed., 1837); Ralph R. Gurley, *Life of Jehudi Ashmun* (1835), with an appendix containing a biographical sketch of Cary.]

B. B.

CARY, PHOEBE (Sept. 4, 1824–July 31, 1871), poet, was the sixth child of Robert and Elizabeth (Jessup) Cary, and shared with her sister Alice [*q.v.*], the hardships of the farm just outside Cincinnati, and felt the same inner music and passion for self-expression. In 1849 she contributed her part to the slender volume, *Poems of Alice and Phœbe Cary*. After she had joined her sister in New York, to her fell most of the domestic duties of the home, and the increasing invalidism of Alice threw more and more responsibility upon her. In the large circle of friends who frequented the Sunday evening receptions she was considered one of the wittiest women in America. By temperament more buoyant and vigorous than her sister, she held her poetic talent in less command. The elder worked ceaselessly, the younger was more the servant of her mood. Her literary output was much less, but there is an ampler variety of feeling, more humor and spirit. Alice Cary was more generally read by contemporaries, but Phœbe Cary's verses seem to have more of that quality which keeps poetry alive, and it would not be without reason if she had in the future the greater number of admirers. Certainly her poem "One Sweetly Solemn Thought" has won for itself a permanent place in the religious poetry of the country. It was composed one Sunday morning in 1852 when the mood of the church service still possessed her. It was soon set to music and became popular and effective as an anthem. After the publication of their first volume of poems, the two sisters worked independently and published their poetry under separate covers. Although the two differed quite widely in temperament, endowments, and methods of work, they perfectly supplemented each other. Their devotion was complete and when Alice died in February 1871 her sister, weakened by constant anxiety and deprived of the one who had been the steadying and controlling influence of her life, followed in July of the same year. Phœbe had published *Poems and Parodies* (1854) and *Poems of Faith, Hope and Love* (1868), and had assisted Dr. Charles F. Deems, pastor of the Church of the Strangers in editing *Hymns for all Christians* (1869).

[*Poetical Works of Alice and Phœbe Cary: with a Memorial of their Lives* by Mary Clemmer (1876); Horace Greeley, "Alice and Phœbe Cary" in *Eminent Women of the Age* (1868) by Jas. Parton and others; R. W. Griswold, *Female Poets of America* (1859).]

C. A. D.

CASANOWICZ, IMMANUEL MOSES (July 25, 1853–Sept. 26, 1927), orientalist, archeologist, was born at Zhaludok, Province of Vilna, Russia, the son of Jekuthiel and Sara (Tanowsk) Casanowicz. His parents, though in moderate circumstances, intended that the youth should become a learned man, perhaps a rabbi. Being set apart with this purpose in view, he received such instruction as could be given in his

native town. At twenty-three years of age he was a student in the Evangelische Predigerschule at Basel, Switzerland, in which he later became a teacher. Emigrating to America about 1882, he took the position of teacher in Hebrew and church history in the German Theological School of Newark, at Bloomfield, N. J., remaining there four years (1883–86). He then studied at Johns Hopkins where he was awarded the degree of Ph.D. in 1892. In the same year he was appointed to the division of Oriental studies originated by Dr. Paul Haupt and under the immediate supervision of Dr. Cyrus Adler in the United States National Museum in Washington. Gradually rising in usefulness in this work, he was appointed assistant curator of Old World archeology in 1906 and held this position at the time of his death. He was a member of the American Oriental Society and of the Anthropological Society of Washington. He was unmarried. Short of stature, slender, and ascetic, he gave an impression of reserve force far beyond the physical. His manner declared him to be kind, considerate, and helpful, inspiring confidence and friendship. The history of religions absorbed a great part of his energies and on this subject he was an authority. His knowledge of the Semitic group of languages, as well as of several other ancient and modern tongues, rendered him one of the first students in Biblical exegesis. He arranged, in the National Museum, exhibits,—unique in America—illustrating the cult or external side of religious activities. Writing on subjects relating to religion formed the bulk of his publications. Of these his inaugural dissertation *Paronomasia in the Old Testament* (1894) attracted much attention from scholars on account of its erudition. Of his descriptive catalogues of material in the United States National Museum, *Ecclesiastical Art* (1919), *Buddhist Art* (1921), *Rosaries* (1909), and *Old World Archeology* (1924) are the most important. He left a large manuscript on the collection of objects of religious ceremonial in the United States National Museum, which may be regarded as a summation of his studies, and which is to be published.

[*Who's Who in America*, 1927–28; *Am. Anthropologist*. n.s., XXX, no. 2, 359; personal acquaintance.]

W. H.

CASE, JEROME INCREASE (Dec. 11, 1818–Dec. 22, 1891), manufacturer, was born in Williamstown, Oswego County, N. Y., where his parents, Caleb and Deborah (Jackson) Case, were among the pioneers from the eastern part of the state. As soon as he was old enough, Jerome helped in clearing and cultivating the wilderness and went to school when he could. His interest in machinery was of local comment. When he was sixteen, his father purchased a horse-treadmill threshing-machine of which Jerome was placed in charge, conducting a threshing business for five years. With his earnings he then attended an academy at Mexico, N. Y., for a year. Upon completing an elective course there, he decided to go West and start another threshing business. He purchased six horsepower threshers on credit and took them to Racine, Wis., in 1842, where he soon found buyers for five of the machines. He kept the sixth with which to earn his living and in the hope that by study and experiment he might improve it. Success crowned his efforts and in 1844, while in Rochester, Wis., he designed, built, and put into practical operation a combined thresher and separator, thus eliminating the fanning mill. He immediately rented a small shop in Racine to build the machine, and, after three hard years during which he succeeded in selling a few units, his machine was generally accepted and he had accumulated sufficient capital to erect a manufacturing plant. His business, in which he displayed much sagacity, grew rapidly. The fact that he was a practical thresher himself was of great advertising value. His plant was the largest west of Buffalo and within ten years, by 1857, was producing 1,600 machines a year. In 1863 he took in three former employees to form the J. I. Case Company, and in 1880 this company was incorporated as the J. I. Case Threshing-Machine Company. Besides his original organization Case formed the J. I. Case Plow Works, and in 1871 established the Manufacturers' National Bank of Racine and the First National Bank of Burlington, Wis. He was president of these institutions at the time of his death and was also a member of the Board of Trustees of the Northwestern Mutual Life Insurance Company of Milwaukee. As successful in banking as in manufacturing, he was later identified with national banks in Minnesota, South Dakota, and California. He was twice Republican mayor of Racine (1856, 1859), was a state senator for one term, was one of the Wisconsin State commissioners at the Centennial Exposition in 1876, and was one of the founders of the Wisconsin Academy of Science, Art, and Letters. His lifelong love of fine horses was gratified in his ownership of the Glenview Stock Farm in Louisville, Ky., where many famous racers were bred, notably Jay-Eye-See. He was married in 1849 to Lydia A., daughter of De Grove Bull of Yorkville, Wis. Three daughters and a son were born to them, all of whom as well as Case's widow survived him.

[*Milwaukee Sentinel*, Dec. 23, 1891; *Western Mo.*, vol. IV, no. 21; *National Mag.*, vol. XV, no. 5.]

C. W. M.

CASE, LEONARD (July 29, 1786–Dec. 7, 1864), Western Reserve land agent, lawyer, was born in Westmoreland County, Pa., the oldest son in a family of eight children. His father, Meshach Case, was of Dutch, and his mother, Magdalene Eckstein, of German descent. They were farmers, and Leonard passed his time as did other country boys between short terms at school and long periods of farm work. One of his early recollections was of the Whiskey Insurrection in his neighborhood. In his autobiography he makes the observation that a cause of the insurrection was the scarcity of currency, and that the presence of the Federal army soon placed in circulation a supply which relieved the situation. In the spring of 1800, tales of the country west of Pennsylvania attracted the Cases to Warren, Ohio, where they obtained a two-hundred-acre farm. In October 1801, Leonard was prostrated with fever, possibly as a result of exposure while ranging the woods for cattle. Complications left him a cripple for life, necessitating the use of a cane and a crutch. He faced the handicap with courage, purchased a Dilworth arithmetic, borrowed *Gibson on Surveying*, and set about their mastery as the first step in his new plan of life. In 1806 he secured a place as assistant to the clerk of courts at Warren and in 1807 he was appointed clerk of the supreme court. He also began the study of law and was employed for a time in the office of the Connecticut Land Company. In the latter office his association with Gen. Simon Perkins, chief agent of the company, proved to be the foundation for much of his later business success. He continued his study of law and in 1814 received his certificate of admission to the bar. In 1816, the Commercial Bank of Lake Erie was founded in Cleveland, and Case became cashier. The next year he was married to Elizabeth Gaylord. The years immediately after 1816 were precarious for the banking business in the West, and in 1819 the bank closed. Some years later, in the thirties, it was rehabilitated with Case as president, but in the meantime he had returned to his law practise and to the real estate business, with intervals in public office. From 1820 to 1824, he was auditor of Cuyahoga County; from 1821 to 1825, president of Cleveland Village. In 1824 he was elected to the state legislature where he distinguished himself for his work in behalf of the Ohio canals. From 1826 to 1830, he was prosecuting attorney of Cuyahoga County, and in 1838, after Cleveland became a city, he was elected a member of the council. When Cleveland's first railroad project, the Cleveland, Columbus & Cincinnati, was organized in 1847, Case was a director and vice-president, and for two years, until his health prevented, he took an active part in the building of the railroad. From 1827 to 1855, he was agent for the Connecticut Land Company. After closing out the land agency, Case spent the remaining years of his life caring for his own properties. His claim for remembrance by posterity rests upon his part as a builder of early Cleveland,—the advancement of its material well-being and the promotion of civic pride.

[The chief source for the life of Case is his unpublished autobiography now in possession of a relative, Mr. Eckstein Case. The latter also contributed a biographical sketch to S. P. Orth, *A Hist. of Cleveland*, I (1910), 556 ff. There is a biographical sketch in the *Western Reserve Hist. Soc. Tract 79* (1891), p. 221, by Jas. D. Cleveland, written with the use of the autobiography, aided by personal recollections.] E. J. B.

CASE, LEONARD (June 27, 1820–Jan. 6, 1880), philanthropist, was the second son of Leonard Case [*q.v.*] and Elizabeth (Gaylord) Case. He attended the schools of Cleveland; for a time the Academy of the Rev. Colley Foster, and later that of Franklin T. Backus. Following the advice of the latter, a Yale graduate, Leonard entered Yale in 1838, and graduated with the class of 1842. The following two years he studied law in the Cincinnati Law School. After admission to the bar he opened a law office in Cleveland. His practise was never large, for he gave his attention chiefly to the real estate business which his father had developed. Meanwhile he found time to pursue mathematical, scientific, and literary studies. He and his brother, William, together with a group of friends, turned the Case office into a miniature natural-history museum. They called themselves the "Arkites" and the office, the "Ark." The "Arkites" formed a stimulating informal natural-history club. In 1845, Case went to Europe in company with Prof. St. John of Western Reserve College and Prof. Loomis, then of the University of the City of New York, formerly of Western Reserve. While in Switzerland he became seriously ill and the effects lasted the remainder of his life, necessitating constant care of his health. He was very fond of travel and though he made only one trip to Europe, he traveled extensively in the United States. He remained unmarried. His tastes were never satisfied with either his law practise or business. As soon as he came into his father's large estate he turned the active management over to another and devoted himself to his lit-

erary pursuits, to writing, to a wide correspondence, and to his growing interest in philanthropic enterprises in Cleveland. On his travels he wrote lengthy descriptive letters. He also wrote a good many poems, usually of a humorous turn, many of which were published in *Western Reserve Historical Society Tract No. 79*. His "Treasure Trove," a mixture of comedy, tragedy, and satire, about medieval knights and kings, was published in the *Atlantic Monthly*, July 1860 (reprinted in book form, 1873).

Of a kindly nature, Case was a generous giver to charities. To the Cleveland Library Association (later Case Library) he gave an endowment of $20,000. Some years later this was very largely increased by the gift of the Case building, where the library had been housed since 1866, and which was valued at the time at $300,000. When the Western Reserve Historical Society was founded in 1867, Case became one of its benefactors. His greatest work was the founding of the Case School of Applied Science, his plan for which seems to have been fully perfected by 1876. There is some evidence that his father and brother had had in mind some use of their fortune for the benefit of their fellow townsmen, but it is probable that Case's own interest in scientific matters was the main cause of this particular project. In February 1877 the trust deed was signed giving a large share of his fortune to endow a school "to teach mathematics, physics, engineering, mechanical and civil, chemistry, geology, mining, and metallurgy, natural history, languages," and such other subjects as the trustees should consider necessary. The gift consisted of real property in the business center of Cleveland and was valued at that time at about one and one-half million dollars. Case disliked publicity and the knowledge of the gift was withheld from the public until after his death. In the fall of 1881, the school opened its doors in the Case homestead on Rockwell St.

[A biography of Case, prepared by Judge Jas. D. Cleveland, is printed in the *Western Reserve Hist. Soc. Tract 79*; *Biog. Record of the Class of 1842 of Yale Coll.* (privately printed, 1878); Mr. Eckstein Case, in *Notes on the Origin and Hist. of the Ark* (Cleveland, 1902), reprints some Case letters.] E. J. B.

CASE, WILLIAM SCOVILLE (June 27, 1863–Feb. 28, 1921), lawyer, jurist, born in Tariffville, Conn., was the son of William Cullen Case and Margaret (Turnbull) Case, and was a descendant in the eighth generation of John Case, who came to America from the southern part of England. William Cullen Case was for many years a lawyer of Connecticut, distinguished, among other things, for his oratorical ability and for his mastery of the art of cross-examination. The fragmentary early education of William Scoville Case in the local schools was supplemented by extended reading. He entered Hopkins Grammar School in New Haven in 1877, was admitted to Yale University, and graduated with his class in 1885 after four happy and well-spent years, during which he had found opportunity for the expression of his literary gift as editor of the *Yale Record.* On leaving college he studied in his father's office until his admission to the bar in 1887. On Apr. 8, 1891, he married Elizabeth Nichols of Salem, Mass., daughter of Nathan and Elizabeth Rodman Nichols. Shortly after his marriage he wrote a novel, *Forward House,* which evinced imagination and unusual powers of description. In July 1897 he became judge of the court of common pleas in Hartford County, and entered upon a judicial career that was to end only with his death twenty-four years later. Promoted to the superior court in 1901, he served there most acceptably until August 1919, when he became a justice of the supreme court of errors. Possessed of a keen, discriminating, and cultured mind, he readily mastered legal principles, and by a sort of flashing intuition rather than by studied processes— at least so it seemed—he was able to select the one that pointed out the judgment to be rendered. But this instinctive method was never permitted to dictate finality in his conclusions, until their correctness had been verified by a course of reasoning,—a test which his logical mind was abundantly able to supply. His memoranda of decisions and later his opinions in the supreme court had a felicity of style rarely equaled in law reports. He also had other means of expression, as many lifelike and clever caricatures of lawyers, witnesses, and jurors, imbedded in his evidence-books, testify; but they, unfortunately, were kept for the delectation of a few friends. A quiet dignity pervaded his court-room, and one was conscious of the firm but unobtrusive control which he exercised over its proceedings. Any deliberate violation of the proprieties met with quick rebuke, uttered occasionally in caustic and witty phrase which members of the bar delighted to recall. His varied gifts would have been certain to bring him ever greater distinction as a justice of the court of last resort, and his death before completing two years of work on that tribunal was deplored by bench and bar, and by a public he had served with conspicuous ability and fidelity.

[*Yale Univ., Quarter-Centenary of the Class of 1885* (1913); 95 *Conn. Reports,* 743; *Hartford Courant,* Mar. 1, 1921; *Who's Who in America,* 1920–21; information from Mrs. Wm. Scoville Case; personal acquaintance.]

J.P.A.

CASEY, JOSEPH (Dec. 17, 1814–Feb. 10, 1879), jurist, was the son of Joseph Casey, a native of Wicklow, Ireland, and a graduate in medicine of Edinburgh University, who in 1792 emigrated to the United States, settled in Pennsylvania, and there married Rebecca, daughter of Thomas McLaughlin of Franklin County. The younger Joseph was born at Ringgold's Manor, Washington County, Md. While he was yet a child misfortune beset his parents, the various members of the family separated, and Joseph was placed with a blacksmith's family in Newville, Pa. In 1828, having received little education, he rejoined his father at Shippensburg, Cumberland County, Pa. He there attended the common schools for about a year, but his father was in financial straits, and in 1831 Joseph was apprenticed to a hat manufacturer at Shippensburg. For the next five years he was employed in this industry, also studying at home to complete his education. In 1836, in Carlisle, Pa., he entered the law office of Charles B. Penrose, grandfather of Senator Boise Penrose, and a very astute politician. In November 1838 he was admitted to the bar at Carlisle. For four years he practised at Bloomfield, Perry County, Pa., but in 1845 moved to New Berlin, Union County, Pa., a place which offered better opportunities. There he commenced to take an active part in politics. In 1848 he was elected as Whig representative of his district in the Thirty-first Congress and served till Mar. 3, 1851, but declined a renomination. He was a moderate opponent of slavery and voted for the compromise measures of 1850 but against the fugitive-slave law. On the conclusion of his term he received the Whig nomination for judge of the district court for Mifflin and Union counties, but was defeated. In 1855, prompted by the exigencies of his growing practise, he opened an office at Harrisburg, and was appointed by Gov. Pollock commissioner to investigate and terminate the "Erie Railroad War," a somewhat difficult and delicate undertaking which he brought to a successful conclusion. In the same year he was appointed reporter of the decisions of the supreme court of Pennsylvania, a position which he occupied for six years, in the course of which he prepared and published 25–36 *Pennsylvania State Reports* (1856–61), covering the years 1855 to 1860. They are frequently cited as "Casey's Reports," and have been uniformly accepted as able and accurate. In May 1861 President Lincoln appointed him judge of the United States Court of Claims, necessitating his removal to Washington, D. C., and in 1863, when the Court was reorganized, he became its first chief justice. He went on the bench at a critical time.

Owing to the outbreak of the Civil War the business of the Court of Claims assumed an importance which hitherto it had lacked, and it fell to his lot to consider and decide many cases involving new problems of vital interest. Eminently fair to both the Federal Government and the private citizen, he enjoyed the confidence and respect of the public, and performed his judicial duties with complete success. Failing health induced his resignation, Dec. 1, 1870. During the last nine years of his life he was a professor in the National University at Washington, and took a deep interest in its success. He was married to Mary A. Krettle of Carlisle.

[*Polit. Reg. and Cong. Dir., 1776–1878* (1878), comp. by B. P. Poore; *Biog. Encyc. of Pa. of the Nineteenth Century* (1874), p. 471; *Nat. Republican*, Feb. 11, 12, 1879.]   H. W. H. K.

CASEY, SILAS (July 12, 1807–Jan. 22, 1882), Union soldier, was born at East Greenwich, R. I. He was appointed to a cadetship at West Point in 1822, graduated in 1826, and was commissioned second lieutenant in the 2nd Infantry. For the next ten years he served with his regiment at posts on the Great Lakes and on the frontier, and from 1837 to 1842 was engaged in the Florida War against the Seminole Indians. He was promoted to first lieutenant in 1836 and to captain in 1839. He was with Gen. Scott's army in its campaign against the City of Mexico, 1847, took part in the battles of Contreras, Churubusco, Molino del Rey, and Chapultepec, and was twice brevetted for gallantry in action. He was severely wounded at the storming of Chapultepec while heading a "forlorn hope" of some 265 selected officers and men (Justin H. Smith, *The War with Mexico*, 1919, II, 153–57). Between the Mexican War and the Civil War he was stationed chiefly on the Pacific coast. For a time he was a member of a board of officers to revise the manual of infantry tactics, and later he prepared the manual adopted in 1862. "Casey's Tactics" remained in use in the army for many years. In 1855, several new regiments were organized, the field officers being chosen from among the ablest officers of the old organizations. Casey was thus appointed lieutenant-colonel of the new 9th Infantry, and became its colonel in 1861. Recalled from the Pacific coast upon the outbreak of the Civil War, he was appointed brigadier-general of volunteers, Aug. 31, 1861. He served with the Army of the Potomac during its formative period and in the Peninsular campaign, where he commanded a division. For distinguished service at the battle of Fair Oaks, where his division bore the first shock of the Confederate attack, he received a brevet in the regular army and was

appointed major-general of volunteers, May 31, 1862 (*Battles and Leaders of the Civil War*, 1884, II, 230–33). From August 1862 until the end of the war he commanded a division of the troops assigned to the defenses of the city of Washington. He was also, for two years, president of the board for the examination of candidates for commission as officers of colored troops. He was a member of the court martial for the trial of Fitz-John Porter. Mustered out of the volunteer service on Aug. 24, 1865, he served in command of his regiment and on special duties until retired from active service, July 8, 1868, upon his own application. He died at Brooklyn. Gen. Cullum says of him: "Casey was a reserved, unassuming gentleman, a gallant soldier, a skilled tactician, and a proficient scholar in the higher mathematics, particularly the application of calculus and quaternions."

[G. W. Cullum: *Biog. Reg.* (3rd ed., 1891); *Official Records (Army)*, 1 ser., vols. II (pts. 1, 2, 3), LI (pt. 1).]   T. M. S.

CASILEAR, JOHN WILLIAM (June 25, 1811–Aug. 17, 1893), engraver and landscape painter, was the third of the nine children of John and Rebecca (Stevens) Casilear. The Stevenses were a prominent family in New Jersey. Casilear's paternal grandfather, Francis Casilear, as a young man came from Barcelona, Spain, to New York City, where he died in 1796, and was buried in St. Paul's churchyard. John William Casilear was born in New York City. Like many artists of the Italian Renaissance period, a number of the men who became eminent as painters in the United States through the first half of the nineteenth century found a safe starting point for their more ideal flights in the practise of engraving, and especially in producing the portraits and pictorial embellishments used on both federal and state bank notes. Peter Maverick, engaged in this phase of engraving, was an early member of the National Academy of Design and it was with him that Casilear at the age of sixteen began his apprenticeship. As the only support of a widowed mother and several brothers and sisters, he worked steadily and advanced to hold an interest in the American Bank Note Company, which he did not relinquish till 1857, thus acquiring a handsome competence. Intimately associated with Asher B. Durand, Edmonds, Kensett, and Rossiter, he was in close touch with the National Academy of Design as a student and exhibitor, becoming an associate in 1835, at a time when, as he modestly said, "The Academy took in anybody." In his case, however, the producing of graceful designs for bank notes, with more than ordinary skill in the use of the graver, and the painting of landscapes, gave probably well-founded reasons for such a distinction. He knew and received advice from Thomas Cole and, in 1840, he was afforded an opportunity to go to Europe with Durand, Kensett, and Rossiter, where he visited the galleries with them and gathered a harvest of sketches and studies. Returning to New York the following year, he did not yet allow the brush entirely to displace the burin, which had so far assured his material well-being. He produced one of the finest American engravings of the period, a reproduction of Daniel Huntington's "Sibyl," which was published by the American Art Union. In sharpness and decision of line it has been considered worthy of the old master engravers. In 1851 he was elected to full membership in the National Academy of Design and after 1854 gave most of his time to landscape painting, spending his summers in the hills of Vermont, about Lake George, in the Genesee Valley, N. Y., and in the Adirondacks. During another trip to Europe in 1857, he visited Switzerland, making a number of studies and sketches of romantic landscapes, from which he afterward painted pictures. One of his earlier exhibits at the Academy, "Storm Effect"—wind and rain passing over a summer landscape—drew attention as a forceful presentation of this striking phase of natural phenomena. "Moonlight in the Glen" depicted the rushing waters of a stream between forest-clad banks, reflecting the light of a full moon rising in the clear sky above. But as a whole, Casilear's pictures, in subject and treatment, harmonized with the even tenor of his life. After he had completely relinquished his engraving interests about 1857, his studio in New York during the latter part of his career was at 51 West Tenth St., where a number of distinguished painters lived and worked. Having acquired the means that assured relief from material cares by the steady industry of his earlier years, he was now able to undertake the production of a series of pictures that reflected usually the more peaceful aspects of American landscape. He was an active member of the Artists' Fund Society which held yearly exhibitions, and at each succeeding exhibit of the National Academy of Design, his landscapes were remarked for their sunny skies, silvery clouds, quiet reaches of rivers and lakes between broad meadows and distant hills. "Lake George," "Adirondack Scenery," "Genesee Meadows," and a "Connecticut Riverside," alternated with reminiscences of European trips that would occasionally appear as "Lake Leman," "Swiss Scenery," or "The Jungfrau" by which he was represented in the Centennial Exhibition of the National Academy of Design, held at

Washington and New York in 1926. Casilear's work, like that of his companions who began their art in the precise school of engraving, was marked by careful finish, contrasting with the more self-assertive technique of the impressionists who followed. He and his associates may not have been as dexterous as their followers in the free use of the brush, and like Cole were directly or indirectly influenced by the classical landscapes of Claude Lorraine; but they were deeply in love with nature, which they approached in a reverent and poetic spirit. They produced pictures remarkable for their simple, unaffected beauty, and have a definite place in the development of American landscape art. Casilear was married in 1867 to Ellen M. Howard of Tamworth, N. H. He died of apoplexy at Saratoga, in his eighty-third year, and was buried from Dr. Houghton's church in Twenty-ninth St., New York.

[H. T. Tuckerman, *Book of the Artists* (1867), pp. 521–22; *Art Jour.* (N. Y.), II, 16–17; Mantle Fielding, *Dict. of Am. Painters, Sculptors and Engravers* (1926); various catalogues and *Academy Notes* of the National Academy of Design Exhibitions, N. Y.; information as to certain facts from Casilear's son, John W. Casilear of Brooklyn, N. Y.]   R. J. W.

CASS, GEORGE WASHINGTON (Mar. 12, 1810–Mar. 21, 1888), engineer and railroad executive, was born on a farm near Dresden, Muskingum County, Ohio. His parents were George W. and Sophia Lord Cass, both of New England stock. In 1824 he was sent to Detroit to attend the Detroit Academy, making his home with his uncle, Gen. Lewis Cass [*q.v.*], who was then governor of Michigan Territory. Appointed from Ohio to the United States Military Academy in 1827, he graduated in 1832 with special honors in mathematics. He was then appointed brevet second lieutenant in the 7th Infantry, but never joined that regiment because of assignment to duty with the Topographical Engineers in the making of a survey of Provincetown Harbor, Mass., from Sept. 12 to Dec. 5, 1832. He was next detailed for duty with the Corps of Engineers as assistant to the superintendent in charge of the construction of the Cumberland Road, east of the Ohio River, and remained on this duty until Oct. 26, 1836, when he resigned his commission as first lieutenant in the 7th Infantry; but continued in the service of the Corps of Engineers as a civil engineer until 1840. During his service (1837) he erected the first cast-iron tubular-arch bridge to be built in the United States. In 1840 he established a mercantile business in Brownsville, Pa., but soon began to turn his attention to the transportation enterprises growing out of the development of the railways. He became one of the engineers in charge of the improvement of the Monongahela River and when this work was suspended because of the inability of the State of Pennsylvania to finance it, he was instrumental in forming a private company which completed the work in 1844. He organized the first steamboat line on the Monongahela and the first fast stage lines across the mountains. In 1849 he established the Adams Express Company from Baltimore to Pittsburgh and in 1854 effected the consolidation of all the company lines between Boston and St. Louis and south to Richmond. The next year he was elected president of the consolidated company, which position he held until 1857. On July 31, 1856, he was elected president and director of the Ohio & Pennsylvania Railroad Company, which later consolidated with the Ohio & Indiana and Fort Wayne & Chicago Railroad companies under the name of the Pittsburgh, Fort Wayne & Chicago Railroad Company, of which he was elected the first president. He held this position, except for a short interval, until May 25, 1881, when, the road being leased to the Pennsylvania Railroad Company, he resigned but continued one of the directors until his death. He was also president of the Northern Pacific Railroad Company from 1872 to 1875. Besides his business activities he was interested in politics. Twice, in 1863 and again in 1868, he was the Democratic candidate for governor of Pennsylvania. In 1859 he was a member of the board of visitors to the United States Military Academy. He was an able business man although sometimes inclined to be too conservative. He possessed simple tastes and being ingenuous in all his methods scorned pretense in others. His nature was generous and he gave very largely to his church and to charities.

[G. W. Cullum, *Biog. Reg.* (1891), I, 499–501; Jas. Parton and others, *Sketches of Men of Progress* (1870–71), pp. 469–73; E. V. Smalley, *Hist. of the N. P. R. R.* (1883), pp. 190–97; *Hist. of the P., F. W. & C. R. R.* (MS.), p. 70; *N. Y. Tribune*, Mar. 22, 1888; *Railway Age*, Mar. 23, 1888; memorial resolutions passed by the P., F. W., & C. R. R., May 16, 1888, in their *Annual Report*, pp. 8–9.]   J.H.F.

CASS, LEWIS (Oct. 9, 1782–June 17, 1866), soldier, diplomat, statesman, was the eldest of the six children of Jonathan Cass, a skilled craftsman with an excellent record in the Revolution, and was descended through his mother, Mary Gilman, from the best New England stock. He was born at Exeter, N. H., while the peace negotiations were still pending. His childhood coincided with the "Critical Period" in American history. In 1786, serious rioting occurred in Exeter, in which the senior Cass upheld the cause of law and order, a cause his son was des-

tined to maintain throughout his life. In 1792, Lewis entered the academy at Exeter, where he won the good will of Daniel Webster, a schoolmate (McLaughlin, *post,* p. 38). Having finished his education, he taught school at Wilmington, Del., for a time in 1799, but in the same year he crossed the Alleghanies to the West and a career.

He was at Marietta, Ohio, in 1800, where he established a law practise in 1802, soon removed to Zanesville, successfully defended Judge Brown, a presiding circuit judge, in impeachment proceedings before the Ohio Senate, married Elizabeth Spencer, the daughter of a Revolutionary general, spent his honeymoon with Mr. and Mrs. Harman Blennerhassett, and was elected at the age of twenty-four to the Ohio legislature, its youngest member, but a leader. Here he opposed Aaron Burr and drew up resolutions of loyalty to Thomas Jefferson, thus early identifying himself with the cause of union, in a fashion which led Jefferson to appoint him marshal for Ohio.

Cass unquestionably felt the enthusiasm of the times for the War of 1812. As colonel of the 3rd Ohio, he went promptly to the rendezvous at Dayton, and accompanied the forces leaving for Detroit in June. His military career is inseparably connected with that of Gen. William Hull. Cass spurred his reluctant chief to action, urged him to attack Malden, himself took part in an engagement near-by, and protested against orders to abandon a strategic position. "To Col. Cass," it is related, "belongs the honor not only of being the first man to invade the enemy's territory, but also of having opened the campaign with a victory" (Young, *post,* p. 27). He was considerate of his men, shared their hardships, and won their affection. He was on a relief expedition to the River Raisin when Hull surrendered at Detroit. Cass himself was included in the capitulation. He broke his sword rather than surrender it. His indignation at Hull's conduct was vented in a letter to the Secretary of War which is one of the sources for the period (*Ibid.,* pp. 49–52). While on parole in Washington, Cass was made a colonel in the regular army and a major-general of volunteers. On his release in January 1813, he was soon brevetted and in April was given joint command with Harrison and McArthur over the Eighth Military District, including Kentucky, Ohio, Indiana, Michigan, Illinois, and Missouri. When Harrison undertook an advance on Malden, Cass arranged the troops in line, and fought with conspicuous gallantry at the battle of the Thames, Oct. 5, 1813. He led the pursuit of Procter, and was highly praised in

Harrison's dispatches. Before the month was out he was appointed governor of the Territory of Michigan, and that winter made the tedious trip to Albany to testify at Hull's court martial.

Returning to Detroit, Cass confronted a difficult task. The *habitants* were impoverished; the Indians were menacing; but present problems did not monopolize the Governor's attention. He pioneered in developing an empire. With a view to overcoming their land titles he met the Indians at Fort Meigs, Sept. *29*, 1817, where they ceded their remaining lands in Ohio, in a part of Indiana, and in a portion of Michigan. Cass signalized the year 1820 by a 5,000-mile trip, mostly by canoe, to visit tribes within his jurisdiction. The itinerary included Mackinac; Sault Ste. Marie, where he procured from the Chippewas the cession of a military post; and, on his return, Chicago.

In 1825, Cass and Gov. Clark of Missouri met the Indians at Prairie du Chien, where on Aug. 19 a treaty was sealed with numerous tribes. The liquor which customarily on such occasions was given to the Indians, Cass poured upon the ground, a courageous manifestation of his lifelong hatred of intemperance (*Ibid.*, p. 90). In this year he settled certain difficulties with the Winnebagoes in his territory, and procured, besides, a right of way for a military road from Detroit to Chicago. He had previously urged a road from Sandusky to Detroit. In helpful, firm, and constructive service, Cass labored eighteen years in his proconsulship of Michigan, to the entire satisfaction of the people whom he governed and of his superiors at Washington (*Ibid.*, p. 98).

The foundation was laid, meanwhile, for an ample personal fortune through the purchase in 1816 of 500 acres near the mouth of the Detroit River, paid for in cash in the sum of $12,000, then deemed exorbitant (Smith, *post*, p. 142), and through the acquisition as a bounty of a further 1,200 acres similarly located. Throughout his political career Cass was far removed from all pecuniary temptation.

The shake up in President Jackson's cabinet caused by the Eaton affair brought Cass into the War Department. Here he was peculiarly fitted for the problems of his office by his previous experience with the Indians. He believed their removal beyond the Mississippi a practical necessity but advanced humane ideas for organizing the new Indian territory. He acted efficiently for the suppression of the Black Hawk War, 1832, and carried his views on temperance over into army regulations. In the trouble of Georgia with the Cherokees, he sympathized with the State in its opposition to the Supreme Court. Toward

similar trouble in Alabama he assumed a corresponding stand. Toward a peaceful outcome in the Nullification crisis he is believed to have exercised a powerful but anonymous influence (McLaughlin, pp. 149–50). He advocated a strong navy and coast defense. After a five years' tenure he left the cabinet because of ill health, but was promptly sent to France as minister in October 1836.

Cass brought to his mission deep anti-British prejudice, the product of his past. All his life he fought the British. When he perceived their efforts to win French acceptance of a quintuple treaty designed to legalize the right of search, acting independently he voiced a protest. (For documents in this important case, see "The Appeal of Gen. Cass to the People of France," in Smith, *post*, pp. 403–27; and "The Right of Search," in Young, pp. 136–66.) Guizot accepted Cass's advice, but Webster, the United States secretary of state, was enraged. Cass resigned. An acrimonious correspondence followed, in which Webster had the advantage of position; Cass, of argument (Young, pp. 172–207). The strong stand of Cass won the admiration of Jackson, his former chief, and undoubtedly contributed to his prestige as a national figure.

Henceforth Cass took a stand on all important issues. Revival of a national bank he did not favor. He opposed distribution to the States of funds derived from public lands. When Texas proved the campaign issue in 1844, he wrote the Hannegan Letter, May 10, strongly urging annexation. It was a bid for the Democratic nomination. When this fell instead to Polk, Cass was loyal to the party ticket. Michigan sent him to the Senate in 1845. Here he assumed a characteristically anti-British attitude toward the Oregon question: "Now the Oregon I claim is all Oregon, and no vote of mine in this Senate will surrender one *inch* of it to England" (*Ibid.*, p. 252).

Toward Mexico Cass was frankly an imperialist. On Feb. 10, 1847, he declared, "We must continue our occupation of Mexico, and push the invasion still farther" (*Ibid.*, p. 309). Opposing the Wilmot Proviso, he anticipated the Squatter Sovereignty of Douglas when he said, "Leave to the people who will be affected by this question, to adjust it upon their own responsibility and in their own manner . . ." (*Ibid.*, p. 327). This was the doctrine of the Nicholson Letter, Dec. 24, 1847, a bid for the nomination of 1848 (Smith, pp. 607–16).

Cass opposed a system of general public improvements under national auspices, but was favorable to river and harbor development, and in

1848 advocated a land grant to Illinois for the encouragement of railroads. He approved of the French Revolution of 1848, esteemed Pius IX a liberal, and introduced a resolution favoring the Hungarian revolutionists. He advocated national relief for the Irish famine, and wished to occupy Yucatan. Upon securing the Democratic nomination for the presidency in 1848, he resigned from Congress, and, had not Van Buren Democrats set up a factional ticket, would almost certainly have defeated Taylor (Young, p. 368). Defection in New York and Pennsylvania cost him the election.

In the Senate, his powerful speech against the Wilmot Proviso reveals nationalism as his dominating principle. All other issues, slavery included, were subordinate. He approved the compromise measures of 1850, to the extent, even, of defending the Fugitive-slave bill (Young, pp. 400–03). Michigan upheld him, and in 1851, he was reëlected to the Senate. Though at first accepting it, he became unfriendly to the Clayton-Bulwer Treaty. He was half-heartedly a candidate for nomination to the presidency in 1852. He lost his wife, Mar. 5, 1853, and wholly declined to be considered for the nomination in 1856.

The career of Cass reached its apex between 1857 and 1860, when as secretary of state in the Buchanan Administration he finally secured from Great Britain abandonment of all claims to a right of visit and search. He also scored a diplomatic victory against Paraguay, although the Administration's policies in Mexico and Cuba were frustrated (McLaughlin, pp. 328–40). But diplomatic issues paled before domestic. In the winter of 1860, Cass's fears for the Union became acute (Auchampaugh, *post*, pp. 71–72). His influence slightly stiffened the tone of Buchanan's message of Dec. 3, 1860. On Dec. 12 he resigned in protest against the decision not to reinforce the Charleston forts. It is now understood that Cass was willing to retract his resignation (*Ibid.*, p. 72), but Buchanan preferred to let it stand. Their rupture was complete (*Ibid.*, pp. 73, 109, 117, 154).

Throughout the Civil War, Cass was an old man and retired, but he counseled the surrender of Mason and Slidell, and in his last public speech, delivered at Hillsdale, Mich., on Aug. 13, 1862, he urged enlistment for the Federal army. In retirement his scholarly interests afforded him much solace. As early as 1827 he had read before the Detroit Historical Society a paper on the "Early History of Detroit and the Conspiracy of Pontiac," which won the acknowledgments of the historian, Parkman. To the

North American Review he contributed several serious studies on Indian and Western subjects. Even as secretary of war he found time for a description of the siege of New Orleans for the *American Quarterly Review*. Essays, written during his mission to France, were gathered into book form in *France, its King, Court, and Government By an American* (1840). A study of "The Modern French Judicature" appeared in the *Democratic Review*. In later life his literary output lessened, but his reading continued unabated.

Cass had a notable career. What appeared to his enemies as equivocations in dealing with sectional controversies, seem in the retrospect of history the wise concessions of a moderate. These failing, the Union was preserved in blood. He lived just long enough to see the outcome.

[W. L. G. Smith, *Fifty Years of Public Life. The Life and Times of Lewis Cass* (1856), and Wm. T. Young, *Sketch of the Life and Public Services of Gen. Lewis Cass: With the Pamphlet on the Right of Search, and Some of his Speeches on the Great Political Questions of the Day* (1852), are sound contemporary estimates, rather richly documented. Andrew C. McLaughlin, *Lewis Cass* (1899), in the American Statesmen Series, is written from a broader viewpoint than the preceding. *The Works of Jas. Buchanan,* ed. by John Bassett Moore (12 vols., 1908–10), contains source material for Cass. Philip G. Auchampaugh, *Jas. Buchanan and his Cabinet on the Eve of Secession* (privately printed, 1926), corrects some previous misconceptions. Interesting if unfriendly references to Cass occur in the "Autobiography of Martin Van Buren," ed. by John C. Fitzpatrick, *Am. Hist. Ass. Annual Report,* 1918, vol. II, especially pp. 603, 608. "The Correspondence of Robert Toombs, Alexander H. Stephens and Howell Cobb," ed. by Ulrich Bonnell Phillips, *Ibid.,* 1911, vol. II, is somewhat rich in Cass material; as is also "The Correspondence of Robt. M. T. Hunter," *Ibid.,* 1916, vol. II. Other allusions to Cass in the same series occur in "The Diplomatic Correspondence of the Republic of Texas," *Ibid.,* 1908, vol. II, pt. II, especially pp. 1243, 1252, 1265–66, 1433; and in the articles by H. B. Learned on "Cabinet Meetings under President Polk," and St. George L. Sioussat on "Tennessee and National Political Parties, 1850–60," *Ibid.,* 1914, vol. I.]

L. M. S.

CASSATT, ALEXANDER JOHNSTON (Dec. 8, 1839–Dec. 28, 1906), civil engineer, president of the Pennsylvania Railroad system, was born in Pittsburgh, Pa., the son of Robert S. and Katharine Kelso (Johnston) Cassatt. He was descended from one Cossart, a Frenchman, who in 1662 settled in Holland and whose grandson emigrated to America. On the maternal side, his ancestors were Scotch-Irish and settled in Chester County, Pa., in 1706. His father was a man of wide influence in financial and business affairs in western Pennsylvania, and was the first mayor of Allegheny City.

After beginning his education in the public schools of Pittsburgh, Cassatt went with his family to Europe, and attended Continental schools and Darmstadt University. Upon returning to this country he was enrolled in Rensselaer Polytechnic Institute where he was graduated as a civil engineer in 1859. Born into wealth he had no need to engage in hard work, yet he at once entered upon the practise of his profession. After a short apprenticeship as an engineering assistant in locating railroad right of way in Georgia, he returned to Philadelphia on the outbreak of the Civil War and entered in 1861 the service of the Pennsylvania Railroad with which his entire career was destined to be associated. His executive officer was Col. Thomas A. Scott, then vice-president of the road, and also assistant secretary of war. The training he received at this time was invaluable in the duties of his later career. His marked ability led to his rapid advancement through the engineering department to positions of responsibility in management, and by 1870 he was general superintendent of the Pennsylvania Railroad. He was one of the first of the railroad managers to see the immense possibilities of the air brake and its introduction by him after exhaustive tests served as an encouragement to other railroad officers.

In 1873 he became general manager of all the Pennsylvania lines east of Pittsburgh and Erie just at the time when the road was beginning its metamorphosis from a local state line into a system covering most of the principal traffic points east of the Mississippi and north of the Ohio. In other words, Cassatt's career as a railroad executive was coincident with the period of rapid expansion, not only of his own road but of railroads in general. In 1874 he was elected third vice-president in charge of transportation and traffic. It was while he was holding this position that the Philadelphia, Wilmington & Delaware was purchased, and Cassatt is given the credit for snatching it from under the nose of the Baltimore & Ohio. In 1880 he was made first vice-president, and then was in direct line for the presidency, but in 1882 at the age of forty-two he retired from active duty, retaining only a directorship. Although he had intended to devote his time wholly to recreation, which had largely to do with his stock-farming interests, he nevertheless associated himself with Col. Scott in the construction of the New York, Philadelphia & Norfolk Railroad and was its president from 1885 to 1899. The road runs to Cape Charles and operates a ferry service from Cape Charles to Norfolk which at the time was the longest and most difficult seagoing ferry service yet attempted.

In 1899, after seventeen years of retirement, Cassatt was called to the presidency of the Pennsylvania Railroad, which position he held until his death. His engineering training was at once put at the disposal of the road, and in many ways which could only be appreciated by railroad men he cleared up traffic difficulties and improved the physical and operating condition of the property. This meant the extension and increase of lines, stations, equipment, and facilities, the provision of necessary terminals and yards, the revision of grades and their elimination, the elevation of track and improvement of alignment, electrification, acquirement of interest in other roads, and all that goes to make up an efficient railroad system. Cassatt did not meddle with the rate structure, but picked out particular kinds of traffic that furnished the bulk of the business and made increases that accomplished the result without arousing the antagonism of the business community. During his administration, earnings nearly doubled, and traffic density increased by half. It was, of course, a period of great prosperity but Cassatt had the foresight to prepare his road to take advantage of it. His attitude toward his employees is shown in the establishment of the Pension Fund to provide for retirement from active service and in the broadening of the Relief Fund so as to include superannuation. Twice during his administration he voluntarily advanced the wages by ten per cent of all the men receiving less than $200 a month, to enable them to share in the increased prosperity of the company.

The greatest achievement of his career, in the opinion of many of his contemporaries, was his solution of the rebate problem. He came to the presidency at the close of the decade which included the panic of 1893. Railroad traffic as a result had reached a low ebb. As markets became stagnant, shippers sought the aid of the railroads in reduced rates, and everywhere the requests were granted because the interests of railroad and shipper were identical. This aid sometimes took the form of open concessions in rates, but more often rebating was resorted to, because the roads were disinclined to make general reductions in rates at a time when they were sorely in need of revenue. By 1899, the year in which Cassatt took the helm in the Pennsylvania organization, the average freight rate had reached its lowest point in the history of the company. In their anxiety to secure business, the railroads had put themselves at the mercy of shippers, and were being played off against one another in an endeavor to get the lowest rate possible. The growth of industrial combinations, which took place on an enormous scale as business recovered from the panic, had greatly strengthened the strategic power of the shipper.

No one railroad could meet the pressure alone and the roads could look for nothing but moral support from the Interstate Commerce Commission. Although the Interstate Commerce Act had been on the statute book for over a decade, all that had come from attempts to prescribe rates had been warnings from the Supreme Court that the Commission lacked the necessary power. If anything was to be done at this time, the railroads must do it themselves, but again they had just been deprived by the Supreme Court of any right to combine if such combination constituted restraint of trade. Pooling was prohibited by the Interstate Commerce Act.

Cassatt, while general manager and vice-president, had had opportunity to observe the pressure that large shippers could bring to bear upon railroads, especially in the relation of the Eastern roads to the Standard Oil Company. In the hearings conducted by the Commonwealth of Pennsylvania in 1879 Cassatt's testimony was startling in its candor and completeness and substantiated the claim of the oil men that the Pennsylvania had become the creature of the Standard Oil Company (Ida M. Tarbell, *History of the Standard Oil Company*, 1904, I, 227). It is not unreasonable to assume that this experience made a deep impression on Cassatt and turned his mind toward possible solutions of the problem. During the seventeen years that he was free from official responsibility he was by no means out of touch with railroad affairs, and his position as director gave him leisurely opportunity to mature plans which he was able to put into execution when he took the reins of management into his hands.

His plan was that of purchasing a sufficient amount of stock in competing roads to give a voice in management and was known as "community of interest." It involved an agreement with the New York Central which through the Lake Shore was to buy some of the stock of the Reading. The Pennsylvania made large investments in the Baltimore & Ohio, Chesapeake & Ohio, and Norfolk & Western. The Baltimore & Ohio in turn bought into the Reading. The strategic roads were thus so interlocked as to be able to present a united front to the industrial combinations that were depleting their revenues. The roads then announced that no further rebates would be granted. This announcement was not received kindly and the Carnegie interests especially refused to comply, first diverting traffic from the Pennsylvania and then threatening to build a road of their own to the seaboard, but the railroad combination refused to be frightened, and the worst of the discrimination in this territory was over. In 1903 the Elkins Anti-Rebate law was passed, largely at the instance of the railroad, and Cassatt was a powerful factor in the movement for its enactment. While the "community of interest" plan did not at the time appeal to the people of the country as a sound solution of the problem, and while the Northern Securities decision of 1904 and later decisions of the Supreme Court led to the dissolution of many of these corporate relationships, it must be conceded that Cassatt's plan accomplished much at the time and that it was a bold adventure and demanded ability of the highest order. That he yielded to popular opinion and sold many of his holdings did not mean that he was in agreement with the prevailing view. Up to the time of his death he held to the belief that co-operation between railroads was essential to a sound and stable rate system, but, at the time, the country, led by Roosevelt, was hostile to combination in any form, and it was not until 1920 that it came round to Cassatt's point of view. Cassatt took prompt action to eliminate the improper use of railroad passes on his lines. He believed in clothing the Commission with power to fix rates and put himself and his company behind the Roosevelt railroad program. He died a few months after the Hepburn Act had been signed which was to put real power for the first time into the hands of the Commission.

Another of Cassatt's achievements was the construction of the Pennsylvania Terminal in New York, the most gigantic project of railroad enterprise that has ever been undertaken. The disadvantageous location of the Pennsylvania Terminal on the west bank of the Hudson had been a matter of concern for thirty years before Cassatt's presidency, and many plans for crossing the river had been suggested; but all for one reason or another had been rejected. In 1901 Cassatt studied the extension of the Orleans Railway in Paris and became so impressed with the possibilities of electric traction that, upon his return, he set actively to work upon the New York tunnel and terminal project which, however, was not brought to completion until after his death. For the bold conception and for the inauguration of the work, however, the credit must be his. His statue was unveiled in the new Terminal in 1910 and on it are inscribed the words: "Whose foresight, courage, and ability achieved the extension of the Pennsylvania Railroad into New York City."

His life outside the railroad was an active one. He was a constant advocate of good roads and for nineteen years was road supervisor of

Merion Township in which he lived. He also served from time to time as director of insurance and trust companies. He was an enthusiastic horseman and was one of the two or three leading patrons of the American turf. He was associated with others in the construction of the race track at Monmouth Park and raced horses there with great success. When the sport fell into disrepute he transferred his attentions to breeding at his Chesterbrook stock farm at Berwyn, Pa., where he raised sheep, cattle, draft horses, and hackneys. He was one of the pioneers of coaching and an enthusiast over cricket, hunting, and yachting.

In 1869 Cassatt married Lois, daughter of Rev. Edward Y. Buchanan, and a niece of President James Buchanan. They had four children.

[The *Biog. Sketch of A. J. Cassatt, Dec. 28, 1906*, was issued by the authority of the Pa. R. R., at the time of Cassatt's death and reissued with addendum in 1910, at the time of the unveiling of his statue in the Pa. Station in N. Y. The *Mo. Bull. Pa. R. R. Dept. Y. M. C. A. of Phila.*, Feb. 1907, is a memorial number devoted to him. Wm. B. Wilson, *Hist. of the Pa. R. R. Dept. of Y. M. C. A. of Phila.* (1911), contains an estimate of his personality and his work. Another appraisal is to be found in an address of one of his successors to the presidency, Samuel Rea, entitled *Engineering and Transportation,* delivered before the Princeton School of Engineering in 1926, and privately printed.]   F. H. D.

CASSATT, MARY (May 22, 1845–June 14, 1926), artist, was descended from a Frenchman named Cossart, who in 1662 emigrated from France into Holland, and whose grandson emigrated to America. She was the daughter of Robert S. Cassatt, a banker, and Katharine Kelso (Johnston) Cassatt. Her eldest brother, Alexander Johnston Cassatt [*q.v.*], became president of the Pennsylvania Railroad. She was born in Allegheny City, Pa. When she was a little girl, her parents took her to Paris where they lived for five years, returning finally to Philadelphia. In 1868 she went again to Paris with her mother, who spoke and wrote French fluently. It was then that Mary Cassatt decided definitely to become an artist. She went to Italy and lived at Parma for eight months studying Correggio, then to Spain where she became filled with such admiration for Rubens that she went to Antwerp to study his work further. In 1874 she returned to Paris permanently. Her studio was in the Rue de Marignan just off the Champs-Élysées, but she spent much of her time in her Château de Beaufresne at Mesnil-Théribus dans l'Oise, seventy miles from Paris. She became a devoted disciple of Degas, with whom she enjoyed long years of friendship and mutual criticism. Degas suggested that she exhibit with his friends of the Impressionist School, and she

accepted with joy. She hated conventional art and with this group, Manet, Courbet, Degas, and others, she departed from the academic tradition, working out her personal interpretation, untrammeled by precedent. She exhibited with Impressionists from 1879 to 1886. Degas's admiration for her was unbounded. Before one of her pictures he said, "I will not admit a woman can draw like that." Mellerio wrote that she "possesses an original inspiration, representative of her epoch and her race, . . . a direct and significant expression of the American character." In 1893 she gave her first independent exhibition, in the Gallery of Durand-Ruel in Paris. She was chosen among women artists to decorate the Woman's Building in the Chicago Exposition. Puvis de Chavannes and Whistler were among her close friends. She painted a number of portraits with admirable results, notably those of her mother and her devoted friend Mrs. Henry O. Havemeyer. For almost every picture and print, she chose the world-old theme of motherhood, depicting mothers and babies in intimate scenes in sunny gardens and quiet interiors, not sentimentally, but in an original and simple manner. Her pastels are not so well known, but they are in soft, light tones, and some of her best work was done in this difficult medium. Her etchings, dry-points, and color prints are of great delicacy, yet firm in line and perception. By competent critics she is esteemed the most distinguished etcher, after Whistler, that America has produced. She was, however, regarded more as a member of the French impressionist school than of any American group. She became honorary president of the "Hostel" for Girl Students, established in Paris by Mrs. John Hoff, to which she contributed money to be distributed between the two girls evincing the most talent, requiring them to study for a year the French Pastellists of the seventeenth and eighteenth centuries in the Musée St. Quentin, said to be the finest collection in France. She possessed wealth and an enviable position in the social as well as the art world. She was above the average height, dark and slender. Her voice was low, soft, and pleasantly modulated, her manner quiet, except when she was roused in some heated art discussion. During the latter years of her life, she was an invalid, becoming almost blind. She died at Mesnil-Théribus. The only portrait of her known to exist is a small sketch made many years ago by Degas, now in a private French collection. Although she did not care for medals or honors, she received many. Her work has been exhibited widely, and she is represented in the Luxembourg, and in the leading galleries and museums of America as well as in important private collections. The Memorial Exhibition held in the Pennsylvania Museum, Philadelphia, April 1927, was a valuable showing of her work in all media. It included forty oils and pastels, over a hundred prints and a series of fifteen water-colors and drawings.

[Achille Segard, *Un Peintre des Enfants et des Mères, Mary Cassatt* (Paris, 1913) ; Y. Rambaud, "Mary Cassatt," *L'Art dans les Deux-Mondes*, Nov. 19, 1890 ; Wm. Walton, "The Art of Mary Cassatt," *Scribner's Mag.*, Mar. 1896 ; Camille Mauclair, "Un Peintre de l'Enfance," *L'Art Décoratif*, Aug. 1902 ; Elisabeth L. Cary, "The Art of Mary Cassatt," *Scrip*, Oct. 1905 ; Christian Brinton, "Concerning Miss Cassatt and Certain Etchings," *Internat. Studio*, Feb. 1906 ; *Arts*, Aug. 1926 ; André Mellerio, "Mary Cassatt," *L'Art et les Artistes*, Nov. 1910 ; Frank Weitenkampf, "The Drypoints of Mary Cassatt," *Print-Collector's Quart.*, Dec. 1916 ; Arsène Alexandre, "Miss Mary Cassatt, Aquefortiste," *La Renaissance de l'Art Français*, Mar. 1924 ; *Metropolitan Museum of Art Bull.*, Jan. 1927 ; *Art News*, May 7, 1927 ; *Pa. Museum Bull.*, May 1927 (Memorial Number).]   H. W.

CASSIDY, WILLIAM (Aug. 12, 1815–Jan. 23, 1873), journalist, politician, was a son of John and Margaret Cassidy. He was named for his paternal grandfather who had migrated from Ireland late in the eighteenth century and had settled in Maiden Lane, Albany, N. Y. John Cassidy, proprietor of a meat-market, won the esteem of the Albanians and represented them as alderman. William, being a studious youth, completed his work at the Albany Academy and entered the senior year at Union College, Schenectady, where he graduated with high honors in 1833. He was trained for the law in the office of John Van Buren and Judge James McKown, and was admitted to the bar but never practised, as his tastes were markedly literary and journalistic. He devoured the contents of books amazingly fast, became conversant with Latin, French, and German, and impressed Henry James as being the best-read man of his time in French ballads. At the age of twenty-five years he was writing caustic articles for the radical *Plaindealer and Rough Hewer*, an Albany newspaper which supported the Azariah Flagg faction of the New York Democracy. His political leanings, and his satirical and witty pen, made him acceptable to the Van Buren group, who had him chosen state librarian for 1841–43, after which he became joint editor with Henry Van Dyke of the Albany daily *Atlas*. His editorials, much shorter than those of many other partisan editors, were written in a dirty corner amidst the confusion of the composing room. His drafts were never transcribed, were seldom revised, and had few erasures, though they were "a very lunacy of hieroglyphics." When the Albany *Argus* deserted Van Buren on the issue of the

annexation of Texas, Cassidy attacked its editor, Edwin Croswell [*q.v.*], in an editorial duel which was long remembered. Croswell finally sued Cassidy for libel, succeeded in having the office of state printer abolished, and bid in the state printing free of charge to prevent Cassidy's election as printer. After the factional fight of 1848, Cassidy turned to Pierce (1852) and through the influence of Horatio Seymour, united the *Atlas* and *Argus* (1856) to fight the Republican party. He bitterly opposed Frémont and denounced the Republican leaders as demagogues, while he urged the support of Pierce and Buchanan. Lincoln seemed to him an uncouth and dangerous man to be elected president. The *Atlas and Argus* was classed as a copperhead sheet during the Civil War, and was barred from the mails. Cassidy's bitter opposition to Lincoln did not prevent him, however, from dashing off, in the heat of the hour, one of the best eulogies on the assassinated president. He ardently supported McClellan, Johnson, and Seymour, and reluctantly aided Greeley in 1872. He served as a member of the constitutional convention of New York (1867), as secretary of the State Democratic Committee (1868–73), as president of the Argus Company (1865–73), and as a member of a commission on revision of the New York state constitution (1872).

An Irish Catholic, he was a life-long enemy of Great Britain. His paper bristles with anti-English editorials, but for consistent foreign news it fails the reader. It was simply a state partisan newspaper. The combative Cassidy was, however, courtly, dignified, and suave in manner. He became the Nestor of Democratic journalists in up-state New York, and was a lover of society, to the last. Death came to him at his birthplace, the Cassidy homestead on Maiden Lane. An estate estimated at well over $150,-000 was left to his wife, née Lucie Rochefort, and to his sons.

[The Albany *Atlas*, *Argus*, *Evening Jour.*, the *Atlas and Argus*, and the N. Y. City newspapers are the chief sources. See also Amasa J. Parker, ed., *Landmarks of Albany County* (Syracuse, 1897) ; Herbert D. A. Donovan, *The Barnburners* (1925) ; M. V. Dolan, *Centenary of the Argus* (1913) ; *Memoir of Wm. Cassidy* (1874).]   W. E. S.

CASSIN, JOHN (Sept. 6, 1813–Jan. 10, 1869), ornithologist, son of Thomas Cassin, a Quaker, was born on a farm in Upper Providence Township, Delaware County, Pa., about a mile from the present town of Media. He was educated at the near-by Quaker school, Westtown. Here, as in all educational institutions conducted by the Friends, natural history received especial attention, and young John Cassin was strongly influenced in this direction. Removing to Philadelphia at the age of twenty-one, he engaged in mercantile pursuits and later held a position in the United States Custom-House. Finally upon the death of Bowen, head of one of the principal engraving and lithographing establishments of the day, Cassin succeeded him in the management of the business and later produced the illustrations for many government and other scientific publications.

Soon after removing to Philadelphia, Cassin joined the Academy of Natural Sciences. The collection of birds especially attracted him and he devoted much of his spare time to its study. Dr. Thomas B. Wilson, patron and later president of the Academy, was at this time beginning to assemble the enormous collection of birds that was to make the institution famous in ornithological centers throughout the world, and upon Cassin devolved the work of arranging and identifying the 26,000 specimens which Wilson had brought together, and which formed the largest collection then in existence. Cassin's opportunities were unequaled, but unfortunately business responsibilities took so much of his time that he was forced to pursue his studies in spare hours, evenings, and holidays. He had the constant support of Dr. Wilson, who procured for the Academy's library practically every book and journal that Cassin needed in his work. Cassin published the results of his researches in many papers in the *Proceedings* of the Academy and soon established a reputation throughout the scientific world. Unlike Audubon and Alexander Wilson, he was what has been termed a "closet naturalist," his publications being mainly technical monographs or descriptions of new species dealing with taxonomy and questions of synonymy and nomenclature. Probably no ornithologist of his day had such a knowledge of the literature of the subject, and Elliott Coues has truly said of him that he was the only ornithologist the United States had produced up to that time who was as familiar with the birds of the Old World as with those of America.

Perhaps Cassin's most notable papers published by the Academy were those based upon the collections of Du Chaillu made in the then unknown regions of West Africa, which abounded in rare and curious novelties. He also contributed the ornithological portions of a number of United States Government publications: *Mammalogy and Ornithology*, being Volume VII (second edition, 1858) of the *United States Exploring Expedition*; "Narrative of the Expedition of an American Squadron to the China Seas and Japan, Volume II," published as *Senate Executive Document No. 79* and *House Executive Document, No. 97*, 33 Cong., 2 Sess.; "United States Naval Astronomical Expedition to the Southern Hemisphere, Volume II," published as *House Executive Document No. 121*, 33 Cong., 1 Sess.; and part of the classic volume on the birds of North America, "Reports of Explorations and Surveys . . . Route for a Railroad from the Mississippi River to the Pacific Ocean, Volume IX, Part II," published as *Senate Executive Document, No. 78* and *House Executive Document, No. 91*, 33 Cong., 2 Sess. He also published a notable work, *Illustrations of the Birds of California, Texas, Oregon, British, and Russian America* (1856), covering the species discovered since the appearance of Audubon's *Birds of America* (1827–38).

[Witmer Stone, "John Cassin," in *Cassinia, a Bird Annual*, 1901, pp. 1–7; T. M. Brewer in *Proc. Boston Soc. Nat. Hist.*, Jan. 1869, reprinted in *Am. Jour. Sci.*, Mar. 1869.]   W. S.

CASTLE, VERNON BLYTHE (May 2, 1887–Feb. 15, 1918), dancer, aviator, the son of William and Jane Blythe, was born in Norwich, England. When a small boy he surprised his parents by wiring the entire house with electric bells. The family immediately planned for him a career as an electrical engineer, and he later received training as a civil engineer in London. In 1906 he came to the United States with his father and his sister, Coralie Blythe, who was to take part in a play in New York. Through association with his sister's friends Vernon was given a small unimportant part in Lew Field's *The Girl Behind the Counter*, in 1907. It was at this time that he assumed the name Castle. The short freakish dance which he did in the show was singled out by the public as unusual and eccentric. Castle soon found himself creating dances for various occasions. On May 28, 1911 he married Irene Foote, the daughter of a New Rochelle physician. His wife proved to be a competent dancing partner and appeared with him a few times in small dance acts. About a year later they went to Paris, and because of lack of funds started dancing in a Paris café. They proved a sensation to the Parisians, and when news of their success reached New York, café owners and theatrical producers besieged them with offers. They returned to America in a few months, and at times, during the next two years, were drawing as much as $6,000 a week for their performances. In 1914 they published a book of instruction in dancing, called *Modern Dancing*. Castle originated the one-step, turkey-trot, Castle-walk and many other dances, some of which have lasted and many of which have not. In February 1916 he enlisted in the Royal Flying Corps. He received the commission of lieutenant and served in the French army under Gen. Foch. He held the respect of officers for his daring and spectacular movements in the air. The Croix de Guerre was awarded him for bringing down two German planes. In 1918 he was sent to Fort Worth, Tex., to teach aviation and was as highly praised as an instructor of aviation as he had been as an instructor of dancing. He was killed in a collision with another airplane, flown by a cadet. His courage in maneuvering to save the cadet's life was highly praised by officers who witnessed the accident. He was a tall, slender, rather frail-looking man, extremely sympathetic, and above all else a lover of animals. He did well the only two things which he attempted during his short lifetime.

[*N. Y. Times, N. Y. Herald*, Feb. 16, 1918; Irene F. Castle, "My Memories of Vernon Castle," in *Everybody's Mag.*, Nov., Dec., 1918, Jan., Feb., Mar., 1919, and *My Husband* (1919).]   M.S.

CASWELL, ALEXIS (Jan. 29, 1799–Jan. 8, 1877), college president, scientist, was a twin son of Samuel and Polly (Seaver) Caswell. He came of a line of farmers which went back to Thomas Caswell, an Englishman, one of the incorporators of Taunton, Mass., in 1639. His maternal grandmother, Zibiah White, was descended from Peregrine White, born on the *Mayflower*. After three years in Taunton Academy Caswell entered Brown University, graduating in 1822 at the head of his class. For five years he taught in Columbian College, Washington, the last two years as professor of ancient languages, meanwhile studying theology with the president. He entered the ministry in 1827, and served as pastor of a Baptist church in Halifax, Nova Scotia, for nearly a year. But in 1828 he accepted the chair of mathematics and natural philosophy in Brown University, where he taught continuously for thirty-five years except for a year abroad in 1860–61. His professorships (mathematics and natural philosophy, 1828–50, mathematics and astronomy, 1850–55, natural philosophy and astronomy, 1855–63) forbade him to confine himself to one science, but his favorite field was astronomy. His lectures on this subject at the Smithsonian Institution in 1858 "were of the highest order of popular instruction," wrote Prof. Joseph Lovering of Harvard, who adds that "he was never superficial." He published admirable reviews of William Whewell's *Astronomy and General Physics* (1833) and of J. P. Nichol's *Architecture of the Heavens* (1838),

his easy, lucid style presenting scientific subjects pleasantly yet with precision (*Christian Review*, June 1836, December 1841). In 1855 he was chosen vice-president of the American Association for the Advancement of Science; in 1858, the president and vice-president being absent, he was called to the chair, and therefore gave the address as retiring president the next year, reviewing the problems of astronomy and forecasting the part American astronomers might have in solving them. His standing as a scientist is also shown by his election as associate fellow of the American Academy of Arts and Sciences in 1850, and by the government's choice of him as one of fifty incorporators of the National Academy of Sciences in 1863. His most important publication was, perhaps, the account of his own meteorological observations at Providence, R. I., from December 1831 to May 1860, in *Smithsonian Contributions to Knowledge*, vol. XII (1860).

After his retirement in 1863, he became president of the National Exchange Bank and of the American Screw Company, in Providence. In 1868 he was called to the presidency of Brown University, to meet an emergency caused by two declinations. He was sixty-nine at the time. A man of that age, called obviously to fill a gap, might only have discharged the routine duties of the office, with which Caswell was already familiar as president *pro tempore* in 1840–41, and as regent, or dean, from 1852 to 1855. But he did more, vigilantly maintaining the scholarship of the university and making some advance. Long before, in 1836, in an article in the *North American Review* he had attacked the prevailing system of higher education in America, referring to the "practise of conferring degrees on easy terms" with the result that "with us, degrees are not distinctions," adding that in England examinations "are conducted with a severity, at which, in this country, all our college fraternities [*i. e.*, the colleges] would stand aghast." In his president's report, in 1872, he spoke of "the weary task" of educating youths "who were not born to study." He retired from the presidency in 1872, but served as trustee from 1873 to 1875 and as fellow the next two years. From 1875 till his death he was president of the Rhode Island Hospital, of which he had been a trustee since its founding.

In all his work Caswell is revealed as a Yankee of the best type, cool, shrewd, kindly, able to turn his hand with confidence to varied tasks. "Dr. Caswell is universally known to be a man of imperturbable good nature," wrote President Wayland to an angry parent. "He never told your son that he was a liar, but he did tell him that he found great difficulty in believing the account which he had given." He was untroubled by the supposed conflict between science and religion; "the legitimate results of all true science, and all discovery," he wrote in 1841, "will be to fix the truths of Christianity upon a broader and deeper foundation." "Inflexible in his own peculiar theology," said Prof. Lovering, "he had no taint of illiberality in his intellect or his heart." He was married in 1830 to Esther L. Thompson, who died in 1850, and in 1855 to Elizabeth B. Edmands, who survived him.

[*New Eng. Hist. and Geneal. Reg.*, July 1877; Jos. Lovering in *Proc. Am. Acad. Arts and Sci.*, 1877, vol. XII, and J. L. Lincoln in *Providence Daily Jour.*, June 20, 1877.]
         W. C. B.

CASWELL, RICHARD (Aug. 3, 1729–November 1789), Revolutionary soldier and politician, was born in Cecil County, Md. Owing to the financial misfortunes of his father, who was a merchant, he was early thrown upon his own resources and at the age of seventeen removed to Raleigh, N. C., where he became a surveyor. He was also a lawyer, and, being a versatile man, a good speaker, and highly regarded, he held political offices at an early age. He was deputy-surveyor of the colony, clerk of Orange County, and in 1754–71 a member of the North Carolina Assembly. During this long term of legislative service he was very active, particularly in reforming the courts of law. In the last two years he was speaker of the Assembly. During the insurrection of the Regulators in 1771 he served under Gov. Tryon at the battle of Alamance, commanding the right wing.

During the Revolution, Caswell was prominent in various lines. He presided over the provincial congress, and also over the convention which prepared the state constitution, being a member of the committee which framed that document. He was a delegate to the Continental Congress 1774–76. In the army he was colonel of North Carolina Partisan Rangers 1776–77, and was major-general of the state militia from 1780 to the end of the war. His military opportunity came at the battle of Moore's Creek, Feb. 27, 1776. In this action Colonels Caswell and Lillington with about 1,100 men repulsed a Loyalist army of about 1,600 led by the Scotch Highlander McDonald. The victory was complete, and decisive—for some years—of the war in North Carolina. McDonald and about 900 of his army were taken prisoners, and the captures included money, arms, and ammunition (see, for the numbers, R. D. W. Connor, *Revolutionary Leaders*, and *North Carolina Colonial Records*). Caswell had shown skill, and received the thanks of Congress.

He was governor of North Carolina, 1776–80, and helped in the organizing and equipping of troops. While governor in 1777 he received a letter from Washington, urging strong measures in dealing with deserters. His popularity suffered a temporary eclipse after the battle of Camden (Aug. 16, 1780). In this disastrous action Caswell commanded the North Carolina militia. When his men broke and fled, Caswell, having attempted vainly to rally them, shared in Gates's rapid flight northward. He was superseded for a while by Gen. Smallwood in the command of the state militia, but his influence in the state was soon recovered. He held the offices of speaker of the Senate, comptroller-general, and governor for a second time, 1785–87. While governor he was chosen delegate to the Federal Convention, but declined to serve. He showed his interest in its actions, however, by asking for information that might be of use to the Convention, and by correspondence with the delegates from his state in regard to the proceedings. When the state convention met for ratification, Caswell's influence was thrown against the new Federal Constitution. While holding his last political office as speaker of the Assembly, he was stricken with paralysis, and died a few days later at Fayetteville.

[R. D. W. Connor, *Revolutionary Leaders of N. C.* (1916); Eugene C. Brooks, "Richard Caswell," in S. A. Ashe, ed., *Biog. Hist. of N. C.*, vol. III (1905), 65; John H. Wheeler, *Hist. Sketches of N. C.* (1851).]
         E. K. A.

CATESBY, MARK (*c.* 1679–Dec. 23, 1749), naturalist and traveler, was born late in 1679 or early in 1680, it is believed at Sudbury, in Suffolk, England. He developed an early interest in natural science and went to London the better to study it. He first landed in America in 1712, in Virginia, where he had relatives living. He remained there seven years, sending back to England collections of seeds and plants; then returned to England, and planned, with the assistance and encouragement of (among others) Sir Hans Sloane, Dr. William Sherard, the botanist, and Gov. Nicholson of South Carolina, an examination of the natural history of the Southern colonies and the Bahamas. He landed at Charleston, S. C., in May 1722, and spent about three years studying and collecting the fauna and flora of South Carolina, Georgia, and Florida. He also visited the Bahamas, returning to England in 1726. He then settled at Hoxton; mastered the art of etching; and wrote and illustrated his most considerable work, *The Natural History of Carolina, Florida, and the Bahama Islands*. Published in parts, in large folio, with the text in French and English, the first volume was completed in 1731, the second in 1743, and an appendix in 1748. The book was illustrated with over 200 plates, the figures etched by Catesby himself, from his own paintings, and the first colored copies tinted under his inspection. Some of the work was later reproduced on the Continent at Nürnberg. It drew considerable interest, both among the wealthy dilettanti to whom it was addressed, and also among the learned. Catesby was elected to the Royal Society in 1733, and in 1747 read a paper before that body (printed in *Philosophical Transactions* the same year) upon the migration of birds, in which he rightly refuted the belief in their hibernating under water, although so good a naturalist as Gilbert White hankered after the theory, more than a generation later. Catesby gave examples from among the South Carolina birds. He wrote, also, *Hortus Britanno-Americanus; or, a Curious Collection of Trees and Shrubs,* which illustrated work, issued posthumously in 1763–67, encouraged the introduction into Europe of North American trees and shrubs. He enjoyed many friendships, notably in the Royal Society, by "his modesty, ingenuity and upright behavior" (Pulteney, *post*). On Dec. 23, 1749, he died at his home in Old St., London, leaving a widow and two children.

[See Catesby's own preface to the *Natural Hist. of Carolina*; R. Pulteney, *Hist. and Biog. Sketches of the Progress of Botany in England* (London, 1790, II, 219–30); Britten and Boulger, *Biographical Index of British and Irish Botanists* (London, 1893, p. 32), where the reference to *Nichols' Lit. Anecdotes* should be VI, 78; Catesby's correspondence with John Bartram reprinted in W. Darlington, *Memorials of John Bartram and Humphry Marshall* (1849), pp. 319–24.] W. H. B. C.

CATHCART, JAMES LEANDER (June 1, 1767–Oct. 6, 1843), consul, was born at Mount Murragh, County of Westmeath, Ireland, the son of Malcolm Hamilton Cathcart, who had married the daughter of Edward Humphreys of Dublin. The family surname is taken from the Barony of Kethcart, County of Renfrew, now the town of Cathcart, Scotland. The founder of the family, Col. Gabriel Cathcart, accompanied the Rev. Malcolm Hamilton (later Bishop of Cashel) to Ireland in 1641. James Leander Cathcart was brought to America as a child by Capt. John Cathcart. In October 1779 he became a midshipman on the Continental frigate *Confederacy,* Capt. Seth Harding, where he served until captured by the British some months later. He was taken to New York and confined on the prison ships *Good Hope* and *Old Jersey* but escaped in March 1782 and entered the merchant service. While he was a seaman on the schooner *Maria,*

of Boston, the vessel was captured (July 25, 1785) by an Algerine xebec off Cape St. Vincent. The crew was sold into slavery in Algiers. Although a prisoner, Cathcart became clerk of the Marine (1787–88), clerk of the Bagnio Gallera (prison of the galley slaves), keeper of the prison tavern, clerk to the prime minister, and, in March 1792, chief Christian secretary to the Dey and Regency of Algiers. He seems to have had some influence with the Dey and claimed that it was only after much effort on his part that the Dey agreed to receive Joseph Donaldson, sent by the United States to negotiate for peace and the release of prisoners (1795). The treaty signed, Cathcart sailed for Philadelphia (May 8, 1796) in the barque *Independent,* which he had purchased, carrying dispatches from Joel Barlow [*q.v.*], and a letter from the Dey to President Washington. He was appointed consul at Tripoli (July 10, 1797), but remained in Philadelphia to select the presents and naval stores for the tribute to Algiers. On June 5, 1798, he married Jane Bancker Woodside of Philadelphia, by whom he had twelve children. In December 1798 he was appointed a special diplomatic agent, and accompanied William Eaton [*q.v.*] to Tunis, where they obtained alterations in the unsatisfactory treaty that had been negotiated by Joseph E. Famin in August 1797. The treaty concluded (Mar. 26, 1799), Cathcart proceeded to Tripoli and procured a settlement with the Pasha by distributing $1,500 in bribes. Later, the Pasha, observing the flourishing condition of the unprotected American commerce in the Mediterranean, made further demands, and declared war on the United States in May 1801, Cathcart retiring to Leghorn. It was upon Cathcart's suggestion that Eaton espoused the cause of Hamet Karamanli, rightful Pasha of Tripoli, then exiled in Tunis (Charles Prentiss, *Life of the Late Gen. William Eaton,* 1813, p. 225). In 1802 Cathcart was authorized to treat with the Tripolitan government, but the Pasha treated his proposals with contempt. Cathcart was then appointed consul-general at Algiers (1802), but the Dey refused to receive him and he was appointed instead consul at Tunis (1803). The Bey of Tunis, who had twice refused to receive Cathcart, whom he characterized as an *embroglione* (translated by Eaton as "troublesome litigious trifler"), rejected both consul and the terms offered and denounced Cathcart to the President, to which Jefferson made an apologetic answer. Cathcart later served as consul at Madeira (1807–15), and at Cadiz (1815–17), and after he returned to the United States became naval agent for the protection of live oak timber in Florida (1818–20). During the last twenty years of his life he was employed in the United States Treasury at Washington, D. C. He received a Revolutionary pension in 1833. Mrs. Jane B. Newkirk, Cathcart's daughter, compiled and published the journal of his Algerine captivity, *The Captives* (La Porte, Ind., 1899), and a volume of his official correspondence, *Tripoli . . . Letter-Book by James Leander Cathcart* (La Porte, 1901).

[In addition to the above: *Am. State Papers, Foreign Relations*, vols. I and II (both 1832) and *Naval Affairs*, IV (1861), 107; S. C. Blyth, *Hist. of the War between the U. S. and Tripoli, and Other Barbary Powers* (1806); *Jour. of the Captivity and Sufferings of John Foss* (1797); *Memoirs of John Quincy Adams*, vol. V (1875); G. W. Allen, *Our Navy and the Barbary Corsairs* (1905); *Daily National Intelligencer* (Washington, D. C.), Oct. 9, 1843; Revolutionary pension records in the Dept. of the Interior and records of the Dept. of State, Washington, D. C.; Cathcart MSS. in the N. Y. Pub. Lib.]   F.E.R.

CATHCART, WILLIAM (Nov. 8, 1826–July 8, 1908), Baptist minister, historian, son of James and Elizabeth (Cously) Cathcart, was born in the county of Londonderry, Ireland, where he was brought up in the strict Presbyterian faith. At about the time of his nineteenth birthday, he had a personal religious experience which he considered a conversion, and in January 1846 he was baptized by immersion. He obtained the rudiments of a classical education at a school near his home, but continued his studies at the University of Glasgow and at the Baptist school (now Rawdon College) in Horton, Yorkshire. In 1850 he married Eliza Caldwell, who was to survive him eight years. Ordained pastor of the Baptist church at Barnsley, but chafing under the restraints of a society dominated by an established church, he determined to migrate to America. Reaching New York on Nov. 18, 1853, he became, the next month, pastor at Groton, Conn. Soon after his thirtieth birthday, he was called to the Second Baptist Church of Philadelphia, beginning on Apr. 1, 1857, a pastorate of twenty-seven years. From the beginning of this ministry, its vigor was conspicuous. Cathcart participated in the broader activities of his denomination and aggressively supported the Bible Union movement in its interest in the translation rather than transliteration of the words referring to baptism. His preaching was largely a scholarly exposition of the Scriptures with an incisive application of evangelical principles, occasionally cutting across cherished views. Early in this pastorate, he assailed the prevalent Sabbatarianism of the strongly Protestant community; for this a group of fellow ministers denounced him as holding heretical views. His announcement that a recurrence of the accusation would lead to a suit for slander stifled these irresponsible charges. The blend of rigor and urbanity in his temperament is revealed in the remark of an officer of his church after his retirement, "We had a master and did not know it."

Early in 1884, on account of his health he retired from the pastorate to his farm at Gwynedd, Pa., where he was able to continue historical activities which he had commenced more than a decade earlier. If his critical acumen lagged behind that of some of the more advanced historians of his day, ne often delved deep for source material. He was best known as editor of the *Baptist Encyclopædia* (1883); its fulsome praise of living subjects may perhaps be ascribed to the poor taste of the period. He wrote other popular works: *The Papal System from Its Origin to the Present Time* (1872); *The Baptists and the American Revolution* (1876); *The Baptism of the Ages and of the Nations* (1878); *The Ancient British and Irish Churches Including the Life and Labors of St. Patrick* (1894).

[John B. Filson, *Hist. of the Second Baptist Ch., Phila.* (1886); Elmer W. Powell, a memorial sketch in the *Baptist Commonwealth*, July 16, 1908.]
     W.H.A.

CATHERWOOD, MARY HARTWELL (Dec. 16, 1847–Dec. 26, 1902), novelist, was the daughter of Marcus and Phœbe (Thompson) Hartwell. There lay behind her a rather significant tradition of culture. Marcus Hartwell, his brother Cyrus, and his three sisters had all received from their father a small fortune and such advanced education as the Ohio of their day afforded—the girls at the Granville Female Seminary, the boys at Marietta College. Marcus, after studying medicine at Columbus, practised in the little settlement of Luray in Licking County, where Mary was born. In the latter part of the 1850's the Hartwells moved to Illinois. The young doctor had barely established a new practise at Milford when he died, his wife following him a few months later. Mary and her brother and sister were separated and cared for by maternal relatives. By the aid of school-teaching, Mary managed to work her way through the Granville Female Seminary (also called the Granville Female College). Her ambition to become a writer by this time firmly fixed, she varied her teaching at Danville, Ill., and elsewhere, by writing various stories, poems, and articles, one of them a prize story published in *Wood's Household Magazine* of Newburgh, N. Y. On Dec. 27, 1877, she was married to James Steele Catherwood. Her husband for a time conducted a confectionery store in Indianapolis, where she was a part of the little literary circle of the city. Erect and graceful, with auburn hair and bright hazel eyes, she was an attractive figure. The major part of her married life was spent at Hoopeston, Ill., where Catherwood was postmaster under Cleveland and member of a real-estate firm. Later, having separated from her husband, she spent her summers in writing, at Mackinac, her favorite resort, or in gathering material in Canada or abroad. Her last years were spent in Chicago.

Throughout her life, Mrs. Catherwood was exceptionally ambitious and prolific, carrying on several pieces of work at one time. She had, for instance, two serials, "Lilith" and "Cracque-o'-Doom," running in the 1881 numbers of *Lippincott's* and a third, "Stephen Guthrie," in the next volume. Her first novel, *A Woman in Armor,* had appeared in 1875. During the eighties she produced a number of children's books. Widespread recognition first came with her historical novel, *The Romance of Dollard* (1889), based largely on Francis Parkman. This she followed with numerous other tales dealing with the French in America: *The Story of Tonty* (1890), *The Lady of Fort St. John* (1891), *Old Kaskaskia* (1893), *The Chase of St. Castin and Other Stories of the French in the New World* (1894), *The Little Renault* (published with *The Spirit of an Illinois Town,* 1897). *The Days of Jeanne D'Arc* (1897) she regarded as in part the result of a divine hint. *The White Islander* (1893) shows the transition from French control. *The Spirit of an Illinois Town* (1897); *Spanish Peggy* (1899); *The Queen of the Swamp and Other Plain Americans* (1899); *Mackinac and Lake Stories* (1899), one of the best of her books; and an unfinished novel about Owen's colony, all treated of the Anglo-Saxon settlement of the West. Her last book, *Lazarre* (1901), dealt with the legend of the Dauphin in America. Since her death, her works have sunk into relative obscurity. It must be admitted that she fell into the pitfalls inherent in her favorite *genre* when she invented for Dollard and her other heroes loves befitting their courage, youth, and chivalry; that she was inclined to refine or sentimentalize her characters too much; and that her longer novels were marred by structural weaknesses. Nevertheless her books show careful research, a feeling for the untamed background of forest and prairie, and an intelligent sympathy with the past.

[M. L. Wilson, *Biography of Mary Hartwell Catherwood* (1904); F. L. Pattee, *Hist. of Am. Lit. since 1870* (1915); D. A. Dondore, *The Prairie and the Making of Middle America; Four Centuries of Description* (1927).]

D. A. D.

CATLIN, GEORGE (July 26, 1796–Dec. 23, 1872), artist, author, was born at Wilkesbarre, Pa., the fifth of the fourteen children of Putnam and Polly (Sutton) Catlin. When eight years

old, Polly Sutton, along with her mother, had been captured by the Indians at the surrender of Forty Fort. George's early life was filled with stories, legends, and traditions of the Red Men, not only from his family but from Revolutionary soldiers, Indian fighters, trappers, hunters, and explorers, who were constant guests of the family. His scanty education was obtained at home. He loved fishing and hunting, became an accomplished sportsman, and in his early years collected Indian relics. In 1817–18 he read law in the office of Reeves & Gould in Litchfield, Conn., where he became celebrated as an amateur artist. Until 1823 he practised law at Luzerne, Pa., and in adjoining counties, but then moved to Philadelphia to devote himself to portrait painting in oil and miniature. In 1828 he visited Albany, where he painted portraits of Gov. DeWitt Clinton and many members of the legislature. While there he met and married Clara B. Gregory, who was to be an enthusiastic aid in his later western work, accompanying him on many of his trips. From 1824 to 1829 he resided mainly in Washington, D. C., painting many portraits, among others that of Dolly Madison. His painting of the Constitutional Convention at Richmond (1829–30) contains 115 figures. During all these early years he had been seeking for an idea to which he could devote the remainder of his artistic life. Upon seeing at Philadelphia a delegation of from ten to fifteen dignified-looking Indians from the wilds of the Far West, he resolved, as he wrote later, "to use my art and so much of the labors of my future life as might be required in rescuing from oblivion the looks and customs of the vanishing races of native man in America." To this one purpose he devoted enthusiastically the rest of his life and that without aid, governmental or individual. He spent his summers among the Indians; in the winters he would return to civilization, paint portraits, and save enough money to take him back to his beloved Indians in the ensuing summer. One of the most difficult things which he had to overcome was the superstition of the Indians, who believed that they would die or that the white medicine man would have power over them, if their portraits were painted. If anything did happen to the tribe, if a person died or was killed, it was supposed to be the fault of the painter, and Catlin several times escaped death only through wise counsel or by fleeing. From 1829 to 1838 he painted some 600 portraits of distinguished Indians of both sexes, in their native costume, accompanied with pictures of their villages, domestic habits, games, mysteries, and religious ceremonies. This original collection he exhibited in many cities in the United States and in Europe during a period from 1837 to 1852. In the latter year he was induced to enter into speculations which ended in financial disaster. Joseph Harrison of Philadelphia advanced him money and took the collection as security, but Catlin was never able to redeem it. Eventually the collection was given by Mrs. Harrison to the United States National Museum. There is also another collection known as the "Catlin Cartoon Collection," which consists of copies and original paintings of North and South American Indians and scenes painted between 1852 and 1870. This is the property of Catlin's heirs, and consists of 603 numbers. Catlin's writings related largely to his own experiences. They consist of: "Notes of Eight Years Travel Amongst the North American Indians," published in the New York *Daily Commercial Advertiser* from 1830 to 1839; *Letters and Notes on the Manners, Customs, and Condition of the North American Indians* (2 vols., 1841); *Catlin's North American Indian Portfolio: Hunting, Rocky Mountains and Prairies of America* (1845); *Catlin's Notes of Eight Years' Travels and Residence in Europe* (1848); *Life Among the Indians* (1867); *Last Rambles Amongst the Indians of the Rocky Mountains and the Andes* (1867). Besides the above, Catlin wrote the various catalogues of his collections and numerous articles for papers and magazines.

[Thos. Donaldson, "The Geo. Catlin Indian Gallery in the U. S. Nat. Mus.," in *Annual Report of the Board of Regents of the Smithsonian Institution*, 1885; W. Matthews, "The Catlin Collection of Indian Paintings," *Ibid.*, 1890; *U. S. Mag. and Democratic Rev.*, July 1842; *N. Y. Herald*, Dec. 24, 1872; *Nature* (London), Jan. 23, 1873; *Am. Bibliopolist*, Jan. 1873; *Pop. Sci. Mo.*, July 1891.]   R. P. T.

CATON, JOHN DEAN (Mar. 19, 1812–July 30, 1895), jurist, was born in Monroe, Orange County, N. Y. He was a son of Robert Caton, a Virginian of English descent, who, after serving through the Revolutionary War with the American forces, moved to Monroe, and married Hannah Dean. When, on the death of his father, the family moved to Oneida County, John worked as a farm hand, attending the district school in winter. In 1827 he was apprenticed to a harness maker, but was compelled to abandon this owing to impaired eyesight. He then became a common carrier between Waterville and Utica, N. Y., studying in the evenings, and in 1829 he was, for a short time, a pupil at the Utica Academy. The following summer he engaged as a farm laborer, and studied classics during the winter. In 1831 he attended the Grosvenor High School at Rome, N. Y., intermittently studying law there and at Utica and

Vernon. Two years later he went west, arriving in Chicago,—then a place of 300 inhabitants—June 19, 1833. The town had no lawyer, so he determined to locate there, and, obtaining a license to practise, opened the first law office. He instituted the first civil suit in the circuit court of the county, prosecuted the first criminal tried in a court of justice there, for which he received a fee of ten dollars—"the greatest fee he ever received," he was wont to say—and also appeared in the first jury case heard in that neighborhood. He was a member and secretary of the first political convention held in Illinois, which met at Ottawa, Mar. 4, 1834. This was followed by his election as justice of the peace. In July 1835 he married Laura Adelaide, daughter of Jacob Sherill of New Hartford, Oneida County, N. Y. In the same year he was admitted to the Illinois bar. Much of his time was taken up in traveling the circuit on horseback, which took him through practically unexplored country, involving much hardship and no little adventure. The financial panic of 1837 seriously affected him, and, his health breaking down, he retired to a farm near Plainfield, where he remained for three years, not resuming practise in Chicago till 1841. In August 1842 he was appointed associate justice of the supreme court of Illinois by Gov. Carlin, holding the office till March 1843, when he was defeated. Two months later a vacancy occurring, he was again appointed to the bench, and on the expiration of his term was unanimously nominated and elected to succeed himself. Under the new Illinois constitution of 1848, he was elected to one of the three supreme court judgeships thereby created, becoming chief justice in 1855 on the resignation of Chief Justice Treat. Reëlected in 1857, he remained chief justice till his retirement, Jan. 9, 1864. Though not a great lawyer, since he lacked the erudition which can come only through deep reading, he was an excellent judge. His opinions were always logical and expressed with great common sense and vigor. He had little respect for precedent, relying more on principles. Endowed with good business instincts, he was "one of the most practical men that ever sat upon the bench" (James B. Bradwell). Chief shareholder in the Illinois & Mississippi Telegraph Company, it is said that at one time he controlled all the telegraph lines in the state. Ultimately these were leased to the Western Union Telegraph Company, and Caton disposed of his holdings in 1867. The last thirty years of his life were spent in retirement. He had a large estate at Ottawa, where he gratified his taste for the amenities of country life. He traveled widely in the United States, Europe, and the East. He died in Chicago.

Caton contributed a number of papers on nature subjects to the Ottawa Academy of Science, and was the author of: *Matter and a Supreme Intelligence* (1864), *A Summer in Norway* (1875), *The Antelope and Deer of America* (1877), and a volume of *Miscellanies* (1880). He also contributed a series of papers to the *Chicago Legal News* in 1888–89, which were subsequently published with additional material under the title *The Early Bench and Bar of Illinois* (1893).

[A judicious study of Caton's career by M. M. Follansbee will be found in *Great Am. Lawyers*, ed. by Wm. D. Lewis (1909), VI, 307. Appreciative sketches appeared in *The Bench and Bar of Ill.*, ed. by J. M. Palmer (1899), I, 39, II, 604, and in the *Green Bag*, III, 230. See also Robt. Fergus, *Biog. Sketch of John Dean Caton* (1882); *Ill. State Bar Ass. Report*, 1896, pt. II, p. 176; 31 *Ill. R.*, p. viii; 162 *Ill. R.*, pp. 15–20.]

H. W. H. K.

CATRON, JOHN (*c.* 1786–May 30, 1865), jurist, was of German descent, at least on his father's side. His birth has been credited to both Pennsylvania and Virginia, and the date put as early as 1779 and as late as 1786. Considering all sources of information, it is believed that he was a descendant of German settlers in Pennsylvania, was born in that state about 1786, spent a part of his childhood in Virginia, and grew to manhood in Kentucky where he resided until 1812. Nothing is known of his life during this time except that his parents were poor and his educational opportunities exceedingly limited.

In 1812 he removed to Tennessee and settled near the Cumberland Mountains, and later became a prominent figure in the pioneer days of that state. He enlisted and served as a soldier under Jackson in the War of 1812. In 1815 he was admitted to the bar and, until 1818, practised on what were known as the mountain circuits, becoming, in the meantime, prosecuting attorney for one of these circuits. He was recognized as unusually proficient in land law, then the chief source of litigation. In personal appearance, he was large and well proportioned, with dark complexion, black eyes, and strong face, indicating determination and confidence in himself. He was not a pleasing or graceful speaker, having an unpleasant voice and being given to awkward and rather violent gesticulation. But his arguments were strong and convincing. As a lawyer he was studious, painstaking, and unusually successful. In 1818 he removed to Nashville where he soon enjoyed a lucrative practise, won distinction, especially as a Chancery lawyer, and acquired, for those times, a comfortable fortune. In 1824 the legislature increased the number of the judges of the supreme court of errors and appeals (then the court of last resort) and elected Catron to the new judgeship. The bar has an apparently well-founded tradition that both the increase in the membership of the court and the election of Catron were due to the fact that land titles were unsettled to a disturbing degree on account of a division in the court as to the effect of certain statutes of limitations. Catron's views on this question were well known and insured a majority of the court for the ruling that has ever since served to quiet titles.

In 1831 the office of chief justice was created, and Catron became Tennessee's first chief justice. He held this office until a new constitution, adopted in 1834, abolished the court of which he was a member, after which he resumed his practise at Nashville. His service as a judge was of great value in developing the system of land laws which has ever since prevailed in the state. Perhaps his most noted opinion was delivered in 1829 in a case in which a lawyer was disbarred for fighting a duel and killing his man. This opinion had much to do with discrediting the then rather prevalent practise of dueling. After a most scathing arraignment of dueling and the false ideas of honor and bravery which led to it, Catron said: "We are told this is only a kind of *honorable* homicide! The law knows it as a wicked and wilful murder" (I *Yerger*, 237).

Besides being a successful lawyer, Catron was an astute politician as he showed while directing the campaign, in Tennessee, of Martin Van Buren for the presidency in 1836. He was an ardent supporter of President Jackson and had a large part in creating a sentiment in Tennessee in favor of Jackson's fight against the Bank of the United States. On Mar. 3, 1837, the day before Jackson's retirement from the presidency, Congress passed an act adding two justices to the membership of the Supreme Court. On the next day, among his last acts as president, Jackson appointed Catron. Several traditions are connected with this appointment. One is that Mrs. Catron went to the White House and personally solicited it. Another is that it was procured through the influence of Van Buren whose friendship Catron had gained. The truth probably is that, knowing his friend and supporter to be well qualified, Jackson was very glad to make the appointment when it was suggested by Mrs. Catron and possibly by Van Buren. Being self-educated, Catron was not a ripe scholar, but he had a good knowledge of the law, a keen insight into human nature, and strong common sense.

His opinions have been considered particularly strong when dealing with the common law and equity jurisprudence. In the great Dred Scott case, he was one of the justices who concurred in holding the Missouri Compromise unconstitutional. At the outbreak of the Civil War, he, as associate justice, presided over the circuit composed of Missouri, Kentucky, and Tennessee. In cooperation with the circuit judges, he was firm and determined in the effort to maintain the authority of the United States. When the Supreme Court adjourned in the spring of 1861, he hurried to Tennessee in the hope that he could aid in holding his state loyal to the Union. Tennessee had not then seceded. An election had been held and the vote had been against secession. But another election had been called. His efforts and those of many other Tennesseans, however, were unavailing and the state voted to secede.

After secession, it was Catron's purpose to remain in Tennessee, endeavor to maintain the authority of the Federal courts, and induce his friends to adhere to the cause of the Union. But this was impossible. Excitement was running too high and feeling was too bitter. Upon his return from Missouri where he had been holding court, a committee waited on him with the friendly advice that he leave the state, since otherwise he would be subjected to indignities. The state was then in control of the Confederate authorities, and, influenced, as was said, by the ill health and entreaties of his wife, he reluctantly yielded. As soon, however, as the fortunes of war made it possible to resume his judicial duties, he returned. But he was then in failing health, was near eighty years old, and soon died.

[Memorial published in 3 *Wallace* IX–XIV (1866); Joshua W. Caldwell, *Sketches of the Bench and Bar of Tenn.* (1898); Josephus C. Guild, *Old Times in Tenn.* (1878); Chas. Warren, *The Supreme Court in U. S. Hist.* (1922).]   W. L. F—n.

CATTELL, ALEXANDER GILMORE (Feb. 12, 1816–Apr. 8, 1894), banker, politician, was descended from Huguenot ancestors who settled in Scotland, moved to Leamington, England, and reached southern New Jersey, via Rhode Island, about 1700. He was the eldest son of Thomas W. and Keziah (Gilmore) Cattell, his father a merchant and banker of Salem, N. J., whose notes were war-time money along the lower Delaware in 1812. Owing to family reverses, Alexander left school for his father's store, but he continued his reading and wrote verses, his favorite poet being Keats. In 1840 he was elected to the legislature, in 1841–42 was clerk of the lower house, and in 1844 was the youngest member of the state constitutional con-

vention. Moving to Philadelphia, 1846, he served on the Common Council, 1848–54, became a director of the Mechanics Bank, president of the Corn (later the Commercial) Exchange Association, 1857, and in 1858 organized the Corn Exchange Bank which he headed for thirteen years. He "did much to build up and extend the grain trade of the city" (Scharf and Westcott, *History of Philadelphia*, 1884, III, 2224). He presided at the opening of the new post-office, Feb. 23, 1863, and at the meeting to relieve Chambersburg, Aug. 3, 1864, and he headed the committee of twenty-one (July 24, 1862) to raise and equip the "Corn Exchange Regiment." He had maintained a residence in New Jersey since 1855, having interests around Merchantville, near Camden. The local Democratic victory of 1864 and the impending necessities of Republican reconstruction brought him into New Jersey politics, as a patriot with a righteous cause and money to back him.

Early in 1865 the "Union Party" (Republican) leaders of the first and second New Jersey congressional districts, "unexpectedly" urged Cattell's nomination for governor, it being understood that "a very large amount of means would be provided for the canvass" (Smith Papers, journal, pp. 159–60). But Marcus L. Ward, "the Soldier's Friend," was nominated and elected, despite knifing by the "Cattell Cabal." A little later when John Potter Stockton's election as United States senator was challenged because he had received only a plurality of the votes of the legislature, Cattell and his friends grasped the chance to seize the office. Stockton was unseated Mar. 27, 1866, and Cattell was elected in the face of an opposition which declared him mentally and morally unfit and only financially qualified (*Ibid.*, p. 124). He was seated, Dec. 3, and gave his vote for the conviction of President Johnson. Allied with Jay Cooke and other Philadelphia interests, a sound banker, a warm friend of Grant as he had been of Lincoln, Cattell now entered his most crowded years. He did constructive work concerning tariff, taxing, national debt, and sound money; but he also became involved in the naval scandals under George M. Robeson. With his brother, Elijah G. Cattell, he "engaged in speculations in which the secretary of the navy was also involved. They gave or lent him money. They built him a house at Long Branch, purchased him horses and carriages, and managed expensive campaigns to make him a United States senator from New Jersey" (Oberholtzer, *post*, III, 182). In 1871 Cattell secured the shifting of the navy deposits in London (over a million) from Baring's to Jay Cooke's. Declining another senatorial candidacy, also a District of Columbia commissionership, he served on Grant's ineffective Civil Service Commission and, on Apr. 24, 1873, took up his headquarters at Rothschild's in London as the United States Treasury financial agent. He refunded $100,-000,000 of bonds from six per cent to five per cent, devised methods still used for quoting exchange between Great Britain and the United States, and transferred the *Alabama* claims payments to Washington. Secretary of the Treasury Bristow refused to reappoint him, because "he had positive evidence to prove that the appointment would be in the interest of dishonesty" (H. V. Boynton, "The Whiskey Ring," *North American Review*, October 1876, p. 287). Cattell served thereafter on various civic bodies, notably as president of the State Board of Assessors, but his health was none too good, partly from overstrain, partly from "a bundle of black cigars" per day (interview with nephew, E. J. Cattell). His end came while under treatment for "dementia." His wife, Eliza (Gillmore) Cattell, and an adopted daughter, had died before him.

[Cattell's letters and papers are scattered. His national career was followed with acid comment by the N. Y. *Sun*, with admiring approval by the Trenton *Daily State Gazette*. His New Jersey politics, later period, were bitterly noted by Chas. Perrin Smith in The Smith Papers (MSS.), in N. J. State Lib., Trenton. C. M. Knapp, *N. J. Politics During the Period of the Civil War and Reconstruction* (1924), and E. P. Oberholtzer, *Hist. of U. S. Since the Civil War* (1917–26) and *Jay Cooke, Financier of the Civil War* (1907) give the best view of his senatorial-financial period. For the Philadelphia navy-yard scandals see *House Misc. Docs., No. 170*, 44 Cong., 1 Sess., pt. III. Obituaries were published in Philadelphia *Evening Telegraph*, Apr. 9, 1894, and Trenton *Daily State Gazette*, Apr. 10, 1894.]   W. L. W.

CATTELL, WILLIAM CASSADAY (Aug. 30, 1827–Feb. 11, 1898), Presbyterian clergyman, college president, was the son of Thomas W. Cattell, descended from an old family of New Jersey Quakers, and Keziah (Gilmore) Cattell. He was born at Salem, N. J., graduated from the College of New Jersey (now Princeton University) in 1848 and from the Princeton Theological Seminary in 1852, and was ordained in 1856. He began his career as an educator in 1853, as associate principal of the Edgehill Preparatory School. In 1855 he became professor of Latin in Lafayette College, Easton, Pa. On Aug. 4, 1859, he was married to Elizabeth McKeen. In 1860 he accepted the pastorate of the Pine Street Presbyterian Church at Harrisburg, Pa., where he was soon active in war work in the camps and hospitals. In 1861 he had become a trustee of Lafayette College, which, embarrassed financial-

ly and suffering from an exodus of students to join the army, was in a condition such that the trustees met to consider a suspension of operations. Instead, they elected Cattell to the presidency, which he held from 1863 to 1883. He began with thirty-nine students, a deficit, and an income insufficient to pay the $4,900 per year due the nine faculty members. A dozen years later the college, with an enrolment above 300 and proportionate increases in faculty, equipment, and endowment, was a first-class institution. Besides unusual gifts as a scholar, teacher, and administrator Cattell had a personal charm that endeared him to both faculty and students. In 1883 he was forced to resign because of ill health. While recuperating in Europe he was elected corresponding secretary of the Presbyterian Board of Ministerial Relief, in which capacity he devoted himself from 1884 to 1886 to the care of retired ministers and their dependents. From 1890 to his death he was president of the Presbyterian Historical Society. He was several times a delegate of the Presbyterian General Assembly to churches in Scotland, Bohemia, and Moravia, and he is said to have been the founder of the Sunday-school system of the Bohemian Reformed Churches. On several of these occasions he acted as a special United States commissioner of education. He was a director of the Princeton Theological Seminary, vice-president of the American Philological Society, and a councillor of the American Philosophical Society. He contributed an article on the "Tunkers" to the *Schaff-Herzog Encyclopædia*, and collected materials for a life of Lafayette and an edition of Lactantius.

[*Memoir of William C. Cattell* (1899), pp. 7–26; the *Journal* (Elmira, N. Y.), Mar. 1895; obituaries in the Phila. *Public Ledger*, Feb. 11, 1898, and in the *Presbyterian*, Feb. 16, 1898. His published addresses contain autobiographical material. See also Donald G. Mitchell, "Lafayette College," *Scribner's Mo.*, Dec. 1876; *An Hist. Sketch of the Presbyt. Board of Ministerial Relief* (1888); *Annual Report of the Presbyt. Hist. Soc.*, 1890–98.]   D. L. M.

CAWEIN, MADISON JULIUS (Mar. 23, 1865–Dec. 8, 1914), poet, was born in Louisville, Ky. His father, William Cawein, descended from Jean de Herancour, a Huguenot who fled Paris at the time of the revocation of the Edict of Nantes, was born near Mannheim, Germany; his mother, born Christiana Stelsly, was of German parentage (fragment of autobiography prepared by Madison Cawein for W. W. Thum, Louisville, 1914). From his father, who gathered herbs and compounded patent medicines, Cawein learned to love the outdoors and to observe so accurately that his poems exhibit a fairly comprehensive catalogue of Kentucky flora and fauna; from his mother, who was interested in spiritualism, he probably acquired his feeling for the supernatural. His first strong impressions of wild nature were gained between the ages of nine and thirteen, the Cawein family having moved from Louisville to a house near the South Fork of Harrod's Creek and later to one near New Albany, Ind. Returning in 1879 to his native city, Cawein graduated as class poet from the Louisville Male High School in 1886. In these student days he became fond of poetry, especially that of Shelley, Tennyson, and Browning (Louisville *Courier-Journal*, Jan. 24, 1901). Working as a cashier in the Newmarket pool-room, he contrived to write verse and to have it published. His first volume, appearing when he was twenty-two, was *Blooms of the Berry* (1887). Almost accidentally it came to the notice of William Dean Howells, who praised it generously in his Editor's Study (*Harper's Monthly*, May 1888). Encouragement from such a source meant much to Cawein, and he showed his gratitude by dedicating his second book, *The Triumph of Music* (1888) to Howells. To escape from the associations of the pool-room Cawein began to dabble in real estate and in stock operations which he made lucrative and to which he devoted most of his time not given to composition. In the morning he watched stock market reports; in the afternoon he repaired to a stretch of forest a few miles south of Louisville where he could write most easily (*Louisville Herald*, Oct. 2, 1910). So tirelessly did he work that to-day his name appears on thirty-six volumes. Of the 2,700 poems included in these volumes, however, almost half are reprints or revisions. In time he came to feel that there was a disproportion between his efforts and their rewards, and at the turn of the century a note of dissatisfaction crept into his correspondence—an arraignment of his time and compatriots as being too much occupied with the materialistic. "Never in the whole history of English literature," he wrote, "was there ever less encouragement for the writing of serious poetry than there is at the present time" (*Louisville Courier-Journal*, Dec. 14, 1902). But recognition came to him, though slowly. Sir Edmund Gosse wrote the introduction for a carefully selected edition of his poems in one volume (*Kentucky Poems*, London, 1902) and in 1907 the introduction was reprinted in a five-volume edition of *The Poems of Madison Cawein* illustrated with seventeen photogravures after paintings by Eric Pape. Cawein was made an overseas member of the Authors' Club of London and a member of the National Institute of Arts and Letters.

He became the friend of many of his contemporaries who ranked high as makers of American literature. Critics were obliged to reckon with him as a sincere if over-prolific worker in a *genre* almost abandoned at that time. But increasing respect on the part of the few for his productions did not win for him a very wide public, and, having married Gertrude Foster McKelvey, on June 4, 1903, he had added reason to wish that his pen might win a large following with a consequent income sufficient to free him from business. In 1906 he met his first sharp reverse in losses incurred by the San Francisco earthquake, but it was not until some seven years later that his modest fortune began to shrink alarmingly. His health, undermined by illnesses and early carelessness, failed; his appearance, never impressive, became that of a man prematurely aged— bald, thin, stooping, with hazel eyes often clouded in sadness. Although usually modest and cheerful, he began to show, in letters from 1911 on, concern about himself and hints of concealed tragedy. He struggled against approaching poverty, opposed sickness with his pen, tried to get an appointment as United States consul in some healthful location, and attempted a scenario for a photodrama. His sudden death at the age of forty-nine rounded out the unity of ironic failure; he fell in his bath-room and struck his head against the railing of the tub, but the question whether his decease was due to the fall or to a stroke of apoplexy preceding the fall caused a long controversy with an insurance company, ultimately compromised with the question still unsettled.

Howells said of Cawein's first volume that it did not echo "any of the poets who are apt to reverberate in the pages of beginners," but this remark was more kind than just. There are unmistakable echoes of Keats and Swinburne in this sophomoric work, and Cawein never entirely threw off the spell of the Romantics and of the best known Victorians. The great bulk of his poetry—and it is unnecessary to argue that he wrote too much—displays the fields and forests, springs and flowers of Kentucky and the fairies and mythical creatures that he somewhat incongruously placed there and in whom he protested belief. The *Christian Science Monitor* declared him "the greatest nature poet his country has produced" (Jan. 24, 1920) and Joyce Kilmer adjudged him "the greatest nature poet of his time" (*Catholic World*, March 1917). Very gradually he accepted the criticism that his poetry was too unearthly, and his latter work shows that he had busied himself in understanding the problems of the modern world even to the extent of experimenting with the newer fashions in verse forms (see *The Cup of Comus*, 1915). Although nature charmed him most, he manifested an inclination toward the Arthurian romances and the Oriental. *The Giant and the Star* (1909) was written to entertain his son; *The White Snake* (1895) is a translation from the German; *The Poet and Nature and the Morning Road* (1914) reveals his horror of the war just beginning in Europe at the time of his death. His poetry is represented in some fifty anthologies of American verse.

[The chief source of information is Otto Rothert, *The Story of a Poet: Madison Cawein* (Filson Club Publications No. 30, 1921), which, not strictly a biography, is a storehouse of facts. Jessie B. Rittenhouse, *The Younger Am. Poets* (1904), ch. IX; and "Memories of Madison Cawein," *Bookman*, Nov. 1922, contain critical and personal material of interest. The best obituary was printed by the *Boston Transcript*, Dec. 19, 1914. Some information was supplied by Madison Cawein, Jr.]

G. C. K.

CAYVAN, GEORGIA (1858–Nov. 19, 1906), actress, was born in Bath, Me. Going to Boston in childhood with her parents, she early began to appear in public, giving recitations and readings before she was fourteen. By the time she was twenty, and for some years thereafter, she was frequently engaged for entertainments by societies, clubs, and lodges in Boston and vicinity. During this period she was also taking part in amateur dramatic performances, one of her earliest recorded appearances being at Union Park Hall, Boston, May 7, 1874, when, under the auspices of the Mercantile Library Association, she played Miss Mortimer in *Naval Engagements*, and Georgiana in a condensed version of *Our American Cousin*. She studied elocution at a private school in Boston, and her first professional acting was with the Boston Ideal Opera Company as Hebe in *H. M. S. Pinafore* at the Boston Theatre, Apr. 14, 1879. On the tenth of the next month she acted Sally Scraggs in *Sketches from India* for her professional début in the drama.

Thereafter her advance was rapid. She went to New York in 1880, making her début there on May 7, at the Madison Square Theatre, as Dolly Dutton in *Hazel Kirke*, later replacing Effie Ellsler in the title character. The next year, after playing Daisy Brown in *The Professor* at the same theatre, she gained considerable added repute by her acting, in Boston and New York, of Jocasta in an English version of *Œdipus Tyrannus*, with George Riddle as *Œdipus*. She went to San Francisco to become leading lady at the California Theatre, and when she returned to New York she replaced Sara Jewett at the Union Square Theatre, playing Marcelle

in *A Parisian Romance* and Jane Learoyd in *The Long Strike*. At the Madison Square Theatre in 1885, she appeared in *Alpine Roses, Young Mrs. Winthrop,* and *May Blossom,* also playing on tour in *Divorce, Impulse,* and *La Belle Russe*. Joining the Lyceum Theatre Stock Company, then newly organized, on Nov. 1, 1888, she remained with it as leading lady until the fall of 1894, enlarging her reputation throughout the country, as well as in New York. A list of the plays in which she acted would be simply a list of the Lyceum Theatre productions, among her more important rôles being those of Helen Truman in *The Wife*, Ann Cruger in *The Charity Ball*, Minnie Gilfillan in *Sweet Lavender*, Katherine Thorpe in *Squire Kate*, and Lady Noeline in *The Amazons*. After retirement on account of ill health she returned to the stage as a star in the season of 1896–97, but with limited success. Her permanent retirement came a little later, and during her last years she was an invalid, her death occurring at Flushing, N. Y. At the height of her career she was one of the most popular American actresses of the "leading lady" type. With an attractive personality, she could always be relied upon to act a character with a certain satisfactory amount of comedy feeling and dramatic insight. She was of dark complexion, with expressive eyes that were often more eloquent even than her voice.

[Sketch by Ralph Edmunds in *Famous Am. Actors of Today* (1896), ed. by F. E. McKay and C. E. L. Wingate; J. B. Clapp and E. F. Edgett, *Players of the Present* (1899); Percy MacKaye, *Epoch, the Life of Steele MacKaye* (1927); *Brooklyn Mag.,* Feb. 1887; *Boston Herald,* Jan. 6, 1886; *N. Y. Dramatic Mirror,* July 11, 1896, Feb. 22, 1902, Dec. 1, 1906; *Toledo Globe,* Aug. 20, 1898.]

E. F. E.

CAZENOVE, THÉOPHILE (Oct. 13, 1740–Mar. 6, 1811), financier and agent of the Holland Land Company, was born in Amsterdam, Holland, the fourth of nine children. His father, Théophile, belonged to a French Protestant family long resident in Switzerland; his mother, Marie, was the daughter of Paul de Raspin-Thoyras, a French Protestant historian and soldier. The younger Théophile by his marriage in 1763 to Margaretha Helena van Jever became connected with a prominent trading family of Amsterdam. For the next twenty-five years he carried on a brokerage and commercial business in Amsterdam. At the end of the period, in 1788, he was coöperating with Clavière, a Swiss banker of Paris, and Pieter Stadnitski, a wealthy financier of Amsterdam, in an unsuccessful attempt to convert the American debt to France into obligations which could be sold to private holders. By the end of 1788 he was bankrupt. Nevertheless he was now selected by Stadnitski and three other Amsterdam firms, who were speculating in American state and federal securities, to go to the United States as their purchasing agent. Arriving in America early in 1790, he established himself in Philadelphia, the seat of the federal government upon whose action largely depended the fate of the state bonds. At first he bought such securities exclusively. Then he invested for his principals in various canal and manufacturing companies, more fruitful in the development of the new country than in profits for the investors. He then persuaded his employers, who had made large profits from their bond operations, to invest in wild lands, a field in which American speculative fever was running high. Having enlarged their combination and laid the foundation for what became in 1796 the Holland Land Company, the Dutch bankers between 1792 and 1794 bought directly or through Cazenove over five million acres of land in western New York and in northern and western Pennsylvania. Cazenove's advice had determined the lands selected, but his judgment left much to be desired. The investment in New York lands, realized only forty years later, proved moderately successful; that in Pennsylvania led to heavy losses. From 1794 to 1799 Cazenove was engaged in perfecting his employers' title to the lands, in providing for their survey, and in opening some of them for sale through sub-agents. Accustomed to good living, he was something of a *grand seigneur* in Philadelphia where he kept a coach and four, a coachman, postillion, and valet. In spite of the gout, which kept him to a régime of water and vegetables, he was entertained much in the political circles of the federal capital. Hospitable and generous, he shared his own well-filled table not alone with the natives whose official positions might supply information valuable to the foreign investor but with many unfortunate French émigrés. One of them, Talleyrand, describes him as an "homme d'un esprit assez éclairé, mais lent et timide, d'un caractère fort insouciant" (*Mémoires*, 1891–92, vol. I). Timid he certainly was not in his American business dealings, but there is no doubt of his extreme carelessness. He kept almost no accounts and he carried his insouciance to the point of confusing his employers' money with his own. Early in 1799 he returned to Europe. Three years later he left the employ of the Dutch bankers and spent most of his remaining years in Paris, where renewed relations with Talleyrand, now in charge of French foreign affairs, helped him to eke out a precarious existence. He died in Paris in 1811. He had become an

American citizen in 1794, and his name is perpetuated in the village of Cazenovia in central New York. His portrait by St. Memin hangs in the Corcoran Gallery in Washington.

[R. W. Kelsey, ed., "Cazenove Journal 1794" (pub. in *Haverford Coll. Studies*, No. 13, 1922) is a diary kept by Cazenove on a trip through Pa. Two books by his descendants give some biographical data : Raoul de Cazenove, *Rapin-Thoyras, sa famille, sa vie et ses œuvres* (1866), and Q. M. A. de Cazenove, *Quatre Siècles* (1908). See also E. and E. Haag, *La France protestante* (2nd ed., Paris, 1877–88), vol. III. For Cazenove's business life and especially his relations with the bankers of the Holland Land Company see P. J. Van Winter, *Het aandeel van den Amsterdamschen handel aan den opbouw van het Amerikaansche Gemeenebest* (1927) and Paul D. Evans, "The Holland Land Company" in *Buffalo Hist. Soc. Pubs.*, vol. XXVIII (1924).]   P. D. E.

CÉLORON DE BLAINVILLE, PIERRE JOSEPH de (Dec. 29, 1693–Apr. 12, 1759), French officer and explorer, was born in Montreal. The family of Céloron de Blainville originated in Paris, whence Jean-Baptiste, the Canadian founder, emigrated to Canada in 1684. There he married, Nov. 29, 1686, Hélène Picoté de Bellestre, widow of Sieur de Brucy. Pierre Joseph was their fifth child and the oldest son. Bred like his father to the career of arms, he obtained his first commission in 1715, and was promoted to a lieutenancy in 1731. Engaged in military duties until 1734, he was in that year chosen commandant of the important post of Michilimackinac where he was so successful in his administration, that he was returned for a second term of three years (1737–40), and was again at this post in 1741–42. He was beloved by the Indians about his station, and governed them firmly, with regard to justice.

While Céloron was stationed at Mackinac, the governor of Louisiana undertook a punitive expedition against the Chickasaw tribe, which had entrapped and destroyed a contingent of French from the Illinois. The Canadian authorities agreed to cooperate and in the autumn of 1739 sent a considerable body of troops from Montreal by way of the Ohio, at the same time ordering Céloron to gather the traders and tribesmen of his post and join the expedition. He met the other contingents on the Mississippi near Memphis, where a fort was built and winter quarters prepared. It was Céloron and his detachment who saved the expedition from entire futility. In the spring of 1740 he penetrated to the Chickasaw towns, forced the Indians to make a treaty, and exacted a partial reparation. About this time he obtained a captaincy and was characterized as "intelligent, a very good officer."

In the summer of 1742 he visited Montreal with the Indians from his post; the governor told them that they could no longer keep their favorite officer. "He has been very kind to us," said the Ottawa chief regretfully. In July of that year Céloron was transferred to Detroit, where he remained somewhat over a year. In 1744 he was in command of the important fortress of Niagara, but because of some differences with the lessees was soon transferred to Fort St. Fréderic, now Crown Point. After a short term (1746–47) he was recalled, and in 1748 took command of a convoy destined to relieve Detroit, which was in danger from a revolt of the Hurons and allied tribes.

After the close of King George's War, La Gallissonnière sent Céloron on an expedition to the Ohio to expel the English traders from this region and to assert French claims. The expedition of about two hundred regulars and militia and thirty domesticated Indians left Lachine on June 15, 1749, going by way of Lake Chautauqua to the upper waters of the Allegheny River. As Céloron passed down that river and the Ohio he buried at strategic points leaden plates, with inscriptions asserting French sovereignty; some of these plates were found in the nineteenth century. He also drove off several English traders, sending by one a letter to the governor of Pennsylvania (*Pennsylvania Colonial Records*, V, 425). The ultimate object of the expedition was to break up the Miami Indian town called Pickawillany, where the English had a trading house. Céloron went up the Miami River to this place; but he was unable to induce the rebel tribesmen to return to the French alliance. He then took his way eastward by way of Detroit and the Great Lakes. The next year he was promoted to a majority and sent to command at Detroit; there he failed to reclaim the recalcitrant Miami; and after a term of three years (1750–53), he was relieved, becoming major of Montreal.

Céloron's share in the French and Indian War was not great; he was with Dieskau in 1755 on Lake George, and must have been in other battles, since his death was due to wounds. He was an able and popular officer, and left by his three wives a considerable progeny, most of whom returned to France after the British conquest of Canada. His son Paul Louis, who was born at Detroit, served as a French officer under Washington during the American Revolution.

[The best sketch of Céloron's life is in *Mich. Pioneer & Hist. Colls.*, XXXIV, 327–33; see also *Wis. Hist. Colls.*, XVII, 207, 367, XVIII, 28. The *Am. Cath. Hist. Researches*, II, 113–95 gives a sketch preliminary to the account of his voyage of 1749. His journal of that voyage has been published several times; the French original is in Margry, *Découvertes et Établissements des Français dans l'Amérique Septentrionale* (Paris, 1886), VI, 666–726; it is translated in *Wis. Hist.*

Colls., XVIII, 36–58; the chaplain's journal is in *Jesuit Relations* (Thwaites ed., 1896–1902), LXIX, 150–199; one plate is in the collections of the Am. Antiquarian Soc., and another in those of the Va. Hist. Soc.]
                                                      L. P. K.

CERRÉ, JEAN GABRIEL (Aug. 12, 1734– Apr. 4, 1805), merchant, fur-trader, son of Joseph and Marie (Picard) Cerré, was born at Montreal, Canada. Little is known of his childhood, except that he received a good education. In 1755 he was established at Kaskaskia, Ill. He pursued the vocation of merchant and trader, spending fifty years in the fur trade. In his extensive operations he went annually from Kaskaskia to Montreal. His many adventures, and the strategies used by him in dealing with Indians and protecting his goods, form an interesting story of pioneer life. The earliest hunters in the Missouri River country, excepting some occasional parties of adventurers, were men sent by Cerré from Kaskaskia. He became one of the wealthiest men in the Illinois country; a man of such eminence and influence among the people, that his assistance was enlisted by both the British and the Americans during the Revolution. Although he may have felt the traditional hatred of the French for the English, and is supposed to have served under Montcalm in defense of Quebec, he received many favors from the English commanders. Even after his espousing the American cause the British sought to break him away from his new alliance. George Rogers Clark in his "Memoir" devotes a great deal of space to his experiences with Cerré. Clark says that he had heard that Cerré was a man of great importance; that he was one of the most inveterate enemies of the American revolutionists. He also states that Cerré ultimately allied himself with the Americans, took the oath of citizenship, and was of infinite service to the United States. He gave financial aid to Clark and furnished provisions to the troops. From Clark's account of the measures taken to gain the cooperation of Cerré, there is room for suspicion that it was first gained through a species of mental coercion.

When the Virginia commandant, Col. John Todd, who had jurisdiction over the Illinois country, caused an election to be held by the people to choose magistrates, Cerré headed the list of those elected. It is doubtful if he served very long, as he appears to have turned his face westward soon thereafter and to have made St. Louis his home. If he moved in order to get out of the United States he was doomed to disappointment, as he lived to see St. Louis ceded by France. He was a soldier in the first company of St. Louis militia in 1780, and one of eight syndics in 1782. In answer to questions propounded to him by a committee of Congress in July 1786, he stated that although the people had chosen magistrates in 1779, the power of the magistrates had been annihilated and everything had fallen into a state of anarchy and confusion after the withdrawal of Todd's troops.

He was a man distinguished for his courtesy, humor, and kindness of heart. When he came to St. Louis many of his relatives in Canada joined him, and these, with his family connections, were so extensive, and his band of employees was so numerous, that he became the patriarch of a considerable portion of the inhabitants. In 1780 he founded New Madrid, Mo., when he established a trading post at that point, then called L'Anse-à-la-Graisse, and in 1781 he sent a trader to the Indians in Tennessee. He was married in 1764 to Catherine Giard and had four children, one of whom, Marie Thérèse, married Auguste Chouteau [q.v.].

[C. Tanguay, *Dictionnaire Généalogique des Familles Canadiennes*, VII (1890), 171, in which the name is spelled Séré; Kaskaskia and St. Louis Church Registers; *Report on Canadian Archives* (1882), p. 21; *Mich. Pioneer and Hist. Soc. Colls.*, XIX, 472; "Geo. Rogers Clark Papers, 1771–81," being *Colls. Ill. State Hist. Lib.*, VIII, 235, 361; W. B. Douglas, "Jean Gabriel Cerré: A Sketch" in *Mo. Hist. Soc. Colls.*, II, 58–76.]   S. D.

CESNOLA, LUIGI PALMA di (June 29, 1832–Nov. 20, 1904), soldier, archeologist, author, and museum director, was born at Rivarolo, near Turin, Italy. He was the second son of an Italian count who had served under Napoleon and whose family had come from Spain to Piedmont in 1282. His mother was Countess Eugenia Ricca di Castelvecchio. The young count was educated at the Royal Military Academy of Turin (1843–48), where he had an English tutor. His military experience began at seventeen in the Sardinian Army of Revolution. He became its youngest commissioned officer when promoted to a second-lieutenancy for bravery on the field of Novara (Mar. 23, 1849). In 1851 he graduated as full lieutenant from the Royal Military Academy of Cherasco, later becoming a staff officer in the Crimean War.

In 1860, we find him in New York for the first time, where he married (1861) Mary Isabel Reid, daughter of Capt. Samuel C. Reid, U. S. N.; taught languages; and—when the Civil War broke out—founded a military school for officers, instructing over 700 students. Strongly in sympathy with the Northern cause, he enlisted in October 1861 as a major in the 11th New York Cavalry of which he became lieutenant-colonel. He excelled as a drill-master

and a disciplinarian. In September 1862 he became colonel of the 4th New York Volunteer Cavalry, was wounded and taken prisoner at the battle of Aldie (June 17, 1863), and was confined in Libby Prison until the spring of 1864. He fought under Sheridan throughout the Shenandoah Valley Campaign, and served till the end of the war, when Lincoln brevetted him brigadier-general of volunteers and offered him the consulship at Cyprus on condition that he would become an American citizen. This he did (1865), and on Christmas Day he landed on that island with his family.

Of his eleven years there, he has himself given us an entertaining account, in excellent English, in *Cyprus, Its Ancient Cities, Tombs, and Temples,* published in London (1877) and New York (1878). He soon made himself so respected and feared by the Turkish Government, and so trusted by the natives, that he was enabled to undertake the excavations which constitute his claim to lasting remembrance. Singlehanded, save for native diggers, with no capital but his own slim purse, without training or experience, he explored sixty-five necropoli (60,-932 tombs) and at least twenty-three other sites, digging up 35,573 objects. Of these, about 5,000 were lost at sea, a selected series went to the Turkish Government, and a few were sold in Europe before he decided, in the interest of science, to keep his collection a unit. The great mass of the objects was ultimately purchased by the Metropolitan Museum of Art in New York, in three instalments, for a moderate sum, less than a quarter of what experts told Cesnola it should bring if auctioned by the piece. He finally left Cyprus in 1876 because of his wife's health, going first to London, where he brought out his book, and later to New York, where he was elected secretary of the Metropolitan Museum in 1877, and director in 1879. Both these posts he held until his death a quarter of a century later, in the face of constant fire on the authenticity of his collection, his personal honor, and his museum administration. The *Art Amateur* in August 1880 contained an attack on his collection by Gaston L. Feuardent, a well-known art dealer, and at once the press took sides with the most intolerant partisanship. In 1882 Clarence Cook, the critic, wrote for Feuardent a scathing pamphlet. Cesnola had meanwhile printed counter-attacks on Feuardent, who sued him for libel. The trial lasted from Oct. 31, 1883 to Feb. 2, 1884. The jury voted unanimously for Cesnola on the counts affecting the standing of the collection, and he had a majority of ten to two on the count which concerned his business dealings with Feuardent—this being technically a disagreement. His collection had been sustained also by the examinations of an investigating committee and by those of sculptors and stone-cutters, but the public remained skeptical and there was another attack by Dr. Max Ohnefalsch-Richter. (See *New York Herald,* May 16, 1893; *Sun,* May 23, 1893.) Later researches in Cypriote archeology have been the most satisfactory vindication of the authenticity and value of the Cesnola collection. (See John L. Myres, *Handbook of the Cesnola Collection of Antiquities from Cyprus,* 1914, for the best history and bibliography of the collection. Cesnola published *A Descriptive Atlas of the Cesnola Collection,* in three volumes, 1885–1903.) As museum director, Cesnola was accused of being hostile to the public and students, ignorant of modern art, and afraid of experts. The trustees, for the most part, credited him with laying the firm foundation on which the Museum was built by his administrative ability and tireless, devoted supervision. In the memory of his associates on the staff, he left a warm glow of affection and admiration.

Throughout his life, he gave and inspired intense loyalty and bitter enmity. Tall, martial, with dark hair (later, iron-gray), a ruddy color and a piercing eye, he dearly loved a fight. He retained the Italian excitability and a slight accent. When he traveled in Italy in 1900, the press featured his progress as that of a conquering hero. Among his thirteen medals and knightly orders was one struck in his honor by special order of the King of Italy (1882). Among his American decorations was the Congressional Medal of Honor.

[*Bulls. Metropolitan Mus.,* IV, 95–96, 153–54; V, 229–33, XXI, 88; *N. Y. Times, N. Y. Tribune,* Nov. 22, 1904; Henry Murray Calvert, *Reminiscences of a Boy in Blue* (1920).]   F. B. H.

CHACE, ELIZABETH BUFFUM (Dec. 9, 1806–Dec. 12, 1899), anti-slavery and woman-suffrage advocate, was born in Providence, R. I., the second daughter of Arnold Buffum [*q.v.*] and Rebecca (Gould) Buffum. She passed her childhood in Smithfield, R. I., and in Connecticut, where she attended the common schools, later studying at the Friends' School, Providence. In June 1828, at Fall River, Mass., she married Samuel Buffington Chace, a cotton manufacturer of that city, like herself an orthodox Friend. Under her father's influence she early interested herself in anti-slavery activities, and in Valley Falls, R. I., whither the Chaces removed in 1840, they conducted an Underground Railroad station. Mrs. Chace gave val-

ued counsel to officers of the New England Anti-Slavery Society, and was their agent for arranging meetings in Rhode Island, entertaining in her home Garrison, Phillips, Frederick Douglass, and other lecturers. In 1843 she resigned from the Society of Friends, alleging their indifference to the abolition cause. Thereafter she was unaffiliated with any religious sect; she retained belief in the "Inner Light," but her views became increasingly liberal. For some years she was a spiritualist, reading assiduously the *Banner of Light* and the writings of Andrew Jackson Davis, but in later life spiritualism ceased to influence her. She helped to sponsor the Woman's Rights convention held in 1850 in Worcester. With Mrs. Paulina W. Davis she organized, in 1868, the Rhode Island Woman Suffrage Association, of which she was president from 1870 till her death. For many years she was also an officer of the American Woman Suffrage Association. She worked ardently for suffrage, writing, speaking, and securing petitions for legislative action. Temperance and humanitarian activities also engaged her. In 1870 her efforts secured the passage of a state law providing for a board of women visitors to inspect Rhode Island penal and correctional institutions where women or children were confined; on this board she served for several years. At the International Congress on the Prevention and Repression of Crime, Including Penal Reformatory Treatment, in London (1872), she was a delegate and active participant. She brought about the establishment of the Rhode Island Home and School for Dependent Children (1884), and several years later reform of abuses in its management. Her wide range of interests brought her many friends, including Julia Ward Howe, Moncure D. Conway, John Weiss (Shakespearean scholar), Thomas Davidson, and Andrew Carnegie. She contributed to the *New England Magazine* and extensively to the *Providence Journal.* Her summer home at Wianno, on Cape Cod, became a literary center for reformers. After 1893 feebleness confined her to her home at Central Falls, where she died. The mother of ten children, she was the affectionate center of her home, which, amid all her activities, she never neglected. Three children only survived her; of these Lillie (Mrs. John C. Wyman) became her mother's biographer, and Arnold B. Chace chancellor of Brown University.

[Sources are Mrs. Chace's vivid *Anti-Slavery Reminiscences* (1891) and *Elizabeth Buffum Chace* (2 vols., 1914), by L. B. C. Wyman and A. C. Wyman. A shorter sketch appears in L. B. C. Wyman's *Am. Chivalry* (1913), pp. 35–50.]   R. S. B.

CHADBOURNE, PAUL ANSEL (Oct. 21, 1823–Feb. 23, 1883), college president, eldest child of Isaiah and Pandora (Dennett) Chadbourne, was born in the town of North Berwick, Me. Orphaned at the age of thirteen, he soon acquired habits of industry in working on a farm and in a carpenter's shop in his native village, meanwhile attending school. Removing to Great Falls, N. H., he became a druggist's clerk and medical student, remaining three years. Then, having prepared for college at Phillips Academy, Exeter, supporting himself by copying law papers, he entered Williams College as a sophomore, and graduated in 1848 valedictorian of his class. As an undergraduate he displayed those habits of intense application and thorough inquiry which characterized him in later years. While pursuing his theological studies at the Theological Seminary at East Windsor Hill, Conn., he was a tutor at Williams College and principal of high schools or academies in New Jersey, New Hampshire, and Connecticut. On Oct. 9, 1850, he was married to Elizabeth Sawyer Page of Exeter, N. H. In 1853 he accepted his first professorship, that of botany and chemistry at Williams College, where afterward he filled the chair of natural history. With the exception of an interval of five years, 1867 to 1872, he was closely identified with that institution till his resignation of the presidency in 1881. While discharging the duties of his professorship at Williams College, he held, for six years, subsequent to 1858, the professorship of the same branches at Bowdoin College, at the Maine Medical School, of which he was dean, and also at the Berkshire Medical Institute till its discontinuance. For twelve years he delivered courses of lectures at Mount Holyoke Seminary, and for a time taught the natural sciences at Western Reserve University.

His passion for scientific research awakened a responsive interest among his pupils, and groups of students attended him upon expeditions, the objects of which were exploration and the collection of specimens. The first was to Newfoundland in 1855, the second to Florida in 1857. In 1859 he made geological studies in Greenland, Iceland, Sweden, Norway, and Denmark, being received as a member of the Royal Society of Northern Antiquaries at Copenhagen. His last scientific expedition was to Greenland in 1861. His lectures at the Smithsonian Institution, given in 1859, were published in 1860, as *Lectures on Natural History; its Relations to Intellect, Taste, Wealth and Religion*. His Lowell Institute lectures were published under the title of *Lectures on Natural Theology* (1867)

and *Instinct, its Office in the Animal Kingdom, and its Relation to the Higher Powers in Man* (1872).

Chadbourne was by nature a practical man. His first cotton manufacturing enterprise was in 1865, and in that year and the following one came service in the Massachusetts Senate. He attended national conventions of the Republican party, once as a delegate-at-large, and was a presidential elector. While a senator he was chosen president of the then recently created Agricultural College at Amherst. During his brief incumbency he selected the site, settled the plans and contracted for the erection of three of the buildings. He also systematized the course of study, largely on the basis of President Hitchcock's classic report on the agricultural schools of Europe. He next became president of the University of Wisconsin, and from 1867 to 1870 administered its interests successfully. After leaving Wisconsin he spent nearly two years among the Rocky Mountains in the pursuit of health and the investigation of mines.

Returning to Williamstown in 1872, he followed the revered Mark Hopkins as president of Williams College, and with rare teaching and executive skill fulfilled the duties of that office for nine years, the period of his stewardship forming a significant chapter in the history of the institution. They were years of upbuilding and growth. Upon its material interests he brought to bear his unusual administrative powers. "He was the most versatile and incessantly active of Williams Presidents," but like his immediate predecessor, he was at his best in the classroom. Although he was rather short of stature and slender, his fine head, keen restless eyes, and gray, flowing beard lent impressiveness to his appearance. A strict disciplinarian, he was nevertheless affable and gracious.

In January 1882 he accepted, for the second time, the presidency of the Massachusetts Agricultural College. The institution then needed all the energy, executive ability, ripe experience and educational resources which such a man could supply. He imparted to the college an impetus which became a vigorous internal life. Even more valuable were his services in securing to it the interest and confidence of the people. In 1874 he succeeded Louis Agassiz as a member of the Massachusetts State Board of Agriculture, a position to which he had first been appointed by Gov. Andrew in 1865. He died in New York, Feb. 23, 1883, at the age of fifty-nine.

Chadbourne published some nine volumes, including *The Public Service of the State of New York* (3 vols., 1882), twelve educational addresses, and twenty-two agricultural addresses. He also contributed a series of articles to the *Congregationalist* and the *Springfield Republican,* and elsewhere articles on his scientific expeditions and was a contributor to Johnson's and other cyclopedias. His pen was seldom idle.

[S. H. Carpenter, *Hist. Sketch of the Univ. of Wis.* (1876), p. 53; A. B. Bassett, "Obituary Sketch of Paul A. Chadbourne," *Alumni Record, Mass. Ag. Coll.,* 1883, pp. 15–20; *Obit. Record of Alumni of Williams Coll.,* 1875–85, pp. 312–20; *Mass. Ag. Coll. Gen. Cat.,* 1862–86, pp. 99–101; A. L. Perry, *Williamstown and Williams Coll.* (1899), *passim*; J. M. Barker, "Memoir of Paul A. Chadbourne," *Proc. Mass. Hist. Soc.,* 2 ser., XXIII, 448–53; L. W. Spring, *Hist. of Williams Coll.* (1917), pp. 227–41; W. M. Emery, *Chadbourne-Chadbourn Genealogy* (Fall River, Mass., 1904); J. F. A. Pyre, *Wisconsin* (1920); E. H. Botsford, *Fifty Years at Williams: Bk. I, The Story of P. A. Chadbourne* (privately printed, 1928).]   F.T.

CHADWICK, FRENCH ENSOR (Feb. 29, 1844–Jan. 27, 1919), naval officer, was born in Morgantown, W. Va. (then Virginia) of good pioneer stock. He was the son of Daniel Clark and Margaret Eliza (Evans) Chadwick. His maternal grandfather was Col. John Evans, a Revolutionary soldier. He received his early schooling at the Monongalia Academy, in his native town. As a boy he read the naval classic, *History of the Navy of the United States of America* (1839) by J. Fenimore Cooper, and was fascinated by it. Entering the Naval Academy (at Newport, R. I., during the Civil War) on Sept. 28, 1861, he was graduated three years later, the fifth in a class of thirty-one members. In the summer of 1864, before his graduation, he served on the sloop of war *Marblehead,* during her pursuit of the Confederate steamers *Florida* and *Tallahassee.* Passing rapidly through the grades of ensign, master, and lieutenant, he was in 1869 promoted lieutenant commander. After serving as a junior officer on board the ships *Juniata, Sabine,* and *Tuscarora* he was in 1870–72 attached to the steamer *Guerrière,* of the European squadron. Three years of teaching at the Naval Academy as assistant professor of mathematics were followed by a tour of sea duty, 1875–78, as the executive officer of the steamer *Powhatan.*

During the two decades that preceded the Spanish-American War, Chadwick developed a great facility in investigating foreign navies and in procuring information useful in the work of constructing the new American navy. In 1879 he made an investigation in Europe, the results of which he embodied in a report on foreign systems for training seamen for the navy (*Senate Executive Document, No. 52,* 46 Cong., 2 Sess.), still a standard work on the subject. The next two years, 1880–82, were spent in "special

light-house duties," including the preparation of a valuable paper entitled "Aids to Navigation," which gave a brief history of lighthouses. In 1882 he was sent to London, where he remained almost continuously until 1889 with the American legation as naval attaché (the first American thus designated) and as the representative of the newly-organized Office of Naval Intelligence. By reason of his expert knowledge, tact, and adroitness he served his superiors so well that they were loth to displace him. Secretary of the Navy Tracy in his annual report for 1889 singled out Chadwick for especial commendation and said that his extraordinary ability and judgment had had a lasting influence upon naval development in the United States. Having been promoted commander in 1884, Chadwick, on being detached from the legation, was placed in command of the cruiser *Yorktown,* of the European station. In 1892 his services as naval attaché received recognition by his appointment as chief of the Naval Intelligence Office and a year later he was advanced to the headship of the Bureau of Equipment where he remained for the full term of four years.

A few days after his promotion to a captaincy, Nov. 7, 1897, he was made commander of the armored cruiser *New York,* the flagship of the North Atlantic squadron. When the battleship *Maine* was sunk in Havana harbor, Feb. 15, 1898, he was off the Florida coast with the squadron. His nearness to the scene of the disaster led to his selection as a member of the court of inquiry on the destruction of the *Maine,* of which Capt. W. T. Sampson [*q.v.*] was the senior member. When late in March Sampson became commander-in-chief of the squadron, Chadwick was appointed his chief of staff, retaining the command of the flagship. In this capacity he served during the eventful summer of 1898 and during the culminating action of the Spanish-American War, the battle of Santiago, July 3. When the Spanish vessels began to emerge from the harbor, the *New York* was several miles away, carrying the commander-in-chief to a conference with Gen. W. R. Shafter [*q.v.*]. She turned about and reached the scene of battle in time to join in the chase and to enable Sampson to give the final orders to his ships (*House Document, No. 3,* 55 Cong., 3 Sess., App., pp. 520–22). In recognition of his services on this day Chadwick was advanced five numbers for "eminent and conspicuous conduct in battle." Chadwick reached the climax of his naval career as president of the Naval War College, 1900–03, and as commander-in-chief of the South Atlantic squadron in 1905. On Feb. 28,

1906, he was retired as rear admiral, a rank to which he had been promoted on Oct. 11, 1903.

Admiral Chadwick belonged to a small group of learned or scientific naval officers, of which Mahan and Sampson were conspicuous members. As an author he attained considerable note, based upon the numerous articles and books which he wrote between 1892 when his first work, *Temperament, Disease and Health*, made its appearance, and 1916 when his last, *The Graves Papers and Other Documents Relating to the Naval Operations of the Yorktown Campaign*, was issued. His scholarly interest lay chiefly in the field of military and diplomatic history, in which he read widely. His most significant contributions are found in four volumes: *Causes of the Civil War* (American Nation Series, vol. XIX, 1906), *Relations of the United States and Spain: Diplomacy* (1909), and *Relations of the United States and Spain: the Spanish-American War* (2 vols., 1911). Believing that the past may serve as a guide for the present, he was inclined to draw definite conclusions, to criticize sharply historical characters, and to dwell upon the lessons of sea power. His style was clear, dignified, and vigorous.

On Chadwick's retirement to Newport in 1906 he actively interested himself in all that pertained to that city and its development, serving on its park commission and also on its representative council. He was largely instrumental in providing the city with a new charter. His wife Cornelia J. (Miller) Chadwick, formerly of Utica, N. Y., whom he married on Nov. 20, 1878, shared the intellectual interests of her husband. The admiral died in New York City, leaving no children, and was buried in Morgantown. He was somewhat above the average in height and weight, with a commanding presence. Direct and forceful in speech, he was a close observer of even the smallest details.

[Record of Officers, Bureau of Navigation, 1862–1919; *Navy Reg.*, 1862–1919; obituary in *N. Y. Times*, Jan. 28, 1919; *Report of Secretary of the Navy*, 1889–99; *Who's Who in America*, 1918–19; letters of Thos. Ray Dille, Morgantown, W. Va., to C. O. P., Nov., Dec. 1928.]
                          C. O. P.

CHADWICK, HENRY (Oct. 5, 1824–Apr. 20, 1908), sportsman, the son of James Chadwick, editor of the *Western Times*, published in Exeter, England, was born in Exeter but came to America when he was thirteen. The rest of his life was spent in and about Brooklyn and New York. After a good education he began contributing in 1844 to the *Long Island Star*. In 1848 he married the daughter of Alexander Botts of Richmond, Va. Turning his attention to sports, he became the first important sports writer in America. The beginnings of his career fell at the period when, owing to the rise of cities, the vogue of field games in America, as distinct from rural pastimes, was beginning. Chadwick made it his work to promote this new outdoor life in the interest of health and good fellowship. Beginning in 1856, he reported and wrote on cricket and baseball for the *New York Times*, the *Brooklyn Eagle*, and other great dailies. For thirty-one years he was on the staff of the *New York Clipper*, a famous sporting sheet of that day. In 1886 he gave up reporting but continued to contribute to periodicals. During the Civil War he was a correspondent for the *New York Tribune*.

Heir to the best English sporting traditions, Chadwick always remained an ardent admirer and close student of cricket, but his greatest contribution to American life was in fostering interest in baseball. In the eighteen-fifties his attention was attracted to this sport, and, after playing as an amateur, he became convinced of its great possibilities and worked earnestly to develop it into a worthy national game. He had much influence in organizing professional baseball and in keeping it distinct from the amateur game. As chairman and member of the rules committee of the first National Association he dominated the development of the playing rules. The system of scoring is also practically his work. In the battle to prevent the national game from being ruined by rowdyism and gambling he did heroic service. Author of numerous athletic hand-books, he prepared, beginning in 1869, an annual baseball hand-book which developed into Spalding's *Official Baseball Guide*, a storehouse of records, edited by Chadwick from 1881 to 1908. In his later life he was widely known as "the Father of Baseball." Tall and powerful in physique and of a certain commanding presence, he was a striking exponent of the beliefs for which he stood. To a surprising degree he retained his vigor and interest to the end of his long life. Copies of Chadwick's pamphlets on various sports as well as the *Baseball Guides* are preserved in the Spalding Baseball Collection in the New York Public Library. Chadwick left his great collection of materials on the history of baseball and other sports to his friend A. G. Spalding. It constitutes the nucleus of the Spalding Collection and upon it was based in part Spalding's valuable book, *America's National Game* (1911). In the Spalding Collection are Chadwick's unpublished diaries from 1873 to 1907, relating largely to the history of sport, as well as a score of books recording baseball games from 1860 to 1907.

[*Brooklyn Eagle*, Apr. 20, 1908; *N. Y. Tribune*, Apr. 21, 1908; A. G. Spalding, *America's National Game* (1911), pp. 339–44; G. C. Richter, *Hist. and Records of Baseball* (1914), p. 278.]
                          E. P. T.

CHADWICK, JAMES READ (Nov. 2, 1844–Sept. 23, 1905), physician, librarian, was born in Boston, Mass., the son of Christopher Chadwick, a merchant of English extraction, who married a daughter of James Read (1789–1870). Graduated from Harvard College in 1865, and from the Harvard Medical School in 1871, in the latter year Chadwick married Katherine, daughter of Dr. George H. Lyman. After a few years of study in Berlin, Vienna, Paris, and London, he returned to Boston and began the practise of a then newly-developed department of medicine, gynecology. He assisted in the foundation of the gynecological department of the Boston City Hospital (1874) and for many years taught this specialty to the students of the Harvard Medical School. In 1876, with his father-in-law, he played an important part in the organization of the American Gynecological Society and served as its secretary for seven years; in 1897 he was president. He was largely instrumental in the publication of the early volumes of the annual *Transactions.*

Although Chadwick was greatly interested in the practise of medicine, he was at heart a book-lover. He established, with the help of a few friends, the Boston Medical Library in 1875, and served as the librarian from its inception up to the time of his death. In the early days he arranged the books in the library and did all the cataloguing. Aided by an exceptional memory, he succeeded in obtaining volumes missing from many important sets of medical journals. His "want book" was always with him in his travels in this country and abroad, and it made him a familiar figure in bookshops and libraries throughout the world. He also began an excellent collection of pamphlets, autographs, paintings, and photographs. His generosity in exchanging books and journals was one of his striking characteristics and served to make his name well-known and popular in all important medical libraries.

Chadwick was active in other fields as well. He founded the Harvard Medical Alumni Association in 1890 and for three years served as its president. Always interested in the subject of cremation, in 1892 he reorganized the decadent New England Cremation Society, assisted in the building of a model crematory and chapel near Boston, and in later years was president of the Massachusetts Cremation Society. His bibliography contains over sixty titles, dealing largely with gynecology, medical libraries, and cremation. Among his publications are a translation of Winckel's *Puerperal Fever*; a translation of two early works of J. D. Schoepff (1874–75); a study of Schoepff's life (1905); his papers on the Boston Medical Library (1876, 1896, 1899) and the *Life of James Read* (1905).

Chadwick was artistic, even Bohemian, in temperament, generous, kind, and sympathetic, but when necessity demanded, he could be sufficiently combative to obtain a point that seemed of importance to him. He had a strong sense of the joy of living, and an equally strong sense of the joy of labor. He is perhaps best described by Oliver Wendell Holmes, as the "untiring, imperturbable, tenacious, impressible, all-subduing agitator, who neither rested nor let others rest until the success of the library project was assured." He was a good public speaker and debater and made numerous addresses throughout the country on medical libraries and on cremation.

[Obituary, with portrait and bibliography, by W. L. Burrage, in *Trans. Am. Gyn. Soc.*, XXXI, 437–45; a series of articles in the *Medic. Lib. and Hist. Jour.*, IV, 113–25; the collection of "memorials" in the Boston Medic. Lib.; John W. Farlow, *Hist. of the Boston Medic. Lib.* (Norwood, Mass., 1918).]   H.R.V.

CHADWICK, JOHN WHITE (Oct. 19, 1840–Dec. 11, 1904), Unitarian clergyman, author, came of fisher-folk, who had been settled for several generations in Marblehead, Mass., where he was born. He was the son of John White Chadwick, mentioned as a seaman or sea-captain, and Jane (Standley) Chadwick. Early apprenticed to a shoemaker, he felt a desire for more learning, entered the State Normal School at Bridgewater in 1857, and while there determined to become a minister. After studying at Phillips Exeter Academy, he entered Harvard Divinity School, from which he graduated in 1864. Immediately thereafter came an invitation to supply for three months the pulpit of the Second Unitarian Church of Brooklyn, N. Y. Chadwick accepted and made so favorable an impression that he was called to the permanent pastorate, which he held for the rest of his life. In 1865 he married Annie Horton Hathaway of Marblehead. Chadwick had a frank, open, weather-beaten countenance, and a breezy manner. Alert and eager, he had the courage of his convictions, and spoke from his pulpit against oppression, privilege, and corrupt government. But he had also a real tenderness and sympathy under his rugged exterior, and a poetic vein, in which a certain touch of mysticism was not wanting. His sermons attracted attention, and he soon became well-known as a preacher and lecturer. He called himself a Radical Unitarian, meaning thereby that he rejected the miraculous and the superhuman character of Jesus and the Bible. He welcomed the doctrine of evolution while it was still generally under suspicion in religious circles. A great lover of literature, especially of biography, with a ready pen, he became a reviewer for the *Nation* from its first volume till the last year of his life, though he wrote also for other journals. His first book to attract attention was *A Book of Poems* (1876), which ran into ten editions. It was a little book, reminiscent of earlier poets, but showed real poetic feeling. Other volumes followed in rapid succession, consisting of discussions of leading topics of religion, biographies of leaders of thought, and more poems. Of these works the most noteworthy were: *The Bible of To-Day* (1878); *The Faith of Reason* (1879); *Some Aspects of Religion* (1879); *Belief and Life* (1881); *The Man Jesus* (1883); *Origin and Destiny* (1883); *In Nazareth Town and Other Poems* (1883); *A Daring Faith* (1885); *Charles R. Darwin* (1889); *Evolution and Social Reform* (1890); *Evolution as Related to Citizenship* (1892); *The Old and New Unitarian Belief* (1894); *Theodore Parker* (1900); *Wm. E. Channing* (1903); *Later Poems* (1905).

[*Christian Reg.*, Dec. 22, 1904; *Congregationalist*, Dec. 17, 1904; *Brooklyn Eagle*, Dec. 12, 1904; *Nation*, Dec. 15, 1904; *Outlook*, Dec. 17, 1904; *Who's Who in America*, 1903–05.]   T.D.B.

CHAFFEE, ADNA ROMANZA (Apr. 14, 1842–Nov. 1, 1914), soldier, was born at Orwell, Ashtabula County, Ohio. His father, Truman Bibbins Chaffee, was descended from Thomas, who was settled at Hingham, Mass., by 1683; his mother, Grace (Hyde) Chaffee, was of Connecticut ancestry. In the summer of 1861 young Chaffee set out from home to enlist in a volunteer regiment, but encountering a recruiting party of the newly organized 6th Cavalry, of the regular army, he enlisted, July 22, 1861, in that regiment, and remained a member of it for twenty-seven years. He was with his regiment only a few weeks before being appointed a sergeant, and after serving through the Peninsular and Antietam campaigns, he was made first sergeant of his troop, Sept. 26, 1862. In the operations of the following winter and spring, reports on his conduct resulted in a note scribbled by Secretary Stanton on an envelope, still preserved in the War Department, directing his appointment as second lieutenant. This, his first commission, was dated May 12, 1863. For the remainder of the war the regiment was with the Army of the Potomac (except while serving under Sheridan in the Shenandoah Valley in the fall of 1864). In 1863 Chaffee was twice wounded, once at Fairfield, Pa., in the Gettysburg campaign, and once at Brandy Station, Va. On the first occasion he fell into the hands of the enemy, but refused to accept parole, and as his captors found themselves unable to

carry him away he did not remain a prisoner. He was promoted to first lieutenant, Feb. 22, 1865. After the war he considered giving up his military career, and finally sent in his resignation, intending to engage in business. The colonel of the regiment, absent at the time, upon his return induced Chaffee to change his mind, and telegraphed to the War Department that "he is too valuable an officer to lose and his place cannot well be filled." The resignation had taken effect on Mar. 13, 1867, but on Mar. 20 Chaffee's restoration was approved. He was promoted to captain, Oct. 12, 1867. For some twenty-five years he served with his regiment in the Southwest, except for a few periods of absence on recruiting duty or while acting as Indian agent, and was engaged summer and winter in innumerable skirmishes with Comanches, Cheyennes, Kiowas, and Apaches. One night march across the Staked Plains, in December 1874, was made in a temperature of twenty-five degrees below zero. With his promotion to major, July 7, 1888, Chaffee left his old regiment for the 9th Cavalry. He was serving as an instructor in the service school at Fort Leavenworth, when promoted to lieutenant-colonel of the 3rd Cavalry, June 1, 1897. At the outbreak of the war with Spain he was appointed brigadier-general of volunteers, May 4, 1898, and assigned to the 5th Corps, then at Tampa. He landed in Cuba, June 22, commanding the 3rd Brigade in the 2nd (Lawton's) Division. In his plan for the battle of Santiago, Gen. Shafter charged Lawton with the task of taking the fortified post of El Caney, on the right of the American line. The garrison consisted of only about 520 men, assisted by a few inhabitants of the village, but it was well entrenched, and under the command of Gen. Vara de Rey held out (July 1) for ten hours. The place was finally taken only when half its defenders, including the heroic Vara de Rey himself, were killed or wounded. The brunt of the fighting fell on Chaffee's brigade. His services were recognized by his appointment on July 8 as major-general of volunteers. After the fall of Santiago, he returned to the United States, but was sent back to Cuba in December as chief of staff of the military governor and remained there until May 1900. Meanwhile, the reduction of the volunteer army deprived him of his major-generalcy, but he was at once reappointed brigadier-general of volunteers, Apr. 13, 1899. He became a colonel in the regular army, May 8, 1899. Upon the Boxer outbreak in China, Chaffee was selected to command the American contingent of the relief expedition, and was again appointed major-general of volunteers. He commanded the American troops in the advance on Peking, the capture of the city, and the occupation of the surrounding territory. His able leadership during the fighting, and his just and considerate treatment of the inhabitants afterward, won him the admiration of the members of the invading forces and of the Chinese as well. He was made major-general in the regular army, Feb. 4, 1901. After leaving China he commanded in the Philippines until October 1902. In January 1904, he was appointed lieutenant-general, and detailed as chief of staff of the army. He retired from active service, Feb. 1, 1906, and made his home in Los Angeles, where for several years he was president of the board of public works. He died on Nov. 1, 1914, and was buried at Arlington. In appearance and in character he was a grim and determined man, but always just and humane. He possessed military abilities beyond anything demanded by the operations in which he commanded. Wholly devoid of selfish ambition, his rise was due to outstanding merit alone.

[*The Life of Lieut.-Gen. Chaffee* (1917), by his friend, Gen. W. H. Carter, is based on personal knowledge and on Chaffee's own papers. H. H. Sargent's *Campaign of Santiago de Cuba* (1914) and A. S. Daggett's *America in the China Relief Expedition* (1903) give detailed accounts of these campaigns. "The Regulars at El Caney," by A. H. Lee, British military observer, in *Scribner's Mag.*, Oct. 1898, has a very vivid description of Chaffee in action.]   T. M. S.

CHAFFEE, JEROME BONAPARTE (Apr. 17, 1825–Mar. 9, 1886), political leader, mining man and banker, second child of Warren and Elizabeth (Otto) Chaffee, was born on a farm near Lockport, Niagara County, N. Y. He received a common school education in Lockport and later in Adrian, Mich., to which place the family moved in his early youth. His subsequent career was varied, for he clerked in stores, taught school, and kept books in a bank. He married Miriam Comstock in Adrian in 1848 and had four children, all of whom died while young, save Fannie Josephine, later Mrs. U. S. Grant, Jr. In his early thirties Chaffee went to St. Joseph, becoming a banker and manager of a real-estate company. After the death of his wife, he migrated to the Pike's Peak gold region in 1860. The firm of Smith & Chaffee operated a stamp-mill in Gilpin County with profit, but the partners made more money through their investments in mines, especially in the rich Bobtail mine. After amassing a fortune in the mountains, Chaffee left them in 1865 to live in Denver. In that year he with others bought the banking house of G. T. Clark & Company and founded the First National Bank of Denver, of which he was president until 1880. While retiring from the mountains, he never gave up his interest in mining. His investments in Colorado mines were widespread, large, and usu-

ally fortunate. For a time he shared in the rich proceeds of the Little Pittsburgh in the Leadville district.

Though a successful business man, Chaffee was best known as a political leader. He was elected to the lower house of the territorial legislature in 1861 and 1863 and became its speaker in 1864. Recognized as a leader of the Republican party, he was chosen as United States senator in 1865, at a time when Colorado hoped to become a state. With John Evans, his colleague, he went to Washington and labored in vain to convert this hope into a reality. As territorial delegate from 1871 to 1875 he spent both time and money freely upon what had now become his main object in life, the admission of Colorado to statehood. Finally on Mar. 3, 1875, when President Grant signed the enabling act, his dreams came true. At the time he was given the chief credit for this accomplishment; in most ways it was the greatest moment of his life. The grateful caucus of the Republican members of the Colorado legislature nominated him by acclamation as its first choice for United States senator and he served in that capacity for the short term from 1877 to 1879. He declined to run again because of ill health. While territorial delegate and senator he was able to secure the passage of several acts benefiting his district, especially a new mining law. After years of directing the Republican party organization in Colorado, he was selected in 1884 as chairman of the national executive committee of the same party. This was his final political honor.

Chaffee was always a man of few words. He was an able organizer, open-handed in generosity to friends and party, blunt in speech, and a bitter foe to his enemies. His massive head, broad shoulders, and height made him a noticeable figure. Despite his splendid physique, his health broke in the late seventies, and he spent much of his time at his daughter Fannie's home in Westchester County, N. Y. On his last trip to Leadville in 1886, he caught a severe cold, returned to his daughter's home, and died there. His body lies beside that of his wife in Adrian.

[Sketch in the *Encyc. of Biog. of Colo.* (1901); *Denver Tribune*, Sept. 13, 1883; *Denver Tribune-Republican*, Mar. 10, 1886; Frank Hall, *Hist. of the State of Colo.* (1891); *Chaffee Geneal.* (1909), comp. by Wm H. Chaffee.]   J. F. W.

CHAFIN, EUGENE WILDER (Nov. 1, 1852–Nov. 30, 1920), temperance leader, Prohibition candidate for president, was born at East Troy, Wis., the son of Samuel Evans and Betsey A. (Pollard) Chafin. He attended the public schools, studied law at the University of Wisconsin, from which he was graduated in 1875, and began to practise his profession in Waukesha. He took an active interest in local affairs and served as justice of the peace, police magistrate, member of the Waukesha board of education, member of the public library board, and three times as president of the Waukesha County Agricultural Society. On Nov. 24, 1881, he married Carrie A. Hunkins of Waukesha. Early in life he became interested in temperance work and joined the Good Templars at the age of fourteen. His work within the organization was soon recognized and he was elected District Chief Templar of Waukesha County. In 1885 he became Grand Counselor and in the following year Grand Chief Templar of Wisconsin. From 1893 to 1901 he was Grand Electoral Superintendent and represented his state in the International Supreme Lodge of Good Templars. He was also interested in the Epworth League, of which he was twice elected state president. In politics he was originally a Republican but in 1881 he joined the Prohibition party and ran for district attorney of Waukesha County (1881), for Congress (1882), for attorney-general (1886 and 1900), and for governor (1898). In October 1901 he moved to Chicago, where he became superintendent of the Washingtonian Home for Inebriates. His interest in politics continued unabated, and he was a candidate for Congress (1902) and for attorney-general of Illinois (1904). His law practise he gradually relinquished, and from 1904 on spent most of his time on the lecture platform, campaigning for prohibition. Within his party he had been a delegate to the Prohibition national conventions since 1884, was chairman of the Committee on the Platform in 1900, and was a member of the Prohibition National Committee from 1888 to 1896. In the Prohibition National Convention of July 1908 it seemed that William B. Palmore of Missouri had the nomination for the presidency almost within his grasp, but Chafin was put forward as a dark horse and received the nomination. He campaigned vigorously, but the result was a foregone conclusion, no Prohibition candidate having any chance of success. Four years later he was again nominated for the presidency, without opposition, but as in 1908, the Prohibition candidate received little attention, the election being for the most part a three-cornered struggle between Taft, Roosevelt, and Wilson. Nevertheless the efforts of Chafin and his colleagues did much to prepare public sentiment in the United States for Prohibition. With the adoption of the Eighteenth Amendment to the Constitution, Chafin turned his attention to world temperance and in the spring of 1919 went to Australia and New Zealand on a lecture tour in support of the Australian temperance organizations. He died in 1920 at his home in Long Beach, Cal. His writings include *The Voters' Hand-Book* (1876); *Lives of the Presidents* (1896); *Lincoln: the Man of Sorrow* (1908); and *The Master Method of the Great Reform* (1913), to which was attached a biographical sketch of the author.

[*Who's Who in America*, 1912–13; Samuel Dickie, "The Prohibitionists and Their Cause," in the *Rev. of Revs.* (N. Y.), Sept. 1908; *Los Angeles Times, Chicago Daily Tribune, Milwaukee Sentinel*, Dec. 1, 1920.]

F. E. R.

CHAILLÉ-LONG, CHARLES (July 2, 1842–Mar. 24, 1917), African explorer, was born at Princess Anne, Somerset County, Md. His ancestor, Pierre Chaillé, a French Huguenot, had settled on the Eastern Shore after the revocation of the Edict of Nantes. Pierre's grand-daughter Margaret Chaillé married Levin Long and became the mother of Littleton Long (of Chaillé). Charles Chaillé-Long was the son of the latter and of Anne Mitchell (Costen) Long. While he was a student at Washington Academy, the Civil War broke out and he left his studies and enlisted in the 1st Eastern Shore Regiment, Maryland Infantry. He was soon transferred and promoted to a captaincy in the 11th Maryland Infantry in which he served throughout the war with distinction. His war experiences and his pioneering spirit then led him to seek an appointment as an officer in the Egyptian army. He was appointed in 1869 and five years later, Feb. 19, 1874, he became chief of staff to "Chinese" Gordon who was engaged in suppressing the slave traffic in the region of the White Nile. Chaillé-Long was now charged by Khedive Ismail with a secret mission: to make a treaty with M'tesa, King of Uganda. On this journey, a vivid account of which is given in his *Naked Truths of Naked People* (1876), he conducted explorations in the upper Nile basin. Their importance in adding to the world's store of geographical knowledge was set forth in Gordon's letter published in the *New York Herald*, Jan. 23, 1880, which said, "Col. Chaillé-Long of the Egyptian staff passed down the Victoria Nile from Nyamyongo where Speke was stopped to Mooli; thus at the risk of his life settling the question, before unsolved, of the identity of the river above Urondogani with that below Mooli." On Feb. 15, 1910, the American Geographical Society conferred upon Chaillé-Long the Charles P. Daly Gold Medal which is given only to those who have made a marked contribution to geography. In 1875 he made another trip from Gondokoro which led him westsouthwest along the Congo-Nile divide region carrying him across the upper tributaries of the

Bahr-el-Ghazel system and linking his route with that of the explorer Schweinfurtter of 1870. Shortly after this last trip his health became impaired and he decided to leave Egypt. Returning to New York, he studied law at Columbia University and graduated in 1880. Two years later he went back to Alexandria to begin the practise of international law. Soon after his arrival, the Alexandria revolt of June 11 occurred. This outbreak, followed by the British bombardment of the city, caused considerable anti-foreign feeling and hundreds of lives were in jeopardy. In the absence of United States consular officials, Chaillé-Long endeavored to reëstablish the consulate and with the aid of American sailors in the harbor was able to offer protection to the refugees. For this service he was later decorated. After being relieved of his post as acting consul-general in August 1882, Chaillé-Long went to Paris where he engaged in the practise of international law. After five years he reëntered the consular service, this time as consul-general and secretary of the legation to Korea. During his two years' stay in that country he took part in a scientific expedition to Quelpart Island.

Familiar with French from his childhood, Chaillé-Long wrote a number of books in that language, including *L'Afrique Centrale* (1877); *Les Sources du Nile* (1891); *L'Égypte et ses Provinces Perdues* (1892); *La Corée ou Chosen* (1894). He also translated and edited *Les Combattants Français de la Guerre Américaine 1778-83*. Among his writings in English were *The Three Prophets; Chinese Gordon, Mohammed-Ahmed (El Maahdi), Arabi Pasha* (1884), and *My Life in Four Continents* (1912). Besides his books he made many contributions to French and American magazines and reviews, principally upon Egyptian and African subjects.

[Chaillé-Long's *Naked Truths of Naked People* (1876) and *My Life in Four Continents* (1912); articles in *Bull. Am. Geog. Soc.*, XLI, 223, XLII, 205–06; obituaries in the *N. Y. Times*, Mar. 26, 1917, and in the *Geog. Rev.*, Apr. 1917.]   G. H. B.

CHALKLEY, THOMAS (May 3, 1675–Nov. 4, 1741), Quaker minister, merchant, and mariner, son of George and Rebecca Chalkley, was born in Southwark, England. When about nine years of age he was sent for a time to a private day school, and was later apprenticed for seven years to his father, "a dealer in meal." In 1699 he decided to marry and was "inclin'd to make Choice of Martha Betterton," who like himself was an English Friends' minister. (She died in 1717, and two years later he married Martha Brown, a widow, who survived him.) Chalkley first came to America in 1698, on a preaching journey, and in 1700 brought his family over to Maryland. The next year he removed to Philadelphia, and in 1723 to a plantation he had purchased in the near-by suburb of Frankford, later a part of the city. He was a busy, successful trader, on land and by sea, dealing principally in foodstuffs. The sea voyages apparently brought the best returns, for in times of financial stress he took to the sea to recoup his fortunes. Soon after removing to America he began, in 1701, to make trading voyages to Bermuda and Barbados. In 1716 he wrote: "My family increasing, I traded a little to sea for their support." Occasionally he made the three-cornered voyage to Barbados, thence to England, and back to Philadelphia. He accumulated a moderate fortune sufficient to enable him in 1724–25 to weather losses considerably over $10,000. During his busiest seafaring years, 1729–35, his usual voyage was from Philadelphia to Barbados and return, although he sometimes called at St. Christopher, Antigua, Anguilla, and other islands of the Windward and Leeward groups. He made, in all, at least fifteen voyages to Barbados.

His greatest enthusiasm, however, was for journeys "in the ministry." He had begun visiting meetings "under a religious concern" as early as 1695 in connection with a business trip for his father into Essex, and soon afterward had gone on a preaching tour through southwestern England into Cornwall, and a little later northward as far as Edinburgh, "where our Meeting was in the Street, we being lock'd out of our Meeting-house by the then Power." In America his religious travels took him again and again up and down the country from New England to the Carolinas. In 1703 he "went thro' *Maryland*, and visited Friends in *Virginia* and *North Carolina*, to the river Pamphlico, where no travelling, publick [*i.e.* preaching] Friends (that ever I heard of) were before, and we had several Meetings there on each Side of the River." The next year he was in New England again, disputing with Congregational "priests" and encouraging the Quaker brethren. His religious journeys in the middle colonies near his home were too numerous to mention in particular. There are few chapters of his *Journal* that do not record preaching trips among Friends in Pennsylvania, Maryland, New Jersey, and New York. He left a valuable account of a visit made in 1706 by himself and a group of fellow Quakers to the Susquehanna Indians at Conestoga, Pa. He preached earnestly to these Indians and to the neighboring Shawnee. The Conestogas were of Iroquoian stock, and Chalkley was impressed with the fact that women spoke in their councils. He asked the interpreter the reason for the custom and the reply was:

"That some Women are wiser than some Men" (*Journal*, p. 49). He returned to England on several occasions, once remaining away from his American home for a period of three years, 1707-10. During this time he held religious meetings in Ireland, Scotland, Wales, England, and on the continent of Europe. In his continental journey, lasting for about nine weeks, in 1709, he traveled through Holland and northwestern Germany, visiting Rotterdam, Amsterdam, Hamburg, and Emden, and holding forty-five religious meetings. Next he spent a full year in England and Wales traveling, as he estimated, about 2,500 miles and attending nearly three hundred public meetings. In later life he suffered much hardship and some persecution in the course of his religious work—on one occasion (1734 or 1735) being shot and painfully wounded in Barbados for urging the islanders to treat their slaves more humanely (*Journal*, p. 273). As master of a ship he sought to engage sailors of good character, and to influence them with prayers and preaching aboard. More than once he narrowly escaped capture by privateers, or death by shipwreck. At one time, when provisions ran low and starvation seemed imminent, he offered his own body as food for the crew, but shortly afterward the capture of a dolphin ended the danger. He always ascribed his escapes to divine interposition. Even in his last years he continued his religious pilgrimages. He was in New England in 1737, rejoicing at the growth of Friends, especially on Nantucket Island. The following year he made his last journey into Virginia and North Carolina, and returned "more broken in the long and hard Travelling in this Journey, than in divers Years before" (*Journal*, p. 310). Only one more voyage awaited him. He made a religious visit in 1741 to Tortola, one of the Virgin Islands. There, after preaching zealously, he died of a fever.

Chalkley's *Journal* contains some information on the trade of the time, but deals largely with his religious activities. It displays an elevation of thought and a simple beauty of style that make it, in places, comparable to John Woolman's *Journal*. It became staple reading in Quaker families, which accounts for the reference in Whittier's *Snowbound* to "Chalkley's Journal old and quaint,—Gentlest of skippers, rare sea-saint."

[The basic source for the life of Chalkley is his *Journal*, in three parts. The original MS. of Parts I and II, covering his life to 1724, is preserved in the library of the Hist. Soc. of Pa. The *Journal* has been printed with other writings of Chalkley, under the title, *A Collection of the Works of Thos. Chalkley*. Citations above are to the first edition, printed at Phila. 1749, by Benj. Franklin and David Hall. For the various editions of the *Journal*, the *Works*, and separate epistles and exhortations, see Jos. Smith, *Descriptive Cat. of Friends' Books* (2 vols., 1867) and *Supplement* to same (1893). There are biographical sketches in the following: *Dict. of Nat. Biog.*, vol. IX (1887); *Friends Ancient and Modern* (London, 1903); *Quaker Biogs.* (First Series), vol. III (Phila., 1909); Jas. Bowden, *Hist. of the Soc. of Friends in America, 1750–54*, II (1854) 264. See also R. M. Jones, *Quakers in the Am. Colonies* (1911), *passim*. There is also valuable material on Chalkley's last days, including reprints and bibliographical notes, in Chas. F. Jenkins, *Tortola* (London, 1923).]

R. W. K.

CHALMERS, JAMES RONALD (Jan. 11, 1831–Apr. 9, 1898), lawyer, Confederate soldier, congressman, was the son of Joseph Williams and Fannie (Henderson) Chalmers. His grandfather, a Scotch planter, was a near relative of the celebrated minister, Dr. Thomas Chalmers; his father, born in Halifax County, Va., and educated at the University of Virginia, practised law in his native state, in Jackson, Tenn., and in Holly Springs, Miss. The younger Chalmers was also born in Halifax County, Va., and graduated in 1851, from South Carolina College, Columbia, S. C. After engaging in the practise of his profession for a few years at Holly Springs, he entered politics and was elected district attorney (1858). In 1861 he was chosen a delegate to the Mississippi secession convention and became chairman of the committee on military affairs. When hostilities began he entered the military service of the Confederacy, and rapidly rose from the rank of captain (March 1861) to that of colonel (April 1861), and then to that of brigadier-general (February 1862), taking part in the engagements at Santa Rosa Island. Pensacola, and in the battle of Shiloh. He was then transferred (1863) to the cavalry service, and participated in the attack on Munfordville and in the battle of Murfreesboro, gaining some distinction in the latter engagement. In April 1863 he was given command of a cavalry force in Mississippi, where he served during the remainder of the war. When he surrendered, in May 1865, he was commander of the first division of Forrest's Cavalry Army Corps. After the war he made his home at Friar's Point, Miss., and resumed the practise of law. He was married to Rebecca Arthur, by whom he had one daughter. In the upheaval by which the Democratic party regained control of the government of Mississippi in 1876, he became a member of the state Senate, and his younger brother, Judge H. H. Chalmers, was raised to the supreme bench of the state. About this time, Senator Chalmers led a force of white men that quelled an incipient negro riot at Friar's Point and drove the leader, a mulatto from Ohio who was then sheriff, out of the county. In the Congressional election, which followed, the aggressive young state senator was elected to the lower house of the Forty-fifth Congress from the celebrated "shoestring district," formed by the reapportionment act of 1876. He then moved to Vicksburg, and was elected to the Forty-sixth Congress. Two years later he received a certificate of election to the Forty-seventh Congress, but his seat was successfully contested by John R. Lynch of Natchez, Miss. (Chester H. Rowell, "Historical and Legal Digest of Contested Election Cases," *House Document, No. 510*, 56 Cong., 2 Sess., pp. 375–78). Chalmers was then appointed a special assistant to the federal district attorneys for the northern and southern districts of Mississippi. Meantime, he moved out of the "shoestring district" and made his home in Sardis, in an adjoining district, which had been represented in Congress since 1876 by Van H. Manning, a Democrat living in Holly Springs. Chalmers ran for Congress in this district (1883), on the independent ticket, with the indorsement of the Republican and Greenback conventions. He claimed a majority of the votes cast, but the Mississippi secretary of state gave a certificate of election to Manning, whose commission was duly signed by the governor. This brought on another contest before the House. After much discussion, Chalmers was finally seated, June 25, 1884 (*Ibid.*, pp. 396–98). Having been succeeded in the Forty-ninth Congress by James B. Morgan, a Democrat living in Hernando, Chalmers ran against him for the Fiftieth Congress. The election was followed by Chalmers' third contest over a seat in the House. This time he lost to his Democratic opponent (*Ibid.*, pp. 457–58). He then retired from politics and moved to Memphis, Tenn., where he engaged in the practise of law until his death, Apr. 9, 1898.

[Sketches of Chalmers in *Biog. and Hist. Memoirs of Mississippi* (1891), I, 535–56, and in Dunbar Rowland, *Mississippi* (1907), I, 390–91; a report of his cavalry operations, 1863, in *Southern Hist. Soc. Papers*, VIII, 222 ff.; a sketch of his father in J. D. Lynch, *The Bench and Bar of Mississippi* (1881).]   F. L. R.

CHAMBERLAIN, ALEXANDER FRANCIS (Jan. 12, 1865–Apr. 8, 1914), anthropologist, son of George and Maria (Anderton) Chamberlain, was born in Kenninghall, Norfolk, England, and was brought to America as a child, the family first settling in New York State near Rochester, but soon moving to Peterborough, Canada, where Alexander was prepared for college in the Collegiate Institute. The family then moved to Toronto that he might attend the University of Toronto, from which he graduated in 1886 with honors in languages and ethnology. While an undergraduate he had come under the influence of Sir Daniel Wilson, vice-chancellor of the University and a Canadian pioneer in anthropology, and it was doubtless due to this con-

tact that young Chamberlain turned from modern languages to anthropology. After his graduation, he made field studies among the Mississuga Indians, the results of which were presented in his thesis for the M.A. degree in 1889. This work was of such merit that he was granted a fellowship in anthropology at Clark University, where he was awarded the Ph.D. degree in 1892. This was the first such degree given for work in anthropology at an American university. Chamberlain remained at Clark until his death, beginning as lecturer in anthropology, 1893, and reaching the grade of professor in 1911. In 1898 he married Isabel Cushman. At the outset of his academic career he made field studies among the Kootenai Indians in western Canada, giving special attention to their language, but he did not carry his field-work further, devoting his time to the printed materials available. In addition to numerous special papers on anthropological subjects, he wrote two books on childhood: *The Child: A Study in the Evolution of Man* (1893); *The Child and Childhood in Folk-Thought* (1896). For many years he was editor of the *Journal of American Folk-Lore* and the *Journal of Religious Psychology,* and he contributed to each number of the *American Anthropologist,* brief comments on current articles. Mention should also be made of his work on the Indian languages of South America, and the preparation of a linguistic map for the same.

Chamberlain took a deep interest in his neighbors and the community, served as an alderman in Worcester, Mass., and as chairman of the Democratic Committee. He believed in prohibition and woman suffrage, was a follower of Henry George, and was a firm adherent of the Unitarian Church. The rights of oppressed peoples and classes was a favorite topic with him, and he was in demand as a local campaigner, and speaker in the people's forums, addressing his audiences in English, French, German, or Italian, as the occasion required. Large-limbed and awkward in appearance, with a high-pitched voice and quick jerky gestures, he was nevertheless an effective speaker. A lover of literature, especially poetry, not only did he treasure the lines of his favorite poets, but himself broke into verse at every opportunity. A volume of his poems, among which were a number of hymns, was issued in 1904.

[Albert N. Gilbertson, sketch in *Am. Anthropologist,* Apr.–June 1914, containing bibliography of Chamberlain's writings; F. Boaz, sketch in *Jour. of Am. Folk-Lore,* July–Sept. 1914; *Pubs. of the Clark Univ. Lib.,* Oct. 1914; *Proc. Am. Antiquarian Soc.,* n.s., vol. XXIV (1914); *Science,* June 5, 1914; *Who's Who in America,* 1914–15.]   C. W.

CHAMBERLAIN, DANIEL HENRY (June 23, 1835–Apr. 13, 1907), governor of South Carolina, was the ninth child of Eli and Achsah (Forbes) Chamberlain. As a boy he worked on the farm of his birth at West Brookfield, Mass., and attended in desultory fashion the country schools. Later he had fragmentary experiences with several secondary schools, in 1849–50 at Amherst Academy, in 1854 at Phillips Academy, Andover, and for more than one session, at Worcester High School, where he graduated in 1857. The next year he taught, as he had done intermittently since 1852. In 1858 he entered Yale. His diploma, which he received four years later, indicated special distinction in oratory and English composition. At the Harvard Law School, to which he went in the same fall, he was restless, and, withdrawing in November 1863, he received his commission as lieutenant in the 5th Massachusetts, a regiment of colored troops. In December 1865, he was mustered out as captain. Visiting South Carolina in 1866 to settle the affairs of a dead classmate, he thought he saw opportunity to earn money to repay what he had borrowed for his education. Although cotton-planting on John's Island proved unprofitable, he remained in the state. In 1867 he was chosen a member for Berkeley County of the constitutional convention. Before this body opened in January 1868, he had returned North to marry, on Dec. 16, Alice Ingersoll of Bangor. In the motley convention he gained some prominence as a member of the judiciary committee and earned the favor of party leaders. In the April election of 1868 he was chosen attorney-general. Nothing of his record in this office was notable, but in the most corrupt quadrennium of South Carolina history, though an *ex-officio* member of several thieving boards, he was never charged with personal dishonesty.

After two years of law practise in Columbia, Chamberlain in 1874 won first the nomination and then the election for governor of the state. Immediately undertaking the reforms which he had promised to effect, he reduced public expenditures, revised taxation and assessment laws, eliminated abuse of the pardoning power, and curbed sharply the predatory aspirations of the state boards. His most conspicuous work was his refusal, often in the face of party insistence, to commission corrupt officials. The whites of the state gave for a time indorsement to his administration. Charleston publicly thanked him in 1875 for barring from the bench Whipper and Moses, elected by the legislature.

In the summer of 1876, looking toward renomination, he aligned himself again with the un-

worthy faction of his party. He also adopted stern measures in connection with racial clashes, especially the Hamburg riot of July. His support among Democrats weakened; and though a minority of the August Democratic convention urged his claim, Wade Hampton was nominated. The contest, unprecedentedly bitter, was marked by charges and counter-charges. Both sides claimed victory. Chamberlain was inaugurated on Dec. 7, and a few days later Hampton was sworn in by a rival government. The issue was not settled until April when President Hayes, having called a conference of the competing governors, withdrew the federal troops. His government having fallen, Chamberlain engaged in law practise in New York. Honored by Cornell with appointment as non-resident professor of constitutional law in 1883, he continued an active life until 1897 when he sought retirement on the old homestead at West Brookfield. The death of a son in 1902 made that residence unhappy. Chamberlain spent a few months in South Carolina, had a year in Europe, returned for a brief stay near Charleston, lived twenty months in Egypt, and in 1906 settled at Charlottesville, Va., where he spent his remaining days.

[Biographical data are found in a prefatory note to Chamberlain's "Some Conclusions of a Free-Thinker," *North Am. Rev.*, Oct. 1907, and in the Allen, Thompson, and Reynolds references below. The standard defense of Chamberlain is Walter Allen, *Chamberlain's Administration in S. C.* (1888). Less friendly appraisals are: E. L. Godkin, "The Republican Party in S. C.," *Nation*, Apr. 19, 1877; John S. Reynolds, *Reconstruction in S. C.* (1905); Henry T. Thompson, *Ousting the Carpet-Bagger* (1926); and F. A. Porcher, "The Last Chapter in Reconstruction in S. C." in *Southern Hist. Soc. Papers*, vols. XII, XIII. The *Atlantic Monthly*, Feb. 1877, had an anonymous résumé, "Political Conditions of S. C."; the same journal for Apr. 1901 carried Chamberlain's "Reconstruction in S. C."]

F. P. G.

CHAMBERLAIN, GEORGE EARLE (Jan. 1, 1854–July 9, 1928), lawyer, governor of Oregon, senator, was born near Natchez, Miss. His father was Charles Thomson Chamberlain, a leading physician of Natchez, whose father had been one of the foremost physicians of Newark, Del. Chamberlain's mother was Pamelia H. Archer, whose father was in turn congressman from Maryland, judge of Mississippi territory with gubernatorial powers, and at the time of his death one of the justices of the court of appeals of Maryland. Chamberlain's early education was received from private tutors and in the schools of Natchez. From sixteen to eighteen he clerked in a store, but with consciousness of his abilities and his family traditions he naturally struck out for a professional career, and, attending Washington and Lee University, he received the degrees of bachelor of arts and bachelor of law in the same year, June 1876.

On arriving in Oregon late in 1876 he first taught school in Linn County. From 1877 to 1879 he served as deputy county clerk in the same county. He then returned to Natchez and on May 21, 1879 was married to Sallie M. Welch, of New England ancestry. In 1880 Chamberlain was elected to the House of Representatives of the Oregon legislature, and, having entered upon the active practise of law, he was in 1884 elected district attorney of the 3rd judicial district. In 1891 the office of attorney-general of Oregon was created and Chamberlain was appointed by the governor to that position. At the succeeding general election he was chosen, as the Democratic candidate, running some 10,000 ahead of his party's ticket. In 1900, having taken up his residence in Portland, he was chosen district attorney of Multnomah County, his vote leading that of the party ticket by about the ratio with which he had won his previous victories. Chamberlain was twice elected governor, first in 1902 and again in 1906. As governor he moved quickly to rescue for the people valuable timbered school lands that were being rapidly filched away from them through dummy entrymen. He also used his veto freely to prevent frustration of the people's aims. The federal amendment providing for popular election of United States senators was anticipated in Oregon through the so-called "Statement No. I," submitted to candidates for election to the legislature in 1908 through which each could be pledged to vote for the man receiving the highest popular vote. This brought about the unique spectacle of a legislature strongly Republican casting its vote in 1909 for Chamberlain, a Democrat, as United States senator. In 1915, with direct election of United States senators provided by federal amendment, Chamberlain was again elected. As senator his attitude and ability had secured immediate recognition and in 1913 he had become chairman of the committee on military affairs. This position during the years immediately preceding and during American participation in the World War placed weighty responsibilities on Chamberlain's shoulders. He is credited with a large part in the formulation and the handling of the measures providing for the selective draft, food control, and the financing of the war. Dilatoriness of movement in the War Department in the early months of the war aroused him to pronounce a sharp judgment upon it in a New York City speech and to ask for an emergency organization to take over some of that department's duties.

Those nearest Chamberlain are inclined to believe that "he considered his efforts in behalf of the boys in service during the late war to have been the finest thing—the thing most fruitful of benefit to humanity—that he ever did." His action, however, was bitterly resented by President Wilson and from that time on he was out of favor with the administration. In 1920, he was defeated for reëlection. This ended his political career. He was large and impressive in appearance; an excellent speaker, whose manner inspired confidence. After his defeat his friends, both Republican and Democrat, secured his appointment as a member of the United States Shipping Board.

[*Ore. Blue Book*; *Ore. Daily Jour.*, and *Morning Oregonian*, July 10, 1928; Jos. Gaston, *Portland, Ore., Its Hist. and Builders* (1911); *Cong. Record*, 1909–20.]

F. G. Y.

CHAMBERLAIN, HENRY RICHARDSON (Aug. 25, 1859–Feb. 15, 1911), newspaper editor and foreign correspondent, was born in Peoria, Ill., where his father, Thomas Chamberlain of Boston, was spending a few months with his family. Educated in the public schools of Boston, Henry first began his newspaper work by hunting up news independently and turning it over to the *Boston Journal*. At eighteen he was a full-fledged reporter on that newspaper. Attracted by the larger salaries paid in New York City he came to the metropolis in 1888 as managing editor of the *Press*,—a position he later resigned to make a tour of Europe. Returning to New York, he became associated with the *Sun*, for which he had done considerable work as special correspondent while in Boston. This connection with the *Sun* lasted until 1891 when Chamberlain went back to Boston to become managing editor of the *Journal*. A year later he again returned to the *Sun* as its correspondent stationed in London,—possibly the highest reportorial honor in the power of any newspaper to bestow. Here he achieved his greatest distinction as a reporter of the political situation in England and also as an expert commentator upon European politics in general. In addition to his work as London correspondent for the *Sun*, he had general oversight of the European news service of that newspaper, a service that was syndicated to many papers throughout the United States. Important crises in European history Chamberlain reported in person, such as the Russian political crisis of 1906. For him the Balkans and their petty feuds had tremendous interest: he was constantly forecasting the possible results of these feuds because the quarrels of the little states were so entangled with the relations of the great European nations. Not only in London, but also in New York, newspaper men were inclined to smile over the seriousness of "H. R. C.'s war-cloud articles," even though their author was not a wailing Jeremiah. In press circles the remark was frequently made, "H. R. is always seeing things." Even his friends, believing that a general war in Europe was impossible, were often skeptical of the dispatches which Chamberlain cabled to America. He died in London in 1911, still in active service for the *Sun,* and to the very last he insisted that the great war was coming. In 1883 he married in Boston Abbie L. Sanger. Author of many short stories, he left only one book, *Six Thousand Tons of Gold* (1894). His best work as a reporter may be found in his accounts of the Macedonian disturbances, the Messina earthquake, and the Panama Canal scandal in France. He was one of the foremost representatives of the brilliant type of reporter that Charles A. Dana secured for the *Sun* when that journal was known as the newspaperman's newspaper.

[*The Story of the Sun* (1918) by Frank M. O'Brien contains a somewhat detailed sketch of Chamberlain as a newspaper man. In the *Sun,* Feb. 16, 1911, appeared an extended obituary.]   J. M. L.

CHAMBERLAIN, JACOB (Apr. 13, 1835–Mar. 2, 1908), Dutch Reformed missionary to India, was the son of Jacob Chamberlain, a farmer of Sharon, Conn., and his wife Anna Nutting. He grew up at Hudson, Ohio, where the family settled in 1838; studied at the Academy at Lodi, Mich.; graduated at Western Reserve College in 1856, and studied theology at Union Seminary and at Rutgers where he graduated in 1859. He also studied medicine at the College of Physicians and Surgeons in New York and at Western Reserve. He was ordained a missionary of the Dutch Reformed Church in May 1859, married Charlotte Close Birge of Hudson in September, sailed for India, and began his life work in the Arcot Mission in April 1860. Beginning with the Tamil language, he soon took up the Telugu in which he became proficient. His first missionary activities consisted of extensive preaching tours on which he distributed vast quantities of Bibles and tracts; but he soon added to these labors those of the medical missionary, in which he was very successful. Many thousands of natives were reached by the hospitals and dispensaries which he established. He compiled a Telugu Bible, being chairman of the revision committee from 1873 to 1896. Early in his career he began to prepare a Telugu Bible dictionary, a task that was left

uncompleted at his death. He was a pioneer champion of the union of churches on the mission field and the notable Reformed and Presbyterian unions in India have been the result of his work. The first theological seminary on the mission field, that of the Arcot mission, founded in 1887, owes its origin to him. Ill health resulting from jungle fever compelled him to spend ten years, at various periods, in the United States and other English-speaking countries where he became a most effective advocate of foreign missions.

Besides his annual reports, written in simple and beautiful English, and his numerous articles in the religious press, he wrote: *The Bible Tested in India* (1878); *In the Tiger Jungle* (1896); *The Religions of the Orient* (1896); *The Cobra's Den* (1900); *The Kingdom in India, Its Progress and its Promise* (published in 1908, with a biographical sketch of the author by Henry N. Cobb). Chamberlain combined in himself the scholar, the preacher, the physician, the inventor, and the advocate, but the missionary motive was always central. He had a sense of humor, was genial and cheerful, and was greatly beloved by his family and associates.

[Cobb's sketch (*ante*) is reprinted in the *Missionary Rev. of the World,* Aug. 1908. The same publication for May 1908 contains autobiographical material. Further material is found in *Acts and Proc. of the Gen. Synod of the Reformed Ch. in America* (1908), and in *Who's Who in America,* 1908–09.]   F. T. P.

CHAMBERLAIN, JOSHUA LAWRENCE (Sept. 8, 1828–Feb. 24, 1914), Union soldier, governor of Maine, educator, was born at Brewer, Me., the son of Joshua Chamberlain and Sarah D. Brastow. On his father's side he traced his descent from William Chamberlain, who migrated from England about 1648 and settled at Woburn, Mass.; his first maternal ancestor in this country was Jean Dupuis, a Huguenot who came to Boston from La Rochelle about 1685. His great-grandfather served in the colonial and Revolutionary wars, his grandfather was a colonel in the War of 1812, and his father acted as second in command on the American side in the so-called Aroostook War in 1839. He was educated at a military academy at Ellsworth, Me., graduated from Bowdoin College, Brunswick, in 1852, and in 1855 completed a course at the Bangor Theological Seminary. On Dec. 7, 1855, he was married to Frances Caroline, daughter of Ashur Adams of Boston and Emily (Wyllis) Adams of Hartford. In the same year he was appointed instructor in natural and revealed religion at Bowdoin; from 1856 to 1862 he was professor of rhetoric; from 1857 to 1861 instructor in modern languages; from

1861 to 1865 professor of modern languages. In 1862 he was granted leave of absence for study abroad, but, abandoning the plan in spite of the protest of the college faculty, he enlisted as lieutenant-colonel of the 20th Maine Infantry, becoming colonel in May 1863, and continuing in active service until the end of the Civil War. He took part in twenty-four engagements (among them Antietam, Fredericksburg, Chancellorsville, Gettysburg, Spottsylvania, Cold Harbor, Petersburg, and Five Forks) and was six times wounded. For his gallant defense of Little Round Top in the battle of Gettysburg he received the Congressional Medal of Honor "for daring heroism and great tenacity." On June 18, 1864, in the operations before Petersburg, where he was wounded, he was made a brigadier-general on the field by Grant, the promotion being later confirmed by the Senate. His distinguished conduct on Mar. 29, 1865, in an assault on Lee's right, caused him to be brevetted major-general of volunteers, and in the operations which ended with Lee's surrender he commanded two brigades of the 1st Division of the 5th Army Corps, and was designated to receive the surrender of the Confederate army. On June 16, 1866, he was mustered out, having declined, on account of his health, an offer of a colonelcy in the regular army and a command on the Rio Grande. In the fall of that year he was elected governor of Maine, and served in that office by reëlection for four successive annual terms. From 1871 to 1883 he was president of Bowdoin, and in addition, from 1874 to 1879, professor of mental and moral philosophy and lecturer on political science and public law, continuing to lecture on the latter subjects until 1885. During the winter of 1878–79, when the Democratic and Greenback parties, under the lead of Gov. Alonzo Garcelon, had combined to get possession of the state legislature, and the Republicans had organized a rival body, Chamberlain, acting as major-general of the state militia, kept the peace until the supreme court of the state affirmed the legality of the Republican organization. He was one of the American commissioners to the Universal Exposition at Paris in 1878, and made a valuable report on the educational exhibit. From 1884 to 1889 he was occupied with railway and industrial enterprises in Florida. In 1900 he was appointed surveyor of the port of Portland, Me., and held that office until his death. His best known and most important writings are *Maine: Her Place in History* (1877), originally prepared as an address at the Centennial Exposition at Philadelphia, Nov. 4, 1876, and *The Passing of the*

Armies (1915), a book of reminiscence dealing with the final campaigns of the Army of the Potomac. Of a number of occasional addresses or papers which were printed the best known is an address at Philadelphia on Feb. 12, 1909, before the Military Order of the Loyal Legion, Pennsylvania Commandery, on the hundredth anniversary of Lincoln's birth (published in the *Magazine of American History*, 1914, Extra No. 32). To *Universities and their Sons* (6 vols., 1898–1923), of which he was for a time editor-in-chief, he contributed a history of New York University.

[N. Cleaveland, *Hist. of Bowdoin Coll.* (1882), ed. by A. S. Packard; Louis C. Hatch, *Hist. of Bowdoin Coll.* (1927); *Gen. Cat. of Bowdoin Coll., 1794–1912* (1912); a biographical note signed G. H. P. (George Haven Putnam?) prefixed to *The Passing of the Armies* (1915); an excellent brief account of the fighting at Little Round Top in W. H. Powell, *Hist. of the Fifth Army Corps* (1896), pp. 526–31; *Official Records (Army)*; obituary in Portland *Eastern Argus*, Feb. 25, 1914.]
W. M.

CHAMBERLAIN, MELLEN (June 4, 1821–June 25, 1900), historian, was born in Pembroke, N. H., the second of the five children of Moses and Mary (Foster) Chamberlain. He attended the district schools and the Academy in Pembroke; later he assisted his father on the farm and in the business of a country store until 1836, when the family moved to Concord, N. H. He prepared for college at the Literary Institute of that place, taught in the district schools during the winters, and aided his father on the farm; he graduated from Dartmouth College in 1844 with special distinction in classical studies. During the college course he taught school three winters in Danvers, Mass., and was principal of the High School in Brattleboro, Vt., until late in 1846, when he entered the Dane (Harvard) Law School; he was soon made librarian of the school, and received his LL.B. degree in 1848. Admitted to the bar in Boston, in January 1849, he married Martha Ann Putnam on June 6 of the same year, and went to live in Chelsea, where he passed the remainder of his days. From 1849 his life was a busy one; while his chief occupation was that of a conveyancer, he soon entered public service as, successively, school committee man, selectman, alderman, and city solicitor. He was elected a representative to the General Court from the thirteenth Suffolk district in 1858 and in 1859, and was appointed a member of the special committee on the revision of the statutes. In 1863 and again in 1864 he was elected a member of the state Senate, and in the latter year was chairman of its judiciary committee. On June 29, 1866, Gov. Bullock appointed him associate justice of the newly created municipal court of

Boston; this office he held until December 1870, when Gov. Claflin appointed him chief justice of the municipal court. He remained in this position until August 1878, when he was made librarian of the Public Library of the City of Boston. His special attainments in the study of early American history proved of essential advantage to the Library in bringing that department of the institution up to the high standing already reached in other branches of knowledge. Because of failing health Chamberlain resigned in September 1890. His collection of autographs and manuscripts, begun in 1836, by will became the property of the Boston Public Library and has proved one of the richest sources of information for students of American history. From 1873 on, Chamberlain played a prominent part in the Massachusetts Historical Society and contributed valuable and interesting papers to its publications. He also wrote the chapter on "The Revolution Impending" in Justin Winsor's *Narrative and Critical History of America,* vol. VI (1888). In 1890 a selection of his writings, edited by Lindsay Swift, was published under the title of *John Adams, the Statesman of the American Revolution, with Other Essays and Addresses, Historical and Literary.* Under the auspices of a committee of publication of the Massachusetts Historical Society, there was published in 1908 *A Documentary History of Chelsea, 1624–1824,* in two volumes, from Chamberlain's incomplete manuscript and from ten folio volumes of manuscripts, plans, engravings, photographs, etc., collected and arranged by him. Uncommon literary quality, combined with judgment, sagacity, and ripe scholarship, marked the style not only of Chamberlain's writings but of his public addresses. His keen memory supplied him, when speaking, with an abundance of illustrations to strengthen and enliven his arguments. In person he was tall and erect; in bearing dignified; in nature companionable and affectionate. His strong and commanding countenance gave additional weight and meaning to his words.

["Memoir of Mellen Chamberlain," by Henry W. Haynes, in *Proc. Mass. Hist. Soc.,* 2 ser. XX, 119–46 (repr. in *Doc. Hist. of Chelsea*) ; "Tribute to Mellen Chamberlain," by Geo. B. Chase, in *Proc. Mass. Hist. Soc.,* 2 ser. XIV, 271–81.]   C. F. D. B.

CHAMBERLAIN, NATHAN HENRY (Dec. 28, 1828?–Apr. 1, 1901), Episcopalian clergyman, author, the son of Artemas White and Lydia Smith (Ellis) Chamberlain, was born in that part of Sandwich, Mass., now called Bourne, and he died about seventy-two years later in the same house. The date of his birth is uncertain. The conventional date is Dec. 25,

1830. Samuel S. Shaw, secretary of the class of 1853 (Harvard), says it is not certain whether Chamberlain was born Dec. 25, or Dec. 28, in the year 1828, '29, '30, or '31, but after careful and exhaustive study he decides on Dec. 28, 1828, as most probable. Chamberlain's early life was one continual struggle with poverty. His father was the keeper of the poor-house in Sandwich and later became a policeman in Cambridge, whither the family moved during Nathan's school-days. By mowing lawns, shoveling dirt, and snaring rabbits, the boy earned money for his needs while in Hopkins Classical School. During his college days at Harvard he taught days and studied nights in bed, being too poor to maintain a fire. He graduated from Harvard in the class of 1853 and completed his professional studies at Harvard Divinity School and at the University of Heidelberg. Ordained to the Unitarian ministry, Apr. 22, 1857, at Canton, Mass., he served Unitarian churches there and in Baltimore, Md. His convictions then led him into the Episcopal church and he was ordained priest at Middletown, Conn., in 1864. For twenty-five years he served as an Episcopalian rector in Birmingham (now Derby), Conn.; Morrisania, N. Y.; Milwaukee, Wis.; Somerville and East Boston, Mass. In 1889 he resigned from the ministry, became a teacher of elocution, and devoted much of his time to writing. He was a master in the use of the English language, lucid, direct, and graphic. His range of interests and study was broad and his themes were varied. Independent as a political thinker, in *What's the Matter? or Our Tariff and Its Taxes* (1890), he protested against protection as "anti-American, anti-republican, aristocratic and the tool of tyranny," and demanded economic as well as political freedom. Though keenly critical of Puritanism as a system of applied religion, he was liberal enough to see the elements of its power in the nation's life and paid a tribute to the same in *Samuel Sewall and the World He Lived In* (1897). A picture of life in the Pilgrim colony toned and colored by the sea is given in *The Autobiography of a New England Farm House* (1864) in which he analyzed the Tory mind and enunciated a philosophy of sorrow. During his last few years his health was seriously impaired, and he lived in retirement on Cape Cod until his death. He was married twice: first, on Feb. 19, 1855, to Hannah Simonds Tewkesbury; and, second, on Apr. 6, 1869, to Mariette Cleveland Hyde.

[*Jour. of the One Hundred Sixteenth Annual Meeting of the Convention of the Diocese of Mass.,* 1901; *Report of the Class of 1853 (Harvard), 1849–1913; Churchman,* Apr. 20, 1901.]   T. C. R.

CHAMBERLAIN, WILLIAM ISAAC (Feb. 11, 1837–June 30, 1920), agriculturist, son of Jacob and Anna (Nutting) Chamberlain, was born in Sharon, Conn. Following the tide of Connecticut movement to the Western Reserve, his parents with their two infant children moved to Ohio in 1838 and settled in Hudson. Having graduated from the public school of the town, Chamberlain entered Western Reserve College and graduated in 1859. His proficiency in the classics led to his immediate appointment as instructor of Latin and Greek in the College. On July 16, 1863, he was married to Lucy Jones Marshall. Two years later, his health and the needs of his parents made it advisable for him to give up teaching and take over the home farm. To the art of farming he applied the scholarly habits of the student, reading and testing by experiments whatever scientific facts might find practical application in the management of soils, crops, and orchards. These tests and experiments formed the basis of his frequent contributions to agricultural journals. His knowledge of Ohio agriculture led to his election as secretary of agriculture of Ohio in 1880 and to his removal to Columbus, Ohio, where he served in this capacity for six years. During this time he was instrumental in organizing throughout the state a system of farmers' institutes and of monthly crop reports, and in securing the passage of a fertilizer law and the equipment of an agricultural fair ground. In 1886 he was called to the presidency of the Iowa Agricultural College, but in 1890 he resigned to return to his experimenting, lecturing, and agricultural writing. He served as a trustee of Ohio State University and as a member of the board of control of the Ohio Agricultural Station. He was an associate editor of the *Ohio Farmer*, 1891–1908, of the *National Stockman and Farmer*, 1908–18, and published a book for practical farmers, *Tile Drainage* (1891). In 1908–09 and again in 1912 he traveled in Europe. While most of his life-work was devoted to the interests of the farmer, his love of the classics never lessened and to the end of his life, with his mind still clear and active, he read almost daily from his favorite Greek authors.

[L. S. Ivins and A. E. Winship, *Fifty Famous Farmers* (1924), pp. 309–14; *Cleveland Plain Dealer*, July 1, 1920; C. R. Aurner, *Hist. of Ed. in Iowa*, vol. IV (1916), pp. 250–57; private information.]   E. H. J.

CHAMBERLIN, THOMAS CHROWDER (Sept. 25, 1843–Nov. 15, 1928), one of the outstanding contributors to constructive thinking in the geologic sciences of the past half-century, was born in Mattoon, Ill., the son of the

Rev. John Chamberlin, a Methodist minister, and of Cecilia (Gill) Chamberlin. When he was three years old the family moved to Wisconsin where he grew to manhood. In 1866 he received the degree of A.B. at Beloit College, and for the next two years was principal of the high school at Delevan, Wis.; meanwhile, in 1867, he was married to Alma Isabel Wilson. He was a graduate student at the University of Michigan, 1868–69; professor of natural sciences at the State Normal School, Whitewater, Wis., 1870–72; professor of geology at Beloit, 1873–82. It was while he was at the latter institution that his really important work began. The fact that he resided in a region of notable glacial deposits was of great importance in the development of his career as a student of earth history. The climatic conditions in past ages, as revealed by traces of ancient glaciers, contrasted sharply with the situation obtaining to-day, and presented a series of questions for which no fully adequate answer had been obtained. His study naturally directed itself, first, to intensive examination of the material remains upon which must be based any research into the physical or climatic conditions through which these relics had been produced. Armed with the evidence secured by his investigations and stimulated by the continually increasing complexity of the problem, he extended his studies to consideration of earth climates through the known range of geological time.

In 1878 he made a special study of the glaciers of Switzerland. By 1883 he was recognized as the leading American glacialist (H. L. Fairchild, *post*, p. 611). During these years he was also the assistant state geologist of Wisconsin, 1873–76, and the chief geologist, 1877–82. Here he had the task of publishing the results of a geological survey of the whole state, made by himself and his associates, in *The Geology of Wisconsin* (4 vols., 1873–82). Volume I contained his summary of the geological history of Wisconsin, beginning with a discussion of the origin of the earth. The work attracted so much attention that a Division of Glacial Geology, of which he was appointed chief, was established in the United States Geological Survey at Washington, D. C., in 1882. He was also professor of geology in Columbian University, Washington, from 1885 to 1887. In the latter year he was called to succeed John Bascom [*q.v.*], in the presidency of the University of Wisconsin. His incumbency fell in the period when the college of liberal arts developed by his predecessor was beginning to expand into the later university. Chamberlin foresaw the future clearly and outlined the policy to be pursued. In his initial year, through the foundation of eight university fellowships, he took the first formal step toward the encouragement of graduate study; he improved the law school; and in his fifth and last year he inaugurated a university extension movement.

In 1892 Chamberlin was appointed head of the department of geology and director of the Walker Museum in the new University of Chicago. Here he remained until his death, becoming professor emeritus in 1919. In 1893 he founded the *Journal of Geology* of which he was editor-in-chief until 1922 when he became senior editor. In 1894 he accompanied the Peary Relief Expedition. In 1897 he published his first non-glacial paper, "A Group of Hypotheses Bearing on Climatic Changes," which contained the germ of his later "planetesimal hypothesis." In 1898 he outlined in "The Ulterior Basis of Time Divisions and the Classification of Geologic History" a line of approach which was to culminate in "Diastrophism as the Ultimate Basis of Correlation" (1909) and "Diastrophism and the Formative Processes" (1913, 1914, 1918). He discussed the nebular hypothesis in "An Attempt to Test the Nebular Hypothesis by the Relations of Masses and Momenta" (1900). In 1906 he published his *General Treatise on Geology,* written in collaboration with R. D. Salisbury. In 1916 his epoch-making volume, *The Origin of the Earth,* appeared, and in 1928 his last work, *The Two Solar Families.*

"Chamberlin was regarded in the profession as without question the ranking geologist of America" (C. K. Leith, in *Wisconsin Alumni Magazine,* Dec. 1928). His outstanding contributions are generally recognized as threefold: first, his detailed researches on glacial phenomena as illustrated in the relics of glaciation so widely spread through the northern United States; second, his investigations of geological climates, arising naturally out of the study of exceptional climatic conditions in the glacial period; third, the contribution to cosmic geology represented in his "planetesimal hypothesis" of the origin of the earth.

The trend of Chamberlin's researches into the geological history of the more remote ages made necessary his inquiry not only into the evolution of climates, but into questions concerning the origin of the atmosphere itself. In examination of the variation in atmospheric conditions the proportion of carbonic acid in the atmosphere appeared a critical factor. Investigation of these particular phenomena reached beyond the study of the origin of the earth climates, and involved groups of inferences relating to the development of life under varying conditions in past periods, and the possibility of linking a wide range of diverse elements in earth history through their relation to atmospheric conditions. The study of climatic changes and the origin of the atmosphere carried Chamberlin ultimately into discussion of the dynamics of the earth, with problems relating to the nature and degree of regularity of earth movements in past time. In another direction it led directly to a consideration of the origin of the earth, which could be discussed only in association with problems relating to the development of the solar system.

Always characterized by exceptional broad-mindedness, and by recognition of the need for utilization of all available materials and application of every possible hypothesis for a study of each specific case, Chamberlin illustrated to an extraordinary degree the development of these qualities in his study of problems relating to the origin of the earth. Drawing into cooperation with him a wide range of investigational efforts in the field of mathematics and astronomy, he brought practically the whole of organized study in cosmic physics to bear upon this interesting problem. In connection with these researches, special mention should be made of his long association with Forest R. Moulton, whose expression of the problem in terms of mathematics and astronomy supplemented in an extremely important manner the constructive thinking of Chamberlin.

It was clear that the widely-recognized hypotheses represented by that of La Place were not competent to account for the development of the earth and other planets, and effort was made to secure an interpretation which would fit the requirements of physics. The result was the theory that the earth and the planets owed their birth to the approach of another sun or star bringing about the partial disruption of the sun, and the expulsion of a great mass from which ultimately the earth was derived. This evolution was defined as by way of a swarm of minute, solid particles, the "planetesimals," swinging in orbits about the sun, and ultimately gathering to build the earth. Checked from every point of view, this became the "planetesimal hypothesis" of the earth's origin.

[H. L. Fairchild, "Thos. Chrowder Chamberlin—Teacher, Administrator, Geologist, Philosopher," *Science,* LXVIII, 610 ff., Dec. 21, 1928; Chas. Schuchert in *Am. Jour. Science,* ser. V, no. 98, vol. XVII, pp. 194–96, Feb. 1929; *Univ. Record* (Chicago), Jan. 1929; *Geographical Rev.,* Jan. 1929; *Sci. Mo.,* Jan. 1929; *Jour. Washington Acad. Science,* XVIII, 564, Dec. 4, 1928; *Bull. Geol. Soc. of America,* XXXVIII, 6–7, Mar. 1927; R. G. Thwaites, *The Univ. of Wisconsin* (1900), pp. 129–40; G. F. A. Pyre, *Wisconsin* (1920).]

J.C.M.

CHAMBERS, CHARLES JULIUS. [See CHAMBERS, JAMES JULIUS, 1850–1920.]

CHAMBERS, EZEKIEL FORMAN (Feb. 28, 1788–Jan. 30, 1867), jurist, born at Chestertown, Kent County, Md., was the son of Benjamin and Elizabeth (Forman) Chambers. His father fought both in the Revolution and in the War of 1812. Ezekiel likewise distinguished himself during the War of 1812, in a militia company which was defending the Eastern Shore, Maryland, at Bel Air, against the British attack under Sir Peter Parker (*Baltimore Sun*, Feb. 2, 1867, *National Intelligencer*, Feb. 4, 1867). After a classical education in Washington College he studied law and was admitted to the bar in March 1808. After the interlude of the War of 1812 he practised until 1822 when he was elected against his will to the Maryland Senate. The famous case of *Prigg* vs. *The State of Pennsylvania*, which involved the right to recover fugitive slaves, was at this time discussed in the Senate and gave him an opportunity to pronounce his Southern state-rights views on slavery and secession. His activities in this case led the State of Maryland to appoint him commissioner to enter into negotiations with Pennsylvania regarding the return of fugitive slaves; the result of these negotiations was satisfactory to his state. Chambers served in the United States Senate from 1826 to 1834, during which time he became an ardent Whig, opposed to "Jacksonism." But he had little taste for politics and probably rejoiced when, in 1834, he was appointed chief judge of the then 2nd judicial district and judge of the court of appeals. In 1850 he was sent to the state convention which framed a new constitution. There he made himself unpopular by his unsuccessful fight against the provision that the people elect their judges. As a result, under the new constitution he was not elected to his old position. President Fillmore in 1852 offered him the appointment of secretary of the navy, which he seriously considered but declined on the ground of ill health. Instead, he turned his attention again to the bar and became celebrated as a *nisi prius* lawyer. When the menacing talk of secession grew at length into a distinct threat his sympathies were unmistakably with the movement, but like most Marylanders he advocated a calm and judicial view, advising compromise. He was in 1864 a member of the constitutional convention of Maryland where his state-rights ideas could but make his efforts ineffective, since the state was at this time controlled by the Unionists under military force. His candidacy for governor in the same year against Thomas Swann ended in fail-

ure, as it was bound to do. At the time of his death he was president of the board of trustees of his alma mater, Washington College.

[*Baltimore Sun*, Feb. 2, 1867; *Md. Hist. Mag.*, vols. XVI, XVII; *Tercentenary Hist. of Md.* (1925), IV, 852–53.]
                        C. W. G.

CHAMBERS, GEORGE (Feb. 24, 1786–Mar. 25, 1866), lawyer, was the grandson of Benjamin Chambers, a native of Antrim, Ireland, but of Scotch descent, who landed at Philadelphia in 1726 and settled near the present site of Chambersburg, Pa. Benjamin's son, also Benjamin, married Sarah, daughter of George Brown, a neighbor, and their eldest son, George, was born at Chambersburg. The family was well off, and George received a good classical education, proceeded to Princeton in October 1802, and graduated with honors in 1804. He then studied law at Chambersburg and Carlisle, and on his admission to the Cumberland County bar, Nov. 9, 1807, opened an office at Chambersburg, with every advantage which respected parentage and large local interests can confer. Devoting himself more particularly to the law of conveyancing and real property, probably because of his father's extensive land holdings, he in time acquired the reputation of being an expert in the intricate and obscure land laws of Pennsylvania. He entered public life through municipal channels, being elected a member of the Chambersburg town council in 1821, and serving as burgess from 1829 to 1833. In 1832 he was elected to Congress as Whig representative of Adams and Franklin counties, and served two terms, being reëlected in 1834. He was a delegate from Franklin County to the Pennsylvania state constitutional convention which met at Harrisburg, May 2, 1837. A bitter controversy arose in the convention anent the judiciary article, it being proposed to substitute a short tenure for judges in place of the original tenure during good behavior. This change Chambers resolutely but unsuccessfully opposed. In April 1851 he was appointed associate judge of the supreme court of Pennsylvania by Gov. Johnson, and held this office till the following December, when the new constitution came into force. Nominated by the Whig state convention of that year for continuance in office, he suffered defeat in common with the whole Whig ticket, and thereafter neither sought nor held any public position. He did not resume his law practise, but devoted much time to the promotion of education and agricultural science in his community. He was the largest landowner in Franklin County, and is said to have known every boundary line and tree throughout his extensive properties. He also engaged in literary work, publishing *A Trib-*

ute to the *Principles, Virtues, Habits and Public Usefulness of the Irish and Scotch Early Settlers of Pennsylvania* (1856). In addition, he prepared a biography of the Rev. John McDowell and an elaborate local history, with particular reference to the laws and usages appertaining to land. The manuscripts of these works, together with a mass of valuable private papers, were destroyed when the Confederate forces burned Chambersburg, July 30, 1864. Chambers was married to Alice A., daughter of W. Lyon, of Cumberland County. "He did not often appear in the trial of criminal cases, but led all other members of the Bar in civil suits and Orphans' Court business . . . was dignified, reserved and courteous. He had few intimates, and perhaps the general public regarded him as aristocratic, and but little disposed to concern himself about his fellow men" (John M. Cooper, *post*).

[Details of the ancestry and life of Chambers are contained in the *Kittochtinny Mag.*, I, 136, 279, 290. Further material will be found in: J. McDowell Sharpe, *Memoir of Geo. Chambers* (1873, repr. in *Hist. of Franklin County, Pa.*, 1887, p. 625); John M. Cooper, *Recollections of Chambersburg, Pa.* (1900), p. 104; W. D. Chambers, *Chambers Hist.* (1925), pp. 46–49).]

H. W. H. K.

CHAMBERS, JAMES JULIUS (Nov. 21, 1850–Feb. 12, 1920), journalist, born at Bellefontaine, Ohio, was the son of Joseph and Sarabella (Walker) Chambers. When he was eleven years old he decided he would work in a newspaper office and thereafter spent most of his vacations in the office of a Bellefontaine newspaper. In 1870 he was graduated from Cornell University and immediately became a reporter on the *New York Tribune* under Horace Greeley. Illness forced him to leave New York for a time, and in the summer of 1872 he explored the headwaters of the Mississippi River in a Baden-Powell canoe, going above Lake Itasca to discover Elk Lake, connected with Itasca by a stream since named Chambers Creek (see *Minnesota Historical Collections*, vol. XI, 1904). For this discovery he was made a fellow of the Royal Geographical Society. His trip furnished material for a series of letters published in the *New York Herald*, and later a book, *The Mississippi River and Its Wonderful Valley* (1910). Returning to New York and the service of the *Tribune* in August 1872, with the connivance of the city editor he arranged to be committed as insane to the Bloomingdale Asylum in order to obtain authentic information as to alleged abuses of the inmates. His friends secured his release after ten days, and his reports and stories in the *Tribune* resulted in the release of some twelve sane persons, in a general readjustment of the authorities of the institution and eventually, it is said, in the

revision of the state lunacy laws. These experiences were later published in *A Mad World and Its Inhabitants* (London, 1876; New York, 1877), an excellent piece of colorful and descriptive reporting. In 1873 he joined the staff of the *New York Herald*, serving as correspondent in various parts of the world, and for a time as city editor. In 1886 Bennett appointed him managing editor and in the following year called him to Paris to launch the Paris *Herald*. This done, Chambers returned to the managing desk in New York. In 1889 he was offered by Joseph Pulitzer the managing editorship of the New York *World*, which he retained until 1891. His remaining years were devoted to travel, literature, and many incidental jobs which offered themselves. He was non-resident lecturer on journalism at Cornell University in 1903–04 and at New York University in 1910. He published two hundred short stories and several volumes of fiction and had two plays produced in New York. In 1904 he began a column in the *Brooklyn Eagle*, called "Walks and Talks," which he continued until the day before he died. In 1912 he brought out a large volume called *The Book of New York*, containing his recollections of personal contacts with important personages during his newspaper career. At the time of his death he was engaged in revising a book for the press, *News Hunting on Three Continents* (1921), a good human-interest account of a reporter's life. Chambers was married twice: first, to Ida L. Burgess, and second, to Margaret Belvin.

[In addition to the autobiographical works cited above, see *Biog. Hist. of Cornell* (1916); *Who's Who in America*, 1918–19; obituaries in the *Brooklyn Eagle* and *N. Y. Times, Tribune, Herald, World,* and *Evening Post* for Feb. 13, 1920. Chambers wrote as Julius Chambers but stated in a letter to the Lib. of Cong. that his full name was James Julius; the "Charles Julius" given in some reference works is an error.]   M. S.

CHAMBERS, JOHN (Oct. 6, 1780–Sept. 21, 1852), congressman, governor of the territory of Iowa, was born at Bromley Bridge, Somerset County, N. J. His parents were Rowland Chambers, a veteran of the American Revolution, and Phœbe (Mullican) Chambers of Long Island. When John was fourteen years of age the family removed to Washington, then the county seat of Mason County, Ky. Shortly after the family settled in their new home John found employment in a store. During the following March he was sent by his brother to Transylvania Seminary at Lexington, Ky., where he remained until the summer vacation, a period of four months which constituted the sum total of his higher education. Upon his return to Washington he again worked in a store until he was appointed deputy clerk of the district court. During the time unoccupied in performing the duties of his new office he studied law, and applied himself so diligently that in November 1800, one month after reaching the age of twenty, he was given a license to practise. On June 16, 1803, he married Margaret Taylor of Hagerstown, Md., who died on Mar. 4, 1807. On Oct. 29, 1807, he married Hannah Taylor, a sister of his first wife. Two ivory miniatures made about this time show him as a sturdy young man with short brown hair, and his second wife as a young woman of unusual beauty. Twelve children were born of their union. During the War of 1812 he served with distinction on the staff of Gen. William Henry Harrison. As a civil officer he held many positions. In 1812 he was chosen to represent his county in the state legislature of Kentucky, and in 1815 was reëlected. In 1828 he was chosen to fill a vacancy in the House of Representatives at Washington, D. C. In 1830 and 1832 he was again elected to the state legislature. In 1835 he was returned to Congress and was reelected in 1837. On Mar. 25, 1841, he was commissioned governor of the territory of Iowa by President Harrison. He arrived at Burlington, Ia., on May 12 where he succeeded Robert Lucas in the dual capacity of governor and superintendent of Indian affairs in the territory. Despite the fact that the Democratic party predominated at that time in Iowa and Chambers was a Whig, he succeeded in administering the affairs of the territory in a way that won both local approbation and the commendation of the administration at Washington. He gave much attention to the management of Indian affairs; and as the commissioner of the United States government concluded a treaty with the Sauks and Foxes in 1842 whereby these Indians agreed to give up the remainder of their land in Iowa and to remove to Kansas. In 1844 he was reappointed to the office of governor of Iowa territory by President Tyler, but in 1845 he was removed from office by President Polk. White-haired, somewhat stooped, and with impaired health, he retired to his farm "Grouseland," a few miles west of Burlington. Shortly afterward he returned to Kentucky. In 1849 he made a journey to Minnesota to serve as a commissioner with Gov. Alexander Ramsey to treat with the Sioux. Three years later during a visit to his daughter at Paris, Ky., he was taken ill and, after a few weeks, died on Sept. 21, 1852.

[The chief source of information about Chambers is his *Autobiography* (1908), ed. by John Carl Parish (repr. from the *Iowa Jour. of Hist. and Politics,* Apr. 1908). An excellent sketch written, but not signed, by his oldest son, Jos. Sprigg Chambers, appears in the *Annals of Iowa,* ser. 1, IX, 553–61. *John Chambers* (1909), written by John Carl Parish, is a critical study.]

B. E. M.

CHAMBERS, JULIUS. [See CHAMBERS, JAMES JULIUS, 1850–1920.]

CHAMBERS, TALBOT WILSON (Feb. 25, 1819–Feb. 3, 1896), Dutch Reformed clergyman, theologian, was born at Carlisle, Pa., the son of William C. Chambers, a physician, and of Mary Ege. He was of Irish stock on his father's side and of German on his mother's. At the age of eleven he entered Dickinson College but transferred at the end of two years to Rutgers so as to study under Dr. Alexander McClelland, formerly of Dickinson, whose vigorous intellect and vivid personality exercised a decisive influence over his pupil. Upon graduating from Rutgers in 1834, he continued to study under McClelland at the New Brunswick Theological Seminary until ill health—he was frail from childhood and subject to pulmonary trouble—compelled him to leave. The year 1836–37 he spent at the Princeton Seminary. This time his course was interrupted by the financial difficulties of his parents, and in order to support himself and a younger brother he tutored in private families in Mississippi from 1837 to 1839. On Oct. 21, 1838, he was licensed to preach by the Presbytery of Clinton, Miss., but, finding himself almost immediately involved in a theological controversy in which his family was on one side and he on the other, he withdrew from the Presbyterian Church and united with the Dutch Reformed, which he had come to know during the years in New Brunswick. From 1840 to 1849 he was pastor of the Second Reformed Church of Raritan, at Somerville, N. J. On May 21, 1841, he married Louise Mercer Frelinghuysen, a daughter of Gen. John Frelinghuysen, by whom he had eleven children. During the Somerville years he dabbled surreptitiously in Whig politics, writing political editorials for a local newspaper. In December 1849 he became one of the ministers of the Collegiate Reformed Church in New York City, which he served till the end of his life. The sudden death of his wife in 1892 visibly weakened his hold on mortality, and he succumbed to pneumonia on Feb. 3, 1896.

His ministry of over half a century was active and influential. Although diligent in discharging his pastoral duties, he was chiefly interested in scholarship. He was a good linguist, with a mastery of Hebrew that made him for ten years a member of the Old Testament Company of the American Committee on the Revision of the English Bible, and with a knowledge of numerous other languages that helped him materially as chairman of the committee on versions of the American Bible Society. He was well versed in theology and in church history, and for short periods taught at Union, Lane, Alleghany, Hartford, and New Brunswick Theological Seminaries. In 1863 he was president of the General Synod of the Reformed Church. Together with Philip Schaff and James McCosh he helped to organize the Alliance of Reformed Churches Holding the Presbyterian System; in 1884 he became chairman of the Western Section and in 1892 president of the Alliance. Although his books are few and unimportant, he was a prolific writer of articles on theological and ecclesiastical topics. In his theology he was a thorough-going conservative, believing unreservedly in the integrity and sufficiency of the Bible as the revelation of God's will, and holding to the doctrines of his church as they were formulated in the early years of the Reformation. Thus cherishing the faith of his fathers, he would have seen no reproach in the fact that he displayed no originality of thought. His conservatism also manifested itself in more personal forms. He was the last minister of the Collegiate Church to maintain the use of the *exordium remotum* in the Sunday morning service, and the last to wear a dress-coat on the street in the daytime. As a divine of a now vanishing type, able, learned, devout, kind, and generous, he deserved the affection and veneration in which he was held.

[E. T. Corwin, *Manual of the Reformed Ch. in America* (4th ed., 1902); *Acts and Proc. of the 90th Regular Session of the General Synod of the Reformed Ch. in America*, June 1896, pp. 496–99; E. B. Coe, *Discourse Commemorative of the Rev. Talbot Wilson Chambers* (1896); J. P. Searle, "The Rev. Talbot Wilson Chambers," in *Presbyt. and Reformed Rev.*, VII, 577–94; bibliographies in Coe and Corwin.]   G. H. G.

CHAMPLAIN, SAMUEL de (*c.* 1567–Dec. 25, 1635), explorer and founder of Canada, was the son of a naval captain, Antoine Champlain, and his wife Marguérite, née Le Roy. He was born at Brouage in Saintonge (now Charente Inférieure), at present a neglected hamlet ten miles from Rochefort on the Bay of Biscay but in the latter half of the sixteenth century an important port, frequented by many vessels from overseas. All we know of Champlain's early life is that he eagerly listened to tales of the New World, and had a vivid curiosity to see the trans-Atlantic lands, of which he heard so much. He also had a good, practical education, was well versed in navigation, and was posted on the discoveries being made by Spanish and English vessels on the high seas. He was early drawn into the vortex of the religious wars of France,—for Brouage was the prize contended for by both Huguenot and Catholic leaguers, at one time sustaining a siege of several months, and being fortified after capture by Condé, the great Huguenot

leader. By 1589 Champlain was serving in the army of Henry of Navarre, and later joined the naval arm of Navarre's forces. Finally when peace came and the treaty of Vervins was signed in 1598, Champlain's coveted opportunity came. An uncle was chosen to pilot home a Spanish contingent in the ship *St. Julien,* and took his nephew with him. In Spain the vessel was impressed to accompany the annual Spanish flotilla to New Spain, and Champlain was selected as its commander. The Spanish as a rule excluded foreigners from their overseas possessions; this was, therefore, an unusual opportunity for a Frenchman, and one of which Champlain took full advantage. The fleet left San Lucar in January 1599, and the *St. Julien* was absent from Spain for two years and eight months; its commander visited the West Indies, Mexico, Cartagena, and the Isthmus of Panama. At the latter place he remarked on the utility of a possible canal. He made careful observations and drawings of the plants, animals, and products of New Spain, and upon his return to France drew up an elaborate report for the King. (The manuscript of this report with the original illustrations is now in the John Carter Brown Library, Providence, R. I.)

Henry IV was pleased with Champlain's observations, and gave him a pension and a patent of nobility, so that he was thereafter the Sieur de Champlain. The King also persuaded his young subject to join a French expedition setting forth to explore in the region discovered by French navigators two generations earlier. Although several of his projects had come to naught, the King, interested not only in exploration but in colonization, was eager to have Champlain attempt another. The voyage of 1603 was a preparatory one. Champlain accompanied a fur-trading expedition, which under the patronage of Aymer de Chastes, governor of Dieppe, was sailing to the Gulf of St. Lawrence under command of François Gravé, Sieur du Pont (usually called Pontgravé). After reaching Tadoussac, at the mouth of the Saguenay, where Pontgravé had already established a post, and where many natives came from the interior bringing rich furs to trade, Champlain in a pinnace ascended the St. Lawrence River, noting its natural features and its availability for a colony. He was stopped by the Lachine Rapids, but not before he had heard from Indian comrades of the great bodies of water lying at the source of the river, a report which stimulated his desire to explore interior North America. Upon his return to France in the autumn he published his first book entitled *Des Sauvages,* descriptive both of his voyage and of the inhabitants of the St. Lawrence Valley.

Chastes, the patron of the North American enterprise, had died during the summer of 1603, but the King found for the enterprise another patron in Sieur de Monts, a Huguenot noble of Champlain's own province of Saintonge. Monts was determined to found a colony in a more genial climate than that of the St. Lawrence, and, despite Champlain's protests, he directed the expedition of 1604 to a more southerly region. The first colony was founded on Douchet Island in the mouth of the St. Croix River, New Brunswick, and, that proving unhealthful, the entire enterprise was transferred in 1605 to Port Royal near the modern Annapolis Royal, Nova Scotia. Champlain was the steadying influence in the little group of exiles which maintained a precarious hold on this shore until 1607; he founded the Order of Good Company, and by his example and good cheer kept the colony alive. During these years, also, he made three exploring expeditions along the coast of New England. In the first he discovered and named Mount Desert Island, and ascended the Penobscot to the site of Bangor. In 1605 he went farther along the coast, discovered the Kennebec, Androscoggin, and Saco Rivers, sighted the White Mountains from Casco Bay, passed Cape Ann and entered Plymouth Harbor —which he named for St. Louis—and finally turned back from Nauset Harbor on Cape Cod. His third survey followed the track of the second, going as far as Stage Harbor off Vineyard Sound, where a hostile attack by the natives forced the French navigators to return to Nova Scotia.

In 1608 Champlain attained the wish of his heart when he persuaded the King to permit him to found a colony on the St. Lawrence. He and Pontgravé sailed in the ship *Le Don de Dieu*, and on July 3 Champlain laid the foundation of what proved to be the first permanent French colony in America, at Quebec. In what he called the "habitation," with twenty-eight companions, he spent the ensuing winter. In the spring he was visited by a group of Huron Indians on their way to attack their enemies the Iroquois, in central New York. Champlain consented to accompany them and on the way entered the beautiful lake that still bears his name. There, on July 30, 1609, occurred the first clash with the Iroquois, in which the French firearms put them to flight.

The assassination of Henry IV in 1610 recalled Champlain to France, where he was obliged to make new arrangements to sustain his colony and his own personal fortune. In behalf of the latter, he entered late in 1610 into a marriage contract with Hélène Boullé, twelve-year-old daughter of one of the royal secretaries. Be-

cause of the youth of the bride it was stipulated that she should remain some time with her parents. She finally came to Quebec with her husband, and passed there four years, 1616–20, after which she separated from Champlain, and ultimately entered a French convent. They never had children. Hélène Champlain's name is retained by St. Helen Island, south of Montreal, which her husband named in her honor. For the colony Champlain arranged a new charter, taken out in 1611, and found for Canada a royal patron in the person of the Prince de Condé. He then determined to undertake explorations westward and to find if possible a route to the western sea. One of his subordinates, whom he had left among the Indians, came to France with the story of a journey to the northern ocean, and in 1613 Champlain set forth to ascertain the truth of this report. He advanced up the Ottawa River, noting its rapids and portages, as far as Morrison Island, where was the Indian village his man had previously visited. There he learned to his sorrow that he had been deceived, and that his informant had never been beyond this point. He learned here, however, more of the inland lakes and planned to explore them at his first opportunity.

This came in 1615 when he accompanied a band of Huron Indians to their home on Georgian Bay. As he had been preceded to Huronia by several traders and a Recollect missionary all of the Great Lakes had been seen by white men before him; he was, however, the first to describe, map, and name Lake Huron, and may well be called its discoverer. He reached it by the Ottawa River, Lake Nipissing, and its outlet into Georgian Bay, and called it *La Mer Douce,* the Fresh Sea. Coasting southward along the bay to the Huron habitat he encountered Ottawa Indians, whom, because of the crests they wore, he spoke of as the "Nation of the Staring Hairs." Arrived at Huronia he was welcomed with acclaim, and soon set out with his Indian allies on another excursion against the Iroquois. Leaving the Huron villages, Sept. 1, the war party passed southeastward to Lake Ontario, which Champlain named "Great Lake of the Entouhonorons," and recognized as the source of the St. Lawrence.

The party then crossed the eastern end of the lake and went inland along the Oneida River until on Oct. 10 they came in sight of an Iroquois fort, located probably on Nichols Pond, Madison County, N. Y. A siege began, in which after desperate fighting—Champlain being severely wounded by poisoned arrows—the French and Hurons were repulsed. They rapidly retreated by the way they had come, and although

Champlain had planned to go to Quebec via the St. Lawrence, his wounded condition made it necessary for him to accompany the Hurons home. There he recovered during the winter, and explored for some distance beyond Huronia to the west. After returning to France in 1616 he embodied his knowledge of the Great Lakes in a map, which was published with the edition of his *Voyages* in 1632.

This voyage of 1615–16 marks the extent of Champlain's personal explorations. Thenceforward he devoted himself to the upbuilding of the colony of New France, and to its economic and agricultural development. From 1620 to 1624 he remained in Canada, and in 1625 succeeded in interesting Cardinal Richelieu in France's overseas domain so that two years later this minister formed the Company of One Hundred Associates to provide and equip colonists for New France. Meanwhile Champlain succeeded in making a treaty of alliance with the formidable Iroquois, and all promised well for the colony's progress. Suddenly, while France and England were engaged in a petty war, a fleet of British freebooters descended upon the St. Lawrence and captured Quebec. Champlain and all his officials were transported. During his exile of four years (1629–33) in Europe, he brought out the final edition of his *Voyages*.

In 1632 France and England signed the treaty of St. Germain by which Canada was restored to the French Crown. Early in the succeeding year Champlain returned as governor of his colony, never more to leave it during life. His arrival was hailed with acclaim both by colonists and tribesmen. With the latter he rebuilt his alliances and arranged in 1634 to send his envoy Jean Nicolet to explore the West. Nicolet's return the next year, with the news of the discovery of Lake Michigan and Green Bay, cheered the veteran governor. By this expedition New France was extended westward many leagues. This was the last important act of Champlain's administration. His death on Christmas Day was deplored by the entire colony, for he had no enemies. He was buried in a new chapel of the parish church of Quebec.

As none of the so-called portraits of Champlain are authentic, we have no knowledge of his physical appearance. His characteristics appear in his writings: he was simple, sincere, and steadfast, without ostentation or pride; he preferred life in the open to that of courts, yet he was no mean courtier and was respected by king and nobles alike. His appreciation of the natives of America was deep and sincere, and by his sympathy for them he had much influence over the savages. His vision and foresight for the colony's needs earned for him the title of Father of New France.

[Champlain's writings were voluminous and appeared at frequent intervals during his lifetime. After *Des Sauvages* describing his voyage of 1603, appeared *Les Voyages du Sieur de Champlain* (Paris, 1613), in which was included his map of 1612. *Voyages et Descouvertes faites en la Nouvelle France* (Paris, 1619), carried his account to 1618. While in exile from his colony (1629–33) he prepared a third volume entitled: *Les Voyages de la Nouvelle France Occidentale dicte Canada . . . depuis l'an 1603 jusques en l'an 1629* (Paris, 1632), including a map of the St. Lawrence and its sources. He also wrote a treatise on navigation entitled *Traitté de la Marine et du Devoir d'un bon Marinier de la Navigation.* His *Brief Discours* of his West Indies voyage was not published until the 19th century. *Œuvres de Champlain,* edited by Abbé C. H. Laverdière (6 vols., Quebec, 1870) is the standard edition. *The Works of Samuel de Champlain* published by the Champlain Society (Toronto, 1922–27) contains the French text and English translation. His biographers are C. W. Colby, *The Founder of New France* (Toronto, 1915); Edwin A. Dix, *Champlain* (N. Y., 1903); Ralph Flenley, *Samuel de Champlain* (Toronto, 1924); Gabriel Gravier, *Vie de Samuel Champlain* (Paris, 1900).]

L.P.K.]

CHAMPLIN, JOHN DENISON (Jan. 29, 1834–Jan. 8, 1915), editor, author, traced his ancestry to Geoffrey Champlin who settled at Newport, R. I., in 1638. He was the son of John Denison and Sylvia (Bostwick) Champlin. The name Denison, borne by his father and himself, was derived from William Denison, of Bishop Stortford, Hertfordshire, England.

He received his early education at the Hopkins Grammar School, New Haven, Conn., whence he entered Yale College in 1852, graduating in 1856. With a strong leaning toward law, he began its study in the office of Gideon H. Hollister at Litchfield, Conn., where in 1859 he was admitted to the bar. After practising for a time in Milwaukee, he became a member of the law firm of Hollister, Cross, & Champlin in New York City, whither Hollister had removed. Champlin's literary interests were, however, already gaining the ascendency, and he collaborated in the writing of a tragedy, *Thomas à Becket* (1866), produced by Edwin Booth in New Orleans in 1861. After a period of free-lancing, in 1864 he became associate editor of the Bridgeport *Evening Standard.* Finding himself hampered in his work by his associates, he decided to remove to Litchfield, and start a paper of his own. So in 1865 he established the *Litchfield Sentinel,* a weekly newspaper devoted to Democratic interests. After four years, he sold this paper in order to remove to New York and engage in other literary enterprises. From the Journal of J. F. Loubart, he wrote a *Narrative of the Mission to Russia, in 1866, of the Honorable Gustavus Vasa Fox,* which occupied him during the years 1872–73. Toward the end of the latter year, he became one of the revisers of the *American Cyclopædia*, becoming associate editor in 1875, especially in charge of the maps and engravings. Between the years 1878 and 1881 he originated and edited a series of Young Folk's Cyclopædias covering common things, persons and places, astronomy and history. Going to Europe in 1884, he accompanied Andrew Carnegie on a coaching trip along the south coast of England, and this he described in his *Chronicle of the Coach* (1886). In conjunction with Arthur E. Bostwick, he published the *Young Folk's Cyclopædia of Games and Sports* in 1890. As an editor of books he was first engaged by Charles Scribner's Sons, producing for that firm the *Cyclopædia of Painters and Paintings* (1886–87) and the *Cyclopædia of Music and Musicians* (1888–90). He then joined the editorial staff of the *Standard Dictionary* (1892–94). In 1901 he added to the Young Folk's Cyclopædia series a volume on *Literature and Art*, and in 1905 one on *Natural History*. In 1910 he edited the *Orations, Addresses, and Speeches of Chauncey M. Depew*. His "One Hundred Allied Families of the Seventeenth Century in England and New England," and "Anne Hutchinson: Her Life, Her Ancestry and Her Descendants," both written in 1912, remained unpublished. He was married, on Oct. 8, 1873, to Franka Eliza, daughter of Capt. George M. Colvocoresses [*q.v.*], of the United States Navy.

[*Records of the Colony of R. I. and Providence Plantations*, I, 91; "John Denison Champlin," by his son John D. Champlin, Jr. in *N. Y. Geneal. and Biog. Record*, Oct. 1915; *Records of the Class of 1856 of Yale College* (1878, 1892); *Obit. Record of Grads. of Yale Univ.* (1915); *Who's Who in America*, 1914–15.]
F. H. V.

CHAMPLIN, JOHN WAYNE (Feb. 7, 1831–July 24, 1901), jurist, was a descendant in the direct line of Geoffrey Champlin, who, coming from England to Rhode Island, settled at Newport. John's father, Jeffrey Champlin, married Ellis Champlin, a member of a collateral branch of the family, and resided at Kingston, Ulster County, N. Y., where John was born. Shortly afterward the family moved to a farm at Harpersfield, Delaware County, where John spent his early youth, attending the village school in winter and working on the farm in the summer. In 1844 he went to Stamford Grammar School, proceeding later to Rhinebeck and Harpersfield Academies, and then taking a course of civil engineering at Delaware Literary Institute, Franklin, N. Y. In 1852 he began to practise as a civil engineer in Delaware County but two years later, seeking a wider field, joined his

brother Stephen G. Champlin in Grand Rapids, Mich., and took up the study of law in the latter's office. On his admission to the Michigan bar in June 1855 he commenced practise in Grand Rapids, with which city he continued associated for the remainder of his life. Evincing at the outset a deep interest in municipal problems he was retained in 1856 to draft the charter of the City of Grand Rapids which was passed by the legislature in the following year. Champlin was also appointed city solicitor in 1857, continuing as such for three years, in the course of which he became recognized as the leading authority in the state on the subject of municipal law and practise. He retired in 1861 and became judge of the recorder's court of Grand Rapids, retaining that position for two years. In 1863 he was an unsuccessful candidate for the position of circuit judge, but in 1864 was elected prosecuting attorney for Kent County and as such displayed great efficiency and impartiality. In 1867 he was elected mayor of Grand Rapids on the Democratic ticket. During his tenure of office he incurred great unpopularity by opposing the issue of bonds of the city for the purpose of bonusing railways, and failed of reëlection, but was subsequently vindicated by the supreme court of Michigan which pronounced the city's action unconstitutional. In 1883 he was nominated by the Fusion party for the office of justice of the supreme court, was elected by a large vote, and took his seat on the bench, Jan. 1, 1884. Becoming chief justice in 1890, he retired, Dec. 31, 1891, and resumed practise in Grand Rapids. In 1892 he was appointed professor in the law department of the University of Michigan where he lectured on corporations and torts, but resigned in 1896. He died at Grand Rapids, July 24, 1901. He was married to Ellen, daughter of John B. More of Roxbury, N. Y.

In legal circles he was esteemed as a competent, conscientious, careful judge, though not distinguished by any deep learning except in relation to municipal law, in which he was an expert. His opinions were marked by extreme clarity of thought, and both at the bar and as a judge he was the essence of courtesy, exhibiting marvelous patience on the bench in listening to arguments of counsel. Politically, he was a Democrat, but never extreme in his convictions, and he supported the Lincoln administration in its war measures. In his later years he abstained from active participation in public affairs.

[*Mag. of Western Hist.*, IV, 692; *City of Grand Rapids and Kent County, Mich. up to Date* (1900), p. 25; *Green Bag*, II, 394; 91 *Mich.*, 47; *Grand Rapids Herald*, July 25, 1901.]
H. W. H. K.

CHAMPLIN, STEPHEN (Nov. 17, 1789–
Feb. 20, 1870), naval officer, was born at South
Kingston, R. I. His father, Stephen, had served
in the Revolution, probably at sea, and his mother Elizabeth Perry was an aunt of Commodores
O. H. and M. C. Perry [*qq.v.*]. About 1795 the
family moved to a farm near Lebanon, Conn.,
where Stephen worked and went to school till
he was sixteen, when he ran away to sea. By
1812 he had risen to captain and made numerous
voyages, one with his cousin Oliver Perry, a
midshipman on leave. When war was declared
he became a sailing master in the navy, May 22,
1812, serving in Perry's gunboats at Newport
and then accompanying him to the Great Lakes
in February 1813. As second in command of the
Asp on Lake Ontario he engaged in the expeditions against York and Fort George. In
command of the small, fast schooner *Scorpion*
(2 guns) at the battle of Lake Erie, he was in
the van throughout the action and in the thick
of the fighting, firing the first shot and also the
last. His narrative of the battle, in strong support of Perry, figures in the literature of the
Perry-Elliott controversy. The *Scorpion* was
later engaged in transporting Harrison's army
to Malden and accompanying it up the Thames;
and during the winter Champlin had charge of
the prizes *Detroit* and *Queen Charlotte* at Put-
in-Bay. In command of the *Tigress* he took part
in the unsuccessful attack on Mackinac, Aug.
4, 1814, and was afterward left to blockade the
post. On the night of Sept. 3 an overwhelming
enemy force in batteaux and canoes surprised
and captured his schooner in the St. Mary's
River. Though perhaps negligent in permitting
the surprise, Champlin and his men defended
their vessel vigorously, all the officers being
wounded, and Champlin receiving a canister shot
through the thigh, shattering the bone. After
detention for thirty-eight days, with great suffering, he was paroled to Erie, and thence went
to Connecticut, arriving in March 1815. During 1816–18 he commanded the *Porcupine* on the
upper lakes, surveying the Canadian boundary.
Thereafter, owing to recurrent trouble from his
wound, he saw little active service, living in
Connecticut until 1834 and then in Buffalo. For
a month in 1828 he was attached to the steam
battery *Fulton* in New York; in 1838 during the
"Patriot War" he commanded two steamers,
operating to prevent movement of armed men
into Canada; and in 1845–48 he commanded
the lake station ship *Michigan*. He remained
on the active list until 1855, being promoted lieutenant, Dec. 9, 1814, captain, 1850, and commodore, retired, 1867. At his death he was the last

officer survivor of the battle of Lake Erie. He
was a stout, thickset man, thoroughly upright in
character, strictly abstemious, simple and rather
rough in manner and dress. Generally esteemed,
he was spoken of for mayor of Buffalo, but declined the nomination because of his naval position. He was married to Minerva L. Pomeroy
of Buffalo on Jan. 5, 1817, and was survived by
three sons and two daughters.

[Geo. Clinton, in *Buffalo Hist. Soc. Pubs.*, VIII,
381 ff., an excellent sketch based on Champlin's private
papers; the "Dobbins Papers" in the same volume;
Usher Parsons, "Brief Sketches of the Officers Who
Were in the Battle of Lake Erie," in *New Eng. Hist.
and Geneal. Reg.*, Jan. 1863; J. B. Lossing, *Pictorial
Field-Book of the War of 1812* (see index).]   A. W.

CHAMPNEY, BENJAMIN (Nov. 17, 1817–
Dec. 11, 1907), painter, born at New Ipswich,
N. H., was one of the seven children of Ebenezer
and Rebecca (Brooks) Champney. The father,
a lawyer, died young, leaving his widow poor.
Benjamin at the age of ten was sent to an aunt
at Lebanon, N. H., where he attended the district school twelve weeks each winter and
worked in a cotton-mill forty weeks. After four
years he returned to his mother and entered
Appleton Academy, intending to take advantage
of a West Point cadetship promised him by
Franklin Pierce, then a representative. "Like
many other congressmen he made too many
promises," Champney afterward wrote of Pierce.
Disappointed, the boy obtained a clerkship with
Henry L. Daggett, a Boston shoe-dealer. From
the shop's back window he looked into a lithographer's studio where he saw artists and engravers at work. For years he had drawn pictures and he was now emboldened to think of
this as a means of livelihood. He went one day
into the lithographic place, but, receiving only
discouragement, resumed selling shoes. A little
later, however, Robert Cooke, head draftsman
at the lithographer's, took a room at Champney's boarding-house and the two became friends.
Cooke directed Champney's drawing and aided
him in securing admittance as an apprentice
in Moore's lithographic establishment. Here
Champney did commercial work, having among
his associates William Rimmer [*q.v.*]. Then,
together with Cooke, he opened a studio for portraiture. The two had success, and saved money
for study abroad, sailing May 1, 1841. At Paris
they studied with Boudin, and copied at the
Louvre. Champney became friendly with J. F.
Kensett and the veteran John Vanderlyn, the
latter employing him as assistant in painting
"The Landing of Columbus," for the Capitol at
Washington. Kensett and Champney made trips
to Fontainebleau, where they painted from na-

ture, then an unusual practise. Champney exhibited in the Salon and sent to Boston copies from old masters which were sold. In 1846 he returned to America in the *Anglo-Saxon,* wrecked off Nova Scotia. After a brief stay, he sailed back to Europe with W. Allan Gay to paint a panorama of the Rhine. Though interrupted by the political upheaval of 1848 they finished the gigantic piece which was exhibited in 1849 at the Horticultural Building, Boston. It was financially unsuccessful and in 1853 was destroyed in the Crystal Palace fire in New York. Turning his attention to landscape, Champney in 1850 discovered North Conway, N. H., as painting ground. He was joined by Kensett, Alfred Ordway, and others. "By 1853," he wrote, "the meadows and banks of the Saco were dotted all about with white umbrellas." In 1853 he married Mary C. Brooks and bought at North Conway a house which was their summer home. Their winters were spent at Woburn. In 1855 Champney was one of the founders of the Boston Art Club, of which he became president in 1856 and in whose exhibitions he was frequently represented. His later life was quiet and uneventful. As a painter he followed the formula of the so-called Hudson River school which lost its vogue in the late nineteenth century. He was a catholic critic of other artists' work,— an admirer of the Barbizon painters long before their merits were generally appreciated and of Claude Monet before the impressionists' theory of values was popularly understood. He is well represented at the Boston Art Club and the Woburn Public Library.

[Champney's autobiographical *Sixty Years' Memories of Art and Artists* (1900), and the *Boston Post,* Dec. 12, 1907.]   F. W. C.

CHAMPNEY, JAMES WELLS (July 16, 1843–May 1, 1903), painter, illustrator, a son of James H. and Sarah (Wells) Champney, was born at Boston where when he was sixteen years old he was apprenticed to a wood engraver. He enlisted in the 45th Massachusetts Volunteers and saw service at Gettysburg. After the war he taught drawing at Dr. Dio Lewis's school in Lexington, Mass., and then, in 1866, went to Paris, where he studied with Edouard Frère, a genre painter. He had also a year at Antwerp under Van Lerius. He exhibited in the 1869 Salon, signing his pictures "Champ" to distinguish himself from the other American Champneys. Back in Boston in 1870, he returned to France in 1871 in time to witness the excitement of the Commune. He then made a sketching tour of Germany which included studies of the Passion Play at Ober-Ammergau,—

a topic on which he afterward lectured. In 1873 he accompanied Edward King to make drawings for a series of *Scribner's Monthly* articles on the "Great South." They traveled about 20,000 miles and Champney did more than 500 sketches. During the same year he married Elizabeth Williams. As illustrator and war correspondent he visited the camp of Don Carlos, then campaigning for the Spanish crown. In 1877 he accepted the professorship of art at Smith College, a position which he held seven years. For *Scribner's* he made a sketching tour of South America in 1878, illustrating articles by Herbert Smith. He directed the art classes of the Hartford Society of Decorative Art, and maintained a winter studio at New York. In 1885 he began to make pastel portraits, having among his sitters Hon. John Bigelow, Henry M. Stanley, William Winter, and many theatrical people. He was represented at the Chicago Exposition, 1893, by his portraits of the Rev. Robert Collyer, Miss Suzanna Sheldon, and his wife. He painted many "translations" into pastel of famous masterpieces in the European galleries. In 1898 he did important decorations for the Hotel Manhattan, New York. As a painter he was one of the first Americans to understand and apply the theory of "values" which the French impressionists, Manet, Monet, and others, had developed. Among pastellists he was ranked in his own day with Whistler and Robert Blum.

[S. G. W. Benjamin, *Our Am. Artists* (1881), pp. 32–35; G. C. de Soisson, "J. Wells Champney, an Am. Pastellist," in the *Artist,* XXIX, 159–61.] F. W. C.

CHANCHE, JOHN MARY JOSEPH (Oct. 4, 1795–July 22, 1852), first Roman Catholic bishop of Natchez, Miss., was the son of John Chanche, a merchant and, it was said, a man of considerable wealth, who, fleeing from the negro disturbances in San Domingo, came to Baltimore with his wife Catherine Provost. There John Mary Joseph was born. He entered St. Mary's College at the age of eleven and presently joined the Sulpician community which conducted it, receiving Holy Orders at Baltimore, June 5, 1819. Following some years of teaching he was made vice-president and, in 1834, president of his alma mater. After twice refusing nomination as bishop-coadjutor of eastern sees, he accepted (Dec. 15, 1840) appointment to the newly-erected diocese of Natchez. Soon after his consecration at Baltimore by Archbishop Eccleston, Mar. 14, 1841, he set out for the South. Though the church in Mississippi was then over a century old and had received the support of the Spanish government probably until 1791, its state was such that Bishop Chanche virtually had to found it anew. The land and buildings in Natchez with which Spain had provided the mission had been lost when the American government took possession of the region, probably because title to them had been vested in the Spanish government. No claim was entered until Bishop Chanche came in May 1841. The search for evidence of ecclesiastical right to these properties led the bishop to Cuba in 1844 and to other parts of Spanish America. He presented the evidence which he discovered to Congress and petitioned that the church be indemnified in money or in lands of equal extent or value with those originally granted. His petition was never returned. Bishop Chanche was, however, too practical a man to wait the issue of this claim. He drew immediately on funds which the Association for the Propagation of the Faith had prior to his coming annually deposited with the bishop of New Orleans for the support of the Natchez mission. He solicited contributions from European missionary societies. He pressed the congregation which had led a precarious existence at Natchez during the American period. His determination to succeed was plainly stated in his first address to it the day after his arrival. "If I meet encouragement I will stay with you; if not I seek a home elsewhere. I am not bound to Natchez, but to the state of Mississippi." His success may be concretely measured by the progress of his cathedral, in its day a large church, and noted for its Gothic architectural beauty. The corner-stone of the edifice was laid on Feb. 28, 1842, and it was dedicated on Christmas Day. At this time however Bishop Chanche had but two priests and a hundred communicants. The Catholic population was thinly distributed over about fifty thousand square miles of territory. When he died he had eleven priests, and he had laid the foundations of an educational system that would indirectly develop vocations. In 1848 he had introduced Sisters of Charity from Emmitsburg, Md., and they promptly opened a school and presently an orphan asylum in Natchez. In the state at large there were on his death eleven churches and seventeen attendant missions, and missionary activity among the negroes also was well under way. Returning to Natchez from the First Plenary Council of Baltimore, of which he had been an earnest promoter, Bishop Chanche fell ill of cholera morbus, and died at Frederick City, Md., July 22, 1852. His was a tall and commanding figure, graceful and dignified of carriage, and an attractive and winning personality, urbane and cultivated of manner.

[See John G. Shea, *Hist. of the Cath. Ch. in the U. S.* (1892), IV, 275–79; Richard Henry Clarke, *Lives of the Deceased Bishops of the Cath. Ch. in the U. S.* (1872), II, 166–90; Francis Janssens, *Sketch of the Cath. Ch. in the City of Natchez . . .* (1886); *Metropolitan Cath. Almanac and Laity's Directory . . . 1853* (1852). *The Am. Cath. Hist. Researches* (1884) printed Bishop Chanche's memorial to Congress (IV, 146–47) and other items relating to the Natchez mission prior to his coming (IV, 147–51; XIX, 64; XX, 48). Scattered data of value may be found in the *Catholic Almanac* for 1853, and the *Annalen der Verbreitung des Glaubens* (Einsiedeln-Mainz, 1832).]   F.J.T.

CHANDLER, CHARLES FREDERICK (Dec. 6, 1836–Aug. 25, 1925), industrial chemist, was born in Lancaster, Mass., in the house of his grandfather, and his boyhood was spent with his parents, Charles and Sarah (Whitney) Chandler, at New Bedford, Mass., where his father owned and conducted a dry-goods store. A few lectures by Louis Agassiz that he heard as a boy aroused his scientific curiosity, and at the age of sixteen he was a student of chemistry at the Lawrence Scientific School of Harvard University. As a youth he had been diligent in making chemical experiments and in collecting minerals, and when in 1855, acting on the advice of Charles A. Joy, professor of chemistry at Union College, he sailed for Europe to study under Woehler at Göttingen, he took his collection with him, having learned that it would be likely to interest Woehler. This Yankee shrewdness, together with Chandler's earnestness and personal attractiveness, soon won for him the favor of being made Woehler's private assistant for the semester. He then went to Berlin to study analytical chemistry under Heinrich Rose, whose private assistant he became, while also studying mineralogy under Gustav Rose. Later he returned to Göttingen where he obtained his doctorate. Coming home, he first sought consulting practise in New Bedford among the whale-oil merchants, but could not make a living at it. He offered an article to the *Scientific American* on the preparation and use for lamps of mineral oil obtained from shale in Scotland, but it was rejected on the ground that the use of mineral oil in lamps was too fantastic a notion for publication. He then heard that Prof. Joy needed an assistant at Union College, and he made the journey thither to apply for the post in person, only to learn that, while Prof. Joy did need an assistant the trustees had decided to secure a janitor instead. So Chandler accepted the position of janitor at a wage of $400 a year, swept and cleaned the laboratory before and after hours, and meanwhile acted as Prof. Joy's assistant during the day. As a side issue, the janitor taught mineralogy. Soon fortune rewarded him. Prof. Joy was called to Columbia College, and the twenty-year-old janitor became full professor of chemistry.

Chandler had a tiger's appetite for work. He taught chemistry (including assaying), geology, and mineralogy; he made an outstanding collection of minerals; and for eight years he did important consulting work in regard to water supplies and other subjects at Schenectady. In 1864 he was invited by Prof. Egleston, theretofore a mining engineer, to join him in establishing a school of mines at Columbia. Professors were to get their living from tuition fees, and $3,000 had been raised to equip the laboratories. This, in 1864, was the beginning of the Columbia School of Mines, of which Chandler was dean for many years. On Prof. Joy's death he took over his work for the College, remaining at the head of the department of chemistry at Columbia after it became a university, until his retirement in 1910.

Few teachers have exercised so great an influence on so many students. They were like sons to him, he was jealous for their welfare, was always available for advice and help, and constantly took the position that to study chemistry was easy and intensely interesting rather than hard or dull. He worked day and night with extraordinary intensity, and yet never seemed hurried. And he regarded physical science as the grandest sport of his day. At the time of his retirement grateful alumni established in his honor the Chandler Lectureship and the Chandler medal for research in chemistry.

Chandler's work at Columbia, however, was only a small part of his total achievement. The New York College of Pharmacy, then a struggling little school, had no one to teach chemistry, and no money to pay for it. Chandler gave the lectures and laboratory instruction at nights, free, until the school grew and could pay. Later he became president of the College of Pharmacy which was eventually taken over by Columbia. In 1866 he had an income of $1,500 a year and he needed more. Without giving up any of his teaching, paid or unpaid, he engaged with Booth & Edgar, sugar refiners, to do their chemical work and conduct research as to improvement in their methods. This he did from 6 to 8 a. m. daily in a laboratory in the refinery at King and West Sts., some four or five miles distant from Columbia. Thus he doubled his income to $3,000 a year. In 1872 the College of Physicians and Surgeons invited him to become adjunct professor of chemistry. Soon he was made full professor of chemistry and also professor of medical jurisprudence.

He became a leading authority on water supplies, sanitation, oil refining, and assaying. The system of assay weights now in general use, whereby the amount of metal in a ton of ore is easily and quickly computed in grams or ounces, was worked out by him in 1866. He served the United States government on many commissions, but his outstanding public service was to New York City as president of its Board of Health. In 1866 members of the Board had asked him to make scientific studies of their sanitary problems. They had no appropriation for the purpose, but that did not deter the young professor, who was then but twenty-nine years of age, working from six to eight every morning in the laboratory of a sugar refinery, struggling all day to build up the School of Mines, and lecturing and teaching several nights a week without pay at the College of Pharmacy. In time a modest honorarium was appropriated by the city for his services, and in 1873 he was appointed to the presidency of the Board by Mayor Havemeyer, the appointment being renewed for a term of six years more by Mayor Ely in 1877. Chandler immediately addressed himself to the food and water supplies of the city, the adulteration of liquors, poisonous cosmetics, and gas nuisances. The water was good, foods were fair, adulteration of liquors less than anticipated, but poisonous cosmetics, kerosene accidents, and gas nuisances were common. Milk he found generally adulterated with one-third water after some of the cream had been removed. He established flash-point tests for kerosene and reduced lamp explosions in such a marked degree that he was invited to appear before the House of Lords to enlighten the British government on the subject. His war against milk adulteration and his subsequent control of the supply was probably the hardest battle of his life, but he succeeded and became a pioneer in municipal milk control. He fought the gas companies and made them put a stop to their nuisances. Another battle against offenses was with slaughterhouses and rendering establishments, and still other difficult undertakings were the control of contagious diseases and the establishment of compulsory vaccination. He reduced the child death rate so as to save 5,000 young lives annually. Plumbing was crude and very defective. He designed the flush closet now in general use and made no attempt to patent the idea, giving it to the plumbing trade in the hope of more healthful homes. He was, as Elihu Root said, "one of the most effective crusaders of his time in behalf of the public good." Eminent as a sanitarian, he was equally eminent as an industrial chemist. He established the 66° Baumé test for sulphuric acid when standards were in a state of conspicuous confusion, and in the early development of the petroleum industry he was the foremost consultant in America. In 1920 the Perkin Medal of the Society of Chemical Industries was conferred on him because he had made "such valuable contributions to applied chemistry" as to place the entire world in his debt.

Chandler was married twice. His only child, the first wife of the present Viscount Exmouth, died before him.

[*Columbia Alumni News*, June 15, 1926, being the Chandler Memorial Number ; *Industrial and Engineering Chem.*, Oct. 1925 ; *N. Y. Times*, Aug. 26, 1925.]

E. H.

CHANDLER, ELIZABETH MARGARET (Dec. 24, 1807–Nov. 2, 1834), author, born at Centre, Del., was the youngest of the three children of Thomas Chandler, descended from English Quaker settlers along the Delaware River, and his wife, Margaret Evans of Burlington, N. J. Her mother died while Elizabeth was a baby, and Thomas Chandler removed to Philadelphia, where he placed his daughter in the care of her grandmother Evans. Elizabeth attended schools managed by the Society of Friends and was strictly trained in religion by her grandmother. When she was nine her father died, and this loss, combined with her religious education, made her unchildishly reflective. At thirteen she left school, but she had acquired the habits of reading and writing, which were her favorite occupations throughout her short life. Friends published some of her essays and poems, anonymously, for she was timid and feared publicity. At sixteen she was writing much for the press and her articles were copied by various newspapers. She had never cared for the amusements of her day and seldom went out except to meetings of the Friends. She had become much interested in philanthropy, especially in the anti-slavery cause, and most of her writing was now concerning the wrongs of slavery. Her best known poem, "The Slave Ship," published in the *Casket,* received a prize and was copied by Benjamin Lundy, editor of the *Genius of Universal Emancipation,* who asked its author to become a regular contributor. Many of her poems on slavery appeared in the *Genius,* among them "The Wife's Lament," "The Recaptured Slave," and "The Slave's Appeal." In 1829 she took charge of the "female department" of the *Genius,* where she soon published an "Appeal to the Ladies of the United States" concerning slavery, which is said to have caused some women to emancipate their slaves. In 1830 she went with her brother and aunt to make a new home in the Territory of Michigan. There on a farm, which they christened "Hazelbank," in Lenawee County, she continued by mail her editorial work for the *Genius.* Her work was interrupted by an illness, called

"remittent fever," which after some months ended in her death. A portrait of her shows a full oval face, with large dark eyes under heavy arching brows, dark hair piled high on her head, a bow mouth, and an expression of happy alertness not suggestive of her serious nature. Two volumes of her writings were published after her death : *Essays, Philanthropic and Moral* (1836) and *Poetical Works of Elizabeth Margaret Chandler; with a Memoir of Her Life and Character* (1836), by Benjamin Lundy. Her work is inspired by a burning moral purpose, but viewed as literature, her best poetry is not her slavery verse but that expressing her love of beauty and tenderness for associations, as in "The Brandywine," "Schuylkill," "The Sunset Hour," and "Summer Morning."

[Benj. Lundy, *ante* ; Rufus W. Griswold, *The Female Poets of America* (1859) ; *Phila. Am. Sentinel*, Nov. 28, 1834.]

S. G. B.

CHANDLER, JOHN (Feb. 1, 1762–Sept. 25, 1841), soldier, senator, a descendant of William Chandler, who settled in Roxbury in 1637, and the son of Capt. Joseph and Lydia (Eastman) Chandler, was born in Epping, N. H. In 1777, a year after the death of his father, who was a veteran of the Seven Years' War and a soldier of the Revolution, Chandler enlisted in the patriot army for three months, participating in the battle of Saratoga. In January 1779 he joined the crew of the privateer *Arnold,* which was later captured by the British ship-of-war *Enterprise.* Chandler escaped from the prison ship on which he was confined and made his way home to New Hampshire. In 1780 he served a further term of six months in the army. Influenced by a fellow townsman and faithful friend who afterward was a great help to him in business, politics, and military affairs, he took part in the "Epping exodus" and purchased land in the plantation of Wales in the District of Maine (incorporated as the town of Monmouth in 1792). He settled there late in February 1784 with his wife, Mary Whittier (also spelled Whitcher) whom he had married on Aug. 28, 1783. In a community of poor men, he was perhaps the poorest, but by constant industry—shoeing horses, keeping tavern and store, building and operating sawmills, farming —he soon acquired a competence, shrewd practises, according to his neighbors, aiding his natural diligence and frugality. His scanty education had been added to after he reached manhood by studies under the local schoolmaster. He therefore filled acceptably various local offices, including those of postmaster and town clerk. During 1803, 1804, and 1819 he was a Massachusetts state senator, and in 1805 and 1806 a member of the national House of Representatives. As sheriff of Kennebec County, 1808–12 (John Chandler, *post*, p. 2), he performed with credit the difficult task of bringing harmony and order out of the animosities resulting from land controversies. Having all this time been a zealous member of the Massachusetts militia, in which he had risen to be major-general of the 17th Division, he resigned on Nov. 18, 1812, to accept a commission as brigadier-general in the United States Army. During the War of 1812 he served for the most part in New York and Upper Canada, being injured and captured in the battle of Stony Creek, June 6, 1813. His conduct during the battle was the cause of some controversy, from which he emerged with credit, although it cannot be said that his attainments as a military officer were exceptional. He was exchanged on Apr. 19, 1814, but his injuries, from which he suffered the remainder of his life, did not permit him to engage in service again until August, when he took charge of the United States forces in Maine. Later he had charge of the defenses of Portsmouth, N. H., performing his duties tactfully with due regard to militia politics. After the treaty of peace he retired from the army and returned to Monmouth to devote himself to business and politics. Influenced to favor the separation of Maine from Massachusetts by political considerations and by the dilatory conduct of Massachusetts while the coast of Maine was being ravaged in the war, he was a member of the convention which met at Portland, Oct. 11, 1819, to form the constitution of Maine. The first state legislature elected him and his political friend, John Holmes, to the United States Senate. In 1823 he was reëlected. As a Jacksonian he opposed internal improvements and the United States Bank. He took a prominent part, however, in the debate which resulted in the construction of the military road from the Penobscot River to Houlton, Me. He was also a member of the board of directors of the United States Branch Bank at Portland in 1829 and 1830. By appointment of President Jackson he served eight years as collector of customs for the district of Portland and Falmouth, declining reappointment at the age of seventy-five.

[The most important account of Chandler's life is his manuscript autobiography owned by the Me. Hist. Soc. Extracts from this have been printed with many changes in punctuation and grammar in the *Me. Hist. Soc. Colls.*, IX, 167–206. The references to Chandler in H. H. Cochrane's *Hist. of Monmouth and Wales* (1894), vol. I, *passim*, successfully counterbalance the fulsome eulogy of W. H. Smith in the *Granite Mo.*, VII, 5–12. Geo. Chandler's *Chandler Family* (1883), gives the Chandler ancestry in detail and contains a short sketch of John Chandler on pages 401–04.]   R. E. M.

CHANDLER, JOSEPH RIPLEY (Aug. 25, 1792–July 10, 1880), journalist, congressman, the son of Joseph and Saba (Ripley) Chandler of Kingston, Mass., was educated in the common schools of Kingston and at the University of Pennsylvania. He taught in the common schools for a time and in 1815 opened a seminary for young ladies in Philadelphia. This he conducted for a number of years. In 1822 he became editorial writer on the *Gazette of the United States*, the celebrated Federalist organ started in 1780 by John Fenno. In 1826, together with two others, Chandler purchased the paper (later merged with the *North American*), editing it until 1847 when he resigned because of ill health. From October 1843 to December 1849, he edited *Graham's American Monthly Magazine of Literature, Art and Fashion*. When Girard College was established, he became president of the first board of directors in 1848. The same year he published his *Grammar of the English Language* for use in the public schools. A Freemason from his early manhood, he had become Grand Master of Pennsylvania when in 1849 he was converted to Catholicism. The same year he was elected as a Clay Whig to Congress where he served three terms. In 1855 he delivered in the House a brilliant speech on "The Temporal Power of the Pope" (*Congressional Globe*, 33 Cong., 2 Sess., App.), which was an attack on the movement to deny full rights of citizenship to Roman Catholics. Abhorring religious intolerance, he delivered an equally commendable oration in 1855 at the celebration of the landing of "the Pilgrims of Maryland." Both speeches were published in book form. In 1858 he was appointed by President Buchanan minister to the Two Sicilies, where he remained for three years. On his return, he became deeply interested in a variety of philanthropic enterprises, especially in the reform of county prison conditions, personally visiting many prisons every year. In 1872, the Philadelphia Society for Alleviating the Miseries of Public Prisons sent him as representative to the international Congress in London. He visited many European penal establishments and upon his return wrote a most comprehensive report of the Congress, with discriminating criticism and explanatory remarks—all in the space of one hundred pages. In 1847 he published an essay entitled *Outline of Penology*, written for the Social Science Association of Philadelphia, and in 1875 he brought out a book of fiction called *The Beverly Family or Home Influence of Religion*, which was of no literary value but perhaps aided in spreading his philosophy of religious tolerance.

[Phila. *Press, Phila. Inquirer, North American,* all of July 12, 1880; Grand Lodge of Pa., *Abstract of Proceedings for 1880; Biog. Dir. of the Am. Congress* (1928).]
M.S.

CHANDLER, PELEG WHITMAN (Apr. 12, 1816–May 28, 1889), lawyer, was descended from Edmond Chaundeler who settled at Duxbury, Mass., in 1633. His grandfather, Peleg Chandler, became one of the pioneers of New Gloucester, Me.; his father, also Peleg, married Esther, daughter of Col. Isaac Parsons. The third Peleg was born at New Gloucester, received his early education at Bangor Theological College, and graduated from Bowdoin in 1834. He then studied law in his father's office at Bangor for a short time, later entering the Dane Law School at Harvard and reading with a relative, Prof. Theophilus Parsons. At the same time he reported legal cases for the Boston *Daily Advertiser.* On Nov. 30, 1837, he was married to Martha Ann Bush, daughter of Prof. Parker Cleaveland of Brunswick, Me. In the same year he was admitted to the Suffolk County bar and commenced practise in Boston, continuing to maintain his association with the press. In 1838 he established a monthly law journal, the *Law Reporter,* remaining its editor for a number of years. He also commenced work on a series of twelve volumes of *American Criminal Trials,* the first of which was published in 1841, followed by a second in 1844, but the subsequent growth of his law practise prevented the completion of his design. In addition to his legal and literary work he threw himself with ardor into the civic life of Boston, being elected a member of the common council in 1843, and president of that body in 1844 and 1845. He had been elected a member of the Massachusetts House of Representatives in 1844 and served one term. In 1846 he became city solicitor. He held the position of United States commissioner in bankruptcy for a time, during which he published *Bankruptcy Laws of the United States, and the Outline of the System with Rules and Forms in Massachusetts* (1842). He was also engaged in collecting and revising the civic ordinances, and these, in their revised form, were published in 1850, together with a digest of the law pertaining to them, under the title *Revised Ordinances, Boston.* He resigned the city solicitorship in November 1853, but always remained closely associated with the legal interests of Boston, advising on legislative projects and preparing the revised charter. He took a prominent part in the "Back Bay Improvement" scheme and devoted a large amount of his time and ability to the advancement of projects for the beautifying and adornment of the city. In 1854 he became a member of the executive council of the commonwealth and in 1862–63 was again a member of the state House of Representatives. Endowed with a strong constitution, capable of intense application, and always at work, in spite of his other varied interests he enjoyed one of the largest practises in the state. An expert in municipal and commercial law, he confined himself to civil cases. He was an excellent speaker with a fund of anecdote and humor. His arguments were distinguished by their appeal to common sense and his presentation of facts was invariably simple, concise, and devoid of ornament. Judge Rockwood Hoar, a competent authority, said that in his prime Chandler was the best jury lawyer in Massachusetts with the possible exception of Choate. Unfortunately, at the very height of his career Chandler became almost entirely deaf and was compelled to retire from jury work, gradually withdrawing from active business and during his last years being more or less of an invalid. He was the author of *Observations on the Authority of the Gospels, By a Layman* (2nd ed., 1867); *Memoir of Gov. Andrew, with Personal Reminiscences* (1880), a work of considerable biographical value; and a number of legal, political, and historical articles.

[Mary C. Lowell, *Chandler-Parsons & Allied Families* (1911), p. 44; T. H. Haskell, *New Gloucester Centennial* (1875); *Am. Law Rev.,* XXII, 280–84, XXIII, 824–27; N. Cleaveland, *Hist. of Bowdoin Coll.* (1882), p. 453; Conrad Reno, ed., *The Judiciary and the Bar of New Eng.* (1900), I, 592; *Green Bag,* I, 270.]
H.W.H.K.

CHANDLER, SETH CARLO (Sept. 17, 1846–Dec. 31, 1913), astronomer, was born in Boston, a son of Seth Carlo and Mary (Cheever) Chandler. He was educated in the Boston public schools (finishing with the English High School), and at Harvard College. During his senior year in college he did some computing for Prof. Benjamin Pierce. After graduation in 1861 he became a private assistant of the astronomer Benjamin A. Gould. This was the beginning of a lasting friendship. From 1864 to 1870 he held a position in the United States Coast Survey. In the latter year he married Caroline Herman of Boston, and soon accepted a position as actuary with the Continental Life Insurance Company of New York, but in 1877 returned to Boston to a similar position which he held for several years. In 1881 he moved to Cambridge, where he became associated with the Harvard College Observatory, and resumed his astronomical work. He was at this time interested in the computation of cometary orbits. Together with John Ritchie, Jr., he devised a telegraphic code for the distribution of astronomical news. He also constructed the almucantar—an instrument for finding time by equal-altitude observations—which constituted his chief contribution to instrumental astronomy. Leaving the Observatory in 1885, he continued privately his work in astronomy, becoming especially interested in variable stars, on which subject he was soon a leading authority. He was the discoverer of several variable stars, and the author of many papers on the classification and general laws of stellar variation. He compiled three catalogues of variable stars, and shortly before his death was engaged in the discussion of a standard system of magnitudes. His greatest work was the demonstration of the variation of latitude, a subject on which he worked many years. His first paper on this subject appeared in 1891. He succeeded Dr. Gould in the editorship of the *Astronomical Journal,* which became an absorbing interest to him. He received the degree of LL.D. from De Pauw University in 1891, the Gold Medal of the National Academy of Sciences in 1895, and the Gold Medal of the Royal Astronomical Society in 1896. The University of Glasgow desired to confer upon him the doctor's degree in 1901, but he was unable to go abroad. With a brilliant creative mind and great nervous energy, he worked at high speed. In his later years his health was broken, chiefly by his excessive zeal. He was unpretentious and social, kind and constant in friendship. He died in Wellesley, Mass., whither he had moved in 1904.

[*Science*, XXXIX, 348–50; *Nature*, XCII, 611–12; *Astronomical Jour.,* XXVIII, 101–02; *Pubs. Astronomical Soc. of the Pacific*, XXVI, 39–41; *Popular Astronomy*, XXII, 271–75; *British Astronomical Ass. Jour.*, XXIV, 221.]　　　　　　　R.S.D.

CHANDLER, THOMAS BRADBURY (Apr. 26, 1726–June 17, 1790), Anglican clergyman, Loyalist, was the eldest of the ten children of Capt. William and Jemima (Bradbury) Chandler. He was born in Woodstock, Conn., where, on his father's farm, he spent his early years. Entering Yale College he came under the strong Episcopalian influence that had clung to the institution since 1722 when its first president, Timothy Cutler [*q.v.*], had publicly announced his doubt of the validity of Presbyterian ordination and had joined himself to the Church of England. After his graduation in 1745 Chandler taught school at Woodstock for two years, at the same time reading theology under the guidance of the Rev. Samuel Johnson [*q.v.*], first president of King's College. In 1747 St. John's Church at Elizabethtown, N. J., being deprived by death of the ministry of the Rev. Edward Vaughan, called Chandler to its service. He accepted the invitation, and being yet too young for ordination undertook the duties of lay reader and catechist. Four years later he went to London to receive orders, returned to Elizabethtown, and long served St. John's Church and adjacent missionary stations with ability and devotion. In 1750 he married Jane M. Emott of Elizabethtown, by whom he had one son and five daughters. In 1753 he received the degree of M.A. from the University of Oxford and was admitted to the degree of D.D. in 1766 and 1767 at Oxford and Columbia respectively. His refusal to allow George Whitefield to speak in his church in 1763 caused resentment and division within his flock, but in spite of many defections he would not compromise.

The clergy of New York, New Jersey, and Pennsylvania delegated him as a leading advocate of American episcopacy to prepare a plea for the sending of bishops to America, and in 1767 he published *An Appeal to the Public in Behalf of the Church of England in America,* which provoked wide controversy. He also wrote *An Address from the Clergy of New York and New Jersey to the Episcopalians in Virginia* (1771). Although he had advised the repeal of the Stamp Act, he was as ardent a Loyalist as churchman, and the events of the next few years moved him to vigorous protest against the drift toward revolution. In 1775 appeared his pamphlet *What Think Ye of Congress Now?* which was a spirited attack upon the authority and actions of the Continental Congress. The occurrences of April 1775 were too much for his Loyalist fervor and he departed for England the following month. During the next ten years he labored for the family he had left behind him, for his destitute brethren, and for an American episcopate. Returning in 1785 he rejoined his family in St. John's rectory, but failing health would not permit him to undertake any but the lightest parochial duties, nor to accept elevation to the episcopate of Nova Scotia, an honor tendered him in 1786. He died at Elizabethtown, June 17, 1790, and was buried in the church whose minister he had been for forty-three years.

[F. B. Dexter, *Biog. Sketches Grads. Yale Coll.*, vol. II (1896); A. H. Hoyt, *Sketch of the Life of the Rev. Thos. Bradbury Chandler, D.D.* (1873), a reprint from the *New Eng. Hist. and Geneal. Reg.*, XXVII, 227–36; J. C. Rudd, *Hist. Notices of St. John's Ch.* (1825); J. D. McVickar, *The Early Life and Professional Years of Hobart* (1838); S. A. Clark, *Hist. of St. John's Ch.* (1857); W. S. Perry, *Hist. of the Am. Episc. Ch.* (2 vols., 1885); Arthur Lyon Cross, *The Anglican Episcopate and the Am. Colonies* (1902).]　　H.J.T.

CHANDLER, WILLIAM EATON (Dec. 28, 1835–Nov. 30, 1917), secretary of the navy, senator, was during his entire life identified with Concord, N. H., where he was born, and where he died. His parents, Nathan S. and Mary Ann (Tucker) Chandler, gave him an education at the local schools and academies, and sent him to the

Harvard Law School, where he received his degree in 1854. After a few years as court reporter, he turned politician and journalist; and with the Concord *Monitor and Statesman* (which he controlled for many years) for an ally, he justified the nickname of the "stormy petrel" of New Hampshire politics. Slight, lithe, bearded, and agreeable, he had great talents as a manager and controversialist, which brought him to power in the rough and tumble of the Civil War. Elected to the legislature in 1863, he was reëlected in the two succeeding years, in both of which he was also speaker of the New Hampshire Assembly. It was no disadvantage that his father-in-law, Joseph A. Gilmore, was at the same time, 1863–65, governor of the state. Chandler established his character as a war Republican, advocating a confiscation of the property of rebels, and the right of soldiers in the field to vote. He gave vigorous support to the Lincoln administration, and was appointed, first, to prosecute frauds in the Philadelphia navy-yard, and then, at the beginning of Lincoln's second administration, to be solicitor and judge-advocate general of the navy department. President Johnson transferred him to the treasury, where he was assistant secretary, 1865–67; after which he returned to the practise of law and politics in his native state. As national committeeman from New Hampshire he assisted in directing party strategy in the four presidential campaigns, 1868, 1872, 1876, and 1880. In the first two of these he was secretary of the Republican National Committee.

Immediately after the election of 1876, although he had ceased to be secretary, he appeared at the headquarters of the national committee in New York City, and took a large share in the maneuvers that secured the outcome of the election. He refused to concede the election of Tilden, inspired the fights before the returning boards of Florida, Louisiana, and South Carolina, and was counsel for the Florida electors before the electoral commission. The installation of Hayes as president was commonly regarded as a triumph of his tactics. He was not, however, appointed to important office in the government, and was soon disgusted with the friendliness shown by Hayes to the South, and with the somewhat non-partisan course of the administration. The Hayes circular directing office-holders to refrain from the official management of political campaigns seemed to him hypocrisy. After the refusal of the Senate to confirm the Hayes appointees to the New York Custom-House, Chandler came out with a public manifesto (*New York Times*, Dec. 27, 1877) addressed to the Republicans of New Hampshire. In this he charged that Hayes was guilty of a corrupt bargain with the Democrats, whereby he received the presidency in return for a pledge to relax Northern control over the South.

In 1880 Chandler led the Blaine faction of the national Republican committee against Cameron, who was manager for Gen. Grant. When Garfield eventually secured the nomination from the Republican convention, Chandler gave him his support, and was rewarded in the spring of 1881 by a nomination to be solicitor-general, which, however, the Senate refused to confirm. In the next winter he was appointed secretary of the navy by President Arthur after the retirement of William H. Hunt. The appointment was interpreted as a civil gesture toward the friends of James G. Blaine; and it gave to Chandler a chance to preside over the navy in a momentous period of its history. He reminded Congress in his first annual report, as Arthur had done in the annual message of the preceding year, that the navy of the United States, as a fighting force, was extinct. Its leading warship was the *Tennessee,* a wooden ship of 4,840 tons displacement. Only the United States, among major nations, had refrained from profiting by the new methods of naval architecture. In Chandler's first year of office, on Aug. 5, 1882, Congress authorized the preparation of plans for two steel cruisers; and on Mar. 3, 1883, it made appropriations for constructing these, and for adding two more steel vessels to the new navy. Under Chandler's direction the plans were drawn and the keels were laid for the *Chicago, Boston, Atlanta,* and a despatch boat, the *Dolphin.* The contracts were let to John Roach who had been building steel ships on the Delaware for several years. It was determined to proceed no more rapidly than American building resources would justify, but to manufacture the new ships and their armament in the United States rather than attempt to buy them abroad. Several years elapsed before the American shipyards and gun foundries were ready for contracts for armored cruisers or battleships. Naval architecture was not beyond the point at which it was possible to argue that the ships should possess complete sailing equipment as well as steam; and at which it was possible to mount the boilers over brick furnaces (as was done in the *Chicago*). As might have been expected, none of these four vessels was a triumph. The *Dolphin* was a scandal. Chandler was publicly charged with favoritism; but he had established the new program of steel construction before he handed over his office to William C. Whitney in 1885.

After 1885, Chandler continued active with his newspaper, fought vigorously against the great railroad combinations of his state, and secured in

1887 election to the United States Senate for the last two years of the term of Austin F. Pike. In 1889 he was elected for a full term, after a bitter fight with Jacob H. Gallinger in the New Hampshire legislature. He was again reëlected in 1895, but was defeated in 1901 by Judge Henry E. Burnham, whereupon President McKinley made him chairman of the Spanish Treaty Claims Commission. Chandler's style of speech and writing may be judged from his *New Hampshire A Slave State* (1891), popularly known as the "Book of Bargains." He was married twice: in 1859 to Ann Caroline Gilmore (d. 1871), and in 1874 to Lucy Lambert Hale, daughter of a former senator, John P. Hale.

[There is a good obituary in the *New Eng. Hist. and Geneal. Reg.*, LXXII, 54, and several less important sketches are to be found in the *Granite Mo.*, vols. VI, X, XII, and XXXIV; the *Daily Patriot* (Concord, N. H.), Nov. 30, 1917, and the *Manchester Union*, Dec. 1, 1917.]

F. L. P—n.

CHANDLER, ZACHARIAH (Dec. 10, 1813–Nov. 1, 1879), senator, Republican boss, was born at Bedford, N. H. His father, Samuel Chandler, was a descendant of William Chandler, who emigrated from England and settled at Roxbury, Mass., about 1637 (George Chandler, *The Chandler Family*, 1872, p. 818). His mother, Margaret Orr, was the oldest daughter of Col. John Orr. He received a common school education, and in 1833 removed to Detroit, where he opened a general store, and eventually through trade, banking, and land speculation became one of the richest men in Michigan. On Dec. 10, 1844, he was married to Letitia Grace Douglass of New York. He made campaign speeches for Taylor in 1848, served for a year (1851–52) as mayor of Detroit, and in 1852 offered himself as a Whig candidate for governor and was defeated. He was one of the signers of the call for the meeting at Jackson, Mich., July 6, 1854, which launched the Republican party, and "the leading spirit" of the Buffalo convention called to aid free state migration to Kansas (George F. Hoar, *Autobiography*, 1903, II, 75). In 1856 he was a delegate to the Republican national convention at Pittsburgh, and was made a member of the national committee of the party. In January 1857, he was elected to the United States Senate in succession to Lewis Cass [*q.v.*], and held his seat until Mar. 3, 1875. In the Senate he allied himself with the radical anti-slavery element of the Republicans, although hostile to Charles Sumner, and was later recognized as one of the most outspoken enemies of secession. From March 1861 to 1875 he was chairman of the Committee on Commerce, to whose jurisdiction

the appropriations for rivers and harbors, later known as the "pork barrel," were assigned. At the outbreak of the Civil War he exerted himself to raise and equip the first regiment of Michigan volunteers. He was a member of the Joint Committee on the Conduct of the War; initiated acts for the collection and administration of abandoned property in the South (Mar. 3, 1863) and for the further regulation of intercourse with the insurrectionary states (July 2, 1864); bitterly denounced the incompetence of McClellan in a speech at Jackson, Mich. (July 6, 1862) which he regarded as one of his most important public services; supported the proposal of a national bank; voted for greenbacks as an emergency measure while strongly resisting inflation of the currency; and approved of the Reconstruction acts although criticizing them as in some respects too lax. His aggressive Republicanism was matched by his clamorous jingoism in regard to Great Britain; on Jan. 15, 1866, he offered a resolution, which was tabled, for non-intercourse with Great Britain for its refusal to entertain the *Alabama* claims, and in 1867, when the question of recognizing Abyssinia as a belligerent in its war with Great Britain was under consideration, he submitted (Nov. 29) a resolution "recognizing to Abyssinia the same rights which the British had recognized to the Confederacy" (*Congressional Globe*, 40 Cong., 1 Sess., p. 810). He was one of the promoters and most influential members of the Republican Congressional Committee, serving as its chairman in the campaigns of 1868 and 1876. From the beginning of his senatorial career he used his Federal patronage to strengthen his political power, and by methods openly partisan and despotic if not actually corrupt obtained control of the Republican machine in Michigan, and was for years the undisputed boss of his party in the state. The Democratic landslide of 1874, however, broke his power, and he was defeated for reëlection to the Senate. In October 1875, he became secretary of the interior, retaining the office until the close of Grant's second administration. His reorganization of the department was attended by wholesale dismissals for alleged dishonesty or incompetence. He was again elected to the Senate in February 1879, to fill a vacancy caused by the resignation of Isaac P. Christiancy [*q.v.*].

[Aside from the *Biog. Cong. Dir.* (1913), the *Journals of the Senate*, the *Cong. Globe*, and *Cong. Record*, the chief source is the anonymous *Zachariah Chandler: an Outline Sketch of His Life and Public Services* (1880), which is supplemented in a number of details by Wilmer C. Harris, *Public Life of Zachariah Chandler, 1851–75* (1917), a doctoral dissertation of the University of Chicago.]

W. M.

VOLUME II, PART 2
CHANFRAU - CUSHING

(VOLUME IV OF THE ORIGINAL EDITION)

CROSS REFERENCES FROM THIS VOL-
UME ARE MADE TO THE VOLUME
NUMBERS OF THE ORIGINAL EDITION.

CONTRIBUTORS

VOLUME II, PART 2

Thomas P. Abernethy . . . . . T. P. A.
Adeline Adams . . . . A. A.
James Truslow Adams . . . J. T. A.
Randolph G. Adams . . . . . R. G. A—s.
Robert G. Albion . . . . . . R. G. A—n.
Edmund K. Alden . . . . . . E. K. A.
Edward E. Allen . . . . E. E. A.
William H. Allison . . . . . W. H. A.
Katharine H. Amend . . . . . K. H. A.
John C. Archer . . . . J. C. A.
George B. Armstead . . . . . G. B. A.
John Murray Atwood . . . . J. M. A.
Benjamin W. Bacon . . . . . B. W. B.
Theodore D. Bacon . . . . . T. D. B.
James C. Ballagh . . . . . . J. C. B.
Albert H. Barclay . . . . . . A. H. B.
George A. Barton . . . . . . G. A. B.
Ernest Sutherland Bates . . E. S. B.
John O. Beaty . . . . J. O. B.
Elbert J. Benton . . . . . . E. J. B.
Arthur R. Blessing . . . . . A. R. B.
George Blumer . . . . G. B.
Roger S. Boardman . . . . . R. S. B.
Ernest F. Boddington . . . . E. F. B.
Herbert E. Bolton . . . . . . H. E. B.
Milledge L. Bonham, Jr. . . . M. L. B.
Archibald L. Bouton . . . . A. L. B.
Sarah G. Bowerman . . . . . S. G. B.
Claude G. Bowers . . . . . . C. G. B.
William K. Boyd . . . . . . W. K. B.
Jeffrey R. Brackett . . . . . J. R. B.
Benjamin Brawley . . . . . . B. B.
Edward Breck . . . . E. B.
John E. Briggs . . . . J. E. B.
Denis W. Brogan . . . . . . D. W. B.
Walter C. Bronson . . . . . W. C. B.
R. P. Brooks . . . . R. P. B.
John S. Brubacher . . . . . J. S. B.
W. B. Cairns . . . . W. B. C.
Isabel M. Calder . . . . . . I. M. C.
Robert G. Caldwell . . . . . R. G. C.
Robert C. Canby . . . . . . R. C. C—y.
Harry J. Carman . . . . . . H. J. C.
Benjamin Catchings . . . . . B. C.
Charles J. Chamberlain . . . C. J. C.
Wayland J. Chase . . . . . . W. J. C.
Russell H. Chittenden . . . . R. H. C.
Robert C. Clark . . . . . . R. C. C—k.
Rudolf A. Clemen . . . . . R. A. C.
Katherine W. Clendinning . K. W. C.
Oral S. Coad . . . . O. S. C.

Charles F. Coan . . . . . . C. F. C.
Frederick W. Coburn . . . . F. W. C.
Lane Cooper . . . . L. C.
Edward S. Corwin . . . . . E. S. C.
R. S. Cotterill . . . . R. S. C.
E. Merton Coulter . . . . . E. M. C.
Isaac J. Cox . . . . I. J. C.
Marshall P. Cram . . . . . M. P. C.
Verner W. Crane . . . . . . V. W. C.
Samuel M. Crothers . . . . . S. M. C.
Edward E. Curtis . . . . . . E. E. C.
S. Foster Damon . . . . . . S. F. D.
Marjory Hendricks Davis . . M. H. D.
Floyd Dell . . . . F. D.
Davis R. Dewey . . . . . . D. R. D.
John Dickinson . . . . . . J. Di.
Frank Haigh Dixon . . . . . F. H. D.
Gilbert H. Doane . . . . . . G. H. D.
Eleanor Robinette Dobson . . E. R. D.
Dorothy Anne Dondore . . . D. A. D.
Stella M. Drumm . . . . . . S. M. D.
Raymond S. Dugan . . . . . R. S. D.
Joseph Dunn . . . . J. Du.
W. F. Durand . . . . W. F. D.
James H. Easterby . . . . . J. H. E.
Edward D. Eaton . . . . . . E. D. E.
Walter Prichard Eaton . . . W. P. E.
Edwin F. Edgett . . . . . . E. F. E.
Arthur Elson . . . . A. E.
Ephraim Emerton . . . . . E. E.
Harold U. Faulkner . . . . . H. U. F.
Ellen Douglass Fawcett . . E. D. F.
William W. Fenn . . . . . . W. W. F.
G. J. Fiebeger . . . . G. J. F.
Carl Russell Fish . . . . . . C. R. F.
Percy Scott Flippin . . . . . P. S. F.
Blanton Fortson . . . . . . B. F.
Harold N. Fowler . . . . . H. N. F.
Dixon R. Fox . . . . D. R. F.
Early Lee Fox . . . . E. L. F.
John H. Frederick . . . . . J. H. F.
Robert D. French . . . . . R. D. F.
Claude M. Fuess . . . . . . C. M. F.
John F. Fulton . . . . J. F. F.
Francis P. Gaines . . . . . F. P. G.
Katharine Jeanne Gallagher . K. J. G.
Ruth A. Gallaher . . . . . . R. A. G.
Curtis W. Garrison . . . . . C. W. G.
George Harvey Genzmer . . . G. H. G.
William J. Ghent . . . . . . W. J. G—t.
Lawrence H. Gipson . . . . . L. H. G.

Contributors

Armistead Churchill Gordon, Jr.	A. C. G., Jr.	William C. Lane	W. C. L.
Harris P. Gould	H. P. G.	Charles H. LaWall	C. H. L.
Gladys Graham	G. G—m.	John J. Leary, Jr.	J. J. L.
Garland Greever	G. G—r.	James Melvin Lee	J. M. L.
Joseph Grinnell	J. G.	Charles Lee Lewis	C. L. L.
Wren Jones Grinstead	W. J. G—d.	John V. Lewis	J. V. L.
Charles W. Hackett	C. W. H.	Thomas O. Mabbott	T. O. M.
Le Roy R. Hafen	L. R. H.	Raymond G. McCarthy	R. G. M.
Percival Hall	P. H.	Thomas Denton McCormick	T. D. M.
Philip M. Hamer	P. M. H.	P. B. McDonald	P. B. M.
George L. Hamilton	G. L. H.	William MacDonald	W. M.
J. G. deR. Hamilton	J. G. deR. H.	Reginald C. McGrane	R. C. M.
Talbot Faulkner Hamlin	T. F. H.	A. C. McLaughlin	A. C. McL.
John L. Haney	J. L. H.	Anne B. MacLear	A. B. M—r.
Alvin F. Harlow	A. F. H.	J. H. T. McPherson	J. H. T. M.
Thomas L. Harris	T. L. H.	Archibald C. Malloch	A. C. M.
Louis C. Hatch	L. C. H.	Dumas Malone	D. M.
Frances B. Hawley	F. B. H.	Newton D. Mereness	N. D. M.
Fred E. Haynes	F. E. H.	George P. Merrill	G. P. M.
George H. Haynes	G. H. H.	John Calvin Metcalf	J. C. M.
George S. Hellman	G. S. H.	Douglass W. Miller	D. W. M.
V. A. C. Henmon	V. A. C. H.	Clinton Mindil	C. M.
Frederick C. Hicks	F. C. H.	Broadus Mitchell	B. M.
J. D. Hicks	J. D. H.	Samuel Chiles Mitchell	S. C. M.
Homer Carey Hockett	H. C. H.	Carl W. Mitman	C. W. M.
M. M. Hoffmann	M. M. H.	Frank Monaghan	F. M.
Arthur Hornblow	A. H—w.	Robert E. Moody	R. E. M.
Walter Hough	W. H.	Albert B. Moore	A. B. M—e.
L. O. Howard	L. O. H.	Mary A. Moore	M. A. M.
Theodora Kimball Hubbard	T. K. H.	Samuel E. Morison	S. E. M.
Charles H. Hull	C. H. H.	Richard B. Morris	R. B. M.
Edgar Erskine Hume	E. E. H.	Edwin G. Nash	E. G. N.
E. F. Humphrey	E. F. H.	Allan Nevins	A. N.
W. J. Humphreys	W. J. H.	Lyman C. Newell	L. C. N.
Albert Hyma	A. H—a.	Robert H. Nichols	R. H. N.
Lewis M. Isaacs	L. M. I.	Ellis P. Oberholtzer	E. P. O.
Theodore H. Jack	T. H. J.	V. F. O'Daniel	V. F. O'D.
Joseph Jackson	J. J.	John R. Oliver	J. R. O.
J. A. James	J. A. J.	Francis R. Packard	F. R. P.
E. H. Jenkins	E. H. J.	Henry R. Palmer	H. R. P.
Allen Johnson	A. J.	William B. Parker	W. B. P.
Edgar A. J. Johnson	E. A. J. J.	Fred Lewis Pattee	F. L. P—e.
Rufus M. Jones	R. M. J.	Charles O. Paullin	C. O. P.
William Jones	W. J.	Frederic Logan Paxson	F. L. P—n.
Charles H. Judd	C. H. J.	C. C. Pearson	C. C. P.
Marie A. Kasten	M. A. K.	Donald C. Peattie	D. C. P.
L. F. Kebler	L. F. K.	Hobart S. Perry	H. S. P.
Louise Phelps Kellogg	L. P. K.	Benjamin H. Pershing	B. H. P.
R. W. Kelsey	R. W. K.	Frederick T. Persons	F. T. P.
W. W. Kemp	W. W. K.	A. Everett Peterson	A. E. P.
William J. Kerby	W. J. K.	James M. Phalen	J. M. P.
Alice M. Keys	A. M. K.	Francis S. Philbrick	F. S. P.
William Bruce King	W. B. K.	Paul C. Phillips	P. C. P.
Alexander Klemin	A. K.	Ulrich B. Phillips	U. B. P.
H. W. Howard Knott	H. W. H. K.	Lewis F. Pilcher	L. F. P.
Ralph S. Kuykendall	R. S. K.	Edward Preble	E. P.
Leonard W. Labaree	L. W. L.	Leo B. Pride	L. B. P.
		Herbert I. Priestley	H. I. P.

Contributors

RICHARD J. PURCELL	R. J. P.	HENRY P. TALBOT	H. P. T.
CHARLES W. RAMSDELL	C. W. R.	JEANNETTE R. TANDY	J. R. T.
JAMES G. RANDALL	J. G. R.	EDWIN P. TANNER	E. P. T.
BELLE RANKIN	B. R.	FRANK A. TAYLOR	F. A. T.
RUTH REDFIELD	R. R.	FRANK THILLY	F. T—y.
WILLIAM NORTH RICE	W. N. R.	DAVID Y. THOMAS	D. Y. T.
THOMAS C. RICHARDS	T. C. R.	R. P. TOLMAN	R. P. T.
IRVING B. RICHMAN	I. B. R.	F. E. TOURSCHER	F. E. T.
FRANKLIN L. RILEY	F. L. R.	FRANCIS J. TSCHAN	F. J. T.
WILLIAM A. ROBINSON	W. A. R.	FREDERICK TUCKERMAN	F. T—n.
WILLIAM M. ROBINSON, JR.	W. M. R.	WILLIAM T. UTTER	W. T. U.
WILLIAM H. ROEVER	W. H. R.	CARL VAN DOREN	C. V–D.
J. MAGNUS ROHNE	J. M. R.	MARK VAN DOREN	M. V–D.
VIRGINIA RONSAVILLE	V. R—e.	HENRY R. VIETS	H. R. V.
VICTOR ROSEWATER	V. R—r.	EUGENE M. VIOLETTE	E. M. V.
FRANK EDWARD ROSS	F. E. R.	ALBERT T. VOLWILER	A. T. V.
CONSTANCE M. ROURKE	C. M. R.	JOHN D. WADE	J. D. W.
RALPH LESLIE RUSK	R. L. R.	JAMES ELLIOTT WALMSLEY	J. E. W—y.
JOSEPH SCHAFER	J. S.	J. BARNARD WALTON	J. B. W.
HERBERT W. SCHNEIDER	H. W. S	LUTHER ALLAN WEIGLE	L. A. W.
ROBERT F. SEYBOLT	R. F. S.	ALLAN WESTCOTT	A. W.
MURIEL SHAVER	M. S.	W. L. WHITTLESEY	W. L. W.
WILLIAM B. SHAW	W. B. S.	ROBERT J. WICKENDEN	R. J. W.
FLOYD CALVIN SHOEMAKER	F. C. S—r.	JEANNE ELIZABETH WIER	J. E. W—r.
E. W. SIKES	E. W. S.	CLARENCE RUSSELL WILLIAMS	C. R. W.
DAVID EUGENE SMITH	D. E. S.	MARY WILHELMINE WILLIAMS	M. W. W.
J. M. POWIS SMITH	J. M. P. S.	STANLEY T. WILLIAMS	S. T. W.
MARION PARRIS SMITH	M. P. S.	WALTER WILLIAMS	W. W.
W. E. SMITH	W. E. S—h.	H. PARKER WILLIS	H. P. W.
THOMAS M. SPAULDING	T. M. S.	GEORGE GRAFTON WILSON	G. G. W.
CHARLES WORTHEN SPENCER	C. W. S.	JAMES E. WINSTON	J. E. W—n.
HARRIS ELWOOD STARR	H. E. S.	CARTER G. WOODSON	C. G. W.
HENRY P. STEARNS	H. P. S.	THOMAS WOODY	T. W.
WAYNE E. STEVENS	W. E. S—s.	HELEN WRIGHT	H. W.
WITMER STONE	W. S.	LAWRENCE C. WROTH	L. C. W.
FREDERICK C. SWANSON	F. C. S—n.	EDNA YOST	E. Y.

DICTIONARY OF
AMERICAN BIOGRAPHY

—

Chanfrau — Cushing

CHANFRAU, FRANCIS S. (Feb. 22, 1824–Oct. 2, 1884), actor, was the son of a French naval officer who settled in America, and of his wife, Mehitable Trenchard of Westchester County. He was born at the corner of the Bowery and Pell St., New York City, in a wooden tenement known as the Old Tree House. After receiving a fair education he left home and went adventuring out west. For a time he was a driver on the Ohio Canal, subsequently he learned the trade of carpentry, but eventually an inclination toward acting led him, first, into amateur organizations, and finally back to New York to the Edwin Forrest Dramatic Association. His début on the professional stage was as a super at the Bowery Theatre. Mimicry appears to have been his forte, and his imitations of Forrest won him considerable popularity. His reputation as an actor became established when as Jeremiah Clip in *The Widow's Victim,* at Mitchell's Olympic, he gave imitations of every actor of note. Henceforth he had no difficulty in finding engagements, playing Laertes to the Hamlet of James W. Wallack, Jr., at the Chatham (July 17, 1844), and Cedric in *Ivanhoe* at Palmo's Opera House (Apr. 7, 1845).

The first great hit of Chanfrau's career was at Mitchell's Olympic, New York (Feb. 15, 1848), when in Benjamin A. Baker's sketch *A Glance at New York* he took the part of Mose—a typical fireman of that period of hand engines, a half-ruffian, half-hero dare-devil, ever ready for an adventure or a fight. His performance of this rôle raised Chanfrau to stardom, and he carried the play to nearly every theatrical town in America. Identified with the character of Mose, he later had some difficulty in freeing himself from it. "Mr. Chanfrau's immense success in this character," writes J. N. Ireland,

"has been somewhat detrimental to his standing in his native city in a more elevated range of the drama; some squeamish connoisseurs insisting that an artist cannot excel in lines dissimilar. The conclusion, however, is unwarrantable and unjust, for his versatility, although unbounded in aim, is almost unequaled in merit, and his name is ever a reliable source of attraction and profit in almost every other city of the Union in a much higher grade of character" (*Records of the New York Stage,* 1866, II, 419).

Meanwhile Chanfrau undertook various managerial ventures. In 1848, in conjunction with W. Ogilvie Ewen, he leased the Chatham, opening it as Chanfrau's National Theatre; from this he withdrew in 1850. Subsequently he had a disastrous managerial experience at the Brooklyn Museum. In 1851 he went to California. Returning a year later, he again tried his hand at management. Taking a lease of the historic Astor Opera House, the scene of the fatal Forrest-Macready riots, he reopened it with James Stark in *Lear* (Aug. 27, 1852); the following month he changed the name of the house to New York Theatre. He was also the manager of White's Varieties, opened the same year at 17–19 Bowery.

In 1858 he married Henrietta Baker of Philadelphia, already an actress of reputation, who later became, as Mrs. F. S. Chanfrau, one of the most noted actresses on the American stage (see sketch of Henrietta Baker Chanfrau). They preferred for the most part to star separately but in *London Assurance* he appeared as Sir Harcourt Courtley and she as Lady Gay Spanker. Chanfrau's last stage success was in *Kit the Arkansas Traveller.* The rôle of Kit proved as popular throughout the country as

John T. Raymond's Colonel Sellers or Mayo's Davy Crockett, and Chanfrau played it for twelve consecutive seasons, from Sept. 23, 1872, to the time of his death, Oct. 2, 1884.

[Newspaper clippings in N. Y. Pub. Lib.; T. Allston Brown, *Hist. Am. Stage* (c. 1870); *N. Y. Clipper*, Oct. 11, 1884; *N. Y. Tribune*, Oct. 3, 1884.]   A. H—w.

CHANFRAU, HENRIETTA BAKER (1837–Sept. 21, 1909), actress, was born in Philadelphia of good family. She was named Jeannette Davis (Henrietta Baker being a stage name). Her début was made at the age of sixteen when, in the summer of 1854, she appeared as a vocalist at the Assembly Buildings, Philadelphia, under the management of Prof. Mueller. She was first seen as an actress on Sept. 19 of that year at the City Museum, Philadelphia, as Miss Ashley in *The Willow Copse*. Soon afterward she became a member of the Arch Street Theatre where she remained two seasons. Later she was seen at the Walnut Street Theatre. When Lewis Baker opened the National Theatre in Cincinnati, the season of 1857–58, she became a member of the company and was a great favorite with her audiences. It was while with this organization that she married Francis S. Chanfrau [*q.v.*], on June 23, 1858. Considered one of the most natural actresses on the American stage, for many years she was one of the most popular performers in the country. She was the original representative in America of Dora (in Charles Reade's play); was very successful as Esther Eccles in *Caste* and as May Edwards in *The Ticket of Leave Man,* and starred in *East Lynne.* She played Ophelia to the Hamlet of Edwin Booth in a long New York run and also supported Mrs. John Drew and Charlotte Cushman. She was the Portia in the noted production, Nov. 25, 1864, of *Julius Cæsar,* in which the three Booth brothers, Edwin, Junius, and Wilkes, appeared together, and she played Ophelia in the hundred nights' run of *Hamlet* at Booth's Theatre. For some years she was with Forrest and later with the elder Davenport, Wallack, Fechter, and William Warren. While lessee and manager of the old Varieties in New Orleans in the early seventies, she "discovered" Mary Anderson, then playing Julia in *The Hunchback* in an obscure theatre, and introduced her to the public. She scored one of her greatest successes, June 5, 1876, at the old Eagle Theatre, New York, as Grace Shirley in the drama called *Parted* in which she later starred. After her husband's death in 1884, she temporarily retired from the stage, but in 1886 she made a European tour and afterward reappeared at the Union Square Theatre, New York. Subse-

quently she purchased the *Long Branch News,* but withdrew to carry on the work of a Christian Science leader, and was active in that sect in Philadelphia until she moved to Burlington, N. J., where she died at the age of seventy-one.

[Newspaper clippings in N. Y. Pub. Lib.; *N. Y. Clipper*, Oct. 9, 1909; *Theatre Mag.*, Nov. 1909; *N. Y. Tribune*, Sept. 23, 1909; Thos. Allston Brown, *Hist. N. Y. Stage* (3 vols., 1903).]   A. H—w.

CHANG AND ENG (May 1811–Jan. 17, 1874), "the Siamese Twins," were born in Meklong, Siam, the sons of a Chinese father and of a mother who was half Chinese. They owed their future celebrity to the fact that they were joined at the waist by a cartilaginous structure, which grew to be about four inches long and eight in circumference. Their parents were poor, and the death of the father in 1819 compelled the boys to fend for themselves. After various makeshifts they went into the duck and egg business and were doing well when in 1824 a British merchant, Robert Hunter, espied them stripped to the waist and realized at once their educational value. He bargained with their mother for their services, and a brother fell heir to the poultry yard. In charge of an American, Capt. Coffin, they left Bangkok on Apr. 1, 1829, and on Aug. 16 arrived in Boston. The public was assured unctuously that the moral character of the youths was irreproachable and that "the most fastidious female [would] find nothing in the exhibition to wound her delicate feelings." To those who suggested the feasibility of a sundering operation it was answered that the twins were so attached to each other, sympathetically and morally as well as physically, that they heard such suggestions with dismay; and their movements, marvelously accommodated to each other, and their unfeigned solicitude for one another's comfort seemed to testify to the truth of this. After astounding and edifying the North Atlantic seaboard for eight weeks, Chang and Eng embarked for England and for further triumphs. On Mar. 4, 1831, they landed once more in New York, but the rest of their extensive travels here and abroad need not be told. On reaching their majority they began to profit by their tours, the receipts having previously gone to their owner. When they had acquired a fortune of some $60,-000 they settled as farmers in Wilkes, and later in Surry, County, N. C., took out naturalization papers, received by act of the legislature the surname of Bunker, and in April 1843 were united in marriage to the Misses Sarah and Adelaide Yates, daughters of David Yates of Wilkes County. Chang had ten children and Eng nine, but their collateral domestic life was unhappy. The wives quarreled so that the brothers were forced to maintain separate establishments, which they visited alternately for three days at a time. The Civil War deprived them of their slaves and of much of their money and made it necessary for them to resume their travels for a while. Chang, the more intelligent but also the more irritable of the two, began to drink heavily and when intoxicated would smash furniture and toss the pieces on the fire. Frequently the twins came to blows and once were bound over to keep the peace. Among their neighbors, however, they continued to maintain their reputation for honesty and fair dealing. Their end was hastened by Chang's intemperance. In August 1870, on a voyage back from Liverpool, he suffered a paralytic stroke. In the night of Jan. 16–17, 1874, Eng awoke to find his brother dead beside him; he himself died, perhaps from fright, a few hours later.

[See "Siamese Twins" in *Index Cat. Surgeon-General's Office, U. S. A.*, vol. XIII (1892).]   G. H. G.

CHANNING, EDWARD TYRRELL (Dec. 12, 1790–Feb. 8, 1856), editor, educator, was born in Newport, R. I., the son of William and Lucy (Ellery) Channing and brother of William Ellery Channing and Walter Channing [*qq.v.*]. At the age of thirteen he entered Harvard College. Owing to his participation in the student rebellion of 1807, he did not receive his degree in course, but was awarded an honorary A.M. in 1819. He studied law with his elder brother, Francis. George Ticknor says regarding him: "In 1813 I was admitted to the bar, at the same time with my friend, Edward T. Channing, who knew, I think, just about as much law as I did, and who afterwards deserted it for letters" (*Life, Letters and Journals of George Ticknor*, 1909, I, 9). In 1814–15, Channing, Willard Phillips, President Kirkland of Harvard, Richard H. Dana, and a few others, formed an association, of which Channing was secretary, for the publication of a bi-monthly magazine, to be called the *New England Magazine and Review*. When, however, it was learned that William Tudor was projecting a periodical, they transferred their labors and good will to him, and in May 1815 the first number of the *North American Review* appeared. In 1817 Tudor retired from the editorship, and the publication passed into the hands of a club composed of the members of the original association with some additions. In May 1818 Channing succeeded Jared Sparks as editor and, assisted by Richard H. Dana, edited the seventh, eighth, and ninth

volumes, until his appointment in October 1819 as Boylston professor of rhetoric and oratory at Harvard. In 1826 he married his cousin, Henrietta A. S. Ellery. His sketch of his grandfather, William Ellery [*q.v.*], in Jared Sparks's *Library of American Biography* (vol. VI, 1836), opens with the remark that "there are men who exercise an important influence within a limited sphere, in a thousand nameless ways, and, it may be, without a distinct consciousness of it on their own part, or that of others, who pass out of life without one strong result, one striking manifestation to make them of public importance." In the main this was true of Channing himself. For thirty-two years his life was strictly academic. Except for the sketch just mentioned and an occasional magazine article, he published practically nothing. After his death his *Lectures Read to the Seniors in Harvard College* (1856) appeared. Their wisdom and charm make them profitable reading still. Indirectly, Channing's influence was far reaching. He had sound scholarship, exquisite taste in literature, and ability to teach. He "probably trained as many conspicuous authors," wrote T. W. Higginson, "as all other American instructors put together" (*Old Cambridge*, 1899, p. 14), and Edward Everett Hale declared, "I had but four teachers in college, Channing, Longfellow, Peirce, and Bachi. The rest heard me recite but taught me nothing" (*James Russell Lowell and his Friends*, 1899, p. 128). "He deserves the credit of the English of Emerson, Holmes, Sumner, Clarke, Bellows, Lowell, Higginson, and other men whom he trained" (*Ibid.*, p. 19). He retired from his professorship at the age of sixty, as he had long before decided he would do, and died at Cambridge five years later.

[R. H. Dana, Jr., memoir in Channing's *Lectures* (1856); Sidney Willard, *Memoirs of Youth and Manhood*, vol. II (1856); H. E. Scudder, *Jas. Russell Lowell*, vol. I (1901); Samuel Longfellow, *Life of Henry W. Longfellow* (1886).]   H. E. S

CHANNING, WALTER (Apr. 15, 1786–July 27, 1876), physician, was born in Newport, R. I., the son of William Channing, who at one time served as United States district attorney, and of his wife, Lucy, daughter of William Ellery [*q.v.*], a signer of the Declaration of Independence. He was a brother of William Ellery Channing and Edward Tyrrell Channing [*qq.v.*]. In 1804 he entered Harvard College in the same class with his cousin, Richard Henry Dana [*q.v.*]. He took part in the undergraduate "Rebellion of 1807" and consequently failed to receive his bachelor's degree in the regular course. (In 1867 it was granted to him as a member of the class of 1808.) His M.D. degree was obtained from the University of Pennsylvania in 1809. After a few years of study abroad, principally in Edinburgh and London, he returned to Boston in 1812 and began to practise obstetrics. In the same year, Harvard conferred upon him the degree of M.D. In 1815, he was appointed the first professor of obstetrics and medical jurisprudence in the Harvard Medical School, a position which he held for nearly forty years. He also acted as dean of the Medical School from 1819 to 1847. His professional interests were many. He assisted in the founding of the Boston Lying-In Hospital in 1832. When the *New England Journal of Medicine and Surgery* expanded into the *Boston Medical and Surgical Journal* (1828), he became co-editor with John Ware, M.D. (1795–1864). He served as librarian of the Massachusetts Medical Society from 1822 to 1825 and treasurer from 1828 to 1840. He was also a member of the American Academy of Arts and Sciences.

Channing's chief contribution to medicine came soon after the introduction of anesthetics at the Massachusetts General Hospital (1846). He began to use ether in cases of childbirth the next year and published his first report of two cases, in the *Boston Medical and Surgical Journal* for May 19, 1847. Later in the same year he was able to issue a small pamphlet on the subject, *Six Cases of Inhalation of Ether in Labor*. His *Treatise on Etherization in Childbirth* (1848) reported over 500 cases. In addition to his work on the use of ether in labor, he published many papers on obstetrics and also various addresses of a more general nature. He wrote brief biographies of Enoch Hale, M.D., John Revere, M.D., John D. Fisher, M.D., and Joshua Fisher, M.D., and an anonymous volume of poems, *New and Old* (1851). His long letter to Dr. J. V. C. Smith, which was later published in pamphlet form as *Professional Reminiscences of Foreign Travel*, gave a graphic account of the prevalence of puerperal fever in Europe in 1852 and of the ether-chloroform controversy. In 1856, he published *A Physician's Vacation*, the record of another extensive European tour.

Channing was a devout Unitarian, an ardent temperance reformer, a pacifist, and an active educationalist. He was full of exuberant vivacity and humor; his gayety was irrepressible and he was a brilliant conversationalist. He was married twice: first, in 1815, to Barbara Higginson Perkins, daughter of Samuel G. Perkins of Brookline, Mass.; second in 1831, to Elizabeth Wainwright of Boston.

[*Boston Medic. and Surgic. Jour.*, XCV, 237; Jas. Freeman Clarke, "Walter Channing and Some of his Contemporaries," in *Memorial and Biog. Sketches* (1878); *Unitarian Rev. and Religious Mag.*, VI, 553–56; Thos. F. Harrington, *Harvard Medic. School* (1905), II, 730; *N. Y. Tribune*, July 31, 1876; *Boston Transcript*, July 28, 1876; *Boston Advertiser*, July 29, 1876.]   H. R. V.

CHANNING, WILLIAM ELLERY (Apr. 7, 1780–Oct. 2, 1842), Unitarian clergyman, was born in Newport, R. I. His ancestors on both sides were of the best New England stock. The earliest American Channing was John, who came from Dorsetshire, England, in 1711. His wife was Mary Antram, a fellow passenger on the voyage hither. Their son John became a prosperous merchant of Newport, R. I., but lost his fortune in later life. John's son William, born in Newport in 1751, was graduated from Princeton College in 1769 and entered at once upon the study of the law. In 1773 he married Lucy, daughter of William Ellery [*q.v.*], who was graduated from Harvard College in 1747. The son of this marriage inherited thus a double academic tradition; on one side the stern Presbyterianism of Princeton, on the other the already threatening liberalism of Harvard. The father would have sent the boy to his own *alma mater*, but the stronger influence of the family connection with Cambridge decided the matter. The boy's maternal grandmother, Ann Remington, was of Cambridge origin, and Francis Dana, chief justice of Massachusetts, whose wife was a sister of Lucy Ellery, was living there. The boy was received into this uncle's family and spent the four years of his college life there, enjoying the benefits of a refined home but deprived of the rough-and-tumble discipline of dormitory life. Contemporary accounts describe him as a serious, over-thoughtful youth, inclined to self-inspection but acutely sensitive to the conditions of life about him. After graduation from college in 1798 he accepted a position as tutor in the family of David Meade Randolph in Richmond, Va., and spent a year and a half there. Up to this time he had been in good health, fond of exercise, and a cheerful if rather serious companion. During this Southern residence among people of alien sympathies he acquired habits of overwork and ascetic discipline which undermined his health. Returning to Newport he applied himself with characteristic fervor to the study of theology. In 1802 he was called to Cambridge as "Regent" of Harvard College, a kind of proctorial office which left him abundant leisure for his chosen studies. In 1814 at the age of thirty-four he married his cousin Ruth Gibbs. On June 1, 1803, he was ordained and installed as minister of the Federal Street Church in Boston, and continued in this pastorate until his death in 1842. Channing's semi-invalidism accounts in a large measure for the social aloofness which was one of his great limitations. He was compelled to husband his physical energy very carefully, and he was shielded by his wife and by his admiring friends from many of the ruder contacts with the world. Only a strong will prevented him from becoming a recluse, and he constantly struggled, not always with conspicuous success, against a valetudinarian habit.

On the pedestal of the statue of Channing in the Public Garden of Boston is the inscription, "He breathed into theology a humane spirit." This expresses his real contribution to theology. He had no novelties of doctrine to propose. He was no innovator. He accepted historic Christianity as a way of life and was eager only to persuade others to walk in it. He was by nature a Broad Churchman of the type common in the Church of England. It is one of the ironies of history that he should have had an important part in some of the bitterest religious and political controversies of his time. A man whose temper was altogether catholic was forced by circumstances to appear as the standard bearer of a new sect.

The "Unitarian Controversy" in which the young minister of the Federal Street Church was destined to take a prominent part was the result of forces which had long been working among the Congregational churches of New England. There had come to be Calvinists, moderate Calvinists, Arminians, and even some ministers darkly suspected of Arianism. About 1815 the differences became acute and the orthodox party, alarmed at the progress of "heresy," insisted upon a thorough house-cleaning. "If Socinians and Arians are among us," they said, "let them show their colors!"

The challenge was promptly accepted, and the word "Unitarian" became henceforth the rallying point for the gathering opposition. New England was in a welter of theological pamphleteering at just the time when Channing was maturing his own thought upon religion. His importance lies in the fact that he refused to identify himself with any of the numerous shades of opinion in the community about him. He committed what, in the eyes of his critics, was the unpardonable sin of doing his own thinking. Starting with a profound conviction of the sufficiency of the Christian Scriptures as the guide of faith, he sought there a basis for the creed of Calvinism in which he had been reared. A "jealous" God; a mankind conceived in iniquity; the vicarious sacrifice of an innocent victim as atone-

ment for "sin" in which man's will had no part; election by grace:—for all these Channing searched the Scriptures in vain. He did not enter the controversy by the barren method of textual criticism, but by the preaching of a gospel founded upon precisely opposite ideas: the goodness of God, the essential virtue and perfectibility of man, and the freedom of the will with its consequent responsibility for action. The effect of his preaching and writing was to bring to a focus all the unrest and dissatisfaction that had long been gathering within the sects, more especially among the Congregationalists.

The name "Unitarian" was borrowed from England but it was some time before the independent thinkers of America could bring themselves to adopt it. Channing himself hesitated, fearing that if a new party with a distinctive name were to be formed, it would soon produce a "Unitarian orthodoxy" with all the limitations and petty tyrannies of the old. He deplored the necessity of organizing a new denomination. "I desire," he said, "to escape the narrow walls of a particular church, and to live under the open sky, looking far and wide and seeing with my own eyes and hearing with my own ears." Soon, however, he recognized that the movement had gone beyond his control and then he not only threw himself heartily into it, but became its acknowledged leader. In 1819 he preached a sermon defining the position of the Unitarian party and defending their right to Christian fellowship. The disruption that followed grieved him, but he accepted it as inevitable. In the following year, 1820, he organized the Berry Street Conference of liberal ministers, at a meeting of which in May 1825 there was organized the American Unitarian Association. The first number of the *Christian Register*, the weekly unofficial organ of the Unitarian denomination, appeared in 1821. Associations and publications alike became vehicles for Channing's thought. "Channing Unitarianism" came to be and has remained the recognized term for that form of religious liberalism which, while unwavering in its assertion of the right of the human reason as a part of the essential dignity of human nature, still clung fondly to the supernatural element of the Christian tradition.

Channing's objection to the Trinitarian orthodoxy of the time was not so much to its doctrine about the nature of the Godhead, as to its view of the nature of man. This he made clear in his epoch-making sermon, "The Moral Argument against Calvinism." The idea that human nature was essentially depraved and incapable of natural growth into goodness was abhorrent to him.

His conception of Christ linked him with Arians like John Milton. He did not reject the New Testament miracles, but they became less and less important to him as evidences of the truth of Christianity.

Those who heard Channing preach testify to the arresting quality of his voice and the charm of his manner. His style was unadorned by illustration. To the modern reader he seems unnecessarily didactic, but this was a characteristic which did not impress his contemporaries. He steadily grew away from the stilted manner of his earlier discourses. There are few of his sermons which do not have their moments of real eloquence.

But though he attained a place of great power as a preacher, it was not from the pulpit of the Federal Street Church that he exerted his widest influence upon his generation. In 1822 the state of his health required a prolonged vacation in Europe. After his return, Rev. Ezra Stiles Gannett, himself a man of distinction in the Unitarian body, became his colleague and took upon himself an increasing part of the ministerial work. From that time Channing addressed the public directly through the press. His essays on Milton, Fénelon, and Napoleon had a wide circulation. In his address on Self-Culture he made a plea for adult education, denying the academic distinction between cultural and vocational studies and insisting on the possibility of attaining true culture by means of one's vocation intelligently pursued. It is interesting, as illustrating the sweep of Channing's mind, to find him in this address delivered in 1838 advocating the policy of setting apart the funds derived from the sale of public lands to support public education.

The influence of Channing on American literature was very direct. The term "Channing Unitarians," while not precise when applied to a theological party, was very apt when applied to the group of New England writers who flourished in the middle of the nineteenth century. Emerson, Bryant, Longfellow, Lowell, Holmes were all closely associated with the Unitarian movement, and acknowledged their indebtedness to Channing. If "he breathed into theology a humane spirit" it may with equal truth be said that he breathed into literature a religious spirit.

Channing's *Remarks on American Literature*, published in 1830, is still worth reading. He defines literature as "the expression of a nation's mind in writing." Then he criticizes the tendency among American writers to imitate English models rather than to find inspiration in what is characteristic of their own land. Amer-

ican literature must become national instead of colonial. The time has come for a literary Declaration of Independence. "We think that the history of the human race is to be rewritten. Men imbued with the prejudices which thrive under aristocracies and state religions cannot understand it. . . . It seems to us that in literature immense work is yet to be done. The most interesting questions of mankind are yet in debate. Great principles are yet to be settled in criticism, in morals, and in politics; and above all, the true character of religion is to be rescued from the disguises and corruptions of ages. We want a reformation. . . . The part which this country is to bear in that intellectual reform we presume not to predict. We feel, however, that if true to itself, it will have the glory and happiness of giving new impulses to the human mind. This is our cherished hope. We should have no heart to encourage native literature did we not hope that it would be instinct with a new spirit. We cannot admit the thought that this country is to be only a repetition of the old world" (*Works*, 1903 edition, p. 134).

To those who are familiar only with Channing's sermons there is something amusing in his serious denial of the charge that he cherished political ambitions and was desirous of becoming a member of Congress. But he never looked upon politics with indifference. All questions were to him moral questions. Politics was the native air he breathed in childhood. His father, William Channing, was a politician so successful that he was at the same time attorney-general of Rhode Island and United States district attorney. His grandfather, William Ellery, whose companionship he enjoyed to middle life, was one of the most ardent of the Sons of Liberty and one of the signers of the Declaration of Independence. His classmate and intimate friend, Judge Story, tells of Channing's intense interest in political questions while in college. During the exciting year 1798, Channing secured a meeting of his fellow students in Harvard "for the purpose of expressing their opinions on the existing crisis in public affairs." The youthful politician was given the principal part at Commencement and assigned the subject "The Present Age" with the stipulation that all reference to present politics should be avoided. Channing resented the restriction and won the plaudits of the audience by stopping in the midst of his address and declaiming, "But that I am forbid I could a tale unfold that would harrow up your souls." His early associations were with the Federalists. His family was connected with the Cabots, the Lees, Jacksons, and Lowells whose names counted for much in the society of those days. George Cabot, the leader of the New England Federalists and president of the Hartford convention, was a friend for whom he cherished the most profound respect. Nevertheless, the trend of his own thought allied him with Jefferson rather than with Hamilton, and he soon outgrew fears of the "Jacobins." His account of the failure of the Federalist party and the reasons for it is full of discriminating sympathy. "A purer party than the Federalists, we believe, never existed under any government." But their fear of the French Revolution destroyed their confidence in their own institutions. "We apprehend that it is possible to make experience too much our guide. . . . There are seasons in human affairs of inward and outward revolution, when new depths seem to be broken up in the soul, when new wants are unfolded in multitudes and a new and undefined good is thirsted for. These are periods when the principles of experience need to be modified, when hope and trust and instinct claim a share with prudence in the guidance of affairs, when in truth to *dare* is the highest wisdom" (*Ibid.*, p. 641).

Unlike the members of the society in which he lived, Channing was conscious of the tremendous revolutionary forces which were at work. He distinguished between the outer and the inner revolution, and his aim was to make the outer revolution peaceful and beneficial, by the timely release of the moral forces which he believed to be stored up in the individual soul. This is emphasized in his pamphlets and addresses on the slavery question. Slavery, he insisted, is an unspeakable evil. But so also is war and of all wars the most dreadful to contemplate is a civil war. He could not dismiss as did many abolitionists the possibility of a war between the states. His residence in Virginia had given him a deep respect for the courage of the Southerners and their willingness to fight in defense of state rights. In his discussions of slavery he addressed himself to the conscience of the South rather than to the New England conscience. He was attacked from both sides, but his addresses did much to prepare people to understand and follow Abraham Lincoln. (See his *Slavery*, 1835; *The Abolitionist*, 1836; *Open Letter to Henry Clay*, 1837; *Duty of the Free States*, 1842.)

In the modern movement against war, Channing may be counted as a pioneer. He began with an outspoken sermon against the War of 1812. In this he voiced the general feeling of Massachusetts. The great aim of his essay on Napoleon was to destroy the romantic glamour that invests the successful warrior. The Massachusetts Peace Society was organized in his study. His lecture on War delivered in 1838 is almost Tolstoyan in its anti-militarism. Unlike Tolstoy, however, he could not follow literally the injunction "Resist not evil." He admitted the right of a nation to use force in self-defense, but insisted that it must be as carefully defined by law as the similar right of an individual. It is possible for a nation to commit murder.

In his discussion of temperance, the condition of laborers, and public education, Channing was clearly in advance of his time. His viewpoint was surprisingly anticipatory of the thought of present-day social workers. Intemperance he treated as a vice for which the community was largely responsible. The law might properly be invoked to prohibit the sale of intoxicants as of other harmful drugs, but improvements in hygiene, food, and recreation were more needed. "I have insisted on the importance of increasing the innocent gratifications in a community. Let us become more cheerful and we shall become a more temperate people" (*Ibid.*, p. 112). In prophetic words, he warns the advocates of temperance against the attempt to coerce. "We want public opinion to bear on temperance, but to act rationally, generously and not passionately, tyranically and with a spirit of persecution. Men cannot be driven into temperance" (*Ibid.*, p. 116).

[Wm. Henry Channing, *Life of Wm. Ellery Channing* (1848; Centenary ed., 1880); John White Chadwick, *Wm. Ellery Channing, Minister of Religion* (1903); Elizabeth Palmer Peabody, *Reminiscences of Rev. Wm. Ellery Channing* (1880); Chas. Wm. Eliot, *Four Am. Leaders* (1906); Ezra Stiles Gannett, *An Address at the Funeral of Wm. Ellery Channing* (1842).]

S. M. C.

CHANNING, WILLIAM ELLERY (Nov. 29, 1818–Dec. 23, 1901), poet, was born in Boston, the son of Walter Channing [*q.v.*] and his wife, Barbara Perkins. His father was an eminent physician and a professor in the Harvard Medical School. His mother died while he was yet young, and Ellery—often so called to distinguish him from his uncle, William Ellery Channing [*q.v.*]—spent an unhappy childhood in the home of a great-aunt, Mrs. Bennett Forbes of Milton, and was sent rather young to the Round Hill School in Northampton. Later he attended the Boston Latin School and a private school and in the summer of 1834 entered Harvard College. There he remained for only a few months. Already as fractious and incalculable as he was brilliant, he soon found chapel tiresome, and stayed away; then the whole program became a bore, and young Channing walked out. When his family discovered his whereabouts, he was at

Curzon's Mill, on the Merrimac, about four miles west of Newburyport, writing poetry. The college authorities took a sensible view of the escapade, but Ellery did not return. About this time he seems to have decided that poetry was his vocation and that any other activity of his must be subordinate to it. His first verses to appear in print were "The Spider," in the *New England Magazine* for October 1835. With a friend, Joseph Dwight, he moved out to Woodstock, McHenry County, Ill., in 1839; but learning, as Hawthorne did at Brook Farm, that prolonged bodily labor is not conducive to writing, he sold his quarter-section within a year. Next he sojourned in Cincinnati, where his uncle, James H. Perkins, was minister of the Unitarian Church. There he gave private lessons, wrote for newspapers, dallied over law books, and fell in love with the demure, pretty younger sister of Margaret Fuller. In the East he met Emerson, who read some of his poems in manuscript and wrote an appreciative critique of them for the *Dial,* I, 220–32 (1841). Channing and Ellen Fuller were married in the autumn of 1842 and settled in Concord in order to be near Emerson. In 1844 Channing was in New York writing for Horace Greeley's *Tribune;* in 1845 he made a visit of a few months to France and Italy; from 1855 to 1858 he was absent from Concord again as an editor of the *New Bedford Mercury.* Except for these excursions he made Concord his home till the end of his long life. His personality, which was both elfin and elvish and "as naturally whimsical," according to Thoreau, "as a cow is brindled," lives in the writings of his friends, Hawthorne, Emerson, Thoreau, and F. B. Sanborn. To Thoreau he was especially devoted, for they had much in common. He was his almost invariable companion in his walks around Concord and accompanied him also on his trips to Cape Cod, Maine, and Canada. He wrote the first biography of Thoreau and edited several of the posthumous volumes of his friend's writings. Separating from his family, he lived alone for a number of years in a small house in Concord. His old age was passed in the home of Franklin B. Sanborn.

Channing's published works are: *Poems* (1843); *Poems, Second Series* (1847); *Conversations in Rome between an Artist, a Catholic, and a Critic* (1847); *The Woodman and Other Poems* (1849); *Near Home, a Poem* (1858); *The Wanderer, a Colloquial Poem* (1871); *Thoreau, the Poet-Naturalist* (1873; enlarged edition, 1902); *Eliot, a Poem* (1885); *John Brown and the Heroes of Harper's Ferry, a Poem* (1886), and *Poems of Sixty-Five Years*

(selected and edited by F. B. Sanborn, 1902). Several occasional poems were also published separately, and he contributed prose and verse to the *Dial* and to other magazines. As a poet Channing was and is almost completely unknown. Edgar Allan Poe greeted his first volume with a merciless review in *Graham's Magazine* for August 1843, and the rest was silence. The faults of diction, meter, and syntax for which Poe excoriated him were deplored by Channing's friends also. Emerson complained that Channing should have lain awake all night to find the true rhyme for a verse instead of availing himself of the first that came. Thoreau recommended that he discipline himself by writing in Latin and described his companion's style with matchless adequacy as "sublimo-slipshod." But Channing's case was beyond help; a thoroughgoing Transcendentalist in his poetic practise, he could only improvise, he could not revise and polish. Yet in spite of his uncertain technique he is a genuine poet, capable of long passages and whole poems of complete felicity. His poetry, moreover, has atmosphere. It is as indigenous to New England as the russet apple, and has the russet's tang and homely flavor. All that it needs is the anthologist who will separate the sound fruit from the culls.

[Channing's papers were left by his will to F. B. Sanborn, who wrote much about him, especially the "Biographical Introduction" to *Poems of Sixty-Five Years* (1902) and "A Concord Note-Book" in the *Critic,* vol. XLVII (four of the five papers in this volume dealing with Channing). The *Dial,* G. W. Cooke's *Hist. and Biog. Introduction to Accompany The Dial* (Cleveland, The Rowfant Club, 1902), II, 75–86; Emerson's *Journals,* practically the whole canon of Thoreau's work, and Hawthorne's *Mosses from an Old Manse* and the *Am. Note Books* contain material for Channing's biography. Minor sources of information are also numerous.]

                                 G.H.G.

CHANNING, WILLIAM FRANCIS (Feb. 22, 1820–Mar. 19, 1901), inventor, was born in Boston, Mass., the son of William Ellery Channing [*q.v.*] and Ruth (Gibbs) Channing. He attended the Boston schools and then entered Harvard College but he did not complete his course there, as his interest in medicine led him to change to the University of Pennsylvania, from which he received his M.D. degree in 1844. Following his graduation he settled first in Boston and subsequently in Providence, but did not practise, his engrossing interest in science causing him to engage in a variety of scientific activities instead. He was an assistant on the first geological survey of New Hampshire, made between 1841 and 1842, and the following year was assistant editor, under Dr. Henry Bowditch, of the *Latimer Journal,* published in Boston. In 1847, he served as an assistant on the geological survey of the Lake Superior copper region. During the same year he was associated with Dr. John Bacon, Jr., in the editing and publication of *Davis' Manual of Magnetism* (1848).

Channing's interest in electricity began as early as 1842 when he called attention to the value of applying electric current to the giving of alarms of fire, and the year after his graduation from college he became intermittently associated with Moses G. Farmer [*q.v.*], one of America's pioneer electrical experimenters, in the perfection of a fire-alarm telegraph. Channing and Farmer gradually developed their idea between 1845 and 1851, and in June 1851 the city of Boston voted $10,000 to test their device. A short time thereafter the system was in operation with Farmer as superintendent. It was crude and unreliable but was basally correct, and the partners, after many trials and tribulations, gradually obtained public favor. It was not, however, until 1857 that they applied for patents. On May 19 of that year they received Patent No. 17,355, entitled "magnetic electric fire-alarm telegraph for cities." Shortly thereafter the patents were purchased by Gamewell & Company, which organization has since developed the present-day electric fire-alarm system universally in use. On Mar. 5, 1859, Farmer and Channing obtained a second patent on an improvement in their system which was turned over to the purchasing company. Thereafter Channing applied himself in other directions. In 1865 he patented a ship railway for the inter-oceanic transport of ships, and in 1877 invented a portable electro-magnetic telegraph. He was the author of *Notes on the Medical Applications of Electricity* (1849); "On the Municipal Electric Telegraph," in the *American Journal of Science and Arts*, 1852; "The American Fire Alarm Telegraph," in *Smithsonian Institution Annual Report*, 1854; "Inter-Oceanic Ship Railway," remarks before a select committee of the House of Representatives, Mar. 27, 1880. Channing was married to Mary Jane Tarr whose death preceded his by many years.

[Edward H. Knight, *Am. Mechanical Dict.* (1876); *Boston Herald*, Mar. 20, 1901; *Electrical Rev.*, May 6, 1901; Patent Office records; records of Harvard Coll. and Univ. of Pa.]   C.W.M.

CHANNING, WILLIAM HENRY (May 25, 1810–Dec. 23, 1884), Unitarian clergyman, reformer, author, was born in Boston, the son of Francis Dana and Susan Higginson Channing. His father died the year he was born, and he was brought up by his mother, a woman of strong mind and character, who relied much upon the advice of the boy's uncle, William Ellery Channing [*q.v.*]. His ancestors, near and remote, had been distinguished in literature, religion, and

public service, and the youth, high-strung, imaginative, and chivalrous in the extreme, early showed a tendency toward all three. He studied at the Boston Latin School, graduated from Harvard College in 1829, and from the Harvard Divinity School in 1833.

Due to a certain amount of temperamental instability, an unwillingness to confine himself to fixed forms and institutions, and especially to the utter unpracticality of the man, his career was one of constantly shifting scenes. After supplying several churches, he spent a year (1835–36) in Europe. Upon his return he married, in December 1836, Julia Allen of Rondout, N. Y. He then went to New York City where, under the auspices of the Unitarians, he attempted to establish a free church among the industrial classes. He abandoned the project in August 1837. In September of the following year he accepted an invitation to supply the Unitarian church at Cincinnati, was called to the pastorate in March 1839, and in May was ordained. From June of this year until March 1841, he also edited the *Western Messenger*, the organ of Unitarianism in the West. Convinced that the Gospels are unreliable as history and that Christianity is not a divine institution, he resigned his pastorate in 1841. As his views clarified, however, he came to have a jubilant and abiding faith in God as the universal Father, and in the human race as an expression of the divine will, destined to attain a state of harmony, righteousness, love, and felicity. "Transfigured humanity" came to be for him the symbol of Christianity, and in the prevailing spirit of reform, he saw a "heavenly hope." From 1843 to 1845 he was the leader of an independent society in New York, the members of which were "fellow-seekers after a higher holiness, wisdom, and humanity." It broke up when Channing felt called to go to Brook Farm, where, however, he remained but a few months. On Jan. 3, 1847, the Religious Union of Associationists was formed in Boston, including among others George Ripley, John S. Dwight, Francis G. Shaw, and Albert Brisbane, with Channing at its head. Its object was mutual sympathy and aid in striving to spread among mankind the reign of love. It came to an end in 1850. In the summer of 1852, Channing went to Rochester to preach for the Unitarian Society and remained there until August 1854.

His convictions being what they were, it was inevitable, that on the platform and by his writings he should give aid to a variety of reforms. He demanded substantial equality for all men, accepted Fourierism as the scientific form of his own social ideal, and, from September 1843 to

April 1844, edited *The Present,* a Socialistic organ. From July 1849 to April 1850 he edited *The Spirit of the Age.* He was an ardent advocate of the abolition of slavery, opposed the Fugitive Slave Law, and at Rochester was interested in the operation of the "underground railroad." He also labored for the emancipation of women and the promotion of temperance.

After 1854 the most of his life was spent in England. From October 1854 to October 1857 he was in charge of Renshaw Street Chapel, Liverpool, and then succeeded James Martineau at Hope Street Chapel. The Civil War brought him back to the United States in 1861. He became pastor of the Unitarian society in Washington, served in camp and hospital under the Sanitary Commission, and in 1863–64 was chaplain of the House of Representatives. He made a trip to England and Scotland in 1863 and gave public addresses in behalf of the Union. Soon after the close of the War he resumed his residence in England, but made occasional visits to the United States. His son became a member of Parliament, and a daughter, the wife of Sir Edwin Arnold. He died in London and his body was brought to Boston for burial.

He was a person of singular purity of character, radiant faith in man and his divine destiny, unbounded enthusiasm, humble but unflinching honesty and courage. Though his learning was extensive and his mind acute, feeling subordinated reason, and he was a most unpractical idealist and mystic; nevertheless, he lent strength to the causes he championed.

He wrote numerous articles for periodicals, and published sermons and addresses. His most important literary work is his *Life of William Ellery Channing* (3 vols., 1848), which attracted wide notice and went through several editions. He translated Jouffroy's *Introduction to Ethics* in 1841, published *Memoir and Writings of James Handasyd Perkins* in 1857, with Emerson and James Freeman Clarke edited *Memoirs of Margaret Fuller Ossoli* in 1852, and published, in Liverpool, *The Civil War in America, or the Slaveholder's Conspiracy* in 1861. In 1873 he edited from manuscripts a volume of William Ellery Channing's sermons, under the title, *The Perfect Life.*

[See *Gen. Cat. Divinity School Harvard Univ.* (1910); O. B. Frothingham, *Memoir of Wm. Henry Channing* (1886), and *Transcendentalism in New Eng.* (1903); Jas. Freeman Clarke in *Unit. Rev.,* Mar. 1885; review of Frothingham's *Memoir* in *Unit. Rev.,* Mar. 1887. A sketch by T. W. Higginson in *Heralds of a Liberal Faith: The Preachers* (1910), ed. by S. A. Eliot, is inaccurate in some details.]   H.E.S.

CHANUTE, OCTAVE (Feb. 18, 1832–Nov. 23, 1910), civil engineer, aerial navigator, was born in Paris, the son of Joseph and Eliza (De Bonnaire) Chanute. His parents emigrated to the United States in 1838, and he was educated in private schools in New York City. Without any formal instruction in engineering, for none was then to be had, he began his career with employment by the Hudson River Railroad, and from 1853 to 1863 served in various capacities with Western railroads. On Mar. 12, 1857, he married Annie James of Peoria, Ill. From 1863 to 1867 he was chief engineer of the Chicago & Alton Railroad. In the two years 1867–68 he planned and superintended the construction of the first bridge across the Missouri River, at Kansas City. He subsequently constructed several railroads in Kansas and from 1873 to 1883 he was in private practise as a consulting engineer, mainly on the construction of iron railroad bridges. But though his successful career as a civil engineer brought him many distinctions, his main claim to fame rests on his work in aerial navigation. The honor of the first scientific gliding experiments made in the United States probably belongs to him. The great exponents of gliding, who really learned how flight could be accomplished, at great personal risk paved the way for the achievements of the Wright brothers. The famous Germans, Otto and Gustav Lilienthal, began their gliding experiments in 1867. Pilcher brought the art to England. From the year 1889, Chanute devoted to aerodynamic theory the greater part of his energies, studying Lilienthal's experiments very carefully. In the year before Lilienthal's death, he himself began to make gliding flights. In 1896 and 1897, he and his assistants made hundreds of glides from a hill ninety-five feet high on the sand dunes of Dune Park, near Lake Michigan. The courage of a man of sixty in undertaking such work is remarkable. In a truly scientific spirit, Chanute tabulated the results of all his experiments and made many notes on the strength and variations of air currents. His actual glides through the air were less impressive and daring than those of Lilienthal and Pilcher, but he had a better scientific training, and more ability as a designer. He was also an acute observer. The airplane of to-day lands tail low. Chanute learned this practise by watching the sparrow. "When the latter approaches the street, he throws his body back, tilts his outspread wings nearly square to the course, and on the cushion of air thus encountered he stops his speed and drops lightly to the ground. So do all birds. We tried it with misgivings, but found it perfectly effective."

His first glides were made with a Lilienthal monoplane which he found unsafe and treacherous. He then designed a five-plane glider, with the surfaces vertically superposed, the flier below them, and a rudder in the rear. An important advance lay in the fact that the wings on either side could swerve fore and aft, so as to bring the center of lift always over the center of gravity, to maintain balance. It was no longer necessary to indulge in violent body movements or undignified kicking of the feet. This glider was tractable in a twenty-mile wind and sailed down a slope of one in four. The five-plane glider was later simplified to a three-decker, and finally there emerged the famous Chanute biplane of novel and exquisite design. It consisted of two arched surfaces, held together by vertical posts and diagonal wires, in the form of a Pratt truss. It weighed only twenty-three pounds, had an area of 135 square feet, and readily carried 178 pounds at twenty-three miles per hour. It was steady in flight even when the wind was blowing seventeen miles an hour over ground.

The first glider the Wrights built was largely modeled upon Chanute's biplane, and they also followed his principle of inherent stability, in conjunction with the use of movable surfaces for control in lieu of shifting weights. In 1901 Chanute visited the camp of the Wrights, watched their experiments and gave them every encouragement; particularly because they were interested in the art without thought of pecuniary gain. The Wrights never failed to acknowledge the help they received from Chanute, and considered him one of the greatest pioneers in the engineering problems of flight.

Always full of enthusiasm and animal spirits, Chanute wrote, at the age of sixty or more, "There is no more delightful sensation than that of gliding through the air. All the faculties are on the alert, and the motion is astonishingly smooth and elastic." He was an exceedingly able, scientific, and inventive engineer, with a generous, courageous, humorous spirit, and a Gallic power of clear and forceful expression. His writings include *Aerial Navigation* (1891); *Progress in Flying Machines* (1894); "Gliding Experiments," in *Journal of the Western Society of Engineers,* October 1897; "Recent Progress in Aviation," *Ibid.,* April 1910 (reprinted in *Annual Report of the Board of Regents of the Smithsonian Institution,* 1910), a remarkable review of power-driven flight experiments from 1904 to the great Rheims Meet of 1909.

[*Who's Who in America,* 1910–11; *Men and Women of America,* 1910; E. C. H. Vivian and W. L. Marsh, *Hist. of Aeronautics* (1921); C. L. M. Brown, *Conquest of the Air* (London, 1927); A. F. Zahm, *Aerial Navigation* (1911); *Bull. Am. Inst. Mining Engineers,* Feb. 1911; *Chicago Inter-Ocean,* Nov. 24, 1910.] A. K.

CHAPELLE, PLACIDE LOUIS (Aug. 28, 1842–Aug. 9, 1905), Catholic Archbishop of New Orleans, La., was born at Runes, Lozère, France. His parents, Jean Baptiste Chapelle and Marie Antoinette de Viala, were noted for their piety and devotion to the Church. An uncle, afterward bishop of Port-au-Prince in Haiti, sent the young Chapelle, when his father died, to the college of Enghien in Belgium, and brought him to the United States in 1859 where he entered St. Mary's Seminary, Baltimore. In this institution he pursued the philosophical and theological courses with distinction, receiving ordination to the priesthood at the hands of Archbishop Spalding in Baltimore, June 28, 1865, and a doctorate in divinity, *maxima cum laude,* in 1869. From 1865 to 1869 he was occupied with pastoral work at St. John's Church, Rockville, Md., whence he was transferred to St. Joseph's Church, Baltimore, and, in 1882, to St. Matthew's Church, Washington, D. C. To this important post he brought both competence as a pastor and experience as a man of affairs. He had acted as secretary of the diocesan council of Baltimore (1869) and as Archbishop Spalding's theological adviser at the Vatican Council (1870). In Washington he attracted many members of the diplomatic corps to St. Matthew's and won warm friends in official circles. Preferment in the ecclesiastical world also attended his career in Washington. He accompanied Cardinal Gibbons to New Orleans in 1888, was secretary of the Bureau of Catholic Indian Missions, and a promoter of the movement which led to the founding of the Catholic University of America. On Aug. 21, 1891, he was appointed to assist Archbishop Salpointe of Santa Fé, New Mexico, as coadjutor with right of succession, and as titular bishop of Arabissus. He was consecrated by Cardinal Gibbons in the cathedral at Baltimore, Nov. 1, 1891, was made titular archbishop of Sabaste, May 10, 1893, and was inducted as Archbishop Salpointe's successor, Jan. 9, 1894. He was not, however, to be long in the Southwest. Transferred to New Orleans by a papal brief (Dec. 1, 1897), he took charge of the see on Mar. 24, 1898. A few weeks later the United States and Spain clashed, with results that diverted the attention of the Archbishop from the affairs of his diocese. His familiarity with the ideals and laws of the Church, as well as with those of the United States, caused Leo XIII to commission him to represent ecclesiastical interests at the peace conference at Paris, where he secured the recognition of ecclesiastical concerns in the peace treaty. He was appointed, on Oct. 11, 1898, apostolic delegate to Cuba and Porto Rico and envoy extraordinary to the Philippine Islands, and on Aug. 9, 1899, apostolic delegate to the Philippine Islands. There he was confronted by a situation full of obstacles. American officials in the islands not only had difficulty in understanding the principles of the old Spanish order, in which the temporal and spiritual powers had been closely associated, but also naturally tended to sympathize with the revolutionists, who were anti-clerical. Archbishop Chapelle tactfully and successfully adjusted ecclesiastical affairs to fit the new régime. Though his insular commissions drew him from his diocesan work in New Orleans for months at a time, he remained always active in the affairs of the Church and community there. He founded a Catholic Winter School in New Orleans. Closing the little seminary at Ponchatoula, La., he induced the Lazarists to take charge of the present Seminary of St. Louis. On his accession the diocesan debt amounted to $135,000; this he had wiped out by the end of the year 1903. His last days were spent in making a visitation of the parishes of his diocese while the yellow fever was claiming victims on all sides. Of this disease he himself died, on Aug. 9, 1905. The New Orleans *Picayune* characterized him editorially the following day: "The archbishop possessed a sweet and most pleasing manner and was the charming center of the intellectual and social gatherings that were at rare intervals able to secure his presence. He was not only a great prelate . . . but he was also a statesman, a scholar and a citizen of the highest quality, devoted to the public interests and teaching patriotism as well as religion."

[The Rev. J. T. Alexis Orban, who was close to Archbishop Chapelle and who was to have written his biography, contributed a short sketch of his life to the *Cath. Encyc.* (1908), but furnished no bibliography. References (with ample bibliographies) to the archbishop's work occur in the *Cath. Encyc.*, in articles on New Orleans, Philippine Islands, Porto Rico. See also the files of the diocesan organ, the *Morning Star,* and the local press, especially the *Picayune* and the *Times-Democrat.* The issues of Aug. 10, 1905, contain extended biographical notices and appreciations. The *Cath. Dir. and Clergy List* (Milwaukee, pub. annually) is valuable for information concerning the dioceses which Archbishop Chapelle administered. The writer is also under obligations to the Archbishop's niece for other data.]

F.J.T.

CHAPIN, AARON LUCIUS (Feb. 6, 1817–July 22, 1892), Congregational clergyman, college president, a son of Laertes and Laura (Colton) Chapin, was born of New England stock in Hartford, Conn. Both of his grandfathers were deacons in the Congregational Church. He prepared for college at the Hartford Grammar School and graduated with honor at Yale College in the class of 1837. He graduated in 1842 at Union Theological Seminary,

New York, and went to Milwaukee, Wis., in 1843, to become pastor of the First Presbyterian Church, where he was ordained Jan. 24, 1844. From the outset keenly interested in the educational development of the Territory, he attended in the summer of 1844 a conference held at Cleveland, Ohio, to consider the religious and educational needs of the Mississippi Valley, and was one of seven men who, while returning to Wisconsin together, resolved to initiate a movement for the establishment of a college of the New England type in southern Wisconsin or northern Illinois. The convention which they called for this purpose, consisting of fifty-six delegates from Wisconsin, Illinois, and Iowa, met in Beloit, Wis., as the most important town educationally in the region. The third of a series of four conventions decided in May 1845 upon the establishment of the college at Beloit; the fourth, in October, elected a board of trustees of whom Chapin was one, as he was also a member of its executive committee, an office which he held throughout his life. From the beginning one of the most influential and trusted members of the board, he was called in 1849 to become the first president of the college and entered upon his official duties in February 1850. As president for thirty-six years (1850–86) of the first institution for higher education in all that part of the country extending from Lake Michigan to the Pacific Ocean, Chapin was for over a generation the center of the efforts to equip and endow the young college as well as the guiding spirit of its educational administration. He also gave his influence freely beyond the bounds of the college; was trustee of Chicago Theological Seminary, 1858–91; of Rockford Seminary (later College), 1845–92; corporate member of the American Board for Foreign Missions, 1851–89; director of the American Home Missionary Society, 1850–83; trustee of the Wisconsin Institute for Deaf and Dumb, 1865–81, and president of its board 1873–81; one of the founders (1870) of the Wisconsin Academy of Sciences, and its president, 1878–81; member of the National Council of Education from its foundation in 1881 to 1888. As associate editor of *Johnson's Cyclopedia,* 1875–78, he contributed articles on social science and political economy. He was editor of the *Congregational Review,* 1870–71, and associate editor of the *New Englander,* 1872–73. In 1878 he published a revision of Francis Wayland's *Political Economy* (1837). His own *First Principles of Political Economy* (1879) was praised by experts for its lucidity and balance. He was twice married: in 1843, to Martha Colton of Lenox, Mass., who died in 1859; and in 1861, to

Fanny Learned Coit of New London, Conn. Tall and of vigorous physique, he possessed quick discernment and sound judgment, and the power of prompt leadership without dictation or vanity.

[A. L. Chapin, "Beloit College, Its Origin and Aims," *New Englander*, Apr. 1872; addresses at *Beloit Alumni Memorial Service* (1893); Edward Dwight Eaton, *Hist. Sketches of Beloit College* (1928).] E. D. E.

CHAPIN, ALONZO BOWEN (Mar. 10, 1808–July 9, 1858), Episcopal clergyman, descended from Deacon Samuel Chapin of Springfield, Mass., whose statue by Saint-Gaudens is widely known as "The Puritan," was born at Somers, Conn., the eldest son of Reuben and Lovisa (Russell) Chapin. His father was educated for the ministry and was licensed to preach, but never became a pastor because of poor health. The son also was delicate, and, relinquishing on that account his early intention to enter the Congregational ministry, studied law in a lawyer's office. Admitted to the bar in 1831, he established himself in Wallingford, Conn. The following year he married Hannah B. Waldo. Coming into contact with some New Haven lawyers who were Episcopalians, he was led to inquire into the claims of their church, and, after diligent study, became himself an ardent Episcopalian. He contributed to the various Church periodicals and in 1836 was chosen as editor of the newly-founded *Chronicles of the Church*, holding the position for eight years. Having regained his health, he fulfilled his early desire to enter the ministry, and was ordained deacon in 1838 and priest a year later. For twelve years he was rector of Christ Church, West Haven. Pamphlets and magazine articles, mostly on local or Biblical history, came forth from his pen in a steady stream. In 1841 he issued *An English Spelling Book,* on new philological principles, but it had no special success. A year later appeared his *View of the Organization and Order of the Primitive Church* (New Haven, 1842), his most important work. It passed through several editions, being regarded by Episcopalians as an arsenal of unanswerable facts and references. But Chapin had not the equipment to make a real historical contribution in this field, and the work has passed from view. His favorite thesis appears from the titles of two pamphlets which he issued soon after, *A Churchman's Reasons for Not Joining in Other Worship* (1844), and *Puritanism Not Genuine Protestantism* (1847). The Episcopal Church, that is, he regarded as genuinely Protestant, but a branch of the Catholic Church, as other Protestant bodies were not, by virtue of its Order, Ministry, and Worship. Individuals of other Protestant bodies he considered Christians by

virtue of their baptism; but their organizations he looked upon as schismatic, and with such he could have no fellowship. He was not however ritualistic, and he viewed the modern Church of Rome with mingled pity and abhorrence. In 1850 he became rector of St. Luke's Parish in South Glastonbury, Conn., but two years later was so crippled with rheumatism as to be obliged to engage an assistant. He obtained the editorship of the *Calendar,* a Church paper, which enabled him to defray the expense. In 1853 he published a local history entitled *Glastonbury for Two Hundred Years.* In 1855 he resigned his cure and removed to Hartford, continuing there his work as editor to the last week of his life.

[The principal sources are the *Calendar* (Hartford), July 17, 1858; and the *Am. Quart. Ch. Rev. and Ecclesiastical Reg.* (New Haven), Oct. 1858.] T. D. B.

CHAPIN, CALVIN (July 22, 1763–Mar. 16, 1851), Congregational clergyman, was the fourth son of Deacon Edward Chapin of Chicopee, Mass., and his wife Eunice Colton. His early years were spent after the manner of farmers' sons of the period, and at the age of fifteen he served for six months as a fifer in a Revolutionary militia company. His preparation for college, which was delayed somewhat by the war, was completed under Rev. Charles Backus of Somers, Conn. At Yale he was one of the best scholars of his class, winning the Berkeleian scholarship or "Dean's Bounty," and graduating in 1788. After two years as a successful and popular teacher in Hartford, he began the study of theology under Rev. Nathan Perkins of West Hartford, at the same time continuing to teach. He was licensed to preach by the Hartford North Association in October 1791 but instead of going directly into the ministry, served as tutor at Yale from 1791 to 1794. This was an eminently successful period of his life, and one upon which he always looked back with much satisfaction. On Apr. 30, 1794, he was ordained pastor of Stepney Parish, Wethersfield (now Rocky Hill), Conn., where he remained for life. His salary during his entire ministry was $333 per year. From 1805 to 1831 he was a trustee of the Missionary Society of Connecticut in whose interests he was very active, making in 1806 a journey to Ohio to investigate certain difficulties that had there arisen in connection with the work. He was prominent in forming the Connecticut Bible Society in 1809, and in 1810 was one of the five founders of the American Board of Foreign Missions, serving as its recording secretary for thirty-two years. He was one of the founders of the Connecticut Society for the promotion of Good Morals, in 1813, and was active in its affairs till its dissolution. In 1816 he became a member of the board of visitors of Andover Seminary and was clerk of that board till 1832. He was a member of the Yale Corporation from 1820 to 1846, and was on its prudential committee for twenty-five years. A pioneer in the temperance cause, he took an extreme stand as early as 1812 and for a time went so far as to persuade his people to abolish the sacramental use of wine. His published works consist of several sermons and an essay on *Sacramental Wines* (1835). Although tall and well proportioned, he made a rather ungainly appearance in the pulpit. He was practical, possessed marked independence of character, and had a pithy and telling way of putting things. In the pulpit he was very solemn. But on all other occasions his wit was much in evidence, often subjecting him to criticism. His tastes were scholarly, and he read the Latin and Greek classics all his life. On Feb. 2, 1795, he was married to Jerusha, daughter of Rev. Jonathan Edwards of New Haven.

[F. B. Dexter, *Yale Biogs.*, 4th ser. (1907); W. B. Sprague, *Annals Am. Pulpit*, vol. II (1857); Am. Board of Foreign Missions, *Memorial Volume* (1861); E. P. Parker, *Appreciation of Calvin Chapin, D.D. of Rocky Hill, Conn.* (1908); *Hist. of Ancient Wethersfield, Conn.*, ed. by Henry R. Stiles (1904), I, 854–62.]

F. T. P.

CHAPIN, CHESTER WILLIAM (Dec. 16, 1798–June 10, 1883), railroad promoter, was descended from Deacon Samuel Chapin who settled in Springfield in 1642. He was born at Ludlow, Mass., the youngest of the seven children of Ephraim and Mary (Smith) Chapin. His formal education was limited to a few winters at the district school and a season at Westfield Academy. This meager schooling was in part due to his father's early death which necessitated a boyhood of arduous toil. As a young man, Chapin was employed with a yoke of oxen in constructing the foundations of the Dwight mill, the first of Chicopee's manufacturing concerns, and for a short time after reaching his majority he tended bar for his brother Erastus, a Springfield inn-keeper. Returning to Chicopee, he conducted a country store, took contracts for building construction, and married Dorcas Chapin, daughter of Col. Abel and Dorcas Chapin. His subsequent career was tied up closely with the development of transportation in the Connecticut Valley. His first connection with the transportation business was as driver of his brother's ox-team which carried merchandise from the river wharves to the Springfield stores. The next step was the purchase from Horatio Sargeant, who owned most of the Springfield

stages, of a part interest in the Northampton line, and the two men soon became partners in the Brattleboro and Hartford line. No sooner had the practicability of steamboat navigation on the Connecticut been demonstrated than Chapin and Sargeant entered aggressively into the building and operation of steamboats until they became not only the chief concern operating river steamboats, but enjoyed for a long time a practical monopoly of the passenger business between Springfield and Hartford. Chapin's steamboat interests eventually included the ownership of boats running from Hartford and New Haven to New York.

With the coming of railroads Chapin sold his steamboats operating north of Hartford and entered enthusiastically into the development of steam railroads. He was a prime mover in getting the New York & New Haven Railroad to extend to Springfield, and soon became a large stockholder in the Western Railroad (the present Boston & Albany) and in the Connecticut River Railroad. He was president of the latter (1850–54) when he was called to head the Boston & Albany. His presidency, which extended to 1877, was a time of prosperity and wise development and included the period of consolidation with the Boston & Worcester which insured through western connection with Boston. Notwithstanding the fact that the Massachusetts legislature censured him because of the leasing by the Boston & Albany of the Ware River Railroad, an enterprise in which he was personally interested, the *Springfield Republican* said that "He had no sympathy with the modern gambling school which waters stocks and preys upon corporations without regard to the public interest" (June 11, 1883, p. 4).

Chapin was reputed to be the wealthiest resident of Springfield. He was founder of the Chapin Bank and the Agawam Bank and vice-president of the Hampden Savings Bank as well as a director of the Springfield Fire & Marine Insurance Company and the Massasoit Insurance Company. He was also interested in various manufacturing establishments and a large landowner. A transportation enthusiast to the end, he participated prominently in the building of the first street car line in Springfield.

A life-long Democrat in a Republican district, Chapin had the confidence of his fellow citizens sufficiently to be elected to several town and city offices, to the state legislature in 1844, to the Massachusetts constitutional convention of 1853, and on a reform wave to the Forty-fourth Congress in 1874. He was one of the seceders at the Democratic convention at Baltimore in 1860 and was later a Breckenridge and Lane elector. He became a war Democrat and largely paid for the uniforms of the city guard when that body joined the 10th Regiment. In appearance he is described as a man of "commanding presence with a firm impassive face whereon the stubby grey moustache covered the lines of a strong mouth" (*Springfield Republican*, June 11, 1883, p. 5).

[*Springfield Republican, ante*; Chester Wells Chapin, *Sketches of the Old Inhabitants and Other Citizens of Old Springfield* (1893); *Railroad Gazette*, June 15, 1883; Mason A. Green, *Springfield 1836–68* (1888); *Chapin Book* (1924), comp. by Gilbert W. Chapin.]

H. U. F.

CHAPIN, EDWIN HUBBELL (Dec. 29, 1814–Dec. 26, 1880), Universalist clergyman, was one of the many descendants of Deacon Samuel Chapin, Puritan, of Springfield, Mass. Born in Union Village, Washington County, N. Y., he was the son of Alpheus and Beulah (Hubbell) Chapin. For four years (1828–32) he studied in Pioneer Academy, Bennington, Vt., and was post-office clerk in this town for two years. He studied law for a time in Troy, N. Y., and then removed to Utica. His soul was revolted by the severer aspects of the orthodox religion in which he had been reared, and, becoming acquainted with Universalism in the office of the *Evangelical Magazine and Gospel Advocate* of which he was associate editor, he entered the Universalist ministry, being ordained on Sept. 27, 1838. During the same year he married Harriet Newland of Utica. He was pastor in Richmond, Va., and Charlestown, Mass., and was the colleague of Hosea Ballou [*q.v.*], at the School Street Church, Boston. In 1848 he became pastor of the Fourth Universalist Society in New York. Twice the church moved to larger quarters on Broadway and then to Fifth Ave., in order to accommodate ever growing congregations. The Church of the Divine Paternity remains as the monument of his life work. He was a friend and contemporary of Henry Ward Beecher, who said of him, "I have never met or heard a man who in the height and glow of his eloquence surpassed or equalled him." Although he was rather awkward in movement and his clothes were never a happy fit, his voice was well rounded, and he was a master of climaxes and brilliant and original in his metaphors. His emphasis was on Christ, not on the Christianity of the creeds. He had great sympathy with and deeply enjoyed Kingsley, Maurice, and Martineau. A lyceum orator of power, an earnest advocate of temperance, he gave his heart and voice to any benevolent or patriotic enterprise. One of the founders of Chapin Home for indigent men and women, he was also a trustee of Bellevue College and Hospital. He was a voluminous writer, his chief publications being: *Duties of Young Men* (1840); *Discourses on Various Subjects* (1841); *The Philosophy of Reform* (1843); *Hours of Communion* (1844); *The Crown of Thorns* (1848); *Duties of Young Women* (1848); *Discourses on the Lord's Prayer* (1850); *Characters in the Gospels* (1852); *Moral Aspects of City Life* (1853); *Discourses on the Beatitudes* (1853); *True Manliness* (1854); *Humanity in the City* (1854); *Select Sermons* (1859); *Extemporaneous Discourses* (1860); *Living Words* (1860); *Lessons of Faith and Life* (1877); *The Church of the Living God* (1881).

[Sumner Ellis, *Life of Edwin H. Chapin, D.D.* (1882); John Ross Dix, *Pulpit Portraits* (1854); Charles Follen Lee and T. T. Sawyer, *In Memoriam, Edwin Hubbell Chapin, D.D.* (1881); Richard Eddy, *Universalism in America* (1886), containing complete bibliography.]

T. C. R.

CHAPLIN, JEREMIAH (Jan. 2, 1776–May 7, 1841), Baptist clergyman, and college president, was born in Rowley (later Georgetown), Mass., the son of Asa and Mary (Bailey) Chaplin. Brought up in a deeply religious atmosphere, at the age of ten he joined the Baptist Church. He remained at home assisting on his father's farm until he was nearly of age, but at the same time he prepared himself for college and finally entered Brown, where he graduated in 1799 with the highest honors. For a year he was a tutor at Brown and then his early religious interests asserted themselves. He studied theology under the direction of Dr. Baldwin of Boston and probably in the summer of 1802 assumed his first pastoral charge, the Baptist church in Danvers, Mass., where he remained for fourteen years. Seldom has a minister been as revered as Chaplin evidently was. One of his parishioners said he felt toward him as he would have felt toward St. Paul or St. Peter, an attitude shared by many in the community. While he was at Danvers he gathered about him for instruction a group of young men who were preparing to enter the ministry. When in 1817 he was asked to become principal of the Maine Literary and Theological Institution, he took the entire group with him. In 1820 this school was given a college charter and in the next year was known as Waterville College. Here Chaplin remained for thirteen years as president and under his "wise and efficient administration" the foundations of the later success of Colby College were laid. He was a thin, spare, tall man, according to one of his students, with a rather sepulchral voice. At early chapel services when it was actually too dark to read, this student wondered how Chaplin managed to see the Bible chapters until he discovered that he knew by heart practically the entire Bible and merely repeated from memory. In 1833 he resigned, owing to difficulties with the students who resented his characterization of a noisy mass meeting as "the braying of wild asses." He returned to the ministry, preaching for a time at Rowley, Mass., and then at Willington, Conn. His last years were spent in Hamilton, N. Y., where he died suddenly at the age of sixty-five. He published: *The Greatness of Redemption* (1808); *Memoir of William Carey* (1837), with an introduction by Jeremiah Chaplin; *The Evening of Life* (new edition, 1859); *The Memorial Hour* (1864). He was married to Marcia S. O'Brien of Newburyport, Mass., and had ten children.

[C. P. Chipman, *The Formative Period in Colby's Hist.* (1912); J. T. Champlin, *Hist. Discourse delivered at the Fiftieth Anniversary of Colby Univ.* (1870); E. C. Whittemore, *Colby College, 1820–1925* (1927); W. B. Sprague, *Annals of the Am. Pulpit*, vol. VI (1860).]   M. A. K.

CHAPMAN, ALVAN WENTWORTH (Sept. 28, 1809–Apr. 6, 1899), botanist, physician, was for fifty years the leader in Southern botany, as Asa Gray was leader in the North. Born at Southampton, Mass., a son of Paul and Ruth (Pomeroy) Chapman, he entered Amherst College in 1825, graduating with the degree of A.B. in 1830. From 1831 to 1833 he was the tutor of a family on Whitemarsh Island, near Savannah, Ga., and in 1833 was elected principal of the academy at Washington, Ga. It was there that he began the study of medicine, and upon his removal to Quincy, Fla., he began the practise of surgery, which he continued for more than half a century, there, at Marianna, and particularly at Apalachicola. In November 1839 he married Mrs. Mary Ann Hancock, daughter of Benjamin Simmons of New Bern, N. C. He had received no formal training in botany, but as early as 1838, Torrey and Gray began to receive specimens of Southern plants from him, and they named the genus *Chapmania* in his honor. The semi-tropical vegetation of western Florida was at that time practically unknown, and Chapman, whose mind it fired, was its pioneer investigator. During the Civil War he and his wife separated, owing to their divergent allegiance. Though strongly a Unionist, he remained in Apalachicola. His popularity as a surgeon preserved the respect of his fellow citizens, and when guerrillas entered the town, he was always warned by his neighbors, fleeing from his pharmacy to spend a night of hiding in a church. His negro slave boy kept watch

in some marshes near the city, through which Northern prisoners escaping from a military prison had to pass, and the boy or the doctor himself would row the prisoners out to the Federal blockaders outside the harbor.

When the war was over, he and his wife became reconciled, and he gradually began to relinquish his practise, because, he humorously says, his growing deafness prevented him from hearing his patient's groans, so that they lost interest in sending for him, but really because botany more and more absorbed his attention. The first edition of his *Flora of the Southern States* had appeared in 1860, and was for nearly fifty years the only manual of Southern botany. It was not only patterned after Gray's *Manual* but followed Gray's dictates and judgments in practically all matters. As Chapman's reputation grew he came into personal touch with Torrey and Gray, who visited him and his hunting grounds around Apalachicola, as well as with M. A. Curtis, Charles Mohr, and C. S. Sargent. Botanists of the South came to look to him as their leader and to think of him as a Southern man. Actually he was extremely proud of his New England ancestry, and in his vigorous, upright, almost stern character he certainly bore the marks of the Puritan, though in religious matters he remarked of his "damnation and predestination" ancestry that they had swung the pendulum too far and made him what he was.

A picturesque incident is that of the excursion with Gray in search of a rhododendron which Chapman said was new to science. Gray was skeptical as always, but when he beheld the plant he shook hands with Chapman, saying, "Congratulations on *Rhododendron Chapmanii!*" The only slip was that Chapman had reported it as white whereas it turned out to be pink, for its discoverer, unfortunately for a botanist, was color-blind to reds. His deafness, too, in his old age grew upon him and made him a recluse. He published little but his *Flora* which, considering that he put forth its third edition in his nineties, was task enough. His death at Apalachicola was the result of too arduous a trip through impassable swamps in search of a rare species of ash. He had outlived his friend and preceptor, Gray; he had almost outlived his entire generation of scientists; and he was among the last of the old school botanists. In appearance he was tall but a little stooped, he had rugged and powerful features, and throughout his life enjoyed exceptional powers of endurance; his long stride, his enthusiasm on botanical excursions, and his stoic endurance of hardships were familiar to all who knew him. He had a phenomenal memory for events, places, and plants.

[The fullest accounts are Charles Mohr in *Bot. Gaz.*, VII, 473–78 (1899) and F. H. Knowlton in *Plant World*, II, 141–43 (1899). A picturesque personal reminiscence is that of Winifred Kimball in *Jour. N. Y. Bot. Gard.*, XXII, 1–12.]   D. C. P.

CHAPMAN, HENRY CADWALADER (Aug. 17, 1845–Sept. 7, 1909), physician, biologist, was born in Philadelphia, the son of Lieut. George W. Chapman, U. S. N., and his wife Emily Markoe. He was a grandson of Nathaniel Chapman [*q.v.*], the distinguished physician. After receiving his preliminary education in the Faires Classical Institute, then the best known private school in Philadelphia, he entered the College Department of the University of Pennsylvania, from which he graduated in 1864. He then studied medicine in the Medical Department, receiving his M.D. in 1867. After serving two years as a resident physician in the Pennsylvania Hospital, he went abroad and for three years studied under the leading teachers of his time, Sir Richard Owen in London, Alphonse Milne Edward in Paris, Emile Du Bois-Reymond in Berlin, and Joseph Hyrtl in Vienna. Before his departure he had been elected a member of the Academy of Natural Sciences of Philadelphia and from his return in 1872 he took the most active interest in its affairs, contributing to its *Proceedings* and serving at various times as curator. In 1874 he became prosector to the Zoological Society of Philadelphia and thereby secured a great supply of various types of animals for dissection. Nolan states that he made two important contributions to original research. One was his study of the pregnancy and delivery of an elephant which he observed in the winter quarters of a circus in Philadelphia. The other was a study of the placenta of the kangaroo. From 1873 to 1876 he was Leidy's assistant in teaching anatomy at the University of Pennsylvania and in 1877 he became demonstrator of physiology in Jefferson Medical College. After the death of Prof. J. A. Meigs [*q.v.*], in 1879, Chapman was appointed professor of the institutes of medicine and medical jurisprudence at Jefferson. From 1878 to 1888 he was also professor of physiology in the Pennsylvania College of Dental Surgery. For a few years he was coroner's physician of Philadelphia. He published *The Evolution of Life* in 1873, an immature performance which according to his friend Nolan he subsequently regretted. In 1887 he published a *Treatise on Human Physiology*, reprinting in it a brochure on the *History of the Discovery of the Circulation of the Blood* which

had been privately printed in 1884. In 1891 he wrote a Memoir of Joseph Leidy for the *Proceedings* of the Academy of Natural Sciences. In 1892 appeared his *Manual of Medical Jurisprudence and Toxicology*. He was a fellow of the College of Physicians of Philadelphia, and a member of the Franklin Institute and the American Philosophical Society. In 1876 he married Hannah N. Megargee, daughter of Samuel Megargee. He died at his summer home in Bar Harbor, Me., and was buried in Laurel Hill Cemetery, Philadelphia.

[Edward J. Nolan, "A Biog. Notice of Henry Cadwalader Chapman," *Proc. Acad. Nat. Sciences Phila.*, LXII, 255, containing bibliography.]   F. R. P.

CHAPMAN, JOHN (*c.* 1775–Mar. 11, 1847), pioneer, was popularly known as "Johnny Appleseed." His parentage and the exact time and place of his birth have not been discovered. It is generally inferred that he was born in 1775, either in Boston or Springfield, Mass. All that is known of his boyhood is that he had a habit of wandering away on long trips in quest of birds and flowers. His first recorded appearance in the Middle West was in 1800 or 1801, when he was seen as he drifted down the Ohio past Steubenville, in an astonishing craft consisting of two canoes lashed together and freighted with decaying apples brought from the cider presses of western Pennsylvania. His first nursery is claimed to have been planted two miles down the river, and another up Licking Creek. It is believed that he returned frequently to Pennsylvania for more apple seeds, but by 1810 he appears to have made Ashland County, Ohio, his center of activity, living some of the time in a cabin with his half-sister, near Mansfield. It is said that he would travel hundreds of miles to prune his orchards scattered through the wilderness. His price for an apple sapling was a "fip penny bit," but he would exchange it for old clothes or a promissory note which he never collected.

Wherever he went he read aloud to any who would listen from the works of Emanuel Swedenborg, or the Bible, lying on the floor and rolling forth denunciations in tones of thunder, so that he came to be accepted as a sort of Border saint, and the stories of his quixotic kindness to animals, even to insects and rattlers that bit him, are characteristic of the growth of a folk legend. Indians regarded him as a great medicine man; he did indeed scatter the seeds of many reputed herbs of healing, such as catnip, rattlesnake weed, hoarhound, pennyroyal, and, unfortunately, the noxious weed dog-fennel which he believed to be anti-malarial.

In 1812, when the Indians around Mansfield were incited by the British to attacks upon the American frontier settlements, Chapman volunteered to speed through the night to Mt. Vernon, Ohio, to get help from Capt. Douglas, warning many lonely homesteads on the way. This incident is authenticated; there is a wider tradition that he traversed much of northern Ohio apprising settlers of the surrender of the American forces under Hull at Detroit and of the imminence of Indian massacres. The most famous tale about him is of a pharisaical minister who demanded from the pulpit, "Where is the man who, like the primitive Christian, walks toward heaven barefoot and clad in sackcloth?" "Johnny Appleseed," clad in short ragged trousers and a single upper garment of coffee sacking with holes cut for head and arms, barefoot, with a tin mush pan on his head for a hat, approached the pulpit, saying, "Here is a primitive Christian!"

About 1838 Chapman crossed gradually into northern Indiana and continued his missionary and horticultural services. But after a long trip to repair damages in a distant orchard he was overtaken by pneumonia, and presented himself at the door of William Worth's cabin in Allen County, Ind., where he died. He was buried in Archer's graveyard near Fort Wayne. A monument to him was erected by the Hon. M. B. Bushnell, at Mansfield. His legendary life has inspired numerous literary works such as Denton J. Snider's *Johnny Appleseed's Rhymes* (1894), Nell Hillis's *The Quest of John Chapman* (1904), Eleanor Atkinson's *Johnny Appleseed, the Romance of a Sower* (1915), and Vachel Lindsay's "In Praise of Johnny Appleseed" in the *Century Magazine*, August 1921.

[As the life of Chapman survives largely in reminiscences and hearsay, most of the accounts are little more than collections of current anecdotes. Gen. Brinkhoff and O. E. Randall were the orators upon the dedication of the Mansfield monument; their speeches are reprinted in *Ohio Archaeol. and Hist. Quart.*, IX, 303–17 (1901). A biographical sketch of value is *Johnny Appleseed, an Ohio Hero*, by W. A. Duff (1914); W. D. Haley's account in *Harper's Mag.*, XLIII, 830–36, gives many legends concerning Chapman.]   D. C. P.

CHAPMAN, JOHN GADSBY (Dec. 8, 1808–Nov. 28, 1889), painter, was born in Alexandria, Va. He was assisted in his early art studies by George Cooke and C. B. King. At sixteen he tried his first oil painting and at nineteen went to Winchester, Va., as a professional artist. The same year, 1827, found him studying at the Pennsylvania Academy of Fine Arts. Through the aid of friends he was enabled to visit Europe, studying at Rome and Florence. He made numerous copies of the old masters and painted

"Hagar and Ishmael Fainting in the Wilderness," with life-size figures. This was the first American painting to be engraved in Italy; it was published in 1830. In 1831 Chapman returned to America, held a successful exhibition of his copies and original pictures in Alexandria, and was soon after working in New York. He was one of the founders of the Century Club, and was an honorary associate of the National Academy in 1832 and a full member in 1836. He taught and practised wood-engraving, painted portraits, and made drawings for publications, furnishing 1,400 drawings for the Harper's Bible published in 1846. In 1847, he brought out *The American Drawing Book* which is said to be the finest drawing book ever published; it went through many editions. This book contains 304 pages and about an equal number of fine illustrations. It treats the various subjects thoroughly, clearly, and sensibly; besides showing the methods of drawing, perspective, and painting, Chapman included accurate directions for etching and engraving as well as composition. About the same time he completed "The Baptism of Pocahontas," one of the eight large paintings in the rotunda of the Capitol at Washington.

In 1848 he returned to Rome, where he lived during most of the remainder of his life. He was one of America's first etchers, reproducing his own designs. His best known paintings, with the exception of "The Baptism of Pocahontas," are his landscapes. An indefatigable worker, he must have made a great many pictures, but few if any are owned by public galleries. "The Israelites Spoiling the Egyptians," "The Etruscan Girl," and "The Donkey's Head" were owned by R. L. Stuart of New York; "The Last Arrow," and "Childhood" after Lawrence, by J. C. McGuire of Washington; "Rachel," by Marshall O. Roberts; "Pifferini" and "The First Italian Milestone," by James Lenox. Where these are at present is unknown. Other pictures which Chapman painted are "The Valley of Mexico," "Sunset on the Campagna," "Harvest Scene," "Stone Pines in the Barberini Valley," "Vintage Scene," and "Views out of the Porta Salara and over the Lake of Albano." His "Landing at Jamestown" was engraved by M. I. Danforth, and his "Montpelier, Va. The Seat of the Late James Madison" was engraved by Prudhomme. He is known to have painted portraits of James Madison and Horatio Greenough, and his portrait of Alexander Anderson [q.v.] belongs to the National Academy of Design. As at least half of his life was spent in Europe, much of his work must still be there. From the paintings, etchings, and illustrations that are known, he was an artist of great ability, whose work has quality, charm, and skill.

[W. S. Baker, *Am. Engravers and their Works* (1875); D. M. Stauffer, *Am. Engravers on Copper and Steel* (1905); Chas. E. Fairman, *Works of Art in the U. S. Capitol Building* (1913); Henry T. Tuckerman, *Book of the Artists* (1867); Wm. Dunlap, *Hist. of the Rise and Progress of the Arts of Design in the U. S.* (rev. ed. 1918).]   R. P. T.

CHAPMAN, JOHN WILBUR (June 17, 1859–Dec. 25, 1918), Presbyterian evangelist, was born in Richmond, Ind., a son of Alexander Hamilton Chapman and his wife Lorinda Mc-Whinney. At sixteen years of age he united with the Presbyterian Church. He spent one year at Oberlin College but graduated from Lake Forest University in 1879 and from Lane Theological Seminary in 1882. He was ordained the same year to the Presbyterian ministry. His principal pastorates were the First Reformed Church, Albany, N. Y.; the Bethany Presbyterian Church, Philadelphia; and the Fourth Presbyterian Church, New York. Eventually he gave up the pastorate for evangelism. He served as executive secretary of the General Assembly's Committee on evangelistic work for the Presbyterian Church and also as the moderator of the national body. On his evangelistic tours he traveled to Australia, Asia, and Great Britain, and he had an international reputation in his chosen field. He was above the average height, with a strong compact frame and great capacity for sustained labor. His voice was mellow, musical, and appealing. His sermons were lucid and definitely outlined. He insisted on the divine nature of Christ, his atoning work and personal return. To secure allegiance to Christ was the purpose of each address. With burning conviction and consuming zeal he preached the gospel; he never spared himself and suffered thirteen serious breakdowns in health. He was married three times: to Irene E. Steddom, May 10, 1882; to Agnes Pruyn Strain, Nov. 4, 1888; to Mabel Cornelia Moulton, Aug. 30, 1910. His writings were largely evangelistic and echoes of his preaching. Chief among them were *The Secret of a Happy Day* (1899); *The Surrendered Life* (1899); *Spiritual Life in the Sunday School* (1899); *From Life to Life* (1900); *Received Ye the Holy Ghost* (1900); *And Peter* (1900); *Revivals and Missions* (1900); *Life of D. L. Moody* (1900); *Present Day Evangelism* (1903); *The Problem of the Work* (1911); *Present Day Parables* (1911); *Chapman's Pocket Sermons* (1911); *Revival Sermons* (1911); *When Home is Heaven* (1917).

[*J. Wilbur Chapman, A Biography* (1920), by Ford C. Ottman, a friend and associate. *Revivals and Missions* (1900), by J. Wilbur Chapman, containing his own account of his methods of evangelism; *When Home is Heaven* (1917), by J. Wilbur Chapman, which gives light on his early home training; "An Appreciation of a Great Evangelist" by Chas. R. Erdman, in the *Congregationalist*, Jan. 9, 1919, a careful characterization; personal acquaintance.]   T. C. R.

CHAPMAN, MARIA WESTON (July 25, 1806–July 12, 1885), reformer, daughter of Warren and Anne (Bates) Weston, was born in Weymouth, Mass., of Pilgrim descent. She was married in 1830 to Henry Grafton Chapman, a Boston merchant. Her husband's parents were enthusiastic abolitionists, and in 1834 Maria Weston Chapman went into the movement. She became the soul of the Boston Female Anti-Slavery Society, editing (1836–40) its reports published annually under the title *Right and Wrong in Boston*. Her services to Garrison were said to have been inestimable, her cooperation with him perfect. She was present at the meeting in Boston in 1835 at which Garrison was mobbed, and it was to her house that the meeting adjourned. Of the Boston gathering she said that when the women left the hall a roar of rage and contempt went up which increased when it was evident that they meant to walk in a regular procession, "each with a colored friend." The next year she spoke for the first time in her life in a public meeting, the day before Pennsylvania Hall was destroyed. She became one of the editors of the *Non-Resistant,* and, with Edmund Quincy, she edited the *Liberator* at various times during Garrison's illness or absence. In 1840 she was made a member of the executive committee of the Anti-Slavery Society, with Lucretia Mott and Lydia Maria Child, and in the same year, the Massachusetts Society chose her as one of its delegates to the World's Convention. In 1842 her husband died. In the two months after his death, she was very busy with the Anti-Slavery Fair, in supporting the Latimer fugitive slave case agitation and with writing almost weekly for the *Liberator*. She edited the *Liberty Bell* (1839–46).

She published *Songs of the Free, and Hymns of Christian Freedom* (1836) and *How Can I Help to Abolish Slavery* (1855), and in 1877 edited, with a memoir, the autobiography of Harriet Martineau, whom she had known for many years.

[*Wm. Lloyd Garrison, the Story of His Life, Told by His Children* (1885–89); files of the *Liberty Bell, Liberator, Right and Wrong in Boston*.]   M. A. K.

CHAPMAN, NATHANIEL (May 28, 1780–July 1, 1853), physician, was born at Summer Hill, Fairfax County, Va., the son of George and Amelia Chapman. His mother was a daughter of Allan Macrae, a wealthy merchant of Dumfries, Va. His early education was received at the

Alexandria Academy, founded by George Washington. At the age of fifteen he commenced reading medicine under Dr. John Weems of Georgetown, Md., and Dr. Dick of Alexandria, Va., and in 1797 he went to Philadelphia, where he became the private pupil of Dr. Benjamin Rush [*q.v.*]. He spent several years in studying the classics along with his medical reading, after which he entered the Medical School of the University of Pennsylvania, from which he was graduated with honors in 1801, having presented a dissertation on hydrophobia as his thesis. He then went to Europe and first spent a year in London under Abernethy, after which he was for two years in Edinburgh, then the medical center of the world. In 1804 he returned to Philadelphia to practise medicine.

He had many of the qualifications which ensure success in that calling. He was of good family, of delightful personality, sparkling with wit, gay and jovial to an unusual degree. He had been made much of in Edinburgh, where he had been a social lion. In Philadelphia he almost immediately became the favorite physician of a large section of the wealthy class. He was as socially popular as he was scientifically eminent. His successful career continued for a period of fifty years during which he became the acknowledged leader of a group of great physicians. From 1810 to 1850 he was actively connected with the Medical School of the University of Pennsylvania as a teacher, beginning first as an assistant to Dr. T. C. James in the chair of midwifery, and within three years thereafter being made professor of materia medica, and, later, professor of the theory and practise of medicine. He combined a profound knowledge of his subjects with a delightful style of presentation. As a raconteur he was famous. In 1817 he founded the Medical Institute of Philadelphia, the first post-graduate medical school in the United States, and conducted summer courses therein for twenty years. In 1820 he became the editor of the *Journal of Medical and Physical Sciences,* later the *American Journal of the Medical Sciences.* He was clinical lecturer in the Hospital of the Philadelphia Almshouse, now the Philadelphia General Hospital, for a number of years. He was president of the Philadelphia Medical Society for six successive yearly terms. In 1848 he was elected the first president of the American Medical Association by acclamation, no other name being placed before the meeting. One of the honors which he most appreciated was his presidency of the American Philosophical Society founded by Benjamin Franklin. He was the author of several important medical works: *Elements of Therapeutics and Materia Medica*

(1817); *Lectures on the More Important Diseases of the Thoracic and Abdominal Viscera* (1844); *Lectures on the More Important Eruptive Fevers, Hemorrhages, and Dropsies, and on Gout and Rheumatism* (1844); *A Compendium of Lectures on the Theory and Practice of Medicine* (1846). In 1850 he retired from his official positions and from active practise and on July 1, 1853, he died. He was married in 1808 to Rebecca Biddle, daughter of Col. Clement Biddle. His grandson, Henry Cadwalader Chapman [*q.v.*], also attained distinction in medicine.

[Samuel Jackson, *A Discourse Commemorative of Nathaniel Chapman* (1854); Samuel D. Gross, ed., *Lives of Eminent Am. Physicians and Surgeons* (1861), pp. 663–78; Jas. G. Mumford, sketch in *Dict. of Am. Medic. Biog.* (1928), ed. by Kelly and Burrage; *Medic. Examiner,* Aug. 1853; *N. Y. Medic. Gazette and Jour. of Health,* Sept. 1853.]   C. H. L.

CHAPMAN, REUBEN (July 15, 1802–May 17, 1882), governor of Alabama, was the son of Col. Reuben Chapman and Ann Reynolds of Virginia. Col. Chapman, son of a Scotchman, fought in the Revolution and afterward acquired considerable wealth. The younger Reuben received his education in a school at Bowling Green, Va. In 1824 he located at Huntsville, Ala., which was then the abode of large planters and the most promising town in the state. After a year of reading in the office of his brother, Judge Samuel Chapman, he was admitted to the bar and practised law for a time at Sommerville, Morgan County. In 1832 he was elected to the state Senate, and in 1835 to the national House of Representatives, to which he was returned for five successive terms. In 1847 he retired from Congress to accept the nomination of the Democratic party for the governorship. He was put forward as a compromise candidate by the Martin and Terry factions of the party, and although the Whigs, heartened by the rift in the opposing party over the state bank question, nominated Nicholas Davis of Limestone County, a popular planter with a distinguished public career, Chapman was victorious by a handsome majority. As governor, he pursued an economical and business-like policy, which was fortunate for the state, at a time when its finances were in a deranged condition. But the breach in Democratic ranks produced by the bank issue was scarcely closed before another, quite as serious, was occasioned by William L. Yancey's bold "Alabama Platform." Yancey supported Chapman for reëlection, but an alliance between the opponents of Yancey and Ex-Governor Martin's friends, who were disgruntled because their hero had not been allowed a second term, prevented Chapman from polling the required two-thirds majority. He retired to his estate at Huntsville, but entered the political arena again in 1855 to help defend the Democracy against the onrush of the Know-Nothings. He was elected to the lower house of the legislature, defeating Jeremiah Clemens [*q.v.*]. When the crisis of 1860 came he ranged himself on the side of the conservatives. He attended the Democratic convention at Baltimore and did his utmost in a vain attempt to bring about a reconciliation between the Northern and Southern wings of the party which shortly before had split asunder at Charleston. During the war the Federal troops burned his handsome residence, laid waste his property, annoyed and imprisoned him, and finally drove him beyond their lines. When the war was ended, he returned to Huntsville and affiliated with the Democratic and Conservative party. He remained faithful to the white man's cause during the Reconstruction period, and after it was over he settled down to a quiet and unobtrusive life. He was married on Oct. 17, 1838, to Felicia Pickett, daughter of Col. Steptoe Pickett, a Limestone County planter who had come down from Virginia.

[W. Brewer, *Alabama* (1872); J. W. Dubose, *Life and Times of Wm. Lowndes Yancey* (1892); Wm. Garrett, *Reminiscences of Public Men in Ala.* (1872); Thos. M. Owen, *Hist. of Ala. and Dict. of Ala. Biog.*, vol. III (1921).]   A.B.M—e.

CHAPMAN, VICTOR EMMANUEL (Apr. 17, 1890–June 23, 1916), first pilot of the Escadrille Lafayette to be killed in action, was one of the American youths who at the outbreak of the World War offered their services to France. Born in New York, the son of John Jay Chapman, lawyer and littérateur, and Minna (Timmins) Chapman, child of an Italian mother by an American father, he grew up in advantageous surroundings. He studied at the Fay School, Southboro, Mass., spent several years at St. Paul's School, Concord, N. H., lived for a time in France and Germany, and after a year at the Stone School, Boston, entered Harvard from which he graduated in 1913. A love for scenery and talent for decoration seemed to fit him for architecture or painting, and he went to Paris where in the atelier of M. Gromort he prepared for admission to the Beaux Arts.

From childhood he had been fond of outdoor life. Strong physically but with no aptitude for sports, he nevertheless took keen delight in hazardous exploits. In perilous circumstances he was imperturbable, and all his faculties were at their best. Several life-saving incidents had already marked his career. He was by nature chivalrous and generous-hearted, with a deep-lying strain of mysticism, and to any opportunity for

service he gave himself with reckless abandon. It was inevitable that he should offer his life to France. In August 1914 he enlisted in the Foreign Legion. For a year he served with the infantry in the trenches, where he showed himself a natural soldier, adaptable, amenable to discipline, fearless, cheerfully performing any assigned duty whether "kitchen police" or trench-digging. Eager for more aggressive action than was afforded by the comparatively quiet sector which he was helping to defend as *aide-chargeur* to a *mitrail,* he transferred in August 1915 to the aviation corps. After preliminary training as a bomb-dropper and at aviation schools, on Apr. 20, 1916, he joined the newly formed Escadrille Lafayette. In the dangerous Verdun section he now had opportunity for service suited to his nature, playing hide and seek among the clouds in flights which he describes as an artist and poet, and engaging in fierce individual combats with enemy planes. He soon had the reputation of being the most determined hard-working member of the squadron and as second to none in aerial dueling. During an encounter, June 17, 1916, he received a severe scalp wound, and brought his machine to the ground riddled with bullets and with parts of the command severed. He treated the affair with characteristic indifference, and on June 23, his head bandaged, he put oranges into his plane to take to his comrade, Clyde Balsley, lying desperately wounded in the hospital; but they were never delivered. Seeing Capt. Thenault, Norman Prince, and Lufbery [*q.v.*] engaged with five German planes, he sped to their assistance. The first three escaped, but Chapman's plane was seen to fall, no longer controlled by the pilot, within the German lines northeast of Douaumont. The death he had expected had come to him in the clouds. His final rank was sergeant, and the French government honored him with the *médaille militaire* (given posthumously, June 24, 1924), and the *croix de guerre* with two palms.

[*Victor Chapman's Letters from France* (1917) with memoir by John Jay Chapman; M. A. DeWolfe Howe, *Harvard Volunteers in Europe* (1916), and *Memoirs of the Harvard Dead in the War Against Germany*, I (1920), 91–103; Georges Thenault, *Story of the Lafayette Escadrille* (1921), translated by Walter Duranty; Laurence LaTourette Driggs, *Heroes of Aviation* (1918); James R. McConnell, *Flying for France* (1916); *Bellman*, July 20, 1918; *Century Mag.*, Feb. 1919.]   H.E.S.

CHAPPELL, ABSALOM HARRIS (Dec. 18, 1801–Dec. 11, 1878), lawyer, historian, son of Joseph and Dorothy (Harris) Chappell, was born in Hancock County and died in Columbus, Ga. His mother's father, for whom he was named, was a soldier in the Revolutionary army. His father, born most likely in Virginia, the descendant of Englishmen who came to America in the seventeenth century, died in Georgia in 1807, when about forty years of age. Absalom attended the Mt. Zion Academy near his home, and then read law for two years in New York City. Later, he returned to Athens, Ga., and read law further in the office of Judge Augustin Smith Clayton before being admitted to the bar in 1821. He lived in several places, at times approximately as follows—in Sandersville (1821–24), in Forsyth (1824–36), in Macon (1836–58), and in Columbus (1858–78). During 1836–37 he helped organize the Monroe and the Western & Atlantic railways, and devised schemes for promoting foreign trade directly through Georgia ports. In May 1842, he was married to Loretto Rebecca Lamar, daughter of John Lamar, of Putnam County, Ga., sister of Mirabeau Buonaparte Lamar [q.v.] and of the Lucius Quintus Cincinnatus Lamar whose son of the same name became a justice of the Supreme Court. His successful activities as a lawyer were constantly interrupted by his participation in politics, and, during his Columbus residence, by his farming interests in Alabama. He was for many years a trustee of the state university, a state legislator and senator, and, in 1843–44 a congressman in Washington. In local politics he was of the Troup faction. Nationally, he was a state-rights Whig, but his party loyalty came under such suspicion while he was in Congress that he felt obliged to issue in justification of himself his letter *To the People of Georgia* (1844). He was a member from time to time—always with distinguished associates—of many public commissions in Georgia. In 1839 he was appointed in this capacity to perfect a system of finance—in 1849, to suggest improvements for the school system—in 1853, to report on public institutions —and, in 1867, to prepare an address to Georgians and to Americans in general on the political abuses then current in the South. When he went to live in Columbus, he thought of himself as withdrawing from public life, but he took part in the agitation for secession. And even when he was past seventy—reduced by the war to poverty, and by Reconstruction to something like despair—his patriotism asserted itself in his *Miscellanies of Georgia* (1874), a series of reminiscent and historical essays. This book is written in a grandiose style, and is of comparatively little worth as history. It remains valuable for the impression it gives of its author who, though perhaps too consistently grave, was always dominated by a sort of classic integrity and fortitude.

[Sketch in 1928 edition of A. H. Chappell's *Miscellanies of Ga.; Biog. Souvenir of Ga. and Fla.* (1889);

T. J. Chappell, "Absalom Harris Chappell," in W. J. Northen, *Men of Mark in Ga.* (1910), vol. II; P. E. Chappell, *Genealog. Hist. Chappell, Dickie and Other Kindred Families of Va.* (1900).]   J.D.W.

CHARLES, WILLIAM (1776–Aug. 29, 1820), etcher, engraver, caricaturist, is said to have been a native of Edinburgh, on the authority of Dr. Alexander Anderson who knew him in America (B. J. Lossing, *Pictorial Field Book of the War of 1812,* 1896, p. 228 n.). The earliest etched caricatures of his seen were issued from his shop in London, in 1803 and the first half of 1804. The majority of these were aimed at Bonaparte's threatened invasion of England. He engraved two line plates for the *Edinburgh Cyclopædia,* and in July 1804, he issued a print from "Charles's Emporium of Art and Fancy's Produce, Edinburgh." He is said to have emigrated in order to avoid the consequences of prosecution for caricaturing "one or more magistrates" of the city (*Ibid.*). The offending caricature was probably that entitled *A Fallen Pillar of the Kirk* which was published in 1805. Charles was in New York City from the time of his arrival in this country until 1814, practising his art without success (*Ibid.*). He illustrated *The American Magazine of Wit,* in New York, in 1808. In 1814 he went to Philadelphia, continued a series of etched caricatures on the War of 1812, then in progress, and opened a print and book-shop. In addition to publishing caricature prints, he also issued a series of chap-books, illustrated by himself and by Joseph Yeager, then a young engraver. He contributed three plates to the American edition of *Rees's Cyclopædia* (Philadelphia, 1810–24), but his line-engraved plate of "Quadrapeds" was so unsatisfactory that afterward it was reëngraved by George Murray. For *Pinkerton's Travels* (Philadelphia, 1810–12) he made two illustrations in line. His first considerable work in Philadelphia was an edition of *The Tour of Doctor Syntax in Search of the Picturesque,* with the Rowlandson aquatints rather crudely copied. He also issued an edition of *The Vicar of Wakefield,* copying the Rowlandson plates. He died in Philadelphia, and was buried in the yard of the New Market Street Baptist Church. His widow, Mary, continued his business for several years and then opened a boarding-house. Frank Weitenkampf (*American Graphic Art,* 1924, p. 213) writes: "The most noteworthy caricatures of the War of 1812 were prints by William Charles. . . . His caricatures were typical of the Rowlandson-Gillray period . . . whilst not remarkable they have a rough humor which no doubt made them popular." Although Charles made a few line plates, and many aquatints, he was especially fond of the etching needle, and all his caricatures and chap-book illustrations were made by that means. His work, when found colored, usually displays the same crudity as that exhibited by his drawing.

[The chief sources of information respecting Wm. Charless are the footnote in Lossing's book (above), inscriptions on the engraver's plates, City Directories of New York and Philadelphia (although his name appears in the latter for 1821) and the burial records of the Philadelphia Board of Health. If his career influenced his contemporaries, none of them, excepting Anderson, has left any comment upon it.]   J.J.

CHARLESS, JOSEPH (July 16, 1772–July 28, 1834), pioneer printer and newspaper publisher, came from a family which originally lived in Wales but which emigrated in 1663 to his birthplace, Westmeath, Ireland. His willingness to risk his life for principles he regarded as fundamental early showed itself, for he was implicated with Lord Edward Fitzgerald and others in the Irish rebellion of 1795. Forced to flee Ireland, he first went to France, from which he embarked for the United States, landing in New York in 1796. Unable to find work in that city, he followed in the footsteps of Benjamin Franklin and went to Philadelphia where he secured work with Matthew Carey [q.v.]. Because his fellow printers did not pronounce his name with the Hibernian quota of syllables he added an extra "s" to the name which had been Charles in Ireland. In Carey's print-shop he met many of the political leaders of the Jeffersonian republicanism. Acting on the advice of Henry Clay, he went West and found employment on the *Gazette* at Lexington, Ky., in 1800. From Lexington he went to Louisville where he remained two years. He then went to St. Louis where he made his home henceforward. There on July 12, 1808, he brought out the first issue of the *Missouri Gazette,* a pioneer newspaper of the West which changed its name a year later to the *Louisiana Gazette.* When, however, Congress created the Missouri territory, Charless, in 1812, changed the name of his newspaper back to the *Missouri Gazette.* It exerted a wide influence in support of Henry Clay and his policies. Always Charless was a fighter for his political principles, even though at times he set them forth in an injudicious way. Hampered by lack of transportation facilities, he frequently found great difficulty in bringing out his newspaper. But through his resourcefulness he was able to meet such emergencies, even though he had to print his paper on foolscap. In 1798 he was married to Mrs. Sarah McCloud (*née* Jordan) who came originally from Wilmington, Del. In 1822 his son Edward changed the name of his father's paper to the

Missouri Republican, but the guiding principle of its editorial policy still remained that of his father, "To extinguish party animosities and foster a cordial union among the people on the basis of toleration and equal government."

[Walter B. Stevens in *St. Louis, the Fourth City, 1764–1911* (1911, I, 147 ff.), records the activity of Charless in St. Louis. Details about the *Missouri Gazette* under both father and son appear in Jas. Melvin Lee, *Hist. of Am. Journalism* (1917, p. 178 ff.).]

                           J.M.L.

CHARLEVOIX, PIERRE FRANÇOIS XAVIER de (Oct. 24, 1682–Feb. 1, 1761), French explorer and historian, was born at St. Quentin, the son of François de Charlevoix and his wife Antoinette, *née* Forestier. The Charlevoix were an ancient family of Picardy of noble stock, and Pierre was well educated, early showing a vocation for the religious life. When not quite sixteen years of age he began at Paris his novitiate in the Jesuit order, and he was a student at the Collège Louis le Grand from 1701 to 1704. Then he was ordained to the diaconate, and the next year was sent to Canada as professor of rhetoric in the Jesuit college at Quebec. On his outward passage he was on the same ship with the Sieurs de Raudot and the Marquis de Vaudreuil, Canadian officials, and young Charlevoix by his good manners and pleasing address secured their friendship; thus during his stay at Quebec he was a member of the highest social circle in that place. Recalled to France in 1709 he taught at his Alma Mater, and there had for a pupil the boy Voltaire. Later he became prefect of his college, and when in 1719 the Regent of France desired to send a messenger to New France for the double purpose of ascertaining the boundaries of Acadia and of finding a new route to the West, Father Charlevoix was chosen for the mission.

As the Regent did not wish that the world should know the objects of Charlevoix's visit, the latter disguised his journey as one to examine the Jesuit missions of the New World. He set out late in 1720, and arrived in Canada in time to prepare for his expedition the succeeding spring. In a single canoe he made the voyage up the St. Lawrence, through the Great Lakes, visiting Detroit, Mackinac, and Green Bay en route; he then entered Illinois River by way of the St. Joseph-Kankakee portage, spent some time at the Illinois settlements, and finally reached New Orleans and Biloxi early in 1722. He was wrecked in the Gulf of Mexico, and then returned to France after an absence of two years and a half.

The journal in which Charlevoix recorded his American experiences consists of a series of letters to a noble patroness, the Duchess de Lesdiguièrres. This form of writing was, however, a fiction; the letters were never sent, and were compiled to afford information not only about the country through which he passed, but also about the customs and manners of the Indians. The importance of this *Journal historique,* as it was called, lies in the dispassionate and accurate observation of the writer, and in the fact that he was the only traveler of the first part of the eighteenth century who describes interior America.

After his return from his voyage of inspection, Charlevoix never traveled more; he was offered but declined the position of missionary at a new post to be built on the upper Mississippi, having no desire for the hardship or possible martyrdom consequent upon a Jesuit's residence at a frontier post. He continued to teach until about the age of fifty, when he withdrew from active work and devoted himself to authorship, dying at the Jesuit convent of La Flèche. He was essentially a scholar, never a zealot; a man of the world, received at court and in good society. His histories were popular and had large sales. He was careful and accurate according to the standards of his time, and in his *Histoire et description de la Nouvelle France* he wrote of what he knew and had learned from documents and contemporaries. He edited for twenty-two years (1733–55) *Le Journal de Trevoux,* a publication of his order, begun in 1701.

[Charlevoix's first work was *Histoire de l'établissement, des progrès, et de la decadence du Christianisme dans l'Empire du Japon* (Rouen, 1715), it was based on previous works of Jesuits in the Far East. It was rewritten and reissued as *Histoire et description générale du Japon* (Paris, 1736). His first book after returning from America was *La Vie de Mère Marie de l'Incarnation* (Paris, 1724), published anonymously. The next volume was *Histoire de l'Isle Espagnole ou de Saint Domingue Ecrite particulierement sur les memoires et description manuscrit du P. Jean-Baptiste le Pers, S. J.* (Paris, 1730). His *Histoire de la Nouvelle France* did not appear until 1744; in the appendix was the journal of his American voyage, also published separately under the title *Journal historique;* the first English edition of the journal was published in London in 1761; this was edited by Louise P. Kellogg and reprinted for the Caxton Club (Chicago, 1923). A translation was published by J. G. Shea (N. Y., 1866–72) in six volumes; a new edition of Shea's translation was issued in 1900. Charlevoix's last work was *Histoire du Paraguay* (Paris, 1756). He has had few biographers; the best sketch is by J. Edmond Roy, "Essai sur Charlevoix" in Canadian Royal Soc. *Trans.,* 1907, sec. 1, 3–25.]　　L. P. K.

CHARLTON, THOMAS USHER PULASKI (Nov. 1779–Dec. 14, 1835), jurist, author, was born at Camden, S. C., the son of Thomas and Lucy (Kenan) Charlton. The elder Thomas was a physician who served both as a surgeon and as a lieutenant of the line in the Revolutionary army. He did not live long after the war, and in 1791 his widow moved to Savannah, where the younger Thomas was educated and where he made his home for the rest of his life. He was ad-

mitted to the bar and elected to the state legislature soon after attaining his majority, and at twenty-five he became attorney-general for the State. He was elected by the general assembly judge of the Eastern circuit in 1807, served until 1811, was again elected in 1821 and served until 1822. In 1804 he published his life of Gen. James Jackson, Revolutionary soldier and statesman, who had been his intimate friend. This is a standard biography, well written, of a prominent figure in early Georgia history. Charlton served as chairman of the committee of public safety during the War of 1812, was a member of the committee which compiled the Georgia statutes in 1825, and for six terms was mayor of Savannah. He married twice: first, Emily, a daughter of Thomas Walter, well-known South Carolinian and author of the botanical work *Flora Caroliniana;* and second, Ellen Glasco.

Charlton is chiefly remembered as the compiler of the first volume of Georgia court decisions— *Reports of Cases Argued and Determined in the Superior Courts of the Eastern District of the State of Georgia* (1824)—but his contemporaries also admired him as an orator and held him in high esteem as a judge. His written opinions reflect an independent spirit and a confidence in his own powers of correctly applying abstract principles to concrete cases not always met with in judges of courts of last resort. In the case, *Ex parte* Paul Grimball (*T. U. P. Charlton,* 153), decided in April 1808, he pronounced the unusual doctrine that hard times brought about by governmental action formed good ground for a court of equity to restrain a judgment creditor from selling his debtor's property. Frankly admitting that so far as he knew there was no precedent to sustain him (and all subsequent decisions on the subject are against him), he restrained the holder of an execution from selling the defendant's property because the national Embargo Act had brought about conditions making it impossible for the property to bring its fair value. In sum, he decided that, if during such a time the legislative department failed to do so, courts of equity should, upon proper case made, declare a *moratorium,* placing his ruling upon the fundamental principle that it was required by equity and good conscience. Startling as the ruling appears to us now there is nothing to indicate that it was regarded as unsound at the time, or that it was adversely criticised. But it may be inferred with reasonable safety that Charlton was not perturbed by the reception his rulings received. Again and again he pronounced judgments he believed to be unpopular, and in his opinions are to be found many such expressions as: "If this act . . . (is) . . . unconstitutional I shall say so, and at the same time feel perfectly tranquil under the clamour of the consequences which may result" and "I am aware of the sensations this opinion may produce. . . . I have obeyed only the principles of the law."

[See Wm. J. Northen, ed., *Men of Mark in Ga.*, vol. II (1910); *Cyc. of Ga.* (Atlanta, 1906); *1 Ga. Reports Annotated* (Charlottesville, Va., 1903). All of Charlton's written opinions are to be found in his volume of *Reports* (above), or in the similar volume issued by his son, R. M. Charlton, in 1838.]   B.F.

CHASE, GEORGE (Dec. 29, 1849–Jan. 8, 1924), law professor, son of David T. and Martha E. (Haynes) Chase, and descendant of Aquila Chase, was born at Portland, Me. He received a good primary education at the public schools, and, proceeding to Yale University, graduated in 1870, being valedictorian of his class. After leaving Yale he taught for three years in the classical department of the University Grammar School in New York City. During the last two of these years he also attended the Columbia Law School, where he graduated LL.B. in 1873, winning also the Townsend Prize. He was admitted to the New York bar but never practised. At Columbia he had come under the influence of Prof. Theodore W. Dwight, who was at that time the head of the Law School, and on the invitation of the latter he joined the faculty as instructor in municipal law, becoming shortly after assistant professor. In 1878 he was appointed professor of criminal law, torts, and procedure, and occupied this post for thirteen years. He was admirably equipped for academic work; a fluent graceful speaker with great powers of exposition and analysis, he was distinguished for accuracy of statement and aptness of illustration. On Nov. 25, 1884, he was married to Eva R. Hawley of Boston. In 1891, when the Columbia Law School was reorganized, he was not in sympathy with the policy which was about to be implemented. He accordingly resigned and founded the New York Law School, with the avowed object of developing the method of instruction devised by Dwight, viewing "the law as a system of principles and not as a mere aggregation of cases decided by the courts" (*New York Law School Catalogue*). The new institution opened Oct. 1, 1891, with Chase as dean, a position which he retained for over thirty-two years. Steadfastly pursuing the policy that the major subject of study ought to be treatises, the reading of reported cases being merely supplementary, he achieved a notable success. Many of his pupils subsequently attained high positions in public life, among them being Theodore Roosevelt, Charles E. Hughes, and

Benjamin Cardozo. In 1920 his health gave way, but, though unable to leave his home, he continued to direct the work of the school until his death.

Chase was the author of *The American Students' Blackstone* (1876–77), an abridgment retaining such of the original as he considered of historic or practical value; *Leading Cases Upon the Law of Torts* (1892); *Leading Cases Upon the Law of Wills* (1892); *The Code of Civil Procedure of the State of New York as Amended* (1909–20); a *Supplement to the Public Statutes of New Hampshire* (1914); and *Pocket Code of the New York (State) Laws, Statutes, etc.* (1919). He edited Johnson's *Ready Legal Advertiser* (1880) and an American edition of Sir James Stephen's *Digest of the Law of Evidence* (1886). For a time he was editor of the *New York Law Journal* and also assisted in the preparation of *Johnson's Universal Cyclopædia*.

[Unsystematic details of Chase's ancestry are contained in a series of articles entitled "Chase Genealogy" by W. E. Gould in the *Daily Eastern Argus* (Portland, Me.), Mar. 2, 1812, *et seq.* Obituaries appeared in the *N. Y. Times* and *N. Y. Herald* of Jan. 9, 1924, and a sympathetic sketch of his career will be found in the *Law Student*, Feb. 15, 1924. See also *Cat. Officers and Grads. Columbia Univ.* (1916); *N. Y. Law School Cat.*, 1923; Lewis W. Hicks, *Biog. Record Class of 1870, Yale College, 1870–1911* (n.d.).]   H. W. H. K.

CHASE, IRAH (Oct. 5, 1793–Nov. 1, 1864), Baptist educator, was descended from Aquila Chase who came from England and had settled in Hampton, N. H., by 1640. Irah's father, Isaac Chase, served in the Revolution, receiving five bayonet wounds in a battle near New York, where he remained a prisoner of war for almost a year; his mother, Sarah Bond, was a descendant of William Bond who came at an early age to Watertown, Mass., and was speaker of the General Court four times between 1691 and 1695. Irah, the second son, was born at Stratton, Vt. The family soon moved to Westford, however, and Irah attended school in the neighboring towns of Milton and St. Albans. In 1811 he entered the second year class at Middlebury College, taking several honors and being graduated in 1814. He then attended Andover Theological Seminary and upon graduation was ordained to the Baptist ministry, Sept. 17, 1817. Accepting a missionary appointment for western Virginia, late that fall he journeyed thither on horseback. Within a few months he was offered a chair in a theological seminary being organized in Philadelphia. The Philadelphia enterprise was soon transferred to Washington as the theological department of Columbian College, where Chase labored amid great discouragements until 1825, with the exception of a little more than a year, 1823–24, which he spent in travel and study in Europe. Personal contacts, with short residences at the Universities of Halle and Göttingen, strengthened his position in advocacy of scientific study of the Bible; he also negotiated in London the solution of a troublesome problem of property rights in the Rangoon mission.

Chase touched educational movements at many points, but his greatest specific contribution to ministerial education was in and through Newton Theological Institution, where he served as professor from November 1825 until 1845. While yet a student at Andover, he had assisted Rev. James M. Winchell of Boston in drafting a plan for a theological institution, and upon resigning at Washington he soon turned to Boston as the place where he might find opportunity to carry on the work for which he had a real passion. At first he was the only instructor at the new seminary. His ideas for the curriculum were developed and became the basis for the organization of the departments of theological study as new chairs became possible. The scientific study of the Scriptures was the central organizing principle, with linguistic requirements which represented an advance step for the Baptist ministry of that day. Within a decade and a half there came to work in this curriculum such outstanding men as Barnas Sears and Horatio B. Hackett [qq.v.]. Chase wrote many articles of a historical and theological character and four volumes of his writings were published. He was twice married, first, to Harriet Savage, Mar. 15, 1821, who died May 2, 1834; second, to Martha Raymond, Oct. 13, 1835, who died Oct. 25, 1846. There were nine children born of these marriages.

[Chase prepared by request an autobiographical sketch for the *Baptist Memorial & Monthly Record* (N. Y.), II, 71–82. A memorial volume, a *Tribute of Affection to the Memory of Prof. Irah Chase* (1865), contains a list of his published works. See also S. F. Smith, *Hist. of Newton* (1880); J. C. Chase and G. W. Chamberlain, *Seven Generations of the Descendants of Aquila and Thomas Chase* (1928); *Cat. Officers and Students of Middlebury Coll., 1800–1915* (1917); *Andover Theol. Sem. Gen. Cat.* (1909).] W. H. A.

CHASE, PHILANDER (Dec. 14, 1775–Sept. 20, 1852), Episcopal bishop, was born in Cornish, N. H., the last of the fifteen children of Dudley and Allace (Corbett) Chase. He graduated from Dartmouth College in 1796, and began his labors by the conversion of his family from Congregationalism. He was ordained deacon in the Episcopal Church in 1798, and priest in 1799. After holding several charges in northern New York, he moved in 1805 to New Or-

leans for the health of his wife, Mary Fay, whom he had married in 1796. In 1811 he was again in the North, connected with Christ Church, Hartford, Conn. He made his first journey into Ohio in 1817. Wherever he found Episcopalians he organized parishes. Mrs. Chase soon joined him, but frontier life was too arduous for her, and she died in 1818. In July 1819, he married Sophia May Ingraham. The struggling parishes of Ohio organized into a diocese in June 1818 and Chase was elected bishop. He was consecrated in Philadelphia on Feb. 11, 1819, and returned to the West. In 1821–22, partly to augment his meager income, he added to his Episcopal duties the presidency of Cincinnati College. He soon discovered that the West must breed its own clergy who could thrive in its peculiar atmosphere of buoyant promises and small realizations. He, therefore, decided upon a theological seminary for Ohio. Undaunted by opposition from the East he determined to solicit money in England. British interest in frontier America was keen, and the pioneer bishop was an appealing figure with his unbounded zeal and his unquenchable faith. He returned in 1824 with something less than $30,000. The site of his new college he named after Lord Gambier, one of his British patrons, and the school itself after Lord Kenyon.

Unfortunately Chase was less successful in managing his college and diocese than in founding them. The clergy of Ohio and the faculty of Kenyon College soon raised complaints against his arbitrary rule. Much of the difficulty lay in the undisciplined nature of the Western clergy. Some of the trouble, however, was undoubtedly in the temperament of the Bishop. In 1831 he resigned the bishopric of Ohio, and settled on a farm which he suggestively named the Valley of Peace. From there he moved to Gilead, Mich. In 1835 the newly organized diocese of Illinois put an end to a delicate question as to the status of a bishop without a see, by electing him to its episcopate. Chase began his new duties with plans for a new theological seminary. A second journey to England for funds was less successful than the first, but he was able to lay the corner-stone of Jubilee College in 1839. In this year he succeeded, in spite of hard times, in raising a considerable sum in the South. With accustomed vigor he championed the low church contentions in the forties, combatting all "idolatrous innovations." He became presiding bishop of the Church in 1843. In 1852 he was thrown from his carriage and died on Sept. 20. To the end he remained an indefatigable warrior who never dipped his colors.

[The chief source of information is Chase's auto-biography, *Reminiscences of Bishop Chase, an Autobiography* (2 vols. 1848). He also wrote *A Plea for the West* (1826); *Star in the West or Kenyon College* (1828); *Defence of Kenyon College* (1831); *A Plea for Jubilee* (1835). He was a frequent contributor to the Church publications, especially the *Spirit of Missions*, 1835–52. Much material concerning him is found in the *Jour. Annual Convention Prot. Epis. Ch. in Ohio* to 1831; *Ibid., Illinois*, 1835–52; and in the *Jour. General Convention Prot. Episc. Ch. in America* (Triennial). See also Laura Chase Smith, *Life of Philander Chase* (1903); Wm. B. Sprague, *Annals Am. Pulpit*, V (1859), 453–62; G. M. Royce, "Kenyon College" in the *Churchman*, Nov. 14, 1896; Geo. F. Smythe, *Kenyon College, Its First Century* (1924); Geo. T. Chapman, *Sketches Alumni Dartmouth College* (1867).]

K. J. G.

CHASE, PLINY EARLE (Aug. 18, 1820–Dec. 17, 1886), scientist, was born in Worcester, Mass. His father, Anthony Chase, for thirty-four years treasurer of Worcester County, was of a family honorably prominent in New England public affairs from the earliest settlements; his mother, Lydia Earle, of Leicester, was the daughter of Pliny Earle, who introduced the manufacturing of machine-card clothing into America. Brought up a Quaker, he was educated in the Worcester Latin School, in the Friends' School in Providence, R. I., and at Harvard University. Entering college when fifteen years old, he stated as his object the acquisition of "honorable fame." After graduation, honor but hardly fame attended him as principal of district schools in Leicester and Worcester. In 1843 he married Elizabeth Brown Oliver of Lynn, niece of Goold Brown [*q.v.*]. From 1841 to 1848 he taught in Philadelphia. A severe hemorrhage of the lungs made necessary a break in this profession and for ten or twelve years he was a member of a stove and foundry firm. While so occupied, an old college friend found him "engaged in solving a problem and selling a Franklin stove, with considerable friction between the two occupations." The same friend says: "Upon my asking him, with unaffected wonder, what induced the scholar of our class to dissipate in hardware, he assuaged my indignation with the softly spoken 'Thee must see, Edward, the multiple of bread and butter.'" In 1861 Chase resumed his teaching, which he continued with success until his death. He was appointed professor of natural sciences at Haverford College in 1871 and was transferred to the chair of philosophy and logic in 1875. In 1886 he acted as president of the College during the absence of his brother, Thomas Chase [*q.v.*], who was its president. He was a prolific writer, his subjects covering a wide range. Among his early publications were arithmetic text-books, one of which was written in conjunction with Horace Mann. In meteorology he collected data, published mostly by the American Philosophical Society, and produced one book, *Elements of Meteorology for Schools and Households* (1884). In the *Proceedings of the American Philosophical Society* alone he published more than one hundred and twenty articles. In 1864 the Society presented him with the Magellanic Medal for his paper on "Numerical relations between Gravity and Magnetism." Chase contributed also to the *American Journal of Arts and Sciences* (Silliman's); to the *London, Dublin and Edinburgh Philosophical Magazine*; to *Comptes Rendus* of Paris; to the *Journal of the Franklin Institute*; and to other periodicals, all of such contributions numbering over one hundred and fifty. As to subject, about one-tenth were philological and the rest mostly meteorological, cosmical, and physical. In later life he was especially interested in the cosmical subjects, striving to establish a common law that "All physical phenomena are due to an Omnipotent Power, acting in ways which may be represented by harmonic or cyclical undulations in an elastic medium." An able linguist, he spoke six or seven languages and with dictionary help could read one hundred and twenty, including dialects. As a lecturer, principally in the fields of astronomy and meteorology, he was notable.

[Pliny Earle, comp., *Ralph Earle and his Descendants* (1888); *Am. Philosophical Soc. Proc.*, vols. IX, XVIII, XIX, XXII, XXIV; contrib., *Journal Franklin Institute*, vol. CXXIV; *Am. Antiquarian Soc. Proc.*, vol. IV, n.s., pt. 4 (Apr. 1887); Wm. Lincoln and Chas. Hersey, *Hist. of Worcester, Mass.* (1862); *Worcester Daily Spy*, Feb. 9, 1887.]

M. H. D.

CHASE, SALMON PORTLAND (Jan. 13, 1808–May 7, 1873), statesman, secretary of the treasury under Lincoln, and chief justice during Reconstruction, was born at Cornish, N. H. His line can be traced through nine generations to Thomas Chase of Chesham, England, and through six generations to the American emigrant, Aquila Chase, who settled at Newbury, Mass., about 1640. From Newbury the Chases moved to Sutton, Mass., and later to Cornish, a frontier community on the Connecticut River. The Cornish farmer, Ithamar Chase, father of Salmon, held various state and local offices and was in politics a Federalist; the mother, Janette Ralston, was a woman of vigorous Scotch ancestry. Salmon was the eighth of eleven children. In his childhood the family moved to Keene, N. H., where Ithamar became a tavern keeper. The boy received his early training in the Keene district school and in a private school kept by a Mr. Dunham at Windsor, Vt.

The death of his father occurred when the boy

was nine years old, and shortly after this he was placed under the stern guidance of his uncle, Philander Chase [*q.v.*], bishop of Ohio, a vigorous pioneer leader in the Protestant Episcopal Church. For two years the boy lived with the bishop at Worthington, near Columbus, Ohio, entering the church school which the bishop conducted. His days at Worthington were devoted to classical studies, and he was at this time confirmed in the Episcopal Church; but his uncle's hope of making him an Episcopal clergyman was not realized. When Bishop Chase became president of Cincinnati College in the fall of 1821 Salmon entered the college; and a very serious student he seems to have been, to judge by his own statement that he had little to do with college pranks but spent much time "in reading, either under the bishop's direction, or at my own will." "I used to meditate a great deal," he added, "on religious topics; for my sentiments of religious obligation and . . . responsibility were profound" (Schuckers, p. 16). Leaving Cincinnati after less than a year, he spent some months in preparatory study, and then entered as a junior in Dartmouth College, from which he graduated without marked distinction in 1826. He then solicited the influence of another uncle, Dudley Chase, United States senator from Vermont, for a government clerkship; but, this being refused, he conducted a school for boys in Washington, having at one time under his charge sons of all but one of the members of John Quincy Adams's cabinet. In Washington and Baltimore he frequently visited in the cultured home of William Wirt [*q.v.*]; and his otherwise sombre diary glows with youthful romance and sprightliness as it records the evenings spent in the company of the charming Wirt daughters.

Having determined upon his career, he read law under the nominal supervision of Wirt; and with scant legal preparation he was admitted to the bar on Dec. 14, 1829. The following year he settled in Cincinnati, where in addition to legal duties he was soon occupied with anti-slavery activities and with various literary ventures. In 1830 he assisted in organizing the Cincinnati Lyceum which presented a series of lectures, and became himself a lecturer and magazine contributor. In his lecture-essay on the "Life and Character of Henry Brougham" (*North American Review*, July 1831) his reforming instinct was manifest in his pointed comments on legal abuses of the time. While waiting for clients the lawyer-author sought unsuccessfully to establish a literary magazine for the West, and then turned his energies into the compilation of the *Statutes of Ohio* (3 vols., Cinn., 1833–35), a standard

work which required heavy labor in the preparation and proved most serviceable to lawyers.

The events of Chase's private life are intimately related in his diary and family memoranda. Three marriages are recorded: the first to Katherine Jane Garniss (Mar. 4, 1834), who died Dec. 1, 1835; the second to Eliza Ann Smith (Sept. 26, 1839), who died Sept. 29, 1845; and the third to Sarah Bella Dunlop Ludlow (Nov. 6, 1846), who died Jan. 13, 1852. Six daughters were born to him, of whom four died when very young. The births and deaths of his children, and the loss of his wives, are recorded in his diary with a revealing tenderness and a grief which takes refuge in religion. Two children reached maturity: the brilliant Katherine, daughter of his second wife, who became the wife of Gov. William Sprague of Rhode Island, and Janette, daughter of his third wife, who became Mrs. William S. Hoyt of New York City.

Despite scornful opposition, Chase prominently defended escaping slaves, and was called the "attorney-general for runaway negroes." He labored unsuccessfully to obtain the release of Matilda, a slave woman befriended by J. G. Birney; and when Birney himself was indicted for harboring a fugitive, Chase carried the case to the supreme court of Ohio, where he made a vigorous argument, contending that Matilda, having been voluntarily brought into a free state by her master, became free (*Birney* vs. *Ohio*, 8 *Ohio*, 230). Unwilling to commit itself to the Chase doctrine with which it was evidently impressed, the court directed the dismissal of the indictment against Birney on merely technical grounds. On another occasion Chase defended Vanzandt (the original of John Van Trompe in *Uncle Tom's Cabin*), prosecuted for aiding the escape of slaves from Kentucky. This case was appealed to the United States Supreme Court, and in its argument Chase was associated with William H. Seward, both giving their services without compensation. Chase contended that the federal government under the Constitution had "nothing whatever to do, directly, with slavery"; that "no claim to persons as property can be maintained under any . . . law of the United States"; and that the fugitive-slave act of 1793 was unconstitutional. The case was lost for his client; but it did much to bring Chase into prominence.

In politics Chase subordinated party interests to the central issue of slavery. Though formerly a Whig, he joined the Liberty party after the nomination of Birney in 1840; and in various of the conventions of this party, state and national, he was an outstanding leader. The resolutions of the Buffalo convention of August 1843 came chiefly from his pen; and the Southern and Western Liberty Convention at Cincinnati in 1845 (designed as a rallying point for anti-slavery sentiment in the Middle West) was mainly his work. He was active in the Free Soil movement of 1848, presiding at the Buffalo convention, and drafting in part the platform which declared for "no more slave states and no more slave territory." The power of the new party in the nation at large was shown by the defeat of Cass, whose choice had angered the anti-slavery Democrats; and in the Ohio legislature the Free Soilers used their balance of power in alliance with the Democrats to elect Chase to the United States Senate (Feb. 22, 1849). By this time he had come to realize the weakness of a party grounded on a purely anti-slavery basis, and was turning his attention to the possibility of capturing the Democratic party for the anti-slavery cause.

Chase entered upon his senatorial career at the time of the mid-century crisis over the slavery question. Unwilling to temporize on this issue, and resenting the Southern leanings of the Democratic party, he opposed the compromise measures of 1850; and in 1854 he issued his "Appeal of the Independent Democrats," denouncing Douglas's Nebraska bill as a "criminal betrayal of precious rights," warning the people that the "dearest interests of freedom and the Union" were in "imminent peril," and imploring all Christians to protest against "this enormous crime." In this "Appeal" we have the key-note of Chase's senatorial policy—a policy of writing slavery restrictions into national law wherever possible, and of paving the way for a new Democratic party that would be free from pro-slavery "domination." He introduced an amendment to Douglas's Kansas-Nebraska bill affirming the right of the people of a territory to prohibit slavery if they wished (as seemed to be implied in Douglas's "popular sovereignty" doctrine); but the amendment was emphatically rejected.

In the altered political horizon produced by the dissolution of the Whig organization and the rise of the Republican party, Chase naturally cast his lot with the Republicans. Meeting in Columbus in July 1855 the new party (perhaps best designated as an "anti-Nebraska" party) nominated Chase as governor; and in a triangular contest in which he had to combat the old Whigs and the old-line Democrats, while suffering embarrassment from his Know-Nothing friends, he was victorious. In 1857 he was reëlected as Republican governor; and by this time he had become committed to the new party. As governor his administration was embarrassed by interstate conflicts over the fugitive-slave question, by a threat of Gov. Wise of Virginia to invade Ohio in order to suppress alleged attempts to rescue John Brown (to which Chase sent a vigorous reply), and by corruption in the office of state treasurer. One of his achievements as governor was a reorganization of the militia system which added greatly to the state's military preparedness in 1861.

In 1856 Chase was an avowed aspirant for the Republican presidential nomination; but he did not even command the support of the full Ohio delegation, and his position at Philadelphia was much weaker than that of Frémont. Again in 1860 his wide prestige and his consistent record of anti-slavery leadership caused him to be prominently mentioned for the presidency; but his expected strength did not materialize in the convention at Chicago, since the Ohio delegation was again divided, and the firmness of his outspoken opinions caused him to be rejected from the standpoint of "availability." With only 49 votes out of 465 on the first ballot, and with dwindling support as the voting proceeded, his friends gave up the struggle in his behalf; and when the break for Lincoln became apparent, they threw their votes to the Illinois candidate, thus putting Chase in favor with the incoming administration.

When Virginia, in an effort to avert impending war, called the Peace Convention at Washington in February 1861 Chase attended as one of the Ohio commissioners; but he refused to compromise as to slavery extension, and his speeches in the convention, though disclaiming any intention to invade state rights, probably tended to confirm the Southerners' worst fears.

Chase was again chosen United States senator in 1860, but resigned to become Lincoln's secretary of the treasury, which office he held from March 1861 until July 1864. As director of the country's finances during the Civil War it was his task to borrow money from reluctant bankers and investors; to labor with congressional committees in the formulation of financial legislation; to devise remedial measures for a deranged currency; to make forecasts and prepare estimates in days when financial responsibility was diffused and scientific budgets were unknown; to trim the sails of fiscal policy to political winds; to market the huge loans which constituted the chief reliance of an improvident government; and to supervise the enforcement of unusual laws, such as that which provided for the seizure of captured and abandoned property in the South. The low state of public credit was reflected in the suspension of specie payments at the close of the year 1861; the high interest rate (over seven per cent) on government loans; the marketing of the bonds at a discount; the difficulty of obtaining loans even on these unfavorable terms and the height and instability of the premium on gold. Chase was fortunate in having the valuable assistance of Jay Cooke who, as "financier of the Civil War," performed the same kind of service in marketing bonds that Robert Morris and Benjamin Franklin did for the Revolutionary War. When the bill to provide for immense issues of paper money with the legal tender feature was under consideration in Congress, Chase at first disapproved, endeavoring to obtain support among bankers for his national banking system; but when this support failed he grew non-committal and later gave a reluctant approval. The country was thus saddled with the "greenback" problem without such active opposition as his judgment would have dictated. The national banking system, first established by law on Feb. 25, 1863, was originated by Chase, who formally submitted his proposal in December 1862 in order to increase the sale of government bonds, improve the currency by providing reliable bank notes backed by government security, and suppress the notorious evils of state bank notes. This was perhaps his most important piece of constructive statesmanship.

On the major questions of the war Chase was called upon, as a member of the President's official family, to assist in the formulation of policies. He favored, in a qualified manner, the provisioning of Fort Sumter; urged the confiscation of "rebel" property; approved the admission of West Virginia (the legality and wisdom of which was doubted by certain members of the cabinet); gave reluctant consent to the surrender of Mason and Slidell; urged McClellan's dismissal; approved Lincoln's suspension of the *habeas corpus* privilege, and, in general gave support to those measures which were directed toward a vigorous prosecution of the war. The closing paragraph in Lincoln's Emancipation Proclamation, invoking the "gracious favor of Almighty God," was penned by him; but he considered the President's policy of liberation weak, and did not approve the exceptions of whole states and large districts from the proclamation as issued. Chase never had that easy comradeship with Lincoln which Seward had; and the President never got on well with his minister of finance. To Chase Lincoln seemed to lack force; and he frequently complained of the chief's lax

administration. He spoke with disparagement of the "so-called cabinet," considered its meetings "useless," and privately expressed distrust of the President's whole manner of conducting the public business. Often he was at odds with his colleagues, and many difficulties arose because of the presence of both Seward and Chase in the President's household—Seward the easy-going opportunist, and Chase the unbending apostle of righteousness and reform. In December 1862 the most serious cabinet crisis of Lincoln's administration arose when, in a Republican caucus of the upper House, certain radical senators, partisans of Chase, expressed lack of confidence in the President and demanded a "reconstruction" of the cabinet, by which was intended primarily the resignation of Seward. One of the senators thus wrote of the designs of the Chase men: "Their game was to drive all the cabinet out—then force upon him [the President] the recall of Mr. Chase as Premier, and form a cabinet of ultra men around him" (*Diary of Orville Hickman Browning*, 1925, I, 604). Lincoln handled the situation by arranging a meeting in which the intriguing senators were asked to give open expression to their complaints in the presence of the cabinet. In this meeting Chase was placed in a very embarrassing position. With Lincoln and his colleagues in the room he felt impelled to speak favorably of cabinet harmony in the presence of senators to whom he is said to have remarked that "Seward exercised a back stair and malign influence upon the President, and thwarted all the measures of the Cabinet" (*Ibid.*, p. 603). As a result of these bickerings both Seward and Chase resigned; Lincoln promptly refused to accept either resignation, and matters proceeded as before, except that, as the months passed, Chase's official position became more and more difficult. He honestly differed with Lincoln on essential matters; chafed at the President's inaction and "looseness"; became increasingly impatient at the slow progress of the war, and probably came to believe in his own superior ability to guide the ship of state. Though not quite disloyal to the President, he nevertheless became the center of an anti-Lincoln movement while retaining his position in the cabinet.

Early in 1864 many zealous Unionists, including Horace Greeley, Henry Ward Beecher, William Cullen Bryant, and Theodore Tilton, had reached the conclusion that Lincoln's administration was a failure; and a congressional committee of which Senator Pomeroy of Kansas was chairman sounded the call for Chase in a paper known as the "Pomeroy Circular," which was at first distributed confidentially but soon found its way into the press. The paper declared that it was practically impossible to reëlect Lincoln; that his "manifest tendency toward temporary expedients" would become stronger during a second term, and that Chase united more of the needful qualities than any other available candidate. Chase, it appears, did not know of the circular until he saw it in a Washington paper; but his criticisms of the administration, as well as his willingness to rely upon the good judgment of those who thought that "the public good" would be promoted by the use of his name, were well known. An element of bitterness was injected into the Chase boom when Gen. Francis P. Blair, Jr., of Missouri, delivered an abusive speech against Chase in Congress in April 1864; and the friendliness of the President toward Blair was misconstrued, adding a further strain to the relations between Chase and Lincoln.

When the publication of the Pomeroy circular required an explanation, Chase wrote Lincoln of his entirely passive attitude toward the movement in his behalf, assured the President of his respect and affection, and offered to resign his secretaryship if the President should desire it. Lincoln's reply indicated that he had not been offended and that he desired no change in the treasury department. The Chase movement soon collapsed, partly from mismanagement, and partly for the lack of any solid foundation. The President's party managers played a trump card by setting an early date (June 7) for the Republican or "Union" nominating convention at Baltimore; and when a caucus professing to speak for the Union members of the Ohio legislature indorsed the President, Chase withdrew his candidacy.

He did not long remain in the cabinet. After various differences over appointments, he submitted for the office of assistant treasurer at New York the name of M. B. Field whom Lincoln found unacceptable because of influential opposition in the state. When Lincoln suggested that the appointment would subject him to "still greater strain," Chase replied that he had thought only of fitness in his suggested appointments, referred to the "embarrassment and difficulty" of his position, and, as on various other occasions, presented his resignation. Chase's diary indicates that he could have been induced to remain in the cabinet (Warden, *post*, p. 618); but, somewhat to his chagrin, Lincoln accepted the resignation, and he unexpectedly found himself out of office. "Of all I have said in commendation of your ability and fidelity," wrote the President, "I have nothing to unsay; and yet you and I have reached a point of mutual embarrassment in our official relations which it seems cannot be overcome or long-

er sustained consistently with the public service."

In the depressing summer of 1864 certain factors seemed to be working for a revival of the Chase candidacy. Distrust of the President, combined with anger at his veto of the Wade-Davis reconstruction bill and depression due to the unfavorable military situation, caused certain anti-Lincoln men to launch a movement for another nominating convention "to concentrate the Union strength on some one candidate who commands the confidence of the country" (New York *Sun*, June 30, 1889, p. 3). The plan contemplated that Lincoln, renominated in June, should be induced to withdraw. On Aug. 18, 1864, Horace Greeley wrote: "Mr. Lincoln is already beaten. He cannot be elected. And we must have another ticket to save us from utter overthrow" (*Ibid.*). Charles Sumner approved the movement; and various men who had been active in the earlier effort toward Chase's candidacy, notably Henry Winter Davis, gave it support. Whitelaw Reid, who was very close to Chase, induced the *Cincinnati Gazette* to come out for Lincoln's withdrawal. Chase's own attitude was at first receptive and non-committal. In September, however, the entire political situation changed with the fall of Atlanta and Republican success in Vermont and Maine. The proposed convention was not held; the whole "radical" movement was abandoned; its sponsors came out for the Baltimore candidates, and Chase himself participated in the campaign for Lincoln, making various speeches in the West.

When Chief Justice Taney died, Oct. 12, 1864, Lincoln's choice fell upon Chase in spite of misgivings as to the former secretary's presidential ambitions—or, as some thought, the President may have felt that he was putting a perpetual candidate in an office where presumably his ambition would be silenced. The years of Chase's chief justiceship fell during the turbulent period of Reconstruction. Occupied with problems of unusual complexity in his judicial capacity, he by no means held aloof from political controversies; and the most determined efforts to put him in the presidency came while he wore the toga of judicial office. Though these years witnessed the fruition of cherished hopes in the eradication of slavery and the restoration of the Union, the satisfaction he might have felt in the accomplishment of these objects was clouded by post-war excesses and corruption which put him out of tune with the party of his later choice, while in his own person he suffered disappointment, affront, and injured dignity. He was probably the least happy of our chief justices. At the time of Lincoln's assassination his life was considered in danger and he was protected by military guard. On Apr. 15, 1865, he administered the presidential oath to Johnson; and it seemed for a time that he might become a sort of mentor to the new president. On various occasions he approached Johnson with advice on Reconstruction policies, at times even drafting public statements to be delivered or issued by the President. Warmly advocating negro suffrage, and favoring the radical policy of Reconstruction, he started in May 1865 on an extended Southern tour which occupied two months and was devoted to confidential investigations concerning conditions in the states lately in "rebellion." At Charleston, S. C., and elsewhere he addressed colored audiences, advocating the enfranchisement of their race.

After the war Chase was confronted with the question of reopening federal courts in the South; but he delayed because of the conviction that subordination to the military authorities would be inconsistent with judicial independence; and when at length he did open the United States circuit court at Raleigh, N. C., on June 6, 1867, he carefully explained in his address to the bar that this was done only after the *habeas corpus* privilege had been restored and assurances given that the "military authority [did] not extend in any respect to the courts of the United States." When planning to reopen the circuit court at Richmond, Va., he declined military protection for himself and the court, with the comment: "If I go to Richmond at all, I intend to have no relations with the military, except those which spring from the good-will which subsists between myself and some of the officers" (Warden, *post*, p. 659).

A painful duty confronting Chase in his capacity as circuit justice was that of presiding at the proposed trial of Jefferson Davis, who, after two years in military custody, was released to the civil authorities in May 1867 and placed under indictment for treason against the United States. The earlier stages of the case cannot be traced here; but on Mar. 26, 1868, in the United States circuit court at Richmond, a grand jury brought in an elaborate indictment against Davis, charging treason under the federal law of 1790, which prescribed the penalty of death. Chase's reluctance to preside at the Davis prosecution may well have explained his repeated postponements in coming to Richmond to hold court. When he did appear he was annoyed by association on the bench with John C. Underwood [*q.v.*], federal district judge in Virginia, a man whose pronounced anti-Southern prejudices destroyed his judicial impartiality. In December 1868 a motion to quash the indictment was argued before Justices Chase and Underwood, Davis's counsel

contending that any prosecution of the Confederate leader for treason would be inconsistent with the fourteenth amendment of the Federal Constitution, in which disability from office-holding, not death, was prescribed for those in Davis's position. Favoring the quashing of the indictment, Chase disagreed with Underwood; the disagreement was certified to the United States Supreme Court; and the Davis case was pending there when, on Dec. 25, 1868, President Johnson issued an unconditional and universal pardon to all who had participated in the "rebellion." The consequent termination of the case, both at Richmond and at Washington, gave genuine relief to Chase (R. F. Nichols, "United States vs. Jefferson Davis," *American Historical Review,* XXXI, 266 ff.).

When the peak of radical fury was reached in the attempt to remove President Johnson, it fell to Chase as chief justice to preside over the Senate sitting as a court of impeachment. The flimsiness of the charges betrayed the whole movement as a partisan attack upon the President because of his opposition to the Stevens-Sumner-Wade policy of Reconstruction; and the great danger was that the judicial character of the whole proceeding would be a mere pretense. Denying that the Senate was a court, the anti-Johnson group sought to subordinate the chief justice as a figurehead, to exclude ordinary rules of evidence, to suppress essential testimony, to deny adequate opportunities for defense, to intimidate individual senators, and to rush the whole proceeding through with railroad speed. Chase, however, refused to accept the rôle of puppet and effectively asserted his prerogatives as presiding judge. Characteristically, he began by lecturing the Senate for receiving articles of impeachment and framing rules of procedure before being organized as a court. For this he was criticized; and even Warden states that his "hero" erred in this respect; but the question was essentially a judicial one to which the Chief Justice had given earnest study, and his unwillingness to surrender his own functions is more to be admired than censured. He considered himself a part of the court, with the presiding judge's function of seeing that its proceedings from the outset were properly conducted. The Senate radicals were minded to deny him the casting vote; but he successfully defended this right, taking the opportunity, on the occasion of the first tie on a question of adjournment, to announce his vote and declare the tribunal adjourned. He was attacked as a partisan of the President, accused of seeking converts for acquittal, and assailed for playing politics in allowing his name to be used as a candidate for the presidency during the impeachment proceedings. As to the "stories" of rides in which he advised senators on their duty, he himself said that there was a "grain of fact sunk in gallons of falsehood" (Warden, *post*, p. 696). He did profoundly disapprove of the whole impeachment movement and did not entirely suppress his views; but there is no reason to reject his own statement that he did not seek to influence or convert any one (not even Sprague, his son-in-law), and that until the final vote he had no idea what the result would be.

Chase's incurable ambition for the presidency found its most striking manifestation in 1868, when, after obtaining no notice in the Republican convention, he became the center of a determined boom among the Democrats. Though certain papers, such as the *New York Tribune*, put forth his name, he made no effort for the Republican nomination. One should perhaps discount his statements in private letters that he would not take the nomination; for he had no chance whatever in that party, whose radical leaders had repudiated him, and whose emotional swing to Grant was irresistible. From the standpoint of party regularity it seemed to many a shocking thing that so prominent a Republican should not only fail to support his party's candidate, but should seek the leadership of the opposing party. For Chase, however, party regularity had never been an imperative motive; he had often described himself as an independent Democrat, and his attitude toward Grant was that of thorough disapproval and lack of confidence. Newspapers and influential leaders began to work for him; and he decided to allow his name to be used. In correspondence and interview he again showed a receptive attitude, and when asked for a public statement he defined his policy, emphasizing universal amnesty and universal suffrage, though realizing that such an attitude would injure his prospects (Schuckers, *post*, pp. 584–86). In the Democratic convention at New York an active group of Chase managers labored early and late ("Kate" Sprague turning politician and exerting her personal and social influence); and a "Chase platform" was circulated among the delegates. When it came to the voting, however, his platform was rejected; Ohio declared for Seymour of New York; and in an atmosphere of pandemonium Seymour was unanimously chosen for the presidential candidacy, with Chase's factious enemy, Blair, as running mate. In his disappointment Chase bore himself in silence and dignity and gave no countenance to efforts of his friends to obtain Seymour's withdrawal or launch a third-party movement.

Meanwhile the court over which Chase presided was faced by a menacing Congress and subjected to unusual strain in deciding a series of perplexing cases. In the Milligan case (4 *Wallace*, 2), it was held that military commissions for the trial of citizens are illegal, except where invasion or war actually deposes the civil courts. On the main point of this decision Chase concurred; but he dissented from that portion which held that Congress could not have provided for such trials if it had wished. At various times it seemed that the court would have to decide on the constitutionality of the Reconstruction Acts; but such a result, which would have precipitated an unseemly contest with Congress, was avoided. In *Mississippi* vs. *Johnson* (4 *Wallace*, 475) and *Georgia* vs. *Stanton* (6 *Wallace*, 50), the court refused to enjoin the President or a member of the cabinet from enforcing the Reconstruction Acts. This was in keeping with the court's practise of avoiding political questions. In the McCardle case (6 *Wallace*, 318), which again involved the legality of Reconstruction legislation, a decision was avoided by an act of Congress which deprived the court of jurisdiction; and the court permitted its functions thus to be limited. Further questions concerning reconstruction were considered in *Texas* vs. *White* (7 *Wallace*, 700), *Cummings* vs. *Missouri* (4 *Wallace*, 277) and *Ex parte Garland* (4 *Wallace*, 333). In these controversies the court held the Union to be indissoluble, declared secession a nullity, and denied the validity of test oaths intended to exclude ex-Confederates from office-holding. The application of the Fourteenth Amendment to certain state legislation was considered in the Slaughterhouse Cases (16 *Wallace*, 36), in which the court refused to set itself up as a censor of state laws or invade the domain of civil rights theretofore belonging to the states. Preferring a broader application of the amendment, Chase dissented from this opinion, whose main doctrine has since been abandoned by the court.

In 1870 Chase delivered the opinion declaring unconstitutional that part of the Legal Tender Act of 1862 which made the "greenbacks" legal tender as to contracts existing at the time the act was passed (*Hepburn* vs. *Griswold*, 8 *Wallace*, 603). As secretary of the treasury he had issued these government notes; and he was now roundly abused for holding them illegal. When the Hepburn decision was reversed in 1871 (Legal Tender Cases, 12 *Wallace*, 457), Chase dissented.

It appears that Chase would have accepted a presidential nomination by the Liberal Republicans in 1872; but, aside from other factors, the state of his health would have prevented such a nomination. His vote this year was given to Greeley (Schuckers, *post*, p. 593). On May 7, 1873, he died of a paralytic stroke in New York.

Chase was tall, massive, handsome in feature, and distinguished in figure and bearing. His portraits show a large head, with deep-set, blue-gray eyes, prominent brow, spirited nostrils, and firm lips. He was near-sighted and may have lacked magnetism and approachableness; but there was something in his mien that bespoke a determined will. His religious convictions were genuine and earnest. Reading his diaries we find how he chided himself on his sinfulness; how at times he declined communion from self-distrust; how he was equally disturbed if at other times his unworthiness failed to oppress him; how he repeated psalms while bathing or dressing; how he pursued his Scripture reading and prayer as a pure matter of conscience. He considered it sinful to waste time. Though fond of chess, he foreswore cards and avoided fashionable society. He once described a charming young lady as one with whom he would have fallen in love had she not been "fond of the gay world" and "disinclined to religion," which he valued "more than any earthly possession" (Warden, *post*, 190). Though he was socially at ease, a sense of humor was denied him; and when telling a story he would usually spoil it. Schuckers speaks of his "modesty"; but others considered him conceited and accessible to flattery. Though hardly the scholar in politics, he was of a literary turn; and in early life he sometimes expressed himself in verse. There are purple patches in his usually grave diaries to which the historian turns with real delight.

Having the "defects of his virtues," he was self-righteous, opinionated, and difficult to work with. Ambition colored all the more prominent phases of his career. That it diminished his usefulness, impaired his dignity, and blinded his judgment as to currents of public opinion, may be conceded; but it did not prompt unworthy bargains nor excessive electioneering. His moral courage was manifest in his opposition in the Cincinnati council to saloon licenses, his defiance of threatened violence, his advocacy of unpopular causes, and his refusal to truckle for the presidency. As war-time minister of finance he resisted alluring opportunities for private gain. Though puritanical, he was not a fanatic. His anti-slavery activities were held within bounds; and he never affiliated with the Garrison or Phillips type of abolitionist. The antagonism between him and Wade was of long standing; and he disliked the excesses of the radical school of Reconstruction while partly approving its program. His mental operations were steady rather than rapid; his public statements precise and devoid of verbiage. As a speaker he commanded attention rather by conviction and intellectual force than by the orator's art. His opinions as chief justice were characterized by a practical emphasis upon main principles rather than by brilliance or fondness for legal lore.

[Portions of Chase's elaborate diaries and letters have been published in Robert B. Warden, *Account of the Private Life and Public Services of Salmon Portland Chase* (1874), in J. W. Schuckers, *Life and Public Services of Salmon Portland Chase* (1874), and in the *Annual Report, Am. Hist. Ass.*, 1902, vol. II. The last mentioned volume includes some interesting letters from Chase to Sumner and a large number of letters from George S. Denison, who, as treasury official at New Orleans during the Civil War, wrote in full concerning conditions in Louisiana. The bulk of the original manuscript of the diary, together with letters and miscellaneous material, is to be found in the library of the Pa. Hist. Soc. at Philadelphia; and another large collection of Chase manuscripts (over one hundred volumes) is deposited in the division of manuscripts of the Lib. of Cong. The biographical work by Warden is garrulous, extravagantly eulogistic, and of negligible importance, except as a source book; that of Schuckers, though of somewhat more value, is far from satisfactory. The short volume by A. B. Hart in the *Am. Statesmen* series (1899), though not free from error, is the best biography. The amusing campaign biography by J. T. Trowbridge, *The Ferry Boy and the Financier* (1864), is based in part upon a series of autobiographical letters written by Chase himself; but Chase's recollections were often dim, and Trowbridge drew freely upon his own fancy. A series of letters bearing upon the movement in 1864 to displace Lincoln in favor of Chase appeared under the title "Unwritten History" in the N. Y. *Sun*, June 30, 1889. The following titles may also be noted: Donn Piatt, *Memories of the Men Who Saved the Union* (1887); Arthur M. Schlesinger, "Salmon Portland Chase, Undergraduate and Pedagogue," in *Ohio Archæol. and Hist. Quart.*, vol. XXVIII, no. 2 (1910); Norton S. Townshend, "Salmon P. Chase" (*Ibid.*, vol. I, 1887); Elbridge G. Spaulding, *A Resource of War: . . . Hist. of the Legal Tender Paper Money Issued During the Great Rebellion* (1869); Chas. Warren, *The Supreme Court in U. S. Hist.* (1922); Hugh McCulloch, *Men and Measures of Half a Century* (1888).]

J.G.R.

CHASE, SAMUEL (Apr. 17, 1741–June 19, 1811), Revolutionary leader, signer of the Declaration of Independence, justice of the United States Supreme Court, was born in Somerset County, Md. His father, the Rev. Thomas Chase, was an emigrant from England, and for many years rector of St. Paul's, Baltimore. His mother, Martha [or Matilda] Walker Chase, daughter of a farmer, died when Samuel was still very young, and his education till he was eighteen devolved upon his father. It was largely in the classics. In 1759 young Chase entered upon the study of the law in the offices of Hammond & Hall of Annapolis. He was admitted to practise in the mayor's court in 1761, and in chancery and certain of the county courts two years later. He was married twice: first on May 21, 1762, to Anne Baldwin; second, on Mar. 3, 1784, to Hannah

Kilty Giles. Till 1786, when he moved to Baltimore, his home was in Annapolis.

From 1764 to 1784 Chase was a member of the Maryland Assembly. At the outset he aligned himself with the opposition to the royal governor, going so far as to support a measure regulating clerical salaries which cut his own father's salary in half. His activity in riotous demonstrations of "The Sons of Liberty" against the Stamp Act caused him to be denounced by the mayor and aldermen of Annapolis as a "busy, restless incendiary, a ringleader of mobs, a foul-mouthed and inflaming son of discord." He, in turn, characterized his critics as "despicable tools of power, emerged from obscurity and basking in proprietary sunshine" (Sanderson, IX, 191).

Chase was a born leader of insurrection. In 1774 he was a member of the Maryland Committee of Correspondence, and a delegate to the First Continental Congress. Next year he was a member of the Maryland convention and of the Council of Safety, and attended both Congresses at Philadelphia. Here he urged a total embargo upon trade with Great Britain, arguing that such a measure must speedily force Great Britain to submission or bankruptcy. At first he opposed the suggestion of an American navy as the "maddest idea in the world," but later took the opposite view. According to John Adams, Chase was the member selected to move an effort to secure foreign alliances. He was also an early advocate of confederation, and was the first to develop Maryland's position on the question of the Western Lands. On Feb. 15, 1776, he was appointed, along with Franklin and Charles Carroll of Carrollton, a member of the commission to win over Canada. The commission reached Montreal at the end of April and returned to Philadelphia in June, having accomplished nothing. Proceeding at once to Maryland, Chase conducted a vigorous campaign which led to the Maryland convention's rescinding its previous instructions and ordering its delegates to vote for independence. Chase arrived in Philadelphia with the new instructions on the eve of the decisive vote, having ridden one hundred and fifty miles in two days. He signed the enrolled Declaration on Aug. 2; and from this time on till the end of 1778 was reappointed regularly to the Maryland delegation. In 1777, he served on twenty-one Congressional committees; in 1778, on thirty. The most important of these was a committee consisting of himself, R. H. Lee, and Gouverneur Morris to prepare a circular to discredit the British peace proposals of 1778. The resultant document is said to have been largely Chase's handiwork. Throughout he steadily opposed Congressional intrigues against

Washington, a fact which Washington was later to remember.

Toward the end of 1778 Chase's reputation fell suddenly into shadow. Utilizing information gained as a member of Congress, he combined with others to attempt a corner on flour in view of the approach of the French fleet. In the *New York Journal* Hamilton, as "Publius," addressed "The Honourable —— Esquire" in an invective modelled on that of "Junius": "It is your lot to have the peculiar privilege of being universally despised. . . . Were I inclined to make a satire upon the species I would attempt a faithful description of your heart" (*Works of Alexander Hamilton*, 1904, I, 199–209). The object of Hamilton's attack has been certainly identified as Chase (W. C. Ford in *New York Evening Post*, Nov. 1, 1886). In the following two years he was omitted from the Maryland delegation to Congress; and though he was later reappointed, he rarely attended and bore only an inconspicuous part. In 1783 the cloud began to lift. That year he was sent by the governor to England to recover from two fugitive loyalists Maryland's holdings in stock of the Bank of England. He remained abroad a year but achieved little. The matter in issue was tied up in Chancery proceedings from which it was only extricated years afterward by Chase's one-time protegé, William Pinkney.

Meanwhile, Chase, still practising his profession, had also entered trade. He was a member of two partnerships which sold supplies to the state and purchased shipping, cannon, and powder for it. Chase himself also purchased an extensive interest in confiscated coal and iron lands. These enterprises resulted disastrously. In 1789, confessing himself insolvent, Chase petitioned the legislature to relieve him from liability for his partnership debts, which was done upon his pledge to turn over certain property to another of the partners. In 1785 he attended the Trade Convention which met at Mt. Vernon and drafted the compact of that year between Maryland and Virginia regarding the navigation of the Potomac. Next year at the urging of friends he removed to Baltimore, where in 1788 he became chief judge of the criminal court. In 1791 he also assumed the post of chief judge of the general court of Maryland. This accumulation of offices, together with a tumultuous episode of the kind that seems to have dogged his footsteps as judge, led to an attempt in the Assembly to remove him from office; and while the motion failed of the necessary two-thirds vote, the majority declared its sense that the constitution had been violated.

Writing over the signature "Caution," Chase opposed the adoption of the Constitution of the United States (*Essays on the Constitution of the United States,* ed. by P. L. Ford, 1892), and was one of the eleven members of the Maryland ratifying convention who cast an adverse vote. He was also one of a committee of the convention to propose amendments to the new instrument, among which were clauses protective of trial by jury and of freedom of the press. He was subsequently to be reckoned an enemy of both these institutions. Just why Chase turned Federalist is something of a mystery, especially in view of his strong anti-British prejudice which he voiced as late as 1793. At any rate, in a letter dated June 14, 1795, we find Washington's close friend, Joseph McHenry, suggesting Chase for federal office. McHenry refers to Chase's past "errors (which no longer exist)," and says that his services and merits far overbalance these. "I need not tell you," he adds, "that to his professional knowledge he subjoins a very valuable stock of political science." McHenry also questions what sort of impression "an appearance of neglect is apt to produce in minds constructed like his." Washington's first inclination was to appoint Chase attorney-general; but on Jan. 26, 1796, he nominated him to the Supreme Court. The following day the nomination was unanimously ratified and Chase commissioned.

Chase's performance on the Supreme bench was the most notable of any previous to Marshall. Opinions were then delivered seriatim, and being the justice of latest appointment, Chase was required for several terms of court to give his opinions first. This accident of position, together with the colorful quality of his judicial utterances, their positiveness of expression, their richness in "political science," have all contributed to give his opinions predominant importance in this period. In his opening term (February 1796) he delivered two notable opinions: that in *Hylton* vs. *United States* (3 *Dallas,* 171) and that in *Ware* vs. *Hylton* (*Ibid.,* 198). In the former, in sustaining a specific tax on carriages as an excise, Chase laid down a definition of "direct" taxes which prevailed until *Pollock* vs. *Farmer's Loan and Trust Company* attempted ninety-nine years later to correct "a century of error" (157, 158 *U. S.*). His opinion in *Ware* vs. *Hylton* remains to this day the most impressive assertion of the supremacy of national treaties over state laws. Another outstanding opinion of his is that in *Calder* vs. *Bull* in 1798 (3 *Dallas,* 386). It is still cited for its definition of *ex post facto* laws; but is even more important for its suggestion that there are unwritten, inherent limita-

tions on legislative powers. This doctrine was presently taken up by the state courts and may be fairly regarded as the germ of the modern doctrine of due process of law as "reasonable law." In *Hollingsworth* vs. *Virginia* (*Ibid.,* p. 378), Chase expressed informally the opinion that Congressional resolutions for amending the Constitution of the United States do not have to be submitted to the president; and this seems to have been the only utterance of the Court on the subject down to the National Prohibition Cases (253 *U. S.*). His opinion in *Cooper* vs. *Telfair* (4 *Dallas,* 14) contains interesting testimony as to the conversion of bench and bar by that date to the doctrine of judicial review. He had himself previously expressed skepticism. On circuit, Chase's most important utterance was delivered in *United States* vs. *Worrall* (2 *Dallas,* 384), in which, traversing the previous views of his brethren, he held that the courts of the United States have no jurisdiction over crimes at common law. This view was later accepted by the Supreme Court in *United States* vs. *Hudson and Goodwin* (7 *Cranch,* 32) and is still in the main the law of the land (see *Ex parte Grossman* 267 *U. S.*).

The most famous incident of Chase's judgeship was his impeachment and trial. This was partly the outgrowth of his high-handed conduct in 1800 at the trial of Fries for treason (F. Wharton, *State Trials,* 610–48) and of Callender for sedition (*Ibid.,* 688). On both of these occasions Chase's evident disposition to play the "hanging judge" brought him into serious collision with counsel who threw up their briefs. The immediate occasion of the impeachment was an intemperate charge to a Baltimore grand jury, May 2, 1803. Assailing the recent repeal of the Judiciary Act of 1801 and the adoption of manhood suffrage in Maryland, Chase predicted the deterioration of "our Republican Constitution ... into a mobocracy." He was also reported, though probably falsely, with having assailed the administration as "weak, pusillanimous, relaxed." On May 13 Jefferson wrote Nicholson, a Maryland member of the House, suggesting impeachment; and on Mar. 12, 1804, under the leadership of Randolph, the House complied by a vote of 73 to 32. Of the eight articles presented against him, six had to do with the Fries and Callender trials while the last dealt with the grand jury charge. The trial formally opened Jan. 3, 1805, but did not really get under way until a month later. Among Chase's counsel were Joseph Hopkinson and Luther Martin; the leader of the House "managers" was Randolph. The fundamental question raised was that of the scope of the term "high crimes and misdemeanors" of Article III, section 4 of the Constitution; did this refer only to indictable offenses or was it broad enough to reach any conduct which the House and Senate might judge to fall short of "good behaviour" (Article III, section 1)? Notwithstanding that Jefferson brought a great deal of secret pressure to bear and that twenty-five of the thirty-four members of the Senate were of his party, the impeachment failed. Five of the articles commanded less than a majority; one failed to receive a single vote; the last received the heaviest vote, 19 votes to 15. It is generally agreed that Chase's acquittal probably saved Marshall; it is therefore of fundamental importance in our constitutional history.

From Marshall's accession, Chase's rôle on the Court became decidedly subordinate. The Chief Justice himself now spoke for the Court, and Chase delivered but one "opinion of the Court" during this whole period, and that in a case which had been appealed from Marshall's own decision on circuit (see 4 *Cranch,* 328). He also delivered a brief concurring opinion (2 *Cranch,* 127), and once announced his dissent (4 *Cranch,* 293). Indeed, through ill health, more specifically gout, he was absent from the bench the entire term of 1806 and probably also that of 1810; and in 1811, the year of his death, no Court was held.

At his prime Chase was a man of striking appearance, over six feet tall and large in proportion. "His face was broad and massive, his complexion a brownish red. 'Bacon face' was a nickname applied to him by the Maryland bar. His head was large, his brow wide, and his hair thick and white . . ." (Beveridge, *Marshall,* III, 184). Story found him "the living image" of Dr. Johnson "in person, in manners, in unwieldy strength, in severity of reproof, in real tenderness of heart; and above all in intellect." At another time Story compared him to Lord Thurlow. His intellectual grasp is fully attested by his judicial opinions; his turbulent disposition appears at every turn in his career.

[For Chase's early life see John Sanderson, *Biog. of the Signers to the Declaration of Independence* (1817); also J. T. Scharf, *Hist. of Md.,* vol. II (1879). On his services in Congress in connection with Independence see especially *Jours. Continental Congress,* vols. I–XII (1904–08); and J. H. Hazelton, *The Declaration of Independence—Its Hist.* (1906). Something of his business activities is revealed in the "Jour. and Corres. of the State Council of Md., 1778–80," in *Archives of Md.,* vols. XXI, XLIII. His period on the Supreme Court is covered by the *Reports* from 2 *Dallas* to 6 *Cranch,* inclusive. The *Official Jour.* of his impeachment trial is available in *Senate Doc.* No. 876, 62 Cong., 2 Sess. See also Wm. Plumer's *Memorandum of Proc. in the U. S. Senate* (1803–07), ed. by E. S. Brown (1923). Miscellaneous items of interest regarding Chase occur in Chas. Warren, *The Supreme Court in U. S. Hist.,* vol. I (1922); A. J. Beveridge, *Life of John Marshall,* vol. III (1919); and Gustavus Myers, *Hist. of the Supreme Court* (1918).]   E. S. C.

CHASE, THOMAS (June 16, 1827–Oct. 5, 1892), classical scholar, college president, was a son of Anthony and Lydia (Earle) Chase, and a brother of Pliny Earle Chase [*q.v.*]. He was of the eighth generation in descent from Ralph Earle, who was admitted in 1638 an inhabitant of Aquidneck, R. I., and in 1655 a freeman of the Colony of the Town of Portsmouth. By descent on both sides, and also by education, he was a Quaker. Worcester, Mass., where he was born, was in 1827 a pretty rural town. In its public schools object lessons and the methods of Pestalozzi were already introduced when the child's school days began before he was three years old. He was studying Latin when he was nine, and Greek when he was ten. English composition was not neglected, and physics, mathematics, ancient and modern history, French, and some general subjects completed the curriculum. His was the last class to enter Harvard College which read the entire Greek Testament as an entrance requirement. He entered Harvard College in 1844 and was graduated with high honors in 1848. He was, to use his own words, "a hard and not unsuccessful student, enjoying more than words can tell the instruction of great men."

After his graduation he was master of the Cambridge High School, but in 1850 was appointed to the professorship of Latin in Harvard College, which he was to hold for one year, until George Martin Lane returned from Europe. He remained, however, a year and a half longer, first as instructor in history and chemistry, then as tutor in Latin. Early in 1853 he went to Europe. He visited classic sites in Greece and Italy, then studied nearly a year at the University of Berlin and attended lectures at the Sorbonne and the Collège de France for one term. He also heard, by courtesy, lectures at the University of Athens and at several universities of Italy and Germany, besides visiting Oxford and Cambridge.

Upon his return to the United States, in 1855, he was urged to resume his place at Harvard College, but accepted the offer of the chair of philology and classic literature at Haverford College, with the understanding that he was at liberty to leave at the end of the year. He consented, however, to remain and, in 1875, was elected president of the college. In 1885 he obtained leave of absence, and in 1886 he resigned. After a year abroad he settled at Providence, R. I., where for a time he gave instruction in the classics in the Moses Brown School and for a year before his death temporarily occupied the chair of Greek in Brown University. He died at Providence, of Bright's disease. He was married on Feb. 8, 1860, to Alice Underhill Cromwell of New York.

Chase was a handsome man, with thick brown hair, a slightly aquiline nose, and an alert and kindly expression. He was not only an admirable teacher and college president but a noted scholar. An early work is *Hellas, Her Monuments and Scenery* (1861). Perhaps his most important work was performed as a member of the New Testament Company of the American Committee for the Revision of the Bible. He was appointed in 1871 and aided the Committee greatly by his translations and criticisms. He contributed a scholarly essay on "The Use of Italics in the English Bible" to a pamphlet on *Bible Revision* issued by the Committee in 1879. He was senior editor of the Chase and Stuart series of Latin texts which were widely used in schools and colleges, making several contributions to the series. He also published a *Latin Grammar* in 1882.

[Pliny Earle, comp., *Ralph Earle and his Descendants* (1888); *Hist. of Haverford Coll. for the First Sixty Years of its Existence* (1882); Phila. *Public Ledger*, Oct. 7, 1892; *R. I. Hist. Soc. Proc.*, 1892–93; *Friends' Intelligencer*, XLIX, 665; *Haverfordian*, Nov. 1892.]　　　　　　　　　　　　　　H. N. F.

CHASE, WILLIAM MERRITT (Nov. 1, 1849–Oct. 25, 1916), artist, was born at Williamsburg, Johnson County, Ind., the eldest of seven children of David Hester and Sarah (Swaim) Chase. He began as a child to copy woodcuts and other pictures, making profile portraits of members of the family and of friends. After a removal to Indianapolis in 1861, he soon outstripped his drawing-teacher at school, and as clerk at his father's shoe store, spent much time studying pictures at an art shop near by. At nineteen, a romantic impulse started him to Annapolis, Md., where he joined the U. S. school-ship *Portsmouth* for a cruise of three months. This proved unsatisfactory, and he returned to Indianapolis and chose a career in art. He was placed with the painter Benjamin Hayes, who, after some months, advised his going to New York (1869), giving him a letter to J. O. Eaton. At first he worked in Eaton's studio, at the same time following the classes of the National Academy of Design, and then set up his own studio in the Y. M. C. A. Building, Fourth Ave. and Twenty-third St., painting still-life studies. One of these, "Catawba Grapes," was exhibited at the National Academy. After two years he returned West to St. Louis, where his family now lived, and shared the studio of J. W. Pattison, painting flowers and fruit. In 1872 four gentlemen sent him to Munich to study.

Entering the antique classes at the Royal Academy at Munich he made rapid progress during the succeeding years, winning several medals. He worked under F. Wagner and later Karl von Piloty, at the same time studying the art of Leibl. After he had gained a prize for a composition, "Columbus before the Spanish Court," Piloty wished him to paint it on a large canvas for Washington, but Chase preferred to paint single figures and portraits, among the latter, those of Piloty's five children and another of his friend, Baron von Haberman. During this period he painted "The Dowager," exhibited at the Academy Exhibition in New York (1875), "The Court-Jester," shown at the Centennial in Philadelphia in 1876, and "Ready for the Ride," exhibited at the first Society of American Artists' Exhibition in 1878, and now at the Union League Club, New York. In 1877 he spent nine months in Venice with Duveneck and Twachtman, painting a "Fishmarket in Venice" and the "Antiquary's Shop." The Art Students' League, recently organized, now requested his services as a teacher, and returning to New York in 1878, he brought with him a remarkable collection of curios and pictures which were installed in a large gallery and studio at 51 West Tenth St. It became famous as a meeting place for artists and students. His classes were frequented by a large number of pupils, and Chase, as president of the Society of American Artists, was a leader among the younger painters dissatisfied with the conventions governing the National Academy. He was a prominent member of the celebrated "Tile Club," joining their excursions and visiting Europe during the summers with Beckwith, Blum, and other congenial friends. In London, 1885, he painted the portrait of Whistler now at the Metropolitan Museum, which the subject qualified as a "lampoon," despite Chase's assurances of sincerity. In 1886 he married Alice Gerson, daughter of a Brooklyn friend; by her he had eight children. Living for a time in Brooklyn, he painted some brilliant views in Prospect Park, as well as others in Central Park, Manhattan. After several changes of residence he decided in 1893 to give up his large studio on West Tenth St., and disposing of its valuable contents at auction, he bought a house on Stuyvesant Square, retaining it as a permanent residence for life. At the same time a studio was taken on Fifth Avenue at Thirtieth St., and after some years another in the Tiffany Building on Fourth Ave. About 1891–92, he organized a school on the Shinnecock Hills near Southampton, Long Island, where for eleven seasons he taught principally landscape painting to large classes. In 1903 he took a party of students to Europe, supplementing practical work with study in the galleries and studios, and this was continued through succeeding summers until 1914. In the latter year he held his first class in California at Carmel-by-the-Sea. No American painter taught such a large number of pupils, while at the same time rapid methods of execution enabled him to paint many portraits, landscapes, and still-life subjects. He rarely surpassed, however, the remarkable qualities of his earlier paintings done at Munich and Venice. A number of otherwise ably-executed portraits show the limitations of one dealing with exterior appearances rather than with imaginative ideals or spiritual suggestion. His still-life studies, especially those of fish, on the other hand, are veritable masterpieces. His portrait, by Sargent—a commission from Chase's pupils—is at the Metropolitan Museum, New York, where a number of his works are to be seen.

[Katherine M. Roof, *Life and Art of W. M. Chase* (1917), with an introduction by Alice Gerson Chase; Mrs. M. G. Van Rensselaer, in *Am. Art Rev.*, II, 91–98, 135–42; H. R. Butler and G. Beal in *Scribner's Mag.*, LXI, 255–58; J. W. McSpadden, *Famous Painters of America* (1907); personal acquaintance.]   R. J. W.

CHATARD, FRANCIS SILAS (Dec. 13, 1834–Sept. 7, 1918), Roman Catholic bishop of Indianapolis, was a grandson of Pierre Chatard. The latter, an emigrant from Santo Domingo, whose slaves and plantation were lost in the negro insurrection, had settled in Baltimore, married the daughter of a fellow emigrant, and won local prestige by writing and practising medicine, in which he had been trained in Paris. His son, Ferdinand, had studied medicine in Paris, London, and Edinburgh, practised in Baltimore, and married Eliza Anne, daughter of Silas Marean of Brookline, Mass., who had served in the War of 1812 and as consul in Martinique, where he had married an Irish widow of an English gentleman. Francis Chatard, son of Ferdinand and Eliza Anne, thus came of a distinguished Baltimore family proud of a diversified French, Irish, and native American ancestry. Expecting to follow the paternal profession, on his graduation from Mount St. Mary's, Emmitsburg, in 1853, he studied medicine under Dr. Donaldson of Baltimore and in the University of Maryland where he obtained his medical degree. After serving two years as an interne in the Baltimore infirmary and as physician of the city almshouse, he heard the religious call and enrolled under Archbishop Kenrick. Nativist rioting and anti-Catholic charges quickened his faith, and close contact with suffering influenced his decision to enter the religious life.

For six years Chatard pursued courses in philosophy and theology in the Urban College of the Propaganda at Rome before he was ordained (1862) and awarded the doctorate of divinity (1863). He was then named vice-rector of the American College at Rome under Dr. W. G. McCloskey, later bishop of Louisville. Succeeding to the rectorship in 1868, he headed the College for ten interesting years during which the Vatican Council of 1870 was held. As the nephew of Admiral Chatard of the Confederacy, he took special pride in presenting Grant, Sherman, and Sheridan to Pius IX with whom as a papal chamberlain he was on intimate terms. During his incumbency, he gathered funds in America to pay off the debts and endow the College whose scholastic standards had decidedly improved.

Named by Pope Pius to the See of Vincennes, he was consecrated (1878) by Cardinal Franchi, prefect of the Propaganda, in the presence of civil and ecclesiastical visitors of high degree. Later he was installed in his bishopric by Archbishop Purcell. Vincennes welcomed in him a man of polished appearance, a good linguist, an attractive conversationalist, an inspiring preacher, and a deep student of foreign politics. In a sense, due to his wide circle of European friends, he was an international figure in Catholic affairs. He ruled his diocese well and took an active part in civic life. In 1898, on removal of his See to Indianapolis, he built a new cathedral, St. Vincent's Hospital, schools, and a convent. On his twenty-fifth anniversary, he was honored by the whole state in ceremonies in which Cardinal Gibbons, forty archbishops and bishops, and three hundred priests took part. Although seven years later Joseph Chartrand was appointed coadjutor, the aged bishop continued active. During the World War, as a stout pro-ally he followed the fortunes of the American Expeditionary Force the more intently because of the enlistment of a favorite nephew in the medical corps. Inactive for the last few months of his long life, he passed away in 1918. Newspapers stressed the unusual fact that he was born at the same time and in the same cathedral parish in Baltimore as Cardinal Gibbons and Bishop John Foley of Detroit.

He translated from the French, *The Memoirs of a Seraph,* published a book of essays and a treatise, *Christian Truths,* and wrote a number of articles for the *American Catholic Quarterly* and the *Catholic World,* including in the latter publication, "Letters from the Vatican in 1870" which attracted wide attention.

[H. Alerding, *Hist. of Cath. Ch. in Diocese of Vincennes* (1883), pp. 211–25; H. A. Brann, *Hist. of the*

Am. College in Rome (1910); *Biog. Hist. of Eminent Men of Indiana* (Cincinnati, 1880); *Indianapolis News,* Sept. 7, 1918; *Indianapolis Sunday Star,* Sept, 8, 1918.]

R. J. P.

CHAUMONOT, PIERRE JOSEPH MARIE (Mar. 9, 1611–Feb. 21, 1693), Jesuit missionary, was the son of peasants of Burgundy who gave him a good education under an uncle who was a priest. He studied Latin and music and showed much aptitude, but as a youthful prank he stole money from his uncle, ran away, and became a vagabond. Finally, in Italy, he repented of his evil ways, and on May 18, 1632, was received as a novice in the Society of Jesus at Rome. He then took the names Joseph Marie, and is usually spoken of as Father Joseph Chaumonot. A fellow student showed him one of the *Jesuit Relations,* whereupon he greatly desired to become a missionary in New France. This wish was granted, and on Aug. 1, 1639, he arrived at Quebec, and immediately set out for Huronia on the shores of Georgian Bay. There he evinced great ability in learning the Indian language, and soon became so useful that he was sent to the Petun tribe with Father Daniel, and to that of the Neutrals with Brébeuf. Upon the destruction of the Huron missions by the Iroquois, Chaumonot escaped martyrdom, and came with the fugitive Christian Hurons to Quebec, where in 1650 they were given a grant of the Isle d'Orleans.

In 1655 Chaumonot was chosen to go with Dablon to open a mission among the Iroquois, who professed to be ready to receive the "black robes." There he found many captive Christian Hurons and ministered to them. The sites of some of the villages where he ministered are now marked: at Indian Hill, Pompey, N. Y., where he held the first mass; near Mud Creek, Ontario County, where the Hurons dwelt; on Cayuga Lake, where he preached in 1656 to the Cayuga tribe. The mission to the Iroquois was abandoned in 1658, the colonists and missionaries escaping death by flight to Canada. Thereafter Chaumonot dwelt among the Hurons, who had been driven from Isle d'Orleans, and lived successively at Beauport, Notre Dame de Sainte Foy, and Lorette. This last settlement was named at the request of Chaumonot, who had always had a strong devotion for the Casa Loretto in Italy. In all he lived with the refugee Hurons over forty years, with the interval of the Iroquois mission 1655–58, and two years as chaplain (1663–64) at Fort Richelieu.

In 1688, at the request of his superior, he wrote his autobiography. He also compiled a Huron grammar, and several sacred writings for the Hurons. In 1692 he retired to the house of his order in Quebec, where he died, much beloved and respected. A simple, naïve, unambitious man, he made an ideal missionary, patiently enduring hardships of every kind, counting all his afflictions to the glory of God and the Holy Family.

[The sources for Chaumonot's life are abundant. His autobiography was published by J. G. Shea, *La Vie du R. P. Pierre Joseph Marie Chaumonot* (Nouvelle York, Cramoisy Press, 1858). There is also a Paris edition of 1885. Shea also publshed a Supplement called *Suite de la Vie* etc. (Nouvelle York, Cramoisy Press, 1858). Chaumonot's Huron grammar was translated from the Latin and printed in *Trans. Lit. and Hist. Soc. of Quebec,* vol. II (1831). His missions in Canada and New York are described in *Jesuit Relations* (Thwaites ed., Cleveland, 1896–1902), with a biographical sketch in XVIII, 255.]

L. P. K.

CHAUNCEY, ISAAC (Feb. 20, 1772–Jan. 27, 1840), naval officer, was born in Black Rock, Fairfield County, Conn. Descended from Charles Chauncy [*q.v.*], the second president of Harvard College, he was the fifth of nine children born to Wolcott and Ann (Brown) Chauncy. Manifesting a liking for the sea, when a mere youth he entered upon his chosen calling and, such was his proficiency, at the age of nineteen he was given command of the ship *Jenny,* belonging to the Schermerhorns, wealthy New York shipowners. It is narrated that during one of his voyages between Charleston and New York the crew and all the officers except himself were taken sick with yellow fever and that single-handed he brought the vessel into port. On June 11, 1799, he was appointed a first lieutenant of the frigate *President,* then building at New York, taking rank from Sept. 17, 1798, and during the last year of the naval hostilities with France he made a cruise in her in the West Indies, with Commodore Truxtun in command. Chauncey was retained under the peace establishment of 1801, ranking sixth in the list of lieutenants, and in the war with Tripoli he found employment during the period 1802–05, first as acting commander of the flagship, *Chesapeake,* and later as commander, successively, of the *New York* and the *John Adams.* While he was in command of the *New York* an explosion of gunpowder near the magazine threatened the destruction of the vessel and all on board. Chauncey coolly and bravely led a party of volunteers below who put out the fire and saved the ship. Joining temporarily the flagship *Constitution* he participated in the attack on Tripoli made by the fleet of Commodore Preble, Aug. 28–29, 1804, when much damage was done to the enemy. His services on this occasion were especially commended by his commodore. He was promoted master-commandant on May 18, 1804, and captain on Apr. 24, 1806—the highest statutory rank in the navy. About the time of the latter promotion he was furloughed, with permission to make a voyage to the East Indies. This he did in command of a vessel belonging to John Jacob Astor. A year later he returned to the navy and took command of the New York navy-yard, where he was stationed until early in the War of 1812.

Possessing the confidence of President Madison and Secretary of the Navy Hamilton, and having the reputation of being one of the most efficient officers in the navy, Chauncey, early in September 1812, was made commander of the naval forces on Lakes Ontario and Erie, with power to build, purchase, and hire vessels, appoint officers, enlist seamen, buy naval stores, and establish navy-yards. This was the most important command at the disposal of the Navy Department. In October 1812, he arrived at Sackett's Harbor, N. Y., where he made his headquarters for upward of three years. An excellent organizer, he established a navy-yard, with a naval hospital, naval school, and rope walk, and built or otherwise procured a fleet of more than twenty vessels. The objectives of his naval operations on Lake Ontario were three in number and more or less interrelated: the reduction of fortified places in conjunction with the army, the capture or destruction of the ships of the enemy (commanded by Sir James L. Yeo), and the obtaining of a naval superiority on the lake. In 1813 he ably assisted the army in the reduction of York and Fort George. During that year both fleets did considerable cruising, but little fighting. On Sept. 28, in an engagement with Yeo, Chauncey won a victory but failed to make the best use of the force under his command (Roosevelt, *post,* p. 253). Both commanders proved to be wary and excessively cautious. The year ended indecisively. In the campaign of 1814 Chauncey appeared in an even less favorable light. At critical moments he was inactive (Mahan, *post,* II, 298–99). Throughout the war he failed, except for brief periods, to establish a naval superiority on Lake Ontario. At last the confidence of President Madison was shaken, and he ordered Commodore Decatur to relieve him. The proposed change, however, did not take place, and Chauncey remained on the lake. It is obvious that among the naval commanders of the War of 1812 he is not of the first rank.

Soon after leaving Sackett's Harbor in the summer of 1815 he took command at Portsmouth, N. H., of the *Washington,* one of the first ships of the line in the navy. With this vessel as his flagship, he commanded the Mediterranean squadron in 1816–18, and, together with Consul William Shaler [*q.v.*], negotiated a treaty with Algiers. During the years 1821–24 he was stationed in Washington as one of the three post-captains comprising the Board of Navy Commissioners, which assisted the secretary of the navy in administering the navy; and in the years 1825–32 he was again commandant of the New York navy-yard. In 1832 he returned as navy commissioner to Washington where he remained until his death, serving for the last three years of his life as president of the board. He is buried in the Congressional Cemetery in that city. He was married to Catharine Sickles of New York. Two of his sons, Charles W. and John S., were naval officers. His portrait (*Analectic Magazine,* III, 177) shows him as large and corpulent.

[Record of Officers, Bureau of Navigation, 1799–1840; *Navy Reg.,* 1815–40; Captains' Letters, and Letters of Officers Ships of War, 1812–14, Navy Dept.; Wm. C. Fowler, *Memorials of the Chaunceys* (1858), pp. 215–21; Theodore Roosevelt, *The Naval War of 1812* (1882); A. T. Mahan, *Sea Power in Its Relation to the War of 1812* (1905); G. W. Allen, *Our Navy and the Barbary Corsairs* (1905).]   C. O. P.

CHAUNCY, CHARLES (1592–Feb. 19, 1671/2), non-conformist clergyman, second president of Harvard, was a son of George Chauncy and his wife Agnes Welch, widow of Edward Humbertson. Notwithstanding the statement in Mather's *Magnalia* that the date of Chauncy's birth was 1589, it is probable that he was born shortly before Nov. 5, 1592, when his baptism was registered in Yardley-bury, Herts, England. A pupil in Westminster School at the time of the Gunpowder Plot, he matriculated at Trinity College, Cambridge, at Easter, 1610, received the B.A. degree in 1613–14, the M.A. in 1617, and B.D. in 1624. He became a fellow of Trinity in 1614 and was Greek lecturer in the same college in 1624 and 1626 (Zachary Grey, *An Impartial Examination of Mr. Daniel Neal's History of the Puritans,* II, 183). On Mar. 17, 1630, he was married to Catharine, daughter of Robert Eyre. He was vicar of St. Michael's in Cambridge in 1626; of Ware, Herts, in 1627–33; of Marston St. Lawrence in 1633–37. Because of his opposition to some of Archbishop Laud's regulations, he was twice summoned before the high commission court,—in 1630 while he was in Ware (*Proceedings Massachusetts Historical Society,* XIII, 337–40; *Calendar of State Papers, Domestic Series,* 1629–31), and again, in 1634 while he was in Marston St. Lawrence (*Calendar of State Papers, Domestic Series,* 1635–36). On the second occasion he was imprisoned for some months. In each case he submitted only to regret his submission later. On June 12, 1637, Dr. S. Clerke wrote to Sir

John Lambe: "Mr. Chauncy . . . mends like sour ale in summer. He held a fast on Wednesday last, and . . . he with another preached some six or eight hours. The whole tribe of Gad flocked thither, some three-score from Northampton; the Lord Say, with his lady, honoured them with their presence" (*Calendar of State Papers, Domestic Series,* 1637). Evidently a new storm was brewing and Chauncy fled before it, reaching New England a few days before the great earthquake, which occurred on June 1, 1638. Before leaving England he wrote a *Retraction* of his submission which was published in London in 1641. In New England he went first to Plymouth as a helper to Mr. Reyner, the pastor. Trouble soon arose on account of his theory concerning baptism which he seems to have believed should be by immersion even in the case of infants. On Nov. 2, 1640, Hooker of Hartford wrote to Shepard of Cambridge: "Mr. Chancy and the church [at Plymouth] are to part. . . . At a day of fast . . . he openly professed he did as verily believe the truth of his opinions as that there was a God in heaven, and that he was settled in it as the earth was upon the center . . . I profess how it is possible to keep peace with a man so adventurous and pertinaceous, who will vent what he list and maintain what he vents, its beyond all the skill I have to conceive" (Lucius R. Paige, *History of Cambridge,* 1877, pp. 49–50). In 1641, he removed to Scituate where he found some remnants of Mr. Lothrop's party who sympathized with him but also others who were inclined to the Church of England. The result was a schism and the two churches wrangled until conditions became unbearable (Samuel Deane, *History of Scituate,* 1831). In 1654, Chauncy left for Boston, intending to return to his former parish in Ware, which had invited him back. At the moment, however, Harvard College was without a president owing to the enforced withdrawal of Henry Dunster because of his Baptist convictions, and the Overseers appointed Mather and Norton a committee to invite Chauncy to the vacant office. Since his views had become well-known, the Committee was instructed to signify to him that the Overseers "expected and desired that he forbear to disseminate or publish any tenets concerning the necessity of immersion in baptism and celebration of the Lord's Supper at evening or to expose the received doctrine therein" (*Publications of the Colonial Society of Massachusetts,* vol. XV, p. 206). Accepting these humiliating conditions, and the meager stipend of £100, Chauncy became, on Nov. 29, 1654, the second president of Harvard College and continued in

that office until his death on Feb. 19, 1671/2. As president, he seems to have been eminently successful. His naturally impulsive temper was curbed by the responsibilities of his position. and, although he disagreed with Jonathan Mitchell, pastor of the Cambridge church, upon the Half-way Covenant (see Chauncy's *Anti-Synodalia Americana,* Cambridge, 1664), their personal relations seem to have continued friendly. His faults of temper were more than offset by his acknowledged erudition, to which Ezra Stiles of Yale bore glowing testimony (*The Literary Diary,* 1901, I, 133). In addition to works already mentioned, Chauncy published: *The Doctrine of the Sacrament* (1642); *God's Mercy Shewed to His People* (1655); *Sermon on Amos* (1665); *The Plain Doctrine of the Justification of a Sinner in the Sight of God* (1659). He also wrote, in Latin prose and verse, various productions for state occasions at Cambridge, England, most of which are in William Chauncey Fowler, *Memorials of the Chaunceys, Including President Chauncy, His Ancestors and Descendants* (1858).

[For the date of Chauncy's birth, see (in favor of 1589) Cotton Mather, *Magnalia Christi Americana* (ed. 1853), I, 463–76; "Chas. Chauncy," *Mass. Hist. Soc. Colls.,* 1 ser., vol. X, pp. 171 ff.; (in favor of 1592) Fowler, above, pp. 1, 337; *Mass. Hist. Soc. Colls.,* 2 ser., vol. VI, p. 607.]   W.W.F.

CHAUNCY, CHARLES (Jan. 1, 1705–Feb. 10, 1787), clergyman, was a great-grandson of Charles Chauncy [*q.v.*], second president of Harvard College, and the son of Charles Chauncy, a Boston merchant, and of Sarah (Walley) Chauncy, daughter of Judge Walley of the supreme court of Massachusetts. He was prepared for college, probably, at the Boston Latin School, graduated from Harvard in the Class of 1721, and received its A.M. degree in 1724. He was thrice married: on Feb. 14, 1727, to Elizabeth Hirst; on Jan. 8, 1738, to Elizabeth Townsend; on Jan. 15, 1760, to Mary Stoddard. Ordained minister of the First Church in Boston on Oct. 25, 1727, as colleague of Thomas Foxcroft who died in 1769, he spent in all sixty years in the service of this church. John Clarke was ordained as his colleague in 1778. Dr. Howard of Springfield, an intimate friend, says of him: "He was, like Zaccheus, little of stature . . . God gave him a slender, feeble body, a very powerful and vigorous mind, and strong passions, and he managed them all exceedingly well" (William B. Sprague, *Annals of the American Unitarian Pulpit,* p. 12).

He was undoubtedly the most influential clergyman of his time in Boston, and, with the exception of Jonathan Edwards, in all New England, becoming the acknowledged leader of the liberals of his generation. His literary activity may be grouped around the three controversies in which he was engaged: Revivalism, Episcopacy, and the Benevolence of God. The first arose out of the Great Awakening, of which Edwards was the theological defender as Whitefield was its popular preacher. Chauncy was thoroughly prosaic, wishing that some one would translate "Paradise Lost" into prose that he might understand it; despising rhetoric to the point of praying that he might never be an orator (which prayer as one of his friends remarked was unequivocally answered); a man of the intellect utterly distrusting the emotions as calculated to befog and pervert the mind; plainly, he could have no sympathy with either Edwards or Whitefield. Undoubtedly the Revival was open to all his criticisms, but Jonathan Edwards was more judicial than he and, while acknowledging the faults which Chauncy condemned, believed in the Revival, nevertheless, as a manifestation of divine grace and power. In this controversy, Chauncy published *Seasonable Thoughts on the State of Religion in New England* (1743), besides a *Sermon on Enthusiasm* (1742), a *Letter to a Friend on the French Prophets* (1742), and two *Letters to Whitefield* (1744, 1745).

The second controversy had to do with Episcopacy as the only divinely instituted form of church polity. After the original charter of Massachusetts had been revoked and the colony had become a province, Episcopacy, favored by the royal governors, gained headway, and the argument was advanced that the established religion of England was that of its dependencies also. English bishops wrote as if Congregationalism were no religion at all and there was demand for an American bishop, and even for a college in which young men might prepare for the Episcopal ministry. All this alarmed the sons of the Puritans, and Chauncy devoted nine years to contending against Episcopal claims, beginning with his *Dudleian Lecture* of 1762 and ending with his *Complete View of Episcopacy* in 1771. The last mentioned book is the work of a diligent and intelligent scholar who had covered the field so far as one could do so at the time and whose conclusions command respect even when they do not carry conviction. Besides these works, Chauncy contributed to this controversy *A Letter to a Friend* (1767), *A Reply to Dr. Chandler* (1768) and a *Reply to Dr. Chandler's Rejoinder* (1770).

The third controversy was more theological in character. Before the Great Awakening, nearly all the New England ministers had been preaching drowsily an attenuated Calvinism. Edwards started a theological movement designed to support the Revival by restoring the Calvinistic doctrine of grace but his teachings concerning God, man, and their mutual relations were presented in forms which many deemed dishonoring to both God and man. This led to the publication by Dr. Chauncy in 1782 of an anonymous tract entitled *Salvation for All Men Illustrated and Vindicated as a Scripture Doctrine* and, in 1784, *The Benevolence of the Deity* and also (anonymously) *The Mystery Hid from Ages . . . or the Salvation of All Men*. Chauncy also published, in 1785, *Five Dissertations on the Fall and Its Consequences,* dealing with the doctrine of depravity.

[See W. C. Fowler, *Memorials of the Chaunceys Including President Chauncy, His Ancestors and Descendants* (1858), pp. 49–70; Wm. B. Sprague, *Annals Am. Unitarian Pulpit* (1865), pp. 8–13; Wm. Emerson, *Hist. Sketch of First Church in Boston* (1812), pp. 181–214; Williston Walker, *Ten New Eng. Leaders* (1901), pp. 267–310. There is a notable letter from Dr. Chauncy to President Stiles of Yale in *Mass. Hist. Soc. Colls.,* 1 ser., vol. X, pp. 154 ff.]   W. W. F.

CHAUVENET, WILLIAM (May 24, 1820–Dec. 13, 1870), astronomer, mathematician, was a son of William Marc Chauvenet, a native of Narbonne, France, who came to Boston, where he was married to Mary B. Kerr, and later removed to Milford, Pa., and still later to Philadelphia. William Chauvenet, an only child, was born at Milford. From his father he inherited his love for music and from his mother his logical mind. In his youth he cared little for outdoor sports, but was interested in mechanical constructions and feats of legerdemain. He attended a private school in Philadelphia conducted by Dr. Samuel Jones. Here he manifested such marked ability that Dr. Jones prevailed upon the elder Chauvenet to send him to Yale College. He entered at sixteen, and graduated in 1840 with high honors in classics and mathematics. He was a frequent contributor to the college paper and was the pianist of the Beethoven Society. For a short time after graduation he assisted Prof. Alexander Dallas Bache [*q.v.*], in observations on magnetism at Girard College in Philadelphia. His career was also influenced by Sears C. Walker [*q.v.*], to whom he attributed his interest in astronomy. In 1841 he married Catherine Hemple of Philadelphia, and in the same year was appointed professor of mathematics in the navy, serving on the U. S. S. *Mississippi.* Previous to this, however, the plan of instructing on shipboard had proved so unsatisfactory that a school for midshipmen had been established (1839) at the Naval Asylum in Philadelphia. Upon the death of Prof. David McClure in 1842, Chauvenet was placed in charge of this school. Not satisfied with the eight-months' course, he drew up a program for a two-years' course. This was approved by Secretary of the Navy Henshaw, but before his order could be put into operation, it was revoked by his successor, Secretary Mason. The attempt nevertheless established a precedent for the exercise of power by the Department, and it was to this power that Prof. Chauvenet directed the attention of several successive secretaries of the navy. Finally, in October 1845, Secretary George Bancroft, by the exercise of this power, established the Naval School (later called the U. S. Naval Academy) at Annapolis without going to Congress for either legislation or money. The new two years' course, rendered ineffective by the appointment and withdrawal of midshipmen at any time, was finally changed in 1851 to a regular four years' course. The actions resulting in this change were recommended to Congress by a board, appointed by Secretary Preston, consisting of Chauvenet and several high officers of the navy and army. Chauvenet also recommended post-graduate study and in his own department offered inducement thereto by the equipment of an astronomical observatory. This resulted in 1853 in a separate department of astronomy and navigation with him in charge. He did more than any one else to establish the U. S. Naval Academy on a firm and scientific basis.

In 1855 Yale offered him the position of professor of mathematics and in 1859 that of astronomy and natural philosophy. Simultaneously with the second offer came a similar one from Washington University, then recently established in St. Louis. He accepted the position at Washington University to which was added the chancellorship in 1862. His address, delivered upon his inauguration as chancellor, revealed a broad vision of the function of education, as well as a broad general culture and a deeply religious nature. His name conferred early distinction upon the University, which grew and prospered during his connection with it. Among Chauvenet's noteworthy labors in St. Louis, Prof. C. M. Woodward records in his *History of the St. Louis Bridge* (1881), a contribution on "The theory of the Ribbed Arch" and the design of a device for measuring modulus of elasticity, both of which were of service in the construction of this famous bridge. While in St. Louis his health became impaired so that in 1869 he was obliged to resign his position. He died the next year in St. Paul, Minn., and was buried in Bellefontaine Cemetery in St. Louis.

In addition to a number of papers on astronomical and mathematical subjects, Chauvenet published several text-books of great scientific merit. Of these, *A Treatise on Plane and Spherical Trigonometry* (1850), pp. 256, is regarded by the *Journal of Franklin Institute* (ser. III, vol. XX, p. 215) as "the most complete treatise on trigonometry extant in the English language." His greatest work, *A Manual of Spherical and Practical Astronomy* (1863), I, 708, II, 632, had as great a reputation in Europe as in America. Prof. Herman Struve, director of the Königliche Sternwarte in Berlin, considered it the best work in existence on practical astronomy (*Science*, LXIII, 126). These two works are classics in their respective fields. Chauvenet's last work, *A Treatise on Elementary Geometry, with Appendices Containing a Collection of Exercises for Students and an Introduction to Modern Geometry* (1870), p. 368, was also outstanding in its field.

Chauvenet was elected to the American Philosophical Society and the American Academy of Arts and Sciences, was one of the incorporators of the National Academy of Sciences, of which he was elected vice-president in 1868, and was president of the American Association for the Advancement of Science at the time of his death. On July 31, 1916, a memorial in the form of a bronze tablet was placed in the Naval Academy Library at Annapolis. In 1925 the Mathematical Association of America honored his memory by establishing "The Chauvenet Prize for Mathematical Exposition" to be awarded every five years (*American Mathematical Monthly*, vol. XXXII, 8, p. 439).

[J. H. C. Coffin in *Biog. Memoirs Nat. Acad. of Sci.* (1877), I, 227–44; J. R. Soley, *Hist. Sketch U. S. Naval Acad.* (1876); P. Benjamin, *U. S. Naval Acad.* (1900); A. P. Stokes, *Memoirs of Eminent Yale Men* (1914), II, 1, 43–47; W. H. Roever in *Washington Univ. Studies*, vol. XII, sci. ser., No. 2 (1925), pp. 97–117 and in *Science*, July 9, 1926; F. Cajori, *Teaching and History of Mathematics in the U. S.* (1890), pp. 239–44; C. M. Woodward, in *Bull. Washington Univ. Ass.* (1905), III, pp. 123–28; G. W. Littlehales, in the *Proc. U. S. Naval Institute*, XXXI, 605–12.]   W.H.R.

CHAVIS, JOHN (*c.* 1763–1838), preacher, educator, was born either in the West Indies or near Oxford in the County of Granville, N. C. He was a full-blooded negro of dark brown complexion and as a free man was sent to Princeton to study privately under President Witherspoon of the College of New Jersey, according to tradition to demonstrate whether or not a negro had the capacity to take a college education. That the test was successful, then or later, appears from a record in the manuscript Order Book of the Rockbridge County, Va., Court of 1802, which certifies to the freedom and character of the Rev. John Chavis, a black, who "as a student at Washington Academy" (the former "Liberty Hall

Academy" of William Graham, now Washington and Lee University) passed successfully "through a regular course of academic studies." Through the influence of the Rev. Samuel Davies, a Presbyterian divine, Chavis became connected as a licentiate with the Presbyteries of Lexington and Hanover, Va. The Hanover records state that in 1801 he was "riding as a missionary under the direction of the General Assembly." About 1805 he migrated to North Carolina, joining in 1809 the Orange Presbytery and ministering to whites and slaves in various churches in at least three counties. He was distinguished for his dignity of manner, purity of diction, simplicity and orthodoxy in teaching. Familiar with Greek and Latin, he established a classical school, teaching sometimes at night, and prepared for college the sons of prominent whites in several counties, sometimes even boarding them with his family. Among his pupils were the subsequent United States Senator Willie P. Mangum, Gov. Charles Manly, Rev. Williams Harris, two sons of Chief Justice Henderson, and others who became lawyers, doctors, teachers, preachers, and politicians. He was respectfully received in the families of his former pupils. Advised by his Presbytery to yield to the law of 1832 prohibiting negro preaching, the old white-haired black man wrote and published a sermon, *The Extent of the Atonement,* which, widely sold and read, aided in the support provided for him, and for his wife after his death, by his Presbytery. Chavis died in 1838, aged about seventy-five years, a conspicuous example of merit rewarded by slave-holding whites.

[The chief sources are: Manuscript Order Book, Rockbridge County Court, VI, 10; *Lexington* (Va.) *Gazette,* Nov. 27, 1879; Chas. Lee Smith, *Hist. of Ed. in N. C.* (1888), pp. 138–41; Jas. Curtis Ballagh, *Hist. of Slavery in Va.* (1902), p. 110.]

J.C.B.

CHEATHAM, BENJAMIN FRANKLIN (Oct. 20, 1820–Sept. 4, 1886), Confederate soldier, was born at Nashville, Tenn., the son of Leonard Pope and Elizabeth (Robertson) Cheatham. His mother was a descendant of James Robertson, "the father of Tennessee." He served as captain of Tennessee volunteers at Monterey, and as colonel in the campaign against the City of Mexico. In the gold rush of 1849 he went to California but returned to Tennessee in 1853, engaged in farming, and became major-general of militia. After Tennessee passed the ordinance of secession he was appointed brigadier-general in the state forces, May 9, 1861, and then in the Confederate army, July 9, 1861. For three years he commanded a division, at first in Polk's and later in Hardee's corps. He fought at Belmont,

Shiloh, Perryville, Murfreesboro, Chickamauga, and Chattanooga, and throughout the Atlanta campaign. In March 1862 he was appointed major-general. When Hood undertook his Tennessee campaign, late in 1864, Cheatham was assigned to the command of a corps. Sherman was on his march to the sea, and only the Army of the Ohio (Schofield) confronted Hood, though Thomas, at Nashville, was improvising an army with troops drawn from every available source. Hood hoped to overwhelm the forces in front of him before they should be prepared to fight, and then, by invading the North, to counteract the effect of Sherman's campaign in Georgia. Schofield's task was to delay Hood until Thomas should be ready to meet him, falling back as slowly as he could without risking the destruction of his army. At Spring Hill, Nov. 29, its withdrawal was deferred so long that Hood gained a position to cut it off. Why he did not do so remains a mystery. A controversy on the subject between Hood and Cheatham lasted the rest of their lives. Each gives a circumstantial and explicit account of events, and the two flatly contradict each other. Hood declares that he personally pointed out to Cheatham the enemy moving along the road and indicated the position his corps should take, that he repeatedly sent urgent orders to attack, which Cheatham disregarded until the golden opportunity was lost, and that Cheatham afterward "frankly confessed the great error of which he was guilty." Cheatham, on the other hand, says that at the time referred to "only a mirage would have made possible the vision" of the enemy on the road, that he disposed his troops exactly as directed, that to his astonishment Hood told him to postpone the attack until daybreak, that he made no such confession as alleged, and that Hood assured him, "I do not censure you for the failure at Spring Hill. I am satisfied you are not responsible for it." Whatever the reason, Schofield made good his escape, and stood in position the next day (Nov. 30) at Franklin, where Hood delivered the furious and unsuccessful attack which broke the strength of his army. Cheatham fought here and at Nashville, and then joined Johnston's army in North Carolina, where he surrendered, and resumed life as a farmer. In 1866 he married Anna Bell, daughter of A. B. Robertson. He was an unsuccessful candidate for Congress in 1872, was for four years superintendent of state prisons, and was appointed postmaster of Nashville a year before his death. As a soldier, he bore a reputation for boldness and hard fighting. If he was remiss at Spring Hill, a point which is unlikely ever to be settled, it was from no dislike for combat.

[*Confed. Mil. Hist.* (1899), VIII, 302–04; *Official Records* (*Army*), 1 ser., vols. III, X (pts. 1, 2), XVI (pts. 1, 2), XVII (pt. 2), XX (pts. 1, 2), XXIII (pts. 1, 2), XXX (pts. 2, 4), XXXI (pts. 2, 3), XXXVIII (pts. 3, 4, 5), XXXIX (pt. 3), XLV (pts. 1, 2), XLVII (pts. 1, 2, 3), XLIX (pt. 1); 4 ser., vol. I; *Battles and Leaders of the Civil War* (1887–88), IV, 425–39, where extracts quoted from Hood's and Cheatham's writings give their respective versions of the Spring Hill affair.]

T.M.S.

CHECKLEY, JOHN (1680–Feb. 15, 1754), Anglican clergyman, controversial writer, was born in Boston of English parents. He was an only son and his one sister died at the age of seventeen. Educated at the Boston Latin School under Ezekiel Cheever [*q.v.*], he later studied at Oxford although he did not matriculate. He learned Greek, Latin, and Hebrew well and traveled extensively through Europe, collecting paintings, books, and manuscripts. He remained in Europe some fifteen years, but about 1710 was again in Boston where in 1717 he bought a house and opened a shop for books, medicines, and small merchandise. On May 28, 1713, he married Rebecca Miller, daughter of Samuel Miller, a prosperous innkeeper of Milton, Mass.

Checkley had read widely in the theological literature of the day and had become a firm believer in the Apostolic origin of Episcopacy. A somewhat dangerous notoriety began to attach to him from his expressions of religious opinions in his shop. In 1719 he published an edition of the Rev. Charles Leslie's treatise, *The Religion of Jesus Christ the Only True Religion*. Apparently one of his objects was to give currency to the testimony of Ignatius to prove the existence of bishops in Apostolic days. The same year he issued another volume, without his name, called *Choice Dialogues between a Godly Minister and an Honest Countryman Concerning Election and Predestination*, which assailed the foundations of the Congregational Church. In December a law was passed providing that two justices could tender the oaths of allegiance and abjuration to any one suspected of disaffection to the king or government. Almost immediately Checkley, alone of all Boston, was tendered the oaths, which, in a fit of annoyance, he refused to take. Later he refused again and was fined six pounds and costs. In 1722 he went to England for eight months and it is said took steps to receive Holy Orders, but did not succeed, possibly because of his having refused the oaths. A few months later he wrote his *Modest Proof of the Order and Government Settled by Christ and His Apostles* (1723) which had a wide circulation, was answered by Edward Wigglesworth, and started a war of pamphlets in which Checkley again joined. He next republished (1723) Leslie's *Short and Easy Meth-*

od *with the Deists*, to which was added "A Discourse Concerning Episcopacy," for which he was proceeded against by the General Court, found guilty of publishing a seditious libel, and fined fifty pounds. About this time he founded the Boston Episcopal Charitable Society which has had a long record of active work. In 1727 he again went to England and again failed to receive Orders as a clergyman. The next year he wrote to the Bishop of London an account of the hardships suffered by Episcopalians in Massachusetts. In 1730 he published the argument he had made at his trial. In 1738 he went to London for the third time in search of Orders and this time was successful. He became deacon and priest, and the Society for the Propagation of the Gospel made him a missionary. He was assigned as rector of King's Church, Providence, R. I., where he ministered for more than ten years. The last two years of his life he was incapacitated by infirmities.

[There are many references to Checkley in Wilkins Updike, *Hist. of the Episc. Ch. in Narragansett, R. I.* (2nd ed., 1907). A. L. Cross also comments on him in *Anglican Episcopate and the Am. Colonies* (1902). There is a brief account of Checkley's family in *New Eng. Hist. and Geneal. Reg.*, II, 349–54. The standard life, with reprints of many of his writings, is that by E. F. Slafter, *John Checkley* (Prince Society, 2 vols., 1897).]

J.T.A.

CHEESMAN, FORMAN (Dec. 11, 1763–Oct. 10, 1821), ship-builder and naval architect, was the son of Thomas and Elizabeth (Forman) Cheesman. His father, one of the first ship-builders in New York, may have been engaged in this occupation even prior to the Revolutionary War for he is recorded as the owner of seventy-five feet of shore front in 1772 between the present Pike and Rutgers Sts. Cheesman's shipyards were variously located. Part of the time he was established on the site of his father's old yards. At another time (during his partnership with Charles Brownne, builder of the *Clermont*) he was farther uptown at Clinton and Cherry Sts. At that period of American history naval constructors did not make contracts to build vessels but were employed by the Government, and were "detached from all private pursuits by a liberal compensation at the rate of $2,000 per annum." Under such an agreement Cheesman received the contract for the famous 44-gun frigate *President*, which was, however, built and launched in the yards of Christian Bergh [*q.v.*]. It is impossible to-day exactly to apportion the credit due each of the two men in the construction of this model of naval architecture. Prior to the launching of the *President* in 1800 Cheesman had already built the *Briganza* and the *Draper*, each of 300 tons, and the *Ontario* of 500 tons. Later, during his partnership with Brownne, some of the finest vessels of the day came from his yards, such as the *Silenus,* the *Triton,* and the *Illinois.*

In the day of Cheesman's father, New York had been an unsuccessful competitor with Philadelphia in the shipbuilding industry. But during the younger Cheesman's life New York came to be recognized for the first time as the equal, at least, of her sister city in that particular industry. Cheesman was one of those most responsible for the growth of the shipbuilding industry in New York City during the first twenty years of the nineteenth century.

He was married at St. Peter's Church in Philadelphia on Feb. 16, 1786, to Ann Cummings of that city.

[Arthur H. Clark, *The Clipper Ship Era* (1910); John H. Morrison, *Hist. of N. Y. Shipyards* (1909), and *Ships and Shipping of Old N. Y.* (1915); *N. Y. Times,* Mar. 18, 1888; *N. Y. Evening Post,* Oct. 11, 1821; family records in the possession of Mrs. T. Matlack Cheesman.]   E.Y.

CHEETHAM, JAMES (1772–Sept. 19, 1810), journalist, was born probably in or near Manchester, England. At the end of the eighteenth century Manchester was restless under the first stirring of the Industrial Revolution and the disquieting news from France. Men of liberal and revolutionary mind were organizing societies for criticism of the government. Of these the most important perhaps was the Constitutional Society, of which Thomas Cooper and Thomas Walker were the leading spirits, and James Cheetham, then a young hatter of Manchester, one of the humbler members. On July 23, 1793, he was arrested with other members of the society charged with conspiracy to overthrow the government. He was freed the following April because of the failure of evidence against him (*Proceedings on the Trial . . . against James Cheetham . . . for a Conspiracy . . . 1794*). He continued to live in Manchester until the riots of 1798 forced him to remove to America at a time when the United States was passing through the changes incidental to the political revolution of 1800.

Inclined by sympathy to the side of the victorious Republicans Cheetham found employment in their interest in New York. He bought a half interest in Greenleaf's *Argus,* and on May 1, 1801, in partnership with D. Denniston, a cousin of DeWitt Clinton, issued it under the name of the *American Citizen,* a daily newspaper devoted to the furtherance of Republican policies. They published also the *American Watchman* as a weekly paper. The tradition is that Burr was interested in the establishment of the paper, expecting to use it as political support. The breach between the Burr and Clinton factions of the party made it necessary for Cheetham to choose whom he would serve, and in spite of the probability that his first support had come from Burr he decided to follow the fortunes of the Clintons, and became Burr's bitter political enemy. It was he who first made the suggestion in *A View of the Political Conduct of Aaron Burr* that Burr had not dealt honorably in his efforts to obtain the presidency in 1800. The language of the charges is vindictive, and the style pretentious and verbose. Cheetham based these charges that the Vice-President had made a treacherous alliance with the Federalists on the fact that Burr had ordered suppressed a libelous anti-Federalist work by one John Wood, called *A History of the Administration of John Adams.* The battle of uncivil words went on; Peter Irving of the *Morning Chronicle* and William Coleman of the *Evening Post* opposed the Clinton editor. Bad feeling brought Cheetham and Coleman to the verge of a duel, averted only by the action of Brockholst Livingston in arresting both of them.

In 1802 Cheetham made the acquaintance of Thomas Paine, "an intercourse," he says, "more frequent than agreeable." Respect for Paine, enduring from the impressionable Manchester days, turned to contempt for the unpleasant old man Paine had become, and Cheetham's distorted and partisan *Life of Thomas Paine* (1809) makes no concealment of his feeling.

Cheetham gathered up such crumbs of patronage as he could, feeling that all good Republicans were in duty bound to give their printing business to his establishment. His letters to Jefferson are filled with minor complaints of neglect and with political tattlings. As time went on he figured less prominently in New York politics; his opposition to the embargo cost him the favor of the Clintons, and his paper was supplanted by the *Columbian.* He died on Sept. 19, 1810, of a congestion of the brain brought on by walking hatless in the September sun.

[Cheetham's connection with the Constitutional Society and the Walker Trial is established by an account of the trial, *The Whole Proceedings of the Trial of Indictment against Thos. Walker of Manchester . . . Jas. Cheetham . . . for a Conspiracy to Overthrow the Constitution and Govt. . . . tried at the Assizes at Lancaster, Apr. 2, 1794.* John W. Francis who knew Cheetham gives some information about his later life in *Old N. Y.* (1866) and in *Griswold's Mag.,* vol. V. Cheetham's letters to Jefferson, among the Jefferson papers in the Lib. of Cong., and printed in the *Proc. Mass. Hist. Soc.,* 3 ser., vol. I, throw light on his life as editor. His writings are to be found in numerous political pamphlets and in the files of the *Am. Citizen* and the *Am. Watchman.*]   M.A.M.

CHEEVER, EZEKIEL (Jan. 25, 1614/15– Aug. 21, 1708), educator, classicist, was born in London, the son of William Cheaver, spinner.

At Christ's Hospital (1626) and Emmanuel College, "that Seminary of Puritans in Cambridge," which he entered in 1633, were laid the classical foundations of his life-long service as teacher. He came to Boston in June 1637, and in 1638 removed to New Haven, where he was almost immediately appointed master of the public school, and, during the same year, was married to Mary ——. Though he was possessed of but twenty pounds and a few acres of wild land, he was among the important men who signed "the Plantation Covenant" in Newman's Barn, June 4, 1639. When Davenport ordered the church to name twelve of the most godly, "fit for the foundation work," who in turn were to choose "seven out of their own number for the seven pillars of the church," Cheever was one named. That he was highly esteemed is shown by the fact that he represented the free burgesses as deputy to the General Court in 1646, and occasionally occupied the pulpit of the First Church. In 1649, he was censured for failing to vote for clearing certain elders of "partiality and usurpation" and was accused of "uncomely gestures and carriage before the church." His defense rings much better than the charges against him; indeed, his arguments caused considerable uncertainty on the part of Davenport and others. His superb independence of mind is reflected in his declaration, upon dissenting from the judgment of the church, "I had rather suffer anything from men than make shipwreck of a good conscience, or go against my present light." During the same year, 1649, his first wife died, and in 1652 he was married to Ellen Lathrop.

In 1650 he had removed to Ipswich whose Free School he made "famous in all the country," and caused the town itself to "rank in literature and population" above all the rest. In 1661 he removed to Charlestown, where he taught nine years, though he complained that other masters took away his scholars, the house was not kept in repair, and the "constables" were "much behind with him" in the payment of salary. His material rewards were never large. At New Haven he received twenty, then thirty pounds; Ipswich provided a dwelling-house and two acres of land besides salary; Charlestown paid thirty pounds, if he could get it. In 1670 he became master of the Boston Latin School where he received sixty pounds a year and "possession and use of ye schoole-house." Though his discipline was strict, supported now and then by the rod, his reputation and venerable years inspired love, obedience, reverence and even awe, for when he stroked his long white beard to the point, it was

"a sign for the boys to stand clear." With eight and thirty years at Boston, his life and seventy years' toil as "a skillful, painful, faithful schoolmaster" came to an end. He was buried, says Sewall, from the school-house, honored by the presence of the governor, councillors, ministers, justices and gentlemen whom, and their fathers and grandfathers, he had been at great pains to teach.

Of his religious writings three essays on *Scripture Prophecies Explained* have been preserved in an edition of 1757. He was long credited with several Latin poems and dissertations, thought to have been composed by him before coming to Boston, but Hassam has shown conclusively that they were not of his making. Far more famous was his *Accidence, a Short Introduction to the Latin Tongue,* in less than a hundred small pages, which, by 1785, had gone through twenty editions and was republished again in 1838. It has been called the "wonder of the age." It was prepared at New Haven and intended for the lower forms of the Latin School. Its content was doubtless an abridgment of larger works Cheever had known in London, with such modifications as were dictated by the experience of Master Cheever. The form and name were probably suggested by the work of Brinsley. In "simplicity, comprehensiveness and exactness" Quincy declared it had not been "exceeded by any other work"; Walker believed it had "done more to inspire young minds with the love of the Latin language than any other work of the kind since the first settlement of the country." So great was its author's reputation that Mather asserted:

> "Do but name *Cheever,* and the Echo straight
> "Upon that Name, *Good Latin,* will Repeat."

[The best sources are: Cotton Mather, *Corderius Americanus, . . . A Funeral Sermon upon Mr. Ezekiel Cheever* (1708); J. T. Hassam, articles in *New Eng. Hist. and Geneal. Reg.,* Apr. 1879, July 1882, Apr. 1884, Jan. 1887, Jan. 1903, and *The Cheever Family* (privately printed, 1896); Elizabeth P. Gould, *Ezekiel Cheever, Schoolmaster* (1904); B. A. Gould, *Some Account of the Free Schools in Boston* (1823); S. A. Green, *Remarks on Thompson's Elegy on John Woodmancy and Ezekiel Cheever* (1889); Thos. F. Waters, *Ipswich in the Mass. Bay Colony* (1905); Edward E. Atwater, *Hist. of the Colony of New Haven* (1881); Henry Barnard, *Memoirs of Teachers and Educators* (1859). An account of Cheever's trial is given in the *Conn. Hist. Soc. Colls.,* I, 22–51.]   T. W.

CHEEVER, GEORGE BARRELL (Apr. 17, 1807–Oct. 1, 1890), clergyman, reformer, was the son of Nathaniel Cheever, a publisher and bookseller of Hallowell, Me., and his wife, Charlotte Barrell. He prepared for college at Hallowell Academy, graduated at Bowdoin in 1825 and at Andover Seminary in 1830. After preaching for two years at Newburyport and in Boston, he was ordained and installed at the Howard Street Congregational Church in Salem, Mass., in 1833. He was pastor of the Allen Street Presbyterian Church in New York, 1838–44, editor of the *New York Evangelist,* 1845, and pastor of the Church of the Puritans, Union Square, New York, 1846–67, after which he was engaged in literary work in New York and in Englewood, N. J., where he died. He was married on Nov. 21, 1845, to Elizabeth Hoppin Wetmore of New York City.

Cheever was an uncompromising reformer and controversialist. Early in his Salem pastorate he attacked the predominant religious faith of that town in a Fourth-of-July oration, maintaining "the inadequacy of the Unitarian faith to produce the highest excellence in literature." This produced a violent newspaper controversy and much local excitement. Soon after this there appeared from his pen "The True History of Deacon Giles' Distillery" in the *Salem Landmark,* in which with changed names he told the story of a distillery in Salem whose proprietor was a church deacon who sold Bibles. This produced a violent upheaval. The press was destroyed by a mob and Cheever was assaulted on the street by the foreman of the distillery. He was sued for libel, fined $1,000, and imprisoned for one month. In 1841, after his removal to New York, he engaged in a controversy in which he took the stand of a pronounced advocate of capital punishment, which he defended on biblical grounds; and a little later in another with the Roman Catholics against the abolition of compulsory Bible reading in the public schools. He was violently opposed to the running of Sunday trains and an outspoken critic of the ritualistic tendencies in the Episcopal Church. During the entire slavery agitation he was a fearless champion of the cause of abolition and the full citizenship and education of the negro. His large library was bequeathed to Howard University.

He was a brilliant writer and his literary work covered the entire period of his active life. His writings deal with such a wide variety of subjects as literature, biography, travel, theology, religion, and politics. He was a frequent contributor to the *Independent, Bibliotheca Sacra,* and to newspapers. His *Lectures on the Pilgrim's Progress* went through repeated editions and were translated into several foreign languages. As a preacher he was a pronounced Evangelical and an orthodox exponent of that variety of Calvinism known as the "New England Theology." To be at his best in the pulpit he needed the stimulus of a gripping cause and so his ser-

monic output inclined to unevenness in quality. There was in his preaching more of the terrors of the law than of the compassionate spirit of the gospel.

His works consist of twenty-three bound volumes and fifty pamphlets, reviews, and addresses. The following is a list of his more important books: *The American Commonplace Book of Prose* (1828); *The American Commonplace Book of Poetry* (1829); *Studies in Poetry* (1830); *Select Works of Archbishop Leighton* (1832); *God's Hand in America* (1841); *The Hierarchical Despotism* (1844); *Sophisms of the Apostolical Succession* (1844); *Lectures on the Pilgrim's Progress* (1844); *Wanderings of a Pilgrim in the Shadow of Mt. Blanc* (1845); *A Defense of Capital Punishment* (1846); *The Pilgrim Fathers: or, the Journal of the Pilgrims at Plymouth* (1849); *The Voyage to the Celestial Country* (1852); *The Voices of Nature to her Foster Child, The Soul of Man* (1853); *The Right of the Bible in our Public Schools* (1854); *Lectures on the Life, Genius, and Insanity of Cowper* (1856); *God against Slavery* (1857); *The Guilt of Slavery and the Crime of Slave-Holding, Demonstrated from the Hebrew and Greek Scriptures* (1860); *God's Vouchers for His Written Word, with Critical Illustrations from the Autobiography of Dr. Franklin* (1881); *God's Time-Piece for Man's Eternity* (1888).

[*Obit. Record Grads. Bowdoin College* (1891); H. Fowler, *The Am. Pulpit* (1856); H. T. Cheever, *Memorial Address . . . upon the Life, Character and Influence of Dr. Geo. Barrell Cheever* (1892); H. T. Cheever, ed., *Memorabilia of Geo. B. Cheever* (1891); *Congreg. Year Book,* 1891, with full bibliography of Cheever's writings.] F. T. P.

CHEEVER, HENRY THEODORE (Feb. 6, 1814–Feb. 13, 1897), theologian, was born at Hallowell, Me., the fifth child of Nathaniel and Charlotte (Barrell) Cheever. The Cheevers, of Huguenot stock, who had settled in Canterbury, England, came to Salem, Mass., early in the seventeenth century. Nathaniel Cheever having learned the printer's trade in Worcester, became the founder and first editor of the Hallowell *American Advocate* in 1810. Removing to Augusta, Ga., where he died in 1819, he left his widow to rear a family of seven children. She, a cultured woman of great piety and strength of mind, was of English ancestors who reached America in the seventeenth century. Henry Theodore Cheever was educated at Hallowell Academy, and at Bowdoin College where Longfellow was his instructor in French and German. Graduating in 1834, he accompanied his younger brother, who was in poor health, through France and Spain, wintering with an uncle, George

Barrell, then United States consul at Malaga. Returning home, he taught in Louisiana and, after one year at Andover Theological Seminary, entered Bangor Theological Seminary. After graduation in 1839, he spent one year as resident licentiate at Bangor; then he went for his health as a passenger on a whaling ship round Cape Horn to the Hawaiian Islands where a college friend was a missionary, meanwhile writing letters of travel, such as he had written from Spain and France, to the New York *Evangelist*, of which he was editor, 1849–52, and gathered material for his *Life in the Sandwich Islands: or the Heart of the Pacific* (1851). His experiences homeward in the *Commodore Preble* he recorded in *The Whale and His Captors* (1849). He then entered actively into the Congregational ministry, being ordained June 4, 1847, and holding pastorates in New Jersey, New York City, Long Island, Connecticut, and, finally, Worcester, Mass. (1863–72). Before the Civil War he was, like his distinguished brother, George Barrell Cheever [*q.v.*], greatly interested in anti-slavery, and as secretary of the Church Anti-Slavery Society, 1859–64, he wrote tracts and articles. He was also a voluminous writer for periodicals, mainly on religious subjects. Other works of his were: memorials of his brother Nathaniel Cheever, M.D. (1851), of a shipmaster, Capt. Obadiah Congar (1851), and of his brother-in-law Ichabod Washburn, inventor, manufacturer, and philanthropist (1878); *Correspondences of Faith and Views of Madame Guyon* (1885); and *The Bible Eschatology* (1893). He also edited the travel books of Walter Colton, chaplain, U. S. Navy, published Colton's literary remains with a memoir, and edited some of his brother George's works. In 1857 he married Jane Tyler of Jewett City, Conn., who died in 1885. He was a Republican and an ardent prohibitionist, advocated women's rights and home rule for Ireland, and criticized England's attitude toward Turkey. He was an early supporter of the liberal movement in the Congregational Church. His physical and mental vigor was retained until his death, after a short illness, on Feb. 13, 1897, in Worcester, Mass.

[*Obit. Record Grads. Bowdoin College* (1897); *Worcester Daily Spy*, Feb. 15, 1897; "Published Writings of Cheever, Class of 1834" in *Bowdoin College Lib. Bibliographical Contributions*, No. 7, Mar. 1898; information from Cheever's daughter, Miss Louisa Sewall Cheever, associate professor of English, Smith College.]
C.L.L.

CHENEY, BENJAMIN PIERCE (Aug. 12, 1815–July 23, 1895), pioneer in the express business, was born at Hillsborough, N. H., the son of Jesse and Alice (Steele) Cheney. He came of early New England stock. His great-grandfather, Deacon Tristram Cheney, born in Dedham, Mass., was one of the first settlers of Antrim, N. H., and his grandfather, Elias Cheney, served four years in the Revolutionary War. His father was a blacksmith, a man of no material wealth, and young Cheney completed his formal education when, at the age of ten years, he left the common schools to work in his father's blacksmith shop. Before two years had passed he had gone to Francistown where he found employment in a tavern and later in a store. At the age of sixteen he had purchased his time from his father and begun his career in the transportation business by driving a stage between Nashua and Exeter, N. H. On his next route, between Keene and Nashua, he covered a distance of fifty miles a day for a period of six years. In 1836 he was sent to Boston to be stationed as agent at No. 11 Elm St., the old-time stage center for northern stage routes. Six years later, in partnership with Nathaniel White of Nashua, and William Walker, he established Cheney & Company's Express between Boston and Montreal. The route was covered by rail to Concord, N. H., which was as far as the Boston & Lowell Railroad was built at that time, thence by four-horse team to Montpelier, thence by messengers on the stage to Burlington, and finally by boat to Montreal. In spite of difficulties, the venture was successful and at the end of its first ten years Cheney & Company bought out Fisk & Rice's Express, operating over the Fitchburg Road to Burlington, which was the first of the companies to be consolidated with Cheney's. Future consolidations resulted eventually in the formation of the United States & Canada Express Company which, with its many branches, covered the northern New England States. When, after thirty-seven years of business, Cheney merged his company with the American Express Company, he became one of the largest stockholders of the new concern, its treasurer, and one of its directors. He retained these offices until his retirement from active business life.

Cheney did not confine all his interests to New England, however. He was one of the pioneers in promoting the Northern Pacific Railroad and a little later embarked in the Atchison, Topeka & Santa Fé project. He was interested in the "Overland Mail" to San Francisco and in the Wells, Fargo & Company's Express. Through his business ventures he amassed a great fortune. In the early days of transcontinental transportation there were periods of decline as well as of prosperity, but Cheney had a tenacity of purpose and a conviction as to the worth and future of his projects, which, coupled with an inherent shrewdness and business ability, brought success to his undertakings. For many years he served as a director of the Market National Bank of Boston, and from the time of its foundation was a director of the American Loan & Trust Company. He was a man of erect appearance, easy of approach. He lost an arm in a railroad accident but was otherwise unmarked by it. On June 6, 1865, he married Elizabeth Stickney Clapp of Boston, whom, as the daughter of his most intimate friend, he had seen grow up from infancy. He had a beautiful country estate at Wellesley, extending for a mile or more along the Charles River, and remarkable for its conservatories and gardens. He made Dartmouth College a gift of $50,000, and presented to his native state a bronze statue of Daniel Webster, one of his early stage-coach passengers, which now stands in State House Park in Concord.

[Edwin M. Bacon, ed., *Men of Progress . . . Commonwealth of Mass.* (1896) ; Chas. Henry Pope, *Cheney Genealogy* (1897) ; W. R. Cochrane, *Hist. of the Town of Antrim, N. H.* (1880) ; *Boston Evening Transcript*, July 23, 1895.]   E. Y.

CHENEY, CHARLES EDWARD (Feb. 12, 1836–Nov. 15, 1916), bishop of the Reformed Episcopal Church, was born in Canandaigua, N. Y., the son of Ephraim Warren and Altie (Chipman) Cheney. He graduated from Hobart College in 1857, spent a year at the Virginia Theological Seminary, and then became assistant rector of St. Luke's Church, Rochester, N. Y. He was ordained deacon in the Protestant Episcopal Church at Utica, N. Y., Nov. 21, 1858, was for a brief time in charge of St. Paul's Church, Havana, N. Y., and on Mar. 4, 1860, was ordained presbyter at Rochester. The same year he became rector of Christ Church, Chicago, which office he held until his death. On Apr. 25, 1860, he married Clara E. Griswold of Chicago. He was a magnetic and lovable person, popular and successful in his parish, intense in his convictions, and as low church and evangelical as his bishop, Henry J. Whitehouse, was high church and sacerdotal. He was a signer of the "Chicago Protest" of Feb. 18, 1869, directed against the "unprotestantizing" tendencies in the church, thus bringing upon himself the disfavor of the bishop, who, learning that he was accustomed to omit the word "regenerate" from the baptismal service, brought him to trial before five of the clergy. This was the beginning of litigation which attracted wide attention. An injunction stayed the trial for a time, and it proceeded with four of the original triers, against the protest of Cheney's attorney, Melville W.

Fuller [*q.v.*]. The accused was found guilty and deposed from the ministry until he should express contrition and promise future conformity. He paid no attention to the judgment, was tried again for contumacy, and deposed. An attempt to oust him from the church property was contested in the circuit court of Illinois, which decided that the property belonged to the parish and not to the diocese, and that the original ecclesiastical court which began with five members and ended with four was not a court according to the canons of the church, and therefore that Cheney had not been legally deposed (*Inter-Ocean*, Chicago, Aug. 17, 1874). In the meantime, December 1873, he had joined with Bishop George D. Cummins [*q.v.*], and others in organizing the Reformed Episcopal Church into which body his congregation accompanied him. He was consecrated missionary bishop of the Northwest by Bishop Cummins, Dec. 14, 1873, and was made bishop of the Synod of Chicago in 1878, still retaining his rectorship. His publications include *Sermons* (1880) ; *A Neglected Power and Other Sermons* (1916) ; *What Do Reformed Episcopalians Believe* (1888) ; and several historical brochures, *A King of France Unnamed in History* (1902) ; *The Second Norman Conquest of England* (1907) ; *The Barefoot Maid at the Fountain Inn* (1912) ; *A Belated Plantagenet* (1914).

[W. W. Foster, *Some Descendants of Arthur Warren of Weymouth, Mass. Bay Colony* (1911) ; Diocese of Western N. Y., *Jour. of Convention* (1859–60) ; Annie D. Price, *Hist. of the Formation and Growth of the Reformed Episc. Ch.* (1902) ; Benj. Aycrigg, *Memoirs of the Reformed Episc. Ch.* (1880) ; *Chicago Tribune*, Mar. 11, 12, 1894, Nov. 16, 1916 ; *Who's Who in America*, 1914–15.]   H. E. S.

CHENEY, EDNAH DOW LITTLEHALE (June 27, 1824–Nov. 19, 1904), author, reformer, born in Boston, wrote of herself, "I belong to humble folks, and can trace my descent to neither William the Conqueror nor the Mayflower." Her mother was Ednah Parker (Dow) Littlehale, daughter of an Exeter, N. H., tanner ; her father, Sargent Smith Littlehale, the exception in a Gloucester family which followed the sea, was working in a store at the age of twelve and later became a partner in a leading Boston grocery business. He was a Universalist and did not believe in restraint either in religion or in family life. Never a popular girl, and disliking most of the amusements of youth, Ednah attended successively the schools of the Misses Pemberton, William B. Fowle, and Joseph H. Abbot, but was requested to leave the last because her influence was "not helpful to discipline." On May 19, 1853, she married Seth Wells Cheney [*q.v.*], an artist, and went with him to

Europe. Death had been a frequent visitor in the Littlehale family, removing four of the children, and it pursued Ednah Cheney into her married life as her husband died in 1856, leaving her with an infant daughter. Henceforth, living in Boston or the vicinity, she interested herself actively in social service and in writing. She aided in forming the Boston School of Design for Women, the New England Hospital for Women and Children, the New England Woman's Club, and a horticultural school for women. The anti-slavery cause and later the Freedman's Aid Society and woman suffrage were among her foremost interests. She visited colored schools in the Southern states and attended many Freedman's Aid and Woman's Rights conventions. She lectured on horticulture for women before the Massachusetts State Agricultural Society and on the history of art at the Concord School of Philosophy. Through membership in Margaret Fuller's conversation classes she became acquainted with Emerson, the Alcotts, James Freeman Clarke, and Theodore Parker. The variety of her interests is shown by her writings, which include a *Handbook for American Citizens* (1860), *Patience* (1870), *Faithful to the Light and Other Tales* (1871), *Social Games* (1871), *Sally Williams* (1873), *Child of the Tide* (1875), *Life of Susan Dimock* (1875), *Gleanings in Fields of Art* (1881), *Selected Poems from Michelangelo Buonarroti* (1885), *Life of Louisa May Alcott* (1888), *Memoir of John Cheney* (1889), *Nora's Return* (1890), *Stories of the Olden Time* (1890). In 1882 she lost her daughter Margaret and was left completely alone. Her appearance in age, when she was handsomer than in youth, was not unlike that of Susan B. Anthony. White hair parted and drawn plainly back over the ears framed a rather heavy large-featured face of seriousness and strength, from which looked deep-set, weary eyes. Her writings show simplicity and directness of style, with considerable humor, but no great distinction. It was as a speaker and an organizer in educational, religious, and social causes that she accomplished her most useful work.

[Ednah Dow Cheney, *Reminiscences* (1902), *Memoir of Seth Wells Cheney* (1881), and *Memoir of Margaret Swan Cheney* (1889); *Who's Who in America*, 1903–05; *Boston Herald*, Nov. 20, 1904; *Boston Evening Transcript*, Nov. 19, 1904.] S. G. B.

CHENEY, JOHN (Oct. 20, 1801–Aug. 20, 1885), engraver, the second son of George and Electa (Woodbridge) Cheney, and brother of Seth and Ward Cheney [*qq.v.*], was born at South Manchester, Conn. Little is known regarding his youth. He attended school and helped with the work on the farm and at the mill. He was interested in drawing and learned engraving from books; his first engraving was made on a piece of copper cut from an old kettle. He also constructed his own press. About 1820 he went to Hartford where he worked with the engraver Willard but did not think that he learned anything. In 1826 he was in Boston, working at Pendleton's lithographic shop, but it is not until 1827 that his first engraving was published as the frontispiece of *The Poetical Works of Thomas Campbell*; it was entitled "Or lisps with holy look his evening prayer," being 2¼ x 2¾ inches. All his finished engravings are small: probably if his whole output were averaged up, the longest dimension would not be over four inches. In 1829, he moved to New York where his brother Seth Wells joined him, studying drawing. In 1830, through the kindness of Joseph Howard of Providence, he was enabled to go to England, where he stayed for two years. The following year Seth joined him in Paris but fell ill, and the brothers thereupon returned to America. During his stay abroad John had made engravings for his publishers in Boston and Philadelphia. On his return he settled in Boston, 1834–37; in the following years he was in New York, in Philadelphia or, when tired of engraving, back at the old homestead. He continued to engrave until 1857, when the demand for fine small engravings was about over. The remainder of his life was spent at the old home or in travel, with a little time devoted to drawing and to his collection of engravings. He never married. Rendered financially independent by his share in the silk-mill of his brothers at South Manchester, he passed his years calmly and serenely with little excitement or adventure. He liked to travel, and visited the upper Mississippi in 1837, Europe again in 1854, California in 1872–74 and in 1882. He died in the house in which he was born.

Among his best engraved works are such plates as "The Guardian Angels," "The Young Princess," "Lesbia," "The Orphans," "The Torn Hat," "Egeria," "Martha Washington," "Mrs. Blodgett," and many others; these were published in annuals and similar books which up to about 1845 were much in vogue. S. R. Koehler says of them that they "are unexcelled of their kind—in delicacy where needed, in force and in suggestion of color where these are called for, in nobility and simplicity of workmanship always . . . he stands at the head of the engravers of his time in this country, and shoulder to shoulder with those of Europe." His work is undoubtedly of very high quality and if he had lived in the sixteenth century he would have been one of the "Little Masters," but living in the nineteenth century when line engraving was on the down grade he has been almost forgotten. He produced a few over a hundred finished plates and lithographs and with his brother Seth, twenty-one, after the outlines and sketches of Washington Allston, these being the largest plates which he worked on. Some of these were photographed by the daguerreotype method on to the engraver's plate and there fixed by tracing the line through the silver. A memorial exhibition of the work of John and Seth Wells Cheney was held in the Museum of Art, Boston, in 1893. This museum also owns a large collection of John Cheney's engravings; other collections are in the United States National Museum and in the Pennsylvania Academy of the Fine Arts.

[Ednah D. Cheney, *Memoir of John Cheney* (1889); Mantle Fielding, *Dict. Am. Painters, Sculptors and Engravers* (1926); S. R. Koehler, *Cat. Engraved and Lithographed Work of John Cheney and Seth Wells Cheney* (1891); *Cat. Memorial Exhibition Work of John and Seth Wells Cheney* (Museum of Art, Boston, 1893).]   R. P. T.

CHENEY, JOHN VANCE (Dec. 29, 1848–May 1, 1922), author, librarian, belonged to a New England family of singers who with self-assertiveness might have won wealth and fame. His father, Simeon Pease Cheney, a traveling singing-school teacher, produced in *Wood Notes Wild* (1891) a pioneer volume of notations of bird music. His mother, Christiana Vance Cheney, taught the piano and sang. Cheney himself was gifted musically and during much of his life earned a subsistence by playing church organs. Born at Groveland, N. Y., he grew up at Dorset, Vt., attended Temple Hill Academy, Geneseo, N. Y., and Burr and Burton Seminary, Manchester, Vt., and read law in Woodstock, Vt., Haverhill, Mass., and New York City. He was admitted to the bar but found legal work irksome. From 1873 he was a frequent contributor of poetry to periodicals, especially to the *Century* under Gilder's editorship. But he wisely resolved not to rely upon his pen for bread. In the thirty-five years of 1877–1912 he obtained only $5,000 for the three hundred and seventy poems published in magazines, and his prose volumes and hackwork brought his total literary earnings only up to $13,636. In 1876 he married his cousin Abbey Perkins, a teacher of music. Her brilliant and imposing personality was never congenial to Cheney's quiet nature, and in 1902 they were divorced.

After moving to Sacramento, Cal., in 1876, Cheney encountered lean years in which he was unsettled as to residence and occupation. From 1887 to 1894, however, he was librarian of the Free Public Library of San Francisco. Not technically trained himself, he had the expert assistance of A. J. Rudolph, and the library showed steady advancement under their management. Cheney wore with grace the social prominence now thrust upon him. He was tall, full-bearded, and refined in appearance, had urbanity of manner, and possessed mellow-voiced readiness of speech. He was at his best, however, in a small company to which he could discourse about books or bring delight with his powers as a raconteur. Among his literary associates of the period were Muir, Markham, and especially Joaquin Miller. He was librarian of the Newberry Library, Chicago, 1894–1909. In 1903 he married Sara Barker Chamberlain, a versatile woman whose devotion did much to brighten his days. But it was in a mood somewhat saddened by the trend of affairs and the passing of old literary fashions that he retired to San Diego, Cal., to spend the remainder of his life. He as always attracted friends and did occasional lecturing, but reserve had grown upon him and he often retired to a cabin in the hills or took solitary walks with his little dogs trotting at his heels.

His verse was primarily lyric. He wrote with dignity and taste, was an accomplished technician, but lacked the vision and the faculty divine. Only once, in "The Happiest Heart," did he strike off stanzas that became at all popular. His volumes of poems—*Thistle-Drift* (1887), *Wood Blooms* (1888), *Poems* (1905), and others—were soon out of print. Of his prose the edition of Derby's *Phœnixiana* for the Caxton Club of Chicago (1897) is a scholarly work, and *The Golden Guess* (1892) and *That Dome in Air* (1895) are collections of critical essays marked by insight, candor, and discrimination. He was, however, a conservative in literature, distrusted Browning and Whitman, and abhorred free verse.

[Cheney's correspondence, papers, and manuscripts, including an unpublished autobiography written in 1914, in the possession of his former secretary, Miss Jessie Sherk of San Diego, Cal.; *Who's Who in America*, 1922–23; information from personal and professional associates.]   G. G—r.

CHENEY, OREN BURBANK (Dec. 10, 1816–Dec. 22, 1903), Baptist clergyman, college president, was the son of Moses Cheney, a member of the New Hampshire legislature, and of Abigail (Morrison) Cheney, a woman of great energy and strength of character. His early education consisted of a few terms at private schools, a few at public schools, and a year when he was thirteen at New Hampton Institute. When he was sixteen he was sent to Parsonsfield Seminary, the first school founded and maintained by Free Baptists, where, as a student, he helped organize a temperance society, believed to be the first school society of that kind in the world. He was present in the same year at the organization of the Free Baptist Foreign Missionary Society. From this school he went again to the New Hampton Literary Institute. A year at Brown in 1835 was followed by a period at Dartmouth where he took his B.A. degree in 1839, and his M.A. in 1842. He taught the Indians who camped near the college, preached at a Free Will Baptist church at Grantham, ten miles away, and taught a school during the winters at Peterboro to pay his college expenses. In the fall after his graduation he was principal at the Farmington (Maine) Academy with Caroline Adelia Rundlett as his assistant. They were married a few months later. The following year he taught at Greenland, N. H., walking to Northampton on Sundays to preach. Soon after he was licensed to preach. At this time he began to contribute articles to the *Morning Star* which appeared more or less regularly for sixty years. Called subsequently to be principal of Parsonsfield Seminary, he remained there for two years. Then, as he felt that he needed more theological preparation, he went to Whitestown, N. Y., to study. At the end of a year he accepted a country pastorate at West Lebanon, Me., at a salary of $175 a year. His wife had died, and in 1847 he married Nancy S. Perkins, daughter of a Baptist clergyman. At Lebanon, with his customary energy, he founded an academy. After six years here in the church and at the academy, he was called to the Augusta (Maine) Baptist pastorate. In 1851, he was elected to the Maine legislature by a combination of the Free Soil, Independent, and Whig parties. He secured $2,000 from the legislature for the Lebanon Academy and voted for the first prohibition measure introduced in the Maine legislature by Neal Dow. In 1852 he was elected a delegate to the Maine Free Soil Convention at Pittsburgh, Pa., which nominated John P. Hale for the presidency. When Parsonsfield Seminary was burned in 1854, he was deeply stirred and at this time began to consider an ideal school in which students could depend on their own efforts to pay their way. The result was the Maine State Seminary in Lewiston, Me., which opened Sept. 1, 1857, with Cheney as principal. In 1863, the trustees were induced to vote to establish a course of collegiate study, the legislature was petitioned for an enlarged charter, received the ensuing year, and the name was changed to Bates College in honor of its most generous patron.

Women as well as men had attended the seminary, but when the college was opened the feeling was so strong against women that all but one withdrew, the one, however, stayed and obtained her degree, and Bates as a result has remained a coeducational institution as its charter first provided. Cheney remained president of the college until 1894 and was president emeritus until his death in 1903. He was married a third time in 1892 to Emeline S. (Aldrich) Burlingame who had been much interested in Christian and reformatory work.

[*Gen. Cat. Bates College and Cobb Divinity School, 1863–1915* (1915); E. Burlingame-Cheney, *Story of the Life and Work of Oren B. Cheney, Founder and First President of Bates College* (1907).] M.A.K.

CHENEY, PERSON COLBY (Feb. 25, 1828–June 19, 1901), manufacturer, governor of New Hampshire, was born at Holderness (now Ashland), N. H. He was the son of Moses and Abigail (Morrison) Cheney, his father being one of the pioneer paper manufacturers of the state, a business with which he himself was identified throughout the greater part of his life. The family then moved to Peterboro in 1835, and after completing his education at Hancock Literary and Scientific Institution and the academy at Parsonsfield, Me., Cheney entered business in the same town, becoming in 1853 a partner in the firm of Cheney, Hadley & Gowing, paper manufacturers. In 1863, he served as quartermaster in the 13th New Hampshire Infantry, but was discharged because of ill health after a few months' service. A year later he was elected railroad commissioner for a three-year term. In 1866 he moved to Manchester. He now reorganized and extended his business, engaging in paper-making at Goffstown and the manufacture of wood pulp at Peterboro. Mills at both these places were under the same corporate organization and operations were later extended to several other towns as well. The business prospered, and Cheney became known as one of the leading industrialists of the state. He was also interested in banking in Manchester and was for some time president of the People's Savings Bank.

In 1872 he was elected mayor of Manchester and in the same year a trustee of Bates College of which his brother, Oren Burbank Cheney [*q.v.*], was president. He served one year as mayor, refusing renomination because of the pressure of private business. He was interested, however, in Republican activities and was an influential leader in party matters. In 1875 he was nominated for the governorship and after a campaign so closely contested that final choice rested with the legislature, was elected. In 1876 he was again elected, this time by the popular vote. He was a successful executive. His terms fell in a period of unemployment and business depression, and his efforts were largely devoted toward economy, improved administration, and the reduction of the public debt. In 1876 when the state was about to hold a constitutional convention he urged the adoption of a simplified amending process, a reduction in the size of the lower house, a larger Senate, the abolition of the religious test for office, and biennial elections. On the liquor question, then an active issue in the state, he declared that the most effective effort was that which "untiringly seeks to write on men's hearts the law of individual self control." After retirement from office he devoted himself to business affairs but in 1886 served out the unexpired term of Austin F. Pike in the United States Senate (Nov. 24, 1886–June 14, 1887). From December 1892 to June 1893 he served as envoy extraordinary to Switzerland. He was from 1892 until his death a member of the Republican National Committee. In both business and politics he represented the better type of the period, and in both won its conventional rewards for successful effort. He was twice married: on May 22, 1850, to Annie, daughter of Samuel M. Moore of Bronson, Mich., and after her death in 1858, on June 29, 1859, to Mrs. Sarah W. Keith.

[G. F. Willey, *Semi-Centennial Book of Manchester* (Manchester, N. H., 1896), pp. 257–58; Albert Smith, *Hist. of the Town of Peterborough, N. H.* (1876); *Manchester* (Manchester, N. H., 1875); J. N. McClintock, sketch in *Granite Mo.*, III, 65, and obituary, *Ibid.*, XXXI, p. 60.]
                                              W. A. R.

CHENEY, SETH WELLS (Nov. 26, 1810–Sept. 10, 1856), crayon artist and engraver, was the fifth son of George and Electa (Woodbridge) Cheney and was born at what is now known as South Manchester, Conn. He was not a robust healthy child and on this account was more at home than his seven brothers, but he was earnest and thoughtful. He had an inventive mind and enjoyed mechanical work. His school education ended at high school where he learned a little French and Latin. His art education was largely experience and association with engravers and artists, especially with his brother John [*q.v.*], of whom he once said, "He taught me all that ever I knew." They were very closely associated, working together on the same engravings, studying at the same schools, traveling together, working for the same publishers. Seth had a position when he was about twenty-two at the Athenæum, where he was able to work and study. It was probably while he was here that he engraved "Mother and Child," after the painting by Washington Allston (Ednah D. Cheney, *post*, p. 10). But as this is considered his best engraving and as it was not published until 1837, it has been sometimes thought a later work (S. R. Koehler, *post*). While Cheney did only a few engravings, they are mentioned as the equal of and occasionally as superior to those of his brother, John. Beside the ones he finished himself, he and his brother were associated as well in making twenty-one from the outlines and sketches of Washington Allston. He joined John in Paris in 1834 but worked so hard that his health gave way and his brother was obliged to bring him home. About 1835 the raising of mulberry trees for the use of silk worms became a great speculation: three of Cheney's brothers, Ward [*q.v.*], Rush, and Frank, were in the business and they sent Seth abroad to buy trees in 1837. He was still there in the spring of 1840, when the mulberry-tree bubble burst, but fortunately the brothers had started a silk-mill at South Manchester in 1838 and they turned their energies with great success to developing this industry which was ultimately to make both John and Seth financially independent. Seth returned home in 1840, settled at the old homestead and made crayon drawings. In the autumn of 1841 he determined to give up engraving and devote his time to portraiture. He moved to Boston where in 1841 and 1842 he did 150 heads, mostly of children. His prices ranged from $10 to $50. Ednah D. Cheney says of the drawings of this period, "There is an exquisite beauty in these early portraits unsurpassed even by the work of his later life, in perception of character and spiritual grace. His execution was free and delicate, and it seemed as if his spirit had breathed itself into form on paper." Having had a very successful two years, and the family being in excellent financial condition, on account of the silk business, in the summer of 1843 Cheney went abroad, studying with Ferrero in Rome, where he was also associated with a number of American artists, such as Daniel Huntington and S. F. B. Morse. In January 1845 he returned to Boston and to his profession, orders were numerous, and his prices were raised to $75 and $100. The work, however, proved exhausting, and he spent the summers in recuperating at South Manchester. Beside his black and white crayon drawings, he made a few paintings, a few engravings, and a few pieces of sculpture. In September 1847 he was married to Emily Pitkin, who died in 1850. In 1853 he married Ednah D. Littlehale (see sketch of Ednah D. Littlehale Cheney). In 1854, together with his wife and a few friends, he visited Europe again, but it was of slight pleasure as he was ill much of the time. Little artistic work was done in the last years of his life.

[Ednah D. Cheney, *Memoir of Seth Wells Cheney* (1881) and *Memoir of John Cheney* (1889); Mantle Fielding, *Dict. Am. Painters, Sculptors and Engravers* (1926); S. R. Koehler, *Cat. Engraved and Lithographed Work of John Cheney and Seth Wells Cheney* (1891); Theodore Bolton, *Early Am. Portrait Draughtsmen in Crayons* (1923); *Cat. Memorial Exhibition Work of John and Seth Wells Cheney* (Museum of Art, Boston, 1893).]   R.P.T.

CHENEY, WARD (Feb. 23, 1813–Mar. 22, 1876), pioneer silk manufacturer, was born at South Manchester, Conn., the sixth of nine children born to George and Electa (Woodbridge) Cheney. His boyhood days were divided between attendance at the village school and work on his father's farm. At the age of fifteen he left for Providence, R. I., where for the next six years he worked in the capacity of clerk for his brother, Charles, who was partner in a dry-goods firm in that city. Here the young man mastered the rudiments of business, and here, also, he married Caroline Jackson, by whom he had three children. In 1834 Charles Cheney moved to a farm in Ohio, and Ward returned to South Manchester. When he arrived at the family homestead he found several of his brothers experimenting with the *morus multicaulis* tree, a variety of the mulberry, which appears to have been first introduced in America in 1826. During the thirties there was a mania for the raising of this type of mulberry and into the speculation the Cheney brothers plunged headlong. Their nursery at South Manchester proving successful, Ward, with his brothers, Frank and Rush, leased a farm in 1836 at Burlington, N. J., where they operated a nursery and cocoonery until 1841. By the latter date the boom had collapsed and with it the hope of profitably producing raw silk in America. Fortunately while the boom was at its height, four of the brothers, Ralph, Ward, Rush, and Fred, together with Edward Arnold, had organized in 1838 the Mount Nebo Silk Manufacturing Company at South Manchester with a capital stock of $50,000, an organization which has had a longer continuous history than any other similar enterprise in the United States. With the collapse of the Burlington project, Ward returned to South Manchester, where he devoted the remainder of his life to the manufacture of silk.

The early years were difficult ones and "the mechanical genius of Frank Cheney and the business acumen of his brother Ward, seem to have been largely responsible for the survival of the business" (M. Spiess and P. W. Bidwell, *History of Manchester, Conn.*, 1924, p. 100). As the industry developed each of the brothers specialized in some branch, Ward not only looking after the financial end but devoting himself to a study of silk-dyeing, the fundamentals of which he learned from Edward Valentine of Northampton. When the organization was incorporated in 1854 as Cheney Brothers Silk Manufacturing Company, Ward became president, serving until his death in 1876. His administration was progressive, and immense strides were made not only in enlarging the units already in operation but in developing such new lines as the manufacture of ribbons and grosgrains. During the Civil War the Cheneys financed a gun factory in Boston where Christopher W. Spencer, one of their mechanics who had invented a repeating rifle, turned out 200,000 rifles for the Federal government.

Cheney was not only a man of great executive capacity and business ability, but was endowed with a splendid physique, a vivid personality, and warm human sympathy. As an employer he would have stood out in any age. "It was the constant delight of this remarkable man," said William Alfred Hinds, "to minister to the happiness and prosperity of his thousand employees. Their homes, the facilities for education and religious improvement, their amusements, all had his sympathetic, practical interest. There was nothing he would not do for them, even to nursing their sick, and laying in the grave with his own hands the body which others, fearing contamination, were unwilling to touch" (*American Communities*, 1908, p. 513).

[On family history consult Chas. Henry Pope, *Cheney Genealogy* (1897), pp. 331, 411. On the Cheney silk industry, see Albert H. Heusser, ed., *Hist. of the Silk Dyeing Industry in the U. S.* (1927), VIII, and H. H. Manchester, *Story of Silk and Cheney Silks* (rev. ed., 1924).]   H.U.F.

CHESEBROUGH, CAROLINE (Mar. 30, 1825–Feb. 16, 1873), author, was descended from William Chesebrough, the first white settler and founder of Stonington, Conn., about 1649, who came in 1630 from Boston, England, to the Massachusetts Bay Colony and settled first in Salem. His descendant, Nicholas Goddard Chesebrough, who was born in Stonington, removed to Canandaigua, N. Y., where he was a hatter, wool dealer, and postmaster. He married Betsey Kimball of Covendish, Vt. Their daughter Caroline was born in Canandaigua and always lived there with her family until 1856. She was educated in the Canandaigua Seminary. About 1848 she began writing stories and articles for magazines, first contributing to *Graham's Magazine* and *Holden's Dollar Magazine*. Two of her stories took prizes offered by newspapers and in a short time she was writing for the *Knickerbocker*, *Putnam's Magazine*, and *Harper's Magazine*. Her first publication in book form was a volume of tales and sketches, *Dream-Land by Daylight* (1852). Other volumes followed: *Isa, a Pilgrimage* (1852), *The Children of Light* (1853), *The Little Cross-Bearers* (1854), *Susan, the Fisherman's Daughter* (1855), *The Beautiful Gate and Other Tales* (1855), *Getting Along* (1855), *Philly and Kit* (1856), *Victoria, or the World Overcome* (1856), *Peter Carradine* (1863), *Blessings in Disguise* (1863), *The Sparrow's Fall and Other Stories* (1863), *Amy Carr, or the Fortune Teller* (1864), *The Foe in the Household* (1871). Most of these books were novels, some for children, some for adults, and she had a novel ready for the press at the time of her death. Her plots are emotional but slow in action and her dialogue is carried on by the continual use of "he said," "she exclaimed," "answered he," "returned she," and similar expressions. The sentiments expressed are old-fashioned and the moralizing is tedious. The scenes are laid in different parts of the United States, chiefly the East, during her own time, and some of the descriptive passages are vivid and realistic. From 1865 until the time of her death Miss Chesebrough was a teacher of English composition at Packer Collegiate Institute, Brooklyn, N. Y. There she was known as a woman of gentle, serious personality, quiet in voice and manner, but accustomed to the attention of her pupils. As a teacher she had initiative, logical insight, and practical resources, and under her direction were trained several brilliant students who later became teachers in the Institute. One of these students recalls her as "of slight build, with blue eyes that could flash, full brows framed by brown wavy hair, features that indicated sensitiveness and ideality." Miss Chesebrough was a devoted daughter and in a period of family adversity showed herself not only unselfish but heroic. When she went to Packer Institute she acquired a home near Piermont, N. Y., where she died. She was buried in the family lot at Canandaigua.

[Anna Chesebrough Wildey, *Genealogy of the Descendants of William Chesebrough* (1903); *N. Y. Times*, Feb. 18, 1873; *N. Y. Daily Tribune*, Feb. 19, 1873; information from Miss Adelaide E. Wyckoff of Brooklyn, N. Y., one of Miss Chesebrough's students at Packer Institute.]
　　　　　　　　　　　　　　　　　　　S. G. B.

CHESNUT, JAMES (Jan. 18, 1815–Feb. 1, 1885), lawyer, planter, senator, Confederate soldier, came of Irish ancestors who left Virginia, their original abode in America, during the French and Indian War, and ultimately settled at Camden, Kershaw County, S. C., where he was born. His father, James, Sr., of the third generation, owned large plantations (said to have aggregated five square miles) in this vicinity,

sat for several sessions in the state legislature, and was intendant of Camden in 1806–07. His mother was Mary Cox, of Philadelphia, a sister-in-law of Horace Binney [*q.v.*]. James, Jr., was the youngest of thirteen children (T. J. Kirkland and R. M. Kennedy, *Historic Camden, Colonial and Revolutionary*, 1905, pp. 366–71). Like his father he was educated at Princeton where in 1835 he was graduated with an honorary oration (*Princeton College Faculty Minutes*, 1832–35). Having read law in Charleston, S. C., under the guidance of James Louis Petigru (J. P. Carson, *Life, Letters and Speeches of James Louis Petigru*, 1920, p. 287), he was admitted to the bar in 1837 and shortly afterward commenced practise in Camden. On Apr. 23, 1840, he married Mary Boykin Miller, daughter of Stephen D. Miller, governor of South Carolina from 1828 to 1830.

Chesnut entered the lower house of the General Assembly as a member for Kershaw in 1840. With the exception of the sessions of 1846–47 and 1848–49 he was regularly returned to this body until 1852. For the next six years he was a member of the state Senate, and its president from 1856 to 1858. Having become a leader of that party in South Carolina which advocated secession, he was sent to the Nashville convention in 1850 and was elected in 1858 to the United States Senate where his ability as an orator made him at once a conspicuous figure among the representatives of the Southern states. His chief efforts were directed to a defense of slavery. "Commerce, civilization, and Christianity go hand in hand," he said, "and their conjoint efforts receive their chief earthly impulse from this reviled institution" (*Congressional Globe*, 36 Cong., 1 Sess., pp. 1613–1619).

When secession became imminent Chesnut resigned his seat in the Senate (Nov. 10, 1860). In the South Carolina convention he was a member of the committee which drafted the ordinance of secession. In the Provisional Congress of the Confederate States he was a member of the committee which drafted the permanent constitution. As an aide on the staff of Gen. Beauregard he, together with Capt. S. D. Lee, bore the messages to Anderson demanding the evacuation of Fort Sumter. The charge that the impetuosity of these messengers was responsible for the firing on the fort (J. F. Rhodes, *History of the United States from the Compromise of 1850*, 1895, III, p. 237) is not sustained by the evidence (see *Official Records (Army)*, 1 ser., I, Index, and N. W. Stephenson, *The Day of the Confederacy*, 1919, pp. 17–18). Chesnut was again an aide to Beauregard during the first battle of Manassas. Subsequently he was a member of the executive council of South Carolina, but resigned in October 1862 to become an aide with the rank of colonel of cavalry on the staff of President Davis. In this capacity his duties were varied and extensive. Davis placed great confidence in the judgment of his "cool, quiet, self-poised colonel." At length, however, Chesnut's desire for field service was recognized, and he was appointed (April. 23, 1864) brigadier-general in command of the reserve forces in South Carolina (*Official Records (Army)*, 1 ser., XXXV, pt. II, p. 456). He was serving at this post when the war ended.

Though disfranchised during the period following the war Chesnut took an active part in the reconstruction of South Carolina. He was president of the convention of 1867 which protested against military rule, a delegate to the Democratic national convention in 1868 and to the state Democratic convention two years later, and chairman of the executive committee of the Taxpayer's conventions of 1871 and 1874. In the campaign of 1876 he was chairman of the Kershaw County Democratic convention. His death occurred at Saarsfield, his plantation near Camden, in 1885.

[The private papers of Chesnut have been destroyed. Some of his letters as well as other intimate material of the war period are preserved in his wife's journal (Mary Boykin Chesnut, *Diary from Dixie*, 1905, ed. by I. D. Martin and M. L. Avary). His correspondence with President Davis is to be found in D. Rowland, *Jefferson Davis, Constitutionalist, His Letters, Papers and Speeches* (1923). Brief accounts of his life occur in *Confed. Mil. Hist.*, vol. V (1899), and T. J. Kirkland and R. M. Kennedy, *Historic Camden, Nineteenth Century* (1926). Chesnut's part in the secession movement is the subject of a careful study by C. W. Jenkins, Jr., a student in the College of Charleston.]   J. H. E.

CHESTER, GEORGE RANDOLPH (1869– Feb. 26, 1924), author, was born in Ohio in 1869. In an interview reported by Herbert Corey (*Cosmopolitan*, May 1911), he stated that he had worked as a boy, left home early, and drifted about for several years; ran an engine in a planing mill, was a pen-and-ink artist in Davenport, Iowa, cook and waiter in a restaurant, plumber, paper-hanger, ribbon salesman, chain dragger for a civil engineer, bill clerk and also "chair designer" in a chair factory. He began newspaper work on the Detroit *News*, where there is an office tradition that he was a brilliant fictionist but poor reporter, omitting the victim's name in a vivid murder story. For seven years thereafter, until 1908, he was on the Cincinnati *Enquirer*, becoming Sunday editor. He also organized a syndicate which supplied weekly humorous stories to some twenty-five papers. From 1905 on his stories appeared frequently in the *Cosmopoli-*

tan, McClure's, Everybody's, and elsewhere. He scored his great success with the *Get-Rich-Quick Wallingford* stories of 1908, sub-titled "a cheerful account of the rise and fall of an American business buccaneer." Magazine readers delighted in these clever tales mingling slang and schemes of high finance, with their fat, rascally, likable Falstaffian hero and his companion "Blackie" Daw. Many novels and short-story sequences in the same vein followed, notably *The Cash Intrigue* (1909), *The Making of Bobby Burnit* (1909), *Young Wallingford* (1910), *Five Thousand an Hour* (1912), *Wallingford and Blackie Daw* (1913); *Wallingford in His Prime* (1913). With his wife he wrote *The Ball of Fire* (1914), *Cordelia Blossom* (1914), *The Son of Wallingford* (1921), *On the Lot and Off* (1924), and several plays. After the war Chester entered the moving picture field as a writer, editor, and director at a salary of $25,000 a year, and directed the scenarios of *Black Beauty* and *The Son of Wallingford*. He returned to magazine writing in 1921 and at the time of his death lived in New York contributing his "Izzy Iskovitch" stories to the *Saturday Evening Post* every three weeks at $2,000 each. "Talk literature little, and work at it much; earn money, and spend it"—these precepts, from his *Art of Writing* (1910), Chester practised. He was a tremendous worker, kept preposterous hours, never took exercise or vacations willingly. Five feet ten, slender, clean-shaven, with quick, prominent blue eyes and round face, he had the alert, good-natured, shrewd expression of a successful journalist. By his first wife, Elizabeth Bethermel of Connersville, Ind., to whom he was married in 1895, he had two sons, George Randolph, Jr., and Robert Fey. In 1911 he secured a divorce and in Paris married Lillian De Rimo of Cincinnati. He died of a heart attack in New York and was buried in Spring Grove Cemetery, Cincinnati.

[Obituary notices of Chester appeared in the New York papers of Feb. 27, 1924, and more extended accounts in the Cincinnati *Enquirer* of Feb. 27, Mar. 2, and Mar. 15. See also "The Author of Wallingford," with portrait, by Herbert Corey, *Cosmopolitan*, May 1911, and brief article in *Saturday Evening Post* (editorial), May 10, 1924.]   A. W.

CHESTER, JOSEPH LEMUEL (Apr. 30, 1821–May 26, 1882), genealogist, antiquarian, was born in Norwich, Conn., son of Joseph and Prudee (Tracy) Chester. His first immigrant ancestor was Capt. Samuel Chester who settled in New London, Conn. (c. 1663), and was engaged in West India trade. The boy was only eleven when his father died; the mother with most of her children soon (1835) moved to Ohio. One of his Norwich teachers spoke of him as "a handsome bright boy," but his school days gave no evidence of "budding genius." After a brief experience as a school-teacher at Ballston, N. Y., he went to New York City, at the age of eighteen, to undertake a law course, but this was soon abandoned for business in the house of Tappan & Company, silk merchants. This firm was unusual in its stress on the moral conduct of its employees, all of whom were aroused to efforts in the causes of temperance and anti-slavery. Before reaching his majority, Chester was lecturing on temperance to audiences all the way from Massachusetts to Ohio. His leisure hours were also given to writing verse, the merit of which was recognized by the *Knickerbocker,* then the leading literary magazine in the United States. The issue for January 1843 printed his poem "Greenwood Cemetery" under the pseudonym, Julian Cramer, a name he assumed many times. Later in the year a volume, *Greenwood Cemetery and Other Poems,* was published, which carried his true name as the author. One poem of his collection, "Lonely Auld Wife," attracted the attention of the composer, William Richardson Demster, who set it to music and included it in his concert repertoire in his tours through the country. Soon after 1845 Chester became a Philadelphian. He spent the business hours in a counting room on Market St., "a quiet unpretending business man," but devoted himself in spare time to literature and music. *Godey's Lady's Book* (March 1850) prints a portrait of him as "our musical editor," who is described as "still on the sunnyside of thirty." In 1852, he appears to have left the counting room for journalism, becoming associated with the *Philadelphia Inquirer* and the *Daily Sun;* his newspaper connections brought him into the political field for the first time, and he was elected to membership in the Philadelphia City Council as a representative from the Sixth Ward, in 1855. He continued to have strong anti-slavery convictions, being responsible for the publication, in 1854, of *Educational Laws of Virginia; The Personal Narrative of Mrs. Margaret Douglass, a Southern Woman who was Imprisoned for One Month in the Common Jail of Norfolk, Under the Laws of Virginia, for the Crime of Teaching Free Colored Children to Read.* During the next two years when Congress was the scene of exciting debates on the question of slavery, Chester spent much time in Washington as corresponding editor for the Philadelphia papers; indeed, during the spring of 1856, he was one of the assistant clerks in the House of Representatives. It was during these years also that he served on the staff of Gov. Pollock of Pennsylvania and acquired his much treasured title, "Colonel." In September 1858, he went to England to try to sell some patent rights, at the same time keeping his connection with the *Philadelphia Inquirer,* to which he contributed a weekly letter.

Up to the time of his arrival in England it does not appear that he had ever given any attention to genealogical research. Capt. Uriah Rogers of Norwich, his great-grandfather, believed that he carried in his veins the blood of John Rogers, who was burned at the stake for his heresy during the English Reformation and whose picture in the old *New England Primer* was doubtless familiar to Chester. "To establish, if possible, the correctness of these claims," his visit to England became "protracted." He found the family tradition incapable of proof, but he "became thoroughly imbued with the convictions that historical justice had never yet been done" the martyred preacher. Hence his first genealogical contribution, *John Rogers: the Compiler of the first authorized English Bible: the Pioneer of the English Reformation; and its first martyr* (London, 1861). The reader is referred to the *Dictionary of National Biography* for information regarding Chester during his continued residence in London. He is credited there with a long list of publications and with research so successful as to gain for him this tribute: "When he died, he had no superior as a genealogist among English speaking people." Further British tributes to this "master in genealogy and biographical history" were an honorary degree (D.C.L.) from Oxford in 1881, and a tablet to his memory in Westminster Abbey. He remained to the last a citizen of the United States (*Notes and Queries,* London, 1882, p. 440) and ever maintained that his prodigious labors in making extracts from parish registers, in copying matriculation registers at Oxford, marriage licenses, wills, books of pedigree, etc., had as their primary object the publication of a "general and detailed account of the character, social status, etc., of the English emigrants to New England prior to the Restoration" (*Biograph and Review,* London, May 1881). His work was well known also in his native country. Columbia University anticipated Oxford in honoring him (LL.D., 1877). He was a frequent contributor to the *New England Historical and Genealogical Register,* and many articles which appeared first in England were reprinted in the *Boston Evening Transcript.* Further, he was a highly important and most generous medium through whom American investigators in the same field could obtain accurate information about the English ancestry of American families.

His first volume of verse was dedicated "To his wife (not knowing a better friend)"; she was Catherine Hendrickson Hubbard, of New York, whom he married, June 26, 1839 (Reuben Hyde Walworth, *Hyde Genealogy*, 1864, I, 443).

[Biographical sketches of Chester by John J. Latting, in *N. Y. Geneal. and Biog. Record*, Oct. 1882; by John Ward Dean, in *New Eng. Hist. and Geneal. Reg.*, Jan. 1884; by W. P. Courtney in the *Academy*, June 3, 1882. An appreciation of his work, prior to his death, appears in the *Biograph and Review*, May 1881. The inscription on the Westminster tablet, as also that on his gravestone at Nunhead Cemetery, Surrey, is printed in Jos. Foster, ed., *London Marriage Licenses, 1521–1869* (1887), preface. Paternal ancestry in U. S. in "Chester Genealogy" in *Old Northwest. Gen. Quart.* (1907), pp. 154–66; maternal ancestry, in both U. S. and England, in *Hyde Genealogy*.]   A. E. P.

CHETLAIN, AUGUSTUS LOUIS (Dec. 26, 1824–Mar. 15, 1914), Union soldier, banker, was born in St. Louis, Mo. His parents, Louis and Julia Droz Chetlain, who were Swiss of French extraction, came in 1821 to the Selkirk settlement in western Canada, and left there in 1823. In 1826 they removed to the neighborhood of Galena, Ill., where the father engaged in mining and teaming, later bought a farm, and prospered in all these undertakings. The son attended school in Galena, and then was employed as clerk by a wholesale merchant. In 1852, with but little capital, he started in business for himself and soon built up a good trade. He sold out in 1859, traveled extensively in Europe, and returned in time to take an active part in the political campaign of 1860. At the outbreak of the Civil War, Galena raised a volunteer company of which Chetlain, at the suggestion of U. S. Grant, was elected captain. He was mustered into service as such on May 2, 1861, and the next day became lieutenant-colonel of the 12th Illinois Infantry, in which the Galena company was incorporated. The regiment remained in camp in southern Illinois until September, when it moved into Kentucky as part of the force with which Grant occupied Paducah. As the colonel was absent in charge of a brigade, the command of the regiment devolved upon Chetlain, and he continued in command as long as he remained with it, although not promoted to the colonelcy until Apr. 27, 1862. He took part in the capture of Forts Henry and Donelson, in the battle of Shiloh, and in the operations which culminated in the battles of Iuka and Corinth. He was then assigned to the command of the post of Corinth. He was appointed brigadier-general of volunteers, Dec. 18, 1863, and put in charge of the organization and recruitment of colored troops in Tennessee and Kentucky, a work in which he was eminently successful. Later he held administrative commands in Tennessee and Alabama

until he was mustered out of service, Jan. 15, 1866. From 1867 to 1869 he was United States collector of internal revenue for Utah, and lived in Salt Lake City. For the next three years he was consul at Brussels. Returning to the United States in 1872, he established himself in Chicago, where he organized the Home National Bank and became its president. In 1892, he also organized the Industrial Bank of Chicago, but a year later poor health obliged him finally to withdraw from business. He traveled widely in the United States, Canada, and Europe. Before his retirement he was a director of the Chicago Stock Exchange and a member of the board of education, and was active in many philanthropic enterprises. He was always prominent in the affairs of the Loyal Legion, Grand Army of the Republic, and similar organizations. Besides a pamphlet on *The Red River Colony* (1893), he published a volume of *Recollections*, in which he records his personal estimate of many eminent men whom he knew intimately. His range of acquaintance was wide, especially among the prominent generals of the Civil War and the political and business leaders of Illinois. Grant and Sherman, John M. Palmer and Shelby Cullom, George M. Pullman and Cyrus McCormick, Lyman Gage and Franklin McVeagh were among his friends. He married, first, Emily Tenney of Elyria, Ohio; and second, Mrs. Melancthon Smith.

[Chetlain's *Recollections of Seventy Years* (1893); *Official Records (Army)*, 1 ser., vols. VII, X (pt. 1), XVII (pt. 1), and 3 ser., vol. IV; *Who's Who in America, 1912–13*.]   T. M. S.

CHEVER, JAMES W. (Apr. 20, 1791–May 2, 1857), privateersman, sea captain, the son of Capt. James and Sarah Browne Chever, was born at Salem where the family, sometimes called Cheever, had been prominent for more than a century. His father, a master mariner, had served as lieutenant on the Salem privateer *Grand Turk* in the Revolution. Young Chever went to sea at thirteen as cabin boy on the *America*. By 1810, he was mate of the *Fame* and at nineteen, he was given command of the ship *Belisarius*. At the outbreak of the War of 1812, the Crowninshields converted their crack ship *America* into a privateer, mounting twenty guns, manned by a crew of 150, and cut down so that she was probably the fastest ship afloat. On her first two cruises, Chever served as prize master and lieutenant under Captains Joseph Ropes and John Kehew, respectively. Late in 1813, he was made captain of the ship, at twenty-two. He cruised between the English Channel and the Canary Islands, able to outsail any of the British frigates. On this third cruise of the ship

(Dec. 13, 1813–Mar. 31, 1814) she captured twelve prizes, three of which were burned and a fourth used as a target. The fourth cruise, starting Oct. 31, 1814, lasted only six days, as she struck a derelict and had to return to port. The final cruise (Nov. 24, 1814–Apr. 8, 1815) carried her again to European waters under Chever's command, netted thirteen prizes, and involved a sharp and victorious fight with a well-armed English packet. In less than three years, the *America* had sent in prizes worth $1,100,-000, half of which went to the owners and the rest to officers and crew. For success, this record was approached only by the *Grand Turk* of Salem, and for boldness, by Capt. Thomas Boyle of Baltimore in the *Chasseur*. Chever's subsequent career was less spectacular, but he continued for many years in command of Salem ships, later retiring as wharfinger at Salem, where he died. At first he called himself James Chever, Jr., but later assumed the middle initial. A portrait, taken in his last years, shows a strong, smooth-shaven face with prominent nose and curly black hair. General tribute was paid to his straightforward, cheerful, guileless character, free from all rough and coarse qualities.

[A detailed account of the *America*, with notes on Chever's life, by B. B. Crowninshield, is found in the *Essex Institute Hist. Colls.*, XXXVII, 1–76. Notes on his father are in the same collections, IV, p. 131. A briefer account of the *America* is in R. D. Paine's *Ships and Sailors of Old Salem* (revised ed. 1923), 326–34. There is also an account in E. S. Maclay's *Hist. of the Am. Privateers* (1899), ch. IX. An obituary appeared in the *Salem Gazette*, May 5, 1857.]

R. G. A—n.

CHEVERUS, JOHN LOUIS ANN MAGDALEN LEFEBRE de (Jan. 28, 1768–July 19, 1836), first Catholic bishop of Boston, born in Mayenne, Lower Maine in France, was the son of a lieutenant of police with judicial powers, John Vincent Lefebre, and his pious wife, Anne Lemarchand des Noyers. No local family was more respected; the mayor was his uncle and the pastor was another uncle. As a day scholar, he attended the local college until at the age of twelve years he accepted the priestly call and received tonsure. Thereupon, he was sent to the College of Louis-le-Grand in Paris, but suffered no ill effects in its radical atmosphere. In public competition, he was selected for the Seminary of St. Magloire (Oratorians) in Paris where he had the advantage of attending lectures at the Sorbonne. Ordained in the last pre-Revolutionary public ordinations in Paris (1790), he was assigned to assist his uncle in Mayenne. To enter orders at this time was courting persecution. He soon succeeded to the pastorate, but on refusal of an oath to support the civil con-

stitution of the clergy, he was deprived of his parish. Sent to Paris, he was imprisoned in the ill-fated convent of the Cordeliers. In June 1792 he escaped and found a hiding place in the city. Thus he avoided the September massacres when so many of his clerical associates were put to death. In disguise, Cheverus made his way to Calais and thence to London where he found a hospitable asylum. He refused the usual bounty and found employment as a French tutor in a Protestant private school and in a gentleman's family. He also preached to a congregation of refugees. In 1795 Dr. Francis Matignon, his former seminary professor, urged him to come to Boston, where Abbé La Poitrie, a chaplain with the French troops, had gathered a small French and Irish congregation in 1784, to which the erudite Matignon had succeeded in 1792. Renouncing his patrimony, Cheverus sailed for Boston in the fall of 1796. He wrote to Bishop Carroll to send him anywhere with no worry concerning his support for he was both able and willing to earn his own livelihood. For a time, he served among the Penobscots of Maine, living on an annuity of $200 appropriated by the Massachusetts General Court for a Catholic Indian missionary. He also made visitations to scattered New England congregations and isolated families, frequently tramping long distances to save the cost of transportation. Carroll offered him St. Mary's Church in Philadelphia, but the missionary preferred to serve his New England people as priest and doctor. In 1800, when Matignon and Cheverus planned Holy Cross Church, their Protestant admirers headed by President Adams signed the subscription list. Three years later Bishop Carroll consecrated the church and Cheverus preached to a curious crowd. Thereafter Matignon and Cheverus attracted auditors of every creed. The scholarly, urbane, humble Frenchmen were confessors to Catholics but often advisers to Protestants in matters of conscience. No incident suggested the affection in which Cheverus was held more than his seat of honor at a banquet tendered President Adams by his aristocratic fellow-townsmen.

On the conclusion of the Concordat, friends urged Cheverus to return to France but Carroll asked him to remain at his post. Of personal persecution there was none, but even the beloved priest faced annoyances. On marrying two Catholics in Maine, though he sent them to a justice for a second civil ceremony, Cheverus was tried in a criminal action but declared not guilty. The civil action was soon dropped. With the aid of two rich Irish merchants of Newcastle,

Me., he built a chapel, but the superior court declared that even if there was a resident priest the Catholics of the region must continue paying Congregationalist tythes. Again in 1820, when he brought the Ursuline nuns to Boston, there was an outburst which he silenced by a communication to the press. He soon forgot these inconveniences, for in later years he extolled American toleration to King Charles X. He occupied Protestant pulpits on invitation; when an oath of allegiance was framed he was appealed to by the legislature lest Catholic conscience be violated; he was a patron of learned societies, assisting in founding the Athenæum to which he left his library. Harrison Gray Otis and Quincy were among his warmest friends, as were Lemuel Shaw and Col. Samuel Lorenzo Knapp, the litterateur, for whom he procured an honorary degree from Paris.

In 1808, at the request of Matignon, Archbishop Carroll recommended that Cheverus be made bishop of Boston with New England for a diocese. Pius VII made the appointment and Cheverus was consecrated by Carroll (1810). This elevation brought no change in his mode of life. His dress was still shabby. He walked on his visitations. He occupied a humble cottage. His house became a seminary, and in the cholera days a hospital. He continued his missionary labors. Frequent were his visits to the Maine Indians, the lowly Irish construction camps, and religious functions in Canada. After Bishop Concanen's death, he ministered to the New York diocese. He conferred the pallium on Archbishop Neale in Georgetown but refused a possible selection as his coadjutor. He urged the selection of Maréchal, whom two years later he consecrated as Neale's successor in the See of Baltimore. Cheverus was too active to write much even if he had not had a distaste for what he termed the "scribomania" of his age: a few letters, an occasional journalistic contribution, a manual of hymns and prayers, and a French edition of the New Testament formed his literary contribution.

Cheverus was not destined to end his career in his "dear Boston." Matignon died in 1818 and Romagne after twenty years with the Indians returned to France; Cheverus missed their association. Hardship and exposure brought an attack of chronic asthma which physicians believed would be fatal if he did not seek a milder climate. This Cheverus would not do, but the French minister in Washington urged the King of France to nominate him to a vacant see. Bishop Cheverus refused the appointment to Montauban (1823). The Catholics were worried; two

hundred Protestants petitioned the grand almoner of France against his removal; the press in eulogistic notices urged that he remain. Dr. Ellery Channing spoke the mind of Boston: "Has not the metropolis of New England witnessed a sublime example of Christian virtue in a Catholic bishop? Who among our religious teachers would solicit a comparison between himself and the devoted Cheverus?" But the king demanded Cheverus and, with hopes of returning, he obeyed. Three hundred carriages—and few Catholics had carriages—are said to have escorted him out of Boston. Threatened by shipwreck in the Channel, he gained the esteem of the passengers by his heroism. In France, his reputation spread, and even the Huguenots of Montauban became "bishop's men." In 1826, he was elevated to the archbishopric of Bordeaux and made a peer by Charles X, but declined the ministry of ecclesiastical affairs. In 1828, he was named a counselor of state, and two years later a commander of the Order of the Holy Ghost. When the July Revolution broke forth, he maintained order in Bordeaux, which accepted the *de facto* government. All France clamored for his elevation to the cardinalate, and Louis Philippe gladly urged the appointment in Rome. In 1836, he became a peer of the Church. On July 7, 1836, he fell prostrated at the conclusion of a day's preaching, and when he died all France mourned.

[Wm. Byrne, Jas. H. O'Donnell, W. A. Leahy, and others, *Hist. of the Cath. Ch. in the New Eng. States* (1899), vol. I; J. H. Doubourg, *Life of Cardinal de Cheverus* (trans. by Robt. Walsh, 1839); *Vie du Cardinal de Cheverus*, par M. le Curé de Sulpice (Paris, 1858); Hamon, *Vie du Cardinal Cheverus*, trans. by Stewart (1839); F. X. Karker, *Der Cardinal de Cheverus* (Freiburg, 1876); James Fitton, *Sketches of Establishment of the Church in New Eng.* (1872); J. G. Shea, *Hist. of Cath. Ch. in U. S.*, III (1890), 107–28; Thomas O'Gorman, *Hist. of Roman Cath. Ch. in U. S.* (1895); R. H. Clarke, *Lives of the Deceased Bishops of Cath. Ch. in U. S.* (1872). See *Boston Monthly Mag.*, June 1825; *U. S. Cath. Mag.*, IV, 261–67; J. S. Loring, *The Hundred Boston Orators* (1852); *Cath. Encyc.* (1913).]   R. J. P.

CHEVES, LANGDON (Sept. 17, 1776–June 26, 1857), congressman, financier, was the son of Alexander Chivas, of Buchan, Aberdeenshire, Scotland, son of John Chivas, or Chivis. [The name is still pronounced Chivis]. In 1762 "honest Sandy Chivas," then twenty-one years of age, came to America and began life as a trader in the Ninety Six district of South Carolina on the frontiers of the Cherokee and Creek nations. In 1774 he married Mary Langdon, daughter of Thomas Langdon, who was a refugee after the "Braddock War" from Augusta County, Va. Alexander Chivas was a lieutenant in Col. Hamilton's Loyal Regiment, and Thomas Langdon was a captain on the American side in the Ninety Six Regiment. Langdon Cheves was born in Abbeville District, in Bull Town Fort, a stockaded blockhouse, where his mother had taken refuge from the Cherokee Indians after the British attack on Charleston. After the death of Mary Langdon Chivas in 1779, this only son of a brilliant mother was brought up in the home of his aunt, Mrs. Thomas Cheves, for six years, and attended Andrew Weed's school. In 1785 he was taken to Charleston by his father and sent to a school kept by a severe old Scotchman who flogged him for his "up country" twang and tried to teach him his broad Scotch. Beyond this and the help from his pastor, Dr. Buist, his education was obtained by his own untiring study. After serving an apprenticeship in a factor's supply store and showing the genius for accurate accounts that served him so well in his banking days, he read law under Judge William Marshall and was admitted to the bar in 1797. His success was pronounced and his law firm was soon the best paid in the city. He early entered politics and held in succession the offices of warden for his city ward in 1802, member of the state legislature from 1802 to 1809, attorney-general in 1809, presidential elector in 1809, congressman from 1811 to 1815, and speaker of the national House of Representatives in the Thirteenth Congress. On May 6, 1806, he married Mary Elizabeth Dulles, a school girl of barely seventeen, with whom he lived for thirty years a life of peculiar domestic charm, and who was the mother of his fourteen children. His favorite recreation was house building, and he planned and built at least six houses of architectural distinction, the most interesting of which was a summer house near Pendleton, S. C.

Cheves's national service began with his election in 1810 to fill a vacancy in the Eleventh Congress. He was one of that brilliant quartet of South Carolina statesmen which included John C. Calhoun, William Lowndes, and D. R. Williams. He served on the Committee on Naval Affairs and later as chairman of the Ways and Means Committee and of the Select Committee on Naval Establishment. When Henry Clay was appointed one of the peace commissioners to Ghent, Cheves succeeded him in 1814 as speaker of the House and served until his retirement from Congress in 1815. Though little interested in expansion, he was a prominent member of the group which precipitated the War of 1812 (J. W. Pratt, *Expansionists of 1812*, pp. 49, 127), and he was one of the Republicans who did not attend the caucus to renominate Madison in 1812. As speaker he cast the deciding vote to

defeat Dallas's bill for rechartering the United States Bank. He was one of the most effective debaters in the House. Massive and striking in appearance, dignified and yet forceful in delivery, he was described by Washington Irving as the first orator he ever heard who satisfied his idea of Demosthenes. After the peace of 1815, believing that his national service was accomplished, he declined reëlection to Congress and returned to his law practise in Charleston, refusing the position of secretary of the treasury to succeed Gallatin. In 1816 he was elected a justice of the court of appeals of South Carolina and served for three years with distinction.

In January 1819, Cheves was elected a director of the United States Bank and on Mar. 6, 1819, its president. At the urgent request of the friends of the Bank he accepted the position, although it involved the sacrifice of what would have been to him a preferable position, that of associate justice of the United States Supreme Court, for which, he was informed by Senator Middleton, President Monroe had selected him. He found the affairs of the Bank in a deplorable condition. In a little over two years from its opening in 1817 it had done an enormous business but had so exceeded its resources in the purchase of drafts, especially on Southern and Western banks, that its demand liabilities exceeded the specie in its vaults by $100,000. On Apr. 5, at the time when Cheves was taking entire control of the situation, John Quincy Adams wrote in his diary: "The Bank is so drained of its specie that it is hardly conceivable that it can go to June without stopping payments. . . . The state of our currency is perilous in the highest degree, and threatens to terminate in a national convulsion." Three weeks after this the Bank was safe and sound again and able to help other solvent but needy concerns. Cheves accomplished this by continuing for a short time the policy of his predecessor, Jones, of curtailing circulation and especially forbidding banks in the South and West to issue notes when exchange was against them, and by a European loan of $2,000,000. Both of these policies were severely criticized but were fully justified by results. By 1822 an accumulation of $3,500,000 had been made to replace past losses of the Bank, and the capital, $28,000,000, again stood whole and untrammeled. Cheves then resigned his place to be succeeded by Nicholas Biddle.

At this time he was appointed chief commissioner of claims under the Treaty of Ghent and filled that office until all claims were adjusted. He resided for a time in Philadelphia and then at Lancaster, Pa., where he practised law. In the fall of 1829 he returned to South Carolina, which was then in the throes of the Nullification struggle. Though believing thoroughly in the right of secession, he opposed separate state action as "dangerous and ineffectual" and said that "the metaphysics of *Nullification* is the worst shape in which its bad principle of separate action can be embodied." But his long absence from the state in national service had weakened his influence with his countrymen, his opinions clashed with those of their leaders, and, rather than abjure his convictions, he withdrew from public life. He wrote "occasional reviews," keen analyses of current situations, was a delegate to the Nashville convention of 1850, and advocated a Southern Confederacy but strongly opposed separate action on the part of any state. When about sixty years of age he took up agriculture seriously, built a new and handsome house, "The Delta," near Savannah, and in the last twenty years of his life amassed a large fortune. He died June 26, 1857, at the home of his daughter Mrs. D. J. McCord, in Columbia, and was buried in Magnolia Cemetery, Charleston. His close friend, Judge Huger, said, "Cheves loved truth; and to it he sacrificed everything." He was a man of clear and accurate vision, broad sympathies, balanced judgment, and both moral and intellectual honesty.

[The most accurate and discriminating study of Cheves is the sketch in John B. O'Neall, *Biog. Sketches Bench and Bar of S. C.* (1859). Gov. Benjamin Perry gives a rather critical estimate in his "Reminiscences of Public Men—Langdon Cheves," in the *Nineteenth Century* for Aug. 1869, and this is answered by Mrs. D. J. McCord in the *Nineteenth Century*, Apr. 1870. Of especial value for his banking career is Louisa Porter Haskell, "Langdon Cheves and the U. S. Bank," in *Am. Hist. Ass. Report*, vol. I, 1896. Valuable manuscript sources are Leverett, "Sketches of Langdon Cheves," and "Hon. Langdon Cheves," by Langdon Cheves, both in the possession of Cheves's grandson, Mr. Langdon Cheves, of Charleston, S. C., who has also numerous letters of Cheves, including his *Exposition of the Bank*, published in 1822. There is also a manuscript sketch of Langdon Cheves, by Mrs. Mildred W. Lewis, of Charleston. Theodore D. Jervey, *Robt. Y. Hayne and His Times* (1909), contains numerous references to Cheves, under whom Hayne studied. There are good obituaries in the *Charleston Courier* and Charleston *Mercury* for June 27, 1857.]   J. E. W—y.

CHEW, BENJAMIN (Nov. 29, 1722–Jan. 20, 1810), jurist, son of Dr. Samuel Chew, chief justice of the District of New Castle, was born at his father's seat on West River, Md. Reared a Quaker he subsequently joined the Anglican Church. Sent to Philadelphia to read law under Andrew Hamilton, who died in 1741, Chew, when barely nineteen, went abroad to study at the Middle Temple, where many of his contemporaries were educated. His father dying in 1743, he returned to Philadelphia and was ad-

mitted to the bar of the supreme court in September 1746 but did not practise there until about nine years later. Living at Dover, Del., he practised there and at New Castle. He was included (1751) in the Boundary Commission representing the lower counties, and secured a legislative appointment (1752) as trustee to sell certain lands. Removing to Philadelphia about 1754, he became prominent, succeeded Tench Francis as attorney-general and held this office from 1755 to 1769. He was also recorder of Philadelphia until June 25, 1774, and member of the Council, 1755 till the Revolution. He was made speaker of the Assembly of the lower counties (1756) and register-general of the Province of Pennsylvania (1765) in charge of probates for Philadelphia County with deputy-registers for Bucks, Chester, New Castle, and other counties. Resigning as attorney-general (1769) he devoted himself to private practise until 1774 when he became chief justice of the supreme court of Pennsylvania succeeding William Allen. The Revolution swept away his offices with provincial authority, but Chew continued register-general until an Act of Assembly, Mar. 14, 1777, which provided registers of wills for each county but legalized Chew's activities. When after the Declaration of Independence he did not show evidence of undoubted patriotism, a warrant was issued for him, but he was allowed to remain a prisoner in his house until he was paroled with John Penn, and they were allowed to live at Union Iron Works, N. J., until Congress ordered him with others to be returned to Pennsylvania without paroles. Washington was friendly with Chew and celebrated at Chew House, "Cliveden," Germantown, May 23, 1787, the wedding dinner of Peggy, Chew's daughter, and Col. John E. Howard. Commissioned (Oct. 3 and 4, 1791) respectively judge and president of the high court of errors and appeals of Pennsylvania, Chew held these positions till the court was abolished in 1808, shortly before his death. He was characterized by William Rawle, prominent attorney, as of "solid judgment, tenacious memory, persevering industry," with perhaps no superior in accurate knowledge of the common law or in sound exposition of the statutes. At the bar his language was pertinent and correct but without oratory, his arguments close and logical, designed to carry conviction not to win applause. He was married twice: first to Mary Thomas (died 1755), then to Elizabeth Oswald who outlived him.

[Frank M. Eastman, *Courts and Lawyers of Pa.* (1922), I, 255 ff.; *Pa. Mag. Hist. and Biog.*, vols. XXII, XXIII, XXV, XXVI, XXVII, XL, XLVI, XLVII, XLVIII, XLIX; John C. Fitzpatrick, ed., *The Diaries of Geo. Washington* (1925), III, 218; David P. Brown, *The Forum* (1856), I, 8, 235, 589.]   J.C.B.

CHICKERING, JONAS (Apr. 5, 1798–Dec. 8, 1853), piano manufacturer, was born at Mason Village, N. H., the third child of Abner and Eunice (Dakin) Chickering. Shortly after his birth the family moved to New Ipswich, N. H., where Jonas spent his boyhood in his father's blacksmith shop and on the family farm. Of a decided mechanical bent, the boy apprenticed himself at the age of seventeen to a cabinet-maker, and toward the end of his apprenticeship undertook to repair the only piano in the village. In this task his skill as a cabinet-maker was happily combined with his passion for music and he discovered his life work. Soon after, at the age of twenty, he left for Boston where he secured employment in the shop of a certain John Osborne, one of the few Americans who were then making pianos.

For five years Chickering labored to master every detail in the art of piano making, and then in 1823 in partnership with a Scotchman, James Stewart, commenced to manufacture pianos under the firm-name of Stewart & Chickering. Stewart soon returned to Europe and Chickering for some years conducted the enterprise alone. Needing capital he established a partnership in 1830 with Capt. John Mackay, a capitalist and sea-captain, whose faith in Chickering led him to invest heavily in the concern. Mackay not only furnished the needed money, thus allowing his partner to devote his whole energy to the technical end, but himself transported and sold pianos in South America, loading on the home voyage with rosewood and mahogany. Mackay was lost at sea in 1841, and Chickering bought out his heirs, supervising until his death the financial as well as the mechanical end of the rapidly growing business.

Chickering's fame, however, rests not so much upon the fact that he founded and developed one of the earliest and largest of the American piano manufacturing houses, but upon the numerous improvements which he introduced. The difficulty of keeping the earlier grand pianos in tune was conquered by Chickering in 1837 when he succeeded in casting an iron frame built to sustain the great tension necessary to a piano of good quality. In that year he built the first grand piano with a full iron frame in a single casting. Samuel Babcock, it is true, had already experimented with the iron frame but Chickering first perfected it and first applied it to the grand piano. This opened a new era in the making of pianos and justified William Steinway in describing Chickering as the "father of American piano forte-

making." In 1843 the firm patented a new deflection of the strings and in 1845 Chickering invented the first practical method of over-stringing grand pianos. In 1852, the Chickering factory on Washington St., Boston, burned, but with characteristic energy, Chickering laid the foundation of a greater establishment on Tremont St., which, when finished, was thought to be the largest building in the United States with the exception of the Capitol at Washington.

Chickering was an indefatigable worker and until the end of his life could be found in his immense factory clad in his mechanic's apron and engrossed in the technical end of piano production. As he was shy and retiring in disposition, his rise was due almost solely to his industry and genius. He was beloved for his unostentatious charity, and in his quiet way influenced the development of musical appreciation in America. He had joined the Handel and Haydn Society in 1818 upon his arrival in Boston and later served as trustee and as president (1843–50). His mechanical ability was recognized by his election to the presidency of the Massachusetts Charitable Mechanics Association. On Nov. 30, 1823, he was married to Elizabeth Sumner Harraden who with four children survived him. The business was carried on by his three sons.

[The best account of Chickering is the biography written by his friend and protegé, Richard G. Parker, *Tribute to the Life and Character of Jonas Chickering* (1854); see also Freeman Hunt, *Lives of Am. Merchants* (1858), I, 493–537. For English ancestry see *New Eng. Hist. and Geneal. Reg.*, VIII, 96–97. The American line is traced in F. C. Torrey, *One Branch of the Chickering Family* (1919).]   H.U.F.

CHILD, DAVID LEE (July 8, 1794–Sept. 18, 1874), journalist, was born in West Boylston, Mass., the son of Zachariah and Lydia (Bigelow) Child. He was graduated from Harvard College in 1817. The following year he became sub-master of the Boston Latin School. In 1820 he served as secretary of legation at Lisbon, Portugal. Later in Spain he engaged in the war against the French, saying that he felt it was always his duty to help secure and defend liberty. From then on he engaged in many struggles for freedom of various sorts. He returned to the United States in 1824 and began the study of law with his uncle, Tyler Bigelow, in Watertown, Mass., being admitted to the Suffolk County bar in 1828. During the same year he was a member of the Massachusetts state legislature, edited the *Massachusetts Journal,* a leading Adams paper, and, in October, married Lydia Maria Francis [see Lydia Maria Francis Child], an author who later became prominent in the anti-slavery movement. Child was himself an early member of the anti-slavery society and in 1832 addressed a series of letters on the subject to Edward S. Abdy, an English philanthropist. He was a trustee of Noyes Academy at Canaan, N. H., in 1834, and was instrumental in opening the institution to colored youths at that time. In 1836 he went to Belgium to study the beet-sugar industry. He returned and erected in Northampton, Mass., the first beet-sugar factory in this country. The factory failed financially and was closed in 1844. But Child had proved the value of the commodity. He published a pamphlet in 1840 called *Culture of the Beet, and Manufacture of Beet-sugar.*

About 1843–44, he for a time assisted his wife in editing the *National Anti-Slavery Standard* in New York. The remainder of his life was spent in bettering conditions among the freed people and in writing on various subjects having to do with freedom. The best examples of his writing and of his political interests are the two pamphlets, *The Texan Revolution* (1843) and *The Taking of Naboth's Vineyard* (1845). He died in Wayland, Mass.

[Information concerning Child is to be found in *Professional and Industrial Hist. of Suffolk County, Mass.* (1894); *Bench and Bar Commonwealth of Mass.* (1895); Elias Child, *Geneal. Child, Childs and Childe Families* (1881); and *Letters of Lydia Maria Child* (1883). An account of Child's experiments with sugarbeets is given in F. S. Harris, *The Sugar-Beet in America* (1919).]   M.S.

CHILD, FRANCIS JAMES (Feb. 1, 1825–Sept. 11, 1896), philologist, was born in Boston, the third of the eight children of Joseph Child, a sailmaker, and his wife, Mary James. He played as a boy on the wharves and along the water-front and, expecting no opportunity to go to college, attended the English High School. There his powers of mind attracted the attention of Epes Sargent Dixwell, principal of the Boston Latin School, who had him transferred to his charge and lent him money to go on to Harvard College. At Harvard, Child took first place in a class that numbered Fitzedward Hall, George Frisbie Hoar, George Martin Lane, Charles Eliot Norton, and Charles Short among its members, was elected class orator, and was noted for his friendships, his wide reading, and his participation in amateur theatricals. After his graduation in 1846 he remained at Cambridge as tutor in mathematics 1846–48 and in history and political economy 1848–49. His real interest, however, was in English philology, and his edition of *Four Old Plays —Three Interludes: Thersytes, Jack Jugler, and Heywood's Pardoner and Frere: and Jocasta, a Tragedy by Gascoigne and Kinwelmarsh* (Cambridge, 1848) shows that he was already a scholar in that field and ripe for further study abroad. Fortunately, he was able to go, and from 1849 to 1851 he studied philosophy, the classics, and

Germanic philology at the Universities of Göttingen and Berlin. Upon his return to Harvard he succeeded his old teacher, Edward Tyrrel Channing [*q.v.*] as Boylston professor of rhetoric and oratory. In 1854 the University of Göttingen conferred on him the degree of doctor of philosophy *honoris causa*. On Aug. 23, 1860, he married Elizabeth Ellery Sedgwick, daughter of Robert Sedgwick of New York, who with four daughters survived him. In 1876, after twenty-five years of reading freshman themes, he was made professor of English and devoted himself wholly thereafter to the teaching and study of literature. The last few years of his life were saddened by the deaths of friends, especially of James Russell Lowell, whom he loved, and by the thought that his own death might come before his work was finished. In 1895–96 he met all his classes and other academic appointments with his usual punctuality, but he died before college reopened in the fall.

His chief works are five in number. His edition of the *Poetical Works of Edmund Spenser* (5 vols., 1855) presented the best text and the fullest biography of Spenser then available, and was not superseded until after Child's death. *English and Scottish Ballads* (8 vols., 1857–58) was the largest collection of ballads before Child's own *magnum opus.* "Observations on the Language of Chaucer" (*Memoirs of the American Academy of Arts and Sciences,* VIII, 1863, ii, 455 ff.), of extraordinary importance, laid a solid foundation for the study of Chaucer's language and versification and began a new era in Chaucerian scholarship. "Observations on the Language of Gower's 'Confessio Amantis'" (*Ibid.,* IX, 1873, ii, 265 ff.) applied the same principles to the study of Chaucer's friend and fellow-poet. *English and Scottish Popular Ballads* (5 vols., originally issued in 10 parts, 1883–98) was planned "to include every obtainable version of every extant English or Scottish ballad, with the fullest possible discussion of related songs or stories in the popular literature of all nations." The tenth part was virtually complete, except for a general introduction to the whole work, at the time of his death. This great achievement seems destined to endure as long as the ballads themselves; few scholars have left so lasting a monument. It was as a result, too, of his kindly insistence and generosity that Frederick James Furnivall founded the Chaucer Society and that the owners of the Percy Folio Manuscript finally permitted its publication. The most notable English philologists of the succeeding generation were trained in his classroom, and his total influence on the cultural life of the nation was large indeed. His power lay not merely in his learning but in his character. "He had a moral delicacy and richness of heart that I never saw and never expect to see equaled," William James wrote to his brother Henry. It is worth remembering of him, also, that his sense of humor played over every subject that he touched and that he cared as much for roses as for ballads. "The keenest, soundest, most loved of American scholars," as Francis Barton Gummere called him, he was one of the most significant men of his generation in America, and his fame since his death has become legendary.

[G. L. Kittredge, "Francis Jas. Child" in the *Atlantic Mo.*, LXXVIII, 737–42 (1896), reprinted with additions in the *English and Scotch Popular Ballads*, I, xxiv–xxxi (1898); C. E. Norton, "Francis Jas. Child" in *Procs. Am. Acad. Arts and Sciences*, vol. XXXII, reprinted with additions in the *Harvard Grads. Mag.*, VI, 161–69 (1897); Ewald Flügel, "Francis Jas. Child" in *Anglia Beiblatt*, Siebenter Jahrgang, pp. 377–81 (Halle A. S., 1897); S. L. Wolff in *Cam. Hist. Am. Lit.*, IV, 484–85; Morgan Callaway, Jr., in *Univ. of Texas Bull. No. 2538* (Oct. 8, 1925), pp. 31–36; *Boston Evening Transcript*, Sept. 11 (p. 1), 12 (pp. 4, 6, 14), 14 (p. 1), 1896; Barrett Wendell, "During Vacation" in same, Sept. 17, 1896 (p. 6); *A Scholar's Letters to a Young Lady: Passages from the Later Correspondence of Francis Jas. Child* (1920); Gamaliel Bradford, *As God Made Them* (1929); *Quinquennial Cat. Harvard Univ.* (1915); *Nation*, LXIII, 209–10 (1896)—unsigned art. by A. G. Sedgwick; *Critic*, XXIX, 181 (1896)—unsigned art. by J. H. Morse; W. D. Howells, *Literary Friends and Acquaintance* (1900); Henry James, *Notes of a Son and Brother* (1914); *Letters of Jas. Russell Lowell* (1894); *Letters of Chas. Eliot Norton* (1913); *Letters of Horace Howard Furness* (1922); *Letters of Wm. James* (1922).]

G.H.G.

CHILD, FRANK SAMUEL (Mar. 20, 1854–May 4, 1922), Congregational clergyman, author, a son of Henry Horatio and Betsy (Brand) Child, was born in Exeter, N. Y. He studied at Whitestown Seminary, graduated at Hamilton College in 1875, and at Union Theological Seminary, N. Y., three years later. His inheritance from his parents was intellectual rather than one of money, and he was largely dependent on himself for support while in college and seminary. He was ordained in Greenwich, Conn., Feb. 27, 1879, where, on Oct. 21, 1880, he married Elizabeth J. Lilley, and where he was pastor till 1881. After a charge in New Preston, Conn., from 1884 to 1888, he was installed at the First Church in Fairfield, Conn., where he remained till his death, becoming pastor emeritus in 1920. Child was an accomplished student of the life of colonial New England. Perhaps his best known work in this field is *The Colonial Parson of New England* (1896), a study of various clerical types illustrated by the lives of eminent members of the profession. His ability to use his knowledge of the same period is further displayed in the following works of history and fiction: *A Colonial*

Witch (1897); *A Puritan Wooing* (1898); *The House with Sixty Closets* (1899); *An Unknown Patriot* (1899). The ancient town of Fairfield, which was a place of importance in Colonial and Revolutionary times and was burned by the British in 1779, was the especial subject of his study. The following books are the fruitage of this work: *An Old New England Town* (1895); *Fairfield, Ancient and Modern* (1909); *An Old New England Church* (1910); *A Country Parish* (1911). In addition he was the author of many historical pamphlets and often lectured on historical subjects. In person he was tall and thin, dignified and somewhat reserved in bearing, but having a genuineness and sympathy that won respect and confidence. He was an intellectual as well as a spiritual leader in his community, a founder and president of the Fairfield Historical Society and one of the founders of the Public Library. He was a leader in all movements for civic betterment and had large responsibilities in the management of charitable and educational foundations both at home and in other states. Theologically he might be classed with the center party of his denomination, but he held his beliefs with tolerance and open-mindedness and in practise knew no denominational lines.

[Elias Child, *Genealogy Child, Childs and Childe Families* (1881); *Who's Who in America*, 1922–23; *Congregational Year Book for 1922*; *Hamilton College Necrology* for 1923; *Congregationalist*, June 8, 1922; personal information from Child's daughter and others.]

F.T.P.

CHILD, LYDIA MARIA FRANCIS (Feb. 11, 1802–Oct. 20, 1880), author, abolitionist, was descended from Richard Francis, who settled in Cambridge, Mass., in 1636. Her paternal grandfather, a weaver, fought at Concord in 1775; her father, Convers Francis, a baker, of West Cambridge and Medford, Mass., was a strong character, a reader, and a foe of slavery; her mother, Susannah Rand, had "a spirit busy in doing good." Lydia, youngest of six children, was born in Medford, where she attended the public schools and for one year a seminary; but her chief mental stimulus in youth came from her brother Convers, a Unitarian clergyman and later a professor in the Harvard Divinity School. As an author she was precocious, publishing two popular novels in 1824 and 1825—*Hobomok*, on early Salem and Plymouth, and *The Rebels, or, Boston before the Revolution*. From 1825 to 1828 she had a private school in Watertown, Mass., and in 1826 started *Juvenile Miscellany*, a bi-monthly magazine. She married David Lee Child [*q.v.*], a Boston lawyer, in October 1828. They soon joined the abolitionists, and in 1833 Mrs. Child threw a bomb into the pro-slavery camps North and South, with *An Appeal in Favor of That Class of Americans Called Africans.* The little book made many converts; Channing, Sumner, Higginson, and other prominent opponents of slavery, acknowledged its influence on them then or later. It also aroused intense hostility: the sale of Mrs. Child's other books fell off badly, and *Juvenile Miscellany* died in 1834; the Boston Athenæum cancelled her free membership. But she kept on undaunted, attacking slavery in work after work, and attending tumultuous abolition meetings; in old age she remembered "collaring and pulling away a man who was shaking his fist in Mr. Phillips's face at a Music Hall mob—and her surprise when he tumbled down." From 1841 to 1849 she, with for a time the assistance of her husband, edited the *National Anti-Slavery Standard,* a New York weekly newspaper. In 1852 they retired to a small farm she had inherited in Weyland, Mass., henceforth their home. Their interest in public affairs remained as keen as ever: out of a modest income they gave liberally to the anti-slavery cause; and when John Brown lay wounded and in prison, after Harper's Ferry, Mrs. Child asked the governor for permission to come to Virginia and nurse him. The ensuing correspondence, including a fiery letter from a Southern lady, Mrs. Mason, and a calm survey of slavery by Mrs. Child, was published in 1860 in pamphlet form as *Correspondence between Lydia Maria Child and Gov. Wise and Mrs. Mason of Virginia,* and reached a circulation of 300,000 copies. During the Civil War she was dissatisfied because the abolition of slavery was not made the prime issue, and even the Emancipation Proclamation disappointed her as "merely a war measure"; but after Lincoln's reëlection she wrote, "I have constantly gone on liking him better and better." Her later life was uneventful; she survived her husband six years, remaining intellectually alert to the end.

Mrs. Child had a wholesome diversity of interests, best shown by her vivacious private correspondence and by her *Letters from New York* (2 vols., 1843, 1845). "My natural inclinations," she said, "drew me much more strongly toward literature and the arts than toward reform." Beauty remained a life-long passion; "I hang prisms in my windows," she wrote in old age, "to fill the room with rainbows." Her early novels, however, show a strong didactic bent; and *The First Settlers of New England* (1829), written before she became an abolitionist, contains the germs of her later ideas. At all events American literature lost little by her interest in reforms, for her creative gift was not great. Her

stories and poems for children are notable only as pioneer work; some of her tales and sketches for adult readers have fanciful beauty or realistic force, but all lack the final touch; and even her later novels (*Philothea,* 1836, on the Age of Pericles; *A Romance of the Republic,* 1867, on slavery and the Civil War) are weak in structure and character-drawing. Mysticism and rationalism, which ran parallel in her nature, early freed her from accepted creeds. Although she never went wholly over into spiritualism, she believed in second sight and saw a profound dualism in all things. Her *Progress of Religious Ideas through Successive Ages* (3 vols., 1855) lacks a basis of adequate scholarship, but was for its time a remarkable attempt to see Christianity in its relation to other religions. Her practical books show great good sense and some advanced ideas. *The Frugal Housewife* (1829), packed with useful information and shrewd hints to thrift, seems the work of a female Franklin; it went to a twentieth edition in seven years. *The Mother's Book* (1831) urged that parents frankly instruct their children on "delicate subjects." Mrs. Child's writings on slavery are compounds of emotional idealism, cool logic, historical and economical truth, and anthropological error. She assumes that negroes and whites differ merely in "complexion," and infers an ancient negro civilization from Homer's reference to "the blameless Ethiopians." *The Freedmen's Book* (1865) abounds in hopeful counsels of perfection, including a daily cold tub and rub. The *Appeal* sometimes pictures appalling cruelties without names of witnesses or details of time and place, and the chapter on the slave trade is irrelevant in a discussion of domestic slavery as it then was; yet the style is strong, the tone calm, and the arguments against the moral and economic evils of slavery unanswerable. The crushing reply to Mrs. Mason avoids the faults of the *Appeal,* and is drawn largely from the laws of the Southern states. *The Right Way the Safe Way* (1860) is a solid piece of work, based on detailed knowledge of emancipation in the British West Indies. The best parts of Mrs. Child's writings on slavery make credible Whittier's statement: "She was wise in counsel; and men like Charles Sumner, Henry Wilson, Salmon P. Chase, and Gov. Andrew availed themselves of her foresight and sound judgment of men and measures."

[The chief sources of information about Mrs. Child are the following: Elias Child, *Geneal. Child, Childs and Childe Families* (1881); *Letters of Lydia Maria Child* (1883), with a biographical introduction by John G. Whittier, Wendell Phillips's remarks at her funeral, a portrait of her at sixty-three, and a list of her works; *Letters from N. Y.* (2 vols., 1843, 1845); a biographical sketch by T. W. Higginson in *Contemporaries* (1899).

reprinted with a few changes from *Eminent Women of the Age* (1869); T. W. Higginson, *Cheerful Yesterdays* (1898) and *Letters and Journals* (1921); G. T. Curtis, "Reminiscences of N. P. Willis and Lydia Maria Child," in *Harper's Mag.*, Oct. 1890. Estimates of her work and personality may be found in the *Atlantic Mo.*, Dec. 1882, and the *N. Y. Nation*, Jan. 25, 1883. Her more important works, in addition to those named above, are the following: *Biogs. of Lady Russell and Madame Guion* (1832); *Biogs. of Madame de Staël and Madame Roland* (1832); *Good Wives* (1833); *Hist. of the Condition of Women in Various Ages and Nations* (2 vols., 1835); *The Oasis* (1834), an anti-slavery miscellany; *Authentic Anecdotes of Am. Slavery* (1835); *The Evils of Slavery and the Cure of Slavery* (1836), in part a compilation of statements by Southerners; *Fact and Fiction* (1846), containing her best story, "The Children of Mount Ida"; *Isaac T. Hopper* (1853), life of a Quaker Abolitionist; *Autumnal Leaves; Tales and Sketches in Prose and Rhyme* (1857); *Aspirations of the World* (1878), selections from the religious books of the world, with introduction by Mrs. Child.]

W.C.B.

CHILDE, JOHN (Aug. 30, 1802–Feb. 2, 1858), pioneer civil engineer, was born in West Boylston, Mass., one of the twelve children of Zachariah and Lydia (Bigelow) Child. During his boyhood he worked upon his father's farm, with only such educational advantages as those of the district school, except for two years which he spent with an older brother in Canada and one year at Georgetown College, D. C. He was, however, an exceptionally studious boy, and in 1823 he entered West Point Academy, from which he was graduated in 1827 with the commission of second lieutenant. In 1835 he resigned from the army to enter the profession of civil engineering, and from that time on was actively engaged in survey, location, construction, and consulting work in connection with the establishment of new railroad lines. One of his earliest and most difficult tasks was the location of the route for the Albany & West Stockbridge Railroad between Springfield and Pittsfield across the Green Mountain Range. Theretofore no attempt had been made in the United States to run a line through a district with such formidable obstacles. Childe entered upon his work with the greatest professional enthusiasm, and to the amazement of layman and engineer alike, accomplished it most satisfactorily. This achievement, in 1844, resulted in a constant demand for his services by one railroad or another. His connection with the Southern lines began in 1848 when he became chief engineer of the Mobile Railroad Company. The road to be built was from Mobile to the mouth of the Ohio River, about 500 miles. It was the longest that had been attempted in the United States at that time. Running across four states, through a region where railroads were unknown, many difficulties were anticipated—and found. Childe not only superintended the field workers but he, in order to obtain subscriptions for stock,

canvassed the whole country through which the line was to run; through his efforts at Washington, Congress passed in its session of 1849–50 the first of a series of acts donating about one million acres of land to aid the company; he visited the legislatures of the various states and obtained valuable privileges from them for the road. He even made two trips to England to dispose of large issues of bonds. Owing to a change of directors in 1856, his professional connection with this work terminated in that year, and when in 1857 the Board of Harbor Commissioners was established for constructing an extensive harbor at Montreal, Canada, Childe was placed at the head of a corps of engineers to make the necessary examination and report. While occupied in arranging the large amount of statistical data for this report, he was taken seriously ill and died at his home in Springfield, Mass. Childe's character, enormous capacity for work, his unusual executive ability, and his genius for solving difficult railroad problems made him an outstanding figure of his time. Of fearless independence and absolute honesty, his decisions were respected alike by employer and employee. He was married in 1832 to Laura Dwight of Springfield, Mass. She and their oldest daughter were lost on board the fated *Arctic* in 1854 while returning from Europe. In 1856 Childe was married to Ellen W. Healy of Boston, Mass., who survived him.

[Chas. B. Stuart, *Biog. Sketch of John Childe* (1861), later included in *Lives and Works of Civil and Military Engineers of America* (1871); editorial in *Springfield Republican*, Feb. 3, 1858.] K.W.C.

CHILDS, CEPHAS GRIER (Sept. 8, 1793–July 7, 1871), engraver, editor, publisher, was one of the pioneers in establishing lithography on a commercial basis in the United States. Born in Plumstead Township, Bucks County, Pa., the son of a farmer, Cephas Childs, and his wife, Agnes Grier, at an early age he lost both his parents. He was placed with a wholesale grocer in Philadelphia, and in 1812 was apprenticed to Gideon Fairman, an eminent engraver in the same city. The following year he enlisted in the Washington Guards, a Philadelphia military organization, and served during the remainder of the War of 1812. For the next twenty years he was prominently identified with military organizations in Philadelphia, and in 1834 was commissioned colonel of the 128th Regiment of Pennsylvania Militia. At the same time he was becoming widely known as an engraver, publisher, and lithographer. Between 1827 and 1830 he engraved and published *Childs's Views in Philadelphia*. In 1829 he became a founder of the lithographic establishment of Pendleton, Kearny &

Childs, Philadelphia, and the following year formed a partnership with Henry Inman, a portrait painter, for the production of lithographs. During a visit to Europe in 1831 in the interest of this business, he suffered an accident on shipboard the results of which forced him to discontinue his engraving. On his return from Europe in 1832 he took renewed interest in his lithograph house, which continued as Childs & Inman until 1833, when with George Lehman the firm became Childs & Lehman. In 1832 Childs became an editor of the *Commercial Herald,* Philadelphia, and, when this was merged with the *North American* in 1840, he became the commercial editor. With Walter Colton he purchased the *North American,* in 1842, but sold his interest in 1845. He was proprietor and editor of the *Commercial List and Philadelphia Price Current,* from 1835 to 1852, and did not retire from the commercial editorship of the *North American* until 1847. He was president of the New Creek Coal Company from 1855 to 1864, with the exception of a short interval in 1858–59. From 1839 to 1851 he was secretary of the board of directors of the Philadelphia Board of Trade, of which body he was a charter member. He also was a director of the Bank of Northern Liberties and of the Pennsylvania Academy of the Fine Arts, to which he bequeathed several important paintings by American artists. Childs began business on his own account as an engraver in 1818, and first exhibited his work in the Academy of the Fine Arts in 1824. Three plates for the American edition of *Rees's Cyclopædia* were engraved by Childs, several subjects being assigned to a plate.

[*Phila. Ledger,* July 10, 1871 ; Eugene Munday's "The Press of Phila. in 1870" in the *Proof-Sheet,* Phila., May 1870 ; a manuscript "Hist. of Lithography in Phila.," by the writer; and facts furnished by a relative of Childs.]   J. J.

CHILDS, GEORGE WILLIAM (May 12, 1829–Feb. 3, 1894), publisher, philanthropist, was born in Baltimore, the unacknowledged child of a father belonging to a prominent family of that city. His early years are hidden in mystery save for the few statements he and his biographers have made. At the age of thirteen he entered the United States Navy, and passed fifteen months at Norfolk (*Recollections by George W. Childs,* 1890, p. 10). When not quite fifteen he went to Philadelphia and worked in a stationery and book-store. In 1848 he started a confectionery business there, under the firm name of George W. Childs & Company but after a few months parted with the store and sold toilet preparations in a small shop in the Ledger Building. In July 1849 he became connected with the book-selling business of R. E. Peterson, who was a silent partner in a firm then dissolved, and who, having been accused of being an infidel, thought it policy to place the business in his clerk's name. In 1853 the firm became R. E. Peterson & Company and undertook Dr. Samuel Austin Allibone's *Critical Dictionary of English Literature.* In November 1854, the name was changed to Childs & Peterson, whose first great success was Dr. Elisha Kent Kane's *Arctic Explorations* (1856). Dr. Kane received royalties amounting to $70,000. Childs prevailed upon the author to make his narrative popular rather than scientific, and it owed "a great part of its success to Mr. Childs's skill in engineering and obtaining medals and resolutions complimentary to Dr. Kane from the legislatures of various states, and especially to his labor in Washington" (*Review, post,* p. 9). The death of Dr. Kane in Cuba the following year was seized upon by the enterprising publisher to keep alive the book's interest, and the body of the explorer was brought back with ceremonies and processions in every city through which it was carried. Upon the dissolution of the firm of Childs & Peterson, in 1860, Childs became a member of that of J. B. Lippincott & Company which took over and completed Allibone's *Dictionary.* A year or so later he retired from that house and began the publication of several books connected with the war then in progress. In January 1863 he took the Philadelphia agency of the Wheeler & Wilson sewing machine, while still continuing the publishing business, and in May of that year founded the *American Publishers' Circular and Literary Gazette,* edited by R. Shelton Mackenzie. This publication he continued until 1870. His greatest success and the foundation of his fortune had to do with the *Public Ledger,* Philadelphia, which newspaper he bought in December 1864, his partners in the enterprise being Anthony J. and Francis A. Drexel, of the banking house of Drexel & Company. When the newspaper was purchased it was losing $3,000 a week. Within a very short time after coming under the proprietorship of Childs, its circulation increased enormously. It reached 90,000 copies a day in 1876, and spread the fame of its proprietor and editor, owing to its high standard of accuracy, decency, and enterprise. Childs was the author of *Recollections of General Grant* (1885) and *Recollections by George W. Childs* (1890). He gave the Shakespeare Memorial Fountain, in Stratford-upon-Avon, 1887; a memorial window to the poets Herbert and Cowper, in Westminster Abbey, 1876; a memorial window to Milton, in St. Margaret's Church, Westminster, 1888; the reredos in St. Thomas's Church, Winchester, as a memorial to Bishop Ken, 1889. To the West Point Military Academy, of which he was a member of the board of visitors, he presented the portraits of Generals Grant, Sherman, and Sheridan. He gave his valuable collection of manuscripts to the Drexel Institute, Philadelphia. From 1870, when his mansion was opened, until his death in 1894, he entertained many distinguished visitors to Philadelphia, including the Emperor Dom Pedro of Brazil, the Duke of Veragua, and President Grant. His remains are in a mausoleum in Laurel Hill Cemetery, Philadelphia. He was married to Emma Bouvier Peterson, daughter of his former partner, Robert E. Peterson.

[For the early career of Childs the anonymous and suppressed pamphlet, *A Review*, etc., understood to have been issued by his father-in-law R. E. Peterson about 1873 is most useful. His own *Recollections* is authority for his later history. The personal knowledge of the writer has supplied the facts both have omitted. See also Jas. Parton, *Geo. W. Childs, A Biog. Sketch* (1870); J. W. Forney, "Anecdotes of Public Men, No. C," *Public Ledger* (Phila.), supplement, Mar. 1, 1873; Frederick Hudson, *Journalism in the U. S. from 1690 to 1872* (1872); *Every Saturday*, Sept. 10, 1870; *Critic*, Feb. 10, 1894; Talcott Williams in *Am. Rev. of Revs.*, Mar. 1894; E. J. Edwards in the *Chautauquan*, Apr. 1894. Obituaries appeared in newspapers all over the world, Feb. 4, 1894.]   J.J.

CHILDS, THOMAS (1796–Oct. 8, 1853), soldier, was born at Pittsfield, Mass., the son of Dr. Timothy and Rachael (Easton) Childs. He was appointed to the United States Military Academy in 1813. Graduated and promoted in the army to third lieutenant of artillery, Mar. 11, 1814, he served in the Niagara campaign of that year. For spiking the enemy's guns in the successful sortie that raised the siege of Fort Erie (Sept. 17, 1814) he was presented with a captured British quadrant "by order of the President." After the war Childs settled into the routine life of an officer in the regular army, becoming in due course first lieutenant (1818) and captain (1826). On Jan. 5, 1819, he married Ann Eliza Coryton, of Alexandria, Va., by whom he had nine children. In order to restore the interrupted communication between the military posts in the second Seminole War, he planned the successful attack on Fort Drane (Aug. 21, 1836), for which he was brevetted major. He was later brevetted lieutenant-colonel "for gallant conduct and repeated successes" in the Florida War. In the Mexican War he was brevetted colonel for his conduct in the battles of Palo Alto and Resaca de la Palma. Ordered by Gen. Worth to take Loma de Independencia, which towered seven or eight hundred feet above the Bishop's Palace at Monterey, Childs led six companies of artillery and infantry and 200

Texas riflemen, up the rocky, chaparral-covered hillside. The almost vertical ascent was begun at 3 A. M. (Sept. 22, 1846) in the midst of a torrential rain, and by daybreak Childs was within 100 yards of the breastwork of sandbags, a position considered impregnable by the Mexican generals. The Mexican battery was stormed and Worth's troops enabled to capture the western gate of the city. In the following year, Childs, with a strong garrison, was stationed at Jalapa as military governor (April to June 1847) by Gen. Scott, with orders to keep open as long as possible the line of communication with Vera Cruz. With Scott's advance on Mexico City Childs was called to Puebla, where he was besieged by Santa Anna. In the siege "the chief element of the defence was the large, robust, fine-featured Childs" (Smith, *post*, II, 174). For his defense of Puebla he was brevetted brigadier-general (1847). There were some complaints of his administration as civil and military governor of Puebla (September–October 1847), but the Bishop of Puebla admitted that Childs did everything he could to prevent abuses. Childs was in command of military operations in East Florida from 1852 until his death from yellow fever at Fort Brooke, Fla.

[*Senate Doc. No. 1* and *House Ex. Doc. No. 4, 29 Cong. 2 Sess.*; *Senate Ex. Doc. No. 1* and *House Ex. Doc. No. 8* and *No. 60, 30 Cong. 1 Sess.*; *Hist. Mag.*, Nov., Dec. 1873, Jan., Mar. 1874, Apr. 1875; G. W. Cullum, *Biog. Reg.* (3rd ed. 1891); J. T. Sprague, *Origin, Progress and Conclusion of the Fla. War* (1848); Justin H. Smith, *The War with Mexico* (1919); S. C. Reid, *Scouting Expeditions of McCulloch's Texas Rangers* (1847); A. G. Brackett, *Gen. Lane's Brigade in Central Mexico* (1854); *Memoirs of Lt.-Gen. Scott* (1864); E. Child, *Geneal. Child, Childs and Childe Families* (1881); *Daily National Intelligencer* (Washington, D. C.), Oct. 26, 1853; information from Mrs. Walter C. White, Sumter, S. C.]   F.E.R.

CHILTON, WILLIAM PARIS (Aug. 10, 1810–Jan. 20, 1871), jurist, was descended from an English family of that name which settled upon the Potomac River about 1650. His father, Thomas John Chilton, a Baptist minister of some note, married Margaret, sister of Jesse Bledsoe, a Kentucky jurist, and William was born near Elizabethtown, Adair County, Ky. His parents died while he was a child, and little is known of his early life beyond the fact that he was brought up by a maternal relative. His education was scanty; nevertheless at the age of seventeen he was earning his living by teaching. In 1828 he went to Nashville, Tenn., where he studied law for three years, and in 1831 removed to Alabama. After some preliminary prospecting he opened a law office at Mardisville, Talladega County, and finally settled at Talladega, the county seat. In 1839 he was elected as Whig representative of his county in the state legislature, where he established a reputation for ability out of the ordinary, and was regarded as a rising force in politics. In the presidential campaigns of 1840 and 1844 he was much to the fore, addressing meetings in all parts of the state on behalf of Harrison and Clay, and in 1843 was an unsuccessful candidate for Congress. In 1846 he removed to Tuskegee, Ala., where he established and conducted a law school, also continuing in practise till his election by the state legislature to the position of judge of the supreme court of Alabama, Dec. 31, 1847. This action of the legislature was a signal testimony to his standing in the community, since he was a strong Whig and its membership was predominantly Democratic. He was chief justice from Dec. 2, 1852, until Jan. 2, 1856, when he retired, and resumed practise. In 1859 he was elected as state senator for Macon County. He considered secession unwise but when the step became inevitable he resigned, and, having taken up his residence in Montgomery, was elected to represent that district in the provisional Confederate Congress. Secession having become a *fait accompli* he threw himself with vigor into the contest, and was an influential member of both regular Confederate Congresses. He acted on important committees and his energy was such that it earned for him the reputation of being "the most laborious member" of the Southern legislative body. The fall of the Confederacy left him in poor financial circumstances, but engaging in law practise he to a large extent retrieved his losses before his death at Montgomery, Jan. 20, 1871. He was twice married: first to Mary Catherine, daughter of George Morgan of Nashville, Tenn., and later to Elvira Frances Morgan, his deceased wife's sister.

A contemporary says of him: "Justice Chilton was of a rather robust figure with well-formed features and a grave but cheerful manner. A profound lawyer and a dignified and impartial judge—distinguished by pure unselfish patriotism, an incorruptible integrity and a capacity and willingness to work which seemed inexhaustible" (W. Brewer, *post*). Fluent in speech, attractive in manner, and possessed of an imposing platform appearance—being over six feet in height—he was a favorite speaker at public meetings, and in the legislature had the reputation of being the ablest debater of his period.

[W. Brewer, *Ala.: Her Hist., Resources, War Record and Public Men* (1872), p. 471; Wm. Garrett, *Reminiscences of Pub. Men in Ala.* (1872); *Memorial Record of Ala.* (1893), II, 641; B. F. Riley, *Makers and Romance of Ala. Hist.* (n. d.); *Centenary Sketches of Wm. P. Chilton* (privately printed, 1910), by C. L. Chilton, his son.]   H. W. H. K.

CHINI, EUSEBIO FRANCISCO. [See KINO, EUSEBIO FRANCISCO, 1645–1711.]

CHIPMAN, DANIEL (Oct. 22, 1765–Apr. 23, 1850), lawyer, author, was descended from John Chipman of Dorchester, England, who came to Boston on the *Friendship*, July 14, 1631, and settled at Barnstable, Mass. John's great-grandson, Samuel Chipman, a farmer and blacksmith of Salisbury, Conn., married Hannah, daughter of Dr. Nathaniel Austin of Suffield, Conn., and their seventh son, Daniel, was born at Salisbury. Daniel's early education was received at home and after his father's removal to Tinmouth, Vt., he studied under his elder brother Nathaniel, assisting also in the farm work. In 1784 he entered Dartmouth College and graduated in 1788. He then took up the study of law in his brother's office at Rutland, and was admitted to the bar of Rutland County in 1790. He first opened an office in Rutland and was a delegate from that place to the state constitutional convention in 1793, but in 1794 moved to Middlebury, where he practised law for twenty-five years. In 1796 he marred Eleutheria, daughter of Rev. Samuel Hedge, of Warwick, Mass., and the following year became state attorney for Addison County, a position which he continued to occupy till 1817. He had, at an early age, taken an active interest in politics, and in 1798 was elected to represent Middlebury in the General Assembly, being reëlected almost continuously till 1808. In that year he was elected to the governor's council and remained a member thereof for seven years, being speaker of the legislature in 1813 and 1814. In 1814 he was elected a representative in Congress, but after serving one session was compelled to resign owing to protracted illness. On regaining his health in 1818 he was once more elected to the Assembly for Middlebury, serving for the sessions of 1818 and 1821. In the latter year he terminated his long connection with the Vermont legislature. He had, in addition to his legal and political engagements, been professor of law at Middlebury College from 1806 till 1816, and on his retirement from active politics devoted part of his time to writing *An Essay on the Law of Contracts for the Payment of Specifick Articles,* which was published in 1822. In 1823 he was appointed by the legislature the first reporter of the supreme court of Vermont, and prepared volume I of *Reports of Cases Argued and Determined in the Supreme Court of . . . Vermont,* covering the years 1789–1824, which was issued in 1824. Another attack of serious illness compelled him to resign, and in 1829 he retired to Ripton, where he was able to give free rein to his literary proclivities. On two occasions, however, he emerged from his retirement, being a delegate to the state constitutional conventions of 1843 and 1850. His matured judgment had always carried weight with all parties in Vermont, and he exercised great influence in the five constitutional conventions which he attended. It was at his suggestion that the legislature was divided into a House of Representatives and a Senate. During his last years three valuable biographical works came from his pen: *The Life of Hon. Nathaniel Chipman, formerly Member of the U. S. Senate and Chief Justice of the State of Vermont, with Selections from his Miscellaneous Papers* (1846); *The Life of Colonel Seth Warner, with an Account of the Controversy between New York and Vermont from 1763 to 1775* (1848); *A Memoir of Thomas Chittenden, the First Governor of Vermont, with a History of the Constitution during his Administration* (1849). While attending the constitutional convention of 1850, he collapsed, and was taken to his home at Ripton where he died.

[*Vt. Hist. Gazetteer* (1868), I, p. 87; Bert Lee Chipman, *Chipman Family: Geneal. Chipmans in America 1631–1920* (1920).]   H. W. H. K.

CHIPMAN, NATHANIEL (Nov. 15, 1752–Feb. 15, 1843), jurist, the son of Samuel and Hannah (Austin) Chipman, was born at Salisbury, Conn. He was fourth in descent from John and Hope (Howland) Chipman, who settled in Barnstable, Mass., in 1631. In 1773, after nine months of preparation under a local minister, he entered Yale College, where he received his degree (in absentia) in 1777. That spring he received an ensign's commission in Col. Charles Webb's Second Connecticut Continental Line. After some eighteen months of service, including the winter at Valley Forge where he was promoted to a first lieutenancy, he resigned. In March 1779 he was admitted to the bar in Litchfield County, Conn., but went immediately to Vermont, where his father had settled at Tinmouth. In June, he was admitted to the bar of Rutland County, Vt., and began the practise of law. Two years later, when the Vermont leaders—Thomas Chittenden [*q.v.*] and others—were involved in secret negotiations with Gen. Haldimand, and rumor was current regarding their treason, Chipman was called into conference with them, regarding certain letters, which the legislature demanded be read in session. It is said that Chipman expurgated the letters in such a manner that the legislators were satisfied that the negotiations were not treasonable (Daniel Chipman, *post*, pp. 37–38). In 1784, he was a member of the legislature, and was appointed to a committee to revise certain acts. Three years

later, his legal capacity won him an appointment as assistant justice of the supreme court of Vermont—the first lawyer to sit on that bench.

When the ratification of the Federal Constitution was being considered by the various states in 1788, Chipman, who was anxious to see Vermont admitted to the Union, took up the matter with Alexander Hamilton and exchanged several letters with him. In 1789 he was appointed to the Boundary Commission, whose agreement brought about a settlement of the dispute between New York and Vermont in 1790. At this same time he became chief justice of the supreme court of Vermont. When the constitutional convention met at Bennington in January 1791, he took a prominent part in its actions, and his influence was instrumental in securing ratification. He was sent, with Lewis R. Morris, to Congress to negotiate for the admittance of Vermont to the Union. Their efforts were successful, and the State was soon admitted.

Within a short time he was appointed judge of the United States court in the district of Vermont, an office he held only two years. In 1793 he resigned and took up his private practise, publishing in that year his *Sketches of the Principles of Government* (revised edition, 1833), and his *Reports and Dissertations*, consisting mainly of reports of cases before the supreme court of Vermont. In 1796, he again became chief justice of the supreme court. At the same time he was made a member of a committee to revise the state code, and the statutes of 1797 were almost entirely his work. In 1798 he was elected to the United States Senate, where he served six years. His work there was not of a spectacular nature, but his judicial mind, with its legal background, proved a valuable asset in Senate affairs. Upon the expiration of his term, he returned to private practise in Tinmouth, but was soon sent to the legislature, representing the town in 1806–09, and in 1811. In March 1813 he became one of the Council of Censors, a committee of thirteen, having power to examine the constitution of the state and institute revision of it. In this same year he was again appointed chief justice. In 1816, he succeeded his brother, Daniel, as professor of law in Middlebury College, where he delivered a series of lectures (printed in part in Daniel Chipman's *Life*) during the ensuing collegiate year. Owing to serious deafness he never returned to public life, but spent the remainder of his days in Tinmouth, where he died Feb. 15, 1843. A large monument, erected there in 1873, commemorates his service to the state. He was married, in 1781, to Sarah Hill, of Tinmouth, who bore him nine children.

He was a thorough student of the law. His heritage of a good mind, his careful training in the classics, and his keen interest in the political affairs of his time made him one of the ablest men of his day in Vermont. In politics he was a Federalist, of the school of Hamilton.

[Daniel Chipman, *Life of the Hon. Nathaniel Chipman* (1846), which is essentially accurate and well written; *Vt. Hist. Soc. Colls.* (2 vols., 1870–71) ; F. B. Dexter, *Biog. Sketches Grads. Yale College,* III (1903), 660–64; *Vt. Hist. Gazetteer* (1877), III, 1154–60; B. L. Chipman, *Chipman Family: Geneal. Chipmans in America* (1920).]   G. H. D.

CHIPMAN, WARD (July 30, 1754–Feb. 9, 1824), Loyalist, the son of John Chipman, a lawyer of Essex County, and Elizabeth (Brown) Chipman, was born in Marblehead, Mass. (*Vital Records of Marblehead, Mass.,* I, 102). He graduated from Harvard with the degree of M.A. in 1770 and, after serving for a short time as preceptor of the free school at Roxbury, studied law under Daniel Leonard and Jonathan Sewall in Boston. He was one of the signers of a loyal address to Gov. Gage on Oct. 14, 1775, and upon the evacuation of Boston in March 1776 removed to Halifax with the British army (Stark, *post,* pp. 132, 133). From there he went to England where he was granted a pension but, dissatisfied with a life of inactivity, he resigned it and returned to America in 1777. He joined his friend Edward Winslow, muster-master general, at New York, and was appointed deputy muster-master general, an office which he held for the duration of the war. Upon the conclusion of peace, Winslow removed to Nova Scotia, but Chipman remained at New York as secretary of a commission to receive claims for supplies furnished to the British government. He was one of the signers of a petition to the commander-in-chief, asking for a grant of lands in Nova Scotia, but later dissociated himself from this enterprise and wrote to Winslow to provide for him "a very romantic, grand-water-river-falls-lake-prospect with a good cold spring of water" (*Winslow Papers,* p. 115). Chipman left New York for England with Sir Guy Carleton on Dec. 4, 1783. Winslow favored a separate government for that part of Nova Scotia lying north and west of the Bay of Fundy and in England Chipman did what he could to bring this about. The province of New Brunswick was set off from Nova Scotia in 1784, and Chipman applied for the office of attorney-general in the new government. He failed to receive it but was appointed solicitor-general, an office which he held for many years without pay because he had retained the half-pay of £91 *per annum* of deputy muster-master general. Chipman sailed from England in August 1784,

and took up his residence at St. John, New Brunswick, where he resumed the practise of law. He was elected to the first House of Assembly of New Brunswick for St. John in 1785, and to the second, for Northumberland County, in 1793. He again represented St. John in the fourth legislature, which met in 1802. He was appointed a member of the Council in 1806, and a judge of the supreme court of New Brunswick in 1809. The treaty of 1794 between Great Britain and the United States provided for a commission to locate the St. Croix River, and Chipman served as agent of the Crown. The treaty of 1814 provided for a commission to determine points between the source of the St. Croix and the point of intersection of the St. Lawrence and the forty-fifth parallel, and Chipman again served as agent of Great Britain. Upon the death of Lieutenant-Governor Smyth in 1823, Chipman succeeded as president and commander-in-chief of the province of New Brunswick, an office which he held at the time of his death. He was married, at St. John on Oct. 24, 1786, to Elizabeth, daughter of William Hazen, a fellow Loyalist. An only son, Ward Chipman, Jr., became chief justice of the supreme court of New Brunswick.

[Lorenzo Sabine, *Biog. Sketches Loyalists of the Am. Revolution* (2 vols., 1864) ; Jas. H. Stark, *Loyalists of Mass.* (1910) ; Bert Lee Chipman, *Chipman Family* (1920) ; Jos. Wilson Lawrence, *Judges of New Brunswick* (1907) ; *Winslow Papers, 1776–1826* (1901), ed. by W. O. Raymond.]   I. M. C.

CHISHOLM, HUGH JOSEPH (May 2, 1847–July 8, 1912), paper manufacturer, was born on the Canadian side of Niagara Falls, the son of Alexander Chisholm, who had come from Scotland as a boy, and his wife, Mary (Phelan) Chisholm. Young Chisholm's education at the local schools terminated with the death of his father, and at the age of thirteen he commenced his business career as a newsboy on the Grand Trunk Railway. His unusual industry and thrift enabled him by the time he was sixteen to secure control of newspaper distribution along the whole Grand Trunk system, and in partnership with his brothers, he was a pioneer, if not the originator, in this country "of the transportation publishing business, producing railroad maps, tourists' guides and albums descriptive of routes of travel" (*Paper,* July 10, 1912, p. 30). In 1865 he moved his residence to Portland, Me., and in 1872 married Henrietta Mason of that city. Shortly after his arrival in Portland he became interested in the manufacture of pulp, and this industry in connection with his railway news business drew his attention to the manufacture of paper. He organized the Somerset Fibre Company, in 1881 the Umbagog Pulp Company at Livermore Falls on the Androscoggin River, and in 1887 the Otis Falls Pulp Company on the Androscoggin. In the early eighties he became convinced that the upper reaches of this river offered unlimited water power and excellent advantages for the manufacture of paper. With a group of associates he purchased an eleven-hundred-acre tract, founded the Rumford Falls Power Company (1890), and then, to provide an outlet, took over the moribund Rumford Falls & Buckfield Railroad, which he speedily rehabilitated and opened to traffic as the Portland & Rumford Falls Railway in 1892. Thus were laid the foundations of a town, which by that year had a population of three thousand and all of the features of an up-to-date industrial community. On the site of the new town were established the Rumford Falls Paper Company, the Oxford Paper Company, the Continental Paper Company, and other concerns which Chisholm organized or in which he was heavily interested.

As a prominent figure in the paper industry of the late nineties he took an important part in the formation in 1898 of the International Paper Company, a combination which controlled about thirty of the leading Eastern newspaper and pulp mills as well as large areas of forest land. Shortly after its organization he became president, holding that office from 1899 to 1910 and serving as chairman of the board of directors, 1907–09. In addition to his interests in paper manufacture and railroads, he was a director of banks, power companies, and many other concerns.

Chisholm not only had the ability to create communities, but he was desirous that his mill villages should be decent places in which to live. In the neighborhoood of one of his plants at Strathglass Park, near Portland, Me., he established a community of model houses for his employees, and at Rumford Falls he was instrumental in founding Rumford Mechanics' Institute, a center dedicated, Nov. 9, 1911, to "physical and mental development, social and moral improvement and the cultivation of an equality or more intimate relationship and acquaintanceship between employed and employer" (*Paper*, Nov. 15, 1911). The extent of his interests led him to move to New York City, which was his headquarters for a number of years prior to his death.

[In addition to references above see *N. Y. State's Prominent and Progressive Men* (1900), ed. by Mitchell C. Harrison, I, 67–69; *Men of America* (1908), ed. by John W. Leonard, p. 442; *Men of Progress . . . in the State of Me.* (1897), ed. by P. W. McIntyre and Wm. F. Blanding; *Sun* (N. Y.) and *N. Y. Times*, July 9, 1912; *Who's Who in America*, 1912–13.]   H. U. F.

CHISOLM, ALEXANDER ROBERT (Nov. 19, 1834–Mar. 10, 1910), soldier, financier, was the son of Edward Newfville Chisolm of Beaufort and Chisolm's Island, S. C., who married, Dec. 14, 1831, Mary Elizabeth, daughter of Maj. William Wigg Hazzard of Hazzard's Neck, Port Royal, S. C. His father was the owner of an extensive estate on the coast near Charleston, which had descended to him through four generations from his ancestor, Alexander Chisholm (*sic*), a lowland Scot, who emigrated to Carolina in 1717. Alexander Robert was born at Beaufort, but both parents died while he was still a child, and his youth was passed in New York City under the guardianship of relatives. He studied for a short time at Columbia College but in 1852 returned to South Carolina, and, taking up his residence on Chisolm's Island a short distance from Charleston, assumed charge of the plantations which he had inherited from his father, together with the 250 slaves thereon. When the Civil War became imminent he joined the South Carolina forces, being commissioned lieutenant-colonel by Gov. Pickens, Mar. 2, 1861. Because of his intimate knowledge of the approaches by water to Charleston, he became personal aide to Gen. Beauregard who was in command of the troops in that neighborhood. He was the bearer of the first communication from Beauregard, Mar. 26, to Maj. Robert Anderson, commanding Fort Sumter, relative to the impending evacuation of that post, and, Apr. 11, personally conveyed to Anderson Beauregard's demand for its surrender. The following day he was present when the first gun of the war was discharged— some accounts stating that he personally gave the order to open fire upon the fort. Thenceforth, throughout the war, he remained on Beauregard's personal staff, being actively engaged in the battles of Bull Run, Shiloh, and Drury's Bluff, and in the sieges of Charleston and Petersburg. At Bull Run he was conspicuous by reason of taking part, though a staff officer, in the Black Horse Cavalry charge, and during the battle of Shiloh all Beauregard's orders were transmitted through him. He "was seldom at a loss for resources in an emergency," and at all times he enjoyed the complete confidence and friendship of his chief (Roman, *post*, II, 411). At the close of the war he signed at Greensboro, N. C., on behalf of Gen. Joseph E. Johnston the parole of the latter's troops east of the Mississippi.

On returning to private life, he established a cotton and shipping firm in Charleston in partnership with Maj. Edward Willis, but in 1869 he moved to New York City where he entered into the stock brokerage business, trading as A.

R. Chisolm & Company, and being one of the promoters of the New York Consolidated Stock Exchange. On Apr. 7, 1875, he was married to Helen Margaret, widow of William Irving Graham and daughter of Gen. Richard L. Schieffelin. In March 1877 he founded the *Mining Record,* a weekly paper devoted to the mining resources of the country, with Gen. Thomas Jordan, a former army colleague, as editor, becoming himself co-editor in December 1882. The scope of the paper was subsequently enlarged to cover the financial, railway, and petroleum fields and its name changed to the *Financial and Mining Record,* novel features being the creation of assay and law departments—the latter expressly stated to be "in the interests of the capitalists who are willing to invest their money for the development of the mines." Later Chisolm was the subject of adverse criticism, the suggestion being that his position as proprietor of an ostensibly impartial financial publication was incompatible with that of an active member of the stock exchange, and in July 1890 he disposed of his interest in the *Record* and retired from the editorship. He contributed to *Battles and Leaders of the Civil War* the following articles, "Notes on the Surrender of Fort Sumter" (I, 82), "The Shiloh Battle-Order and the Withdrawal Sunday evening" (I, 606), and "The Failure to Capture Hardee" (IV, 679).

[Family history of W. G. Chisolm, *Chisolm Genealogy* (1914), which also contains (p. 31) a sketch. See also A. Roman, *Military Operations of Gen. Beauregard* (1884), *passim;* S. W. Crawford, *Genesis of the Civil War* (1887); announcements in *Mining Record* and *Financial and Mining Record;* obituaries in *N. Y. Times* and *N. Y. Daily Tribune,* Mar. 11, 1910.] H. W. H. K.

CHISOLM, JOHN JULIAN (Apr. 16, 1830–Nov. 2, 1903), surgeon and oculist, born in Charleston, S. C., was the son of Robert Trail and Harriet Emily Chisolm, and a descendant of Alexander and Janet (Fraser) Chisolm of Inverness, Scotland, who came to South Carolina about 1717. Having received the degree of M.D. at the Medical College of South Carolina (1850), he continued his studies in London and Paris. He returned to Charleston in 1852 and soon demonstrated great skill as a surgeon. He conceived the idea of following the European custom of having gratuitous lectures on medical topics delivered at night for the benefit of all students and covering the school work and lectures of the previous week. The plan was successful and Chisolm was selected to deliver the lectures on surgery. From this system there developed the summer school of medicine (1853), one of the first of its kind. During this period Chisolm conducted a free hospital for slaves. In 1858 he was appointed professor of surgery at his alma mater and is said to have been the youngest professor of surgery in the United States. At the outbreak of the Civil War he received from the Confederacy the first commission issued to a medical officer and attended the wounded at Fort Sumter. He began at once the preparation of his *Manual of Military Surgery* (1861) and was able to present the first copy to the surgeon-general while the battle of Bull Run was being fought. This text, based on the author's experience in Italy in 1859, when he saw many of the wounded from Magenta and Solferino in the hospitals of Milan, became the standard of the Confederate army and appeared in several editions. He was for a time chief surgeon of the military hospital at Richmond and later directed the plant for the manufacture of medicines at Charleston until it was burned by the Union forces under Sherman during the Civil War. After the war he returned to his professorship and was made dean (1865). He spent 1866 in Europe and in 1868 declined the chair of surgery at New Orleans. He removed to Baltimore in 1869, and within a few months a chair of eye and ear surgery was created for him at the University of Maryland. Before the end of the year he was elected dean. He retained active connection with the University until 1895 after which time he was professor emeritus. He declined professorships at the Universities of St. Louis and Louisville. In 1870 he organized the Baltimore Eye and Ear Institute and in 1877 the Presbyterian Eye and Ear Charity Hospital, of which he was chief surgeon. Beginning in 1873 he limited his practise to ophthalmology which he continued until 1898 despite an attack of apoplexy with aphasia in 1894. He was married, first, to his cousin Mary Edings Chisolm at Charleston, Feb. 3, 1852; and, secondly, to Elizabeth Steel, at Petersburg, Va., on Jan. 14, 1894. He died in Petersburg and was buried in Greenmount Cemetery in Baltimore.

Chisolm was a prolific writer (more than a hundred papers), not only of original articles but of résumés of the literature on special surgical topics to which he added his views and experiences. He was among the first to use cocaine in eye surgery and his operative treatment of cataract was well known. He was one of the first users of chloroform anæsthesia. One of the ablest instructors the University of Maryland ever had, he was the recipient of many honors.

[*Va. Medic. Mo.,* Jan. 1879 (including list of publications and portrait); notes on surgical cases with comments, *Charleston Medic. Jour. and Rev.,* May 1857; *Jour. Am. Medic. Assn.,* Nov. 14, 1903, p. xli; *Hospital Bull.,* Baltimore, Mar. 15, 1910, p. 13; Wm. G. Chisolm, *Chisolm Genealogy* (1914). Dates and spellings, given variously in published accounts, have been verified by Wm. G. Chisolm, a nephew.]   E. E. H.

CHISUM, JOHN SIMPSON (Aug. 15, 1824–Dec. 23, 1884), cattleman, was born in Hardeman County, Tenn., the son of Claiborne C. and Lucy (Chisum) Chisum. The family was of Scotch origin. The father's name had been Chisholm, and the altered spelling is said to date from the time of the battle of New Orleans. Claiborne Chisum with his family moved to Texas in 1837. The boy had no advantages and began to work at an early age. He was diligent and determined, and success followed his efforts. He became a contractor and builder and constructed the first court-house in Paris, Tex. For eight years he was the county clerk of Lamar County. In 1854, with a partner, he started in the cattle business in the same county, but three years later moved to Denton County, where he remained until 1863. In that year he drove a herd, estimated at 10,000 head, into Concho County, where he engaged in business with a number of other men on shares. He was one of the first of the Texas cattlemen to shift their operations to the ranges of New Mexico. In the late fall of 1866 he drove a herd up the Pecos to Bosque Grande, about thirty miles north of Roswell, and in the following spring disposed of it to government contractors for the Navajo and Mescalero Apache reservations. He then formed a connection with Charles Goodnight by which for three years he continued to drive cattle from Texas to Bosque Grande, Goodnight contracting for their sale in Colorado and Wyoming. Indian raids were frequent, and later came the depredations of white "rustlers," but in spite of heavy losses in cattle and horses Chisum prospered. In 1873 he made South Spring his home, establishing a ranch there. His herds multiplied; estimates of the number of cattle owned by him at the peak of his prosperity vary from 60,000 to 100,000. It seems certain that he was the largest individual owner in the United States and may well have held the same title for the world.

His part, if any, in the famous Lincoln County War of 1878–79 is a subject of dispute. This war, growing out of alleged thefts of cattle from Chisum and others by employees of Maj. L. G. Murphy, and breaking into savage conflict on the killing (Feb. 12, 1878) of J. H. Tunstall, a friend of Chisum, involved most of the cattleman's partisans. It is denied, however, by Anderson (see below) that either Chisum or any man employed by him participated in any of the acts of violence that followed. Neutrality under the circumstances would have been difficult, and that it was not wholly attained is indicated, in a statement

quoted by Burns, in *The Saga of Billy the Kid,* which asserts the payment by Chisum of $500 to the Kid for his services in the war. The evolution of the Kid into a cattle thief, an indiscriminate killer, and the leader of a gang of desperadoes brought Chisum to the front in the movement to end lawlessness in New Mexico. He was largely instrumental in 1880 in having Pat Garrett elected sheriff, and it was Garrett who a few months later ended the young bandit's career. A popular belief long associated Chisum, in spite of his disclaimer, with the great Chisholm cattle trail, but it is now generally conceded that the trail, which probably he never even saw, takes its name from Jesse Chisholm, a half-breed Cherokee trader and government agent, who was not related to the cattleman.

Chisum was unmarried. He died at Eureka Springs, Ark., leaving an estate valued at about $500,000. For many years he had been known as the "cattle king of America." He was a man adventurous and brave, resolute in purpose and cool in the face of danger, who in the most lawless period of New Mexican history often risked his life. In his community he was, except for the brief period of the ascendancy of the Murphy faction in the time of the Lincoln County war, a dominating influence, and there is no evidence that he used his power for unworthy ends. By his many friends, among whom in his later days he was familiarly known as "Uncle John," and by the community generally, he was regarded as honest, truthful, and public spirited.

[Geo. B. Anderson, ed., *Hist. of New Mexico* (1907); Ralph Emerson Twitchell, *Leading Facts of New Mexican Hist.,* vol. V (1917); Chas. F. Coan, *Hist. of New Mexico* (1925); Walter Noble Burns, *Saga of Billy the Kid* (1926); J. Marvin Hunter, ed., *Trail Drivers of Texas* (2nd ed., 1925), p. 950; *Frontier,* June, Nov., 1925.]   W. J. G—t.

CHITTENDEN, HIRAM MARTIN (Oct. 25, 1858–Oct. 9, 1917), military engineer, historian, was born at Yorkshire, in the Chautauqua Lake region of New York, the son of William F. and Mary Jane (Wheeler) Chittenden. He was a student at Cornell when appointed to West Point from which he graduated with high honors, June 15, 1884, as a second lieutenant of engineers. On Dec. 30, after entering the Engineer School of Application for the usual three years' course, he married Nettie M. Parker of Arcade, N. Y. He was made a first lieutenant on Dec. 31, 1886, and on his graduation was ordered to Omaha as engineer officer of the Department of the Platte. A two years' detail followed (June 1891–March 1893) as assistant to the officer in charge of road construction in Yellowstone National Park. It marked the awakening in him of a deep and abiding interest in the history and the topography of the Great West and a wish to preserve its chief wonderland, unaltered except by new trails and roadways, "as a genuine example of original nature." Out of this experience came his book, *The Yellowstone National Park,* the first edition of which appeared in 1895. Other details took him for a time elsewhere; as a captain (commissioned Oct. 2, 1895) he had charge of improvement work on the Osage and Gasconade Rivers in Missouri, and in the Spanish-American War he served as chief engineer of the 4th Army Corps. But in the spring of 1899 he was back in the Park, this time in full charge of road construction and with an adequate appropriation; and he kept to the task, in spite of other calls, for the seven years necessary to complete the first stage of the work.

During this period he was promoted to the rank of major (Jan. 23, 1904) and was appointed a member of the Federal Commission on Yosemite Park. In the midst of his arduous duties he somehow found time for much writing. Two technical works on reservoir systems had appeared in 1897 and 1898. *The American Fur Trade of the Far West* was published in 1902, *The History of Early Steamboat Navigation on the Missouri River* a year later, and *The Life, Letters and Travels of Father Pierre Jean de Smet* (written in collaboration with Alfred T. Richardson) in 1905. From 1906 to 1908 he was engaged in engineering projects on the Pacific Coast. In the latter year overwork brought on a stroke of partial paralysis, from which he never fully recovered. On Feb. 10, 1910, he was retired, with the rank of brigadier-general, for disability incident to the service. Despite his infirmity, however, he continued his labors both as an author and an engineer. From Sept. 5, 1911, to Oct. 15, 1915, he was president of the Port Commission of Seattle, and under his charge the excellent docking and terminal facilities of that city were planned and constructed. In 1911 he produced *War or Peace,* in 1915 *Flood Control,* and in 1916 *Letters to an Ultra-Pacifist.* Perhaps his last literary labor was given to a thorough revision and considerable expansion of *The Yellowstone National Park,* a new edition of which appeared after his death. He died in Seattle.

Chittenden was a man of the highest character. He had great energies, an exceptional intensity of purpose, and unflagging industry. Despite his somewhat dignified reserve he was genial and companionable. In the field of engineering, wherein his chief interests were the Park, flood control, and the storage of waters, he was known as a "practical idealist"—one whose imagination and vision were guided by a matter-of-fact regard for the attainable with the means at hand. To his work as a historian he brought an eager spirit of inquiry, a critical judgment, and a passion for exactness; and to these were added a rare art of presentation. In his invaluable history of the fur trade he not only recovered from court records, newspapers, letters, and the musty papers of the fur companies the unknown or long-forgotten data of the period but he so vitalized his material that he recreated an era. The work has not escaped criticism for an occasional omission or misplacing of emphasis (as, for instance, in T. M. Marshall's paper, "St. Vrain's Expedition to the Gila in 1826," in *The Pacific Ocean in History,* 1917); but the wonder must remain that in this pioneer venture so few defects have been found. Though later discoveries have greatly augmented the documentation of the era, they have not served to impair the basic excellence of this epochal work.

[*Who's Who in America,* 1916–17; G. W. Cullum, *Biog. Reg.*; obituary by Jas. C. Sanford in *Forty-Ninth Annual Report, Assn. Grads. U. S. Mil. Acad.,* 1918.]

W. J. G—t.

CHITTENDEN, MARTIN (Mar. 12, 1763–Sept. 5, 1840), governor of Vermont, son of Thomas [*q.v.*] and Elizabeth (Meigs) Chittenden, was born at Salisbury, Conn. When he was about five years old his family removed to Vermont and settled at Williston, where he grew to manhood. He was sent to Dartmouth College, receiving his degree in 1789. On Sept. 7, 1790, he was elected to the General Assembly as the representative of the town of Jericho, where he had taken up his residence. For eight years he held this office, and, upon his removal to Williston in 1798, he was immediately elected to the same office from that town. In 1791 he was a delegate from Jericho to the Bennington convention, called to ratify the Federal Constitution; and, in 1793, he attended the constitutional convention held at Windsor. He was clerk of the Chittenden County Court, later an assistant justice, and finally chief judge, an office he resigned upon his election to Congress, as a Representative, in 1803. He was reëlected four times. In 1811 and again in 1812 he was a candidate for the governorship of the state, but was defeated both times by his brother-in-law, Jonas Galusha (who married Mary Chittenden). The next year he ran again, as a Federalist, against Galusha. As neither candidate had a majority of the votes cast, the election was decided by the House, who chose Chittenden by a majority of one. The following November he issued his proclamation, recalling the Vermont militia from New York, where it had been taken under the command of Elias Fassett, who was removed from command by the Assembly at the instance of the Governor, and replaced by Jacob Davis. Chittenden maintained that the militia should not leave the state, and that an officer of the United States Army (Fassett held also a federal commission) did not have the power to call the militia for service outside of the state. The matter was brought up in Congress the following January, when resolutions were presented ordering the prosecution of Chittenden before the Supreme Court of the United States, but, as they failed to carry, nothing further was done. Later in the war, however, Chittenden coöperated with the officers of the army in calling for volunteers for the defenses of Plattsburg. In 1814 he was a candidate for re-election, with Galusha as a rival. This time he polled more votes than his opponent, but not a majority, so, once more, he was elected by the House.

During this second term Governor Chittenden presented to the Assembly the proposal of the Massachusetts legislature that delegates be sent to Hartford to consider certain proposed amendments to the Federal Constitution. The Assembly decided that it was unwise, but the secretary of state, William Hall, Jr., went unofficially. In 1815, Galusha defeated Chittenden in the election for governor, and the latter, except for a term as judge of probate in 1821–23, practically retired from active political life, and spent the remainder of his years on his farm in Williston. He was married, in 1796, to Anna Bentley, by whom he had twelve children.

[*Records Gov. and Council State of Vt.*, vols. III–VI (1875–78), especially vol. VI, which covers his terms as governor; A. M. Hemenway, *Vt. Hist. Gazetteer*, vol. I; MSS. in state archives at Montpelier; Alvan Talcott, *Chittenden Family* (1882); *Hist. of Jericho, Vt.* (1916), ed. by C. H. Hayden and others; *Men of Vt.* (1894), comp. by J. G. Ullery.]   G. H. D.

CHITTENDEN, SIMEON BALDWIN (Mar. 29, 1814–Apr. 14, 1889), merchant, congressman, was descended from William Chittenden, one of the founders of the town of Guilford, Conn., in the early seventeenth century. He was the son of Abel and Anna Hart (Baldwin) Chittenden. When he was twelve years old his father died and it was impossible for him to obtain the college education that had been planned. He continued his studies, however, until he received an offer of a clerkship in a New Haven store. This he accepted at the age of fourteen, and served a seven-years' apprenticeship during which the material rewards were scant and appreciation lacking. On coming of age he was able to engage

in business for himself at New Haven. Hardly had he begun to prosper in that undertaking when the panic of 1837 brought a check to trade expansion throughout the country; but having weathered that storm Chittenden was soon in a position to embark on a more ambitious venture. In 1842 he went to New York and entered the wholesale dry-goods field on a modest scale. His quick success there seems, when considered in the light of modern conditions, remarkable. He was a shrewd business man, whose sound judgment carried him far, and he excelled most of his contemporaries in the knowledge of the principles on which legitimate trade is based. He early became a student of economics, investigating and testing propositions that were put forward in the name of the "dismal science." Up to the campaign of 1860 he had never taken a public stand in politics. In that campaign a demand from the South that his mercantile house be boycotted because of his known opposition to slavery caused him to come out for the election of Lincoln and after the Civil War began he supported the Administration vigorously. Having made Brooklyn his home, he joined with a group of his neighbors in founding a daily newspaper, the *Union*, to uphold the government at Washington. The journal was a financial success. Chittenden was elected to Congress in 1874 as an independent Republican and although a member of the minority party in the House of Representatives he made a distinct impression in the debates of that body. In the period preceding the resumption of specie payments, when it was commonly remarked that few members of Congress had any expert knowledge of currency questions, Chittenden quickly took a prominent position in opposing the nostrums put forward by "cheap money" advocates in both political parties. He was a defender of the National Banks and generally in accord with Republican policy, but in several matters he held views in advance of the party's declarations. In formulating a program for resumption he proposed, as a first step, restoration of the privilege of funding legal tender payments at par in government securities; as a second step, the abolition of the legal tender quality; as a third, the perfect freedom of issue for bank notes thoroughly secured and constantly redeemed; and finally, the payment and cancellation of United States notes after a time fixed. Years afterward it was pointed out by conservative authorities that the adoption of these proposals would probably have saved the Administration considerable trouble and embarrassment in the process of resumption. Chittenden's record in Congress on the whole was noteworthy; it led the *Brooklyn Daily Eagle,* opposed to him in politics, to characterize him as "the most distinguished and in national respects the most influential representative Brooklyn has ever had in Congress." Chittenden was known for many years as one of Brooklyn's public-spirited citizens. The Academy of Music, the Free Library, and the Polytechnic Institute were among the Brooklyn institutions to which he gave liberally of his time and money. Outside of Brooklyn, Yale University received important gifts from him, including the building that long housed the university library. He was married (1) to Mary Elizabeth Hartwell and (2) to Cornelia Baldwin Coltons.

[*Wm. Chittenden of Guilford, Conn., and His Descendants,* comp. by Alvan Talcott (1882); *Brooklyn Daily Eagle,* Apr. 15, 1889; *N. Y. Times,* Apr. 15, 1889.]

W. B. S.

CHITTENDEN, THOMAS (Jan. 6, 1730–Aug. 25, 1797), governor of Vermont, the son of Ebenezer and Mary (Johnson) Chittenden, was born at East Guilford, Conn. He was fourth in descent from William and Joanna (Sheaffe) Chittenden, who came from Cranbrook, Kent, England, and settled in Guilford in 1639. Chittenden received a common-school education. At the age of eighteen, he shipped on a West Indian merchant vessel, which was captured by the French. After several months of privation, he worked his way back to Connecticut, and gave up the sea. In October 1749 he married Elizabeth, daughter of Lieut. Janna and Elizabeth (Dudley) Meigs, and settled in Salisbury, Conn., where he lived for the next twenty-five years. Here he became a man of affairs, holding various public offices and representing the town in the colonial Assembly. In 1774, having received a grant of land on the Winooski River, in Williston, Vt., he removed his family thither. Two years later he represented Williston at the Dorset convention, being, it is said, the only member who had ever sat in a legislative assembly before. His sagacity was soon recognized, and he took a prominent part in this and the succeeding conventions, the outcome of which was the formation of the State of Vermont. There had been a controversy of several years' duration over the jurisdiction of that territory, as both New York and New Hampshire claimed control and the governors of both provinces made grants therein. The situation had become intolerable to the settlers, hence their declaration of independence and the establishment of the state. At the convention of September 1776, Chittenden, with twelve others, was appointed to attend this convention at its next sitting, thus forming what

was to become the Council of the State. The following January, Chittenden helped to draw up the "declaration for a new and separate state" and was asked, with others, to present the petition for recognition to the Continental Congress, which was unsuccessful. Between 1777 and 1787, Chittenden and his family lived in Pownal, Williamstown (Mass.), and Arlington, before finally returning to his farm in Williston.

Chittenden, who was president of the Council of Safety, helped Ira Allen [*q.v.*] draw up the constitution of Vermont, which was closely modeled on that of Pennsylvania; and, in the general election of March 1778, he was chosen first governor of the state, an office he held, with the exception of the year 1789–90, until 1797. His level-headed attitude in a crisis, his ability to make a wise decision, his firm character, and his general disarming friendliness, made him one of the strongest men in the state, and enabled him to conduct successfully the affairs of the young government. He apparently rarely made a mistake in judging men. In 1780–83 he was closely associated with Ethan Allen [*q.v.*], and others, in the secret negotiations with Gen. Haldimand, commander of the British forces in Canada. The intentions of these men have never been determined. Documentary evidence supports the idea that they were attempting to make the state a British province, but, on the other hand, there is also evidence to confirm the belief that they were merely attempting to force Congress to recognize the independence of the state. When, in 1781, rumor was rife regarding the negotiations, Chittenden wrote a letter to Gen. Washington, which some have claimed as evidence for the loyalty of the Vermonter. It is, however, a carefully worded document, in which very little is said that was not publicly known (the letter and Washington's reply may be found in *Records of the Governor and Council,* II, 350–55). In 1785–87, as an aftermath of the War, there was a crisis in Vermont affairs. Chittenden suffered a period of unpopularity, owing to which he lost the election of 1789; but the following year he took the chair again. In 1791 he saw the culmination of his efforts to procure the recognition of Vermont and her admission to the Union. He continued in the governor's chair until 1797, when he resigned just a few weeks before his death.

By his wife he had ten children, of whom Martin [*q.v.*] became governor, and the other sons, Noah, Giles, and Truman, each sat in the Assembly and held various public offices. One of the daughters, Mary, became the wife of Gov. Jonas Galusha.

[Records Gov. and Council State of Vt., vols. I–IV (1873–76); Wm. Slade, Vt. State Papers (1823); Vt. Hist. Soc. Colls. (1870–71); Ira Allen, Natural and Political Hist. State of Vt. (1798); Samuel Williams, Natural and Civil Hist. of Vt. (1794); Vt. State Papers, vol. III (1924–25); E. B. O'Callaghan, Documentary Hist. State of N. Y., vol. IV (1851), pp. 531–1034; Benj. H. Hall, Hist. of Eastern Vt. (1858); Archives in Montpelier, Vt., and Ottawa, Canada; Stevens MSS. in Montpelier; Alvan Talcott, Chittenden Family (1882). Daniel Chipman, Memoir of Thos. Chittenden (1849) consists of but a very brief sketch of his life, followed by a lengthy discussion of the Constitution of Vt.; there is a good sketch by Hon. David Read in A. M. Hemenway, ed., Vt. Hist. Gazetteer, I, 905–29; see also J. B. Wilbur, Ira Allen, Founder of Vt. (1928).]

G. H. D.

CHIVERS, THOMAS HOLLEY (Oct. 18, 1809–Dec. 18, 1858), poet, was the grandson of Thomas Holley Chivers, who emigrated to Virginia in the mid-eighteenth century but eventually became one of the first settlers of Georgia; and the son of Col. Robert Chivers, who in 1806 married a Miss Digby. He was born on his father's cotton-farm a few miles south of the recently founded Washington, Ga. The date is determined by a poem in Conrad and Eudora, written Oct. 18, 1834 "on the Anniversary of my Twenty-fifth Year." Toward the end of his life, Chivers claimed 1807 as the year of his birth, and his tombstone speaks of his dying æt. 52 in 1858; but possibly Chivers antedated his birth, so that he would appear older than his rival Poe, who was actually his senior by nine months.

Having been trained at a Georgia preparatory school, he studied medicine at Transylvania University, Lexington, Ky.; in 1830 he wrote his thesis on Intermittent and Remittent Fevers, obtained his M.D. with distinction, and began to practise. Meanwhile he had been writing verse. Though as late as 1856 he refused a chair in physiology at a Southern university, he seems to have given up his medical career soon after graduation. About this time, while recovering from an illness, he had a vision of harp-playing angels and a fountain of water, which his mother could not see (Univercœlum, Dec. 9, 1848). In 1831 he traveled in "the West," visiting in March the Cherokees, with whose sufferings he sympathized strongly; some of the Indian material in his later poems may have been collected then. In 1832 he printed privately, for distribution among friends, The Path of Sorrow, or the Lament of Youth: A Poem, written while studying medicine in 1828–29. These verses are his defense for a rash marriage, which had broken up much as Byron's was supposed to have broken up; Chivers even rephrases Byron's "Dream" for the title-poem. Later, in his will, he cut off his first wife and her daughter with a dollar apiece. In 1833 he was writing more poems, in the Mississippi Valley, and St. Louis. In 1834 he came North (the date is sometimes given as 1832—an error which arose in calculating from the erroneous birth-year 1807). While in Springfield, Mass., he met and married Harriet Hunt, daughter of George and Jerusha (Smith) Hunt of that city, a famous beauty aged sixteen at the time of her marriage. In the latter part of 1834 Chivers printed privately at Philadelphia his Conrad and Eudora; or, the Death of Alonzo, a five-act version of the Sharpe-Beauchamp murder of 1826, which follows (at times almost verbatim) a pamphlet, The Confession of Jereboam O. Beauchamp (Bloomfield, Ky., 1826); the second half of the volume consists of twenty-nine lyrics grouped together as Songs of the Heart. The verse is either bad or indifferent, with some lines characteristic of his exalted mysticism, but with none of the Poe-esque music which he developed later. In 1837 he went to New York, where he published Nacoochee; or, the Beautiful Star, his third book and first published volume, which evidently contains all the juvenilia which he thought worth preserving. The title-poem is an unfinished Indian legend, with a symbolic metaphysics that may have suggested Poe's later "Ulalume," though otherwise the two poems are unlike, "Nacoochee" being written in rather Keats-like Spenserians. The preface is a curious though nebulous statement of Chivers's beliefs as to the transcendental nature of poetry. On Apr. 1, 1838, at Philadelphia, he wrote a sonnet on receiving the news of the death of his mother, and went South for the funeral. In 1839, he was at New York again, preparing a play for presentation: Leoni; or, the Orphan of Venice (never produced or published; manuscript at Harvard). The plot was a complete reworking of the Sharpe-Beauchamp murder, somewhat in the manner of Otway, though with Drydenesque metaphors. It is dignified and well-sustained throughout. On June 25, 1839, his daughter, Florence Allegra, was born; a year later, his son Aster; in these two children he recognized the harp-playing angels of the vision of a decade before.

In 1840 he received a prospectus for the Penn Magazine from Poe, to whom he wrote on Aug. 27, with much enthusiasm but no money. In Graham's Magazine (which eventually published thirteen of Chivers's poems) Poe published in his "Autography" (December 1841) a brief critique of Chiver's manuscripts submitted for publication but not published, in which Chivers was characterized as "one of the best and one of the worst poets in America." Chivers protested twice by letter, and was answered at last on June

6, 1842: Poe had revived his plans for the *Penn Magazine* and apologized for the squib. Chivers promised to get subscribers, but complained that the squib had confirmed a popular rumor that he was mad. The correspondence continued, and Poe accepted three poems for *Graham's Magazine*. Henceforth Chivers's work appeared regularly in various magazines, until about five years before his death. On his thirty-third birthday, Oct. 18, 1842, Florence Allegra was struck down by a virulent form of typhoid, and died in her father's arms that night; he took her body to Georgia and wrote a long rhapsody on the occasion, "The Lost Pleiad"; on Dec. 12, 1842, he wrote another elegy, "To Allegra Florence in Heaven" (rejected with quotations and comments in the *Orion*, March–April, 1843). Another daughter was born to him, but within a year he lost his three other children. The death of these four children furnished subjects for several poems. In the spring of 1845, he went to New York, to publish a new volume, *The Lost Pleiad and Other Poems*. While there he met Poe several times (helping him home in an intoxicated condition on the first occasion), and after his return to Georgia there ensued a correspondence between the two poets—Poe crying desperately for ready money and Chivers, apparently, giving only good advice and an invitation to come South to be taken care of by him for the rest of Poe's life. In his last letter Poe, sincerely or otherwise, wrote: "Except yourself I have never met the man for whom I felt that intimate *sympathy* (of intellect as well as soul) which is the sole basis of friendship." Attracted by the visions of Andrew Jackson Davis [*q.v.*], Chivers, in 1848, contributed liberally to Davis's *Univercœlum*, both poems and prose, including the "Scene from Via Cœli; or, the Way to Heaven, a Moral Drama in Five Acts," which contains an account of his own visions. In the same year he published a pamphlet, *Search After Truth; or a New Revelation of the Psycho-Physiological Nature of Man*. After Poe's death he wrote a "New Life of Edgar Allan Poe," a rhapsody intended to place Poe as a great poet, without concealing his weakness; the manuscript remains unpublished, except for fragments edited by Prof. Woodberry in the *Century Magazine* (January–February, 1903).

In the latter part of 1850, Chivers published at New York his *Eonchs of Ruby, A Gift of Love*, a mixture of ultra-musical verse and gorgeously extravagant imagery, with verse collected from the magazines, and much stuff that should have been destroyed. The very evident influence of Poe immediately caused various charges of plagiarism, and there began a controversy which cannot be said to have ended yet. Chivers defended himself at first in private letters with considerable heat, and finally broke out, under the signature of "Fiat Justitia," in the *Waverly Magazine* (1853), accusing Poe with much blindness and fury of stealing the "Raven" from "To Allegra Florence in Heaven," and quoting the very worst stanza from it as proof. At last the editor closed the controversy with justifiable harshness. The truth of the matter seems to be that Poe and Chivers at first developed their melodic theories of verse independently; that Chivers later followed Poe's lead for some time; that Poe saw in Chivers's more careless work material which he could entirely make over; while Chivers, gaining courage from Poe's example, freely helped himself to Poe's rhymes and names and tricks of refrain. But after Poe's death, Chivers continued his experiments far beyond anything that Poe had ever done. In 1853 he published three more volumes of poetry. *Memoralia; or, Phials of Amber Full of the Tears of Love* was nothing but the unsold copies of *Eonchs,* the first twenty-six pages of which were replaced with a new title-page, index, preface, and six poems. *Virginalia, or Songs of my Summer Nights,* though less known than *Eonchs,* is Chivers's most extraordinary volume; it contains his wildest and most successful experiments in meter. His third volume for 1853 was *Atlanta, or the True Blessed Island of Poesy,* "a Paul Epic in Three Lustra," which appeared as a pamphlet at Macon, Ga. The preface includes many ideas apparently taken from Poe's *Poetic Principle* (1850), but is dated July 18, 1842; and elsewhere Chivers insisted on his priority. In 1854 he wrote a five-act play, *The Sons of Usna: a Tragi-Apotheosis* (published, 1858), which is the first literary treatment in English of the famous legend of Deirdre (barring mere translations and paraphrases, as well as Macpherson's "Darthula"). In 1856, he returned South; was asked by a committee to write a Fourth-of-July Oration; and wrote and published in pamphlet form, but did not recite, his *Birth-day Song of Liberty. A Pæan of Glory for the Heroes of Freedom*. On Dec. 18, 1858 he died at his home, Villa Allegra, Decatur, Ga. His influence on Swinburne has been demonstrated by Prof. A. G. Newcomber (*Sewanee Review,* January 1904). He always was utterly unable to judge his own productions; and Poe's original squib about him still holds. Yet his best work is frequently poetry of a high order, and his originality (despite any question of plagiarism) is unquestionable.

[Besides the sources mentioned above, see W. C. Richardson, "Who Was Chivers?" *Boston Transcript*, Apr. 24, 1897; *Passages from the Correspondence and other Papers of Rufus W. Griswold* (1898); L. T. Hodges, "Thos. Holley Chivers," *Alkahest Mag.*, Oct. 1898; Joel Benton, *In the Poe Circle* (1899); J. W. Townsend, "Thos. Holley Chivers," *Lib. Southern Lit.*, vol. II (1907); Jas. Huneker, *Pathos of Distance* (1913); and T. O. Mabbott's edition of Poe's *Politian* (Richmond, 1923).]   S. F. D.

CHOATE, JOSEPH HODGES (Jan. 24, 1832–May 14, 1917), lawyer, diplomat, was born at Salem, Mass., the youngest son of Dr. George Choate and Margaret Manning Hodges. He was the seventh in descent from John Choate who came from England in 1643 and settled in Ipswich, Mass. On the maternal side, his grandparents were Capt. Gamaliel Hodges and Sarah Williams. Joseph H. Choate had two sisters, Elizabeth and Caroline (Mrs. E. B. de Gersdorff); and three brothers, Charles F., president of the Old Colony Railroad, George C. S., a physician, and William G., United States district judge. Rufus Choate [*q.v.*] of Boston was the first cousin of Dr. George Choate, and therefore a first cousin once removed of Joseph H. Choate.

"The lives of my father and mother," says Choate, "were truly heroic in the matter of the training of their own children. Having four sons and two daughters, they determined at all hazards to give them the best education that the times afforded, and in so doing they set them a wonderful example of self-control, self-denial, and self-sacrifice" (*Boyhoood and Youth*, p. 31). The father, himself a graduate of the academic and medical departments of Harvard, sent his four sons there also, with the result that in 1848–49, one was a medical student, one was a senior in the college, and two were freshmen. In the Commencement of 1852, William gave the Valedictory oration, and Joseph H. the Salutatory oration. The latter always remained devoted to his college, returned often to it at the annual graduation period, and was a president of the Harvard Alumni Association and of the Harvard Club of New York. He entered the Harvard Law School in 1852, where, until his graduation in 1854, he earned his living by tutoring boys preparing to enter the college. A third year was spent in Boston in the office of Hodges & Saltonstall, after which, in October 1855, he was admitted to the Massachusetts bar.

Bearing a letter of introduction from Rufus Choate to William M. Evarts, Choate moved to New York in 1855, and in the following year entered the office of Butler, Evarts & Southmayd. After a three years' apprenticeship, and a brief interval of practise on his own account, he was invited to join the firm as partner, and retained that relationship for the rest of his life. The firm now survives as Evarts, Choate, Sherman & Léon. Although Choate was the junior in this firm, and therefore, for ten years or more, played an inconspicuous rôle before the legal public, this period shaped his career in two respects. It taught him, under the wise judgment of Southmayd, how to form the theory of a case, and under Evarts, how to present it effectively in court; and second, it gave him opportunity to take an interest in social intercourse and in projects for the public welfare. He acquired a facility and grace in public utterance to which much of his success in life must be attributed. In 1861, he married Caroline Dutcher Sterling, daughter of Frederick A. Sterling, of Cleveland, Ohio. Their married life extended over fifty-five years.

The life of Choate may be said to present five major aspects which, however, cannot be viewed chronologically, and are not mutually exclusive. They may be labeled as the social, political, public-welfare, legal, and international aspects.

It was not an accident that he became president of the New England Society of New York; the Union League Club; the Pilgrim Society; the Harvard College Alumni and Law School associations and the Harvard Club of New York; the Century Association; and various legal societies; and that the list of his other club memberships was extensive. He was a "club man," enjoying association with his fellows, getting along well with them, and being often chosen as their leader. His skill as an after-dinner speaker is still a tradition, and his published speeches, models of their kind. For years he divided the laurels in this field with Chauncey Depew, who said of him, "Mr. Choate believed, with me, that the mind is fresher and more capable of grasping the questions arising in one's vocation or profession, if there is relief in some other direction. We both found that in after-dinner speaking" (*Speeches and Literary Contributions*, 1918, p. 246).

Politics, compared to his other activities, played a minor rôle in Choate's life, yet he was an active party man and a life-long Republican. He made his first political speech for Frémont in 1856, and his last for Hughes in 1916. In 1871, he was a leader in arousing New York City against the Tweed Ring. At the mass meeting in Cooper Union, Sept. 4, 1871, as chairman of the Committee on Resolutions, he presented the resolution calling for the organization of the Committee of Seventy; and, on Nov. 3, 1871, when that committee reported, he made a notable speech which roused the public to definite action. Twenty-three years later, in 1894, he was again an active crusader as a member of the Committee of Thirty in opposition to Tammany Hall and Richard Croker. In the previous year he had been elected delegate-at-large to the New York Constitutional Convention of 1894. The Republicans had a majority in that convention and Choate was selected as its president. His influence, during the five months of this convention, according to Elihu Root, who was leader of the majority on the floor of the convention, was very great, and he played a conspicuous part in the election of November 1894, in bringing about the adoption of the new constitution by the electorate. The only political office for which he was ever a candidate was that of United States senator in opposition to Thomas C. Platt. He consented to run as a protest against boss rule within his own party, but without expectation of election. "I told them I would run," he said, after the legislature had reëlected Platt, "if I only got one vote. In fact I got seven, and I regarded this as a real triumph" (Strong, *post,* p. 88).

Not only was he a party man and an active worker in the ranks to bring about political action which he believed would be for the public good, but he was a leader in non-political cultural and humanitarian activities. It was this side of his career which in later life, added to his legal and diplomatic careers, made him stand out as first citizen of the City of New York. He was a founder and from 1869 to 1917 a trustee of the American Museum of Natural History; an incorporator and for forty-seven years a trustee of the Metropolitan Museum of Art, being at times its vice-president, chairman of its Law Committee and a member of its Executive Committee; governor of the New York Hospital for forty years (1877–1917); president of the board of directors of the New York State's Charities Aid Association (1895–99, 1905–17); president of the New York Association for the Blind; vice-president of the Carnegie Endowment for International Peace; president of the American Society for the Judicial Settlement of International Disputes; and honorary president of the National Security League and of the National Defense Society.

Choate's legal career was remarkable for its length (over fifty-five years), for the variety of its activities, for the number of cases won, and for the sustained reputation that it brought him. Honors directly connected with his professional work were showered upon him. He was a member of the Commission on revision of the judicial system of New York State in 1890; president of the Association of the Bar of the City of New York, of the American Bar Association, of the New York State Bar Association, of the New York County Lawyers' Association, and of the Harvard Law School Association, and in 1905 he was elected a Bencher of the Middle Temple, London.

Being blessed with a strong constitution and unusually good health, he was very active during his whole legal career. A mere catalogue of the important cases in which he participated would be too long for a biographical article. Probably the public knew him best as a jury lawyer; for he was himself a dramatic figure and both in the examination of witnesses and in speeches to juries, as well as in passages at arms with opposing counsel, he displayed wit, sarcasm, and an audacity which produced continual surprises. "Whatever the printed brief or the prepared address," says William V. Rowe, "the oral presentation was bound to be filled with new ideas, a new point of view, a personal emphasis." Another writer describes him as "physically tall, with a relatively large head, plentiful hair, often somewhat tousled, handsome in features, but manly of line and giving an impression of health and physical strength, carefully but not obtrusively dressed, apt to assume careless attitudes, standing with one hand in a trousers' pocket as he spoke, and with a musical voice of tenor quality, flexible, well-controlled, not loud, but of great carrying power."

Although he was popularly known as an advocate, rather than as a lawyer conspicuous for legal learning, he was in fact an all-round lawyer capable of effectively handling any legal problem. He was engaged in the contests over the wills of Cruger, Vanderbilt, A. T. Stewart, Samuel J. Tilden, Hoyt Drake, Hopkins-Searles, Vassar, and Vanderpoel; in the anti-trust cases involving the Standard Oil Company, the Trenton Potteries, and the "Tobacco Trust"; in two famous cases dealing with the law of clubs, *Loubat* vs. *Union Club,* and *Hutchinson* vs. *New York Stock Exchange*; in libel suits, including that of *Funk* vs. *Godkin*; in admiralty cases, such as the *Republic* (steamship) case; in railroad cases; in two famous court-martial proceedings, the McCalla naval case and the Fitz-John Porter case; in the controversy of Lord Dunraven with the New York Yacht Club over the race between the *Defender* and *Valkyrie III*; in the Goff contempt proceedings; and in numerous arguments before the United States Supreme Court, including the Neagle case arising out of the attempted assassination of Mr. Justice Field by

Judge Terry of California, the Leland Stanford case, the California Irrigation Law cases, the Massachusetts Fisheries case, claims under the *Alabama* awards and the Spanish Treaty, and the Income Tax cases.

Probably his most important arguments were in the Income Tax cases before the United States Supreme Court in March and May 1895, in which he and his associates convinced the court that the income tax law of 1894 was unconstitutional. His argument at the time was compared to that of Webster in the Dartmouth College case. Choate himself, however, once said that he considered the task of proving Gen. Fitz-John Porter innocent of the charge of treason was his most difficult exploit and greatest victory, because two courts martial had decided adversely to Porter, and the true facts were hard to gather and get before the court after the lapse of fifteen years.

Early in 1899 Choate was appointed Ambassador at the Court of St. James's. Being sixty-seven years old, he had already crossed the traditional threshold of old age. He had lived a singularly full life, successful according to the highest social and professional standards, and had reached a peak from which for most men only descent in declining years could have been expected. But for him, unimpaired in health, mind, and spirit, a new career was just beginning. He acquitted himself in the field of international affairs so as to add measurably to the prestige of the United States and to his own reputation. Three matters of major importance were brought to a successful issue by him.

When he went to England, the Joint High Commission of 1898 for the settlement of questions between Canada and the United States had just been dissolved without reaching an agreement. The Commission was in deadlock over the critical question of the Alaskan boundary, the location of which might determine the ownership of gold-bearing lands. Choate and Secretary Hay obtained agreement upon a treaty providing for the submission of the boundary question to a tribunal composed of an equal number of members from each country, charged to hear evidence, and decide according to law. The conference of the tribunal, held in London in 1903, resulted in a determination of the boundary question, and paved the way for the disposal of all the questions which had been unsuccessfully considered by the Joint High Commission.

The Spanish American War, resulting in the acquisition by the United States of Porto Rico and the Philippines, and in responsibility for the protection of Cuba, brought to the United States a realization of the necessity for a canal across Central America. The need was emphasized by the growth of population and commerce on the Pacific coast, and by political development in the Far East. A canal under exclusive American control was wanted; but the way to it was blocked by the Clayton-Bulwer Treaty of 1850, under which the United States and Great Britain had stipulated for joint control of any such canal. One of the achievements of Choate, under Hay's direction, was the abrogation of this treaty, and the substitution of an agreement that any American-controlled canal should "be free and open to the vessels of commerce and war of all nations on terms of entire equality."

Another accomplishment of far-reaching effect was that of securing Great Britain's agreement to the Hay doctrine of the open door in China, resulting in checking the partition of that country by the Great Powers.

These three were large diplomatic achievements, but, in the judgment of many, the most important result of Choate's six years in London was the good feeling engendered by him as representative of the people of the United States to the people of Great Britain. He was uniquely equipped for this undertaking by his personality, his humor, his skill as a speaker both at formal and informal occasions, and by his power of unwearied attention to the details of social intercourse.

Two years after his return to the United States, at the age of seventy-five, he went as head of the American delegation to the Second Hague Conference of 1907. His ambassadorship had made him the logical choice for this mission, for he had become known and respected throughout Europe as a man who, to use the words of Elihu Root, "had learning without pedantry, power of expression which never sacrificed accuracy to rhetoric, or sense to sound, courage saved from rashness by quick perception and long experience, the lawyer's point of view and the statesman's point of view, the technique of forensic debate, and the technique of diplomatic intercourse" ("Memorial of Joseph H. Choate," in *Association of the Bar of the City of New York Year Book*, 1918). He undoubtedly was one of the great leaders of the Conference, bringing to his work earnestness, technical skill, and knowledge of the history, implications, and probable results of proposed projects, and yet overriding tradition when it stood in the way of progress. Few men without offense could have made the speech, reminiscent of the judicial forum rather than of diplomatic intercourse, which he made on Oct. 10, 1907, in opposition to the proposition of the First Delegate of Austria-Hungary regarding the Anglo-American project for international arbitration. Such episodes justify the comment of the foreign press that he was the *enfant terrible* of the Conference. "He seems aware," wrote Saint Maurice, "neither of the grandeur of the mission intrusted to the delegates, nor of the personal majesty of their excellencies. He is barely a diplomat. He it is who, with an air of innocence, inserts into a discussion a few cold words which effectively shatter the grandiloquent bubbles of his colleagues. He it is who unsmilingly emphasizes some imposing puerility. It is he, always he, whose brief logic brings back to earth again discussions which have drifted into the pacific ether" (*Ibid.*, pp. 98–99).

The period from 1908 to 1914 was as active in Choate's life as would have been appropriate for a man of middle age. He resumed participation in projects for public welfare, took part in politics, accepted innumerable invitations to speak, was director in many corporations, was active in associations of the bar, and in interpreting his profession to the public, and practised law not only as counsellor and advisor, but also sometimes in the courts. When the European war broke out, he threw himself into the task of arousing the United States to the gravity of the situation and the necessity for entering the war. His speeches had great weight because of his reputation and experience, and more than that because of an enthusiasm and emotional intensity which coming from a man in his ninth decade presented a moving example of patriotism and self-sacrifice. He devoted himself wholly to his self-imposed task, and after the United States had entered the war, served as chairman of the New York Committee for the reception of the Commissions from England and France under Balfour and Viviani and Marshal Joffre. At the end of an arduous week, after the closing exercises at the Cathedral of St. John the Divine, he said to Mr. Balfour, "Remember, we meet again to celebrate the victory" (Martin, *post*, II, 391). The next day he died.

[The chief sources of information are Choate's autobiography, *Boyhood and Youth of Jos. Hodges Choate* (N. Y., privately printed, 1917); Theron G. Strong, *Jos. H. Choate; New Englander, New Yorker, Lawyer, Ambassador* (1917); Edward S. Martin, *Life of Jos. Hodges Choate as Gathered Chiefly from His Letters* (2 vols., 1920); and *Arguments and Addresses of Jos. Hodges Choate, collected and ed. by Frederick C. Hicks* (St. Paul, West Publishing Co., 1926).]

F. C. H.

CHOATE, RUFUS (Oct. 1, 1799–July 13, 1859), lawyer, statesman, was descended from sturdy Puritan stock, his immigrant ancestor, John Choate, having settled in the town of Ipswich, Mass., in 1643. Rufus, the fourth child and second son of David Choate, a veteran of the

Revolution, and of his second wife, Miriam Foster, was born in the family homestead on Hog Island, off the Atlantic coast, in a district then called Chebacco but now part of the town of Essex. When he was six months old, however, his parents moved to a farm on the mainland. Both his father, who had been a teacher, and his mother, who is described as a woman "of strong sense and ready wit," were fond of books; and he was a precocious lad, who read *The Pilgrim's Progress* at the age of six and exhausted the village library before he was ten. He studied under local clergymen or in grammar schools until he was fifteen, following this with a year of formal instruction at an academy in Hampton, N. H. His father having died in 1808, Rufus had to borrow money to take him through Dartmouth College, where he made a brilliant scholastic record, graduating as valedictorian of the class of 1819. He showed little interest in games at Hanover, but sat with his books far into the night, coming to his lectures haggard and worn. Although he was diffident and modest, he was the most romantic undergraduate of his period at Dartmouth, and his intellectual supremacy was conceded by his classmates. In his senior year, because of over-study, he suffered a nervous breakdown, and it was feared that he might not be able to speak at the Commencement exercises; but he rose from his bed at the last moment and delivered an address which amazed his audience, among whom was Daniel Webster.

Webster's argument in the famous Dartmouth College Case (Mar. 10, 1818) made a lasting impression on Choate and determined him, in emulation of the great orator, to take up the law. For a year after his graduation, however, he remained in Hanover as a tutor, mainly in order to earn enough to pay off his debts. He then spent a few months as a student in the Dane Law School, in Cambridge, going from there to Washington, where he was, for nearly a year, in the law office of William Wirt [*q.v.*]. After additional preparation under Asa Andrews of Ipswich, and Judge Cummins of Salem, he was admitted, in September 1822, to practise in the Massachusetts court of common pleas and started on that career which was to make him perhaps the most successful pleader of his day. He opened an office in Danvers, only a few miles from Salem, and, in November 1825, was admitted to practise in the supreme judicial court. In the same year he married Helen Olcott, daughter of Mills Olcott of Hanover, N. H., by whom he had seven children.

Throughout his life Choate's chief interest was always in his profession. From time to time he was drawn reluctantly into public affairs, but he invariably returned joyfully to the law. Even with such rivals as Webster, Cushing, and Rantoul, he quickly made a reputation in Essex County and moved gradually to wider fields of activity—to Salem in 1828 and from there to Boston in 1834. He was, from the beginning, primarily a court-room attorney, and most of his cases were tried before a jury. It has been said that, while he was practising in Essex County, no verdict was brought in against any person whom he was defending in a criminal action.

In 1825, rather against his wishes, Choate was elected to the lower house of the Massachusetts General Court. His first speech was in favor of educating teachers for the common schools. Because of the pressure of his legal business, he attended the sessions of the legislature only intermittently, but, on the rare occasion when he addressed his colleagues, his opinion carried weight. In 1827 he was chosen as state senator. Like most Massachusetts leaders of that period, he was an anti-Jackson man. In October 1830 he was nominated by the National Republicans of Essex South District for Congress, and was elected by a majority of 500 over Benjamin W. Crowninshield [q.v.], who had represented that district for eight years. During his first session, which opened in December 1831, he made but two speeches—one favoring Revolutionary pensions and the other defending a protective tariff. In 1832 he was reëlected, but resigned within a few months in order to take up residence in Boston. With Webster, Everett, and Cushing, he assisted in organizing the Whig party in Massachusetts, and, when the anti-Masonic mania was at its height in the summer of 1834, he rode with Cushing through the eastern part of the state trying to persuade Masonic lodges to give up their charters in order to keep the Whigs from breaking up on that issue.

Choate's advancement at the Boston bar was rapid, and his position with leaders like Jeremiah Mason, Franklin Dexter, and even Daniel Webster was soon established. He resisted many efforts to draw him into politics, but he was an ardent supporter of Harrison in 1840, and, when Webster resigned his senatorship (Feb. 22, 1841) in order to become secretary of state, Choate, in spite of the opposition of such abolitionists as John Greenleaf Whittier, was chosen to fill the vacant seat. Although his senatorial duties often proved irksome, he took them very seriously. He was a loyal member of the Whig party, opposing the annexation of Texas and favoring the protective tariff and a National Bank. His first speech on the floor of the upper house was made (June 11, 1841) in defense of Webster's conduct in the case of the indictment of Alexander McLeod, a British subject, by the United States courts for the burning of the steamer *Caroline*. A few days later, Choate, in advocating an amendment to Clay's bill for a National Bank, stated that, unless such an amendment were passed, the measure would be vetoed by President John Tyler. Clay, in his dictatorial manner, insisted on hearing the source of Choate's information, which the latter, quite properly, refused to disclose. On the following morning Clay made a courteous explanation and apology to Choate. Choate spoke forcefully for the confirmation of Edward Everett as minister to England, and made three speeches in 1843 for the Webster-Ashburton Treaty. He was eager to retire in 1844, before the expiration of his term of office, and efforts were made to induce Webster to take his place; but Choate eventually completed his term in March 1845, and gladly returned to private life, resuming the law partnership which he had formed in 1834 with B. F. Crowninshield. This was dissolved in 1849, and a new firm was formed consisting of Choate and his son-in-law, Joseph M. Bell. If he had wished them, he could have had many honors. Gov. Briggs offered him a seat on the bench of the supreme judicial court of Massachusetts, and, on the death of Levi Woodbury, in December 1851, Webster urged Choate to accept a nomination as justice of the Supreme Court of the United States; but Choate declined both places, feeling that he was not temperamentally fitted to be a judge. He was also tempted, in 1848, to accept a professorship in the Dane Law School in Cambridge, but he preferred to remain untrammeled.

Sheer physical and mental weariness led him, in 1850, to make a hurried trip to Europe, where he spent three months traveling restlessly through England, Belgium, France, Germany, and Switzerland—his only experience abroad. He thoroughly approved of the compromise measures of 1850 and of Webster's Seventh-of-March Speech, and he spoke at a Union Meeting in Faneuil Hall (Nov. 6, 1850) in praise of Webster and in justification of his policies. He was invited to deliver the address of welcome to Webster in April 1851, but the mayor and aldermen of Boston, incensed at Webster's alleged "treachery" to the North, refused at the last moment to let Faneuil Hall be opened. At the Baltimore convention in June 1852, Choate made a dramatic but futile appeal to the Whigs for the nomination of Webster for the presidency. Webster died on Oct. 24, 1852, and Choate, who had always idolized him, prepared a eulogy of the dead statesman, over which he toiled longer and harder than over any address which he had ever made. It was spoken at Dartmouth College, the alma mater of both Choate and Webster, in August 1853. In the same year Choate was a member of the Massachusetts constitutional convention, at which he spoke effectively in opposition to a proposal to have judges elected by the people.

Choate's attitude toward the unavoidable issue of negro slavery had from the first been conservative, like that of Webster, Everett, and the "old Whigs." Opposed though he was on moral grounds to human servitude, he never advocated abolition, and stated on one occasion, "I do not believe it is the greatest good to the *slave* or the *free* that four millions of slaves should be turned loose in all their ignorance, poverty, and degradation, to trust to luck for a home and a living." As the controversy grew violent, Choate insisted that the rights of the South should be respected, and expressed the opinion that the federal government could do nothing to compel a sovereign state to remain within the Union. In the campaign of 1855 in Massachusetts, he wrote a letter (Oct. 1) to the Whig convention at Worcester denying that the party was dead, denouncing the newly formed Republican party, and closing with the sentence, often quoted, "We join ourselves to no party that does not carry the flag and keep step to the music of the Union." In the presidential campaign of the following year, Choate said that the Republicans were "a new geographical party . . . a sectional, anti-Union party, and nothing should be left undone to defeat them." In a long and carefully reasoned letter to the Maine Whig Central Committee (Aug. 9, 1856), he said, "The contest in my judgment is between Mr. Buchanan and Col. Frémont. In these circumstances, I vote for Mr. Buchanan." It was a statement which turned many Whig voters to the Democratic side and marked the death of the Whig party. In making this choice, Choate incurred the animosity of many of his Boston friends, but even those who criticized his course most vigorously were careful not to impugn the honesty of his motives.

In the spring of 1855 Choate had an accident to his leg, resulting in an operation from which he never fully recovered. His strength slowly waned, and in 1859, at the insistence of his physician, he started with his son on a voyage to Europe. When his vessel, the *Europa,* touched at Halifax, he was so ill that he was removed to lodgings in the town. There, on July 13, 1859, he died, the immediate cause of his death being Bright's disease. His body was brought back to Boston and buried in Mount Auburn Cemetery.

A memorial meeting was held on July 23, in Faneuil Hall, with Edward Everett as the principal speaker. His only son, Rufus Choate, Jr., served through the Civil War in the Northern ranks and died, Jan. 15, 1866, from illness contracted in the field.

Choate was a picturesque figure, about whose personality and career many legends have gathered. Physically he was nearly six feet in height, robust and broad-chested, with a deeply wrinkled face, an olive complexion, a profusion of wild and fantastic hair, thick bushy eyebrows, and deep spectral eyes. His contorted lips, disheveled locks, and somber expression gave him a weird, exotic appearance, as if he were the product, not of staid New England, but of some far-off planet. Naturally strong, he habitually overworked and suffered from violent sick headaches of an exhausting kind. For an hour or two before breakfast he read, making the most of his free time, and he was tireless in his labors. He once defined a lawyer's vacation as the period between putting a question to a witness and the answer. He was animated by a prodigious nervous energy, which drove him on even when his jaded body protested against its abuse. He was a reckless, dashing, impetuous person, with no serenity of mind, and the stormy working of his brain showed itself in "the unearthly glance of his eye." After a great speech he was always prostrated for a few hours. His nervousness was revealed in the carelessness of his dress and the jerkiness of his movements, as well as in his handwriting, which, with the possible exception of Horace Greeley's, is probably more illegible than that of any other famous man. E. P. Whipple describes it as resembling "the tracks of wildcats with their claws dipped in ink, madly dashing over the surface of a folio sheet of white paper."

Books were Choate's chief relaxation, and he possessed a private library of more than 8,000 volumes. All his spare hours were spent in reading, even when he was dressing and undressing, and he learned some lines of poetry every day. His library table was covered with the latest publications, and he loved to frequent second-hand book-shops, from which he seldom emerged without some treasure. He was especially fond of the Greek and Latin classics, from which, with his retentive and accurate memory, he could quote long passages. He even planned an authoritative work on Greek history, but the appearance of Grote's masterpiece prevented him from carrying his project through.

Choate belongs among the really great orators. He had a pleasing voice—"now like a flute for softness, and now like a clarion"—a ready command of language, and a logical faculty which never forsook him even when he was most swayed by emotion. He was persuasive, even magnetic, in his manner, and his impassioned fervor when he was aroused stirred even sluggish hearts. The busts in his library were those of Demosthenes and Cicero, and he labored constantly, as his journal indicates, to model his style on theirs. He paid especial attention to his diction, leaning perhaps too obviously toward the Latin derivatives. His sentences were likely to be long—there is one covering four pages in his eulogy on Webster—but it was seldom that his audience could not follow him, and he never tired his hearers. His spectacular appearance contributed to the dramatic effect when he spoke. He gesticulated with his whole body, and Wendell Phillips described him facetiously as "a monkey in convulsions." Some of his occasional lectures became famous, particularly one on "The Romance of the Sea," which was stolen from his hand-bag and has never been published. He spoke frequently on the lyceum platform, on such subjects as Washington, Sir Walter Scott, Kossuth, and other eminent men. Among the greatest of his addresses was "The Age of the Pilgrims" (1843), delivered in New York City before the New England Association and described by one of the audience as coming "like a series of shocks." Other speeches which attracted attention were his "Eulogy on William H. Harrison" (1841) in Faneuil Hall (printed in the *Boston Daily Advertiser,* Apr. 22, 1841); "The Annexation of Texas" (1844), in Tremont Temple, Boston; "The Position and Functions of the American Bar" (1845), and "The Eloquence of Revolutionary Periods" (1857).

It is, however, as a practising lawyer that he will be longest remembered. In February 1842, Charles Sumner wrote to Dr. Lieber, "I am glad you like Choate so well. His position here is very firm. He is the leader of our bar, with an overwhelming superfluity of business." George F. Hoar said that his power over a jury was like the fascination of a bird by a snake. He knew instinctively the basic principles of human psychology, and he was always something of an actor, his sentiment, his humor, and his sarcasm being all directed to the one end of winning the twelve men in the box to his side. He did not, moreover, rely on inspiration, but gave to each case, no matter how seemingly trivial, the most careful scrutiny, often sitting up all night before an important trial. Some of his critics were disposed to minimize his knowledge of the law, but he was actually a profound scholar, who neglected no details and was industrious in searching for precedents. His management of a case was usually flawless, and his cross-examinations were appallingly clever. In argument with his opponents he was uniformly courteous, even under strong provocation, and his urbanity became a tradition with the Boston bar. His manner was adapted to the situation—sometimes conversational, sometimes theatrical—but in the full swing of his discourse he spoke with a rapid rush of words and ideas, his mind seeming to sweep along with startling velocity. A shorthand reporter, sent to take down an argument by Choate, came back saying, "Who can report chain lightning?" When he was wrought up, he made ordinary persons appear like great tragic figures. One of his contemporaries said of him, "He dressed the common and mean things of life with a poetic charm and romance." Yet the basis of his argument was usually Yankee common-sense. His wit was unfailing, and stories of his brilliant repartee passed from mouth to mouth in legal circles. Few lawyers in this country have ever been more talked about, and it is no exaggeration to state that he has had no superior as an advocate.

Some of his cases have become part of legal history, among them being the Tirrell murder trial, in which he employed somnambulism as a defense and secured an acquittal for his client; the Gillespie case, in which he obtained the exoneration by a Protestant jury of a Roman Catholic priest accused by a girl of criminal assault; and the Dalton divorce case, in which he blocked the attempt by a husband to procure a separation from his wife whom he had deserted and wrongfully accused. No one of his cases, however, was as important in legal history as some of those which gave Webster his reputation as a constitutional lawyer. Choate was almost absurdly indifferent to money, and his fees were for years ridiculously low. Indeed, he often defended cases for nothing when he saw that a client had little property. After his partnership with his son-in-law, however, his affairs were arranged more systematically, and his income increased. His largest recorded fee for a single case was $2,500, and his heaviest receipts for any one year were $22,000.

In his private life Choate was kind and gentle, a thoughtful husband and father. To those in need he was charitable, often giving away more than he could afford. He was not a sociable person, and hated formal dinners and conventional entertainments. He liked to take solitary walks, and he did not seek or need the companionship of others. He had no vices, and the legend that he took opium as a stimulant has long been disproved. He was a man of sound character, against whose integrity no one cast the slightest suspicion. President Buchanan described him accurately when he said, "He was an unselfish patriot, devoted to the Constitution and the Union."

Although Choate stirred the imaginations of his contemporaries, his reputation has in some degree shared the fate of those of most great lawyers—such advocates, for instance, as Jeremiah Mason and William Pinkney and Sergeant S. Prentiss. Choate's indifference to politics has been unfortunate for his fame. Had he been politically ambitious, he might have taken Webster's place as the leader of the Unionist party, but he was not to be lured from the law. As a statesman, then, he exercised no important influence. The days of great jury trials, moreover, have gone by, and forensic eloquence is seldom to-day a factor in deciding the issue of a case. But Choate's romantic personality, his fiery energy, his devastating wit, and his almost hypnotic power over other men have lent a fascination to his name, and he is praised and remembered by those who would be unable to point to anything definite which he contributed to our national history.

[*Works of Rufus Choate with a Memoir of his Life* (2 vols., 1862), ed. by Samuel Gilman Brown; *Addresses and Orations of Rufus Choate* (1878); Edward G. Parker, *Reminiscences of Rufus Choate* (1860); Jos. Neilson, *Memories of Rufus Choate* (1884); E. P. Whipple, *Some Recollections of Rufus Choate* (1879; repr. in *Recollections of Eminent Men,* 1887); John B. Cogswell, sketch in *Memorial Biogs. of the New Eng. Hist. Geneal. Soc.,* vol. III (1883; E. O. Jameson, *The Choates in America, 1643–1896* (1896); Claude M. Fuess, *Rufus Choate* (1928).]   C.M.F.

CHOPIN, KATE O'FLAHERTY (Feb. 8, 1851–Aug. 22, 1904), author, was descended through her mother from a French family which settled at old Kaskaskia in the early part of the eighteenth century, and through her father, Thomas O'Flaherty, from an honorable Irish family which had for generations been land agents in the County Galway. Thomas, who had come to St. Louis a lad of eighteen, was markedly successful in business, but his death in the Gasconade Bridge disaster when his daughter Kate was a mere child prevented his influencing her. His lavish hospitality was continued by his wife Eliza (Faris) O'Flaherty, a society-loving woman of unusual beauty and force. From the perpetual callers and entertainments as well as from the troubles of the Civil War period the daughter's favorite refuge was a stepladder in the attic where she pored over the works of Scott, Fielding, and Spenser. Her schooling was rather irregular, and she herself attributed more of her education to her wide reading than to the music,

French literature, theology, and elementary science which she was taught at the Sacred Heart Convent. After her graduation from there in 1868 she was for two years one of the belles of St. Louis. In June 1870, she married Oscar Chopin, a native of Louisiana, who was then working in a bank owned by relatives. After a honeymoon in Europe, the move to the Southland which was undoubtedly the most important influence in Mrs. Chopin's literary development was made. In view of the fact that five sons were born in the ten years in which her husband acted as a cotton factor in New Orleans and that she was immediately drawn into the social life of the city, it is not surprising that her début as a writer was still postponed. Her husband's decision to manage his own and his younger sister's large plantations on the Red River brought her to a new and fascinating world, the world which is even yet best described in her short stories. At this home in Cloutiersville her only daughter was born and her husband died from a swamp fever in 1882. The difficulties of managing a large estate and her mother's desire to have the family reunited in St. Louis caused Mrs. Chopin first to rent and then to sell the plantation although she always loved and frequently revisited Natchitoches Parish.

One of the most modest and retiring of women, in her new leisure she was induced to take up writing by friends who had been charmed by her letters. As she herself realized, her first novel, *At Fault,* published in her home city in 1890, is distinctly amateurish, its chief interest being in the fact that the central character represents her mother. Her critical faculty, however, and her study of the French masters whom she admired and translated, notably De Maupassant and Daudet, produced in a short time an amazing development in technique. The *Youth's Companion, Harper's Young People,* and *Wide Awake* took all her children's stories; her work for mature readers appeared in such magazines as the *Century* and *Harper's.* She is known to-day, however, through her interpretations of the Creoles in her collections, *Bayou Folk* (1894) and *A Night in Acadie* (1897), and her second novel, *The Awakening* (1899). A new edition of the best of her work is now in preparation by her daughter, Mrs. Lelia Hattersley.

Unquestionably Mrs. Chopin's stories rank very high in the local color movement of the nineties. Although some of them are mere sketches, a tale like "Désirée's Baby" could scarcely be excelled. All of her shorter pieces are marked by sympathy, a delicately objective treatment, and endings poignant in their restraint. These same qualities make *The Awakening* almost exotic. The sensuous loveliness of the description, the subtle symbolism, the jewel-like polish of each haunting episode, the masterly manner in which are unveiled the tumults of a woman's soul, all are Gallic in effect. It is one of the tragedies of recent American literature that Mrs. Chopin should have written this book two decades in advance of its time, that she should have been so grievously hurt by the attacks of provincial critics as to lay aside her pen. Always a self-sacrificing mother, she devoted herself with special solicitude at this time to her son Jean. Renewed plans for work were prevented by her sudden death from a brain hemorrhage.

Mrs. Chopin's early photographs show her a charming girlish figure in the quaint costume of the mid-century. At the time she was writing, the premature whitening which often accompanies black hair and which formed a marked contrast to her brilliant brown eyes and delicate complexion as well as her small plump figure caused her friends to compare her to a French marquise. Always quiet and unassuming, she is said to have been a most stimulating listener; undoubtedly to this fact, even though she never consciously sought for materials, must be attributed the range of her characterizations—from the cotton-picking negro to great Creole ladies. As for her method of composition, the effortless ease of her style makes plausible the account of how she wrote a story as soon as the theme occurred to her, recopied it, and sent it off with practically no revision.

[Mrs. Chopin's work has been treated by F. L. Pattee in *Hist. of Am. Lit. since 1870* (1915) and by D. A. Dondore in *The Prairie and the Making of Middle America: Four Centuries of Description* (1926). Biographical accounts are found in Wm. Hyde and H. L. Conard, *Encyc. of the Hist. of St. Louis* (1899); in the *Lib. of Southern Lit.*, II (1909), 863 ff.; in A. N. De Menil, *Lit. of the La. Territory* (1904); and in the *Writer*, Aug. 1894. This latter article by Wm. Schuyler, a personal friend, is the best of the contemporary accounts.]   D. A. D.

CHORPENNING, GEORGE (June 1, 1820– Apr. 3, 1894), pioneer western mail man, the second of the seven children of George Chorpenning and Elizabeth (Flick) Chorpenning, was born in Somerset, Pa. His first American ancestor came to North Carolina with the French Huguenots in colonial days. As a young man he assisted his father in various enterprises and became manager of a store. He was tall and well-built, active and ambitious (data from Mrs. Frank G. Chorpenning, Clearfield, Pa.). When the United States mail between Salt Lake City and California was to be established, young Chorpenning and Absalom Woodward joined in offering a bid for the service. A contract was made with them which provided for a monthly service over the emigrant trail at $14,000 per year. They at once went to California and on May 1, 1851, set out from Sacramento with the first mail. Great obstacles were encountered in crossing the Sierras. For sixteen days they struggled through deep drifts, beating down the snow with mauls. Throughout the summer Indians threatened, and in November Woodward and several of his men were killed by them. The winter of 1851–52 brought renewed difficulties; horses were frozen and carriers endured frightful sufferings. For some years thereafter the mail was carried from San Francisco via Los Angeles and the Mormon Trail to Salt Lake City. Indian depredations continued, and Chorpenning made an appeal to Congress which in 1857 resulted in an appropriation for his relief. In 1858 he changed from pack-horses to coaches and improved the service to a weekly schedule. The following year he changed to a more direct course across the Nevada desert—the route now followed by the Lincoln Highway. Friction with the Department developed and resulted in the annulment of his mail contract in May 1860. Thus ended nine years of pioneering from Utah to the Pacific Coast over three different routes. Chorpenning now went east to present his claims. When the war broke out he assisted in recruiting and organizing two Union regiments in Maryland and was commissioned major of the 1st Maryland Infantry, June 11, 1861. But in order to remain in Washington and prosecute his claims against the government he tendered his resignation and was discharged from the service in September 1861. Now began his long attempt to obtain compensation for the losses sustained in his overland mail service. Congress responded in 1870 by ordering an adjustment of the claim and in conformity therewith the postmaster-general awarded him $443,010.60. Just before this was to be paid it was assailed in Congress as fraudulent; payment was suspended and then revoked. Testimony given at a criminal case in 1878 indicated that the persons primarily responsible for revoking payment were extortioners. The matter was again presented to Congress and was still unsettled when Chorpenning died. He was married twice: on Jan. 19, 1841, to Mary Margaret Pile, and, after her death, to Mrs. Carrie Dunlap.

[L. R. Hafen, *The Overland Mail, 1849–69* (1926), which gives an account of Chorpenning's mail service and cites the primary sources in government documents and elsewhere; *The Case of Geo. Chorpenning vs. the U. S.* (1874), a 56-page pamphlet published by the claimant; *Statement and Appendix of Claim of Geo.*

Chorpenning Against the U. S. (1889), a more extensive statement in 103 pages; an article on the Chorpenning claim and implication of high officials in the *Nation*, XV, 228; family data furnished by Mrs. Frank G. Chorpenning of Clearfield, Pa., and by Harry Chorpenning McGee of Berkeley, Cal.]   L. R. H.

CHOUART, MEDART. [See GROSSEILLIERS, MEDART CHOUART, SIEUR DES, 1621?–1698?]

CHOUTEAU, AUGUSTE. [See CHOUTEAU, RENÉ AUGUSTE, 1749–1829.]

CHOUTEAU, AUGUSTE PIERRE (May 9, 1786–Dec. 25, 1838), fur trader, was born in St. Louis, the son of (Jean) Pierre and Pelagie (Kiersereau) Chouteau. He entered West Point Academy July 17, 1804, and graduated June 20, 1806, as an ensign in the 2nd Infantry. He served for a short time as aide to Gen. James Wilkinson on the southwestern frontier, but resigned from the army Jan. 13, 1807. In the same year, at the head of a trading party, he accompanied the military expedition led by Ensign Nathaniel Pryor in the first attempt to restore the Mandan chief, Big White (Shehaka), to his people, and for his gallantry in the disastrous battle with the Arikaras, Sept. 9, was commended by Gen. Clark in a report to the secretary of war. He was one of the ten partners of the Saint Louis Missouri Fur Company and accompanied the expedition of 1809 to the mouth of Knife River, returning to St. Louis the following May. In the War of 1812 he served as a captain of the territorial militia, and though on Mar. 1, 1813, he took his seat as judge of the court of common pleas, he appears not to have retained the place, but to have continued in the military service till the peace. In 1815, with Jules de Mun, he conducted a trading and trapping expedition to the upper Arkansas, meeting with great success until the spring of 1817, when the party was captured by Spanish soldiers and taken to Santa Fé. The two leaders were put in chains and imprisoned for forty-eight days, and their property, valued at $30,000, was confiscated.

After his release and return he traded for a time with the Osages in western Missouri and middle Kansas. In 1823 he bought the trading house of Brand & Barbour, on the Verdigris, near its junction with the Arkansas, and in this region he spent the greater part of his remaining days. It was the country of the Arkansas Osages, whom his father had colonized there more than twenty years before—a country soon to be shared by them with the Creeks, the Choctaws, and the Cherokees. The Dwight Mission, on the Grand, had been established in 1820, and a military post, Fort Gibson, was built in 1824. To this region, thronging with savages often at war, came Indian agents, soldiers, missionaries, traders, and land speculators; and it remained for many years the theatre of the most stirring and colorful drama to be found anywhere on the old frontier. Not the least of its notables was Sam Houston, who from 1829 to 1832 lived with the Cherokees and became an intimate friend of Chouteau's. On the Grand, near the present Salina, Chouteau built a two-story log palace, and here, in the midst of his Indian family and attended by retainers and slaves, he lived the life of a frontier baron, the arbiter of numberless disputes and the dispenser of a lavish hospitality. From St. Louis, where he happened to be in September 1832, he led the party of Commissioner Ellsworth, Gen. Clark, Washington Irving, Count de Pourtales, and Charles Latrobe on their long ride over the prairies to his home, and often he was the host of other travelers, eager for a view of the West in its most picturesque setting. In 1835 he built, on the abandoned site of Camp Holmes (near the present Purcell), another trading post, which he put in the charge of an agent. Two years later, appointed by the secretary of war to negotiate treaties among the warring Indians, he visited this post, where he remained for the winter and the following spring. He died in the vicinity of Fort Gibson and was buried at the fort with military honors.

By common consent Chouteau was a colonel, and in distinction from his uncle, "Colonel Auguste," during the latter's lifetime, he was known as "Colonel A. P." He was married at St. Louis in church on Aug. 13, 1814 (a civil ceremony having preceded this one), to his cousin Sophie Labbadie, who with one son and five daughters survived him. He also had an Indian wife, Rosalie, born an Osage but naturalized a Cherokee, by whom he had several children, and he also had children by three other Indian women. "For however it may be considered as a reproach on his character," wrote Indian Agent Montford Stokes to the Commissioner of Indian Affairs, Mar. 19, 1839, "almost all Traders who continue long in an Indian Country have Indian wives." He died heavily in debt, and he was no sooner gone than Indian and white creditors began to seize his property, which would have been wholly dispersed but for the intervention of friends. His personal qualities and his worth as a citizen have been highly extolled by many writers.

[F. B. Heitman, *Hist. Reg.*; W. B. Douglas (ed.), *Three Years Among the Indians and Mexicans*, by Thos. James (1916); Grant Foreman, *Pioneer Days in the Early Southwest* (1926); *Annals of Iowa*, 3rd series, I, no. 8. (Jan. 1895), containing official documents relating to the Shehaka expedition of 1807; C. J. Latrobe, *The Rambler in North America* (1835); Washington Irving, *Tour on the Prairies* (1835).]

W. J. G—t.

CHOUTEAU, JEAN PIERRE (Oct. 10, 1758–July 10, 1849), fur trader, Indian agent, was born in New Orleans, the son of Marie Thérèse (Bourgeois) Chouteau and Pierre Laclede [q.v.]. The surname Chouteau he bore in accordance with French law, while the given name Jean he appears to have dropped at his majority. With his mother he arrived in the new village of St. Louis in September 1764. What formal schooling he received is not known; in his age he used to say that his chief school had been *l'académie osage,* though his ability to quote Horace in the original is evidence that he had training not obtainable among the Osages. His connection with these Indians began at an early day; in 1792 they formally presented him with a tract of land in gratitude for his services "of many years." From 1794 to 1802, while his half-brother held the monopoly of Osage trade, he was stationed with the tribe, both as a trader and as a commandant of Fort Carondelet. In the latter year, when the monopoly was given to a company headed by Manuel Lisa [q.v.], he induced the majority of the tribe, numbering some 3,000 souls, to move to the vicinity of the "Three Forks of the Arkansas" where he had a trading privilege of his own. He gave hearty accord to the American rule on its establishment and shortly afterward sent his eldest son, Auguste Pierre [q.v.], to West Point. In the same year President Jefferson appointed him United States Agent for the Osages, and as the government terminated Lisa's monopoly, he was soon again the dominant influence among the Missouri Osages. He organized the first troop of horse for the territorial militia and was made its captain, later becoming major.

His business interests developed separately from those of his half-brother, though in many projects the two continued to be allied. On Mar. 7, 1809, he joined with his rival, Lisa (who, though distrusted, had become too powerful to be ignored), William Clark, and eight others in the formation of the Saint Louis Missouri Fur Company. This historic company, the first important organization formed to exploit the beaver regions of the West, was at once intrusted by the government with the mission of restoring the Mandan chief, Big White (Shehaka), to his people. Appointed by Gov. Lewis to command the expedition, Chouteau, at the head of a force of 172 well-armed men, left Fort Osage, at the mouth of the Osage River, toward the end of June, and in September, without loss or serious incident, accomplished his mission. By Nov. 20 he was again at home. The company, for all its enterprise and the prestige of its partners, did not thrive, and in January 1814, dissolved. Chouteau had several trading houses in the lower Missouri region, each in the charge of an agent; and for several more years he continued active in business, making frequent trips to the frontier. From about 1820, however, he lived in semi-retirement on a "plantation," as it was called, which he developed on the outskirts of St. Louis. It was a noted place, where hospitality was shown to all visiting celebrities, among whom was Lafayette, a guest there in 1825. The red man also was welcome, and often his tepee decorated the scene. Chouteau still found time for an occasional journey, and in the year that he was eighty-two he voyaged to New Orleans and back. During his nearly ninety-one years he saw St. Louis grow from a mere camp in the wilderness to a great modern city. Death came to him at the loved plantation.

Chouteau was twice married: to Pelagie Kiersereau on July 26, 1783, and to Brigitte Saucier on Feb. 17, 1794. He had eight sons (of whom Auguste Pierre and Pierre, Jr. [qq.v.] were the most noted) and one daughter. He was one of the leading citizens of his community; from the time of the American occupation to the time of his retirement probably no one, except his half-brother, outranked him in civic importance. An excitable and sometimes tempestuous man he may have been in his younger days: Thomas James, who as a boatman and trapper, accompanied the expedition of 1809, pictures a scene in which Chouteau, "frantic with passion and raging like a mad bull," would have precipitated a bloody encounter among his men had he not been restrained by a group of bystanders, including two of his sons. But his basic nature was genial and companionable, and he mellowed with time.

[For references see René Auguste Chouteau; also Walter B. Douglas (ed.), *Three Years Among the Indians and Mexicans,* by Thos. James (1916).]

W. J. G—t.

CHOUTEAU, PIERRE (Jan. 19, 1789–Sept. 6, 1865), merchant, fur trader, financier, was born in St. Louis, son of Jean Pierre and Pelagie (Kiersereau) Chouteau. Although in business he was referred to as Pierre Chouteau, Jr., he was familiarly known among his friends and relatives as "Cadet," meaning second born. He received his early education from the village school-master, Jean Baptiste Trudea. Before reaching the age of sixteen he became a clerk in his father's store. In 1808 he accompanied Julien Dubuque to the lead mines on the upper Mississippi, remaining there for two years. In 1809 he joined his father on one of the St. Louis Missouri Fur Trading expeditions. Soon after reaching his majority he went into business on his own account, and in 1813 formed a partnership with his brother-in-law, Bartholemew Berthold, in the Indian trade and general merchandising business. This partnership terminated in 1831, when Chouteau became a member of the firm of Bernard Pratte & Company; later the firm name was changed to Pratte, Chouteau & Company. This company having had the agency of the Western Department of the American Fur Company for some years finally, in 1834, purchased the Western Department. Four years later the firm name was changed to Pierre Chouteau, Jr. & Company, which name it carried for more than twenty years. As his business expanded, Chouteau was drawn into other fields, and for many years resided mainly in New York. He was at this time one of the leading financiers in the country. His business operations during the whole of his life were extensive; his trading area extended over an immense territory, embracing the whole country watered by the upper Mississippi and Missouri rivers, as well as the tributaries of the latter. In 1843 he joined the American Iron Company to work the Iron Mountain deposits in St. François County, Mo., and in 1850 the firm of Chouteau, Harrison & Valle to operate a rolling-mill in North St. Louis. He was also one of the original incorporators of the Ohio & Mississippi Railroad of Illinois in 1851. In 1820 he was elected as one of the delegates from St. Louis County to the constitutional convention of Missouri. He was generous and helpful toward scientific expeditions seeking to go into the Far West, and contributed in no small degree to their success. At the time of his death, which occurred in St. Louis, he had accumulated a fortune amounting to several millions. He was married in church on Aug. 13, 1814 (a civil ceremony having preceded this one) to his cousin Emilie Gratiot, daughter of Charles Gratiot, by whom he had five children.

[H. M. Chittenden, *Am. Fur Trade of the Far West* (1902), I, 382–84; Louis Houck, *Hist. of Mo.* (1908), III, 254; Richard Edwards, *Great West* (1860), p. 538; Chouteau papers in Mo. Hist. Soc. (St. Louis); *Mo. Republican* (daily), Sept. 7, 1865.]   S. M. D.

CHOUTEAU, PIERRE. [See CHOUTEAU, JEAN PIERRE, 1758–1849.]

CHOUTEAU, RENÉ AUGUSTE (September 1749–Feb. 24, 1829), trader, assistant to Pierre Laclede [*q.v.*], in the founding of St.

Louis, was born in New Orleans, the son of René Auguste and Marie Thérèse (Bourgeois) Chouteau. He was baptized on Sept. 7, 1749, and was probably born on the same day or at most a day or two earlier. Soon after his birth, the mother, alleging gross cruelty on the part of her husband, separated from him taking her infant with her. In 1757 she formed an unsanctioned but generally approved union with Laclede, by whom she had four children, all of whom, in observance of French law, bore the surname of the undivorced husband. In August 1763 Laclede with his family left New Orleans for the Illinois country, reaching Fort de Chartres in November. Auguste, now a sedate, intelligent, and disciplined lad of fourteen, who enjoyed the utmost confidence of his stepfather, accompanied him in December on a tour of the west bank of the river, where a site was selected for a new settlement. Two months later Laclede sent him in command of a party of thirty men to begin the building of the village, to which the founder, who followed in April, gave the name of St. Louis.

Until the death of Laclede, June 20, 1778, Chouteau was his chief lieutenant in all the many activities in which he was engaged. Succeeding to the management of the business, he built up, by his energy, ability, and tactfulness, a large trade. A connection with the Osage Indians, then on the Osage River, in the present Vernon County, Mo., had been made apparently as early as the eighties, his half-brother Pierre acting as his representative with the tribe. In 1794 he obtained a monopoly of the Osage trade, which he retained until 1802, adding considerably to his fortune. On the transfer of Louisiana to the United States, March 10, 1804, he cordially cooperated with the officials in establishing the new order. He was appointed one of the three justices of the first territorial court, and in 1808 became a colonel of the St. Louis militia, a title which clung to him for the rest of his life. In the following year, when St. Louis was incorporated as a town, he was made chairman of its board of trustees. In 1815, with Governors Edwards of Illinois Territory and Clark of Missouri Territory, he served as a federal commissioner in negotiating treaties with the Sioux, Iowas, Sauks, and Foxes. He was also the United States pension agent for Missouri Territory, 1819–20. He had, however, small inclination toward public office, giving his time chiefly to his many business interests. Others of the family sought the remoter frontier, but "Colonel Auguste" spent most of his days in St. Louis. In this isolated village, insignificant in itself, but the chief mart of furs and skins, the frontier capital and the radial point of exploration and settlement, he became the wealthiest citizen and the largest landholder. The humble Laclede cottage he rebuilt and enlarged, adding to it a beautiful garden and making it one of the town's show places. He died at his home.

Chouteau was married, Sept. 26, 1786, to Marie Thérèse Cerré, who with four sons and three daughters survived him. His character was of the highest. The French inscription on his tomb characterizes his life as a model of the civic and social virtues, and contemporary records attest its truth. Delassus, the Spanish lieutenant-governor, wrote of him (May 31, 1794), as "a man of incorruptible integrity." He was of less than medium height, with a high forehead, light brown hair, an oval face which he shaved smooth, straight nose and classic mouth, and his expression was quiet and grave. He left a narrative of the founding of the village which family tradition says is only a fragment of a work embracing the local annals of many years, the larger portion having been accidentally burned.

[Chouteau MSS. in the Mo. Hist. Soc.; "Jour. of the Founding of St. Louis," *Mo. Hist. Soc. Colls.*, vols. III, no. 4 (1911), and various notes and references in other volumes; Louis Houck, *Hist. of Mo. from Earliest Explorations and Settlements Until Admission of the State into the Union* (1908); Paul Beckwith, *Creoles of St. Louis* (1893); J. Thos. Scharf, *Hist. of St. Louis City and County* (1883); Wm. Hyde and H. L. Conard, *Encyc. of the Hist. of St. Louis* (1890); Frederic L. Billon, *Annals of St. Louis in its Early Days* (1886).]
W. J. G—t.

CHOVET, ABRAHAM (May 25, 1704–Mar. 24, 1790), surgeon, anatomist, was the son of David Chovet, a wine merchant of London. In 1720 he was apprenticed for seven years to Peter Gougeux Lamarque, a foreign brother of the Company of the Barber-Surgeons of London, paying Lamarque one hundred and five pounds for the privilege. At the expiration of his apprenticeship he went to France, where he studied anatomy, having Winslow as one of his teachers. In 1732 he was back in London giving demonstrations of anatomy on wax models. At that time teachers of anatomy had the greatest difficulty in procuring subjects for dissection, the lack being supplied by means of wax models and other preparations. Chovet was particularly skilled in constructing such material. An advertisement appeared on Dec. 27, 1733 in the *London Evening Post*: "To be seen this day and for the future, price 5 s., at Mr. Lamark's, Surgeon, in Orange Street, Leicester fields, Mr. Chovet's the surgeon's, New Figure of Anatomy, which represents a woman chained down upon a table, suppos'd opened alive; wherein the cir-

culation of the blood is made visible through glass veins and arteries: the circulation is also seen from the mother to the child, and from the child to the mother, with the Systolick and Diastolick motion of the heart and the action of the lungs. All which particulars, with several others, will be shewn and clearly explained by Mr. Chovet himself. Note, a Gentlewoman qualified will attend the ladies." In 1734 Chovet became a foreign brother of the Company of the Barber-Surgeons of London, and in the same year he was chosen one of the Demonstrators of Anatomy at Surgeons' Hall. (The term "foreign brother" does not necessarily imply that its holder was a foreigner or alien, but that he was "a surgeon who practised within the jurisdiction of the Company of Barber-Surgeons of London and was not 'free' of the Company by patrimony, servitude or redemption.") Sidney Young states that judging from his residence in Leicester Fields and his position in the Company, Chovet must have acquired some eminence (*Annals of the Barber-Surgeons of London*, 1890). In 1736 Chovet resigned his position of Demonstrator of Anatomy, and as after 1740 his name no longer figures on the lists of the Company, Young thought he must have died. In reality he had only transferred his activities to other fields. He next appears in the Barbados, pursuing his anatomical labors with the same enthusiasm. Peachey found his name as a resident of Antigua in a list of subscribers to the Protestant schools in Ireland. In 1759 he was practising surgery at Kingston, Jamaica. Thence he fled with his wife and daughter to escape a threatened uprising of the blacks and sometime before 1774 he settled in Philadelphia, as on Oct. 12, 1774 he advertised a course on anatomy in that city. His advertisements all stress the fact that studying his preparations is unattended with the disagreeable smells and sights unavoidable in the dissecting room. Many laymen seem to have attended his demonstrations. When John Adams arrived in Philadelphia as a delegate to the Congress of 1774 he was taken to see the anatomical paintings which Dr. Fothergill had presented to the Pennsylvania Hospital to be used by Dr. Shippen in his lectures on anatomy. The statesman was much impressed with what he termed their "exquisite art," but when a little later he saw Chovet's wax preparations he writes, "This exhibition is more exquisite than that of Dr. Shippen at the Hospital." In 1793 after the death of Chovet, the managers of the hospital purchased his collection of preparations and wax models, which in 1824 they presented to the University of Pennsylvania, where it remained until utterly destroyed by fire in 1888. From many contemporary pen portraits Chovet seems to have been an eccentric character. Chastellux terms him "a perfect original." When the English were in Philadelphia he was a Whig, after they left he proclaimed himself a Tory. John F. Watson says he was "licensed to say and do what he pleased, at which no one took umbrage," and that he was noted for possessing much sarcastic wit and for using expletives which were "neither useful nor ornamental" (*Annals of Philadelphia*, 1830, pp. 609, 611). He gives a pathetic picture of him as he appeared on the streets of the city in his old age. Coste the chief medical officer of Rochambeau's army is quoted as speaking most highly of Chovet's skill in anatomy and surgery. He was one of the founders of the College of Physicians of Philadelphia in 1787. S. Weir Mitchell depicts him, quite unfairly, in one of the characters of his novel *The Red City* (1908).

[*Annals Medic. Hist.*, Sept. 1922, Dec. 1926; T. G. Morton, *Hist. Pa. Hospital* (1895); G. W. Norris, *Early Hist. of Medicine in Phila.* (1886); Geo. C. Peachey, *Memoir of Wm. and John Hunter* (1924); W. S. W. Ruschenberger, "Account of the Institution of the Coll. of Physicians of Phila.," *Trans. Coll. Phys. of Phila.*, ser. 3, vol. IX.]   F. R. P.

CHRISTIAN, WILLIAM (*c.* 1743–Apr. 9, 1786), soldier, politician, was a descendant of a Manx family that had settled in Ireland, whence his parents, Israel and Elizabeth (Stark) Christian, came to Virginia in 1740. They soon afterward opened a general store at Staunton, Augusta County, where William was born. He must have begun his military career early, for at the age of twenty he had risen to the rank of captain in Col. William Byrd's regiment. About four years later he entered the law office of Patrick Henry as a student, with more success in wooing and marrying Henry's favorite sister, Anne, than in acquiring a profession. He resided successively in Botetourt and Fincastle counties, represented the latter in the lower house of the Virginia legislature in 1773, 1774, and 1775, and both counties in the state Senate during sessions of 1776 and 1780–83. In 1775 he was a member of the Committee of Safety, a member of the conventions of Mar. 20 and July 17, and a member of the committee named to provide plans for the execution of Patrick Henry's famous resolutions of Mar. 23, 1775. During Dunmore's War Christian commanded a regiment of Fincastle militia. He was appointed lieutenant-colonel of the 1st Virginia Regiment, Continental Line, on Feb. 13, 1776, and on Mar. 18 following he was promoted to the rank of colonel, a position he held until July,

when he resigned and accepted a commission as colonel of militia from the Virginia Council of Defense (Aug. 1, 1776), with orders to organize and lead a punitive expedition against the Cherokee Indians, whose raids, under the leadership of the chiefs Dragging Canoe and Oconostoga, had terrorized the settlements in the upper Holston and Wautaga river valleys. Christian collected a force of about seventeen hundred militiamen from Virginia and North Carolina at Long (also called Great) Island, now Kingsport, on the Holston River, while the Indians retired beyond the French Broad River. The militia followed by the way of Chimney Top Mountain and Lick Creek to the French Broad, destroying crops and a few villages with a show of force that overawed the Indian leaders. Without giving battle, the Indians agreed to a truce which was to be followed by a "permanent" treaty of peace the next year. The army returned to Long Island, where they rebuilt Fort Robinson and renamed it Fort Patrick Henry, and then disbanded after a three months' bloodless campaign. Christian received the official thanks of the governor and council and was appointed one of the three commissioners on the part of Virginia to negotiate the Cherokee treaty which was signed at Long Island July 20, 1777 (T. W. Preston, *Historical Sketches of the Holston Valleys*, 1926, pp. 56–59). In August 1785 he moved his family to Kentucky, where his Virginia land grants amounted to nine thousand acres, and located on Bear Grass Creek, near Louisville. The following year he was killed, near the present site of Jeffersonville, Ind., while leading a pursuit party against marauding Wabash Indians.

[J. A. Waddell, *Annals of Augusta County, Va.* (2nd ed., 1902), p. 125; *Colonial Va. Reg.* (1902), comp. by W. G. and Mary N. Stanard; W. J. Carrington, *Hist. of Halifax County, Va.* (1924), pp. 143–44; W.W. Henry, *Patrick Henry* (1891), vols. I and II, *passim*; Lewis and R. H. Collins, *Hist. of Ky.* (1874), II, 127, 496; *Official Letters Governors State of Va.*, vol. I, "Letters of Patrick Henry" (1926), ed. by H. R. McIlwaine; *Calendar Va. State Papers and Other MS.*, vols. I (1875), II (1881), III (1883), ed. by W. P. Palmer; J. G. M. Ramsey, *Annals of Tenn.* (1853); *Porterfield vs. Clark, 2 Howard 76*; *Colonial Records of N. C.*, vol. X (1890), ed. by W. L. Saunders; W. R. Jillson, *Ky. Land Grants* (1925); E. G. Swem and J. W. Williams, *Reg. of General Assembly Va., 1776–1918, and Constitutional Conventions* (1918).]   T. D. M.

CHRISTIANCY, ISAAC PECKHAM (Mar. 12, 1812–Sept. 8, 1890), lawyer, senator, was descended from forebears named Christiaanse, who emigrated in 1614 from Leyden to New Amsterdam. He was the son of Thomas and Zilpha (Peckham) Christiancy, and was born in Johnstown, Fulton County, N. Y. His father was a blacksmith until Isaac was eight years old; after that he cleared a piece of land and cultivated a farm. He was always poor, but did all he could to maintain his family. When Isaac had reached the age of twelve, his father had a serious accident, and it devolved upon the boy to help support the family. He could only attend school three months in winter, two miles from home. His mother, however, taught him a great deal, and at eighteen he began to teach school. For a few months each year he attended first the academies at Johnstown and Kingsborough, and later the one at Ovid. In the fall of 1834 he took up the study of law with John Maynard in Ovid. On May 12, 1836, he left Ovid for Monroe, Mich., where in the same month he became clerk in the United States land office. He kept up his studies, with the result that he was admitted to the bar in 1838. In November 1839 he was married to Elizabeth McClusky. His ability and diligence won for him the position of prosecuting attorney of Monroe County for three terms (1841–46). In 1844 he brought his father, mother, sister, and two brothers to Monroe. Having become a prominent lawyer, he naturally felt a strong interest in politics. Till 1847 he was a staunch Democrat, but the slavery issue impelled him to join the Free-Soil party, whose convention he attended in 1848 at Buffalo. From 1850 to 1852 he was a member of the Michigan Senate, while in 1852 he ran for governor, securing 5,850 votes out of a total of 83,308. When in 1854 the consolidation of the Free-Soil and Whig parties resulted in the formation of the Republican party, Christiancy turned Republican. He issued the call for the convention at Jackson, Mich., in 1854, and was a delegate to the first national convention at Philadelphia in 1856. During the latter year he purchased the *Monroe Commercial*, and as its editor vigorously supported the Republican cause. Early in 1858 he became one of the first four justices of the supreme court of Michigan. Volumes V–XXXI of the *Michigan Reports* amply testify to his keen sense of justice and equity, his thorough acquaintance with the fundamental principles of law, and his great industry. He was continuously reëlected, until in 1874 he resigned the office, in order to go to Washington as senator from Michigan. He owed his selection largely to a split in the Republican party. Within eight days after entering the Senate he made a speech on the Louisiana election (*Congressional Record*, 44 Cong., Spec. Sess., pp. 39–41) which won for him the respect of his colleagues. But his career as senator was not a success, and he resigned in 1879; whereupon President Hayes appointed him minister to Peru. Returning to the United States two years later, he passed his declining years in the home of his daughter, Mrs. Thomas O'Brien, in Monroe, Mich.

[I. P. Christiancy, "Recollections of the Early Hist. of the City and County of Monroe," in *Mich. Pioneer and Hist. Colls.*, VI, 361–73 ; sketch in J. E. Wing, ed., *Hist. of Monroe County, Mich.* (1890) ; obituary in the *Detroit Tribune*, Sept. 9, 1890.]   A. H—a.

CHRISTY, DAVID (b. 1802), anti-slavery writer, geologist, was a resident of Cincinnati who was active in the colonization movement in Ohio and the author of a number of pamphlets on slavery and scientific subjects. From 1824 to 1836 he was a newspaper man, and it was probably owing to this early training that he acquired his later skill in presenting his views on public questions in an interesting and striking manner. In 1848 he was appointed an agent of the American Colonization Society in Ohio and was instrumental in inducing Charles McMicken of Cincinnati and others to contribute toward the purchase of a tract of land in Africa for the colonization of the free colored laborer. This land lay between Sierra Leone and Liberia and was known as "Ohio in Africa." In his capacity as agent he visited Columbus in January 1849 where he found the legislature in heated discussion over the repeal of the Black Laws which were designed to prevent the immigration of colored men into Ohio. A memorial was presented by the friends of colonization to send emigrants to Liberia, and Christy was asked to deliver lectures on African colonization before the House of Representatives in Ohio, which he did on Feb. 19, 1849, and again on Jan. 19, 1850. These were subsequently published at Columbus as well as a pamphlet, *On the Present Relations of Free Labor to Slave in Tropical and Semi-Tropical Countries,* which he had prepared for the Ohio Constitutional Convention. In 1852 he published *The Republic of Liberia : Facts for Thinking Men,* which was originally addressed to the citizens of Cleveland and printed in the columns of the *Herald* and the *Plain Dealer.* The agitation over the Kansas-Nebraska Act and the attacks of the Abolitionists on slavery caused Christy in 1855 to publish his most important work. This was entitled *Cotton Is King: or the Economical Relations of Slavery* (1855). The author's name was withheld in the first edition although it was given in later editions. Christy's object in writing the essay was "to convince the abolitionists of the utter failure of their plans" (Elliott, *post*, p. 22). The essay ran through three editions and *De Bow's Review* declared that it was "cogent, well-informed, and temperate" (*De Bow's Review*, September 1855). This work was followed in 1857 by a pamphlet on *Ethiopia: Her Gloom and Glory* (1857). In the meantime, due to the fact that his duties as agent compelled him to travel extensively in the eastern and middle sections of the country and because he had a natural aptitude for the sciences, Christy began to make geological observations. These he reported in a series of letters first published in the *Cincinnati Gazette* and later issued in pamphlet form and addressed to Dr. John Locke, assistant to the chief geologist of Ohio. According to Locke, no one else had "actually drawn approximate sections of the strata from the Atlantic to Iowa and from Lake Erie to the Gulf of Mexico" (*Letters on the Geology of the West and Southwest*, Rossville, 1848). Christy's interest in geology led him to correspond with M. de Verneuil of Paris and to be employed as the geologist of the Nantahala & Tuckasege Land & Mineral Company of North Carolina. In 1867 he was engaged in writing a book on "Geology Attesting Christianity" (*De Bow's Review*, November 1867).

[E. N. Elliott, *Cotton Is King and Pro-Slavery Arguments* (Augusta, 1860); H. N. Sherwood, "The Movement in Ohio to Deport the Negro" in *Quart. Pub. Hist. and Philosophical Soc. of Ohio*, VII, 51–102; G. P. Merrill, *First Hundred Years of Am. Geology* (New Haven, 1924).]   R. C. M.

CHRISTY, EDWIN P. (1815–May 21, 1862), minstrel, was a native of Philadelphia. Of his early life until 1842, when at Buffalo, N. Y., he originated the Christy Minstrels, little is known. The troupe was first called the Virginia Minstrels, and in addition to its founder, its leading members were George Christy (born Harrington), Lansing Durand, and T. Vaughn. They traveled at first principally through the West and South, and were later joined by Enom Dickerson and Zeke Backus, well-known minstrel performers. They first appeared in New York at Palmo's Opera House, Apr. 27, 1846, and during the following six years they gave more than twenty-five hundred performances in Mechanics Hall and other theatres and entertainment places, winning great favor, and establishing a record for their type of program. In all these performances Edwin P. Christy took the part of interlocutor. It has been claimed that he was the originator of modern negro minstrelsy. All that his announcements asserted, however, was that he was "the first to harmonize and originate the present type of minstrelsy," meaning thereby the singing in harmony and the introducing of various acts, such as wench dancing and solo playing. The Christy Minstrels went to London at one period, and were so cordially received by English audiences that they set the fashion, musical entertainments of that form remaining popular, especially in London, for many years. Christy's two sons were E. Byron Christy (1838–66) and William

A. Christy (1839–62), both of whom were members of their father's profession during their short lives. He acquired a considerable fortune, and lived in retirement after 1854. During his later years, he was subject to attacks of melancholia, suffering from delusions that he was without adequate means of support. While in a period of temporary insanity he jumped from the window of his residence in New York, receiving injuries which proved fatal. His name stands among the first in point of time, and at the head of his profession, as a master in the art of providing the public with that peculiar and now almost non-existent type of entertainment known as blackface or negro minstrelsy.

[Laurence Hutton, "The Negro on the Stage," *Harper's Mag.*, June 1889; *N. Y. Herald*, May 22, 1862; H. P. Grattan, "The Origin of the Christy's Minstrels," in the *Theatre* (London), Mar. 1882.]   E. F. E.

CHURCH, ALONZO (Apr. 9, 1793–May 18, 1862), educator, the son of Reuben and Elizabeth (Whipple) Church, was born near Brattleboro, Vt., where his father was engaged in farming. His grandfather, Timothy Church, had fought in the French and Indian War and was a colonel in the Revolution, also taking an active part in the attempt of New York to secure control of Vermont. His father was a lieutenant in the Revolution. Alonzo was ambitious for an education and as soon as he could prepare for entry he was off to Middlebury College where he graduated in 1816. Having helped himself through college by teaching at odd times, he had learned to like such work, and immediately after graduating he joined that train of young college men in the North who had begun to drift southward. Following the practise of most of the migrating Middlebury College graduates, he set out for Georgia. Like his fellows he was bent on teaching and soon appeared in Eatonton, Putnam County, where he became the head of an academy.

As Church was afflicted with "pulmonary infirmity," he felt that he should make his home permanently in a warm climate. Hence he looked upon Georgia as his fixed abode. The year after his arrival he acquired another element of permanency in his marriage to Sarah J. Trippe, the daughter of a Putnam County planter. So great was his success both in teaching and in impressing himself upon the educational leaders of the state that in 1819 he was elected to teach mathematics in the State University at Athens. Undoubtedly another important element aided him in this promotion: he was genuinely religious and had in 1817 placed himself in the care of the Hopewell Presbytery. This move recommended him to the Presbyterians, who now controlled the

University and were largely to continue to do so until the Civil War. In 1820 he was licensed to preach and four years later he was ordained an evangelist at Bethany Church in Greene County. At the time when he came to the University as professor of mathematics, Moses Waddel, another Presbyterian preacher and academy teacher, arrived as the new president. When Waddel left ten years later (1829), Church was his natural successor. By this time the Methodists and Baptists had become powerful enough and self-conscious enough to resent the control of the University by the Presbyterians; the latter especially made a bitter fight against Church solely because he was a Presbyterian. Nevertheless he was elected and for the next thirty years he molded and controlled one of the principal ante bellum Southern universities. Although founded in 1801 (chartered in 1785) the University had never been able to gain strength until Waddel had given it ten years of faithful service. With this basis Church built the University into an institution of great usefulness to Georgians as well as to the youth of surrounding states. He ruled with a firm will both trustees and faculty; he believed in a scrupulous attention to duties; and he held that whatever the rules required was a sacred obligation. His piercing black eyes, dark complexion, graceful and dignified carriage, together with a quick temper, marked him as a positive character. In 1834 he became involved in a long and heated controversy with Stephen Olin, a classmate at Middlebury College, who had recently been a member of the faculty at the University. His most famous dispute was with John and Joseph LeConte, teachers at the University in the early fifties. The issues were varied and confusing but centered in the attempt of the LeConte brothers to remake the University in curriculum and organization along more modern lines. The fight resulted in the departure of the LeContes and the complete reorganization of the faculty in 1856 with Church reëlected as president. Worn out and weak, Church informed the trustees in 1858 that he would resign the next year. After his resignation he moved into the country near Athens to spend the last years of his life. His wife died in 1861 and the following year he himself passed away in an atmosphere tense with a civil conflict in which the sons and sons-in-law of this former New Englander were vigorously fighting on the side of the South.

[E. M. Coulter, *College Life in the Old South* (1928); A. L. Hill, *Hist. Sketch Univ. of Ga.* (1894); *Minutes Board of Trustees Univ. of Ga.*; *Minutes Faculty Univ. of Ga.*; files of the *Athenian*, 1829, *Southern Banner*, 1834, 1845, *Ga. Telegraph*, 1855, and *Southern Watchman*, 1862.]

E. M. C.

CHURCH, BENJAMIN (1639–Jan. 17, 1718), soldier, was born at Plymouth, Mass., the son of Richard and Elizabeth (Warren) Church. He was brought up to follow his father's trade of carpentry, which, especially in his early years, carried him to many parts of the Plymouth Colony. On Dec. 26, 1671, he married Alice Southworth. By 1674 he had bought land and was engaged in building a house at Sogkonate (Little Compton, R. I.), where he became well acquainted with the Indians and was soon "in great esteem among them." The outbreak of King Philip's War, in June 1675, found Church living on the frontier, where his first act was to dissuade Awashonks, squaw-sachem of the Sogkonate Indians, from joining the Wampanoags. During the summer, commanding small detachments of Plymouth troops, Church fought numerous skirmishes of no great importance aside from their value in teaching methods of Indian warfare. He constantly urged his superior officers to pursue the enemy, instead of building forts, but his suggestions were ignored. In the "Great Swamp Fight" of Dec. 19, 1675, near South Kingston, R. I., he played a prominent part as captain of a Plymouth company, and was twice wounded. Had his advice, that the troops be allowed to remain and recuperate in the Narragansett fort, been followed, the English losses from exposure on the return march might have been greatly diminished. During the following spring and summer the troops of the United Colonies undertook the systematic destruction of the Indians' corn, and the capture of warriors, with their women and children. By offering his captives their choice between slavery or fighting against their kinsmen, Church enlisted many Indians in his forces and, with their assistance, took additional prisoners, including a squaw and son of Philip. The sachem himself, with his remaining followers, took refuge in a swamp near Mount Hope (Bristol, R. I.). Betrayed by a deserter, he was ambushed by Church on Aug. 12, 1676, and shot in attempting to escape, by Alderman, one of Church's Indians. During the following twelve years Church lived at various places within the Plymouth Colony, where he bought lands and served occasionally as magistrate or selectman. During King William's and Queen Anne's wars he served as major, and later colonel, in five expeditions against the French and Indians in Maine and Nova Scotia, in the last of which, in 1704, he plundered the French town of Les Mines and, in his blustering manner, ordered the governor of Port Royal to discontinue the raids on the English settlements. These expeditions accomplished little, since the enemy avoided decisive engagements, and Church, poorly compensated for his services, retired in disgust in 1704. He seems to have been a man "of uncommon activity" even in his later years, when he had grown so fat that the aid of a stout sergeant was needed to lift him over fallen trees. On one occasion his impetuosity caused some of his French prisoners to be "knocked on the head," an act which he found difficult to explain on his return to Boston. He died Jan. 17, 1718, near Little Compton, R. I., from injuries sustained in a fall from his horse.

[Thos. Church, a son of Benj. Church, was the author of *Entertaining Passages Relating to King Philip's War* (1716). The book describes his father's part in King Philip's War and in the later expeditions to Maine, was written from his notes, and received his approval. The best edition, that of Henry M. Dexter (1865), is in two volumes, and contains in the Introduction a detailed account of Benj. Church's life. Numerous references to him appear in the *Plymouth Colony Records* (1855).]

H.P.S.

CHURCH, BENJAMIN (Aug. 24, 1734–1776), physician, traitor, poet, and author, was a grandson of Col. Benjamin Church [*q.v.*], who was conspicuous in the Indian and French Wars, and a son of Benjamin, deacon of Mather Byles's church (Boston). He was born at Newport, R. I., entered the Boston Latin School in 1745, and graduated from Harvard College in 1754. Soon after graduation he wrote two poems which appeared in a collection in celebration of the accession of George III. He studied medicine with Dr. Joseph Pynchon, later going to London where he married Hannah Hill of Ross, Herefordshire. About 1768 he built a fine house at Raynham, Mass., which some think threw him into debt. Seemingly his pen supported the Whig cause vigorously, but it is said that he parodied the patriotic songs in favor of the British and that his political essays were answered from the Tory side by his own pen. *The Times* . . . "by an American" (Boston, 1765), a satire upon the Stamp Act, has been attributed to him. He examined the body of Crispus Attucks, killed in the Boston Massacre, 1770, and his deposition was printed in the narrative of the town (James Spear Loring, *The Hundred Boston Orators* . . . 4th ed., Boston, 1855, p. 37). He is said to have written for the Loyalist paper, *The Censor,* but on Oct. 28, 1772, being a member with Adams and Warren of a committee of correspondence, he was appointed to draft a letter to the other towns about the colony's rights (Justin Winsor, editor, *Memorial History of Boston,* 1881, III, 44). On Mar. 5, 1773, he delivered *An Oration . . . to Commemorate the Bloody Tragedy of the Fifth of March, 1770,* which ranks high amongst these utterances. In 1774, after a caucus of Whigs, sworn to secrecy, it was learned, according to Paul Revere, that the proceedings had been divulged to the Tories, and Revere did not doubt that Church had supplied the information to Hutchinson (see letter in *Massachusetts Historical Society Collections,* ser. I, vol. V, pp. 106–12). Church, nevertheless, continued in the confidence of the Whigs, for, with Dr. Joseph Warren and others, he was appointed a delegate in 1774 to the Provincial Congress. According to Samuel Kettel, soon after the battle of Lexington, Church told his confreres that he must go into Boston, to see about medicines. On his return, he said he had been made prisoner and taken before Gen. Gage, but it was learned later that he had paid Gage a voluntary visit. In May 1775, on the other hand, he went to consult the Continental Congress, Philadelphia, about the defense of the colony. He was unanimously elected director and chief physician of the first Army Hospital (at Cambridge), July 25, 1775, at a salary of four dollars a day, but his management of its affairs seems to have been not altogether successful, finally causing an inquiry to be held into his conduct. It must be admitted, however, that he had rivals seeking his position (see Church's letter to Gen. Sullivan, *American Archives,* ser. IV, vol. III, p. 712). He evidently wrote to Washington, Sept. 20, seeking permission to leave the army (*American Archives,* ser. IV, vol. III, p. 780).

Church was tried by court martial, Oct. 4, 1775, Washington presiding, and was found guilty of "holding criminal correspondence with the enemy." In July 1775, he had sent a cipher letter to the commander of a British vessel at Newport. The correspondence had been intercepted, Henry Ward taking it to Washington at the end of September. The Massachusetts Provincial Congress unanimously expelled Church from their body on Nov. 4. He defended himself ably but was not convincing. He admitted that he wrote the letter, but said he was not acting traitorously as he purposely had exaggerated the numbers of the Continental Army in order to frighten the British and quickly end hostilities. The Continental Congress resolved on Nov. 6 that he should be imprisoned at Norwich, Conn., but, because of illness, he was removed to Massachusetts and put on parole not to leave the colony (Richard Frothingham, *History of the Siege of Boston,* 3rd ed., 1872, pp. 259–60). Eventually allowed by the Massachusetts Council to depart for the West Indies, he sailed from Boston probably in 1778, but the ship was never heard from again. Church's family was pensioned by the Crown.

[Richard Frothingham, *Life and Times of Jos. Warren* (1865), p. 225 n.; *New Eng. Hist. and Geneal. Reg.*, Apr. 1857, p. 123; Wm. O. Owen, *The Medical Department of the U.S. Army, . . . 1776–1886* (1920); Lorenzo Sabine, *Biographical Sketches of Loyalists of the Am. Revolution* (1864), I, 313; J. M. Toner, *The Medical Men of the Revolution . . .* (1876); Justin Winsor, *Narr. and Crit. Hist. of America* (1888), vol. VI; Church's original cipher letter, as well as the letter as deciphered, in the Lib. of Cong., Washington.]
A.C.M.

CHURCH, FREDERICK EDWIN (May 4, 1826–Apr. 7, 1900), landscape painter, born at Hartford, Conn., was descended in a direct line from Richard Church, one of the earliest settlers of that city, who arrived with the Rev. Thomas Hooker, in June 1636 by way of Newton, Mass., having emigrated from Braintree, Essex, England, a few years previously. Frederick's father was Joseph Church a prominent citizen of Hartford and his mother's maiden name was Eliza Janes. Notwithstanding certain misgivings as to the boy's choice of art as a profession, his parents, in view of marked evidences of his talent, placed him with Benjamin A. Coe to learn drawing, and for six months with A. H. Emmons to study color. He was also encouraged by the sculptor E. S. Bartholomew who had studied at the National Academy of Design in New York. Thomas Cole [*q.v.*] was induced to receive Church as a pupil in 1844, and from that time till Cole's death in 1848, Church was an inmate of his house and studio. After his master's death, Church continued his studies from nature and painted a number of pictures for which he found subjects in the mountains and along the rivers and coasts in the vicinity of New York—effects of storm in which the sky and clouds play an important part, or striking masses of rock, such as "View of West Rock near New Haven" (bought by Cyrus W. Field), or the hills that border the Hudson. These gave evidence of a love for the exceptional, cultivated by association with Cole, though he did not share that painter's story-telling and allegorical tendencies. He had read of Humboldt's travels in South America and desiring to realize pictorially that naturalist's eloquent descriptions, he visited South America in 1853 and again in 1857, occupying at Quito the house Humboldt had lived in fifty years before. He brought back to New York an ample supply of studies and sketches, and in 1859 exhibited successfully his famous picture, "The Heart of the Andes," besides a number of other realistically painted tropical landscapes, "The Falls of Tecemdama," "Cotopaxi" (1854), and "The Mountains of Ecuador" (1855). In the mean-

time, he had visited Niagara Falls and from near Table Rock on the Canadian side, painted, in 1857, the Horse-shoe and American Falls, on an oblong canvas, seven by three feet in size. It has been considered his masterpiece, and was the first satisfactory delineation of the Falls in art. At the Paris Exposition of 1867, it was awarded a second medal. From the collection of John Taylor Johnston it was purchased for the Corcoran Gallery in Washington. As a complete change from tropical subjects, he sought the effects of extreme cold in the north, going to Labrador, where he made studies for "Icebergs" (1863) and "Aurora Borealis" (1865). A trip to Jamaica yielded "The Vale of St. Thomas" (1867) and other West Indian subjects. Emulating in painting what Washington Irving had accomplished in literature, he turned from America to Europe in 1871, finding in Greece and the Near East inspiration for "The Parthenon,"—a truly noble picture,—and the decorative "Ægean Sea," now at the Metropolitan Museum, New York. He also visited Palestine and made studies at Jerusalem and Damascus. Returning to New York, he continued painting from his ample supply of studies, notes, and sketches till about 1877, when an attack of inflammatory rheumatism deprived him of the use of his right arm and hand. He learned to use his left hand, till that also failed him, and he was obliged to cease work "in the maturity of his powers and still retaining the enthusiasm of his youth." He was a member of the National Academy of Design, where he often exhibited, and was also represented in 1852 at the Royal Academy in London. Of his exhibits at the Paris Exposition (1867), a celebrated critic wrote, "The originality of this artist, more than his technical skill with the brush, entitled him to the leading position,"—and Ruskin wrote to Charles Eliot Norton of Church's "Cotopaxi," now at the Public Library Galleries, New York, "Church's 'Cotopaxi' is an interesting picture. He can draw clouds as few men can . . . he has a great gift of his own." After a forced inactivity of over twenty years, Church died at New York on the eve of his seventy-fourth birthday, after returning from Mexico, where he had spent a number of winters.

[H. W. French, *Art and Artists in Conn.* (1879); H. J. Tuckerman, *Book of the Artists* (1867); *Cat. Memorial Exhibition, Metropolitan Museum, N. Y.* (1900), preface by Chas. Dudley Warner; L. L. Noble, *Life and Works of Thos. Cole* (1856), and *The Heart of the Andes* (1859).]
R.J.W.

CHURCH, FREDERICK STUART (Dec. 1, 1842–Feb. 18, 1924), painter, son of Thomas B. and Mary Elizabeth (Stuart) Church, was born at Grand Rapids, Mich. As a young boy he was taught to draw by a local painter and engraver named Hartung, a native of Holland. His parents, however, destining him for business, he was sent at thirteen years to Chicago to enter the employ of the American Express Company. While in the office his clever caricatures made him known as "the art chap." At seventeen he enlisted as a private in Company A, Chicago Light Artillery, and saw honorable service in the Civil War, including participation in Sherman's march to the sea. After he was mustered out he went to New York where he studied drawing and painting with Walter Shirlaw and L. M. Wilmarth. He began to show pictures at the National Academy of Design and to make illustrations for *Harper's Weekly* and other publications. For three years he was employed by the Elgin Watch Company as commercial illustrator. He began at this time to make studies of animals which, as he generally endowed them with human and humorous attributes, proved popular and salable. He took an active part in 1875 in the formation of the Art Students' League of New York, called by his friend and associate William St. John Harper "the most democratic and American of art academies." Of Church himself Harper wrote: "Himself one of the most unconventional and least academic of draftsmen, he has always maintained the importance of thorough academic training." Church showed his sympathy with both the radicals and the conservatives in painting by belonging simultaneously to the Society of American Artists and to the National Academy and he helped to effect the union of these societies. He was active in the American Water Color Society and the New York Etching Club, and he served as a trustee of the Harper Fund to help young students through the art schools. He was a member of the Lotus Club and of the Architectural League of New York, and for several years was chairman of the art committee of the Union League Club. Though resident at New York during most of his professional life he retained characteristics of the Middle West. Notably American in aspirations and reactions, he was an old man when he first visited Europe, and he created a mild newspaper sensation on his return by announcing that European art could teach Americans little or nothing. But while he painted pictures in which subject seemed to be of primary consideration, he was a thoroughly artistic technician whose work was remarkable for its refined tonality, broad handling, and truth of tone relations. He is represented in the National Gallery, Washington; in the Metropolitan Museum, New York; in the City Art Museum, St Louis; and in other public and private collections.

[Wm. St. John Harper, "F. S. Church: a Painter of the Ideal," in the *Outlook*, Nov. 25, 1905; *Art News*, Feb. 23, 1924; *Outlook*, Mar. 5, 1924; *Who's Who in America*, 1920–21.]   F. W. C.

CHURCH, GEORGE EARL (Dec. 7, 1835–Jan. 5, 1910), civil engineer, explorer, writer, was born in New Bedford, Mass., the son of George Washington and Margaret (Fisher) Church. On his father's side he was descended from Richard Church who came from Oxford, England, to Plymouth, Mass., in 1632; on his mother's side he was a lineal descendant of Edward Winslow who came over on the *Mayflower* and was several times governor of the colony at Plymouth. When he was a small boy, Church's family moved to Rhode Island where he attended the Providence High School. His father had died before this, so when the boy decided to become a civil engineer he was obliged to make his way by means of practical experience instead of by going through college. After some experience in helping to make a topographical map of the state of Massachusetts, as an assistant engineer on the Hoosac Tunnel, and in the construction of railways in Iowa, in 1857 he went to Buenos Aires to serve as chief engineer on a railway project for the Argentine Republic. The work was postponed, and he was appointed a member of a scientific commission which was to explore the Republic's southwestern border and report on a system of defense against the savages on the slopes of the Andes. This commission, which covered a distance of 7,000 miles in nine months, had many exciting adventures with the Indians and on one occasion it was reported that Church had been captured and burned to death. In 1860 and 1861 he acted as chief assistant engineer on the construction of the Great Northern Railway of Buenos Aires which he had previously surveyed and located; but at the outbreak of the Civil War he gave up his position to return to the United States and enlist in the army. He was commissioned captain in the 7th Rhode Island Infantry and sent to the front. His service was with the 7th, 11th, and 2nd Regiments, Rhode Island Volunteers, and as a brigade commander in the Army of the Potomac. He earned special distinction in the battle of Fredericksburg where his regiment suffered heavy losses. He entered it as a captain and came out a lieutenant-colonel in command of what was left of his regiment. Afterward he was promoted to a colonelcy.

Soon after the war Church went to Mexico

where he acted as special war correspondent for the *New York Herald* during the revolution against Emperor Maximilian. He attached himself to the army of President Juarez and shared its fortunes until the capture of Maximilian in 1867. Then, in 1868, he went back to South America where his greatest work was accomplished in connection with the Madeira & Mamoré Railway. For ten years, at the request of the Bolivian Government, he engaged in the task of opening Bolivia to trade by way of the Amazon River and its tributaries. He obtained from Brazil a concession to construct a railway in order to avoid the falls of the Madeira River, conducting not only the negotiations with the Brazilian Government but persuading European capitalists to finance the undertaking. The concession, and the companies formed in connection with it, became involved in legal proceedings and eventually had to be abandoned for many years, but the enterprise was eventually resumed and the terminus of this railway which Church had done so much to promote was named Villa Church in his honor. In 1880 he was appointed United States commissioner to report on the political, financial, and trade conditions of Ecuador. His report, "Ecuador in 1881," was published as a special message of the President to Congress. On the completion of this mission he took up his residence in London. Although he retained his United States citizenship, he lived the remainder of his life in London. He was connected with various Argentine railway undertakings, and with some in North America which brought him back frequently but only for short periods. After taking up his residence in London he devoted much time to literary pursuits and to the scientific societies of which he was a member. His experiences in South America, supplemented by a lifetime of study of the experiences of other travelers on that continent, gave him the knowledge which led the *Geographical Journal* to speak of him as "one of the foremost authorities on the history and geography of South America" (XXXV, 203). The *Transactions of the American Society of Civil Engineers* says of him: "Colonel Church probably possessed a wider and more complete knowledge of the history, geography, and resources of South America than any other authority" (LXXI, 407). His presidential address, "Argentine Geography and the Ancient Pampean Sea," before the Geographical Section of the British Association was pronounced by the London *Times* to be "the most scientific paper ever read before that section." He was the first, and until his death, the only Fellow of the Royal

Geographical Society not a British subject to be elected a member of its Council. He was a frequent contributor to its *Journal*. His book, *Aborigines of South America,* which he was still working on at the time of his death, was published in 1912. He died and was buried in London but left his library, a valuable collection of 3,500 volumes, to Brown University. He was married twice: first, in 1882, to Mrs. Alice Helena Carter who died in 1898; second, to Anna Marion Chapman, daughter of Sir Robert Harding. He had no children.

[In addition to references above, see John A. Church, *Descendants of Richard Church of Plymouth* (1913).]

E. Y.

CHURCH, JOHN ADAMS (Apr. 5, 1843– Feb. 12, 1917), metallurgist, son of Pharcellus [*q.v.*] and Chara Emily (Conant) Church, was a native of Rochester, N. Y., and a member of the first class (1867) to receive the degree E.M. from the Columbia School of Mines. After graduation he went to Europe, and while pursuing a course at Clausthal visited numerous continental metallurgical establishments. His technical observations were embodied in a publication, *Notes on a Metallurgical Journey,* which he published in 1873, at which time he was assistant editor of the *Engineering and Mining Journal* (1872–74). For one semester, after his return from Europe, he took over Prof. Egleston's course at the Columbia School of Mines, and again (1878–81) resumed the teacher's rôle as professor of mining and metallurgy at the Ohio State University. In 1877 he became a member of the United States Geological Survey West of the 100th Meridian, and produced a monograph on the Comstock Lode, containing an ingenious theory that kaolinization was the cause of the high temperature of the ore body. The publication of this theory (*Transactions of the American Institute of Mining Engineers,* vol. VII) led to an interesting and spirited discussion, Church's view being opposed notably by G. F. Becker of King's Survey (*Ibid.,* vol. VIII). In 1881 Church resumed his metallurgical work as superintendent of the Tombstone Mining & Milling Company, in which capacity he established a record by his utilization of manganese instead of iron in silver-lead furnace slags, developing successfully a slag with 43 per cent MnO, a classic example of its kind. On July 30, 1884, he was married to Jessie A. Peel, by whom he had one son. Accompanied by his wife, Church went to Ku Shanza, Manchuria, in 1886, under contract with Li Hung Chang, then viceroy, to introduce American methods into certain mining districts in China, taking with him a few

Americans to act as mine and smelter foremen. In sharp contrast with the spirit of modern development shown by Li Hung Chang was the unwillingness of the Chinese officials to disregard an ancient superstition as to a sacred dragon supposed to dominate a conveniently located coal mine. This made it necessary for Church to obtain the fuel for his Ku Shanza smelting operations from a coal deposit, at an almost prohibitive distance, located beyond the reach of the imagined dragon. The Chinese metallurgical operations, at the time of Church's arrival, were as primitive, in their way, as was such a belief in the existence of the dragon. The smelting furnaces were about the size of ordinary washtubs, the air being supplied by the most crude hand bellows. One can therefore imagine the initiative, patience, and resourcefulness which were required to develop commercially successful metallurgical operations under such conditions, especially when hampered, as Church was, by deep-seated prejudices and unreasonable demands on the part of his native labor, and by the constant danger of depredations from marauding robber bands. Nevertheless he successfully fulfilled his contract with Li Hung Chang. He returned to the United States in 1890 and established a consulting practise which he continued until his death.

[*Eng. and Mining Jour.*, Mar. 10, 1917; *N. Y. Herald*, Feb. 13, 1917; *N. Y. Tribune*, Feb. 14, 1917; *Who's Who in America*, 1916–17.]   R. C. C—y.

CHURCH, PHARCELLUS (Sept. 11, 1801– June 5, 1886), Baptist clergyman, was born in Seneca, N. Y., the son of Willard and Sarah (Davis) Church. His early education was meager. His mother encouraged him at the age of twelve to read the Bible through, and his contact with the Gospel of John brought a religious interest. When a Baptist church was formed near his home, he united with it and soon began to preach. In 1824 he graduated from the Hamilton Literary and Theological Institution (now Colgate University), where he was especially influenced by Dr. Nathaniel Kendrick. His early pastorates were at Poultney, Vt. (1825–28), Providence, R. I. (1828–34), and (temporarily) New Orleans, where he wrote his first book, *The Philosophy of Benevolence* (1836). He then was called to the First Baptist Church of Rochester, N. Y., where his most important ministerial work was accomplished (1835–48). Here also he wrote his most significant volume, *Antioch: or, Increase of Moral Power in the Church of Christ* (1843), which anticipated somewhat the argument of Henry Drummond as to the unity of natural and spiritual law, while

his attempt to establish a *via media* between Augustinianism and Pelagianism was prophetic of the later working compromise between Calvinistic and Free Baptists. Although he left Rochester before the University there was established, he was an influential leader in the preliminary efforts; his participation in the attempt to bring the college and seminary from Hamilton is traced somewhat in detail in Jesse L. Rosenberger's *Rochester and Colgate; Historical Background of the Two Universities* (1925). Although Church had two more pastorates— Bowdoin Square, Boston (1848–52), and the Second Baptist, Brooklyn (1853–55), during both he was engaged in journalistic activities, first with the *Watchman and Reflector* (Boston), and then with the *New York Chronicle* (purchased in 1854 by Church and Dr. Jay S. Backus). The latter magazine, devoted especially to the Bible translation cause, Church edited until its merger into the *Examiner* (1865). Among his more important writings may be mentioned a prize essay, *Religious Dissensions* (1838); a novel, *Mapleton* (published anonymously, 1853), in the interest of prohibition; *Seed-Truths* (1871), written in Bonn, Germany, during one of several sojourns in Europe. Church was married in 1828 to Chara Emily Conant, sister of Thomas J. Conant [*q.v.*], the eminent Hebraist (John A. Church, *Descendants of Richard Church of Plymouth, Mass.*, 1913). William Conant and John Adams Church [*qq.v.*] were two of his sons.

[Thos. Armitage, sketch in the *Examiner*, June 17, 1886; obituary in the *Watchman*, June 10, 1886; *First Half Century of Madison Univ. 1819–69* (1872).]
         W. H. A.

CHURCH, WILLIAM CONANT (Aug. 11, 1836–May 23, 1917), editor, born in Rochester, N. Y., was the son of Pharcellus Church [*q.v.*] and Chara Emily (Conant) Church. At the age of nineteen, he received editorial experience when he assisted his father to edit the *New York Chronicle*. After five years of this, he became publisher of the New York *Sun* but withdrew in 1861 for a European trip. Abroad at the outbreak of the Civil War, he returned in July and became a member of the joint military-naval expedition under Gen. W. T. Sherman and Admiral S. F. Dupont, and was present at the capture of Port Royal. He was the first bearer to the North of the news of the victory and wrote the account of it for the New York *Evening Post*. Later he became a volunteer aide on the staff of Gen. Silas Casey and was wounded in the battle of Williamsburg. He also took part in the battle of Fair Oaks. During 1861–62 he was Washington correspondent for the *New*

York Times but gave this up when he was appointed inspector and mustering officer of provisional brigades with the rank of captain. He was rapidly promoted to major and lieutenant-colonel of volunteers. Resigning in order to start a military paper, together with his brother, Francis P. Church, he began the publication of the *Army and Navy Journal* in 1863. During the same year he was married to Mary Elizabeth Metcalf. Soon after the draft riots broke out in New York, he joined the Civilian Committee which assisted in putting them down. In 1866 the *Galaxy Magazine* was started by the two brothers. This publication lasted for twelve years and was then merged with the *Atlantic Monthly*. Henry James's first stories appeared in it, also a novel by Charles Reade, and the early writings of Mark Twain. "The Claverings," by Anthony Trollope, began in the first number, May 1866. With Gen. George W. Wingate, Church established the National Rifle Association and was its first president as well as an honorary director for life. He was one of the founders and a fellow in perpetuity of the Metropolitan Museum of Art, a life member and director of the New York Zoological Society, an original member of the Military Order of the Loyal Legion of the United States, of which he was also senior vice-commander. He was a member of the National Council of the National Economic League, and of the Executive Committee of the National Security League. He was also chairman of the committee in New York which erected a monument to John Ericsson and he delivered an oration at the dedication. He ranked, according to a statement in the *New York Times* at the time of his death, as among the foremost journalists of the country. He had been a newspaper man for more than sixty years. His paper, which was largely the result of his military training and experience, supported an extreme military policy. He was a constant contributor to the *Century, Scribner's,* the *North American Review* and other leading magazines; the *New York Times* and other newspapers. Appointed literary executor of John Ericsson, he published his biography in two volumes (1890). He also wrote *Ulysses S. Grant and the Period of National Preservation and Reconstruction* (1897).

[John A. Church, *Descendants of Richard Church of Plymouth, Mass.* (1913); *Who's Who in America,* 1914–15; *N. Y. Times,* May 27, 1917; *Galaxy,* 1866–76.]   M. A. K.

CHURCHILL, THOMAS JAMES (Mar. 10, 1824–Mar. 10, 1905), Confederate soldier, governor of Arkansas, was born in Jefferson County, Ky., the son of Samuel and Abby (Oldham)

Churchill, and the grandson of Samuel Churchill, who came from Bushey Park, near London, and settled in Albemarle County, Va. Thomas received his academic training in Saint Mary's College (1844) and his training in law at Transylvania University. In the Mexican War he served as lieutenant in the 1st Kentucky Mounted Riflemen under Col. Humphrey Marshall. In January 1847 he was taken prisoner and was not exchanged until the war was virtually over. On returning from Mexico he moved to Arkansas (1848), acquired a large plantation near Little Rock, and engaged in planting. He was married, on July 31, 1849, to Ann, daughter of Ambrose H. Sevier. In 1857 he was appointed postmaster at Little Rock and served until the outbreak of the Civil War. He then raised a regiment called the 1st Arkansas Mounted Riflemen and entered the Confederate army. In the battle of Oak Hills (Wilson's Creek) he rendered notable service. By December 1862 he had risen to the rank of brigadier-general and was assigned to the defense of Arkansas Post. This was considered a key position for blocking the progress of the enemy up the river toward Little Rock and as a menace to Sherman, who was trying to capture Vicksburg. After Sherman's failure, Gen. John A. McClernand superseded him and gave orders for the capture of Arkansas Post so as to remove any menace in the rear of a second move on Vicksburg. Churchill had but 5,000 men, of whom only 3,000 were really effective, against a much larger force and a fleet. He was poorly equipped with guns and munitions, but fought desperately the first day and held the enemy at bay. That night he received a telegram from Gen. T. H. Holmes ordering him to hold the fort "until help arrives or all are dead." Next day the enemy attacked with such fury that some of Churchill's men raised the white flag without his knowledge and he was forced to surrender. His loss in dead and wounded was only 135 while that of the attacking party was 1,061 (D. Y. Thomas, *Arkansas in War and Reconstruction, 1861–74,* 1926, pp. 175–81). Later he took part in the attack upon Banks's Red River expedition and on Steele at Jenkins's Ferry. He followed Kirby Smith's fortunes into Texas and finally surrendered there unwillingly, having risen to the rank of major-general. With the return of the Democrats to power in Arkansas, in 1874 he was elected state treasurer and served until 1880, when he was nominated for governor by the Democrats on a platform indorsing the submission of an amendment repudiating the state debt. This, however, was not an issue between him and his Greenback opponent, W. P. Parker, whom he defeated by a vote of 84,088 to 31,284. He withheld his signature from a legislative bill virtually repudiating, but not vetoing it. Soon after he became governor a shortage of $233,616 in his accounts as treasurer was discovered, and the attorney-general brought suit to recover this sum. Churchill declared that the shortage was due to bad bookkeeping and was able to establish, before the master in chancery, credits for large sums. Final judgment was rendered for $23,973 in currency and $56,548 in scrip. Gov. Churchill claimed that the latter had been burned by mistake by the state debt board and, as none of it ever was presented for payment, he probably was correct. Settlement was made for the currency.

[*Confed. Mil. Hist.*, vol. X (1899); *Ark. Leg. Jours.* (1881); Fay Hempstead, *Hist. Rev. of Ark.*, vol. I (1911); D. Y. Thomas, *Ark. in War and Reconstruction, 1861–74* (1926).]   D. Y. T.

CHURCHILL, WILLIAM (Oct. 5, 1859– June 9, 1920), philologist, ethnologist, son of William and Sarah Jane (Starkweather) Churchill, was born in Brooklyn, N. Y. He received all the advantages of early education and entered Yale College with the class of 1881. Owing to ill health, he was obliged to leave in the middle of his sophomore year, but, after a voyage to England on a sailing vessel, he returned and finished his course with the class of 1882. After graduation he taught school for one year in Indianapolis, and then went on a trip to Australia and the South Sea Islands. On his return, he was for two years librarian of the Academy of Sciences at San Francisco. He next held a position in the Signal Service Bureau in Washington, D. C., and in 1891 he became an editor of the *Brooklyn Daily Times*. A way opened for him as a philologist and ethnologist when he was appointed United States consul-general to Samoa (1896–99). Here in the house where Robert Louis Stevenson died he engaged in the fascinating study of Polynesian languages, a prerequisite in ascertaining the natives' point of view. The amount of data collected by him in these few years is beyond calculation, and formed the basis of his scientific work. On Aug. 14, 1899, he was married to Llevella Pierce. Back in the United States at the beginning of the century, he began a new line of duties as a department editor of the New York *Sun* (1902–15), then a giant in the newspaper field. In the coterie of brilliant men summoned by Dana, Churchill as a writer of trenchant and pure English was a well-known member. In spite of the exacting work on the *Sun*, his philological studies were continued and his house in Brooklyn became a

transplanted bit of Samoa containing an outstanding library of works on Polynesia. He brought out the results of his years of study in *Polynesian Wanderings* (1910), in which Polynesian migrations were traced ingeniously by loan words among the Melanesian. Not only was the first application of this method fruitful of results, but as a by-product it was ascertained that Polynesian is a language in process of formation. *Polynesian Wanderings* was followed by *Beach-la-Mar* (1911), a study of the trade speech of the Western Pacific, and this by *Easter Island, Rapanui Speech and the Peopling of Southeast Polynesia* (1912). In 1915 he became an associate in primitive philology of the Carnegie Institution of Washington, D. C. The Great War summoned him to government work in which a knowledge of various languages was requisite, and he performed an exacting bit of war service as director of the division of foreign language publications of the Committee on Public Information. Many other papers and monographs on ethnological and philological topics also came as the result of Churchill's assiduous labors. His conclusions are especially valuable since it is likely that it will be long before any one with Churchill's groundwork will attempt the problem of the most widespread migration ever known, that of the Polynesian to the islands in the west Pacific.

[*Who's Who in America*, 1918–19; *N. Y. Sun*, June 10, 1920; *Carnegie Inst. of Washington Year Book No. 19*, 1920; *Yale Univ. Obit. of Grads.* (1920); *Hist. Class of '82, Yale College, 1878–1910* (1911).]   W. H.

CHURCHMAN, WILLIAM HENRY (Nov. 23, 1818–May 18, 1882), educator of the blind, was born in Baltimore, Md., of Quaker parentage, the son of Micajah and Eliza Churchman. When he was fifteen years old his eyesight began to fail, according to family tradition from overtaxing in reading and the study of languages and mathematics; in manhood he was totally blind. When eighteen he entered as an advanced student the new school for the blind in Philadelphia, where he came under the influence of Friedlander, and where he was graduated after three years as a pupil in whom "the institution has reason to be proud." Within a few months he was teaching music and mathematics in the school for the blind at Columbus, Ohio; and when he was only twenty-six he was given full charge of the school at Nashville, Tenn., thus early illustrating in his own person what he later said of some blind men, that they succeeded "by dint of irrepressible energy of character." Thereafter he successively headed similar institutions at Indianapolis, Janesville, Wis., and again at Indianapolis. Having everywhere shown himself a first-rate planner, organizer, and administrator, he was chosen in his forty-eighth year as the one best fitted by experience to shape the plans and policies of the projected New York State Institution for the Blind. Accepting the call as a duty, he as superintendent-elect submitted his matured views in an elaborate discussion of the whole question involved. Circumstances, however, kept him as superintendent of the Indiana institution until 1879 when he, in company with other heads of the state institutions, lost his position through political change. Here as elsewhere his trustees recorded their satisfaction with him as superintendent. He was at one time president of the American Association for Instructors of the Blind.

The Indiana Institution for the Education of the Blind was his particular child. Having searched out pupils on tour, he showed the need of a school, addressed the legislature, and more than anybody else brought the institution into being. He was the planner of its buildings, a member of its building committee, the organizer of its routine, and he made it "the model for other and older states" (*Twentieth Annual Report of the Indiana Institute*, 1866, p. 9). He claimed for Indiana the credit of first recognizing an institution of this character as officially a department of public instruction (*First New York Annual Report*, p. 50), and for himself the plan of having his school industrial department run by a contractor on the business principle of self-interest.

Churchman married Mary Marshall who became a real helpmeet to him. He was described by one who knew him well as having a keen sense of humor; as cheerful, hopeful, dignified in bearing, imaginative, resourceful, wise and generous, but firm in judgment, and as having a good physique and a winning personality.

[For Churchman's ideas and the testimonials of his trustees, see the early reports of the Tenn., Wis., and Ind. Institutes for the Blind, especially the Ind. reports for 1862 and 1867. The *Proc. Am. Asso. Instructors of the Blind*, 1878, portray him as a presiding officer; those of 1882 contain an obituary.]   E. E. A.

CILLEY, JOSEPH (1734–Aug. 25, 1799), Revolutionary soldier, judge, and politician, was born in Nottingham, N. H. His father, Capt. Joseph Cilley, who came from the Isles of Shoals, was one of the early settlers of Nottingham; his mother was Alice Rollins (or Rawlins). The younger Joseph was married on Nov. 4, 1756, to Sarah Longfellow, by whom he had ten children. He combined the occupations of farmer, lawyer, and business man. In December 1774 he came into notice in an act which has been styled by an enthusiastic historian "the beginning of the Revolution." He was a member of Sullivan's party which entered Fort William and Mary (later Fort Constitution) near Portsmouth, took out fifteen cannon, and by hard labor, breaking the ice in the river, transported them to Durham. Langdon, another patriotic leader, had carried away about 100 pounds of powder, and these, too, were taken up-stream. The action was just in time, as British vessels directly afterward entered the harbor of Portsmouth. The ammunition was stored at Nottingham and other villages, some of it in a meeting-house.

Cilley was a member of the provincial congress of New Hampshire, and was employed on coast guard duty. His regiment was ordered to Cambridge, and he took part in the siege of Boston. In August 1775 he was assigned to the task of transporting the Portsmouth powder to Winter Hill (Medford). After the evacuation of Boston he accompanied Sullivan's brigade to New York, and thence to the St. Lawrence for the relief of Gen. Thomas. He shared the retreat of the unfortunate expedition from Canada, and reached New York in time to take part in the battle of Long Island. In that disaster Sullivan himself and many others were captured, but Cilley succeeded in fighting his way through the lines. He participated in the retreat from New York, and in the battles of Trenton and Princeton. Meanwhile he had been commissioned major of the 2nd New Hampshire, May 20, 1775, and of the 8th Continental Infantry, Jan. 1, 1776, lieutenant-colonel of the 1st New Hampshire, Nov. 8, 1776, and colonel, Feb. 22, 1777. In the summer of 1777 Cilley was at Ticonderoga. He was engaged in the skirmishing and retreat from that fortress. More fortunately, he fought under Arnold at Bemis Heights, and was distinguished at the battle of Stillwater in the capture of cannon. He was at Valley Forge and in the operations which preceded the battle of Monmouth. He was present at that battle, and accompanied his old commander Sullivan in the expedition against the Indians in 1779. In the latter year he received from his state legislature the gift of a pair of pistols, and he was promoted brigadier-general of militia. He retired from the army Jan. 1, 1781, with a reputation as a good disciplinarian, and he became one of the original members of the Cincinnati. After the Revolution he was made justice of the peace and of the quorum for Rockingham County, and held the position for life. In the first year of his term (1786–92) as major-general of militia, a movement developed in New Hampshire similar to Shays's Rebellion. Cilley, collecting troops, repelled the attempt of insurgents to intimidate the legislature at Exeter, and personally arrested the ringleader. In politics he was a Jeffersonian Republican. He was a member of the state Senate, 1790–91, and of the House, 1792, and was a councillor 1797–98. He was a fluent speaker, a good man of business, and attractive in manner. He died at Nottingham.

[John Scales, *Life of Gen. Jos. Cilley* (1921); Wm. Abbott, *Crisis of the Revolution* (1899); E. C. Cogswell, *Hist. of Nottingham, Deerfield, and Northwood* (1878); *Maine Genealogist and Biographer*, Mar., June, Dec. 1877, Mar. 1878.]
E.K.A.

CIST, CHARLES (Aug. 15, 1738–Dec. 1, 1805), printer, publisher, son of Charles Jacob Sigismund Thiel and Anna (Thomasson) Thiel, was born in St. Petersburg, Russia. He received a good education and was trained in pharmacy and medicine, graduating from the University of Halle as a doctor of medicine. He was probably connected with the court of Catherine the Great where he apparently became involved in difficulties which made it necessary for him to leave the country. In 1769 Thiel determined to emigrate to America and at the same time changed his name to Cist which the initials of his own name formed. He settled in Philadelphia where he was employed by Henry Miller as a translator of English into German. While so engaged he acquired a knowledge of the printer's trade and finally in December 1775 he entered into partnership with Melchior Styner (Steiner) who was the son of the Reform Minister Conrad Steiner of Philadelphia, and who had likewise learned the printer's craft under Miller's tutelage. The new firm of Styner & Cist published works in English and German and was located in Second St. at the corner of Coats's Alley. They soon acquired the reputation of being good and correct printers of books and job work (I. Thomas, *History of Printing in America*, 1810, II, 80–81). Among their more important publications may be listed Thomas Paine's *The American Crisis* (1776); William Brown's *Pharmacopœia Simpliciorium* (1778), the first pharmacopœia of the United States (O. Seidensticker, *First Century of German Printing in America, 1728–1830*, 1893, p. 103); and the issuance of a German newspaper which owing to an insufficient number of subscribers they were forced to discontinue in April 1776. With the advance of the British army on Philadelphia during the Revolutionary War they were compelled to leave Philadelphia but with the evacuation of the city they returned. Shortly thereafter, in 1781, the firm dissolved, but Cist continued the enterprise and by careful management acquired wealth. In

1784 he undertook the publication of the *American Herald* and in 1786 that of the *Columbian Magazine*. He is best remembered, however, as being one of the organizers of the Lehigh Coal Mine Company which was formed in 1792 for the purpose of mining "stone coals" (anthracite) in the Lehigh district. In his efforts to market his product he was threatened with mob violence (*Pennsylvania Magazine of History and Biography*, April 1915). During the administration of John Adams he was appointed public printer and established in Washington a printing office and book bindery at great expense. He later returned to Philadelphia where he had already married Mary, the daughter of John Jacob and Rebecca Weiss of that city, on June 7, 1781. He died at Bethlehem and was interred in the Moravian cemetery.

[In addition to references above, see C. R. Hildeburn, *A Century of Printing, Issues of the Press in Pa., 1685–1784* (1885–86).]
R.C.M.

CIST, CHARLES (Apr. 24, 1792–Sept. 5, 1868), editor, the son of Charles [*q.v.*] and Mary (Weiss) Cist, was born in Philadelphia. He received his education in the public schools of Philadelphia and served in the United States army during the War of 1812. At the close of this conflict he moved to Pittsburgh and later on to Harmony, Pa. On Nov. 18, 1817, he married Janet, daughter of Edward and Sarah White of Whitestown, Pa., by whom he had thirteen children. "His duties as a parent he took care not to make secondary to any other business" (*Cincinnati Gazette*, Sept. 8, 1868). In 1827 he removed to Cincinnati and until 1840 was engaged in mercantile pursuits. He soon displayed, however, an interest in movements of social welfare by opening and superintending the first Sunday-school in Cincinnati which he managed until its growth necessitated its division among the churches. He likewise was one of the most earnest advocates of the free-school system, which was then being discussed throughout the country. His connection with the taking of the census of 1840 in his district gave him an opportunity to collect a mass of valuable statistical information about Cincinnati which he determined to utilize in book form. He had acquired a taste for literary work and the publishing business owing to his association with his father's printing establishment; and in 1841 appeared his first book based upon his census data entitled *Cincinnati in 1841* (1841), which drew heavily upon Daniel Drake's *Natural and Statistical View, or Picture of Cincinnati and the Miami Country* (1815). This was followed by *Sketches and Statistics of Cincinnati in 1851* (1851) and *Sketches and Statistics of*

Cincinnati in 1859 (1859). These three works are valuable as they disclose the growth of the city during these years and recount many events "of a local and statistical nature." Of these three, the last is considered the most valuable since it covers the material included in the two former books and contains an interesting account of the early settlement of this area (Peter G. Thomson, *A Bibliography of the State of Ohio,* 1880, pp. 64, 65). In 1843 Cist began *The Western General Advertiser* which recounted the early pioneer history of the West and included statistics pertaining to the state of Ohio and to Cincinnati. Two years later the name was changed to *Cist's Advertiser* and though the enterprise was never profitable to himself "he labored assiduously to make it so to his patrons and to promote the reputation of the city abroad" (*Cincinnati Chronicle,* Sept. 7, 1868). It was a gossipy paper but it breathed the kindly personality of the editor and his love for his adopted city (Henry Howe, *Historical Collections of Ohio,* 1891, I, 831–32). In 1845 and 1846 historical sketches from this paper were published in Cincinnati under the title of *The Cincinnati Miscellany, or, Antiquities of the West.* In 1853 the paper was discontinued and Cist retired from active affairs. He was a Presbyterian and originally a Democrat in politics but like many other northern Democrats he ultimately found himself within the Republican fold. He died at his home in College Hill, a suburb of Cincinnati.

[In addition to above references, see H. A. and Mrs. Kate B. Ford, *Hist. of Cincinnati* (1881); *Cincinnati Daily Gazette,* Sept. 7, 1868; *Cincinnati Commercial,* Sept. 7, 1868.]   R.C.M.

CIST, HENRY MARTYN (Feb. 20, 1839– Dec. 17, 1902), Union soldier, military historian, was born in Cincinnati, Ohio, the son of Charles Cist [*q.v.*]. He graduated in 1858 at the Farmers' College (later Belmont College) in Hamilton County, studied law in the office of George Hoadly, afterward governor of Ohio, and was admitted to the bar shortly before the outbreak of the Civil War. He entered the army as a private in the 6th Ohio Infantry, Apr. 20, 1861, and served through the West Virginia campaign of that summer and fall, including the battles of Carrick's Ford and Cheat Mountain. On Oct. 22, 1861, he was appointed first lieutenant in the 74th Ohio. The assignment to his new regiment took him to the (old) Army of the Ohio, later renamed Army of the Cumberland, with which he was identified throughout the remainder of the war. He was soon detailed as an assistant adjutant-general, and as such served on the staff of a brigade at the battle of Murfreesboro, and

on the staff of the commander of the army—first Gen. Rosecrans and then Gen. Thomas—in the Chickamauga, Atlanta, and Nashville campaigns. He was promoted captain, Apr. 20, 1864, and major, Mar. 13, 1865. Upon his muster out of the service, Jan. 4, 1866, with the brevet rank of brigadier-general of volunteers, he took up the practise of law, and was for a time mayor of College Hill, Ohio. His avocation was military history, especially of the Civil War, on which he accumulated one of the best private libraries in the country. He wrote extensively on the subject, for periodicals and encyclopedias, and published one book of some importance, *The Army of the Cumberland* (1882), in Scribner's Campaigns of the Civil War series. This is a detailed account of the operations of the army from its organization as Buell's Army of the Ohio until the spring of 1864, after which time it no longer operated independently, but as one of the group of armies under Sherman's personal control. Cist was one of the most active members of the Loyal Legion and of the Society of the Army of the Cumberland, and for twenty-three years served as corresponding secretary of the latter organization. Failing eyesight finally compelled him to abandon both his professional and his literary work. He was married twice: on Sept. 22, 1868, to Mary E. Morris of Urbana, Ohio; and on Apr. 12, 1882, to Jennie E. Bare of Cincinnati. His later years were largely spent in travel. He died in Rome.

[F. B. Heitman, *Hist. Reg.* (1903), I, 302; obituary published as *Circular No. 11* (1903), *Commandery of Ohio, Mil. Order Loyal Legion; Who's Who in America,* 1901–02.]   T.M.S.

CIST, JACOB (Mar. 13, 1782–Dec. 30, 1825), naturalist, anthracite coal pioneer, inventor, was born in Philadelphia, Pa., the son of Charles Cist [1738–1805, *q.v.*] and of his wife, Mary Weiss. After attending the Philadelphia public schools and Nazareth Hall, Nazareth, Pa., he entered his father's printing establishment at the age of fifteen and three years later became manager of a similar business newly founded by his father in Washington, D. C. Some months later this establishment was forced to close by reason of the change of Federal administration and Jacob entered the United States Post Office Department. He served in clerical capacities for eight years, then resigned to settle in Wilkes-Barre, Pa., and was appointed postmaster there, which office he held for the rest of his life. Through his father, educated as a physician and apothecary, Cist became interested in the natural sciences, particularly geology. He was also clever at sketches, both in ink and oils, and was apt at writing, having from an early age published in magazines and newspapers essays in prose and verse on a variety of subjects—"Morning"; "Noon"; "Ode on Hope"; "Eve's Cotton Gin." With this background, Cist in his leisure studied and "geologized" a large part of the country about Wilkes-Barre and became thoroughly familiar with its mineral resources, especially anthracite coal. With friends he undertook the mining and marketing of this commodity between 1813 and 1815, acquiring a lease on the defunct Lehigh Coal Mine Company's land near Mauch Chunk, Pa. Like its predecessor, Cist's company was unsuccessful in convincing either the domestic or industrial consumer of the value of this new fuel and abandoned the project. Cist's scientific interest did not flag, however, and between 1815 and 1821 he collected and distributed both in this country and France fossil plants and flora, described many of the coal formations, and corresponded with various scientists on the general subject, most of his data being published in the *American Journal of Science,* in 1822. Cist's interest in the general development of his new environment prompted him to endeavor to organize a glass-works and pottery in 1808 and an iron works in 1820, but without success. He was one of the founders and first corresponding secretary of the Luzerne County Agricultural Society and did much to introduce the finer grades of fruit trees. He spent many years in the preparation of a work on American Entomology, making hundreds of drawings for the same. This was not completed at his death and was subsequently lost. Three inventions are credited to him: one patented in 1803 of an artist's paint-mixing mill; another in 1808 of a printer's ink made from anthracite coal; and a third in 1814 of a stove to burn anthracite. He was treasurer of Luzerne County for 1816; a founder and treasurer of the Wilkes-Barre Bridge Company, 1816–18; and a charter member and first cashier of Wilkes-Barre's first bank in 1817. He married Sarah Hollenback of Wilkes-Barre on Aug. 25, 1807, and was survived by two daughters.

[H. Hollister, *Hist. of the Lackawanna Valley* (5th ed., 1885); *Proc. and Coll. Wyoming Hist. and Geological Soc.,* I and II; Geo. B. Kulp, *Families of the Wyoming Valley,* vol. III (1890).] C.W.M.

CLAFLIN, HORACE BRIGHAM (Dec. 18, 1811–Nov. 14, 1885), merchant, was born at Milford, Mass., of Scotch descent, the son of John and Lydia (Mellen) Claflin. He attended the common schools and Milford Academy. His father was the owner of a country store and in 1834 he loaned Horace $1,000 with which to

start in business at Worcester, Mass., then a small place. The son prospered in his enterprise and within five years had a trade of $200,000 a year. In 1843 he went to New York City and engaged, with others, in the wholesale dry-goods business. There the Worcester experience was repeated on a far greater scale. The Claflin firm was soon selling to retail merchants all over the United States. At the outbreak of the Civil War Southern merchants were owing the house millions of dollars. It was impossible to realize on these credits and the firm had to make an assignment, but its creditors were paid in full within two years. Later, Claflin and his partners weathered the panic of 1873 without disaster or loss to any with whom they had dealings. During that period their business had grown by leaps and bounds, successfully rivaling that of A. T. Stewart, commonly called New York's merchant prince, and in one year passing the $70,000,000 mark in volume. Claflin had been a pioneer in making the jobbing house a manufacturer, as well as an importer and distributor of merchandise. This gave him an advantage in disposing of large stocks of goods in times of crisis. He could undersell competitors and still realize a small profit. Unquestionably the excellent reputation enjoyed by the firm for a long term of years was due in great part to the sound business sense and personal integrity of the senior partner. At one time an effort was made in the federal courts to prove the Claflin firm guilty of defrauding the Government in the payment of customs, but the accusers were charged with attempted blackmail and the trial resulted in a vindication of the firm. Claflin at seventy was a familiar figure in the New York financial district —a ruddy, white-haired man, unusually active for his years. In public affairs he early identified himself with the Republican party and supported the Government in the Civil War. He was a presidential elector in 1872. In the campaign of 1884 he worked for the election of Grover Cleveland as president. For thirty-eight years he was a trustee of Plymouth Church, Brooklyn, in Henry Ward Beecher's pastorate. He gave liberally for many public causes and to relieve individual distress. He was married on Nov. 28, 1836, to Agnes Sanger of Sherborn, Mass., who, with two sons, survived him.

[C. H. Wight, *Geneal. Claflin Family* (1903); *Brooklyn Daily Eagle,* Nov. 16, 1885; *Horace B. Claflin* (1885).] W.B.S.

CLAFLIN, TENNESSEE (1845–1923). [See WOODHULL, VICTORIA, 1838–1927.]

CLAFLIN, WILLIAM (Mar. 6, 1818–Jan. 5, 1905), governor of Massachusetts, descended from Robert Mackclothlan (or Mackclaflin), a townsman of Wenham, Mass., in 1661, was the eldest of the three children of Lee and Sarah Watkins (Adams) Claflin. He was born in Milford, Mass., where his father was a prosperous boot and shoe manufacturer. After preparation in the local schools and Milford Academy William entered Brown University in 1833 but was obliged to leave before completing the course. After learning the details of his father's business, he went west to St. Louis in 1838, and organized there a wholesale boot and shoe business, in which he held a large interest even after his return East in 1844. In 1845 he entered into business with his father under the firm name of Lee Claflin Company. He was one of the founders and for years president of the Hide and Leather National Bank of Boston and was also one of the organizers of the New England Trust Company, and the Five Cent Savings Bank.

While in Missouri, Claflin had been much interested in the question of slavery extension. His human sympathies had revolted at the sight of the slave block; on one occasion he had purchased with his scanty funds a slave whom he immediately freed. He was one of the members of the Free-Soil Party of Massachusetts on its formation in 1848. As a member of that party he represented the town of Hopkinton in the state legislature from 1849 to 1853. He was a member of the state Senate from 1859 to 1861, being president of that body in 1861. From 1866 to 1868 he was lieutenant-governor and from 1869 to 1871 governor of Massachusetts. In the three gubernatorial elections he had a substantial majority over his Democratic opponent, John Quincy Adams. He was the first governor of Massachusetts to believe in the legal right of female suffrage and he was also an active prohibitionist. While he was governor, legislative bills were enacted extending the rights of women, bettering the condition of criminals, establishing a bureau of statistics for labor, protecting destitute children, and regulating divorce. His messages were straightforward and business-like, as one would expect from a business man. As governor in 1871, he signed the charter of Boston University, of which his father was a founder. Of this institution's board of trustees, he was for many years president. He was also a trustee of Wellesley College, of Mount Holyoke College, and of the New England Conservatory, and was interested in Claflin University, a negro institution in Orangeburg, S. C., which had been named for his father. From 1877 to 1881 he was a representative in the Forty-fifth and Forty-sixth Congresses. He was married

twice: first to Nancy Warren Harding in October 1840, who died in January 1842; and second to Mary Bucklin Davenport on Feb. 12, 1845. He numbered among his intimate friends such notables as Henry Wilson, John Greenleaf Whittier, and Henry Ward Beecher. Their visits to the Claflin home and other events have been described by Mrs. Mary B. Claflin in her books, *Brampton Sketches* (1890), *Real Happenings* (1890), *Personal Recollections of John G. Whittier* (1893), and *Under the Old Elms* (1895).

[A brief memoir by C. S. Ensign is in the *New Eng. Hist. and Geneal. Reg.*, LXI, 111–16. See also *Ibid.*, LXXVIII, 437–38; C. H. Wight, *Geneal. Claflin Family* (1903); *Boston Transcript*, Jan. 6, 1905; R. E. Moody, "A Short Biog. of Wm. Claflin," *Boston Univ. Alumni Mag.*, Feb. 1929.]   R. E. M.

CLAGETT, WYSEMAN (August 1721–Dec. 4, 1784), lawyer, was born at Bristol, England, the son of Wyseman Clagett, a barrister at law. He received an excellent education, became an articled student in a law office, and was admitted as an attorney of the Court of King's Bench. In 1748 he left England, went to the West Indies, and settled in Antigua, where he practised with success for ten years, becoming secretary of the colony. In 1758 he came to New England, established his home in Portsmouth, N. H., and was admitted as an attorney of the superior court of that province. Shortly afterward he was appointed a justice of the peace and in this position proved efficient, exacting, severe, and overbearing, so much so that a new figure of speech was added to the vernacular, the expression "I'll prosecute you," giving way to "I'll Clagett you." In 1765 he was appointed King's Attorney for the province, continuing as such till 1769, when he went with his family to England. On returning to America in 1771 he moved to Litchfield, N. H. Aligning himself with the colonists in the pre-revolutionary struggle with Parliament, he represented Litchfield and Nottingham West in the last General Court under the British crown. He was an active member of the provincial congresses, and had a large share in drafting the constitution of the new state, becoming in 1776 a member of the Council and Committee of Public Safety. In 1778 he was made a special justice of the superior court, which position he resigned in November 1781 in order to become solicitor-general under the temporary form of government then adopted by New Hampshire. He was the only person who ever held this office, since the new constitution of 1784 abolished it. He died at Litchfield, Dec. 4, 1784. He was married in 1759 to Lettice, daughter of Dr. Mitchell of Portsmouth

Clagett was a man of striking personality. Possessed of great learning, "he wrote the Latin language with ease and elegance, and spoke it with fluency" (Adams, *post*, p. 281). He had a fine taste for poetry, was generous, and enjoyed society. On the other hand, his manners were rude, and his habitual profanity of speech was appalling. He never obtained any considerable practise, except in criminal cases. He was not a profound lawyer, yet in the constitutional discussions anent the post-revolution government of New Hampshire he displayed much statecraft and exercised great influence. In his later years he was often embarrassed financially, but never relinquished his full bottomed wig and laced hat, and, in his once fine clothing "he exhibited a striking picture of delapidated importance" (C. W. Brewster, *post*).

[A full account of Clagett's life and career appeared in *The Bench and Bar of N. H.*, by C. H. Bell (1894), p. 204. His personality is vividly pictured in *Annals of Portsmouth*, by Nathaniel Adams (1825), p. 279. See also *Rambles About Portsmouth*, by C. W. Brewster (1st ser., 1859), p. 234, and *Hist. of Hillsborough County, N. H.*, ed. by D. H. Hurd (1885), pp. 8, 495.]

H. W. H. K.

CLAGHORN, GEORGE (July 6, 1748–Feb. 3, 1824), Revolutionary soldier, ship-builder, born in Chilmark, Mass., was a descendant of James Claghorn, a Scotchman who settled in or near Barnstable in the seventeenth century. His father was Shubael Claghorn, a soldier in the Louisburg expedition of 1745; and his mother was Experience Hawes. He himself served in the Revolutionary War as first lieutenant and then captain in the second Bristol regiment, and was wounded at Bunker Hill. Subsequently he became major and then colonel; and Colonel Claghorn he remained after he became a well-known ship-builder at New Bedford. There, in 1785, he built and launched the *Rebecca,* said to have been the first American whaler to double Cape Horn and obtain cargo oil in the Pacific (*New England Historical and Genealogical Register,* XXV, 127). She was a vessel of 175 tons and aroused much interest because of her size (Daniel Ricketson, *The History of New Bedford,* 1858). In 1794 he was appointed naval constructor of the *Constitution,* one of the four 44-gun frigates authorized by Congress to protect commerce against the Algerine corsairs. The design was drawn by Joshua Humphreys [*q.v.*] of Philadelphia, and the keel was laid at Hartt's naval yard in Boston. The frigate was nearing completion when a treaty was signed with Algiers in November 1795, and work was then suspended. The threatened rupture with France, however, moved Congress to provide for completion of three frigates—the *Constitution,* the *United States,* and the *Constellation.*

Wednesday, Sept. 20, 1797, was the day set for the launching of the *Constitution,* when the president, the governor, and other notables were to attend. Solicitous that no accident should mar the launching, Claghorn issued a circular, Sept. 18, 1797, warning his fellow citizens not to allow their curiosity to carry them too near the frigate or the water's edge. "The loss of life of a single citizen," he declared, "would mar the satisfaction and pleasure that the constructor would otherwise enjoy of building and constructing for the ocean a powerful agent of national justice which hope dictates may become the pride and ornament of the American race" (Circular in possession of the Brookline Public Library, reprinted in *The Claghorn Family,* pp. 38–39). To the chagrin of the builder, the vessel moved only a few feet, when the props were knocked away, and refused to budge farther. Two days later a second attempt was made to launch her and again she stuck on the ways. Finally, on Oct. 21, "she descended into the bosom of the ocean with an ease and dignity" gratifying to thousands of spectators (*Commercial Gazette,* Boston, Oct. 23, 1797). No blame was attached to Claghorn for these failures. On the contrary he was commended for his skill, intelligence, and circumspection (*Independent Chronicle,* Boston, Sept. 21, 1797). He had erred, if at all, from excessive caution. Desiring to avoid a repetition of the accident to the *United States,* which had been damaged at the launching by a premature and too rapid descent, he had given a smaller declivity to the ways of the *Constitution* (*Columbian Centinel,* Boston, Sept. 23, 1797). The excessive pressure on her keel amidships, however, gave the *Constitution* a permanent hog or sag (F. A. Magoun, *The Frigate Constitution,* p. 67). Further records of Claghorn's shipbuilding have not been found. He married Deborah Brownell, who bore him four sons and four daughters. He died at Seekonk, R. I.

[Newspapers and books cited above; *The Claghorn Family* (n.d.), comp. by W. C. Claghorn; Ira N. Hollis, *The Frigate Constitution* (1900).]

A. J.

CLAIBORNE, JOHN FRANCIS HAMTRAMCK (Apr. 24, 1807–May 17, 1884), congressman, editor, historian, born near Natchez, Miss., was descended from William Claiborne [*q.v.*]. His father was Gen. Ferdinand Leigh Claiborne, who married a daughter of Col. Anthony Hutchins, a retired British officer who had settled on a large royal grant in what was then West Florida. The name, John Francis Hamtramck was bestowed on Gen. Claiborne's eldest son in honor of a German officer under whom the general had served in the American Revolution. Young Claiborne studied law in the office of his cousin, Benjamin Watkins Leigh in Richmond, Va., until a slight hemorrhage caused him to return to the warmer climate of his childhood home. He resumed his studies in the office of Griffith & Quitman of Natchez, Miss., but again gave up and went to Cuba for his health. Six months later he returned to Virginia and completed his studies under the direction of Gen. Alexander Smythe, at Wytheville. His delicate constitution, however, caused him to abandon his intention of living in Virginia, and he once more returned to Mississippi. In December 1828 he was married to Martha Dunbar of Dunbarton, near Natchez. Being an ardent Democrat, he took charge of a Jackson paper, published in Natchez. He was then elected to the legislature from Adams County for three successive terms. In 1835 he removed to Madison County, and in the same year was nominated for Congress by the first Democratic convention held in Mississippi and was elected by a large majority. When he entered Congress he was the youngest member of that body, and the only one who was a native of the West. Although he was in feeble health during his brief congressional career, his speeches established his reputation as an orator and debater. He was reëlected to Congress in July 1837, an extra session having been called to meet in September of that year. He and his colleague Gholson were seated by the House not only for the special session, but for the regular session which was to follow in December. They did not, therefore, enter the November election, and Prentiss and Ward, the Whig candidates, were elected. As a result there was a spirited contest between the two sets of representatives for seats in the House, when the regular session of Congress began in December. Claiborne, being very ill, was not able to participate in the debate, and under the influence of Prentiss's eloquence the House "rescinded" its former action, but refused to seat Prentiss and Ward, and notified the governor of Mississippi that the seats were vacant (Chester H. Rowell, *A Historical and Legal Digest of All the Contested Election Cases in the House of Representatives of the United States, 1789–1901*, 1902).

Upon the advice of his physician, Claiborne then retired from public life and went to Cuba a second time for his health. Later he returned to Natchez, and in July 1841, became one of the editors of the *Mississippi Free Trader,* an influential organ of the Democratic party. In 1842 he was appointed president of a commission to adjudicate the claims of the Choctaw Indians to several thousands of acres of valuable land, which were also claimed by speculators, whose designs he thwarted. In 1844 he removed to New Orleans and became editor of the *Jeffersonian,* published in French and in English, and of the *Statesman,* published in German and in English. Several years later, he became editor of the *Louisiana Courier,* which supported Franklin Pierce for the presidency. After the election of Pierce he accepted a position as custodian of the public timber in Alabama, Mississippi, and Louisiana, a position which he held until these states seceded from the Union. His opposition to secession caused him to hold aloof from all official connection with the Confederacy, though his only son, Willis Herbert, entered the Confederate Army and died from wounds received in the service. Having inherited a large collection of "time-worn papers and documents" from his father, his uncle and his grandfather, all of whom were connected with the early history of Mississippi, Claiborne set himself to work to add thereto from every available source. His manuscript history of the Southwest, "when ready for the press," was lost by the sinking of a steamboat on the Mississippi. He then reproduced from memory part of this book under the title, *Life and Times of Sam Dale,* which was published in 1860. In the same year appeared his *Life and Correspondence of John A. Quitman,* in two volumes. Shortly after the Civil War, warned by declining health, he retired from all other pursuits and devoted his energies to writing a history of Mississippi, the first volume of his *Mississippi as a Province, Territory and State* appearing in 1881. He completed the second volume of this work, but the manuscript was destroyed by the burning of his home, Mar. 2, 1884. The shock and grief caused by the double loss hastened his death, which occurred on May 17, 1884.

[Probably the most detailed sketch of Claiborne is Franklin L. Riley's "Life of Col. J. F. H. Claiborne" in *Miss. Hist. Soc. Pubs.,* VII, 217–44. See also "Choctaw Land Claims," by the same author in *Ibid.,* VIII, 345–95, and his sketch with extracts from Claiborne's writings and speeches in *Lib. of Southern Lit.,* II (1908), 891–914. Other sketches are to be found in Jas. D. Lynch, *Bench and Bar of Miss.,* pp. 516–29, and in *Biog. and Hist. Memoirs of Miss.,* vol. I (1891), 544–46.]   F.L.R.

CLAIBORNE, NATHANIEL HERBERT (Nov. 14, 1777–Aug. 15, 1859), congressman, descended from William Claiborne [*q.v.*], was the youngest son of Mary (Leigh) Claiborne and Col. William Claiborne of King William County, Va., a veteran of the Revolutionary War. He was born in Sussex County, Va.; received a classical education at the Richmond Academy; settled in Franklin County, where he soon entered public life, and there spent his remaining days. In 1815 he married Elizabeth Archer Binford, of Goochland County, by whom he had eleven children. He represented his district in the Virginia General Assembly, in the House of Delegates (1810–12) and in the Senate (1821–25), achieving reputation as a "watchdog of the treasury" and as a reformer of various abuses in the state government. During the War of 1812 he was a member of the Virginia Executive Council. In 1818 he was on the special board whose report to the legislature resulted in the establishment of the state university. From 1825 to 1837 he was a member of the House of Representatives from Virginia, but seldom entered into debate, speaking from the floor only three or four times during his incumbency. In his opposition to internal improvements at national expense he was in perfect accord with President Jackson; his disapproval of pension or relief bills was another phase of his concern for governmental economy. He stood with his Southern colleagues against increased tariffs, although he supported the tariff bill of 1832 which provoked South Carolina to nullification and, while opposing the Force Bill, supported Clay's compromise tariff of 1833. After voting against the rechartering of the United States Bank he broke with the Administration's fiscal policy, indorsing the proposal for an Independent Sub-Treasury and condemning as derogatory to laws and constitution Jackson's action in removing the deposits. His *Notes on the War in the South, with Biographical Sketches of . . . Montgomery, Jackson, Sevier, the Late Governor Claiborne and Others* (1819), is an account of the campaign against the Creek Indians and the operations about New Orleans in the War of 1812, written with clearness and vigor but with little concern for nuances of style. It is an artless and often personal narrative, composed that the author's family "may see the part their relations have taken in the contest through which we have just past" (p. 79), but despite its vehemently anti-British temper, a confessed carelessness of dates, and occasional moralizings, it is reasonably accurate history.

[See autobiographical portions of Claiborne's *Notes on the War in the South*; *Va. Mag. of Hist. and Biog.*, vols. I, II, *passim*; Geo. Mason Claiborne, *Claiborne Pedigree* (1900); John Herbert Claiborne, *Wm. Claiborne of Va.* (1917); *Richmond Standard*, Aug. 28, 1880.]
A. C. G., Jr.

CLAIBORNE, WILLIAM (*c.* 1587–*c.* 1677), colonist, was descended from a family which possessed the manor of Cleburne, or Cliburne, in Westmoreland County, England, as early as 1086. He was the second son of Edmund Cliburne, lord of the manor, and his wife, Grace, daughter of Sir Alan Bellingham. In June 1621 he was appointed surveyor for the colony of Virginia, where he arrived in the following October. In March 1625/26 he was appointed secretary of state for the colony and a member of the Council. He continued to serve as secretary until 1637, and again from 1652 to 1660. In April 1642 King Charles appointed him treasurer of the colony. He led an expedition against the Indians in 1629 and again in 1644. In recognition of his services he was granted large tracts of land. With the governor's license he was active in Indian trade along the shores of the Chesapeake in 1627 and 1628. He was one of the Virginians who tendered Lord Baltimore the oaths of supremacy and allegiance in 1629. Following him to England, he opposed his application for territory within the limits of the grant of 1609 to the Virginia Company, associated with him a firm of London merchants known as Cloberry & Company, and obtained a commission signed by William Alexander, secretary of state for Scotland, which licensed him to trade for corn, furs, or other commodities in all parts of New England and Nova Scotia where there was not already a patent granted to others for sole trade. With this license, dated May 16, 1631, he returned to Virginia and in August of the same year commenced the establishment of a trading settlement on Kent Island in the Chesapeake Bay and within the limits of the grant, the following year, to Lord Baltimore. He purchased the island from the Indians, stocked it with cattle and hogs, planted corn and tobacco, and within a few months the settlement had a representative in the Virginia House of Burgesses. Upon the arrival of the Maryland colonists, in 1634, Claiborne spurned an offer from the proprietor to promote his welfare should he recognize the proprietary jurisdiction over the island. He had previously asked the advice of the Council of Virginia in the matter and that body had answered, "They knew no reason why they should render up the right of the Isle of Kent, which they were bound in duty to maintain." Hearing that Claiborne was charged with inciting the Indians against the Maryland colonists, Lord Baltimore, in a letter dated Sept. 4, 1634, instructed the governor to arrest him and reduce the island to submission. A petty warfare followed, both sides in the meantime petitioning the king for a redress of grievances against the other. Claiborne and his associates contended that the grant to Lord Baltimore embraced only land not cultivated or planted. In 1635 discord arose between Claiborne and his London associates, and subsequently each blamed the other for failure to overthrow the Maryland charter. In May 1637, Claiborne departed for England for an accounting, and during his absence the governor of Maryland reduced the island to submission. This was in February 1637/38, and in the following month the Assembly passed an act for the attainder of Claiborne. On Apr. 4, 1638, the Commissioners of Plantation decided wholly in favor of Lord Baltimore. "The Isle of Kent," they declared, "is wholly within the bounds and limits of Lord Baltimore's patent and Captain Claiborne's commission is only a license under the signet of Scotland to trade with Indians where the sole trade had not been formerly granted by the king to any other."

During the next decade when anti-Catholic feelings were strong in Maryland, Claiborne, claiming to have a commission from King Charles, together with Richard Ingle, claiming authority from Parliament, incited an insurrection, drove Gov. Calvert into Virginia, and held the province from October 1644 to December 1646. In September 1651, Claiborne was appointed a member of a commission of the Puritan Parliament for the government of "the plantations within the Bay of Chesapeake," and from 1652 to 1657 the affairs of Maryland were subject to the control of this body. Although Claiborne did not at this time lay hands on Kent Island, one of the last records of his career is a petition, in 1676–77, to King Charles II for that island.

Claiborne was a strong man with a successful career in Virginia; but his zeal for that colony, his associates, and his strong dislike of Catholics led him astray in Maryland. In a painting in the State Capitol of Virginia he appears with long flowing hair, high forehead, penetrating eyes, large straight nose, agreeable mouth, pointed mustache, and short narrow beard.

[Much has been written about Claiborne, but the most reliable sources of information are B. C. Steiner, *Beginnings of Md.* (1903); *Archives of Md.*, vols. I, III, IV, and V; *Va. Mag. of Hist. and Biog.* (1893–); and The Calvert Papers. J. H. Claiborne, *Wm. Claiborne of Va.* (1917), is dominated by pride of ancestry.]
          N. D. M.

CLAIBORNE, WILLIAM CHARLES COLES (1775–Nov. 23, 1817), governor of Louisiana, was born in Sussex County, Va., son of William and Mary (Leigh) Claiborne, and brother of Nathaniel Herbert Claiborne [*q.v.*]. After a brief period of instruction at the Richmond Academy and at William and Mary College, at the age of fifteen he secured a position under the clerk of Congress and continued therein for a few years. Upon the advice of John Sevier [*q.v.*], having already displayed some oratorical ability, he returned to Virginia and studied law. Thence he moved to Sullivan County, Tenn., where he speedily gained a large criminal practise. He was a member of the convention that in 1796 framed a constitution for Tennessee. Under the new state government he was appointed a judge of its supreme court by Gov. Sevier. In August 1797, he was elected to Congress to fill out the term of Andrew Jackson and was reëlected for the next regular period, although still under the constitutional age. In his second term he held the vote of his state for his friend Jefferson in preference to Aaron Burr. Shortly thereafter the President made him governor of Mississippi Territory. He married his first wife, Eliza W. Lewis of Nashville (who died in 1804), and reached his new post at Natchez, on Nov. 23, 1801. In the new territory he had to intervene in the factional quarrels that had divided the people under his predecessor and was obliged to organize new counties, settle land claims, and suggest measures for public health, for controlling the negroes and for public instruction. Most of his initial measures stood the test of time. He also acted as superintendent of Indian Affairs and sought to maintain peaceful relations with the Spaniards to the southward. The ordinary difficulties of his task were greatly increased by the prospective cession of Louisiana to France and by the closing of New Orleans, in the fall of 1802, to American trade from up the river. Nevertheless his course as territorial executive proved satisfactory to his superiors.

In the latter part of 1803 he was associated with Gen. James Wilkinson as commissioner to receive the province of Louisiana from the French, and was sent to New Orleans as its governor. Here he found himself in a far more difficult position. For a few months he was a sort of proconsular representative of Jefferson. He had no precedents to guide him, little knowledge of the habits, customs, and laws of the people over whom he was placed and no acquaintance with their language. The Creole population felt resentful at their unexpected transfer to American rule, distrusted their new executive and, when disappointed, were inclined to berate and ridicule him (J. Q. Adams, *Memoirs,* I, 315). Their discontent was further increased by the action of Congress in dividing the territory of Louisiana and in prohibiting the slave trade. Claiborne was a man of good motives, pleasing appearance, mild temper, scrupulously honest and diligent. At times he seemed irresolute and was likely to magnify the difficulties that confronted him. His kindly disposition, his evident honesty and his later marriage alliances with Creole families, by his second wife Clarissa Duralde, and his third wife, Suzette Bosque, did much to remove these initial handicaps; but he never escaped bickerings with his legislative and administrative associates. In the early years of his administration he had to meet the puzzling problems caused by Burr's uncertain movements and the hostile advance of the Spaniards, in 1806, beyond the Sabine. In the ensuing complications at New Orleans he acquiesced in the arbitrary course of Gen. Wilkinson and shared in the opprobrium visited on that general. He was severely wounded in a duel with Daniel Clark [*q.v.*] in the summer of 1807. When Madison determined to annex West Florida, in 1810, Claiborne was selected to take possession of the district of Baton Rouge and later to incorporate it with Louisiana, of which state he had become governor. On the eve of the War of 1812, he found his measures for defense of the new state complicated by the activities of political refugees from Mexico, by filibusters who wished to take part in the revolt there, and by smugglers and pirates operating along the coast. The people at large and the legislators failed to respond to his urgings in behalf of adequate defense. Thus when invasion actually occurred he and his fellow officials received little consideration from the impetuous Jackson. Claiborne's own letters may have given the General an unfair view of the situation, but after the repulse of the British, he warmly defended the loyalty of the state, which had finally rallied to the defense of New Orleans, and thus strongly commended himself to his fellow citizens, whom Jackson had flouted. On Jan. 13, 1817, he was elected to the United States Senate, but died before he could take office. At his premature death he had at least achieved an honorable record on a disturbed frontier during a transitional period of uncertainty and turmoil.

[The principal sources for Claiborne's activities are *The Official Letter Books of W. C. C. Claiborne* (6 vols., 1917), and *The Mississippi Territorial Archives, 1798–1803* (1905), both ed. by Dunbar Rowland. The original documents on which these volumes are based are to be found in Jackson, Miss., and in the State Dept. and the Lib. of Cong., together with supplementary material lacking in the printed text. The correspondence, both printed and manuscript, of Claiborne's contemporaries, particularly of Jefferson, Madison, and Jackson, contains many important references to him, as do the volumes of the *Am. State Papers* and the *Annals of Congress*. For secondary works the most important are: N. H. Claiborne, *Notes on the War in the South* (1819); J. F. H. Claiborne, *Miss. as a Province, Territory, and State* (1881); I. J. Cox, *The West Fla. Controversy* (1918); Chas. Gayarré, *Hist. of La.*, IV (1885); and W. F. McCaleb, *The Aaron Burr Conspiracy* (1903).]
                                                      I. J. C.

CLAP, THOMAS (June 26, 1703–Jan. 7, 1767), Congregational clergyman, for more than twenty-six years head of Yale College, first as rector, and afterward, under the revised charter of 1745, as president, was born in Scituate, Mass., the son of Stephen and Temperance Clap, and a descendant in the third generation of Thomas Clap, who came to Dorchester, Mass., from England in 1633, moved to Weymouth, and later settled in Scituate. He prepared for college in part under Rev. James McSparran [*q.v.*] an Episcopal missionary of Rhode Island, graduated from Harvard at the age of nineteen, and later, it is said, studied theology with McSparran. He was called to the Congregational Church, Windham, Conn., Feb. 22, 1726, and was ordained on Aug. 3. On Nov. 23, 1727, he married Mary, fifteen-year-old daughter of his predecessor, Rev. Samuel Whiting. She died Aug. 9, 1736, and on Feb. 5, 1740, he married Mary (Haynes), twice a widow, first, of Elisha Lord; and second, of Rosewall Saltonstall. He was elected rector of Yale College Oct. 31, 1739, and installed Apr. 2, 1740. While at Windham he had become known as a rigid Calvinist, and a strict disciplinarian. "He impressed himself upon the community by his scholarly accomplishments, his force of character, and his indomitable will." He ruled with a rod of iron and his people endured it, although it was remarked that when in 1739 he accepted the presidency of Yale College, "they acted like boys let out of school" (*Windham's Bi-Centennial, 1692–1892*, 1893, p. 25).

These characteristics gave him success as an administrator, but made his career a stormy one. Under his rule the college had notable expansion. He drafted a more liberal charter, granted in 1745; drew up a code of laws, approved in 1745; prepared catalogues for the library; and secured the erection of new buildings. His stiff theological convictions and high-handed methods, however, brought trouble to himself and unpopularity to the college. He was unfriendly to Whitefield and the movement he inaugurated. Owing to dissatisfaction with the preaching and theology of the Rev. Joseph Noyes of the First Church, which the students attended, in 1753 at the corporation's request President Clap undertook to preach Sundays in the college hall until a professor of divinity could be secured. This alleged irregular proceeding, which resulted in

1757 in the establishment of the Church of Christ in Yale College, together with the corporation's requirement that every future officer of the college should publicly assent to the orthodox faith as stated in the Westminster catechism and the Saybrook Confession, awakened violent resentment in the colony. President Clap defended his position in *The Religious Constitution of Colleges, Especially of Yale College in New Haven* (1754). Bitterly attacked by Dr. Benjamin Gale [*q.v.*], he replied in *The Answer of the Friend in the West to a Letter from a Gentleman in the East, Entitled The Present State of the Colony Considered* (1755); and further supported his own and the corporation's action in *A Brief History and Vindication of the Doctrines Received and Established in the Churches of New England* (1755). Opposition to his policies culminated in a memorial to the General Assembly in 1763, praying for an act authorizing appeal from the authority of the college to the Governor and Council, and the appointment of a commission of visitation to inquire into the affairs of the college. To this attempt at state control President Clap made an elaborate and effective reply. Dissension arose among the tutors and students, however, and the latter petitioned the trustees for his removal on the ground that he was in his dotage. Conditions became chaotic, and in the summer of 1766 the president finding himself "tired and fatigued," his health "not so firm as formerly," and desirous of enjoying the "sweets of retirement and private life," he resigned. The corporation urged him to continue in office, but at commencement in September he retired. He lived but a few months longer.

"As to his person," writes President Stiles, "he was not tall; yet being thick set, he appeared rather large and bulky. . . . He was a calm, still, judicious, great man." His learning was extensive, and he was especially versed in algebra, optics, and astronomy. His publications include a sermon preached at the ordination of Rev. Ephraim Little (1732), and *An Introduction to the Study of Philosophy* (1743); *A Letter to Mr. Edwards Expostulating with Him for his Injurious Reflections in a Late Letter to a Friend* (1745); *An Essay on the Nature and Foundation of Moral Virtue and Obligation* (1765); *The Annals or History of Yale College to the Year 1766* (1766); *Conjectures upon the Nature and Motion of Meteors* (1781).

[Ebenezer Clapp, *Record Clapp Family in America* (1876); Ebenezer Baldwin, *Annals Yale College* (1831); F. B. Dexter, *Biog. Sketches Yale College with Annals College Hist.*, vols. I (1885), II (1896), III (1903); *Lit. Diary of Ezra Stiles* (1902); Wm. B. Sprague, *Annals Am. Pulpit*, vol. I (1857); Naphtali Daggett, *The Faithful Serving of God and Our Generation, the only Way to a Peaceful and Happy Death, a Sermon occasioned by the Death of Rev. Thos. Clap* (1767).]   H. E. S.

CLAPP, ASA (Mar. 15, 1762–Apr. 17, 1848), shipmaster and merchant, the second son of Abiel and Bathsheba (Pratt) Clapp, was born in Mansfield, Mass. His father, a farmer, was accidentally killed while Asa was still a boy, thus depriving the latter of an opportunity for more than a rudimentary education. He enlisted in the Revolutionary army on May 23, 1776, and thereafter served several short terms of enlistment, for the most part in Rhode Island. Near the end of the war, he went to Boston, there taking up the life of a mariner. He served as an officer on a letter-of-marque, probably the *Charming Sally,* commanded by Capt. Dunn, being wounded in one of several desperate engagements. Later, while in the merchant service, he was at Port-au-Prince during the negro revolution, and gave aid to the white residents. In 1787 he was married to Eliza Wendell Quincy, daughter of Dr. Jacob Quincy of Boston and niece of Dorothy (Quincy) Hancock. After passing several years at sea, gaining necessary capital in the West Indian trade, he settled down as a merchant in 1798 in Portland in the District of Maine (until 1820 a part of Massachusetts). In this business he was so successful, in spite of some eccentricities and the lack of formal education, that in 1809 he paid taxes in Portland second only to those of his senior partner, Matthew Cobb. Although his trade, which extended to Europe, the East and West Indies, and South America, was seriously affected by the embargo of 1807, Clapp supported the Government. In the unsettled days after the embargo was lifted, his ships were detained in the Sound by the Danes (*American State Papers, Foreign Relations*, III, 523, 529–31, 562–63), suffering damages for which, in 1831, he submitted a claim totaling with interest $124,520.50 (Manuscript Letter-book). When war came in 1812, he again supported the Government, subscribing, it is said, half his fortune to the national loan. He was one of nine owners of the privateer *Mars*, commissioned Jan. 4, 1815. Appointed one of the commissioners to obtain subscriptions to the capital stock of the Second Bank of the United States in 1816, he became the largest subscriber in Maine. In politics, he was first a Jeffersonian and later a Jacksonian. In 1811 he was a member of the council of Massachusetts. Having strenuously advocated the separation of Maine from Massachusetts, he was a member of the convention which framed the constitution of the new state in 1819. From the records it appears that he did not take a prominent part. He was a member of the House of Representatives of Maine from 1820 to 1823. As the wealthiest man in Maine and a lavish dispenser of hospitality, he entertained many notables at his mansion (built 1794, taken down 1925) on Congress St., Portland. The *Eastern Argus* for July 22, 1817, describes his reception to President Monroe. When Lafayette visited Portland, Clapp was a member of the reception committee. In 1847 President Polk and his Secretary of State, James Buchanan, called on the aged merchant.

[See Ebenezer Clapp, *Record Clapp Family in America* (1876), 158–62; Freeman Hunt, *Lives of the Merchants* (1856), 539–53; *Portland Advertiser*, Apr. 22, 1848; an article by C. H. Farley in the *Portland Sunday Press and Times*, Oct. 27, 1918. The Me. Hist. Soc. owns an oil portrait of Clapp as well as his business papers, 1825–48. The family Bible and other relics are owned by a descendant, Mr. Gist Blair of Washington, D. C.]   R. E. M.

CLAPP, GEORGE ALFRED. [See Dockstader, Lew, 1856–1924.]

CLAPP, WILLIAM WARLAND (Apr. 11, 1826–Dec. 8, 1891), journalist, author, was born in Boston and died in that city. His father, descended from Thomas Clapp who arrived in New England in 1633, was William Warland Clapp, and his mother Hannah W. Lane. There is little record of the boy's early training. He spent much of his youth about the office of one of his father's papers, the *Saturday Evening Gazette,* and "he was educated partly in France." He was back in America at the age of twenty-one, in time to be put in charge of the paper with which he had in a sense come to maturity. He owned and operated this publication from 1847 to 1865, when he abandoned it for the editorship of the *Boston Journal,* a position which he occupied till within a few months of his death. He was most successful as a journalist whether judged as executive or editor. A staunch Republican in his affiliations, he was so just in what he wrote for his paper that he was listened to with interest by people of all parties; throughout New England and especially in the districts north of Boston it may be said that the *Journal* was for many years the standard newspaper. Aside from his profession, his most notable interest was in the theatre. In 1853, collecting some articles of his that had appeared in the *Gazette,* he published *A Record of the Boston Stage,* a solemn but full and dependable history. The Puritans, he said, held the theatre to be "the abode of a species of devil, who, if allowed once to exist, would speedily make converts,"

but he himself was of no such opinion. He implied, indeed, that "a first class theatre in Boston, properly built and conducted, would prove a boon to the public and a fortune to the manager." Around 1857, he wrote or adapted several plays, *La Fiaminna* (from the French); *John Gilbert and his Daughter, A Dramatic Trifle*; and *My Husband's Mirror, A Domestic Comedietta.* His literary methods were not subtle, and the moral at the end of one of his compositions, at least, was driven in with drastic obviousness, but the effect in general was light and pleasing. In 1880, he printed privately a short monograph on Joseph Dennie. He was keenly interested in flowers; he participated in philanthropic and scholarly organizations, and in politics to such a degree that he became an officer in the militia, an alderman of Boston, and a state senator. He was married in 1850 to Caroline Dennie, by whom he had three children.

[Ebenezer Clapp, *Record Clapp Family in America* (1876); *Boston Post,* Dec. 9, 1891; *Boston Transcript,* Dec. 9, 1891.]   J. D. W.

CLARK, ABRAHAM (Feb. 15, 1726–Sept. 15, 1794), surveyor, lawyer, farmer, signer of the Declaration of Independence, was a leader of the dour, sensible American middle-class. About 1678 one Richard Clark, shipwright, of Southold, Long Island, moved to Elizabethtown, N. J. His grandson Thomas, charter alderman and patriotic magistrate of Elizabethtown, became in due time the father of Abraham, his only child, locally known later as "Congress Abraham" to distinguish him from others of the same name. Studious by nature, too frail for farm work, and much indulged by his parents, the boy got only a local smattering of "education in the English branches" (*Sanderson's Biography of the Signers to the Declaration of Independence,* edited by R. T. Conrad, 1847). A natural bent for mathematics led him into surveying and this to an informal study of the law as a means of arbitrating and settling land disputes. His zeal in giving legal advice free, and his preference for the common law, made him known as "The Poor Man's Counsellor" and deepen the suspicion that he never was admitted formally to the bar. The New Jersey legislature (1784) passed "An Act for Regulating and Shortening the Proceedings of the Courts of Law." This was popularly known as "Clark's Law," and he was quoted as saying, "If it succeeds it will tear off the ruffles from the lawyers' wrists." His social-political point of view, through life, resembled that of a seventeenth century English "Leveller."

About 1749 he married and brought home to

his father's house near Elizabethtown, Sarah Hatfield, by whom he had ten children, none of whom rose to eminence. Ten years after his death she was thriftily conducting his ancestral farm located at what is now Chestnut St. and Ninth Ave., Roselle, N. J. With her solid cooperation he was able to take part in nearly thirty years of public service. Under the Crown he was high sheriff of Essex County and clerk of the Colonial Assembly. In December 1774, adhering to the patriot cause, he became a member of the New Jersey Committee of Safety and later its secretary. In May 1775, he sat in the New Jersey Provincial Congress which drafted the State's first constitution, and appointed him, June 22, 1776, a delegate to the Second Continental Congress. He had been outspoken for separation from Great Britain and was sent to uphold that view at Philadelphia where he voted for and later signed the Declaration of Independence. Despite continued "want of health" and numerous domestic distractions, the British forces on Staten Island being only a few miles from his home, he was thrice rechosen to Congress, besides interim service in the New Jersey legislature. His opposition to lawyers' privileges, to "commutation of pay" for army officers, and to the unlimited issue of paper money, had made him numerous and formidable enemies in politics, but these seem to have affected neither his industry nor his influence. He served on innumerable committees, prepared many reports in his own hand, and was almost invariably present to vote. He was especially active in keeping the disaffected out of public office and in raising supplies for Washington's army.

After the Revolution, New York discriminations against New Jersey commerce led Clark to remonstrate with Gov. Clinton, to urge closer union among the states, and to go as a delegate to the Annapolis Convention in 1786. Representing the broader views of his state as to the constitutional problem confronting the nation, he was elected to the Philadelphia Convention of 1787, but ill-health prevented his attendance. Opposed to the new Constitution until after the adoption of the Bill of Rights, he was kept out of the First Congress, serving 1789–90 as a commissioner to settle New Jersey's accounts with the Federal Government, but was elected to the Second and Third Congresses. In these his hard-sense industry persisted. His pungent and invariably brief remarks are still worth reading and give a clear picture of the man.

While watching the erection of a bridge in his meadow on Sept. 15, 1794, he suffered sun-stroke, drove his cousin home, and died two hours later. His grave and monument are in the cemetery of the Rahway Presbyterian Church of which he was long a member.

[Clark's letters and papers are not published. The usual accounts of him are from the *Hatfield Manuscript* (N. Y. Hist. Soc.). The best single source is *Abraham Clark* by Ann Hart Clark (San Francisco, 1923), a somewhat confused genealogical compilation.]

W. L. W.

CLARK, ALVAN (Mar. 8, 1804–Aug. 19, 1887), astronomer, maker of astronomical lenses, was born in Ashfield, Mass., the fifth of the ten children of Alvan and Mary (Bassett) Clark. He was a direct descendant of Thomas Clark of the *Mayflower*. The farm of one hundred acres, on which he was reared, was "one of the roughest and most rocky in that rough and rocky town." But two fine trout brooks ran through the farm and on these were a sawmill and a grist-mill. The first school-house in the district was built on the farm. The school, the farm, and the mills gave the boy occupation until he was about seventeen. He then (1824–25) put himself "at work in good earnest to learn alone engraving and drawing" and made small portraits with "a pretty satisfactory measure of success." In a newspaper used as a wrapper for some brushes that he had ordered from Boston he found an advertisement, headed, "Engravers wanted." He at once set off for Boston and secured a position as engraver of rolls for calico printers in East Chelmsford (now Lowell) at eight dollars per week. Soon thereafter he married Maria Pease of Ashfield, on Mar. 25, 1826. He was able to supplement his income "a little by painting and cutting stamps," and was fortunate enough to meet his "money promises all along, and have a fair reserve for a rainy day." While working at his trade in Lowell, and later in Providence, New York, and Fall River, he kept up his painting. He finally gave up engraving and opened a studio in Boston, where he successfully followed the profession of portrait painter for many years.

At the age of forty he took up the study of optics. His son George Bassett Clark was then at Andover studying to be an engineer. He found that the boy had become greatly interested in the casting and grinding of mirrors for telescopes and had already cast a small mirror. And then, in his own words, "I was at some pains to acquaint myself with what had been done, and how done, in this curious art, that my son could have the benefit of my maturer judgment, in giving effect to his experiments." This was the start of the renowned firm, Alvan Clark & Sons, makers of the world's largest telescopes. Although they began with reflectors they soon turned to the manufacture of refractors. Their 6-inch and 8-inch lenses were marvels of excellence, "but the encouragement was small" until Clark aroused the interest of W. R. Dawes of England, by reporting the discovery of two difficult double stars. As soon as it became known how good the glasses were there was no difficulty with the sales. Soon the firm was making 12-inch objectives. One went to the Vienna Observatory, one to Wesleyan at Middletown, Conn., and one to the Lick Observatory. Then came the 18-inch, originally intended for the University of Mississippi, but now at the Dearborn Observatory in Evanston, Ill. A 23-inch for Princeton, 26-inch telescopes for the Naval Observatory and for the University of Virginia, and a 30-inch for the Pulkovo Observatory soon followed. Clark lived to see the completion, but not the installation, of his greatest objective, the 36-inch for the Lick telescope. His firm not only made objectives but completely mounted telescopes as well. During the thorough testing to which the telescopes were subjected before being delivered, Clark discovered a number of difficult and interesting double stars. He received the Rumford medal of the American Academy of Arts and Sciences.

["Autobiography of Alvan Clark," *New Eng. Hist. and Geneal. Reg.*, Jan.–July 1889; Wm. W. Johnson, *Clarke-Clark Geneal.* (1884); Wm. W. Payne, "The Life and Achievements of Alvan Clark," *Sidereal Messenger*, Sept. 1887; "The Late Mr. Alvan Clark," *Observatory*, Sept. 1887; August Krisch, *Astronomisches Lexikon* (Vienna, 1901).]   R. S. D.

CLARK, ALVAN GRAHAM (July 10, 1832–June 9, 1897), maker of astronomical lenses, astronomer, son of Alvan [*q.v.*] and Maria (Pease) Clark, was born in Fall River, Mass., and educated in the public schools of Cambridge, Mass. As a boy he was apt at everything requiring keen vision and exactness, and he showed a deep interest in astronomy while still at school, where he received prizes for essays on casting and grinding mirrors. At the age of twenty he was taken into partnership with his father and brother George, in the firm of Alvan Clark & Sons, makers of astronomical lenses. In 1865 he was married to Mary Mitchell Willard. When the 18-inch glass now in the Dearborn Observatory was finished, Clark turned the telescope upon Sirius and discovered the companion which had already revealed its presence by its effect upon the motion of Sirius. For this discovery he was awarded the Lalande Medal of the French Academy of Sciences. He was also the discoverer of sixteen double

stars. After the death of his father and of his brother, he carried on the business of the firm and under him it achieved its greatest fame, in the construction of the 40-inch lenses of the Yerkes telescope, the largest in the world. The making of these lenses was a much greater undertaking at that time than it would seem now, and the shipping of them in a carefully padded box, fixed on springs, in a parlor car, was a source of much anxiety. When they were delivered, Clark said he felt as if he had been relieved of a crushing load. Less than ten days after he returned from the trip with the lenses he died.

[*N. Y. World*, June 10, 1897 (repr. in *Observatory*, XX, 291–93); *Astronomische Nachrichten*, CXLIV, 31; E. S. Holden, "Death of Alvan G. Clark," in *Pub. Astronomical Soc. Pacific*, IX, 152; S. W. Burnham, "Double Stars Discovered by Mr. Alvan G. Clark" in *Am. Jour. Sci.*, Apr. 1879.]   R. S. D.

CLARK, ARTHUR HAMILTON (Dec. 27, 1841–July 5, 1922), master mariner, historian, was born in Boston. His father, Benjamin Cutler Clark, was a leading merchant-shipowner, and one of the earliest yachtsmen of New England. Arthur graduated from the Boston Latin School in 1857, helped to win a famous regatta on the Charles as member of the *Volant* crew, and in December shipped as apprentice seaman on the clipper ship *Black Prince*. He returned as her third mate in March 1860, after a voyage around the world. The following summer he attended a commercial school in Boston, rowing up twelve miles from Nahant every pleasant day, and winning three races for single wherries in rowing regattas. In December 1860 he became second mate of the clipper ship *Northern Light* on a voyage to San Francisco, and on returning joined the *Black Prince* as first mate on a government transport charter, staying with her on a China voyage. Clark got his master's certificate in 1863 in Far Eastern waters, where he remained two years, then traveled in Europe, and in July 1866 sailed the 27-ton sloop yacht *Alice* from Nahant to the Isle of Wight in twenty days. That winter he took out the S. S. *Manchu* from New York to China, commanded her in the China seas for two years, and became a well-known figure in the Treaty Ports. His presence of mind once saved his next command, the paddle steamer *Suwonada*, from foundering; but in January 1872 she struck an uncharted rock in Haitan Straits. Clark promptly ran her aground on a sand spit, and beat off a flotilla of Chinese pirates until rescued by the U. S. S. *Ashuelot*. He commanded the *Indiana* of the American Line (New York-Liverpool) from 1874 to November 1876, when he resigned to become the London representative of several American marine insurance companies (1877–90). Returning to America as passenger on the *William R. Grace,* he survived a shipwreck off the Delaware Capes. He organized the marine transportation department of the World's Columbian Exposition, and in 1895 was appointed Lloyd's agent in New York, where his wide knowledge of marine affairs, good judgment, and sense of honor made him universally respected. From early life he had been a collector of ship pictures, models, and maritime history. He now tried his hand at writing, publishing *The History of Yachting, 1600–1815* (1904), and *The Clipper Ship Era, and Epitome of Famous American and British Clipper Ships . . . 1843–1869* (1910), a brilliant and accurate work containing some of the best description and narrative in the literature of the sea. After retiring from the Lloyd's agency in 1920 he purchased a house at Newburyport, Mass., where he died, July 5, 1922.

[Manuscript memoir by Robt. J. Clark; Capt. Clark's scrap-books in Essex Institute; Fred. A. Wilson, *Some Annals of Nahant, Mass.* (1928).]   S.E.M.

CLARK, CHAMP (Mar. 7, 1850–Mar. 2, 1921), speaker of the House of Representatives, was born near Lawrenceburg, Anderson County, Ky., the second child and only son of John Hampton Clark of New Jersey and Alethea Jane Beauchamp of Kentucky. He early dropped his baptismal names James Beauchamp, adopting Champ. He was educated at Kentucky University, Lexington, and at Bethany College, W. Va., graduating from the latter institution in 1873. In college he laid the foundations of a wide acquaintance with classical and other literature which was later one of his distinctions as a public man. Following his graduation, he was for a year president of Marshall College, Huntington, W. Va., the first normal school of the state; then he turned to law, and in 1875 completed a course at the Cincinnati Law School. After brief residences at Wichita, Kan., and Kansas City, he removed in 1876 to Louisiana, Mo., and in 1880 to Bowling Green, in both of which places he was city attorney. At Louisiana he also edited the *Daily News,* and subsequently bought, and edited for a year, the *Riverside Press,* a Democratic paper. His first incursion into national politics was as a Democratic presidential elector in 1880. From 1885 to 1889 he was prosecuting attorney for Pike County. He sat in the Missouri legislature in 1889–91, where he was chairman of the Committee on Criminal Jurisprudence and took a prominent part in the reorganization of the state university, whose administration had become a political issue.

At the Trans-Mississippi Congress at Denver in May 1891 he headed the Missouri delegation. Elected as a Democrat to the Fifty-third Congress (1893–95), he continued to sit in the House until his death, except for the Fifty-fourth Congress (1895–97), when he met defeat in the Republican wave which swept over his state. He entered the House with a local reputation as an orator, and won a wider recognition by a much-applauded speech at Tammany Hall, New York, on July 4, 1893, before he took his seat, but his later manner in debate, while witty and forcible, often trenched upon the bounds of courtesy. His standing in the House was attested by long service on the committees of Foreign Affairs and Ways and Means, but he showed his political independence by ardently supporting the war with Spain and strongly opposing the annexation of Hawaii. For several years he was the trusted lieutenant of John Sharp Williams [*q.v.*], the Democratic minority leader of the House, and succeeded to the leadership of his party in the Sixtieth Congress (1907–09). His most conspicuous achievement in Congress was his successful leadership of the fight against Speaker Joseph G. Cannon [*q.v.*], and the arbitrary control of legislative procedure which had come to be known as Cannonism. At the opening of the Sixty-second Congress (Apr. 14, 1911) he was elected speaker by a House which, for the first time since 1893, had a Democratic majority, and he held the office by successive elections until March 1919. In the pre-convention campaign of 1912 he had the support of Illinois, Iowa, Nebraska, and California as a Democratic candidate for president at the state primaries, and at the Baltimore convention in June received 440½ votes on the first ballot against 324 for Woodrow Wilson, his nearest competitor. He continued to lead until after the 14th ballot, when he lost the support of William J. Bryan, who dominated the convention, and who charged him with representing reactionary interests. Thereafter his vote fell off, and on the final ballot he received only 84 votes. Bryan's allegation was later admitted to have been unfounded. Notwithstanding his defeat, Clark supported Wilson in the ensuing campaign. In May 1917 he took the floor in opposition to the Selective Draft Act. He was again minority leader in the Sixty-sixth Congress (1919–21), but was defeated for reëlection in the "great and solemn referendum" called for by Wilson in 1920. He was married, on Dec. 14, 1881, to Genevieve Bennett of Aux-Vasse, Calloway County, Mo.

[The main authorities for Clark's life, aside from an official sketch in the *Biog. Cong. Dir.* (1913) and the

Jour. House of Representatives and *Cong. Record*, are W. R. Hollister and H. Norman, *Five Famous Missourians* (1900), and a sketch by W. D. Bassford in M. G. and E. L. Webb, *Famous Living Americans* (1915). Both are uncritical and laudatory. Clark's own reminiscences, *My Quarter Century of Am. Politics* (2 vols., 1920), is chiefly valuable, save for his comments on persons and events, for his earlier years. Obituaries were published in the *N. Y. Times* and *N. Y. Tribune*, Mar. 3, 1921. The former paper also contains, under date of Mar. 6, 1921, Chas. W. Bryan's account of the elimination of Clark in the 1912 convention.]

W.M.

CLARK, CHARLES (1810–Dec. 18, 1877), Confederate soldier, governor of Mississippi, belonged to a family which reaches back to the first settlement of Maryland. His grandfather was a Revolutionary soldier, and his father was a pioneer settler in what is now the city of Cincinnati, Ohio. Here Charles Clark was born. After finishing his education in Kentucky, he removed (about 1831) to Mississippi, and engaged in teaching in Natchez and in Yazoo and Jefferson counties. In the latter county he became a devoted friend of Gen. Thomas Hinds, an ex-congressman and a hero of the War of 1812, who was one of the most influential men in south Mississippi. Clark entered politics as a Whig, and was elected on that ticket to represent Jefferson County in the legislative sessions from 1838 to 1844. At the beginning of the Mexican War he organized the Thomas Hinds Guards, which became part of the 2nd Mississippi Regiment of Volunteers, of which he later became colonel. In the great party and sectional conflicts which culminated in the Compromise of 1850, Clark followed the lead of Henry Clay. About that time, he removed to a plantation in Bolivar County, Miss. His new constituents elected him to represent them in the legislative sessions from 1856 to 1861. Meantime (1857), he was defeated as the Whig candidate for Congress by his old commander, Reuben Davis. In the late fifties he changed his views on secession, and became a Democrat. He was chosen a delegate to the Democratic State Convention of 1860, and to the national conventions at Charleston and Baltimore, in which latter conventions he supported the Breckinridge faction. As a candidate for delegate to the Mississippi Secession Convention, Clark declared for secession without delay, but was defeated by Miles H. McGehee, who insisted that before taking such a step Mississippi should await the cooperation of other Southern states. In the convention, McGehee found the sentiment for immediate secession so strong that he changed his position and voted with the majority. After the state seceded, Clark was elected one of the first four brigadier-generals of Mississippi, and was later advanced to the rank of major-general. When the state troops were turned over to the Confederacy, he became brigadier-general in the Confederate army. He was wounded in the battle of Shiloh, but was soon able to reënter the service. In the attack on Baton Rouge (July 1862), he was wounded so severely that his comrades could not move him from the field, and he became a Federal prisoner. He was taken to New Orleans for treatment, and his wife (Ann Eliza Darden) was allowed to pass through the lines to nurse him. As he was never afterward able to walk without crutches, he had to retire from military service. He was elected governor of Mississippi, practically without opposition in 1862, and was reëlected in 1864. When Gen. Richard Taylor surrendered at Meridian (May 4, 1865), Clark issued a call for the legislature to meet in special session. In his last message to this body he referred to the assassination of President Lincoln as follows: "For this act of atrocity, so repugnant to the instincts of our hearts, you feel, I am sure, in common with the whole people, the profoundest sentiment of detestation." The legislature was in session only about an hour, when the report came that Gen. Osband, of the Federal army, had received orders to arrest the members. Clark was taken to Fort Pulaski, near Savannah, Ga., as a prisoner, but was soon released and permitted to return to his home. In reply to an invitation to address the new legislature (Oct. 18, 1865), he wrote that he was "still a prisoner of State and on parole," and that it would be improper for him to accept the invitation, but he expressed a hope that the State would soon be restored to "equal political rights with her sister States." When his party returned to power (1876), he was appointed chancellor of his district, which position he held until his death a year later.

[Sketches will be found in Dunbar Rowland, *Mississippi* (1907), I, 437–45; *Biog. and Hist. Memoirs of Miss.* (1891), I, 549–62; R. Lowry and Wm. H. McArdle, *Hist. of Miss.* (1891), 350–53. Important facts may be gleaned from Jas. W. Garner, *Reconstruction in Miss.* (1901); Reuben Davis, *Recollections of Miss. and Mississippians* (1889). Manuscript sources may be found in the Miss. Dept. of Archives and Hist., though some important papers are still in the hands of Clark's descendants.]

F.L.R.

CLARK, CHARLES EDGAR (Aug. 10, 1843–Oct. 2, 1922), naval officer, was born at Bradford, Vt., the son of James Dayton and Mary (Sexton) Clark, the latter being the daughter of Maj. Hiram Sexton of Vermont, an officer in the War of 1812. On the paternal side, Clark was descended from a prominent Massachusetts colonial family. Appointed to the U. S. Naval Academy, Sept. 29, 1860, through the influence of Senator Morrill of Vermont, he made his first voyage on board the historic frigate *Constitution,* when the midshipmen were transferred from Annapolis to Newport in 1861. Under the stress of war, promotion came fast. Joining the *Ossipee* of Farragut's fleet, Clark commanded the forward gun division of that vessel in the furious fight on Aug. 5, 1864, with the powerful Confederate ironclad *Tennessee* and her consorts in Mobile Bay, resulting in her capture and the sealing up of the important port of Mobile. He also shared in the bombardment of Fort Morgan. In 1865 he was assigned to the steamer *Vanderbilt* of the Pacific Squadron, and in 1867 was transferred to the *Suwanee,* witnessing in her the bombardment of Valparaiso by the Spanish fleet and its defeat by the batteries at Callao. The *Suwanee* was wrecked July 7, 1868, near the northern extremity of Vancouver Island, and Clark was left in command of a party of rescued sailors on Hope Island until taken off by the steamer *New World.* On Apr. 8, 1869, he was married to Marie Louise Davis, daughter of W. T. Davis of Greenfield, Mass. Between this time and the beginning of the Spanish-American War, he followed the usual routine of alternating periods of sea and land service. Promoted to commander, Nov. 15, 1881, he commanded the steamship *Ranger* and was in charge of the survey of the west coast of Mexico and Central America from 1883 to 1886, and ten years later was at the head of a squadron of six war vessels and two revenue cutters, which cruised in Bering Sea to enforce the regulations agreed upon by the Paris Tribunal. Promoted captain, June 21, 1896, he was assigned, a short time before the outbreak of the war with Spain, to the command of the battleship *Oregon.*

As "Clark of the *Oregon,*" he became one of the best-known and most admired officers of the United States Navy. In the expectation that war might break out at any moment, and in doubt regarding the strength of the Spanish naval resources, the Navy Department ordered the *Oregon,* then in the Pacific, to join the fleet in the Atlantic with all possible dispatch. In accordance with this, Clark left San Francisco on Mar. 19, 1898, and on May 25 reported to Admiral Sampson off the coast of Florida after a voyage through Magellan Strait, his ship arriving in first-class condition and ready to go into battle immediately. This voyage, while its actual significance was exaggerated in the eyes of the public, is still considered to have been a triumph of naval discipline, engineering, and planning.

Joining the fleet of Admiral Sampson off San-

tiago de Cuba, the *Oregon* took part in the ensuing efficient blockade of that port, in which the cruisers of the Spanish Squadron under Admiral Cervera were contained. In the battle of July 3, in which the Spanish Squadron was annihilated, the *Oregon's* part was noteworthy. In the pursuit of the fleeing Spanish cruisers along the coast she outstripped all her sister ships except the fast cruiser *Brooklyn,* overhauling and causing the beaching of the fleetest of the enemy's ships, the *Colon,* after a successive exchange of fire with the other enemy cruisers, all of which felt the accuracy and power of her guns. Clark was highly commended by naval experts for the condition and the masterly handling of his ship, and, together with his fellow battleship commanders, was promoted five numbers in his grade.

On July 7, 1898, after the removal of the Spanish menace to the American coast, Clark, still in command of the *Oregon,* was appointed chief of staff to Commodore J. C. Watson [*q.v.*], who was ordered to command a special squadron of the battleships *Iowa* (replaced by the *Massachusetts*) and *Oregon,* the auxiliaries *Yosemite,* *Dixie,* and *Yankee,* three colliers, and the flagship *Newark.* This Eastern Squadron, or "Flying Squadron," as it was popularly called, was to proceed to the coast of Spain for the purpose of compelling the fleet under Admiral Camara to abandon its voyage to the Philippines and to return to Spain, where it could be easily destroyed by the more powerful American force, and the war thus brought to a close. The Eastern Squadron, however, never put to sea, as the mere threat of its departure caused the return of Camara to Spain, where he remained in idleness until the close of the war. In the autumn of 1898 Clark was granted leave of absence to regain his impaired health, but returned to active duty in March 1899, as commandant of the League Island Navy Yard, Philadelphia, afterward becoming governor of the Naval Home near that city. He was promoted rear admiral June 16, 1902, and retired for age Aug. 10, 1905.

[The chief source is Clark's autobiography, *My Fifty Years in the Navy* (1917). See also F. E. Chadwick, *Relations U. S. and Spain: Spanish-American War* (1911); L. R. Hamersly, *Records Living Officers U. S. Navy and Marine Corps* (7th ed., 1902); *House Doc. No. 3,* 55 Cong., 3 Sess.]
E. B.

CLARK, CHARLES HEBER (July 11, 1847– Aug. 10, 1915), author, was born at Berlin, Md., the son of an Episcopalian clergyman, William J. Clark, who as an abolitionist and Northern sympathizer drifted unprosperously from one Maryland parish to another and finally withdrew from the ministry. His son, "brought up on sweet potatoes and among negroes," got his schooling at Georgetown, D. C., began life at fifteen as an office boy in a Philadelphia commission house, later served two years in the Union army, and on his return to Philadelphia in 1865 found work as a reporter on the *Philadelphia Inquirer,* where by luck and some ability he rose in two months' time to be editorial writer and book reviewer. The rest of his life was given to Philadelphia journalism, with authorship and politics as by-products. At different times he wrote for the *Evening Bulletin* as musical and dramatic critic, for the *North American* as editorial writer during the presidential campaign of 1904, and for the *Textile Record,* of which he was for some years sole proprietor. His literary repute depended almost entirely on his first book, *Out of the Hurly Burly* (1874), a collection of humorous sketches of life in a suburban town. For thirty years the horseplay and labored extravagance of the book found an appreciative audience both in America and in England. He followed it with *Elbow Room* (1876), *Random Shots* (1879), and *The Fortunate Island* (1882), a volume of short stories, and after a long interval brought out three novels, *Captain Bluitt: a Tale of Old Turley* (1901), *In Happy Hollow* (1903), and *The Quakeress* (1905), and a second collection of stories, *By the Bend in the River* (1914). Many of these works were written under the pseudonym of "Max Adeler." As a novelist Clark was not very competent, his chief merit being a genuine fondness for his backgrounds, which were either his boyhood Maryland or Conshohocken, on the Schuylkill, where he made his home. He was one of the organizers of the Manufacturers' Club of Philadelphia and for ten years its secretary, much of his own income being derived from investments in the enterprises of his former Sunday-school pupil, J. Elwood Lee. In political economy he called himself a disciple of Henry C. Carey [*q.v.*], and as an advocate of a high protective tariff, for which he harangued voters and lobbied before the Ways and Means Committee at Washington, he was recognized by other manufacturers as a profound student of their problems. In person he was tall and gaunt, with the preternaturally sober face popularly attributed to humorists. He loathed his reputation as a humorist and tried to live it down. His first wife was Clara Lukens of Conshohocken, who died in 1895; in 1897 he married Emily K. Clark, who survived him.

[*Who's Who in America,* 1914–15; C. H. Garrett in *Book Buyer,* Sept. 1902; E. P. Oberholtzer, in *Book New. Mo.,* Jan. 1916; Phila. *Evening Bulletin,* Aug. 10, 1915; Phila. *Inquirer, North American, Public Ledger,* and *Press,* Aug. 11, 1915.]   G.H.G.

CLARK, CHARLES HOPKINS (Apr. 1, 1848–Sept. 5, 1926), editor, son of Ezra and Mary (Hopkins) Clark, came of a long colonial ancestry. He was born at Hartford, Conn., was graduated at the Hartford Public High School in 1867 and at Yale College, with the B.A. degree in 1871. On Oct. 1 after graduation he entered the office of the *Hartford Courant,* published and edited by Gen. Joseph R. Hawley and Charles Dudley Warner. Gen. Hawley had a predilection for politics amounting to infatuation. His associate editor, Warner, devoted his life to letters. Thus Clark received his journalistic training where passionate political thought went hand in hand with good writing. Hawley fired the young recruit's native delight in politics and fixed his enthusiasms upon the Republican party. Warner blue-penciled his copy. When Hawley was elected United States senator in 1881, Clark became the paper's chief political writer. In 1890 Hawley retired as publisher, Warner became president of the Hartford Courant Company and Clark its secretary. In 1892 he was made vice-president. Warner's death in 1900 made Clark editor of the paper while Hawley became president of the publishing company. Hawley died in 1905 and the next year the editor became president and publisher as well.

Clark made his newspaper the medium for expressing his own individuality, and by a selection of news and by impassioned editorials, a daily brief for his party. Like Dana, Greeley, and Watterson, he became a forceful and militant practitioner of that dogmatic personal journalism which now is almost entirely a thing of the past among daily newspapers. So trenchant was his pen, so devastating his wit, so delicious his sarcasm and irony, that his dynamic and imperious personality stood out in every issue. Men in public life and fellow editors spoke of "Charlie Clark's paper" as frequently as they called it by name. In fact the *Courant* was Clark and Clark was the *Courant.* Never caring to be a candidate for office, still he fought the battles of the Republican party each day of every year. His newspaper became a power in Connecticut and an influence far beyond the borders of his state.

From 1910 until his death Clark was a director of the Associated Press, and from 1910 to 1925 a fellow of the Corporation of Yale University. He delivered the Bromley Lectures on Journalism at Yale in 1906 and contributed to the *Critic, Scribner's Magazine,* and the *North American Review.* Eight consecutive Republican national conventions, beginning with that of 1888, Clark attended as a reporter, and at all subsequent conventions of the party he was a delegate-at-large from Connecticut. He was a director of three large insurance companies and long a devoted officer in many quasi-public institutions for cultural development or social betterment. He was married twice: first, on Dec. 15, 1873, to Ellen Root of Hartford, who died on Feb. 28, 1895; second, on Nov. 15, 1899, to Matilda Colt Root, a sister of his first wife. He died in Hartford, having completed fifty-four years of continuous service with his paper.

[*Hartford Courant*, Sept. 6, 1926; I. O. Woodruff, *Biogs. Class of 1871, Yale Coll.* (1914); *Yale Univ. Obit. Record Grads.* (1927); *Encyc. of Conn. Biog.* (1917); *Biog. Record Hartford County* (1901).]

G. B. A.

CLARK, DANIEL (1766–Aug. 16, 1813), merchant and territorial delegate, was born in Sligo, Ireland, and for a time attended Eton and other English schools. In December 1786 he came to New Orleans, where he was associated with an uncle of the same name as merchant and landholder. The two owned properties in the neighboring districts of Baton Rouge and Natchez, and formed commercial connections with the upper Ohio and with Philadelphia. The younger Clark also served as clerk in the local office of the Spanish governor and was looked upon as an enterprising man of wealth, who was socially and politically ambitious but thoroughly honest and public-spirited. In 1798, when the Natchez district was transferred to the United States and organized as the Territory of Mississippi, both men renewed with Gen. Wilkinson, who accompanied the American troops thither, a business and social connection that had been established some ten years before. The younger Clark then became an American citizen. For a few months the Spanish governor permitted him to act in New Orleans as temporary American consul. In that capacity he submitted a partial report on the early commerce between Kentucky and New Orleans (*Annals of Congress*, 10 Cong., 1 Sess., p. 2731). He served as intermediary between the governor and Wilkinson and Andrew Ellicott, the American boundary commissioner, and helped to bring the trading activities of Philip Nolan to the attention of Jefferson.

On July 16, 1801, Jefferson appointed Clark regular consul at New Orleans. Some months later, after a visit to the seat of government, where he dropped some hints of Wilkinson's earlier intrigues with the Spaniards, he made a hurried trip to France, and held interviews with the officials who were about to take possession of Louisiana (*American State Papers, Foreign Relations*, II, 526). After his return, early in 1803,

he continued his efforts to establish American control in New Orleans. He concerted measures with friends in that city to thwart the French Commissioner, Laussat, and tried to prevail upon Wilkinson and Gov. Claiborne to embody the regulars and the militia of Mississippi Territory and occupy New Orleans before the French arrived in force. Later, during the brief interregnum of the French Commissioner, he organized in connection with that official a local force to guard the city. He made two trading voyages to Vera Cruz in 1805–06 that were popularly supposed to have some connection with the Burr Conspiracy. When Burr first visited New Orleans in 1805, he bore a letter of introduction from Wilkinson to Clark, and the latter soon warned Wilkinson of the wild rumors that were beginning to cluster around Burr's movements. In the following year Claiborne at first charged Clark with complicity in the conspiracy but later retracted the charge. At that time, as earlier, he was a bitter opponent of Claiborne, and their animosity finally brought about a duel in the summer of 1807, in which the Governor was seriously wounded.

In 1806 Clark was elected as delegate to Congress from Orleans Territory. While serving in that capacity he openly broke with Wilkinson and later secured for the committee of Congress that investigated the General's conduct much of its material. This service provoked a bitter attack on him and in reply he published his book, *Proofs of the Corruption of Gen. James Wilkinson* (1809), which furnishes much evidence of the General's treachery. Clark served only one term in Congress and withdrew from mercantile activities during the closing years of his life. Between 1801 and 1806 he had formed with Madame Zulime Des Granges an irregular connection, of which two daughters were born and which gave rise some twenty years after his death to a half-century of litigation over his estate.

[The most important source for Clark's services and character is his *Proofs of the Corruption*. This may be supplemented by Chas. Gayarré, *Hist. of La.*, vol. III (1854), vol. IV (1866); *Am. Hist. Rev.*, XXXII, 801–24; XXXIII, 331–59; *Quart. Tex. State Hist. Asso.*, VII, 308–17; Jas. Wilkinson, *Memoirs of My Own Times*, vol. II, *passim* (1816). The essential facts as to his personal relation with the mother of his children are given in *Gaines* vs. *New Orleans*, 6 *Wallace*, 642–718. For his correspondence with Wilkinson preceding the acquisition of Louisiana, consult in the War Dept., "War Office, Letters Received, 1804 and Prior Years."]

I. J. C.

CLARK, DANIEL (Oct. 24, 1809–Jan. 2, 1891), politician, jurist, was the son of Benjamin and Elizabeth (Wiggin) Clark. He was born at Stratham, N. H., and educated in the district school, Hampton Academy, and Dartmouth College, graduating from the latter in 1834. His father was a farmer and blacksmith and because of limited means, Daniel, like many other young men of that period, was obliged to pay for his own education by teaching school during the winter months. After graduation he studied law, was admitted to the bar, began practise at Epping, and in 1839 moved to Manchester. This town was about to enjoy a prolonged period of industrial development, and he soon acquired a considerable practise. For the rest of his life he was active in Manchester affairs, holding several local offices and trusteeships and between 1842 and 1855 serving five times as representative in the legislature, being in charge of the bill for the incorporation of the city in 1846. He was also active in various business enterprises and was for some years a director of the Amoskeag Corporation. Politically, he was a Whig, and when that party disintegrated he was one of the active organizers of the Republican party. In 1857 he was chosen to serve out the unexpired term of Senator James Bell and, being reëlected for a full term, was for nine years one of the prominent figures in Washington affairs. He was an accomplished speaker and debater, ranked by S. S. Cox, a veteran member of the lower house, with Sumner, Fessenden, Seward, Trumbull, and other notables in "a galaxy of ability" (*Union-Disunion-Reunion: Three Decades of Federal Legislation,* 1885). Early in his senatorial career, in the course of the Kansas debate, he declared, "We have had enough of bowing down, and the people in my region have got sick of it" (*Congressional Globe,* 35 Cong., 1 Sess., App., p. 107). These words are the key to his subsequent course. He was an uncompromising foe of slavery and secession and his attitude in 1861 was criticized by many who believed that reconciliation was still possible. He was prominent throughout the war period and his service on the committees on finance, claims, and judiciary was especially important in view of their war-time responsibilities. In 1866 he failed to receive renomination, apparently largely because of New Hampshire's adherence to the doctrine of rotation in office. On July 27, 1866, President Johnson appointed him United States judge for the district of New Hampshire, although Gideon Welles remarked "On every Constitutional point that has been raised, Clark has opposed the President . . . and has been as mischievously hostile as any man in the Senate" (*Diary,* 1911, II, 565). Clark resigned from the Senate and spent the remainder of his life on

the bench, declining at the age of seventy, because of excellent health, to take advantage of the provisions of the retirement act. He had an excellent standing as a jurist and frequently was called to sit in other courts on the New England circuit. His political activity was, of course, largely at an end but he served as president of the constitutional convention of 1876. He was married twice: on June 9, 1840, to Hannah W. Robbins, daughter of Maxcy Robbins of Stratham, who died in 1844; and on May 13, 1846, to Anne W., daughter of Henry Salter of Portsmouth.

[C. H. Bell, *Bench and Bar of N. H.* (1894); J. B. Clarke, *Manchester* (1875); I. W. Smith, *Granite Mo.,* July 1887; J. O. Lyford, *Life of Edward H. Rollins* (1906).]

W.A.R.

CLARK, FRANCIS EDWARD (Sept. 12, 1851–May 26, 1927), Congregational minister, founder of the Young People's Society of Christian Endeavor, the son of Charles Carey Symmes and Lydia (Clark) Symmes, was descended on both sides from old Massachusetts Puritan stock. He was born at Aylmer, Quebec, where his father, a citizen of Massachusetts, was located as a civil engineer and timber surveyor. Bereft of father, brother, and mother before he was eight years of age, the boy was adopted by his uncle, the Rev. Edward W. Clark, then pastor of the Congregational Church of Auburndale, Mass., and his name was legally changed to Francis Edward Clark. He prepared for college at Kimball Union Academy in Meriden, N. H., and was graduated from Dartmouth College in 1873, and from Andover Theological Seminary in 1876. He then married Harriet E. Abbott, daughter and grand-daughter of ministers, and a descendant of John and Priscilla Alden.

Clark became pastor of the Williston Church at Portland, Me., a small offshoot which began to grow rapidly under his vigorous leadership. Here, on Feb. 2, 1881, he organized the "Williston Young People's Society of Christian Endeavor." This was planned, he said, "to be an *out-and-out* Christian society." Its characteristic features were the pledge taken by members, not only to endeavor to lead a Christian life, but to pray to God and read the Bible every day, and to attend and "take some part, aside from singing," in every meeting; the monthly consecration meetings; and the committees through which the young people undertook active participation in the work of the church. The plan immediately transformed the young people's prayer-meeting, hitherto a relatively formal and lifeless affair. The idea spread rapidly, partly because there was general interest in the more effective organization of young people for Christian service, partly because of Clark's ability as an advertiser. In August 1881 he contributed to the *Congregationalist* an account of his society, and in 1882 he published a pamphlet and a book describing the plan. In 1883 he became pastor of the Phillips Church in South Boston; but he resigned the pastorate four years later, to devote his whole time to Christian Endeavor work. The United Society of Christian Endeavor was incorporated under the laws of Maine in 1885, and transferred to Massachusetts in 1887. The *Golden Rule*, a religious weekly, was purchased in 1886 by Clark and a group of friends, who organized the Golden Rule Company. Clark became editor of the paper, which he made the organ of the Christian Endeavor movement, though not owned by the United Society. Its name was changed to *Christian Endeavor World* in 1897. Clark's income from this paper, together with the proceeds of his other writings, enabled him to give his services without salary to the promotion and oversight of the Christian Endeavor movement. He was, in 1887, made president of the United Society of Christian Endeavor, an office which he held for thirty-eight years. In 1888 he went to England, at the invitation of the British Sunday School Union, to tell of the new organization for young people. That was the first of many journeys to many lands in the interest of his cause. A World's Christian Endeavor Union was organized in 1895, and incorporated in 1902; of this he was president from the beginning. In 1919 he resigned as editor of the *Christian Endeavor World* and was made honorary editor. His last European journey was to preside at the convention of the World's Christian Endeavor Union at London in 1926, where delegates from forty nations, many of which had been at war a decade before, gathered in the interest of Christian fellowship and international good-will.

Clark was a prolific and interesting writer. Thirty-seven titles are contained in the list of books written by him which is appended to his autobiography, published in 1922. Among the more important are: *The Children and the Church* (1882); *Our Journey Around the World* (1894); *World-Wide Endeavor* (1895); *A New Way Around an Old World* (1900); *Christian Endeavor in All Lands* (1906); *The Continent of Opportunity* (1907); *Old Homes of New Americans* (1913); *The Holy Land of Asia Minor* (1914); *In Christ's Own Country* (1914); *In the Footsteps of St. Paul* (1917); *Our Italian Fellow Citizens* (1919); *Memories of Many Men in Many Lands* (1922).

[The best sources are the files of *Golden Rule* and *Christian Endeavor World* and Dr. Clark's own books, cited above. Interesting side-lights are given in *The Evolution of an Endeavorer* (1924), the autobiography of his long-time associate, Wm. Shaw.]   L.A.W.

CLARK, GEORGE ROGERS (Nov. 19, 1752–Feb. 13, 1818), conqueror of the Northwest during the American Revolution, was the son of John and Ann (Rogers) Clark, both of them native Virginians. He was born two miles east of Charlottesville. When he was five years of age, his parents, after selling their farm, returned to the southwestern corner of Caroline County. Here, for a quarter-century, they lived on a small plantation which was bequeathed to them by an uncle, John Clark. Until the age of nineteen when he began the study of surveying under the direction of his grandfather, George had acquired little in the way of a formal education. He read history, however, and geography. and took a marked interest in natural phenomena, to which there are frequent references in his letters.

Early in June 1772, having already achieved a reputation for courage, Clark set out from Pittsburgh with a few other adventurers on an exploring expedition in canoes, down the Ohio River. He was then six feet in height, strong of body, and is further described as having red hair and black penetrating sparkling eyes. After spending some time in locating parcels of land at the mouth of the Kanawha, he returned to his home. The next spring he returned with a company of men to the mouth of Fish Creek, on the Ohio, one hundred and thirty miles below Pittsburgh. With a single companion, he then descended the river on an exploring trip, an additional one hundred and seventy miles. The two spent the winter alone on Fish Creek devoting their time to hunting, cutting rails, girdling trees, and burning brush in preparation for the cultivation of the land. The next season Clark gave attention also to surveying farms for the settlers who were coming to the region in increasing numbers. In 1774, as captain of militia, he took part in Dunmore's War, and, after the treaty at Camp Charlotte, set out for the Kentucky River, where he was engaged in surveying lands for the Ohio Company.

Quickly accorded a place of leadership among Kentuckians, he devoted his energy to the establishment of orderly government; to offsetting the design of Judge Richard Henderson who aimed to set up a proprietary colony (Transylvania) with Boonesborough as its capital; and to acquainting Patrick Henry, the governor of Virginia, with the necessity of placing Kentucky under the protection of that State. Should this be done, he declared, not only would the population of Kentucky increase rapidly but trade would develop and a respectable body of fine riflemen would furnish an effective guarantee for the safety of the interior counties against the attacks of Indians. In response to Clark's challenge that "if a country was not worth protecting, it was not worth claiming," the Virginia Council voted five hundred pounds of powder for the protection of Kentucky. This assistance was timely, for at the close of the year 1776, Kentuckians, cooped up in their three stockaded forts, Harrodsburg, Boonesborough, and Logan's Fort, were forced to defend themselves against a succession of Indian expeditions which had been organized at Detroit by Lieutenant-Governor Henry Hamilton. Thus, it was hoped, at the opening of the Revolution, to establish British control over the country west of the Alleghany Mountains. To Clark, who was commissioned a major, was entrusted the organization of the militia for defense. Having conceived a plan for the conquest of the Illinois country, he secured the approval of Gov. Henry and the Assembly for the enlistment of troops. As lieutenant-colonel, he set out with his little army of one hundred and seventy-five men from Fort Massac, ten miles below Louisville. An overland march of six days, two of them without food, through unbroken forests and trackless plains, brought them to Kaskaskia which was surprised and captured July 4, 1778. By early August, the American flag was also floating over Cahokia and Vincennes and with rare tact Clark had won the allegiance of the French villagers and neighboring Indian tribes. Detroit was his next goal.

Upon hearing of Clark's success, Hamilton prepared an expedition consisting of one hundred and seventy-five white troops, two-thirds of them being French volunteers, and sixty Indians, with which he set out on Oct. 7, for the recapture of the Illinois posts. On the way, his force was increased to the number of five hundred by accessions from the Indians. Panic seized the French at Vincennes on the approach of the enemy and Capt. Leonard Helm, having only a single American soldier to guard the fort, surrendered. Had Hamilton pushed forward at once, it seems probable he could have regained control over the other Illinois villages. But he delayed on account of the midwinter floods. Clark, on the contrary, resolved to risk all he had gained by at once taking the offensive and attempting the reduction of Vincennes. The winter march of one hundred and eighty miles, at times across plains and through overflowing

rivers, of this army of one hundred and seventy men, one-half of them French volunteers; the capture of Vincennes; and the surrender of Hamilton with seventy-nine of his followers, Feb. 25, 1779, have furnished topics for many historians and novelists. In the well-known letter to his friend, George Mason, a leading lawyer of Virginia, Clark wrote: "If I was sensible that You wou'd let no Person see this relation I wou'd give You a detail of our suffering for four days in crossing those waters, and the manner it was done; as I am sure You wou'd Credit it; but it is too incredible for any Person to believe except those that are as well acquainted with me as You are or had experienced something similar to it" (*Illinois Historical Collections*, VIII, 140).

The undertaking of such a project, the skill with which it was executed, and the perseverance in overcoming obstacles, seemingly insurmountable, excited the praise even of Hamilton. Courage born of desperation was manifested by men and leaders alike, for all were fully conscious that failure would mean the loss not alone of the Illinois country but also of Kentucky.

The summer following, Clark was forced to forego the march against Detroit. As he expressed the situation, "Detroit lost for want of a few men." While establishing his headquarters in the newly erected Fort Nelson, at the falls of the Ohio (Louisville), his plans comprehended two main objectives—to raise a force in Kentucky, "with the hopes of giving the Shawnees a drubbing" and to make a "bold push" and reduce Detroit and Michilimackinac. During the year 1780, he was engaged in foiling the plan instituted by the British for the recapture of the Illinois country and the Falls of the Ohio and then of Pittsburgh and Fort Cumberland. If successful, the whole region west of the Alleghany Mountains would have become British territory. Moreover, conditions east of the mountains must have been materially changed, for the British rangers and their hordes of Indian allies would then have been free to join the ranks of the British in Virginia and the South. In response to entreaties from St. Louis and Cahokia, Clark hurried to the latter post with a small body of troops. He claimed for his men and himself the honor of having saved St. Louis and the rest of Louisiana for the Spanish—Spain having entered the war as an enemy of Great Britain. After the retreat of the main body of the enemy, Clark set out for Harrodsburg, in order to prevent the advance of an even more formidable force of British and Indians under Col. Henry Bird. Within seven weeks after leaving

Cahokia, one thousand volunteers responded to his orders to assemble at the mouth of the Licking River. By a forced march, they reached Piqua where they overtook several hundred Indians. After a fierce engagement, the Indians fled and Col. Bird also retreated.

For upward of two years after the surrender of Cornwallis, Oct. 19, 1781, war in the West continued. After the terrible defeat of the Kentuckians at the battle of the Blue Licks, Aug. 18, 1782, Clark, who had taken no part in the engagement, instituted a plan for a retaliatory expedition against the Shawnee. On Nov. 4, as brigadier-general under Virginia, he led an expedition against their stronghold at Chillicothe which was completely successful. By this stroke, he not only saved the frontier settlements from the danger of attack but he held the British on the defensive at Detroit.

By the terms of the treaty concluded at Paris, Sept. 3, 1783, the old Northwest was ceded to the United States. No reference is made in the diplomatic papers to the conquest of Clark as a factor in reaching the final agreement. If his position at the close of the Shawnee campaign is considered, it is evident he was virtually in military control of the Northwest during 1782 and 1783. This stroke marked the final aggressive movement in his offensive-defensive policy. At no time were the British prepared to reduce Fort Nelson although they were aware that it constituted the key between the East and the Illinois Country and Kentucky; that it dominated western trade; and was the center for operations against Detroit.

For a number of years after the Revolution, Clark served as a member of the Board of Commissioners (much of the time acting as chairman) which supervised the allotment of lands in the Illinois grant. These lands, one hundred and fifty thousand acres, located north of the Ohio across from Louisville, were granted by Virginia to the soldiers of Clark for their services during the Revolution. Clark also served with Richard Butler and S. H. Parsons on a commission for making a treaty with the Indians of the Northwest, and at Fort McIntosh, January 1786, the Indians acknowledged the sovereignty of the United States over the territory ceded by Great Britain.

Because of depredations by the Wabash tribes at Vincennes and in Kentucky, Clark led a retaliatory expedition against them during the summer of 1786. Owing to a mutiny of certain of the Kentucky troops, it proved a failure. Before returning to Kentucky he provided a force of one hundred men for the protection of Vincennes. To secure the necessary food and clothing for this garrison, he ordered the seizure of goods which had been brought by three Spanish merchants to Vincennes for trade. The act was, in general, approved throughout the West, for no progress had been made by the Government of the United States toward securing their demands for the free navigation of the Mississippi River. The opportunity was seized by James Wilkinson, former brigadier-general in the Continental Army, to make an attack on the reputation of Clark, who stood in his path toward preferment in Kentucky. A man of daring and selfish ambition, proficient in corruption and intrigue, Wilkinson succeeded in his scheme. Public favor was never again accorded Clark by Virginia nor by the federal government. Thus, at thirty-five years of age, Clark was without means of support, although the State of Virginia was in his debt some twenty thousand dollars for his pay as an officer and for money he had advanced to secure supplies for his troops. Early in 1788, with the hope of improving his condition, he proposed founding a colony in Louisiana opposite the mouth of the Ohio. But his demand that political and religious freedom should be granted the colonists was not acceptable to the Spanish government. During the summer of 1791, Dr. John O'Fallon, an adventurer, proposed to take possession of lands which had been granted by the State of Georgia to the South Carolina Yazoo Company. This grant, over which the Spanish claimed jurisdiction, extended from the mouth of the Yazoo River along the Mississippi almost to Natchez. Clark was to lead an armed force of one thousand men on this expedition, but President Washington issued a proclamation forbidding the project.

In 1793, the French government accepted the proposal made by Clark that he should lead an expedition on behalf of France, for the conquest of Louisiana. It failed because of the demand by Washington that Genêt, the French minister to the United States, should be recalled. The President also issued a proclamation which forbade any American citizen to enlist for such a project. When, in 1798, as a result of the X. Y. Z. affair, war between France and the United States seemed imminent, a strong minority of the Republican party were opposed. Any seeming alliance with Great Britain was especially obnoxious to them. This spirit was particularly notable in the communities west of the Alleghanies where the influence of Thomas Jefferson was marked. Once more, the French government planned for the reconquest of Louisiana. Clark, as general in the French army, was to raise volunteers for the purpose. Refusing to surrender this appointment, on the demand made by United States officers, he took refuge in St. Louis.

Upon his return to Louisville he lived for a time in the home of his youngest brother William. In 1803 he built a cabin at Clarksville. This village near the falls, on the Indiana side of the Ohio River, was located on the land which had been assigned by Virginia to Clark's Illinois Regiment. Here he spent his time, as chairman of the commission, in apportioning lands and in running a grist-mill. That he at times drank to excess and lost some of his power and influence cannot be denied. Evidence is lacking, however, to prove that he was, for the most part, a "sot" after the Revolution, a statement which has been concurred in by some historians. During the year 1791 he completed the writing of his *Memoir* which consists of one hundred and twenty-eight closely written pages of manuscript. This document, now in the possession of the Wisconsin Historical Society, is essential to a full understanding of the conquest of the Northwest. About the same time, he prepared a lengthy statement on the origin of the mounds in the Ohio and Mississippi valleys. In this letter, published for the first time by H. R. Schoolcraft, in *Archives of Aboriginal Knowledge*, IV (1860), he developed a theory which, unknown for three-fourths of a century, is now universally accepted by archæologists, namely, that the builders of the mounds were the ancestors of Indian tribes then occupying that region. Another significant letter was written by him (1798) which has always been accepted as proof regarding the statements made in the famous speech of Logan, an Indian chief at the time of Dunmore's War.

Because of a stroke of paralysis and the amputation of his right leg, Clark went to live with his sister Lucy, the wife of Maj. William Croghan, at Locust Grove, near Louisville (1809). There he died and was buried with marked ceremonial on the part of his former companions in arms and by other citizens of Louisville. The funeral oration was given by Judge John Rowan who also wrote an obituary which is a summary of the significance of the conquest of the Northwest (*Western Courier*, Louisville, Feb. 21, 1818). A marble tablet about two feet high marks his grave in Cave Hill cemetery. The United States Government in 1928 appropriated $1,000,000 for a memorial to Clark at Vincennes.

[H. W. Beckwith, *Colls. Ill. State Hist. Lib.*, vol. I (1903); F. J. Turner, "Geo. Rogers Clark and the Kaskaskia Campaign, 1777–1778," *Am. Hist. Rev.*, VIII, 491–506; J. A. James, "Geo. Rogers Clark Papers," *Ill. Hist. Colls.*, vol. VIII (1912) and vol. XIX (1926), containing copies of the original Clark letters which are in the *Draper Coll.* of the *Wis. State Hist. Soc.*, in the *Va. Archives*, and in a number of other places; W. H. English, *Conquest of the Northwest, 1777–83, and Life of Geo. Rogers Clark* (1896); Temple Bodley, *Geo. Rogers Clark* (1926), notably eulogistic; J. A. James, *Geo. Rogers Clark* (1928); Theodore Roosevelt, *Winning of the West*, vols. I, II (1889); E. G. Mason, *Chapters from Ill. Hist.* (1901); R. G. Thwaites, *How Geo. Rogers Clark Won the Northwest* (1903).]
J.A.J.

CLARK, GEORGE WHITEFIELD (Feb. 15, 1831–Nov. 10, 1911), Baptist clergyman, was born in South Orange, N. J. He was related to Abraham Clark [*q.v.*], signer of the Declaration of Independence from the State of New Jersey. His parents, John B. and Rebecca (Ball) Clark, were loyal Baptists and gave their son strict religious training. He was converted and joined the Northfield Baptist church, at the age of twelve. In the public schools of his native town he prepared for college, but taught school at the age of seventeen. He graduated from Amherst College in 1853, and received the degree of A.M. from the college three years later. In 1855 he graduated from Rochester Theological Seminary, was ordained to the Baptist ministry, and married Susan C. Fish, a minister's daughter, of Halifax, Vt. His pastorates included New Market, Elizabeth, and Somerville, N. J., and Ballston, N. Y. An indefatigable student, his persistent and ardent studies brought about a failure in his health, and he resigned his pastorate at Somerville in 1877. From 1880 he was a missionary colporteur of the American Baptist Publication Society in New Jersey. From house to house he plodded, selling and giving away Bibles, tracts, and religious books and earnestly carrying the gospel into homes—preaching and holding prayer-meetings as opportunity offered. To the end of his life he was a real home missionary, carrying on work among Sunday-schools and weaker churches, native and foreign, white and colored. But by instinct and training he was a scholar and a writer. In the theological seminary he was an enthusiastic student of Hebrew and Greek under Prof. T. J. Conant [*q.v.*], the celebrated Oriental scholar. This study he kept up all his life. At Amherst College he was class poet and a year after graduating from the seminary he edited a Baptist hymn-book, *The Harp of Freedom* (1856). He also wrote *The History of the First Baptist Church, Elizabeth, N. J.* (1863). His life ambition and chief work was the writing of a complete commentary on the New Testament. His object was to prepare a popular commentary on a critical basis for Sunday-school teachers and others not able to go to the original sources. There resulted his *New Harmony of the Four*

Gospels (1870); *Notes on the Gospel of Matthew* (1870); *Notes on the Gospel of Mark* (1872); *Notes on the Gospel of Luke* (1874); *Notes on the Gospel of John* (1879); *Harmonic Arrangements of the Acts of the Apostles* (1884); *Brief Notes on the New Testament,— The Gospels* (1884); *Notes on the Acts* (1892); *Commentary on Romans and Corinthians* (1897); *Galatians to Philemon* (1903). This whole New Testament work was combined into *Clark's People's Commentary* in nine volumes, O. P. Eaches writing the last two volumes on *Hebrews to Second Peter* and *1 John to Revelation*. This, Clark's *magnum opus,* was completed in 1910 just before his death.

[Geo. Whitefield Clark's autobiographical *Struggles and Triumphs of a Long Life* (1914); *Amherst College Bull., Obit. Rec.,* June 1912; *Rochester Theol. Sem. Gen. Cat.* (1910); *Biog. Rec. Alumni Amherst College* (1883); *Ann. Reports Bapt. Pub. Soc.* from 1880 onward.]

T.C.R.

CLARK, GREENLEAF (Aug. 23, 1835–Dec. 4, 1904), jurist, born in Plaistow, N. H., was of Puritan stock, being a lineal descendant of Nathaniel Clarke who settled in Newbury, Mass., early in the seventeenth century. His parents were Nathaniel Clark, a resident of Plaistow, prominent in public affairs, and Betsey (Brickett) Clark. He received his early education there and at Atkinson Academy, N. H., from which he proceeded in 1851 to Dartmouth College, graduating in 1855. After reading law for a short time at Portsmouth, N. H., he completed his course at the Harvard Law School, graduating LL.B. in 1857, and was admitted to the Suffolk bar the same year. He commenced practise at Roxbury, Mass., but in the fall of 1858 removed to St. Paul, Minn. At first entering a law office as clerk, he was connected with several firms during the next seven years. In 1865 he became a partner of Horace R. Bigelow, and was joined in 1870 by Judge Flandrau, the firm name becoming Bigelow, Flandrau & Clark. From the outset they were associated with important corporation interests. They held a retainer as general counsel for the St. Paul & Pacific Railway Company and its subsidiaries, prior to and throughout its reorganization as the St. Paul, Minneapolis & Manitoba Railway Company in 1880. They were attorneys for the Minnesota Central, the St. Paul & Chicago, and the Southern Minnesota Railway companies, and also the Milwaukee & St. Paul system, later known as the Chicago, Milwaukee & St. Paul Railway Company. The majority of these were "land grant" companies, and the volume of legal business accruing in connection with their operation was enormous. Clark's special province

was in connection with organization, acquisition of rights of way, and construction contracts, including the preparation of trust deeds, securities, and contracts. His draftsmanship was superb, and "his important railway contracts and mortgages were models" (H. H. Stevens, *post*). He was appointed associate justice of the supreme court of Minnesota, Mar. 14, 1881, but retired on Jan. 12, 1882. During his tenure of office, the attempted repudiation of the state railroad bonds came before the court and the decision that the state must recognize and pay them was in great measure due to his opinion. On leaving the bench he resumed practise in St. Paul, and, though not holding any general retainers, was again engaged mainly in legal work for railroad corporations. He retired from practise in 1888, and died on Dec. 4, 1904, at Lamanda Park, near Los Angeles. As a lawyer he was not erudite but eminently safe. Endowed with an infinite capacity for taking pains, he explored and exhausted every contingency and possessed remarkably sound judgment.

[Geo. K. Clarke, *Geneal. Descendants Nathaniel Clarke of Newbury, Mass.* (2nd ed., 1885); *Colls. Minn. Hist. Soc.,* XII, 697; H. H. Stevens, ed., *Hist. of Bench and Bar of Minn.* (1904), p. 16; W. B. Hennessy, *Past and Present of St. Paul, Minn.* (1906), p. 770; C. C. Andrews, ed., *Hist. of St. Paul, Minn.* (1890), p. 257; *Green Bag,* IV, 109.]

H.W.H.K.

CLARK, HENRY JAMES (June 22, 1826–July 1, 1873), zoölogist and botanist, son of Rev. Henry Porter and Abigail Jackson (Orton) Clark, was born at Easton, Mass. His father was a Swedenborgian clergyman and a life-long friend of the Rev. Henry James [*q.v.*], father of Henry and William James. While the young Clark was still a lad his father removed to Brooklyn, N. Y., where he lived many years and where the son received much of his early training and was fitted for college. Entering the University of the City of New York he was graduated there in 1848. From college he went as a teacher to White Plains, and while engaged in the study of botany, made observations upon the structure of *Chimaphila* and *Mimulus*. These and subsequent observations upon the flora of the neighborhood attracted the favorable notice of Asa Gray, who invited him to Cambridge. Thither he went in 1850, and for a time was a pupil and private assistant at the Botanic Garden. While a student there he taught, for a single term, the academy at Westfield. Soon after this the lectures of Louis Agassiz developed in him a taste for zoölogical studies. He was graduated from the Lawrence Scientific School, *summa cum laude,* in 1854, and during the same year was married to Mary Young Holbrook of

Boston by whom he had eight children. Immediately after graduation he became the private assistant of Prof. Agassiz. Three years later Agassiz called him "the most accurate observer in the country." "Clark," says Jules Marcou, "was the favourite pupil of Agassiz. . . . In the eyes of Agassiz everything and every one in his laboratory was second to Mr. Clark. . . . In fact Clark was his right hand during almost twelve years" (*Life, Letters and Works of Louis Agassiz,* 1896). In June 1860 he was appointed assistant professor of zoölogy in the Scientific School at Harvard, a position which he held until 1865. Following this appointment he went abroad for a time mainly in pursuit of health, traveling in England, France, Germany, and Switzerland, visiting the leading universities and museums, and meeting many scientific workers, including Gegenbaur, Haeckel, Huxley, and Owen.

After Clark became a student of Agassiz his love for botany remained undiminished. He studied it in later years from the side of plant histology and morphology in connection with and as illustrating the histology and morphology of animals. It prepared him for his studies on spontaneous generation, on the theory of the cell, on the structure of the protozoa and the nature of protoplasm. His discovery of the flagellated cells of living sponges and demonstration of their animal nature was a great step in advance of previous observers, and his work on the protozoa and cœlenterata was a valuable contribution to science. Notwithstanding his constant researches, and lectures at the Museum of Comparative Zoölogy, Clark found time to prepare a course of lectures—embodying the results of his micro-physiological studies—which he delivered at the Lowell Institute in 1864. These were published the following year, under the title of *Mind in Nature; or the Origin of Life, and the Mode of Development of Animals.* This work, based on structure and development in the animal kingdom, is crowded with original observations and testifies to years of the severest labor and independent thought. Between 1856 and 1862 he was associated with Agassiz in the preparation of the anatomical and embryological portions of the great work entitled *Contributions to the Natural History of the United States of America* (4 vols., 1857–62). To these volumes he was a large contributor, most of the histological and embryological portions of the work being his; more than half the plates illustrating the embryology and histology of the turtles and acalephs bear his name. Unfortunately, a controversy arose between Agassiz and himself over the authorship of this work, which led Clark to publish a pamphlet entitled *A Claim for Scientific Property* (1863). At the expiration of his term of office he finally left Cambridge.

In 1866 he accepted the chair of botany, zoölogy, and geology at the Pennsylvania State College, where he remained for three years, leaving it in 1869 for similar duties at the University of Kentucky. Neither of these posts was agreeable to his taste, chiefly because of the pressure of college work, which left him but little time for abstract investigations. It was, therefore, with great readiness that he accepted the call to the Massachusetts Agricultural College in 1872. But his work was now interrupted by a severe illness. Never robust, his assiduous and confining labors had seriously impaired his health. After much suffering, he died on July 1, 1873, at the age of forty-seven.

Clark was admirably adapted by nature for doing histological work of the highest order. He possessed that philosophic insight of the true naturalist which often enables him to *divine* much further than he can perceive in the tracing of relationships and to anticipate what the microscope is to reveal. In the use of the microscope itself, he showed not only mechanical skill and ingenuity, but a patience, caution, and experience in difficult points in histology, which undoubtedly placed him at the head of observers in this country and rendered him perhaps inferior to few in Europe. He suggested many improvements in the microscope which were carried out by Spencer and Tolles. Five years after his death, the Smithsonian Institution published, as one of its Contributions to Knowledge, his monograph of *The Lucernariæ and Their Allies* (1878)—a beautiful memoir, though a fragment of what was designed to cover at least fifteen parts, two parts only having an actual existence. A list of Clark's published writings will be found in the first volume of the *Biographical Memoirs* of the National Academy of Sciences, and in the *Catalogue of Scientific Papers* compiled by the Royal Society of London.

[W. S. Clark, *Eleventh Report, Mass. Ag. College,* 1874, pp. 14–15; A. S. Packard, Jr., in *Nat. Acad. Sci.; Biog. Memoirs,* I, 317–28; *Proc. Am. Acad. Arts and Sci.,* IX, 328–30; *Gen. Cat. Mass. Ag. College* (1886), pp. 103–07; F. Tuckerman, in *Science,* May 10, 1912.]

F. T—n.

CLARK, HORACE FRANCIS (Nov. 29, 1815–June 19, 1873), lawyer, banker, railroad executive, was born in Southbury, New Haven County, Conn., the son of the Rev. Daniel A. Clark, a Presbyterian minister, and of Eliza (Barker) Clark. His early education was obtained at the Mount Pleasant Classical Institution at Amherst, Mass. He then entered Williams College and graduated in 1833. Soon adopting law as a profession he studied in the office of Prescott Hall, and was admitted to the New York bar in 1837 making his home in New York City. In 1856 he was elected a member of the Thirty-fifth Congress and was reëlected, as an independent candidate, to the Thirty-sixth Congress. Identified with the "Hardshell" wing of the Democratic party, he nevertheless dissented from the policy of President Buchanan in regard to Kansas, and supported the views of Senator Douglas. On leaving Congress he resumed the practise of law but abandoned it when railroad interests began to occupy most of his attention. In 1857 he became a director in the New York & Harlem Railroad and at the same time began to acquire stock in other railroads in the management of which he soon began to exert an influence. He became president of the Lake Shore, Michigan Southern & Northern Indiana Railroad and of the Union Pacific Railroad Company, besides being a director in five other railroads and holding much stock in still others. His railroad holdings were so large that his operations exerted an influence upon the New York Stock Exchange, the term "Clark Stock" being applied to those companies in which his holdings were the largest. He was also a member of the executive committee of the Union Trust Company of New York and was chairman of the executive committee of the Western Union Telegraph Company. In many of his railroad ventures he was associated with Commodore Cornelius Vanderbilt, having married his daughter Marie Louise on Apr. 13, 1848.

[Calvin Durfee, *Williams Biog. Annals* (1871); Henry K. White, *Hist. of the Union Pacific Ry.* (1895), p. 55; Nelson Trottman, *Hist. of the Union Pacific* (1923), pp. 53–54, 69, 100; Clark's testimony before the Congressional Committee investigating the Union Pacific Railroad Co. and the Crédit Mobilier in *House Report No. 78*, 42 Cong., 3 Sess.; *N. Y. Herald*, June 20, 1873; *N. Y. Times*, June 21, 1873; *Harper's Weekly*, July 12, 1873.]   J.H.F.

CLARK, JAMES (Jan. 16, 1779–Sept. 27, 1839), congressman, judge, governor of Kentucky, was born in Bedford County, Va., near the Peaks of Otter. When a boy, he was brought by his parents, Robert and Susan Clark, to Kentucky where the family settled in Clark County on a farm near the Kentucky River. He received his education from Dr. Blythe who later made a name for himself on the faculty of Transylvania College (*Biographical Cyclopedia of the Commonwealth of Kentucky*, 1896, p. 577). He returned to Virginia to study law with his brother, Christian, and after completing his studies made an extended trip into the West looking for a suitable place in which to begin the practise of his profession (Lewis and Richard Collins, *History of Kentucky, 1877*, p. 133). He finally came back to Winchester, Clark County, Ky., and was admitted to the bar there in 1797. He was a successful lawyer, but politics attracted him. In 1807 he was elected to the state House of Representatives, and was reëlected in 1808. In this he was following in the footsteps of his brother, Robert, who had represented Clark County in the legislature for several years. In 1810 he was appointed a judge of the Kentucky Court of Appeals and remained on the bench for two years. In 1813 he was elected to the lower house of Congress and was reëlected for a second term in 1815. His two terms were without distinction, and he brought them to a close by resignation in 1816 (*Debates and Proceedings*, 14 Cong., 2 Sess., p. 230). In 1817 he was appointed judge of the circuit court of Kentucky and served in that position until his resignation in 1824. He attracted national attention by a decision declaring the popular replevin law of Kentucky unconstitutional. For this decision he was summoned before the Kentucky legislature but refused to appear, making his defense in writing. A subsequent attempt to remove him by legislative action was defeated (Charles Kerr, editor, *History of Kentucky*, vol. II, 1922, p. 623). In 1825 he was again elected to Congress to fill the place made vacant by Clay's acceptance of a position in the cabinet, and was reëlected in 1827 and 1829. The *Debates and Proceedings* of Congress indicate that he was not an active member, rarely speaking, and apparently exerting no influence upon legislation. As a neighbor and friend of Clay he became a bitter enemy of Andrew Jackson and was active in organizing the Whig party in Kentucky. In 1831 he declined a nomination for Congress and the next year was elected to the Kentucky Senate, holding the position for four years. Here he made his best legislative record and definitely contributed to state history by his work as chairman of the committee on internal improvements (*Senate Journal*, 1832–33, 1834–35). He was chosen speaker of the Senate in 1835. In 1836 he was elected governor of Kentucky on the Whig ticket but died in 1839 before the completion of his term. His administration was a good one without being brilliant. He was married to a widow, Mrs. Thornton (*née* Buckner). His long public career, unbroken from 1808 to 1839, made him the best known man in Kentucky after Henry Clay. He was a man of culture and independence, courageous, of considerable logical powers, and, in the last part of his life, a bitter partisan. His most definite impression on his time was made as circuit judge.

[The brief sketch of Clark in the *Biog. Cong. Dir.* is of value because it supplies the day and month of his birth, otherwise practicably unobtainable. The year given for his birth (1757) is a palpable absurdity, the correct date being that given by Collins. His political attitude is revealed in the *Circular Address of Jas. Clark to his Constituents* (1831), while information as to his judicial conduct is to be found in *Niles' Reg.,* June 22, 1822. There is considerable material on Clark in the possession of the Clark County Hist. Soc. at Winchester, Ky.]   R. S. C.

CLARK, JOHN (Feb. 28, 1766–Oct. 12, 1832), governor of Georgia, was born in Edgecomb County, N. C. As a boy he came with his distinguished father, Elijah Clarke [*q.v.*], to Wilkes County, where most of his life was spent. He served under his father in campaigns against the Tories, was a lieutenant at fifteen and a captain at sixteen years of age. After the Revolution he received, as did his father, a generous grant of bounty lands. At twenty-one he was made major in the state militia, and fought in a battle against the Creek Indians, named in his honor the battle of Jack's Creek. Shortly after, he married Nancy Williamson, daughter of Micajah Williamson, a prominent man of some substance before the losses of the Revolution.

The main interest of posterity in the career of Clark centers in the long and bitter strife of the Clark and Troup parties in Georgia, in which Clark, almost unlettered, and followed by the democratic, small-farmer, frontier element of the population, maintained himself and his faction successfully against the redoubtable James Jackson, William H. Crawford, and George M. Troup, aristocratic and cultured champions of the wealthy planters of the coast and large farmers of the uplands.

Gen. Elijah Clarke—the son dropped the final "e," perhaps as an affectation of democratic sentiment—was more or less implicated in the Yazoo affair, and James Jackson's scathing arraignment of all Yazooites drove them into a sort of defensive organization under Clark. This became more defined as time went on, and when Jackson won to his cause the adhesion of William H. Crawford, then a brilliant and prominent young lawyer of the uplands, the Clark faction hitherto supreme in that section began to fear for their laurels. A deliberate plot seems to have been hatched to dispose of Crawford by a duel. Peter Lawrence Van Allen of Elberton, a young New Yorker, Federalist, and Yazooite, was put up to goad him into an encounter. The duel came off, but it was Van Allen who fell. In 1806, new ground of offense having arisen

from a sarcastic speech of Crawford in the Georgia legislature, Clark challenged and met Crawford in a famous duel at High Shoals. At the first fire Clark was untouched, and Crawford's left wrist, which should have been held in safety behind him, was painfully shattered. Clark insisted on proceeding, but the seconds objected. Before Crawford's wound had healed, Clark sent him another challenge, but as no new *casus belli* had arisen Crawford, under the code, could without loss of honor decline.

In the following year Crawford was sent to the United States Senate, to enter upon his brilliant national career. The place left vacant in Georgia politics was filled by George M. Troup. The two factions soon became known as the Troup and Clark parties, violent antagonists contesting every election with varying success. The War of 1812 brought a lull, but on the return of peace the strife broke out with increased bitterness. It became intense in 1819, when Clark announced himself as a candidate for governor. Troup, now a United States senator, resigned his seat in order to oppose him. Clark won on the ballot of the legislature by thirteen votes. Two years later the Troup forces made a strenuous effort to defeat Clark for a second term. Clark won again, by a margin of only two votes. The ensuing two years were made a continuous intensive campaign. The Clark party put up Matthew Talbot against Troup. On the day of election, amid breathless excitement, the ballots stood 81 to 81 with four still to be counted. These, one after another, proved to be for Troup. In 1825 Clark again in person became a candidate against Troup. In the meantime a constitutional amendment had transferred the election from the legislature to the people. The Clark faction claimed credit for this democratic change. The older centers in general voted for Troup; the newer and frontier settlements for Clark. After weeks of waiting, as the returns came slowly in to Milledgeville it was learned that Troup had received a majority of 683 votes. Curiously enough the newly elected legislature contained a majority of Clark men, indicating that Clark would have triumphed if the system had not been changed. Although the two factions continued their antagonism for years to come, Clark ceased henceforth to take any active share in it. His party assumed the name "Union Party" and later were absorbed in the Democrats, while the Troup party called themselves first the "States Rights" party and later, singularly enough, became Whigs. Clark accepted from the President an appointment as Indian Agent and in 1827 removed to Florida,

He and his wife both died of yellow fever at St. Andrew's Bay in 1832.

[Contemporary newspapers, especially the *Ga. Jour. of Milledgeville* (file 1810–37 in the Univ. of Ga. Lib.) ; Edward J. Harden, *Life of Geo. M. Troup* (1859) ; G. R. Gilmer, *Sketches of Some of the First Settlers of Upper Ga.* (1855) ; Wm. H. Sparks, *Memories of Fifty Years* (1870) ; W. F. Northen, ed., *Men of Mark in Ga.*, II (1910), 163–67 ; U. B. Phillips, *Ga. and States Rights* (1902) ; L. L. Knight, *Ga.'s Landmarks, Memorials and Legends*, II (1914).] J. H. T. M.

CLARK, JONAS (Dec. 14, 1730 o.s.–Nov. 15, 1805), Congregational clergyman, patriot, was for fifty years pastor of the First Parish Church, Lexington, Mass. Born in Newton, Mass., the son of Thomas and Mary (Bowen) Clark, and a descendant of Hugh Clark, an early settler of Watertown, Mass., later of Roxbury, he graduated from Harvard in 1752, and was called to Lexington, May 19, 1755. Here he was ordained Nov. 5, 1755, and here he spent the remainder of his days. In appearance and behavior he was the typical New England parson, friendly to all but never forgetful of his clerical dignity. He preached sermons considered long even in his time, and it is said that he once prayed in public for two hours. His voice was an organ of power which could be heard far beyond the walls of the meeting-house. On Sept. 21, 1757, he married Lucy Bowes, daughter of Rev. Nicholas and Lucy (Hancock) Bowes, by whom he had thirteen children, one of whom died in infancy. Early each morning he stood at the foot of the stairs in his homestead, and summoned his family in these words, "Polly, Betsey, Lucy, Liddy, Patty, Sally, Thomas, Jonas, William, Peter, Bowen, Harry— Get up ! Woe to the delinquent !" (F. H. Bowen, *Lexington Epitaphs*, 1905). He was a man of method and industry, able to support his large family only by supplementing his salary of eighty pounds and twenty cords of wood with the income of a well-managed sixty-acre farm.

Back of almost everything of importance that happened in Lexington during the Revolutionary period lurked the influence of Jonas Clark. It also extended beyond the town. He was the close friend and adviser of Samuel Adams and John Hancock, who were frequently at his house, where, indeed, they slept, strongly guarded, on the night before the battle of Lexington. The spirit his parishioners displayed on that occasion has ever since been attributed in no small degree to the ideas and feelings he had inculcated. To him they looked for guidance on every political question that arose. It was he who prepared the instructions to the representative of the town with respect to the Stamp Act (Charles

Hudson, *History of the Town of Lexington*, 1913, I, 69). These were the first of a notable series of papers written by him, expressing the sentiments of the town, the last of which was one condemning "Jay's Treaty." All are inscribed on the town records. In 1799 he was appointed delegate to the convention for drawing up a state constitution, where he served on important committees. Some knowledge of his views and ability may be gathered from his published sermons which include : *The Importance of Military Skill, Measures for Defense, and a Martial Spirit in a Time of Peace* (1768) ; *The Fate of Blood Thirsty Oppressors and God's Tender Care of His Distressed People* (1776), an appendix to which contains an account of the battle of Lexington; *A Sermon Preached Before John Hancock . . . May 30, 1781, being the First Day of General Election* (1781) ; *A Sermon Preached to a Religious Society of Young Men in Lexington* (1761) ; *A Sermon on the Use and Excellency of Vocal Music in Public Worship* (1770) ; a sermon on the death of Rev. Samuel Cooper, and several ordination sermons.

[Chas. Hudson's *Hist. of Lexington* (1913) contains a number of Clark's writings. See also *Vital Records Newton, Mass. to 1850* (1905) ; Wm. B. Sprague, *Annals Am. Pulpit*, vol. I (1857) ; *Proc. Lexington Hist. Soc.*, vol. IV (1912) ; *Proc. . . . Commemoration Two Hundredth Anniversary Incorporation Lexington* (1914) ; John Clark, *Records Descendants Hugh Clark, of Watertown, Mass.* (1866).] H. E. S.

CLARK, JONAS GILMAN (Feb. 1, 1815– May 23, 1900), philanthropist, a descendant of Hugh Clark, who settled at Watertown, Mass., early in the seventeenth century, was the son of Elizabeth and William Smith Clark. He was born at Hubbardston, near Worcester, Mass. One of a family of eight children, he absorbed what learning he could from the district school in the winters and toiled early and late on his father's farm in the summers. From sixteen to twenty-one he served an apprenticeship in the carriage-maker's trade and after he came of age he set up for himself in the manufacturing of carriages, exchanging his product with the nearby farmers for hard wood that he made into chairs to sell in Boston and elsewhere for cash. Later he found the tinware business profitable and opened hardware stores at Lowell and Milford ; but in 1851–53 he sold these and engaged in the shipping of furniture and other goods to California and the selling of miners' supplies during the gold excitement in that state. He accumulated money and invested it in San Francisco and New York real estate. A temporary breakdown in health caused him to take a European trip in 1861. He had been a member of the famous

Vigilantes, organized to put down lawlessness in San Francisco, and was one of the five men who formed the Union League of California during the Civil War, thus cooperating with those who were active in holding the state loyal to the Union. He was prominent also in the work of the United States Sanitary Commission. During and after the war he invested heavily in government bonds. His investments in New York and Boston real estate were increasingly profitable. During the fifteen years following the Civil War he lived much of the time in New York City, and in 1881, he sold to John D. Rockefeller nine lots on Fifth Ave., New York City, at a profit of over sixty-six per cent.

A series of journeys to Europe opened Clark's eyes to some of the benefits of schooling to the individual and the state. As his contacts with educated men increased there gradually took form in his mind certain more or less definite plans for a contribution to higher education in America. These began with nothing more ambitious than a scheme to enable young men in Massachusetts towns to have the advantage of college training at lower cost than was possible in existing New England colleges. Conversations with President Eliot of Harvard, President White of Cornell, and other university authorities expanded these ideas as time went on. In 1880 Clark became a resident of Worcester, Mass., and soon decided that the school or schools which he intended to found should be in that city. During eight years he spent all his leisure time in visiting foreign universities and technical schools. The purpose to found an institution that should aim definitely at the expansion of knowledge came to possess his mind. By 1887 he was ready to name his board of trustees and to announce the founding of Clark University. His original gifts for this purpose, including notes and buildings and grounds, totaled $1,000,000—the largest amount ever given in New England, up to that time, by any individual for education. The university was to be, in the words of its founder, "without any religious, political or social tests." The corner-stone of the first building was laid in October 1887; in the following year Dr. G. Stanley Hall [*q.v.*], of Johns Hopkins University, was called to the presidency, and on Oct. 2, 1889, the institution was formally opened. The members of the faculty brought to their tasks an unusual zest, which quickly gave the infant university a renown that became more than national. Yet for an institution that promised and attempted great things the available money resources were painfully inadequate. The founder's extreme reticence and

refusal to take his trustees into his confidence helped to bring about a situation that appeared to president, trustees, and faculty alike as nothing less than tragic. After the death of Clark in 1900, however, it was found that his will left the residue of his estate to the University and provided for the establishment of Clark College, with a separate president. Early in life Clark had married Susan Wright of Hubbardston, who was a most loyal and helpful companion throughout his career. She was devotedly interested in the University and herself founded fellowships and scholarships in it.

[John Clark, *Records Descendants Hugh Clark, of Watertown, Mass.* (1866); *In Memoriam: Jonas Gilman Clark* (1900), authorized by the widow; Calvin Stebbins, *Pubs. Clark Univ. Lib.*, Apr. 1905; Edmund C. Sanford, *Ibid.*, Feb. 1924; G. Stanley Hall, *Life and Confessions of a Psychologist* (1923), pp. 260 ff.]

W. B. S.

CLARK, JOSEPH SYLVESTER (Dec. 19, 1800–Aug. 17, 1861), Congregational clergyman, a descendant of Thomas Clark of the *Mayflower,* and the son of Seth and Mary (Tupper) Clark, was born and brought up on the ancestral farm at Manomet Ponds, South Plymouth, Mass. He began teaching at seventeen, and this with study and farm work occupied his time till he was twenty-two, when he entered the Amherst Academy and a year later Amherst College where he graduated with the valedictory in 1827. He graduated at Andover Seminary in 1831, his course being interrupted by a year spent as tutor at Amherst. On Dec. 27, 1831, he was married to Harriet B. Bourne of New Bedford, Mass. Six days previously he had been ordained at the Congregational Church in Sturbridge, Mass., where he remained until Dec. 20, 1838. From 1839 to 1857 he was secretary of the Massachusetts Missionary Society. He became corresponding secretary of the Congregational Library Association in 1853, and its financial agent in 1857, devoting the remainder of his life to its interests. His understanding of people and his rare tact made him a successful pastor. As a preacher he was practical and helpful rather than brilliant. His knowledge of rural life contributed to his efficiency as a secretary. He was a strong Congregationalist and was saturated with the civil and ecclesiastical history of New England. While at Sturbridge he wrote a careful and painstaking *Historical Sketch* (1838) of that town. The literary monument of his secretaryship was *A Historical Sketch of the Congregational Churches of Massachusetts from 1620 to 1858* (1858), a thorough and scholarly work of permanent value. He did not live to complete the further volume or the same subject for which he had gathered the materials. Although a Calvinist, he was opposed to controversy and inclined to be charitable toward the beliefs of others. His interests were historical rather than theological. The Congregational Library, founded by him, became a great source collection of denominational history. He was editor-in-chief of the *Congregational Quarterly,* to whose first number, January 1859, he contributed three articles. From 1852 he was alumni secretary of Andover Seminary. A devoted Amherst alumnus, he was a trustee from 1852, secretary of his own class, and was appointed, just before his death, to write the history of the college.

[Edwards A. Park of Andover, a classmate of Clark and life-long friend, wrote a thorough and comprehensive article on him in the *Cong. Quart.,* vol. IV, no. 1, Jan. 1862. A briefer article is in the *Congregationalist,* Aug. 23, 1861.]   F. T. P.

CLARK, LEWIS GAYLORD (Oct. 5, 1808– Nov. 3, 1873), editor, twin brother of Willis Gaylord Clark [*q.v.*], was born in Otisco, N. Y. Eliakim, his father, a descendant of Lieut. William Clark of Massachusetts, after serving in the Revolutionary War, migrated to Onondaga County, N. Y., and married the daughter of Lemon Gaylord, an early settler in the same region from Connecticut. The twin brothers spent a happy, rural childhood, acquiring a lasting love for nature. They won an early reputation for ingenious pranks and for prodigious feats of memory. The formal education at the local school was supplemented by paternal instruction at home, Eliakim Clark being a man of philosophical and literary tastes. The Rev. George Colton, a maternal relative, furnished additional training in the classics. Probably the chief influence on their youthful ambitions was that of their uncle, Willis Gaylord, locally celebrated as editor of the *Genesee Farmer and Albany Cultivator.* Upon reaching maturity, both brothers determined upon literary careers. By 1830 Willis had established himself in Philadelphia, and two or three years later Lewis reached New York City, an obscure aspirant to fame. Early in 1834 he contributed an article to the *Knickerbocker Magazine,* the periodical with which his career was henceforth to be associated. Established in 1833, the *Knickerbocker* (originally *Knickerbocker) Magazine* had been successively under the editorships of Charles Fenno Hoffman, Timothy Flint, and Samuel D. Langtree. Learning that the magazine was in the market, Clark and his friend Clement M. Edson secured financial backing, and in the spring of 1834 became the proprietors

of the *Knickerbocker.* Under Clark's editorship, which was to cover more than a quarter of a century, the periodical rapidly won popularity and prestige. Its avowed policy of promoting "a national literature" attracted to its pages most American writers then prominent. Clark soon inaugurated his monthly Editor's Table, which became a permanent and favorite section of the magazine. Subscriptions increased; but undercapitalization and "delinquent subscribers" kept the financial status of the *Knickerbocker* insecure.

In October 1834, Clark married Ella Maria Curtis, then in her eighteenth year. The marriage was a happy one, Mrs. Clark devoting herself to their growing family, which eventually numbered four daughters and two sons. Their home was also the frequent scene of festive gatherings. Clark, always fond of social intercourse, had become a popular citizen of literary New York, and a thorough-going metropolite. He was elected to the St. Nicholas Society (1840), and in 1846 was one of the founders of the Century Club. At public dinners and literary assemblages the presence of "Clark of the *Knickerbocker*" became indispensable. His literary friendships were numerous, including a congenial intimacy with Irving. His friendship with Dickens, begun by correspondence, was personally cemented during the latter's American tour in 1842 (W. G. Wilkins, *Charles Dickens in America,* 1911). Through the forties and fifties the *Knickerbocker Magazine* flourished. Its policy of avoiding controversial issues won favor. In its pages names of established writers mingled with those of the rising generation. The Editor's Table, with its sub-section of local Gossip, grew in importance and size. Success (except financial) was attained. To remedy the single deficiency, a group of *Knickerbocker* contributors collaborated upon a memorial volume, published in 1855 as *The Knickerbocker Gallery,* the proceeds from which helped to buy a tasteful cottage at Piermont, N. Y., where Clark spent his last years. In 1861 the *Knickerbocker* succumbed to the financial panic of the War, a change of proprietorship keeping it precariously afloat. New editors failed to improve matters, and in 1863 Clark was invited to reassume his duties. This arrangement lasted for several issues only; his second retirement barely anticipated the end of the magazine. He continued to write, contributing to *Harper's* and other publications personal and reminiscent articles. For a period he held a position in the New York Custom House. A brief illness following a paralytic stroke in 1873 resulted in his death. He is buried in Nyack Cemetery. His widow survived him twenty years.

Clark's editorial duties allowed him little leisure for independent authorship. The following books bear his name on the title-page: *The Literary Remains of the Late Willis Gaylord Clark* (1844), with an Introductory Memoir; *The Knickerbocker Sketch-Book* (1845), a volume of selections; *Knick-Knacks from an Editor's Table* (1852); *The Life, Eulogy, and Great Orations of Daniel Webster* (1854). His literary characteristics were sentimental tenderness, gentle humor, and leisurely philosophizing, in a graceful and sometimes patrician style.

[W. W. Clayton, *Hist. of Onondaga County, N. Y.* (1878); D. H. Bruce, *Onondaga's Centennial* (1896); *Harper's New Mo. Mag.*, Mar. 1874; N. Y. *Evening Post*, Nov. 4, 1873; *N. Y. Times*, Nov. 5, 1873; *N. Y. Tribune*, Nov. 5, 1873; personal information from Mr. Clive Mecklem of New York City, grandson of Clark.]
C. M.

CLARK, MYRON HOLLEY (Oct. 23, 1806–Aug. 23, 1892), governor of New York, was born on a farm in the town of Naples, Ontario County, a son of Maj. Joseph and Mary (Sutton) Clark. His family was of New England origin, his grandfather, Col. William Clark, having migrated from Berkshire County, Mass., to western New York after the Revolution. As a boy he had only the meager schooling that was obtainable in new settlements. He served an apprenticeship as a cabinet-maker. Early in life he was married to Zilpha Watkins. A successful campaign for sheriff, in 1837, helped to make him known to the voters of the county. After completing his term of office, he entered the hardware business in Canandaigua, the county seat, but retained his interest in public affairs and in taking an advanced position in the temperance and other reform movements of the day gradually extended his reputation beyond local bounds. He was one of a small group of Whig politicians prepared to unite the several diverse groups of radical voters to at least a temporary victory. His opportunity came when his Senate district sent him to Albany to uphold the cause of prohibition in the legislature. He was joined then by other legislators equally zealous but not all as convincing speakers as he. Out of this situation came a prohibition bill which passed both Senate and Assembly (1854) and for which Clark received the chief credit. Gov. Seymour promptly vetoed the measure, chiefly on the ground that it deprived persons of property unconstitutionally. Early in the summer Clark was proposed for the governorship by some of the temperance groups. An anti-Nebraska mass-meeting at Saratoga in Au-

gust adopted a platform written by Horace Greeley. Clark expressed his adhesion to that platform and in the following month was nominated not only by the regular Whig convention at Syracuse but by the Free Democracy, the Anti-Nebraska party, and the Temperance party, each holding its own delegate convention at Auburn. Clark accepted all four nominations and always held that the Republican party of New York was thereby originated (Myron H. Clark to A. N. Cole, Aug. 12, 1884, quoted in F. Curtis, *The Republican Party . . . 1854–1904*, 1904, I, 204). The ensuing campaign for the governorship was one of the most complicated in the history of New York politics. The Clark coalition won the election by a plurality of 309 votes. Clark thus came to the governor's chair as an avowed radical in the politics of that day, bent on the placing of a prohibitory liquor law on the statute-books. Back of him stood about one-third of the state's voters and a legislature in sympathy with his aims. A prohibition bill was passed, signed by Clark, and partially enforced for about eight months, until it was declared unconstitutional by the court of appeals. Clark was not renominated at the end of his term because the leaders of his party were convinced that he could not be elected. Sentiment on the liquor question had undergone a change. Clark was appointed collector of internal revenue under the Lincoln administration. After serving in that office for some years he lived in retirement at Canandaigua. Once he emerged as a third-party Prohibitionist candidate for the governorship, but that was his last public appearance.

[See Chas. F. Milliken, *Hist. of Ontario County, N. Y. and its People* (1911); obituary in *Ontario County Times* (Canandaigua, N. Y.), Aug. 24, 1892. An account of the campaign of 1854 is given in the *Memoir of Thurlow Weed* (1884), p. 247. Reasons for the support of Clark's candidacy for the governorship by the temperance press are given in the *Jour. Am. Temperance Union*, July 1854. Clark's defense of the prohibitory law which he signed as governor is contained in his annual message of 1856 (*State of N. Y.: Messages from the Governors*, 1909), vol. IV, ed. by Chas. Z. Lincoln. The adverse decision of the court of appeals is in *Wynehamer vs. People* (1856), 13 *N. Y.*, 378.]
W. B. S.

CLARK, SHELDON (Jan. 31, 1785–Apr. 10, 1840), friend of learning, was born and spent practically his entire life in Oxford, Conn., a farming community about fifteen miles from New Haven. He had a mind of unusual vigor, and from boyhood was eager for an education; but his father having died, he was brought up by his grandfather, Thomas Clark, a hard-headed, parsimonious farmer, who regarded schooling as a waste of time. Except for a brief period of instruction at Litchfield in 1805–06, his only opportunity to acquire knowledge was through his own reading on Sundays, stormy days, and in the long nights of winter. His respect for his grandfather's wishes was rewarded, however, at the former's death; for he left his grandson an estate valued at $20,000. Being now about twenty-six years old, he went to Prof. Benjamin Silliman [q.v.] of Yale and asked if he might have any of the advantages of the college without being a regular member of the institution. Through the latter's influence, he was permitted in 1811–12 to pursue a course of study connected with President Dwight's classes and the lectures in natural philosophy and chemistry.

While engaged in this he determined that he would devote his life to the encouragement of literature and sciences in the only way circumstances had made possible for him. Returning to his farm, he plowed his stony fields, fatted his calves, lent his money, and, spending little upon himself, accumulated thousands of dollars, all of which he devoted to the cause of education. In 1823 he gave to Yale the sum of $5,000 to be placed at interest until it should become the foundation of a professorship. It is now the foundation of what is known as the Sheldon Clark Professorship of Philosophy. For the establishment of a scholarship Clark donated in 1824 $1,000, to be invested and allowed to accumulate for twenty-four years. To replace, by a better one, the telescope of the college which was lost in the wreck of the packet-ship *Albion* in 1822, he gave sums of money amounting finally to $1,200. In 1835 he had the satisfaction of learning that Halley's comet had been first observed in this country through the telescope he had provided. He also remembered the college liberally in his will, becoming at his death by far the largest individual contributor thereto.

He was respected and influential in his community, representing it in the General Assembly of 1825 and in several subsequent sessions. He read and wrote much, leaving behind numerous manuscripts on economic matters and more especially upon moral and metaphysical subjects; some of these had been printed and sent to eminent men. His death which came when he was but fifty-five years old was caused by a fall from a scaffolding in his barn. Letters and papers left by him are preserved in the library of Yale University.

[This sketch is based chiefly upon an article by Benj. Silliman in the *Am. Jour. Sci.*, July–Sept. 1841, which is accompanied by portrait. See also Henry Barnard, *Am. Jour. Ed.*, XXVIII, 887.]

H. E. S.

CLARK, THOMAS MARCH (July 4, 1812–Sept. 7, 1903), bishop of the Episcopal Church, bore his father's name, and was a descendant of Nathaniel Clark who settled in Newbury, now Newburyport, Mass., sometime before 1670. Here Thomas was born, and among his early recollections was that of seeing his father's richly laden ships come in from distant lands. His mother, Rebecca, was a daughter of Abraham Wheelwright, who had been a Revolutionary soldier, a seafaring man, and later a partner in a profitable business with the West Indies. He was a descendant of John Wheelwright [q.v.], banished with Anne Hutchinson from Massachusetts in 1637. Both Clarks and Wheelwrights were rigid Presbyterians, and Thomas was brought up under Calvinistic teachings, which came back to trouble him even in his later years. Educated in his home town, in an academy in Framingham, and in Phillips Andover, at the age of fourteen he was a freshman at Amherst. Here, he says, "I neglected my studies to such a degree during the first two terms as to render it disadvantageous for me to remain there." In 1828 he entered Yale, graduating in 1831. After a period of teaching, during which he was the first principal of the Lowell, Mass., high school, he entered Princeton Theological Seminary, and in 1835 received, in his old home church, Presbyterian licensure to preach. He supplied the Old South Church, Boston, for a few months, but on Feb. 3, 1836, was ordained deacon in the Episcopal Church, and priest the following November. This change was precipitated, he says, "by consciousness of my unfitness to express in extemporaneous prayer the sentiments of an intelligent congregation whose Christian experience had in a great many cases been matured before I was born" (*Reminiscences*, p. 33). He had outgrown Calvinism, however, and the ancient liturgy appealed to him strongly. From 1836 to 1843 he was rector of Grace Church, Boston, where, Oct. 2, 1838, he married Caroline, daughter of Benjamin Howard. Called to St. Andrews, Philadelphia, in 1843, he remained there till 1847, when he returned to Boston to become assistant at Trinity, thinking that Bishop Eastburn, then in charge, was about to relinquish the parish. After "four years of mossy quietude" and waiting, he accepted a call to Christ Church, Hartford. In 1854, greatly to his surprise, he was elected bishop of Rhode Island, and on Dec. 6, was consecrated at Grace Church, Providence, of which he also acted as rector until 1866.

For forty-nine years he filled the office of bishop, and from 1899 till his death, that of presiding bishop of the Episcopal Church in the United States. His simplicity, genuineness, sane judgment, broad sympathies, and irenic temper made him trusted and beloved by all classes, and during his administration his diocese had peace and growth. His humor and wit were irrepressible, but always kindly. A massive, magnetic person, with a deep rich voice, and unfailing resourcefulness, he became one of the most popular preachers and lyceum lecturers of the country. He was among the first to discard the old-fashioned pulpit style, and speak directly and plainly. Succeeding Henry Ward Beecher, he contributed an article a week to the *New York Ledger,* for ten years, receiving a hundred dollars for each. During the Civil War he was an active member of the Sanitary Commission, and an occasional consultant with President Lincoln. He was a representative of this country at the first Lambeth Conference in 1867, and in 1876 officiated in many of the American churches in Europe. He was a Broad-Churchman and one of Bishop Brooks's most intimate friends, but evangelical in his faith and preaching, and while condemning excesses of ritual, not intolerant toward the High Church party. Among his publications are a series of lectures to young men, *Early Discipline and Culture* (1855); and *Primary Truths of Religion* (1869), designed to meet unsettled conditions of mind. Widely read once, it has little help for doubters of a later day. Worthy of mention, also, is *John Whopper,* a tale of the extraordinary adventures of a newsboy, published anonymously in 1871, and sometimes credited to Edward Everett Hale. It was republished in 1905 with an introduction by Bishop Henry C. Potter. In 1895 Clark published his *Reminiscences,* a book of much charm and value. He died in Newport, and was buried in St. Mary's churchyard, South Portsmouth, R. I.

[Mary C. Sturtevant, *Thos. March Clark* (1927); Henry C. Potter, *Reminiscences of Bishops and Archbishops* (1906); *Who's Who in America,* 1903–5; *Providence Jour.,* Sept. 8, 9, 1903.]   H. E. S.

CLARK, WALTER (Aug. 19, 1846–May 19, 1924), jurist, was the son of David Clark, later brigadier-general of North Carolina militia, and of Anna M. (Thorne) Clark. He was born in Halifax County, N. C., where the Clarks and Thornes had lived and prospered since leaving Virginia three generations before. Broad lands, books, and influential connections were his heritage, and with them a keen sense of personal and civic responsibility. Eager and quick of mind, the lad at six had read the Bible through, "standing at his mother's knee." At fourteen, aided by

a year (1860–61) at Capt. Tew's Military Academy, he was drill-master in the Confederate army; at sixteen he was adjutant of the 35th North Carolina Regiment, with a reputation for coolness and capacity won at Antietam and Fredericksburg. Leaving the army from February 1863 to June 1864, he graduated at the state university. Reënlisting immediately, he was thenceforth major (temporarily lieutenant-colonel) in the fighting Junior Reserves, and thus was skirmish commander against Sherman in the state's biggest battle. After the war, turning promptly to the law—at the state university, in a Wall St. office, and at the Columbia Law School— Clark had graduated and was practising at twenty-one. He served as Halifax magistrate, as aide to Gov. Worth, as counsel to local railroads, and as editorial director of the Democratic *Raleigh News;* he attracted attention through his "Mudcut Circular" (1880) and his sketch of Methodism in North Carolina (1881); he married (1874) Susan Washington Graham (daughter of the former secretary of the navy), by whom he had seven children; he toured Europe (1881); and he built up—in Raleigh after 1873—an extensive law practise. Appointed in 1885, and elected the next year, a superior court judge, in 1888 he threatened to contest the governorship but accepted instead a place on the supreme court bench, by appointment in 1889 and election in 1890. Toying with the Populists in 1894 and thus, alone of the Democrats, holding over under the Fusionist régime, he was unbeatable in his campaign for chief justice in 1902 notwithstanding opposition of business interests which supported the Republican candidate. He continued chief justice until his death.

During these forty years Clark's was always "the youngest mind on the bench." "Every age," he said, "should have laws based upon its own intelligence and its own ideas of right and wrong." Authorities and precedents, accordingly, suffered severely at his hands; and when his colleagues refused to follow, men said, "Judge Clark's dissenting opinion of to-day becomes the law of to-morrow." Taxation of railroads despite old exemptions, adequate local support of public schools despite apparent constitutional limitations, inclusion of water supply among the "necessary" expenses of municipalities, a severe narrowing of the doctrine of "contributory negligence," legislative control over offices notwithstanding office-holders—these illustrate his peculiar influence and its direction. During this period were prepared his *Annotated Code of Civil Procedure* in several editions, his highly commended "Appeal and Error" running a thousand pages in the *Cyclopedia of Law and Procedure* (1901), and his standard *Supreme Court Reports,* with annotations and index, in 164 volumes. Permitting himself social life only in the Church and in Masonry and toiling far into early morning hours, he translated Constant's *Memoirs of Napoleon* in three volumes (1895), collected and edited sixteen volumes of the *State Records* (1895–1901), and inspired as well as edited the *Histories of North Carolina Regiments* in five volumes (1901). A clear and incisive writer, his political thinking was formulated in multitudinous addresses and magazine and newspaper articles. Although he was an extensive farmer and always identified with progressive farm movements, his radicalism was probably motivated by his intellectual committal to democracy. In behalf of this he branded Blackstone and Coke as bad influences, condemned "usurpation" by an irresponsible federal judiciary, advocated woman's suffrage, and justified Taft's playful remark that he would not "trust the Constitution with Judge Clark over night." "Big Business" was his *bête noir.* He still-hunted for the peanut trust in Halifax, fought the tobacco trust's influence in Trinity College, tried to curb the power trust—wished, indeed, to outlaw the nefarious things. The tremendous significance of the state's economic regeneration seemed to escape him. Lacking personal attractiveness to the masses, he met overwhelming defeat in the Senatorial primary of 1912; and having then fought the state party machine, he received only the minor recognition of appointment to the National War and Labor Board from President Wilson. But his place as the progressive intellectual leader of his people during a most plastic period seems assured.

[Sketches appear in S. A. Ashe, ed., *Biog. Hist. of N. C.* (1908), pp. 67–76; in the *Charlotte Observer,* and the Raleigh *News and Observer,* May 20, 1924; and in the *N. C. Bar Ass. Report,* 1925. A campaign biography by D. P. Waters appeared in the *Carolina Democrat* and was reprinted in 1912; *Some Campaign Letters* deal with the opposition to Clark in 1902. His numerous private papers are with the Historical Commission in Raleigh; they contain few letters by him and no autobiographical material.]   C.C.P.

CLARK, WILLIAM (Aug. 1, 1770–Sept. 1, 1838), explorer, governor of Missouri Territory, Indian agent, was the ninth child of John and Ann (Rogers) Clark of Virginia. He was born at the family home in Caroline County, Va., whither his parents had removed fifteen years earlier from Albemarle County. There was a family tradition that the children inheriting the red hair of a certain ancestress would become persons of force and vitality; of the red-headed Clarks—George Rogers [*q.v.*], Lucy (mother of

George Croghan), William, and Frances (mother of John O'Fallon)—the tradition proved true. In later life William's name among his Indian wards was "Red Head." The boy grew up in his Virginia home, the customary home of a planter with many acres and slaves, enjoying life in the open, with little formal education, but trained by contact with men of affairs, and by constant observation of natural phenomena. He learned to ride and hunt, to survey a piece of land, to notice acutely the habits of wild birds and animals, to draw a little, to make maps, and to manage men. He acquired without knowing it the manners and accomplishments of a Virginia gentleman, yet there was always about him something of the frontiersman, a bluff, direct manner of speaking and acting, which made him at home in the backwoods, where much of his life was spent.

Clark grew up in the stirring times of the Revolutionary War; he was not six years old when his oldest brother Jonathan became a major in the Virginia line. At Germantown his brother John was taken prisoner by the British, and lingered many months in prison, finally dying in 1783 of the effects of his imprisonment. From over the mountains came echoes of the daring deeds of his second brother George Rogers Clark, of his capture of the Illinois and Vincennes; then in the spring before "Billy" was nine his cousin John Rogers passed through Caroline County escorting the British officers taken at Fort Sackville by the audacious courage of the conqueror of the Northwest. The next year Brother George came home himself, was commissioned a general and sent back to protect the western settlements. Finally after the close of the Revolution the Clark family, greatly to the joy of its younger members, decided to remove to Kentucky. They left their Caroline County home in the autumn of 1784, were detained during the cold months near Redstone on the Monongahela, and in the lovely spring days of 1785 floated down the Ohio in a flat boat, taking horses, stock, negroes, furniture, and all the equipment for a new home. At Louisville Gen. Clark received his parents, brothers, and sisters with great pleasure. Soon a house was built on a large tract of land outside of the town, which was called thenceforward "Mulberry Hill"; there young William grew strong and tall until he was over six feet in height. This home he inherited by the will of his father after both parents died in 1799, and there he lived until he started on the expedition to Oregon.

Although the war with Great Britain was over and the United States was no longer a group of colonies but an independent nation, Indian war continued on the western border and took its toll of the lives of many men who were neighbors of the Clarks at "Mulberry Hill." In 1785 Gen. George Rogers Clark was one of a commission of three to draw up a treaty with the tribesmen beyond the Ohio; but in spite of all their efforts the peace was a fictitious one and the next year Gen. Clark led a punitive expedition against the Indians on the Wabash. It is probable, but not certain, that William, then a large strong lad of sixteen, accompanied his brother on this occasion. Certain it is that he went on a similar excursion in 1789 when Col. John Hardin led two hundred militia against the White River Indian towns near the Wabash. They left Louisville on Aug. 5 and were away sixteen days, falling in with a party of Indians with whom they had a skirmish, and carrying the wounded whites back to Vincennes. All the following winter was spent in defense of the Kentucky settlements, when William was associated with his brother-in-law, Col. Richard Clough Anderson, with Col. Hardin, and with other experienced Indian fighters (Clark's manuscript diary of this year is in the Missouri Historical Society at St. Louis).

The next year (1791) Clark was again on an excursion with notable soldiers. A letter to his eldest brother says, "Your brother William has gone out as a cadet with Gen. Scott; he is a youth of solid and promising parts and as brave as Cæsar" (Draper Manuscripts, 2L28, Wisconsin Historical Library). With Charles Scott on this expedition were John Hardin, James Wilkinson, and other soldiers with whom Clark was associated for several years. The army crossed the Ohio at the mouth of the Kentucky and started across country to the Ouiatanon towns; it was gone from May 23 to June 16 and returned home without loss (William Clark's manuscript diary in the Wisconsin Historical Library). That fall occurred Gen. St. Clair's disastrous defeat on the Miami, and all the frontier was defenseless before the attacks of the marauding Indians. Clark's traditions and training were military; he offered himself for the regular service, was commissioned Mar. 7, 1792, lieutenant of infantry, and was attached to the 4th Sub-legion on the army's reorganization in September of that year.

For four years Clark was an army officer under the command of Gen. Wayne. In September 1793 he was placed in charge of a rifle corps, in which were several Chickasaw Indians, for in June of that year Clark had been ordered to take ammunition and provisions to the Chickasaw tribesmen near Memphis, who were wavering between allegiance to the Americans or to the Spanish. The Spanish governor reported of him on this occasion that he was "an enterprising youth of extraordinary activity" (Spanish manuscripts in Draper Collection 42AJ76; Clark's manuscript journal in Missouri Historical Society at St. Louis).

During the winter of 1793–94 Clark was in charge of a detachment at Vincennes and on an excursion up the Wabash was frozen in for twenty days, and had to depend upon his rifle for subsistence. He was then stationed at Cincinnati and, when Wayne began his march into the Indian country, was ordered to bring up provisions. About eighteen miles north of the Ohio his detachment was attacked by an Indian party with which he had a severe but successful skirmish, finally joining Wayne at Greenville before the last of May (Draper Manuscripts, 2L33). Then Clark continued with Wayne until his victory in August over the allied Indians at Fallen Timbers, a campaign minutely described in Clark's journal and letters (Draper Manuscripts, 2L34, 35, 36, 37; 5U33). On this campaign Meriwether Lewis [q.v.], having just entered the army, served in the same division with Clark.

Before resigning from the army, Clark was sent on a second mission down the Mississippi, this time with a flag of truce to the Spanish officers at Natchez, protesting against the fortification of Chickasaw Bluffs by Spain (Clark's manuscript journal in Missouri Historical Society at St. Louis; Spanish manuscripts in Draper Papers, 42J200). Clark made friends with the Spanish governor, Gayoso de Lemos, who three years later granted him a passport to visit New Orleans.

Army life had begun to pall upon Clark even before the Indian submission, but at the earnest request of his superiors, he remained in commission until July 1, 1796, when he resigned and returned to "Mulberry Hill" and to the leisure of private life. During the next few years he travelled widely, visiting Virginia, New Orleans, and the new capital at Washington City. Most of these travels were in the interest of his brother George Rogers Clark, who had lost heavily during his Revolutionary services, and whose accounts Virginia refused to settle. Thereupon he was sued, his lands attached, and William had much difficulty in saving anything from the wreck of his brother's fortune.

In 1803 Clark received an unexpected letter from his friend Capt. Lewis, which changed his whole life; by the acceptance of the invitation it carried, his service for his country expanded to important proportions. Lewis proposed that

Clark should accompany him in leading an expedition which President Jefferson was sending to explore the continent and to find a route to the Pacific Ocean. The plan made an instant appeal to Clark, and he threw himself into the preparations with all the enthusiasm and vitality he possessed.

During the winter of 1803–04, the expedition was recruited in Illinois, nearly opposite St. Louis, and on May 14, 1804, it set out in several boats up the Missouri River. The entire summer was occupied in reaching the home of the Mandan Indians in North Dakota. At these villages the explorers wintered, sent back superfluous men and possessions to St. Louis, and as early as possible in the spring of 1805 began the ascent of the upper Missouri. Fortunately they obtained as a guide, Sacajawea [q.v.], an Indian woman from an upper river tribe, who not only piloted the expedition, but secured the good-will of her tribal friends. From them the explorers obtained horses and crossed the continental divide. Then, having reached the head-waters of the Columbia, they built canoes and descended that river to its mouth. There they made camp almost within sound of the ocean and spent the ensuing winter.

It had been planned to return to the states by sea, but no merchant vessels having come to the mouth of the Columbia, Lewis and Clark were obliged to retrace their route by land. On the return journey they found other mountain passes, and Clark descended the Yellowstone River, meeting Lewis at its mouth. They reached St. Louis Sept. 23, 1806, to the great delight of the whole country which had given them up for lost.

The success of the expedition, although Lewis was in ultimate command, was really due to the combined qualities of the two leaders, who worked in complete harmony and supplemented each other at every point. Clark had more enterprise, daring, and resource than Lewis, as he had had more frontier experiences. By his quick thought and action he more than once saved the expedition from disaster. He was the map-maker, and also the artist, drawing birds, fish, and animals with meticulous care. The explorers kept separate diaries, as did several of their men, and immediately upon their return Clark began putting these records into definite shape for publication. The issuance of the book was delayed until 1814, when after careful editing by Nicholas Biddle and final revision by Paul Allen the journals of the expedition were given to the world.

Clark resigned from the army Feb. 27, 1807, and was at once appointed brigadier-general of militia for Louisiana (later Missouri) Territory and superintendent of Indian affairs at St. Louis, where he thereafter made his home.

Thither in January 1808, he brought his bride Julia Hancock of Fincastle, Va., for whom he had named the Judith River in far distant Montana. Occupied with the new community in which he had cast his lot, with his Indian wards who continually sought him out in his St. Louis home, and with the cooperation he was giving to his friend Gov. Lewis, he was startled to learn of the latter's death on a journey to Washington, and gratified that the President should appoint him as Lewis's successor, an honor he felt at this time obliged to decline. He was appointed governor of Missouri Territory in 1813.

His duties and responsibilities were greatly increased by the War of 1812, when it became his duty in conjunction with Gov. Edwards of Illinois and Gov. Harrison of Indiana to protect the frontiers from the incursions of the Indians, most of whom were allied with the British. Harrison had every confidence in Clark's military skill; in 1813 he wrote of him, "Having served several years with this gentleman and having a perfect knowledge of his character and talents, I do not hesitate to say that in the kind of warfare in which we are engaged I had rather have him with me than any other man in the United States"; and when it was decided that Clark should stay at St. Louis, Harrison declared that, "Missouri may be safely confided to the military talents of Governor Clark" (Draper Manuscripts, 3X31, 4X73).

In 1814 Clark led an expedition into what was then the enemy's country by advancing up the Mississippi River with about fifty regulars and three times as many volunteers, to Prairie du Chien, at the mouth of the Wisconsin River. There he threw up a log fort and ran up the American flag, the first one to float over any building in what is now Wisconsin. Clark named the little post Fort Shelby in honor of the veteran governor of Kentucky; then the time of many of his volunteers being about to expire he retired to St. Louis, leaving a gunboat named the *Governor Clark* and a small garrison to defend the place. Fort Shelby was attacked a month later by a large force of British and Indians and forced to surrender. Two supporting expeditions were also defeated near Rock Island.

With the close of the war it fell to Clark's lot, in connection with Auguste Chouteau and Ninian Edwards, to reconcile the western Indians by a series of treaties. This was successfully accomplished, and for years thereafter Clark was greatly occupied with Indian affairs. He received delegations of chiefs at his home, held councils with them, occasionally escorted some of them to Washington; he appointed agents and factors; sent messages to the various tribes; and in 1825, in conjunction with Gov. Lewis Cass, attempted to bring about permanent peace by the treaty of Prairie du Chien, which defined the tribal boundaries and arranged for conciliation among many tribes. This peace was often broken; twice when in 1827 the Winnebago, and in 1832 the Sauk tribe led by Black Hawk, went on the war-path. Clark was instrumental in subduing these uprisings, and in checking other incipient ones by his prestige with the red men and his skill in treating with them. He had a large collection of Indian and natural curiosities, which formed a kind of museum in his St. Louis home.

His first wife died in 1820 leaving four children of whom only two sons, Meriwether Lewis Clark and George Rogers Hancock Clark, survived their parents. In 1821 William Clark married a cousin of his first wife, Harriet Kennerly, widow of Dr. Radford. Their son was Jefferson Kennerly Clark, who died in St. Louis in 1902, leaving a considerable sum for a monument to his father, which was dedicated in 1908.

Clark passed his last years peacefully in his St. Louis home, which was the center of hospitality for both red men and white. In 1820 he was talked of for state governor, but was not elected; in 1824–25 he was surveyor general for Illinois, Missouri, and Arkansas; in 1828 he laid out the town of Paducah, Ky.; throughout all the period he held his Indian superintendency, and made constant pleas to the government at Washington for humanity and justice to the aborigines. He died at the home of his eldest son, his wife having passed away before him. He was buried with military and Masonic honors (having joined the order in 1809). His collections were given to the St. Louis Natural History Society and have been for the most part lost.

[There is no adequate biography of Clark but his career is sketched in the several editions of his travels, and Wm. R. Lighton has a brief biography of both Lewis and Clark in the Riverside Series (1901). See also Harlow Lindley, "Wm. Clark, the Indian Agent," in *Miss. Valley Hist. Asso. Proc.,* 1908–09, pp. 63–75; also R. G. Thwaites, "Wm. Clark," in *Mo. Hist. Soc. Colls.,* II, 1–24. After the *Hist. of the Expedition under the Commands of Captains Lewis and Clark* (Phila., 1814; Dublin and London, 1817) appeared, no good edition was issued until that of Elliott Coues, *Hist. of the Expedition under the Command of Lewis and Clark* (4 vols., 1893). R. G. Thwaites edited the *Original Jours. Lewis and Clark Expedition* (8 vols., 1904–05). Clark manuscripts are in the Wis. Hist. Lib., Draper MSS.; the Mo. Hist. Soc. at St. Louis; and in the Kan. Hist. Soc., Topeka, which has the letter-books for his Indian agency. The journals of the expedition are in the Am. Philosophical Soc., Phila.]   L. P. K.

CLARK, WILLIAM ANDREWS (Jan. 8, 1839–Mar. 2, 1925), senator, was born in Fayette County, Pa. His parents, John and Mary (Andrews) Clark, were of Scotch-Irish ancestry. His boyhood was spent on a farm and was varied in winter by attending short sessions of school. In 1856 the family moved to Iowa. William entered an academy at Birmingham and later studied law at Iowa Wesleyan College. In 1856 he went to Missouri to teach school. Three years later, when civil war was devastating the state, he drove a team to Colorado and started to work in the gold quartz mines there. In 1863 he went to Bannack in what is now Montana, attracted by reports of rich discoveries of gold on Grasshopper Creek. He soon joined a stampede to Horse Prairie Creek where he washed out $1,500 in gold. With this for capital he shipped in a load of provisions from Salt Lake City and started a store at Virginia City. There was a heavy demand for tobacco in Montana, and the price was high. Clark went in search of a supply and at Boise City, Idaho, found it. He bought several thousand pounds and hauled the cargo to Last Chance Gulch (now Helena) where he sold it at a good profit. In the fall of 1866 he went on horseback to the Pacific Coast and bought a large stock of goods which he took to a new store at the mining camp of Elk City. He had learned the trails, and the next year he obtained the contract for carrying the mails between Missoula and Walla Walla. This was a hazardous enterprise, as the route lay over rugged mountains and across the lands of hostile Indians, but Clark made a success of the undertaking. By this time he had become wealthy. He entered into partnership with R. W. Donnell of New York and S. E. Larabie of Montana in banking and wholesale merchandise. The firm's first bank was established at Deer Lodge in 1870 and another bank was started at Butte in 1877. With prosperity attending him, Clark in March 1869 married Kate L. Stauffer from near his old home in Pennsylvania. In 1872 he bought the Original, Colusa, Mountain Chief, and Gambetta mining claims at Butte. He then went to the School of Mines at Columbia University for a year to study mining. Upon his return he built the "Old Dexter" stamp mill, the first of its kind in Butte, then formed the Colorado and Montana Smelting Company, and built the first smelter in Butte. He established the huge Butte Reduction Works; he acquired the Elm Orlu, the greatest of the Butte mines; and he extended his mining interests to Arizona where he purchased the United Verde mine and its wonderful smelter. Other projects also claimed his attention. He built the

San Pedro, Los Angeles & Salt Lake Railroad and sold it to the Union Pacific, of which company he became a director. He organized the Los Alamitos Sugar Company and built a large sugar factory near Los Angeles.

Clark early became active in Montana politics. His prestige as a miner made him a leader of the mining interests, but he found a rival in Marcus Daly [q.v.], once his friend but eventually his implacable enemy. Both men were Democrats and both fought to control the Democratic party. This rivalry dominated the mining and political history of Montana during the 80's and 90's. Clark began his political career as president of the constitutional convention of 1884 and presided with dignity and fairness. In 1888 he was nominated for delegate to Congress. Opposed by Thomas H. Carter, then unknown, he believed that he had the support of Marcus Daly, but when the returns came in, he was found to be defeated by about 5,000 votes and where Daly's influence was strong his defeat was overwhelming. In 1889 Clark again presided over a convention that was to frame a constitution for the new state; and again he presided with fairness, although there was complaint from the small number of farming members that the miners were running the convention in their own interests (*Proceedings and Debates of the Constitutional Convention*, 1889, pp. 472–74). When the state was admitted, Clark was indorsed by the Democrats for United States senator. The legislative vote was close and both parties claimed the election. The United States Senate however seated the Republicans. In 1893 Clark was again a candidate for the Senate and now Daly was openly fighting him. It appears that both sides spent money lavishly. On the last day of the session Clark had six Republican votes but was three votes short of election, and amid cries of fraud from the Daly group the legislature adjourned and left the state with but one senator. The next episode in the feud was the fight over the state capital. Daly had been crowded out of Butte and had built Anaconda only a few miles away, desiring to make this city the capital. Clark was willing to further this ambition if Daly would support him for United States senator; but they could come to no agreement and Clark threw his support to Helena, which was eventually chosen. In the legislature which met in 1899 the Democrats had a large majority, but neither Clark nor Daly controlled it. There was a deadlock for many days, and stories were rife of huge bribes offered for votes for Clark (see testimony of Fred Whiteside and Henry L. Myers in *Senate Report No. 1052*, Pt. I, 56

Cong., 1 Sess.). One member dramatically produced $30,000, which he said had been given him with which to purchase votes. The Daly men stood firm, but finally eleven Republicans voted for Clark, and he was declared elected. Petitions against seating him were presented to the United States Senate. Clark denied any fraud but admitted the expenditure of $140,000 in the campaign. After an exhaustive investigation the Senate committee on elections reported unanimously, "That William A. Clark was not duly and legally elected to a seat in the Senate of the United States . . ." Before action could be taken on this report Clark resigned. He was immediately appointed by Acting-Governor A. E. Spriggs to fill the unexpired term but did not present himself for the oath of office. In 1901 he was elected to the Senate without much opposition. As senator he ably opposed the Roosevelt conservation policy, urging that the federal government turn over its forests to the states wherein they were located (*Congressional Record*, 59 Cong., 2 Sess., p. 3724). He also opposed that provision of the Hepburn Act which prohibited railroads from carrying the coal produced in their mines (*Ibid.*, 59 Cong., 1 Sess., p. 6564). He was one of the leaders in defeating the bill to organize Arizona and New Mexico as one state. When his term was over he quietly retired from the Senate. His first wife having died in 1893, he married, on May 25, 1901, Anna E. La Chapelle, of Butte, Mont.

In his palatial but much-ridiculed home in New York, popularly called "Clark's Folly," he built up a notable art gallery. Along with some indifferent material, it contained a number of works by Titian, Van Dyck, Rembrandt, Franz Hals, and Rubens; a representative collection of the best work of the English school, with outstanding paintings by Reynolds, Hogarth, Gainsborough, and Raeburn; some of the finest products of the Barbizon School in France; and an especially fine Cazin collection. The gallery also held a small but fine group of sculpture, some rare Gobelins and Beauvais tapestries, and many specimens of antique lace, and rare rugs (from statement of C. Powell Minnigerode, director of the Corcoran Gallery of Art, which now possesses the Clark collections).

Clark was a man of unusual and contradictory characteristics. Refined and even fastidious in manner, he could nevertheless deal with all classes of people. With intellectual and artistic dreams he was coldly practical in finance and politics. He was self-reliant and always formed his policies and directed their execution with little regard for the opinions of others. He owned outright practically every enterprise in which he was interested, and he built up one of the greatest mining businesses in the West.

[The most detailed sketch of Clark is in *Progressive Men of the State of Mont.* (1901). A biased and unfriendly view is given by C. P. Connolly in "The Story of Mont.," *McClure's Mag.*, vols. XXVII, XXVIII. There is a sketch by H. R. Knapp in the *Cosmopolitan*, Feb. 1903. Much valuable information is contained in the files of the *Butte Miner*. The *Cong. Record*, 56 to 59 Congresses, contains a number of Clark's speeches. Information as to his art collection may be found in *Bull. Metropolitan Mus. of Art*, N. Y., May 1925; *Art News*, Apr. 11, Aug. 15, Dec. 5, 1925; Mar. 31, 1928; Frank Jewett Mather in *The Arts*, Apr. 19, 1928; *N. Y. Times*, Mar. 11, 1928.]   P. C. P.

CLARK, WILLIAM BULLOCK (Dec. 15, 1860–July 27, 1917), geologist, son of Barna A. and Helen (Bullock) Clark was born at Brattleboro, Vt. His earliest American ancestors were Thomas Clark who arrived at Plymouth in 1623 on the ship *Ann*; Richard Bullock who came to Salem in 1643; and John Howland who came to Plymouth on the *Mayflower*. Clark received his early training under private tutors and at the Brattleboro high school, from which he graduated in 1879, entering Amherst College in 1880 and graduating in 1884. Prof. B. K. Emerson of Amherst was an inspiring force in turning Clark's mind toward geology. Immediately after graduation, Clark went to Germany, where he devoted himself to geological studies under Professors Groth, Rothpletz, and Zittel and received his degree of Ph.D. at the University of Munich in 1887, after which he gained experience in field work with the official surveys of Prussia and Great Britain. He returned to America in the fall of 1887, and entered at once upon the duties to which he had been appointed as instructor in geology in Johns Hopkins University in Baltimore, advancing rapidly through the academic grades until in 1894 he became full professor and head of the department, a position he continued to occupy until his death. In addition to his professional duties, Clark became in 1888 an assistant geologist on the United States Geological Survey, and in 1892 was appointed director of the Maryland State Weather Service. In 1896 he was elected State Geologist of Maryland, in 1906 executive officer of the State Board of Forestry, and in 1910 State Road Commissioner; these offices he continued to hold for the remainder of his life. In addition, he was appointed in 1900 to represent the state in the resurvey of the Maryland-Pennsylvania or Mason-Dixon line and in 1908 was adviser to the governor at the White House conference on conservation. He also rendered efficient service for sixteen years as president of the Henry Watson Children's Aid Society and was a member of the executive committee of the Maryland Association for the Prevention of Tuberculosis and vice-president and chairman of the executive committee of the Alliance of Charitable Agencies of Baltimore. He was president of the Association of American State Geologists, a foreign correspondent of the Geological Society of London, and a member of the National Academy of Sciences, the American Philosophical Society, the Philadelphia Academy of Natural Sciences, the American Academy of Arts and Sciences, the Deutsche Geologische Gesellschaft, the Paleontologische Gesellschaft, Mining and Metallurgical Society of America, and the American Association for the Advancement of Science. He died suddenly and unexpectedly at his summer home in North Haven, Me., July 27, 1917. He was married on Oct. 12, 1892, to Ellen Strong, daughter of Edward A. Strong of Boston.

Clark's early geological work involved a study and exploration of the sedimentary deposits of southern Maryland. For several years he carried on this work at his own expense; later, under the auspices of the United States Geological Survey, he prepared a bulletin on the *Eocene Deposits of the Middle Atlantic Slope in Delaware, Maryland, and Virginia* and monographs on the Mesozoic and Cenozoic Echinodermata of the United States. During his administration of the state survey, there were issued over thirty volumes of reports dealing with building stones, clays, coals, limestones, and other mineral deposits, and in cooperation with the federal bureaus there were prepared and published fifty-seven county maps. As a teacher Clark was eminently successful. "There are not a few graduates of his department who have said that he was the most potent influence in their lives" (J. M. Clarke, *post*). He insisted on thorough groundwork and permitted no specialization until the student had covered the entire broad field of science, organic as well as inorganic. He was a man of wide interests, with a large and influential circle of acquaintances, and of such varied accomplishments that it was more than once said of him that he would have succeeded in life whatever calling he might have adopted.

[E. B. Mathews, *Report Geol. Survey of Md.*, vol. X; J. M. Clarke, *Bull. Geol. Soc. of America*, vol. XXIX (1918), p. 21; personal recollections and correspondence; full bibliography of Clark's publications in Nickles, *Bull. 746, U. S. Geol. Survey*.]   G. P. M.

CLARK, WILLIAM SMITH (July 31, 1826–Mar. 9, 1886), Union soldier, scientist, college president, son of Dr. Atherton and Harriet (Smith) Clark, was born in the town of Ashfield, Mass., and received his early education there and at Williston Seminary, Easthampton. Graduating from Amherst College in 1848, he returned to Williston Seminary, where he taught the natural sciences from 1848 to 1850. He then went abroad and for the next two years devoted himself to the study of chemistry and botany at Göttingen, receiving from that university the degree of Ph.D. in 1852. On his return to the United States, he was offered by Amherst College the professorship of chemistry in 1852, to which was added the chair of zoölogy in 1853 and that of botany in 1854, the two latter being relinquished in 1858. He was also a member at large of the Massachusetts State Board of Agriculture from 1859 to 1861. On the outbreak of the Civil War he hastened to offer his services in the field, and in August 1861 received a commission as major in the 21st Massachusetts Volunteers. A born leader of men, he was quickly promoted lieutenant-colonel in February 1862 and colonel in May 1862, and was recommended by Gen. Burnside "for a well-deserved promotion" as brigadier-general in September of the same year. He took part in many engagements. At the battle of Chantilly, losing his way and becoming separated from his regiment, accompanied by only a handful of men, he was surrounded by the Confederates and ordered to surrender. Rather than encounter the horrors of Andersonville or Libby, a desperate effort was made to escape, but all were shot down except himself. Bullets whistled through his cap and clothing, but unhurt he reached the cover of the woods, and lay concealed within the enemy's lines for three days, suffering from hunger and exposure, until finally he reached the Union forces in safety, and was welcomed as one returned from the dead, for he had been reported among the fallen. After his military service was over, he returned to his professorship at Amherst, and was also a presidential elector and secretary of the electoral college in 1864, and a representative to the General Court in 1864, 1865, and 1867.

In the latter year he accepted the presidency of the Massachusetts Agricultural College. This and the professorship of botany and horticulture he held from 1867 to 1879. Since he was a forceful and persuasive speaker, it was largely owing to his efforts in town meeting and in the General Court that Amherst was selected as the seat of the Massachusetts Agricultural College. He was virtually its first president, as his predecessors, French and Chadbourne, had been able to do little more than take the initiatory

steps. It was left for Clark therefore to organize and establish the new college, and during his administration it greatly prospered. A man of ardent temperament, active mind, enterprising spirit, and boundless energy, he brought to the lecture-room intense enthusiasm and personal magnetism, which quickly established a bond of sympathy between teacher and pupil. While still connected with the Massachusetts Agricultural College, he was invited by the Japanese government to establish and organize the Imperial College of Agriculture, at Sapporo, Japan, and during the years (1876–77) of his residence there continued to preside over the interests of both colleges. He then became interested in the project of a "floating college," and being made president, bent all his energies during the next two years to develop the scheme of uniting scientific study with a tour around the world. This enterprise, owing to the death of its originator, was abandoned. Clark subsequently engaged in mining operations, but these proved disastrous to himself and others.

The author of several chemical papers in Liebig's *Annalen* in 1851 and 1852, he contributed not a few articles to the reports of the Massachusetts State Board of Agriculture, and also published a monograph on *The Phenomena of Plant Life* (1875), a work in which he received valuable aid from the investigations of two of his colleagues, Prof. Peabody and Dr. Goessmann. He was married, on May 25, 1853, to Harrietta Keopuolani Richards, daughter of the Rev. William Richards, of the Sandwich Islands, and adopted daughter of Hon. Samuel Williston of Easthampton. He had eleven children, eight of whom survived him.

[*Mass. Ag. College Reports, 1868–79; Ibid., 1887;* W. S. Tyler, *Hist. of Amherst College* (1873), pp. 421–23, 426, 581; *Amherst College Biog. Record, 1821–1921* (1927); *Proc. Am. Acad. Arts and Sci.,* vol. XXI, pt. II, pp. 520–23; D. P. Penhallow, in *Science,* n.s., XXVII, 172–80.]   F. T—n.

CLARK, WILLIAM THOMAS (June 29, 1831–Oct. 12, 1905), Union soldier, carpet-bag representative from Galveston, Tex., was born in Norwalk, Conn., the son of Levi and Fanny Clark. His school life was cut short at the age of thirteen, when on account of the poverty of his parents he was thrown on his own resources. For a few years he did odd jobs in his home town, then taught school and studied law. In 1854 he removed to New York and was admitted to the bar. Two years later he was married to Laura Clark of Hartford, and went to Davenport, Iowa, where he practised law in the firm of Judge Dillon, later one of the counsel for the Gould interests. At the beginning of the

Civil War, with the assistance of a chaplain, a drummer, and a fifer, he raised the 13th Iowa Regiment and went to the front, himself as adjutant of the command with the rank of captain. He took part in many of the western battles, receiving in 1864 a gold medal inscribed "Shiloh, Siege of Corinth, Corinth, Port Gibson, Raymond, Jackson, Champion's Hill, Vicksburg." Almost from the beginning he was a staff officer. When Gen. McPherson took command of the Army of the Tennessee he made Clark his adjutant-general, and it was Clark who brought to Sherman the first news of the tragic death of McPherson before Atlanta. As chief of staff, Clark seems to have been energetic and efficient. In the fall of 1865, now a brigadier-general by brevet (July 22, 1864), he was transferred to Texas, where the Americans were watching the progress of the war against Maximilian. On the Rio Grande he became interested in a scheme by which the liberal general, Mejia, was to hand over Matamoras to the Americans in return for a subsidy of $200,000 (*Official Records*, ser. I, vol. XLVIII, pt. 2, p. 1259). The plan, eagerly advocated by Clark, won the initial favor of Sheridan in New Orleans and of Grant in Washington, both of whom were anxious for intervention against Maximilian, but was blocked by President Johnson and Secretary Seward, who preferred the slower and less dangerous methods of diplomacy.

Clark now resigned from the army, and in 1866 was in Galveston, helping to organize one of the first national banks in Texas, of which he became cashier. About this time he began to take an active part in the creation of union leagues among the negroes and came into close affiliation with G. T. Ruby, the mulatto leader of the Galveston negroes. In 1869, Clark was elected to Congress from the Third District of the now "reconstructed" State of Texas. In Congress his speeches were frank and complete expositions of the political philosophy of the carpet-baggers but had little influence on legislation. His plan to sell a vast region in western Texas to the nation for a sum of forty millions of dollars, to be used to subsidize various railroads (in which Clark was reputed to be interested) and to advance negro education, was regarded by conservative newspapers as a mere attempt to add to the resources of a corrupt administration. When he came up for reëlection in 1871, the conservative forces were for the first time well organized and ably led, and the election resulted in a plurality of more than three thousand votes in favor of the Democratic candidate, D. C.

Giddings of Brenham. E. J. Davis, the Republican governor, had, however, small difficulty in changing these figures into a narrow victory for Clark, who was seated pending an investigation. But, largely owing to the wide publicity given the whole matter by Horace Greeley of the *Tribune,* on May 13, 1872, Clark was expelled by the unanimous vote of a Republican House and Giddings was seated in his stead. The incident was an important step in what was later to be called the "regeneration of the South."

At the close of his congressional career, Clark secured a post in the Bureau of Internal Revenue, in which he served until his death in 1905. The old general was justly proud of his army record and his military bearing. For forty years he always wore the same type of slouch hat and the same type of high top boots. In Texas, he will be remembered as "the last of the carpet-baggers."

[Clark's speeches in Congress, 1870–72, and especially his farewell address on May 13, 1872 contain biographical references; his life in the army has been traced in the *Official Records,* especially after he became chief of staff; for his life in Texas see the state newspapers, especially the *Galveston Daily News* and *Flake's Daily Galveston Bull.*; the story of the contested election of 1871–72 may be followed in the *Cong. Globe,* 42 Cong., 2 Sess., and the *N. Y. Tribune,* Jan.–May 1872; these may be supplemented by N. G. Kittrell, *Governors Who Have Been and Other Public Men of Tex.* (1921), pp. 95–96, and C. W. Ramsdell, *Reconstruction in Tex.* (1910), p. 286; for his later life see *Who's Who in America,* and an obituary in the *N. Y. Tribune,* Oct. 13, 1905.]　　　R. G. C.

CLARK, WILLIS GAYLORD (Oct. 5, 1808–June 12, 1841), poet, editor, and publicist, was the son of Eliakim Clark and the twin brother of Lewis Gaylord Clark [*q.v.*]. He was named after his uncle, Willis Gaylord, whose father, coming to Otisco in 1801, was the third settler in that hamlet (Joshua V. H. Clark, *Onondaga,* 1849, II, 339–44). In his early education he was materially aided by the Rev. George Colton, a maternal relative, and found in his father's library a somewhat remarkable collection of books on philosophical subjects and on poetry. Going to Philadelphia, he found employment in an editorial capacity on several literary and religious periodicals before he became permanently associated with *Relf's Philadelphia Gazette* as editor. In 1836 he married Anne Poyntell Caldcleugh, a niece of Samuel Relf, formerly publisher of the *Gazette* (Frederic Hudson, *Journalism in the United States from 1690–1872,* 1873, p. 79). After Clark became the chief editor he changed the paper from an advocacy of Jacksonian democracy to a championship of Whig principles. A leader in Philadelphia journalism, he became through his contributions to the leading literary monthlies the foremost Philadelphia poet of his day. Writing in *Graham's Magazine* Edgar Allan Poe remarked that in all that Clark wrote there was "a deep abiding sense of religion" and that Clark was "almost the first poet to render the poetry of religion attractive" (E. P. Oberholtzer, *The Literary History of Philadelphia*, 1906, p. 301). Possibly Clark's most distinguished poems were "The Spirit of Life," read before the Franklin Society of Brown University, Sept. 3, 1833, and "The Past and Present," read before the Athenian Society of Bristol College, July 23, 1834. Always a popular speaker before college audiences, he last appeared in this rôle, on July 4, 1840, when he delivered an address on the characters of Lafayette and Washington before the Washington Society of Lafayette College. Some of his best prose works may be found in the department, "Ollapodianna," which he conducted in his brother's magazine, the *Knickerbocker*. His name appears frequently as a contributor to American annals such as the *Souvenir*, the *Token*, the *Keepsake*, etc. In one special field his services should not be overlooked: he was the first to advocate in print an international copyright (*Knickerbocker Magazine*, vol. XIX, No. 4, p. 384). His published volumes include *The Literary Remains of the Late W. G. Clark*, edited by L. G. Clark (1844), and *The Poetical Writings of Willis Gaylord Clark* (second and complete edition, 1847). Unusually sad must be the concluding note because both Clark and his wife died of consumption when both should have been in their prime.

[The best account of Willis Clark is unquestionably that by his brother, Lewis Clark, in the *Knickerbocker*, Apr. 1842. An extended review of some of his poetry appeared in 1837 in the *Am. Quart. Rev.*, XXII, 459–72. An obituary together with an editorial appreciation may be found in the *Phila. Ledger and Daily Transcript*, June 14, 1841.]   J.M.L.

CLARKE, Sir CASPAR PURDON (Dec. 21, 1846–Mar. 29, 1911), architect, archeologist, art connoisseur, and museum administrator, although born a British subject at his father's home in Richmond, County Dublin, Ireland, and retaining his nationality after coming to New York to live, nevertheless played an important rôle in the art history of the United States. The second son of Edward Marmaduke Clarke, of an old Somerset family, and Mary Agnes, daughter of James Close of Armagh, Ireland, he studied at Gaultier's Collegiate School, Sydenham, and at a private school in Boulogne, and graduated in 1865 from the architectural department of the National Art Train-

ing School, South Kensington; but is said to have owed most to his contact in early life with Sir Woolaston Franks. For his forty years of service to the South Kensington Museum and other departments of his Government—not only at home, but in Europe, India, and the Orient—for his principal buildings, published work, honors received by him, and portraits painted of him, the reader is referred to a two-column article in the *Dictionary of National Biography* (Second Supplement, ed. by Sir Sidney Lee). Passing to 1905, the trustees of the Metropolitan Museum of Art in New York were then seeking a man to fill the vacant directorship who should be a recognized art expert and in sympathy with the educational side of museum work, especially as it touched the arts and crafts. These were all among the specialties of Sir Purdon, whose versatility seemed unlimited. It was said that with him judgment was an instinct; "were he blindfolded, he would know spurious objects from their odour." He was also expert in technical processes, knew how everything was made, and enjoyed taking infinite pains, saying, "I could make a cobweb without breaking it." He seldom had to answer, "I don't know," and his memory was perfectly indexed. He had been the patron saint of artisans since at the age of twenty-four he had organized and conducted evening art classes for them in various parts of England. Knighted in 1902, he had been director of the great Victoria and Albert Museum (formerly the South Kensington) since 1896, and was in his fifty-ninth year; but to the surprise of his compatriots he accepted, in January 1905, the New York position—lured chiefly by its constructive possibilities. American criticism at the choice of a Britisher soon evaporated under his charm of personality, simplicity, and kindliness. Soon every branch of the art fraternity was frequenting the Museum and interviewing its always genial and entertaining director; the industrial art education began; the public acquired the Museum habit; the critics became friendly. But his health broke. In 1909 he was given a year's leave of absence from which he never returned, resigning in June 1910, but remaining the Museum's European correspondent until his death about eight months later. In 1866 he had married Frances S. Collins, who survived him. He left but a modest estate and his widow was pensioned by the British government. He was a Mason of high degree. In appearance, he was of medium height, very active, bright of eye, ruddy of countenance, "smiling pleasantly over his gold-rimmed glasses." A fascinating talker, a ready and lucid writer, a fluent lecturer, a tactful gentleman.

[Harry Furniss, "Some Walking Encyclopædias," *Windsor Mag.*, Mar. 1905; John Lane, *Sir Caspar Purdon Clarke* (1905); *Metropolitan Museum of Art Bull.*, I, 3–5, V, 164–65, VI, 73, 108; *Quatour Coronati Lodge*, XXIV, 118–24; Frank Jewett Mather, Jr., in *Burlington Mag.*, VII, 479–80.]   F.B.H.

CLARKE, ELIJAH (1733–Jan. 15, 1799), Revolutionary soldier, adventurer, was born in Edgecombe County, S. C. He was probably of Scotch-Irish origin, and had the characteristics of a pioneer; he was strong and active, brave and resolute, uneducated, but a leader in stirring times. In 1774 he had removed to Wilkes County, Ga., and when the war shifted to the South, he became one of the leading partisan commanders. He was colonel of militia, serving at times under Pickens, and was brigadier-general in 1781–83. His name occurs in various skirmishes of the far South, at Alligator Creek in 1778 where he was wounded; at Kettle Creek in 1779, where he shared with Pickens the credit of the victory, displaying foresight in occupying the higher ground; at Musgrove's Mill in August 1780, where he was severely wounded and had a narrow escape; at Fish Dam and Blackstocks in October 1780; at Long Cane, where he was again wounded; and at Beattie's Mill, where he defeated the British leader Dunlap. He served at both sieges of Augusta—in September 1780 when he was repulsed, and the next year when he cooperated with Pickens and Lee in the reduction of the town. In recognition of his services Wilkes County and the legislature of Georgia granted him an estate.

After the war Clarke by turns negotiated with the Indians and fought against them, inflicting a defeat at Jack's Creek, Walton County, Ga., in 1787. In 1793 he became involved in the schemes of Genêt, the intriguing minister of France, directed against Spain. Clarke entered the French service and received a commission as major-general, a salary of $10,000, and some means for the carrying out of the plans. It was his part to enlist Georgians, Creeks, and Cherokees, but there was little fighting; Genêt was soon recalled, and Fauchet his successor stopped the undertaking. The next year Clarke was implicated in a still more serious affair. He led a force into Creek territory across the Oconee River. His motives, according to a biographer, were "not quite clear." But the Georgians were "land-hungry"; they were irritated with the Creeks and with the attitude of the Federal government, and Clarke claimed to be defending the rights of his state. A few forts were erected, and some towns were laid out. These proceedings

brought him to the notice of the law, but he was popular with Georgians, and was acquitted by a Wilkes County tribunal. He continued his project, and the "Trans-Oconee State" received a constitution and a committee of safety. The Federal government, through a letter from Hamilton to the governor of Georgia, then made representations. A blockade along the Oconee was established by Georgia troops, and Clarke, deserted by most of his followers, surrendered. At a time subsequent to 1794 he was accused (probably without foundation) of scheming, with British encouragement, against Florida. He was also charged with complicity in the Yazoo land frauds. His general reputation in the state did not suffer, however, in consequence of these events. On his death, in Wilkes County, the commander of militia issued a general order for mourning. A county in the state bears his name, and a monument at Athens stands in his honor. He was married to Hannah Arrington and was the father of John Clark [*q.v.*].

[E. M. Coulter, "Elijah Clarke's Foreign Intrigues and the 'Trans-Oconee Republic,'" *Proc. Miss. Valley Hist. Asso.*, X, 260–79; Absalom H. Chappell, *Ga. Miscellanies* (1874); C. C. Jones, *Hist. of Ga.* (1888); W. F. Northen, ed., *Men of Mark in Ga.*, I (1907), 40–45; G. R. Gilmer, *Sketches of Some of the First Settlers of Upper Ga.* (1855), p. 39.]   E.K.A.

CLARKE, FRANCIS DEVEREUX (Jan. 31, 1849–Sept. 7, 1913), educator of the deaf, was the eldest of the four children of William J. and Mary Bayard (Devereux) Clarke [*q.v.*] of Raleigh, N. C. His father, an eminent lawyer and judge of the state courts, was also distinguished for bravery as an officer in the Mexican War, and later became a colonel in the Confederate army. His mother was a brilliant writer of both prose and poetry. The family was descended on the father's side from Scotch ancestry, and on the mother's from Scotch and from French Huguenot strains. Both families appeared in the Carolinas in the seventeenth century, and were prominent in theology, teaching, and the law. Francis began his education in the primary schools of Raleigh, but moved with the family to San Antonio, Tex., when he was seven years old. Here he was under the instruction of Oliver D. Cooke, a former teacher in the American School for the Deaf. His mother's failing health improved and the family returned to Raleigh at the opening of the Civil War. Francis entered Davidson College, but after two years of study left to join the Confederate navy as a midshipman, at the age of thirteen. He served with distinction on various ships, including the battleship *Tennessee*. At the close of the Civil War, though only sixteen years of age, he had risen to the rank of lieutenant. For three years he engaged in business in North Carolina with a brother, but felt a call to sea service, and went to New York City with the purpose of joining the merchant marine. His old tutor, Oliver D. Cooke, then a teacher in the New York Institution for the Deaf, persuaded Francis to call upon Dr. Isaac L. Peet, principal of the New York Institution, and to observe the work being done for the education of deaf children in this institution. Dr. Peet was so pleased with the young man's intelligent questions that he offered him a place as instructor in his school, and Clarke accepted.

On Sept. 24, 1873, Clarke was married to Celia Laura Ransom of Kalamazoo, Mich., niece of the then chief justice of the state, who later became governor. Miss Ransom was a teacher of the deaf at the time of their marriage. Although Clarke was also much interested in engineering, receiving the degree of Master of Arts in course from Columbia University in 1873 and the degree of Civil Engineer in 1875, and working for a brief time as a civil engineer in North Carolina, he nevertheless remained with Dr. Peet until 1885, and then accepted the superintendency of the Arkansas Institute for the Deaf at Little Rock. He found there a small school, not well provided with buildings or equipment. He revised the course of study, increased the pupilage, and rebuilt the plant in the seven years that he remained. In September 1892 he was invited to take charge of the State School for the Deaf at Flint, Mich. Here again he showed his energy in rebuilding and enlarging an institution. He added a kindergarten department, a physical education department, a normal department, a farm of 350 acres, and he introduced poultry raising, farming, and gardening for the students. He revised the course of study and made many additions to the buildings and equipment, so that the Michigan School took first rank among the state institutions for the education of the deaf in the United States. One of his last acts was the laying of the corner-stone of the handsome new administration building for which he had obtained sufficient funds after a hard fight in the state legislature. He died a few weeks later from heart failure, leaving this excellent school, with its many successful graduates, as a monument to his energy and wisdom.

Clarke was honored by election to the Executive Committee of the Conference of Superintendents and Principals of American Schools for the Deaf in 1900. He was one of the incorporators of the Convention of American Instructors of the Deaf and was a regular contributor of articles on the education of the deaf to the *American Annals of the Deaf.* Among these are "Courses of Study and Textbooks," "Foundation Work in Arithmetic," "Kindergarten for the Deaf," "The Training of Teachers." One of his most important works was a book entitled *Michigan Methods,* which is a valuable treatise on primary work for deaf children.

[Jas. M. Stewart in the *Am. Annals of the Deaf,* LVIII, 534–41; A. S. Eickhoff in the *Mich. Mirror,* Oct. 23, 1913; *Detroit Free Press,* Sept. 8, 1913; personal acquaintance.]
P. H.

CLARKE, GEORGE (1676–Jan. 12, 1760), colonial official, was the son of George Clarke of Swainswick, Somersetshire, near Bath. He was in early youth articled to an attorney. In 1701 he was a resident of Dublin where he became involved in a quarrel with a merchant, for which he had to pay damages of three guineas. He was a nephew of William Blaithwait whose well-known influence in matters of patronage in connection with plantation affairs was doubtless responsible for Clarke's appointment to the office of Secretary of the Province of New York. Arriving in New York on July 23, 1703, he remained, except for a brief visit to England in 1705, for forty-two years. He was therefore very far from being an absentee sinecure-holder. Of no brilliance of gifts or striking force of character, it was rather by a long course of steady attention to the opportunities of his position in the province, coupled with painstaking assiduity in keeping contact with important sources of political and social influence in England, that he finally became a significant figure in New York provincial history. On his journey to England in 1705 he was married to Anne Hyde, who was distantly related to the Clarendons and so to Queen Anne and to Lord Cornbury, who was at that time governor of New York. Subsequent to his marriage he took up his residence on Long Island where he purchased nearly 100 acres of land and erected a villa. Here he spent a great portion of his time, leaving the details of his office to be attended to by his deputy. As landmarks in his official career may be mentioned his appointment in 1716 to membership in the Council of New York, and, in 1718, to the commission to run the Connecticut boundary line, and as deputy for New York to the Auditor General of the Plantations, Horace Walpole. Probably through this latter connection he became a frequent correspondent of the Duke of Newcastle. By 1736 he had amassed a considerable fortune, in small part from the fees of his offices, but much more as a result of extensive dealings in land, for which those offices afforded peculiarly favorable opportunities. Throughout these same years he had consistently made himself useful to the successive governors in the domain of provincial politics, and yet, till Cosby's administration, 1732–36, he had managed to keep on fairly good terms with the provincial leaders. The peculiar circumstances of his accession to the headship of the provincial government as lieutenant-governor in 1736, after the violent excesses of the Cosby administration, brought him, however, to the center of a local situation full of dangerous popular passion. By adroit management, made possible by his acquaintance with the local scene, he was able after a time to reduce the tension. But he was obliged to yield entirely to the ambitions of the Assembly for complete control of provincial finance. It was while he was lieutenant-governor that the precedent was firmly established of supporting the provincial government by annual grants of revenue instead of for terms of three or five years, and of making specific appropriations by legislative act instead of appropriations in general terms supplemented by resolves requesting particular applications. The attainment of this precedent by the Assembly constituted a crisis of the first order of importance in the constitutional development of New York as a royal province. Clarke also abandoned the practise, formerly prevalent, of presiding in the Council when the latter sat as a legislative body. His "interest" at home proved insufficient to obtain for him more than the commission as lieutenant-governor and he was succeeded in the headship of the province by George Clinton to whom the seals and commission were delivered September 1743. Henceforth Clarke took no further part in public affairs. On his voyage home in 1745 he was taken prisoner by the French, but his losses incident to this occasion as well as those from the "Negro Plot" fire in New York in 1741 were made up—and more, according to his enemies—by a Parliamentary donation. He was said to have made a fortune of £100,000 in America. He certainly was able to purchase a handsome estate in Cheshire, and at his death was buried in Chester Cathedral.

[*Voyage of Geo. Clarke, Esq. to America,* with introduction and notes by E. B. O'Callaghan (Albany, 1867), being vol. II of N. Y. Colonial Tracts; *Letters of Isaac Bobin, Esq., Private Secretary to Hon. Geo. Clarke,* ed. by E. B. O'Callaghan (Albany, 1872), being vol. IV of N. Y. Colonial Tracts; J. W. Leonard, *Hist. of the City of N. Y.* (1910), pp. 199–203; Wm. Smith, *Hist. of the Province of N. Y.* (1829); H. L. Osgood, *Am. Colonies in the Eighteenth Century* (1924).]

C.W.S.

CLARKE, HELEN ARCHIBALD (Nov. 13, 1860–Feb. 8, 1926), author, editor, musician, was born in Philadelphia, the daughter of Hugh Archibald and Jane (Searle) Clarke. On her father's side she was of Scotch ancestry; on her mother's of English. Hugh Clarke, who was born in Hamilton, Ontario, was a music-teacher and later professor of harmony in the University of Pennsylvania; his father and grandfather had been musicians in Edinburgh. His wife was born in London and was brought when a child to Canada; she too had musical tastes. Their daughter was trained in music almost from babyhood, received a certificate for proficiency in that art from the University of Pennsylvania in 1883, and played and composed music her life long. The best known of her compositions is probably "The Hidden Dark." Music, however, was to be her avocation, editing and writing her main occupation. Deeply interested in poetry, she and her friend Charlotte Endymion Porter in 1888 launched a periodical called *Poet Lore,* which was to be "devoted to Shakespeare, Browning, and the Comparative Study of Literature." The coupling of the names of Shakespeare and Browning, and the broad program implicit in the third object of the magazine's devotion, indicate the inclusive enthusiasms of its editors and the atmosphere of American Victorian culture in which *Poet Lore* was to flourish. It was started amid the benedictions of Walt Whitman, Edmund Clarence Stedman, Richard Hovey, and Bliss Carman, and, besides numerous articles on Shakespeare and Browning, delighted and thrilled its readers by printing translations of Maeterlinck, Strindberg, Gorky, D'Annunzio, Ibsen, and other European writers, who, at that time, were known only as names to most American readers. Early in the nineties Miss Porter and Miss Clarke transferred their paper to Boston, where Dana Estes, the publisher, had offered them office room in exchange for three pages per issue of advertising space. There the two lived until Miss Clarke's death, spending their summers regularly at Miss Porter's estate on Isle au Haut, Me., and giving themselves whole-heartedly to editing, writing, lecturing, and Browning. In 1896 they edited a two-volume edition of Browning's poems, in 1897 a volume of *Clever Tales,* translated from several languages, and an edition of *The Ring and the Book,* in 1898 an edition of Browning's complete poetical works in twelve volumes, in 1900 a volume of *Browning Study Programmes* and an edition in six volumes of Mrs. Browning's complete works, and in 1912 an edition of Shakespeare in twelve volumes. Miss Clarke also aided her friend with the first three volumes of a larger undertaking, the *First Folio Shakespeare* in forty volumes. They sold *Poet Lore* in 1903 to Richard G. Badger, but continued to edit it for some time thereafter. Once her editorial responsibilities were over, Miss Clarke gave more time to writing. Her chief publications are: *Browning's Italy: a Study of Italian Life and Art in Browning* (1907); *Browning's England: A Study of English Influences in Browning* (1908); *A Child's Guide to Mythology* (1908); *Longfellow's Country* (1909); *Hawthorne's Country* (1910); *A Guide to Mythology for Young Readers* (1910); *Ancient Myths in Modern Poets* (1910); *The Poets' New England* (1911); and *Browning and His Century* (1912). In 1915 appeared *Balaustion's Euripides,* a dramatic version of "Balaustion's Adventure" and "Aristophanes' Apology." Miss Clarke was an honorary member of the Boston Browning Society and of the New York Browning Society, and had lectured at the Boston Public Library only a week before her sudden death.

[Charlotte E. Porter, "A Story of Poet Lore," *Poet Lore,* XXXVII, 432–53; *Who's Who in America,* 1926–27; *Boston Transcript,* Feb. 9, 1926; *Gen. Alumni Cat. Univ. of Pa.* (1917); birth certificate from the Phila. Dept. of Public Health; letter from Miss Porter, Mar. 6, 1928.]
        G.H.G.

CLARKE, JAMES FREEMAN (Apr. 4, 1810–June 8, 1888), Unitarian clergyman, was named after his step-grandfather, Dr. James Freeman, minister of King's Chapel, Boston (1787–1835), who had married the widow of Samuel Clarke. His mother, Rebecca Parker Hull, was a daughter of Gen. William Hull [*q.v.*]. His father, Samuel Clarke, seems to have been a "handy man," able to do many things passably but to make a living at none. Shortly after the birth of his son in Hanover, N. H., he removed to Newton, Mass., and established himself near the families of James Freeman and the Hulls so that although the boy was brought up in Dr. Freeman's household, there was scarcely any separation from his immediate family. His grandfather also took charge of his early education, kindling intellectual interests and teaching him right methods of study. He entered the Boston Latin School in 1821 and there prepared for Harvard, from which he graduated in the class of '29 celebrated in the poems of Oliver Wendell Holmes. After graduating from the Harvard Divinity School in 1833, and receiving ordination in Boston (July 21, 1833), he went directly to Louisville, Ky., where he was minister of a Unitarian church from Aug. 4, 1833, to June 16, 1840. During his residence in Louisville he was editor from April 1836 to October 1839 of the *Western Messenger* in which appeared notable contributions from many of Clarke's eastern friends, including Dr. Channing and Emerson.

Returning to Boston, he founded there a new Unitarian church modestly named The Church of the Disciples, of which he became pastor on Feb. 28, 1841. The founding of this church made almost as much stir in Boston as that of the Brattle Street Church nearly a century and a half earlier and for similar reasons, the chief of which was its exceptional recognition of the power of the laity. The value of this innovation was signally shown during the period from Aug. 11, 1850, to Jan. 1, 1854, when notwithstanding the sale of the church property and the absence of the minister on account of ill health, the organization held together with occasional services, especially the communion services, conducted by lay members of the church. These years, broken by a trip abroad, were spent by Clarke in Meadville, Pa., where he acted as minister of the local Unitarian church which had been founded in 1825 principally by Harm Jan Huidekoper whose daughter Anna he had married in August 1839. With restored health, he returned to Boston in 1854 and resumed his duties as minister of the Church of the Disciples. In this position he speedily won the full and unbroken confidence not only of his clerical colleagues, but also of the community which he served in various ways. He was a member of the State Board of Education (1863–69); trustee of the Boston Public Library (1879–88); non-resident professor in the Harvard Divinity School (1867–71), and lecturer on ethnic religions (1876–77); member of the Board of Overseers of Harvard College (1863–72, 1873–85, 1886–88). In addition, he was active in behalf of temperance, anti-slavery, and woman suffrage. Such labor he refused to regard as "outside activity," deeming it rather his part, as minister of the church, of its due contribution to the life of the city.

Dr. Clarke's most notable characteristic was a remarkable balance and wisdom. He was rightly numbered among the Transcendentalists, but his thought was simple and his style lucid. His Transcendentalism appeared chiefly in his confidence in the universality of truth and goodness among men, and in his earnest efforts to discover it in all persons, sects, and religions. A convinced and devout Christian, he studied appreciatively other religions also (*Ten Great Religions,* pt. I, 1871, pt. II, 1883); a loyal Unitarian, he was sympathetic with other denominations, aiming to give full credit to all that his fellow Christians of whatever name were contributing to human welfare. The same discriminating insight taught him to discern the best in individuals and to labor to free it from base entanglements. He was a wise, discriminating, sympathetic and irenic friend and teacher; quick to praise, slow to blame; more eager to cherish good than to crush evil; a rare combination of particular loyalties and universal sympathies. He was a prolific writer: sermons, newspaper and review articles streamed from his facile pen almost beyond enumeration. Besides *Ten Great Religions,* he published: *The Christian Doctrine of Forgiveness of Sin* (1852); *The Christian Doctrine of Prayer* (1854); *Orthodoxy: Its Truths and Errors* (1866); *Common Sense in Religion* (1874); *Essentials and Non-Essentials in Religion* (1878); *Self-Culture* (1882); *Anti-Slavery Days* (1884); *The Problem of the Fourth Gospel* (1886).

[The beginning of an Autobiography is contained in the first six chapters of *Jas. Freeman Clarke* (1891) by Edward Everett Hale. See also the sketch by Clarke's daughter Lilian Freeman Clarke, in *Heralds of a Liberal Faith,* III, 67–75; a memoir by Andrew Preston Peabody in *Mass. Hist. Soc. Proc.,* Mar. 1889; tributes from friends and contemporaries in the *Christian Reg.,* June 14, 1888.]   W. W. F.

CLARKE, JAMES PAUL (Aug. 18, 1854–Oct. 1, 1916), governor of Arkansas, United States senator, was the son of Walter and Ellen (White) Clarke. He was born in Yazoo City, Miss., and was educated in the schools of Mississippi and in the law school of the University of Virginia, where he received the degree of LL.B. in 1878. The next year he opened a law office in Helena, Ark. On Nov. 10, 1883, he was married to Mrs. Sallie (Moore) Wooten of Moon Lake, Miss. From 1887 to 1895 he served as representative, senator, attorney-general, and governor. His administration as governor was uneventful except for the passage of some populistic legislation, such as a law to tax national-bank notes and United States treasury notes in circulation as currency. He declined a second term and in 1897 moved to Little Rock and resumed the practise of law. In 1903 he was elected to the United States Senate as a Democrat to succeed J. K. Jones and was reëlected in 1909. In 1914, under popular election, he narrowly missed defeat in the Democratic primary, but was triumphantly elected at the general election. In 1913 he was elected president *pro tempore* of the Senate and was reëlected in 1915, although he had opposed some of the administration measures and did not always vote with his party. During his first term in the Senate his "unqualified independence" caused him to break with his party in its opposition to Roosevelt's policy on Panama Canal legislation, and the President declared that Clarke was largely instrumental in securing its passage. He support-

ed the Bristow amendment for popular election of United States senators with federal control, although his party was for state control. He contributed largely to the defeat of the Ship Purchase Bill (1915), an administration measure, and secured several important modifications in the bill before it was finally passed. He bitterly opposed the Adamson eight-hour law (1916), another administration measure, in which he was supported by only one Democratic senator. He was an ardent advocate of Philippine independence and pushed through the Senate a bill promising independence in a short time, but it failed in the House. Although Clarke was somewhat conservative in certain things he was progressive in others. He favored full control of the railroads. When the Hepburn Bill (1906) was under consideration he advocated physical valuation as a basis for rate making, the giving of the Interstate Commission final power over rates without any right of appeal to the courts, and the prohibition of any preliminary injunction against the enforcement of new rates proclaimed by it (*Congressional Record,* 59 Cong., 1 Sess., pp. 6104–27). In 1908 he opposed the Aldrich Currency Bill as premature. He voted for the exclusion of Reed Smoot and William Lorimer. He supported employers' liability and workmen's compensation legislation, the exemption of farmers and laborers from the anti-trust law, the literacy test for immigrants, and the taxation of trading in cotton futures. He served on several important committees, being chairman of the Committee on Commerce. He made few set speeches, but participated freely in debate and exercised considerable influence on legislation. He died at Little Rock and was buried in Oakland Cemetery.

[D. T. Herndon, *Centennial Hist. of Ark.,* vol. I (1922); Ark. Senate and House *Journals,* 1887–95; memorial addresses on the life and character of Jas. P. Clarke, in *Cong. Record,* 14 Cong., 2 Sess., p. 3546; *Who's Who in America,* 1916–17; *Biog. Dir. Am. Cong.* (1928); *Ark. Gazette* and *Ark. Democrat,* Oct. 2, 1916.]
D. Y. T.

CLARKE, JOHN (Oct. 8, 1609–Apr. 28, 1676), Baptist clergyman, statesman, was the son of Thomas and Rose (Kerrich) Clarke. His maternal grandfather was William Kerrich, of a Suffolk family, while the Clarkes belonged to Bedfordshire. John was born in Westhorpe, Suffolk, the sixth of eight children and the midmost of five sons, four of whom ultimately settled in Newport, R. I. No definite contact with any educational institution has been traced unless a John Clarke of the University of Leyden is to be identified with him; but his intellectual outlook reveals a breadth of view not entirely ascribable to self-training, while various evidences point to some erudition. He was probably married before he left England; his first wife, Elizabeth Harris, may have brought him some dowry. Much later a legacy came from her father out of the manor of Wrestlingsworth.

Clarke landed in Boston in November 1637, just after the General Court had taken its last rigorous action against the Antinomians. His unselfishness stands out clearly as he placed himself among the defeated supporters of the "covenant of grace," who recognized him at once as a leader. He and the others went first to Exeter, N. H., and in the next spring he went with a party to Providence, where they were courteously received by Roger Williams, with whom they conferred about their plans. The result, after Clarke had consulted with the Plymouth authorities, was the decision to settle at Aquidneck. Clarke was one of eighteen who on Mar. 7, 1638, signed a compact incorporating themselves into a body politic. Although Coddington was selected as governor, Clarke, as physician and preacher, was equally a leader. A year later, these two with a few others moved to the southern end of the island, settling Newport. Clarke's original relations with the Baptists are as obscure as is the early history of the church at Newport. He may have had contact with Anabaptists in Holland; he may have been among those in Rhode Island who, according to Winthrop, "turned professed anabaptists" in 1641. From 1644, at the latest, he was pastor of the Baptist Church in Newport.

The best-known incident in the career of Clarke was his visit with John Crandall and Obadiah Holmes to Lynn, Mass., when on July 20, 1651, while holding a religious service in the house of William Witter, a non-resident member of the Newport church, they were arrested. Brought first to the public service of worship, where Clarke expressed "his dissent from their order," the next day they were taken to Boston for trial. The specific charges against Clarke were unauthorized preaching, disrespect in the assembly of worship, administering the Lord's Supper to persons under discipline, and denying the lawfulness of infant baptism. All three were sentenced to be fined or be whipped. A friend, without Clarke's knowledge, paid his fine of £20.

Later that same year, Clarke was sent with Roger Williams to England to protect the interests of the colony. In this they were so successful that Williams soon returned to America, but Clarke remained for ten years or more. In the

fall of 1654 the assembly of freemen sent him a letter of thanks. A recent writer ("The English Career of John Clarke," *Baptist Quarterly*, 1923, pp. 192 ff.) ingeniously identifies Clarke with a man who was somewhat implicated in the Fifth Monarchy movement, but by the time of the overthrow of the Venner rebellion had completely dissociated himself from the extremists. It seems doubtful, however, whether the Rhode Islander would have proceeded so rapidly in his task of securing the charter for that colony if he had not been quite free from political suspicion. Of greater importance is the charge that Clarke was willing to use unworthy methods to advance the interests of Rhode Island. The basis of the charge is probably the pique of some Massachusetts leaders at his diplomatic successes, and at the worst, it represents his enemies' interpretation of an attitude capable of a quite different explanation. It is possible that Clarke returned to America for a short time in 1661; he was in England on Apr. 7, 1663, when he had in his possession the agreement with Connecticut as to the boundary between that colony and Rhode Island. During this year he was largely instrumental in securing the royal charter for Rhode Island. He returned to Newport in 1664, when he again received the thanks of the colony. While continuing to serve as minister and physician, he was elected to the General Assembly and thrice was elected deputy governor. He retired from political activity in 1672. The previous year he had married, as his second wife, Jane Fletcher, who died within about a year; soon thereafter he married Sarah Davis, who survived until 1692.

The democratic character of the charter of Providence Plantation (1647) and of the Code of Laws at once adopted is traceable fully as much to Clarke as to Williams. Captious criticism has interpreted the recognition of the authority of Christ in the Compact of Mar. 7, 1638, as a limitation even upon toleration; but Clarke's attitude in Boston earlier and his influence later upon the legislation in Rhode Island show that for him nothing less than liberty of conscience was compatible with that authority; while his petition to King Charles II (probably 1662) contained the immortal sentiment—"a most flourishing Civill State may stand, yea, and best be maintained . . . with a full liberty in religious concernments" (*Records of the Colony of Rhode Island and Providence Plantations*, vol. I, 1856, pp. 485–91).

[*The Story of Dr. John Clarke* (1915), by T. W. Bicknell is more pretentious than satisfying. Clarke's

Ill Newes from New Eng. (London, 1652, reprinted in *Mass. Hist. Soc. Colls.*, 4th ser., vol. II, 1854) is to some extent autobiographical and embodies his account of the Lynn episode. This affair is most fully treated in H. M. King, *A Summer Visit of Three Rhode Islanders to the Mass. Bay in 1651* (1896). The criticism of Clarke's conduct in England may best be traced in Jas. Grahame, *Hist. of the U. S.* (2nd ed., 1856, I, 224 ff.) ; there is nothing to substantiate Chalmers's statement upon which Grahame relied. A *Concordance of the Bible* which Clarke prepared and which was licensed for printing seems not to be extant ; it has sometimes been confused with *Holie Oyle for the Lampes of the Sanctuarie* (London, 1630), an earlier work by an Anglican divine of the same name. The Newport Hist. Soc. has considerable material, including Clarke's will and a Life of Clarke (MS.) by the Rev. Samuel Adlam, but this contains little information not otherwise available.]   W. H. A.

CLARKE, JOHN MASON (Apr. 15, 1857–May 29, 1925), paleontologist, was born one of six children, in Canandaigua, N. Y. His father was Noah Clarke whose ancestors William Clarke and his wife Sarah came to America in 1630 on the sailing vessel *William and John* and settled in 1636 in Dorchester, Mass. His mother was Laura Mason (Merrill) Clarke of Castleton, Vt., whose ancestors were among the *Mayflower* company. John Clarke's scientific tendencies were early manifested and doubtless in part inherited, for his father for fifty years taught the sciences in Canandaigua Academy of which he was principal. Environment was, however, also favorable. "Born of a father who was a lover and teacher of nature, and in a village whose rocks are replete with Devonian fossils, he began collecting the latter when he was but six years of age" (Schuchert, *post*). He received his early training at the Canandaigua Academy and entered Amherst College in 1874 to graduate in 1877. During the following year he taught in the Canandaigua Academy, but in 1878 returned to Amherst as a temporary assistant to Prof. B. K. Emerson. In 1880 he taught science classes in the Utica Free Academy whence he was called to become instructor in geology, mineralogy, and zoölogy at Smith College. At the end of the college year (1883) he went abroad, studying with Prof. von Koenen in Göttingen, returning in the autumn of 1884 with the expectation—unrealized—of resuming his teaching at Smith. The year was spent in lecturing on science and teaching German in the Massachusetts Agricultural College. On Jan. 1, 1886, he received an appointment as assistant to Prof. James Hall, state paleontologist, at Albany, N. Y. Here he continued for the remainder of his life, teaching also in the Rensselaer Polytechnic Institute, and on Hall's death in 1898 succeeding him as state paleontologist. He was instrumental in bringing about the mapping of nearly one-half the sta-

tion on a scale of one mile to the inch and brought the knowledge of New York geology and its mineral industry to a condition of which it may be said that "no equal area in America is so completely known and understood." He was also in 1904 made director of the State Museum and of the Science Department, University of the State of New York. Under his direction was completed the new museum building in 1913 and the installation of its collections, forming what has been said to be the best State Museum in America, containing upward of 7,000 types of specimens of invertebrate fossils invaluable to the scientific worker, and a remarkably fine series of restorations of early geological invertebrate forms. A reproduction to scale of the Gilboa Devonian forest furnishes an unrivaled picture of the oldest forest known.

Clarke was a man of culture, a ready speaker and toward the latter part of his life a writer of no ordinary charm and ability. He became one of the world's authorities on the Devonian Age and the author of some 150 papers on various scientific subjects. He received the Hayden Gold Medal of the Philadelphia Academy of Sciences, the Spindiaroff prize of the International Geological Congress in Stockholm, the Thompson Medal for distinguished service in geology from the National Academy of Sciences and the gold medal of the Wild Life Permanent Protective Fund. He was the recipient of numerous honorary degrees and belonged to nearly a score of learned societies. A delightful conversationalist and good raconteur, he was usually in amiable mood but was capable of intense likes and dislikes and was a master of sarcasm. He was twice married: first to Mrs. Emma Sill, née Emma Juel of Philadelphia; second to Mrs. Fannie V. Bosler, also of Philadelphia.

[Chas. Schuchert, *Bull. Geol. Soc.*, vol. XXXVII, no. 1, 1926, pp. 49–93, containing full bibliography of Clarke's publications ; C. R. Keyes, *Pan American Geologist*, vol. XLIV, no. 1, 1925, pp. 1–16 ; personal information.]   G. P. M.

CLARKE, JOHN SLEEPER (Sept. 3, 1833–Sept. 24, 1899), actor, theatrical manager, was born in Baltimore, Md., of English parents, the grandson of Stephen Clarke, a London merchant. He was educated in a private school and studied law in the office of a Baltimore attorney, but having acquired a taste for dramatics, he began his career as a comedian at the Howard Athenæum (Boston) in *Paul Pry* (1851) and in 1852 appeared in *She Would and She Would Not* at the Chestnut Street Theatre in Philadelphia, where he later succeeded the elder John Drew [*q.v.*], as principal comedian (1853). He then became low comedian at the Front Street Theatre in Baltimore (1854), took the rôle of Diggory in *The Spectre Bridegroom* at the Metropolitan Theatre in New York (May 15, 1855) and returned to Philadelphia as leading comedian at the Arch Street Theatre (August 1855), which theatre was afterward leased by Clarke and William Wheatley (June 1858). On Apr. 28, 1859, Clarke married Asia, daughter of Junius Brutus Booth [q.v.]. Retiring from the management of the Arch Street house in 1861 he went to New York, where he appeared in *Babes in the Wood* (Apr. 1, 1861) and *The Toodles* (Aug. 19, 1861), which latter performance established his reputation. The Winter Garden reopened Aug. 18, 1864 under the management of William Stuart, with Clarke in the rôle of Maj. Wellington de Boots in Stirling Coyne's *Everybody's Friend*. Clark and Edwin Booth [q.v.] then went into partnership with Stuart, Clarke selling out to Booth shortly before the destruction of the theatre by fire in March 1867. For a number of years Booth and Clarke controlled the Walnut Street Theatre in Philadelphia, where Clarke frequently appeared in *The Toodles,* as Asa Trenchard in *Our American Cousin,* and in many other plays, occasionally making trips through the South. For one season (1866–67) the two controlled the Boston Theatre. On Oct. 16, 1867 Clarke made his first London appearance at the Royal St. James's Theatre as Maj. de Boots in a new version of *Everybody's Friend*, rewritten for him by Coyne and renamed *A Widow Hunt.* He then played Bob Tyke in *The School of Reform* (Nov. 20, 1867) and appeared at the Royal Princess's Theatre as Salem Scudder in *The Octoroon* (Feb. 10, 1868), after which he made a tour of Great Britain and Ireland. Returning to London for an engagement at the Royal Strand Theatre (Nov. 6, 1868–Mar. 18, 1870), he played Maj. de Boots in *A Widow Hunt,* Gosling in *Fox v. Goose,* Babington Jones in John Brougham's *Among the Breakers* (166 nights), Timothy Toodles in *The Toodles* (201 nights), and Dr. Pangloss in *The Heir at Law.* He then crossed the Atlantic to play *The Toodles* and *A Widow Hunt* at Booth's Theatre in New York (Apr. 18, 1870), made a tour of the principal American cities, and returned to London to appear in *The Heir at Law* (July 29, 1871) for 150 nights and in the ever popular *Toodles* at the Royal Strand. He then made another trip to the United States, after which he played Dr. Ollopod in *The Poor Gentleman* at the Royal Strand (Mar. 9, 1872) and opened the Charing

Cross Theatre, Nov. 7, 1872, playing Bob Acres in *The Rivals.* He later took over the Holborn Theatre, which he opened Apr. 4, 1874, appearing as Phineas Pettiephogge in *The Thumbscrew.* In the autumn of 1878 he assumed the management of the Theatre Royal, Haymarket, where he resuscitated *The Rivals* (Oct. 3, 1878), after which he produced *The Crisis* (Dec. 2, 1878) and Albery's adaptation of *Les Fourchambault* (Apr. 14, 1879), the latter being a failure. Rewritten and produced as *Brag* (June 12, 1879), its immediate failure caused a sudden revival of Dion Boucicault's *The Life of an Actress* four days later. Clarke then sold the Haymarket and later went to Philadelphia to take over the Broad Street Theatre (1881). In England once more he divided his time between English country theatres and the Royal Strand in London, where his occasional appearances included *The Heir at Law* (Nov. 18, 1882), *The Comedy of Errors* (Jan. 18, 1883), *A Widow Hunt* (Apr. 25, 1885), and *Cousin Johnny* (July 11, 1885). He retired from the stage in 1887 but ten years later assumed the management of the Strand, where he produced *The Prodigal Father* (Feb. 1, 1897).

Clarke had a rare command of an audience, his spectators delighting in his exuberant humor, droll transitions of expressions and oddities of accent. His intense earnestness made a ludicrous, eccentric character seem natural, for his mimicry was not merely of clothes but of character and modes of thought and feeling. He was more successful in presenting characters in old comedy than in creating new parts.

[D. Cook, *Nights at the Play* (London, 1883); *Actors and Actresses of Gt. Britain and the U. S.,* ed. by B. Matthews and L. Hutton (1886), vol. V; J. B. Clapp and E. F. Edgett, *Players of the Present,* Pt. I (1899); *Atlantic Mo.,* June 1867; *Lippincott's Mag.,* Nov. 1881; *Theatre* (London), Feb. 1883, Sept. 1885; *Athenæum* (London), Feb. 6, 1897, Sept. 30, 1899; *Era* (London), Sept. 30, 1899; *N. Y. Tribune,* Aug. 21, 1861, Aug. 19, 1864, Apr. 19, 1870; London *Morning Post,* Oct. 17, 1867; London *Daily Telegraph,* Oct. 17, Nov. 21, 1867, Feb. 11, 1868, May 10, 1869, Feb. 7, 1870, Mar. 11, Nov. 9, 1872, Apr. 6, 1874, Oct. 4, Dec. 4, 1878, Apr. 15, June 12, 1879, Nov. 20, 1882, Jan. 19, 1883, Apr. 27, July 15, 1885; see also sources for Edwin Booth.]   F. E. R.

CLARKE, JONAS. [See CLARK, JONAS, 1730–1805.]

CLARKE, JOSEPH IGNATIUS CONSTANTINE (July 31, 1846–Feb. 27, 1925), journalist, playwright, was born at Kingstown, near Dublin, Ireland, the son of William and Ellen (Quinn) Clarke. His father, a barrister, died while James was still a small boy, and in 1858 the mother moved with her children to

London. James had attended several Catholic schools in Ireland; in London he managed to get a little more instruction, including some French and Latin, before going to work in the shop of the Queen's Printers. In spare hours he explored the city, delighting as an imaginative boy would in its museums and galleries, its venerable buildings, and its ceaseless, surging crowds. In his sixteenth year he obtained, by a stroke of good luck, a sinecure in the Civil Service, and a career of unruffled though frugal respectability seemed opening before him when his Irish patriotism drew him in 1865 into the Fenian movement. For a time he was by day a sleek, top-hatted young clerk in the Home Office, and by night a hirsute, collarless ruffian who was one of the two "head centers" in London of the Irish Republican Brotherhood. He was working with admirable impartiality and efficiency for both Government and its enemies when the disastrous Clerkenwell explosion of Dec. 13, 1867, which according to his own story (*post*, pp. 43–59) he had done his best to prevent, aroused the authorities. Before long the trail led to his door. Clarke, however, was foolhardy enough to continue in his position, and when he did make his escape to Paris in February 1868 it was by a nip-and-tuck race with the police.

Paris offering at best a precarious livelihood, he went in April to New York, where he was met by his eldest brother Charles, and soon found work on the *Irish Republic,* a weekly paper. That autumn he was inveigled half-jokingly into making a speech or two for Grant and Colfax, attracted the attention of Republican managers, and was sent to Missouri on a speaking campaign. After the election he began writing at space rates for the *New York Herald,* was taken on the staff, went to the Pacific coast in 1871 to report a murder trial and to interview Brigham Young, and continued on the *Herald* until 1883, acting in turn as night, dramatic, literary, musical, and sporting editor, and displaying a resourcefulness and versatility that gave him a high reputation among newspapermen. He was managing editor of Albert Pulitzer's *Morning Journal* 1883–95, editor of the *Criterion,* a literary and social weekly, 1898–1900, Sunday editor of the *Herald* 1903–06, and publicity director of the Standard Oil Company 1906–13. His career as a playwright began with *Heartease* (in collaboration with his friend Charles Klein) in 1896; his other stage plays were: *For Bonnie Prince Charlie, The First Violin, Her Majesty, Lady Godiva, The Great Plumed Arrow,* and *The Prince of India.* He was

also the author of: *Robert Emmet, A Tragedy* (1888), *Malmorda, a Metrical Romance* (1893), *The Fighting Race and other Poems and Ballads* (1911), various occasional poems, and *Japan at First Hand* (1918), based on materials gathered during a trip to the Orient in 1914. His best-known poem, "The Fighting Race" (in the New York *Sun,* Mar. 17, 1898) was prompted by the list of Irish dead in the battle-ship *Maine.* Its refrain: "Well, here's thank God for the race and the sod! Said Kelly and Burke and Shea," was greatly admired in Irish-American literary circles. His last public appearance was at a dinner given in his honor at the Hotel Astor, Feb. 28, 1924, by the American Irish Historical Society, of which he had been president 1913–23. He died a year later, after a lingering illness, and was survived by his wife, Mary Agnes Cahill, whom he had married in New York, June 18, 1873.

[The chief source is Clarke's posthumously published autobiography, *My Life and Memories* (1925). See also E. J. McGuire, "Memorial of Jos. I. C. Clarke," in *Jour. Am. Irish Hist. Soc.,* vol. XXIV, 227–40; *N. Y. Times,* Feb. 28, Mar. 6, 1925; *Who's Who in America,* 1924–25.]   G. H. G.

CLARKE, MARY BAYARD DEVEREUX (May 13, 1827–Mar. 30, 1886), author, was born in Raleigh and died in New Bern, N. C. Her parents were Thomas Pollock Devereux, of North Carolina, and Katherine Anne Johnson of Connecticut. She was descended from many distinguished ancestors, among whom, in addition to five colonial governors, were Jonathan Edwards and Dr. Samuel Johnson, first president of what is now Columbia University. When her mother died the child was still young, and her father, a lawyer and planter of considerable wealth, employed an English governess to superintend her education. It is said that this personage at length subjected her charge to the full course of instruction prescribed at Yale. She learned to read with discrimination and to write gracefully. She had some command of modern languages, and she conversed with so much erudition, yet so much gaiety, that she impressed acquaintances as one of the few women in America who, "without being a blue-stocking, was thoroughly educated." In 1848, she married William J. Clarke. In 1854, she published *Wood Notes,* a collection of North Carolina poetry, some of which, under her pseudonym, Tenella, she had written herself. Her contributions are romantic and imitative, but at times, in their reference to North Carolina, they give evidence of a wholesome clarity of outlook. An indisposition which was declared tubercular in origin caused her to spend the winter of 1854–55 in Havana—a residence described in her "Reminiscences of Cuba," published in the *Southern Literary Messenger,* September–December, 1855. Here she danced much, rode horse-back, and attended countless plays and parties, but she was none the less glad, when the climate of San Antonio was judged better for her, to forsake a "land of despotism for the home of liberty and equal laws." That liberty, under the frontier and half-military surroundings in which she and her family found themselves, proved in the event sometimes more inclusive than she had anticipated. At the outbreak of the Civil War, her husband went into the Confederate army, and she with her four children returned to North Carolina. Here she wrote quantities of patriotic verse, which appeared from time to time in the newspapers. Much of this, along with other work, was published in 1866 as *Mosses from a Rolling Stone or Idle Moments of a Busy Woman.* The war having destroyed her family's one-time affluence, she recognized that she was under the necessity of earning money, and followed this necessity arduously but bravely for the remainder of her life. In 1865 she became for a while an editor of the *Southern Field and Fireside.* Later she contributed to *The Old Guard* and *The Land We Love,* and she reviewed books for Harper, Appleton, and Scribner. She published a long narrative poem, *Clytie and Zenobia* (1871), translated a French novel, composed a libretto, *Miskodeed,* and wrote "Sunday-school hymns at five dollars a piece." Poverty and illness caused her great despondency, from which, though always a faithful Protestant, she sought relief at times from Rome and at other times from the Ethical Culture Society. She became paralyzed, and a month before her death her husband succumbed to an illness which had long held him powerless.

[E. G. Reade in J. Raymond, *Southland Writers* (1870); W. Hall, in M. B. Clarke, *Poems* (1905); B. L. Whitaker in E. A. Alderman and J. C. Harris, *Lib. of Southern Lit.* (1907), II, 915–35.] J. D. W.

CLARKE, MARY FRANCIS (Mar. 2, 1803–Dec. 4, 1887), Roman Catholic nun, was born in Dublin, Ireland, the daughter of Cornelius and Catherine (Hyland) Clarke. Her mother was the daughter of an English Quakeress; her father was a prosperous dealer in leather. A fire, however, destroyed most of his property, and anxiety brought on a paralytic stroke that left him for the rest of his life an invalid. On Mary, the eldest of his four children, fell the burden of supporting the family. She took charge of the leather business and carried it on successfully. While ministering to victims of the cholera epidemic of 1831 she became acquainted with Margaret Mann, Rose O'Toole, Elizabeth Kelly, and Catherine Byrne, who like herself were inclined toward the life of a religious. Under her leadership they opened "Miss Clarke's School" on Mar. 19, 1832, for Catholic children who were too poor to attend a convent school. Their undertaking prospered, but persuaded by an American priest that in the New World was a larger opportunity to serve God the little group migrated in 1833 to America, the voyage from Liverpool to New York occupying fifty-one days. As they were about to land at New York their store of money rolled out of their purse and was lost overboard. Undaunted by this misfortune they proceeded to Philadelphia, as they had planned, and there on Sept. 10, 1833, they first met Terence James Donaghoe, an Irish priest and a man, among other virtues, of remarkable discernment in things spiritual. He secured their services as teachers in his parish, and under his inspiration and guidance the informal community became, with the consent of Bishop Kenrick, the Sisters of the Blessed Virgin Mary. The act of consecration was performed on All Saints' Day, 1833. Father Donaghoe became Director of the Order, and Sister Mary Clarke its Superior. Father Donaghoe drew up the constitutions of the Order. Until 1843 the Sisters lived in Philadelphia, maintaining their school and contending with a poverty that sometimes meant actual hunger. In June 1843, at the pressing invitation of Bishop Matthias Loras, five of the Sisters went to Dubuque, Ia., and so evident was the need of them in the western diocese that the rest followed before the end of the year. Father Donaghoe was made vicar-general of the diocese. Dubuque was then a frontier settlement of some 700 people; wolves and Indians still roamed the prairie. Amid these primitive conditions the Sisters devoted themselves to teaching, and although their convent was burned by a crazed incendiary May 22, 1849, the Order grew in numbers and effectiveness. It received several testimonies of Papal favor, the Decree of Final Approbation and Confirmation being issued by Pope Leo XIII on Mar. 15, 1885. Mother Clarke led a life hidden entirely from the world and largely even from her own Sisters, but the order that she founded is some index of her character. Charity, simplicity, and humility are the virtues enjoined on its members, with absence of censoriousness as the form of charity especially to be cultivated.

[*In the Early Days: Pages from the Annals of the Sisters of Charity of the Blessed Virgin Mary* (1912) ; minor accounts in E. T. Dehey, ed., *Religious Orders of Women in the U. S.* (1913), and in F. T. Oldt, ed., *Hist. of Dubuque County, Iowa* (n.d.).]   G. H. G.

CLARKE, McDONALD (June 18, 1798–Mar. 5, 1842), the "Mad Poet," was born in Bath, Me.; but, by the age of nine, he was living in New London, Conn., sheltered by his mother, with John G. C. Brainard [*q.v.*] as playmate. In manhood, Clarke remembered his boyhood as an unhappy one, on account of peculiarities of his own that made him subject to the taunts of other boys. When he was twelve, the death of his mother left him alone, grief-stricken, and apparently without resources. Nothing is known of the interval following until his appearance on Broadway in New York on Aug. 13, 1819. Here he soon became a familiar figure about town: tall and slight in body, with a striking face, well-formed mouth, aquiline nose, grayish-blue eyes shadowed with melancholy, characteristically clad in a long dark-blue frock coat with a large turn-over collar enlivened by a red silk neckerchief. His personality was vivid and his temperament volatile. Music could affect him to tears, social injustice or fashionable folly to wrath; and suffering to sympathy or sentimentality. Terse and witty in repartee, he easily routed those who attempted to make sport of his eccentricities. Not even his friends knew where to draw the line in his case between mild insanity and deliberate pose, but the character of his madness in later life dispels the idea that he was a mere *poseur*. His insanity, however, was harmless to others and he possessed no vices. He attended the fashionable Grace Church on Broadway regularly. His marriage to Mary Brundage, an actress, which was opposed by her mother, was accomplished by elopement. Their extreme poverty finally made separation necessary. Clarke, constantly penniless and living often on the bounty of his friends, impoverished himself by a generosity, frequently freakish, to those more in need than himself. Friendly by nature, he sought to cultivate companionships which his mental disorder intervened to limit. Nevertheless he won a measure of regard from Fitz-Greene Halleck who frequently helped him over hard places, and commemorated him in a humorous poem, "The Discarded." During the last year of his life, Clarke became almost constantly insane; and, on Mar. 5, 1842, he was drowned in water running from an open faucet in a cell of the Asylum on Blackwell's Island. He seems to have been a prolific writer, but much of his verse received only ephemeral publication, and in consequence most of the editions are now rare. Any object or incident in his neighborhood could form the nucleus of a poem, and many a belle of the town, not always to her delight, found herself the subject of his writings. His verse is frequently grotesque in its irregularity, expressing scornful and even violent indignation against snobbery or social injustice; but it is also often genuinely humorous, tender, or intelligently satirical. Little or none of his verse is remembered to-day save the couplet:

> "Now twilight lets her curtain down
> And pins it with a star."

[A brief essay on Clarke is to be found in Jas. Grant Wilson, *Bryant and His Friends* (1886), pp. 398–99. The most complete biographical account is contained in an article by Wm. Sidney Hillyer in the *Mo. Illustrator*, XII, 357. Some facts may also be gleaned from Clarke's prefaces to his publications, which include the following: *A Review of the Eve of Eternity and other Poems* (1820) ; *The Elixir of Moonshine* (1822) ; *The Gossip; or, a Laugh with the Ladies, a Grin at the Gentlemen and Burlesques on Byron, a Sentimental Satire; with Other Poems: in a Series of Numbers, No. 1* by McDonald Clarke (1823) ; *Sketches* (1826) ; *Afara, a Poem* (1829) ; *Death in Disguise; a Temperance Poem, from The Mss. of Mr. McDonald Clarke* (1833) ; *Poems of McDonald Clarke* (1836) ; and *A Cross and a Coronet* (1841). Duyckinck also lists *Afara, or the Belles of Broadway* (2nd series, 1836).]
          A. L. B.

CLARKE, REBECCA SOPHIA (Feb. 22, 1833–Aug. 16, 1906), writer of children's books under the pseudonym Sophie May, was born in a white-columned, red brick house, with a background of hills, in Norridgewock, Me., on the Kennebec River, and there she made her home during her seventy-three years of life. Her parents were Asa and Sophia (Bates) Clarke, both descended from pioneer settlers of that portion of the Massachusetts Colony which later became Maine. She attended the Norridgewock Female Academy where she was considered a precocious child, and her journal, kept between the ages of nine and eleven, contains comments on sermons, debates, and lectures on astronomy and phrenology. An early tendency to verse-making was discouraged by her mother, for which she was afterward grateful. Tutors of Greek and Latin completed her formal education. At eighteen she secured a position to teach in Evansville, Ind., the home of a married sister. Growing deafness caused her resignation and her return to her birthplace, where, at the age of twenty-eight, she wrote her first article, at the request of a friend in Memphis, Tenn., using the *nom de plume* Sophie May. Her first stories were written for the *Little Pilgrim*, edited by Grace Greenwood, and became the Little Prudy series, which when published in book form brought her only fifty dollars a volume. Other stories were written for the *Congregationalist*. When her Dotty Dimple books were ready for publication, she was offered a hundred dollars a volume, but by this time she had become more sophisticated and secured a ten per cent basis. She wrote over forty books for children, of which the most successful, in six volumes each, are: Little Prudy Stories (1863–65) Dotty Dimple Stories (1867–69); Little Prudy's Flyaway Series (1870–73); Quinnebasset Series (1871–91); Flaxie Frizzle Stories (1876–84); Little Prudy's Children Series (1894–1901). Several novels for adults, among them *Drone's Honey* (1887) and *Pauline Wyman* (1897), met with slight success. The characters in her stories were all drawn from life, the adults from Norridgewock people, the children from her own nephews and nieces, and Norridgewock furnished nearly all her settings. The boys and girls of her books are natural, fun-loving, sometimes naughty beings, instead of the stiff perfections of most juvenile literature of her time. Thomas Wentworth Higginson said: "Real genius came in with Little Prudy." Children of a later day, however, care little for Sophie May's books, with their lack of plot, their "baby talk," and their obvious moralizing. Rebecca Clarke was in her youth considered beautiful; she had wavy black hair, very dark blue eyes, and an expression which showed kindly interest in others and zest in life on her own account. She and her sister, Sarah J. Clarke, with whom she lived, were concerned in all activities for the welfare of their native town. They often spent their winters in Baltimore, or California, or Europe, but the summers always brought them back to Norridgewock. Shortly before her death in the old family home, Rebecca Clarke purchased and presented to Norridgewock a handsome building for a public library.

[*Who's Who in America*, 1906–07; Florence Waugh Danforth, "Sophie May, a Pioneer Writer of Juvenile Books," in the Magazine Section of the *Lewiston* (Me.) *Jour.*, Feb. 2, 1924; a typed article, with extracts from Rebecca Clarke's childhood journal, by Mrs. Henrietta Wood, a summer resident of Norridgewock, in the Me. State Lib.; Frances Willard and Mary A. Livermore, *Am. Women*, vol. I (1897), pp. 178–79; *Boston Transcript*, Aug. 17, 1906, *Daily Kennebec Jour.*, Aug. 18, 1906, *Portland Daily Press*, Aug. 18, 1906.]
S. G. B.

CLARKE, RICHARD (May 1, 1711–Feb. 27, 1795), Boston merchant, Loyalist, was the son of William and Hannah (Appleton) Clarke of Boston, where he was born, and not, as sometimes stated, of Francis Clarke of Salem. On May 3, 1733 he married Elizabeth Winslow who has been variously said to be the daughter of Edmund, Isaac, and Col. Edward Winslow. It is probable that she was the Elizabeth, daughter of Edward Winslow and Elizabeth his wife, whose birth of Feb. 16, 1712 is recorded in the Boston records (*Boston Births, 1700–1800*, p. 87). Both Richard Clarke and his wife were of distinguished ancestry and occupied high social position. Richard had graduated from Harvard in 1729 and became one of the most prominent merchants in Boston, his firm at the time of the Revolution including his two sons, Jonathan and Isaac, under the name of Richard Clarke & Sons. Jonathan was in London in 1773 and Richard Clarke & Sons were named as factors for the East India Company and were among the consignees of the tea which was thrown into Boston Harbor in December of that year. On Nov. 2, they had received a letter signed "O. C.," ordering them to appear at the Liberty Tree the following Wednesday at noon to make a public resignation of their commission as factors. On Wednesday morning some of the other consignees, including Thomas Hutchinson, Benjamin Faneuil, and Joshua Winslow, met the Clarkes at their warehouse in King St. A mob of about five hundred had gathered at the Liberty Tree and, as the merchants did not appear, a considerable number gathered in front of the warehouse. Nine of them went in as emissaries to induce the merchants to yield, and, when they refused to do so, the mob attempted to storm the building but was repulsed. When Jonathan arrived from England there was a gathering of friends at the Clarkes' house in School St. to welcome him, which was the occasion of another attack by the mob. The Clarke firm at first refused to sign the Non-Importation Agreement, but afterward consented. Richard Clarke was also one of the signers of the Address to Gen. Gage. The family had become extremely unpopular with the Whigs, and when, on one occasion, Isaac went to Plymouth to collect some debts, he was attacked and forced to make a midnight escape. Susannah Farnum Clarke, one of Richard's four daughters, had married John Singleton Copley [*q.v.*], the artist, in 1769 and had gone to live with him in London. In view of the growing difficulties in Boston, Clarke decided to go to England also, and after a remarkable voyage of only twenty-one days landed there on Dec. 24, 1775, and, until his death, lived at Copley's house. With one of his sons he joined the Loyalist Club of London. The family was on the American proscription lists, but in his will Clarke disposed of considerable property, including Bank of England stock and American securities.

[J. H. Stark, *Loyalists of Mass.* (1910); L. Sabine, *Loyalists of the Am. Revolution* (1864); *Mass. Colonial Soc. Pubs.*, vols. VII (1905), XIII (1912), in which Clarke's will is given in full, XIX (1918); *New Eng. Hist. and Geneal. Reg.*, vols. V (1851), XXXIII (1879), XXXIV (1880), XLVI (1892); "Letters and Papers of John Singleton Copley and Henry Pelham," *Mass. Hist. Soc. Colls.*, vol. LXXI (1914); *Proc. Mass. Hist. Soc.*, XVI, 475; David-Parsons Holton, *Winslow Memorial* (1877).]   J.T.A.

CLARKE, ROBERT (May 1, 1829–Aug. 26, 1899), publisher, the son of Peter Clarke and Margaret (Henderson) Clarke, was born in Annan, Dumfrieshire, Scotland. In 1840 he came with his parents to Cincinnati where he was educated at Woodward College. He soon displayed an interest in literary and scientific subjects, and as bookkeeper for William Hanna probably developed the neat, methodical habits so characteristic of the later man. His first venture into the business field was the opening of a second-hand book-shop at the corner of Sixth and Walnut Sts., which in time became the favorite resort of literary men in the city. With the retirement of the publishing firm of H. W. Derby in 1858 Clarke succeeded to their business and organized the firm which in 1894 was incorporated as the Robert Clarke Company. The directors of the new company were all members of the old firm. Under the skilful guidance of its organizer, the Robert Clarke Company became an influential power in the publishing world, especially in the West. It was the first company "to import books in any considerable number from Europe to the Ohio Valley" and "the leading firm in the West for the publication of law books." One of Clarke's business proverbs was: "Keep a little ahead of the public," and this he endeavored to carry out (W. H. Venable, *post*, p. 21). He specialized in bibliographies, especially in the fields of American history and archeology, and how well the firm succeeded in its efforts is evidenced by the fact that Justin Winsor declared that the Americana catalogues of the Robert Clarke Company were the most complete published in America (Winsor, *Narrative and Critical History of America*, vol. IV, 1884, p. 198). In addition to his activities in the printing, binding, and bookselling trade Clarke was both author and editor. He wrote a pamphlet entitled, *The Pre-Historic Remains Which Were Found on the Site of the City of Cincinnati, Ohio, with a Vindication of the Cincinnati Tablet* (1876), and edited, in large part, the *Ohio Valley Historical Series*, in seven volumes (1868–71), published over the protests of his partners. The collection and publication of this series was probably his best work. His love of books caused him to be an indefatigable collector of rare Americana. Ex-President R. B.

Hayes was the purchaser of one of his collections and another, consisting of over 6,000 volumes, was sold to William A. Proctor who presented it to the University of Cincinnati. In 1896 Clarke retired from business, made a tour of the globe, and devoted his remaining years to study and writing. Always interested in furthering the advancement of history and literature, he made his home in Glendale a center of intellectual activity; his modest, unassuming manner attracted a host of friends. He died unmarried.

[The best sketch of Clarke's life is the article by Wm. H. Venable in *In Memoriam: Being a Condensed Account of a Meeting of the Members of the Glendale Lyceum and Other Friends of the Late Robert Clarke Held in His Memory at Glendale, Oct. 7, 1899*; see also C. F. Goss, *Cincinnati, the Queen City* (4 vols., 1912); article on Clarke in *Ohio Archeol. and Hist. Quart.*, Apr. 1900; *Cincinnati Enquirer*, Aug. 27, 1899.]   R.C.M.

CLARKE, THOMAS SHIELDS (Apr. 25, 1860–Nov. 15, 1920), sculptor and painter, son of Charles J. and Louisa (Semple) Clarke, was born in Pittsburgh, Pa. He entered the School of Science at Princeton in 1878 where he remained for the full four years though he did not receive his degree of B.S. until 1892. While at Princeton he was instrumental in establishing the college comic paper, the *Tiger*, and later when studying at the Art Students' League in New York he did illustrations for various magazines. After a year in New York he went to Paris where he studied drawing at the Académie Julien under Boulanger and Lefebvre. For three years he was at the École des Beaux Arts studying under Gérôme, after which he sought instruction under Dagnan-Bouveret. He likewise spent some time in Rome and Florence. But painting soon became of secondary importance to him, and sculpture began to occupy more and more of his time. He exhibited at a number of Salons, at first only paintings: "The Milk Path, Holland," Salon of 1885; "A Fool's Fool" (now in the Pennsylvania Academy), Salon of 1887; "Night Market, Morocco" (Philadelphia Art Club), Salon of 1892. To the Salon of 1893 he sent a plaster fountain group, "The Cider Press," the bronze of which is now in Golden Gate Park, San Francisco. A smaller group of the same subject had been awarded a medal of honor at the Madrid International Exhibition of the year before. To the Chicago Exposition of 1893 he sent, besides the bronze group of "The Cider Press," a number of paintings: "A Fool's Fool" and "The Night Market," which had already been exhibited in Paris; "A Gondola Girl"; "Portrait of Madame d'E."; "Morning, Noon and Night," a triptych which was awarded a medal. Medals were also given him at Atlanta, San Francisco, and

Charleston. For the temporary arch erected in New York in honor of Admiral Dewey's return he executed the statue of Commodore McDonough. He designed, for the gunboat *Princeton*, a bell which was given by the Princeton alumni. One of his most important commissions was for four caryatids, representing the seasons, on the Appellate Court Building, New York (*c.* 1899). Belonging to his maturer style also is the "Alma Mater" at Princeton. Work of a different sort was the mural decoration of the library of a private house in Pittsburgh.

In 1887 Clarke had married Adelaide Knox at Geneva, Switzerland. There is still record of a painting in which he used her and their little girl as models. Although he did not have to depend on his profession for his means of support, he was extremely industrious. At one time he had a home at Lenox, Mass., but he never lost touch with New York, where he became a member of the National Sculpture Society in 1893, of the Architectural League in 1898, and an associate of the National Academy of Design in 1902. He was a member of the Princeton, Century, and Salmagundi clubs. It was in New York, at the Post-Graduate Hospital, that he died.

[Arthur Hoeber, in *Brush and Pencil*, Aug. 1900; Lorado Taft, *Hist. of Am. Sculpture* (1903); *Am. Art Annual* (1920); *Who's Who in America*, 1920–21; Thieme-Becker, *Allgemeines Lexikon der Bildenden Kunstler*, vol. VII (1912); *Princeton Alumni Weekly*, Dec. 15, 1920.]   E.G.N.

CLARKE, WALTER (*c.* 1638–May 23, 1714), colonial governor of Rhode Island, was the son of Jeremiah (or Jeremy) Clarke and his wife Frances (Latham) Dungan, the former of East Farleigh, Kent, and the latter of Kempston, Bedford, England. Jeremiah came to New England about 1637 and settled at Newport, R. I., where Walter was born. The son became prominent in the colony and was an office-holder most of his life. He was a deputy in 1667, 1670, 1672 and 1673; an assistant in 1673–75 and 1699; deputy-governor from May 1679 to May 1686 and from May 1700 to his death in 1714; he also served as governor from May 1676 to May 1677, from May 1686 to June 29, 1686 (when the charter was suspended), and from January 1696 to March 1698.

On Dec. 22, 1686, Sir Edmund Andros [*q.v.*] named him as one of the seven men from Rhode Island to serve on his Council, and eight days later demanded of them the delivery of the colonial charter. Clarke and his colleagues replied that it could not be brought from Newport because of the bad weather. In November of the following year when Andros went to Rhode Island with the intention of obtaining possession of

the charter, Gov. Clarke sent it to his brother with orders that it should be hidden in some place outside the Governor's knowledge, and when Andros was courteously entertained at the Governor's house, the document could not be found. The Governor, however, surrendered the seal of the colony, which Andros broke. When Andros left, the charter was returned to Clarke, who retained it until the fall of Andros. He declined to surrender it to a committee of the Assembly (though he told them they might break into the chest which contained it) and he did not deliver it up until after the election of May 1690.

After the fall of Andros, Clarke was one of the two men to sign a call to the people to meet and consult as to whether or not they would resume their former charter government (Apr. 23, 1689), and on May 1 signed the declaration proclaiming that they had done so. He was, however, extremely cautious and when called upon to serve as governor declined to do so, the colony remaining without a chief executive for ten months, during which time, the Deputy Governor, who had more courage, acted in that capacity. In 1698 when Lord Bellomont [Richard Coote, *q.v.*], was examining into conditions in Rhode Island, he inquired closely into Clarke's possible connection with piracy. As a Quaker, Clarke had refused to take the required oaths under the Acts of Trade and it was suggested that he be impeached as an example. He resigned his office in 1698 in favor of his nephew, and the Quaker régime came to an end. In that same year a small tract, called *Lithobolia, or the Stone Throwing Devil*, was published in London, recounting the remarkable and terrifying happenings in the home of George Walton in New Hampshire where devils or witches had been throwing around stones, cooking utensils, crowbars and other objects. Clarke was one of the witnesses who attested the truth of the facts (*New England Historical and Genealogical Register*, October 1870). Clarke was married four times: first, in 1660, to Content Greenman, who died Mar. 27, 1666; second, in February 1667/8, to Hannah Scott, who died July 24, 1681; third, in March 1682/3, to Freeborn (Williams) Hart, who died Dec. 10, 1709; fourth, on Aug. 31, 1711, to Sarah (Prior) Gould, who died in 1714. He had, in all, nine children, three by his first wife and six by his second, but all of his male issue died in infancy. He was buried in the Clifton burial ground at Newport.

[S. G. Arnold, *Hist. of the State of R. I.* (2 vols., 1859–60); *New Eng. Hist. and Geneal. Reg.*, vol. LXXIV (1920); *R. I. Court Records*, vol. II (1922); *Records Colony of R. I. and Providence Plantations* (1856–62); G. A. Morrison, *The "Clarke" Families of*

Clarke

R. I. (1902) ; Robt. N. Toppan, "Andros Records" in *Proc. Am. Antiq. Soc.*, n.s., vol. XIII ; *Newport Hist. Mag.*, Jan. 1883.] J.T.A.

CLARKE, WILLIAM NEWTON (Dec. 2, 1841–Jan. 14, 1912), Baptist clergyman, theologian, son of the Rev. William and Urania (Miner) Clarke, was descended from Jeremiah Clarke, one of the founders of Newport, R. I., and from Thomas Miner, who came with Winthrop to Massachusetts Bay. He was born in the Baptist parsonage in Cazenovia, N. Y., and spent his boyhood in that village except during the short pastorate of his father at Whitesboro, which intervened (1852–54) between two pastorates at Cazenovia. Clarke entered the Oneida Conference (Cazenovia) Seminary, graduating in 1858, the youngest of his class. He was admitted to sophomore standing in Madison University, received the degree of A.B. in 1861 and graduated two years later from the Theological Seminary. The spiritual and scholarly character of his first pastorate, at Keene, N. H., led to his call to the First Baptist Church in Newton Center, Mass., where the faculty and students of Newton Theological Institution formed a part of his congregation. He began his Newton pastorate in May 1869 and on Sept. 1 married Emily A. Smith at Waverly, Pa. From the beginning of his pastorate, he was making that independent study of the doctrine of the Atonement which was to lead him away from the traditional static view of theology and make him a recognized interpreter of a new day. He remained eleven years at Newton, but sensing some dissatisfaction among the older parishioners whose ideas were too fixed for change, he accepted a call to the Olivet Baptist Church, Montreal. Here was the most cosmopolitan environment of any place of his residence and his mind expanded with the broader outlook upon life. The main scholarly task of his Montreal pastorate was a *Commentary on Mark* (1881), which he had been requested to write. Early in 1883, he fell on icy steps and injured a knee which treacherously caused several later falls in which his right elbow also suffered, producing handicaps of motion and considerable suffering, very real but to which he rarely alluded. A call to the chair of New Testament interpretation at the Baptist Theological School in Toronto seemed providential and he began teaching there in the autumn of 1883. These were quiet years spent largely in the intimate study of the New Testament; but his duties included the teaching of homiletics and he was in constant demand to preach in the churches. In the spring of 1887, Clarke returned to the pastorate, going to the scene of his college days,

Hamilton, N. Y. On the death of President Ebenezer Dodge, he undertook to carry on some of his work in theology in the Seminary and in June 1890 accepted the election to the J. J. Joslin Professorship of Christian Theology.

On assuming full charge of the course in systematic theology, Clarke began at once to write out his own views, furnishing his students manifolded copies of the material as needed. During two periods of absence, chiefly in California, he was able to prepare his lecture manuscript for printing (1894) for limited circulation; after careful revision, it was published as *An Outline of Christian Theology* (1898). This was an epoch-making book, for it was the first broad survey of Christian theology which frankly accepted the modern view of the world, substituted vital, dynamic phraseology for the mechanical and static, and subordinated theology to the Christian religion itself, which was to be discerned both by a historical approach to the Scriptures and by the experiential evidence of all times. From August 1901 to June 1902 Clarke was in Europe. At Oxford he began his treatise on *The Christian Doctrine of God* (1909), but he made an entirely new start after returning home. Much of the next seven years was devoted to this work in addition to his regular teaching. In 1903 he gave a Dudleian lecture at Harvard and in 1905 the Taylor lectures at Yale. In 1908, he resigned his professorship, but a lectureship in Christian Ethics was provided that the Seminary might continue to have his services. On account of the frailty of his own and Mrs. Clarke's health, they spent his last winters in Florida, where, at Deland, he died suddenly on the forty-eighth anniversary of his ordination. Among his more important works not previously mentioned are : *Can I Believe in God the Father?* (1899) ; *What Shall We Think of Christianity?* (1899) ; *A Study of Christian Missions* (1900) ; *The Use of the Scriptures in Theology* (1905) ; *Sixty Years with the Bible* (1909), a spiritual autobiography; *The Ideal of Jesus* (1911).

[*Wm. Newton Clarke; a Biography, with Additional Sketches by His Friends and Colleagues* (1916), written and edited by his widow, outlines Clarke's career and interprets his life and thoughts. Evaluations of his work will be found in the *Outlook*, Jan. 27, 1912, and by Shailer Mathews in *Am. Jour. Theol.*, July 1912.] W.H.A.

CLARKSON, COKER FIFIELD (Jan. 21, 1811–May 7, 1890), editor, born at Frankfort, Me., was the son of Richard Perkinhon and Mary (Simpson) Clarkson. His paternal grandfather came to America in 1779, settling in New Hampshire, where his son Richard was born in 1782. Richard Clarkson married the daughter of a

Continental soldier and moved to Maine in 1806; he served in the War of 1812. In 1820 the family removed to Indiana settling about thirty miles northwest of Cincinnati. At seventeen years of age, Coker Clarkson began to learn the printer's trade and in a few years he became the owner of a newspaper (the *Indiana American*) which he conducted successfully until 1854. In the following year he moved to Iowa and settled in Grundy County where he developed a highly cultivated farm. On Apr. 2, 1833, he married Elizabeth Goudie, who died in 1848; in 1849 he married Elizabeth Colescott, who survived him. In the summer of 1856 he was chosen a delegate to the state constitutional convention but declined to accept because of his brief residence in the state. He was a member of the Iowa delegation to the Republican convention of 1860 and was one of the earliest supporters of Lincoln. In 1863 he was elected to the state Senate and served four years.

In 1870 with his sons, Richard and James S., Clarkson purchased the *Iowa State Register,* published at Des Moines. As its agricultural editor, in which capacity he served for two decades, he was one of the pioneers in agricultural education in Iowa, becoming known to the people of the state as "Father" Clarkson. He was the leading spirit in the notable contest between the farmers and the Barbed Wire Syndicate, which, supported by capitalists, had formed a combination to control the manufacture and sale of barbed wire. Clarkson understood the situation, and in concert with others called a public meeting, at which he made a vigorous opening speech. He described the controversy and proposed the organization of a Farmers' Protective Association to resist the syndicate. The Association was formed and a factory established to supply the farmers without purchase from the syndicate. The legal contest which followed was the most stubborn in the history of the state, the farmers being represented by Albert B. Cummins [*q.v.*], later governor and senator. The struggle lasted for several years, but the syndicate was finally broken.

Clarkson continued to live in Grundy County until 1878 when he removed to Des Moines. He continued his editorial work until his last illness, although he disposed of his interest in the paper to his sons a few years after the purchase. In physique he was large and commanding; his convictions were deep and abiding, and his opinions were held with tenacity. His morals were rigid, but he prescribed for others nothing that he was not willing to require of himself. For nearly seventy years he was a loyal Methodist. In early

life a Whig, a friend of Henry Clay and zealous opponent of Andrew Jackson, he joined the Republican party when it was organized, and remained an ardent supporter of it for the rest of his life. In one of his letters he declared, "I never split my ticket to vote for a Democrat in forty-four years."

[E. H. Stiles, *Recollections and Sketches of Notable Lawyers and Pub. Men of Early Iowa* (1916), pp. 504–06; B. F. Gue, *Hist. of Iowa* (1903), vol. IV, pp. 53, 54 (portrait); C. Cole, *Hist. of the People of Iowa* (1921), p. 435; *Daily Iowa State Reg.,* May 7, 8, 10, 14, 1890.]

F. E. H.

CLARKSON, JOHN GIBSON (July 1, 1861–Feb. 4, 1909), baseball player, was born in Cambridge, Mass. His father, Thomas Clarkson, an enthusiastic sportsman, gave his sons valuable athletic coaching. John G. Clarkson early displayed ability as pitcher for the Beacons and other baseball teams about Boston, and of his three brothers two, Arthur and Walter, were also professional pitchers of ability. Attracting the attention of A. C. Anson [*q.v.*], manager and captain of the Chicago Club of the National League, John Clarkson was induced by him in 1884 to sign a contract. On Mar. 4, 1884, he was married to Ella M. Barr. From the beginning of his professional career, he met success and speedily became the winning pitcher of Anson's white-hosed champions. In 1885 he won fifty-five out of the seventy games which he pitched for Chicago, one of the best records ever made. In 1889, together with his catcher, the aggressive Michael J. Kelly [*q.v.*], he was sold by the Chicago management to Boston for what was then regarded as the phenomenal price of $10,-000. The transaction aroused much discussion, and Clarkson and Kelly became famous as "the Ten Thousand Dollar Battery." For Boston Clarkson won that year fifty-three games out of seventy-two. And in 1891 and 1892 the work of Clarkson and Kelly virtually gained the pennant for Boston. In 1892 Cleveland secured the services of Clarkson, but he soon afterward retired. Later he conducted a cigar store in Bay City, Mich., until his health failed in 1906. He died at Waltham, Mass. For several years before his death he is said to have been insane.

This famous athlete was not an unusually large man, standing but 5 feet 9 inches and weighing 168–170 pounds. His hair was very dark, but his eyes were gray. In the history of baseball Clarkson stands as the first great exponent of the modern school of pitchers who study the weaknesses of batters and secure their results by control, change of pace, and outguessing their victims rather than by mere speed and curves. Clarkson possessed great speed when he chose to use it, but he was a clever baseball general who preferred to win by intelligence. At that time pitchers were forced to work day after day, and Clarkson was one of the first to demonstrate that something other than physical strength was necessary to carry on and win games. His coolness at critical stages was proverbial, and he was never more deadly than "in the pinches." Clarkson's chief rival was Tim Keefe of the New York Giants, a pitcher who used somewhat similar methods, and the duels between these two real artists were famous. But though Clarkson played "inside ball" he remained a thorough sportsman who would not tolerate trickery or deception. This high conception of sporting ethics made him one of the most popular players of his generation.

[The Spalding and Reach Baseball Guides for the years of Clarkson's activity contain his records. Obituaries appeared in the *N. Y. Times, N. Y. Herald,* and *Sun,* Feb. 5, 1909. Valuable information for this article was furnished by Walter Clarkson and by the veteran sportsman George Wright of Boston.]   E.P.T.

CLARKSON, MATTHEW (Oct. 17, 1758–Apr. 25, 1825), Revolutionary soldier, New York philanthropist, was the son of David and Elizabeth (French) Clarkson, and the great-grandson of Matthew Clarkson, who came from good family connections in England to New York in 1690, as secretary of the province. The descendants of the Secretary intermarried with leading provincial families and otherwise won a strong position in the mercantile and political affairs of the community. In the Revolutionary period they early took a strong patriotic stand, and young Matthew participated as a volunteer in the battle of Long Island. Later he was aide-de-camp to Arnold, was wounded at Fort Edward, and behaved with gallantry in the battle of Saratoga. (His likeness is among the figures in Trumbull's painting in the Capitol rotunda at Washington.) Following his chief to Philadelphia, he became involved in a heated newspaper controversy with Thomas Paine over the Silas Deane affair, his precise relationship to the matter in dispute being somewhat obscure. In the early part of 1779, owing to his refusal in disrespectful terms of a summons from the President and Executive Council of Pennsylvania, he received a reprimand from Congress, which body, however, at the same time granted his request for opportunity to serve in southern territory. He was attached to the staff of Gen. Lincoln, and served with him until the end of the war, and also as assistant to the latter during his term as secretary of war. Clarkson's military career included later service as brigadier-general and then as major-general of New York state militia. Naturally he was called

Gen. Clarkson and was an early member of the Cincinnati. He was married twice: first, on May 24, 1785, to Mary Rutherfurd; second, on Feb. 14, 1792, to Sarah Cornell. His life after retirement from active military service was that of a public-spirited citizen of means and leisure. He was a regent of the State University of New York; a member of the Assembly for one term (1789–90), during which he introduced a bill for the gradual abolition of slavery in the state; United States marshal (1791–92); a member of the state Senate for two terms (1794 and 1795); one of the commissioners to build a new prison (1796–97); president of the New York Hospital (1799); and president of the Bank of New York (1804–25). He was the Federalist candidate for the United States Senate in 1802, but was defeated on the joint ballot by DeWitt Clinton.

Aside from his military record perhaps the most characteristic aspect of his career concerns his connection with the numerous societies and "movements" for public improvement which were coming into existence in New York City in the half-century after independence. His integrity, his high social position, personal amiability, and ample means all combined to give him prominence in this relation. The long and extremely varied list of organizations in which he was a leading figure quite justifies DeWitt Clinton's remark: "Whenever a charitable or public-spirited institution was about to be established Clarkson's presence was deemed essential. His sanction became a passport to public approbation."

[W. W. Spooner, ed., *Historic Families of America* (1907), pp. 282–85; *The Clarksons of N. Y.* (2 vols., privately printed, 1876); *Jours. Continental Cong.,* vol. XIII; Martha J. Lamb, *Hist. of City of N. Y.* (1881).]
                                                        C.W.S.

CLAUSEN, CLAUS LAURITZ (Nov. 3, 1820–Feb. 20, 1892), pioneer Lutheran clergyman, was born on the island of Aerö, Denmark, the son of Erik and Karen Pedersen Clausen. He was destined for the law, but abandoned it for theology after he had fallen under the influence of the Grundtvigian (Lutheran) awakening. Interrupted in his studies by a recurrence of ill health, he went to Norway where he hoped to qualify as missionary to Africa. Failing in this, he undertook to go to Muskego, Wis., as a teacher. There he was ordained to the American Lutheran ministry on Oct. 18, 1843. He lost no time in entering upon the strenuous duties of his ministry. On the day after his ordination he "conducted the first of fifty-four funerals in a period covering the four last months of 1843. This terrible toll of death was taken from the small Muskego settlement alone' (J. Magnus

Rohne, *Norwegian American Lutheranism up to 1872,* 1926, p. 60). His field covered practically all of Wisconsin, and, later, much of northern Iowa and southern Minnesota. In spite of severe headaches from which he suffered constantly, he was a minister in every sense of that word; he could draw a deed or draw a tooth; he was as good a judge of land as of human nature; yet he always remained a worthy and democratic man of God.

Clausen remained at Muskego less than three years; at Luther Valley, seven years. There, in 1846, his first wife, Martha F. Rasmussen, died. Within a year he married Mrs. Bergette Hjort (*née* Brekke), who died in 1887.

In 1851 he joined Rev. H. A. Stub and Rev. A. C. Preus in forming a synod of which he was elected "superintendent." Forced to undo this work, he took a perfunctory part in organizing the so-called Norwegian Synod in 1853. In the same year he led a party of immigrants to St. Ansgar, Iowa, serving as pastor to this group which expanded into a settlement fifty miles wide and two hundred miles long. From 1856 to 1859 he served as immigrant commissioner of Iowa. At the outbreak of the Civil War he enlisted as chaplain for the 15th Wisconsin Regiment, but had to retire in 1862 after suffering shell shock in the bombardment of Island No. 10. Estranged from the Norwegian Synod over questions of Sabbath observance, he left it in 1868, and helped to form the Norwegian-Danish Conference in 1870, being elected first president. Frequent strokes and hemorrhages in the head forced him to resign his pastorate at St. Ansgar in 1872. After three years of complete mental rest in Virginia, he preached for two years in Philadelphia, and then took up active work at Blooming Prairie, Minn., where he served until his retirement from the ministry in 1885. In 1890 he took active interest in the formation of the United Norwegian Lutheran Church, one of the contracting parties being his beloved Conference. His last years were spent at Austin, Minn., or in travel, of which he was very fond. He died on a visit to his son at Paulsbo, Wash.

Clausen established and edited the religious journal *Maanedstidende* (Monthly Times) and the secular paper *Emigranten,* and was a lifelong contributor to the secular and religious press. He wrote two brochures, the so-called *Gjenmäle* (Rebuttal) to the church council of the Norwegian Synod in the slavery controversy, and his *Tilsvar* (Reply) to Prof. Sverdrup's attack in the struggle between the "old" and "new" tendencies in the Conference.

[In English there are, besides the work by Rohne quoted above, biographies by "H" in Jens C. Jensson (Roseland), *Am. Lutheran Biogs.* (1890); R. B. Anderson, *The First Chapter of Norwegian Immigration, Its Causes and Results* (2nd ed., 1896); O. N. Nelson, *Hist. of the Scandinavians and Successful Scandinavians in the U. S.* (1897); O. M. Norlie, *Hist. of the Norwegian People in America* (1925). In Norwegian there are biographies by Svein Strand in *Symra* (Decorah, Iowa, 1913); Thrond J. Bothne, "Kort Udsigt over det Lutherske Kirkearbeide blandt Nordmändene i Amerika," appended to Hallvard G. Heggtveit, *Illustreret Kirkehistorie* (Chicago, Takla ed., 1898); Johan Arndt Bergh, *Den Norsk Lutherske Kirkes Historie i Amerika* (Minneapolis, 1914); O. M. Norlie, *Norsk Lutherske Prester i Amerika 1843–1913* (Minneapolis, 1914), a translation and revision of which was published as *Who's Who Among Pastors in All the Norwegian Lutheran Synods of America, 1843–1927* (1928).]

J.M.R.

CLAXTON, KATE (1848–May 5, 1924), actress, was born in Somerville, N. J., the daughter of Spencer Wallace Cone, a lawyer whose literary inclinations led him to spend more time in the writing of plays, editorial work, and speaking in public, than at the bar. Her grandfather, the Rev. Spencer H. Cone [*q.v.*], had been an actor before he became a clergyman. Her mother was Josephine Martinez, daughter of a Spaniard, Tomas Martinez, and of Margaret Terry. Kate was educated at private schools in New York, and at the age of seventeen, according to her own statement, was married "ill advisedly" to Isadore Lyon (*New York Dramatic Mirror,* interview, Dec. 8, 1894; W. W. Cone, *Some Account of the Cone Family,* 1903). Her early stage aspirations received no parental encouragement, and she went to Chicago, where she thought there would be less family opposition to her desire to become an actress, and in that city, at the Dearborn Street Theatre, on Dec. 21, 1869, she made her début as Mary Blake in *Andy Blake.* A week later she joined Lotta's company at McVicker's Theatre in Chicago, and before long she was back in New York, a full-fledged actress. She joined Augustin Daly's company at the Fifth Avenue Theatre, where she first appeared on Sept. 13, 1870, as Jo, in *Man and Wife.* She remained there through more than two seasons, but rarely played anything but inconspicuous characters. An engagement by A. M. Palmer at the Union Square Theatre, during which she acted Georgette in *Fernande* and Mathilde in *Led Astray,* resulted in her being cast for the part of Louise, the blind girl, in *The Two Orphans.* This melodrama from the French, in which there is abundant action, pathos, bitter anguish, and a conflict between love and duty, was produced on Dec. 26, 1874. For the rest of her life she was identified with this play throughout the country. She was acting in it in 1876, at the Brooklyn Theatre on the evening it was destroyed by fire with a loss of more than two hundred lives. She sought other plays and characters, notably: *The World Against Her, Bootles's Baby, The Sea of Ice,* and *Cruel London,* but the public invariably demanded her Louise in *The Two Orphans* and nothing else. In that character she had the advantage of the sympathy of impressionable audiences for a hapless girl, placed in a series of overwhelming misfortunes from which she emerged triumphant, and she played it always, in later life as well as in youth, with a simplicity that won the hearts of multitudes. In 1878 she was married to Charles A. Stevenson, an English actor whose professional life was passed almost wholly in this country and who was for many years a member of her company. The marriage was annulled in 1911. She died in New York City.

[T. Allston Brown, *Hist. of the N. Y. Stage* (1903); J. B. Clapp and E. F. Edgett, *Players of the Present* (1901); Arthur Hornblow, *Hist. of the Theatre in America* (1919); *N. Y. Commercial Advertiser,* July 30, 1885; obituaries in *N. Y. Herald-Tribune, N. Y. Sun,* and *N. Y. Times,* May 6, 1924; *Who's Who in America,* 1924–25.]   E. F. E.

CLAY, ALBERT TOBIAS (Dec. 4, 1866– Sept. 14, 1925), Orientalist, the son of John Martin and Mary Barbara (Sharp) Clay, was born at Hanover, Pa. He was graduated from Franklin and Marshall College in 1889 and from the Lutheran Theological Seminary at Mount Airy, Pa., in 1892. He entered the graduate school of the University of Pennsylvania in 1892, working under Professors Hilprecht, Peters, and Jastrow, and received the degree of Ph.D. in 1894. From 1892 to 1895 he was also instructor in Hebrew in the same university. In 1893 he was ordained to the ministry in the Lutheran Church and in 1895–96 was pastor of St. Mark's Church, South Bethlehem, Pa. On June 11, 1895, he was married to Elizabeth Sommerville McCafferty of Philadelphia. In 1896 he became instructor in Old Testament theology in the Lutheran Theological Seminary, Chicago. In 1899 he was recalled to the University of Pennsylvania as lecturer in Assyriology and assistant curator of the Babylonian section of the University museum. Here he remained until 1910, being promoted through the various grades of professorships until in 1909 he became professor of Semitic philology and archeology. From 1904 to 1910 he was instructor in Hebrew at Mount Airy Lutheran Seminary. When, through the gift of the late J. Pierpont Morgan, the Laffan Professorship of Assyriology was founded at Yale, Clay was called in 1910

to fill the chair, a position which he occupied until his death.

Clay was chiefly noted as an editor of cuneiform texts. His first volume, *Business Documents of Murashu Sons of Nippur dated in the Reign of Artaxerxes I* (1898), was published conjointly with Prof. Hilprecht, but he afterward published three other volumes in the series of the Babylonian Expedition of the University of Pennsylvania, edited by Hilprecht, and two in the Publications of the University Museum, Babylonian Section, which succeeded it. He also published four volumes of texts in the library of J. Pierpont Morgan. At Yale he organized and built up the Babylonian Collection, in connection with which he inaugurated the publication of a series of volumes of texts, to which he himself contributed two volumes. A third volume, prepared by him, appeared after his death. All these texts were copied with accuracy and beauty. In addition to these publications, Clay brought out a valuable volume on the proper names of the Cassite Period in Babylonia, and, in connection with the late Prof. Jastrow, *An Old Babylonian Version of the Gilgamesh Epic on the Basis of Recently Discovered Texts* (1920). Four volumes of which he was especially proud were: *Amurru, the Home of the Northern Semites* (1909); *The Empire of the Amorites* (1919); *A Hebrew Deluge Story in Cuneiform* (1922); and *The Origin of Biblical Traditions* (1923). In these he developed an original theory of the antiquity of the Amorites and their importance as the originators of the civilization of western Asia. His training had not fitted him for such historical investigations, and it is sufficient to say that the theory is already disproved. In addition to his books, he contributed to many scientific journals and publications, and by his enthusiasm and encouragement stimulated scientific activity in others. Several rising Assyriologists were his pupils and contributed to the Yale Oriental Series which he founded. He also projected a series of translations of Semitic inscriptions, to which a large number of American scholars had promised to contribute volumes. His untimely death occurred, however, before the first volume was published. The American Oriental Society has arranged to carry forward the enterprise as a memorial to him.

Clay was twice annual professor in the American School in Jerusalem; once in 1919–20, and again in 1923–24. On the first of his visits to the East he was sent to Iraq by the Mesopotamian Committee of the Archeological Institute of America to ascertain the practicability of establishing an American School of Oriental Research in that country, and on the second he was sent by the American Schools of Oriental Research as the first annual professor, and professor in charge of the school in Bagdad, which he formally opened in November 1923. During the first of his sojourns in Jerusalem, by his enthusiasm and tact, he brought together the Orientalists resident there, differing as they did both in race and religion, and persuaded them to form the Oriental Society of Palestine, patterned on the American Oriental Society. The Society has ever since published a quarterly journal which contains much valuable scientific work. Clay's training, while giving him a keen appreciation of all evidence which bore on textual interpretation, prevented him from attaining a similar scientific point of view with reference to questions of ethnology and history. On these he was to the end a dogmatist and propagandist. His youthful enthusiasm, which he retained all his life, made him many friends to whom he was devoted. He did much for the advancement of Oriental studies in the United States, and especially for his own subject, Assyriology.

[Who's Who in America, 1924–25; C. C. Torrey, "In Memoriam Albert T. Clay," Bull. Am. Schools Oriental Research, no. 19, Oct. 1925; J. A. Montgomery, "In Memoriam Albert T. Clay," with a selected bibliography by Ettalene M. Grice, Jour. Am. Oriental Soc., no. 4, vol. XLV, Dec. 1925; G. A. Barton, "Albert Tobias Clay," Am. Jour. Archeology, No. 1, XXX, 97–99, Jan.–Mar. 1926; W. F. Albright, "Prof. Albert T. Clay," Jour. Palestine Oriental Soc., VI, 175–77; P. Dhorme, "A la mémoire du professeur Albert Clay," Ibid., 169–72.]   G. A. B.

CLAY, CASSIUS MARCELLUS (Oct. 19, 1810–July 22, 1903), abolitionist, the youngest son of Green Clay [q.v.], and Sally (Lewis) Clay, was born on his father's estate, "White Hall," in Madison County, Ky. His ancestry was Scotch, English, and Welsh; and in him was so strange a mixture of manly vigor, unfaltering honesty, indiscreet pugnacity, and the wild spirit of the crusader, as to make him one of the most remarkable of the lesser figures in American history. When very young he fought his mother, his schoolmaster, and a slave companion; the day before his wedding he caned a rival in the streets of Louisville; and when ninety-three years old, suffering under the hallucination that people were plotting against his life, he converted his ancestral mansion into a fortified castle, protected by a cannon. His career was turbulent in politics, in the army, within the circle of his family, and in all his social and diplomatic relations. In 1841 he fought a duel in Louisville with Robert Wickliffe, Jr.;

four years later he so mutilated with a bowie knife Sam M. Brown as to be indicted for mayhem; in 1850 he stabbed to death Cyrus Turner; and in his old age he shot and killed a negro. In all his early political campaigns he carried a bowie knife and two pistols.

Clay was given the best opportunities of his day for an education, first receiving instruction from Joshua Fry in Garrard County, and later under the same master at Danville. He was then sent to the Jesuit College of St. Joseph in Nelson County. He attended Transylvania University for a time, and in 1831 with letters of introduction to President Jackson and to the principal men of note in the East he entered the junior class in Yale College, where he was graduated the next year. He returned to Kentucky and studied law at Transylvania but never took out license to practise. Wealthy and ambitious for a political career, he was elected to the state legislature from Madison County in 1835 and in 1837, being defeated in 1836 on his advocacy of internal improvements. He now moved to Lexington and in 1840 was elected to the legislature to represent Fayette County. The following year he again ran, contrary to the advice of his distant kinsman, Henry Clay, and was defeated on the question of slavery. Though his father had been a large slaveholder, Clay had early developed a bitter hatred toward the institution, and, inspired by William Lloyd Garrison whom he had heard at Yale College, this hatred became a crusading passion. In his defeat for the legislature he saw the blatant tyranny and implacable opposition of the slaveholders, and he resolved to rid Kentucky of the evil. In June 1845 he set up in Lexington a newspaper which he called the *True American* and began his campaign. Foreseeing trouble he fortified his office with two four-pounder cannon, Mexican lances, and rifles, and strategically placed a keg of powder to be set off against any attackers. In August a committee of sixty prominent Lexingtonians visited his establishment while he was absent, boxed up his equipment, and sent it to Cincinnati. He continued to publish his paper from this new location, and later, changing its name to the *Examiner,* he moved it to Louisville.

Although Clay had opposed the annexation of Texas, in 1846 he volunteered among the first of those who were to invade Mexico, believing that since his country was at war it was his duty to fight, and feeling that a military record would help him politically. He fought with bravery in a number of engagements and was taken prisoner at Encarnacion in January 1847. After many harrowing experiences he was set free, returning to Kentucky to share in a resolution of commendation by the legislature and to receive a sword presented by his fellow citizens. In politics he began a strong follower of Henry Clay, but, during the campaign of 1844, became estranged from him on the issue of abolitionism. In the next presidential campaign he supported Taylor from the beginning, and in 1849 he made a determined effort to build up an emancipation party in Kentucky by holding a convention in Frankfort and running for governor. In the election he received 3,621 votes, enough to defeat the Whig candidate. On the birth of the Republican party he joined it, voting for Frémont in 1856 and for Lincoln in 1860. In this latter year he had a considerable following for the vice-presidency. He was on terms of close friendship with Lincoln, and, having been led to understand that he might have the secretaryship of war, was greatly chagrined when he did not receive it. To pacify him Lincoln offered him the diplomatic post at Madrid, which he refused. Later he accepted the Russian post. On his way east he reached Washington in April, at the time when it was cut off and undefended. He quickly grasped the situation and raised 300 men for the protection of the city and government, for which service he might have received appointment as major-general in the Federal army had he not preferred to continue to Russia. In 1862 he was recalled and made a major-general, but he refused to fight until the government should abolish slavery in the seceded states. He returned to Kentucky in the fall of 1862 on a mission to the legislature, did some fighting, and left for Russia again in 1863, where he remained until 1869. He fell out with President Grant and joining the Liberal Republicans supported Greeley in 1872. Disagreeing with the policy of reconstruction, he supported Tilden in 1876, but in 1884 he was for Blaine. After returning from Russia he retired to his estate in Madison County and in his old age, a few weeks before his death, the Richmond court adjudged him a lunatic. He was married to Mary Jane Warfield of Lexington in 1832, but was divorced from her in 1878. On his final return from Russia he brought to his home a Russian boy, whom he named Launey Clay, refusing to disclose his parentage. Shortly before his death he married a young girl from whom he soon secured a divorce.

[A vivid account of Clay's career is set forth in his *Life of Cassius Marcellus Clay; Memoirs, Writings and Speeches* (1886), vol. I. A second volume was projected but never published. *Biog. Memoranda Class of 1832 Yale Coll.* (1880) contains sketch "communicated

by himself." In 1848 his speeches were brought out by Horace Greeley under the title of *Speeches and Writings of C. M. Clay.* All of Clay's papers prior to the Civil War were burned during the conflict. Incomplete sketches of him may be found in R. H. and L. R. Collins, *Hist. of Ky.* (1874), and *Biog. Encyc. of Ky.* (1877). A short sketch is in *Who's Who in America,* 1901–02. An account of the last days of his life and an obituary appear in *Lexington* (Ky.) *Leader,* July 6–9, 23, 1903. Files of his *True American* are preserved in the Lexington Pub. Lib.]   E. M. C.

CLAY, CLEMENT CLAIBORNE (Dec. 13, 1816–Jan. 3, 1882), lawyer, senator, Confederate diplomat, a member of a distinguished family in the Tennessee Valley of Alabama, was born near Huntsville, the son of Clement Comer Clay [*q.v.*], and Susanna Claiborne (Withers) Clay. He was graduated from the University of Alabama in 1834, served as private secretary to his father, the Governor, engaged for a time in editorial work on the *Huntsville Democrat,* and entered the University of Virginia as a law student under the celebrated John B. Minor, receiving his degree in 1839. After a brief service in the state legislature (1842, 1844, 1845), he became judge of the county court of Madison County, resigning in 1848 to resume the active practise of his profession. He made an unsuccessful campaign for a seat in the lower house of the federal Congress in 1853 but soon afterward won election as a Democrat to the United States Senate, defeating his fellow townsman, R. W. Walker. He was unanimously reëlected in 1859. In the Senate, he was an ardent defender of the principle of state rights and a vigorous supporter of the political philosophy of John C. Calhoun. While a member of the state legislature, he had married, on Feb. 1, 1843, at Tuscaloosa, Virginia C. Tunstall, who became "one of the brightest ornaments" of Washington society during her husband's service, a member of a coterie comprising Mrs. James Chesnut of South Carolina, and Mrs. Roger A. Pryor of Virginia.

With the secession of his state from the Union, Clay withdrew from Congress in February 1861, and returned to Alabama. On the organization of the Confederate government, Jefferson Davis, with whom he had served in the United States Senate, tendered him the post of secretary of war, but Clay declined and secured the appointment for his fellow townsman, Leroy Pope Walker. The legislature of Alabama elected him to the Confederate Senate, but at the end of his two years' term he failed of reëlection. In April 1864, he was appointed by Davis a member of a secret and confidential mission to Canada, the other members being Jacob Thompson of Mississippi and James P. Holcombe of Virginia.

This mission was directed to initiate informal negotiations with the Federal government which, it was hoped, would lead to formal negotiations of peace between the United States and the Confederacy. Early in July the commissioners entered into correspondence with Horace Greeley, seeking through him a safe-conduct to Washington and an interview with President Lincoln. At first Lincoln seemed to favor such a conference but soon decided against it, on the ground that the commissioners were not authorized to treat. For nearly a year Clay was in Canada, but, despairing of any result from his mission, he returned South just before the war closed. While he was preparing to set out on horseback for Texas with Gen. Wigfall, to join Gen. Richard Taylor, he learned in Lagrange, Ga., where he was the guest of Benjamin H. Hill, that Lincoln had been assassinated and that President Johnson had offered a reward for his arrest. Clay was accused, with Davis and others, of inciting and encouraging the assassination of Lincoln, of conspiring, while in Canada, to release Confederate prisoners of war on Johnson's Island, and of plotting raids from Canada against the territory of the United States. Though urged to attempt an escape, Clay refused, rode 170 miles to Macon, Ga., and surrendered to the commanding officer of the United States troops. He was taken with Davis and others to Fortress Monroe, where he was kept in solitary confinement for nearly a year. Mrs. Clay and his friends were zealous in their efforts to secure a trial for him, and Clay appealed directly to President Johnson, a former colleague. He was finally released, a broken man, on Apr. 17, 1866, without opportunity to defend himself against the charges preferred against him. The remaining years of his life were spent quietly in the practise of the law and in efforts to restore his health. Apparently he took no active part in the struggle over the reconstruction of the state and did not enter again actively into political life.

[See Willis Brewer, *Alabama* (1872); Wm. Garrett, *Reminiscences of Public Men in Ala.* (1872); Thos. M. Owen, *Hist. of Ala. and Dict. of Ala. Biog.*, vol. III (1921); Virginia Clay-Clopton, *A Belle of the Fifties* (1905), edited by Ada Sterling, a eulogistic and highly colored picture of Clay by his wife. Clay's experiences in Canada are set out in the *Official Records* (Army), 2 ser., VIII; accounts of his prison life in Fortress Monroe may be found in John J. Craven, *Prison Life of Jefferson Davis* (1866), and in F. H. Alfriend, *Life of Jefferson Davis* (1868). The story of his arrest is in *Trans. Ala. Hist. Soc.* (1897-98), vol. II. For the genealogy of the Clay family, see J. E. Saunders, *Early Settlers of Ala.* (1899). Mrs. Clay's efforts to secure the release of her husband are recounted in D. S. Freeman, *Calendar of Confed. Papers* (1908).]   T. H. J.

CLAY, CLEMENT COMER (Dec. 17, 1789–Sept. 7, 1866), governor of Alabama, United States senator, son of William Clay, a Revolutionary soldier, and Rebecca Comer, was born in Halifax County, Va., and removed as a boy to Grainger County, Tenn., where his early education was obtained. He was graduated from the East Tennessee College (now the University of Tennessee) in 1807, read law under Hugh Lawson White, in Knoxville, and was admitted to the bar in 1809. Two years later he removed to Huntsville, then in the Mississippi Territory, the center of Virginian influence in the Tennessee Valley, where he engaged successfully in the practise of his profession and where, in 1815, he married Susanna Claiborne Withers. Clement Claiborne Clay [*q.v.*], also a lawyer and man of affairs, was his son.

Though primarily devoted to the practise of law, Clay gave much time to public service for more than thirty years of his life. He was first a private and then adjutant of a battalion in the Creek War of 1813; he was a member of the territorial legislature of Alabama in 1817-19; and he was chosen in 1819 as a delegate to the first constitutional convention of Alabama, serving notably as chairman of the committee which drafted the first organic law of the state. Immediately upon the organization of the judiciary of the new commonwealth, he became chief justice (1820-23), resigning to resume his private practise. In 1827 he was elected to the state legislature and served as speaker of the lower house. He was elected to membership in the lower house of Congress in 1829 and served thereafter by successive reëlection without opposition until 1835. He was instrumental in securing the passage of preëmption laws for settlers and "relief laws" for the benefit of distressed purchasers of government lands in Alabama. He took an active part in the debates on national affairs during his six years of service in the House, supporting Jackson in his attacks on the Bank, in his removal of the deposits, and in his opposition to nullification in South Carolina, though he refused, as a believer in state sovereignty and state rights, to vote for the Force Bill. After his nomination by the Democrats for the governorship in 1835, he gave his support to Van Buren for the presidency, although his personal preference was for his friend and law teacher, Judge Hugh Lawson White. Because of this, the supporters of White in Alabama made a determined fight against him, but Clay was successful before the people, defeating Gen. Enoch Parsons by 13,000 votes, the largest majority given up to that time to any candidate for the governorship. In the spring of 1836, during the first year of Clay's term as governor, the state had serious difficulties with the Creek Indians, and, though Clay was charged with inactivity and neglect of duty in his handling of the situation, he appears to have been active and energetic in cooperating with the federal troops in removing the Indian peril from the state. In the latter part of his administration, he was seriously hampered by the bad economic conditions, culminating in the panic of 1837. Despite these difficulties and criticisms, he was chosen before the expiration of his term as governor to the seat in the Senate made vacant by the appointment of Senator McKinley to the Supreme Court bench. Clay supported the administration and served satisfactorily but without notable distinction till 1841, when financial stress and illness in his family caused his resignation.

On his return to Alabama, he was commissioned by the legislature to prepare a digest of the Alabama laws, which he completed in 1843; in that year he served for a few months by appointment as a member of the state supreme court; and, in 1846, he was one of the commissioners appointed to wind up the affairs of the state bank. He then returned to his private law practise in which he was engaged without further interruption for the remainder of his life. Though he was an ardent advocate of the secession movement, he took no active part in the Civil War. When Huntsville was occupied by Federal troops, Clay's home was seized, his property was dissipated, and he himself was kept for some time under military arrest. He died in Huntsville in 1866.

[W. Brewer, *Alabama* (1872); Wm. Garrett, *Reminiscences of Public Men in Ala.* (1872); Thos. M. Owen, *Hist. of Ala. and Dict. of Ala. Biog.*, vol. III (1921).]
             T. H. J.

CLAY, EDWARD WILLIAMS (Apr. 19, 1799–Dec. 31, 1857), etcher, engraver, caricaturist, the son of Robert Clay and Eliza Williams, was born in Philadelphia of well-to-do parents. His father was a sea captain, and his grandfather, Curtis Clay, a merchant of his native city. It is asserted (Scharf and Westcott, II, 1063), that Edward Williams Clay was a midshipman under Commodore Perry, but his name does not appear in the Navy Register. While studying art he was for a time an accountant (*Philadelphia Directory*, 1824). The following year, on Mar. 12, he was admitted to the Philadelphia bar as an attorney. His name does not appear in the Philadelphia directories for 1825 or 1828, but in that of 1829 he is de-

scribed as "artist," and evidently practised art there until 1836. Very few examples of his etching or other work survive. For the *American Monthly Magazine*, 1824, he furnished a drawing, engraved by C. G. Childs, and in 1827 he made the drawing of Sedgeley Park, for *Childs's Views of Philadelphia*, but did not engrave it. In 1828–29, he made a series of comic etchings, entitled *Life in Philadelphia*, which were published by W. Simpson and S. Hart & Son, Philadelphia. They pictured with good-natured but telling satire the efforts of the negroes of that day to imitate the extravagant conduct of the whites. After the manner of Cruikshank, he projected in 1829 a series of oblong caricatures, entitled *Sketches of Character*, published by R. H. Hobson, Philadelphia. Only No. 1 appears to have been issued. This is a biting, almost savage attack upon the careless, shiftless militia of his time. It is entitled, "The Nation's Bulwark—A Well Disciplined Militia," and shows a nondescript body of militiamen being drilled. For the same publisher in 1830 he etched four pages of a comic song, "Washing Day," the vignettes illustrating the verses. There is also in existence a single lithographed caricature by Clay which bears the date 1831, and indicates that he was experimenting with the new process, having produced two lithographs the preceding year for the *Memoirs of the Old Schuylkill Fishing Company*. The caricature mentioned, which shows Henry Clay, who had been nominated by the national Republicans, in the guise of a simian, is entitled, "The Monkey System or every one for Himself." Joseph Hopkinson is introduced grinding out "Hail Columbia!" on a hand organ. In 1837 Clay went to New York where in 1839 he was drawing on stone for John Childs, lithographer. Later he went to Europe to study art, but his eyesight failed him and he abandoned his profession on his return to this country. From 1854 to 1856 he was register of the court of Chancery and clerk of the orphans' court of Delaware. He died in New York City in 1857, and was buried in Christ Church burial ground, Philadelphia. He engraved several plates, the best being the portrait of the Rev. Joseph Eastburn. Clay was an artist who had a fresh, original manner and a fancy that was not bound by convention; his only fault was that he made far too few drawings.

[The chief authorities are David M. Stauffer, *Am. Engravers* (1907); J. T. Scharf and T. Westcott, *Hist. of Phila.* (1884), vol. II; a manuscript "Hist. of Lithography in Phila.," by Jos. Jackson; directories of Phila. and N. Y.]
             J. J.

CLAY, GREEN (Aug. 14, 1757–Oct. 31, 1826), soldier, legislator, son of Charles Clay of Welsh descent, was born in Powhatan County, Va. His opportunities for schooling were meager, but he obtained from experience an education of great practical value. Because of a disagreement with his father and lured on by the stories he had heard of Daniel Boone's exploits beyond the Alleghanies, he migrated to Kentucky about 1777. Having some knowledge of surveying and liking it, he entered the office of James Thompson, a surveyor, where he learned his subject well. In 1781 he was made a deputy surveyor for Lincoln County. Impressed by the ease with which good land might be obtained, he immediately began to make use of his opportunities. A system that permitted any number of surveys of the same tract brought about much confusion, and Clay, with his expert knowledge of former surveys and his unusual memory for markers, was in great demand. As was the custom of the day he exacted a half of the land called for by the warrants he surveyed. When the lands in central Kentucky were largely taken up, he carried on surveys in the western part of the state, suffering great hardship and many dangers. As a result of his sagacity and good business sense he amassed a fortune. He settled in Madison County and built up an estate which he called "White Hall." In 1787 he was made one of the trustees for the town of Boonesborough. Though not primarily interested in politics, he was elected to the Virginia legislature in 1788 and in 1789. When Kentucky became a state he represented Madison County in 1793 and in 1794 in the lower house of the legislature and was a member of the Senate from 1795 to 1798. In 1807 he was again a member of the Senate and was elected its speaker. When in 1799 a second constitution for Kentucky was to be made, he represented Madison County in the convention and took an active part in the proceedings. Upon the outbreak of the second war with Great Britain he became a major-general in the state militia, and after Winchester's defeat at Frenchtown he was placed at the head of 3,000 Kentuckians and sent to the relief of the American forces at Fort Meigs. Cautious in his movements, on reaching the fort he constructed flatboats with side protections and floated down the Maumee. A detachment, through rashness, was cut to pieces by the Indians, but the main forces reached the fort and raised the siege. Clay was now in command of the fort, and a little later beat off an attack by Proctor and Tecumseh. As the enlistment of his troops expired within a short time he did not participate in the invasion of Canada. After going as far as Detroit, he returned to Kentucky. He was an able business man and an excellent farmer, using the best

methods of his day. He married Sally Lewis who bore him three sons and four daughters,—the best-known of his children being Cassius Marcellus [q.v.] and Brutus J. Clay. Clay County in Kentucky was named in his honor.

[*Life of Cassius Marcellus Clay; Memoirs, Writings and Speeches* (Cincinnati, 1886) ; Lewis and R. H. Collins, *Hist. of Ky.* (1882) ; *Biog. Encyc. of Ky.* (1877).]   E. M. C.

CLAY, HENRY (Apr. 12, 1777–June 29, 1852), congressman, senator, secretary of state, was descended from English ancestors who came to Virginia shortly after the founding of Jamestown but did not rise to any position of importance in the colony. His father, John Clay, was a Baptist minister, who moved from Henrico County to the frontiers of Hanover County in search of a district more hospitable to the practise of his religion. His mother was Elizabeth Hudson, who came of a family of no greater prominence than the Clays. Henry Clay was born in the midst of the Revolution in a region overrun by war, in that part of Hanover County generally referred to as The Slashes. He was the fourth son, and next to the youngest child, in a family of eight—three daughters and five sons. Of these children only two sons besides Henry lived far beyond the age of maturity. His father died in 1781 leaving the family little more than the respectability of his name. As Henry was only four years old at the time the influence of his father could have affected him very little. To his mother he owed much. He always held her in affectionate remembrance. His formal education consisted of three years before the master of The Slashes log school, Peter Deacon, whom Clay always pleasantly recalled. In 1791 Clay's mother married Henry Watkins, a man who came to regard his step-children kindly and who took a particular interest in Henry. He moved the family to Richmond where he was a resident, and soon secured for Henry a position in a retail store kept by Richard Denny, where the young clerk remained for a year. Feeling that Henry's capacities recommended him for a higher position, his step-father secured work for him in the office of the clerk of the High Court of Chancery, and here Clay remained for the next four years, until 1796. Though somewhat ungainly in appearance, he attracted attention by his open countenance and industry, and thereby recommended himself to Chancellor George Wythe, who made him his amanuensis to copy the court's decisions when not busied in the clerk's office. In his contact with Wythe, Clay secured good counsel and intelligent direction of the reading which he had begun in Denny's store. All his surroundings and his proclivities suggested to him the study of law. This he began in 1796 in the office of Attorney-General Robert Brooke, and within a year he secured his license to practise. During this time he lived in the home of the Attorney-General and had unusual opportunities to meet the people of prominence in the Virginia capital.

While his introduction to Richmond had been far more fortunate than he could have had reason to expect, he felt that conditions were settled there and competition too keen. The same lure that had drawn so many others to the new state of Kentucky also tempted him. Added to this was the fact that his mother was now living there, having left Virginia the year Kentucky became a state. In 1797 Clay moved to Lexington, the outstanding city of all the West in culture and influence. His reputation as an attorney-at-law was soon made and his clients became numerous. As a criminal lawyer, he came by common consent to have no equal in Kentucky. It has been repeatedly stated that no person was ever hanged in a trial where Clay appeared for the defense. He used every trick in argument and procedure in addition to his great skill as an orator. Infrequently he appeared as prosecutor for the state, once serving under protest for a short time as attorney for Fayette County, but by preference he usually acted for the defense. It was not long before the law became to him the means to a much more important end, the regulation of the political and constitutional relations of Kentucky. His first appearance in a political capacity was in 1798 when he followed George Nicholas in a denunciation of the sedition law before a great throng in Lexington. This speech, which was never forgotten by those who heard it, was a fitting introduction to his new constituents. In 1803 in a contest against Felix Grundy, he was elected to the legislature, where he continued until 1806. He had by this time become typically Western in his point of view, and when it seemed that the United States might at the last moment be cheated by Spain out of the prize of Louisiana, he became as greatly excited as any other Kentuckian over the possibility of marching on New Orleans.

In this new community, so little acquainted with the sanctity of law and of established usages, Clay generally took a conservative stand. In 1804 when a fight was made to repeal the charter of the Kentucky Insurance Company in which banking powers had been secured by a stratagem, he championed the cause of the corporation by arguing that a contract was involved and could not be broken except by the agreement of both parties; and in 1807 when the animosity against

England was so bitter that the legislature was about to exclude from Kentucky courts the citation of English precedents, he was able to limit the application of the law to the period after July 4, 1776. While Clay was still completely identified with Kentucky affairs, Aaron Burr made his second visit to the West (1806) and came violently into conflict with Joseph Hamilton Daveiss [q.v.], a Federalist and the federal district attorney for Kentucky. When Daveiss sought an indictment against Burr, Clay agreed to come to the defense of the latter who appeared to be the object of persecution. Clay was also moved to take this course because he did not like Daveiss, with whom he had come near fighting a duel in 1803. Before the first hearing was held, Clay had been elected to the United States Senate to fill the unexpired term of John Adair and now felt that he should have double assurance of Burr's innocence in the form of a written statement. This Burr gave him. Later when, on going to Washington, he was persuaded by Jefferson of Burr's guilt, he felt that he had been tricked, and never afterward spoke to Burr. In the meantime, when Burr's associate, Harman Blennerhassett, came through Lexington and was proceeded against in a civil matter, Clay defended him. Although Clay's enemies later attempted to implicate him in the Burr schemes, he never suffered in the eyes of the people on account of these charges.

Clay spent the short session of 1806–07 in the United States Senate, where he appeared on the floor as a supporter of internal improvements. When he returned to Kentucky, it was with a pleasant feeling toward national politics. The importance which the legislature had attached to him in 1806 had by this time been increased; and when the next year Fayette County returned him to the legislature he was elected speaker. He remained in this body until he was reëlected in 1809 to fill out another unexpired term in the United States Senate. His interests were unmistakably becoming national; and when in 1809 he introduced in the Kentucky House a set of resolutions praising Jefferson's embargo measures and the general accomplishments of the President, Humphrey Marshall brought in a substitute set and started a debate which soon became acrimonious. Later, when Clay introduced a resolution in favor of home manufactures, Marshall's language became so obnoxious that Clay challenged him to a duel, which was fought in Indiana, across the river from Louisville. Both were wounded.

In 1809 Clay returned to Washington, never again to serve his state officially in any other than a national capacity, except in 1822 when he went to Richmond in company with George M. Bibb to secure an agreement with Virginia on the occupying claimants' law, and in the following year when again with Bibb he appeared for Kentucky before the Supreme Court in Washington in the case of *Green* vs. *Biddle* and lost. From the beginning he took an active part in the discussions in the Senate, here supporting some policies from which he never after swerved and others upon which he completely changed his views. He laid the beginnings of the foundations of his celebrated American system in 1810 when he spoke in favor of promoting home manufactures; also, following the instructions of the Kentucky legislature as well as carrying out his own views, he opposed the re-chartering of the United States Bank, charging it with being a money power dangerous to free institutions and holding it to be unconstitutional. These doctrines he later entirely abandoned. He made his first entry into matters of foreign policy when he upheld the Perdido River as the eastern boundary of the Louisiana Purchase. Much of his enthusiasm and inspiration in official life came from his feeling that he was a direct agent and defender of the people; hence it was only natural that in 1810 he should decide to exchange the Senate for the House of Representatives and should make the following announcement: "In presenting myself to your notice, I conform to sentiments I have invariably felt, in favor of the station of an immediate representative of the people" (*Lexington Gazette,* May 15, 1810). He was elected from the district of which Fayette County was a part, and which came to be known as the Ashland district, from the name of his home near Lexington. His strong nationalism was by this time unmistakable and was by no means incompatible with his equally strong advocacy of Western interests. He entered the Twelfth Congress as the leader of the young, unterrified "war hawks," determined to uphold the national honor against Great Britain whether on the high seas or west of the Alleghanies. He was elected speaker, and intrenched in this position he proceeded to prepare for war by appointing "war hawks" to prominent committees, urging President Madison on to a stern course, advocating military preparation, and arousing general enthusiasm with such flourishes as the assertion that the Kentucky militia alone could take Montreal and Upper Canada. He pushed Madison into war and stood valiantly behind him. When in 1814 it seemed that Great Britain might be willing to engage in peace parleys, Madison added Clay and then Gallatin to the commission composed of Adams, Russell, and Bayard, and

the negotiations at Ghent were started. As Clay had had Western interests in mind in getting into war, he was not now going to forget them in getting out of the war, especially when it came to trading them for Eastern benefits. The conference almost collapsed when Adams insisted on giving England the free navigation of the Mississippi in exchange for the Newfoundland fisheries. Clay saved the Mississippi, won a certain secret contempt in the mind of Adams, and after visiting Paris and London, returned in 1815, convinced that the United States was now one of the powerful nations of the earth. He was reëlected to his position in Congress, which he had abandoned the year before, and was again made speaker, to both of which positions he was reëlected until 1821, resigning the latter in October 1820, and refusing to stand for election to the former after Mar. 4, 1821.

Unquestionably Clay had been greatly broadened by his European experiences, and his power and influence were much increased. Madison sought to reward him by offers of the Russian post and the secretaryship of war, both of which he refused, largely because he was now intent on consolidating his position of leadership in Congress. He hoped to receive the secretaryship of state from Monroe, who became president in 1817, but this had been reserved for Adams, who thereby became, according to the custom of the times, the designated successor to the presidency. Instead, Monroe successively offered Clay the ministry to England and the secretaryship of war, both of which he declined. He soon found easy means to become a critic of the national administration and with one exception maintained this rôle for the rest of his life. His position in Kentucky being now paramount, his confidence in himself and in his country awakened in him an ambition for the presidency which haunted him to his dying day, making of his life an unending series of disappointments. He developed and set forth a program of nationalism, including surveys for canals and highways and the building of them, the re-chartering of the United States Bank, protection for American industries, and a policy of national defense in keeping with the grandeur and glory of his country. The Bank was re-chartered and the protective principle was incorporated in the tariff of 1816, but Clay was never to see his program of internal improvements carried out.

His impetuosity soon precipitated him into conflicts with the President and various other prominent leaders. He incurred the most momentous and bitter enmity of his life when in 1819 he left the speaker's chair to attack Andrew Jackson for his invasion of Florida. Jackson never forgave him for his offense. Already critical of Monroe's administration and impelled by a sympathy for the South American revolutionists, Clay began in 1818 his campaign for the recognition of their independence, and by his eloquence and persistency made himself a hero in South America second only to Simon Bolivar. Not being a part of Monroe's administration, he was unconcerned with the effect his speeches were having on the Florida treaty which was then being negotiated with Spain, and when this document came up for ratification he attacked it for its failure to include Texas. His sympathy for the Greeks struggling against Turkey for their independence he strongly expressed in 1824, regardless of the fact that American interference in European affairs was incompatible with the position his country had taken in the recently announced Monroe Doctrine.

In the Missouri Compromise debate the dangers of a divided country first rudely shocked the nation, and propelled Clay into a new rôle, which he was to play thereafter. The essence of the struggle to him was not the extension or restriction of slavery, but the continuance of the Union of equal states. If Congress could lay restrictions on slavery in Missouri, its power might extend to any subject. Herein lay the fundamental danger to the Union. Through the compromise suggested by Senator Thomas, Clay saw the question practically settled, and in 1820 he returned to Kentucky to look after his private affairs, and to be absent from much of the session beginning in the fall. Trouble broke out anew when Missouri sought to exclude free negroes from her boundaries. Clay hastened back to Washington in January 1821 and succeeded in pushing through the House a compromise plan, substantially the same as that which Senator Eaton had introduced in the Senate. He returned to Kentucky at the end of the session, in March 1821, not to reappear in Congress until he should come as an avowed candidate for the presidency. His private affairs in Kentucky engaged his attention for the next two years, during which time he enjoyed the almost universal acclaim of Kentuckians. In 1822 a joint meeting of the legislature nominated him for the presidency, and other states soon followed. He was also reëlected to Congress, where he served from 1823 to 1825, being again the choice of that body for speaker. He now set about consolidating a national program calculated to secure his election. It was during this period that he developed fully his American system of protective tariffs and internal improvements. The tariff bill of 1820 had

failed, but in 1824 he secured the passage of the highest protective tariff enacted up to that time. In the presidential election of 1824 he received the smallest number of votes cast for any of the four candidates and was thereby eliminated by the Constitution from those to be voted upon by the House, which body chooses the president when no one receives a majority of the electoral college. Clay had carried Kentucky by an overwhelming vote against Jackson, his nearest competitor, who had received a plurality in the nation. Jackson had grievously wounded the feelings of Kentucky in 1815 when he had accused the Kentucky troops at New Orleans of cowardice, but even so he was much more attractive to Kentuckians than Adams, whose enmity shown at Ghent was well known. The legislature instructed Clay to vote for Jackson when the House should take up the election of the president, instructions which Clay ignored by voting for Adams and effecting his election. For this rebellious conduct Clay suffered his first eclipse in Kentucky, temporary though it was. Jackson and his friends were furious, charged Clay with making a bargain with Adams, and when Clay accepted the secretaryship of state were irretrievably convinced of his duplicity. Clay and his friends labored throughout the rest of their lives to disprove this slander, but it dogged his tracks in every subsequent campaign. When he returned to Kentucky he found considerable hostility, but the warmth of the welcome extended by his friends soon convinced him of the solidarity of his position. He bitterly attacked Jackson, and repeatedly asked how the winning of a military victory and the possession of an imperious and dictatorial spirit could possibly be a recommendation for the civil leadership of the nation. Yet many of Clay's friends could never shake off the feeling that the alliance with Adams was a most unnatural one.

As secretary of state, Clay was thoroughly loyal throughout to the Administration. He served the full term and perhaps never spent a more miserable and uninteresting four years in all his life. He was by nature opposed to the routine of administrative work, finding his chief delight in the excitement of debate and parliamentary maneuvers. Much of the time he was ill, and but for his loyalty would have resigned. No problems of great importance in foreign affairs arose, though he made a host of minor commercial treaties. The best-known incident of his incumbency was the Pan-American Congress, in which he sought to have the United States participate. The enemies of the Administration started an acrimonious debate in Congress over the instructions to the delegates, which delayed their departure so long that they arrived too late. Out of this controversy grew a harmless duel between Clay and John Randolph of Roanoke, precipitated by the cutting sarcasm of the latter.

In the election of 1828 Clay supported Adams, though he was unable to convince his own Kentucky of the New Englander's worth. Jackson carried the state and the nation, and Clay was temporarily disheartened when he saw the government handed over to a military chieftain. He refused to accept a position on the Supreme Court, and returned wearily over muddy roads to Kentucky, with his simple faith in the good sense of the people much shaken. The ardor of his reception, however, soon brought a return of the warm glow and enthusiasm that were characteristic of him. In company with his friend, John J. Crittenden, he toured western Kentucky, where he was received with unexpected acclaim. He also visited New Orleans twice within the next two years, his progress up and down the Mississippi reaching the proportions of a triumphal procession. Yet with all this manifestation of support, he was tempted to become a quiet country gentleman. At this time he wrote a friend, "My attachment to rural occupation every day acquires more strength, and if it continues to increase another year as it has the last, I shall be fully prepared to renounce forever the strifes of public life" (Calvin Colton, ed., *Private Correspondence of Henry Clay*, 1856, p. 261). But in 1830 the legislature again nominated him for the presidency and in order to place him in a more strategic position sent him to the Senate in 1831. Crittenden resigned to make a place for him. Clay now began to weld together all the elements of protest against Jackson and to develop his program. In the debate leading to the tariff of 1832 Clay restated at great length the protectionist argument. He presented to Jackson a bill which to his amazement the President signed. As another move in his campaign he decided that the Second United States Bank should be re-chartered. He pushed the bill through Congress, and Jackson vetoed it. Finally, he wished to settle the question of public lands and the problem of the surplus by distributing the proceeds of land sales among all the states according to population. The bill was finally passed (1833), but Jackson met it with a pocket veto, and at the beginning of the next Congress gave the reasons for his action. Clay then attacked Jackson from every angle and harassed him by leading the Senate to reject the President's nominations, the most conspicuous example being that of Van Buren as minister to London. Clay was nominated by the anti-Jackson men in Baltimore in December 1831, but in the election the next year he was disastrously defeated. The popular appeal of the vigorous Jackson and the activities of the anti-Masons combined to bring about his discomfiture. Again Clay almost despaired of the popular good sense, but he soon found a menacing problem that required his best thought and efforts. South Carolina had assumed a threatening attitude toward the tariff, and when the law of 1832 was passed, nullified it. Jackson's threats disturbed Clay almost as much as did Calhoun's nullification, for he feared lest Jackson should precipitate a civil war. He soon had ready the compromise tariff of 1833, which gradually reduced the rates. Substituting it for the administration bill, he secured its passage with the aid of Calhoun and his friends. Again he had effected a compromise in a menacing situation and perhaps saved the Union from disruption.

Throughout the rest of Jackson's official life Clay battled against him, as an overwhelming threat to the liberties of the people. For the purpose of curtailing Jackson's power, he advocated amendments to the Constitution which if adopted would have been of lasting harm to the country. When the President sought to hurry the destruction of the bank by the removal of the deposits, Clay in 1834 introduced and secured the passage of resolutions of censure. In January 1837, however, these were expunged from the record, an event which so unstrung Clay that he gloomily declared, "The Senate is no longer a place for a decent man." When Jackson's brusque language angered the French and came near precipitating war, Clay as chairman of the Committee on Foreign Relations in the Senate smoothed out the affair satisfactorily. In 1836, however, he felt that no one could stop the headlong course of the Jackson party, and looked upon the election of Van Buren as so inevitable that he did not offer himself to the Whigs as a candidate. He chose to remain in the Senate, to which the Kentucky legislature elected him for another term.

Following the panic of 1837, which soon burst upon the country, Van Buren brought forward the sub-treasury system to take the place of Jackson's "pet banks." Clay opposed the measure, here parting company with Calhoun who supported it and rejoined the Democrats. Thereafter Clay and the South Carolinian engaged in many tilts on the floor of the Senate. Van Buren's administration proved so unsatisfactory to the country that the Whigs felt certain of victory in 1840 and Clay fully expected the nomination. But a new schemer with new tricks now appeared prominently in American politics.

Thurlow Weed, by his astute maneuvers in the Whig convention at Harrisburg, threw the nomination to William Henry Harrison, a questionable military hero thirty years removed from his exploits and an incomparably less able leader than Clay. John Tyler, a Democrat of the old school and an admirer of Clay, became the vice-presidential candidate. Though Clay was enraged when he learned of Weed's trickery he campaigned vigorously for the ticket. The Whigs won and Clay rejected the offer of the secretaryship of state in order better to assume the leadership of the new administration. He introduced in the Senate a set of resolutions which he expected to be accepted as the party program, consisting of the repeal of the sub-treasury system, the re-chartering of the United States Bank, the distribution among the states of the proceeds from the public lands sales, and the passage of a new tariff. But when Tyler succeeded to the presidency on the death of Harrison exactly one month after assuming office, he soon showed the Whigs how completely they had been cheated out of their victory. Clay, indeed, succeeded in getting the sub-treasury system repealed, but when he sought to have the United States Bank re-chartered he found Tyler unsympathetic. He so amended his measure that he thought it would secure the President's approval, and after putting it through Congress was almost stupefied to see Tyler veto it. He had no better success with the tariff, and in 1842 resigned his position in the Senate, making on Mar. 31 a farewell address which created a profound effect on his auditors.

If Clay had revived the idea of retiring to Ashland and settling down to the stock farming which he so much enjoyed, he was soon dispossessed of the thought, for his reception in Kentucky was so vigorous as to constitute a mandate for the presidency in 1844. Enthusiasm for him was equally marked throughout the rest of the country. The year he retired from the Senate, two years before the election, various states began to nominate him. He made a few trips out of Kentucky, notably one to the states north of the Ohio. In Dayton it was estimated that 100,000 people gathered to hear him. Long before 1844 it was conceded that Clay would be the Whig nominee, and it was no less an accepted fact in Clay's mind that Van Buren would receive the Democratic nomination. When Van Buren chanced to visit Ashland, the two prospective candidates appear to have agreed to eliminate the question of Texas from the campaign. Accordingly, on the same day in the latter part of April, after Clay had made a trip through the lower South, both he and Van Buren issued statements opposing immediate annexation (for Clay's letter, see *Niles' Register,* LXVI, 152–53). A few days later Clay was nominated by acclamation in the Whig national convention. Van Buren, however, lost the Democratic nomination to Polk, as the Democrats were determined on expansion. The apparent enthusiasm of the country for annexation and the widespread impression that he was favoring the abolitionists, led Clay to restate his position in what came to be called the "Alabama letters." In these he declared that slavery was not involved one way or the other in the Texas question, and that he would be glad to see Texas annexed, if it could be done "without dishonor, without war, with the common consent of the Union, and upon just and fair terms" (*Ibid.,* LXVI, 439). Owing to this ill-advised maneuver, Clay lost New York, and thereby the election, to Polk. "Never before or since has the defeat of any man in this country brought forth such an exhibition of heartfelt grief from the educated and respectable classes of society as did this defeat of Clay" (James Ford Rhodes, *History of the United States,* 1902, I, 84).

Polk's success brought annexation, at the hands of Tyler, and war with Mexico. Clay felt that the declaration of war was an outrage, yet after war was declared he supported it. His favorite son, Henry, was killed at Buena Vista. Much concerned over the ultimate outcome of the war, Clay made a speech in Lexington on Nov. 13, 1847, in which he called upon Congress to disclaim any intention of annexing Mexico and to announce the purposes of the war. During this period of retirement he made two trips to the East and was received with almost unbounded enthusiasm in New York, Philadelphia, and in other cities. Again the clamor began to arise for his nomination in 1848. Convinced of support, he announced his candidacy in April 1848. But there were many Whigs who felt that he could not be elected, and some of these were in Kentucky. A Kentucky Whig wrote John J. Crittenden, Jan. 2, 1847, that "the Whig party cannot exist, or with any hope of success, so long as Mr. Clay continues his political aspirations" (Mrs. C. Coleman, *Life of John J. Crittenden,* 1871, I, 266). Crittenden's desertion brought to an end a long-standing friendship. Gen. Zachary Taylor was nominated, and Clay, disconsolate because he did not control even the Kentucky delegation, felt that the Whig party had destroyed itself by its own act. The folly of nominating a military hero who had no qualifications for civil leadership had been repeated. Clay definitely refused to take part in the campaign.

After Taylor's election, when the problems growing out of the war and the sectional struggle had nearly driven the country to disunion, he returned to the Senate (1849) in a last effort to ward off disaster. Spurning Taylor's weak course, he set forth in detail his plan for gradual emancipation in the Pindell letter of 1849 and introduced in the Senate his well-known series of resolutions. In the debate in the Senate he made his greatest and last effort to save the Union, begging the radicals, in both North and South, to abandon a course which could mean only disruption. He particularly warned the South against secession, declaring that no such right existed and that he would advocate force in opposing it. Clay hoped that the compromise measures would definitely settle the sectional struggle; but to make doubly sure he with forty-four other members of Congress signed a pledge to oppose for public office any one who did not accept the settlement. In the summer of 1851 he returned to Kentucky by way of Cuba, hoping the Southern climate would help a racking cough with which he was now afflicted, but he found no relief. In the fall he was back in Washington, determined, it seemed, to die in the service of his country. On the following June 29, death closed his career. His remains were taken to Lexington by way of Baltimore, Philadelphia, New York, Albany, Buffalo, Cleveland, and Cincinnati, amid national mourning. He was buried in the Lexington cemetery.

No man in American public life has had more ardent supporters or more bitter enemies than Clay, and no one has depended more for his happiness on the friendship of the people. His mastery of Kentucky's emotions and reason was complete and lasting on every public question except that of slavery. Kentucky absorbed his strong Unionism but refused to adopt his plan of emancipation. Clay obtained much pleasure from his Ashland home with its six hundred acres and fifty slaves; but however often he might resolve to abandon public life, the importunities of his friends and his love of debate changed his mind. When his home was in danger of being sold for his debts, unknown friends throughout the country raised $50,000 with which which they settled his obligations. He was not by nature a religious man, though he joined the Episcopal Church in later life (1847). He fought duels, but he afterward came strongly to oppose that method of vindicating honor. In common with his contemporaries, he played cards, was fond of horse-racing, and liked good liquors, though he did not drink to excess. In appearance he was tall, with a high forehead, gray eyes, and a large mouth. His voice was engaging, and in debate he employed every movement of his body with grace and skill, even using his snuff box to great advantage. His personal magnetism was remarkable; he seemed never to be without a proper word or expression, and always seemed to be perfectly at ease. Enthusiasm and warmth characterized his speaking, getting the best of his reason at times and leading him into untenable positions. His knowledge was not characterized by the profundity of Webster's, nor did he have the philosophical powers of Calhoun or the acquaintance with the classics which Adams and Sumner possessed. But in his understanding of human nature, in his ability to appeal to the common reason, and in his absolute fearlessness in stating his convictions, he was unexcelled by any of his contemporaries. He was married in 1799 to Lucretia Hart, a daughter of Col. Thomas Hart of Henderson's Transylvania Company, by whom he had eleven children—six daughters and five sons. All his daughters and one son died before him. Another son became insane from an accident. Of the others, Thomas H. Clay was minister to Guatemala under Lincoln and died in 1871; James B. Clay was chargé d'affaires at Lisbon under an appointment from Taylor, was later elected to Congress, and died in 1863; and John M. Clay became a farmer and was the last surviving member of the family, dying in 1887.

[The letters and papers of Henry Clay are voluminous. Many of them have been scattered among his descendants, but the largest single collection is in the Lib. of Cong. Among his published letters and speeches are the following: Richard Chambers, ed., *Speeches of the Hon. Henry Clay, in the Cong. of the U. S.* (1842); Daniel Mallory, ed., *Life and Speeches of Henry Clay* (2 vols., 1843); Calvin Colton, ed., *Private Correspondence of Henry Clay* (1856); *Works of Henry Clay* (6 vols., 1856, repub., with additional matter, in 7 vols., 1896), and *Monument to the Memory of Henry Clay* (1857). The principal biographies of Clay are: Geo. D. Prentice, *Biog. of Henry Clay* (1831); Epes Sargent, *Life and Public Service of Henry Clay* (1842, repub. with additions, 1848); Calvin Colton, *Life and Times of Henry Clay* (2 vols., 1846); Calvin Colton, *The Last Seven Years of the Life of Henry Clay* (1856); Carl Schurz, *Henry Clay* (2 vols., 1887); Thos. H. Clay and E. P. Oberholtzer, *Henry Clay* (1910); Jos. M. Rogers, *The True Henry Clay* (1902). An estimate of Clay's service as speaker of the House of Representatives is in M. P. Follett, *The Speaker of the House of Representatives* (1909) and H. B. Fuller, *Speakers of the House* (1909). The ancestry of Clay has been most fully set forth by Zachary F. Smith and Mrs. Mary Rogers Clay in *The Clay Family* (1899), being no. 14 of the Filson Club Publications.]

E. M. C.

CLAY, JOSEPH (Oct. 16, 1741–Nov. 15, 1804), merchant, Revolutionary officer, and member of the Continental Congress, was prominent among those young colonials of property and position who espoused the Revolutionary cause in Georgia. His father, Ralph Clay, was a native of Yorkshire, England, and there, at Beverley, Joseph was born. His mother, Elizabeth Habersham, was a sister of James Habersham who emigrated to Georgia some five years before Joseph's birth, became a leading citizen, and served as royal governor during the absence in England of Sir James Wright. It was at the instance of this uncle that Joseph, in his nineteenth year, sailed for Savannah. A few years after his arrival, Joseph was placed by his uncle in the general commission business in partnership with his cousin James Habersham, Jr., and a little later, still in association with his Habersham relatives, he acquired interests in rice plantations. He prospered from the first, both as a merchant and as a planter, and at various times was a member of the firms of Joseph Clay & Company, Seth John Cuthbert & Company, Clay, Telfair & Company, all of Savannah, and a co-partner in the house of William Fox & Company of Newport, R. I., although he always lived in Savannah. He has been described as being prompt, energetic, and competent. Early in his career, Jan. 2, 1763, he was married to Ann Legardère, and one of his sons, Joseph Clay [q.v.], attained some distinction in his state. Although Clay's fourteen years out of England had been spent for the most part in a loyal atmosphere under the tutelage of a royalist uncle, he threw himself actively into the conflict on the side of the revolutionists. From the time when as a member of a committee appointed by the Savannah republican mass-meeting of July 27, 1774, he helped draft the resolutions expressing the determination of Georgia to associate herself with the sister colonies in opposition to the acts of the British Parliament, until the end of the war, he held positions of responsibility in the civil government and in the army. There is evidence that he was considered by his contemporaries to be a valuable member of the Council of Safety which took over the administration of the city of Savannah in 1775, and he was placed upon the important committees of the Provincial Congress of that year. He also participated in the secret raid upon the King's powder magazine on the night of May 11, 1775, with a party which seems to have been restricted in its personnel to the *corps d'élite* of the revolutionary faction. As paymaster-general of the Continental Army for the Southern Department—to which position he was appointed in 1777—he was both honest and efficient, and it appears that he had the confidence

and esteem of Gen. Nathanael Greene, his commanding officer. He was included among the twenty-five rebel leaders who were attainted for treason by the royalist Assembly of 1780 in retaliation for similar action taken by the republican Assembly of 1778. He was a member of the Continental Congress in 1778, 1779, and 1780, but was not conspicuous there.

At the cessation of hostilities he served for one year (1782) as state treasurer, and in the following year he was made a justice of his county. In 1785 he was made a member of the board created by the General Assembly to establish an institution of higher education, and thus became one of the fathers of the University of Georgia, the first state university to be chartered in America. Most of his time after the war, however, was devoted to his private business.

[C. C. Jones, Jr., *Biog. Sketches Delegates from Ga. to the Continental Congress* (1891); *Ga. Official and Statistical Reg.*, 1923; "Letters of Jos. Clay," *Ga. Hist. Soc. Colls.*, vol. VIII (1913).]   B. F.

CLAY, JOSEPH (Aug. 16, 1764–Jan. 11, 1811), a Baptist clergyman who attained prominence as such after having had a distinguished career as a lawyer and jurist, was born in Savannah, Ga., the son of Joseph [q.v.] and Ann (Legardère) Clay. He had natural gifts of a high order and the advantage of belonging to a family of means, social standing, and political influence. When twenty years old he graduated from Princeton with highest honors, and later studied law at Williamsburg, Va., under the celebrated jurist and teacher, George Wythe (*Georgia Historical Quarterly*, September 1923, p. 211). On Nov. 25, 1789, he was married to Mary, daughter of Thomas and Mary (Butler) Savage, of Charleston, S. C.

He was a man of fine personal appearance, above the average height, with a kindly face, and eyes of singular beauty. His ability and eloquence soon brought him into prominence in his native state, where he engaged in the practise of his profession. He was one of the most influential members of the convention of 1795, which revised the Georgia constitution, and the original draft of the constitution which was framed in the convention of 1798 was from his pen. On Sept. 16, 1796, he was commissioned United States district judge for the District of Georgia. Letters to President Washington from the great Carolinian, Chancellor DeSaussure, from the Postmaster-General at that time, Joseph Habersham, and from Representative Abraham Baldwin, indorsing Clay for this office have been published (*Ibid.*, pp. 209–12). On Feb. 24, 1801, he was commissioned United States circuit judge for the 5th Circuit, under the "Midnight Judges Bill." By the repeal of this act which took effect July 1, 1802, he was legislated out of office (30 *Fed. Cas.,* 1367).

An Episcopalian by early training, he was converted to Baptist doctrines in 1803, and joined the church in Savannah of which Dr. Henry Holcombe was pastor. He was soon called to be his assistant, and in 1804 he was ordained. From this time on, he devoted himself almost wholly to religious work. As a member of the General Committee of the Baptist Association of the state, he worked to promote education and missionary effort. A visit to New England in the autumn of 1806, where he preached in various cities, resulted in his being called to become an associate of the aged Dr. Samuel Stillman of the First Baptist Church, Boston, with right of succession. He accepted, and on the death of Dr. Stillman became pastor, being installed Aug. 19, 1807. Mr. Clay himself preached the sermon, which was on the nature and duties of the ministry (*A Discourse, Delivered in the First Baptist Meeting House in Boston . . . by Joseph Clay, A.M., on the Occasion of His Installation,* 1807). Failing health caused him to resign in 1809. Death came to him in his forty-seventh year, and he was buried in the Granary Burying Ground, Boston.

[Montgomery Cumming, *Table of the Descendants of Joseph Clay of Savannah, Ga.* (1897); Lawrence Park, *Maj. Thos. Savage of Boston, and His Descendants* (1914); *Gen. Cat. Princeton Univ.* (1908); *Jour. of the Convention of the State of Ga.* (1795); Jas. M. Winchell, *Two Discourses Exhibiting an Hist. Sketch of the First Bapt. Ch. in Boston* (2nd ed., 1820); *Hist. of the Bapt. Denomination in Ga.* (1881, comp. for the *Christian Index*), esp. chs. v and vi; N. E. Wood, *Hist. of the First Bapt. Ch. of Boston* (1899); Wm. B. Sprague, *Annals Am. Pulpit,* VI (1860).]   H. E. S.

CLAY, MATTHEW (Mar. 25, 1754–May 27, 1815), congressman, the son of Charles and Martha (Green) Clay, was born in Halifax County, Va., before the establishment of Pittsylvania County out of the western portion of Halifax. His father and Henry Clay's grandfather were brothers and were the sons of Henry Clay, one of the confederates of Nathaniel Bacon, the colonial Virginia rebel (*Virginia Magazine of History and Biography,* VII, 124–25). In the Revolution, Matthew served as ensign in the 9th Virginia Regiment in 1776, being promoted second lieutenant in 1777 and first lieutenant in 1778. In the latter year he was transferred to the 1st Virginia Regiment, and served as regimental quartermaster. Transferred once more, to the 5th Virginia, in 1781,

he retired in 1783. He was a member of the Society of the Cincinnati.

After representing Pittsylvania County in the House of Delegates from 1790 to 1794 he was elected to the national House of Representatives as a member of the Republican party, and served from 1795 to 1813, and from Mar. 4, 1815 until his death. In a "sensible speech," as Benton called it, in which he urged a reorganization of the militia, Clay declared, "I defy any man to say that I ever gave other than a republican vote, or did any other than a republican act, while acting as a public man" (T. H. Benton, *Abridgment of the Debates of Congress from 1789 to 1856,* 1857–61, III, 659–63). He was apparently much interested in the military organization, notwithstanding his republicanism. He urged that enlistments should be made for a longer period than was customary at the time (*Annals of Congress,* 12 Cong., 2 Sess., p. 490). He believed firmly that the United States was justified in entering upon the War of 1812, and declared: "I am not for stopping at Quebec or anywhere else; but I would take the whole continent from them, and ask no favors. . . . If we get the continent, she must allow us the freedom of the sea" (*Ibid.,* p. 498). He supported Jefferson in the purchase of Louisiana and in the establishment of a government for that territory (*Ibid.,* 8 Cong., 1 Sess., p. 550) and opposed the re-charter of the United States Bank (*Ibid.,* 11 Cong., 2 Sess., p. 826). From the personal property and land tax books of Pittsylvania County (Manuscripts in Virginia State Library) it appears that in 1813 Clay was the owner of fifteen slaves and held land in the county to the extent of 1,176 acres, valued, for taxation purposes, at $1,058.57, and on which, with all of his personalty, he paid $20.14 tax. He was twice married, his first wife being Polly Williams and his second, —— Saunders. He died at Halifax Court House, Va., and was buried in the family burying-ground in Pittsylvania County.

[A portrait of Matthew Clay, marked no. 39, came into the possession of Hampton L Carson of Philadelphia in 1898, as one of the St. Memin Collection (*Wm. and Mary Coll. Quart.,* IX, 146). For biographical data see: W. H. Powell, *List Officers Army U. S., 1779–1900* (1900), p. 22; *Lineage Hist. Reg. Officers Continental Army* (1914); *Biog. Dir. Am. Congress* (1928).]   E. L. F.

CLAYPOLE, EDWARD WALLER (June 1, 1835–Aug. 17, 1901), geologist, educator, was born at Ross, Herefordshire, England, the eldest of the six children of Edward Angell Claypole, a Baptist minister, and Elizabeth (Blunt) Claypole. His early training is said to have been severe and protracted and largely in classical lore, in which his father was very proficient. In 1852, at the age of seventeen, he passed the matriculation examination of the University of London, but owing to certain restrictions did not receive his B.A. degree until ten years later. His first inspiration toward natural history was due to the influence of two sisters of his mother who encouraged him to collect plants and fossils from near-by quarries. He began teaching while quite young (in 1852) at Abingdon, and in 1866 became tutor in the classics and mathematics at Stokescroft College in Bristol. His liberal tendencies in matters pertaining to evolution soon brought him into difficulties. This, together with the death of his wife in 1870 and his failure to procure a professorship in mathematics, caused him in 1872 to cross the Atlantic in the hope of finding a more liberal atmosphere. In 1873 he was appointed professor of natural history in Antioch College, Yellow Springs, Ohio, where he remained for eight years, leaving in 1881 to accept an appointment on the staff of the Geological Survey of Pennsylvania under Lesley. He remained here but two years, accepting in 1883 an appointment as professor of natural sciences in Buchtel College, Akron, Ohio. In 1898 he was appointed professor of geology and biology at the Throop Polytechnic Institute at Pasadena, Cal.

Claypole was more a naturalist of the old school than a modern geologist, as is very evident from his bibliography in which are titles ranging over nearly the whole gamut of the sciences. A large portion of his geological papers dealt with stratigraphic and paleontologic matters, though he wrote also on glacial questions and occasional physical problems, like the "level of no strain" in the earth, the conditions of the earth's interior, and Pennsylvania before and after the elevation of the Appalachian Mountains, in this last attempting to show that the distance along a straight line crossing the range had been actually reduced by some 65 miles by the process of folding. Perhaps his most epoch-making discovery was that of fish remains in Silurian rocks in Pennsylvania. His paper on "The Devonian Formation of the Ohio Basin" was awarded the Walker prize of the Massachusetts Institute of Technology. He is represented to have been of a modest and retiring disposition, caring nothing for display, thoroughly unselfish, and, though of a serious temperament, full of good-fellowship. As a teacher he had a genuine interest in his pupils, willing to go to any length to help but demanding the best in return. "Teaching was his profession and

he taught all his working life except two years when he was on the Geological Survey of Pennsylvania. For nearly a third of a century he taught many things, nearly the whole curriculum of an ordinary college at different times, and everything with equal facility, but his specialty was the natural sciences and particularly geology. His early ambition was to be a civil engineer, not a teacher. He might have made a good engineer, but it is certain he was a teacher born, as truly as men are born gentlemen or geniuses" (*American Geologist, post*).

Dr. Claypole was a member of the Geological Societies of London, Edinburgh, and America, the American Philosophical Society of Pennsylvania, the American Society of Psychical Research, and several smaller and local societies devoted to various subjects. He married first, in 1865, Jane Trotter of Coleford, England, who died in 1870 before his coming to America, leaving a young son and twin daughters but a few weeks old; in 1879, while at Antioch College, he married Katharine Benedicta Trotter of Montreal, a second cousin of his first wife, who survived him but a few days. He died suddenly of a cerebral hemorrhage at Long Beach, Cal., Aug. 17, 1901.

[Memoirs by J. B. Comstock and others in the *Bull. Geol. Soc. of America*, XIII, 487, and the *Am. Geologist*, vol. XXIX; the former containing full bibliography of Claypole's publications.]   G. P. M.

CLAYTON, AUGUSTIN SMITH (Nov. 27, 1783–June 21, 1839), lawyer, congressman, born at Fredericksburg, Va., was the fourth child of Philip and Mildred (Dixon) Clayton. In 1784 the family removed to Georgia and settled in Richmond County. After being graduated from the University of Georgia in 1804, in the first class graduated by that institution, which opened in 1801, he studied law, was admitted to practise (1806), and settled in Athens. He was married in 1808 to Julia Carnes, daughter of Judge Thomas P. Carnes of Augusta. In 1810 he was commissioned by the legislature to compile the Georgia laws from 1800 to 1810; his compilation was published in 1812. After terms in the General Assembly (1810–12) and three years as clerk of the lower house, he was elected judge of the western superior circuit court. He held this office from 1819 to 1825, when he was defeated for reëlection. He was again elected to the judgeship in 1828. At that time the northern portion of Georgia was still in the possession of the Cherokee Indians, and the state had begun to take steps to acquire the Cherokee lands. In 1827 the Cherokees adopted a written constitution and claimed to be a sovereign state, denying the right of Georgia to interfere in any way with their autonomy. The state's answer to this move was promptly made in 1828 in the form of legislation extending the jurisdiction of Georgia laws and courts over Cherokee land and making it illegal for Cherokee courts to sit or their processes to be executed. Jurisdiction over the Indian land was divided between neighboring Georgia counties, a part of the area being assigned to counties in Clayton's circuit. A bitter struggle followed between Georgia and the Cherokees over the constitutionality of the state's legislation. Clayton vigorously upheld the state's position. The difficulty of the problem was accentuated in 1829 by the discovery of gold in the Indian land. The country was invaded by a turbulent, lawless element, some three thousand men going there within the year. With the idea of controlling the disorder the General Assembly enacted a law (1831) making it illegal for any white men to reside in Cherokee land unless a license from the state were first obtained. Such migrants were also required to swear allegiance to the constitution of Georgia. Among these white residents was a missionary named Worcester. He and others refused either to apply for a license and take the oath of allegiance or to leave the Cherokee nation. They were indicted (1831) by the grand jury of Gwinnett County, which was in Clayton's circuit. In the subsequent trial, the defendant, Worcester, denied the jurisdiction of the court, contending that the Cherokee nation was an independent state and that Georgia was without authority to extend the jurisdiction of state law over them. Clayton overruled this plea; the defendants were convicted and sentenced to four years in the penitentiary. The Governor offered a pardon if they would agree to abide by the law in future. All accepted the offer of clemency except Worcester and one other missionary. Worcester appealed his case to the Supreme Court of the United States. Clayton expressed in no uncertain terms his resentment of the decision of that court, which declared that the Georgia law with reference to the Cherokees was unconstitutional, null and void. Clayton was defeated for reëlection to the judgeship in 1831 because of an unpopular decision in connection with the Cherokees. The General Assembly had enacted a law prohibiting Indians from digging gold on their own land. In a test case Clayton declared this law unconstitutional. The decision was rendered shortly before the General Assembly was called upon to elect a judge of the circuit. There was no opposition to Clayton

until the decision was rendered, but another candidate saw fit to take advantage of his momentary unpopularity and Clayton was defeated. Many Georgians of the period held that the Indians had no rights that a white man was bound to respect when conflict arose between whites and Indians. In politics Clayton was an uncompromising adherent of the state sovereignty school. His attitude toward the national government was clearly shown by his defiance of the Supreme Court in connection with the Worcester case. It was natural, therefore, that when he entered Congress (1831) at a critical moment in national history, he should throw himself with great zeal into the tariff and bank matters, always championing the strictest state-rights position. His opposition to the tariff rested on constitutional grounds and on the claim that it fostered manufacturing at the expense of agriculture. He had been a member of the company which, in 1828, erected at Athens the first cotton-mill in Georgia (the mill is still operating), and in buttressing his arguments he was able to point to his own excessive profits, the company having doubled its capital within two years. On returning to Georgia in the summer of 1832, Clayton, Berrien, and others organized an anti-tariff convention to meet in the fall. When the convention assembled, Clayton was made chairman of a committee to prepare resolutions on the tariff situation. The resolutions, denouncing the tariff, Jackson's proclamation, and the Force Bill, were adopted. Clayton was in entire agreement with Calhoun as to the right of a state to nullify acts of Congress which the state thought exceeded the powers that had been delegated to Congress. Indeed, he was the only Georgia politician of the first rank who was an avowed nullifier. On the other important question of the period, that of rechartering the second Bank of the United States, he was equally radical. Both in Congress and in numerous communications to the press (writing under the pseudonym "Atticus"), he denounced the Bank as a money monopoly, as interfering in politics, as a subsidizer of the press to gain support, as guilty of oppression, extortion, and fraud, and as being largely foreign-owned. In fact, he reflected the views current in all agricultural sections about centralized banking. He pointed out with great vigor the faults of the Bank, but was totally unable to see any of its virtues. He retired from Congress at the end of the session in March 1835. Personally he was an agreeable and popular man and was regarded by his contemporaries as a jurist and statesman of ability. He was deeply interested in the University of Georgia, serving for many years as trustee and secretary of the board. Late in life he became a member of the Methodist Church. In 1838 he was stricken with paralysis and died the following year.

[S. F. Miller, *Bench and Bar of Ga.* (1858), contains a reliable, though brief account of Clayton's life and reproduces numerous extracts from his speeches, judicial decisions, political pamphlets, and writings of literary character. Wilson Lumpkin, *Removal of the Cherokee Indians* (Savannah, 1907), treats fully Clayton's connection with that interesting phase of Georgia history. For an account of his activities in relation to the tariff and Bank, see U. B. Phillips, "Ga. and States Rights" in *Ann. Report Am. Hist. Asso. for 1901* (1902), vol. II.]   R. P. B.

CLAYTON, JOHN (c. 1685–Dec. 15, 1773), botanist, was born in Fulham, England, the son of John Clayton, appointed attorney-general for Virginia by the Crown. His uncle was Gen. Jasper Clayton, governor of Gibraltar, and his grandfather, Sir John Clayton, a barrister of London belonging to a Yorkshire family. These points are important in establishing the identity of the botanist, who has been confused with Rev. John Clayton, the rector of Crofton Church, Wakefield, Yorkshire. The latter also went to Virginia, and communicated to the Royal Society of London papers relating to the medical botany and the ethnology of that colony, but he left Virginia in 1686, nineteen years before John Clayton the botanist arrived.

Soon after his coming to Virginia in 1705, John Clayton was appointed assistant to the clerk of Gloster (now Gloucester) County, though he lived in what is now Mathews County, on the Piankatank River, at an estate called "Windsor." Later, he became first clerk of the county, a position he held until his death. It is said that he planted a fine botanical garden. He was in correspondence with Gronovius, Linnæus, Alexander Garden, and, probably, with Peter Kalm and Peter Collinson, and sent seeds and plants to John Bartram and others, and was constantly collecting Virginia plants. After many delays the results of his work were embodied in the *Flora Virginica* by John Frederick Gronovius. Because Clayton's herbarium specimens formed the basis of this work it is often asserted that it should be called Clayton's *Flora Virginica,* but the final identification of the specimens, the science and system of the book, and the Latinity, were largely the work of Gronovius. Nevertheless Gronovius's *Flora Virginica* may be said to be also Clayton's masterpiece. It was printed by C. Haak at Leyden, the first part appearing in 1739; the second not until 1743. In that same year there was a second imprint issued, which explains why some copies

of the first part bear the date 1743. A second revised edition, edited by the elder Gronovius and put through the press by Laurans Theodore Gronovius, appeared in 1762, and represented Clayton's more mature work. This edition is important as appearing after the 1753 edition of Linnæus's *Species Plantarum,* which is taken as the dividing line between medieval and modern botany. According to the rules of modern botanical nomenclature the first edition of the *Flora Virginica* is of merely historical interest, but the second edition takes rank as true, modern systematic work. It contains a map of Clayton's travels which shows that he was seldom north of the Rappahannock or south of the James, and that his knowledge of the mountains did not extend beyond the Blue Ridge. He was thorough, however, in his exploration of the middle Tidewater districts, and recent botanical work shows that as a field botanist he was more astute than has been realized. In the last year of his life, though of advanced age, he made his most extended trip, as far as Orange County.

Two volumes by Clayton's own hand, with many drawings and a fine supporting herbarium, were left by him at his death, but were destroyed during the British raids in Virginia in the last part of the Revolution. His letter-book, containing his copies of letters to scientists, was known to be in the possession of his descendants until about thirty years ago. All efforts by Virginia antiquarians to trace it since have failed. Most of the herbarium specimens which formed the basis of the *Flora Virginica* and which were of great importance to Linnæus are now in the National Herbarium in England.

Concerning Clayton's personal life not much has been established. His public duties were discharged faithfully and Gov. Page of Virginia in a letter to B. S. Barton (Jan. 18, 1808) said Clayton was "a strict but not ostentatious observor of the practices of the church of England." Though parsimonious, he would pay money for a new species of plant brought to him. He was personally known to Benjamin Franklin and Thomas Jefferson, and highly esteemed by them.

[Confusion of Clayton the botanist with his distant relative Clayton the cleric appears in the notice in the *Dict. of Nat. Biog.* (James Britten in *Jour. of Botany,* XLVII, 1909, 297–301). R. M. Slaughter's account in H. A. Kelly and W. L. Burrage, *Am. Medic. Biogs.* (1920) is not free from some of this confusion, and J. M. Toner's *Contributions to the Annals of Medic. Educ. in the U. S. Before and During the War of Independence* (1874) cannot be accepted as wholly authoritative. The best general account is still B. S. Barton, "Memorandums of the Life and Writings of Mr. John Clayton the celebrated Botanist of Va." in *Phila. Medic. and Physical Jour.,* II (1806), 139–45, which was prepared with the assistance of notes by Galt, Jefferson, Madison, and Page. Clayton's letters are found only in scattered collections. E. G. Swem, who has rendered assistance in the preparation of this notice, published in the *Wm. and Mary Quart.*, Oct. 1924, the only letter of Clayton to Linnæus in the collection of the Linnæan Society of London, and in the same periodical for Oct. 1926, printed one letter never before made public.]   D. C. P.

CLAYTON, JOHN MIDDLETON (July 24, 1796–Nov. 9, 1856), farmer, lawyer, statesman, was a descendant of the Quaker, Joshua Clayton, who accompanied William Penn to America. From his mother, Sarah Middleton of Annapolis, Md., he derived conversational fluency and charm; from his father, James Clayton of Delaware, an interest in law and politics. His birthplace was the little village of Dagsborough, Sussex County, Del., but when he was still an infant the family removed to Milford, Kent County, where James Clayton engaged in the milling and tanning business as well as in farming. At home, John was well grounded in the Bible and Shakespeare, and in academies at Berlin, Md., and Lewes and Milford, Del., he secured his early schooling and preparation for Yale College, from which he graduated in 1815 with the highest honors. Following this, he spent some time in the law office of his cousin, Thomas Clayton [*q.v.*], after which he attended the famous law school at Litchfield, Conn., for almost two years. At Georgetown, Del., in November 1819 he was admitted to the bar, and soon began practise in Dover. In 1822 he married Sarah Ann, daughter of James Fisher, a physician of Kent, Del.

Clayton's superior training, remarkable memory, great eloquence, charming manners, and rare skill as a cross-examiner, won him a reputation unrivaled in Delaware. He was counsel in more than a thousand cases, some of them nationally famous. He reached his majority in the politically dull "era of good feeling," and at first took little interest in partisan politics, though, following family tradition, he allied himself with the Federalist group. He early developed, however, a deep love for his native Delaware, and served it while still very young in various state offices. The bitter Adams-Jackson strife made him an ardent partisan. A Whig, he remained loyal to the party until it went to pieces, when he joined the embryonic Republican group. His services to the local Whigs in 1828 won him a seat in the national Senate. Though the youngest member of that body, he at once became very active, and soon established his reputation as an orator, his first notable speech, made in 1830, being in favor of the Foote Resolution. The next year he began an investigation of the abuses in the Post Office Department, which resulted in reform and reorganization. He had strong affection for the Union, and supported Jackson in the nullification controversy; but opposed the President's bank policy, and voted for the resolution of censure against the removal of the deposits. An intense advocate of protection, he aided Henry Clay greatly in putting through the tariff bill of 1833. As chairman of the Senate Judiciary Committee, he facilitated the settlement of the boundary dispute between Michigan and Ohio, which left the Upper Peninsula to the former. In 1834 he was reëlected to the Senate, but, feeling that his family needed him, he resigned in 1836 and became chief justice of Delaware. After two and a half years he left the state bench to campaign for William Henry Harrison, and for some time following Harrison's election he devoted most of his energies to scientific farming near New Castle, and became noted as an agriculturalist far beyond the borders of Delaware.

Though rather disgusted with the political trend, in 1845 Clayton again accepted election to the federal Senate, where he favored peace with England and Mexico, but supported the Mexican War after it had begun. From his position in the Senate he took an active interest in the presidential election of 1848. Though long a close friend of Henry Clay, he felt that the latter had no chance of election, and so gave his support to Gen. Zachary Taylor. His reward was the portfolio of the State Department. But the defection brought a permanent coolness between himself and Clay, and thereafter his closest political friend and adviser was Gov. John J. Crittenden of Kentucky. He was also in close confidential relations with Richard Montgomery Bird, editor of the Philadelphia daily, the *North American*. In this paper, Clayton had a large financial interest, and from it he usually received hearty support for his policies.

When he joined Taylor's cabinet, Clayton was one of the most attractive personalities in the Capital. He was more than six feet tall and well-built, with good features, dominated by large, friendly gray eyes shaded by dark, bushy brows, but his hair, worn brushed back in pompadour style, was prematurely white. In conversation he was brilliant; in manners, polished. He was unusually kind-hearted and unselfish; but was known at times to use questionable methods to gain political ends; and was somewhat wanting in tact and patience, as well as in firmness and stability of character.

As secretary of state, it was his policy to pay strict regard to international obligations, as well as to the rights of his own country, and to promote assiduously American commerce. He, accordingly, did his utmost to prevent the departure of filibustering expeditions for Cuba, but when a group of alleged filibusters were unjustifiably seized on the Mexican coast by a Spanish vessel, he vigorously contended for and ultimately secured their release. Nevertheless, due largely to the influence of Taylor, he made upon Portugal extreme demands for indemnity for the destruction of American vessels, refused arbitration, and presented what was virtually an ultimatum of war; and with France the United States was brought to the very brink of conflict over the merest trifle, by the Secretary's undiplomatic language and the arbitrary stand of the President.

Clayton's commercial plans were more successful and made for national progress and continental well-being. The program prepared at his instruction for opening up trade relations with the Orient was used a few years later by Perry in his expedition to Japan. With England, he made the famous Clayton-Bulwer Treaty, which was doubtless his most important work. The agreement, which perhaps averted war with England, provided for a neutralized international canal across Central America, and contained pledges that ultimately forced Great Britain to withdraw from large tracts of territory which, in plain violation of the rights of the Central-American nations, it had been occupying upon the Isthmus.

Taylor died, however, before the treaty could be put into effect, and Clayton gave up his office, July 22, 1850, and retired to his farm. But when in 1852 Cass, Douglas, and others began to attack the treaty which he had made with Bulwer, Clayton again returned to the Senate, and ably defended the document. He now worked with great effort, for his health was rapidly declining from kidney disease, and he realized that his career was drawing to a close. The end came in Dover, at the home of his niece, and he was buried beside his wife and sons in the cemetery of the local Presbyterian Church.

[The chief printed sources for the biography of Clayton are the state documents of Delaware, the *Cong. Record, Cong. Globe, British Parliamentary Papers,* and U. S. documents, but a number of important letters appear in C. Coleman's *Life of John J. Crittenden* (1871), and in the Appendix to John Bigelow's *Breaches of Anglo-American Treaties* (1917). The most important sources are, however, still in manuscript form, in the British and American archives, in the Papers of Clayton himself, and in those of John J. Crittenden, Geo. P. Fisher, and Wm. Larned Marcy, in the Lib. of Cong., and those of Richard Montgomery Bird, in the Lib. of the Univ. of Pa. No satisfactory biography of Clayton exists. The most inclusive life, Jos. P. Comegys's *Memoir of John Middleton Clayton* (1882) is frankly eulogistic and contains many errors of fact. The brief sketches by Wm. Elbert Wright in W. D. Lewis, *Great Am. Lawyers* (1907), vol. III, and by J. T. Scharf, in his *Hist. of Del.* (1888), vol. I, are based upon Comegys's work. The most comprehensive account of Clayton's career as secretary of state is Mary W. Williams's "John M. Clayton" in vol. VI of *Am. Secretaries of State and Their Diplomacy* (1928).]   M. W. W.

CLAYTON, JOSHUA, (Dec. 20, 1744–Aug. 11, 1798), physician, governor of Delaware, was a descendant of Joshua Clayton who accompanied William Penn on one of his visits to this country (H. F. Hepburn, *The Clayton Family*, 1904, and T. J. Clayton, *Rambles and Reflections at Home and Abroad*, 1893, p. 399). The younger Joshua's father, James Clayton, settled with his wife Grace in Cecil County, Maryland, where their son was born. At one time the father was engaged in milling in Kent County, Del. (H. C. Conrad, *History of the State of Delaware*, 1908, III, 826, 903). The parents early destined their son for medicine, but where he received his degree of M.D. is not known. He was a student at the University of Pennsylvania, however, from 1757 to 1762 (*A Biographical Catalogue of the Matriculates of College*, 1894). About this time, he married Rachael McCleary, an adopted daughter of Richard Bassett [*q.v.*], former governor of Delaware. He practised his profession quietly until he was interrupted by the Revolution. His Quaker antecedents did not hinder him from taking part in the war and on Jan. 6, 1776, he was elected second major of Bohemia Battalion, a body of militia recruited from the inhabitants of Bohemia Manor where he was then living. The battalion was later incorporated into the Continental Army, Clayton being commissioned colonel by Washington and placed on his staff. His active participation in the war seems to have been limited to the battle of Brandywine (George Johnston, *History of Cecil County, Maryland*, 1881, pp. 323, 326). After the war his career as a statesman began with his election to the Delaware House of Assembly in 1785 and again in 1787. A year previous to the last election he had been made state treasurer. His rise to position was rapid, for on May 30, 1789, he was elected president of Delaware, to succeed Thomas Collins, deceased. He held office in this capacity until 1792, when a new constitution was adopted and the title of president changed to governor. Under this new constitution Clayton sought a second term and in the fall of 1792 was victorious by a majority of 307 over his opponent, Thomas Montgomery. At the end of his second term, Jan. 13, 1796, he resumed his practise at Bohemia Manor in Delaware (Conrad, *op. cit.*, p. 826). A great part of his influence must have resulted from his immense land holdings, some of which were acquired as early as 1791. It is estimated that he and Richard Bassett, his wife's foster father, owned about 20,000 acres in Bohemia Manor (Johnston, *op. cit.*, pp. 184–85; Hepburn, *op. cit.*, p. 26). Clayton was again pressed into public service with his election as United States senator on Jan. 19, 1798. While in Philadelphia in the summer of that year he was in frequent consultation with Dr. Rush and other physicians on the yellow-fever epidemic then prevalent. He contracted the disease and retired at once to his estate, where he died (Conrad, p. 827). Medical men may know of him principally for his discovery of a substitute for Peruvian Bark which became very scarce during the Revolution. This consisted of a mixture of poplar bark, the bark of dogwood root, and the bark of white oak, and was said to be efficacious as a remedy for gangrene and mortifications (James Thacher, *American Medical Biography*, 1828, I, 225–26).

[In addition to references given above see sketch by Douglas F. Duval in H. A. Kelly and W. L. Burrage, *Am. Medic. Biogs.* (1920), and *Biog. Dir. Am. Cong.* (1928).]
                                            C. W. G.

CLAYTON, POWELL (Aug. 7, 1833–Aug. 25, 1914), politician, governor of Arkansas, was born in Bethel County, Pa., a son of John and Ann (Clark) Clayton. He was educated in the common schools, the Partridge Military Academy at Bristol, Pa., and in an engineering school in Wilmington, Del. In 1855 he moved to Kansas where he engaged in civil engineering, becoming city engineer of Leavenworth in 1859. When the Civil War began, he volunteered, serving first as captain of the 1st Kansas Infantry (May 29, 1861), later as colonel of the 5th Kansas Cavalry. He served in Missouri and Arkansas and was assigned to the command of Pine Bluff after the capture of Little Rock (1863) and repulsed an attack there by Gen. Marmaduke. On Aug. 1, 1864, he was made brigadier-general and was mustered out, Aug. 24, 1865. As a military officer he was fairly capable, but showed no remarkable abilities. On retiring from the army, he bought a plantation near Pine Bluff and became a cotton planter. He was married, on Dec. 14, 1865, to Adaline McGraw of Helena. When the new constitution was drawn up by the convention under the congressional plan of Reconstruction (1868), he campaigned for its adoption and was elected governor as a Republican for a term of four years. Upon his election, he became Republican boss of the state, a position which he virtually held for the rest of his active life. He became a member of the Republican National Committee in 1872 and

served, with the exception of two years, until his death.

Clayton was an able man, neither the worst nor the best of the carpet-bag governors. Among his acts which were severely criticized was the institution of martial law under which he used negro militia to hunt down the Ku Klux Klan at a cost of $330,675, but he claimed that he stamped out the order. He was also accused of corrupt management of the bond issues authorized in aid of railroads, and of aiding in election frauds. On the last two counts he was impeached by the Arkansas House in 1871, but the Senate was friendly and the prosecution was dropped. On Jan. 10, 1871, he was elected to the United States Senate, but he refused to resign the governorship because he did not want J. M. Johnson, the lieutenant-governor, to succeed him. A way out was found by "persuading" R. J. T. White to resign as secretary of state and appointing Johnson to this more lucrative position. Soon afterward White received $5,000 in money and $25,000 worth of railroad bonds as compensation for giving up his position. Who supplied the funds was never known, but Clayton sent White the certificate of deposit. Clayton was again elected Senator and now accepted, resigning the governorship in March 1871. Many Democrats supported his election to get him out of the governor's chair. Soon after he reached Washington, he was indicted. A majority of a Senate investigating committee gave him a qualified exoneration, and the prosecution was dropped (*Congressional Record*, 43 Cong., Spec. Sess. of the Senate, vol. I, 169–182). When the Democrats returned to power in 1874, the bonded debt of the state was $10,618,166, of which $6,900,000 had been issued in aid of railroads under the law passed in Clayton's administration and indorsed at the polls by a very large majority. The complaint was, not against the loaning of the credit of the state, but against the corruption connected with it. Clayton's defense was that 315 miles of railroad had been built. It was never proved that he got any of the bonds. In the Brooks-Baxter "War" he at first supported Baxter, but later turned to Brooks and did all in his power to prevent President Grant from recognizing the Baxter government. In Congress he was not a prominent leader, neither was he an inconspicuous member. He introduced a bill to repeal the tax on state bank-notes (1874) and voted for Sumner's civil rights bill. Returning to Arkansas in 1877, he established his residence in Little Rock, but moved in 1882 to Eureka Springs, where he constructed and became the manager of the Eureka Springs Railway, president of the Crescent Hotel Company, and a director in the Missouri & North Arkansas Railroad. In 1884 he was nominated by the Republican National Committee as temporary chairman of the National Republican Convention, but was defeated by John R. Lynch, colored, of Mississippi, who was put up by Lodge, Roosevelt, and other supporters of Edmunds. In 1897 he was appointed ambassador to Mexico and held the position until 1905. About 1912 he moved to Washington, D. C., and resided there until his death.

[See the *Official Records* (*Army*) for Clayton's military career. T. S. Staples's *Reconstruction in Ark.* (1923) gives the most scholarly account of his administration. His own defense is contained in his book, *The Aftermath of the Civil War in Ark.* (1915). See also *Who's Who in America*, 1912–13; D. Y. Thomas, *Ark. in War and Reconstruction* (1926); *Foreign Relations U. S.*, 1897–1905.]   D.Y.T.

CLAYTON, THOMAS (July 1777–Aug. 21, 1854), jurist, was the son of Joshua Clayton [*q.v.*]. Although his father was in 1777 a resident of Delaware, Thomas was born at Massey's Cross Roads, Md., to which place his mother, Rachael (McCleary) Clayton, had been removed to avoid the excitement occasioned by the march of the British across Delaware. Thomas was given a classical education at Newark Academy, and then three years' legal instruction at Dover, Del., after which he was admitted to the bar. After completing his education he married Jeanette Macomb, and practised his profession for about eight years, building up a considerable reputation. The first recognition of his talents was an appointment to the secretaryship of state of Delaware under Gov. Truitt. Three years later he was made attorney-general. In 1814 he entered the field of national politics as representative in Congress from Delaware, but he was defeated at the next election, having placed himself in the field as an Independent. An examination of the debates reveals not only his character but the probable reasons for his defeat. Clayton said that although "he would always regard the wishes of his constituents with the highest respect, when he had once made up his mind on any question of great national policy, no consideration would induce him to surrender his conscience to their keeping" (*Annals of Congress*, 14 Cong., 2 Sess., pp. 648–49). In 1824, however, he was elected by a Federalist legislature to the United States Senate to fill the unexpired term of Caesar Rodney. In 1828 he was appointed chief justice of the court of common pleas. In 1832, after his office had been abolished by constitutional amendment, he was nominated chief justice of Delaware under exceptional circumstances. The constitution required that the su-

preme court be composed of three judges, one from each county in the state. With Clayton's nomination, Kent County, his residence, had two representatives and the county of New Castle was unrepresented. It was therefore necessary to nominate a judge from New Castle in order to abide by the constitutional provision. This added a fourth and superfluous judge to the supreme court. Many interesting stories are told of Clayton's impartiality, sternness, and uprightness. His decisions bespeak a thorough knowledge of the law and a power of keen analysis in seizing upon the fundamental principles. In January 1837 he was chosen to fill the unexpired term of his cousin, Senator John M. Clayton [*q.v.*]. His senatorial service continued until 1847. The record of his remarks indicates that he was a moderate but independent Whig. Pennsylvania iron manufactures received his solicitous support, for he at one time introduced a resolution stating that a duty of twenty per cent was not high enough (*Congressional Globe*, 27 Cong., 2 Sess., p. 281). When the Oregon question was discussed he declared for preparedness (*Ibid.*, 29 Cong., 1 Sess., p. 59). The close of this term marked the close of his public life. He retired to his home in New Castle where he remained until his death.

[Henry C. Conrad, *Hist. of Del.* (1908), pp. 961 ff; H. F. Hepburn, *Clayton Family* (1904), p. 27; *Del. Gazette* (Wilmington), Aug. 25, 1854; J. T. Scharf, *Hist. of Del.* (1888), I, 528 f.]   C.W.G.

CLEAVELAND, MOSES (Jan. 29, 1754–Nov. 16, 1806), pioneer, was born at Canterbury, Conn., the second son of Col. Aaron and Thankful (Paine) Cleaveland. He was descended from Moses Cleaveland who migrated from Yorkshire to Boston in 1635, and a few years later, in company with some companions, founded Woburn, Mass. Two uncles, the Rev. John Cleaveland and the Rev. Ebenezer Cleaveland, were expelled from Yale College in 1745 for having violated its laws and those of the Colony by attending "Separatist" meetings, but were later given their degrees. To Yale Moses was sent, graduating in 1777. In 1775, for about a month, he had held a commission as lieutenant in a group drawn "from sundry places to the relief of Boston in the Lexington Alarm." In January 1777, before his graduation from Yale, he was commissioned ensign in the 2nd Connecticut Continental Regiment. In the following fall he entered active service with Washington's army where he continued until 1781. In December 1777, he was commissioned lieutenant and in August 1799, captain in the corps of sappers and miners. After the Revolution he maintained his interest in military affairs by membership in the Connecticut Society of the Cincinnati and in the Connecticut militia in which he rose to the rank of brigadier-general. In 1781 he entered upon the practise of law in Canterbury. From 1787 until his death more than eighteen years later, he represented Canterbury in the General Assembly. He was also a member of the state convention (1788) that ratified the Federal Constitution. On Mar. 21, 1794, he was married to Esther Champion, daughter of Col. Henry Champion of Colchester, Conn.

With the return of prosperity, three or four years after the Revolution, projects for settlement of the West and for speculation in frontier land were numerous. Cleaveland took a conspicuous part in this movement. He held two shares in the Ohio Company which founded a settlement at Marietta on the Ohio River. It was, however, due to his part in the enterprise of the Connecticut Land Company that he was to link his name inseparably with the development of the West. In 1795, the Connecticut Land Company purchased about three million acres of Connecticut's Western Reserve, agreeing to pay $1,-200,000, interest to begin in two years, principal due in five years. Each purchaser gave bond with securities to meet his own obligation. Cleaveland was one of the thirty-six who formed the company. His share amounted to $32,600. He was chosen one of the seven directors, and superintendent of the agents and men sent to survey and settle the land. Accordingly, in June 1796, he led out to the south shore of Lake Erie a party of fifty-two persons, surveyors, commissary, physician, boatmen, laborers, and settlers, two of whom were women. The mouth of the Cuyahoga River was selected for the principal settlement and a plan for a city prepared and surveyed. The surveyors named it Cleaveland. At the close of the summer, Gen. Cleaveland's party returned to Connecticut, reporting that three inhabitants had been left in Cleaveland, a similar group at Conneaut, and that progress had been made with the survey of the company's lands. Cleaveland never returned to the Western Reserve. Until his death ten years later, his life was devoted to his legal practise, his lands, and an ever active interest in political and military affairs. In appearance he was of medium height, thick-set, muscular. His complexion was so swarthy that the Indians were inclined to regard him as one of their own race. His companions on the western expedition called him Paqua, the name of an Indian chief. His qualities of leadership are evident in his expedition to the West, and in his public life in Connecticut. If some of the stories about him are to be credited, he possessed a keen sense of humor.

[The chief sources have been compiled and published in part by Chas. Whittlesey in *Early Hist. of Cleveland* (1867), pp. 250–52, *passim,* and more fully by Elbert J. Benton in *The Conn. Land Company and Accompanying Papers* (1916). H. P. Johnston, ed., *Record of Conn. Men in the Military and Naval Service During the War of the Revolution* (1889) ; F. B. Dexter, *Biog. Sketches Grads. Yale Coll.,* III (1903), 664–66, give material not otherwise accessible. See also Edmund J. and Horace G. Cleveland, *Geneal. Cleveland and Cleaveland Families* (1899). Cleaveland published *Oration Commemorative of the Life and Death of Gen. Geo. Washington* (1800). Unfortunately large portions of his Journal and other papers known to have existed have been lost.]   E.J.B.

CLEAVELAND, PARKER (Jan. 15, 1780–Oct. 15, 1858), scientist, was born in Byfield, Essex County, Mass., of ancestry noted for adherence to old Puritan principles and discipline. His grandfather, Rev. John Cleaveland, and his great-uncle, Ebenezer Cleaveland, were expelled from Yale in 1745 for having attended religious services conducted by a lay exhorter of the Whitefield stamp, but they were later given their degrees. His father, also Parker Cleaveland, was a physician in Byfield, who achieved only small success in medicine but more in politics, having been the representative of the town of Rowley in the Massachusetts convention of 1780; his mother was Elizabeth Jackman. He attended Dummer Academy, situated about two and a half miles from his home, and in 1795, before he was sixteen years old, entered Harvard. After being graduated in 1799 he taught school in Haverill, Mass., for a few months, and then in York, Me., for three years. During this time he read law, but in 1803 decided to study for the ministry. After a few months of theological reading, he received an offer from Harvard College of a tutorship in mathematics and natural philosophy. This he accepted with alacrity, and remained at Harvard until 1805, when he was chosen professor of mathematics and natural philosophy in Bowdoin College, an institution opened three years before in Brunswick, Me. This position he held until his death.

He shortly undertook to give instruction in chemistry, and in 1807, as a result of some questions asked him by local lumbermen, he became interested in mineralogy. His *Elementary Treatise on Mineralogy and Geology,* published in 1816, was the first American work upon the subject, and attained a considerable degree of popularity in this country and abroad. This was due to the citation of American localities for minerals not previously given in European works, and to the author's having followed the model of Brongniary in classifying minerals according to chemical composition rather than according to crystal form. A second edition was published in 1822, but since no later revision was made, the book, which for a time had been the leading American authority, was soon supplanted. Upon the establishment of the Medical School of Maine under the administration of Bowdoin College in 1820, Cleaveland began to give instruction in materia medica in that institution, and at the same time to attend to much of its administrative work. The mineral cleavelandite, a variety of the feldspar albite, discovered by Brooke at Chesterfield, Mass., in 1823, was named after him (*Annals of Philosophy,* London, V, 381, May 1823). In 1827 he published a pamphlet, *Agricultural Queries,* and between 1807 and 1859 he kept a record of his meteorological observations which, reduced and discussed by Charles Schott, were published in Vol. XVI of the *Smithsonian Contributions to Knowledge* (1870).

Cleaveland was an example of that type of college teacher, of pronounced personality, not without idiosyncrasies, which was more common then than it is to-day. The sonnet by Longfellow beginning "Among the many lives that I have known," written in 1875, refers to him (*Complete Poetical Works,* Cambridge Edition, p. 319).

[The chief source is an address delivered by Leonard Woods, president of Bowdoin College, and published in the *Me. Hist. Soc. Colls.,* VI (1859), 381. Shorter accounts, drawn largely from the above, are to be found in Nehemiah Cleaveland and Alpheus S. Packard, *Hist. of Bowdoin Coll.* (1882), p. 126, and in L. C. Hatch, *Hist of Bowdoin Coll.* (1927).]   M. P. C.

CLEBURNE, PATRICK RONAYNE (Mar. 17, 1828–Nov. 30, 1864), Confederate soldier, was born in the county of Cork, Ireland, son of Joseph Cleburne, physician and farmer. On the side of his mother, Mary Ann Ronayne, he was alleged to be descended from Maurice Ronayne who helped to wring from Henry IV greater liberties in 1406. Young Patrick was instructed by tutors and in a private school and at the age of eighteen apprenticed himself to a druggist to learn the trade. Because of his deficiencies in Greek, Latin, and French he failed to pass the examination set for him in the Apothecaries' Hall, Trinity College, Dublin. This proved a great humiliation, and Cleburne decided to hide himself by enlisting in the 41st Regiment of Infantry. After three years of service he obtained enough cash from his father's estate to purchase his discharge and started for America, accompanied by a sister and a half-brother. He landed at New Orleans in 1849 and went to Cincinnati, where he became a druggist's clerk. After six months he moved to Helena, Ark., to a similar position. and two years later he became a part-

ner. Here he found much time for study, conversation, and debate in association with congenial friends, several of whom rose to distinction; indeed, this small town later furnished seven generals to the Confederate army. In 1855, during an epidemic of yellow fever, Cleburne remained to nurse the sick when others fled. In 1856 he was admitted to the bar and continued in practise until the Civil War, by which time he had acquired considerable property, chiefly in land. In politics he was at first an ardent Whig, but when that party gave place to the Know-Nothings, with their anti-foreign principles, he went over to the Democrats. In 1860 he helped to organize the Yell Rifles, a military company, and the following January went with it to Little Rock to seize the Federal arsenal. Gov. Rector had not planned to seize it just at that time, but now demanded its surrender to avoid further trouble. When Arkansas seceded, the Yell Rifles volunteered and Cleburne was soon made captain, then colonel of the 1st (later the 15th) Regiment of Infantry. Early in 1862 he was made a brigadier-general. At Shiloh he won commendation for his valor and skill. He was wounded while leading his men in a fierce charge at Richmond, Ky., but was nevertheless able to participate in the battle of Perryville. On Dec. 12, 1862, he was made a major-general and a few days later showed at Murfreesboro that the confidence of his superiors had not been misplaced. But his most distinguished service was during the fighting around Chattanooga; at Chickamauga his men captured and held a position which had resisted several other attacks, and at Missionary Ridge he repulsed Sherman. At Ringgold Gap, at his own peril, he saved Bragg's artillery and wagon train from capture by pursuing the enemy for which he received a vote of thanks from the Confederate Congress.

The Confederate ranks were now being more rapidly depleted than they could be filled. Laying aside his rank and appealing to his men, Cleburne succeeded in getting ninety per cent of them to reënlist, but others were not equally successful. Many foresaw disaster, unless something could be done. Because of this Cleburne wrote a carefully prepared paper, advising that the slaves be freed and used as soldiers. This was read to his fellow officers, some of whom approved, but Gen. Johnston, who had succeeded Bragg, declined to forward it to Richmond on the ground that the question was more political than military in character. Cleburne was greatly disappointed, but had no idea of sending it over the head of his superior. A fellow officer, however, thought that so incendiary a paper should be reported, asked for a copy, and sent it to Richmond. President Davis returned it with the indorsement that he approved and appreciated the patriotic motive of the signers—thirteen besides Cleburne had signed—but that he deemed it inexpedient to make the paper public and asked that it be suppressed. Had this paper never been written, Cleburne, instead of Hood, might have succeeded Johnston at Atlanta. His attention was called to the fact that it might stand in the way of advancement, but he persisted in putting what he believed to be the good of his adopted country above personal ambition. He followed Johnston on to Atlanta, fought with Hood in his three battles for that city, retreated with him to Tennessee, and died on the field at Franklin after his men had carried two lines of the enemy works, a useless sacrifice to Hood's ill-advised determination to fight whenever the opportunity presented itself. Lee compared him to "a meteor shooting from a clouded sky," and he was known as the "Stonewall Jackson of the West." While not as demonstratively religious as Jackson—he was a member of the Episcopal church—he was no less scrupulously honest. He is said to have paid out of his own pocket for chickens captured by his men from loyalists in Kentucky. He was modest, never pushing himself or his opinions forward. He was a strict disciplinarian, yet commanded the love and confidence of his men. He never married.

[*Official Records (Army)*, 1 ser.; C. A. Evans, ed., *Confed. Mil. Hist.*, X, 396–98; I. A. Buck, *Cleburne and His Command* (1908); D. Y. Thomas, *Ark. in War and Reconstruction, 1861–74* (1926), pp. 341–47.]

D.Y.T.

CLEMENS, JEREMIAH (Dec. 28, 1814– May 21, 1865), soldier, novelist, senator, came of a well-to-do cultured Southern family. He was born at Huntsville, Ala., the son of a Kentuckian, James Clemens, who had migrated to the Tennessee Valley in 1812 while it was yet a part of the Mississippi Territory, and had married a sister of Archie E. Mills. Clemens received excellent educational advantages for the times, studying at La Grange College, in the Valley, and being among the first students matriculated at the University of Alabama on its opening in 1831 at Tuscaloosa. But he seemed never to know just what he really wanted to be or to do. His first choice was the law, and, on account of family connections, he completed a law course in Transylvania College, Lexington, Ky., and returned to Alabama to practise his profession. Not yet twenty years old, he married, on Dec. 4, 1834, a Huntsville girl, Mary L. Read. Before he was well established at the bar, but not before his promise as a lawyer had been recognized, he

was appointed a federal district attorney, served for a short time in a volunteer company engaged against the Cherokees, and represented his county in the state legislature from 1839 to 1844, with the exception of one term. These circumstances seem to have shaped his life. Thereafter his law practise was seriously interfered with by his penchant for politics and his desire for a military career. When the war for Texan independence started, he left Alabama in 1842, in command of a company of volunteers, and won promotion to a lieutenant-colonelcy. A few years later, on the outbreak of the war with Mexico, he entered the regular army (Mar. 3, 1847) as major of the 13th United States Infantry, served effectively in Mexico as chief of the depot of supplies, and retired to civil life with the rank of colonel in 1848. On his return to Alabama, he aspired to high political honors, and, though he suffered a rebuff at the hands of the people of his own district when he attempted to displace an Alabama war-horse, Cobb, as representative in Washington, he was successful later in the same year (1849) in winning, as a Democrat, election to the seat in the United States Senate vacated by the death of Dixon H. Lewis, defeating Benjamin Fitzpatrick, an ex-governor and one of the strongest men in the state. In the Senate, Clemens earned a reputation as an able and eloquent debater, though his name was not connected with any legislation of national moment. He lost favor with the people of Alabama by his ardent support of the candidacy of Fillmore for the presidency in 1856 and did not again seek public office for several years. In the meanwhile, his interests changing, he turned eagerly to the writing of historical novels. In rapid succession he published: *Bernard Lile: an Historical Romance of the Texan Revolution and the Mexican War* (1856); *Mustang Gray: a Romance* (1858); and *The Rivals: a Tale of the Times of Aaron Burr and Alexander Hamilton* (1860). The year of his death (1865), *Tobias Wilson: a Tale of the Great Rebellion,* appeared, and it was generally understood that in the last months of his life he was engaged in preparing a history of the war in northern Alabama, a book which was never completed. For a brief time during 1859 he lived in Memphis, where he edited the *Memphis Eagle and Enquirer,* with no great success. When he returned to Alabama, the people were seriously divided on the question of immediate secession or delay and cooperation with sister states of the South. Elected to the convention called to decide the question, Clemens, with Robert Jemison, Jr., assumed leadership of the cooperationists. At the organization of the convention he controlled 46 of the

100 delegates, but as other states acted his strength ebbed, and, when the secession ordinance was put on its passage, he could muster only 39 in opposition. Having lost the fight, Clemens then signed the ordinance, and, because of his military prestige and in an effort to heal the breach in the state, he was appointed major-general of the "Republic of Alabama," a position in which he never rendered any active service. His Unionist tendencies brought him increasing unpopularity as the war progressed, and, an avowed Unionist in 1862, he moved to Philadelphia where he conducted a pamphlet campaign against his state and advocated the reëlection of Lincoln in 1864. He returned to Huntsville toward the close of the war and died a few weeks after peace was declared. He was a man of genuine ability, gifted, but erratic and over-ambitious, and at times his career was seriously affected by his dissipated habits.

[Details of Clemens's career are furnished by Willis Brewer, *Alabama* (1872); Wm. Garrett, *Reminiscences of Public Men in Ala.* (1872); T. M. Owen, *Hist. of Ala. and Dict. of Ala. Biog.*, vol. III (1921). His position on secession is found in Wm. R. Smith, *Hist. and Debates Convention People of Ala.* (1861). For his activities during the war see letter from Hon. Jeremiah Clemens issued in pamphlet form by the Union League of Phila. (1864). Descriptions of his appearance and personality are found in Virginia Clay-Clopton, *A Belle of the Fifties* (1905).]   T.H.J.

CLEMENS, SAMUEL LANGHORNE (Nov. 30, 1835–Apr. 21, 1910), humorist, novelist, better known by the pseudonym Mark Twain, was born in the village of Florida, Mo., the son of John Marshall Clemens and of Jane Lampton his wife. The father, of Virginia stock, had been married in Kentucky, had gone to Tennessee, and after various removes had settled in Missouri. Always full of visions of great wealth which he expected sooner or later to acquire through the rise in land values, he lived long enough to educate his son in such expectations, but died in 1847, leaving his wife and children little besides a tract of land in Tennessee which for many years kept them in a restless state of hope. The mother, a woman of more practical energy than her husband, was, however, a member of a family which had an earldom in one of its English branches and which not only included certain American claimants to the title but which also, in the person of a cousin (James Lampton), furnished the model for Col. Sellers of *The Gilded Age*. Samuel Clemens was thus brought up in circumstances which early gave direction to a form of optimism probably native to him, as it was native to many residents of that frontier. At the same time, these circumstances kept him during his youth in the slack casual society which was to serve as the background for most of his best writings, and they deprived him of the regular schooling which might have had important, and possibly unfortunate, effects upon his mind and style.

From 1839 till 1853 the boy lived at Hannibal, Mo., to which the father had followed his delusive star on his last move before his death. Hannibal was on the Mississippi and was larger than Florida so that it met the needs of a nature which, though not precocious, widened rapidly in experience. Some record of this boyhood, rearranged for the purposes of comedy, is to be found in *Tom Sawyer* and *Huckleberry Finn*, though these books have to be often corrected by reference to the facts before they can be looked upon as in any sense autobiographical. This being understood, it may be said that the Judge of the stories owes something to Mark Twain's father; Aunt Polly, to his mother; Sid Sawyer, to his brother Henry; the Negro Jim to a slave known as Uncle Dan'l; Huckleberry Finn, to Tom Blankenship; and Tom Sawyer, to "a combination of three boys whom I knew"— one of whom was the author himself. Many of the incidents of the books were taken over from actual happenings, and the setting offers a reasonably faithful description of Hannibal and the neighborhood. On the whole it was a boyhood marked by adventure, not too dangerous, and by unrestraint, not without touches of conscience and punctilio.

The death of the elder Clemens when his third son was only twelve years old forced the boy to leave school in order to earn a part of the small amount of money on which the widow and her children had to live. Apprenticed to a printer, he became expert at his trade, mastering therewith certain of the niceties of composition which many writers learn late, if ever. Printing led him to reading, and reading to writing, first for the newspaper which his elder brother Orion edited and published in Hannibal, and then for other papers elsewhere. More noteworthy was his turn through the world as a journeyman printer. During 1853 and 1854 he worked his way to St. Louis, New York, Philadelphia, and back to Keokuk, Iowa, where he was again employed by his brother, who had left Hannibal. By this time the youth's restlessness had become a habit which was, presumably, a sign that he needed some larger occupation. In 1856 he made plans to go to South America to seek his fortune collecting cocoa along the Amazon, paying part of his expenses by letters to a Keokuk weekly. He got only as far as Cincinnati and wrote only three instalments of *The Adven-*

tures of Thomas Jefferson Snodgrass, which was tiresome country journalism, quite without value. The next year, on the way to New Orleans by boat, he got himself apprenticed to a river pilot, and thus entered what has been called his university.

The resemblance of the Mississippi to a university lay in the fact that it compelled the young pilot to become erudite in all that concerned the course and behavior of the river, in the midst of actual events, under the pressure of serious responsibilities. Perhaps the degree of actuality and of responsibility in this training destroys the resemblance. At any rate, Mark Twain learned another craft which called for precision of knowledge. And beyond that, he became familiar with a world full of diversity and color, a world which was very nearly an epitome of the United States of the time, and which furnished him an epic theme when afterward he gave his version of it in *Life on the Mississippi.* But his year and a half of apprenticeship and his two years and a half as a licensed pilot brought him, at the time, apparently no closer to authorship. He was gathering material, not using it.

When the outbreak of the Civil War had closed the river, the former pilot was obliged to look for another occupation, and discovered another world of adventure. He joined a volunteer company of young enthusiasts who were not quite sure which side they meant to choose and who broke up as soon as the war took on professional aspects. By that time, Mark Twain, tired of military life, had found a semi-official post in civil life, as secretary to his brother Orion, who in turn was secretary to the territorial governor of Nevada. In 1861 the brothers set out from St. Louis, by boat and overland stage, for Carson City. *Roughing It* gives the classic account, not only of Mark Twain's Far Western experiences, again heightened for the sake of comedy, but of the new frontier to which the son of an older frontier was introduced. The young Clemens, finding neither duties nor salary attached to his position, became an ardent prospector but an unsuccessful miner, and then, in 1862, a reporter in Virginia City, with the pseudonym Mark Twain, a river term (meaning two fathoms deep) which had already been used by an obscure pilot on the Mississippi.

At last his true career had begun. Few writers have ever had so much experience of life with so little purpose to turn it into literature as the printer-pilot had had during his preparatory years. Even if there were no records to prove this, it would be clear from his early ventures into writing as a livelihood. Having no particular literary principles, he adapted himself to the modes of frontier journalism, wrote burlesques full of topical allusions, and played with hoaxes and such trivialities. The birth in him of a larger ambition came with the visit to Virginia City of Artemus Ward (Charles Farrar Browne, *q.v.*), already famous as a humorous lecturer. The Yankee encouraged the Westerner and made him believe that he too might find a hearing outside the narrow world which had hitherto been all he aimed at. This encouragement, as well as an absurd duel in which Mark Twain became involved, sent him in 1864 to California, where he again found work as a reporter and where he met Bret Harte [*q.v.*], already, however little known, a conscious man of letters. There, in 1865, was written the story of the *Jumping Frog,* which appeared in a newspaper in New York and which promptly ran through the newspapers of the entire country.

California, eager to be known for its native literature, clutched at this small success. Mark Twain was sent by a newspaper to the Sandwich Islands on a roving commission to write about whatever interested him. He did this so well that he greatly increased his personal reputation, to which he added, on his return, by delivering lectures which their Rocky Mountain audiences instantly declared to be as good as Artemus Ward's. Recognition, in those days and in that community, could not be fuller. On the crest of it, Mark Twain set out to make a journalistic tour around the world for another California newspaper, traveled east by way of the Isthmus, and in New York characteristically changed his plans. After publishing his first book, *The Celebrated Jumping Frog of Calaveras County, and Other Sketches* (1867), and giving a triumphant lecture at Cooper Union, he sailed on the *Quaker City* with a party of excursionists bound for the Mediterranean and the Holy Land. The reports which he sent back form the basis for the book which made him a national figure, *The Innocents Abroad* (1869).

Probably no other book in American literature has ever been more representative than *The Innocents* was of the age which produced it. The United States, having arrived at something like a settlement of its domestic affairs by a civil war, was turning once more to thoughts about the rest of the universe. The *Quaker City* excursion was a straw in the wind. Its members were not many of them the sort of Americans who had hitherto visited the Old World, but instead were plain citizens, little addicted to history and yet hungry, in the defiant American way, for the sight of ancient things. They were typical of a whole stratum of the American population which had been thrown up by the war to a level on which traveling was a possibility. Mark Twain, though a man of genius and frequently bored by his fellows on the voyage, was nevertheless very close to them, as he was to the public at home which read what he wrote about their adventures. He too, though now and then genuinely awed by the monuments of antiquity, was also defiantly American, disposed, if only to strengthen his self-confidence, to laugh at what he saw and to boast of the New World in comparison with the Old. This was a traditional habit of Americans, and the readers of his book greeted in his narrative a quality which they would have displayed themselves in the same situation. Nor did the fact that they themselves, displaying it, might have been merely peevish and dull, make them less willing to be delighted in a writer who was hilarious, surprising, and eloquent, with a vast if irregular comic force.

The Innocents Abroad at once brought its author a reputation and a fortune. Indirectly it brought him a wife. During the voyage he had become acquainted with a young man named Langdon who had with him a miniature of his sister Olivia. With the picture Mark Twain virtually fell in love, and on his return late in 1867 he completely fell in love with the original, to whom he was married in 1870 at her father's house in Elmira, N. Y. The effect of this marriage upon the career of Mark Twain has been much discussed. (See, particularly, *The Ordeal of Mark Twain*, 1920, by Van Wyck Brooks.) Without going too far into controverted details, it may be agreed that his marriage put an end to his Bohemian days, that it brought him into contact with a very conservative bourgeois society, that his great affection for his wife probably led him to consider her opinions more tenderly than they always deserved, and that several of his most striking works were not published until after her death. There is, however, little reason for claiming that he resented or hated the pressure which his marriage put upon him. Toward women he had the conventional attitude of his time. After a cheerful bachelorhood, without a single recorded love affair, he settled down as any other American Victorian might have done, accepted the supremacy of his wife in all that concerned his private existence, and proceeded to make, for his family, as large a use of his talents as he could. He was not by temperament a lone wolf prowling the forests of the intellect. He was a frontiersman who, having had his fill of the wilds, adapted himself gratefully to the comforts of civilization.

The civilization into which he settled did, however, greatly condition his work for the next two decades. All around this native Southerner, now living and prospering in the North, was the spectacle of a flushed, triumphant nation engaged in a tremendous exploitation of its natural resources. Mark Twain saw in his experience a resource to be exploited by his talents. His world wanted to hear about the Old South, which was just then a favorite subject with writers in both parts of the united country, and about the Far West, which likewise stirred the national imagination. Of these two subjects he had a wide knowledge. Moreover, he had an unusual range of talents. He could give lectures; he could write for newspapers and magazines; he could sum up what he had to say in books for larger and longer audiences. Out of each of these literary processes he could take a profit. His plans eventually ran to the manufacture of a type-setting machine which, he thought, would enable him to profit by everybody's printing. His inherited instinct for speculation was so fostered and stimulated by his environment that he could have directed it into other activities only if he had been sustained by a profound culture, which he was not, or guided by a ruthless critical code, which he did not have.

Having made a magnificent success with *The Innocents Abroad,* he proceeded in *Roughing It* (1872) to exploit another chapter of his experiences. This he followed with *The Gilded Age* (1873), written in collaboration with Charles Dudley Warner [*q.v.*], which was called A Tale of To-Day but which actually made not a little use of Mark Twain's recollections of Hannibal in the days of his own youth. *The Gilded Age,* however, touched upon contemporary life with a vigor of satire which did not reappear in its next important successor, *The Adventures of Tom Sawyer* (1876). Astringent critics have found in the turning away from satire, particularly in the turning to boyhood reminiscences, an evidence that the humorist had been intimidated by his conservative family and friends and had for that reason shirked his obligations to be drastic. The question is one about which debate can go on as long as Mark Twain continues to be an issue with critics. He himself would pretty certainly have been surprised if anybody at the time had called his change of subject-matter a change of front. The impulse to satirize was only a part of his mental constitution, so far as he was then aware.

His theological, political, economic, and social opinions were at best rough-and-ready, the spontaneous radicalism of the frontier, always susceptible to influence by the more intricate conditions of a settled society, because not grounded in any thoroughgoing set of principles. Nor were Mark Twain's opinions, on any subject, all that he had to work with. There was also an immense delight in life in general, an omnivorous relish for all the phases of comedy, a tenderness too quick to be invariably well-judged, and an eager disposition to please his hearers and readers as well as he pleased himself with the exercise of his robust art. His comic energy, while his powers were at their height, was his nature rather than his purpose or his weapon.

To say, as it may be said, that his comic energy remained at its height for the twenty years between *The Innocents Abroad* and *A Connecticut Yankee in King Arthur's Court* (1889) is not to insist that he was by any means always at his best during that period. He was an uneven writer, who poured out many pages as they came and had later to decide, or to have it decided for him, whether they deserved to be kept and published, and how much they needed to be edited. Besides his wife there was also William Dean Howells [*q.v.*] to restrain him. If there was about this pair of critics a good deal that must have tended to keep Mark Twain's genius within decorous bounds, it is likewise true that he wrote with a violence which frequently drove him into burlesque so fantastic as to be dull. Until the unpublished manuscripts have been exhumed and studied, whatever loss there may have been can only be guessed at. But certain of the published writings, such as *Mark Twain's Sketches, New and Old* (1875) and similar collections are plainly inferior to *Roughing It, The Gilded Age, Tom Sawyer, A Tramp Abroad* (1880), and *The Adventures of Huckleberry Finn* (1884), which themselves are not of equal merit. To this period also belongs *1601* (written 1876), a pamphlet often surreptitiously printed for no particular reason except that its report of fireside conversation in the time of Queen Elizabeth contains numerous obscenities which are common in speech but not in print. Like most memorable writers, Mark Twain could not be forever writing classics. He had to write as he was driven to, and posterity has had to choose what to remember him by.

Without much question he touched his peak for these middle years in the first part of *Life on the Mississippi* and in *Huckleberry Finn*. They were both concerned with the river which ran as preëminently through his life as it runs through its own valley. The subject liberated him from the flat lands on either side. Remembering this section of his youth, he could work at his best resource with his best talent. It was his best resource because he knew more about the Mississippi than about anything else and because he had learned what he knew at a time when his perceptions and his memory were keenest. It was his best talent that he employed in both books, the talent for humorous autobiography. From the beginning of his career, whether in conversation, lecturing, or writing, he had always tended to this form. A traveler and a man of adventures, he told, or pretended to tell, what he had gone through. The aim of his method, of course, was not history but amusement. A joke told at his own expense was twice as good as a joke about somebody else. Events which he had, or claimed to have, witnessed could be made twice as interesting as events he had only heard about. Nor did he necessarily think of the narrator as strictly himself, that is, as Samuel Langhorne Clemens. The "I" of his lectures and books was Mark Twain, a personage who, however often identified with the man who used the pseudonym, was occasionally a mere fiction of the comedy. The narrator of Huckleberry Finn is, indeed, neither the actual Clemens nor the invented Mark Twain, but he also delivers himself in the first person, so that the devices and effects are much the same as in the avowedly autobiographical chapters of Mark Twain's history.

It should here be pointed out that the element of humorous autobiography in Mark Twain goes a long way toward accounting for his style. It was a style largely governed by his ear. While he need not be called first a speaker and second a writer, yet he had learned as a speaker to fit his rhythms and his diction, his tempo and his pauses, to listening audiences, and he appears always to have written to the sound of his own words. This everywhere colors his work, particularly when he becomes angry or eloquent. And it serves also to explain certain defects of taste which appear. Speaking, he could verge upon burlesque or rodomontade with comparative safety, able with his matchless voice and his smiling presence to make his hearers understand that he too saw the danger and that he enjoyed the perilous edge. Writing without this advantage, he too often took the same risks, with the consequence that a reader out of hearing and out of sight has only a part of the writer's endowment to judge by and so notices faults which naturally seem greater as each decade removes the reading public a little further from the idiom in which the lecturer spoke.

The custom of adapting himself so closely to his audiences might have had one fatal effect on him if he had been no more than the entertainer he was for a long time thought to be. Like Bret Harte, Mark Twain, introduced to the world as a curiosity from the Far West, encountered the temptation to go on indefinitely working a single vein at the insistence of his readers and his editors. But Mark Twain had too much energy and too wide a range of interests to fall into that familiar American trap. He refused to confine himself to the Mississippi cycle. *The Prince and the Pauper* has its scene laid in the England of the Elizabethan age. *A Tramp Abroad* returned to the method of *The Innocents Abroad* with an account of a walking trip which the author took with Joseph H. Twichell [*q.v.*] through the Black Forest and the Alps in 1878. *A Connecticut Yankee in King Arthur's Court* extended this method to an investigation of the chivalric past. The Yankee is only another figurehead used to vary the method of humorous autobiography. But the Yankee is close enough to Mark Twain to have his sympathy throughout his adventures. As *The Innocents* drew comedy from the presence of simple, rowdy Americans in remote places, so the Yankee drew comedy from the presence in an ancient world of an intensely modern, utilitarian, scientific American. Though scholars and romancers have been hurt by the liberties which Mark Twain took with the Arthurian legend, his comic estimate of chivalry is perhaps not so far from justice as it has been called. In any case, it is comedy, not history.

The Yankee marks the last appearance of the rough, sky-larking vigor of this middle period. Possibly the frontier humorist had been subdued by the various influences engaged in reducing him to something more easily measurable. Certainly he had won increasing consideration from sober critics, and he had received academic recognition in the form of an honorary degree of Master of Arts from Yale in 1888. But more possibly all that had happened was that Mark Twain, now several years past fifty, had begun to lose some of that energy which, hitherto, had furiously impelled him. What looks like the rise of his critical faculties may have been only the decline of his bodily powers. There can be no question that he had been under a heavy strain. His pretense of idleness in all the chapters of his autobiography was only humorous. After *The Innocents* he had lived for two years (1869–71) in Buffalo, writing for the Buffalo *Express,* a newspaper of which he was part owner, and for the *Galaxy,* a magazine published in New York. For the next seventeen years he had lived in Hartford, from which several of his books were issued by subscription. All that time he wrote constantly as well as violently. He poured out his strength in numerous lectures, traveling to Europe as well as through much of the United States. He accumulated personal relationships which drained off much of his energy. He experimented with the stage, on which the dramatic versions of his novels had some success. He invested heavily in various speculative schemes with no success at all. He became his own publisher by putting money into the firm of Charles L. Webster & Company, which prospered for a time but which was to fail disastrously in the end. It is no wonder that the teeth of life, gnawing at even so powerful a figure, gradually began to wear it away.

The decade of the nineties saw Mark Twain working with less steady nerves and therefore with less steady and unified an output than he had shown during the two previous decades. He returned to the saga of Col. Sellers in *The American Claimant* (1892), and to the saga of Tom Sawyer in *Tom Sawyer Abroad* (1894) and in *Tom Sawyer, Detective* (1896). In them, as in *The Tragedy of Pudd'nhead Wilson and the Comedy, Those Extraordinary Twins* (1894), there was that large element of the incredible or the melodramatic to which the humorist resorted when he was not working with his hands full of familiar material. Either he had exhausted the vein of boyhood reminiscence or else, as is more likely, he had lost the kind of interest in it which could fully arouse his imagination. Now a citizen of the whole world, he was a long way from the Mississippi, so far that he could imagine himself into feeling at home in medieval France, and could put profound emotions into his *Personal Recollections of Joan of Arc* (1896). In various respects, however, this book is evidence that there was a mood of youth still persisting in Mark Twain. Joan was the character in history who had first made him want to read. For years he had planned to write something about her, and had put more conscious research into the theme than he had ever put into any other. She was the supreme illustration of a type of woman which he had adored as a child and which as a young man on a rough frontier he had continued to reverence in the fashion of such frontiers in the United States. Nor was his attitude toward Joan as a virgin, his sort of secular Mariolatry, a mere obedience to a fashion. It was the quintessence of that tenderness which was as much a part of him as his early boisterousness and his later bitterness. And of course his tenderness was only intensified, in the *Personal Recollections,* by the contrast which he had to draw between Joan and the malign stupid forces which overwhelmed her.

Writing to Howells in 1899 Mark Twain said: "I have been reading the morning paper. I do it every morning—well knowing that I shall find in it the usual depravities and basenesses and hypocrisies and cruelties that make up civilization, and cause me to put in the rest of the day pleading for the damnation of the human race." The teeth of life had been gnawing cruelly for a decade. He had not only wasted a fortune in money on the type-setting machine before, after many years of hope, the venture was abandoned at the end of 1894, but he had wasted, what was more valuable to an artist, time and energy which could never be recovered. That same year had seen likewise the failure of his publishing house and his own bankruptcy. Determined to pay his debts, Mark Twain had promptly set off on a tour around the world, to lecture as he went, though by now he hated lecturing with all the distaste of a man who, at odds with the human race, was obliged to live by making it laugh. His daughter Susy had died during his absence. Besides these personal shocks there had been the philosophical disturbances likely to come to an American in Asia, in the spectacle of societies too old and disillusioned to have any confidence in the future, resigned to the endless repetition of a barren and meaningless process. Each chapter of *Following the Equator* (1897), the record of the tour, is opened with a maxim of Pudd'nhead Wilson, that village unbeliever whose unbelief, in this book as in the one devoted to him, embraces the universe. "Prosperity is the best protector of principle." "Let me make the superstitions of a nation, and I care not who makes its laws or its songs either." "Everything human is pathetic. The secret source of humor is not joy but sorrow. There is no humor in heaven." "Pity is for the living, envy is for the dead."

The year 1898, in which Mark Twain finished paying off his debts, was nevertheless the darkest year of his life, if his writings may be allowed to furnish the evidence. Then he wrote *The Man That Corrupted Hadleyburg* (published 1900), *What is Man?* (first printed, privately, 1906), and *The Mysterious Stranger* (not published till 1916). The first is a story exhibiting the effects of greed in a smug provincial town—a story which on the surface is specific enough but which manages, thanks to the inclusive contempt and pity with which it was written, to have the general bearings of allegory. The second is a kind of theological dialogue in which it is argued that the behavior of men is entirely without freedom of choice, each act like each decision following irresistibly from precedent circumstances, and all to be ascribed, evil and good alike, to whatever gods may have bungled their creation and have refused to correct or destroy it. The third brings a devil into human affairs, in sixteenth-century Austria, lets him comment upon the bad workmanship of the heedless gods, and through him prophesies the time when life shall have been bettered by passing into nothingness. As a work of art *The Man That Corrupted Hadleyburg* is the best of the three. *The Mysterious Stranger* is only a fragment, and *What is Man?* is by no means so novel or so troubling a discourse as Mark Twain thought it. In his dialectic he did not know how to go beyond such self-made skeptics as Paine and Ingersoll, just as, when in 1868 he wrote *Captain Stormfield's Visit to Heaven* (published 1909), he had carried his criticism of the idea of immortality no further than to a burlesque of the vulgar conceptions of heaven. But of course the dialectic of Mark Twain is less to be considered than the presence in him of this natural pessimism. It was the pessimism of a representative American who, without the aid of subtle philosophies, had drawn his doctrines from his observations. It is as typical of one mood of the United States as the standard optimism is of another.

If no one of Mark Twain's remaining years was apparently so dark as 1898, it is because after that midnight of his mind he grew in resignation, not despising mankind less but pitying it more. He continued to be a restless traveler, both in America and Europe, and he allowed himself now to comment freely upon numerous contemporary matters, often with a fury which must have been increased by his knowledge that the public found something humorous in the most serious things he had to say about even the Philippines, the Boxer indemnities, the Belgian rule in the Congo. The demand for his books was great, many of his short pieces were issued as separate volumes, and consequently he seemed to be even more active a writer than he was. His only full-length books written after 1900 were *Christian Science* (1907), his analysis of what he thought a menacing new cult, and *Is Shakespeare Dead?* (1909), an unimportant addition to the Baconian controversy

But he delivered many speeches on all sorts of occasions, and after 1906 he worked steadily at dictating his autobiography upon which was to be based the official life. The death of his wife in 1904 and of his daughter Jean in 1909 caused him a grief too great to be eased by any bitterness. He gradually let go of the world, which during his last days gave him as many honors as he could endure or would accept. What he most valued was perhaps the degree of Doctor of Literature conferred upon him by Oxford in 1907. His death, at his house "Stormfield," in Redding, Conn., caused a more universal regret than has ever followed the death of any other American man of letters.

This regret was accompanied by a revaluation of Mark Twain's work which has made the posthumous figure very different from the living figure of the humorist. Alive, he could never correct the first impression of him, that he was chiefly a fun-maker. Dead, he has come to be regarded, at least by one school of opinion, as a tragic character, a victim of a national misconception, an artist cheapened by an overpowering demand for cheap wares. Though his early writings are still read, nearly as much as ever, his later writings are held to be the truer expressions of his mind and art. The change is due in part to the books published after his death. *The Mysterious Stranger, What is Man? and Other Essays* (finally published, not merely printed, in 1917), *Mark Twain's Letters* (1917), *Mark Twain's Autobiography* (1924), with its Preface as from the Grave—all have served to reveal the inner life of rage and contempt, of dissent and disillusion, of despair and pity which he chose to cover up from most of the world during most of his career. Yet these documents by themselves would not have been enough without the evidence furnished in the authorized biography which, published in 1912, not only touched a high point in biographical writing but also raised an issue. A newer generation, engaged in a critical study of American culture, seized upon Mark Twain's life as proof of the claim that the United States seldom produces authentic genius and subdues or neglects it when the phenomenon occurs. The debate called a special attention to the posthumous books and continues to make them seem intrinsically more valuable than they perhaps are. In the long run they are almost certain to be fused, in the reputation of Mark Twain, with his life rather than with his completed work. They supply the undertones which, without them, might never have been detected in the earlier books, but which, no matter how much they may have been sup-

pressed, are actually there, and which make it easier to be sure that Mark Twain, despite the dissipation of his energies, belongs with the great humorists—even with the great humorists who have known, better than he did, how to direct their powers.

[The principal source of information about Mark Twain is the authorized *Mark Twain: A Biography* (1912, 3 vols.) by Albert Bigelow Paine, who condensed this material in *A Short Life of Mark Twain* (1920), and in *Mark Twain's Letters* (1917, 2 vols.) and in *Mark Twain's Autobiography* (1924, 2 vols.) printed the chief written sources. Further material is to be found in *Wm. Dean Howells: Life in Letters* (1928, 2 vols.), ed. by Mildred Howells. Full lists of Mark Twain's publications are given in the Paine *Biography* (III, 1674–84) and in *The Cambridge Hist. of Am. Lit.* (1921, IV, 635–39), the second giving also a list of biographical and critical works. Of these *My Mark Twain* (1910), by Wm. Dean Howells, and *The Ordeal of Mark Twain* (1920), by Van Wyck Brooks, are indispensable. See also Friedrich Schönemann, *Mark Twain als literarische Persönlichkeit* (Jena, 1925); F. W. Lorch, "Mark Twain in Iowa," in *Iowa Jour. of Hist. and Politics*, XXVII, 408–56 (1929).]

C. V–D.

CLEMENT, EDWARD HENRY (Apr. 19, 1843–Feb. 7, 1920), journalist, son of Cyrus and Rebecca Fiske (Shortridge) Clement, was born in Chelsea and died in Concord, Mass. His connection with the Civil War being limited to visits to a brother at the front in South Carolina, it was possible for him to be duly graduated from Tufts College in 1864. He had such great faith in the development of the negro under freedom that in 1865 he took up residence where he could observe that development at first hand, in Savannah. Journalism had fascinated him for many years, and the state of Georgia being at the moment under alien control, he was able to procure work with the *Savannah Morning News*. In 1867 when the ex-Confederates had to a degree come back into power, the editor regretfully sent the boy home,—the paper's clientele, he explained, would not countenance a reporter from Boston. Despair over the South was soon alleviated by a succession of journalistic enterprises which took Clement in 1867 to New York with the *Tribune,* in 1869 to Newark with the *Daily Advertiser,* and in 1873 to Elizabeth with the *Daily Journal.* In 1875, he returned to Boston as associate editor of the *Transcript,* and in that capacity, before becoming editor-in-chief in 1881, he acquired a lasting interest in dramatic and artistic criticism. His retirement in 1906 was not for the sake of inactivity. He followed sedulously the fortunes of various oppressed races; he took part in societies to prevent imperialism and vivisection, and to better the condition of Boston work horses; and, in addition to a play, *The Princess Matilda,* he wrote poetry and magazine articles on subjects ranging from the social ideals dominant on the planet Mars, to Boston journalism in the nineteenth century. To the day of his death he contributed to the *Transcript* a column called the "Listener," and in his old age he devoted himself fervently to painting,—especially to portraiture. He was radical to the extent of opposing the trusts and many aspects of organized religion, but in matters that touched more intimately upon his affections,—the integrity of the family, for instance, and the supremacy of Tennyson as a poet—he was conservative enough to hate Samuel Butler with a perfect hatred. The *Transcript* spoke of him at the time of his death as mild but determined, fluent and expository rather than forceful, an idealist, a typical example of the "Boston upbringing." He was married twice: in 1869, to Gertrude Pound of New York, who died in 1895; and in 1898 to Josephine Hill Russell of Boston.

[E. H. Clement, "Vinland," a poem in something like Old English meter, in H. S. Harsford, *Discovery of the Ancient City of Norumbega* (1889); "Warren of the West," *New England Mag.*, Oct. 1906; "Boston Journalism in the Nineteenth Century," *New England Mag.*, Nov. 1906–Sept. 1907; "At the Needle's Eye," sonnet, *Cosmopolitan*, Jan. 1908; *The Bull Run Rout* (1909); "The Martian Gospel," *N. Y. Nation*, June 27, 1907; *Who's Who in America*, 1920–21; Boston *Evening Transcript*, Feb. 9, 1920.]   J.D.W.

CLEMENTS, JUDSON CLAUDIUS (Feb. 12, 1846–June 18, 1917), congressman, judge, the son of Dr. Adam Clements and Mary (Park) Clements, was born on his father's farm in Walker County, in the extreme northwestern corner of Georgia. After attending the ordinary schools of the time and serving in the Confederate army (1864–65), he matriculated in the law school of Cumberland University at Lebanon, Tenn., in 1868. He was admitted to the bar in Georgia in 1869. Locating in La Fayette, Walker County, he there practised his profession until 1892. Between 1872 and 1876 he was a member of the Georgia legislature; was a state senator for one year, 1877; and from 1881 to 1891 represented his district in Congress. At the time of his election to Congress, he was president of the Rome & Northern Railway Company, and it was natural that in Congress his primary interest should be in transportation matters. He helped perfect the Interstate Commerce Act and was appointed by President Cleveland to membership on the Interstate Commerce Commission in 1892. Cleveland's successors reappointed him four times, so that he had twenty-five years' consecutive service in that important regulatory body. On Mar. 17, 1917, the officers and employees of the Commission celebrated the completion of Clements's quarter-century of service. The speeches made

by the chairman and others, and the numerous telegrams received by Clements, attest the value placed upon his work by those best fitted to judge it. Three months later he died in his seventy-first year. All witnesses agree that his official conduct was characterized by a high degree of strength, courage, fairness, and sagacity. In an obituary notice the Washington *Evening Star* bracketed him with Henry G. Turner and Charles F. Crisp, as the ablest men Georgia had sent to Congress since the Civil War, and said that "he had mastered as perhaps no other person the large, complicated and important question of railroad transportation." He was twice married: first, to Elizabeth Wardlaw, who died in 1875 (W. J Northen, *Men of Mark in Georgia*, vol. IV, 1908, pp. 14–20), and second, on Dec. 2, 1886, to Lizzie Dulaney of Louisville, Ky., by whom he had three daughters.

[The Interstate Commerce Commission has preserved a record of the services of Clements, as well as a check list of his more important speeches and writings. Among the records is a pamphlet entitled *Testimonial of the Officers and Employees of the Interstate Commerce Commission to Hon. Judson C. Clements upon the Completion of Twenty-five Years of Service with the Commission*. This publication contains the speeches referred to above. See *Who's Who in America*, 1916–17, and obituaries in *Atlanta Jour.* and *Evening Star* (Washington), June 18, 1917.]   R.P.B.

CLEMMER, MARY (May 6, 1839–Aug. 18, 1884), author, was born in Utica, N. Y. She was the daughter of Abraham Clemmer, a descendant of Alsatian Huguenots settled in Pennsylvania about 1685, and of Margaret (Kneale) Clemmer, born on the Isle of Man. During Mary Clemmer's girlhood, her father removed to Westfield, Mass., and she received her education at the Westfield Academy, an excellent school. Abraham Clemmer, with the temperament of a poet, had been obliged to enter business, in which he never attained success. Family poverty and rapidly-arriving younger brothers and sisters brought early responsibilities and shortened Mary Clemmer's childhood. These causes also had something to do with her marriage when she was only sixteen to a man much older than herself, the Rev. Daniel Ames, a Presbyterian minister, from whom she was divorced in 1874. She lived successively in Massachusetts, Minnesota, New York City, Harper's Ferry where she witnessed the entrance of the Confederate army in 1862 and was herself for a brief time a prisoner, and in Washington, where she worked in army hospitals.

Mary Clemmer's literary work began early, with a poem sent by her Westfield teacher to the *Springfield Republican* and there published. When barely twenty, she began contributions to newspapers, in her effort, successful from the start, to provide support for herself and her parents. While living in New York she became the friend of Alice Cary [*q.v.*], between whose character and her own there were many resemblances. From this friendship resulted the *Memorial of Alice and Phœbe Cary* (1873), a sympathetic and well-written work. Mary Clemmer always desired to write novels and felt that she was capable of writing better ones than she ever achieved. Her first novel, *Victoire* (1864), though crude and emotional, shows some ability in interpretation of character; her second, *Eirene; or a Woman's Right* (1871), introduces war scenes about Harper's Ferry; her third, *His Two Wives* (1874), diffuse and unconvincing, was often credited with being partly autobiographical, but without justification. When health began to fail, she was writing another novel, which was never finished. What was probably her best work took the form of letters to newspapers on topics of public interest. In 1866 she began contributions to the New York *Independent,* called "A Woman's Letters from Washington." These continued until within a few months of her death and furnished some of the material for her two books, *Outlines of Men, Women, and Things* (1873), and *Ten Years in Washington* (1874). In 1869 she entered into a three-year contract to write a daily column for the *Brooklyn Daily Union,* and at the end of the time was proud that she had not once failed to send her column. During the last year she received a $5,000 salary, at that time large for a woman. In 1882 her collected poems were published under the title *Poems of Life and Nature.* Her poetry is characterized by deep religious feeling and love of nature but not by originality of imagination or technique.

In 1876 Mary Clemmer brought her parents to Washington and established a home on Capitol Hill, where on Mondays her drawing-room was always filled with callers. In 1878 she was injured in a runaway accident, and henceforth suffered continuously from severe headache and carried on her literary work with difficulty. In 1883 she was married in St. John's Church, Washington, to Edmund Hudson, editor of the *Army and Navy Register,* and went with him on a European trip. On her return her health seemed better, but improvement was brief and she soon died, after a cerebral hemorrhage. She is buried in Rock Creek Cemetery, Washington.

Mary Clemmer was slender, graceful, dignified. She liked to trace her blue eyes, light-brown hair and high coloring to her Manx ancestry. Her extreme sensitiveness was perhaps an inheritance from her idealistic father. A conscientious, thorough worker, she was also fearless and vehement in expressing her opinions on political and social questions and because of this often aroused antagonism. She was intensely patriotic, intensely Northern. She felt keenly the various forms of injustice from which women suffered and wrote much on the subject, but was not greatly interested in the suffrage and took no part in organized movements. Her style is sometimes ornate and sentimental.

[*A Memorial of Mary Clemmer* (1886), by her husband, Edmund Hudson; "Mary Clemmer," in *Our Famous Women* (1884), based on material supplied by Mary Clemmer herself; obituaries in the *Nation,* Aug. 21, 1884; the N. Y. *Commercial Advertiser,* Aug. 19, 1884.]   S.G.B.

CLEMSON, THOMAS GREEN (July 1, 1807–Apr. 6, 1888), mining engineer, founder of Clemson College, was born in Philadelphia where his father was a merchant. As a student in the Philadelphia public schools and in a laboratory he became deeply interested in chemistry, an interest which took him to Paris about 1826. There he entered a practical laboratory and attended lectures at the Sorbonne by Thénard, Gay-Lussac, and DuLong. In 1827 he entered the laboratory of Robiquet. Through the influence of the American Consul at Paris he was admitted as *auditeur libre* to the École des Mines Royale (1828–32). He was examined at the Royal Mint of France and received a diploma as assayer. From about 1832 to 1839 he was engaged in Paris, Philadelphia, or Washington as consulting mining engineer, developing a profitable practise, and during this period he contributed numerous articles to the publications of various learned societies. In Washington he came to know the family of John C. Calhoun, in 1838 was married to Calhoun's eldest daughter, Anna Maria, and became associated with his father-in-law in Southern agriculture and gold mining. In 1844 he left his plantation upon being appointed by President Tyler to the post of chargé d'affaires in Belgium. In this post, which he held until 1851, he negotiated important commercial treaties, attempting to promote direct cotton trade between Southern ports and the German states through Antwerp (Letters to Calhoun). He was a keen observer of the growing European interest in agricultural and technical education. From 1853 to 1861 he made his residence at "The Home," near Bladensburg, Prince Georges County, Md., near Washington. He was engaged in planting and assaying, and probably was representing the Belgian government in a professional way. During this time he was a frequent contributor of articles on scientific agriculture and agricultural education, and was influential in the establishment of the Maryland Agricultural College in 1856. Three years later he was appointed superintendent of agriculture by Jacob Thompson, secretary of the interior. In this position he urged both the establishment of an independent bureau of agriculture and the establishment of land grant colleges. Resigning his post Mar. 4, 1861, because of his Southern sympathies, Clemson soon entered the service of the Confederate government. When he was paroled four years later he was supervisor of mines and metal works of the Trans-Mississippi Department. From 1865 to 1888 he lived in South Carolina at Pendleton or at Fort Hill, the latter being the home of the Calhouns. During the greater part of these years he was engaged, with almost passionate zeal, in an attempt to raise funds "for aid to found an institution for the diffusion of scientific knowledge that we may once more become a happy and prosperous people." Finally, despairing of attaining his end during his life, he left by will to the State of South Carolina the bulk of his estate, including Fort Hill, which he and his wife had purchased. When the State of South Carolina accepted his bequest and Clemson College was established, there was brought to fruition the great aim of his life.

Clemson had a very striking personality. He was six feet six inches in height, well proportioned physically, and a man of broad intellectual interests. He was a member of many learned societies, and received the decoration of the Order of Leopold and the French Legion of Honor. Something of a violinist, he was also an amateur in oil painting, and collected in Belgium about forty paintings, some of which are considered of rare value.

[*Am. Farmer*, 1855–98; *Charleston News and Courier*, Apr. 9, 1888; Yates Snowden, ed., *Hist. of S. C.*, vol. II (1920); Patent Office Reports, 1859–60; manuscript letters of Clemson to Calhoun, in Clemson Ag. College; recollections of personal acquaintances.]

E. W. S.

CLERC, LAURENT (Dec. 26, 1785–July 18, 1869), educator of the deaf, was the third of a family of five children born to Joseph François Clerc and Marie Elizabeth Candy, at La Balme, near Lyons, France. His father and a number of ancestors before him had served as mayors of La Balme, and his father also held the offices of notary public and judge. A fall into the fire when Laurent was about a year old resulted in deafness. At the age of twelve his formal education was begun at the Institute for the Deaf and Dumb in Paris, presided over by the Abbé Sicard. Clerc's first teacher was a brilliant deaf man, Massieu, but during most of his eight years of

schooling he was under the instruction of the Abbé himself. An apt scholar, at twenty he was an assistant teacher in the Paris Institute, where he finally became an instructor of the highest class.

In 1815, during a trip to London by Sicard, Massieu, and Clerc, to exhibit their methods, they met Thomas Hopkins Gallaudet, who had come from America to study the art of teaching the deaf. The latter was invited to visit the Paris Institute, and did so in 1816, after he had found he could get little help in England. Gallaudet, after finishing his study of the Paris school, asked permission of Abbé Sicard to take back young Clerc with him to aid in establishing a permanent school for the deaf in the United States at Hartford, Conn. Finding that Clerc wished to go, Sicard released his brilliant young teacher, who left with Gallaudet on June 18, 1816, arriving in New York on Aug. 9. During the voyage of almost two months Clerc studied English with Gallaudet, who in turn received lessons in the language of signs from Clerc. Within three months after beginning the study of English, Clerc was able to present a written address in this language in Boston on the needs of the deaf, which was clear, convincing, and grammatically correct. He spent several months with Gallaudet in visiting the large cities of New England and the middle states, and in appearing before state legislatures, for the purpose of showing the possibilities of educating the deaf and the need of establishing an institution for their instruction in America. He was everywhere received with attention and kindness, and in a short time a considerable sum of money was raised by Gallaudet and Clerc for opening the first permanent school for the deaf at Hartford, now known as the American School for the Deaf. This school opened its doors on Apr. 15, 1817. Gallaudet was made principal of the school and Clerc a teacher, and within a year thirty-two deaf pupils were under their instruction. In 1819, largely owing to the favorable impression made by Clerc upon Congress, the latter granted to the school 20,000 acres of wild land, later sold for $300,000. During the same year Clerc married Eliza Crocker Boardman of Whiteborough, N. Y., a beautiful and brilliant young woman who had lost her hearing in early childhood and had studied at the school. Although he visited his native land in 1820, and again in 1835 and 1846, he returned each time to his labors. In 1858, at the age of seventy-three, he closed his active work as teacher and retired, though he was constantly in attendance at meetings of deaf people throughout New England, and continued his interest in the Hartford school. He was the author of a number of addresses and articles in regard to the education of the deaf, which appeared in the *American Annals of the Deaf* (I, 62, 113, 170; II, 84, 203; III, 56; VI, 57, 95; VII, 23; and X, 51).

[W. W. Turner, "Laurent Clerc," *Am. Annals of the Deaf*, XV, 14–25; information furnished by Mrs. Charlotte G. Heaton, grand-daughter of Laurent Clerc.]

P.H.

CLEVELAND, AARON (Oct. 29, 1715–Aug. 11, 1757), clergyman of the Congregational and later of the English Church, was born in Cambridge, Mass., the son of Aaron and Abigail (Waters) Cleveland. His father kept a tavern in Cambridge, was a contractor and builder, and in time grew well-to-do by speculating in land at Charlestown and elsewhere. In 1738 he moved to East Haddam, Conn., where he rose to be captain in the militia and was described in the tax list as a "gentleman." At the time when his son entered Harvard College, however, he was still a publican. Students were graded according to their social position, and accordingly young Aaron Cleveland ranked only thirty-second in a class of thirty-eight. To compensate him for his lowly station he had inherited from his father a large, powerful, and handsome body. His feats of strength and his popularity with the belles of Cambridge and vicinity eclipsed the fame of whatever intellectual attainments he may have displayed. He swam from Cambridge to Boston and back again without resting, knocked senseless a bully who had journeyed all the way from Boston to try the manhood of the collegians, and excelled in general as a swimmer, wrestler, and skater. He graduated in 1735; on Aug. 4, 1739, married Susannah, daughter of the Rev. Aaron Porter of Medford, Mass.; and in the same year accepted a call to the Strict Congregational Church of Haddam, Conn. There he proved to be a witty, scholarly, and earnest pastor, but his Whitefieldian tendencies were too much for some of his parishioners, dissension arose, and in 1746 he resigned, much to the regret, it would seem, of most of his congregation. He was pastor of the South Church in Malden, Mass., 1747–50, when he went to the newly settled town of Halifax in Nova Scotia to organize the congregation known as Mather's Church. By 1754 he had become convinced of the correctness of the Episcopal position, resigned his charge, went to England, where he was ordained by the Bishop of London, and became a missionary of the Society for the Propagation of the Gospel. The ship on which he returned went aground on Nantucket Shoals; while assisting the sailors Cleveland was struck by a wave and injured severely. He

sought to organize a parish at Lewes, Del., but abandoned the field as unpromising. On July 1, 1757, he was commissioned by the Venerable Society to take charge of the church at New Castle, Del. He proceeded thither, was received with cordiality, and set out for Norwich, Conn., to bring his family. At Philadelphia he became ill and found shelter and care at the home of his friend Benjamin Franklin, who was then absent in Europe. He died in Franklin's house.

[B. Rand, "Rev. Aaron Cleveland," in *New Eng. Hist. and Geneal. Reg.* (1888), XLII, 73–78; E. J. and H. G. Cleveland, *Geneal. Cleveland and Cleaveland Families* (Hartford, Conn., 1899); "C. D. Cleveland," in W. B. Sprague, *Annals Am. Pulpit*, vol. V (1859); *Harvard Quinquennial Cat., 1636–1915* (1915).]

G.H.G.

CLEVELAND, BENJAMIN (May 26, 1738–Oct. 1806), Revolutionary soldier, was born in Prince William County, Va., the son of John and Martha (Coffee) Cleveland. His parents later moved to Orange County, Va., where Benjamin married Mary Graves and showed great fondness for gambling and horse racing. About 1769 Benjamin, his brother Robert, and his father-in-law moved to North Carolina, settling on Roaring Creek, near the Blue Ridge, where Benjamin began farming, assisted by his father-in-law's servants. Much of his time was spent in hunting and about 1772 he and some equally adventurous friends went to Kentucky on a hunting expedition, but near the Cumberland Gap they were plundered by the Cherokees and ordered off the Indian hunting grounds. With the outbreak of the Revolution he became ensign, and later lieutenant and captain, of the 2nd Regiment of North Carolina militia. Later serving with the county militia in the local warfare of western North Carolina, he commanded "Cleveland's Bull Dogs," called by the Loyalists "Cleveland's Devils." Administering stern justice, his harsh treatment of Loyalists earned for him a reputation for brutality in a partisan warfare characterized by inhumanity, summary hangings, and mutilation. In the summer of 1776 he acted as a scout on the western frontier and served as a captain in Gen. Rutherford's campaign against the Cherokees (*Colonial Records of North Carolina*, X, 882). He also acted as chairman of the Surry County Committee of Safety and after the organization of Wilkes County he became justice of the county court and was elected to the House of Commons (1778). During the winter campaign of 1778–79 in Georgia he served with Gen. Rutherford but returned home after the defeat of Gen. John Ashe [*q.v.*], at Briar Creek, was promoted colonel, and was elected to the state Senate. With the invasion of North Carolina by Maj. Patrick Ferguson of the 71st Highlanders in September

1780, Cleveland, with 350 militia, joined Col. William Campbell, Col. Isaac Shelby, Col. John Sevier [*qq.v.*], and other militia leaders at Quaker Meadows, near the Catawba River. As the officers were of equal rank it was agreed that the command should rest with the board of colonels, and Col. Campbell was elected officer of the day to execute the board's decisions. Ferguson evaded battle and began withdrawing toward Charlotte, hoping to rejoin Lord Cornwallis, but was pursued and defeated in the battle of King's Mountain, Oct. 7, 1780, Cleveland commanding the left flank of the Continental forces. After the battle the army encamped at Bickerstaff's, where Cleveland was conspicuous in securing the execution of a number of captured Loyalists who were accused of being thieves, house-burners, parole-breakers, and assassins. At the close of the Revolution, Cleveland, having lost his plantation, "Round About," on the Yadkin, "by a better title," moved to the Tugaloo region of western South Carolina, where he served for many years as a justice of the Pendleton (now Oconee) county court. As a judge he had great contempt for technicalities and the arguments of lawyers and often slept while on the bench, his colleagues prodding the enormously fat judge whenever his snoring interfered with litigation.

[Jas. Ferguson, *Two Scottish Soldiers* (Aberdeen, 1888); Wm. Moultrie, *Memoirs of the Am. Revolution* (1802); H. Lee, *Memoirs of the War in the Southern Dept. of the U. S.* (1812); *Southern Lit. Messenger*, Sept. 1845; *Am. Rev.*, Dec. 1848; *N. C. Univ. Mag.*, Sept. 1854; B. F. Perry, *Biog. Sketches of Eminent Am. Statesmen* (1887); L. C. Draper, *King's Mountain and Its Heroes* (1881); F. Moore, *Diary of the Am. Revolution* (1860); E. J. and H. G. Cleveland, *Geneal. Cleveland and Cleaveland Families* (1899).]   F.E.R.

CLEVELAND, CHAUNCEY FITCH (Feb. 16, 1799–June 6, 1887), lawyer, governor, congressman, was born at Hampton, Conn., the son of Silas and Lois (Sharpe) Cleveland. After receiving a common-school education, he studied law with Daniel Frost of Canterbury, Conn., for three years, and in August 1819 was admitted to the Windham County bar. He became clerk of the probate court (1827), probate judge (1829), prosecuting attorney (1833), and state bank commissioner (1837). Between 1826 and 1866 he was twelve times elected to the General Assembly from the town of Hampton and was speaker of the House in 1835, 1836, and 1863. Elected governor of Connecticut in 1842 and 1843, he interested himself in social reform and recommended and carried through an act abolishing imprisonment for debt, a child-labor law, and appropriations for a "Retreat" for the insane poor at Hartford. During the Dorr insurrection in Rhode Island, he twice refused to honor the requisition of Charter Governor King for Thomas W. Dorr [*q.v.*], charged with treason against the State of Rhode Island, on the ground that Dorr was a political refugee and not a fugitive from justice (*Providence Daily Journal*, Sept. 2, 1842). Nominated for Congress, he was defeated in 1838 and 1840 but was elected to the Thirty-first and Thirty-second Congresses, where he defended the United States Supreme Court, asked that the franking privilege of members of Congress be curtailed, and opposed Clay's compromise measures of 1850 including the Fugitive Slave Bill. He was strongly anti-slavery, twice receiving the nomination of Free-Soilers for Congress, simultaneously with the Democratic nomination, and went so far in obeying the resolutions of the Connecticut legislature against extension of slavery as to compare Daniel Webster with Benedict Arnold. A leader of the Democrats in Connecticut, he bolted his party in the mid-fifties, joined the new Republican party, acted as one of the vice-presidents of the Republican conventions of 1856 and 1860, and served as Republican presidential elector in 1860. In the following year he was appointed by Gov. Buckingham to the delegation representing Connecticut in the peace conference that met in Washington, Feb. 4–27, 1861, at the invitation of the State of Virginia. After the war he returned to the Democratic fold and was a Democratic presidential elector in 1876. He abandoned his law practise about 1879 and died at Hampton of apoplexy at the age of eighty-eight. He was married, first, to Diantha Hovey, Dec. 13, 1821, by whom he had two children. She died, Oct. 29, 1867, and on Jan. 27, 1869, he was married to Helen Cornelia Litchfield.

[*Pub. Acts, State of Conn., May Sess. 1842*, chapters xxiii and xxviii; *Resolutions and Priv. Acts, State of Conn., May Sess. 1842*, p. 52, *May Sess. 1843*, p. 28; *Cong. Globe*, 31, 32 Cong.; *Roll State Officers and Members of Gen. Assembly of Conn.* (1881); L. E. Chittenden, *Report Debates and Proc. . . . Conference Convention* (1864); E. J. and H. G. Cleveland, *Geneal. Cleveland and Cleaveland Families* (1899); E. D. Larned, *Hist. of Windham County, Conn.*, vol. II (1880); *Hartford Daily Courant*, May 8, Oct. 27, 1842, May 6, 1843; *Hartford Times*, June 7, 1887.]

                               F.E.R.

CLEVELAND, GROVER. [See CLEVELAND, STEPHEN GROVER, 1837–1908.]

CLEVELAND, HORACE WILLIAM SHALER (Dec. 16, 1814–Dec. 5, 1900), landscape architect, writer, was born and brought up in Lancaster, Mass., a direct descendant of Moses Cleveland who came from Ipswich, England, in 1635. Horace's father, Richard Jeffry Cleveland [*q.v.*], who had married his cousin Dorcas Cleveland Hiller in 1804, was a skilled and daring sea captain gifted with no little literary ability. Although his early prosperity was occasionally interrupted, he lived in ample and hospitable fashion; and with his wife, whose interest in education was exceptional, was instrumental in securing superior educational advantages for his boys by bringing about the establishment of a classical school in Lancaster first presided over by Jared Sparks. Horace therefore had both an hereditary and inculcated taste for writing. A further literary influence was his near relative, Henry R. Cleveland, one of the members of the famous "Five of Clubs," to which Longfellow and Sumner belonged. As a young man, fond of reading, Horace Cleveland deeply appreciated the advantage of frequent intercourse with these older men (mentioned in his *Social Life and Literature Fifty Years Ago,* published anonymously in 1888).

While his father was vice-consul at Havana, Cleveland saw active service on a coffee plantation. On his return he studied civil engineering, but after a few years devoted himself to agriculture, settling on a farm near Burlington, N. J. Almost immediately (Sept. 4, 1842) he married Maryann Dwinel at Bangor, Me., by whom he had two sons. In 1854 he removed with his family to the vicinity of Boston, living first in Salem and then for ten years in Danvers. He formed a partnership with R. Morris Copeland to pursue the profession of "Landscape and Ornamental Gardening." In 1857 the firm entered the competition for the design of the newly acquired Central Park in New York, but lost to Olmsted & Vaux. With Frederick Law Olmsted, Cleveland later formed a warm friendship. In 1864 he published a pamphlet, *Hints to Riflemen.* In 1869, he established himself in Chicago, and published his first Western professional paper, *Public Grounds of Chicago; How to Give Them Character and Expression.* His early work in Chicago was especially on South Park and Drexel Boulevard.

Some of his most important contributions to civic improvement were made at this time, especially in his practise outside of Chicago, which extended to Indiana, Michigan, Wisconsin, Iowa, and Kansas. A pamphlet, *A Few Hints on Landscape Gardening in the West* (1871), in the nature of a professional announcement, records a loose partnership with W. M. R. French, for the civil engineering phases of Cleveland's practise. In 1873 he published a little book, *Landscape Architecture as Applied to the Wants of the West; with an Essay on Forest Planting on the Great Plains,* which shows the deep insight into civic needs which twenty years of professional

practise had developed. In 1882 he published a pamphlet, *The Culture and Management of Our Native Forests,* giving his further experience. In 1886 he removed to Minneapolis where his public park and private work had been increasing steadily. A notable fruit of his efforts was the scenic preservation of the Falls of Minnehaha, although his recommendations for a regional park system comprising both St. Paul and Minneapolis were too far in advance of public opinion to succeed. There are two pamphlets on this subject (1885 and 1887) interesting in the history of American city planning. Minneapolis proved a far more congenial home than Chicago, and Cleveland's activities radiating from there were astonishing for a man over seventy. In 1886 he published *Voyages of a Merchant Navigator,* an extremely interesting account of his father, based on the latter's *Narrative of Voyages and Commercial Enterprises* (1842). In 1898, having returned to the vicinity of Chicago, he contributed a paper, *Influence of Parks on the Character of Children,* to the second meeting of the American Park and Outdoor Art Association, of which he was made an honorary member. He died in Hinsdale, Ill., and was buried in Minneapolis.

Among Cleveland's best known works were designs for Roger Williams Park in Providence, R. I.; the Minneapolis park system; the Omaha park system; the grounds about Natural Bridge, Va.; Sleepy Hollow Cemetery, Concord, Mass.; Washington Park, Chicago; Como Park, St. Paul; Brookside Suburb, Indianapolis; and a design for Jekyll Island, Ga., as a winter resort. Cleveland was a broad-minded, far-seeing pioneer, who, aligning himself with and drawing constant inspiration from the leadership of Olmsted, helped to spread the gospel of foresight and planning in the rapidly developing West.

[A brief autobiographical notice may be found in E. J. and H. G. Cleveland, *Geneal. Cleveland and Cleaveland Families* (1899), vol. II. *The Voyages of a Merchant Navigator* contains autobiographical material. Many of the facts here given have been gleaned here and there in Cleveland's other writings and from unpublished letters written to Frederick Law Olmsted in the eighties. See also A. T. Andreas, *Hist. of Chicago* (1884); I. Atwater, *Hist. of Minneapolis, Minn.* (1893); *Chas. Eliot, Landscape Architect* (1902); *Frederick Law Olmsted, Landscape Architect* (1922); *Chicago Tribune,* Dec. 7, 1900. The Codman Collection at the Boston Pub. Lib. contains most of Cleveland's professional publications.]   T. K. H.

CLEVELAND, RICHARD JEFFRY (Dec. 19, 1773–Nov. 23, 1860), merchant navigator, was born in Salem, Mass., the eldest child of Stephen and Margaret (Jeffry) Cleveland. His father, when sixteen years old, had been kidnapped on the streets of Boston and impressed into the British navy; later he helped to design and equip Revolutionary privateers and held one of the first naval commissions issued by the Continental government. At fourteen his son left school to enter the counting-house of Elias Hasket Derby [q.v.], and at eighteen went to sea as captain's clerk. A year later he completed a voyage as second mate, the first mate, Charles Derby, being nineteen, and the captain, Nathaniel Silsbee [q.v.], not yet twenty. He himself was a full-fledged captain at twenty-four. In 1797, finding himself footloose in Havre with $2,000 in his pocket, and eager to provide for the comfort of his aging father, he embarked on the series of daring voyages and trading ventures to which he owes his fame. When he returned to Salem, May 13, 1804, he brought with him a fortune of $70,000. In the interim he had sailed twice around the globe, had engaged in a number of successful commercial transactions, had matched wits with Indians on the Alaskan coast and with British, French, and Spanish officials and naval men on the high seas and in a half-dozen far-flung ports, had had a close escape from Malay pirates, had quelled a mutiny on the China coast, and—most brilliant of all—had performed three extraordinary feats of navigation in small sailing vessels. With a crew of four miscellaneous incompetents and an inexperienced Nantucket boy as mate, he had taken a cutter-sloop of forty-three tons from Havre to the Cape of Good Hope (Dec. 21, 1797–Mar. 21, 1798). In a vessel only slightly larger, with a short-handed, disaffected crew, he beat his way, in midwinter, in the monsoon season, from Canton to Norfolk Sound on the Alaskan coast (Jan. 10–Mar. 30, 1799). Finally, in a boat of only twenty-five tons, he sailed from Balasore Roads, near Calcutta, to the Isle of France (now Mauritius) in forty-five days (Mar. 29–May 14, 1800). It was at Mauritius that he met his life-long friend and partner, William Shaler [q.v.]. He married his cousin, Dorcas Cleveland Hiller, Oct. 12, 1804, bought a beautiful estate in Lancaster, Mass., and looked forward to a serene domestic life amid his books and flowers; but in 1806 he was compelled to go to sea again, the enterprises in which his winnings were invested having come to grief, and at sea he remained, except for short intermissions, until the end of 1821. During these years he made and lost several fortunes. Twice his ship and cargo were confiscated: in the Caribbean by the notorious Admiral Cochrane of the British navy, at Naples by Napoleon. Throughout these years he acted with his old foresight and competence, but his luck was almost uninterruptedly bad. When his

friend Shaler was made consul at Havana in 1828, Cleveland went with him as vice-consul and shared equally in the perquisites of the office. Shaler died there of cholera in 1833; Cleveland was ousted from his post by President Jackson, and found a berth for a while in the Boston Customs House. From 1845 till his death he made his home with his son, Horace W. S. Cleveland [q.v.], first at Burlington, N. J., and after 1854 at Danvers, Mass., where he died. Cleveland was no mere trader and adventurer. He was one of the greatest of the great race of New England sea captains—intrepid, skilful, clean, temperate, honest—but regard for Spanish trade regulations and for the nice conduct of neutrals in wartime was no part of his code. He was interested in art, literature, and education, was a thorough gentleman, and a born writer.

[The chief source is Cleveland's own *Narrative of Voyages and Commercial Enterprises* (2 vols., 1842), a fascinating book. There is additional information in H. W. S. Cleveland, *Voyages of a Merchant Navigator . . . comp. from the Jours. and Letters of the Late Richard J. Cleveland* (1886). See also R. D. Paine, *The Ships and Sailors of Old Salem* (rev. ed. 1924). The *Narrative* was republished in 1855 anonymously as *Voyages and Commercial Enterprises of the Sons of New Eng.*]   G. H. G.

CLEVELAND, STEPHEN GROVER (Mar. 18, 1837–June 24, 1908), President of the United States, was the fifth child of a country clergyman of the Presbyterian Church. His father, Richard Falley Cleveland, a graduate of Yale College and of the theological seminary at Princeton, was descended from a Moses Cleaveland who arrived in Massachusetts in 1635. His mother, Ann Neal, was born in 1806 and married in 1829 in Baltimore. She met her husband while he was tutor in that place. Her father was a publisher of whose antecedents little is known except that there was an Irish strain in his blood. Cleveland was born in the parsonage at Caldwell, N. J. (*Americana*, VII, 150), and was named for the parson who had preceded Richard Falley Cleveland there. In 1841 he was taken by his family to Fayetteville, N. Y., where his father had a church. The family moved again in 1850 to Clinton, N. Y.; and here when the father died in 1853 Grover was forced to undertake the larger part of his own support. He had already worked in a general store, and now he found a position in the New York Institution for the Blind; but life was hard and living was rather precarious for him until he entered the family of an uncle of his mother, Lewis Allen, at Black Rock, near Buffalo. He resisted the Whig tendencies rife in western New York, and became a Democrat before he became a voter. He studied law, was admitted to the bar in

1859, and in 1863 became assistant district attorney of Erie County. Financial burdens, and the need to aid his mother, kept him out of the army in the Civil War—to his political disadvantage. But he helped make it possible for two of his brothers to serve. His practise of law grew reasonably, as did his repute as a dependable, steady workman. The post of sheriff of Erie County came to him unsought—to his further political disadvantage since the necessity of the post required him to execute two murderers. He began his long career of making friends through his enemies by relieving Erie County of the burden of dishonest contractors. "We love him most for the enemies he has made," said Gen. Edward S. Bragg of Wisconsin, in seconding the nomination of Cleveland for the presidency in 1884 (*Wisconsin State Journal*, July 10, 1884).

Grover Cleveland was forty-four years old, a bachelor lawyer of moderate means and slight prominence when in 1881 the Democratic party "catered to the better class" by nominating him for mayor of Buffalo. Elected to reform the city administration, he reformed it. Before his term was out he began to be known as the "veto mayor," and his partisan associates were somewhat dismayed by the degree of reform that had let loose in electing him. His reputation served him well in 1882. In this year, foreseen as a Democratic year because of the scandals that had injured the Republican party, and the Star Route trials that were immediately before the public, young Democrats were in many places brought to the ticket to make it easier for Republicans to vote it. In New York, in the perennial struggle to control the Republican state organization, where the grip of Conkling was now broken, the secretary of the treasury, Charles J. Folger, was nominated for governor as an Arthur man. Cleveland was no more than a local favorite for the Democratic nomination until it occurred to the state organization (and to Daniel Manning of Albany, in particular) that the best strategy for the campaign would be the nomination of a new man, little known, and dissociated from the taint of membership in the inner ring. Cleveland was nominated at Syracuse, Sept. 22, 1882, and was elected with the aid of many thousand Republican votes as an "unowned candidate" (McElroy, *Grover Cleveland*, 1923, I, 45). He became governor of New York on Jan. 3, 1883.

For the next two years Albany, as often, was a vestibule to the White House. Cleveland was under scrutiny as any man must be who overturns political order in New York. His admirers watched for, and saw evidence of the same stubborn honesty that had given them satisfaction and him local prominence in Buffalo; his political associates watched with less comfort his independence of judgment and his refusal to play politics as a game of spoils, patronage, and party regularity. One of his vetoes (*New York Times*, Mar. 3, 1883), that of a five-cent-fare bill for the elevated railroads of New York City, brought him into opposition to a popular movement that had for the moment the support of young Theodore Roosevelt, then in the Assembly. The lowering of the rate from ten cents to five was desired; but was unfortunately an obvious violation of the State's charter contract with the companies, and to Cleveland's simple and direct mind there was no alternative to a veto. Roosevelt, on his second thought, sustained the veto and made apologies for his indorsement of the measure; and together Roosevelt and Cleveland worked for municipal reform legislation for New York City which, when passed in March 1884, became at once useful for the metropolis and proof of Cleveland's willingness for non-partisan cooperation. In his relations with Tammany Hall Cleveland made valuable enemies while governor. His fight with John Kelly, then leader of Tammany, turned upon the continuance in politics of state Senator Thomas F. Grady. Cleveland won the fight, as well as the hostility of the Tammany organization. The latter proceeded, in the spring of 1884, to oppose the drift of the Democratic party toward the nomination of the governor as president of the United States.

It is unlikely that Cleveland would have been nominated or elected president had it not been for James G. Blaine. That Republican statesman, outstanding among the leaders as the Civil War receded, had a record that was defaced by suspicions of near-corruption that he had never been able to dispel. An ambitious aspirant for the presidency, Blaine found that these charges, supported by the Mulligan letters, interfered with his chances in 1876. The deadlock of the convention in 1880 blocked Blaine, so that there was no occasion for his enemies to make great use of the charges in this campaign. As 1884 approached, Blaine was the great aspirant again; and the group that had opposed him for eight years was vigorous in attack and threat. The threat was that in the event of his nomination they would lead a secession into the Democratic party, if only that party would nominate a suitable man. Blaine was, in spite of this, nominated; the insurgents seceded and were given the enduring name of "mugwumps" (M. Sullivan,

Our Times, II, 1927, 382, traces the word to the New York *Sun,* Mar. 23, 1884) ; and when the Democratic convention came together in Chicago, July 8, 1884, the delegates knew that if Cleveland should be their choice there would be a chance of enough Republican support to elect him. They also beheld the Tammany delegation opposing him at every point. The opposition was as valuable as the promise of support, for Tammany had a bad name ; and Cleveland was nominated on the second ballot, with Thomas A. Hendricks of Indiana for the vice-presidency.

The hope of the mugwumps for a canvass in which the spotted record of Blaine could be opposed by the clean name of Cleveland was soon destroyed. The mugwump attacks on Blaine had gone far beyond the evidence in viciousness and bitterness, and had inspired his supporters to eager search for similar material for a counter-attack. On July 21, 1884, a Buffalo paper gave first publication to what had been found. The story, which had been hawked among the newspapers for several days, purported to show that some eight years previously the Democratic candidate had become the father of an illegitimate child, which he had since supported (*Chicago Tribune,* July 22, 23, 1884). For the rest of the canvass much of the Republican press published, enlarged, and falsified the case of Maria Halpin (who was the woman named) ; and made much of the alleged personal immorality of Cleveland. When the Democratic managers, dismayed at the scandal, inquired of Cleveland what they should do, he answered, briefly for once, "Tell the truth" (*Harper's Weekly,* Aug. 16, 1884, p. 528). A novel, embodying parts of the situation, and presenting its hero in an heroic light, became a best-seller a few years later when Cleveland had been made president for a second term (P. L. Ford, *The Honorable Peter Stirling,* 1894). How far the scandal hurt him or affected the campaign cannot be known ; it was at least partly offset by the accident that befell Blaine when on Oct. 29 the indiscreet Dr. Burchard used the fatal words "rum, Romanism, and rebellion" as a description of the common bond among Democrats. Cleveland was attacked, also, for his failure to serve in the Civil War and for the substitute he hired to take his place when he was drafted ; in spite of the fact that Blaine had equally abstained from service. Cleveland was, however, elected by a plurality of about 23,000 votes over Blaine, although he had a minority of all the votes cast. His administration of the presidency must be judged in light of the fact that although the Democrats controlled a majority in the new House of Repre-

sentatives, the Senate continued Republican. At no time was there a possibility of a one-party control of the government, with President, Senate, and House of the same political faith (H. C. Thomas, *The Return of the Democratic Party to Power in 1884,* 1919).

At the age of forty-eight Grover Cleveland took office, the first Democratic president after the Civil War. "He is a truly American type of the best kind," wrote James Russell Lowell, who was acquainted with enough types to know (to R. W. Gilder, Dec. 26, 1887, in C. E. Norton, *Letters of James Russell Lowell,* 1894, II, 344). He was still a bachelor, and his unmarried sister, Rose Elizabeth Cleveland, lived with him in the executive mansion. A rather short and unimpressive man, he made up in bulk what he lacked in height and weighed over 250 pounds when inaugurated (C. R. Lingley, "Characteristics of President Cleveland," in *Political Science Quarterly,* XXXIII, 255). He was clean-shaven, except for a small mustache, at a time when American statesmen generally went bearded. He was reticent and unexpansive, except in the private society of his intimates ; but the actor Joseph Jefferson, with whom he fished and near whom he lived in his summer place, "Gray Gables" on Buzzard's Bay, testified that he was a mimic of high order, told a good story, and might have been a great actor (O. S. Straus, *Under Four Administrations. From Cleveland to Taft,* 1922, p. 115). The close friendship that he maintained for many years with Richard Watson Gilder suggests that although he was without much formal education he had traits that made him companionable to cultivated men ; his choice of Princeton as a home for his years of retirement confirms this. But it was the task of his friends constantly to combat the hostile, and apparently untruthful, gossip, that he was habitually intemperate. More than once, after he had married, it was necessary for the wife of one of his cabinet members to assert the untruthfulness of the slander that in drunken fits he beat his wife (Mrs. William C. Whitney, *Milwaukee Sentinel,* Dec. 13, 1888) ; and even Mrs. Cleveland was driven to assert that she was happy (to Mrs. Maggie Nicodemus, June 3, 1888. McElroy, *Grover Cleveland,* I, 286). The persistence of slander and attack showed the resourcefulness of the political opposition (which was as likely to be Democratic as Republican), and the craving of the press for sensation. Cleveland's marriage, June 2, 1886, to Frances Folsom, daughter of his former law partner Oscar Folsom, was "news" interesting to the public and oppressive to the persons concerned. No detail was too small for the ubiquitous reporters, and Cleveland was outraged by the "colossal impertinence" with which his private life was pried into by the press (McElroy, I, 187). There were five children by this marriage, of whom all but one survived him.

The history of the Democratic party for the twenty-five years before 1885 was not such as to produce a large group of recognized and available party leaders from whom might be selected an impressive cabinet. Only Thomas F. Bayard, who became secretary of state, and who had been Cleveland's chief rival for the nomination, had a name that meant much to Americans at large; and his prominence owed much to the generations of service rendered by his forebears in Delaware. Daniel Manning, the anti-Tammany New Yorker who had "invented" Cleveland, received the Treasury. William C. Endicott of Massachusetts went to the War Department and paid part of Cleveland's debt to the independents. William C. Whitney, New York business man and son-in-law of the Ohio Standard Oil magnate, Senator Henry B. Payne, took over the Navy. The Post Office was given to William F. Vilas of Wisconsin, railroad magnate and orator. To the southern Democrats, who had seen little of office for so many years, went the Interior Department, to Lucius Q. C. Lamar of Mississippi; and the office of attorney-general, to Augustus H. Garland of Arkansas. The last two appointments received violent denunciation from the Republican press; but Cleveland subsequently promoted Lamar still further to the Supreme Court. In 1888 Melville W. Fuller of Chicago was appointed to be chief justice of the United States. The minor appointments tested the sincerity of Cleveland's pledge for a "practical reform in the civil service" (to G. W. Curtis, Dec. 25, 1884, McElroy, I, 124). His party had advocated this reform for many years, so long as there was no prospect of success; but with the inauguration of Cleveland the political "bread line" formed at once, and Democrats of every order demanded jobs, to throw Republicans out, or as party rewards, or for the health of their wives, or frankly because they needed the money. They had been kept away from such opportunities for twenty-four years. Cleveland had made no promise of such complete disregard of political considerations as would have lifted him out of all contact with the standards of his time; but his slow and reluctant compliance with partisan demands, and the steady support that he gave to the work of the Civil Service Commission mark a definite break from the practise of presiden-

tial politics that had long prevailed. He induced Congress to repeal the Tenure-of-Office Act that had hobbled presidents since 1867, and he maintained with acidity and success the independence of the president in appointments. But the devoted civil-service reformers were not satisfied, and the party politicians were enraged. Cleveland disliked and suffered under the criticism of disappointed politicians but was not diverted by it from his chosen course, and could never understand why the public would not see his duty as he saw it.

An even more unpopular duty than that which guarded the public offices led Cleveland to protect the Civil War pensioners from the attack of fraudulent claimants and cheap political sentimentalists. The Arrears of Pensions Act (1879) had made it profitable for veterans to search for excuses that would place them on the lists. They could now receive not only current pensions, as allowed by law, but back pensions from the time of discharge until the time of going on the pension list. In many cases these arrears ran into hundreds or thousands of dollars. A swarm of astute attorneys discovered the easy money to be made by aiding veterans to get pensions; and the more dubious the evidence, the larger were the fees. Congress was willing, with the surplus in the treasury, to pass in the form of private bills many claims that, for lack of authority, or lack of fact, could not be granted through the ordinary channels of the pension bureau. No congressman liked the unpleasant notoriety that might attach to a refusal to vote a pension to a soldier, however undeserved. Such bills descended upon Cleveland in a flood. In the spring of 1886 he began to read these bills and the papers that accompanied them, and to veto those that were without merit. Many were so completely bad as to be a scandal upon the Congress that voted them; pensions to deserters, pensions to men who had not been in the army, pensions for injuries received many years after the war was over. In February 1887, he vetoed a general pension bill based upon the new principle of allowing relief to veterans, not because of wounds incurred in the service, but "upon the ground of service and present disability alone" (J. D. Richardson, *Messages and Papers of the Presidents*, VIII, 549). The persons interested in such legislation turned upon Cleveland as an enemy to old soldiers; and many of them, running for office, promised friendship as a bait for soldier votes. In May 1887, Cleveland made a damaging error in judgment. Upon a recommendation from the War Department he ordered the return to the states of their origin of such

Confederate battle-flags as were in the possession of the government. In 1905 President Roosevelt accomplished this return with general approval, but the time was not ripe for it in 1887; and a Democrat was not the proper agent for such a friendly gesture. In Ohio a soldier candidate for governor gained votes by asserting that "No Rebel flags will be surrendered while I am Governor" (J. B. Foraker, *Notes of a Busy Life,* 1916, I, 242); and the commander of the Grand Army of the Republic declared, in violent denunciation, "May God palsy the hand that wrote the order!"

The great surplus revenue that began to accumulate in the United States Treasury after the resumption of specie payments (1879) constituted the most embarrassing of the problems of internal policy for President Cleveland. It was a certain incentive to extravagance, and invited the opposition to attack the government for overtaxing the people; yet it could not well be lessened without legislation revising and reducing many of the customs duties and thereby stirring up the same opposition to resist a departure from the principles of protection. Within the Democratic party the years 1881–87 brought about the overthrow of the Randall Democrats, who were generally protectionists, and the rise to power of the Carlisle-Mills group who indorsed varying degrees of tariff reform. Cleveland, never a free trader, was led to an attack upon the tariff because he was embarrassed by the surplus, and because he believed that tariff rates had come to be evidence of improper favoritism to the protected industries. He gave his support to Carlisle, who had been elected speaker of the House in 1883, and who was reëlected in 1885 and 1887; and when Congress met for the session of 1887–88 the message of the President was a comprehensive broadside against the existing rates, and an invitation to revise them. The debates of 1888 over the proposed Mills bill were the result; a second result was the decision of the Republican party to undertake an aggressive movement in favor of even more protection. The conventions of 1888 were held before the tariff debate was over. Cleveland was renominated (with Allen G. Thurman of Ohio as vice-president), and his friends were able to persuade the convention to indorse the Mills bill as a proper Democratic tariff. Benjamin Harrison and Levi P. Morton were nominated by the Republican convention. The political waters were muddied in the closing days of the canvass, as they were in 1884, by a political trick or *roorback* that this time took the form of the Murchison letter. This letter, released to the press at Los Angeles, Oct. 21, 1888, was the consequence of a trap that had been baited for Sir Lionel Sackville-West, the British minister in Washington. Sir Lionel incautiously fell into it, and gave great glee to Republicans by writing to an unknown correspondent, Murchison, that a vote for Cleveland would be useful to England. Cleveland dismissed the minister for his indiscretion; but the damage was done, for the letter appeared to sustain one of the Republican contentions, that tariff reduction was a British policy, and was perhaps inspired by British gold. In spite of having a plurality of the popular vote, Cleveland lost the election.

In 1889 Cleveland retired to New York, to resume the practise of law and to seek such privacy as is allowed to ex-presidents. He was forced to undertake gainful work, because he had no private fortune; but his associates testified that he was indifferent to fees and profits. He enjoyed his family, his fishing trips, his summer home, and an increasing amount of respect and attention from his fellow citizens. In 1890 the revulsion against the protective tariff moved on of itself to an overwhelming defeat of the Republicans at the polls. The extreme McKinley Tariff (1890) had uncovered dangerous discontent in the West and the South; and tariff opponents turned more and more to Cleveland to resume his leadership. There was much spontaneity in the popular demand that he should be the Democratic candidate again in 1892, although some of his friends played a skilful hand in nursing it (G. F. Parker, *post,* p. 136). The movement gained such volume in 1891 that Cleveland's great New York rival, David B. Hill, sought to head it off by holding the Democratic convention to select delegates to the national convention early in the year. The "snap" convention did its work Feb. 22, 1892, and was a boomerang for Hill. He gained control of the New York delegation with ease, but his opposition did now what John Kelly's had done in 1884. It advertised Cleveland not only among tariff reformers but also among friends of the Australian ballot and enemies of "boss" rule. The Cleveland movement swept the party, and the Chicago convention approved it on the first ballot. Adlai E. Stevenson of Illinois was nominated for vice-president. Tariff reduction was confirmed as the major issue of the canvass. In the ensuing struggle it was not hard to defeat the Republican ticket, Benjamin Harrison and Whitelaw Reid, for Harrison had lost control of the party leaders. He was losing votes as well, for Republicans in the western states were still angry about the McKinley bill and were seeking financial relief through the agency of free-silver coinage. Some of them turned Democrat, and more than one million of them seceded for the time and voted in the new People's party. But it was impossible for Cleveland, when reëlected, and reinaugurated in 1893, to satisfy the voters who had chosen him. A great financial panic was imminent, and the sufferers from it were calling for impossible relief; there was still a protectionist minority within his own party, ably led by Senator A. P. Gorman of Maryland; and the free-silver coinage that was demanded by western and southern populist elements was a form of currency inflation that he bitterly disapproved.

As far back as 1885, Cleveland had gone squarely on record against inflation (Letter to A. J. Warner, Feb. 24, 1885, *New York Herald,* Feb. 28, 1885). He now continued this attitude in the face of the financial crisis that broke in April 1893, and instead of surrendering to the demand for free silver he summoned the Fifty-third Congress, Democratic for once in both Houses, to repeal the Sherman Silver Purchase Act 1890, which was the most visible and concrete of the elements of financial unsoundness. He secured the repeal of this act, with the support of many Republican votes, but thereby he broke his party and drew upon himself the permanent hostility of the inflationist wing. It was not, for many years, common knowledge that at the moment when the special session of 1893 was called, the life of the President was uncertain because of the diseased condition of the roof of his mouth. This was successfully operated on, and his convalescence was concealed from the public (Dr. W. W. Keen, in *Saturday Evening Post,* Sept. 22, 1917). When, in the winter after the panic, Congress undertook the fulfilment of the Democratic pledge for tariff reduction, the animosities left from the fight on silver prevented harmony on any program. The protectionist Democrats stood out against revision and forced the drafting of a bill (the Wilson bill) that was so little a compliance with the pledge that Cleveland openly denounced it as "party perfidy and party dishonor." He was not willing to sign it; but the situation of the treasury was such that he did not dare veto it and thus forego the chance of improving revenue. He permitted the Wilson bill to become a law without his signature; and he himself became a president without a party for the remaining years of his term.

The cabinet of the second administration showed a greater familiarity with the problem of government and a wider acquaintance among Democratic leaders than did that of the first term. It was not bitterly partisan, for at its head was Judge Walter Q. Gresham, who had only recently left the Republican party. John G. Carlisle, as secretary of the treasury, had to wrestle with the panic. The War Department was given to Daniel S. Lamont, private secretary of the first administration. Richard Olney of Massachusetts was attorney-general; Wilson S. Bissell, an old law partner of the President, was postmaster-general; Hilary A. Herbert, who while in Congress had been chairman of the committee on naval affairs, was secretary of the navy; Hoke Smith of Georgia was at the Interior; J. Sterling Morton of the Nebraska sound-money wing was secretary of agriculture. But Cleveland himself was unquestionably the dominant figure of the cabinet, and he still continued somewhat to slow down administration by his inability to delegate authority, or to act upon any judgment but his own. The typical stories tell of his long hours of patient work over papers in minor cases, and of his briefs and notes upon matters that, soundly administered, would never have got beyond the desk of some subordinate. In his first term he often answered White House telephone calls; he never grew to be entirely comfortable with secretaries. The voluminous long-hand memoranda that he drew up would have been invaluable sources for the historian, had he not regarded them as personal, taken them into retirement with him, and destroyed many of them.

Out of the treasury, whose plethoric condition had caused him so much care in his first term, came the problem of a shrinking balance, that threatened even to disappear. Receipts fell away because of business depression. Gold was hoarded by its nervous owners, who paid their debts to the government in paper money whenever they could. It was not only impossible to make receipts balance expenditures in any fiscal year of the second term, but it was uncertain whether the treasury could continue its policy of redeeming on demand every type of currency in gold. The gold reserve, upon which this policy depended, fell below 100 millions in April 1893. Thereafter Cleveland, through Carlisle, kept it alive only by the desperate means of four bond issues, aggregating $293,000,000. Even with these it was difficult to draw gold into the treasury as rapidly as it was drained out. The Republican opposition made much of this embarrassment, charging Cleveland with running the government on borrowed money in time of peace; the Democratic opposition, desirous of a silver or a paper basis, made equal use of it to indicate Cleveland's close alliance with the great financial interests. His large capacity for taking punishment was needed, and was adequate.

An aftermath of the panic of 1893 was the railroad strike of 1894, in which the American Railway Union, engineered by Eugene V. Debs, undertook to tie up railway traffic by a strike in sympathy with the employees of the Pullman Company. The center of the strike was in the vicinity of Chicago, where the boycott on the Pullman palace cars originated. There was violence in the train yards, but the governor of Illinois, John P. Altgeld, believed that the violence was under control. The federal government intervened in two ways, both of which were novel: an injunction was issued by a federal court restraining the strikers, and Cleveland, upon application of federal officials, sent troops from the regular army to Chicago, to enforce the laws. The strikers had interfered with the free flowing of the mail service. Altgeld asked in vain for the withdrawal of the troops from his state, and criticized their presence as "this uncalled for reflection on our people"; but Cleveland had his way.

Cleveland's dominance of the State Department revealed itself first in Gresham's withdrawal of American recognition from the revolutionary government in Hawaii, and in his refusing to have anything to do with the overturning of the native monarchy there. The American residents had engineered the revolution in the final weeks of the Harrison administration, believing that prompt recognition and speedy incorporation in the United States would follow. Had the phrase then been current, Cleveland would have been correctly described as vigorously anti-imperialist. He showed the same temper between 1895 and 1897, during the Cuban insurrection, when American filibustering expeditions were organizing for Cuban service, and American arms salesmen were trying to make deliveries of consignments of munitions of war. Part of the American press whipped up an enthusiasm for the Cuban patriots, and played in detail upon the excesses of the royalist troops and the sufferings of non-combatants. Congressmen were openly sympathetic. But the President tried to enforce the neutrality law, and refused to be driven by sentiment into a war with Spain. Even with both houses joining in concurrent resolutions for Cuban recognition, he declined to be forced. He was strongly American, however, when he believed that the facts called for sharp action; and he brought England and the United States to the verge of war by intervening in the old quarrel between England and Venezuela over their joint boundary. In this, in a message to Congress,

Dec. 17, 1895, Cleveland gave new precision to the interpretation of the Monroe Doctrine, maintaining the hegemony of the United States in the Americas, and the vital interest of the United States in having boundary disputes with European countries settled without risk of aggrandizement. England yielded the point, believing that Cleveland was correctly interpreting American opinion; and the matter was steered into an amicable arbitration. In the reaction of relief at the passing of this danger, Cleveland and Olney, now secretary of state, negotiated a general arbitration treaty with England; but the Senate mutilated this until it was no longer useful.

Long before the end of the second term, Cleveland and his official family were outside the dominant currents of the Democratic party, and western and southern demands were driving the party into a campaign for free silver. There was much denunciation of him before and during the convention of 1896. After the nomination of William J. Bryan, the Cleveland Democrats, who could not bring themselves to vote for Maj. William McKinley the Republican candidate, and who would not vote for Bryan, organized a gold Democratic convention that nominated independent candidates. For these they voted, in protest to the course of their party. In the following March, Cleveland retired to a modest home in Princeton, N. J., and here maintained his residence for the rest of his life.

As a private citizen, Cleveland became a public and impressive figure. After a very few months the animosities began to fade, and opinion began more and more to turn to him as one of the few independent and disinterested voices in America. He was in demand for speeches and articles, and spent much of his time in preparing the autobiographical essays which he delivered as lectures, and later printed as *Presidential Problems*. He found time for friendship and recreation, and for active participation in the affairs of Princeton University, which had made him one of its trustees. On three more occasions he came prominently into the circle of great events. In 1902, during the anthracite coal strike, President Roosevelt turned to him for aid, and sought his cooperation in a public commission that was to investigate this phase of the labor controversy (J. B. Bishop, *Theodore Roosevelt and His Time*, 1920, I, 204). The project fell through because of difficulties over personnel, but for a moment it brought together in a common non-political purpose the outstanding figures of the two great parties. In 1904 there was talk of a third term for Cleveland, not so much because of a change among radical Democrats as because the enemies of Bryan saw little chance of a victory without the use of Cleveland's name. Cleveland enjoyed the anxiety that this talk caused among the friends of Bryan (McElroy, II, 321), but had no intention of trying to profit by it. In 1905 he undertook the heavy duty of assisting in the reorganization of the Equitable Life Assurance Society after the damaging revelations that had been brought out by Charles E. Hughes for the Armstrong investigation in New York. Thomas F. Ryan had purchased the control of the stock in the company, in order that reorganization might have a free hand; and Cleveland became one of the three trustees to whom the management was intrusted. With these affairs on his hands, his life was full until, in his seventy-first year, he died. His death came in the interval between the Republican and Democratic conventions of 1908, and brought about a pause in the preparations of partisanship. There were gestures of esteem from nearly every American group, but these were fewest from the radical followers of Bryan who were preparing to nominate him for a third campaign. In the ensuing canvass much use was made of a forged letter in which Cleveland was made to indorse William H. Taft instead of the Democratic candidate (*New York Times,* Sept. 12, 1908).

[Robert McElroy, *Grover Cleveland the Man and the Statesman* (2 vols., 1923), is easily the most important work on Cleveland, and has been executed with conscience and intelligence. It reveals that Cleveland kept a diary of his fishing trips, but left his files of correspondence in deliberate disorder (II, 389). The most important writing by Cleveland, apart from his state papers which may be found in J. D. Richardson, *Messages and Papers of the Presidents* (1920), vol. VIII, was his *Presidential Problems* (1904). There are many campaign and fugitive biographies, listed by McElroy (II, 400), and there is a multitude of special articles on him; but the best of the personal books are Geo. F. Parker, *Recollections of Grover Cleveland* (1900), and Richard Watson Gilder, *Grover Cleveland, A Record of Friendship* (1910).]   F. L. P—n.

CLEVENGER, SHOBAL VAIL (Oct. 22, 1812–September 1843), sculptor, was born on a farm near Middletown, Ohio, where his father, a New Jersey weaver, had settled in 1808. His mother is said to have been related to John Hancock. The year following Shobal's birth his parents moved to Ridgeville and later to Indian Creek. Shobal was the third child of a family of ten, and until his fifteenth year he worked on the farm in summer and attended school occasionally in winter. When fifteen he was sent to learn stone-cutting with his brother who was employed on the canal at Centerville. Here young Clevenger contracted a fever and was forced to return home. When he had recovered he went to Louisville and then to Cincinnati. On the market house of the latter city was a female figure in wood

which aroused his admiration and a desire to emulate it. He placed himself under a stonecutter, David Guion (Guiou, Guino, Guio) with whom he remained about four years. Tradition records that Clevenger criticized an angel's head carved by his master who thereupon challenged him to do better. Clevenger did, and was thereafter entrusted with the ornamental work of the shop. In order to procure models to study he crept into the graveyard on moonlight nights and took impressions in clay from some of the sculptured tombstones, especially of allegorical reliefs and a statue of Grief by John Airy, on the monument to Gen. Ganno. Soon after he left Guion he married Elizabeth Wright of Cincinnati and went to Xenia where he set up for himself, but receiving only a few commissions he returned to Cincinnati and again worked for his former master. He soon, however, formed a partnership with a man named Basset. E. S. Thomas, editor of the *Evening Post,* attracted by some of his work, gave him a commendatory notice in his paper. When Hiram Powers [*q.v.*] was about to return from Washington with a model of Chief Justice Marshall from which he was to carve a bust, Clevenger said he "would cut the first bust from stone in Cincinnati, if he couldn't cut the best," and accordingly made one of Thomas, cut directly from the stone without any model (*c.* 1836). From this time on his reputation seems to have increased, and commissions multiplied. Nicholas Longworth became interested in him and enabled him to follow a course of anatomical lectures at the Ohio Medical College. During this period he made a number of busts from the fine-grained freestone of the region, among them one of William Henry Harrison. At Lexington, Ky., he made those of Clay and Gov. Poindexter. Visiting Washington, Philadelphia, New York, and Boston, he modeled, in plaster, busts of Washington Allston, Isaac P. Davis, and Joseph Hopkinson which are in the Pennsylvania Academy of the Fine Arts; and busts of Clay, Edward Everett, W. H. Harrison, Philip Hone, and Webster, plaster casts of which are in the New York Historical Society's collection. Marbles of Allston, John Davis, and Lemuel Shaw, the two latter dated 1839, are in the Boston Athenæum. Besides these he is said to have made busts of J. Q. Adams, Van Buren, Biddle, Woodbury, Dr. James Jackson, Jeremiah Mason, H. G. Otis, and Joseph Tilden. His bust of Webster was represented on the fifteen-cent stamp.

In the spring of 1840 he went again to New York where he made busts of Samuel Ward, Ward's daughter, Gov. Wolcott of Connecticut, and Chancellor Kent (plaster casts of the last two are in the New York Historical Society's collection), and in October 1840, Longworth having supplied the means, he sailed for Havre. After spending a few days in Paris he went on to Florence. In the spring of 1842 he had trouble with his eyes, but after visiting Rome he returned to Florence and made busts of Powers and Louis Bonaparte as well as an idealized bust called "The Lady of the Lake." He began, in October of that year, what was to prove his last work. It was a nude, life-size figure of an Indian warrior, which has since entirely disappeared. On account of the subject it caused, at the time, a considerable sensation and was even called the first distinctively American sculpture. When the model was practically completed, the sculptor's health failed, and in June 1843 his physician pronounced the disease consumption, brought on, some say, by the inhalation of marble dust. On Sept. 17 he sailed for home with his wife and his three children. A day or two after passing Gibraltar he died. His youngest son, Shobal Vail Clevenger [q.v.], attained some distinction as a psychiatrist.

Clevenger's work consisted almost entirely of busts, and in these he showed a carefulness and exactitude in portraiture and a skilful use of the chisel. Though somewhat deficient in general education, he profited by association with his sitters, some of whom were men of culture. They were attracted by his personality, for he was frank and unaffected, industrious and patient in the pursuit of his art. In appearance Tuckerman described him as "a compact and manly figure, with a certain vigor of outline [that] promised more continuity of action than is often realized by artists."

[The exact date of Clevenger's death is variously given as Sept. 23, 27, and 28. The more important sources of information concerning him are: *Southern Lit. Messenger,* Apr. 1839; *Sculpture and the Plastic Art* (1850); H. T. Tuckerman, *Book of the Artists* (1867); Lorado Taft, *Hist. of Am. Sculpture* (1903); *Boston Transcript,* Nov. 13, 1843; *N. Y. Tribune,* Nov. 11, 1843; *U. S. Mag. and Democratic Rev.,* Feb. 1844; and the biography of his son, *The Don Quixote of Psychiatry* (1919), by Victor Robinson.]   E.G.N.

CLEVENGER, SHOBAL VAIL (Mar. 24, 1843–Mar. 24, 1920), psychiatrist, son of Shobal Vail Clevenger [q.v.] and his wife, Elizabeth Wright of Cincinnati, was born in Florence, Italy. But six months old when his father died, he was cared for during part of his early childhood by relatives in the United States. He joined his mother and stepfather Thwing in New Orleans to begin his schooling, but a visitation of yellow fever in 1853 scattered this family, and a relative in St. Louis put him to work as a bank messenger (1855). Several years later he served as clerk and interpreter for Señor Aguirre who

was engaged in freighting goods between Kansas City and Mexico; and when the Civil War broke out he enlisted in a Kansas City company but was soon transferred, at Nashville, to the United States Engineer Corps, in which he had much experience in building railways and bridges. Having secured some money after the close of the war by service as a claims agent, he married a college girl, Mariana Knapp, and migrated to Montana where he functioned as justice of the peace, probate judge, court commissioner, and revenue collector. He was later a government surveyor in the Dakotas and civil engineer in charge of building the South Dakota Railway. He also installed telegraph lines and telegraphed weather reports to the Smithsonian Institution. He contributed articles on scientific subjects to *Van Nostrand's Engineering Magazine* and published a *Treatise on Government Surveying* (1874) which went through several editions. For years he had collected evidence of corruption in the Land and Indian departments and early in the seventies made a trip to Washington for the joint purpose of securing contracts and submitting his evidence, but the results were so unsatisfactory that he returned home determined to change his profession. Although he was made superintendent of the government observatory at Fort Sully, he began to read medicine with an army post surgeon, Dr. Bergen; then, having lost his government position through politics, he worked as a steamboat clerk to get funds for his medical project. He finally obtained his M.D. from the Chicago Medical College (1879), and with his large family settled in that city as a general practitioner. He began to specialize in neurology and psychiatry and to write articles under these heads. In 1883 he secured the position of special pathologist to the Cook County Insane Asylum at Dunning and began to make case records and autopsies on the brains of the insane. The corruption which prevailed in such institutions was shameless, and, although he was an appointee of the political machine, he began to expose the abuses in the *Chicago Inter-Ocean* but was unsuccessful in obtaining the cooperation of the press, pulpit, bar, clubmen, business men, or any other group. He resigned when a pistol bullet had imperilled his family and devoted himself to private practise, serving for a time as neurologist to the Alexian Brothers' and Michael Reese Hospitals. In 1884 appeared his *Comparative Physiology and Psychology,* and his classic work, *Spinal Concussion* (1889), gave him an international reputation. He lectured in various capacities at the Art Institute, School of Pharmacy, and Law School, but never held a chair in a medical college, although he received offers from eastern institutions. In 1893 Gov. Altgeld appointed him superintendent of the Illinois Eastern Hospital for the Insane at Kankakee and he planned great reforms in the treatment of the insane, based on the belief that insanity is often due to or aggravated by physical ailments. He gave up his private practise and hospital appointments for this work, but, as he would not adjust himself to political exigencies, he was soon forced to resign and return once more to private life. He wrote much and testified in many cases involving medical jurisprudence, also maintained a large correspondence with Eastern psychiatrists and brain specialists, and published the following works: *Medical Jurisprudence of Insanity* (2 vols., 1898) ; *The Evolution of Man and His Mind* (1903) ; *Therapeutics, Materia Medica and the Practice of Medicine* (1905), and the autobiographical *Fun in a Doctor's Life* (1909). Tiring of the city, he lived for many years at Park Ridge, Ill. When finally he sought to resume his practise it was without success, and his last days were spent in narrow circumstances. His wife died in the autumn of 1910 and he married an orphan whom the Clevengers had taken into their home. He died of cerebral hemorrhage on his seventy-seventh birthday.

Clevenger had the usual defects of versatility. Numerous patented inventions brought him but little money, the best known being his book-typewriter and his brain model for teaching. As a psychiatrist he was ahead of his time and popularized new concepts of mental disease such as paranoia and katatonia. As a biologist he ranked high and added to the conception of evolution, especially in connection with the difficulty of man in adapting himself to the upright position. In his hatred of sham he sometimes went too far, as when he condemned certain neurologists for belief in the efficacy of electrotherapy. He was often inconsistent, for he testified in court cases while deploring the principle of factional expert testimony and fought the spoils system of which he was the beneficiary. His reform efforts were always single-handed and hence foredoomed to failure.

[Clevenger received the distinction of an extensive biography entitled *The Don Quixote of Psychiatry* (1919), by Victor Robinson. See also *Western Medic. Reporter*, 1893, p. 151 ; *Jour. Am. Medic. Asso.*, Apr. 3, 1920, p. 963 ; article by H. A. Kelly and W. L. Burrage, *Dict. Am. Medic. Biog.* (1928).]   E. P.

CLEWELL, JOHN HENRY (Sept. 19, 1855– Feb. 20, 1922), Moravian clergyman, educator, was born in Salem, N. C. His father, John David Clewell, was of Huguenot ancestry; his mother was Dorothea Shultz. John Henry passed through the elementary schools of Salem and entered the Moravian College and Theological Seminary in Bethlehem, Pa., from which he graduated, receiving the degrees of A.B. and B.D. in 1875 and 1877 respectively. He planned to enter the Moravian ministry but before doing so he spent two years at Union Theological Seminary in New York. Upon his ordination as a deacon of the Moravian church in 1879 he went to Ohio to take charge of the Uhrichsville church. While serving here he also founded the Port Washington (Ohio) church in 1880, and became a presbyter in the Moravian church. In June 1882 he married Alice Cornelia Wolle of Bethlehem, Pa., by whom he had five sons. In 1884 he was called to the place of his birth to become the assistant principal of Winston-Salem Academy and College, a Moravian institution for girls; in 1888 he became principal, and later president. For twenty-five years he labored in this institution, traveling extensively in the West and the South in the interest of the school. In 1899 he went to Europe to attend the General Synod of the Moravian church. In 1900 he received the degree of Ph.D. from his alma mater. Among his outstanding achievements in the South was the organization of the Association of Presidents of Women's Colleges in the South. That he was effectively assisted by Mrs. Clewell is testified by the beautiful Alice Clewell Memorial dormitory on the Winston-Salem campus. He was so successful in raising the academic standards of Winston-Salem and in building it up generally that he was offered the presidency of the Moravian Seminary and College for Women at Bethlehem, Pa., and accepted the position in 1909. His problem at Bethlehem was to develop a strong institution in spite of restricted financial resources. This he succeeded in doing through a working arrangement with Lehigh University whereby certain members of its faculty were able to give a portion of their time to teaching in the Moravian College for Women. He remained president of the school to the time of his death. In 1902 he published his *History of Wachovia in North Carolina,* which is an account of the Moravian church in this region for a period of 150 years. Though not a great scholar or one of the country's foremost educators, Clewell played a rather important rôle in the education of women in the United States for almost forty years.

[Files of the *Moravian,* the official publication of the Moravian church ; Clewell's own *Hist. of Wachovia* (1902), which gives a sketch of his activities at Winston-Salem ; the bulletins of the two colleges ; and an unprinted memoir by his son, Clarence E. Clewell of the Univ of Pa.; *Who's Who in America,* 1922–23 ; obituaries in the *Moravian,* Mar. 1, 1922, the *Globe* (Bethlehem, Pa.), and *Evening Bull.* (Phila.), of Feb 21, and the *Public Ledger* (Phila.) of Feb. 22, 1922.]   L. H. G.

CLEWS, HENRY (Aug. 14, 1834–Jan. 31, 1923), financier, author, was one of the seven children of James Clews, a Staffordshire potter, who chanced to visit the United States about the year 1850. He had been intended from birth for the ministry. His father's visit, on which Henry accompanied him, was designed for the purpose of obtaining data for the manufacture of his china and of establishing a plant in the United States. This china bore, on various of the graceful pieces, now much sought by collectors, early colonial scenes. It was of a beautiful delft blue. To-day it is held principally by connoisseurs and museums. Henry Clews, however, was interested neither in china nor in the ministry. Becoming attached to the conditions of life in New York, he persuaded his father to place him in business in that city. His education, obtained in English public schools, had been better than the average; and it was not difficult for him to obtain an immediate start as a clerk with the firm of Wilson G. Hunt & Company, which at that time was one of the largest firms of woolen importers in New York. The experience proved to be all that he had expected, and he remained engaged in it some eight years; but long before the end of that period, it became obvious that he was more interested in the financial side of the establishment than in its merchandising activities. He acquired a thorough knowledge of credits, discounts and commercial paper and became so well-known in this field that he eventually left the woolen business, and opened an office in Wall Street as a note broker and private banker in a firm organized as Stout, Clews & Mason. Before the opening of the Civil War he had become well-known both in that business and in ancillary branches of banking and investment, and his reputation had gained some foothold in Europe.

Civil War finance offered to Clews, as it did to many other investment bankers of the day, a great opportunity for large turnover and substantial profits. Secretary Chase, the war head of the Treasury Department, gave a substantial part of the public business to the firm, which had become Livermore, Clews & Mason (later Livermore, Clews & Company), located at 32 Wall St., now the site of the United States Assay Office. By the close of the war, this firm ranked second only to the house of Cooke & Company, in the amount of government bonds taken and disposed of to investors. The prestige obtained in this way, and the new clientele which appeared with the fresh industrial growth after the close of the war, still further enlarged the business of the house of Clews. In 1877 the firm name became Henry Clews & Company. In 1882 the establish-

ment was transferred to the Mills Building just opposite the Stock Exchange on Broad St., where it remained for forty-one years. The outstanding characteristic of the firm's policy was abstention from commitment to new promotions, flotations and the like, the business being steadily conducted along rather limited lines, though on a large scale, as a stock-trading and banking establishment, with emphasis upon the customer's margin phase of the business. In furtherance of his position as a student of, and leading dealer in, stocks, Clews published a weekly circular which for years was widely known as an authoritative interpretation and forecast of market conditions.

Partly as a result of his youthful education and partly as a matter of business development, Clews early interested himself in public questions, chiefly of a financial nature, and at one time acted as currency adviser to the Government of Japan, later receiving a decoration for his service. His *Twenty-eight Years in Wall Street* (1887, revised and enlarged as *Fifty Years of Wall Street,* 1908), is a collection of connected reminiscences, sketches, and discussions on various matters which attracted his attention in the course of his business and his *Wall Street Point of View* (1900) was an exposition of the financial attitude of New York toward public questions. A volume of *Speeches and Essays Financial, Economic and Miscellaneous* (1910) was also issued under his name. Owing to his increasing prominence in the community he was, during the life of President Grant, close to the administration and was offered an appointment in it, and, although he never accepted public office, he continued to play a part behind the scenes in connection with the affairs of the Republican party. He became associated with numerous charitable and civic societies and was at one time president of the Peace and Arbitration Society, the forerunner of later and better-known efforts to promote the causes indicated. He married, during his early years, Lucy Madison Worthington of Kentucky. Of about average height, he possessed a gravity and sobriety of mien which gave the impression of membership in the ministerial profession, for which he had been intended, rather than the more mundane occupation of a broker.

[See, in addition to the writings of Clews himself, Chas. Morris, *Makers of N. Y.* (1895), p. 115; *Men of Affairs in N. Y.* (1906), p. 55; *Jour. of Commerce* (N. Y.), Feb. 1, 1923; *N. Y. Times,* Feb. 1, 1923.]

H. P. W.

CLIFFORD, JOHN HENRY (Jan. 16, 1809–Jan. 2, 1876), lawyer, railroad president, was born in Providence, R. I., the son of Benjamin and Achsah (Wade) Clifford. After graduating in 1827 from Brown University, he studied law with Timothy G. Coffin of New Bedford, Mass. In 1830 he was admitted to the bar of Bristol County, and became an attorney in New Bedford, with which city he was closely identified during the remainder of his career and in which he built up an extensive practise. In 1835 he made his entry into politics, being chosen as a representative to the General Court, and consequently made the acquaintance of Gov. Edward Everett. In 1839 Everett appointed him district attorney for southern Massachusetts, an office which he held for ten years. Gov. Briggs named him in 1849 as attorney-general of the Commonwealth, and Clifford won a reputation a year later for his clever prosecution of Prof. Webster of Harvard College, for the murder of Dr. Parkman.

In 1853 Clifford ran for governor on the Whig ticket, and, although he did not receive a majority of the popular vote, he was afterward elected by the legislature and served one term. Declining a renomination, he was reappointed by Gov. Emory Washburn as attorney-general and continued in that office until 1858. During the Civil War he vigorously supported Lincoln's policies. In 1862, when he was elected to the state Senate, he was at once made president of that body. He retired in 1867 from his profession and became president of the Boston & Providence Railroad, a position which he retained until his death. It was under his administration that a new terminal was erected in Boston.

Clifford declined appointments from President Grant as minister to Turkey and minister to Russia, but consented to be a member of the United States Commission on the Fisheries under the Arbitration Treaty with Great Britain. He was an Overseer of Harvard College, 1854–59 and 1865–68, and president of the Board of Overseers, 1869–74. As governor, he officiated at the induction of President Walker in 1853, and, as president of the Board of Overseers, at the inauguration of President Eliot in 1869, giving an address on each occasion. He was a trustee of the Peabody Education Fund and an intimate friend of its founder, George Peabody.

His long experience in public affairs eventually broke his health. A trip to Florida in 1873 and another to Europe in 1875 brought him relief, but on Thanksgiving Day 1875, he had a sudden attack of heart trouble, and died in New Bedford, Jan. 2, 1876. He was married on Jan. 16, 1832, to Sarah Parker Allen, daughter of William Howland Allen of New Bedford, and a lineal descendant of Myles Standish. Naturally genial and urbane, he possessed a high degree of personal magnetism which drew friends to him.

Although he was not in any sense a hard worker, he had rare facility in acquiring knowledge and was a man of broad interests and culture.

[The best account of Clifford is a memoir by Robert C. Winthrop in *Proc. Mass. Hist. Soc.*, 1876–77. See also *Proc. Am. Acad. Arts and Sci.*, 1875–76; *Providence Daily Jour.*, June 21, 1876.]   C.M.F.

CLIFFORD, NATHAN (Aug. 18, 1803–July 25, 1881), jurist, was born in Rumney, N. H., where the Cliffords had been settled for three generations. His father, Deacon Nathaniel Clifford, remembered as a serious man even by the standards of that serious part of the country, was a small farmer; his mother, whose maiden name was Lydia Simpson, possessed the enterprise and energy which her son is said to have inherited from her. At fourteen Nathan, the oldest child and only son of a family of seven, having finished the village school course, was permitted, after some opposition from his family, to attend Haverhill (N. H.) Academy, where he earned his living by teaching district school and giving singing lessons. His father's death in 1820 ended his hopes of entering Dartmouth College, but he found means to spend a year at the "Literary Institution" at New Hampton, N. H. He then studied law in his native village in the office of a local practitioner, Josiah Quincy. Admitted to the bar in 1827, he determined to commence practise in Maine and he selected as a permanent place of settlement Newfield, a village of about a thousand inhabitants in the southwestern corner of the state. During his first year of residence he married Hannah, the seventeen-year-old daughter of Capt. James Ayer, one of the leading citizens.

In 1830 Clifford entered politics as a successful candidate on the Democratic ticket for the lower house of the Maine legislature. In an Assembly largely composed of new men, Clifford, with his huge physique, robust health and aggressive willingness to work, forced his way rapidly to the front. Consciousness of his lack of higher education made him a painstaking student, and he developed marked ability for formulating and defending the philosophy of Jacksonian democracy. He was thrice reëlected to the Assembly, serving during his last two terms as speaker, and in 1832 was a delegate to the National Democratic Convention in Baltimore. In 1834 the office of attorney-general of the state becoming vacant, Clifford successfully sought it as a reward for his party services. In 1837 he was an unsuccessful candidate in the party caucus for the nomination for United States senator. In 1838 he was elected to the national House of Representatives where he served two terms. Here he displayed the same activity and devotion to duty as in the legislature. Many of his speeches on economic questions were prepared with great care and showed far more than the usual grasp of principles and statistical data. In 1843 when Maine was redistricted he failed of renomination and retired to Newfield, somewhat disgruntled at his treatment by his party. Three years later President Polk appointed him attorney-general of the United States at the instance of the Maine senators.

When Clifford came to Washington at forty-three, he was still a New England countryman. His interests centered in his Newfield home where his wife and family remained because the smallness of his means would not permit their living in Washington. Several days before the opening of the Supreme Court term at which he was to make his first appearance as attorney-general, he surprised the President by tendering his resignation. "I told him," wrote Polk, "if he resigned now it would be assumed by his political opponents that he was not qualified and would ruin him as a public man" (*Diary*, Dec. 13, 1846). Clifford accordingly withdrew his resignation and in a few days regained his self-confidence by winning his first case before the Supreme Court. In addition to his legal duties, Clifford found himself involved in delicate political tasks. Polk and his secretary of state, Buchanan, were at variance over the conduct of the Mexican War. Clifford enjoyed Buchanan's confidence, but agreed with the President's policy, so that he became a helpful intermediary between the two. Polk showed appreciation of his tact and fidelity by entrusting him at the close of the war with a diplomatic mission to Mexico. The treaty of peace which had been concluded by Commissioner Trist had been amended by the Senate, and it became necessary to secure the Mexican government's consent to the amendments. A. H. Sevier, chairman of the Foreign Relations Committee of the Senate, was designated to conduct the negotiations, and Clifford was joined with him in the commission and ordered to proceed at once to Mexico. After ratifications of the amended treaty were exchanged, Clifford was commissioned to remain in Mexico as minister plenipotentiary to inaugurate the relations between the two countries on a peaceful footing. With the defeat of the Democrats at the presidential election of 1848 and the coming of the Whigs into power, he was recalled.

On his return, Clifford moved to Portland, Me., where he practised law for the next eight years. His practise does not seem to have brought him financial independence and his means continued small, but he was retained in a number of important cases, including *Luther* vs. *Borden* (7 *Howard* 1), in which he made an argument before the United States Supreme Court for the losing side. In 1850 and in 1853 he was an unsuccessful candidate for the United States Senate, long the object of his ambition. His close connection with Buchanan made it natural that when the New England seat on the Supreme Court became vacant during Buchanan's presidency through the resignation of B. R. Curtis, Clifford should have been named as his successor. But since his affiliations were with the pro-slavery wing of the Democrats, the nomination aroused bitter opposition. In the end it was confirmed by the Senate by the narrow margin of 26 votes to 23, and on Jan. 21, 1858, he took his seat on the Court of which he was to be a member for the remaining twenty-three years of his life. He set about his new duties with the same thoughtful and studious industry which he had displayed in his previous offices, and from the beginning most of his opinions were elaborate legal essays which because of their comprehensiveness and learning were widely cited as authorities by other courts.

In all, Mr. Justice Clifford wrote the opinion of the Supreme Court in 398 cases. He also wrote 8 concurring and 49 dissenting opinions and dissented without opinion in 42 cases, an unusual proportion of dissents which indicates the hard-headedness of his character. He wrote no opinion for the Court on a question of foremost constitutional importance, his specialities being commercial and maritime law, Mexican land grants and procedure and practise. Some of his dissenting opinions, however, express decided constitutional views, and in one case he established on circuit a major constitutional precedent affirmed on appeal by the Supreme Court in *Collector* vs. *Day* (11 *Wallace* 113), holding that the national government may not tax the salary of a state officer. He was unwilling, however, to extend this principle as far as the Court and dissented from the holding in *U. S.* vs. *B. & O. R. R. Co.* (17 *Wallace* 322) that railroad bonds owned by a municipality are exempt from federal taxes; and in the Franchise Tax Cases (6 *Wallace* 594, 611, 632), following Marshall's view that the subject of a tax is the criterion of its constitutionality, he upheld the validity of a state tax laid upon franchises although the measure of the tax was assets which included United States bonds. This tendency to seek sharp dividing lines of power between federal and state authority led him to differ from his colleagues in taking the position, likewise inspired by Marshall, that federal power over interstate and foreign commerce absolutely excludes regulation by the states (*Hall* vs. *De Cuir*, 95 *U. S.* 485). The same tendency toward definiteness inspired his dissent in *Loan Association* vs. *Topeka* (20 *Wallace* 655), perhaps his major constitutional contribution, in which he denied the power of the courts to set aside legislative acts as contrary to "natural justice" or on any other ground than clear-cut constitutional provision. From the same point of view his dissent in the Legal Tender Cases (12 *Wallace* 457) was based not on the ground that Congress was prevented from making greenbacks legal tender by any vague projection of the "obligations of contracts" clause, but that the power could not be deduced from any definite constitutional grant. On the great constitutional issues growing out of the Civil War and Reconstruction he voted naturally with the "conservative" majority of the court which after 1870 became a minority. He concurred without opinion in *ex parte Milligan* (4 *Wallace* 2), *ex parte Garland* (4 *Wallace* 333), and *Hepburn* vs. *Griswold* (8 *Wallace* 603), and dissented without opinion in the cases like *ex parte Virginia* (100 *U. S.* 371) allowing federal interference with state authorities to protect the political rights of negroes. Although attacked by Blaine in a political speech in 1876 as "an ingrain hungry Democrat, double-dyed and dyed-in-the-wool, and coarse wool at that," his judgments were never regarded by competent members of the profession as marred by party bias, and even the *New York Tribune* referred to him as "a jurist of learning and integrity."

After the death of Chief Justice Chase on May 7, 1873, a long wrangle ensued over the selection of a successor, during which Clifford presided over the Supreme Court as senior associate justice until Chief Justice Waite took his seat on Mar. 4 of the following year. In 1877 he was again called upon as senior associate justice to preside over the Electoral Commission which canvassed the votes in the disputed Hayes-Tilden election. On the first question submitted to the Commission, that involving the vote of Florida, Clifford wrote a careful dissenting opinion in favor of the view that it was within the province of the Commission to examine extrinsic evidence to determine the validity of the returns. The decision of the Commission to the contrary by a strict partisan vote apparently convinced him of the hopelessness of what he regarded as a fair outcome, and he wrote no more opinions. He considered Hayes a usurper of the presidential office and refused to enter the White House during his administration. While free from bias in his judicial duties, Clifford always remained a loyal party man, and hope for the election of a Democratic president who might appoint his successor. For this reason he refused to avail himself of his legal right to retire, and went on carrying the burden of his heavy duties, the last link between the Court and the days of Democratic ascendency before the Civil War. Even after he had been incapacitated by an apoplectic stroke in 1880 he refused to resign. He lingered as an invalid for a year and died July 25, 1881.

[Philip Q. Clifford, *Nathan Clifford, Democrat* (N. Y., 1922), includes many of Clifford's letters, and an adequate account of his political career and private life. His judicial career can be traced only through the contemporary Supreme Court Reports and the three volumes of Clifford's Reports, containing his opinions delivered on circuit.]   J.Di.

CLIFFTON, WILLIAM (1772–December 1799), poet, was born of Quaker stock at Philadelphia. His father was a "wealthy mechanic" of Southwark who perhaps had an interest in shipbuilding. The boy was well educated, but of delicate frame, and the rupture of a blood-vessel at the age of nineteen caused him to abandon hopes of an active commercial career. Possessed of a competency, he seems to have devoted the rest of his brief life to literary and social pursuits. His favorite pleasure was shooting, which probably contributed to prolong his life. He was a skilled musician, and an accomplished painter. We are told that he was of medium height, well-proportioned, that his eye was animated, and his face handsome. These last details are certainly confirmed by a portrait painted by Robert Field, of which D. Edwin's engraving (D. M. Stauffer, *American Engravers*, 1907, no. 729) is given as the frontispiece to Cliffton's *Poems* (N. Y., 1800) and in the *Analectic Magazine*, June 1814—and in which the woodcut in Duyckinck's *Cyclopedia* is a bad reversed copy. Though living a retired life, Cliffton could not escape the political excitement of his times, and sided naturally enough with the more conservative party in Pennsylvania, which supported Washington, and favored the mother-country England in her struggle with regicide, Jacobin, and free-thinking France. When the more radical politicians were urging the United States to join France against Great Britain, Cliffton was a member of the Anchor Club, a small band of literary gentlemen who met for social purposes and to advocate war with France. For this body he wrote some prose papers upon the necessity of an established American navy and "Some Account of a Manuscript . . . entitled Talleyrand's Descent into Hell"—a mixture of prose and verse, which pictures the pains of the revolutionary leaders in the next world, and the happiness of the martyr Louis XVI in Elysium. The Anchor Club soon dissolved. But Cliffton wrote other poems—chief among them *The Group,* which was published as a pamphlet at Philadelphia (1796). It is a savage attack on Gallatin, containing much of the wit and coarseness to be expected in a follower of Pope and Churchill. "Rhapsody on the Times" recounts the adventures of an Irish ne'er-do-weel agitator who is kicked into the water for his pains in pointing out the faults of America to some citizens—all showing the influence of Peter Pindar's *Odes* and the poetry of the Anti-Jacobin. "The Chimeriad" is a satire on the ideal republics, so pleasing in the books of philosophers, that they have been happily left there. "The Address of the Devil to the United Irishmen," and their "Reply," poems first printed in the Philadelphia *Gazette of the United States,* wittily parody the style of councils with the Indians—instead of belts of wampum the chieftain of Hell and his earthly followers exchange halters, and "strings of lies and blasphemies." Upon Lord Nelson's victory of the Nile, Cliffton wrote a "Song" to the "hearts of oak," to be sung at a Philadelphia festival. It shows considerable lyric gift, as does the warlike "Soul of Columbia." In gentler vein are his "Il Penseroso," which reminds one of Gray and Collins, "The Flight of Fancy," which has a foretaste of Joseph Rodman Drake, the song, "Mary will smile," written for Miss Broadhurst to sing at the theatre, and the lyrical "To a Robin," "To Fancy," "To Sleep," and the song on "Friendship, Love, Wine, and Song." For the Philadelphia edition of William Gifford's *Baviad and Mæviad,* Cliffton wrote an introductory "Epistle" to the critic author, a piece showing his poetic gifts of smooth and forceful verse at their best. It is dated May 13, 1799. In December Cliffton died at the age of twenty-seven. A collected volume of *Poems, Chiefly Occasional,* was printed at New York the next year. Cliffton had perhaps more feeling, more quality, than any other American writer of his day save Freneau, and though inferior in genius to Drake and E. C. Pinkney, he ranks with them among the chief losses to American literature by early death.

[The source of most of our knowledge of Cliffton is the anonymous introduction to the edition of 1800. See also G. C. Verplanck's article in the *Analectic Mag.,* June 1814; E. P. Oberholtzer's *Lit. Hist. of Phila.* (1906), and Wm. Abbatt's edition of *The Group* published as *Mag. of Hist.,* Extra No. 92 (1923).]

T.O.M.

CLIFTON, JOSEPHINE (1813–Nov. 21, 1847), actress, was born in New York. She was the daughter of a Mrs. Miller, but was reared in the home of Thomas Hamblin, manager of the Bowery Theatre, where she made her début on Sept. 21, 1831, as Belvidera in Otway's *Venice Preserved.* This was followed by appearances in the same rôle at the Chestnut Street Theatre, Philadelphia, and as Lady Macbeth at the Walnut Street Theatre in the same city. In 1834, after a successful tour of the United States, she set out for London, the first American actress to attempt to star in England. She appeared as Belvidera at Drury Lane, thus breaking the ground for Charlotte Cushman a decade later, and then for Mrs. Mowatt. In 1837, Nathaniel P. Willis wrote a tragedy for her, *Bianca Visconti,* which she produced at the Park Theatre, New York City. H. P. Phelps (*post*) records her season in Albany in 1837, and lists her parts as Bianca, Mrs. Haller, Clari, Juliet, Lady Freelove, and Jane Shore. He also records that "she seemed likely at one time to rival Charlotte Cushman," but that as she grew older, "she became so lymphatic as almost to preclude study." Possibly her physical condition in later years was brought on by the revival of a long-dead scandal concerning her mother which was dug up by a scurrilous sheet called the *Polyanthus,*—the revelations so preying on the mind of Miss Clifton's younger sister, Louisa Missouri, as to cause her death at the age of seventeen in 1838. From this time the scattered records of Miss Clifton's appearances grow fewer and fewer. In July 1846, she married Robert Place, manager of the American Theatre in New Orleans, and died suddenly the following year. Her body was taken to Philadelphia and laid in the same grave with that of her sister. There was no reference to her in either the New York or Philadelphia papers at the time of her death. The New Orleans *Picayune* (Nov. 22, 1847), had a short editorial notice, in which it remarked on the fact that she had not acted "in late years," but added that no player had enjoyed a career "less checquered by the vacillation of public taste," and that she was popularly styled "The magnificent Josephine." This appellation, and the fact that she was once regarded as a rival of Charlotte Cushman, suggest a woman of beauty, talent, and forceful personality. But no adequate critical descriptions of her acting are available, and she remains a forgotten and faintly tragic figure.

[T. Allston Brown, *Hist. of the Am. Stage* (1870); H. P. Phelps, *Players of a Century* (1880); F. C. Wemyss, *Chronology of the Am. Stage* (1852).]

W.P.E.

CLINCH, CHARLES POWELL (Oct. 20, 1797–Dec. 16, 1880), author, was the son of

James Clinch, a wealthy ship-chandler of New York City. After a public school education, he obtained a post as secretary to Henry Eckford [*q.v.*], prominent marine architect and father-in-law of Joseph Rodman Drake [*q.v.*], the poet. Through his employer he met Drake, Fitz-Greene Halleck [*q.v.*], and other New York writers with whom he formed warm friendships. In 1835 he was elected a member of the state legislature, and his absences in Albany on this duty made the only break in his life-long residence in New York City and its environs. In that same year, fire plagued the city, and Clinch, who had invested heavily in insurance stocks, lost a fortune. In 1838 he obtained a place as inspector in the New York Custom House, becoming deputy collector and then assistant collector. He rendered indefatigable and faithful service for forty years, refusing on principle to act upon cases arising out of the importations of A. T. Stewart [*q.v.*], his brother-in-law. In 1876 he retired and moved from Staten Island back to New York City, where he died on Dec. 16, 1880. A likeness, taken late in life, pictures an exceedingly handsome man with bushy white hair, a clear eye, and a determined mouth.

During the long years of a busy life, Clinch acted as literary and dramatic critic and editorial writer for the press, prepared public addresses, and wrote plays, including *The Spy* (1822), a dramatic romance based on Cooper's novel of that name; *The Expelled Collegians*; and *The First of May,* which was produced at the Broadway Theatre. The manuscript of *The Spy* bears the marks of practical use, but it is uncertain that the play was professionally produced. The stiffness of its dialogue and its use of formal soliloquies sufficiently account for any want of marked appeal to the public taste. Clinch's critical prose possesses ease of manner, and his public addresses must have had a certain rhetorical force in delivery. On July 4, 1823, he delivered before the Fire Department of the City of New York an *Oration on the 47th Anniversary of American Independence,* which was subsequently published.

When in 1819 Drake and Halleck were writing the clever series of verse satires, known under the collective name of *The Croakers,* upon the political and social life of New York City, Clinch, with four other friends, assisted in preserving the anonymity of the two poets by copying the verses before they were sent to the New York *Evening Post* in which they received publication. He especially admired the poetry of Halleck and Bryant and dedicated a poem to the memory of the latter. The Knickerbockers, in turn, apparently considered him a clever and worthy member of their group. Clinch's relationship to them did not prohibit, now and then, a certain rivalry, as when both Halleck and Clinch submitted manuscripts, published in 1821, in competition for the prize address on the occasion of the opening of the Park Theatre in New York City.

[References to Clinch occur in Jas. Grant Wilson, *Life and Letters of Fitz-Greene Halleck* (1869), and, at greater length, in his *Bryant and His Friends* (1886). See also Hamilton W. Mabie, *The Writers of Knickerbocker N. Y.* (1912); *Evening Post* (N. Y.), Dec. 16, 1880; *N. Y. Times, Herald, Tribune, World, Sun,* all of Dec. 17, 1880.]   A. L. B.

CLINGMAN, THOMAS LANIER (July 27, 1812–Nov. 3, 1897), political leader in North Carolina during the ante bellum period, was born in Huntersville, Surry (now a part of Yadkin) County, N. C. His ancestry represents various racial strains. His father, Jacob Clingman, was of German stock; his mother, Jane, was the daughter of Capt. Francis Poindexter, of French descent, and Jane (Patillo) Lanier, daughter of Rev. Henry Patillo, Scotch Presbyterian clergyman of North Carolina and widow of Col. Robert Lanier. There was also Indian blood in the Poindexter family, Thomas Poindexter, father of Capt. Francis Poindexter, having married Elizabeth Pledge, daughter of a Cherokee chieftain. When Thomas Clingman was four years old his father died, and his early training was directed by his mother and uncle, Francis Alexander Poindexter. In 1832 he graduated at the University of North Carolina, leading his class. He then studied law at Hillsboro under William A. Graham [*q.v.*]. Returning to his native county, he represented Surry in the legislature of 1835, but soon after removed to Asheville, Buncombe County, where he resided for sixty years. He devoted his life to politics and the development of the mountain region of North Carolina. In 1840 he was a member of the state Senate from Buncombe and in 1843 was a member of the Twenty-eighth Congress from the mountain district. In the following Congress he did not appear but from the Thirtieth to the Thirty-fifth (1847–58) he continuously represented his district and from 1858 until the opening of the Civil War was in the Senate.

In the earlier part of his career he was a staunch Whig, inclined to independent action. Thus he was one of the few Southern Whigs who voted against the exclusion of abolition petitions. At various times he denounced the Democratic party and John C. Calhoun in strong language. As a result of one of these outbursts he fought a duel with William L. Yancey in 1845,

Yancey missing fire and Clingman firing over his opponent's head. In the discussion on the Wilmot Proviso, Clingman upheld the theoretical right of Congress to regulate slave property in the territories and also the practical necessity of making half the new territories slave and half free. In 1848 he began to distrust the attitude of the Northern Whigs toward the slavery question and his distrust was confirmed on a visit to the Northern states in the autumn of 1849. On his return to Washington in December of that year he undertook to arouse Southern sentiment by a letter to Senator Foote of Mississippi, a Democrat, urging preparation for resistance "in a manner commensurate with the violence of the attack." He did not, however, support Calhoun in the effort to form a Southern *bloc* in Congress, but was instrumental in the filibustering which resulted in the election of Howell Cobb [*q.v.*] as speaker of the Thirty-first Congress. As an adjustment of the slavery controversy he favored the extension of the northern boundary of Missouri to the Pacific as the dividing line between free and slave territories, and did not support any of the compromise measures of 1850, except the fugitive-slave law. In the next election, his failure to vote for the compromise measures and his inclination to support the right of secession cost him many votes, and he was reëlected by a reduced majority. In 1852 he definitely left the Whig party, carrying his district with him into the ranks of the Democracy. In 1861 he was a delegate from North Carolina to the Confederate States convention at Montgomery, Ala. In August 1861 he was appointed colonel of the 25th North Carolina Volunteers, and in 1862 he became a brigadier-general. After the close of the Civil War he attempted to resume his seat in the Senate, from which he had been expelled after the opening of hostilities, but he was not allowed to do so. Thereafter he served in no political capacity save as member of the North Carolina constitutional convention of 1875. He devoted much of his energy in his later years to exploiting the resources of western North Carolina. He never married.

[No formal biography of Clingman exists, but his niece, Mrs Jane P. Kerr, contributed an excellent personal sketch, "Brig.-Gen. Thos. L. Clingman," to the *Trinity Archive*, Mar. 1899. Supplementing this is John S. Bassett, "Cong. Career of Thos. L. Clingman," in *Papers of Trinity Coll. Hist. Soc.*, 4 ser., 1900. *The Speeches and Writings of Thos. L. Clingman* (1877), is a selection of his speeches and essays, and J. M. Huger, *Memorandum of the Late Affair of Honor* (1845), treats of the duel with Yancey.]   W. K. B.

CLINTON, DeWITT (Mar. 2, 1769–Feb. 11, 1828), statesman, philanthropist, savant, was born at Little Britain, Orange County, N. Y. Charles Clinton, a scion of an English family long domiciled at Longford, Ireland, had led a party of immigrants to America in 1729 and to this region of New York in 1731, where he set up as a surveyor, farmer and land speculator. Two of his sons were destined to fame: George [*q.v.*], as the first governor of New York State and his elder brother James [*q.v.*], a major-general in the Revolutionary War. The latter was father of DeWitt Clinton, second son of his marriage with Mary DeWitt, daughter of an old Dutch family. DeWitt was educated at Rev. John Moffat's grammar school, then for two years at the Kingston Academy which, under John Addison, was the leading school of that grade in the state, and finally at Columbia College, where he graduated A.B. at the head of his class in 1786. The college as he knew it is described in his address delivered in 1827 before the alumni (W. W. Campbell, *post*, pp. 1-19). He studied law with Samuel Jones, Jr., and was admitted to the bar, but made little immediate use of his legal learning except in his private land transactions in western New York. Accustomed from earliest youth to the discussion of public affairs, while still a law student he enlisted actively in the interest of his uncle, the Governor; in November 1787 he published through the *New York Journal* a series of letters over the signature "A Countryman" opposing the proposed United States Constitution, and wrote a report of the ratifying convention at Poughkeepsie with a strong Anti-Federalist bias. Shortly after he had completed his three years of legal study, he accepted the post of private secretary to his uncle, and soon to these duties were added those of secretary of the board of regents and of the board of fortification. Thus at about the age of twenty he had arrived at a position of considerable political influence without having been obliged to serve an apprenticeship in the humble ranks of party workers, a circumstance which may account for certain defects as a tactician which he showed in later life.

With the fall of his party in 1795 he lost his offices and thereupon carried forward a program of study in natural science under the impulse and guidance of Professors S. L. Mitchill and David Hosack of Columbia, but still found time actively to oppose the administrations of President Adams and Gov. Jay. In 1797 he was elected to the Assembly and the following year to a four-year term in the state Senate. Under the constitution of 1777 the Assembly chose annually four senators to sit with the governor as a council of appointment, having at its disposal some fifteen thousand offices, civil and military. To this Clinton was elected in 1801. It had been customary for the governor to propose appointments and for the other members of the council to advise, ratify, or reject. Clinton vigorously disputed this interpretation of the constitution, claiming that any member could introduce names, and he and Gov. Jay debated their respective positions in written argument before the Assembly. The matter was left to a constitutional convention which, controlled by the governor's opponents, sustained Clinton's interpretation, he having made the principal speech before it on that side. Now virtually in control of the council, he took the lead in supplanting Federalists with Republicans, on principle, and thus has been blamed by historians as the father of the spoils system in the United States. As a matter of fact such practises in the government of New York date from a hundred years earlier; under Clinton's direction the system was doubtless more radical, and yet even this was partially justified by the exclusive policy which had been pursued by the retiring Federalists (H. L. McBain, *DeWitt Clinton and the Origin of the Spoils System in New York*, 1907, p. 158). "The meekness of Quakerism," he remarked, "will do in religion, but not in politics" (letter quoted in S. P. Orth, *Five American Politicians*, 1906, p. 90).

On the resignation of John Armstrong from the United States Senate, Clinton was appointed (Feb. 19, 1802) to be his successor. He served through two annual sessions, making a long and creditable speech against the proposal introduced by the Federalists to seize New Orleans, whose Spanish governor had lately denied to Americans of the Mississippi Valley the necessary right to land goods on those wharves preparatory to ocean shipping (*Annals of Congress*, 7 Cong., 2 Sess., pp. 105–56), and introducing the Twelfth Amendment providing for the present method of electing president and vice-president (*Ibid.*, 8 Cong., 1 Sess., p. 16). Though he had made an excellent beginning as a senator he resigned his office in October 1803 to accept that of mayor of the City of New York. He was moved to do this, apparently, by the feeling that he could be of use to his uncle, that the office was one of dignity and importance, proportionately greater then than now, and possibly because the emoluments, which through accumulation of fees then amounted to about $15,000 annually (D. R. Fox, *Decline of Aristocracy in the Politics of New York*, 1918, p. 111), would restore his finances then, as frequently, disordered by

generosity and neglect. At any rate it removed him from national politics when he might have played a great rôle, and made New York the theatre of his effort. It was, as his contemporaries came to realize, the turning point in his career (J. D. Hammond, *History of Political Parties in the State of New York*, 1842, I, 197–200; W. H. Seward, *Works*, 1884, IV, 211).

He was mayor of New York from 1803 to 1815 with the exception of two annual terms (1807–08 and 1810–11); no mayor since has served so long; probably no mayor has done more for the city. Just as when an assemblyman he had concerned himself with better laws on sanitation, the relief of prisoners for debt, the abolition of slavery, the promotion of steam navigation, the encouragement of agriculture, etc., so now he was the chief organizer of the Public School Society (1805), the chief patron of the New York Orphan Asylum, and of the New York City Hospital (Hosack, *post*, pp. 46–50). He was faithful in attendance upon fires, a requirement of his office, fearless in quelling mobs, and indefatigable in inspecting markets, docks, etc. (Renwick, *post*, pp. 73–74). He obtained $100,000 as an appropriation for defense and supervised the erection of fortifications on Governor's Island and elsewhere about the city. He adopted a firm tone in dealing with officers of British war-ships who attempted to impress sailors in the harbor (on the *Leander* affair of 1805, see manuscript letters to Clinton) and to blockade the Narrows in order to prevent the escape of French ships. It was during his administration that the city adopted the plan followed in its subsequent development over Manhattan Island. He was the last mayor to preside in the mayor's court, subsequently made into the court of common pleas (*New York Civil List*, 1884, p. 258). While mayor he was also a state senator (1806–11) and then lieutenant-governor (1811–13).

After his return to New York in 1803 Clinton was considered the most powerful political leader in the state. He virtually dictated the nomination of Morgan Lewis for governor in 1804. In 1800 the three factions of the Republican party, the Clintonian, the Livingstonian, and the Burrite, had united behind Jefferson. To DeWitt Clinton, indeed, is attributed a pamphlet then published by "Grotius," *A Vindication of Thomas Jefferson* from charges of infidelity. But the Burrites had been read out in 1804, and before Lewis's three-year term was finished Clinton had broken with the Livingston faction which the Governor represented, and in 1807 he succeeded in electing his candidate, Daniel

D. Tompkins, over Lewis. He was now considered somewhat of a heretic by the national administration. Influenced by the New York merchants, he at first opposed the embargo, but retreated from this position before a definite break with Jefferson had been forced. In 1809, fearing the influence of the Tammany Society, always in harmony with Virginia leadership, he attempted to win over the old Burrites and approached their leader, John Swartwout—albeit he had once fought a duel with him (Clinton-Post letters, *Harper's Magazine,* Mar. 1875)—but again drew back, because of the jeers of the Tammany "Martling," or "Bucktail," faction which quoted his utterances on Burr in 1804. He was thus earning a reputation as a political trader (D. S. Alexander, *A Political History of the State of New York,* 1906–09, I, chaps. XIV–XVI).

This impression was deepened in the presidential campaign of 1812. Clinton was enough of an insurgent to have attracted the attention of certain Federalists. His strong dislike of "mob rule," expressed in a charge in his mayor's court during the Columbia College riot case (D. R. Fox, *Decline of Aristocracy,* pp. 162–66), had pleased such observers, as well as his supposed favor of a Federalist project, the Merchants' Bank. About seventy Federalist leaders from many states gathered in New York, Sept. 15, 1812, for consultation as to a candidate; they were not strictly delegates and they kept the privacy of a caucus, yet they more closely resembled a modern nomination convention than any gathering before (J. S. Murdock, *American Historical Review,* July 1896). Led by H. G. Otis, the meeting passed resolutions favorable to Clinton as a candidate, though they did not formally nominate him, owing to the opposition of Rufus King and others. He had already been nominated by the Republicans of the New York legislature, the first important challenge to the mode of nomination by congressional caucus. His position seemed equivocal; his agents recommended him among New England Federalists as a man who would stop the war with England which had begun in June, while with Republicans they maintained that he would fight it more vigorously than his rival, Madison (J. D. Hammond, *History of Political Parties in the State of New York,* 1842, I, 353, 399–450). He was defeated by an electoral vote of 128 to 89, getting all votes east of the Delaware except the eight from Vermont, together with five of Maryland's eleven. Had Pennsylvania voted with her northern neighbors, Clinton would have been president. His consorting with

Federalists seemed to ruin his prestige with his own party in New York. He was not renominated for lieutenant-governor; in 1815 he was removed from his office of mayor.

The politician being rebuked, the statesman emerged. Clinton now devoted himself to promoting the project of a state canal from the Great Lakes to the Hudson. The advantages of some such scheme had been apparent to many minds, but it was Clinton who by calculation and by effective presentation established its practicability. He had been appointed one of the canal commissioners in 1810 and with some of his colleagues had journeyed across the state to Buffalo when they satisfied themselves that a canal could be built to Lake Erie, a safer route in case of war with Great Britain than would be one which included Lake Ontario. In 1811 with Gouverneur Morris he tried unsuccessfully to gain federal aid for the project; the War of 1812 necessitated postponing its serious consideration either at Washington or at Albany. Now in 1816, however, Clinton believed the time propitious and, aiding in the organization of public meetings throughout the state, he presented a memorial to be sent to the legislature favoring the enterprise as a state work.

After obtaining many signatures he went personally to Albany to urge the acceptance of his plan, which outlined not only the main features of the engineering process, but the commercial benefits to be expected and the method by which it might be financed, all the result of long study. On Apr. 17, 1816, the legislature adopted the plan, and a new canal commission, of which Clinton was also a member, set to work to survey in detail the ways and means by which Lakes Erie and Champlain might be connected with the Hudson. Clinton and Stephen Van Rensselaer, though like the others giving full time to these duties, would accept no compensation. Gov. Tompkins resigning in March 1817 to become vice-president, Clinton was nominated as his successor by the first state convention, made up of Republican legislators supplemented by delegates from districts not so represented by Republicans, and, despite the opposition of the Tammany Society, he was elected by a vote of 43,310 against Peter B. Porter with 1,479.

As governor he prosecuted the building of the canal both by his writing, as in the "Tacitus" papers published in 1821, and by constant personal contact with the work. He stood here for constructive leadership and active government, thus drawing many old Federalists to his support; inevitably he acknowledged this in official favor. Martin Van Buren, now leading the Tammany-Virginia wing of the party, seized upon this circumstance to brand Clinton as a Federalist, built up a strong opposition of disgruntled politicians, and, supporting Rufus King, long disliked by Clinton, for reëlection to the United States Senate, even pulled into these opposition ranks a group of "high minded Federalists," who soon berated Clinton in their organ the *New York American*. As a result Clinton was reëlected governor in 1820 over Vice-President Tompkins by only a narrow margin of 1,457 votes out of 93,437. Party strife was at high pitch. Though Clinton appreciated that the constitution of 1777 had grave defects, especially the council of appointment, he hesitated to recommend a new convention, then being proposed, which almost certainly would be in the hands of his opponents; and though he finally indorsed the project, he found that his hesitation had still further impaired his popularity. He did not attempt a campaign for reëlection in 1822, retiring on Jan. 1, 1823, the strongest man in the public life of New York, but the weakest, for the moment, in partisan support. The "Albany Regency" directed by Senator Van Buren was supreme.

On Apr. 12, 1824, in a wave of party frenzy the Regency men removed Clinton from his office of canal commissioner which he had held since 1810, an act so wanton as to develop a strong reaction in Clinton's favor throughout the state (Hosack, *Memoir*, pp. 464–81). The Anti-Regency element, now organized as the People's party promptly adopted him as candidate for governor and he was elected in November by a vote of 103,452 against 87,093 for Samuel Young. Thus, appropriately, he was governor when the canals were completed in 1825—the Erie, 362 miles, and the Champlain, 71 miles—and took a prominent part in the celebration of the event by which New York City rather than New Orleans became the port of the Northwest. President Adams offered him the post of minister to England, but he declined. He apparently had presidential aspirations and was later (1827) put in nomination by a convention at Steubenville, Ohio. But he could hardly have commanded support throughout the North, because of his state-rights views.

He offended many by his distribution of patronage, others by his choice of local-improvement projects to advocate; he disliked Adams and favored Jackson, though many of his sturdiest supporters were Adams men; he was an active Mason, having been elected to the highest station in the American order in 1816, and hence was objectionable to many in the western coun-

ties affected by the Anti-Masonic excitement beginning in 1826. Consequently in the election of that year his former majority was much reduced, the vote standing, Clinton, 99,785, and William B. Rochester, 96,135. His messages to the legislature reveal an energetic and highly intelligent mind, though some of his recommendations, as for normal schools and a legal code, were made long before the state was ready for them.

A picture of Clinton as a politician only would be singularly distorted. He was perhaps the most effective personal force for public education in the history of the state. Besides his work in the Public School Society of New York City of which he was the first president, he was probably the leading promoter of the Lancasterian schools in America (J. F. Reigart, *The Lancasterian System*, 1916, p. 17). He was a naturalist of real attainment, discovering a native American wheat, and a new fish, the Salmo Otsego, and publishing papers on pigeons, swallows, rice, etc., and he was a member of many scientific societies in this country and abroad. His *Introductory Discourse* (1814) was certainly one of the best summaries of the state of scientific knowledge in America that appeared in the early years of the century. He was the second president of the American Academy of Art, pronouncing an "elegant" discourse before it in 1816. In 1817 he was elected president of the New York Historical Society of which he had been a founder, and in 1811 delivered before it an address on the Six Nations. He had secured its charter in 1809 and five years later a grant of a lottery fund from the state. While governor he inaugurated the work of translating the state's Dutch archives. He was co-founder of the Literary and Philosophical Society in 1816, New York's first attempt to rival the American Philosophical Society in Philadelphia, and continued as its president until his death. He was also actively identified with the Lyceum of National History, the Humane Society, the Society for the Promotion of Useful Arts, etc. In 1820 he published a *Memoir on the Antiquities of the Western Parts of the State of New York*. He was vice-president of the American Bible Society (Address in Campbell, 297–308), where he several times presided in the absence of the president John Jay, and held the same office in the Education Society of the Presbyterian Church. Yet he was no bigot; in 1806 he succeeded in having removed the political disabilities of Roman Catholics in New York, and while mayor set a precedent by respecting the secrets of the confessional when a priest was on the witness stand (Renwick, p. 91).

His sudden death, Feb. 11, 1828, at his residence in Albany simplified political alignments in New York, restoring the clear distinction of a dozen years before, but it removed a great leader. He was inept in intrigue, overbearing in manner, demanding support but indifferent to supporters, cynical as to the virtue of others, and hence personally unpopular. At the same time he was generally admired and respected as a man of liberal ideas and administrative competence. His principles associated him with democrats, his tastes with aristocrats. He expressed himself on all occasions as the friend of state rights, yet other interests that he cherished, such as internal improvements and the growth of manufacturing, demanded another theory of government. Having long disliked Virginia, he could not easily gain great influence in the Democratic party; even had his principles allowed him he could not have risen to leadership among the National Republicans since that would have meant cooperation with Adams, of whom he was inordinately jealous. Death came, perhaps, when he had done what he was fitted best to do.

After some partisan wrangling the legislature voted $10,000 for his minor children. He had been married twice, first on Feb. 13, 1796, to Maria Franklin, daughter of the prominent New York Quaker merchant, Walter Franklin, by whom he had ten children, four sons and three daughters surviving at the time of her death in 1818. On May 8, 1819, he married Catharine Jones, daughter of a New York physician, Thomas Jones, who survived him. In appearance he was impressive, being six feet tall and of such proportions as to give him the sobriquet "Magnus Apollo."

[David Hosack, *Memoir of DeWitt Clinton* (N. Y., 1829), the first biography published, is a mere memorial discourse, but the Appendix, pp. 136–530, has much indispensable material. Jas. Renwick, *Life of DeWitt Clinton* (N. Y., 1840), is the best narrative. W. W. Campbell, *Life and Writings of DeWitt Clinton* (N. Y., 1849), devotes but ten pages to the life, being valuable chiefly for the Private Journal of 1810, pp. 27–204, not published elsewhere. Cuyler Staats, *Tribute to the Memory of DeWitt Clinton* (Albany, 1828) contains a collection of editorial comments upon his death. Clinton's writings, mentioned in the sketch, are published separately and in Campbell. His communications to the legislature are printed in C. Z. Lincoln, ed., *Messages from the Governors* (Albany, 1909), vols. II, III. His manuscript correspondence is largely in the Columbia Univ. Lib. and the N. Y. Pub. Lib. His diary is in the N. Y. Hist. Soc. E. A. Fitzpatrick, *Educational Views of DeWitt Clinton* (1911), analyzes his cultural contribution in general.]   D.R.F.

CLINTON, GEORGE (c. 1686–July 10, 1761), colonial governor, came of a family long distinguished for public service. He was a younger son of Francis Clinton, sixth earl of Lincoln, and of Susan, daughter of Anthony Penniston of Oxfordshire. Through his brother, the seventh earl

of Lincoln, and his nephew, the ninth earl, he was connected by marriage with the Pelham family, the most prominent members of which, Thomas Pelham-Holles, Duke of Newcastle, and Henry Pelham, were leaders of the Whig aristocracy of the eighteenth century. It was through this connection with Newcastle that Clinton secured most of the important appointments of his career. He entered the navy in 1708 (British Museum, Additional MSS., 32,693, fos. 245–48) and attained his captaincy in 1716. During the next twenty-five years he received various naval assignments, the most important of which were those of commodore of the convoy to Newfoundland and governor of that island in 1731 and of commodore and commander-in-chief of the squadron in the Mediterranean in 1737. On Dec. 10, 1743, Clinton was promoted to be rear admiral of the red squadron and on the following June 23 was advanced to be vice admiral of the white. On Apr. 23, 1745, he rose to be vice admiral of the red, and on July 15, 1747, he received his final promotion to the rank of admiral of the white. From 1757 until his death he was the senior flag officer of the navy. As a naval officer he had almost no opportunities to distinguish himself, and apparently his abilities in this direction were little above the ordinary. After attaining the rank of rear admiral he never served at sea.

During the latter years of his captaincy, he had become increasingly dissatisfied with his prospects and especially with his meager income. Although he had expressed a desire to "live by the sea," he began, about 1739, to press Newcastle for the governorship of New York, a post in which he believed he might live at ease on shore while ridding himself of the heavy debts which he had incurred. At first Newcastle was inclined to put him off, but Clinton's financial situation grew steadily worse and his fear of his creditors increased until he wrote that he was "obliged to a way I never knew before, of going out very early in a morning and not returning till dark night, afraid what may happen" (Additional MSS., 32,693, fo. 268). Finally Newcastle yielded, and on July 3, 1741, Clinton's commission as governor passed the seals. After an unusually long delay in departure, he arrived in the province on Sept. 20, 1743, and at once assumed the administration. One of the greatest weaknesses of his character—his entire dependence on others for advice and support—immediately displayed itself. Largely through the influence of James De Lancey [*q.v.*], chief justice of the province and its leading politician, he endeavored to conciliate the Assembly by permitting the passage of an annual revenue law, instead of one of perpetual duration or for a term of years as his instructions directed. The outbreak of war with France in the following year and the exigencies of civil administration, enabled the Assembly to gain further advantages, especially in financial matters. A personal quarrel with De Lancey in the spring of 1746 threw the Governor into the hands of Cadwallader Colden [q.v.], the senior councillor and a bitter enemy of the chief justice. For the next four years Colden controlled the Governor's policy and drafted most of his messages to the Assembly with unfortunate results to Clinton's popularity. Always more interested in military than in civil affairs, Clinton permitted the legislature to assume entire control of all appropriations, contrary to his instructions, and even to dictate the appointment of officers. On the other hand, the Assembly's refusal to advance the money necessary for the pay of the troops raised for the abortive expedition to Canada in 1746 and 1747 or for gifts needed to secure the cooperation of the Iroquois, gave the Governor an excuse to draw upon the home government for about £84,000, a large part of which, according to his opponents, found its way into his own private fortune. The truth of this charge cannot now be fully determined, but it seems certain that Clinton was not entirely scrupulous in the methods he employed to gain that financial profit which was his chief incentive in securing the governorship. At the close of the war in 1748 he made a gallant attempt to regain the authority which he had lost. Fortified by the advice of Gov. Shirley of Massachusetts, he put aside his naturally indolent and easy-going ways and refused to approve the Assembly's money bills unless it would surrender the executive powers which it had seized. But his frantic appeals for help from home went unanswered, due to the incompetence of the Board of Trade and its concern with other matters. After two years of deadlock, without salary from the province or encouragement from England, Clinton gave way and conceded all the advances which the Assembly had made. The last three years of his administration were passed in comparative quiet. But, meanwhile, the Board of Trade had revived under the leadership of the Earl of Halifax and had determined upon a vigorous effort to restore the prerogative in New York. For this purpose a new governor was deemed necessary. Clinton was therefore superseded on Oct. 10, 1753, by Sir Danvers Osborn, a brother-in-law of Halifax. Subsequent governors, however, never recovered more than a small part of the authority which Clinton had lost, and his administration

thus brought a permanent weakening of the royal government in the province and a corresponding increase in popular control. His failure was due in part to conditions brought by the war, but more particularly to his own dependence on ill-chosen advisers, to his reluctance to exert himself in a struggle with the Assembly, and to the absence from his character of those qualities which make a successful politician. "Easy in his temper but uncapable of business," wrote a son of a member of his council, "he was always obliged to rely upon some favorite. In a province given to hospitality, he erred by immuring himself in the fort, or retiring to a grotto in the country, where his time was spent with his bottle and a little trifling circle, who played billiards with his lady and lived upon his bounty" (Smith, post, II, 158). He returned to England with £80,-000, was made governor of Greenwich Hospital and sat in parliament from 1754 to 1760 as a member for the borough of Saltash. He died July 10, 1761, survived by his widow, Anne, daughter of Major-General Peter Carle, by one daughter, and by a son, later distinguished as Major-General Sir Henry Clinton, K.B., commander-in-chief of the British forces during a large part of the American Revolution.

[The most important body of material on Clinton's administration in New York is in *Docs. Relative to the Colonial Hist. of the State of N. Y.*, ed. by E. B. O'Callaghan, vol. VI, which contains his correspondence with the English officials as well as other documents, including an exhaustive report by the Board of Trade on his relations with the Assembly. Other letters relating to his governorship are printed in "The Letters and Papers of Cadwallader Colden," *N. Y. Hist. Soc. Colls.*, vols. L–LVI (1917–23), and in *The Papers of Sir Wm. Johnson*, vol. I (1921). The unpublished papers of the Clinton family are located at the William L. Clements Lib., Ann Arbor, Mich. Clinton's letters to Newcastle regarding his appointment as governor are in the Brit. Mus., Additional MSS., 32,692–32,699 (Newcastle Papers VII–XIV). Extended notice of Clinton's family and of himself is given in Arthur Collins's *Peerage*, of which the best editions for this purpose are those of 1756 (II, 128–68) and 1779 (pp. 243–79), and a generally accurate sketch of his naval career appears in John Carnock's *Biographia Navalis* (1796), IV, 59–62. Wm. Smith's "Hist. of N. Y.," *N. Y. Hist. Soc. Colls.*, 1829–30, contains a vivid and, on the whole, fair account of Clinton's administration. Since Smith was the son of a contemporary political leader and was in after years himself a member of the provincial council, his work is especially valuable. The best recent account of part of Clinton's administration is in H. L. Osgood, *Am. Colonies in the Eighteenth Century*, vol. IV (1924), Chap. X.]   L. W. L.

CLINTON, GEORGE (July 26, 1739–Apr. 20, 1812), Revolutionary soldier, statesman, served seven times as governor of the State of New York and was twice elected vice-president of the United States. His father, Charles, born in 1690 in the county of Longford, Ireland, organized a group of colonists, came to America, and finally, in 1731, settled at Little Britain in Ulster

County, N. Y. Here, eight years later, George was born. During a short period in 1758 he served on the *Defiance,* a privateer sailing from New York. As a subaltern in his father's regiment he was a member of the successful expedition led by Col. John Bradstreet against Fort Frontenac on Lake Ontario. After having studied law under William Smith in New York he returned to Ulster County where he practised with reputation if not with distinction. Elected to the Provincial Assembly in 1768, he became the rival of Philip Schuyler in the leadership of a revolutionary minority. His ostentatious defense of Alexander McDougall, who posed as the John Wilkes of America, augmented his reputation as a fiery young radical and defender of freedom of speech and of the press. By his marriage to Cornelia Tappen on Feb. 7, 1770, he allied himself with the Wynkoops, a family politically powerful in Ulster County.

Having been a member of the corresponding committee appointed by the Assembly, Clinton was elected a delegate to the Second Continental Congress, and in December 1775 he became brigadier-general of militia. He voted for separation from Great Britain, but military duties in New York caused his absence at the signing of the Declaration of Independence. At the beginning of the war he was one of the few leaders in the colonies who possessed military experience, and he was entrusted with measures necessary to the defense of the Hudson River. He was a man of vigor and courage, but he proved to be deficient in military ability. His defense of Fort Montgomery was so unskilful that its capture was easily accomplished by the British; nor did he make any serious efforts to prevent the burning of Esopus by the enemy in the fall of 1777. In March of that year he had written the New York Convention that he contemplated resigning his military command because "from fatal Experience I find that I am not able to render my Country that Service which they may have Reason to expect of me" (*Public Papers,* I, 643). In the same month he was commissioned brigadier-general in the Continental Army. In the elections to state office in June 1777, Clinton, despite the plans of political leaders, defeated Philip Schuyler and was elected both governor and lieutenant-governor. The election was a surprise to the ruling class; John Jay wrote that "Clinton's family and connections do not entitle him to so distinguished a pre-eminence." He resigned the lieutenant-governorship and, after a series of delays incident to his military duties, he was inaugurated governor at Kingston on July 30, 1777. This was the beginning of a series of six successive terms as governor. Although he had failed to win renown on the battle-field he had been able to inspire the people with confidence and to urge them on to significant efforts in the revolutionary struggle. He managed the difficult finances of the state adroitly and dealt with the troublesome Indian situation in western New York with considerable success. He was also popular because he dealt severely with the Loyalists in New York.

Clinton is chiefly remembered as a great war governor and as the father of his state; but he was also one of the most vigorous of the opponents of the adoption of the Federal Constitution. As early as 1781 he had disapproved of the legislative grant to Congress of the import duties collected in the port of New York and in 1783 he secured the passage of a law providing that, although the duties were to be given to Congress, they were to be collected by officials of the state. This unfriendliness to a national revenue was later to become a determined opposition to a national government. Many facts contributed to his advocacy of state sovereignty. He well understood the commercial advantage of New York state's geographical situation and believed that it made too great a sacrifice for the few advantages it would gain from union. Nor did he wish to diminish the state's and his own political power. Clinton had used the immense patronage that the constitution conferred upon the governor to build up a powerful political machine. He "preferred to remain the most powerful citizen of New York rather than occupy a subordinate place under a national government in which his own state was not foremost" (John Fiske, *Essays Historical and Literary,* 1902, I, 118). In September 1787 Congress submitted a draft of the proposed federal constitution to the legislatures of the various states. Writing under the name of "Cato," Clinton published seven letters against adoption in the *New York Journal* from September until the following January. The author of these letters was attacked by Hamilton in two letters written by "Cæsar" to the *Daily Advertiser* in October. In his opening address to the legislature Clinton did not even mention the ratification of the constitution, the important question for legislative consideration. It was under the leadership of Egbert Benson that a resolution providing for a convention was finally passed. Of this convention, held at Poughkeepsie the following June, Clinton was president. It was not until the constitution had been ratified by the necessary number of states and he had lost the support of Melancthon Smith that he acquiesced in the ratification by the New York convention.

With the possible exception of that offered by

Jay in 1786, there had been no considerable opposition to the various elections of Clinton to the governorship. In 1789, however, the contest between Robert Yates [q.v.] and Clinton was sharp and bitter. A large majority in Ulster County, whose vote he controlled, gave Clinton a total majority of over four hundred votes, but he was alone in surviving the close election. Preparations were at once begun for the next election; here Clinton displayed the abilities of a master politician. He appointed his late opponent chief justice; and in his attempt to attach brilliant and promising young men to the ranks of the Anti-Federalists he made Aaron Burr attorney-general. In 1791 he was able to obtain the election of Burr as United States senator, and it was partly through Burr that he was able to secure the support of the powerful Livingston family. The 1792 election was the most bitter that the state had yet experienced. Jay was again the opponent of Clinton and received a majority of the votes cast for the governorship; but through a notoriously unjust and partisan decision, the state canvassers ruled out the ballots of three counties on technicalities and awarded the election to Clinton. If Clinton had thus established a vicious precedent in usurping the governorship, it was the conversion of the Council of Appointment into a great political machine by his opponents under the leadership of Philip Schuyler that led to twenty years of political corruption and scandal. Clinton was quickly shorn of his great powers as governor by the Federalist Assembly. In 1795, when defeat would have been inevitable, he declined to become a candidate for governor again. He sensed the changes that were about to come in the politics of New York; and he dreamed of offices of greater honor and prestige.

He did not again participate actively in politics until 1800, when political control of the state passed from the Federalists to the Republicans. This was brought about partly by the election of Jefferson to the presidency and partly by the strength of the coalition ticket that Burr had selected against Hamilton. Clinton was elected to his seventh term as governor. As early as 1804 his friends began to work for his election as vice-president and in February 1804 he replaced Burr on the Republican ticket; while in the state elections Morgan Lewis, supported by the Clinton and Livingston factions, defeated Burr for the governorship. Clinton was elected vice-president and went into comfortable retirement until 1808 when he definitely entered the presidential contest, as an insurgent Democrat with a policy highly acceptable to the Federalists, for whose support on a coalition ticket he was bidding. This

alliance the Federalists seriously considered, but with the reëstablishment of Democratic harmony in Pennsylvania the strength of Clinton outside of New York vanished and there was little that the Federalists could gain by a coalition (see S. E. Morison in *American Historical Review*, XVII, 744–58). Clinton was returned to the vice-presidency on the Republican ticket with James Madison, whom he held in contempt and toward whom, in 1809, he was openly hostile. His last conspicuous act was to break the tie in the Senate (Feb. 20, 1811) by casting his vote against the bill to re-charter the Bank of the United States (Henry Adams, *post*, V, 336–37). He died in office, Apr. 20, 1812.

[No adequate biographical treatment of Clinton exists. Hugh Hastings's introduction in vol. I of the *Public Papers of George Clinton* is discursive and incompetent, as are the twenty-one papers on Clinton by Benj. Meyer Brink in *Olde Ulster*, vols. IV–VI (1908–10). Vol. X of the *Public Papers* contains a list of biographical articles and of Clinton MSS.; to the former should be added scattered references in *Papers* and *Annual Reports* of the Am. Hist. Asso., and to the latter, MSS. in the Henry E. Huntington Lib. and in the Lib. of Cong. The *Public Papers of George Clinton* (10 vols., printed by the State of N. Y., 1899–1914) print many MSS., since destroyed by the fire of 1911. Valuable are Henry Adams, *Hist. of the U. S.* (1889–91); J. D. Hammond, *Hist. of Political Parties in the State of N. Y.* (2 vols., 1846 ed.) and D. S. Alexander's *Political Hist. of the State of N. Y.* (2 vols., 1906); see also *Essays on the Constitution of the U. S.* (1892), ed. by P. L. Ford and the *Works of Alexander Hamilton* (1885–86), ed. by H. C. Lodge.]   F.M.

CLINTON, GEORGE WYLIE (Mar. 28, 1859–May 12, 1921), negro bishop, was born in Cedar Creek Township, Lancaster County, S. C. In the midst of the Black Belt where negroes were reduced to a lower plane than in the case of those better circumstanced in the border states, he had little opportunity for mental development. Having an intelligent father, however, he learned some of the fundamentals before the Civil War. Immediately after freedom, his mother, having also the same interest in the thorough education of her son, engaged in hard labor that he might be properly equipped for life. Desiring more thorough training than that which he had obtained immediately after freedom, he was among the first to become a student at the University of South Carolina when its doors were thrown open to negroes. He remained there from 1874 until 1877 when the negroes were ejected as a result of legislation restricting the use of the university to the whites. Interrupted thus in his studies, Clinton entered upon teaching and continued in this work for twelve years. Believing that he would have to perform other duties of importance, he always had the impression that he should have a professional career. While engaged in teaching, therefore, he read law for some months in the of-ice of Allison & Connors of Lancaster County. Uniting with the study of Blackstone that of the Bible, he became more deeply interested in the latter. While he learned sufficient law to be useful in drafting papers in one or more cases, he tended to restrict himself to the study of the Scriptures. Experiencing a call to the ministry, he was licensed as the local preacher of the A. M. E. Zion Church in 1879, and was admitted to the Traveling Association, Nov. 21, 1881. As a minister, he held some of the most important appointments in the South Carolina Conference and served also with distinction in Pittsburgh. Meanwhile, he was also making a number of literary contributions to various newspapers and magazines. In connection with his pastorate in Pittsburgh, he edited the *Afro-American Spokesman,* a paper devoted to all matters of interest to the negro. In this capacity he impressed upon the public opinions which were helpful to negroes throughout the nation in shaping a new program for their future. He was, therefore, able to induce his denomination to establish in 1890 the homiletic publication, the *Quarterly Review* of the A. M. E. Zion Church. After developing this magazine to the extent that it was recognized as important in filling a distinct place in the religious life of the denomination, he was made editor of the *Star of Zion,* a weekly organ. Becoming a stronger factor in his church as a result of his increasing influence, he was elected and consecrated bishop in 1896. In this commanding position among his people he became a national figure with influence extending far beyond the limits of his denomination. Educators and social uplift workers of both races sought his opinion on matters of policy and procedure. His simplicity, his common sense, and his sympathy for humanity endeared him to those who knew him. He participated in the Southern Sociological Congress, and was conspicuous in the work of the Interracial Commission of the South and in that of the Federal Council of the Churches of Christ in America.

[J. W. Hood, *One Hundred Years of the African M. E. Zion Church* (1895), pp. 268–74; I. G. Penn, *Afro-Am. Press* (1891), pp. 309–12.]   C.G.W.

CLINTON, JAMES (Aug. 9, 1733–Dec. 22, 1812), Revolutionary soldier, was born in Ulster (now Orange) County, N. Y. He was the sixth child of Charles and Elizabeth (Denniston) Clinton, and the brother of George Clinton [*q.v.*], Revolutionary governor of New York. At the time of the French and Indian War he was a captain in the militia and accompanied Bradstreet's expedition against Fort Frontenac. By 1775 he was a lieutenant-colonel. He was elected deputy to the Provincial Congress of New York from Ulster County in May 1775. On Oct. 25, 1775, he was commissioned colonel in the New York state troops and was assigned in command of the 3rd Regiment. During the preceding summer he had accompanied Gen. Montgomery's expedition to Quebec, leading six badly equipped companies. He participated in the disastrous attack on Quebec in December 1775. When the American troops withdrew from Canada in the following spring, Clinton returned to New York, and was commissioned brigadier-general in the Continental Army in October. He was stationed at Fort Clinton in the highlands of the Hudson, where he remained superintending the erection of defensive works until the following summer. In Oct. 1777, the British under Sir Henry Clinton made a desperate effort to cooperate with Burgoyne's expedition which was marching south from Canada. Sir Henry with three thousand British attacked and captured Forts Clinton and Montgomery which were defended by James Clinton with six hundred Americans. James Clinton was wounded by a bayonet during the assault, but escaped capture, drawing off most of his troops. In November 1778, he was ordered to Albany to act against the Tories and Indians harrying the frontier. He remained at that post until June 1779, when, the activities of the Indians and Tories having culminated in the massacres at Cherry Valley, N. Y., and Wyoming, Pa., Washington determined to take action against them. Gen. Sullivan was detached from headquarters with a force which marched across Pennsylvania, and Gen. Clinton was directed to march a similar force across New York. By July Clinton had his troops and baggage intact at Otsego at the foot of the lake which he dammed. Washington expressed some concern at Clinton's elaborate preparations, but when the word came from Sullivan, Clinton broke the dam and on the force of the accumulated waters floated his whole force down-stream into Pennsylvania and effected a junction with Sullivan's troops. Together the two completely defeated the Indians under Brant and the Tories under Butler near Newton, Pa. (probably the present Elmira, N. Y.), devastated the Indian country and destroyed the Indian crops as far north as the Finger Lakes. In the next year Clinton was placed in command of the Northern Department with headquarters again at Albany. Here he remained until Washington and Rochambeau completed their plans for the great coup of the summer of 1781. As they started south, Clinton and his brigade joined the main army and participated in the siege of Yorktown. Clinton's force was attached to Lincoln's division, and, according to the newly discovered Register of the Continental Army, counted at this time over 1,110, a much larger number than heretofore has been allowed by historians. Clinton's brigade received the surrendered British colors at Yorktown. In 1785, he was appointed a member of the Commission to settle the boundary between New York and Pennsylvania. Clinton married, first, Mary DeWitt in 1764, by whom he became the father of DeWitt Clinton [q.v.]; and, second, Mrs. Mary Gray. He was a member of the New York convention called to ratify the Federal Constitution, and voted against the ratification because the constitution contained no bill of rights. He died and was buried at Little Britain, Orange County, N. Y.

[Sources for Clinton's military career are: letters in the *Calendar of Hist. MSS. Relating to the Revolution Office Secretary of State N. Y.* (1868); *The Writings of Geo. Washington*, ed. by Jared Sparks (1834); *Writings of Geo. Washington*, ed. by W. C. Ford (1889–93); *Am. Archives* (4 and 5 ser., 1837–51); Manuscript Reg. of the Strength of Forces of the Continental Army in the Wm. L. Clements Lib.; *Public Papers of Geo. Clinton* (1899–1914); *Corres. Am. Rev.*, ed. by Jared Sparks (1853). Additional biographical information is contained in John Frost, *The Am. Generals* (1852); Wm. W. Campbell, *Lecture on the Life and Military Services of Gen. Jas. Clinton* (1839; read before N. Y. Hist. Soc. in February of that year); and in works on DeWitt Clinton.]   R. G. A—s.

CLOPTON, DAVID (Sept. 29, 1820–Feb. 5, 1892), jurist, was a member of a well-known Virginian planter family. Dr. Alford Clopton, a physician and a member of the Georgia legislature, married Sarah Kendrick, and their son David was born in Putnam County, Ga., where his father was practising. His early education was obtained at the county schools, and at Eatonton and Vineville, Macon County, to which latter place his father moved in 1831. He entered Randolph-Macon College in 1836 and graduated with honors in 1840. Taking up the study of law at Macon, he was admitted to the Georgia bar in 1841 and commenced practising in Griffin, Ga. In 1844 he removed to Tuskegee, Ala., where he practised for a period of twenty-two years. Few details of his professional labors at this period have been preserved; but he was active in political circles. In 1859 he was, despite his written protest, nominated by the Democratic party to represent Montgomery district in Congress, and was elected after a spectacular contest. He sat in the House till Jan. 21, 1861, when, Alabama having passed the ordinance of secession, he retired together with the other Alabama members. On the outbreak of war he enlisted as a private in the 12th Alabama Infantry, subsequently becoming assistant quartermaster and captain. That autumn he was

elected as representative of his district in the Confederate Congress, was reëlected in 1863, and continued in that body till the collapse of the Confederacy. In March 1866 he moved from Tuskegee and made his home in Montgomery. In 1874, he took a vigorous part in the anti-carpet-bag campaign of that year, addressing meetings in every quarter of the state. In 1878, he was, without his knowledge, nominated by the Montgomery County Democrats for the state House of Representatives and elected by a phenomenal majority. He was chosen speaker of the House but at the conclusion of his term declined reëlection. This was in accord with the life-long distaste for legislative honors which had been expressed on several occasions in his reluctance to accept nomination for office. In 1884 he was appointed associate justice of the supreme court of Alabama by Gov. O'Neil, and at the end of his term in 1886, being nominated by the Democratic party, was elected without opposition, continuing to hold office till his death. Judicial office was the measure of the only ambition he ever felt, and on the bench he displayed qualities of mind which commanded confidence. A finished speaker, he was careful, patient, receptive, eminently fair, and an indefatigable worker. He died in Montgomery. He was married first, to Martha E. Ligon, sister of Robert F. Ligon, lieutenant-governor of Alabama; second, to Mrs. Mary F. Chambers; and third, to Mrs. Virginia Clay, widow of Judge C. C. Clay.

[Willis Brewer, *Alabama* (1872); T. M. Owen, *Hist. of Ala.* (1921), III, 352; *Ala. State Bar Asso. Report*, 1895, p. xc; *Green Bag*, IV, 141; *Memorial Record of Ala.* (1893), II, 644.]   H. W. H. K.

CLOPTON, JOHN (Feb. 7, 1756–Sept. 11, 1816), congressman, was born in St. Peter's Parish, New Kent County, Va. He was son, grandson, and great-grandson of three generations of William Cloptons, the first of whom came as an immigrant into the colony and settled in York County, where he was constable in 1682. John Clopton entered the University of Pennsylvania in 1773, graduating in 1776. During the Revolution he served as captain of Virginia militia and became a member of the Cincinnati. He married Sarah Bacon, a descendant of Nathaniel Bacon, the rebel (*William and Mary Quarterly*, X, 268–70). Representing New Kent County in the Virginia House of Delegates for three sessions, 1789, 1790, 1791, he was elected to the national House of Representatives in 1795 from the district including Richmond, though the election was contested and the committee declared him elected by only six votes over Burwell Bassett, in an election in which 854 votes were cast—70 of which were defective. Beginning in 1795 he sat in Congress until his death, with the exception of the Sixth Congress, when John Marshall defeated him by 108 votes. The campaign between Clopton, Republican, and Marshall, who at the earnest solicitation of Washington became the Federalist candidate, is considered by many Virginians to have been the most stirring congressional election ever held in the state (*Virginia Magazine of History and Biography*, XXIX, 176–77). In December 1799 Clopton was elected a member of the privy council of Virginia. As a member of Congress he consistently supported the Jeffersonian program. He advocated the revision of the Federalist judiciary act and denied the existence of judicial vested rights, held out to the last for the embargo "until a majority of the great body of the people . . . should prefer war itself to a longer continuance of it," reversed his position of 1798 by voting for an army in 1808 upon Jefferson's recommendation, denied the power of the federal government to charter banks, and strongly supported the War of 1812. Fearing the tendency toward enlargement of federal powers, he proposed in 1806 an amendment to the "necessary and proper" clause to the effect that it "shall be construed so as to comprehend only such laws as shall have a natural connection with and immediate relation to the powers enumerated in the said section, or to such other powers as are expressly vested by the Constitution in the Government of the United States or in any department or office thereof" (H. V. Ames, *Proposed Amendments to the Constitution of the United States*, pp. 167–68). He also transmitted from the Virginia General Assembly a proposed amendment providing for the recall of senators by their state legislature (*Ibid.*, pp. 64, 328). The personal property and land tax records of Clopton's county indicate that in 1810 he owned 18 slaves and 450 acres of land, and that he paid a tax of $18.59.

[In addition to references above, see short sketch in *Encyc. of Va. Biog.*, ed. by L. G. Tyler, vol. II (1915).]

E. L. F.

CLOSSON, WILLIAM BAXTER (Oct. 13, 1848–May 31, 1926), painter, engraver, was born at Thetford, Vt., a son of David Wood and Abigail (Palmer) Closson. As a youth he was clerk in a Vermont railroad office when, during a visit to Boston, he saw some wood-engravers' tools which he borrowed, and with which in the early morning before going to work he taught himself to engrave. Having sent some proofs to a Boston engraver he was invited to

become an apprentice at three dollars a week— one-third of the salary he was already earning in Vermont. Closson accepted the offer and lived on his stipend until it was considerably increased. He studied in the evening drawing classes of the Lowell Institute and gained facility in portraiture. His employer S. G. Kilburn sent him to New York to solicit work. At the Century Company's office young Closson's engravings were highly approved, but he learned that the company dealt only with individual artists, not with firms. Returning to Boston he opened a studio and began engraving independently for the Century Company, Harpers, and Boston book publishers. A friendship formed with George Fuller led to Closson's engraving "Winifred Dysart," a very popular work. In 1882 Harper & Brothers sent him to engrave masterpieces in European galleries. This employment lasted several years. Closson in each case familiarized himself with his subject by making at the gallery a painted copy from which he engraved at his studio. In 1886 appeared L. Prang & Company's *Homes and Haunts of the Poets*, with etched portraits by Closson. He also engraved many of his own compositions, such as "The Water Nymph," "Night Moths," and "Evening in the Woods." About 1888 he devised a method of printing from intaglio plates, examples of which were exhibited at the Keppel Gallery, New York, in 1890. Two circumstances caused Closson rather abruptly to give up his burin: the close application required of the engraver had affected his eyesight, and the development of the half-tone practically ended in this country opportunities for artistic engraving on wood. The artist, who had been awarded medals for his engravings at the Paris Exposition, 1889, and the World's Columbian Exposition, 1893, and who as a member of the Society of American Wood Engravers participated in the award of a Grand Diploma of Honor for a joint exhibition at Vienna, began to devote himself to painting in pastel and oil. He married in 1907 Grace W. Gallaudet of Washington, D. C. Of quiet unassertive personality, he was liked by fellow artists. His style of painting, usually festive and somewhat reminiscent of Watteau and Monticelli, found general appreciation. An important exhibition of his paintings and wood engravings was hung at the Worcester Art Museum, July 10–Aug. 10, 1914. A Closson Memorial Exhibition was held at the Robert C. Vose Galleries, Boston, May 9, 1924.

[The best appreciation of Closson as a painter is by his friend Wm. Howe Downes in the *Catalogue Closson Memorial Exhibition*, 1927. He is evaluated as engraver by Geo. Howes Whittle. *The Printing Art* Apr. 1918.

See also Frank T. Robinson, *New Eng. Artists* (1888);
W. J. Linton, *Hist. of Wood-Engraving in America*
(1882); *Boston Evening Transcript,* June 1, 1926.
Date of birth supplied by Mrs. Closson.] F. W. C.

CLOUD, NOAH BARTLETT (Jan. 26, 1809–
Nov. 5, 1875), planter, politician, was born at
Edgefield, S. C., the son of Noah and Margaret
(Sweringen) Cloud. He prepared himself at
Philadelphia for the practise of medicine, and
at the age of twenty-six married Mary M. Barton, also of Edgefield. His father having died
in 1838, he set out for Alabama in 1846. He
made his new home at La Place, Macon County, and became a cotton planter of the Black
Belt. He immediately took an active interest in
the Chunnenugga Horticultural Society of Macon County, one of the oldest organizations of its
kind in the Southwest. In 1852, at a convention in Macon, Ga., held for the purpose of forming an agricultural society for the Cotton States,
Cloud and a group of Alabama friends decided
to establish an agricultural monthly at Montgomery. The first number of the *American Cotton Planter* accordingly appeared in January
1853. In 1857 the magazine was combined with
the *Soil of the South* and continued its career
until the war put an end to its existence in 1861.
Cloud's work as editor was of primary importance in the agricultural history of Alabama.
An agricultural society for the state was organized, and the formation of county societies and
the holding of county fairs was urged upon the
people. The importance of raising more stock
and of using more fertilizer upon cotton plantations was stressed. The question of education
also engaged the editor's attention, and he advocated more practical instruction for the agricultural part of the population than was afforded by the colleges and academies of the time.

Cloud opposed secession, but served as a surgeon in the Confederate army (Records Division, Adjutant General's Office, Washington, D.
C.). In 1868 he was elected superintendent of
public instruction in Alabama under the carpet-bag government. In this capacity, it became
his duty to establish a system of free schools for
the state, including schools for the negroes. It
is not surprising that Cloud was the object of
much local hostility, for the carpet-bag administration was thoroughly honeycombed with corruption. That his work was not on a higher
level than that of his associates is shown by
the fact that the judiciary committee of the
carpet-bag Senate accused him of malfeasance in
office (*Alabama Senate Journal,* 1869–70, p.
419). Failing of reëlection in 1870, he passed
from the public view, and died at Montgomery
in 1875, unnoticed by the community in which
he had spent the active years of his life.

[Cloud's political activities in the Reconstruction period have caused him to be neglected by local historians,
and no previous biographical notice of his life has appeared. The principal sources for this sketch are the
files of the *Am. Cotton Planter* (1853–61), Walter L.
Fleming's *Civil War and Reconstruction in Ala.* (1905),
and the Cloud family Bible in the possession of Mr. S.
R. Cloud of Montgomery.] T. P. A.

CLOUGH, JOHN EVERETT (July 16, 1836–
Nov. 24, 1910), Baptist missionary, was born
near Frewsburg, Chautauqua County, N. Y.
His father, Cyrus Clough, was of Welsh descent, and his mother, Mariah Sturgeon, Scotch-
English. They were both pioneers by disposition, and in 1844 the family moved westward
and settled for two or three years in Winnebago
County, Ill., where they suffered hardship and
poverty. Moving on to Strawberry Point, a
claim staked by them in Iowa, they found better
fortune. There John acquired a little schooling
and a taste for more. From 1853 to 1857 he
worked with a party of surveyors in Minnesota
and Dakota and saved money for further education. In the fall of 1857 he entered the Burlington (Iowa) Institute, but owing to the loss of his
savings in the financial crisis of that winter,
he was soon "working his way." An interest in
religion developed in him and he joined the
Baptist Church in February 1858. The Civil
War interrupted the work of the Institute.
Clough was not drafted, however, nor did he
wish to enlist. On Aug. 15, 1861 he married
Harriet Sunderland, with nothing very definite
in mind as to a career. His family persuaded
him to finish his college course at the newly
founded Upper Iowa University. Entering the
senior class there in the fall of 1861, he graduated the following June with the B.A. degree.
For a year he taught at Colesburg, Iowa, public
school, and then took up the work of colporteur-
age with definitely religious service in mind.
In quest of theological training he attended a
"Ministers' Institute" in Chicago, and while
there offered himself for foreign missionary
work. He was accepted and assigned to the
Telugu Mission, India. After ordination on Nov.
20, 1864 in Burlington, Iowa, he started at once
with his wife for the East, sailing from Boston
Nov. 30 on the *James Guthrie,* and arriving at
Nellore, Madras Presidency, Apr. 22, 1865.

At Nellore, Clough began at once the study of
the vernacular and early set about the writing
of tracts, such as *Where are You Going?* and
Messages for All. In the midst of this work
there came to Nellore a letter from one Yerra-
guntla Periah, a Madiga leather-worker, of a

village near Ongole, asking for Christian teaching. It was decided that the Cloughs should accept the invitation. Thus was his own life-work determined as a missionary among the outcastes, and a large body of converts made possible for the Mission. On Sept. 17, 1866 Mr. and Mrs. Clough arrived to take up residence in Ongole. Within a month he organized a Baptist church and began to receive numerous members into it. A "mass movement" was soon under way. The converts came at first by tens, then, in 1869, by hundreds, and after that by thousands. The terrible famine of 1876–78 spread its distress over the Telugu area, affecting the lower classes most of all, but Clough was able to enrol his Madigas in Government famine-relief projects. During this period he deemed it wise to refuse baptism to many thousands who sought admission to the Church. In June 1878, however, he began again to exercise the rite, and within six weeks 9,000 converts were baptized. At the close of the year the total membership of the Ongole Church was nearly 13,000, representing some four hundred villages, and in 1883 there were 21,000 members over a field so large that division became necessary.

Clough's service in India was interrupted by several furloughs in America. In 1873 he raised $50,000 for the founding of a Telugu theological institution; in 1883 he secured $10,000 to build the Ongole mission high school, and $15,000 for mission houses in Ongole and Madras; and in 1890 he raised $50,000 for sending out new missionaries to new stations, and $50,000 to establish Ongole College. His first wife died in 1893, leaving two sons and three daughters, and in 1894 he married Emma Rauschenbusch, of the Mission. Until 1902 he continued active missionary service but during 1901 and 1902 he suffered painful accidents which led to the curtailment of his work and a visit to America. In 1905 he was forced to retire from India altogether. He died in Rochester, N. Y., and was buried in Newton Center, Mass.

[Clough's autobiography entitled *Social Christianity in the Orient* (1914), ed. by his second wife; Emma R. Clough, *John E. Clough* (1902); C. C. Creegan, *Pioneer Missionaries of the Ch.* (1903); H. C. Mabie, in *Missionary Rev. of the World*, Feb. 1911.]   J. C. A.

CLOUGH, WILLIAM PITT (Mar. 20, 1845–Aug. 17, 1916), lawyer, railroad executive, was descended from John Clough of Watertown, Mass., who came from England in the ship *Elizabeth* in 1635. He was born at Freetown, Cortland County, N. Y., the son of William Parks Clough and Sabrina (Vunk) Clough, a member of an old Dutch family. In 1848 the family moved to Erie County, Pa., where his early education was received. He later entered the Northwestern State Normal School at Edinboro, Pa., taking a classical course, and graduating in 1862. He then became a school-teacher, reading law at intervals, following which he went to Oil Creek, Venango County, Pa., in 1865 and spent two years in that region. He was married on May 19, 1867 to Dacia Alathea Green of Erie County, Pa. In June of the same year he removed to Minnesota, settling at Rochester, where he entered a law office. Admitted to the bar of Olmstead County, Minn., July 3, 1868, he practised in Rochester till June 1872, when he moved to St. Paul, and, in association with John M. Gillman, acquired an influential legal connection. In 1873 he was an unsuccessful Democratic candidate for the office of state attorney-general, but the nomination was made in his absence and without his acquiescence. In 1880 he became western counsel for the Northern Pacific Railway. In this position his outstanding ability attracted the attention of James J. Hill [*q.v.*], then president of the St. Paul, Minneapolis & Manitoba Railway, who induced him to join the executive of the latter as assistant to the president, June 1, 1887. From that time he continued a close associate with Hill in all his enterprises, and was one of his most trusted legal advisers. He became second vice-president Jan. 1, 1888, remaining with the company until its absorption early in 1890 by the Great Northern Railway Company, of which he was then elected vice-president. For some years Hill and J. Pierpont Morgan were considering means whereby the Great Northern, Northern Pacific, and Chicago, Burlington & Quincy railroads might be brought under a unified control. Finally with that object in view the Northern Securities Company was formed in November 1901, and Clough, who had taken a leading part in the formulation and working out of the plans, became its fourth vice-president and general counsel, with headquarters in New York City. On the dissolution of the Northern Securities Company he continued in New York City as Hill's personal representative, and, when the latter resigned the vice-presidency of the Northern Pacific Railway in July 1912, was elected to that office, becoming two years later chairman of the board of directors. Of a retiring disposition, he avoided publicity, and in later life was little known outside his immediate circle of business associates.

[C. C. Andrews, ed., *Hist. of St. Paul, Minn.* (1890), pt. II, p. 50; *St. Paul Hist. and Progress* (1897), p. 39; *Minn. Hist. Soc. Colls.*, vol. XIV; *Railway Age Gazette*, Aug. 25, 1916; B. H. Meyer, *Hist. of the Northern Securities Case* (1906).]   H. W. H. K.

CLYMAN, JAMES (Feb. 1, 1792–Dec. 27, 1881), trapper, pioneer settler, and chronicler, was born in Fauquier County, Va. He grew up a farm boy, acquiring little education but becoming an adept in woodcraft and marksmanship. About 1806 the family moved to Pennsylvania and then to Stark County, Ohio. Young Clyman served as a mounted ranger throughout the Indian campaigns of the War of 1812, returning to farm work at its close. In 1818 he left home, drifting westward and working at various occupations. Early in 1823 he went to St. Louis, where, as a clerk, he joined Ashley's second expedition to ascend the Missouri. He was in the battle with the Arikaras, June 2, when he barely escaped with his life, and also in the second battle, Aug. 11. In September he left the Missouri with the Smith-Fitzpatrick party that reached Green River in February or March 1824—probably the first whites to traverse South Pass and certainly the first to traverse it from the east. Returning by the pass, and becoming separated from his companions on the Sweetwater, he walked the 600 miles through a hostile and unknown region back to the Missouri, arriving at Fort Atkinson in September. Here he seems to have met Ashley's first overland expedition, with which he again went to the mountains. He was one of the four men who in the early spring of 1826 circumnavigated Great Salt Lake.

In October 1827 he returned to St. Louis. With the proceeds from the sale of his furs he bought a farm near Danville, Ill., and with a partner started one of the first stores in the town. He was a soldier in the Black Hawk War of 1832, for a time with Abraham Lincoln in Jacob Earley's company, and continued in the service until 1834. His roving disposition led him next to the Wisconsin frontier, where he acquired his title of colonel at the hands of Gen. Henry Dodge and where he was severely wounded in an encounter with an Indian. The Danville and Milwaukee settlements alternately claimed him until after the winter of 1842–43, when he started on a horseback trip for his health. At Independence, Mo., in the spring of 1844, he decided to try the West again and accordingly set out with one of the emigrant trains. Arriving at the Willamette in October, he remained in Oregon for a time, but in the following year went to California. In the spring of 1846, learning of Frémont's difficult position, he offered to raise for the Pathfinder a company of mounted men, but on the declination of the offer started east with a party of disappointed emigrants.

Arriving at Independence in July, he spent the next eighteen months in visiting friends. But in 1848 he again headed west, this time as guide to an emigrant party which included the Mecombs family. Arriving in California in September, the Mecombs settled at the town of Napa, and Clyman remained with them. On Aug. 22, 1849, in the first marriage performed in the town, he was united to Hannah Mecombs, thirty years his junior. His thirty-seven years of roving, trapping, and fighting were done. In 1850 he acquired the land on which he established his own ranch, and his subsequent life was uneventful. He died at his Napa home.

Clyman was more than six feet tall, rawboned and angular, with stooping shoulders and a long, narrow head. His hair was dark brown, his complexion ruddy, and his eyes were small, dark blue, and piercing. In manner he was dignified and courteous, and his disposition was exceptionally generous and helpful. Except at the hands of H. H. Bancroft he had received little attention from historians until Mr. C. L. Camp assembled and annotated his manuscripts, which have proved one of the richest sources of early Western history.

[C. L. Camp, "Jas. Clyman, His Diaries and Reminiscences," *Cal. Hist. Soc. Quart.*, vol. IV, nos. 2–3, vol. V, nos. 1–4, vol. VI, no. 1 ; reprinted and enlarged as *Jas. Clyman, Am. Frontiersman* (1928).]

W. J. G—t.

CLYMER, GEORGE (Mar. 16, 1739–Jan. 24, 1813), signer of the Declaration of Independence and of the Constitution, was a prosperous and well-connected Philadelphia merchant of indefatigable energy in the service of his state and nation in the early formative period. Descended from a Bristol, England, immigrant grandfather (Richard Clymer) and father (Christopher Clymer) and a Philadelphia mother (Deborah Fitzwater Clymer), he lost both parents in 1740, and came under the guardianship and educational direction of an uncle, William Coleman, a friend of Franklin and prosperous merchant. Living in Coleman's house with access to his large library, he acquired an early taste for reading. He began a business career first as clerk, then partner, then successor and legatee of his uncle's business. After association with Robert Ritchie, he was later taken into partnership by Reese Meredith and his son, establishing the firm of Merediths & Clymer, and continuing as partner, after the death of the elder Meredith, until 1782. He had married Reese Meredith's daughter Elizabeth in 1765, and at the Meredith home had become acquainted with the young George Washington who was a frequent visitor there. A contact was thus established that lasted through the Revolution and Clymer's subsequent career in public service. An early and ardent patriot, Clymer attended all revolutionary meetings, becoming captain of volunteers in Gen. Cadwalader's brigade, and, as chairman of a committee of the "Philadelphia Tea Party" (1773), forcing the resignation of the merchants appointed by the British to sell the tea. He became a member of the Pennsylvania Council of Safety, was one of the two first continental treasurers (July 29, 1775–Aug. 6, 1776), and then entered Congress as a Pennsylvania delegate. He supported the continental loan, was one of the first subscribers and solicitors for it, exchanged all his specie for continental currency, and paid a special visit to Boston to gain further revolutionary information and inspiration. Appointed with Rush, Wilson, Ross, and Taylor (July 20, 1776) to replace Pennsylvania delegates who refused to sign the Declaration of Independence, Clymer, though not present when it was adopted, realized "his dearest wish" when he signed the document, for he had been among the first to advocate complete independence from Britain. His valuable business acumen was utilized on varied special and standing committees in both the Continental and the first United States congresses. Commissioned (Sept. 26, 1776) with Stockton to inspect the Northern Army at Ticonderoga he advocated expansion of Washington's powers. Left with Robert Morris and George Walton as a committee for congressional business in Philadelphia when the advance of the British drove the government to Baltimore (December 1776), he worked so incessantly that if he visited his family, twenty-five miles distant in Chester County, it was only for a night and he was back at his desk the next morning. After his reëlection to Congress (Mar. 12, 1777), his service on the boards of war and of the treasury and on the committee to protect Philadelphia was so strenuous that after three months he was obliged, temporarily, to retire. He was again on duty with Livingston and Gerry as a commissioner to investigate and remedy the difficulties in Washington's commissariat (July 11, 1777), and he continued to serve in Congress until after Sept. 14, 1777, although then not reëlected. As commissioner of prisoners he received the Hessian captives and sent to Allentown those able to travel. The British after their victory at Brandywine ransacked his house, on a detour from their march to Philadelphia, for the purpose of terrorizing his family and destroying his furniture and store of liquors. The expedition organized by Congress to reduce Detroit and prevent an Indian war was the result of a report made by Clymer and two fellow commissioners sent, Dec. 11, 1777, to Fort Pitt to investigate disorders inspired by the British. From Nov. 24, 1780 to Nov. 12, 1782 he was for the third time in Congress, laboring almost continuously as chairman or member of special or standing committees, such as those of commerce or finance. Called from a brief retirement at Princeton, whither he had gone to educate his children, as a legislator of Pennsylvania he wrote the report for mitigating the penal code, lessening capital crimes, and restricting public employment of convicts. He was one of the petitioners for a bicameral legislature and a supporter of the old constitution of the Confederation. As a Pennsylvania delegate to the Federal Convention he spoke little but to the point, served upon important financial committees, and signed the Constitution. He carried his rigid republicanism into the first United States Congress (November 1788), supporting Washington, but favoring liberal naturalization, and a pro-French and Jeffersonian economic policy. Declining reëlection, he fulfilled two successive commissions to which Washington appointed him and retired from public life July 31, 1796, after an almost unbroken service of over twenty years, and preferment which he had never solicited. Subsequently he promoted community interests as first president respectively of The Philadelphia Bank and of the Academy of Fine Arts, and in 1805 as vice-president of the Philadelphia Agricultural Society, retaining these offices till his death in 1813. Diffident, retiring, no orator, speaking seldom and briefly but with deep reasoning, he never sought nor bought office, and "was never heard to speak ill of any one."

[John Sanderson's verbose and monotonous sketch of Clymer in his *Biog. Signers Declaration of Independence* (2nd ed., Philadelphia, 1826, III, 145–95; rev. ed., Philadelphia, 1865) remains the chief source. Scattered information may be gleaned from Max Farrand's *Records Federal Convention* (1913), II, 322, 328, 363, 366, 375, 415, 442, 450, 477, 562, 563, 664; *Jours. Continental Cong.*, XVIII, 1090–94, 98; 1100–14, 15, 21, 55, 65, 66; 1203; 1229; *Pa. Mag. of Hist. and Biog.*, XI, 300, 301, 304; XIV, 92; XVIII, 41, 347; XXII, 286; J. C. Fitzpatrick, ed., *Geo. Washington's Diary* (1925), III, 221, 223; IV, 72; Jared Sparks, ed., *Writings of Geo. Washington* (1838–39), IV, 253, 256, 552; D. R. B. Nevin, *Continental Sketches of Distinguished Pennsylvanians* (1875), pp. 51–59. See also Jas. R. Macfarlane, *Geo. Clymer ... His Family and Descendants* (1927).]   J. C. B.

CLYMER, GEORGE E. (1754–Aug. 27, 1834), inventor, was born on his father's farm in Bucks County, Pa., of a Swiss family which had emigrated from Geneva early in the eighteenth century. He attended the district schools and at the same time assisted with the farm work in which he showed a particular skill in the maintenance of the mechanical equipment. When sixteen years old he took up carpentry and joining, and within a short time devised a unique plow especially adapted to the local soils. He continued at his chosen trade in his home neighborhood for at least twenty-five years, during which time he applied his ingenuity and inventive skill in numerous ways. About 1800 he moved to Philadelphia and became much interested in the erection of the first permanent bridge across the Schuylkill River, particularly in the construction of the piers. To clear the coffer-dams he devised a pump superior to any then available. It had a capacity of 500 gallons of water per minute and was capable of transporting sand, gravel, and stone. For this he received a United States patent Dec. 22, 1801, and later obtained a British patent. He then turned his attention to the improvement of the printing-press, particularly the iron hand-press devised by the Earl of Stanhope. After sixteen years of concentrated effort he introduced his improved press, which he called the "Columbian," and which exhibited the greatest amount of improvement ever attained in any one instance in hand-printing machines. It was also the first real American invention in printing. Its elbowed pulling bar and diagonal connecting rod which changed a horizontal movement into a perpendicular one, combined with its main lever, applying its force directly to the form, commended it to all pressmen as it required considerably less strength and effort on their part to obtain perfect work. Another unusual feature of Clymer's press and one that made it always recognized was its ornamentation, all of cast-iron—a Hermes on each pillar, alligators and other reptiles on the levers, and, surmounting the whole, an American spread eagle. The eagle, however, was more than an ornament for it acted as a counterweight to lift the platen after printing. Much as the press was desired by American printers they were too poor at this early date to pay the price ($400), so Clymer took it to England in 1817 where it was immediately taken up by experienced printers and was in great favor for many years. For this invention Clymer received from the King of the Netherlands a gold medal valued at one hundred golden ducats and a present from the Czar of Russia following the introduction of the Columbian press in that country. Somewhat later, a few of the presses were used in the United States. For business reasons, presumably, Clymer spent most of his time after 1818 in Europe, particularly England, and died in

London in his eightieth year. He was married to Margaret Backhouse, daughter of Judge Backhouse of the Durham Iron Works in Pennsylvania and was survived by three daughters.

[*Am. Dict. Printing and Bookmaking* (1894); J. L. Ringwalt, *Am. Encyc. Printing* (1871); J. W. Moore, *Moore's Hist., Biog., and Misc. Gatherings—Relative to Printers, Printing, Publishing and Editing* (1886); W. F. Cleaver, *Five Centuries of Printing* (1927); Waldemar Kaempffert, *Pop. Hist. of Am. Invention* (1924).]
                                                    C. W. M.

COALTER, JOHN. [See COLTER, JOHN, c. 1775–1813.]

COAN, TITUS (Feb. 1, 1801–Dec. 1, 1882), missionary to Hawaii, was the youngest child of Gaylord Coan, a farmer of Killingworth, Conn., and of Tamza (Nettleton) Coan, an aunt of Asahel Nettleton [q.v.], a distinguished evangelical preacher. From the age of four until twelve he attended district school, and was later among the pupils of the local pastor, the Rev. Asa King. In time he went to the academy at East Guilford (now Madison), Conn. After graduation from the academy and until the spring of 1826 he taught school in his own and neighboring towns. He then went to western New York and took charge of the school at Riga, where on Mar. 2, 1828, he was received into the fellowship of the Presbyterian Church, then under the pastoral care of his oldest brother, George. Coming under the influence of the evangelist Charles G. Finney [q.v.], he decided upon the ministry as his life-work and entered, in June 1831, the middle class of Auburn Theological Seminary. On Apr. 17, 1833 he was licensed by the Cayuga County Presbytery as a minister of the Gospel. On Aug. 4 he was ordained as a missionary of the American Board and was dispatched on an expedition to Patagonia, sailing Aug. 16, 1833. He returned on May 7, 1834 and reported the futility of missionary endeavor there. He was married on Nov. 3 to Fidelia Church, and on Dec. 5 he and his wife sailed from Boston on the ship *Hellespont* for service in the Sandwich Islands. They landed at Honolulu on June 6, 1835, and were entertained at the home of the Rev. Hiram Bingham [q.v.]. During the meeting of the Hawaiian mission which was then in session at Honolulu the Coans were assigned to Hilo on the east coast of the island of Hawaii. Thither they proceeded at once.

Coan's work in Hilo and in Puna, the district contiguous on the south, was mainly evangelistic and pastoral. He was soon master of the new language and able to give himself to preaching. On Nov. 29, 1836 he set off on his first tour of the island. His thirty-day trip kindled a movement similar in many ways to the work of Nettleton and Finney in America. Succeeding tours added impetus. Shortly the natives began flocking into Hilo, and throughout the island a great revival took hold. At Hilo in particular the situation took on in 1837–38 the character of a huge camp meeting with daily services, prayer meetings, classes, and the like. Coan himself reports "men praying, confessing, and breaking off their sins by righteousness . . . thieves brought back what they had stolen . . . quarrels were reconciled . . . The lazy became industrious. Drunkards stopped drinking . . . Adulteries ceased, and murderers confessed." The largest number of converts was gathered in during 1838–39. All told, from April to April, 5,244 were admitted to baptism. Reckoning up to 1880, however, the net total for the Hilo Church was only some 1,200, for dismissals, deaths, and a general reaction took a heavy toll. Coan seemed to some of his colleagues to exercise less caution than circumstances required in the reception of new members. He was among the first to advocate a native mission to the Marquesas Islands, and as a delegate of the Hawaiian Missionary Society made two voyages thither (1860, 1867). He took an interest also in the natural phenomena about him. His observations recorded in his *Adventures in Patagonia* (1880) and *Life in Hawaii* (1882) were written in a "lucid, direct, and virile" style, somewhat in contrast with his frequently conventional and exclamatory treatment of religious subjects (W. F. Blackman, *The Making of Hawaii*, 1899, p. 80). He returned but once to America, and then (1870) in the interest of his wife's health. She died in 1872 on their return to Hilo, and in 1873 he married Lydia, the youngest daughter of the elder Hiram Bingham. Nine years later he died, smitten with paralysis toward the close of his eighty-second year.

[R. Anderson, *Sandwich Islands Mission* (1870); Lydia Bingham Coan, *Titus Coan* (1884).] J.C.A.

COATES, FLORENCE EARLE (July 1, 1850–Apr. 6, 1927), poet, was born in Philadelphia, the daughter of George H. and Ellen Frances (Van Leer) Earle. Her father, a noted lawyer, was the son of Thomas Earle, a philanthropist descended from a Rhode Island family dating from the migration of Ralph Earle in 1634. Florence was educated at private schools in New England and at the Convent of the Sacred Heart in Paris. For over a year she studied music in Brussels with the tenor Dupré, intending to devote herself to music and art. In 1872 she was married to William Nicholson, who died in 1877. Her interest in poetry began several years after

her marriage on Jan. 7, 1879, to Edward Horner Coates (1846–1921), financier and publicist, who from 1890 to 1906 was president of the Pennsylvania Academy of the Fine Arts. They both took an active interest in local literary affairs, entertained Matthew Arnold at their Germantown home, and were among the founders of the Contemporary Club (1886). Mrs. Coates was president of the Browning Society of Philadelphia from 1895 to 1903, and again in 1907–08. Eager to promote Anglo-American friendship, she participated in the activities of the Transatlantic Society of America, the Society of Mayflower Descendants, and the Colonial Dames of America. She wrote an *Ode on the Coronation of King George V* (1911). In 1915 she was elected poet laureate of Pennsylvania by the state Federation of Women's Clubs. For many years she contributed short poems to leading American magazines and to the London *Athenæum*. Her only prose works of interest were two essays on Matthew Arnold, one appearing in the *Century Magazine* for April 1894, the other in *Lippincott's Magazine* for December 1909. The poems appeared in collected editions in 1898 and (two volumes) in 1916, many early poems being omitted from the latter edition. Other volumes of verse were: *Mine and Thine* (1904); *Lyrics of Life* (1909); *The Unconquered Air and Other Poems* (1912); and *Pro Patria* (1917). Some of her best poetry is found in the fine nature poems inspired by her Adirondack summer home, "Elsinore," at St. Regis Lake, and among the patriotic poems written during the Great War. Her work was essentially lyrical in quality. She took her literary life rather seriously. "The business of art," she held, "is to enlarge and correct the heart and to lift our ideals out of the ugly and the mean through love of the ideal. . . . The business of art is to appeal to the soul" (*New York Times*, Magazine Section, Dec. 10, 1916). With her finished workmanship and careful technique, there was also an element of restraint, characteristic of a lyric talent that develops relatively late in life. Her occasional poems were usually most felicitous and justified her state laureateship, but her appeal was to the understanding minority. In other days Mrs. Coates, with her distinctive social standing, her keenness of mind, her sense of humor, and her stately suavity of manner, would have presided as a *grande dame* over a literary *salon*. Her portrait by Violet Oakley, entitled "The Tragic Muse," won the gold medal of honor at the San Francisco Exposition. During her later years, Mrs. Coates entertained Mrs. Humphry Ward and other noted visitors at her town home on Spruce St., Philadelphia. She died in Philadelphia in her seventy-seventh year.

[*Who's Who in America*, 1926–27; *Book News*, Dec. 1898 and Dec. 1917; *Public Ledger* (Phila.), May 11, 1913, Apr. 29, 1917; obituaries in Phila. and N. Y. newspapers, Apr. 7, 1927; *Mentor*, June 15, 1920; *Public Ledger* (Phila.) Dec. 12, 1915; Pliny Earle, *The Earle Family* (1888).]   J.L.H.

COATES, GEORGE HENRY (June 23, 1849–Oct. 18, 1921), inventor, manufacturer, was born in Windsor, Vt., the only son of Henry Moss and Orra Natalia (Cone) Coates. After attending the local public schools and Windsor Academy, during which time he developed a marked mechanical bent (his father being the village blacksmith), Coates left home at the age of eighteen to secure a better education and experience in the mechanical arts. He went to Worcester, Mass., found employment with the Ethan Allen Firearms Company, and because of his aptitude quickly rose to the position of shop foreman. From the very beginning, too, of his residence in Worcester he attended night school at Worcester Polytechnic Institute, studying machine design and mechanical drawing. His ability in the latter is evidenced by the fact that he won several prizes for his drawings at public exhibitions in Boston, receiving on one occasion the highest award for a colored drawing of a Corliss engine. Upon completing eight years' service with the Ethan Allen company, Coates resigned about 1875 and went into business for himself as an expert machinist. One of his first jobs was that of repairing hair-clippers then imported from England and France, and so skilful was his work that his fame spread, his jobs multiplied, and he made clipper-repairing his specialty. Coates soon saw that there were opportunities for making improvements on the imported clipper and from the extent of his repair business realized that a market existed for such a product. He had some slight experience in invention and in securing patents in that in 1874 he was a co-patentee of a fire kindler. Accordingly in 1876 he devised and received his first patent for an adjustable hair-clipper, which was so much better than the imported variety that one of his New York repair customers immediately ordered five hundred. This marked the beginning of Coates's clipper business which he immediately established in Worcester and which under his direct administration developed from a basement shop to a modern manufacturing plant of well over an acre of floor space and with established markets all over the world. In addition to managing the plant Coates continued active in experimental and inventive work. Between 1880 and 1905 he obtained eight patents for clipper improvements. He devised an animal hair shears in 1885 and a fingernail cutter in 1886, but his most important invention was that of a flexible shaft. This he patented in 1892, but he made numerous improvements on it in the succeeding years. The device made it possible to transmit power to a machine tool to do work in difficult places such as drilling holes under water or grinding the inside of a complicated steel casting. Through Coates's several improvements of his flexible shaft as much as 150 horse-power have been transmitted, while shafting to transmit power to clippers as well as to delicate dental machinery became available also. The last patent, issued to him in 1920, when he was seventy-one years old, was an improvement on this device. He also perfected and patented a number of unique tools all of which found a waiting market. Amongst these were a breast drill, drill press, mechanical hummer, and screw-driver. The latter is power-driven at high speed through a flexible shaft and is used by chair builders and others having to insert large numbers of screws. Coates was much interested in civic matters in Worcester and served for five years on the board of aldermen, one year as president. He married Adelaide Long of Biddeford, Me., on June 23 1872, who with a son survived him.

[Ellery Bicknell Crane, *Geneal. and Personal Memoirs of Worcester County, Mass.*, vol. I (1907); Chas Nutt, *Hist. of Worcester and Its People*, IV (1919), 800 ff.; *Boston Transcript*, Oct. 19, 1921; Patent Office Records.]   C.M.

COATES, SAMUEL (Aug. 24, 1748–June 4, 1830), merchant, philanthropist, was more successful as a citizen than as a merchant. He was born in Philadelphia of an old Quaker family descended from Thomas Coates who emigrated from England probably after the year 1680. His father, also Samuel Coates, died when Samuel, Jr., was nine weeks old, and his mother, Mary Langdale Coates, allowed his uncle, John Reynell, to adopt him. He was given a good classical and business education and at nineteen was put in charge of a small commercial business which he handled so well that at the end of three years it was terminated so that he might enter into partnership with his uncle as a member of the firm of Reynell & Coates. His first wife, Lydia Saunders, whom he had married in 1775, died in 1789; and in 1791 he married Amy Hornor.

After the withdrawal of his uncle from active business life, Samuel Coates formed a partnership with his brother, Josiah Langdale Coates; but the brother withdrew to establish himself as a grocer, and after 1785 Samuel Coates was in business for himself. He prospered, but after he became interested in philanthropic enterprises he neglected his business and it dwindled away. When he finally paid all his debts and gave up his business he had but a small competence instead of a fortune.

One of his chief interests was the Pennsylvania Hospital. He was elected a manager in 1785 and president of the board of directors in 1812. He gave forty-one years of unremitting attention to the affairs of this hospital and during the fearful yellow-fever epidemic of 1793 was one of the few citizens of means who remained in the city to gather together the forces with which to combat the scourge. His portrait, by Sully, is still in the possession of this institution. For a period almost as long, 1786–1823, he gave his services to the body entitled "The Overseers of the Public Schools, founded by charter in the town and county of Philadelphia," which was the ruling authority managing what were called "the Quaker Schools." In 1800 he was elected a director of the first Bank of the United States and was still a director at the time its affairs were wound up in 1812. He was under the average size, but of an athletic figure, with a large chest and head, and heavy hair. He was cheerful and sociable, genial and entertaining, fond of children, who were also fond of him. His death occurred in the house at the corner of Walnut and South Front Sts., which had been his place of business since 1791.

[Mary Coates, *Family Memorials and Recollections* (1885); Stephen N. Winslow, *Biogs. of Phila. Merchants* (1864); Henry Simpson, *Lives of Eminent Philadelphians* (1859).]   E. Y.

COBB, ANDREW JACKSON (Apr. 12, 1857–Mar. 27, 1925), jurist and teacher of law, was born at Athens, Ga., at a time when his father, Howell Cobb [*q.v.*], was a member of the cabinet of President Buchanan. His mother, Mary Ann Lamar, was a cultured member of a distinguished family. In his youth Andrew acquired a taste for study and graduated from the University of Georgia with honors (Phi Beta Kappa) at nineteen; within the following year he completed the law course of the same institution and, soon after, began the practise of law in Athens. On Mar. 3, 1880, he was married to Stark Campbell, a daughter of Col. Jesse Campbell of Griffin, Ga. She died in 1901.

At twenty-seven Cobb became a professor of law at the University of Georgia where he remained until 1893, when he moved to Atlanta to practise law and also to become dean of the Atlanta Law School. At thirty-nine he was made an associate justice of the supreme court of Georgia, and almost at once became conspicuous for the lucidity of his opinions. He was especially capable in clarifying adjective law and did much to simplify and systematize the rules of pleading and practise. His decisions have been cited and followed more often, within a similar period of time, than those of any other Georgia jurist. Outside of his state he is perhaps best known for his opinion in the case of *Pavesich* vs. *New Eng. Life Insurance Company* (122 *Ga.* 190), which established for the first time in America the principle that an individual has "a right of privacy" for the invasion of which he may recover damages without proof of any special loss.

After serving twelve years upon the supreme bench Cobb returned to Athens and resumed the practise of law. In 1917, however, he again accepted judicial appointment, this time as judge of the superior courts for the western circuit of Georgia. His judicial temperament, ripe experience, and great learning were ideal qualities for a trial judge, and he served with distinction, but the western circuit then was the most populous in the state and the task proved too great a burden for his waning strength, so he resigned in January 1921 and resumed his work as a teacher of law at his alma mater.

He was a slender man of medium height and with classical features. His manners were gentle, his nature tranquil, but at times he could become aroused to impetuous action. During the World War, when opposition appeared in Georgia to the selective service act and other administrative measures, he vigorously denounced all who opposed the policies of President Wilson and contributed no little to the defeat of a Georgia senator who had allied himself with the "irreconcilables" in the Senate. It is perhaps not too much to say that his words carried more weight with the people during the critical years 1917 and 1918 than those of any other person in Georgia. He died suddenly in his sixty-ninth year.

[Memorial to Judge Cobb, 162 *Ga.* 843; *Atlanta Constitution*, Mar. 28, 1925; private information. Cobb's opinions are to be found in 100–128 *Ga. Reports*.]   B.F.

COBB, DAVID (Sept. 14, 1748–Apr. 17, 1830), Revolutionary officer, judge, politician, was born at Attleborough, Mass. His parents were Thomas and Lydia (Leonard) Cobb. Graduating at Harvard in 1766, he studied medicine in Boston, and practised his profession at Taunton. In the opening scenes of the Revolution, he was secretary of the Bristol County convention, member of the General Court, and of the provincial congress. Serving for a while as surgeon of a Massachusetts regiment, he became, Jan. 12, 1777, lieutenant-colonel of Henry Jackson's regiment (later the 16th Massachusetts) ; he was promoted to be colonel, was appointed to the 5th Massachusetts, Jan. 7, 1783, and was made brevet brigadier-general, Sept. 30, 1783. He took part in the battles of Monmouth, Quaker Hill, and Springfield, and during the last two years of the war he was one of Washington's aides. In this capacity he had the honor of going to meet Rochambeau with letters from the Commander-in-Chief in June 1781, and of treating with Sir Guy Carleton in regard to the evacuation of New York in 1783. His active service ended in November of that year, though he was made major-general of militia in 1786. After the war he held a number of public offices. During his term as judge of the court of common pleas in Bristol County, 1784–96, Shays's Rebellion broke out. Attacks on court-houses were made by mobs, in Taunton as in other towns, and Cobb's attitude was pronounced. It is reported that he said, "I will hold this court if I hold it in blood; I will sit as a judge, or I will die as a general"; and again, drawing a line as he placed a field-piece in front of the court-house, he said, "If you want these papers you must come and take them, but I will fire on the first man that crosses the line" (quoted in *Proceedings of the Massachusetts Senate, post*). Cobb was speaker of the Massachusetts House of Representatives, 1789–93, and a Federalist member of Congress, 1793–95. Removing to Maine (then a part of Massachusetts), he settled as a farmer in Gouldsboro, and promoted the opening of lands for colonists from Massachusetts. He continued to be active in politics; president of the state Senate, 1802–05; member of the council; lieutenant-governor 1809; and member of the Board of Military Defence in 1812. His last judicial office was that of chief justice of Hancock County. He died at Boston in 1830.

[Francis Baylies, memorial address delivered July 2, 1830, at the Taunton Lyceum, printed in the *New Eng. Hist. and Geneal. Reg.*, Jan. 1864; Samuel C. Cobb, biog. sketch in *Memorials of the Soc. of the Cincinnati of Mass.* (1873); S. W. Williams, *Am. Med. Biog.* (1845); *Barnstable* (Mass.) *Patriot*, Aug. 5 to Sept. 2, 1862; Jared Sparks, *The Writings of Geo. Washington* (1834–37); *Proc. of the Mass. Senate*, Feb. 23, 1882.]

E. K. A.

COBB, ELIJAH (July 4, 1768–Nov. 2, 1848), sea captain, took an active part in the events which made American commerce at once exciting and lucrative during the first three decades after the Revolution. He was born on Cape Cod in the part of Harwich which later became Brewster, Mass., the son of Capt. Scottow and Mary Freeman Cobb. His father died at sea in 1774, leaving his mother nearly destitute with six small children. In 1783, Elijah packed his wardrobe in a gin case and set out for Boston, where he signed as cook and cabin boy on a ship to Surinam. He continued at sea and by 1794 he was captain of a ship bound for Cadiz. After dodging the Algerine pirates, he was captured by a French ship and taken into Brest. With his characteristic determination and acumen, he hurried to Paris and secured the release of the ship from Robespierre, whom he later saw guillotined. He returned to France again with a cargo of grain and then engaged in rum-running off the Irish coast, dropping hogsheads of rum into the Cove of Cork and hoisting aboard a bag of guineas in return. Loading at Malaga, in 1808, he first heard of the Orders in Council and his ship was held up by the British at Gibraltar, but he escaped by bribing an official. In 1812 he arrived at Norfolk, Va., to learn that the Embargo was to go into effect in thirty-six hours. Hastily unloading his ship in a storm, he rushed aboard a cargo of flour and secured a last-minute clearance from the collector of customs who vainly pursued him into Hampton Roads on the hour when the act went into effect. The flour sold at Cadiz at a very high price. On a return voyage he received his first news of the War of 1812 off Newfoundland, when his ship was seized by the British and he was carried into St. John's, later being released on a cartel. After this he remained ashore at Brewster until the end of the war, when he resumed trade with Europe and then made two trips to the African coast in 1818 and 1819. His cargo seems to have been oil and ivory, with no trace of rum or slaves. In 1820, he retired from the sea and settled at Brewster where he became one of the leaders of the community, serving as town clerk, state representative and senator and inspector-general, with the rank of brigadier-general. He was a devoted Universalist. His memoirs bear the laconic entry that in 1793 he "went to the Cape & got married," but the records give no further details of his wife than that her name was Mary and that she bore him four children. A pastel drawn in France in 1794 tallies with the description of Cobb's "tall, straight fine figure." He was credited with sturdy integrity in addition to the unusual shrewdness and determination which he showed.

[The principal source for Cobb's life is his interesting, matter-of-fact autobiography to 1812, edited with a foreword by Ralph D. Paine under the title *Elijah Cobb, 1768–1848, a Cape Cod Skipper* (1925). The book includes a sketch of the remainder of his life, written by his grandson, and numerous original letters. The pastel portrait serves as a frontispiece and also appears in J. Henry Sears, *Brewster Ship Masters* (1906), with abridged extracts from the autobiography, pp. 10–20. Genealogical details will be found in *Vital Records Brewster, Mass.* (1904), pp. 25, 87, 236, and in *Mayflower Descendant*, Jan. 1910, p. 156, Apr. 1911, p. 98.]

R. G. A—n.

COBB, FRANK IRVING (Aug. 6, 1869–Dec. 21, 1923), newspaper editor, was the son of Minor H. Cobb and his wife Mathilda, who left a farm in New York State to settle in Shawnee County, Kansas, the birthplace of their son, Frank. Unable to make the new farm pay because of a plague of grasshoppers, the Cobb family moved to a new settlement in the wilds of Michigan where the son grew up amid the rough men of a lumber camp. His education came from rural schools—supplemented by a course at the Michigan State Normal. Pedagogue for a term or two at Martin, Mich., he sought and secured a position as school superintendent. Under twenty-one when he presented himself, he was greeted with, "We expected a man of at least thirty." His reply was, "If I were thirty I wouldn't work for you at fifteen hundred a year." With these words he turned on his heel, walked out, and accepted a position as reporter on the *Grand Rapids Herald* at a salary of six dollars a week—later becoming a political correspondent and finally city editor. After working on a rival newspaper, the *Grand Rapids Daily Eagle,* he went to the *Evening News* of Detroit where his first job was that of political correspondent. At twenty-seven an editorial writer, he was scarcely past thirty when appointed its chief editorial writer—a position held for four years. His editorials were so terse that they attracted the attention of Joseph Pulitzer of the New York *World* who, suffering from an affliction of the eyes, was seeking some one to take charge of the editorial department. Coming to New York in 1904, Cobb became the confidential adviser to Pulitzer, who soon put him in control of the editorial page, though the title of editor-in-chief was not his until after Pulitzer's death (Oct. 29, 1911). The *World,* being a fighting organ or campaign sheet, was exposing corruption in the insurance world as well as in municipal affairs. Into these conflicts Cobb thrust his pen with telling effect—often at the risk of libel suits. The Democratic convention at Baltimore in 1912 found Cobb fighting against odds, local and national, to make Woodrow Wilson the Democratic nominee for president. Editorials printed in the *World* at this time made Wilson a life-long friend. About eight years later (Mar. 4, 1920), Cobb broke his office rules of short editorials to print "Woodrow Wilson—An Interpretation." The editorial, which later appeared in pamphlet form, was considered by many Democratic leaders an exceptionally able pen portrait of the war president. This pamphlet and editorials in the *World* were about all that came from Cobb's pen except two magazine articles. To the *Atlantic Monthly* for November 1921 he

contributed an article dealing with the military expenditures still made though the Great War had ended, and in *Harper's Magazine* for June 1923 he printed an article which showed that the self-governing nations, emerging from the World War, were rejecting congressional government in favor of parliamentary government. Offered a cabinet position by President Wilson, he declined it but did go with Colonel House to report the situation overseas. Asked by his wife whether the cabinet offer had not tempted him, he replied, "That kind of power is merely temporary anyhow and I have as much as I want on the *World.*" He declined many honorary positions which were offered to him. He was, however, a Chevalier of the French Legion of Honor and the Belgian Order of Leopold, but never displayed their ribbons on the lapel of his coat. Interested in promoting higher journalistic standards, he was active in the American Society of Newspaper Editors of which he was a director and the first vice-president. To his editorial room, always open, came great political leaders but his most cordial welcome was saved for the ordinary man of the street. To put the latter at ease he wore a shabby office coat. He was married first in 1897 to Delia S. Bailey, and second, on Oct. 2, 1913, to the well-known newspaper woman, Margaret Hubbard Ayer. Living and working in New York City, his heart was always at the little farm which he owned near Westport, Conn.

[Lindsay Denison contributes to *Cobb of "The World"—A Leader in Liberalism* (1924) an opening chapter, "Cobb, The Man." The book is a collection of editorials selected by John L. Heaton with a foreword by Woodrow Wilson. Obituaries may be found in the leading newspapers of New York City and of Detroit for Dec. 22, 1923, see especially the *World* (N. Y.) and the *Detroit Free Press.* There are many references to Cobb in Don C. Seitz, *Jos. Pulitzer, His Life and Letters* (1924).]

J.M.L.

COBB, HOWELL (Sept. 7, 1815–Oct. 9, 1868), senator, was the son of John A. and Sarah (Rootes) Cobb. The elder Cobb was an extensive planter in Jefferson County, in the cotton belt of middle Georgia, and it was there that Howell was born. While he was yet a small boy the family removed to Athens, Clarke County, the seat of the University of Georgia. The Cobbs, therefore, while retaining their farming interests in Jefferson and other counties, became identified with northeast Georgia. Howell Cobb was born into a family which, by reason of its wealth, social prestige and the ability of its members, occupied a secure position in the small group of planters who dominated the political life of the South throughout the ante bellum period. His formative years were spent in an atmosphere of culture and among people in whom there was a long tradition of public service. His grandfather (John Cobbs) came to Georgia from Virginia in 1783 and immediately assumed a position of importance in politics, serving six years in the House of Representatives, being a member of the Executive Council of the state and a delegate to the Constitutional Convention of 1795. John Cobbs's sons (John A. and Howell) dropped the "s" from the name. John A. (the father of the subject of this biography) served several terms in the state legislature; Howell, the elder, was a member of Congress (1807–13) and his son, Thomas W., was a United States Senator (1824–28). Furthermore, Howell Cobb's kinspeople, the Jacksons, Lamars and others, had long been among the leading families in the state, socially and politically. His early marriage (1834), immediately after graduating from the University of Georgia, to Mary Ann Lamar, daughter of another wealthy middle Georgia planter, materially strengthened his resources. Leisure and comparative freedom from financial worries enabled him to devote his life to public affairs. After two years' private study he was admitted to the bar in 1836. His opportunity to enter public life came in 1837. In that year the legislature elected him to the office of solicitor-general of the Western Circuit. This circuit lay in the northeastern portion of Georgia. It was economically a poor section, occupied by the small white farmer element, but these sturdy people were politically well educated. They took a keen interest in national and state politics, and, though removed from the politically dominant plantation areas, they kept informed of the trend of affairs. They were strongly Unionist in feeling and had little economic interest in slavery. During Cobb's three years as solicitor he came constantly before the people. On the expiration of his last term as solicitor-general, he entered the race for Congress in the last election on a general ticket, and was successful (1842). Congress during the same year established the district system and at the 1844 election Cobb was returned for the sixth district, which was practically coterminous with the judicial circuit in which he had been solicitor. He was not yet twenty-seven years of age when first elected, and he represented this district at various times until he became a member of Buchanan's cabinet in 1857. His freedom from rancorous sectional outbursts, the broad national spirit that he showed on all occasions, coupled with his thorough knowledge of constitutional questions, and his ability as a debater, quickly established him in Congress, and, on the death of Drumgoole of Virginia, he was elected (1848) as parliamentary leader of his party in the House.

During the entire period of Cobb's service in Congress territorial expansion and the sectional struggle over the extension of slavery was the dominating issue. He upheld the constitutionality of the annexation of Texas; he defended Polk's administration for the declaration of war against Mexico; and as soon as it became apparent that the United States would defeat Mexico and demand a huge cession of territory, he urged that the slavery question be settled by the extension of the Missouri Compromise line to the Pacific. Calhoun, meanwhile, was urging the Southern members of Congress to dissociate themselves from the Northern wings of the two parties and form a Southern *bloc* for the protection of their interests. At a meeting of Southern senators and representatives in January 1849, he produced his well-known "Southern Address," calling for united action of all Southerners. But the Whig members refused to cooperate, only two of them signing the Address. Cobb and three other Democrats also declined to fall in with Calhoun's plan, and issued another address, written by Cobb. The gist of it was that the united national Democracy was a far better guarantee of justice to the South than any sectional party could be. The position thus taken alienated large numbers of Cobb's Southern Democratic colleagues, but increased his popularity with the Northern wing of the party. So much so, indeed, that, after one of the most spectacular fights ever seen in Congress, Cobb was elected speaker of the House in December 1849, on the sixty-third ballot. He was, therefore, presiding officer of the House during the critical debates on Clay's compromise measures. Shortly after the passage (in September 1850) of the various measures, Cobb, alone of Southern Democrats, signed a paper circulated among members pledging its signatories not to support any candidate for office who was not opposed to the renewal in any form of the slavery agitation. When news of the passage of the compromise measures reached Georgia, Governor Towns immediately summoned a state convention to meet in December 1850 to deliberate on Georgia's course. The campaign which followed was as stirring as any in Georgia history. Whigs and Union (or Cobb) Democrats, were arrayed against the Southern Rights wing of the Democratic party. Cobb took the stump along with notable Whig leaders, such as Toombs and Stephens, for the Union and compromise. The result was an overwhelming Unionist victory. It is significant to note that, while the Whig leaders in this movement were following the natural tendencies of their party and, therefore, risked nothing, Cobb staked his entire political future,

The popularity thus lost was never regained. He was pursued by the relentless hatred of the Southern Rights Democrats for many years.

During the convention the Unionists organized themselves into a new party, taking the name "Constitutional Union." It was composed of Whigs and Cobb Democrats. The bulk of the Democratic party likewise reorganized under the name of "Southern Rights Party." The next year, 1851, was an election year in Georgia. The Southern Rights Democrats named Charles J. McDonald, an extremist, as their candidate for governor, and in their state convention (in May) declared for the sovereign (*i.e.*, constitutional) right of a state to secede from the Union. The Union Party held its convention in June and was immediately confronted by this question of the abstract right of secession. The convention declined to commit itself on the issue, because there was a serious difference of opinion among the leaders. Some upheld the constitutional right to secede; others thought that such a right was merely revolutionary in its nature and not constitutional. Cobb was nominated for governor. The ensuing campaign was quite as heated as that for the election of the delegates to the convention in the preceding year. The same ground was fought over anew, that is to say, secession and the "finality" of the compromise were the issues. Cobb was constantly heckled about the secession question and his position has generally been regarded as a straddle. Though he spoke all over Georgia for the Union cause, he yet could not bring himself to the point of avowing that, if elected governor, he would use force to put down a secession movement. Nevertheless he was elected by the greatest majority that had ever been given a candidate up to that time, and the result of the election was taken to mean that Georgia had spoken emphatically against disunion and secession. This is the high point of Cobb's career. Some of the leaders, in organizing the Union Party in the state convention of 1850, had hoped to make the new party a national organization. Cobb, however, regarded the Georgia Union Party as a temporary organization to meet the emergency presented by the compromise measures, and after Georgia had been brought to accept the compromise he preferred to resume the old alliance with the national Democracy. For this and other reasons the idea of a national Union Party failed. The Southern Rights wing of the Georgia Democracy had arrogated to itself the position of sole Democratic regularity. They had control of the machinery and read Cobb out of the party. The Whig element in the Union Party returned to their normal affiliation and

Cobb was thus left stranded with few followers except the North Georgia Union Democrats. It so chanced that at the expiration of his term as governor the legislature was called upon to elect a successor to Senator Dawson, the Whig incumbent, and a candidate for reëlection. Cobb entered the contest, but was overwhelmingly defeated by the Whigs and the Southern Rights Democrats (1854).

The following year Cobb was returned to Congress by the 6th District. He was instrumental in the nomination and election of Buchanan, his close personal friend, and the President named him secretary of the treasury. During his incumbency the crisis of 1857 occurred and Cobb's handling of treasury matters received high praise from the New York papers. After the election of Lincoln to the Presidency in 1860, Cobb, in a letter to the people of Georgia (Dec. 6, 1860, "Toombs, Stephens and Cobb Correspondence," pp. 505 ff.) advocated immediate secession; and he was one of the most prominent supporters of secession in the campaign preceding the Secession Convention, which met in January 1861, though he was not a member of the Convention. When the seceding states met in convention in Montgomery to organize the Southern Confederacy, Cobb was made its chairman. Many thought he would have been a better choice for the presidency than Jefferson Davis. Want of military training and the enmity which had been engendered against him because of his former Unionist principles stood in the way of his election. During the following summer he organized the 16th Georgia Regiment, and went to the front as a colonel. Though temperamentally and by training unfitted for the life of a soldier, he yet served with distinction, was promoted to a brigadiership, and in 1863 became a major-general. He was at that time assigned to the command of the District of Georgia. Political motives seem to have determined this step. Conflict between Gov. Joseph E. Brown [*q.v.*] and President Davis made it necessary that a strong supporter of the government should be on the ground. When the Confederacy collapsed Cobb surrendered at Macon to Gen. Wilson. After the war he formed a law partnership at Macon with James Jackson, a relative and close friend, and resumed the practise of his profession, practically abandoned for politics twenty-five years before. He was an uncompromising opponent of the Congressional Reconstruction policies. During this period, while on a visit to New York, he died suddenly on Oct. 9, 1868.

[Cobb left a great collection of letters and papers now in the possession of his daughter, Mrs. A. S. Erwin of Athens, Ga. This collection has been twice gone through, once by U. B. Phillips, in whose "Toombs, Stephens and Cobb Correspondence," *Am. Hist. Asso. Annual Report,* 1911, vol. II, were included the most important documents in the Erwin Collection, and later by R. P. Brooks, who printed in "Howell Cobb Papers," *Ga. Hist. Quart.,* vols. V, VI, a large number of papers and letters unused by Prof. Phillips. In his "Plantation and Frontier," *Doc. Hist. Am. Industrial Soc.,* vol. I (1910), Prof. Phillips incorporated many letters bearing on plantation and slavery conditions, written to or by Cobb and taken principally from the Erwin Collection. Files of the *Southern Banner,* a weekly published in Athens, and commonly regarded as Cobb's organ, are available for part of the ante bellum period. The best sketch of Cobb is that written by his kinsman, Jos. R. Lamar, Associate Justice of the United States Supreme Court, for *Men of Mark in Ga.,* III (1911), 566 ff. Judge Lamar in a footnote (p. 569) gives a list of biographical sketches of Cobb preceding his own. R. P. Brooks in "Howell Cobb and the Crisis of 1850," *Miss. Valley Hist. Rev.,* IV, 279–98, has made a study of Cobb's part in the compromise agitation.] R.P.B.

COBB, JONATHAN HOLMES (July 8, 1799–Mar. 12, 1882), lawyer and silk manufacturer, was born at Sharon, Mass., the eldest of the ten children of Jonathan and Sibbel (Holmes) Cobb. His father was a prosperous innkeeper and farmer and the eldest son had the advantage of an excellent preparation at Milton Academy and a college course at Harvard. He graduated from that institution in 1817 in a class which included George Bancroft, Caleb Cushing, and Stephen H. Tyng. After graduation he commenced the study of law in the office of William Dunbar of Canton, Mass., where he remained about a year, when he went to Charleston, S. C. In that city he pursued his studies in the office of Benjamin S. Dunkin and at the same time opened a classical and English school. An outbreak of yellow fever in 1819 led him to return to Massachusetts and enter the law office of Jabez Chickering. From there he was admitted in 1820 to the Norfolk County bar, the commencement of a distinguished legal career. In addition to a legal practise in Dedham and Boston, Cobb was register of probate for Norfolk County, 1833–79, and town clerk of Dedham for thirty consecutive years, declining a reëlection in 1875. For forty years he was an active magistrate in Norfolk County. He was widely known in his own day as an expert in the production and manufacture of silk. When the *morus multicaulis,* a new form of the mulberry tree, was introduced into the United States in the decade of the twenties, he was among the earliest and most enthusiastic experimenters. After a period of intensive experimentation he so convinced the state legislature of the practicability of silk production in Massachusetts that they commissioned him to write a manual on the subject and appropriated $600 to cover publication. The result was *A Manual Containing Information Respecting the Growth of the Mulberry Tree with Suitable Directions*

for the Culture of Silk (1831). This little book came out at the height of the *morus multicaulis* boom and was widely read. The Congress of the United States ordered the printing of 2,000 copies for distribution, and the book went through four editions by 1839. Before the last edition was printed Cobb was in a position to give directions as to the production of silk from the tree to the finished product for he had successfully accomplished the whole process in Dedham. In 1837 he established a silk-mill which in the following year operated sixteen throwing machines of one hundred spindles each and turned out $35,000 worth of sewing silk as well as a "considerable quantity of narrow goods" (*Manual,* 4th ed., p. 152). This factory, which was destroyed by fire in 1844, was one of the earliest in the United States, and to Cobb as much as to any single individual must go the credit of arousing an interest in the manufacture of silk.

Cobb was active in many local projects. He was a founder and treasurer (1831–34) of the Dedham Institution for Savings, editor for some years of the *Village Register* and for forty years a deacon in the First Church of Dedham. He was married on Sept. 26, 1822, to Sophia Doggett of Roxbury.

[Wm. R. Cutter, *Geneal. and Personal Memoirs Relating to Families of Boston and Eastern Mass.* (1908), III, 1220. See also *New Eng. Hist. and Geneal. Reg.,* XXXVI, 231; D. H. Hurd, *Hist. of Norfolk County* (1884), and the *Manual* mentioned above.] H.U.F.

COBB, LYMAN (Sept. 18, 1800–Oct. 26[?], 1864), educator and author, the son of Elijah William and Sally (Whitney) Cobb, was born in Lenox, Mass., but lived chiefly in New York State. Little is known of his early life and education, but in some of his publications Cobb mentions himself as "Master of Arts." He was author of numerous texts, chiefly in spelling, reading, and arithmetic, millions of copies of which are said to have been sold. His spelling-books created the greatest stir. The first of these appeared about 1821 (*American Journal,* Ithaca, Oct. 17, 1821), and was followed at intervals by revisions, introductions, and sequels. He published a *Critical Review of Noah Webster's Spelling Book,* which many held was inspired by malice and a desire to increase his own sales. This he stoutly denied. The *Critical Review* was answered by Webster in an eight-page pamphlet, *To the Friends of American Literature.* Each side was able to point out numerous errors in the other, though Cobb's agents defied "anyone to show a variation from the true dictionary of Walker," an abridgment of which, by Cobb, was published at Ithaca in 1829. In the early forties Cobb had another controversy over spelling-books, this time with Charles W. Sanders [*q.v.*].

Among his most significant books was *The Evil Tendencies of Corporal Punishment* (1847), wherein he discussed thirty "objections" to, and offered forty "substitutes for and preventives of, the use of the rod." This work was warmly commended by Gallaudet, Mann, Russell, and Griscom; and Cobb's views were reëchoed in hundreds of articles opposing the old practise. His Pestalozzian bias is also seen in a statement that he did not want pupils to "become disgusted or fatigued" with monotonous reading. The *Juvenile Reader No. 1* (1830) was recommended as "interesting, moral and instructive"; illustrations were used in some of his books; but it must be admitted that by the time the *New Sequel or Fourth Reading Book* (1843) was reached, an excessive aridity and formality had crept in, despite the author's ambitious efforts. In the *North American Reader* (1835) he made a patriotic appeal, the "pieces" being "chiefly American." Most readers, he said, do not include "a single piece or paragraph written by an American citizen. Is this good policy? Is it patriotism?" Though his books were widely used and received favorable comment, as in the *American Journal of Education,* their merits were perhaps exaggerated and excessively advertised (*e.g., Maine Palladium,* May 16, 1827, p. 4). Cobb married Harriet Chambers of Caroline, Tompkins County, N. Y., in 1822. He died at Colesburg, Pa., where he lies in an unmarked grave. His books are the most reliable evidence of his life, and his only monument.

[*Am. Annual Cyc.,* 1864; J. T. Scharf, *Hist. Westchester County* (1886); Chas. E. Allison, *Hist. of Yonkers* (1896); *Hist. Genealogy of the Lawrence Family* (1858); numerous letters from members of the family to the writer; obituary in the *Ithaca Jour.,* Mar. 1, 1865.]
T. W.

COBB, SYLVANUS (July 17, 1798–Oct. 31, 1866), Universalist clergyman, was the son of Ebenezer and Elizabeth Cobb, both descendants of Elder Henry Cobb who came to Plymouth on the second voyage of the *Mayflower*. The year before Sylvanus was born his parents went in an ox-wagon as pioneers to Norway, Me. As a boy he cut hoop-poles at a cent each to provide himself with books and stationery. During the War of 1812 he early exhibited his journalistic and political tendencies by writing poetry and prose in support of the Republican or War party. The first Universalist Church in Maine was built in Norway and in his sixteenth year he espoused that faith. It was a controversial era when hostility to Universalist doctrine was strong and vigorous. When Cobb received his first certificate to teach school the "orthodox" preacher wrote a "P. S." that the young man was legally qualified but he could not consistently commit a child to the care of one of his religious sentiments. In 1820 the young man went to Portsmouth, N. H., to study with Rev. Sebastian Streeter preparatory to entering the Universalist ministry, to which he was ordained in Winthrop, Me., June 28, 1821. While pastor at Winthrop and Waterville, he became the chief pioneer and missionary of Universalism in the state of Maine. The first Parish Church of Malden, Mass., became Universalist instead of Unitarian by calling Cobb to its ministry in 1828. All the time he was at heart a journalist and he began to publish in Waltham, Mass., *The Christian Freeman and Family Visiter* in 1839. In religion it stood for the Universalist faith and also for total abstinence and anti-slavery. Both were unpopular causes. He was accused of mixing politics and religion, as he had been accused in his pulpit. Already he had served two terms each in the Maine and Massachusetts legislatures, and in politics and reform he was always found with the advanced liberals. He became champion and confessor of the Universalist faith, and carried on his polemics with earnestness and ability. He reviewed in his paper Dr. Edward Beecher's *Conflict of the Ages.* Two great debates were also conducted in the *Freeman,* one with the orthodox Calvinist, Dr. Nehemiah Adams, on "The Scripturalness of Future Endless Punishment," and the other on "Human Destiny" with Rev. C. F. Hudson who supported the annihilationist theory. These were republished in book form. After twenty-three years he sold out the *Freeman,* which soon became the property of the Universalist Publishing House. While editing the paper he had also preached in Universalist churches in Waltham and East Boston. One of his constructive contributions was his *Compend of Divinity* (1846), a thorough and concise epitome of the Universalist doctrine, while his *New Testament of Our Lord and Savior Jesus Christ: with explanatory notes and practical observations* (1864) shows his ability as a theologian. Standing well over six feet in height, broad shouldered, full chested, he had a commanding presence and a massive head. He had not the characteristics of a popular preacher, but rather strength and solidity of thought, closely knit and logical. Weight of argument was his chief weapon instead of brilliance or elegance of style. Severe in denunciation and condemnation of error or evil, he was kind of heart and of large charity. The last years of his life were spent in Boston where he died. He was married on Sept. 10, 1822 to Eunice Hale Waite of Hallowell, Me., by whom he had nine children, one of whom, Sylvanus Cobb [*q.v.*], was his father's biographer.

[The chief source is *The Autobiography of the First Forty-One Years of the Life of Sylvanus Cobb, D.D.; to which is added a Memoir by his eldest son, Sylvanus Cobb, Jr.* (1867). *The Christian Freeman and Family Visiter* also has much autobiographical material.]

T. C. R.

COBB, SYLVANUS (June 5, 1823–July 20, 1887), novelist, the eldest of the nine children of the Rev. Sylvanus Cobb [*q.v.*] and his wife, Eunice Hale Waite, was born in Waterville, Me. From his parents, who were of deep-rooted New England stock, he acquired certain Yankee and Puritan traits—resourcefulness, thrift, uprightness, and piety—that, softened by the sentimentality of the period and undisciplined by any intellectual or æsthetic training, shaped his character and colored his writing. His boyhood and youth were spent in Malden, Mass. He was scribbling fiction at the age of eleven and displayed his lifelong regard for grammar and the mechanics of style almost equally early by getting himself expelled from high school for disputing with the teacher over a nice problem in parsing. His father had him learn the printer's trade, but at seventeen the boy ran away from home and enlisted at Boston (February 1841) in the navy. Service on the United States frigates *Brandywine* and *Fairfield* gave him glimpses of various Mediterranean ports and a nautical vocabularly that later was a useful part of his literary paraphernalia. Discharged from the navy at Hampton Roads (March 1844), he returned home and on June 29, 1845, was married to Jane Head of Waltham, Mass.

In May 1846, with his brother Samuel he started the *Rechabite,* a paper devoted—apparently in the order of decreasing intensity—to "temperance, moral elevation, literature, and general intelligence." Although Cobb's fiction began to appear in the second number, the real feature of the *Rechabite* was its amazingly vituperative attack, in the name of temperance, on innumerable prominent New Englanders and on such national figures as Henry Clay, Daniel Webster, and President Polk, who was accused of turning the executive mansion at Washington into "a free tippling house."

From 1850 on Cobb devoted himself assiduously to the manufacture of popular fiction. His stories invariably contained the maximum amount of excitement compatible with strict morality. A facile style, an unfailing knack for simple characterization and for devising melodramatic incident against romantic backgrounds, and complete harmony in sentiment and ideas between the author and his enormous—and enormously naïve—audience, made his work immediately and continuously popular. From 1850 to 1856 he was on the staff of Gleason's *Flag of Our Union* and *Pictorial Drawing Room,* writing 36 novelettes and 200 short stories for the two magazines, besides doing much work for other publications. From March 1856 till his death (July 20, 1887) he wrote for Robert Bonner's *New York Ledger.* To the *Ledger* he contributed 130 novelettes, 30 Forest Sketches, 72 Forest Adventures, 102 Sketches of Adventure, 57 Scraps of Adventure from an Old Sailor's Logbook, 573 other short stories, and 2,305 shorter items. Not content with writing for a living, for thirty-five years he kept a diary, in which he never failed to note the state of the weather. He was almost six feet tall and weighed almost two hundred pounds. With his broad, smooth forehead, long hair, and flowing beard, he was an impressive figure. From 1869 till his death he made his home in Hyde Park, Mass.; previously he had lived at Norway, Me. As literature his work is of no value, but as the first American to apply quantitative methods to the production of fiction, he has his place in the general history of American printed matter.

[The only account of Cobb's life is a *Memoir of Sylvanus Cobb, Jr.* (1891), by Ella Waite Cobb (his daughter).]

G. H. G.

COBB, THOMAS READE ROOTES (Apr. 10, 1823–Dec. 13, 1862), lawyer, soldier, was the son of John A. and Sarah (Rootes) Cobb and was born in Jefferson County, Ga. Like his elder brother, Howell Cobb [*q.v.*], after being graduated from the University of Georgia he studied law and was admitted to the bar (1842). His reputation as an advocate and constitutional lawyer was high. To talent he added a truly prodigious capacity for work. Few men of his age made so many books. From 1849 to 1857 as a supreme court reporter he edited twenty volumes. His digest of Georgia Laws (1851) was in fact a codification of the laws of the state. It was unique in America both by reason of its method, its comprehensiveness, and the clearness of its language. In addition he wrote *An Inquiry into the Law of Negro Slavery* (1858) and *A Historical Sketch of Slavery from the Earliest Periods* (1859). He was a regular contributor to newspapers in Georgia and the North.

In November 1860, after the election of Lincoln was definitely known, Cobb addressed the General Assembly of Georgia advocating immediate secession. It is said that, because of his force and eloquence, he was the most potent influence in taking Georgia out of the Union (Alexander H. Stephens, *A Constitutional View of the Late War Between the States*, 1870, II, 321). The legislature declined to take upon itself the responsibility for so momentous a step in the absence of any expression of popular opinion, but passed an act requiring the governor to summon a special convention in January following. Thereupon Cobb went about preaching a crusade for secession. He was elected to membership in the convention and took an active part in its proceedings. After the convention had adopted the ordinance of secession, it proceeded to revise the constitution of Georgia. Cobb was made chairman of the committee for that purpose, and internal evidence in the proceedings of the convention indicates that he practically controlled the work of revision. The convention elected both the Cobbs as delegates to represent Georgia in the Montgomery convention of the seceding states. There Thomas Cobb was made a member of the committee on the permanent constitution, and contributed his wide knowledge of constitutional law to the making of the constitution. But, though without military training, he felt a call to the active service of the Confederacy. He retired from the Montgomery convention, receiving a commission as colonel (August 1861) and organized "Cobb's Legion." In November 1862, he was promoted to brigadier-general, and was killed at the battle of Fredericksburg in December of that year. Gen. Lee spoke in terms of high praise of his character, accomplishments, and ability as an officer. He was married to Marion, the daughter of Chief Justice Joseph Henry Lumpkin of the Georgia supreme court. The Lucy Cobb Institute, founded by Cobb, was named for a daughter who died when fourteen years of age. Only three of Cobb's children reached maturity, all daughters—Callendar, married to A. L. Hull of Athens; Belle, married to Harry Jackson of Atlanta, and Marion, married to Hoke Smith, senator and member of Cleveland's cabinet.

[The *Southern Hist. Asso. Pubs.*, vol. II, 1907, Nos. 3–6, contain numerous Cobb letters edited by his son-in-law, A. L. Hull. R. P. Brooks, of the Univ. of Ga., has a much larger mass of Cobb papers in typed form, the originals having in some way been lost. There is not in print any life of Cobb beyond inadequate sketches in various biographical dictionaries. The most ambitious of these is that of A. L. Hull in *Men of Mark in Ga.*, vol. III (1911). Cobb's famous speech of Nov. 12, 1860, was printed by the state in *Confed. Records State of Ga.*, I (1909), 157–82. This volume also contains the full proceedings of the secession convention in which Cobb played a leading part. Cobb's *Digest Statute Laws State of Ga.* (1851) is in all large law libraries. His other works are hard to locate.]   R. P. B.

COBB, WILLIAM HENRY (Apr. 2, 1846–May 1, 1923), clergyman, librarian, was the descendant of Massachusetts Puritan and Pilgrim ancestors, and the son and grandson of Congregational clergymen. His parents were Rev. Leander and Julia Ann (Scribner) Cobb. He was born and received his early education in Marion, Mass., but completed his preparation for college at Rochester Academy, Rochester, Mass. He graduated from Amherst in 1867. After teaching for two years in Wilmington, Del., he studied at Princeton Theological Seminary, 1869–70, and graduated at Andover in 1872. He was pastor of Congregational churches at Chiltonville, Mass., 1872–76; Medfield, Mass., 1876–78; Uxbridge, Mass., 1878–87. From 1887 to his death he was librarian of the Congregational Library in Boston. Cobb was master of many languages including Hebrew, which was his specialty. As an Old Testament scholar he had an international standing, his especial field being the book of Isaiah, upon which he left an unfinished work at the time of his death. He was an authority on the history of Congregationalism and an indefatigable collector of the literature of the Puritan and Pilgrim movements, in which department the Congregational Library became under his headship one of the most complete collections in existence. He was a member of the Society of Biblical Literature and Exegesis, 1890–1915, and its recording secretary for the same period. On his retirement he declined an election to the presidency of the society. He was an editor of the *Journal of Biblical Literature*, 1889–1915. His publications include: *A Criticism of Systems of Hebrew Metre* (1905), which was awarded a prize by Manchester College, Oxford; *The Meaning of Christian Unity* (1915); and *Seven Centuries Illustrated in the Congregational Library* (1921). He also published many articles in the *Bibliotheca Sacra* and the *Journal of Biblical Literature*, as well as the article "Metre in the Bible," in the *Jewish Encyclopedia.*

Cobb was slight in stature, below the medium height, with reddish hair and beard which became gray in his latter years. His portrait painted toward the close of his life may be seen in the Congregational Library. His memory was remarkable, and his habits were those of the methodical and painstaking scholar. He was mild and modest in demeanor, had a fine sense of humor, and qualities that secured for him warm and enduring friendships. On Oct. 30, 1872, he married Emily W. Wiggins of Philadelphia, who survived him with two sons and two daughters.

[*Princeton Theol. Sem., Necrological Report*, 1924;

Congreg. Year Book, 1923; Nation (N. Y.), Feb. 10, 1916; Congregationalist, May 10, 1923; and the Minutes of the Society of Biblical Literature and Exegesis; information as to certain facts from a daughter.]   F. T. P.

COBBETT, WILLIAM (Mar. 9, 1763–June 18, 1835), journalist, publicist, was born at Farnham, Surrey, the third of the four sons of George and Ann (Vincent) Cobbett. His career as a whole belongs to English history, but from October 1792 till June 1800 and again from May 1817 till the end of October 1819 he lived as a political refugee in the United States. He is one of the founders of American party journalism. The United States occupied a large place in his imagination though not in his affection; he had friends there; and his interest in the country was life-long.

On his first arrival in America he settled with his bride, Ann Reid, at Wilmington, Del., but soon moved to Philadelphia, where he lived in decent obscurity by teaching English to French *émigrés*. The ovations and oratory attendant on Joseph Priestley's landing at New York ignited his British patriotism. The *Observations on the Emigration of Dr. Joseph Priestley* (Philadelphia, Thomas Bradford, 1794) created a furore the greater because the author of the pamphlet remained anonymous. Republicans were aghast; Federalists applauded; and Cobbett bounded gleefully into vituperative journalism. His partisan rivals retaliated and he was blackguarded in pamphlet after pamphlet, but he was pleased rather than abashed by such attentions and inundated his enemies in his own incomparable Billingsgate. *A Bone to Gnaw for the Democrats* (2 pts., 1795), *A Kick for a Bite* (1795), *A Little Plain English Addressed to the People of the United States* (1795), *A New Year's Gift for the Democrats* (1796), *The Life and Adventures of Peter Porcupine* (1796)—he had adopted the name, on an opponent's suggestion, in 1795—and *The Gros Mousqueton Diplomatique or Diplomatic Blunderbuss* (1796) exemplify in their titles the spirit of his writing but do not exhaust the list of his publications. Having quarreled with the grasping Bradford, he opened on July 11, 1796, a bookseller's shop of his own and advertised the occasion by filling his window with portraits of George III, Lord Howe, and other obnoxious personages. The mob threatened to tar and feather him and to burn the house over his head, but his effrontery was unconquerable. On Mar. 4, 1797, he launched *Porcupine's Gazette and Daily Advertiser* to advocate alliance with England, war against France, and perdition for Republicans. The savage, sarcastic humor of the paper ex-

ceeded anything that Philip Freneau had done or that Benjamin Franklin Bache could do. It attained a large circulation but made little money. Meanwhile he had several narrow escapes from prosecution; such powerful men as Thomas McKean [q.v.] and Edward Shippen were among his enemies; and President John Adams thought seriously of deporting him. Catastrophe finally came. During the yellow-fever epidemic of 1797 Dr. Benjamin Rush treated his patients to violent purges and copious bleeding, and Cobbett on politico-medical grounds made a terrific onslaught upon him. Rush sued for libel, and after a delay of two years the case came to trial and Cobbett was mulcted of $5,000. It is clear that Rush was libeled and deserved to be libeled, but the trial was unfair. Anticipating the worst, Cobbett had already retreated to New York, whence he issued a new paper, *The Rush-Light*, which the philosophical Priestley found very amusing. Cobbett, however, was tired of the game, homesick, and uncertain about his future. Assured of a friendly reception, he returned in June 1800 to England.

He was driven from England again by the suspension on Mar. 4, 1817, of the Habeas Corpus Act. Landing at New York on May 5, he retired the next day to an inn on Long Island, rented a small farm at Hyde Park in North Hempstead, and settled down to his favorite routine of agriculture and authorship. He had little appetite now for American affairs. He did try, however, to get the Pennsylvania legislature to reimburse him for the losses he had suffered in the courts; and he disputed vehemently with Morris Birkbeck [q.v.] over the feasibility of colonizing Englishmen on the prairie lands of the West. Birkbeck's accusation, repeated by certain historians (E. E. Sparks, *The English Settlement in the Illinois*, 1907, p. x; T. C. Pease, *The Frontier State 1818–48*, 1918, p. 14), that he was in the pay of eastern land dealers, rests only on hearsay. Cobbett himself was happy only when his feet were planted on English soil; he could not conscientiously urge any Englishman to seek liberty and happiness in the States. During these two years of comparatively undisturbed work he came to his full stature as a writer. *A Journal of a Year's Residence in the United States* (pt. I, 1818; pts. II and III, 1819) records some of his experiences. On May 20, 1819, his house burned; and the next autumn, with the unblessed bones of Thomas Paine [q.v.] in his baggage, he returned home.

[E. I. Carlyle, *Wm. Cobbett: A Study of his Life as Shown in his Writings* (1904), and G. D. H. Cole, *The Life of Wm. Cobbett* (1925), are excellent and indispensable and between them furnish ample guidance to Cobbett's own writings and to other writings about him. See also Jasper Yeates, *Reports of Cases Adjudged in the Supreme Court of Pa.*, vol. II (1818; 1871); Francis Wharton, *State Trials of the U. S. during the Administration of Washington and Adams* (1849); J. T. Rutt, *Life and Corrcs. of Jos. Priestley* (1831–32), II, 432; *A Memorial . . . of Dr. Benjamin Rush . . . Written by Himself* (privately printed, 1905), pp. 72–74; *The Poems of Philip Freneau* (Princeton, N. J., 1902–07), III, 167–69; J. V. N. Ingram, *Check List of Am. Eighteenth Century Newspapers in the Lib. of Cong.* (1912).]   G. H. G.

COBURN, ABNER (Mar. 22, 1803–Jan. 4, 1885), business man, governor, philanthropist, was born in that part of the town of Canaan, Me., now a part of Skowhegan. His father, Eleazar Coburn, was a skilful land-surveyor and an owner of large tracts of timberland. He also took considerable interest in politics, was a Federalist and a Whig, and served several terms in the legislature. He married Mary Weston, a grand-daughter of one of the earliest settlers of Somerset County, Me. Of their fourteen children, Abner was the second. He spent most of his youth on his father's farm but attended the common schools, studied for a few terms at Bloomfield Academy and taught a winter school before he was twenty. For a few years he assisted his father in surveying and thus acquired a good knowledge of the art and also of the timberlands of central Maine. In 1825 he set up for himself but in 1830 joined his father and a younger brother, Philander, in forming the firm of E. Coburn & Sons, for buying lands and dealing in lumber on the Kennebec River. In 1845 Eleazar Coburn died and the firm was reorganized under the name of A. & P. Coburn. The firm became the largest landowner in the state. It also acquired large timber holdings in Wisconsin, and Abner Coburn obtained fifty thousand acres of timberland by virtue of connection with the Northern Pacific Railroad. The Coburn brothers were held in the highest regard by the vigorous, independent woodsmen in their employ, whom they always treated fairly and many of whom they helped to go into business for themselves and then by timely aid in periods of financial stringency, saved from ruin. In 1854 the Coburns began to interest themselves actively in the railroad development of central Maine, by their personal influence and business prestige turning failure into success. Abner Coburn is said to have instantly granted a request for a loan of $200,000 to save the Maine Central Railroad from bankruptcy. When a Boston interest obtained control of the Maine Central it made Coburn president of the new subsidiary, probably expecting him to be little more than a rubber stamp whose use would conciliate local feeling. Coburn, however, not only

managed the Maine Central with great efficiency and economy but firmly resisted attempts to sacrifice the interests or the dignity of his road.

Like his father, he took considerable interest in politics. He served three terms in the state legislature as a Whig, helped found the Republican party of Maine, and was twice a member of the Executive Council. In 1860 he was a formidable candidate for the Republican nomination for governor, having the special support of the friends of James G. Blaine, but he was defeated by Congressman Israel Washburn. In 1863 Gov. Washburn declined to run again and Coburn received the Republican nomination on the first ballot and was elected. It was, however, a year of Democratic reaction throughout the country and Coburn's majority was much smaller than that received by Washburn at either of his elections. As governor Coburn gave Maine a clean, honest, business-like administration, making appointments and awarding contracts with regard to the interest of the state rather than that of the politicians. This helped to deprive him of the renomination usually given to governors; even some men who admired his independence believed that it would be unwise to present as a candidate a man who had aroused such opposition. More important was the fact that the Republican party gave way to a "Union" convention and that the chairman of their state committee, James G. Blaine, strongly favored the choice of a worthy War Democrat, Samuel Cony, who was nominated and elected. Coburn held no other important political office but was chosen presidential elector in 1884 and while attending the meeting of the Maine electors was seized with an illness from which he did not recover.

Among Coburn's chief characteristics were calmness, self-reliance, and generosity. He once received news of the loss of hundreds of thousands of dollars, without giving the slightest sign of agitation. His closest friend, whom he made an executor of his will, knew no more of his affairs than did a mere acquaintance and was not even informed of his appointment as executor until after Coburn's death. Coburn was generous to a fault in helping individuals in distress but he never spoke of the aid which he gave. By his will he left over a million dollars to religious, educational, and charitable institutions, much the greater share going to Baptist foundations. Three institutions in which Coburn took great interest during his life and which he remembered generously in his will have given special evidence of their gratitude. Colby College and the University of Maine have each a

Coburn Hall and the Waterville Classical Institute changed its name to that of the Coburn Classical Institute.

[Chas. E. Williams, *Life of Abner Coburn, A Rev. of the Pub. and Private Career of the Late Ex-Gov. of Maine* (1885), is a mere compilation of a eulogistic nature but contains valuable material. Consult in L. C. Hatch, *Maine, A History* (1919), II, 447–54; Gaillard Hunt, *Israel, Elihu and Cadwallader Washburn: A Chapter in Am. Biography* (1925), p. 108; G. A. Gordon and S. R. Coburn, *Geneal. Descendants of Edward Colburn-Coburn* (1913); *Bangor Daily Whig and Courier*, Jan. 5, 6, 15, 1885.]   L. C. H.

COBURN, FOSTER DWIGHT (May 7, 1846–May 11, 1924), agricultural editor, author, and administrator, was born at Cold Springs, Jefferson County, Wis., the son of Ephraim W. and Mary (Mulks) Coburn. His early life was spent on the farm and his formal education was such as his home town supplied. At the age of eighteen he served in the Civil War as corporal in an Illinois regiment and soon after, in 1867, moved to Kansas and became a farm laborer and farmer in Franklin County. But as his character and ability were soon widely recognized, his engagement in farming was largely superseded by other work as a writer, adviser, and administrator. Thus from 1882 to 1887 he was editor-in-chief of the *Livestock Indicator,* published at Kansas City, Mo. Later he became an editorial writer on the *Kansas City Gazette* and one of the editors of *Country Life in America.* He prepared and published some thirty volumes of the reports of the Kansas State Board of Agriculture with special papers on certain subjects.

He was the author of *Swine Husbandry* (1877); *Alfalfa* (1901); *The Book of Alfalfa* (1906); *Swine in America* (1909); *Uncle Sam's Farm Book* (1911), a manual; *Coburn's Manual; a Complete Guide to the Farmer's Cyclopedia* (1915); and *How to Make Money with Hogs* (1915). His *Swine in America* was translated into Portuguese in 1913, by the ministry of agriculture of Brazil. His official positions, too, were many. Thus from 1894 to 1914 he was secretary of the Kansas State Board of Agriculture; for a time he was a member of the Board of Regents of the State Agricultural College and president of the Board. He was also a member of various state commissions, agricultural societies, and philanthropic organizations. He was a director of various financial institutions, the Prudential Trust Company, Prudential State Bank, and the Bank of Topeka. Believing that he could be of greater service in his chosen field for which he was admirably equipped, he refused to be a candidate for the governorship in 1898 and declined the appointment of the governor as United States senator. On Sept. 8, 1869 he married Lou Jenkins of Franklin County, Kan. He was a man "of the people," devoted to the advancement of agriculture, with a natural ability and integrity which, without preliminary discipline in educational institutions, made him a wise leader in agricultural affairs. Quiet and unassuming, understanding his limitations, he was a man of high ideals and of deep religious feeling. He devoted himself solely to the interests of a business which he loved and understood, in a state of whose advancement he was proud. In 1909 he received the honorary degrees of M.A. from Baker University and of LL.D. from the Kansas Agricultural College, and after his death a tablet to his memory was placed in the Memorial Hall at Topeka.

[*Kansas, a Cyc. of State Hist.,* vol. III (1912); *Twenty-fifth Biennial Report Kan. State Board of Ag.* (1926), pp. 272–78; *Breeder's Gazette,* May 29, 1924; *Topeka Daily Capital,* May 12, 1924; Geo. A. Gordon and Silas R. Coburn, *Geneal. Descendants of Edward Colburn-Coburn* (1913), pp. 359–61.]   E. H. J.

COCHRAN, ALEXANDER SMITH (Feb. 28, 1874–June 20, 1929), manufacturer, sportsman, philanthropist, was born in Yonkers, N. Y., where his father, William Francis Cochran, owned an estate of some six hundred acres. His mother, Eva (Smith) Cochran, was the daughter of the founder of Alexander Smith & Sons Carpet Company. Cochran attended St. Paul's School, Concord, N. H., and was graduated from Yale College in 1896. Some years after graduation, he told William Lyon Phelps that "the thing he missed most in his undergraduate days was good conversation" (letter from W. L. Phelps to the *New York Times,* June 24, 1929). For fourteen years he devoted himself to the affairs of the carpet company which had made the fortunes of his family, serving as president from 1902 until 1910. Liberal policies won him the loyalty of his workmen. He shortened their hours of labor and inaugurated a system by which they received semi-annually a bonus of from five to fifteen per cent of their wages. After his resignation from the presidency, he served as a director of the company until 1919. He inherited great wealth from his parents and uncle, and newspaper writers used to refer to him as "the world's most eligible bachelor." The title was revived, not without malice, at the time of his marriage, in September 1920, to Mme. Ganna Walska, the Polish singer. They were divorced in 1922. Wealth and leisure enabled him to indulge a taste for travel and to pursue his interests as sportsman and collector. A journey through Persia, in 1907, bore fruit in a collection of illuminated manuscripts of Persian poetry, which he presented to the Metropolitan Museum of Art. His library of rare editions in the field of English literature of the sixteenth and seventeenth centuries was one of the finest in the world. Distinction as a sportsman often brought his name before the public. In 1910 he sailed his schooner yacht *Westward* across the Atlantic, raced her at Cowes, and defeated the Kaiser's *Meteor* for the Jubilee prize at Kiel. His yacht *Vanitie,* built to defend the America's cup in 1914, did not race against the *Shamrock,* as he had hoped, for the war prevented the meeting. Late in 1914, he volunteered to carry dispatches between the American embassies at London and Berlin, but on his first trip he was arrested at Bentheim and spent a night on the guard-room floor (J. W. Gerard, *My Four Years in Germany,* 1917, p. 424). Subsequently he turned his steam yacht *Warrior* over to the British navy, was commissioned commander in the Royal Naval Reserve (February 1916), and served as captain of the *Warrior* in West Indian waters and the North Atlantic. At the close of the war, he received the decoration of Commander of the Order of the British Empire. He died at Saranac Lake, N. Y., of pulmonary tuberculosis, which had threatened his life for many years. One of his classmates has described him as "a reserved, unassuming sort of chap, with a face that may strike you as cold until you see his smile . . . generous but not to be imposed upon; very pleasant; conscientious; decisive; only moderately social; only moderately happy" (Clarence Day, Jr., *The '96 Half-Way Book,* 1915, p. 86).

He gave large sums for the founding of the Sprain Ridge Memorial Hospital, the Sherman Memorial Dispensary of Saint John's Riverside Hospital, and the College of Preachers of the Washington Cathedral, to which he left a bequest of $1,000,000. His will provided for gifts of from $1,000 to $10,000 to employees of the Alexander Smith & Sons Carpet Company; and he left a quarter of a million to Saint Paul's School, Concord. Perhaps his most interesting monument is the Elizabethan Club at Yale, established in 1911 in accordance with ideas formulated by Cochran himself. He provided the club with a house, a generous endowment, and a library consisting of his own magnificent collection of rare editions in the field of Elizabethan and Jacobean literature. The club has been an unqualified success, and on every afternoon the portrait of Queen Elizabeth, which was part of the founder's gift, looks down upon an animated company of undergraduate and faculty members, enjoying the sort of conversation that Alexander Cochran had missed in his own college days.

[Accounts of Cochran's activities, with photographs and personal impressions, are to be found in the unusually well edited publications of the Class of 1896 at Yale, particularly in the volume cited above and in the *Quarter-Century Record* (1924). His talents as a collector are reflected in the list of rare editions in the club library, included in *The Book of the Yale Elizabethan Club,* 1912, pp. 29–40, and in the *Cat. of the Coll. of Persian MSS. . . . Presented to the Metropolitan Museum by Alexander Smith Cochran* (1914), prepared by A. V. Williams Jackson and Abraham Yohannan. The collections are described, in some detail, in the *Yale Alumni Weekly,* Dec. 8, 1911, and in the *Nation* (N. Y.), June 19, 1913. Obituary notices appeared in the leading New York newspapers on June 21, and in the *Yale Alumni Weekly* on July 5, 1929.] R.D.F.

COCHRAN, JOHN (Sept. 1, 1730–Apr. 6, 1807), physician, was born in Sadsbury, Pa., of Scotch-Irish ancestry. His father, James, and his mother, Isabella, were akin, both Cochrans who had emigrated from Ireland. John was fortunate in having his early schooling under that remarkable classical scholar and Presbyterian divine, Dr. Francis Allison [q.v.]; his study of "physic and surgery" was under Dr. Thompson at Lancaster, Pa. During the French and Indian War (1754–63), he entered the British service as surgeon's mate in the hospital department, and was with Bradstreet when he marched against Fort Frontenac. Acquaintance with Maj. Philip Schuyler in this campaign led him to settle at Albany and to marry (Dec. 4, 1760) Mrs. Gertrude Schuyler, widow of Peter Schuyler. He soon moved to New Brunswick, N. J., where he became one of the founders of the New Jersey Medical Society and later (1769) its president. A devout Presbyterian and a zealous Whig he could not remain an idle spectator of the American Revolution, and volunteered his assistance in the hospital service. He collaborated with Dr. Shippen in preparing a plan for establishing military hospitals (Papers of the Continental Congress, in the Library of Congress, No. 22, folio 9) that was submitted to Congress Feb. 14, 1777. Washington observed his diligence and fidelity particularly in the case of smallpox patients and wounded soldiers, and recommended him to Congress as "highly deserving of notice, not only on account of his abilities, but for the very great assistance which he has afforded . . . merely in the nature of a volunteer." He was appointed physician and surgeon-general in the middle department, Apr. 10, 1777, and subsequently chief physician and surgeon. He was vehement in his denunciation of the inefficiency which at first characterized the hospital department. "It grieves my soul," he wrote (letter to Jonathan Potts, dated Mar. 18, 1780, in *Chronicles of the Cochrans,* 1915, p. 97), "to see the poor, worthy, brave fellows pine away for want of a few comforts, which they have dearly earned. I shall wait on the Commander-in-Chief, and represent our situation, but I am persuaded it can have little effect, for what can he do? He may refer the matter to Congress; they to the Medical Committee, who will probably pow-wow over it awhile and nothing more be heard of it." Director-General of the hospitals of the United States was the final responsibility (Jan. 17, 1781) given to him by Congress. His experience in British service enabled him to make great improvements in the army hospitals.

The war over, he removed to New York. When Washington became president "a cheerful recollection of his (Cochran's) past services" suggested his appointment (1790) as commissioner of loans, and he was provided with office space in Federal Hall for this work (*Minutes of the Common Council of the City of New York*, May 27, June 3, 1793, II, 10–11, 13). Finally compelled by a paralytic stroke to resign the office, he retired to Palatine, N. Y., where he died.

["Biog. Memoir of the Late John Cochran" (with portrait) in *Am. Medic. and Philosophical Reg.* (1814), 2nd ed., I, 465–68; E. J. Marsh, "Biog. Memoir of John Cochran, M.D.," in *N. J. Medic. Reporter* (Burlington, 1849), II, 25–28; Ida Cochran Haughton, *Chronicles of the Cochrans* (2 vols., 1915–25); Jas. E. Pilcher, *Surgeon-Generals of the Army of the U. S. A.* (1905). There are frequent references to Cochran in *Jour. of the Cont. Cong.*, 1777–81, and a few original documents in Papers of the Cont. Cong. in the Library of Congress.]

A. E. P.

COCHRANE, ELIZABETH. [See SEAMAN, ELIZABETH COCHRANE, 1867–1922.]

COCHRANE, HENRY CLAY (Nov. 7, 1842–Apr. 27, 1913), officer of the United States Marine Corps, was born at Chester, Pa., the son of James L. and Sarah Jane (Gillespie) Cochrane. He was educated in the Upland Normal School and the Friends' Central High School at Philadelphia. Appointed to the Naval Service and sworn in as a second lieutenant in the late summer of 1861, because of his youth he was not formally commissioned until Mar. 10, 1863. He was in almost constant action, however, and in January 1863 was officially commended for coolness and courage. He continued in active duty throughout the Civil War and received several official commendations for meritorious services. He was commissioned first lieutenant on Aug. 20, 1865.

As with all marines, his duty included tasks in times of peace as well as war, and in October 1867 he rendered exceptional service during an epidemic of Asiatic cholera. The Commandant of the Marine Corps, Gen. Zeilin, commended him in the following words: "The moral courage displayed by yourself and command is as praiseworthy as the most conspicuous gallantry on the field of battle" (L. R. Hamersly, *Records of Living Officers of the U. S. Navy and Marine Corps*, 7th ed., 1902, p. 483). During the following decade, Cochrane performed his work faithfully in various parts of the world and in July 1877 had command of the United States Arsenal at Washington, D. C., during the labor riots. He received his captaincy on Mar. 16, 1879, and about the same time published "The Naval Brigade and the Marine Battalions in the Labor Strikes of 1877" (*United Service*, January and October 1879). From 1881 to 1884 he was Fleet Marine Officer in the European Station, and in July 1882 he was present at the British bombardment of Alexandria, Egypt, where he later aided in the reëstablishment of the United States consulate.

Cochrane had command of the Marine detachment sent by the United States to the Paris Exposition in 1889, receiving the order of Chevalier of the Legion of Honor and an official compliment from the Secretary of the Navy. The end of the century found him a major (promoted Feb. 1, 1898) and in active and meritorious service in the Spanish-American war. On Jan. 11, 1900, he was commissioned colonel and the same year was appointed governor of the Peninsula of Cavite. So beloved was he by the natives that one of the cities requested permission to name a street for him. After service in the Boxer trouble in China and routine duties in this country, he was retired with the rank of brigadier-general on Mar. 10, 1905. After returning to his native city, he became actively identified with many civic enterprises and for several years was president of the board of trade. He was a member of many societies, both civilian and military, the latter including the Military Order of Foreign Wars. He was also a noted lecturer and orator. On June 30, 1887, he married Elizabeth F. Lull, daughter of Capt. E. P. Lull, U. S. N., and they had a daughter and a son, the latter becoming an officer in the United States Navy.

[*Who's Who in America*, 1912–13; U. S. Navy Reg., 1913, 1914; R. S. Collum, *Hist. of the U. S. Marine Corps* (1903); obituaries in the *Army and Navy Jour.*, May 10, 1913, and *N. Y. Times*, Apr. 28, 1913.]

A. R. B.

COCHRANE, JOHN (Aug. 27, 1813–Feb. 7, 1898), politician, was born in Palatine, Montgomery County, N. Y., the son of Walter Livingston Cochrane and Cornelia Wynchie (Smith) Cochrane and grandson of John Cochran [*q.v.*], surgeon-general in the Revolutionary War. Walter Livingston Cochrane added the final "e" to the family name. John was educated in the New York schools, and in Union and Hamilton Colleges, graduating from the latter in 1831. He was admitted to the bar in 1834, and after 1846 practised law in New York City. Beginning his political life as a Democrat, he belonged to the Barnburner wing of New York Democracy and with that faction favored the Free-Soil movement in the late 1840's. Within the next few years, however, he returned to the regular Democratic ranks, campaigning in 1852 for the election of Pierce. For this service he was appointed surveyor of the port of New York. As a state-rights Democrat he was elected to the House of Representatives of the Thirty-fifth and Thirty-sixth Congresses (Mar. 4, 1857–Mar. 3, 1861). Here he was at one time chairman of the Democratic Caucus. He spoke frequently on routine matters as well as on matters of public interest, was especially concerned with the burning questions of slavery, and national versus state sovereignty, and on these issues always upheld the Southern view-point.

In 1860, he was a delegate to the Charleston-Baltimore Convention of the Democratic party, a member of the Cagger-Cassidy Delegation which that convention seated. Though personally opposed to the nomination of Douglas, Cochrane voted for him, forced to do so by the unit rule governing the delegation. After the nomination, as a loyal Democrat he promised to support the nominee, hoping, he said, to "compensate the reluctance of the past by the cordiality of the future." Believing that the North was responsible for the discontent of the South, he favored conciliatory measures to heal the breach between the two sections of the country. As late as Mar. 14, 1861, while speaking in Richmond, Va., he promised that if Virginia "would present her ultimatum to New York" that state would "sustain her" (*New York Tribune,* Mar. 15, 1861). He did not favor secession, however, and when the war came he supported the Union. At the great Union Square meeting on Apr. 20, 1861, he stated his views in words that gave great offense to his Southern admirers (*New York Herald,* Apr. 21, 1861). He joined the army, raising a regiment of which he was made colonel. In 1862 he was made a brigadier-general of volunteers but was forced by ill health to retire on Feb. 25, 1863. Shortly after this, a war Democrat, he was elected attorney-general of New York on the ticket of the Republican-Union party, whose platform indorsed the administration of Lincoln. But he became dissatisfied with many of Lincoln's policies, and in 1864 joined some equally dissatisfied Republicans in the movement that resulted in the Cleveland Convention of May 31, 1864. By this convention he was nominated for vice-president with John C. Frémont for president. Their nomination and platform met with little

response from the country, so in September both withdrew. Cochrane immediately campaigned for Lincoln, speaking in Philadelphia and attacking the Chicago platform (*New York Tribune,* Oct. 11 and 12, 1864). In 1872, he joined the Liberal Republican party and went as a delegate to the Cincinnati Convention where he was largely responsible for the nomination of Horace Greeley.

Cochrane held city offices, and in 1869 was collector of Internal Revenue in the sixth New York district. He was a member of Tammany Hall and in 1889 its Sachem. He belonged to various patriotic societies, among them the Society of the Cincinnati of which he was president at the time of his death.

[De Alva Stanwood Alexander, *Political Hist. of N. Y.* (3 vols., 1906–09), shows his connection with N. Y. politics. The obituary notice in the *N. Y. Times,* Feb. 9, 1898, gives a complete account of Cochrane's life. See also Gustavus Myers, *Hist. of Tammany Hall* (1901); and M. Halstead, *Hist. of the National Political Conventions of the Current Presidential Campaign* (1860); J. G. Nicolay and John Hay, *Abraham Lincoln* (1890), IX, 42–44; E. McPherson, *Political Hist. of the U. S. A. During the Great Rebellion* (1864); *Biog. Dir. Am. Cong.* (1928); Ida Cochran Haughton, *Chronicles of the Cochrans,* II (1925), 80.]   A. B. M—r.

COCKE, JOHN HARTWELL (Sept. 19, 1780–July 1, 1866), planter, publicist, was born in Surry County, Va., son of John Hartwell and Elizabeth (Kennon) Cocke, and sixth in descent from Richard Cocke, who first appeared in Virginia from southern England in 1628. He inherited a fortune as well as refinement and native ability from his forebears, and after attending William and Mary College (1794–99), he chose the life of a country gentleman at "Bremo" in Fluvanna County, to which he removed about 1803. He married on Dec. 25, 1802, Ann Blaus Barraud of Norfolk, by whom he had several children, among them Philip St. George Cocke [*q.v.*]. Progressive and prescient in all things, he promoted new agricultural methods, the founding of agricultural societies, the developing of waterways and steam navigation, and various public improvements. He attacked the practise of making tobacco the principal crop and published a monograph, *Tobacco* (1860), to prove it ethically and economically "the bane of Virginia husbandry." During the War of 1812 he rose in eighteen months from captain to brigadier-general, commanding the Virginia soldiery guarding Richmond, 1814–15, at Camps Carter and Holley on the Chickahominy River. "I find Gen. Cocke universally respected," wrote his secretary, "and looked up to by the officers under his command—a striking instance of the triumph of talents and perseverance in the cause of duty" (A. C. Gordon, *William Fitzhugh Gor-*

don, 1909, p. 82). His conduct as a soldier brought him such reputation that his name was canvassed for governor in the General Assembly of 1814 until Cocke positively forbade its use (Bruce, *post,* I, 158). In religious and social movements his activities were unceasing and influential. He abetted Bible, Tract, and Sunday-school societies, and served on the American Board of Commissioners for Foreign Missions. Slavery he denounced as a curse to commonwealth and nation, predicting that Virginia would make no progress toward prosperity until it and tobacco tillage should be ended. From its organization in 1819 until his death he was senior vice-president of the American Colonization Society, formed to settle the slavery problem peaceably by colonizing the negroes of the South in Africa. He favored federal intervention and a constitutional amendment providing funds for this purpose; and in 1831 wrote of slavery as "the great cause of all the great evils of our land." Duelling and intemperance he likewise detested and warred against with cogent reasoning or acid satire. In a drinking age, his was the most insistent voice in his state demanding nation-wide prohibition; and when the American Temperance Union succeeded the United States Temperance Union in 1836, Cocke was elected president of the new society. A friend to popular education, he sponsored sounder primary and secondary school systems, but his greatest service lay in his efforts toward a state university, his share in its physical development, and his thirty-three years (1819–52) on its Board of Visitors. Without playing so conspicuous a part in founding the University of Virginia as did Jefferson and Joseph C. Cabell, Cocke's contribution was subordinate only to theirs. He cooperated with Jefferson on the important building committee, and, though disapproving of various particulars of Jefferson's architectural plan which contravened his economical and conservative bent, never interposed his objections; his suggestions were uniformly constructive, and his experience and practical counsel during the institution's infancy proved invaluable. His inordinate modesty and refusal to hold political office have helped undeservedly to obliterate his name from public memory. Although in his day he was widely known and though his erect figure and impressively determined countenance compelled respectful consideration, few realized the solidity of his talents and even enlightened contemporaries considered his attitude toward slavery, tobacco, and temperance extreme. Conscientious, tenacious of opinion, boldly independent, and devoid of partisanship, sectarian or sectional, he was impervious

to the derision and contempt which his convictions occasionally provoked: he formed conclusions deliberately, and before his death saw established many of the causes which he had upheld against incisive opposition. Without being either a prig or a Puritan, he was a zealous reformer; yet even those who impugned his principles admired his sincerity, catholic benevolence, and alertness to civic responsibility. The causes which he supported indicate him to have been one of the most remarkable Virginians of his generation in power of foresight, a pioneer of modern social reform.

[Little has been written about John Hartwell Cocke, the only adequate sketch of him being that in Philip A. Bruce, *Hist. of the Univ. of Va.* (1920–22), I, 157–64. His correspondence in MSS., now in possession of the Cocke family of University, Va.; the correspondence in MSS. of Wm. Cabell Rives, his aide-de-camp in the War of 1812, in the possession of the Rives family of Washington, D. C.; the correspondence in MSS. of Jos. C. Cabell, in the Univ. of Va. Library; and the reports and minutes of the University's Board of Visitors are the most fertile sources of information about him. For the Cocke genealogy, see Jas. C. Southall, "A Memoir of the Cocke Family," in the *Va. Mag. of Hist. and Biog.,* vols. III, IV, and V. An editorial notice of Cocke was published in the Richmond *Whig,* July 4, 1866.]
A. C. G., Jr.

COCKE, PHILIP ST. GEORGE (Apr. 17, 1809–Dec. 26, 1861), soldier, planter, writer on agriculture, was born at "Bremo," Fluvanna County, Va., third child of John Hartwell Cocke [*q.v.*] and his wife Ann Blaus Barraud. Inheriting the military and agricultural aptitude without the reforming instinct of his father, after attending the University of Virginia he entered the United States Military Academy, where he graduated with distinction in 1832; served as second lieutenant and as adjutant in the 2nd Artillery at Charleston, S. C., 1832–33; and resigned, Apr. 1, 1834, to manage his extensive plantation interests in Virginia and Mississippi. To this occupation he devoted his energies until the outbreak of the Civil War, but conducted his seven plantations so systematically that he found opportunity to advance Southern agriculture by precept as well as practise. He had an elevated conception of agriculture as a profession, and while indorsing sound technical training insisted that general culture was scarcely less desirable for the planter. As president of the Virginia Agricultural Society (1853–56) he stimulated interest in progressive farming, and pointed out the opportunity of such a body not only for collecting and disseminating useful farming knowledge but also for serving as a farmers' protective association. Besides publishing one volume, *Plantation and Farm Instruction* (1852), and his *Address to the Virginia Farmers' Assembly* (pamphlet, 1856), he contributed numerous short articles to the press. From its beginnings he gave freely of time and money to the welfare of the Virginia Military Institute, served for nine years on its board, and founded there the first school of scientific agriculture in the state. When Virginia seceded he was appointed brigadier-general in the state service and was assigned, Apr. 21, 1861, the command of the important military district along the Potomac. Commissioned a colonel in the Confederate provisional army, after having charge of the mustering of volunteer forces throughout Piedmont Virginia, on May 9 he began the concentration of troops at Manassas Junction. He commanded the 5th Brigade of Beauregard's army in the Manassas Campaign, and was thanked by Beauregard for strategic skill at Blackburn's Ford. At First Manassas, with Evans's demi-brigade and unattached companies also under his command, he was assigned to the Confederate left, along Bull Run. Although his projected advance upon Centreville was abandoned because of the Federal flanking movement, he sustained Schenck's attack on the Stone Bridge and Lewis's Ford, sent regiment after regiment to the support of Johnston, and in the afternoon "led his brigade into action on the left with 'alacrity and effect'" (*Confederate Military History*, III, 586). After eight months' active service, during which he was appointed brigadier-general in the Confederate provisional army, he returned in shattered health to his home, "Belmead," in Powhatan County, where, overwrought and naturally impetuous, he took his own life. His untimely death evoked widespread regret, official and personal, for he was known as a skilful and chivalrous soldier, a modest and benevolent citizen. He married, June 4, 1834, Sally Elizabeth Courtney Bowdoin, by whom he had four sons and seven daughters.

[Sources of information about Cocke are necessarily varied. P. A. Bruce, *Hist. of the Univ. of Va.*, 5 vols. (1920–22); J. C. Wise, *Mil. Hist. of the Va. Mil. Institute* (1915); and the *Special Report Superintendent Va. Mil. Institute to the Gov. of Va.*, Feb. 4, 1862, trace his relations with these two institutions. *Confed. Mil. Hist.*, ed. by Clement A. Evans (1899), III, 585–86, Beauregard's report of the first battle of Manassas in *Confed. Official Reports* and elsewhere, and R. M. Johnston, *Bull Run: Its Strategy and Tactics* (1913), furnish an account of his military activity. His manuscripts, papers, and letters are in the possession of his grand-daughters, the Misses Cocke, University, Va. For his ancestry, see Southall, "Memoir of the Cocke Family," in *Va. Mag. of Hist. and Biog.*, V, 78, July 1897. See also obituary in the Richmond *Whig*, Dec. 28, 1861. An oil portrait of him hangs in the Va. State Lib., Richmond.]

            A. C. G., Jr.

COCKE, WILLIAM (1748–Aug. 22, 1828), soldier, legislator, Indian agent, lived a long and colorful life on the frontier of the Old Southwest. He was born in Amelia County, Va., the son of Abraham Cocke, a descendant of Richard Cocke who had come to Virginia from England as early as 1628. William Cocke studied law but never learned the rules of English grammar and his spelling was his own. He was twice married; to Sarah Maclin and to the widow Kissiah Sims.

About the year 1774 he moved to the frontier of settlement in the Holston Valley near the present boundary between Virginia and Tennessee. As captain of militiamen he helped guard the frontier during Lord Dunmore's War. He fought the Indians and the Tories during the Revolution but was charged with cowardice. In 1775 he had followed Daniel Boone into Kentucky and was there a member of the House of Delegates of the abortive colony of Transylvania. Two years later he served with his "Dear Old & ever admired friend," Thomas Jefferson, in the Virginia Assembly. In 1778 and on several subsequent occasions he sat in the legislature of North Carolina. When some of the western counties of North Carolina (the present East Tennessee), attempted during the years 1784–88 to establish themselves as the State of Franklin, Cocke was a leader in this movement for separate statehood. He helped form the constitution for the short-lived state; he was a member of its legislature; he served on its Council of State; he was one of its brigadier-generals; he negotiated in its name with the Cherokee Indians; he was its unseated delegate to the Congress of the United States, where unsuccessfully he presented its memorial for recognition; and he was also its commissioner to North Carolina in a futile attempt to persuade the mother state to recognize its existence. When the State of Franklin had ceased to exist, he returned as a member to the North Carolina legislature. When his western counties became the Southwest Territory, Cocke was a member of the territorial legislature and sponsored the bill for the creation of Blount College (the present University of Tennessee). In 1796 he was a member of the convention that transformed the territory into the State of Tennessee, and was sent by this state to Congress as one of its first senators. In 1809 he was defeated by Willie Blount for governor of Tennessee, but the legislature immediately chose him to be a judge of the circuit court. For this office he was temperamentally unfitted. He was emotional, passionate, quick-tempered, intolerant. He loved his friends and hated his enemies and quarreled with both. He was an able orator but a poor judge. He was charged with showing partiality to his friends, impeached, and in 1812 removed from office. Nothing daunted, he volunteered for the campaign in East Florida, returned to take a seat in the Tennessee legislature, and from this rushed off at the age of sixty-five to fight as a private in the Creek War with such bravery as to win the praise of Andrew Jackson. In 1814 he was appointed United States Agent to the Chickasaw Indians, but he failed to gain their confidence and was soon superseded. He spent his remaining years in Mississippi, and to round out his experience as a law-maker, he served in 1822 in the legislature of that state.

[Wm. Goodrich in *Am. Hist. Mag.* (Nashville), July 1896, Apr. 1897; *Jour. Am. Hist.*, V (1911), 97–104; Samuel C. Williams, *Hist. of the Lost State of Franklin* (1924); *State Records of N. C.* (1895–1914); *Am. State Papers, Indian Affairs*, vol. II (1834); *Va. Mag. of Hist. and Biography*, Apr. 1897; *Knoxville Gazette*; Draper Papers at Madison, Wis.; Monroe Papers, Jefferson Papers, and Jackson Papers in the Lib. of Cong.]

P.M.H.

COCKERILL, JOHN ALBERT (Dec. 4, 1845–Apr. 10, 1896), journalist, was born in Adams County, Ohio, the son of Joseph Randolph and Ruth (Eylar) Cockerill. During the Civil War his father was colonel of the 70th Ohio Volunteers. Enlisting at fifteen, John saw service as a drummer boy with the 24th Ohio Regiment, 1861–63, and upon being mustered out by the War Department, reënlisted as a bugler in the artillery. Before the war he had played "devil" in a small printing office and after he left the army he went to the *Scion of Temperance,* published at West Union, Ohio. His first practical work as a printer was with C. L. Vallandigham [*q.v.*], publisher of the *Empire* (later the *Ledger*) at Dayton, Ohio, and his first reportorial work was in 1870 in Cincinnati on the *Cincinnati Enquirer* of which, in 1872, he became managing editor. Four years later he left the editorial desk to become a correspondent for the *Enquirer* in the Russo-Turkish War. On his return to the United States he joined the staff of the *Washington Post* before going to Baltimore to become managing editor of the *Gazette* in 1878. From that city he was taken to St. Louis by Joseph Pulitzer to aid in publishing the *St. Louis Post-Dispatch.* In editorial charge while Pulitzer was in New York, Cockerill had, in 1882, criticized editorially the conduct of the law firm of Broadhead, Slayback, & Haeussler for accepting a retainer of $10,000 from St. Louis in a suit against the Laclede Gas Company only to abandon the city and defend the corporation. On Oct. 5, he shot and killed Col. A. W. Slayback after a fist fight started by the latter to force an editorial retraction. Cockerill insisted that he had shot in self-defense, but because of the bitter feeling the affair aroused left on an extended trip. In the spring of 1883 he resumed work with Pulitzer who, after the purchase of the New York *World,* wanted his former associate to take charge of the news end. Fertile

in suggestions, Cockerill rose to be editor-in-charge—a position he resigned in 1891 when his request for a controlling share in the *World* was refused. Then he purchased an interest in the New York *Commercial Advertiser* with which he remained until Sept. 28, 1894. He joined the staff of the *New York Herald* early in 1895, and was assigned to the Far East as a special correspondent in China and Japan. Homeward bound by way of Egypt, he was stricken with apoplexy in Cairo where he died. Fearless and fiery, a typical Southwesterner "upon whom the wear and tear of newspaper management made no abrasion," he was a great fighting editor in the period of the sensational press.

[Western chapters in Cockerill's life are given in *Encyc. of the Hist. of St. Louis* (1899), ed. by Wm. Hyde and Howard L. Conard, while Eastern chapters are found in *Jos. Pulitzer: His Life and Letters* (1924), by Don C. Seitz. *This Is the Life!* (1926), by Walter H. McDougall, pp. 205 ff., contains the financial arrangement between Pulitzer and Cockerill. See also Elizabeth Bisland, *Life and Letters of Lafcadio Hearn* (1906); *Bill Nye, His Own Life Story* (1926); obituaries in the *N. Y. Herald* and the *World* (N. Y.), Apr. 11 and 12, 1896; sketch in *Mil. Order of the Loyal Legion, Ohio Commandery, Circular No. 20,* series of 1897.]

J.M.L.

COCKRAN, WILLIAM BOURKE (Feb. 28, 1854–Mar. 1, 1923), lawyer, congressman, was born in County Sligo, Ireland, the son of Martin and Harriet (Knight) Cockran. He was educated in the schools of Ireland and later studied in France. Although his parents intended him to enter the Church, he was not so disposed, and at the age of seventeen he came to New York to live his own life. He first worked as a clerk in a department store, then became principal of a public school in Tuckahoe, N. Y., and devoted his nights to the study of law. He was admitted to the bar in 1876, practised for two years in Mount Vernon, and then moved to New York. Leaders of the Irving Hall Democracy, a faction opposed to Tammany, made him their spokesman at the Democratic State Convention at Albany in 1881. Two years later, John Kelly, leader of Tammany, invited him to join the Wigwam, and he was made counsel to the sheriff of New York County.

In the Democratic National Convention of 1884, Cockran, a Tammany delegate, forced a hostile convention to listen to his speech attacking the nomination of Grover Cleveland. His greatest dramatic triumph occurred during the turbulent convention of 1892, when he was forced to place David B. Hill in nomination at two o'clock in the morning. Outside a terrible storm was raging. Rain was pouring through the leaking roof. Above the thunder and the jeers of the impatient Cleveland majority was heard the bold defiance of Cockran: "If New York's candidate and his supporters cannot receive fair treatment, New York will withdraw from this convention." Thereafter the Hill speakers were heard (Arthur Wallace Dunn, *From Harrison to Harding,* 1922, vol. I, 95–96).

Cockran was first elected to the House of Representatives in 1886, and again in 1890 and in 1892. In the following year he delivered an eloquent address against the free coinage of silver (*Congressional Record,* 53 Cong., 1 Sess., App., p. 113), which was a forerunner of his break with Bryan and the Democratic party on the silver issue in the campaign of 1896. In that year he campaigned for William McKinley. His "Sound Money" speech in Madison Square Garden is regarded by many as the peak of his oratorical efforts. His switch to McKinley and his return to the Democratic fold in 1900 were made the target for charges by the press that he was paid well for his speeches (*New York Journal,* Oct. 26, 1897). Cockran denied the charges on the floor of the House emphatically and with dignity (*Congressional Record,* 58 Cong., 2 Sess., pp. 5460, 5646, 5750).

In 1900 he returned to the Democratic party and supported Bryan for president, making "the brutal imperialism of McKinley" the issue. He was elected to Congress again in 1904 and served until the end of 1909. He had, in the meantime, broken with Charles F. Murphy, who had become leader of Tammany Hall, and he once more found himself outside the party. He then embraced the cause of Roosevelt, whom he had frequently denounced in unsparing terms (see *e.g., Congressional Record,* 58 Cong., 2 Sess., pp. 5654, 5656). He campaigned effectively for the Progressive ticket in 1912, although he himself was unsuccessful in seeking election to Congress. After a period of comparative political inactivity, he returned to the Democratic party once more, and, at the National Convention at San Francisco in 1920 delivered a ringing oration nominating Gov. Alfred Smith of New York for the presidency (*New York Times,* July 1, 1920). Later in the year he was returned to Congress, where he served until his sudden death, which occurred on Mar. 1, 1923, the morning after his sixty-ninth birthday dinner. He was married three times; first, to —— Jackson, sister of the Rev. Father Jackson of St. Anne's Church, New York; second, to Rhoda E. Mack. daughter of Jonathan Mack; third, to Anne L. Ide, daughter of Gen. Henry C. Ide.

Cockran was a friend of organized labor and opposed compulsory arbitration and labor injunctions ("The Law's Delays," *Ohio Law Reports,* VI, 381–416). Himself an immigrant, he fought against any restrictions on immigration or naturalization (*Congressional Record,* 59 Cong., 1 Sess., p. 9192, 1906; 67 Cong., 1 Sess., p. 518, 1921). He was outspoken in his condemnation of the Eighteenth Amendment and the Volstead Act, and led an unsuccessful attempt to place a plank in the Democratic platform at the 1920 convention permitting the manufacture in homes of cider, light wines, and beer (*New York Times,* July 3, 1920; see also last public statement in *New York Times,* Feb. 11, 1923).

He was a picturesque and commanding figure. Tall, burly in his later years, with a leonine head, deep-set eyes, a thoughtful forehead, a mobile face, described as containing "something Spanish, Celtiberian as well as Celtic," he possessed in addition a deep and resonant voice. An Irish brogue gave an exotic quality to his speech. He was a lawyer of ability. The most celebrated case with which he was associated was that of Thomas J. Mooney, in whose behalf in 1918 he successfully besought the intervention of President Wilson to prevent execution of the death sentence by the state of California.

[In addition to sources mentioned above, see *W. Bourke Cockran, Memorial Addresses Delivered in the House of Representatives,* 68 Cong., May 4, 1924 (1925); *N. Y. Times, N. Y. Herald,* Mar. 2, 1923. Cockran papers, sixty-two portfolios and four bundles of MSS. in the N. Y. Pub. Lib., comprise chiefly his speeches and a collection of newspaper clippings relative to his death.]

R. B. M.

COCKRELL, FRANCIS MARION (Oct. 1, 1834–Dec. 13, 1915), Confederate soldier, senator, son of Joseph and Nancy (Ellis) Cockrell, was born near the little village of Columbus, fifteen miles from Warrensburg, Mo. His father came from Kentucky to Missouri in 1831 and was the first sheriff of Johnson County. Francis was reared on a farm, attended the rural log school-house, entered Chapel Hill College, Lafayette County, Mo., and graduated with honor in 1853. He then studied law, was admitted to the bar in 1855, and began the practise of his profession at Warrensburg. At the outbreak of the Civil War he allied himself with the Southern cause and enlisted. In a single year he rose from the rank of private to that of brigadier-general. He took part in many of the important battles of the Civil War from Carthage to Vicksburg and from Vicksburg to Mobile, was five times wounded, and was three times taken prisoner. When not in battle, he drilled his troops so well that "Cockrell's Brigade" of fighting Missourians was said to be one of the best-drilled and most courageous brigades in the Southern army. After the war, he returned to Missouri and again began the practise of his profession in partnership with Gov. Thomas T. Crittenden [*q.v.*], but his ambition soon led him into politics. In 1872 he became a candidate for governor of Missouri and although he was defeated in the Democratic state convention by Charles H. Hardin it was only by one-sixth of a vote. He made such an earnest campaign for his successful rival that in 1874 he was chosen United States senator to succeed Carl Schurz. He served in this capacity from 1875 to 1905. In the latter year, a Republican legislature, after a factional deadlock, elected William Warner to succeed him. President Roosevelt's comment on this change was that the people of Missouri had lost a faithful servant but that the government would not lose him. On the day Cockrell left the Senate, he was appointed by Roosevelt a member of the Interstate Commerce Commission and remained a member until Dec. 31, 1910. He was appointed United States commissioner to adjust the boundary between Texas and New Mexico in March 1910. Later he served as a civilian member of the Board of Ordnance and Fortifications. In the Democratic National Convention in St. Louis in 1904 he was nominated for the presidency by Champ Clark and William J. Bryan.

While the greater part of Cockrell's service in Congress was as a minority member his opinion was valued as much by his Republican colleagues as by those of his own party. There was something about the man that drew people to him and made them repose confidence in his integrity, honesty, and ability. His political opponents in Washington were glad to grant him any personal favor, while in Missouri he was idolized. He was intelligent and far-seeing and his indorsement of any enterprise was evidence of its merit. An uncompromising Democrat, he held positions of honor and trust under two Republican administrations. He was commanding in appearance, being over six feet tall and weighing two hundred pounds. He usually wore a linen duster and preferred a corn-cob pipe. He had a remarkable memory and could call his acquaintances by their first names without hesitating. Simple in manner and dress, his figure was a familiar one in every county in his state. He was married three times: first, in 1853 to Arethusa D. Stapp; second, in 1866 to Anna E. Mann; third, to Anna Ewing.

[W. B. Davis and D. S. Durrie, *Illus. Hist. of Mo.* (1876), pp. 488–89; *Bench and Bar of St. Louis, Kansas City, Jefferson City and Other Mo. Cities* (1884), pp. 19–20; *St. Louis Globe-Democrat*, Dec. 14, 1915; *Kansas City Star*, Dec. 13, 1915; *Warrensburg Standard-Herald*, Dec. 17, 1915; *Mo. Hist. Rev.*, X, 136–39.]
F. C. S—r.

CODDINGTON, WILLIAM (1601–Nov. 1, 1678), governor of Aquidneck, was born in Boston, England. By his thirtieth year he had achieved substance and position. At about the same time as John Winthrop (1630), he came to Massachusetts as an Assistant (director) in the Bay Company. He himself relates that he built in Boston the first good (brick) house. On Aug. 6, 1633 he was chosen with others to oversee the building of a sufficient cart bridge over Muddy River and another over Stony River. On Mar. 14, 1635 he was appointed to the committee on military affairs. During 1634–36 he was the Bay Company's treasurer, and in 1636–37 was a deputy. In a secular way he was of the John Winthrop order, shrewd and conservative; but in the way of religion he differed therefrom, being touched with the new spirit—a spirit found rather among the poor and lowly than among the rich and mighty: the spirit of Antinomianism or salvation by grace. A devotee of this spirit in the Bay Company was Mistress Anne Hutchinson [*q.v.*], and when in 1637 she was haled before the Massachusetts General Court for "traducing the ministers and their ministry in this country," Coddington was bold enough to enter protest in her behalf. Anne Hutchinson was banished. As for Coddington, banishment did not at once overtake him, but in 1638 he, together with Dr. John Clarke and other liberals, withdrew to the island of Aquidneck (Rhode Island) which by help of Roger Williams had been purchased from the Narragansett Indian chiefs Canonicus and Miantonomo. Here at Pocasset (Portsmouth) they set up an Old Testament government of Judge and Elders, electing Coddington judge. But hither straightway came Anne Hutchinson and that arch-heretic of early New England, Samuel Gorton [*q.v.*]; whereupon in 1639 the Coddington party in some dismay betook themselves to the south side of Aquidneck and on May 16 founded Newport.

For a time Portsmouth and Newport maintained a divided life, but in 1639–40 they combined, formally declaring the new commonwealth a "Democracie or Popular Government" under the "Powre of the Body of Freemen orderly assembled, or the major part of them"; and "none [was to] be accounted a delinquent for Doctrine." Coddington was then elected governor. His steadfast aim thenceforward was to keep his colony of Aquidneck an independent factor, and of that factor to keep himself the head. In 1644 Roger Williams secured from Parliament a patent uniting Aquidneck, or Rhode Island, to his own mainland settlement of

Providence Plantations. This patent Coddington in 1651 succeeded in having set aside, so far as Aquidneck was concerned, by obtaining a patent creating Aquidneck a distinct colony with himself as governor in perpetuity. In consequence, not only were Williams and Providence Plantations alienated, but in large degree Coddington's own followers, and, in October 1652, Parliament annulled the grant. Coddington thereupon fled to Boston and temporized; but at length in 1656, during the régime of Oliver Cromwell, resigned *in toto* his high pretensions. "I, William Coddington," he wrote, "doe freely submit to ye authoritie of his Highness in this colonie as it is now united and that with all my heart."

As a would-be autocrat, Coddington tried every shift and failed. He made divers overtures to be taken, with his colony, under the shelter of the New England Confederation, and he sought the support of the Dutch of New Netherland under Peter Stuyvesant. Failure, however, did not attend him as a merchant. At Newport, prior to 1651, he built a "towne house," and he conducted a large Newport estate on which he bred sheep, cattle, and horses; the latter for shipment to Barbados. Late in life he espoused Quakerism, and thus having clarified himself anew, was, in 1674, 1675, and 1678, honored with the chief magistracy of Rhode Island and Providence Plantations as reconstituted under Charles II in 1663. He was thrice married: (1) to Mary Mosely, who died in 1630; (2) to Mary ——, who died in 1647; (3) to Anne Brinley, who died in 1708. He had thirteen children. In 1678 he died. Roger Williams (ever to Quakers little charitable) says of him during King Philip's War: "A poor man came to Mr. Coddington in these late bloody distresses and offers to buy a bushel of corn for his poor Wife and Children in great want. Mr. Coddington, though abounding, would not let this poor soul have a bushel except he would pay him a week's work for it. . . . Alas why doth the Pope, Cardinals, Bishops, Doctors, Presbyters, Independents, Baptists, Foxians prate of the Christian's name, and new and old England talk of Religion?"

[J. O. Austin, *Geneal. Dic. of R. I.* (1887); S. G. Arnold, *Hist. of the State of R. I. and Providence Plantations, 1636–1780* (1859), vol. I; *State of R. I. and Providence Plantations at the End of the Century* (1902), ed., by Ed. Field, Index; I. B. Richman, *R. I.: its Making and its Meaning* (2nd ed., 1908); H. E. Turner, *Wm. Coddington in R. I. Affairs* (1878); *New Eng. Hist. and Geneal. Reg.*, XXVIII, 13, XXXVI, 138.]
                 I. B. R.

CODMAN, JOHN (Oct. 16, 1814–Apr. 6, 1900), sea captain, author, was born in Dorchester, Mass., the son of John and Mary (Wheelwright) Codman. His father, son of a prosperous Boston merchant of the same name, was pastor of the Second Parish in Dorchester from 1808 till his death in 1847 and a sturdy upholder of the old orthodoxy against Unitarians and other schismatics. His hospitable mansion was a favorite gathering place for clergymen, who would stop there on their way to Boston and furnish the children of the family with an extensive though disorderly theological education by arguing doctrinal questions hot and heavy from dinner till bedtime, the while making devastating inroads into their host's supplies of rum and smoking tobacco. To them young Codman listened with interest, but with even more interest to the reminiscences of his maternal grandfather, a Newburyport sea captain. After two years (1832–34) at Amherst College he went to sea in a clipper ship. His nautical career lasted till the close of the Civil War. He made numerous trips to China and the East Indies, during the Crimean War commanded the *William Penn*, which carried troops from Constantinople to the Crimea, and during the Civil War was captain of the *Quaker City*, which transported stores to Port Royal, S. C. Once, when his ship had been run down in mid-ocean by a larger vessel, he nevertheless succeeded in bringing his command safely to New York; for this feat the underwriters presented him with a silver service. In December 1864 he took the steamer *Cotopaxi* to Rio de Janeiro and sold her to the Brazilian government. The next year he returned to Brazil and for a few months engaged in the coastwise trade. On many of his voyages he was accompanied by his wife, Anna G. Day of New York, whom he had married Nov. 3, 1847. Throughout his active life he was an enthusiastic horseman, sometimes traveling from Boston to New York on horseback. At one time he owned a ranch in Idaho. He wrote vigorous English, his books being *Sailors' Life and Sailors' Yarns* (1847), "*By* Captain Ringbolt," *Ten Months in Brazil* (1867), *The Round Trip* (1879), describing a tour of the western states, *Winter Sketches from the Saddle* (1888), and *An American Transport in the Crimean War* (1896). He was also the author of numerous pamphlets in favor of free ships and shipbuilders' materials and against subsidies for the merchant marine. He died at his daughter's home in Boston after a short illness.

[W. D. Orcutt, *Good Old Dorchester* (1893); *Boston Transcript*, Apr. 7, 1900; W L. Montague, ed., *Biog. Record Alumni Amherst Coll. 1821–71* (1883). For his father cf. also *Hist. of the Town of Dorchester, Mass.* (1859), by a committee of the Dorchester Antiquarian and Hist. Soc., and *New Eng. Hist. and Geneal. Reg.*, LXVIII (1894), 409–13.]
                 G. H. G.

CODY, WILLIAM FREDERICK (Feb. 26, 1846–Jan. 10, 1917), scout, showman, better known as "Buffalo Bill," was born on a farm in Scott County, Iowa, the son of Isaac and Mary Ann (Leacock) Cody. The parents were from Ohio. The father, abandoning his farm, turned to stage-driving for a time, afterward (1854) moving with his family to Salt Creek Valley, in the vicinity of Fort Leavenworth, Kan. On his death, in the spring of 1857, the eleven-year-old son undertook to fill his place as breadwinner. He got work as a "cavvy boy" to one of the supply trains of the expedition against the Mormons, and later as a mounted messenger with the freighting firm of Russell, Majors & Waddell. Until his twelfth year he had resisted all efforts to induce him to learn his letters, but in the winter of 1857–58 he entered school, where he acquired the art of writing his name and of reading simple words. In the following spring he again found employment. The gold fever drew him to Denver in 1859, but he came back penniless. In April 1860, he was hired as a rider for the Pony Express, but it is uncertain how long he continued. In the summer of 1861 he joined a local organization of Jayhawkers, and in 1863 he served as a scout with the 9th Kansas Cavalry in operations against the Kiowas and Comanches. In the winter of the same year his mother died. In the following February he enlisted in the army, serving as a scout for Gen. A. J. Smith in Tennessee, and later as a trooper in the operations against Price in Missouri and as a scout on the plains.

On Mar. 6, 1866, he was married to Louisa Frederici in St. Louis. From some time in 1867 to May 1868, he was employed by Goddard Brothers, food contractors to the Kansas Pacific railway construction camps, to furnish buffalo meat, and by his remarkable exploits with the rifle earned the nickname which he adopted and by which he was ever afterward known. For the next four years he did further service with the army, becoming chief of scouts of the 5th Cavalry. He had a nominal residence at Omaha, and in the fall of 1872 was elected to the lower house of the Nebraska legislature, but he declined to serve. His friend, Col. Judson, "Ned Buntline," who had already glorified some of his adventures in popular fiction, now wrote a play, *Scouts of the Prairies* (or *Plains,* as it was sometimes billed), and Cody produced it, taking the leading rôle for himself. During the first season, which opened in Chicago, Dec. 16, 1872, he had with him in the cast "Texas Jack" Omohundro, and in the next season "Wild Bill" Hickok. In this play and in its two or three

successors, he kept to the stage, except for an interval of scouting in 1874, until the close of the season of 1875–76. The Sioux War brought him back to the frontier, and he again became chief of scouts of the 5th Cavalry. On July 17, 1876, at War Bonnet Creek, west of the Red Cloud agency, occurred the famous duel between Cody and Yellow Hand, son of the Cheyenne chief Cut-Nose. On the junction of Merritt with Crook and, later, of the combined force with Terry and Miles, Cody continued for a short time to scout, performing some of the most daring exploits of his career. In the fall he was again on the stage, playing to large audiences in various parts of the country.

He had in the meantime formed a partnership in the cattle business with Maj. Frank North, and a large ranch was established sixty-five miles north of North Platte, Nebr. About the same time he bought a farm on the outskirts of North Platte, and there for many years he made his home. He continued on the stage until 1883, when, in association with Maj. John M. Burke and Dr. W. F. Carver, he started his "Wild West" exhibition. In the following year Carver withdrew, and Nate Salsbury became a partner with whom Cody was to remain more or less continuously for the rest of his life. In 1894 he acted as guide to Prof. O. C. Marsh's fossil-hunting expedition to the Big Horn Basin. Here Cody determined to settle. He received a large land grant from the state, on which a town was laid out which his friends insisted on naming Cody, and he began soon afterward the development of his famous ranch. His subsequent years were divided between the ranch and the show, which was frequently in financial difficulties. At the close of the season of 1916 he and his wife went to Denver. His health broke in December, and in January the end came suddenly. His body was carried to the capitol, and after being viewed by immense throngs, was placed in a temporary vault. On June 3, in accordance with his expressed wish, it was buried on the top of Lookout Mountain, near Golden. His wife died in 1921 and was buried beside him.

Much of the material for a biography of Cody is found only in his own statements. It is no derogation of his many substantial qualities to say that he was an untrustworthy chronicler of events. He dealt with facts in a large, free way, and he had a tendency after he became famous to make himself the central figure in the episodes he recounted. Most of his statements are inaccurate; many are preposterous; and he sanctioned on the part of his publicity agents a gross indulgence in fiction. He was better in action than in narration. His merits as a scout have been widely attested, perhaps by no one more authoritatively than by Gen. Eugene A. Carr, onetime commander of the 5th Cavalry. In a letter of July 3, 1878, Carr wrote that the eyesight of Cody was better than a good field-glass; that he was the best trailer within the writer's knowledge—a perfect judge of distance and of the "lay" of a country—and that he never tired, but was always ready to go. He was conspicuous in his attire, and until late in life he remained lithe and active, a masterful rider and an expert shot.

[The most dependable work on Cody is that of Richard J. Walsh, *The Making of Buffalo Bill* (1928). Other sources are *Who's Who in America*, 1916–17; *The Life of Hon. Wm. F. Cody, Known as Buffalo Bill; An Autobiography* (1879), republished in many guises; Helen Cody Wetmore and Zane Grey, *Last of the Great Scouts* (1899); Louisa Frederici Cody and Courtney Ryley Cooper, *Memories of Buffalo Bill* (1919); Jos. Mills Hanson, *Conquest of the Missouri* (1909); Homer W. Wheeler, *Buffalo Days* (1925); various newspaper obituaries. See also the bibliography in Walsh's work.]   W. J. G—t.

COE, GEORGE SIMMONS (Mar. 27, 1817– May 3, 1896), banker, son of Adam Simmons and Ann (Pease) Coe, was a descendant in the sixth generation from John and Priscilla Alden, and was born at Newport, R. I. His father was a cabinetmaker, and could afford only a common schoool education for his son. At fourteen the latter began working in a general country store; in 1835 he transferred to a local bank and there became a "general clerk," whose duties involved sweeping out the establishment and acting as messenger as well as keeping books. Throughout these early years, however, the boy maintained the habit of study and was able to educate himself much beyond the point at which he had been obliged to leave school. In 1838 he was offered a place in the private banking house of Prime, Ward & King in New York City. There he remained until 1846, at which time his firm sent him to Cincinnati as their representative in the development of new business. Returning to the East after a comparatively short stay, he became cashier of the Ohio Life Insurance & Trust Company in New York City, an enterprise with which he had been acquainted during his residence in Ohio. This connection, however, did not continue long, for he found himself less interested in general finance than he was in actual banking. After a venture as partner in the private banking house of Gilbert, Coe & Johnson which failed in 1854, in 1856 Coe was elected cashier of the American Exchange Bank, at last finding himself in a connection which enlisted his full interest and en-

thusiasm. Within a few months he became vice-president, and in 1860 was elected president, continuing to hold that office for thirty-four years. In this capacity he was prominent among those New York bankers who came to the aid of the government in the disposal of bonds at the critical period after the battle of Bull Run.

During the years after Coe's return to New York from Cincinnati, he was greatly interested in the project then under discussion for the organization of a clearing house in New York. It is often stated that the idea originated with Coe, but the various plans for organization of a clearing house which have been carefully collected by the New York Clearing House Association do not include any by him. This fact probably indicates that he acted in company with others to develop and round out a notion which was, in a certain sense, common property. He served the organization in various important phases of committee work and eventually became president of it, and encouraged the steady expansion of its service.

Besides this major interest and an active membership for thirty-seven years in the Chamber of Commerce, he was a trustee or a director of a number of New York corporations, president of the American Bankers Association in 1881, and a member of the Presbyterian Board of Foreign Missions. On June 15, 1843, he was married to Almira Stanley of New Britain, Conn., who died in 1880; his second wife was Mary E. Bigelow of Englewood, N. J. It was in Englewood that he died.

[The files of the New York Clearing House; *Ann. Report Chamber of Commerce State of N. Y.*, 1896–97, pp. 18–20; *N. Y. Times, Evening Post* (N. Y.), May 4, 1896; H. Hall, *America's Successful Men of Affairs* (1895), I, 145; Henry F. Coe, *Descendants of Matthew Coe* (1894). Of his own writings, the lengthy and careful address, *Is Resumption Complete?* delivered before the Am. Bankers Asso., Aug. 7, 1879, and published in that year, is probably the best example.]   H. P. W.

COE, ISRAEL (Dec. 14, 1794–Dec. 18, 1891), brass manufacturer, was born at Goshen, Conn., the eldest son of Abijah and Sibyl (Baldwin) Coe, and a descendant in the eighth generation from Robert Coe, Puritan, who came to America in 1634, and settled with the first colony at Wethersfield, Conn., in 1635. Abijah Coe, a blacksmith, was successful enough to afford his oldest son (who was seriously handicapped by the loss of his right arm through a hunting accident) an education in the district school at Winsted, Conn., with two additional years (1811–12) at Winsted Academy. In 1813 Israel made his first venture in business as a clerk in the office of the Torrington Cotton Factory. When this firm failed, the new proprietors, Wadham & Thompson, made Coe their resident manager in charge of the factory. In this position Coe became rather prominent in the affairs of the town and served as constable and collector. On Sept. 17, 1817, he married Nancy Wetmore, daughter of Ebenezer and Elizabeth (Miller) Wetmore of Torrington. Wadham & Thompson failed in 1821, and Coe moved to Waterbury, Conn., where he kept a public-house and took an active part in local politics, representing Waterbury in the Connecticut House in 1824 and 1825. In this latter year he also made his first connection with the brass industry as a bookkeeper in the firm of "A. [Aaron] Benedict," manufacturer of gilt buttons. In 1829 he purchased the interest of one of the partners, and a new partnership was formed under the name of Benedict & Coe, with a capital of $20,-000. This partnership expired in 1834, and Coe withdrew to organize a business under his own name, with Anson Phelps, John Hungerford, and Israel Holmes as partners. The firm which was soon called the Wolcottville Brass Company, was one of the earliest to roll brass for its own use and for sale. It was also the first in the country (1834) to make brass-ware by the "battery" process. In this process kettles were hammered into shape by repeated blows of a trip-hammer under which the workman held the cast brass blank in a concave anvil. Many pieces were spoiled by cracking, and after workmen brought from England by Holmes proved no better than the native workers, Coe decided that the trouble lay in the metal used. He accordingly, in 1842, visited the two European establishments using this process and obtained the proper mixtures and annealing methods. Applying this information to the battery process he made it the most satisfactory method of manufacture until it was superseded by the spinning process in 1851. In 1843 Coe again entered politics and represented the Wolcottville district in the Connecticut Senate. In 1845 he sold his interest in the brass business and moved to Detroit where he engaged in banking and the lumber business. While in Detroit (1850) he was instrumental in interesting Waterbury manufacturers in the establishment of a copper smelter there. To this end the Waterbury & Detroit Copper Company was formed, and built the first smelter to handle copper from the Lake Superior mines. In 1853 Coe moved to New York where he engaged in other business and lost his fortune. He then (1867) went to live in Bloomfield, N. J., where he remained twenty years, serving most of that

time as a justice of the peace and commissioner of deeds for Essex County. About 1887 he returned to Waterbury, Conn., where he died at the age of ninety-seven. Coe's first wife by whom he had seven children, died on Aug. 30, 1838, and on Oct. 16, 1839, he married Huldah DeForest.

[J. G. Bartlett, *Robt. Coe, Puritan, His Ancestors and Descendants* (1911); W. G. Lathrop, *Brass Industry* (1926); Joseph Anderson, *Hist. of the Town and City of Waterbury* (1896); Samuel Orcutt, *Hist. of Torrington, Conn.* (1878).]   F. A. T.

COERNE, LOUIS ADOLPHE (Feb. 27, 1870–Sept. 11, 1922), composer, teacher, the son of Adolphe M. and Elizabeth (Homan) Coerne, was born in Newark, N. J. His father, of Dutch and Swedish extraction, was a man of brilliant mind and an accomplished linguist. After receiving his early education in Germany and France, young Coerne moved with his family to Boston, where he graduated from the Latin School in 1888. He then spent two years at Harvard studying harmony and counterpoint with John Knowles Paine, and violin, outside, with Franz Kneisel. In 1890 he went to the Royal Academy of Music at Munich, where he took organ and composition with Rheinberger, and violin and conducting with Abel. In 1893 he graduated with highest honors. Returning to Boston, he led a concert performance of his symphonic poem "Hiawatha." He was then called to Buffalo, as musical director of the Vocal Society, the Liedertafel, and the Church of the Messiah. From 1897 to 1899 he filled similar positions at Columbus, Ohio. On Dec. 14, 1897, he was married to Adele Turton. From 1899 to 1902 he was abroad, composing various works, and completing and editing Rheinberger's posthumous Mass in A Minor. Returning late in 1902, he headed the music department at the next Harvard summer school, and became associate professor at Smith College (1903–04). During the years 1904–05 he did research work at Harvard and in New York, as preparation for his book, *The Evolution of Modern Orchestration* (1908)—a subject for which he was well fitted by his own orchestral technique and modern style. This research won its author a Ph.D. degree (1905), the first given at Harvard for special work in music. Another sojourn abroad (1905–07) enabled him to hear his opera *Zenobia,* which was given at Bremen five times. This is said to have been the first American grand opera to be performed in Germany. Coerne returned to Troy, N. Y., being an active leader there for two years. He then became director of the conservatory at Olivet College, where he received the degree of Mus. Doc.

His later wanderings took him to the University of Wisconsin, as professor and director of the music school, with outside work as church organist and chorus leader. A last change, in 1915, led him to New London, as professor in the Connecticut College for Women. For the final three years of his life he was also editor of the school and college department of the Oliver Ditson Company. His death took place in Boston.

As a composer, Coerne was very active, with 150 opus numbers to his credit, and many other works in manuscript. His melodic line is always well defined, and his harmonic settings rich in character, though they have something of the sameness of style that goes with a constant attempt at modernist effects. His best work was *Zenobia*, showing that queen first presiding at a celebration of victories won by her generals, then defeated by Aurelian, and finally spurning his love, to die, rather unhistorically, with her chancellor Selenos, the real object of her affections. The first act, which includes priestly rites, military display, dances of rejoicing, and triumph over prisoners and tribute-bearers, contains many clearly effective and beautiful numbers, and has been classed with the tonal pageantry of *L'Africaine* and *Aida*. The second and third acts, however, show a lack of characterization, the modernist chords creeping in throughout, where a contrast of emotional styles would have been preferable. Coerne's earlier opera, *A Woman of Marblehead*, like his cantata *Skipper Ireson's Ride*, owes its inspiration to the history and literature of the old colonial town. *The Maiden Queen* and *The Bells of Beaujolais* are operettas. Another ambitious work was the ballet *Evadne*, a concert suite from it consisting of a melodious introductory march, a droll "Clowns' Dance" in bolero rhythm, a varied and well-contrasted introduction to Act II, a "Valse de Salon," a spicy "Devils' Dance," and a strong waltz finale, working up to a great climax with the sudden introduction of voices. The melodrama *Sakuntala* was a success in a field that deserves more attention from composers, the spoken text against a musical background being not only effective, but well suited to concert performance. Coerne's incidental music to *The Trojan Women* deserves mention also. For orchestra, besides "Hiawatha," there are two overtures, a "Fantaisie," a "Tone Picture," a "Tone Poem," and "On Mountain Crests." A "Jubilee March" for military band became well known. For violin Coerne wrote the "Romantic" concerto, a "Swedish Sonata," and a "Concertino" with piano. Other chamber works include various trios,

concertos for small forces, a string quartet, and a striking set of three piano trios in canon. Among vocal works, his cantatas (mostly with orchestra) include *Beloved America, Until the Day Break, The Landing of the Pilgrims*, a *Dedication Ode, A Song of Victory*, etc. The *Man of Galilee* and *The First Christmas* are in the sacred field, as are the Morning and Communion Services, and a six-voiced Mass. Many songs and piano pieces, with some anthems, part-songs, organ pieces, and violin works, complete a long and worthy list.

[*In Memoriam: Louis Adolphe Coerne* (n.d.); *Who's Who in America*, 1922–23; Rupert Hughes, "Music in America," *Godey's Mag.*, Oct. 1897, pp. 424–25, and *Contemporary Am. Composers* (1900), pp. 262–66; *Grove's Dict. of Music and Musicians, Am. Supp.* (1928); *Boston Transcript*, Sept. 12, 1922.] A. E.

COFER, MARTIN HARDIN (Apr. 1, 1832–Mar. 22, 1881), Confederate soldier, jurist, the son of Thomas and Mary Cofer, was born at Elizabethtown in Hardin County, Ky. His mother was a daughter of Martin Hardin, for whom he was named and from whom the county took its name. His grandfather, William Cofer, came from Virginia and settled in Bullitt County, Ky., in 1781. Martin's boyhood was spent upon a farm and what little education he received at this time came largely through his own efforts. When twenty years of age he began teaching in the common schools and at the same time commenced the study of law. The next year he married Mary E. Bush and removed to Illinois where he remained three years, not returning however before he had been admitted to the Illinois bar. In 1856 he began to practise his profession in Elizabethtown and continued there until the beginning of the Civil War.

Being a Democrat and a Southern sympathizer of pronounced views, he began to take an active part in the heated controversy in 1860. In this year he became the editor of the Elizabethtown *Democrat* and after the election of Lincoln tried to bring about the secession of Kentucky. He ran for the legislature in the August (1861) election on the Southern Rights ticket and was defeated. Seeing no possibility now of forcing the secession of the state, he took the short cut of raising volunteers for the Confederacy. He helped to organize the 6th Kentucky Infantry, C. S. A., became its lieutenant-colonel, and fought with it in every engagement except Murfreesboro up to Aug. 30, 1864, being severely wounded at Shiloh in 1862. He was promoted to a colonelcy in 1863 and the next year, when Hood's army retreated from Atlanta into Tennessee, he was made provost-marshal of the Army of Tennessee. He showed great skill in reorganizing the scattered remnants of Hood's army after the disastrous defeat before Nashville. He then helped to lead them into North Carolina, there to join Gen. Joseph E. Johnston in time for the surrender near Durham.

After the war Cofer returned to Kentucky and took up his practise of law at Elizabethtown. In 1867 he published *A Supplemental Digest of Decisions of the Court of Appeals of Kentucky, 1853–67*, which became the standard authority for the state. After serving as judge of the circuit court (1870–74), in August 1874 he was elected associate justice of the state court of appeals and held this position until 1881 when he became the chief justice. Cofer was broad in his sympathies and attitudes and exact in his information. Not until March 1871 were his federal disabilities removed, by an act of Congress, yet two months later he violated Kentucky laws and court decisions by admitting negro testimony against white persons, holding that the Fourteenth Amendment so required. He died in Frankfort while yet in office.

[*Lawyers and Lawmakers of Ky.* (1897), ed. by H. Levin; *Biog. Encyc. Ky.* (1888); E. P. Thompson, *Hist. of the First Ky. Brigade* (1868) and a new edition entitled *Hist. of the Orphan Brigade* (1898). For further facts concerning his life see R. H. and L. Collins, *Hist. of Ky.* (1874), I, and S. Haycraft, *Hist. of Elizabethtown, Ky., and Its Surroundings* (1869).]   E. M. C.

COFFEY, JAMES VINCENT (Dec. 14, 1846–Jan. 15, 1919), jurist, was born in New York City, the son of James and Catherine Coffey. His father was an Irish Nationalist and his mother a devout Catholic. Her Catholicism permeated and influenced Coffey's entire career. He had some ten years of formal schooling, in New York, Bridgeport, Conn., and Nevada City, Cal. His legal education he received in law offices in New York City, Virginia City, Nev., and San Francisco, being admitted to the bar of California in 1869. Despite his brief formal education he became a master of Latin classics. He never married.

Coincident with the commencement of his legal career, Coffey engaged in journalism, being for six years the leading editorial writer on the *San Francisco Examiner*. His editorials won recognition from many Eastern journals. He had a quality of rightness and of fair judgment that showed itself in this field of his labors as it later did in his legal career. His early editorials, like his later legal papers, were ably written in pure English.

He was a staunch Democrat, spending two sessions in the California legislature (1875–78) where he was notable as a fighter against special privilege. He sponsored many important measures during these sessions, such as those which placed the police and fire departments on a civil service basis, which reduced the car-fare from ten cents to five cents, and which subjected the rates of common carriers to state regulation. Few better speeches have been made on the question of protecting the public from corporate greed than that by Coffey in resisting the attempted "grab" of the San Francisco waterfront by railroads. His party never forgot his record in the legislature and proffered him many favors, among others: the Democratic nomination for the California constitutional convention; the nomination for attorney-general in 1879, which he declined; the judgeship of the superior court of San Francisco; the nomination for justice of the supreme court in 1890; and the nomination for Congress in the 4th California district in 1900, which he declined. He was also the choice of Democratic members of the legislature for United States senator in 1899, but failed of election. In 1882 he was elected judge of the superior court of San Francisco County and was assigned to the probate department. He held this position continuously for thirty-six years and was responsible for many new features of probate administration. He established the practise of setting attorney's fees by using a regular schedule based upon the value of the estate. Over $600,000,000 in estates was administered in his court during his career on the bench. Among these estates were those of Spreckles, Sharon, DeLaveaga, Leland Stanford, and Mark Hopkins. Coffey wrote several articles urging reforms—many of them since adopted—to decrease the cost and complexity of legal procedure. His opinions as trial judge were published in six volumes known as Coffey's Probate Reports (*Reports of Decisions in Probate*, 1894–1916). Had it not been for their partial destruction in the San Francisco fire of 1906, these decisions would have filled twenty volumes. They are extensively used as authority in California courts to-day. They reflect a noble and generous nature combined with a mastery of English diction and law.

[An outline of Coffey's career may be found in *Who's Who in America*, 1918–19; the *Recorder*, a San Francisco legal newspaper, contains several short sketches of him. The Bar Asso. of San Francisco published in 1920 a memorial pamphlet dealing with his life. The *Nation*, a San Francisco Catholic newspaper, contains in the issue for Feb. 1919, a ten-column *résumé* of his career and character. See also *San Francisco Examiner*, Jan. 16, 1919.]   J. V. L.

COFFIN, CHARLES ALBERT (Dec. 30, 1844–July 14, 1926), president of the General Electric Company, son of Albert and Anstrus (Varney) Coffin, was born in Somerset County, Me. He graduated from the Bloomfield (Me.)

Academy, and began his business career in Boston. His interest centered in the shoe and leather industry, and he soon helped to found the firm of Coffin & Clough, a shoe-manufacturing establishment at Lynn. He was married in 1872 to Caroline Russel of Holbrook, Mass. In 1883 he became one of the Lynn Syndicate, formed for the purchase of the American Electric Company of New Britain, Conn., the head of which was Elihu Thomson. The plant was moved to Lynn and the name of the Company changed to the Thomson-Houston Electric Company. Coffin himself knew little about electrical matters at this time, but he had a genius for organization and the ability to surround himself with the very best men in the technical field. He interested himself keenly in the work of such men as Elihu Thomson, Edwin J. Houston, and E. W. Rice. In 1892 the Thomson-Houston Company was consolidated with the Edison General Electric Company of New York in which all the activities and interests of Edison's incandescent lamp development had been merged. Coffin was elected president of the new firm, which took the name of the General Electric Company, and he held this office until 1913. From 1913 to 1922 he was chairman of the board of directors. The growth of the General Electric Company under Coffin's leadership was phenomenal. In 1873 the Company's gross business was twelve million dollars a year; in 1920 it was almost a million dollars a day. Coffin supported the work of the Company's engineers in developing the Curtis Steam Turbine which revolutionized the primary power sources in electric light and power stations. He indorsed the movement in 1901 to establish the research laboratory which has contributed not only to electrical development but to the advancement of pure science. T. C. Martin and S. L. Coles say: "Coffin stands supreme in contributing more to create the magnitude of the whole electrical industry than any one or many men, by his encouragement of invention along useful lines, by his financial powers, by his talent for organization, by his tireless energy, by his course in introducing and his abilities in selling new apparatus" (*Story of Electricity*, 1919, I, 82).

During the World War (1915) Coffin created the War Relief Clearing House. After this was consolidated with the Red Cross, he transferred his tireless energy to the latter. In recognition of his war work he was made an officer of the Legion of Honor (France); commander of the Order of Leopold II of Belgium; and a member of the Order of St. Sava of Serbia. He aided in the establishment of American scholarships for France and was generous in assisting young peo-

ple, both in America and abroad, in their efforts toward an education. The Charles A. Coffin Foundation, created by the Board of the General Electric Company at the time of his retirement from active participation in its affairs, carries on some of his educational work through the award of fellowships to college graduates interested in continuing their research activities. He was a modest man who shunned publicity always and who found joy in his domestic life, his books, and his flowers.

[*Electrical Record*, Aug. 1926; *Eng. News-Record*, July 22, 29, 1926; the *Link* (Gen. Electric Co.).] E. Y.

COFFIN, CHARLES CARLETON (July 26, 1823–Mar. 2, 1896), war correspondent, writer, gained fame under his pen-name, Carleton, and found a direction for his later writing by his success as a correspondent in the Civil War. He was born in Boscawen, N. H., son of Thomas Coffin and Hannah Kilburn, grew up on a farm, and had only the education of village school and academy. After his marriage to Sallie Russell Farmer, Feb. 18, 1846, he worked at farming and surveying for a time. In 1852, in association with his brother-in-law, Moses Gerrish Farmer [*q.v.*], he installed in Boston the first electric fire-alarm system. He had already tried his hand at writing, and in 1853 definitely took up newspaper work, serving as assistant editor of the *Boston Atlas*, 1856–57, and as correspondent of the *Boston Journal* in the Middle West in 1854 and again in 1857 and 1860. He was in Washington at the outbreak of war, made his first great success by his eye-witness account of Bull Run, and from then until the close of the war was almost constantly at the front, with Grant in the West from December 1861 to June 1862, with the ironclads off Charleston in April 1863, and with the Army of the Potomac in almost all the important engagements from the Wilderness to the fall of Richmond. More than once, as at the capture of Fort Donelson, at Gettysburg, and at the occupation of Charleston, his telegraphic dispatches to the *Journal* gave the first definite news. Nearly six feet in height, an abstainer from liquor and tobacco, with handsome, open face, and a reputation for courage and absolute trustworthiness, he had also the assurance essential to his profession. "He was the cheekiest man on earth for the sake of the *Journal* and the people of New England. ... He would talk to the commander as no civilian could or would ... and Grant always welcomed it" (soldier's statement, Griffis, p. 94). "Carleton" exploited his war experience in many volumes: *My Days and Nights on the Battlefield* (1864), *Following the Flag* (1865), *Four Years of Fighting* (1866, republished, 1881 and 1896, as *The Boys of '61*), and a series entitled *Drumbeat of the Nation, Marching to Victory, Redeeming the Republic, Freedom Triumphant* (1888–91). He was in Europe for sixteen months, 1866–67, and thence went eastward through India, China, and Japan to San Francisco and thus home, describing his journey in *Our New Way Round the World* (1869). A popular book, *The Seat of Empire* (1870) was the outcome of a subsequent tour in the West. Turning to books for youth, Coffin employed his vigorous, graphic style and familiarity with New England life in *The Boys of '76* (1876), *The Story of Liberty* (1879), *Old Times in the Colonies* (1881), *Building the Nation* (1883), and *Daughters of the Revolution* (1895). He wrote also lives of Garfield (1880) and Lincoln (1892); two novels, *Winning His Way* (1866) and *Caleb Krinkle* (1875); and a *History of Boscawen and Webster* (1878). His children's books, especially *The Boys of '76,* had a tremendous and deserved popularity; several have been reissued in recent years. Genial and warm-hearted, Coffin had a host of distinguished friends, and was in great demand as a popular lecturer, giving in his lifetime some 2,000 public addresses. From Boston he was elected to the Assembly, 1884–85, and to the state Senate, 1890. He was a gifted organist and musician, a devoted worker in the Shawmut Congregational Church, Boston. In February 1896 friends gathered in his newly built home in Brookline to celebrate the fiftieth anniversary of his happy though childless marriage. His death from apoplexy came a fortnight later.

[W. E. Griffis, *Chas. Carleton Coffin* (1898); shorter sketches in the *Granite Mo.,* Apr. 1885; *Book News* (Phila.), Feb. 1891; and in F. L. Bullard, *Famous War Correspondents* (1914), pp. 380–86. *In Memoriam: Chas. Carleton Coffin* (1896) contains addresses and biographical memoirs at the time of his death.] A.W.

COFFIN, CHARLES FISHER (Apr. 3, 1823–Sept. 9, 1916), Quaker minister, was descended from Tristram Coffyn, Massachusetts colonist (1642) and one of the original settlers of Nantucket. Tristram's grandson, Samuel, was the first of the family to join the Society of Friends, from which date onward this branch of the Coffin family produced many notable Quaker leaders. William, son of Samuel, removed to North Carolina in 1773. His grandson Elijah Coffin (1798–1862) was a man of distinction and influence. He was a school-teacher in his youth in North Carolina, where he married Naomi Hiatt, a highly gifted woman of an important Quaker family. With her and his one-year-old son, Charles Fisher Coffin, he migrated to Indiana in 1824, where he was a pioneer school-teacher. He was later a banker in Cincinnati (for one

year, 1833), and in Richmond, Ind.; and for thirty-one years was clerk of Indiana Yearly Meeting of Friends. Charles Fisher Coffin was educated at first by his father and later in the early Quaker schools of the pioneer period. He began his career in the Richmond Bank, a branch of the State Bank of Indiana, when he was twelve years old, continuing his education during the evenings. When he was twenty-one he took an extensive journey of great educational value through the Eastern states, becoming acquainted with many distinguished persons, especially with the spiritual leaders in the Society of Friends. In 1847, he was married to Rhoda M. Johnson of Waynesville, Ohio, a woman of grace and talent, who, like her husband, made a large contribution to the moral and spiritual causes of their time. Charles succeeded his father in the Richmond Bank in 1859, in which position he had a distinguished business career until 1885, when he retired and removed to Chicago. He was clerk (presiding officer) of Indiana Yearly Meeting of Friends (succeeding his father in this position also) from 1857 to 1885, and during this period he came to be recognized as one of the leading Quakers in America. He was recorded a minister of the Gospel in the Society of Friends in 1866, and continued to preach, with effect and charm and power, until his death at the age of ninety-three. He had a large part in the development of the Sunday-schools in Indiana, and took a foremost place in the early evangelical movement in the Society of Friends. He and his wife were leaders in the creation of the Indiana Reform School and he was first president of the board of control of the Indiana House of Refuge for Juvenile Offenders, a position which he held from 1867 to 1880. He spent the last thirty years of his life in Chicago with the exception of two years in London, England. At his death he left many valuable papers and reminiscences about western pioneer life, as well as extensive correspondence with public men. These are in the library of Earlham College, Richmond, Ind.

[*Life of Elijah Coffin* (1863), ed. by his daughter, Mary C. Johnson; *Rhoda M. Coffin, Her Reminiscences and Addresses* (1910); *Chas. F. Coffin, A Quaker Pioneer* (1923), comp. by Mary C. Johnson and Percival B. Coffin; the files of the *Friends Rev.* and the *Am. Friend.*] R.M.J.

COFFIN, Sir ISAAC (May 16, 1759–July 23, 1839), British admiral, born in Boston, Mass., was a son of Nathaniel and Elizabeth (Barnes) Coffin. He was a descendant in the fifth generation from Tristram Coffyn who emigrated to Massachusetts in 1642 and settled in Nantucket in 1660. When eight years old he was sent to the Boston Latin School where he excelled in nautical science and in the school sports. His father was the King's Cashier of the Customs at Boston and was a man of great wealth. Isaac entered the Royal Navy at the age of fourteen and was assigned to the brig *Gaspee,* then commanded by Lieut. William Hunter. He advanced rapidly and in 1778 was made a lieutenant and placed in command of the cutter *Placentia.* He took part in many naval engagements of the American war, notably in Rodney's brilliant victory over De Grasse in April 1782. The following June he became captain of the *Shrewsbury* of 74 guns. A month later he refused to receive three youthful lieutenants appointed by Rodney. He was tried by court martial for contempt and disobedience but was acquitted. The end of the war found the royalist Coffin family scattered and his father dead of the gout. Coffin went to England, had his prize money invested judiciously, and spent much of his time in France. In 1786 he was appointed to the *Thisbe* to take Lord Dorchester and his family to Quebec. Upon his return it was discovered that he had failed to comply with a technicality that currrent abuse had made obsolete and he was suspended (David Hannay, *Naval Courts Martial,* 1914, pp. 98–104). Resenting what he considered unjust treatment, he went to Flanders and joined the Brabant patriots against Austria. An appeal set aside his suspension and restored his rank. Coffin had seriously crippled himself while rescuing a sailor who had fallen overboard; a further injury incapacitated him for active service and he became resident commissioner at Corsica and later at Lisbon. In April 1804 he was appointed rear admiral and the following month was created a baronet. By regular seniority he became a full admiral in 1814. In March 1811 he married Elizabeth Browne, the only daughter of William Greenly of Titley Court in Herefordshire. Coffin had wished for an heir to his title and his fortune, but his jovial manners and rough humor so distressed his father-in-law and his wife's habit of writing sermons far into the night so distressed him that a separation was soon arranged. In 1818, through the influence of Lord Darlington, Coffin was returned to Parliament for the borough of Ilchester. He remained there seven years and distinguished himself by his rough, salty humor and his Latin quotations. He was deeply interested in America and his visits were frequent. He sent many English race-horses to improve the American breed. He imported rare fruits and plants and brought the first European turbot to New England waters. His most notable philanthropy was the Coffin school at Nantucket. Started in May 1827, it was first restricted to the descendants of Tristram

Coffyn but was later opened to the children of Nantucket.

[Thos. C. Amory, *Life of Admiral Sir Isaac Coffin, Bart.* (1886) ; *N.Y.Geneal. and Biog. Record,* vol. XVII (1886) ; Allen Coffin, *Life of Tristram Coffyn* (Nantucket, 1881) ; John Marshall, *Royal Naval Biography,* vol. I (London, 1823) ; J. K. Laughton in *Dict. Nat. Biog.*]
                        F.M.

COFFIN, JAMES HENRY (Sept. 6, 1806– Feb. 6, 1873), mathematician, meteorologist, was the third child of Matthew and Betsy (Allen) Coffin, both of Martha's Vineyard, and sixth in descent from Tristram Coffyn who came from England in 1642. Matthew Coffin died in 1820 and the family, being destitute, soon was scattered among relatives. James, who during his earlier years had been feeble and sickly, had now become strong enough to work on a farm, which he did at times, though he planned soon to enter the trade of musical-instrument and cabinet-maker. In September 1821, however, while visiting his uncle, the Rev. Moses Hallock of Plainfield, Mass., his cousin, William Hallock, persuaded him to come and live with them and get an education. He entered Amherst College in September 1823, but an attack of the measles during the first session injured his eyes for several years and prevented his graduation until Aug. 27, 1828. During this period he supported himself mainly by tutoring at college and by teaching during vacations. In 1829 he opened at Greenfield, Mass., a select school for boys and the next spring added to it a manual labor department for which he rented some 200 acres of land and hired a farmer-superintendent. This was the beginning of the Fellenberg Manual Labor Institution, probably the first of its kind in the United States. The results were excellent in every particular save in respect to his own remuneration. This was so meager that in 1837 he accepted the headship of an academy in Ogdensburg, N. Y., which he retained until Aug. 10, 1839. From 1840 to 1843 he was a tutor in Williams College. Here he installed on the peak of Mt. Greylock an apparatus for automatically recording the direction and velocity of the wind, and continued his meteorological studies begun in 1838 at Ogdensburg. In October 1843, he became principal of the academy at South Norwalk, Conn., where he remained until Oct. 16, 1846, when he moved to Lafayette College to take the chair of mathematics and natural philosophy, where he remained for the rest of his life.

In that year he became a collaborator in the work of the Smithsonian Institution, which published the two works: *Winds of the Northern Hemisphere* (1853) ; and *Winds of the Globe* (1875), on which his scientific reputation chiefly rests. The second of these studies, a large quarto volume involving years of work, was by far the most exhaustive collection and the fullest analysis of wind data that had been made, and its main conclusions are good for all time. Coffin was a highly respected and successful teacher, and always, as from childhood, exceptionally pious. He was twice married: to Aurelia Medici Jennings in 1833; and to Abby Elizabeth Young in 1851.

[J. C. Clyde, *Life of Jas. H. Coffin* (1881); A. Guyot, "Memoir of Jas. Henry Coffin," in *Biog. Memoirs Nat. Acad. Sci.*, I (1877), 257–64.] W.J.H.

COFFIN, JOHN (1756–June 12, 1838), Massachusetts Loyalist, was born in Boston, a son of Nathaniel and Elizabeth (Barnes) Coffin. He went to sea as a small boy and by the time he was eighteen had been given command of a ship. In 1775, while in an English port, his ship was engaged by the British government to carry troops to Massachusetts, and arrived at Boston, with nearly a whole regiment in command of Gen. Howe, on June 15. Two days later the troops were landed directly at Bunker Hill and Coffin himself took part in the fight. For gallant conduct he was made an ensign on the field and after the battle was presented to Gen. Gage, being made a lieutenant shortly afterward. Howe promised him the command of 400 men if he could raise them in New York. Coffin went to that town upon the evacuation of Boston in March 1776, and there succeeded in raising the required number among the Loyalists. He was thereupon made commander of the "Orange Rangers," a mounted rifle corps. With these he took part in the battle of Long Island. In 1778 he exchanged into the New York Volunteers and the same year transferred to the South where he raised a corps of cavalry in Georgia. He distinguished himself in the battles of Savannah, Hobkerk's Hill, and Eutaw Springs, in which last his gallantry and good judgment won the praise of his Continental opponent, Gen. Greene. He was of assistance to Cornwallis at Yorktown and at the close of the war that officer gave him a handsome sword. It is said that the Colonials had offered $10,000 for his head. At any rate, failing to secure what he considered protection when Cornwallis surrendered, he cut his way through to Charleston, where, during the war, he had already met the girl who was to become his wife, Ann Mathews, the daughter of William Mathews of St. John's Island. On his first stay there, he was almost caught by the Colonials and there is a story that he escaped only by hiding under a hoop-skirt.

When Charleston was evacuated by the British, Coffin succeeded in getting to New York where he met old comrades and on Dec. 25, 1782, was made major in the King's American Regiment by Sir Guy Carleton. Before the evacuation of New York he went to New Brunswick, Canada, where he was joined by his young wife and four negro slaves. Here at twenty-seven he started a new life as a pioneer, clearing his farm himself. In 1783 he bought a considerable tract of land and the next year was settled about twelve miles from St. John on his estate, which he called Alwington Manor, after the family home in England. This comprised about 6,000 acres and became a valuable property. He remained in the army on half-pay, being made lieutenant-colonel, Oct. 12, 1793; colonel, Jan. 26, 1797; major-general, Sept. 25, 1803; lieutenant-general, Oct. 25, 1809; and general Aug. 12, 1819. In the War of 1812 he raised 600 men. He also served as member of the Assembly, chief magistrate of King's County, and member of the Council. He alternated his residence between New Brunswick and England and at his death, which occurred in New Brunswick, was the oldest general in the British army. His widow died at Bath, England, in 1839.

[L. Sabine, *Biog. Sketches Loyalists of the Am. Revolution* (1864); J. H. Stark, *Loyalists of Mass.* (1910); Brit. Army Registers; *Gentleman's Mag.* (London), Sept. 1838.] J.T.A.

COFFIN, LEVI (Oct. 28, 1789–Sept. 16, 1877), a leader in operations of the "Underground Railroad," was descended from Tristram Coffyn, who came to New England in 1642 and was one of the nine original purchasers from the Indians of the Island of Nantucket. Levi was born on a farm at New Garden, N. C., the youngest of the seven children of Levi and Prudence (Williams) Coffin. His mother's family was of Welsh descent. Both of his parents were Quakers. The boy, who was the only son, could not be spared from necessary work on the farm except for short intervals at the district school. He was mainly taught by his father at home. When he was twenty-one, he left for a session at a distant school. He then taught for a winter, attended school the following year, and taught at intervals for several years thereafter. In 1821, together with his cousin Vestal Coffin, he organized at New Garden a Sunday-school for negroes. This succeeded for a time but eventually the masters, becoming alarmed at Coffin's methods, kept their slaves at home, and the school was closed. On Oct. 28, 1824, Coffin was married to Catharine White, a Quaker. Two years later, he moved to Newport (now Fountain City), Wayne County, Ind.—a village of about twenty families

—where he was to live for more than twenty years. Here Coffin opened a store. Very soon after he came to Newport, he found that he was on a line of the Underground Railroad through which slaves often passed. Coffin let it be known that his house would be a depot and immediately fugitives began to arrive. When his neighbors saw his fearlessness and success, they began to help in clothing and sending the negroes on their way, but they would not take the risk of sheltering them. The Railroad was attended with heavy expenses. These Coffin could not have borne had he not been prosperous. He kept a team and wagon always ready to carry slaves. Sometimes one or two other wagons and teams were required. Journeys had to be made at night, often through deep mud and bad roads and along seldom traveled by-ways. A week seldom passed without his receiving passengers. Coffin was also at this time a member of a Committee on Concerns of People of Color to look after their educational interests, treasurer of a fund raised to sustain schools and aid the poor and destitute, and an active participant in the temperance movement. Almost twenty years after he had gone to Newport to live, he became interested in the free labor question. In 1847, he agreed to go experimentally to Cincinnati for five years and open a wholesale free-labor goods store. A Quaker Convention at Salem, Ind., had voted in 1846 to raise $3,000 to begin such a project. A year after the outbreak of the Civil War, Coffin began his work for the freedmen and devoted his entire time to this for the rest of his life. In May 1864 he went to England for this purpose, and an English Freedmen's Aid Society was formed. Over $100,-000 in money, clothing, and other articles was forwarded in one year from England and the Continent. In 1867, Coffin was appointed delegate to the International Anti-Slavery Conference in Paris, which was held on Aug. 26 and 27. The last ten years of his life were passed in retirement.

[*Reminiscences of Levi Coffin, Reputed President of the Underground R. R.* (1876, 2nd ed., 1880); S. B. Weeks, *Southern Quakers and Slavery* (1896); W. H. Siebert, *The Underground R. R. from Slavery to Freedom* (1898); *A Woman's Life-Work: Labors and Experiences of Laura S. Haviland* (1882); *Hist. Mag.*, Sept. 1868; *New Eng. Hist. and Geneal. Reg.*, Oct. 1848, Apr., July 1870; *Am. Hist. Rec.*, Jan. 1872, Jan., Feb. 1873; *Internat. Rev.*, Aug. 1880; *Cincinnati Daily Gazette*, Sept. 17, 20, 1877; *Cincinnati Enquirer*, Sept. 18, 1877.]   M.A.K.

COFFIN, LORENZO S. (Apr. 9, 1823–Jan. 17, 1915), philanthropist, was born on a farm near Alton, N. H., the son of the Rev. Stephen and Deborah (Philbrook) Coffin. His father was a Baptist clergyman and farmer. Lorenzo attended Wolfboro Academy, Wolfboro, N. H., and then studied for two years in the preparatory department of Oberlin Collegiate Institute (later Oberlin College). For a year he taught at Geauga Seminary, a Free-will Baptist institution in Chester, Ohio, where James A. Garfield and Lucretia (Randolph) Garfield were among his pupils. He married Cynthia T. Curtis in 1848, moved to Iowa in 1855, and bought government land near Fort Dodge. His first wife died on Apr. 20, 1856 and in February 1857 he married Mary C. Chase. On Sept. 8, 1862, he enlisted in the 32nd Regiment of Iowa Volunteer Infantry and within two months was promoted from quartermaster-sergeant to chaplain. He left the service in July 1863. Soon after his return to Fort Dodge he was elected superintendent of schools in which position he had the opportunity to develop ideas of improvement in educational methods and in farming. He contributed often to the agricultural journals, conducting in one of them a column of advice on farm problems. Gov. Sherman appointed him railroad commissioner in 1883, a position he filled for five years. His interest in railroad men had been awakened two years before his appointment, when he was instrumental in securing the right of way for the Fort Dodge & Des Moines Railroad to Ruthven. His position as commissioner made frequent trips necessary, and these he took, by preference, on freight trains. He learned much of the lives of railroad men and the hazards to which they were exposed. The accident rate was very high at that time, and he determined to do what he could to lessen what seemed an unpardonable loss of life. He found that the majority of fatal accidents on freight trains were due to the hazards involved in coupling the cars or in applying the brakes. Self-couplers and air-brakes had been installed on passenger cars, and he felt that they should be established on freight trains as well. He wrote articles on the subject, spoke from many platforms, and sent letters to every religious and family periodical in the country, until at last tests were made in 1886 and again in the following year. Westinghouse became interested and devised a brake sufficiently strong to hold fifty freight cars. These brakes were required by an act of the Iowa legislature passed in 1890, and Coffin turned his attention to national legislation. With the aid of D. B. Henderson and W. B. Allison of Iowa, he had bills introduced in Congress which were eventually passed. Accidents to railroad employees had averaged from 20,000 to 30,000 annually. This number was reduced by sixty per cent after the safety devices were installed. Coffin started a Temperance Association among railroad men in 1893, was its president after it was founded, and helped found near Chicago, a Home for Aged and Disabled Railroad Men of which he was president for twelve years. On his farm near Fort Dodge he built Hope Hall, No. 3, modeled on the Hope Halls of Chicago and Flushing, N. Y., established originally for discharged convicts by Mrs. Maud Ballington Booth. He was the candidate of the Prohibition party for governor in 1907, and of the United Christian party for vice-president of the United States in 1908.

[*Hist. of Fort Dodge and Webster County, Iowa* (1913), II, 148–62; B. F. Gue, *Hist. of Iowa* (1903), vol. IV; *Annals of Iowa*, 1901–03; *Roster and Records Iowa Soldiers in the War of the Rebellion* (1908–11); *Chicago Daily Tribune*, Jan. 5, 1894; *Reg. and Leader* (Des Moines), Oct. 25, 1905, Dec. 6, 1908, Jan. 18, 1915; *Who's Who in America*, 1914–15.] M.A.K.

COFFIN, WILLIAM ANDERSON (Jan. 31, 1855–Oct. 26, 1925), painter, art critic, was the son of James Gardiner and Isabella Catharine (Anderson) Coffin of Allegheny, Pa., where William was born. He was graduated from Yale in 1874 when, as he told F. W. Coburn (*American University Magazine*, May 1895), "finding the business life to which his father had destined him intensely disagreeable, he could think of nothing more pleasant than to return to New Haven." Not knowing just what he wanted to do, Coffin registered at the Yale Art School, and became fascinated by the allurements of the painter's profession. In 1877 he went to Paris where he was a pupil of Léon Bonnât. In 1882 he opened a studio in New York, intending to be a portrait painter. His devotion to landscape, in which he attained his special distinction, resulted from some successful exhibition pieces which he painted in 1886 and 1887. His honors and prizes were numerous, beginning with a Hallgarten prize of the National Academy of Design in 1886. He won a medal at the Paris Exposition in 1889; the Webb prize of the Society of American Artists, 1891; the gold medal of the Art Club of Philadelphia, 1898; silver medals of the Charleston Exposition, 1902, and the Louisiana Purchase Exposition, 1904. In 1901 Coffin served as director of fine arts at the Buffalo Exposition. He was a member of the advisory board of the art department, Panama-Pacific Exposition, 1915. During the World War he was president of the American Artists' Committee of One Hundred to raise relief funds for the families of artist-soldiers of France. He became a Chevalier of the Legion of Honor in 1917. He was appointed by the French government in 1919 president of a committee to arrange an exhibition of American paintings and sculptures at the Luxem-

bourg Museum. Coffin's influence as lecturer and writer was considerable. He served as art critic of the New York *Evening Post* and the *Nation*, 1886–91, and of the New York *Sun*, 1896–1900. His landscapes, many of them painted in Pennsylvania, were made intelligently and artistically; his experiments with formal and decorative landscape were not uniformly successful. Examples of his work may be seen at the Metropolitan Museum of Art, New York City; Brooklyn Museum of Arts and Sciences; National Museum, Washington; Albright Art Gallery, Buffalo; Brooks Memorial Art Gallery, Memphis; and in other public collections. He was never married.

[*The Art News*, Oct. 31, 1925; *Biog. Record of the Class of 1874 in Yale Coll.* (1912); *Yale Univ. Obit. Record* (1926); *Who's Who in America*, 1924–25.] F.W.C.

COGDELL, JOHN STEVENS (Sept. 19, 1778–Feb. 25, 1847), sculptor, painter, and lawyer, was born in Charleston (or Georgetown), S. C. The son of George Cogdell, a captain in a South Carolina regiment, and Elizabeth Stevens, mistress of a girls' school, he received his grounding in English from his mother and later was graduated from the College of Charleston. When about seventeen, he entered the law office of William Johnson, Jr., and in 1799 was admitted to the bar. In June of the following year, for the sake of his health, he made with his brother Richard an eight months' voyage to the Mediterranean. Prior to this trip he had shown no great inclination for art although he had at times found amusement in making copies of prints in watercolor. In Italy, however, his ambition was fired by the paintings he saw, and by a visit to Canova. Though handicapped by ill health, he took up oil painting and drawing from plaster casts and soon tried painting from life, doing portraits of many of his friends as gifts. On his return to Charleston from Europe he began the practise of law. He was successful and, in 1806, he married Maria Gilchrist. In spite of his profession he found time to paint. As a gift to a former instructor, the Rev. Simon Gallagher, he painted a "Crucifixion" which the latter placed in St. Mary's Church. He likewise did a picture for the orphanage and numerous heads and landscapes for his friends. He made several visits to northern cities and on one of his trips to Boston, in 1825, he was persuaded by Washington Allston to attempt modeling in clay. In the following year he studied anatomy and made a clay head of his professor. A number of his earliest busts were exhibited at the Athenæum in Boston—Dr. Holbrook, Stephen Elliott, Lafayette, Gen. Moultrie (one cast given to Congress, one also in the National Academy of Design), Scott (cast, dated 1834, owned by Charleston Library Society), and Washington. He also made busts from memory of Judge De Saussure, Judge Elihu H. Bay, and Bishop England. Greatly desirous of visiting Europe with his wife, he had nearly accumulated the necessary funds when a prominent New York banker induced him to invest in his bank, which failed and left Cogdell ruined. Fortunately he could fall back on his profession and his position in the customs. He had been elected to the state House of Representatives in 1810, 1814, 1816, and 1818. In this last year he was made comptroller general of South Carolina but resigned during his second term to become naval officer of the custom-house in 1821. From 1832 until his death he was president of the Bank of South Carolina. He seems not to have given up his art, however, for he made a tablet to the memory of his mother in St. Phillip's Church. The National Academy of Design, besides the bust already mentioned, has one of Gen. Ruckney and the Pennsylvania Academy has two. Failing health compelled Cogdell to give up active employment some time before his death which took place in Charleston. As a sculptor he is interesting in that he belongs to an early epoch of American art and in that, coming from a section where sculpture was little known, he acquired through his own effort a certain proficiency in that art.

[Wm. Dunlap, *Hist. of the Rise and Progress of the Arts of Design in the U. S.* (new ed., 1918); A. S. Salley, Jr., article in the Charleston *Sunday News*, July 14, 1901; *Charleston Courier*, Feb. 26, 1847. Cogdell's middle name is variously given as Stevens and Stephano. The date of birth is taken from C. Jervey, *Inscriptions on the Tablets and Gravestones in St. Michael's Church and Churchyard, Charleston, S. C.* (1906).]   E.G.N.

COGGESHALL, GEORGE (Nov. 2, 1784– Aug. 6, 1861), sea captain, author, was born in Milford, Conn., the son of William and Eunice (Mallett) Coggeshall. His father, an ardent Revolutionary patriot, suffered on land and sea the privations of the common soldier, was captured by the enemy, and endured the winter of 1779–80 in the prison ship *Jersey,* where, famished and half-frozen, he nearly succumbed to smallpox. After the war he throve for a while as a shipmaster; but, for trading with Martinique one of his schooners with its cargo was seized and sold by the British, for trading with a British island another was taken and sold by the French, and William Coggeshall was reduced to poverty. His son, therefore, came naturally by his patriotism and his hatred of foreign oppression, and equally so by his democratic principles, his piety, his pride and skill in his calling. Too poor to go to school, he began his seafaring as soon as he was old enough to carry a message

from the quarter-deck to the forecastle; at fifteen he made his first long voyage—to Cadiz as cabin-boy in a schooner built at Milford and commanded by a Milford captain; in 1809 he received his first command. For almost sixty years he followed the sea. During the War of 1812 he distinguished himself as captain of the privateers *David Porter* and *Leo.* The *Leo* was captured off Lisbon by the frigate *Granicus,* whose commander, Capt. William Furlong Wise (see article on Wise in *Dictionary of National Biography*) treated him courteously and delivered him a prisoner to the authorities at Gibraltar. By good luck and mother wit Coggeshall made his escape from the fortress within two days and got back safely to New York on May 9, 1815. The career of an American sea captain, though hardly less strenuous in peace than in war, had its domestic side: Coggeshall was able to return to Milford from time to time to visit his widowed mother; he gave employment as mates or captains under him to several of his brothers; and on some of his voyages he was accompanied by his wife. He was twice married; his first wife, Sarah, died Oct. 3, 1822, his second, Elizabeth, Mar. 6, 1851. In the long hours of inactivity at sea he read diligently and kept a careful journal, and on his retirement from the sea he turned author. His books are: *Voyages to Various Parts of the World* (1851); *Second Series of Voyages to Various Parts of the World* (1852); *Voyages to Various Parts of the World* (2nd ed., 1853, in two volumes, but only one volume ever issued); *Thirty-Six Voyages to Various Parts of the World* (3rd ed., 1858, revised, corrected, and enlarged, the best edition); *History of the American Privateers and Letters-of-Marque* (1856; 3rd ed., 1861); and *An Historical Sketch of Commerce and Navigation from the Birth of the Saviour down to the Present Date* (1860). A volume of *Religious and Miscellaneous Poetry* has also been ascribed to him. Coggeshall wrote a clear, terse, seamanly English flavored with a dash of quaint elegance. His strength lies in his details, which he drew in abundance from his journals and records; his best writing, in fact, can stand comparison with the novels of Daniel Defoe. His *History of American Privateers* is still useful to students of naval history and contains two stirring chapters on his own exploits. As a compiler, however, he is generally tedious. His last book, by its sanctimonious tone and hodge-podge arrangement, shows that the captain's health was failing. He died soon after its publication and was buried in his native town.

[Coggeshall's own writings are the only accessible source of information about him. Mr. Clarence S. Brigham of the Am. Antiq. Soc., and Coggeshall's cousin,

Miss Martha Coggeshall of Milford, Conn., have collected some additional facts for this article. E. S. Maclay, *A Hist. of Am. Privateers* (1899) retells the story of the *David Porter* and the *Leo*.]   G. H. G.

COGGESHALL, WILLIAM TURNER (Sept. 6, 1824–Aug. 2, 1867), journalist, author, seems to have been a direct descendant of that John Coggeshall who came to America in the *Lyon* in 1632, suffered some persecution in Massachusetts Bay because of his support of Anne Hutchinson, and later became first president of Rhode Island (*Rhode Island Historical Magazine*, October 1884, and W. T. Coggeshall, Record of Facts, *post*, p. 14). William Turner was born at Lewistown, Pa., the third of the twelve children of William C. Coggeshall, a coachsmith, and Eliza Grotz, whose father had come from Germany (Record of Facts, pp. 25–28). On Oct. 6, 1842, he left Lewistown for Ohio, arriving at Akron in November. Here he became (1844–46) an editor and part owner of a temperance paper, which underwent rapid changes of name (Samuel A. Lane, *Fifty Years and Over of Akron and Summit County*, 1892, p. 225). Meantime on Oct. 28, 1845 he had married Mary Maria Carpenter; and in the spring of 1847 (Coggeshall, *Stories of Frontier Adventure*, "Dedicatory Letter") he removed to Cincinnati, where he was connected with a number of newspapers and magazines, the most important of which was the monthly *Genius of the West* (1853–56). During this Cincinnati period he also published his earliest books; and in 1852 he accompanied Kossuth from Cincinnati on the remainder of his American tour, reporting his speeches for the press (Kossuth to Coggeshall, June 17, 1852). From May 31, 1856 (13th *Annual Report* of the library) to Mar. 24, 1862, he was librarian of the Ohio State Library at Columbus, and in 1858–59, editor of the *Ohio Educational Monthly*. During the first year of the Civil War he also acted as military secretary to Gov. Dennison, and was assigned for a time to secret service. Removing to Springfield, Ohio, he was owner and editor of the *Republic,* 1862–65 but was at Columbus as editor of the *Ohio State Journal* during the greater part of the latter year. Early in 1866 he served as private secretary to Gov. Jacob D. Cox.

On May 4, 1866, he was appointed American minister to Ecuador, and officially announced his arrival at Guayaquil on Aug. 2 and at Quito on Sept. 8. The only notable event of his ministry was his successful appeal to the government of Ecuador, in opposition to the papal nuncio and other authorities of the church, for the right of Protestant burial for foreigners. Coggeshall himself was already so ill of consumption that his

daughter Jessie (1851–68), who had accompanied him from the United States and served as interpreter and secretary, was practically in charge of the legation; and on Aug. 2, 1867, he died at a country place near Quito. His body was at first buried in consecrated ground, but when the clerical revolution occurred soon afterward, was disinterred and placed in a public warehouse. Later the remains of both Coggeshall and his daughter, who had died at Guayaquil on her way home, were returned to the United States at the public expense, and buried at Columbus, Ohio.

As a writer, Coggeshall addressed himself generally to the young, and fell naturally into a strain of conventional moralizing. In his controversial speaking and writing, however, he was often vigorous: he argued effectively in support of Lincoln in his political pamphlets and appealed skilfully to popular interest in his tract, *Need and Availability of the Writing and Spelling Reform* (1857). Other works, like his *Lincoln Memorial* (1865), were mere compilations. His fiction, as in *Oakshaw* (1855), was awkward and too intent on moralizing, but made some attempt to avoid the easy appeal of blood and tears popular in that day, and was concerned to a considerable extent with character. *The Protective Policy in Literature* (1859), a plea for sectionalism as a fruitful motive in literature, was, in effect, an announcement of what was by far his most important work, *The Poets and Poetry of the West* (1860), a comprehensive anthology for the years 1789–1860, with brief biographical sketches. His estimates of Western verse writers are not critical, but the book is nevertheless a valuable record. It was designed as the first of a series of volumes, never continued, which should constitute a survey of Western literature and so offset the neglect which, as he thought, the West had suffered at the hands of Griswold and the Duyckincks. Both this work and *The Protective Policy* mark Coggeshall as a disciple of William D. Gallagher [*q.v.*], who, with James Hall and Timothy Flint [*q.v.*], was a pioneer partisan of a distinctly sectional literature for what in those days was called the West.

[Perhaps the best, as well as the most detailed, notice is that in W. H. Venable's *Beginnings of Literary Culture in the Ohio Valley* (1891), based, to a considerable extent, upon information furnished by Coggeshall's widow. A portrait is to be found in *Ohio Arch. and Hist. Quart.*, Jan. 1919, p. 104. Coggeshall's papers and diaries, including his Record of Facts Pertaining to Coggeshall Family, are in the possession of his son-in-law, Mr. T. A. Busbey of South Vienna, Ohio, who has supplied some of the dates given above. For the events of 1866–69, see *N. Y. Times*, Jan. 25 and Sept. 9, 1867; *Cincinnati Daily Gazette*, Sept. 6, 1867; *Ladies' Repository*, Nov. 1867; *House Ex. Doc. No. 1*, 39 Cong., 2 Sess., pt. II, p. 477; and especially *Cong. Globe*, 40

Cong., 3 Sess., 232–35 and 321. For the burial of Cogeshall and his daughter at Columbus, see *Ohio State Jour.*, Oct. 19, 1870.]

R. L. R.

COGSWELL, JOSEPH GREEN (Sept. 27, 1786–Nov. 26, 1871), teacher and librarian, was the son of Francis and Anstis (Manning) Cogswell and was born in Ipswich, Mass., where his immigrant ancestor, John Cogswell, had settled soon after having been wrecked off Pemaquid in 1635. His father died in 1793. Cogswell was educated at the grammar school in Ipswich and at Phillips Exeter Academy. He entered Harvard College at sixteen and graduated in 1806. From 1807 to 1809 he studied law under Fisher Ames and Judge Prescott, but a restless disposition and a love of travel led him to engage in a succession of mercantile ventures in Southern Europe, 1809–11, in which he experienced dangers from bandits and pirates and from the confiscation of ships and cargoes in Naples.

On Apr. 17, 1812 he married Mary F. Gilman, daughter of Gov. John T. Gilman, of New Hampshire, and began the practise of law in Belfast, Me. His wife dying in July 1813, he gave up the law and for two years was tutor in Latin at Harvard, but resigned on account of ill health. The next five years (1815–20) were spent for the most part in travel and study in Europe. At Göttingen (1817), Cogswell with Edward Everett and George Ticknor [*qq.v.*] constituted the first group of American scholars to resort to a German university (T. W. Higginson in *Harvard Graduates' Magazine*, VI, 1897, 6–18). At this time he became somewhat intimate with Goethe, with whom he corresponded for several years. It was evidently due to his high regard for Cogswell that Goethe presented a set of his works to Harvard in 1819 (Mackall, *post*). During the following years (1817–20) in Italy, Switzerland, France, and England, Cogswell was in close touch with the best society and with literary men. Having intimate relations with Israel Thorndike, a wealthy Boston merchant, whose son was under his care, he was instrumental in purchasing for the Harvard Library in 1818 the valuable American library of C. D. Ebeling, the librarian of Hamburg. In 1819 (February, March) he contributed to *Blackwood's Edinburgh Magazine* two anonymous essays: "On the Means of Education and the State of Learning in the United States of America," and "On the State of Learning in the United States of America." (These were reviewed, in the *North American Review* for September 1819 by Sidney Willard, who considered them a gross exaggeration of American deficiencies.) Returning to America in the fall of 1820, Cogswell was appointed librarian of the Harvard Library and

professor of mineralogy and geology. He reclassified the library, following Göttingen as a model, and was eager to introduce further improvements (*Life as Sketched in Letters*, pp. 133–35), but, discouraged by lack of support and understanding on the part of the College government, he resigned in 1823, and with George Bancroft [*q.v.*] established the Round Hill School in Northampton, Mass., a school well known for its strict but kindly discipline, its thorough instruction on the plan of the German *gymnasium*, and the vigorous outdoor life and manly spirit it fostered. Financial difficulties brought the school to an end in 1834. Hoping to free himself from debt, Cogswell took charge of a boys' school in Raleigh, N. C., but ill health and lack of sympathy with Southern habits and standards turned him again to the North after two years.

From 1836 to 1838 he lived in the family of his friend Samuel Ward in New York and tutored his children. At the former's suggestion he bought an interest in the quarterly *New York Review* to which he had already contributed a long anonymous article on "National Education" (July 1838). He partly edited the number for January 1839, soon after became sole proprietor, and conducted the *Review* until it was discontinued with the number for April 1842. While with the Wards he formed an acquaintance with John Jacob Astor [*q.v.*], and, gaining his respect and confidence, became his adviser with regard to the public library which Astor proposed to establish in New York. Until Astor's death in 1848 Cogswell continued in close association with the old man, who kept him occupied in buying books and making plans but never succeeded in arriving at final decisions and in establishing the library. In 1848, the trustees having organized, Cogswell was appointed superintendent and devoted himself to the purchase of books (involving four visits to Europe), to the erection of the building (opened in January 1854, with a stock of 90,000 volumes), and to the preparation of printed catalogues, the latter a task which he performed almost entirely by himself. The preliminary *Alphabetical Index to the Astor Library . . . and of the Proposed Accessions* (1851), was not only compiled entirely by Cogswell, but was also printed privately at his personal expense. He occupied rooms in the Library and his labors were unceasing. In December 1861, at the age of seventy-five, he resigned, being unable longer to perform his duties to his own satisfaction, yet within a year he undertook the compilation of a supplement to the catalogue, which demanded long days of persistent work and was not completed until October 1866. On his trips abroad in the interests of the library he had gratified a taste for art by accumulating for himself a collection of drawings of the old masters (see *Original Drawings by the Old Masters: The Collection formed by Joseph Green Cogswell 1786–1871*; with Introduction and notes by George S. Hellman, 1915).

Having built a house in Cambridge for a beloved niece of his wife (Mrs. David G. Haskins), he made his home there when not visiting his friends. In June 1871 he went for the last time to New York to advise the trustees of the Astor Library on the selection of a new librarian. He died in Cambridge, in November of that year, and was buried in Ipswich, his birthplace. His later years were made happy by the loyalty and affection of his former Round Hill pupils and other old-time friends, who appreciated his intellectual hospitality, his quick and keen perceptions, his wide attainments in literature and bibliography, and his firm principles of duty.

[An intimate view of Cogswell is given in the privately printed volume, *Life of Jos. Green Cogswell as Sketched in His Letters* (1874), ed. by Anna Eliot Ticknor; the earlier portion of his life is well told in T. F. Waters, "Augustine Heard and His Friends" (*i.e.*, J. G. Cogswell and Daniel Treadwell), *Ipswich Hist. Soc. Pubs.*, No. 21 (1916) and the later portion in H. M. Lydenberg, *Hist. of the N. Y. Pub. Lib.* (1923), pp. 1–55. For an account of the Round Hill School, see the *Prospectus of a School to Be Established at Round Hill, Northampton* (1823); *Some Account of the School for the Liberal Education of Boys Established on Round Hill* (1826), by Cogswell and Bancroft; and Cogswell's *Outline of the System of Education at the Round Hill School* (1831); also J. S. Bassett in *Proc. Am. Antiq. Soc.*, n.s., XXVII (1917), 18–62; and F. C. Shattuck in *Proc. Mass. Hist. Soc.*, LVII (1924), 205–09. Glimpses of Cogswell's life are found in Geo. Ticknor's *Life, Letters and Journals* (1876). His relations with Goethe are treated by Leonard L. Mackall in *Goethe-Jahrbuch*, 1904, and in *Essays Offered to Herbert Putnam by His Colleagues and Friends* (1929), ed. by Wm. Warner Bishop and Andrew Keogh; see also *Goethes Gespräche*, ed. by von Biedermann (5 vols., 1909–11), with further notes by Mackall. Other references are noted in A. C. Potter and C. K. Bolton, "The Librarians of Harvard College," *Harv. Univ. Bibliog. Contributions*, no. 52 (1897), p. 36, and in H. M. Lydenberg, "A Forgotten Trail Blazer," in *Essays Offered to Herbert Putnam*.]   W.C.L.

COGSWELL, WILLIAM BROWNE (Sept. 22, 1834–June 7, 1921), mining engineer, was born at Oswego, N. Y., the son of David and Mary (Barnes) Cogswell. His parents moved to Syracuse when he was four years old. His early education was acquired in private schools at Syracuse and Seneca Falls and at Hamilton Academy. When he was about twelve years old he took some lessons in architecture under Luther Gifford of Syracuse and plans drawn by Cogswell were used for the Globe Hotel, erected in Syracuse in 1846–47. His fourteenth year was spent with a railroad surveyor's party. He stud-

ied civil engineering at the Rensselaer Polytechnic Institute for three years, but left in 1852 without a degree. In 1884, however, the Institute conferred upon him the degree of C.E. After his work at Rensselaer he spent three years as an apprentice in machine-shops at Lawrence, Mass., and from then until 1860 he was actively engaged in responsible positions in foundries or machine-shops where his mechanical engineering abilities were marked. During the Civil War he held an appointment as civil engineer in the United States navy. He fitted out five repair shops for stations on the Atlantic seaboard, assembled equipment, and then converted an old whaler into a floating machine-shop, of which he took command. This enabled warships to be repaired without leaving the spots where they were participating in blockades of Southern ports. In 1862 Cogswell was transferred to the Brooklyn Navy Yard where he remained until 1866. After the war, supervision of the construction and operation of the blast furnaces of the Franklin Iron Works in Oneida County and the completion of the Clifton Suspension Bridge at Niagara Falls occupied him until 1873.

It is because of his share in the introduction into this country of the Solvay Process of manufacturing soda, however, that Cogswell is best known. His interest in "things under the earth" was awakened in 1874, when he was placed in charge of some lead mines at Mine La Motte, Mo. In 1879, at a meeting of the American Institute of Mining Engineers, he heard a paper by Oswald J. Heinrich on "The Manufacture of Soda by the Ammonia Process" (*Transactions*, VII, 294 ff.). He conceived the idea of applying the process patented by the Solvay brothers of Brussels to the exploitation of the salt lands of Onondaga County, N. Y. Going to Europe, he succeeded in persuading Ernest and Alfred Solvay of the soundness of his plan, and became treasurer and general manager of the Solvay Process Company formed in 1881. Later he became its vice-president and managing director. His company became the largest manufacturer in the United States of soda ash and its derivatives, and the production of soda became one of the major industries of Onondaga County. It was largely due to Cogswell's personal effort (and in the face of much opposition) that the vein of rock salt, fifty to a hundred feet in thickness, and 1,200 feet below the surface, was located twenty-two miles south of Syracuse at Tully. He was interested also in other local enterprises, especially in the development of the Hannawa Falls Power Company.

Cogswell built the Hospital of the Good Shepherd in Syracuse, and did much charitable work in a quiet way. He had a deep interest in astronomy, and found recreation and pleasure in gathering together a remarkable collection of precious stones. He was married twice: in 1856 to Mary N. Johnson, who died in 1877, and on Apr. 29, 1902, to Cora Louise Brown of New York City.

[*Trans. Am. Inst. Mining and Metallurgical Engineers*, LXVI (1922), pp. 838–40; H. B. Nason, *Biog. Record Officers and Grads. Rensselaer Polytechnic Inst.* (1887); *Railway Machinery*, Sept. 1906; Franklin H. Chase, *Syracuse and Its Environs* (1924), III, 380–83; W. M. Beauchamp, *Past and Present of Syracuse and Onondaga County, N. Y.* (1908), vol. II; *Who's Who in America, 1920–21*; *N. Y. Times*, June 8, 1921.]

E. Y.

COHEN, JACOB DA SILVA SOLIS (Feb. 28, 1838–Dec. 22, 1927), physician and physicist, was born in New York City, the eldest son of Myer David Cohen and his wife Judith Simiah da Silva Solis. His maternal grandmother was Charity Hayes, daughter of David Hayes, Jr., of Mount Pleasant, N. Y., and of his wife Esther Etting, of Baltimore, so that Cohen was descended from an old Jewish family and from an old colonial family. In 1840 his parents moved to Philadelphia, where he received his early education, graduating from the Philadelphia Central High School. During the session of 1857–58 he attended the Jefferson Medical College. In 1858–59 he spent a year in Memphis, Tenn., returning to Philadelphia in 1859 and resuming his medical studies at the University of Pennsylvania, from which institution he graduated in 1860. After graduation he was appointed one of the resident physicians of the Philadelphia Hospital, but resigned on the outbreak of the Civil War to enlist in the United States army as a private, soon being commissioned assistant surgeon in the 26th Pennsylvania Regiment. He served with this regiment in Hooker's brigade, but resigned in September 1861 to accept an appointment as acting assistant surgeon in the United States navy. He accompanied Du Pont's expedition to Port Royal and served in the South Atlantic Blockade Squadron, for a time as acting fleet surgeon. He resigned from the navy in January 1864 and was requested by the surgeon general of the United States to act as visiting surgeon to the two military hospitals in Philadelphia. *The Medical and Surgical History of the War of the Rebellion*, part III, vol. II (1882), indicates that he successfully carried out this work. He resigned in 1865, and, after a brief residence in New York, returned to Philadelphia in 1866 and entered private practise. On Feb. 10, 1875, he was married to Miriam Binswanger, by whom he had nine children.

Among his first patients was a young girl with an obscure disease of the throat, and this led him to make a study of the use of the laryngoscope, then just becoming known to the medical profession. He soon gained recognition as an expert in this work. In 1867 he was appointed by the American Medical Association chairman of a committee to investigate the value of treatment by inhalation. He accumulated so much material on the subject that he decided to publish it in book form, which he did, as *Inhalation; Its Therapeutics and Practice* (1867). In 1872 he published his well-known work *Diseases of the Throat*, for a time the only work of its scope in English, which he revised in 1879, under the title, *Diseases of the Throat and Nasal Passages*. Subsequent to this he published a small monograph on croup. During the remainder of his life he contributed a number of articles to medical literature, the best known being his articles on the operative treatment of cancer of the larynx (*Medical News*, vol. XLIII, 1883; *New York Medical Journal*, vol. XLV, 1887, p. 682). He also contributed chapters to various medical encyclopedias and systems. During this period he taught in the Jefferson Medical College and in the Philadelphia Polyclinic, of which he was one of the founders. Cohen had two interests outside of his professional work, the scientific aspect of acoustics and the religious life of his sect. He gave many popular lectures on acoustics and taught that subject for many years at the Stevens Institute of Technology in Hoboken. He was greatly interested in the traditional melodies of the Sephardic and Minhag, and for many years took part in the services of the Philadelphia synagogue which he attended.

[Information as to certain facts from Dr. Myer Solis-Cohen. See also *Who's Who in America, 1926–27*; *The Jeffersonian* (Phila., 1901); H. S. Morais, *The Jews of Phila.* (1894); *Jour. Am. Medic. Asso.*, Jan. 7, 1928; *Public Ledger* (Phila.), Dec. 1927.]

G. B.

COHEN, MENDES (May 4, 1831–Aug. 13, 1915), civil and railway engineer, was born in Baltimore, his home throughout his life. His first American ancestor settled in Lancaster, Pa., in 1773. The close of the Revolution found the family in Richmond, Va., and it was from that city that David I. Cohen went to Baltimore to enter the banking business. He was one of seven persons who founded in 1844 the (second) Baltimore Stock Board, which later became the Baltimore Stock Exchange. He married Harriet Rahmah Cohen, of Swansea, Wales, and Mendes was their eldest son. Upon the death of his father in 1847, Mendes, who had been under the instruction of a private tutor, entered the works of Ross Winans [*q.v.*], builder of locomotives. In 1851 he was made assistant to the engineer of the

Baltimore & Ohio Railroad, and while there worked out the method adopted for handling traffic on the ten per cent temporary grade over the Kingwood Tunnel, a remarkable achievement in railroad operation. Another task assigned him at that time was that of studying the alteration of wood-burning locomotives to coal-burning, and on Aug. 29, 1854, he presented a most comprehensive report on that subject. When only twenty-four years old, he had already become known as an especially capable railroad official, and was appointed assistant superintendent of the Hudson River Railroad. He was with that company until 1861, when he succeeded Gen. George B. McClellan as operating head of the Ohio & Mississippi Railroad, first as superintendent and later as president and superintendent. Soon after the close of the Civil War he was engaged for a short time on special work for the Philadelphia & Reading Railway. From 1868 to 1871 he was comptroller and assistant to the president of the Lehigh Coal & Navigation Company, and from 1872 to 1875 was president of the Pittsburgh & Connellsville Railroad, which was subsequently consolidated with the Baltimore & Ohio system. He retired in 1875 from official connections with any companies, but continued his practise in Baltimore as consulting engineer. The standard of ethics which he maintained in all his work is illustrated by his resignation from the presidency of one road when figures which he had furnished were altered before being presented to the stockholders of the company.

A prominent figure among civil engineers, Cohen was elected president of the American Society of Civil Engineers in 1881, an honor which he greatly appreciated. Nor in after years did he ever lose interest in the many problems arising in its affairs as a growing institution. He was a member of the board appointed in 1894 by President Cleveland to report on a route for the Chesapeake and Delaware Ship Canal. From 1893 to 1904 he was chairman of the Baltimore Sewerage Commission. He was a member of the Municipal Art Commission of Baltimore for thirty-three years, and for many years also an active member of the board of trustees of the Peabody Institute. His acquaintance with history, especially that of Maryland, was remarkable. For twenty-one years he was secretary of the Maryland Historical Society, serving for nine years as its president. He was also vice-president of the American Jewish Historical Society from 1897 to 1902. Cohen was a serious, religious man; socially of the best, and a strong and influential citizen in Baltimore. He was consulted in all matters of great importance, and his judgment, always given after deliberate consideration, had great weight. He was survived by his wife, Justina Nathan Cohen, who died in 1918.

[*Trans. Am. Soc. Civil Engineers*, vol. LXXXI (1917); files of the Md. Hist. Soc. and the *Md. Hist. Mag.*, Mar. 1924; *Engineering News*, Aug. 19, 1915; *Am. Jewish Hist Soc. Pubs.*, no. 25 (1916); the *Sun* (Baltimore), Aug. 14, 1915; *Jewish Comment* (Baltimore), Aug. 20, 1915.]   K. W. C.

COIT, HENRY AUGUSTUS (Jan. 20, 1830– Feb. 5, 1895), Episcopal clergyman, schoolmaster, was born in Wilmington, Del., the second of the nine children of Joseph Howland and Harriet Jane (Hard) Coit, and the seventh in descent from John Coite, a Welshman, who landed at Salem, Mass., in 1636 and established a shipyard at New London, Conn., in 1650. His father, a graduate of Columbia College, was converted to Episcopalianism while a student in Princeton Theological Seminary and served as pastor of churches in Wilmington, Del., Plattsburg, N. Y., and Harrisburg, Pa. By a happy choice Henry Coit was sent at fifteen to St. Paul's College at College Point, Flushing, L. I., where he felt to the full the moral and religious power of William Augustus Muhlenberg [*q.v.*]. No other man so influenced his life and thought. He matriculated at the University of Pennsylvania in 1847 but was soon compelled to leave because of illness. To recruit his health he went to Georgia as tutor in the family of Bishop Stephen Elliott. Subsequently he taught under John Barrett Kerfoot in St. James College at Hagerstown, Md., and in a parish school at Lancaster, Pa. He was ordained deacon by Alonzo Potter at Lancaster Jan. 22, 1854, and priest in Philadelphia Dec. 3, 1854, and began home missionary work at Ellenburg, Clinton County, N. Y. Meanwhile George Cheyne Shattuck the younger and some associates projected a church school for boys to be opened in Concord, N. H. Their first choice having declined, they offered the rectorship of the school to Coit, who accepted it. On Mar. 27, 1856, he was married in Philadelphia to Mary Bowman Wheeler, and one week later he entered on his duties as the first rector of St. Paul's School in Concord, N. H. He held the rectorship until his death thirty-nine years later. His school, which on its opening day consisted of the rector and his bride with three pupils in a lonely farmhouse, became one of the most successful and most often imitated of American boys' schools. Coit gave himself to the work with complete singleness of purpose and with the energy and resources of a man of genius. St. Paul's School was his lengthened shadow; without striving to do so or even intending to do so, he dominated the pupils, the masters, and the board of trustees. To him the purpose of education was the formation of character, and character that Miltonic union of true virtue and the heavenly grace of faith which make up the highest perfection. What he actually accomplished was, he knew, inexpressibly below his aims and ideals, but it was sufficient to rank him with Arnold of Rugby, Fellenberg of Hofwyl, and his own teacher, Muhlenberg. He had a profound understanding of boys, and a rich gift of humor; and his strong, exquisite, unselfish, deeply religious personality left an enduring impress on their minds. He made no innovations in the course of study or the methods of instruction; it was his moral and religious influence over those in immediate contact with him that made him a great educator.

Coit had few intimate friends, lived much within himself, and avoided the world. Calls to various influential parishes and to the presidency of Hobart and Trinity Colleges he declined. Once he wrote a letter to a newspaper, and once he was persuaded to contribute to *The Forum* an article on boys' schools. The death in 1888 of his wife was a grievous loss to him; his own health visibly declined during 1894, and on Feb. 5, 1895, he died after a brief illness. He was buried in Concord. A volume of his *School Sermons* was published in 1909. Joseph Howland Coit, his brother, succeeded him as rector of the School; another brother, James Milnor Coit, was for years one of the masters of the School and later conducted the Coit School for American Boys in Munich.

[J. H. Coit, *Memorials of St. Paul's School* (1891); *Univ. of Pa. Biog. Cat. of the Matriculates of the Coll. 1749–1893* (1894); obituary in *Church Eclectic*, Mar. 1895; J. P. Conover, *Memories of a Great Schoolmaster* (1906); J. J. Chapman, "The Influence of Schools" in *Learning and Other Essays* (1910); J. C. Knox, *Henry Augustus Coit* (1915); O. Wister, "Dr. Coit of St. Paul's" in the *Atlantic Monthly*, Dec. 1928.]

G. H. G.

COIT, HENRY LEBER (Mar. 16, 1854–Mar. 12, 1917), physician, was born at Peapack, N. J., the son of John Summerfield and Ellen (Neafie) Coit. His father, a Methodist minister, died while Henry was still a boy, and his mother moved to Newark to bring up her children. There Coit attended the public schools and went from them to the New York College of Pharmacy, from which he graduated as valedictorian with the class of 1876. After working for a few years as a chemist with Tarrant & Company, he entered the College of Physicians and Surgeons, and upon his graduation in 1883 began his practise of medicine in Newark. In 1886 he married Emma Gwinnell of that city. Pediatrics had already become his chief interest when in 1889 the difficulty of obtaining cows' milk of a uniform high standard was forcibly brought home to him. In seeking clean milk for his own dying baby he saw the forty-quart cans from which the city's milk was being casually ladled. The experience indicated to him his life-work. He lost his own son, but his unremitting efforts to raise the standards of cleanliness for milk and to impress on the public and on the medical profession the relation between milk and infant mortality have saved the lives of countless children. Failing, after persistent appeals, to obtain help from the New Jersey legislature, he enlisted the voluntary aid of physicians and dairymen. In a paper read before the Practitioners' Club of Newark on Dec. 5, 1890, he coined the term "certified milk" and outlined the method by which the initial cleanliness of milk might be insured. His plan "provided for a commission of medical men who, with the support of physicians generally, should, by voluntary supervision, paid expert inspection, and final certification, endeavor to influence a supply of milk produced under regulations imposed by themselves." He formulated minute regulations for securing clean hands, clean udders, clean pails, sterile containers, healthy cows, safe workingmen, good feed and fodder, suitable bedding, and proper housing. In 1893 his plan was put into effect on a dairy farm near Fairfield, N. J., and was shown to be practicable, in spite of the greatly increased cost of production. To the dairyman the principal danger came from the unscrupulous opposition of large milk distributing companies. The example of the Essex County Medical Milk Commission was imitated in New York in 1896 and in Philadelphia in 1897; at the time of Coit's death there were sixty such commissions in the United States, and the movement had spread to Canada, Europe, and Asia. An American Association of Medical Milk Commissions, of which Coit was twice president, kept the commissions in touch with one another. The indirect effect of these commissions in raising the general standard of cleanliness among dairymen has been enormous. Coit was also vice-president of the International Society of Milk Dispensaries, with headquarters in Brussels, and visited Europe four times as a delegate to medical congresses.

The other great work of his life began in 1896 with the opening in Newark of the Babies' Hospital, the second institution of its kind in the United States. He had done much to make the hospital possible, and to its welfare he gave time and attention without stint, his last visit to it as attending physician being made on the day before his death from pneumonia. His death was undoubtedly hastened by overwork. An epidemic of infantile paralysis had visited Newark and its vicinity the previous summer. Sacrificing his vacation, Coit had taken active charge of the medical relief work and had accomplished a task that alone would entitle him to the gratitude of his fellow citizens. His published papers are: *The Feeding of Infants* (1890); *The Care of the Baby* (1894); *Causation of Disease by Milk* (1894); *Clean Milk in its Economic and Medical Relations with Special Reference to Certified Milk* (1908); *The Public School as a Factor in Preventing Infant and Child Mortality* (1912); and *Certified Milk* (1912).

[H. A. Kelly in Kelly and Burrage, *Am. Med. Biogs.* (1920); *N. Y. Times*, Mar. 14, 1917; *Newark Evening News*, Mar. 13, 14, 15, 1917; *Newark Sunday Call*, Mar. 18, 1917; *Archives of Pediatrics*, XXXIV, 212.]

                              G.H.G.

COIT, THOMAS WINTHROP (June 28, 1803–June 21, 1885), Episcopal clergyman, theologian, was born in New London, Conn., the son of Thomas and Mary Wanton (Saltonstall) Coit. On both sides of the family he was of early New England stock. His father and his father's father were physicians in New London. Coit graduated from Yale College in 1821, taught school for several years, attended Andover Theological Seminary 1823–24 and Princeton Seminary 1824–25, was led by his studies to withdraw from the Congregational Church and to join the Episcopalian, was ordained a deacon by Bishop Brownell at Newton, Conn., June 7, 1826, and a priest by Bishop Griswold at Salem, Mass., Nov. 15, 1827. On June 28, 1828, he married a widow, Eleanor (Forrester) Carlile of Salem, Mass. He was rector of St. Peter's, Salem, until 1829 and of Christ Church, Cambridge, until 1835. In 1834 he began his career as a theologian by measuring himself against no less an antagonist than Andrews Norton; his *Remarks on Mr. Norton's "Statement of Reasons"* was, however, a belated rejoinder, for *Norton's Statement of Reasons for Not Believing the Doctrine of Trinitarians* had appeared in 1819, when Coit was still a student in college. In 1834 he also published his *Holy Bible . . . Arranged in Paragraphs and Parallelisms with Philological and Explanatory Annotations,* which was long prized by students for the trustworthiness of its text. In October 1834 he was called to the presidency of Transylvania University at Lexington, Ky., on a salary of $2,000 a year; he was inaugurated July 1, 1835, and resigned in September 1837—presumably with relief, for the institution was dying

of inanition and of denominational squabbles among its trustees, and Coit had been unable to ameliorate the situation. He edited in 1837 an American edition of Townsend's *New Testament Arranged in Historical and Chronological Order* and followed it in 1838 with a similar edition of Townsend's *Old Testatment.* Subsequently he was rector of Trinity Church, New Rochelle, N. Y., 1839–49, professor of church history in Trinity College, Hartford, Conn., 1849–54, rector of St. Paul's, Troy, N. Y., and lecturer in the Berkeley Divinity School, Middletown, Conn., 1854–72, and professor of church history in the Divinity School from 1872 until his death in 1885. In that year he was able to report to his bishop that he had performed all his teaching duties punctually and had also preached regularly in neighboring churches. In 1844 he submitted to the joint committee which the General Convention had appointed to prepare a standard *Prayerbook* a report (reprinted in *Jour. of the Gen. Convention of the P. E. Church in the U. S. 1868*) that displays minute liturgical scholarship and excellent taste. His *Puritanism, or a Churchman's Defence against its Aspersions by an Appeal to its own History* (1845) was his best-known work. The book combined sarcasm and solid, well-documented learning in a way difficult to answer; it had its day of fame and is still readable. Coit also published lectures on the *Early History of Christianity in England* (1859) and various sermons. He was an able student of the Bible, of liturgics, and of church history, a zealous churchman, and the master of a dignified, vigorous English. His theological library of 14,000 volumes now belongs to the Berkeley Divinity School.

[F. W. Chapman, *The Coit Family* (1874); L. Saltonstall, *Ancestry and Descendants of Sir Richard Saltonstall* (1897); *Cat. of Grads. of Yale Univ. 1701–1892* (1892); *Gen. Cat. of the Theol. Sem. Andover, Mass., 1808–1908* (n.d.); *Necrological Reports . . . of the Alumni Association of Princeton Theol. Sem. 1875–89* (1891); R. Peter, *Transylvania University* (1896); W. S. Perry, *Hist. of the Am. Epis. Ch. 1587–1883* (1885); *Churchman*, June 27, 1885; Hartford, Conn., *Daily Courant*, June 23, 1885.]   G.H.G.

COKE, RICHARD (Mar. 13, 1829–May 14, 1897), governor of Texas, United States senator, was born in Williamsburg, Va. Descended from John Coke who emigrated from England to Virginia in 1724, he was the son of another John and Eliza (Hawkins) Coke. He received his early education in the common schools of Williamsburg, entered William and Mary College in 1845, and graduated in 1849 with honors. He studied law and was admitted to the bar. In 1850 he removed to Waco, Texas, then a new village on the frontier. Here his personality, ability, and industry speedily won him recognition and he became known as one of the leading lawyers of his section of the state before he was thirty years old. In 1852 he married Mary Elizabeth Horne of Waco. In 1858 difficulties arose between the settlers on the frontier and the reservation Indians on the upper Brazos and a general war was threatened. In 1859 Coke was a member of a commission, appointed by Gov. Runnels, which induced the Indians to remove to the Indian Territory, and restored peace. When the great crisis of 1860 arose, Coke favored secession and was a member of the Texas secession convention of 1861. In 1862 he raised for the Confederate service an infantry company which became a part of the 15th Texas Regiment, and as captain of this company he served throughout the rest of the war in Arkansas, Louisiana and Texas. When the war ended, he returned to the practise of law at Waco. Soon afterward he was appointed by Provisional Governor A. J. Hamilton judge of the district court. When the government of Texas had been reorganized in 1866 under President Johnson's policy, he was elected an associate justice of the state supreme court on the conservative ticket. He served only one year, for in the summer of 1867, after the passage of the Reconstruction acts, he was included in the wholesale removal of state officials by Gen. Sheridan, the military commander, as "an impediment to reconstruction." During the next six years he added to his reputation as a lawyer and became one of the leaders of the reorganized Democratic party which was seeking to recover control of the state from the radical Republicans. In 1873, as the Democratic nominee for the governorship, he defeated the Republican candidate, Gov. E. J. Davis, by a vote of two to one. The Republicans sought to retain control by contesting the legality of the election, and the Republican state supreme court in the case *ex parte* Rodriguez actually declared the election void. The newly-elected state legislature assembled, and Gov. Davis stationed negro militia in the state-house and appealed to President Grant for military support. Grant refused to interfere, and Davis, to avoid armed conflict, vacated his office. Coke was inaugurated on Jan. 15, 1874. His administration was beset with many difficulties. The retiring heads of departments had made no reports; the state government was in debt and without funds; the frontiers were unprotected; Indians ravaged the western settlements; and Mexican bandits raided the valley of the lower Rio Grande. The whole state was suffering from lawlessness, the product of years of war and civil disturbances during the Reconstruction period.

Coke set himself to remedy these evils. By appealing to the United States military authorities and by the judicious use of rangers and state militia he obtained protection against the Indians and broke up the bands of outlaws. By encouraging rigid economy he reduced the expenses of the government and made a new beginning of the public-school system. Reëlected governor, he was inaugurated in April 1876, and in the following month he was elected United States senator. As senator he endeavored to obtain federal protection for the Rio Grande frontier against Mexican bandits and to assist in deepening the harbors of Texas ports. He supported the free-coinage silver bill of 1878 and advocated the repeal of the Resumption Act. He seconded the efforts of John H. Reagan to bring interstate railways under federal control, and worked for the Interstate Commerce Act of 1887. He opposed the Blair Bill for federal aid to local schools on the score of constitutionality; and fought the protective tariff, the suspension of silver coinage, and the Force Bill. In all these matters he had the confidence and support of the great majority of his Texas constituents. He was reëlected without opposition in 1882 and again in 1888. In 1894 he declined reëlection and spent the short remainder of his life at his home in Waco, near which he had an extensive plantation. Coke was a man of spotless integrity, strong common sense, and unwavering fidelity to every trust reposed in him.

[Jas. D. Lynch, *The Bench and Bar of Texas* (1885); C. W. Ramsdell, *Reconstruction in Texas* (1910); D. G. Wooten, *Comprehensive Hist. of Texas* (1898), vol. II; *Dallas News*, May 14, 15, and 16, 1897.]

C. W. R.

COKE, THOMAS (Sept. 9, 1747–May 3, 1814), Methodist bishop, was the only surviving child of Bartholomew and Anne Phillips Coke. He was born in Brecon, Wales, where his father was a prosperous apothecary and small office-holder. He looked back upon his youth as a period of indiscretion, for he had been gay and handsome and fond of dancing, cards, and liquor. A troubled conscience at times caused him to wrestle with the prevalent infidelity at Oxford, but when he graduated from Jesus College in 1768 he was merely an academic Christian. When his patient hopes of church preferment were dashed, he obtained a small curacy at Road, Somersetshire, in 1770, and later at South Petherton in the same county. There, from the eloquence and vehemence of his preaching, his parishioners suspected that he was tainted with Methodism. Meetings with Thomas Maxfield, one of Wesley's lay preachers, and with Hull, a dissenting minister of South Petherton, further attracted him to the Methodist group. In August 1776 he met Wesley. His preaching became more fervent and evangelical, and he was dismissed from his church by the ancient ceremony of chiming. He then joined Wesley and attended the Bristol conference in 1777. During his ministry in London, he assisted Wesley in his vast correspondence. In 1782 he became the first president of the Irish conference, an office which he held for many years. Two years later he outlined the first Methodist scheme for the establishment of missions among the heathen, a work in which he was later to become preëminent.

After long deliberation, Wesley drew up a plan for the necessary organization of the Methodist church in America, which he revealed to Coke in February 1784. So unprecedented a measure startled Coke and two months of reflection were necessary to overcome his doubts. At Bristol, on Sept. 2, Wesley ordained Richard Whatcoat and Thomas Vasey as presbyters for America and appointed Coke the first superintendent; several weeks later these three sailed from England "to go and serve the desolate sheep in America." Arriving in New York on Nov. 3, Coke preached several times before proceeding to Philadelphia where he was entertained by the governor. He traveled southward into Delaware and at Barratt's Chapel in Kent County he was met by Francis Asbury [q.v.]. When he had explained the instructions of Wesley, Asbury professed to be shocked and for a time refused to be ordained. With his astute political sense, Asbury realized what Coke hardly suspected: that the trend of Methodism in America was away from Wesley. Hence Asbury refused to exercise the duties of his office unless elected by a majority of the American itinerants. A general conference to be held in Baltimore during Christmas week was determined upon, and Coke went on a thousand-mile preaching tour in Maryland and Virginia. On Dec. 17 the leaders assembled near Baltimore to prepare for the work of the conference, and a week later, in Baltimore, the conference, presided over by Coke but dominated by Asbury, was opened. Coke and the two presbyters ordained Asbury on successive days a deacon, an elder, and general superintendent, a title that Asbury himself changed to bishop.

From 1784 to 1803 Coke made nine voyages to America. He was tireless in his labors for American Methodism; and his lengthy and arduous preaching tours were fruitful. Yet his career in America was a series of conflicts and misunderstandings. In his numerous disputes with Asbury he was inevitably unsuccessful. His solitary triumph over Asbury, who desired mere-

ly a Methodist school, was Cokesbury College, founded at Abingdon, Md., in 1787; but even this was not lasting, for in December 1795 the college was completely destroyed by fire. When, during the third conference, Coke suggested that the continent be divided between himself and Asbury as bishops, Asbury secured the passage of a resolution "consenting" that Coke remain in England until recalled and limiting the exercise of his duties as bishop. Although the control of Coke in American Methodism was merely nominal, Asbury remained jealous of the empty priority of consecration that he enjoyed. A storm of criticism broke upon both Asbury and Coke when they, with considerable courage, took a firm stand against slavery. In 1785 they presented an anti-slavery petition to George Washington at Mount Vernon. In June of 1789 Coke committed a serious indiscretion when he assisted Asbury in preparing a congratulatory address to Washington as president of the United States; for this the English conference at Bristol formally rebuked him. His efforts to unite the Methodist and Episcopal churches in America in 1791 produced great indignation and were as fruitless as were his similar efforts in England eight years later. He did not return to America after 1803. In 1790 the first Methodist missionary committee had been formed in England with Coke as its head; when the missionary organization was revised in 1804 Coke was made its president. His conspicuous success in the work of the foreign missions gained him a high and enduring place in the history of Methodism.

[*Extracts of the Journals of the Rev. Dr. Coke's Five Visits to America* (London, 1793); Samuel Drew, *Life of the Rev. Thos. Coke* (London, 1817); J. W. Etheridge, *Life of the Rev. Thos. Coke* (London, 1860); W. A. Candler, *Life of Thos. Coke* (1923); Herbert Asbury, *A Methodist Saint: the Life of Bishop Asbury* (1927). For his later career, see Alexander Gordon, "Thomas Coke," in *Dictionary of National Biography*.]
F.M.

COKER, JAMES LIDE (Jan. 3, 1837–June 25, 1918), manufacturer, philanthropist, was born on a large plantation near Society Hill, S. C., an old Welsh settlement, the son of Caleb and Hannah (Lide) Coker. He early manifested fondness for agriculture, which remained one of the primary interests of his life. After preliminary training at a local academy and at the South Carolina Military Institute of Charleston, he entered Harvard in 1857 for special work in soil analysis and plant development. His courses under Agassiz and Asa Gray delighted him, but when he was given by his father a substantial estate near Hartsville, he returned the following year to undertake actual farming. He organized at once an agricultural society for the dissemination of scientific ideas. On Mar. 28, 1860, he married Susan Stout of Alabama. At the outbreak of the war he volunteered and was commissioned captain of Company E, 6th South Carolina Infantry. After two years of hard fighting in Virginia, he was transferred to Tennessee, wounded at Lookout Mountain, promoted major, and at Missionary Ridge was captured. Paroled in July 1864, he returned to his ruined plantation.

A brief experience in the legislature, 1864–66, taught him that he had no desire for public life. He thereupon devoted himself to business. His ventures were varied and uniformly successful. He continued to farm for fifty years after his return and never once had an unprofitable season. In 1866 he opened a small country store at Hartsville which grew in time into one of the largest department stores of the state. From 1874 until 1881 he was a member of Norwood & Coker, dealers at Charleston in cotton and naval supplies. In 1884 he organized the Darlington National Bank. Five years later he built a small railroad from Darlington to Hartsville, subsequently purchased by the Atlantic Coast Line. In the same year he organized, with the aid of his son, James L. Coker, Jr., the Carolina Fiber Company, first corporation to make on a practical scale wood pulp from the pine wood so common in that section. A few years later he promoted the Southern Novelty Company, manufacturing from paper the cones and parallel tubes used by yarn mills for shipping the yarn. In the nineties he organized the Hartsville Cotton Mill, the Hartsville Cotton-Seed Oil Mill, and the Bank of Hartsville. Meantime, cooperating with his son, David R. Coker, he developed on his farm one of the South's principal experimental agencies for seed-testing and plant development. With the exception of four years spent in Charleston from 1877, he lived at Hartsville.

Deeply though tolerantly religious, Coker was interested in all phases of social welfare, particularly in education. In 1908 he made an initial subscription of $85,000 in land and $150,000 in cash for the establishment of a college for women in Hartsville. He added further donations; and it was due almost exclusively to his efforts that this institution, now called Coker College, was able to meet the requirements for standard colleges for women. Virtually bankrupt at the close of the war, he accumulated one of the largest private fortunes in the history of South Carolina. He was the state's most versatile business man, one of its most cultivated gentlemen, and the foremost South Carolina philanthropist of his generation.

[J. W. Norwood, "Major James Lide Coker" in H. T.

Cook, *Rambles in the Pee Dee Basin* (1926), App.; Edwin Mims, "The South Realizing Itself" in the *World's Work*, Oct. 1911; James Lide Coker, *Memorial Exercises, Founder's Day, Coker Coll.* (1919).]

F. P. G.

COLBURN, DANA POND (Sept. 29, 1823–Dec. 15, 1859), educator and author of numerous school books, was born in West Dedham, Mass. He was the youngest of a family of fifteen born to Isaac and Mary Colburn (*Dedham Records of Births, Marriages and Deaths,* vols. I and II, 147) both hardy New Englanders who reared their children "to subsist by honest toil." His early annals are brief. He obtained "a good English education" in the town school, showing an early marked preference for mathematics and exhibiting a philosophical turn of mind. The neighborhood Lyceum, the school of Joseph Underwood, and the Bridgewater (Mass.) Normal School, where he came under the powerful influence of Nicholas Tillinghast [*q.v.*], furnished the rest of his formal education.

Fresh from the discipline of the normal school, he plunged into teaching, a profession he never relinquished. First at Dover and Sharon, Mass., then at East Greenwich, R. I., and, finally, at Brookline, Mass., he exhibited such a mastery of common-school problems and such skill as a teacher that he drew the attention of Horace Mann. He was invited in 1847 to begin institute work, which he carried on with the greatest success till his death. He gave lessons in orthography and geography, but in arithmetic he excelled as a teacher. The path soon opened which led him to become a teacher of teachers. After 1848, when he became assistant in the Bridgewater institution, his work centered in normal schools. After 1852, he taught in a private normal school at Providence, becoming its principal in 1854, when it was changed to the Rhode Island Normal School. Three years later he transferred, with the State Normal School, to Bristol, where, in 1859, at the height of his success, he was accidentally killed, a few days before he was to have been married.

Colburn's popularity as a teacher owed much to his keen imagination, boundless enthusiasm for his subject, and love for those whom he taught. His chief contribution to teaching was in his emphasis on the rational rather than the memory method. With him study was to be a pleasure. As a true Pestalozzian, he surveyed the Hill of Knowledge and sought to lay out new approaches, avoiding unnecessary crags which impeded the progress of beginners. In his textbooks illustrations relieved the usually tedious pages. He published *First Steps in Numbers* (1845), *Decimal System* (1852), *Interest and*

Discount (1853), *Arithmetic and Its Applications* (1855), *Common School Arithmetic* (1858), *Child's Book of Arithmetic* (1859), and *Intellectual Arithmetic* (1859). Numerous articles and accounts of demonstration lessons by Colburn appeared in the *Rhode Island Schoolmaster* (1855–59) and other educational periodicals. In his brief life he outstripped the accomplishments of most contemporaries. His elaborate plans for the improvement of the teaching of mathematics, which included more advanced arithmetics, a geometry, and an algebra, were frustrated by his death.

[The best published account is the *Memoir of Dana P. Colburn,* republished from Barnard's *Am. Jour. of Education,* March 1862. Sketches, with notices of his death, appeared in the *R. I. Schoolmaster,* vol. VI, 1860, 26–28; *Bristol Phenix,* Dec. 17, 1859; *R. I. Pendulum,* Dec. 17, 24; and the *Providence Jour.,* Dec. 16, 1859. The file of the *R. I. Schoolmaster* (1855–59) throws light on many of Colburn's activities; and Thos. W. Bicknell, *Hist. of the R. I. Normal School* (1911), gives an account of his service there.]   T. W.

COLBURN, IRVING WIGHTMAN (May 16, 1861–Sept. 4, 1917), manufacturer, inventor, was born in Fitchburg, Mass., the eldest son of Henry Joseph and Eliza Ann (Siner) Colburn, both of English ancestry. The early history of Massachusetts records the pioneer activities of three Colburn brothers in textile manufacture and their mathematical and inventive abilities. Early in Irving's life these inherited characteristics were revealed. His father, manager of a machine works and an inventor of wood-working machinery, had a well-equipped mechanical shop in his home, and here Colburn after school spent all of his time. Electrical experimentation especially attracted him, even before graduating from high school, and after spending a few years in the machine works with his father, he established at the age of twenty-two Fitchburg's first agency for the sale of electrical equipment. Within a year or two he began in a small way and as a side issue, the manufacture of dynamos and motors of his own design and, using one of his machines, made the first electric lighting installation in Fitchburg. He also installed the city's first telephone system. In 1891 Colburn organized the Colburn Electric Company in Fitchburg to engage in electrical equipment manufacture. The business thrived so well that four years later a new and larger plant was built. Difficulties then arose in securing working capital, chiefly because Colburn was financially unknown, his manufactured products having been sold under the name of his distributor; and after three years of unsuccessful effort to correct this error, the business was discontinued. Colburn then went to Toledo, Ohio, and like his father who

had preceded him there, became interested in glass manufacture. His innate inventive turn led him to experimentation in the fashioning of glass by mechanical means and eventually to drawing continuous sheets; and for the succeeding nineteen years until his death, he was engrossed in the solution of these problems. His work attracted to him world-wide attention and was crowned with success just a year before he died, when his process became the basis of the commercially successful Libbey-Owens Sheet Glass Company. While his headquarters were in Toledo, Colburn conducted his preliminary work from 1899 to 1907 in Frankford, Pa., patenting a number of glass-working machines as they were developed. For the next four years he was at work in Franklin, Pa., chiefly on a process for blowing tumblers and lamp chimneys, and it was while thus engaged that he began his experiment of mechanically drawing continuous sheets of glass. His basic patent, No. 876,267, was granted Jan. 7, 1908 and assigned to the Colburn Machine Glass Company. After several years of experimentation and the expenditure of much money with no appreciable financial return to his backers, Colburn sold his patents in 1912 to large financial glass interests in Toledo. With his assistance the process was brought to perfection in 1916 and a $2,000,000 plant was built near Charleston, W. Va. Colburn was married to Ida E. Hamlin of Toledo, who survived him.

[Fitchburg Hist. Soc., correspondence; J. M. Killits, *Toledo and Lucas County, Ohio,* vol. II (1923); *Scientific American, Supp.,* May 16, 1908.]   C. W. M.

COLBURN, WARREN (Mar. 1, 1793–Sept. 13, 1833), author, was the firstborn of Richard Colburn, a farmer of Dedham, Mass., and Joanna Eaton, his wife. At the age of four he began summer district school, and at seven or eight, winter school at Milford, whither by that time his parents had moved. About 1806 they moved again to Uxbridge where he continued to attend the winter terms of the district school. In the course of this schooling he had revealed his interest and expertness in arithmetic, and his father to encourage this bent took into his family an infirm schoolmaster, who was known as a "good cipherer." The instruction Warren got from him and at the district school constituted all the book-learning he had until 1815. By that time he had mastered the trades of weaver and machinist and had been employed for five years at the latter occupation. In the summer of that year he began to prepare for Harvard College which he entered in 1816. Here, too, he showed a strong interest in mathematics along with physical science. His graduation thesis was "On the

Benefit Accruing to an Individual from a Knowledge of the Physical Sciences." He included in his mathematical study calculus and the recently published works of Laplace. During his college course he taught winter terms of school at Boston, Leominster, and Canton, and on graduation in 1820 opened a private school in Boston. It was while he was teaching there that he wrote his text-books in arithmetic. The earliest of these bore the title, *First Lessons in Arithmetic, on the Plan of Pestalozzi, with some improvements* (1821). This remained the title till 1826 when it was changed to *Colburn's First Lessons. Intellectual Arithmetic upon the Inductive Method of Instruction.* This title was retained thereafter. In 1822 his second arithmetic appeared, *Arithmetic; Being a Sequel to the First Lessons in Arithmetic.* In 1825 he published *An Introduction to Algebra upon the Inductive Method of Instruction.* His arithmetics, which almost immediately leaped into public favor and came to be used very widely both in this country and abroad, are still being published. Though he profited by Pestalozzi's theories, these books were the product of his own experience as a teacher and of his own genius. They transformed the school study of arithmetic from a blind following of rules to a reasoned solution of problems excellently adapted to the stages of development of the child's power, and marked the beginning of a new epoch in the teaching of this study. In 1823 Colburn gave up teaching to accept the superintendency of a cotton-mill at Waltham and in the following year became superintendent of the mill of the Merrimack Manufacturing Company at Lowell, Mass., remaining in this position until his death. In the last years of his life, 1830–33, he published a graded series of *Lessons in Reading and Grammar*. In 1826 he was elected to the first school-board of Lowell and was twice reëlected. He was one of the founders of the American Institute of Instruction in Boston and made before them many addresses, that of 1830 on "The Teaching of Arithmetic" being especially memorable. He was elected a fellow of the American Academy of Arts and Sciences and a member of the examining committee for mathematics at Harvard. From year to year he delivered before local lyceums and mechanics' associations, which he helped much to promote, lectures upon scientific subjects. From 1827 on he was a communicant in the Episcopal Church which he served as warden. On Aug. 28, 1823, he married Temperance C. Horton, whom he had had as a pupil while as college student he was teaching in Canton. By her he had four sons and three daughters. His disposition was char-

acterized by its unvarying cheerfulness and serenity. Rather tall and well-proportioned, he was attractive in appearance, suggesting intelligence, refinement, and benevolence.

[The best sources are a biographical sketch by a contemporary, Theodore Edson, in Henry Barnard's *Am. Jour. of Educ.*, Sept. 1856, pp. 294–316; and Walter Scott Monroe's monograph on the "Development of Arithmetic as a School Subject," *U. S. Bureau of Educ. Bull.*, 1917, no. 10. See also *Boston Transcript*, Aug. 8, 1884.]

W. J. C.

COLBURN, ZERAH (Sept. 1, 1804–Mar. 2, 1839), mathematical prodigy, son of Abiah and Elizabeth (Hall) Colburn, was born in Cabot and died in Norwich, Vt. When he was less than six years old, it was discovered that he could solve rapidly in his head any problem of arithmetic that was assigned to him. His father, a poor man already nearing fifty, recognized in the child's unique ability a means of gaining a livelihood for his wife and nine children. He exhibited the prodigy throughout New England, and as far south as Richmond, and in April 1812, leaving only a small debt-incumbered farm as support for the family, set out with him for England. In London, erudition, nobility, and even royalty acclaimed the marvel of Zerah's faculty; but Paris, "owing," Zerah thought, "to the native frivolity and lightness of the people" (*Memoir, post*, p. 74) received him without enthusiasm. His schooling was spasmodic, and no more than moderately effective even in mathematics. His French residence of eighteen months, beginning July 1814, was financially disastrous, but half of it was spent under regular instruction at the Lycée Napoléon.

During 1816–19, public interest in mathematical prodigies having ceased, the boy attended Westminster School, under the patronage of an earl, a period in which he distinguished himself chiefly by his rebellion against "fagging." Angered because funds which he thought properly destined for himself were being diverted elsewhere, the father quarreled with the Earl of Bristol who had favored him. Soon, plagued by poverty, he urged his son to redeem their fortunes by a career on the stage. Zerah complied as usual, but poverty still followed them, and in his extremity the boy turned school-master. The father died in 1824 and soon afterward the son returned to America. Here he gave his attention so earnestly to religion that to his surprise he was early pronounced "a child of grace" and received into the Congregational Church (*Ibid.,* pp. 155–56). Doctrinal questions of free-will and foreordination continued unanswered, and he could not feel spiritually at home, until, affiliating himself with the Methodists and becoming a minister, he set out on a nine years' itinerancy in

Vermont. In 1833, he published *A Memoir of Zerah Colburn Written by Himself*, and in 1835, he ended his official career as a minister to become professor of languages in Norwich University. His prowess in mental arithmetic, though somewhat impaired, remained with him always. He was married on Jan. 13, 1829 to Mary Hoyt, by whom he had six children. He died from tuberculosis.

[In addition to Colburn's *Memoir*, see G. A. Gordon and S. A. Colburn, *Geneal. of the Descendants of Edward Colburn-Coburn* (1913); P. C. Dodge, *Encyc. Vt. Biog.* (1912).]   J.D.W.

COLBY, FRANK MOORE (Feb. 10, 1865–Mar. 3, 1925), editor, author, was born in Washington, D. C., of New England stock, the son of Stoddard Benham and Ellen Cornelia (Hunt) Colby. He graduated from Columbia University in 1888; took his master's degree the next year in political science; was Seligman Fellow at Columbia, 1889–90, and acting professor of history in Amherst College, 1890–91; returned to Columbia as lecturer in history in the College and instructor in Barnard College, 1892–95; and then went to New York University as professor of economics. Meanwhile, to eke out his salary as a teacher, he had begun to write for encyclopædias and so drifted into what proved to be his life-work. His first staff position was as editor, 1893–95, of the history and political science department of *Johnson's Encyclopædia.* He married Harriet Wood Fowler of Amherst, Mass., Dec. 30, 1896, and in 1898 became editor of the *International Year Book,* later named the *New International Year Book,* of which he remained editor until his death. In 1899 appeared his *Outlines of General History,* a succinct, well-devised text-book, which in 1921 went into a fourth edition. In 1900 he gave up his academic post in order to give all his attention to editing and writing. He was an editorial writer for the New York *Commercial Advertiser,* 1900–02, was on the staff of the *International Encyclopædia,* and was American editor of *Nelson's Encyclopædia.* With Daniel Coit Gilman and Harry Thurston Peck he was editor of the *New International Encyclopædia,* 1900–03, and with Talcott Williams supervised the publication of the second edition, 1913–15. He also edited the two supplementary volumes of 1924 besides doing his annual work on the *Year Book.* The bulk of the editorial responsibility was in each case his. The merits of the *New International* were largely due to his genius for planning and organization and to the high standards of literary expression to which he held his contributors. Through his editorial labors he exercised a salutary influence on popular educa-

tion in America. Though he once maintained that it would be no homicide to shoot a man with an "encyclopædic mind" and was fond of comparing himself to a chute down which tons of general information plunged annually in a long, deafening roar, leaving only a trail of dust behind, he was a man of broad and accurate learning. That learning came as a surprise at times to readers of certain popular magazines who never guessed that the author of witty, pungent brief essays on books, plays, and manners was anything besides a literary journalist. At one time or another Colby wrote either as regular contributor or as member of the staff for the *Bookman, Harper's Weekly,* the *New Republic, Vanity Fair,* the *North American Review,* and *Harper's Magazine.* He collected some of his magazine work in several volumes of essays: *Imaginary Obligations* (1904), *Constrained Attitudes* (1910), and *The Margin of Hesitation* (1921). His literary work is best represented, however, in a two-volume collection of excerpts and whole essays, gleaned from the entire range of his magazine writing, which appeared after his death. In his personal essays he is revealed as an original, masculine mind expressing itself with remarkable vigor and precision. He was consciously a stylist, often rewriting his ideas to bring them nearer to perfection. He was reserved almost to the point of shyness, though an excellent talker with those he knew well.

[*International Year Book,* 1925; *Who's Who in America,* 1924–25; *Columbia Univ. Gen. Cat. 1754–1912* (1912); *Saturday Rev. of Lit.,* I, 615, Mar. 21, 1925; *N. Y. Herald-Tribune* and *N. Y. Times,* Mar. 4, 1925; C. Day, Jr., ed., *The Colby Essays* (1926).]   G.H.G.

COLBY, GARDNER (Sept. 3, 1810–Apr. 2, 1879), merchant, railway-president, philanthropist, was the son of Josiah C. Colby, of Bowdoinham, Me. His fortune and ship-building business swept away by the War of 1812, the elder Colby died, leaving his widow, Sarah Davidson of Charlestown, Mass., with four children to support, of whom Gardner was the second. At the age of twelve the latter was at work in a potash factory at Waterville, Me. Lacking time for school, he looked up at the Waterville Literary and Theological College with longing. After failing in her small store ventures at Bath and Waterbury the mother removed her children to Boston, where Gardner was sheltered and boarded by a Mr. Stafford in exchange for such work as he could do. After a year or so his mother managed to establish a home once more. Gardner had a few months at school and worked for Phelps & Thompson, grocers, after school hours. At fourteen his school days ended and for three years he was a clerk in a dry-goods store at $150 a year and his board. His interest in education for others was demonstrated by his successful solicitation of two scholarships of $75 each on one Thanksgiving Day, while he was still a clerk. With his savings and a small loan he rented a store in Boston and immediately prospered in the retail dry-goods business. Soon Gardner Colby & Company were wholesale jobbers and importers, interested in navigation and trade with China. In 1850 Colby became a manufacturer of woolens by the purchase of a half-interest in the Maverick Mills at Dedham, Mass. During the Civil War he was successful bidder on many government contracts for clothing. He retired from business and established his home at Newton, but becoming restless in retirement, undertook the presidency of the Wisconsin Central Railroad. His own money and that of many friends went heavily into this venture. Troublous times came upon the country and he encountered great difficulties, but lived to see the 340 miles of road completed to Lake Superior. When urged by friends to give up, his reply was, "if I'm good for anything, I'm good in a storm." The road being completed in 1878 Colby returned to Newton, where he died in the following April. In 1836 he had married Mary Low Roberts of Gloucester, Mass. Four sons and two daughters survived him.

As treasurer of the Baptist Education Society, treasurer of the Newton Theological Institute, trustee of Brown University at Providence, he rendered valuable personal service and contributed to these institutions constantly and progressively as his wealth increased. The Waterville Literary College was in desperate circumstances in 1864, with the student body either at war or kept on the farms. Colby contributed $50,000 upon condition that a total of $200,000 be raised. This timely act enabled the college to continue, and in 1867 its name was changed by the legislature of Maine to Colby University (now Colby College).

[A Tribute to the Memory of Gardner Colby (Boston, 1879), containing a sketch of his "Life and Characteristics" by his son the Rev. Henry F. Colby; Boston Herald, Apr. 3, 1879; E. C. Whittemore, Centennial Hist. of Waterville (1902), pp. 78, 86, 302–03.] B.C.

COLBY, LUTHER (Oct. 12, 1814–Oct. 7, 1894), spiritualist, was born at Amesbury, Mass., the son of Capt. William Colby, a shipmaster, and of Mary Colby, who survived her husband many years. From boyhood he was the intimate friend of his fellow townsman John Greenleaf Whittier. At the age of fifteen he completed his education in the common schools of his native town and went to Exeter, N. H., to learn the

printing trade. In the light of his subsequent interests, it is worth noting that his first work in printing was done on an edition of Scott's Family Bible. In 1836 he moved to Boston and began his twenty years' connection with the *Boston Daily Post,* during which time he advanced from journeyman printer to night editor. Through a fellow printer, William Berry, with whom he became familiar while in the service of the *Post,* he was introduced to Charles Crowell, Mrs. J. H. Conant, and other spiritualist mediums. As a result of noting the reports of manifestations of the spirit world and of attending séances where he received what appeared to him indubitable testimony to the truthfulness of spiritualism, Colby joined with Berry and in 1857, "in obedience to a company on high, unfurled the *Banner of Light,*" a weekly spiritualist paper, "devoted to the advocacy of the Spiritual Philosophy and Phenomena." The avowed purpose of the paper was the publication of spirit messages through the mediumship of Charles Crowell. Colby firmly believed that truth could best be served by a careful publication of all alleged communications from the "sphere of light" to the "mortal state," together with the supposed evidence for them, and that thereby man could come to know himself truly as a spiritual being in his eternal relations, instead of confining himself to sense knowledge of his temporary material bonds. He had a fervent conviction that the revelation of spiritual truth by the *Banner of Light* would revolutionize the world. Berry was killed in the Civil War; Colby continued to serve as editor of the *Banner of Light* until his death.

The whole life of "Luther the veteran," was centered in this paper and in his defense of the unpopular cause of spiritualism. Though not personally a prominent man or a writer of books, his influence as editor of the *Banner of Light* was widespread. The paper was his pride both as to its high moral tone and as to its attempt to serve nothing but the truth. Its typographical form received his close attention, and the paper was a model of neatness and accuracy. Personally, Colby was genial, honest, upright to the core, and, though excitable and impetuous, extremely generous. He was of large stature, robust physique, and temperate habits. Of his sincere belief in spiritualism there can be no doubt. He possessed a mind comparatively free from conventional dogmatism and narrowness, and was given neither to theological speculation nor to church practises. Throughout his editorship he followed the liberal policy enunciated in his first statement, that we "shall not believe everything but shall not refuse to listen to what is said." The *Banner of Light,* through Colby's instrumentality, was the foremost organ of spiritualism until its discontinuance in 1907.

[John W. Day, *A Biographic Memorial of Luther Colby* (1895); The *Banner of Light,* esp. for Oct. 13, 20, 1894, in which memorial articles on Colby appeared; personal letter from Mary T. Longley, associated with Colby in editorial and spirit message service 1879–93.]

          H.W.S.
          R.R.

COLDEN, CADWALLADER (Feb. 7, 1688 n.s.–Sept. 28, 1776), Loyalist, lieutenant-governor of New York, philosopher and scientist, was born in Ireland, while his mother was visiting there, though he was of Scotch ancestry and the son of Alexander Colden, a minister of Duns, Berwickshire, Scotland. He was destined for the church, but after he had received the degree of A.B. from the University of Edinburgh in 1705, he followed his stronger inclinations and went to London to study medicine. From there, at the suggestion of an aunt, he made his way to Philadelphia in 1710, where he practised medicine and carried on a mercantile business. Except for short business trips and a return to his native country in 1715, when he married Alice Christie (daughter of David Christie of Kelso, Scotland) on Nov. 11 of that year, his stay in Philadelphia was uninterrupted until 1718, when he moved his family to New York. The Governor of that province had met him, been well impressed, and promised to make him the next surveyor-general of the colony if he would make his home there—a promise which was accordingly fulfilled in 1720. This proved to be only the beginning of Colden's long public career. In 1721 he was appointed to the Governor's Council and in 1761 he became the lieutenant-governor of the colony, offices which he held until his death in 1776. Whether straightening out with industrious skill the tangle with which colony lands; demonstrating the ease with which huge patents could be automatically reduced by the exaction of legal quit-rents, which, in turn, could be used as a salary fund to insure the independence of crown officials; formulating an Indian policy; or, discredited, living in watchful retirement at his Orange County manor, Coldengham, he never ceased to fight colonial aggression with the same indomitable resolution which characterized everything he did.

His official duties, however, did not smother his other interests, for the scope of his attainments displays a remarkable versatility of mind. He not only wrote treatises which embraced history, applied mathematics, botany, medicine, and philosophy, but he carried on a correspondence which included Linnæus, Gronovius, Benjamin Franklin, Peter Collinson, Alexander Garden, and Samuel Johnson. Of his writings, *The History of the Five Indian Nations Depending on the Province of New York* was his first important work, published originally in 1727, but enlarged and reprinted in later editions. Strangely enough, though Colden was closely associated with the Indian tribes of New York, the book was based on French sources, and is both dull and confused. It was widely read, however, and is still an authority on the subject. He was also impressed with the great superiority of the French in their knowledge of the country, due to their superior instruments for map-making. He devoted much time, therefore, though without success, to the improvement of his own map-making instruments and compiled a set of astronomical tables from his own observation. He also invented, though others had probably preceded him, the process now known as stereotyping, an explanation of which is contained in "An original paper of the late Lieut. Gov. Colden, on a new method of Printing discovered by him; together with an original letter from the late Dr. Franklin, on the same subject; and some account of Stereotyping, as now practised in Europe, &c. by the Editors of the Register" (*American Medical and Philosophical Register,* vol. I, April 1811, pp. 439–50).

Colden's interest in botany led him to master the Linnæan system, according to which he classified the flora of the country surrounding Coldengham. The results of his study he sent to the Swedish master who published in the *Acta Societatis Regiæ Scientiarum Upsaliensis* for 1743 (1749), *Plantæ Coldenghamiæ in provincia Novaboracensi Americes sponte crescentes, quas ad Methodum Cl. Linnæi sexualem, anno 1742 &c. observavit et descripsit* Cadwallader Colden," and a supplement with a corresponding title in the *Acta* for 1744–50 (1751). As for medicine, his first choice for a career, his published works include an "Account of the Climate and Diseases of New-York" (*American Medical and Philosophical Register,* vol. I, January 1811, pp. 304–10), "Observations on the Fever which prevailed in the City of New-York in 1741 and 2 written in 1743" (*Ibid.,* pp. 310–30), "Observations on the Yellow Fever of Virginia, with some remarks on Dr. John Mitchell's Account of the Disease" (*Ibid.,* vol. IV, January 1814, pp. 378–87), and an "Extract of a letter from Cadwallader Colden, esq. to dr. Fothergill concerning the throat distemper. Oct. 1, 1753" (*American Museum,* vol. III, January 1788, pp. 53–59). In addition to these he wrote two papers on the treatment of cancer, and another on the medical properties of tar-water, which gained him much local reputation.

In mental and moral philosophy he found further outlet for his mind. "The First Principles of Morality or the Actions of Intelligent Beings," "An Introduction to the Study of Phylosophy wrote in America for the use of a young Gentleman" (Peter De Lancey), and his translation of Cicero's letters were all worthy products of his pen. But it was in physics that he found his chief joy. His pamphlets: *Light and Colors, An Inquiry into the Principles of Vital Motion, The Cohesion of the parts of Bodies,* and *An Introduction to the Doctrine of Fluxions or the Arithmetic of Infinities,* show the catholicity of his mind, but to him his *magnum opus* was *An Explication of the First Causes of Action in Matter, And, of the Cause of Gravitation* (New York, 1745; London, 1746). The theorem had been promulgated by James Bernonilli toward the close of the preceding century, but Colden seems, as Franklin believed, to have been quite unaware of that fact. In 1748 an edition with notes was printed at Leipzig and Hamburg. In 1751 a revised edition, *The Principles of Action in Matter, the Gravitation of Bodies, and the Motion of the Planets explained from those Principles,* was published in London. The edition was well-launched, but its implied criticism of Newton was resented and there was much counter criticism which Franklin attributed to the reluctance of Europeans to learn from "us Americans." Once more revising and enlarging the *Principles,* he sent the manuscript in 1762 to Robert Whyte, professor of medicine at the University of Edinburgh, asking him to deposit it in the university library if he thought it unworthy of publication. Dr. Whyte advised against immediate publication and there our knowledge of this revision rests. The old edition, however, continued to be read, Buffon in 1778 asking Thomas Jefferson to replace his own lost copy.

In August 1760, the death of Colden's keenest opponent, James De Lancey, who had been made lieutenant-governor despite Colden's many requests for the office, called the latter to take command of the government, a summons eagerly obeyed by this indomitable man of seventy-three. Because he immediately undertook to enforce the laws against smuggling merchants and grasping landowners, and was determined to hold the judiciary under some restraint, he was soon fighting as he had never fought before. Meanwhile, his commission as lieutenant-governor had come, under which he ruled the province for fourteen years save for the brief ad-

ministrations of several governors. Late in 1764 came the news of the Stamp Act and Colden was asked by a most restrained assembly to join it in requesting a repeal. He replied evasively, and later refused to sign addresses to King, Lords, and Commons, for, notwithstanding the precedent set by the other colonies and the disrespect shown him in public, he proposed to enforce the law. The result was that on Nov. 1, 1765, a mob burned Colden's effigy along with one of the devil and destroyed some property. Urged by prominent citizens, Colden then promised to leave the stamps alone and later under some pressure yielded them to the mayor, an action promptly censured by the home government. The Stamp Act was shortly after repealed, but no reply came to Colden's claim for damages for nearly three years. Yet, despite his difficulty in getting his financial claim satisfied, the excitement caused by further taxation and the quartering of the regulars, Colden succeeded in keeping a fair balance between radicals and conservatives until the Boston Port Act led to the Continental Congress at Philadelphia. The next Assembly was controlled by the Loyalists, but they were defeated by the popular demonstration which elected the delegates to the second Congress. Soon after, the battle of Lexington virtually ended British government in the colonies, and Colden retired to his Long Island estate, "Spring Hill," where he died. He was devoted to his family, and attributed his labors to a desire to give his children leisure for scholarly pursuits. His daughter Jane [*q.v.*] achieved unusual distinction for a woman of her time, and his son David was a scholar of recognized standing. His daughter Elizabeth married Peter De Lancey with whose brother, James De Lancey [*q.v.*], Colden had contended for the office of lieutenant-governor.

["The Colden Letter Books," *N. Y. Hist. Soc. Colls.,* vols. IX, X (1877–78); "Letters and Papers of Cadwallader Colden . . . 1711–1775," *N. Y. Hist. Soc. Colls.,* vols. L–LVI (1918–23); E. B. O'Callaghan, *The Documentary Hist. of the State of N.-Y.* (4 vols., 1850–51); Wm. Smith, *The Hist. of the Late Province of N.-Y., from its Discovery, to the Appointment of Gov. Colden in 1762* (2 vols., 1829); "Letters on South's Hist. of N. Y." by Cadwallader Colden in *N. Y. Hist. Soc. Colls.,* vol. I (1868), pp. 179–235; Edwin R. Purple, *Geneal. Notes of the Colden Family in America* (1873); Alice M. Keys, *Cadwallader Colden, a Representative Eighteenth Century Official* (1906); L. Woodbridge Riley, *Am. Philosophy, the Early Schools* (1907), pp. 329–72; Proc. of the Exec. Council (MS.); Jour. and Proc. of the Gen. Assembly.]   A. M. K.

COLDEN, CADWALLADER DAVID (Apr. 4, 1769–Feb. 7, 1834), lawyer, mayor of New York City, was the grandson of Cadwallader Colden [*q.v.*], Loyalist lieutenant-governor of New York on the eve of the Revolution.

He was born at Flushing, N. Y., the son of David and Ann (Willett) Colden. He received his early education at Jamaica, N. Y., and, in the year 1784, at a classical school near London. Upon the death of his father in that year, he returned to New York City and began the study of law, which he subsequently pursued intensively at St. John, N. B., under the expert guidance of the crown counsel, William Wylly, Loyalist émigré (Colden letters; Edward A. Jones, *American Members of the Inns of Court,* 1924, p. 227), and again, on his return to New York, at Kinderhook. Colden was admitted to the bar in 1791, and two years later he married Maria, daughter of Rt. Rev. Samuel Provost, first Protestant Episcopal bishop of New York. Down to the War of 1812 he practised law in Poughkeepsie, N. Y., and in New York City; and served in the capacity of district attorney of New York City in 1798 and 1810 (Hugh Hastings, ed., *Military Minutes of the Council of Appointment of the State of New York, 1783-1821,* 1901, pp. 1109 ff.). The New York law reports (see, for example, 1 *Caines,* 9 *Johnson, passim*) bear tribute to his ability and growing reputation in the stalwart age of Emmet, Wells, and Ogden. As a member of the committee on the judiciary in the state Senate in 1825, Colden made a vigorous plea for the simplification of procedure and the codification of the law. Although in his earlier years he had manifested a reverence for the English system of jurisprudence, he now assailed its "useless and antiquated" formalities and fictions (*Journal,* 48 Senate, 1825, pp. 320–21). The report of the committee foreshadowed the legal revolution of the next decade.

Though a Federalist, Colden supported the War of 1812, and served as colonel in the state militia, subsequently (1819) being raised to the rank of major-general (*Council of Appointment,* pp. 1748, 2013). Elected to the state Assembly in 1818 with the indorsement of Tammany Hall, he openly supported Gov. DeWitt Clinton, who, as head of the council of appointment, was wreaking political vengeance on that organization. Colden was rewarded by being appointed mayor of New York City to succeed Jacob Ratcliffe (*Council of Appointment,* pp. 1858–59). In this capacity he served from 1818 to 1820. In 1821 he successfully contested the election of Peter Sharpe to Congress (*Annals of Congress,* 17 Cong., 1 Sess., p. 520). During his term he seldom departed from his "usual course of silence," but in 1822 he made a vigorous address in the House attacking the fugitive-slave law (*Ibid.,* p. 1379), in line with his earlier indorsement of the plan of Gov. Tompkins for the

emancipation of slaves in New York (*Journal,* Colden letters, 40 Assembly, pp. 126, 137, 239). In his term in the New York state Senate, 1825–27, Colden actively sponsored relief for the poor, and juvenile welfare, and his expert knowledge was marshalled in attacks on fanciful canal projects, and in urging further development of the port of New York (see, for example, *Journal,* 48 Senate, pp. 64, 75, 93; 50 Senate, 1 Sess., pp. 33, 490).

Colden was intensely interested in navigation and internal improvements. In 1825 he drew up for the city of New York a *Memoir* on the completion of the New York canals. In this (p. 51) he expressed his conviction that the Erie Canal would make New York the greatest commercial metropolis in the world. His *Life of Robert Fulton* (1817), is an uncritical but detailed survey of the inventor's career, which minimizes the contributions of earlier pioneers in the field of steam navigation. During the years 1817-19, Colden was engaged in the production of a number of polemical tracts supporting the patent rights of Fulton and the steamboat monopoly. He died in Jersey City, N. J.

[Edwin R. Purple, "Notes Biog. and Geneal. of the Colden Family," in *N. Y. Geneal. and Biog. Record,* vol. IX (1873), pp. 161–83, contains a brief note on Colden, as does Lorenzo Sabine, *Biog. Sketches of the Loyalists of the Am. Revolution,* vol. I (1864). The N. Y. Hist. Soc. has a number of important Colden letters. For specific sources see references in the body of the article.]   R. B. M.

COLDEN, JANE (Mar. 27, 1724–Mar. 10, 1766), was the first woman in the New World to be distinguished as a botanist. Both her parents were Scotch, and members of families wherein education was a tradition and not a luxury. Her father, Cadwallader Colden [*q.v.*], was a graduate of Edinburgh University, a correspondent of Linnæus, and distinguished as a scientist as well as a statesman. Her mother was Alice Christie, the daughter of a clergyman at Kelso, Scotland. Gov. Colden took up his residence at Coldengham, nine miles from Newburgh, N. Y., when his daughter Jane was four years of age, and she grew up on this great estate, whose hospitable owners were hosts to all the notable visitors of the day. Her father was an ardent botanist, and made a special study of the flora of Orange County in which there is evidence of his daughter's collaboration. From Coldengham John Bartram and his son William [*qq.v.*] explored the near-by mountains, and made a survey of the flora of the Catskills, and to Coldengham came Peter Kalm, the celebrated traveler and favorite pupil of Linnæus.

Jane, the fifth child in a family of ten, received her entire education from her father and mother. She early showed a love of botany and shared with her father an enthusiasm for the great Swedish botanist, Linnæus, and a mastery of his system which is recorded with admiration in many contemporary letters. Peter Collinson wrote to Linnæus (May 12, 1756), "I but lately heard from Mr. Colden. He is well; but, what is marvellous, his daughter is perhaps the first lady that has so perfectly studied your system. She deserves to be celebrated." And Dr. Alexander Garden wrote to John Ellis (Mar. 25, 1755), "not only the doctor himself is a great botanist, but his lovely daughter is greatly master of the Linnæan method, and cultivates it with assiduity." John Ellis hinted to Linnæus (Apr. 25, 1758) that, as he had named a plant *Coldenia* after the father, it would be a compliment to call *Fibraurea* or Yellow Root for the daughter. He suggested "Coldenella or any other name that might distinguish her among your genera." Linnæus had already named the plant in question *Helleborus Trifolius*, but apparently said "civil things" about Jane Colden in a letter to Ellis.

Gov. Colden taught his daughter to take the impression of the leaves of plants in printers' ink, and she seems also to have made drawings. Ellis wrote to Linnæus (Apr. 25, 1758) that "she has drawn and described 400 plants in your method only," and she may have been the author of other articles. Peter Collinson notes that in the second volume of *Edinburgh Essays* "is published a Latin botanic dissertation by Miss Colden," and mentions in another letter to Linnæus "a curious botanic dissertation by Miss Jane Colden" which may refer to the same work. The records of her life are fragmentary; on Mar. 12, 1759, she married Dr. William Farquhar, described by her brother as "An old widower, but very worthy good Scotchman," by whom she had a child who died in 1766. Her husband practised medicine in New York City and long survived her.

[Edwin R. Purple, *Geneal. Notes of the Colden Family in America* (1873); *A Selection from the Correspondence of Linnæus*, etc. (1821), edited by Sir Jas. Edward Smith; *Memorials of John Bartram and Humphrey Marshall* (1849); Dr. Howard A. Kelly, "Some American Medical Botanists" (1914); Samuel W. Eager, *An Outline Hist. of Orange County* (1846–47); "Account of Jane Colden," by S. W. Eager in *The Newburgh Telegraph*, Apr. 25, 1861; "The Colden Letter Books" and "Letters and Papers of Cadwallader Colden," in *N. Y. Hist. Soc. Colls.*, vols. L–LVI (1918–23).]   M. P. S.

COLE, CHESTER CICERO (June 4, 1824– Oct. 4, 1913), jurist, teacher of law, was born in Oxford, N. Y., the youngest of the eleven children of Samuel and Alice (Pullman) Cole. He attended the public schools and academy at Oxford until he was thirteen, and for five years was a clerk in a general store. He read law in the office of a local lawyer for two years, then entered the Harvard Law School, from which he graduated in June 1848. The same month he was married to Amanda M. Bennett of Oxford, by whom he had seven children. After his graduation he went to Marion, Ky., was admitted to the bar, and during a period of nine years gained a high reputation in criminal law. The campaign of 1856 and the controversies that followed led Cole to move to Des Moines, Iowa, where he lived until his death. He associated himself with the Democratic party in Iowa and continued with that party throughout the campaign of 1860. In 1859 he was a candidate for the state supreme court and in 1860 for Congress, but was defeated in both contests. At the outbreak of the Civil War he allied himself with the Union men in support of the government and left the Democratic party, which was dominated by Southern sympathizers. He supported William M. Stone for governor on the Republican ticket in 1864, and in recognition of his labors in behalf of the Union, he was appointed a judge of the supreme court. He was twice reëlected and served for twelve years. In 1876 he returned to the practise of law.

With Judge George G. Wright, his associate in the supreme court, he organized the Iowa Law School in Des Moines in September 1865. The school was conducted with marked success for three years, after which it was merged with the law department of the State University at Iowa City. Cole served as professor for seven years. Upon his return to Des Moines in 1875, leading citizens urged upon him the organization of a law school in the capital city, pointing out that every consideration of convenience and advantage to students required the establishment of such a school. It was opened in September 1875. In 1881 Drake University was established in Des Moines and at the request of its founders the law school was affiliated with it. For all but about five or six years from 1875 to 1907 Cole was dean of the school. During all of this time he was actively engaged in the practise of law. In 1907 after a service of forty-two years, he was awarded a retiring allowance by the Carnegie Foundation, in recognition of his work as a teacher of law, and was made dean emeritus of the law school. He continued his practise until he was eighty-seven years of age. Cole was one of the most widely known lawyers in Iowa. At his best he had few equals and no superiors as a trial lawyer. As a judge his opinions were models—terse, well phrased, pointed and strong.

He was remarkable for his talents, and for his unceasing industry, not only in his prime, but in his old age. When he received the announcement of the Carnegie award in 1907, he described himself as "only eighty-three years of age" and as not feeling "any necessity of retiring."

[E. H. Stiles, *Recollections and Sketches of Notable Lawyers and Public Men of Early Iowa* (1916), pp. 472–80; *Proc. Iowa Bar Asso.* (1914), vol. XX, pp. 18–20; B. F. Gue, *Hist. of Iowa* (1903), vol. IV, pp. 56–57; the *Register and Leader* (Des Moines), Oct. 5, 7, 1913; *Who's Who in America*, 1908–09; *Bench and Bar of Iowa* (1901), pp. 68–71.]   F. E. H.

COLE, FRANK NELSON (Sept. 20, 1861–May 26, 1926), mathematician, the son of Otis and Frances Maria (Pond) Cole, was born at Ashland, Mass., of old New England stock. His father was a farmer, an expert judge of standing timber, and for a time interested in manufacturing. Moreover, he had a taste for mathematics and was a lover of flowers and trees. From both parents Cole inherited a taste for learning and a stability of character which showed themselves all through his life. After graduating from the high school he was tutored for a short time by a clergyman and then, with financial assistance from a friend, he entered Harvard in 1878. Here he was soon recognized as a man of unusual ability and was granted scholarships which not only made it possible to secure the A.B. degree with highest honors (1882), but to go to Leipzig for the purpose of pursuing his studies in the seminar of Prof. Felix Klein (1883–85), and to return to Harvard where he received the degrees of M.A. and Ph.D. in 1886. He was married in Germany on July 26, 1888, to Martha Marie Streiff.

Cole lectured at Harvard from 1885 to 1887, from 1888 to 1895 was instructor and then assistant professor at the University of Michigan, and was professor of mathematics at Columbia from 1895 to the time of his death. From 1908 to 1923 he was secretary of the Faculty of Pure Science at Columbia. He was secretary of the American Mathematical Society for more than twenty years, and was editor-in-chief of its *Bulletin* from 1897 until shortly before his death. His published contributions to mathematics began with an essay on the general equation of the sixth degree (1885), and included memoirs on Klein's *Ikosaeder* (1889); the linear functions of a complex variable (1890); the theory of groups (1891–1924); number theory (the factoring of $2^{67} - 1$ by the aid of quadratic remainders); and triad systems. He also translated Eugen Netto's work on the theory of substitutions (*The Theory of Substitutions and Its Applications to Algebra*,

1892). As a man Cole was admired by all who penetrated a certain reserve that was natural to him; as an executive he was faithful to every duty; as a teacher he was lavish of the time that he would give to those who proved their worth; and as a friend he was loyal to the last. He loved to take long walks in the country, studying trees and wild flowers, and at the time of his death was planning to retire from his university work and lead a rural life.

[Information as to certain facts from members of the family and from a colleague, Prof. Thomas S. Fiske of Columbia. See also obituaries in *Am. Mathematical Monthly*, XXX, 238; *Am. Math. Soc. Bull.*, 2 ser., XXXII, 300, 580 f.; E. D. Harris, *A Geneal. Record of Daniel Pond* (1873), p. 122; *Who's Who in America*, 1920–21.]   D. E. S.

COLE, JOSEPH FOXCROFT (Nov. 9, 1837–May 2, 1892), painter, was, "after Hunt, the first Boston artist who studied in Paris." When he returned from Paris, Hunt bought four of Cole's paintings and helped him to a career that was eminently successful (Knowlton, *post*, p. 33). While Hunt's priority as "the first Boston artist to study in Paris" may be denied, it is unquestionable that he and Cole were pioneers in calling the attention of New England people to the merits of French painting. Cole's part in this service has had, perhaps, less general recognition than it deserves. He was born at Jay, Me., a son of Samuel and Selinda (Allen) Cole. His parents moved to Boston when he was seven years old. After public-school education Cole served an apprenticeship at the Bufford Lithograph establishment, where he had as associates Joseph P. Baker and Winslow Homer (William Howe Downes, *Winslow Homer*, 1911, p. 27). While he worked at lithography Cole saw in Boston many English and German paintings but "had no desire to become an artist" (Robinson, *post*, p. 45). Once, however, he saw a landscape by Constant Troyon which aroused in him an intense desire to paint after the French formula. In 1860 his savings permitted him to go to Paris where he enrolled himself as a pupil of Lambient. After a sketching tour in Italy he returned to Boston where he sold enough pictures to enable him to continue his studies. In 1865 Charles Jacques received him as an advanced student and assistant, employing him to paint from pencil sketches pictures which the master finished and signed. Cole exhibited pictures of his own at the 1866 Salon and the International Exposition of 1867. His summers were spent in Normandy and Belgium. In the latter country he married Irma de Palgrom, a singer of international celebrity. Returning to the United States he occupied a studio in the Century Building, Boston, and a house at Melrose.

In 1873 the family went to Paris where they remained four years. During this time Cole exhibited paintings in the Salons of 1873, 1874, and 1875. He sent to the Philadelphia Centennial three pictures: "Cows Ruminating," "Scene in Normandy," and "Melrose Twilight." Returning home, in 1877 he built a house and a studio on Mystic Lake, Winchester, Mass., where, except for brief trips to Europe and to California, he passed the rest of his life. Here he painted his serious, low-toned landscapes, and advocated among his professional associates and friends the formation of collections of nineteenth-century French art. "One can hardly estimate," says F. T. Robinson, "the influence which Cole, in connection with Hunt, 'Tom' Robinson, A. H. Bicknell and Henry Sayles, has had on the arts of the two continents." Among those whom Cole instructed was his daughter, Adelaide Cole Chase, a distinguished portrait-painter of Boston. He belonged to the Society of American Artists and was well represented in public and private collections when he died in middle life. He was buried in Wildwood Cemetery, Winchester. The Winchester library owns two of his most successful landscapes: "Coast of Normandy" and "The Aberjona."

[Frank T. Robinson, *Living New England Artists* (1888) ; Helen M. Knowlton, *Art Life of Wm. Morris Hunt* (1899) ; obituaries in *Boston Evening Transcript* and *Boston Daily Globe*, May 3, 1892.]　　F. W. C.

COLE, THOMAS (Feb. 1, 1801–Feb. 11, 1848), artist and poet, one of the first painters to interpret the romantic beauty of American landscape, and a pioneer of the "Hudson River School," was born in England at Bolton-le-Moor, Lancashire, the seventh of eight children of James and Mary Cole. His father, a woolen manufacturer, was a man of fine tastes but poor business ability, born at Haynford, Norfolk. Failing in business, he moved to Chorley, and Thomas was sent to school at Chester. His father wished to make him a lawyer or iron manufacturer, but he preferred to enter a calico factory as an engraver of simple designs, where association with an old Scotsman developed his romantic tastes. Accompanied by his youngest sister Sarah, Thomas enjoyed wandering about the parks and old ivy-mantled halls in his leisure moments, playing his flute in picturesque solitudes, while Sarah added the charm of song. An omnivorous reader, he came upon a book which awakened his interest in the beauties of the North American states. Influenced by the boy's enthusiasm and thinking that he might repair his shattered fortunes, the elder Cole sailed with his family for Philadelphia, arriving July 3, 1819. Here, with

a stock brought with him, he opened a small dry-goods shop, while Thomas took up wood-engraving which he had already practised at Liverpool. In the fall, the family moved by way of Pittsburgh to Steubenville, Ohio, while Thomas remained at Philadelphia enjoying the brilliant colors of his first American autumn along the banks of the Schuylkill and Delaware rivers. On Jan. 4, 1820, with a companion, he sailed for St. Eustatius in the West Indies. In this mountain island of the tropics, which appeared to him a dream of paradise, he made a number of sketches. He returned home in May to join his family at Steubenville, making the entire journey from Philadelphia on foot. For two years he aided his father in the manufacture of wall-paper, engraving the blocks and relieving these tasks by wanderings in the then primeval wilderness along the Ohio.

Although addicted to literary and poetic composition, he now decided to make the brush rather than the pen his chosen means of expression. With materials procured from a chair-maker whose wares he decorated, he made several experimental portraits of his father and friends. His real delight was in landscape, but portraiture then offered the only means of gaining a livelihood. When twenty-one, in February 1822, with a green baize bag containing a few clothes, colors, brushes, and a stone muller for grinding paint, slung over his shoulder, and not forgetting his beloved flute, he started on foot for St. Clairsville, thirty miles away. Here his experiences lacked financial success, and another walk of three days brought him to Zanesville, whence, after an even more discouraging sequel, he went on seventy-five miles to Chillicothe. An encouraging beginning here ended in disappointment, and, hearing of his family's intended removal to Pittsburgh, he joined them at Steubenville, where he painted some scenery for a local dramatic club. The following spring found him in Pittsburgh helping his father in the manufacture of oilcloth, and sketching along the banks of the Monongahela. In November 1823 he went to Philadelphia and there passed what he called "the winter of my discontent," working meanwhile at the Pennsylvania Academy of the Fine Arts, and writing, besides poems, a story, "Emma Moreton," which appeared in the *Saturday Evening Post*. His family had moved to New York and he joined them, painting in the garret of his father's house in Greenwich St. Several paintings placed in a shop kept by a Mr. Dixey were sold, and three others, the results of excursions up the Hudson to Weehawken, the Palisades, and the Highlands, found notable purchasers in the artists Col. John Trumbull, A. B. Durand, and William Dunlap ; and the poet William Cullen Bryant added his appreciation and patronage. Durand said, "His fame spread like wildfire." He took rooms at Catskill, painting from nature in the mountains beside the Hudson. His poetic bent found expression in two Miltonic landscapes, "The Garden of Eden," and "Expulsion from Paradise," which he exhibited at the National Academy Exhibition of 1828.

The generosity of Thomas Gilmor of Baltimore enabled him to visit England in 1829. There he met the poet, Samuel Rogers, and the painters, Sir Thomas Lawrence and Turner, who received him kindly, and his pictures were exhibited at the Royal Academy and British Institution. Otherwise, however, his English visit, which lasted nearly two years, was somewhat depressing. He went on to Paris, and from Marseilles to Genoa and Leghorn (1831–32). Florence he found "a painter's paradise," and at Rome he took a studio on the Pincian Hill formerly occupied by Claude Lorraine. From Naples he went to Paestum, sketching its ancient temples. Sailing from Leghorn, he returned to New York in November 1832. He exhibited his works in rooms at the corner of Wall St. and Broadway, and Luman Reed commissioned him to paint "The Course of Empire": five canvases depicting growth from "Primeval Nature" through "Pastoral Life" to "Wealth and Glory," and decline through "War" and "Desolation." These pictures, which Bryant considered "the most remarkable and characteristic of his works," and which Fenimore Cooper said, "ought to assure the reputation of any man," were completed in October 1836. They are now in the museum of the New York Historical Society. He married Maria Bartow on Nov. 22, 1836, and settled at Catskill, painting from nature and occupied with his allegorical works. For Samuel Ward, in 1839, he began "The Voyage of Life," four subjects: "Childhood," "Youth," "Manhood" and "Old Age," afterward in possession of John Taylor Johnson. These became well known through engravings by Smillie, and are still found in many American homes. Of simpler and less elaborate design than the "Course of Empire," they are more purely imaginative.

In 1841 Cole again visited England, thence going to France, Switzerland, Rome, and Sicily, where he painted studies of Mount Etna. He returned to America by way of the Rhine and Rotterdam in 1842. He visited the Adirondacks in 1846 and Niagara in 1847, dividing his time between the direct study of nature and the composition of pictures which became more abstractly religious in character. A series, "The Cross and the World," was begun, but while painting "The Pilgrim of the Cross" he was seized with inflam-

mation of the lungs and died at Catskill. Cole holds an important place in the development of American art. He was the master of F. E. Church [q.v.]. William Cullen Bryant, in an oration delivered before the National Academy of Design in New York, May 4, 1848, eulogized him not only as a successful painter of actual landscapes, but also as giving evidence of "an ardent imagination" in the more symbolic productions of his brush.

[Louis L. Noble, *Life and Works of Thomas Cole* (1856); W. C. Bryant, "Eulogy," in *Orations and Addresses* (1873); H. T. Tuckerman, *Artist Life or Sketches of Am. Painters* (1847), p. 116; G. W. Greene, *Biog. Studies* (1860), pp. 74–120.]   R.J.W.

COLEMAN, CHARLES CARYL (Apr. 25, 1840–Dec. 4, 1928), painter, was born in Buffalo, N. Y., the son of John Hull and Charlotte Augusta Coleman. He early evinced talent as an artist and began his study with William H. Beard [q.v.], who had a studio in Buffalo. When he was nineteen years old, he went abroad for further study in Paris, but returned to America after three years to serve in the Union army during the Civil War. He was badly wounded and suffered intensely, but he returned to Europe in 1866 and worked in Paris and Rome with William Hunt and Elihu Vedder [q.v.], the latter a close friend. They made a trip together into Brittany stopping first at Dinan and at Vitré on their way back to Paris. Although Paris had become the favorite place for study for young Americans, Eugene Benson [q.v.], Vedder, and Coleman found charm in the classic dignity of Rome. Here Coleman lived with George Simmonds, occupying the Keats apartment which has now become a shrine, sacred to the two poets Shelley and Keats. Though keeping his apartment in Rome, Coleman made his home finally on the Island of Capri. Vedder lived near by, each choosing for his home an old villa snuggled against steep hills, with terraces vine-clad, orange trees on the slopes, wide windows that swept the Bay, where to "see Naples and die, means to live in God's Paradise." Coleman was particularly interested in Vesuvius. Whenever the old volcano burst forth, he was ready with canvas and brush to record the various atmospheric effects and changes made by the volcano on the clouds and the surface of the Bay of Naples. His picture of the last great eruption which continued for several days is a historic record of real value. It is owned by the Brooklyn Museum. His "Vesuvius from Pompeii" is in the Detroit Institute of Arts. One of his earliest pictures was a study of Vedder in Coleman's studio. He painted a portrait of Walter Savage Landor, through the influence of Kate Field. Elihu Vedder in his *Di-*

gressions, told many interesting stories of sketching with him. On one occasion at Bordighera, Coleman had put a "chalk mark" on some particularly attractive view. They apparently respected each other's "chalk marks," but when he began his sketch Vedder sat down behind him to paint the same scene. Vedder said: "I made one of my best sketches and had finished it before Coleman had hardly begun to draw his in. Whereupon Coleman was enraged, shut up his box and left, but he claimed *my picture* as his own, since *he* had discovered the place." His work, not only in oil but in water-color and pastel, covers a wide range of subjects. Portraits and figure pieces occupied him in the early part of his career; later, landscapes and architectural subjects. He also painted flowers very successfully, understanding color and mass arrangement, and he became famous for his religious pictures and picturesque views throughout Italy. One of his most charming paintings, bought by the Buffalo Fine Arts Academy, is a moonlight view of the village of Capri. He was an associate of the National Academy of Design, New York; a member of the National Arts Club and the Players, New York; and an associate member of the Newspaper Artists Association. He received a Bronze Medal at the Columbian Exposition at Chicago in 1893, and the Silver Medal at the Pan-American Exposition in Buffalo in 1901. Soon after his death the Brooklyn Museum gave a special memorial exhibition of his work for which they assembled a large collection. His funeral at Capri, where he died in his villa "Narcissus," was attended by the public officials and the American colony at Capri.

[Samuel Isham, *Hist. of Am. Painting* (1927); Elihu Vedder, *Digressions of V.* (1910); Ulrich Thieme, *Allgemeines Lexikon der Bildenden Künstler* (1912), VII, 197; Lars Gustaf Sellstedt, *Art in Buffalo* (1910), p. 120; *N. Y. Times*, Dec. 6, 1928; *Art News*, Dec. 15, 1928; *Am. Art Annual*, 1917; *Who's Who in America*, 1910–11.]   H. W.

COLEMAN, LEIGHTON (May 3, 1837–Dec. 14, 1907), Episcopal bishop, son of the Rev. John and Louisa Margaretta (Thomas) Coleman, was born in Philadelphia where his father was rector of Trinity Church. After attending St. James's Grammar School and the Episcopal Academy of Philadelphia, he spent five years in business, and then entered the General Theological Seminary in New York where he graduated in 1861. From 1860 to 1862 he was missionary at Randall's and Blackwell's Islands, N. Y. Being ordained priest in the latter year, he was for the next seven years successively rector at St. Luke's, Bustleton, Pa.; St. John's, Wilmington, Del.; St. Mark's, Mauch Chunk, Pa.; and Trinity, Toledo, Ohio. Going

abroad in 1879 on account of his wife's health, he remained for nearly seven years, residing chiefly at Oxford, engaging in clerical work, and serving for three years as organizing secretary of the Church of England Temperance Society. Returning to the United States, after a brief pastorate at Sayre, Pa., he was elected bishop of Delaware and was consecrated Oct. 18, 1888. He was the first incumbent of the office who was not at the same time rector of a church, and consequently he was able to devote all his energies to diocesan and other public interests. With a strongly-developed journalistic instinct he wrote much for the daily press. He was also the author of the following books: *History of the Lehigh Valley* (1872); *The Church in America* (1895); *A History of the American Church* (1902). A staunch upholder of temperance and law and order, he was a prominent Mason and a member of numerous historical, patriotic, educational, and social organizations within and outside of the Episcopal Church. He was a stiff churchman of the Oxford type and outspoken in the expression of his views. But his genial humanity put him on a friendly footing with all schools and classes, making for him a large place in the hearts of the people of Delaware. In his latter years, on account of his flowing white beard and venerable appearance, he was affectionately called "Santa Claus" by the children of Wilmington. He was a confirmed pedestrian, making long walking trips in the states of Maryland and Virginia, on which he concealed his identity and made friends among all classes of people. His portrait in oil may be seen at "Bishopstead," the Episcopal Residence in Wilmington. He was married in 1861 to Frances Elizabeth du Pont of Wilmington, who died Mar. 17, 1902. One son survived his parents.

[The entire number of the *Delaware Churchman* for Jan. 1908 is devoted to Bishop Coleman. An outline of his life is also found in *Who's Who in America*, 1906–07. The *Outlook* for Dec. 28, 1907, has an appreciative editorial, and large space is devoted to his life and services by the *Churchman* of Dec. 21, and the *Living Church* for Dec. 21 and 28 of the same year.]   F. T. P.

COLEMAN, LYMAN (June 14, 1796–Mar. 16, 1882), educator, writer of theological works, was born in Middlefield, Mass., the son of Dr. William Coleman and his wife Achsah Lyman. With only a common-school foundation he prepared himself for college while working on his father's farm, entered Yale against strong paternal opposition, maintained himself there largely by his own exertions, and graduated in 1817. For three years he was principal of the Latin Grammar School in Hartford, and for the next four years tutor and student of theology at Yale.

His contact during these years with eminent scholars and theologians did much to overcome his shyness and to shape his life purposes. On Oct. 19, 1825, he was ordained at the Congregational Church at Belchertown, Mass., where he remained till Sept. 4, 1832. This, his only pastorate, under which the church prospered greatly, was marked by activities on behalf of the Sunday-school (then a new institution), the cause of missions, and temperance reform. Returning to what he considered his true vocation, Coleman was for five years principal of Burr Seminary, Manchester, Vt., and for five years the head of the English department, Phillips Academy, Andover, Mass. In 1842–43 he spent nearly two years in Europe, studying for seven months under Neander in Berlin. He then became instructor in the classics at Amherst for three years, professor of German in the College of New Jersey (now Princeton) for two years, and then principal of the Presbyterian Academy in Philadelphia for nine. In 1856 he paid his second visit to Palestine and Egypt, and in 1861 he became professor of the classics at Lafayette College, Easton, Pa., where he remained till his death. He was married twice: on Sept. 21, 1826, to Maria Flynt of Monson, Mass., who died on Jan. 11, 1871; and in October 1873 to Marion B. Philleo, who survived him.

His principal publications are: *The Antiquities of the Christian Church,* largely translated from the German (1841); *The Apostolic and Primitive Church,* with a preface by Neander under whose inspiration it was written (1844); *An Historical Geography of the Bible* (1849); *Ancient Christianity Exemplified* (1852); *Historic Text-Book and Atlas of Biblical Geography* (1854); *Prelacy and Ritualism* (1869); *Genealogy of the Lyman Family* (1872). He also wrote many articles on miscellaneous subjects and his *Wall Map of Palestine* issued in the latter fifties was long a standard authority. For some years the oldest active college professor in the United States, he was a man of commanding presence, courteous demeanor, warm sympathies, and strong convictions. Firmly grounded in the old faith, he was nevertheless hospitable to new ideas in theology.

[Autobiographical sketch in Lyman Coleman, *Genealogy of the Lyman Family* (1872); A. H. Kellogg, *A Sermon Commemorative of the Life and Character of the Rev. Lyman Coleman* (1882); P. W. Lyman, *Sermon Delivered in Belchertown, Mass.,* Mar. 19, 1882; *Obituary Record Grads. Yale College, 1882.*] F.T.P.

COLEMAN, WILLIAM (Feb. 14, 1766–July 14, 1829), the most effective Federalist journalist of the period of Hamilton's leadership, was born in Boston in poverty and, according to Jeremiah Mason, in the poorhouse. His unusual promise attracted the attention of people of means who made it possible for him to enter Andover Academy, where he acquired a taste for standard authors, and a love for Sterne and Junius. He then studied law under Robert Treat Paine at Worcester, interrupting his studies to march with the militia in Shays's Rebellion, and began the practise of his profession at Greenfield, Mass. His tastes being literary and political, he wrote much for the *Impartial Intelligencer,* which he established, and served in the Massachusetts House in 1795 and 1796. Financially ruined through speculations in the Yazoo land frauds, he moved to New York City, with no other recommendation than an honorary degree from Dartmouth College, a letter from Robert Treat Paine, and a slight personal acquaintance with Hamilton. A partnership of short duration with Aaron Burr was followed by a more advantageous one with John Wells, who introduced him into literary and political circles. A vacancy occurring in the clerkship of the circuit court, at the instance of Hamilton he was appointed over an applicant with superior claims. Thenceforth until Hamilton's death he was intimately identified with the political fortunes of his benefactor. Swept out of office by the Democrat victory of 1800, he was made editor and proprietor of the *Evening Post,* established for political purposes by Hamilton and his friends. It immediately began to fashion the thought of the Federalist press, particularly through its semi-weekly edition, the *New York Herald,* which had a national circulation. Coleman had made promises to abstain from scurrility in his prospectus, but he was soon assailing Jefferson and his policies with as much abandon as had characterized Duane's attacks on Adams, and his insinuations against Jefferson's private morals were as indecent as they were false. He persevered in the pro-English policy of his party, advocated a strong navy, ridiculed Gallatin as a financier, but supported Jefferson in the Louisiana Purchase, while seeking to deprive him of the credit. During the first Jefferson administration, Coleman was under the direct influence of Hamilton, who frequently met him by appointment at late hours in the night to dictate editorials; and Hamilton contributed anonymous articles, such as the series of Lucius Crassus on Jefferson's first message to Congress. However, after Hamilton's death there was no marked deterioration in the editorial discussions of the *Post.*

During Jefferson's second administration, Coleman bitterly denounced his foreign policy as anti-English: fought the embargo; attacked Clay.

the leader of the war party, as "a liar and demagogue"; and sought to discredit and prevent the floating of the Gallatin loan. With war declared, he editorially discouraged the recruiting of federal regiments and called the war "unjust." He did not, however, participate in the Hartford Convention, albeit charged by Theodore Dwight, secretary of the convention, with having sought admission. After 1816 he ceased to be an uncompromising partisan. He had supported the state administration of DeWitt Clinton and favored him for the presidency in 1812. Four years later he was persuaded that the Jeffersonian policies were too popular to make war upon them wise, and he was soon defending Monroe as one "more generally acceptable to all classes . . . than any other man . . . since . . . Washington." Coming under the spell of the personality of Vice-President Tompkins in 1819, his antipathy for Democrats faded, and he supported William H. Crawford for president in 1824, largely because of a dislike for John Quincy Adams, and in 1828 he supported Jackson against Adams because of the more moderate tariff views of the former. His death occurred in the first year of the Jackson régime.

A ready writer, much given to literary allusions, trained by the law to an intelligent discussion of legislative and constitutional questions, Coleman made his influence widely felt. An excellent conversationalist, jovial, naturally kindly, and easily moved to pity, he was much loved by his associates. Despite his opposition to dueling, he was forced to fight Capt. Thompson, harbor-master of New York, in 1803 and the encounter at the foot of Twenty-first St. resulted in the death of the Captain. After Hamilton's death, Coleman, at Mrs. Hamilton's request, published a compilation of tributes, *Facts and Documents Relative to the Death of Major General Hamilton*; and in 1810 he published a pamphlet of 123 pages attacking Madison for refusing further communications from the British minister.

[There is no biography of Coleman. The most satisfying sketch is that by Allan Nevins in *The Evening Post: A Century of Journalism* (1922). A good characterization is that of Wm. Cullen Bryant in "A Brief Hist. of the Evening Post" in *N. Y. Evening Post: One Hundredth Anniversary* (1902). The *Memoir of Jeremiah Mason* (1917) contains Coleman's confession to Mason of Hamilton's dictation of editorials. Frederick J. Hudson, *Hist. of Journalism in the U. S.* (1873), and Geo. Henry Payne, *Hist. of Journalism in the U. S.* (1920), throw light on Coleman's rôle in the journalism of his time.]   C.G.B.

COLEMAN, WILLIAM TELL (Feb. 29, 1824–Nov. 22, 1893), merchant, San Francisco Vigilante, was born near Cynthiana, Harrison County, Ky. His father was Napoleon B. Coleman, a lawyer and at one time a member of the

legislature. Of his mother little is recorded. The boy was but nine when his father died, a bankrupt; and thereafter, with few opportunities for schooling, he had to work for the support of the family. At fifteen he went to Jacksonville, Ill., where he was employed by an uncle, one of the chief engineers for a system of railroads projected by the State; but the collapse of the State's program the following year threw him adrift. At St. Louis he found work in the lumber trade, leaving it two years later to enter St. Louis University as a preparation for the career of a lawyer. His health failing, he went to Louisiana in 1844, but shortly afterward returned and then went to Wisconsin. Regaining his health after several years, he decided on an overland journey to California. With his brother he arrived at Sutter's Mill, Aug. 4, 1849, and at once engaged in the buying and selling of cattle, making also some ventures in real estate. For several months he kept a store at Placerville, and later, with two partners, at Sacramento. In June 1850 he closed the Sacramento store and with one of his partners started the merchandising firm of William T. Coleman & Company in San Francisco. He was for a time a member, and sometimes the presiding officer, of the executive committee of the Committee of Vigilance of 1851, where he opposed the extremism of Sam Brannan and others. Though resigning from the executive committee after two months' service, he continued to be a member of the general organization and also of its mysterious and shadowy Committee of Thirteen which five years later was to bring another vigilance movement into being. In August 1852, in Boston, he married Carrie M. Page, and thereafter for about three years made his home in New York, where he established an eastern branch of his firm.

He returned to San Francisco in January 1856, to find that social conditions had relapsed into a state similar to that which preceded the citizens' uprising of 1851. The assassination of James King of William, editor of the *Bulletin*, by a New York ruffian, James Casey, on May 14, brought on a new crisis. A call from the old Committee of Thirteen was published, and on the following day a new Committee of Vigilance was formed, and Coleman was made president of its executive committee. In an article in the *Century Magazine*, published thirty-five years later, he makes the doubtful statement that absolute authority was given him and that without this grant of power he would not have accepted the place. The Committee began work promptly. On May 18 the sheriff, realizing the popular strength of the movement, surrendered Casey and another murderer, Charles Cora, to the Committee. They were put on trial on the 20th, found guilty on the 21st, and publicly hanged on the 22nd. For three months the Committee, with every evidence of general approval, though facing the proclamation of Gov. Johnson, who on June 3 declared San Francisco County in a state of insurrection, continued its work of trying criminals. On Aug. 18, after having hanged four of them, exiled twenty-three, and frightened many others into leaving the city—a record curiously similar to that of 1851, it held a great parade and then disbanded.

Coleman again became a resident of New York City, remaining there for several years. At the conclusion of the Civil War he returned. On Dec. 16, 1865, he received the complimentary vote of 26 legislators for the United States senatorship. He was frequently besought to accept public office, but always declined. During the anti-Chinese agitation of 1877, which brought on rioting and some destruction of property, he came to the front as the head of a Committee of Safety. Arming his volunteers at first with weapons from the War Department, but immediately thereafter discarding these arms and substituting hickory pick-handles, he organized a large force for the preservation of order. It was a brief episode, for the danger, which had become acute on July 23, had passed by the 26th, and by the 28th the Pick-Handle Brigade was dissolved. Coleman's various activities had brought him into national prominence. In the months immediately preceding the national campaign of 1884 he was enthusiastically supported for nomination as a presidential candidate by Charles A. Dana in the New York *Sun*. In 1886 his house failed with large liabilities. Though by a temporary adjustment the creditors were paid at forty cents on the dollar, Coleman declared that he would in time pay every one in full, a promise he fulfilled in the year before his death. He died in San Francisco, survived by his widow and two sons. Coleman is described by Bancroft as "tall, large, symmetrical in form, with a high intellectual forehead and eyes of illimitable depth and clearness" and of a presence "always imposing." The dedication of the second volume of the historian's *Popular Tribunals* (1890) addresses the Vigilante as "the chief of the greatest popular tribunal the world has ever witnessed"; and the work praises him in high terms.

[H. H. Bancroft, *Popular Tribunals* (1890); G. W. Sullivan, *Early Days in Cal.* (1888); S. S. Eldredge, ed., *Hist. of Cal.* (1915); Wm. Tell Coleman, "San Francisco Vigilance Committees," *Century Mag.,* Nov. 1891; "Sherman and the San Francisco Vigilantes," *Century Mag.,* Dec. 1891; T. H. Hittell, *Hist. of Cal.* (1897); Mary Floyd Williams, ed., "Papers of the San Francisco Committee of Vigilance of 1851," *Pubs. Acad. Pacific Coast Hist.,* vol. IV (1919), and "Hist." of the San Francisco Committee of Vigilance of 1851," *Univ. of Cal. Pubs. in History* (1921); *San Francisco Examiner,* Nov. 23, 1893.]
      W. J. G—t.

COLES, EDWARD (Dec. 15, 1786–July 7, 1868), abolitionist, governor of Illinois, was born on a plantation, "Enniscorthy," in Albemarle County, Va. His father, Col. John Coles, who was a slaveholder and of good family, had served in the Revolution and enjoyed the friendship of many of the foremost Virginia statesmen of the time. Edward was given an exceptional education and training, even for an aristocratic Virginian of that period. After being prepared by private tutors, he first attended Hampden-Sidney College, and later William and Mary, where he failed to graduate, however, owing to a physical injury. From 1809 to 1815 he served as private secretary to President Madison and in 1816 he was sent by the President to Russia on a diplomatic mission. His European journey also afforded him opportunity for travel in Germany, France, and the British Isles. The trend of Coles's later career was determined by a strain of idealism in his character which led him early in life to champion the anti-slavery cause, on moral and humanitarian grounds. Upon the death of his father in 1808, he had fallen heir to a plantation and a number of slaves, but this did not alter his attitude. In 1814 he corresponded with Jefferson on the subject of slavery and a letter of Jefferson's, dated Aug. 25, 1814, has become famous as one statement of the anti-slavery view-point (Washburne, *Coles,* Alvord ed., pp. 24–27). Being, as one of his friends expressed it, "an experimental philosopher," Coles determined to remove to free soil and emancipate his slaves. He had made two preliminary journeys to the Northwest, first in 1815 and again in 1818, and had decided to settle at Edwardsville, Ill., the state having been admitted to the Union in 1818.

He set out in the spring of 1819, carrying his negroes with him. With an instinct for the dramatic, he informed them of their emancipation during the journey down the Ohio River. Upon arriving in Illinois, he executed formal deeds of emancipation and assisted his former slaves to make a new start in life. On Mar. 5, 1819, he was appointed register of the Land Office at Edwardsville, a position which enabled him to extend his acquaintance among the people of the state. He is described at this time as "a young man of handsome, but somewhat awkward personal appearance, genteelly dressed, and of kind and agreeable manners" (*Ibid.,* p. 49). In 1822, only three years after his arrival in the state,

Coles was elected governor, though by a very narrow margin. His success may be attributed in part to the appearance of slavery in Illinois politics. Though nominally free territory, slavery virtually existed, and there was evidence of a desire to extend the institution. Coles naturally represented the forces opposed to this movement. In his first message to the Assembly, he urged the adoption of measures which would abolish slavery in fact as well as in name. The challenge was taken up by the pro-slavery faction, which passed a resolution calling for a referendum upon the question of holding a convention to amend the constitution. It was understood that one purpose of this move was to legalize slavery. A bitter struggle ensued, with Coles leading the anti-convention forces. In a letter to a friend he wrote at this time, "I assure you, I never before felt so deep an interest in any political question. It preys upon me to such a degree, that I shall not be happy or feel at ease until it is settled" (*Ibid.*, p. 122). The convention project was decisively defeated at the polls in August of 1824, and the menace of slavery was averted. As governor, Coles was greatly interested in the furthering of internal improvements and in the promotion of agriculture. As early as 1819 he had taken the initiative in organizing the first state agricultural society. In national politics he was at first a Republican. In 1824 he favored Crawford for the presidency, but later he became an opponent of Jackson. Aside from his career as governor he met with little success in state politics, being defeated for the United States Senate in 1824 and for Congress in 1831. Apparently he did not find life in a frontier state congenial, for a few years after retiring from the governorship in 1826, he removed to Philadelphia, probably in the fall of 1832. There he passed the remainder of his life, years which were happy, prosperous, but uneventful from a political standpoint. On Nov. 28, 1833, he was married to Sally Logan Roberts. He died in 1868 at the age of eighty-two, having witnessed the fulfilment of his life-long hope, though at the cost of civil war. In helping to prevent the extension of slavery into the Northwest, it is evident that he himself played no small part in the emancipation movement.

[The best account of Coles's life is Elihu B. Washburne's *Sketch of Edward Coles* (1882). It includes a full history of the convention struggle of 1824 and is valuable for the documents which it contains. This *Sketch* has been reprinted, along with additional documentary material, under the title "Gov. Edward Coles," as vol. XV (1920) of the *Colls. of the Ill. State Hist. Lib.*, edited by C. W. Alvord. Some of Coles's correspondence as governor is contained in E. B. Greene and C. W. Alvord, *Governors' Letter Books, 1818–1834*

(1909), vol. IV of the *Ill. Hist. Colls.* See also Solon J. Buck, *Illinois in 1818* (1917), and Theodore C. Pease. *The Frontier State, 1818–1848* (1918), the latter being vol. II of the Centennial History of Illinois. In the absence of any considerable body of manuscript material, early Illinois newspapers constitute one of the most valuable sources regarding his political activities.]
                    W. E. S—s.

COLFAX, SCHUYLER (Mar. 23, 1823–Jan. 13, 1885), vice-president of the United States, was born in New York City. His paternal grandfather, William Colfax, was commander of Washington's body-guard during the Revolutionary War (William Nelson, in the *Proceedings of the New Jersey Historical Society*, 2 ser., IV, 145–52). His maternal grandmother, Hester Schuyler, was a cousin of Gen. Philip Schuyler [*q.v.*]. His father, Schuyler Colfax, who married (Apr. 15, 1820) Hannah Stryker of New York, died Oct. 30, 1822, and in 1834 his mother married George W. Matthews of Baltimore. In 1836 the family removed to New Carlisle, Ind., where Matthews, who became auditor of St. Joseph County in 1841, appointed his stepson deputy auditor at South Bend, an office which he held for eight years. Colfax found time to serve as assistant enrolling clerk of the state Senate (1842–44) and as correspondent of the *Indiana State Journal* (Indianapolis) and also studied law, but was never admitted to the bar. Having bought an interest in the South Bend *Free Press* in 1845, he changed the name of the paper to *St. Joseph Valley Register*, made it the Whig organ of northern Indiana, and retained his interest in it until shortly after he became speaker of the House of Representatives. His political activities began early. He made campaign speeches for Clay in 1844, was secretary of the Chicago Rivers and Harbors Convention in 1847, delegate to the Whig national convention of 1848, and sat in the state constitutional convention of 1850. In 1851 he was defeated as a Whig candidate for Congress, notwithstanding a unanimous nomination, but was a delegate to the Whig national convention of 1852. When the Republican party was formed he joined it, and took an active part in organizing the new party in Indiana. In December 1855, he entered the House of Representatives of the Thirty-fourth Congress (1855–57) as a Republican, and served continuously until the end of the Fortieth Congress (Mar. 3, 1869). From the Thirty-eighth to the Fortieth Congress, inclusive (1863–69), he was speaker of the House. On June 21, 1856, he made a speech, of which more than a million copies were said to have been circulated, opposing the use of the army in Kansas until the laws of the Territory should have received congressional approval. His longest and most important service, prior to the speakership, was as chairman of the Committee on Post Offices and Post Roads, in which capacity he directed the reorganization and extension of the overland mail service to California. He was strongly urged for postmaster-general under Lincoln, but was passed over on the ground, as Lincoln wrote, that he was "a young man, is already in position, is running a brilliant career, and is sure of a bright future in any event" (Hollister, *post*, p. 175). On Apr. 8, 1864, he left the speaker's chair to move the expulsion of Alexander Long of Ohio, who had spoken in favor of recognizing the Confederacy. The resolution was later changed to one of censure.

His position as speaker, together with his "advanced ideas on Negro suffrage" (W. A. Dunning, *Reconstruction Political and Economic*, 1907, p. 129), commended Colfax as a candidate for vice-president in 1868, and at the Chicago convention, after the fifth ballot, when he received 541 votes, his nomination was made unanimous (E. Stanwood, *History of the Presidency*, I, 321), and he was later elected. An offer of the secretaryship of state in August 1871 was declined. Consideration of his availability as a presidential candidate by the Liberal Republicans in 1872 aroused the opposition of administration leaders, and at the Philadelphia convention he was defeated for renomination on the first ballot, the vote standing 321½ for Colfax and 364½ for Henry Wilson (*Ibid.*, I, 348). Shortly thereafter he declined an offer of the editorship of the *New York Tribune*. He was implicated in the Crédit Mobilier scandal, the investigation showing that he had agreed to accept twenty shares of stock in the company and had received a considerable sum in dividends. His denial of the charge was not convincing, and in his examination before the committee "it is impossible to believe that he told the truth" (Rhodes, VII, 13–15). He escaped formal censure on the ground that his misconduct, if any, had been committed before he became vice-president, but although he claimed to have been "fully exonerated" (*Biographical Directory of the American Congress*, 1928, p. 834), his political standing was ruined. His part in the Crédit Mobilier affair was somewhat overshadowed by the disclosure that he had received in 1868 a campaign gift of $4,000 from a contractor who had supplied envelopes to the government while Colfax was chairman of the Committee on Post Offices and Post Roads. He continued after his retirement to be in demand as a lecturer, and devoted much time to the Odd Fellows, of which

order he had been a member since 1846. He died suddenly at Mankato, Minn., and was buried at South Bend. His first wife, Evelyn Clark of New York, whom he married Oct. 10, 1844, died at Newport, R. I., July 10, 1863. On Nov. 18, 1868, he married Ellen W. Wade, a niece of Benjamin F. Wade of Ohio [*q.v.*].

[The chief authority, aside from the *Jour. of the House of Representatives*, the *Cong. Globe*, and the reports of House committees, is O. J. Hollister, *Life of Schuyler Colfax* (1886), able and thorough but over-friendly. A. Y. Moore, *The Life of Schuyler Colfax* (1868), a campaign biography, is valuable for the texts of speeches, letters, newspaper comment, etc. The Poland and Wilson reports on the Crédit Mobilier scandal form *House Report No. 77*, 42 Cong., 3 Sess.; their facts and findings are judiciously summarized and appraised in J. F. Rhodes, *Hist. of the U. S.*, VII (1906), ch. 40.]
W. M.

COLGATE, JAMES BOORMAN (Mar. 4, 1818–Feb. 7, 1904), stock-broker, philanthropist, was the son of William [*q.v.*] and Mary (Gilbert) Colgate and was born in New York City. He attended school in the city and in Connecticut until he was about sixteen, when he began work in the commission house of Boorman, Johnson & Company. He went to Europe in 1841, and on his return the following year was employed by a wholesale dry-goods house. In 1852 he formed a stock-brokerage partnership with John B. Trevor, under the firm name of Trevor & Colgate. Five years later the firm added a bullion department, to which Colgate gave most of his time. During the Civil War the firm served in some degree to regulate the ratio of value between gold and paper, thus preventing the hoarding of specie, and in various ways helped to sustain the credit of the government. In 1873 the name was changed to James B. Colgate & Company, which is still retained. During the earlier stages of the resumption of specie payments the firm conducted the largest specie and bullion business of any house in the United States. Colgate was one of the founders, and for a number of years the president, of the New York Gold Exchange and in his last years vice-president and a director of the Bank of the State of New York. He was an advocate of the remonetization of silver during the years 1890–97, and despite the adverse sentiment of nearly all his business colleagues, vigorously maintained his position with tongue and pen. He was married twice: first, about 1847 to Miss Hoyt of Utica, N. Y., who died a few years later, and, in 1857 to Susan F. Colby, who, with a daughter and a son, survived him. Like his father, he was a Baptist. Becoming prosperous at an early period of his business career, he followed his father's example of contributing generously to educational and religious institutions.

With his partner Trevor he built the Warburton Avenue Baptist Church in Yonkers. He made many gifts to Madison University in Hamilton, N. Y., and in 1873, with the assistance of his brother Samuel, built and endowed in the same village Colgate Academy, thereafter serving for a number of years as the president of its board of trustees. On the combining, in 1890, of the University and the Academy, the institution was named, in honor of his father, Colgate University. He is said to have made a substantial gift to it every year, and during the period of thirty years to have given to it and to its predecessors more than a million dollars, as well as a substantial donation to Colby Academy, at New London, N. H., the home of his wife. He had a wide range of interests and was a member and supporter of several societies for the furtherance of knowledge and art.

[*Who's Who in America*, 1903–05; *N. Y. Times, N. Y. Tribune*, and *N. Y. Herald*, Feb. 8, 1904; information as to certain facts from Jas. C. Colgate.]

W. J. G—t.

COLGATE, WILLIAM (Jan. 25, 1783–Mar. 25, 1857), manufacturer of soaps and toilet preparations, was born in the parish of Hollingbourn, Kent, England, the son of Robert and Sarah (Bowles) Colgate. In March 1795, the father, threatened with arrest for his too ardent advocacy of the French Revolution, sailed with his family for Baltimore. He bought and cultivated a farm near Baltimore, but lost it through a defect in the title. His son William had some schooling both in England and in America. At fifteen he went to work, probably for a tallow-chandler, and in 1804 he left Baltimore for New York, finding employment with Slidell & Company, then the largest tallow-chandlers in the city. Before long he became business manager of the firm. In 1806 he started his own establishment in Dutch St., which from the first was successful. He was married, in 1811, to Mary Gilbert, a woman highly praised for her cultivation, charm, and benevolence. By 1812, worth $5,000, he considered himself wealthy, and his after-years are said to have been of uninterrupted prosperity. About this time he began the manufacture of starch, subsequently abandoned, and for many years his establishment included one of the largest starch plants in America. Though the manufacture of soap in this country was then in its crude beginnings, the finer qualities being made by secret process in England and France, the industry grew enormously during the first four decades of the century, and Colgate's business shared in this expansion. The discoveries of Chevreul in 1841, revealing the true principles of saponification, were quickly utilized by Colgate and others, greatly transforming the industry and prompting the manufacture of many new varieties of toilet and shaving soaps. In 1847 the factory was moved to Jersey City, and three years later the making of "fancy" soaps was established on a large scale, to be followed in later years by a wide range of toilet preparations.

Out of his first profits Colgate bought a farm in Delaware County, N. Y., for his father. When he began business he resolved to devote ten per cent of each year's net earnings to benevolence—a resolve adhered to throughout the remainder of his life, though the percentage was often doubled and even trebled. His main interests were education, religion, and temperance. He was a liberal supporter of the Hamilton Literary and Theological Seminary, at Hamilton, N. Y., and its successor (1846), Madison University, which in 1890 became Colgate University. In his twenty-fifth year he joined the Baptist Church. He aided in organizing the first Bible society formed in New York and in 1816 in organizing the American Bible Society. In 1836, however, objecting to some of the methods of the latter society, he resigned and helped to organize the American and Foreign Bible Society, of which for thirteen years he was the treasurer. By 1838 he had come to regard sectarianism as an obstacle to the progress of Christianity. Withdrawing from his church, he joined with others in organizing the society which built the Tabernacle, a society which adopted no creed, but only a simple covenant. In the same year he admitted to partnership his son Samuel. Until about a year before his death he continued actively in business. He died at his home in New York City, leaving three sons: Samuel (1822–97), who succeeded to the business and greatly extended it, James Boorman [*q.v.*], and Robert.

In the manufacture of soaps and toilet preparations in the United States Colgate was a pioneer. He combined shrewd judgment with clear vision, and he seems never to have made a serious commercial blunder. Even during the ruinous times of the War of 1812 he prospered. He was noted, among other things, as the possessor of an exceptionally sunny temperament. He was just in his dealings; to his employees he was liberal, and he was known as a friend of the workingman. His hospitality was lavish, and to the causes he had at heart he was a generous contributor.

[Samuel Colgate, "Am. Soap Factories," in *One Hundred Years of Am. Commerce* (1895), ed. by C. M. Depew; *N. Y. Tribune*, Mar. 26, 1857; W. W. Everts, *Wm. Colgate, the Christian Layman* (1881); information as to certain facts from Jas. C. Colgate.]

W. J. G—t.

COLLAMER, JACOB (Jan. 8, 1791–Nov. 9, 1865), judge, United States senator, postmaster-general, was born in Troy, N. Y., third of the eight children of Samuel Collamer, member of an early Massachusetts family, and Elizabeth Van Ornum, of colonial Dutch descent. The family moved to Burlington, Vt., when Jacob was about four. Here he prepared for college under members of the faculty, and graduated from the University of Vermont in 1810. At once he began the study of law at St. Albans, Vt., under Mr. Langworthy and later under Benjamin Swift, afterward senator. His studies were interrupted by his being drafted into the detailed militia service in 1812. He served as lieutenant of artillery and as aide to Gen. French, with whom he went to Plattsburg, arriving in the evening after the battle was over. Admitted to the bar in 1813 he practised at Randolph Center until he removed to Royalton in 1816. He married Mary N. Stone of St. Albans, daughter of Abijah Stone, on July 15, 1817. He served four terms in the legislature as representative of Royalton, and was one of the assistant judges of the supreme court of Vermont from 1833 until 1842 when he declined reëlection. As delegate to the Vermont constitutional convention (1836) he actively supported the movement to substitute a state Senate for the old Governor's Council. "That amendment has been largely attributed to the ability and zeal with which he urged it" (Barrett, *post*). This year he moved to Woodstock, Vt., his home for the rest of his life. His national career began in 1842 when, after a close and hotly contested election, he was chosen member of the House of Representatives for the 2nd Congressional District. Reëlected in 1844 and 1846, he declined a fourth election. As representative he made speeches on the annexation of Texas, the Mexican War, and the tariff, his address on "Wools and Woolens" attracting most attention. Recommended for a cabinet position by a legislative caucus, he became postmaster-general in the cabinet of President Taylor (1849). His service was short, for upon the death of President Taylor in July 1850 he resigned with the rest of the cabinet.

A few months after his return home, the Vermont legislature elected him, under the recently remodeled judicial system, circuit judge for the 2nd judicial circuit. In 1854, a candidate of the young Republican party as an anti-slavery Whig, he was elected senator. As a Republican he belonged to the conservative wing. In the Thirty-fourth Congress he served on the Committee on Territories under the chairmanship of Senator Douglas, and on Mar. 12, 1856 made a vigorous minority report on the disorders in Kansas, defending the character of the free-state leaders. He was one of three New England senators to vote against the tariff bill of 1857. In 1860 Vermont presented his name to the Republican convention for the presidential nomination, but after the first ballot, on which he received ten votes, his name was withdrawn. In the same year he was reëlected to the Senate "with almost unprecedented unanimity." He and Fessenden refused to vote against the Crittenden compromise of the winter of 1861, though they did not vote for it. He drafted the bill, enacted July 13, 1861, which, according to Senator Sumner, "gave to the war for the suppression of the rebellion its first congressional sanction and invested the President with new powers" (Address of Senator Charles Sumner, Dec. 14, 1865). On the problems of Reconstruction he held that Congress should control. While not an orator, and rarely speaking in the Senate, he was always listened to with attention, the logic of his arguments commanding respect. From June 1855 to October 1862 he was president— the last—of the Vermont Medical College at Woodstock, in which he had lectured on medical law. He died at his home in Woodstock after a brief illness. Judge James Barrett, long his law partner, said of Collamer, "His mind was made up of a clear and ready perception, acuteness of discrimination, a facile faculty of analysis, an aptness and ease in rigid and simple logic, excellent commonsense, and withal a most tenacious memory of facts."

[The chief source is the *Memorial Address* read by Judge Jas. Barrett before the Vt. Hist. Soc., Oct. 20, 1868 (Rutland, 1868; Woodstock, 1868). Consult also *Addresses on the Death of Hon. Jacob Collamer delivered in the Senate and House of Representatives*, Dec. 14, 1865 (1866) and *Addresses on the Presentation of the Statue of Jacob Collamer of Vermont*, by Jas. M. Tyler, Geo. B. Long, and Alexander H. Stephens, delivered in the House of Representatives Feb. 15, 1881 (1881); and Henry Swan Dana, *Hist. of Woodstock, Vt.* (1889).]   C. R. W.

COLLENS, THOMAS WHARTON (June 23, 1812–Nov. 3, 1879), jurist, writer, known to his contemporaries as T. Wharton Collens, was born in New Orleans, the son of John Wharton Collens and Marie Louise de Tabiteau. For a while he was employed as a printer. As a young man he contributed to the city papers a number of articles dealing with social problems in which he had become interested. Some of these appeared in the *True American*, edited during the thirties by his kinsman, John Gibson, "the faithful and bold." At this time Collens was a follower of Robert Dale Owen in his peculiar deistical doctrines and social theories. The philosophy of Fourier also made a deep appeal to him. Turning to the study of law, young Collens was admitted to the bar in 1833. His rise to prominence in the courts of his native city was rapid. The following year (1834) he held the position of clerk and reporter of the state Senate. He further served as chief deputy clerk of the federal circuit court (1836–38), and as district attorney for the Parish of Orleans (1840–42). As a result of his ability, industry, and fidelity, criminal law was administered during this time with marked vigor. His reward came in being designated as presiding judge of the city court of New Orleans (1842–46). Later he served as judge of the first district court (1856), and after the Civil War he was twice elected judge of the seventh district court (1867–73). He then resumed the practise of his profession. He was also a member of the convention which framed the constitution of 1852. Though opposed to secession, Collens cast in his lot with the Confederacy. A close student, with quick and penetrating faculties, and habits of unusual methodical industry, his decisions while judge were accepted by the bar with marked respect. As a writer Collens is remembered by his "Lines to the Memory of Father Turgis," printed among other places in the *Living Writers of the South* (1869). At the age of twenty-four he brought out an historical tragedy in five acts entitled *The Martyr Patriots; or Louisiana in 1769* (see *The Louisiana Book: Selections from the Literature of the State,* 1894, ed. by Thomas McCaleb). This drama was performed in the old St. Charles Theatre in 1836. In addition to "Humanics" and the "History of Charity," his most pretentious work is *The Eden of Labor; or the Christian Utopia* (1876). In the introduction to this volume the author states that his intention is "to carry to legitimate and ultimate consequences, the fundamental principles admitted by all economists, viz., 'Labor is the real measure of the exchangeable value of all commodities and services,' and to show that the principle and its application rest still deeper upon the rights of God, and the law of *neighborly love* propounded by our Lord Jesus Christ." From this it is seen the author had left far behind the theories of his youth. At one time he had attained the rank of grand master in masonry, but for a number of years before his death he was a devout Catholic. His wife, Amenaide Milbrou, by whom he had eight children, died before him. In person Collens was a man of courtly manners and address, making himself an agreeable social companion. He spoke French by choice, saying that it was impossible to converse well in any other lan-

guage. A little above medium height in stature, with dark hair and eyes, indicative of his Creole origin, his features were prepossessing, if not handsome.

[There is a brief sketch in McCaleb's book referred to above. The bare facts of Collens's career are listed in *The South in the Building of the Nation* (12 vols., 1909–10), VII, 323; XI, 221, where his name is misspelled Collins. See obituaries in the *Daily Democrat* (New Orleans), and *New Orleans Times,* Nov. 9, 1879.]
         J. E. W—n.

COLLES, CHRISTOPHER (1738–Oct. 4, 1816), engineer, inventor, and promoter of internal improvements, was born in Ireland probably in 1738. His education, which appears to have been thorough, was directed by Richard Pococke, Anglican bishop and distinguished oriental traveler. After the bishop's death in 1765 Colles, who early manifested an interest in science, came to America. In 1772 he lectured in Philadelphia on pneumatics and the following year in New York on inland navigation. Always planning new devices and new ways of doing things, he suggested in 1774 that New York City replace its wells and springs with a water system. To this end he proposed the erection of reservoirs and the piping of the city's streets. All his proposals in this connection were seriously considered but the state of the city's finances and the disturbances occasioned by the Revolution resulted in their indefinite postponement. From 1775 to 1777, when Baron von Steuben arrived, Colles was an instructor in the artillery department of the Continental Army and taught the principles of projectiles. He was one of the first persons in America to design a steam-engine and was also one of the first to attempt to build one; although the undertaking failed for want of adequate funds, the design was heartily approved by David Rittenhouse and the American Philosophical Society.

From early manhood Colles was deeply interested in internal improvements, particularly canals. He seems to have been the first to propose linking the Great Lakes with the Hudson River by means of natural and artificial waterways and to point out the great social, economic, and political advantages that would accrue from such an improvement. The scheme received wide publicity. In 1785 its author memorialized the legislature in its behalf, and shortly afterward the project was enthusiastically indorsed by the New York Chamber of Commerce. This indorsement, together with the support which the proposal received in other quarters, resulted in the introduction in both Houses of the state legislature of a bill "for improving the navigation of the Mohawk River, Wood Creek and Onondaga

River, with a view to opening an inland navigation to Oswego and for extending the same if practicable to Lake Erie." Many were in favor of passing the bill and putting Colles in charge of the work. Incidentally, he had already traversed much of the territory through which the proposed waterways would extend and had surveyed a portion of the Mohawk River. Many years later (1808) he proposed construction of a canal between New York and Philadelphia which would be built entirely of timber and would be above ground. He was also deeply interested in roads and road-building and during the late eighties made an extensive personal survey of the roads of New York and Pennsylvania. In 1796 he went into business in New York City where he manufactured such articles as rat and mouse-traps, paper hangings, fireworks, band-boxes, and colors. He also dealt in furs and Indian goods. But he was too much interested in invention and science to make a success of either merchandising or manufacturing. During these years he supplied Blanchard & Brown, publishers of the *Mathematical Correspondent*, with astronomical calculations, made proof glasses, and invented a number of useful devices. During the War of 1812 he constructed and operated a semaphoric telegraph on Castle Clinton.

A man of lovable character, pleasing personality, and absolute honesty, Colles stood in high esteem. Unfortunately, he was usually in pecuniary difficulties, and was, therefore, compelled to rely on the assistance of friends. An appointment in the customs service, where he was assigned the duty of testing the specific gravity of imported liquors, helped to relieve the financial strain; and eventually, through John Pintard, one of his closest and most influential friends, he was made superintendent of the American Academy of Fine Arts. As a publisher of scientific and semi-scientific essays and pamphlets Colles was fairly prolific. His chief works were: *Syllabus of Lectures on Natural Philosophy* (1773); *Proposals for the Settlement of Western New York and for the Improvement of Inland Navigation between Albany and Oswego* (1785); *A Survey of the Roads of the United States of America* (1789); *The Geographical Ledger and Systematized Atlas; Being a United Collection of the Topographaical* [sic] *Maps Projected by One Universal Principle and Laid Down by One Scale* (1794); *Proposals of a Design for Inland Communication of a New Construction* (1808); and *Description of the Universal Telegraph* (1813).

[Little biographical material regarding Colles is to be had other than that found in his own writings and in the newspaper publicity which his numerous inventions and proposals received. Brief mention is made of him and his work in histories of New York City, the more important of which are Mrs. Martha J. Lamb's *Hist. of the City of N. Y.: Its Origin, Rise and Progress* (1877–80), II, 577, and *The Memorial Hist. of the City of N. Y. from Its First Settlement to the Year 1892* (1893), ed. by Jas. Grant Wilson, scattered references in vols. III and IV. New York City newspapers of the time also contain brief obituaries, of which that in the N. Y. *Evening Post*, Oct. 5, 1816, is typical.]

H.J.C.

COLLIER, HENRY WATKINS (Jan. 17, 1801–Aug. 28, 1855), jurist, governor of Alabama, was the son of James and Elizabeth (Bouldin) Collier, both members of prominent Virginia families. He was born on the ancestral plantation in Lunenburg County, but when he was a year old his parents removed to the Abbeville District of South Carolina, and, in 1818, to the newly opened cotton lands of the Tennessee Valley, in Madison County, Ala. Henry received his basic education in the famous school of Dr. Moses Waddel [*q.v.*] at Willington, S. C., where Calhoun, McDuffie, Petigru, and Longstreet also were instructed. After the removal to Huntsville, Ala., he took up the study of law at Nashville under the tutelage of Judge John Haywood of the supreme court of Tennessee. He was admitted to the Huntsville bar in 1822, and the following year went to Tuscaloosa, Ala., to practise law. Here, in 1826, he married Mary Ann Battle of North Carolina, a sister of one of his Tuscaloosa colleagues. Collier was at this time a well-knit young man with ample brow and kindly gray eyes. His bearing was dignified, his manner reserved, and his temperament judicial. Though apparently lacking in the qualifications of a Western politician, he espoused the Democratic cause, and was elected to the legislature in 1827. During the next year he was elected by that body to membership in the highest court of the state. When the supreme court was separately organized for the first time in 1832, Collier was retained on the circuit bench. In 1836 the governor gave him an appointment *ad interim* to the supreme court, and at its next session the legislature confirmed the governor's choice and elected him to the place. He was elected the following year to the chief justiceship and served in that capacity for twelve years. Lacking brilliant mental qualifications, he performed his judicial duties with laborious care and left himself little time to look after his private interests as a planter (Garrett, *post*, p. 718). He was a faithful Methodist, and became one of the leading supporters of his denomination in Tuscaloosa.

That a man lacking in oratorical or political gifts should be nominated for the governorship in 1849 and elected by a vote of 36,350 to 364 indicates not only the dominance of the Democratic party in the state at that time, but also the power within the party of its conservative leaders. This was not the brand of democracy which Andrew Johnson represented during the same period in Tennessee. As governor, Collier retained the placid dignity which had characterized him as judge. When he was renominated in 1851, he refused to take the stump, saying that he would stand on his record alone. The question of the compromise measures of 1850 was the leading issue in the campaign. William L. Yancey represented the extreme Southern faction which opposed compromise, while B. G. Shields stood for unconditional submission to the Union. Collier stood for the compromise and the Georgia platform, refusing to go to either extreme represented by the other two men. He was elected by a large majority. In matters of state policy, Collier stood for the free banking system, and for educational and judicial reforms. He took a keen interest in the humanitarian movement which was in progress at the time, and, visited by Dorothea L. Dix [q.v.], used his influence to secure in the state penitentiary system some of the reforms which she advocated. On his retirement from the governorship he was offered a seat in the Senate of the United States, but his health had been undermined by hard work and he died while seeking to regain his strength at Bailey Springs, Ala., in 1855.

[Thos. M. Owen, *Hist. of Ala.* (4 vols., 1921); W. Brewer, *Alabama* (1872); Wm. Garrett, *Reminiscences of Public Men in Ala.* (1872), pp. 718–20; B. F. Riley, *Makers and Romance of Ala.* (n.d.); obituary in the *Independent* (Gainesville, Ala.), Sept. 8, 1855. The *Journal* of the Ala. House of Representatives for 1849–50 contains Collier's message for that year.]

T.P.A.

COLLIER, HIRAM PRICE (May 25, 1860–Nov. 3, 1913), author, was the son of Robert Laird Collier, a distinguished Unitarian clergyman of Maryland stock, and Mary Price. He dropped his first name and was generally known as Price Collier. He was born in Davenport, Iowa, at the home of his mother's parents. After the death of his mother in 1872, his father took him to Europe, where he spent five years at school in Geneva and Leipzig and became proficient in French and German. After graduation from the Harvard Divinity School in 1882, he was for nine years a Unitarian minister at Hingham and elsewhere in Massachusetts. In 1891 he left the ministry to take up writing. Of slender but athletic build, five feet eleven inches in height, he was a good shot, played all games well, and loved outdoor life. For a time after 1891 he was in the West, and his first book, *Mr. Picket Pin and His Friends* (London, 1894), was an account of the Sioux Indians and reservation life. On Aug. 8, 1893, he married Katharine D. Robbins and sailed for England, where he was European editor of the *Forum*. Returning to America in 1895 he made his permanent home in Tuxedo Park, N. Y., and devoted himself to writing and study. A sharply critical volume purporting to be written by a Frenchman, *America and the Americans from the French Point of View*, was published, at first anonymously, in 1897; *A Parish of Two*, a story told in letters and written in collaboration with Henry G. McVickar, appeared in 1903. Collier also contributed the chapters on riding to a book on *Driving and Riding* (1905) for Macmillan's Sportsman's Library. During the Spanish War he was in active service as an ensign in the navy. Afterward he was secretary of the Outing Publishing Company. His book *England and the English from an American Point of View*, published serially and in book form in 1909, was the first to gain him a wide audience, and suggested the direction of his later writing. His subsequent years were spent largely in travel with Mrs. Collier in Europe, South America, India, China, and Japan. In 1911 appeared *The West in the East from an American Point of View*, followed in 1913 by *Germany and the Germans from an American Point of View*. At the time of his death he had spent the summer with his wife and two daughters in Scandinavian countries, contributing articles to *Scribner's*. He died suddenly of heart failure while shooting on the estate of Count Wedell on the island of Fünen, Denmark. Appearing just before the World War, his book on Germany attracted general attention. Though not unfriendly or intentionally unfair, it was, like all his other writing, plain-spoken, incisive, a trifle over-positive. In his earlier book on England he had declared that "the Germans since 1870 have taken the place of the English as the boors of Europe," and he also predicted their defeat in a war against England. Hence there was a furor when he was received with special favor by the Kaiser. He had a faculty for presenting a wealth of information in popular, attractive style, spiced with sharp observation and comment. His zest for fact appears in his own statement that he got more keen enjoyment out of a census report than from a novel (*Germany and the Germans*, p. 185). He stated his beliefs vigorously, and some of his characteristic beliefs were in capital punishment, athletics, war, the Kaiser, and the House of Lords. He attacked socialism, and though intensely patriotic, was critical of much in modern American life.

[Obituaries in the *N. Y. Times*, Nov. 4 and Nov. 9

(editorial), 1913; *Outlook,* Nov. 15, 1913; brief sketch and portrait in *Rev. of Revs.* (N. Y.), June 1911. Collier's writings contain some biographical material, and Mrs. Collier has supplied information as to certain facts.]					A. W.

COLLIER, PETER (Aug. 17, 1835–June 29, 1896), agricultural chemist, a son of Jacob and Mary Elizabeth Collier, was born at Chittenango, N. Y., where he passed his childhood and youth. Between the ages of fourteen and nineteen he was engaged for some portion of his time, first in a drug store and then in selling merchandise. Fitted for college at Late's Polytechnic Institute in his home town, he entered Yale College and graduated in the class of 1861. He then took graduate work in chemistry at Yale and became a special student under Prof. S. W. Johnson. Here he acquired his interest in the applications of chemistry to agriculture. He was made an assistant in chemistry and took the degree of Ph.D. in 1866. In the following year he was appointed professor of chemistry, mineralogy, and metallurgy in the University of Vermont, and of toxicology and chemistry in the medical school. In 1870 he received the degree of M.D. and became the dean of the medical faculty. His special interest in agriculture and knowledge of the relations of chemistry to this and other commercial interests was recognized by his election the next year as secretary of the state board of agriculture, mining, and manufacture. He became more and more engaged in the problems of the farm and in promoting agricultural education; and with all his other duties found time to conduct a series of farm institutes throughout the state. In 1873 he visited the International Exposition at Vienna as one of the United States commissioners and made an extended report on the fertilizer materials in the exposition.

He resigned his positions in Vermont in 1877 to become chief chemist in the United States Department of Agriculture. His chief work here, besides a study of grasses and forage crops made jointly with the department botanist, was an elaborate and careful investigation of sorghum, the problems of its growth and the commercial production of sugar from it, which was the first really important chemical research work done in the department. In 1883, with a change in the administration, he left the agricultural department and devoted his time to writing a work embodying the results of his investigations: *Sorghum, Its Culture and Manufacture, economically considered as a Source of Sugar, Syrup and Fodder* (1884). After four years of residence in Washington, D. C., he was chosen in 1887 director of the New York Agricultural Experiment Station at Geneva, N. Y., succeeding Dr. E. Lewis Sturtevant. His management of the station directed investigation along lines which, without impairing its scientific character and value, made very direct appeal to the farmers of the state because of its practical applications. His labors resulted in finally fixing the character and great practical value of the institution in the minds of its patrons and supporters. During his administration the equipment of the station was much increased, its staff increased three-fold, and work on special projects was begun in different parts of the state. Attacked by a fatal and lingering illness, he resigned in 1895 and went to Ann Arbor, Mich., where he died. On Oct. 18, 1871 he had married Caroline Frances, daughter of Hon. Andrew A. Angell of Scituate, R. I. His wife and a daughter survived him. An excellent portrait of Collier, the gift of a classmate, is owned by Yale University. In private life he was a man of personal charm, ready wit, and prized either as a casual acquaintance or as a familiar friend.

[Records of Yale Class of 1861, especially *Second Supp. to the Twenty-five Years' Record* (1897); *Reports of the U. S. Commissioner of Agriculture,* 1877–83; *Reports of the N. Y. Agric. Station,* 1888–95; sketch by W. H. Jordan in L. H. Bailey, *Cyc. Am. Agriculture,* vol. IV (1909), pp. 563–64.]					E. H. J.

COLLIER, PETER FENELON (Dec. 12, 1849–Apr. 24, 1909), publisher, son of Robert C. and Catherine (Fenelon) Collier of Myshall, County Carlow, Ireland, came to America at the age of seventeen. He had studied in Irish schools, and his parents had wished him to prepare for the priesthood. Arriving in the United States shortly after the close of the Civil War, he went to Ohio and in the course of time entered St. Mary's Seminary at Cincinnati, maintaining himself meanwhile by doing carpentry work at Dayton. Before he became of age, however, he had given up the idea of following the priesthood as a career. Early in the seventies he went to New York City and engaged himself to a firm of publishers of Catholic books as a salesman. While in that employment he developed a plan of selling on instalment payments, but as this did not commend itself to his employers he went into business independently and as a publisher of Catholic books was notably successful. He then, with a limited capital, undertook the publication of standard works of popular appeal at low prices, with instalment payments. Himself a man of literary taste, he was not content to purvey books of inferior quality. He began in 1877 with sets of Dickens and Shakespeare. These were manufactured under contracts with New York printers and binders, but about 1880

Collier began to assemble a plant of his own and this shortly grew into one of the most complete and best-equipped printeries in the country. During the last thirty years of his life, his firm printed and sold more than 50,000,000 books. Many standard works sold at an average price of from fifty to sixty cents a volume. More than seventeen per cent of the total sales were histories. Among novelists, Dickens alone accounted for nearly 6,000,000 volumes and Cooper for 1,500,000. Of encyclopedias, nearly 2,000,000 volumes were printed and circulated. Branch offices in thirty-two of the chief cities controlled ninety-six sub-branches, with managers, salesmen, deliverers, collectors, and clerical force. The manufacturing plant in New York employed over 700 persons and had a capacity of 20,000 volumes a day. The presses were equipped with new improvements as fast as they could be installed. To the end of his life, Collier was the driving force in this huge establishment. In 1888 he founded a periodical called *Once a Week,* which was replaced in 1896 by *Collier's Weekly,* a journal that quickly attained, through able editorship, a commanding rank among publications of its class. It "discovered" a number of short-story writers of distinct merit and by its independent attitude in politics won a constituency of serious readers throughout the country. It refused advertisements of beer, whiskey, or alcoholic liquors, as well as of patent medicines and articles making claims to medicinal effects, and investments promising extraordinary returns. For its comment on the course of a "society" publication in New York the publisher and editors of *Collier's* were sued for libel. In the case against the writer of the offending article the jury found for the defendant. The other actions were dropped.

Collier was always known as an "out-of-doors" man. For years he was master of the Meadowbrook Hunt on Long Island and later was active in a New Jersey hunting club, the owner of noted horses, and a polo enthusiast. It was often said of him that he played as hard as he worked. It was his pride to be the circulator of meritorious books in humble homes, and hardly less was it his ambition to live as a true sportsman. Collier was married in 1873 to Katherine Dunn, of County Carlow. Their son, Robert, was responsible editor of *Collier's Weekly* in its early years.

[*In Memoriam: Peter Fenelon Collier* (privately printed, 1910); editorial, *Collier's Weekly,* May 8, 1909; data supplied by George J. Kennedy, of Peter F. Collier & Son.]
                          W. B. S.

COLLIER, PRICE. [See COLLIER, HIRAM PRICE, 1860–1913.]

COLLINS, EDWARD KNIGHT (Aug. 5, 1802–Jan. 22, 1878), ship-owner, was descended from Joseph Collins, son of a starch maker, who in 1635 came from Ireland with his family and settled in Lynn, Mass. One of Joseph's sons moved to Cape Cod where for several generations his descendants followed the sea. About 1800, Capt. Israel Gross Collins on a trip to England married Mary Ann Knight and brought her back to Truro. There she died five months after the birth of her only son, Edward Knight Collins, who was to become the leader of the most ambitious and spectacular attempt of the American merchant marine to challenge British supremacy (Shebnah Rich, *Truro-Cape Cod,* 1883, pp. 391, 522). At fifteen, Edward went to New York where he was to reside for the rest of his life. After serving as a clerk for the house of McCrea & Slidell, he went to the West Indies as supercargo in a joint venture. For a while, he and his father conducted a general commission business before he entered on his important life-work, the management of packet lines. He took over and improved the line to Vera Cruz and in 1831 secured control of the New Orleans line. Five years later, he started the "Dramatic Line" from New York to England, so called because the ships were named after famous actors. His continued success in these ventures gave him a high reputation for ability and made him one of the wealthiest men in New York.

Foreseeing that steam would soon replace sails, Collins began to study its possibilities. When England made its subsidy mail contract with Samuel Cunard in 1838, he is reported to have urged upon Van Buren the need of a steam navy of subsidized mail steamers. The President is said to have replied curtly that this country needed no navy at all, much less a steam navy (*New York Herald,* Jan. 23, 1878). The Cunard Line prospered from its very first trip to Boston in 1840. Congress, convinced that American subsidies were necessary to combat this "monopoly," in 1845 authorized government aid through mail contracts to lines which would build potential warships (*Statutes at Large,* V, 748–50). Contracts were soon made for lines to Bremen and Havre and to the Pacific coast via Panama, but the most important effort to "drive the Cunarders out of business" developed from a proposal made by Collins on Mar. 6, 1846 (*Senate Document 237,* 29 Cong., 1 Sess., p. 6). On Nov. 1, 1847, Collins and his associates, James and Stewart Brown, made a contract with the postmaster general. They were to build, under naval supervision, five steamships of specified size, which were to make twenty round trips annually, carrying mails between New York and Liverpool. For this, they were to receive $385,000 annually for ten years, dating from the first trip (*Statutes at Large*, IX, 187, 378; *House Executive Document 91*, 32 Cong., 1 Sess., p. 36). Five weeks later, they organized the United States Mail Steamship Company, generally known as the "Collins Line" (*Ibid.*, p. 76). Collins spent more than two years building four ships which were to surpass in size, speed, and splendor anything then afloat. Sparing no expense and exceeding the government requirements, he gave them hulls of oak and pine averaging nearly 2,800 tons and engines of 1,500 horse-power (C. B. Stuart, *On Naval and Mail Steamers*, 1853, *passim*). Service began on Apr. 27, 1850 when the *Atlantic* sailed from New York, followed in the course of the year by the *Pacific, Arctic,* and *Baltic.* Their superior speed was at once apparent, and American periodicals proudly published records, showing that their average runs were shorter than the Cunarders' by a full day (*Hunt's Merchant's Magazine*, September 1851, p. 380; March 1852, pp. 379–81; April 1853, p. 506). They attracted the cream of the passenger trade and their competition forced a radical reduction of the British freight rates. Such speed and service were expensive, and in 1852 Congress increased the Collins subsidy to $33,000 a round trip for fortnightly service, a total of $858,000 annually (*Statutes at Large*, X, 21). During their first four years, the Collins ships outstripped all rivals and were the pride of the American merchant marine, which was then at its peak and nearly equal to that of Great Britain.

Then came a series of disasters, caused perhaps by the emphasis on speed. On Sept. 27, 1854, the *Arctic* collided in the fog with a small French steamer off Cape Race. The liner soon sank with nearly all on board, the victims including the wife, son, and daughter of Collins. In spite of this blow, he continued his service and in 1855 launched the *Adriatic* of 4,114 tons. Then came the second disaster. The *Pacific* sailed from Liverpool in January 1856 and was never heard from again. Seven months later, Congress gave Collins the *coup de grâce*. On the motion of Representative Norton of Illinois, the extra subsidy granted in 1852 was withdrawn with six months' notice, and the same motion stipulated that a contract be made with Cornelius Vanderbilt to run a rival line at about the original rate (*Congressional Globe*, 34 Cong., 1 Sess., pp. 2162–66, 2219–22; *Statutes at Large*, XI, 102). Crippled by the heavy loss in ships and subsidy, Collins struggled to maintain the ser-

vice but missed several sailings. The panic of 1857 hastened the end of the company, which had never paid a dividend, and on Apr. 1, 1858, the three remaining ships were sold at auction for $50,000 to satisfy creditors (*Hunt's Merchant's Magazine*, May 1858, p. 630). Collins survived this failure twenty years, living in somewhat reduced circumstances and turning his attention to the development of coal and iron properties in Ohio. Scoville described him in 1860 as "rosy, hearty and not careworn as when he had those mighty American steamships resting on his single shoulders" (*Old Merchants of New York*, 1863, p. 140). In 1876 he sold his country seat at Larchmont and bought the house on Madison Avenue where he died. His first wife, lost on the *Arctic,* was Mary Ann Woodruff. He later married a widow, Mrs. Sarah Browne, who survived him with three sons.

[The best account of Collins's life is the detailed obituary in the *New York Herald,* Jan. 23, 1878. In addition to sources cited above see Congressional documents, particularly *Sen. Report 267*, 32 Cong., 1 Sess., and files of New York newspapers for the period. A very good secondary account of the Collins Line may be found in the *Hist. of Merchant Shipping* and *Ancient Commerce*, vol. IV (1876), pp. 202–28, by Wm. S. Lindsay, a contemporary British ship-owner. The *Catalogue of Portraits in the Chamber of Commerce of the State of N. Y.* (1924) contains a reproduction of Collins's portrait.]   R. G. A—n.

COLLINS, FRANK SHIPLEY (Feb. 6, 1848–May 25, 1920), botanist, unlike most Americans of his calling did not gain his love of the natural sciences through direct and intimate contact with nature, but had an urban upbringing into which a certain amount of botanical training entered as a formal part of his education. Born in Boston of an old New England family, the son of Joshua Cobb and Elizabeth (Carter) Collins, he was largely educated at home, his health being very delicate, by two aunts who added to their knowledge of literature and languages a distinct interest in botany. The boy attended high school, graduating in 1863, and tried several small mercantile positions, but from 1864 he was practically an invalid because of violent asthma, and occupied himself in studying harmony and musical classics. Then, to quote his wife, Anna Lendrum Holmes, whom he married in 1875, "at twenty-five, and out of a job, he borrowed a thousand dollars from a scandalized grandfather and took a seven months' vacation in Europe," principally to attend concerts in the chief musical centers. Shortly after his return he entered the Malden Rubber Shoe Company as a bookkeeper, and rapidly rose to the position of manager, a post which he held till 1913, when he retired, only to be recalled to it in the wartime pressure of 1918 as an efficiency expert.

About 1875, on a visit to Magnolia, Mass., his attention was attracted by some "sea mosses" or marine algae, which were being sold on postal cards as souvenirs of the seaside resort, and which bore scientific names so palpably wrong that Collins amused himself by trying to set them right. This led rapidly to an intensive study of the algae, a subject which had engaged no prominent specialists in America for more than a generation. His first note-books record the species found in the tidal pools no farther away than Lynn Beach. In the next forty-five years his interests broadened and intensified, so that he became the authority upon the algae of the New England coast. His personal knowledge of the flora of the Bermudas and his studies upon the collections of other workers from all the North American coasts brought him greater fame in his avocation than he ever achieved in his business life. He began to lecture and write on the algae in 1879. His series of New England algological studies appeared in *Rhodora* from 1899 to 1911. *The Green Algae of North America,* with its subsequent supplements, first issued in 1909 by Tufts College, was a notable work which opened the most neglected branch of algology, while his *Working Key to the Genera of North American Algae,* published by Tufts College in 1918, went far toward popularizing the whole subject.

Collins achieved recognition in Europe as the foremost American algologist of his time; he completely revised the algological collections of Harvard, the Missouri Botanical Garden, and the Boston Society of Natural History; and he issued, at great labor and expense, many complete sets of typical specimens of all the American marine algae. His works upon the life histories of algae, a subject fraught with especial importance in the biological theories of sex, were pioneering studies of great value. He never possessed college training himself, but his instinct for languages and his natural scientific ability made him as valued a member of the marine biological stations at Woods Hole, Mass., and South Harpswell, Me., as the most academic of students. In person he was urbane, cultivated, and courteous. He died at New Haven, while still in the service of his business house. The names *Collinsiella tuberculata,* Setchell and Gardener, a genus of green algae, and *Phæosaccion Collinsii,* Farlow, a species of brown algae, commemorate his many years of scientific devotion.

[Sketch by W. A. Setchell in *Am. Jour. Botany,* Jan. 1925; obituary in *Jour. N. Y. Botanical Garden,* July 1920; *Who's Who in America,* 1920–21.]   D.C.P.

COLLINS, JOHN (Nov. 1, 1717–Mar. 4, 1795), third governor of the State of Rhode Island, was born at Newport, the son of Samuel and Elizabeth Collins. He stood forth as a staunch advocate of the independence of the British colonies in America. An admirer of George Washington, he was selected by the governor of Rhode Island in 1776 to carry a letter to Washington soliciting counsel. Later (1782) he was made bearer to the President of Congress of a statement of Rhode Island's reasons for rejecting the Impost Act. During the American Revolution, Rhode Island was for the most part an agricultural community and as such opposed the restrictions of a national government. Within the state the agriculturists contended vigorously for a paper currency. Collins espoused their cause and in 1786 was elected governor. During his encumbency the issuance of paper money, which had been intermitted since 1750, was resumed. It was provided by law that should any creditor refuse to accept the bills of the state the debtor might secure a discharge by depositing the amount of his debt with one of the judges of the state superior court or the court of common pleas. This law led to the suit of *Trevett* vs. *Weeden,* one of the most remarkable cases in the history of American jurisprudence, which resulted in a decision looking toward the right of courts to declare legislative enactments unconstitutional (I. B. Richman, *Rhode Island, A Study in Separatism,* 1905, pp. 78–81). Collins represented Rhode Island in the Continental Congress in 1778 where he served until May 1781, when he was superseded by William Ellery. He was, however, reëlected in 1782 and held the position until 1783. Rhode Island, up to 1790, vigorously fought against the calling of a convention to decide upon entering the Federal Union, but in that year (Jan. 17) gave its sanction to such a call by a majority of one vote in the Senate. This vote was cast by Collins, who had come to realize the importance of a Federal connection. The vote cost him his popularity and the governorship. Later, however, he was elected to Congress but did not take his seat. He was married to Mary, daughter of John Avery of Boston.

[*Biog. Cyc. of Representative Men of R. I.* (1881); Samuel G. Arnold, *Hist. of the State of R. I. and Providence Plantations* (1860), vol. II; Edward Field, ed., *State of R. I. and Providence Plantations* (1902), vol. I; J. R. Bartlett, ed., *Records of the State of R. I. and Providence Plantations* (1863), vol. VIII; *Vital Record of R. I.,* VII (1895), 53; XII (1901), 45, 288.]
                    I.B.R.

COLLINS, JOHN ANDERSON (fl. 1810–1879), abolitionist and social reformer, was born at Manchester, Vt., attended Middlebury College in his twenty-fifth year, and left it, without graduating, to enter Andover Theological Seminary. This was the period of the rising tide of sentiment against slavery. Feeling, both bitter and warm, with regard to the question ran high at Andover. Collins is said to have played a leading part in revealing the so-called "Clerical Plot" to the abolitionists. This incident probably had an influence in his ensuing abrupt departure from the seminary and his installation as general agent of the Massachusetts Anti-Slavery Society. The Society sent him abroad to try to rouse sympathy for its work in England and to try to raise funds for carrying on propaganda. He carried letters of introduction from William Lloyd Garrison, commending him as "a free spirit, a zealous advocate" who had made large sacrifices for the cause. But his lot was no more easy than that of the other abolitionists. A group that included one particularly virulent clergyman went to great lengths to discredit him abroad, and on his return, accused him of importing "foreign gold to destroy the government" and of "disloyal and subversive propaganda."

From July 1840 to November 1841, Collins edited the *Monthly Garland,* a small magazine dealing with slavery, for which he wrote most of the material. Like many others of his enthusiastic temperament he was particularly attracted to the various Utopian doctrines newly imported from Europe, and he came to feel that the abolition of physical slavery was only a small part of a greater social reformation that was to free mankind. In 1843 he planned a series of "picnics" and the "hundred conventions" that were designed to rouse the country to the cause of the abolitionists. To the dismay of his backers, he began to follow the anti-slavery meetings with "constructive meetings" at which he preached a kind of Fourieristic doctrine. For reasons both diplomatic and conservative, he was reprimanded. He then decided to resign in order to devote himself to the founding of a commune. Garrison parted from him with regret. Collins, with two or three other enthusiasts, selected a farm at Skaneateles, N. Y., for the experiment, and he made a large part of the cash payment on the farm, giving his note for the rest. He then issued a call in the newspapers to others "of like mind" to join him, announcing a creed in which he denied all religious doctrines, denounced individual property, and advocated a social system founded on the negation of all force, admitting marriage only if accompanied by the right of easy divorce, and prescribing universal education and vegetarianism. This creed, which was some-

what modified later, aroused the usual stormy discussion far and wide. A group gathered about Collins, composed chiefly of those who saw an opportunity for free maintenance. The colony did not prosper, and Collins's disillusionment and disappointment were keen. In May 1846, he decided to liquidate. He next appears in California in 1849. In 1852, with John Wilson, he organized a company to mine the sands of the Klamath River. Many unfortunate investors lost all they had in the scheme. J. S. Hittell (*History of City of San Francisco,* 1878, p. 273) gives Collins credit for honestly believing in the plan. He was living in California as late as 1879 but he seems to have abandoned his schemes of philanthropy and social improvement (Noyes, *History of American Socialisms*).

[See the files of the *Liberator*; F. J. and W. P. Garrison, *William Lloyd Garrison*: the Story of His Life Told by His Children, 4 vols., 1885–89; Edmund N. Leslie, *Hist. of Skaneateles and Vicinity* (1882).]

K. H. A.

COLLINS, NAPOLEON (Mar. 4, 1814–Aug. 9, 1875), naval officer, was born in Pennsylvania, and appointed midshipman from Iowa on Jan. 2, 1834. Promoted lieutenant, Nov. 6, 1846, he was on the sloop *Decatur* in the Mexican War, taking part in the attacks on Tuxpan and Tabasco. In the Civil War he commanded the gunboat *Anacostia* in the Potomac, May 28–Aug. 30, 1861, and then the gunboat *Unadilla* in the south Atlantic blockading squadron, participating in the capture of Port Royal and subsequent operations on the southeastern coast until the summer of 1862. He was promoted commander July 16, 1862, and afterward cruised in the Bahamas in the *Octorara*. In this service he was notably energetic, making twelve captures from November 1862 to June 1863. One of these, the British schooner *Mont Blanc,* taken near the tiny British possession Sand Key, brought protests from England and a reprimand, in Secretary Welles's opinion unjustified, for Collins (*Diary of Gideon Welles,* 1911, I, 417–23). Sent to Brazilian waters in the steam-sloop *Wachusett* in January 1864, Collins there performed the exploit for which he is chiefly remembered, the capture of the Confederate raider *Florida.* The *Florida* entered Bahia, where the *Wachusett* was lying, Oct. 5, 1864. While her captain and many of her crew were ashore, Collins at dawn of the 7th attempted to ram her, and after striking only a glancing blow, fired several volleys of small arms and forced her surrender. Then, despite remonstrances from a Brazilian corvette anchored near-by, he towed her out of the harbor and brought her to Hampton Roads. On Brazil's protests Collins was ordered to take the *Florida* back to Bahia, but she was leaking, and after collision with an army transport she sank on Nov. 28, the sinking being declared accidental by a court of inquiry. Collins's action was what his government wanted, and he found some excuse in privileges permitted the *Alabama* in Brazilian waters. Apologies, however, were necessary, and Collins on Apr. 7, 1865, was sentenced to dismissal. This sentence was not approved by the secretary, and in July 1866, he was made captain. In June 1867, while cruising in Eastern waters, his vessel, the *Sacramento,* was wrecked without loss of life on a shoal in the Bay of Bengal. Collins was suspended, but was reinstated Mar. 13, 1869, Secretary Welles commenting that he was "an honest, straightforward, patriotic man," though without, in his opinion, "particular love or aptitude for the service" (*Ibid.,* III, 120, 554). Collins was commissioned commodore Jan. 16, 1871, and was lighthouse inspector until August 1874, when he became rear admiral and took command of the South Pacific Squadron. He died of malignant pustula at Callao, Peru. During his last cruise Admiral Collins made himself very popular in Latin-American countries, a Panama paper remarking that "no visitor ever produced such a feeling of fondness." He was buried in Callao, but in 1876 his body was brought home.

[*Official Records* (*Navy*), esp. 1 ser., vols. I–III, and see general index; obituary notes in *Army and Navy Jour.,* Aug. 28, Sept. 11, 18, 1875, June 17, 1876.]

A. W.

COLLINS, PATRICK ANDREW (Mar. 12, 1844–Sept. 14, 1905), politician, was born at Ballinafauna, near Fermoy, County Cork, Ireland. His mother was the second wife of Bartholomew Collins, a "strong farmer," who leased two hundred acres. Among the more opulent members of the Irish peasantry, Bartholomew Collins was a man of some education and was active in local Nationalist and Catholic politics. He died in 1847 and in March 1848 Mrs. Collins landed in Boston, having disposed of her rights in the lease. Patrick was then too young to remember his native land but his knowledge of it, gained from his elders, must have been colored by the catastrophe of the famine in the midst of which his father died. Mrs. Collins settled in Chelsea, Mass., and there Patrick went to school. His first school days were unhappy: his schoolmates and their elders were affected by the prejudices of the "Know-Nothing" period and the boy suffered verbal and physical assaults on his faith and race. Thenceforward, intolerance ranked with English tyranny in Collins's mind.

In 1857 Mrs. Collins moved to Ohio and for two years Patrick worked in the fields and around the coal-mines. In 1859 he returned to Boston and became apprenticed to an upholsterer. He quickly became a capable and highly paid workman, and, as a charter member of the local union, acquired a reputation for loyalty to his fellows that later stood him in good stead when labor troubles threatened Democratic unity. He became a Fenian in 1864 and soon attained some prominence, but the collapse of the movement convinced him Ireland had little to hope from violent conspiracy. His ability as a speaker becoming known, Collins was chosen delegate to the Democratic State Committee and elected to the General Court in 1867. He served in the lower house in 1868 and 1869, and in the Senate 1870 and 1871, where he strove to abolish the special "Catholic Oath" and to secure Catholic chaplains for jails and hospitals. In 1867 he entered the law office of a Boston Democrat, James A. Keith, and began to attend the Harvard Law School. He graduated LL.B. in 1871 and opened his own office that year. In 1874 his services in the election of Gov. William Gaston were rewarded by the rank of judge-advocate-general, from which office came the title "General" which Collins had too much sense to like. He was a delegate to the convention which nominated Tilden for the presidency, but his chief services to his party were on behalf of Charles Francis Adams, Democratic candidate for governor, who was distrusted by the Irish because of his alleged neglect, while minister to London, of Irish-American prisoners detained as Fenians by the British government. Collins, in an able speech at Marlboro, recanted his own previous utterances and declared that Irish-Americans should vote on American issues only. When, in 1880, Parnell toured the United States on behalf of the Irish Nationalist Party, Collins actively associated himself with the appeal for funds. As president of the American Land League, he was a conservative influence, setting himself against all incitement to crime or palliation of it (J. J. Roche, *Life of John Boyle O'Reilly,* 1891, p. 218).

Rather against his will Collins was elected to Congress in 1882. He found Washington expensive and his work in the House futile, rendered more so by the loose procedure. He served three terms but escaped in 1888. In the election of 1884 Collins at first shared the dislike of many Irish Democrats for Cleveland, but won over in a personal interview, campaigned for the party's candidate in speeches at Albany and elsewhere, taking the same position he had at Marlboro, eight years before. His services in staying the desertion were very great and his friends expected for him a place in the cabinet, which was not offered. There was no breach, however, and Collins had abundant minor patronage to distribute. He was chosen to preside over the convention which renominated Cleveland in 1888. After the latter's defeat, Collins was active in Massachusetts politics in the election of Gov. Russell. In 1892 he again helped to nominate and elect Cleveland (Michael E. Henessy, *Twenty-Five Years of Massachusetts Politics*, 1917, p. 31). The consul-generalship in London was the only reward Collins could afford to accept and, after assurances that the ex-Fenian would be *persona grata* to the British government, he was appointed. His office enabled him to save a little and kept him out of the election of 1896 fortunately, as he had little sympathy with the silver doctrines of Bryan. He entered heartily into the anti-imperialist campaign of 1900, and in 1904, put Olney's name before the Democratic convention.

By this time, however, his interests were chiefly in Boston politics. Defeated in his first mayoral campaign in 1899 by a split in the Democratic ranks, he was elected in 1901 and in 1903, the support of many independents offsetting disaffection bred in some members of his own party by his strict notions of public duty. As mayor, he stood for economy, probity, and home rule. He resisted all attempts to plunder the public, whether engineered by city workers or by corporations, and opposed the imposition by the legislature of special burdens on the city. Failing health limited his activities but his sudden death, at Virginia Hot Springs, was a surprise and shock even to his intimate friends. He was survived by his wife, Mary Carey of Boston, whom he had married in 1873. Though Collins was neither a great lawyer nor statesman his probity of character and his loyalty to his church, his party, his native and adopted countries, gained him general esteem. A monument was erected to him in Boston by public subscription in 1908.

[Collins's friend and secretary, M. P. Curran, published *The Life of Patrick A. Collins with Some of His Most Notable Public Addresses* (1906). It is uncritical but honest. Collins wrote a brief autobiography for the *Boston Globe* in 1893, which was first published on Sept. 15, 1905. All the Boston newspapers devoted much space to his career on the days immediately following his death. The *Globe* and the *Herald* articles are the best of these. Some of Collins's speeches, *e.g.*, those at Marlboro (1876) and Albany (1884), were printed as campaign leaflets. Others are to be found in the *Proceedings* of the Democratic Conventions of 1888, 1892, 1904.]   D.W.B.

COLLYER, ROBERT (Dec. 8, 1823–Nov. 30, 1912), clergyman, was born in Keighley, England. He was the son of Samuel and Harriett

(Norman) Collyer, originally workhouse children from London and Norwich respectively, bound out till their majority in a cotton-mill at Blubberhouses in Yorkshire. Robert was brought up in Blubberhouses, where he went to school about two years in all, and at the age of eight was set to work in the cotton-mill where he remained until fourteen. He was then apprenticed to a blacksmith at Ilkley, seven miles distant, and for many years followed blacksmithing as an occupation. In June 1846 he married Harriet Watson of Ilkley, who died on Feb. 1, 1849, leaving one son. Her death turned his thoughts toward religion. He had been reared in the Church of England; but he now became a Methodist, and soon discovered that he had a talent for preaching which he exercised constantly, meanwhile continuing to work at the forge. On Apr. 9, 1850 he married Ann Armitage of Ilkley and the same day set sail for America, where he obtained work as a blacksmith at Shoemakertown, seven miles from Philadelphia. There he worked constantly at his trade, read incessantly, and ridding himself of his Yorkshire dialect, became widely acceptable as a Methodist lay-preacher. During these years he became a strong abolitionist. He also began to find himself out of line with the current orthodox doctrines of Hell, Total Depravity and the Atonement, and under the influence of Lucretia Mott and Dr. William H. Furness of Philadelphia, moved toward Unitarianism. His Methodist license was withdrawn in January 1859 and in February he was called to Chicago to be minister-at-large to the First Unitarian Church. He was ordained to the Unitarian ministry in May and became pastor of the new Unity Church on the North Side. Here his success was immediate. The earlier buildings were outgrown and an elaborate stone structure, one of the largest Protestant churches in Chicago, was dedicated in 1869. This was destroyed in the great fire and rebuilt on a larger scale. All the different social classes of Chicago were represented in the congregation. In 1860 Collyer was appointed to administer relief to the victims of the Iowa cyclone. During the Civil War he was a staunch upholder of the Union and prominent in the work of the Sanitary Commission, visiting many southern battlefields. After the great Chicago fire of 1871 he was an outstanding leader in the work of relief and reconstruction. He was a prime mover in establishing the Liberal Christian League in 1866, to promote the welfare of the masses and to provide for them popular religious services. In 1862 and 1863 he received calls from Theodore Parker's congregation in Boston, and in 1864 from the

Second Unitarian Church in Brooklyn and the Church of the Messiah in New York City. All these he declined but in 1879 accepted the second call of the latter church, where he was pastor until 1903 and then pastor emeritus until his death. He always preached on the simple themes of the personal religious life, reading his sermons from manuscript in English of Anglo-Saxon purity. As a lecturer he was very active, among his well-known lectures being "The True George Washington," "From Anvil to Pulpit," and "Clear Grit." Besides several volumes of sermons, his works include: *Life of A. H. Conant* (1868); *Ilkley; Ancient and Modern* (1885); *Father Taylor* (1906), and his lecture, *Clear Grit* (1913). Large and tall, he had a massive head crowned with an abundance of gray hair, and his ruddy face of almost classic symmetry expressed the strength, sweetness, and light of his character.

[Dr. Collyer published an autobiography, *Some Memories* (1905). Other biographical works are, John H. Holmes, *The Life and Letters of Robt. Collyer* (1917); *Robt. Collyer; A Memorial* (pub. by Unity Church, Chicago, 1914), and a pamphlet with the same title (pub. by the Church of the Messiah, N. Y., 1914).]   F.T.P.

COLMAN, BENJAMIN (Oct. 19, 1673–Aug. 29, 1747), Boston clergyman, was the second son of William and Elizabeth Colman who emigrated from England and settled in Boston shortly before his birth. He attended school under Ezekiel Cheever [*q.v.*], entered Harvard in 1688, and graduated with high honors in 1692. After having supplied the pulpit at Medford for six months, he returned to Harvard to continue his theological studies and remained there until he received his degree of A.M. in 1695. In July of that year he sailed for England, having en route the diverting experiences of capture by a French privateer and incarceration for a short time in a French prison. In England he became acquainted with many prominent non-conformist divines and preached regularly at Bath.

Meanwhile at home in Boston a somewhat radical religious movement had been begun under the leadership of certain laymen such as the Brattles. They decided to organize a new church differing from the three already in existence in certain points of worship. Among other points, they advocated doing away with the public relation of personal religious experience, and instituting the reading of the Bible and the reciting of the Lord's Prayer. William Brattle, John Leverett, Simon Bradstreet [*qq.v.*], and others in the movement sent urgent letters to Colman in England inviting him to become the minister of the new Brattle Street Church. He accepted, and, knowing that the ministers of the other three churches in Boston would not welcome

him into fellowship, he had himself ordained by the London Presbytery (Aug. 4, 1699), as suggested by his Boston correspondents. He sailed soon after and by Nov. 1 was in Boston, a clergyman in good standing according to Presbyterian ideas but not in the eyes of the stricter Congregationalists. On Nov. 17 the associates of the Brattle Street Church issued a manifesto proclaiming their firm adherence to the doctrines of the Westminster Confession and stating that they were desirous of fellowship with the other Boston churches. The Mathers and others of the conservative group were bitterly opposed to the innovators, but by Jan. 31, 1700 a partial reconciliation was effected and Colman himself soon became a conservative, though the controversy continued. In itself the episode amounted to little and the various churches became indistinguishable in doctrine but the later effects were important, for the movement was the apparent cause of the attempt on the part of the Mathers and others to secure a stricter ecclesiastical government in Massachusetts, an attempt later checked by John Wise [*q.v.*].

Colman was one of the most prominent clergymen of his day and place, active in civil as in religious affairs. He was a Fellow of Harvard from 1717 to 1728 and an Overseer until his death, was offered and refused the presidency in 1724, and was the main instrument in securing for the college the Hollis, Holden, and other benefactions. He also assisted Yale College, was much interested in the mission among the Housatonic Indians and other charities, was a defender of inoculation, and a strong believer in the evangelistic movement known as the Great Awakening. He was well known in England where his correspondents included such men as Isaac Watts, and in 1731 he was given the degree of D.D. by Glasgow University. His writings were prolific and number over ninety separate titles. On June 5, 1700 he married Jane, daughter of Thomas and Jane Clark, who died Oct. 26, 1731; on May 6, 1732 he married the thrice widowed Sarah (Crisp) Clark who died Apr. 24, 1744; and on Aug. 12, 1745, he married another widow, Mary Frost, who survived him.

[W. B. Sprague, *Annals Am. Pulpit*, vol. I (1857), containing a detailed bibliography; "Memoir of Rev. Benj. Colman, D.D.," *New Eng. Hist. and Geneal. Reg.*, III, 105–22, 220–32; "Colman Papers," *Ibid.*, IV, 57–61; J. Quincy, *Hist. of Harvard Univ.* (1840); Ebenezer Turell, *Life and Character of Benj. Colman* (1749), with bibliography; S. K. Lothrop, *Hist. of the Church in Brattle St.* (1851) and *Memorial of the Church in Brattle Square* (1871); W. Walker, *Creeds and Platforms of Congregationalism* (1893), which cites many authorities; a number of other references in *Proc. Mass. Hist. Soc.*; *Colonial Soc. of Mass. Pubs.*; and *New Eng. Hist. and Geneal. Reg.*]   J.T.A.

COLMAN, HENRY (Sept. 12, 1785–Aug. 17, 1849), Unitarian minister and agricultural writer, was born in Boston, Mass., the son of Dudley and Mary (Jones) Colman. He graduated from Dartmouth College in 1805, studied theology under the Rev. James Freeman of Boston and the Rev. John Pierce of Brookline, Mass., and on June 17, 1807, was ordained pastor of the Congregational Church in Dedham, Mass. He resigned in 1820, and the same year published a volume of sermons, *Sermons on Various Occasions,* widely circulated in this country and reprinted in England. Until 1825 he taught a school in Boston. He gave vigorous expression to his Unitarian views in controversy with Trinitarians. An attempt to place him over a church in Salem, Mass., creating a dissension, his followers withdrew and organized the Independent Congregational Church in Barton Square. A church edifice was built, where he was installed pastor in February 1825. Here he served until 1831 when, partly because of impaired health, he resigned. In 1833 he published a second volume of sermons, *Sermons on Various Subjects Preached at the Church in Barton Square, Salem.*

Having a decided taste for farming, Colman took a farm in Deerfield, Mass., and proceeded to give practically his entire attention to agriculture. His published articles and addresses on that subject soon attracted attention. Appointed commissioner by Gov. Edward Everett in 1837 to make an agricultural survey, he visited all parts of the state and extended his inquiries into neighboring states. Much valuable material was secured, presented in four reports covering over 1,100 pages, printed by the state from 1838 to 1841. In 1843 Colman published a treatise on raising swine which is included in H. L. Ellsworth's *Improvements in Agricultural Arts . . . of the United States.* His experience in the survey of Massachusetts had admirably equipped him for a larger project. In April 1843 he went to England and spent three and one-half years in studying the agricultural conditions of Great Britain. In November 1846 he went to the Continent and made similar studies in France, Holland, Switzerland, and Italy, returning to England in 1848, and to America in the fall of that year. The report of the agricultural survey is partly contained in his *European Agriculture and Rural Economy from Personal Observation.* The first edition appeared in 1844, a second in 1849, a third in 1850 in two volumes containing 972 pages, and three further editions were issued, the sixth in 1857. There was, also, separately printed, *Agriculture and Rural Economy in France, Belgium, Holland, and Switzerland*

(London, 1848). After his return Colman published *European Life and Manners in Familiar Letters to Friends* (2 vols. 1st ed. 1849, 2nd ed. 1850). His health now failed and his eyesight became impaired. Hoping to improve his physical condition, he went to England, but without benefit. He died in Islington, now a part of London. He was tall and well proportioned, of commanding presence, active mind, and keen intelligence. Although not without faults of temper, he displayed great kindness of heart. He was married on Aug. 11, 1807, to Mary, daughter of Thomas Harris of Charlestown, Mass.

[Geo. T. Chapman, *Sketches of the Alumni of Dartmouth College* (1867); *Hist. of the Town of Hingham, Mass.,* vol. I (1893); L. H. Bailey, ed., *Cyc. of Am. Agriculture,* IV, 564; *Cultivator,* n.s., VI, 321; *Mo. Religious Mag.,* VI, 481–501.]   E.H.J.

COLMAN, JOHN (Jan. 3, 1670–*c.* 1753), merchant, in Boston, Mass., was the son of William and Elizabeth Colman of London, and the grandson of Matthew and Grace of Satterly, Suffolk, England. The father, William, migrated to the Bay Colony in 1671 in the ship *Arabella.* John early engaged in mercantile pursuits and apparently was a merchant of some standing, though not preëminent. In 1698 Colman was one of a group of twenty to whom Thomas Brattle conveyed Brattle's Close, upon which was built in 1699 the Brattle Street Church. He was also a member of the committee of proprietors who, in the same year, invited his brother, Benjamin Colman [*q.v.*], to become their minister. He was active in town affairs, served as selectman, as a member of various town committees, and was justice of the peace. In the second decade of the century the currency disorder in Massachusetts overshadowed all other public questions, with sharp division of opinion as to methods of reform. Colman identified himself with those who would permit private banks to be organized with power to issue and loan bills on real-estate mortgages. In 1714 he was one of the eight signers of *A Vindication of the Bank of Credit Projected in Boston from the Aspersions of Paul Dudley, Esqr. in a Letter by him Directed to John Burril, Esqr., Late Speaker to the House of Representatives for the Province of the Massachusetts Bay in New England.* In 1720 he published *The Distressed State of the Town of Boston, etc. Considered In a Letter from a Gentleman in the Town, to his Friend in the Countrey.* He recognized the evils of a fluctuating currency, but opposed any severe restriction of credit. He favored a private bank, and if this were not feasible, the emission of bills of public credit for the construction of public works and encouragement of industries. In particular he criticized a recent law giving creditors the right to charge interest on book debts, and designed to break up the practise of trusting debtors for long periods of time. This pamphlet was advertised in the *News-Letter*, Apr. 11, 1720. The Council of the province held that the pamphlet reflected upon the government and had a tendency to disturb the public peace. Colman was arrested and gave bonds. On July 5 his recognizance was discharged. This pamphlet provoked several replies. Colman again entered the controversy in July 1720, with a second brochure, *The Distressed State of the Town of Boston Once More Considered—With a Scheme for a Bank Laid Down; and Methods for Bringing in Silver Money Proposed*. In it he recommended the establishment of a land bank open to partnership by all in the province who owned land; and that, on pledge of land or mortgage, notes be given equal to two-thirds of the land value, for which six per cent interest in notes be charged. The profits from the loans were to be devoted to the purchase of silver which in turn was to be held as a fund until it equaled the original value of the notes. This would be accomplished, it was estimated, in twenty years. The proposal, however, made no headway. In 1739 the plan of a land bank was revived. Several hundred persons formed a partnership to issue notes to be loaned to the shareholders at three per cent interest and annual payment of one-twentieth of the principal, either in notes or commodities at fixed prices, and the project received the approval of the provincial legislature. It was quickly suppressed by the English government, but not until 150,000 or more of notes had been issued. It is not clear how large a part Colman had in the administration of the bank. He was one of the partners, and his name was intimately associated with its brief career. On July 19, 1694, Colman was married by the Rev. Cotton Mather to Judith Hobbey, daughter of William Hobbey, a merchant, and sister of Sir Charles Hobbey (*Boston Births, Baptisms, Marriages, and Deaths, 1630–99*, 1908, p. 217). He died at the age of eighty-three (*New England Historical and Genealogical Register*, XXXVII, 58).

[Scattered references may be found in Andrew McFarland Davis, ed., *Colonial Currency Reprints, 1682–1751* (4 vols., 1910–11); in the indexes of the *New Eng. Hist. and Geneal. Reg.*, and in *Proc. Mass. Hist. Soc.* Colman's writings are most conveniently found in the edition of *Currency Reprints* referred to above, and in *Tracts Relating to the Currency of the Mass. Bay* (1902), pp. 233–46; 347–82, also edited by Davis.]

D. R. D.

COLMAN, LUCY NEWHALL (July 26, 1817–Jan. 18, 1906), abolitionist, lecturer, descended from Nicholas Danforth, an English-man emigrating to New England in 1634, was born at Sturbridge, Mass., the second of four daughters of Erastus and Hannah (Newhall) Danforth. Her mother was a descendant of John and Priscilla Alden. Her father, a fur-trader and blacksmith, was a prominent Universalist layman and she early entered that church; later, dissatisfied with the dogmas of all Christian churches, she became a Spiritualist. Her education in public schools was scanty; at the age of twelve, thrown on her own resources, she became a teacher. When eighteen she married John Mabrey Davis, who died of tuberculosis six years later. They lived in Boston, where Mrs. Davis supplemented her education through the cultural advantages there available. After her husband's death she taught in a girls' school in Philadelphia. In 1843 she married a railroad engineer, Luther N. Coleman (he apparently spelled his name thus although his widow later used the name Colman). In 1852 Coleman was killed in a railroad accident; the circumstances following upon this tragedy were such as to embitter his widow and intensify her sympathies with the cause of woman's rights. After much effort she secured a position as teacher of "the colored school" of Rochester, N. Y., at a meager salary. A year later, unaided, she accomplished its abolition, thereby removing educational discrimination against the negroes of Rochester. In another position she publicly used her influence against corporal punishment in schools. A long-standing desire to strike at slavery led her to abandon teaching and to secure through friends appointments as an anti-slavery lecturer. She spoke in New York, Pennsylvania, Michigan, Illinois, Indiana, and Ohio; endured various hardships in the crude homes and country hotels of ante-bellum days; attacked slavery always in vigorous, even violent language; defied social and religious conventions; exposed sham. Though encountering determined opposition—misrepresentation, insults, and grave perils—she escaped actual physical harm. She adopted a young colored woman for a time as a fellow traveler. Sometimes she mingled in her protests the wrongs of blacks and the wrongs suffered by woman. After the outbreak of the Civil War she became matron of the National Colored Orphan Asylum at Washington, where she substituted kind treatment and sanitation for mismanagement. She served as superintendent of certain colored schools supported by the New York Aid Society in the District of Columbia, instructing the pupils in morals and cleanliness. She secured interesting interviews for Sojourner Truth with Presidents Lincoln and Johnson. Later she returned to New York State, making her home after 1873 in Syracuse, where she was active in the Spiritualist Society and as a Freethinker. She joined the J. S. Mill Liberal League, becoming a contributor to the *Truth Seeker*. In appearance she was a small woman, whose face gave evidence of intelligence, independence, and determination. She died in Syracuse after a five years' illness, and was buried in Rochester.

[Sources for Mrs. Colman's career are her own *Reminiscences* (1891); John J. May, *Danforth Genealogy* (1902); Frances E. Willard and Mary A. Livermore, *Am. Women* (1897); Syracuse (N. Y.) directories, 1873–1906.]   R.S.B.

COLMAN, NORMAN JAY (May 16, 1827–Nov. 3, 1911), agricultural journalist, first secretary of agriculture, was born near Richfield Springs, N. Y., the son of Hamilton and Nancy (Sprague) Colman. He attended an academy in a neighboring town, and then went to Louisville, Ky., where he taught school. While there he also studied law and received the degree of LL.B. from the law department of the University of Louisville. After graduating from law school he went to New Albany, Ind., and began the practise of his profession. Within three years he was elected to the office of district attorney, but as he had never intended to follow the law as a permanent profession, he resigned his office and removed to St. Louis. He was a Unionist during the Civil War, serving as lieutenant-colonel of the 85th Missouri Militia. As a boy Colman had read the old *Albany Cultivator* to which his father was a subscriber and had made up his mind that some time he would publish such a paper. He purchased a country house, and in 1865 began the publication of an agriculture paper, *Colman's Rural World*. In the same year he was elected to the Missouri legislature, and after serving with distinction in that body received the Democratic nomination for lieutenant-governor of Missouri in 1868. He was defeated in the election as was the entire Democratic ticket, but in 1874 he was again nominated for the same office and elected. Colman interested himself in the welfare of the Missouri state university at Columbia, and was for sixteen years a member of the board of curators of that institution. At the same time he served as the head of many agricultural organizations, some of state, some of Middle Western, and some of national character. He was a member of the Missouri state board of agriculture from the time of its organization in 1865 until his death in 1911. Because of his broad and practical knowledge he was appointed United States commissioner of agriculture by President Cleveland in 1885. As commissioner he so improved the work of the bureau and so enlarged its scope that on Feb. 11, 1889, it was elevated in dignity and power to an executive department, with its secretary as a member of the president's cabinet. During his term of office Colman was author of the Hatch Bill, creating experiment stations in states and territories, supported by federal aid, and thus has sometimes been called the "Father of the Experiment Station." After his retirement as secretary of agriculture he lived at his country home and devoted his time to the editorial management of his journal. His election as president of the National Editorial Association and of the Missouri Press Association is evidence of the esteem in which he was held by the profession of journalism.

[W. B. Davis and Daniel Durrie, *An Illus. Hist. of Mo.* (1876), pp. 489–91; *Mo. Hist. Rev.*, XIX (1925), 404–08; H. L. Conard, *Encyc. of the Hist. of Mo.*, II (1901), 53–54; biographical sketch and obituary notice in *Colman's Rural World*, Nov. 15, 1911.]   F.C.S.—r.

COLMAN, SAMUEL (Mar. 4, 1832–Mar. 26, 1920), painter, was born in Portland, Me., the son of Samuel and Pamela Atkins (Chandler) Colman. His father, a bookseller and publisher in Portland in comfortable circumstances, moved to New York and opened a publishing house on Broadway, where he published, among others, the poems of Willis and Longfellow, well printed and illustrated with engravings which aroused interest in this form of art. The place was a popular resort of authors and artists and may have had the effect of directing the dawning talents of the boy who often spent his time there after school. He early became a pupil of Asher B. Durand [*q.v.*], one of the successful landscape painters, and he made rapid progress, when only eighteen exhibiting at the New York Academy of Design a painting which was highly commended. At twenty-seven he was elected an associate of the National Academy. He painted Hudson River and Lake George scenery, and was a close friend of many painters belonging to the Hudson River school. In 1860 he went abroad for two years, studying in Paris and Spain.

When he returned to the United States he was made a full Academician and in 1866 was elected first president of the American Water-color Society, of which he was one of the founders. He went again to Europe in 1871, visiting Holland, Normandy, Brittany, Switzerland, and England, and remaining four years. On his return he exhibited forty-five sketches from nature. At one time he lived at Irvington-on-Hudson, where he painted some charming river views, impressed by the effect of veils of fog and smoke and long masses of boats. His "Tow-boats in the Highlands, Hudson River" has a Turneresque quality. His style both in oil and water-color was broad and effective, and his coloring was brilliant. He made many contributions to the exhibitions of the National Academy and the Water-color Society, and three of his pictures were exhibited at the Paris Exhibition of 1878. He was one of the original members of the Society of American Artists. His studio in New York was in the building on the corner of Twenty-fifth St., and Fourth Ave. It is described as richly decorated with rare tapestries, Chinese pottery, and Japanese armor. He was a collector and connoisseur of Oriental art. In his later years he lived and painted at Newport, R. I. Publications by Colman include *Nature's Harmonic Unity* (1912), edited by C. A. Coan, and in collaboration with Coan, *Proportional Form* (1920). He is represented in the Metropolitan Museum, New York Public Library, Union League Club, Chicago Art Institute, and in many notable private collections. In 1862 he was married to Anne Lawrence Dunham, and in 1903 to Lillie Margaret Goffney. He died in New York City.

[G. W. Sheldon, *Am. Painters* (1881); C. E. Clement and L. Hutton, *Artists of the Nineteenth Century* (1884); editorial, *Art World*, July 1917; *Am. Art News*, Apr. 3, 1920; *Who's Who in America*, 1920–21.]
H.W.

COLQUITT, ALFRED HOLT (Apr. 20, 1824–Mar. 26, 1894), statesman, soldier, was the eldest son of Walter T. Colquitt [*q.v.*] and Nancy (Lane) Colquitt. He was born in Walton County in the north central section of Georgia. He graduated from the College of New Jersey (Princeton) in 1844, studied law, and was admitted to the bar. On the outbreak of the Mexican War he entered the army and served throughout as a staff officer with the rank of major. Returning to Georgia at the conclusion of the war he settled in Macon and entered upon the practise of his profession. He was married in May (1848) to Dorothy Tarver, daughter of Hartwell Tarver, his father's step-brother. She died in 1855 and he then married Sarah, the widow of Fred Tarver. The first Mrs. Colquitt received from her father a plantation in Baker County. The Colquitts removed there and Alfred H. Colquitt was identified with Baker County throughout the remainder of his life. Like many another Georgian of the ante bellum period, Colquitt was at once lawyer, politician, and farmer. His father, Senator Walter T. Colquitt, had just finished his political career with an effort to bring about secession in connection with the struggle over the compromise measures of 1850. The father was always an extreme pro-Southern Democrat and the son took the same position. With a reputation already established as a brilliant orator, he entered politics in 1853 as a Dem-

ocratic candidate for Congress from the 2nd District, opposing the incumbent, James Johnson, who was a Unionist. Colquitt defeated Johnson easily and took his seat in the thirty-third Congress. During his term in Congress Colquitt made one set speech, on the Kansas situation, in which he presented a historical account of the long struggle over the extension of slavery (*Congressional Globe*, 33 Cong., 1 Sess., App., pp. 749 ff.). On account of his wife's poor health he did not offer himself for reëlection. In 1859 he was again in the political arena as a member of the Georgia legislature. He became an elector on the Breckinridge and Lane ticket in the presidential campaign of 1860. Elected to membership in the secession convention, he helped carry the state out of the Union and when the war broke he immediately entered the Confederate army as a captain of infantry. He developed considerable military ability and was promoted to colonel, then to brigadier-general, and finally to the rank of major-general. His most noteworthy service was in command of the Confederate forces at the battle of Olustee in Florida in 1864, in which he won a signal victory.

On the return of peace Colquitt resumed his vocations of law and farming. He was a bitter opponent of the congressional Reconstruction policies and of ex-Gov. Joseph E. Brown [*q.v.*]. He continued active in state politics, serving as president of the Democratic state convention in 1870. During the same year he was elected president of the state agricultural society, strong evidence of his popularity. In 1876 he received the Democratic nomination for governor and was elected by the greatest majority ever given a gubernatorial candidate up to that time. His four-year term of office was characterized by able reorganization of the state finances, large reduction in the floating debt and the bonded debt, economy in administration and reduction in the tax rate. Colquitt made many enemies during his incumbency of the governorship. Few public officials have been subjected to more scandalous misrepresentation. Largely for the purpose of obtaining public vindication of his policies, he again became a candidate for the governorship in 1880. The ensuing campaign is memorable in Georgia history for its rancor. The public excitement was much heightened by an incident that occurred in May 1880. Gen. John B. Gordon suddenly resigned from the United States Senate and immediately Colquitt appointed ex-Gov. Joseph E. Brown, who at that time was held in general detestation by thousands of Georgians. The cry of bargain and corruption was raised. The allegation was that Gen. Gordon resigned in return for a promise of the presidency of the state-owned Western & Atlantic Railroad, then under the control of Brown, and that Colquitt won ex-Gov. Brown's political support by appointing the latter as senator. These charges seem to have been groundless. After a hard fight in the Democratic state convention, Colquitt secured the nomination and was later elected. On the expiration of his second term (1882) he was appointed to fill the unexpired term of United States Senator Benjamin H. Hill, who died in office, and he served from 1883 to his death in 1894. A contemporary historian who knew intimately nearly all the public men of his time, says that Colquitt was an unusually astute politician, true to his friends, and governed by a strong sense of duty. Like his father, he was a licensed Methodist preacher. He was an early champion of temperance, and took keen interest in all religious and moral issues. He was president at one time of the International Sunday School convention.

[Wm. J. Northen, *Men of Mark in Ga.* (1911), vol. III; *Memoirs of Judge Richard H. Clarke* (1898), ed. by L. B. Wylie. I. W. Avery, *Hist. of the State of Ga. from 1850 to 1881* (1881), is an account of the period by a Colquitt partisan; Mrs. Wm. H. Felton, in *My Memoirs of Georgia Politics* (1911), gives a view unfavorable to Colquitt. See also *Atlanta Constitution*, Mar. 26, 27, 1894.]   R. P. B.

COLQUITT, WALTER TERRY (Dec. 27, 1799–May 7, 1855), lawyer, statesman, was born in Halifax County, Va., the son of Henry and Nancy S. (Holt) Colquitt. While he was still a small boy he was taken by his father to Georgia, where they settled in Hancock County, later moving to Walton County. After attending the College of New Jersey (Princeton) for a time, Walter Colquitt studied law in Milledgeville, Ga., then the state capital, and was admitted to the bar. After a brief residence in Sparta, Ga., he removed to Cowpens in Walton County. His entrance into politics was as a candidate for Congress (1826) on a "Troup Party" ticket; he was defeated by a plurality of thirty-two votes. In the same year he was appointed judge of the Chattahoochee superior court circuit, was reëlected in 1829, and returned to the private practise of law in 1832. After two terms (1834 and 1837) in the state Senate, Colquitt was elected (1838) to the Twenty-sixth Congress as a state-rights Whig. The Troup party was a state-rights organization controlled by the planter aristocrats. In the early thirties it was merged with the national Whig party, which, in its inception, was a coalition of Andrew Jackson's enemies. When Calhoun in 1840 returned to the Democratic party, he was followed by Colquitt, who became a leader of the radical wing of the

Georgia Democracy, the Union wing being led by Howell Cobb. The Democrats returned Colquitt to Congress in 1842 and shortly thereafter he was elected to the United States Senate. In the House Colquitt made "an exceedingly eloquent speech of great length" in opposition to the reception of Abolition petitions. He favored the establishment of the Independent Treasury system, incidentally taking occasion to denounce the Second Bank of the United States as "a great moneyed institution for the support of men who were too idle to earn their bread by industry and too proud to work." He opposed as an infringement on state rights the bill to district states for the purpose of choosing congressmen. As a senator he favored the annexation of Texas, the Mexican War, and the acquisition of territory from Mexico. He advocated congressional non-interference with slavery in the territories.

In January 1848, for some reason now unknown, Colquitt resigned his seat in the Senate. Two years later he was one of a dozen eminent Georgians who participated in the Nashville Convention, in opposition to the pending territorial settlement. Thoroughgoing resolutions were adopted against Clay's Omnibus Bill, and Colquitt advised the Southern states to prepare for war. After the adjournment of the Nashville Convention the Georgia campaign of 1850 occurred for the election of members to the important convention of that year. It was this convention that was called upon to decide whether Georgia would or would not support the compromise measures. In the campaign Colquitt was a crusader for the Southern rights position. He advocated secession ("Correspondence of Robert Toombs, Alexander H. Stephens, and Howell Cobb," *House Document No. 968*, 62 Cong., 3 Sess., pp. 207, 214), but after this campaign took no further part in the turbulent politics of the period. A contemporary historian regarded him as the most versatile and brilliant public man the state had produced. In addition to his political activities, he was a local Methodist preacher and a very impressive speaker. Three times married, on Feb. 3, 1823, to Nancy H. Lane; in 1841 to Mrs. Alphia B. (Todd) Fauntleroy, who died a few months later; and in 1842 to Harriet W. Ross, Colquitt had twelve children. Among the six of the first union was Alfred H. Colquitt [*q.v.*], governor and United States senator.

[I. W. Avery, *Hist. of the State of Ga. from 1850 to 1881* (1881), is the most important source; *Memoirs of Judge Richard H. Clarke* (1898), ed. by Lollie Belle Wylie, contains a brief account of the Colquitts, father and son; Stephen F. Miller, *Bench and Bar of Ga.* (1858), contains a sketch based on family information.]
R. P. B.

COLSTON, RALEIGH EDWARD (Oct. 31, 1825–July 29, 1896), Confederate general, was born and received his early education in Paris, where Dr. Raleigh Colston, Sr., a former resident of Berkeley County, W. Va. (then in Virginia), lived for many years with his wife, Elizabeth Marshall. In 1842 young Colston was sent to the United States, and the next year entered the Virginia Military Institute, where he graduated in 1846. While still a student he acted as an instructor in French, and upon his graduation he was immediately appointed assistant professor. In the same year he married Louise Meriwether Gardiner, widowed daughter of John Bowyer of "Thorn Hill," near Lexington, Va. He was advanced to a full professorship in 1854. At the outbreak of the Civil War he was appointed colonel of the 16th Virginia Infantry, and on Dec. 24, 1861, was made brigadier-general. He commanded a brigade in the Peninsular campaign from April to June 1862, when he was disabled by illness from which he did not recover until December. In April 1863, on the application of his former fellow professor, he was assigned to a brigade in Stonewall Jackson's corps. He commanded the division at Chancellorsville. He afterward served under Beauregard in the defense of Petersburg in 1864, and then commanded at Lynchburg. Left without resources upon the return of peace, he established a military school at Wilmington, N. C., and conducted it successfully until offered an appointment as colonel in the Egyptian army, in which several veterans of the late war, both Union and Confederate, held commissions. He served for six years in Egypt. Twice during that period he conducted extensive exploring expeditions in the Soudan. On the second of these, while in the heart of the desert, he was injured by a fall from his camel, and paralyzed from the waist down. He refused to return to Cairo, however, for he was the only American with the command, and knew that if he abandoned it the expedition would fail. For days he was carried forward in a litter, until he reached El Obeid, where he connected with another force sent out from lower Egypt, to whose leader, Maj. Henry G. Prout, afterward distinguished as an engineer, he turned over his command. After six months' rest at El Obeid he started back, and reached Khartoum after a three-hundred-mile journey, in a litter as before. He returned to the United States in 1879, when the American officers were discharged. His savings, unwisely invested on the advice of friends, were soon completely lost. Impoverished and crippled, he secured a clerkship in the War Department in Washington, which he held until complete disability overcame him in 1894. There was no pension system for civil servants in those days, and he spent the last two years of his life in the Confederate Soldiers' Home in Richmond, suffering greatly, but always patient, cheerful, and companionable. A man of wide culture, kindly nature, and high character, he had the faculty of winning the ardent devotion of those who knew him. He was revered alike by his college students, his brother officers and soldiers of the Confederate army, and his Arab followers in Egypt.

[*Confed. Mil. Hist.*, III (1899), 586–87; L. G. Tyler, *Encyc. Va. Biog.* (1915), III, 49–50; *Official Records (Army)*, 1 ser., vols. XI (pts. 1, 3), XVIII, XXV (pts. 1, 2), XXXV (pt. 1), XXXVI (pt. 2); information furnished by Col. Jos. R. Anderson of Lee, Va., from personal knowledge and extensive collection of materials for the history of Va. Mil. Inst.]   T. M. S.

COLT, LeBARON BRADFORD (June 25, 1846–Aug. 18, 1924), jurist, senator, was born at Dedham, Mass., the son of Christopher and Theodora Goujand (DeWolf) Colt. He traced his ancestry to John Colt of England, who came to America with Rev. Thomas Hooker in 1636 and settled in Hartford, Conn., in 1638. On his mother's side he was descended from the DeWolf family of Bristol, R. I. His maternal grandfather was Gen. George DeWolf, who in 1810 built the beautiful mansion, "Linden Place," at Bristol, where the grandson lived many years, and where he died. His father was engaged in the silk business at Dedham, Mass., and afterward at Paterson, N. J. Later the household was moved to Hartford, where LeBaron and his younger brother Samuel Pomeroy, between whom and himself there existed a life-long devotion, grew up. LeBaron attended the public schools in Hartford, prepared for college at Williston, and was graduated from Yale in 1868 with the degree of A.B. He was graduated in law at Columbia in 1870, spent a year abroad, and began the practise of law in Chicago as a member of the firm of Palmer & Colt. On Dec. 17, 1873, he married Mary Louise Ledyard, daughter of Guy Carlton and Elizabeth (Morris) Ledyard of Chicago. In 1875 he moved to Bristol, R. I., and from that time to 1891 was a law partner of Francis Colwell at Providence. He was elected as a Republican to the lower branch of the General Assembly in 1879 and again in 1880, and on Mar. 21, 1881, though not yet thirty-five, was appointed by President Garfield judge of the United States district court for the district of Rhode Island. On July 5, 1884, President Arthur made him judge of the United States circuit court for the 1st judicial district (Maine, New Hampshire, Massachusetts, and Rhode Island), and in 1891 he became presiding judge of the new circuit court of appeals for the 1st circuit. Among the important cases which he decided were the Bell telephone suits. He remained on the bench till 1913. He made an extraordinary impression upon his legal contemporaries by his judicial mind, broad knowledge of the law, fondness for his work, and intellectual clarity.

Elected to the United States Senate from Rhode Island, as a Republican, by the General Assembly in 1913 and by the people in 1918, he served from Mar. 4, 1913, to the day of his death. He immediately took rank in the Senate as an authority on legal and constitutional questions. He did not often address the Senate, but was an eloquent and impressive speaker, as a published volume, *Addresses* (1906), testifies. As chairman of the Committee on Immigration he was in charge of a new immigration bill, but refusing to acquiesce in its provision for Japanese exclusion, which he considered to be in violation of the "gentleman's agreement" between Japan and the United States, he turned over the direction of the bill to Senator Reed of Pennsylvania, and with one other senator, voted against the exclusion provision. He favored the acceptance of the League of Nations Covenant with the Senate reservations and opposed the Panama Canal Toll bill as an attempt to settle a judicial matter by statute. When it was proposed to appropriate $20,000,000 for Russian relief, he answered the argument that the proposal was unconstitutional by declaring that the Constitution must be elastic enough to supply the great fundamental wants of society. A confirmed student of history and the science of government, Colt believed that "America's solution of the great problem of government is based upon the realization of the common sense of the average man, or the collective sense of the multitude of average men, as the active, controlling force," and was confident of the future prosperity of the Republic. Possessed of a remarkable combination of humor and charm, he was tall, spare, dignified in bearing, and looked the part of a judge and a senator.

[Information as to certain facts from the family; personal acquaintance and talks with friends; *Providence Journal*, Bristol *Phœnix* and other papers, August 1924; memorial addresses in Congress in *Cong. Record*, 68 Cong., 2 Sess., pp. 2079, 3782; H. P. Wright, *Hist. of the Class of 1868, Yale Coll.* (1914); *Yale Univ. Obit. Record*, 1925.]   H. R. P.

COLT, SAMUEL (July 19, 1814–Jan. 10, 1862), inventor, manufacturer, the third child of Christopher and Sarah Caldwell Colt, was born in Hartford, Conn., where his father, a manu-

facturer of cotton and woolen fabrics, was prosperous and well known. The first six years of his life were happy and normal, but before he was seven his father failed in business, and his mother died of consumption. Upon his father's second marriage less than two years later, a real home was lost to him. For three years after his mother's death he lived about with his father and paternal aunt, avoiding school as much as he possibly could. In 1824, his father sent him to Ware, Mass., to the dyeing and bleaching establishment which he operated. Here he led a varied existence, working in the factory, attending school, and laboring on various farms. In spite of himself he progressed in school and when he was thirteen he was sent to a college preparatory school at Amherst, Mass. His mischievousness was his eventual undoing, however, for in 1830 he was taken from school and sent to sea as a plain seaman. A voyage of one year, to India, apparently sufficed, and upon his return he again went to work in his father's bleaching establishment in Ware. This time he took great interest in the chemical work of the plant, but a year later he told his father that he was leaving to "paddle his own canoe." For the next three years nothing was heard of him directly, but from newspaper accounts throughout the East, it was learned that Colt, under the name "Dr. Coult," was making a livelihood by giving popular lectures in chemistry, with practical demonstrations of the effects of laughing-gas. From his earliest youth explosives and firearms had always interested him, and on his voyage to Singapore he whittled out of wood a model showing his idea of a multi-shot firearm of the revolving barrel type. The perfection of this idea seems to have been uppermost in his mind from the time he made this first wooden model. In 1831 he constructed two pistols, one of which exploded; in 1832 he sent a description of his idea to the Patent Office in Washington; and in 1833 he constructed, in Baltimore, both a pistol and a rifle on the principle for which he subsequently obtained patents in England and France, when he wandered over there in 1835. Within a month after his return from Europe, on Feb. 25, 1836, he secured his first United States patent. His invention was the first practical revolving fire-arm and embodied as its leading feature the automatic rotation of the cylinder in cocking by a pawl on the hammer engaging a ratchet on the end of the cylinder. Within three months a company was formed to manufacture the revolver at Paterson, N. J. While it was accepted by individuals, Colt was unsuccessful in persuading the army and navy to adopt it. His business failed in 1842, and he lost his patent rights to others. Following this he turned his attention to the development of the submarine battery upon which he had been working. During the next five years, with the aid of government funds, he successfully demonstrated his system of destroying vessels even when under sail. He introduced electricity as the agent for igniting the powder, and advanced the submarine a step forward. At this time, too, he engaged in submarine telegraphy and put into operation a system from New York to Coney Island and Fire Island Light in 1843. At the outbreak of the Mexican War, Colt received an order for one thousand pistols from the Federal Government. He immediately began their manufacture at Whitneyville, near New Haven, and bought back his patent rights as quickly as possible. Following his initial invention he obtained further patents for improvements on Aug. 29, 1839, and on Sept. 3 and 10, 1850. In 1848, after a year at Whitneyville, he returned to Hartford and began to manufacture his revolver there, renting a three-story building for the purpose. The business grew rapidly and between 1854 and 1855 he built his own immense armory at Hartford and continued to direct its affairs until his death. On June 5, 1856, he married Elizabeth H. Jarvis, the oldest daughter of Rev. William Jarvis of Middletown, Conn.

[J. D. Van Slyke, *Representatives of New Eng.* (1879); *Armsmear, A Memorial* (1866), ed. by Henry Barnard; Henry L. Abbott, *The Beginning of Modern Submarine Warfare* (1881); F. von Ehrenkrook, *Hist. of Submarine Mining and Torpedoes*, in Professional Papers of the Engineer School of Application U. S. Army, vol. I; *Submarine and Land Telephone Systems of the World* (U. S. Treasury Dept., Bureau of Statistics, Jan. 1899); E. W. Byrn, *Progress of Invention in the Nineteenth Century* (1900).]   C. W. M.

COLTER, JOHN (c. 1775–November 1813), trapper, explorer, was born in or near Staunton, Va., the son of Joseph and Ellen (Shields) Colter. His grandfather Michael and great-grandfather Micajah seem to have spelled the name Coalter. The earliest record of him is that of his formal enlistment in Lewis and Clark's company, Oct. 15, 1803, at Louisville. The captains mention him frequently in the journals, and he was repeatedly chosen for especially hazardous services. On the return journey, at the Mandan villages, he asked to be released in order to join two trappers; and the captains, as a token of appreciation, consented, Aug. 16, 1806. In the following summer he was met at the mouth of the Platte by Manuel Lisa's trapping party and was persuaded to return with them.

On their arrival at the mouth of the Big Horn, Nov. 21, where Lisa began the building of a trading post, Fort Raymond, Colter was dispatched on a mission to the Crows and other tribes south of the Yellowstone. Afoot and alone, "with a pack of thirty pounds weight, his gun and some ammunition" (Brackenridge), he set out on this daring venture, through a region wholly unknown to white men. The tracing lettered "Colter's route in 1807," on Clark's map in the Biddle-Allen edition of the journals, credits Colter with penetrating to a point southwest of Jackson Lake and with traversing Yellowstone Park. Defects of the map have prompted considerable speculation regarding this journey, but it seems safe to conclude that since the charting is based upon information not only from Colter, but from Lisa, Drewyer, and Maj. Andrew Henry (the last-named of whom had wintered to the west of Jackson Lake in 1810–11), the route traced is approximately correct. How much of the journey was motived in a passion for discovery and how much in mere obedience to Lisa's orders cannot be said, but Chittenden chooses to stress Colter's merit as an explorer (*American Fur Trade of the Far West*, 1902, p. 717).

From Fort Raymond, in the spring of 1808, Colter journeyed to the Three Forks of the Missouri, a region rich in beaver. It was guarded from intrusion, however, by hostile Blackfeet, and in a battle between these Indians and a party of Crows and Flatheads, on whose side he fought, Colter was badly wounded. The encounter in this locality by which he is most widely known and in which his companion, John Potts, was butchered, occurred in the fall of the same year. Dangers, however, according to Thomas James the trapper and trader, "had for him a kind of fascination"; he had no sooner recovered from his injuries than he again ventured to the place, and again he had a narrow escape. Later he descended the Yellowstone and the Missouri to the Hidatsa village, at the mouth of the Knife, to recuperate. Here the great expedition of the St. Louis Missouri Fur Company found him in September 1809, and he was engaged to guide the party of Menard and Henry, which James joined at Fort Raymond, to the Three Forks. It arrived Apr. 3, 1810, and began the erection of a stockade. An escape, nine days later, from an attack in which five men were killed, at last decided Colter to quit. With two companions he started for St. Louis about the 21st, arriving there before the end of May.

He was not again to see the wilderness. After reporting to Clark and telling his story to Bradbury, Brackenridge, and others, he took up a farm, probably on his bounty land, near the present village of Dundee, on the Missouri

River. He married a young woman whose first name was Sally but whose surname has not been discovered. His death, which according to James was due to jaundice, probably occurred at the farm. Colter, says James, "was about . . . five feet ten inches in height and wore an open, ingenious [ingenuous] and pleasing countenance of the Daniel Boone'stamp. Nature had formed him, like Boone, for hardy indurance of fatigue, privations and perils." James says further that "his veracity was never questioned among us," and that "his character was that of a true American backwoodsman."

[Researches of the writer, 1922–23, in collaboration with Miss Stella M. Drumm; Thomas James, *Three Years Among the Indians and Mexicans* (1846, republished in 1916); John Bradbury, *Travels in the Interior of America*, etc. (1817); H. M. Brackenridge, *Views of Louisiana* (1814); information from Colter's great-grandniece, Mrs. Janet Logan of Salt Lake City, and Dr. E. B. Trail of Berger, Mo. H. M. Chittenden, both in his history of the fur trade and in *The Yellowstone National Park* (1920 ed.), devotes considerable space to Colter. See also *John Colter*, by Stallow Vinton (1926).]   W. J. G—t.

COLTON, CALVIN (Sept. 14, 1789–Mar. 13, 1857), journalist, politician, author, was a member of a family of some distinction in colonial Massachusetts. Quartermaster George Colton had represented Springfield in the General Court (1677) and his son married the sister of Roger Wolcott, governor of Connecticut, 1750–54. Capt. Simon Colton, grandson of the Quartermaster and grandfather of Calvin Colton, served as an officer in the French and Indian War. Luther Colton (1756–1803) was a major in the American army during the Revolution. He married Thankful Woolworth, and Calvin Colton, their son, was born at Longmeadow, Mass. He prepared for college at Monson Academy and was graduated from Yale in 1812. Entering Andover Theological Seminary, he completed the three-year course in two years. He served as missionary in western New York and then held Presbyterian pastorates at LeRoy and Batavia. The death of his wife, Abby North (Raymond) Colton (Feb. 1, 1826) and the failure of his voice led him to give up the ministry. Later, having taken orders in the Episcopal Church (1836), he served for one year, 1837–38, as rector of the Church of the Messiah in New York City. His numerous religious writings, which include *History and Character of American Revivals of Religion* (1832), *Church and State in America* (1834), *Protestant Jesuitism* (1836), *The Genius and Mission of the Protestant Episcopal Church in the United States* (1853), are of small value either as history or as theology. In 1831 he went to England where he remained four years as correspondent for the *New York Observer*. His descriptive narratives of travel are of much real value. He wrote a *Manual for Emigrants to America* (1832); *The Americans* (1833), a defense of his country against the criticisms of Capt. Basil Hall and Mrs. Trollope; *Tour of the American Lakes, and Among the Indians of the North-West Territory, in 1830* (1833), personal observations on aboriginal life accompanied by facts relative to the origins of the Indians, details of their wars, and of their treaties with Great Britain and the United States; and *Four Years in Great Britain* (1835).

Next Colton played with political pamphleteering. He wrote much under the *nom-de-plume* "Junius," in support of Whig policies, and was editor of the *True Whig* in Washington, 1842–43. Among his pamphlets, some of which appeared over his pseudonym "Junius," are: *Abolition a Sedition* (1839); *Colonization and Abolition Contrasted* (1839); *Reply to Webster* (1840); *One Presidential Term* (1840); *The Crisis of the Country* (1840); and *The Junius Tracts* (1843–44), a series of ten essays on public lands, the currency, the tariff, expansion, etc. Summoned to Ashland, Ky., in 1844 he became the official biographer of Henry Clay, and editor of his works. *The Private Correspondence of Henry Clay* (1855), and *The Works of Henry Clay* (1856–57) are still standard. His *Life and Times of Henry Clay* (1846), and *The Last Seven Years of the Life of Henry Clay* (1853) are superseded by later biographies. Already known as an advocate of protection, in 1848 he published a protectionist work, *Public Economy for the United States*. It was a strange mixture of views gained through earlier experiences—religious, editorial, and political—but was favorably received and resulted in the establishment of a chair of Public Economy at Trinity College, Hartford, which was offered to Colton and which he held from 1852 until his death. Here his main endeavor was to "give form to" the various phases of the protective system. In *A Lecture on the Railroad to the Pacific* (1850), delivered at the Smithsonian Institution, Aug. 12, 1850, he advocated a transcontinental railroad on the religious ground that through it the human family, dispersed at the Tower of Babel, might be reunited. Yankee acquisitiveness and a facile pen made Calvin Colton a prodigious writer—prolific, rather than profound. A protagonist of the Anglican Church, the protective tariff, slavery, and the Whig party, he was a man of moment in the "Fabulous Forties" of American history. Colton died in Savannah, Ga.

[F. B. Dexter, *Biog. Sketches Grads. Yale Coll.*, vol. VI (1912); Nathan Crosby, *Ann. Obit. Notices*, 1857, pp. 96–97; J. H. Hotchkin, *Hist. of Western N. Y.* (1848), pp. 547–48; *Am. Ch. Rev.*, X, 309–10 (1857–58); *International Monthly Mag.*, Aug. 1851; *Long-meadow Centennial* (1884), Geneal. app., 27, 29, 33, 30; Geo. W. Colton, *Quartermaster Geo. Colton and His Descendants, 1641–1911*, Lancaster, Pa., 1912.]

E. F. H.

COLTON, ELIZABETH AVERY (Dec. 30, 1872–Aug. 26, 1924), educator, was the daughter of James Hooper Colton, a Confederate soldier of Massachusetts ancestry and of Eloise Avery, a descendant of a North Carolina family of some distinction. Her father was a missionary to the Choctaws in the Indian Territory, where Elizabeth was born, the eldest of eight children. In her later life are to be seen the influence of the minister's home, with its cramped means and large demands, and its traditions of conscientiousness, altruism, and love of learning. She prepared for college in the public schools of Jonesboro, N. C., and in a private "college" at Statesville. A year or two of teaching, to support herself and get means to go to college, preceded her entrance to Mount Holyoke in 1891. After two years her father died, and Elizabeth undertook in part the support and education of the younger children. She taught three years in various places, and then became head of the department of English in Queen's College at Charlotte, N. C. The six years spent here seem to have determined her later career. The low standards of the school contrasted painfully with what she had seen in the East, and she felt the inadequacy of her own training to remedy the situation. In spite of her responsibilities and her limited means she attended summer school in the universities of North Carolina, Tennessee, and Chicago. By 1902 she was able to return to college. She received the B.S. degree at Teachers College in 1903, and the A.M. at Columbia in 1905, teaching meanwhile for a year in the Horace Mann School. She then spent three years as an instructor at Wellesley.

Meanwhile she was evidently cherishing her ambitions to aid in the educational regeneration of the South. In 1903 she had become a charter member of the Southern Association of College Women; and in 1908 an invitation to Meredith College (Raleigh, N. C.) as head of the department of English furnished her opportunity. She was personally well fitted for the leadership of college women. She was of slight build and attractive appearance, well-groomed and modish in dress, vivacious and witty, and buoyant and carefree in temperament even in her years of heavy responsibility and physical pain. To generosity and disregard of her personal welfare,

which won intense personal devotion, she added unbending devotion to principle as she saw it, and a keen relish for a fight in a righteous cause. In 1910 she became chairman of the committee on college standards of the Southern Association of College Women, and for the next eight years was a recognized leader in the campaign. She became secretary in 1912, and president in 1914. In a series of incisive pamphlets she exposed the pretensions of the many so-called colleges for women in the South, insisting upon standards of equipment, faculty scholarship and recording, and fully recognizing such merit as she found. Her chief papers were on "The Approximate Value of Recent Degrees of Southern Colleges" (*Meredith College Bulletin*, 1914), and one which largely superseded it, "The Various Types of Southern Colleges for Women" (Bulletin 2 of the *1916 Publications of the Southern Association of College Women*). These evoked a storm of criticism and "more than one presidential threat of a libel suit" (*Journal of the American Association of University Women*, January 1925). The opposition alleged that her findings were based on inadequate data, were contradicted by the results of official inspection, were unfairly discriminatory, and were prompted by personal motives (Letters of H. E. Stout, R. R. Thompson and J. C. Guilds). Even in her own school a faction thought her a fanatic and a pedant. Time has, however, largely justified her. In 1919 her health broke down and she resigned her public leadership. Two years later she gave up teaching and spent the rest of her life in a vain search for health. Before her death she had the satisfaction of knowing that her campaign was on the road to success.

[The only important published sources for the life of Elizabeth Avery Colton are obituary notices. One in the *Jour. of the A. A. U. W.*, Jan. 1925, is reprinted, with supplementary eulogies, in the *Meredith Coll. Quart. Bull.*, June 1925. It appears also in the *Mount Holyoke Alumnæ Quart.*, Apr. 1925. The notice in the *Biblical Recorder*, Sept. 3, 1924, is independent. The official records of Columbia University, of Teachers College, and of the Mount Holyoke Alumnæ Asso. furnish a partial chronology. Certain personal data are from letters of her brother, H. C. Colton of Nashville, and of her associates, Emily H. Dutton, Dean of Sweetbriar College, and Sophie C. Hart of Wellesley.]

W. J. G—d.

COLTON, GARDNER QUINCY (Feb. 7, 1814–Aug. 9, 1898), anæsthetist, younger brother of Walter Colton [*q.v.*], was the tenth son and twelfth child of Walter and Thankful (Cobb) Colton. The father, a poverty-stricken weaver of Georgia, Vt., was descended from George Colton, who came from England about 1650 and settled in Springfield, Mass., and from his son, Capt. Thomas Colton, the Indian fighter. Owing to eye trouble Gardner Colton received a scanty education and, at sixteen, he was apprenticed for five years to a chairmaker of St. Albans, Vt., at five dollars a year, after which he went to New York City as journeyman maker of cane-seated chairs. With his brother's financial assistance he later (1842) studied medicine under Dr. Willard Parker of New York but did not take a degree. During his studies he learned of the exhilarating effects of nitrous oxide inhalation, and in 1844, with borrowed money, he gave in New York a public demonstration of its effects at which the gate receipts were $535. With this encouragement he set out to give demonstrations in other cities. On Dec. 10, 1844, at Hartford, Conn., a similar demonstration aroused the interest of a dentist, Horace Wells [q.v.], who, after Colton had extracted one of his teeth "under" nitrous oxide, used the anæsthetic in his dental practise and thus became one of the claimants in the subsequent controversy on anæsthesia (see sketch of W. T. G. Morton). Colton always gave Wells the credit of first suggesting the practical use of nitrous oxide. He gave many other public demonstrations, and in 1863, lectured again in New Haven. On this occasion Dr. J. H. Smith, a dentist, became interested, and together he and Colton extracted 1,785 teeth in twenty-three days, with the use of nitrous oxide. Colton then removed to New York (July 1863), where he established, with John Allen, the "Colton Dental Association," which had for its sole object painless extraction of teeth under nitrous oxide. No records were kept during the first six months, but from Feb. 4, 1864, to Jan. 1, 1867, 17,601 individuals registered, and two or three teeth were extracted from each. In 1866 branch associations were opened in Philadelphia, Baltimore, St. Louis, Cincinnati, Brooklyn, and Boston. Colton probably administered nitrous oxide gas, or caused it to be given, at least 25,000 times, without a fatality. While lecturing on the telegraph for its inventor, S. F. B. Morse [q.v.], Colton devised an electric motor which was exhibited at Pittsburgh in 1847. The model is fully described in G. B. Prescott's Dynamo-Electricity (1885) and is now preserved in the Smithsonian Institution but it was never patented. Though the idea of using electricity for propulsion was probably original with Colton, it was not new, for Thomas Davenport [q.v.] had patented an electric railway motor in 1837. In February 1849 Colton joined his brother in the gold fields of California and for a few months practised medicine there. Later he was appointed by Gov. Riley justice of the peace at San Francisco. He accumulated a small fortune while in California,

but on his return to the East he soon lost it by a bad investment and had to support himself by reporting sermons for the Boston Transcript. In 1860 he published a series of war maps, which bore his name. He died in Rotterdam, Holland. Though a wide reader, he wrote only a few ephemeral pamphlets, and he is to be remembered chiefly for his services in perfecting the use of anæsthesia.

[Obituary by C. S. McNielle in Dental Cosmos, Oct. 1898, pp. 874–75; J. H. Hunt, "Who Discovered Anæsthesia?" in Tri-State Medic. Jour., Mar. 1897, pp. 128–30; three pamphlets by himself: A True Hist. of the Discovery of Anæsthesia; A Reply to Elizabeth Whitman Morton (1896); Boyhood and Manhood Recollections: the Story of a Busy Life (1897); and Boyhood Recollections: a Story with a Moral (1891); L. W. Nevius, The Discovery of Modern Anæsthesia (1894); G. W. Colton, A Geneal. Record of the Descendants of Quartermaster Geo. Colton (1912); private information.]

J.F.F.

COLTON, GEORGE RADCLIFFE (Apr. 10, 1865–Apr. 6, 1916), governor of Porto Rico, customs expert, was a son of Francis and Frances A. (Garey) Colton and was born in Galesburg, Ill. He was a descendant in the eighth generation of Quartermaster George Colton who emigrated from England before the middle of the seventeenth century, served in King Philip's War, and lived to become a trusted and prominent citizen of Massachusetts. At an early age young Colton went West where he worked as a ranchman in New Mexico; then, when about twenty years old, he moved to Nebraska and entered the banking business, eventually becoming cashier and manager of the Central Nebraska National Bank of David City, Nebr. He served a term as a member of the state House of Representatives from David City and in 1897 was a national bank examiner. In October 1889 he was married to Jessie T. McLeod. He had affiliated himself with the National Guard of his state and at the outbreak of the Spanish-American War was one of those instrumental in organizing the 1st Regiment of Nebraska Volunteer Infantry. He saw service in the Philippine Islands as lieutenant-colonel of his regiment and, upon the American occupation of the Islands, organized the customs service at Manila and remained in this work until 1905 when he was sent to Santo Domingo to organize a customs receivership under the modus vivendi between the United States and the Dominican Republic. In 1907 he was reassigned to the Philippines where for two years he acted as Insular Collector of Customs. While in this position he drafted and presented to Congress a new tariff for the Philippines. This was enacted at a special session of Congress in 1909. In November of that year Colton went to Porto Rico as governor of the Island. He held this post for four years, returning to the United States in November 1913. He then became connected with banking interests in this country. He was regarded as an authority on matters relating to customs duties and tariffs. He rendered valuable service to his country at the time when tariff revision was a pressing need, and brought his expert information to the problems of tariff protection or free trade, especially as they pertained to the insular possessions of the United States, and the Pan-American countries.

[Geo. W. Colton, *A Geneal. Record of the Descendants of Quartermaster George Colton* (1912) ; the *Neb. Blue Book,* 1926; *Bull. of the Pan-American Union,* Apr. 1916; *Evening Star* (Washington, D. C.), Apr. 7, 1916; the *N. Y. Times* and *Washington Post,* Apr. 8, 1916.]

E. Y.

COLTON, WALTER (May 9, 1797–Jan. 22, 1851), theologian, journalist, author, was born in Rutland County, Vt., the third of twelve children of Deacon Walter Colton and Thankful (Cobb) Colton, and brother of Gardner Quincy Colton [*q.v.*]. He was descended in the fourth generation from Quartermaster George Colton, a prominent citizen of colonial Massachusetts, who came from England before 1650. When Walter was an infant, his father, a weaver by trade, moved his family to Georgia, a village on Lake Champlain. As a lad, young Colton was sent to an uncle in Hartford, Conn., to learn cabinetmaking. Here, in 1816, he was received into the church and soon thereafter entered the Hartford Grammar School to prepare for college and the ministry. He pursued his studies in Yale College with credit from 1818 to 1822, winning the Berkeleyan Prize in Latin and delivering the valedictory poem at graduation. He then entered Andover Theological Seminary, where he devoted much time to literature, writing a sacred drama and a "News Carriers' Address" for which a Boston newspaper gave him a two-hundred-dollar prize. Graduating in 1825, he was ordained an evangelist in the Congregational Church and then made professor of moral philosophy and belles-lettres in the Scientific and Military Academy at Middletown, Conn. As chaplain, he often preached to the students; his eulogy, delivered at the Academy after the funeral of Commodore Macdonough, is particularly noteworthy. Meanwhile, he wrote several articles for the Middletown *Gazette,* thus becoming initiated into journalism. Resigning his professorship in 1830, he went, at the request of friends of the American Board of Commissioners for Foreign Missions, to Washington to edit the *American Spectator and Washington City Chronicle.* This paper had been established to prevent President Jackson from removing the

Indians from Georgia, where the Board had a mission. Jackson prevailed, however, and the newspaper came to an end. Colton sometimes preached at the church where Jackson worshipped. A friendship developed notwithstanding their political differences, and Colton was frequently a White House guest. The President, learning that Colton's health had been impaired, offered him a naval chaplaincy. This was accepted, and on Jan. 29, 1831, he began his first cruise, on the *Vincennes* to the West Indies. Early in 1832 he went to the Mediterranean in the *Constellation,* Commodore George C. Read. The experiences and observations of this three-years cruise Colton recorded in his *Ship and Shore; or Leaves from the Journal of a Cruise to the Levant* (1835), and *A Visit to Constantinople and Athens* (1836). In the spring of 1835 he was assigned to the naval station at Charlestown, Mass., where he prepared his manuscripts for publication, ministered to seamen, and often preached in the pulpits of Charlestown and Boston. He was appointed, in 1837, historiographer and chaplain of the South Sea Surveying and Exploring Squadron, and while in Washington preparing for his new duties he edited the *Colonization Herald* for several months. The personnel of the exploring expedition had to be reorganized and Colton resigned his post largely on the score of health. Then, early in 1838, he became chaplain of the naval station at Philadelphia, where with the consent of the Navy Department he was also co-editor of the *Independent North American.* But the change of politics at Washington incident to President Harrison's death prevented his editing a paper hostile to the new administration, and he then devoted himself exclusively to his chaplaincy. On June 26, 1844, he married a distant relative, Cornelia B. Colton of Philadelphia. In the late summer of 1845, he was ordered to sea in the *Congress,* Commodore Robert F. Stockton, bound for the Pacific. This voyage in the Pacific Squadron flagship afforded Colton material for another book, *Deck and Port; or Incidents of a Cruise in the United States Frigate Congress to California* (1850). Though a chaplain, he was appointed, July 28, 1846, alcalde, or chief judge, of Monterey and neighboring territory, by the military authorities; and on Sept. 15, the citizens confirmed his appointment with the votes. During his tenure of office, he established *The Californian,* the first newspaper to be published in California; built its first school-house, and a public building, which was named "Colton Hall" in his honor; and in a letter to the Philadelphia *North American and United States Gazette,* first publicly announced to the East the discovery of gold in the Sacramento Valley. On his return home in the summer of 1849, he prepared for the press his *Three Years in California, 1846–1849* (1850), and tried to regain his health, but after a long period of severe illness, he died in Philadelphia. Colton wrote numerous sermons and other addresses, newspaper articles, and pamphlets; but his travel books on Constantinople, Greece, and California constitute his most important writings.

[The chief sources of information concerning Colton are, in addition to his books of travel, the "Memoir" by Henry Theodore Cheever in his edition of Colton's *The Sea and the Sailor, Notes on France and Italy, and Other Literary Remains* (1851); George Woolworth Colton, *A Geneal. Record of the Descendants of Quartermaster George Colton* (1912); and obituary in the *North American and United States Gazette* (Phila.), Jan. 23, 1851; the *United States Navy Register*; Laura B. Everett, "A Judge Lindsey of the Idle Forties," in the *Survey* for Apr. 5, 1913.]

C.L.L.

COLVER, NATHANIEL (May 10, 1794–Sept. 25, 1870), Baptist clergyman, reformer, was born in Orwell, Vt. His father and grandfather both bore the same name, and both were Baptist preachers and pioneer farmers, descendants of Edward Colver, who came to Massachusetts from England in 1635. His mother, Esther Dean, daughter of John and Thankful Dean, was also of early Colonial stock. When he was a year old his parents moved to northeastern New York, near what is now Champlain, and in 1810, to West Stockbridge, Mass. The family was large and the boy was brought up under the toughening conditions of frontier life. Two winters' schooling comprised his education, and the only books in his home were the Bible, Psalmbook, and speller. He learned the tanner's trade, joined the troops assembled to defend New York against the British in 1814, and, on Aug. 27, 1815, married Sally Clark. Soon after he was converted and became a preacher. He was ordained in West Clarendon, Vt., his first regular parish, in 1819, and for the next twenty years served small churches in Vermont and New York. His first wife died Jan. 27, 1824, and Jan. 26, 1825, at Plattsburg, N. Y., he married Mrs. Sarah A. Carter.

He had natural oratorical ability, derived probably from his mother whose family was noted for its public speakers, herself, it is said, a woman of unusual intellectual qualities. His mind was vigorous, and quick to acquire, and he possessed a ready wit and platform resourcefulness. From the start he drew large audiences. Inheriting through his paternal ancestors a restless, independent, fighting spirit, he naturally became a vigorous champion of reform. Having joined the Masons and finding that he disapproved of some of their principles and requirements, he repudiated the order in 1829, and thereafter opposed secret societies as wrong morally and dangerous politically. He was also active in the cause of temperance, and especially in behalf of abolition, to which he gave practically all his time in 1838 and a part of 1839, serving for a period as an agent of the American Anti-Slavery Society.

Addresses delivered in New England brought him to the attention of certain Boston Baptists who desired to establish a church with free seats, and particularly opposed to slavery and intemperance. Such a church, the First Free Baptist, later known as Tremont Temple, was organized, with Colver as minister. Here from 1839 to 1852 he had a notable pastorate, and acquired an enviable reputation as a preacher, being regarded as one of the attractions of the city. He was recognized also as one of the ablest advocates of abolition. John Quincy Adams said he was the best off-hand speaker he had ever heard. A delegate to the World Anti-Slavery Convention at London in 1840, he attracted favorable attention there. In a sermon published in 1850, *The Fugitive Slave Bill, or God's Laws Paramount to the Laws of Men,* he urged disobedience to the law as a sacred duty.

Pastorates in South Abington (Whitman), Mass.; Detroit; Cincinnati; and Chicago followed. He kept up his attacks upon slavery, and a sermon, preached in Cincinnati, Dec. 11, 1859, *"Slavery or Freedom Must Die." The Harper's Ferry Tragedy a Symptom of Disease in the Heart of the Nation,* was published in 1860. Appreciating the need of theological education in the West, both in Cincinnati and Chicago, he gathered together groups of young men contemplating the ministry and instructed them. He was active in the establishment of the Chicago Baptist Theological Institute in 1865, the object of which was the creation of a theological seminary in connection with the first University of Chicago, and pending its opening he was appointed to give instruction in doctrinal and practical theology at the University. In 1867 he established at Richmond, Va., the Colver Institute for the training of colored ministers, which survives in the theological department of the Virginia Union University. An oil painting of Colver hangs in one of the halls in Tremont Temple, Boston; another in the Divinity School of the University of Chicago, bearing the inscription "A Founder of the Divinity School."

[J. A. Smith, *Memoir of Rev. Nathaniel Colver, D.D.* (1873); F. L. Colver, *Colver-Culver Genealogy* (1910), from which some dates, differing from those given elsewhere, are taken; J. L. Rosenberger, *Through Three Centuries* (1922); T. W. Goodspeed, *Univ. of Chi. Biog. Sketches*, vol. I (1922).]   H. E. S.

COLVER, WILLIAM BYRON (Sept. 26, 1870–May 28, 1926), editor, chairman of the Federal Trade Commission, was the son of Byron Henry and Josephine (Noble) Colver and was born at Wellington, Ohio. He attended the public schools of Cleveland and later studied law at Ohio State University. He practised law for only a short time, however, before he became reporter on the *Cleveland Plain Dealer* in 1894. In 1897 he was married to Pauline Simmons of Cleveland. From the *Plain Dealer* he went to the *Cleveland Press* and in 1898 became New York and Washington correspondent for the old Scripps-McRae League. When Tom L. Johnson [*q.v.*], a close personal and political friend, launched his famous three-cent-fare fight, Colver withdrew from journalism for a few years to devote his energy to the civic cause in Cleveland. He was one of a group of a half-dozen men who, under Johnson's leadership, fought for the public control of street-car lines. He served for a year of this period as tax inquisitor for Cuyahoga County, and for another year as secretary of the Municipal Traction Company of Cleveland. In 1907 he returned to newspaper work as editor of the Newspaper Enterprise Association. Five years later he resigned to become editor-in-chief of the "Clover Leaf" publications of the Northwest. In 1917 he was appointed by President Wilson to the Federal Trade Commission of which he was a member for three and a half years, serving for one year as chairman. This position developed into a war-time post of grave responsibility and his associates gave him great credit for his practical vision in setting up principles to govern competition and prevent unfair practises in trade. Concerning his work here the *New York Times* said (May 29, 1926): "Outstanding in Mr. Colver's incumbency of the Federal Trade Commissionership were his fight against the excess profits tax which he believed to be uneconomic, and his opposition to the great packing interests which he felt had an unwholesome control of the meat industry." He served also as a member of the Price Fixing Committee of the War Industries Board. In 1919 he organized the Scripps-Howard Newspaper Alliance, the Washington editorial bureau for all Scripps-Howard papers, and until his retirement from active work in 1924 he served as general editorial director of the Scripps-Howard newspapers, in which position he assisted in starting or inspiring many of the policies of these papers.

It was in newspaper work rather than in public office that Colver achieved his greatest suc-cess. As a writer of editorials which bristled with purpose and were packed with solid and accurate information, he waged many a campaign for public causes. During the Taft administration his editorial skill exposed the celebrated power-site and forest exploitation. He wrote stirring editorials on the Teapot Dome exposures and chided the newspapers that they had done so little to expose the unfair practises for which the public continually suffered and which every newspaper man in Washington knew existed. He was of the firm belief that the publisher and the editor had different functions, and that it was the editor's duty to get all the news and then really serve the public by giving it all the news in the most readable and interesting way. He preached the gospel of terse, bright newswriting and saw vast possibilities for the tabloid sheets. These, he believed, need not be sensational papers but should offer an attractive economical form in which brevity could be conserved and displays made without waste of material.

[Information from Mr. Lowell Mellett, editor, the Scripps-Howard Newspaper Alliance, Washington, D. C.; article by Marlen Pew in *The Editor and Publisher*, June 5, 1926; *Who's Who in America*, 1926–27; *Evening Star* (Washington), and *Washington Daily News*, May 29, 1926. For his connection with Tom Johnson see Tom L. Johnson, *My Story* (1911), ed. by E. J. Hauser.]   E. Y.

COLVIN, STEPHEN SHELDON (Mar. 29, 1869–July 15, 1923), educator, author, was the son of Stephen Colvin, a loom manufacturer, and Clara Turner Colvin. He was born in Phenix, R. I., and received his early education in private schools, completing his preparation for college in Worcester Academy. He graduated from Brown University with the degrees of Ph.B. (1891) and A.M. (1894). During a part of the period of his graduate work at Brown he was engaged in reporting for the *Providence Journal* and the *Evening Bulletin*. He became instructor in rhetoric at Brown in 1892, serving in this position until 1895. He was married in 1891 to Edna F. Boothman of Riverpoint, R. I. She died in 1893. He was married again in 1895 to Eva M. Collins of Providence. During the next two years he studied philosophy at the universities of Berlin and Strasburg and prepared a thesis on *Schopenhauer's Doctrine of the Thing-in-Itself and his Attempt to Relate it to the World of Phenomena* (published 1897). He received the degree of Ph.D. at Strasburg in 1897.

After his study in Germany, he filled the position of instructor in English in the Worcester high schools for four years, from 1897 to 1901. During this period he attended the seminars of G. Stanley Hall [*q.v.*] at Clark University, where he became absorbed in the applications of psychology to education. His later interest in high-school education is to be traced to his studies with Hall. In 1901 he became assistant professor of psychology at the University of Illinois and remained in this position until 1903. After a year (1903–04), during which he served as assistant professor of philosophy at Brown University, he returned to the University of Illinois as associate professor of psychology. He was later promoted to a professorship and to the headship of the department, which position he held until 1912. At the University of Illinois he was associated intimately with William C. Bagley, in collaboration with whom he prepared a book entitled *Human Behavior* (1913). Much of his writing during this period dealt with problems in the field of educational psychology, the most important being *The Learning Process* (1911). In this book he stated his position on the subject of formal discipline, which was at that time much discussed. He vigorously defended the position that there are general mental habits and that through these transfer of training takes place.

In 1912 he was called back to Brown as professor of educational psychology. He continued in this position until 1923, assuming in 1919 the duties of director of the School of Education in addition to those of his professorship. At Brown University he inaugurated the plan of administering intelligence tests to all students and of following these tests with personal guidance on an extended scale. He also assisted the State Department of Education of Rhode Island as inspector of high schools in developing the secondary schools of the state. He published a book entitled *Introduction to High School Teaching* (1917), which is extensively used as a text-book in teacher-training institutions in all parts of the country. In 1923 he went as professor of education to Teachers College, Columbia University, where he had for a number of years given courses during the summer. He had suffered from a heart lesion for some time, and during his first year at Teachers College he died suddenly of a severe angina. In addition to the books mentioned, Colvin published a number of important papers, especially on mental tests of college students and high-school seniors. All his writings are characterized by careful attention to details and by a strict empiricism. He exercised a strong influence in the direction of a conservative use of mental tests as substitutes for the conventional college-entrance examinations. His contributions to the literature of methods of teaching have done much to systematize and improve instruction in American high schools

[*Jour. Nat. Educ. Asso.*, Nov. 1923, p. 379; *Teachers Coll. Record*, Nov. 1923, p. 504; *Brown Alumni Mo.*, Oct. 1923, p. 83.]   C.H.J.

COLVOCORESSES, GEORGE MUSALAS (Oct. 22, 1816–June 3, 1872), naval officer, was born in Chios, Greek Archipelago, son of Constantine and Franka (Grimaldi) Colvocoresses. Brought to Smyrna by the Turks after a massacre on the island in 1822, he was ransomed by relatives and sent with nine other boys in the American brig *Margarita* to Baltimore. Through the Greek Relief Committee, Capt. Alden Partridge, head of Norwich (Vt.) Academy, took the lad and entered him in his school, where he gained a good education, remaining until his appointment as midshipman, Feb. 21, 1832. As a passed midshipman he accompanied the Wilkes Exploring Expedition (1838–42) in the South Seas and Antarctic, making also an overland journey from Oregon to San Francisco in connection with the expedition, September–October 1841, and returning by the East Indies. These experiences are described in his *Four Years in a Government Exploring Expedition* (1852), a popular book at the time, which went to five editions. Commissioned lieutenant, Dec. 7, 1843, he was in the Pacific Squadron during the Mexican War; in the Mediterranean, 1847–49; on the African Coast, 1851–52; and then, after two years' duty in New York, executive of the *Levant* in the East India Squadron, where he led a landing force in the capture, Nov. 20–22, 1856, of the barrier forts below Canton. In the Civil War, with the rank of commander (July 1, 1861), he commanded the storeship *Supply* until 1863, and then the sail-sloop *Saratoga*. Though the *Saratoga* was of little value for blockading, Colvocoresses drilled his large crew thoroughly, and when sent to the Georgia coast in the spring of 1864 he led three landing parties, Aug. 3, 16, and 25, breaking up a coast-guard organization meeting on the 3rd and taking twenty-six prisoners, and on the 16th capturing twenty-nine cavalrymen. For these exploits he was thanked in general orders by Admiral Dahlgren (*Official Records, Navy*, XV, 637), who also protested to the department upon the withdrawal of Colvocoresses in September. In 1865–66 he commanded the *St. Mary's* on the west coast of South America, and on one occasion by a sharp warning against injury to American property protected Valparaiso from bombardment by a Spanish squadron. He was retired as captain Jan. 11, 1867. Five years later he was shot and killed by thieves on a street in Bridgeport, Conn., while about to take a steamer on a business trip from his home in Litchfield, Conn., to New York. Colvocoresses had a quick mind and attractive personality and in later years often gave lectures on his voyages and subjects from natural history. On May 17, 1846, he married Eliza Halsey, niece of Commander T. Freelon, U. S. N., by whom he had three daughters and a son, George Partridge, born at Norwich, Vt., who entered the navy and rose to rear admiral. On July 19, 1863, after his first wife's death, he married Adeline Swasey, a sister of Mrs. Alden Partridge.

[An account of Captain Colvocoresses appears in G. M. Dodge and W. A. Ellis, *Norwich Univ., 1819–1911* (1911), II, 85; *Official Records (Navy)*; Navy Registers 1833–69; N. Y. *Herald* and other papers, June 5–9, 1872; letter describing his coming to America, by his son, Portsmouth (Va.) *Star*, May 2, 1923.]   A.W.

COLWELL, STEPHEN (Mar. 25, 1800–Jan. 15, 1871), political economist, was born in Brooke County, Va. (now W. Va.), and graduated from Jefferson College, Pa., at the age of nineteen. He studied law under Judge Halleck, in Steubenville, Ohio, was admitted to the bar, and practised for seven years in St. Clairsville, Ohio, and then in Pittsburgh until 1836. In that year he gave up the practise of law and became an iron manufacturer, first at Weymouth, N. J., and later at Conshohocken on the outskirts of Philadelphia. For twenty-five years he had particular occasion to weigh the results of the tariff policy as it affected iron manufacturers, and this practical experience vitalized much of the writing on economics to which his legal training gave precision of thought and expression. In his studies pertaining to the technical side of the science, especially the treatment of the subject of money and exchanges, Colwell's view-point was that of the school of Henry C. Carey [*q.v.*]; he set forth always the advantage of protection to industry, and assailed the quantity theory of money. With him, however, economics was also a theory of benevolence. He was an active Presbyterian, and the close interrelation of his economics and his religion was signalized by his attacks upon current orthodoxy in both fields. His religion was infused with the guiding principle of human helpfulness; his strictures on the merely pious (in such works, for instance, as *New Themes for the Protestant Clergy*, 1851) drew sharp comment from his critics, though the course of years brought general acceptance of his contentions. He was a trustee of the University of Pennsylvania and of Princeton Theological Seminary. To the former institution he bequeathed his library of political economy, composed of upward of 6,000 items, almost half of them pamphlets separately bound. He coupled with this gift the condition that the University should found a chair of social science, but his family waived the con-

dition. He secured the establishment at Princeton of a chair of Christian ethics; and was hopeful that this chair should develop and popularize the social implications of Christianity. His interests were many, and increased with his marked success in business. He was a director of the Camden and Atlantic, the Reading, and the Pennsylvania Central railroads. An active member of the Colonization Society, he strove to persuade the South that slavery was an unwise and unprofitable institution. During the Civil War he did his best to support the Union cause; he was active in the work of the Sanitary Commission and the Christian Commission, guaranteeing funds for the relief of the wounded and sick, and himself visiting the battle-fields and hospitals. He presided over the first formal meeting which led to the organization of the Union League. Afterward he gave generously of time and money to the Freedmen's Aid Society. His life was probably shortened by intensive work on the preparation in 1865 of six reports on the subjects of trade and taxes for the United States Revenue Commission, of which he was a member. He died in Philadelphia.

[Henry C. Carey, "A Memoir of Stephen Colwell," in *Proc. Am. Philos. Soc.*, XVII (1871–72), 195–209; this contains a list of Colwell's writings: see also, obituary in Phila. *Public Ledger*, Jan. 17, 1871.]   B.M.

COMAN, CHARLOTTE BUELL (1833– Nov. 11, 1924), artist, was born in Waterville, N. Y., the daughter of Chauncey Buell. She early evinced great artistic talent and began her studies in America with James R. Brevoort [*q.v.*], a successful landscape painter and a member of the National Academy. She went abroad and studied in Paris with Émile Vernier and Harry Thompson, later going to Holland. She devoted herself chiefly to painting landscapes, after the manner of the great landscapists, Corot, Daubigny, and others, but was not imitative, having her own distinct manner in color and conception. She sent to the Centennial Exposition in Philadelphia in 1876 a picture entitled "A French Village," which received loud praise and to the Paris Exposition in 1878 another landscape, "Near Fontainebleau." She remained abroad six years. Many awards and prizes came to her, among them a medal at the Midwinter Exposition in San Francisco in 1894, the Shaw Memorial Prize at the exhibition of the Society of American Artists in 1905, the second prize at the exhibition of the Society of Washington Artists in 1906, the Burgess Prize from the New York Woman's Art Club in 1907. She was made an Associate Academician in 1910 and was a member of the New York Watercolor Club and of the National Association of Women Painters and Sculptors. Her pictures are owned in Boston, New York, and Paris, and several exhibits of her work have been held. She is represented in a number of permanent collections: in the Metropolitan Museum, New York; in the National Gallery, Washington, by a landscape "Early Summer"; in Dallas, San Antonio, Fort Worth, the Artists Club, and elsewhere. She died at Invalid's Rest Sanitarium, Yonkers, in her ninety-first year.

[Clara E. Clement and Laurence Hutton, *Artists of the Nineteenth Century and Their Works* (1907) ; *Am. Art Annual*, 1923–24 ; *Who's Who in America*, 1912–13 ; Ulrich Thieme, *Allgemeines Lexikon der Bildenden Künstler*, VII (1912), 266 ; *Art News*, Nov. 15, 1924 ; *N. Y. Times*, Nov. 13, 1924.]   H.W.

COMBS, LESLIE (Nov. 29, 1793–Aug. 22, 1881), soldier, politician, was the son of Capt. Benjamin Combs of Stafford County, Va., and of Sarah Richardson of Annapolis, Md. His father first went to Kentucky in 1775, returned to Virginia to fight in the Revolution, and going again to Kentucky in 1782 settled in Clarke County across the Kentucky River from Boonesborough (*Biographical Encyclopedia of Kentucky*, 1878, p. 79). Leslie was educated by Rev. John Lyle, a well-known Presbyterian minister and teacher. He was serving as deputy county clerk of Jessamine County when the War of 1812 began. He joined the Kentucky troops and was a scout in the River Raisin campaign (A. C. Quisenberry, *Kentucky in the War of 1812*, 1915, p. 53). On the expedition to relieve Fort Meigs in May 1813 he was captain of a company of scouts, was severely wounded, and taken prisoner (L. and R. H. Collins, *History of Kentucky*, 1874, II, 196). After the war he read law in a private office in Lexington and was admitted to the bar in 1818 (Robert Peter and Wm. H. Perrin, *History of Fayette County, Kentucky*, 1882, p. 349). After practising law for a short period, he was elected to the lower house of the Kentucky legislature in 1827 and remained a member through 1829. He was later a member of the House in 1833, 1845–47, and 1857–59 (Collins, II, 170). In 1846 he was speaker of the Kentucky House of Representatives. He was a candidate for congressman in 1851 but was defeated by John C. Breckinridge [*q.v.*]. In 1836 he was appointed colonel of the ten companies of Kentucky militia raised to protect the Sabine frontier, but the troops were ordered discharged before they began their march (*Niles' Weekly Register*, Aug. 27, 1836, 431). Combs was a Whig in politics as long as that party existed in Kentucky. In Aug. 1860 he was a candidate, on the Bell-Everett ticket, for clerk of the court of

appeals and was elected by an overwhelming majority. This position he held for six years. He was a pronounced Unionist at the beginning of the Civil War and exerted himself to prevent the secession of Kentucky. He was not an extremist, however, and as the war went on he became very bitter in his protests against military rule in Kentucky (*Official Records, Army*, I ser., vol. XXXIX, pt. 2, p. 240). After the war he lived in retirement at Lexington until his death. Combs was an able lawyer of rather wide reputation. His service in the Kentucky legislature was without special incident although he was active in internal-improvement measures. He was a useful legislator though not a brilliant one, and his popularity was attested by his huge majority for clerk of the court of appeals in 1860. In 1819 he was married to Margaret Trotter of Fayette County and after her death married (1849) Mary Elizabeth Brownell of Connecticut. There were eleven children of the first marriage and three of the second.

[In addition to references given above see "Narrative of the Life of Gen. Leslie Combs of Ky." in *Am. Whig Rev.*, Jan., Feb. 1852, repr. in pamphlet form; obituary in the *Courier-Journal* (Louisville), Aug. 23, 1881; Robt. B. McAfee, *Hist. of the Late War in the Western Country* (1816). The *Official Records* spell his name "Coombs."]   R.S.C.

COMBS, MOSES NEWELL (1753–Apr. 12, 1834), manufacturer, philanthropist, was a native of Morris County, N. J. Toward the end of the Revolutionary War, a veteran of "several severe engagements," he took up his residence in the village of Newark. As a tanner and shoemaker, he quickly attained success, and with a shipment in 1790 of 200 sealskin shoes from his shop to Georgia the export trade of the city of Newark may be said to have started. Although not the first tanner or shoemaker in the community, Combs has been called the "Father of Newark industries," for "it was through him that the town's industrial system was formed" (Urquhart, *post*, I, 516). In later years he received as high as $9,000 for a single order of shoes, and "silver was showered on him so plentifully," he said, that he did not know what to do with it (W. H. Shaw, *post*, I, 572). The shoe and leather business has always been a basic Newark industry, and many men, such as Luther Goble, later prominent in Newark buisiness life, served their apprenticeship under Combs. In addition to his leather interests Combs was treasurer of the Springfield-Newark Turnpike Company (1806) and one of the founders and directors of the Newark Fire Insurance Company. Of a philanthropic turn of mind, Combs "strenuously advocated three things many years ahead of his time: emancipation of slaves, temperance and universal education" (Urquhart, *post*, I, 517). In 1794 he opened an evening school for his own and other apprentices, the tuition fee being $2.50 for each scholar from November to March. This nominal tuition fee was soon abolished and for years Combs supported the institution as a free school. It was in existence as late as 1818 when announcement was made of a "School for Educating the Children of the Poor in Newark," with Moses N. Combs as president, one of his sons, David, as treasurer, and another son, Isaac, as a trustee. It is stated (Urquhart, *post*, I, 518) that this school "was probably the first night school in the United States, and was one of the first free schools in the country, (and possibly the first)."

The religious interests of Combs were very deep. Differing with Dr. Alexander MacWorter and the majority of the First Presbyterian Church of Newark because of their willingness to accept the "half-way covenant," Combs led an exodus from the Newark church to the Presbyterian Church of Orange. Finding the distance to Orange too great, Combs and his associates after several years held services in one of the buildings attached to his tanning plant, and here Combs preached to them. During 1797 he issued a few numbers of a magazine containing a variety of essays on the Bible. His church after some years disintegrated, the members returning to their original Newark communion. Combs was a man of strong personality and extreme individuality bordering on eccentricity, but was conceded to have been one of the most valuable citizens of his community in his day. Soon after his arrival in Newark, he fell in love with Mary Haynes, daughter of one of the leading men of the village and married her against her father's will. She bore him thirteen children.

[Frank J. Urquhart, *A Hist. of the City of Newark, N. J.* (1913), I, 514-20 and Wm. H. Shaw, *Hist. of Essex and Hudson Counties, N. J.* (1884), I, 571-72, contain material on Combs. See also the *Newark Evening News*, Nov. 24, 1914, and the *Newark Sunday Call*, Oct. 24, 1915. The *Newark Daily Advertiser* for Apr. 16, 1834, notes his death.]   H.U.F.

COMER, BRAXTON BRAGG (Nov. 7, 1848–Aug. 15, 1927), business man, governor of Alabama, was the fourth son of John Fletcher Comer, judge of the superior court of Georgia, and Catherine Drewry. The Comers came of English and Irish stock, said to have been supporters of the Cromwellian régime. They settled in Virginia in colonial times and moved to Georgia in the early part of the nineteenth century, and thence to Barbour County, Ala., where they engaged in planting, lumbering, and grist-milling, achieving marked business success. Braxton received his early education in a private school, and attended the University of Alabama during the last year of the war, taking part in the student defense of the University against Gen. Croxton's invasion. After the burning of the University, he returned to his father's plantation. The following year he entered the University of Georgia, but was soon forced to retire because of ill health. After recovering his health, he entered Emory and Henry College, Va., where he received the A.B. and A.M. degrees with distinction in natural science. From college he returned to Barbour County and engaged in planting and merchandising at Comer Station. There he demonstrated his business capacity by developing large and successful farming and country-store interests, during the difficult years immediately following the Reconstruction régime. He was married on Oct. 4, 1872, to Eva Jane Harris, member of a prominent family of Cuthbert, Ga. In 1890 he moved to Birmingham from Anniston where he had for five years been engaged in the wholesale grocery and commission business. He became president of the City National Bank and engaged in corn and flour milling and in farming. As the cotton-manufacturing industry grew, and Comer's alert mind envisaged the possibilities of it, he abandoned banking and concentrated upon cotton-milling.

As merchant, manufacturer, and shipper, Comer had first-hand knowledge of the deleterious results of railroad rate discriminations. In 1904 he plunged into politics with a view to removing this abuse, being elected president of the railroad commission upon a platform of railroad rate regulation. Not contented with the work he was able to do as commissioner, he entered the race for governor in 1906 and won, after a heated and colorful campaign. In a manner that was typical of his blunt business methods and his implacable spirit, he called upon the legislature to abolish the "debauching lobby" maintained by the railroads at Montgomery and to pass laws for a thorough regulation of the railroads in the interest of equity as between them and the people. In compliance with his instructions, the legislature passed a series of acts, known as the "railway code," and taxed the property of railroads and other public-service corporations on the same principle that other property was taxed. He also secured the adoption of a tax-adjusting system in order to obtain a fairer assessment of property values. A state-wide prohibition law and a child-labor law were passed; and large appropriations were made to the state schools and to eleemosynary institutions. His most enduring achievement however was in the field of public education. Operating upon the principle that the future citizens of the state must be considered as well as the contemporary tax-payers, he led the legislature into making unprecedentedly large appropriations for colleges and schools. A system of county high schools was established which constitutes the backbone of the state's secondary-school system. In recognition of his services to education, some of the college buildings, erected out of funds provided by his administration, were named for him and he is known in Alabama as the "educational governor."

At the end of his term, in 1911, Comer retired from politics, devoting his time to his large business interests. He sought the governorship again in 1914, but in a second, or "run off," primary his conservative enemies combined against him and defeated him. He gave the remainder of his life, save the year 1920 when he served by appointment in the United States Senate in a vacancy caused by the death of Senator J. H. Bankhead, to business, earning a fortune from his cotton-mills. He was born a fighter, a man of incorrigible independence and individuality, and possessed of an imposing figure and a vivid personality. He throve on contest, and at the time of his death was pronounced by an opposition paper (*Montgomery Advertiser*) as "easily the most audacious executive who ever ruled Alabama."

[A. B. Moore, *Hist. of Ala. and Her People*, vols. I, II (1927); T. M. Owen, *Hist. of Ala. and Dict. of Ala. Biog.* (1921), vol. III; manuscript prepared by Gov. Comer a few months before his death.]   A. B. M—e.

COMSTOCK, ANTHONY (Mar. 7, 1844–Sept. 21, 1915), reformer, born in New Canaan, Conn., was the son of Thomas Anthony Comstock and Polly (Lockwood) Comstock. His father was a farmer and owner of a sawmill in New Canaan. His mother bore ten children and died when he was ten years old, being always thereafter the chief object and image of his devotion. He was brought up under strict Congregational discipline, and attended the public schools until his eighteenth year. In that year he became a clerk in a general store at Winnipauk, Conn., where an incident occurred which in his later life he liked to consider prophetic of his whole career. He shot and killed a mad dog which was running the streets; and shortly afterward he conducted a solitary crusade against the owner of the dog, who illegally took groceries in exchange for whiskey. Comstock broke into the premises one night and emptied all the liquor on the floor. He often referred to the persons he subsequently prosecuted as mad dogs endanger-

ing the community. On Dec. 31, 1863, he enlisted as a volunteer in the Union army, taking the place of his brother Samuel who had been killed at Gettysburg. He served a year and a half quietly in Florida, where in his intervals of leisure he kept a diary which has been preserved. He kept a similar record of his thoughts and deeds in later years, but this early document (frequently quoted in the biography by Broun and Leech) is particularly interesting as showing him possessed of a curious, vague sense of sin. A photograph of Comstock dating from this period (Broun and Leech, p. 30) reveals a set of severely contracted facial muscles of the sort associated with acute conscience and the determination to exorcise sin from the whole of the subject's environment. After Comstock was mustered out in the summer of 1865 he returned home to New Canaan, but soon became clerk in a store at New Haven. Satisfied neither with this position nor with one which he held for a few months at Lookout Mountain, Tenn., he finally found his way to New York, where he worked as shipping clerk and salesman for various dry-goods houses until in 1873 he abandoned business for the profession of reforming. He was married in January 1871 to Margaret Hamilton, ten years his senior, whom he likened to his mother and who bore him one daughter, Lillie, in December 1871. The child died the following summer; an adopted daughter, Adele, took her place. The family lived first in Brooklyn and later in Summit, N. J.

As early as 1868, Comstock, inspired by a campaign of the Young Men's Christian Association against obscene literature, had secured the arrest of two publishers, one of whom, Charles Conroy, he pursued for many years. He wore to his grave, under his famous divided whiskers, a scar inflicted by Conroy's knife in 1874. In 1871 he offered his services as crusader to the Y. M. C. A. and helped form a committee for the Suppression of Vice which subsidized him in his many operations against publishers and booksellers. In 1873 he went to Washington, forced the passage of new postal legislation preventing the communication of obscene matter through the mails, received an appointment as special agent of the Post Office Department, returned to New York, and was made secretary of the newly created Society for the Suppression of Vice. He remained agent and secretary until his death, taking no pay from the government until 1906, when he was required to accept $1,500 a year. Utterly incorruptible and tirelessly zealous in the pursuit of what he considered his duty, he spent the rest of his years in furious raids upon publishers of obscene and fraudulent literature, quacks, abortionists, gamblers, managers of lotteries, dishonest advertisers, patent-medicine venders, and artists in the nude. It is clear that he did not know how to distinguish between good art and bad, or indeed between art and morals. He was a notably unsubtle man, and has been rightly called an enemy of much that is valuable in literature and life. But as a prosecutor of frauds and quacks he did useful work, and as a censor of books and post-cards he removed from circulation many items which have not been missed.

His fame grew rapidly until he was a national figure, generally lauded for his work but in certain quarters ridiculed and reviled. His first conspicuous drive was against Victoria C. Woodhull [q.v.] and Tennessee Claflin, two gifted and emancipated sisters of New York who in 1872 used their *Weekly* to attack Henry Ward Beecher, then in the limelight of the Tilton scandal. Comstock had them arrested and angrily pursued their defender, George Francis Train [q.v.], a wealthy and eccentric New Yorker. The case won him notoriety mingled with derision; but he was never daunted. His labors against what he defined as vice took him over the country as far as St. Paul and St. Louis; he inspired the founding of the Watch and Ward Society in Boston in 1876; he made New York the headquarters of all effort in the nation to exterminate the forces believed to be undermining American youth; and when necessary he wrote books to vindicate his calling. His methods of attack were direct and ruthless. When Madam Restell, a wealthy abortionist and contraceptionist of New York whom he had tricked into a confession of her trade and imprisoned, took her own life in 1878, she was the fifteenth suicide he was willing to place to his credit; and there were several others. He encountered effective opposition first in the eighties, when his persecution of such men as Ezra Heywood and De Robigné M. Bennett [qq.v.] for their advanced opinions as expressed in certain pamphlets aroused the articulate ire of freethinkers in the National Liberal League and the National Defense Association. The word "liberal" was always synonymous for him with "quack" and "libertine," and although the opposition from this source gained a certain popular strength he was not deterred in 1905 from proceedings against Bernard Shaw's *Mrs. Warren's Profession,* partly perhaps in pique because the author of the play had coined in his honor the opprobrious word "comstockery." He was ever an active enemy of Col. Robert G. Ingersoll. In 1887 he raided Knoedler's Art Gallery in

New York in order to suppress certain paintings he had decided were indecent; and in 1906, this time in the face of widespread criticism, he took action against the Art Students' League. His death occurred soon after his return from California, where he had been the United States delegate, appointed by President Wilson, to the International Purity Congress. His personal features—a thick, powerful trunk, short legs, bald head, whiskered chin, and uncompromising eyes—are preserved in countless cartoons. He ate heavily, collected stamps, and loved children.

[Comstock published two books, *Frauds Exposed* (1880) and *Traps for the Young* (1883), and several pamphlets, of which *Morals Versus Art* (1888) is the most interesting. His activities are fully described in the Annual Reports of the Society for the Suppression of Vice (1874–1916). Charles Gallaudet Trumbull's *Anthony Comstock, Fighter* (1913) is mostly adulation; *Anthony Comstock, Roundsman of the Lord* (1927), by Heywood Broun and Margaret Leech, is informing and critical.]   M. V–D.

COMSTOCK, ELIZABETH L. (Oct. 30, 1815–Aug. 3, 1891), Quaker minister, philanthropist, was born at Maidenhead, Berkshire, England, daughter of William and Mary Rous. It was a gifted family, with a long line of Quaker ancestors. One of Elizabeth Comstock's sisters, Lydia Rous, was a prominent educator in the English Quaker schools and for many years governess in John Bright's home in Rochdale. Elizabeth Rous was educated in a Quaker school in Croydon and afterward taught both in Ackworth School and in her old school in Croydon. She was married in 1847 to Leslie Wright, who died two years later, leaving one daughter, Caroline. In 1854, the mother and daughter emigrated to Canada and settled in Belleville, Province of Ontario, where there was a meeting of the Society of Friends, and it was in this community that Elizabeth Wright (as she then was) began her public ministry. In 1858 she was married to John T. Comstock. They moved that year to the United States and settled in Rollin, Mich., where there was a pioneer Quaker community. Here Elizabeth Comstock's striking gifts of speech and spiritual leadership were quickly recognized and she was recorded a minister of the Society of Friends. Rollin was on one of the lines of the famous Underground Railroad for the transmission of fugitive slaves from the South to Canada, and Mrs. Comstock threw herself with passionate zeal and moral fervor into the work of helping slaves to gain their freedom. She became from this date, a devoted Abolitionist and life-long helper of the colored race. Meantime, she was developing her powers as a public speaker. In the Quaker gatherings in the western states, she was learning to hold and move large audiences. She threw herself in this period of development into the "causes" of the day and became a vigorous advocate of peace, of temperance, of prison reform, and of enlarged rights and privileges for women. She early discovered that she had a peculiar gift for working effectively with prisoners. She traveled extensively, carrying on this work of kindness and friendship and she influenced many lives in the jails and prisons of the country.

She proved to be even more effective during the Civil War in the hospitals and in the prison camps, where she comforted and brought mental relief to thousands of distressed soldiers. As the progress of the war liberated the slaves, Mrs. Comstock spent much of her time visiting the "contraband" camps, alleviating the distress of the destitute, and helping to organize the extensive work of relief undertaken by the Society of Friends. In 1864, she had a remarkable visit at the White House, ending in a favored season of divine worship with President Lincoln, conducted after the manner of the Quakers (see *Life and Letters*, ch. XI).

Elizabeth Comstock was regarded at the close of the war as one of the foremost of the noble women of the country who had dedicated themselves to the work of spiritual ministration, both among the wounded soldiers and among the vast throngs of "contrabands." She had become also a powerful platform speaker in behalf of great causes and reform movements. When the great migration of negroes into Kansas occurred in 1879–80, Elizabeth Comstock, under Gov. St. John of that state, took a very important part in organizing the temporary relief and in providing for the permanent care of the refugees. Her work takes a high rank in the long story of Quaker contribution to the welfare of the colored race. In 1885, she settled in Union Springs, N. Y., where she had her home until her death in 1891. She traveled extensively in the United States and in England in her service of preaching and she continued her spiritual work with prisoners well on into old age.

[The chief sources are *Life and Letters of Elizabeth L. Comstock*, comp. by C. Hare (1895); files of *Friends Review*, 1855–91; R. M. Jones, *Later Periods of Quakerism* (1921).]   R. M. J.

COMSTOCK, GEORGE FRANKLIN (Aug. 24, 1811–Sept. 27, 1892), jurist, was the son of Serajah Comstock, a native of Litchfield, Conn., who, after serving through the Revolutionary War, settled on a farm near Williamstown, Oswego County, N. Y. Here George Franklin was born. His early education at the district school was scanty and at the age of fourteen when his father died, he had to earn his own living. He taught school, attended Ellisburg Academy in Jefferson County for a short time, and by heroic measures saved sufficient money to enter Union College, Schenectady, Apr. 28, 1832, where he graduated with high honors in 1834. He then obtained a position as classical instructor in a private school at Utica, studying law at the same time, but shortly after moved to Syracuse, N. Y., where he entered the law office of Noxon and Leavenworth, also engaging in private tuition in order to pay his way. On his admission to the bar in 1837, he was taken into partnership by his principals. In 1847 he was appointed reporter of the New York court of appeals—being the first to occupy that position—and acted as such for three years, publishing *Reports of Cases Argued and Determined in the Court of Appeals of the State of New York* (vols. 1–4, 1849–51). In 1850 President Fillmore nominated him solicitor for the treasury, but he held the position only a few months, retiring with the change of administration. He had always been a consistent Whig and was nominated by that party and elected a judge of the state court of appeals, Nov. 6, 1855. He held office till Dec. 31, 1861, being chief justice during the last two years of his term, but on seeking reëlection lost in the Republican sweep of that time. Though only on the bench six years "he left an indelible impress upon the jurisprudence of the State." His professional contemporaries pronounced him a great judge and posterity has confirmed the verdict. He was not "safe" in the sense of adhering to formula and he was original inasmuch as he evinced no reverence for precedent, but his judgments were always luminous, framed with a logical precision which carried conviction, constructed with the utmost care, and distinguished on occasion by an unusual research. It is said that he devoted an entire vacation to preparing his masterly opinion in *Bissell* vs. *Michigan, etc. R. Co.* (22 *N. Y.* 258) *re* the liability of a corporation for an act *ultra vires* causing personal injury. He resumed active practise at Syracuse, where for the ensuing thirty years he had an undisputed monopoly of the important legal business. Such was his reputation that, though he never had an office in New York, he was frequently retained in that city in cases involving big interests in vital issues. Not an advocate in the popular sense, he did not show to great advantage in jury causes, perhaps because, as he said, "as a general thing I have no faith in juries." He was, however, a profound equity lawyer, particularly on the subject of trusts and was retained in all the big testamentary litigation of the period, including the contest involving Commodore Vanderbilt's will. Perhaps the most spectacular of his legal triumphs was in connection with William M. Tweed, whose cumulative sentence to the penitentiary for one year on each of twelve counts of the indictment was reduced on *habeas corpus* to one year only with a corresponding diminution of the fine which had accompanied the sentence. He was a delegate-at-large to the state constitutional convention of 1868 and took an outstanding part in the proceedings, being largely responsible, with Folger and Andrews, for the new judiciary article as it subsists to-day. Always intensely interested in educational matters, in 1869 he initiated the movement which resulted in the removal of Genesee College to Syracuse and its re-organization as Syracuse University. He contributed munificently to its endowment and was a member of the Board of Trustees for over twenty years. He also actively cooperated in many commercial enterprises in Syracuse, the ill success of some causing him serious embarrassment in his later years. He died at Syracuse, Sept. 27, 1892. His wife was Cornelia, daughter of his partner, B. D. Noxon of Syracuse. His only excursion into the realm of letters was an edition of Kent's *Commentaries on American Law* (1867), undertaken at the request of the Chancellor's heirs.

[The best commentary on his life and career is that by Prof. Thaddeus David Kenneson in W. D. Lewis, ed., *Great Am. Lawyers*, vol. VI (1909). An intimate personal sketch, perhaps too eulogistic, is contained in *Landmarks of a Lawyer's Lifetime* (1914), by Theron G. Strong, pp. 228–40. See also *N. Y. State Bar Ass. Report*, 1893, p. 130; *Green Bag*, II, 286, IV, 548, and *Memorial Hist. of Syracuse, N. Y.*, by Dwight H. Bruce (1891), pp. 79 and 438.]   H. W. H. K.

COMSTOCK, HENRY TOMPKINS PAIGE (1820–Sept. 27, 1870), for whom the Comstock Lode at Virginia City, Nev., was named, was born in Trenton, Ont., Canada, the fifth and youngest child of Noah and Catherine (Tompkins) Comstock. Contrary to statements usually made about him, he came from one of the best families in Connecticut and had good blood on both sides of his family. His father was born in Warren, Conn., about 1790, the son of a Congregational minister at that place, a descendant of William Comstock who came from England in 1635 and was the founder of all the Comstock lines in America. This ancestor was in the Pequot War (1637), being one of the twenty-six from Wethersfield, Conn., in Capt. John Mason's company, which took the Indian fort at Mystic, Conn., May 1, 1637. The old New London mill which is still in operation was built in 1650 by Comstock and others. Noah Comstock went in early life to Cooperstown, N. Y., then to Trenton in Ontario, and thence to Cleveland, Ohio,

and to Blissfield, Mich. He was engaged in the lumber and hotel business. Thus Henry grew up amidst constantly renewed pioneer surroundings and inherited a desire for frequent removals ever farther and farther to the West. He first went to Nevada from Santa Fé in 1856, having been previously engaged in trapping for the American Fur Company and having served in the Black Hawk, Patriot, and Mexican wars. He was drawn into the mad rush of fortune hunters on the Pacific Coast which resulted from the discovery of gold at Sutter's Mill in California. Early in the fifties prospectors found gold near Dayton in the "Washoe" mining area and in search of more precious metal they followed up the wash of Mount Davidson. The Grosch Brothers of Philadelphia are commonly credited with the first discovery of silver, but they met an untimely death before the world had become acquainted with these happenings. Possibly Comstock learned of the ledge from them. At any rate, after their death he claimed by right of discovery and previous location the ground where the Comstock lode was found. He soon sold his holdings for small sums, the Burning Moscow going for only forty dollars. He left Nevada in 1862 and seems to have followed the life of a prospector and road-builder in eastern Oregon, Idaho, and Montana. He accompanied the Big Horn expedition in 1870 and in the same year testified as a witness for the Ophir Company in a law suit in Nevada. For this latter service he was well paid. As he was going back to Bozeman, Mont., on horseback he met his death. The report was circulated that he had committed suicide, but those who knew him best have always believed that he was murdered for the money he carried. He was buried at Bozeman, Mont.

[Correspondence of L. W. Comstock of Wellesley Hills, Mass.; *Second Biennial Report Nev. Hist. Soc.* (1911); H. H. Bancroft, *Hist. of the Pacific States of North America*, Vol. XX, *Nev., Colo., Wyo.* (1890), pp. 97 ff.; popular accounts in Myron Angell, *Hist. of Nev.* (1881) and Sam P. Davis, *Hist. of Nev.* (1913).]   J. E. W—r.

CONANT, ALBAN JASPER (Sept. 24, 1821– Feb. 3, 1915), artist, archæologist, second of the five children of Caleb and Sarah (Barnes) Conant, was born in Chelsea, Vt. His ancestor, Roger Conant, came over from England in 1623, and became an important functionary in the government of colonial Massachusetts. As a child, Alban helped his father both on his farm and—at sign painting—in his trade as carpenter. Later, by teaching in a country school he accumulated a little money and "attended a first-class institution in St. Lawrence County, where he took an eclectic course" (Barns, p. 704). He was given to writing poems and drawing little sketches, and in June 1844, fired by the talk of a rusticating landscape artist, he went down to New York. Then, having studied art for about a year, he went to Troy, N. Y., in order to practise it and teach it to others—or, if the client preferred, to teach either vocal or instrumental music. In 1845 he was married to Sarah M. Howes of Chelsea, Vt., and in 1857, he and his wife, having gone West for the benefit of her health, determined to settle in St. Louis. He found plenty of work to do, and a rising interest in art which needed only some one like himself as a leader. Largely through his influence the Western Academy of Art was established in 1860. Aside from acting as a promoter of such interests, he made himself valuable in Missouri as a curator of the state university, especially in connection with its courses in agriculture and mining. During the Civil War, largely in Springfield and Washington, he did several portraits of distinguished people—Lincoln, Stanton, and, perhaps at this time also, Henry Ward Beecher. His wife died in 1867, and in 1869 he married Brianna Constance Bryan of San Francisco. He was for many years interested in archæology. In 1876 he published *The Archæology of Missouri,* and in 1879 *Footprints of Vanished Races in the Mississippi Valley,* carefully written essays which, in spite of his lack of scientific training, have yet a value as among the first investigations along these lines undertaken in America. At the time of their publication they were widely read and even translated in Europe. In 1893 he contributed to a sort of "album," *Liber Scriptorum,* a reminiscent but not especially unique section called "My Acquaintance with Abraham Lincoln." Toward 1885 he transferred his residence to New York, where he lived for the remainder of his life. His last picture, "The First Gun at Fort Sumter," was completed in 1910. In religious matters he was a devout Baptist, but so "catholic" withal, says an old account, "so much of a Presbyterian, so much of a Methodist, and so much of a Christian [*i.e.* Campbellite], that all good Christians recognize his brotherhood and bid him Godspeed" (Barns, p. 706).

[*Commonwealth of Mo.* (1877), ed. by C. R. Barns; F. O. Conant, *Hist. and Geneal. of the Conant Family* (1887); *Who's Who in America,* 1914–15; *N. Y. Times,* Feb. 4, 1915.]   J. D. W.

CONANT, CHARLES ARTHUR (July 2, 1861–July 5, 1915), journalist, author, economic adviser, was born in Winchester, Mass., son of Charles E. and Marion (Wallace) Conant, and direct descendant in the ninth generation of Roger Conant, acting governor of the Massachusetts Bay Colony, 1632. Educated in the public schools and by private study, he early entered journalism on the *Boston Post* and from 1889 to 1901 was Washington correspondent of the *New York Journal of Commerce, Springfield Republican,* and other newspapers, specializing in finance and banking. He was also early interested in politics and in 1893 was the Democratic candidate in his district for Congress and in 1896 delegate to the Gold Democratic Convention. Throughout his journalistic career he was an earnest advocate of "sound currency" and in opposition to the silver wing of his party. He enjoyed the acquaintanceship and confidence of treasury officials and international bankers and was recognized as an expert on topics relating to banking and currency, and a staunch upholder of the gold standard. In 1901 he was selected by Elihu Root, secretary of war, and appointed by President McKinley to investigate and report upon the monetary system of the Philippines, recently acquired from Spain. His recommendations were adopted by Congress and the system so established is still in effect. The new silver pesos of the Philippines were long called "Conants," and at one time the paper currency issued carried his vignette. His interest in the Islands was further seen in his service on the Board of Directors of the Manila Railway, and a journey in financial diplomacy brought him into relations with the Vatican and a personal interview with Pope Pius X with reference to compensation for the friars' lands in the Philippines. From 1902 to 1906 he served as treasurer of the Morton Trust Company, New York, but he was constantly being called upon for service in public affairs. In 1903 he went to Mexico as an adviser in changing the monetary system from a silver to a gold basis. In the same year he was made member of the Commission on International Exchange which was constituted, at the request of the governments of Mexico and China, for the cooperation of the United States in an effort to bring about a fixed relationship between the moneys of the gold-standard and silver-standard countries. The report of this Commission was published as *House Document No. 144, 58 Cong., 2 Sess.* Three years later, in 1906, he was chosen a member of the special committee of the Chamber of Commerce of New York on currency reform which made a report advocating the establishment of a central bank. His active interest in sound monetary practise was again shown when he was an official delegate of the United States to the International Conference on Bills of Exchange held at The Hague in 1910 and 1912. His report of the conference of 1910 was published as *House Document No. 768, 61 Cong., 3 Sess.* In 1911–12 he assisted Nicaragua in reforming its currency, and a similar service for the Republic of Cuba occupied his energy for several months before his death.

For many years he was editor of the department devoted to foreign banking and finance of the *Bankers Magazine,* and in addition to a continuous flow of articles in magazines and proceedings of conventions and associations, he wrote *A History of Modern Banks of Issue* (1896), one of the earliest histories in this field, which passed through five editions; *The United States in the Orient* (1900); *The Nature of the Economic Problem* (1900); *Alexander Hamilton* (1901); *Wall Street and the Country* (1904); *Principles of Money and Banking* (2 vols., 1905), translated into French by Dr. Georges-Levy; *Banking System of Mexico* (1910), published by the National Monetary Commission; *National Bank of Belgium* (1910), also published by the National Monetary Commission. Conant was unmarried. He had a strong personality, was modest, very diligent in application to his duties, enterprising, a devoted public spirit, and witty. His independence was shown in bolting the Democratic Bryan ticket in 1896. Besides membership in numerous societies in the United States he was a member of the Société d'Économie Politique de France. He died in Havana, and was buried at Winchester, Mass.

[Published data are found in *Who's Who in America,* 1903–05, in the obituaries in *Jour. of Commerce* (N.Y.), and *N. Y. Times,* July 7, 1915; *Bankers Mag.,* Sept. 1915; and in F. O. Conant, *Hist. and Geneal. of the Conant Family* (1887). The date of Conant's death is given variously as July 4, 5, and 6.]　　　D.R.D.

CONANT, HANNAH O'BRIEN CHAPLIN (Sept. 5, 1809–Feb. 18, 1865), writer, translator, was the eldest daughter of the Rev. Jeremiah Chaplin, D.D., first president of Waterville (now Colby) College, Waterville, Me., and his wife, Marcia S. O'Brien. She was born in Danvers, Mass., where her father was pastor of the Baptist church before his removal to Waterville. On July 12, 1830 she was married in Waterville to Rev. Thomas Jefferson Conant [*q.v.*]. Her education was obtained in the public schools and through private study with her father, under whose tuition she became a proficient scholar in the oriental languages. After her marriage she assisted her husband in his work, besides doing a vast amount of writing for the papers and periodicals. In 1839, while the family was living at Hamilton, N. Y., she became editor of the *Mother's Monthly Journal*

of Utica, which she continued for practically the remainder of her life. She was the author of *The Earnest Man; a Sketch of the Character and Labors of Dr. A. Judson, the First Missionary to Burmah* (1855) and *The English Bible; a Popular History of the Translation of the Holy Scriptures into the English Tongue* (1856). In addition, she translated a number of works from the German, the more important of which are: *Lea; or, The Baptism in Jordan* (1844), by G. F. A. Strauss; *The Epistle of Paul to the Philippians Practically Explained* (1851), by A. Neander; *The First Epistle of John Practically Explained* (1852), by A. Neander; *Erna, the Forest Princess; or Pilgrimage of the Three Wise Men to Bethlehem* (1855), by G. Nieritz; *The New England Theocracy; a History of the Congregationalists in New England to the Revivals of 1740* (1859), by F. H. Uhden. Mrs. Conant was a woman of strong intellectual powers and a well-trained classical scholar who used the French and German languages with almost the familiarity of a native. In matters of art she had wide knowledge, sound judgment, and excellent taste. She was a lover of nature and had a deep sense of the moral meanings of the natural world. But she was modest and sensitive and made no display of her learning. She had a great capacity for friendship and the family home in Brooklyn was the center of a choice social circle. In spite of her scholarly occupations, she was a woman of domestic tastes, and was the mother of ten children.

[Materials for the life of Mrs. Conant are in part the same as those for her husband. The best bibliography of her writings is found in *Allibone's Dictionary of Authors,* suppl. vol. I (1891). Articles on her life and character are found in the *Watchman* (Boston), Mar. 2, 9, 1865. In the latter number is an excellent and informing tribute by Henry Ward Beecher. There is also an article in the *Examiner* (N. Y.), Feb. 23, 1865.]
　　　　　　　　　　　　　　　　　　F.T.P.

CONANT, HEZEKIAH (July 28, 1827–Jan. 22, 1902), inventor, manufacturer, was the son of Hervey and Dolly (Healy) Conant and was born on his father's farm in Dudley, Mass. He was descended from Roger Conant who came to America in 1623, founded Salem, Mass., and was the first governor of that colony. Up to the age of seventeen Conant's life was divided between school and farm work. He left his home in 1844, went to Worcester, Mass., and entered a newspaper office where in the course of the succeeding two years he learned the printer's trade. Finding this not entirely to his liking, Conant next entered a machine-shop in Worcester and in two years learned the machinist's trade. He had saved a little money during this time and with his savings reëntered his former school, Nichols

Academy, for a year's additional study. He then returned to the machine-shop and devoted his evenings to the study of mechanical engineering, acquiring by the time he was twenty-five a local reputation as a professional mechanical expert. On Aug. 24, 1852, he took out his first patent, a pair of "lasting pinchers" for the use of shoe-makers. Following this he became a journeyman machinist, working in shops in Boston and Worcester, and finally, about 1855, in Hartford, where he entered the Colt Firearm manufactory. Here he assisted Christian Sharp, the rifle inventor, and devised an improvement in projectile molds. The following year Conant invented and patented the "gas check" for breech-loading fire-arms which was immediately adopted by the United States and British governments. That same year, too, he devised a machine for Samuel Slater & Sons for sewing the selvage on doe-skins. In 1857 Conant became interested in thread manufacture, devising and patenting in 1859–60 one machine for dressing sewing-thread and another automatic machine for winding thread on spools. Within two months after securing these patents, about Feb. 1, 1860, he succeeded in selling a half-interest to the Willimantic Linen Company in Willimantic, Conn., which concern engaged him as its mechanical expert. Here he remained nine years, in the course of which time he instituted many improvements in the plant of his company and went abroad to study thread-manufacturing methods, especially in England and Scotland. In 1868 he removed to Pawtucket, R. I., and organized the Conant Thread Company. Less than a year later he succeeded in effecting a combination with the leading thread manufacturers of Europe, the J. & P. Coats Company of Paisley, Scotland, by which that firm became a partner in his Pawtucket enterprise. With the additional capital thus made available, Conant's plant was immediately enlarged to manufacture the Coats thread, and between 1870 and 1881 five additional mill buildings were erected. Until 1893 the establishment was known as the Conant Thread Company, but thereafter it was operated as one of the branches of the J. & P. Coats Company, Ltd. At the time of Conant's death the works covered forty acres, employed 2,400 persons, and represented a capital investment of close to $5,000,000. While much of the machinery in the plant was of English manufacture, Conant devised many improvements, some of which he patented. He was largely interested in a variety of Rhode Island enterprises, being a prominent director of industries allied to his as well as of banks. He was married three times: first, on Oct. 4, 1853, to Sarah Williams

Learned; second, in November 1859, to Harriet Knight Learned, to whom were born a son and daughter; and third, on Dec. 6, 1865, to Mary Eaton Knight. He was survived by his widow and two children and was buried in Dudley, Mass.

[*Representative Men and Old Families of R. I.*, vol. I (1908), pp. 69–71; *Pawtucket Past and Present* (1917), by Slater Trust Co.; obituary in Pawtucket *Evening Times,* Jan. 22, 1902; F. O. Conant, *Hist. and Geneal. of the Conant Family* (1887), pp. 465–69; Patent Office records.]
C.W.M.

CONANT, ROGER (c. 1592–Nov. 19, 1679), early settler of New England, was the youngest of the eight children of Richard and Agnes (Clarke) Conant of East Budleigh, Devonshire, England. He was baptized on Apr. 9, 1592 in All Saints' Church in East Budleigh. The family seems to have been of the lower middle class, in fairly comfortable circumstances. Roger appears to have gone to London when about eighteen years old, and there he became a salter. On Nov. 11, 1618 he married a certain Sarah Horton of whose family nothing has been ascertained. By her he had at least nine children, the youngest being named Exercise. In 1623 he emigrated to Massachusetts with his wife and his son Caleb, the latter subsequently returning to England and dying there. It is probable that they sailed for America on the *Ann,* which carried Roger's brother Christopher and which arrived at Plymouth Colony, with John Oldham, as "particulars," that is as independent of the "common stock" system of the first settlers. Before long, there was trouble between some of the newcomers and the original group. Oldham and Lyford were ordered out of the community, and Conant soon followed voluntarily. In religion he was not a Separatist but merely a Non-Conformist and he seems not to have been altogether happy with the Pilgrims. In 1624 he settled at Nantasket and it was probably while there that he used the island in Boston Harbor which long bore his name. Becoming acquainted with the Rev. John White and other members of the Dorchester Company who had been trying to establish a settlement on Cape Ann, late in the autumn of 1625, at their request, he removed to their fishing settlement as manager or governor. He did not like the location and in the next autumn about forty of the settlers joined him in settling at Naumkeag (Salem). Conant continued as governor. In 1627 the colonists sent an agent to England to solicit a patent. It was obtained, however, in March 1628, by an English group with more ambitious ideas, and John Endicott [*q.v.*] came over with about fifty settlers, superseding Conant as governor. There was much ill-feeling at first but Conant submitted and became a loyal member of the new organization. In 1634 he was elected to represent Salem in the General Court. Two years later he moved to Beverly. He acquired a moderate amount of land, tried various adventures, such as trading with the Indians, and besides being for a while justice of the quarterly court, occupied many minor public offices, indicative of the deserved confidence and esteem of his neighbors. He was an honest, conscientious man who did useful work in the seedling days of the colony, and his self-control when Endicott arrived saved the colony from what might have been a ruinous struggle.

[F. O. Conant, *Hist. and Geneal. of the Conant Family* (1887); J. W. Thornton, *The Landing at Cape Ann* (1854); J. B. Felt, "Notice of Roger Conant," *New Eng. Hist. and Geneal. Reg.*, II, 233–39, 329–35.]

           J.T.A.

CONANT, THOMAS JEFFERSON (Dec. 13, 1802–Apr. 30, 1891), philologist, translator of the Bible, was descended from Roger Conant who came to Massachusetts in 1623 and became one of the founders of Salem. A descendant of the sixth generation was John, a Vermont pioneer and leading citizen of Brandon, whose wife was Charity Waite Broughton. Their son Thomas Jefferson was born in Brandon, educated at Brandon Academy and graduated at Middlebury College in 1823. After two years spent in the study of philosophy with Prof. R. B. Patton in New York, he became tutor in the classics at Columbian College, Washington, D. C. From 1827 to 1833 he was professor of languages at Colby College, Waterville, Me. He spent the period 1833–35 in the neighborhood of Boston engaged in the study of Hebrew and other oriental languages, and it was during this period (May 1834) that he was ordained to the Baptist ministry. From 1835 to 1841 he was professor of Hebrew and Biblical Criticism at the Hamilton Literary and Theological Institution at Hamilton, N. Y. During this period (1841–42) he spent more than a year in Europe investigating methods of university teaching and in philological study. From 1850 to 1857 he was professor of Biblical Literature and Criticism at Rochester Theological Seminary. In the latter year he moved to Brooklyn, N. Y., where he resided till his death. Here he engaged in the revision of the English Bible for the American Bible Union. In 1873 he was chosen a member of the American Revision Committee, cooperating with the Old Testament Company of the Convocation of Canterbury, which produced the Revised Version of 1881. His first elaborate production, *The Laws of Translation*, was the keynote of his whole career. His translation of Roediger's edition of the *Hebrew Grammar* of

Gesenius first appeared in 1839, and, enlarged and revised in subsequent editions, became for many years the standard in Europe and America. His great work was the translation of the Bible, upon which all his scholarly energies were spent. As an interpreter of the text in pure, simple, and forceful English, he has no equal. In addition to those mentioned, his principal works are as follows: *The Book of Job* (1857); *The Gospel of Matthew* (1860); *The Entire New Testament* (1867); *The Book of Genesis* (1868); *The Book of Psalms* (1868); *The Book of Proverbs* (1872); *The First Thirteen Chapters of Isaiah* (1874); *The Historical Books of the Old Testament, Joshua to II Kings* (1884). He was a thorough and inspiring teacher, a man of unaffected piety, genial, tender and affectionate in his family circle, and loyal to his friends. On July 12, 1830 he married Hannah O'Brien, eldest daughter of Rev. Jeremiah Chaplin, D.D. [*q.v.*], first president of Waterville (now Colby) College, Waterville, Me.

[Material for the life of Conant is found in the *Catalogue of the Officers and Students of Middlebury College 1800–1900* (1901); *Laurea* (Middlebury College, 1900), containing portrait; *Watchman* (N. Y.), May 7, 1891; F. O. Conant, *Hist. and Genealogy of the Conant Family* (1887).]

           F.T.P.

CONATY, THOMAS JAMES (Aug. 1, 1847–Sept. 18, 1915), Roman Catholic prelate and educator, the son of Patrick Conaty and Alice (Lynch) Conaty, was born in Kilnalec, Ireland, the eldest of eight children. When he was three years of age his family emigrated to the United States and settled in Taunton, Mass. He attended the public schools there and entered Montreal College in 1863 where his high-school education was completed. He qualified as a student of Holy Cross College, Worcester, in 1866 and was graduated in 1869. He made his theological studies immediately thereafter in the Sulpician Seminary of Montreal and was ordained to the priesthood for the diocese of Springfield in 1872. After seven years of service in the ministry he was appointed pastor of the Sacred Heart parish of Worcester where he served until 1897. During this period he displayed an active interest in civic as well as ecclesiastical life. His gifts as an orator attracted wide attention. He became a leader in his community and exerted far-reaching influence in movements that dealt with educational, moral, and social problems. He was particularly active in the work of total abstinence and was president of the Catholic Total Abstinence Union of America from 1888 to 1890. He was an ardent supporter of constitutional efforts for the freedom of Ireland. Conaty served on the Board of Education of Worcester for fourteen years and on its Library Board for six years. He was one of the founders and president, 1893–97, of the Catholic Summer School of America established originally at New London, Conn., and later permanently located at Cliff Haven, N. Y. He was active in founding the association of Catholic colleges later known as the National Catholic Education Association, and was its president, 1899–1903. He established in 1892 and edited until 1897, the *Catholic Home and School Magazine* and he published a volume, *New Testament Studies* (1898), for secondary schools. Appointed Rector of the Catholic University of Washington in 1897, Conaty was made Domestic Prelate in 1898 and was consecrated Titular Bishop of Samos by Cardinal Gibbons in 1901. At the expiration of his term as Rector of the Catholic University he was appointed to the See of Monterey and Los **Angeles**. During his twelve years as Bishop there, Los Angeles developed with great rapidity. The traditions of broadmindedness and civic activity which had characterized Conaty's earlier life were continued with notable effect throughout the entire period of his incumbency of the See of Monterey and Los Angeles. At the same time he multiplied parishes, developed Catholic secondary schools, created a Catholic Teachers' Institute, and multiplied agencies of social service in keeping with the rapid growth of the city. In addition to these local activities, Conaty took particular interest in the preservation of the Old Missions and other historical Catholic landmarks of California. He personally aided in much of the restoration work to which popular interest led, and cooperated heartily with other agencies in the state that aimed to develop an interest in its history and its monuments of Christian civilization. His death called forth notable tributes to his character and his work from all sides.

[Obituaries in *N. Y. Times*, Sept. 19, 1915 ; *Los Angeles Times* of the same date. See also *Official Catholic Directory*, 1916 ; *Who's Who in America*, 1914–15.]

W.J.K.

CONBOY, SARA AGNES McLAUGHLIN (Apr. 3, 1870–Jan. 7, 1928), the first woman to be admitted to the inner councils of the American labor movement, was born in Boston, Mass., to Michael and Sara (Mellyn) McLaughlin. At the age of eleven she went to work in a candy factory to help her widowed mother support her smaller brothers and sisters. There for **sixty** hours of work a week she received $2.50. Thence she went into a button factory where wages were slightly higher and work steadier, and, after that, into a carpet mill. As a highly skilled weaver she eventually received eighteen dollars for a sixty-hour week that might, as the law then

stood, call for night as well as day work. She was in the mill when she married Joseph P. Conboy, a Boston letter carrier. Within two years she was a widow, working at a loom in a Roxbury mill to support herself and her infant daughter. Shortly thereafter under her leadership the poorly-organized operatives struck for recognition of the United Textile Workers and higher wages. The strike was bitterly fought, but ended in victory for the strikers and Mrs. Conboy was started on what was to win for her international recognition as a labor leader and a proponent of legislation to protect child life and women in industry. Following the strike she became first an organizer of the United Textile Workers and later secretary-treasurer. In the latter capacity most of her time was spent raising money for an organization usually in need of funds. Just how much she raised she herself could not tell, but it is no exaggeration to say that the total was well in excess of $1,000,000. Between times she pleaded with legislators, and more than any other woman was responsible for legislation limiting the hours of labor for women and prohibiting their employment at night. To the American Federation of Labor, in whose conventions she was a prominent figure for more than twenty years, Mrs. Conboy brought the view-point of the woman. In it she early gained the confidence of men like Samuel Gompers, John Mitchell, and James Duncan [*qq.v.*], who depended much upon her judgment. From her there were no secrets. In token of its appreciation of her service the Federation in 1920 gave her the highest honor ever extended a woman— that of delegate to the British Trades Union Congress—an honor for which heads of the most powerful unions contest year in and year out. At the beginning of her career as a labor leader Mrs. Conboy was in her early thirties, a trim, upstanding, blue-eyed woman, full of energy and enthusiasm. With the years came weight and gray hair, but to the end she was handsome. With the years also came polish and a knowledge of practical economics of which many a university man might be proud. "Aunt Sara," as she was affectionately termed by men years older than she, was always essentially feminine, soft-voiced, and smiling. Perhaps it was as a conciliator of warring groups of hard-fisted and harder-headed men that she was of greatest value to organized labor.

[*Who's Who in America*, 1926–27 ; *World* (N. Y.), Jan. 8, *Brooklyn Eagle*, *N. Y. Times*, Jan. 9, 1928.]

J.J.L.

CONDIT, JOHN (July 8, 1755–May 4, 1834), surgeon, congressman, was descended from one John Condit, Condict, Conduit, or Cunditt, who left Wales and came, about 1678, to Newark, N. J., where later he bought land from the Lawrences on the Mill Brook Plain. His descendants were active in New Jersey politics, jail reform, medicine, and constitution-making. One of them, Samuel, married in 1754 Mary, daughter of Joseph Smith of Orange, N. J., and became the father of John Condit, born in 1755. Educated in local schools, he studied medicine privately with Dr. Jonathan Dayton of Springfield. On June 29, 1776, the New Jersey Provincial Congress "Ordered That Dr. John Condit be Surgeon" in Van Cortlandt's regiment of Heard's Brigade (*American Archives*, 4 Ser., VI, 1633). He soon resigned, having married Abigail, daughter of Joseph Halsey, by whom he had four sons and one daughter. She died in 1784 and in 1785 he wed her sister Rhoda, by whom he had two sons and one daughter. Being of "sterling integrity and of amiable disposition, fearless, energetic and thorough in everything he undertook" (Shaw, *post*, I, 304), he attained "a large success as a physician" (Wickes, *post*), though he did not join his fellow practitioners in the New Jersey Medical Society until 1830, when he was made an honorary member. He was also something of a sportsman, raised fine horses and "was perpetually on the road" (*Ibid.*). In 1785 he was influential in founding the Orange Academy of which he became a trustee. Condit entered politics after the Revolution, serving as assemblyman in the New Jersey legislature 1788–89, as Council member 1790–98, in the United States House of Representatives 1799–1803, in the United States Senate 1803–17, and in the House again, 1819–20. Few men have served twenty years in Congress so inconspicuously, the normal entry being, "Mr. John Condit of New Jersey appeared and took his seat." His politics were consistently anti-Federalist and Republican (Democratic), favoring strict administration and less government but opposed to popular excitement or mob rule in affairs of state. Nevertheless, in opposition to the stand of his party, in 1811 he favored the re-charter of the United States Bank. In the New Jersey legislature Condit usually came late to sessions but served on road and boundary committees and had charge (1791–95) of counting and burning cancelled loan-office certificates and old State money in the treasury. His twenty-four line report (Nov. 2, 1795) on "the prerogative and secretary's office" (*Journal of the New Jersey Council, 1794–99*, 1st and 2nd sitting of 20th session, p. 7) shows the quality of the man and the quiet methods of work which inspired such long confidence. A typical

eighteenth-century legislator he outlived his age. Public service having broken up his practise, he was appointed assistant collector of the port of New York, in Jersey City, but was removed from office in 1830 because of his criticism of President Jackson's financial policies. Long a skeptic, he "cordially embraced the truths of the Gospel" as paralysis ended his days in peace.

[Jotham H. and Eben Condit, *Geneal. Record of the Condit Family* (rev. ed. 1916); Wm. Shaw, *Hist. of Essex and Hudson Counties, N. J.* (1884), I, 304; Stephen Wickes, *Hist. of Medicine in N. J. and of its Medic. Men from the Settlement of the Province to A. D. 1800* (1879); David L. Pierson, *Hist. of the Oranges to 1921* (1922), II, 112, 249, 284 f.] W. L. W.

CONDON, THOMAS (Mar. 3, 1822–Feb. 11, 1907), Congregational clergyman, geologist, was born at Ballinafana, near Fermoy, Ireland, the son of John and Mary (Roach) Condon. His father was a stone-cutter. When Thomas was eleven years old, the Condons emigrated to the United States, settling first in New York City and later on a farm in Michigan. At one time the boy worked for a florist whose gardens occupied the present site of the New York Public Library. Later he attended Cazenovia Seminary, taught school at Camillus and at Skaneateles, made a collection of paleozoic fossils, and in 1849 entered Auburn Theological Seminary. He helped support himself in Auburn by teaching inmates of the state penitentiary. Owing to his Irish origin he was unable to secure a call to a congregation. Upon his graduation in 1852 he offered himself therefore to the Home Mission Board of the Congregational Church and was assigned to Oregon Territory. On Oct. 31, 1852, he married Cornelia J. Holt of Colden, Erie County, and that same autumn he and his bride sailed from New York on the clipper *Trade Wind*. In spite of storms and a fire in the hold the *Trade Wind* carried them safely round Cape Horn and north again to San Francisco, whence they proceeded by steamer to Portland. The rest of their lives was spent in Oregon. Condon was ordained immediately and entered on twenty years of missionary and pastoral labor: at St. Helen's 1853–54, Forest Grove 1854–57, Albany 1857–62, and The Dalles 1862–73. Gentle, earnest, simple, resourceful, friendly, he won the regard of every one, even of the gamblers and saloon-keepers of The Dalles, and his wife proved an able helper in his work. Meanwhile, however, a Bible was no more essential to his kit than a geologist's hammer. Accompanying parties of soldiers, he made excursions into the Indian country and succeeded in recording, though not with complete accuracy, the geology of a large part of eastern Oregon. He was made professor of geology and natural history in Pacific University of Forest Grove in 1873 and in the University of Oregon at Eugene in 1876. He was a beloved and influential teacher. At first he was obliged to give instruction in a variety of subjects, but as the University grew he was able to devote himself more and more to his favorite subject of paleontology. His first important discovery was made in 1867, when a well-digger brought him a fossil bone which he recognized as the distal end of the humerus of a horse; his last was in 1906, when he found a fossil sea-lion which he named *desmatophoca oregonensis*. He was the first paleontologist to explore the rich fossil-bearing formations of the John Day Valley. To railroad builders, land-owners, the state legislature, and visiting geologists he gave freely of his time and knowledge, never expecting compensation and seldom getting it. Several well-known scientists importuned him for fossils, failed to return specimens that had been entrusted to them as loans, and even neglected in their publications to give him proper credit for his discoveries. Condon, on the other hand, was unfailingly generous to them and either ignored or never noticed their attempt to deprive him of his due. Apparently he found it an effort to write: he contributed a few articles to the *Overland Monthly* and to the *Portland Morning Oregonian,* as state geologist presented a *Preliminary Report to the Legislative Assembly* (Salem, 1874), and gathered these few writings into his one book, *The Two Islands and What Came of Them* (Portland, 1902; revised as *Oregon Geology,* 1910). In him the scientist, the teacher, and the lover of men were blended. What he learned through patient and minute study of the rocks, he taught with an enthusiasm and sweep of general knowledge that kindled the minds of his students. But the wider public, he believed, also had claims upon him. He delivered lectures up and down the coast, in which the new scientific knowledge centering in the doctrine of evolution was winningly presented to audiences that dreaded the effect of such theories upon established beliefs. More than any other man, he was to the Pacific Northwest the interpreter of the fruits of Darwinism and the conserver of the best in revealed religion. In his later years he was venerated as one of the grand old men of the state. His wife died in September 1901; in 1905 he was made professor emeritus; he died two years later at the home of his daughter. Condon Butte, in Lane County, is named for him.

[*Gen. Biog. Cat. of Auburn Theol. Sem. 1818–1918*

(1918); C. W. Washburne, "Thomas Condon" in *Jour. of Geology,* XV, 280–82 (1907); E. S. Meany, "Professor Thomas Condon" in *Pacific Monthly,* XVI, 565–69 (1906); L. M. Scott, *Hist. of the Oregon Country* (1924), III, 86, 87, 169; *Portland Morning Oregonian,* Feb. 12, 14, 1907; L. A. McArthur, *Oregon Geographical Names* (1928); E. C. McCornack, *Thomas Condon, Pioneer Geologist of Oregon* (1928); letter to author from Condon's daughter, Ellen Condon McCornack, Dec. 6, 1928. Prof. Jos. Schafer is authority for the characterization of Condon as scholar and lecturer.]

G. H. G.

CONE, MOSES HERMAN (June 29, 1857– Dec. 8, 1908), merchant, manufacturer, was the son of Herman Cone, who was born in 1828 at Altenstadt-on-the-Iller, Bavaria, and came to America as a youth, settling at Richmond, Va. Here he married Helen Guggenheimer, who as a child had come with her parents from Huerben, Würtemburg, and settled near Natural Bridge, Va., where her father was a merchant. Herman Cone later engaged in the retail general merchandise business at Jonesboro, Tenn., where his son Moses, eldest of thirteen children, was born. Herman Cone moved to Baltimore in 1870 and, after two partnerships in the wholesale grocery business, he bought a business of his own and associated his four oldest sons with him in the firm of H. Cone & Sons. Moses, who had attended the public schools of Baltimore, entered his father's business at an auspicious time for his later career. Baltimore then enjoyed the bulk of the Southern wholesale trade, and the South was on the eve of the industrial development which has since become conspicuous. Among the customers of H. Cone & Sons were many Southern cotton-mills which maintained mill villages and company-owned stores for trade with the operatives. The connection between the Cones in Baltimore and the Southern cotton-factories began in the incidental acceptance of bale goods by the wholesale grocers in payment of accounts of mill stores. Gradually mills came to ask the Baltimore firm to sell their product through the South on commission, and this increased the intimacy of Moses Cone with the cotton manufactures of the section. He was struck with the lack of standardization and the difficulties attending the marketing of "negro plaids," a favorite product of the Southern mills. He spent the year 1890—a year of marked depression in the cotton-goods trade—in the first significant attempt to combine Southern mills in a selling organization intended to control the product to the extent of making the goods more uniform and improving the styles. The Cone Export & Commission Company was consequently formed in 1891, establishing its office in New York City. After much organizing work and many disappointments on the part of

Moses Cone, about forty mills in the Carolinas and Georgia and other Southern states joined the venture. The wholesale grocery firm in Baltimore was dissolved, Herman Cone joining his sons in the new undertaking. The selling agency did not succeed in the completeness with which it was planned, but the Cones soon began to acquire interests in Southern cotton-mills, the first being at Asheville, N. C. In 1893 the main office of the Cone Export & Commission Company was established at Greensboro, N. C., and two years later Moses Cone, particularly in association with his brother Cæsar, began the erection of denim-mills on a large tract on the edge of the town. These are now the largest denim-plants in the world. The company has been conspicuous for the extent and completeness of its welfare work in the villages established for its operatives. Cone married Bertha M. Lindau of Baltimore in 1888. In 1901 he acquired an estate of 3,750 acres at Blowing Rock, N. C., and was one of the pioneers in the western part of the state in the growing of apples on a large scale.

[See *Commercial and Financial Chronicle*, Sept. 12, 1891; *Daily Commercial Bulletin* (N. Y.), May 14, 1891; *Dry Goods Economist*, May 23, 1891; obituaries in *Jewish Comment* (Baltimore), Dec. 11, 1908; *Charlotte* (N. C.) *Daily Observer*, Dec. 9, 10, 1908; *Asheville* (N. C.) *Gazette-News*, Dec. 10, 1908; *News and Observer* (Raleigh, N. C.), Dec. 10, 1908.] B. M.

CONE, ORELLO (Nov. 16, 1835–June 23, 1905), New Testament scholar, author, was born in Lincklaen, Chenango County, N. Y. His parents, Daniel Newton and Emily (Sadd) Cone, early recognized that he was a natural student, and sent him for his schooling to the academy at New Woodstock, and later to Cazenovia Seminary in Madison County. His intellectual appetite thus whetted, young Cone undertook to pursue college studies by himself, while teaching in private schools. Later he was enabled to supplement this study by a partial course at St. Paul's College at Palmyra, Mo. In this institution he was also for three years (1858–61) an instructor. After further study he entered in 1864 the Universalist ministry and became pastor of the Universalist Church of Little Falls, N. Y. While serving here, he met and married (Oct. 4, 1864) Mariamne Pepper, daughter of Luke Pepper, one of his parishioners. In 1865 he became professor of Biblical Languages and Literature in the Theological School of St. Lawrence University, Canton, N. Y. This appointment determined his career. In this new and agreeable relation he soon established within his own denomination a reputation for accurate and critical scholarship. For many years no volume of the *Universalist Quarterly* appeared that did not contain one or more articles from his pen. Within his own communion Cone was considered as belonging to the progressive wing. He edited a volume entitled *Essays Doctrinal and Practical by Fifteen Clergymen* (1889) which was supposed to present the views of the more liberal scholars of his church. Higher Criticism was far from popular, even in a so-called liberal communion. He was frequently assailed as a "destructive" critic but he refused to be involved in controversy or to be deterred from his studies and research. In 1880 he became the president of Buchtel College, Akron, Ohio (now the Municipal University of Akron). Here he remained until 1897, as president and professor of philosophical subjects. His heart, however, was still with his New Testament studies. While at Buchtel he commenced bringing out the series of books that gave him a reputation, internationally, as a thorough scholar and critic of rare acumen. His first work in this field, *Gospel Criticism and Historical Christianity* (1891), was dedicated "To the believers who fear criticism and to the unbelievers who appeal to it." This was repeatedly declared by competent scholars to be the ablest work in its field that had, up to that time, appeared on this side of the Atlantic. It was followed by *The Gospel and its Earliest Interpretations* (1893). During 1897–98 Cone pursued his studies in Berlin, Paris, and London. While in London he published his chief work, *Paul, the Man, the Missionary, and the Teacher* (1898). This was pronounced by Dr. H. J. Holtzmann of Strasburg, himself a foremost New Testament scholar, to be the ablest monograph on Paul and his teaching that had ever appeared in any language—an unusual encomium.

After a brief pastorate at the Unitarian Church of Lawrence, Kan. (1898–99), he returned in 1900 to the Theological School of St. Lawrence University as Richardson Professor of Biblical Theology. During the remaining six years of his life he published *Rich and Poor in the New Testament* (1902), was editor of the International Handbooks of the New Testament, and himself contributed one volume to the series (*Epistles to the Hebrews, Colossians, Ephesians and Philemon*, 1901). He also collected and translated, in part, essays by his friend Dr. Otto Pfleiderer of the University of Berlin and published them under the title *Evolution and Theology and Other Essays* (1900). He was a constant contributor to various periodicals. In conjunction with progressive scholars in this country, he helped in 1892 to launch a religious quarterly called *The New World* and was one of its editors. During the seven years of existence of this journal, he wrote frequently for its pages. In 1902 he was a professor at the Harvard Summer School of Theology. Cone was a man of dignified bearing and urbane manners. "He loved the quiet and serious tasks of learning," and was not so much a teacher as a remarkable scholar and a keen, discriminating critic. At home in many languages, especially the German, he was "a theologian of wide reading and rational conviction" (Forbes, *post*).

[The most adequate and appreciative sketch of Cone's life is that by a New Testament scholar, his former pupil and friend, H. P. Forbes, in *The Necrology of St. Lawrence Univ.*, 1904–06. See also: Wm. Whitney Cone, *Some Account of the Cone Family in America* (1903); *Who's Who in America*, 1903–05; an article by Forbes in the *Universalist Leader*, July 1, 1905.]

J. M. A.

CONE, SPENCER HOUGHTON (Apr. 30, 1785–Aug. 28, 1855), Baptist clergyman, noted as a preacher, and long a leader in his denomination, was born in Princeton, N. J., a descendant of Daniel Cone who settled in Haddam, Conn., in 1662, and son of Conant and Alice (Houghton) Cone. As a boy he displayed a liking for poetry and could recite long passages from Shakespeare, Milton, and Dryden. At Princeton, which he entered when he was twelve, President Smith told him his voice would be his fortune. After he had been two years in college, his father, a Revolutionary soldier, respectable but improvident, found himself reduced to poverty and went mad. As the eldest son young Spencer undertook to support the family by teaching, finally becoming assistant to Dr. James Abercrombie at his academy in Philadelphia. He also studied law, but his elocutionary ability finally led him to go upon the stage, and he made his début at the Chestnut Street Theatre as Achmet in the tragedy of *Mahomet*. During the next seven years, he played regularly in Philadelphia, Baltimore, and Alexandria, where he enjoyed considerable popularity. In 1812 he turned to journalism, first entering the office of the *Baltimore American* as treasurer and bookkeeper, and later joining with his brother-in-law, John Norvell, in conducting the *Baltimore Whig*. In this capacity he was a vigorous supporter of President Madison's administration and the War of 1812. He also served under arms, being with Pinckney's rifles in the battle of Bladensburg, and acting captain of the company by whose fire Gen. Ross was killed in the advance upon Baltimore.

The end of the war found him with a wife, Sally, daughter of Robert and Mary Price Morrell of Philadelphia, whom he had married May 10, 1813, and in financial difficulties. Friends secured him a position in the Treasury Department, Washington. A lively interest in religion had taken possession of him in 1814, when he had been converted to the Baptist faith, and immersed in the Patapsco River through a hole cut in the ice. He began to preach in a small Baptist church at the Navy Yard, and soon attracted such attention that in 1815 he was licensed and made chaplain of Congress. In 1816 he became pastor of the Baptist Church in Alexandria, where in spite of calls to much larger places he remained seven years. From 1823 to 1841 he was associated with the Oliver Street Church, New York, first as co-pastor and later as pastor, and from 1841 till his death, was pastor of the First Baptist Church of that city. Besides being popular and effective as a preacher, he took a leading part in the administrative work of his denomination. From 1832 to 1841 he was president of the Baptist General Convention, a representative body which shaped the denominational activities at home and abroad. He was prominent among those who in 1836 protested against the action of the American Bible Society in refusing a grant for the publication of the Bengali New Testament, which translated *baptizo* according to Baptist usage, from which action resulted the American and Foreign Bible Society of which he was a founder, and the head from 1837 to 1850, when he became president of the American Bible Union. In 1824 he brought out an edition of William Jones's *The History of the Christian Church*. He published *The Backslider* (1827); and was joint author with William H. Wyckoff of *The Bible Translated* (1850); *The Bible, Its Excellence,* and *The New Testament ... According to the Commonly Received Version ... with Several Hundred Emendations* (1850).

[W. W. Cone, *Some Account of the Cone Family* (1903); Edward W. Cone, *Some Account of the Life of Spencer Houghton Cone* (1856); W. B. Sprague, *Annals Am. Pulpit*, vol. VI (1860); Thos. Armitage, *Funeral Sermon on the Death of Rev. Spencer Houghton Cone* (1855); *Christian Rev.*, Jan. 1856.] H. E. S.

CONEY, JABEZ (Oct. 21, 1804–Jan. 23, 1872), millwright and engineer, was born in Dedham, Mass. One of the sixth generation of Coneys descended from John Coney of Boston, Lincolnshire, who settled in Boston, Mass., prior to 1628, he was the second of eight children of Jabez and Irene (Gay) Coney. His father was a carpenter and builder ("housewright") and the boy not only came to be an expert in his father's trade but a machinist as well. He commenced business on his own account in Dedham at an early age and before he was twenty-one had established a high reputation as a millwright. Later he removed his shop to South Boston where he set up as a machinist, developed a large business, and performed heavy contracts for his day. The two largest contracts of his concern were the building for the United States government of the iron steamer *McLean* in 1843 and five years later the machinery for the warship *Saranac,* the first vessel to which the navy applied steam. He is believed to have constructed the first iron vessel ever built in New England, the first large marine engine, and the first gravel excavator. Overwork brought a physical collapse and a paralytic stroke in 1850, which forced him to suspend his business at the height of its prosperity. Although confined to his house as a cripple for twenty-two years, he established a school for mechanics where he fitted many for the navy and for other positions. Harrison Loring, who built up a foundry for marine engines and iron ships after Coney's retirement, had served his apprenticeship in Coney's shop. In 1847 and 1850 Coney represented Ward 10 (South Boston) in the Boston City Council. His wife was Mary Whiting (July 4, 1807–Feb. 20, 1847), whom he married Oct. 25, 1827, and by whom he had three children.

[Mary L. Holman, *Coney Genealogy* (in press); J. J. Toomey and E. P. B. Rankin, *Hist. of South Boston* (1901), p. 235; T. C. Simonds, *Hist. of South Boston* (1857), p. 209, and *Boston Post,* Jan. 24, 1872.]

H. U. F.

CONEY, JOHN (Jan. 5, 1655–Aug. 20, 1722), silversmith, was the first child of John Conney [*sic*] and Elizabeth Nash, the daughter of the butcher Robert Nash, who were married on June 20, 1654, in Boston. It is thought that John Coney learned his trade from Jeremiah Dummer [*q.v.*], whose wife's sister, Mary Atwater, became Coney's second wife. His first wife, Sarah, died in 1694. Coney's silver displayed fine workmanship and his house had a number of apprentices, among them Apollos Rivoire, lately arrived from France, David Jesse, and Thomas Millner. The remaining records of his life are few. He engraved the first plates for paper money issued by Massachusetts Colony. He was a member of the Second Church of Boston. In 1677 he signed a petition with his fellow "Handycraftsmen, a very considerable part of the town of Boston," praying trade protection in their several callings "whose outward substance doth depend on God's blessings, and many of us not having estates any other way to advantage us." In September 1689 he was one of the number of "Hogg-Reeves" of whom it was recorded in the proceedings of the Town Meet-

ing: "Ordered, that ye Selectmen send for and quicken the Hogg-Reeves to the faithful discharge of their offices, which is of late much neglected." In 1666 he was one of twenty-six signers of a petition to the elected Government to "acknowledge the King's authority." In 1693 he was one of the fourteen "Tythingmen" chosen to represent the fourteen militia companies, his company being that of Capt. Penn Townsend. His funeral sermon, still preserved, and dedicated to his widow, was preached by his son-in-law, the Rev. Thomas Foxcroft. A loving-cup made by him and given to Harvard College by Justice William Stoughton [*q.v.*], who presided at the witchcraft trials, is considered one of the finest examples of the art of the New England silversmiths of colonial days. Coney's marks were crude capitals, in a heart with a cross below, or in a shield crowned, with a coney below, or (probably Coney's) crude capitals in an oval or a rectangle.

[Hollis French, *A List of Early Am. Silversmiths and their Marks* (1917); E. Alfred Jones, *Old Silver of Am. Churches* (1913); Thos. Hills, *The Parentage and English Progenitors of Nathaniel Coney* (1906); Francis Hill Bigelow, *Hist. Silver of the Colonies and its Makers* (1917); C. Louise Avery, *Am. Silver of the XVII and XVIII Centuries* (1920), being a catalogue of the Clearwater Coll. in the Metropolitan Museum; S. G. Drake, *Hist. and Antiquities of Boston* (1856).]

K. H. A.

CONGDON, CHARLES TABER (Apr. 7, 1821–Jan. 18, 1891), poet, author, born in New Bedford, Mass., was the son of Benjamin Taber and Deborah (Hartt) Congdon. He began his career by sweeping out the office of the *New Bedford Courier,* the weekly paper published by his father. Later, while carrying papers on the village route, he composed his first poem, "Ode to Commerce." From the local school he went in 1837 to Brown University for three years, which he has described in detail in *Reminiscences of a Journalist* (1880). Without graduating from Brown (though he received the honorary degree of A.M. in 1879) he returned to New Bedford as reporter on the *Daily Register,* but went back to Providence to edit the *New Age,* a suffrage paper. He then made New Bedford his home again, being first, editor of the *Daily Bulletin* and later, associate editor of the *Daily Mercury.* His success on the latter paper explains his call to Boston in 1854 to edit the *Atlas,* then the leading Whig organ of New England. At the personal request of Horace Greeley he went to New York in 1857 to work on the *Tribune,* where he became known as "Greeley's right hand man." Some of his best work on that newspaper may be found in *"Tribune" Essays* (1869), leading editorials contributed during the exciting years from 1857 to 1863. At the close of his college days he published a poetical volume with the sophomoric title, *Flowers Plucked by a Traveler on the Journey of Life* (1840). During his editorial years on the *Tribune,* from which he resigned in 1882, he brought together a somewhat remarkable library which attracted considerable attention for its Americana when it was sold in 1891. Associates on the *Tribune* said that Congdon wrote from the head while Greeley wrote from the heart. On his arrival in New York he became a constant contributor to the periodicals of the day. His published articles ranged from those in *Vanity Fair,* the great humorous weekly edited by Artemus Ward, to those printed in the serious, dignified *North American Review.* A kinsman of William Cullen Bryant, he was naturally a contributor to the *Knickerbocker Magazine* then edited by Lewis Gaylord Clark [*q.v.*]. For many years he was the New York correspondent of the *Boston Courier* in which his contributions were signed with the *nom de plume* "Paul Potter." Possibly the most meritorious of all his poems was *The Warning of War* (1862), which he delivered before the United Societies of Dartmouth College on July 30, 1862. While engaged in newspaper work in New Bedford he married Charlotte M. Bayliss who died at the birth of their only child, Alice B. Congdon. Beloved by all newspapermen, he spent his declining years in a New York hotel near Washington Square. After his death from heart failure his body was taken to his old home, New Bedford.

[Congdon's own *Reminiscences of a Journalist* (1880); obituary in the *N. Y. Tribune,* Jan. 19, 1891. Rare and unusual volumes in his library are described in the catalogue printed just before its sale (1891). See also *Hist. of New Bedford* (3 vols., 1918), ed. by Z. W. Pease; L. B. Ellis, *Hist. of New Bedford and its Vicinity* (1892); Jas. M. Hartt, *Geneal. Hist. of Samuel Hartt . . . and Descendants* (1903).] J.M.L.

CONGER, EDWIN HURD (Mar. 7, 1843– May 18, 1907), soldier, congressman, diplomat, was the son of pioneering parents, born near Galesburg, Ill. Both his father, Lorentus E. Conger, and his mother, Mary Hurd Conger, were of thrifty American stock, endowed with the ambition and common sense of a long line of New York and Vermont ancestors. Having prospered at farming and banking, they sent Edwin to Lombard College, a Universalist school in Galesburg, where he graduated from the classical course in 1862. Reared as a Universalist, he never departed from that faith (*Progressive Men of Iowa,* 1899, vol. II, p. 93). As soon as he was out of college he hastened to enlist, and on Sept. 2, 1862, was mustered into the United States service as a first lieutenant of

Company I, 102nd Illinois Infantry. In October 1863 he was promoted to the rank of captain and served in that capacity until the end of the war. Although he was regarded as "an intelligent officer" (*Official Records, Army,* 1 ser., XXIII, pt. 1, p. 323) and marched with Sherman to the sea, the records credit him with no particularly notable military achievements (Records in Adjutant General's office, War Department). Having graduated from the Albany Law School, he married Sarah Pike on June 21, 1866, and straightway opened a law office in Galesburg. Two years later he moved to Madison County, Iowa, where he operated a large stock farm and engaged in banking so successfully that he accumulated a modest fortune, most of which was lost, however, through the failure of friends and relatives whose notes he had endorsed (*Register and Leader,* Des Moines, May 19, 1907).

The same traits of character which made him successful in business—a genial disposition, honest dealing, and a knack for remembering people, together with a wide personal acquaintance—were essential factors in his political career. Beginning as a Madison County supervisor (1870–73), he afterward served two terms as treasurer of Dallas County and held the office of state treasurer for two terms. Meanwhile, in 1884, he was elected to the Forty-ninth Congress from the 7th district of Iowa, and was twice reëlected (*Iowa Official Register*). Like most members of the Grand Army, he devoted much of his energy to securing pensions for old soldiers, but in the Fifty-first Congress, when the Republicans resumed control, he became chairman of the Committee of Coinage, Weights and Measures, and ranked second on the committees on agriculture and banking and currency (*Congressional Directory,* 51 Cong., 1 Sess., pp. 137, 138). As a member of the conference committee on the Silver Purchase Act of 1890 he agreed to the elimination of the free coinage provision. In harmony with his constituents he favored the suppression of trusts and advocated the taxation of "compound lard" (*Congressional Record,* 51 Cong., 1 Sess., pp. 235, 7167, 9077). On Sept. 27, 1890, Conger resigned from Congress, his appointment as minister to Brazil being that day confirmed by the Senate (*Ibid.,* pp. 10573, 10794). After three pleasant and rather uneventful years at Rio, he was displaced by a deserving Democrat, but in May 1897, he was reappointed by his friend, President McKinley. Then, in less than a year, he was unexpectedly transferred to China (*Ibid.,* 55 Cong., 1 Sess., p. 1304; 2 Sess., p. 758). Arriving in Peking in the early summer of 1898, he observed the development of the anti-foreign feeling and, during the terrible weeks from June 20 to Aug. 14, 1900, when the Boxers besieged the legations, he conducted himself with the courage and firmness of a veteran soldier. After the uprising, as before, Conger steadfastly refused to demand concessions or aid other schemes for the exploitation of the Chinese, with the result that he won their confidence, respect, and high esteem. For a few months he served as ambassador to Mexico, but the expense of that post and his need for rest caused him to quit the diplomatic service on Oct. 18, 1905. "In zeal, efficiency and single-minded devotion to public duty," wrote President Roosevelt, "you have been the kind of official of whom Americans have a right to feel proud, and I congratulate the country on having had your services" (*Register and Leader*, May 19, 1907).

[The most intimate biographical sketch of Edwin Hurd Conger was printed in the Des Moines *Register and Leader*, May 19, 1907, on the occasion of his death. *Letters from China* (1909), written by his wife, Sarah P. Conger, presents a vivid account of his activities as minister to China. For a survey of his diplomatic career, see John E. Briggs, "Iowa and the Diplomatic Service," *Iowa Jour. of Hist. and Politics*, XIX, 347–52.]

J. E. B.

CONKLIN, JENNIE MARIA DRINK-WATER. [See DRINKWATER, JENNIE MARIA, 1841–1900.]

CONKLING, ALFRED (Oct. 12, 1789–Feb. 5, 1874), congressman, judge, author, was born at Amagansett, two and a half miles from Easthampton, Suffolk County, Long Island. His ancestor, John Conkling of Nottinghamshire, England, married Elizabeth Allseabrook in 1625 and ten years later emigrated to Salem, Mass., thence removing to Long Island. Here a descendant, Benjamin Conkling, married Esther Hand and Alfred was their second child. He had a normal, healthy, happy childhood with his two brothers and two sisters. The district schoolmaster is said to have exclaimed, when very angry with a culprit, "You are as bad as Alfred Conkling!" From the district school Alfred went to the village clergyman to be tutored for college. He was graduated from Union College in 1810, and after graduation entered the law office of Daniel Cady [*q.v.*] of Johnstown, Fulton County. Two years later he was admitted to the bar and married Eliza, the daughter of James Cockburn, a civil engineer. Of this union three daughters and four sons were born, the most noted of whom was Roscoe [*q.v.*]. In 1813 the Conklings removed to Canajoharie in the adjoining county of Montgomery. Five years afterward Conkling was elected district attorney for this county. It is related that as he was prosecuting a man for murder the defendant made

the Masonic signal of distress. This debasing of the principles of the order so disgusted Conkling that he resigned forthwith from his lodge. Elected to Congress in 1820 as an anti-Jackson Democrat, he served but one term, after which he settled in Albany and resumed the practise of his profession. When the "Albany regency" removed DeWitt Clinton from the canal commission in 1824, Conkling wrote the vigorous resolutions denouncing this outrage which were adopted by an indignant mass-meeting. In 1825 Conkling was appointed by President Adams federal judge for the district of northern New York and discharged the duties of this office with ability and justice for twenty-seven years. His opinion in the case of *Bradstret* vs. *Huntington* (1834) so impressed the Utica bar that sixteen members petitioned for leave to print it, which was granted. At the suggestion of William H. Seward, Conkling moved in 1839 from Albany to Auburn, where he received visits from many eminent persons, including Chancellor Kent, Ex-Presidents Adams and Van Buren, Governors Throop and Seward, and Thurlow Weed. This last described Conkling as "a tall, handsome man with graceful manners." He varied his judicial duties with social pleasures, with addresses before colleges and literary societies, and with the composition of works on legal and political subjects. His publications include a eulogy on DeWitt Clinton (1828); *The Young Citizen's Manual* (1836); *Treatise on the Organization and Jurisdiction of the Supreme Circuit and District Courts of the United States* (1842); *Jurisdiction Law and Practise in Admiralty and Maritime Causes* (1848); *Powers of the Executive Department of the United States* (1866). The last three were revised and republished at later dates, the *Powers of the Executive* going through five editions. Roscoe Conkling studied law under his father, was admitted to the bar in 1850, and argued his first case in his father's court that same year. His brother said: "Although the Judge was a very Brutus in his utter want of partiality toward his son under the circumstances, young Conkling won his case." President Fillmore appointed Conkling minister to Mexico in 1852. Upon his return in August 1853, he went to Omaha, Nebr., where he practised law for eight years. Returning to his native state he lived first at Rochester, whence he moved to Geneseo in the adjacent county of Livingston. Literary pursuits occupied most of his time. He had the gratification of seeing his son Frederick win a colonel's commission in the Union army and Roscoe become United States senator. The last years of Alfred Conkling were spent in Utica, which was also Roscoe's home. Here he died in his eighty-fourth year. A man of considerable ability and high character, he also possessed unusual personal charm.

[There are a few letters to and from Conkling in the N. Y. Hist. Soc. Other sources are the *Autobiography of Thurlow Weed* (1884); A. R. Conkling, *Life and Letters of Roscoe Conkling* (1889); I. B. Conkling, *Conklings in America* (1913). Consult also the following: D. McAdam, *Hist. of the Bench and Bar of N. Y.* (1897–99); *Biog. Encyc. of the State of N. Y.* (1916); W. F. Johnson, *Hist. of the State of N. Y. Political and Governmental* (1922).]   M.L.B.

CONKLING, ROSCOE (Oct. 30, 1829–Apr. 18, 1888), senator, was born at Albany, N. Y., but lived most of his life in Utica, N. Y. His father was Alfred Conkling [*q.v.*]; his mother, Eliza Cockburn, was of Scotch extraction and was noted for her beauty. His older brother, Frederick, was congressman for a single term, and a colonel in the Civil War. The family removed to Auburn, N. Y., in 1839 and in 1842 Roscoe entered the Mount Washington Collegiate Institute in New York City. He went to Utica in 1846 to study law in the office of Spencer & Kurnan, was admitted to the bar in 1850, and was immediately appointed district attorney of Albany. At the close of the term he entered into partnership with Thomas H. Walker of Utica. One of the great "spread eagle" orators of his day, before he was thirty years of age he was a familiar and valued figure at the Whig conventions of his county and state. He became mayor of Utica in 1858, was elected to Congress in the autumn of the same year, and represented his district at Washington, 1859–67, except for the single term 1863–65. He married in 1855 Julia, a sister of Horatio Seymour, Democratic governor of New York in 1853 and 1863. He remained temperate in a day when strong drink was a pervasive enemy of American men, he detested tobacco, and he built up his body by systematic exercise and boxing, so that he enhanced the dignity and impressiveness of a figure of which he was inordinately proud, and which his jocose critics described as the "finest torso" in public life. On a notable occasion soon after his entry into Congress, and not long after the attack on Sumner in the Senate, he stood up beside the crippled and sharp-tongued Thaddeus Stevens as a body-guard, and discouraged interference. He not only protected Stevens, but he agreed with him, becoming a sturdy War-Republican, and an advocate of vigorous repressive measures in the Reconstruction period. His ambitions in Congress and in the Republican party collided more than once with those of James G. Blaine, and produced a biting description by the latter, who jeered at Conkling's "haughty disdain, his gran-

diloquent swell, his majestic, super-eminent, overpowering, turkey-gobbler strut" (*Congressional Globe*, Apr. 30, 1866, p. 2299). The words could not be forgotten.

The decision of William H. Seward, leader of the New York Republicans, to remain loyal to President Andrew Johnson, and to support the latter in his Reconstruction policy, caused a break in the party and gave opportunity for the appearance of a leader among the radical Republicans of the state. Conkling was elected senator in 1867, and in the following autumn dominated the Republican convention, establishing an ascendancy over Gov. Reuben E. Fenton. In the next ten years, with the support of the federal patronage and the New York City "custom-house crowd," he became the almost undisputed leader of his party in the state, and an aspirant to greater things. He was reëlected to the Senate in 1873 and 1879. In 1876 he was the favorite son of New York as a candidate for the Republican presidential nomination, in rivalry to James G. Blaine, but met with disappointment when Gov. Rutherford B. Hayes of Ohio secured the nomination and became president in 1877. Conkling's intimacy with and support of President U. S. Grant, to which he owed much of his strength as leader of New York, had procured for him in 1873 an offer of the post of chief justice of the United States, to succeed Salmon P. Chase. He had declined the honor, recognizing that his talents were those of a partisan rather than of a judge. He was again later to be offered an appointment to the Supreme Court by his friend Chester A. Arthur, and was again to decline.

Conkling was a bitter opponent of President Hayes. He claimed to believe that the latter had no right to his position, he had reason to fear that the power of the Grant dynasty was broken, and he was outraged by Hayes's selection of a New Yorker whom he hated, William M. Evarts, as secretary of state. He regarded the New York patronage as his special preserve, and fought to defend it when the treasury department under John Sherman began to inquire into the management of the custom-house and the services therein of Chester A. Arthur and Alonzo B. Cornell [*qq.v.*], who were Conkling's chief assistants in the control of the party organization. He led the opposition to the desires of Hayes to separate civil service officials from the direction of party affairs, and his presence and spirit pervaded the New York Republican convention of September 1877, where the President was openly flouted. In substance he asserted the privilege of a senator to control the federal administration in his own state; and he denied to a president the right to select and direct his subordinates. The Tenure of Office Act, passed in 1867 to restrain Andrew Johnson, made it harder for the President to win his point; but eventually in 1879 Hayes had his way and got rid of Conkling's friends. New York, however, remained loyal to its leader. Cornell was made governor, Conkling was triumphantly reëlected to the Senate, and another of his lieutenants, Thomas C. Platt [*q.v.*], was chosen as the other senator in 1881. Arthur had meanwhile risen to greater rewards.

Disgusted with Hayes, and anxious for the return of the old order of politics, Conkling was a leader in the movement for the renomination of Grant in 1880. His success went only far enough to deadlock the Republican convention, and prevent the nomination of either Blaine or Sherman. Garfield, who was chosen after a long and destructive fight, represented the anti-Conkling or "Half-Breed" wing of the Republicans; and the selection of the "Stalwart," Arthur, for vice-president failed to heal the breach. It was only after much persuasion that Conkling ceased to sulk in the canvass of 1880, and gave any support to the ticket of Garfield and Arthur. His friends and he believed, that as the price of his final and lukewarm support, Garfield had made him sweeping promises of presidential patronage; but to this belief the selection of Blaine as secretary of state gave contradiction. Within a few days after the organization of the new administration, Conkling was again in opposition, and again over the right to control the jobs in the New York custom-house. He fought the confirmation of Garfield's appointees until defeat came to him in May 1881. He then resigned his Senate seat in protest, May 14, 1881, and induced his colleague to resign with him. He turned to the usually pliant legislature at Albany for vindication and reëlection, but discovered that his power to dominate it had departed. Even the open support of Arthur, now vice-president, was in vain. For the remainder of his life, Conkling was outside of politics. He removed to New York City, and entered into the practise of his profession, where he made a large fortune and a great name. He died in the spring of 1888, as the result of over-exertion during a severe snow-storm. His personal character and integrity were never challenged; he was, said the *New York Times* (Jan. 18, 1879), on the occasion of his third election to the senate, "a typical American statesman—a man by whose career and character the future will judge of the political standards of the present."

[Robt. G. Ingersoll, *Memorial Address on Roscoe Conkling* (1888), includes many obituary notices. There is a family biography by Conkling's nephew, Alfred R. Conkling, *The Life and Letters of Roscoe Conkling,*

Orator, Statesman, and Advocate (1889). Many of the details of his career may be traced in De Alva S. Alexander, *Political Hist. of the State of N. Y.* (3 vols., 1906–09), but no one has yet assembled and evaluated the material upon his public life that fills the press from 1859 to 1881.]   F.L.P—n.

CONNELLY, CORNELIA (Jan. 15, 1809– Apr. 18, 1879), foundress of the Society of the Holy Child Jesus, was born in Philadelphia, Pa., daughter of Ralph Peacock, a merchant of means, and Mrs. Mary (Swope) Bowen. She was of English and Spanish ancestry, and displayed the strong will and sound judgment of the former, and the emotional traits of the latter. Both her father and mother died during her girlhood, and she was reared with every social advantage by her half-sister, a Mrs. Isabella Montgomery. Her religious training was in the Episcopal Church, and on Dec. 1, 1831, she married Pierce Connelly, a young Episcopal clergyman, who shortly became rector of Trinity Church, Natchez, Miss. An interest in convent life led Mrs. Connelly to make a study of Catholicism, and in 1835 both she and her husband decided to embrace the Roman Catholic faith. This same year they started for Rome. Delayed in New Orleans, Mrs. Connelly was received into the Church at the Cathedral there by Bishop Blanc, but her husband deferred the ceremony until their arrival at Rome. After two years' residence in Italy, Mr. Connelly became professor in the College of St. Charles, Grand Coteau, La., while his wife taught music in a near-by convent, where her interest in such institutions was intensified. With self-abnegating devotion, she took up the practises of the religious life. In 1840 her husband announced his desire to enter the priesthood. She had then had four children, two of whom were living, and a few months later another son, Pierce Francis [*q.v.*], the sculptor, was born. The accomplishment of her husband's desire was dependent upon her willingness formally to separate from him, enter a convent, and take a vow of perpetual chastity. Although devoted to her family, she consented to make the sacrifice. Journeying to Rome again, husband and wife met the preliminary requirements, and the former was ordained priest, July 6, 1845.

At this time Bishop Wiseman was urging upon church authorities the need of education for Catholic girls in England. Mrs. Connelly was chosen as peculiarly fitted to provide for that need. Acting upon instructions she drew up rules and constitution for a new Order, basing them upon those of the Society of Jesus. Its principal object was to be the education of girls of all classes, and she chose for its name the Society of the Holy Child Jesus. In 1846 she went to Derby, England, under the direction of Bishop Wiseman, and founded the first House of the Order there, later transferring it to St. Leonards-on-Sea, Sussex. The rest of her life was dedicated to insuring the permanence and extension of the Order. Trying obstacles arose, among them the attempt of her husband to obtain control of the Society through her, and later, after he had apostatized, to compel her by legal process to live with him. Her faith, persistence, and unselfishness overcame all difficulties, however, and the Society prospered and received the approval of Rome. Much to her satisfaction, it was established in the United States in 1862, and in 1867 she visited its convents there.

[A detailed account of her career is given in *The Life of Cornelia Connelly* (1922), by a member of the Society. See also sketch in *Records of the Am. Cath. Hist. Soc.*, vol. XXXI, pp. 1–42 (Mar. 1920).]   H.E.S.

CONNELLY, HENRY (1800–July 1866), governor of the Territory of New Mexico, pioneer trader, was the son of John Donaldson and Frances (Brent) Connelly, and was born in Nelson (now Spencer) County, Ky. He was a descendant of Thomas Connelly of County Armagh, Ireland, who settled near Charleston, S. C., in 1689. He was trained in a school kept by a locally noted teacher, James Dozier, and later attended Transylvania University, from which he graduated as a doctor of medicine in 1828. In the same year he began practise in Liberty, Mo., then one of the outermost towns of the frontier, but in a few months closed his office and left with a trading party for Santa Fé and Chihuahua. In the latter city he became a clerk in the store of a Mr. Powell, whom subsequently he bought out. He seems to have been naturalized as a Mexican citizen about 1832. He is said to have made many trips between Chihuahua and Independence, Mo., at first with pack mules and later with his own wagon trains, and to have been the first merchant to take a wagon train (Apr. 1839–Aug. 1840) from Chihuahua to Fort Towson and back. He was married in Chihuahua about 1836 to a Mexican woman, by whom he had three sons. She died, probably in 1843, and Connelly took the two surviving sons to the east to be educated. He was in Santa Fé Aug. 12, 1846, when Capt. Philip St. George Cooke entered the city in advance of Kearny's army, and he was chosen by Gov. Armijo as his emissary to return with Cooke and negotiate with the general. After the flight of Armijo and the establishment of American rule he proceeded south. Arrested by the Mexican authorities as the bearer of a letter from Kearny to James Magoffin, he was taken to Chihuahua, but was soon released. He then moved to Peralta, in the present Valencia Coun-

ty, N. Mex., resuming his American citizenship. There he married Dolores Perea Chavez, a widow, by whom three children were born to him. In the period following the conquest he induced the Mexican inhabitants, in spite of the ugly mood evidenced by the Taos uprising in 1847, to accept and cooperate with the American rule. In the movement to establish a state government he was elected governor, June 20, 1850, but as Congress ignored the action and made New Mexico a territory, he did not serve. During the following ten years he and Edward J. Glasgow, his partner since 1843, built up the largest business in New Mexico. In 1861 he was appointed governor of the territory, and at the outbreak of the Civil War his influence was decisive in moulding public opinion against the maneuvers of the Confederates. During the panic caused by the Confederate invasion, under Gen. H. H. Sibley, and the Union disaster at Valverde, Feb. 21, 1862, he acted with coolness and determination, and his indefatigable efforts in support of the army of defense contributed greatly to the rout of the invaders. At the close of his four-year term, President Lincoln reappointed him. For some time his health had been failing, and in 1863 he had visited the east for medical treatment. Believing himself cured, he resumed his duties, but before long his illness returned. He died in office, at Santa Fé, from an overdose of an opiate. H. H. Bancroft regards him as "a man of good intentions, of somewhat visionary and poetic temperament, of moderate abilities and not much force." W. E. Connelly, on the other hand, praises him warmly, and his general estimate is supported by R. E. Twitchell. As a pioneer trader Connelly was, according to the former, "to this commercial new world what Kit Carson, Frémont and others were in their spheres of action." He was, moreover, "a gentleman of refinement and intelligence, honorable and upright in all the relations of life."

[Hubert Howe Bancroft, *Hist. of the Pacific States of North America* (1887); Wm. Elsey Connelly, ed., *Doniphan's Expedition and the Conquest of New Mexico and Cal.* (1907); Ralph Emerson Twitchell, *The Leading Facts of New Mexican Hist.* (1917); Stella M. Drumm, ed., *Down the Santa Fé Trail and into Mexico: the Diary of Susan Shelby Magoffin, 1846–47* (1926).]
W.J.G—t.

CONNELLY, PIERCE FRANCIS (b. Mar. 29, 1841), sculptor, was born at Grand Coteau, La., the son of Pierce Connelly and Cornelia Peacock; the latter, as "Mother Cornelia Connelly" [*q.v.*], later became the foundress of the Order of the Holy Child Jesus. A few months prior to Frank's birth his father, formerly an Episcopal clergyman, had announced his desire to enter the Catholic priesthood. The little boy lived with his mother in a convent; then with his father in Italy where the Prince Borghese became interested in him, and at five he was placed in a school for boys at Hampstead, England. In 1850 his father renounced the Catholic faith and reëntered the Protestant Episcopal ministry, taking his three children to Italy with him and settling in Florence, where for some years he was rector of the American Protestant Episcopal Church. Frank's artistic talent manifested itself early and he was sent to Paris to study painting; there he was a medalist of the École des Beaux-Arts. He later went to Rome to study and then returned to Florence where, at the age of twenty, he was so profoundly impressed by the sculpture of Hiram Powers [q.v.] that he turned to that medium. After working in Florence for a number of years he settled for a while in England where he seems to have enjoyed somewhat of a vogue, for he did numerous portraits of members of the aristocracy. To the Royal Academy Exhibition of 1871 he sent busts of Henry George, Earl Percy, and Algernon George, sixth duke of Northumberland. Besides these he did a full-length statue of the Duchess of Northumberland; a bust of Princess Louise; and a bust of the Marchioness of Lorne, a replica of which is preserved in the Inner Temple in London. Busts of the Duke of Northumberland and Lady Percy are said to be in Alnwick Castle.

During the Centennial year, 1876, Connelly came to America and was largely represented at the exposition in Philadelphia, where he was greeted as one of the most significant of American sculptors. The most important of his works there was a bronze group, "Honor Arresting the Triumph of Death," a reference to the fallen soldiers of the Civil War, which he had worked on from 1866 to 1869 and which had been exhibited in his studio in Florence the year of its completion. It is now in the Pennsylvania Academy. "Ophelia" was a romantically treated and elaborately detailed figure. Among his other works were "St. Martin and the Beggar," "Thetis" (1874, now in the Metropolitan Museum, New York), "Queen Philippa," "Lady Clare," "Diana Transforming Actæon," "Viola," and "The Thread of Life." At this period also he made busts of the Countess Von Rosen, Mr. Lippincott, and Mr. McKean. Most of his works are done in marble with high finish and often with minute detail. The very subject of the majority of them illustrates his romantic tendency. After a few months in America Connelly went to New Zealand where he reverted to painting again, and made many sketches of the craters, lakes, and glaciers of the country. An exhibition of his paintings was held in Auckland in 1877. He likewise took up mountain climbing and explored some hitherto almost unknown mountains. In the early eighties he returned once more to Florence where his father died in 1883. Little of the sculptor's later career is recorded; he was in Florence in January 1900, at the deathbed of his sister Adeline who had turned Catholic again, after their mother's death, and died praying for her brother's conversion.

[*The Life of Cornelia Connelly* (1922); "Sketch of the Life of Mother Cornelia Connelly," in *Records Am. Cath. Hist. Soc.,* XXXI, pp. 1–42 (Mar. 1920); Algernon Graves, *Royal Acad. of Arts,* vol. II (1905); C. E. Clement and L. Hutton, *Artists of the Nineteenth Century* (3rd ed., 1885); Lorado Taft, *Hist. of Am. Sculpture* (1903).]

E. G. N.
E. R. D.

CONNER, CHARLOTTE MARY SANFORD BARNES. [See BARNES, CHARLOTTE MARY SANFORD, 1818–63.]

CONNER, DAVID (1792–Mar. 20, 1856), naval officer, was born in Harrisburg, Pa., son of David Conner, an Irishman who came to the Wyoming Valley about 1750, and Abigail Rhodes, of longer-settled English stock. At fourteen the boy found employment with his brother in a Philadelphia counting-house, while still continuing his studies. Appointed midshipman, Jan. 16, 1809, he took one or two merchant voyages and then served from August 1811 to May 1817, in the famous sloop *Hornet.* Upon the capture of the privateer *Dolphin,* July 9, 1812, Conner entered her as prize-master, but the ship was soon afterward retaken by the British. Exchanged and back in the *Hornet,* he was third lieutenant in her victory over the *Peacock,* Feb. 24, 1813, being sent to the captured ship to rescue her crew and if possible keep her afloat, and narrowly escaping when she sank. He was first lieutenant in the victory over the *Penguin,* Jan. 22, 1815, suffering a grapeshot wound through the hip which necessitated crutches for nearly two years. His conduct in both actions won particular commendation from his commanders, Lawrence and Biddle, and he was awarded two Congressional Medals. During 1817–18 he was first lieutenant in the *Ontario,* which took formal possession of Oregon. After two years' duty in Philadelphia he rounded the Horn in the little brig *Dolphin,* and had later commands in the West Indies and Mediterranean. Made captain Mar. 3, 1835, he was Navy Commissioner, 1841–42, and then until May 30, 1843, head of the newly created Bureau of Construction, Equipment, and Repair. From December 1843 to March 1847, he commanded American naval forces in the Gulf and Caribbean. The soul of courtesy, Commodore Conner was excellently suited for the diplomatic problems preceding hostilities with Mexico, and, though broken in health by the climate, he gave himself unreservedly to the greatly increased administrative tasks created by the war. A blockade was established, and in the summer and autumn of 1846 expeditions were undertaken against Alvarado, Tobasco, Tampico, and other Mexican ports. Hampered, however, by lack of light-draft steamers and other means, he operated with a caution which aroused great dissatisfaction in the fleet and at home. What the navy could do was little, but the weak opposition doubtless justified bolder measures. The verdict of his subordinate, W. H. Parker, will probably stand, that Conner was "an educated man and a brave officer . . . but would not take the responsibilities that his position imposed upon him" (*Recollections of a Naval Officer,* 1883, p. 53). Credit is due him for the admirably managed landing of Scott's army, Mar. 9, 1847, in which the navy put ashore over 10,-000 men in five hours, and for the plan of naval cooperation in the capture of Vera Cruz; but on Mar. 21, the day before the final attack, he turned over the squadron to his former second-in-command, M. C. Perry [*q.v.*], in accordance with orders brought by Perry from home. This change was explicable as routine procedure, for Conner was ill and had been at sea beyond the usual period, but it was prompted also by desire for more aggressive leadership. Upon the fall of Vera Cruz, Mar. 29, Conner returned home, where he declined a position as bureau chief, and was made honorary member of the Cincinnati. After recuperation in Florida he was commandant of the Philadelphia Navy Yard, October 1849–June 1850. He was put on the Reserved List in 1855 and died shortly afterward at his home in Philadelphia. Conner is described as slightly above medium height, erect and active, with a presence commanding respect. He was survived by his wife, a daughter of the celebrated Philadelphia surgeon Philip Syng Physick, whom he married in 1828, and by two sons.

[An account of Conner's life and the chief documents of his Mexican War service appear in his son P. S. P. Conner's *The Home Squadron under Commodore Conner in the War with Mexico* (1896). See also R. Semmes, *Service Afloat and Ashore in the Mexican War* (1851); H. Simpson, *Lives of Eminent Philadelphians* (1859); an excellent obituary sketch in the *National Intelligencer,* Apr. 25, 1856; and controversial notes on his work in the Mexican War in *Army and Navy Jour.,* Feb. 2, Feb. 23, Apr. 19, 1884. Three vols. of MS. letters to Conner, chiefly 1842–47, are in the Lib. of Cong.]   A.W.

CONNER, JAMES (Sept. 1, 1829–June 26, 1883), lawyer, Confederate soldier, attorney-general of South Carolina, was a grandson of

James Conner, who came from the north of Ireland to America about 1776, fought in the Revolutionary War, and subsequently settled in Mecklenburg County, N. C., where he rose to considerable prominence, and a son of Henry Workman and Juliana (Courtney) Conner. He was born in Charleston, S. C., where his father had established himself as a successful banker in the early nineteenth century (see letters of H. W. Conner to J. C. Calhoun in "Calhoun Correspondence," *American Historical Association Report for the Year 1899,* vol. II). Having chosen to follow the legal profession in a commercial community, he spent several months in a counting house before entering college, and after graduation from the South Carolina College (1849) studied law under James L. Petigru [*q.v.*]. Admitted to the bar in 1851 he soon acquired a large practise. In these early years he published three legal works: *A Digest of the Cases Decided in the Law Court of Appeals of the State of South Carolina, 1835–54* (1855); *A Digest of Equity Reports of the State of South Carolina, from the Revolution to December, 1856* (1857) in collaboration with C. H. Simonton; and *The History of a Suit at Law* (1857), a manual for the guidance of students. In 1856 he was appointed United States attorney for the district of South Carolina. In this office he drew national attention by his vigorous prosecution of the operators of the *Echo,* a vessel which had violated the slave-trade law (*The Case of the Slaver Echo,* reported by D. A. Levein, 1859).

Believing that the time had come for South Carolina to secede, Conner resigned the attorneyship early in December 1860. Though for a time he occupied a seat in the secession convention and consented to become titular district attorney under the Confederate government, he devoted himself chiefly to preparation for military service. Having been elected captain of the Washington Light Infantry when that company was made a part of Hampton's Legion, he distinguished himself at the first battle of Manassas and was soon afterward promoted major (*Official Records, Army,* I ser., II, 567). Because he was not willing to be advanced in the Legion at the expense of a superior officer he withdrew (June 1862) to become colonel of the 22nd North Carolina Regiment. Except for a short period when he was convalescing from a severe wound, he served with this command until June 1, 1864 when he was commissioned brigadier-general. He was assigned temporarily first to McGowan's, then to McGowan's and Lane's brigades, and finally as acting major-general to McGowan's, Lane's, and Bushrod Johnson's brigades. In

August 1864 he assumed permanent command of Kershaw's brigade. In one of the actions at Cedar Creek, Oct. 12, 1864 (*Ibid.*, XLIII, pt. 1, p. 579), he suffered the loss of one of his legs and in consequence was incapacitated for further active duty.

After the war he married Sallie Enders (1866) and resumed the practise of law. He was solicitor for the South Carolina Railroad and receiver for the Greenville and Columbia Railroad Company. Except for the campaign of 1870 when he supported the Union Reform party, he deliberately abstained from politics until 1876 when, although he opposed the "Straightout Movement," he was a candidate for the office of attorney-general on the successful Hampton ticket. During the heated campaign which followed, his prudence averted serious trouble with the negroes in Charleston. As attorney-general he performed his most outstanding public service. It fell to him to establish the legality of the Hampton government. This having been accomplished and his health failing, he resigned in December 1877. His death occurred in 1883 in Richmond, Va.

[A volume of obituary articles from leading Southern newspapers, memorial addresses, etc., was published shortly after Conner's death under the title *James Conner, In Memoriam.* Permission to consult a quantity of private papers was generously granted by his son, Henry W. Conner, and a daughter, Mrs. Geo. H. Moffett, both of Charleston, S. C. See also J. B. O'Neall, *Biog. Sketches of the Bench and Bar of S. C.* (1859); J. F. J. Caldwell, *Hist. of a Brigade of South Carolinians Known First as "Gregg's" and Subsequently as "McGowan's Brigade"* (1866); D. A. Dickert, *Hist. of Kershaw's Brigade* (1899); *Confed. Mil. Hist.* (1899), vol. V.]
                                J.H.E.

CONNEY, JOHN. [See CONEY, JOHN, 1655–1722.]

CONNOLLY, JOHN (1750–Feb. 6, 1825), Roman Catholic bishop, was born at Slane, Ireland. Nothing seems to be known of his parents; yet the fact that he began his education at an early age indicates that they were in good circumstances. He entered the Dominican Order in youth and was sent to Rome, where, after brilliant studies and ordination (about 1775), he remained until 1814. The first years of his priesthood were spent in teaching. Later he held various posts of importance in his Order—among them that of assistant to its General. He was also a director of the Casanate Library, established by Cardinal Jerome Casanate, which now belongs to the government and is one of the most noted in the Italian capital. Many of the Roman Catholic hierarchy, especially those in English-speaking countries, made him their agent at the papal curia. Every charge entrusted to him he executed with a prudence, fidelity, and

success which not only won confidence and made friends, but also caused him to be an outstanding character among the clergy of Rome. His letters reveal a clear, trained, and orderly mind. More than once Father Connolly was mentioned for a bishopric in his native land. In 1808, when four new dioceses were erected in the United States, Rome seriously considered him for that of New York. His confrère, Richard Luke Concanen, who received the appointment, was held in Europe by the French embargo, and died there two years later. Meanwhile Pius VII was exiled. One of his first acts on regaining his freedom, however, was to nominate Connolly the second bishop of New York. Although consecrated on Nov. 6, 1814, he could not, because of the war with England, reach his diocese for a twelvemonth.

The aged prelate set about his new task with characteristic courage and vigor. His diocese embraced all New York State and half of New Jersey. He was pastor, missionary, and bishop all in one. Racial antagonism combined with lay trusteeism to give him considerable trouble in New York City. The French and the Irish were especially arrayed in hostile parties. Those who held that the management of the temporalities of the Church should rest with laymen, allied themselves with the French, and even sought to interfere in matters purely spiritual. Despite the opposition, acrimony, and unjust accusations of the malcontents, Connolly maintained the even tenor of his ways, defended his Episcopal rights, accomplished much good for religion, and left a name that is still cherished. One of his early acts was to establish an orphan asylum and introduce Sisters of Charity. The sick and poor were special objects of his goodness. Particularly did he show himself a father to all during several epidemics of yellow fever. He was the first Roman Catholic prelate to urge the erection of a diocese in each state and the promotion to the miter only of clergymen adept in the English language. Some historians, following the misrepresentations of Connolly's enemies, have been unfair to him. Yet even these writers not only admit that he was without personal blemish, but also say that he was a man of great virtue. He was held in high esteem by all classes and creeds (*New York Gazette and General Advertiser,* Feb. 10, 1825).

[Archives (ecclesiastical): Propaganda and San Clemente, Rome; Dublin and Tallaght, Ireland; Baltimore, Md. Published sources: J. R. Bayley, *A Brief Sketch of the Cath. Ch. on the Island of N. Y.* (1853); R. H. Clarke, *Lives of the Deceased Bishops,* vol. I (1872); A. Cogan, *Diocese of Meath* (Dublin, 1862–70); Henry De Courcy and J. G. Shea, *Hist. of the Cath. Ch. in the U. S.* (1856); J. G. Shea, *Hist. of the*

Cath. Ch. in the U. S. 1808–43 (1890) ; Peter Guilday, Life and Times of John Carroll (1922), and Life and Times of John England (1927) ; Cath. Miscellany, Charleston, for 1824–25.]   V.F.O'D.

CONNOR, HENRY GROVES (July 3, 1852– Nov. 23, 1924), judge, the sixth child of David and Mary Catherine (Groves) Connor, was born in Wilmington, N. C. His parents, the one of Irish and the other of English descent, were both natives of Florida. Three years after his birth the family moved to Wilson, N. C. There he began his education in a private school, but the death of his father cut short his formal schooling, and at fifteen he began to aid in the support of his family. Entering a law office as clerk, he began preparation for the bar and secured his license in 1871. In the same year he married Kate Whitfield of Wilson, by whom he had twelve children. He was quickly successful in practise and in 1884 was elected to the state Senate where he was chairman of the judiciary committee and secured the passage of the Connor Act, requiring registration of deeds, which, more than any statute in the history of the state, has brought security of land titles. In 1885 he was appointed superior court judge and served with distinction, resigning in 1895 to return to practise. The following year the Republican and Populist parties which had fused nominated him for associate justice of the supreme court, but he declined to take any part in a movement to which he was politically opposed. In 1899 he was a member and speaker of the lower house of the legislature where he was a leader in formulating the suffrage amendment to the constitution, which, by imposing an educational qualification coupled with the "grandfather clause," was designed to eliminate the negro vote. In the succeeding legislature he was again a member, and as chairman of the committee on education he fought boldly and successfully to aid Governor Aycock in carrying out the party pledge that educational opportunity would be given to all. He opposed the majority of his party on the question of impeaching three justices of the supreme court. All were later acquitted by the Senate. Party feeling was strong, but he lost no strength, for his party nominated him in 1902 for associate justice. Elected, he served until 1909 when President Taft, disregarding politics, appointed him federal district judge, a position which he filled until his death.

Connor was a man of striking charm of personality combined with much strength. Warmly human and cordial in personal intercourse, his quiet and genial humor, mental alertness, wide information, and breadth of interest, made association with him an experience to be prized. His varied contacts, extensive reading, and eager intellectual curiosity combined to keep him essentially youthful. He looked, picturesquely, every inch a judge, and though full of natural dignity, there was about him no hint of aloofness. As a trial judge he gained the confidence and affection of the state. As an appellate judge, by his poise and balance, his humanity, and his well-reasoned opinions, progressive, yet untouched by radicalism, he confirmed the popular estimate of him. As federal judge he performed undoubtedly his greatest judicial service. Federal courts, since Reconstruction, had been viewed with dislike and distrust in North Carolina, as alien and hostile agencies of government. But so great was the confidence felt in him by all classes and parties that during his service prejudice rapidly disappeared. In addition to his numerous opinions Connor wrote many valuable historical monographs. He was the author of *John Archibald Campbell, Associate Justice of the United States Supreme Court* (1920) which is an excellent piece of biographical and historical work. He also collaborated with J. B. Cheshire, Jr., in preparing *The Constitution of North Carolina, Annotated* (1911). All his writings were marked by an easy, graceful style and by clarity of thought and expression.

[Frank A. Daniels, Henry Groves Connor: An Address (1926) ; Reports of the N. C. Bar Asso., vol. XXVII, 135–50 ; N. C. Reports ; N. C. newspapers, esp. News and Observer (Raleigh), Nov. 24, 1924.]
                                        J.G.deR.H.

CONNOR, PATRICK EDWARD (Mar. 17, 1820–Dec. 17, 1891), pioneer, soldier, Indian fighter, was born in County Kerry, Ireland. His parents brought him to New York when he was a child. Beginning to work at an early age, he had few opportunities for education. At nineteen he enlisted in the army, serving in the Seminole War and in various garrisons. In 1844 he returned to New York, but early in 1846 went to Texas, where he enlisted in the Texas Volunteers. He fought in the battles of Palo Alto and Resaca de la Palma (May 8–9) ; was commissioned a first lieutenant on July 7, a captain on Feb. 12, 1847, and eleven days later took part in the battle of Buena Vista. He resigned from the army on May 24. In the winter of 1849–50 he moved to California, where he engaged in mining. At Redwood City, in August 1854, he married Johana Connor, a native of his own County Kerry.

On the opening of the Civil War he enlisted, and the governor appointed him colonel of the 3rd California Infantry. Directed to assume command of the Military District of Utah (including Nevada), he entered Salt Lake City with 700 men on Oct. 20, passing on a few miles to a commanding site, where he established Camp (afterward Fort) Douglas. The Mormons looked upon the action as an intrusion, but Connor, convinced that in the main they were unfriendly or even seditious, disregarded their protests; and in several subsequent clashes between the church and the government he compelled peace with a threat of force. Indian depredations were frequent, most of them traceable to a hostile band of Bannocks and Shoshones. Learning the location of their village, a fastness on Bear River, near the present Franklin, Idaho, Connor set out with 300 men during a spell of exceptionally severe weather and on the morning of Jan. 29, 1863, with two-thirds of his force, attacked them, capturing the village and killing most of the warriors. For this feat, which brought peace and opened to settlement a region that had been harassed for fifteen years, he was appointed (Mar. 30) a brigadier-general of volunteers. In March 1865 he was assigned to a newly created command, the District of the Plains, with instruction to cooperate, in a movement to be known as the Powder River Indian Expedition, with two columns from the Missouri River against the hostile Sioux, Cheyennes, and Arapahos. With about 900 men and with James Bridger as guide, he set out from Fort Laramie on July 30, reached the Powder near the Dry Fork, in the southeastern part of the present Johnson County, Wyo., where he established Fort Connor (later Fort Reno), and then pushed on to the Tongue. Here, on Aug. 29, he surprised a large village of Arapahos, winning a signal victory. But the other two columns, unprovided with equipment, supplies, or accurate maps, lost their way, and, after suffering terrible privations, disintegrated. On Sept. 6 Connor started to return. Before reaching Fort Connor he learned that he had been made the scapegoat for the failure of the campaign and had been relieved of his command. Incensed at this treatment, he returned to Utah without making an official report. In the general promotions dated Mar. 13, 1865, he had been brevetted a major-general of volunteers. On Apr. 30, 1866, he was honorably mustered out of the service.

Connor established the first daily newspaper in Utah, the *Union Vidette;* he was the owner of the first steamboat on Great Salt Lake; and he was an indefatigable promoter of the mining industry of the territory. Reverses came to him, for his business judgment was unequal to the task of conducting the many and ambitious enterprises he initiated. In territorial affairs he was steadfastly anti-Mormon. The Mormons

disliked him greatly; and Mormon histories, while conceding his courage and military skill, portray him as prejudiced, bellicose, and overbearing. The Gentiles, on the other hand, made him their leader and acclaimed him with the titles, "Father of the Liberal Party," and "Liberator of Utah." He was, said the *Salt Lake Tribune,* the day after his death, "a mighty factor in the last twenty-five years' history of Utah."

[F. B. Heitman, *Hist. Reg.* (1903); Grace R. Hebard and E. A. Brininstool, *The Bozeman Trail* (1922); Hubert Howe Bancroft, *Hist. of Utah, 1540–1886* (1889); Orson F. Whitney, *Hist. of Utah* (1893); *Salt Lake Tribune,* Dec. 18, 1891; "The Powder River Expedition of 1865," *U. S. Army Recruiting News,* Aug. 1, 15, Sept. 1, 15, Oct. 1, 1928.]   W.J.G—t.

CONOVER, OBADIAH MILTON (Oct. 8, 1825–Apr. 29, 1884), educator, lawyer, was born at Dayton, Ohio, of Dutch ancestry, being seventh in line of descent from Wolfert Gerretsc van Kouwenhoven, who came to the first Dutch settlement with Patroon van Rensselaer. By some unknown process the name took on its present form. His mother, Sarah Miller, came from an old Kentucky family. He was graduated from the College of New Jersey at Princeton in 1844; taught Latin and Greek at Lexington, Ky., and Dayton, for two years, meanwhile studying law in the office of Gen. Robert C. Schenck; and then returned to Princeton, being graduated from the theological seminary in 1849. After graduation he removed to Madison, Wis., where the remainder of his life was spent. He became editor of a literary and educational monthly, the *North-Western Journal,* of which only a few numbers were issued. When the first class was organized at the University of Wisconsin, in August 1850, there were two members of the faculty, Chancellor Lathrop and Professor Sterling, but in the second term Conover was appointed general tutor, being thus the third member of the faculty in order of appointment. Two years later he was made professor of ancient languages and literature, which position he held until 1858, when he was removed with his colleagues in the revolution and reorganization which the University underwent in that year. Renewing an earlier interest in the law, he was admitted to the Dane County bar in 1859, and two years later became assistant reporter to the Supreme Court of Wisconsin. In 1864 he was appointed reporter, which office he held for twenty years. His continued interest in educational matters is indicated by the fact that he was a member of the Board of Regents of the University, 1859–65; was for some years State Librarian; and was commissioned to collect books, pictures, and busts for the University abroad. In the later years of his life the condition of his health did not permit him to undertake any but his routine duties as reporter to the Supreme Court. His chief interest lay in Greek literature, but his relations to it were those of enjoyment and culture. Apart from the published reports of the Supreme Court, his writings consisted of occasional papers prepared for the Madison Literary Club. Two poems, "Via Solitaria" and "Reconciliation," often quoted, and frequently attributed to Longfellow, were products of his pen. He was twice married: in 1849 to Miss Julia Darst, who died in 1863, and in 1882 to Mrs. Sarah Fairchild Dean. His death occurred in London while on his return from a two years' sojourn in Greece.

[Stephen H. Carpenter, *Hist. of the Univ. of Wis. 1849–76* (1876); biographical sketches in C. W. Butterfield, *Hist. of the Univ. of Wis. up to 1879* (1879), and in R. G. Thwaites, *The Univ. of Wis., Its History and Alumni* (1900); memorial by Wm. F. Allen in *Trans. Wis. Acad. of Sciences, Arts and Letters*, vol. VII (1883–87); family records kept by Conover's descendants in Madison.]   V.A.C.H.

CONRAD, CHARLES MAGILL (Dec. 24, 1804–Feb. 11, 1878), lawyer and statesman, was born in Winchester, Frederick County, Va. On the side of his father, Frederick Conrad, he was descended from German stock that had come into the Shenandoah Valley in the early eighteenth century. On the side of his mother, Frances Thruston Conrad, who was the daughter of Charles Mynn Thruston, an Episcopal minister in Virginia and a colonel in the Revolutionary army, he was descended from English stock that had settled in Virginia in the seventeenth century. While he was a boy his father's family moved to Mississippi and later to Louisiana, settling near New Iberia. Charles was educated in a school in New Orleans maintained by a Dr. Huld, said to have been the founder of the first English school in that city. He studied law in the office of Abner L. Duncan in New Orleans and began the practise of his profession in 1828. He entered politics as a supporter of Andrew Jackson but shortly withdrew from the Democratic party and became a Whig over the Bank issue. At that time the Whigs were very strong in Louisiana and Conrad soon began to take high rank among them. He was a member of the Louisiana state legislature for several terms and was serving in that capacity when he was appointed to the United States Senate in April 1842, in place of Alexander Mouton who had resigned. He was defeated by the legislature for reëlection in January 1843, and hence retired in the following March. In 1844 he was sent as a delegate to the Louisiana state constitutional convention, and in 1848 he was elected to Congress from the Louisiana 2nd District. He took his seat on Dec. 3, 1849 and served until Aug. 13, 1850 when he resigned to accept appointment by President Fillmore to the office of Secretary of War. He retired from that position at the close of Fillmore's administration in March 1853.

During his brief term in Congress, the chief issue before that body was the admission of California as a free state. Conrad opposed the measure except as one of the conditions of a general compromise on the subject of slavery (*Daily New Orleans Crescent*, Mar. 11 and Apr. 6, 1850). He had resigned his seat, however, before the compromise measures of 1850 were agreed upon. In the memorable political campaign of 1860 he was active as a member of the Constitutional Union Party and was appointed one of the delegates from New Orleans to a state convention in June, to ratify the Bell and Everett national ticket and nominate candidates for state offices. During the Civil War he played a prominent political part in the Confederacy, serving first as a delegate from the 1st district of Louisiana to the Provisional Confederate Congress that met at Montgomery in February 1861, and later as a representative from Louisiana to the first and second Confederate Congresses, 1862–64. His large estate was confiscated but after the close of the war he resumed the practise of law in New Orleans and soon amassed a competency.

Conrad was very intense in his convictions and tenaciously persistent in support of whatever cause he espoused. In his earlier years he was somewhat belligerent in disposition and fought a duel with a Dr. Hunt of New Orleans, brother of Randall Hunt, a noted lawyer of the time, in which he killed his antagonist. He had, nevertheless, a profound reverence for the majesty of the law and the sanctity of the courts. He was a man of small stature but of abounding energy. Stricken with paralysis while testifying in the federal circuit court at New Orleans, he died a few days later. Conrad's wife was M. W. Angela Lewis of "Woodlawn," Fairfax County, Va., the grand-daughter of Fielding Lewis and Elizabeth, sister of George Washington. On her death she was buried at Mt. Vernon.

[Brief sketch in Alcée Fortier, *Louisiana* (1914), I, 251–52; obituaries, not altogether reliable, in newspapers of New Orleans for Feb. 12 and 13, 1878; *Biog. Dir. of the Am. Congress* (1928); some family data from Wm. Meade, *Old Churches, Ministers, and Families of Va.* (1851).]   E.M.V.

CONRAD, HOLMES (Jan. 31, 1840–Sept. 4, 1916), lawyer, was born at Winchester, Va. His father was Robert Young Conrad, a prominent lawyer of Winchester, and state attorney-general from 1857 to 1862; his mother was Elizabeth Whiting, daughter of Burr Powell. Holmes Conrad's education was received at the primary schools and Virginia Military Institute, whence he proceeded in 1858 to the University of Virginia, graduating in 1860. He then became a school-teacher, but, on the outbreak of civil war, enlisted as a private in Company A, 1st Virginia Cavalry, Apr. 17, 1861, and saw active service throughout the contest. Commissioned lieutenant, he was appointed adjutant in August 1862, and in 1864 became major and assistant inspector-general of Rosser's cavalry division, serving as such till the termination of hostilities. In 1865 he commenced the study of law in his father's office at Winchester, and on his admission to the Virginia bar in January 1866, joined his father in practise. A strong Democrat, the active interest he displayed in political affairs assisted in bringing him to the front, and in 1878 he was elected to the Virginia legislature, serving till 1882. In the course of the next few years he became one of the leaders of the Virginia bar, and acquired an influential position in the councils of the Democratic party. In 1893 President Cleveland appointed him assistant attorney-general of the United States and in 1895 he became solicitor-general. On his vacating office in 1897 he was retained by President McKinley on behalf of the federal government in *Morris* vs. *United States,* the "Potomac Flats Case," which involved the title to the shore front of Washington (174 *U.S.* 196). In October 1901 he joined the law faculty of Georgetown University as lecturer on the history of English law, at a later date taking over in addition the lectureship on the history and development of law and comparative jurisprudence. In 1904 he was again retained on behalf of the federal government as special prosecutor in the Postal Fraud Cases. During the last twenty years of his life he was constantly engaged in appeals before the Supreme Court where his outstanding ability had wide scope. He achieved his greatest success in the last case he was engaged on, *Commonwealth of Virginia* vs. *State of West Virginia,* involving the amount of the contributive share that the latter state should pay toward the public debt of the former. Appearing as counsel for Virginia, Conrad's argument upon the demurrer in the United States Supreme Court (206 *U.S.* 290) was in professional circles considered remarkable. Judgment was ultimately given against West Virginia for $12,393,929.50 principal and interest up to June 14, 1915 (238 *U.S.* 202). For this complicated and long-drawn-out litigation he was specially retained by the bond-holding creditors. Conrad was of striking appearance, tall of stature with an erect military bearing throughout his life. Though wielding great political influence in his state, he did not care for public office. By nature somewhat of an aristocrat and reserved in manner, he was never what the politicians termed a "good mixer." As a lawyer he excelled in discussing constitutional questions, and was at his best in appellate work before the Supreme Court. He had an extreme distaste for the routine of office work. He died at Winchester. His wife was Georgia Bryan, daughter of Thomas Bryan Forman of Brunswick, Ga.

[A good summary of Conrad's life and professional career appeared in *Virginia State Bar Ass. Report,* 1916, pp. 101–06. See also Jas. S. Easby-Smith, *Georgetown University* (1907), and J. M. Callahan, *Hist. of W. Va.* (1923), I, 623–27.]   H.W.H.K.

CONRAD, ROBERT TAYLOR (June 10, 1810–June 27, 1858), journalist, jurist, and dramatist, son of John and Eliza Conrad, was born in Philadelphia, Pa. His father, a prosperous publisher who printed Charles Brockden Brown's *Literary Magazine* and brought out Joel Barlow's *Columbiad* in sumptuous form, had Robert trained for a legal career. Although young Conrad was admitted to the bar in 1831, he was more interested in journalism and literature than in law. Accordingly he became associated (1831–34) with the *Daily Commercial Intelligencer* and wrote plays and poetry in his spare time. Before he was twenty-two he saw his first play, *Conrad, King of Naples,* successfully produced (Jan. 17, 1832), at the Arch Street Theatre by James E. Murdoch. It was afterward played by John R. Scott. Realizing the dramatic possibilities offered by Jack Cade's Rebellion (1450), Conrad worked on a blank-verse play with Cade as hero, which he intended to name *The Captain of the Commons* or *The Noble Yeoman,* but which was announced for production by A. A. Addams at the Walnut Street Theatre on Dec. 7, 1835 as *Aylmere.* Unfortunately Addams was intoxicated that evening and the première was postponed until the 9th, when David Ingersoll played the part of Cade. Addams essayed the rôle on Feb. 1, 1836, but failed. About this time Conrad was appointed judge of the court of criminal sessions in Philadelphia, which diverted his attention from literature for several years. He found time eventually to rewrite *Aylmere* as *Aylmere, or The Kentish Rebellion,* for Edwin Forrest [*q.v.*], who produced it at the Forrest Theatre in New York, May 24, 1841, and at the Arch St. Theatre, Philadelphia, on June 16, 1841. The clumsy title was soon changed to *Jack Cade,* under which name the play had a permanent place in Forrest's repertoire. Forrest was most successful in the rôle, which he also played in Europe (1868). After his death *Jack Cade* was produced by John McCullough and as late as 1888 by Edmund Collier. Others who assumed the part were Edward Eddy (1862, 1874) and Albert Roberts (1877).

The success of *Jack Cade* made Conrad a literary figure in Philadelphia. In 1843 he was chairman of the committee of judges that awarded to Edgar Allan Poe a prize of $100 for "The Gold Bug" as the best story submitted to the *Dollar Magazine*. He became (1845) an associate editor of the *North American* and in 1848 assisted George R. Graham in editing *Graham's Magazine*. He edited (1846) a revised, abridged edition of *Biography of the Signers to the Declaration of Independence*, by John Sanderson and others, originally published (1820–27) in seven volumes. In 1847 Joseph Reese Fry prepared a *Life of General Zachary Taylor* from material collected by Conrad; that work was reprinted in 1850 as *Our Battles in Mexico*. During those years Conrad wrote various poems, including "The Sons of the Wilderness," on the wrongs of the Indians, and a series of sonnets on the Lord's Prayer. These were published (Philadelphia, 1852) with the text of *Jack Cade* as *Aylmere, or the Bondman of Kent; and Other Poems.*

In 1853 the Pennsylvania legislature passed an Act enlarging the City of Philadelphia by adding to it the twenty-nine districts, boroughs, and townships comprising the rest of Philadelphia County. Judge Conrad, as he was always called, became the candidate of the combined Whig and American parties for mayor of the newly consolidated city. At the election (June 1, 1854) he defeated Richard Vaux, the Democratic candidate, by 29,507 votes to 21,011. Conrad was sworn in as the first mayor of greater Philadelphia on the first Monday of July, 1854. He not only handled with skill the difficult problems associated with the consolidation, but enforced the rigorous Sunday laws that were now effective in all parts of the newly acquired territory. He gained some adherents by his strong support of current Know-Nothing politics, requiring even his policemen to be native-born Americans, but he aroused bitter opposition by his strict administration of the law. He served as mayor until the expiration of his term in 1856, when he was appointed to the bench of quarter sessions by Gov. Pollock and served until the following year. He died at his home in Philadelphia. His *Devotional Poems* (1862) were published posthumously with an introduction by George Henry Boker

lauding Conrad's character and literary achievements. Among these later verses is "Sinai," a series of poems in Spenserian meter on the Ten Commandments. There is record of a third play by Conrad, entitled *The Heretic,* written for Forrest, produced at the Howard Athenæum, Boston, on June 1, 1863, and at the Broadway Theatre, New York, on Sept. 17, 1866 (T. A. Brown, *A History of the New York Stage,* 1903, I, 516). It was also played at the Arch Street Theatre, Philadelphia, with Mrs. John Drew in the cast. The text, like that of *Conrad of Naples,* has not survived. Though impulsive at times, Conrad had a gracious manner and an attractive scholarly bearing. He was an accomplished orator of the old school, fond of sonorous verbiage and rhetorical flights. His rather stilted speeches on many notable occasions are available in pamphlet form. Contemporaries hailed him as a dramatic poet of Shakespearian quality; fortunately he did not live to witness the eclipse of his fame.

[See obituary sketches in *Public Ledger* (Phila.), June 28, 1858, and other daily papers; J. T. Scharf and T. Westcott, *Hist. of Phila.* (1884), I, 715–20; Jas. Rees, *Life of Forrest* (1874), pp. 431–39; F. C. Wemyss, *Twenty-six Years of the Life of an Actor and Manager* (1847), II, 245–52; A. H. Quinn, *Hist. of the Am. Drama from the Beginning to the Civil War* (1923), pp. 251–52. M. J. Moses, *Representative Plays by Am. Dramatists* (1925), II, 425–520, reprints *Jack Cade* with an introduction.]
                        J.L.H.

CONRIED, HEINRICH (Sept. 13, 1855–Apr. 27, 1909), actor, producer, and impresario, was born at Bielitz, Austria, of Jewish parentage, the son of Joseph and Gretchen Cohn. He early exhibited talent as an actor and was enrolled with the company of the Hofburg Theatre in Vienna at the age of eighteen, later becoming a leading character actor with traveling companies. For one season he managed the Stadt Theatre in Bremen. In 1877 or 1878 he came to America to take charge of the Germania Theatre in New York City, where he used the name Heinrich Conried both on and off the stage. He soon became co-manager of the Thalia Theatre, bringing over the famous German actor, von Possart, the first of a number of German stage celebrities for whose introduction to the American public he was responsible. In 1892 he took over the Irving Place Theatre, making it the center of theatre-going activity for the German-Americans of the city, then sufficiently numerous to support an excellent German stock company. To add lustre to the regular repertory, which included German classics and modern comedy, Conried invited as guest players some of the foremost German actors of the day, among them Sonenthal, Barney, Sorma, Odilon, and Schratt.

The excellence of the productions at the Irving Place Theatre gained him a large American support for his company, and he secured country-wide recognition through performances of the classics at the larger universities, interest in which was enhanced through lectures which he delivered. During this period, he also gave occasional spirited performances of operettas by Strauss, Milloecker, Suppé, and others, and in 1898 staged an elaborate production of Humperdinck's *Die Koenigskinder,* in its original form as a drama with incidental music and songs. In addition to this, he found time to assist Rudolph Aronson in the production of light opera at the Casino Theatre in its best days.

In 1903 he was appointed manager of the Metropolitan Opera House (succeeding Maurice Grau), a position which he filled for five years. He inherited from his predecessor a brilliant list of singers, and added to the roster many others of equal renown, including Caruso, Chaliapin, Ternina, Fremstad, and Farrar. He also brought over Mottl and Mahler as conductors. His outstanding single achievement at the Opera House was the first performance, outside of Bayreuth, of Wagner's *Parsifal,* which took place on Dec. 24, 1903. The publicity surrounding this event was unprecedented in the annals of opera; praise and dispraise were about equally distributed. There was, moreover, some futile litigation by the Wagner heirs to restrain the production. But all of this helped to make the production a financial success of the first magnitude. There were eleven performances in all, outside of the regular season, the receipts for which are reported to have been $186,308. Next in importance was his production of *Madame Butterfly* by Puccini, brought out with an excellent cast under the inspiring presence of the composer, and Humperdinck's *Hänsel und Gretel,* to which the composer also lent the dignity of his presence. Conried's use of the Opera House for elaborate productions of light opera—Johann Strauss's *Die Fledermaus* (in his second season) and *Zigeunerbaron* (in his third)—aroused considerable criticism.

As years wore on, there appeared dissension in the ranks of the directors of the Opera, which came to a head with the production of Richard Strauss's *Salomé.* This was performed only once, and the directors of the real-estate company owning the Opera House put their caveat on its repetition. In the last two years of his régime, Conried encountered competition from Oscar Hammerstein who had set up a rival company in the Manhattan Opera House, near by, which threatened serious results to the monopoly theretofore enjoyed by the Metropolitan. The competition was enlivened by personal quarrels over some of the artists who were enticed away from Hammerstein. The increasing difficulties of the situation, and his own ill health, led Conried to resign his position in February 1908, leaving soon for Austria in quest of renewed health. He died there at Meran, in the Austrian Tyrol, a year later. He had married Augusta Sperling in 1884, who, with her son, brought his body back to be interred in this country. While the forces of partisanship for and against Conried were active during his régime at the Metropolitan Opera House, it now seems fair to say that his lack of background, so far as the opera world is concerned, militated against his complete artistic success as an impresario, in spite of a record of interesting events. But posterity will undoubtedly accord him unstinted praise for his years of fruitful achievement at the Irving Place Theatre and the invigorating influence of that theatre's standards on the dramatic history of the country.

[Montrose J. Moses, *Life of Heinrich Conried* (1916); *Grove's Dict. of Music and Musicians, Am. Suppl.* (1920); *The Art of Music* (1915–17), ed. by Daniel Gregory Mason and others, vol. IV, pp. 149–51; H. E. Krehbiel, *Chapters of Opera* (1908), and *More Chapters of Opera* (1919); Henry T. Finck, *My Adventures in the Golden Age of Music in New York* (1926); *N. Y. Clipper* and *N. Y. Dramatic Mirror,* both May, 1909; *Neue Freie Presse, Abendblatt* (Vienna), *N. Y. Times, Evening Post* (N. Y.) and *N. Y. Tribune,* all Apr. 27, 1909.]
L.M.I.

CONSIDÉRANT, VICTOR PROSPER (Oct. 12, 1808–Dec. 27, 1893), Fourierist, founder of a Utopian community in Texas, was born at Salins (Jura), a remarkable son of a remarkable father. The latter, Jean-Baptiste Considérant, learned professor of the humanities and librarian at Salins, in his efforts to preserve the college buildings during a fire, deliberately permitted two houses of his own, constituting his entire fortune, to burn to the ground. His son was equally public-spirited. Educated in the École polytechnique (Paris) and the École de Metz, and quickly advanced to captain in the engineering division of the army, taking part in the war against Algiers in 1830, he sacrificed a promising military career at the call of a philanthropic ideal. On Mar. 13, 1830, he published in the *Mercure de France* his adherence to the unpopular communistic theories of Fourier, and therewith, at the age of twenty-one, began his life-work. He resigned from the army and soon made the personal acquaintance at Lyons of Fourier himself, whose trusted lieutenant he became, assisting him to establish a monthly magazine, *Le Phalanstère* (which became with No. 15 *La Reforme Industrielle* and in 1836 *La Phalange*).

In fact, Considérant was the real founder of the French cooperative movement, in a practical sense, as Fourier himself had remained a theorist with but few disciples. In a long series of works Considérant expounded the philosophy of his master, pruned of its extravagancies and patent absurdities. Of these writings the most important were: *Destinée sociale* (3 vols., 1834–44); *Manifeste de l'école societaire* (1841); *Exposition abrégée du système Phalanstérien de Fourier* (1845); *Principes du socialisme* (1847); *Théorie du droit de propriété et du droit au travail* (1848); *Socialisme devant le vieux monde* (1849). After Fourier's death in 1837 Considérant became the acknowledged leader of the movement, winning many previous followers of Saint-Simon, such as Jules Lechevalier and Abel Transon. He established a Fourierist library in Paris, and, in 1843, a Fourierist daily, *La Democratie Pacifique*. He was much ridiculed by the conservative press, which, taking advantage of an unfortunate speculation of Fourier to the effect that human beings in a state of perfection would become endowed with tails equipped with eyes, always portrayed Considérant, really a man of much dignity, with a caudal appendage, and delighted to tell of English visitors who came desiring to witness his "perfection." Nevertheless his influence increased, and through the financial assistance of Arthur Young, an Englishman, he established short-lived phalansteries at Condé-sur-Vesgres and elsewhere. After the Revolution of 1848 he was elected to represent the Department of the Loire in the Constitutional Assembly in which he introduced an abortive measure to confer the franchise on women. In 1849 he was elected deputy of the Seine, but having taken part in Ledru-Rollin's armed demonstration, on June 13, 1849, against Louis Napoleon's Roman expedition, he was accused of treason and fled to Brussels.

In 1852 he paid a visit to America, where, in New York, he obtained the support of Albert Brisbane [*q.v.*] and subsequently journeyed, largely on horseback, as far as the western part of Texas. On his return he published *Au Texas* (1854), full of extravagant enthusiasm for the land, climate, and inhabitants of the new region. Plans for colonization, temporarily halted by Considérant's brief imprisonment in Belgium on a charge of conspiracy against a neighboring state, were completed immediately after his release, and a company was formed with a capital of $300,000, which purchased 57,000 acres in various parts of Texas. Headed by Considérant himself, the first colonists in April 1855 formed the settlement of Reunion, on the bank of the

Trinity River three miles west of Dallas, Tex. Subsequent arrivals brought the number up to between 350 and 500 settlers. Most of these were artisans, with a large sprinkling of writers, musicians, and artists; there were only two farmers in the entire company. As might have been anticipated, with two successive years of drought, the cooperative community was soon in financial difficulties. The opposition of a partially Know-Nothing legislature was overcome by Considérant's eloquent *European Colonization in Texas, an Address to the American People,* but the cooperative feature was abandoned, and Considérant with his wife and mother-in-law, Mme. Clarice Vigoureux, herself a gifted Fourierist writer, withdrew in disgust to San Antonio where he became an American citizen. In 1869 he returned to Paris and died there in poverty and obscurity in 1893. His colony had perished even earlier, the company finally selling all its assets in 1875. To-day an old cemetery with crumbling headstones is the only vestige of Reunion, but many of its descendants became notable in the subsequent history of the state.

[E. de Mirecourt, *Les Contemporains* (1853–58), sketch no. 99 (1858); René Samuel, article in *La Grande Encyclopédie*, vol. XII; Pierre Larousse, *Grand Dictionnaire Universel du XIXe Siècle*, vol. IV; Claude Augé, ed., *Nouveau Larousse Illustré*, vol. III; Athanase Cretien, *Dictionnaire Universel* (1849), ed. by Maurice Lachatre; *Revue des Deux Mondes*, Aug. 1, 1845; Louella Styles Vincent, "The Story of Old Frenchtown," *Dallas Morning News*, Nov. 23, 1919; W. S. Adair, "Old French Settlement near Dallas," *Ibid.*, Mar. 26, 1922; Eusibia Lutz, "Almost Utopia," *Southwest Rev.*, vol. XIV, no. 3 (Spring 1929).]
E. S. B.

CONVERSE, CHARLES CROZAT (Oct. 7, 1832–Oct. 18, 1918), composer, lawyer, was born at Warren, Mass., the son of Maxey Manning and Anne (Guthrie) Converse. After student days he went abroad to take up theory and composition with Richter, Hauptmann, and Plaidy, at Leipzig, where he stayed from 1855 to 1859. He met Liszt, but was more influenced by Spohr, who was interested in his work. Returning to America, he entered the Albany Law School, graduating in 1861, with the degree of LL.B. From 1875 on he practised law at Erie, Pa., receiving a doctor's degree from Rutherford College in 1895. He was also a partner in an organ manufacturing concern. In composition, Converse began with a set of six German songs, composed abroad, which included the elegiac "Täuschung" and the expressive "Ruhe in der Geliebten." More ambitious was his "American Concert Overture," which treated the tune of "Hail, Columbia" with a full orchestral setting and development. This was performed at peace jubilees and expositions, as well as at various concerts, but did not become a permanent classic because of the somewhat simple conventionality of the song. A "Festouvertüre" won some success in 1870. His American national hymn, "God for us," was written in rather obvious contrary motion to "God Save the King." A cantata setting of the 126th Psalm, given by Thomas in 1888 at a teachers' convention, won much notice. It is closed with a five-voiced double fugue, of such excellence that Sterndale Bennett, impressed by its mastery, persuaded Cambridge University to offer the composer the degree of Mus. Doc., which, however, Converse did not accept. His other cantatas, such as *Spring Holiday,* were less ambitious in style. Many of his works remained in manuscript including two symphonies, the oratorio *The Captivity,* several suites, some overtures, three symphonic poems, and a number of string quartets. Of these, the overtures "Im Frühling" and "Christmas" received concert performances. Most widely known was his hymn "What a friend we have in Jesus," which must have been printed many thousand times if collections are included. Converse wrote many other hymns, and made several compilations. Among his songs, such examples as "The Death of Minnehaha" and "The Virgin's Cradle Song" show expressive intensity, but such lyrics as "We miss thee at home," and "My poor lost Geraldine," are frankly popular in style. Converse published also a successful guitar method. He wrote many articles on various subjects, sometimes using the pen name Karl Redan, or anagrams such as C. O. Nevers or C. E. Revons. Among these were "A Symposium on Church Music: How can the New Music profit most from the Old?" in the *Homiletic Review* (April 1899); "Music's Mother-tone and Tonal Onomatopy" (*Monist,* April 1895); "The Verse of the Future" (*Open Court,* December 1905); "Reminiscences of Some Famous Musicians" (*Etude,* October 1912); and an attempt to introduce a new pronoun, "thon," condensed from "that one," to take the place of "he or she" and "him or her" (see "thon" in *Standard Dictionary*). The idea was good, even though the article caused no linguistic change. The composer's last years were spent at Highwood, N. J., where he died.

[Rupert Hughes, *Contemporary Am. Composers* (1900); *Musical Observer,* Dec. 1909; *Grove's Dict. of Music and Musicians, Am. Supp.* (1928); *Who's Who in America,* 1918–19.] A. E.

CONVERSE, EDMUND COGSWELL (Nov. 7, 1849–Apr. 4, 1921), inventor, capitalist, philanthropist, was born in Boston, the son of James Cogswell and Sarah Ann (Peabody) Converse. He graduated from the Boston Latin School in 1869 and went to work as an apprentice in the McKeesport, Pa., plant of the National Tube Works, of which his father was founder and president. On Jan. 10, 1882, he was granted Patent No. 252,020 for a lock-joint for tubing. During the next six or seven years he perfected his invention in its details and extended its application, taking out eleven other patents of his own and gaining possession of a number of others. His coupling was the best on the market for water and gas systems, and once it became known it brought millions of dollars of business to the company, of which he had become general manager in 1889. He now turned his attention from coupling tubes to coupling tubing companies, with even greater benefits to himself. In 1892 he consolidated various tube manufacturing companies under a New Jersey charter with a total capitalization of $11,500,000. In 1899 he and William Nelson Cromwell, acting as agents for J. P. Morgan & Company, succeeded in merging about twenty iron and steel tube companies, with others acquired later, into the National Tube Company, which was incorporated at $80,000,000. When the United States Steel Corporation was organized in 1901, Converse retired from the field and gave himself to banking and its ramifications. By this time he was a power in financial circles, doing much to make New York the banking center of the nation and responsible for the rise of such men as Henry P. Davison, Benjamin Strong, and Seward Prosser, who with others were known as "Converse boys." He was president of the Liberty National Bank 1903–07, of the Bankers' Trust Company 1903–13, and of the Astor Trust Company from its organization in 1907 till its merger with the Bankers' Trust in 1917. During the World War he again was head of the Liberty National Bank, while its regular president, Harvey D. Gibson, engaged in Red Cross activities in Europe. He was a director of many corporations (see *Who's Who in America,* 1920–21). His first wife, Jessie Macdonough Green of New York, whom he had married Jan. 2, 1879, died in 1912; and on Jan. 30, 1914, he married Mary Edith Dunshee of New York. In these latter years he withdrew, so far as circumstances would allow, from his financial interests, played golf, joined genealogical societies, and experimented with possibilities of life that hitherto he had left untried. Conyers Manor, his 2,000 acre estate in Greenwich, Conn., became a show place; apples from its orchards won prize after prize at pomological fairs. In 1910, when the district between Rye, N. Y., and Sound Beach, Conn., was suffering from a water famine, he proved himself a good neighbor by turning over his large private lake at Stanwich to the use of the public. In 1912 he bought for $75,000 the Gainsborough portrait of Count Rumford, who was a member of his mother's family, and in the same year he gave $125,000 to the Harvard Graduate School of Business Administration. In 1915 he gave the Converse Memorial Library to Amherst College. In 1915, also, he made his Greenwich estate into a bird sanctuary. The winters he spent in a Pasadena hotel, where he died unexpectedly of a heart attack. His will was equally generous to public institutions and to numerous friends and employees. According to the inventory and appraisal filed in the Probate Court of Greenwich, his estate was valued at $30,769,867.

[*N. Y. Times,* Apr. 5, 13, 29, June 26, 1921, May 18, 26, June 8, 1922; *N. Y. Tribune, World, Wall Street Jour.,* Apr. 5, 1921; *Who's Who in America,* 1920–21; *New Eng. Hist. and Geneal. Reg.,* vol. LXXVI (1922); *N. Y. Geneal. and Biog. Record,* vol. LIII (1922); S. H. Peabody, *Peabody Geneal.* (1909), p. 98; J. J. Putnam, *Family Hist. in the Line of Joseph Convers of Bedford* (1897), pp. 55, 58–59; E. O. Jameson, *The Cogswells in America* (1884), p. 157; *U. S. Pat. Off. Gazette,* vols. 21, 22, 24, 27, 29, 33, 36, 39, 41, 42, 44, 46, 49, 50, and 52.]
                                      G.H.G.

CONVERSE, JAMES BOOTH (Apr. 8, 1844–Oct. 31, 1914), Presbyterian clergyman, author, was born in Philadelphia, the son of the Rev. Amasa Converse and of Flavia Booth. His father, who was of New England birth and education but had lived in the South, was proprietor of a church paper, the *Christian Observer,* which was suppressed by the federal government in 1861 because of Converse's vehement opposition to "the spirit of anti-slavery infidelity." After a short incarceration at Fort Delaware, Amasa Converse made his way through the Union lines and reëstablished his periodical in Richmond, Va. In spite of his father's difficulties James managed to graduate from the College of New Jersey (Princeton) in 1865 and in 1870 completed his preparation for the ministry at the Union Theological Seminary in Richmond. He was ordained the next year by the Presbytery of East Hanover, was pastor for a short time on the Eastern Shore of Virginia, helped to edit his father's paper, which had been removed to Louisville, Ky., 1872–79, engaged in evangelistic work, and was pastor at Blountville, Ky., 1881–87. On June 30, 1874, he married Pamelia Hopkins Campbell of Paducah, Ky. In the summer of 1877 he visited the British Isles, Paris, and Switzerland, publishing his impressions the next year as *A Summer Vacation—Sketches and Thoughts Abroad.* His wife had died in October 1875, and on Feb. 14, 1881 (or 1882) he married Eva Almeda Dulaney of Blountville. The turn-

ing point of his life came in 1886. Confined indoors by a snow-storm he happened upon Henry George's *Progress and Poverty.* To him it was still a new book and more than a mere book—a revelation. His thought quickened and his enthusiasm kindled by his reading of it, he turned for further enlightenment, not to other treatises on economics, but—as habit and culture made inevitable—to his Bible. The results of his inquiry were published privately at Morristown, Tenn., in 1889 as *The Bible and Land,* in which he adopts as much of George's natural-rights philosophy and theory of taxation as he was able, by his exegesis, to find authority for in Holy Writ. Few people could have read the book; its only visible effect was to bring down on the author such disrepute as a subversive thinker as kept him for fifteen years from occupying a regular pulpit. Converse, however, with the support of his wife, was resolutely true to his mission. From 1890 to 1895 he published a periodical, the *Christian Patriot,* to advocate the authority of the Bible in civil affairs; he printed notes on Exodus in the *New Era* of Springfield, Ohio; in 1899 he summarized his doctrines in *Uncle Sam's Bible, or Bible Teachings about Politics.* The little book is written as a series of discussions among two clergymen, a lawyer, their wives, and several other characters; it contains a slight tincture of autobiography and is written with simplicity, reasonableness, and good humor. Though a man of one idea, Converse was no crank. During the last ten years of his life he labored as a missionary in the valleys of East Tennessee, where he set up schools and Bible study classes and made himself beloved by the mountaineers. His last appeal to a generation too sophisticated, or too heedless to listen, was *There Shall Be No Poor* (1914) published by his wife after his death.

[C. A. Converse, *Some of the Ancestors and Descendants of Samuel Converse,* etc. (1905); *Who's Who in America,* 1914–15; *Who's Who in Tenn.* (1911); *Christian Observer,* Nov. 11, 1914; *Knoxville* (Tenn.) *Jour. and Trib.,* Nov. 1, 1914; *Gen. Cat. of Princeton Univ. 1746–1906* (1908).]
                                      G.H.G.

CONVERSE, JOHN HEMAN (Dec. 2, 1840–May 31, 1910), locomotive builder, was born in Burlington, Vt., the son of a Presbyterian minister, Rev. John Kendrick Converse. His mother was Sarah Allen, daughter of Hon. Heman Allen, member of Congress from Vermont. John prepared for college in the Burlington High School. In 1861 he received the degree of A.B. from the University of Vermont. In 1864 he was employed as a railway clerk by the Chicago & Northwestern Railway Company. Two years later he entered the employ of the Pennsylvania

Railroad Company where he made the acquaintance of Edward H. Williams, a General Superintendent. Williams took an interest in the young man and when he became one of the proprietors of the present Baldwin Locomotive Works offered Converse a desirable position in the concern. Three years later, in 1873, upon the retirement of one of the firm's members, Converse became a partner. In the same year he married Elizabeth Perkins. When on July 1, 1909 the partnership was dissolved and the Baldwin Locomotive Works was incorporated as a stock company under the laws of Pennsylvania, he was elected its first president, which office he held until the day of his death. Although he was deeply interested in every development of locomotive design and construction, from the beginning he was primarily concerned with general financial and commercial administration. Perhaps his greatest single financial coup occurred when, as president of the Baldwin Locomotive Works, he floated successfully $10,000,000 of first mortgage bonds, bearing interest at five per cent.

Converse's activities were not confined solely to locomotive construction, for he was a leader in many financial, patriotic, benevolent, religious, and educational projects. His financial contributions to many institutions, particularly the University of Vermont, were notable. He was elected president of the trustees of the General Assembly of the Presbyterian Church and vice-moderator of the Presbyterian General Assembly at the St. Louis meeting in 1901. For a long time he served as a trustee of the theological seminaries at Princeton and the University of Vermont. His educational policy was far-sighted. By his writings and lectures, during the last fifteen years of his life, he advocated widespread public intellectual guidance by the universities of the country, believing that the universities could accomplish this result through the medium of circulating libraries, extension schools, and a change in the course of studies. He was interested in educational institutions, not only for the general culture obtained from the study of the humanities but for the specialized courses dealing with the social, political, and economic problems affecting the well-being of society; he believed that the relative importance of the general-culture courses had diminished because of the increasing number of college graduates who were entering business as their life-work, and because of the changed nature of the methods of conducting business enterprises. Some of his theories are expressed in an address, *The Twentieth Century University,* delivered before the Associated Alumni of the University of Vermont in 1898, and in a paper "Higher Education for Business Pursuits and Manufacturing," in the *Annals of the American Academy,* vol. XXVIII (1906). Those who knew him well declared that Converse realized the enormous power which his great wealth conferred upon him and that he always tried to use "his splendid talents and large resources in the Service of God and man."

[*History of Baldwin Locomotive Works 1831–1923* (1923); *Obituary Record, University of Vermont,* I, 157 (pub. 1895, *Suppl.,* June 1910); John W. Jordan, *Colonial and Revolutionary Families of Pa.* (1911), II, 1099.]   H.S.P.

CONWAY, ELIAS NELSON (May 17, 1812– Feb. 28, 1892) was born in Greene County, Tenn., the youngest of seven sons of Thomas and Ann (Rector) Conway. The family traced its history back to the Conways resident upon the Conway River in north Wales during the thirteenth century. The first member of the family to come to Virginia was Thomas, who arrived about 1740. He had only one son, Henry, who was an officer in the Revolutionary War. To preserve his slaves and other property from capture and confiscation by the British, Henry put them in charge of his son Thomas and John Sevier, son of a companion in arms, and sent them into Tennessee. Here Thomas made his home and became a member of the Senate of the State of Franklin during its brief life. To him were born seven sons and three daughters. To his sons he gave all the educational advantages possible, not the least of which was association with Andrew Jackson. All who lived beyond young manhood attained some distinction. The three daughters married into the Sevier family. When Elias was only six years old his father moved with his family to St. Louis and later settled in Saline County, Mo. Here Elias was given the best educational advantages to be found in Saline, Boone, and Howard Counties. In 1833 he went to Arkansas, whither his older brothers Henry W. and James Sevier [*q.v.*], had gone in 1820, and at once engaged in surveying the northwestern counties. In 1835 President Jackson appointed him auditor of the territory. When the territory became a state, with his brother James as governor, he was continued in this office, which he held for fourteen years. A part of his duties as auditor was to administer the public lands of the state. The federal government was still issuing military-bounty land warrants and a good many of these were issued on lands located in Arkansas. Many of the beneficiaries never saw their grants and in course of time their lands were sold for taxes. In 1840 Conway laid before the legislature a well-prepared plan for giving these lands to actual settlers. His plan was adopted by the legislature. It attracted a good deal of attention outside the state and probably furnished a model for the bills which finally led to the Homestead Act of 1862.

In 1852 Conway was nominated for governor by the Democrats and was elected by a majority of 3,028 over Bryan H. Smithson, Independent Democrat-Whig. He served two terms of four years each. The chief problem confronting him was to wind up the affairs of the Real Estate Bank and the State Bank, and save the credit and honor of the state. The bank had been chartered during the administration of his brother, James S. Conway. No doubt some of the men connected with the banks were honest, but contemporary investigations revealed a good deal of corruption and the historian Hallum (*post*, pp. 52, 57) reached the conclusion that the whole affair was a swindle from the beginning. Both banks suspended specie payments soon after opening, but they controlled some of the most influential newspapers, kept friends in the legislature, and through mortgages brought pressure to bear on officials, including a member of the supreme court, so that it was impossible to bring them to book. Soon after his inauguration Gov. Conway determined to wind up their affairs and kept at the job for eight years without fear or favor, though great efforts were made to block the way. At the close of his administration (1860) he was able to report that $1,090,000 out of $3,199,000 in state bonds issued to these banks had been retired. Conway took an active interest in internal improvements, such as good roads, levees to protect overflowed lands, and railroads. Several railroad companies received land grants and a part of the line between Little Rock and Memphis was in operation by the close of 1860. The Governor urged the legislature to improve educational conditions, but saw little accomplished beyond the organization of the state school for the blind. He worked on the principle of economy and at the close of his second term reported a handsome surplus in gold and silver. Although reared by a mother religiously austere, he never joined any church. Drinking and gambling were common in his day, but he neither drank nor gambled. His success in public life was due to his character and not to "politics," for he refused to campaign. After his term expired he took no further part in public life. He never married.

[Dallas T. Herndon, *Centennial Hist. of Ark.* (1922), esp. vol. I, pp. 479–504; John Hallum, *Biog. and Pictorial Hist. of Ark.* (1887), which gives the family genealogy and biography as gathered from Gov. Conway, but needs to be checked for accuracy; *Report of the Accountants Appointed under the Act of Jan. 15, 1855, to Investigate the Affairs of the Real Estate Bank of Ark.*

(1856); *Report of the Accountants of the State Bank of Ark. Made to the Governor in Pursuance of Law* (1858); W. B. Worthen, *Early Banking in Ark.* (1906); Legislative Jours.; Acts of 1840, 1844, 1846.]

D. Y. T.

CONWAY, FREDERICK BARTLETT (Feb. 10, 1819–Sept. 7, 1874), actor, was born at Clifton, England. His father, William A. Conway, also an actor, came to the United States in 1821, and committed suicide by leaping from a steamship off Charleston, S. C., in 1828. Frederick Bartlett had developed a "fair position" on the English stage before he came to America to try his fortunes. He opened here as Charles Surface in *The School for Scandal*, at the Broadway Theatre, New York, on Aug. 19, 1850. In October he appeared at the Walnut Street Theatre, Philadelphia, as Claude Melnotte. His acting attracted attention, and he was engaged by Edwin Forrest to play Iago to that star's Othello, and De Mauprat to his Richelieu (*N. Y. Times*, Sept. 8, 1874). His first wife having died, in 1852 he married an American actress, Sarah Crocker, the sister of Mrs. D. P. Bowers (Elizabeth Crocker) [*q.v.*], also well known on the stage. They were daughters of William Crocker, a Methodist preacher of Ridgefield, Conn. (D. W. Teller, *History of Ridgefield, Conn.*, 1878, p. 134). Two years later he played Armand to the Camille of Jean Davenport Lander, whose production of that play was the first in America, preceding the more famous one by Matilda Heron. Conway, not E. A. Sothern, was accordingly the original Armand in America. Thereafter Mr. and Mrs. Conway played much together, making joint starring tours, and, as was then the fashion, appearing with the local stock companies. In 1855 they played an engagement at the Boston Museum, for example, being "supported" by such actors as William Warren—a far finer player than Conway. Here they acted Morton's *All That Glitters Is Not Gold*. In 1859 they leased Pike's Opera House in Cincinnati, and endeavored to conduct a stock company there, but the venture failed. In 1861 they visited London, acting at Sadler's Wells. In 1864, Mrs. Conway, who appears to have been the executive member of the family, leased the Park Theatre in Brooklyn, which became known as Conway's Theatre, and was for many years thereafter a fashionable amusement resort in that city. Here they both appeared in the majority of the bills, and here their two young daughters, Lillian and Minnie, made their débuts. Programs of the theatre show that Conway played Malvolio to his wife's Viola in 1864, but that evidently Irish plays were more popular than the classics, for we find records of *The

Colleen Bawn, Peep o' Day, or Savourneen Dee-lish (its nature indicated by such scene descriptions as "The dark valley—terrific leap for life !" or "Twine the dear green flag with the Stars and Stripes"), and Green Bushes, or the Hunter of the Mississippi—a Romantic Irish Drama. In the absence of the text, the connection between Ireland and the Mississippi is not entirely clear. There was also a "sensational drama" made from the popular American story, Cudjo's Cave, and Conway played Richelieu in The Three Guardsmen. The programs suggest rather the work of a routine stock company catering to a romantic public taste than the productions of original and creative artists. T. Allston Brown (A History of the New York Stage, vol. I, 1903, p. 384) says that Conway was "a good all-round actor. He was considered the best John Mild-may in Still Waters Run Deep ever seen on the American stage, and he was excellent as Armand in Camille." Quite evidently he was popular, too, in romantic Irish rôles. But there is little in his record to indicate more than the proficient, routine leading man. A contemporary described him as "somewhat pompous in manner." He died at his summer home, Manchester, Mass. A grandson, Conway Tearle, carried the name into the moving pictures.

[T. Allston Brown, Hist. of the Am. Stage (1870) ; J. N. Ireland, Records of the N. Y. Stage from 1750 to 1860, vol. II (1867) ; Eugene Tompkins, The Hist. of the Boston Theatre, 1854–1901 (1908) ; Laurence Hutton, Plays and Players (1875) ; obituaries and other articles in Evening Post (N. Y.), Sept. 7, N. Y. Herald and N. Y. Tribune, Sept. 8, and N. Y. Times, Sept. 8, 9, 10, 11, 1874; programs of Conway's Theatre, Brooklyn.]   W. P. E.

CONWAY, JAMES SEVIER (Dec. 9, 1798–Mar. 3, 1855), governor, was born in Greene County, Tenn., a son of Thomas and Ann (Rector) Conway. He went from Missouri to Arkansas in 1820 with his brother under contract to survey public lands, and became the first surveyor-general of Arkansas Territory. In 1829 he was reappointed by President Jackson and continued in office until the territory was admitted to statehood. He soon became master of a large cotton plantation and more than a hundred slaves on the Red River in Lafayette County, but continued his work in surveying, marking a part of the western boundary of the territory in 1825 and cooperating with a commission from Louisiana in 1831 in surveying the southern boundary. In both cases his work was well done. On Dec. 21, 1826, he married Mary J. Bradley, formerly of Nashville. Conway's great ambition, to become the first governor of the state, was realized in 1836. No real parties had existed in the territory, but small groups and mass conventions

meeting in different counties asked him to run for office. The ticket he headed was called "Democratic-Republican," though this hyphenated form was no longer used in the East. It supported Van Buren. Absalom Fowler was nominated in the same way on the "People's" ticket, which supported Hugh L. White for president. It is interesting to note that, while Conway received 5,338 votes and Fowler 3,222, Van Buren received only 2,400, and White 1,238. The most notable event of Conway's administration was the passage of the acts chartering the State Bank and the Real Estate Bank, and the issuance of state bonds to put them on their feet. The speaker of the House became the president of the Real Estate Bank, but continued to hold his place as speaker until he was expelled for killing a member on the floor of the House. Gov. Conway has been severely criticized (John Hallum, Biographical and Pictorial History of Arkansas, 1887, p. 52) for allowing "this piratical crew of fortune seekers" to take the helm from him at the start and "scuttle the financial fame of the state," but the most pressing need of the state was capital ; this was the only way the embryonic statesmen knew to get it, and other states were doing the same thing. The failure of the banks and their subsequent dark history could not be foreseen. No one has ever questioned the integrity of Conway in connection with them; he was a man of unchallenged probity. In 1836, federal funds to the amount of $25,000 were turned over to him to pay Arkansas volunteers called into federal service. These funds he, because of illness, turned over to an army officer who proved careless in his accounts, and a judgment was secured against Conway for a considerable sum unaccounted for. Congress, however, upon the recommendation of Reverdy Johnson, chairman of a committee to investigate, cancelled the debt (Senate Document No. 126, 29 Cong., 2 Sess; Statutes at Large, IX, 687). Twice Gov. Conway urged the legislature to enter upon an educational policy. Upon the expiration of his term (1840) he retired to his plantation, where he died and was buried. His brother, Elias N. Conway [q.v.] became governor in 1852 and undertook to restore the credit of his state.

[Ark. Hist. Asso. Pubs., vol. I (1906), p. 233 ; Fay Hempstead, Hist. Rev. of Ark. (3 vols., 1911) ; D. T. Herndon, Centennial Hist. of Ark. (3 vols., 1922) ; Biog. and Hist. Memoirs of Southern Ark. (1890) ; obituaries in the True Democrat (Little Rock), Mar. 14, 1855, and State Gazette and Democrat (Little Rock), Mar. 23, 1855.]   D. Y. T.

CONWAY, MARTIN FRANKLIN (Nov. 19, 1827–Feb. 15, 1882), free-state leader, first congressman from Kansas, was the son of Dr.

W. D. Conway and Frances, his wife, who lived in Harford County, Md. He left school at the age of fourteen and went to Baltimore, where he learned the printer's trade. While working as a compositor he aided in founding the National Typographical Union, studied law, and was admitted to the bar. He was married to Emily Dykes in June 1851. Three years later they removed to Kansas. As correspondent for the Baltimore *Sun* he reported conditions in the new territory for some time after his arrival. His letters attracted attention and he soon became one of the recognized leaders of the free-state movement. He was elected a member of the first territorial legislature but resigned without taking his seat. He took an active part in the Big Springs convention, Sept. 5, 1855, which formulated the platform of the free-state party. A few weeks later he was elected a delegate to the Topeka constitutional convention and wrote the resolutions offered by that body. State officers were elected under this constitution, and Conway was chosen one of the supreme court justices of the territory. In 1858 he was elected a delegate to the Leavenworth constitutional convention of which he was made president. In 1859 he was nominated for representative in Congress by the Republicans and elected by a majority of 2,107 votes over John Halderman, his opponent. Kansas did not become a state until Jan. 29, 1861, and the Congress to which he had been elected expired on Mar. 4 following. He served during this short interval, being the first congressman from Kansas, was promptly renominated, and elected again in June 1861. Conway was dubbed "the silver tongued orator of the West" and "the Patrick Henry of Kansas" (*Kansas Historical Collections*, V, 45; X, 186). In the Thirty-seventh Congress he was noted for his radical utterances on the slavery question. Soon after the first session began he made a speech in which he declared that the paramount object of the federal government should be immediate and unconditional emancipation. Until such a policy should be adopted, he said, he would "not vote another dollar or man for the war." "Millions for freedom but not one cent for slavery," was one of his epigrams (*Congressional Globe,* 37 Cong., 2 Sess., pt. 1, p. 87).

Failing to be renominated at the end of his term in the Thirty-seventh Congress, he retired to private life but kept up his interest in public affairs. In the struggle between President Johnson and Congress, he strongly supported the former. The President appointed him United States consul at Marseilles, France, in June 1866. After his term of service ended he made

his home in Washington, D. C., where, on Oct. 11, 1873, he fired three shots at former Senator Pomeroy, slightly wounding him. When arrested Conway said, "He ruined myself and family." The former Senator declared that there had never been any trouble between them. Undoubtedly Conway was becoming unbalanced; later his mind gave way entirely as a result of disappointed ambition, and he was confined in St. Elizabeth's Hospital for the Insane, at Washington, where he died.

[D. W. Wilder, *The Annals of Kan.* (1886); Andreas, *Hist. of Kan.* (1883); F. W. Blackmar, *Cyc. of Kan. Hist.* (1912); The *Cong. Globe,* 37 Cong., 2 Sess., pt. 1; *Kan. Hist. Coll.,* vols. V (1896); VI (1900); VIII (1904); X (1908); XI (1910); XIII (1915); and XVI (1925).]   T. L. H.

CONWAY, MONCURE DANIEL (Mar. 17, 1832–Nov. 15, 1907), preacher, author, was born near Falmouth, Stafford County, Va., the son of Walker Peyton and Margaret E. Daniel Conway. Through his mother he was descended from the Moncures, and he was related to other distinguished Virginia families. His father was a slave-owner, but unlike most neighbors of equal prominence in the community was a devout Methodist, and Moncure was brought up in the strict traditions of that sect. After studying at Fredericksburg Academy he entered Dickinson College, Carlisle, Pa., as a sophomore at the age of fifteen, and four months later was advanced to the junior class. Here he was converted to Methodism, somewhat deliberately, as he would have us believe, since he knew that his family wished him to have the experience. After his graduation at the age of seventeen he studied law for a time, but the reading of Emerson turned his thoughts toward the ministry. He first entered a Methodist conference in Maryland and served two circuits there, travelling about with perhaps as odd a collection of books as Methodist preacher ever carried in his saddlebags: the Bible, Emerson's *Essays,* Watson's *Theology,* Carlyle's *Latter Day Pamphlets,* Jeremy Taylor's *Holy Living and Dying,* the *Methodist Discipline,* and Coleridge's *Aids to Reflection.* The young circuit rider soon grew out of sympathy with some of the doctrines of his denomination, and at the age of twenty-one, much to the disappointment of his family, he entered Harvard Divinity School. While here he saw something of Emerson, and met most of the leaders of the Concord and Cambridge intellectual groups.

On his graduation from the Divinity School he became pastor of the Unitarian Church in Washington. His views on slavery had changed as rapidly as his theological views—in one of his early writings he had maintained that the negro is not a man—and his outspoken anti-slavery utterances in the pulpit finally led to his dismissal from the Washington church in 1856. He was at once called to the First Congregational Church of Cincinnati. On June 1, 1858 he was married to Ellen Davis Dana, of Cincinnati, to whose influence he credits much of his accomplishment to her death in 1897. During his residence in Ohio he wrote on all sorts of subjects for all sorts of periodicals, including the *Atlantic Monthly*. Through the year 1860 he edited *The Dial, a Monthly Magazine for Literature, Philosophy, and Religion*—a journal for which he secured contributions from such diverse men as Emerson and W. D. Howells. In 1862 he removed to Concord, Mass., and edited the *Commonwealth* (Boston), an anti-slavery paper with more literary tendencies than Garrison's *Liberator*. He had published several books and pamphlets dealing with the slavery question, and in 1863 he went to England to lecture in behalf of the North. Early the next year he accepted the pastorate of South Place Chapel, Finsbury, London, an ultra-liberal congregation; and he maintained this connection until 1884. In these years he traveled much and wrote much, even serving as correspondent from the front for the *New York World* during part of the Franco-Prussian War. Among other activities were researches in demonology, a subject on which he delivered a series of lectures before the Royal Institution. Conway early rejected all supernaturalism from his theology. His religious views continued to become more free and radical, and his political ideas were individual, if not erratic. He advocated a unicameral government, seeing grave evils in a president and a second chamber. He never admitted the wisdom of Lincoln's policies, maintaining that Lincoln was something of an apostate on the slavery question, that Virginia would not have seceded if it had not been for his unwise call for troops, and that he might have ended the struggle and slavery at once, without bloodshed, if he had issued an emancipation proclamation in 1861. His *Autobiography*, while not written in the tone of an *apologia*, shows how his extreme changes of opinion and some of these erratic views came naturally to a man of his ancestry, temperament, and experiences. In 1884 he resigned his London pastorate and returned to America, though he often visited Europe, and from 1892 to 1897 was again pastor of South Chapel. His later years were spent in study, writing, and travel. He died in Paris. Perhaps his most scholarly work is his *Life of Thomas Paine* (2 vols., 1892) and his edition of Paine's works

(*The Writings of Thomas Paine,* 4 vols., 1894–96). Wherever he was Conway came in contact with the leading men of the day—a fact that has led some critics to accuse him of tuft-hunting; but published correspondence seems to indicate that those who knew him valued his acquaintance. Among his more than seventy separately published books and pamphlets are several on slavery, on oriental religions, on demonology, two novels, lives of Paine, Hawthorne, Carlyle, Edmund Randolph, and others, his *Autobiography, Memories and Experiences* (1904) and his last important work, *My Pilgrimage to the Wise Men of the East* (1906).

[The chief source of information concerning Conway is his *Autobiography*. Both the appearance of this work and the author's death called out many articles in reviews and magazines. The *South Place Mag.*, vol. XIII, no. IV (London, 1908?) is a Conway memorial number. See also Edwin C. Walker, *A Sketch and an Appreciation of Moncure Daniel Conway* (1908). *Addresses and Reprints* (1909), a collection of some of his shorter works, contains a bibliography of over seventy titles of books and pamphlets. No bibliography of his contributions to periodicals has been compiled.]

W. B. C.

CONWAY, THOMAS (Feb. 27, 1735–c. 1800), sometimes known as Count de Conway, general in the Revolutionary War, was born in Ireland. Taken to France at the age of six, he was educated in the latter country and joined the French army in 1749. In 1772 he had reached the rank of colonel in this service, having served in the campaigns in Germany, 1760–61. In 1776 Silas Deane, then representative of the United States in France, recommended Conway, with a number of other French officers, for service in America (Wharton, *post*, II, 202). He was said to have been a skilful disciplinarian, particularly with infantry. Conway came to the United States from Bordeaux in April of 1777, and on May 13 he was appointed brigadier-general in the Continental Army. He was present at the battles of Brandywine and Germantown. In October of 1777, Washington strongly opposed the promotion of Conway to be major-general, on the ground that it was unjust to the abler and older American officers. He felt that Conway was a general of no particular distinction, and somewhat of a braggart (Washington, *Writings,* Ford ed., VI, 121). Upon his failure to be promoted, Conway offered his resignation. The Continental Congress refused to accept it, commissioned him major-general, and on the same day, December 14, 1777, appointed him inspector-general. Emboldened by this evidence of his influence in Congress, Conway entered into correspondence with Gates and others in which he criticized Washington. The contrast between the victories of Gates and the defeats of Washington in the summer of 1777 caused dissatisfaction in Congress and a movement to oust the Commander-in-Chief in favor of the victor at Saratoga.

Through a leak in Gates's official family, for which James Wilkinson was probably responsible, the affair came to Washington's knowledge. Wilkinson apparently told a Col. McWilliams, who told Lord Stirling, who passed on to Washington, the statement that Conway had said to Gates, "Heaven has been determined to save your country, or a weak General and bad counsellors would have ruined it." Washington informed Conway in a brief letter what had been reported. In a longer letter to Gates, which Washington sent through Congress, the Commander-in-Chief apprized both Gates and Congress of what had happened (*Ibid.*, VI, 278; see also Washington, *Writings,* Sparks ed., V, 516). The conspirators in Congress seem at once to have taken cover. Though the conclave who desired the removal of Washington has gone down in history as the "Conway Cabal," Conway was probably not the prime mover in the conspiracy but simply the one who was caught. The cabal failed utterly of its purpose, and did no good to either Gates or Conway. Meantime, in January of 1778, Congress proposed to send an expedition to Canada, under the command of Lafayette, with Conway as second in command. Lafayette came immediately to headquarters, and, according to Henry Laurens, "discovered a noble resentment for the affront offered to his commander Genl. Washington" (Burnett, *post,* III, 64). Lafayette refused to take Conway as his second, and said if the matter was pressed, he would return to France and take with him the whole French contingent. So Kalb went as second in command, superior to Conway, who finally accompanied the expedition. On arriving in New Hampshire, Conway began to intrigue for a separate command, and was directed on Mar. 23, 1778, to return to Peekskill and put himself under the command of Major-General McDougall. Meanwhile his friends in Congress turned against him, and Henry Laurens, who had at first thought highly of him, wrote that Conway's "conduct respecting General Washington is criminal and unpardonable, severely censured by all the foreign officers" (*Ibid.*, III, 209). On Apr. 22, 1778, Conway again threatened to resign. Congress, to his chagrin, accepted his resignation, Apr. 28.

His conduct subsequent to this still further outraged the friends of Washington, so that on July 4, 1778, he had to fight a duel with General Cadwalader. The latter's bullet struck Conway in the mouth and passed through the upper part of his neck. It seemed at first that the wound would be fatal, and while hovering between life and death on July 23, Conway wrote Washington a complete apology for all the injury he had done (Washington, *Writings,* Sparks ed., V, 517). However, he recovered and returned to France, where he rejoined the army and in 1779 was stationed on the staff of the Army of Flanders. In 1781 he went out in command of a regiment to Pondicherry in India, where he became a maréchal-de-camp in 1784 and finally in 1787 governor-general of the French possessions in India. In December of 1787 he was made a Commander of the Order of St. Louis. In 1793 he was back in France where he espoused the Royalist cause, for which he was compelled to flee the country. He died in exile. He married the daughter of Maréchal Baron de Copley.

[The documents on the "Conway Cabal" were gathered by Jared Sparks in his *Writings of Washington,* appendix, vol. V (1834). To this certain others were added by W. C. Ford in his edition of Washington's *Writings,* vol. VI (1890), and by the publication of the *Journals of the Continental Congress* for 1777 and 1778 (Lib. of Cong., 1907–08). A more substantial addition was made by Dr. E. C. Burnett's investigation in the Laurens Papers and his *Letters of the Members of the Continental Congress,* vols. II and III (1923–26). See also Francis Wharton, *Revolutionary Diplomatic Correspondence of the U. S.,* vol. II (1889) ; James Wilkinson, *Memoirs* (1811) ; J. T. Austin, *Life of Elbridge Gerry* (1828).]

R. G. A—s.

CONWELL, HENRY (*c.* 1745–Apr. 22, 1842), Roman Catholic bishop, was born in Moneymore, Londonderry, Ireland. His studies for the priesthood were made in Paris. He was ordained priest in 1776, and for twenty-four years before coming to America he was vicar-general in the ancient metropolitan see of Armagh. Appointed bishop of Philadelphia by papal letters dated Nov. 26, 1819, he was consecrated in London by William Poynter, the vicar apostolic of the Southern District, on Sept. 24, 1820, and arrived in Philadelphia about the end of November in the same year. Soon after his arrival some domestic difficulties with a rebellious priest, William Hogan, opened a long-drawn-out controversy which was, unhappily, the significant episode of Conwell's career. The lay trustees at St. Mary's, which was then the cathedral church, claimed the right to retain Hogan in his pastoral office despite the fact that the bishop had deprived him of the exercise of faculties of the priesthood. Litigation followed in which it was shown definitely that the charter granted by the legislature of the state gave the trustees no powers to choose or name their own pastors. It was proved also that the canon-law title to "Patronage" claimed by the trustees did not exist in the churches of America. The trustees now endeavored to have the charter changed, but a decision of the state supreme court in January 1822 rejected the proposed amendment. After the middle of May 1821, the Cathedral, St. Mary's, was closed to the bishop and the Catholic congregation, the trustees taking the stand that they had the sole right to the control and administration of temporalities. Those who remained loyal to the bishop were forced to recede to St. Joseph's Chapel which was enlarged for their accommodation. Later it was found that legal title to ground and buildings was still held in the name of the original purchasers and their successors by will, not in the name of the corporation or its trustees. In October 1826 an endeavor was made to come to an understanding and terms of peace. An agreement was drawn up defining the rights of each of the contending parties. This pact was by previous consent submitted to the Propaganda at Rome to be judged according to the rules of the general law of the Church. The agreement was rejected by the Sacred Congregation as harmful to the rights of Church government and the sacred ministry. Bishop Conwell was now called to Rome to give an account of the causes of the troubles in Philadelphia, and discuss a remedy. In the meantime the first Provincial Council of Baltimore made a request that Francis Patrick Kenrick be appointed coadjutor to the aged prelate and administrator of the diocese. This request was granted. Bishop Conwell returned, retaining the title Bishop of Philadelphia but with no powers of administration. He lived in retirement. During the closing years of his life he was almost blind and quite deaf. He died in Philadelphia at the age of ninety-six.

[M. I. J. Griffin, "Life of Bishop Conwell of Phila.," in *Records of the Am. Cath. Hist. Soc.*, vols. XXIV–XXIX (1913–18); *The Works of the Right Rev. John England* (5 vols., 1849), ed. by I. A. Reynolds; pamphlets printed during the Hogan Schism, 1821–27, a series of about seventy; copies of unpublished correspondence between Bishop Conwell, the Trustees at St. Mary's, and the Congregation de Propaganda Fide, 1816–40; obituaries in *Public Ledger, North American and Daily Advertiser*, and *U. S. Gazette* of Phila., Apr. 23, 1842.]
F. E. T.

CONWELL, RUSSELL HERMAN (Feb. 15, 1843–Dec. 6, 1925), clergyman, was the son of Martin and Miranda Wickham Conwell of South Worthington, Hampshire County, Mass. The father was an Abolitionist and their farm home was a station of the "Underground Railway" and sheltered many a runaway slave. It was a plain home of poverty and hard work, but it had a certain intellectual atmosphere and Russell developed early into an extensive reader. At the age of fifteen he ran away and worked his

way to Europe on a cattle ship. In 1859 he graduated at Wilbraham Academy where he supported himself largely by his own exertions. After a year spent in teaching, he entered Yale, taking the academic and law courses together and earning his expenses by work in a hotel. In the fall of 1862 he raised Company F, Massachusetts Volunteer Militia in the Hampshire region of the state. This company, of which he became captain, was known as the "Mountain Boys." His term of service was spent in North Carolina and Virginia, and so great was his reputation as a recruiting officer that he was asked to raise Company D, 2nd Massachusetts Heavy Artillery, of which he was elected captain. He became lieutenant-colonel on the staff of Gen. McPherson, where he saw much service and was severely wounded at Kenesaw Mountain. He was admitted to the bar in 1865, and went to Minneapolis where he practised law and founded the *Daily Chronicle*. After three years of professional and civic activity his health failed and he went abroad as immigration agent for Minnesota. After the recovery of his health he began a career of intense activity in Boston as lawyer, editor, lecturer, and author. He founded the *Somerville Journal* and the Boston Young Men's Congress.

In college he had become an avowed atheist, but after his wound at Kenesaw Mountain he turned to religion, and after the death of his wife in 1872, this experience deepened. Taking up a decadent Baptist church in Lexington, Mass., he achieved a remarkable success. He was ordained there in 1879, and after eighteen months was called to the Grace Baptist Church of Philadelphia, which was struggling with debt and discouragement. Under his leadership this church entered on a great career of prosperity, and in 1891 dedicated its new home, the great Baptist Temple, seating 3,000 people. Out of a night school in the basement of the church, with a corps of volunteer teachers, grew Temple University, a college for working people, which had instructed more than 100,000 pupils in Conwell's lifetime. He was also responsible for the foundation of three hospitals. His famous lecture, *Acres of Diamonds*, whose proceeds were devoted to the education of more than 10,000 young men, was given more than 6,000 times. He was prominent as a lecturer on a great variety of subjects for more than sixty years. Among his numerous books are campaign lives of Grant, Hayes, Garfield, and Blaine, and biographies of Spurgeon, Bayard Taylor, and John Wanamaker. Other titles are: *Lessons in Travel* (1870); *History of the Great Fire in Boston*

(1873) ; *Woman and the Law* (1876) ; and *Why Lincoln Laughed* (1922). In 1923 he was awarded the Bok Prize of $10,000 by the people of Philadelphia. Conwell had the gifts of the popular orator and his appeal was preëminently to the plainer sort of people. It has often been pointed out that his ideals of success were nothing more than the popular materialistic ideals of his day, though he always coupled philanthropy with money-getting, in precept and practise. In 1865 he married Jennie Hayden of Chicopee Falls, Mass., who died in 1872. In 1874 he married Sarah Sanborn of Newton Center, Mass., who died in 1910. The children were a son and a daughter by the first marriage and a daughter by the second.

[The authorized life of Conwell is *Russell H. Conwell and his Work* (1917) by Agnes Rush Burr. This book contains portraits and his famous lecture, *Acres of Diamonds.* Other biographies are Albert H. Smith, *The Life of Russell H. Conwell* (1899) ; Robert J. Burdette, *The Modern Temple and Templars* (1894) ; and R. Shackleton, *Life and Achievements of Russell H. Conwell* (1915). In addition to the above, a radically different view of Conwell and his work is presented by W. C. Crosby in "Acres of Diamonds," an article in the *American Mercury* for May 1928. Probably the truth about him in some important respects lies somewhere between the view of this writer and that of the more laudatory biographies.]   F. T. P.

CONYNGHAM, GUSTAVUS (*c.* 1744–Nov. 27, 1819), naval officer, was born in County Donegal, Ireland. He was the son of Gustavus Conyngham and his wife, a cousin, and the daughter of Gabriel Conyngham. The family was a landed one, of gentle origin, having descended from William Cunningham, fourth earl of Glencairn (d. 1547), in the peerage of Scotland. A member of this family, Redmond Conyngham, founded the shipping house of Conyngham and Nesbitt in Philadelphia. He was a cousin of the younger Gustavus, who emigrated to Philadelphia in 1763 and entered the service of his relative as an apprentice. Going to sea, he learned navigation on board one of his cousin's vessels, and within a few years was given the command of another, the ship *Molly.* In September 1775, he sailed from Philadelphia as master of the brig *Charming Peggy,* for Europe, with a cargo of flax-seed, intending to return with a ship-load of military supplies. The desired articles were purchased in Holland, but unfortunately the British consul in Ostend was informed of their character and prevailed upon the Dutch government to prevent the sailing of the *Charming Peggy.* Conyngham was stranded in Europe, but being of a resourceful character was not long unemployed. On Mar. 1, 1777 the American commissioners in Paris, filling out one of the blank commissions of the Continental Congress, ap-

pointed him to the command of the American lugger *Surprise,* and two months later he sailed from Dunkirk on a cruise. Within a few days he returned to port with two valuable prizes, the British packet *Prince of Orange* and the brig *Joseph,* with a cargo of wine, lemons, and oranges. As the result of a protest made by the British ambassador in Paris, the French government seized the *Surprise,* released the prizes, and arrested the American commander and his crew. Conyngham soon obtained his release, however, and on July 16 sailed on another cruise, under a new commission from the American commissioners, appointing him captain and commander of the Continental cutter *Revenge.* He cruised in the North and Irish seas and in the Atlantic Ocean, taking many prizes, burning some, and sending others into Spanish ports. This bold adventuring into waters where British supremacy had been seldom challenged caused much excitement in London, greatly alarmed the coast towns, increased the cost of insurance, and made the name of Conyngham to be more dreaded than had been that of Thurot, the famous French corsair, in the Seven Years' War. Prints were issued in London and Paris caricaturing him. One of these represented him as a ferocious pirate of gigantic and powerful frame, with a belt full of pistols, and in the right hand a sword of great size. The legend beneath it described the American captain as *"la terreur des Anglais."*

During the early part of 1778 Conyngham cruised with much success out of Spanish ports. One of his cruises extended as far as the Azores and the Canary Islands. Finally, owing to British protests, the Spanish government became less hospitable and Conyngham sailed for the West Indies. Off St. Eustatius he captured two British privateers, with valuable cargoes. Turning his prow homeward, he arrived in Philadelphia on Feb. 21, 1779, with a ship-load of military supplies. In eighteen months he had taken sixty prizes (Neeser, *post,* p. xlvi). The *Revenge* was now sold to some Philadelphia merchants, fitted out as a privateer, and sent to sea with Conyngham in command. Leaving the Delaware, he sailed for a cruise off New York and soon after arriving at his cruising grounds, was captured Apr. 27, 1779, by the British naval vessel *Galatea,* and later imprisoned in the "condemned dungeon." In the following July he was sent to England in irons and confined first in Pendennis Castle, Falmouth, and later in Mill Prison, Plymouth. As a punishment for what the British chose to regard as piratical depredations on their commerce, his confinement was made unusually severe. At first put in irons, often lodged at night in the "black hole," and at no time supplied with proper and sufficient food, he underwent sufferings from which he never fully recovered. The Continental Congress retaliated by subjecting an officer of the Royal Navy to close confinement in the American prison in Boston. Twice Conyngham attempted to escape. Finally, on Nov. 3, 1779, he made a third attempt and succeeded in digging his way out of Mill Prison—"committing treason through his Majesty's earth," as he expressed it. Reaching London he found friends and money, went to Holland, and at Texel embarked on the *Alliance*, flagship of John Paul Jones, which after a cruise put into Corunna. Here Conyngham took passage for America on board the *Experiment*. On Mar. 17, 1780, this vessel fell into the hands of the enemy and shortly the adventurous captain once more found himself within the confines of Mill Prison. A year elapsed before he was exchanged. He was preparing at Nantes for a cruise in the ship *Layona* when the news of peace arrived. After the Revolution Conyngham returned to the merchant service. He tried to reënter the navy, but failed. He petitioned Congress for compensation for his Revolutionary services, but his prayer was not granted. During the War of 1812 as a member of the Common Council of Philadelphia he assisted in the defense of that city. He and his wife, Ann (Hockley) Conyngham, whom he married in 1773, are buried in St. Peter's churchyard, Philadelphia.

[The best account of Conyngham is found in R. W. Neeser, "Letters and Papers relating to the Cruises of Gustavus Conyngham" (*Naval Hist. Soc. Pubs.*, vol. VI, 1915), introduction. This book and "The Tragedy of the Lost Commission" by James Barnes in the *Outlook*, LXXIII, 71–83 (1903), contain excellent portraits and illustrations. Other sources are H. E. Hayden, *The Reminiscences of David Hayfield Conyngham* (1904); C. H. Jones, *Capt. Gustavus Conyngham* (1903); G. W. Allen, *A Naval Hist. of the Am. Revolution* (1913); S. Hazard, *Hazard's Register of Pa.*, vols. V and VI (1830); and R. W. Neeser, *Les Croisières du Capitaine Conyngham* (1928).]   C. O. P.

COODE, JOHN (d. 1709), adventurer, emerged from obscurity when, in 1676, he took a seat in the Maryland Assembly as a delegate from St. Marys County. He immediately became active in proceedings for the protection of the frontier from the Indians. Subsequently he was charged with accusing Catholics of committing murders that were usually laid to Indians. He became an associate of Josias Fendall as early as 1681. The two were arrested that year on a charge of attempting to stir up mutiny and sedition. Coode was not found guilty but was reproved for his "love to amaze the ignorant and make sport with his wit." The governor and council requested that Coode, while under indictment, be suspended

from his seat in the lower house of the Assembly. In the dispute that arose from this request it was stated that at a session of the St. Marys county court in which Coode was sitting as a justice of the peace he, who had once been a clergyman, behaved so debauchedly and profanely that the court issued an order to put him under bonds to keep the peace; that he contemptuously tore and disobeyed the order; that the proprietor then vacated his commission as a justice of the peace; and that since then Coode had for revenge persisted in spreading false scandalous reports, uttering mutinous and seditious speeches, and threatening a force of ten thousand men to subvert the government. Coode's opportunity came in 1689 when a messenger's death caused delay in an official recognition of the new Protestant monarchs of England by the Catholic government of Maryland, which the preceding year had joyfully acclaimed the birth of a Catholic heir to the English throne. The failure of such recognition gave credence to an oft repeated rumor that the Catholics were in a conspiracy with the Indians to massacre the Protestants, and in July of this year Coode, as captain of the militia of a "Protestant Association" with about seven hundred men at his command, seized the government. In a series of falsehoods, mixed with some truth, he represented to the King that the proprietor had forfeited his rights and that the Association had acted only in the interest of his Majesty's service and the Protestant religion. Assuming the title of general he, in the name of the King, called for the election of an Assembly and to this body he and his associates surrendered the supreme authority which they had usurped. In August 1690 he sailed for England to prove his charges against the proprietor, saying on the way over that what he had done "was in prejudice or revenge to the Lord Baltimore." He was among those recommended by the first royal governor to a seat in his council, but was not appointed. He was elected to the Assembly in 1696 but was denied a seat, on the ground that he had once been a Roman Catholic priest and was therefore ineligible. He then hatched a plot against the governor, was indicted by grand jury, and fled to Virginia. At this time he was characterized as "so hainously flagitious and wicked scarce to be paralleled in the Province." In 1701 he was pardoned on his own abject petition. He was again elected in 1708, but, after sitting a few days, was again excluded. He died in March 1709, leaving a widow (Eliza), three sons, three daughters, and four plantations.

[The *Archives of Maryland* contain about all that is known of Coode. The most important secondary sources are B. C. Steiner, "Protestant Revolution in Maryland" in the *Annual Report of the Am. Hist. Asso. for the Year 1897,* being *House Doc. No. 577,* 55 Cong., 2 Sess., and W. H. Browne, *Md., the Hist. of a Palatinate* (1884).]   N. D. M.

COOK, ALBERT STANBURROUGH (Mar. 6, 1853–Sept. 1, 1927), scholar, was seventh in descent from Ellis Cook, who was settled at Southampton, L. I., by the year 1644, and whose great-grandson, Ellis, removed to Morris County, N. J., about 1747. Albert's father, Frederick Weissenfels Cook (1802–74), of Montville, Morris County, had by a second wife, Sarah Barmore (1824–96), three children, of whom Albert, the eldest, owed qualities of heart to his mother, and intellectual powers to his grandfather, Silas Cook (d. 1852). At the age of five he had read the Bible through, and used a dictionary. At six he began an interrupted schooling, first under a Mr. Whittlesey; at twelve he had some weeks, with a little French and German, at Miss Crane's school in the neighboring Boonton. He spent a year or more of his frail boyhood working in New York City. At fifteen he taught in a country school at Towaco; at Taylortown some of his pupils were older than he. In after years he said that he would not take a million dollars for his experience of poverty. He graduated from the Latin-scientific course in Rutgers College, at the head of the class of 1872, and remained for a year as tutor in mathematics. Thereafter (1873–77) he taught at the Freehold (N. J.) Institute, continued reading poetry, privately studied Greek, and hoped to become a teacher of English at Rutgers. On his return from a year (1877–78) at Göttingen and Leipzig, the promised position was refused him because he had censured the mismanagement of the Rutgers Grammar School. Jacob Cooper [*q.v.*] now recommended him to the Johns Hopkins University; Cook here became associate in English, and organized the department. Again he went abroad (1881–82) to study Old English, first in London with Sweet, and then with Sievers in Jena, where in 1882 he won the doctorate with honors. He returned to a professorship in the University of California, whence he exerted a yet visible influence upon the schools of the state. In May 1889, he was called to Yale; at his request, in October he was entitled professor of the English language and literature. For thirty-two years he was active in the professorship, not lecturing, but employing an inductive dialectic that was effective in turning graduate students into scholars. He was himself indefatigable in productive scholarship. When he retired in 1921 some of his best research, in the background of Old English poetry, and in Chaucer, was yet to be done. Gradually beset by

angina pectoris, he still produced virtually to the end, taking his work for a patriotic as well as a Christian and universal duty. He was twice married: in 1886 to Emily Chamberlain (d. 1908); and in 1911 to Elizabeth Merrill. Latterly he spent his summers at Greensboro, Vt., and there did much of his constructive work— with intensive hay-farming as an avocation.

Apart from travel abroad, numerous calls to university chairs, honorary degrees, and the establishment of prizes in poetry and philosophy, the chief items in his life were his scholarly publications. Though seldom working at night, in productive capacity he was amazing; and his effect upon his pupils was catalytic. Some seventy-five Yale Studies in English (1898) partly show his stimulus in training doctors of philosophy, who have diffused his eclectic method. A bibliography of over 300 titles speaks for his own research. In Old English, besides adapting Sievers's *Grammar* (1885, 1903), he published an excellent *First Book* (1894, 1903) for beginners, and edited *Judith* (1888, 1889, 1904), the *Christ of Cynewulf* (1900), *The Dream of the Road* (1905), *Elene, Phœnix, and Physiologus* (1919). His *Literary Middle English Reader* (1915) was a welcome innovation. He did much for the study of the English Bible in its origins and influence; much also for the art of poetry by editing the treatises of Sidney, Shelley, Horace, Vida, Boileau, Addison, Hunt, and Newman. A sample of his scholarly method is *The Date of the Ruthwell and Bewcastle Crosses* (1913). His philosophy of scholarship may be seen in a presidential address to the Modern Language Association, *The Province of English Philology* (1898); his ideals in *The Artistic Ordering of Life* (1898); his style and personal quality in his tribute to Jacob Cooper (1906). A complete *Bibliography* of his writings up to 1923 was "printed for private circulation" at New Haven in that year. His publications from then on (some posthumous) are chiefly found in *Speculum, Modern Language Notes,* the *Philological Quarterly,* and the *Transactions of the Connecticut Academy of Arts and Sciences.* This list gives no hint of his many briefer articles and notes. His interests ranged from ancient to modern literature, and in English from Caedmon to Kipling. He regarded the study of language and literature as inseparable. He united contrary powers, moving patiently, yet, where possible, swiftly. Tender-hearted, he was uncompromising enough not to be popular. He had loyal friends, but was not prone to mingle with scholars of his own age, although he maintained a large and spirited correspondence. He lavished himself on his accepted pupils, and, hating folly and pretense, was quick to recognize intelligent endeavor. His occasional praise was remembered. The scholar and teacher in him were at one; the affair of his life was the advancement of learning, for the enrichment of private and communal well-being.

[*Speculum*, II (1927), 499–501; Kemp Malone in *The Johns Hopkins Alumni Mag.*, XV (1927), 116–18; C. H. Whitman in *Rutgers Alumni Mo.*, VII (1927), 28–30; C. G. Osgood in *Jour. Eng. and Germanic Philology*, XXVII (1928), 289–92; information from Mrs. Elizabeth Merrill Cook; personal acquaintance.]

L. C.

COOK, CLARENCE CHATHAM (Sept. 8, 1828–June 2, 1900), art critic, author, journalist, was born in Dorchester, Mass. He was the fourth son of Zebedee and Caroline (Tuttle) Cook, both of early American families. Graduating from Harvard in 1849, he studied architecture at Newburgh, N. Y., but gave it up for teaching and journalism. In September 1853, he was married in New York to Louisa (De Windt) Whittemore, a widow, and great-great-grand-daughter of President John Adams. She was intellectual and of artistic tastes, and the marriage proved exceptionally happy. Cook first attracted attention in 1863 by a series of bold and satirical criticisms of a loan collection of paintings at the Sanitary Fair, New York. His spirited art column in the *New York Tribune*, 1863–69, was read by every one, but so scathing, almost brutal, were his attacks on contemporary work that a delegation of his victims visited Horace Greeley to protest (to that editor's amusement), and Cook was feared, rather than loved, by American artists. In 1869 Greeley sent him to Paris as special correspondent, but war broke out in 1870 and drove Cook home, after some months in Italy. His *Tribune* connection ceased in the early seventies, owing partly to his resentment that Greeley's successor, Whitelaw Reid, had curtailed his space. In 1869 had been published his pamphlet on *The New York Central Park*. Now came the following: a translation of Viardot's *Wonders of Sculpture*, with a chapter by Cook on American Sculpture (1873); the text for a heliotype reproduction of Dürer's *Life of the Virgin* (1878); an American edition of Lübke's *History of Art* (1878); *The House Beautiful* (1878), his most successful book; *What Shall We Do With Our Walls?* (1881); *Art and Artists of Our Time* (3 vols., 1888); besides various contributions to magazines and art books and, in 1882, a pamphlet savagely attacking the Cypriote antiquities of the Metropolitan Museum of Art and the character of Cesnola under the title

Transformations and Migrations of Certain Statues in the Cesnola Collection. He and Feuardent, his friend and publisher, succeeded for some years in shaking the confidence of the public in the collection and the collector; but they were not archeologists and later Cypriote scholarship has sustained Cesnola (see sketch of Luigi Palma de Cesnola). Cook failed to testify in the lawsuit of *Feuardent* vs. *Cesnola* which grew out of the controversy, writing the *New York Times* that "he had no evidence to give as to facts within his own knowledge"—certainly a reflection upon his pamphlet—yet he continued his vindictive attacks on Cesnola and the Museum from the editorial chair of *The Studio*, which he occupied from 1884 to 1892, when his name disappeared as editor. The magazine was financially unsuccessful and often unable to appear, but from 1886 it was beautifully illustrated by a variety of new processes, including photo-etching, and Cook helped to introduce the use of etching as a reproductive art. Publication ceased in November 1894.

Clarence Cook ranks as a brilliant pioneer in the professional criticism of art in America. If his pen was dipped in gall, it may have been his reaction to the undiscerning praise then in vogue. He was among the first in America to appreciate the Impressionists. His style was lucid and when he was not on the war-path it was also graceful and urbane. He was much in demand as a drawing-room lecturer. Personally, he was charming. All who knew him recall his pleasant voice and manner, his gentleness and culture, the atmosphere, altogether gracious and graceful, that enveloped him.

[*Internat. Studio*, Nov. 1900, Supp., p. ii; N. Y. *Sun*, N. Y. *Tribune*, *Evening Post* (N. Y.), June 3, 1900; interviews and correspondence with neighbors and acquaintances.]

F. B. H.

COOK, FLAVIUS JOSEPHUS (Jan. 26, 1838–June 24, 1901), lecturer, was descended from Francis Cook, one of the Pilgrim fathers. He was born in Ticonderoga, N. Y., the son of William Henry and Merett (Lamb) Cook, and grandson of Warner Cook of New Milford, Conn. A farmer's boy, he attended schools in the neighborhood of his birthplace, and read every book he could obtain. To complete his preparation for college he went to Phillips Academy, Andover, and entered Yale in 1858. In 1861 he broke down in health and was obliged to leave, but later went to Harvard, where he graduated with honors in 1865. Graduating three years later from Andover Theological Seminary, he remained there for another year of post-graduate study. For two years he preached in the vicinity of Boston and then went abroad for another two years, studying at several German universities and traveling in Southern Europe, Egypt, and Palestine. On his return, having modified "Flavius Josephus" into plain "Joseph," he resumed preaching and also started to lecture. In 1874 he was invited to lead the Monday noon prayer-meetings in Tremont Temple. He accepted, and under his leadership they increased so amazingly in attendance that a year later they became the Monday Lectures. In 1877 he married Georgiana Hemingway of New Haven, Conn. For nearly twenty years, Cook's Boston Monday lectures were one of the striking features of that city. Year after year, on Monday noon, Tremont Temple was thronged to hear the lecturer "present the results of the freshest English, German, and American scholarship on the more important and difficult topics concerning the relation of Religion and Science," together with "Preludes on Current Reform." As their fame increased the lectures were repeated elsewhere, were published in newspapers in the United States and in England, were again published in book form, and were translated into various foreign languages. A great, burly man, with a massive head covered with reddish hair and beard, Cook spoke in an oracular manner which greatly impressed his audience. The doctrine of evolution and the philosophical theories connected with it were then disturbing the faith of many. It was a great comfort to such to listen to one who was ardently orthodox in his sympathies, who seemed to have all knowledge at his fingers' ends, and who made so clear and plain that what the scientists and philosophers were saying was either incorrect or entirely in harmony with revealed religion. But his statements were not allowed to go unchallenged either by theologians or by scientists. The latter were especially severe, as may be inferred from the titles of two criticisms of Cook, viz., "Spread Eagle Philosophy" in *The Popular Science Monthly Supplement,* June 1878, and "Theological Charlatanism," by John Fiske in the *North American Review,* March 1881. There is no reason to doubt Cook's sincerity, but his learning was not accurate or profound, and he was often unfair to those whose views he opposed. Even his friends also acknowledged that his belief in his own learning and ability was exaggerated. He was sensational in his methods; but, in his own fashion, he helped to convince his hearers that science and philosophy are not at enmity with religion and thus helped to combat obscurantism. Of the eleven volumes of his lectures that were published in book form, the most popular was his *Biology* (1877). The others were *Transcendentalism* (1877), *Orthodoxy* (1877), *Conscience* (1878), *Heredity* (1878), *Marriage* (1878), *Labor* (1879), *Socialism* (1880), *Occident* (1884), *Orient* (1886), and *Current Religious Perils* (1888). Cook made a lecturing tour of the world, speaking to great crowds in the British Isles, India, Australia, and Japan. In 1895 he started on a second world tour, but in Australia he suffered a sudden stroke, from which he never fully recovered. Brought back to America, he was able after 1899 to lecture a few times, but in 1901 he died as a result of the grippe.

[The chief sources for the life of Cook are articles in the *Congregationalist,* July 6, 1901, and *Zion's Herald,* June 21, 1911. Obituaries were published in the *N. Y. Tribune,* June 26, 1901, and various other journals of the day; but his popularity had greatly declined, so that his death did not attract widespread notice.]

T. D. B.

COOK, GEORGE CRAM (Oct. 7, 1873–Jan. 14, 1924), founder and director of the Provincetown Players, had a New England ancestry and a Middle-Western background. His father, Edward Everett Cook, was a lawyer in Davenport, Iowa; his mother, Ellen Katherine Dodge, a woman of unworldly nature and liberal sympathies. From her the son inherited qualities which were to make him part artist and part seer. Educated at the University of Iowa, Harvard, Heidelberg, and Geneva, he taught English literature at the University of Iowa and later at Leland Stanford. In 1902 he married Sara Herndon Swain of Chicago, and the following year published a quasi-Nietzschean romance, *Roderick Taliaferro, a Story of Maximilian's Empire.* Then, spurning the academic realm, he went to the gardener's cottage on the family estate and sought to support a literary life by chicken-raising and truck-farming, to the chagrin of his young wife and the scandal of local respectable society. The marriage did not long survive this experiment. An enthusiasm for Nietzsche had led him to an aristocratic Anarchism. Now, drawn toward the local group of Socialists, he revised upon Marxian lines his hopes of the Superman, and in 1911 produced a Socialist novel, *The Chasm.* A second mariage, in 1908, with Mollie A. Price of Chicago, who bore him two children, Nilla and Harl, was broken up a few years later. He went to Chicago, where he was associate literary editor of the *Evening Post,* and then to New York, where in 1913 he married Susan Glaspell of Davenport, a fellow writer. Their summers were spent in Provincetown, Mass., seasonally inhabited by artists and writers; and these, under Cook's leadership, organized the Provincetown Players, establishing in

1915 a tiny Playwrights' Theatre in New York, which within a few years had a profound influence upon the American stage. There had been "little theatres" in America before; the special distinction of this one was its complete break with the tradition of producing exotic European plays, and its program of discovering and encouraging vigorous American talent of a sort not welcome on Broadway. Its success was such that Broadway proceeded presently to enrich itself with many of the talents thus brought to light in the stable-theatre on Macdougal St.

What to another would have been a sufficient achievement remained for Cook a disappointment. Seer more than artist, he had never been fully articulate either in his novels or in his plays, despite the grandeur of their conceptions; meanwhile his creative energies spilled over in talk so luminous and profound, in friendships so stimulating, that they conveyed to all who knew him an impression of true greatness far exceeding his tangible achievements. The little theatre, too, fell short of his dream. "I am forced to confess," he wrote, "that the attempt to build up, by our own life and death, in an alien sea, a coral island of our own, has failed." Haunted by a sense of frustration, he left the scene of what appeared to be his triumph, and went away on his last pilgrimage. The Greece of Pericles had been the earliest, and it was to be the final, symbol of his hopes for a beautiful world to be achieved by the travail of humanity. Accordingly it was to Greece that he went, with his wife, in 1921; and in Greece the seer was instinctively recognized and honored. He fraternized with poets and scholars and peasants; he adopted the peasant costume; he built a wall of Cyclopean rock; that was all: but when he died, in 1924, the shepherds left their flocks and gave him a funeral. "He belongs to us," they said. At the petition of the poets of Greece, the government gave a stone from the sacred ruins of Delphi to mark his grave; the Pythian games were reinstituted in his honor; and he has passed into the legends and songs of the Greek peasantry.

[Susan Glaspell, in *The Road to the Temple* (1926), has written a romantic but faithful and documented biography of her husband. *Greek Coins* (1925), poems by George Cram Cook, with Memorabilia by Floyd Dell, Edna Kenton, and Susan Glaspell, contains prefatory information concerning the Davenport, Provincetown, and Greek periods of his life, and the poems have autobiographic value. The English and modern Greek edition of his play, *The Athenian Women* (1926), published in Athens, contains a biographical sketch by Leandros K. Palamas. *Who's Who in America, 1922–23*, records the chief dates of his career. Personal memories dating from 1904 to 1921 are also drawn upon here.]   F. D.

COOK, GEORGE HAMMELL (Jan. 5, 1818–Sept. 22, 1889), geologist and educator, the third son of John and Sarah Munn Cook, was born at Hanover, Morris County, N. J. His paternal ancestors were English who settled in Lynn, Mass., in 1640, but soon after removed to Southampton, L. I., and later to Hanover. His early training was gained at the common country schools. At eighteen years of age, he was employed in surveying for the Morris & Essex and Catskill & Canajoharie railroads. In 1838 he entered the Rensselaer Polytechnic Institute at Troy, N. Y., where Amos Eaton [q.v.] was teaching geology as he understood it. It is a fair assumption that it was through Eaton's influence that Cook's attention was turned toward geology. On his graduation, in 1839, he was employed first as tutor at the Institute, during which time he pursued graduate studies and received the degree of B.N.S. and M.S. Later he became adjunct professor, and after 1842 senior professor. On Mar. 6, 1846, he married Mary Halsey Thomas. In the same year apparently in doubt as to his calling, or for lack of opportunity, he abandoned teaching and for two years was engaged in the business of glass-making in Albany. In 1848, however, he returned to his profession and was appointed professor of mathematics and natural philosophy in the Albany Academy, of which he became principal in 1851. In 1852 his geological qualifications received recognition through his being sent under state auspices to study salt deposits in Europe, with a view to the development of those of Onondaga County. In 1853, he accepted the chair of chemistry and natural science in Rutgers College, with which institution he retained connection for the remainder of his life. In 1854 he was appointed an assistant to William Kitchell on the geological survey of the state. In 1864, by act of the legislature, he was made state geologist, an office he continued to hold in connection with his professorship in the college until his death. While state agricultural colleges were being established under the Morrill Act, Cook was successful in having the New Jersey institution connected with Rutgers, and became vice-president of the combination. He was also active in the formation of a State Board of Agriculture and became permanently a member of the executive board. In 1879 he interested himself in the subject of agricultural experiment stations and brought the matter before the state legislature, succeeding, the year following, in having one established in New Jersey. He was made director of this station, and was of influence later in promoting the Act of Congress of 1887 creating like stations in all the states.

Among Cook's chief geological accomplishments while on the Kitchell Survey were his reports on the Greensand beds and the apparent recent subsidence of the coast which was still in progress, a fact made apparent by the buried stumps and logs in the coastal swamps. As state geologist, he worked out the structural relationships of the beds of iron ore and of the fine and potter's clays. Both of these were matters of economic importance by means of which he might have profited financially, had he been willing to sacrifice his profession. Under his survey too, important work was done in tracing out the continuation of the great terminal moraine in the northern part of the state. The topographic and geologic maps issued under his administration were among the best of any survey up to that date. The water power and water supply of the state were made the subject of investigation and he early advocated the drainage and reclamation, for the purpose of agriculture, of the swamp lands along the Pequest and Passaic rivers. In connection with this work he was made president of the New Brunswick Board of Water Commissioners and a member of the State Board of Health.

His most important publications were his *Geology of New Jersey* (1872), a volume of 900 pages, and his *Report on the Clay Deposits of Woodbridge, South Amboy, and other places in New Jersey* (1878), the latter in collaboration with J. C. Smock. His work, with the exception of that on the glacial moraine and the sinking of the coast, was almost wholly of a practical nature. "His reports had the rare merit of plain, concise, yet clear statement of the facts which were understood by those for whom they were written" (Smock, *post*, pp. 325–26). As a teacher, Cook was beloved by his pupils to whom he had the faculty of imparting confidence in themselves and enthusiasm for their work. With the public at large, he was respected as a thoroughly upright and honest Christian gentleman, one who was ever helpful and humane. He won the confidence of legislatures by his earnestness and honesty of purpose. He worked hard, continuously, and faithfully with never a selfish motive and died suddenly of heart failure in the midst of his labor.

[G. K. Gilbert, "Memoir of Geo. Hammell Cook," in *Nat. Acad. Sci. Biog. Memoirs*, vol. IV (1902); *Commemorative Addresses* by James Neilson, A. S. Hewitt, J. W. Powell and others, June 17, 1890; an obituary notice in the *Bull. Geol. Soc. of America*, vol. I (1890); J. C. Smock, in the *Am. Geologist*, vol. IV (1889); correspondence and personal information. Full bibliography of Cook's publications in J. M. Nickles, "Geol. Literature on North America, 1785–1918," in *Bull. 746, U. S. Geol. Survey* (1923).]   G. P. M.

COOK, ISAAC (July 4, 1810–June 23, 1886), politician, wine merchant, was born at Long Branch, N. J. His father, Stephen Cook, a Quaker farmer, was a Tory during the Revolution. His mother was the daughter of Daniel Denniston, a patriot of some military note. Cook's education must have been curtailed, for before he was twenty he had served several years in a New York mercantile establishment. With a small amount of capital in hand he went to Chicago about 1834. He invested his money in the Rialto, a boarding-house with saloon attached, on North Dearborn St. As his capital grew he kept it invested in city property and he soon became well-to-do. He became identified with the Democratic politics of the city and state, and from 1838 he was one of Senator Douglas's foremost lieutenants. He was favored by the party: in 1844 he was made agent of the canal lands; he served Cook County four years as sheriff and a like term as treasurer. In 1854 he had a hand in founding the *Chicago Daily Times*, a paper which came to the defense of Douglas when other Democratic papers were repudiating him for his part in the repeal of the Missouri Compromise. Cook was appointed postmaster in March 1855 by President Pierce. He was succeeded by William Price shortly after the inauguration of Buchanan. When the break came between Douglas and the administration in 1858, Cook supported President Buchanan. He was reappointed postmaster on Mar. 9, 1858. In May he was associated with others in the founding of the *Daily Chicago Herald* in opposition to the *Times*, the Douglas organ. In 1860 rival Democratic conventions were held in the state for choosing delegates to the Charleston convention. The so-called "Danite" faction, led by Cook, repudiated Douglas and the Freeport doctrine, and upheld the Dred Scott decision and Buchanan's stand on Kansas. A delegation, headed by Cook, went to Charleston, but Douglas prevented their being seated. Cook took up the cause of Breckinridge in the election of 1860. Lincoln's victory in that election brought an end to Cook's career as a politician.

Cook's business interests were highly successful. In 1853 he built the Young American Hotel (later the Revere House) at the corner of Dearborn and Randolph Sts. This was the first five-story brick building in the city. For a time he was assistant treasurer of the Chicago, Rock Island & Pacific Railroad. In 1859 he became president of the American Wine Company of St. Louis, and in 1861 removed to that city. Under his energetic direction the company attained a leading place in the wine industry of the country.

Extensive vineyards in northern Ohio were owned by the Cook interests. His name was given to a variety of wine grape developed through his selection. He was a connoisseur of wines and maintained that his vintages did not suffer by comparison with the more famous European wines. He continued in the direction of the wine interests until his death at Eureka Springs, Ark., in 1886. Cook's wife was Harriet Norton of English parentage. They had three children, one of whom carried on the business of the American Wine Company.

[Wm. Hyde and Howard L. Conard, *Encyc. of the Hist. of St. Louis* (1899), I, 479 ff.; the *Times* (Chicago), June 25, 1886; F. W. Scott, *Newspapers and Periodicals of Illinois* (1910), p. 65; A. C. Cole, *The Era of the Civil War* (1919).]   W. T. U.

COOK, JAMES MERRILL (Nov. 19, 1807– Apr. 12, 1868), capitalist, politician and financial officer, was the son of James Cook, the head of an established New York family settled in Saratoga County, N. Y. The father was a lawyer and judge living in Ballston Spa, where James Merrill Cook was born. His family had the tradition of education and professional training, and a general liberal education was offered to James. As his earlier schooling drew to a close, however, a preference for business manifested itself, and resulted in a transfer to New York City, where the young man was appointed to a clerkship in a commercial house. He retained close relationship with affairs in his own town, nevertheless, and when about thirty-one years of age returned to Ballston Spa to live, where he became conspicuous in party politics, strongly advocating Whig principles. Much of his time thereafter was spent in running for, and in holding, elective offices. He was chosen a member of the constitutional convention of 1846, and his service in that connection was followed by an election to the state Senate in 1848. He served as state senator 1848–51. From that position he passed to a place as state treasurer. An election contest led to a decision in favor of his opponent, but after a brief period out of office he was named state comptroller, a place which he held from 1854 to 1855.

At this time, New York, in common with a good many other states, was passing through a period of banking disturbance. While the panics and commercial stringencies of the decade 1850–60 were not, even locally, due to the banking system of the State of New York, that system at least did not much alleviate them. Leading citizens rightly ascribed an important influence upon the financial stability of the State to the management and supervision of the banks. In these circumstances Cook was offered and accepted the position of superintendent of the state Banking Department in the year 1856. He was at that time president of a local institution, the Ballston Spa Bank, and, being a man of substantial means, was a large stockholder both in it and a number of other institutions. He was thus in a very distinct way representative of the country banking interests which have always been powerful in New York. His five years of service proved a notable period in the history of the Banking Department. He was able to restore a very substantial degree of order among the banks and to repress and punish many frauds. Moreover his annual reports showed an increasing mastery of financial theory and his last two, those of Dec. 31, 1859, and Dec. 10, 1860, were rightly viewed as documents well above the prevailing level of financial discussion. In these he furnished a thoughtful discussion of the panics of 1857 and 1859 and a keen analysis of the characteristics of the banking law of the state. His notable success in the department of banking was followed by another election to the state Senate in 1864. In 1858 he had been considered by the Republican state convention as a candidate for the governorship, for he represented the same ideas that were entertained by William H. Seward, with whom he was closely associated, but at his own suggestion the candidacy was withdrawn. He was throughout his life largely interested in the local affairs, both business and political, of his own county, and was in a real sense its leading citizen.

[*Hist. of Saratoga County, N. Y.* (1899), esp. p. 196; De Alva S. Alexander, *A Political Hist. of the State of N. Y.* (1906), II, 188, 247; E. A. Weimer, *Civil List and Constitutional Hist. of the Colony and State of N. Y.* (1889); obituaries in *Albany Evening Jour.*, Apr. 13, 1868; *N. Y. Tribune*, Apr. 14, 1868; *N. Y. Herald*, Apr. 15, 1868; *Banker's Mag.*, May 1868.]
H. P. W.

COOK, JOHN WILLISTON (Apr. 20, 1844– July 16, 1922), educator, was born near Oneida, N. Y. His father, Harry Dewitt Cook, decided to seek his fortune in the new state of Illinois upon learning that Congress had authorized the construction of the Illinois Central Railroad. In 1851, when John was seven, the family established a home near Bloomington, and his father engaged in the building of bridges for the railroad. When the road was completed, he became a station-master and grain-dealer. Later, he served two terms in the Assembly, was a cavalry officer in the Union army, and at the time of his death in 1873 was chairman of the State Railroad and Warehouse Commission. His various interests were not without formative influence on his son who, outside of school-hours, assisted him in his office work and accompanied him to political meetings. In the companionship of his father and the latter's numerous acquaintances, John Williston Cook acquired the readiness of address and genial manner which were so characteristic of him in later life. His mother, Joanna Hall Cook, who had been a school-teacher, instilled in him early a love of books and study. After a period of elementary schooling, he entered the Illinois State Normal University. Graduating in 1865, he became principal of the public school at Brimfield, Ill. A year later he returned to his alma mater, where he remained for thirty-three years —the first two as instructor in the training department, one as instructor in geography and history, seven as instructor in reading, and fourteen as head of the department of mathematics. In 1890 he became president of the school, and remained in that office until he resigned nine years later. On Aug. 26, 1867, Cook married Lydia Farnham Spofford of North Andover, Mass. The daughter of a schoolmaster, she was quite familiar with her husband's problems and gave him much intelligent encouragement. The period 1866–99 was crowded with plans and accomplishments. In 1874, Cook purchased an interest in the *Illinois Schoolmaster,* which he edited for two years in collaboration with Edwin C. Hewett. With the purchase of the *Illinois School Journal* in 1883, Cook again essayed the rôle of editor. At the end of the first year, he invited R. R. Reeder to collaborate with him, and this arrangement continued until 1886 when the magazine was sold. Cook was an untiring worker, and the tremendous energy for which he was noted served him in good stead during this period of engrossing activity. His frequent articles on all phases of educational theory and practise and his numerous addresses in many states won him national recognition as an educator. In 1880 he was elected president of the Illinois State Teachers Association; in 1896, president of the Normal Department of the National Education Association; and in 1904, president of the Association. When the Northern Illinois State Normal School was established at De Kalb in 1899, Cook was chosen as its organizer and first president. Here he emphasized the training department, and won his reputation as a teacher of teachers. During this period he published his *Educational History of Illinois* (Chicago, 1912), and collaborated with Miss N. Cropsey in the publication of a series of arithmetics. The varied activities of his earlier years were continued with unabated vigor until his resignation on Aug. 1, 1919. His death followed three years later.

[The chief source is Cook's own book, *Educ. Hist. of Ill.* (1912), pp. 215, 216, 245, 246, 248, 249, 251, 259, 278, 447, 450, 451, 519, 540–41. See also *Who's Who in America,* 1922–23; obituary notice in the *Illinois Teacher,* Sept. 1922.]   R. F. S.

COOK, JOSEPH. [See COOK, FLAVIUS JOSEPHUS, 1838–1901.]

COOK, MARTHA ELIZABETH DUNCAN WALKER (July 23, 1806–Sept. 15, 1874), author, editor, and translator, was born in Northumberland, Pa., the daughter of Jonathan Hoge and Mary (Duncan) Walker. Her father had been a soldier in the Revolution, and was afterward in succession, a judge of the common pleas, of the high court of errors and appeals of Pennsylvania, and of the federal district court. Robert J. Walker [*q.v.*], her brother, was governor of the territory of Kansas under President Buchanan, secretary of the treasury under President Polk, and, during the Civil War, a prominent supporter of the Union cause. The family moved to Pittsburgh when Martha was about fourteen. She received most of her education from her father, who had a classical as well as a legal training. From him she derived intellectual and literary tastes and a passion for justice which she was never to lose. Her marked social qualities made her an excellent conversationalist and correspondent, and enabled her to draw out the best qualities of those who came in contact with her. At the age of eighteen she married Lieut. William Cook, later chief engineer of the Philadelphia & Trenton Railroad (1836–65) and brigadier-general of New Jersey militia from 1848 until his death (G. W. Cullum, *Biographical Register of the Officers and Graduates of the U. S. Military Academy,* 3rd ed., 1893). Mrs. Cook, unsatisfied with a life filled solely with social duties, devoted herself to study, the instruction of her children, and literary pursuits. From 1863 to 1864 she was editor of the *Continental Monthly,* founded in 1862 by James R. Gilmore "to advocate emancipation as a political necessity," and published in New York. To this periodical she contributed numerous poems, sketches, and tales of transitory interest.

Her admiration for the music and literature of Poland, her sense of outraged justice in the political sufferings of that country, and of the debt of America for the services of Polish *émigrés* in the Revolution made her a warm if occasionally a somewhat sentimental advocate of Poland's cause. She was ready at all times with sympathy and with practical assistance and advice in aid of Polish emigrants, thus rendering a service which endeared her name to Poles at home and in America. In 1871 she wrote an indorsement of the *Appeal to the Friends of Poland in the United States of America* by Count Ladislas Plater, for aid in establishing the Polish Historical Museum at the Château of Rapperswyl, Switzerland. She translated for American readers several works, including, from the French, Franz Liszt's *Life of Chopin* (Boston, 1863); from the German, Guido Goerres's *Life of Joan of Arc* which she published as a serial in the *Freeman's Journal*; and, from the French and German, *The Undivine Comedy and Other Poems* of Count Sigismund Krasinski. This last work was published in 1875, after her death, "in accordance with her desires and as a tribute of honor to disinterested labor and love of abstract justice." With the exception of her rather desultory verse, Mrs. Cook's literary activities seem to have been founded in practical humanitarian aims rather than in the pure joy of writing. Such examples of her style as are available display a vigorous if somewhat rhetorical manner. Her work, as a whole, bears the stamp of sincerity rather than of great literary value. She died in Hoboken, nine years after the death of her husband.

[A brief character study and biographical sketch of Mrs. Cook is contained in "In Memoriam," an editorial note appended to her translation of *The Undivine Comedy and Other Poems* (1875). In addition to the publications mentioned above there is an eight-page pamphlet in verse *Affectionately addressed to Robert J. Walker, Governor of Kansas, by his Sister, Mrs. Martha Walker Cook* (1857). Family history is found in material on Robt. J. Walker. An extended obituary was published in the *N. Y. Tribune*, Sept. 17, 1874.]

A. L. B.

COOK, PHILIP (July 30, 1817–May 20, 1894), lawyer, Confederate soldier, congressman, was the son of Philip and Martha (Wooten) Cook. The elder Cook was born in Brunswick County, Va., in 1775, and was taken as a boy to Georgia. He served as a major in the 18th United States Infantry in the War of 1812 and at the close of that war set up as a cotton planter in Twiggs County, Ga., where he died in 1841. His son Philip received his college training at Oglethorpe University, an institution then located near Milledgeville, the capital of the state, and was subsequently graduated (1841) from the University of Virginia Law School. For a good many years after he took up his residence at Oglethorpe in Madison County, Cook's life seems to have been uneventful. On the outbreak of the Civil War he volunteered as a private with the Macon County Volunteers, his company being assigned to the 4th Georgia Regiment at Portsmouth, Va. There he was made adjutant of his regiment. After the Seven Days' battles about Richmond he was commissioned lieutenant-colonel. His regiment passed through the battles of Second Manassas and Sharpsburg, and he was promoted to colonel. He was in the brigade of Gen. George Doles, who was killed at the battle

of Cold Harbor in August 1864. Cook, promoted to brigadier-general, succeeded Doles in the command of the brigade. He was several times wounded, the last time at Petersburg. He was captured there and remained in the Petersburg hospital until the close of the war. After the return of peace, Cook changed his residence to Americus, Ga., where he practised law until his retirement in 1880. He was a member of Congress from 1873 to 1883. In 1890 he became secretary of state of Georgia and was holding that position at the time of his death in 1894. In public service for twenty-three years, he had held other offices, among them those of a state senator, 1859–60, and 1863–64, member of the constitutional convention of 1865, and member of the commission which erected the present capitol of Georgia. In 1842 he married Sara, daughter of Henry H. Lumpkin, of Monroe County. His son Philip was secretary of state of Georgia from 1898 to 1918. One of Cook's contemporaries said of him: "No man in Georgia was more entirely beloved by the people of the state."

[W. J. Northen, *Men of Mark in Ga.* (1907–12), III, 298–300; *Atlanta Constitution*, May 21, 1894. There is a good deal of confusion in the numerous sketches of Cook with reference to the exact dates of his birth and death. The figures here given were supplied from family records by his grand-daughter, Mrs. Phinizy Calhoun of Atlanta.]

R. P. B.

COOK, ROBERT JOHNSON (Mar. 21, 1849–Dec. 3, 1922), publisher, rowing coach, originator of the Bob Cook stroke, was born near Cookstown, Pa., the son of John Bell and Matilda (Cunningham) Cook, both of Scotch-Irish ancestry and descendants of pioneers of Western Pennsylvania. When he was twenty years of age, inspired and encouraged by his mother, he quit his father's prosperous farm and enrolled at Phillips Academy, Andover, Mass. He entered Yale with the class of 1875, but had to drop back to the class of 1876, with which he graduated. After graduation, he read law in Greensburgh, Pa., and in Pittsburgh and was admitted to the Allegheny County bar in 1879. After two years in law, and a year abroad he became business manager of the *Philadelphia Press,* a position which he held until 1897, during that time changing a bankrupt paper to one of the most prosperous journals in the country. He was married on Apr. 26, 1881, in Allegheny City, Pa., to Annie Glyde Wells, daughter of Calvin Wells, then owner of the *Philadelphia Press.* They had three daughters but were divorced in 1897.

In the spring of his freshman year at Yale, Cook wandered down to the boat-house, and asked for a chance to row. The Yale boat club in those days was an exclusive organization, in spite of the fact that the crew was being defeated regularly. Cook's request was curtly refused and he was told to keep away. His fighting spirit was roused and day after day he haunted the club. He had already established himself as the best wrestler and boxer in college and no one seemed eager for the job of throwing him out. Finally the captain turned to diplomacy and put Cook in a pair-oar with the strongest and best oar in Yale, hoping in this way to discourage him. In less than a quarter of an hour, Cook, who had never before had his hands on an oar, was pulling the veteran around in a circle. Two weeks later, he was in the varsity boat. That year Yale was again defeated and Cook was elected captain for 1873. All summer and all fall he brooded over the defeat. College rowing in America was then in a very crude state and what little style it possessed had been acquired from professional scullers. The sliding seat was a novelty and most of the crews were still sliding on boards greased with tallow. It was not until the Christmas vacation when Cook, too poor to afford the expense of the trip home, sat in his room reading *Tom Brown at Oxford* that he had an inspiration which still guides American college rowing. He resolved to go to England, somehow, to study English rowing, interviewed President Porter, and won the reserved and scholarly old president's consent. The boat club did not have a dollar in its treasury with which to finance the expedition, but Cook and the same undergraduates who six months before had shut the door of the boat-house in his face, pawned their watches and overcoats and sold their spare furniture, and within a week he was on his way to England. The square-jawed, broad-shouldered young American was cordially received at Cambridge, at Oxford, and by the London Rowing Club. For six weeks he rowed every day and spent the evenings with the coaches. He decided that he would have to modify the orthodox English stroke to fit American boys, that they would not be able to master the exaggerated body swing without a waste of effort and exhaustion. He therefore shortened it and counter-balanced this by emphasizing the form in-board and the finish of the stroke. He returned to New Haven and produced a victorious crew in June. The same year he won the single scull race. From 1876 to 1897, Cook coached thirteen Yale eights, twelve of which were victorious over Harvard. Including the crews he coached as an undergraduate, he won fourteen out of seventeen races against Harvard; two of these races were triangular events in which Cook's crews were de-

feated by Cornell eights coached by Charles E. Courtney [*q.v.*].

In 1896 when Yale and Harvard broke off athletic relations, Cook took the Yale crew to Henley. The Leander Boat Club, composed of former Oxford and Cambridge "Blues," called from as far as South Africa their best oars. Yale was beaten by a fraction of a boat length. The experience convinced Cook that he had refined his stroke too much and on his return he attempted to follow the English stroke more closely. About the same time new policies in his business led to his retirement. He took the change philosophically and became a traveler, spending much of his time in Paris but returning to the house at Belle Vernon, Pa., built by his great-grandfather Col. Edward Cook more than one hundred and fifty years before, to spend his last days. Cook was not only a great teacher of rowing but also of men. Industrious, courageous, and honest, he left with hundreds of boys who came under his teaching, an imprint of sturdy character which they carried through life. Many offers of generous remuneration from other colleges came to him during the years of his success, but he scorned them and gave to Yale, with no thought of reward, his time and his services for twenty-seven years.

[Richard M. Hurd, *A Hist. of Yale Athletics* (1888); Lewis S. Welch and Walter Camp, *Yale, Her Campus, Class-rooms and Athletics* (1899); *Thirty-five Year Class Book of Yale, '76*; *Yale Alumni Weekly*, Dec. 8, 15, and 22, 1922; *Public Ledger* (Phila.), and *N. Y. Times*, Dec. 4, 1922; *Obit. Record of Yale Grads 1922–23*; *Biog. and Portr. Cyc. of Fayette County, Pa.* (1889).]
                           A. H. B.

COOK, RUSSELL S. (Mar. 6, 1811–Sept. 4, 1864), clergyman, was born in New Marlboro, Mass. After a diligent childhood, he set out on the study of law. His main interests shifting to religion, he entered the theological seminary at Auburn, N. Y., and in January 1837 became pastor of the Congregational Church at Lanesboro, Mass. Trouble with his throat caused him in 1838 to abandon the ministry and engage in work for the American Tract Society. Cook brought to it a new spirit—a tireless and explosive determination not only to disseminate publications but to implant principles everywhere, and instantly. He was made corresponding secretary in 1839. During his term of office he put into circulation more than a million volumes. He visited here and there over the widest areas, encouraging sales by appeal sometimes to pure rivalry and sometimes to pure altruism. He merged (1843) the bi-monthly *Trust Magazine* with his new monthly *American Messenger*, and in twelve years increased the circulation from 10,000 to 200,000 copies, not counting 2,500 copies in German. He instituted *The Child's Paper* in 1852 and in two years was printing 300,000 copies. He popularized "colportage," a system by which evangelical itinerants went about the sparsely settled country selling books where possible and giving them away if that course seemed preferable. The scheme was suited to the America of 1841 in which it originated, but it was also adopted in parts of Europe. The Tract Society was widely condemned in the fifties for its evasive attitude regarding slavery, and indeed, while from a large view-point its course may have been defensible, it was actually shown in small and tangible matters to have handled facts loosely. Cook did not find time to reply. Personally, he was moving hither and thither, like a shuttle, about America, and in 1853 and 1856 he visited Europe. During his second visit, in Switzerland, he was seized with an affection of the lungs which necessitated his resigning from his duties with the Tract Society, but, returning home, he still devoted much energy to a Committee for a Better Observation of the Sabbath, with headquarters in New York. He fought his disease stubbornly, visiting in search of relief now Florida, now Maine. He died at Pleasant Valley, N. Y. He was married four times: to Ann Maria Mills of Auburn, in 1837; to Harriet Newell Rand of Pompey Hill, N. Y., in 1841; to Harriet Ellsworth, and to a Miss Malan.

[R. S. Cook, "Sketch of the Sabbath Reform," *The Christian Sabbath* (1863); Am. Tract Soc., *Am. Colporteur System* (1843); *Brief Hist. of the Organization and Work* (1855); W. Jay, *Letter to the Am. Tract Soc., in Relation to Slavery* (1857); *Unanimous Remonstrance of the Fourth Congreg. Ch., Hartford, Conn., against the Policy of the Am. Tract Soc.* (1855); *Tables Turned* (1855); *Ann. Report Am. Tract Soc.,* 1865; *Gen. Biog. Cat. Auburn Theol. Sem.* (1918).]

J. D. W.

COOK, TENNESSEE CELESTE CLAFLIN, Lady (1845-1923). [See WOODHULL, VICTORIA, 1838-1927.]

COOK, WALTER (July 23, 1846–Mar. 25, 1916), architect, was born at Buffalo, N. Y., the son of Edward and Catherine (Ireland) Cook. He entered Yale as a freshman but transferred to Harvard and there received the degree of A.B. in 1869 and A.M. in 1872. He then went to Paris and was one of the earliest Americans to take advantage of the opportunities for architectural training in the École des Beaux-Arts, where he came under the influence of the gifted Vandremer, whose atelier was a center of inspirational instruction. His preparation was broadened by further study in the Royal Polytechnic School at Munich. Returning to New York in 1877 he became the dominating factor successively of the architectural firms of Babb, Cook & Willard; Willard, Babb, Cook & Welch; and Cook & Welch. During his long career many commissions were executed, the most notable among which, designed wholly or in part by him, were the De Vinne Press Building, the New York Life Insurance Building, the residence of Andrew Carnegie, and branch libraries for the New York Public Library in New York City, the stadium of the Pan-American Exposition in Buffalo, and many residences. The Choir School of the Cathedral of St. John the Divine characterizes his mature style. In all of his designs there is an evident fitting of the means to the conditions, an application of modern methods and their utilization in the most efficient manner. He brought to the career of architecture a great fund of collateral knowledge, administrative ability, and educational ideals. His professional performance was thorough and distinguished. It notably influenced the achievement of his time. These characteristics were recognized by his fellow architects in elevating him to the position of president of the New York Chapter of the American Institute of Architects and of the Society of Beaux-Arts Architects; of fellow in the Institute (1891); and finally of president for two terms of the American Institute of Architects (1912–14). His intimate interest in the affairs of the Institute was continued to the time of his death, as a member of the Board of Directors. The city of New York made him a member of the Municipal Art Commission (1905–07), consulting architect of the Board of Estimate and Apportionment, and of the Court House Board. As an architectural adviser he was a member of the competition juries for the selection of architects for the New York Public Library and for the University of California. He was also signally honored by election as a member of the National Institute of Arts and Letters, and as Academician and Chevalier of the Légion d'honneur, France.

Walter Cook was "a man of rare qualifications, of wide and genial culture, imbued with that kind of personal dignity and charm which well fitted him to represent the architects of this country on all occasions requiring tact and judgment, executive and administrative ability. . . . He was always simple and 'get-attable' [*sic*] with a delightful sense of humor, gentle and kindly though ever ready to fight when a principle was involved" (Hastings, *post*). He was married in Paris on Nov. 18, 1876, to Marie Elizabeth Hugot of Fresnes, Yonne, France. She died in 1888, and on Feb. 25, 1890, he was married to

Louise Sprague Oakey. He died in New York City.

[E. H. Bradford, in *Eleventh Report of the Class of 1869 of Harvard Coll.* (1919); Thos. Hastings, editorial in the *Am. Architect*, Apr. 19, 1916; Ralph Adams Cram, "Walter Cook—an Appreciation," in *Jour. Am. Inst. of Architects*, June 1916; obituary in *N. Y. Times*, Mar. 26, 1916; portrait in *Arch. Record*, Feb. 1912.]   L. F. P.

COOK, ZEBEDEE (Jan. 11, 1786–Jan. 24, 1858), insurance man, horticulturist, was the son of Zebedee and Sarah (Knight) Cook. He was born in Newburyport, Mass., where his father was a mast-maker, spent most of his active business life in Boston, was a resident of New York City for some years, and after his retirement from business, returned to his native state. Cook entered the insurance business in its infancy in this country, opening a private office in Boston after his commission business had failed. From 1822 to 1827 he was president of the Eagle Insurance Company of Boston. Nearly as great as his interest in insurance, to which throughout his life he devoted a large part of his energies, was his interest in horticulture. On Jan. 9, 1829, a letter written by him appeared in the *New England Farmer*, calling attention to the fact that New York, Philadelphia, and other cities had horticultural societies and that Massachusetts would benefit from such an organization. The editor, as a result of this letter, called for a meeting of interested citizens at Cook's insurance office. A snow-storm filled the streets five or six feet deep, on the day appointed for the meeting, but sixteen men came in sleighs or on foot and the Society was founded with Cook as one of its vice-presidents. Later meetings were also held in his office. He became the second president of the organization, and his presidential address, delivered before the second annual festival of the Society on Sept. 10, 1830, may be found in the *History of the Massachusetts Horticultural Society*. It was during the period of Cook's activity in the Society that Mount Auburn was purchased and an experimental flower garden and cemetery established. His interest in horticulture found outlet in personal experiments, too. At his home in Dorchester he had a large garden where he grew successfully several kinds of foreign grapes, apricots, peaches, and pears (Justin Winsor, *Memorial History of Boston*, vol. IV, 1883, pp. 618–19). He was a zealous member of the Whig party and served in the Massachusetts House of Representatives from 1835 to 1838. In the latter year he went to New York to become president of the newly established Mutual Safety Insurance Company of that city, and later became president of the Astor Insurance Company there. Upon his retirement from business he returned to his native state, making his home in South Framingham, where he died.

[*Hist. of the Mass. Horticultural Soc. 1829–78* (1880), ed. by R. Manning; Wm. H. Sumner, *A Hist. of East Boston* (1858); obituary notice from *Boston Courier*, reprinted in *N. Y. Times*, Jan. 27, 1858; obituary in *Boston Daily Advertiser*, Jan. 27, 1858; Wm. Armstrong, *The Aristocracy of N. Y.* (1848); *Vital Records of Newburyport, Mass.*]   E. Y.

COOKE, ELISHA (Sept. 16, 1637–Oct. 31, 1715), political leader, was the son of Richard Cooke, tailor, who with his wife Elizabeth arrived at Boston in 1634 or 1635, probably from Gloucestershire, England. A man of some ability, Richard Cooke became freeman of the colony, lieutenant in the artillery company, selectman and deputy, and acquired a moderate estate. Elisha, the second of his five children, entered Harvard College and took his first degree in 1657, standing fifth in a class of seven. His marriage in June 1668 to Elizabeth, daughter of Gov. Leverett [*q.v.*], gave him the highest social standing. He practised medicine and "was esteemed as a physician," but from 1673 when he was made a freeman, his principal interest was in public affairs. As deputy of Boston in the General Court 1681–84 (speaker 1682–84), his opposition to the extension or even the recognition of royal prerogative was so pronounced that Edward Randolph [*q.v.*] recommended (June 14, 1682) that he be summoned to answer the "Articles of High Misdemeanor" against the colony. His uncompromising position against surrendering the charter won popular approval, and election as assistant in place of Joseph Dudley [*q.v.*] in 1684. He continued to serve on the Board of Assistants until the arrival of Dudley's commission as president of New England. In 1689, Cooke took a leading part in the overthrow and imprisonment of Andros and Dudley, became a member of the Council of Safety and resumed his office of assistant when the old government restored itself. Randolph while imprisoned wrote Cooke, "Your treating Sir Edmund Andros like a gentleman when you were last at the Castle, shall be remembered with respect." As colony agent in London (1690–92) Cooke stood stiffly on his instructions to insist on the old charter, and refused to approve the new Province Charter. Accordingly his name was omitted by Increase Mather [*q.v.*] from the first Council of the Province, which was appointed by the King, and although chosen to the Council in 1693 by the General Court, he was negatived by Gov. Phips whose appointment he had opposed. Reëlected in 1694, he obtained the seat by reason of Phips's absence, and retained it through his administration and that of Lord Bellomont. Cooke at this time was one of the wealthiest men of Boston, and through his family connections wielded considerable influence; his home in School St. still was the recognized center of a party equally opposed to clerical domination and royal prerogative. He took a leading part in thwarting Increase Mather's efforts to obtain a new charter for Harvard College, and in forcing him to resign the presidency. When Cooke's old adversary Dudley became royal governor (1702), he was remembered in a sense contrary to Randolph's promise, for Dudley not only ousted him from the superior court bench where he had served capably for seven years and from the probate court to which he had been appointed the previous year, but negatived his annual election to the Council until 1715, when he was seventy-seven years old. Five months later on Oct. 31, Cooke died, leaving his son, Elisha Cooke, Jr. [q.v.] to carry on the political influence of the family.

[The chief sources are Thos. Hutchinson, *Hist. of the Colony of Mass. Bay* (3 vols., 1764–1828) and *A Collection of Papers Relative to the Hist. of the Colony of Mass. Bay* (1769); and John L. Sibley, *Biog. Sketches of Grads. of Harvard Univ.* (1873), vol. I. See also E. Kimball, *Public Life of Jos. Dudley* (1911) and Kenneth B. Murdoch, *Increase Mather* (1925). A red chalk drawing of Cooke is in the gallery of the Am. Antiquarian Soc.]   R. G. M.

COOKE, ELISHA (Dec. 20, 1678–Aug. 24, 1737), physician and statesman, was the "great Darling of his Countrey" for over twenty years (*Publications of the Colonial Society of Massachusetts*, XVII, 93n). Born in Boston, the grandson of Gov. John Leverett and the son of Elisha Cooke [*qq.v.*], he was placed first in his class at Harvard College in 1697. Like his father, he became a physician, but his political service began the year after his graduation when he was appointed clerk of the superior court. His marriage to Jane Middlecott, great-granddaughter of Gov. Edward Winslow [*q.v.*], occurred in 1703. He inherited his father's controversy with the Dudley family and this flamed out anew in 1714 when the "private bank" was attacked by Paul Dudley [*q.v.*], in a pamphlet *Objections to the Bank of Credit lately Projected at Boston*. Cooke as one of the directors of the proposed bank signed the *Vindication . . . from the Aspersions of Paul Dudley*. Elected representative from Boston by the land-bank party in 1715, Cooke began a service of eighteen years. He was chosen to the Council five years (1717, 1724–26, 1728). In 1716 he began his controversy with Gov. Shute [*q.v.*], whose first official act approved the issue of £100,000 in bills of

credit. After it reached the Governor's ears that Cooke in conversation had called him a blockhead and intimated that the Governor was a tool of Dudley, he removed Cooke "from his Clark's place" and negatived him as councillor in 1718. Meantime a violent quarrel had broken out between Cooke and John Bridger, Surveyor-General of the Woods, concerning the right to cut timber in Maine. Cooke maintained that no royal reservation of timber had been made when Maine was purchased from Gorges and that the acts of Parliament regarding naval stores did not bind Massachusetts under the province charter. The House, after sustaining this advanced position, chose him speaker (1720). Gov. Shute declared, "He has treated me ill and I do negative him." When the House refused to elect another speaker, the Governor dissolved the assembly. Before the new House convened (July 1720), Cooke published a pamphlet (*A Just and Seasonable Vindication*) in which he insisted that the House had an "indubitable, fudamental Right to Chuse their Speaker" [*sic*] and denied the governor's right of veto. Upon the departure of Gov. Shute and the presentation of his grievances before the Privy Council, Cooke was sent to England (1723) to controvert the charges. This mission was fruitless (*Acts of the Privy Council of England, Colonial Series*, vol. III, 1720–45, pp. 93 ff.) and the Explanatory Charter of 1726 definitely gave the governor the right to disapprove the choice of the speaker. Cooke was again chosen to the Council and when Gov. Burnet [*q.v.*] arrived, directed the opposition to a fixed salary. In 1731 Gov. Belcher [*q.v.*] appointed Cooke to the court of common pleas of Suffolk County. He remained a member of the House of Representatives but his popularity, which had kept the people "steady in the applause of his measures" (Hutchinson, *post*, II, 378), began to decline because he seemed to favor a fixed salary for Gov. Belcher. This inconsistency is difficult to explain, since Belcher's confidential letters repeatedly refer to Cooke as his "inveterate enemy" and since the Governor in 1733 dismissed him from his judicial post. In his opposition to royal prerogative, Cooke was not an entirely impartial and disinterested champion of liberty, for he was involved in speculative ventures in Maine timber lands; but Belcher asserted that he had "a fixt enmity to all Kingly Governments." His death in 1737 and the departure of Gov. Belcher mark the end of a political period in Massachusetts Bay. Cooke and his father inherited independent traditions of the old colony and transmitted them to the era of Adams and Otis. The younger Cooke was truly a leader, and the "masterly hand from School Street" directed the political events of his generation.

[Cooke's *A Just and Seasonable Vindication Respecting some Affairs transacted in the late General Assembly at Boston* (1720), *News from Robinson Cruso's Island with an Appendix relating to Mr. Cooke's late Pamphlet* (1720), Dudley's pamphlet, and the *Vindication of the Bank of Credit* are reprinted in Andrew McF. Davis, *Colonial Currency Reprints*, vol. I (1910). The chief other sources of information about Cooke are Thos. Hutchinson, *Hist. of the Colony of Mass. Bay*, vol. II (1767); J. L. Sibley's MSS. relating to Harvard Graduates, Mass. Hist. Soc.; Emory Washburn, *Sketches of the Judicial Hist. of Mass.* (1840).]

E. A. J. J.

COOKE, GEORGE WILLIS (Apr. 23, 1848–Apr. 30, 1923), Unitarian clergyman, writer and lecturer on religious, social, and literary subjects, was born in Comstock, Mich., the son of Hiram and Susan (Earl) Cooke. Although he became noted for the extent and variety of his knowledge, his scholastic training was meager. Until he was nineteen years old he attended district school and worked on his father's farm. Later he took a preparatory course at Olivet College, Mich., spent two years at the Liberal Institute, Jefferson, Wis., and studied for a time at the Meadville Theological School, Meadville, Pa. On June 20, 1872, he was ordained as a Unitarian minister, and the same year he married Lucy Nash of Rochester, Wis. He held pastorates at Sharon, Wis., Grand Haven, Mich., Indianapolis, Ind., Lexington, Mass., and at Dublin and Francestown, N. H. He died in Revere, Mass., at the home of his second wife, Rev. Mary (Leggett) Cooke, to whom he had been married but a week.

All his life he was an apostle of liberalism in religion and active in social reform. In his first parish he published a small but able paper, *The Liberal Worker*, which indirectly led to his being one of the founders and first editors of *Unity* (Chicago), started in 1878. After 1899 he devoted practically his entire time to writing and lecturing, giving courses at the Rand School of Social Science, New York, the Boston School of Social Science, and single lectures and courses throughout the country. Regarding the present industrial and economic system as unjust, and believing in what he called "collectivism" (*i.e.*, in politics, democracy; in industry, cooperation; and in religion, brotherhood), he supported the socialist movement.

He was a keen, appreciative, widely informed literary critic, and in his day was considered the best living authority on New England Transcendentalism. In 1881 he published *Ralph Waldo Emerson, His Life, Writings, and Philosophy*, which soon became a standard work. He also prepared *A Bibliography of Ralph Waldo Emerson* (1908). His *Early Letters of George William Curtis to John S. Dwight* (1898) and his *John Sullivan Dwight* (1898) give an excellent picture of Brook Farm. He published *The Poets of Transcendentalism, an Anthology* (1903) and *An Historical and Biographical Introduction to Accompany the Dial*, 2 vols. (1902). Other literary works of his include *George Eliot, a Critical Study of her Life, Writings, and Philosophy* (1883); *Poets and Problems* (1886), a critique of Tennyson, Ruskin, and Browning; and *A Guide Book to the Poetic and Dramatic Works of Robert Browning* (1891). He also wrote the notes and introduction to the Riverside edition of Browning (1899). In the theological and religious field, he edited three volumes of Theodore Parker's works, wrote *Unitarianism in America* (1902), which was generally adopted as the standard historical work on that subject, and in 1920 published *The Social Evolution of Religion*. He was a clear and vigorous writer, and his work is marked by careful scholarship, keen discernment, and good spirit. It is mainly expository and interpretative, but as such has much value. He contributed numerous articles to periodicals, among them ten to *The Chautauquan* (September 1909–May 1910) on "Woman in the Progress of Civilization," from material for an elaborate book on this subject, which he left unfinished.

[In *Unity*, June 14, 1923, there is an extensive and informing appreciation of Cooke's character and work by J. T. Sunderland. See also *Who's Who in America*, 1923–24; *Unitarian Year Book* (1923–24); *Christian Register*, May 10, 17, and July 12, 1923; and *Boston Transcript*, May 1, 1923.]

H. E. S.

COOKE, HENRY DAVID (Nov. 23, 1825–Feb. 24, 1881), journalist, banker, was born in Sandusky, Ohio, a son of Eleutheros and Martha (Carswell) Cooke, and a brother of Jay Cooke [*q.v.*]. Henry went to Allegheny College, Meadville, Pa., and then to Transylvania University, Lexington, Ky. Upon graduation (1844) he was sent to Philadelphia to study law, for which he had little liking. He contributed minor articles to various publications and in 1846 went to Valparaiso to a place in the office of his brother-in-law, William G. Moorhead, the consul. On his way to Chile he was forced to stop a month in St. Thomas and there became enthusiastic over the possibilities of connection with California by way of Panama. He wrote to newspapers on this subject, and persuaded Moorhead later to make an official report on it to Washington. His stay in Chile was brief and he went on to California. There he had some success in trade but lost what money he made in unfortunate speculations and in fires.

Returning East in 1849 he was for a time financial editor of the *United States Gazette* in Philadelphia, and then went back to Sandusky to edit the *Register,* which his brother Jay later helped him to buy. He made many friends, among them being Salmon P. Chase and John Sherman [*qq.v.*]. In 1856 he went to Columbus to edit the *Ohio State Journal.* This journal was politically powerful but financially unprofitable, and only party favors kept Cooke with it until 1861. At that time his friend Chase became secretary of the treasury. As the Civil War began, Jay Cooke, feeling the need of a personal representative close to the administration, persuaded Henry to sell his paper and move to Washington. There with Harris C. Fahnestock, he was placed in charge of the Washington office of Jay Cooke & Company. Soon afterward he piloted through Congress the bill authorizing the construction of the first street railway in the District of Columbia; then Jay Cooke organized the Washington and Georgetown Street Railway Company, with Henry as first president, and by the summer of 1862 the railway was in operation. Henry Cooke resigned shortly after to organize the First National Bank of the District, another Jay Cooke enterprise, and later helped to form the National Life Insurance Company. More and more of the business of financing the war came to the company of Jay Cooke. Henry went into the field with much success in the placing of one bond issue and in 1864 went abroad to interest foreign investors, a move he had long urged as a means of drawing foreign sympathy to the side of the North. All through the war he was most valuable to the firm because of his Washington contacts; and his lavish entertaining of newspaper correspondents brought countrywide publicity for, and faith in, the bond issues.

After the war he strongly urged his brother to assist in the financing of the Northern Pacific Railroad, and in 1870 he conducted the Northern Pacific lobby before Congress. He had become increasingly prominent in Washington affairs, and when the District was given territorial government in 1871 he was appointed the first governor. This position he resigned in 1873 at his brother's urging, because he was involving the firm too heavily in projects for the expansion and improvement of the District. After Jay Cooke & Company closed its doors in the panic of 1873, Henry Cooke continued to reside in Washington, participating in local affairs and assisting various charities. Grace Chapel in Georgetown was his gift. Bryan, the District historian, described him as "an agreeable man of high personal character." His wife was Laura Humphreys of Utica.

[W. B. Bryan, *Hist. of the National Capital* (1916); E. P. Oberholtzer, *Jay Cooke, Financier of the Civil War* (1907); *National Republican* (Washington, D.C.), Feb. 25, 1881.]   K. H. A.

COOKE, JAY (Aug. 10, 1821–Feb. 16, 1905), banker, financier, came, in the paternal line, of a family of which record is found in Salem, Mass., as early as 1638. The Cooks, or Cookes, removed to Connecticut, then to New York State, and then to the Western Reserve, where, in a place which is now Sandusky, Ohio, Jay Cooke, the third child and second son of Eleutheros and Martha (Carswell) Cooke, was born. Eleutheros Cooke was a lawyer and was sent to Congress, but life in the "West" at this time offered few favorable opportunities to youth. Ambition, if not need, inclined Jay when he was but fourteen to seek employment as a clerk in a store in his native town. In 1836 he found a position in St. Louis, then little more than a French trading post. But, his employers having been ruined in the panic of 1837, he left in a few months to become a clerk on a canal packet line in Philadelphia. This move determined his career, for from this employment in 1839 he passed to the banking house of E. W. Clark & Company, and henceforward banking was his business and Philadelphia was his home. He retired from the Clark firm after the panic of 1857 and was quite at liberty in 1861 to form a partnership of his own, Jay Cooke & Company, which, until 1873, was one of the most widely known banking houses in the country.

The acquaintance which Jay Cooke's younger brother, Henry David Cooke [*q.v.*], who had conducted a newspaper in Columbus, had formed at that place with Gov. Chase [*q.v.*] of Ohio, in 1861 appointed secretary of the treasury, led to relationships with the government which developed rapidly. Chase soon came to rely upon the kindly, open, confident, and optimistic counsel of the Philadelphia banker, as the financial problems arising out of the Civil War multiplied. The credit of the government was low, and the Treasury was wanting in the funds to meet ordinary public expenses, without taking into account the extraordinary demands which were made upon it by the raising and equipment of an army. The first attempt at selling bonds and short-term notes was not very successful, but the battle of Bull Run, in July 1861, awakened the country, and, upon receipt of the news, Cooke put on his hat, left his office, and visiting the bankers of Philadelphia, in a few hours collected over $2,000,000 on the security of three-year treasury notes, bearing interest at the rate of 7.30 per cent, or $7.30 a year for $100. In a few days Chase, in company with Cooke, met the bankers of New York, and, as a result of their negotiations, the Associated Banks agreed to advance $50,000,000 to the government, to be repaid out of the sales of "seven-thirties." Cooke at once converted his office into an agency for advertising the loan and receiving public subscriptions, a business which he later developed to proportions attracting widespread notice.

In February 1862, Jay Cooke & Company opened an office in Washington that the firm might the better care for business growing out of its connections with the government. In October 1862, when Chase's attention was occupied with the "five-twenty" loan (a 6 per cent loan which could be paid at the expiration of five, and must be paid in twenty years) which he had not been able to sell even at a discount, he appointed Cooke a treasury agent for the disposition of the bonds at par. From this time on the "five-twenties" and their merits, said John Sherman [q.v.], were made to stare "in the face of the people in every household from Maine to California." The entire loan of $500,000,000 was distributed before Jan. 21, 1864, when, indeed, after all the orders were received through the mails, it was considerably oversubscribed. More than 600,000, perhaps a million, citizens had been persuaded to take shares in the public debt.

Chase resigning in June 1864, William P. Fessenden [q.v.] became secretary of the treasury. The pecuniary straits of the government were again severe, and necessity induced the new secretary to turn in an obvious direction for relief. He had been giving his attention to the sale of a new issue of "seven-thirties," but it proceeded slowly, and Cooke was again on Jan. 28, 1865, appointed "fiscal agent" of the Treasury Department. The machinery which had been constructed for the distribution of the five-twenties was reorganized. In seven months Secretary Fessenden had, with difficulty, sold $133,-000,000 of the seven-thirties; Cooke, in less than six months, sold $600,000,000 in government securities of this issue.

The war having ended and business for the government having been concluded, except for some funding operations, Cooke found himself with an organization not fully employed, and he resolved to develop a large general banking business, which, in 1866, led to the establishment of a branch in New York, and in 1870, of a house in London, where Hugh McCulloch [q.v], who

had been secretary of the treasury in the last months of the Lincoln and during the Johnson administrations, became the resident partner. Many of the enterprises which after the war sought the favor of bankers and capitalists, were brought to Cooke's attention. One in particular attracted him—the project for a Pacific railroad over a northern route. The Central Pacific was being advanced with government subvention from Omaha to San Francisco. Cooke's support was secured for a road having for its eastern terminus a town called Duluth, at the head of Lake Superior, for its western terminus, Tacoma, a site which was being prepared in a forest of fir trees, on a fine harbor in Puget Sound. Thus would the navigation of the Great Lakes be connected overland with navigation of the Pacific. The avidity of the nation for speculation was spent, however, before the important object in view could be realized. The road was completed to the Missouri River in the east and some miles of the way had been finished on the Pacific coast when, on Sept. 18, 1873, Jay Cooke & Company were compelled to close their doors, out of which event developed a general panic. Cooke's misfortune, in view of valuable services to the government during the war and the national character of the enterprise which bore him down, awakened general sympathy, and public gratification was not withheld when, in later life, he recovered the estates which he had surrendered to his creditors, and a substantial income, through his connection with mines in Utah and by other successful investments. On Aug. 21, 1844 Cooke married Dorothea Elizabeth Allen, a daughter of Richard Allen. Four children, two sons and two daughters, were born to them.

[The chief source is Ellis Paxson Oberholtzer, *Jay Cooke, Financier of the Civil War* (2 vols., 1907), based upon the papers of Jay Cooke, a large collection, carefully arranged and preserved by the financier, and now on deposit in the Library of the Hist. Soc. of Pa.]

E. P. O.

COOKE, JOHN ESTEN (Mar. 2, 1783–Oct. 19, 1853), physician, was the first of eight children born to Dr. Stephen Cooke of Philadelphia, a surgeon in the Revolutionary War, who was captured by the British and taken to the Bermudas, where he married, June 7, 1782, Catherine, daughter of John Esten, chief justice, and at one time acting governor. He was the elder brother of John Rogers and Philip St. George Cooke [qq.v]. The family continued to dwell in the Bermudas until 1791 when it moved to Alexandria, Va., and later to Leesburg, in Loudoun County in the same state. Cooke received a good education although his biographers mention no schools. He read Latin and used a Greek Testament throughout his life. Having begun the study of medicine under his father in Loudoun County, he obtained his medical degree from the University of Pennsylvania in 1805, his graduation thesis, which was published, being devoted to an account of an epidemic of fever that prevailed in his county in 1804. He practised for years at Warrenton, Va., but in 1821 moved to Winchester. His *Essays on the Autumnal and Winter Epidemics* (1829) which appeared in the *Medical Recorder* in 1824 attracted much attention. With Dr. McGuire and others he had planned to start a medical college at Winchester, when, in 1827, he was called to the chair of theory and practise of medicine at the Transylvania University Medical School, Lexington, Ky., to succeed his old classmate, Daniel Drake. In the next year he published the first volume of his *Treatise on Pathology and Therapeutics,* which was later followed by the second volume. This work is said to have been the earliest American systematic text-book on medicine. With C. W. Short he began in the same year the *Transylvania Journal of Medicine and the Associate Sciences,* and to this journal and the *Medical Recorder* he contributed sufficient papers to form, had they been republished, a large volume. His design seems to have been to emancipate the United States from servile dependence on European medicine and to establish an American medical literature, but this attitude was ridiculed by the Eastern leaders of the profession. While in Lexington he changed his old creed of Methodism to Episcopalianism and defended this departure in his *Essay on the Invalidity of Presbyterian Ordination* (1829). In 1832, when his church established a theological seminary, he was made professor of church history and polity and he also assembled an excellent library for the seminary. In 1837 he moved to Louisville where he was co-founder of the Louisville Medical Institute, later known as the University of Louisville, and was made its professor of the theory and practise of medicine. He was never popular either with the faculty or the students. He made the liver responsible for most of human ailments and insisted that the chief remedies must be those which act upon that organ. He gave enormous doses of calomel and other purgatives, and he bled his patients freely. His colleague Drake in the chair of clinical medicine opposed such teachings, and Cooke's withdrawal, which was a foregone conclusion, took place in 1844. The rest of his life was spent on a farm near the Ohio River. He had a total disregard for the opinions of others and an intolerance toward all that he regarded as error.

He took great pains to get at the truth and his reasoning powers were unusual, but he was unable to comprehend that his premises might be at fault. He was wrapped up in clerical matters, wrote on the ailments of the clergy, and at one time contemplated publishing a popular manual on disease.

[*Memoir* by Jas. Craik (also published in pamphlet form) was printed in the *Church Rev. and Ecclesiastical Reg.,* July 1856, and reprinted in the *Southern Literary Messenger,* Apr. 1857. See also biography by L. P. Yandell in *American Practitioner,* July 1875; *Western Jour. Med. and Surg.,* Oct. 1854; and Jas. Craik, *Hist. Sketch of Christ Church, Louisville, Diocese of Ky.* (1862).]   E. P.

COOKE, JOHN ESTEN (Nov. 3, 1830–Sept. 27, 1886), novelist and historian of Virginia, was born in Winchester, Va., the son of John Rogers Cooke [*q.v.*], and Maria, daughter of Philip Pendleton of Berkeley County and a grandniece of Judge Edmund Pendleton [*q.v.*]. After a boyhood in the Valley, chiefly at "Glengary" where he roamed the farm with his younger brothers, and admired the varied talents of his elder brother, Philip Pendleton [*q.v.*], John Esten was taken to the family's new home in Richmond. Here he attended school and was prominent in a literary society. Unable to realize his hope of attending the University of Virginia, he studied law in his father's office and was admitted to the bar in 1851. In practise as in study law was irksome and Cooke was constantly writing and resolving not to write. The ready acceptance of his work by the *Southern Literary Messenger* and a check from *Harper's* (1852) led him definitely to adopt a literary career. In the next eight years, Cooke produced a great number of fugitive poems, essays, stories, and seven volumes of fiction. His first novel, *Leather Stocking and Silk* (1854), reflects his knowledge of the Valley. *The Virginia Comedians* (1854), a story of late Colonial Virginia, is distinguished alike by dramatic quality and charm of diction, and is probably the best work of its author. *Henry St. John* (1859) is a sequel. Before Cooke was thirty, his recognition was nation-wide, but his success was clouded by the deaths, within a decade, of his mother, father, and three brothers.

Cooke was an ardent secessionist, was a special friend and admirer of Stuart, and served through the entire war, surrendering with Lee at Appomattox. His advocacy of winning the war rather than defending Richmond may have cost him the majority for which he was recommended by Stuart and by Lee. In the intervals of campaigning, Cooke wrote a *Life of Stonewall Jackson* (1863), and after the surrender used his experiences as the basis of literature. *Surry of Eagle's Nest* (1866) and its sequel *Mohun* (1869) combine stories of love and adventure with an essentially authentic account of the struggle in Virginia. *Wearing of the Gray* (1867) and *Hammer and Rapier* (1870) are collections of essays on military subjects. *A Life of General Robert E. Lee* (1871) is a military rather than a personal biography.

After Appomattox, Cooke had returned to his boyhood surroundings in the Valley. On Sept. 18, 1867 he married Mary Francis, daughter of Dr. Robert Page of "Saratoga," Clarke County. Soon he moved to a near-by estate, "The Briars," which became his home for the remainder of his life. Here, in the happy society of his wife, his three children, and many visitors, he divided his time between farming and writing. When his Civil War vein was exhausted, he sought in many fields the material for his romances. Most interesting to-day is *The Heir of Gaymount* (1870) which urges intensive farming as the salvation of the post-war South. After Mrs. Cooke's death (1878) the novels strike a deeper human note, but show less of the enthusiastic dash which characterized the author's best manner. Most widely known is *My Lady Pokahontas* (1885), a pleasing story of the settlement of Virginia. *Stories of the Old Dominion* (1879) is a fascinating book for boys and *Virginia* (1883) is a history, chiefly of the colonial period. While his energy was still undiminished, Cooke was stricken with typhoid fever, and died, in his fifty-sixth year. He was at heart a chivalric Cavalier, who idealized the past and was unreservedly devoted to Virginia. His books are what he wished them to be—entertaining and pure. His popularity has suffered somewhat from the unwinnowed abundance of his writings, but his best romances of colonial Virginia and of the Civil War will unquestionably survive.

[There is a sketch of Cooke by A. A. Link in *Pioneers of Southern Literature*, no. 5 (1898), and one by M. J. Preston in the *Critic*, Oct. 16, 1886; the only biography is *John Esten Cooke, Virginian* (1922), by John O. Beaty.]   J. O. B.

COOKE, JOHN ROGERS (1788–Dec. 15, 1854), lawyer, was the third child of Dr. Stephen Cooke and Catherine (Esten) Cooke, and brother of John Esten and Philip St. George Cooke [*qq.v.*]. In 1791 he accompanied his parents to Alexandria and thence to Leesburg, Loudoun County, Va., where he received his early education. In 1807 he held a commission in the Frederick troop, which was raised in consequence of the *Chesapeake* incident, and in 1812 saw service in the coast defense. Having taken up the study of law, probably at William and Mary College law school, on his being admitted to the bar (*c.* 1812) he commenced practise at Martins-

burg (now W. Va.). Esteemed "the glass of fashion of the scarcely more than border town" (J. O. Beaty, *post*), his marriage, Nov. 18, 1813, with Maria, daughter of Philip and Agnes (Patterson) Pendleton of Martinsburg, and grand-niece of Judge Edmund Pendleton, assured him a prominent position socially and otherwise, and he established himself at Winchester, where he practised for twenty-five years. In 1814 he represented Frederick County in the House of Delegates, but served only one term. Great intellectual endowments joined to remarkable powers of speech fortified by wide reading quickly made him the leading lawyer in transmontane Virginia. Elected a delegate from Frederick and Jefferson counties to the Virginia constitutional convention 1829–30, he was a conspicuous figure in "one of the greatest assemblies of intellect ever held on Virginia soil" (Chandler, *post*, p. 32). On the major question before the convention, *i.e.*, the future basis of representation in the legislature, he and Doddridge were the leaders of the Western party and his speeches, dealing with the matter from the philosophical standpoint of the natural rights of man and displaying deep constitutional study, were among the ablest in a brilliant series of arguments (see *Proceedings and Debates of the Virginia State Convention of 1829–30*, pp. 53, 337, 342, 433, 549, 678, 691). A member of the select committee of seven, including Madison and Marshall, which drafted the resulting compromise constitution, he was the only western delegate who voted for it on its final submission to the convention, his action being bitterly assailed by Doddridge who accused him of betraying the West. A contemporary describes him at this juncture as "thin in stature, the full expression of a good face neutralized by green glasses; unknown in federal politics and as yet in state . . . his mind thoroughly imbued with the logic of the schools, and feeding on abstractions as its daily bread; versed in the minute history of the state, and famous for the provoking pertinacity with which he worried an opponent, a dog-eared Hening in his hand" (H. B. Grigsby, *post*). The prominent part taken by him in the convention brought a state-wide reputation and in March 1840 he moved to Richmond where he confined himself to work before the superior and appellate courts, holding retainers in almost every case of importance, including the Randolph Will litigation. His speech in the latter case before the court of appeals was said by one of the judges to have been the ablest ever delivered in that court. Of his children, Philip Pendleton Cooke [*q.v.*] and John Esten Cooke [*q.v.*] attained high distinction.

[Information as to Cooke's career has been supplied by his grand-daughters, Miss M. P. Duval of Charles Town, W. Va. and Mrs. Carter Harrison of University, Va. The allusions to John Rogers Cooke in J. O. Beaty, *John Esten Cooke, Virginian* (1922), should be revised in the light of this information. It is a family tradition that Cooke attended Wm. and Mary College and the College of New Jersey (Princeton) but no record of such attendance has been found. H. B. Grigsby, "The Virginian Convention of 1829–30," *Va. Hist. Reporter*, vol. I (1854), p. 15, is appreciative. See also Mary S. Kennedy, *Seldens of Va. and Allied Families* (1911), II, 265–67; Toner Coll., "Medical Men in the American Revolution," vol. VIII, in MSS. Div., Lib. of Cong.; C. H. Ambler, *Sectionalism in Va. from 1776 to 1861* (1910), esp. pp. 166–77; Julian A. C. Chandler, *Representation in Va.*, Johns Hopkins University Studies in Historical and Political Science, 14 ser., VI, VII (1896); *Daily Richmond Enquirer*, Dec. 16, 1854.]

H. W. H. K.

COOKE, JOSIAH PARSONS (Oct. 12, 1827–Sept. 3, 1894), chemist, teacher, author, was born in Boston, Mass., and died in Newport, R. I. His early life was spent in Boston where his father, also Josiah Parsons Cooke, was a successful lawyer. When he was six years old he lost his mother, Mary (Pratt) Cooke, and was brought up by a faithful friend of the family. As a boy he was frail, reserved, and disinclined to outdoor sports. He spent his spare time in reading and in studying chemistry, in which his interest had been aroused when as a lad he heard some lectures by Benjamin Silliman before the Lowell Institute of Boston (1839–43). Like all lovers of chemistry he read Mrs. Marcet's *Conversations on Chemistry*, but the experiments performed by Silliman kindled in him such enthusiasm that he also fitted up a little laboratory in the cellar of his father's home. Here he performed many experiments, guided by Turner's *Chemistry*. In this way he studied the science by the toilsome method of individual experiment, which he rigorously followed and made his students follow during his forty-four years of association with Harvard University. He entered Harvard in 1844, pursued the regular course, and after graduation in 1848 spent a year in Europe where he attended lectures in chemistry by Dumas and Regnault. Upon his return he was appointed tutor in mathematics at Harvard. He had decided to devote his life to chemistry, however, although his knowledge of the subject was almost entirely self-acquired. Elected Erving Professor of Chemistry and Mineralogy in 1850 at the age of twenty-three, he founded the two departments, developed courses, procured teaching equipment, and won the respect of his classical colleagues and the financial support of the corporation. In 1858 Boylston Hall, the new chemistry laboratory, was completed, largely through the zealous efforts of Cooke, and chemistry started on a widened path. Assistants were appointed, the first one being Charles W. Eliot, and laboratory instruction was offered for the first time to a class of undergraduates.

During the manifold duties incident to establishing and administering the department of chemistry, Cooke found time to write and investigate, and between 1855 and 1893 to deliver eight courses of lectures before the Lowell Institute. He also taught chemistry for a few years in the Harvard Medical School. Of his eight books, the more important are: *Elements of Chemical Physics* (1860), which went through three editions; *Principles of Chemical Philosophy* (1868), four editions; *The New Chemistry* (1874), five editions and several translations; and *Laboratory Practice* (1891). Several of his other books deal with the relation between religion and science. He published over forty papers on his original investigations. Some early papers were devoted to mineralogy, and one, "The Numerical Relations between the Atomic Weights" (*American Journal of Science,* 2 ser., XVII, 1854), dealt with the classification of the elements. This was the first scientific attempt to classify the elements by their atomic weights, and foreshadowed the investigations on atomic weights which occupied Cooke in later life and prepared the way for the superior work in this field done at Harvard. The first investigation of the latter type was on the atomic weight of antimony, and it led to three fundamental papers (*Proceedings of the American Academy of Arts and Sciences,* XIII, 1; XV, 251; XVII, 1; 1877–81) and several subsidiary ones. The second (in cooperation with Theodore W. Richards, *Ibid.,* XXIII, 149, 182; 1887–89) was on the relative atomic weights of oxygen and hydrogen, and was a helpful contribution to the experimental procedure in this exacting work. Cooke wrote about thirty other papers, which include fourteen on chemical topics and nine on the biography of celebrated men. His annual reports as director of the chemistry laboratory contain helpful contributions on the construction of laboratories, arrangement of mineralogical specimens, contents of courses, and methods of teaching science.

In 1860 he married Mary Hinckley Huntington, of Lowell, Mass. They had no children, but a nephew and a niece of Mrs. Cooke were members of the family for many years. Cooke was a member of many scientific societies including the National Academy of Sciences and the American Academy of Arts and Sciences. He was active in the latter, being corresponding secretary for nineteen years (1873–92), and president for three years (1892–94). He was also a resident fellow for forty-one years and librarian for eight. As a college lecturer he was luminous, and despite a tremulous hand his experiments were uniformly successful; he was especially popular with younger students. As a teacher he was convincing in the lecture room, patient in the laboratory, and persistent in making students think for themselves. He exerted a wholesome influence on American education, secondary and collegiate, by his determined and energetic championship of the study of science. As an investigator he was singularly clear in thought, undismayed by experimental difficulties, ingenious in devising apparatus and methods, and keen in his enthusiasm for research.

[*Proc. Am. Acad. Arts and Sci.*, XXX (1894), 513–47; *Nat. Acad. Sci., Biog. Memoirs*, IV (1877–1909), 175–83; *Popular Science Monthly*, X (1877), 491–95; brief articles in the *Am. Chem. Jour.*, XVI, 566–68, and the *Harv. Grads. Mag.*, III (1894–95), 195–97.]

L. C. N.

COOKE, PHILIP PENDLETON (Oct. 26, 1816–Jan. 20, 1850), poet, story-writer, was the eldest child of John Rogers Cooke [*q.v.*], a distinguished Virginia lawyer, another of whose sons was John Esten Cooke [*q.v.*], the novelist. His mother was Maria Pendleton. Philip was born at Martinsburg, Berkeley County, Va. (now W. Va.). In his boyhood the family lived at and near Winchester ("Glengary") and at Charles Town; his later years were passed in the adjoining county of Clarke, near Millwood, at his home "The Vineyard," in the beautiful Shenandoah Valley. At fifteen he entered Princeton College, where he devoted more time to reading poetry than to the prescribed studies. Chaucer and Spenser were favorites. After his graduation (1834) at Princeton, he read law with his father. Before his twenty-first birthday he was married to Willie Anne Burwell of Clarke County, and admitted to the bar. Law was his profession but literature and hunting were his master passions. His frequent letters to his father show that he was intermittently reading Blackstone and writing verse and prose romances, frequently hunting, and daily enjoying the noble scenery of mountain and stream with a poet's fine sense for the beauty of landscape and legend. The region was lovely, society was merry, and the lawyer-poet was handsome and popular. Above the average height, with "deep hazel eyes, dark chestnut curling hair," and a musical voice, he must have looked the poet far more than the sport-loving country gentleman and village barrister. His manly and affectionate nature is reflected in his letters to his father, upon whom he relied for counsel and often for money. He was singularly happy in his own family life. For writing, however, he had little encourage-ment. Literature was looked upon as only an elegant pastime. Toward the law he had good intentions and for literary production he had a positive urge, but he showed no sustained diligence in the pursuit of either. If one takes into account his social nature, the demands of an uncongenial profession, his struggle to support a growing family on an uncertain income, and the lack of incentive to literary effort in the old leisurely plantation life, the slenderness of Cooke's achievement is not to be attributed mainly to lack of ambition. Under all the circumstances his accomplishment in letters is not inconsiderable for his brief span of thirty-three years. There is evidence, indeed, that he was turning more and more to literature and that, had he lived another score of years, he might have been one of the major poets and romancers of the older South.

His earliest poems, written at Princeton, were published in the *Knickerbocker Magazine* in 1833. From 1835 to his death in 1850 he occasionally wrote for the *Southern Literary Messenger* of Richmond, beginning with a series of essays on English poetry. A famous poem, "Florence Vane," which appears in most anthologies of American verse, was first published in Burton's *Gentleman's Magazine*, Philadelphia, for March 1840, and was soon translated into several languages. In 1847, at the suggestion of his cousin, John Pendleton Kennedy [*q.v.*] of Baltimore, Cooke collected some of his magazine verses into a volume, *Froissart Ballads and Other Poems*, which was published by Carey and Hart, Philadelphia. He called the ballads "versified transcripts from Froissart," but only three are directly from the old chronicler. The poems in this volume show a delicate sense for form and rhythm and a rare freshness of imagery in descriptions of nature. Cook's four short prose romances, "The Gregories of Hackwood," "The Two Country Houses," "John Carper the Hunter of Lost River," and "The Crime of Andrew Blair," and his satirical story of whimsical humor, "Erisicthon," appeared in the *Southern Literary Messenger* during 1848–49. His one novel, or historical romance, "The Chevalier Merlin" (unfinished), highly praised by Poe, was running in the *Messenger* at the time of his death. His stories have rapid movement, vivid delineation, and the usual romantic coloring of our earlier fiction. Both his poetry and prose reflect his acute interest in nature and outdoor sport, which he always depicts with sureness and sincerity. The one memorable lyric, "Florence Vane," and several meritorious ballads form his slight but real contribution to our literature.

[The chief sources of information on Philip Pendleton Cooke are: Letters to his father, now owned by his nephew, Dr. Robt. P. Cooke of Lexington, Va.; autobiographical fragment of John Esten Cooke, quoted in John O. Beaty's *John Esten Cooke, Virginian* (1922); editorial tribute by John R. Thompson in *Southern Literary Messenger,* Feb. 1850; "Philip Pendleton Cooke," by Rufus W. Griswold, in the same for Oct. 1851 (reprinted from *Internat. Mag.*); "Recollections of Philip Pendleton Cooke," in *Messenger* for June, 1858; "Philip Pendleton Cooke," by F. V. N. Painter, *Lib. of Southern Literature,* vol. III (1909).]

J. C. M.

COOKE, PHILIP ST. GEORGE (June 13, 1809–Mar. 20, 1895), soldier, author, the son of Dr. Stephen and Catherine (Esten) Cooke, was born at Leesburg, Va. He was the younger brother of John Esten Cooke (1783–1853) and of John Rogers Cooke (1788–1854) [*qq.v.*]. He was named St. George in deference to his mother's nationality, but he was appointed a cadet at West Point under the name of Philip St. George, through a mistake somewhat similar to that by which Gen. Grant's name was altered when he entered that institution. Graduating in 1827, Cooke was commissioned in the 6th Infantry, joined his regiment in Missouri, and served with it for nearly six years at various western stations and on expeditions into the Indian country. He was engaged in the Black Hawk War of 1832. The next year he was appointed first lieutenant in the newly organized 1st Dragoons (now the 1st Cavalry), and two years later (May 31, 1835) became a captain. From frontier stations, generally Fort Leavenworth, he went on many expeditions into the remote West, including one in 1845 through the South Pass of the Rocky Mountains, when his command covered twenty-two hundred miles in ninety-nine days. In the war with Mexico, his service was with Kearny's Army of the West, which achieved the conquest of New Mexico and California by hard marching more than by fighting. With an escort of twelve men, Cooke preceded the army from the rendezvous at Bent's Fort, on the Arkansas River, to Santa Fé, three hundred miles distant. It was intended that he should negotiate under a flag of truce, but Mexican resistance collapsed without much negotiation. Meanwhile reinforcements for the army had been started forward, including a battalion enlisted among the Mormons who had recently been driven from Nauvoo. Cooke was assigned to its command, with the rank of lieutenant-colonel. His impression of his battalion, when it arrived at Santa Fé, was not favorable. "It was enlisted too much by families; some were too old, some feeble, and some too young; it was embarrassed by many women; it was undisciplined; it was much worn by travelling on foot" (*Conquest of New Mexico and*

California, p. 91). When he left it in California nine months later, however, he had made it into an efficient organization. He was promoted to major of the 2nd Dragoons in 1847, lieutenant-colonel in 1853, and colonel in 1858, being employed usually on the frontier as before, skirmishing occasionally with Apache and Sioux Indians, and taking part in the Utah expedition of 1857–58. He prepared a new system of calvary tactics for the army, and was an observer of the war in Italy in 1859–60.

His family "followed the State" in 1861. His son, John R. Cooke, and his son-in-law, J. E. B. Stuart, became general officers in the Confederate army. On both sides it was supposed that he would probably do likewise, but his loyalty was unshaken, and when a letter from a Confederate general was secretly delivered to him in Washington he promptly handed it over to the War Department. He was appointed a brigadier-general in the regular army, Nov. 12, 1861, and commanded a brigade of cavalry at Washington until the Army of the Potomac entered upon the Peninsular campaign, in which he commanded the so-called Cavalry Reserve—a division of two brigades. This was his only actual field service during the war. He commanded the district of Baton Rouge for a time, and later was general superintendent of recruiting for the regular army. After the war, besides other duties, he commanded successively the departments of the Platte, the Cumberland, and the Lakes. He retired from active service in 1873. Besides his *Cavalry Tactics* (2 vols., 1861; many later editions) he published *Scenes and Adventures in the Army* (1857) and *The Conquest of New Mexico and California* (1878). The former is his autobiography from the time of his first commission until 1845, interspersed with curious reflections, frequently thrown into the form of dialogue, on subjects of every conceivable nature. It is useful as a picture of life in the far West during the period. The second of these books is a strictly historical narrative, the more valuable because largely made up of extracts from the diary which he kept at the time. Cooke was a stern disciplinarian, with a high sense of honor and sincere religious feeling. He did not lack a sense of humor, and was notably fond of young people. His wife was Rachel Hertzog of Philadelphia.

[In addition to Cooke's own publications see G. W. Cullum, *Biog. Reg.* (3rd ed., 1891); *Bull. Ass. Grads. U. S. Mil. Acad.,* 1895, pp. 79–86; Frank A. Golder, *March of the Mormon Battalion* (1928); Daniel Tyler, *Concise Hist. of the Mormon Battalion in the Mexican War* (1881); *Official Records* (*Army*), 1 ser., vols. XI (pts. 1, 2, 3), XXVI (pt. 1), XXXIV (pts. 2, 3), LI (pt. 1).]

T. M. S.

COOKE, ROSE TERRY

COOKE, ROSE TERRY (Feb. 17, 1827–July 18, 1892), story-writer, poet, was born on a farm near Hartford, Conn. Her father, Henry Wadsworth Terry, was the son of a Hartford bank president and member of Congress; her mother, Anne (Hurlbut) Terry, was the daughter of John Hurlbut, the first New England shipbuilder to sail around the world. When Rose was six, her parents removed to one of the finest houses in Hartford, owned by Henry Terry's mother, and there the girl learned to become a thorough New England housekeeper. The life and festivals in this home are described in some of her stories. Because of a serious illness, she was not a strong child and so was kept much outdoors where, through the companionship of her father, she became learned in the lore of woods, garden, and sky. She could read at the age of three, and was graduated from the Hartford Female Seminary when she was sixteen. The same year she joined the church and throughout her life was devoted to church association. Following graduation, she taught in Hartford, then in a Presbyterian school in Burlington, N. J., then as a governess in a clergyman's family. A call came for her service at home and from this time her first interest was domestic. The death of a sister threw upon her the care of the sister's children, who became like her own. At home, in her spare time, she began to write stories and verse, but her literary work was always of secondary importance in her own estimation. Charles A. Dana introduced her verses to the *New York Tribune,* and they were later published in one volume, *Poems* (1860). They show considerable variety both in subject and metrical form, and include ballads and translations as well as poems on travel, the Civil War, festival occasions, nature, religious subjects, and subjective experience. It is the work of one sensitive to beauty, both physical and spiritual, but not over-emotional. Her meters, though conventional, are free from stiffness. Perhaps the best poems are those on New England scenes, such as "My Apple Tree," "The Sheepfold," "The River," "The Snow-Filled Nest," "The Two Villages," "Trailing Arbutus." Many of her short stories, contributed to *Harper's Magazine,* the *Atlantic Monthly,* and other periodicals, were collected into the volumes *Happy Dodd; or, She Hath Done What She Could* (1878), *Somebody's Neighbors* (1881), *Root-Bound and Other Sketches* (1885), *The Sphinx's Children and Other People's* (1886), *Huckleberries Gathered from New England Hills* (1891). She also wrote a novel, *Steadfast* (1889). Her best stories are those of New England life and character, which show a keen perception of human motives and appreciation for the meaning in even a humdrum life. Her subjects are similar to those of Mary Wilkins Freeman, but her outlook is free from morbidity and full of humor. Her style is simple and spontaneous. Her characteristic humor showed in the expression of her rather large mouth and deep-set, dark eyes, and a phrenologist would have read intellect in her high forehead. Tall, with Spanish coloring and black hair, she was striking, and in her youth was considered beautiful. Her wit and interest in people and things brought her many friends. In 1873 she married Rollin H. Cooke, an iron manufacturer, and removed to Winsted, Conn. She continued writing and attempted novels, without great success. In 1887 she and her husband removed to Pittsfield, Mass. An attack of pneumonia in 1889 left her an invalid and her home was broken up. Successive attacks of influenza followed and she died at Pittsfield in 1892.

[Harriet Prescott Spofford, who knew her, wrote an article on Rose Terry Cooke published in *Our Famous Women* (1883). See also Fred. L. Pattee, *The Development of the Am. Short Story* (1923); brief mention in Edward O'Brien, *The Advance of the Am. Short Story* (1923), and in J. L. Onderdonk, *Hist. of Am. Verse, 1610–1897* (1901); sketch in *Am. Women* (1897), ed. by Frances Willard and Mary Livermore; obituaries in *Boston Transcript,* July 19, *Boston Herald,* July 20, and *Critic,* July 23, 1892.]   S. G. B.

COOLBRITH, INA DONNA

COOLBRITH, INA DONNA (Mar. 10, 1842–Feb. 29, 1928), poet, the daughter of New England parents, was born near Springfield, Ill., and died in Berkeley, Cal. Her father died when she was a child and she went with her mother to live in St. Louis. There the young widow married a newspaper man named William Pickett. In 1849 the Pickett family went to California and settled in Los Angeles. Ina attended such public schools as the place afforded, read many books, and delighted herself with the conversation of pioneering miners. About 1865 the family moved to San Francisco. Ina was by this time definitely "literary," and she accordingly went into teaching as a means of contributing to the family income. Her writings attained a local reputation, and when in 1868 Bret Harte founded the *Overland Monthly,* he engaged her as one of his co-editors. To the first issue of the publication she contributed the poem "Longing," restating the doctrine that one hour in a vernal wood is more instructive than all the sages. In the next issue, she published "Blossom Time," a lyric exultant over the approach of spring. This poem is typical of her work, and it remains the specimen of it which is perhaps most generally known. While associated with the *Overland Monthly* she gave encouragement to the young poet Cincinnatus Heine Miller, to whom she is said to have suggested his pseudonym, "Joaquin Miller." A volume of poems under the title, *A Perfect Day and Other Poems* appeared in 1881; *The Singer of the Sea,* a brief elegy, in 1894; and *Songs from the Golden Gate,* a collective edition of her work, in 1895. Her writings were from the first popular, though never, it appears, remunerative. She was acclaimed by critics in England as well as in America, and she was about to set out for New York and eventually London, when she was suddenly left with the responsibility of rearing a niece and a nephew. From 1893 to 1897 she was ill, but with that exception she worked from 1873 to 1906 as librarian in Oakland and San Francisco—for twenty-one years at the Oakland Public Library, for two years at the San Francisco Mercantile Library, and for eight years at the San Francisco Bohemian Club. The San Francisco fire destroyed quantities of her manuscript and left her without employment. Appreciative friends, however, soon made provision for her. When the exposition was held in San Francisco in 1915, she contributed to the occasion by summoning a World Congress of Authors. In the same year, with elaborate ceremony, she was crowned poet laureate of California, pursuant to an act of the state legislature. Though not a poet of high rank she phrased beautifully some worthy and agreeable thoughts, and she exemplified throughout her life personal traits which have for a long time been held admirable.

[Marian Taylor, "A Poet-Laureate Hostess," in *Sunset Mag.,* Jan. 1915; Marian Taylor, "Congress of Authors and Journalists," and Josephine C. McCrackin, "Ina Coolbrith Invested with Poet's Crown," in *Overland Monthly,* Nov. 1915; A. K. Lynch, "Ina D. Coolbrith as the Literary Associate of Bret Harte," in *Overland Monthly,* Nov. 1920; *Who's Who in America,* 1922–23; *Oakland Tribune,* Feb. 29, 1928; *N.Y. Times,* Mar. 1, 1928.]   J. D. W.

COOLEY, LYMAN EDGAR (Dec. 5, 1850–Feb. 3, 1917), civil engineer, was born in Canandaigua, N. Y., the son of Albert Blake and Achsah (Griswold) Cooley. He was graduated from the Rensselaer Polytechnic Institute in 1874 with a degree in civil engineering, and in December of the same year was married to Lucena McMillan. Making his home in Chicago, Cooley became one of the city's best-known consulting hydraulic engineers. He began his professional life as a teacher of engineering subjects at Northwestern University (1874–77) and acted as the associate editor of the *Engineering News* for most of that period. After a year's work as assistant engineer on the construction of a bridge over the Missouri River at Glasgow, Mo., he had his first experience on waterway problems when, from 1879 to 1884, he served as assistant engineer on the Mississippi and Missouri river improvements. In September 1884 he began a year's work as editor, with Merrick Cowles, of the *American Engineer.* But at the end of a year he left the editorial field to devote himself to engineering features of waterway problems. He first achieved prominence in promoting the undertaking of the Chicago Sanitary and Ship Canal. He was the first chief engineer of the enterprise and when, through a political combination, he was replaced by another, he was elected one of the trustees of the district. His work in connection with the Sanitary District in Chicago was almost continuous from 1885 till within a year of his death, when failing eyesight gave him difficulty. He gave the initial form to the solution of the problems pertaining to the Chicago Sanitary Canal, its relation to lakes and rivers, its sanitary and constructive features; and his opinions and work met the test of experience and time. In 1913, following the refusal of the Secretary of War to permit an increase in the diversion of water to 10,000 cubic feet per second through the Canal, he prepared a volume containing a brief of the facts and issues, published under the title *The Diversion of the Waters of the Great Lakes by Way of the Sanitary and Ship Canal of Chicago* (1913).

In 1895 Cooley had been appointed by President Cleveland a member of an International Commission to make investigations for a ship canal between the Great Lakes and the Atlantic Ocean, and with James B. Angell of Michigan and John E. Russell of Massachusetts made the report that gave the first substantial basis to the engineering merits of that enterprise. From that time until his death he was prominent in connection with plans for deep-water navigation to the Lakes. He was consulting engineer for the Lakes-to-the-Gulf Deep Waterway Association for several years; served as an advisory engineer in an investigation for the Erie Canal; was a consultant for the Denver Union Water Company on the Cheesman Dam; and did notable work in connection with water-power enterprises and water storage at Keokuk, Iowa. He was interested in the Isthmian Canal problem, visited Panama and Nicaragua as consulting engineer with the contractors' and engineers' expedition, and in 1902 published *Isthmian Canal.* He also served as a member of the United States Postal Committee on Pneumatic Tubes for mail in cities. Cooley was a prolific writer on engineering subjects, and his papers, particularly on waterway problems, appeared for years in the technical press. He also lectured on waterway problems. He was active in the Society of Western Engineers, serving a year as its president, and in the American Waterworks Association.

[Files of the Am. Soc. of Civil Engineers; *Engineering News*, Feb. 8, 1917; *Engineering Record*, Feb. 10, 1917; *Who's Who in America*, 1916–17; Cooley's published books and papers.]   E. Y.

COOLEY, THOMAS McINTYRE (Jan. 6, 1824–Sept. 12, 1898), jurist, was descended from Benjamin Cooley, one of the selectmen of Springfield, Mass., in 1646. He was born on a farm near Attica, N. Y., the eighth of the thirteen children of Thomas Cooley and his second wife Rachel Hubbard. That part of New York, then being rapidly peopled, was as yet not far advanced beyond the frontier stage; comfort depended on hard work and much of it. In later life, when Cooley had won fame and pecuniary competence, he rarely spoke, and even then reluctantly, of early hardships. Still, he had the advantage of reasonably good schooling, supplemented by his own reading; he apparently read everything he could obtain, especially works of history. He attended the public schools, which were probably of a very simple character, and later the Attica Academy, from which he was graduated in 1842. There his formal education ended, but through a long and busy life he enriched his mind and spirit with books beyond the borders of his profession. It appears that for some months each year, he taught school in the neighborhood of Attica, even before leaving the academy. In 1842 he began the study of law, chiefly at Palmyra. The next year, determined to test his fortunes farther afield, he moved to Adrian, Mich., where he continued his studies, supporting himself by doing tasks of various kinds till his admission to the bar in January 1846. In December of that year, he married Mary Elizabeth Horton, a woman of unusual charm and character.

The next ten years had their share of anxiety. Cooley was ambitious and at that time restless; at all events, not content with opportunities at Adrian, he thrice tried other places, living for brief periods in Tecumseh and Coldwater, Mich., and later in Toledo, Ohio; but after each venture he returned to the town where he had begun the practise of his profession. His early connections were with the Democratic party, but soon after the formation of the Republican party he entered its ranks and was thenceforth associated with it though never as an extreme partisan. In 1855 he formed a partnership in Adrian with Charles M. Croswell, later governor of the state. His fortunes began to brighten somewhat, his law business increased, and in 1857 he was chosen by the legislature of Michigan to compile the state statutes. This work he did with

great thoroughness and skill, and his success doubtless brought his appointment (1858) as official reporter of the supreme court of the state. Though he had appeared but seldom before the supreme bench, there is probably truth in what was said later by one of the justices: "We appointed him because we had noticed in his management of cases, even in his early standing at the bar, a very great discrimination in picking out and enforcing the strong and important points in the case." Certainly that discrimination was characteristic of everything Cooley did; and in his work as reporter it was peculiarly exemplified. He held the position till 1865, and edited eight volumes (5–12 *Michigan Reports,* covering the years 1858–64). The impression made by his scholarship and industry won for him election to the state supreme court (1864). The years of uncertainty and of struggle were now behind him; ahead lay unceasing toil, but also reputation and notable accomplishment. He was successively reëlected till his defeat in the spring of 1885. During his more than twenty years of service, the court as a whole had a reputation for ability and vigor. Cooley's own work was of high order. At the time of his death a writer in the *American Law Review* (XXXII, 917) declared that his "numerous judicial opinions . . . are in every respect models; they have been rarely equaled, never surpassed by English or American judges." When asked to select what he himself thought his best opinion, Cooley named *Park Commissioners* vs. *Detroit,* 28 *Mich.,* 228 (1873).

Even before his judicial duties had begun, he had taken another momentous step. When the Law Department of the University of Michigan was established in 1859 Cooley was chosen one of the three professors of law, and in that year he moved with his family to Ann Arbor, to be associated with the University for the remainder of his life. For a time he was secretary, later dean of the department. His lectures were characteristically clear, thoroughly organized, and so straightforward and even apparently simple, that the art and the drudgery involved in preparation were concealed from the listener. They were commonly written and read to his classes; they were condensed, terse and telling, but doubtless because of their very merits the students often failed to realize that they were being led unerringly by a master. In 1884 he gave up his professorship in the law school, and the next year reluctantly accepted the position of professor of American history and constitutional law in the Literary Department. This title he held until his death, but after the first few years his connection with the University was not much more than nominal or honorary.

Cooley wrote unceasingly, and his reputation largely rested then, and rests to-day, on his success as a publicist. The first work of importance, still an indispensable companion for every one interested in constitutional problems, was *A Treatise on the Constitutional Limitations which Rest Upon the Legislative Power of the States of the American Union* (1868, 8th ed. 1927). The volume is characterized by clarity of style and perfection of organization; though based on precedent and authority, it is by no means lacking in philosophic grasp or wanting in the presentation of fundamental principles of jurisprudence and of social order. His presentation of constitutional provisions designed to protect individual liberty was especially strong and influential. A much smaller work, *The General Principles of Constitutional Law* (1880, 3rd ed. 1898), was for years widely used as a college text-book. In 1870 he finished his edition of *Blackstone's Commentaries* (1871) with introduction and notes covering the main developments of English Law since the author's time and indicating the differences between American law and the English system. Next to his *Limitations*, Cooley's most influential work was his *Treatise on the Law of Torts* (1879, 3rd ed. 1906). It was long considered the authoritative American treatment. Cooley himself thought this book his best. He published an edition of Story's *Commentaries on the Constitution* (1873); and *The Law of Taxation* (1876, 4th ed. 1924). For the series of American Commonwealths he wrote *Michigan, a History of Governments* (1885, rev. ed. 1905), a readable and accurate state history. A considerable number of articles in periodicals and a few public addresses of importance also came from his pen. Of these and other miscellaneous writings a list is given in the *Michigan Law Journal*, V, 373.

The later years of Cooley's life were largely taken up with railroad affairs. He was called on several times to act as arbitrator in disputes. At the end of 1886 he was appointed receiver of the Wabash lines east of the Mississippi, and entered upon the task with characteristic energy, showing marked administrative capacity. In the spring of 1887 he was asked by President Cleveland to become a member of the Interstate Commerce Commission, then being organized. He accepted the position, became chairman of the commission, and at once devoted to the difficult task his customary labor and interest. It is plain from his letters, his diary, the reports he prepared, and the testimony of his associates, that he bore the chief burden and in great degree shaped the policy of the commission. To state in brief compass the nature and effect of his work is quite impossible; it is fair to believe that one of the Commission, writing at the time of Cooley's retirement, did not exaggerate in saying, "You have organized the National Commission, laid its foundations broad and strong and made it what its creators never contemplated. a tribunal of justice, in a field and for a class of questions where all was chaos before." Worn out with labor, he resigned in September 1891. The *Reports of the Interstate Commerce Commission* in its early years, all of them—except in their purely statistical portions—presumably written by Cooley, should be included among his important contributions.

In great degree Cooley's essential character was visible in his appearance; his face bore a look of earnestness and thought not uninfluenced by a certain benignity. Quiet, even retiring, very self-contained, he loved the companionship of intelligent people, was fond of children, and was interested in young men and their problems. His most marked qualities, aside from calmness and a dominating sense of justice, were his capacity for unremitting toil and the supreme care with which he performed his tasks. He died at Ann Arbor Sept. 12, 1898. His wife had died eight years before.

[Diaries and letters covering a portion of Cooley's life are in the library of the Univ. of Mich., where also is a typewritten and incomplete biography by Henry Wade Rogers, Cooley's successor as dean of the Law School. In W. D. Lewis's *Great Am. Lawyers*, vol. VII (1909), is an excellent sketch by H. B. Hutchins. A trustworthy summary and estimate is C. A. Kent's *Address* (pub. by the Univ. of Mich., 1899). Of value are *Am. Law Rev.*, XXXII, 916; *Report Am. Bar Asso.*, 1898, p. 674; Jerome C. Knowlton in *Mich. Law Rev.*, vol. V, Mar. 1907, p. 309.]   A. C. McL.

COOLIDGE, ARCHIBALD CARY (Mar. 6, 1866–Jan. 14, 1928), historian, was born in Boston, Mass., the son of Joseph Randolph and Julia (Gardner) Coolidge. He came of a family that included many names distinguished in the social and commercial life of Boston. His paternal grandmother was Eleonora Wayles Randolph, a grand-daughter of Thomas Jefferson. On his mother's side was a strain of French Huguenot blood which added strength to the sturdy independence of the father's Scotch-Irish inheritance. He was graduated *summa cum laude* from Harvard College in the class of 1887, and almost immediately decided to devote himself to the scholar's life. Ample means, which in a less resolute character might have tempted to waste of energy, were to him only a stimulus to thoroughness and persistent effort. Family connections enabled him to spend the six years following graduation in a preparation of unusual breadth and variety, not, however, excluding the normal academic routine of study leading to the degree of Ph.D. in history at Freiburg in Germany in 1892. During these years he served as acting secretary of legation at St. Petersburg, 1890–91; as private secretary to his uncle, the United States minister to France, 1892; and as secretary of the American Legation at Vienna, 1893. In this period also he acquired the command of European languages which was to serve him so well in the varied activities of later life. Returning to America in 1893 he accepted an appointment as instructor in history at Harvard. As a teacher of large classes his method was formal, inclining to dryness, but revealing always a personal judgment of men and affairs and enlivened by rare touches of sedate humor. In the closer intimacy of smaller student groups he found his real opportunity and called forth here the permanent loyalty of the choicer spirits.

This long experience in making great historic periods intelligible to unprepared students bore fruit in the writings which made Coolidge's literary reputation. He was not a prolific writer, but as in personal conversation he held himself in reserve until he could speak with decision, so he was never tempted into writing until he had something definite to say. His most important books, *The United States as a World Power* (1908), *Origins of the Triple Alliance* (1917), *Ten Years of War and Peace* (1927), were the outcome of lectures or the summary of previously printed articles. His style was clean-cut without ornament, almost conversational in its directness and its half-humorous allusions. In the year 1906–07 he went as Harvard Exchange Professor to France where he delivered at the Sorbonne and at other French universities the substance of his later volume, *The United States as a World Power*. Widely read and translated into French, German, and Japanese, this may fairly be described as a classic in its field. It was a timely reminder to Americans and foreigners alike that our traditional policy of aloofness in world affairs is no longer feasible and must give place to a larger participation in the common interests of the present day. At the same time it avoided with excellent judgment all dogmatism as to the forms which such participation should take.

Coolidge's interest in books was not that of the "collector" in the ordinary sense of the word. He was rather concerned with the gathering of books as the tools of scholarship. He began early in his academic career to keep himself in-

formed on the activities of the Harvard library, then housed in an ancient building quite inadequate to its needs. He conceived then that ideal of a university library to which he devoted a great part of his energies as long as he lived. He would be satisfied with nothing less than a collection of books so large and so carefully chosen that scholars in every field should find there all printed material necessary for their work. To this end he worked incessantly officially and unofficially, contributing largely of his own wealth and convincing others of the importance of the object he had in view. The lack of a suitable building delayed the fulfilment of his plans until in 1913 the large-minded generosity of Mrs. Eleanor Elkins Widener came half-way to meet them. In the long and sometimes delicate negotiations necessary to combine the architectural problem with the memorial purpose of the donor, the needs of scholars, and the convenience of the library staff, his grasp of the whole situation and his unfailing tact contributed largely to the final result. The Widener Memorial Library stands as his most enduring monument. It was eminently fitting that the office of Director of the University Library, created in 1910, should be entrusted to him. From then until his death he guided with admirable judgment the work of the group of trained assistants in whose hands were placed the details of library administration.

In 1922, when the Council on Foreign Relations decided to start a new quarterly review on a higher plane than had heretofore been attempted, it selected Coolidge as editor-in-chief, and for five years he conducted *Foreign Affairs* with eminent success. His own articles, generally unsigned, dealt in authoritative fashion with topics of immediate interest to thoughtful readers. His gifts of learning and his personal quality found their natural expression in public service. In 1908–09 he went as delegate of the United States and of Harvard University to the Pan-American Scientific Congress at Santiago, Chile. In 1918 he served as special agent of the United States in Sweden and Northern Russia. During the Peace Conference of 1919 he acted as chief of mission in Paris and Vienna. In 1921 he was selected by Secretary Hoover as negotiator for the Red Cross with the Soviet government in Russia, to arrange for its distribution of supplies to the famine-stricken people. Dignified and friendly in manner, modest but unabashed in any society, he attached pupils and subordinates to him by the sincerity and openness of his character.

[C. K. Bolton, in the *Boston Evening Transcript*,

Jan. 18, 1928; R. B. Merriman, in *Harvard Grads. Mag.*, June 1928; *Reports* of the Harvard College Class of 1887; official Minute of the Faculty of Arts and Sciences in Harvard University; personal acquaintance.]

E. E.

COOLIDGE, THOMAS JEFFERSON (Aug. 26, 1831–Nov. 17, 1920), merchant, financier, diplomat, was born in Boston, the youngest child of Joseph Coolidge, Jr., and Eleanora Wayles Randolph. His father was seventh in descent from John Coolidge, the immigrant, who settled about 1630 in Watertown. His great-grandfather on his mother's side was Thomas Jefferson, third president of the United States. Beginning his travels at an early age, Coolidge attended boarding school in London, in Geneva, and in Dresden. At the age of sixteen he returned and entered the sophomore class at Harvard College "without difficulty." His European ideas, formed during his early education abroad, persisted for a number of years. "I believed myself," he later wrote, "to belong to a superior class, and that the principle that the ignorant and poor should have the same right to make laws and govern as the educated and refined was an absurdity." Graduating seventeenth in a class of sixty-odd (1850), he decided to devote himself to the acquisition of wealth. Beginning his business career in foreign commerce, he soon showed a capacity for mercantile affairs. In 1852 he married Hetty Sullivan, daughter of William Appleton of Boston. They had three daughters and a son. Weathering the commercial crash of 1857, he was persuaded by his father-in-law to accept the treasurership of the Boott Mills, thus embarking on a life-long activity in the cotton-spinning industry of New England, holding at different times the treasurership of the Lawrence Manufacturing Company, and of the Amoskeag Mills, and directorships in other New England manufacturing companies. In touch with the banking world, he became director of the Merchants National Bank of Boston, of the New England Trust Company, and of the Bay State Trust Company, and one of the original incorporators of the Old Colony Trust Company of Boston. His business enterprise engaged him in the management of various railroads, and he served for a short time as president of the Atchison, Topeka & Santa Fé road. He also devoted himself to the public interest, serving as a member of the first Park Commission, which laid out the park system of the City of Boston. He was the donor to Manchester-by-the-Sea of a town library, and to Harvard College of the Jefferson Physical Laboratory. He also established a fund for research in physics and served for eleven years as a

member of the Board of Overseers of Harvard University. In 1889 he was appointed a member of the Pan-American Congress. In 1892 he became minister to France, where his ability to speak the language as a native, and his tact, courtesy, and sound judgment won him the high consideration of his associates. A change of administration brought him home, where in 1896 he was appointed member of a Massachusetts Taxation Commission. In 1898 he was appointed to the Joint High Commission of the United States, Great Britain, Canada, and Newfoundland, to examine the question of the Alaskan boundary, the fisheries, the destruction of fur seals, armaments upon the lakes, and transportation of goods in bond. His distinguished life of business achievement and public service closed in his ninetieth year.

[*T. Jefferson Coolidge, 1831–1920, An Autobiography* (1923), *Proc. Mass. Hist. Soc.*, LIV, 141–49; *Harvard Grads. Mag.*, Mar. 1921.]

G. G. W.

COOMBE, THOMAS (Oct. 21, 1747–Aug. 15, 1822), Anglican clergyman, Loyalist, poet, was born and educated in Philadelphia, being graduated from the College of Philadelphia in 1766. While still in college, he evinced some measure of literary ability by assisting, with others of his fellow pupils, in translating some of the Latin poems of his master, John Beveridge, which appeared in the latter's *Epistolæ Familiares* (1765). Two years after graduation, Coombe went to England, and one year later, in 1769, was ordained in the Church of England by the Bishop of London. In 1771 he was appointed chaplain to the Marquis of Rockingham, but he left England in 1772 to return to America. In Philadelphia, serving as assistant minister to the congregations of Christ Church and St. Peter's, he soon distinguished himself as a preacher. His sermon delivered on July 20, 1775, a general fast-day appointed by the Continental Congress, in which he advocated the cause of the Colonies, aroused much attention and received wide circulation in several editions. Coombe's ordination oath did not permit him conscientiously to go the whole length of the Declaration of Independence, and his deportation to Staunton, Va., was decreed in 1777, together with that of other Tories. Coombe, however, pleaded ill health, and the order, in his case, was not enforced. In 1778 he was granted permission to go to New York, and in the following year sailed for England where he passed the remainder of his life. After a period of service as chaplain to the Earl of Carlisle, Coombe was appointed chaplain in ordinary to the King and, in 1800, became prebendary of Canterbury.

Eight years later, the Dean and Chapter of Canterbury appointed him rector to the united London parishes of St. Michael's Queenhithe and Trinity the Less. In these livings he gave respected service for fourteen years, until his death.

Both in America and in England Coombe developed considerable contemporary reputation for scholarly, eloquent, and forceful speaking. Josiah Quincy, Jr., said of one of Coombe's extemporary prayers, that "in point of sentiment, propriety of expression, and true sublimity" it excelled anything of the kind that he had ever heard. A number of his sermons and addresses were published. On Apr. 14, 1771, during his first sojourn in England, Coombe preached at St. Stephen's, Walbrook, for the benefit of the children belonging to the St. Ethelberg Society, a sermon which was published in London in 1772. After his return to America, his first publication, *The Harmony between the Old and New Testaments Respecting the Messiah* (Philadelphia, 1774), was a consolidation of two sermons preached before the united congregations of Christ Church and St. Peter's on Christmas Day, 1773, and "on the Sunday when the collection was made for the relief of the poor of those congregations." One other discourse was published in London in 1790, the *Influence of Christianity on the Condition of the World*, delivered at Trinity Chapel, Conduit St., London, on Dec. 13, 1789.

Coombe's claim to the title of poet is based primarily on *The Peasant of Auburn; or, the Emigrant* (London, 1783). The poem is in content and form an imitation of the *Deserted Village* of Goldsmith, to whom it was dedicated, and was designed to recount the unhappy fortunes of the emigrant from "sweet Auburn" when, later, on the banks of the Ohio, his bright hopes darkened to desolation, war, and death. The volume included also a number of shorter poems. He no doubt impressed his contemporaries more as an Englishman than as an American; and more as clergyman of character and ability than as a poet.

[An obituary, printed in the *Gentleman's Mag.* (London), Aug. 1822 gives the primary facts of Coombe's professional career and of his publications in England. See also Benj. Dorr, *A Hist. Account of Christ Ch., Phila.* (1841); Jas. S. M. Anderson, *Hist. of the Ch. of England in the Colonies and Foreign Dependencies of the British Empire* (London, 1845–56); Wm. S. Perry, *Hist. of the Am. Episc. Ch. 1507–1883* (1885). In addition to the edition of *The Peasant of Auburn* specified in the text, there was one limited to 150 copies privately printed for the Auungervyle Society in 1887. *The Peasant of Auburn and Other Poems*, "attributed to J. Coombe, D.D. circa 1786." Copies of either edition are now rare.]   A. L. B.

COOPER, EDWARD (Oct. 26, 1824–Feb. 25, 1905), manufacturer, public man, was born in New York City, the son of Peter Cooper [*q.v.*], and Sarah Bedell. He attended the New York public schools and entered Columbia University, but before taking a degree he went abroad for travel with his classmate Abram S. Hewitt [*q.v.*], suffered shipwreck on the return voyage, was rescued by a sailing vessel, and came back to New York resolved to enter business. Together with Hewitt, he organized Cooper, Hewitt & Company for the manufacture of iron and steel in which he became expert, rising to a high rank among the metallurgical engineers of America. From his father he inherited marked inventive talent which he cultivated by scientific study of the iron and steel industry, with fruitful results. Perhaps the most notable of these was the invention of the regenerative hot-blast stove for blast furnaces, one of the most important improvements made in iron manufacture in America up to that time, as it greatly increased the iron output of a furnace and lessened the cost. Neither for this nor for his other inventions did he apply for patents; thus many noteworthy improvements designed by him, such as the Durham double bell and hopper, are not generally known as his. Recognition, however, meant little to him. He preferred that his colleagues and the public should benefit by his ingenuity and have free use of his discoveries.

Keeping pace with the development of the iron and steel industry in the United States, the firm of Cooper, Hewitt & Company grew rapidly. It succeeded to the iron interests of Peter Cooper and added also the Trenton, Ringwood, Pequest, and Durham Iron Works. In consequence Edward Cooper was sought for places of responsibility and at various times served as a director of the United States Trust Company, American Sulphur Company, New Jersey Steel & Iron Company, New York & Greenwood Lake Railway, American Electric Elevator Company, Chrysolite Silver Mining Company, and the Metropolitan Opera House. His public career began when, in 1860, he was chosen a delegate to the National Democratic Convention held in Charleston. In 1871, he suggested to Gov. Samuel Tilden, to whom he was a valued counselor, that the accounts of "Boss" Tweed and his associates, who then dominated New York City politics, be subjected to examination. The Governor approved, and a vigorous investigation was ordered which ended in the complete downfall of the "Tweed Ring." As a member of the Committee of Seventy, Cooper played a prominent part, not only in the prosecutions but also in the reform that followed. Although always a Democrat, he was chosen in 1879 fusion candidate for mayor by the Republicans and a wing of the Democrats, and after an exciting campaign was elected. During his administration he worked energetically toward municipal reform. Like his father, he devoted himself generously to the public interests. Of Cooper Union, which was established and endowed by his father, he became a trustee and president of the board of trustees, and labored unsparingly for its advancement. He was married in 1863 to Cornelia Redmond, who died in 1894. Cooper died in New York City in his eighty-first year.

[R. W. Raymond, "Biog. Notice of Edward Cooper," in *Trans. Am. Inst. Mining Engineers*, XXXVII (1907), 349–56; New York newspapers, Feb. 26, 1905. See also sketch of A. S. Hewitt in vol. XXXIV (1904), and an article on hot-blast stoves and hot-blast furnaces in vol. XIV (1886) of *Trans. Am. Inst. Mining Engineers*; M. H. Howe, *Metallurgy of Steel* (2nd ed., 1891), vol. I.]　　　　　　　　　　　　　　W. B. P.

COOPER, ELIAS SAMUEL (Nov. 25, 1820–Oct. 13, 1862), surgeon, was born on a farm near Somerville, Butler County, Ohio, the son of Jacob and Elizabeth (Walls) Cooper, and a brother of Jacob Cooper [q.v.]. Following a course in medicine at Cincinnati, which he began at the age of sixteen, he attended St. Louis University at St. Louis, Mo., where he obtained his M.D. degree in 1841. He began practise at Danville, Ill., and at the age of twenty-two had become the leading surgeon of the community. In 1844 he moved to Peoria in the same state, where he practised for ten years. Following a year spent in European surgical clinics, he went to San Francisco in 1855. Soon after his arrival, he was instrumental in organizing the Medical Society of the State of California. In 1858 Cooper founded in San Francisco the first medical college on the Pacific coast, known as the Medical Department of the University of the Pacific. In 1860 he began the publication of the *San Francisco Medical Press,* a quarterly journal of medicine and surgery, which was continued after his death by his nephew, Dr. Levi Cooper Lane, who was associated with his uncle in practise. It is in this journal that most of Cooper's published writings appear.

From the time of his arrival in San Francisco, Cooper was recognized as a surgeon of skill and originality. As professor of surgery his teaching was marked by earnestness, without oratory. It is noteworthy that he conducted a course in operative surgery upon animals. His claims to permanent recognition in surgery rest upon his use of alcoholic dressings of wounds, the treatment of diseased joints by free incision, the use of metallic sutures for un-united fractures and free exploration of the thoracic cavity after rib resection. Such aggressive leadership could not fail to arouse jealousies and Cooper's later years were somewhat embittered by a long-drawn-out suit for malpractise in a case of Cæsarian section. The suit never came to trial. Cooper was a large, powerful man, intensely earnest, vigorous in language and quick to resent what he considered injustices. He read and wrote only medicine, he thought only medicine and talked only medicine. He slept little, saying that sleep was so much time stolen from life and from his work. Such utter neglect of the laws of health brought the usual penalty of an early death. Soon after arriving in California he had developed an obscure nervous affection which later caused a bilateral facial paralysis and intense neuralgic pains. In the spring of 1862 he went to the mountains on account of his condition; in May he went suddenly blind, but later recovered some vision. He died in San Francisco in October of that year. He was never married. His medical school lived until 1864, two years after the death of its founder. It was reorganized in 1870 as the Medical College of the Pacific; again in 1880, as Cooper Medical College, when Dr. Levi Cooper Lane donated a site and erected an imposing building for the school; and in 1908 it was taken over by Stanford University.

[Sketches of Cooper's life and works by Levi C. Lane in the *San Francisco Medic. Press,* Oct. 1862; by Washington Ayer, in the *Occidental Medic. Times* (Sacramento), Oct. 1893; and by Emmet Rixford, in *Am. Medic. Biogs.* (1920), ed. by H. A. Kelly and W. L. Burrage; information as to parentage from Prof. Lane Cooper. A portrait of Cooper is contained in the collection of the Army Medical Library in Washington.]

　　　　　　　　　　　　　　J. M. P.

COOPER, EZEKIEL (Feb. 22, 1763–Feb. 21, 1847), clergyman, a pioneer in the establishment of Methodism in the United States, was born in Caroline County, Md., the son of Richard and Ann Cooper, whom he describes as "plain people, in easy and plentiful circumstances." He was brought up in the Church of England, but when thirteen years old became interested in the type of religion exemplified by the Methodists, through the preaching of Freeborn Garrettson [q.v.]. It was not until several years later, however, after having experienced the inner struggle which the evangelical theology of the day was likely to engender, that he joined a Methodist society. Garrettson made him a class-leader in Talbot County, but he long hesitated to become a preacher, though, he says, "I was bold in reproving, and zealous in inviting sinners in private to turn to the Lord and seek the salvation of their souls. My earnestness in this soon had such an effect that it was seldom that any of my acquaintances would sin within my sight or hearing." Finally, in 1784, he was brought to the attention of Francis Asbury who appointed him to the Caroline circuit. At the conference of 1785, held at Baltimore, he was admitted on trial, and on June 3, 1787, at John Street Church, New York, he was ordained deacon by Bishop Asbury. His ministry extended over sixty-four years, and covered a wide era, including Long Island, East Jersey, Trenton, Baltimore, Annapolis, Alexandria, the Boston district, of which he was superintendent, New York, Brooklyn, Philadelphia, and Wilmington. Throughout this long period of the church's growth he was a recognized leader, effective as a preacher, powerful as a debater, noted for his encyclopedic knowledge, and having the confidence and warm affection of Bishop Asbury until the latter's death. Physically he was a man to attract attention, being over six feet tall and heavy of frame, with large head, high forehead, sharp features, and a large wen suspended from his right jaw. He was extremely frugal, some said penurious, and succeeded in leaving an estate of $50,000. It was his business ability, no doubt, which in 1779 led to his being appointed agent of the Methodist Book Concern. When he took charge it had no capital, and debts equaling its assets; when he left in 1808 it was on a firm foundation with assets of $45,000. Even when in a slave-holding community he vigorously opposed slavery, publishing in the (Annapolis) *Maryland Gazette* in 1790–91 a series of letters in advocacy of freedom, under the signature of "A Freeman." A letter by him on the same subject, dated Apr. 18, 1791, appeared in the *Maryland Journal,* another in the *Virginia Gazette* of Nov. 17, 1791, and one dated Nov. 28, 1791, in the same paper. His only other publications seem to have been, *A Funeral Discourse on the Death of that Eminent Man the Late John Dickens* (1799) and *The Substance of a Funeral Discourse . . . on the Death of the Rev. Francis Asbury* (1819).

[Geo. A. Phœbus, *Beams of Light on Early Methodism in America* (1887) is based on a diary, letters, and other MSS. left by Cooper. The appendix reprints several of his letters on slavery. Standard histories of Methodism contain numerous references to him. See also Wm. B. Sprague, *Annals Am. Pulpit,* vol. VII (1861); and W. F. Whitlock, *The Story of the Book Concerns* (1903).]   H. E. S.

COOPER, HENRY ERNEST (Aug. 28, 1857–May 14, 1929), lawyer, leader in the Hawaiian revolution, minister of foreign affairs of the Republic of Hawaii, was of New England ancestry, though born in New Albany, Ind., the son of William Giles Cooper and Harriet A. (Weller) Cooper. The elder Cooper having enlisted in the Union army when the Civil War came on,

Mrs. Cooper took her children back to her old home in Boston. Henry was educated in the schools of that city and graduated from Boston University in 1878 with the degree of LL.B. In the same year he was admitted to the bar. His first professional employment was with a syndicate organized in Boston for the construction of a railroad in the southwestern part of the United States. Through this circumstance he became a resident of San Diego, Cal., where he was for a time attorney for the Santa Fé Railroad. During the "boom" in that section he organized an abstract and title company and made some real-estate investments. On Oct. 2, 1883, he was married to Mary E. Porter; eight children were born to them.

Cooper first visited Hawaii in 1890, returning there a year later with his family to take up his residence. During the stormy reign of Queen Liliuokalani (1891–93), he became a member of the annexation party and in the beginning of 1893 helped to organize the revolution which deposed the queen and set up a republican government. On the day of the overthow, as chairman of the Committee of Safety, he read from the steps of the government building the proclamation of the Provisional Government. His services in this movement were rewarded by his appointment as one of the judges of the circuit court for the island of Oahu, a position which he filled with satisfaction. In November 1895 he was appointed minister of foreign affairs of the Republic of Hawaii and entered upon eight years of service in the executive branch of the government, during which period he administered, at one time or another, either regularly or *ad interim,* most of the important executive offices, including those of acting president of the Republic and acting governor of the territory. He held as many as three positions simultaneously. On one occasion he was minister of foreign affairs, superintendent of public instruction, and acting president; at another time he was secretary of the territory, superintendent of public works, and treasurer *ad interim.* He clearly demonstrated his capacity for effective administration of public office. A competent observer said of him, "He is positive and active and as a rule has progressive views on public matters." He had some bitter enemies, however, chiefly among the native Hawaiians and those who composed the old royalist party, who disliked him not only because of his share in the overthrow of the monarchy but because he was a recent arrival thrust prominently into Hawaiian politics, being about the only important leader in the revolutionary movement who was not born in Hawaii or long resident in the country.

After the inauguration of the territorial government a newspaper representing this faction once spoke of him as the Mark Hanna of Hawaii.

As minister of foreign affairs Cooper had to carry on a diplomatic controversy with Japan, arising mainly from the attempt of the Hawaiian government to limit the immigration of Japanese laborers into Hawaii, and to handle the somewhat delicate relations between Hawaii and the United States during the years 1896–98. In the Japanese controversy—which was never judicially settled on its merits—he maintained that Hawaii's position was correct in its entirety and only consented to the payment of an indemnity in order to clear the way for annexation to the United States. To the policy of annexation he was ardently devoted and he sought in every proper way to promote American interests. It is believed that he, more than any one else, was responsible for the decision of the Hawaiian government to disregard neutrality at the outbreak of the Spanish-American War and to place Hawaii squarely on the side of the United States. He was the first secretary of the Territory of Hawaii (1900–03) and was one of the two men most seriously considered by President Roosevelt for appointment as governor in 1903. After retirement from public office in that year, he engaged in the practise of law. He had an important part in the founding of the College (now University) of Hawaii and was the first chairman of its board of regents (1907–14). From 1910 to 1914 he was first judge of the first circuit court (Oahu) and then retired permanently to private life. The last years of his life were spent on his walnut ranch in California. He died at Long Beach, Cal.

[*Men of Hawaii*, vol. II (1921), ed. by J. W. Siddall; contemporary notices in Honolulu newspapers, especially obituary in *Honolulu Advertiser*, May 16, 1929; reports of Hawaiian government departments; correspondence in Archives of Hawaii and Dept. of State.]

R. S. K.

COOPER, JACOB (Dec. 7, 1830–Jan. 31, 1904), college professor, was born on a farm near Somerville, Butler County, Ohio, the son of Jacob and Elizabeth (Walls) Cooper, and a brother of Elias Samuel Cooper [*q.v.*]. Working by day and studying at night he prepared for college. After some time at other institutions he entered Yale in the Junior class and graduated with high honor in 1852. The next year he was licensed in the Presbyterian ministry. From Berlin in 1854 he received his Ph.D., and then studied theology at Halle and Edinburgh. In 1855 he became professor of Greek in Centre College, Danville, Ky. This town was then rife with anti-slavery agitation, and when the Civil War broke out it became the center of opposition to the se-

cession of Kentucky. To uphold the Federal cause some professors of the college and of Danville Theological Seminary established the *Danville Review* (1861–65). Cooper was an editor, and wrote fervent outspoken articles. In 1862 he became chaplain of the 3rd Kentucky Infantry, composed chiefly of mountain men, whom he served with signal devotion. The next year he returned to the college, which had before it several years of extreme disturbance. His Kentucky experiences gave Cooper a life-long intense interest in politics, with a zealous attachment to the Republican party.

In 1866 he joined the faculty of Rutgers College. For twenty-seven years he was professor of Greek, and for eleven, till his death, professor of mental and moral philosophy. Besides teaching, he gave the service of college pastor, preaching often in the chapel, and also constantly in churches. He impressed himself deeply on generations of students, and became in a remarkable way identified with the life of the college. He had large and various learning, and contagious intellectual enthusiasms. A rare gift of personal sympathy and many kindly acts won for him the hearts of his students. His individuality of speech and manner gave spicy interest to his teaching and his other relations, and made him vivid in memories. His influence in the college was increased by his high place as a citizen of New Brunswick. While decided and indeed militant in his opinions, he was and is remembered for great Christian goodness and friendliness. For two years from 1883 he was importuned to become professor in the University of Michigan, but Rutgers would not release him. He received the degree of D.C.L. from Jena in 1873. He was an editor of *Bibliotheca Sacra* from 1897 to 1903. He was married in 1855 to Caroline Macdill of Oxford, Ohio, who died two years later. In 1865 he married Mary Linn of Cincinnati. Cooper's published writings were chiefly his numerous periodical articles, philosophical, theological, political, and biographical, covering forty years. Many were reprinted as pamphlets. His list of separate publications includes *The Eleusinian Mysteries* (Berlin Ph.D. thesis 1854, revised editions 1876, 1895), *The Loyalty Demanded by the Present Crisis* (reprinted from the *Danville Review*, 1862), *The Natural Right to Make a Will* (Jena D.C.L. thesis 1874, 1894), *Biography of George Duffield, Jr., D.D.* (1889), *Biography of President Theodore Dwight Woolsey* (1899), all pamphlets.

[*Who's Who in America*, 1903–05; *Obit. Record Grads. Yale Univ.*, 1904; E. T. Corwin, *Manual of the Reformed Ch. in America* (1902), containing a partial list of Cooper's articles in periodicals; W. H. S. Demarest, *Hist. of Rutgers Coll.* (1924); A. S. Cook, *Address on . . . Presenting to Rutgers Coll. a Portrait of Prof. Jacob Cooper* (1906); H. A. Scomp in *Bibliotheca Sacra*, Apr. 1904; *The Targum* (Rutgers Coll., Feb. 4 and 11, 1904); *Rutgers Alumni Mo.*, Jan. 1928; Cooper's writings.]   R.H.N.

COOPER, JAMES (May 8, 1810–Mar. 28, 1863), lawyer, United States senator, was born in Frederick County, Md. Owing to the straitened financial circumstances of his parents he was not able to go to college until 1829, when he entered Mount St. Mary's College, Emmitsburg. Three years later he was graduated from Washington and Jefferson College, after which he entered the law office of Thaddeus Stevens at Gettysburg, Pa. He was admitted to the bar in 1834. As a Whig in the federal House of Representatives, where he served from Dec. 2, 1839, to Mar. 3, 1843, he was a strong supporter of the measure providing for the distribution of the funds from the sales of public lands among the states for internal improvements and of the Preëmption Act of 1841 (*Congressional Globe*, 27 Cong., 1 Sess., p. 143). From 1844 to 1848 he was in the state legislature and he became speaker of the Assembly in 1847. He was an aggressive candidate against Gen. Irvin for the Whig nomination for governor but was not successful. In 1848, he was appointed attorney-general of the state by Gov. Johnston, in which position he served until the legislature met in January 1849, when he appeared again as a representative from Adams County and was again chosen speaker. In this year he was elected United States senator. As senator probably his greatest claim to national distinction was his membership on the Committee of Thirteen which framed the famous compromise measures of 1850. Ill health prevented him from taking an active part in the work of the Senate during the latter half of his single term. He opposed the bill in 1853 granting federal aid for a Pacific railroad on the ground that the bill conferred too extensive powers on a corporation (*Ibid.*, 32 Cong., 2 Sess., App., p. 183). He spoke against the Kansas-Nebraska Bill on Feb. 27, 1854 (*Ibid.*, 33 Cong., 1 Sess., App., p. 505). At the outbreak of the Civil War he became a member of the Brengle Home Guard of Frederick, Md., where he had returned to reside at the close of his senatorial term. He was authorized by the War Department to raise and organize a regiment of infantry in Maryland (*Official Records, Army*, 3 ser., I, 138, 618). On May 17, 1861, he was commissioned a brigadier-general in the volunteer service and was placed in command of Camp Wallace near Columbus, Ohio, which had been established by Gen. Lew Wallace as a camp for paroled soldiers organized for service against the Indians in the Northwest. Later he was made

commander of Camp Chase, near Columbus, where he died.

[In addition to references given above see some mention, not wholly favorable, of Cooper's political life in A. K. McClure, *Old Time Notes of Pa.* (1905), written by a contemporary of Cooper, who characterizes him as a "weak man . . . and unbalanced by the distinction he had attained. He was a fluent and adroit speaker, but he was not a man of forceful intellect and was greatly lacking in well balanced judgment." Obituaries appeared in the *Ohio State Journal*, Mar. 31, 1863, and the *Capital City Fact*, Mar. 28, 1863, both of Columbus.]
         F.C.S—n.

COOPER, JAMES FENIMORE (Sept. 15, 1789–Sept. 14, 1851), novelist, was born in Burlington, N. J., the son of William Cooper [*q.v.*] and of Elizabeth Fenimore his wife. William Cooper was descended from a Quaker ancestor who had crossed the Atlantic in 1679 and had founded the family tradition of landowning on a large scale. Elizabeth Fenimore was of Swedish descent. The father of the novelist at the close of the Revolution had acquired a tract of land along the upper Susquehanna and had established a settlement called Cooperstown. To it in 1790 he brought his family, and there between 1796 and 1799 he built Otsego Hall, which was long the most notable private residence in that part of New York state. A man of fortune and standing, he represented his district in Congress, and in his mode of life maintained the dignity expected of a border aristocrat. His son, the eleventh of twelve children, grew up in circumstances which were as near to being manorial as the age and place could afford. At the same time, since the village of Cooperstown lay on the very edge of the forest, was indeed surrounded by it, the future romancer early became familiar with the magic of the wilderness as well as with the rough makeshifts of the frontier. The divided elements of the pioneer and of the gentleman, which were always to struggle in his mind, were equally developed by his childhood.

His formal education tended to confirm him in a kind of Federalist pride. From the village school in Cooperstown he was sent in 1800 to Albany, where he was a pupil in the household of the rector of St. Peter's and the companion of young gentlemen much like himself in upbringing and in prospects. The rector, a good scholar and a good churchman, was also a man of the world who was neither republican nor even American in his sympathies, and who cherished a special prejudice against New England. When Cooper, after two years at Albany, went to Yale to enter the class of 1806, he carried with him his own pride and, apparently, some of his late teacher's prejudice. He took college lightly, resisted its obligations, got little out of its advantages, and was dismissed in his third year. It was then decided that the boy, now sixteen, should go to sea in preparation for entering the navy, which at the time had no naval academy. Accordingly he shipped before the mast in 1806, on board a vessel which sailed from New York, changed cargo in London, proceeded to the Straits of Gibraltar, returned to England, and reached America again in 1807. With this training in seamanship Cooper was able to get a commission as midshipman. He served for a brief period on the *Vesuvius* in 1808, and spent the winter on Lake Ontario with a party engaged in building a brig for inland use against the British in Canada. During 1809 he visited Niagara Falls with his commanding officer, was for a short time himself in command on Lake Champlain, and was ordered back to the Atlantic, to the *Wasp*. The next year he was granted a furlough for twelve months, at the end of which he resigned his commission and left the navy for good.

These years, which submitted Cooper to all the technical discipline he was ever to have, had not won him away from his impulse toward the life of a country gentleman, and he seems to have felt no regret at giving up his profession. His immediate excuse was that on Jan. 1, 1811, he had been married to Susan Augusta De Lancey at Mamaroneck, N. Y. Not only was the young wife unwilling to share her husband with the sea, but she was also, as a member of a land-holding family, predisposed to a country life. The two settled at once into a domestic serenity not easy to match in the history of literature. Cooper managed to hold the firmest principles in general respecting his rights over his household and yet to yield them in the gentlest way on any special occasion. That is to say, he loved and admired his wife, who was a woman of tact, who made him comfortable and happy, and let him work as much as he wished, provided he did it where she chose. After their marriage they lived until 1814 with or near the elder De Lanceys at Heathcote Hill in Mamaroneck. In that year they moved to Cooperstown, where Cooper selected a farm, "Fenimore," just outside the village and began to build a house. In 1817, however, his wife persuaded him to go back to Westchester, a more civilized county. There he lived at Scarsdale, in a house on Angevine Farm overlooking Long Island Sound, until 1822, when he left the country for New York in the interest of his new career as writer.

Up to the age of thirty Cooper had never even thought of the literary profession. His family and his farms had sufficiently occupied him, and he had been content to live as did other men in his class. There must have been, however, some growing restlessness in him, some longing for the life of movement and adventure which he had given up on his marriage at twenty-one. Almost any accident might have suggested to him that he could combine domestic peace with heroic activity by becoming a writer of romances. The particular accident which did suggest it was one which must have happened to many men. Reading a novel aloud to his wife one day, Cooper said he could write a better one. She challenged him to do it. Here, in most instances, the matter would have ended. But this restless squire was one case in ten thousand, a man of genius whose gifts were none the less real because they were unsuspected by him or by anybody else. He first tried his hand at *Precaution* (1820), a conventional novel with its scene laid in England and with all its action mere gentility and propriety. The reception of the book did little to encourage its author, but he did not need encouragement. His gathered energy, which had to have an outlet, had found one, and for the next thirty years it poured itself into a powerful stream of novels, romances, and criticism.

Having no definite literary aims of his own when he wrote *Precaution*, Cooper had fallen into a familiar mode without any sense that he was misdirecting his talents. With his next book he vigorously asserted himself. His setting was to be American, his chief character the very essence of native patriotism. Starting with the story of an actual spy who during the Revolution had served John Jay against the British, then in possession of New York, Cooper enlarged this somewhat shadowy figure with all the additions of romance. Harvey Birch in *The Spy* (1821) is cunning, mysterious, eloquent in both words and silences, dedicated to his cause, driven by patriotism as by a demon, and lonely as a hero in a Byronic poem. The fact that Birch plays like a shuttle of secrecy back and forth between the British and the American lines allowed Cooper to exhibit both sides in the struggle and to represent the topography and manners of Westchester County in considerable detail. He had already hit upon the formula of flight and pursuit which recurs in most of his romances, keeping up the characteristic suspense and displaying the characteristic panorama. He had also revealed his attitude toward characters from the lower social classes: he thought he looked upon them as one democrat upon another, but there was really an element of condescension, however generous, in his evident gratification at being able to prove that a plain man may be as much a hero as a gentleman. What was most important of all, Cooper had found in himself and had shown to his readers that large vigor of narrative without which no man can be a great romancer and on account of which any man can be forgiven any minor defect.

The Spy met with a prompt success. New editions were called for, in England as well as in America; a dramatic version was on the New York stage within a few months; a French translation appeared in less than a year. The first outstanding American novel, it did not then suffer from its stately, not to say stilted, language and its lofty sentiments, not to say top-heavy affectations. Contemporary readers took such qualities in a romance as much for granted as they took contemporary costumes on men and women. They saw only the flesh and blood of heroic actions, set in a new world not hitherto seen under any such heroic light. Cooper, who hardly guessed he was writing in a fashion, and who believed that he was dealing with a life full of reality, was stimulated by his audience to go on as he had begun. He never used any narrative method but that of rapid improvisation, and his only concern was to hit upon some new and interesting story to tell.

This must not be taken to mean that he thought of fiction as existing for its own sake. He was a country gentleman, not a Bohemian, and he was constitutionally didactic. Literature in those days of the Republic could not easily help feeling that it had duties to perform. But Cooper, though he did lard his plots with incidental morals, had such a wilderness of life to transform into fiction that he had to work on a scale which kept him in motion. After the *Spy* he again struck out somewhat at random. *The Pioneers* (1823) owes more of its continued fame to its connection with the Leather-Stocking series than to its individual merits. Cooper had not yet imagined Natty Bumppo and Chingachgook to the plane of romantic elevation on which they were subsequently to move. He regarded them as picturesque figures rather than as universal symbols, and he gave them only a reasonably important part in his drama of that frontier which he remembered from his childhood in Cooperstown and which he now depicted, as he said, exclusively to please himself. Next he turned to yet another region of his youthful memories and wrote *The Pilot* (1823), avowedly to prove that a sailor could write a better novel than the landsman Scott had written in *The Pirate,* but actually, no doubt, to make a fresh escape into a lost world of adventure. Once more Cooper used conventional, Byronic elements, in his John Paul Jones, and he flamed with patriotism as in *The Spy.* But *The Pilot* contained another exciting pursuit and

flight, another arresting simple hero, Long Tom Coffin, and another thrilling background, exhibited with such contagious magic that Cooper, though he could not know it, was setting the mode for all later stories of the sea, and more or less determining their tone.

These three successes made him a personage in the new, tentative literature of the age. He founded the Bread and Cheese Club in New York, a literary society which his reputation no less than his vigorous character enabled him to dominate. He served on the committee which welcomed Lafayette back to the United States in 1824, and he received in that year the honorary degree of Master of Arts from Columbia College. In the expansive mood which came to him with such recognition he planned to become a national romancer by writing the Legends of the Thirteen Republics, one story for each of the original states. He wrote, however, only *Lionel Lincoln* (1825), dealing with Boston in the days of Bunker Hill. His account of the battle was admirable, but on the whole the book was dull, and it generally failed to please. The dislike which Cooper felt for the New England character, a dislike which he formed early and which he seems to have encouraged in himself, handicapped him when it came to writing a romance. The idea of satire had not occurred to him, nor was he, as his later work was to show, happy in that vein. He was obliged to create largely out of his affections, with the help of knowledge which he had picked up before he began to write. His first three experiments, after *Precaution,* had indicated most of the ground on which his imagination was at home: the New York past, the Northern frontier, the high seas. Outside of these territories he was seldom to show his capacities at their best.

Although the Natty Bumppo of *The Pioneers* had been only a preliminary sketch, he had so interested the public that Cooper, urged by his friends, decided to go further with his most striking character. It must be borne in mind that Daniel Boone had died in 1820, and that he had been glorified by Byron in *Don Juan* shortly after *The Pioneers* appeared. While Boone cannot strictly be said to have been the original of Natty, they were at least alike in that each of them had chosen the wilderness in preference to the settlements. This, at a time when Americans were becoming sharply conscious of a clash between the wilderness and the settlements, seemed intensely dramatic. About Boone there was not much more to tell; at any rate, his biographers did not tell it. Natty Bumppo, bound by fewer limits of actuality, could be freely elaborated. In *The Last of the Mohicans*

(1826), Cooper took the hero back to the deeds of his prime, during the French and Indian War. In *The Prairie* (1827), Leather-Stocking was made to appear in his old age, sunk from scout to trapper, beyond the Mississippi in the wilderness where Boone had taken refuge from the crowding world. In the one, the scout is endowed with all the finished competence which in Cooper's time it was already traditional to ascribe to frontiersmen. In the other, the trapper has assumed the wide benevolence which it was then traditional to think of as the result of living and reflecting in the wilderness. As Cooper had thought more and more about his childhoood, the magic of the forest had grown upon him. It had become the symbol of whatever was spacious and elevated, and so naturally the breeding-ground of heroism and wisdom. The prairie he did not know from experience, but he imagined it as a sea of land, a kind of combination of the two wildernesses he did know. With as much movement and adventure as in any of the previous romances, *The Last of the Mohicans* and *The Prairie* had also a dignity and a poetry which were new. Still another enrichment came from the various Indians in the stories. They have never, even by Cooper himself, been considered realistic, nor have they needed to be. They have always stood as figures of romance, creatures of the wild, dark aborigines neither lifted nor corrupted by civilization. Conceived in that universal mood of chivalry which, when an enemy has ceased to threaten, impels the descendants of the victors to pay homage to the defeated, Cooper's Indians have been accepted in the same mood. Their craft, their nobility, their eloquence—these are the tribute and compensation given them in a sort of poetic justice. It will, however, be noted that Chingachgook and Uncas, to whom Cooper devoted his chief praise and sympathy, are the allies of Leather-Stocking.

Having touched the peak of his accomplishment and having won international fame, Cooper entered another chapter of his career. *The Prairie,* indeed, had been written in Paris, to which he had taken his family in 1826. He went, nominally, as United States consul at Lyons, in order not to seem an expatriate, but he soon allowed this nominal appointment, which involved no duties and no fees, to lapse, and gave himself up to travel, authorship, and controversy over the relative virtues of America and Europe. His travels included brief stays in England in 1826 and 1828, a longer visit to Switzerland in 1828, temporary residences in Italy during 1828–30, an excursion to Munich and Dresden in 1830, and a return after the July revolution to Paris, where he lived until his return to New York in 1833. Besides *The Prairie* he published, during his absence, *The Red Rover* (1828), *The Wept of Wish-ton-Wish* (1829), *The Water-Witch* (1831), romances all of which have their scenes laid in America or on the sea in American ships; and the European romances, *The Bravo* (1831), *The Heidenmauer* (1832), and *The Headsman* (1833), "in which," he said, "American opinion should be brought to bear on European facts." His *Notions of the Americans* (1828), purporting to be a series of letters written home by an Englishman traveling in the United States, was the work of a homesick American defending his country from the misunderstandings he had met in Europe. His *Letter of J. Fenimore Cooper to General Lafayette* (1831), a pamphlet arguing that republics are more economical than monarchies, was the work of an enthusiastic partisan. There can be no question that Cooper, educating himself in cosmopolitanism, remained all the time a genuine, even a bumptious, patriot, so far as he was conscious of his own feelings. But neither can there be any question that at the same time he was being stiffened in certain of his early prejudices, to a degree that promised trouble when he should once more be back among the people whom he had tended to romanticize while he was away from them. The matter is important, not merely because the shock of reality affected Cooper as a citizen, but because it affected him as an artist also. Writing from Paris to his brother in 1831 he had said: "Now my longing is for a wilderness—Cooperstown is far too populous and artificial for me, and it is my intention to plunge into the forest, for six months in the year, at my return. I will not quit my native state, but shall seek some unsettled part of that." At his actual return two years later Cooper found that not only Cooperstown but the entire country repelled him. He suddenly missed the simplicity, the decorum, the private and public virtue, the enlightened patriotism which he held to be innate in republicans and which during his absence he had declared to be natural to Americans. He failed to realize that he, more than American society, had changed. Those elements in him which had imagined Leather-Stocking now longed for the wilderness. Only, he discovered that the wilderness of his fantasy had ceased to exist, if it had ever existed. He was imprisoned in the settlements. Had Cooper been a pure romancer, able at will to lose himself in the universe of his creation, he might have endured his disappointment and his prison. But his temper was by no means so detached. A man of action, he had to take a hand when he saw things, as he thought, going badly. For the next ten years he devoted much of his strength to angry criticism, suppressing the pioneer in himself while the gentleman in him fought to reform the settlements.

The trouble started with Cooper considerably in the wrong. Always sensitive to adverse criticism, he had bitterly resented it from his countrymen while he was abroad defending them, and, little of it as he had really to endure, he came home smarting with what he believed to be many grievances. He declined the public dinner at once proposed for him in New York, thus letting slip an opportunity to learn of the esteem in which he was genuinely held by the very persons whose opinion he cared for. Stubbornly aloof, he insisted that there were no longer any Americans of the old breed. Unfortunately, in the first book after his return, *A Letter to his Countrymen* (1834), he wrote too much like a man vexed by reviewers, and, more unfortunately still, like a gentleman angry at being dealt with by mere journalists. Thereafter, even when he was less petulant in his disquisitions, he had the disadvantage of having formerly made himself ridiculous. But he did not stop with answering his reviewers. In a rush of savage books he poured out his judgments concerning Europe, to which he had preferred his mythical America, and concerning America, to which he now preferred a mythical republic such as has never had a place on any map: *The Monikins* (1835), a leaden satire on England and America, *Sketches of Switzerland* (1836), *Gleanings in Europe* (1837), devoted to France, *Gleanings in Europe: England* (1837), *Gleanings in Europe: Italy* (1838). He tried direct exposition of his thesis in *The American Democrat* (1838), and he illustrated it at length in the two novels *Homeward Bound* (1838) and *Home as Found* (1838), in which a family of Americans, returning to their native land after a patriotic absence, suffered a disillusionment like Cooper's. In all these works he displayed the energy which was his essential characteristic, and he produced the effect which invariably follows when a powerful man lays about him without regard to consequences. In many of his accusations of vulgarity, stupidity, dishonesty, and cruelty he was more than justified, but he was almost always wrong at least to

the extent of being wrong-headed. *Homeward Bound* and *Home as Found,* for instance, offered him a fine occasion for showing high illusions in a tragic downfall. Instead, they showed a patriotism so confused with snobbishness in the returning Americans as to be beyond sympathy or respect. Gentlemen and ladies who assert their claims too volubly cannot be taken as quite authentic.

In the touchy state of American opinion which then prevailed Cooper was bound to rouse the fury of his compatriots, and he would have been overwhelmed if he had been less robust. The public took its revenge by neglecting his books for half a dozen years after his return, as indeed they more or less deserved. The newspapers replied to him in the manner of the day, increasing their violence to the point of libel. Cooper, who was a Democrat in politics, thereupon began to bring suits against the Whig papers of New York State, argued his cases himself with remarkable skill and vigor, and between 1837 and 1842 was so regularly victorious that he taught the press to speak with caution about his character and his motives. At the end of the period he stood vindicated but alone. Even in Cooperstown, where after 1834 he had made his residence in Otsego Hall, he had quarreled with his fellow townsmen over the possession of a piece of land which was his but which they believed to be theirs. Moreover, his earnings had been cut down, not only by the nature of his controversial books but by the movement of taste away from the type of romance to which his earlier books belonged. Nevertheless, he had somehow managed to keep alive those elements in his mind which were profoundly concerned with the world of adventure. Litigation or no litigation, he had written a solid work of scholarship on *The History of the Navy of the United States of America* (1839). More remarkably still, he had been able to abandon himself to his imagination long enough to write *The Pathfinder* (1840) and *The Deerslayer* (1841).

Opinions differ as to whether *The Pathfinder* and *The Deerslayer* are better than *The Last of the Mohicans* and *The Prairie.* Certainly, however, the element of poetry is not so great in the later pair as in the earlier, written before Cooper had suffered his disillusionment. Any gain must be looked for in the characterization, in the skill with which new qualities in Leather-Stocking are displayed. For this gain, which does appear, there was a reason connected with the fact that the books carried on a kind of epic. Cooper had now gone far enough from the original conception of his hero to realize that there was still much to be brought out or explained. Though it was impossible to make the mature conception uniform throughout, it was possible to put into the series, as a whole, the same total of characteristics that it might have had if the whole could have been foreseen from the beginning. The fourth and fifth stories of the cycle have therefore rather more than their share of deliberate craft in portraiture. In *The Pathfinder* the scout is seen falling in love, failing to win the girl of his choice, and surrendering her to another with a good grace which shows that, after all, he was properly married to his wilderness. In *The Deerslayer* he is seen in the fresh morning of his youth, resisting the temptations of the world with the integrity of a forest saint, and for the first time finding human blood on his blameless hands. Between them the two novels complete the outline and add the light and shade to the most truly epical figure in American fiction.

The Leather-Stocking Tales should of course be read in the order in which they take up successive episodes in their hero's life: *The Deerslayer, The Last of the Mohicans, The Pathfinder, The Pioneers, The Prairie.* Thus read, they reveal the unfolding character of Natty Bumppo without serious discrepancies, though *The Pioneers* remains the weakest link in the chain. Since Leather-Stocking's nature was in no way complex, it could be represented only in its relation to outward events, only through the deeds with which he rose to meet the circumstances which assailed him. Cooper, consequently obliged to discover or invent a multitude of circumstances, did not hesitate to invent. He not only regarded the frontier as somewhat barren of materials for his purposes; he consciously held, as he said in discussing the work of Scott, that invention in a romancer is a higher faculty than that "of creating a *vraisemblance.*" The amount of history in the series, indeed, should not be underestimated, for it is considerable. But the real triumph of Cooper is the variety of his invention, the power with which, isolating his few characters in the wilderness, he contrives to fill their existences, at least for the time being, with enough actions, desires, fears, victories, defeats, sentiments, thoughts to make the barren frontier seem a splendid stage. How relatively dry was his original matter may be noted in *The Pioneers,* which itself marks a long advance upon what any previous writer had been able to do with the frontier, and perhaps an advance upon the reality itself. The later novels in the series did more than transcribe; they transmuted.

Taking what he wanted from a region in which his imagination moved happily, Cooper did with it what he wanted, until he had added a new classic territory to the heroic world.

If, in the fresh burst of creative energy which succeeded his quarrelsome digression, he had turned again to other of his characters besides Leather-Stocking and his companions there might have been another series to stand with Cooper's masterpiece. Instead, he ranged widely during the prodigious years from 1840 to 1846. *Mercedes of Castile* (1840) went back to the first voyage of Columbus. *The Two Admirals* (1842) concerned itself with the British navy before the American Revolution. *The Wing-and-Wing* (1842) told the story of a French privateer in the Mediterranean at the end of the eighteenth century. *Ned Myers* (1843) was the biography of an actual sailor who had served with Cooper before the mast and who long afterward had come to the famous novelist with the story of his life. *Lives of Distinguished American Naval Officers* (1846) made further use of the studies begun for the *History of the Navy.* The two parts of *Afloat and Ashore* (1844—now known respectively as *Afloat and Ashore* and *Miles Wallingford*) dealt with the evils of impressment but also with the charms of life in the New York of Cooper's own youth. *Wyandotte* (1843) recounted the siege of a blockhouse on the upper Susquehanna. *Le Mouchoir* (1843) was a chronicle of fashionable life in Manhattan. Only in the three novels called, as a whole, the *Littlepage Manuscripts,* did Cooper try to repeat the cyclic scheme employed with Natty Bumppo. Of these the third, *The Redskins* (1846), which touched upon the question of anti-rentism then stirring in New York, was both fantastic and dull. The second, *The Chainbearer* (1845), was better by only one striking character, the squatter Thousandacres. The first, *Satanstoe* (1845), ignored at first by the press and neglected ever since by the public, was the only novel of Cooper outside the Leather-Stocking series which had the good temper and the strong illusion of his work at its best. Tracing the history of the Littlepage family through three generations, Cooper seems to have been the less tempted to wrangle the farther off he was from his contemporaries. *Satanstoe,* representing the life of the New York gentry in the mid-eighteenth century, must still be considered, for both its matter and its manner, one of the most distinguished of American historical novels.

Rarely, however, during this last decade of his life was Cooper so amiable. The venom of controversy persisted in him. He grew more and more bigoted in his theological opinions, which were both orthodox and aristocratic. He cultivated his animosity toward New England, which furnished most of his later villains. He was always ready to turn aside from his narrative to harangue the age for its shortcomings. Even the plots of his latest novels—*The Crater* (1848), *The Oak Openings* (1848), *The Sea Lions* (1849), *The Ways of the Hour* (1850)—were at the mercy of his various doctrines. He had lost all touch with the magical, philosophical wilderness which had so long been a refuge for his imagination. Yet it must be pointed out that his rages were in some respects only a literary habit into which he had slipped. In his private life he was reasonably serene. Though he reduced his fortune by unsuccessful speculations, he was never in any serious distress. He was devoted to his wife and children, one of whom, Susan Fenimore [*q.v.*], published an agreeable book, *Rural Hours,* the year before her father's death and afterward edited his collected novels with valuable prefaces. Cooper kept up relations with a few old friends, now and then left his home on matters of business, and in 1847 traveled as far west as Detroit; but for the most part he remained in Cooperstown, where he died and was buried. Irving acted as chairman of the committee which arranged a memorial meeting in New York, Bryant delivered the eulogy, and Webster presided. These were great names, and their presence on the occasion meant that Cooper's countrymen would doubtless have made peace with him if he had permitted it. He himself was responsible, through his dying injunction against any biography of him whatever, for the fact that his memory has continued to be involved with the tradition of his quarrels, instead of being lifted out of that, as it might have been, to a level on which his creative qualities would alone have seemed important.

[*A Discourse on the Life and Genius of Jas. Fenimore Cooper* (1852) by Wm. Cullen Bryant was published shortly after Cooper's death. This was superseded by the prefaces furnished by Susan Fenimore Cooper to the collected edition of the novels—the prefaces being later collected in *Pages and Pictures from the Writing of Jas. Fenimore Cooper* (1861). Thos. R. Lounsbury in his *Jas. Fenimore Cooper* (1883) brought together all the facts then known and produced a biographical and critical study of genuine merit. Some anecdotal information was added by Mary E. Phillips in *Jas. Fenimore Cooper* (1913). The most extensive source of original information about Cooper is the *Correspondence of Jas. Fenimore-Cooper* (2 vols.; 1922), edited by his grandson Jas. Fenimore Cooper. There is a careful bibliography of the writings by and about Cooper in *The Cambridge Hist. of Am. Lit.* (1917), I, 530–34).]   C. V–D.

COOPER, JAMES GRAHAM (June 19, 1830–July 19, 1902), naturalist, was born in New York City, son of William and Frances (Graham) Cooper, and was the eldest of six children. When the boy was seven years of age his father moved to New Jersey and established his home near Hoboken. On his walks to and from school the child availed himself of his ample opportunities to study natural history, and in the home he was equally fortunate. His father, having inherited a competence, devoted himself to a life of study and drew about him such friends as Lucien Bonaparte, Thomas Nuttall [*q.v.*], and John J. Audubon [*q.v.*], ornithologists, John Torrey [*q.v.*], the botanist, and Henry Schoolcraft, the historian. The elder Cooper was a central figure of the group which founded the Lyceum of Natural History of New York, the forerunner of the New York Academy of Sciences. In 1851 Cooper graduated from the College of Physicians and Surgeons, New York. He spent the next two years in the hospitals of the city. The active period of Cooper's life as a field naturalist began in 1853, when he signed a contract with Gov. Isaac I. Stevens [*q.v.*], of Washington Territory, to act as one of the physicians of the Pacific Railroad Survey Expedition, detailed to explore for two years the route along the forty-seventh and forty-ninth parallels. Government employ as contract surgeon in the army, private collecting expeditions, occupation as zoölogist of the Geological Survey of California, and the writing of reports filled his time thenceforth for a period of years and brought him close familiarity with the geographic and biologic features of the Pacific Coast region. As in his father's home Cooper had been surrounded by noted men of science, so here during his pioneer labors in the West he was equally fortunate, sharing his rich experiences in the field with such gifted interpreters of science as Hayden, Gibbs, and Asa Gray [*qq.v.*]. The writing of reports brought him into correspondence with Spencer F. Baird and Elliott Coues [*qq.v.*]. Baird characterized Cooper's work, published in conjunction with the Geological Survey of California, as "By far the most valuable contribution to the biography of American birds that has appeared since the time of Audubon" (S. F. Baird, T. M. Brewer, and R. Ridgway, *History of North American Birds,* 1874, Preface, p. v); while Coues, in 1866, referred to Cooper as "sc well known as an indefatigable and accurate naturalist."

On Jan. 9, 1866, Cooper was married to Rosa M. Wells at Oakland, Cal., and during that year established himself in the practise of medicine at Santa Cruz, Cal. In 1871 he removed to Ventura County where he remained until 1875, returning then to the vicinity of Oakland, where he spent his declining years at Hayward. He published many articles on conchology, botany, ornithology, mammalogy, geology, and paleontology. The authoritative chapter upon zoölogy in T. F. Cronise's *Natural Wealth of California* (1868), is by Cooper, as acknowledged in the preface of the book. A pioneer collector of scientific materials and writer on the natural history of California and Washington, Cooper left an impress for all time on the records of these Western states, by setting down painstakingly the facts of geographic distribution in the days when original conditions were untrammeled.

[W. O. Emerson, "Dr. Jas. G. Cooper, a Sketch," *Bull. Cooper Ornith. Club* (Jan., Feb. 1899); W. O. Emerson, "In Memoriam: Dr. Jas. G. Cooper," and J. Grinnell, "The Ornithological Writings of Dr. J. G. Cooper," in *Condor*, IV, 101–05 (Sept.–Oct. 1902); W. P. Taylor, "Notes on Mammals collected principally in Washington and California between the years 1853 and 1874 by Dr. Jas. Graham Cooper," *Proc. Cal. Acad. Sci.*, vol. IX, no. 3 (July 12, 1919), pp. 69–121.]
J.G.

COOPER, JOSEPH ALEXANDER (Nov. 25, 1823–May 20, 1910), soldier, was the son of John Cooper, a native of Maryland and a veteran of the War of 1812. The latter removed to Kentucky and settled as a farmer near Cumberland Falls in Whitley County, where his son Joseph Alexander was born. A few years later the family moved across the Tennessee line to the adjoining county of Campbell where they settled on Cove Creek and carried on farming. In September 1847 Cooper enlisted in the 4th Tennessee Infantry and served for the remainder of the war against Mexico. After the war he returned to Tennessee and engaged in farming near Jacksboro in Campbell County until the outbreak of the Civil War. He was a Whig in politics and in common with the great majority of his East Tennessee neighbors he opposed the secession of his state. He was a delegate to the union convention at Knoxville in 1861 and took a prominent part in its deliberations and activities. After its adjournment he busied himself with recruiting and drilling men in his county for the Union army. In August 1861 he enlisted at Whitesburg, Ky., and was mustered into service as captain of the 1st Tennessee Infantry (Temple, *post*, p. 105). Before the Civil War, Cooper had been little more than a poorly educated, impecunious farmer without any great significance even in his own county, but his war record was brilliant and he rapidly rose to prominence. As captain he fought in the mountains of Kentucky and Tennessee during the fall of 1861 and the spring of 1862, and in March of the latter year was made colonel of the 6th Tennessee Infantry. His command saw hard service in the battles of Murfreesboro, Chickamauga,

and Chattanooga. He became involved in a quarrel with his brigade commander, Brigadier-General Spears, and finally joined with his fellow officers in having Spears court-martialed for Southern sympathies (*Official Records*, 1 ser., vol. XXXII, pt. 2, p. 34). In July 1864 Cooper was made brigadier-general and led the 2nd Division of the 23rd Corps in Sherman's attack on Atlanta. From this time to the end of the war he took part in the operations in East Tennessee. In May 1865 he was made brevet major-general. Throughout the war Cooper's services were greatly appreciated by his superior officers, not only for his ability as a fighter but even more for his influence among the East Tennesseans and his personal knowledge of East Tennessee geography.

He was mustered out of service at Nashville, Jan. 15, 1866 (F. B. Heitman, *Historical Register and Dictionary of the United States Army*, 1903). In 1868 he was an unsuccessful candidate for senator from Tennessee (J. T. Moore, *Tennessee, the Volunteer State*, 1923, I, 534). In 1869 Grant appointed him collector of Internal Revenue for the Knoxville District, in which position he continued for ten years. In 1880 he removed to Stafford County, Kan., and engaged in farming until his death. Cooper was a member of the Baptist church and for more than thirty-five years was a deacon. He helped organize the South-Central Baptist Association of Kansas in 1889 and served for many years as moderator of the Association. He was twice married: on Apr. 9, 1846, to Mary J. Hutson, who died in 1874, and on Jan. 21, 1875, to Mary J. Polston. He died in his eighty-seventh year, and was buried in the National Cemetery at Knoxville, Tenn.

[Full details of the war record of Cooper are to be found in the *Official Records* (*Army*); Oliver P. Temple, *Notable Men of Tenn.* (1912), deals largely with his part in the Knoxville Convention. Details of his life in Kansas have been supplied by the Kan. State Hist. Soc. See also tribute to Gen. Cooper in *Daily Jour. and Tribune* (Knoxville), Sept. 13, 1895; obituary in *Leavenworth Times*, May 21, and *Chattanooga Daily Times*, May 22, 1910, and extensive obituary material in *Daily Jour. and Tribune* (Knoxville), May 22 and 26, 1910.]
R. S. C.

COOPER, MARK ANTHONY (Apr. 20, 1800–Mar. 17, 1885), business man, politician, came of a Virginia family which migrated to Georgia and settled in Hancock County in the heart of the black belt. His father was Thomas Cooper; his mother, Sallie Cooper, a descendant of an Italian who, having been driven out of his native land, perhaps for religious reasons, settled in Holland. His son, Mark Anthony, was sent back to Italy to be educated, but ran away to sea, was captured by Algerian pirates, escaped to an English ship, and eventually reached Virginia where he became the progenitor of an important American family.

Mark Anthony Cooper was born in Hancock County, Ga. He was prepared for college at a noted private academy in the neighborhood, attended the University of Georgia for a time, then migrated to the University of South Carolina, where he was graduated with an A.B. degree in 1819. Leaving college he studied law and was admitted to the bar at Eatonton, Ga., in 1821. Though successful in the practise of law, his real bent was toward a business career. He was one of the few who foresaw the great possibilities that lay in the state's natural resources and set to work to develop them, at a time when nearly everybody was interested primarily in farming. In 1833 he organized a cotton-mill company and erected near Eatonton the second water-driven cotton factory in the state. It was capitalized at $50,000. Two years later he sold his stock in this concern, removed to Columbus, Ga., and organized a bank, capitalized at $200,000. As a member of the state legislature in 1833 he was a warm advocate of the project to charter a railroad. The charter was granted to the Georgia Railroad & Banking Company, which built a road connecting Augusta with Atlanta. Later Cooper was an important factor in the building of the East & West Railroad in northwest Georgia. His work as a developer spread from cotton-milling, banking, and railroading to the production of iron. Purchasing an interest in a small furnace near Etowah, in Bartow County, he renovated and extended the plant, and supplemented it by erecting a rolling mill and a nail factory. In conjunction with this enterprise he erected a flour mill. He connected his settlement by a four-mile railway with the Western & Atlantic to Chattanooga, and proceeded to develop coal mines. The entire business, occupying some 12,000 acres and embracing these various industries, in time became his sole property.

In 1836 he volunteered for the Seminole War, and was commissioned major of a battalion raised in Macon, Ga. He entered the Twenty-sixth Congress (1839) as a Whig, but when Calhoun led an important Whig group back into the Democratic party in 1840, Cooper with W. T. Colquitt [q.v.] and others, having become dissatisfied with the growing nationalistic and anti-slavery tendencies of the national Whig party, followed him. Cooper was reëlected to the next two Congresses, but resigned in 1843 to become the Democratic candidate for governor. He was defeated by George W. Crawford [q.v.], and thereafter he took no further part in politics.

Cooper was married to Mary Evalina Flournoy, in 1821, but his bride lived only three or four months after the marriage. In 1826 he was again married, this time to Sophronia A. R. Randle, and to them there were born seven daughters and three sons, two of whom were killed in the Civil War. Cooper died at Etowah, Ga., in his eighty-fifth year.

[There is an account of Cooper by his grandson, W. G. Cooper, in W. F. Northen, *Men of Mark in Ga.*, vol. II (1910), which is reproduced almost verbatim in L. L. Knight, *Ga. and Georgians*, IV (1917), 2097. See also L. L. Knight, *Georgia's Landmarks, Memorials, and Legends* (1913), I, 290; obituary in *Atlanta Constitution*, Mar. 20, 1885.]   R. P. B.

COOPER, MYLES (February 1737–May 20, 1785), clergyman, Loyalist, second president of King's College, N. Y., was the son of William and Elizabeth Cooper of Wha House Estate, seven miles from Millom, in Cumberland County, England. At the age of sixteen he entered Queen's College, Oxford, and received the degree of B.A. in 1756, and M.A. in 1760. In the latter year he became an usher in Tonbridge School. On Mar. 2, 1760, he was ordained a deacon; and a year later was elected chaplain of Queen's College, Oxford, and ordained priest. In this same year (1761) he published a volume of poems, written by himself and others, with the title *Poems on Several Occasions*. He was acting as the curate of a church near Oxford, when the Archbishop of Canterbury named him, in response to an inquiry of the governors of King's College, as a man capable of serving as vice-president and succeeding to the presidency. In the expectation of receiving this appointment he sailed for New York in 1762; but the governors, finding no authority in the charter for appointing a vice-president, made him an assistant to the president, professor of moral philosophy, and a fellow of the College. After the resignation of President Samuel Johnson [q.v.] in 1763, he was chosen president (Apr. 12, 1763). His administration was notably successful. Changes in the curriculum and the rules of discipline to conform to Oxford ideas were made; a grammar school was started as a feeder for the College; a medical school and a hospital were founded; and large grants of land were secured. It was Cooper's ambition to change the College into a royal American university. In 1771 he went to England to secure a charter and endowment for such an institution, but the most that he could accomplish at the time was a remission of quit-rents on certain tracts of land held by the College and a gift of books from Oxford for the library.

Meantime he had become one of the outstanding churchmen in the American Colonies. In 1765 he presided at the convention of Episcopal clergymen of New York and adjoining colonies. He thrice toured the southern colonies to secure the support of the clergy for an American Episcopate. He was also an active member of the Society for the Propagation of the Gospel in Foreign Parts. When the *Whip For The Whig* was started in 1768, he contributed to the paper, never losing an opportunity to promote the interests of the Church and to give vent to his intense dislike of dissenters. He thought Whitefield a "common disturber of the peace of the Church" and his disciples either "Knaves or Madmen."

Cooper was a not less ardent supporter of the royal government. As local opposition increased, he put his pen at the service of those Loyalists who believed that nothing should pass unanswered "that had a tendency to lessen the respect or affection that was due to the Mother Country." In 1772 he and John Vardill, a tutor in the College, published two pamphlets, "Causidicus" and "Causidicus Mastix," in reply to an address of President Witherspoon of Princeton in which, they asserted, he had spoken disparagingly of the English universities. He and Vardill were also the authors of "A Series of Papers Signed Poplicola." In the bitter controversy that preceded the break with England, Cooper was accused of writing nearly every Loyalist pamphlet; but none of the pamphlets usually accredited to him were his work (see correspondence of Dr. T. B. Chandler and his memorial to the Royal Commission on Loyalist Claims). It is possible that he wrote the poem entitled "The Patriots of North America" (1775). Certain it is that he became one of the most detested Loyalists in New York. When, then, news came of the bloodshed at Concord and Lexington, he fled for his life to a British frigate in the harbor; and again on May 10, 1775, while Alexander Hamilton, then a pupil, harangued the mob from the College steps. On May 25, 1775, he sailed for England never to return. Of this last experience he wrote a dramatic description in some "Stanzas" published in the *Gentleman's Magazine*, July 1776 (see also MS. diary of Dr. T. B. Chandler in General Theological Seminary, N. Y.).

For a time Cooper returned to Oxford as Fellow at Queen's College. From 1778 until his death he was senior minister of the new English Chapel at Cowgate near the University of Edinburgh. He also was given various church livings in England and a pension by the Crown for his services to state and church. Though he himself never married, he bore heavy financial burdens to aid the families of his widowed sister and of his elder brother. Cooper had a jovial and sociable nature. He always lived well, keeping his garret well stocked with liquors "ot a most delicate Texture"; and he seems to have paid for his love of the table by a chronic ailment which caused his sudden death at luncheon.

[An unpublished monograph by Clarence H. Vance, Esq., of New York, based on extensive use of manuscript material, supersedes other accounts of Cooper's career. Two anonymous articles in *Analectic Mag.*, July 1819, and *Am. Medic. and Phil. Reg.*, Jan. 1813, contain some information about his "life and character." See also Jos. Foster, *Alumni Oxonienses*, vol. I (1887).]

A. J.

COOPER, PETER (Feb. 12, 1791–Apr. 4, 1883), manufacturer, inventor, philanthropist, the son of John and Margaret (Campbell) Cooper, was born at Little Dock St., New York. The Cooper family was of English stock. Obadiah Cooper, Peter Cooper's great-great-grandfather, came to America and settled at Fishkill-on-Hudson in 1662. John Cooper, Peter's father, born about 1758, a lieutenant in the Continental Army, at the close of the war went into business, first in New York, later in Peekskill, Catskill, and Newburgh. He was successively a hatter, a brewer, a store-keeper, and a brick-maker—in all of which he was aided by his son Peter, who, by the time he was sixteen years old, was already a veteran in experience. Though the lad was lacking in formal education, for he had attended school for only a year, his varied training in affairs fitted him well for business success. At seventeen, he was apprenticed at twenty-five dollars a year and board to John Woodward, a New York coach-maker, who voluntarily paid him fifty at the end of the third year and seventy-five at the end of the fourth, and when his apprenticeship was over, offered to lend him money to start a business of his own. Peter declined the offer, and instead found employment, first in a manufactory of cloth-shearing machines, then as traveling salesman, and later as owner of a new cloth-shearing machine. He continued prosperously in this business until the close of the War of 1812, and, when peace was followed by smaller profits, he sold out and opened a retail grocery store at the corner of the Bowery and Rivington St. On Dec. 18, 1813, being then twenty-two years of age, he married Sarah Bedell of Hempstead, a Huguenot, educated by the Moravians of Pennsylvania, with whom he lived happily for fifty-six years until her death in 1869.

Deciding that manufacturing was his field, Cooper bought a glue factory, together with a twenty-one-year lease of the ground on which it stood, near the site of the old Park Avenue Hotel. With this business he found his opportunity and was soon supplying the American market with American-made glue and isinglass which bettered the foreign imports. So complete was his success that he won a monopoly of the trade in this line, but he continued his frugal ways, and was, for many years, his own stoker, secretary, bookkeeper, executive, and salesman. Eventually the business outgrew even his energy, and he entrusted part of the direction to his son Edward and his son-in-law, Abram S. Hewitt [*qq.v.*]. If the glue factory was the foundation of his fortune, the bulk of the latter came originally from the iron works which he set up at Baltimore. There, in 1828, with two partners, he bought 3,000 acres of land within the city limits and erected the Canton Iron Works. The Baltimore & Ohio Railroad upon whose success much of the value of this land depended, was on the verge of failure. The route followed by the few miles of track was so twisting and hilly that Stephenson, the English engineer, declared it impossible for an engine to run on it. Cooper was not dismayed. "I'll knock an engine together in six weeks," he said, "that will pull carriages ten miles an hour." The engine—the first steam locomotive built in America—was made, and, in spite of its diminutive size which gave it the nickname of "Tom Thumb" and the "Teakettle," actually pulled a load of over forty persons at more than ten miles an hour. On Sept. 18, 1830, it raced with a noted horse from Riley's Tavern to Baltimore and would have won but for a leak in the boiler caused by excessive pressure.

The Canton Iron Works afforded a striking example of Cooper's good judgment and good fortune in business matters. When he sold the property in 1836 he accepted in payment stock of the Baltimore & Ohio Railroad at forty-five dollars a share which he soon afterward sold for two hundred and thirty dollars. His interests now expanded rapidly, until within two decades they included a wire manufactory in Trenton, N. J., blast furnaces in Philipsburg, Pa., a rolling mill and the old glue factory in New York, foundries at Ringwood, N. J., and Durham, Pa., and iron mines in northern New Jersey. In 1854, in his Trenton factory, the first structural iron for fireproof buildings was rolled—an achievement which contributed to the winning of the Bessemer Gold Medal awarded him in 1870 by the Iron and Steel Institute of Great Britain.

To Cooper belongs much of the credit for the final success of the New York, Newfoundland & London Telegraph Company, which he served as president for twenty years, during which he was the chief supporter of Cyrus Field [*q.v.*]. His confidence in the ultimate success of the project never weakened notwithstanding repeated failures and many deficits which it fell to him to meet when every one else drew back. He be-

came president, likewise, of the North American Telegraph Company which at one time owned or controlled more than half of the telegraph lines of the country. As an inventor, Cooper possessed genius which might have made him an earlier Edison had it been joined to the necessary technical training. His first invention was a washing machine, followed by a machine for mortising hubs, and others for propelling ferry-boats by compressed air, for utilizing the tide for power, and for moving canal barges by an endless chain run by water-power. He made use of gravity as a source of power in an endless chain of buckets in one of his mines.

It is, however, chiefly as a philanthropist that Cooper is remembered. During his service on the Board of Aldermen of New York, he was an early advocate of paid police and fire departments, sanitary water conditions and public schools. In the broader field of national politics, he supported the Greenback party and consented to run on its ticket for president in 1876, with, it would appear, little hope of election, in order to bring before the public his views on the currency. His greatest monument is the Cooper Union or Cooper Institute at Astor Place, New York City, which he founded in 1857–59 "for the advancement of science and art." It is unique in the combination it offers of the ideal and practical in education. Free courses are given in general science, chemistry, electricity, civil, mechanical, and electrical engineering as well as in art. There are also free lectures of a very high order and the Institute maintains an excellent reading-room and library service. Cooper died on Apr. 4, 1883, and was sincerely mourned by the city which he had so well served. At a reception given in his honor in 1874, he said: "I have always recognized that the object of business is to make money in an honourable manner. I have endeavoured to remember that the object of life is to do good." To this creed he remained faithful.

[R. W. Raymond, *Peter Cooper* (1901); John Celivergos Zachos, *Sketch of the Life and Opinions of Peter Cooper* (1876); W. Scott, *Peter Cooper, the Good Citizen* (1888); Howard Carroll, *Twelve Americans, Their Lives and Times* (1883); C. Edwards Lester, *Life and Character of Peter Cooper* (1883).]   W. B. P.

COOPER, SAMUEL (Mar. 28, 1725–Dec. 23, 1783), clergyman, was a son of Rev. William and Judith Sewall Cooper and was born in Boston where he attended a grammar school and entered Harvard College from which he graduated in 1743. In December of that year he was elected to the pastorate of the Brattle Square Church in Boston which was the scene of his life-work. This, the fourth church of the Puritan order to be established in Boston, was founded in 1699 and was frequently called the "Manifesto" Church from the title of the document which set forth the principles of its founders. Dr. Benjamin Colman [q.v.] was the first pastor. In 1715 Rev. William Cooper was chosen as his colleague, and at his death in 1743, apparently at the earnest desire of the aged Senior Pastor, Samuel was called to succeed his father, doing part duty till his ordination, May 21, 1746. On the death of Dr. Colman, Aug. 29, 1747, he became sole pastor, and remained such till his death. He was given the degree of D.D. by the University of Edinburgh in 1767.

Cooper was an able and eloquent preacher, a sympathetic and untiring pastor, and under him Brattle Church was strong and flourishing. His orthodox Calvinism showed signs of softening at certain points, and in his pulpit style also he was accounted in advance of his time. His only literary output consists of a small number of sermons and miscellaneous pamphlets of which Palfrey rates his sermon of 1780, *On the Commencement of the Constitution*, as his best, and his Dudleian Lecture of 1774, *The Man of Sin*, a diatribe against the Papacy, as "the most indifferent." It was during his pastorate, in 1773, that the society built its second edifice on the old site. This building, regarded at its erection as the most splendid and costly church in Boston, was used by the British as a barrack during the siege, and was struck by a cannon ball the night before the evacuation. It was restored and used as a house of worship until its removal in 1871.

Cooper was active in the cause of American freedom and intimately associated with its leaders. As early as 1754 he wrote a pamphlet, *The Crisis*, against a government excise, and before and during the Revolution he was a constant contributor to the newspapers and an orator on the popular side. The celebrated inflammatory *Hutchinson Letters* passed through his hands, but were published against his advice. He became obnoxious to the British authorities and an order was issued for his arrest along with other leaders. But being warned, he fled from Boston on Sunday, Apr. 8, 1775, and did not return until after the evacuation (W. H. Sumner, *History of East Boston*, 1858). It is commonly asserted that Cooper did not allow his political activities to interfere with his pastoral duties. Some doubt is thrown on this in William Tudor's *Life of James Otis* (1823) where it is stated that because of his neglect of his sermon preparation he became notorious in clerical circles for his frequent pulpit exchanges.

His portrait represents the typical clergyman of the period, in wig, gown, and bands. But the face indicates less austerity of character than is commonly associated with the eighteenth-century New England divines. He had polished manners, an elegant diction, and a voice of great sweetness and power. He was a fluent speaker and would probably have been a fine extemporaneous preacher had he chosen to cultivate that art. His learning was extensive rather than deep (Emerson Davis, "Sketches of Congregational Ministers in New England," manuscript in the Congregational Library). He was prominent in public affairs and had a wide circle of friends. His intimacy with Adams and Franklin brought him foreign friends and correspondents, and he was much sought after by visitors who came to New England from France and other European countries. He was the first vice-president of the Academy of Arts and Sciences, instituted by the General Court in 1780. The Society for the Promotion of the Gospel among the Indians found in him a constant patron. He declined the presidency of Harvard College in 1774, but was a member of the Corporation from 1767 and was active in raising funds for the restoration of the Library after the fire of 1764. Several portraits of Cooper were painted by Copley, the best known of which is in the possession of the Massachusetts Historical Society. He married Judith, a sister of Dr. Thomas Bulfinch [q.v.], by whom he had two daughters.

[The principal authorities for the life of Cooper are: W. B. Sprague, *Annals Am. Pulpit*, vol. I (1857); S. K. Lothrop, *A Hist. of the Church in Brattle St.*, Boston (1851); J. G. Palfrey, *A Sermon Preached in the Church in Brattle Square, Boston, July 18, 1824*; *Records of the Church in Brattle Square* (1902).] F.T.P.

COOPER, SAMUEL (June 12, 1798–Dec. 3, 1876), Confederate general, was born at Hackensack, N. J., the son of Samuel and Mary (Horton) Cooper. His great-grandfather had come from Dorsetshire to Massachusetts, and his father, also a Massachusetts man, served as a major of artillery in the Continental Army. Cooper entered the Military Academy from New York on May 25, 1813, and was commissioned in the artillery, Dec. 11, 1815. He served in garrison with troops at intervals, and was promoted to first lieutenant and captain of artillery in 1821 and 1836. He was early selected for staff duty at headquarters of the army, however, and most of his service, aside from an expedition against the Seminoles in 1841–42, was in Washington. He was appointed an assistant adjutant-general, with the rank of major, in 1838, was made lieutenant-colonel in 1847, and was appointed adjutant-general of the army, with the rank of colonel, in 1852, partly in consequence of his highly efficient conduct of business in the War

Department during the Mexican War. Having married a grand-daughter of George Mason, he acquired a country place in Fairfax County, Va., near the homes of his wife's' relatives and also convenient to his duties in Washington. These family connections, together with a close friendship with Jefferson Davis which had grown up when the latter was secretary of war, had made him wholly Southern in his feelings and sympathies, in spite of his Northern birth and ancestry, so that on the outbreak of the Civil War he resigned his commission, Mar. 7, 1861, and went to Montgomery to offer his services to the Confederacy. To a newly established government, which had to create a complete military organization while engaged in fighting a great war, Cooper's long administrative experience was invaluable. He was at once made adjutant- and inspector-general of the army, and was appointed to the full rank of general as soon as that grade was created by Congress. He was the senior officer of the Confederate Army throughout the war. When the Confederate government left Richmond in April 1865, he accompanied the President and cabinet until the party finally broke up, and then surrendered himself, turning over to his captors all of the records of the War Department which he had been able to remove and transport. The preservation of a great quantity of valuable historical material was thus due to his foresight and care. After his parole and release he returned to his estate at Cameron, near Alexandria, Va., where he resided in retirement until his death.

[G. W. Cullum, *Biog. Reg.* (3rd ed., 1891); *Confed. Mil. Hist.* (1899), I, 616–17; article by Gen. Fitzhugh Lee in *Southern Hist. Soc. Papers*, vol. III (1877), pp. 269–76; F. B. Heitman, *Hist. Reg. and Dict. of the U. S. Army* (1903), I, 326.]   T.M.S.

COOPER, SARAH BROWN INGERSOLL (Dec. 12, 1836–Dec. 11, 1896), philanthropist, founder of kindergartens, was born at Cazenovia, N. Y., the daughter of Capt. Samuel Clark Ingersoll and Laura (Case) Ingersoll. She was a cousin of Robert G. Ingersoll [*q.v.*], and possessed a gift of eloquence almost equal to his. She was graduated from Cazenovia Seminary, one of the earliest coeducational institutions in the country. One of her classmates was Leland Stanford [*q.v.*], founder of Stanford University. At the age of fourteen she began school-teaching but soon thereafter entered the Troy Female Seminary for further study. From here she moved to Atlanta, Ga., and accepted a position as governess in the family of Gov. Schley. In Atlanta, on Sept. 4, 1855, she married Halsey Fenimore Cooper, formerly a professor at Cazenovia, sometime editor of the *Chattanooga Advertiser,*

who held during his life various offices under the federal government. In 1869 Mr. and Mrs. Cooper, with their daughter Harriet, located in San Francisco, where Mrs. Cooper began her career of public work. Following Cooper's death in 1885, mother and daughter became constant companions and co-workers, imbued with a devotion passing all ordinary affection. Entirely self-forgetful, no sacrifice was too great for these women. But the strain finally told on Harriet, who developed intermittent attacks of profound melancholia until her mind gave way. After several unsuccessful attempts to take her own and her mother's life, the daughter succeeded in asphyxiating them both on the eve of her mother's sixtieth birthday.

Mrs. Cooper's public work was of wide scope. She was president of the Women's Press Association, treasurer of the World's Federation of Women's Clubs, and a director of the Associated Charities. She was one of five eminent women elected to the Pan-Republican Congress during the Chicago World's Fair. Returning to San Francisco, she helped to organize the Woman's Congress, serving as president for two years preceding her death. Her title to national recognition, however, rests primarily on her organization of the Golden Gate Kindergarten Association in 1879, and her founding of some forty-four free kindergartens throughout San Francisco. For this she collected an endowment fund of $300,000. Her work marked the first attempt at kindergarten training on so large a scale and it acted as a stimulus to similar activity in a number of American cities. It was her aim "to lay the foundation for a better national character by founding free kindergartens for neglected children." During her life the Association had conferred its benefits upon eighteen thousand children. The years 1870–95 mark the period of the introduction and extension of kindergarten education in America. Throughout the period Mrs. Cooper was an outstanding figure among five or six of the notable workers in the United States. When, in 1892, the International Kindergarten Union was organized at Saratoga, N. Y., she was elected its first president as a recognition of her leadership.

[*Annual Reports,* 1888–91, 1899, of the Golden Gate Kindergarten Ass., also *Kindergarten Mag.*, Feb. 1897; Gertrude De Aguirre, "A Woman from Altruria," in *Arena*, May 1897; *Portraits and Biographies of Prominent Am. Women* (1901), ed. by Frances E. Willard and Mary A. Livermore; Lillian Drake Avery, *A Genealogy of the Ingersoll Family in America* (1926); *San Francisco Chronicle,* Dec. 12, 1896.]   W.W.K.

COOPER, SUSAN FENIMORE (Apr. 17, 1813–Dec. 31, 1894), the child of James Fenimore [*q.v.*] and Susan (De Lancey) Cooper, was for nearly half her life very closely associated with her father, accompanying him on his travels, and acting as his amanuensis for all his later books. During the last years of his life she kept a journal (1848–50), extracts from which formed her most important work, *Rural Hours* (1850). There is little of biographical interest in these notes. Their popularity rested on the freshness and pleasantness of her observations of signs and seasons. There is a natural grace and sincerity in her records of melting snow, bluejays and woodpeckers, old Dutch superstitions, house-cleaning, and "fresh lettuce from the hot-beds." An observation of haymaking leads her to reflections on the position of women in America. She is chronicler of the county fair, and of the disappearing Indian. In the four years between its publication and that of Thoreau's *Walden* (1854) her book ran through six editions, and new editions appeared in 1868 and 1887. Her later volumes of nature notes, *Rhyme and Reason of Country Life* (1854), and *Rural Rambles* (1854), seem to have had only single editions. The superiority of *Rural Hours* may be ascribed to its birth from the last years of association with her father, for, she tells us, "In his own garden he took very great pleasure, passing hours at a time there during the summer months. . . . It was his great delight to watch the growth of the different plants, day by day. His hot beds were always among the earliest in the village" (J. F. Cooper, *The Crater*, Household Edition, 1880, Preface, pp. 10–11). The author of *Rural Hours* was invited to edit the American edition of *Country Rambles*, by the well-known English naturalist, John Leonard Knapp. This volume, with her notes, appeared in 1853. She published *Mount Vernon, a Letter to the Children of America* in 1859, and two years later prepared *Pages and Pictures From the Writings of James Fenimore Cooper* (1861). She also wrote prefaces for the Household Edition of her father's works (1876–84). A study of her comments and interpretations reveals the intensity of her daughterly devotion. In her old age she published *William West Skiles, a Sketch of Missionary Life in Valle Crucis in Western North Carolina, 1842–1862* (1890).

Meanwhile she had devoted herself to numerous charitable works, the most important of which was the Orphan House of the Holy Savior which she founded in 1873 in Cooperstown. This institution, beginning with five inmates, in ten years grew under her personal superintendence to a large institution with buildings for the housing and education of nearly one hundred boys and girls. It has been stated that the or-ganization of the Girls' Friendly Society in America grew out of and was suggested by Miss Cooper's work in the Orphan House of the Holy Savior (*Evening Post,* New York, Dec. 31, 1894), but the official publications of the Girls' Friendly Society ascribe its origin in this country to other causes.

[Throughout Miss Cooper's prefaces and notes to her father's works, and her comments on excerpts in *Pages and Pictures,* may be found reminiscences of her family life. See also John S. Hart, *Female Prose Writers of America* (1855), p. 413; *Correspondence of Jas. Fenimore Cooper* (1922), ed. by J. F. Cooper; Ralph Birdsall, *Fenimore Cooper's Grave and Christ Churchyard* (1911), pp. 70–72; *The Critic,* Jan. 5, 1895; *Harper's Monthly Mag.,* Mar. 1895; *Boston Transcript* and *Evening Post* (N. Y.), Dec. 31, 1894; *N. Y. Times* and *N. Y. Herald,* Jan. 1. 1895.]
                     J.R.T.

COOPER, THEODORE (Jan. 13, 1839–Aug. 24, 1919), civil engineer, bridge-builder, was born at Cooper's Plain, Steuben County, N. Y., where his father, John Cooper, Jr., was a physician. Both his father and his mother, Elizabeth M. (Evans) Cooper, were from Pennsylvania. Theodore attended the Rensselaer Polytechnic Institute and was graduated from it in 1858 as a civil engineer. After his graduation he acted as an assistant engineer on the Troy and Greenfield Railroad and the Hoosac Tunnel. At the outbreak of the Civil War, he enlisted in the United States navy as an assistant engineer. The gunboat, *Chocura,* on which he was stationed, took part in the siege of Yorktown and the battles of West Point and York River, and acted as a guardship in the Potomac during the Chickahominy campaign. At the cessation of hostilities, Cooper was detailed as an instructor in the department of steam engineering at the Naval Academy. He remained in the service of the navy until 1872. In that year he began his work in bridge construction, to which profession he was to contribute worthily. He was appointed by Capt. James B. Eads [*q.v.*] as inspector, at the Midvale Steel Works, for the steel being made for the St. Louis bridge, and afterward went to St. Louis to take charge of the erection of the bridge. After some further experience with the Delaware Bridge Company and the Keystone Bridge Company, Cooper established himself as a consulting engineer in New York City. Some of the bridges he designed were the Seekonk Bridge at Providence, the Sixth Street Bridge at Pittsburgh, the Second Avenue Bridge over the Harlem River, New York City, the Newburyport Bridge over the Merrimac River, and the Junction Bridges over the Allegheny River. He was one of five engineers appointed by President Cleveland in 1894 to determine the span of the Hudson River Bridge. He acted as a consultant for the New York Public Library and the Quebec Bridge, and did work for the Suburban Rapid Transit Company, the New York and Boston Rapid Transit Commissions, and the Harlem River Commission. The results of his experience were put in permanent form through his contribution of several papers on phases of bridge construction to the *Transactions* of the American Society of Civil Engineers. The *Engineering News-Record* said of Theodore Cooper: "His name became universally familiar to bridge engineers through his system of locomotive and train loading for bridge design. Composed of a wheel system, representing the heaviest locomotive of that time, followed by a uniform load whose amount in pounds per foot bore a simple relation to the driving-axle load, this system proved so convenient, and was so excellently adapted to modification for increasing weight of trains and engines by simple multiplication, that it quickly won a commanding position. . . . Theodore Cooper also exerted a strong influence toward bringing about the adoption of wheel-load analysis for railway bridges instead of uniform-load or other methods, and the moment tables which he published made it possible to carry out the analysis rapidly and conveniently."

[*Trans. Am. Soc. Civil Engineers*, vol. LXXXIV (1921); *Engineering News-Record*, Aug. 28, 1919; *N. Y. Times*, Aug. 25, 1919.]   E.Y.

COOPER, THOMAS (Oct. 22, 1759–May 11, 1839), agitator, scientist, educator, was born in Westminster, England, the son of Thomas Cooper, a man of means and standing. He was thoroughly grounded in the classics and sent to Oxford, where he was matriculated from University College in February 1779. His failure to take a degree was perhaps due to his unwillingness to sign the Thirty-nine Articles. But for his father's insistence upon the law, he would probably have become a physician. He attended anatomical lectures in London, took a clinical course in the Middlesex Hospital, and later at Manchester attended patients under direction. His mature life in England was spent chiefly in Lancashire, where he became a member of a firm of calico-printers which ultimately failed, traveled the northern circuit as a barrister, and dabbled in philosophy and chemistry. His scientific attainments doubtless warranted his nomination to the Royal Society by his friend Joseph Priestley [*q.v.*] but his radical philosophy rendered him unacceptable to that body. Certain ponderous essays of his, published at Manchester, reveal him as a materialist in philosophy, a Unitarian in theology, and a revolutionist in political theory. Temperamentally an agitator rather than a phi-

losopher, he soon identified himself with the movements, which proved unsuccessful, for the abolition of the slave-trade and the repeal of the Corporation and Test Acts. Upon the occasion of a visit to Paris in 1792, he instituted correspondence between the Manchester Constitutional Society, in which he was prominent, and the Jacobins. Attacked in the House of Commons by Burke for this action, he replied in a vehement pamphlet which was at the same time a tirade against the "privileged orders." The conservative reaction in England against the French Revolution did not directly endanger him but convinced him that freedom of thought and speech were no longer possible in the land of his birth. Disgusted also with the Terror in France, he looked to America as the land of promise. After a preliminary visit, he removed to the United States in 1794 with his friend Priestley and settled near him at Northumberland, Pa.

Here he practised law, served unofficially as a physician, and remained for several years in relative obscurity. By 1799, however, he was definitely associated with the Jeffersonian opposition to the Federalist administration, and during 1800 was conspicuous as a pamphleteer. He attacked chiefly the Sedition Law, under which he was himself convicted in May 1800 and sentenced to serve six months in prison and pay a fine of $400. Throughout the rest of his life he sought the repayment of this fine, which, after his death, was refunded to his heirs with interest. Republican success brought him no political reward commensurate with his abilities and deserts, but he served as commissioner in Luzerne County, Pennsylvania, from 1801 to 1804, and as a state judge from 1804 to 1811. A chief feature of state politics during this period was the attack made upon the judiciary by the more radical democrats. Cooper, for the first time in his life, was identified with the conservative faction. His observation of the practical operations of democracy, indeed, had served to chill his ardor and modify his political philosophy. The hostility of the radical faction to him resulted in his removal from the judiciary by the governor in 1811 on joint address of the two houses of the legislature, following charges of arbitrary conduct for which there was some foundation.

Driven from politics and disgusted with practical democracy, he returned to science and entered upon the profession of teaching. Through his long association with Priestley, he had been afforded unusual opportunities for the study of chemistry, which appealed to him as the most useful of the sciences. Elected in 1811 to the chair of chemistry in Carlisle (now Dickinson)·

College, he remained here until 1815. The following year he became professor of applied chemistry and mineralogy in the University of Pennsylvania, where he remained until 1819. This period of his life, devoted to science and learning to the exclusion of politics, was very fruitful in publication. He was a skilful, and might have become a great, investigator, but served chiefly as a disseminator of useful scientific information. The American Philosophical Society had earlier welcomed him into its membership, and (*c.* 1817) a "University of New York" conferred on him the honorary degree of M.D., which he ever afterward flaunted. Jefferson, whose friendship with him had ripened with the years and who described his abilities in superlatives, was desirous that he become the "corner-stone" of the new University of Virginia, and procured his election to its faculty. Owing, however, to clerical opposition and the delay in the opening of the university, Cooper never assumed the position, greatly to the disappointment of his patron.

In January 1820 Cooper entered upon the last and most fateful period of his life, when he became professor of chemistry in South Carolina College (now University of South Carolina). Elected president shortly afterward, he maintained his connection with the college until 1834 and added greatly to its distinction. Besides chemistry and mineralogy, he taught political economy, in which he was distinctly a pioneer in America. He was a prime factor also in the establishment of the first school of medicine and the first insane asylum in the state. Throughout his tenure of office, he was the target of clerical attack, chiefly on the part of the Presbyterians. The controversy was an episode in the age-long conflict between science and theology, but was accentuated by Cooper's ill-concealed contempt for the clergy as a class. He was nominally successful in the struggle, not so much because of any general acceptance of the principles of biblical criticism and the doctrines of materialism that he championed, but because of his identification with the extreme state-rights party, to which he had rendered conspicuous service. Now a realist and a utilitarian in politics, though still a foe to tyranny, he defended slavery, repudiated the social philosophy of his old friend Jefferson, and supported with powerful economic arguments the Southern position on the tariff. He became the academic philosopher of state rights and, as a teacher and writer, exerted a profound and lasting influence. In 1827, in a speech against the tariff, he urged that South Carolina calculate the value of the Union, and aroused thereby a tempest of protest within the state and out of

it. He favored nullification and regarded the outcome of the famous controversy as unsatisfactory because it was a compromise. Valuing union too little because he loved liberty too well, he was one of the first to sow the seeds of secession. After his retirement from the college in 1834, he edited the statutes of the state, supported the second Bank of the United States against Jackson, and carried on a lengthy intrigue with Nicholas Biddle looking toward the candidacy of the latter for the presidency in 1840. Vigorous almost to the end, he died May 11, 1839, and was buried in Trinity Churchyard, Columbia, where a stone was later erected to his memory by a "portion" of his fellow citizens.

The influence of Cooper on his generation was exercised chiefly by means of an extraordinarily vigorous, versatile, and prolific pen. His political pamphlets, of which his *Reply to Mr. Burke's Invective, etc.* (1792), his *Political Essays* (1799), *Consolidation* (1824), and *On the Constitution* (1826) have greatest significance, are distinctly controversial in tone and are of interest chiefly in connection with the specific events and circumstances which called them forth. All of them, however, have a certain permanent value in that they are characterized by a passionate hostility to tyranny in any form. His *Lectures on the Elements of Political Economy* (1826) served as a pioneer American text-book, but even this work emphasized contemporary questions. His various anti-clerical pamphlets are far from philosophical, but are extremely interesting as an expression of aggressive modernism. His *Tracts* (1789) represent the most systematic statement of his religious philosophy, which remained essentially unmodified throughout his life.

Even his controversial works attest his notable scholarship, and his *Institutes of Justinian* (1812) and *Statutes at Large of South Carolina* (5 vols., 1836–39) remain as monuments to his legal learning. His presidential addresses which have been preserved disclose a noteworthy and prophetic educational statesmanship. Most of his scientific writings were designed to extend popular scientific information on subjects of practical concern. Thus he edited the *Emporium of Arts and Sciences* (1813–14), published practical treatises on dyeing and calico printing, gas lights, and the tests of arsenic, and edited several European text-books in chemistry for the use of American students. The most interesting of his more theoretical writings are his description of the scientific discoveries of Priestley (in Appendix 1 of the latter's *Memoirs*, 1806), his *Introductory Lecture* on Chemistry (1812), and his

Discourse on the Connexion between Chemistry and Medicine (1818), in which, as usual, he was forward-looking. These writings serve as a valuable index to the state of American scientific knowledge in his day and reveal his own persistent faith in salvation by enlightenment.

Cooper was twice married: first, in London, to Alice Greenwood, who before her death in 1800 bore him five children; second, about 1811, to Elizabeth Pratt Hemming, also an Englishwoman, who bore him three children and survived him. Physically, Cooper was small but impressive. His head was so large that he is said to have resembled a wedge. Brilliant in conversation and loyal in friendship, he was terrible in controversy. Too belligerent and forward-looking to be agreeable to his age, he none the less taught it the truth as he saw it, embodied most of its noblest hopes and aspirations, shared its disillusionments, and deserves to be ranked at least among its minor prophets.

[The materials for this sketch have been drawn from Dumas Malone, *The Public Life of Thos. Cooper, 1783–1839* (1926), which contains an extensive bibliography, pp. 403–16, including a list of Cooper's own voluminous writings, with comments. For a discussion of Cooper's scientific work by an eminent chemist, see Edgar F. Smith, *Chemistry in America* (1914), ch. VI, and *Chemistry in Old Phila.* (1919), pp. 62–81. For a discussion of his philosophy of materialism, see I. W. Woodbridge Riley, *Am. Philosophy: the Early Schools* (1907), bk. V, ch. V. The Univ. of S. C. has a portrait of Cooper and a bust, generally regarded as a caricature.]

D. M.

COOPER, THOMAS ABTHORPE (Dec. 16, 1776–Apr. 21, 1849), actor, theatrical manager, was born at Harrow-on-the-Hill, England, the son of Thomas Cooper, a prominent physician of Irish descent, and of his wife Mary Grace Cooper. He received, according to one who knew him, "an excellent English education at a principal seminary" (W. B. Wood, *Personal Recollections of the Stage,* 1855, p. 410). When Dr. Cooper died in 1787, leaving his family destitute, William Godwin, whose mother was Mrs. Cooper's first cousin, assumed the care and education of Thomas. At sixteen the boy resolved to be an actor. Godwin, approving this choice, sought the advice of his friend Thomas Holcroft, and on the latter's recommendation Cooper approached Stephen Kemble, then at Edinburgh. After being sent on in very minor parts, he essayed Malcolm in *Macbeth,* in which rôle he distinguished himself by forgetting the last speech of the play. He was summarily dismissed. For about three years he played with various provincial companies, and was then taken in hand by Holcroft, who carefully coached him and secured for him an opportunity to appear at Covent Garden as Hamlet in October 1795. The critics

warmly praised his efforts, but the manager offered him an engagement for secondary characters only, which he indignantly refused. In 1796 Thomas Wignell, the Philadelphia director, engaged him for three years.

Cooper made his American début Nov. 11, 1796, at Baltimore, where the company was temporarily stationed. He first faced a Philadelphia audience, Dec. 9, as Macbeth and was favorably received. Relations with Wignell becoming strained, largely because Fennell was given more important rôles than himself, Cooper broke his contract and, after some legal complications, went over to the New York theatre in February 1798. Here he was at once recognized as the unrivaled tragic actor of America, despite a faulty memory and careless study, which sometimes caused him to appear at a disadvantage. After a temporary return to Philadelphia he was back in New York in 1801. From this time on, Cooper was a star —one of the first in this country—rather than a regular stock actor. His career was an important step in the evolution from the stock to the starring system.

When John Kemble retired from Drury Lane, Cooper was secured to succeed him. He made his first appearance Mar. 7, 1803, but he failed to attract well-filled houses and was soon released. His return to the Park Theatre, New York, in November 1804, was rapturously welcomed. After spending the season of 1805–06 largely at Boston, he became lessee of the Park Theatre. In the fall of 1808 he sold a share of his interests to Stephen Price, and, being thus partially relieved of managerial duties, contracted to play half of each week at Philadelphia, the other half to be devoted to New York. Driving his own fast horses, he was able, by a relay arrangement, to leave one town after the evening performance and be in the other in time for morning rehearsal. In June 1810 he again sailed for England, where he acted with success in some of the provincial towns, and engaged the celebrated George Frederick Cooke for a series of appearances in America, a project which proved extremely profitable to the New York managers.

Cooper's first wife, formerly Mrs. Joanna Johnson Upton, having died in 1808, he was married on June 11, 1812, to Mary Fairlie, daughter of Maj. James Fairlie. She was said to be the most brilliant and beautiful belle of New York. This marriage gave Cooper a prominent position in the society of the town, and, having made a fortune through the theatre, he took up his residence in a fashionable section of the city, where he lived and entertained in a most lavish style and associated with the leading literary and professional people of the day. About 1815 he withdrew from the management of the Park and gave himself entirely to starring engagements. Again, in 1827, he appeared at Drury Lane, but was received with discourtesy, perhaps because of prejudice against American talent, and he refused to play a second night. By degrees enthusiasm for Cooper in the United States waned as younger actors arose and his own powers declined through advancing years and, it may be, a too great fondness for stimulants. His once large fortune having been dissipated by extravagant living, and the receipts from his profession having sadly shrunk, friends came to his aid by arranging, in 1833–34, a series of notably successful benefits in several cities to provide a fund for the support of his family. In 1834 Cooper brought his daughter Priscilla before the public, but her stage career was cut short by her marriage to Robert Tyler, son of John Tyler, later president of the United States. Cooper last appeared on the New York stage on Nov. 24, 1835, at Hamblin's benefit; his retirement from the theatre is thought to have occurred in 1838 (Odell, *post*, IV, 72, 74). During his final years he held several government posts, which he secured through the patronage of President Tyler, among them an inspectorship in the New York Custom House. He died at Bristol, Pa., at the home of his daughter, Mrs. Tyler, after an illness of four months. He was survived by six daughters and one son, all children of his second wife.

During a period of at least thirty years Cooper was the most conspicuous figure on the American stage. His hold is not difficult to explain. He possessed extraordinary beauty of face and form, and a magnificent voice. In his great rôles, such as Macbeth and various Roman characters, he was remarkable for the majesty and grandeur of his acting. If he was at times addicted to shouting and rant, if he relied upon impulse more than art, at his best he created an impression of unforgettable power. One qualified critic said: "I still think his Macbeth was only inferior to Garrick's, and his Hamlet to Kemble's; while his Othello, I think, was equal to Barry's itself" (John Bernard, *Retrospections of America*, 1887, p. 268). Cooper did not confine himself wholly to tragic characters; Charles Surface in *The School for Scandal* was one of his most effective parts, and he even attempted Falstaff with considerable success. His energy was as great as his gifts: he is known to have appeared in at least 164 different plays and is said to have acted, prior to 1830, in every state then in the Union. Off the stage as well as on, Cooper was a favorite. His utter fearlessness, his tire-

less vitality, his astonishing skill with a guıı and a horse, his prodigal liberality, his devotion to his family, even his reckless betting, all contributed to make him one of the most engaging of American actors.

[The date of Cooper's birth is taken from his tombstone at Bristol, Pa. The names of his parents are from the baptismal record of the parish church at Harrow-on-the-Hill. Nearly all that is known about his life is found in the writings of his associates, such as *A Hist. of the Am. Theatre* (1832) by Wm. Dunlap, and the works of Wood and Bernard cited above. This material with additions is assembled in *A Memoir of the Professional Life of Thos. Abthorpe Cooper* (1888), by J. N. Ireland. See also G. C. D. Odell, *Annals of the N. Y. Stage*, vols. I–IV (1927–28).]

O.S.C

COOPER, WILLIAM (Dec. 2, 1754–Dec. 22, 1809), jurist and extensive landowner, was born in Byberry, Pa., where his great-grandfather, James, coming from Stratford-on-Avon in 1679, purchased a plantation in addition to other land in and around Philadelphia. After his marriage to Elizabeth Fenimore of Rancocus, N. J. (Dec. 12, 1775), he lived in Burlington, N. J., until he settled (1789) on the shores of Otsego Lake, and founded the town that bears his name. When he was ready to start for this wilderness in central New York, his wife refused to budge from the chair where she was sitting and holding her infant son, James. Picking up the chair, he placed it, with its occupants, on the waiting wagon. In securing tenants for his land he adopted the policy of instalment payments instead of annual rents, on the theory that a man having a proprietary interest would stick to the soil in spite of hardships. In lean years he accepted payments in maple sugar and wood-ash; to improve the morals in a "rough and ready" community, he persuaded Trinity Church (New York) to grant $1,500 for a church in Cooperstown; through donations, headed by his own, he erected a seminary; by judicious use of a little rum he built roads and bridges; he furnished the money to buy a printing-press and type for a newspaper. An advertisement in the *Otsego Herald* (December 1797) showed that he was selling land not only for himself but also for the Hartwick, the Hillington, the Jew, and the Schuyler patents. He later bought land both in the northern and the western parts of the state. In his real-estate transactions Alexander Hamilton was his attorney. Defeated once but twice elected to Congress (1795–97; 1799–1801), he was the first judge of Otsego County (1791). An ardent Federalist, he always campaigned next to the ground, was said to have won votes by embracing "the toothless and the decrepit," and after the election of 1792, when votes from Otsego and other counties were, at the instigation of Aaron Burr, rejected by the official canvassers in order to elect Clinton governor, he was charged, in a petition presented to the state legislature, with unduly influencing the voters in Otsego County, a charge later dismissed as frivolous and vexatious. Cooper died in Albany as the result of a blow struck from behind, by a political opponent; he was buried at Cooperstown. A curious mixture of silk hose and leather stockings, he made Otsego Hall the finest home west of the Hudson, but he was always willing to go to any shanty on his settlements to show his ability as a wrestler. Portraits by Gilbert Stuart, John Trumbull, and an unknown artist, show that he was unusually handsome. He failed to foresee that canals would supplant natural water routes and that streams would shrink with banks cleared of timber, but he said truthfully, "I have settled more acres than any other man in America. There are forty thousand souls holding directly or indirectly under me."

[A genealogy prepared by W. W. Cooper (c. 1885) gives interesting facts about Cooper's ancestors. *The Chronicles of Cooperstown* (1838), by his son, Jas. Fenimore Cooper [q.v.], record his struggles to establish his "pioneer" town. A chapter, "Some Old Letters," in *The Legends and Traditions of a Northern Country* (1921), by his great-grandson, Jas. Fenimore Cooper, tells about his extensive real-estate transactions. A scarce volume, *A Guide in the Wilderness; or the Hist. of the First Settlements of the Western Counties of N. Y., with Useful Instructions to Future Settlers* (Dublin, 1810), by himself, though published after his death to aid settlers, contains much autobiographical material told with a charm rarely surpassed by the tales of his son. The best notices about his last days are found in the December issue of the *Cooperstown Federalist*, the paper for which he bought the press and the type. In *To Commemorate the Foundation of the Village of Cooperstown* (1907) there is a sketch of Wm. Cooper by his great-grandson, J. F. Cooper.] J.M.L.

COOPER-POUCHER, MATILDA S. (Feb. 2, 1839–Apr. 5, 1900), educator, was a native of Blauveltville, N. Y. She received her education at Hardcastle's Institute at Nyack, Clinton Liberal Institute, and the Albany State Normal School. After graduating from the latter in 1856 she was immediately retained by the Oswego board of education to teach in one of the senior schools of that city. Although shortly transferred to work in the primary grades, she was recognized at once as a teacher of unusual ability. Thus, when the city training school, later to be recognized as the famous Oswego State Normal School, was organized under Dr. Sheldon, Miss Cooper was secured as one of the critic teachers. At a somewhat later date she was made teacher of language and methods. She became active in the National Education Association and her services as an institute lecturer were in demand beyond the borders of the state. She was almost a right hand to Dr. Sheldon while

she was in charge of the records of scholarship and attendance and of the teacher placement work. In the latter work she distinguished herself by her uncanny ability to remember details about students past and present. Along with her other duties she undertook those of preceptress of the Normal Boarding Hall, a post most exacting in its demands on tact, sympathy, and judgment. In this office she came into very close personal contact with many of the students and through it exercised a significant influence over their characters. She contributed no small share toward the success of the Normal School. When the Quarter-Centennial Anniversary of the Oswego Movement was celebrated in 1886 her experience was of great value in furnishing biographical material. On this anniversary she resigned from active work in the school. After the conclusion of the semester of 1886 she returned to her home in Nyack, N. Y., to comfort and care for her parents in their declining years. When these both died in 1889, she returned to Oswego, as the wife of Dr. Sheldon's successor, Isaac B. Poucher, whom she married Feb. 4, 1890. They had been co-workers at Oswego for a long time. The same exactness and orderliness which had characterized Miss Cooper's work as critic, teacher, statistician, and preceptress were now transferred to home making. She now found time to take an active interest in church and social affairs of the town. It was while performing her duty as a director of the Oswego Hospital that death came upon her suddenly after only a few hours of illness.

[Sketch by Mary Sheldon in *Hist. of the First Half Century of the Oswego State Normal and Training School* (1913); *Hist. Sketches Relating to the First Quarter Century of the State Normal and Training School at Oswego, N. Y.* (1888); *Oswego Daily Times,* Apr. 5, 14, 16, 1900. N. H. Dearborn, *The Oswego Movement in Am. Educ.* (1925) and Nat. Educ. Asso., *Jour. of Proc. and Addresses,* 1900, add little. Brief estimates of Miss Cooper's work are found in A. P. Hollis, *The Contribution of the Oswego Normal School to Educ. Progress in the U. S.* (1898), and *Autobiography of Edwin Austin Sheldon* (1911), ed. by Mary Sheldon Barnes.] J.S.B.

COOTE, RICHARD (1636–Mar. 5, 1701), Earl of Bellomont, colonial governor, was the son of Richard Coote and Mary, daughter of Sir George St. George, Bart. He succeeded his father as Baron Coote of Coloony, in the Irish peerage, in July 1683. His father, uncle, and grandfather had distinguished themselves as soldiers in Ireland, and as supporters of the Restoration in 1660. In corresponding fashion Richard, the second baron, was an early and warm supporter of the movement in favor of the Prince of Orange in 1688, attained to friendly personal relations with William, and received substantial marks of his favor. He was sworn treasurer and receiver-general to the Queen, Mar. 27, 1689, and having been attainted by the Jacobite Parliament at Dublin, was advanced, Nov. 2, 1689, to the dignity of Earl of Bellomont, in the Irish peerage, receiving also extensive grants from the Irish forfeited estates. By his marriage to Catherine, daughter of Bridges Nanfan, landowner, of Bridgemorton, he acquired an interest in Worcestershire, and he was member of Parliament for Droitwich from 1688 to 1695. His appointment in 1697 to be governor of New York, Massachusetts, and New Hampshire, with command of the militia during the war in Rhode Island, Connecticut, and the Jerseys (*Documents Relative to the Colonial History of the State of New York*, IV, 261–62), was said to have been due to the King's high estimate of his integrity and resolution (William Smith, *History of New York*, 1814, p. 150). A more unified conduct of the affairs of the English plantations on the northern frontier of the American continent, particularly in matters of defense, was regarded as imperative, while scarcely less pressing were the problems presented by the American disregard of the imperial trade laws, and the encouragement said to be given to piracy, especially in New York.

Bellomont's administrations in New England, where he spent fourteen months, May 1699 to July 1700, were comparatively uneventful, and through no fault of his own the cause of intercolonial union cannot be said to have been advanced by his lordship's tri-provincial governorship. The situation in New York, where he arrived on Apr. 2, 1698, after a long and stormy passage, was one of extreme difficulty. In that province evasion of the trade regulations and complicity with piratical operations were complicated with the political consequences of the passionate Leislerian feud, which had been raging for over seven years. This internal disturbance was of perilous significance for all the English colonies on the American continent by reason of the close connection of the New York government with the Iroquois confederacy, the pivot upon which turned the fate of the issue between the French and the English in North America.

The precipitate vigor of the Earl's proceedings soon aroused the antagonism of the mercantile community, the landed interest, and the few but highly placed Anglicans of the province. Though personally of aristocratic bearing, he found himself maneuvered into the appearance of leading the Leislerian "democracy" against the pillars of provincial society as that had hitherto developed. Moreover his opponents had powerful friends in England, and spared no efforts in their attempt to undermine the Earl's support from home. In this they failed, but Bellomont was obliged, as indeed was every governor who tried to realize the imperial ideal, to carry on a struggle on two fronts. By unrelenting exercise of executive prerogatives he was able to put a considerable restraint on the dealings of New York merchants with pirates. But for the enterprise of promoting an orderly development of provincial affairs in accordance with the aims of the English government, it would seem that he was not especially well fitted. Free from personal avarice, high-spirited, prone to quick judgment and action, he was lacking in the deliberate prudence, the capacity for indirect methods, and especially the patience, which the conditions in New York at that time seemed to require. On the other hand, the observations expressed in his voluminous correspondence with the English authorities displayed alertness of perception and far-sighted imagination in estimating the potentialities of the "plantations," and on several important features of colonial policy his representations bore fruit in orders later issued from Whitehall. Regulations for the granting of land and for facilitating the policy of naval-stores production are cases in point. Especially comprehensive and far-seeing were his ambitions for the development of Indian relations, but, in this matter, as in regard to his whole administrative career, the shortness of his time in America precludes definitive judgment. For the student of English colonial administration in America Bellomont's administration is exceedingly significant and suggestive, but its actually permanent results elude exact estimate. Bellomont died Mar. 5, 1701, and was buried with public honors in the chapel of the fort, near the site of the present Bowling Green in New York. When this building was demolished in the late eighteenth century, his coffin was interred in St. Paul's churchyard, but without monumental notice.

[The chief sources of information concerning Bellomont's American career are to be found in the archives of the provinces concerned, and in the Public Record Office in London. Much of this material is accessible in the *Calendar of State Papers, America and West Indies*, and *Calendar of Treasury Papers*, and in the *Docs. Relative to the Colonial Hist. of the State of N. Y.*, vol. IV (1854). The chief biographical sketches are F. de Peyster, *Life and Administration of Richard, Earl of Bellomont* (1879); and the chapter by A. G. Vermilye in Jas. G. Wilson, *Memorial Hist. of the City of N. Y.*, vol. II (1892). See also Herbert L. Osgood, *The Am. Colonies in the Eighteenth Century* (1924), vol. I, ch. VIII and pp. 466–72, 499–504, 530–42. For facts as to his family and peerage, see J. B. Burke, *A Geneal. Hist. of the Dormant ... and Extinct Peerages of the British Empire* (1866), pp. 133–35; A. de Vlieger, *Hist. and Geneal. Record of the Coote Family* (1900).] C.W.S.

COPE, CALEB (July 18, 1797–May 12, 1888), merchant, financier, son of William and Elizabeth (Rohrer) Cope, was born in Greensburg, Pa. His father died when Caleb was very young and he was cared for by his mother and maternal grandfather. He received a rudimentary education in a one-story log-cabin school-house and at the age of twelve or thirteen was bound out by his mother to John Wells, a storekeeper, with whom he served a four-year apprenticeship. In 1815 he went to Philadelphia where his uncles, Israel and Jasper Cope, well-known merchants, had offered him a home. To their training he attributed much of his success. In 1820 his uncles discontinued their part of the business and conveyed all their merchandise to Caleb Cope and his cousin. The firm of Caleb Cope & Company, dealing principally in silks, became one of the wealthiest in the country. In 1857, however, came a panic and the failure of the firm. Cope was forced to sell his country seat, "Springbrook," near Holmesburg, and then removed to the St. Lawrence Hotel. He was one of the founders and for many years president of the Merchants Hotel Company, which in 1861 opened the Continental Hotel, where Cope made his residence thenceforth. When the Civil War broke out, the government selected him to represent it in Europe for the purchase of supplies, but he was unable to accept the post. In 1864 he was elected president of the Philadelphia Saving Fund Society in which he had been a director since 1841, and to its service he successfully devoted the best efforts of the remaining years of his life, living to see it become the largest institution of its kind in America.

In his earlier years Cope had served as a director of the United States Bank, acting as its president in the temporary absence of Nicholas Biddle. He was one of the original trustees of the Lehigh Coal & Navigation Company, and the Philadelphia agent for the Bank of Kentucky. He was a manager of the Pennsylvania Hospital, of the Institution for the Instruction of the Blind, and an active worker for other charitable organizations. He had an ardent interest in horticulture and at his country place was raised for the first time in America the *Victoria Regia,* or great American water-lily. He was twice married: first, in 1835, to his cousin Abby Ann Cope who died in 1845, and in December 1864 to Josephine Porter of Nashville, Tenn. He was one of the best-known and most highly respected men of Philadelphia and though frequently pressed to accept political honors, always refused them.

[Sketch of Caleb Cope prepared by his son Porter F.

Cope for *Encyc. of Contemporary Biog. of Pa.* (1889), vol. I, with corrections by Porter F. Cope; Jas. M. Willcox, *Hist. of the Phila. Saving Fund Soc., 1816–1916* (1916), pp. 118–23; Gilbert Cope, *Record of the Cope Family* (1861); J. W. Jordan, *Encyc. of Pa. Biog.* (1914), II, 697.]　　　　　　　　　　　　　　　E. Y.

COPE, EDWARD DRINKER (July 28, 1840–Apr. 12, 1897), zoölogist, paleontologist, a lineal descendant of Oliver Cope who came from Wiltshire, England, about 1687, was born in Philadelphia. His parents, Alfred and Hannah (Edge) Cope, were wealthy members of the Society of Friends, and at the age of thirteen he was sent to the Friends' School at Westtown, where he received his early training, supplemented by a single year at the University of Pennsylvania, and by the assistance of private tutors. As a mere boy he showed a strong love for the natural sciences, extraordinary powers of observation, and unusual ability in the discrimination of characteristics essential in classification. His note-books made before reaching the age of ten were filled with sketches from life and notes that would have done credit to one of twice his years. In 1859 he went to Washington and studied reptiles under S. F. Baird [*q.v.*] at the Smithsonian Institution, and while there made his first contribution to scientific literature in a paper "On the Primary Divisions of the Salamandridæ, with a Description of Two New Species," which appeared in the *Proceedings of the Academy of Natural Sciences* of the same year. Returning to Philadelphia, he entered upon his course at the University under Joseph Leidy [*q.v.*] and at the same time worked almost daily at the Academy, paying particular attention to the reptiles and pursuing his studies with such diligence that at the age of twenty-two he was recognized as one of the country's leading authorities in his field (King, *post,* p. 2). In 1863–64 he spent several months in study abroad. On his return he accepted the chair of comparative zoölogy and botany at Haverford College, but he was obliged by ill health to abandon the position in 1867. He devoted the following twenty-two years wholly to exploration and research. His studies in vertebrate paleontology, the branch in which he became most proficient, began in 1866 with the reptilian (dinosaur) remains from the Greensand of New Jersey and the Cetaceans and the other vertebrate remains of the Miocene deposits of Maryland and Virginia. In 1868 he began studies on the air-breathing vertebrates of the upper Mississippi Valley and in 1870 became associated with Leidy in the description of fossils collected by the Hayden Survey in Wyoming, making in this, as it proved, the beginning of his connection with the National Survey which lasted throughout the life of the organization. In 1874 he became connected for a single year, as paleontologist, with the Wheeler Survey west of the one-hundredth meridian. In 1889, through bad investments and loss of a considerable portion of his fortune, he was led to accept the professorship of geology and mineralogy in the University of Pennsylvania, and in 1895, after the death of Leidy, he assumed the chair of zoölogy and comparative anatomy, which position he held until his death.

Cope in his early youth was precocious almost to the danger point. He became a tremendous force in the anatomical world, an active, tireless, and rapid worker, carried away by the impetuosity of his thoughts, the immensity of the work to be done, and the excitement of competition with O. C. Marsh, a rival in his field. His haste occasionally led him into superficiality; Leidy once charged him with having described a new form which was without a skull, "wrong end to." Nevertheless, it was said of him that his intuition was better than his logic.

His literary fecundity was remarkable, amounting in some cases to as many as fifty papers within a single year. In all, he is credited with 600 separate titles, one of which, a monograph of the Hayden Survey familiarly known as "Cope's Primer," was a pudgy quarto volume of 1,009 pages and 137 plates. From January 1878 he was owner and senior editor of the *American Naturalist*. Concerning his work as a whole one cannot do better than quote from a contemporary: "The greatest and most enduring monument to his fame will prove to be the gigantic work which he accomplished among the extinct vertebrates of the far West. . . . It was in the unraveling of the complexities of the freshwater Tertiaries that Cope's most splendid services to geology were rendered" (W. B. Scott, *post*, pp. 32, 35).

Cope's first honor was his election to membership in the Philadelphia Academy of Natural Sciences in 1861 when he was but twenty-one years of age. In 1865 he became a curator and in 1879 was elected a member of the council, holding the office until 1880. He was a member of the National Academy of Sciences and of the American Association for the Advancement of Science, and president of the latter in 1896. He was married, on Aug. 14, 1865, to Annie Pim, a daughter of Richard Pim of Chester County, Pa. (*The Friend*, Oct. 14, 1865), by whom he had one child, a daughter. His domestic ties were not strong, however, and he died amidst the clutter of his work rooms and surrounded by the objects of his life study, in Pine St., Philadelphia.

[*Addresses in Memory of Edward Drinker Cope* (1897), by Theodore Gill, Henry F. Osborn, and Wm. B. Scott; Helen King, "Edward D. Cope," accompanied by a full bibliography of Cope's publications, in *Am. Geologist*, Jan. 1899; Persifor Frazer, "Life and Letters of Edward Drinker Cope," *Ibid.*, Aug. 1900; J. S. Kingsley in *Am. Naturalist*, May 1897; Henry Fairfield Osborn, *Impressions of Great Naturalists*, rev. ed., 1928.]

G. P. M.

COPE, THOMAS PYM (Aug. 26, 1768–Nov. 22, 1854), merchant, philanthropist, the son of Caleb and Mary (Mendenhall) Cope and a descendant of Oliver Cope who emigrated from England to Pennsylvania about 1687, was born in Lancaster, Pa. He was given an education, good for his time, which included the study of English and German and a foundation in Latin. His parents were both Quakers, and when he was a boy of twelve, his father gave shelter to Major André and other British prisoners who, sent to Lancaster by Gen. Montgomery, could find no one else willing to give them a place in which to live. The populace grew so excited at this act of their Quaker neighbors that they broke every window in the Cope house. In later years they redeemed themselves by assisting liberally in the reconstruction of the house when it had been accidentally destroyed by fire.

In 1786 Thomas Cope went to Philadelphia and began a four-year apprenticeship to his uncle, Thomas Mendenhall, a merchant. In 1790 the firm of Mendenhall & Cope was formed, but it was dissolved two years later. Then Cope began business for himself, importing his own goods and selling them. He was a prudent man, and his rise in the business world was not as rapid as it was sure and sound. In 1803 he again formed a partnership in the firm of Cope & Thomas. While thus engaged in business, he laid the foundation for a line of packets to Europe. His first ship, the *Lancaster*, was built in 1807, and in 1821 he established the first regular line of packet ships between Philadelphia and Liverpool. His mercantile success was such that he became possessed of one of the large fortunes of his day and his business passed on to his sons and grandsons. He lived his long life in the Quaker faith, creditably discharged many positions of public trust, and did much for the development of Philadelphia. Having been ill with yellow fever in the epidemic of 1793, on his recovery, and again during the return of the scourge in 1797, he rendered much service, being a manager of the Almshouse and one of the "Guardians of the Poor" who carried food to the homes of the sufferers. At the close of the century he was a member of the City Council, and as such was a promoter and staunch advocate of the introduction of Schuylkill River water into the city, one of the most important health measures devised in his day. He served in the state legislature in 1807, later refusing overtures which might have led him to Congress, and was an important member of the state constitutional convention of 1837. He was one of the founders, and for many years president, of the Mercantile Library Company, and one of the first members of the city's Board of Trade of which he was the first, and for a period of twenty-two years ending with his death the only, president. He was instrumental in bringing about the completion of the Chesapeake & Delaware Canal, and was active in promoting the construction of the Pennsylvania Central Railroad. A close friend of Stephen Girard, he was one of the executors of the Girard will and later a director of Girard College. Influential in securing Henry J. Pratt's estate, "Lemon Hill," for a park for the city and contributing heavily toward the purchase of the Sedgeley estate for a similar purpose, he also gave $25,000 to the Zoölogical Society, and $40,-000 to the Institute for Colored Youth to found a scientific school. He took great delight in social life, and his buoyancy of spirit made him a favorite at the social gatherings of his day. He was twice married, his first wife being Mary Drinker of Philadelphia.

[Obituary in *North American* (Phila.), Nov. 23, 1854; Freeman Hunt, *Lives of Am. Merchants* (1857), I, 103–31; Henry Simpson, *Lives of Eminent Philadelphians* (1859); Gilbert Cope, *Record of the Cope Family* (1861); S. N. Winslow, *Biogs. of Successful Phila. Merchants* (1864); *Makers of Phila.* (1894), ed. by Chas. Morris.]
E.Y.

COPE, WALTER (Oct. 20, 1860–Nov. 1, 1902), architect, was born in Philadelphia, the son of Thomas P. and Elizabeth Waln (Stokes) Cope. He was given the finest type of old-fashioned Quaker training, in which strictness and culture were combined. Upon graduating from the Friends' School at Germantown, he entered the office of a builder named Hutton and, subsequently, the architectural office of T. P. Chandler, where he received his professional training. In 1884 he went abroad for a year, bringing back many sketches which showed his skilful draftsmanship, sense of composition, and grasp of details. In 1886 he formed an association, later a partnership, with John Stewardson [q.v.]. Emlen L. Stewardson became a partner in 1887.

The earliest important commission of the firm of Cope & Stewardson was Radnor Hall at Bryn Mawr College (1886). They subsequently designed Pembroke, East and West, and Denbeigh Halls at Bryn Mawr. This work, with which the elder Stewardson had much to do, revolutionized college building in America; at

Bryn Mawr, for the first time, the English collegiate Gothic was adapted freely, beautifully, and successfully to the problems of modern American collegiate architecture (Seeler, *post*, p. 289). Cope & Stewardson were given the commission for the University of Pennsylvania dormitory group in 1897, where they developed further the use of the English collegiate Gothic, this time in brick and stone, with details rich, but occasionally, to the modern eye, heavy. The quadrangle scheme adopted was carried out in a masterly manner with a just balance of informality and directness. Later (1900) Cope & Stewardson were made official architects of the University. They began an epoch-making work at Princeton in 1896 with Blair Hall and its great arched tower (now containing memorial tablets to both Cope and Stewardson) and the low dormitories which flank it. This was the last of the firm's designs prior to the death of John Stewardson, who was drowned in January 1896. Later work at Princeton included the Ivy Club (1897), Stafford Little Hall (1899–1901), and the enormous gymnasium (1903); and at the University of Pennsylvania the Archeological Museum (done in association with Frank Miles Day and Wilson Eyre) and the Law School, a great brick and stone building in a modified Georgian style. Probably the finest of the educational work was that done for Washington University in St. Louis, which was awarded to the firm after a competition in 1899. This is characterized by the most admirable restraint; there are none of the facile tricks to which the Tudor lends itself; everything is of the most direct simplicity, distinguished by exquisite proportion and refined detail. Cope used many styles with equal ease and freedom: for instance, the Law School of the University of Pennsylvania is Georgian; the Lady Chapel of St. Mark's Church and the choir screen of St. Luke's (both in Philadelphia) are in the richest type of intimate late Gothic; the winning design in the competition for the Municipal Building in Washington is in a severe classic of French character; and the Cassatt house at Rosemont, Pa., with its quiet stone and stucco walls and high slate roofs, is a perfect example of Normandy inspiration. In 1895 Cope spent several months in Spain. The results appeared shortly in the Pennsylvania Institute for the Instruction of the Blind, at Overbrook, Pa., one of the earliest successful adaptations in America of the more informal type of Spanish renaissance. It is not obviously stylistic, Italian motives abound, but the Spanish influence is dominant in the quiet dignity of its courts and in its broad, stucco wall surfaces.

Cope was made a Fellow of the American Institute of Architects in 1893, he was chairman of the committee appointed by the Philadelphia chapter to restore Congress Hall, the result of his intense interest in the preservation and restoration of Philadelphia colonial relics, and he directed the restoration of Stenton for the Colonial Dames. He was a manager of the Stewardson Travelling Scholarship in Architecture (named after his partner), and was one of a small group who volunteered their services as lecturers on architecture in the early days of the University of Pennsylvania School of Architecture. He was also largely responsible for the foundation of the T-Square Club in Philadelphia.

Cope was distinguished by his love of nature, his frankness, his larger grasp of a problem, his charm and hospitality. He was "simple, direct, sincere, and . . . studious" (Editorial in the *Architectural Review*, IV, 273). In 1893 he married Eliza Middleton Kane. They made their home in Germantown.

[Editorial in *Arch. Rev.*, Oct. 1902, p. 273; Edgar V. Seeler, "Walter Cope, Architect," an analysis of Cope's work and personality, *Ibid.*, Dec. 1902, p. 289; *Am. Art. Annual*, 1903, p. 138; R. C. Sturgis in the *Outlook*, Apr. 4, 1903; Memorial Address by President M. Carey Thomas of Bryn Mawr in the Bryn Mawr *Lantern*, Feb. 1905.]   T. F. H.

COPELAND, CHARLES W. (1815–Feb. 5, 1895), naval engineer, was born in Coventry, Conn., the son of Daniel Copeland, a builder of steam-engines and boilers in Hartford. Under his father's guidance Charles received his first lessons in the profession which was to become his life-work. These were followed by a course at Columbia College, after which, at the age of twenty-one, he was appointed superintendent of the West Point Foundry Association. There he began the design of the machinery of the *Fulton*, the first steam war-vessel to be constructed under the direct supervision of the United States Navy Department. In 1839 he received an appointment from the government under which he signed himself "Naval Engineer" and was entrusted with the designs of the machinery for the *Mississippi* and *Missouri* and later for the *Susquehanna, Saranac,* and *Michigan.* In 1850, this work for the government completed, he was appointed superintendent of the Allaire Works in New York City, where he designed and supervised the construction of a large number of merchant steamers, two of which, transatlantic steamers of the Collins line, broke the record of their day. During the Civil War, his experience as a marine engineer was used by the government in the adaptation of merchant steamers for service in the Southern blockade. At the close

of the war, he became the constructing engineer for the United States Lighthouse Board, which position he held nearly to the time of his death.

Copeland was simple and kindly in manner, frugal in personal economy, untiring in industry even to his latest days. His professional work by no means absorbed all of his interest. He was a lover and a reader of books and a discriminating collector. He was a charter and life member of the American Society of Mechanical Engineers and maintained an interested and helpful relation to the work of this society.

[*Trans. Am. Soc. Mechanical Engineers,* XVI (1895), 1191–92; obituaries in *N. Y. Tribune, Hartford Times,* Feb. 7, 1895.]   W. F. D.

COPLEY, JOHN SINGLETON (1738–Sept. 9, 1815), painter, was born, presumably, at Boston, Mass., a son of Richard and Mary Singleton Copley, both Irish. Allan Cunningham gives the date of his birth as July 3, 1737 (*The Lives of the Most Eminent British Painters, Sculptors, and Architects,* 1830–33, V, 162), but the published *Boston Records* have no entry confirming this date. Copley himself wrote, Sept. 12, 1766, to Peter Pelham, his step-brother, that he had had "resolution enough to live a bachelor to the age of twenty-eight" ("Copley-Pelham Letters," *post,* p. 48). His daughter, Elizabeth Clarke Greene (in a letter quoted by William Dunlap, *post,* I, 119) spoke of her father as "born in 1738." Worthington C. Ford, editor of the Copley-Pelham correspondence, and Frank W. Bayley, a biographer, accept the evidence as indicating that the artist "was born in 1738, and not in 1737 as usually stated" ("Copley-Pelham Letters," p. 48).

Copley's mother in his early boyhood kept a tobacco shop on Long Wharf (Dunlap, III, 323). The parents, who according to the artist's grand-daughter, Martha Babcock Amory, came to Boston in 1736, were "engaged in trade, like almost all the inhabitants of the North American colonies at that time" (Amory, *post,* p. 4). The father was of Limerick; the mother, of the Singletons of County Clare, a family of Lancashire origin. Letters from John Singleton, Mrs. Copley's father, are in the Copley-Pelham collection. Richard Copley, described as a tobacconist, is said by several biographers to have arrived in Boston out of health and to have gone, about the time of John's birth, to the West Indies where he died. William H. Whitmore (*Notes Concerning Peter Pelham,* 1867, p. 13) gives his death as of 1748, the year of Mrs. Copley's remarriage. James Bernard Cullen (*The Story of the Irish in Boston,* 1889, p. 190) says: "Richard Copley was in poor health on his arrival in America and went to the West Indies to improve his failing strength. He died there in 1737." Neither of the foregoing dates has been either confirmed or disproved.

Except for a family tradition of his precocity in drawing, nothing is known of Copley's schooling or of the other activities of his boyhood. His letters, the earliest of which is dated Sept. 30, 1762, reveal a fairly well educated man. He may have been taught various subjects, it is reasonably conjectured, by his future step-father, who besides painting portraits and cutting engravings eked out a living in Boston by teaching dancing and, beginning Sept. 12, 1743, by conducting an "Evening Writing and Arithmetic School," duly advertised. Certain it is that the widow Copley, May 22, 1748, was married to Peter Pelham [q.v.] and that at about that time she transferred her tobacco business to his house in Queen St., at which the evening school also continued its sessions. In such a household young Copley may have learned to use the paint brush and the graver's tools. Whitmore says plausibly (p. 29): "Copley at the age of fifteen was able to engrave in mezzotint; his step-father Pelham, with whom he lived three years, was an excellent engraver and skillful also with the brush." Extant portraits by Peter Pelham, both painted and engraved, excite admiration and prove how unnecessary it is to surmise that Copley had lessons from John Smibert, who died in 1751 or Joseph Badger (1708–65), the latter distinctly inferior as a craftsman to the elder Pelham.

The artistic opportunities of the home and town in which Copley grew to manhood should be emphasized because he himself, and some of his biographers, taking him too literally, have made much of the bleakness of his early surroundings. His son, Lord Lyndhurst, wrote (Amory, p. 9) that "he (Copley) was entirely self taught, and never saw a decent picture, with the exception of his own, until he was nearly thirty years of age." Copley himself complained, in a letter to Benjamin West, Nov. 12, 1766: "In this Country as You rightly observe there is no examples of Art, except what is to [be] met with in a few prints indifferently exicuted, from which it is not possable to learn much" ("Copley-Pelham Letters," p. 51). Variants of this thesis are found almost everywhere in his earlier letters. They suggest that while Copley was industrious and an able executant he was physically unadventurous and temperamentally inclined toward brooding and self-pity. He could have seen at least a few good paintings and many good prints in the Boston of his youth.

The excellence of his own portraits was not accidental or miraculous; it had an academic foundation. A book of Copley's studies of the figure, now at the British Museum, proves that before he was twenty, whether with or without help from a teacher, he was making anatomical drawings with much care and precision. It must be believed that through the fortunate associations of a home and workshop in a town which had many craftsmen he had already learned his trade at an age when the average art student of to-day is beginning to draw.

Copley was fourteen or thereabout and his step-father had recently died, when he made the earliest of his portraits now preserved, a likeness of his half-brother Charles Pelham, good in color and characterization though it has in its background accessories which are somewhat out of drawing. It is a remarkable work to have come from so young a hand. The artist was only fifteen when (it is believed) he painted the portrait of the Rev. William Welsteed, minister of the Brick Church in Long Lane, a work which, following Peter Pelham's practise, Copley personally engraved to get the benefit from the sale of prints. No other engraving has been attributed to Copley. A self-portrait, undated, depicting a boy of about seventeen in broken straw hat, and a painting of "Mars, Venus and Vulcan," signed and dated 1754, disclose crudities of execution which do not obscure the decorative intent and documentary value of the works. Such painting would obviously advertise itself anywhere. Without going after business, for his letters do not indicate that he was ever aggressive or pushing, Copley was started as a professional portrait-painter long before he was of age. In October 1757, Capt. Thomas Ainslie, collector of the port of Quebec, acknowledged from Halifax the receipt of his portrait, which "gives me great Satisfaction" (Ibid., p. 23), and advised the artist to visit Nova Scotia "where there are several people who would be glad to employ You." This request to paint in Canada was later repeated from Quebec, Copley replying: "I should receive a singular pleasure in excepting, if my Business was anyways slack, but it is so far otherwise that I have a large Room full of Pictures unfinished, which would ingage me these twelve months if I did not begin any others" (Ibid., p. 33).

Besides painting portraits in oil, doubtless after a formula learned from Peter Pelham, Copley was a pioneer American pastellist. He wrote, Sept. 30, 1762, to Jean Étienne Liotard (1702–90), the Swiss painter whose "Chocolate Girl" now in the Dresden Gallery is internationally celebrated, asking him for "a sett of the best Swiss Crayons for drawing of Portraits." The young American anticipated Liotard's surprise "that so remote a corner of the Globe as New England should have any demand for the necessary eutensils for practiceing the fine Arts" by assuring him that "America which has been the seat of war and desolation, I would fain hope will one Day become the School of fine Arts" (*Ibid.*, p. 26). The requested pastels were duly received and used by Copley in making many portraits in a medium congenial to his talent.

Copley's fame was established in England by the exhibition, in 1766—not in 1760, as stated by Mrs. Amory, and not in 1774 as stated by Michael Bryan in *Dictionary of Painters and Engravers* (1898)—of "The Boy with the Squirrel," which depicted his half-brother, Henry Pelham, seated at a table and playing with a pet squirrel. This picture, which made the young Boston painter a Fellow of the Society of Artists of Great Britain, by vote of Sept. 3, 1766, had been painted the preceding year. Copley's letter of Sept. 3, 1765, to Capt. R. G. Bruce, of the *John and Sukey*, reveals that it was taken to England as a personal favor in the luggage of Roger Hale, surveyor of the port of London. A familiar story is to the effect that the painting, unaccompanied by name or letter of instructions, was delivered to Benjamin West (whom Mrs. Amory describes as then "a member of the Royal Academy," though the Academy was not yet in existence). West is represented as having "exclaimed with a warmth and enthusiasm of which those who knew him best could scarcely believe him capable, 'What delicious coloring worthy of Titian himself!'" The American squirrel, it is said, disclosed the colonial origin of the picture to the Pennsylvania-born Quaker artist. A letter from Copley was subsequently delivered to him. West got the canvas into the Exhibition of the year and wrote, Aug. 4, 1766, a letter to Copley in which he referred to Sir Joshua Reynolds's interest in the work and advised the artist to follow his example by making "a viset to Europe for this porpase (of self-improvement) for three or four years."

West's subsequent letters were considerably responsible for making Copley discontented with his situation and prospects in a colonial town, and the consequences were such that this may be thought to have been a disservice to American art. Copley in his letters to West of Oct. 13, 1766, and Nov. 12, 1766, gleefully accepted the invitation to send other pictures to the Exhibition and mournfully referred to himself as "peculiarly unlucky in Liveing in a place into which

there has not been one portrait brought that is worthy to be call'd a Picture within my memory." In a later letter to West, of June 17, 1768, he displayed a cautious person's reasons for not rashly giving up the good living which his art gave him. He wrote: "I should be glad to go to Europe, but cannot think of it without a very good prospect of doing as well there as I can here. You are sensable that 300 Guineas a Year, which is my present income, is a pretty living in America. . . . And what ever my ambition may be to excel in our noble Art, I cannot think of doing it at the expence of not only my own happyness, but that of a tender Mother and a Young Brother whose dependance is intirely upon me" (*Ibid.*, pp. 68–69). West replied, Sept. 20, 1768, saying that he had talked over Copley's prospects with other artists of London "and find that by their Candid approbation you have nothing to Hazard in Comeing to this Place."

The income which Copley earned by his brush in the seventeen-sixties was extraordinary for his town and time. It had promoted the son of a needy tobacconist into the local aristocracy. The foremost personages of New England came to his painting-room as sitters. He married, Nov. 16, 1769 (not 1771, as stated by Dunlap) Sussannah Farnum Clarke, daughter of Richard [*q.v.*] and Elizabeth (Winslow) Clarke, the former being the agent of the East India Company in Boston; the latter, a New England woman of *Mayflower* ancestry. The union was a happy one, and socially notable. Mrs. Copley was a beautiful woman of poise and serenity whose features are familiar through several of her husband's paintings. Copley had already bought land on the west side of Beacon Hill extending down to the Charles River (concerning his purchases of which see Allen Chamberlain, *post,* pp. 50–96). The newly married Copleys established their Lares and Penates in "a solitary house in Boston, on Beacon Hill, chosen with his keen perception of picturesque beauty" (Amory, p. 24). It was on the site, approximately, of the present Boston Women's City Club. Here were painted the portraits of dignitaries of state and church, graceful women and charming children, in the mode of faithful and painstaking verisimilitude which Copley had made his own. The family's style of living at this period was that of people of wealth. John Trumbull (1756–1843) told Dunlap (I, 120) that in 1771, being then a student at Harvard College, he called on Copley who "was dressed on the occasion in a suit of crimson velvet with gold buttons, and the elegance displayed by Copley in his style of living, added to his high repute as an artist, made a permanent impression on Trumbull in favor of the life of a painter."

In town and church affairs Copley took almost no part. He referred to himself (letter to West, Nov. 24, 1770) as "desireous of avoideing every imputation of party spirit. Political contests being neighther pleasing to an artist or advantageous to the Art itself." His name appeared Jan. 29, 1771, on a petition of freeholders and inhabitants to have the powder house removed from the town whose existence it imperiled. Records of the Church in Brattle Square disclose that in 1772 Copley was asked to submit plans for a rebuilt meeting-house, and that he proposed an ambitious plan and elevation "which was much admired for its Elegance and Grandure," but which on account of probable expensiveness was not accepted by the society. Copley's sympathy with the politicians who were working toward American independence appears to have been genuine but not so vigorous as to lead him to participate in any of their plans.

It was known to earlier biographers (as to Dunlap, see his vol. I, p. 121) that Copley at one time painted portraits in New York. The circumstances of this visit, which was supplemented by a few days in Philadelphia, were first disclosed through Prof. Guernsey Jones's discovery of many previously unpublished Copley and Pelham documents in the Public Record Office, London. From these letters and papers, published by the Massachusetts Historical Society in 1914, it appears that in 1768 Copley painted in Boston a portrait of Myles Cooper [q.v.], president of King's College, who then urged his visiting New York. Accepting the invitation later, Copley between June 1771 and January 1772, painted in New York thirty-seven portraits, setting up his easel, according to Dunlap (I, 121) "in Broadway, on the west side, in a house which was burned in the great conflagration on the night the British army entered the city as enemies." Copley's letters to Henry Pelham, whom he left in charge of his affairs in Boston, describe minutely the journey across New England, his first impressions of New York which "has more Grand Buildings than Boston, the streets much cleaner and some much broader," and the successful search for suitable lodgings and a painting-room; thereafter they give detailed accounts of sitters and social happenings. The correspondence also contains Copley's careful instructions to Pelham concerning the features of a new house then building on his Beacon Hill "farm," giving elevations and specifications of the addition of "peazas" which the artist saw for the first time in New York. Copley

at the time had a lawsuit respecting title to some of his lands. His letters reveal a man who allowed such disputes to worry him not a little.

Mr. and Mrs. Copley in September 1771 visited Philadelphia where, at the home of Chief Justice William Allen they "saw a fine Coppy of the Titian Venus and Holy Family at whole length as large as life from Coregio" ("Copley-Pelham Letters," p. 163). Returning they viewed at New Brunswick, N. J., several pictures attributed to Vandyck. "The date is 1628 on one of them," wrote Copley; "it is without dout I think Vandyck did them before he came to England." Back in New York Copley wrote, Oct. 17, requesting that a certain black dress of Mrs. Copley's be sent over at once. "As we are much in company," he said, "we think it necessary Sukey [his wife] should have it, as her other Cloaths are mostly improper for her to wear" (*Ibid.*, p. 168). On Dec. 15 Copley informed Pelham that "this Week finishes all my Business, no less than 37 Busts; so the weather permitting by Christmas we hope to be on the road." Thus ended Copley's only American tour away from Boston. Accounts of his having painted in the South are without foundation. Most of the Southern portraits popularly attributed to him were made by Henry Benbridge [*q.v.*].

His correspondents in England continued to urge Copley to undertake European studies. He saved an undated and unsigned letter from some one who wrote: "Our people here are enraptured'd with him, he is compared to Vandyck, Reubens and all the great painters of Old." His brother-in-law Jonathan Clarke, already in London, advised his "comeing this way." West wrote, Jan. 6, 1773: "My Advice is, Mrs. Copley to remain in Boston till you have made this Tour [to Italy], After which, if you fix your place of reasidanc in London, Mrs. Copley to come over."

Political and economic conditions in Boston were increasingly disturbed. Copley's father-in-law, Mr. Clarke, was the merchant to whom was consigned the tea that provoked the Boston Tea Party. Copley's family connections were all Loyalists. He defended his wife's relatives at a meeting described in his letter of Dec. 1, 1773. He wrote Apr. 26, 1774, of an unpleasant experience when a mob visited his house demanding the person of Col. George Watson, a Loyalist *mandamus* counselor, who, fortunately, had gone elsewhere. The patriots having threatened to have his blood if he "entertained any such Villain for the future," Copley exclaimed: "What a spirit! What if Mr. Watson had stayed (as I pressed him to) to spend the night. I must either have given up a friend to the insult of a Mob or had my house pulled down and perhaps my family murthered" (*Ibid.,* p. 219).

With many letters of introduction, all of which are published in the Copley-Pelham correspondence, Copley sailed from Boston in June 1774, leaving his mother, wife, and children in Henry Pelham's charge. He wrote, July 11, from London "after a most easy and safe passage." An early call was upon West, to "find in him those amiable qualitys that makes his friendship boath desireable as an artist and as a Gentleman." The American was duly introduced to Sir Joshua Reynolds and was taken to "the Royal Accademy where the Students had a naked model from which they were Drawing." In London Copley took no sitters at this time though urged to do so. Shortly before leaving for Italy he "dined with Gov'r Hutchinson, and I think there was 12 of us altogether, and all Bostonians, and we had Choice Salt Fish for Dinner."

On Sept. 2, 1774, Copley chronicled his arrival at Paris where he saw and painstakingly described many paintings and sculptures. His journey toward Rome was made in company of an artist named Carter, described by Cunningham (V, 167) as "a captious, cross-grained and self conceited person who kept a regular journal of his tour in which he set down the smallest trifle that could bear a construction unfavorable to the American's character." Carter was undoubtedly an uncongenial companion. Copley, however, may at times have been both depressing and bumptious. He found fault, according to Carter, with the French firewood because it gave out less heat than American wood, and he bragged of the art which America would produce when "they shall have an independent government." Copley's personal appearance was thus described by his uncharitable comrade: "Very thin, a little pock-marked [presumably a souvenir of the Boston smallpox epidemic described by Copley in a letter of Jan. 24, 1764], prominent eyebrows, small eyes, which after fatigue seemed a day's march in his head." Copley afterward wrote of Carter (Dunlap, I, 129): "He was a sort of snail which crawled over a man in his sleep and left its slime, and no more." Mrs. Amory relates that "both parties were undoubtedly glad to separate on their arrival at their destination." Oct. 8, 1774, found Copley at Genoa where he wrote to his wife describing, among other things, the cheapness of the silks: "The velvet and satin for which I gave seven guineas would have cost fourteen in London." He reached Rome, Oct. 26. "I am very fortunate," he wrote, "in my time of being here, as I shall see the magnificence of the

rejoicing on the election of the Pope; it is also the year of jubilee, or Holy Year."

Copley's plan of study and mode of living at Rome are described in several letters. He found time for excursions. He visited Naples in January 1775, writing to his wife: "The city is very large and delightfully situated but you have no idea of the dirt, . . . and the people are as dirty as the streets,—indeed, they are offensive to such a degree as to make me ill" (Amory, p. 44). The excavations at Pompeii greatly interested him and in company with Ralph Izard of South Carolina (whose family portrait he later painted) he extended his journey to Paestum. At Rome early in 1775 he copied Correggio's "St. Jerome" on commission from Lord Grosvenor, and other works for Mr. and Mrs. Izard. About May 20 he started on a tour northward through Florence, Parma, Mantua, Venice, Trieste, Stuttgart, Mayence, Cologne, and the Low Countries. From Parma he wrote to Henry Pelham urging that the whole family leave America at once since, "if the Frost should be severe and the Harbour frozen, the Town of Boston will be exposed to an attack; and if it should be taken all that have remained in the town will be considered as enimys to the Country and ill treated or exposed to great distress." This anxiety was groundless, for Mrs. Copley and the children had already sailed, May 27, 1775, from Marblehead in a ship crowded with refugees. She arrived in London some weeks before Copley returned from the Continent, making her home with her brother-in-law, Henry Bromfield. Her father, Richard Clarke, and her brothers came soon after. Copley happily rejoined his family and set up his easel, at first in Leicester Fields (*Ibid.,* p. 99) and later (not immediately, as related by Dunlap, I, 129) at 25, George St., Hanover Square, in a house built by a wealthy Italian and admirably adapted to an artist's requirements. Here Mr. and Mrs. Copley and their son Lord Lyndhurst lived and died.

As an English painter Copley began in 1775 a career promising at the outset and destined from personal and political causes to end in gloom and adversity. His technique was so well established, his habits of industry so well confirmed, and the reputation that had preceded him from America was so extraordinary, that he could hardly fail to make a place for himself among British artists. He himself, however, "often said, after his arrival in England, that he could not surpass some of his early works" (*Ibid.,* p. 76). This was in effect the painter's own confession that the pictures of his maturity did not always reach the standard of the best of those of his youth. The deterioration of his talent was gradual, however, and some of the "English Copleys" are superb paintings.

Following a fashion set by West and others, Copley began to paint historical pieces as well as portraits. His first essay in this genre was "A Youth Rescued from a Shark," its subject based on an incident related to the artist by Brooke Watson. Engravings from this work achieved a popularity that has continued until the present. For a place over the fireplace of the George St. dining-room was painted the great family picture now at Boston, which, when first publicly shown by Lord Lyndhurst at the Manchester exhibition, 1862, was "pronounced by competent critics to be equal to any, in the same style, by Vandyck" (*Ibid.*, p. 79). But the artist's fame as a historical painter was made by "The Death of Lord Chatham." The painting, however, brought him denunciation from Sir William Chambers, president of the Royal Academy, who objected to its being exhibited privately in advance of the Academy's exhibition. In an open letter Chambers accused Copley of purveying his picture like a "raree-show" and of purposing "either the sale of prints or the raffle of the picture." To this censure, obviously unfair to one newly arrived in London and uninformed as to the professional ethics of exhibiting, Copley one morning wrote a caustic reply, and at evening wisely threw it into the fire. Engravings from the Chatham picture later sold well in England and America.

Copley's adventures in historical painting were the more successful because of his painstaking efforts to obtain good likenesses of personages and correct accessories of their periods. He traveled much in England to make studies of old portraits and actual localities. At intervals came from his studio such pieces as "The Red Cross Knight"; "Abraham Offering up Isaac"; "Hagar and Ishmael in the Wilderness"; "The Death of Major Pierson"; "The Arrest of Five Members of the Commons by Charles the First"; "The Siege of Gibraltar"; "The Surrender of Admiral DeWindt to Lord Camperdown"; "The Offer of the Crown to Lady Jane Grey by the Dukes of Northumberland and Suffolk"; "The Resurrection"; and others. He continued to paint portraits, among them those of several members of the royal family and numerous British and American celebrities. Between 1776 and 1815 he sent forty-three paintings to exhibitions of the Royal Academy, of which he was elected an associate member in the former year. His election to full membership occurred in 1783 (Cunningham, IV, 145).

The industry with which Copley labored over his compositions was exemplary save that it may at times have injured his health and disposition. "He has been represented to me by some," wrote Cunningham (Dunlap, I, 142), "as a peevish and peremptory man while others describe him as mild and unassuming." Both descriptions probably fitted Copley according as he was nervous from overwork and worry or was in a normal condition. His grand-daughter, Mrs. Amory, recalls that he usually painted continuously from early morning until twilight. In the evening his wife or a daughter read English literature for his benefit. He took but little exercise—probably not enough for health. (See his wife's letter, Amory, p. 301.)

He would have liked to return to America but his professional routine prevented this. He was politically more liberal than were his relatives. He painted the Stars and Stripes over a ship in the background of Elkanah Watson's portrait, Dec. 5, 1782, after listening to George III's speech formally acknowledging American independence. "He invited me into the studio," wrote Watson in his Journal (Bayley, p. 255), "and there, with a bold hand, a master's touch, and I believe an American heart, attached to the ship the Stars and Stripes; this was, I imagine, the first American flag hoisted in Old England." Copley's contacts with New England people continued to be many. He painted portraits of John Adams, John Quincy Adams, and other Bostonians who visited England. His daughter Elizabeth was married in August 1800 to Gardiner Greene of Boston, a wealthy gentleman whose descendants have preserved much of the correspondence of the Copley family.

Prior to this marriage of his daughter, Copley had sold his Beacon Hill estate to a syndicate of speculators headed by Dr. Benjamin Joy. He felt himself victimized when he learned that the purchasers knew of a project of building the State House at the top of the hill, and he sent his son John Singleton Copley, Jr. (see sketch in *Dictionary of National Biography*), then at the beginning of his brilliant legal career, to Boston in 1796 seeking to annul the arrangement. The letters which the future lord chancellor wrote during his visit to the United States are interesting reading but his quest was unsuccessful. "I do not believe," he wrote to his father, "that any person could have obtained from them one shilling more." Despite this report the artist made further efforts to recover his "farm." The subject of his grievance frequently recurs in the family correspondence, but it is not certain that Copley had any reason to feel himself defrauded. A memorandum prepared for him by Gardiner Greene stated (Amory, p. 144) that long after the land "had passed out of Copley's possession it, or a part of it, was offered at no higher price than was paid to his son." Allen Chamberlain, whose *Beacon Hill* gives an admirable summary of the complicated negotiations consequent upon this purchase, holds that Copley was fairly compensated at a price three times what he had paid for property from which he had had rents of considerable amount.

In his last fifteen years, though painting persistently, Copley experienced much depression and disappointment. The Napoleonic wars brought hard times. The household at 25, George St., was expensive to maintain. The education of a talented son was costly. It grieved the father that after the young barrister began to earn his way it became necessary to accept his help in carrying the home. Lord Campbell (*Lives of Lord Lyndhurst and Lord Brougham,* 1869) quotes the jurist as saying that "his father, having lived rather expensively, accumulated little for him." Mrs. Amory (p. 176) makes out a case for Mrs. Copley's admirable management, but it appears that a standard of living difficult to maintain in the changed circumstances made much borrowing inevitable. Copley was chagrined by the failure of his "Equestrian Portrait of the Prince Regent" to "bring a financial return." Cunningham says, "No customer made his appearance for Charles and the impeached members." Other canvases involving years of labor were unsold. Troubles with engravers were many, whether the fault was theirs or the painter's. Copley's letters to his son-in-law in Boston usually concerned loans made to him and frequently extended.

The aging artist's physical and mental health gave anxiety. In 1810 he had a bad fall which kept him from painting for a month (*Ibid.,* p. 300). He incessantly bewailed the loss of his Boston property. Mrs. Copley wrote Dec. 11, 1810: "Your father has been led to feel this affair [his unsuccessful litigation to recover the "farm"] more sensibly from the present state of things in this country where every difficulty of living is increasing and the advantages arising from his profession are decreasing" (*Ibid.,* p. 301). In October 1811, Copley wrote to Greene in distress, craving an additional loan of £600. And on Mar. 4, 1812 he wrote: "I am still pursuing my profession in the hope that, at a future time, a proper amount will be realized from my works, either to myself or family, but at this moment all pursuits which are not among the essentials of life are at a stand" (*Ibid.,* p. 304).

In August 1813, Mrs. Copley wrote that, although her husband was still painting, "he cannot apply himself as closely as he used to do." She reported in April 1814: "Your father enjoys his health but grows rather feeble, dislikes more and more to walk; but it is still pleasant for him to go on with his painting." In June 1815, the Copleys entertained as visitor John Quincy Adams with whom they jubilantly discussed the new terms of peace between America and England. In the letter describing this visit the painter's infirmities are said to have been increased by "his cares and disappointments." A note of Aug. 18, 1815, informed the Greenes that Copley while at dinner had had a paralytic stroke. He seemed at first to recover. Late in August his prognosis was favorable to his painting again. A second shock occurred, however, and he died on Sept. 9, 1815. "He was perfectly resigned," wrote his daughter Mary, "and willing to die, and expressed his firm trust in God, through the merits of our Redeemer." He was buried at Croydon in a tomb belonging to the Hutchinson family.

How sadly embarrassed Copley was in his latest years was disclosed in Mrs. Copley's letter of Feb. 1, 1816, to Gardiner Greene in which she gave details of his assets and borrowings and predicted: "When the whole property is disposed of and applied toward the discharge of the debts a large deficiency must, it is feared, remain." The estate was settled by Copley's son, later Lord Lyndhurst, who maintained the establishment in George St., supported his mother down to her death in 1836, and kept the ownership of many of the artist's unsold pictures until Mar. 5, 1864, when they were sold at auction in London. Several of the works then dispersed are now in American collections.

[Copious as is the Copley documentation no authoritative and exhaustive life of John Singleton Copley, covering both the American and the English periods, has been published to date. The chief source book for the artist's early years is the collection of "Letters and Papers of John Singleton Copley and Henry Pelham," edited by a committee of the Mass. Hist. Soc. consisting of Chas. Francis Adams, Guernsey Jones, and Worthington Ford, and published in *Mass. Hist. Soc. Colls.,* vol. LXXI (1914). The letters in this volume are printed entire and the explanatory footnotes are numerous and accurate. Martha Babcock Amory's *Domestic and Artistic Life of John Singleton Copley* (1882) is a grand-daughter's tribute to a great artist's memory, marred by a few minor inaccuracies and some inferences not justified by the data presented, but replete with well-selected extracts from the family correspondence of the years 1800–15. The collection of documents which Mrs. Amory used in writing her biography was the subject of litigation among descendants in 1922. Augustus Thorndike Perkins in 1873 printed privately his *Sketch of the Life and Some of the Works of John Singleton Copley,* containing a list, generally accurate, of Copley's paintings as then owned. Perkins's work was the basis of *The Life and Works of John Singleton Copley* (1915), by Frank W. Bayley, which lists and describes many canvases attributed to Copley. Since 1915 several works by Copley not then known have been discovered and many changes in ownership have been reported in the bulletins of the art museums, in *Am. Art News*, and in other periodicals. Wm. Dunlap's *Hist. of the Arts of Design in the U. S.*, published in 1834, had an entertaining, gossipy, and not altogether reliable account of Copley, some of the mistakes of which are corrected in footnotes of the Bayley and Goodspeed edition, 1918. The accounts of Copley in Michael Bryan's *Dictionary of Painters and Engravers* (1898) and in the *Dictionary of National Biography* (1923) contain inaccuracies and lacunæ. One of the best literary appreciations of Copley is in Chas. H. Caffin's *The Story of Am. Painting* (1907). Descriptions of several of his most famous paintings are in *The Boston Museum of Fine Arts* (1924) and *The Art of the National Gallery* (1906), both by Julia DeWolf Addison. The Boston Pub. Lib. has a large scrapbook of correspondence and newspaper cuttings relating to the purchase of the painting of "Charles I Demanding the Surrender of the Five Members," now in the trustees' room at the library. The fifth report of the Record Commissioners of Boston, 1880, contains many references to Copley's real-estate transactions and lawsuits. These are summarized and explained in Allen Chamberlain's *Beacon Hill*, 1925.]

                                                F.W.C.

COPLEY, LIONEL (d. Sept. 9, 1693), colonial governor, was commissioned a captain of royal foot-guards in 1676. Before this his home had been in Wadsworth, Yorkshire, England. When first stationed at the fortress of Hull, about 1681, he was commended by the Duke of York as an honest man. He was a Protestant. The governor of the fortress was a Catholic. During the English revolution of 1688 the governor purposed to fill all the offices with Catholics. Copley, hearing of this, sent for the other Protestant officers, and they unanimously agreed to call the Protestant soldiers privately to arms to seize the governor and his principal adherents. The plan was successfully executed, the town and fortress were secured for King William, and Copley, promoted to the rank of colonel, was made lieutenant-governor. He was commissioned as the first royal governor of Maryland on June 27, 1691, but his earliest instructions are dated two months later, and he did not arrive in the province until late in March or early in April 1692. He was sworn in at a meeting of the Provincial Council Apr. 6, 1692, and met the Assembly on the 10th of the following month. In his brief address to this body he urged that the heats and animosities which had been rife during the overthrow of the proprietary government be laid aside and that adequate provision be made for his salary. He approved bills for the establishment of the Church of England, for granting the Governor an annual revenue, for the limitation of officers' fees, for the administration of justice, for regulating the militia and providing for defense, and for regulating trade with the Indians. He refused to permit one of the nominees for the Council to take a seat in

that body on the ground that he was the leader of a small hostile faction. Three separate treaties of peace were concluded by him with the Piscataway, Mattawoman, and Choptico Indians, all dated May 14, 1692. In a dispute between the Governor and the Secretary of the Council over the right to the fees derived from the appointment of county clerks and over the right of their removal, the home government decided in favor of the Secretary. The Secretary also claimed the fees derived from the sale of ordinary licenses, but the assembly gave these to Copley as part of his annual revenue as governor. Copley stated that it was morally impossible for one in his position to serve the king without bringing complaint from Lord Baltimore, who under the royal government was supposed to enjoy all the territorial rights that had been his under the proprietary government. Lord Baltimore's chief grievance was that, by Copley's permission, the Assembly had passed an act depriving him of a fourteen-pence tonnage duty. Copley's wife died in March 1692/93 and he himself in the September following, leaving two sons, Lionel and John, and a daughter, Ann.

[Nearly all that is known of Copley is contained in vols. VIII (1890) and XIII (1894) of *Archives of Md.*, but see *Calendar of State Papers, Colonial Ser., 1693–96*, pp. 572, 573; and for a secondary account of Copley's administration, J. T. Scharf, *Hist. of Md.* (1879), vol. I. For an account of the seizure of Hull see John Tickell, *Hist. of the Town and County of Kingston upon Hull* (1796).]

                                                N.D.M.

COPLEY, THOMAS (1595–c. 1652), Jesuit missionary, appears in the domestic records of the Society of Jesus as Philip Fisher, which name he assumed upon joining the Order. His grandfather, Thomas Copley, was, at the close of the reign of Mary I, a wealthy and influential Protestant of Surrey, England, but became a Catholic early in the reign of Elizabeth and was driven into exile. William Copley, son of the exile, married Magdalen, daughter of Thomas Prideaux, and they were in Madrid, Spain, in 1595, when Thomas was born. The family returned to England in 1603, the year of the accession of James I, and there Thomas was educated as a Catholic until 1611, when he went to Louvain for the study of philosophy. Five years later he joined the Society of Jesus. He returned to England about 1623 and soon became prominent in the affairs of the Society's London mission. When, in 1633, Lord Baltimore was preparing to send out the first colonists for a plantation in Maryland, Father Copley was the business manager for the Society in cooperating with Lord Baltimore and in founding a Maryland mission. He remained in London "putting heat and spirit of action" into the business until 1637, when he sailed for Maryland to give personal direction to the missionary activities there.

Within a few months after his arrival in the province, he was engaged in a struggle with Lord Baltimore over the relation of church and state. In founding Maryland, Lord Baltimore was governed chiefly by economic motives and to that end he sought religious toleration and the complete subordination of all sects to the civil authorities. Father Copley contended that none had done so much in "peopling and planting this place" as he and his fellow missionaries, and he desired for the mission many of the exemptions from lay jurisdiction that had formerly been enjoyed by the Church of Rome. He asked that the missionaries be permitted to receive lands as gifts from converted Indians; that their churches and their houses have the privileges of sanctuary; that they be exempted from the jurisdiction of lay courts, from taxes, and trade regulations; and he warned that he who placed restrictions on ecclesiastical liberties might incur danger of excommunication. Lord Baltimore was alarmed. He suspected that the missionaries designed his temporal destruction by forming an opposition party or by arming the Indians. He appealed to the English Provincial for the Society, and Copley was superseded as head of the Maryland mission. In 1645, during the Claiborne and Ingle rebellion, Copley was seized and carried to England where he was kept in prison for two years. He was then tried on the charge of coming to that country to seduce subjects of the Commonwealth, and was banished. He returned to Maryland and there the record of his activities terminated in 1652. As head of the Maryland mission Copley was characterized by a contemporary as a man of good talents but deficient in judgment and prudence.

[The *Calvert Papers* (1889) contain important information relative to Copley as head of the Md. mission. Katharine C. Dorsey, *Life of Father Thos. Copley* (1885), is valuable chiefly for information relative to the Copley family. Thos. Hughes, *Hist. of the Society of Jesus in North America*, vol. I (1907), contains a more scholarly account of the conflict between Lord Baltimore and the Jesuit missionaries than that by Bradley T. Johnson in *The Foundation of Md. and the Origin of the Act concerning Religion* (1883). Consult also Alfred P. Dennis, "Lord Baltimore's Struggle with the Jesuits, 1634–49" in the *Annual Report Am. Hist. Ass. for 1900*, and W. P. Treacy, *Old Cath. Md. and Its Early Jesuit Missionaries* (1889).]   N. D. M.

COPPÉE, HENRY (Oct. 13, 1821–Mar. 21, 1895), soldier, educator, was the son of Edward and Carolina Eugenia Raingeard DeLavillate Coppée, who fled from Santo Domingo during the great slave insurrection. His father, a physician, took up the practise of medicine in Georgia, was one of the founders of the First Presbyterian Church in Savannah in 1827, and was a charter member of the Georgia Historical Society in 1839. Henry was born in Savannah, and lived there until his fifteenth year, when he entered Yale with the class of 1839. After two years, however, he ceased to attend college. He was employed in the construction of the Central of Georgia Railroad, from Savannah to Macon, and in the study of engineering until the age of nineteen, when he entered West Point, from which institution he graduated in 1845, eleventh in his class. As brevet second lieutenant of artillery he was assigned to garrison duty at Fort Columbus, N. Y., until the outbreak of the war with Mexico, when he was transferred to the 1st Artillery which was with Scott. In the progress of the campaign he was promoted to the rank of first lieutenant and after the storming of Chapultepec was brevetted captain "for gallant and meritorious conduct" in the battles of Contreras and Churubusco.

In 1848 upon the conclusion of the war he was married to Julia de Witt and returned to West Point as assistant professor of French. After a year he was transferred again to garrison duty, this time at Fort McHenry, but the year following saw his return to the military academy as assistant professor of geography, history, and ethics. Here he taught and also had charge of the library until his resignation from the army in 1855 and his acceptance of the chair of English literature and history at the University of Pennsylvania. For eleven years he held this post with distinction. During this period he became identified with the American Philosophical Society, of which he was an honored member; he also published a number of text-books and collections of literature, among them: *Elements of Logic* (1857); *Elements of Rhetoric* (1858), which ran through eleven editions; *Gallery of Famous English and American Poets* (1859); and *Gallery of Distinguished English and American Female Poets* (1860).

When the secession crisis preceding the Civil War made the question of loyalty an imperative one, Coppée made his choice for the Union rather than for his native state. Although he did not reënter the army, he threw himself with great zeal into the cause for the Union and through various writings on military science he sought to contribute to the efficiency of the Northern armies, publishing in 1862 his *Manual of Battalion Drill* and a translation of Marmont's *Esprit des Institutions Militaires* and in 1863 his *Manual of Evolutions of the Line* and *Manual of Courts-Martial*. In 1864 he became the editor of a new publication, *The United States Service*

Magazine, a military periodical conceived along broad and scholarly lines, which, however, went out of existence two years later when Coppée was led to relinquish the editorship as well as his chair at the University of Pennsylvania to accept the presidency of the newly founded Lehigh University.

From 1866 to 1875 Coppée acted not only as the first president of Lehigh but also as professor of history and literature. His chief interests, however, were in teaching and writing, and he therefore resigned the presidency in 1874, continuing in office another year until a successor could be found, and then taking the title of professor of English literature and international and constitutional law. Upon the death of President Lamberton in September 1893, Coppée became acting president and continued to serve until the time of his death. During his connection with Lehigh University he published *Grant and his Campaigns. A Military Biography* (1866); *Lectures in English Literature* (1872); *English Literature Considered as an Interpreter of English History* (1873), which ran into nine editions; an American edition of *La Guerre Civile en Amérique* by the Comte de Paris, in four volumes (1875–78); and *General Thomas* (1893), in the Great Commander series. His most pretentious and solid literary effort was the *History of the Conquest of Spain by the Arab Moors,* which first appeared in *The Penn Monthly,* a short-lived literary magazine of that period, in 1873, and in 1881 was published in two volumes, a second edition appearing in 1892 (see, for critical reviews, C. K. Adams, *A Manual of Historical Literature,* 1882, and the *Nation,* Apr. 21, 1881). He also was a contributor to the *North American Review,* the *Princeton Review* and the *Church Quarterly.* These various literary efforts bespeak the breadth of Coppée's knowledge and the wideness of his intellectual interest. His manner of writing was easy and flowing, if sometimes a little over-ornate; his mentality was distinctly Gallic in its enthusiasm, its imagination, its logical trends. His *History of the Conquest of Spain* shows his strength and weakness as a writer and scholar. It is delightfully written and a really valuable contribution, but it will hardly take rank with the very best contributions to historical literature both because new sources have been made available since he wrote and because he was occasionally inclined to come warmly to the defense of the traditional rather than submit it to the cold test of supportable evidence.

As a young man Coppée was strikingly handsome and during his latter years he made a most impressive and venerable appearance with his white hair and flowing beard. By all testimony he possessed an unusual charm of presence. He was fond of reading Shakespeare, and the élite of the Lehigh Valley eagerly gathered to hear him interpret that master. He was a man of simple faith and a devout churchman as is attested by his *Songs of Praise in the Christian Centuries* (1866); for many years before his death he served as the warden of the Church of the Nativity in Bethlehem. At the time of his death he was a regent of the Smithsonian Institution.

[The chief sources for the life of Coppée are the publications of the various institutions with which he was identified during the periods of his connection; G. W. Cullum, *Biog. Reg.* (3rd ed., 1891); *Centennial of the U. S. Mil. Acad. at West Point* (1902); *Proc. Am. Philosophical Soc.* (1895); *The Twenty-Year Book of the Lehigh Univ.* (1886); the memorial number of the *Brown and White* of Lehigh Univ., Mar. 1895; information from personal acquaintances.]   L. H. G.

COPPENS, CHARLES (May 24, 1835–Dec. 14, 1920), Roman Catholic priest, educator, was born at Turnhout, Belgium, the son of Peter Hubert and Caroline (Vaes) Coppens. He began his training in the Jesuit college of St. Joseph in his native town and came to the United States to continue it in the scholasticates at St. Louis and at Fordham universities. He entered the Society of Jesus in 1853 at Florissant, Mo., and was ordained in New York by Cardinal McCloskey in 1865. He was professor of Latin and Greek in St. Louis University 1855–59 and in St. Xavier's College, Cincinnati, 1860–62, taught rhetoric in the normal school at Florissant, Mo., 1863–75, and in St. Louis University 1876–80, was president of St. Mary's College at St. Mary's, Kan., 1881–84, was professor of rhetoric again at Florissant, 1885–86, and of philosophy in Detroit College, 1887–95, in Creighton University at Omaha, 1896–1905, in St. Louis University, 1906–08, and finally in Loyola University in Chicago, where he died. His sixty years in the classroom exerted a strong influence on Jesuit education in America. Besides contributing to the *American Catholic Quarterly Review,* the *American Ecclesiastical Review,* the *Messenger of the Sacred Heart,* the *Messenger, Men and Women,* and the *Catholic Encyclopedia,* Father Coppens was the author of numerous text-books and devotional works: *The Art of Oratorical Composition* (1885); *A Practical Introduction to English Rhetoric* (1886); *A Brief Text-Book of Logic and Mental Philosophy* (1891); *A Brief Text-Book of Moral Philosophy* (1895); *The Living Church of the Living God* (1902); *A Systematic Study of the Catholic Religion* (1903); *Mystic Treasures of the Holy Mass* (1904); *The Protestant*

Reformation: How It was Brought About in Various Lands (1907); *Choice Morsels of the Bread of Life, or Select Readings from the Old Testament* (1909); *A Brief History of Philosophy* (1909); *Who Are the Jesuits?* (1911); *Spiritual Instruction for the Religious* (1914); *The Spiritual Exercises of St. Ignatius Adapted to an Eight Days Retreat and Six Triduums* (1916); and *A Brief Commentary on the Little Office of the Immaculate Conception of the Blessed Virgin Mary* (1916). Several of his textbooks have been widely used in Catholic schools and colleges. They are admirably suited to their purpose and are written in a style of unusual lucidity and ease. In them, as in his devotional works, Father Coppens made no significant departures from Jesuit tradition as regards style and matter. More originality was displayed in his most important book, *Moral Principles and Medical Practice* (1897; new and enlarged edition by H. S. Spalding, 1921). He was the first to treat medical ethics and medical jurisprudence from the Catholic point of view. His book deals with matters highly controversial in a way to provoke thought if not to secure assent. He was slight of stature and seemingly fragile, delicate of health, and so zealous and humble that "he never lost a moment of time or spoke an uncharitable word."

[*Who's Who in America*, 1920–21; *Am. Cath. Who's Who* (1911); *Cath. Encyc. and its Makers* (1917), with portrait; brief obituary in *America*, Dec. 25, 1920.]   G. H. G.

COPPET, EDWARD J. de. [See DE COPPET, EDWARD J., 1855–1916.]

COPWAY, GEORGE (1818–*c.* 1863), Chippewa (Ojibway) chief, Wesleyan missionary, author, was born in the fall of 1818 near the mouth of the river Trent in Ontario, while his parents were attending the government's yearly distribution of presents. His Indian name was Kah-Ge-Ga-Gah-Bowh and his father belonged to the Crane, his mother to the Eagle tribe. His great-grandfather was the first Chippewa to settle in the Rice Lake district, which had formerly been territory of the Hurons. His father was an hereditary chief of the Rice Lake Chippewas, a medicine man, and an excellent hunter. The family, like the other Indians of the region, were able by hunting, fishing, and farming to gain only a bare subsistence. One winter, while on a fur-gathering expedition, they were snowed in in their wigwams and nearly perished of hunger. Copway was taught to read by the Rev. James Evans, an English Wesleyan missionary, and in the summer of 1830 was converted to Methodism. His mother, who had died

the previous February, and his father nad both become Christians. In June 1834 Copway was sent as missionary's helper to the region south of Lake Superior, and from that time till his death he was engaged either in actual missionary work among his scattered people or in lecturing and gathering funds for the cause. His field extended over what are now Michigan, Minnesota, Wisconsin, Iowa, and Illinois. He attended Ebenezer Academy near Jackson, Ill., 1838–39 and after finishing his schooling there made an extensive, somewhat unceremonious, tour of the East. On the journey from Boston to New York he had for a traveling companion Father Edward Taylor (*Life*, p. 136). Copway was tall, handsome, and muscular, and had fine manners. Once he carried more than 200 pounds of flour, shot, coffee, and sugar on his back for a quarter of a mile without resting; at another, in 1835, in order to fetch flour to his starving companions he traveled 185 miles on foot in two days. In the early summer of 1840 he married Elizabeth Howell of Toronto. In 1850 he visited Europe, attended the Peace Congress at Frankfurt, and took back books from Freiligrath, the German poet, to his friend Longfellow (S. Longfellow, *Life of Henry Wadsworth Longfellow*, 1891, II, 212). For a while he engaged in journalism in New York City. His books are: *The Life, History, and Travels of Kah-Ge-Ga-Gah-Bowh* (Albany, 1847, 2nd to 6th eds., Philadelphia, 1847; revised as *Life, Letters, and Speeches of Kah-Ge-Ga-Gah-Bowh*, New York, 1850, and as *Recollections of a Forest Life*, London, 1850, 1851); *The Traditional History and Characteristic Sketches of the Ojibway Nation* (London, 1850, Boston, 1851; later published under the title *Indian Life and Indian History*, 1858, 1860); *The Ojibway Conquest, a Tale of the Northwest* (1850); *Organization of a New Indian Territory East of the Missouri River* (1850); and *Running Sketches of Men and Places in England, France, Germany, Belgium, and Scotland* (1851). He also helped the Rev. Mr. Hall of Lapointe, Mich., in translating the Gospel according to Luke and the Acts into Ojibway. His own style is an amalgam of Washington Irving, St. Luke, and elements derived from Methodist exhorters. In his earnest advocacy of a new Indian territory he displayed the vision of a statesman. He is said to have died near Pontiac, Mich., about 1863.

[F. W. Hodge, *Handbook of Am. Indians* (1907); Copway's own writings.]   G. H. G.

COQUILLETT, DANIEL WILLIAM (Jan. 23, 1856–July 8, 1911), entomologist, was the sixth child of Francis Marquis LaFayette Coquillett and his wife Sara Ann. He was born on a farm at Pleasant Valley near Woodstock, Ill. He was educated at the country school and taught there for one or two terms. While helping his father on the farm he began collecting, rearing, and studying insects. He bought books on entomology with all of his spare money, and began corresponding with A. R. Grote of Buffalo. He also studied birds, and in 1876, with his brother's help printed on a hand-press *The Oology of Illinois*. His first paper was on the larvæ of Lepidoptera, and was published in the *Canadian Entomologist* for 1880. This article attracted the attention of Cyrus Thomas, state entomologist of Illinois, and Coquillett was engaged to prepare an article on these larvæ for the entomologist's *Annual Report*. He was then employed by Thomas until his health failed in 1882, when his parents took him to Anaheim, Cal., where he recovered and continued his studies of insects. In 1885 he was appointed a field agent of the Division of Entomology of the United States Department of Agriculture. During this employment he experimented with hydrocyanic-acid gas as a remedy for scale insects and perfected its use. In 1887 he cared for the first shipments sent by Koebele from Australia of the beneficial ladybird beetle (*Vedalia* or *Novius cardinalis*). He handled them with extreme care and succeeded in bringing about their acclimatization, with the result that they saved citrus culture in California, by destroying the white or cottony cushion scale which threatened ruin to the growers. In 1893 he was brought to Washington, and in 1896 was appointed custodian of the Diptera in the United States National Museum, holding this position until his death.

Aside from his important work with hydrocyanic-acid gas and his help in the acclimatization of the Australian ladybird beetle, his achievements were mainly in the taxonomic study of the true flies (Order Diptera). He was a tireless worker, and his bibliography covers more than two hundred and fifty titles. He was an extremely shy, retiring man, and although he belonged to several scientific societies and contributed frequently to their proceedings and transactions, he never read a paper at a meeting. At the time of his death he was probably the foremost dipterologist of the United States.

[*Proc. Entomological Soc. of Washington*, XIII (1911), 196–210, including a list of Coquillett's published writings; *Canadian Entomologist*, Sept. 1911; and *Entomological News*, Oct. 1911.]   L. O. H.

CORAM, THOMAS (1668–Mar. 29, 1751), merchant, colony promoter, was the son of a mariner of Lyme Regis, Dorsetshire, England. Left motherless, he went to sea "at 11 years and [a] half old until 5 years after" his father apprenticed him to a London shipwright. It was as a shipbuilder, a factor for Thomas Hunt of London, that he began an acquaintance with the colonies which led Horace Walpole to describe him in 1735 as "the honestest, the most disinterested, and the most knowing person about the plantations, I ever talked with" (Coxe, *Walpole*, 1798, III, 243). In 1693 he carried over a party of shipwrights to Boston; and in 1697 he removed for a time to Taunton, and set up a shipyard in South Dighton, drawn thither by "the Vast great plenty of oak and fir Timber, and Iron oar." But his forthright personality and sturdy Anglicanism soon involved him in quarrels and litigation in that primitive Puritan community—a "generation of vipers," as he afterward described his neighbors. He won his lawsuits, upon appeal, and escaped two murderous assaults. In 1703 he took characteristic revenge by deeding in trust fifty-nine acres—awarded him as indemnity by the Superior Court—for building a Church of England edifice, "if ever hereafter the inhabitants of the town of Taunton . . . should be more civilized than they now are" (Compston, *post*, p. 32).

Those ten stormy years served, however, to fix Coram's interest in the material and spiritual development of the colonies. He naturally supported various efforts to extend the Church of England in New England, and himself projected a King's College at Cambridge. But his Anglicanism was not inflexible. At Boston he married (June 27, 1700) a Puritan wife, Eunice Wayte (1677–1740). For years he corresponded with the Boston divine, Benjamin Colman, and enlisted the Associates of Dr. Bray and other agencies to supply books for the New England missionaries to the Indians, and for other dissenting ministers. The American projects of this "indefatigable schemist" ranged from missionary efforts "to Beat down the Old Goliah's [the] French Jesuits," and plans for the relief of distressed New England seamen in foreign ports, to full-fledged enterprises of colonization. Probably no contemporary promoter showered so many memorials upon the Board of Trade. He returned to England in 1704, and at his own expense, so he claimed, solicited the act to encourage the making of tar and pitch in the plantations (3 and 4 Anne, c. 10). For several years he was employed in supplying the Admiralty with American naval stores. He was a strong mercantilist; as his first biographer remarked, "He loved the daughters dearly: but he loved them as daughters." In a memorial of 1732 he recommended the suppression of various colonial manufactures in their infancy, though at other times he pressed the claims of the colonial iron manufacture. He vigorously espoused the complaints of the London Company of Felt Merchants against colonial competition, and lobbied for the Hat Act of 1732 (5 George II, c. 22). In Hogarth's portrait of Coram there appears conspicuously the hat which he accepted from time to time as his sole fee from the Company.

For some years after the Peace of Utrecht, Coram was engaged in the shipping trade, but increasingly he devoted himself to philanthropic projects: to his famous scheme for the Foundling Hospital, chartered in 1739, and to his less successful colonial plans. In 1713 he incited a group of officers and soldiers, unemployed after the wars, to petition for a grant of the eastern lands between the Kennebec and the St. Croix, from the Atlantic to the St. Lawrence. For thirty years this was the favorite scene of his projects, in which he proposed to employ Chelsea pensioners, Huguenots, convicts, Palatines, Ulster Scots, and the "graduates" of the Foundling, to raise hemp and provide naval stores. Several times the Board of Trade indorsed his designs, but after 1717 the opposition of Massachusetts and of rival claimants defeated his obstinate efforts to prove the Crown's title to the Sagadahoc lands. From the beginning, moreover, the Board of Trade had preferred, for strategic reasons, that he colonize Nova Scotia. Accordingly in 1735 Coram turned his energies toward the settlement of unemployed artisans in Nova Scotia and in one of the Bahamas. Meanwhile, as a friend and parishioner of Dr. Thomas Bray [q.v.], he had been drawn into the Georgia Trust. But he had soon quarrelled with the "Oglethorpians" for neglecting the religious aims of Bray, and over their land-tenure system and "military rule"; and he now hoped to draw off the Georgia malcontents to his northern colony. In his own schemes, though he had proposed as early as 1717 that the soil be vested in eminent trustees, he had consistently urged a singularly free government under the Crown, "the Nearest to the English Government in America." But such an establishment was ill-adapted to a frontier colony. The Board of Trade indorsed his Nova Scotia plan in 1737, but the approach of war gave it the quietus. Coram lived to see Halifax settled, but upon a footing contrary to his generous proposals.

[For a fuller account of Coram's career and his great English philanthropy consult H. F. B. Compston, *Thos. Coram* (1918). See also sketch in the *Dict. of Nat. Biog.*, XII, 194–95. On Coram in New England see an essay by Hamilton A. Hill in *Proc. Am. Antiquarian Soc.*, n.s., VIII, 133–48, Apr. 1892; and another by Chas. A. Reed in *Old Colony Hist. Soc. Colls.*, II, 5–36. A contemporary eulogy of some interest is [Richard

Brocklesby?], *Private Vertue and Public Spirit Display'd. In a Succinct Essay on the Character of Capt. Thomas Coram* (1751). The correspondence of Coram with Benj. Colman, 1734–40, was printed by W. C. Ford in *Proc. Mass. Hist. Soc.*, LVI, 15–56. A memorial on colonial manufactures is in *Archives of the State of New Jersey*, 1 ser., V, 308–14. The Colonial Office Papers, Public Record Office, contain much unpublished material. On Coram and Georgia see also the *Diary of John Lord Viscount Percival* (3 vols., 1920–23).]
V. W. C.

CORBETT, HENRY WINSLOW (Feb. 18, 1827–Mar. 31, 1903), merchant, banker, railroad promoter, politician, the son of Elijah and Melinda (Forbush) Corbett, was descended from seventeenth-century English settlers of Massachusetts. He was born at Westboro, Mass., but spent his boyhood on a farm in Washington County, N. Y., where he enjoyed the advantage of a common school. He then attended an academy at Cambridge, N. Y., during parts of two years, at the same time working in a store. Later he received a few months more of formal schooling and another year of apprenticeship in the mercantile line. In 1843 he entered the dry-goods establishment of Williams, Bradford & Company in New York City, remaining until 1850. During his seven years' service he so completely won the confidence of his employers that they were prepared to fit him out with an extensive line of merchandise for the far West, and in October 1850 he sailed "round the Horn," arriving, Mar. 4, 1851, in Portland, Ore., then a small river town of some four hundred inhabitants. The venture proved highly successful and made the beginning of Corbett's business career in Oregon which was to continue for more than half a century. In company with Henry Failing, he established a large wholesale hardware business, and also secured control of the First National Bank of Portland. He promoted the building and operation of river steamboats; he assumed important responsibility in the work of completing the Northern Pacific Railroad; he was deeply interested in the Oregon-California Railroad; he was, for a time, the contractor for carrying the United States mail between Sacramento, Cal., and Oregon. He was a great builder, having at the time of his death more structures to his credit in Portland than any one else. He was always ready to invest in worthy business enterprises in his home city and finally, as a crowning service to Portland and the Pacific Northwest, he took the lead in working out plans for the Lewis and Clark Exposition to which he also contributed a large sum of money. He was first president of the exposition but died before the work was completed. He was married twice: in 1853 to Caroline E. Jagger of Albany, N. Y., and in 1867 to Emma L. Ruggles of Worcester, Mass.

Corbett was a man of extraordinary personal force. He was of conservative temper, and of rare business acumen. He was always interested in politics, transferring his allegiance early from the Whig to the Republican party, and taking a prominent part in insuring the triumph of Republicanism in Oregon. In 1862 he was urged to become a candidate for governor but refused. In 1866 the legislature, in order to break a deadlock, elected Corbett to the United States Senate where he served a single term, from Mar. 4, 1867, to Mar. 4, 1873. He was a member of the Committee on Finance, of which John Sherman was chairman, and his work centered in that committee's activities. The records show that Corbett spoke almost exclusively on financial questions, such as resumption, the repeal of the tax on raw cotton, and the tariff. His speeches were always informal, usually brief, but often crammed with statistics. It cannot be said that he exhibited remarkable qualities as a debater, a tactician, or parliamentary leader. His forte was business rather than statesmanship; he had the gifts of the executive, not those of the legislator.

[See the *Cong. Globe* for the years of Corbett's service in the senate. Chas. Henry Carey, *Hist. of Ore.*, gives in very concise form Corbett's business and political career. The best sketch of Corbett's life is by Harvey W. Scott, as reprinted from the *Oregonian* in *Hist. of the Oregon Country*, ed. by Leslie M. Scott (1924), V, 183–88.]
J. S.

CORBIN, AUSTIN (July 11, 1827–June 4, 1896), capitalist, railroad executive, a descendant of Clement Corbin who had settled in Connecticut during the first half of the seventeenth century, was born at Newport, N. H. His parents, Austin and Mary (Chase) Corbin, were well-to-do and had enjoyed educational advantages better than the average, but until he reached his twentieth year their son had no formal instruction beyond that afforded by the common schools of the neighborhood. About that time, however, he obtained employment in a Boston store and later entered the Harvard Law School, from which he graduated in 1849. He began law practise, but did not long continue in it. At that time the West was calling to the young men of New England in persuasive tones. Corbin was attracted to Davenport in the new state of Iowa and located there in 1851. Three years later the firm of Macklot & Corbin opened a bank that was to have a successful career during the period of "wild-cat" banking that preceded the Civil War. In the panic of 1857 it remained one of the few unshaken financial institutions in Iowa. Corbin had induced friends in the East to loan money on Iowa farm lands as security. In a short time he built up in this way a profitable business,

which was managed on conservative principles. On the establishment of the national banking system of 1863, the First National Bank of Davenport, organized by Corbin, was one of the earliest in the country to receive a charter and is said to have been actually the first to open its doors for business. Corbin's reputation for sound banking soon extended beyond Iowa. His Eastern connections continued to grow in importance and in 1865 led to his removal to New York City, where Austin Corbin & Company (after 1874 the Corbin Banking Company) opened an office. At that time Corbin was well started on the road to wealth, and, without great exertion, he might have achieved his ambitions so far as his personal fortune was concerned. A man of initiative and vision, however, he was forming constructive objectives that involved far more than his individual profit. Not long after coming to New York his attention was directed to the advantages of Coney Island as an ocean resort within a short distance from the city. Thinking of New York's population in terms of millions, instead of the hundreds of thousands then dwelling on Manhattan Island, Corbin looked forward to a day when those millions would be carried safely, cheaply, and quickly from the midsummer heat of the tenements to the breeze-swept beaches of Long Island. Transportation between New York and the ocean-side resorts was a problem that had never been worked out. The Long Island Railroad at that time was an inefficient and unproductive system that failed to meet even the modest requirements of the day. Corbin got control of it, energized its operation, and in time made it a useful servant of the public. Through that and other rail connections he developed transportation to Coney Island and neighboring beaches so effectively that within a few years they were the most popular resorts in the metropolitan area. For a time, especially in the development of the Manhattan Beach Railway, his brother, Daniel Chase Corbin [*q.v.*], was associated with him. His reorganization of the Long Island Railroad having restored the earning power of that corporation, Corbin began to be regarded as a successful railroad executive. Under his management, in the years 1886–88, the Philadelphia & Reading, which had been in a receivership, was rehabilitated and made a paying enterprise. Corbin's railroad operations were all broadly constructive and planned for the future of communities and industries. Some of his projects were regarded as ahead of his time. He was interested in a transatlantic steamship port at the eastern end of Long Island, with a view to cutting the time required for the passage from

Europe to New York Harbor. He gave much thought to a scheme of metropolitan subway transit, even having borings made and bringing an engineer from England to make plans, at his own personal expense. He could obtain no consideration for his project, however, and died long before the New York subway had been built. The last great enterprise of public interest in which he engaged was the establishment near Newport, N. H., of a game park eleven miles long and four miles wide, embracing 26,000 acres. He spent $1,000,000 in stocking this preserve with animals and providing for their maintenance and increase. Thrown from his carriage in a runaway accident near his New Hampshire birthplace, he died within a few hours from the injuries thus received. He was married in 1853 to Hannah M. Wheeler, who, with a son and a daughter, survived him.

[Harvey M. Lawson, *Hist. and Geneal. of the Descendants of Clement Corbin* (1905) ; *N. Y. Times,* June 5, 1896; *Hist. of Scott County, Iowa* (1882) ; *Iowa State Register* (Des Moines), July 18, Aug. 22, 1860 ; *Century Mag.,* Oct. 1897; Wm. T. Bonner, *N. Y., the World's Metropolis* (1924).]   W.B.S.

CORBIN, DANIEL CHASE (Oct. 1, 1832– June 29, 1918), financier, railroad president, son of Austin and Mary (Chase) Corbin, was born at Newport, N. H. He received a common-school education and in 1852 secured a government contract for surveying lands in Iowa. In 1858 he began similar operations in Nebraska and laid the foundations of a substantial fortune by purchasing land in the latter territory. The important mining developments in Colorado in the early sixties aroused his interest in the overland trade and in 1862 he moved to Denver. He secured important contracts for supplying the quartermaster's department at Fort Laramie, Wyo., and operated wagon trains from the Missouri River, via Denver, to places as far inland as Salt Lake City. After three years in Denver he moved to Helena, Mont., where for the next ten years he was actively engaged in mercantile business and also in banking as cashier and part owner of the First National Bank, one of the pioneer institutions of the Territory. In 1876 he moved to New York and until 1882 was associated with his brother Austin Corbin [*q.v.*] in the financing and active management of the Manhattan Beach Railway. This project was a success, and Daniel Corbin also established financial connections which were of great importance in subsequent projects.

The approaching completion of the Northern Pacific Railway brought about his return to the Northwest to begin the most significant and constructive part of his career. In 1883 the great importance of recent silver-lead discoveries in the Cœur d'Alène district attracted his attention to the Idaho Panhandle, and, three years later, under contract with the Bunker Hill & Sullivan Mining Company, he constructed one of the first concentrating plants in the region. About the same time he became interested in the transportation problems of the district and organized the Cœur d'Alène Railroad & Navigation Company, operating steamers on Lake Cœur d'Alène, and constructing a railroad from the head of navigation to the adjacent mining town. This line was completed in 1887 and was sold a year later to the Northern Pacific, becoming a feeder of the latter system and making an important contribution to the upbuilding of Spokane, Wash. Corbin moved to Spokane in 1889 and was associated with its various activities and those of the adjacent region for the rest of his life. He grasped the importance of the site as a strategic center for transportation and distributing developments, based on the great agricultural, mineral, and timber resources of the Inland Empire. In 1889 he began the construction of the Spokane Falls & Northern Railway, building the line northward through Colville to Northport on the Columbia. Within a few years, in spite of the acute financial stringency, he was able to secure capital for the extension of the line to Rossland, B. C., thus opening up another great mineral area. In 1899 this line was absorbed by the Great Northern.

Corbin was active in various local projects and developments including British Columbia mining, and organized the Corbin Coal & Coke Company to handle his extensive properties in the southern part of the province. He attempted to promote sugar-beet culture in the lands south of Spokane, but this development proved unsuccessful, largely because of the scarcity of labor. He was a director in the Old National Bank and Union Trust Company, the leading financial institutions in eastern Washington. In 1905 he began the construction of the Spokane International Railway, extending from Spokane through the Panhandle to Eastport, Idaho, and connecting with the Canadian Pacific Railway at Yahk, B. C., thus giving the city another transcontinental outlet, opening up a great stretch of productive territory, and tapping important coal areas. After ten years of independent operation this line was purchased by the Canadian Pacific in 1916.

Corbin spent almost sixty years in various development projects beginning at a time when frontier conditions still prevailed. He had the shrewdness, sound judgment, tenacity of purpose, and integrity characterizing many New

England business men in the unprecedented growth of the West. He avoided publicity and was reputed to be irritable and brusque in manner, although his associates testified to his loyalty to friends and employees, and also to a great deal of unostentatious or anonymous charity and kindness on his part. His business operations were constructive in character and likely to leave a permanent impress on the history of the Northwest. He married in 1860 Louisa M. Jackson of Iowa, who died in August 1900. In 1907 he married Mrs. Anna (Larsen) Peterson, who survived him.

[The *Spokesman-Review* (Spokane), June 30 and July 1, 1918, contains interesting obituary material and editorial comment, as does *Ry. Age* (July 19, 1918), p. 154; see also H. M. Lawson, *Hist. and Geneal. of the Descendants of Clement Corbin* (1905); Edmund Wheeler, *Hist. of Newport, N. H., from 1766 to 1878, with a Geneal. Reg.* (1879); Nelson W. Durham, *Hist. of the City of Spokane and Spokane County, Wash.* (1912), vol. III; *Post-Intelligencer* (Seattle), and *Daily Colonist* (Victoria, B. C.), June 30, 1918.] W.A.R.

CORBIN, MARGARET (Nov. 12, 1751–Jan. 16, 1800), Revolutionary heroine, was the daughter of Robert Cochran, a Scotch-Irish pioneer in western Pennsylvania. She was born in what is now Franklin County. In 1756, at a time when she was away from home, her father was killed by Indians, and her mother carried off. She lived during the rest of her childhood at the home of an uncle. In 1772 she married John Corbin. When the Revolution began he joined the First Company of Pennsylvania Artillery as a matross (*Pennsylvania Archives,* ser. V, vol. III, p. 948). Margaret accompanied him, a custom not unusual at that period. At the battle of Fort Washington, Nov. 16, 1776, where Corbin was in charge of a small cannon on a ridge later named Fort Tryon, he was killed during an assault by the Hessians. Margaret, who witnessed his fall, took his place and courageously performed his duties until she was severely wounded. After the surrender of Fort Washington, she was not included among the prisoners, but was allowed to go to Philadelphia. Her injuries completely incapacitated her, and her serious condition came to the attention of the Executive Council of Pennsylvania, which, on June 29, 1779, granted her $30 for her immediate necessities and referred her case to the Board of War (*Minutes of the Supreme Executive Council of Pennsylvania,* XII, 34). The Board reported favorably (*Papers of the Continental Congress,* no. 174, vol. III, folio 501), and Congress, on July 6, 1779, voted her "during her natural life or the continuance of said disability the one-half of the monthly pay drawn by a soldier in the service of these states . . . and now . . . one complete

suit of cloaths, or the value thereof in money" (*Journals of the Continental Congress,* XIV, 805). This act enrolled her in the Invalid Regiment, organized for garrison purposes, and her name appears several times on the pay-roll, and finally on the list of those discharged when it was mustered out in April 1783 (*Pennsylvania Archives,* ser. V, vol IV, pp. 40, 59, 65, 79, 90). She spent the remainder of her life in Westchester County, N. Y., near the scene of her husband's death and her own heroism.

[*Fort Washington* (pub. by the Empire State Soc., S.A.R., 1902); G. M. Pierce, "Three Am. Women Pensioned for Mil. Service" in *D.A.R. Mag.,* LI, 140; J. C. Pumpelly, "Some of the Women Who Skillfully Planned and Heroically Suffered in the Revolution" in *Americana,* X, 818; R. Keim, "Heroines of the Revolution" in *Jour. Am. Hist.,* XVI, 31.] V.R—e.

CORBY, WILLIAM (Oct. 2, 1833–Dec. 28, 1897), Roman Catholic clergyman, president of the University of Notre Dame, Indiana, was the son of Daniel Corby, a native of King's County, Ireland, who came to America as a young man and settled in Detroit. There William was born and reared. After a boyhood in the common schools and practical experience in his father's business, he entered Notre Dame in 1853. Impressed by the religious atmosphere of the place, he joined in 1854 the Congregation of the Holy Cross, an order of priests and brothers devoted to education and charity, and decided to dedicate his life to the cause of Christian education. He pursued his studies with ardor, made his religious profession as a member of the congregation in 1858, and was appointed Prefect of Discipline in the University. Upon his ordination to the priesthood in 1860, he was made a professor and director of the Manual Labor School at Notre Dame, at the same time having charge of the mission at South Bend, where he was the first resident Catholic clergyman. In December 1861, along with six other priests from Notre Dame, he was commissioned by the Governor of New York and served for three years as chaplain of the famous Irish Brigade, with the rank of captain of cavalry. He performed faithful service in all the campaigns of the Army of the Potomac, his most conspicuous act being his general absolution pronounced under fire on the field of Gettysburg on the afternoon of July 2, 1863. At the close of the war he took up vigorously his work at South Bend, but was made vice-president of Notre Dame in 1865 and in the following year was elected its president and local superior of his order. After an administration of six years, marked by the establishment of a law school and great general prosperity, he was transferred to the presidency of the young and struggling Sacred Heart College at Watertown, Wis., which he placed on a firm footing. In 1877 he was again made president of Notre Dame and became a powerful factor in its progress and advancement. He rebuilt its buildings on a larger scale after the fire of 1879, added a number of new departments, broadened the standards of learning, and earned for himself the title of second founder of the University. Retiring from the presidency in 1881, he became the Provincial General of his order in the United States, and later First Assistant General in All Parts of the World. He was commander of the Indiana commandery of the Loyal Legion and founder and commander of Notre Dame Post, No. 569, G. A. R., the only post composed entirely of members of a religious order.

Father Corby was a modest man whose character combined simplicity and strength. He had a high forehead, kindly eyes, and a distinguished bearing. His portrait in oil may be seen at Notre Dame. A bronze statue of Corby in the act of pronouncing absolution was dedicated at Gettysburg in 1910, and its replica stands on the campus at Notre Dame. His *Memoirs of Chaplain Life* (1894) is a vivid narrative of camp and battlefield.

[*Notre Dame Scholastic*, vol. XXXI (1898); *The Class Day Book of '80* (Notre Dame, 1880); *The Corby Monument Committee* (Phila., 1910); *Ave Maria*, vol. XL (1898); J. G. Shea, *The Cross and the Flag* (1899); David P. Conyngham, *The Irish Brigade and Its Campaigns* (1867).]   F.T.P.

CORCORAN, JAMES ANDREW (Mar. 30, 1820–July 16, 1889), Catholic priest, theologian, editor, was born in Charleston, S. C. At the age of fourteen he went to Rome to attend the Propaganda College, and there, eight years later, he was ordained by Cardinal Fransoni, being the first native son of the Carolinas to enter the priesthood. He had made a brilliant record, especially in languages. Latin came as fluently as English, and he was thoroughly familiar with the European tongues. A year's added study gained for him the degree S.T.D., and he was ready to return to Charleston in 1843, to begin his notable services to the Church in America.

After a seasoning tour of teaching in the Charleston Seminary, with the rectorship of the cathedral and other pastoral duties added, when preparations began for the Eighth Baltimore Provincial Council of 1855, Corcoran came to national prominence as a theologian. He was made secretary of the Council and was so successful that he was given a like post at the Ninth Council in 1858. Charged with supervising the progress and drawing up the decrees at these Councils, which were in effect national gatherings, he left his stamp on the results of both. Thus when the Second Plenary Council was held at Baltimore, eight years later, he was promptly chosen secretary-in-chief. Seven archbishops, thirty-nine bishops or their procurators, and two abbots signed the fourteen decrees of this Council, all of which bore the mark of Corcoran's deep knowledge and exactness as an interpreter of conciliar decisions recognized by the whole body of the Church as binding precedents. In 1868, the American hierarchy unanimously named him their theologian on the preparatory commission for the Twentieth Ecumenical Council at the Vatican, which he later attended. It was he who drew up the "Spalding formula" on Papal Infallibility, the chief matter dealt with at this gathering. Following this period, he became professor of theology at Overbrook Seminary near Philadelphia, which had just been opened. This post he held until his death. When, however, the American archbishops went to Rome in 1883, preparatory to the Third Plenary Council, they took Corcoran as their secretary, and at their request he attended their sessions. Returning, he brought his experience and learning to bear once more at the Council's meetings in Baltimore.

Corcoran's editorial periods were two in number. Immediately after his return from his studies in Rome, he became a co-editor of the *United States Catholic Miscellany*, the pioneer Catholic literary journal of the country. He continued with the *Miscellany* for fifteen years, from 1846 to 1861, and it was in this period that an accident denied him the authorship of a great work. Having become engaged in an editor's controversy over Luther, he gathered a wealth of material and was well advanced in writing a life of the outstanding figure of the Reformation when his library burned, destroying both manuscript and material. His second editorial period began in 1876, when he was chosen chief editor of the newly-founded *American Catholic Quarterly Review*. His contributions to this journal were notable and successful. He was one of the editors of the works of Bishop England (1849). In 1883 he was made a Domestic Prelate and the Propaganda College conferred on him the degree D.D.

Corcoran was a pastor as well as a scholar. When in 1862, Gen. Beauregard sent four doctors to Wilmington, N. C., which was swept by yellow fever, Corcoran unhesitatingly accompanied them. He labored with great fortitude amid his disease-smitten flock, and continued as their pastor until 1868.

[John J. Keane, "Monsignor Corcoran," in *Am. Cath. Quart. Rev.* (Phila.), Oct. 1889; *Rosary*, vol. I (1891–92); *Cath. Encyc.*, vol. IV.]   E.F.B.

CORCORAN, WILLIAM WILSON (Dec. 27, 1798–Feb. 24, 1888), banker, philanthropist, was the son of Thomas and Hannah (Lemmon) Corcoran of Baltimore. His father was born in Ireland in 1754, emigrated to America in 1783, settled in Georgetown, D. C., in 1788, was magistrate, member of Levy Court, and postmaster. William was educated in private schools, and for one year at Georgetown College, now Georgetown University. In 1815 he insisted upon going into the dry-goods store of two brothers, James and Thomas Corcoran, in Georgetown. In 1817, they established him in the same business under the name of W. W. Corcoran & Co. In 1819, the firm added a wholesale auction-and-commission business which suspended in 1823 with debts of $28,000, which were then settled at fifty cents on the dollar. Corcoran attended to his father's affairs until 1830. From 1828 to 1836 he was engaged with business of the branch Bank of the United States and Bank of Columbia. In 1837 he began a brokerage business in Washington and in 1840 formed the banking firm of Corcoran & Riggs, which has continued under various changes of name and organization to the present time. He served in the militia of the District of Columbia as lieutenant, captain, lieutenant-colonel, and colonel. On Dec. 23, 1835, he married Louise Amory Morris, daughter of Commodore Charles Morris, U. S. N.

The business of Corcoran & Riggs prospered to such an extent that, in 1847, Corcoran paid the creditors of W. W. Corcoran & Co. in full the balance of the indebtedness existing at the failure of that firm in 1823, with interest to date. In 1848, Corcoran & Riggs bid 103.02 for the entire issue of $16,000,000, of the bonds of the United States issued under act of Mar. 31, 1848, and were awarded $14,065,550. On a trip to England, in spite of discouraging initial experiences, Corcoran succeeded in placing $5,000,000 of these bonds in London, with great enhancement of the public credit. This success caused such a rise in the market price of the bonds as to net a handsome profit to his firm, making the foundation of his fortune. On Apr. 1, 1854, he retired from active business and devoted himself until the time of his death to the management of his properties and to his philanthropic interests.

As was the case with a majority of the old and leading residents of the District of Columbia, his sympathies were with the South during the Civil War, but this did not extend to any act of opposition to Federal authority. He left the United States in 1862 and remained abroad until the close of the war. The Government's proposed seizure of his residence in Washington was prevented by the French Minister, who claimed the right to occupy it under lease. Corcoran had begun the construction of the Corcoran Gallery of Art in 1859. During the Civil War the building was occupied by the Quartermaster-General's Office. This delayed the completion and inauguration of the gallery until Feb. 22, 1872. The act of Congress of May 24, 1870, incorporated the Gallery and provided compensation to the corporation for the use of the building by the Government. Corcoran's gifts, including a bequest, amounted to $1,600,000. His own considerable collection formed the nucleus of the Gallery collection. The building at Pennsylvania Ave. and Seventeenth St. was purchased by the Government by act of Mar. 3, 1901, and is now occupied by the United States Court of Claims. The new Gallery on Seventeenth St. between E St. and New York Ave. was opened in 1897.

The Louise Home was founded by Corcoran in 1869 as "an institution for the support and maintenance of a limited number of gentlewomen, who have been reduced by misfortune." His donations for this purpose, including a bequest, were $550,000. Other considerable gifts during his lifetime were to The Columbian (now George Washington) University, Ascension P. E. Church toward a new church building, the University of Virginia, William and Mary College, Virginia Military Institute, Washington and Lee University, Episcopal Theological Seminary near Alexandria, Va., Protestant Orphan Asylum of Washington, and the convent and Academy of the Visitation of Washington. Besides these larger benefactions, he continually gave to regular and occasional beneficiaries a large aggregate of gifts, of which a large proportion were to residents of Virginia and other Southern states who had been impoverished by the Civil War. In 1883 he caused the remains of John Howard Payne [q.v.], author of "Home, Sweet Home," to be removed from Tunis and reinterred in Oak Hill Cemetery in Georgetown, and there erected a monument to his memory.

A portrait of Corcoran by Charles Loring Elliott is in the Gallery of Art. He was of medium height, heavy set; of agreeable, kindly, and dignified bearing and courtly manners. He dressed with care and always wore gloves, carried a gold-headed cane, and wore a red rose in his button-hole. His wide circle of friends, extending over a long period of years, included Stephen Decatur, George Bancroft, George Peabody, Daniel Webster, William H. Prescott, Jefferson Davis, Winfield Scott, Edward Everett, Charles Sumner, and Presidents Millard Fillmore and James Buchanan.

[*A Grandfather's Legacy* (1879), containing a biographical sketch and letters; *Evening Star* (Washington), Feb. 24, 1888; M. E. P. Bouligny, *A Tribute to W. W. Corcoran* (1874); W. B. Bryan, *Hist. of the National Capital* (1916); *U. S. Statutes at Large*, IX, 217, XVI, 139, XXXI, 1135; Report of Secretary of Treasury on state of finances, Dec. 11, 1848, *House Ex. Doc. No. 7*, 30 Cong., 2 Sess.; *House Doc. No. 46*, 23 Cong., 2 Sess.]

W.B.K.

CORLISS, GEORGE HENRY (June 2, 1817–Feb. 21, 1888), inventor, manufacturer, was the only son of Hiram and Susan (Sheldon) Corliss. He was born at Easton, Washington County, N. Y., where his father practised medicine and surgery. To permit him to be properly educated, Corliss's family moved to Greenwich, N. Y., when he was eight years old. He proved to be a very apt student and showed a marked inclination toward mathematics and mechanics. He remained at school until he was fourteen, when, as the field for mechanical pursuit was quite limited, he entered the employ of William Mowray & Son as their general storekeeper. In this service he was clerk, bookkeeper, salesman, and official inspector and measurer of cloth turned out by the factory. After four years, he was sent by his father to Castleton Academy in Vermont. Here he remained for three years, after which he returned to Greenwich and started a store of his own. His first real opportunity to apply his natural mechanical instincts was afforded him about this time as a result of persistent complaints of customers over the stitching in the shoes he sold. At an outlay of about $100 he devised, in a crude way, a machine for sewing boots, which consisted, in the main, of passing needles and thread through the heavy leather in opposite directions at the same time. A United States patent was granted him in 1842. Two years later he went to Providence, R. I., to try to market his invention. The firm of Fairbanks, Bancroft & Company, machine and steam-engine builders, undertook to assist him, and it was not long before they recognized his genius. To secure his services they offered him a position as a draftsman, provided he dropped the sewing machine idea. Corliss accepted, sold out his store in Greenwich, and moved with his young wife and two children to Providence. In less than a year he was admitted to the firm, and before another year had elapsed he had devised mechanisms that very soon revolutionized the construction and operation of steam-engines. His first ideas for improvements in the steam-engine were formulated in 1846 when he was twenty-nine years old, and his first United States patent embodying his ideas was granted Mar. 10, 1849 and reissued July 29, 1851. In 1848, and before receiving his patent, Corliss left Fair-

banks, Bancroft & Company and joined with John Barstow and E. J. Nightingale of Providence, organizing a new company under the name of Corliss, Nightingale & Company. It was this company that built the first steam-engine embodying the Corliss features. His invention consisted of rotary valves (separate ones for steam and exhaust ports) and a governor which by a system of levers controlled the valves and the admission of steam to the engine cylinder. Reciprocating steam-engines have not been greatly bettered either in steam or fuel or fuel economies since the introduction of engines operated with Corliss's valve gear and drop cut-off, as the invention is called. By the technical world Corliss is ranked equally with Watt in the development of the steam-engine. Corliss's company bought land in Providence for the erection of a steam-engine factory; by 1856 the new plant was completed, and the company was incorporated under the name of the Corliss Engine Company. Corliss as president not only directed all the business activities but at the same time devised all the subsequent improvements in his engine mechanism. His first type of valve gear was improved in 1850, a second type was devised in 1852, a third in 1858, a fourth in 1867, a fifth in 1875, and a sixth and seventh in 1880. During this time, too, the business of the company grew at a prodigious rate until over one thousand men were employed in the plant. The principal features of the engine were copied by engine manufacturers, both in the United States and Europe, and Corliss had many infringements to fight. Besides his steam-engine inventions, he received patents for a gear-cutting machine, an improved boiler with condensing apparatus, and a pumping engine for water-works. Although he had little taste for politics he represented North Providence in the General Assembly of Rhode Island in 1868–70 and was a Republican presidential elector in 1876. He was twice married: first, in January 1839, to Phœbe F. Frost of Canterbury, Conn., who died in 1859; second, in 1866, to Emily A. Shaw of Newburyport, Mass., who survived him.

[*Biog. Cyc. of Rep. Men of R. I.* (1881); Dwight Goddard, *Eminent Engineers* (1906); Edward W. Byrn, *Progress of Invention in the Nineteenth Century* (1900); Robt. H. Thurston, *Hist. of the Growth of the Steam Engine* (4th ed., 1902); J. D. Van Slyke, *Representatives of New Eng.* (1879); U. S. Patent Office Records.]

C.W.M.

CORNBURY, EDWARD HYDE, Viscount (1661–Apr. 1, 1723), governor of New York and New Jersey, was the eldest son of Henry Hyde, second earl of Clarendon, and the grandson of Edward Hyde, first earl of Clarendon, famous as Lord Chancellor under Charles II and historian of the Civil War. Cornbury was first cousin to Queen Anne. He was educated at Geneva and in 1688 married Katherine, daughter of Lord O'Brian. "Early taught to consider his relationship to the Princess Anne as the groundwork of his fortunes," he came under the influence of John Churchill (later Duke of Marlborough) and at his suggestion was one of the first officers of the army to desert James II at the time of the Revolution (T. B. Macaulay, *The History of England,* edited by C. H. Firth, 1913–15, III, 1147). He thus ingratiated himself with William of Orange. Since 1685 he had been a member of the Commons, but owing to straitened financial circumstances he sought office in the Colonies. Appointed governor of New York and later of New Jersey, he arrived at his post, May 3, 1702 (*Documents Relative to the Colonial History of the State of New York,* IV, 955). Because of his relationship to the Queen he was received with unusual deference, but his administration in both provinces was a complete failure. "Careful inquiry into the course of Cornbury's administration in New York on the whole substantiates the legend which portrays him as a spendthrift, a 'grafter,' a bigoted oppressor and a drunken, vain fool" (Spencer, *post,* p. 309). Throwing his influence to the aristocratic Anti-Leislerian faction in New York, he secured from an assembly dominated by them a gift of £2,000. As the second Intercolonial War was raging, he obtained grants for the raising of men and supplies, but on the embezzlement of a large part of the money he was drawn into bitter conflict with the Assembly. He was eventually compelled to submit to the naming of a treasurer, elected by and responsible to the Assembly, through whom the public funds were to be expended. In spite of his peculations, he showed great zeal for the Church of England. He seized the church at Jamaica from the Presbyterians and unjustly prosecuted one Francis Mackemie [*q.v.*], a Presbyterian minister, for preaching without the governor's license. Finally the Assembly, Sept. 11, 1708, unanimously adopted resolutions condemning various features of his rule.

Cornbury's administration in New Jersey was even more disastrous. Great importance was attached to his policy there because after the surrender by the proprietors it rested with Cornbury to initiate royal rule. His Lordship took bribes, however (*Archives of the State of New Jersey,* ser. I, vol. III, pp. 198 ff.), oppressed the Quakers, and came into collision with leading proprietors like Lewis Morris and Samuel Jen-

ings. In May 1707 the Assembly of the Jerseys adopted an outspoken remonstrance against Cornbury's policy which was read to the Governor in person by Jenings as speaker (*Ibid.,* pp. 173 ff.). Among the charges brought by the Governor's critics was the strange accusation that he forfeited respect by publicly appearing in woman's attire (Smith, *post,* I, 194). This has been put down as a mad prank due to Cornbury's vanity in imagining that he resembled his royal cousin, but Stanhope (*History of England,* 3rd ed., 1853, I, 79) declared that Cornbury endeavored in this way actually to represent Queen Anne (see also *The Memorial History of the City of N. Y.,* edited by James Grant Wilson, vol. II, 1892, p. 86, note). Finally, in December 1708, Cornbury was recalled. His numerous creditors at once caused his arrest, however, and he remained in the custody of the Sheriff of New York until the death of his father made him Earl of Clarendon and enabled him to return to England. In 1711 he was raised to the Privy Council and in 1714 served as Envoy Extraordinary in Hanover (Stanhope, *op. cit.,* I, 79). Lady Cornbury died in New York, Aug. 11, 1706 in her thirty-fifth year. Apparently she also had shown peculiarities of character (Wilson, *op. cit.,* II, 78, note). The impression left in America by Lord Cornbury is indicated by Smith, the Tory historian of New York, who wrote "We never had a governor so universally detested" (*post,* I, 194).

[The career of Cornbury as governor may be traced in the *Docs. Relative to the Colonial Hist. of the State of N. Y.,* vols. IV and V (1854–55); *Archives of the State of N. J.,* vols. III (1881) and XIII (1890); Wm. Smith, *Hist. of the Late Province of N. Y.* (1830), vol. I. Modern critical estimates are found in Herbert L. Osgood, *The Am. Colonies in the Eighteenth Century* (1924), vol. II, and Chas. Worthen Spencer, "The Cornbury Legend," *Proc. N. Y. State Hist. Asso.,* vol. XIII (1914), p. 309.]

E. P. T.

CORNELL, ALONZO B. (Jan. 22, 1832–Oct. 15, 1904), politician, governor of New York, was born at Ithaca, the eldest son of Ezra Cornell [*q.v.*] and Mary Ann (Wood) Cornell. Before his sixteenth birthday the boy had exchanged home and school for a telegrapher's key in Troy. There he discovered the possibility of reading by sound, and upon passing from the control of his father's lines in Montreal to take charge of the main western office in Cleveland he organized it as the first to dispense with the recording tape. Marriage led him to prefer less confining employment in an Ithaca bank (1852–56). After a term as manager of the Wall Street telegraph office he returned to Ithaca (1859) and bought the line of steamboats plying on Cayuga Lake, but soon sold them to participate in organizing the first national bank there, of which he was cashier 1864–66. In 1868 he began a thirty-year directorship of the Western Union Company. During 1870–76 he was its vice-president and in 1875 its acting president. He was apprenticed to politics in 1858 as the youngest member of the Tompkins County Republican committee. Next year he became its chairman and in 1864 and 1865 was also supervisor for Ithaca. Mounting Republican majorities in "talismanic Tompkins" drew the attention of larger politicians. He was placed on the Republican state committee (1866); nominated, and defeated, for lieutenant-governor (1868); appointed by President Grant, at Senator Conkling's desire, to be surveyor of customs for the port of New York (March 1869); and, in September 1870, advanced to the chairmanship of the state committee. In this capacity he carried through, and defended in the Syracuse convention of 1871, a reënrolment of the city Republicans, whose central committee, under the ornamental chairmanship of Horace Greeley, he had found to be "subsidized by Tammany plunderers." In the Liberal nomination of Greeley for the presidency in 1872 Cornell saw a continuation of this contest between the Conkling and Fenton factions for control of the Republican organization and summoned all his energies to hold the state against the party traitor. In return, his Republican colleagues in the Assembly of 1873 elected him to be speaker despite his entire lack of legislative experience. As state chairman in the campaign of 1876, although the state was lost to Tilden, Cornell was judged by the organization to have made a good fight. In February 1877, President Grant, about to retire, rewarded him with the lucrative post of naval officer in the New York customs house. In June, President Hayes issued his executive order forbidding federal office-holders to engage in party management. Cornell, being under no charges of official misconduct (C. R. Williams, *Life of Hayes*, 1914, II, 94), refused either to resign his office or to relinquish what he professed to consider his duty to his party. Hayes therefore suspended him and in February 1879, the Senate, against Conkling's persistent opposition, confirmed his successor. The state organization, in reply, marked its approbation of Cornell's stand by nominating him for governor and he was elected.

Discharge of executive office was to work a change in Alonzo Cornell's reputation. He had determined to give the state the best administration he could. His appointees for the purpose were men of his own choice, many of them active

politicians whose qualities he knew. The reformers inferred that he was repairing the Conkling machine, the Conklingites that he was building a machine of his own. In any event it did the state's work without scandal. His recommendations to the legislature concerned chiefly elections and state finances. Not all of them were accepted, but the state government began to receive a modern stamp. More spectacular was Cornell's use of the veto power. Over three hundred loosely drawn acts were returned for amendment; over four hundred others, deemed unconstitutional, subversive of local government, or extravagant, failed to receive his signature, including much-lobbied measures desired by New York's traction-mongers. From this stream of vetoes great irritation arose in the legislature, but so little outside that not one of them was overridden.

On May 19, 1881, Cornell sent in his briefest message, and the most momentous for his political career: "The Legislature is hereby respectfully notified that the two Senatorial offices by which the State of New York is entitled to representation in the Congress of the United States, are now vacant by the resignations of the late incumbents." Thus was indicated his determination to keep clear of the spoils squabble with President Garfield into which Senators Conkling and Platt had plunged upon the nomination of the "half breed" William H. Robertson [q.v.] to be collector of customs at New York. Defeated in Washington, they had transferred their grievance to Albany, counting on the legislative influence of the Governor to secure them a political vindication. The senior senator chose to attribute his collapse to the ingratitude of "that lizard on the hill."

Cornell openly sought renomination in 1882. His chances seemed good. Independents who had resented his first nomination had been converted by the merits of his administration, the rank and file of Republican voters were pleased, and there were experienced political managers in what the administration press called his machine. But contests were decided against Cornell delegates and the administration candidate, Charles J. Folger [q.v.], was nominated. Cornell took no farther part in politics. He engaged in business in New York, wrote a biography of his father, published in 1884, and at length returned to Ithaca, where he died on Oct. 15, 1904. He was twice married: on Nov. 9, 1852 to Elen Augusta Covert, and after her death in 1893 to her widowed younger sister.

[The materials for Cornell's life are scattered. In 1889 he wrote a reticent autobiography still in MS. His *Public Papers* were printed by the state in three volumes, 1880–82. The sketches in P. A. Chadbourne, *Public Service of the State of New York* (1882), and in J. H. Selkreg, *Landmarks of Tompkins County, N. Y.* (1894), were probably revised by him. He had no knack of dealing with newspaper men and seldom enjoyed a good press. If any editors were in his confidence they were J. N. Matthews of the *Buffalo Express* (until the break with Conkling), C. E. Smith of the *Albany Evening Jour.* and J. H. Selkreg of the *Ithaca Jour.* The editorials of the *N. Y. Times, Harper's Weekly,* and the *Nation* in 1879–82 reveal the gradual shift of opinion in the state to his favor.]   C.H.H.

CORNELL, EZEKIEL (Mar. 27, 1733–Apr. 25, 1800), Revolutionary soldier, the son of Richard Cornell and Content Brownell, was born in Scituate, R. I. He was a mechanic before he entered the army, and largely self-educated. In 1760 he married Rachel Wood of Little Compton. He took a lively interest in the affairs of Scituate, representing it in the Assembly in 1772, 1774, and 1775, serving on its Revolutionary Committee of Correspondence; helping to draft for it a remarkable paper respecting colonial independence; and serving as moderator of its town meeting. He was the first to promote the establishment of a public library and the cause of education in his native town. When the Rhode Island Assembly, on receipt of the news of the battles of Lexington and Concord, voted to raise an "army of observation," Cornell was appointed (May 3, 1775) lieutenant-colonel of Hitchcock's regiment. He participated in the siege of Boston, and after the British evacuation accompanied his regiment (known in 1776 as the 11th Continental Infantry) to New York, where he took part in the battle of Long Island and presumably in the operations following it. From Oct. 1 to Dec. 31, 1776 he served as deputy adjutant-general.

In December 1776 the Rhode Island Assembly voted to enlist a brigade of three regiments of infantry and one of artillery to serve principally in defense of the colony. Thus originated the Rhode Island State Brigade of which Cornell, after acting in a subordinate position, was appointed commander, Dec. 19, 1777, with the rank of brigadier-general. Under his leadership the brigade rendered valuable service in protecting the colony against British marauders, and especially distinguished itself at the battle of Rhode Island, Aug. 29, 1778, which was fought near the Cornell homestead. Gen. Sullivan in his dispatch to Congress lauded Cornell's "good conduct" and "indefatigable industry" in preparing for the retirement of the colonial forces to Tiverton on the day following the battle. During this period, Cornell was chosen by the Assembly to act on various committees of a military character, and was for a time a member of the Council of War which supervised arrangements for the defense of Rhode Island. On May 1, 1780 he resigned his commission, and having received the thanks of the Assembly for his military services, was shortly after elected by that body delegate to Congress. Twice reëlected (May 1781 and May 1782), he proved a useful member, acting on various committees and serving on the Board of War from December 1780 until its abolition in October 1781. He favored the establishment of a stronger national government and in opposition to the general sentiment of his state was willing to confer upon Congress authority to tax imports. After serving as inspector of the main army under Washington from Sept. 19, 1782 until the formal conclusion of the war, he retired to his farm at Scituate. He was a strict disciplinarian, was cool in battle, and brought to the management of both military and civil affairs an unusual fund of common sense. He died at Milford, Mass.

[Sketches in Benj. Cowell, *Spirit of 1776 in R. I.* (1850); John Cornell, *Geneal. of the Cornell Family* (1902). Many of Cornell's letters as a member of Congress are printed in W. R. Staples, *R. I. in the Continental Congress* (1870). See also R. I. *Colonial Records,* vols. VII–IX (1862–64); C. C. Beaman, *Historical Address* (1877); S. G. Arnold, *Hist. of the State of R. I.,* vol. II (1860); E. Field, *State of R. I. and Providence Plantations at the End of the Century,* vol. I (1902); F. B. Heitman, *Hist. Reg.* (1914).]   E.E.C.

CORNELL, EZRA (Jan. 11, 1807–Dec. 9, 1874), capitalist, founder of Cornell University, was born of New England Quaker stock, the son of Elijah and Eunice (Barnard) Cornell, the former a farmer and pottery maker, at Westchester Landing on the Bronx River in New York. Elijah Cornell failing to prosper at earthenware manufacture, the family in 1819 removed to De Ruyter in Madison County, N. Y. Here Ezra attended the village school, helped manage his father's farm and earthenware manufactory, and learned carpentry. At eighteen he set out for himself, working as a laborer and mechanic at Syracuse and Homer, N. Y., exhibiting mechanical ingenuity, tenacity, and Yankee shrewdness. Hearing of Ithaca as a town rising in commercial importance through its connection with the Erie Canal by Lake Cayuga, in the spring of 1828 he secured employment as a carpenter and millwright there—thenceforth his lifelong home. His practical abilities shortly raised him to the general managership of the flouring and plaster mills of J. S. Beebe. Here he planned and built an enlarged flouring mill; devised many mechanical improvements; dug a tunnel through solid rock for water-power; and built a difficult dam. Fortunately for his future, the conversion of the mills into a woolen factory in 1841 cost him his place and threw him into a larger sphere.

Temporary occupation in promoting a patent plow in Maine shortly brought Cornell in contact with F. O. J. Smith, editor of the *Maine Farmer* and member of Congress, who was interested in Morse's magnetic telegraph. Congress having appropriated $30,000 to enable Morse to test the invention, Smith contracted to lay a pipe with wires from Washington to Baltimore, and appealed to the enterprising Cornell to build a machine for the purpose. Cornell devised a successful machine and supervised the pipe-laying near Baltimore, but, when underground insulation was found impracticable, at Morse's bidding he wrecked the device to gain time for further experiment. He then furnished Morse a satisfactory method of insulating the wires on poles, and aided in erecting the Washington-Baltimore line. Shrewdly confident of the great commercial future of the telegraph, he at once threw himself into the work of demonstrating it, enlisting capital, and building lines, and became within a few years the chief figure in this field. He helped organize the Magnetic Telegraph Company to connect New York and Washington, and in 1845 built the line from the Hudson to Philadelphia. He followed this by constructing a New York-Albany line, on which he made $6,000, his first large profit. Other remunerative contracts for lines in parts of New York, Vermont, and Quebec were completed. With his accumulated capital he then launched in 1847 his Erie & Michigan Telegraph Company, which after many discouragements linked together Buffalo, Cleveland, Detroit, Chicago, and Milwaukee; this was followed by the New York & Erie Telegraph Company, which connected New York City with Dunkirk. Subsidiary lines were rapidly constructed, especially in the Middle West, where the telegraph preceded rather than followed the railroad. Meanwhile, numerous rival companies appeared, and many towns soon had three or four competing telegraph offices. The cut-throat competition made some form of combination indispensable, and in 1855 Cornell and other leading owners of Middle Western lines formed the Western Union Telegraph Company, a consolidation of seven major and several minor systems. This company rapidly extended its operation to most parts of the United States and Canada. Cornell was for twenty years a director and in limited degree active in the management; for more than fifteen years he was the largest stockholder. As the company grew rich his dividends rose above $100,000 a year, and his son said that

"he was enabled to realize for his telegraph interests in the aggregate probably more than two millions of dollars."

Thus achieving wealth and leisure, Cornell, with his usual calm energy, turned his attention to public affairs. He built in 1863 a free public library in Ithaca, for which he ultimately gave more than $100,000. He established a model farm, with imported Shorthorn cattle and Southdown sheep, and in 1862 became president of the State Agricultural Society. For six years beginning in 1861 he sat in the legislature, two years in the Assembly and four in the Senate, and in his rugged way became a force there. As a trustee of the feeble State Agricultural College just founded at Ovid, N. Y., he was struck with the unrealized potentialities of such an institution. The result was a hasty offer to endow it with $300,000 on condition that it be removed to Ithaca and that half the Morrill land grant, provided by Congress in 1862, be given it. This suggestion met the opposition of Andrew D. White [*q.v.*], a member of the state Senate from Syracuse, who vehemently objected to dividing the federal endowment. Cornell had imagination as well as practical grasp, and White's enlarged views of university education and of the need for a new institution in New York devoted to the liberal and mechanic arts opened a new vista before his mind. As a result of much conversation and thought he was aroused to ardor and agreed to pledge a site and $500,000 to such a new institution. He cooperated with White in drafting and carrying the legislation to found Cornell University; and he was White's unwearied co-worker, counselor, and financial supporter in all the labors which led to its opening in the fall of 1868. Both inside and outside the legislature he met obstacles, misunderstanding, and abuse, but his dour and unflinching patience matched the liberality of his principles and the shrewdness of his foresight. The university bore the impress of his democratic and practical ideas in its total freedom from religious ties, its provision for the education of women, its emphasis on advanced training in agriculture and engineering, and its facilities for poor students. It was he who was mainly instrumental in the choice of Andrew D. White for the first president. Not less important than his endowment of the university was his wise resolve, carried out with grim determination, to prevent the premature sale of the land grant: he agreed in 1866 to purchase the land-scrip, locate the land at his own expense, pay all taxes and other charges, and bind himself to turn into the state treasury for the benefit of the "land-poor" university all the profits realized. This plan within twenty years yielded the university approximately two and a half millions. Cornell also gave numerous special gifts to the classical and scientific departments. As White wrote, "He felt that the university was to be great, and he took his measures accordingly." He was sometimes irritatingly taciturn as to his plans, he was always stern and austere, and he was not broadly educated; but he needed only to be convinced of the rightness of any purpose to support it with immovable resolution. His friendship with Goldwin Smith, Agassiz, Lowell, and other lecturers gave him special pleasure. Till his death in 1874 his tall spare figure, set off with frock coat and stovepipe hat, was a familiar sight on the campus. He was married to Mary Ann Wood on Mar. 19, 1831. Alonzo B. Cornell [q.v.], governor of New York, was their son.

[The fullest account of Ezra Cornell is in *"True and Firm": Biography of Ezra Cornell* (1884), published anonymously but written by Alonzo B. Cornell. This is supplemented by eight chapters in *Autobiography of Andrew Dickson White* (1905), I, 287–426. Goldwin Smith's *Reminiscences* (1910), ed. by Arnold Haultain, offer interesting pages. Andrew D. White published a separate pamphlet, *My Reminiscences of Ezra Cornell* (1890). Addresses by White, Andrew Carnegie, and others are contained in *Centennial Anniversary of the Birth of Ezra Cornell* (1907). A sketch published in the *N. Y. Geneal. and Biog. Record*, Jan. 1875, was reprinted in the *Am. Bibliopolist*, Feb. 1875. Many of Cornell's letters on the telegraph are in the N. Y. Hist. Soc. An autobiographical fragment, letters, and other papers are in the Cornell Univ. Lib. Histories of Cornell Univ. afford scattering material.]   A. N.

CORNING, ERASTUS (Dec. 14, 1794–Apr. 9, 1872), prominent in railroad development in the state of New York, was born in Norwich, Conn., the son of Bliss and Lucinda (Smith) Corning. His father was a Revolutionary soldier and was a descendant of Ensign Samuel Corning who emigrated from England to Beverly, Mass., in 1641. Erastus served his apprenticeship in business as a clerk in the hardware store of his uncle, Benjamin Smith, in Troy, N. Y. In 1814 he removed to Albany and there began his career as an iron manufacturer. Starting in a small way in a partnership in a hardware store, he took advantage of an opportunity to purchase a small foundry and rolling-mill for the making of nails from imported bar iron. In 1837 he associated himself with John F. Winslow [q.v.], a genius in the working of metals, and the business under their management became one of the most extensive in the country.

Corning's active business life was coincident with the birth and early development of railroads, and he seemed from the beginning to grasp their significance for the industrial development of the country. The Mohawk & Hudson had been chartered in 1826 and opened for operation in 1831, paralleling the Erie Canal from Albany to Schenectady. Its opening, although attended by many difficulties, due to working in a pioneer field, at once demonstrated the feasibility of this form of transportation and led to an avalanche of railroad charters, many of which were of course wholly impracticable. Among them, however, was one for the incorporation of the Utica & Schenectady, dated Apr. 29, 1833, with an authorized capital stock of $2,000,000, which was to extend the Mohawk & Hudson to Utica, a distance of about seventy-eight miles. It is a fair inference that Corning was one of the chief promoters of the enterprise, for he was elected one of the thirteen original directors and was the road's first and only president, serving for twenty years until it became a part of the New York Central in 1853. The road was opened on Aug. 1, 1836. It was built in a productive region along a natural line of travel and proved very profitable to its stockholders. For his long and efficient service as president, without compensation, Corning was presented by the stockholders in 1850 with a service of plate costing $6,074.10.

By the early forties the desirability of consolidating the short stretches of road across the state into a continuous system had become obvious and various overtures in that direction had been made. At a convention of the interested companies in 1851, a resolution was adopted on Corning's motion, appointing a committee to apply to the legislature for a law, authorizing any two or more companies to consolidate into a single company. When the consolidation act was finally passed in 1853, the only question left to consider was the terms of consolidation; the principle had long since been agreed upon. Committees from the roads met in convention for the purpose and from them was chosen a subcommittee of one from each road, consisting of the ablest men present, to devise the actual plan of consolidation. Corning was made chairman of this committee. Following the consolidation he was elected first president of the New York Central Railroad, a position which he held until he resigned in 1864. He was a director for a few years longer and ceased his connection with the road in 1867. He was for some years a director of the Michigan Central Railroad and from 1849 to 1863 of the Hudson River road.

He did not confine his interest in transportation to this one railroad system. The Corning Land Company was organized by him in 1835 for the purpose of establishing a commercial center at the head of navigation on the Chemung River. The village of Corning at this location was named in his honor. A railroad was built south into Pennsylvania to the coal region at Blossberg for the purpose of diverting traffic to the new Chemung Canal, and thence through the Erie Canal and the Hudson to New York, an answering challenge to the commercial rivalry of Baltimore and Philadelphia.

Corning was four times elected mayor of Albany, resigning during his fourth term in 1837. He was a state senator from 1842 to 1846, was twice elected a Democratic Representative in Congress, in 1857–59 and 1861–63, and was again reëlected but resigned, presumably on account of ill health. His career in Congress was undistinguished. He was a member of the Peace Conference held in Washington in 1861. A regent of the University of New York from 1833, he was at the time of his death vice-chancellor.

There is a story, not well authenticated, told by John W. Starr in *Lincoln and the Railroads* (1927) to the effect that when Lincoln was in New York in 1860, delivering a political address at Cooper Institute, he was offered by Corning the position of general counsel of the New York Central at an annual salary of $10,000. Whether or not this story is true, Corning had occasion three years later to learn something of Lincoln's power of argumentation. After Vallandigham's arrest, a meeting of Democrats called in Albany, May 16, 1863, in which Corning took a prominent part, passed resolutions denouncing the arrest as unconstitutional. These resolutions were sent in a covering letter to Lincoln. His uncompromising reply, dated June 12, 1863, and addressed to Erastus Corning and associates, constitutes one of his greatest state papers (Nicolay and Hay, *Complete Works of Abraham Lincoln*, 1905, VIII, 298).

[The best source is Frank Walker Stevens, *The Beginnings of the N. Y. Central, A History* (1926). Otherwise material is to be found in various scattered sources, including: Joel Munsell's *Annals of Albany* (1850–59), vols. V–X; *Albany Chronicles* (1906), comp. by Cuyler Reynolds; *Pioneer Days and Later Times in Corning and Vicinity, 1789–1920* (1922), by Uri Mulford; *Encyc. of Biog. of N. Y.* (1916), by Chas. E. Fitch.]

F. H. D.

CORNOYER, PAUL (Aug. 15, 1864–June 17, 1923), painter, was born at St. Louis, Mo., a son of Charles and Marie (Barada) Cornoyer, both of French descent. Paul began to draw and paint as a young boy, and at seventeen he entered the St. Louis School of Art whose director, Halsey C. Ives, befriended and encouraged him. While continuing his art education Cornoyer did reporting for the St. Louis *Republic,* having secured a position through Augustus Thomas. then a news-

paper writer. In 1889, thanks in part to commissions from appreciative fellow townsmen, Cornoyer had accumulated funds sufficient to assure him several years' study at Paris. He entered the Julian Academy where he had criticisms from Jules Lefebvre and Benjamin Constant. He exhibited in the Salon and in 1892 won the first prize of the American Art Association of Paris. In 1894 he returned to St. Louis where, despite his winning the gold medal of the St. Louis Association of Painters and Sculptors in the ensuing winter, he found less encouragement than he had expected. A canvas, meantime, which he had sent to the Pennsylvania Academy of Fine Arts was seen, admired, and bought by the painter William M. Chase [*q.v.*]. The purchase led to correspondence in which Cornoyer was urged by his older confrère to settle in New York City. Cornoyer followed this advice and became in 1899 an instructor at the Mechanics' Institute where he proved himself an able and inspiring teacher. He held summer painting classes at first in Connecticut and then on the Massachusetts North Shore. His own creative work of his best period included many New York street scenes which he rendered with acute appreciation of the picturesqueness of rainy day effects, of dully gleaming pavements, and of the intermingling of natural and artificial lights. He also did notable decorations, of Italianate and other subjects, such as those for the Planters' Hotel, St. Louis, and the residences of W. B. Thompson, Yonkers, N. Y., and Francis J. Oakes, Brookline, Mass. He was elected an associate of the National Academy of Design in 1909. In 1917 he decided to make his permanent residence at East Gloucester, Mass., where he had remodeled an old house to provide a commodious and attractive studio. He was a moving spirit in the formation of the North Shore Arts Association of which he was vice-president when he died. He was a friendly, helpful man, greatly beloved by his fellow artists. He is represented by characteristic street scenes in the collections of the Brooklyn Museum, the City Art Museum of St. Louis, and the Dallas Art Association.

[The *Art Interchange*, Dec. 1903, printed an appreciative biographical sketch of Cornoyer. See *Am. Art News*, June 23, 1923, for a detailed and generally satisfactory obituary. Information as to specific facts has been had from the artist's sister, Miss Julie Cornoyer of Burlington, Ia., and Mr. and Mrs. Charles A. Winter of New York, who were associated with Cornoyer at East Gloucester.]

F. W. C.

CORNSTALK (*c.* 1720–1777) was a Shawnee Indian chief, whose English name was a translation of his Indian cognomen, Keigh-tugh-qua, the blade or stalk of the maize plant. Nothing is known of his early life, although he may have

447

been born in Pennsylvania, where a portion of the Shawnee tribe dwelt before removal about 1730 to the plains of the Scioto. Cornstalk's first known raid against the English settlers was in 1759 during the height of the French and Indian War; in alliance with the French traders he led a party into what is now Rockbridge County, Virginia, and killed ten of a family named Gilmore. Again in 1763 during the Pontiac outbreak Cornstalk raided the Greenbriar settlements of western Virginia, and when Col. Bouquet marched his avenging soldiery into Ohio the next year Cornstalk was one of the hostages exacted from the repentant but sullen tribesmen.

The ten following years (1764–74) there was a state of suppressed war along the Ohio-Virginia frontier. In the spring of 1774 the clashes between the whites and the red men grew so frequent that all backwoods settlements were alarmed. Cornstalk and his brother Silver Heels remained true to their parole and escorted several white traders to safety near the forts. Despite their neutrality, Silver Heels was fired upon as he went back, and was seriously wounded. Cornstalk sent messages to the governors of the neighboring colonies asking for a cessation of hostilities. Nevertheless, the disturbance grew until the governor of Virginia, Lord Dunmore, called out the militia and initiated the hostilities known as Dunmore's War. Cornstalk was compelled to yield to the exigencies of the time. He enrolled his warriors and led them against the western wing of Dunmore's army and fought on Oct. 10, 1774, the battle of Point Pleasant. The frontiersmen led by Col. Andrew Lewis drove back the Indians, not without considerable loss. Throughout the battle Cornstalk could be heard exhorting his warriors to stand.

Dunmore followed the retreating Indians to the plains of the Scioto, where the treaty of Camp Charlotte was made with Cornstalk, and reinforced the next year by a treaty at Fort Pitt. Cornstalk loyally kept his promise of alliance, and returned all white prisoners and stolen horses. In 1777 he went to the fort at the mouth of the Kanawha, where he had fought his battle three years earlier, to warn the whites that the Shawnee were about to take up arms at the instigation of British officers. Capt. Arbuckle thought best to detain him as a hostage. His son Elinipsico came on a visit to his father, when a soldier named Gilmore was shot from ambush. His enraged comrades rushed upon the hostages at the fort, and despite their officers' orders murdered them all. Cornstalk was brave until the last, exhorting his son to meet death as the Great Spirit willed it. Some of his murderers

fled the country to avoid prosecution; others were tried but acquitted. After the loss of their chief the Shawnee tribe became enemies of the whites for nearly a score of years. A monument to Cornstalk stands near the site of the fort where he met his death.

[The best account is in manuscript: Draper MSS. Wis. Hist. Lib. on which is based the sketch in the *Ohio Archaeol. and Hist. Quart.*, XXI, 245–62 (Apr.–July 1912). There are documents on Cornstalk's later career in R. G. Thwaites and L. P. Kellogg, *Documentary Hist. of Dunmore's War* (Madison, 1905); *Revolution on the Upper Ohio* (Madison, 1908); *Frontier Defense on the Upper Ohio* (Madison, 1912); also accounts of him in Jos. Doddridge, *Notes on Indian Wars* (Albany, 1876), pp. 239–41; Alex. S. Withers, *Chronicles of Border Warfare* (Cincinnati, 1895), pp. 172–73.]   L.P.K.

CORNWALLIS, KINAHAN (Dec. 24, 1839– Aug. 15, 1917), lawyer, editor, writer, was born in London, the son of Elizabeth and William Baxter Kinahan Cornwallis, barrister-at-law. Certain branches of the Cornwallis family were of Irish origin but Kinahan Cornwallis said of himself that he never saw or walked on Irish ground until he was fifteen and that his parents were not Irish, but English. After a collegiate education, while still very young, he entered the British Colonial Civil Service and spent two years in Melbourne, Australia. At this time and later he visited the Philippines, Singapore, Ceylon, Suez, Egypt, and various parts of Japan, Australia, Africa, South America, and Canada. In 1860 he came to New York and secured an editorial position on the *New York Herald*, where he continued until 1869, acting much of the time as financial editor. When the Prince of Wales, later Edward VII, visited the United States in 1860, Cornwallis was selected by the State Department, as a representative of the government, to accompany the Prince on his travels through the country. In 1863 he was admitted to the New York bar. He became editor and proprietor successively of the *Knickerbocker Magazine* and the *Albion* and from 1886 until about the time of his death was editor and proprietor of the *Wall Street Daily Investigator*, later the *Wall Street Daily Investor*. During all this time he successfully practised law, with offices in Nassau St. He was twice married: his first wife was Annie Louise Tisdale of New York, his second, Elizabeth Chapman of Hartford, Conn. Before coming to the United States, while still under twenty, Cornwallis had published several books. He continued writing at intervals, novels, verse, travels, history, and works on legal and financial subjects, until he was over sixty. His chief writings are: *Howard Plunkett* (1857), a novel; *An Australian Poem* (1857); *The New Eldorado, or British Columbia* (1858); *Two Jour-*

neys to Japan (1859); A Panorama of the New
World (1859); Wreck and Ruin (1858), a
novel; My Life and Adventures (1860); The
Crosstrees (1859), a medley; Royalty in the
New World (1860); Pilgrims of Fashion
(1862), a novel; Adrift with a Vengeance
(1865), a novel; The Gold Room and the New
York Stock Exchange and Clearing House
(1879); A Marvelous Coincidence (1891), a
novel; The History of Constructive Contempt
of Court (1892); International Law (1892);
Historical Poems (1892); The Song of America and Columbus (1892); The Conquest of
Mexico and Peru (1893); Two Strange Adventures (1897), a novel; and The War for the
Union (1899). When dealing with the New
York Stock Exchange or legal subjects, he
writes as something of an expert but as a historian his work would hardly be considered
scholarly. The institution of slavery, with all
its social results, and its downfall in the Civil
War period furnished material which he used
both in history and novels. His verse is negligible. His travels are interestingly written,
with original personal observations and much
humor. His novels, which he particularly enjoyed writing, are frankly modeled after the
picaresque romances of Sterne and Smollett.
They are stories of wanderings, hardships, and
adventures, melodramatic and frequently interrupted by pages of moralizing. His own travels
are utilized as backgrounds. At the time of his
death Cornwallis was living in East Twenty-
second St., New York City. He died, after a
short illness, at St. Luke's Hospital.

[The chief sources of information about Cornwallis
are: Who's Who in America, 1916–17; the prefaces of
his books; and his book My Life and Adventures which,
though fiction, contains much autobiographical material. An obituary notice appeared in the N. Y. Tribune,
Aug. 18, 1917, and an obituary article in the N. Y.
Times, Aug. 17, 1917.]   S. G. B.

CORONADO, FRANCISCO VÁZQUEZ
(1510–1554), explorer, governor of Nueva Galicia, was a native of Salamanca, Spain. There his
ancestors were Señores de Coquilla y de la
Torre de Juan Vázquez. He came to Mexico in
1535 in the retinue of Antonio de Mendoza, first
viceroy of New Spain. Two years later he married Beatriz de Estrada, "the Saint," daughter
of Alonso de Estrada, former treasurer of New
Spain. With Doña Beatriz he received as dowry an estate near Mexico City described as "the
half of Tlalpa." He took part in suppressing a
negro uprising in the mines of Amatepeque, and
in 1538 he became governor of Nueva Galicia.
In the same year he assisted Fray Marcos de
Nizza [q.v.] with an outfit for his northern ex-

plorations, and escorted him as far as Culiacán.
As governor he did much to improve his capital
city of Guadalajara.

When Fray Marcos returned from the Zuñi
pueblos in New Mexico, Coronado accompanied
him to Mexico City and was appointed commander of an expedition organized to follow up
the friar's explorations. To cooperate with Coronado, Hernando de Alarcón [q.v.], was sent
with two vessels up the Gulf of California. Viceroy Mendoza went in person to the rendezvous
at Compostela on the western coast to review
the forces. Coronado's following consisted of
some two hundred Spaniards on horseback, seventy foot-soldiers, and nearly one thousand Indian allies and servants. So eager were the volunteers that it was feared that the country would
be depopulated. The expedition was equipped at
royal expense with a thousand horses, mules
for pack-trains, cannons, and droves of cattle,
sheep, goats, and swine for food.

The start was made on Feb. 25, 1540. As far
as Culiacán the way was well known. From
there Coronado went ahead with about a hundred picked men and four friars. Following behind, the main army moved up to Corazones in
the Yaqui River valley, where the Spanish town
of San Gerónimo was founded and left in charge
of Melchior Díaz. In July Coronado reached
the Zuñi pueblos, which he conquered with little
difficulty. But the country was disappointing,
and the expedition resulted chiefly in explorations. These, however, were of great importance. Alarcón ascended the Colorado River,
passing the mouth of the Gila. Melchior Díaz
went by land from San Gerónimo to the Colorado
to communicate with Alarcón, but failed and lost
his life. During the journey, however, he crossed
the Colorado and went some distance down the
Peninsula of California. Hearing of the Moqui
pueblos to the north of Zuñi, in July Coronado
sent Pedro del Tovar to find them which the
latter succeeded in doing. Shortly afterward
Garcia Lopez de Cárdenas [q.v.] went further
northwest and discovered the Grand Canyon of
the Colorado. Moving to the Rio Grande, Coronado visited the pueblos in its valley and camped
at Tiguex, above Isleta. In the course of the
winter the Indians revolted and were put down
with great severity.

Meanwhile Coronado heard of a rich country
to the northeastward called Gran Quivira, and
in April 1541, he set out to find it. Crossing the
mountains and descending the Pecos River, he
marched out into the limitless buffalo-covered
plains, the "Llanos del Cíbola," inhabited by roving tribes. Near the upper Brazos River he

turned north, crossed the Texas Panhandle and Oklahoma, and reached Quivira in eastern Kansas. It was probably a settlement of Wichita Indians. Disappointed, he then returned to Mexico. Three fearless missionaries remained behind to preach the Gospel, and soon achieved the crown of martyrdom. Coronado had made one of the epochal explorations of all history but to Viceroy Mendoza he was a disappointing figure. Although he returned to his governorship of Nueva Galicia, his rule there was marked by numerous acts of cruelty to the natives which led to an investigation, conducted by Lorenzo de Tejada, in 1544. Coronado was found guilty of crimes and negligence, was removed from the governorship, and was fined 600 gold pesos. He then went back to Mexico City, where he spent the remainder of his days as a regidor in the municipal administration. His last public appearance was on Jan. 26, 1554 and he died sometime before Nov. 12, 1554.

[Coronado's lineage is treated in Alberto and Arturo García Carraffa, *Diccionario Heráldico y Genealógico de Apellidos Españoles y Americanos*, Tomo XXV, pp. 177–178 (Madrid, 1927). A great deal of light on his career in Mexico has been thrown recently by the researches of Dr. A. S. Aiton, whose results are summarized in his *Antonio de Mendoza* (Durham, N. C., 1927). See also "The Later Career of Coronado" by Dr. Aiton in *Am. Hist. Rev.*, XXX, 298–304 (Jan. 1925). The principal known source for the history of the Coronado expedition is the *Relación de la Jornada de Cíbola*, written several years after the event by Pedro de Castañeda, a member of the expedition. In 1896 this narrative was published in both Spanish and English, with an excellent historical introduction, by George Parker Winship ("The Coronado Expedition, 1540–1542," in the *Fourteenth Annual Report of the Bureau of Ethnology*, pp. 329–613). With the Castañeda narrative Winship published most of the supplementary documents then known. The *Relación* was reprinted in English by Winship in 1904 (*The Journey of Coronado, 1540–1542*); and by Frederick W. Hodge in 1907 (*Spanish Explorers in the Southern U. S., 1528–1543*).]   H. E. B.

CORRIGAN, MICHAEL AUGUSTINE (Aug. 13, 1839–May 5, 1902), archbishop of New York, was born in Newark, N. J., the fifth child in Thomas and Mary (English) Corrigan's household of nine. His father, a cabinetmaker, had emigrated from County Meath, Ireland, in 1828, and about the same time his mother had accompanied her Catholic mother from County Cavan to Newark on the death of her father, who was a member of an Irish Presbyterian family. Thomas Corrigan as a grocer and a frugal man of business made money which enabled him to give advantages to his family. Michael attended a local private school kept by his godfather, Bernard Kearney, a cultured Dublin emigrant, and served as an acolyte at St. John's Church under the distinguished Father Patrick Moran. Studying two years at St. Mary's College in

Wilmington, he proceeded to Mount St. Mary's College at Emmitsburg, Md. (1855), bearing a recommendation from Bishop James Roosevelt Bayley [*q.v.*], as "the son of one of our most respected Catholic citizens." His formal studies were interrupted in 1857 when he spent a year in European travel with his health-seeking sister, who later became an Augustinian nun. Returning to college with some linguistic attainment, Corrigan out-distanced his fellow students in classics and literature and was graduated in 1859. Experiencing a religious call, he was assigned by Bishop Bayley to the newly established American College at Rome as one of its first twelve seminarians. Here he was associated with students who were destined for high stations in the Catholic Church, among them Edward McGlynn [*q.v.*]. Completing the course in theology, he was ordained by Cardinal Patrizi at the Basilica of St. John Lateran (Sept. 19, 1863). A year later on the award of a doctorate from the College of the Propaganda, he was recalled by his ordinary to teach dogmatic theology and sacred scripture at Seton Hall Seminary, South Orange, N. J.

A conscientious teacher, Corrigan continued his studies and subjected himself to the rigorous seminary routine and table. Soon he was named director of the seminary and vice-president of the collegiate department, in this office displaying an unusual blend of strength and executive ability with an effeminate gentleness. In 1868, he succeeded to the presidency on the elevation of his intimate friend and superior, Bernard J. McQuaid [*q.v.*], to the see of Rochester. His brothers, Father James as director of the seminary and Dr. Joseph M. as school physician, assisted in the administration and joined him and Father George, another brother, who was pastor at St. Joseph's, Newark, in founding a Corrigan burse and in developing the library from their personal funds. Corrigan continued as president until 1876 and as a director until 1891. In 1868, he was named vicar-general and in this capacity administered the diocese while Bishop Bayley was at the Vatican Council and on his translation to Baltimore. Indeed Corrigan is said to have been considered for the bishopric of Columbus until the bishop of Newark insisted upon retaining his services.

Corrigan's nomination, therefore, to the see of Newark was no surprise, although he was opposed by Bayley and other bishops on the score of youth, until Bishop McQuaid with characteristic vigor maintained that "they had little comprehension of the capacity and learning and strength of will-power of that mere boy." At all events, his appointment as bishop of Newark by Pius IX was well received by the bishops of the province and the clergy and laity of the diocese, and he was consecrated (May 4, 1873) in St. Patrick's, Newark, by Archbishop Mc-Closkey. For seven years, he administered the diocese which included all of New Jersey. Through the Catholic Union, a religious fraternity, he sought in vain for Catholic freedom of worship in state reform schools, though ultimately the state accepted the principle and named Catholic chaplains in penal and charitable institutions. Thereupon, the bishop built the St. Francis Catholic Protectory for boys at Denville (1874) and established a Good Shepherd home for girls in Newark (1875). Keenly interested in dependents, he founded a newsboys' lodging house. An authority on questions of morals, rubrics, and canon law, he was frequently consulted by various bishops, and he spent some time systematizing the Baltimore archdiocesan records. Calling synods (1878, 1879), he amended and enforced the regulations of his diocese, and thereafter by visitation and inspection kept a methodical record of ecclesiastical affairs, annual parochial reports, and finances. Through his aid and personal contributions, the tremendous debt on the poorly administered parish of St. John's in Orange was lessened and ultimately fully met. In 1875, he ordered a census of Italians whose confessions he was compelled to hear himself because of a lack of Italian-speaking priests. Interested in Catholic education, he aided the Jesuits in establishing a college in Jersey City, fostered academies, orphanages, and hospitals, and compelled pastors in the larger parishes to build schools. In 1874, he encouraged a lay pilgrimage to Rome, the first of its kind from the United States. With an increase of churches and chapels from 121 to 182, the diocese of Newark thrived under Bishop Corrigan's direction.

Meanwhile Cardinal McCloskey counseled with his suffragan bishops concerning a coadjutor with the right of succession, and they agreed upon Corrigan who was forthwith named by Rome with the title of Archbishop of Petra (Oct. 1, 1880). Apparently, Corrigan was loath to undertake the enlarged responsibilities, but he followed the call of duty. In September of 1883, he attended the fourth provincial council of New York for which he had helped prepare the schema, and, in November on a papal invitation, he accompanied a number of American archbishops to Rome to help prepare for the Third Plenary Council of Baltimore, at which he later represented the cardinal. As Cardinal Mc-Closkey's agent, he preserved the American College at Rome from Italian confiscation through skilful negotiations with President Arthur and his friend, Secretary Frelinghuysen (1884). On the death of the Cardinal, Corrigan automatically became archbishop of New York (Oct. 10, 1885), though he was not formally installed by Cardinal Gibbons until May 4, 1886.

Almost immediately Archbishop Corrigan, a conservative, a strict canonist, and a stalwart patron of parochial schools, came into conflict with Father McGlynn of St. Stephen's Church, who disapproved of separate schools, actively interested himself in the Anti-Poverty Society, and associated with advanced social and political thinkers including Henry George whose candidacy for mayor he openly supported. On Jan. 14, 1887, Corrigan removed McGlynn from his pastorate. McGlynn, summoned to Rome, refused on the score of health to make the journey, and was excommunicated, July 4, 1887. Archbishop Corrigan was named "prelate assistant at pontifical throne" as a defender of the faith. McGlynn had strong supporters among the clergy and laity, and as a martyr won outside sympathy, though the press and conservatives supported Corrigan's drastic action. In 1892, Father McGlynn was restored after his economic views had been considered by four professors at the Catholic University and after a hearing before Mgr. Satolli, papal delegate, who had been authorized to settle current disputes between priests and their bishops. On Aug. 15, 1893, Corrigan, in the presence of the delegate, preached a sermon in St. Patrick's Cathedral in which he emphasized his loyalty to the Holy See, thus closing the lips of aggressive critics. McGlynn was assigned to St. Mary's Church at Newburgh (1895), though he continued to be Henry George's friend and was his eulogist at the grave (1897). As Corrigan's severity was due to the rigidity of over-zealousness, rather than personal bitterness, he learned to forget, even presiding over Father McGlynn's requiem mass (1900).

Archbishop Corrigan's lack of interest in the Ancient Order of Hibernians, his faint sympathy for Irish nationalism, and his strict definition of the rule concerning secret societies, which would prevent Catholic membership in the Odd Fellows, Knights of Pythias, and Sons of Temperance as well as in the Free Masons, annoyed various elements. He had no sympathy with Archbishop John Ireland's Faribault experiment. He was quite annoyed by the assistance which Archbishop Ireland gave to the candidacy of Father Sylvester L. Malone for a vacant regency of the State University of New York when he himself favored the selection of Bishop McQuaid, his counselor and life-long friend. Unfortunately these difficulties of Corrigan have been emphasized in the popular mind rather than his successful administration of the great archdiocese with its tremendous problems. A great builder and a careful administrator, Corrigan in his last days could look over his diocese of 1,200,000 communicants and note the advance: churches, chapels, and stations had increased by 188, priests by 284, schools by 75, and charitable institutions (as hospitals, industrial homes, schools for the blind and deaf mutes) by 25. Better still he left an harmonious priesthood and hence a contented flock, who, however, were somewhat disappointed that their bishop had not received the cardinalate. Contracting a cold on a visitation in the Bahamas, Corrigan died, after a short illness, on May 5, 1902.

[Corrigan maintained a voluminous correspondence, but there are no literary published remains save a register of the clergy laboring in the archdiocese from the earliest missionary times to 1885 (*U. S. Cath. Hist. Soc. Records and Studies*, III, 9–13), an occasional printed sermon, pastoral letters, and a manual, *Praxis Synodalist.* For biographical references see J. A. Mooney, *Memorial to M. A. Corrigan* (1902); *Souvenir of the New Seminary of St. Joseph* (1891); J. M. Flynn, *The Cath. Ch. in N. J.* (1904); P. V. Flynn, *Hist. of St. John's Ch., Newark* 1908); H. A. Brann, *History of the American College, Rome* (1910); J. T. Smith, *The Cath. Ch. in N. Y.* (1905); Jas. Cardinal Gibbons, *A Retrospect of Fifty Years* (1916); J. M. Farley, *Life of John Cardinal McCloskey* (1918); S. L. Malone, *Dr. Edward McGlynn* (1918); *U. S. Cath. Hist. Soc. Records and Studies*, I, 14–17; *Catholic Univ. Bull.* (1902); *Harper's Weekly*, XLVI, 610; *Cath. World*, LXXV, 282; *Ecclesiastical Rev.*, XXVI, 642; *Chicago Post*, Jan. 8, 1893.]   R.J.P.

CORROTHERS, JAMES DAVID (July 2, 1869–Feb. 12, 1917), clergyman, poet, was born in Calvin, Mich., and died in West Chester, Pa. His mother, Maggie Churchman, was part negro and part French, and his father, James Richard Corrothers, had a negro mother. The boy was reared by his father's father, whose ancestry was Indian and Scotch-Irish. His upbringing, which involved nine years in the South Haven, Mich., public schools, was penurious but extremely pious. He worked at many tasks for little money, from sailor on Lake Michigan to boot-black in a hotel. His ambitious determination at length attracted the patronage of some white friends, among whom was Frances E. Willard, and he was enabled to spend some time at Northwestern University. He taught school, and under the influence of his friend, Paul Laurence Dunbar, composed dialect verse which was published chiefly in the *Century Magazine*. He wrote for various newspapers, among others for the *Chicago Journal*, for which he did a series of humorous negro "reports" later published in book

form as *The Black Cat Club* (1902). "A sunburst having fallen upon his being," he entered the ministry, and in this capacity traveled over a fair portion of the United States and observed something of its inhabitants. At first he was Methodist, but after some years he was expelled from this body—unjustly, he maintained—on a charge of having "plotted to ruin his bishop's good name." Then he became a Baptist. At last, "for conscience sake, convinced that his race needed religious training along the higher lines," he became a Presbyterian. In 1916 he published an autobiography, *In Spite of the Handicap*. He was at heart an earnest, sentimental American who assumed until he died the ascendency of a social order which even in his youth had passed its zenith. For all his being a spokesman for the negro, the people to whom he attached most importance were usually white—dealers in general merchandise, as likely as not, in a Virginia village. New England as he knew it was disillusioning—ignorant, he complained, of Whittier and Emerson, filled up with "a large and assertive foreign population which has not imbibed any other than the coarser Americanisms." He was married first to Fannie Clemens and later to Rosina Harvey.

[Sources not already referred to: J. D. Corrothers, "Thanksgiving Turkey," *Century Mag.*, Nov. 1900; "Ha'nts," *Century Mag.*, Dec. 1903; M. N. Work, *Negro Year Book*, 1918–19; *Who's Who in America*, 1906–07.]   J.D.W.

CORSE, JOHN MURRAY (Apr. 27, 1835–Apr. 27, 1893), Union general, was born at Pittsburgh, Pa., of Huguenot ancestry. His parents, John L. and Sarah (Murray) Corse, removed in 1842 to Burlington, Ia., where the father was six times mayor. Young Corse was employed, and afterward became a partner, in his father's book and stationery business. At the same time he studied law, and was admitted to the bar. He took an active part in politics, and in spite of his youth received the Democratic nomination for secretary of state of Iowa in 1860, but was defeated. He was appointed major of the 6th Iowa Infantry, July 13, 1861, and served as inspector-general on Pope's staff during the operations at New Madrid and Island No. 10. Promoted to lieutenant-colonel, May 21, 1862, he took command of his regiment, to the colonelcy of which he was promoted, Mar. 29, 1863. In the Corinth and Vicksburg campaigns he established a reputation for able leadership and conspicuous courage, and was appointed brigadier-general of volunteers, Aug. 11, 1863. Desperately wounded at Missionary Ridge, Nov. 25, 1863, he was sent home to recover. Rejoining the army in time for the Atlanta campaign, he acted as Sherman's inspector-general until July 26, 1864, when he was put in command of a division. In October, while Sherman was preparing for his march to the sea, and Hood moved northward to cut his communications, Sherman ordered Corse to hasten to Allatoona Pass and hold it until the army could be brought to its relief. Arriving in the morning of Oct. 5, Corse found himself in command of some 2,000 men, to defend the post against French's division, which was closing around it. To French's demand for an unconditional surrender, "to avoid a needless effusion of blood," Corse replied that "we are prepared for the needless effusion of blood whenever it is agreeable to you." Corse says the fighting which ensued "was of the most extraordinary character"; French calls the battle "one of the most sanguinary conflicts of the war." In spite of the loss of one-third of his command, Corse held out, repelling all attacks, till late afternoon, when news of the approach of the relieving force caused French to withdraw. Corse himself was badly wounded and lay insensible for half an hour, but resumed command as soon as he recovered consciousness, and next day sent the triumphant message, "I am short a cheekbone and one ear, but am able to whip all hell yet." Meanwhile, Sherman had been advancing in great anxiety, for communication had failed for several hours. During the morning, however, a staff officer caught the flicker of a signal flag, and spelled out the message, "We hold out. Corse here," and in the afternoon came news that the attack was repulsed. Sherman issued a general order offering the thanks of the army to the defenders. The hymn, "Hold the Fort" (written by Philip P. Bliss [*q.v.*]), was inspired by this fight at Allatoona, one of the most dramatic incidents of the war. Corse served in the march to the sea and the Carolina campaign; was mustered out, Apr. 30, 1866, declining an offered appointment as lieutenant-colonel in the regular army; and became collector of internal revenue in Chicago. For some years after, he was engaged in railroad and bridge construction. Removing to Massachusetts, he resumed active political work, and was chairman of the State Democratic Committee. As postmaster of Boston during Cleveland's first administration his efficient conduct of the office made it known as the "model office of the United States." He died at Winchester, Mass., and was buried at Burlington. He was twice married: first, in 1856, to Ellen Edwards Prince, and second, in 1882, to Frances McNeil, a niece of Franklin Pierce.

[A biography by Wm. Salter was published in *Annals of Iowa*, vol. II (1895), pp. 1–19, 105–45, 278–304. See also *Official Records* (*Army*), 1 ser., vols. XXIV (pt. 2), XXX (pts. 3, 4), XXXI (pt. 2), XXXII (pt. 3), XXXVIII (pts. 3, 4, 5), XXXIX (pts. 1, 2, 3), XLIV, XLVII (pts. 1, 2, 3); *Battles and Leaders of the Civil War* (1887–88), IV, 322–25.]   T. M. S.

CORSON, HIRAM (Nov. 6, 1828–June 15, 1911), teacher, author, was born in Philadelphia, Pa., and died in Ithaca, N. Y. Until he was fifteen, his education was conducted by his parents, Joseph Dickinson and Ann Hagey Corson, and from fifteen to twenty he attended schools in Montgomery County, Pa. He was notably proficient in mathematics and in classical languages. When twenty-one, he went to Washington, to become for a short time a reporter in the Senate, and later for about seven years, a librarian in the Smithsonian Institution. His associations in the library and his marriage in Boston in 1854 to Caroline Rollin, an erudite lady of European education, stimulated his interest in modern literatures. From 1859 to 1865 he was an unattached lecturer and private teacher in Philadelphia. He did not take part in the Civil War, but at its conclusion, he published, "for the use of the Southern freedmen," *A Revised Edition of Jaudon's English Orthographical Expositor* (1866). During 1865–66 he was professor of moral science, history, and rhetoric in Girard College; from 1866 to 1870, professor of rhetoric and English literature in St. John's College, Annapolis; and from 1870 to 1903, when he was made professor emeritus, he taught literature at Cornell. In the many books which he wrote or edited between 1863 and 1899 he dealt with most of the great phases of English letters. His most important writings were perhaps his critical volumes, *An Introduction to the Study of Robert Browning's Poetry* (1886) and *An Introduction to the Study of Shakespeare* (1889), his *Primer of English Verse* (1892), and, above all, his *Aims of Literary Study* (1895). Through all his scholarly work he insisted on two things as necessary for a true understanding of literature— a disciplined use of the human voice, and a recognition that philosophic and esthetic elements in literature must take precedence over elements that are wholly technical. Among his contemporaries, some of the teachers of literature who considered themselves most advanced believed apparently that his contention relative to beauty in speech was too trivial for notice; and his contention upholding the spirit as against the technique of art was too often the object of their ridicule. Championing his side of this debate firmly —in his writings as well as in his lectures at Cornell, Johns Hopkins, and elsewhere—he induced at last, or helped to induce, a real and valuable, if meager, shift of emphasis in the public estimate of these matters. He knew many distinguished people intimately, among them Walt Whitman, whom he defended when such defense was still dangerously irregular. One of the earliest ardent admirers of Browning, he organized numerous Browning clubs throughout America, and in 1882 lectured before the Browning Society of London, to the high approval of the poet himself. He did not limit his attention purely to letters. He was a zealous opponent of slavery; he publicly deprecated many aspects of organized religion (Corson, *Spirit Messages,* pp. 8, 99); he was strenuously apprehensive of the social effects of concentrated wealth; and as early as 1874, he wrote for a Cornell student publication an essay avowing his faith in spiritualism. This faith grew with years into a dominant passion. He reserved a room in his house for the portraits of people whom he had loved and who were dead, and before each portrait he kept always an offering of flowers. It pleased him to think that disembodied spirits were likely to be about him at any moment. His book, *Spirit Messages,* published posthumously in 1911, sets forth the result of twenty-four daily seances between himself and a ghostly but convivial and extremely famous group organized by his wife in 1901 soon after her death.

[Important sources not already mentioned: H. Corson, *Corson Family* (1906); *Who's Who in America,* 1910–11; *N. Y. Times,* June 16, 17, 1911; *N. Y. Tribune,* June 16, 1911; Murray E. Poole, *A Story Historical of Cornell Univ. with Biogs. of Distinguished Cornellians* (1916); W. T. Hewett, *Cornell Univ., A History,* II (1905), pp. 36–47.]   J. D. W.

CORSON, JULIET (Feb. 14, 1842–June 18, 1897), pioneer teacher of cooking, was born in Roxbury, Mass., the daughter of Peter R. and Mary Ann (Henderson) Corson. When she was six years old her parents moved to New York City. Too delicate to attend school regularly, she spent much of the next ten years in the home of her uncle, Dr. Alfred Upham, in whose library she became well acquainted with Greek and Roman history and classical poetry. Soon after her mother's death, when she was eighteen years old, she started to earn her own living. After assisting in a teaching agency for a short time, she obtained the post of librarian in the Working Women's Library in the New York University building. The pay was very small and she added to her income by writing poems and sketches for various newspapers. She wrote a weekly article for the *New York Leader* and was employed to prepare the half-yearly index of the *National Quarterly Review,* where her work so pleased the editor that she was given a place upon the staff of the publication. Her career as teacher of cooking grew out of her interest in the Free

Training School for Women, which was opened in 1873 in her own home. At first only free instruction in sewing was given, but the institution proved so popular that it was soon moved to larger quarters and the curriculum enlarged to include bookkeeping, short-hand, and proof-reading. Miss Corson saw the need for training in cooking also and set about fitting herself to teach that science. A chef was hired to demonstrate to the classes while she explained the theory.

In 1876, she opened a school of her own in St. Mark's Place, where she taught paying classes and also gave free instruction. Her lessons attracted much attention and in 1878 she was commissioned by John Eaton, United States Commissioner of Education, to prepare a circular for the Bureau of Education on the history and management of cooking schools in Europe and the United States. The following year he arranged for her to lecture before the Training School for Nurses in Washington, D. C., and later, under his patronage, she addressed groups in many other cities, making one trip to the Pacific coast.

Probably the first lessons in cooking given in a public school on this continent were given by Miss Corson in a six weeks' course to high-school girls in Montreal in 1880. There, for the first time, she did the cooking herself, the chef having failed to appear, and thereafter, finding that it appealed to her audience, she always did her own demonstrating. While eager to increase the general knowledge of scientific cookery, her chief interest, always, was in teaching the women of the poorer classes how to prepare nourishing yet inexpensive food. With that end in view, she published, in 1877, *Fifteen Cent Dinners for Workingmen's Families,* and distributed 50,000 copies free, chiefly at her own expense. Always on her lecture tours she gave free lessons to those who could not afford to pay for instruction. In her *Cooking Manual* (1877), which ran into several editions, she said she had endeavored to answer the question of the hour, "How well can we live if we are moderately poor?" (1886 edition), and in 1887 she published *Family Living on $500 a Year.* The material in this book was derived from a series of articles on "Sanitary Living" which appeared in *Harper's Bazar,* 1882–84. Her writings received much favorable comment and her lectures were exceedingly popular. In 1880, the French government requested her to prepare a plan of work and list of books for use in the schools of France. For a few months in 1890–91, she was editor of the *Household Monthly.* At the World's Columbian Exposition in Chicago, she was awarded the prize for scientific cookery and sanitary dietetics. The last years of her life were devoted chiefly to literary work, most of it done in an invalid's chair. She died in New York City and was buried in Greenwood Cemetery.

[Alice Chittenden, "Records of a Busy Life," in *Household Mo.*, Feb., Mar., and Apr. 1890; "The New York Cooking School," in *Harper's Mag.*, Dec. 1879; obituary in *N. Y. Times*, June 20, 1897.]   B.R.

CORSON, ROBERT RODGERS (May 3, 1831–Feb. 19, 1904), merchant, humanitarian, was born at New Hope, Pa., a descendant of Cornelius Corson of Staten Island, who was born in France but emigrated to New York with other Huguenots and was commissioned a justice of the peace and captain of foot (*Calendar of Historical Manuscripts in the Office of the Secretary of State, Albany, N. Y.*, 1865–66). Benjamin Corson, a son of Cornelius and Maritie, his wife, moved from Staten Island to Bucks County, Pa., in 1726, taking with him Benjamin Corson II. From the latter was descended Dr. Richard D. Corson of New Hope, Bucks County, who married Helen Stockton Johnson of Princeton, N. J. Dr. Corson became well-known in his locality as a medical practitioner and as an instructor of medical students who studied under his direction and rode with him in his medical circuits. His son, Robert Rodgers Corson, was educated in the local schools at New Hope and in the Tremount Seminary at Norristown, Pa. At nineteen years of age he went to Pottsville to learn the business of mining and selling coal. In 1856, having leased a coal-mine near Pottsville, he moved to Philadelphia and became active as a coal merchant and shipper, operating three wharves on the Schuylkill. He married Rebecca J. Foulke of Penllyn District, who later shared his humanitarian labors. They had no children. At the outbreak of the Civil War the Union soldiers were largely assembled at and near Philadelphia. With others, Corson established the Union Volunteer Refreshment Saloon and served as its corresponding secretary. The United States government established its military hospitals at Philadelphia, and the activity of Corson in the visitation of the sick soldiers, and his ministrations to the army were of such importance that he was commissioned State Agent by the governors of Connecticut, Indiana, Massachusetts, Maine, Wisconsin, Vermont, New Jersey, New Hampshire, Rhode Island, Delaware, and Maryland. The resolution of the Rhode Island Assembly in January 1866 expressing thanks for his devotion to the interests of "our soldiers," and the Massachusetts General Order No. 13 of July 20, 1865, thanking Corson for his "kindness in watching over the sick and wounded soldiers from this state" are typical of the contemporary appreciation of this work. Cor-

son's little volume, *A Soldiers' Guide,* containing local addresses of army officials, railroad schedules, etc., seems to have been his only publication. It was distributed freely by the Committee of the Union Volunteer Refreshment Saloon. Corson recruited some 14,000 colored troops into the Union service without cost to the Government. He was a member of the Union League of Philadelphia from Feb. 20, 1864, to Sept. 25, 1883, when he resigned. His interests in humanitarian effort were extensive. He served as secretary to the Freedmen's Relief Association, as treasurer of the Association for the Prevention of Cruelty to Animals, as director and treasurer of the Citizens Municipal Reform Association, as inspector for the Deaf and Dumb, for the State of Pennsylvania. His interest in prison reform resulted in his appointment as inspector to the Moyamensing Prison. He took an active part in the work of the Philadelphia Society for Organizing Charity, and various other Philadelphia welfare works. In 1881 he became interested in the Luray Caverns in Virginia. Under his management electric lights were introduced into the caverns and the Luray Inn was built. He later returned to Philadelphia, where he died.

[Hiram Corson, *The Corson Family* (1906), pp. 22, 25, 163–65; *Who's Who in Pa.*, 1904; Frank H. Taylor, *Phila. in the Civil War* (1913), pp. 207, 208, and 224; note of death in *Public Ledger* (Phila.), Feb. 20, 1904.]   B.C.

CORTAMBERT, LOUIS RICHARD (1808– Mar. 28, 1881), author, journalist, was born in Paris, France, the son of a physician. He emigrated to the United States as a youth, making St. Louis his home in the thirties, where he married Susan, daughter of Auguste P. Chouteau [*q.v.*], and became French vice-consul, resigning, however, in 1851 as a protest against the *coup d'état.* From 1855 to 1858 he edited in St. Louis *La Revue de l'Ouest,* a weekly French newspaper. He was an abolitionist, and his philosophy in many respects resembled that of Thoreau. He sought to duplicate Thoreau's Walden experience, but Walden near Concord and the Illinois lowlands differed, and malaria aided in ending Cortambert's experiment. From 1864 to 1881 he edited in New York City *Le Messager Franco-Américain,* a daily French newspaper. He wrote numerous books in his native tongue and came to be regarded by many as the most distinguished writer in French in the United States. To his *Histoire Universelle Selon la Science Moderne* (Paris, 1879), Henri Martin the historian wrote a preface; and Victor Hugo praised his *Religion du Progrès* (New York, 1884). Among his other works are: *Voyage aux Pays des Osages* (Paris, 1847); *Les Trois Époques du Catholicisme*

(Paris, 1849); *Le Catéchisme Rationaliste* (St. Louis, 1855). Jointly with F. de Tranaldos, he wrote: *Le Général Grant: Esquisse Biographique* (New York, 1868) and *L'Histoire de la Guerre Civile Américaine* (Paris, 1867). His *Général Grant* is an enthusiastic, laudatory biography of Grant as a soldier. The two-volume *Histoire de la Guerre Civile Américaine* was written entirely from the Union side as far as sympathy is concerned. Both books are vivid in style, the work of an advocate rather than a historian. Cortambert frequently lectured in French in New York and in Canada. Dr. Alexander N. De Menil, a nephew, described him as a tall, solemn, dignified man, generally dressed in black, adding: "He always seemed to be in a meditative mood, even while on the streets. He was a handsome man, but his solemnity repelled in spite of his courteousness." Cortambert was the brother of Eugene Cortambert, the noted French geographer, and the uncle of Richard Cortambert, a promising young author who died in his early thirties.

[*Encyc. Hist. Mo.*, II (1901), 141–42; *Encyc. of the Hist. of St. Louis* (1899), I, 489; *Mo. Hist. Rev.*, Oct. 1920, pp. 82–83; personal letters.]   W. W.

CORTHELL, ELMER LAWRENCE (Sept. 30, 1840–May 16, 1916), civil engineer, was born in South Abington (now Whitman), Mass., the son of James Lawrence and Mary Gurney Corthell. He prepared for college at the South Abington high school and the Phillips Exeter Academy and then entered Brown University in 1859. At the outbreak of the Civil War he enlisted as a private in the 1st Rhode Island Artillery, serving for the period of the war. He left the army with the rank of captain to return to Brown, from which he was graduated in 1867, taking the degree of M.A. a year later. He was married in 1870 to Emily Theodate Davis of Providence, R. I. She died in 1884, and in 1900 Corthell married Marie Küchler of Berne, Switzerland.

In his youth it was Corthell's desire and intention to become a Baptist minister. Ill health made it advisable, however, for him to enter a more active profession, and he chose civil engineering. He found employment with Samuel Barrett Cushing, a prominent engineer of Providence, and began what proved to be all but a half-century's work devoted to engineering in its various fields and on two continents. His great contribution was the improvement of transportation facilities and at the same time the reduction of transportation costs. In 1868 he was assistant engineer on the construction of the Hannibal & Naples Railroad in Illinois—now a part of the Wabash System—and a year later was engineer on the location and construction of the Han-

nibal & Missouri Railroad. In 1871 he began his work in connection with the levees along the Mississippi River. He was chief engineer of the Sny Island Levee, fifty-one miles in length, and then became assistant to James B. Eads [*q.v.*] in the construction of the jetties at the South Pass mouth of the river. Ill health forced him to go north again in 1880. During his convalescence he wrote his *History of the Jetties at the Mouth of the Mississippi River* (1880).

Some construction work for the New York, West Shore & Buffalo Railroad Company was followed, in 1884, by Corthell's association with Eads in the promotion of the Tehuantepec Ship Railway. In exploiting this railway he visited various cities of the United States and exhibited perfect working models of the railroad and a ship being placed in its cradle on the rails. By this time he had established himself as a consulting engineer and was variously engaged on the construction of railroads, bridges, and harbors all over the country. He was engineer in charge of the design and construction of the substructure and foundation of the St. Louis Merchants' Bridge over the Mississippi, and acted as special consultant in charge of the terminal work in Chicago for the Chicago, Madison & Northern Railroad. In 1889 he examined and submitted plans and a report on an improvement of the harbor at Tampico, Mexico, for the Mexican Central Railroad; later he was chief engineer for the construction of their jetties.

In 1891 Corthell went to Europe to study engineering education as it was administered in the leading universities and technical schools there. This was in conjunction with his work as a trustee of the University of Chicago. He also examined European railroad terminals and harbors in order to fit himself better for solving problems in the United States and Mexico. He revisited Europe in 1897. The results of his investigations were published in the *Engineering Magazine* and presented in a paper which he read before the Fiftieth Anniversary Meeting of the American Association for the Advancement of Science held in Boston in 1898. In 1900 he sailed for Buenos Aires where, for the Argentine minister of public works, he investigated and reported on many problems pertaining to commerce. A few years later he was engaged on important commercial works in Brazil, at Para, and in other South American cities. He maintained his consulting engineering office in New York City.

Corthell was representative for the Department of State of the United States at the International Engineering Congress in Brussels. It was he who suggested and then acted as chairman of the executive committee having charge of the International Engineering Congress held during the Columbian Exposition. He was active in advancing the interests of the national technical and scientific societies and his printed papers on engineering subjects fill many volumes. He had boundless enthusiasm and industry, and was generous not only with advice but with financial aid to younger members of his profession.

[Files of the Am. Soc. of Civil Engineers; *Trans. Am. Soc. Civil Engineers*, vol. LXXXI (1917); *Engineering News*, Feb. 3, 1916; *Who's Who in America*, 1916–17.]

E. Y.

CORWIN, EDWARD TANJORE (July 12, 1834–June 22, 1914), clergyman, historian, was born in New York City, son of Edward Callwell and Mary Ann (Shuart) Corwin. He traced his ancestry to Matthias Corwin, an Englishman who first settled at Ipswich, Mass. (*c.* 1634), and subsequently moved to Southold, L. I. On his mother's side he was related to the Dutch founders of New York. He was graduated from the College of the City of New York in 1853, and from the New Brunswick Theological Seminary three years later. After a year spent in special linguistic studies he was ordained as a minister in the Reformed Church of America (Dutch) in 1857, and was pastor successively at Paramus, N. J., Millstone, N. J., where he spent twenty-five years, and Greenport, N. Y. In an interval of seven years between the last two pastorates he was rector of Hertzog Hall at the Reformed Church Seminary at New Brunswick, N. J. He was married on July 25, 1881 to Mary Esther Kipp at Geneva, N. Y. In each of his pastorates he became immediately interested in local church and town history, an avocation that resulted in the publication of *Manual and Record of Church of Paramus* (1858), *The Millstone Centennial* (1866), and *General Ecclesiastical History of Columbia County, N. Y. on Occasion of the 60th Anniversary of the Church of Greenport, N. Y.* (1896). Research in a wider field enabled him to bring out *A Manual of the Reformed Protestant Dutch Church in North America* (1859), a revised and enlarged *Manual* a decade later, and two subsequent editions (1879 and 1902). A fifth edition, published in 1922, was dedicated to his memory. When a history of the Reformed Church, Dutch, was desired for the American Church History Series, Corwin was selected to write it (see Volume VIII of the Series). These historical instincts coupled with a genius for hard work finally resulted in *The Ecclesiastical Records of the State of New York* (7 vols., 1901–16). Corwin had been commissioned in 1897 by the General Synod

of the Reformed Church to explore ecclesiastical archives in Holland. His report of his findings at Amsterdam and The Hague revealed so much of historic value that the New York legislature, in 1899, made an appropriation for the publication of the records under the general direction of the state historian with Corwin as editor. The Index Volume to this work, which was long delayed, represents the painstaking activity of Corwin's last years; he did not live to see it in print.

[An autobiographical sketch together with a list of Corwin's writings, in *Manual of the Reformed Ch. in America* (4th ed., 1902), pp. 394–95, and a sketch written by Corwin's son, Chas. E. Corwin, in *Eccl. Records of the State of N. Y.*, VII, 9–11, are the best sources of information. For Corwin's research work in Holland see *Eccl. Records*, vol. I (Introduction) and *Report of the General Synod's Agent on his Searches in the Eccl. Archives of Holland*, 1897–98. *The Manual of the Reformed Ch. in America* (5th ed., 1922), is dedicated to him as the "Founder of the Manual," and has his portrait as a frontispiece. See also obituaries in the *Christian Intelligencer*, June 24 and July 1, 1914. His ancestry is traced in *Corwin Geneal. in the U. S.* (1872), compiled by Corwin himself.]

A. E. P.

CORWIN, THOMAS (July 29, 1794–Dec. 18, 1865), governor of Ohio, senator, secretary of the Treasury, traced his ancestry to Matthias Corwin who settled in Ipswich, Mass., about 1634. When Matthias Corwin, a descendant of the first Matthias, settled at Lebanon, Ohio, in 1798, he had only $100 with which to buy a farm, but he possessed qualities of mind and character which brought him to the speakership of the state Assembly, and endowed his children with an excellent inheritance. His wife, Patience Halleck, is reputed to have been a person of marked intellectuality. Thomas, their fifth child, born in Bourbon County, Ky., early exhibited bookish tendencies which the father did little to encourage, less, it appears, through lack of sympathy than through lack of means. From his large family he selected an older son to be educated as a lawyer, leaving Thomas to acquire what learning he could by the diligent use of a scanty leisure and his brother's books. At twenty-one, Thomas began to read law and in due course was admitted to the bar. In 1822 he married Sarah Ross, daughter of a congressman, related on her mother's side to the Randolphs of Virginia. He was elected to the General Assembly in 1821, 1822, and 1829, and became a supporter, in national politics, of the Clay-Adams group, by this path passing into the Whig party. Following Jackson's election, Corwin's party put him forward in his home district, a community favorable to Jackson, as its strongest candidate for Congress, and elected him with one-fourth more votes than his opponent received. During a decade in Congress, a period of Democratic control, his speeches, although infrequent, made an excellent impression. Most notable of these was his reply to Gen. Isaac Crary (Feb. 15, 1840).

His canvass for governor in 1840 made him famous as a campaign orator. He won by a majority of 16,000, but was defeated in 1842, in consequence of party strife over matters for which he had slight responsibility, and he refused renomination in 1844. He campaigned actively for Clay, however, on the Texas issue. The Whigs lost the presidency, but, regaining control of the Ohio legislature, sent Corwin to the United States Senate. Here, during the Mexican War, he reached the climax of his career. Convinced that the war was waged for territory, he besought Webster and Crittenden to stand with him against further appropriations. When they failed him, he pursued his opposition alone, delivering a powerful speech on Feb. 11, 1847, in which he denounced the war as unjust, and with prophetic vision as well as eloquence predicted the sectional conflict which would follow the acquisition of Mexican territory. A few radicals talked of him for the presidency, but most Whigs as well as Democrats regarded such sentiments uttered in actual time of war as traitorous. Petitions to the legislature, however, demanding that his resignation be required, brought forth as a committee report a resolution of confidence.

Taylor's death brought Fillmore to office and Corwin to the post of secretary of the Treasury; this he filled without distinction, retiring with his chief in 1853. As the slavery controversy developed, he reluctantly abandoned the Whig party, being elected to the House in 1858 as a Republican, although he did not wholly accept the party program. He advocated the abolition of slavery in the territories, but upheld the right of each new state to decide the slavery question for itself. After Lincoln's election, he earnestly sought means of allaying the fears of the South, and served as chairman of the House committee of thirty-three. As minister to Mexico during the critical years 1861–64, he filled acceptably his last public office. Returning to Washington, he opened a law office, but died only a few months later.

Corwin's face was remarkably expressive, and his voice, although neither deep nor powerful, was musical and far-reaching. As a lawyer he was brilliant rather than learned; politics diverted his attention from profound study. A natural wit, he came to believe that fun-making had hampered his career, but his brilliant satire seldom left a sting. Though not a church member, he was permanently influenced by the religious atmosphere in which he was reared. His speeches are saturated with Biblical allusions and quotations. His chief fault was laxity in financial affairs. He was careless in collecting fees, and during most of his life was handicapped by a burden of debt. After leaving the cabinet he was impoverished by an unfortunate investment in railway stocks. He suffered loss frequently through becoming surety. He was much loved, and nowhere more so than at home and by his neighbors, for he was kind and generous.

[See E. T. Corwin, *Corwin Geneal. in the U. S.* (1872); Josiah Morrow, *Life and Speeches of Thos. Corwin* (1896); Addison Peale Russell, *Thos. Corwin, A Sketch* (1882), a somewhat laudatory character study containing valuable anecdotal material. Some sidelights are provided by letters of Thos. Corwin to Wm. Greene, 1841–51, in "Selections from the Wm. Greene Papers," ed. by L. Belle Hamlin, in *Hist. and Philosophical Soc. of Ohio Quart. Pub.*, vol. XIII (1918). See also *Speeches of Thos. Corwin with a Sketch of his Life* (1859), ed. by Isaac Strohm; *Ohio Hist. and Philosophical Soc. Quart. Pub.*, vol. IX (1914). The Lib. of Cong. has twelve volumes of Corwin Papers covering the years of Corwin's term as secretary of the Treasury.]   H. C. H.

CORY, CHARLES BARNEY (Jan. 31, 1857–July 29, 1921), ornithologist and author, was, throughout the greater part of his life, contrary to the usual lot of scientific men, surrounded with all the comforts and opportunities that wealth could provide. His father was Barney Cory, a wealthy importer of Boston, a descendant of Philip Cory who settled in Rhode Island early in the seventeenth century, and his mother was Eliza Ann Bell of Newport, R. I. Charles was from early youth deeply interested in all sorts of outdoor sports, especially in hunting, and he soon began collecting specimens of birds. In 1876 he entered the Lawrence Scientific School of Harvard University where he came in contact with J. A. Allen [q.v.], the noted zoölogist, then curator of birds and mammals in the Museum of Comparative Zoölogy. Just before this he had joined the Nuttall Ornithological Club of Cambridge and made the acquaintance of William Brewster [q.v.] and other local ornithologists so that his interest in birds was greatly stimulated and it became his chief pastime. His college course was never completed, but for nearly forty years, beginning in 1877, he devoted his life to travel and the collecting of ornithological specimens, visiting Florida most frequently but also other parts of America, and Europe. He published accounts of his experiences in several volumes, such as *Southern Rambles* (1881), *A Naturalist in the Magdalen Islands* (1878), *Hunting and Fishing in Florida* (1896). In 1878 he visited the Bahamas and then concentrated his interests on the

West Indies, becoming the recognized authority on the birds of these islands. He published *Birds of the Bahama Islands* (1880), *The Birds of Haiti and San Domingo* (1885), and *The Birds of the West Indies* (1889), many papers in *The Auk* and the *Bulletin of the Nuttall Ornithological Club,* and a large folio work with colored illustrations entitled, *Beautiful and Curious Birds of the World* (1880–83).

Cory was married in 1883 to Harriet W. Peterson of Duxbury, Mass. His home at this time was at Hyannis, where he established a spacious game park which he maintained as a bird sanctuary, one of the first in the United States. He was one of the founders of the American Ornithologists' Union in 1883 and later served it as treasurer, vice-president, and president. Upon the establishment of the Field Museum at Chicago he presented to that institution his entire collection of birds, and was made curator of ornithology for life with no residence obligations, an assistant caring for the collections under his direction. He was thus enabled to continue his travels and his collecting. In 1906, when in his fiftieth year, he experienced the crisis of his life—the loss of his entire fortune. He accepted a salaried position in the Museum, and the care-free roving amateur became a hard-working professional ornithologist.

About the time of his first connection with the Field Museum he had published a key to the birds of eastern North America and he now prepared a volume on the *Birds of Illinois and Wisconsin* (1909). He next arranged for the extensive collecting of South American birds by the field force of the museum, and the study and identification of these specimens occupied most of the remainder of his life. In this connection he conceived the *Birds of the Americas,* a synopsis and synonymy of all the birds of North, Middle, and South America. He published two volumes of this, his most important work (1918 and 1919), and the Museum later provided for its completion.

Cory's interest was not confined to his ornithological studies. Among his other publications were *Hypnotism or Mesmerism* (1888); a number of light opera librettos: *The Corsair* (1887), *The Mermaid, or The Curse of Cape Cod* (1888), *A Dress Rehearsal* (1891), *An Amazon King* (1893); and a volume of short stories, *Montezuma's Castle and Other Weird Tales* (1899). His prowess in various athletic sports was notable and he played games with the same concentration and determination to succeed that marked his scientific work. He was kind and generous in disposition and possessed

of a keen sense of humor. The fortitude with which, at middle age, he gave up all the comforts and associates of a luxurious life and set about making a living for his family with no outward show of mental suffering, illustrates better than anything else his strength of character.

[W. H. Osgood, "In Memoriam: Chas. Barney Cory," *The Auk,* Apr. 1922, pp. 151–66; *Who's Who in America,* 1920–21; obituary in *Chicago Tribune,* July 31, 1921; personal acquaintance of over thirty years.]

W. S.

COSBY, WILLIAM (*c.* 1690–Mar. 10, 1735/6), colonial governor of New York and New Jersey, was a member of an influential Irish family. His father was Alexander Cosby of Stradbally Hall and his mother, Elizabeth, who died in 1692, was a daughter of Henry L'Estrange. William Cosby became an officer in the British army and married Grace Montagu, a sister of the second earl of Halifax. During Cosby's régime in New York his daughter was wedded to Lord Augustus, son of the Duke of Grafton. According to hostile critics this match was due to the intrigues of Lady Cosby (Smith, *post,* II, 33). Cosby was one of the placemen who surrounded the Duke of Newcastle. Before coming to America he had served as governor of the Island of Minorca, but had incurred charges of extortion (Smith, *op. cit,* II, 1). Nevertheless, upon the death of Montgomerie in 1731, Cosby secured commissions as governor of New York and the Jerseys. Delaying, however, in order to lobby against the Sugar Act which was hurtful to his colonies, he did not arrive in New York until Aug. 1, 1732. Among his first acts were to appoint his son, "Billy," to a sinecure as secretary of the Jerseys and to send a live beaver to the Duchess of Newcastle (*Documents Relative to the Colonial History of the State of New York,* V, 936–37). With the Assembly of New York he got on fairly well, securing an act for support for five years with additional reward for his services against the Sugar Act. He came into collision, however, with a group of provincial aristocrats of whom the leaders were Chief Justice Lewis Morris and James Alexander [*qq.v.*]. These men foiled Cosby's efforts to wrench from Rip Van Dam [*q.v.*], president of the Council, one-half of the emoluments received for conducting the administration before his arrival, and they supported John Peter Zenger [*q.v.*] in establishing the *New York Weekly Journal* to assail Cosby. The Governor struck back in the famous libel suit but met humiliating defeat when Zenger was acquitted. About a year later Cosby died after a long illness. As governor of the Jerseys he avoided serious trouble. He was the last governor of the united provinces, as after his death New Jersey was given a separate executive. Cosby's correspondence shows him to have been devoid of statesmanship, seeking money and preferment. He was accused of violence and profanity, and ranks with Fletcher and Cornbury [*qq.v.*], among New York's most unenlightened royal governors. His point of view appears in his oft-quoted letter to Newcastle: "I am sorry to inform your Grace, that ye example and spirit of the Boston people begins to spread among these colonys in a most prodigious manner. I had more trouble to manage these people than I could have imagined" (*Ibid.*, V, 937).

[For Cosby's public career the chief sources are the *Docs. Relative to the Colonial Hist. of the State of N. Y.* and the *N. J. Archives*. Wm. Smith, *Hist. of the Late Province of N. Y.* (2 vols., 1830), gives an interesting but partisan account. The best recent study is Herbert L. Osgood, *Am. Colonies in the Eighteenth Century* (1924), II, ch. V. See also P. W. Chandler, *Am. Criminal Trials* (2 vols., 1841–44); Livingston Rutherford, *John Peter Zenger, His Press, His Trial, etc.* (1904); J. B. Burke, *Geneal. and Heraldic Hist. of the Landed Gentry of Ireland* (1912).] E. P. T.

COSTANSÓ, MIGUEL (fl. 1769–1811), Spanish cosmographer and army engineer, was the ensign (*alférez*) of engineers sent under Gov. Gaspar de Portolá to make astronomical observations when José de Gálvez, visitor general of New Spain, and his coadjutor Francisco de Croix the viceroy, decided to send, in 1769, a "Holy Expedition" to occupy Alta California. Costansó sailed from La Paz, Baja California, on Jan. 10, 1769, on the paquebot *San Carlos*, reaching the port of San Diego, Alta California, on Apr. 29 or 30, after 110 terrible days at sea. On July 14 he was a member of Portolá's famous party which set out by land to find Sebastián Vizcaíno's noteworthy port of Monterey, upon which a fort was to be built. On this expedition Costansó and Father Juan Crespi [*q.v.*] took observations of the latitudes, usually with fair agreement; they also participated in bestowal of place names along the coast, many of which survive in use. Costansó returned to Mexico in July 1770. He was the author of the first book which concerned Alta California exclusively, his *Diario histórico de los viages de mar y tierra hechos al norte de la California,* finished at Mexico Oct. 24, 1770, and printed there before 1771. It contains the complete account of Portolá's first expedition promised in the preceding brief pamphlet, the *Extracto de noticias del Puerto de Monterey,* of which two editions were printed at Mexico. The *Diario histórico* was preceded by Costansó's fuller *Diario del viage de tierra hecho al norte de la California,* finished at San Diego, Cal., Feb. 7, 1770, manuscript

copies of which are in the Sutro Library and Archivo Nacional, Mexico City (*Historia,* tomo 396).

Costansó thus made three major contributions to the literature of the Spanish conquest of California; they are full of reasonable scientific accuracy, competent personal experience, and humane observations on the country and the natives. The author's name appears again in connection with this territory when in 1772 he was consulted as an expert on the feasibility of the plan proposed by Juan B. Anza [*q.v.*] to connect Sonora and Alta California by a land route; his affirmative advice contributed to the success of Anza in the founding of San Francisco in 1776. Again in 1794–95 the engineer's opinion was called for when the problem came up of defending the coast from European enemies. He also served as consulting engineer in affairs concerning the drainage of Mexico City through the Huehuetoca Canal, in the fortification of Vera Cruz, and in the matter of the military judgment on Intendant Riaño's strategy in opposing Miguel Hidalgo's attack on Guanajuato in 1811.

[The *Diario histórico* was translated by Wm. Reverley, and printed in English by A. Dalrymple, London, 1790, from a MS. obtained from Dr. Wm. Robertson the historian. It appeared again, edited by C. F. Lummis, in *The Land of Sunshine* (Los Angeles) June and July issues, 1901. The Spanish text with English translation appeared in the *Acad. of Pacific Coast Hist. Pubs.,* vol. I, no. 4, Mar. 1910. There is a manuscript copy in the Sutro Library, San Francisco. The *Diario del viage de tierra* was published as *Acad. of Pacific Coast Hist. Pubs.,* vol. II, no. 4, Aug. 1911, and was there accompanied by a reproduction of Costansó's map of the California coast from Cape Blanco to Cabo de Corrientes on the Mexican coast; the map was drawn in Mexico in 1770 and printed in Madrid in 1771. Our chief knowledge of Costansó is gleaned from his writings already mentioned; Father Francisco Palóu mentions him frequently in his *Noticias de la Nueva Cal.,* as published by the Cal. Hist. Soc. with an introduction by John T. Doyle (4 vols., 1874) and more recently by H. E. Bolton, *Hist. Memoirs of New Cal.* (4 vols., 1926). There is frequent mention of Costansó in Crespi's letters, as edited by Bolton in *Fray Juan Crespi* (1927).] H. I. P.

COTTON, JOHN (Dec. 4, 1584–Dec. 23, 1652), Puritan clergyman, author, was born at Derby, Derbyshire, England. His father, Roland Cotton, was a lawyer and a strenuous Christian, and his mother is also said to have been an extremely religious woman. Little is known of his childhood until he became a student of Trinity College, Cambridge, in his thirteenth year. He received the degree of A.B. in 1603 and that of A.M. in 1606. He had a strong inclination for the life of a scholar and was assisted financially by his father who seems to have been well-to-do. The young student was particularly proficient in Hebrew and in an examination based mainly on that language won a fellowship at Emmanuel College, which had been founded by a Puritan and was the most inclined to Puritanism of all those in Cambridge, the university at that time being strongly Puritan in tone. Cotton remained at Emmanuel for six years, became head lecturer and dean and preached occasionally with great effect at St. Mary's Church. It was during these years at Emmanuel that he experienced his first genuine religious awakening. On July 13, 1610, he was ordained deacon and priest at Lincoln, and in 1613 he received the degree of B.D.

His learning and his ability in preaching had already attracted attention, and on June 24, 1612, when only twenty-seven years old, he was chosen vicar of the large and beautiful parish church of St. Botolph's at the seaport of Boston in Lincolnshire. Cotton Mather tells the odd story that the city council was tied in the election and that Cotton received the appointment only by the mayor's twice casting his vote in favor of him by mistake. The appointment had to be approved by the bishop of the diocese, and it appears that his approval was secured by bribery, although there is no evidence that Cotton had any direct hand in or even knowledge of this transaction (Whiting in Young's *Chronicles,* p. 423). He had been only a few years at St. Botolph's when he began to alter the liturgy by omitting certain forms and ceremonies in accord with Puritan belief and practise. His first change in this direction seems to have been made about 1615. Although there is good evidence that he was beloved by his parishioners, he appears to have carried only a part, possibly a minority, of his congregation with him in gradually abandoning the practises of the Church of England for the simpler Puritan form of worship. As was often done in such cases, an assistant was appointed who held services according to the old forms while Cotton was left free to follow his more Puritanical ideas.

Within three or four years he was in trouble with the ecclesiastical authorities, but no action was taken and throughout almost the entire twenty years that he spent at Boston he was treated with great leniency and consideration by his bishop. It was even said by one of his friends that King James himself had ordered that he should not be molested for his non-conformity (*Ibid.,* p. 426). An incident in 1621, when some unruly Puritans broke all the beautiful stained glass in the church and defaced the monuments and carving, does not seem to have led to anything else, and there is nothing to connect Cotton himself with the outrage. In 1632,

however, Cotton was summoned to appear before the Court of High Commission, and, although the summons was not served, he fled to London, where he was befriended by John Davenport [*q.v.*]. From there he resigned his charge in a letter to the Bishop of Lincoln, dated May 7, 1633.

Cotton had already been interested in Massachusetts, having been a friend of John Winthrop [*q.v.*], and having journeyed from Boston to Southampton to preach the farewell sermon when Winthrop and his party sailed. In July 1633 he embarked for America on board the *Griffin* with his wife, Thomas Hooker, Edmund Quincy, John Haynes, and others who later became prominent in New England. On the voyage his first son was born and named Seaborn. He landed at Boston on Sept. 4 and on Oct. 10 was chosen teacher of the church there, a post he occupied until his death. He at once became a leading figure on the small stage of the colony's public life, taking an active interest in its political as well as religious affairs. Indeed, in the New England theocracy the two were almost identical. So much weight did his opinion carry that it was said that whatever he pronounced in the pulpit soon became either the law of the land or the practise of the church. In one case, however, his influence happily failed and the *Abstract of the Lawes of New England* which he drew up for the General Court in 1636 was rejected by that body in favor of a less drastically Mosaic code.

In the constant disputes which characterized the life of the colony Cotton naturally took a leading part. It is impossible here to attempt to treat of the Antinomian controversy which for several years shook the colony to its foundations, ending in the excommunication and banishment of its protagonist, Mrs. Anne Hutchinson [*q.v.*], in 1638. All of the participants, as C. F. Adams has said, were "lost in a thick fog of indefinable ideas and meaningless phrases" but of the importance of the controversy in the life of the colony there can be no doubt. Cotton at first took the side of the defendant but when he found himself practically alone among the leaders in his attitude he went over to the side of the persecutors. However honest his opinion may have been, from that time on he became more narrow and bitter in his views.

His two controversies with Roger Williams brought forth many pamphlets on both sides. The first of these disputes had to do with the question of church membership, Williams taking the ground that only those who definitely renounced the Church of England should be members of the church in New England, Cotton taking the opposite and more liberal stand. In the second controversy Williams maintained that magistrates should have no power over men's souls, Cotton claiming that their authority should extend to the religious as well as to the secular affairs of the citizens.

Cotton was a man of indefatigable industry. He is said to have remarked that twelve hours should make a scholar's day, and what his church services meant to him and his congregation in mental strain may be inferred from the fact that he sometimes consumed six hours in praying and preaching. In addition he was a voluminous writer. His catechism called *Milk for Babes* (1646) was for long the standard work on which New England children were brought up. He also wrote, besides his controversial pamphlets, many works on prayer, church music, and, most important of all, his works on the theory and methods of Congregationalism as practised in New England. The most widely read of these treatises was *The Way of the Churches of Christ in New England* (1645), although perhaps *The Keyes of the Kingdom of Heaven* (1644) was not less important. In 1648 he answered the opponents of these volumes in *The Way of the Congregational Churches Cleared*. As one of the foremost defenders of Congregationalism it was suggested that he attend the Westminster Assembly in England in 1643 but he did not go. By 1646 he had become the Congregational leader in New England and was one of the three ministers chosen by the Cambridge Synod to frame a model of church government, although his plan was not the one finally adopted.

Cotton was undoubtedly one of the ablest and most influential men of his day in Massachusetts, of much natural sweetness of disposition and a scholar by temperament. Yet in studying his career in America it is difficult to avoid the conclusion that he was more and more warped from his own nature by the unconscious desire to retain his prestige and influence in the narrow and bigoted environment in which he had become great. As he advanced in his career he became more and more reactionary. A nonconformist himself in England, he came in later life, like most of the Massachusetts leaders, to uphold staunchly the power of the civil magistrate over the conscience of citizens and was willing to grant the state power of life and death in order to bring about conformity. "Better," he said, "a dead soule be dead in body, as well as in Spirit, than to live, and be lively in the flesh, to murder many precious soules by the Magistrates Indulgence." Like Winthrop, he

had no faith in the common man and advocated a strong government by the few. "Democracy," he wrote, "I do not conceyve that ever God did ordeyne as a fitt government eyther for church or commonwealth."

Cotton labored to the end of his life. In the autumn of 1652 he caught a heavy cold while preaching to the students of Harvard and this developed into serious trouble with the respiratory organs. He preached in his church for the last time on Nov. 21 and died on Dec. 23. He was married twice: first, on July 3, 1613, at Balsham, Cambridgeshire, England, to Elizabeth Horrocks who died some time after Oct. 2, 1630; second, on Apr. 25, 1632, to Sarah (Hawkridge) Story, widow of William Story, who survived him and married the Rev. Richard Mather [*q.v.*], whom she also survived. Of Cotton's six children by his second wife, his daughter Maria married Increase Mather [*q.v.*], and became the mother of Cotton Mather [*q.v.*].

[Perhaps the best brief life of Cotton is that by Williston Walker in his *Ten New England Leaders* (1901), which has many references to source material. The contemporary life by Samuel Whiting may be found in Alexander Young's *Chronicles of Mass. Bay* (1846). Young also prints a letter of Cotton to his wife, his letter of resignation to his bishop, and his "Reasons for his Removal to New England." John Norton also wrote a contemporary life under the title *Abel Being Dead, Yet Speaketh* (1658) which was reprinted with notes by Enoch Pond (1834). Cotton's grandson, Cotton Mather, also wrote an account of him (first published in 1695) in his *Magnalia Christi Americani* (1702; but see edition of 1853, vol. I). There is a modern estimate of Cotton by Wm. G. Brooks in the *New Eng. Mag.*, for Feb. 1887. For his comparatively little-known farewell visit to Winthrop at Southampton see *Proc. Mass. Hist. Soc.*, 3 ser., I, 101–15. The pamphlets in the Williams controversies may be found in the volumes of the *Narragansett Club Pubs.*, vols. I–IV (1866–70). The Antinomian controversy may best be studied in C. F. Adams, *Three Episodes in Mass. Hist.* (2 vols., 1892) and *Antinomianism in the Colony of Mass. Bay* (Prince Soc., 1894). *The Abstract of the Lawes of New Eng.* has been reprinted many times and may be found in Force's *Tracts.* Nicholas Hoppin's articles in the *Church Monthly*, vols. IV and V (1862–63) should be consulted for Cotton's earlier life in England. Julius H. Tuttle has prepared a bibliography of Cotton's writings in *Bibliographical Essays; a Tribute to Wilberforce Eames* (1924). J. and J. A. Venn, *Alumni Cantabrigienses* (1922) gives dates of baptism, degrees, and ordination.]   J. T. A.

COTTRELL, CALVERT BYRON (Aug. 10, 1821–June 12, 1893), inventor, manufacturer, born in Westerly, R. I., the home of the Cottrell family for many generations, was the son of Lebbeus and Lydia (Maxson) Cottrell. He had the regular education afforded by the local schools and at the age of nineteen began his apprenticeship as a machinist in Phenix, R. I., in the shops of Levalley, Lanphear & Company. Here he remained for fifteen years, most of the time as an employing contractor. While so engaged he made many improvements in machine tools and machinery and saved enough money to start a business of his own. In 1855 he formed a partnership with Nathan Babcock, a skilled mechanic, and rented a shop from the Pawcatuck Manufacturing Company in Westerly. Cottrell & Babcock had intended doing a general machinist's trade but the Pawcatuck Company had just purchased the rights to manufacture a patent oscillating printing-press and prevailed upon the new firm to manufacture this. Press manufacture, however, did not engage their whole time until 1868. In that year it was made the predominating feature, and thenceforward Cottrell's inventive genius began to show itself. Among the first of his press improvements was the air spring for reversing the bed of a press, which lessened the jar and permitted greater printing speeds and hence increased the capacity of a press. He was the first to apply tapeless sheet delivery to the drum cylinder press. He invented and introduced hinged roller frames and devised an attachment for controlling the momentum of the cylinder. After a brief period of minor but valuable inventions, he introduced front sheet delivery which permitted dispensing with both tapes and fly, delivering the sheets of paper to the cylinder, front side up, and at the front end of the press. He also invented a rotary color printing-press, feeding from a roll of paper and printing in three colors 300,000 labels a day. Probably his most valuable invention was the shifting tympan for a web perfecting press. This prevented offset on the second cylinder and enabled a press which had heretofore been capable of printing only the ordinary newspaper to execute the finest class of illustrated printing. The invention contributed much to making the five and ten cent magazines possible. During his life Cottrell received over a hundred patents in the United States and Europe, the first one having been obtained in 1858. Cottrell & Babcock continued in business until 1880 when Babcock retired, Cottrell continuing, however, with the aid of his three sons. Just a year before he died, the business was incorporated with a capitalization of $800,000 as C. B. Cottrell & Sons Company. In the early days of his business, Cottrell traveled a great deal among the trade, and he was known widely for his quick but accurate judgment, geniality, and sincerity. On May 4, 1849 he married Lydia W. Perkins, a descendant of John Perkins of Ipswich who came from England in 1632. Cottrell died in Westerly survived by his widow and five children.

[*Am. Dict. of Printing and Bookmaking* (1894), ed. by W. W. Pasko; J. L. Ringwalt, *Am. Encyc. of Printing* (1871); W. Kaempffert, *Popular Hist. of Am. Invention* (2 vols., 1924); *Am. Bookmaker*, July 1893; *Providence Jour.*, June 13, 1893; correspondence with C. B. Cottrell & Sons Co.]   C. W. M.

COUCH, DARIUS NASH (July 23, 1822– Feb. 12, 1897), Union general, was born on a farm in the town of Southeast, Putnam County, N. Y., to which place his father, Jonathan Couch, had removed from Redding, Conn. His grandfather, Thomas Couch, came to Redding from Fairfield, Conn., where the family had been long established; he served under Montgomery at Quebec (C. B. Todd, *History of Redding, Conn.*, 1906). Couch entered West Point in 1842, and graduated in 1846, in the class with McClellan, Stonewall Jackson, and Reno. The last-named, afterward killed at South Mountain, was his room-mate for three years. Couch was commissioned in the 4th Artillery and sent to Mexico, where he was present at the battle of Buena Vista. Promoted to first lieutenant, Dec. 4, 1847, he served until Apr. 30, 1855, chiefly at stations on the Atlantic coast, and then resigned his commission. While on leave of absence in 1853–54 he made an expedition into northern Mexico, collecting zoölogical specimens, and was then for a time on duty with the Smithsonian Institution. He had married Mary Caroline Crocker, Aug. 31, 1854, and after his resignation entered the employment of the Taunton (Mass.) Copper Company, conducted by the Crocker brothers. He entered the volunteer service, June 15, 1861, as colonel of the 7th Massachusetts Infantry, which arrived in Washington July 13, and camped on the Kalorama estate. Couch remained with it only a few weeks, being assigned to the command of a brigade and appointed brigadier-general of volunteers with his commission antedated to May 17. He commanded a division in the Peninsular campaign with high ability, especially distinguishing himself at the battle of Fair Oaks, although always handicapped by ill health. "During the Rebellion," he says, "my well days were few in consequence of disease contracted during the Mexican War" (unpublished letter). For this reason he offered his resignation in July 1862, but McClellan did not forward it, and he was appointed major-general of volunteers. He commanded his division at Antietam, and the 2nd Corps at Fredericksburg and Chancellorsville. Profound distrust of Hooker's capacity was aroused in him by the plan of the Chancellorsville campaign. He wrote of Hooker: "It hardly seemed possible that a sane General could have talked in this manner" (*Ibid.*). The issue of the battle confirmed his opinion, and he asked to be relieved from duty with the Army of the Potomac. He was therefore assigned to command in Pennsylvania, where he turned out the militia to assist in the Gettysburg campaign, kept order in the coal-mining districts, and opposed, though unsuccessfully, the raid on Chambersburg. He was in charge of the ceremonies at the consecration of the national cemetery at Gettysburg. Late in 1864, he was assigned to a division of the 23rd Corps and joined in time to command it at the battle of Nashville, where his horse was shot under him. After taking part in the Carolina campaign, he resigned, May 26, 1865. He was Democratic candidate for governor of Massachusetts in that year, but was not elected. For a short time he was collector of the port of Boston, under a recess appointment, and then became president of a Virginia mining and manufacturing company. After 1870 he lived in Norwalk, Conn. He was quartermaster-general of Connecticut for two years, and adjutant-general of the state for two years. He died at Norwalk and was buried at Taunton.

[G. W. Cullum, *Biog. Reg.* (3rd ed., 1891), *Bull. Ass. Grads. Mil. Acad.*, 1897, pp. 53–62; *Official Records (Army)*, 1 ser., vols. XI (pts. 1, 2, 3), XII (pt. 3), XIX (pts. 1, 2), XXI, XXV (pts. 1, 2), XXVII (pts. 1, 2, 3), XXIX (pt. 2), XXXVII (pts. 1, 2), XLIII (pts. 1, 2), XLV (pts. 1, 2), XLVII (pts. 1, 2, 3), LI (pt. 1); 3 ser., vols. III, IV; C. M. Selleck, *Norwalk* (1896), pp. 99–101; unpublished records in the War Dept.]
T.M.S.

COUDERT, FREDERIC RENÉ (Mar. 1, 1832–Dec. 20, 1903), lawyer, was born in New York City, the eldest son of Charles Coudert and Jeanne Clarisse du Champ. The father was a native of Bordeaux, France, and was an army officer under Napoleon I. After the restoration, he became allied with Lafayette in a plot to place the Duke of Reichstadt on the throne. He was sentenced to death, escaped, and returned to France two years later; but was again forced to flee, and reached the United States in 1824. Here he set up a school which became widely known, in which his son, Frederic, was prepared for college. The latter entered Columbia College at the age of fourteen, and was graduated with honors in 1850. While in college, he gave Spanish and French lessons to a large class of boys. He studied law in the offices of Edward Curtis and Edward Sandford, contributing to his own support meanwhile by writing for the press, particularly for Porter's *Spirit of the Times,* the leading sporting journal of the period. In 1853, he was admitted to the New York bar, and with his two brothers, Charles and Louis Leonce, formed a law partnership. He married Elizabeth McCredy.

Throughout his life, Coudert was interested in politics as an independent Democrat, but he consistently declined office. He believed it to be "the duty of every citizen to become, at some time or other, and to some extent, an active factor in the working of the governmental machinery," but he thought that this might be "more effectually done by those who ask no reward from the powers that be, and no salary from the public treasury." He exemplified this text in his own life by accepting the presidency of the Young Men's Democratic Club, and of the Manhattan Club. In the presidential campaign of 1876 he was active in support of Tilden, and was one of a committee of citizens who visited New Orleans to influence the Returning Board to render a fair count in Louisiana. In 1892, he successfully led that branch of his party in New York which insisted on the renomination of Cleveland for president.

Coudert's interests were broad. He served as commissioner of public schools of New York City in 1883–84, was president of the Columbia University Alumni Association, and from 1890 until 1901, a trustee of the University. He was devoted to the interests of the Roman Catholic Church; in 1873, gave a series of addresses under the auspices of the Catholic Union; was president of the United States Catholic Historical Society; and for many years aided in the management of the St. Vincent de Paul Orphan Asylum. He was an ardent admirer of France and the French; was president of the French Benevolent Society, and gave the address to the French Delegates, at the presentation of the Statue of Liberty in June 1885.

As a lawyer, Coudert held high place for forty years. In the judgment of his colleagues, he was sound and learned. He was elected seventh president of the Association of the Bar of the City of New York, and was offered, but declined to accept, appointments to the New York court of appeals and to the United States Supreme Court. In 1893 he successfully led the protest against the elevation of Judge Maynard to the New York court of appeals. His practise included a wide range of cases, civil, commercial, criminal; and he demonstrated his practical business capacity as government director (1884–87) and government receiver (1892–98) of the Union Pacific Railroad. His greatest achievements, however, were in international law, public and private. Initiated into this field as associate to Reverdy Johnson in the Civil War blockading cases, he eventually became counsel in the United States to the French, Italian, and Spanish governments. His firm had foreign branches and handled a large volume of patent, trade-mark, and extradition cases. He was a delegate of the New York Chamber of Commerce to the Antwerp conference called to revise the rules of general average, and in 1880 was a member of the International

Conference at Berne, for codification of the law of nations. He was one of the American counsel in the Bering Sea Fur Seal arbitration in 1893–95, and in 1896 was appointed by President Cleveland a member of the commission to investigate and report on the Venezuelan boundary dispute. Coudert had great natural gifts as an advocate, an intuitive insight, power of clear statement, and originality in presentation of arguments. He possessed a withering power of sarcasm, was easily moved, and "took refuge from pathos by unexpected transitions to humor."

[See Frederic R. Coudert, *Addresses: Historical-Political-Sociological* (1905), with an Introductory Note by Paul Fuller; memorial by Judge Edward Patterson in *Report Asso. of the Bar of the City of N. Y.* (1905); Paul Fuller in *U. S. Cath. Hist. Soc., Hist. Records and Studies*, vol. III (Dec. 1904); D. McAdam and others, *Hist. of the Bench and Bar of N. Y.* (1899), II, 102–04; *N. Y. Times*, Dec. 21, 1903.]   F. C. H.

COUES, ELLIOTT (Sept. 9, 1842–Dec. 25, 1899), ornithologist, was born in Portsmouth, N. H., the son of Samuel Elliott Coues, a man of literary and humanitarian interests, and of Charlotte Haven Ladd, a descendant of John Mason, the original grantee of New Hampshire. He was descended from Peter Coues, a native of the island of Jersey, who about 1735 settled in Portsmouth. In 1853, when Elliott was but eleven years of age, his family moved to Washington where the father had secured a position in the Patent Office. The son attended Gonzaga Seminary and Columbian College (now George Washington University) where he received the degrees of A.B. (1861) and M.D. (1863). During the Civil War he enlisted (1862) in the United States Army as a medical cadet and was appointed assistant surgeon in 1864, a position which he retained until his resignation in 1881. In boyhood Coues had shown a marked interest in the study of birds, and his removal to Washington, where he met many naturalists at the Smithsonian Institution, had increased this interest until it became absorbing. His first paper, *A Monograph of the Tringeæ*, published at the age of nineteen, was typical of him. Instead of beginning with some amateurish note on a rare bird seen, or upon some field trip, he wrote a technical treatise of which any ornithologist in America might well have been proud, exhibiting not only knowledge of the subject but remarkable facility of expression. There followed at short intervals a long series of papers, notes, and reviews covering the whole field of ornithology but dealing with the birds of North America. These appeared in the *American Naturalist*, the *Bulletin of the Nuttall Ornithological Club*, the *Auk*, and the *Proceedings* of various societies. Coues's assignments in the army took him to various outposts in the West

at a time when it was as yet little affected by civilization. He was stationed at Fort Whipple, Ariz., in 1864; at Fort Macon, N. C., in 1869–70; at Fort Randall, Dakota, in 1873; and he was appointed naturalist and secretary of the United States Northern Boundary Commission, 1873–76. Wherever he was located he made collections, discovering a number of hitherto unknown bird species and securing a vast amount of information for later publications. Realizing that the exploration of the West had so increased the knowledge of its ornithology as to render all general works on the subject out of date, he conceived and published, in 1872, his famous *Key to North American Birds* which ran through five editions, the last appearing in 1903, several years after his death. A preface to the work covered the history of ornithology and the elements of field and general ornithology, including in small compass the most astonishing amount of ornithological information and illustrating once more the author's remarkable ability to write forcibly and tersely. In 1874 he published his *Birds of the Northwest*, one of the most important works on the bird life of the north central portion of the country. Then came the classic *Birds of the Colorado Valley* (1878) containing some of the finest bird biographies that have ever appeared, as well as some beautiful examples of English prose writing. Unfortunately this work was never completed, but an appendix containing a bibliography of North American Ornithology from 1612 to 1877 is as notable in its way as the text itself. This was a part of a Universal Ornithological Bibliography upon which Coues had spent years of work in the large scientific libraries of the country. He also turned his attention to North American Mammals, publishing a notable volume on the *Fur Bearing Animals* (1877), a monograph of the North American Mustelidae, and later five monographs of Rodentia to accompany others by J. A. Allen, the whole forming the bulky fourth volume of the Hayden Survey. He occupied the chair of anatomy in Columbia University, 1877–86. He became secretary and naturalist of the Geological and Geographic Survey of the Territories under F. V. Hayden in 1880, and wrote many important ornithological papers which appeared in the Bulletin of the Survey. He was one of the founders of the American Ornithologists' Union, in 1883, and served later as vice-president and president, acting also as associate editor of its publications, the *Bulletin of the Nuttall Ornithological Club* and its successor, the *Auk*. He was one of the committee of the Union which prepared the original edition of the *Check List of North American Birds* (1886), and the

Code of Nomenclature by which it was governed. From 1884 to 1891 he became a contributor to *The Century Dictionary* covering the subjects of general zoölogy, biology, and comparative anatomy, and supplying upwards of 40,000 definitions. The ornithological portion has well been termed an "encyclopedia of ornithology."

During the eighties he devoted much time and attention to the subject of psychical research. In 1884, on a visit to Europe, he met Henry Steel Olcott and Mme. Helena Blavatsky [*qq.v.*] and became an ardent theosophist. He soon founded the Gnostic Branch of the Theosophical Society in Washington, D. C., and was elected president of the American Board of Control of the Theosophical Society; he was also active in the formation of the American Society for Psychical Research. He brought out an American edition of Olcott's *Buddhist Catechism* and edited Robert Dodsley's *True and Complete Economy of Human Life,* adding the sub-title "Based on the System of Theosophical Ethics." But his ambition to become head of the entire theosophical movement in America, as well as his skepticism in regard to Mahatmic messages, brought him in May 1888 into conflict with William Quan Judge [*q.v.*] and eventually into conflict with the whole society. As late as Dec. 25, 1888, he could still write to Mme. Blavatsky as "the greatest woman of this age, *who is born to redeem her times,*" and, indeed, on Apr. 16 and 17, reiterated his devotion, but less than a month later, after his failure to be elected president of the American Section, he denounced the Society as "Mme. Blavatsky's famous hoax" (*Religio-Philosophical Journal,* May 11). On June 22 he was formally expelled. An injudicious interview given to the New York *Sun* a year later (*Sun,* July 20, 1890) in which he assailed the characters of Mme. Blavatsky and of Judge, led to a libel suit terminated by the *Sun's* abject apology on Sept. 26, 1892, which stated that the charges of Coues were "not sustained by evidence and should not have been printed" (for a detailed, if partisan, account of these episodes, see *The Theosophical Movement,* 1925, chs. 12–14).

Coues finally turned his attention to the editing of various works on early travel in the West. In turn there appeared *History of the Expedition of Lewis and Clark* (1893), *Expeditions of Zebulon Montgomery Pike* (1895), *Journals of Alexander Henry and David Thompson* (1897), *Journal of Major Jacob Fowler* (1898), *Forty Years a Fur Trader on the Upper Missouri by Charles Larpenteur* (1898), and *Diary of Francisco Garcés* (1900), fifteen volumes in all, and, with the exception of the Lewis and Clark and Pike volumes, consisting of hitherto unpublished matter. All contained copious annotations by the editor. While he was on an arduous journey through New Mexico and Arizona in search of information for the last of the above works Coues's hitherto robust health gave way and a complication of maladies resulted in his death. He was married twice: on May 3, 1867, to Jane Augusta McKenney; and, on Oct. 25, 1887, to Mrs. Mary Emily Bates who survived him.

[D. G. Elliott, "In Memoriam: Elliott Coues," *Auk,* vol. XVIII, no. 1 (Jan. 1901); *Nat. Acad. Sci.,* "Biographical Memoir of Elliott Coues," J. A. Allen, VI, 397–446 (June 1909); personal acquaintance.]   W. S.

COULDOCK, CHARLES WALTER (Apr. 26, 1815–Nov. 27, 1898), actor, was born in Long Acre, London, the son of a compositor who died when the boy was four years old. His mother remarrying, the boy was taken into the carpenter shop of his stepfather. He attended the London High School, and continued his education by going to evening school, while he worked at various trades during the day. When he was sixteen he saw Macready play Werner, and from that time on he was determined to be an actor. The realization of this desire, however, was delayed by the opposition of his grandmother. When she died, young Couldock turned to the stage at the age of twenty-one. He obtained his training by speaking in an elocution class, by acting with a company of strolling players at Farnham in Surrey, and by playing in stock companies at Gravesend, Bath, Southampton, and Edinburgh, arduous work that kept the young actor up many nights studying new parts. Later he was engaged to play leading rôles at Birmingham, appearing on Dec. 26, 1845, as Sir Giles Overreach in *A New Way to Pay Old Debts.* He remained as leading man at the Theatre Royal in Birmingham and at the Theatre Royal in Liverpool for four years, acting with all the stars of the day, Macready, John Vandenhoff, Charles Kean, Madame Vestris, Buckstone, Webster, Ellen Tree, Madame Céleste, Charles Mathews, Fanny Kemble, and many others, including the American actress Charlotte Cushman, with whom he came to America.

In America Couldock's ability was recognized at once. He appeared on Oct. 8, 1849, at the old Broadway Theatre playing the title rôle in *The Stranger* to Charlotte Cushman's Mrs. Haller. He made a brief tour with her company, after which he remained for four seasons at the Walnut Street Theatre in Philadelphia as leading man. During his first engagement in America Couldock played Othello, Macbeth, King Lear, Iago, Hamlet, Cardinal Wolsey, Jacques, St. Pierre, Master Waller, Duke Aranza, Benedict.

and Louis XI, then his greatest success. He also played many parts in stock. At the Walnut Street Theatre he took the part of Luke Fielding in *The Willow Copse* (1853), a new play brought to America by Madame Céleste, who rewarded Couldock's brilliancy as an actor by presenting him with a copy of the drama with the right to produce it (*New York Dramatic Mirror,* Apr. 13, 1895). He traveled for several seasons with this play, starring extensively with his daughter Eliza. In *The Willow Copse* and *The Chimney Corner* he made a national reputation. In 1858 he joined Laura Keene's company, playing the original Abel Murcott in *Our American Cousin.* He originated the character of Dustan Kirke in the popular domestic drama *Hazel Kirke,* and he played the part at the Madison Square Theatre for 486 performances before the play was withdrawn. His name was also among the prominent artists who appeared at the Boston Museum from 1850 to 1870. He appeared on the stage for sixty years, and few actors of his time equaled him in his hold on the public. He earned considerable money, but he gave it away to the poor. A complimentary benefit performance was given him May 10, 1887 (matinée), at the Star Theatre in New York City in celebration of his fiftieth year upon the stage. A profound lover of dramatic art, he knew all the important actors of his time. He was the friend of Edwin Booth, Macready, and Joseph Jefferson, who said of him: "I have known him as a father, a husband, a friend. And during the forty years that I have known him, and longer than that, no living man can say that Charles Walter Couldock ever disappointed a public, deceived his friends, or injured his enemy" (*New York Times,* May 13, 1895). He was a man of fertile mind, of great vitality, and of inexhaustible energy. He was hearty, genial, full of wit, and a good story teller.

[Laurence Hutton, *Plays and Players* (1875); Henry P. Phelps, *Players of a Century: A Record of the Albany Stage* (1880); T. Allston Brown, *A Hist. of the N. Y. Stage* (3 vols., 1903); J. N. Ireland, *Records of the N. Y. Stage* (1866–67); *N. Y. Dramatic Mirror,* Nov. 26, 1898, p. 17; *N. Y. Clipper,* Dec. 3, 1898, p. 672; *N. Y. Times,* Nov. 28, 1898.]   L.B.P.

COULTER, JOHN MERLE (Nov. 20, 1851– Dec. 23, 1928), botanist, was born at Ningpo, China, the son of missionary parents, Moses Stanley and Caroline E. (Crowe) Coulter. He graduated with the degree of A.B. from Hanover College in 1870. In 1872 he was assistant geologist on the Hayden Survey. While the expedition was waiting in the mountains for Hayden, the rest of the party whiled away the time playing cards; but since young Coulter did not know how to play, he collected plants. When Hayden arrived, he was so impressed by Coulter's collections that he appointed him botanist of the expedition. The object of the expedition was to look for the rumored hot springs and geysers of what is now Yellowstone Park. When they found the geysers, each member was assigned one of the holes for study. Since Coulter was the youngest member of the party, they assigned him one of the smaller holes. It turned out to be Old Faithful.

The study of his botanical collections took him to Washington, where he met Asa Gray. The meeting was the beginning of a life-long friendship. Coulter became Gray's most distinguished pupil and with Sereno Watson he edited (1890) the sixth edition of Gray's famous *Manual.* In 1873 he received the degree of A.M. from Hanover College and was professor of natural sciences there, 1874–79, and professor of biology in Wabash College, 1879–91. During this period (in 1884) he received the degree of Ph.D. from Indiana State University. He was a life-long friend of David Starr Jordan, and when Jordan resigned from the presidency of Indiana State University (1891), he persuaded Coulter to succeed him. The politics of a state university and the worry about securing funds from politicians were so distasteful that Coulter resigned in 1893 and became president of Lake Forest University, which he thought was so well endowed that there would be no financial problems. Even at Lake Forest, however, administrative duties interfered seriously with his chosen work and he went to the University of Chicago (1896), where he was able to devote nearly thirty years to building up a strong department and to training young men and women for teaching and research. After retiring from active teaching in 1925 he became adviser to the Boyce Thompson Institute for Plant Research at Yonkers, N. Y., for the foundation of which he was largely responsible.

His early training and teaching in botany were taxonomic; but when the nomenclature controversy promised to make the taxonomy of the next twenty years a quarrel over the names of plants, he turned to morphology, and nearly all of the research done under his direction at the University of Chicago belonged to this field. Nevertheless he was broad-minded and sympathetic in his attitude toward other phases of botany. He called Prof. Charles R. Barnes to Chicago to develop plant physiology and gave to Prof. Henry C. Cowles such an opportunity to develop the new field of ecology that this branch has become recognized as one of the fundamentals of a botanical education.

In 1875, while at Hanover College, he founded the *Botanical Gazette,* which he not only edited, but also managed and often financed. It has become the leading botanical journal of America. Reviews of the critical type, as distinguished from the colorless type of abstracting journals, have always been a feature of the *Gazette,* and Coulter's reviews are models of this kind of writing. He wrote several manuals and botanical text-books, among which were: *Manual of the Botany of the Rocky Mountain Region* (1885), *Manual of Texan Botany* (1893), *Plant Relations* (1899), *Plant Structures* (1899), *Plant Studies* (1900), *Morphology of Gymnosperms* (1910) with Charles J. Chamberlain, *Morphology of Angiosperms* (1903) with the same, *A Textbook of Botany* (1906), *Fundamentals of Plant Breeding* (1914), *Evolution of Sex in Plants* (1914), *Plant Genetics* (1918). Besides these there were taxonomic monographs and shorter articles. What would have been his greatest contribution, a history of botany, will probably never be completed. For years he had been gathering material, and, occasionally, in lectures he had given glimpses of what the work might be. He had just completed a collection of biographical sketches when he died.

Coulter's greatest influence was not through his books and papers, however, numerous and good as they were, but through the men and women he trained. No other American botanist has so many students holding high positions. He belonged to botanical organizations at home and abroad and received all the major honors his fellows botanists could bestow upon him. Before his death, his students had already established the John M. Coulter Research Fellowship in Botany, to support exceptional students engaged in research.

[*Who's Who in America,* 1928–29; *International Who's Who in Science,* 1914; *Am. Men of Science* (1921); Geo. D. Fuller in *Science,* Feb. 15, 1929; H. C. Cowles in *Bot. Gazette,* Mar. 1929; personal acquaintance of thirty years.]   C.J.C.

COUPER, JAMES HAMILTON (Mar. 4, 1794–June 3, 1866), planter, was the son of John and Rebecca (Maxwell) Couper. John Couper emigrated to Georgia from Scotland, and, in partnership with a boyhood friend, James Hamilton, acquired (1804) an extensive tract of land on the southern bank of the Altamaha River about sixteen miles from Brunswick, Ga. The name "Hopeton" was given to this plantation of some 2,000 acres. John Couper also owned a large plantation on St. Simon's Island known as Cannon's Point. He became a wealthy and influential citizen of the community. Indeed he was one of the leaders in the most influential group of seaboard planters.

After graduation from Yale in 1814, James Hamilton Couper spent some time in Holland studying the Dutch methods of water control. On his return to Georgia he was made manager of the Hopeton estate. His father failed in business in 1826. The partner, Hamilton, assumed all of John Couper's liabilities in return for a half interest in the Hopeton property. James Hamilton Couper, the following year (1827), bought from Hamilton a half interest in the Hopeton plantation and remained as manager of the whole. He also in time inherited his father's place at Cannon's Point and acquired other interests in his own right. In his heyday James Hamilton Couper had the supervision of 1,500 slaves and the management of extensive properties owned by others in addition to his own important plantations.

Couper's distinction derives from the fact that he was one of the first American planters to conduct his operations on the basis of scientific research and experimentation. Not content with following time-honored methods, he blazed the way for his contemporaries and successors in the great coastal plantation area. The diking and drainage system established by him at Hopeton became the model followed by all rice planters. Couper's experiments in agricultural lines were of much interest and importance. At first his efforts were devoted principally to the production of sea island or long staple cotton. He found, however, that because of the richness of the soil, the plant grew too late in the season for proper maturing. He thereupon shifted to sugar cane as his leading crop. In 1829 he erected at Hopeton the most complete and modern sugar mill in the South. After 1838 Couper and most other Georgia planters practically abandoned sugar growing for rice. Couper made extensive experiments in the production of olive oil. His father had set out a grove of olive trees at Cannon's Point. The son demonstrated that olive growing was practicable on the Island despite losses from occasional heavy frosts. He was furthermore the pioneer in the crushing of cotton seed for oil. The United States Census states that the first cotton-seed oil mill was established in 1837, but by 1834 Couper was operating two such mills, one at Natchez, Miss., the other at Mobile, Ala. (Couper Letters, January 1834 and Dec. 13, 1834). Couper undertook many other experiments in the way of introducing and acclimatizing exotic plants, notably in the introduction of Bermuda grass, now the principal grass of Georgia. His fame as a scientific farmer, experimenter, geologist, and conchologist spread. Many noted travelers from Europe visited him at Hopeton and Cannon's Point. These visitors were unanimous in their praise of his agricultural system, his management and treatment of slaves, and expressed wonder at the bounty of his hospitality, the extent and beauty of his orchards and gardens. So well did he systematize his time that he had ample leisure for reading and for practising the art of conversation, of which he was a master. His library was large and well chosen.

The Civil War rudely interrupted this life. The slaves were freed, work abandoned, the plantations fell into decay, the primeval forests and the uncontrolled water reclaimed the coastal areas. Every rice plantation on the Savannah, Ogeechee, and Altamaha rivers was ultimately abandoned (Wylly, *Memories*). Couper had been opposed to secession, but all five of his sons went into the Confederate army. Two of them died in the service, the eldest, Hamilton, a graduate of Yale University, and John, a gifted artist. Couper died in 1866, broken in health and fortune. He lies buried at Frederika on St. Simon's Island.

[There is some first-hand material bearing on the life of Couper in the possession of his grand-daughters, Mrs. Franklin B. Screven of Savannah, Ga., and Mrs. W. S. Lovell of Birmingham, Ala. The writings of Capt. Chas. Spalding Wylly, a family connection of the Coupers, may also be ranked as primary sources. His studies are *Annals and Statistics of Glynn County, Ga.* (1897); *The Seed That Was Sown in the Colony of Georgia* (1910); *Memories* (1916). Geo. R. White, *Hist. Colls. of Ga.* (1855), was dedicated to Jas. Hamilton Couper and contains valuable data, particularly with reference to his father. Sir Chas. Lyell, *Second Visit to the U. S.* (1849), vol. I, chs. xviii and xix, gives a full account of the Couper plantations. References to Couper and his work are also to be found in Fredrika Bremer, *The Homes of the New World* (1853), vol. III; Frances Anne Kemble, *Jour. of a Residence on a Georgian Plantation in 1838–39* (1868); and Frances Butler Leigh, *Ten Years on a Georgian Plantation* (1883). Hon. W. G. Brantley, a former congressman from Ga., and a resident of Brunswick (the county seat of Glynn County) delivered a notable address on the life of Couper before the Inter-State Sugar Cane Growers' Association, in Macon, Ga., held May 6, 7, 8, 1903. This address reproduces a number of the Couper letters and other writings.]

R. P. B.

COURTNEY, CHARLES EDWARD (Nov. 13, 1849–July 17, 1920), single sculler, rowing coach, was born at Union Springs, N. Y., the son of James Thomas Courtney, a landscape gardener, who had moved thither from Salem, Mass. Fascinated by yacht-racing, then popular on Cayuga Lake, Charles at the age of twelve years built his first boat. He learned the carpenter's trade and with his eldest brother became a builder and contractor. In August 1868 a New Yorker named Tyler appeared on Cayuga

Lake with a paper scull and issued a challenge for a race. Courtney entered the race, putting oars in a home-made sailing craft which outweighed those of his competitors by over twenty pounds, and won in walk-away style. This was the beginning of his career. On June 25, 1873, at Syracuse, he defeated Charles Smith and William Bishop of New York, by almost a quarter of a mile over a three-mile course. In September of that year, he entered the Saratoga regatta and won against twelve entries in record time. After that as an amateur he won eighty-eight consecutive races. At Saratoga with Frank Yates he rowed two miles in twelve minutes, sixteen seconds, still the world's record for this distance. At Aurora, in a single scull, he rowed two miles in thirteen minutes fourteen seconds, the fastest time on record for a race with a turn. In practise he rowed a mile in six minutes and a mile and a half in nine minutes. In 1877 he turned professional. He had never been beaten until he met Ned Hanlan at Lachine in 1878 and lost in a race which was so close that the sporting world demanded another to determine which man was the better oar. Papers were signed for a return race on Chautauqua Lake on Oct. 8, 1879. On the morning of the race, Courtney's shell was found in his boat-house sawed in two. Courtney was accused, and for a generation an argument, which was never settled, raged between his friends and his enemies. As a professional Courtney rowed forty-six races of which he lost seven.

His career as a trainer and a coach began in 1875 with a class of girls from the seminary at Union Springs. In 1883 he prepared a Cornell four in ten days, which defeated by thirty-two seconds, Pennsylvania, Princeton, and Wesleyan. In this race, Courtney introduced sliding seats on rollers. In 1885 he was made head coach at Cornell, after which he practically withdrew from professional sculling. From 1883 until he retired in 1916 he coached approximately 146 Cornell crews which took part in inter-collegiate races of which they won 101.

In 1895 Cornell sent her eight to the Henley regatta, where an unfortunate incident and Courtney's secretive methods created a bad impression among the English rowing public. Courtney, however, learned a lesson at Henley and afterward lengthened out and improved his stroke, though he always stubbornly denied that he had changed his style in the slightest degree. In his coaching he tried everything that was suggested or invented; he was the first man to use the camera in rowing, and a pressure-recording machine attached to a rowing machine. As a coach he was a martinet, imposing upon his men rules of diet and training to which few college boys would submit. With all his temperamental ways and czar-like methods, however, he was affectionately known to students and faculty as "The Old Man." On his way to Poughkeepsie in 1915 he was thrown against the end of his berth and suffered a serious concussion of the brain, but went on with his coaching until the day of the regatta, when he collapsed. He never fully recovered.

[C. V. P. Young, *Courtney and Cornell Rowing* (1923) ; files of the *Cornell Era* and *The Cornell Alumni News*; obituaries in *Cornell Alumni News*, July 1920, *N. Y. Times* and *N. Y. Tribune*, July 18, 1920.]
A. H. B.

COVODE, JOHN (Mar. 18, 1808–Jan. 11, 1871), congressman, son of Jacob Covode and —— Updegraff, was the grandson of Garrett Covode, who was kidnapped on the streets of Amsterdam by a sea-captain and brought as a child to Philadelphia where he was sold as an indentured servant. John Covode received a scanty education in the public schools of Westmoreland County, Pa. After working for several years on his father's farm and serving an apprenticeship to a blacksmith, he found employment in a wooden-mill at Lockport. Of this mill he became owner in his early manhood and continued in the business of manufacturing for the remainder of his life, although from time to time he was interested in other business enterprises, such as the Pennsylvania Canal, the Pennsylvania Railroad, and the Westmoreland Coal Company. At his death he had a considerable fortune.

Through his conduct in his first public office, that of justice of the peace, Covode gained for himself the sobriquet, "Honest John," which clung to him all his life. He served two terms as a Whig in the Pennsylvania House of Representatives and was twice a Whig candidate for the state Senate, being defeated both times. He was elected to the national House of Representatives as an anti-Masonic Whig in 1854 and reelected as a Republican in 1856. In this position he served continuously until 1863 when he declined the nomination. He reëntered the House in 1867 and remained a member until his death.

In Congress he first became prominent in the spring of 1860 by reason of his chairmanship of the Covode Investigation Committee, appointed by the House on the adoption of Covode's resolution of Mar. 5, 1860, to inquire into the alleged use of improper influence by President Buchanan in attempting to secure the passage of the Lecompton Bill (*Congressional Globe*, 36 Cong.,

1 Sess., p. 997). In moving this investigation Covode was probably retaliating for a charge made by the President that bribery had been used in the Congressional elections in Pennsylvania in 1858; his pretext was the charge by two members of the House that the President had attempted to bribe and coerce them in the Lecompton affair (*Ibid.*, p. 1017). Buchanan sent to the House a protest against this investigation so far as it related to himself, but the House disregarded the protest and the investigation proceeded. It resulted in a majority and a minority report (*House Report 648*, 36 Cong., 1 Sess.), but the House took no action on either. In all probability the investigation was meant to produce nothing more serious than ammunition to be used by the Republicans in the presidential campaign of 1860; Covode was a member of the Republican Executive Congressional Committee for this campaign.

During the war Covode was a strong supporter of Lincoln. In December 1861 he was appointed a member of the Joint Committee on the Conduct of the War and took an active part in its work until his retirement in 1863. In the summer of 1865 he was sent by the War Department into the South, "to look into matters connected with the interests of the government in the Mississippi valley." Upon his return President Johnson declined to accept his report, in which he urged the removal of Gov. Wells of Louisiana and opposed the policy of withdrawing the troops from the South (*Report of the Joint Committee on Reconstruction*, 1866, pt. 4, p. 114). The President suggested that he file it with the War Department under whose authority he had been acting. From this time on Covode was an opponent of the President and upon his return to Congress steadily supported the congressional policy of reconstruction (*Congressional Globe*, 40 Cong., 2 Sess., Appendix, p. 462). He introduced into the House the resolution calling for the impeachment of Johnson. The results of Covode's mission to the South do not appear to have been of any special importance nor does he appear to have exerted any considerable influence in Congress at any time during the Reconstruction period.

[*Memorial Addresses on the Life and Character of John Covode, delivered in the House and Senate* (1871) ; *Cong. Globe*; John M. Gresham, *Biog. and Hist. Cyc. of Westmoreland County* (1890) ; J. M. Boucher, *Hist. of Westmoreland County, Pa.* (1906), vol. I; *Biog. Dir. Am. Cong.* (1928) ; *Press* (Phila.), Jan. 12, 1871.]
R. S. C.

COWAN, EDGAR (Sept. 19, 1815–Aug. 31, 1885), lawyer, United States senator, was born at Greensburg in Westmoreland County, Pa., of Scotch-Irish ancestry. In his childhood he lived with the family of his grandfather, Capt. William Cowan. Through his own efforts he secured funds to attend Franklin College at New Athens, Ohio, from which he graduated in 1839. In 1842 he was married to Lucetta Oliver of West Newton, daughter of Col. James B. Oliver. Admitted to the bar in Westmoreland County in the same year, he soon won recognition as one of the ablest lawyers in western Pennsylvania. At first a follower of Andrew Jackson, he had become a Whig in 1840, and in 1856 he joined the Republican party. In 1861 he became a candidate to succeed William Bigler in the United States Senate. His most dangerous opponent in the Republican caucus was David Wilmot; but Cowan, although not as well known, was believed to be conservative and therefore safe at a time when the people of the state wished to show the South that they did not believe in extreme measures. He was elected by a vote of 98 to 35 for Henry Foster, his Democratic opponent (*Pittsburgh Gazette*, Jan. 15, 1861).

Cowan went into office with the confidence of his constituents (*Philadelphia Press*, Jan. 23, *Pittsburgh Gazette*, Jan. 22, 1861). Unfortunately, however, this soon gave way to the most violent denunciation. His adherence to a strict construction of the Constitution led him in 1862 to oppose the expulsion of Senator Jesse D. Bright [*q.v.*] of Indiana (*Congressional Globe*, 37 Cong., 2 Sess., p. 653). Believing that the purpose of the war was the suppression of a rebellion and not the conquest of the Southern states, he opposed the Confiscation Act (*Ibid.*, pp. 1049, 1862, 1965). He refused also to support the Legal Tender Act (*Ibid.*, p. 804) and the National Bank Act (*Ibid.*, 3 Sess., p. 897). Such a course led him to be bitterly denounced by the Unionists. Ben Wade termed him the "watch-dog of slavery" (*Pittsburgh Daily Post*, June 18, 1862). The Republicans of Allegheny County passed resolutions of censure at their annual convention in 1862 (*Ibid.*, June 25, 1862). This criticism continued to the end of his term and made his reëlection impossible, despite his support of such measures as the suspension of the writ of *habeas corpus*, conscription, and the various acts authorizing loans, increasing taxes, imposing additional revenue duties, and raising the tariff. So complete was the reversal of his political status that in 1867 the Democrats supported him as their candidate for the Senate (*Pittsburgh Gazette*, Jan. 20, 1867). Cowan upheld President Johnson in his contest with Congress. The belief that his selection as minister to Austria in 1867 was a reward for this support led the Senate to refuse to confirm his nomination. He re-

tired to private life at the expiration of his term in the Senate and practised law until his death. He was an able lawyer, a well-trained scholar, and a forceful speaker. In assuming the unpopular position that he took on public questions he contended that he did that which he believed to be constitutional. Possessed of strong convictions, he had the courage to be true to them.

[In addition to sources cited above see: B. H. Pershing, "Senator Edgar A. Cowan," in *Western Pa. Hist. Mag.*, Oct. 1921; *Biog. Dir. Am. Cong., 1774–1927* (1928); *Hist. of the County of Westmoreland, Pa., with Biog. Sketches* (1882), ed. by Geo. D. Albert, pp. 334–41; *Biog. and Hist. Cyc. Westmoreland County, Pa.* (1890), ed. by J. M. Gresham and S. T. Wiley, pp. 68–69; John M. Boucher, *Hist. of Westmoreland County, Pa.* (1906), I, 353–58.]   B. H. P.

COWELL, SIDNEY FRANCES. [See BATEMAN, SIDNEY FRANCES COWELL, 1823–81.]

COWEN, JOHN KISSIG (Oct. 28, 1844–Apr. 26, 1904), lawyer, railroad administrator, was the son of Washington and Elizabeth (Lemmon) Cowen, Pennsylvanians of Scotch-Irish descent. They early moved to Holmes County, Ohio, where Washington Cowen eked out the income from his pioneer farm by blacksmithing for his neighbors. In Holmes County, John Kissig was born, and reared under the discipline which comes from religion, poverty, and hard work. His earliest education was gained in the public schools at home, his preparation for college in private institutions. In the academic year 1863–64 he matriculated at Princeton. A fellow student described him as then being "six feet tall, big-shouldered, and strong-looking all over," with a "big round head covered thickly with reddish hair." This Western youth likewise had a humorous philosophy and an amiable disposition which won him many friends. He soon excelled in his studies, especially in Greek and mathematics, and, in 1866, graduated at the head of his class. Following graduation he studied law, first, by himself, while teaching in the Millersburg, Ohio, high school and while principal of an academy at Shreve, and then as a student in the law school of the University of Michigan. In 1868 he passed the bar examinations at Canton, Ohio, and shortly afterward began to practise in Mansfield.

In addition to the rarely combined qualities of unusual eloquence, clarity of expression, and sound judgment, Cowen had a fine perception of the spirit of the law. He soon became a leading member of the profession in Ohio, and gained an extensive practise, always preferring civil to criminal cases. In 1872 he was offered the position of counsel for the Baltimore & Ohio Railroad Company, which he accepted, and for the remainder of his life he was connected with that railroad and made his home in Baltimore. In 1876 he became general counsel for the company. During the early years in Baltimore he had considerable private corporation practise; and for some time following 1882, he gave attention to politics, usually acting independently on local questions but affiliating, as regards national issues, with the "sound money" Democrats. From 1894 to 1896 he was a representative in Congress from Baltimore, but he had little leisure to give to service in Congress because of the now great burdens connected with his relation to the railroad company.

The financial difficulties of the Baltimore & Ohio had already begun when Cowen joined the company, and in 1896 matters reached a climax. A receivership was necessary, and this position was given by the court jointly to Cowen and Oscar G. Murray. In addition, Cowen was made president of the company. The receivership, which lasted from February 1896 to June 1898, was handled with unusual ability. Under it, the company's property was reorganized and placed in a sound condition, and made a net earning of almost $25,000,000. On a very narrow collateral the receivers were able to borrow approximately $20,000,000, which was necessary for repairing the road. Every bondholder was paid in full, the floating debt was paid, and the fraction of loss to the stockholders of the company was a small one. Cowen's heavy duties, however, caused a serious physical breakdown, and in 1901 he resigned the presidency of the Baltimore & Ohio and was made a member of the board of directors. Most of his time during the few remaining years of his life was given to a futile effort to recover his health. Cowen was married to Helen Woods.

[See the annual Reports of the B. & O. R. R. Co., 1872–1904; A. C. Bond, "My First Glimpse of John K. Cowen," in the *Princeton Alumni Weekly*, Mar. 3, 1915; a memorial speech by Judson Harmon, in *Proc. Md. Bar Asso.*, 1905; W. Irvine Cross, "John K. Cowen," in the *Md. Hist. Mag.*, Mar. 1925; minute regarding Cowen's death adopted Apr. 28, 1904, by the B. & O. R. R. officials; the *Sun* (Baltimore), Apr. 27, 1904; Edward Hungerford, *The Story of the B. & O. R. R., 1827–1927* (1928), vol. II.]
M. W. W.

COWLES, EDWIN (Sept. 19, 1825–Mar. 4, 1890), journalist, was born in Austinburg, Ohio. A Cowles, originally Coles or Cole, had come to Massachusetts in 1635, and a year later had joined the pioneer band that the Rev. Thomas Hooker led from Cambridge to Connecticut. In 1810, a descendant, Dr. Edwin Weed Cowles, settled at Austinburg, Ohio, among Connecticut neighbors who had been lured into the West. When Edwin, the son of Dr. Edwin Weed and Almira (Foote) Cowles, was seven years of age, the family took up its abode in Cleveland. Edwin's education was limited to a few years in the local schools and one at the Grand River Institute in Austinburg. At the age of fourteen, he entered a printer's office. Five years later (1844) he and T. H. Smead became partners in the printing business. In 1853, the partnership with Smead was dissolved and another formed with Joseph Medill and John C. Vaughn (Medill, Cowles & Company). The new organization published the *Forest City Democrat*, a Free-Soil Whig newspaper. In 1854, the name was changed to the *Cleveland Leader*. A year later Cowles became sole owner and shortly afterward editor as well. His enterprise rapidly grew to include both a morning and an evening daily newspaper.

His connection with political history was intimate. He was one of the founders of the Republican party. At the beginning of the Civil War he became an insistent advocate of coercion of the Southern states and immediate emancipation of the slaves. In 1861, Lincoln appointed him postmaster in Cleveland, an office he held five years. In 1876 and 1884, he was a delegate to the National Republican Convention. On the second occasion he was vice-president of the convention. He was a regular party man, loyal to Grant, and throughout his life a believer in Blaine. Finding that Blaine could not be nominated in 1876 and 1880, he threw his influence behind Ohio's favorite sons, Hayes and Garfield. Working all his life under a handicap of deafness that would have baffled a weaker personality, he was an editor of remarkable courage, unchangeable convictions, and relentless dogmatisms, and such qualities made his pen a power in northern Ohio for a generation.

He was married in 1849 to Elizabeth C. Hutchinson of Cayuga, N. Y. In his later years he aided his sons, Eugene and Alfred, in the development of new methods in electric smelting. The aluminum, carborundum, calcium carbide, and acetylene industries grew out of their work. A company was formed for the manufacture of such products and Edwin Cowles, who supplied most of the capital, was its president. His interests in this company kept him in Europe much of the last two years of his life.

[The chief sources are Cowles's newspapers, files of which are in the Western Reserve Hist. Soc. The *Cleveland Plain Dealer*, the *Leader*, and the *N. Y. Times*, Mar. 5, 1890, each published an estimate of his work. See also the *Cleveland Weekly Leader and Herald*, Mar. 8, 1890; Gertrude Van Rensselaer Wickham, *The Pioneer Families of Cleveland* (1914), II, 394 ff. *A Hist. of Ashtabula County, Ohio* (1878), contains a sketch prepared under Cowles's direction.]
E. J. B.

COWLEY, CHARLES (Jan. 9, 1832–Feb. 6, 1908), lawyer, author, was born at Easting-

Cowley

Cox

ton, Gloucestershire, England, his parents being Aaron and Hannah (Price) Cowley. While he was a child, the family came to the United States and settled in Massachusetts, his father establishing carpet factories at Lowell and Woburn. Charles attended the common schools at Lowell and after a short period of private tuition, commenced reporting for the local newspapers. He became editor of the *Lowell Daily Courier*, June 30, 1853, at the same time interesting himself in the early history of the locality and the antiquities of the native inhabitants. He gave up journalism, however, in 1854, studied law, and on his admission to the Middlesex bar, May 16, 1856, commenced practise at Lowell. In the same year he wrote a "History of the City of Lowell" for *A Handbook of Business in Lowell*. This was followed by *Memories of the Indians and Pioneers of the Region of Lowell* (1862). In the meanwhile the Civil War had begun, and Cowley entered the United States navy as a paymaster, being at first stationed at Brooklyn Navy Yard. Later he served in the same capacity on the monitor *Lehigh*, then attached to the South Atlantic Squadron under Admiral Du Pont. When Rear Admiral Dahlgren assumed command in 1863 Cowley was appointed judge-advocate on the latter's staff and transferred to the flagship *Pennsylvania*, later becoming provost judge. He was present at the occupation of Savannah and Charleston. On the termination of the war he opened a law office at Boston, but in a short time returned to Lowell, resuming his historical investigations, and devoting much time to literary pursuits. His *Illustrated History of Lowell* (1868) covered new ground and was written in an attractive style. It displayed thorough research and became the standard work on the subject. He had also interested himself in social welfare work, and acted as legal adviser to the various labor organizations in Lowell. He was counsel for the Grand Lodge of Knights of St. Crispin, and, when its incorporation by the legislature was assailed as unconstitutional, he was successful in establishing the legality of trade unions in Massachusetts (*Snow et al* vs. *Wheeler*, 113 *Mass.* 179). He ardently championed the ten-hour movement through a five years' struggle in the legislature. When that body in 1874 finally passed a penal act restricting the hours of labor of women and children to ten hours a day, he established its constitutionality in the supreme judicial court (*Commonwealth* vs. *Hamilton Manufacturing Company*, 120 *Mass.* 383). In 1875 and 1876 he was a member of the Common Council of Lowell, the only public office he ever held, serving on the commit-

tee which drafted a new city charter and ordinances. His interests were diversified and his literary activity was at this period intense. He edited *Revised Charter and Ordinances of the City of Lowell* (1876) and Dahlgren's *Maritime International Law* (1877), and in rapid succession wrote *Famous Divorces of All Ages* (1878), *Historic Sketch of Middlesex County* (1878), *Leaves from a Lawyer's Life Afloat and Ashore* (1879), *Reminiscences of James C. Ayer* (1879) and *Our Divorce Courts; Their Origin and History* (1879). He later published *Lowell in the Navy during the War* (1894) and *The Siege of Charleston: a History of the Department of the South and of the North Atlantic Blockading Squadron* (1899). He also published in the *Contributions to the Old Residents Historical Association* of Lowell a number of papers on subjects of local interest. He died at Lowell, Feb. 6, 1908.

[Material for the details of Cowley's life is scanty, the best review of his career being in *New Eng. Hist. and Geneal. Reg.*, vol. LXIII (1909), p. lii. See also his *Leaves from a Lawyer's Life Afloat and Ashore*, which however singularly lacks personal detail.] H. W. H. K.

COX, GEORGE BARNSDALE (Apr. 29, 1853–May 20, 1916), Ohio politician, was born in Cincinnati, the son of George Barnsdale Cox, and of a daughter of James Stitt, a Canadian customs official. His father, an Englishman who came to this country in 1847, died penniless when the boy was eight years old and to support his mother Cox left school. He was, in turn, newsboy, bootblack, butcher boy, wagon driver, tobacco salesman, bartender, and ultimately proprietor of a saloon. At eighteen he entered the Republican party as a challenger at the polls because, as he later declared, "my father had been a Republican" (*Cincinnati Enquirer*, May 15, 1911). At twenty-four he was elected to the city council, the only public office he held with the exception of that of state inspector of oil to which he was appointed in 1888. He was, however, twice a candidate for county clerk but in each case was defeated. In 1881 he sold his saloon and devoted his time to real estate and local politics. By 1884 his prominence as a ward politician caused him to be elected chairman of the Republican County Congressional Committee. The success of his candidates in the October election brought his appointment as chairman of the Blaine campaign in Hamilton County. Blaine carried Cincinnati and the county by a large majority, and this further enhanced Cox's prestige. The following year Joseph B. Foraker [*q.v.*] was elected governor, and it was during his administration that the foundation of the Republican machine was laid through the efforts of Dr. Thomas Graydon; R. K. Hynicka, Cox's secretary; August Hermann; and

473

Cox. The Ohio legislature was induced to pass a law replacing the elective Cincinnati Board of Public Works by a Board of Public Affairs appointed by the governor. The new Board proceeded to dismiss all Democratic office-holders, and Cox was given the power to appoint Republicans. By a judicious method of scattering his appointments over all the wards his own power was increased. From 1888 to 1910 "no man had a chance to get on the Republican ticket without the approval of Cox"; and the organization he erected was "in its way, more complete, more exacting, and under more rigid discipline than Tammany Hall" (*Ibid.*, May 21, 1916). To learn the essentials of boss rule, Cox visited New York and studied the Tammany machine; but his success lay largely in the apathy of the individual voter and the press (with the exception of the *Cincinnati Times-Star*) in the early eighties, the inefficiency of the reformers when in office, the decimating of the ranks of his opponents by offers of lucrative positions, his shrewdness in confusing the public by placing "third tickets" in the field, his close association with the corporate interests, his loyalty to his supporters, and the faith they had in his skill. There was always, however, a minority in his party who resented his rule; and this group, combined with the Democrats, frequently attempted to dethrone him. They failed to do so in 1894 but in 1897 the fusionists were triumphant. Cox published a letter of resignation, but the "call of the people" caused his return and in 1899 he elected his full slate. Beaten again in 1905, he regained control in 1907, even though the Drake Committee, appointed by a Democratic state legislature in 1906, had brought out the fact "that various banks had for years been paying interest on vast sums" which had not been paid into the treasury. This disclosure caused the return of $214,998.76 to the treasury (Goss, *post*, I, 264–76). In 1911 the district attorney obtained an indictment against Cox on the ground that he had perjured himself in testifying that he had never received any of this money. These indictments were finally quashed on the ground that Cox had been subpœnaed before the grand jury while under investigation and that "under the constitution of Ohio and the constitution of the United States no one can be compelled to be a witness against himself" (*Cincinnati Enquirer*, May 21, 1911). With the closing of this case Cox retired from active politics and during the remainder of his life devoted his time to his large theatrical and other business enterprises. In a personal interview to the New York *World*, May 15, 1911, he gave his own views on bosses and politics. He acknowledged

the title given him, claimed the boss was a product of American political life, and with due modesty declared that he had evolved into a boss "because of my peculiar fitness." To him politics was a game. "I like it because I am successful. One usually likes to play the game in which one is successful." Yet at the same time he strenuously "advised young men not to enter politics. . . . In the first place there is no money in it for the honest man and in the second place there is only abuse whether you are successful or unsuccessful" (*Ibid.*, May 15, 1911). Cox was physically a large man, fearless in the face of danger (*Ibid.*, May 21, 1916), methodical in his habits, a man of few intimate friends, reticent in speech, and devoted to his wife, Caroline, daughter of Samuel Shields.

[The most illuminating sketch of Cox's life is given in his personal interview to the New York *World* printed in the *Cincinnati Enquirer*, May 15, 1911. Cf. also *Cincinnati Enquirer*, May 21, 1916, for a general résumé of his career. The most complete printed account of his activities can be found in Chas. F. Goss, *Cincinnati, the Queen City* (1912), but this is somewhat biased by the strong feelings of the writer. H. C. Wright, *Bossism in Cincinnati* (1905), is of slight value. Brief accounts can be found in "The Uncovering of the Corrupt Rule of Boss Cox," *Arena*, XXXV, 632–37 (June 1906); Lincoln Steffens, *The Struggle for Self-Government* (1906), pp. 161–208.]   R. C. M.

COX, HANNAH PEIRCE (Nov. 12, 1797– Apr. 15, 1876), Quaker anti-slavery worker, daughter of Jacob and Hannah (Buffington) Peirce, was born in Chester County, Pa. Bayard Taylor praised the peace and beauty of its landscape and Whittier testified to its hospitable air of prosperity. Here she lived, her character influenced by her environment. Of Quaker stock, she was of the fifth generation of her family in America, George Peirce having come over from England with William Penn in 1684, and the Buffingtons also having been early Quaker colonists. In 1731 George Peirce had purchased land in East Marlborough township, Chester County, where seven generations of his family were to live. Jacob Peirce's farm, "Longwood," contained two hundred acres of rich soil and woodland. Prosperous, public-spirited, and intelligent, he built the first school-house in the neighborhood and the brick house where Hannah was born, lived, and died.

Hannah was early left fatherless, and her education was directed by her brother Jacob, "a man of fine intellect and a member of the Philadelphia Academy of Natural Sciences." She studied for a time at the Westtown Boarding School, developing a love of nature, sympathy for the oppressed, and positive ethical views. After a brief career as teacher she married, apparently in 1820 or 1821, J. Pennell, who soon afterward was killed in an accident. In 1823 she married John Cox, of near-by Willistown, a farmer and, like herself, a Friend of high character. Two sons and two daughters were born to them. Four years were passed in Willistown; Cox then purchased "Longwood," the Peirce homestead, which was thereafter their home. *The Liberator* and poems of Whittier's interested them in the anti-slavery movement; the burning of Pennsylvania Hall in 1838 quickened their zeal. Thenceforth Mrs. Cox labored unceasingly for the negro. Her husband and she conducted a station of the Underground Railroad, cooperating with Thomas Garrett at Wilmington, Del. Fugitive slaves were received, generously fed and clothed, and conducted northward by Cox or his sons, often with thrilling attendant incidents. The Coxes formed life-long friendships with Lundy, Garrison, Whittier, Lucretia Mott, and many other anti-slavery advocates who enjoyed their hospitality. From the anti-slavery interest ultimately sprang a liberal movement organized as "The Progressive Friends of 'Longwood.'" Many notable reformers, from as far as Boston, attended its yearly meeting; these Mrs. Cox and her husband gladly entertained, "Longwood" becoming a center of cultured effort for reform. At the Coxes' golden wedding, Sept. 11, 1873, eighty-two guests were present and "The Golden Wedding of Longwood" was contributed by Whittier and "A Greeting from Europe" by Bayard Taylor. Mrs. Cox interested herself in current social movements for emancipation, temperance, peace, the abolition of capital punishment, and woman's betterment, exerting a strong influence on all whose lives touched hers. Garrison testified to her "motherly nature," her eager charity, her unpretentiousness.

[Phebe A. Hanaford, *Daughters of America* (1883); *Kennett News*, Apr. 20, 1876; *Historic Homes and Institutions and Geneal. and Personal Memoirs of Chester and Delaware Counties, Pa.*, II, 530–31; information from Mrs. Cox's grand-daughters, Mrs. W. W. Polk and Miss Isabelle Cox of Kennett Square, Pa.] R.S.B.

COX, HENRY HAMILTON (c. 1769–c. 1821), farmer, poet, religionist, was born in Ireland, son of Joshua and Mary (Cox) Hamilton. He took the name of Cox in 1784 as a condition of inheriting the estate of Dunmanway, County Cork, according to the will of Sir Richard Cox, the second Baronet of that name (Sir Bernard and Ashworth P. Burke, *A Genealogical and Heraldic History of the Peerage, etc.*, 84th edition, 1926, p. 329; George Edward Cokayne, *Complete Baronetage*, 1904, vol. IV, p. 238n.). He married Letitia Elinor, daughter of David Wilson Hutcheson of Dublin, and, after serving in the British army in India, he came to America

about 1799, leaving his Irish estate in the care of a faithful steward until the income should cancel the encumbrances upon it. After settling first near York, Pa., he removed in 1813 to Chester County, near London Grove, where he leased a large farm. He became a member of the Society of Friends and was active in both York and London Grove meetings. He sometimes preached, but not with enough success to be recorded a minister. It is said that he spoke ably in business meetings but at times forgot himself and addressed the assembled Friends as "My Lords." He had a large family of children whom, according to tradition, he brought to the meeting door in a farm cart and then dumped them as he would a load of potatoes. In spite of this eccentricity and others, he was respected by his neighbors and was described by a contemporary (J. J. Lewis, *post*) as a man of superior ability, with an air of authority and the manners of a gentleman.

When Cox first came to America he gave to the Library Company of Philadelphia five volumes of seventeenth-century manuscripts consisting chiefly of official documents relating to affairs in Ireland. These "Irish State Papers" probably came rightfully into Cox's hands but they were gracefully returned to the British government in 1867 by the Library Company to fill an unfortunate gap in a series (see *Calendar of the State Papers Relating to Ireland, 1603–06*, 1872, p. lxxxvii; *The First Report of the Deputy Keeper of the Public Records in Ireland*, 1869, App. no. 31; Herbert Wood, *A Guide to the Records Deposited in the Public Record Office of Ireland*, 1919, p. 285).

Cox's literary efforts resulted in *Metrical Sketches. By a Citizen of the World* (1817). In this little collection his "Pennsylvania Georgics" was the most important poem. His knowledge of farm practise and his skill in verse may be judged from the following apostrophe to clover:

> "Still as the season grows new toils appear,
> Nor least the clover claims the farmer's care;
> Blest plant, tho' latest known, Columbia's pride,
> None ever fail to praise thee who have tried:
> Our mows beneath the swelling burden groan,
> Our furrows wave with fatness not their own;
> In either line thy genuine worth appears,
> Fruitful of hay or nurse of golden ears."

Upon hearing that his Irish estate had been cleared of debt, Cox returned to it in 1817, taking with him a Minute of London Grove Meeting of Friends addressed to Dublin Meeting, Ireland. On shipboard he apparently thought better of his Quakerism, and in Ireland he returned to the Anglican fold. His religious exploits were later capitalized by Bayard Taylor in "The Strange Friend." Cox appears as Henry Donnelly in this story, and liberal embellishments of fiction are added to the facts of history (see Bayard Taylor, "The Strange Friend," in *Beauty and the Beast: and Tales of Home*, 1872, pp. 75–105).

[Apparently the only serious attempt at a biographical sketch of Cox is Jos. J. Lewis, "Sketch of the Life of Henry Hamilton Cox," MS. in the Lib. of the Hist. Soc. of Pa., Phila. There are some errors in this sketch, but it is valuable, partly as a source, since Lewis as a boy knew Cox and later consulted with many others who knew him. See also J. S. Futhey and Gilbert Cope, *Hist. of Chester County, Pa.* (1881), pp. 505–08. The Quaker records of York and Chester counties, Pa., contain scattering references to Cox and his children. His *Metrical Sketches*, 60 pp., was printed for the author by J. R. A. Skerrett, Phila. There is a copy in the Lib. of Cong., and one is owned by the Lib. Co. of Phila., Ridgway Branch.]   R.W.K.

COX, JACOB DOLSON (Oct. 27, 1828–Aug. 8, 1900), Union general, governor of Ohio, secretary of the interior, author, was descended from one Michael Koch, who came from Hanover and settled in New York City in 1705. Jacob Dolson Cox, Sr., received his middle name from his mother, a member of a Dutch family of New York: his wife, Thedia R. Kenyon, was descended from Elder William Brewster and from the Allyns and Kenyons of Connecticut. To them was born, at Montreal, Jacob Dolson Cox, Jr., while the father, a building contractor, was engaged in the construction of the roof of the Church of Notre Dame. Returning to New York City soon after this event, the family suffered business reverses during the crisis of 1837. The boy's hope of obtaining a college education was impaired by the misfortune, and, under the state law, the alternative path to a lawyer's career, to which he aspired, was a seven years' clerkship in a law office. Entering upon such an apprenticeship in 1842, he changed his mind two years later, and went into the office of a banker and broker, where the shorter hours permitted him, with the aid of a friend, to pursue the study of mathematics and the classical languages. After two years more, through the influence of Rev. Charles G. Finney [*q.v.*], then professor of theology at Oberlin College, he was led to enter the preparatory department of that institution. Three years later (1849), while still an undergraduate, he married Helen, the daughter of Finney who was now president of the college. Graduating in 1851, Cox served for two years at Warren, Ohio, as superintendent of schools and principal of the high school, reading law at the same time, and beginning to practise in 1853.

Cox was at this time a Whig, but his Oberlin associations, his marriage, and other influences, combined to make him strongly anti-slavery in principle. He voted for Scott in 1852, but took a prominent part in bringing about the fusion of Whigs and Free-Soilers, and in 1855 was a delegate to the convention at Columbus which organized the Republican party in the state. A few years later his party friends, against his protest, nominated and elected him to the state Senate. Entering the Senate in 1859, he found there his friend James A. Garfield, and Governor-Elect Dennison, with whom he soon became intimate, this trio, together with Salmon P. Chase, then governor, forming a radical anti-slavery group.

With the outbreak of war in 1861, Cox's activity in organizing volunteers brought him a commission as brigadier-general of volunteers. During the summer he had a part in the Kanawha Valley campaign under McClellan, and a year later, in the Army of the Potomac, he participated in the battles of South Mountain and Antietam, commanding the 9th Corps at the former after the fall of Gen. Reno. He was advanced to the rank of major-general on Oct. 6, 1862, but the following April was reduced to his former rank because the number of major-generals permitted by law had been inadvertently exceeded. This bungling, which resulted in the promotion of less deserving officers, was a discouraging episode in his military career; but after repeated urging on the part of his superiors he was at length recommissioned in December 1864. During the winter of 1862–63 he commanded the forces in West Virginia, and from April to December 1863 was in charge of the Ohio military district. During the Atlanta campaign he led a division of the 23rd Army Corps, and after the fall of Atlanta for a time commanded the entire corps. He took part in the battle of Nashville, and early in 1865 was sent into North Carolina to open communications along the coast with Sherman, who was nearing the end of the march to the sea. On this expedition Cox defeated Bragg's troops and effected a junction with Sherman at Goldsboro.

After the war, while engaged in superintending the mustering out of the troops in Ohio, Cox was elected governor of the state. During the campaign in response to the inquiries of friends at Oberlin, he expressed himself as opposed to negro suffrage. He could not assume as they did, he wrote, that the suffrage, while whites and blacks dwelt in the same community, would cure all of the ills of the freedmen. Carrying these ideas further, he declared while governor, that the large groups of whites and blacks in the Southern states could never share political power, and that insistence upon it on the part of the colored people would bring about their ruin. As a remedy, he advocated the forcible segregation of the negroes, a plan which found little or no support. By such views, and by his indorsement of President Johnson's reconstruction policy, which he thought essentially the same as Lincoln's, he lost favor with his party, and was not renominated. He tried in vain to mediate between Johnson and the radical Republicans, and finally himself abandoned the President because of the latter's obstinacy and pugnacity. In 1868 Cox declined Johnson's tender of the post of commissioner of Internal Revenue.

Upon Grant's accession, Cox accepted the office of secretary of the interior. He had become a prominent advocate of the new cause of civil-service reform, and in his own department he put the merit system into operation, resisting the efforts of the party spoilsmen to dictate appointments and to collect campaign assessments. He and Attorney-General Hoar were regarded by the Independent Republicans as the only strong men in Grant's cabinet. When Grant's extraordinary Santo Domingo embroglio forced Hoar from the cabinet—the story of which episode Cox gave to the public twenty-five years later (see *Atlantic Monthly,* August 1895)—Cox lost hope of maintaining his fight without the support of the President. Already he had clashed with Grant over the fraudulent claims of one McGarrahan to certain mineral lands, as well as over the Dominican situation and on Oct. 5, 1870, he submitted his resignation. "My views of the necessity of reform in the civil service," he wrote, "have brought me more or less into collision with the plans of our active political managers, and my sense of duty has obliged me to oppose some of their methods of action" (*New York Tribune,* Oct. 31, 1870).

The breach with Grant hurt Cox deeply. He held Grant's military talent in high esteem, and did not allow his judgment thereof to be affected by their difference (see, *e.g.,* his review of Grant's *Memoirs,* in the *Nation,* Feb. 25, 1886, July 1, 1886); but in private conversation he permitted himself to criticize the President's course severely. Grant on his part, with his military instincts and experience, regarded Cox's independence of mind as a kind of insubordination. "The trouble was," as he put it, "that General Cox thought the Interior Department was the whole government, and that Cox was the Interior Department. I had to point out to him in very plain language that there were three controlling branches of the Government, and that I was the head of one of these and would so like to be considered by the Secretary of the Interior" (Hamlin Garland, *Ulysses S. Grant,* p. 427). Progressive opinion supported Cox, and his political "martyrdom" undoubtedly hastened the triumph of the reform movement.

Upon leaving the cabinet the former secretary

became conspicuously identified with the Liberal Republican movement, and was much talked of as its probable nominee for the presidency in 1872. At the Cincinnati convention, however, he was defeated by the more available Greeley. Meantime he had resumed the practise of law, at Cincinnati; but in 1873 he removed to Toledo to become president of the Wabash Railway. This position he gave up in turn upon being elected to Congress in 1876, from the 6th Ohio District, by an unprecedented majority.

He served but one term in Congress. He seems to have hoped to be able to do something to support President Hayes in his reform efforts, and his helplessness under existing political conditions probably discouraged him. At any rate he abandoned politics, even refraining thereafter from comment on political events, with the exception of a single speech during the Garfield campaign. Resuming his residence at Cincinnati, he became dean of the Cincinnati Law School (1881), a position which he held for the next sixteen years. During part of this time (1885–89) he also served as president of the University of Cincinnati. In addition to high repute as a lawyer, his reputation as a business man was enviable, and brought him in the middle nineties the tender of the post of railroad commissioner in New York City. This offer he declined, preferring to continue his connection with the Law School. In 1897 he declined President McKinley's offer of the Spanish mission, but in the same year he presented his library to Oberlin College and retired thither to write his *Military Reminiscences.* This work was barely completed and still unpublished when his death occurred, after a brief illness, while he was enjoying his customary summer outing along the coast of Maine, in company with a son.

Cox was tall, graceful, and well-proportioned, with erect, military bearing, and a frame denoting great physical strength. A man of many interests, he devoted much time in his later years to the study of microscopy, in which field he won international distinction. He was also a student of European cathedrals. His wide information, conversational gifts, and courteous manners made him an agreeable companion. The artistic genius of a son, Kenyon Cox [*q.v.*], doubtless bears witness to undeveloped talents of the father.

No small part of Cox's reputation rests upon his work as a writer. From 1874 until his death he was the *Nation's* military book critic. In addition to contributions to this and other journals, he wrote several books on military topics, the most important of which are: *Atlanta,* and *The March to the Sea; Franklin and Nashville* (volumes IX and X in the Campaigns of the Civil War series, 1882) ; *The Battle of Franklin, Tennessee, November 30, 1864* (1897) ; and *Military Reminiscences of the Civil War* (2 vols., 1900). He also contributed four chapters to M. F. Force's *Life of General Sherman* (1899). A work of less consequence is *The Second Battle of Bull Run as Connected with the Fitz-John Porter Case* (1882). Some critics of these books regard his attitude toward Rosecrans as unjust and not well informed, and his judgment in the Fitz-John Porter case is open to question. In general, however, he is recognized as an elegant and forceful writer, of fine critical ability and impartial judgment, one of the foremost military historians of the country.

[The autobiographical nature of the *Military Reminiscences* makes it the chief source of information for Cox's life as a soldier. It contains a portrait. See also *Bibliotheca Sacra*, July 1901, pp. 436–68. J. R. Ewing, *Public Services of Jacob Dolson Cox* (1902), is a slight sketch of about twenty pages which contains some data not found elsewhere. Jas. Ford Rhodes touches the high points of Cox's civil career and appraises his personality in "Jacob D. Cox" (*Hist. Essays*, 1909, pp. 183–88). He tells the story of the cabinet controversy in *Hist. of the U. S. from the Compromise of 1850*, VII (1910), 3–7. See also L. A. Coolidge, *Ulysses S. Grant* (1917); Hamlin Garland, *Ulysses S. Grant, His Life and Character* (1898); *Nation*, Aug. 9, 1901, p. 107. Estimates of Cox's writings may be found in the *Am. Hist. Rev.*, III (1898), 578–80, and VI (1901), 602–06.]

H.C.H.

COX, KENYON (Oct. 27, 1856–Mar. 17, 1919), painter, art critic, born at Warren, Ohio, came of a distinguished family. His father, Jacob Dolson Cox [*q.v.*], was a major-general in the Civil War, becoming one of its able historians. His mother was Helen, a daughter of Dr. Charles G. Finney [*q.v.*], theologian and first president of Oberlin College. His youth was clouded by ill health, as he was practically bed-ridden from his ninth to his thirteenth year, and often under the surgeon's knife. This left its physical impress through life. In the meantime his mother directed his studies, and, after a recovery, in view of his taste for art, he entered McMicken's Academy at Cincinnati, where Robert Blum was a fellow student. At that time he shared Blum's enthusiasm for Fortuny. They visited the Centennial Exhibition at Philadelphia together in 1876, and remaining to study at the Pennsylvania Academy of the Fine Arts, then set up a studio at Elbow Lane, where Brennan joined them. In 1877, Cox went to Paris and for a year worked in Carolus Duran's *atelier,* where Carroll Beckwith and John Sargent [*qq.v.*] had preceded him. Desirous of thorough academic training, he entered Gérôme's *atelier* at the École des Beaux-Arts, continuing there until his return to America in 1882. That he benefited by this combined instruc-

tion is made evident by the exhibition of two pictures at the Salons in 1879 and 1882. After his return to New York, his academic studies led to the production of several pictures of classic nudes, which failed to find purchasers. Similar subjects by European artists found places in American collections, but no encouragement was given to native painters who depicted the undraped figure. In portraits, however, of which he painted several, Cox's conscientious drawing and characterization were more appreciated. His academic precision tempered the bolder brush work of some of his associates of the lately formed Society of American Artists who resented the limited conventions of the older National Academy of Design. In 1886 he illustrated Rossetti's "Blessed Damozel," and in such paintings as "Moonrise," and some time later in "Hope and Memory," used landscape as a setting for classic figures of symbolic intent. Not meeting with encouragement in the pictorial treatment of life-size figures, however well and learnedly painted, he turned toward decorative art, and as a preparation made a profound study of the great Venetians, Titian, Tintoretto, Veronese, and Tiepolo, and of the principles underlying the decorative works of Delacroix and Baudry among the moderns. In the meantime his thorough knowledge made him a valuable instructor in the drawing of the human figure, and a more frequent use of the pen and lecture-platform helped to compensate for the lack of financial encouragement. His devotion to high ideals helped others as much as himself, and an era of mural decoration began. He took part in the decoration of the Walker Art Building at Bowdoin College, Me., and was one of the group who went out to Chicago in 1892 to decorate the domes of the Liberal Arts Building for the Exposition of 1893. There he and his clever, sympathetic wife, formerly Louise Howland King, also a painter of distinction, joined a party of notable American artists living at a recently opened hotel near their work at Jackson Park. It was an experiment in which each painter benefited by the free criticism of his fellows, and even though the immediate results of their labors were afterward destroyed by the axe of the wrecker, they served as an object-lesson. Other more permanent buildings throughout the country soon called for the exercise of the growing skill and added experience of the artists. Cox had his share. At the appellate court in New York he did some notable work, and for the Library of Congress at Washington he painted a series of female figures, each bearing emblems of the Arts and Sciences they were intended to symbolize. Based on a formal classicism, these are considered better from the point of view of purely decorative design than from that of their general color effect, and suggest a certain detachment from actuality. Several lunettes were executed for the Iowa State Capitol, and some fine decorations for the court house at Wilkes-Barre, Pa. Cox's decoration at Winona, Minn., "The Light of Learning," is remarkable for beautifully calculated rhythms of color and line. On the walls of the state capitol at St. Paul, Minn., he depicted "The Marriage of the Atlantic and the Pacific," with several mosaics somewhat formal in treatment but beautiful in design. In the meantime, his easel pictures were to be seen at the Metropolitan Museum, at the Lotos and Players Clubs in New York, at the National Gallery, Washington, and at the Carnegie Institute, Pittsburgh, as well as at the various current exhibitions.

As a writer on art subjects, Cox for twenty-five years contributed articles and essays to the *Nation, Scribner's,* and other magazines. These were appreciated as much by professional artists as by a wider circle of readers in search of standard opinions. His various essays and lectures were gathered into succeeding volumes published under the titles of *Old Masters and New* (1905), *Painters and Sculptors* (1907), *The Classic Point of View* (1911), *The Fine Arts* (1911), *Artist and Public* (1914), *Concerning Painting; Considerations Theoretical and Historical* (1917). In these writings his classical preferences in no way precluded a broad appreciation of other points of view or of certain manifestations in modern art. Besides membership in the Society of American Artists, he became an associate of the National Academy in 1900 and a full member in 1903. Medals were awarded him at the Paris Salon and Universal Expositions of 1889 and 1900, and in various American exhibitions, including the National Academy and Architectural League. He was an early and active member of the American Academy of Arts and Sciences, serving also on many art committees and juries. He stood heroically for the authority of tradition in an age of art license. His theory and practise were not only salutary and enlightening while he lived, but will remain as valuable sources of information for future students of art.

[F. J. Mather, Jr., "Kenyon Cox," in *Scribner's Mag.*, June 1919; "Kenyon Cox," *Literary Digest*, Apr. 5, 1919; S. Isham, *Hist. of Am. Painting* (1905), pp. 480, 553–60; C. H. Caffin, *Story of Am. Painting* (1907), p. 323–24; *N. Y. Herald*, Mar. 18, 1919; E. H. Blashfield in *Evening Post* (N. Y.), Mar. 20, 1919; Cox's own writings; personal acquaintance.] R.J.W.

COX, LEMUEL (1736–Feb. 18, 1806), mechanic, bridge-builder, was the youngest son of William and Thankful (Maudsley) Cox. He was born in Boston, Mass. In 1763 he married Susannah, daughter of William and Sarah (Sale) Hickling. Not much is known of Cox's early life. As early as 1765 there are records to show (Suffolk Deeds, vol. CIII, pp. 239, 251) that Cox and his brother Jesse, "wheelwrights all of Boston," purchased land in that city. He was a Loyalist, and in 1775 for that reason he served a term of confinement at Ipswich. His name is numbered in Boston's quota of some two thousand adherents of the King who left Massachusetts temporarily. Later he removed to Taunton, Mass., returning to Boston about 1789 and living there till June 1792 when he moved to Medford before going abroad.

Cox first came into prominence in 1785–86 as the master workman under whose supervision was constructed between Boston and Charlestown the first bridge across the Charles River, a piece of work which at that time was considered very remarkable. Its length was 1,503 feet and its width forty-two feet, and it was especially adapted to withstand tidal currents and ice. Its opening on June 17, 1786 was celebrated with great pomp by a large civil and military procession, including both branches of the legislature, with Cox himself occupying a prominent position. Broadsides were published upon the occasion, one of them being a poem of forty stanzas of which the following is a specimen:

> "Now Boston, Charlestown, nobly join,
> And roast a fatted Ox;
> On noted Bunker Hill combine,
> To toast our patriot, Cox."

Cox was also the architect and builder of the Essex Bridge from Salem to Beverly, a bridge which stood second only to the Charles River Bridge in its size and in the caliber of work involved. Success with these two undertakings and others in Massachusetts and Maine resulted in his being asked to construct the great bridge at Waterford, Ireland, which was built under his direction and supervision in 1793. For many years a bridge in Ireland, near Dublin, bore his name inscribed upon its piers. His stay overseas resulted in a number of works requiring great mechanical and engineering skill. He returned to Massachusetts, and died in Charlestown. He seems never to have acquired great wealth. "In 1796," says Joseph Barlow Felt in his *Annals of Salem* (1845, vol. I, p. 308), "he [Cox] had a grant of 1,000 acres of land in Maine from our legislature for being the first inventor of a machine to cut Card wire, the first projector of a Powder Mill in Massachusetts, the first suggestor of employing prisoners on Castle Island to make nails, and for various other discoveries in mechanical arts."

[John H. Cox, *New Eng. Cox Families* (1898–1904), pp. 77–78; N. B. Shurtleff, *Topographical and Hist. Description of Boston* (1891), pp. 417–18; "Description of Charles River Bridge," in *Mass. Mag.*, Sept. 1789, pp. 533–34; Lorenzo Sabine, *Sketches of Loyalists of the Am. Revolution* (1864), vol. I; S. A. Drake, *Old Landmarks and Historic Fields of Middlesex* (1895); *Columbian Centinel* (Boston), Feb. 19, *Boston Gazette* and *Independent Chronicle*, Feb. 20, *New Eng. Palladium* (Boston) Feb. 21, and *Boston Courier*, Feb. 27, 1806.]
K. W. C.

COX, PALMER (Apr. 28, 1840–July 24, 1924), author, illustrator, was born in Granby, Canada, of Scotch parents, Michael and Sarah (Miller) Cox. He grew up in the little Scotch community and after graduating from the Granby Academy started out to make his own way. He went to San Francisco in 1863, for several years was a railroad employee, and for some time worked as a ship-carpenter. During these years, for his own pleasure, he contributed humorous verse and cartoons to California papers, but none of his productions attracted any special attention. In 1875 he wrote and drew the pictures to accompany a story called *Squibs of California or Everyday Life Illustrated*, which met with no applause. He then went to New York and obtained a place on a weekly comic paper, *Wild Oats*, which struggled along for about five years and then went out of existence. During this time Cox published three stories, *Hans Von Pelter's Trip to Gotham* (1876), *How Columbus Found America* (1877), and *That Stanley* (1878). At the age of forty he began illustrating stories for *St. Nicholas Magazine*, to which he also contributed short poems of his own, with fantastic illustrations. He loved children and enjoyed entertaining them, and the children loved his drawings. As the magazine called for more and more material his brain was taxed for an original idea with which to carry on a series of stories, and eventually the famous "Brownies" were conceived. Suggested by the folklore of the Grampian Mountains, legends which Cox had heard in his childhood from the emigrant Scots at Granby, the "Brownies" were modified to fit the environment of the nineteenth-century American child. He resolved that there should be no pain or crime in the beings of his creation, only laughter for children. He managed, however, to convey a suggestion of reality, and the Brownie Policeman, the Brownie Wheelman, and the other reflections of contemporary life soon found a secure place in the child's imaginary world. The Brownies gave joy to two generations of children. Cox estimated that he drew over a million of them, and of his thirteen Brownie books over a million copies were so'd within his lifetime. His financial success enabled him to return to his old home at Granby and build a huge house which he called "Brownie Castle." Thereafter his summers were spent in Canada, and the major part of his winters on Long Island. He died, unmarried, at Brownie Castle. His publications for children include: *The Brownies, Their Book* (1887); *Queer People* (1888); *Queer People with Wings and Stings* (1888); *Queer People With Paws and Claws* (1888); *Another Brownie Book* (1890); *The Brownies at Home* (1893); *The Brownies Around the World* (1894); *The Brownies Through the Union* (1895); *The Brownies in Fairyland* (1895), a cantata in two acts; *Palmer Cox's Brownies* (1895), a play in three acts, which ran almost five years; *The Brownies Abroad* (1899); *The Brownies in the Philippines* (1904); *The Palmer Cox Brownie Primer* (1906); *Brownie Clown in Brownie Town* (1907); *The Brownies' Latest Adventures* (1910); *The Brownies Many More Nights* (1913).

[*Who's Who in America*, 1924–25; "Palmer Cox, The Brownie Man," in *St. Nicholas*, Oct. 1924; *Current Opinion*, Sept. 1924; *Nation* (N. Y.), Aug. 6, 1924; obituary and editorial in *N. Y. Times*, July 25, 1924.]
M. S.

COX, ROWLAND (July 9, 1842–May 13, 1900), patent lawyer, author, was a direct descendant of Richard Cox who, emigrating from England in 1708 to Newark, Del., ultimately settled in Chester County, Pa., in 1728. His father, John Cooke Cox, who married Ann Johns, daughter of Judge Rowland of the supreme court of Delaware, resided at Philadelphia where Rowland Cox was born. Receiving his early education privately, he entered the College of New Jersey (Princeton) in the class of 1863. The outbreak of the Civil War, however, interrupted his studies and he enlisted as a private in Company B, 15th Pennsylvania Volunteer Cavalry, on Oct. 3, 1862, at Carlisle. He took part in the Stone River and Chickamauga campaigns, and was promoted assistant adjutant-general on the staff of Major-Gen. J. B. McPherson, commanding the 17th Army Corps, Oct. 9, 1863. He remained on McPherson's staff when the latter assumed command of the Army of Tennessee, and was present at the battle of Atlanta, July 22, 1864, where McPherson was killed. He then joined the staff of Major-Gen. F. P. Blair and participated in Sherman's march through Georgia and the Carolinas. At the conclusion of the war he retired with the rank of brevet major, and took up the study of law at Quincy, Ill., being admitted to the Illinois bar in 1868. He practised for a short time at Washington, D. C., specializing in the law of inventions, copyright, and trade-marks, and edited *American Law Times Reports,* volumes II–VI (1869–74), and *American Law Times Reports,* volumes I–IV (1874–77), in addition to preparing *American Trade Mark Cases, a Compilation of all the Reported Trade Mark Cases Decided in the United States Courts prior to 1871, Together with the Leading English Cases* (1871). In 1875 he removed to New York City where he acquired a national reputation as an expert in trade-mark and copyright law. In 1878 in conjunction with Howard Ellis, he edited *The Reporter: Decisions of the Supreme and Circuit Courts, United States, Courts of Last Resort in the Several States and of the English and Irish Courts,* volumes V and VI, being a continuation of *American Law Times Reports, N. S.,* volumes I–IV. In 1881 appeared his *Manual of Trade Mark Cases; Comprising L. B. Sebastian's Digest of Trade-Mark Cases Covering Cases Prior to 1879, with Those of a Leading Character since that Time,* which became the standard work on the subject and passed through several editions. For over twenty years he was engaged in most of the important trade-mark and copyright litigation in the United States. He made it an invariable practise to accept retainers on behalf of complainants only, being thus enabled to employ a systematic method of argument in every instance. Never spectacular, he always appealed to the intellect, and his clear, cold, logical arguments, clothed in unpretentious yet forcible language, always had a powerful effect in cases where the principles of equity were allowed full sway. He died at Plainfield, N. J. On Oct. 29, 1868, he was married to Fanny Cummins, daughter of Robert Hill of Smyrna, Del.

[H. W. Cox, *The Cox Family in America* (1912); "Rowland Cox," prepared by E. C. Perkins in *Asso. of the Bar of the City of N. Y. Report,* 1901; *Hist. of the Fifteenth Pa. Volunteer Cavalry* (1906), ed. by C. H. Kirk.]   H. W. H. K.

COX, SAMUEL HANSON (Aug. 25, 1793–Oct. 2, 1880), Presbyterian clergyman, educator, a man of brilliant but eccentric genius, was born in Rahway, N. J., the son of James Cox, member of a New York importing firm, and Elizabeth (Shepard) Cox. He was of Quaker ancestry, fifth in descent from Isaac Cox of Talbot County, Md., and received his early education privately and at a Friends' academy in Westtown near Philadelphia. In 1813, while studying law under William Halsey at Newark, N. J., the charm of Quakerism in which he had been nur-

tured "was dissolved by the *unmystical* verities of the Bible," and he joined the Presbyterian Church. His experiences at this period he describes at length in *Quakerism not Christianity* (1833), a discursive work of nearly seven hundred pages. He now turned to the study of theology, and, Oct. 10, 1816, was licensed by the New York Presbytery. On July 1, 1817, he was ordained and installed pastor of the Presbyterian Church, Mendham, N. J. His other pastorates were at Spring Street Church (1820–25) and Laight Street Church (1825–35), New York, and the First Presbyterian Church, Brooklyn (1837–54). He was married, Apr. 7, 1817, to Abia Hyde Cleveland (1796–1865), by whom he had fifteen children, the eldest of whom, Arthur Cleveland Coxe [*q.v.*], became a bishop in the Episcopal Church. His second wife, whom he married Nov. 16, 1869, was Anna Fosdick Bacon.

He was noted both for his peculiarities and for his gifts. His utterances, tinged with intellectual arrogance and interlarded with quotations from the Latin, a language he spoke fluently, reveal an amusing fondness for long and uncommon words. His learning was extensive, but his scholarship not profound. Strong sympathies and antipathies led him into extravagances. Nevertheless, his versatility, eloquence, wit, sincerity, and courage, gave him standing and influence. At the outset of his career he came into prominence through being refused an appointment by the Young Men's Missionary Society of New York, because of his Hopkinsian sentiments. In the sharp conflicts of 1836–38 which split the Presbyterian Church, he was one of the New School leaders, and he was moderator of the New School General Assembly in 1846. He was a founder of New York University, and during a thirty-six years' term as director of Union Theological Seminary did much to shape its policies. From 1835 to 1837 he was professor of sacred rhetoric and pastoral theology at Auburn Seminary, and from 1856 to 1863 the head of Ingham University, Le Roy, N. Y., an institution for young women. He died at Bronxville, N. Y.

Although at the anniversary of the British and Foreign Bible Society, London, May 1833, he defended his country when attacked on the score of slavery, his early radical anti-slavery sentiments got him into trouble. His church and house were stoned, and in July 1835, he was hanged in effigy at Charleston along with Garrison and Arthur Tappan. For the London edition of William Jay's *Slavery in America* (1835), a work antagonistic to the Colonization

Society he wrote a vigorous introduction. Later he modified his views, fought the attempted exclusion of slaveholders at the meeting of the Evangelical Alliance in London, 1846, and repudiated his former friendship for Frederick Douglass because of his behavior at a temperance convention they attended there (*Liberator,* Nov. 20, 1846). Violently opposed both to intoxicants and to tobacco, he wrote a long introduction, addressed to John Quincy Adams, for Benjamin I. Lane's *Mysteries of Tobacco* (1851). He edited and brought down to date Archibald Bower's anti-Catholic *History of the Popes* in 1844–47. *Interviews Memorable and Useful* (1853) indirectly reveals many of his characteristics.

[*Gen. Cat. Auburn Theol. Sem.* (1883); John Q. Adams, *Hist. of Auburn Theol. Sem.* (1918); G. L. Prentiss, *The Union Theol. Sem., N. Y., Hist. and Biog. Sketches of its First Fifty Years* (1889); J. L. Chamberlain, ed., *Universities and Their Sons, N. Y. Univ.* (1901); E. J. and H. G. Cleveland, *Geneal. Cleveland and Cleaveland Families* (1899), I, 515–20; W. P. and F. J. Garrison, *Wm. Lloyd Garrison* (1885–89), I, 461, 485; III, 165–66.]   H. E. S.

COX, SAMUEL SULLIVAN (Sept. 30, 1824–Sept. 10, 1889), congressman, writer, was a descendant of Thomas Cox, one of the original proprietors of East Jersey, who came to the Province in 1670. A great-grandson of this pioneer was Gen. James Cox, soldier of Brandywine and Germantown, speaker of the New Jersey legislature, friend of Jefferson, and member of the Tenth Congress. His son, Ezekiel Taylor Cox, removed to Zanesville, Ohio, and became editor of the *Muskingum Messenger,* marrying the daughter of Samuel Sullivan, at one time state treasurer. Of this union were born thirteen children, Samuel Sullivan Cox being the second child.

After attending Ohio University for nearly two years, Samuel entered Brown University, graduating in 1846 with high honors. During his course he distinguished himself as a debater and writer of prize essays in history, economics, and criticism. Returning to Ohio after graduation he read law. Two years of practise in Cincinnati opened prospects of professional success, but his tastes drew him to literature and travel. In 1849 he married Julia A. Buckingham of Zanesville, who was thenceforth his congenial and inseparable companion. With her he visited Europe, publishing upon his return his first book, *A Buckeye Abroad* (1852). Its favorable reception turned his attention to journalism, and he became editor and chief owner of the *Ohio Statesman* at Columbus. A glowing description of a sunset, printed May 19, 1853, won him a sobriquet which clung—"Sunset" Cox.

Journalism led into politics. As chairman of the Democratic state committee Cox showed such efficiency that President Pierce offered him the post of secretary of legation in England (1855). He chose in preference a similar appointment to Peru, but turned back on the way because of ill health. Thereupon he was elected to Congress (1856), defeating his Republican and "Know-Nothing" rivals by a plurality of 355. From 1857, with the exception of the Thirty-ninth and Fortieth Congresses and a year of diplomatic service, he was almost continuously a member of the lower house. Despite reapportionments, gerrymanders, and other vicissitudes of politics, he failed only a few times in thirty years to win reëlection by votes which show an increasing hold upon his constituents. When his career closed, few if any of his associates enjoyed greater distinction for long and useful service. Almost every major issue for a generation had felt his influence.

Entering Congress during the Kansas crisis, while Douglas was attacking the Lecompton constitution in the Senate, Cox's maiden speech was made against it, the first by any member of the House. As war drew near, he supported all measures which promised adjustment of sectional difficulties; and after hostilities began, although he voted consistently for money and men to sustain the Federal authority, he advocated every effort to restore peace and union. He strenuously opposed the resort to martial law outside of the war zone (he was a friend of Clement L. Vallandigham [*q.v.*] and, as he testified on oath, was the author of the words for which Vallandigham was arrested); as a member of the Committee on Foreign Affairs, he aided in settling the *Trent* affair; he influenced Lincoln's decision to treat Southern seamen as prisoners of war instead of pirates; he was among the foremost in efforts to abolish privateering; he was instrumental in bringing about the Hampton Roads Conference in 1865. At the National Democratic Convention of 1864 he seconded McClellan's nomination for the presidency. In 1864 he successfully opposed extreme confiscation measures. Defeated in the autumn election, he removed permanently to New York City, in the belief, it seems, that his Ohio district would thenceforth be Republican. He practised law and wrote *Eight Years in Congress* (1865), while the radicals passed the Thirteenth and Fourteenth Amendments and impeached the President. Returning to Congress in 1868, he labored during many sessions for complete amnesty, and was prominent as an advocate of reform of the tariff and the Civil Service. He was directly responsible for bills establishing the Life Saving Service, securing increased pay and vacation privileges for letter-carriers, and broadening the scope of the census enumeration of 1890. He took pride in the development of the West, promoting legislation for the reclamation of waste lands, and insisting upon statehood for the Dakotas, Montana, and Washington. Appointed minister to Turkey by President Cleveland in 1885, he resigned and returned to America after a year. The literary result of this sojourn was *Diversions of a Diplomat in Turkey* (1887). Almost immediately after reaching home he was sent to Congress again in place of Joseph Pulitzer, resigned. He visited the Northwest in the summer of 1889, following the admission of the "omnibus" states, but his health, never robust, broke down, and his death followed.

Cox was a deeply religious man, a scholar of broad reading and prodigious memory, and an independent thinker who never allowed his party to prescribe his course. He opposed centralizing tendencies in government, and saw in Cleveland's election the promise of a permanent return to early Democratic principles. In debate he was ready, witty, and courteous. He was a prolific writer. In addition to the titles already mentioned the following may be enumerated: *Puritanism in Politics* (1863); *Why We Laugh* (1876); *Free Land and Free Trade* (1880); *Arctic Sunbeams* (1882); *Orient Sunbeams* (1882); *Three Decades of Federal Legislation* (1885).

[The chief source is Wm. Van Zandt Cox and Milton Harlow Northrup, *Life of Samuel Sullivan Cox* (Syracuse, 1899). See also the addresses of fellow members of Congress at the memorial session held on Apr. 19, 1890; *Congressional Record*, 51st Cong., 1 Sess., 3558–90; 7028–33. Cox's own books are also valuable sources, especially the *Three Decades of Federal Legislation*, which contains an engraved portrait of the author on the title-page. A statue erected by the letter-carriers and executed by Louise Lawson, stands in Astor Place, New York City.]   H. C. H.

COX, WILLIAM RUFFIN (Mar. 11, 1832–Dec. 26, 1919), Confederate soldier, politician, was descended from John Cox, a British naval officer of good family and trading inclinations, who settled in North Carolina in the early nineteenth century. His son Thomas, after building up at Plymouth, N. C., an important export business with the West Indies, married Olivia Norfleet and became a planter in Halifax County, the home of his wife. Here, at Scotland Neck, their son William Ruffin was born. On his father's death he was, for family reasons, put to school in Tennessee. After graduating from Franklin College and studying law at Lebanon College, he practised at the Tennessee bar for

five years. In 1857 he married Penelope Battle of Edgecombe County, N. C., and, settling there, began to develop the fine plantation which he retained throughout his life. Soon, however, he became an enthusiastic secessionist. Having organized and equipped a military company at his own expense and having set himself to the study of military tactics, on the outbreak of the Civil War he was appointed by the governor major of the 2nd North Carolina Regiment. During the next four years he was with the Army of Northern Virginia continuously, participating in most of its battles and winning official commendation for ability to keep his command intact and for skill and intrepidity in attack. Eleven times he was wounded, five times at Chancellorsville. The temporary command of a brigade came on May 31, 1864. To Cox fell the honor of leading the last organized attack made by his army. After the war this military record was an asset of first importance when, having begun again the practise of law in Raleigh, he drifted into politics. For a while it seemed that original secessionists and the Holden party might unite in support of Cox as a candidate for governor in opposition to Worth, whom old Unionists supported. Instead, however, the former elected to assist in building a party of out-and-out opposition to the Radical régime by standing, in 1868, for the humble, but at that time peculiarly important, office of solicitor in the heavily Radical Raleigh district. Winning by the narrowest of margins, he continued to serve in this capacity until 1874, when he was made chairman of the state Democratic committee. Emphasizing fairness of nominations, rigid party discipline, and thorough local organization (*Raleigh Daily News*, June 11, 1874), this committee under his leadership "redeemed" the state in the three stirring campaigns of 1874, 1875, and 1876. In 1876 Cox became district judge by appointment. Resigning in 1880 he was elected to Congress from the Raleigh-Durham district, and was reëlected in 1882 and 1884. As chairman of the House Committee on Civil Service he supported President Cleveland's reform policy, declaring in a set speech (June 1886) that the merit system involved "the very essence and genius of Democracy." For this reason chiefly he was defeated for renomination by his party, though not until his friends had deadlocked the convention for 197 ballots. In consonance with common opinion—although Cox indignantly denied that there was any understanding to that effect—President Cleveland offered him a position in the Land Office. This he declined (*News and Observer*, Raleigh,

Aug. 7–10, 1886). In 1893, however, he was elected secretary of the Senate, a position which he continued to hold until 1900. Meantime he was busy with many other affairs. He served as grand master of the Masonic Order, sat in the councils of the Protestant Episcopal Church, served on the executive committee of the State Agricultural Society, and as chairman of the committee that established the *North Carolina Journal of Education*. He often delivered memorial addresses, the most elaborate of which was "The Life and Character of Ramseur." These addresses disclose no unusual learning or eloquence and tend to confirm Gov. Worth's view that Cox was "a man of slender capacity" (J. G. de R. Hamilton, *Correspondence of Jonathan Worth*, II, 707). On the other hand it is recorded that he was of striking physical appearance, cultured and courtly; and his political choices indicate wisdom as well as character. In 1883 he was married to Fannie Augusta Lyman, who bore him two sons, and in 1905 to Mrs. Herbert A. Claiborne of Richmond, Va.

[In addition to references above see sketch by S. A. Ashe, in *Biog. Hist. of N. C.*, vol. I (1905); obituary in the *News and Observer* (Raleigh), Dec. 27, 28, 1919.]

C. C. P.

COXE, ARTHUR CLEVELAND (May 10, 1818–July 20, 1896), Episcopal bishop, writer, was born in Mendham, N. J., the first parish of his celebrated Presbyterian father, Rev. Samuel Hanson Cox [*q.v.*], the son adopting what he deemed an earlier spelling of the family name. His youth was spent principally in New York. He early displayed a liking for the Episcopal Church, which was probably strengthened in the home of his uncle, Dr. Abraham Cox, a prominent New York physician. At twenty he graduated from the University of the City of New York, and in 1841, from the General Theological Seminary. He was ordained priest, Sept. 25, 1842, at St. John's Church, Hartford, Conn., of which he became rector. From 1854 to 1863 he was rector of Grace Church, Baltimore, declining an election to the episcopate of Texas in 1856, and from 1863 to 1865, rector of Calvary Church, New York. On Jan. 4, 1865, he was consecrated assistant bishop of Western New York, and at the death of Bishop De Lancey, three months later, he succeeded him. On Sept. 21, 1841, he married Katherine Cleveland Hyde, a second cousin once removed.

He was long a prominent figure in ecclesiastical councils, and a prolific writer on subjects covering a wide range. In physical vitality, versatility, learning, intensity of feeling, and devotion to reform he resembled his father. In addition he had a gift of versification which enabled him to publish several volumes of ecclesiastical poetry. His best-known work of this kind is *Christian Ballads* (1840), many editions of which appeared both in America and England. The impression of the author created by these is said to have had much to do with his election as bishop (Charles W. Hayes, *Diocese of Western New York*, 1904, p. 245). Theologically and ecclesiastically he was strongly conservative. He was opposed to the consecration of Phillips Brooks as bishop (*Ibid.*, p. 350), and his *Holy Writ and Modern Thought* (1892) shows little sympathy with the scientific tendencies of the day. His efforts at reform were directed chiefly toward Christian unity on the basis of "that constitution of the Church and that profession of faith which were *recognized*, not invented, by the Council of Nicæa." *The Criterion* (1866) and *Apollos, or the Way of God* (1871) state fully his views. After a visit to Dr. John von Hirscher at Freiburg, a precursor of the Old Catholic movement, he published at Oxford (1852) a translation of the former's *On the Actual State of the Church*, under the title, *Sympathies of the Continent*, a work which attracted much attention in England and at home. He participated actively in the formation of the Anglo-Continental Society, an object of which was the promulgation on the Continent of the principles of the English Reformation. His *Letter to Pius the Ninth*, at the calling of the Vatican Council in 1869, was published in Europe in French, German, Greek, Bohemian, and Italian. In 1874 he published in Paris *L'Épiscopat de l'Occident*, a treatise on the history of the Church of England, controverting Roman Catholic attacks. He opposed revisions of the Bible on the ground that the authorized version was a bond that united the churches, and in 1857 published his *Apology for the English Bible*. He organized the Christian Literature Company in 1885 for the publication of the patristic fathers, and during 1885–86 brought out an edition of the *Ante-Nicene Fathers*.

Dignified in bearing and punctilious in deportment, with finely chiseled features, high forehead, waving white hair, and side whiskers, he looked and acted the part of the typical bishop.

[See *Christian Lit.*, Sept. 1896; *Critic*, Aug. 1, 1896; *Churchman*, July 25, 1896; Henry C. Potter, *Reminiscence of Bishops and Archbishops* (1906); Herman G. Batterson, *Sketch-Book of the Am. Episcopate* (1891) lists eighty-one of Coxe's publications.] H. E. S.

COXE, DANIEL (August 1673–Apr. 25, 1739), landowner, politician, was the eldest son of Daniel and Rebecca (Coldham) Coxe of London. His father (1640–1730) was a member of the Royal Society (March 1664/5), a doctor of medicine of Cambridge (1669), one of the physicians to Charles II and to Queen Anne, and a writer on chemistry and medicine. Although he was never in America, Dr. Coxe was a figure of importance in early colonial history. He acquired interests in West Jersey in 1684 and in East Jersey in 1686 and by purchase of land from the heirs of Gov. Billinge he was nominally governor of West Jersey from 1687 to 1692, when he sold the greater part of his proprietary. Dr. Coxe was a large speculator in colonial proprietary rights; by 1698 he had procured the assignment of Sir Robert Heath's patent to Carolana, which included Norfolk County, Va., and the English rights to the Mississippi Valley west of the Carolinas. He agitated many years with partial success for the confirmation of this patent. He conceived the magnificent idea of forming a commonwealth within Carolana, and sent two armed vessels to explore the Mississippi, but, having once abandoned his plan for a settlement there, attempted unsuccessfully to settle a body of Huguenots in Virginia. He collected a large body of documentary information concerning colonial travels and explorations and from these compiled his advertising tracts; in his "Account of New Jersey" he wrote that he had "made greate discoveryes towards the greate Lake . . . and contracted Freinshipp with diverse petty Kings," but these events were experienced where they were written—in the quiet of his library in Aldersgate Street.

Dr. Coxe was ably assisted in his claims and efforts by his son, Daniel, who came to America in 1702 with Lord Cornbury [q.v.], of whom he was a favorite. Appointed by the latter commander of the forces in West Jersey he was thereafter known as Col. Coxe. He was recommended in 1702 and again in 1705 for a seat on the Governor's Council; in 1706, despite the opposition of the Quakers, he was appointed. In the same year he was made one of the associate judges of the supreme court of the province. In 1707, following an elopement, this "fine, flaunting gentleman" married Sarah Eckley, daughter of a Philadelphia Quaker. When Lord Lovelace became governor of the province in 1708 Coxe was again appointed to the Council. He was unable to get along with the succeeding governor, Hunter, and in 1713 was removed from the Council through Hunter's influence. Having obtained the Swedish vote in Gloucester County, he was elected to the Assembly in 1714 and again in 1716, when he was chosen speaker. Hunter at once prorogued the Assembly, and when it convened again Coxe and his followers absented themselves in an un-

successful attempt to obstruct the session. When a majority of the Assembly was finally gathered, Coxe and his friends were expelled and fled to Bristol in Pennsylvania. He returned to London, and his father and his brother Samuel petitioned the Lords of Trade in January and February 1714/15 against the renewal of Hunter's commission, but without success.

While in London in 1722 he published *A Description of the English Province of Carolana, by the Spaniards call'd Florida, and by the French La Louisiane also of the great and famous river Meschacebe or Mississippi,* composed of the memoirs of traders and explorers collected by his father. This book is chiefly remarkable because in the introduction Coxe sets forth what is believed to be the first printed plan for a political confederation of the North American colonies. He proposed that the colonies "be united under a Legal, Regular, and firm Establishment," that a Lieutenant or Supreme Governor be constituted to whom the colonial governors should be subordinate, and that two deputies, elected by the Assembly of each province, should "meet together, consult, and advise for the good of the whole, settle and appoint particular Quotas or Proportions of Money, Men, Provisions that each respective government is to raise for their mutual defense and safety."

He returned to New Jersey and in 1725 was a candidate for the Assembly from Burlington. In 1730 he was deputized as "Provincial Grand Master of the Provinces of New York, New Jersey, and Pensilvania" and thus became the first appointed Grand Master of Masons in America. He was again appointed to the supreme court in 1734 as third judge, a position which he held until his death in 1739.

[See *N. Y. Col. Docs.,* vols. V, VI; *N. J. Archives,* first ser., vols. IV, X, XI; *Calendar of State Papers, Colonial Ser., America and West Indies;* Richard S. Field, "Provincial Courts of N. J.," vol. III of the *N. J. Hist. Soc. Colls.* (1849); G. D. Scull in *Pa. Mag. of Hist. and Biog.,* vol. VII (1883); C. W. Alvord and Lee Bidgood, *First Explorations of the Trans-Allegheny Region by the Virginians 1650–74* (1912); Hamilton Schuyler, *Hist. of St. Michael's Church, Trenton . . . 1703–1926* (1926); Jos. H. Hough, *Origin of Masonry in N. J.* (1870); *Pa. Mag. of Hist. and Biog.,* vols. V, VI (1881–82). A manuscript chart of the descendants of Daniel Coxe, prepared by Mrs. Brinton Coxe, is in the possession of the Geneal. Soc. of Pa.]   F.M.

COXE, ECKLEY BRINTON (June 4, 1839– May 13, 1895), mining engineer, the son of Charles Sidney Coxe, district attorney of Philadelphia and later judge of the district court, and of Ann Maria (Brinton) Coxe, was born in Philadelphia. He was a descendant of Col. Daniel Coxe [q.v.] and a grandson of Tench Coxe [q.v.]. The latter had acquired large tracts of land in the anthracite region of Pennsylvania before the importance of coal was generally realized, and Eckley Coxe was educated with the intention that he should develop them. At the age of nineteen he was graduated from the University of Pennsylvania. After graduation he continued for a time at the University, studying science, French, and bookkeeping. During his college course his summers had been spent in the coal regions and in 1859 he assisted in surveying the family's lands. In 1860 he went to Paris where he spent two years at the school of mines, after which he attended for a year the famous mining academy at Freiberg in Saxony, thus helping to set a fashion which led many American students of mining thither. Prof. Julius Weisbach of Freiberg authorized Coxe to translate the first part of his important treatise on mechanics; this was published in 1870 in New York as *A Manual of the Mechanics of Engineering and of the Construction of Machines, with an Introduction to the Calculus: Vol. I, Theoretical Mechanics,* a volume of 1,112 pages. Coxe spent nearly two years more in Europe studying the actual operations of mines in England and on the Continent; this was during the period of the Civil War in America. In 1864, at the age of twenty-five, he returned to America to take up the development of the coal lands. In 1865 the firm of Coxe Brothers & Company was organized, the name later being changed to The Cross Creek Coal Company. Eckley Coxe made his home at Drifton, near Wilkes-Barre, in the anthracite region, and on June 27, 1868, married Sophia G. Fisher, daughter of Joshua Francis Fisher of Philadelphia.

The problems of Coxe in the development of the coal lands were both administrative and technical. Several leases for mining coal on the family's lands had already been granted. For economy in operation he maneuvered to consolidate these. By 1886 only 1,200 acres of the estate remained outside the control of the Cross Creek Company, of which Coxe was president, and the company controlled about 35,000 acres. The problem of transportation was critical. After controversies with the several railroads serving the region, the Delaware, Susquehanna & Schuylkill Railroad was organized in 1890 with members of the Cross Creek Company as stockholders and Coxe as president. Other problems were labor troubles, fires in the coal-mines, and the waste of coal due to short-sighted policies of operators anxious for quick profits. Coxe's policy in meeting all of these difficulties was commendable and patriotic. Among his technical achievements were the inventions of long steel tapes to use instead of chains for mine-surveying; Coxe's micrometer; an automatic slate-picking chute; corrugated rolls for breaking coal; coal-jigs; gyrating screens; the mechanical stoker; grease-packing for plunger-pumps; and applications of compressed air to machinery. His efforts to reduce the waste of small coal were particularly noteworthy and helped to stop the growth of the great culm heaps that marked the enormous losses in early anthracite mining. Many of Coxe's inventions and improvements were made in conjunction with skilful assistants who worked under his directions. A number of patents in his name or assigned to him were recorded about 1890. Over seventy of these were issued to cover mechanical stoking—an important development in engineering.

Coxe's constructive ability was not confined to his business enterprises. He established and contributed liberally to the support of a technical school at Drifton, for the sons of working miners. He was one of the founders of the American Institute of Mining Engineers and its president in 1878 and 1879, president of the American Society of Mechanical Engineers from 1892 to 1894, member of the American Society of Civil Engineers and of the American Chemical Society, state senator from the Luzerne and Lackawanna district of Pennsylvania from 1880 to 1884, and a trustee of Lehigh University from its inception. He was a Democrat and an Episcopalian. As a politician he was too conscientious to be practical; as a trustee of Lehigh he was active and enthusiastic. He was a robust, forceful man characterized by energy and spontaneity, and had an unusually large number of friends. He died of pneumonia at the age of fifty-four.

[Obituary article by R. W. Raymond in *Trans. Am. Inst. Mining Engineers,* vol. XXV (1896); obituary articles in *Trans. Am. Soc. Mech. Engineers,* vol. XVI (1895); *Trans. Am. Soc. Civil Engineers,* vol. XXXVI (1897); *Biog. Cat. Matriculates of the Coll. 1749–1893* (Univ. of Pa.).]   P.B.M.

COXE, JOHN REDMAN (Sept. 16, 1773– Mar. 22, 1864), physician, a descendant of Col. Daniel Coxe [*q.v.*] and the son of Daniel and Sarah (Redman) Coxe, was born in Trenton, N. J., but brought up by his grandfather, the distinguished physician John Redman [*q.v.*], in Philadelphia. Young Coxe was sent to school in England and then studied medicine in London and Edinburgh. In 1790 he returned to Philadelphia where he resumed his medical studies under Dr. Benjamin Rush [*q.v.*] and at the University of Pennsylvania, from which he received his degree of M.D. in 1794. During the yellow-fever epidemic of 1793 he worked faithfully by the side of his great preceptor. The following year he went abroad again and spent several years studying in the hospitals at London, Edinburgh, and Paris. He returned to Philadelphia in 1796 and started to practise. During the yellow-fever epidemic of 1797 he gave up his private work to serve as resident physician at the Bush Hill Hospital under Dr. Physick and Dr. Cathrall. Coxe was an early advocate of vaccination, naming a son of his Edward Jenner and vaccinating him as well as himself in 1801. He was also an expert pharmacist. The compound syrup of squills of the United States Pharmacopœia was originally prepared by him and was generally known as Coxe's Hive Syrup. He is said to have introduced the Jalap plant into the United States. His lectures on materia medica and pharmacy were the chief source of systematic instruction for prospective apothecaries before the establishment of the College of Pharmacy.

Coxe was editor of the *Medical Museum* which was published from 1805 until 1811. In 1808 he edited the *American Dispensatory* and published a *Medical Dictionary*. His other writings include: *An Inquiry into the Claims of Dr. William Harvey to the Discovery of the Circulation of the Blood with a More Equitable Retrospect of that Event, to Which Is Added an Introductory Lecture Delivered on the Third of November, 1829, in Vindication of Hippocrates from Sundry Charges of Ignorance Preferred Against Him by the Late Professor Rush* (1834); *The Writings of Hippocrates and Galen Epitomized from the Original Latin Translation* (1846). From 1802 to 1807 he was physician to the Pennsylvania Hospital. He was professor of chemistry in the University of Pennsylvania from 1809 to 1819, when he was transferred to the chair of materia medica and pharmacy in the medical department. In 1835 his chair was declared vacant by the Board of Trustees. He seems to have been too conservative in his teachings. According to Carson, "The doctrines and opinions of the earlier fathers of Physic had so superior a value in his estimation as to lead to too exclusive an exposition of them in his lectures."

At the time of Coxe's death his library, according to Gross, who held Coxe's learning in high esteem, contained the "best collection of the Fathers of Medicine and of Theology" in the country. The library was sold by auction; the theological section was purchased for the Princeton Library and the Theological Seminary in Philadelphia, and Gross himself bought many of the medical books. Coxe was married to Sarah, daughter of Col. John Cox, by whom he had six children.

["Records of Christ Church" (Phila.), in *Pa. Archives*, II, 68; Jos. Carson, *Hist. of the Medic. Dept. of the Univ. of Pa.* (1869); Samuel D. Gross, *Autobiography* (1884); T. G. Morton, *Hist. of the Pa. Hospital* (1895); *Am. Medic. Times*, May 7, 1864; *Boston Medic. and Surgic. Jour.*, Sept. 26, 1849.]   F.R.P.

COXE, RICHARD SMITH (Jan. 1792–Apr. 28, 1865), lawyer, was a great-grandson of Col. Daniel Coxe [*q.v.*], and a son of William Coxe [*q.v.*] and Rachel (Smith) Coxe, who at the time of Richard's birth were residing at Burlington, N. J. Richard obtained his early education at the Burlington Academy, was prepared for college by a private tutor, and entered the College of New Jersey (Princeton) in 1805, graduating in 1808. He then read law for three years in the office of Judge William Griffith at Burlington, after which he went to Philadelphia, studied with Horace Binney [*q.v.*], and was admitted to the bar of the supreme court of Pennsylvania, Dec. 11, 1812. He practised for some time in Philadelphia, making a special study of real property law. Early evincing great literary activity, in his leisure he prepared *A New Critical Pronouncing Dictionary of the English Language Compiled by an American Gentleman*, which was published in 1813. He also compiled *Reports of Cases Argued and Determined in the Supreme Court of New Jersey from April Term 1790 to November Term 1795 Both Inclusive*, which appeared in 1816. This work forms the first volume of the series of reports of decisions of the supreme court of New Jersey. On his marriage, Jan. 23, 1816, to Susan B., daughter of Judge Griffith, he returned to Burlington and was admitted to the New Jersey bar in May 1817. Opening an office in Burlington he soon acquired a good practise and was appointed deputy attorney-general for Burlington County. In December 1822, however, he removed to Washington, D. C., and was admitted to the bar of the circuit court of the District of Columbia. At this period much litigation dealing with intricate questions of real property law applicable to the colonies of Great Britain, France, and Spain arose from the cession of Florida and Louisiana, and in due course came before the Supreme Court of the United States. Coxe, owing to his having specialized in real property law, was briefed in a number of suits, and such was the skill which he displayed in handling these cases, involving as they did not only important principles of municipal law but delicate considerations of public international law, that he quickly established himself as a leader of the Supreme Court. Thenceforth his practise was chiefly before that tribunal, where his ability procured for him some years predominance as counsel. It was said of him at one time that he was employed in more cases upon the docket of the Supreme Court of the United States than any other lawyer in the country (Crew, *post*). Despite his heavy professional engagements, he prepared a *Digest of Decisions Supreme, Circuit, and District Courts, United States, 1789–1829,* which was published in 1829. As judge advocate he appeared for the government in many prosecutions before courts-martial. Consistently refusing to enter public life, he confined himself to his professional work, seeking his recreation in literary studies, particularly the English classics. To this avocation may be attributed the attractive scholarly way in which he invariably presented his cases to the Court, his arguments being remarkable for their perfection of language and logic. He was frequently called upon on academic and patriotic occasions to deliver addresses, a number of which were subsequently published, and, in addition to the works previously referred to, he wrote a *Review of the Relations between the United States and Mexico* (1846) and a brochure, *The Present State of the African Slave-Trade* (1858). In 1840 he married as his second wife Mrs. Susan R. Wheeler, daughter of John Warren of New York. He died at Washington.

[John Clement, *Sketches of the First Emigrant Settlers in Newton Township, N. J.* (1877), p. 174; E. M. Woodward and J. F. Hageman, *Hist. of Burlington and Mercer Counties, N. J.* (1883); *Biog. Sketches of Eminent Am. Lawyers* (1852), ed. by John Livingston, p. 692; *Centennial Hist. of the City of Washington, D. C.* (1892), ed. by H. W. Crew; F. R. Noel and M. B. Downing, *The Court House of the District of Columbia* (1919); *Evening Star* (Washington), Apr. 28, 1865.]
H. W. H. K.

COXE, TENCH (May 22, 1755–July 16, 1824), political economist, was the son of William and Mary (Francis) Coxe and grandson of Col. Daniel Coxe [*q.v.*], colonial legislator and judge, and of Tench Francis [*q.v.*], attorney-general of the province of Pennsylvania. Tench Coxe, like his brother William [*q.v.*], was born in Philadelphia. He was educated at the College of Philadelphia, now the University of Pennsylvania, though he seems not to have graduated. He studied law, but instead of undertaking an independent practise entered his father's counting-house, and in 1776 became a member of the firm of Coxe, Furman & Coxe. Friendly writers have said that it was the exigency of the business, of which he was left in complete charge, which made him neutral during the Revolution. Others declare that royalist sympathies made him resign from the militia and leave Philadelphia to join the British, returning in 1777 with the army under Howe, and that with Howe's withdrawal Coxe was arrested, paroled, and turned Whig. At any rate, he did not sacrifice the esteem of patriots, for he was a member of the Annapolis Convention of 1786 and of the Continental Congress in 1788. He supported the adoption of the Constitution in an able pamphlet, *An Examination of the Constitution for the United States* (1788), which was one of the earliest arguments to appear in its behalf, and marks its author in every way a Federalist. He was particularly anxious that the financial difficulties of the Confederation should be cured through adoption of the new instrument. He was made assistant secretary of the treasury in 1789 and became Commissioner of the Revenue in 1792. From the latter post Adams removed him in December 1797 (probably because of Wolcott's dissatisfaction with his subordinate, though no official reason was given), and Coxe altered allegiance again by joining the Republicans. In the campaign of 1800 he added to the Federalist discomfort, already acute through Hamilton's attack upon President Adams, by publishing a letter which he had received from Adams in 1792 openly insinuating that Charles and Thomas Pinckney, both Federalist leaders, were not to be trusted because under British influence. Federalists promptly branded Coxe a traitor to the party, whereupon Jefferson took him up, in 1803 appointing him Purveyor of Public Supplies, which office he held until it was abolished in 1812. Jefferson and Madison remained his friends, and the latter, in 1820 when Coxe was an old man, sought unavailingly to have Monroe give him preferment.

Coxe's shifts in politics were in marked contrast to his steadfastness in adherence to the economic policies which he believed would promote the prosperity of the new nation. Dealing in practicalities rather than in doctrine, he belonged to the nationalist group which later found its full expression in the works of Henry C. Carey [*q.v.*]. He resented the hardships of Britain's colonial policy, realized the necessity of close political union following the weakness of the Confederation, and was moved to action by the flooding of American markets with British goods when peace was concluded. His pamphlet, *An Enquiry into the Principles on Which a Commercial System for the United States of America Should be Founded,* read to a meeting in the house of Benjamin Franklin in 1787 and published in the same year, is a key to his views. While ever mindful of the claims of agriculture (which he calculated embraced seven-eighths of the country's wealth), he thought these would best be served by development of manufactures which would afford a home market for raw materials and foodstuffs. He believed a revenue tariff, combined with the natural advantages of the country, sufficient for the encouragement of

American industry. He was unalterably opposed to commercial restrictions between the states. He urged confining importation to American bottoms and to ships of the country of origin. Coastwise trade, he held, should belong exclusively to American ship-owners. He early (1775) became a member of the United Company of Philadelphia for Promoting American Manufactures, and became president of the Pennsylvania Society for the Encouragement of Manufactures and the Useful Arts (founded in 1787). He has been called the father of the American cotton industry because he was one of the first to urge on the South cultivation of cotton as a staple, and was active in the promotion of cotton manufacture. In 1787, two years before Samuel Slater's arrival, Coxe attempted, though without success, to have models of the Arkwright machinery brought to America by way of France. Early aware of the existence of coal in central and western Pennsylvania, and, apparently, of its future importance (see his *View of the United States of America,* 1794, pp. 70–71), in 1787 and 1793 he purchased extensive tracts of land in the coal areas, which he transmitted to his heirs. A grandson, Eckley B. Coxe [*q.v.*], educated to develop the coal lands, became one of the outstanding mining engineers of the United States.

Tench Coxe was married twice: first, to Catherine McCall of Philadelphia, who died without issue; and second, to Rebecca, daughter of Charles Coxe of New Jersey. He was a handsome, winning person, capable and versatile, high in the second rank of men of his day.

[See Henry Simpson, *The Lives of Eminent Philadelphians* (1859); Lorenzo Sabine, *Biog. Sketches of Loyalists of the Am. Revolution* (1864); *Pa. Mag. of Hist. and Biog.*, vols. V (1881) and XVI (1892); George S. White, *Memoir of Samuel Slater* (2nd ed., 1836); obituaries in Philadelphia papers: *Franklin Gazette* and *National Gazette* for July 16, 1824, and *Poulson's Am. Daily Advertiser* for July 17, 1824. There are numerous references to Coxe in the letters of Jefferson, Madison, and Adams. For his opinions see his *View of the United States* (1794), which is in effect a compilation of a number of his papers published during the years 1787–94, and (also by Coxe) *A Statement of the Arts and Manufactures of the U. S. for the Year 1810*.] B.M.

COXE, WILLIAM (May 3, 1762–Feb. 25, 1831), pomologist, a grandson of Col. Daniel Coxe [*q.v.*], was born in Philadelphia. His parents were William and Mary (Francis) Coxe, and Tench Coxe [*q.v.*] was an older brother. William's schooling was imperfect, but he had a great fondness for reading, and through his own efforts, and with the aid of a member of his family, laid the foundation for an education which eventually fitted him for a wide and influential public service. At the time of his marriage to Rachel Smith in 1789, he was engaged in a mer-

cantile business in Philadelphia, but apparently without results that justified its continuance. He moved to Burlington, N. J., where he materially improved extensive property owned by his wife, and laid out the work which in due course was to make him known as the father of American pomology. There he began the cultivation of fruit, assembling in his orchards varieties not only from all parts of the United States, but from England and France as well. His first-hand observations and experience gained him a position of authority probably held by no other at that time. The demands made upon him for scions and for information became so great that he decided to give the public the benefit of his knowledge in print, which he did in the book entitled: *A View of the Cultivation of Fruit-Trees, and the Management of Orchards and Cider; with Accurate Descriptions of the Most Estimable Varieties of Native and Foreign Apples, Pears, Peaches, Plums, and Cherries, Cultivated in the Middle States of America: Illustrated by Cuts of Two Hundred Kinds of Fruits of the Natural Size.* This book was published in 1817 and undoubtedly had a marked influence on the development of American pomology during the first half of the nineteenth century. Coxe planned a new edition and collected material with it in view. His daughters, Mrs. McMurtrie and her sisters, prepared illustrations in color of about 160 varieties of apples, pears, peaches, plums, and cherries, more than one hundred of the paintings being of apples and crabs. The book was not published, however, and in succeeding years the paintings were lost. A recent search resulted in their discovery in the possession of Mrs. McMurtrie's grandchildren, who gave them, together with a manuscript upon which the original book was apparently based and various notes in manuscript, to the library of the United States Department of Agriculture.

Coxe was recognized abroad as well as at home. He was instrumental in introducing the Seckel pear into England and for this service made an honorary member of the Royal Horticultural Society. He withdrew his membership, however, after a few years, feeling that the recognition was out of proportion to the service. Always public-spirited though in no sense a politician, he was a member of the state legislature, 1796–1804, 1806–09, 1816 and 1817, and speaker of the Assembly from 1798 to 1800, and also in 1802. In 1813 he went to Congress as a Federalist, remaining for one term. For financial reasons he sold his residence in Burlington and moved to his farm located on the Delaware River, near town, where he spent the last years of his life in comparative retirement, devoting himself to his family, his books, the interests of his church, and the welfare of those about him. He was a handsome man, of gentlemanly bearing and kindly spirit, generously sharing with his neighbors his knowledge, his fruit, and his extensive library. One of his daughters married Bishop McIlvaine [*q.v.*], and a son, Richard Smith Coxe [*q.v.*], attained distinction as a lawyer.

[*Horticulturist,* July 1856, pp. 304–07; *Country Gentleman,* Apr. 2, 1857, pp. 225–26; *Science,* July 14, 1916; *Cyc. of Am. Horticulture* (1906) and *Standard Cyc. of Horticulture* (1914), ed. by Liberty Hyde Bailey; *Biog. Dir. Am. Cong.* (1928).]   H.P.G.

COXETTER, LOUIS MITCHELL (Dec. 10, 1818–July 10, 1873), mariner, was the most celebrated of the Confederate privateersmen and one of the most successful of the blockade-runners. He was born in Nova Scotia; but early in his youth made Charleston, S. C., his home port. He entered the Florida trade, and soon rose to the command of a schooner plying between Charleston and St. Augustine. During the Mexican War he was in public service as a transport captain. Upon the termination of hostilities, he returned to Charleston, and initiated the first line of steampackets between that city and Florida ports, commanding in turn the *Florida, Carolina,* and *Everglade.* A few days after President Davis issued his famous letter-of-marque proclamation, a company, composed of men of high standing, was organized in Charleston to send the brig *Putnam* (the one-time slaver *Echo*) to sea as a private-armed cruiser under the Confederate flag; and Coxetter was invited to join this syndicate, as part owner and captain. He received his commission as commander of the vessel, renamed the *Jefferson Davis,* on June 18, 1861, and ten days later ran the blockade, having on board about seventy men and five obsolete guns. He cruised leisurely up the coast into New England waters, taking heavy toll of the West-Indian and South-American trade. The United States sent nine war vessels in search of this raider; but Coxetter successfully eluded his pursuers, transferring his cruising ground to the West Indies, with base at San Juan, Porto Rico. At length he found his crew so reduced by the number of men which he had put on his prizes that he was forced to turn homeward to recruit. In attempting to call at St. Augustine, Aug. 18, 1861, a half-gale blowing, he got aground on the bar and lost his ship. The crew was saved. Upon his return to Charleston, he was presented with a gold watch and fob as a token of the public estimation. Of his prizes only two inured to the benefit of the captors (being regularly condemned and sold by order of a Con-

federate court of admiralty); three were recaptured; one was burned; three released as cartels; and one released on account of her neutral cargo.

His skill and resolution were recognized by the Navy Department, which recommended him to its foreign purchasing agent as a suitable man to run a cargo of supplies through the blockade. In October he left Charleston on the Confederate transport *Theodora* (which also carried Mason and Slidell on the first leg of their famous interrupted voyage). It was generally supposed in Charleston that he had gone to Cuba to get another privateer to sea; but he went on to England *incognito,* using his middle name, and switched to a blockade-running career. He entered the service of John Fraser & Company of Charleston, and Fraser, Trenholm & Company of Liverpool, recognized agents of the Confederate government. His first command was the *Herald,* a fast steamer, which was subsequently renamed *Antonica* in honor of his wife. He also commanded the *Beauregard* of the same line. In the last few weeks of the war, he was engaged by the navy on some secret mission in the Savannah River, near Augusta, probably in connection with the mining of the river against the ascent of Federal gunboats from Savannah.

His humanity as a privateersman is attested by the high character which his captives gave him (see Capt. Smith in *New York Herald,* July 22, 1861, and Mate Jones, *Ibid.,* Aug. 21, 1861). After the war he reëntered the packet service, commanding, until about two months before his death, the side-wheel steamer *Dictator,* of the Charleston-Palatka line. He owned a ninth interest in this vessel and five-sixths of the Cooper River steamboat *Starlight.* He was survived by his wife, Antonica Geiger, and three of his four sons. He was buried from St. Mary's Church (French Catholic) in St. Laurence Cemetery, July 11, 1873.

[*Official Reords* (*Navy*), 1 ser., vols. I, VI–IX, XII, XIII, XVI, XVII, 2 ser., vols. I, II; *Official Records* (*Army*), 1 ser., vol. I, 2 ser., vol. III; war-time files of Charleston *Mercury* and Charleston *Courier;* Charleston City Directories; *The News and Courier* (Charleston), July 11–12, 1873; Charleston County, Records of Probate Court and Bureau of Vital Statistics; W. M. Robinson, *The Confederate Privateers* (1928).]
           W.M.R.

COZZENS, FREDERICK SWARTWOUT (Mar. 11, 1818–Dec. 23, 1869), author and wine merchant, son of Frederick Cozzens, a chemist and naturalist of New York City, was descended from Richard Haywarde who was born in Hampshire, England, in 1693, and emigrated to Rhode Island as a Moravian missionary. Haywarde's great-grand-daughter married Issachar Cozzens, Quaker descendant of Leonard Cozzens, who had been admitted to Rhode Island as a freeman on May 3, 1715, after his emigration from Devizes, Wiltshire, England. Issachar Cozzens, who fought at Bunker Hill, was the paternal grandfather of Frederick Swartwout Cozzens. His maternal grandmother was a native of Carlisle on the Scottish Border and possessed a fund of Border tales and ballads, to his familiarity with which as a boy he later attributed his passion for poetry. As a child he formed studious tastes which led him to turn for recreation to reading, to the theatre, to writing, and to travel. He devoted some attention to mechanics and spent three years in the machine branch of bank-note engraving. At the age of twenty-one, he entered the grocery and wine business in Vesey St., and became an important wine merchant of the city, introducing the native Longworth wines of Ohio. He gave active attention to his business until his failure in 1868, when he retired to Rahway, N. J. His wife was Susan Meyers of Philadelphia.

One of the original members of the Century Club in New York, he enjoyed the friendship of many of the writers of his generation, though literature was with him only an avocation. His first publication, *Yankee Doodle* (1847), was a humorous imitation of Spenser. At this time began his eight years of contribution, anonymous for the most part, to the *Knickerbocker Magazine*. Many of these essays, sketches, and poems were collected in *Prismatics* (1853) under the pseudonym Richard Haywarde, the name of his earliest American ancestor. His greatest popularity grew out of *The Sparrowgrass Papers,* an account with humorous exaggeration of the experiences of the city man in setting up a rural abode at "Chestnut Cottage," the author's summer home in Yonkers. The first chapters appeared in *Putnam's Magazine* in 1854, and their publication in book form in 1856 won Cozzens immediate and wide recognition as a humorist. They were reprinted in at least five editions, of which the latest appeared in 1870.

In 1854 he began the publication of the *Wine Press,* a trade monthly designed primarily to promote the introduction of native wines. This he edited for seven years. The entertaining and instructive essays on various topics by Cozzens and a few of his contemporaries, which had appeared, chiefly, in this periodical, were collected in *The Sayings of Dr. Bushwhacker and Other Learned Men* (1867). The New York Publishers Association, in 1858, sent Cozzens as their representative to the copyright congress in Brussels. Following a tour in Nova Scotia, he published *Acadia; or, a Month with the Bluenoses* (1859), and in the same year contributed to the *New York*

Ledger his "True History of New Plymouth." Primarily a humorist, Cozzens could command at times an unpretentious, dignified style and a manner of simple eloquence. These traits characterize his memorials to Col. Peter A. Porter (1864) and to Fitz-Greene Halleck (1868). His humor was widely copied and even imitated, but his popularity did not survive his century; and his unsatirical pleasantries have passed with the trivial incidents upon which they were expended.

[See the autobiographical *Sayings, Wise and Otherwise* (1880), with an Introductory Note by Donald G. Mitchell (1880); Jas. Grant Wilson, *Bryant and His Friends* (1886), and *Life and Letters of Fitz-Greene Halleck* (1869); Mary Ross, "An Impression of the Fifties," in *Putnam's Mo.,* Jan. 1908; "Leaves from the Jour. of Frederick S. Cozzens," with explanatory comment by Arthur D. F. Randolph, in *Lippincott's Mag.,* May 1890; *N. Y. Herald,* Dec. 25, 28 and *World* (N. Y.), Dec. 28, 1869.]   A. L. B.

CRABTREE, LOTTA (Nov. 7, 1847–Sept. 25, 1924), actress, was born in New York, the daughter of John Ashworth Crabtree, a bookseller, and Mary Ann (Livesey) Crabtree, both of whom came of Lancashire stock. Caught by the gold fever, Crabtree left for California early in the fifties. His wife and Lotta followed in 1853, arriving in San Francisco at a climax in that free outburst of theatricals which had become one of the astonishing features of life on the Coast in those years. Handsome theatres had been built; the major theatrical talent of the period had hastened to California. Mrs. Crabtree was a woman of unusual enterprise, resourcefulness, and native wit. With Lotta she soon joined her husband at the flourishing mining camp of Grass Valley, and there met Lola Montez, who taught Lotta to dance. At Lola's cottage both Lotta and Mrs. Crabtree met traveling players. In 1855, at Rabbit Creek, a remote, wild camp in the Sierras where Crabtree had gone in further search of gold, Lotta made her first appearance on the stage as a child of eight, dancing and singing in a rude hall before the assembled miners, who showered her with gold nuggets. Mrs. Crabtree learned to play the triangle, and with Lotta joined a small company of troupers, setting out in the spring of the same year through the mountains, traveling by wagon or on the backs of mules. For the next few years Lotta made many such tours, with highly-colored adventures on the road and unbroken success in the mining camps. Her tiny figure, bright black eyes, and mop of red hair, her blackface impersonations, her intricate step-dancing, charmed the exacting audiences of miners. In 1859 she began long engagements at the variety halls of San Francisco. Five years later, still hardly more than a child, she left for the East. After a mistaken venture in New York and months of hard travel in the south and middle west, she attracted the attention of John Brougham [*q.v.*], who dramatized for her scenes from *The Old Curiosity Shop,* under the title of *Little Nell and the Marchioness.* With her appearance in the doubled rôles at Wallack's in New York in 1867, her widespread popular triumphs began. Her most successful plays included *Little Nell, The Little Detective, Nan the Good for Nothing, The Ticket of Leave Man, Heartsease*—a California play—*Zip, Musette,* with others bordering upon minstrelsy and comic opera. These were all slight in idea and plot; they were given character by Lotta's gift for extravaganza. Her comic faculty seemed boundless. In the mining camps she had gained a free, infectious humor; she had also learned there the power of intimate communication with an audience. Her dancing and by-play were often considered daring, but she gave an innocent distinction to her most piquant innovations, and became an outstanding figure in the growing native art of burlesque and extravaganza. Almost unbelievably child-like in appearance, known affectionately only as "Lotta," she remained a favorite throughout the country for many years. The only break in her long success came in 1888, when an unfortunate combination of circumstances brought her almost to the brink of failure in England. She triumphed in spite of these, returned to the United States, and continued on the stage until 1891.

Upon her retirement Lotta became a comparatively solitary figure. Her life off stage had always been in marked contrast to her public career. Widely beloved, she had had few close friendships. She had never married. Her single companion had been her mother, who had directed her early stage successes, and had managed her business affairs astutely. Her immense wealth—even at the end of her early California period she had possessed a comfortable fortune—was the cause of a fantastic episode after her death. All the members of her immediate family had died; she left no direct heirs. A woman who claimed to be her daughter by a secret marriage precipitated one of the most remarkable will contests of recent years. The claim was proved wholly fraudulent, however, and Lotta Crabtree's large fortune was bequeathed mainly to charity.

[See Constance Rourke, *Troupers of the Gold Coast, or the Rise of Lotta Crabtree* (1928), which contains a statement of sources.]   C. M. R.

CRADDOCK, CHARLES EGBERT. [See MURFREE, MARY NOAILLES, 1850-1922.]

CRAFTS, JAMES MASON (Mar. 8, 1839–June 20, 1917), chemist, teacher, administrator, was the son of Royal Altemont and Marian (Mason) Crafts, and grandson of Jeremiah Mason, noted lawyer and statesman of Portsmouth, N. H., and Boston. His father was a merchant and manufacturer of woolens in Boston where James attended the Sullivan School, and the Boston Latin School, and studied under the tutorship of Dr. Samuel Eliot. The young boy was of generally serious mien, but vigorous and at times full of fun. He attracted attention among his mates by his mechanical ingenuity and dexterity and his fondness for scientific subjects, a fondness which was fostered by attendance at the Lowell Institute Lectures in Boston, and the personal interest of Prof. William Barton Rogers [*q.v.*], soon to be founder of the Massachusetts Institute of Technology. Crafts was graduated from the Lawrence Scientific School of Harvard in 1858, with chemistry as his major subject, having worked mainly under Prof. Horsford. He remained at Harvard for nearly a year after graduation as a student of engineering, and in 1860 went to Europe. He first studied at the Bergakademie at Freiberg but soon transferred to Heidelberg, where for a year he worked with Bunsen, acting as assistant just at the time when spectrum analysis was a newly discovered tool in the search for and identification of the rare metals. He then went to Paris to take up work under Wurtz, the noted French organic chemist. At this time he published several papers in conjunction with Charles Friedel and a firm friendship was established between them, with important later results. Crafts continued his study at the École de Médecin for four years. In 1865 he returned to America and became an inspector of mines in Mexico at a time when this occupation called for courage and alert resourcefulness as well as expert knowledge. Not long after the opening of Cornell University, Crafts began his teaching career (1868) as professor of chemistry in charge of the department, a position which he held until 1871. Meanwhile, in 1868, he married Clémence Haggerty of New York. From Cornell Crafts returned to Boston where he succeeded Prof. Francis H. Storer at the Massachusetts Institute of Technology, an institution also in its early youth. He threw himself into his new duties with characteristic energy, being "particularly interested in the establishment of advanced courses of study and research in chemistry, physics, and other branches which should lead to a higher degree" (Cross, *post*, p. 161).

In 1874 impaired health made it necessary for him to abandon teaching for a time, and the research resources open to him in Paris led him again to transfer his residence to the latter city, though he retained a non-resident professorship at the Massachusetts Institute until 1880. He remained in France until 1891, spending his time mostly upon research at the École des Mines, again in conjunction with Friedel. Many papers, published in the *Comptes Rendus* and the Bulletin of the Chemical Society of Paris followed. Among these one, published with Friedel, relating to the use of aluminum chloride in organic syntheses (1877), gave permanent distinction to its authors because of the far-reaching applicability of the reaction which they discovered, known to chemists as the "Friedel-Crafts reaction." Other valuable contributions relating to thermometry and to the determination of vapor densities belong to the same time. In all, Crafts was author, or joint author (almost wholly with Friedel), of more than one hundred and thirty-five scientific papers.

After his return to America in 1891 he was elected a member of the corporation of the Massachusetts Institute of Technology and became professor of organic chemistry in 1892. Upon the death of President Francis A. Walker in 1897, Crafts became chairman of the faculty, and subsequently was president for two years. During his presidency the question of the merging of the Massachusetts Institute of Technology with the Lawrence Scientific School of Harvard was the subject of serious, and sometimes acrimonious, discussion. Crafts favored the merger, believing that the two institutions should unite energies and resources to a common end while retaining their independence, but this view was ardently opposed by many of the alumni of the Institute and various difficulties arose which finally led to its abandonment. Crafts soon after (1900) resigned the presidency, the duties of which were never fully congenial to him, and returned to teaching and research, retaining a laboratory at the Institute until his death. His researches at that period concerned themselves chiefly with a study of catalysis and accurate thermometry with reference to the exact determination of boiling points to serve as standards. After several years spent in the design and perfection of elaborate apparatus for this purpose, he began experimentation in 1904.

In the summer of 1911 he suffered a severe attack of neuritis from which he never fully recovered. While he was thereafter debarred from continuously active laboratory work, he devoted himself to the preparation for publication of the collection of exact data resulting from years of activity. During this period, "he divided his time between his Boston residence on Commonwealth Ave. . . . and his beautiful country place at Ridge-

field, Conn., where he had a small laboratory well-fitted for his work, and where he enjoyed quiet and seclusion always more suited to his taste than the publicity and whirl of city life" (Richards, *post*). Crafts was handsome and imposing in appearance, a man of marked culture and refinement, quiet but kindly in manner, yet somewhat difficult on first approach. He was an active worker when his health permitted. As an administrator he was just in his decisions and fertile in suggestion. His short term of office did not permit of the fulfilment of many new policies. He retained the vigor of his mental powers until his death, from heart disease, in his seventy-ninth year.

In 1880 he received the Jecker Prize of 2,000 francs from the Paris Academy of Sciences "for his researches relative to organic chemistry," and in 1885 he was made a Chevalier of the Legion of Honor. In 1911 he received the Rumford Medal of the American Academy of Arts and Sciences, of which he had been a Fellow since 1867, "for his researches in high temperature thermometry and the exact determination of fixed points on the thermometer scale." He was elected a member of the National Academy of Sciences in 1892, a corresponding member of the British Association for the Advancement of Science, and a foreign member of the Royal Institution of Great Britain (1904).

[Chas. R. Cross, "A Biog. Memoir of Jas. Mason Crafts" in *Nat. Acad. Sci. Memoirs*, IX (1920), 159–77; Theodore W. Richards, "Jas. Mason Crafts," *Proc. Am. Acad. Arts and Sci.*, LIII (1917–18), 801–04; personal recollections.]   H.P.T.

CRAFTS, WILLIAM (Jan. 24, 1787–Sept. 23, 1826), author, lawyer, was born in Charleston, S. C., the eldest child of William Crafts (1763–1820) by his first wife, Margaret Tébout, and the sixth in descent from Griffin Craft, who, with his wife Alice, emigrated in John Winthrop's company to Massachusetts in 1630 and settled at Roxbury. His father, born in Boston, became an opulent, public-spirited merchant of Charleston. His mother was the daughter of a Beaufort, S. C., family. Young Crafts was handsome and popular and acquired a precocious reputation as a wit and scholar. Upon his graduation from Harvard College in 1805 he dawdled over Coke and Littleton for three years in a Charleston law office, returned to Cambridge to receive his M.A., and set the college agog with the banter and informality of an oration couched in execrable Latin, was admitted to the South Carolina bar Jan. 9, 1809, and set out to win glory in law, politics, and letters. The glory, however, was never more than local. Born to money and good society, gifted but ind'olent, Crafts was spoiled by a succession of easy triumphs in his early manhood and never learned to work. Entering politics as a Federalist, he was elected to the lower house of the legislature in 1810, was defeated in the next election, but later was reëlected for a term or two. His principal achievement as a legislator was a ringing speech on the necessity of public education, which he delivered in November 1813, when some wiseacres proposed in the interest of economy to suspend the free public schools. For the last six years of his life Crafts was a member of the state Senate. His career as a lawyer was handicapped by the fact that his knowledge of law was negligible; Hugh Swinton Legaré even denied that he was a lawyer at all. Accordingly he drifted into criminal cases, in which his shortcomings were less conspicuous and his talent for dazzling juries with his rhetoric was of great effect. As a literary man he achieved a fuller measure of success. He was in constant demand as an orator for public funerals and anniversary celebrations; and his *Eulogy on the Late Rev. James Dewar Simons, Rector of St. Philip's* (1814) was regarded locally as one of the masterpieces of American eloquence. In 1817 he delivered the Phi Beta Kappa address at Harvard. To the Charleston *Courier* he contributed theatrical criticisms, essays in the manner of Addison, and poems first in the manner of Pope and Gay and later in that of Byron and Moore. His most ambitious effusions were "Sullivan's Island," a descriptive poem modeled too closely on "Windsor Forest," "The Raciad," a pleasing picture of Charleston social life, and a "Monody on the Death of Decatur," which was published the day after the news of Stephen Decatur's death reached Charleston. His anacreontics are the best verse written in South Carolina before William Gilmore Simms. His principal publications are *The Raciad and Other Occasional Poems* (1810), *The Sea Serpent: A Dramatic Jeu d'Esprit* (1819), and *Sullivan's Island, The Raciad, and Other Poems* (1820). On June 19, 1823, he married his cousin, Caroline Crafts Homes of Boston, who survived him. He died at Lebanon Springs, N. Y., whither he had gone for his health, and was buried in King's Chapel churchyard in Boston.

[*A Selection in Prose and Poetry from the Miscellaneous Writings of the Late Wm. Crafts* (Charleston, 1828) with a memoir by the Rev. Samuel Gilman; H. S. Legaré, article in the *Southern Rev.*, I, 503–29 (Charleston, 1828); *Harvard Quinquennial Cat.* (1915); J. B. O'Neal, *Biog. Sketches Bench and Bar of S. C.* (1859), II, 345–67; E. A. and G. L. Duyckinck, *Cyc. Am. Lit.* (rev. ed., 1875), I, 781–82; J. M. and W. F. Crafts, *The Crafts Family* (1893); Ludwig Lewisohn, "The Books We Have Made: A Hist. of Lit. in S. C.,"

II, in the Charleston, S. C., *Courier and News*, July 12, 1903; V. L. Parrington, *Main Currents of Am. Thought*, II (1927), 112–14.]   G.H.G.

CRAIG, AUSTIN (July 14, 1824–Aug. 27, 1881), clergyman, educator, noted as a pioneer advocate of freedom of thought in the church and of the obliteration of denominational lines, was all his life associated with the "Christian connection," joining it, as he states, "before the word 'denominational' came into vogue among us. I do not consider myself as belonging to that word. It is to me a disagreeable word. I like the name Christian far better. That name expresses all I have ever desired to be" (Harwood, *post,* p. 306). Horace Mann, who in his later activities leaned heavily upon him for advice and encouragement, called him a religious genius, and such was his scholarship and ability in exegesis that Henry Ward Beecher declared that "Whenever I have met that man I have felt like taking a stool and sitting at his feet and listening to his words as long as he would talk to me."

Born in Peapack, N. J., the son of Moses and Rachel (Carhart) Craig, he was of Scotch-Irish and English descent. His father, formerly a teacher, was a successful merchant and farmer, and Austin was brought up in a home where both learning and religion were highly regarded. When he was sixteen he entered Lafayette College, but left during his third year, returning in 1846 for the study of Hebrew. He was extremely independent and individualistic, never disciplining himself to a harness of any kind. At college he and a classmate petitioned the faculty to permit the study of Christian writers instead of the usual Greek and Latin authors, and he left because, as he confessed, he would not study what the authorities offered, since they would not let him study what he desired. He had a most vigorous and retentive mind, however, and was always a thorough student of everything pertaining to the Bible. He became one of the best New Testament Greek scholars in the country, and was invited to be one of the American revisers of the Bible. Though he declined because of other duties, he was repeatedly consulted when difficult problems arose.

He began to preach while in college. In May 1844, he was licensed by the New Jersey Christian Conference, and was ordained in 1845. For six years he was an itinerant preacher and supply, serving without pay, since, as he said, he was getting his ministerial education. His principal charge was at Blooming Grove, Orange County, N. Y., where he settled in 1851, and remained with the exception of two or three brief intervals until 1865. It was preceded by a short pastorate at Feltville, N. J., and in 1868–69 he was pastor of the North Christian Church, New Bedford, Mass. While in Feltville he became widely known because of an address delivered at a church conference held at Camptown (Irvington), N. J., May 18, 1850, arraigning sectarianism and setting forth in masterly fashion the basis for Christian union. Horace Greeley published it in the *New York Tribune*, and it was issued in pamphlet form. From this time on Craig was a constant writer of tracts and articles for religious periodicals, many of the former having extensive circulation here and in England. He was the constant adviser of Horace Mann when the latter undertook the establishment of Antioch College, was supply professor of Greek in 1855, and, yielding to Mann's entreaties, became college pastor and professor of logic and rhetoric in 1857, but returned to Blooming Grove in 1858. He was elected president in 1862, but did not take active charge, though he aided in the rehabilitation of the institution, until 1865, and then only for a year. Prior to 1869 he also served for several years as non-resident professor of Christian Life and Experience at the Meadville Theological School. From 1869 until his death he was president of the Christian Biblical Institute, located first at Eddytown, N. Y., and later at Stanfordville, N. Y., established with the aim of helping its students "to search the Scriptures for themselves, with the aids and appliances of modern scholarship, and to qualify them for the free and untrammelled interpretation of the Holy Scriptures according to the individual conscience, without bias or prejudice, and to train them to be efficient ministers of the Gospel of Christ." This statement embodies the spirit and chief interest of Craig's whole life.

He was twice married, first, Aug. 12, 1858, to Adelaide Churchill, who died June 24, 1879; second, in 1880, to Sarah J. McCarn, M.D. Many of his productions may be found in Martyn Summerbell's *Writings and Addresses of Austin Craig*, 2 vols. (1911, 1913). O. O. Wright and Selah Howell published in 1885 *A Memorial of the Rev. Austin Craig, D.D.*, which contains phonographic reports of his lectures.

[In addition to above, see W. S. Harwood, *Life and Letters of Austin Craig* (1908); M. T. Morrill, *Hist. of the Christian Denomination* (1912); and J. F. Stonecipher, *Biog. Cat. Lafayette Coll.* (1913).]   H.E.S.

CRAIG, DANIEL H. (*c.* 1814–Jan. 5, 1895), journalist, was born in Rumney, N. H. His father fought in the War of 1812 and his grandfather was a Revolutionary soldier. After learning the printing trade, Craig went to New York

and then to Baltimore where with Arunah S. Abell [*q.v.*] of the *Sun* he experimented with the use of carrier pigeons to carry news. He next appeared in Boston as an independent news collector, succeeding Samuel Topliff and Harry Blake, pioneers in gathering and selling news to Boston newspapers. He met the Cunard boats with schooners as they approached Boston, received packets of news from the incoming vessels and sent synopses of it to Boston papers by carrier pigeons released sometimes fifty miles from port. News thus forwarded arrived several hours before the boat docked and was published as an extra for the *Boston Daily Mail* and for Bennett's *New York Herald*. The extras bearing the *Herald* title were forwarded to New York where rivalry between the *Herald* and *Sun* was intense.

When the New York newspapers formed the Associated Press in 1848, Craig faced formidable competition which he met by moving his base of operations to Halifax where Liverpool steamers touched en route to United States ports. He had a synopsis of the latest news prepared in Liverpool. This was sealed in a tin can and thrown overboard at Halifax where Craig's representatives met the ships in small boats. The news was then rushed to New York and Boston by carrier pigeons and pony express. When the New York and Boston papers finally combined to charter a steamer to carry dispatches from Halifax in faster time than Craig's system made possible, Craig traveled to Halifax carrying two of his best pigeons in a basket. He got his European news, bought passage on the special steamer, and when it was off the Massachusetts coast secretly released his carrier pigeons with the result that his news was in print before the steamer arrived in Boston. Shortly after, about 1850, the Associated Press employed Craig as its Halifax representative. In 1851, he was brought to New York as general agent of the Associated Press. He succeeded Gerard Hallock as president in 1861 and resigned in 1866. After his retirement from journalism, he was associated with Ezra Cornell [*q.v.*] in development of telegraphic facilities. His later years were spent in quiet comfort at Asbury Park, N. J.

Craig's publications include four pamphlets: *The American Telegraph Company and the Press. A Reply to the Falsehoods of the Executive Committee* (1853), *Letter to F. M. Edson* (*on the House Telegraph Line*) (1853), *Machine Telegraphy of Today* (1888, 1890, 1891), *Startling Facts! Practical Machine Telegraphy. One Thousand Words per Minute* (no place and no date).

[See Frederick Hudson, *Journalism in the U. S.* (1873), pp. 611–13; Melville E. Stone, *Fifty Years a Journalist* (1922), pp. 207–09; Jas. Melvin Lee, *Hist. of Am. Journalism* (1917), pp. 217–18 and 276; *N. Y. Herald, N. Y. Times, World* (N. Y.), Jan. 6, 1895; *Press* (Asbury Park, N. J.), *Sun* (Baltimore), Jan. 7, 1895; *Granite Mo.*, Feb. 1895. The date of Craig's birth is given variously as Nov. 3, 1811 and 1814.]

D. W. M.

CRAIG, THOMAS (Dec. 20, 1855–May 8, 1900), mathematician, was of Scotch descent, his parents, Alexander Craig and Mary Hall, having been born in Ayrshire. The father was a mining engineer and came to America for the purpose of engaging in his profession in the coal regions of Pennsylvania. Thomas Craig was born at Pittston, in that state, and was prepared for college at the Pittston Seminary, showing even in his school days notable ability in his studies. Interested in his father's profession, he entered Lafayette College in September 1871, and was graduated four years later (1875) with the degree of civil engineer. After teaching for a year he entered Johns Hopkins University in 1876, induced by the opportunities offered to study under the guidance of Prof. Sylvester, then beginning his notable (although not his first) work in this country. His abilities were immediately recognized by the grant of a fellowship and by its extension for a period of three years (1876–79). The degree of Ph.D. in mathematics was conferred upon him in 1878, he being one of the first of Sylvester's pupils to receive it. Even before this, however, he was called upon to lecture in the university, and soon after graduating he became connected with the United States Coast and Geodetic Survey, a relationship maintained for three years (1879–81). He was successively a fellow, associate professor, and (1892–1900) professor of mathematics at Johns Hopkins University.

For many years he was a contributor to the *American Journal of Mathematics,* later becoming a member of the editorial staff and finally (1894–99) the chief editor, his wide mathematical interests making him unusually well equipped for such a position. He also contributed to the *Bulletin of the American Mathematical Society,* to Crelle's *Journal,* and to the *Comptes Rendus.* His published works include *A Treatise on Projections* (1882), prepared for the use of the Coast and Geodetic Survey; *Elements of the Mathematical Theory of Fluid Motion* (reprinted from *Van Nostrand's Magazine,* 1879); and *A Treatise on Linear Differential Equations; Vol. I, Equations with Uniform Coefficients* (1889), a work of which he completed only the first volume. At the time of his death he was engaged in preparing a treatise on the theory of

surfaces. His closing years were less productive than those immediately following his graduate days, his failing health having limited his capacity for sustained effort. For some years he had suffered from insomnia and from heart difficulty, and the end came peacefully in his hours of sleep.

Prof. Simon Newcomb, under whose guidance Craig studied Königsberger's *Vorlesungen über die Theorie der elliptischen Functionen, Nebst einer Einleitung in die allgemeine Functionenlehre,* briefly and fairly summed up his abilities as follows: "From the beginning he showed an extraordinary development of the faculty of acquisition, being able to master, almost without effort, the writings of any of the great geometers to which he was attracted."

Craig was married at Washington on May 4, 1880, to Louise Alvord, daughter of Gen. Benjamin Alvord, U. S. A., himself the author of several mathematical works.

[Biog. sketch by F. P. Matz in the *Am. Mathematical Mo.*, Oct. 1901; list (incomplete) of Craig's contributions in J. C. Poggendorff, *Biographisch-Literarisches Handwörterbuch,* vol. IV (Leipzig, 1904), p. 279.]

D. E. S.

CRAIGHEAD, EDWIN BOONE (Mar. 3, 1861–Oct. 22, 1920), educator, was born at Ham's Prairie, Mo. His parents Oliver and Frances (Payne) Craighead were of Scotch-Irish ancestry. They had migrated from Virginia and the father was a prosperous farmer. Edwin was given a good education and graduated from Central College, Mo., in 1883. He then went to Vanderbilt for a year to continue his study of Greek, Latin, and English literature. His enthusiasm for his studies led him to Leipzig, but the methods of research there soon repelled him and he went to Paris and took up the study of French literature. Before going to Europe he had been for a time a teacher in Neosha Collegiate Institute, and upon his return to America he began again to teach. He married Kate Johnson in 1889. In 1890 he became professor of Greek at Wofford College. His broad culture, his grasp of educational and other public affairs, and his powers as a speaker and writer attracted so much attention that in 1893, at the age of thirty-two, he was elected president of the South Carolina Agricultural and Mechanical College at Clemson. At this institution he began a new policy insisting upon higher standards of preparation and attainment than were usual in the South of that day. In 1897 he became president of Central College, his alma mater, and four years later he was elected president of the Missouri State Normal School at Warrensburg. Here he organized the program more in accordance with college curricula and under his administration attendance greatly increased. In 1904 he was elected president of Tulane University, where his first work was to reorganize the medical school, doing away with part-time instructors, raising the standards of admission, and encouraging the study of tropical medicine, which Tulane has continued to make its special field.

In 1912 he was elected president of the State University of Montana, an institution with an enrolment of 230 students. Three years later its registration had increased to about 850 students. He sought to bring to the University men of reputation as scholars, added a school of forestry and a school of journalism, started a premedical course, and formed a plan to consolidate the four small state institutions of higher education into one university. This project was defeated, but his campaign led to the "unification" of the institutions of higher education, under a plan providing for the continuance of their physical separation but allowing a centralized administration under one executive known as the chancellor. Opposition to his policies led to his dismissal, in 1915, in spite of the protests of alumni and students. He was then elected commissioner of education for North Dakota, to act as expert adviser for the board of regents in reconstructing the system of higher education for the state. The Non-Partisan Movement put an end to this plan of reorganization and he returned to Missoula, where he had established a newspaper. The remainder of his life was given to spreading his ideas through this paper, the *New Northwest*. He opposed the influence in politics and education of big business and particularly of the Anaconda Copper Mining Company. He advocated vigorously academic freedom in teaching. His other important service was as trustee (1904–15) of the Carnegie Foundation for the Advancement of Teaching.

Although he was a man of courage and stubbornness Craighead possessed a gentleness and charm that won him great popularity with students and alumni. He was original in planning educational policies and shrewd in carrying them out. Tolerant of opposing opinions, he was uncompromising in his own, and even when failure was inevitable he would not yield. He gave vitality and broader ideals to the institutions he served.

[The writings of Craighead are widely scattered, mostly in newspapers. The Montana newspapers, particularly the *Missoulian* from 1912 to 1915, gave him much attention. Cassius J. Keyser, "No Braver Man," in *Mole Philosophy and Other Essays* (1927) is a fine appreciation of a friend. See also obituaries in *New Orleans States, Montana Record Herald, Anaconda Standard, Helena Independent,* all of Oct. 23, 1920.]

P. C. P.

CRAIGIE, ANDREW (June 7, 1743–Sept. 19, 1819), apothecary, financier, and speculator, was born in Boston, one of the three children of Andrew and Elizabeth Craigie. He was educated in the Boston Latin School. Information is wanting as to whether he was trained as an apothecary or as a physician, but he was known as a man skilled in medicine. His public career began on Apr. 30, 1775, when the Massachusetts Committee of Safety appointed him to take care of the medical stores of the Colony. On May 14 he was empowered to impress beds, bedding, and other hospital necessities. He was present at the battle of Bunker Hill and assisted in taking care of the sick and wounded. Shortly afterward he was appointed by the Provincial Congress medical commissary and apothecary to the army of Massachusetts. He took part in the siege of Boston, and on Aug. 3, 1775 was given charge of the medical store at Watertown, Mass. He was probably the first to fill the office of Continental apothecary, created in July 1775. With the exception of a few months, he served either in this office or in that of apothecary general (created in February 1777) during the entire Revolutionary War. By an act of the Continental Congress, Oct. 27, 1779, the apothecary general was given the military rank of lieutenant-colonel.

The first pharmaceutical laboratory in the United States was established during Craigie's term of office, and the first Pharmacopœia in America, published by Dr. William Brown [q.v.], also came into existence during this time. In 1780 Craigie was "well known to the whole army as a surgeon of the highest character." He served as apothecary general on the general staff to the end of the war and was mustered out about Nov. 12, 1783. He became a member of the Society of the Cincinnati. During his connection with the army he acquired a large fortune by purchasing government certificates and by other speculations. For a time after returning to private life he engaged in the wholesale apothecary trade, but soon broadened the scope of his activity. He was one of the directors of the first United States Bank, and maintained a voluminous correspondence. The American Antiquarian Society has about 600 of his letters bound in three large volumes.

In 1791 Craigie purchased the Vassall house in Cambridge, where Gen. Washington had his headquarters during the siege of Boston. This house came to be known as the Craigie Mansion, and later as the Craigie-Longfellow house. Craigie laid out gardens, built a greenhouse and an ice-house, and maintained a princely bachelor establishment which became a social center. The merchant princes enjoyed his hospitality. Entertainments were on a large scale, and after Craigie's marriage to the beautiful Elizabeth Nancy Shaw, the social functions became even more brilliant. Royalty was entertained. Mrs. Craigie had all the luxury and social prestige money could provide, but it did not bring her happiness and she became estranged from her husband. Craigie continued in his speculations, buying large properties around Cambridge and built the bridge which was the inspiration of Longfellow's poem, "I Stood on the Bridge at Midnight." After a time, however, his glory waned, and he became so heavily involved in debt that he was unable to leave his property for fear of arrest. He was a vestryman of Christ's Church, which was a comfort and solace to him in his reverses. He is buried in the tomb of the Vassall family. Mrs. Craigie survived her husband many years, dying in 1841.

[Lyman F. Kebler, "Andrew Craigie, The First Apothecary General of the U. S.," in *Jour. Am. Pharmaceutical Asso.*, Jan.–Feb. 1928; which contains numerous references; Samuel S. Green, "The Craigie House, Cambridge, during its Occupancy by Andrew Craigie and his Widow," *Proc. Am. Antiquarian Soc.*, n.s., XIII (1900), 312–52; Archer B. Hulbert, "Andrew Craigie and the Scioto Associates," *Ibid.*, n.s., XXIII (1913), 222–26; John Holmes, "Andrew Craigie," *Mass. Col. Soc. Pubs.*, VII (1905), 403–07.]   L. F. K.

CRAIK, JAMES (1730–Feb. 6, 1814), chief physician and surgeon of the Continental Army, was born at Arbigland near Dumfries, Scotland. Of his father we know only that he had an estate on which the father of the famous John Paul Jones [*q.v.*] was the gardener. Craik studied medicine at Edinburgh, and emigrating in 1750 he practised in the West Indies, in Norfolk, Va., and in Winchester, Va., where he was also surgeon at the fort. He was commissioned surgeon in Col. Fry's regiment Mar. 7, 1754. In the following year he was at the battle of Great Meadows, and attended to Braddock's wounds at Monongahela, July 3, 1755. When Col. Washington was made commander-in-chief of the Virginia forces, Aug. 14, 1755, Craik became his chief medical officer. He built a house on a fine plantation at Port Tobacco, Charles County, Md., and, Nov. 13, 1760, married Mariamne Ewell of Prince William County, Va. In the autumn of 1770, Washington and Craik went by horseback and canoe into the wilds along the Ohio and the Kanawha to make a "location" of land granted by the Crown to officers and men who had fought in the French and Indian War.

In 1777 Washington offered Craik the appointment of senior physician and surgeon of the hospital of the middle district which "includes the States between North or Hudson's River and the Potomac," or of assistant director-general (*Writings of Washington*, Sparks ed., vol. IV, 1834, p. 400). Craik became assistant director-general, organizing the hospitals for the French army when Rochambeau arrived at Newport, R. I. When the medical department of the army was reorganized in 1780, he was made one of the chief hospital physicians, and, in 1781, Congress appointed him chief physician and surgeon of the army. He served until Dec. 23, 1783. As a close friend Craik warned Washington of the "Conway Cabal," naming Gen. Mifflin [*q.v.*] as one of the party against him (*Ibid.*, vol. V, 1834, p. 493).

During his first presidential year Washington while ill wrote to the Hon. James McHenry about Craik (*Ibid.*, vol. X, 1834, p. 13): "Could it be made consistent with his advantage to be near me, I am sure it would be highly pleasing to me. . . ." Craik was commissioned director general in the hospital department in 1798. When war with France was feared, Washington became commander-in-chief as lieutenant-general on condition that Craik was to be physician-general. The latter was appointed, July 19, 1798, being honorably discharged, June 15, 1800. On Dec. 14, 1799, about nine in the morning, Craik arrived at Mount Vernon to attend Washington, ill of "acute laryngitis." He saw that little could be done, so rapid was the course of the disease, but bled the patient afresh and prescribed certain medicines. About ten in the evening of the same day Washington died. Craik's only known published writing deals with this illness, *A Sermon Occasioned by the Death of Gen. Washington . . . Preached December 29, 1799. By the Rev. Hezekiah N. Woodruff, A.M. . . . To which is Added,—An Appendix, Giving a Particular Account of the Behaviours of Gen. Washington, During his Distressing Illness, Also of the Nature of the Complaint of which he died. By Doctors James Craik and Elisha C. Dick, Attending Physicians* (1800). The Appendix, signed "James Craik, Attending Physician" and "Elisha C. Dick, Consulting Physician," is dated from Alexandria, Va., Dec. 30. Dr. Gustavus Brown, the other consultant was not present to sign the statement. A clause in Washington's will runs: "To my compatriot in arms, and old and intimate friend, Dr. Craik, I give my bureau (or, as the cabinet makers call it, tambour secretary), and the circular chair, an appendage of my study."

For several years before he died, Craik and his wife lived with their daughter-in-law, Mrs. George W. Craik, near Alexandria. He had a healthy, cheerful old age.

[In addition to references above see H. E. Brown, *The Medic. Dept. of the U. S. Army from 1775 to 1873* (1873); F. B. Heitman, *Hist. Reg. of the Officers of the Continental Army* (1914); Jas. Jackson, "Memoir on the Sickness and Death of Gen. Washington" in *Another Letter to a Young Physician* (1861); Wm. O. Owen, *The Medic. Dept. of the U. S. Army 1776–86* (1920), portr.; J. M. Toner, *The Medic. Men of the Revolution* (1876); J. M. Toner, *Trans. Med. Soc. Va.*, 1879, III, 95–105; Jas. E. Pilcher, *The Surgeon-Generals of the Army of the U. S. A.* (1905); Jas. Thatcher, *Am. Medic. Biog.*, vol. I (1828).]   A. C. M.

CRAMER, MICHAEL JOHN (Feb. 6, 1835–Jan. 23, 1898), Methodist clergyman, diplomat, was descended from Swedish refugees in Switzerland at the time of the Reformation. He was the eldest son of John Jacob and Magdalene (Baumann) Cramer, and was born near Schaffhausen, Switzerland. When he was five years old his mother died. In 1845 the family emigrated to America, making its home first in Pittsburgh and later in Cincinnati, where young Cramer entered the German department of the Methodist Book Concern, learning the printer's trade. He devoted his spare time to preparation for college, entering Ohio Wesleyan University, where by teaching German and Latin he earned his expenses, graduating with honors in 1859. The following year he joined on trial the Cincinnati Conference of the Methodist Episcopal Church. While pastor of the Pearl Street Church of Cincinnati, he married (Oct. 27, 1863) Mary Frances, daughter of Jesse Root and Hannah (Simpson) Grant, and sister of General Grant. In 1864 he reorganized the Methodist churches of Nashville, Tenn, which had been abandoned after the fall of Vicksburg. After serving as chaplain at Newport Barracks, he was appointed (May 1867), by President Johnson, consul at Leipzig. President Grant in 1871 appointed him minister to Denmark, a position which he held for ten years. His chief accomplishments were a naturalization treaty and a series of reports on trade which resulted in a marked increase of exports from the United States to Denmark. A distressing neuralgic difficulty of long standing was aggravated by the rigors of the Danish climate, and, at his own request, he was transferred by President Garfield in 1881 to Berne, Switzerland, where he was resident minister and consul-general for four years. Resigning from office, he returned to the United States in July 1885. For one year he was professor of systematic theology at the Boston University School of Theology. Ill health compelled him to resign this position as the climate caused a recurrence of his old trouble. In 1886–87 he substituted for Dr. George R. Crooks [*q.v.*] as professor of church history at Drew Theological Seminary. He then became assistant editor of a theological magazine published at Cleveland, called *Zeitschrift für Theologie und Kirche*. At the time of his death, which occurred at Carlisle, Pa., he was occupying the chair of philosophy at Dickinson College. His European friendships included such scholars as Christlieb, Tischendorf, Luthardt, and Harnack. He was a member of the Victoria Institute, the Society of Biblical Exegesis, the American Society of Church History, and the American Institute of Christian Philosophy. While Cramer wrote many articles and essays on European affairs, on art and literature, and on theology, his only book is *Conversations and Unpublished Letters of Ulysses S. Grant* (1897).

[See *Minutes Annual Conferences M. E. Ch., Spring Conferences, 1898* (1898), under Newark Conference, pp. 112–13; *Zion's Herald*, Jan. 26, 1898; *N. Y. Times*, Jan. 25, 1898; *Phila. Press* and *Public Ledger* (Phila.), Jan. 24, 1898. Details of the above account have been verified by Cramer's only son, Dr. Jesse Grant Cramer of Pasadena, Cal.]   R. E. M.

CRAMP, CHARLES HENRY (May 9, 1828–June 6, 1913), shipbuilder, was the eldest son of William [*q.v.*] and Sophia (Miller) Cramp. He received his early education in the Philadelphia public schools, attending the Central High School from July 1841 to September 1844. After receiving his first specialized training for his life-work in the shipyard of his uncle John Byerly, he entered the employ of his father in 1846. With the aid of his father and the naval architects employed by him, and by dint of much study on his own part in higher mathematics and in modern languages, he perfected his education in the art of shipbuilding in all its important phases. In 1859 he became an active participant in the management of The William Cramp Shipbuilding Company, sharing, along with his younger brothers who followed him into the company, in the achievement of his father in overcoming the obstacles in naval architecture during the transition period when iron and steel vessels were replacing those of wood. In 1872 William Cramp, appreciating the efforts of his five sons, changed the name of the firm to The William Cramp & Sons' Ship and Engine Building Company. The concern was incorporated at this time. In 1879, upon the death of the father, Charles Cramp became its president continuing in this capacity until his retirement at the age of seventy-five. He retained a considerable interest in the management of the company, as chairman of its board of directors, until his death in 1913.

Cramp's desire for research was great, and as a result he achieved distinction not only as president of one of the most famous shipyards in the world but also as one of the leading naval architects of his day. The shipyard he inherited from his father was relatively small, but by his energy, intelligence, and organization, he developed it into one of the most extensive and complete in the United States. Many important merchant and naval vessels were constructed under his direction. The steamships *St. Louis* and *St. Paul* were among the fastest vessels in their day, holding the world's record for the transatlantic trip. The steamships *Kroonland* and *Finland* were the largest vessels ever built in the United States up to the time that they were launched. Many war-vessels were constructed for the United States navy, ranging through all varieties and types from gunboats to battleships. Among the most famous vessels of the latter type were the U. S. S. *Maine,* which was sunk in Havana Harbor, the U. S. S. *New York,* U. S. S. *Indiana,* and the U. S. S. *Massachusetts.* The U. S. S. *Colorado* and U. S. S. *Pennsylvania,* the construction of which was authorized in 1900, were armored cruisers of the first class. They were powered with twin screw, vertical, triple-expansion engines, the steam being supplied by water-tube boilers, and were fast vessels, developing twenty-two knots per hour. Their normal displacement was 13,680 tons. Cramp's work achieved international reputation, and the Russian, Turkish, and Japanese governments placed orders with his firm for the construction of war-vessels. He was decorated by the Czar of Russia in appreciation of the success of the vessels designed and built for the Russian navy.

Under his skilful guidance Cramp's Ship and Engine Building Company became a pioneer in engine development. The first triple-expansion engine ever constructed in America was installed in the yacht *Peerless.* The U. S. S. *Columbia,* a protected cruiser of 7,350 tons displacement and 21,000 horse-power, was the first American vessel to be propelled by three screws, and previously only one such vessel, of 6,300 tons and 14,000 horse-power, had ever been built in Europe. The U. S. S. *New York's* machinery was composed of four separate engines in independent water-tight compartments, working in pairs on two shifts, and provided with sliding collar couplings by means of which the forward engine on each shaft could be engaged with or disengaged from the after engine in a few minutes. Emperor William II of Germany was much impressed by this achievement, and paid several visits to this vessel.

Cramp believed that the shipping industry was one of the important key industries of the United States. As a result, he did everything possible by speaking and writing to promote an American merchant marine. His attitude on this topic is suggested by his words in a speech before the American Society of Naval Architects and Marine Engineers: "Let me remark that the ships [*St. Louis* and *St. Paul*] are American from truck to keelson. No foreign materials enter into their construction. They are of American model and design, of American material, and they are built by American skill and muscle."

Cramp was married twice: in 1850 to Hannah Ann Cox, and in 1870 to her sister, Amy Jane Cox. He followed the tradition established by his father and took his six sons into the ship-building establishment.

[Augustus C. Buell, *Memoirs of Chas. H. Cramp* (1906); *Who's Who in America,* 1913–14; Lewis Nixon, in *Cosmopolitan,* May 1902; *Public Ledger* (Phila.), June 6, 1913; *Phila. Enquirer* and *Press* (Phila.), June 7, 1913; references in bibliography of Wm. Cramp.]   H. S. P.

CRAMP, WILLIAM (Sept. 22, 1807–July 6, 1879), shipbuilder, was a descendant of Johannes Krampf of Baden, Germany, who settled near Penn Treaty Park, Philadelphia, in 1703. This original homestead of the Cramp family was located not far from the site of the present shipyard of The William Cramp & Sons' Ship and Engine Building Company, whose founder, William Cramp, was born in the Kensington section of Philadelphia. After he had received a good elementary education in the Philadelphia schools he was placed under the instruction of Samuel Grice, the leading American naval architect of the time. In 1827 he married Sophia Miller. Early in life he had conceived the idea of going into business on his own account, and at the age of twenty-three he established The William Cramp Shipbuilding Company. His plant was located at the foot of Otis St., now called East Susquehanna Ave., but this location soon proved to be inadequate, and he moved the plant a short distance down the Delaware River. Here many important sailing and steam vessels were constructed. Under Cramp's able direction the concern was provided with modern mechanical devices, and came to be considered one of the best equipped of shipyards. This factor, combined with his extraordinary capacity for work, his reputation for honest dealings, and the pride he took in his ships made his concern prosperous even through prolonged periods of business depression. The shipbuilding industry itself was in the throes of a transition in the design and construction of vessels. Wooden vessels were replaced by iron and in turn iron vessels were replaced by steel. The changes involved the installation of new machinery, a new industrial organization, and a new science of naval architecture and construction. William Cramp was among the first American shipbuilders to foresee the inevitable change, and his aggressiveness and astuteness enabled him to cope with the situation. By 1872 he had taken into his organization several of his sons, all of whom were taught the art of shipbuilding. In this year he decided to incorporate the concern and to affiliate his sons more closely to its destiny. Accordingly its name was changed to The William Cramp & Sons' Ship and Engine Building Company. Cramp exerted an important influence on America's national and international economic and political affairs, as he was directly responsible for the construction of 207 vessels of all sorts, both merchant and naval. Two foreign countries, Russia and Venezuela, gave him contracts for the construction of war-vessels. The United States Government gave him several contracts for naval vessels of all classes and types. The first of these was completed in 1862, when the U. S. S. *New Ironsides* was launched, the most powerful cruising ironclad of its time, which participated in more naval engagements during the Civil War than any other vessel of the United States. Cramp remained president of the company which he had founded until his death at Atlantic City in his seventy-third year when he was succeeded by his eldest son, Charles Henry Cramp [*q.v.*].

[*Hist. of Cramp's Shipyard, 1830–1902* (1910); Henry Fry, *Hist. of North Atlantic Steam Navigation* (1896); J. T. Scharf and T. Westcott, *Hist. of Phila.* (1884); J. R. Young, *Memorial Hist. of the City of Phila.* (1898), vol. II; C. M. Depew, ed., *One Hundred Years of Am. Commerce* (1905), vol. I; Chas. Blanchard, *The Progressive Men of Pa.* (1900), vol. II; *Press* (Phila.) and *Phila. Enquirer*, July 7, 1879; *Sci. Am.*, July 26, 1879; information from Mr. Francis Le Baron Cramp.]   H. S. P.

CRANCH, CHRISTOPHER PEARSE (Mar. 8, 1813–Jan. 20, 1892), painter, critic, poet, Unitarian minister, was the youngest of the thirteen children of William Cranch [*q.v.*] and Anna (Greenleaf) Cranch. His father, a Massachusetts man, had been appointed by President John Adams to a judgeship in the circuit court of the District of Columbia, and Christopher was born in Alexandria, then part of the District. The boy had early training in drawing from his brother Edward, a topographical draftsman, but, being destined for a learned profession, he attended Columbian College, Washington, from which, after graduation in 1831, he entered the Divinity School of Harvard College. He preached as a Unitarian minister at Andover, Bangor, and Portland, Me., and at Richmond, Washington, St. Louis, Cincinnati, and Louisville. In the last-named city he took James Freeman Clarke's pulpit, and edited the *Western Messenger*. Cranch here illustrated Emerson's *Essays* with comic drawings which caused merriment among literati. The year 1840 found him preaching at South Boston. He became a social favorite in Boston: he was picturesquely attractive, with dark, curly hair and delicately beautiful features, he had a fine baritone voice, and he played several instruments. He wrote poetry (as notably the 200th Anniversary poem, Quincy, Mass., May 25, 1840). Emerson became interested in his poems, several of which he published in the *Dial*. Cranch was in sympathy with the experiment at Brook Farm, and a frequent welcome visitor there.

In 1841, while spending the summer at Washington, he tried landscape painting. He became engaged the following October to Elizabeth De Windt of Fishkill, N. Y., a cousin, who encouraged him to paint. They were married, Oct. 10, 1843, with slender but assured resources, and Cranch took a house on Lexington Ave., New York, to practise his new profession. In 1846 in the congenial company of George William Curtis [*q.v.*] the Cranches went to Italy for study and observation of art. At Rome and Florence they formed many friendships (see Cranch's *Personal Recollections of Robert Browning*, 1891). In August 1849 they returned to New York where they spent several winters. Cranch wrote her "Farewell to America" for Jenny Lind in 1853. In that year he took his family to Paris for a ten years' residence. He painted diligently, studied, and cultivated friendships. In 1856 he recorded his delight at discovering Barbizon and its painters. In 1863 he returned to America, his son George, aged eighteen, having enlisted in the Union army for service which resulted in his death. The family lived for a time on Staten Island but in 1873 they removed to Cambridge, Mass., where the rest of Cranch's life was spent as, so he wrote, "an ignoramus trespassing in the dominion of scholars." Life near Harvard he found stimulating, but he deplored a prevalent indifference to art. As a member of the Boston Radical Club he was associated with many New England liberals. In 1880 he made his third visit to Europe, at Rome meeting Francis Duveneck whose work he admired, and who painted his portrait. Cranch's health began to fail in 1889. After his peaceful death his friend Curtis wrote in "The Easy Chair" of *Harper's Magazine*: "Cranch . . . followed the leading of his temperanient and talent in becoming an artist. . . . He was poet, painter, musician, student, with a supplement of amusing social gifts, and chief of all was the freshness of spirit which kept him always young. . . . It was a long and lovely life, and if great fame be denied, not less a beautiful memory remains." Among Cranch's numerous published works his translation of Vergil's *Æneid* was his monumental achievement. As a painter he won respect and liking without attaining marked distinction or professional leadership.

[Cranch's story is told with copious extracts from his letters and journals in *The Life and Letters of Christopher Pearse Cranch* (1917), by his daughter, Leonora Cranch Scott. For additional criticism and appreciation see: G. W. Cooke, *The Poets of Transcendentalism* (1903); Mary E. F. Sargent, *Sketches and Reminiscences of the Radical Club of Chestnut St., Boston* (1880); J. T. Codman, *Brook Farm, Historic and Personal Memoirs* (1894); Lindsay Swift, *Brook Farm* (1900); H. T. Tuckerman, *Book of the Artists* (1867); *Critic*, Jan. 30, 1892; *Harper's Mag.*, Apr. 1892; *Boston Transcript*, Jan. 20, 1892.]   F. W. C.

CRANCH, WILLIAM (July 17, 1769–Sept. 1, 1855), jurist, was a grandson of Richard Cranch, who coming from Kingbridge, Devonshire, England, settled at Braintree, Mass., in 1720. The latter's son, Richard, was a member of the Massachusetts legislature and judge of the court of common pleas. He married Mary, daughter of the Rev. William Smith of Weymouth, Mass., and sister of Abigail Adams [*q.v.*], wife of the future president. This connection had an important influence on William's future career. Born at Weymouth, and educated privately at Haverhill, he entered Harvard in February 1784, and graduated with honors in 1787, John Quincy Adams being a class-mate. He studied law at Boston and in July 1790 was admitted to practise. Opening an office in Braintree, he moved after a year to Haverhill. The following year he went to Washington, D. C., as agent for a real-estate firm which had made large speculative investments in that city on the strength of its selection as the federal capital. The venture, however, was a disastrous failure, and Cranch himself became involved financially. In 1800 President Adams appointed him a commissioner of public buildings of the District of Columbia, and when, Feb. 27, 1801, the United States circuit court of the District of Columbia was established, he was nominated junior assistant judge by the President, commencing an association with that court which lasted for the unprecedented term of fifty-four years. In 1802 he became reporter of the Supreme Court of the United States, and published *Reports of Cases Argued and Adjudged in the Supreme Court of the United States 1801–15* (9 vols., 1804–17).

These reports have always been highly regarded for their clarity and accuracy, and are of great importance since they contain a large number of Chief Justice Marshall's most vital opinions on fundamental constitutional problems. In 1805, President Jefferson appointed Cranch chief justice of the district court, much to the general astonishment, since he was a Federalist in politics, and his uncle John Adams was the President's political opponent. He remained chief justice for fifty years. During its earlier years the business of the district court had been light, but additional jurisdiction in admiralty and on appeal from the Commissioner of Patents was conferred upon it, and the volume of its work steadily increased. Cranch's opinions were distinguished for their accuracy and logic. During the whole course of his judicial career only two of his decisions were reversed on appeal. An outstanding case before him was *U. S. vs. Bollman & Swartwout*, 1 *Cranch* (*U. S.*) 379, where, resisting presidential pressure and popular clamor, he held the arrest of Aaron Burr's accomplices unjustifiable, and was sustained by the United States Supreme Court. He contributed occasional papers and articles to local periodicals on matters of public interest, and in 1817 delivered before the Columbian Institute a lecture upon his uncle, published as *Memoir of the Life, Character and Writings of John Adams* (1827). He was compelled in 1817, by pressure of judicial work, to discontinue his Supreme Court Reports, but in his later years he assembled the decisions of his own court, which had theretofore existed only in manuscript, and published them as *Reports of Cases Civil and Criminal in the United States Circuit Court of the District of Columbia from 1801 to 1841*, in six volumes (1852–53). The United States Government published a collection of his *Decisions in Cases of Appeal from the Commissioner of Patents 1841–47* (*U. S. Miscellaneous. Law relating to Patents*, 1848, pp. 87–150). The authorship of *An Examination of the President's Reply to the Remonstrance*, signed Lucius Junius Brutus (New York, 1801), relating to President Jefferson's course in removing Federalists from office to make way for Republicans, has been attributed to him (see Cushing, *Initials and Pseudonyms*, 1885, p. 42; Sabin, *Bibliotheca Americana*, IV, 229). He died in Washington, in his eighty-seventh year. He was married to Anna Greenleaf, sister of James Greenleaf, real-estate operator. Christopher Pearse Cranch, the artist [*q.v.*], was his son.

[An excellent survey of Cranch's career by A. B. Hagner appeared in *Great Am. Lawyers* (1907–09), ed. by Wm. D. Lewis, III, 87. See also *The Life and Character of the Hon. Wm. Cranch* (1855), by Moncure D.

Conway, who was an intimate friend; F. R. Noel and M. B. Downing, *The Court House of the District of Columbia* (1919); New-Eng. Hist. Geneal. Soc., *Memorial Biogs.*, II (1881), 446.]   H. W. H. K.

CRANDALL, CHARLES HENRY (June 19, 1858–Mar. 23, 1923), poet, son of Henry Sargent Crandall and Mary Carmichael Mills, was born in Greenwich, N. Y., and died in Stamford, Conn. He lived for seventeen years on the farm where he was born, engaged in mercantile business for five years, and was for five years on the staff of the *New York Tribune*. He also worked for a while with the New York *Globe*. In 1893— following a nervous collapse—he retired to the farm near Stamford on which he spent the remainder of his life. He was married in 1884 to Kate Virginia Ferguson, a New York newspaper woman. After her death, he married in 1891 Mary Vere Davenport of Stamford, from whom he was divorced in 1916. In 1890 he edited an anthology of American sonnets, with an elaborate introduction, and from 1883 to 1918 he published seven volumes of his own poetry, collected in general from magazines in which it had already appeared. These magazines were usually the most distinguished in America, but the verse is not appropriately satisfying. It deals with the conventional subjects of poetry, but, above all, with patriotism. That theme stirred him most— the thrill of seeing one's flag unfurled, the superior bravery of the American military, the divine mission of America as guardian of her neighbors to the south, and as model for the governments of Europe. The Daughters of the American Revolution solicited his verse, Theodore Roosevelt "sympathized cordially" with it, Leonard Wood urged that it be given the "widest circulation." When the United States went into the World War, Crandall's four sons entered the service of the government, one of them to be killed in action. The father's boundless enthusiasm was set forth in 1918 with vigor and sincerity—if without other merit—in his *Liberty Illumined* and *Songs for the Boys in Khaki*. The war was to him a holy and invincible crusade for everything that spiritual men most ardently and most rightfully desire, and at the conclusion of it, he believed, we should all be justly happy. One day, less than five years after the war ended, he killed himself with a pistol.

[C. H. Crandall, *Wayside Music* (1893); *Chords of Life* (1898); *Songs from Sky Meadows* (1909); *Who's Who in America*, 1922–23; *N. Y. Times*, Mar. 24, 1923.]   J. D. W.

CRANDALL, PRUDENCE (Sept. 3, 1803– Jan. 28, 1889), educator and reformer, born at Hopkinton, R. I., was of Quaker descent, the daughter of Pardon and Esther Crandall (J. N. Arnold, *Vital Record of Rhode Island*, vol. V, 1894). The family had a tinge of fanaticism in their blood and her younger brother was imprisoned for nearly a year in Georgetown, D. C., without trial, for spreading Abolitionist doctrines there. Prudence moved from Rhode Island and after a brief career as a teacher at Plainfield, settled at Canterbury, Conn., where in 1831 she opened a school for girls. A colored girl wished to attend and received Miss Crandall's permission. Immediately there were protests, whereupon Miss Crandall decided to keep a school for negroes only. A town meeting was held on Mar. 9, 1833, to prevent her. She was denied opportunity to be heard in defense by counsel, although she offered to retire to a more secluded place if reimbursed for her preparatory expenses at Canterbury. The leader of the movement against her declared that no negro school should be established anywhere in Connecticut, but Miss Crandall continued firm in her resolution and opened her school. Disgraceful forms of intimidation were used against her. Her well was filled with refuse, physicians refused to attend the sick in her home, she was forbidden to enter the church, her house was attacked and narrowly escaped burning, and she was threatened with personal violence. Her opponents secured (May 24, 1833) the passage of an act in the state legislature making it illegal for any one to set up a school for colored people who were not inhabitants of the state without the consent of the selectmen of the town in which the school was to be located (*Public Statute Laws of the State of Connecticut*, 1833, chap. ix). Under this law, she was arrested and imprisoned. By this time the case had attracted very wide attention in Abolitionist circles, the Rev. Samuel J. May and Arthur Tappan [*qq.v.*] took up her cause, eminent counsel were retained in her behalf, and a newspaper, the *Unionist*, of Brooklyn, Conn., edited by C. C. Burleigh [*q.v.*], was established to defend her. The first trial resulted in a divided jury but a new case was made up and she was tried a second time. Her counsel claimed that the law was unconstitutional, as negroes were citizens and it infringed that clause of the Federal Constitution which gave the "citizens of each state . . . all privileges and immunities of citizens in the several states." The case, however, was decided against her. It was then appealed to the supreme court of Connecticut which reversed the decision of the lower court on the ground merely of insufficient evidence and dodged the real issue (see 10 *Conn.* 339). The supreme court decision was rendered in July 1834 and the next month Miss Crandall married the Rev. Calvin Philleo, a Baptist clergyman of Ithaca, N. Y. The project for educating colored girls in Connecticut was obviously hopeless, and the couple moved to Illinois. After her husband's death in 1874, Mrs. Philleo lived with her brother Hezekiah in southern Kansas, dying at Elk Falls in that state. She retained both her mental vigor and her great interest in the colored race until her death.

[A short pamphlet on Prudence Crandall was written by John C. Kimball during her life and privately printed in 1886. See also: S. J. May, *Some Recollections of Our Anti-Slavery Conflict* (1869) ; W. P. and F. J. Garrison, *Wm. Lloyd Garrison* (4 vols., 1885) ; J. C. Hurd, *The Law of Freedom and Bondage* (1862), II, 46 ; *Report of the Arguments of Counsel in the Case of Prudence Crandall* (1834) ; Ellen D. Larned, *Hist. of Windham County, Conn.*, vol. II (1880). A portrait is at Cornell University.]   J. T. A.

CRANE, ANNE MONCURE (Jan. 7, 1838–Dec. 10, 1872), author, was born in Baltimore and died in Stuttgart, Germany. Her father, William Crane, a descendant of Jasper Crane, one of the founders of both New Haven and Newark, came to Richmond, Va., in 1812. He was already married, but his wife died in 1830, and in something less than a year he married Jean Niven Daniel, originally from Falmouth, Va. In 1834 he removed to Baltimore and organized a business in leather. Anne's education was supervised by a Rev. N. A. Morrison, and she was "graduated"—whence, it is not disclosed—in 1855 (Boyle, p. 554). She was intensely fond of music and reading, and her thoughts were always likely to be colored by a sort of mystical piety. When she was about twenty, a group of young women of which she was a member decided that each of them should write a novel. Hers alone seems to have been completed. She wrote under a stimulus perhaps not granted to her companions; she thought herself inspired. "The angel," she was fond of quoting, "said unto me, 'Write'; and I wrote" (Shepherd, p. 72). The resulting composition was held in manuscript for five years. Then, under the title *Emily Chester,* it was offered to some publishers in Boston, who put it out anonymously in 1864. The style is tedious, but the characters, residents of New York and Baltimore, are rich and distinguished, and the plot involves the effort of a married woman to suppress her attraction toward a man not her husband. The book rapidly went through many editions in America and England, it was successfully dramatized, and a translation of it was published in Germany. Indeed it set a literary fashion which for ten or twelve years was widely followed by women writers. Her next novel, *Opportunity* (1867), was also concerned with the denial of passion for the sake of respectability. Late in

1869, she married Augustus Seemüller, a prosperous New York merchant. She had not resided long in her New York City home before she learned many things so "fearful" that she felt constrained, she said, to expose them or "the very stones would have cried out against me" (Boyle, p. 356). But her response, *Reginald Archer* (1871), so dutifully intended, brought against her the outcry of the moralists. The dedication was exemplary, "affectionately, to my husband, in token of the happy days when this was written," but this could not atone for the all too sure occupation of some of the female characters of the book, or for the failure of the author to award sorrow and painful death to all who sinned, or, in general, for a woman's writing openly of matters which seemed clearly a problem for men only. She was ill, and while the protests against her were still sounding, she went to Europe and died in Stuttgart.

[Sources not already named: A. M. Crane, "My Courtship," *Galaxy*, July 15, 1866; "Words to a 'Lied Ohne Worte,'" *Ibid.*, Aug. 1, 1866; E. Boyle, *Biog. Sketches of Distinguished Marylanders* (1877); E. B. Crane, *Geneal. of the Crane Family* (1900); H. E. Shepherd, *Representative Authors of Md.* (1911); Reviews: "Emily Chester," *Littell's Living Age*, Mar. 31, 1865; "Opportunity," *Nation*, Dec. 5, 1867; "Reginald Archer," *Nation*, May 11, 1871, *Southern Mag.*, July 1871; death notice: *Nation*, Jan. 30, 1873.] J. D. W.

CRANE, FRANK (May 12, 1861–Nov. 5, 1928), Methodist and Congregational clergyman, journalist, was born in Urbana, Ill., the son of James Lyons and Elizabeth (Mayo) Crane. In those qualities of heart and head that insured his success as a writer of newspaper homilies he resembled his father, a Methodist minister, whose kindly, strongly marked idiosyncrasies made him one of the best-liked men in central Illinois. The elder Crane, incidentally, was for a few months chaplain of the 21st Illinois Volunteers under U. S. Grant, who in 1869 appointed him postmaster of Springfield. He was noted for his "happy faculty . . . of stoutly maintaining, his own opinions on all subjects, doctrinal, ecclesiastical, or political, in such a way as to give no cause of offence to any one." Young Crane helped his father in the post-office, attended Illinois Wesleyan University 1877–78, read law, taught country schools, and was admitted on trial into the Illinois Conference of the Methodist Church in 1882 and into full connection in 1884. On Sept. 26, 1883, he married Ella C. Stickel of Hillsboro. For twenty-seven years he was in the active ministry, serving congregations at Roodhouse, Ashland, Island Grove, Rantoul, Urbana, Bloomington (First Church), Omaha, Nebr. (First Church), Chicago (Trinity; Hyde Park; and an independent

People's Church), and Worcester, Mass. (Union Congregational). Though effective, popular, and well paid, by 1909 he found his profession tame and cramping and decided to make a change. Borrowing $1,600 on his life insurance to tide him over, he resigned his charge, returned to Chicago, and began haunting newspaper offices. He lost his first job, on the *Chicago Evening Post,* after a few months, but not before his writings had attracted the attention of Edward Bok and other expert judges of the public taste. Before long he was firmly established as a writer for newspaper syndicates and the popular magazines. Although he published a number of books, including *The Religion of To-morrow* (1899); a volume of verse, *Vision* (1906); a disquisition on the 103rd Psalm, *The Song of the Infinite* (1909); *War and World Government* (1915); *Why I am a Christian* (1924); and *The Ten Commandments* (1928), he owed his affluence and renown to his four-hundred word didactic, inspirational, and personal essays, which were long a daily feature of many American newspapers. Some hundreds of these essays were reprinted in three collections: *Four Minute Essays* (10 vols., 1919); *The Crane Classics* (10 vols., 1920); and *Everyday Wisdom* (1927). The shrewd, homely, humorous, tolerant, sentimental, common sense tone of these brief writings, together with their brevity and simple phrasing, won for them a multitudinous audience. Among the plain people their author enjoyed the honors of a sage, while the city wits derided him as the current great prophet of tautology, a mere dealer in weary platitude and facile optimism. A more discerning criticism saw in him an amiable gentleman of decided liberal tendencies, who took a hearty pleasure in being the counselor and spokesman of the average American. Though in his later years he suffered from diabetes, his personal cheerfulness remained unquenchable, and he continued to write his daily article and to answer faithfully every letter addressed to him that bore a legible signature and address. He lived in New York and Los Angeles and traveled a great deal. He admired the French people and lived as much as he could in France. He died at Nice, of a cerebral hemorrhage, while on a tour around the world. His wife and their two children survived him. He left an estate of $200,000 in stocks and bonds.

[*Minutes Annual Conferences M. E. Ch.: Fall Conferences of 1879* (pp. 41–42) and *of 1882–95* (see indexes) ; *Minutes Rock River Conference* (of the M. E. Ch.), 1896–1902; *U. S. Biog. Dict.: Ill. Vol.* (1876), pp. 449–50; *Who's Who in America,* 1899–1929; *The Crane Classics,* III, 16–18, IV, 13–21, VII, 315–17; information from Helen M. Dean, librarian of Ill. Wesleyan Univ.; see also *N. Y. Times Index,* vol. XVI, no. 4.]

G. H. G.

CRANE, JOHN (Dec. 7, 1744–Aug. 21, 1805), Revolutionary soldier, was born at Braintree, Mass., the son of Abijah Crane and Sarah Beverly. At the time of the French and Indian War, although only fifteen years of age, he offered to serve in place of his father who had been drafted by the Massachusetts provincial government and was in poor health. On his return from the war, he learned the trade of housewright. About 1762 he helped to set out a famous row of elm trees opposite the Granary Burying-ground, Boston. In 1767 he married Mehitable Wheeler, and with his brother purchased a house and shop on what is now Tremont St., near Hollis. In the years following the passage of the Stamp Act, Crane was identified with the Sons of Liberty. At his shop some of the men who staged the Boston Tea Party disguised themselves as Indians and set out for Griffin's Wharf, Crane among them. As he was down in the hold of one of the ships, a chest of tea fell upon him and knocked him senseless. His companions believing him to be dead concealed him under a heap of shavings in a near-by carpenter shop, but thanks to a sturdy constitution he recovered. In 1774 owing to the paralysis of trade produced by the Boston Port Bill, he removed to Providence. He had already acquired some knowledge of gunnery when, as a resident of Boston, he had joined a train of artillery composed of mechanics and commanded by Maj. Adino Paddock. On the arrival of the news of the battle of Lexington, he was made captain of the train attached to the Rhode Island "army of observation." Marching to Boston, he joined Gridley's regiment of artillery, and thenceforth saw almost continuous service. During the siege of Boston, he was in charge of a breastwork on the Neck and on July 8, 1775 attacked and routed a British advance post. He also participated in several skirmishes on islands in the harbor. On Dec. 10, 1775 he was commissioned major in Knox's regiment of artillery and later accompanied the army to New York. He was disabled for a time by a wound in the foot received Sept. 14, 1776 at Corlear's Hook while he was bombarding a British man-of-war. On Jan. 1, 1777 he was commissioned colonel and proceeded to raise a regiment in Massachusetts, the 3rd Continental Artillery. Detachments of it were present under Sullivan in the Rhode Island campaign—where Crane's services evoked honorable mention in the dispatches—under Gates at Saratoga, and in the defense of Red Bank. On

Sept. 30, 1783 Crane was brevetted brigadier-general. After the war he went into the lumber business on Passamaquoddy Bay, but, the venture not proving successful, he removed to Whiting, Me., where he had been given a grant of 200 acres for his military services by the legislature of Massachusetts. He was appointed judge of the court of common pleas by Gov. Hancock in 1790. He died Aug. 21, 1805, highly respected by his comrades in arms for his energy, courage, and coolness in the presence of danger.

[There is a manuscript memoir of John Crane by a descendant, Geo. H. Allan, in the library of the New-Eng. Hist. and Geneal. Soc., Boston. Authentic sketches of him are in F. S. Drake, *Tea Leaves* (1884), and Albert Crane, *Henry Crane of Milton, Mass.* (1893). References to his services will be found in *Mass. Soldiers and Sailors of the Revolutionary War* (1896–98); "Heath Papers" in *Mass. Hist. Soc. Colls.*, ser. 5, vol. IV (1878); ser. 7, vol. IV (1904), vol. V (1905); F. B. Heitman, *Hist. Reg. of Officers of Continental Army* (1914).]   E. E. C.

CRANE, JONATHAN TOWNLEY (June 18, 1819–Feb. 16, 1880), Methodist clergyman, was born at Connecticut Farms, now a part of Union, N. J., the youngest of the six children of William and Sarah (Townley) Crane. He was a descendant of Stephen Crane who, coming probably from England or Wales, settled at Elizabethtown as early as 1665. William Crane, who was a farmer, surveyor, and justice of the peace, died June 4, 1830, and his wife, Aug. 18, 1832. While saving money to enter the College of New Jersey (Princeton University), Crane worked in a Newark trunk factory. Upon his graduation in 1843 he prepared himself for the Methodist ministry, for though of Presbyterian stock he had been converted to Methodism at New Providence, N. J., when he was eighteen years old. Licensed as a local preacher in 1844, he spent one year on the Parsippany circuit, six months on the Asbury circuit, six months at Port Richmond, Staten Island, and on Quarantine, was admitted to the New Jersey Conference, and was pastor at Hope 1846, Belvidere 1847, and Orange 1848. On Jan. 8 of that year he was married to Mary Helen Peck of Wilkes-Barre, Pa., daughter of the Rev. George Peck. In 1848 also he published an *Essay on Dancing*, the sentiments of which may have recommended him to the leaders of his church, for in June he was elected principal of the Conference Seminary at Pennington. After ten years of being schoolmaster he returned to preaching as pastor of Trinity Church, Jersey City, 1858–60; at Haverstraw, N. Y., 1860–62; of the Central Church, Newark, N. J., 1862–64; at Morristown 1864–67; and at Hackettstown, 1867–68. Then followed eight laborious years as presiding elder

of the Newark district, 1868–72, and of the Elizabeth district, 1872–76. After that he was pastor of the Cross-street Church, Paterson, 1876–78, and of the Drew Church, Port Jervis, N. Y., from 1878 till his death.

Crane was the author of numerous contributions to the *Methodist Quarterly Review* and the *Christian Advocate* and of *The Right Way, or Practical Lectures on the Decalogue* (1853, 1857); *The Fruitful Bough: the Centenary Sermon preached before the Newark Conference, Mar. 23, 1866* (1866); *Popular Amusements* (1869); *Arts of Intoxication: the Aim and the Results* (1870, 1871); *Holiness the Birthright of All God's Children* (1874); and *Methodism and its Methods* (1876). His style is chaste, well ordered, and economical, and rises on worthy occasions to a sober eloquence. In doctrine he was a strict Methodist of the old stamp, filled with the sense of God's redeeming love, deeply concerned about such sins as dancing, breaking the Sabbath, reading trashy novels, playing cards, billiards, and chess, and enjoying tobacco and wine, and too innocent of the world to do more than suspect the existence of greater viciousness. Even his discussions of theatregoing, smoking, and drinking are strangely academic and derivative; probably he did not know intimately any one who had been defiled by those sins and was consequently unable to study their effects at first hand. In controversy he was gentlemanly, in his judgments charitable. Noah's lapse from temperance principles he was thus able to excuse, "The Scriptures tell us that Noah planted a vineyard and on one occasion drank of the wine until he was drunken. Very possibly the process of fermentation had not before been noticed, the results were not known, and the consequences in this case were wholly unexpected." He leaves the impression of an unusually noble mind straitened by dogma and a narrow education. Of his fourteen children the youngest, the darling of his last years, was Stephen Crane [*q.v.*], who was to write the *Red Badge of Courage*.

[E. B. Crane, *Geneal. of the Crane Family*, II (Worcester, Mass., 1900), 495, 518–19; *Gen. Cat. of Princeton Univ. 1746–1906* (1908); *N. Y. Christian Advocate*, Mar. 18, 1880, pp. 184, 187, Feb. 19, 1880, p. 116.]   G. H. G.

CRANE, STEPHEN (Nov. 1, 1871–June 5, 1900), writer, was the fourteenth, and ninth living child of Rev. Jonathan Townley Crane [*q.v.*] and Mary Peck. He was born in the Methodist parsonage at 14 Mulberry St., Newark, N. J., and named for a New Jersey ancestor who signed the Declaration of Independence. When he began school the family was settled in a pleasant, tree-shaded house in Port Jervis, N. Y. Here his father died in 1880, and the terrors of the village funeral fastened on the boy. "We tell kids," he wrote later, "that Heaven is just across the gaping grave and all that bosh, and then we scare them to glue with flowers and white sheets and hymns . . . I have forgotten nothing about this, not a damned iota, not a shred." There is much of Crane in this outburst, in its revelation of sensitiveness and feeling for children, its hard vividness, its suggestion of other qualities that startled the eighteen-nineties. For most of the next ten years the family lived at Asbury Park, Stephen helping an elder brother, a newspaper correspondent, in gathering summer news. He was at the Hudson River Institute, Claverack, N. Y., 1887–89, at Lafayette a year, and the next year at Syracuse University, where he had work as correspondent of the *New York Tribune.* The record of this period has more of loafing, news-writing, and baseball—he was team captain at Syracuse—than of studies. There are hints of reading: a gift of Tolstoi's *Sebastopol,* praise of Flaubert's *Salammbô,* criticism of American writers as not "sincere." College ended after his mother's death in 1890. She was a talented, religious woman; her counsel in last letters to Stephen was to be good, independent, honest.

Aside from summers in Asbury Park and visits to his brothers, his life in the next two years was that of a struggling writer in New York, actually hungry and sometimes ill in the old Art Students' League on East Twenty-third St., reporting intermittently the *Herald* or *Tribune,* exploring the slums, lounging in Bowery saloons. His first significant writing, *Maggie: A Girl of the Streets,* had all the qualities of his later work, but it was impossibly grim for magazines, and when printed late in 1892 with $700 borrowed from a brother, it was piled in his room unsold. *The Red Badge of Courage* was finished in the following summer, and with it, in William Dean Howells's phrase, Crane's genius seemed to "spring to life fully armed." From reading *Battles and Leaders of the Civil War,* from no actual experience save his own struggles and failures, came this realistic picture of war, its truth vouchsafed for by veterans; but more than this, an extraordinary study of the common man amid the turmoil, clamor, and distortion typified by war. Pushed by his friend Hamlin Garland, the story was serialized in the Philadelphia *Press* and published, October 1895, by Appleton, and by Heinemann in London. It sold amazingly, and Crane rose to sudden fame. Its intensity, its

startling yet inevitable descriptive phrase, struck a new note in American prose. Its success led the publishers, in the following year, to issue *Maggie.*

Meantime the reading of some of Emily Dickinson's poems, at a luncheon with Howells, suggested the manner at least of *The Black Riders and Other Lines,* published in 1895. But readers of that year were ready for neither the form nor the content of poems such as the one which describes the world as set sailing in a careless moment,

"So that forever rudderless it went upon the sea,
And there were many in the sky
Who laughed at this thing."

In the same winter he went West as a writer for the Bacheller Syndicate, traveling from Nebraska to Texas and Mexico, where he was pleasantly thrilled by a bandit attack, and finding color and setting for "The Blue Hotel," "The Bride Comes to Yellow Sky," and others of his best tales. *George's Mother,* a bare, somber story of the *Maggie* type, and *The Little Regiment and Other Episodes of the Civil War* appeared in 1896. Though the success of *The Red Badge* was a matter of observation and expression, not of theme (save as war was a pleasanter subject than slums), Crane was thrust into the groove of his masterpiece, and spent most of his remaining years seeing and writing of war. In December 1896 he sailed for Cuba in a filibustering vessel which sank off the Florida coast, and with four others he experienced the fifty-hour struggle with the "jagged," "boisterously abrupt" waves described later in "The Open Boat." The Turkish war took him in the next year to Greece, where inexperience, ignorance of languages, and indigestion rendered him almost helpless. In the autumn he went to London, meantime having married (Aug. 25, 1898) Cora Taylor, a capable, attractive woman, older than he, whom he had first met in Jacksonville.

At London Crane met Conrad, and a warm friendship was cemented by Crane's devotion to the Conrads' infant boy. Conrad spoke of the younger writer's "intense earnestness," "his very steady, penetrating blue eyes," of "a strain of chivalry which made him safe to trust with one's life." H. G. Wells, another friend made at this time, described him as "very typically American, long and spare, with very straight hair, and straight features, and long quiet hands and hollow eyes, moving slowly and speaking slowly." London lionizing was not altogether escaped in the cottage the Cranes took in Oxted, Surrey, for even here they were overrun by friends and acquaintances who imposed on their hospitality.

In April came the Spanish-American War, and Crane was off for Cuba as a highly paid writer for the *World*. He won official recognition for coolness under fire in a skirmish at Guantanamo, described in his Cuban sketches, *Wounds in the Rain* (1900). In the fighting around Santiago he was dazed by quinine and worn out by bad food and hardship, so that he returned to New York broken in health. In New York the Crane "myth," started perhaps by *Maggie* and his slum adventures, had swollen until he was accused of drugs, drunkenness, and general depravity. Although he had many ardent friends and defenders, Howells, Garland, Huneker, Richard Harding Davis, and others, Crane was disgusted and returned to England after Christmas, 1899. His last year was spent in Brede Place, a great, dilapidated, medieval house in Sussex. *Active Service* (1899) was now finished, like *The Third Violet* (1897) a not very successful adventure in the field of conventional fiction; and the "Whilomville Stories" in which the humors and tragedies of childhood are handled in a manner suggestive of Tarkington's later work, were continued in *Harper's Magazine*. A second volume of verse, *War is Kind* (1899), appeared in this year, and the uninspired "Great Battles of the World." There were welcome visits from H. G. Wells and the Conrads, horseback riding and drives, long nights of writing, and the same wild swarm of guests as at Oxted. Hardly heeded, tuberculosis hung over Crane throughout the winter. He suffered a hemorrhage in March, and died at Badenweiler in the Black Forest, after a hurried journey thither in May. The permanent achievements of these few crowded years are perhaps slender, but Crane will live by *The Red Badge of Courage,* which set fresh standards in descriptive writing, and by the best of his other work, the bulk of which is collected in the volume *Men, Women and Boats* of 1921.

[Crane's writings have been collected and admirably edited by Wilson Follett in twelve volumes (1925–26). The best biography is Thomas Beer's *Stephen Crane* (1923). There is a shorter life by T. L. Raymond, published by the Carteret Club, Newark, N. J. (1923); *Stephen Crane: A Bibliography* by Vincent Starrett (1923); and much useful material gathered by the Stephen Crane Society of Newark, the president of which, Max J. Herzberg, has been indefatigable in Crane research. Valuable reminiscences and criticism are found in articles by H. G. Wells, in *North Am. Rev.*, Aug. 1900; Hamlin Garland, in *Yale Rev.*, Apr. 1914; Jos. Conrad, in *Notes on Life and Letters* (1921); Edward Garnett, in *Friday Nights* (1922); Mrs. Conrad, in *The Bookman*, Apr. 1926; Crane's niece, Edna Crane Sidbury, in the *Literary Digest Internat. Book Rev.*, Mar. 1926; Willis Fletcher Johnson, *Ibid.*, Apr. 1926; Ralph Paine, in *Roads of Adventure* (1922), and Ford Madox Hueffer, in *Thus to Revisit* (1921).]

A. W.

CRANE, THOMAS FREDERICK (July 12, 1844–Dec. 9, 1927), teacher, scholar, and author, was born in New York City, the oldest child of Thomas Sexton and Charlotte (Nuttman) Crane. His father was a merchant, who, after the birth of his son, settled at New Orleans, La., of which the colorful pre-war atmosphere left vivid impressions on the growing boy, who spent the first nine years of his life there. In 1853 Thomas went to live in Ithaca, N. Y., in charge of his mother's mother, and attended the public schools there until 1858, when he rejoined his father in Elizabeth, N. J., where he prepared for college. He graduated from the College of New Jersey (Princeton) in 1864, receiving from the same institution the degree of A.M. in 1867, of Ph.D. in 1883, and of Litt.D. in 1903. He commenced the study of law at the Columbia Law School, but, called to Ithaca, in January 1865, by the illness of a relative, he continued his studies in the law-office of F. M. Finch, later judge of the court of appeals of the State of New York. He was admitted to the bar in May 1866, and began the practise of law, incidentally acting as assistant deputy-collector of Internal Revenue, and as a sort of secretary for Cornell University, on the eve of its formal opening. From boyhood an omnivorous reader, he had continued his study of French, commenced at college, and had made substantial progress in his independent study of German and Spanish. Such unusual interests in a lawyer led Andrew D. White [*q.v.*], the president of the newly founded university, to offer him the position of assistant professor of Spanish and German, on the opening of the University in October 1868. With the intermission of several months in 1869 spent in travel and study in Europe, Crane served in that rank, with various changes in the title of his position, until 1873, when he became professor of Spanish and Italian. In 1882 he became professor of Romance languages, and head of the department, a position he filled efficiently until his retirement in 1909. From 1896 to 1902 he was dean of the College of Arts, and from 1902 to 1909 dean of the University faculty, while in 1898–99 and in 1912–13 he was acting president of Cornell University during the absence of J. G. Schurmann.

Crane was one of the pioneers in America in the study of folk-lore and medieval literature. In numerous reviews and notices contributed to the *Nation*, the *North American Review*, and various journals devoted to linguistic studies, he called the attention of cultured American readers to the publications of European scholars in those two fields. He was a member of the board of editors of the initial volumes of the *Journal of American Folklore* (I–V, 1888–92). His first independent publication dealt with a subject which he was to make peculiarly his own: *Mediæval Sermon-Books and Stories* (1883). This was followed by his edition of *The Exempla, or Illustrative Stories from the Sermones Vulgares of Jacques de Vitry* (1890), the introduction and notes giving it at once the place it holds as a standard work. Later contributions of his own and of others he summed up in his *Mediæval Sermon-Books and Stories and their Study since 1883* (1917), while his last book was a well-edited edition of the *Liber de Miraculis Sanctæ Dei Genitricis Mariæ, Published at Vienna, in 1731 by B. Pez* (1925).

His *Italian Popular Tales* (1885) is not only one of the best selections of stories for young readers, but its introduction and notes make an attractive and informing guide to the comparative study of the genre for older readers. His *Italian Social Customs of the Sixteenth Century* (1920) presents a wide orientation of an important factor in modern social and literary life. The wide range of his interests in literature and history can be appreciated by the bibliography of his writings, published as a supplement to Pez's *Liber de Miraculis,* which includes no less than 331 items.

Crane married on July 10, 1872, Sarah Fay Tourtellot, who died Aug. 21, 1912.

[The principal source of information for his biography down to 1868 is Crane's own article "How I Became a Professor," *Cornell Era,* XLI (1909), 149–58, and his unpublished autobiography covering the same period. See also *Who's Who in America,* 1926–27; W. T. Hewett, *Cornell Univ., A Hist.* (1905); *N. Y. Times,* Dec. 11, 1927; *Nation* (N. Y.), Jan. 18, 1928.] G. L. H.

CRANE, WILLIAM HENRY (Apr. 30, 1845–Mar. 7, 1928), actor, was born at Leicester, Mass., the son of a locksmith, Amaziah Brito Crane, and of his wife, Mary Sophia Masters. At the age of seven or eight he took part in his first theatricals in a barn loft. At sixteen he graduated from the Brimmer School in Boston; and during that same year his name appeared for the first time on a theatrical program when when he acted the part of Hatchet in *Black-Eyed Susan* at Cambridgeport. After leaving school he began working in a furniture store, but was unhappy there and continued rehearsing with amateur companies. At eighteen he joined the Holman Opera and Dramatic Troupe as an "apprentice," receiving no salary at first. He had a fine bass voice, and for several years his forte was thought to be light opera. He sang in the operas of Offenbach, Balfe, Donizetti, and others, though he had also numerous spoken parts in popular plays of the time. He began with serious or "straight" rôles, but, substituting on one occasion for a comedian who was ill, he made such a hit that he continued to play comedy throughout most of his career. He remained with the Holman Company seven years and the Oates Opera Company four years. In 1874 he entered R. M. Hooley's stock company in Chicago, where he played not only in the melodrama and comedy of the period, but in Shakespearian and other classics. In 1877 he made a notable success in a new play, *Evangeline.* That year also marked the beginning of his connection with Stuart Robson. Crane had been engaged to play the lead in a comedy, *Our Boarding House;* then plans were changed, Robson was employed for the leading rôle, and Crane given one less important. Robson, learning the facts, came to Crane and offered to withdraw, but the latter would not permit it; and thus began a partnership which continued for twelve years and a friendship which endured until death. One of their best-remembered hits together was made as the two Dromios in *A Comedy of Errors.* Crane also scored in such parts as Falstaff, 'Squire Hardcastle, Sir Toby Belch, but the partners met with their greatest success in an American comedy, *The Henrietta,* by Bronson Howard. In 1889 they separated amicably, Crane to take the star part in *The Senator,* in which he frankly imitated, in makeup and "business," Senator Plumb of Kansas. During the remainder of his career he was best known as the exponent of a slightly varying, homely, American type, usually a bit uncouth, sometimes gruff and crotchety, but sound and kindly at heart. Such were his parts in *On Probation, The American Minister, Brother John, Fool of Fortune, The Pacific Mail,* and *The Head of the Family.* A notable variation was that of the tight-fisted, heartless screw in *Business is Business* (1906). From 1900 to 1903 he played perhaps his greatest hit, *David Harum,* a dramatization of Edward Noyes Westcott's popular novel. This was followed by *The Spenders* and *Business is Business.* Then came *The Senator Keeps House* and a revival of *She Stoops to Conquer.* George Ade's *Father and the Boys* was successful in the seasons of 1907–10. Crane's last play was *The New Henrietta,* his old comedy rewritten and brought up to date. He retired from the legitimate stage in 1916, though in November of the following year he appeared in vaudeville. The last years of his life were spent in California, where he played in at least two motion pictures. He died at

Hollywood, survived by his wife, Ella Chloe Myers of Utica, N. Y., to whom he was married on Nov. 6, 1870.

[The major source is Crane's autobiography, *Footprints and Echoes* (1927). See also *Who's Who in America*, 1926–27; *Who's Who in the Theatre*, 1922; T. A. Brown, *Hist. of the N. Y. Stage* (3 vols., 1903); obituaries in leading newspapers; especially N. Y. *Evening Post*, Mar. 7, N. Y. *Herald-Tribune*, and *Boston Globe*, Mar. 8, 1928. The obituary in the N. Y. *Times*, Mar. 8, 1928, states that the initial "H" in Crane's name stood for Henry.]   A. F. H.

CRANE, WILLIAM MONTGOMERY (Feb. 1, 1784–Mar. 18, 1846), naval officer, was born at Elizabeth, N. J., son of Gen. William Crane, who fought under Montgomery at Quebec, and of Abigail (Miller) Crane. He entered the navy as midshipman May 23, 1799, served in the *United States* under Barry during the naval war with France, and remained on her until 1803. After promotion to lieutenant, July 20, 1803, he was in the *Vixen* in the Mediterranean, commanding gunboat *No. 7* in the bombardment of Tripoli, Aug. 7, 1804. He was later second lieutenant in the *Chesapeake*, and testified against Captain Barron [q.v.] in his court martial after the *Chesapeake-Leopard* affair of 1807. At the outbreak of the War of 1812 he commanded the brig *Nautilus*, and sailed from New York July 15. Next day at sunrise the *Nautilus* ran into Broke's blockading squadron and surrendered to the *Shannon* after a six-hour chase, during which Crane threw overboard his lee guns, and, according to the verdict of the subsequent court of inquiry, "did everything to prevent capture that a skilful and expert officer could possibly do" (*Naval Monument*, 1840, pp. 9, 210). Exchanged soon afterward at Halifax, he was in temporary charge of the Charlestown Navy Yard in November 1812, and during the next spring commanded the *John Adams* at New York. Then with his crew he was ordered to join Chauncey on Lake Ontario, where he arrived July 3, 1813. In command of the *Madison* he took part in the desultory actions of Aug. 9 and Sept. 27–28 on the lake, and during Chauncey's absence was in charge at Sackett's Harbor through the following winter, showing great energy in pushing new construction in spite of illness among his force and threats of enemy attack. He commanded the *General Pike* in the summer of 1814, and remained on Lake Ontario till the next spring. He was then given the *Independence* (74 guns), flagship of Bainbridge's squadron against Algiers, which left Boston July 3, 1815. In the Mediterranean he transferred to the *Erie*, and took part in the naval demonstration off Algiers in the following April. Noteworthy in his subsequent service was his

command of the Mediterranean Squadron June 1827–October 1829, during which, in the winter of 1828–29 he was joint commissioner with Consul Offley of Smyrna in negotiations for a commercial treaty with Turkey (see C. O. Paullin, *Diplomatic Negotiations of American Naval Officers*, 1912, p. 141). He was Commandant of the Portsmouth (N. H.) Navy Yard, 1832–40; Navy Commissioner, 1841–42; and chief of the Bureau of Ordnance and Hydrography, 1842–46. As ordnance chief he incurred some responsibility for the bursting of the new gun "Peacemaker" on the *Princeton*, Feb. 28, 1844, which killed the secretaries of state and navy and several others (*United States Naval Institute Proceedings*, November 1926). Though Crane had disapproved the gun and refused to witness the trials, his suicide by cutting his throat, in the Navy Department offices two years later, was attributed by his family to brooding over the accident. He was buried in the Congressional Cemetery. Commodore Crane was an upright and dependable officer, popular with his men and greatly loved by family and friends. He had no children. His wife, who survived him, was Eliza King, sister to the wife of Commodore Warrington and daughter of Col. Miles King of Norfolk, Va.

[Master Commandant's and Captains' Letters in the Navy Dept. Lib.; Ellery B. Crane, *Geneal. of the Crane Family*, II (1900), 479; B. J. Lossing, *The Pictorial Field-Book of the War of 1812* (1896), pp. 885–86.]
                    A. W.

CRANE, WINTHROP MURRAY (Apr. 23, 1853–Oct. 2, 1920), manufacturer, governor of Massachusetts, senator, was bred in a family where paper-making and counsel-giving were hereditary activities. The son of Zenas Marshall and Louise (Laflin) Crane, he was the grandson of Zenas Crane who in 1799 established at Dalton, Mass., the first paper-mill west of the Connecticut River. This Zenas Crane, his son, and his grandson, Winthrop Murray Crane, each served in the Massachusetts Executive Council. Winthrop's brief schooling at Wilbraham Academy and Williston Seminary ended when he was seventeen, and he returned to Dalton, where he underwent a thorough training in all branches of the paper business from the crudest processes up to factory management and sales. At twenty-six, in keen competition, he secured for the Crane Company the contract for the silk-threaded paper such as has been used ever since for the United States notes, and then at the mill he personally worked out the novel processes for its production.

In 1892, as delegate-at-large from Massachusetts, he attended the Republican National Convention, and was placed upon the Republican

National Committee. He served upon it for more than twenty years, but would never accept its chairmanship, although he became a most potent influence in nominating conventions and election campaigns. In 1896 he was elected lieutenant-governor; he served three terms as governor, 1900–02, giving the commonwealth a most businesslike administration. He brought about the merging of many commissions, made prompt and discriminating appointments, and upheld the merit system. In the interest of economy and of local self-government he vetoed bills freely, and every veto was sustained. In 1902 a Boston teamsters' strike, which threatened widespread disaster, was settled through the Governor's summoning to the State House the representatives of the contending parties and there acting as the patient intermediary between them. A few months later in personal conference he urged upon President Roosevelt a similar procedure in dealing with the anthracite strike, and this led to the White House conference at which that long deadlock was broken. In that year Crane was urged to accept the position of secretary of the treasury, but declined because of his duties to the state and to his family. On two later occasions he declined President Roosevelt's tender of other cabinet positions—postmaster-general and secretary of the interior. In 1904 Roosevelt's celebrated announcement as to a "third term" was issued after a conference in which Crane had advised such action, and on Nov. 24, 1911, Roosevelt wrote to Crane expressing "extreme pleasure" that Crane took the position that he should not accept the nomination for the presidency.

On Oct. 12, 1904, Crane was appointed to fill the vacancy caused by the recent death of Senator Hoar. He quickly won friendly association with his colleagues of both parties, for no one who knew him could doubt his sincerity and his disinterested public spirit. It was said that not even the official whips knew the trend of opinion on different bills or the attitude of individual senators so well as he. "He was one of the wonders of the Senate. He never made a speech. I do not remember that he made a motion. Yet he was the most influential member of that body. His wisdom, tact, his sound judgment, his encyclopedic knowledge of public affairs and of public men made him an authority" (C. M. Depew, *My Memories of Eighty Years*, 1922, p. 183). A leading Democrat declared that in the last years of Crane's service "no other member had such control in shaping and directing legislation" (Griffin, *post*, p. 125, quoting Hoke Smith). President Taft's opinion was that, although Crane entered the Senate without legislative ex-

perience, "he became its most influential member." In routine work his most important service was on the Post Office and Interstate Commerce Committees. In May 1912, because of ill health and family responsibilities, he announced his intention not to stand for reëlection.

He was profoundly impressed with the opportunity and duty of the United States to enter the League of Nations, and in the Massachusetts Republican convention of 1919 it was his insistence that resulted in the platform's declaration in favor of such entrance, against Lodge's demand for indorsement of the Senate's action. With waning strength but with undaunted spirit, in 1920 he went to the Republican National Convention, but there his utmost efforts could not dissuade the implacable senators on the Resolutions Committee from their determination to pledge the party to approval of their defeat of the League. Broken by this struggle into which he had thrown himself without reserve, he came home to die. To the last he remained convinced that the entrance of the United States into the League was demanded alike by justice and by sound national policy.

Throughout his life he showed himself a man of unfailing friendliness, his strength constantly over-taxed by his will to help. "Arrange your business so as to have time for personal and public service" was his advice to young men. He responded not more generously to the need for financial help than to appeals for business counsel and for intimate human sympathy. He hated publicity. In all his political campaigns he made no speech; he stood upon his record. His gift to his town by will was a community house, for he "desired above all to provide a place where the people of Dalton could spend their evenings in pleasant companionship." He was married twice: in 1880 to Mary Benner of Astoria, N. Y., who died in 1884, and in 1906 to Josephine P. Boardman of Washington, D. C.

[Solomon Bulkley Griffin, *W. Murray Crane: A Man and Brother* (1926) and Ex-President Taft's address at the dedication of the Crane memorial, Dalton, Oct. 2, 1925, are appraisals by intimate friends; see also *Boston Transcript*, Oct. 2, and *Springfield Republican*, Oct. 3, 1920.]
                                                      G. H. H.

CRANSTON, JOHN (1625–Mar. 12, 1680), physician, colonial governor of Rhode Island, was descended from an ancient Scotch family holding lands in Mid-Lothian. He was the eldest son of Rev. James Cranston, M.A., a chaplain of King Charles I, at one time attached to the church of St. Mary Overie, now known as St. Saviour's, in London. At an early age his father placed him in the care of Jeremiah (or Jeremy) Clarke, a London merchant and nephew of Richard Weston, lord high treasurer to King Charles

I. About 1637, Clarke emigrated to the island of Aquidneck (Rhode Island), bringing with him his wife and her four children by a former husband, and his ward, John Cranston. Descended as he was from a long line of Scottish border fighters, and born and brought up in the atmosphere of the English Church and the Stuart court, John Cranston took his place among the Cavalier families who had been driven out of Boston with Anne Hutchinson and were laying the foundations of Portsmouth and Newport. At the General Court of Elections held at Newport on Mar. 13, 1644, when he was eighteen or nineteen years old, he was chosen drummer of the Portsmouth militia and, within a few years, captain of the train band. At a meeting of the General Assembly on May 16, 1654, he was elected "Generall Atturnie," and was reëlected to this office in 1655 and in 1656. He was commissioner from Newport in the General Assembly every year except three from 1655 to 1666. On June 3, 1658, he married Mary Clarke, the eldest daughter of his former guardian.

During these years Cranston was employing his time profitably in gaining a knowledge of medicine and surgery. On Mar. 1, 1664, the General Assembly of the colony unanimously voted that "the said Captayne John Cranston is lycenced and commissioned to administer Phissicke and Practice chirurgery throughout this whole Colony, and is by this Court styled and recorded Doctor of Phissicke and Chirurgery." This was probably the first time that a degree equivalent to that of Doctor of Medicine was granted in the American colonies.

Cranston was Assistant in 1669, 1670, and 1671, and member of many sub-committees chosen to negotiate with other colonies and to deal with other important matters. In 1672 he was elected deputy-governor, and was thrice reëlected. At the time of King Philip's War, in 1676, he was commissioned major. Two years later, in October 1678, Gov. William Coddington died, and John Cranston, who was then deputy-governor, was chosen to fill his place. He was reëlected governor the following year, but did not complete his term of office. He presided at a meeting of the Assembly on Mar. 10, 1680. The following day the Assembly met and adjourned on account of the sudden illness of the Governor, and on the 12th he died. He was buried in the old Common Burial Ground on Farewell St., Newport. His son, Samuel Cranston [q.v.], also served the colony as governor.

[Records of the Colony of R. I. and Providence Plantations, ed. by John R. Bartlett, vol. III (1858) ; letters written by Samuel Cranston, in possession of the R. I. Hist. Soc. in Providence, printed in the New-Eng. Hist.

and Geneal. Reg., LXXX (1926), 370–78. See also Henry E. Turner, "The Two Governors Cranston," in the Narragansett Hist. Reg., July 1889 ; New-Eng. Hist. and Geneal. Reg., LXXIX (1925), 57–66.]   W.J.

CRANSTON, SAMUEL (August 1659–Apr. 26, 1727), colonial governor of Rhode Island, was born in Newport. In spite of the fact that the colony was a chartered democracy, family connections eased his way into office. His father was John Cranston [q.v.], and his mother, Mary Clarke, was the daughter of Gov. Jeremiah Clarke, and sister of Gov. Walter Clarke [q.v.]. Samuel Cranston himself took as his first wife Mary Williams Hart, grand-daughter of Roger Williams, by whom he had seven children. A second wife was Judith Parrott Cranston, widow of his brother Caleb (J. O. Austin, Genealogical Dictionary of Rhode Island, 1887). Tradition has it that as a young husband he went to sea ; was picked up by pirates ; escaped, and, returning, found his wife, by whom he had been given up for dead, on the point of marrying a Mr. Russell of Boston. The wedding guests had assembled, when the lost sailor appeared, declared himself by a scar on his head, and shattered the nuptial scene.

He was chosen governor in 1698 and rechosen thirty years in succession. At no time during the colony's stormy history was the stress greater than during his administration. Under his immediate predecessors (Walter Clarke, his uncle, and John Easton, both Quakers and little active officially), the deputy-governor, John Greene, had been gracious to pirates,—"privateers" they were called,—granting, it was said, commissions to "applicants and their assigns" and exacting no bonds. Selected by England in 1697 to bring about reform, Richard Coote [q.v.], the Earl of Bellomont, was appointed governor of New York, Massachusetts, and New Hampshire, with powers of captain-general over Rhode Island ; while in Rhode Island a royal judge of admiralty was named. In all this, the danger was that Rhode Island might lose its charter and therewith its liberties. When, therefore, the colony was charged by the Lords of Trade with "disorders and irregularities," and when sight was demanded of the commissions and bonds (mostly nonexistent) which John Greene had issued, Gov. Cranston, realizing this danger, tactfully abased himself, praying a "favorable construction of what weakness may appear in us, we being a plain and mean sort of people ... yea, an ignorant and contemptible people." Bellomont died in 1701, but was replaced as inquisitor for Rhode Island by Joseph Dudley [q.v.], governor of Massachusetts, who revived the Bellomont charges and contrived others. Queen Anne's War had now broken out, however, and privateering, wherein Rhode Island excelled, was better thought of. Besides, the Colony had as representative at Court the astute William Penn. Accordingly Gov. Cranston challenged Dudley's charges with noteworthy diligence. Even so, loss of charter rights by Rhode Island was but narrowly escaped, for a bill regulative of chartered governments actually passed the Commons, failing in the Lords.

Following the disposal of the Dudley charges, Gov. Cranston was confronted with ancient disputes with Massachusetts and Connecticut over boundaries. In both cases Rhode Island was successful, that with Connecticut, ended in 1726, being of major consequence, since it involved the whole of the present county of Washington, the famed Narragansett country. A never-ending problem was that of the currency. With both the parties created by the reckless experiment (beginning 1710) in bills of credit not redeemable through taxation but based on mortgages upon land, Cranston seems to have been in favor. In 1714 the hard-money element won the Colony elections, retaining Cranston; but in 1715 the paper-money element reversed the vote, still, however, retaining Cranston. In 1727, the year of his death, he was privileged to look back upon a career checkered, but, as tested by events, highly successful. Population in Rhode Island had trebled; trade had grown; society had improved; and a printing-press had been set up at Newport.

[Henry E. Turner, "The Two Governors Cranston," in *Narragansett Hist. Reg.*, July 1889; S. G. Arnold, *Hist. of the State of R. I. and Providence Plantations* (1859–60); *Records of the Colony of R. I. and Providence Plantations*, vol. III (1858), IV (1859); *Privateering and Piracy in the Colonial Period* (1923), ed. by J. F. Jameson; "Some Correspondence of Samuel Cranston, Esq., Gov. of R. I., 1698–1727" in *New-Eng. Hist. and Geneal. Reg.*, LXXX (1926), 370–78; genealogical material in *New-Eng. Hist. and Geneal. Reg.*, LXXIX (1925); H. M. Chapin, *The First Century of Am. Colonial Privateering* (1926).]   I.B.R.

CRAPSEY, ADELAIDE (Sept. 9, 1878–Oct. 8, 1914), poet, became a legendary figure within a year of her death. In 1915 a slender gray volume, *Verse*, appeared, bearing on its covers a delicately enigmatic device in gold. Scarcely known to the general public, this book became almost immediately a symbol of the initiate to the young poets of the day. Its fragile word etchings, poignant, brief, written during the last year of Miss Crapsey's short life, a year spent in isolation, a conscious prisoner with death, caught by contrast the imagination in a period devoted to realism rather than beauty. She was the daughter of the Rev. Algernon Sidney Crapsey [*q.v.*], a noted Episcopal clergyman, and of his wife, Adelaide Trowbridge. At the time of her birth

her father was on the staff of Trinity Parish, New York City, but in June 1879 he became rector of St. Andrew's, Rochester, N. Y., in which city Adelaide's girlhood was passed. A brilliant student, she stood at the head of her classes in the preparatory school of Kemper Hall (Kenosha, Wis.) as well as in Vassar College, where she graduated in 1901. Her verse of this period —none of it published—is said to have been of a gay, light-hearted character. She spent the years 1903–05 as a teacher of history and literature at Kemper Hall, 1905–06 as a student in the School of Archeology in Rome, and 1907–08 as an instructor in literature and history in Miss Lowe's Preparatory School in Stamford, Conn. In the latter year came the first threat of tuberculosis, and she went abroad to recuperate. While there she planned *A Study in English Metrics* of which only the first part, dealing with the relations of monosyllabic and polysyllabic words, was ever published (posthumously, 1918). In 1911 her health was apparently sufficiently recovered for her to resume teaching, and for the next two years she was instructor in poetics at Smith College: but a too strenuous devotion to her work eventually caused another, and final, break-down. She went to Saranac Lake where her windows overlooked "Trudeau's Garden," as she grimly named the grave-yard; here in exile she lingered for only a little over a year. To this single year of failing health and fading hope she owes her place in American letters. The fastidious concision which marks all of her poems, and which was responsible for the small number which she herself selected and arranged for posthumous publication, led her to create an original verse form which she called the cinquain. This five-line verse with approximately twenty-two syllables achieves a brevity approached only by that of the Japanese *hokku* which there is every reason to suppose was known to Miss Crapsey and may well have influenced her later style. Although she wrote in many meters, the brevity and starkness of the cinquain made it the most perfect form of expression for her poised, unresigned, and valiant spirit.

[A brief sketch by Claude Bragdon appears in *Verse* (1915, 1922), as does a reprint of an appreciation by Jean Webster in the *Vassar Misc.*, Mar. 1915. See also Louis Untermeyer, *Modern Am. Poetry* (1925), p. 258. Carl Sandburg has a poem, "Adelaide Crapsey," in *Cornhuskers* (1918).]   G.G—m.

CRAPSEY, ALGERNON SIDNEY (June 28, 1847–Dec. 31, 1927), Episcopal clergyman, author, was born at Fairmount, five miles west of Cincinnati, Ohio, the son of Jacob Tompkins and Rachel (Morris) Crapsey and grandson of Thomas Morris [*q.v.*]. He went to work in his eleventh year when his father's law practise had gone into a decline; at fifteen he campaigned for four months in Kentucky and Tennessee as a private in the 79th Ohio Infantry and was invalided home to die of a hypertrophied heart; at twenty, while a bookkeeper in a New York printing-office, he joined the Episcopal Church and decided to become a minister. He pursued a special course at St. Stephen's College at Annandale-on-Hudson 1867–69, graduated from the General Theological Seminary in New York in 1872, was ordained deacon that same year and priest in 1873, and until 1879 was on the staff of Trinity Parish in New York, being assigned to the work at St. Paul's Chapel. There he was from the outset so successful that the special position of junior assistant minister was created for him. On June 2, 1875, he married Adelaide Trowbridge of Catskill, N. Y., who with five of their nine children outlived him. Adelaide Crapsey [q.v.] was their third child. In order to have a parish of his own he relinquished his post in New York and in June 1879 assumed the rectorship of St. Andrew's, Rochester, N. Y., a small, impecunious, and spiritually sickly church. Under his guidance it grew to be one of the most frequented and influential in the city and the center of extensive, highly efficient social work. A gentle, soft-spoken, scholarly little man—he was five feet six inches tall and weighed only 120 pounds—he attracted men of all classes to him by his eloquence, still more by his transparent sincerity and consecration. As missioner, conductor of retreats, and occasional preacher, he became one of the best-known clergymen of his denomination. On Apr. 18, 1906, at Batavia, N. Y., he was placed on trial for heresy before the court of the Diocese of Western New York for having said in a lecture that "in the light of scientific research the Founder of Christianity, Jesus the son of Joseph, no longer stands apart from the common destiny of man in life and death, but He is in all things physical like as we are, born as we are born, dying as we die, and both in life and death in the keeping of that same Divine Power, that heavenly Fatherhood, which delivers us from the womb and carries us down to the grave." The trial ended in the conviction of the heretic and the propagation of his heresy. Unable to recant before his bishop, Crapsey was deposed from the ministry, and on the Christmas Eve before his death might have heard the same teaching in regard to the Second Person of the Trinity broadcast over the radio, quite without criticism, by one of the leading Episcopal clergymen of New York City. Friends within and without the Church remained steadfast and manifested their friendship in helpful ways. He continued to live in Rochester, devoting much of his time to lecturing and writing, was a delegate to the International Peace Conference at The Hague in 1907, and in 1914 was appointed one of the state parole officers. As a writer he constantly grew in power; his last book, which ranks well among American autobiographies, is also his best. Crapsey wrote *Meditations on the Five Joyful Mysteries* (1888); *The Greater Love,* a novel (1902); *Sarah Thorne,* memoir (1900); *Religion and Politics* (1905); *The Rebirth of Religion* (1907); *The Rise of the Working Class* (1914); *International Republicanism* (1918); *The Ways of the Gods,* an excellent popular work (1920); *Lewis Henry Morgan* (1923); and *The Last of the Heretics* (1924).

[For Crapsey's life see *Who's Who in America,* 1927–28; Rochester, N. Y., *Dem. and Chron.,* Jan. 1–4, 1928; *Churchman,* vols. 93–94 (1906), and Jan. 14, 1928; *Arguments for Presenters and Defence of Rev. A. S. Crapsey Before the Court of Review of the P. E. Church Upon his Appeal from the Judgment of the Court of the Diocese of Western N. Y.* (1906); J. W. Suter, *Life and Letters of Wm. Reed Huntington* (1925).] G.H.G.

CRARY, ISAAC EDWIN (Oct. 2, 1804–May 8, 1854), educator, first representative in Congress from Michigan, was born in Preston, New London County, Conn., of Puritan stock. He was the oldest son of Elisha and Nabby (Avery) Crary, and had in him some of the adventurous spirit which had impelled Peter Crary to move from Northumberland to Plymouth, Mass., and later to go with 200 armed men to found a colony near Mystic River in New London County, Conn. It was not until Isaac Crary had reached the age of twenty-seven, however, that his adventurous spirit had an opportunity to assert itself. He was educated at Bacon Academy, Colchester, and Trinity College, Hartford, graduating from the latter institution in 1827 (*Catalogue of Trinity College,* 1855). In Hartford he read law with Henry W. Ellsworth, practised law for two years, and assisted G. D. Prentice in editing the *New England Weekly Review.* Early in the year 1832 the tide of westward emigration carried him to southern Michigan, where he bought 240 acres of land (*Michigan Pioneer and Historical Collections,* III, 1881, 401), located in Bellevue, Eaton County. The next year he began to practise law in Marshall, Calhoun County. Here he became intimately acquainted with Rev. John D. Pierce [q.v.], in whose house he lived for a time (*Ibid.,* vol. I, 1877, p. 38). They owned a sawmill in Marshall, and sponsored a plan to have a railroad constructed through Calhoun County (see letter by Crary to Lucius Lyon, dated Marshall, Jan. 7, 1834). In the militia organization of Michigan Crary was nominally a brigadier-general; hence the title of Gen. Crary, so often applied to him. In October 1835 he was elected territorial delegate for Michigan, and two years later he became the first representative of the newly created state. He served in this capacity till 1841. Although a man of considerable ability, he was not a statesman of the first order. Particularly unfortunate was his decision to speak slightingly in Congress of the military career of Gen. Harrison, for he so aroused the anger of John Quincy Adams that the latter permitted Tom Corwin to attack Crary in scathing terms, whereupon Adams and others referred to the representative from Michigan as the "late Gen. Crary" (see B. P. Poore, *Reminiscences*, vol. I, 1886, pp. 234–37; *Congressional Globe*, 26 Cong., 1 Sess., pp. 200–01). From 1842 to 1846 he was a member of the state legislature, and during his last term he was speaker of the House. Throughout his whole career he was an ardent Democrat. He was far more widely known as an educator, however, than as a statesman. He was not only one of the founders of the University of Michigan, but was chairman of the Committee on Education, in the constituent convention of 1835, and prepared the Article on Education. This Article proposed a school system closely patterned after the Prussian model. It provided for the first superintendent of public instruction in any state, which office was first filled by Crary's friend, the Rev. J. D. Pierce. Provision was also made for the founding of a state university "with such branches as the public convenience may hereafter demand." These "branch universities" were established in various parts of the state. In 1837 Crary was appointed a member of the board of regents of the newly created university. Twice he was reappointed; in 1844 he resigned the office. He served as a member of the state board of education from 1850 to the time of his death. Crary was married twice, but left no children. He was cold in temperament, and careless in his dress. It was his habit to walk along the street with swinging gait, his hat cocked on one side. His last years were spent in Marshall.

[In addition to references given above see *Mich. Pioneer and Hist. Colls.*, V (1884), 382–84; XI (1888), 273–74; XIV (1890), 280–83. Crary's letter to Lucius Lyon is in the Lib. of the Univ. of Mich.]   A.H—a.

CRATTY, MABEL (June 30, 1868–Feb. 27, 1928), social worker, was born at Bellaire, Ohio, the daughter of Charles Campbell and Mary (Thoburn) Cratty. Her mother was a sister of Bishop James M. Thoburn [*q.v.*], missionary bishop of the Methodist Episcopal Church in India, and of Isabella Thoburn [*q.v.*], first unmarried American woman foreign missionary. Miss Cratty herself was a life-long Methodist. She was educated in the public schools of Bellaire, at Lake Erie Seminary, Painesville, Ohio, and at Ohio Wesleyan University, where she graduated with the degree of B.L. in 1890. She taught in the Wheeling (W. Va.) Female Seminary and in the high schools of Kent and Delaware, Ohio, and was principal of the Delaware High School, 1900–04. Through the efforts of two of her college friends she became interested in Y. W. C. A. work (1902), and for a time she was a member of the Ohio state committee. She was appointed associate general secretary of the American Committee of the Young Women's Christian Association in 1904, and, with the unifying of Y. W. C. A. movement and the formation of the National Board in 1906, she was made general secretary of the Board. In this position she remained until her death, closely associated, during the early years, with Grace H. Dodge [*q.v.*], first president of the Board. Miss Cratty's interests and activities were not limited to the organization of which she was so important a part, but extended to many other movements, among them the Camp Fire Girls of America, Institute of Pacific Relations, National Social Work Council, Council of Christian Associations, National Council Committee to study relations between the Young Men's Christian Association and the Council of Churches, National Committee on the Cause and Cure of War. In the development of the last organization, she was prominent from its beginning. Miss Cratty attended many meetings of the World's Committee of the Y. W. C. A., and World Conferences; in Paris (1906), Swanwick (1910), Berlin (1912), Stockholm (1914), Champéry (1920), Washington (1924), Oxford (1926). She visited Y. W. C. A. headquarters in Germany, Czechoslovakia, Italy, France, Switzerland, Great Britain, the Scandinavian countries, China, Japan, and Honolulu. In 1922 she was a member of the John D. Rockefeller, Jr., party which spent four months in the Orient. In July 1927 she was a delegate to the Institute of Pacific Relations at Honolulu. Seven months later, after a brief illness from pneumonia, she died at the Rockefeller Institute Hospital, New York City. She was buried in the family lot at Bellaire, overlooking the Ohio River.

Miss Cratty was called the "statesman" of the Y. W. C. A. With great ability for organization and complete understanding of her problems, she preferred to keep herself in the background and to work through others. This she did successfully that in 1928 the Y. W. C. A. had over 1,300 local associations and a membership of about 600,000. In 1906 the National Board employed a few assistants in one small room; in 1928 a twelve-story building, 600 Lexington Ave., was occupied by a staff of 110 women secretaries. Except for her direct, kindly expression, Miss Cratty was not striking in appearance, and her personality was a quiet one, but those who knew her appreciated her uprightness, keen insight, patience in obtaining results, clear vision, practical sense, helpfulness, gift for developing others, and justice. Two aims were hers throughout life and to the accomplishment of them she contributed much: the securing of social justice and improvement in industrial conditions for working women; and the advancement of international sympathy, with the object of world peace.

[Margaret E. Burton, *Mabel Cratty: Leader in the Art of Leadership* (1929), containing a biographical sketch and extracts from her papers; *Who's Who in America*, 1926–27; memorial articles in the *Capital Outlook* (published by the Y. W. C. A. of the D. C.), Apr. 1928, and the *Woman's Press* (official organ of the Nat. Board, Y. W. C. A.), Apr. and May 1928; a typed MS. supplied by the Publicity Dept., Nat. Board, Y. W. C. A.; obituary in the *N. Y. Times*, Feb. 28, and editorial Feb. 29, 1928.]   S.G.B.

CRAVATH, ERASTUS MILO (July 1, 1833–Sept. 4, 1900), clergyman, first president of Fisk University, was born at Homer, N. Y., the eldest son of Oren Cravath, a prosperous farmer, and Betsey (Northway) Cravath. Early influences created in him a hatred of the institution of slavery and a deep sympathy for the slave. His father's house was a station on the Underground Railroad. As a youth in his teens he attended for a year New York Central College, a poorly equipped institution founded by abolitionists. Here some of the students and one of the faculty were negroes, and it is to be presumed that Cravath joined his fellow students in their song, "I am an Abolitionist, I glory in the name" (*The Fisk Herald,* November 1900). In 1851 the family moved to Oberlin, Ohio, where anti-slavery sentiment had for many years been strong. From Oberlin College Cravath graduated in 1857 and three years later he completed the work of the theological seminary. In this same year he married Ruthanna Jackson of Kennett Square, Pa., and assumed the pastorate of the Congregational church in Berlin Heights, Ohio. The Civil War affected Cravath's life profoundly. He became chaplain of the 101st Regiment of Ohio Volunteers in December 1863, served for the remainder of the war, and was mustered out in Nashville, Tenn. Here he began the work of educating the freedmen to which he was to devote the remaining thirty-five years of his life. For ten years, successively as field agent, as district secretary, and as field secretary of the American Missionary Association, he labored with missionary zeal

and with notable success in raising money in the North and establishing and supervising negro schools in the South. One of these schools became Atlanta University; another became Fisk University, in Nashville. He was elected first president of this latter institution in 1875, but because of a tour of Europe with the famed Jubilee Singers of Fisk he did not assume active administration of its affairs until three years later. His ideal of education for the colored race he once expressed in these words: "There must be thoroughly and liberally educated men and women of their own race to fill the high places of influence and responsibility in school and church, in business and professional life, if the masses are to be reached and uplifted" (*The Fisk Herald,* December 1884). He made the university a leader in the field of negro education. Tall, handsome, dignified, he inspired in his students and faculty members deep affection and something of awe, and in his highly critical white neighbors a large measure of respect.

[Brief sketch in W. W. Clayton, *Hist. of Davidson County, Tenn.* (1880); *Nashville Banner*, Sept. 5, 1900; *The Congregationalist*, Sept. 13, 1900; materials in the offices of the Am. Missionary Ass. in New York City and at Fisk Univ.; information as to certain facts from Cravath's daughter, Mrs. Herbert A. Miller of Columbus, Ohio, through her brother Mr. Paul D. Cravath of New York City.]   P.M.H.

CRAVEN, BRAXTON (Aug. 22, 1822–Nov. 7, 1882), first president of Trinity College (now Duke University), was born in Randolph County, N. C. His early years were spent at the home of a farmer, Nathan Cox, and his education was secured mainly by self-help. He attended two sessions at New Garden School (now Guilford College) and in 1850 he passed the examinations on the entire course of study at Randolph-Macon College in Virginia, and received the degree of B.A. In 1841 he became assistant teacher at Union Institute, Randolph County, a local school organized in 1838 by a group of Quakers and Methodists, and in 1842 he was made principal. Desiring to make the institution more than an academy, he undertook the training of teachers for the common schools of North Carolina, and in 1850 he published his *Theory of Common Schools,* the first comprehensive program of teacher training formulated in North Carolina. The same year he began the publication of the *Southern Index,* an educational journal, which was soon converted into a literary magazine, the *Evergreen.* He sought aid from the legislature and in 1851 Union Institute was rechartered as Normal College, those students holding a certificate from the institution being authorized to teach in the common schools without further examination. In 1852 the college was granted a loan of $10,000 from the State Literary Fund. This was the first college for teacher training in North Carolina; but the experiment was not a success and Craven turned to the Methodist Church for aid. In 1856 an agreement was made by which Normal College was transferred to the North Carolina Conference of the Methodist Episcopal Church, South. The Conference agreed to raise $20,000 for the institution, but never fulfilled its promise. In 1859 the name of the institution was changed to Trinity College. Braxton Craven remained its president until his death, with the exception of an interval during the Civil War.

[J. Dowd, *Life of Braxton Craven* (Raleigh, 1896); Thos. N. Ivey, "Braxton Craven," in *Biog. Hist. of N. C.*, IV, 102–11, ed. by Samuel A. Ashe.] W. K. B.

CRAVEN, JOHN JOSEPH (Sept. 8, 1822– Feb. 14, 1893), inventor, physician, was born in Newark, N. J., in such lowly circumstances that he was deprived of even the limited advantages afforded the youth of the time. When he was old enough to work he entered a chemical manufacturing plant in Newark where he continued for a number of years, taking every opportunity for study. About the time of his majority the telegraph had been launched, and, when the construction of the line from New York to Philadelphia was begun in 1845, Craven left the chemical plant and joined the telegraph construction crew. He continued with the Magnetic Telegraph Company, as the organization was called, until after its completion, and had the distinction of being the first man to use the newly invented pole climbers. He is said to have devised a gutta-percha insulation for cables at this time which had the particular advantage of permitting the laying of the telegraph wires in water. It is said further that with his insulated cables successful communication was had between New York and Philadelphia, but a patent for which he applied was denied on technical grounds. His insulation method pointed the way for the later successful ocean cable. In 1849, with a group of friends, he sailed around the Horn for California. He apparently had rather indifferent success in the search for gold and within two years was again back in Newark. His early work in chemistry undoubtedly had a marked influence upon him, for from this time on he devoted himself to the study of medicine, in which he eventually gained success. At the outbreak of the Civil War he joined the 1st New Jersey Infantry as a surgeon, but within a few months was mustered out and became a surgeon of volunteers, serving throughout the war in this capacity. In 1862 he was medical director of the Department of the

South, and in 1864 became director of the 10th Corps. For "faithful and meritorious service during the war" he was made a brevet lieutenant-colonel of volunteers in 1865, and was mustered out of service Jan. 27, 1866. While with the 10th Army Corps, he was in attendance upon Jefferson Davis who was a prisoner at Fortress Monroe, Va., and after the war he published *The Prison Life of Jefferson Davis* (1866, republished in 1905). Craven returned to Newark after the war, served four years as postmaster, and then became a practising physician until 1883, when he retired and removed to Patchogue, L. I. Here he entered energetically into the civic affairs of the town in various capacities, such as health officer, president of the library association and board of education, as well as acting as consultant for several abattoir organizations. His wife was Catherine S. Tichenor, daughter of Samuel Tichenor of Newark.

[F. B. Heitman, *Hist. Reg. and Dict. of the U. S. Army* (1903); Jas. D. Reid, *The Telegraph in America* (1886); *Newark Daily Advertiser*, Feb 15, 1893; *N. Y. Tribune*, *N. Y. Herald*, Feb. 16, 1893; *Biog. Encyc. of N. J.* (1877).] C. W. M.

CRAVEN, THOMAS TINGEY (Dec. 20, 1808–Aug. 23, 1887), naval officer, was born in the District of Columbia. His father, Tunis Craven, who was a native of New Jersey and who early in life was a merchant in Alexandria, Va., was a purser in the navy, 1812–13, and for many years a naval storekeeper, first at Portsmouth, N. H., and later at Brooklyn, N. Y. His mother, Hannah (Tingey) Craven, was a daughter of Commodore Thomas Tingey [q.v.]. Entering the navy as a midshipman from New Hampshire on May 1, 1822, Craven was made a passed midshipman in 1828, and a lieutenant in 1830. In the last-named grade, he served off the Brazilian coast and in East Indian waters, and later, in 1838–39, as first lieutenant of the *Vincennes*, the flagship of the Wilkes exploring expedition. In 1843–44 he assisted Commodore M. C. Perry [q.v.] in suppressing the slave-trade off the coast of Africa, part of the time as commander of the schooner *Porpoise*. For almost eight years, 1850–55 and 1858–60, he was commandant of midshipmen at the Naval Academy. He initiated and elaborated the practise cruise, still regarded as one of the most beneficial features of the course at Annapolis. In 1852 he was promoted commander and in the first year of the Civil War while in command of the Potomac flotilla, he was made a captain. In the following year he commanded the *Brooklyn* of Farragut's squadron on the Mississippi and had an active share in the stirring events that resulted in the opening of that river. In 1863 he was made a commodore and was ordered with the steam frigate *Niagara* to European waters there to perform certain special duties, which included the protection of American commerce. In August 1864 he captured off the coast of Portugal the Confederate steamer *Georgia.* Eight months later off the coast of Spain near Corunna, the commander of the Confederate ironclad ram *Stonewall* challenged Craven to a trial of strength in the open sea. In addition to the *Niagara* the Commodore at this time had under his control the sloop-of-war *Sacramento.* These two wooden ships carried an armament superior in the number of guns, but otherwise much inferior to that of the *Stonewall.* Craven therefore declined the challenge and allowed the *Stonewall* to proceed on her way unmolested. His action was much criticized and on his return to the United States he was brought before a court martial composed of nine of the most distinguished officers of the navy, with Vice-Admiral Farragut as president. The court found him guilty of failing to do his utmost to destroy the *Stonewall* and sentenced him to be suspended from duty for two years on leave-pay. On the ground that the finding was inconsistent, Secretary Welles set aside the proceedings of the court and discharged Craven from arrest. The Secretary, nevertheless, was of the opinion that the Commodore was too cautious an officer (*Diary of Gideon Welles,* vol. II, 1911, p. 267). In 1866 Craven was promoted rear admiral, and, after serving as commandant of the Mare Island navy-yard and commander of the Pacific Squadron, he was in 1869 retired in that grade. In the following year he served as port admiral at San Francisco. He died at the Boston navy-yard. His first wife was his cousin, Virginia Wingate; his second, Emily Truxtun Henderson, by whom he had eight children. Three of his sons graduated at the Naval Academy.

[Record of Officers, Bureau of Navigation, 1823–87; *Record of the Testimony taken in the Trial of Commodore T. T. Craven* (1866); *Official Records (Navy),* I ser., vols. XVII, XVIII; D. D. Porter, *Naval Hist. of the Civil War* (1886), pp. 823–27; and *Army and Navy Jour.,* Dec. 23, 1865.]   C.O.P.

CRAVEN, TUNIS AUGUSTUS MACDONOUGH (Jan. 11, 1813–Aug. 5, 1864), naval officer, son of Tunis and Hannah (Tingey) Craven, was born in Portsmouth, N. H. He was the youngest brother of Rear Admiral Thomas Tingey Craven [*q.v.*]. His early education was acquired at the grammar school of Columbia College, New York, after his father became naval storekeeper at the Brooklyn navy-yard. Entering the navy in 1829 as a midshipman, he

in 1835 was promoted to be a passed midshipman and in the last-named year was for the first time employed in surveying the coast, an employment, chiefly in connection with the United States Coast Survey, which lasted, with intervals of other duties, for more than twenty years. Developing an aptitude for scientific work, he became one of the leading surveyors and hydrographers of the navy, and in 1857–58 was in charge of the expedition that surveyed a ship-canal route through the Isthmus of Darien from the Atlantic to the Pacific Ocean by way of the Atrato River. His report on this survey was published by the Federal Government (*House Executive Documents, No. 63, 46* Cong., 2 Sess.). His surveying duties were interrupted in 1846–49 by his service as a lieutenant, to which grade he was promoted in 1841, on board the sloop *Dale,* of the Pacific Squadron, which cruised during the Mexican War off the coast of Mexico and California. In 1845–46 he was the chief editor of the *United States Nautical Magazine,* one of the first periodicals devoted to the interests of the navy and the merchant marine. While in command of the steamer *Mohawk* of the home squadron, 1859–61, he captured off the coast of Cuba the slaver *Wildfire,* with more than five hundred negroes on board. In 1860 he saved the crew of the *Bella,* a Spanish polacca, that had been wrecked on a Cuban island. As a token of her appreciation, Queen Isabella II presented him with a gold medal and a diploma. For similar aid rendered to American merchantmen in distress, the Board of Underwriters of New York sent him a complimentary letter and gave Mrs. Craven a handsome silver service.

Early in the Civil War as commander of the steamer *Crusader,* Craven had an important share in saving Key West for the Union. In September 1861, soon after he received his commission as commander, he took command of the new sloop *Tuscarora,* with orders to report to the American minister in London, Charles Francis Adams. He cruised in European waters for more than a year in search of Confederate commerce-destroyers. While he made no captures, he kept so close a watch on the *Sumter* that her officers and crew abandoned her at Gibraltar. In the summer of 1863 he was placed in command of the ironclad *Tecumseh* and later joined Rear Admiral Lee's James River flotilla. He was among the first to reach City Point. Ordered to reinforce Rear Admiral Farragut, Craven arrived in Mobile Bay the evening before the attack was made on the Confederate defenses, Aug. 5, 1864. The *Tecumseh,* one of the foremost vessels in the advance, fired the first shot and three-fourths of an hour later struck a mine and went down almost instantly, carrying with her Craven and all on board with the exception of two officers and thirteen men. One of the survivors was the pilot, John Collins, who owed his life to the courtesy of his commander. The two men reached the ladder leading to the top of the turret at the same time, and Craven, stepping aside, said to Collins, "After you, pilot." The delay of a few moments was fatal.

Craven was married in 1838 to Mary Carter of Long Island, who died in 1843. A few years later he married Marie L. Stevenson of Baltimore. He was an able and studious officer and a thorough seaman and gentleman. The United States destroyer *Craven* was named for him.

[Record of Officers, Bureau of Navigation, 1830–64; *Army and Navy Jour.*, Aug. 20, 1864; *U. S. Naval Inst. Proc.*, XIV, 1888, 119–20; *Official Records (Navy)*, 1 ser., vol. XXI; Loyall Farragut, *Life of Rear-Admiral David Glasgow Farragut* (1879), pp. 413–39.]
C. O. P.

CRAWFORD, FRANCIS MARION (Aug. 2, 1854–Apr. 9, 1909), novelist, historian, was born in Bagni di Lucca, Tuscany, the youngest of four children of Thomas Crawford [*q.v.*], an American sculptor long resident in Italy, and of Louisa Cutler Ward, a sister of Julia Ward Howe. He was early sent to relatives at Bordentown, N. J., but on the death of his father was returned to Italy where his mother still made her home. The boy's education from the first was thorough and peculiarly cosmopolitan. "Most of my boyhood," he wrote in later years, "was spent under the direction of a French governess. Not only did I learn her language of her, but all of my studies, geography, arithmetic and so forth were taught me in French and I learned to write it with great readiness as a mere boy because it was the language of my daily tasks. The consequence is that to this day I write French with the ease of English." Between the ages of twelve and fourteen he was a pupil at St. Paul's School, Concord, N. H., and during the following ten years he was successively student of mathematics and Greek at Rome; student with a tutor at Hatfield Broadoak, Essex, England; matriculant at Trinity College, Cambridge, where he pursued courses in German, Swedish, and Spanish; and attendant upon lectures at Karlsruhe and Heidelberg. As a result he became fluent in most of the languages of Europe including the Turkish and the Russian, and later learned to converse in most of the Eastern languages. At twenty-two he was at the University of Rome specializing in the study of Sanskrit in which he had become intensely interested, and it was to perfect himself in this language at its fountain head that in 1879, borrowing the money to pay his expenses, he went to India. In financial straits at length, he turned, like Kipling in later years, to journalism; for eighteen months he served as editor of the *Indian Herald* at Allahabad. He returned to Rome in 1880 and the next year was in America pursuing studies in Sanskrit at Harvard, making his home with his aunt Julia Ward Howe. Unsettled, perplexed as to what was to be his lifework, supporting himself precariously with hackwork sold to papers and magazines, in May 1882, while in New York City the guest of his uncle Samuel Ward, he told at a dinner the story of one Jacobs, a diamond merchant of Simla, whose sale of an unusual stone had called forth a protest from the British government. Recognizing the interest of the story and the graphic power of the telling, his uncle urged him to put it into the form of a novel and publish it. The result was *Mr. Isaacs* which Crawford wrote in less than six weeks, the greater part of it at his aunt's home in Boston. The success of the novel was instant and sensational. It was the most talked of book of its season. Crawford had found his profession. From that time until his death fiction flowed from his pen in a steady stream, often two or three volumes coming in a single publishing season. In less than twenty-five years he produced more than forty novels, not to mention other works historical and critical.

His second book was *Dr. Claudius* (1883), its central character drawn from his uncle Samuel. Then Aldrich asked for a serial for the *Atlantic*, and *A Roman Singer* (1884) resulted. Historical romances laid in the Orient and in Europe, Italian novels, and stories of contemporary life, some of them American, now came in full tide. The titles are suggestive: *To Leeward* (1884); *An American Politician* (1885); *Zoroaster* (1885); *A Tale of a Lonely Parish* (1886); *Marzio's Crucifix* (1887); *Paul Patoff* (1887); *Saracinesca* (1887); *With the Immortals* (1888); *Greifenstein* (1889); *Sant' Ilario* (1889); *A Cigarette Maker's Romance* (1890); *Khaled* (1891); *The Witch of Prague* (1891); *The Three Fates* (1892); *The Children of the King* (1892); *Don Orsino* (1892); *Pietro Ghisleri* (1892); *Marion Darche* (1893); *Katharine Lauderdale* (1894); *Love in Idleness* (1894); *The Ralstons* (1895); *Constantinople* (1895); *Casa Braccio* (1895); *Adam Johnstone's Son* (1895); *Taquisara* (1895); *Corleone* (1896); *A Rose of Yesterday* (1897); *Via Crucis* (1898); *In the Palace of the King* (1900);

Marietta, a Maid of Venice (1901); *Cecilia, a Story of Modern Rome* (1902); *The Heart of Rome* (1903); *Whosoever Shall Offend* (1904); *Soprano, a Portrait* (1905); *A Lady of Rome* (1906); *Arethusa* (1907); *The Little City of Hope* (1907); *The Primadonna* (1908); *The Diva's Ruby* (1908); *Stradella* (1909); *The White Sister* (1909); *The Undesirable Governess* (1909); *Wandering Ghosts* (1911). In addition to these he wrote three historical works of considerable value, *Ave Roma Immortalis* (1898); *Rulers of the South* (1900); *Salve Venetia; Gleanings from Venetian History* (1905), and also a suggestive treatise on the art of fiction, *The Novel—What It Is* (1893). He was the author of a play *Francesca da Rimini*, produced in Paris by Bernhardt in 1902. At the time of his death he left incomplete a series of archeological studies of Italy which were to have eventuated finally in a history of Rome in the Middle Ages.

As a novelist Crawford was primarily a storyteller. He could create character, and could picture with vividness scenes in unusual, sometimes unique, areas which his cosmopolitan life had opened for him. He was a master of dialogue; he excelled in portraying action; his power to hold his reader to the end was unfailing. To him the novel was "a pocket theatre" exclusively for entertainment; propaganda, or moral teaching, or the shedding of light upon the meaning of life was no part of its province. He wrote undoubtedly too much; more than half of his voluminous product could be spared, but the other half, especially those novels like the Saracinesca series which deal with the Italian life he knew so well, has won a secure place.

His life was unusually strewn with the picturesque. The year 1884 he spent mostly in Constantinople where he was married to Elizabeth Berdan, daughter of Gen. Berdan, and the next year he settled at Sorrento, Italy, at "Villa Crawford," on a high bluff overlooking the Bay of Naples. Here he made his home for the rest of his life and here he died. Almost yearly he was in America, sometimes in his own yacht of which he was himself the captain and master mariner. He was commanding in physique, athletic, and handsome, with a melodious voice and polished deportment,—a cosmopolite, an adventurer, romantic, restless, competent, "driving his boats into the most dangerous seas, building his palaces on the Mediterranean shore, travelling over every queer quarter of the globe, fearless and challenging and heroic."

[E. F. Harkins, *Little Pilgrimages Among the Men who have Written Famous Books* (1902), pp. 169–83; M. C. Fraser, "Notes of a Romantic Life," *Collier's,*

Apr. 23, 1910; F. T. Cooper, "Marion Crawford," *Forum,* May 1909; and "The Novels of F. Marion Crawford," *Edinburgh Rev.,* July 1906, reissued in the *Living Age,* Aug, 25, 1906.]   F. L. P—e.

CRAWFORD, GEORGE WALKER (Dec. 22, 1798–July 22, 1872), governor of Georgia, was a member of a family noted in Georgia for ability and devotion to the public service. Though not so well known in national affairs as his second cousin, William H. Crawford [*q.v.*], he was yet a leader in his day and an intimate friend of Toombs, Stephens, and other eminent Whig politicians. His forebears, of Scottish descent, migrated to Georgia from Virginia at an early period. He was the son of Peter and Mary Crawford, whose home was in Columbia County, near Augusta.

After graduation from the College of New Jersey (Princeton) in 1820, Crawford was admitted to the bar (1822) and opened a law office in Augusta. He was a successful candidate (1827) for the office of attorney-general and held the place for four years. From 1837 to 1842 he was, with the exception of one year, a member of the legislature from Richmond County. In 1843 he was elected as a Whig to Congress to fill an unexpired term, but served in Congress only one month (Feb. 1 to Mar. 4, 1843). His brief service was due to the fact that he received the Whig nomination for governor in 1843. He was elected, and reëlected in 1845, serving until 1847. His term as governor was coincident with the period of recovery after the crisis of 1837 and the succeeding depression. The decade of the forties was characterized by great economic activity—railroad construction, building of cotton-mills, improvement in banking facilities, and the extension of cotton culture. Wise handling of the state finances by the Governor contributed materially to the growing prosperity of Georgia in the period. Robert Toombs said of him, "There are but few abler and no purer men in America, and he has administrative qualities of an unusually high order" ("Correspondence," *post,* p. 147). His service to the state as a competent administrator was the most important aspect of his public career.

On the election of President Zachary Taylor the post of secretary of war was tendered to Crawford. He accepted (March 1849), but resigned (July 1850) on Taylor's death. From the time of his resignation to the outbreak of the Civil War he was in retirement. His last public service was as chairman of the state secession convention in 1861.

["Correspondence of Robt. Toombs, Alexander H. Stephens, and Howell Cobb," in *Am. Hist. Asso. Re-*

port for the Year 1911, vol. II; Richard H. Shryock, *Ga. and the Union in 1850* (1926); W. F. Northen, *Men of Mark in Ga.*, vol. II (1910), pp. 229–31; *Memoirs of Ga.* (1895), I, 233.]   R. P. B.

CRAWFORD, JOHN (May 3, 1746–May 9, 1813), physician, was the second of four sons of a North Ireland clergyman. All four became professional men. At seventeen John Crawford entered Trinity College, Dublin, but he took his medical degree at the University of Leyden, in Holland. He acquired his first practical experience as surgeon and agent in charge of the British Naval Hospital in Barbados, where he had opportunities for studying the reactions of the British to a tropical climate. During a fearful hurricane in 1780 he showed himself a generous friend and devoted physician, giving away his own supplies and his entire stock of medicines. Ill as a result of strain and exposure, he went to England on furlough, his wife dying during the voyage. Leaving his infant children in England, he returned to his post to begin a long period of activity and patient investigation. About 1790 he was transferred to Demerara, then a Dutch possession, and was given a hospital of from sixty to eighty beds. Here he made frequent autopsies, studied botany and entomology, and laid the foundation for his later theory, of "animal contagion." He saw and described many cases of hepatic abscess. In 1794, during a visit to Leyden, he discussed with his old teachers his theory of contagion, but it received little attention. Apparently because of some disappointment or because of an antagonism to British methods, he never returned to Demerara, which in 1796 was taken by the British. Instead, in that year, he emigrated to Baltimore with his children. For seventeen years he practised and wrote there, becoming one of the best-known members of his profession. Rather didactic and cock-sure, he seems to have aroused a good deal of antagonism, but in such atmosphere he throve and rejoiced.

In the summer of 1800 Crawford received from Dr. Ring in London (Cordell, *post*, p. 48) some vaccine "on a cotton thread, rolled up in paper and covered with a varnish which excluded the air." This was the first vaccine received in Maryland, but no record of its use appears to have been kept. In 1809 Crawford published in the *Baltimore Medical and Physical Recorder* (I, 40–52, 81–92, 206–21) "A Series of Observations on the Seats and Causes of Disease," in which he set forth the theory of infection or contagion which was his most important contribution to medical science. This he discussed further in a lecture, *Introductory to a Course of Lectures on the Cause, Seat and Cure of Diseases* (1811). He stated his belief in a *contagium vivum* or *animatum*. Man, he said, is an animal having many properties in common with any other animal. He then traced the connection between animals and the vegetable world, especially between vegetables and insects. Everywhere he found parasitism. He held that disease was caused by the introduction into the human body of some form of animal life so minute as to escape observation, and he believed that each of these minute organisms produced its own peculiar disease, just as a seed in the vegetable kingdom produces its own type of plant and no other. In Baltimore he found no interest in his idea, but he said himself in the lecture of 1811: "The difficulties I have met with have only increased my ardour. As long as life and health remain, I shall devote myself strictly to the performance of my duty, and I shall leave the results to the August Being who made nothing in vain." His literary activity was very great, although few of its results were printed and many of his manuscripts were lost or destroyed after his death. In addition to the papers mentioned above he published four letters on yellow fever and quarantine (*Federal Gazette*, Baltimore, September 1802 ff.); four letters on quarantine (*Baltimore Observer*, Nov. 29, 1806 ff.); "An Extraordinary Case of Ascites" (*Baltimore Medical and Physical Recorder*, vol. I, 1808–09, pp. 1–5); "An Account of the Sanicula" (*Ibid.*, pp. 222–31); "A Case of Hepatic Infection" (*Ibid.*, pp. 300–09). He also left a manuscript of 175 pages "On the Means of Preventing, the Method of Treating and the Origin of the Diseases most prevalent and which prove most destructive to the natives of Cold Countries visiting or residing in warm countries." This study, written about 1807, embodied the results of observations made during his service in the tropics.

Crawford's vital personality soon overflowed the bounds of professional life into the civic life of Baltimore. He helped to found a Society for the Promotion of Useful Knowledge, the Baltimore Dispensary, and the Baltimore Library (1798); and he was deeply interested in the building and up-keep of Baltimore's first penitentiary. He gave public lectures, apparently not very successfully; was an active Free Mason and Grand Master of his Lodge in 1801. He was censor, examiner, and orator of the Medical and Chirurgical Faculty of Maryland, and member of the committee appointed to publish its *Transactions*. He was also a member of the board of health. Crawford died after four days' illness and was buried with great pomp by his Masonic brethren, in the Presbyterian cemetery at Fayette and Greene Sts. Apparently he had married a second time, for in the year of his death his library of several hundred valuable books was sold to the University of Maryland by his widow.

[*Johns Hopkins Hosp. Bull.*, Aug.–Sept. 1899; E. F. Cordell, *Medic. Annals of Md.* (1903), *passim*; John R. Quinan, *Medic. Annals of Baltimore* (1884); E. T. Schultz, *Hist. of Freemasonry in Md.* (1885), vol. II.]

J.R.O.

CRAWFORD, JOHN MARTIN (Oct. 18, 1845–Aug. 11, 1916), physician, translator, son of John S. and Clarissa Crawford, was born in Herrick, Pa., and died in Cincinnati, Ohio. He attended public school, and at the age of twenty-two, after teaching school for four years, entered Lafayette College. Completing his course there in 1871, he soon went to Cincinnati, where for eight years he taught Latin and mathematics. In the meantime he studied at three different medical schools in Cincinnati. Having received a diploma from each, he taught and served as registrar at one of them, the Pulte Medical College, during the years 1881–89. In 1884 he is reported to have been at work on a dictionary of medical and scientific terms, and in 1887 he completed the first English translation of the ancient Finnish epic, *Kalevala*. He had become acquainted with the poem while a student in Lafayette College, because of the admiration in which it was held by one of his teachers. As teacher of Latin and as student and teacher of medicine, he diverted himself by turning this poem into English verse metrically imitative of the original. It was a vast undertaking; the poem contains more than 150,000 words, and the translation of it obviously required a faithful study of history and prosody as well as of language. For all that, the translator was not sated. He long anticipated revising the entire work, and as late as 1904 he was busily engaged with a translation of the Esthonian epic, *Kalevipoeg*. From 1889 to 1894 he was United States consul-general in Russia. Here he added to his official responsibilities the somewhat kindred responsibility of negotiating between the Russian government and the administration of the World's Fair in Chicago. In connection with this work, he translated into English, in urgent haste, he complained, the encyclopedic and voluminous *Industries of Russia* (1893). Returning home to Cincinnati, he successfully engaged in merchandising, manufacturing, and banking, but affairs were never so pressing as to obliterate the interest in European affairs which he had acquired during his term as consul. He read much, and lectured from time to time on subjects having to do with Finland and Russia. He was married twice, in 1873 to Nellie Baldwin, and in 1888 to Cora Hayward.

[J. F. Stonecipher, *Biog. Cat. Lafayette Coll. 1832–1912* (1913); S. J. Coffin, *Men of Lafayette, 1826–1893* (1891); C. T. Greve, *Centennial Hist. of Cincinnati* (1904), vol. II; *Biog. Cyc. of the State of Ohio*, vol. II (1884); *Who's Who in America*, 1916–17; *Cincinnati Enquirer*, Aug. 12, 1916.]

J.D.W.

CRAWFORD, JOHN WALLACE (CAPTAIN JACK) (Mar. 4, 1847–Feb. 28, 1917), "the poet scout," was born in County Donegal, Ireland, the son of John Austin and Susie (Wallace) Crawford. The mother claimed descent from the famous chieftain, William Wallace. The father, a Glasgow tailor, when threatened with arrest for some seditious utterance, fled to Ireland, where he met and married Miss Wallace. In 1854 he came to America, finding work as a coal miner at Minersville, Pa., and four years later the mother and children followed. The boy began to work in the mines at an early age and thus had no opportunities for schooling. On the opening of the Civil War the father enlisted in the army, and the boy, after two rejections on account of his youth, was accepted for service in the 48th Pennsylvania Volunteers. At Spottsylvania, May 12, 1864, he was badly wounded. In the Saterlee Hospital, in West Philadelphia, through the efforts of a Sister of Charity, he learned to read and write. He was again sent to the front, and at Petersburg, Apr. 2, 1865, was again wounded. Shortly afterward his mother and father died, his mother exacting a deathbed promise from him that he would never touch liquor.

He married Anna M. Stokes of Numidia, Pa., in 1869, and some time afterward went West, where for several years he was variously employed. He is said to have been one of the first seven men to enter the Black Hills region after the Custer expedition of 1874. A local document dated Apr. 25, 1876, mentions him as a member of the Board of Trustees of Custer City and chief of scouts for a volunteer organization known as the Black Hills Rangers. In the Sioux War of that year he served as a scout and messenger for both Merritt and Crook, and on Aug. 24 succeeded Cody (Buffalo Bill) as Merritt's chief of scouts. He later served as a scout in the campaigns against the Apaches. He was for a time post trader at Fort Craig, N. Mex., and later a special agent of the Indian Bureau. Near San Marcial, on the Rio Grande, in 1886, he established a ranch, which for the remainder of his life was his main home, though he also had a home in Brooklyn. He had by the late seventies become famous as a composer and reciter of verses. His first volume, *The Poet Scout*, was published in 1879 and was succeeded by a revised and enlarged edition of the same work (1886); *Camp*

Fire Sparks (1893) ; *Lariattes* (1904), and *The Broncho Book* (1908). He also wrote three plays, in the production of which he took the leading part, and more than one hundred short stories. As a lecturer and a reciter of his own verses he was a noted figure for many years. He died in his Brooklyn home.

Crawford was a tall man of wiry build, with nervous, sensitive face. He wore his hair and beard after the fashion of his friend Buffalo Bill, and he dressed the part of a "poet scout." His histrionic embellishments seem, however, to have been chiefly a concession to the public demand, for he was at bottom simple and unaffected. "I am simply Jack Crawford," he said, "boy soldier, rustic poet, scout, bad actor, etc." His work as a scout was highly praised by his commanders. His verses, though popular in his day, can by no stretch of courtesy be called poetry.

[*Who's Who*, 1916–17 ; sketches by Jas. E. Smith in *A Famous Battery and Its Campaigns* (1892) ; John G. Scorer in introduction to *Lariattes* (1904) and Irvine Leigh in *The Poet Scout* (2nd ed., 1886) ; obituary in the *Brooklyn Eagle*, Feb. 28, 1917.]   W. J. G—t.

CRAWFORD, MARTIN JENKINS (Mar. 17, 1820–July 23, 1883), judge, congressman, Confederate soldier, was the son of Hardy and Betsy Roberts (Jenkins) Crawford and was born in Jasper County, Ga. This county lay in the heart of the old black belt or cotton plantation area and Hardy Crawford was a prominent and wealthy planter of his community. After a term spent at Mercer University, a Baptist institution at Macon, Ga., Martin Crawford read law and was admitted to the bar (1839), before his twentieth anniversary, by a special act of the legislature. Meanwhile the Crawfords had removed to Harris County, following the westward trend of the planters, and for a time Martin practised law in that county and represented it in the legislature (1845–47). In 1849, however, he made his home at Columbus, Ga., and he was thereafter identified with that city. Throughout the later ante bellum period Columbus was a hot bed of radical state-rights sentiment. Crawford, though a comparatively young man at the time of his removal thither, became at once a leader of the state-rights group. In 1850 he was appointed a delegate to the Nashville Convention. In 1855, after a year's service as judge of the superior court of the Chattahoochee circuit, he was elected to Congress as a Democrat, defeating the Know-Nothing candidate. He held his seat until the Southern congressmen withdrew on the outbreak of the Civil War. Throughout his service in Congress the matter of the territorial expansion of slavery occupied the front of the stage. In the running debate on the Kansas trouble and

after secession had actually begun, he was constantly on his feet, championing the Southern views, but always in a moderate and courteous manner.

After the secession of Georgia, Crawford was elected to represent the state in the Provisional Congress of the Confederacy at Montgomery and participated in the organization of the Confederate government. He was the most important of the three members appointed by Jefferson Davis to serve on the peace commission with which Seward dallied for a brief time. On the failure of this commission, Crawford returned to Georgia, raised a regiment of cavalry, and became its colonel. A year later he joined the staff of Gen. Howell Cobb and was serving there when the war closed. Near the end of the war, Federal troops overran west Georgia, destroying many plantations, including that of Crawford. He was impoverished, but, being comparatively young, resumed the practise of law and continued for many years prominent in state affairs. The year 1875 found him again judge of the Chattahoochee circuit. In 1880 he was appointed by Gov. Colquitt associate justice of the supreme court and was on the bench at the time of his death in 1883.

Crawford was described by contemporaries as tall, slender, well built and of blond coloring, gifted as an orator and possessing a vein of dry humor and keen practical wisdom, qualities which made him a man of considerable influence. His decisions as a supreme-court justice are marked by clear and concise reasoning. In 1842 he married Amanda J. Reese, daughter of Joseph Reese of Morgan County. He died in Columbus.

[Judge Henry R. Goetchius contributed a good article on Crawford to *Men of Mark in Ga.*, vol. III (1911), ed. by W. F. Northen. See also : J. W. Avery, *Hist. of the State of Ga., 1850–81* (1881) ; *Cong. Globe*, 34–36 Congs. ; *Biog. Dir. Am. Cong.* (1928) ; *Atlanta Constitution*, July 24, 1883.]   R. P. B.

CRAWFORD, SAMUEL JOHNSON (Apr. 15, 1835–Oct. 21, 1913), Union soldier, governor of Kansas, of Scotch-Irish descent, was the son of James and Jane (Morrow) Crawford. He was born on a farm near Bedford, Lawrence County, Ind., attended the public schools in that town and later read law there in an office. He was admitted to the bar in 1856 at the age of twenty-one. Desiring better preparation he entered the Cincinnati Law School, from which he was graduated two years later. In 1859 he moved to Garnett, Kan., and began the practise of his profession. In November of that year he was elected a member of the first state legislature, which did not convene, however, until Mar. 26, 1861, two months after Kansas attained statehood. After six weeks of service he resigned his seat in the legislature to become captain of a company assigned to duty with the 2nd Kansas Volunteer Infantry. He served under Gen. Lyon in southwestern Missouri and took part in the battle of Wilson's Creek on Aug. 10, 1861. In March 1862 he was transferred to the 2nd Kansas Cavalry and soon given command of a battalion in that regiment. He served with gallantry and success under Gen. Blunt in Missouri and Arkansas in the fall and early winter of 1862. A year later he became colonel of the second regiment of Kansas Colored Infantry. In July 1864 he conducted an expedition through the Indian territory and later took part in the campaign against the Confederate Gen. Price who led a raid into Missouri and southeastern Kansas.

Crawford's military record attracted the attention of the people of his state and on Sept. 8, 1864, he was nominated for governor by the Republican party. Two months later he was elected by a majority of 4,939 votes in a total of 22,335. On Dec. 2, 1864, he resigned his military commission and five weeks later was sworn into office, being at that time less than thirty years of age. In March 1865 he was made brevet brigadier-general of volunteers "for meritorious services." Toward the end of his first term as governor he was nominated again and reëlected by a large majority. Much useful and important legislation was enacted while he was governor and the interests of the young state were greatly advanced. On Nov. 27, 1866, he was married to Isabel M. Chase of Topeka. In the summer of 1868 Indians began to raid the frontier settlements of Kansas. As the season advanced the savages became bolder and their incursions more destructive. Men were killed, women and children made captives, buildings burned, and stock driven off. On Oct. 10 Gov. Crawford issued a call for the enlistment of a regiment of cavalry for frontier service. On Nov. 4—two months before the expiration of his second term of office—he resigned the governorship to become commander of the new regiment known as the 19th Kansas Cavalry. The campaign against the Indians was entirely successful and the captives were recovered. This ended his military career and his direct participation in Kansas politics. The last half-century of his life was spent in civil pursuits, farming, the practise of law, and acting as claim agent for his state at Washington. His book, *Kansas in the Sixties,* was published in 1911. It deals chiefly with events in which Crawford was a participant. For a short time prior to his death he was the only surviving war governor in the Northern states.

[See *Who's Who in America,* 1912–13; *Kan. Hist.* *Colls.,* vol. XII (1912) and XVI (1925); *Cyc. of Kan. State Hist.* (1912), ed. by F. W. Blackmar; O. W. Wilder, *Annals of Kan.* (1875); Wm. E. Connelley, *Hist. of Kan., State and People* (1928), vol. II; obituary in the *Topeka Daily Capital,* Oct. 22, 1913. Crawford's *Kansas in the Sixties* is based chiefly on an old man's recollections of what had happened half a century before, and should be used with caution.]   T.L.H.

CRAWFORD, THOMAS (Mar. 22, 1813?– Oct. 10, 1857), sculptor, was probably born in New York City, of Irish parents. A writer in the *Albany Knickerbocker* (quoted in the New York *Evening Post,* Dec. 21, 1857) says, however: "We know that he was a native of Ireland, and emigrated with his parents at an early age (about seven years) from Ballyshanen, in the county of Donegal, and the writer of this was well acquainted with his father in the city of New York thirty years ago. Give old Ireland her due." The date of Crawford's birth was either 1813 or 1814. Even when very young, he showed delight in beauty. He gazed tiptoe into print-shop windows, he tinted engravings, he sketched, he drew, sometimes neglecting his routine school lessons, but not the drawing lessons to which his parents sent him. At the age of fourteen, he went to work with a wood-carver; his evenings he spent in his room, modeling in clay. At nineteen, he placed himself as apprentice in the studios of Frazee & Launitz, leading monument-makers of the city. Here his sensitive carvings of marble flowers and his intelligent service in monumental design won approval. He worked also on marble busts, including that of Chief Justice Marshall. Meanwhile he gained some knowledge of architecture from poring over books, he studied art in the evening classes of the National Academy of Design, and he began collecting casts, among them a copy of Thorwaldsen's "Triumph of Alexander." When Launitz disregarded his plea for higher wages, he quietly went back to work in the wood-carver's shop, where Launitz sought him out, inviting him to return, and granting his request. Launitz became his true friend, encouraged him to go to Rome for study, and gave him letters to two residents there, Dr. Paul Ruga and Thorwaldsen. In May 1835, at the age of twenty-two, he set sail for Leghorn in a small merchantman, and in the following September he presented his letter to Thorwaldsen. The famous sculptor received him kindly, giving him the freedom of his studios, and setting him at work on a clay copy of an antique. Naturally the sensitive carver of marble flowers was feeble in his grasp of the ensemble. With the utmost patience Thorwaldsen explained the need of studying mass before detail. A lasting friendship resulted. "These few words of instruction," wrote Crawford, years later, "gave me more insight into my art and were of more service to me than all else put together that I have ever seen and heard."

In Rome, the young man devoted himself heart and soul to his studies, working with even too much eagerness day and night. His vigorous health suffered. "I am alone," he had written from Leghorn to his sister; "I am venturing much." And almost alone as well as unknown he at first remained. He modeled and drew from the nude; he spared time to visit collections, studios, museums. By the purchase of books, casts, and other tools of trade as needful to him as breath, he made serious inroads into his funds, denying himself physical comforts. In ten weeks (1837) he modeled seventeen busts for marble, "at a laborer's wage," he wrote to his sister; and the same year he copied in marble a Demosthenes in the Vatican. His solitary lamp burned nightly in his little studio in the Via del Orto di Napoli. He began to attract consideration. One day Mr. Greene, American consul at Rome, got a tremulous note, "Come and see me." He found Crawford prostrate and delirious from fever, and at once obtained for him through Dr. Ruga the best medical aid and nursing, probably saving his life thereby. Interest was aroused; numerous minor commissions came. Before the end of 1839, Crawford completed two bas-reliefs, the "Centaurs," the "Hercules and Diana," for Prince Demidoff of St. Petersburg; a group, "Lead Us into Life Everlasting," for Mr. Tiffany of Baltimore; also portrait busts of Mr. Greene, of Commodore Hull, of Sir Charles Vaughan, of Kenyon, the English poet, of Charles Sumner, the American statesman. Crawford was then engaged on his "Orpheus," his first group of genuine importance. Sumner, full of faith in the sculptor's genius, created interest in Boston for this work, and pushed a subscription to carry it out in marble. Returning to Rome after a studious visit to the art-treasures of Florence, and oppressed by misgivings as to the fate of the "Orpheus," Crawford found awaiting him Sumner's draft. The next mail brought other orders. From that moment, his anxieties as to bread and shelter were over. Prosperity, no less than adversity, stimulated his mind. An astonishing productiveness ensued. In the Piazza Barberini he fitted up a suite of studios, soon to be peopled with a host of forms created by him, and carved in marble by Italian workmen under his direction. "I regret," he writes to his sister in 1842, "that I have not a hundred hands to keep pace with the workings of the mind." From that remark may be deduced a valid criticism of Crawford's sculpture. He constantly undertook a greater volume of work than he could direct; nay more, he accepted commissions which were beyond his artistic powers. He did not know this, nor did most of his contemporaries. His friends held his genius to be different from that of others, because of his rapid mental processes and his poetic vision. "His 'Orpheus,'" said the painter Thomas Hicks, "an expression of heroic manhood inspired by Genius, had secured to him noble and permanent friendships." This once-famous group, bought in 1840 by the Boston Athenæum, has for modern eyes the characteristic aspect of work done when Thorwaldsen ruled the world of sculpture, and Houdon's sturdy realism was out of fashion. With his marble cloak at his back, with his lyre under his arm, and with Cerberus at his feet, Orpheus strides peering through Hades. The hero's anatomy is slicked rather than understood; unintentionally, Cerberus is thrice grotesque. Yet in the whole work Crawford is as always an eager, aspiring artist, full of lofty thought. Hawthorne, not as a rule sympathetic toward this sculptor, called it his best production, a view often shared by later critics; and without doubt the group was a stimulus to American art. In quick succession came other idealistic conceptions, generally mythological, allegorical, or anecdotical, but not always sculptural. Crawford read avidly and widely, with a special liking for the classics in translation, and his approach to his work was from the literary side. To be seen at New York, in the Metropolitan Museum of Art are his "Dancing Girl" (1844), his "Dying Indian Maiden" (1848), and his "Flora" (1853), all in marble. The Corcoran Gallery has his "Peri," a winged figure, life size. In 1843, a head of "Vesta," extolled for purity of expression, was a sensation of the season in Crawford's studio, then much frequented by interesting visitors. That year, he became engaged to Louisa Cutler Ward, sister of Mrs. Julia Ward Howe [q.v.], and daughter of Samuel Ward, the New York connoisseur; in 1844 he returned to his native city for a marriage which brought happiness to both. Already famous, he carried back to Rome, thereafter his permanent residence, American commissions as well as an American bride. Crawford, who spoke Italian well, had many Italian friends. When the Revolution of 1848 broke out, he joined the Civil Guard as officer, notwithstanding his American citizenship. In 1849, having returned to his country for business reasons, he read by mere chance a newspaper item announcing a competition to obtain for the city of Richmond, Va., a design for a grandiose equestrian monument to Washington. For years he had thought of this theme. In his room in the Via del Orto di Napoli he had made sketches of it, and now, aided by his prodigious memory, he swiftly struck off a model which won the prize. Ingenuity rather than imagination characterizes this work, with its outposts of allegory framing a central equestrian group of Washington precariously set above a six-nosed plinth bearing statues of six great Virginians. Among these, the "Patrick Henry" and the "Thomas Jefferson," modeled by Crawford himself, are by far the most interesting. The four other statues, the "Marshall," "Mason," "Nelson," and "Lewis," were made by Randolph Rogers, who after Crawford's death completed the monument. Hawthorne admits that this Richmond work "will produce a moral effect through its images of illustrious men." Taken as a single part of a pretentious whole, Crawford's "Patrick Henry" deserves praise from others besides the moralist. In the pose, in the use of the cloak, and above all in the eloquent head, an artist's inspiration is manifest. This is true also of Crawford's "James Otis," at Mount Auburn, Cambridge, an authentic sculptural conception finely expressed, and of his massive harmony-haunted bronze "Beethoven," long dominating the old Music Hall in Boston, and by many considered his most poetic work.

On winning the Richmond competition, the sculptor hurried back to Rome, there to spend the next six years (1850–56) in joyous unremitting labor. He had accepted from the United States Government the invitation to compete for sculptural decorations proposed for the Capitol, and as a result, he had received the award of the most extensive commissions of that period. The works thus entrusted to him were the marble pediment and the bronze doors for the Senate wing, and the bronze "Armed Liberty" capping the dome. Charles E. Fairman ("Works of Art in the United States Capitol Building," *Senate Document, No. 169*, 63 Cong., 1 Sess., p. 18) states that the only pieces which were executed under the sculptor's personal supervision are the marble figures of "History" and "Justice" over the Senate doors. On the Capitol grounds, Italian workmen carved in Massachusetts marble Crawford's huge pedimental group with its busy unrelated figures planted at each side of the central subject "America," an America amply draped, secure in her laurel wreaths, eagle, and sun-rays. The theme is "The Past and Present of America." The sculptor has treated it with a literal pioneer simplicity. He is the modeling story-teller, celebrating the vanquished Indian, the sturdy woodman, the hunter with his spoil, the soldier, the merchant, the mechanic, the teacher, the schoolboy. Many of the figures have

power; that of the Indian received great praise both here and abroad. The bronze doors, unfinished at Crawford's death in 1857, were completed years later by Rinehart, and cast at Chicopee, Mass. They capture attention by their stories, not by their sculpture. The colossal "Armed Liberty," cast in bronze by Clark Mills (1860), and hoisted atop the dome to the booming of cannon and the hurrahs of the multitude, is a successful creation, simple, solidly based, and cleaving the sky in a good silhouette. Crawford's letters to Secretary of War Jefferson Davis during the progress of the Capitol models reveal Crawford's clear mind, urbane temper, and grasp of practical details. The spring of 1856 found him once more on native soil, arranging business matters relative to these and other works. In the fall, leaving behind his wife and children, and accompanied by his sister, he returned to Rome. On the voyage one eye troubled him and in Rome a marked protrusion of the eyeball rapidly increased. Absorbed in the supervision of his studios, he paid scant attention to medical advice. Finally an explorative operation, afterward unjustly criticized, discovered a malignant growth behind the orbit of the eye; it "encroached on the sources of life itself." Crawford was sent to Paris for treatment and his wife was summoned. Many months of suffering patiently borne ended in his death in London. The news reached the United States by the same ship that brought his bronze equestrian Washington, cast in Munich for the Richmond monument.

Crawford was tall, handsome, bright-eyed; his portrait medallion shows a head of classic type, with a wholly genuine look of dedication to purpose. He lived his ardent life of forty-four years unassailed by doubts which were afterward to appear on the horizon, doubts as to the value and stability of an American art based largely on imitation of classic forms. Had longer life been granted him, his sensitive temper might have responded valiantly to newer ideals. Better American sculptors came after him, not before.

[Information about Thos. Crawford and his works is found in Lorado Taft, *Hist. of Am. Sculpture* (1903); Wm. J. Clark, Jr., *Great Am. Sculptures* (1878); Samuel Osgood, *Address Before the N. Y. Hist. Soc. Upon the Reception of Crawford's Statue of the Indian*, Presented by Frederic de Peyster (1875); *Passages from the French and Italian Note-Books of Nathaniel Hawthorne* (1883); C. E. Lester, *The Artists of America* (1846); H. T. Tuckerman, *Book of the Artists* (1867), and "Crawford and Sculpture," *Atlantic Mo.*, June 1858; G. S. Hillard, "Thos. Crawford: a Eulogy," *Atlantic Mo.*, July 1869, a painstaking review of the sculptor's career; C. E. Fairman, "Art and Artists of the Capitol of the U. S. A.," *Senate Doc. No. 95*, 69 Cong., 1 Sess.; Thos. Hicks, *Thos. Crawford; his Career, Character, and Works* (1858), valuable not only in itself, but for the Appendix which gives correspondence relating to Crawford's malady and its treatment by celebrated surgeons, also some of the Davis-Meigs and Davis-Crawford letters concerning the Capitol sculptures.]   A. A.

CRAWFORD, WILLIAM (1732–June 11, 1782), Revolutionary soldier, was born of Scotch-Irish parents who migrated from Pennsylvania down the mountain valleys to Frederick County in the northwestern part of Virginia. His father was a farmer, and the son, a tall, athletic fellow, was both farmer and surveyor. In the latter capacity he was for a time associated with Washington. He fought in Braddock's campaign, 1755, and became captain and leader of scouts. He was with Forbes in the successful expedition to Fort Duquesne, 1758, and served in the Pontiac War. In 1766 or the following year he removed with his family to that part of western Pennsylvania which became Fayette County, and settled in New Haven (now included in Connellsville). He was soon a justice of the court of quarter sessions, and a land agent for his friend Washington, who visited him in 1770. Three years later he received a visit from the governor, Lord Dunmore. In Dunmore's War, 1774, Crawford destroyed two Iroquois villages in Ohio. Soon after this he was removed from his office of judge by the Pennsylvania authorities, as the region where he had settled was in dispute between that colony and Virginia.

When the Revolution began, Crawford was a member of the committee of defense at Pittsburgh, and he also aided in raising the West Augusta (Virginia) regiment. He was commissioned lieutenant-colonel of the 5th Virginia, Feb. 13, 1776, and colonel of the 7th Virginia, Aug. 14, 1776. He took part in the battle of Long Island, in the retreat from New York, and in the battles of Trenton, Princeton, Brandywine, and Germantown. Not long after the last of these he went to the West, and thenceforth was engaged in the defense of the frontier. In 1778, he was placed in charge of the militia, under Gen. Lachlan McIntosh [q.v.], and the next year he accompanied Col. Daniel Brodhead [q.v.] on his punitive expedition against the Indians. Among his fortifications were Fort Crawford on the Allegheny River and Fort Fincastle, at the site of the present Wheeling, on the Ohio. He resigned in 1781, intending to pass in quiet the remainder of his life.

From his retirement, however, Crawford was summoned in May 1782 at the urgent request of Gen. Irvine, to take part in an expedition against the Indians of Ohio. The little army of Pennsylvania and Virginia mounted men, about 400 in number, gathered at Mingo Bottom, near the modern Steubenville. The men were "not specially fit"; some of the troops had shared in an outrageous attack upon the Christian Indians shortly before. Crawford was elected commander, and the army marched northward, planning a surprise, and by June 4 reached "Battle Island" near a Wyandot deserted village, three miles from the modern Upper Sandusky in Wyandot County. The Indians, however, were well informed, and about 400 Wyandots and about 200 Delawares had collected. The fighting of the first day was to the advantage of the frontiersmen, but on June 5 reinforcements appeared for the Indians, among others, 200 Shawnees and a force of British, Butler's Rangers. Crawford's army was surrounded, supplies were running low, and the guides advised return to the Ohio. The retreat began that night, and the main force under Williamson reached the river, with a loss of about seventy. One report says, "They had been deceived, out-generaled and caught in a trap" (Hill, *post*). Crawford himself became separated from the main body, and, with a companion, Dr. Knight, fell into the hands of the Delawares. The captives were taken to a point near Crawfordsville, where the unfortunate commander was tortured and burned at the stake. Dr. Knight, who had been a witness of his sufferings, escaped, and eventually reached the settlements and gave a report of the event.

[Knight's narrative, probably first published in the *Freeman's Jour.* (Phila.), Apr. 30–May 21, 1783, was reprinted in pamphlet form the same year and went through many subsequent editions, *Narratives of the Perils and Sufferings of Dr. Knight and John Slover* (a guide) being reprinted in 1867 from a Nashville edition of 1843. See also N. N. Hill, "Crawford's Campaign against the Sandusky Indians," in *Mag. of Western Hist.*, May 1885; Jas. H. Anderson, "Col. Wm. Crawford," in *Ohio Archæol. and Hist. Pubs.*, vol. VI (1898), pp. 1–34; C. W. Butterfield, *An Hist. Account of the Expedition against Sandusky under Col. Wm. Crawford in 1782* (1873); *Washington-Crawford Letters* (1877), and *Washington-Irvine Correspondence* (1882), both ed. by C. W. Butterfield; address by Henry P. Snyder, *Col. Wm. Crawford, Pioneer and Patriot* (1909).]   E. K. A.

CRAWFORD, WILLIAM HARRIS (Feb. 24, 1772–Sept. 15, 1834), senator, cabinet member, presidential candidate, was descended from Thomas Crawford who immigrated from Scotland to Virginia in 1643 and was the progenitor of a numerous family now scattered throughout the South. His descendants of present concern, middle-class folk undistinguished except for tall stature and ruddy faces, seem to have followed the prevailing drift of population up the James River valley, until the eve of the Revolution when Joel Crawford and his wife, who had been Fannie Harris, were settled on Tye River close against the Blue Ridge. Their children eventually numbered eleven, with William Harris in the middle of the list. In his boyhood financial stress prompted another removal which took the then prevailing course to South Carolina, and, after a few years, yet another trek to the clearings in what is now Columbia County, Ga. Between the sessions of an "old field school" the boys worked on the farm; but William soon turned to teaching, and then had the good fortune to continue his studies, like McDuffie and Calhoun, under the talented master, Moses Waddel [q.v.]. This modified the outlook of the youth, which doubtless would otherwise have been that of the plantation squires roughened by contact with a crude frontier. After teaching school again, now in the town of Augusta, and shortly being admitted to the bar, Crawford attained enough prosperity by 1804 to marry Susanna Girardin to whom he had long been engaged, and to build a home near the village of Lexington, Ga. There at "Woodlawn" he spent the rest of his life when not riding the circuit of the courts or absent on public service. The steading was gradually enlarged into a plantation, with a corps sufficient to furnish each of his eight children with several slaves in the division of property after his death.

Before the end of the eighteenth century Crawford had taken some part in politics, denouncing the sale of Yazoo lands by the Georgia legislature and indorsing the stiff attitude of President Adams toward France. Elected to the legislature in 1803, he quickly became the leading upland ally of James Jackson [q.v.] of Savannah in a faction which was known successively as the Jackson, Crawford, and Troup party. This embraced most of the well-to-do Georgians and was differentiated in policy from the opposing Clark faction chiefly by its insistence upon conservative public finance. As episodes in his political career, Crawford killed Peter L. Van Allen in a duel in 1802, and had his left wrist permanently crippled by John Clark [q.v.] at the duello distance of ten paces in 1806. Clark had proposed that the combatants be permitted to advance at will to a distance of five paces and that they continue to exchange shots until one of them could not stand, kneel, or sit (Clark, Considerations, p. 94), but Crawford demurred.

Upon the death of Abraham Baldwin in 1807 Crawford was elected to fill the vacancy in the United States Senate, where, along with his gigantic stature and handsome face, a studious disposition, a clear judgment, a native sagacity, an engaging affability, and a fund of entertaining anecdotes promptly marked him for distinction. He was particularly congenial to John Randolph as an anti-Yazooist, to Nathaniel Macon as an advocate of public frugality, and to Albert Gallatin as a willing promoter of treasury business in the Senate. But Crawford was no man's man, as he took some pains to show. In his "Delphic Oracle" speech in 1810 he censured Madison's message for its ambiguity on military preparations; and the next year he advocated the extension of the national bank's charter against the opposition of most of his Democratic-Republican colleagues, including Henry Clay who denounced it as unconstitutional.

Honors now crowded upon Crawford. He was elected president *pro tempore* of the Senate upon the death of Vice-President Clinton; he declined an offer of the secretaryship of war, only to accept appointment in 1813 as minister to France; and, resigning this in 1815, he was made secretary of war by Madison while yet upon the homeward voyage, and then secretary of the treasury for the better utilization of his financial talents. At this time, indeed, he was the choice of most of the Democratic-Republicans at Washington for the presidency as against Madison's favorite, Monroe. So strong was the movement, despite Crawford's private disavowals of candidacy, that Abner Lacock [q.v.], senator from Pennsylvania but a Virginian by birth and a supporter of Monroe, sought a conference with Crawford with a view to prevent a disruption of the party. Monroe, said he, was the last of the Revolutionary worthies who could have a claim to the presidency, whereas Crawford was young enough to serve after Monroe should have gone to his grave. Crawford answered that his own feelings would not permit him to oppose Monroe for the office, and that Lacock was free to quote him to this effect. Lacock reported the conversation, Feb. 7, 1816, to John Binns [q.v.], editor of the Democratic Press at Philadelphia, who published it (reprinted, with Binns's praise of Crawford's magnanimity, in the Savannah Daily Republican, Jan. 10, 1824). Nevertheless, when the usual congressional caucus was held soon afterward, fifty-four members cast their ballots for Crawford, as compared with sixty-five for Monroe. Crawford continued at the treasury during both of Monroe's administrations, but declined reappointment at the hands of John Quincy Adams.

The election of 1820 went again to Monroe by default, but campaigning for the succession began at once. The disappearance of the Federalist party had now produced the so-called Era of Good Feeling, which from Crawford's point of view was wretchedly misnamed. He was easily the foremost aspirant, supported warmly by Randolph and Macon and also by Madison, Van Buren, and Marcy, with a chorus of newspapers including the New York *Evening Post,* the *Albany Argus,* the *National Intelligencer,* the *Washington Gazette,* and the *Richmond Enquirer.* His group was often styled "the Radicals" because they clung more or less to the rights of the states after most others had become nationalists. But their leader was disposed to sanction moderate protection in tariff legislation, as well as to maintain the national bank. As early as Jan. 7, 1821, James Barbour [*q.v.*] had written from Washington lamenting the rise of opposition: "No one challenges universal support—the candidates multiplying like the leaves upon the forest. The secret plots and but badly disguised schemes already beginning—the progress and catastrophe are concealed by the future" (manuscript in Tait Papers, Alabama Department of Archives). The field, indeed, was becoming full of rivals—Adams, Clay, Jackson, for a while Calhoun, Lowndes until his untimely death, and sundry lesser lights. All of these or their supporters were with one accord striving to weaken Crawford, and they were aided indiscriminately by his inveterate enemy John Clark, now for a time governor of Georgia. Crawford was censured by many penmen for having recommended in 1816 that, as an alternative to the expulsion and extermination of the Indians, they be persuaded to adopt private landholding and agriculture, and that the whites intermarry with them if necessary to promote their civilizing. He was charged by Ninian Edwards [*q.v.*] with having corruptly favored certain banks in the panic of 1819. He was cleared of this charge, disastrously to Edwards, by a congressional investigation, whereupon John Randolph issued a jubilant address to the "freeholders" of his district (printed in the *Richmond Enquirer,* May 25, 1824). At his door was also laid responsibility for the "spoils system"; but it has been well argued latterly that his main purpose in promoting the enactment of the four-year law of 1820 was to increase efficiency in the public service (C. R. Fish, *The Civil Service and the Patronage,* 1905, p. 170). His administrative work, including the initiation of coast fortification, the construction of the "National Road," and the improvement of the public land system, was largely ignored.

Crawford's prospects continued fairly bright until the fall of 1823 when he was stricken with paralysis. For a year and a half he lay in seclusion, almost blind and quite incapacitated

though slowly improving. His friends issued bulletins as favorable as might be, and maintained their plan of nominating him by caucus. All elements of opposition now turned against the caucus as undemocratic, though Adams and Clay, the latter with some protest, had participated in such assemblages in earlier years. As the months passed there were many defections, but Barbour declared that if no one else should attend he would hold the caucus alone and do all the voting. When the meeting was held, Feb. 14, sixty-four votes were cast for the nomination of Crawford, two for Adams, and one each for Jackson and Macon. But the absence or abstinence of the rest of the 261 senators and representatives made of the occasion a fiasco which marked the end of the congressional caucus as an institution. The election in the following November returned Crawford as a poor third among the four surviving candidates, with no one elected under the constitutional provision. With the choice thus thrown into the House of Representatives, Crawford's friends hoped forlornly and labored in a losing cause, for Adams was elected with Clay's assistance.

Crawford's remaining years were those of a Tantalus. Crippled in body and none too clear of mind, he found no solace on the judge's bench upon which his Georgia devotees placed him in 1827, but nursed a fatuous ambition for the White House, though his former following had scattered to new allegiances. With a view to making a rift between Jackson and Calhoun, he said to a visitor in 1828 and repeated in a letter of 1830 that it had been Calhoun and not he who had proposed in the cabinet in 1818 that Jackson be disciplined for having invaded the Spanish province of Florida and having executed there the Englishmen Arbuthnot and Ambrister. This had the desired effect of embroilment, and it revived for a moment the name of Crawford on the lips of men, but with no beneficial result.

[Paralysis played a scurvy trick upon Crawford's person and repute. His rivals for the presidency lived on to great prominence, attracting biographers each of whom wanted a foil for his hero. Crawford was made to serve again and again until by the time of Carl Schurz (*Henry Clay,* 1887, I, 223) he was reduced to a "reputation of a reputation." J. E. D. Shipp in his *Giant Days, or the Life and Times of Wm. H. Crawford* (1909) has tried to redress the balance, but with a tyro's ill success. Among the contemporary pamphlets John Clark's *Considerations on the Purity of the Principles of Wm. H. Crawford, Esq.* (1819, 2nd ed., 1823) and *Some Objections to Mr. Crawford as a Candidate for the Presidency* by "a South-Carolinian" (1824) are offset by the eulogistic *Life and Character of Wm. H. Crawford,* by "Americanus" (1824, reprinted from the *Albany Argus*). There are sketches of Crawford in the *Southern Literary Messenger,* Apr., May 1837; the *Am. Portrait Gallery* (vol. IV, 1839);

J. D. Hammond, *Hist. of Political Parties in the State of N. Y.* (1852); J. B. Cobb, *Leisure Labors* (1858); S. F. Miller, *The Bench and Bar of Ga.* (1858); and W. H. Sparks, *Memories of Fifty Years* (1870). Crawford's diary during part of his ministry to France has been edited by D. C. Knowlton and printed in the *Smith College Studies in History* (vol. XI, no. 2, 1925). See also *Memorials of that Branch of the Crawford Family which Comprises the Descendants of John Crawford of Va.* (1883).]   U. B. P.

CRAZY HORSE (*c.* 1849–Sept. 5, 1877), generally regarded as the greatest military genius of the Sioux Confederacy, was of the Oglala tribe. His name, Tashunca-uitco, translated "Crazy Horse," is said to have been suggested by the incident of a wild pony dashing through the village of his people at the time he was born. Of his youth little is recorded, but it is probable that he took an active part in the campaigns of the noted Oglala chieftain, Red Cloud, against the forts and settlements of Wyoming in 1865–68. Bold, adventurous, and implacable, he early became one of the leaders of the element among the Southern Sioux and Northern Cheyennes who refused to be confined on the reservations and who made frequent forays against the Crows and isolated parties of whites. His marriage to a woman of the Cheyennes brought him into closer affiliation with that tribe, which at various times furnished him with most of his following. With the rest of the "hostiles" he ignored the War Department's order that all roving bands must be back on the reservations by Jan. 1, 1876, and he was the first to feel the shock of the war. Gen. George Crook's early start in the campaign caught him unawares, for on Mar. 17 his village of 105 lodges, with probably 400 warriors, near the mouth of the Little Powder, was surprised by a detachment of 450 men under Col. J. J. Reynolds, who destroyed it and captured his pony herd. Crazy Horse, however, kept up a stubborn resistance, and on the retirement of the force followed it for twenty miles and recaptured most of the ponies. On June 17—his band in the meantime increased to probably 1,200 Oglalas and Cheyennes—he was attacked on the upper Rosebud by Crook's army of 1,300, but after a day's fighting Crook withdrew, with severe losses and baffled at every point. Crazy Horse now moved north and joined the large body under the medicine man, Sitting Bull, in the valley of the Little Big Horn.

In the famous battle of June 25, in which Reno was driven with heavy loss from the upper end of the village and Custer's immediate command of 212 men was annihilated, the Indians had no supreme commander, though Gall, the chief of the Unkpapa Sioux, doubtless exercised a predominant influence. Crazy Horse led a force consisting mostly of Cheyennes, who charged upon Custer from the north and west, while Gall, after routing Reno, assailed Custer from the south and east. In the subsequent siege of Reno and Benteen on the bluffs, which lasted until the afternoon of the 26th, neither Crazy Horse nor any of the other chiefs was conspicuous, the warriors keeping up the fight by fits and starts, with no discipline and little concert of action. On the break-up of the savage horde into bands moving in various directions, some weeks after the battle, Crazy Horse, with about 800 warriors, started in the direction of the agencies, probably intent upon getting recruits, ammunition, and supplies. Crook followed him closely, and on Sept. 9, at Slim Buttes, in northwestern South Dakota, a picked force of 150 men under Capt. Anson Mills surprised the village of American Horse, capturing and destroying it, killing a number of the warriors and mortally wounding the chief. Crazy Horse, with the remainder of his force, hurried to the scene, but Crook was ahead of him, and after some long-range fighting the chief withdrew. His plan of reaching the agencies having failed, he slipped past Crook to the west and took up winter quarters in the Wolf Mountains, near the head of the Rosebud. Here Col. Nelson A. Miles, with a force much inferior in numbers, but with two pieces of artillery, attacked him on Jan. 8, 1877, in one of the most desperate and daring encounters of the war, and broke up his village, though he retired in good order. With ammunition and supplies well-nigh exhausted, the Cheyennes openly resentful over his refusal to succor Dull Knife's band (though he then had nothing to give), and his own tribesmen deserting him, he was now ready to listen to the pleas of his friends that he give up the hopeless contest. Yet for another four months he held out. On May 6, with about 1,100 men, women, and children, he arrived at the Red Cloud agency, near Camp Robinson, Nebr., and surrendered. For a time he was quiet; but in August the officers began to suspect that he was planning another outbreak. On Sept. 5 he was arrested and taken before Gen. L. P. Bradley, commander of the district, with headquarters at the fort. Remanded to the charge of the officer of the day, he suddenly realized that he was to be locked up, and in a frenzy of rage drew a long knife and started to fight his way out. One of his close friends, Little Big Man, grappled with him and attempted to seize his wrists. In the mêlée that followed he was mortally wounded in the abdomen, either by a bayonet thrust from a soldier or (as Little Big Man subsequently told

Capt. John G. Bourke) by an accidental lunge of the knife in his own hand, and at midnight he died. It is certain that orders had been given to convey him to Omaha, and it seems probable that a decision had been made to transport him to the Dry Tortugas. The body was given to his father and mother, who buried it secretly somewhere in the hills near the camp.

Capt. Bourke, who was stationed at Camp Robinson in 1877, described him as a man who "looked quite young, not over thirty years old (he was probably not more than twenty-eight), five feet eight inches high, lithe and sinewy, with a scar in the face. The expression of his countenance was one of quiet dignity, but morose, dogged, tenacious and melancholy. . . . All Indians gave him a high reputation for courage and generosity. . . . He was one of the great soldiers of his day and generation." "He was a born soldier," writes Brady, "whose talents for warfare and leadership were of the highest order, . . . one of the bravest of the brave and one of the subtlest and most capable of captains."

[Unsigned sketch in *Handbook of Am. Indians* (1907); John G. Bourke, *On the Border with Crook* (1891); James McLaughlin, *My Friend the Indian* (1910); Homer W. Wheeler, *Buffalo Days* (1925); Cyrus Townsend Brady, *Indian Fights and Fighters* (1904); Nelson A. Miles, *Serving the Republic* (1911).]

W. J. G—t.

CREAMER, DAVID (Nov. 20, 1812–Apr. 8, 1887), hymnologist, was born in Baltimore, the son of Joshua and Margaret (Smith) Creamer, and the fourth in descent from Henry Creamer, a German emigrant who settled in Westminster County, Md. In 1832 he became a partner in Joshua Creamer & Son, dealers in lumber. On Nov. 27, 1834, he married Eliza Ann, daughter of Judge Isaac Taylor of the orphans' court of the city. For two years (1836–38) he was publisher and co-editor of the *Baltimore Monument*, which described itself as a "weekly journal devoted to polite literature, science, and the fine arts." It was a poor little sheet, ambitious but impecunious, made up largely of snippets from other papers. In it Creamer printed several poetic effusions of his own, and for one or two of them, as a special feature, a musical accompaniment was provided. The financial panic of 1857 almost wiped out his lumber business, and the next year he retired. Thereafter he was for a considerable time in government employ. A staunch Union man, he was foreman of the jury that investigated the deaths in the attack Apr. 19, 1861, on the 6th Massachusetts Infantry, and through him the people of Massachusetts were informed of the care given their dead and injured by the citizens of Baltimore. In August 1862 he was appointed recruiting officer of the state. In September of the same year the governor nominated him to visit the regiments in and near Washington and to report on their needs. In July 1863 he was made an assessor of internal revenue. Later, for some ten or eleven years, he was a clerk in the Post Office Department in Washington.

This none-too-successful merchant and minor government employee was a devout Methodist. Piety and mild taste for poetry led him to read and reread lovingly the hymns of the Methodist Church, and by private study he made himself the first American hymnologist of any note. Through booksellers in England he acquired a set of the poetical publications of the Wesleys, complete except for a single pamphlet, and many rare hymnals and works on hymnology. His collection, numbering in all about seven hundred volumes, was sold at auction in December 1884 and became the property of Drew Theological Seminary at Madison, N. J. In 1848 he published privately in New York his *Methodist Hymnology*, accurately inventoried on its title-page as "comprehending notices of the poetical works of John and Charles Wesley; showing the origin of their hymns in the Methodist Episcopal, Methodist Episcopal South, and Wesleyan collections; also, of such other hymns as are not Wesleyan, in the Methodist Episcopal hymn-book, and some account of the authors; with critical and historical observations." Except for the smaller *Wesleyan Hymnology* (London, 1845) by Burgess, the book was without a precedent. It is still valuable, and the simple piety and enthusiasm of the author linger in its pages. He was one of the two laymen on the committee that prepared the *Hymns for the Use of the Methodist Episcopal Church* (1849). He contributed to the *New York Christian Advocate*, was for twenty-one years a trustee of Dickinson College, and was a pillar of the Monument Street Methodist Church. He died in Baltimore on Good Friday, 1887, in the house where he had lived for fifty years.

[F. J. Metcalf, *Am. Writers and Compilers of Sacred Music* (1925); article on Creamer by Frederic Mayer Bird in *Dict. of Hymnology* (rev. ed., London, 1907), ed. by J. Julian; *Sun* (Baltimore), Apr. 9, 1887.]

G. H. G.

CREATH, JACOB (Feb. 22, 1777–Mar. 13, 1854), clergyman, commonly called Elder Jacob Creath, Sr., to distinguish him from his nephew Jacob [*q.v.*], whose career was somewhat similar, was for thirty-two years a Baptist preacher, and then, excluded from that denomination because of his Campbellite views, was for twenty-seven years more a pioneer promoter of churches of the Disciples of Christ in Kentucky. The Creath family was prolific in preachers and influential in the religious development of the Southwest. At least one of Jacob's brothers and five of his nephews were ministers. He was born near Cumberland, Nova Scotia, the son of Samuel and Susan (Moore) Creath. In 1784 his father, having been in prison for seven years because of his sympathy with the American Revolutionists, was given twenty days to leave Canada or be hanged. He brought his family to New York, from which place they went to Cherry Valley, Pa., and finally in 1786 settled in Grassy Creek, Granville County, N. C. Here Jacob seems to have grown up, for in 1795 he joined the Grassy Creek Baptist Church (Chas. C. Ware, *North Carolina Disciples of Christ,* 1927). According to a contemporary, however, being a spritely lad, he attracted the attention of a Colonel Carter of Culpeper County, Va., who reared him in his own home, where the youth fell in love with his benefactor's daughter whom he married (J. H. Spencer, *A History of Kentucky Baptists,* 1886, I, 310). It is certain that he was married, Jan. 24, 1799, to Milly V. Carter, whose father, Job, however, is said to have hailed from Lancaster County, Va. (Stratton Nottingham, *The Marriage License Bonds of Lancaster County, Va., 1701-1848,* copyright 1927). He began to preach at the age of eighteen, and in April 1798, was ordained at Roundabout Meeting House, Louisa County, Va. After serving as pastor in Mathews County, Va., he migrated to Kentucky in 1803 where he became a member of the Elkhorn Association. For the remainder of his life he was conspicuous in the religious affairs of the state. He was of good appearance, "inclined to be foppish in his dress," and "possessed a fine tact for carrying the populace with him." He was also charged with being bold, aspiring, and ambitious. Thomas Campbell was much impressed with his abilities as a speaker, and Henry Clay is said to have called him "the finest orator that Kentucky has ever produced." In spite of his evangelical effectiveness, however, he proved a disturbing element among the Baptists. A personal difference with Jacob Lewis over a slave trade in which friends of both parties took sides, became a *cause célèbre,* and led Elder Elijah Craig to issue a pamphlet entitled, *A Portrait of Jacob Creath,* written with a pen "dipt in poison." Creath was acquitted of its charges by a council of churches, but the affair disrupted the Elkhorn Association and brought about the formation of the Licking Association. By 1830, he had become one of the leading champions of Campbellism in that section of the state, and his church

with others was dropped from the Baptist connection. Thereafter he did much to organize and build up churches of the Campbellite order, traveling extensively and baptizing large numbers of people. For the last seven years of his life he was totally blind.

[Besides references above see David Benedict, *A Gen. Hist. of the Bapt. Denomination* (1813), esp. II, 293; *The Millennial Harbinger,* May 1854; Robt. Richardson, *Memoirs of Alex. Campbell* (1868–70), II, 116; F. D. Power, *Sketches of Our Pioneers* (1898).]

H. E. S.

CREATH, JACOB (Jan. 17, 1799–Jan. 8, 1886), clergyman, was originally a Baptist, but later became an aggressive champion of Campbellism in the South, especially in Missouri. To distinguish him from his uncle [*q.v.*] who had the same name and was also a pioneer Campbellite, he was known as Jacob Creath, Jr. He was the son of William Creath, a Baptist preacher who was born at sea during the passage of his parents from Dublin, Ireland, to Nova Scotia, and came with them to the United States where they finally settled in Granville County, N. C. Here he married Lucretia, daughter of Thomas and Elizabeth Brame. They had sixteen children, five of whom became ministers. Jacob was born on Butcher's Creek, Mecklenburg County, Va., and throughout his youth was obliged to work upon the farm which helped to support the ever-increasing family. He was licensed to preach, however, on Feb. 15, 1818, and in January of the following year he put himself under the instruction of Prof. Abner W. Clopton of the University of North Carolina. He accompanied him to Milton, Caswell County, N. C., in 1820, where the latter took charge of a seminary, and in September 1820 was ordained at Mill Creek Meeting House. Subsequently he entered Columbian College, Washington, D. C., where he remained until December 1823, soon after which he took up his residence in Kentucky, supplying at various Baptist churches.

There now began a career long, strenuous, militant, often bitterly controversial, but on the whole constructive in its influence. Creath was six feet tall, of remarkable physical and mental energy, bold in defending what he thought was right, but intense in his passions and prejudices, and relentless toward his opponents. After two years in Kentucky he made a long tour through the South as far as New Orleans. So strong was sectarian feeling that his polemic preaching excited violent opposition; his character was assailed; once he was burned in effigy; and he was assured that his life was in danger. Upon returning to Kentucky, he visited Alexander Campbell whom he later accompanied on one or two preaching tours. He served churches in the Elkhorn Association and by 1830 having become one of the leaders of the Campbellite faction among the Baptists within its bounds, was excluded from its fellowship. He continued his labors in Kentucky until 1839, when he removed to Missouri, living first near Monticello, then at Palmyra, later at St. Louis, and finally at Palmyra again. He established churches at Hannibal, New London, St. Louis, and elsewhere, besides making frequent evangelistic tours in Illinois, Tennessee, Mississippi, Alabama, and once up the Mississippi River as far as St. Paul. In 1848 he published a pamphlet entitled *A Blow at the Root of Episcopalianism.* For six years preceding the Civil War he was an agent of the Bible Revision Association for which he raised considerable sums of money. He was twice married, first, in September 1831 to Mrs. Susan Bedford, widow of Sidney Bedford of Bourbon County, Ky., and second, in March 1842 to Mrs. Prudence Rogers.

[P. Donan, *Memoir of Jacob Creath, Jr.* (1872), is based on autobiographical material. Other authorities are J. H. Spencer, *A Hist. of Ky. Baptists* (1886); T. P. Haley, *Hist. and Biog. Sketches of the Early Churches and Pioneer Preachers of the Christian Ch. in Mo.* (1888); F. D. Power, *Sketches of Our Pioneers* (1898); Robt. Richardson, *Memoirs of Alex. Campbell* (1868–70); Chas. C. Ware, *N. C. Disciples of Christ* (1927).]

H. E. S.

CREELMAN, JAMES (Nov. 12, 1859–Feb. 12, 1915), journalist, was the son of Scotch-Canadian parents, Matthew and Martha Creelman, the latter a daughter of Edward Dunwoodie. Born in Montreal, James ran away from home at twelve to follow his mother who had settled in New York City. He walked most of the way and reached the latter city with five cents in his pocket. He rebelled against school and, although his mother was a Scotch-Presbyterian, found a job on an Episcopal paper, the *Star.* In 1878 he joined the staff of the *New York Herald* with which he remained nearly two decades and for which he secured an interview with Pope Leo XIII on labor troubles. His work took him to London in 1890 and a year later to France, to edit the Paris edition of the *Herald.* Securing interviews with King George of Greece and other "crowned heads" for use in the *Herald,* he later used the same material in a book, *On the Great Highway* (1901). Anxious to secure public recognition as a writer, he broke with James Gordon Bennett, proprietor of the *New York Herald,* because the latter insisted that all interviews be anonymous, and in 1893 he became manager of a British edition of the *Cosmopolitan Magazine.* At the request of the New York *World,* he served (1894) as a special correspondent in the Sino-Japanese War. For six months

he was on the staff of Count Field Marshal Oyama in Manchuria, and he was present at the taking of Port Arthur. For the *New York Journal* he reported the Græco-Turkish War in 1897. In Cuba, in 1898, he volunteered to lead the forces to the Fort of El Caney, as he was the only man who knew the back road up the hill. He was wounded in that attack, and returned to the United States to become editorial writer and then Washington correspondent for the *Journal.* Returning to the New York *World* in 1900 for six years of service, in 1906 he became associate editor of *Pearson's Magazine,* and held this position until 1910. In 1902 he published a novel, *Eagle Blood*; his other books include *Why We Love Lincoln* (1908), and *Diaz, Master of Mexico* (1911). For two years (1910–12) he was president of the Municipal Civil Service Commission under Mayor Gaynor of New York, resigning to become associate editor of the *New York Evening Mail.* Early in 1915 he went to Berlin as war correspondent for the *New York American,* but died of pleurisy a few days after his arrival. He was married to Alice L. Buell of Marietta, Ohio, in 1891. His chief peculiarity was an abhorrence of nicknames: for six years he worked beside Robert H. Davis but at the end they were still "Mr. Creelman" and "Mr. Davis" to each other.

[See *Who's Who in America,* 1914–15; J. K. Winkler, *W. R. Hearst: An Am. Phenomenon* (1928). Creelman's own book, *On the Great Highway,* is the best record of his journalistic achievements but needs to be supplemented by obituary notices in the N. Y. newspapers for Feb. 13, 1915.]

J. M. L.

CREESY, JOSIAH PERKINS (Mar. 23, 1814–June 5, 1871), sea captain, came from old colonial stock. He was born in Marblehead, Mass., the eldest child of Josiah P. and Mary Woolridge Creesy. The family surname has been spelled in some twenty-three different ways, with several variations even in the case of Creesy himself—"Cressy" and "Cressey" for instance. Young Creesy shipped before the mast in an East Indiaman while still a boy. Promotion was rapid, and he was commanding a ship at twenty-three. In 1841 he married Eleanor Horton Prentiss, who thereafter accompanied him on many of his voyages. Several fast runs from China in the *Oneida* gave him the reputation of a successful "driver." This led Grinnell, Minturn & Company of New York to give him the command of their new clipper, the *Flying Cloud,* built at East Boston by Donald McKay [*q.v.*]. She left New York for San Francisco on her maiden voyage June 2, 1851, seven weeks after she was launched. Creesy, striving for a record, spared neither his ship, his crew, nor himself. Three days out, three spars were carried away; the mainmast cracked a week later; sails were torn to bits; but repairs were made without slackening speed. Shortly before noon on Aug. 31, Creesy brought his ship to anchor at San Francisco. The voyage had been accomplished in eighty-nine days and twenty-one hours, and shattered all previous records. Creesy then proceeded across the Pacific to China for tea, and returned to New York the following April after a ninety-four day run around Africa from Whampoa. In 1854, he shortened his original record to San Francisco by thirteen hours. No other captain or ship equaled it (claims that the *Andrew Jackson* beat these records in 1860 seem to have been disproved. See O. T. Howe and F. C. Matthews, *American Clipper Ships*, 1926, I, 9, 193). Creesy's records for his five trips to San Francisco—89, 115, 92, 89, and 108 days—average better than those of any other clipper. On her fourth voyage the ship ran into a coral reef a few days out from Whampoa and leaked at the rate of eleven inches an hour, but Creesy kept the pumps going all the way and brought the precious cargo to New York in a run of 115 days. At the end of 1855 he retired to his home for a much-needed rest, but went to sea again for a short naval career in the Civil War, being made a volunteer acting lieutenant on Aug. 2, 1861, and given command of the ship *Ino*. He had been absolute master on his own quarterdeck so long that he did not fit into naval discipline. Early in 1862 when the commander of the squadron ordered him to release two Confederate prisoners taken at Tangier, Creesy bluntly replied, "I positively decline to give these men up," and sailed away without orders. Commander Craven preferred charges against him for this "contemptuous disregard" and Creesy was dismissed on July 18, 1862 (*Official Records, Navy*, 1 ser., I, 319, 392; *Navy Register*, 1863, p. 168). He returned to the China trade and commanded the clipper *Archer* for two voyages. He died at Salem at the age of fifty-seven and was buried at Marblehead.

[In addition to sources cited above see A. J. Clark, *Clipper Ship Era* (1910); B. J. Lindsey, *Old Marblehead Sea Captains and the Ships in Which They Sailed* (1915); T. W. Higginson, *Mass. in the Army and Navy in the War of 1861–65* (1896), II, 36, name spelled Cressey; *Vital Records of Marblehead, Mass., to . . . 1849*, I (1903), 122, II (1904), 102; Town Records (MS.) of Marblehead.]   R. G. A—n.

CREIGHTON, EDWARD (Aug. 31, 1820–Nov. 5, 1874), pioneer telegraph builder, banker, philanthropist, was the fifth of nine children of James and Bridget (Hughes) Creighton, both natives of Ireland, who came to the United States in 1805 and 1808 respectively and were married in 1811. They settled in Belmont County, Ohio,

in 1813, removing subsequently to Licking County. Poverty permitted Edward only a most rudimentary schooling. At fourteen he was put to work as a wagon-driver. When the poles bearing the iron wire began advancing over the Ohio hills, the newly invented magnetic telegraph excited the imagination of the young man. With little capital but his brawn, energy, and vision, he took on contracts to build lines in the Middle West and the Southwest, coming into close touch with the telegraph magnates of that day, especially with Jephtha H. Wade and Hiram Sibley whose complete confidence he won. To Creighton, Sibley entrusted the delicate task of making a pseudo survey of the South to suggest impending construction of a competing telegraph, a performance constituting "the lemon-squeezer" that frightened the company there entrenched into yielding a coveted lease necessary to the success of the budding Western Union. Sibley originated the first practical plan for a transcontinental telegraph to the Pacific and in this, too, assigned Creighton an essential rôle. In 1854, Edward Creighton had associated with him in his work his younger brother, John Andrew [*q.v.*], and the two made their advent two years later in Omaha City, the prairie-outfitting base on the edge of Nebraska Territory, to which they brought the wires from St. Joseph, bridging distance previously traversed only by steed, stage, and steamboat.

About this time, Edward Creighton was deputed by Sibley to examine a cross-country telegraph route by way of Fort Smith, and another by way of Memphis. Both proving unsuitable, he turned to the trail from Omaha to Salt Lake via Fort Kearny, Laramie, and South Pass and over the Sierra Nevadas to Sacramento and San Francisco. He covered the entire stretch personally on muleback, in the winter of 1860, made his report Apr. 12, 1861, and asserted his readiness to undertake construction to Salt Lake. Having procured congressional legislation for a subsidy, Sibley chartered the Pacific Telegraph Company and engaged with the government for completion within ten years. Actual work at both ends began July 4, 1861, the section from Julesburg, Colo., to Salt Lake City falling to Creighton. Connection with Salt Lake City was established Oct. 24, and the section from Salt Lake west was completed two days later. Nov. 15 saw the line in operation from ocean to ocean, only four months and eleven days after its commencement. One of the largest subscribers to the stock, Creighton emerged in possession of a great fortune, further increased by successful ventures in gold and silver mines and large-scale cattle-raising. For a number of years he served as general manager of the telegraph company, then joined in organizing the first national bank in Nebraska Territory and became its president. A devout Roman Catholic, his public spirit paralleled his prosperity and he frequently proclaimed his purpose to provide a free Catholic school for higher education, a project still of the future when he was stricken with paralysis in his fifty-fifth year. His widow, Mary Lucretia Wareham, whose sister had married John Andrew Creighton, determined to carry out the unfulfilled intention of her husband but she died within two years and it remained for John Andrew Creighton as executor of the bequest in her will ($100,000), supplementing it from his own ample resources from time to time, to usher Creighton University into existence. It was incorporated Aug. 14, 1879, and entrusted to the Jesuit order.

[J. D. Reid, *The Telegraph in America* (1886); P. A. Mullens, *Creighton* (1901); *Illus. Hist. of Nebr.* (1905), ed. by J. Sterling Morton and Albert Watkins; J. S. Savage and J. T. Bell, *Hist. of Omaha* (1894); *The Story of Creighton* (1928), souvenir of the fiftieth anniversary of Creighton University; contemporary newspaper obituaries; incidental references in biographies of associates. The date of birth is taken from his tombstone.]   V. R—r.

CREIGHTON, JAMES EDWIN (Apr. 8, 1861–Oct. 8, 1924), philosopher, was born in Pictou, Nova Scotia, the son of Scotch-Irish parents, John and Mary C. (O'Brien) Creighton. He attended school in his native town, helped his father on the farm, and taught in the schools of his Province until he was twenty-two, when he entered Dalhousie College in Halifax. Here he came under the influence of Prof. Jacob Gould Schurman who aroused his interest in philosophy and influenced his entire future life. In 1887 Creighton won his A.B. degree with distinction in philosophy and then entered Cornell University to pursue his graduate studies under the guidance of Schurman, who had been called to Cornell in 1886. He spent the year of 1888 at the universities of Leipzig and Berlin, and upon his return in 1889 was appointed to an instructorship at Cornell which he held until 1892. In that year he received the doctor's degree upon the presentation of his doctoral thesis on *The Will, Its Structure and Mode of Action* (published 1898). This led to his advancement to an associate professorship of logic and metaphysics in the Sage School of Philosophy, which had been established at Cornell in 1891 through the efforts of Schurman, who became its dean. In 1892 Creighton married Katherine F. McClain of Pictou. In 1895 he became the Sage Professor of logic and metaphysics, a chair which he held for the rest of his life. Additional duties, however, were placed upon him in 1893 when he was made co-editor, with President Schurman, of the *Philosophical Review,* a journal devoted to philosophical research which had been established by Cornell University in 1891. In 1902 he assumed full charge as editor-in-chief, retaining the important office until his death in 1924. During this long period he exercised a wholesome influence upon the study of philosophy in the United States: he possessed high ideals of scholarship and fine literary taste, qualities which were supported in his case by an editorial conscience that was satisfied only by good workmanship. From 1896 to 1924 he served as the American editor of *Kant-Studien,* the organ of the German Kant Society. His ability was also shown in the influence which he wielded in the American Philosophical Association, in the founding of which he played a leading part and of which he was the first president (1902–03). All these interests and activities contributed to his success as a teacher, particularly in the field of graduate study. The respect of his students was expressed by the publication of a volume of *Philosophical Essays* published in 1917 under the editorship of Prof. G. H. Sabine, of the Ohio State University. The esteem in which he was held by his own university found expression in his election, in 1914 as dean of the Graduate School and in 1922 as a faculty representative on the Board of Trustees. Creighton's philosophy was greatly influenced by the Hegelian philosophy, as this had been developed in England by Bernard Bosanquet and his following. He became the leading American exponent of the idealistic or speculative philosophy and its most strenuous defender. From this standpoint he reviewed and criticized all the new American systems of his time, the pragmatisms of William James and John Dewey, as well as the neo-realism and materialism of the younger thinkers. His published works include: a translation of Wundt's *Human and Animal Psychology* (1894), with E. B. Titchener; *An Introductory Logic* (1898); a translation of Paulsen's *Immanuel Kant, His Life and Doctrine* (1902), with Albert Lefevre; and *Studies in Speculative Philosophy,* edited by H. R. Smart and published posthumously in 1925.

[W. A. Hammond, "Jas. Edwin Creighton," and Katherine Gilbert, "Jas. E. Creighton as Writer and Editor," in *Jour. of Philosophy,* May 7, 1925; G. W. Cunningham, "In Memoriam: J. E. Creighton," in *Internat. Jour. of Ethics,* Jan. 1925; Frank Thilly, "Prof. J. E. Creighton," in *Kant-Studien,* 1925; articles by Thilly and G. H. Sabine, "The Philosophy of J. E. Creighton," in *Phil. Rev.,* May 1925.]   F. T—y.

CREIGHTON, JOHN ANDREW (Oct. 15, 1831–Feb. 7, 1907), philanthropist, was born in Licking County, Ohio, youngest of nine children. His parents, James and Bridget (Hughes) Creighton, both natives of Ireland, emigrated to the United States in the years 1805 and 1808, respectively, and were married in 1811. James Creighton was employed for a time in a Pittsburgh foundry, but in 1813 he moved to Ohio, where he became a farmer. John received his formal education at the local district school, and at St. Joseph's, a Dominican college at Somerset, Ohio. He had hoped to fit himself for the profession of civil engineering, but in 1854, after only two years of college, he entered the employ of his elder brother, Edward [q.v.], who built telegraph lines and took grading contracts. In 1856 the latter met with some reverses in Missouri and Iowa, after which the two brothers and several of their relatives settled in Omaha. Here John secured temporary employment in a store. It soon developed that the road to fortune lay still farther to the West. In 1860 he took two train-loads of merchandise by ox-team to Denver, where he remained until 1861. On July 4 of that year the construction of a telegraph line to the Pacific was begun. Edward Creighton had contracted to build the section from Julesburg, Colo., to Salt Lake, and John was put in charge of the work. Thereafter for many years the interests of the two men centered in the Far West, where as freighters, traders, contractors, and stockmen they amassed great wealth. John Creighton was active in starting the packing industry in South Omaha. For five years he was located at Virginia City, Mont., and at one time he figured prominently as a member of the famous Vigilantes. In 1868, however, he left the rough life of the western mining camp, was married to Sarah Emily Wareham, the sister of his brother Edward's wife, and once more established himself in Omaha.

In 1874, Edward, by this time reputed to be Omaha's wealthiest citizen, died, and John succeeded to much of his brother's property, including Wyoming cattle interests which sold in 1875 for $700,000. Wisely invested in numerous enterprises both in Omaha and in the West, the Creighton fortune compounded rapidly in spite of the numerous benevolences that were charged against it. Childless, and after 1888 a widower, Creighton took great pleasure in giving liberally, especially to the Catholic Church, of which he was a devout member, and to Catholic institutions. To Creighton University, which his brother Edward's widow had endowed in accordance with a plan of her husband to establish a free Catholic school of higher education, he gave most liberally, and the day (Feb. 7) of John Creighton's death has been adopted as the University's Founder's Day. It is said that the total gifts to the institution from John Creighton and his estate reached nearly a million and a quarter dollars. In recognition of these good works Pope Leo XIII made him a knight of the Order of St. Gregory, and in 1895 conferred upon him the title of Count of the Papal Court. As "Count Creighton" the Omaha capitalist was thereafter generally known. In 1900 Notre Dame University gave him its Laetare medal. Creighton's imposing figure, made almost patriarchal in his later years by silvery hair and a flowing beard, was well-known in Omaha and indeed throughout the entire West. His business connections, his philanthropy, his marked devotion to his church, and his political enthusiasms all brought him before the public. In politics he was an ardent Democrat, and he voted for Bryan in 1896 when most men of wealth, regardless of party, supported the Republican candidate. He remained to his dying day, in spite of his riches, distinctly the Westerner, always fully alive to the interests of the West, and always sympathetic with its point of view.

[The best sketch of Creighton's life is to be found in a little volume dealing appreciatively with the lives of several members of the Creighton family, *Creighton* (1901), by P. A. Mullens. The brief biography in the *Illus. Hist. of Nebr.* (1905), ed. by J. Sterling Morton and Albert Watkins, I, 629, was read and approved by Creighton himself. Local histories such as J. W. Savage and J. T. Bell, *Hist. of the City of Omaha* (1894), contain frequent references to Creighton and his work. See also *World-Herald* (Omaha), Feb. 7, 1907.] J.D.H.

CREIGHTON, WILLIAM (Oct. 29, 1778–Oct. 1, 1851), congressman from Ohio, lawyer, was one of the group of Virginians, "the Chillicothe Junto," who brought about Ohio's statehood. The son of William Creighton, he was born in Berkeley County, Va. (now in West Virginia). At seventeen he was graduated from Dickinson College, Carlisle, Pa. He studied law for two years in Martinsburg, Va. (now W. Va.), and emigrated to Chillicothe, Ohio, in 1799. Shortly afterward he was admitted to the bar. When statehood was achieved Creighton's abilities were recognized by his appointment (Mar. 5, 1803) as the first secretary of state. He continued to hold this office by repeated appointment until his resignation in December 1808. Shortly after his resignation he acted as one of the attorneys in defense of two Ohio judges who were impeached for having declared an act of the legislature void because unconstitutional. The acquittal of the two judges marks the establishment in Ohio of the practise of judicial review. This trial and the subsequent ousting of the judges and other appointive officials through the "sweeping resolution" led to a schism in the Republican party in the state. Creighton was identified with the conservative wing of the party and for a time was the leader of the opposition to Thomas Worthington and Edward Tiffin [*qq.v.*], particularly at the time when these men were seeking to control the state through the medium of a Tammany Society (1810–11). Worthington, prior to this break, had been Creighton's warm friend, and had obtained his appointment as United States district attorney, a position which he held during the years 1809, 1810, and a part of 1811. In 1813 Creighton was elected to Congress to fill a vacancy, and in 1814 was elected to the subsequent Congress. His attention was then directed (1817) to his legal business and it was not until 1827 that he again appeared in Congress. He was elected in 1828 as an Adams man. President Adams sought to recognize Creighton's ability by appointing him federal district judge in August 1828, but his appointment was not confirmed by the Senate. He was sent back to the Twenty-second and Twenty-third Congresses, but, judging by the *Annals of Congress* and the *Congressional Debates,* he played no important rôle. He was identified with the Whig party and continued to serve its interests after his retirement to his legal practise in 1833. His home, which preserved the best traditions of Virginia, was presided over by his wife, Elizabeth Meade Creighton, whom he had married Sept. 5, 1805.

[The fullest sketch of Creighton's life is in N. W. Evans, *A Hist. of Scioto County, Ohio* (1903), pp. 167 ff. See also *A Biog. Dir. of the Am. Congress* (1928). Many of his letters are to be found in the Worthington MSS. in the Ohio State Lib. at Columbus. D. M. Massie, *Nathaniel Massie, a Pioneer of Ohio* (1896), contains many references to Creighton. For the political situation in early Ohio see the article by W. T. Utter, "Judicial Review in Early Ohio," in *The Mississippi Valley Hist. Rev.*, June 1927.]   W.T.U.

CRERAR, JOHN (Mar. 8, 1827–Oct. 19, 1889), financier, philanthropist, was born in New York City and died in Chicago. His parents, John and Agnes Smeallie Crerar, were born in Scotland. His father died in July 1827 when John was only a few months old, but his mother gave him not only the common-school education of the day but also an ardent, reverent affection for herself and for Scotch Presbyterianism. A few years after her husband's death, Mrs. Crerar married William Boyd, whose business was in iron and steel. In his eighteenth year John Crerar began work under his step-father, and after about five years was sent as a bookkeeper to an affiliated branch of his firm in Boston. He returned to New York after a short time and engaged himself, still as bookkeeper, to another business house also dealing in iron. At this time he entered

somewhat fully into social life, joining several clubs, among others, the Mercantile Library Association, as president of which he is said to have induced Thackeray to come to America. In 1856, he formed with Morris K. Jesup [*q.v.*] a friendship which affected his life profoundly as regards both business and philanthropy. He entered Jesup's firm, first as employee and soon as partner, and in 1862 went to Chicago in connection with the branch of the firm inaugurated there in 1859, a manufactory of railroad supplies and contractors' materials. A few months after his arrival, in company with one of Jesup's emissaries who had preceded him, he bought over all the interests of the firm in his locality. Circumstances were propitious and the administration excellent; the complexity and wealth of the new business increased rapidly. In 1867, Crerar was one of the incorporators of the Pullman Palace Car Company organized by his friend G. M. Pullman [*q.v.*]. He remained a director in this company throughout his life. He became also a director of the Illinois Trust and Savings Bank, of the Chicago & Alton Railroad Company, and president of the Chicago & Joliet Railway Company. He was a civic force of great importance, lending his influence and resources to any cause that seemed to him at once sound of itself and conducive to the development of Chicago. In the personal relationships which came as a result of his associations in business, he was characterized by geniality and imagination. His other contacts were restricted. He lived quietly, in hotels, and when he was urged by his friend Jesup to engage in his lifetime in large-scale philanthropies, he demurred, saying, "I am satisfied and content." He professed that he was in love with all women, but he never married. Until the death of his mother in 1873 he continued to regard New York as his home, and he specified in his will that he be buried beside her in Brooklyn. The influence of his mother probably accentuated an hereditary bent toward ecclesiasticism. In this regard he was fervent, an active protagonist of orthodoxy. He could not fancy what the story of Jonah and the whale had to do with religion, but he was careful to make a bequest to a certain church contingent upon its "preserving and maintaining the principles of its faith," and he remembered to ban from the library he founded "all nastiness and immorality," that is, he explained, "dirty French novels and all skeptical trash and works of questionable moral tone." His will, written about three years before his death, made legacies to many friends and to certain cousins related to him through his mother, but omitted mention of other cousins equally related to him through his father. Members of the latter group contested the will vigorously at the time of his death, but it was sustained by the courts in 1893. The major portion of his vast estate was left to the many philanthropic purposes dear to him, to the endowment of scholarships, churches, and mission boards, and, most notably, to the erection of "a collossal statue of Lincoln" (that by St. Gaudens), and to the creation of the John Crerar Library, an institution which in 1918 had total assets of over $5,500,000. It was not he, but his friends, named by him as trustees of this library, who determined to make it primarily a place of scientific and technical reference. They felt that in this way they might best supplement the other library facilities of Chicago, and at the same time might exclude automatically from its collections those classes of books which the great financier had prohibited as incompatible with "healthy, moral and Christian sentiment."

[John Crerar, Will (probated 1889); Wm. M. MacBean, *Biog. Reg. St. Andrew's Soc. State of N. Y.*, II (1925), 266–67; T. W. Goodspeed, "John Crerar" in *Univ. of Chicago Biog. Sketches*, I (1922); C. W. Andrews, *John Crerar Lib.* (1905); *Chicago Tribune* (Oct. 20, 1889); *Biog. Dict. of Chicago* (1892).] J.D.W.

CRESAP, MICHAEL (June 29, 1742–Oct. 18, 1775), border leader and Revolutionary soldier, the son of Col. Thomas Cresap [*q.v.*], was born in what is now Allegany County, Md. At an early age he married Mary Whitehead of Philadelphia and set up as a trader near his father's stockaded house and trading-post at Oldtown. He began in the spring of 1774 to clear land in the neighborhood of Wheeling on the Ohio, but before he had made much progress, the activities of the border were halted by the Indian war sometimes called Cresap's War but described more critically as Dunmore's War. The war was actually brought to an outbreak by the Yellow Creek Massacre on Apr. 30, 1774, an ugly incident which is supposed to have been effected by one Daniel Greathouse. The fatalities included certain members of the family of Tah-gah-jute or Logan [*q.v.*], a Mingo warrior then on friendly terms with the white people. Under a Virginia commission, Cresap took part as a captain in the campaign that resulted in the white man's victory at Point Pleasant on Oct. 10, 1774, and it was at the treaty following this battle that John Gibson [*q.v.*], fresh from an interview with Logan, read that warrior's message accusing Cresap of the murder of his family. Illness prevented Cresap from resuming his land-clearing operations, but he was well enough in the following year to accept a Maryland commission to raise a company of riflemen for the Continental Army, and volunteers from the Ohio and West-

ern Maryland made his recruiting a short task. This company set out from Frederick, Md., on July 18, 1775, and twenty-two days later, the first southern troops on the scene, joined Washington before Boston, having marched the intervening 550 miles at the rate of twenty-five miles a day. Ill for weeks before leaving and exhausted by the march, Cresap gave up his command two months later and on his journey homeward died in New York on Oct. 18, 1775. Cresap's memory has been kept alive by an unusual set of circumstances. Logan's speech, with its pitiable conclusion, "Who is there to mourn for Logan? not one!" was printed in the *Virginia Gazette* for Feb. 4, 1775. Then in 1782 Jefferson printed the "morsel of eloquence" in his *Notes on Virginia,* and in the brief introduction referred to Cresap as "a man infamous for the many murders he had committed on those much injured people" [*i.e.* the Indians]. When assailed for the assertion by his political opponent Luther Martin [*q.v.*], who chanced to be also the son-in-law of Cresap, Jefferson modified his statements somewhat, but brought forward in the 1800 edition of the *Notes on Virginia* much assiduously collected evidence to prove Cresap's guilt. Unhappily for his case in modern eyes, he suppressed evidence to the contrary known to be in his possession, notably the letter in which George Rogers Clark exonerated Cresap from the specific charge of the Yellow Creek Massacre (Clark to Samuel Brown, June 17, 1798, enclosed in letter from Brown to Jefferson, Sept. 4, 1798, Jefferson Papers, Library of Congress). The testimony, in general, points to Cresap's innocence in the Logan matter, and shows him to have been no more brutal in his dealings with the Indians than the normal actor in a scene in which men went day and night in fear of an appalling death. Perhaps the final judgment should be that Cresap, whose interest as a settler of new lands would have impelled him to keep peace with the Indians, was forced to act in defense of his land and of the people who made him their leader, and that in performing this duty he was caught in a snarl of intercolonial politics that has not yet been unraveled.

[John J. Jacob, *A Biog. Sketch of the Life of the Late Capt. Michael Cresap* (Cumberland, Md., 1826, repr., Cincinnati, 1866); Brantz Mayer, *Tah-Gah-Jute; or Logan and Cresap, an Hist. Essay* (1867); Thomas Jefferson, *Notes on Va.* (1782), p. 115, and edition of 1800, App. IV; Wm. F. Poole in Justin Winsor, *Narr. and Critical Hist. of America,* vol VI (1887), pp. 707–14, esp. p. 712 where references are given to numerous periodical articles.] L.C.W.

CRESAP, THOMAS (c. 1702–c. 1790), pioneer, was born at Skipton in Yorkshire and came to Maryland at the age of fifteen. About 1727, he

Cresap

married Hannah Johnson, and two years later removed from the neighborhood of Havre de Grace, Md., to a tract near the present town of Wrightsville, Pa., in the territory then in dispute between Lord Baltimore and the Penns. The murderous little war which now broke out with Cresap as its leader under a Maryland commission as captain of militia came to an end on Nov. 24, 1736 with the burning of Cresap's house by the Pennsylvanians. The year 1740 found Cresap the westernmost occupant of lands in Maryland at a place known as Shawanese Oldtown, where two years later his son, Michael Cresap [q.v.], was born. Thomas Cresap's stockaded house and trading-post lay on the old Indian trail customarily taken by the Iroquois on their war expeditions against the Cherokees, and though frequently at odds with the Indians, he soon became the intermediary between the Maryland government and the friendly Iroquois of the north and the enemy Cherokees of the south. The position of his house, printed in many maps of the day, made it a stage in westward journeys from Virginia, Maryland, and Pennsylvania. He was one of the most prominent men of the Appalachian border, known to Indian and white man alike from Canada to Carolina. When the Ohio Company was chartered in 1749, Cresap's name was found among the organizers, and to him was committed by the Company the practical task of blazing the old Indian trail Gist had followed in his preliminary explorations of the territory. With his Indian friend Nemacolin, Cresap marked and improved the sixty miles of trail that ran from Fort Cumberland to the junction of the Redstone and the Monongahela. He was an active patriot in a private capacity in the Revolution, prominent as a local magistrate, and interested always in schemes of western land development and of western transportation. He died about the year 1790. From personal knowledge of Cresap, John J. Jacob speaks of his benevolence and hospitality, his personal bravery, coolness, and fortitude, but the old frontiersman seems to have possessed an uncertain temper, and the disinterestedness of his motives was never above suspicion in the estimation of his contemporaries. Even with this admitted, however, there is no doubt of the value of Cresap's services to his province and to the whole western border at a time when soft hands, white collars, and the ethical niceties were neither fashionable nor useful in that country.

[Md. Council Proc., Jours. of Assembly, Correspondence of Gov. Sharpe, in various volumes of the printed *Archives of Md.* from 1730 throughout the period in question; John J. Jacob, *Biog. Sketch of the Life of the*

Crespi

Late Capt. Michael Cresap (Cumberland, Md., 1826; reprinted, Cincinnati, 1866); Lawrence C. Wroth, "The Story of Thos. Cresap, a Md. Pioneer," in *Md. Hist. Mag.*, IX, 1–37 (March 1914); Registers of All Saints' Parish, Frederick County, Md., and the published "Earliest Records of All Saints' Parish, Frederick, Md., 1727–81" in G. N. Brumbaugh, *Md. Records*, vol. I (1915).]

L. C. W.

CRESPI, JUAN (1721–Jan. 1, 1782), missionary, explorer, is conspicuous among the diarists who recorded explorations in the New World. For more than three decades he was a pioneer in the wilds of North America. Like Francisco Palóu [q.v.], he was a pupil of the great Junípero Serra [q.v.], and for many years was his close companion. Like them both he was a Mallorcan. In the same mission with them he came to America in 1749. With them he became a member of the Franciscan College of San Fernando in Mexico. Beside them he went as missionary to the Sierra Gorda, that wild mountain fastness northeast of the Aztec capital. With them he was sent to the Peninsula of California on the expulsion of the Jesuits in 1767, and there was put in charge of Mission Purísima Concepción. Two years later he was one of the small band of friars selected by Serra to join the Portolá expedition for the occupation of San Diego and Monterey (see sketch of Gaspar de Portolá). Crespi even preceded Serra on the great march, for he joined Rivera y Moncada, who led the vanguard, while Serra followed with Portolá. Crespi was one of the handful of pioneers who planted the Cross and the banner of Spain at San Diego in the summer of 1769. With Portolá he continued north, accomplishing the first European expedition by land up the California coast. With the mystified Portolá, seeking the harbor of Monterey, he pushed still farther north, and became one of the discoverers of San Francisco Bay, whose existence theretofore was unknown and whose importance he was one of the first to recognize. Returning to San Diego with Portolá he again made the land march to Monterey. With Serra he became one of the founders of Mission Carmel, and there he spent the next twelve years, as Serra's companion. In 1772 he went with Pedro Fages [q.v.], to explore a route around San Francisco Bay. Two years afterward he joined the Pérez expedition to Alaska. In 1782 he died at Carmel.

Gentle character and zealous missionary though he was, Crespi is famous primarily as explorer and diarist. Of all the men of the half decade (1769–74) so prolific in frontier extension up the Pacific Coast by land and sea, he alone participated in all the major path-breaking expeditions. From Vellicatá to San Diego, he journeyed; from San Diego to San Francisco Bay; from Monterey to the San Joaquin Valley; from Monterey by sea to Alaska. In distance he outtraveled Coronado. In all these expeditions he went in the double capacity of chaplain and diarist. Of all of them he kept superb diaries that have come down to us. His precious pages record nearly two thousand miles of land travel and a sea voyage of twice that distance.

[Data for Crespi's career as a whole are contained in Palóu's *Relación Historica de la Vida . . . del Venerable Padre Fray Junipero Serra* (Mexico, 1787), English translation by G. W. James and C. Scott Williams (Pasadena, 1913). Crespi's diaries have been translated and edited by Herbert E. Bolton in *Juan Crespi, Missionary Explorer on the Pacific Coast, 1769–74* (1927). Good secondary accounts are H. H. Bancroft, *Hist. of Cal.* (1890) and Chas. A. Engelhardt, *The Missions and Missionaries of Cal.* (4 vols., 1908–15).]
                            H. E. B.

CRESSON, ELLIOTT (Mar. 2, 1796–Feb. 20, 1854), Quaker merchant and philanthropist, was born in Philadelphia. A representative member of a family of successful merchants and valued citizens, he was in his generation noted more for the distribution of his wealth than for activities in attaining it. The family trace descent from Pierre Cresson, Huguenot refugee from France to Holland and later to New Amstel on the Delaware River in 1657. Elliott Cresson was the eldest son of John Elliott and Mary (Warder) Cresson, and was brought up in the influence of a Quaker home. He became a partner in Cresson, Wistar & Company at 133 Market St., Philadelphia, and resided at 30 Sansom St. (above Seventh) with his mother, who outlived him. Through the grave exterior of a "plain" Friend there could be seen in his countenance a character of kindly sympathy. From the teachings of the Society of Friends he had come to have an interest in the oppressed races, the American Indian and the negro, even thinking at one time of becoming a missionary to the Seminole Indians. His devotion, however, was chiefly given to the cause of colonization. He was one of the organizers, in 1834, of The Young Men's Colonization Society of Pennsylvania and a life member of the American Society for Colonizing the Poor People of Color of the United States. In addition to liberal gifts to the cause himself and helping to buy land for the colony at Bassa Cove, Liberia, he made a trip to New England in the winter of 1838–39 as agent of the American Colonization Society to raise funds and to arouse the spirit of colonization, which had become dormant in those regions (Alexander, *post*, p. 550). He made similar visits to the South and to England.

His interests covered a wide range. In addi-

tion to gifts during his life and bequests to relatives by his will, he left to the American Sunday School Union, $50,000; to the Philadelphia School of Design for Women, $10,000; to the Historical Society of Pennsylvania, $10,000; for a monument to William Penn, $10,000; for Episcopal missions, schools and college, at Port Cresson, Liberia, $10,000; to the Pennsylvania Hospital for the Insane, $5,000; to the City of Philadelphia, for planting trees, $5,000; to the University of Pennsylvania, to endow a professorship in the fine arts, $5,000; for founding a Miners' School in Pennsylvania, $5,000; to the Pennsylvania Agricultural Society, $5,000; to the Protestant Episcopal Seminary, Alexandria, Va., $5,000; and to the Athenæum, Philadelphia, to the Widows' Asylum, Philadelphia, to the Deaf and Dumb Asylum, to the House of Refuge, to the Colored Refuge, to the Refuge for Decayed Merchants and to the Pennsylvania Colonization Society, $1,000 each. He also left land valued at over $30,000 to found and support a home for aged, infirm or invalid gentlemen and merchants. Another line of interest is shown in his founding the Elliott Cresson medal, awarded annually by the Franklin Institute "for some discovery in the Arts and Sciences, or for the invention or improvement of some useful machine, or for some new process or combination of materials in manufacturing, or for ingenuity. skill or perfection in workmanship."

[*Colonial Families of Phila.*, ed. by John W. Jordan, vol. II (1911); Archibald Alexander, *Hist. of Colonization on the West Coast of Africa* (1846); *Annual Reports of the Am. Colonization Soc.*, esp. that for Jan. 1855; *African Repository*, Mar. 1854, p. 65; Henry Simpson, *Lives of Eminent Philadelphians* (1859).]
                         J. B. W.

CRESSON, EZRA TOWNSEND (June 18, 1838–Apr. 19, 1926), entomologist, was the son of Warder and Elizabeth (Townsend) Cresson. His original American ancestor, Pierre Cresson, probably a native of Picardy, was born in 1610, emigrated to Holland, and thence to America, settling at New Amstel on the Delaware in 1657, moving later to Manhattan Island and finally to Staten Island. Ezra T. Cresson was born at Byberry, Bucks County, Pa. His father, Warder Cresson, brother of Elliott Cresson [*q.v.*], was United States consul at Jerusalem in 1844. Ezra Cresson married Mary Ann Ridings in 1859. In the same year, with James Ridings and George Newman, he founded the oldest of the entomological societies of this country, at first called the Entomological Society of Philadelphia, but changed in 1867 to the American Entomological Society. Cresson was an officer of the Society from its beginning until

1924, serving as editor of its Transactions for forty-two years and as treasurer for fifty years. On account of the poverty of the Society in its early days, he acted as compositor and pressman in getting out its publications. He was employed by the Franklin Fire Insurance Company in 1869, and was made its secretary in 1878, holding this position until his resignation in 1910. His scientific life-work was devoted almost solely to the insects of the order *Hymenoptera,* and between 1861 and 1882 he had published sixty-six papers of a descriptive, synoptic, or monographic character. He was undoubtedly the ranking American student of this great order. His work culminated in his *Synopsis of the Families and Genera of the Hymenoptera of America North of Mexico, Together with a Catalogue of the Described Species and Bibliography* (1887). In 1865 and 1866 he was editor of the *Practical Entomologist,* the first journal devoted to economic entomology published in the United States. Cresson himself summarized his work upon the *Hymenoptera* in a paper entitled *The Cresson Types of Hymenoptera* published in 1916 as No. 1 of the Memoirs of the American Entomological Society. In this paper he recorded the types of 2,737 of his species. A bibliography comprising seventy titles was appended to this paper. His influence on the progress of entomological studies in the United States was very great, and, like most of the leading naturalists of the nineteenth century, he was always ready to help and encourage young workers.

[P. P. Calvert, "Ezra Townsend Cresson: A Contribution to the Hist. of Entomology in North America," with a bibliography, *Trans. Am. Entomol. Soc.,* vol. LIII (Supp. issued Feb. 13, 1928); obituaries in *Science,* July 2, 1926, and *Entomol. News,* XXXVII, 161; John W. Jordan, ed., *Colonial Families of Phila.* (1911), II, 945 ff.]   L. O. H.

CRESWELL, JOHN ANGEL JAMES (Nov. 18, 1828–Dec. 23, 1891), postmaster-general, was born at Port Deposit, Md. His father, John G. Creswell, was a Marylander of English ancestry, and his mother, Rebecca E. Webb, a Pennsylvanian, whose forebears were German and English, one of the latter being the famous Quaker missionary, Elizabeth Webb. Creswell received his advanced education at Dickinson College, graduating with honors in 1848. After studying law for two years, he was admitted to the Maryland bar, in 1850, and soon began to practise. Early in his career he married Hannah J. Richardson of Maryland, a woman of considerable wealth.

In politics, Creswell was a strong partisan. He first affiliated with the Whigs, then after that party broke up, was for a short period a Democrat, and attended the Cincinnati convention which nominated Buchanan. After the Civil War opened, however, he became and remained a staunch and influential Republican. In the critical days of 1861 and 1862 Creswell filled his first public office, as loyalist member of the Maryland House of Delegates, and did much toward keeping the state in the Union. A year later, as assistant adjutant-general, he had charge of raising Maryland's quota of troops for the Northern army. From 1863 to 1865 he was a member of the national House of Representatives; but in March of the latter year he was elected to the Senate to fill the unexpired term of Thomas H. Hicks. In January 1865, after Maryland had freed its slaves, he made a strong impression by a speech in the House in favor of general emancipation. As senator, he stood for manhood suffrage, the compensation of loyal owners of drafted slaves, and strict enforcement of the Civil Rights Act.

Creswell's most important public work was done as head of the Post Office Department, to which he was appointed by President Grant in March 1869. The country has had few, if any, abler postmasters-general. The changes made by him in the Department were sweeping, reformatory, and constructive. The cost of ocean transportation of letters to foreign countries was reduced from eight cents to two, and great increase in speed was secured by giving the carriage of the mails to the best and fastest steamers, four of which were to sail each week, and by advertising a month in advance the vessels selected; the pay to railroads for mail-carriage was rearranged on a fair basis; there was great increase in the number of railroad postal lines, postal clerks, and letter-carriers, and in the number of cities having free delivery of mail and money-order departments; one-cent postal cards were introduced; the system of letting out contracts for the internal carriage of the mails was so reformed as ultimately to do away with straw bidding and to secure fair competition among responsible bidders; the laws relating to the Post Office Department were codified, with a systematic classification of offenses against the postal laws; and postal treaties with foreign countries were completely revised. Creswell also denounced the franking system as the "mother of frauds," and secured its abolition, and he strongly urged the establishment of postal savings banks and a postal telegraph.

Pressure of private business led him to resign from the Post Office Department in July 1874, but he later accepted the position of United

States counsel before the court of commissioners on the *Alabama* claims, and served until the court expired by law in December 1876. Thereafter, he spent most of his remaining years at Elkton, Md., where he had his home, and gave his attention to banking and the practise of law. Here, following two years of general ill health, he died of bronchial pneumonia.

[*Jour.* of the Md. House of Delegates, 1861–62; *Cong. Globe,* 1863–69; *Reports* of the Postmaster-General, 1869–74; *Biog. Am. Cong., 1774–1927* (1928); sketch in *Biog. Cyc. of Representative Men of Md. and the D.C.* (1879), based, apparently, upon data furnished by Creswell himself. The short biography included in Sams and Riley, *Bench and Bar of Md.* (1901), was founded upon the account given in the *Biog. Cyc.* just mentioned. An editorial on Creswell's appointment as postmaster-general appears in the Baltimore (Weekly) *Sun,* Mar. 6, 1869, and an obituary in the supplementary issue of the same paper for Dec. 26, 1891.] M. W. W.

CRÉTIN, JOSEPH (Dec. 19, 1799–Feb. 22, 1857), first Roman Catholic bishop of St. Paul, Minn., was born at Montluel, Ain, near Lyons, France, the son of a prosperous bourgeois baker, Joseph Crétin, and his wife, Jane Mary Mery. His early education was received amid the reverberations of the Napoleonic wars, and, while studying at Meximieux, he saw the seminary occupied by Austrian troops after the "Hundred Days' Campaign" in 1815. He attended the colleges at L'Argentière and Alix, and entered the famous seminary of St. Sulpice in Paris in 1820. Ordained at Belley by Bishop Devie on Dec. 20, 1823, he was immediately appointed vicar at Ferney, for many years the home of Voltaire, with the special object of overcoming the rationalistic influences surviving this philosopher. He opened a preparatory college and later became pastor of the parish. The July Revolution of 1830 found him more than sympathetic with the fallen monarchy, and his refusal to offer public prayers for the new king, Louis Philippe, brought him under sharp displeasure at Paris for a time. He had long cherished the desire to enter foreign missions, and in 1838 after meeting Mathias Loras, the first bishop of Dubuque in the Iowa territory and formerly his professor at Meximieux, Crétin slipped quietly away to Havre and left for America.

Arriving in Dubuque in April 1839, he was made vicar-general of the huge pioneer diocese containing over 30,000 Indians, and among these, the Winnebagoes particularly, he labored for a number of years. Strongly recommended by the federal agent and by many others to be principal of the government Indian school on the Turkey River, he was ignored by Gov. Chambers, and in 1845 even forbidden to erect a mission school in the neighborhood, although he was allowed to remain as a missionary. After suc-

cessful work in Dubuque and Prairie du Chien, he was appointed in 1850 the first bishop of St. Paul, which diocese embraced the state of Minnesota, and was consecrated Jan. 26, 1851 at Belley, France, by the same bishop who had ordained him a priest. He pushed vigorously his missionary activities among the Indians and was in Washington in 1852 discussing government Indian schools with President Millard Fillmore. He encouraged the colonization of his state and made heroic efforts to reach the scattered members of his faith throughout his diocese. A strong advocate of the temperance movement and a bitter foe of the frontier saloon, he ordered the cathedral bell to be rung in approval when the Minnesota legislature enacted a "liquor law." Ever active in educational work and parochial organization, he also commenced building a stone cathedral in 1854 but arduous tasks and a prolonged illness brought death upon him before its completion.

[An unfinished life of Crétin from the pen of Archbishop John Ireland appears in the *Acta et Dicta,* vols. IV, V (pub. by St. Paul Cath. Hist. Soc., 1915–17); in the same publication, vols. I–V, are published a number of his letters and in vol. I (1907) are recorded personal reminiscences of the bishop by A. Oster; biographical sketches appear in J. D. G. Shea, *Hist. of the Cath. Ch. in the U. S.,* vol. IV (1892), bk. X, ch. vii; in Shea, *The Hierarchy of the Cath. Ch. in the U. S.* (1886), pp. 377–78, and in *The Cath. Encyc.;* while Louis DeCailly, *Memoirs of Bishop Loras* (1897), and Augustin Ravoux, *Reminiscences, Memoirs and Lectures* (1890) throw interesting side-lights on his life and career. Some material is found in *Berichte der Leopoldinan Stiftung in Kaiserthume Oesterreich,* XXVI Heft (1854), XXV Heft (1853); and in original letters in archives of Columbia Coll., Dubuque, Ia.] M. M. H.

CRÈVECŒUR, J. HECTOR ST. JOHN. [See CRÈVECŒUR, MICHEL–GUILLAUME JEAN DE, 1735–1813.]

CRÈVECŒUR, MICHEL–GUILLAUME JEAN de (Jan. 31, 1735–Nov. 12, 1813), essayist, was born near Caen, in Normandy, the son of Guillaume Jean de Crèvecœur (see birth certificate) and of Marie-Anne-Thérèse Blouet. He later stated that his family name was Saint-Jean, "Crèvecœur" being the name of an ancestral estate which neither he nor his father ever possessed. Though the descendant of families of distinction, the young man chose to become a pioneer and wanderer. He migrated to Canada and served under Montcalm in the last of the French and Indian wars. He had received part of his education in England, which he had left in 1754, and during his services in New France seems to have explored the vast tracts of land near the Great Lakes and the Ohio River. His official duty was, perhaps, that of map-maker. In any case, he acquired a knowledge of the countries of the Scioto and the Muskingum, and of their Indian peoples. These adventures were a mere overture to his later participation in the drama of American colonization and revolution. At the age of twenty-four (1759), he landed in New York. For the next decade he again traveled widely, acquiring a thorough knowledge of Pennsylvania and New York, and, presumably, penetrating into the Carolinas. Now, however, there were anchors for this French voyager. In December 1765 he became a naturalized American citizen; in 1769 he married Mehetable Tippet of Yonkers, and in the same year he settled on his farm, at "Pine Hill," Orange County, N. Y. Though details of his experiences are wanting between 1769 and September 1780, when he embarked for France, it is probable that during this decade he wrote most of the charming and informative essays on which his reputation rests. These are, for the most part, available in *Letters from an American Farmer* (1782) "by J. Hector St. John," a name which Crèvecœur occasionally used simply because he liked it; and in *Sketches of Eighteenth Century America* (1925). It is likely that he sometimes wrote long after the event, and the particular essays cannot be finally dated, but it is reasonable to think that these two volumes present substantially the Farmer's reactions to American life during his stay here.

Immediately after the war he returned to America, arriving in New York, Nov. 19, 1783, only to discover that his home had been burned. His wife had died, and his children had disappeared. "I should have fallen to the ground," he said, "but for the support, at this instant, of my friend Mr. Seton, who had come to conduct me from the French vessel to his house." Eventually he found his children, but the dramatic circumstances of the Indian raid which had caused the catastrophe in his absence seem a startling parallel to the sufferings of the frontier which he himself had described in his essays. He now became French consul at New York and endeavored to cement the friendly relations of his two countries. He corresponded with Washington; he knew Franklin; he wrote for the American newspapers over the signature "Agricola," and at the marriage of his daughter, America-Francès, Thomas Jefferson was present. Perhaps of equal interest to this born farmer was his boast that he had introduced into America sain foin, lucerne (alfalfa), the vetches, vignon, and racine de disette. In 1790 he took final leave of his adopted country. He died at Sarcelles, on Nov. 12, 1813.

Had Crèvecœur written nothing, his life as a Frenchman living through the upheaval of the Revolution would have been remarkable. He was a master of the forest and of the pioneer farm. He studied with the utmost thoughtfulness the vexed question of taxation. He was familiar with the evils of fraudulent titles, heavy mortgages, and imperfect agricultural equipment. He understood the misery of the poor, and he observed the vast reëstablishments in America of feudal systems under the Dutch and other colonial aristocrats. He was particularly interested, since this was his own lot, in the difficulties of the independent family tilling the soil, under cramped methods of husbandry, for a perilous livelihood. Finally, he experienced the despair of the Revolution which set at naught all that he, and those like him, had gained. Though deeply attached to the common people, he became, perhaps because of an innate aristocratic bias, a Loyalist; and he saw in the chicanery of some so-called patriots much to support him in this conviction. In *Landscapes,* an early specimen of American drama, and in various essays, he penetrated shrewdly economic and personal motives that underlay the Revolution. An intense lover of true liberty, he saw clearly the oppressions committed in America in its name, and he could not endure those, as he said, who were "perpetually bawling about liberty without knowing what it was."

All this he set down in vigorous English, in such letters or essays as "What is An American?", or "The American Belisarius." These great issues he viewed with a broad and sane philosophy, but he described also in detail the physical and social conditions of rural life in America. In "Farm Life," "Enemies of the Farmer," "Customs," and "Implements" he at once gives a photographic record of the husbandman's life about the year 1775; and he also destroys finally the popular notion that he was a sentimentalizer concerning agricultural life. Truer than this outworn tradition is the fact that many of the essays reflect the warm humanity which was so strong a part of his own nature. He can describe unforgettably a negro under torture, travelers arriving for the night; children coming home from school in a snowstorm; a woman's cry as the raiders enter her home for massacre; or a family "frolic." In "The Wyoming Massacre" he silhouettes the refugees on their long journey through the forest. On a horse with bedding as a saddle, "sat a wretched mother with a child at her breast, another on her lap, and two more placed behind her." He himself said, "There is something truly ridiculous in a farmer quitting his plough or his axe, and then flying to his pen," but, in spite of oddities in spelling, construction, and style, he has also, by reason of his powers of observation and selection of trenchant detail, some claim to be regarded as a man of letters. Charles Lamb wrote, "Tell Hazlitt not to forget to send the American Farmer." In the simple, strong writing that is the chief characteristic of American literature of the eighteenth century the essays of Crèvecœur have a distinct place.

[The *Letters from an Am. Farmer* were published in London in 1782; the next year the author brought out in Paris his *Lettres d'un Cultivateur Americain*, a translation and expansion of the original essays, and in 1793 another English edition appeared, the latter republished in 1904 with preface by Wm. P. Trent and introduction by Ludwig Lewisohn. Crèvecœur's *Voyage dans la Haute Pensylvanie et dans l'État de New-York* (3 vols.) was published in Paris in 1801. In 1922, new MSS., apparently suppressed in 1782 by Crèvecœur or his publishers, were discovered by H. L. Bourdin. These appeared, with fresh introductory material, as *Sketches of Eighteenth Century America* (1925), ed. by Bourdin, R. H. Gabriel, and S. T. Williams; they form an important supplement to the volume published during Crèvecœur's lifetime. A few other essays have also appeared, ed. by Bourdin and Williams: "Crèvecœur on the Susquehanna," *Yale Rev.*, Apr. 1925; "Hospitals (During the Revolution)," *Philological Quart.*, Apr. 1926; "Crèvecœur, The Loyalist," *Nation*, Sept. 23, 1925; "Sketch of a Contrast Between the Spanish and English Colonies," *Univ. of Cal. Chronicle*, Apr. 1926. The most complete biographical study is *St. Jean de Crèvecœur* (1916), by Julia Post Mitchell. See also Robert de Crèvecœur, *Saint John de Crèvecœur, Sa Vie et Ses Ouvrages* (1883); *Cambridge Hist. of Am. Lit.* (1917), vol. I; "Unpublished MSS. of Crèvecœur," ed by H. L. Bourdin and S. T. Williams, *Studies in Philology*, July 1925, and *The Am. Farmer Returns* (by the same editors), *North Am. Rev.*, Sept. 1925.]   S. T. W.

CRIMMINS, JOHN DANIEL (May 18, 1844–Nov. 9, 1917), contractor, capitalist, was of Irish ancestry. A son of Thomas and Johanna (O'Keefe) Crimmins, he was born and grew up in New York City. His father was a well-to-do contractor, who gave his son educational advantages in addition to what were afforded by the public schools of the period. The lad was graduated at the College of St. Francis Xavier and at once entered his father's contracting business. At twenty-one he was made a member of the firm, which added building to other forms of construction. Under the son's management more than 400 buildings were erected, many of which were private dwellings, but public works continued to occupy an increasing part of the firm's attention. Most of the elevated railway mileage in New York City was built by Crimmins, and later the subways required for electric wiring in the city streets were constructed under his contracts. At times as many as 12,000 men were in his employ at once. Practically all the work that he did was under contracts made with corporations, estates, and individuals, on a percentage basis. His firm did not seek city or county contracts. He was the first to make use of steam drills in excavation work in New York. The fact that he was a large employer of labor, known to have been for years on good terms with his employees, caused him to be sought as an arbitrator in wage disputes. He might also have gone far in local politics if he had been inclined to that kind of career. In 1883–88 he served as Park Commissioner for the city. He was a member of the state constitutional convention of 1894, and was appointed by Gov. Roosevelt a member of the Greater New York Charter Revision Commission. Distinction came to him also as a Roman Catholic layman. He gave generously of his wealth to religious and charitable institutions, and for services to the Church was made a Knight Commander of the Order of St. Gregory by Pope Leo XIII, and a count by Pope Pius X. All his life interested in the history of the Irish people in America, Crimmins, as a member of the American-Irish Historical Society, the Friendly Sons of St. Patrick, and other organizations, sought to popularize a knowledge of that history. His two books, *St. Patrick's Day: Its Celebration in New York and Other American Places, 1737–1845* (1902) and *Irish-American Historical Miscellany* (1905), contain much information not easily to be obtained elsewhere. His zeal in these researches led him to engage in the collection of books and manuscripts on a large scale. At the same time he became purchaser of rare works of art. In 1868 Crimmins married Lily Louise Lalor (like himself of Irish parentage), who bore him eleven children. She died in 1888.

[The *Diary of John D. Crimmins from 1878 to 1917* (privately printed, 1925); *Who's Who in America*, 1916–17; *N. Y. Times*, Nov. 10, 1917.]   W. B. S.

CRISP, CHARLES FREDERICK (Jan. 29, 1845–Oct. 23, 1896), congressman, was the son of William and Elizabeth Crisp, natives of England. They had become American citizens, but were on a visit to England when Charles was born at Sheffield. During his early infancy they removed to Georgia. The Crisps were theatrical people, playing for the most part Shakespearian rôles. William Crisp owned theatres in various parts of the South. Charles seems to have had no formal education except such as was afforded in the public schools of Macon and Savannah. While he was yet a boy the Civil War began, and at sixteen he was at the front. He became a lieutenant in Company K, 10th Virginia Infantry, fought three years in the Confederate army, and passed one year as a prisoner at Morris Island. Released from prison in June 1865, he returned to his old home in Ellaville, Schley County, Ga., and began to study law. He was then twenty years of age, but four years of war had made a man of him. He was admitted to the bar and settled at Americus, an important town in southwest Georgia. In 1872 he was appointed solicitor-general of the southwestern superior court circuit and after five years was elevated to the bench. This position he was holding in 1882 when he resigned to accept the Democratic nomination for Congress. He was elected and entered the Forty-eighth Congress, serving from Mar. 4, 1883, until his death.

On entering Congress, Crisp devoted himself to mastering the rules and methods of procedure. He came to be regarded as an exceptionally able parliamentarian. When John G. Carlisle of Kentucky, went into the Senate, Crisp became the Democratic leader of the House, and, when the control of the House passed in 1891 to the Democrats, he was elected speaker. He held this post through the Fifty-second and Fifty-third Congresses (1891–95). His rise to the leadership of his party in Congress and to the speakership was due, as one of his colleagues put it, to the "sheer force of his remarkable fitness." Perhaps the most important legislation with which Crisp was concerned was the Interstate Commerce Act of 1887. It chanced that the chairman of the committee in charge of this bill was away from Congress and that the burden of championing it fell upon Crisp. He, along with another Georgian, Judson C. Clements, deserves a large measure of credit for the passage of the bill. He was a leader of the silverites, advocating the Sherman Act of 1890 which provided for a limited coinage of silver, and in 1896 announcing his candidacy for the Senate on a free-silver platform. A series of four debates in important Georgia towns was arranged between Crisp and Hoke Smith, another prominent Georgian, and at the time secretary of the interior in Cleveland's cabinet, who stood with the President in his fight to maintain the gold standard. Smith was not a candidate for office, but felt it incumbent upon him to defend the administration in Georgia. The debates occurred early in the summer of 1896 before the meeting of the state Democratic Convention in June and before the nomination of Bryan in Chicago. Georgia, like other agricultural states, was a debtor community and swallowed eagerly the arguments of the inflationists. Public sentiment was, therefore, with Crisp, and he was regarded as having had the better of the contest. The Democratic state convention which met shortly after

the debates indorsed free silver. A silver legislature was elected in the autumn and Crisp would unquestionably have been elected to the Senate but for his untimely death in October of that year. A seat in the United States Senate had been his highest ambition. Once before the opportunity had presented itself, when, on the death of Senator Alfred H. Colquitt [q.v.], Gov. Northen tendered Crisp the post. But at that time his sense of public duty did not permit him to resign the speakership of the House.

Crisp is generally regarded as among the two or three ablest Georgia congressmen since the Civil War. Rising from obscurity, without the advantages of wealth, education, or family influence, he attained eminence through the force of his own ability, character, and efforts. He had a commanding physical appearance, was a convincing speaker, ranks as one of our greatest parliamentarians; and, personally, he won and retained the respect and affection of his colleagues of both parties in Congress. In 1867 he married Clara Belle Burton of Ellaville, Ga.

[This sketch of Crisp's life has been based principally on information supplied by his son, Chas. R. Crisp, who succeeded him in the House of Representatives. A volume of *Memorial Addresses* published by order of Congress in 1897, contains a number of important estimates of Crisp's personal character and work as member and speaker of the House. The debate with Hoke Smith is described in L. L. Knight, *Ga. and Georgians* (1917), II, 999. See also L. L. Knight, *Reminiscences of Famous Georgians* (1908), II, 380–91.]   R. P. B.

CRITTENDEN, GEORGE BIBB (Mar. 20, 1812–Nov. 27, 1880), soldier, eldest son of John Jordan Crittenden [q.v.] and Sally (Lee) Crittenden, was born in Russellville, Logan County, Ky., whither his father had recently moved to take advantage of the prosperity that had come to this part of the state with the opening of new lands. George B. Crittenden was graduated from West Point in 1832, and as brevet second lieutenant saw his first service in the Black Hawk War. He was later stationed at Augusta, Ga., and in Alabama, but as the drab existence at army posts did not appeal to his rather restless nature, he resigned from the army in 1833 to study law. He began under his father, then continued his studies at Transylvania University in Lexington. The law, however, ultimately proved less attractive than the army, especially in view of the excitement then prevailing on the Southwestern border. In 1842 Crittenden decided to cast in his lot with the Texans. In 1843 he enlisted with Col. William Fisher's forces which crossed the Rio Grande and rashly attacked the village of Mier. The small army was soon overwhelmed and captured, and, after an unsuccessful attempt to escape, the prisoners were commanded to draw lots in order to determine which one out of every ten men should be executed. Crittenden was fortunate enough to draw two white beans, the first of which he gave to a fellow Kentuckian, and was carried prisoner to Mexico City. He was later freed through the efforts of Daniel Webster and Waddy Thompson, the American minister to Mexico.

Crittenden returned to Kentucky and on the outbreak of the Mexican War in 1846 volunteered and was made captain of a company of mounted rifles. For bravery at Contreras and Churubusco he was made brevet major, and was promoted full major in 1848. After peace he chose to remain in the army. He was sent to the frontier, and in 1856 was promoted lieutenant-colonel. In June 1861, when the dangers of civil war were upon the country, he resigned from the army in the Territory of New Mexico and returned to Kentucky. Against his father's views he joined the Confederate army, and was made a brigadier-general. In January 1862 he attacked at Mill Springs, Ky., a Federal force much larger than his own and was badly defeated, losing his wagon train and most of his artillery. For his rashness he was put under arrest and later censured. He now resigned his commission, but his heart was with the South, and, though he had a brother, Thomas Leonidas [q.v.], in the Federal army, he joined the Confederate forces again and served without rank for the rest of the war, on the staff of Gen. J. S. Williams. After the war he returned to Kentucky and resided in Frankfort. His bravery and loyalty to the South were soon recognized by a state that had become converted to the Confederacy after the war had ended. In 1867 he was appointed state librarian and continued in that position until 1874. He died in Danville and was buried beside his distinguished father in the Frankfort cemetery.

[R. H. and L. Collins, *Hist. of Ky.* (1874), vol. I; Mrs. C. Coleman, *Life of John J. Crittenden* (1871); *Ky. Gazette*, Dec. 4, 1880; *Battles and Leaders of the Civil War* (1887–88); *Official Records (Army)*, 1 ser., vols. IV, VII, XVII (pt. 2), XXX (pt. 4), XXVII (pt. 1), XXXIX (pt. 2), LI (pt. 2), LII (pt. 2); 2 ser., vol. I; 4 ser., vol. I.]   E. M. C.

CRITTENDEN, JOHN JORDAN (Sept. 10, 1787–July 26, 1863), lawyer, statesman, one of the four sons of John and Judith (Harris) Crittenden, was of Welsh descent on his father's side and of French Huguenot descent on his mother's. His father, a major in the Revolution, the year after the treaty of peace was signed emigrated to Kentucky, settling in Woodford County. Here, near Versailles, John J. Crittenden was born. He was sent to Jessamine County in 1803–04 to be prepared for college, having as school-mates

John C. Breckinridge and Francis P. Blair, Sr. [qq.v.]. He early developed a liking for the law and began its study with George M. Bibb, living in his home at the time. Finishing his course at William and Mary College in 1807, he returned to Woodford County where he first began his practise. Central Kentucky was well supplied with excellent lawyers, however, and Crittenden left for the recently opened western part of the state, settling at Russellville in Logan County. He soon became the best-known lawyer in that section, and in 1809 was appointed attorney-general for the Illinois Territory, holding the position for a year. The approach of the second war with Great Britain led him into military service. He was aide-de-camp to Gen. Sam Hopkins in some operations against the Indians; then (1812) he was appointed by Gov. Charles Scott to a similar position in the 1st Kentucky Militia. In 1813 he was appointed aide-de-camp to Gov. Isaac Shelby and was present at the battle of the Thames, receiving the special commendation of the governor for his faithfulness in carrying out orders.

Crittenden's war service was coincident with the beginning of his political career. In 1811 he was elected to the legislature to represent Logan County, and was reëlected successively six times, being chosen speaker of the House in 1815 and 1816. When in 1817 a vacancy in the United States Senate developed, he was chosen to complete the term. He took an active part in the affairs of the Senate, assuming early his life-long rôle of champion of the downtrodden and defenseless, but left the Senate at the expiration of his term in 1819, believing that his interests and greatest happiness lay in Kentucky, where his private fortune was yet to be made. During the next sixteen years his activities were identified entirely with Kentucky, and it is probable that this was the happiest period of his life. He removed to Frankfort, where his business before the courts could best be served, and here and in the surrounding counties his name became associated with many important trials. He was generally engaged by the defense and generally won his case. He was always in great demand for the defense in murder trials. One of his first public services after returning from the Senate was in connection with the boundary dispute between Kentucky and Tennessee. In 1820 he and John Rowan were appointed to treat with the latter state, but the negotiations failed, principally because the two Kentucky commissioners could not agree. The radical developments that had their climax in the Old and New Court struggle aroused Crittenden's conservative character, and espousing the Old Court, he ran for the legislature in 1825. He was defeated by Solomon P. Sharp, whose assassination on the eve of the meeting of the legislature necessitated a new election. Crittenden ran again and won. Four years later he was elected again and was reëlected successively for the next three terms. Throughout these four years (1829–32) he was speaker of the House, and three times he was elected without opposition.

The presidential election of 1824 saw the beginning of Crittenden's active support of Henry Clay, which was to continue for the next quarter of a century. After Clay had been eliminated and the election had gone to the House of Representatives, Crittenden favored Jackson, though in no decided fashion. On the election of Adams he became the President's staunch supporter and received as a reward (1827) the appointment of United States district attorney for Kentucky. Knowing that Crittenden would be removed by President Jackson in 1829, the former's friends persuaded Adams to nominate him for the United States Supreme Court, but a majority of the Senate, supporting Jackson, refused to let the nomination come up for ratification before Mar. 4, 1829, and so the appointment was never made. When Jackson became president he promptly dismissed Crittenden from the district-attorneyship. In 1834 Crittenden became secretary of state of Kentucky under Gov. James T. Morehead.

In 1835 he was again elected to the United States Senate for a full term of six years, and for the remainder of his life he remained a national figure, being connected with the federal government in some capacity almost all the time. In the Senate he opposed Jackson's bank policy and Van Buren's financial schemes; and in the campaign of 1840 he spoke from one end of Kentucky to the other in favor of Harrison, whom he affectionately referred to in his correspondence as "Old Tip." In December 1840 the Kentucky legislature reëlected Crittenden to the Senate, but he soon resigned to accept from President Harrison the position of attorney-general. Immediately on assuming office he was sent to New York despite his protests, to aid the federal government in preventing a breach with Great Britain over the McLeod trial. He saw Gov. William H. Seward and secured from him a promise to pardon McLeod immediately if he should be convicted. This was Crittenden's only service of note as attorney-general and he insisted that it was an encroachment upon the duties of the secretary of state. Harrison's death one month after he had assumed the presidency placed at the head of the government John Tyler, whose refusal to support the Whig bank policy brought confusion to the party. Unable to agree with Tyler, Crittenden resigned on Sept. 11, 1841, together with all the other members of the cabinet excepting Webster.

Having given up a six years' term in the Senate to serve his party, Crittenden now after six months was left without an office. On his return to Kentucky he was welcomed at a public dinner at Maysville. His Woodford County friends, mindful that his private fortune had dwindled during his public service, bought at a cost of $17,000 the farm on which he had been born, and presented it to him. Kentucky elected him to the Senate again in 1842, to fill the position Clay had resigned, and he was reëlected for the full term beginning Mar. 4, 1843. He now took a prominent part in the discussions on the Texan and Mexican question and on the Oregon boundary dispute. While earlier he had rejoiced to see Texas win her independence, he now strongly opposed her admission into the Union. He was equally opposed to forcing the issue with Great Britain on the Oregon question. Later when the joint occupation agreement was repealed, he insisted that England be given at least two years' notice. In this instance as well as in all other dealings with foreign nations he stood for a conservative, peaceful course of action.

In the campaign of 1844 he loyally supported Clay and stood with him against the annexation of Texas. On the defeat of the Whigs, Crittenden opposed the joint resolution admitting Texas into the Union. Shortly thereafter when Gen. Taylor was attacked by the Mexicans on the Rio Grande and President Polk asked for a declaration of war, Crittenden was skeptical as to the justice of the cause of the United States. Having long stood for peace and friendship with Mexico and South America he saw in this war a great calamity. When his government entered the struggle he was willing to support it with men and money, but he wished to send commissioners along with the army to offer peace with every blow. Throughout the war he kept up a voluminous correspondence with Gen. Taylor on military affairs, now and then interspersed with political matters. As early as 1847 presidential candidates were being discussed. Some of Crittenden's friends suggested his own name but he received the idea coolly, and led Taylor on in his ambitions to secure the Whig nomination. Clay, he was sure, could not possibly be elected if nominated, but he felt that Taylor might win. Clay, hearing of Crittenden's stand, wrote him in September 1847 for an avowal of his position, and received a confirmation of it. Thereafter Clay never communicated with Crittenden until reconciliation came on the former's deathbed. Crittenden felt very keenly the loss of this long-standing and cherished friendship. Taylor after his election visited Frankfort and offered Crittenden his choice of the cabinet positions, none of which he accepted, refusing largely out of respect for Clay's feelings.

In the meantime Crittenden had in 1848 resigned from the Senate to run for governor of Kentucky, believing that only with his assistance could the Whigs carry the state. In November he won Kentucky for Taylor and was himself elected. In less than a year Taylor died, and Fillmore on assuming the presidency offered Crittenden the post of attorney-general, which he now accepted. During an illness of Webster in 1851 he acted as secretary of state. At the end of Fillmore's term Crittenden returned to Kentucky to resume his law practise, but in January 1854 he was elected again to the United States Senate. He saw with much concern the country torn over the slavery question and drifting toward war. He had always, with Clay, been actuated by the hope that slavery might eventually disappear, and had in 1836 been one of the vice-presidents of an anti-slavery society which James G. Birney was promoting. But he at no time embraced the abolition cause or showed patience with abolitionists. He decried the reopening of the slavery debate in the Kansas-Nebraska Bill and felt that a great mistake had been made when the Missouri Compromise was superseded. He opposed the Topeka constitution as irregular and held the Lecompton constitution to be a fraud. He believed that the South could not wish to lend its support to statehood for Kansas, since that would inevitably increase the Northern majority in Congress. He stood for any course of action that would bring peace and compose the slavery turmoil. His position on slavery in the territories was one of congressional non-intervention. With the downfall of the Whig party he came out in support of the Know-Nothings, advocating restriction of the privileges of aliens, especially with regard to their rights to the public lands. In the presidential election of 1860 he supported the Bell and Everett ticket, although he had entertained a good opinion of Douglas since his refusal to support the Lecompton constitution.

Perhaps the most solemn and the greatest effort of Crittenden's life came during his last three years. The Union had always been almost a passion with him, and as governor in 1848 he had said, "The dissolution of the Union can never be regarded—ought never to be regarded—as a *remedy,* but as the *consummation of the greatest evil than can befall us"* (Coleman, *post,* I, 333). The excitement over Lincoln's election produced melancholy forebodings in him. In Buchanan's message to Congress in December 1860 he saw some hope of a solution, though he did not agree with the President that there was no power in the national government to deal with the seceded states. In December he introduced in the Senate the famous "Crittenden propositions," restoring by constitutional amendment the Missouri Compromise line and guaranteeing the protection of slavery in the District of Columbia against congressional action. He saw his compromise defeated in the Committee of Thirteen, and he saw with bewildered amazement the uncompromising attitude of radical senators whose course he believed would deliberately destroy the Union. He even found great difficulty in getting the opportunity to present petitions to the Senate favoring the compromise measures. On Jan. 3, 1861, he introduced a resolution calling for a referendum on his propositions, feeling, as many have felt since, that his compromise would have been overwhelmingly supported by a popular vote. Later he sought to secure the adoption of the program of the Washington Peace Conference, but failed utterly.

Finding himself checked by a determined group of hostile radicals in Congress, he returned to Kentucky to keep his native state from seceding. On Mar. 26, 1861, he addressed the legislature and sought to show the utter folly of leaving the protection of the federal Union to join the weak and untried government of the Confederacy. On Apr. 17, five days after the Fort Sumter bombardment, almost dazed by the quick war movements, he made an address in Lexington in which he still counselled Kentucky to remain in the Union and to refuse to take part in a war she had neither promoted nor desired, but had tried to avert. This was the neutrality which the state adopted a month later. He was a member of the futile conference, May 10, between three Bell and Douglas representatives and three Breckinridge men to decide on some course of united action for Kentucky. On May 4 he was elected a delegate to a Border Slave State convention which met in Frankfort on May 27 and was made chairman. The convention called upon the seceded states to reëxamine their position, and counselled moderation on the part of the North.

In June, Crittenden was elected to the special session of Congress meeting in July. Having failed to prevent the war, he now as a member of the House gave all of his efforts to controlling its purpose. On July 19 he introduced resolutions declaring that the war was not for the conquest or subjugation of the South or to interfere with the established institutions of a state, but "to defend and maintain the supremacy of the Constitution, and to preserve the Union with all the dignity, equality, and rights of the several states unimpaired." He measured the subsequent acts of the Federal government by this standard and soon found many things of which he could not approve. He opposed the dismemberment of Virginia, the confiscation acts, the enlistment of negro troops, the Emancipation Proclamation, and the military régime in his native state, which was bringing about arrests, banishments, and interference with courts, elections, and trade. He was preparing to run for reëlection to Congress when he died in Frankfort in 1863, not yet completely divorced from his sympathy for the national government.

Crittenden was married three times: first, in 1811, to Sally O. Lee, a daughter of Maj. John Lee of Woodford County; second, in 1826, to Mrs. Maria K. Todd, a daughter of Judge "Hary" Innes; and third, in 1853, to Mrs. Elizabeth Ashley, who survived him. He had altogether five sons and four daughters. In the Civil War one son, George B. Crittenden [q.v.], joined the Confederacy, to his father's great sorrow, and another, Thomas L. [q.v.], became a major-general in the Federal army.

Crittenden was never a profound lawyer, but he was one of Kentucky's greatest advocates at the bar. He loved political activities, was intensely honest in his opinions and dealings with people, and had feelings so tender that he could never forgive himself for offending a friend or losing one.

[The records of Crittenden's life are voluminous. Besides the contemporary material in newspapers and in official sources, the Crittenden Papers are in the Lib. of Cong. No critical life of Crittenden has been written, but Mrs. C. Coleman, *The Life of John J. Crittenden* (2 vols., 1871), is a valuable source. Short sketches may be found in R. H. and L. Collins, *Hist. of Ky.* (1874); and in *Lawyers and Lawmakers of Ky.* (1897), ed. by H. Levin; R. M. McElroy, *Ky. in the Nation's Hist.* (1909), is also valuable.]

E. M. C.

CRITTENDEN, THOMAS LEONIDAS (May 15, 1819–Oct. 23, 1893), lawyer, soldier, was the second son of John Jordan Crittenden [q.v.] and Sally (Lee) Crittenden, and a brother of George B. Crittenden [q.v.]. He was born in Russellville, Logan County, Ky., received an education as good as could be obtained outside of a college, and early began the study of law under his eminent father. He was admitted to the bar in 1840 and two years later was elected commonwealth's attorney for his district. At the outbreak of the Mexican War he enlisted, was appointed aide to Gen. Zachary Taylor, a kinsman, and was present at the battle of Buena Vista. A few months later when the 3rd Kentucky Infantry was organized he was made its colonel, with John C. Breckinridge [q.v.] serving as a major under him. He was mustered out of the service in 1848. When Taylor became president he appointed Crittenden consul at Liverpool, where the latter remained until 1853, in that year returning to Kentucky to begin the practise of law in Frankfort. After a few years he removed to Louisville and became a merchant.

When the state's militia laws were reorganized in 1860 and the state guards were set up under the control of Simon B. Buckner [q.v.], Crittenden was commissioned major-general. Following in the footsteps of his father, he opposed secession, and, on Sept. 18, after Buckner had led most of the state guards to the Confederacy, was given command of the state forces. The Kentucky troops were soon mustered into the Federal service, however, and Crittenden joined the Union army, being made a brigadier-general on Oct. 27, 1861. He commanded a unit in the march south through Kentucky and in the invasion of Tennessee. He especially distinguished himself at Shiloh, for which service he was promoted major-general. He was with Rosecrans at Murfreesboro and at Chickamauga, commanding the left wing in the former battle and the 21st Army Corps in the latter. At Chickamauga he was driven back after having weakened his forces to reënforce Gen. Thomas. He was relieved of his command and his conduct investigated. On Dec. 14, 1863 the Kentucky legislature demanded of President Lincoln a rehearing. In February following, Crittenden was honorably acquitted by a court of inquiry at Louisville. He was now transferred to the Army of the Potomac in Virginia and on Dec. 13, 1864 resigned from the service.

In January 1866 he was appointed state treasurer for Kentucky but on Nov. 15, 1867, having been offered a colonelcy by President Johnson, he resigned his civil office to reënter the army. He was stationed at various posts in the West, and finally at Governors Island where he remained until he was retired in 1881. He died at Annandale on Staten Island, twelve years later, and was buried in the Frankfort cemetery. He married Kittie Todd of Frankfort.

[R. H. and L. Collins, *Hist. of Ky.* (1874), vol. I; Mrs. C. Coleman, *Life of John J. Crittenden* (1871), vol. I; and *Morning Transcript* (Lexington, Ky.), Oct. 24, 1893; John Fitch, *Annals of the Army of the Cumberland* (1864); Thos. Speed, R. M. Kelly, and A. Pirtle, *Union Regiments of Ky.* (1897); *Battles and Leaders of the Civil War* (1887–88), vols. I, III, IV· *Official Records (Army)*.]

E. M. C.

CRITTENDEN, THOMAS THEODORE

(Jan. 1, 1832–May 29, 1909), governor of Missouri, was born near Shelbyville in Shelby County, Ky. His father, Henry Crittenden, was a younger brother of John Jordan Crittenden [q.v.]. His mother, Anna M. (Allen) Crittenden, was the daughter of John Allen, an eminent Kentucky lawyer. Young Crittenden received such education in the elementary branches as the schools of the country afforded and in 1852 entered Centre College at Danville, Ky., from which institution he graduated in 1855. He then studied law in the office of his uncle, John J. Crittenden, at Frankfort, and was admitted to practise in 1856. In the fall of the same year, he was married to Carrie W. Jackson, a lady of charming accomplishments, daughter of Samuel Jackson of Kentucky. Crittenden removed to Missouri in the summer of 1857, settled at Lexington in Lafayette County, formed a law partnership with Judge John A. S. Tutt, and very soon attained an active and lucrative practise. Early in the Civil War he entered the Union service and was appointed by Gov. Gamble to be lieutenant-colonel of the 7th Regiment of the Missouri State Militia, a cavalry regiment commanded by Col. John F. Philips. This regiment performed much valuable service and did good fighting in Missouri and Arkansas. Crittenden served to the end of the war and was honorably discharged in 1865. He had already been appointed attorney-general of Missouri by Gov. Hall to fill the vacancy caused by the death of Aikman Welch in 1864. At the close of the war he returned to civil life and formed a partnership with Francis Marion Cockrell [q.v.] for the practise of law at Warrensburg. This partnership existed until Crittenden was elected to the United States Congress from the 7th Missouri congressional district in 1872. He served one term, but in 1874 after 690 ballots he was defeated for renomination by his old military associate, Col. John F. Philips. In 1876 Crittenden received the nomination without solicitation on his part and was elected by the largest Democratic majority ever given in the 7th district. In 1880 he secured the nomination for governor on the Democratic ticket, and in the election defeated the Republican candidate, David P. Dyer, by a plurality of 54,034. The most memorable act of his administration was the institution by the State of Missouri of the suit against the Hannibal & St. Joseph Railroad for the payment, with interest, of the $3,000,000 loaned to that road in 1851 and 1855. The suit was settled in favor of the state, and the road paid the claim in full with accrued interest. Crittenden was persis-

tent in his efforts to suppress outlawry, and succeeded in ridding Missouri of the notorious Jesse James [q.v.] and in breaking up the James gang. During the second administration of President Cleveland, he was appointed consul-general to Mexico. At the time of his death in Kansas City, May 29, 1909, he was referee in bankruptcy for the United States district court. He was a man possessed of an unusually cheerful and genial disposition. In politics he was a Democrat of the conservative type, and in religious belief a Presbyterian of the old school. In Congress he was a conspicuous figure and made friends among the leading politicians. As governor, he was distinguished by his positive and aggressive spirit.

[W. B. Davis and D. S. Durrie, *An Illustrated Hist. of Mo.* (1876); *The Bench and Bar of St. Louis, Kansas City, Jefferson City, and Other Mo. Cities* (1884); *Messages and Proclamations of the Govs. of the State of Mo.*, vol. VI (1924); *Centennial Hist. of Mo.* (1921), vol. III; *Mo. Hist. Rev.*, July 1909; *Kansas City Star*, May 29, and *St. Louis Republic*, May 30, 1909.]

F. C. S—r.

CRITTENTON, CHARLES NELSON

(Feb. 20, 1833–Nov. 16, 1909), "Merchant Evangelist," founder of the Florence Crittenton Missions, was of English and Welsh ancestry, the son of Harvey and Phœbe (Matteson) Crittenton. Born and brought up on a farm in Henderson, Jefferson County, N. Y., he was educated in the common schools, and began his business career as a clerk in the village store. When twenty-one years old he went to New York to make his fortune, and succeeded. First he was office boy for an undertaker, the sexton of St. George's Church; then bookkeeper, cashier, and salesman for W. H. Dunham, later being taken into the firm, which was known as Dunham, Crittenton & Company. In 1861 he withdrew and with sixty dollars capital started a drug business in a little back room on Sixth Ave. Ultimately this became the Charles N. Crittenton Company, capitalized at $800,000. In 1859 he married Josephine Slosson of Lawrenceville, Pa. With his wife he was confirmed in St. Clement's Episcopal Church in 1874, but did not "experience conversion" until after the death of his four-year-old daughter Florence in 1882. Almost immediately he became active in evangelistic and mission work, especially in rescue work for women, and soon retired as the active head of his business in order to give all his time to service. With others he formed an organization for saving unfortunate women, named after his daughter the Florence Mission, which opened at 27 Bleecker St., Apr. 19, 1883. Similar institutions were started elsewhere, so that at the time of his death there were more than sixty in this country and five abroad. In 1895 they were combined under the charter of the corporation known as The National Florence Crittenton Mission, of which he was president until his death. He traveled about continually, visiting these missions and engaging in evangelistic activities, using for a time a special car which he purchased, named the "Good News." His death occurred in a hotel at San Francisco, and he was buried in Woodlawn Cemetery, New York. He left one-half of his estate to the work to which he had previously given liberally of his income. His autobiography, entitled *The Brother of Girls* (1910), reveals a shrewd business man, rather well satisfied with himself, limited in outlook and interests, emotional, sentimental, of naïve religious faith, entirely governed in his later years by the evangelistic motive. Through the work he started, which has continued, his influence has been important and extensive.

[In addition to the autobiography, see *Girls,* the official organ of the National Florence Crittenton Mission, Dec. 1909, Jan. 1910, and obituary notices in the *San Francisco Chronicle* and *N. Y. Times* for Nov. 17, 1909.]   H. E. S.

CROCKER, ALVAH (Oct. 14, 1801–Dec. 26, 1874), manufacturer, politician, and railroad builder, was born in Leominster, Mass., the oldest son of Samuel and Comfort (Jones) Crocker. Both parents were intensely religious; they had been founders of the Baptist church in Leominster, and their seven sons were reared in the strictest traditions of New England Puritanism. As the family was large and the income small, Alvah was put to work in a paper-mill at the age of eight where he worked twelve hours daily at twenty-five cents a day. His schooling was scanty, but was supplemented by wide reading and by a short period at Groton Academy during his sixteenth year. Having given up hope of attending college, he went to work in 1820 in a paper-mill at Franklin, N. H. Removing to Fitchburg, Mass., in 1823, he worked for a while in the mill of Gen. Leonard Burbank. In 1826 he managed to borrow sufficient capital to start paper-manufacturing on his own account. His early years as a manufacturer were hard ones, but unfailing optimism and unremitting toil enabled him so to establish his factory that his business continued to grow even when his own energies were largely consumed in politics and railroad building. Increasing pressure of other affairs led him in 1850 to take in Gardner S. Burbank as his partner, and to reorganize his paper-factory as Crocker, Burbank & Company. This firm expanded rapidly until it became one of the largest paper-manufacturing

concerns in New England. In addition to manufacturing paper Crocker at one time owned a chain factory and a machine-shop (both destroyed by fire in 1849). In 1847 he was prominent in establishing the Fitchburg Mutual Fire Insurance Company; he was on the first board of directors of the Rollstone Bank, and was a trustee of the Fitchburg Savings Bank from 1851 until his death. Perhaps his most significant contribution as a manufacturer was his organization of the Turners Falls Company in 1866 which set itself to develop the water-power at Turners Falls, Mass., and built there a number of mills. Until his death Crocker was a leader in the growth of that community.

He was one of the earliest of the American business men whose imaginations were fired by the possibilities of rail transportation. As a member of the legislature, as a speaker at scores of meetings, and as the leading member of the board of directors he was chiefly responsible for the building of the Fitchburg Railroad (1843–45) between Boston and Fitchburg. His dreams, however, were more inclusive, and he labored for many years to open rail communication with Canada and the West. Hardly had the last spike been driven in the Fitchburg Railroad before a charter was obtained for the Vermont & Massachusetts Railroad which Crocker, as president, built from Fitchburg to Brattleboro, Vt., between 1845 and 1849. In 1848 a bill to incorporate the Troy & Greenfield Railroad was passed. To build this railroad necessitated the tunneling of the Hoosac Mountains and a loan from the state to carry the work to completion. During all of the early stages Crocker was the leader in the movement for the western connection, and when, in 1868, the state was forced to complete the work, he became commissioner in charge.

His interest in politics was life-long. He commenced as "hog-reeve" in 1830, became "tithingman" in 1831, and after holding other local offices was elected to the General Court in 1836. He served three times in the lower house and twice in the upper, his service covering the years 1837–38 and 1842–43. Upon the resignation from Congress of William B. Washburn to become governor of Massachusetts (1872), Crocker was elected on the Republican ticket to complete his term, and was reëlected the same year to the Forty-third Congress. Past seventy when he entered Congress, he refused to be a candidate a third time. He was not only an indefatigable worker and a man of great earnestness of purpose, but a ready debater and excellent orator. A devout Christian, and a vestryman of the Episcopal Church, he left a political and business reputation of the strictest honesty. He was married three times: first, to Abigail Fox of Jaffrey, N. H., on Aug. 14, 1829; second, to Lucy A. Fay of Fitchburg, on Apr. 9, 1851; and third, to Minerva Cushing, on Oct. 20, 1872.

[Wm. Bond Wheelwright, *Life and Times of Alvah Crocker* (1923), is far from adequate biography, but contains the most complete account. There is some material in Wm. A. Emerson, *Fitchburg Past and Present* (1887), and an account of Crocker's early railroad activities in Henry A. Willis, "The Early Days of Railroads in Fitchburg," *Proc. Fitchburg Hist. Soc.,* I (1895), 27–49.]   H. U. F.

CROCKER, CHARLES (Sept. 16, 1822–Aug. 14, 1888), merchant, railroad builder, capitalist, was the son of Isaac Crocker, a merchant of Troy, N. Y., and Eliza Wright, daughter of a Massachusetts farmer, both of whom traced their lineage in this country back to the early seventeenth century. Charles Crocker had few educational advantages and at an early age began to aid his father in the support of the family. In 1836 the family moved to Marshall County, Ind., and soon afterward Crocker began to earn his own living, working first as a farm-hand, then in a sawmill, and then as an apprentice in an iron forge. In 1845 he discovered a bed of iron ore in Marshall County and established a forge under the name of Charles Crocker & Company. When gold was discovered in California this business was sold, and Crocker led a band of young men, including his two younger brothers, Clark and Henry, by the overland route to the Pacific Coast, arriving there in 1850. In 1852 he gave up mining and opened a store in Sacramento, Cal., and in October of the same year returned to Indiana for a short time and married Mary A. Deming. By 1854 he was one of the wealthiest and most prominent men in Sacramento and in 1855 was elected to the City Council. In 1860 he was elected to the state legislature and soon afterward became associated with Leland Stanford [*q.v.*], Collis P. Huntington [*q.v.*], and Mark Hopkins in the building of the Central Pacific Railroad across the Sierra Nevada Mountains to connect with the Union Pacific Railroad then being constructed westward from Omaha, Nebr. Crocker had charge of the actual work of construction, leaving the problems of financing and general policy to his associates. A man of tremendous energy whose strongest point lay in the supervision of large groups, Crocker was well fitted for the task. He lived in the construction camps, faring no better than his men, and seldom left them except on pressing business. He was constantly moving up and down in the line guiding the operations of the army of contractors and their workers. Under his supervision, records for railroad building were established which have never been equaled since. At one time construction averaged three miles per day through rough country. Only a man of extraordinary physique could have endured the great strain without rest or recreation, but Crocker had a constitution of iron without nerves. The work on the Central Pacific was begun on Feb. 22, 1863 and completed on May 10, 1869. During this period Crocker had charge of the construction, and he was president of the Contract and Finance Company until 1869. It was through his efforts that the road was completed seven years ahead of the time allowed by the United States government. In 1871 he was elected president of the Southern Pacific Railroad of California, the construction of which he personally supervised. In 1884 he effected the consolidation of the Central and Southern Pacific roads and later took an active interest in the construction of the California and Oregon road between San Francisco and Portland. In addition to his railroad interests Crocker was concerned in real estate, in banking and in industrial properties throughout the state of California. He was also much interested in the development of various irrigation projects. After the success of the Central Pacific Railroad became certain, he built in San Francisco a mansion said to have cost $1,500,000 with the furnishings. This was long one of the show places of the city, but was destroyed in the fire of 1906. Later a home was also established in New York City. Despite his success Crocker always remained a plain man with simple tastes and was domestic by choice. In 1886 he was seriously injured when thrown from his carriage while driving in New York City and never really recovered his health. He died in Monterey, Cal., and was survived by his wife, three sons, and a daughter. His fortune was estimated at $40,000,000.

[A. Phelps, *Contemporary Biog. of California's Representative Men* (1881), I, 57–61; H. H. Bancroft, *Chronicles of the Builders of the Commonwealth* (1892), VI, 33–69; H. H. Bancroft, *Hist. of Cal.* (1890), VII, 533, 544, 546, 549–50; R. D. Hunt, *Cal. and Californians* (1926), III, 110–11; Z. S. Eldredge, *Hist. of Cal.* (1915), IV, 277–79, 290–91, 454; S. Daggett, *Hist. of the Southern Pacific* (1922), *passim*. The Bancroft Lib. of the Univ. of Cal. possesses considerable material on Crocker, referred to as "Crocker MSS." Obituary notices were published in the N. Y. and San Francisco papers of Aug. 15, and in the *Railroad Gazette* of Aug. 17, 1888. For the Senate investigation of the business methods of Crocker, Huntington, and Stanford, among others, see *Senate Ex. Doc. No. 51,* 50 Cong., 1 Sess.]   J. H. F.

CROCKER, FRANCIS BACON (July 4, 1861–July 9, 1921), electrical engineer, the son of Henry Horace and Anne (Eldredge) Crocker, was born in New York City. He was graduated in 1882 from the School of Mines at Columbia University, and later received the degree of Ph.D. In 1883 with Charles G. Curtis, Crocker formed the firm of Curtis & Crocker, patent attorneys and patent experts. In 1886 the two partners established the C. & C. Electric Motor Company, from which Crocker resigned two years later to join Schuyler S. Wheeler in the formation of the Crocker-Wheeler Company, of which he remained a director throughout his life. His brilliant work in his design of electric motors and the arc furnace and in the chemistry of the primary battery, at a time when these were virgin subjects, resulted in his selection by Columbia University to create and take charge of the department of electrical engineering. He remained in that work for twenty years, poor health alone causing him to retire. His directorship of the department was so successful that many of the technical schools of the United States in the organization of their electrical engineering departments followed the program first mapped out by Crocker at Columbia.

Crocker's most important contribution to the electrical industry was the creation with Charles G. Curtis and Schuyler S. Wheeler of the commercial motor of standard specification, the first of which was put into use in 1886 and which was the forerunner of all the motors now in use. Of this motor Dr. M. I. Pupin said, "It was a wonder of efficiency for those days and for the size of the motor. It is the earliest monument to Crocker's life-long faith that empiricism has no place in the art of designing electrical machinery" (*Electrical World*, July 16, 1921, p. 135). It is as "Father of American electrical standards" that Crocker will probably go down in engineering history. He was chairman of the committee of the American Institute of Electrical Engineers which drew up the original standardization rules for electrical apparatus, and chairman of the committee which revised them. He was also chairman of the conference of insurance and engineering representatives who formulated the National Electric Code. To him is credited the choice of the name "henry" for the international unit of inductance, a name he chose to honor Joseph Henry of the Smithsonian Institution. In the effort to effect complete international standardization of electrical equipment he was one of the two American delegates to the International Electrotechnical Commission in London in 1906. At its most important session he was able to insure the standardization necessary to make world-wide electrical manufacturing successful. On this occasion Lord Kelvin said of him, "He is one of the world's two greatest electrical engineers."

Crocker's writings were numerous, including many papers for the scientific and technical press as well as a two-volume treatise on electric lighting. His last contribution before his death dealt with temperature rating of motors. He had a remarkably easy, interesting, and at the same time clear and concise, method of writing, and this combined with his belief that things should not be made to appear complicated or "technical" to the public, made him much in demand as a lecturer and writer. He was probably the best known of consulting inventors. In 1897–98 he was president of the American Institute of Electrical Engineers. During the World War he was an adviser for the members of the Naval Consulting Board; he had been asked to become a member of the Board but refused because of poor health. In 1917, in company with Peter Cooper Hewitt, he developed the first helicopter in this country which was capable of flight. So important was this invention that the government took it over and was preparing to manufacture it for use in France when the Armistice was signed. Crocker's researches into the problem of curvature for airplane wings were most successful, and many of his discoveries are now in every-day application. He was a man of many friends and his life was one of constant graciousness. At his death there was an outpouring of tributes to his memory from both industrial and scientific leaders in the electrical world.

[Files and *Jour.* (Aug. 1921) of the Am. Inst. of Electrical Engineers; *Electrical World*, July 16, 1921; *Aerial Age Weekly*, July 18, 1921; *N. Y. Times*, July 11, 1921; *Engineering News-Record*, July 14, 1921; *Power*, July 19, 1921.]

K. W. C.

CROCKER, HANNAH MATHER (June 27, 1752–July 11, 1829), writer, early advocate of woman's rights, was born in Boston, the granddaughter of Cotton Mather, and the seventh child of Rev. Samuel and Hannah (Hutchinson) Mather. On Apr. 13, 1779, she became the wife of Joseph Crocker, son of Rev. Josiah Crocker of Taunton, Mass., a graduate of Harvard, and a captain in the Revolutionary War. Her entire life apparently was spent in the vicinity of Boston. As was to be expected in one of the Mather family, she had a vigorous mind, a firm will, and a keen interest in moral and social questions. Her earlier years were necessarily much taken up with domestic duties, for she was the mother of ten children, and it was not until some time after her husband's death in 1797 that any of her publications appeared. She was among the first women in this country to be conspicuously interested in Masonry, making a study of the history of the institution, and herself being matron of a lodge of women founded on its principles. Chief among the objects of this lodge was the cultivation of the mind, since at that period, she says, "If women could even read and badly write their names, it was thought enough for *them*, who by some were esteemed as only 'mere domestic animals.'" In 1810 she wrote some letters in the form of a correspondence between "Enquirer" and "A. P. Americana," in advocacy of Masonry, which at the request of Rev. Thaddeus M. Harris [*q.v.*] she published in 1815 under the title, *Series of Letters on Free Masonry, by a Lady of Boston*. The following year she published *The School of Reform, or Seaman's Safe Pilot, to the Cape of Good Hope,* a little homily addressed to sailors with some use of nautical terms, warning against intemperance and vice. In 1818 appeared her *Observations on the Real Rights of Women, with Their Appropriate Duties, Agreeable to Scripture, Reason and Common Sense*. In it she admits that owing to Eve's having first yielded to temptation, woman was put under subjection to man, though she naïvely remarks that Adam was to blame for letting his mate wander about the Garden unattended; but she argues that with the Christian dispensation woman was restored to an equality with man. Moral and physical differences in the sexes allot to each appropriate duties, and woman should not trespass upon the peculiar sphere of man, but both have equal powers of mind and ability to judge what is true and right, and recognizing this fact should cooperate in mutual respect and fidelity. Mrs. Crocker inherited most of the Mather library and family portraits and transferred them to Isaiah Thomas [*q.v.*] for the American Antiquarian Society, Worcester, Mass. At her death she was buried in the Mather tomb, Copp's Hill, Boston.

[Information regarding Mrs. Crocker, except that to be derived from her writings, is scanty. See Horace E. Mather, *Lineage of Rev. Richard Mather* (1890); *New-Eng. Hist. and Geneal. Reg.*, Jan. 1852, July 1875, July 1893; *Hist. Mag.* (N. Y.), Mar. 1865, p. 93, May 1865, p. 157. *The Diary of Isaiah Thomas, 1805–28* (1909), contains several references.]   H. E. S.

CROCKER, URIEL (Sept. 13, 1796–July 19, 1887), printer, publisher, was born at Marblehead, Mass., a son of Uriel and Mary (James) Crocker, and the third of eight children. He was graduated from the Academy at Marblehead "as first scholar" when barely fifteen. A true son of the old Massachusetts port he felt the urge to go to sea, but "None of my descendants shall go

to sea," was grandfather Capt. James's stern command. Grandfather Crocker took the lad to Harvard for the 1811 Commencement and introduced him to Samuel Parkman, in the hope that the latter would find a job for the grandson in Boston. A few weeks later Uriel was established as "printer's devil" in the office of Samuel T. Armstrong [*q.v.*], in Cornhill, Boston. For the first four years of his apprenticeship he received his board ($2.50 per week), thirty dollars a year for clothes, and twenty-five cents a thousand for all types he set up in a day in excess of 4,000. The lad's account book shows he earned in this way $180.02 in the four years, and at the end of that time he had attained such proficiency that Armstrong promoted him to be foreman of the establishment. "He told me," said Crocker, "to manage the office just the same as if it was my own, and if any of the men did not do what I told them to, I was to order them to go down stairs and get their money" (*Memorial of Uriel Crocker,* p. 32). Such was the kindly manner of the nineteen-year-old foreman that he never had "an unpleasant or unkind word" from any of his fellow apprentices. In 1818 Armstrong took Crocker and Osmyn Brewster [*q.v.*] into partnership with him, and seven years later the firm name became Crocker & Brewster. Religious books in great number bear the imprint of the firm; the "best seller" of them all was Scott's Family Bible (1824) which was the first large work in America to be printed from stereotyped plates. The undertaking was distinctly Crocker's. It required eighteen months of labor and cost $20,000. The work in six volumes retailed at twenty-four dollars. The firm published many school texts also, including Andrews's *First Lessons in Latin,* and a complete set of Latin texts by the same author.

A branch office was established in New York in 1821, but the business there suffered under a dishonest manager and was sold to Daniel Appleton [*q.v.*] and Jonathan Leavitt, a transaction which represents the start of the publishing firm of D. Appleton & Company. The first iron-lever printing-press in Boston was introduced by Crocker & Brewster, as was also the first power press. During the panic of 1837 when all other booksellers failed, Crocker & Brewster continued in business. From 1811 to 1864 the firm was situated at the same place, although the street number was changed from 50 Cornhill to 47 Washington St. Then a move was made to the adjoining building and the business continued till 1876 when the octogenarian partners sold out to Houghton & Company.

Crocker took great interest in railroad development, being a director of the Old Colony Railroad Company for many years, president of the Atlantic & Pacific Railroad Company in 1874, and a director of several other roads at different times. The variety of his interests is shown in his official connection with the Boston Dispensary, the Old South Society, the Bunker Hill Monument Association (he addressed the annual meeting of this organization, June 17, 1885, giving reminiscences of Lafayette's visit to New York and Boston in 1824), the Franklin Savings Bank, the Boston House of Correction, the United States Hotel Company, the South Bay Improvement Company, the Massachusetts Charitable Society, the Massachusetts Charitable Mechanics Association, and Mount Auburn Cemetery. Crocker's wife, whom he married on Feb. 11, 1829, was Sarah Kidder Haskell, daughter of Elias Haskell of Boston.

[*Memorial of Uriel Crocker* (1891), compiled by his son, Uriel Haskell Crocker, is the chief source of information. The book includes Crocker's reminiscences, a number of portraits and letters, a "Crocker Genealogy," and a catalogue of Crocker & Brewster publications. See also obituary in *The Publisher's Weekly*, July 23, 1887.]   A. E. P.

CROCKETT, DAVID (Aug. 17, 1786–Mar. 6, 1836), frontiersman, was the son of John and Rebecca (Hawkins) Crockett, and was born near the present Rogersville, Hawkins County, Tenn. His father, a Revolutionary soldier who fought at King's Mountain, was born either in Ireland or on the voyage to America, and his mother in northern Maryland. His parents moved (probably from Lincoln County, N. C.) to the Hawkins County location about three years before he was born, later settling on the Holston, where the father kept a tavern. Here the boy remained until about his thirteenth year. To escape an anticipated beating he ran away from home, making his way as far as Baltimore and wandering about for nearly three years. On his return he worked for six months for a neighbor to pay off a debt of $36 owed by his father, and another six months for another neighbor to cancel a similar debt of $40. At eighteen, to heighten his chances with the girl of his choice, he went to school for nearly six months, but left when he learned that he had been jilted. Some months afterward he married Polly Findlay, and on a rented tract, with a horse, his bride's dower of two cows with calves, and $15 capital borrowed from a friend, he set up a home of his own. Though a mighty hunter, he was a poor farmer, indolent and shiftless, and he did not prosper. A couple of years later, with his wife and two babies, he moved to a farm in Lincoln County, near the Alabama line. In the Creek War of 1813–14, under the command of Andrew Jackson, he served with distinction as a scout, but retired before the end of the campaign, hiring a substitute to fill out his term of enlistment.

His wife died about 1815, leaving him with three children. He acquired two more by his marriage, some months later, to the widow of a fellow-soldier. He now moved to a settlement eighty miles west, where he was informally chosen a magistrate, and on the incorporation of the district into Giles County was appointed a justice of the peace. In after years he could boast that in reaching his decisions he "relied on natural-born sense instead of law learning" and that none of his judgments was ever reversed. He was elected as colonel of a militia regiment organized in his district, and in 1821 was elected to the legislature. He was then wholly unacquainted with public affairs and did not even know the meaning of the word "judiciary." He moved again, this time to a point in the extreme western part of the state, near the junction of the Obion with the Mississippi, where his nearest neighbor was seven miles distant. Here, among other activities, he hunted bears; and unless he woefully miscounted his victims, he succeeded in killing, during a period of eight or nine months, 105 of them. His new constituency elected him to the legislature in 1823. In the spring of 1826 he attempted to float a cargo of staves down the Mississippi, losing all his cargo and nearly losing his life. A jocular proposal that he run for Congress decided him to make the race in earnest, and after a campaign enlivened by his humorous stories and the ridicule of his two opponents he was elected. He served in the Twentieth and Twenty-first Congresses (1827–31), was defeated for the Twenty-second, but was elected to the Twenty-third (1833–35). In April 1834, he commenced his celebrated "tour of the north," visiting Baltimore, Philadelphia, New York, and Boston, and, after returning to Washington, left for home to prepare for a new campaign. From the time he entered public life he had generally opposed Jackson, having voted in the legislature against him for United States senator, and later having voted against many of the Jackson measures in Congress. An effective rally of the Jackson sentiment in his district caused his defeat. Disheartened by this reverse, he resolved to leave Tennessee. The movement for Texan independence attracted him, and he started for the war front by way of Little Rock. He arrived at the Alamo in February 1836, took part in its heroic defense, and fell, bullet riddled, in the final assault.

Crockett was a brave soldier, an able scout, and an expert rifleman. He was generous and open-handed, frank and upright, of a sterling independence of spirit and blessed with a bubbling good nature and an exceptional degree of self-confidence. His knowledge of public questions, meager at the start of his career, was probably not greatly enhanced by his service in Washington. He was not a student. He rather prided himself on his lack of education—correct spelling appearing to him in the main as something "contrary to nature" and grammar "nothing at all," despite "the fuss that is made about it." To what degree the autobiographical writings published in his name were his own cannot be said; but it is noteworthy that they bear little resemblance, either in substance or manner, to such of his letters as have come down to us.

[Anon., *Sketches and Eccentricities of Col. David Crockett*, etc. (1833) ; David Crockett (?), *A Narrative of the Life of David Crockett . . . Written by Himself* (1834) ; *An Account of Col. Crockett's Tour to the North and Down East* (1834), and *Col. Crockett's Exploits and Adventures in Texas* (posthumous, 1836) being his so-called "Journal" ; "Letters of Davy Crockett," *Am. Hist. Mag.*, Jan. 1900 ; Marcus J. Wright, "Col. David Crockett of Tenn.," *Pubs. Southern Hist. Asso.*, Jan. 1897 ; *Biog. Cong. Dir.* (1928).] W. J. G—t.

CROGHAN, GEORGE (d. Aug. 31, 1782), Indian trader and agent, land speculator, was brought up as an Episcopalian near Dublin, Ireland, and migrated to Pennsylvania in 1741. His relationship to Gen. William Croghan and his son, Col. George Croghan [1791-1849, *q.v.*] is uncertain. He established a home on the frontier near Carlisle, Pa., and made it a base for his trading operations. Here his only white child, Susannah, was born in 1750. Croghan was rapidly transformed into a typical frontiersman. He learned the Delaware and Iroquois languages and had an intimate knowledge of the habits and customs of the Indians. He established trading-posts throughout the upper Ohio country; from them English influence spread among the Indians to such a degree that the French feared that a wedge would be driven between Canada and Louisiana. In the numerous Indian councils and treaties that followed, Croghan, as the representative of Pennsylvania, was the leading English agent. In 1752, the French in self-defense opened hostilities at Pickawillani, and by 1754 Croghan's business in the West was ruined and his employees and fellow traders killed or driven across the mountains. As a captain in charge of friendly Indian scouts, he assisted Washington and Braddock in their attempts to stop the French onslaught

In 1756, Sir William Johnson rewarded Croghan's restless activity and his genius for Indian negotiations by taking him into the imperial service as his deputy superintendent of Indian affairs. As such, Croghan conducted the most important and delicate negotiations with the strong and sullen tribes in the Northwest. He assisted Gen. Forbes in capturing Fort DuQuesne in 1758 and Col. Bouquet in occupying Detroit in 1760. In 1764, he was in England, supporting before the leading English officials a plan for a strong imperial Indian department and also furthering his own and others' plans to exploit western lands. Upon his return Gen. Gage and Sir William Johnson sent him upon his most famous mission, that of opening the Illinois country to English occupation. It was still ruled by the French and thither Pontiac had retreated like a lion at bay. While on the way, Croghan and his party were attacked and he himself tomahawked and taken prisoner. "I got the stroke of a Hatchet on the Head, but my skull being pretty thick, the hatchet would not enter, so you may see a thick skull is of service on some occasions," he wrote to his friend Capt. Murray. Soon, however, he was freed, met Pontiac, and made a final treaty of peace with him. In 1768 he played a prominent part in making the important treaty of Fort Stanwix. The policy of economy and of restricting the imperial Indian department caused him to lose interest in it and finally to resign in 1772. Meantime he had acquired several thousand acres of land around Carlisle, but soon sold most of his holdings at a profit and followed the advancing frontier to Pittsburgh. Here, in 1758, he built "Croghan Hall" and acquired large estates. In central New York he patented over 250,000 acres. He also purchased 200,000 acres near Pittsburgh from the Indians, but failed to perfect his title. His greatest rival here was George Washington. Between 1763 and 1775, Croghan was intimately associated with Benjamin Franklin, Sir William Franklin, Sir William Johnson, Samuel Wharton, and William Trent [*qq.v.*] in organizing western land companies. He was a member of the Indiana Company, which for years vainly tried to secure legal recognition of its grant of 2,500,-000 acres on the upper Ohio, and of the Illinois Company, which tried to secure 1,200,000 acres on the Mississippi and establish a colony there. Most promising of all, however, was his charter membership in the Grand Ohio Company which planned to establish the "fourteenth" English colony, Vandalia, south of the Ohio. The outbreak of the Revolution, however, wrecked all of Croghan's extensive land operations. His last years were spent in poverty. He was unjustly accused of being a Tory, in spite of the fact that he had served as chairman of the committee of correspondence at Pittsburgh in 1775. He died at

Passyunk, near Philadelphia, in 1782. Next to Sir William Johnson, Croghan was the most prominent English Indian agent of his time. His journals and correspondence constitute one of the chief sources for the history of the West from 1745 to 1775 and his career epitomizes it. He was one of the first Englishmen to foresee the future greatness of the wilderness beyond the Appalachians.

[Most of Croghan's journals and many of his letters are found in the *Ill. Hist. Colls.*, vols. X (1915) and XI (1916); *Pa. Archives*; *Pa. Colonial Records*; *Docs. Relative to the Colonial Hist. of the State of N. Y.*, vols. VI to IX (1855); and R. G. Thwaites, *Early Western Travels*, vol. I (1904). A. T. Volwiler, *Geo. Croghan and the Westward Movement, 1741–82* (1926), gives a full bibliography. See also C. W. Alvord, *The Miss. Valley in British Politics* (2 vols., 1917); Francis Parkman, *Conspiracy of Pontiac* (1870) and *Montcalm and Wolfe* (1884).]

A. T. V.

CROGHAN, GEORGE (Nov. 15, 1791–Jan. 8, 1849), soldier, was born near Louisville, Ky. His father, William Croghan, emigrated from Ireland, became a planter in Virginia and then in Kentucky, and made an excellent military record during the Revolution. George's mother was Lucy Clark, sister of George Rogers Clark [q.v.] and of William Clark [q.v.], one of the members of the famous Lewis and Clark expedition. Young Croghan was inspired by his illustrious relatives and read widely in history, biography, and military subjects. He graduated from William and Mary College in 1810. During the War of 1812 Croghan's family prestige, together with efficient service as a volunteer aide-de-camp in the battle of Tippecanoe, led Gen. William Henry Harrison to recommend his appointment as captain in the regular army, even though he was barely twenty-one. His excellent record in the defense of Fort Defiance and Fort Meigs caused Harrison to give him command of Fort Stephenson in northern Ohio. Here on Aug. 1, 1813, with 160 men and only one cannon, this youth successfully defended himself with great skill and gallantry against Gen. Proctor with an overwhelming force of British and Indians. Though the event had no great military significance (Harrison had wisely planned to abandon the fort before the attack), it touched the imagination and thrilled the hearts of the American people at a time when disgraceful incompetency, defeat, and surrender alone filled the newspapers. It was a fit prelude to Perry's victory and the battle of the Thames. Presents were showered on Croghan; he was brevetted lieutenant-colonel and Congress tardily awarded him a gold medal in 1835. Except for the few days at Fort Stephenson his life was commonplace and uneventful. In May 1816 he married Serena Livingston, a daughter of John R. Liv-ingston and a member of the famous Livingston family of New York. He served as postmaster at New Orleans in 1824, and very ably as inspector-general in the regular army. Drink ruined many of his later years. He served under Taylor in the Mexican War and died of cholera at New Orleans in 1849.

["Life of Col. Croghan," by a contemporary, in the *Port Folio* (Phila.), Mar. 1815, pp. 212–20; Official records of the U. S. War Department; C. R. Williams, "Geo. Croghan," in *Ohio. Arch. and Hist. Soc. Pubs.*, vol. XII (1903), pp. 375–410; Lucy E. Keeler, "The Croghan Celebration," *Ibid.*, vol. XVI (1907), pp. 1–105, and "The Centennial of Croghan's Victory" in vol. XXIII (1914), pp. 1–33. *Proceedings at the Unveiling of the Soldiers' Monument on the Site of Fort Stephenson, Fremont, Ohio, with an Account of the Heroic Defense of the Fort by Maj. Geo. Croghan, etc.* (Fremont, 1885).]

A. T. V.

CROIX, TEODORO DE (June 30, 1730–1792), was commandant general of the Provincias Internas of Mexico, 1776–83, and viceroy of Peru, 1784–89. He was descended from a distinguished Flemish family, and at the age of seventeen years entered the Spanish army. Promotion was rapid and before he was thirty years old Teodoro received a colonel's commission. Five years later (1765) he accompanied to New Spain, as captain of the guards, the new viceroy, his uncle, the Marqués de Croix. Soon afterward the royal visitor, José de Gálvez, appointed Teodoro to the important post of collector at Acapulco, the port of arrival and departure for the richly laden vessels in the Manila galleon service. His efficiency and administrative ability are attested by the fact that the port revenues increased greatly during his incumbency. In 1767 Teodoro was entrusted with the supremely important task of collaborating with Viceroy Croix and Gálvez in the execution of the king's secret instructions for the suppression of the Jesuit Order in New Spain. Three years later he was promoted to the rank of brigadier-general and in 1771 he returned to Spain to resume active military service.

Meanwhile, at the suggestion of Gálvez, it had been decided to detach the northern provinces of New Spain—Nueva Vizcaya, Coahuila, Texas, New Mexico, Sinaloa, Sonora, and Upper and Lower California—from the jurisdiction of the viceroy and create of them a new military and political entity, directly under the king, to be known as the Commandancy General of the Provincias Internas. This change, which was virtually equivalent to the creation of a new viceroyalty, was effected by a royal order, dated Aug. 22, 1776, and the same day the king named Teodoro de Croix as the first commandant general. As such he exercised supreme military and civil authority, and, in addition, was invested with the administration of the royal finances and the right, under certain limitations, to appoint to church offices. As commandant general Croix set a high standard for administrative efficiency. De Burgos says: "Law, justice, and finance were thoroughly reformed: agriculture and mining were fomented; population increased; towns were founded; the army was reorganized; the paymasters were regenerated; Indian militia were established; home guards and minutemen were created; California was promoted; prisons were built and hospitals founded; crimes decreased; vagabondage diminished; and respect for Spanish institutions increased." Croix was promoted on Feb. 13, 1783, to the rank of lieutenant-general; two days later he was relieved of his post as commandant general. Upon arriving in Mexico City on Sept. 26, 1783, he learned that he had been named viceroy of Peru, the highest office within the gift of the Spanish monarch. He assumed power on Apr. 6, 1784, and ruled for five years. He left office virtually penniless and returned to Spain. In 1791 he was made colonel in the king's bodyguard and also was promoted to a commandership in the Teutonic Order. He died in Madrid at the age of sixty-two.

[H. H. Bancroft, *Hist. of the North Mexican States*, vol. I (1884); Francis de Burgos, "The Administration of Teodoro de Croix, Commander General of the Provincias Internas de Mexico, 1776–83" (thesis, MS., Univ. of Texas Lib., 1927); Carlo Francisco Croix, Marqués de, *Correspondance du Marquis de Croix, 1757–89, Vice Roi du Mexique* (1891); L. E. Fisher, "Viceregal Administration in the Spanish-American Colonies," being *Univ. of Cal. Pubs. in Hist.*, vol. XV (1926); H. I. Priestley, "José de Gálvez," *Ibid.*, vol. V (1916); A. Salcedo Ruiz, *Historia de España* (1914); the Lib. of the Univ. of Texas possesses transcripts of official documents in the Mexican and Spanish archives relating to the administration of Croix.] C. W. H.

CROKER, RICHARD (Nov. 23, 1841–Apr. 29, 1922), New York City politician, was a native of Ireland, where his family, originally English, had lived for six generations. He was born at Cloghnakilty, County Cork, the son of Eyre Coote Croker. His mother belonged to the Scotch family of Wellstead, which had lived in Ireland perhaps as long as the Crokers had. When Richard was three years old, his father and mother, with their nine children, migrated to America, settling in New York City, where Richard attended a public school irregularly from his eleventh to his thirteenth year. At thirteen he was large for his age and began working as a machinist. At nineteen he was leader of the "Fourth Avenue Tunnel Gang" and a prize-fighter of no slight distinction among the youth of New York's upper East Side. After he reached his majority, he attached himself to

Tammany Hall, which was in control of the city government, under William M. Tweed [q.v.]. He was appointed an attendant in the supreme court, but left that sinecure to become an engineer on a Fire Department steamer. From this comparative obscurity he emerged in 1868 as a member of the "Young Democracy," a faction of Tammany, headed by "Honest John" Kelly [q.v.], which made war on Tweed and all his cohorts. Thirty years later Croker declared that in this fight he was actuated solely by a consuming zeal to release the city from the clutches of Tweed, who had stolen millions of public money, had operated crudely, and had been found out. Croker was elected a member of the board of aldermen and in that capacity he signed, with other members, on Mar. 20, 1870, an agreement to take no official action on any proposition affecting the city government without first obtaining the consent of certain leaders of the Young Democracy, who were named (Fassett Investigation, vol. II, pp. 1711–12). In that year (1870) Croker, with other anti-Tweed aldermen, was legislated out of office by a bill passed through Tweed's influence in the state legislature. Yet Croker's part in the premature attempt to purify Tammany did not stand in the way of his appointment by the comptroller to a lucrative post in the city administration.

After Tweed's downfall and imprisonment in 1871 Croker's star continued in the ascendant. He was elected coroner and in that office received fees amounting to $20,000 or $25,000 a year. He gave whole-hearted support to John Kelly, Tweed's successor as boss. On election day in 1874, a man belonging to a faction opposed to Croker's was shot and killed. Croker was charged with the crime, but the case was dismissed, the district attorney admitting a lack of evidence. In after years Croker declared that the guilty man was one of his own henchmen, that the shot had been fired in self-defense, and that he would not "give away" a friend under such circumstances. It was the law of the gang, not that of the state, which most strongly influenced his decisions throughout his life. After a month in jail he resumed the office of coroner, to which he was reëlected two years later. His next promotion was an appointment by Mayor Edson to a fire commissionership. In 1885 he brought about the nomination of Hugh J. Grant for sheriff. In the following year, after ten years' tutelage under John Kelly, Croker succeeded his old chief in the Tammany leadership. He became chairman of the Tammany Finance Committee (which kept no books) and for sixteen years his word was law in the Democratic

Croker

organization of New York City. As leader, he was shrewd enough to surround himself with advisers who had qualities that he himself lacked. Certain of his traits as a political strategist were displayed in the mayoral campaign of 1886, when the labor vote was an important factor. Croker at first offered the Democratic nomination to Henry George [q.v.], who declined it, but later accepted the United Labor party's nomination after more than 30,000 signatures of voters had been secured. Croker then named as the Tammany candidate Abram S. Hewitt [q.v.], a citizen of high standing who was the choice of the County Democracy. The Republican nominee was Theodore Roosevelt. Hewitt was elected and served a term of two years, but antagonized Tammany by his independent attitude and did not receive a renomination. The next two mayors, Grant and Gilroy, were named by Croker and elected by the efforts of the 90,000 enrolled workers, marshaled by thirty-five district leaders, who now made up the Tammany phalanx. The keystone of Croker's political theory was the spoils system, as developed and practised by Tammany. At the same time he was the first Tammany chieftain to turn over the handling of local patronage to the district leaders, whom he held to a strict accounting. He always maintained that a corrupt official could be dealt with more effectively by a disciplined organization such as Tammany than by any other agency. The last public office held by Croker was that of city chamberlain, in 1889–90, at a salary of $25,-000. The disclosures before the Lexow Committee concerning the Police Department led to a fusion against Tammany in 1894 and the election of Mayor Strong. Croker's leadership was discredited and he went to England to live.

During the campaign of 1896 the organization was in the hands of John C. Sheehan, and McKinley carried the city by 20,000. In the next year occurred the first mayoral election for the newly created Greater New York, including Brooklyn, Staten Island, and portions of Queens and Westchester counties. Croker returned from England in September 1897, and despite the disaffection of three-fifths of the Tammany district leaders, he succeeded in nominating and electing Robert C. Van Wyck as mayor, although a strong anti-Tammany ticket, headed by Seth Low, was in the field. The running of Gen. B. F. Tracy on a Republican ticket contributed powerfully to Tammany success. In 1899 Croker admitted before a legislative committee that the officials in the Van Wyck administration were selected by himself or his close associates. When asked by counsel whether he

was working for his own pocket all the time, he replied that he was doing just that. Although he had been a poor man before he became Tammany's recognized leader, afterward he paid $250,000 for a stock farm and more than $100,-000 for race horses, and later $200,000 for a residence. It was never shown that he acquired this wealth illegally. According to a general belief at the time, it was what an associate of Croker's called "honest graft," stock in contracting companies and other enterprises for which the friendship of men in control of certain city departments was helpful, if not essential. In 1900 the English tax officers assessed Croker's income at $100,000, the tax being fixed at $5,000 (*World*, New York, Dec. 12, 1900). At the end of four years under Van Wyck a genuine fusion movement, with no third ticket in the field, resulted in Seth Low's election. From that time Croker never regained dominance in New York City affairs. He lived for several years at Moat House, Wantage, England, and later bought Glencairn, near Dublin, Ireland, where he maintained racing stables, breeding horses that won a series of Irish races and in 1907 sending Orby, a half-American horse, to win the classic Derby in England, with betting odds of ten to one against him. As an owner of racers, Croker seems to have conformed to the standards of English sportsmanship. He declined to wager money on his own horse in the Derby. His first wife (Elizabeth Frazier of New York) whom he had married in 1873 and from whom he had been estranged for some years, died in 1914. He then married Beula Benton Edmondson, a twenty-three-year-old Cherokee Indian from Oklahoma. His latter years (1920–22), were embittered by disputes and litigation with his children concerning property. All his mature life Croker was a reserved, silent man, at times taciturn. He was called a "good listener" in conferences with his aides. His physical resemblance to President Grant was often noted.

[*Testimony taken before the* (*N. Y.*) *Senate Committee on Cities* (1890), the Fassett investigation, see esp. vol. II, pp. 1690–1767; *Report and Proc. of the* (*N. Y.*) *Senate Committee Appointed to Investigate the Police Dept. of the City of N. Y.* (1895), the Lexow investigation; *Report of the Special Committee of the* (*N. Y.*) *Assembly Appointed to Investigate the Public Offices and Depts. of the City of N. Y., etc.* (5 vols., 1900), the Mazet investigation; Gustavus Myers, *Hist. of Tammany Hall* (2nd ed., 1917); M. R. Werner, *Tammany Hall* (1928); Alfred Henry Lewis, *Richard Croker* (1901), a sketch; Louis Seibold in *Munsey's Mag.*, Aug. 1901; *N. Y. Times*, Apr. 30, 1922; *Who's Who in America*, 1920–21; W. T. Stead, "Mr. Richard Croker and Greater N. Y.," in *Rev. of Revs.* (London), Oct. 1897, is chronologically inaccurate but reflects Croker's opinions at the climax of his career in politics.]
W. B. S.

CROLY, DAVID GOODMAN (Nov. 3, 1829–Apr. 29, 1889), journalist, was born in Cloghnakilty, County Cork, Ireland, the son of Patrick and Elizabeth Croly. He came to America when a very small boy and grew up in New York City. For a time he was apprenticed to a silversmith. He went to the University of the City of New York for one year, and received a special course diploma in 1854. In 1855 he became a reporter on the New York *Evening Post*, receiving a salary of eight dollars a week. After a short time he took charge of the city intelligence department of the *Herald*, which position he held until 1858. In that year, with his wife, Jane Cunningham Croly [*q.v.*], also a journalist, whom he had married in 1857, he moved to Rockford, Ill., and started the *Daily News*. The investment was not profitable financially, but both Croly and his wife were highly regarded in the community, and various persons offered money to keep the paper in existence. Their offers were declined, however; Croly returned to New York in 1860 and became first city editor and then (1862–72) managing editor of the *World*. In 1868 Croly and C. W. Sweet founded the *Real Estate Record and Builder's Guide*, the former being joint owner and manager until 1873. Then Croly became editor of the *Daily Graphic*, a new illustrated paper. He resigned in 1878 because the owners interfered with his editorial management. He was an independent, fearless person who disliked the obvious way of saying or doing a thing and accordingly cultivated the unexpected almost to a fault. He thought and labored as an iconoclast and a reformer. He was the principal author of a book, *Miscegenation* (1864), in which he stated: "All that is needed to make us the finest race on earth is to engraft upon our stock the negro element which providence has placed by our side on this continent. We must become a yellow-skinned, black-haired people, if we would attain the fullest results of civilization." The word "miscegenation" was coined by Croly and first used in this book (Sir James A. H. Murray, *A New English Dictionary*, vol. VI, pt. 3, Oxford, 1908). He published (1868), *Seymour and Blair, Their Lives and Services*, a campaign biography of the Democratic candidates for president and vice-president. In 1872 *Truth*, an attempt to explain the merits of the Oneida Community, was published. The following year Croly started a new magazine, *The Modern Thinker*, which he explained was not a monthly, nor a quarterly, but a periodical with no assured periodicity. A strange typographical make-up was employed, each article being printed on paper of a different color with type of various sizes and ink of various tints to match the paper. Three issues appeared. Another book, *Glimpses of the Future*, dealing with suggestions as to the drift of things, was published in 1888. One of Croly's chief interests was Auguste Comte's theory of Positivism, a philosophy which he did his best to introduce into the United States. In 1871 he published a *Primer of Positivism*.

[See *Real Estate Record and Builder's Guide*, May 4, 1889; *General Alumni Cat. of N. Y. Univ., 1833–1905* (1906); *N. Y. Times*, Apr. 30, 1889. A vivid idea of Croly is obtained by reading his publication, *The Modern Thinker* and his book, *Miscegenation*.]

M. S.

CROLY, JANE CUNNINGHAM (Dec. 19, 1829–Dec. 23, 1901), journalist, was probably the first American newspaper woman. She was born in Market Harborough, Leicestershire, England, the daughter of the Rev. Joseph H. and Jane Cunningham, and came to the United States with her father when she was twelve years old. In her childhood she was taught by her father and brother at their home in Poughkeepsie and later in New York City. In her early girlhood she attended school at Southbridge, Mass., where she edited the school paper, wrote plays, and acted as stage manager. In 1855, she gained a place on the staff of the *Sunday Times and Noah's Weekly Messenger*, writing under the pseudonym, "Jennie June," because she felt the traditional shyness concerning women in public life. She became a special writer on women's fashions and was among the first to "syndicate" her articles. In 1856 she married David Goodman Croly [*q.v.*], a New York journalist. Five children were born to them, but Mrs. Croly departed from the conventional mode of the time and continued her journalistic work. For over forty years she held various editorial positions on newspapers and magazines. In the year of her marriage was called the first Woman's Congress, to meet in New York. She was editor, for a time, of *Demorest's Quarterly Mirror of Fashion*, and in 1860, when that journal and the *New York Weekly Illustrated News* were incorporated into *Demorest's Illustrated Monthly*, she became its editor, remaining as such until 1887. She was also connected with *Godey's* and with the *Home-Maker*. Jane Croly was probably the first woman correspondent in New York for out-of-town papers. For fifteen years she wrote letters for the *New Orleans Picayune* and the *Baltimore American*. She represented in New York the *New Orleans Delta*, the *Richmond Enquirer*, and the *Louisville Journal*. At various times she was editorially connected with the New York *World*,

and the *Graphic Daily Times,* and, for nine years
with the *New York Times.* She was also dramatic critic and assistant editor of the *Messenger*
from 1861 to 1866. In 1868 Mrs. Croly in common with a number of New York women, was
extremely indignant because her sex was completely ignored at the Charles Dickens reception. As a protest, in harmony with her advocacy of everything she considered for the betterment of women, she founded Sorosis, which
was not the first woman's club, but was the
first of any consequence or endurance. Mrs.
Croly was the first president of the New York
State Federation of Women's Clubs. When her
husband attempted to teach in America the philosophy of Positivism originated by Auguste
Comte, Mrs. Croly endeavored to aid him. In
1889 she founded the Women's Press Club in
New York. Of her separate publications the
most notable was *The History of the Woman's
Club Movement in America,* a large volume published in 1898. In 1866 she published *Jennie
June's American Cookery Book,* and in 1875
published *For Better or Worse. A Book for
Some Men and All Women.* In 1898 she met
with an accident which crippled her, and subsequently she spent much of her time in England
seeking rest and cure. She died in New York
City.

[See *Woman's Journal,* Jan. 4, 1902; *Jane Cunningham Croly, "Jenny June"* (1904), containing a description of her personality and activities by her brother, John Cunningham; *Harper's Bazar,* Mar. 3, 1900,
p. 173; *Critic,* Mar. 1904, p. 238; *N. Y. Times,* Dec.
24, 1901.]   M. S.

CROMPTON, GEORGE (Mar. 23, 1829–Dec.
29, 1886), inventor and manufacturer, was the
son of William Crompton [*q.v.*] and Sarah
(Low) Crompton, and was born at Holcombe,
Tottingham, Lancashire, England. In 1839 William Crompton took the family to Taunton,
Mass., where, two years before, he had invented and patented a fancy loom which he now intended to introduce to the mill owners of New
England. George grew up at Taunton and received an education there in private schools and
in the mills and machine-shops which his father's business opened to him. Later, when the
success of his father's loom was established, he
was able to attend Millbury (Mass.) Academy.
After the completion of his course he worked
in the Colt pistol factory at Hartford and in
mills belonging to his father, holding a variety
of positions, clerical and mechanical, and obtaining a knowledge of the textile industry that
very soon proved useful. In 1849 William
Crompton was forced to retire because of ill
health, and in 1851 the patents on his loom ex-

pired and automatically terminated the agreements for its manufacture. George Crompton
succeeded in having the patents extended and,
with M. A. Furbush, began the manufacture of
the loom at Worcester, Mass. He immediately
began to improve the loom, receiving his first
patent, Nov. 14, 1854, for the substitution of a
single cylinder chain for two or more different
patterns. In 1859 Furbush retired and Crompton became sole owner of the business which was
then known as the Crompton Loom Works. In
1861 the war caused a depression in the demand
for looms, and Crompton for two years manufactured gun-making machinery for government
and private arsenals. Returning to the manufacture of looms, he continued his improvements
and found a steadily growing demand that
forced him to enlarge his works. This plant in
time became one of the largest and best-known
of American machine-shops. The success of the
business, and the two hundred patents on which
his name appears, indicate the importance of
George Crompton's work. He improved practically every part of the loom as well as its
appearance, and invented many new textile
fabrics. It is estimated that Crompton added
sixty per cent to the producing capacity of the
loom and saved fifty per cent of the labor formerly necessary for its operation. By making a
simpler loom he greatly reduced the time and
cost of repairs and many of his looms were
capable of more varied work than those before
them. Crompton's looms in world-wide competition at the Paris Exposition received the first
award, and at the Centennial Exposition of 1876
the Commission pronounced them the best looms
for fancy weaving. Crompton was a member
of the board of aldermen and of the common
council of Worcester and in 1871 was a candidate for mayor. He was one of the founders
and the first policy-holder of the Hartford Steam
Boiler Inspection & Insurance Company, a
founder and president of the Crompton Carpet
Company, and a director in various other corporations. He was married on Jan. 9, 1853 to
Mary Christina Pratt, who after his death became president of the Crompton Loom Works.
Two of his sons also took out a large number
of patents, Charles Crompton being one of the inventors of the fancy automatic loom and Randolph Crompton of the first practical shuttle-
changing loom.

[See bibliography of Wm. Crompton; obituaries in
Manufacturer's Rev. and Industrial Record, Jan. 1887,
and *Boston Post,* Dec. 30, 1886.]   F. A. T.

CROMPTON, WILLIAM (Sept. 10, 1806–
May 1, 1891), textile machinery inventor and

manufacturer, was born at Preston, Lancashire, England, the son of Thomas and Mary (Dawson) Crompton. Preston was a textile mill town where the Crompton family had long been associated with the trade,—though Samuel Crompton, inventor of the spinning "mule," was not a family connection,—so that as a matter of course William was taught handloom cotton-weaving and later the trade of machinist. Before he was thirty years of age he was superintendent of a cotton-mill at Ramsbottom, in which position he had the opportunity to experiment with mill machinery and succeeded in increasing production there very materially. On May 26, 1828 he married Sarah Low of Holcombe. In 1836 he came to Taunton, Mass., entered the employ of Crocker & Richmond, and within a year had designed a loom to weave a pattern of goods such as the looms then used would not produce. This loom overcame two great disadvantages of its predecessors. In the early looms the movement of the warp harnesses was controlled by cams which limited the number of harnesses to not more than six and necessitated the changing of the cams to change the pattern. Crompton used an endless pattern-chain upon which rollers or pins could be variously placed to engage the harness levers as had the cams, but which allowed any number of harnesses to be used (usually twenty-four) and permitted an extremely easy change from one pattern to another. The second novel feature was the double motion of the warp, which allowed more space for the shuttle and put correspondingly less strain on the warp threads (Patent No. 491, Nov. 23, 1837). Crocker & Richmond failed in 1837, and Crompton went back to England where he entered into business relations with John Rostran, in whose name he took out British patents on his loom. Returning to America in 1839, he settled his family at Taunton, and then traveled over New England trying to introduce his loom. Finally the Middlesex Mills, at Lowell, Mass., asked him to adapt one of their looms for the production of figured woolens similar to the French goods then being introduced. In 1840 he demonstrated that with his pattern-chain the desired figure could be woven. This was probably the first instance of fancy woolens being woven by power. Crompton spent two years in the Middlesex Mills, remodeling many of their looms and constructing several of his own invention. He then licensed Phelps & Bickford at Worcester to build his looms on a royalty basis, which they did until the expiration of the patent. Crompton then divided his time between the manufacture of cotton and woolen goods at Millbury,

Mass., and travel for the purpose of instructing operatives in the use of his loom, which had rapidly come into use throughout the United States and England. In 1849 he became incapacitated for business and retired to Connecticut where he died years later at Windsor. His loom was greatly improved by his son, George Crompton [q.v.].

[E. B. Crane, *Historic Homes . . . of Worcester County, Mass.*, vol. IV (1907), and *Hist. of Worcester County* (1924), III, 113–14; Chas. Nutt, *Hist. of Worcester* (1919); C. G. Washburn, *Manufacturing and Mechanical Industries of Worcester* (1889); *Bull. Nat. Asso. Wool Mfgrs.*, 1891, pp. 188–90; information as to certain facts from Mr. Geo. Crompton of Worcester.]
F. A. T.

CROMWELL, GLADYS LOUISE HUSTED (Nov. 28, 1885–Jan. 24, 1919), poet, was born in Brooklyn, N. Y., the daughter of Frederic and Esther Whitmore (Husted) Cromwell. Her father was graduated from Harvard at the age of twenty, a conscientious student and something of a dandy. In his mature life he became very rich, and gave much attention to political reform and to the promotion of music and art. His tranquil domestic life of forty-one years was broken in 1909 by the death of his wife, and his own death came in 1914. The youngest of his five children were Gladys and her twin sister Dorothea. They were practically inseparable, eagerly devoted to each other throughout their lives. As girls they traveled extensively in Europe and attended the Brearley School, a private institution in New York City. Both were concerned with the larger phases of social adjustment, and both were writers, Dorothea chiefly in prose, and Gladys in poetry. In spite of their wealth they were in a sense personally frugal, and they had the quality of mind which enabled them to be aware at once of stark actuality and poetic mystery. In 1915, Gladys published *Gates of Utterance,* a collection of admirable but in no sense remarkable verse. The war in Europe from its early stages was considered by both the sisters as unprecedented disaster, a horrid indorsement of philosophies they had long recognized. Their speculations regarding it were ceaseless, and many of them are recorded in Gladys's verse in various magazines. The volume *Poems* (1920), containing nearly everything that she wrote, shows great advance over *Gates of Utterance,* and some of it has the mark of permanence. Two of the lyrics, "The Mould" and "The Crowning Gift," are little short of magnificent, unique in view-point and apparently final in phraseology, but probably too sophisticated ever to be popular; and "The Deep," with its lines "I must have peace, increasing peace, such as dark oceans keep," assumes in connection with its author's death a sorrowful tragicalness. In January 1918 the two sisters went to France to do Red Cross work. There, near the front, at Chalons-sur-Marne, they remained without relief for eight months, exposed to every harrowing consequence of war and giving comfort and sympathy to any who were in pain or grief. In January 1919 they took passage for America on the steamer *Lorraine,* and on the night of the 24th, while the ship was still in the Gironde River making its way seaward, they leapt overboard. Their bodies were buried in France some months later, with special honors from the French government. "Her life," says one who knew Gladys intimately, "was interior, and the delicate charm of her personality was like a slender wreath of smoke that encircled a deep burning fire" (letter of Anne Dunn).

[Harvard College, *Report of the Secretary of the Class of 1863* (1903), *Class of 1863 Memoirs,* June 1914–Mar. 1915; Anne Dunn, "Biog. Note" in G. Cromwell, *Poems* (1919), and letter to present writer, Mar. 20, 1928; L. Untermeyer, *Modern Am. Poetry* (1925); *N. Y. Times,* Jan. 25, 29, 1919; P. Colum, "Poetry of Gladys Cromwell," *New Republic,* Mar. 8, 1919.]

J.D.W.

CROOK, GEORGE (Sept. 23, 1829–Mar. 21, 1890), soldier, son of Thomas and Elizabeth (Mathers) Crook, was born near Dayton, Ohio. His ancestry was Scotch and German. From the public schools he entered West Point on July 1, 1848, and on graduation four years later was commissioned lieutenant of infantry. Until the Civil War he served in the Northwest where he was engaged in explorations and in protecting the settlers from periodic Indian raids. In September 1861 he was commissioned colonel of the 36th Ohio Infantry and with his regiment served in West Virginia, where in May 1862 he received the brevet of major in the regular army for his defeat of a Confederate force under Gen. Heth at Lewisburg. The following August he was made brigadier-general of volunteers and commanded a brigade in the Kanawha Division which was attached to the 9th Corps in the Antietam campaign. He was engaged in the battles of South Mountain and Antietam and for his conduct in the latter received the brevet of lieutenant-colonel. In 1863 he commanded a cavalry division in the Army of the Cumberland and took part in the Chickamauga campaign. Shortly thereafter he undertook the pursuit of Gen. Wheeler's cavalry corps which he engaged successfully at Farmington, Tenn., on Oct. 7. For this he received the brevet of colonel.

In February 1864 he was again in West Virginia, where in the spring of that year, under the orders of Gen. Grant, he undertook to interrupt railway communication between Lynchburg and East Tennessee. In this operation he defeated the Confederates at Cloyd Farm on Walker Mountain, captured the station of Dublin, and destroyed the New River bridge and the railway in its vicinity. For this operation he later received the brevet of brigadier-general. In August of the same year he was placed in command of West Virginia and in personal command of one of the corps of Sheridan's Army of the Shenandoah. He was engaged in the three important battles of that army—Winchester, Fisher's Hill, and Cedar Creek—and in addition to receiving his promotion to the grade of major-general of volunteers he later received the brevet of major-general in the regular army for his conduct in the battle of Fisher's Hill. He now returned to the command of his department. When in March 1865 Sheridan joined Grant in front of Petersburg, he requested that Crook be assigned to the command of one of his cavalry divisions, and in consequence the latter took part in the final battles of the war, being engaged at Dinwiddie Court House, Sailor's Creek, Farmville, and Appomattox.

In the reorganization of the regular army after the war Crook became lieutenant-colonel of the 23rd Infantry and was assigned to the command of the district of Boise, Idaho, where for three years he was engaged in bringing to an end the Indian war which had been raging for several years in southern Oregon, Idaho, and northern California. For this he received the thanks of the legislature of Oregon and the commendation of his superiors. In 1871 he was sent by President Grant to end the war with the Apaches and other hostile tribes in northern Arizona, and this he did with such success that he received the thanks of the legislature of the territory, and in 1873 was promoted from lieutenant-colonel to brigadier-general in the regular army, an unusual advancement at that time. In 1875 he was placed in command of the Department of the Platte, where trouble was expected with the Sioux and Cheyenne tribes of Indians on account of the discovery of gold in the Black Hills of Dakota. Here he took a prominent part in the great Sioux War of 1876, remaining in the field the entire year, and with his troops enduring incredible hardships. In 1882 he was sent back to Arizona where the Apaches were again on the warpath. He had no difficulty in pacifying the tribes with whom he had dealt before. His problem now was the Chiricahua tribe of Apaches whom he had never encountered and who had taken refuge in the Sierra Madre Mountains of Mexico, from which, under their chief Geronimo [*q.v.*], they raided settlements both north and south of the boundary. In 1883 Crook led an expedition into these mountains where no American or Mexican force had ever penetrated, and induced the tribe, some five hundred persons, to return to their reservation. In 1885 Geronimo with a quarter of the tribe again fled to the mountains and was there pursued until he had only twenty-four followers left. These later surrendered to Gen. Nelson A. Miles [q.v.]. In the spring of 1886 Crook returned to the command of the Department of the Platte where he remained until April 1888 when he was promoted to the grade of major-general and assigned to the command of the Division of the Missouri with headquarters at Chicago. Here he died on Mar. 21, 1890. He was survived by his wife, Mary Dailey of Oakland, Md.

As a soldier Crook was fearless both morally and physically, shunning neither responsibility nor personal danger. By nature he was modest and retiring, chary of speech but a good listener. Of a kindly and sympathetic disposition and easy of approach, he made friends in all classes of society. Although he spent most of his life on the frontier he was never profane, indulged in no intoxicating liquors, and was clean of speech. He thoroughly understood the Indian character. Realizing their hopeless struggle to hold their lands against encroachment, he was more prone to pardon than to punish. In his recommendations on the subject of the Indians he was far in advance of his times. He advocated the division of reservations into individual plots, so that the Indians might become self-supporting. He also believed that they should be granted equal rights with the whites in courts of law and all the privileges of citizenship.

[War Department records; *Official Records (Army)*; G. W. Cullum, *Biog. Reg.* (3rd ed., 1891); *Reports* of the Secretary of War; John G. Bourke, *On the Border with Crook* (1891); personal recollections of the author, who served on Crook's staff in the Geronimo campaign.] G.J.F.

CROOKS, GEORGE RICHARD (Feb. 3, 1822–Feb. 20, 1897), Methodist Episcopal clergyman, educator, editor, the son of George Richard Crooks, was born and spent his early life in Philadelphia. He graduated with highest honors from Dickinson College in 1840, and began his ministerial career as a circuit rider on the Illinois frontier. In 1842 he was called back to Dickinson to be classical and mathematical instructor in the Collegiate Grammar School, of which, the following year, he became principal. In 1845 he was made adjunct professor of Latin and Greek in the college. He reëntered the active ministry in 1848, and both in the Philadelphia Conference, which he had first joined, and in the New

York East Conference to which he was transferred in 1857, he held some of the most important pastorates. From 1860 to 1875 he edited *The Methodist,* a weekly paper founded by an association of laymen and clergymen. Surrounding himself with able assistants, he made this paper a powerful influence within the denomination and of acknowledged value without. From 1880 until his death he was professor of historical theology in Drew Seminary. He was married, June 10, 1846, to Susan Frances Emory, daughter of Bishop John Emory. In an unusual degree he possessed scholarly tastes combined with administrative ability and willingness to engage in denominational controversies. He opposed those who would have deprived of membership in the church slave-holding Methodists in the border states, and his influence is said to have done much to save that portion of the country to the church and to the Union. Believing that "the Church of God is not an estate to be carved out among the ministry," he was a leader of those who secured for the laity a share in the control and administration of the Methodist denomination. From the beginning of his career he felt that the Methodists owed more to the intellectual elevation of the country than they had ever achieved, and labored for a better educated ministry. As a member of the Committee on Education in the General Conference of 1856, when the distinction between "God-made" and "man-made" ministers was still drawn, he was prominent in securing the adoption of a resolution sanctioning the establishment of theological seminaries. His own contribution of aids to knowledge was considerable. While a young man at Dickinson he prepared with John McClintock *A First Book in Latin* (1846) and *A First Book in Greek* (1848), and later, 1858, with Alexander J. Schem, *A New Latin-English School Lexicon on the Basis of the Latin-German Lexicon of Dr. C. F. Ingerslev.* In 1852 he published *Bishop Butler's Analogy of Religion,* with analysis, notes, index, and a life of the bishop, a work commenced by Robert Emory. He wrote an elaborate introduction for the Gospel of Matthew (1884) in the American edition of Meyer's *Commentary on the New Testament.* With John F. Hurst, he edited the *Library of Biblical and Theological Literature,* for which he himself prepared *The Theological Encyclopædia and Methodology* on the basis of Hagenbach (1884). He also published the *Life and Letters of Rev. Dr. John McClintock* (1876), the *Life of Bishop Matthew Simpson* (1890) whose sermons he edited in 1885, and *The Story of the Christian Church* (1897).

[Wm. F. Anderson, "George Richard Crooks," *Methodist Rev.*, May 1898; Ezra S. Tipple, *Drew Theological Seminary* (1917); New York Conference, *Minutes*, 1897, pp. 107–11; *Christian Advocate* (N. Y.), Mar. 4, 1897; *N. Y. Times*, Feb. 22, 1897.]   H.E.S.

CROOKS, RAMSAY (Jan. 2, 1787–June 6, 1859), fur-trader, was born in Greenock, Scotland, the son of William and Margaret (Ramsay) Crooks. At sixteen he emigrated to Montreal and at once entered the fur trade. As the clerk of Robert Dickson he went to Mackinaw, and by 1806 he had pushed on to St. Louis. In 1807 he formed a partnership with Robert McClellan, and in the fall of the year, with a force of eighty men, they set out for the upper Missouri. On their way they met the party headed by Ensign Nathaniel Pryor, and learning of its defeat at the hands of the Arikaras, turned back and established a trading-post near the present Calhoun, Nebr. Two years later, with forty men, they started to follow the great expedition of the St. Louis Missouri Fur Company northward, but finding the Sioux hostile gave up the venture. In 1810 the partnership was dissolved and Crooks went to Canada. Here he found Wilson Price Hunt recruiting men for the proposed overland journey to Astoria, and by purchasing five shares of stock became a partner in Astor's Pacific Fur Company. He accompanied the expedition the following spring, but in the Blue Mountains of Oregon, worn out with illness and hunger, he and five others were left behind. In the spring, with a companion, he reached the Columbia, arriving at Astoria May 11, 1812. Four days later, disheartened with the prospects of the enterprise, he relinquished his shares. On June 29 he started on the return east with Robert Stuart's party of seven, which after experiencing many dangers and extreme privations, reached St. Louis Apr. 30, 1813.

Crooks remained in close association with Astor and the American Fur Company, which in 1816 bought out the American interests of the Northwest Company. In this enlarged firm he became a partner. He was appointed general manager of the American Fur Company in 1817. In the winter of 1820–21 he visited Astor, then in Europe, and arranged with him for the next four years' campaign. It was due to his persistent urging that Astor established the Western Department of the company in St. Louis in the spring of 1822. Chittenden considers him to have been the virtual head of the company from this time until Astor's retirement in 1834. Every year he made the long and arduous journey to Mackinaw, frequently going on to St. Louis. He formulated the policies of the company, wrote most of its letters and with an extraordinary grasp of detail managed its business throughout the whole field of its operations. When Astor sold out, he bought the Northern Department, of which he became president, continuing the name of the American Fur Company. He remained in the fur business until his death. He died at his home in New York.

Crooks was married, Mar. 10, 1825, to Marianne Pélagie Emilie Pratte, of the Chouteau clan of St. Louis, and by the union greatly enhanced his position in the fur metropolis. Physically he was a frail man, and the almost incredible hardships of his early days left him a legacy of ill health, contrasting strongly with the sustained vigor with which he carried on his work. His character was of the highest; though a relentless enemy in competition, he was fair, and in an industry notorious for its illicit trading he kept the law. A self-educated man, he wrote letters that are models of force and incisiveness and are besides rich in historical information. He is pictured in his age as a genial companion, fond of reminiscence and often surrounded by groups eager to hear him relate his thrilling adventures. In the still unsettled controversy as to who discovered the famous South Pass he maintained, in a letter written June 26, 1856, that the gap traversed by the Robert Stuart party was this identical pass and that it was thus discovered eleven years before a party of Ashley's men traversed it from the east in 1824. His range of interests was wide. He was the first president of the Mohawk & Hudson Railroad Company, serving until 1835. In his later years he was a trustee of the Astor Library as well as of several learned societies.

[H. M. Chittenden, *The Am. Fur Trade of the Far West* (1902); Stella M. Drumm, "More about Astorians," *Quarterly* of the Ore. Hist. Soc., XXIV, Dec. 1923; Thos. James, *Three Years Among the Indians and Mexicans*, ed. by W. B. Douglas; *N. Y. Herald*, June 8, 1859; Wayne E. Stevens, *Northwest Fur Trade 1763–1800* (1926); Ida A. Johnson, *The Mich. Fur Trade* (1919); J. Ward Ruckman, "Ramsay Crooks and the Fur Trade" in *Minn. Hist.*, vol. VII; Grace L. Nute, "Wilderness Marthas," *Ibid.*, vol. VIII; "The Papers of the Am. Fur Co.," *Am. Hist. Rev.*, vol. XXXII; Anne Ratterman, "The Struggle for Monopoly of the Fur Trade," a master's thesis, Univ. of Minn. Of special importance for the career of Crooks are the papers of the Am. Fur Co. in N. Y. Hist. Soc.; the Ewing Bros. papers in the Ind. Hist. Soc.; the Chouteau papers in Mo. Hist. Soc.; some of the earlier papers of the Am. Fur Co. in Wis. Hist. Soc.]   W.J.G—t.

CROPSEY, JASPAR FRANCIS (Feb. 18, 1823–June 22, 1900), painter, was born in Rossville, N. Y., the son of Jacob Rezeau and Elizabeth Hilyer (Cortelyou) Cropsey. His paternal great-grandfather came from Holland and his mother's family were French Huguenots, but his father and mother were born on Staten Island. He went to the country schools near his home, and early began the study of architecture. At the age of thirteen he received a diploma, from the Mechanics' Institute, for a well-executed model of a house. The American Institute also conferred upon him a diploma for the same model. It attracted so much attention when it was exhibited in 1837, that he was called "the boy that built the House." It secured for him a position in the office of a successful architect, where he studied for five years, at the same time studying landscape painting with Edward Maury. In 1847 he went abroad, visiting London, Paris, Switzerland, and Italy, spending much time in Rome and in traveling with W. W. Story and C. P. Cranch [qq.v.]. In 1857 he went again to Europe and lived in London for seven years, becoming a regular exhibitor at the Royal Academy, and making many sales of his paintings. He was presented at the Court of Queen Victoria by the United States minister, Charles Francis Adams, and among his acquaintances were Ruskin and other literary personages. He was made assistant commissioner to the International Exhibition of 1862 in London and received a medal for his services. He also received a medal and diploma from the Centennial Exposition at Philadelphia in 1876. He was represented there by his picture, "Old Mill," which received an award and was engraved for the Centennial catalogue. He made illustrations for Poe's and Moore's poems. He painted a series of sixteen landscapes of American scenery for E. Gambart & Company, London publishers. He painted a picture, "The Battle of Gettysburg," shortly after the battle. He was one of the founders of the American Water-color Society, a member of the Artists Aid Society, the Century, Union League, and Lotus Clubs, an honorary member of the Pennsylvania Academy of Fine Arts, as well as a Fellow of the Society of Science, Letters and Arts of London, England. He moved to Hastings-on-Hudson, N. Y., where he made studies from nature. His picture, "Greenwood Lake," sent to the National Academy Exhibition, won him election as Associate of the Academy. Most of his paintings depict autumn scenes. His "Autumn on the Hudson River" was highly praised by the London Times. He was perhaps as successful an architect as he was a painter, and is best known as the designer and superintendent of the building of the Sixth Avenue Elevated Railroad Stations of New York. He also superintended the building of George Pullman's house in Chicago and cottages at Long Branch. He is represented in the Metropolitan Museum, in the Corcoran Gallery, Washington, and in private collections in this country and in Europe.

[Clara Erskin Clement and Laurence Hutton, *Artists of the 19th Century* (1907), p. 173; *Am. Art Annual*, 1900–01, p. 58; G. W. Sheldon, *Am. Painters* (1881), pp. 82–84; Ira K. Morris, *Memorial Hist. of Staten Island*, vol. II (1900); Samuel Isham, *Hist. of Am. Painting* (1927).]   H. W.

CROSBY, ERNEST HOWARD (Nov. 4, 1856–Jan. 3, 1907), author, social reformer, son of Rev. Howard Crosby [q.v.] and Margaret (Givan) Crosby, belonged to a family distinguished for its wealth, ability, and philanthropy. His early life was passed in his birthplace, New York City, where he was educated (graduating from New York University in 1876 and from Columbia Law School in 1878), where he was admitted to the bar, and where he was married to Fanny Schieffelin in 1881. He was elected to the legislature in 1887, as the successor of Theodore Roosevelt. Upon his retirement in 1889 he was nominated by President Harrison as a judge of the International Court in Egypt, upon which he served until 1894. Up to this time he had believed that the political problems of the day could be solved without any radical changes in society, but now the reading of Tolstoy led him to more revolutionary views. He resigned his position and started home, stopping on the way to visit the Russian leader, by whom he was bidden to seek out "the greatest living American," Henry George. Crosby followed this advice, with the result that he became an ardent advocate of Henry George's single-tax program. Disowning, and disowned by, his former associates, he again settled in New York and devoted himself fervently to various movements for social betterment. Antimilitarism, industrial arbitration, vegetarianism, and settlement work shared his allegiance with the single tax. He was one of the founders and the first president of the Social Reform Club which was particularly concerned with the interests of labor. His ethical idealism also found expression in *Edward Carpenter: Poet and Prophet* (1901); *Captain Jinks, Hero* (1902), a satirical novel; *Shakespeare's Attitude toward the Working Classes* (1902); *Tolstoy and His Message* (1903); *Tolstoy as a School-Master* (1904); *William Lloyd Garrison, Non-Resistant and Abolitionist* (1905); *Golden Rule Jones, Mayor of Toledo* (1906). Of more permanent literary value were his poems, *Plain Talk in Psalm and Parable* (1899), *Swords and Plowshares* (1902), and *Broad-Cast* (1905), all written in a free verse reminiscent of Walt Whitman, but expressive of a genuine and at times impassioned aspiration. Although a remarkably handsome man himself, Crosby had little appreciation of sensuous beauty; beauty of character, however, he understood and to a high degree exemplified.

[*Addresses in Memory of Ernest Howard Crosby* (Cooper Union, N. Y., Mar. 7, 1907), by Hamlin Garland, Felix Adler, Edwin Markham, and others; *Who's Who in America*, 1906–07.]   E. S. B.

CROSBY, FANNY (Mar. 24, 1820–Feb. 12, 1915), hymn-writer, was born at Southeast, Putnam County, N. Y., the daughter of John and Mercy (Crosby) Crosby. Her given name was Frances Jane. When she was six weeks old a blundering doctor prescribed hot poultices for an inflammation of her eyes. Her sight was destroyed, although as late as 1843, when she visited Niagara Falls, she could still dimly perceive light and color. She enjoyed in spite of her misfortune a happy childhood, the most interesting incident of which is her contact with Daniel Drew [*q.v.*], then a dealer in live stock. He good-naturedly gave her a lamb to replace a pet. At fifteen she entered the New York Institution for the Blind. Her readiness at rhyming, already manifest, was gently discouraged by her teachers until a traveling Scotch phrenologist proclaimed her a potential poet. Thereafter she was the prodigy of the school. After completing the course she was a teacher of English and history in the Institution from 1847 to 1858. Meanwhile she was rapidly becoming a celebrity, appeared frequently on the lecture platform, addressed both Houses of Congress on several occasions, and met many of the literary, political, military, and ecclesiastical notables of the day. Several collections of her verse appeared from time to time: *The Blind Girl and Other Poems* (1844), *Monterey and Other Poems* (1851), *A Wreath of Columbia's Flowers* (1858), which was a miscellany of prose and verse, and *Bells at Evening and Other Verses* (1897). Several of her pieces such as "Rosalie, the Prairie Flower" and "There's Music in the Air," were set to music and sold by the thousand. On Mar. 5, 1858, she married Alexander Van Alstyne, a blind music teacher and church organist, who had been one of her pupils. They made their home in Brooklyn. Not till 1864 did she write her first hymn, but with it she found her vocation, and soon made up for lost time. Although there were days when, she confessed, she could not have written a hymn to save her soul, there were others when she turned out six or seven. No such phenomenon had occurred since the days of Isaac Watts and Charles Wesley. Her productions were widely circulated and were sung by millions of pious people. Some were translated into other languages; at least seventy

came into common use in Great Britain. Her publishers were afraid to credit her with all that she wrote and are said to have issued her hymns under as many as two hundred pseudonyms and initials. When she died in her ninety-fifth year it was conjectured that she had composed about six thousand hymns. Probably her best known is "Safe in the Arms of Jesus," which she wrote in fifteen minutes. Though her popularity in her own day was enormous, the Methodist Church observing for a time an annual "Fanny Crosby Day," her real contribution to hymnody is slight. "It is more to Mrs. Van Alstyne's credit," wrote a competent judge, S. A. W. Duffield, "that she has occasionally found a pearl than that she has brought to the surface so many oyster shells." Julian considers her hymns "with few exceptions very weak and poor, their simplicity and earnestness being their redeeming features. Their popularity is largely due to the melodies to which they are wedded." In her old age, which was as cheerful and healthy as her whole life had been, she wrote two accounts of herself. She died at Bridgeport, Conn.

[*Fanny Crosby's Life-Story by Herself* (1903); Fanny J. Crosby, *Memories of Eighty Years* (1906); *Fanny Crosby's Story of Ninety-Four Years retold by S. Trevena Jackson* (1915); J. Julian, *A Dict. of Hymnology* (rev. ed., 1907); obituary in *N. Y. Times*, Feb. 13, 1915; S. A. W. Duffield, *English Hymns: Their Authors and History* (1886).]   G. H. G.

CROSBY, HOWARD (Feb. 27, 1826–Mar. 29, 1891), Presbyterian clergyman, the son of William Bedlow and Harriet (Ashton) Crosby, was born in New York City. One of his great-grandfathers, William Floyd [*q.v.*], was a signer of the Declaration of Independence; another, Joseph Crosby, was a Massachusetts judge; his grandfather, Dr. Ebenezer Crosby, was a trustee of Columbia College, and an uncle, Col. Henry Rutgers for whom Rutgers College was named, was a regent of the University of New York. The latter left the family a fortune. Howard began at six to study Greek, and entered the University of the City of New York at fourteen, graduating four years later (1844) with first honors in Greek. After a period of ill health during which he helped to run a farm owned by his father, he married Margaret E. Givan and traveled abroad. Upon his return in 1851 he published his first book, *Lands of the Moslem*, and in the same year he became professor of Greek at his alma mater, where he remained until 1859. During this period he taught a Bible class of boys, and helped to organize the New York Young Men's Christian Association, of which he was the second president. In 1859 he went to Rutgers as professor of Greek. Two years later he published *Scholia on the New*

Testament (1861), and was ordained to the Presbyterian ministry, adding to his academic work the pastorate of the First Presbyterian Church of New Brunswick. In the same year President Lincoln offered him the post of minister to Greece, but he declined it. In 1863 he accepted a call to the pulpit of the Fourth Avenue Presbyterian Church in New York City, where he spent the rest of his life. He was moderator of the Presbyterian General Assembly in 1873 and in 1877 a delegate to the first Presbyterian General Council at Edinburgh.

Inheriting traditions both of scholarship and of public service, he united in a rare degree scholarly tastes with zest for public affairs. He was a member of the Council of the University of the City of New York, and its chancellor from 1870 to 1881; a member of the New Testament Company of the American Revision Committee (1872–80); and in 1879–80 he delivered the Yale Lectures on Preaching, which were published in 1880 as *The Christian Preacher*. Among his other published works are: *Social Hints for Young Christians* (1866); *Bible Companion* (1870); *Jesus, His Life and Work* (1871); *Healthy Christian* (1872); *Thoughts on the Decalogue* (1873); *Expository Notes on the Book of Joshua* (1875); *Commentary on Nehemiah* (1877); *The True Humanity of Christ* (1880); *Commentary on the New Testament* (1885); *Conformity to the World* (1891). His keen sense of civic responsibility, however, prompted him to a much wider sphere of activity than study and pulpit afford, while his ardor for righteousness and human well-being made him a champion of numerous reforms. He founded the Society for the Prevention of Crime and served as its president. He was active in the cause of temperance, though opposed to prohibition (see his *Moderation vs. Total Abstinence,* 1881), and, aided by his son, Ernest Howard Crosby [*q.v.*], was prominent in the attempt to secure high-license laws for New York State. He was also much interested in the effort to secure an international copyright law. Though a man of bold courage, and a born fighter, he was always a courteous gentleman, kind even to his foes, so that among all classes he was held in high esteem.

[*Eclectic Mag. of Foreign Lit., Sci., and Art,* 1874; *Critic,* Apr. 4, 1891; *N. Y. Times, N. Y. Tribune,* Mar. 30, 1891; L. L. Doggett, *Hist. of the Y. M. C. A.* (1922); *Presbyt. Jour.* (Phila.), *N. Y. Observer, Christian Advocate* (N. Y.), *Christian Union, Congregationalist,* all of Apr. 2, 1891; *N. Y. Evangelist,* Apr. 2 and 9, 1891; sketch by E. G. Sihler in *Universities and Their Sons: N. Y. Univ.* (1901), ed. by J. L. Chamberlain.]
M. A. K.

CROSBY, JOHN SCHUYLER (Sept. 19, 1839–Aug. 8, 1914), soldier, public official, son of Clarkson Floyd and Angelica Schuyler Crosby, was born in Albany, N. Y., to an inheritance of wealth and aristocratic tastes. Among his ancestors were William Floyd, a signer of the Declaration of Independence, and Gen. Philip Schuyler [*qq.v.*]. Crosby was a freshman in the University of the City of New York, 1855–56. In 1856 he made the venturous and at that time rarely attempted crossing of South America from Valparaiso to Montevideo. He entered the Union army early in the Civil War, and during the course of that conflict engaged in active service from Virginia to the lower Mississippi Valley. By August 1861 he was a first lieutenant, and in June 1863 he was made captain. On account of gallant and meritorious conduct in Louisiana, he was brevetted captain in April 1863 and major in April 1864. In March 1865 he was brevetted lieutenant-colonel. His war services as courier attracted the personal notice and thanks of Lincoln. From March 1869 to July 1870 he was lieutenant-colonel and aide-de-camp to Gen. Sheridan in the campaigns against the Indians. He resigned from the army at the close of 1870. In 1877, in recognition of his bravery in saving life at the time of a yacht disaster, he was awarded a medal by Congress. From 1876 to 1882 he was American consul in Florence, Italy, and during this time he was decorated by the King in gratitude for his having captured a notorious band of criminals. From 1882 to 1884 he was territorial governor of Montana. He gave his zealous attention to the progress of the territory, and even made a special appeal to Congress to put an end to schemes for the commercial exploitation of Yellowstone Park. He had long been much concerned with sports, especially shooting, in which he was most proficient. His residence in Montana gave him opportunity to indulge this taste freely, and, at occasional big-game hunts extending over several days, to indulge also his instinct for grand-scale hospitality. Among his guests on one of these hunts, was President Chester A. Arthur. He was first assistant postmaster-general of the United States during the last four months of the Arthur administration, and from 1889 to 1892 he was a school commissioner of New York City. In January 1914, his health, already bad, was further impaired by the violent struggle which ensued when he was attacked by a suddenly crazed Japanese servant. During the following summer he set out as was his custom on a yachting trip, but illness necessitated his being put ashore at Newport, R. I., where he died. He was married in 1863 to Harriet Van Rensselaer, a daughter of Gen. Stephen Van Rensselaer.

[J. S. Crosby, *Report of the Gov. of Mont.*, 1883, 1884; F. B. Heitman, *Hist. Reg. and Dict. of the U. S. Army* (1903); *Who's Who in America*, 1912–13; *N. Y. Times*, Aug. 9, 1914; *Circular and Cat. of the Univ. of the City of N. Y.* (1856); *Army and Navy Jour.*, Aug. 15, 1914; H. M. Crittenden, *Yellowstone Nat. Park* (1895).]   J. D. W.

CROSBY, PEIRCE (Jan. 16, 1824–June 15, 1899), naval officer, a son of John P. and Catharine (Beale) Crosby, was born in Delaware County, Pa., of English ancestors prominent in Pennsylvania since 1682. He was educated in private schools and entered the navy as midshipman, June 5, 1838. After service in the Mediterranean, he was attached to the Coast Survey and was then in the *Decatur* and *Petrel* in the Mexican War, participating in the operations against Tabasco and Tuxpan. Following three years in the *Relief* on the African coast, he was made lieutenant, Sept. 3, 1853, and until 1857 was in the *Germantown* in the Brazil Squadron. In the Civil War he did energetic work, April and May 1861, in command of tugs protecting trade in the Chesapeake, and then had special duty under Gen. Butler as harbor-master at Hampton Roads. Under Butler and Flag-Officer Stringham he commanded the tug *Fanny* in the capture of Hatteras Inlet, rendering excellent service, Aug. 28, in rescuing two barges laden with troops which had stranded in a heavy sea. After an attack of typhoid, he took command of the steamer *Pinola* at Baltimore, Dec. 18, 1861, and thence joined Farragut below New Orleans. On the night of Apr. 20, 1862, the *Pinola,* under Crosby, and the *Itasca* attempted to break the barrier of chains and hulks stretched across the river below New Orleans. Under a heavy fire from the Confederate forts, later checked by Union mortars, the *Pinola* placed mines in one hulk, but, in the confusion of separating the two vessels, the wires were broken and the charges failed to ignite. Then with much difficulty she released the *Itasca,* which had grappled another hulk and run aground with it above the barrier, and the two steamers retired after making a gap wide enough for passage of the fleet. While running the forts below New Orleans, and again later at Vicksburg, the *Pinola,* being in the rear of Farragut's column, encountered a severe fire. In October, despite Farragut's protests at losing a dependable officer (*Official Records, Navy*, XIX, 338), Crosby was chosen by Admiral S. P. Lee as fleet captain in the North Atlantic Blockading Squadron, in which arduous and responsible position he served from January to October, 1863. Later he commanded the *Florida* from

March to November 1864, the *Keystone State* in the same squadron, capturing nine blockade-runners. He was in the *Metacomet* in the Gulf Squadron from December 1864 to August 1865, participating in the later operations leading to the capture of Mobile and sweeping up 150 torpedoes below the city with nets of his own devising, a service which earned Admiral H. K. Thatcher's praise as requiring "coolness, judgment, and perseverance" (*Ibid.*, XXII, 92). From 1865 to 1868 he was in the *Shamokin* in the South Atlantic, and after promotion to captain, May 7, 1868, held several navy-yard positions until commissioned commodore, Oct. 3, 1874. In March 1882 he became rear admiral. After commanding the South Atlantic Squadron for a year and then the Pacific Squadron, he retired in October 1883, living afterward in Washington. Crosby had a fine military figure, standing over six feet and weighing over two hundred pounds. In Admiral John Upshur's words, he was "brave as a lion and had the tenderness of a woman." He was married four times: on Oct. 16, 1850, to Matilda Boyer of Lexington, Va., who died in 1853; in March 1861, to Julia Wells who died in 1866; on Feb. 15, 1870, to Miriam Gratz, who died in 1878; and on June 24, 1880, to Louise Audenried.

[*Official Records* (Navy); J. H. Martin, *Hist. of Chester, Pa.* (1877), pp. 202–18; obituaries in *Army and Navy Jour.*, June 24, 1899, and *Washington Post*, June 16, 1899.]   A. W.

CROSBY, WILLIAM OTIS (Jan. 14, 1850–Dec. 31, 1925), geologist, son of Francis William and Hannah (Ballard) Crosby, both of English descent, was born in Decatur, Ohio. His father was a school-teacher who shortly after the close of the Civil War went south and became superintendent of a gold-mine in North Carolina. Here the boy gained his first insight into the problems of economic geology. In 1871 he accompanied his father, who had become interested in a silver-mine, to Georgetown, Colo., and while there met President Runkle with a party of students from the Massachusetts Institute of Technology and accompanied them on one of their trips. As was to be expected, such association aroused in him sufficient interest to cause him to enter upon a course of study at the Institute, from which he graduated in 1876. He must have been a student of unusual promise, for in the fall of the same year he received an appointment as assistant in the geological department in the Institute, where in the course of time he became full professor and head of the department.

Crosby was from the start an original worker and an inspiring teacher. He was capable of an amount of patient drudgery in his work that would have been far from congenial to most; and of gathering material, handling and preparing it for his classes or his wider audiences at the Boston Society of Natural History, where he had become a curator, he never tired. Forced by almost total deafness to retire from teaching, he devoted himself after 1906 largely to work pertaining to various phases of economic geology. As an expert in mining problems he covered in more or less detail the whole western mining region, besides many of the states in the East. It was, however, in problems relating to water supply and storage dams in which intricate problems of underground structure were involved, that he became most deeply interested, and widely and favorably known. This work often involved responsibility for large financial outlay, as in his studies of the Muscle Shoals region in Alabama. He served as consulting engineer for the celebrated Arrow Dam in Idaho, the highest in the world; the dams on the Medina River in Texas; the Conchos River in Mexico, and the great dam across the Mississippi River at Keokuk, Iowa, the third longest in the world. He was consulting geologist to the Board of Water Supply of New York City during 1906–12, investigated the conditions for the Ashokan and Kensico dams, the deep Hudson River siphons, and the Catskill aqueduct. He was also called as consulting geologist for three large dams in Spain. Always painstaking and thorough, he became identified with many of the most important hydraulic operations in America.

Crosby's publications cover a considerable range of subjects. Of greatest importance probably from the standpoint of systematic geology, and involving the most detailed field work over a considerable area was his *Geology of the Boston Basin,* pts. 1–3 (1893–1900).

Crosby was married in 1876 to Alice Ballard of Lansing, Mich.

[Sketch by Douglas Johnson in *Science,* June 18, 1926; sketch by H. W. Shimer and Waldemar Lindgren, accompanied by a full bibliography, in *Bull. Geol. Soc. of America,* Mar. 1927; personal recollections.]

G. P. M.

CROSS, EDWARD (Nov. 11, 1798–Apr. 6, 1887), jurist, was born in Virginia where his grandfather, originally from Wales, had settled early in the eighteenth century. His father, Robert Cross, served with the colonial forces in the Revolutionary War, afterward engaging in farming. In 1799 the family moved to Cumberland County, Ky., where Edward spent his youth on a farm, obtaining his education at the common schools. When he became of age he determined to take up law and went to Overton County, Tenn., reading for two years in the office of Adam

Huntsman at Monroe in that county. On being admitted to the Tennessee bar in 1822 he opened an office there and practised for three years. He made progress, but, having been brought up on the frontier, he found the lure of the West irresistible and in 1826 he proceeded to the Territory of Arkansas, settling at Washington, Hempstead County, and entering into partnership with Daniel Ringo, who was later chief justice. In 1828 he became a member of the staff of Gov. Izard and in that position took a prominent part in the organization of the territorial militia. He acquired an extensive practise and had the reputation of being a sound lawyer of sterling character. In 1832 President Jackson appointed him one of the justices of the superior court of the Territory of Arkansas, and he remained on the bench for four years, being reappointed by President Van Buren. On the admission of Arkansas to the Union as a state, June 16, 1836, the court ceased to function, and Cross became surveyor-general of the public lands under the new constitution, a position which he retained for two years. In 1838, as Democratic nominee, he was elected representative in Congress, where he served for three terms, being reëlected in 1840 and 1842. He was extremely active in the presidential election of 1840, taking a leading part in the Democratic campaign and addressing meetings in many parts of the state. As a delegate from Arkansas he attended the National Democratic Convention at Baltimore in 1844, with instructions from his constituents to support Van Buren. The subsequent publication of the latter's letter opposing the annexation of Texas induced Cross to disobey his instructions and vote for Polk, and this action on his part was afterward approved by his party. In 1852, to meet an emergency, he was appointed by Gov. Drew a special justice of the supreme court of the state. He was one of the promoters in 1853 of the Cairo & Fulton Railroad, which was planned to make eastern connection at Cairo, Ill., and continue the line of the St. Louis & Iron Mountain, running south from St. Louis toward Texas, and was its president from 1855 to 1862, during which period it was, in common with the majority of the companies forming the Missouri railroad system, forced into bankruptcy. After 1860 he took no very active part in politics and gradually relinquished practise, though his interest in public affairs continued unabated to an advanced age. Speaking of this period of his life a contemporary said, "His good morals and integrity are of the highest type and the old patriarch is universally esteemed" (Hallum, *post*). He died at Little Rock in his eighty-ninth year. On Aug. 4, 1831, he had married

Laura Frances, daughter of Benjamin Elliott of Washington County, Mo.

[John Hallum, *Biog. and Pictorial Hist. of Ark.* (1887), p. 119; Dallas T. Herndon, *Centennial Hist. of Arkansas* (1922), I, 917, which must be used with caution; obituary and editorial in *Ark. Gazette* (Little Rock), Apr. 7, 1887.]   H.W.H.K.

CROSWELL, EDWIN (May 29, 1797–June 13, 1871), journalist, politician, was of English stock, his paternal ancestor having come from England and settled in Boston in 1655. He was born in Catskill, N. Y., the son of Mackay Croswell and the nephew of the eminent Dr. Harry Croswell [*q.v.*]. Mackay Croswell was a tavern-keeper who was noted for his geniality, his fund of good stories, and boon companionship. He was also editor of the *Catskill Packet* (founded in 1792) and of its three successors. Edwin spent his boyhood about the tavern and in the office of his father's newspaper. He and Thurlow Weed [*q.v.*] were boys together, the one quiet, studious, and of a refined nature, the other a lover of sports and adventure. Croswell educated himself in the English classics; was attracted to Swift's sententious purity, and patterned his style after the Junius Letters. When he was fourteen years old he entered the office of the *Catskill Recorder* and was soon assistant editor. Edwin's future appeared bright while Thurlow hung about Mackay Croswell's office hoping to be apprenticed. Croswell's untiring industry and single-hearted devotion to party soon attracted the attention of the politicians. When Moses Cantine (editor of the Albany *Argus*) died in 1823, the "Albany Regency," especially Martin Van Buren, called Croswell to the editorial chair of the *Argus*. He was elected state printer in 1824 and held the office until 1847, save for one interruption, when Weed, master Whig politician, became state printer (1840–44).

Croswell was one of a trio of great partisan editors of the Democratic party in the thirties, the others being Francis Preston Blair [*q.v.*] of the Washington *Globe,* and Thomas Ritchie [*q.v.*] of the *Richmond Enquirer.* These were the pen-executives for their party until they fell victims to party factions. Croswell was more certain in his judgment than Ritchie, and less vitriolic than Blair. As mouthpiece of the Albany Regency his journal led the way for the New York papers of his faith. He was a conservative who sagaciously labored to keep harmony in the Democracy until the inevitable break came between the "Barnburners" and "Hunkers." He broke with Van Buren on the Texas question, became embroiled in an unfortunate party quarrel with William Cassidy [*q.v.*] of the Albany *Atlas,* which was increasing in strength, and re-tired from the *Argus* in 1854. The Canal Bank failure (1848), his illness, and a desire to enter business of a different nature to improve his financial circumstances, had much to do with his retirement. He engaged in business in New York City, but died a poor man at Princeton, N. J., after friends had come to his aid.

[Files of the Albany *Argus, Atlas,* and *Evening Journal*; obituaries in *Atlas* (Albany) and *N. Y. Tribune,* June 16, 1871; scattering letters in the Van Buren MSS. (Lib. of Cong.); MSS. in the N. Y. Pub. Lib., in the Archives of the N. Y. Hist. Soc., and in the James Watson Webb Papers (in possession of Col. Creighton Webb, Shelburne, Vt.); Herbert D. A. Donovan, *The Barnburners* (1925); De Alva S. Alexander, *A Pol. Hist. of the State of N. Y.* (1906). Croswell was one of the authors of *Reminiscences of Catskill: Local Sketches, by the Late D. Pinckney, Together With Interesting Articles by Thurlow Weed, Edwin Croswell, S. Sherwood Day and Joseph Hallock, Esqrs.* (1868).]   W.E.S—h.

CROSWELL, HARRY (June 16, 1778–Mar. 13, 1858), editor, clergyman, the seventh child of Caleb Croswell and his wife, Hannah Kellogg, was born in West Hartford, Conn. His father had removed to Connecticut from Charlestown, Mass., before the Revolution. The boy received his early education from the Rev. Dr. Nathan Perkins, and had for one winter the advantage of being a member of Noah Webster's household, where he received instruction from Webster in return for his services. He worked for a little time as a clerk in a country store in Warren, but left there to join an older brother who was in charge of a printing establishment in Catskill, N. Y. This was more to his liking than clerking, and he made the most of his opportunity. He was soon sending communications to the *Catskill Packet,* which was printed in the shop, and at the age of twenty-two was made editor of the paper. With this assurance of a livelihood he married Susan Sherman of New Haven, Conn., on Aug. 16, 1800 (New Haven *Register,* Mar. 14, 1858). He soon moved to Hudson, N. Y., however, where he established himself in May 1801 as proprietor of an independent newspaper, the *Balance.* The town had at this time a Republican paper, the *Bee,* for whose sting the local Federalists sought an antidote. Croswell provided this by publishing the *Wasp,* a letter-size sheet first issued in 1802. His caustic pen very soon involved him in difficulties. The Republicans had just placed as judge in Columbia County one of the leading members of their party; and the law of libel in the state did not require that questions of fact be submitted to the jury. Croswell was indicted for libel. The case was sufficiently challenging to the New York Federalists to bring Alexander Hamilton and William Van Ness to the aid of the young editor, but even Hamilton's brilliant speech could not change the foregone conclusion of the trial. Croswell was found guilty, and the publication of the *Wasp* was discontinued. Croswell issued the *Balance* as a Federalist paper in Hudson until 1809 when encouraged by promises of Federalist support he removed with it to Albany. Promises failed, debts accumulated, and he was jailed by a Federalist creditor. He thereupon gave up his career as a journalist and turned to the ministry for refuge from the ingratitude and uncertainties of the political world. He was ordained deacon in the Episcopal Church, May 8, 1814. His first charge was Christ Church in Hudson, N. Y., where he remained only a few months. On Jan. 1, 1815, he was installed as rector of Trinity Church in New Haven, Conn. Here he passed the remainder of his life contentedly, in the faithful performance of his pastoral duties.

[Croswell's diary (MS.) is in the possession of Yale Univ. Lib. A memoir, based upon it, was published by F. B. Dexter in *Papers of the New Haven Colony Hist. Soc.*, vol. IX (1918), and reprinted in Dexter's *A Selection from the Miscellaneous Hist. Papers of Fifty Years* (1918). See also Croswell's life of his son, *A Memoir of the Late Wm. Croswell, D.D.* (1853), and obituaries in New Haven papers, Mar. 14, 1858. An account of Croswell's trial is to be found in *Speeches at Full Length of Mr. Van Ness, Mr. Caines, Mr. Harrison and Gen. Hamilton in the Great Cause of the People against Harry Croswell* (1804). New York and Albany papers of Feb. 19 and 20, 1804, printed notices of the trial.]
      M.A.M.

CROTHERS, SAMUEL McCHORD (June 7, 1857–Nov. 9, 1927), clergyman, essayist, was born at Oswego, Ill. His ancestors, of Scotch-Irish stock, came to America in the seventeenth century and settled in Pennsylvania, their descendants spreading westward and taking their part in the life of the frontier. A strain of French Huguenot blood on the mother's side served to intensify the spirit of adventure and independence that marked the family in successive generations. His grandfather, Samuel Crothers, was a Presbyterian minister; his father, John M., who married Nancy Foster, was a lawyer. In 1873 Samuel M. Crothers was graduated from Wittenberg College, Ohio, and in 1874 from the College of New Jersey (now Princeton). He next spent three years at the Union Theological Seminary, New York, in preparation for the work of the Presbyterian ministry.

After graduation from the Seminary, being then just twenty years old, he began the practical life of the ministry, serving in two frontier parishes in Nevada and for two years in Santa Barbara. Up to this time he had remained satisfied with the Calvinistic theology of his forefathers as handed down by Princeton and Union Seminary. In the freer air of the West, however, the mind of the youth soon found itself expanding into larger and more liberal views upon the fundamental problems of Christian life and thought. Without abandoning the old he began to venture into new ways of interpreting the traditions of Calvinism as he had received them. The consequence was that his preaching became suspect to the authorities of his church, while at the same time it was appealing with increasing attraction to the more open-minded in the community and to the visitors from other states. By the end of the year 1881 he had decided to sever his connection with the Presbyterian body and to spend a year in study and reflection before making new denominational attachments. With this object he entered the Harvard Divinity School and there discovered that he was already prepared to join the Unitarian fellowship. In 1882 he began at once the two happy ventures of the Unitarian ministry and the family life, marrying, Sept. 9, Louise M. Bronson of Santa Barbara, Cal. For forty-five years these were to move on together in parallel ways of singular harmony and increasing usefulness.

With characteristic modesty and good sense the young convert declined several brilliant offers of city parishes and accepted a call to Brattleboro, Vt., where for four years he worked out the problems inevitable to so radical a change of mental attitude. From this semi-rural pastorate he was called to wider service at St. Paul, Minn., and during eight years made the church there a far-reaching center of liberal religion throughout the rapidly developing northwestern country. From St. Paul he made his final change of residence to Cambridge, Mass., as minister of the historic First Parish in 1894. In the congenial atmosphere of the University town and neighboring Boston, he found the keenest stimulation to his ripened powers. His work here became equally fruitful in three lines of activity: first, as pastor of a large, highly organized church already a potent force in the life of the community. Crothers was as far as possible from the type of the bustling, dictatorial church official. Quiet, unobtrusive, hesitating in manner, leaving to others the direct management of every organized effort, he kept his eye and his hand upon the working out of all the plans for social welfare and religious influence of which his church was the center. The traditional forms of worship he accepted as they came to him, approved changes as they were suggested by the parish itself, and sought steadily to infuse all forms with the spirit of true devotion which alone could give them value.

Of his two other functions, those of preacher and writer, it is impossible to speak separately, so closely were they interwoven in the method of his thought. His preaching, as he himself said, had but one subject, and that was "liberty," the freedom of the human soul to think for itself and to act for itself so long as such action does not interfere with the freedom of others. In his writing he developed this doctrine of freedom in his treatment of social habits and institutions. If he had a philosophy, it was the philosophy of common sense, and this meant to him much the same thing as a sense of humor; for, if humor is, as he thought it was, "the perception of the incongruous," it is by the same token the perception of the congruous, the fitting, the sane, the harmonious. It is this sanity, this sense of proportion, that above all else distinguishes the long series of essays which are Crothers's literary monument. Written under the impulse of some popular discussion of educational or social problems and often read before publication to friendly audiences, their whimsical humor, their keen insight, their searching criticism of social foibles and their delivery, clothed in a demure, half apologetic seriousness, made them the most delightful of entertainments. To other audiences, at times, their subtlety of thought and playfulness of language made them quite unintelligible. Printed first in magazines of the higher class and later collected into volumes with suggestive titles, they make their appeal to a choice circle of discriminating readers.

The same quality of balanced judgment penetrated also his pulpit utterances, but with rare discretion and self-control he never allowed his sense of humor to appear in his sermons. The cheap devices of the "popular" preacher to catch the attention of his hearers were abhorrent to him, and it is probably owing to this quality of elevation and refinement that his preaching like his writing appealed rather to a limited group of like-minded followers than to great numbers of casual listeners. He spoke without notes, but after such careful elaboration that, as he expressed it, the work of composition was rather an act of memory than of original thinking. His publications include: *The Understanding Heart* (1903); *The Gentle Reader* (1903); *The Pardoner's Wallet* (1905); *By the Christmas Fire* (1908); *Among Friends* (1910); *Humanly Speaking* (1912); "The Charm of English Prose in the 17th Century: Phi Beta Kappa Oration, Harvard, 1913," in *Harvard Graduates Magazine*, XXII, 1–15; *Meditations on Votes for Women, etc.* (1914); *The Pleasures of an Absentee Landlord* (1916); *Oliver Wendell Holmes, the Autocrat and His Fellow-Boarders* (1909); *The Dame School of Experience* (1920); *Ralph*

Waldo Emerson: How to Know Him (1921); *The Cheerful Giver* (1923); *The Children of Dickens* (1925). Death came to him suddenly at Cambridge in his seventy-first year.

[*The Critic*, Mar. 1906; *Nation* (N. Y.), Nov. 30, 1927; *Outlook*, Nov. 23, 1912, pp. 643–56; *Boston Transcript*, Nov. 10, 12, 1927; *N. Y. Times*, Nov. 10, and editorial Nov. 13, 1927; *Who's Who in America*, 1926–27; personal acquaintance.]   E.E.

CROUNSE, LORENZO (Jan. 27, 1834–May 13, 1909), jurist, governor of Nebraska, was born at Sharon, Schoharie County, N. Y., the son of John and Margaret (Van Aernam) Crounse. His father was of German, his mother of Dutch descent. He received little more than a common school education, but taught school, studied law, and in 1857 was admitted to the bar. In 1860 he was married to Mary E. Griffiths, and the next year went to war as captain of Battery K, 1st Regiment, New York Light Artillery, but his service ended shortly after the second battle of Bull Run, in which he was severely wounded. In 1864 he moved to Rulo, Nebr., later settling at Fort Calhoun, and again turned to law. From the first Crounse was active in Nebraska politics. He served in the legislature, and helped draft the constitution under which the territory was admitted as a state. He was associate justice of the state supreme court for six years following 1867 and wrote many opinions that were of great local importance. Notable among his decisions was that in *Brittle* vs. *The People* (2 *Nebr.* 198), in which he upheld the right of a colored man to sit on a jury. He served for two terms, 1873–77, in the national House of Representatives, and his disregard while he was there of the wishes of the Nebraska railroads probably accounts for his failure to win in 1876 the seat in the United States Senate to which he aspired. For four years after 1879 he was collector of internal revenues for the Nebraska district, in 1880 he attended the Republican National Convention as an ardent Blaine man, and in Harrison's administration he became assistant secretary of the treasury. During these years he spent much time on the fine farm he had acquired near Fort Calhoun.

By this time the Farmers' Alliance had blossomed into the People's party, and in the election of 1890, because of the agrarian uprising, the Republicans lost control of the Nebraska state government. In order to regain their former supremacy the old party leaders decided in 1892 to nominate Crounse for the governorship. This they did, but with some reluctance, for, while Crounse was no friend to Populism, his disdain for machine politics, which in Nebraska was but another name for railroad dictation, was well known. During the campaign the Democratic nominee, J. Sterling Morton, joined with Crounse in attacking the record of Van Wyck, the popular and capable choice of the third party forces, who advocated ardently the regulation of railway rates by the state. Unfortunately for the Populists Crounse was able to show that his own record was more consistently hostile to the railroads than Van Wyck's, and on this showing he won the election.

Crounse probably took the governorship as a stepping-stone to the United States Senate, but in 1893 the coveted seat went to a Populist, and Crounse had to serve out his term as governor. His administration, coinciding as it did with a period of acute hard times, gave him small satisfaction. He was compelled to report at its end a condition of "partial failure of crops in the year 1893, and their total destruction in a large portion of the state in the year just closed." State finances were also in a deplorable state, in spite of the economies he had effected. His colleagues at the state house were for the most part small men under machine control who consistently embarrassed him. Under these circumstances he refused a renomination in 1894, and by so doing paved the way for the choice of a Populist as his successor. Crounse was out of office until 1901 when he became a member of the state Senate. That year the legislature was long deadlocked over the election of two United States senators, and for a time it seemed that Crounse, who was not originally a candidate, would be one of those chosen to break the deadlock, but, when his election was practically conceded, the Burlington and Union Pacific interests, which up to the moment had been fighting each other, joined forces and effected a compromise. Needless to say, they did not choose Crounse.

After this until the time of his death in May 1909 Crounse remained aloof from politics. He traveled, as he had already done previously, both abroad and in this country. Dignified, serious, and in his prime almost austere, he mellowed in his declining years and acquired an "unruffled tranquillity" that endeared him to his associates. He was a great lover of books and liked even to translate the Latin of his school days. From the time of his wife's death in 1882 he remained a widower, and his last years were spent in Omaha with one of his four children.

[A reliable sketch of Crounse's life is in J. S. Morton and Albert Watkins, *Illustrated Hist. of Nebr.* (1905), I, 631–34. Excerpts from his more important speeches in Congress are given in T. W. Tipton, "Forty Years of Nebr.," in *Nebr. State Hist. Soc. Colls.*, 2 ser., IV (1902), 395–409. His message to the legislature, Jan. 3, 1895, is in the *Senate Jour.* of that year, pp. 45–70. A good obituary notice and editorial appreciation were published in the Omaha *World Herald*, May 15, 1909.]
J.D.H.

CROUTER, ALBERT LOUIS EDGERTON (Sept. 15, 1846–June 26, 1925), educator of the deaf, was a member of a Huguenot family which moved to Germany and later to New York City. Loyal to King George, Crouter's ancestors went to Canada during the Revolution, and he was born near Belleville, Ontario. His father was Abraham Lewis Crouter and his mother was Elizabeth Eliza German. After finishing his primary and secondary education in the Belleville schools, he entered Albert College. At seventeen he became a teacher in the public schools in Belleville. At twenty he moved to Kansas, where he taught in an Indian school at Shawneetown. While he was there Thomas Burnside, superintendent of the Kansas School for the Deaf at Olathe, offered him a position which he accepted before his twenty-first birthday. From that time until his death he was actively engaged in the education of the deaf. At the age of twenty-one he was offered the superintendency of the Kansas school. He accepted, however, an offer to teach in the Pennsylvania Institution for the Deaf at Philadelphia, and in 1884 he became its principal. Becoming interested in the oral method of instructing the deaf, he organized a separate department for orally taught pupils, extended the trades teaching of the school, and established a normal department. Later all class work was done orally. In 1892, under Crouter's guidance, the Pennsylvania Institution was moved to Mount Airy, where new grounds and modern buildings with every convenience had been provided by his energy and foresight. The grouping of the buildings into three separate departments according to the ages of the children, and the addition of a manual-training department, have made this a model residential institution for deaf children. The title of principal of this school was changed to that of superintendent without changing the duties, and Crouter remained until his death superintendent of the Pennsylvania Institution. Under his administration it became one of the largest and best-known of schools for the deaf, and was visited and studied by teachers of the deaf from all parts of the world.

He was one of the founders of the American Association to Promote the Teaching of Speech to the Deaf, and became its president in 1904, succeeding Alexander Graham Bell [q.v.]. He was for many years a member of the Executive Committee of the Conference of Superintendents and Principals of American Schools for the Deaf. He represented the United States at the Seventh International Conference of Instructors of the Deaf at Edinburgh, and attended practically every important gathering of instructors of the deaf in the United States throughout the whole term of his connection with the Pennsylvania Institution, which lasted for fifty-eight years. He also found time to attend meetings of the deaf themselves and to address them in the language of signs. A member of the Episcopal Church, he was rector's warden of Grace Church, Mount Airy, for many years, and from 1895 until his death he was a member of the commission in charge of the Episcopal Mission for the deaf in Philadelphia. He wrote many papers dealing with the education of deaf pupils and with the training of teachers of the deaf, among them being "Marriages of the Deaf," in *The American Annals of the Deaf,* October 1889; "The Deaf in Hearing Schools and in Day Schools," *Ibid.,* May 1904; "The Supervision and Care of Pupils," *Ibid.,* January 1905; "The Training of Teachers," *Ibid.,* November 1911. His style was particularly clear and forceful. Crouter was singularly successful as an executive. His presence was commanding but his expression was attractive and kindly, and he was well loved by his pupils and by the members of his profession. On Apr. 30, 1895, he was married to June Yale, a teacher of the deaf at the Clarke School at Northampton, Mass. Three of their nine children have followed their parents' calling.

[*The Mount Airy World,* Nov. 19, 1925; article by Dr. Harris Taylor in the *Volta Rev.,* Nov. 1925; article by Frank W. Booth in *The Am. Annals of the Deaf,* Mar. 1926, pp. 89–96; letter from members of Crouter's immediate family; personal recollections of the writer.]
P.H.

CROWELL, LUTHER CHILDS (Sept. 7, 1840–Sept. 16, 1903), inventor, was descended from Yelverton Crowell, who with his brother Thomas settled on Cape Cod in 1638. Luther was the son of Francis Baker Crowell, a ship's captain, and Mehitable Hall Crowell. Though both parents were of the same surname, they were not related. Both were born on Cape Cod, the father in South Yarmouth and the mother in West Dennis, and it was in the latter place that Luther was born. By the time he was seventeen he had not only completed the courses of the local schools but had also attended an academy and spent a year studying medicine privately with a physician. Following his adventures in higher education he entered the merchant marine service and at the end of four years was offered a captain's commission, which he declined. The reason for this, apparently, was his intense interest in aeronautics, for within a year he had moved to Boston and on June 3, 1862, obtained a patent for an aerial machine. He immediately proceeded to develop the mechanism, but the business failure of his chief backer put a stop to the work. He then turned his attention to the development of another idea

which had been suggested in the course of his work on the aerial machine; namely, a machine to make paper bags. For this he received a patent in 1867. Five years later he devised the square-bottomed paper bag universally used today and also the machine for making it; and while legal proceedings arising out of infringement of this patent were still in progress, he invented the side-seam paper bag and then sold partial rights in all his bag patents to the infringing company. Improvements in printing machinery next attracted Crowell and by 1873 he had devised and patented a sheet-delivery and folding mechanism. This invention marked a distinct forward step in the development of printing machinery and was quite ahead of its time, so that the first opportunity to introduce it did not come until two years later when it was combined wih a new press purchased by the *Boston Herald.* The combination machine was the first rotary folding machine whereby newspaper sheets, singly or collectively, were delivered folded as complete products. For the next few years Crowell devoted his time wholly to improving his mechanism, being unable financially to enter into the general manufacture of it. Meanwhile R. Hoe & Company, in their various printing-press experiments, found that some of their devices encroached upon Crowell's inventions, and offered him not only a substantial sum of money for partial rights in his paper-bag improvements and sheet-delivery mechanism but also a liberal salary to join them. He accepted and in 1879 entered the employ of this firm where he remained until his death. He could now work to his heart's content and during the following ten years he perfected the double supplement press, and followed this with double and quadruple presses and the combined pamphlet-printing and wire-binding machines. He obtained over 280 United States patents for printing machinery alone, including those for the printing of both sides of a web of paper from one cylinder, a rotary printing mechanism, a positive cutting and folding mechanism without tapes, the first sheet-piling mechanism, and many others. One of his last inventions was a machine for pasting labels on bottles, and at the time of his death he was working on a wrapping and mailing machine. Crowell gloried in being a "Cape Codder." He despised shams and expressed himself freely and fearlessly in all matters. He was a member of the American Society of Mechanical Engineers, and of the Franklin Institute. On Aug. 18, 1863, he married Mrs. Margaret D. Howard of Boston. Although a resident of New York City he died at his old home in West Dennis.

[*A Short Hist. of the Printing Press* (1902), printed and published for Robt. Hoe; Stephen D. Tucker, "Hist. of R. Hoe & Co., N. Y.," transcript (MS.) in Lib. of Cong.; W. B. Kaempffert, *A Popular Hist. of Am. Invention* (1924); Records of U. S. Patent Office and of the Franklin Institute; family correspondence.]

C. W. M.

CROWNE, JOHN (1640–April 1712), Restoration dramatist, was the first Harvard College playwright. He was the eldest of the three children of William [*q.v.*] and Agnes Mackworth Crowne and was probably born in Shropshire, England, where the family estates of his mother were situated. He accompanied his father to New England in the summer of 1657 when the latter came with Col. Thomas Temple to take possession of the province of Nova Scotia. In the fall of 1657 his father entered him at Harvard College and proceeded to the Penobscot River country. Crowne was a student at Harvard for three years, but did not graduate. He returned with his father to England early in 1661. When in 1667 by the Treaty of Breda the elder Crowne lost his estates in Nova Scotia he could no longer assist his son, who turned to the theatre for a livelihood. By his own confession it was the loss of his father's fortune that caused him to "run into that Madness call'd Poetry" and to frequent "that Bedlam call'd a Stage."

He began his career with the tragi-comedy *Juliana* (1671) but soon devoted his attention to tragedies. He achieved his first considerable success with *The Destruction of Jerusalem* (1677). He wrote with his eye on the financial rewards and in his efforts to trim his sails to the changing winds of popular favor he attempted all types of drama. Though his tragedies are more numerous than his comedies he is best known to posterity as a comic dramatist. Much of his caustic satire was clever and effective despite its coarseness. His pictures of contemporary London life were often successful. In the summer of 1674, with both Settle and Dryden out of favor, the Earl of Rochester asked Crowne to produce a court masque. His masque, *Calisto*, first performed in December 1674, won him the favor of Charles II. This was increased by the King's hearty enjoyment of *The Countrey Wit*, produced in 1675. In 1679, at the suggestion of his father, he attempted to capitalize this royal favor when he petitioned, unsuccessfully, for Mounthope, near the Plymouth settlements. The following year he attempted to secure the proprietorship of Boston Neck, a valuable tract of land in the Narragansett country, but without success. During the turbulent period following the Popish Plot, Crowne allied himself with the Tory group and produced the comedy, *City Poli-*

tiques, a clever political satire against the Whigs. Having again pleased Charles II he petitioned for a sinecure that would give him financial independence. The king first demanded another comedy. Crowne reluctantly wrote *Sir Courtly Nice,* now the best known of his many plays, but on the day of the last rehearsal the king was seized with a fit and died three days later. During the last years of his life the struggling playwright suffered from poverty and want. He never ceased his attempts to recover his father's lands in Nova Scotia, but, though he sometimes lived upon the royal bounty, he failed to secure compensation for the loss of his valuable patrimony. He died in obscurity in London.

[A. H. Bullen's article on John Crowne in the *Dict. Nat. Biog.* is superseded by Arthur Franklin White's *John Crowne: His Life and Dramatic Works* (Cleveland, 1922), the definitive biographical treatment, and by his "John Crowne and America" in *Pubs. Modern Language Asso.,* Dec. 1920; see also Geo. Parker Winship, *The First Harvard Playwright; a Bibliog. of John Crowne* (Cambridge, Mass., 1922) and Allardyce Nicoll, *Hist. of Restoration Drama 1660–1700* (Cambridge, England, 2nd ed. 1928).]

F. M.

CROWNE, WILLIAM (c. 1617–1683), adventurer, born in England about 1617, first emerges from the obscurity which surrounds his ancestry and early life when, in 1636, as a servant in the retinue of Thomas Howard, Earl of Arundel, he accompanied him on a diplomatic mission to Ferdinand II of Germany. After his return to England Crowne in 1637 published a brief narrative of the journey, *A True Relation of All the Remarkable Places and Passages Observed in the Travels of Thomas, Lord Howard.* . . . Through the favor of the same nobleman he was created Rouge Dragon in the College of Arms in September 1638. It was probably during the year following this event that he married Agnes, daughter of Richard Mackworth and widow of Richard Watts. At the outbreak of the civil wars he joined the parliamentary cause and became secretary to Basil Fielding, Earl of Denbigh. After various services to Parliament he became a lieutenant-colonel of militia for Shropshire and for four years was one of the county commissioners. In 1654 he was returned the sole member of Parliament for Bridgnorth. Crowne had amassed considerable fortune when he first became interested in land speculation in America; in 1656 he supplied the funds by which he and Col. Thomas Temple acquired title to Nova Scotia from Charles de la Tour. The new proprietors came to America in the summer of 1657 and in the fall made a division of their property; Crowne became owner of the lesser half of the tract, including the Penobscot River country. He entered his son

John [*q.v.*], the future dramatist, at Harvard College and himself proceeded to the Penobscot River where, at Negue, he built a trading-post. He later leased the territory to Temple, who after a short time refused to pay the rent or surrender the land.

With the restoration of Charles II the title of Temple and Crowne to Nova Scotia was jeopardized. Early in 1661 Crowne with his son John sailed to England. In London he successfully defended their claim to Nova Scotia and secured the suspension of Thomas Breedon as governor. As Rouge Dragon he participated in the coronation ceremonies in April 1661 and shortly after resigned the office. While in England he was successfully engaged in making the new government more friendly toward Massachusetts. In recognition of his services the General Court of Massachusetts in October 1662 voted him five hundred acres of land. Meanwhile Crowne could secure no settlement from his unscrupulous partner; the courts of New England, to which he appealed, disclaimed jurisdiction. A greater misfortune befell in 1667, when, by the Treaty of Breda, Charles II disregarded the claims of both Crowne and Temple and ceded Nova Scotia to France. In the same year Crowne settled in Mendon, Mass., and became the first town register. There he lived until 1674 when he went to Rhode Island; by August 1679 he was again a resident of Boston where he remained until his death four years later. Efforts to secure compensation for the loss of Nova Scotia were without success; nor did the sale of his land in Massachusetts and a small grant from the General Court keep his declining years free of poverty.

[The scattered writings about William Crowne are brief, inaccurate, and unsatisfactory. Definitive treatment is Arthur Franklin White's *John Crowne: His Life and Dramatic Works* (Cleveland, 1922); see also "John Crowne and America" by the same author in *Pubs. Mod. Lang. Asso. of America* for Dec. 1920.]

F. M.

CROWNINSHIELD, BENJAMIN WILLIAMS (Dec. 27, 1772–Feb. 3, 1851), merchant, politician, brother of George and Jacob Crowninshield [*qq.v.*], was born in Salem, Mass., the son of George and Mary (Derby) Crowninshield. He was a great-grandson of Johannes Kaspar Richter von Kronenshelt (or Kronenscheldt) who for killing his antagonist in a duel (F. B. Crowninshield, *The Story of George Crowninshield's Yacht, 'Cleopatra's Barge,'* 1913, p. 174), was compelled to leave the University of Leipzig somewhat hastily. He established himself as a physician in Boston, married Elizabeth Allen of Lynn, who had been one of his patients, anglicized his name, and became highly respected. George Crowninshield was a sea-captain and merchant of Salem. Each of his six sons was taken from school early, and, after a short period in the counting-house, was sent to sea as cabin-boy, so that he might learn navigation and the art of leadership without serving before the mast. This system of training was completely successful: all the brothers except Edward, who died at Guadeloupe at the age of seventeen, commanded ships before they were twenty, and eventually they displaced the Derbys as the leading merchant family of Salem. Like his brothers, Benjamin was taken from school early and sent to sea as a cabin-boy, commanded a ship before he reached his majority, proceeded from the quarter-deck to the counting-room, and was made a partner in the world-renowned firm of George Crowninshield & Sons. On Jan. 1, 1804, he was married to Mary Boardman, daughter of Francis and Mary (Hodges) Boardman of Salem, and sister-in-law of Nathaniel Bowditch and Zachariah Silsbee. The double misfortune of the Embargo and the death of his gifted brother Jacob caused the dissolution of George Crowninshield & Sons in 1809. Benjamin then went into business with his father and his brother George, but the father's death in 1815 and George's in 1817 terminated the enterprise. He was also president of the Merchants Bank of Salem, which was organized in 1811 in opposition to Federalist banks. Meanwhile Benjamin had succeeded Jacob as the politician of the family, sitting as a member of the Massachusetts House of Representatives in 1811 and of the state Senate in 1812. The fame of his brother lent him a reputation that his own political prowess did not deserve, and on Dec. 19, 1814, the Senate confirmed his appointment by President Madison as secretary of the navy. Crowninshield promptly declined and then, a few days later, dispatched a second letter accepting the office. The weakness revealed in this vacillation marked his whole career in Washington. In deference to his wife, he remained in the capital only while Congress was in session. Consequently, although he discharged the administrative duties of his office with entire competence, he never mastered the complexities of national politics. President Monroe retained him in office, but Crowninshield was evidently dissatisfied with the part he was playing and resigned on Oct. 1, 1818. He was a presidential elector on the ticket of Monroe and Tompkins in 1820 and a member of the Massachusetts lower house again in 1821. In 1823 he returned to Washington as a Democrat in the House of Representatives, was reëlected to the Nineteenth, Twentieth, and Twenty-first Congresses but was defeated in 1830 by Rufus Choate. While in Congress he was a friend and supporter of John Quincy Adams, and an ironical, somewhat bewildered, observer of national affairs. In 1833 he was for the third time a member of the Massachusetts House, but his political career was closed. He moved in 1832 to Boston and lived there in retirement for the rest of his life. His death came suddenly, while he was ascending the steps of a business house. He was buried in Mount Auburn Cemetery.

[*Biog. Direct. of the Am. Cong. 1774–1927* (1928); *Essex Inst. Hist. Colls.*, XV, 285 (1879); *Boston Transcript*, Feb. 3, 1851; *Memoirs of John Quincy Adams* (1874–77); *The Diary of William Bentley, D.D.*, vol. IV (1914); F. B. Crowninshield, ed., *Letters of Mary Boardman Crowninshield 1815–16* (1905); same, *The Story of George Crowninshield's Yacht, 'Cleopatra's Barge'* (privately printed, 1913); letters of Crowninshield among the Warren Papers in the archives of the Mass. Hist. Soc. and in the MSS. Division of the Lib. of Cong.]   G. H. G.

CROWNINSHIELD, FREDERIC (Nov. 27, 1845–Sept. 13, 1918), painter, writer, was born at Boston, a son of Edward A. and Caroline M. (Welch) Crowninshield, and a scion of a famous Salem family. He was prepared for college at the Boston Latin School and was graduated from Harvard in 1866. In the following year he was married to Helen S. Fairbanks of Boston. Possessed of ample means and a taste for art, which had been stimulated by lessons from Dr. William Rimmer, he went to Paris in 1867 and entered the École des Beaux-Arts. He afterward studied in Italy, remaining abroad until 1878. He then returned to Boston and for seven years occupied a studio, a local landmark, in the rear of the Museum of Fine Arts. He served, under Otto Grundmann, as instructor in drawing and painting and lecturer on anatomy in the museum school. In 1886 Crowninshield removed to New York to devote himself to stained glass and mural painting, foreseeing a great development of these arts in the United States. He was one of the organizers of the National Society of Mural Painters. He was a frequent exhibitor with the Architectural League of New York, of which he was a vice-president. His windows included the depiction of "Hector and Andromache" for Memorial Hall, Harvard University, and the Goodrich window, Church of the Ascension, New York, and he did mural paintings for the Municipal Building, Cleveland, Ohio, the Hotels Waldorf and Manhattan, New York, and many other buildings. In 1900 he became president of the Fine Arts Federation of New York. He took interest in training younger artists for decorative work, and served (1900–11) as director of the American Academy in Rome. He spent much time abroad, living and painting at Rome, Naples, Capri, and Taormina. He wrote poetry as an avocation: *Pictoris Carmina* (1900); *A Painter's Mood* (1902), with his own illustrations; *Tales in Metre and Other Poems* (1903); *Under the Laurel* (1907); and *Villa Mirifiore* (1912). Crowninshield's summer studio was at Stockbridge, Mass., and there, in his last year, when his serious illness was reported from Capri, where he died, a special exhibition of his works was arranged by the Stockbridge Art Association. In April 1919, at the Boston Museum of Fine Arts, a Crowninshield Memorial Exhibition was hung. This included some of the many water-colors, usually of architectural subjects, which the artist made in Italy. Of them the *Boston Herald* (Apr. 13, 1919) said: "A cheerful grayness pervades them, for Mr. Crowninshield, like most colorists who learned their art in France in the seventies, was disinclined to overstate the brilliancy of nature."

[Crowninshield put on record some of his precepts and principles in his book, *Mural Painting* (1887). The *Harvard Grads. Mag.*, Sept. 1909, published a good biographical sketch. "L. W. H." wrote from Stockbridge an appreciation printed in the *Boston Transcript*, Aug. 30, 1918. References to Crowninshield's Boston studio are found in H. Winthrop Peirce, *Early Days of the Copley Soc.* (1903). See also obituary in *Boston Transcript*, Sept. 14, 1918.]   F. W. C.

CROWNINSHIELD, GEORGE (May 27, 1766–Nov. 26, 1817), sea-captain, merchant, pioneer yachtsman, was the eldest son of George and Mary (Derby) Crowninshield, and brother of Benjamin Williams and Jacob Crowninshield [*qq.v.*]. Young George, like the rest of his brothers, received a common school education until he was eleven, and then, after studying navigation, was sent to sea as a captain's clerk. He was in command of a ship to the West Indies in 1790 and four years later he was commanding the *Belisarius* to the East Indies. About 1800 he came ashore to assist his father in the counting-house, directing the extensive commercial interests of George Crowninshield & Sons. The firm made great profits from the *America* and their other privateers in the War of 1812. Upon his father's death in 1815, the firm dissolved and George retired to live upon his very ample income. He always had a love of the spectacular, dressing in the extreme of fashion with bizarre waistcoat, shaggy beaver hat, and tasseled Hessian boots. He drove a flashy yellow curricle and attracted attention by taking a ship to Halifax to bring back the bodies of Capt. Lawrence and Lieut. Ludlow of the *Chesapeake*. Most conspicuous, however, were his pioneer activities as a yachtsman. About the time that he settled down in 1800, he built the first American yacht, the little *Jefferson,* in which he cruised around Massachusetts Bay, sometimes making thrilling rescues after storms. After his retirement in 1815 he built a more elaborate yacht, *Cleopatra's Barge,* in which he sailed to the Mediterranean in 1817, carrying with him more than three hundred letters to consuls and other officials in Europe. The yacht was the first sea-going vessel of her class, and aroused considerable wonderment, throngs of visitors coming aboard at every foreign port. The Europeans marveled at the crew where even the negro cook knew the mysteries of navigation. Crowninshield died suddenly at Salem a few weeks after his return from this cruise. He had never married. He was a short man, remarkably robust and strong, with a high reputation for courage.

[B. W. Crowninshield, "Account of the Yacht *Cleopatra's Barge*" in the *Essex Inst. Hist. Colls.,* XXV, 81-117 (1888), includes a biographical sketch of Crowninshield with verbatim quotations from contemporary newspapers. Further biographical details will be found in the same collections, III, 163 (1861), and in F. B. Crowninshield, *The Story of George Crowninshield's Yacht, 'Cleopatra's Barge'* (privately printed, 1913). There is a full account of Crowninshield and his yacht in R. D. Paine, *Ships and Sailors of Old Salem* (revised ed., 1923), pp. 172-81. The history of the *Cleopatra's Barge* is continued in S. E. Morison, *Maritime Hist. of Mass.* (1921), p. 262.]

R. G. A—n.

CROWNINSHIELD, JACOB (May 31, 1770–Apr. 15, 1808), sea-captain, merchant, congressman, was born in Salem, Mass., the son of George and Mary (Derby) Crowninshield, and brother of George and Benjamin Williams Crowninshield [*qq.v.*]. Jacob was the second son and the most gifted member of the family. He was master of the schooner *Active* on a voyage to Europe in 1790. In 1791 he took the *Henry* to the West Indies. On Nov. 3, 1792, he returned from Calcutta and the Isle of France (Mauritius). On Jan. 23, 1793, he sailed again for India in the *Henry,* returning in November 1794. In April 1796 he brought to New York, in the famous armed ship *America,* the first live elephant ever seen in the United States. It was a female six feet four inches high and sold for $10,000. Crowninshield married Sarah, daughter of John and Sarah (Derby) Gardner, June 5, 1796, and remained ashore thereafter, devoting himself to his extensive commercial interests and to politics. Like the other members of his family, he was an uncompromising supporter of Jeffersonian policies. In 1801 he was elected to the Massachusetts state Senate. In the following year he defeated Timothy Pickering [*q.v.*] in a bitterly contested race for the national House of Representatives. He served in the

Eighth, Ninth, and Tenth Congresses and was regarded as one of the ablest members of the Republican party. In 1805 President Jefferson invited him to succeed Robert Smith [*q.v.*] as secretary of the navy. Crowninshield felt compelled to decline, but the President nevertheless sent his nomination to the Senate. It was confirmed, and according to the records of the Department of State Crowninshield was secretary of the navy from Mar. 3, 1805, until Mar. 7, 1809, although he never assumed the duties of the office. On May 18, 1807, his wife died. His own health grew precarious. The rugged young viking, who could take a clipper from Salem round the Cape of Good Hope to Calcutta and back again, succumbed to the stuffy, unventilated atmosphere of the hall of the House of Representatives. Blood gushed from his throat as he brought his last speech to a close. He died while Congress was still in session, and his body was brought back to Salem for burial. "We lament him very much for his Natural Abilities, his great Commercial knowledge, his sincere virtues, & his inflexible patriotism," the Rev. William Bentley wrote in his diary for Apr. 20, 1808. "I have known him from a lad & have nothing to blame in him. He was everything in every domestic, social, & civil relation. Had he not been confined in his early education & early been engaged in the business of the Seas he would have left none before him."

[*Vital Records of Salem, Mass., to the Year 1850,* vols. I, III, V (1916, 1924, 1925); B. W. Crowninshield, "An Account of the Yacht *Cleopatra's Barge*" in *Essex Inst. Hist. Colls.,* XXV, 81-108 (1888); *The Diary of William Bentley, D.D.* (4 vols., 1905-14); *Essex Register* (Salem, Mass.), Apr. 23, 27, 1808; *Salem* (Mass.) *Gazette,* Apr. 26, 1808; T. H. Benton, ed., *Abridgment of the Debates of Congress 1789-1856,* vol. III (1856); Henry Adams, *Hist. of the U. S.* (1889-91); H. R. W. Cooke, *The Driver Family* (privately printed, 1889); F. A. Gardner, *Thomas Gardner, Planter, and Some of his Descendants* (Salem, Mass., 1907); H. S. Tapley, *Salem Imprints 1768-1825* (Salem, 1927); B. B. Crowninshield, "An Account of the Private Armed Ship *America* of Salem" in *Essex Inst. Hist. Colls.,* XXXVII, 1-76 (1901).] G. H. G.

CROZER, JOHN PRICE (Jan. 13, 1793–Mar. 11, 1866), manufacturer, philanthropist, was descended from James Crozier, a French Huguenot, who in 1700 went from France to Antrim, Ireland, whence he emigrated to America and settled in Delaware County, Pa. He married Esther Gleave (J. H. Martin, *History of Chester,* 1877, pp. 454-55). The son James Samuel Crozer married Sarah Price, and John Price Crozer, one of their five children, was born at West Dale, Delaware County, Pa., in the house where some years before Benjamin West, the painter, had been born. Educated locally and surrounded by Quaker and Baptist influences, Crozer gained a religious training which governed his subsequent life. From 1810 to 1820 he farmed the 173 acres left by his father. Average in height, sturdily built, and vigorous, about 1820 he traveled on horseback for 2,700 miles through Ohio, Indiana, Illinois, and Kentucky to see the country, but returned to his native county. About 1822, with his inheritance of $3,400, he bought second-hand machinery and began the manufacture of yarn, but his product was poor and he went in for weaving. A timely loan of $600 saved him from disaster. In 1824 he bought a near-by mill-seat and farm, which he named West Branch. In the new location his business undertaking succeeded, and in 1825 he married Sallie L. Knowles. In 1828 he built his first meeting-house, which served as a church and school-house for his employees. In 1839 he bought power machinery on borrowed capital and succeeded rapidly thereafter. He took great interest in his employees and visited them personally in sickness, but in 1842 he had the leaders of a strike convicted for conspiracy. An overturned sleigh in 1843 crippled him for life. A flood in the same year swept away his mill-dam buildings at a loss of $50,000. Nevertheless, in 1845 he purchased the Flower estate, near Chester, Pa., which he called "Upland," and on it he built a mansion and a meeting-house. In 1847 he retired, admitting his son Samuel to partnership, and thereafter found his chief interest in his philanthropies. He enjoyed the sharing of his wealth and bounty. Crozer's local benefactions were numerous. He founded a normal school at Upland which served the Government as a hospital during the Civil War. In 1861 he and George H. Stewart were selected as the Philadelphia members of the Christian Commission. He contributed to raising a company for service in the Union cause, and his son George K. Crozer was its captain. He entrusted various funds to the American Baptist Publication Society, built a Baptist church at Upland, and endowed a professorship at Bucknell University. A younger brother died in Africa in connection with the work of the American Colonization Society, in which Crozer was greatly interested. His will established a $50,000 Memorial Fund for "Missions among the Colored People of this Country." His widow and children established the Crozer Theological Seminary at Chester, Pa., as a memorial to him by adding $195,000 for buildings, library, and endowment to the normal school property, then valued at $80,000.

[The Am. Baptist Pub. Soc. published the *Life of John P. Crozer* (1868), by Jas. Wheaton Smith, based upon 2,130 pages (ledger) of Crozer's diary. In addition to source cited above see Henry G. Ashmead, *Hist. of Delaware County, Pa.* (1884); *The John P. Crozer Memorial* (1866).]

B. C.

CROZET, CLAUDE (Jan. 1, 1790–Jan. 29, 1864), soldier and engineer, was born at Villefranche, in France, was educated at the École Polytechnique, and in 1807 was commissioned in the artillery. He served with credit at Wagram and in the Russian campaign, was captured during the retreat from Moscow, and remained a prisoner in Russia for two years, being released and allowed to return to France only after the fall of Napoleon. He then resigned his captaincy, but rejoined the army on the Emperor's return from Elba. The second restoration of the Bourbons left him once more out of the service, and in 1816 he determined to seek his fortune in a new country. Gen. Simon Bernard [*q.v.*], the distinguished French military engineer, had just been appointed to a position in the engineer service of the United States army, and Crozet accompanied him to America. On the recommendations of Lafayette and Albert Gallatin, he was appointed, Oct. 1, 1816, assistant professor of engineering at West Point, and on Mar. 6, 1817, was made professor and head of the department. Up to this time instruction in engineering there had been unsystematic and elementary; Crozet improved it greatly, particularly by requiring a much more substantial foundation of mathematics. He introduced the study of descriptive geometry, not hitherto taught in the United States, and prepared the first American textbook on the subject (*A Treatise of Descriptive Geometry for the Use of the Cadets of the United States Military Academy*, 1821). Both at West Point and at the Virginia Military Institute, with which he was later associated, descriptive geometry has continued a specialty up to the present time. Resigning his professorship in 1823, he soon after became state engineer of Virginia. He left that position in 1832, and spent five years in engineering and educational work in Louisiana, but returned to his place in Virginia in 1839. He had the vision and the technical ability to plan a great development of inland communication by road, canal, and railroad, which, though never entirely carried out, gave Virginia one of the best road systems in the country for the time. He urged, though unsuccessfully, the creation of a through route from the seaboard to the West by canalizing the James River from the head of navigation at Richmond up to Lynchburg, and by the construction of a railroad from that point to deep water on the Kanawha. Perhaps his greatest engineering achievement was the location and construction of a railroad through the Blue Ridge between Albemarle and Augusta counties, which later passed into the possession of the Chesapeake & Ohio Company. He is now best remembered, however, for his work in connection with the Virginia Military Institute, formally organized in 1839. Crozet was a member of the original Board of Visitors, was chosen president of the board, and retained that office until 1845. The statute creating the new institution provided that it should be a "military school," and "give instruction in military science and in other branches of knowledge"; also that the students should be "formed into a military corps" and "constitute the public guard of the arsenal." Subject to these very general directions, its character and curriculum were left to the discretion of the Board of Visitors. Crozet's influence caused it to be modeled closely after the pattern of West Point, where he had previously taught, and whose course of study, indeed, was in a considerable degree his own creation. The regulations of the Military Academy were adopted substantially without change, and its uniform was quite closely copied. The course of instruction could not be made identical, partly for lack of funds and partly on account of the difference in the future vocations of the students of the two schools; but the resemblance was strong, military and mathematical subjects being greatly emphasized. In 1857 Crozet was appointed principal assistant to Capt. (afterward Brig.-Gen.) Montgomery C. Meigs [q.v.] for the construction of the aqueduct which supplies the city of Washington with water from the Great Falls of the Potomac. By a natural misapprehension, the building of the Aqueduct Bridge to the Virginia shore is sometimes ascribed to him. He was not employed upon this, however, for the structure was the property of a canal company and had no connection with the city's water-supply system. In 1859, when work on the aqueduct was suspended because of exhaustion of funds, he became principal of the Richmond Academy, and held that position until his death.

[Article by Gen. W. H. Carter in *Jour. of the Mil. Service Inst.*, vol. LIII (July-Aug. 1913), pp. 1–6, republished in *Professional Memoirs, Corps of Engineers*, vol. V (1913), pp. 719–23, and in Nichols's pamphlet mentioned below. Jennings C. Wise, *Mil. Hist. of the Va. Mil. Inst.* (1915); Francis H. Smith, *The Va. Mil. Inst., Its Building and Rebuilding* (1912); E. W. Nichols, *The Va. Mil. Inst., Historical and Traditional* (pamphlet, n.d., apparently 1924).]   T.M.S.

CRUGER, HENRY (Nov. 22, 1739–Apr. 24, 1827), merchant, mayor of Bristol, England, member of Parliament, N. Y. State senator, was born in New York City, son of Henry and Elizabeth (Harris) Cruger. His grandfather, John Cruger, was the first of the family to come to America, and the family association with the

English cousins in Bristol was always intimate. Henry matriculated at King's College in the class of 1758 but he did not complete his course. In 1757 he was sent by his father to the counting-house in Bristol, then a rival of London in the American trade, to familiarize himself with the Cruger business. The young man found it a simple matter to take to wife the daughter of Samuel Peach, a Bristol banker, and settle down to a successful career as merchant. He rose to a high degree of personal popularity, and eminently enjoyed the regard and confidence of his fellow citizens of Bristol" (Van Schaack, *Henry Cruger*, p. 9). Cruger kept in constant touch with the members of his family in New York during the pre-Revolutionary days and felt keenly the mistakes that were being made by the British government in its treatment of the colonies. In 1774 he stood for Parliament and induced his fellow citizens to place Edmund Burke on the ticket with him. "Burke, Cruger, and Liberty" was the party cry. Triumphantly elected and "chaired," Cruger entered Parliament in the session which began Nov. 29, 1774, although his political enemies tried to get the House of Commons to refuse a seat to the American. In his maiden speech (Dec. 16), admirable for its restraint, he deplored the parliamentary measures that had "widened the breach instead of closing it," that "diminished the obedience of the colonies instead of confirming it," that "increased the turbulence and opposition instead of allaying them," and pled for a different plan of conduct which would "secure the colonists in their liberties, while it maintains the just supremacy of Parliament" (*Parl. Hist. of Eng.*, XVIII, 64–67). During the speech, Flood, the Irish orator, was heard to say: "Whosoever he is, he speaks more eloquently than any man I have yet heard in the House" (Van Schaack, *Henry Cruger*, p. 14). At the next election, in 1780, Cruger was "turned out," as he said, "because of his attachment to the Americans during the war." However, he was made mayor of Bristol the following year, and was again successful as a candidate for Parliament in 1784.

The Cruger family bond had been sufficiently strong to bring Henry's father to Bristol (1775) to spend his last years with him. Henry himself declined to run again for Parliament in 1790 in an address "to the Gentlemen, Clergy, Freeholders and Freemen of the city of Bristol," and removed with his family to New York. His political welcome was an election to the Senate of New York State in April 1792, a high compliment to his American sympathies. Cruger's second wife was Elizabeth Blair, who died soon after the family removed to New York. His third wife, whom he married about 1799, was an American woman, Caroline Smith. He was not active in business after his return to America, but overcame ill health to live to a good old age.

[Henry C. Van Schaack, *Henry Cruger: the Colleague of Edmund Burke in the British Parliament* (1859) includes letters to relatives in America and speeches in Parliament; *Knickerbocker Mag.* for Nov. 1842 and Jan. 1843; *Jour. of the First Cong. of the Am. Colonies* (1845), Appendix; Genealogical tables in *The Cruger Family* (1892).]   A.E.P.

CRUGER, JOHN (July 18, 1710–Dec. 27, 1791), mayor of New York, speaker of the last colonial assembly, first president of the New York Chamber of Commerce, was the second of his name to lead a distinguished career as merchant and public official. John Cruger the elder, probably of German origin, who came to New York from Bristol, England, in 1698, had built up a very prosperous shipping business, and as alderman for twenty-two years and mayor from 1739 to his death in 1744, had brought the family to a position of great weight in the affairs of city and province. John, the third son of John and Maria (Cuyler) Cruger, after two years' service as alderman, was appointed mayor in 1756 and held that office till the close of 1765. In the first year of his service the city was thrown into commotion by the demand of the Earl of Loudoun for quarters for large numbers of British troops. The circumstances were new, the behavior of the commander was inexcusably rough, and ugly events were only averted by Cruger's dignified patience, together with his influence in procuring private subscriptions for quarters for the officers. In like manner in 1765, the mayor's cool judgment, aided by the confidence reposed in him by both sides, made possible a popular victory in the delivery of the stamps to the municipality, marred by much less serious breaches of public order than was the case, for example, in Boston in corresponding circumstances.

In the provincial Assembly, in which he served from 1759 to 1775, with an interruption in 1768, he took a prominent part in resistance to the measures of the British ministry. He was a member of the Assembly's Committee of Correspondence and was one of the New York delegation to the Stamp Act Congress. The authorship of the latter's Declaration of Rights and Grievances is claimed for him as well as for John Dickinson [*q.v.*]. He was one of the organizers of the New York Chamber of Commerce in 1768, and on the occasion of his reëlection as its president, May 2, 1769, he conveyed, as speaker of the Assembly, the thanks of that body to the merchants of New York for their proceedings relative to the non-importation of British goods.

Although an opponent of the British policy, Cruger had always a strong sense of his responsibility as an official both of the Crown and of the Province. When the movement of popular resistance developed into revolution, he thus found himself outside the current of what was destined to be the triumphant cause. His name was included in a list of "suspected persons" in the resolution of the Provincial Congress of June 5, 1776. This was doubtless due in part to his course in the Assembly in opposition to the motion to approve and adopt the proceedings of the First Continental Congress and to his refusal personally to sign the Association, and in part to his close business and family connections with certain active Tories. He is said, however, to have contributed to the funds of the Committee of Safety, and he is known to have urged General Gage, after receipt of the news from Lexington and Concord, to order an immediate cessation of public hostilities. At all events, it does not appear that he was ever summoned before the Committee.

Before the British occupation of the city he retired to Kinderhook, returning to New York after 1783 to live with his nephew, Nicholas, who had been conspicuous for patriotic activities. He died, unmarried, Dec. 27, 1791.

[J. A. Stevens, *Colonial Records of the N. Y. Chamber of Commerce, 1768–84* (1867); *Am. Archives*, 4 ser., VI; J. A. Scoville, *The Old Merchants of N. Y. City*, vol. III (1865); *Portrait Gallery of the Chamber of Commerce of the State of N. Y.* (1890), comp. by Geo. Wilson; Chas. King, *Hist. of the N. Y. Chamber of Commerce* (1848); *N. Y. Geneal. and Biog. Record*, Apr. 1875.]   C.W.S.

CRUMP, WILLIAM WOOD (Nov. 25, 1819–Feb. 27, 1897), jurist, was born in Henrico County, Va., his parents being Sterling Jamieson and Elizabeth (Wood) Crump. His father was an importer and the family had been associated with Virginia for some generations. William's early youth was spent in Richmond, where he attended Dr. Gwathmey's school. After passing a short time at Amherst Institute, Mass., he entered William and Mary College in 1835 and graduated there in 1838. Then joining the College Law School, he studied with Prof. N. Beverley Tucker, and was admitted to the Virginia bar in 1840. Opening an office in Richmond, he at the same time commenced to take an active part in political and civic affairs. He had a natural aptitude for public speaking, being fluent, impressive and lucid, as a consequence of which he came to the front rapidly. An ardent advocate of state rights, he was a strong supporter of Calhoun, Polk, and Cass. In 1851 he was elected by the legislature of Virginia judge of the circuit court of the City of Richmond. By virtue of the reorganization of the courts under the state constitution of 1850, however, all existing tenures of judicial office terminated July 1, 1852, and on the expiration of his term Crump returned to practise, stating that the bench did not suit his disposition. He was by nature and temperament an advocate rather than a judge. An expert in the art of cross-examination, he was particularly effective in the conduct of cases before a jury (George L. Christian, *post*), appearing in most of the important civil and criminal cases of his time. He was a strong advocate of secession, and when the Civil War began, became assistant secretary of the treasury of the Confederate States. He represented the city of Richmond in the General Assembly, called at the conclusion of the war, but when the Shellabarger Bill, which put the seceded states under military law came into effect, returned to his law practise. On the arrest of Jefferson Davis, he acted as one of the latter's bondsmen in May 1867, also appearing for the defense in the subsequent trial of Davis for treason. He withdrew, however, from active participation in public affairs, and with the exception of one term in the state legislature, never again held office of any kind. In 1885 he was leading counsel for the defense in the most famous criminal trial in the history of the state, *i.e.*, that of Thomas J. Cluverius for murder. He was also retained in the John Randolph will case. Throughout his life he took a keen interest in the affairs of William and Mary College, and as member and later president of the Board of Visitors, was indefatigable in his efforts to place it on a sound financial basis. He died at Richmond in his seventy-eighth year. His wife was Mary, daughter of Philip Edward Tabb of Waverley, Gloucester County, Va.

[*"Memorial of Judge W. W. Crump by the Bar Asso. of Richmond, Va.," Va. Law Reg.,* Apr. 1897, p. 915; Geo. L. Christian, "Reminiscences of Some of the Dead of the Bench and Bar of Richmond," *Va. Law Reg.,* Dec. 1908, at p. 669; W. A. Christian, *Richmond, Her Past and Present* (1912); *Encyc. of Va. Biog.,* vol. III (1915), ed. by L. G. Tyler.]   H. W. H. K.

CRUNDEN, FREDERICK MORGAN (Sept. 1, 1847–Oct. 28, 1911), educator and librarian, was born in Gravesend, England. His parents were Benjamin Robert and Mary (Morgan) Crunden, of old Saxon, Welsh, and French ancestry. They moved to St. Louis, Mo., in his early childhood, where he was educated in the public schools. He graduated from the high school in 1865, was valedictorian of his class, and won a scholarship to Washington University. By teaching during vacations, he accumulated funds for support during his college career. After receiving degrees of A.B. in 1868, and A.M. in 1872, he was made instructor at Smith Academy.

Six months later he was employed in the public schools as principal of the Jefferson and Benton schools, successively. After two years he was engaged by Washington University as instructor in mathematics and elocution. He became a member of the faculty and remained until 1876, when ill health took him to Colorado. His health restored, Crunden returned to St. Louis and taught in the high school for a short time.

On January 1877 he was appointed secretary and librarian of the Public School Library. He had developed great interest in library work and the new field was most congenial to him. The Library at this time had few books and a small membership. It was not a free library; members were charged for the use of books. The sums thus received, together with a small contribution from the public-school fund, afforded its only support. The new librarian created a sentiment in favor of a free public library, and started the campaign which separated the library from the school board. According to his plan a special tax was provided for the support of the library, and a library board was created to manage the institution and disburse its funds. A prominent member of the board testified that "Mr. Crunden was the life, the soul, and the center of every great advance it made." Before he died St. Louis had a great public library, with six branches and ample support. Over the main entrance to the central building were carved Crunden's words: "Recorded thought is our chief heritage from the past, the most lasting legacy we can leave to the future. Books are the most enduring monument of man's achievements. Only through books can civilization become cumulative."

Crunden regularly attended meetings of the American Library Association, of which he was vice-president (1887), president (1889), and councilor from 1882 almost continuously until his last illness. He was first president of the Missouri State Library Association, and vice-president of the International Library Conference. He served as chairman of the library section of the Louisiana Purchase Exposition, and was selected to arrange and classify the arts and science exhibit. He contributed to various publications, and at his death left unfinished a library textbook. In 1889 he was married to Kate Edmondson. He died after an illness of five years, his funeral services were held at St. Louis, in the Church of the Messiah (Unitarian), and his body was cremated.

[A. E. Bostwick, *Frederick Morgan Crunden: A Memorial Bibliography* (1914); Wm. Hyde and H. L. Conard, *Encyc. of the Hist. of St. Louis* (1899), I, 532; *St. Louis Republic,* Oct. 29, 1911; *Mo. Hist. Rev.,* VI, 101 (Jan. 1912).]   S. M. D.

CUBERO, PEDRO RODRÍGUEZ (1645–1704), Spanish governor of New Mexico, was born at Calatayud, Spain, in the Ebro valley southwest of Saragossa. During the nine years following 1680 he made a world cruise including in his journey parts of America, Asia, and Europe, and he then served for a time at Havana, Cuba. On June 24, 1692, the governorship of New Mexico was granted to him but he was not to take office until the end of De Vargas's term of five years. This should have occurred on Feb. 22, 1696, but on Mar. 3, 1697, Cubero was making demand upon the viceroy of New Spain for the office. An official investigation followed. De Vargas claimed that he had been reappointed by the viceroy, the Conde de Galve, but the records showed no confirmation from the king. The viceroy ordered Cubero to assume the office and his action was confirmed by the king, Jan. 26, 1699. Cubero arrived in Santa Fé on July 2, 1697, and found De Vargas unwilling to surrender the governorship. The latter, as a result of rather arbitrary methods, had made numerous enemies. On charges preferred by the *cabildo* (town council of Santa Fé) Cubero placed De Vargas in prison. The following offenses were said to have been committed by De Vargas and his officers: they had appropriated money belonging to the settlers; they had been responsible for the Pueblo uprisings of 1694 and 1696 and for the famine of 1695. In addition to imprisonment De Vargas was fined 4,000 pesos, his property was confiscated, and he was required to pay the costs of the suit. While the Pueblos of the upper Rio Grande valley had submitted to De Vargas, those west of the river including Ácoma, Zuñi and the Hopi towns were still independent. Cubero succeeded in gaining the submission of Ácoma on July 6, 1699. A week later he persuaded the Zuñi Indians to leave their citadel on Thunder Mountain and return to the valley. The Indians, who had settled in the San José Valley following the Pueblo Revolt, were officially named the Pueblo of Laguna, July 4, 1699, and the Spanish settlement nine miles northeast of Laguna was named Cubero. Several attempts were then made by Cubero to reëstablish the missionary work among the Hopi towns but without success, and the missionary at Zuñi was ordered to return to the Rio Grande Valley because the military force was not large enough to protect him. Meanwhile Cubero released De Vargas in July 1700, and the latter's case was investigated in Mexico City. In 1701 a royal decree was issued providing for De Vargas a second term at the close of Cubero's governorship. Fearing the events that might follow with their positions reversed, Cubero left Santa

Fé in August 1703, and died in Mexico in 1704. The *cabildo* of Santa Fé reversing itself, stated that De Vargas had labored to protect the settlements while Cubero had done nothing to prevent attacks from the nomadic tribes but had been "Solely occupied with drinking and writing papers . . . and ascribing faults and crimes to those who had not committed them."

[R. E. Twitchell, *Leading Facts of New Mex. Hist.* (1911), I, 414–19, and *Spanish Archives of New Mex.* (1914), II, 117–26; C. F. Coan, *Hist. of New Mex.* (1925), I, 108, 112, 119, 199, 223; H. H. Bancroft, *Hist. of the Pacific States of North America*, XII (1888), 218–21, 224–26, 263–64.]   C.F.C.

CUDAHY, MICHAEL (Dec. 7, 1841–Nov. 27, 1910), meat-packer, was born in Callan, County Kilkenny, Ireland, son of Patrick and Elizabeth Shaw Cudahy, and came to America with his parents in 1849. He made his home in Milwaukee and at the age of fourteen left grammar school and entered the employ of Layton & Plankinton, meat-packers, in Milwaukee, where he advanced rapidly in the business. Later he worked for another packer, Edward Roddis, until 1866, when the business was terminated. In 1866, he became private meat inspector for Layton & Company, and three years later superintendent in charge of the packing-house of Plankinton & Armour at Milwaukee. Later still he became a board of trade inspector in the Milwaukee packing plants and after three years plant superintendent for Plankinton & Armour. His ability was widely recognized, and in 1875 he was offered and accepted a partnership in the firm of Armour & Company of Chicago, assuming control of the company's plant operations at the Union Stock Yards as general superintendent. At about this time he was married to Catherine Sullivan of Cedarburg, Wis. Cudahy's outstanding contribution to the development of American meat-packing operations was the epoch-making innovation of summer curing of meats under refrigeration (1870–80). The packing industry had been hitherto a winter season business for the most part. People had eaten cured meats heavily salted, it being necessary to cure the meats in this manner in order to preserve them; and as this had been customary for centuries, no one had thought of eating fresh meat throughout the year. The process of refrigeration revolutionized the industry so that operations could be carried on continuously throughout the year. It prevented premature decay of perishable products, lengthened the period of consumption and thus greatly increased production, enabled the owner to market his products at will, and made possible transportation in good condition from the point of production to point of consumption, irrespective of distance. Cudahy's part in this evolution was that of a captain of industry who understands the significance of a new scientific development and who makes possible its application to commerce. The first step in meeting the new era was provided by stationary refrigeration in the form of cold storage warehouses, or "coolers," as a part of every packing plant. In addition, it was realized that refrigeration had to be applied to transportation. This was accomplished in the middle seventies with the evolution of the refrigerator car now so common in the transportation of all perishable food products. Cudahy's contribution was mainly on the production side, but he was also one of the leaders in the development of the transportation phase.

In 1887 Philip D. Armour, Michael Cudahy, and his younger brother, Edward A. Cudahy, purchased a small packing plant in South Omaha, Nebr., and began a new business there under the name of the Armour-Cudahy Packing Company. There were in Omaha at that time only two small packers, whose business was for the most part confined to the British market, but this was not the best outlet for the rapidly increasing supply of live-stock which was really better adapted to the domestic market. This was more especially true of hogs. The Cudahy brothers very shrewdly saw the opportunity to be developed in packing for the domestic market. In this course they were amply justified, and were later able to develop a foreign outlet on a large scale as well. In 1890 Michael Cudahy sold his interests in the firm of Armour & Company and purchased Armour's interests in the Armour-Cudahy Packing Company, the name of which was subsequently changed to the Cudahy Packing Company. Michael Cudahy was president of the company from the beginning and continued in that office until his death. He was a Roman Catholic and was widely known for his philanthropic and civic activities.

[Obituaries in leading Chicago newspapers following Cudahy's death; see also a short account of his life in Rudolf A. Clemen, *Am. Livestock and Meat Industry* (1923); for personal characteristics see *Patrick Cudahy, His Life* (1912).]   R. A. C.

CUFFE, PAUL (Jan. 17, 1759–Sept. 9, 1817), negro seaman, was born at Cuttyhunk, on one of the Elizabeth Islands not far from New Bedford. He was the seventh of the ten children of Cuffe Slocum, a Massachusetts negro who had purchased his freedom, and of Ruth Moses, an Indian woman. When sixteen years of age he was a sailor on a whaling vessel. On his third voyage he was captured by the British and held in New York for three months. When released he repaired to Westport to engage in agriculture. He

studied arithmetic and navigation, and after various unhappy experiences with small vessels, including the capture of his goods by pirates, he made a successful voyage, in 1795 launched a sixty-nine-ton vessel, the *Ranger,* and by 1806 owned one ship, two brigs, and several smaller vessels, besides property in houses and lands. As early as 1778 he had persuaded his brothers to drop their father's slave name, Slocum, and to take his Christian name, Cuffe, as their surname. In 1780 he and his brother John raised before the courts of Massachusetts the question of the denial of the suffrage to citizens who had to pay taxes. For the moment the two men were not successful, but their efforts helped toward the act of 1783 by which negroes acquired legal rights and privileges in Massachusetts; and especially did they assist in giving to New Bedford a tradition of just and equal treatment for all citizens. On Feb. 25, 1783, Paul Cuffe was married to a young Indian woman, Alice Pequit. In 1797 he bought for $3,500 a farm on the Westport River where he built a public-school house and employed a teacher. In 1808 he was received into the membership of the Society of Friends of Westport; and he later assisted materially in the building of a new meeting-house. As early as 1788 he had been prominent in the suggestion of an exodus of negroes to Africa. On Jan. 1, 1811, with a crew of nine negro seamen, he sailed in the *Traveller* from Westport for Sierra Leone. In Freetown he formed the Friendly Society, which looked toward further immigration from America. Returning to America, Apr. 19, 1812, he planned to make a yearly trip to Sierra Leone. On Dec. 10, 1815, with a total of nine families and thirty-eight persons he set forth, expending not less than $4,000 of his own funds in the venture. He was well received and hoped to do even more, but his health failed in 1817. Tall, well-formed, and athletic, he was a man of remarkable dignity, initiative, tact, and piety, and the unselfishness of his efforts impressed all who knew him. He left an estate of $20,000.

[H. N. Sherwood, "Paul Cuffe," in *Jour. of Negro Hist.,* Apr. 1923, VIII, 153–232; Peter Williams, *Discourse on the Death of Paul Cuffe* (1817); *Memoir of Capt. Paul Cuffee* (York, Eng., 1812).]   B. B.

CULBERSON, CHARLES ALLEN (June 10, 1855–March 19, 1925), lawyer, statesman, born in Dadeville, Ala., was the son of David B. [*q.v.*] and Eugenia Kimbal Culberson. When he was one year old his parents moved to Gilmer, Upshur County, Tex., and five years later to Jefferson, Marion County. Here he received his primary education. In 1870 he entered Virginia Military Institute where he graduated in 1874.

He then studied law in his father's office and later entered the law school of the University of Virginia where he graduated in 1877. He began the practise of law at Jefferson, Tex., and was elected county attorney; but he soon returned to his private practise which grew rapidly. On Dec. 7, 1882, he married Sallie Harrison of Fort Worth; and in 1887 he moved to Dallas. In 1890 he ran for the attorney-generalship of Texas and was elected. In this first race for a state office he displayed that remarkable gift for organization which always marked his political contests. He owed much, no doubt, to the popularity of his father, who was becoming one of the Democratic leaders in Congress; but the son was winning success also on his own merits. When he became attorney-general, James S. Hogg, his predecessor in that office, became governor on a reform platform; and it fell to Culberson to defend before the courts some of the measures which Hogg had enacted into law. The most important of these measures was the railroad commission law, the constitutionality of which the United States Supreme Court upheld in *Reagan* vs. *Farmers' Loan and Trust Company* (154 *U. S.*, 362). Other important cases in which he represented the State were: *The Houston and Texas Central Railroad Company* vs. *Texas* (177 *U. S.*, 66) in which the State recovered a large tract of land in western Texas claimed by this road; and *The United States* vs. *Texas* (143 *U. S.*, 621 and 162 *U. S.*, 1), known as the Greer County case, in which Texas lost its claim to the region between the forks of the Red River, now in Oklahoma. In 1892 he was reëlected attorney-general.

In 1894 he entered the contest for the Democratic nomination for governor and won an easy victory. In this, as in his later campaigns his manager was Col. E. M. House, afterward famous as the political adviser of Woodrow Wilson. In the November election he was opposed by Thomas L. Nugent, the Populist candidate, but after a strenuous contest Culberson won by nearly 60,000 votes. The great issue in this campaign was free silver, and the state Democratic platform had leaned toward gold; but Culberson quickly identified himself with the silver men. His administration as governor was notable for activity and vigor in the enforcement of the laws and for a strong fiscal policy by which expenses were reduced through rigid economy and administrative and judicial reforms. The most spectacular action of Culberson was his calling the legislature into special session in October 1895, to enact a law which prevented the holding of the Corbett-Fitzsimmons prize-fight in Texas. In

1896 he was again the Democratic candidate for governor, and in a hard fight defeated the Populist candidate, Jerome C. Kearby, by some 60,000 votes. In 1898 both Culberson and Roger Q. Mills were candidates for the United States Senate—the latter for reëlection, but Culberson's organization was so effective that Mills withdrew and Culberson was elected by the legislature. He took his seat in March 1899, and served in the Senate for four consecutive terms. He proved a steady and effective party worker; and his ability, united to a fondness for details and a passion for accuracy, soon attracted attention. In 1907 he became the leader of the Democratic minority in the Senate. Although a rather strict constitutionalist, he generally supported progressive measures, especially those for the regulation of great corporations. His chief service was as a member of the Committee on the Judiciary, of which he was chairman during the momentous years 1913–19. Though his health had broken badly he remained steadfastly at his post and continued actively in committee work; and he had a prominent part in framing the important legislation of the Wilson administration, especially the war measures. In 1922 he was defeated for reëlection in the Texas primaries. This was his first defeat and it was largely due to his physical inability to conduct his own campaign. After his retirement in 1923 he remained in Washington, where he died two years later. In his prime he was an unusually handsome man, tall, straight, with regular features and keen twinkling eyes. He was reserved in manner, except among his closest associates, and uncommunicative. It was said of him that he never had to reproach himself for having talked too much. Though he did not speak frequently, he was an accomplished orator, and his prepared speeches are remarkable for literary finish and strength. He is buried at Fort Worth.

[The best sketch is in the *Dallas Morning News*, Mar. 20, 1925. Culberson himself wrote a sketchy autobiography, "Personal Reminiscences," in the form of thirty-two brief letters which were syndicated through a number of Texas newspapers in the winter of 1923–24. His speeches while governor of Texas he collected and republished in an undated booklet. Some information of value may be gleaned from the following: E. W. Winkler, *Platforms of Political Parties in Texas* (1916); "The Claims of the Candidates" in the *North Am. Rev.*, June 1908, pp. 812–17, a favorable appraisal by Tom Finty, Jr.; Charles Seymour, ed., *The Intimate Papers of Col. House* (1926), vol. I. See also J. W. Madden, *Charles Allen Culberson* (1929).]   C. W. R.

CULBERSON, DAVID BROWNING (Sept. 29, 1830–May 7, 1900), lawyer, statesman, was descended from John Culbertson who came from the North of Ireland to Chester, Pa., about 1712. Joseph, the grandson of this John, moved to North Carolina before the Revolution and somewhere dropped the "t" from his name. David Browning Culberson was the son of Rev. David B. Culberson, a well-known Baptist preacher, and Lucy Wilkinson Culberson, daughter of a large planter of Oglethorpe County. He was born in Troup County, Ga. His education was obtained chiefly at Brownwood Institute, Lagrange, Ga. He then read law, after the custom of that day, in the office of the noted lawyer and Whig leader, William P. Chilton of Tuskegee, Ala., who was at that time chief justice of the supreme court of that state. He was admitted to the bar in 1851 and settled at Dadeville, Ala. Here he married Eugenia Kimbal, Dec. 2, 1852. In 1856 he moved to Upshur County, Tex., where he continued the practise of law. In 1859 he was elected to the lower house of the legislature. He had been a Whig until that party disappeared and he seems to have supported the Constitutional Unionist candidates in 1860. He opposed secession and the recognition of the Texas Secession Convention by the legislature, and finding that his constituents disagreed with him, he resigned from the legislature. At about this time he moved to the rising town of Jefferson, in Marion County, which was his home throughout the rest of his life. When the war came he enlisted as a private; but in 1862 he aided in raising the 18th Texas Infantry and became its lieutenant-colonel and later its colonel. This regiment served in Arkansas and Louisiana in J. G. Walker's division, and Culberson distinguished himself for courage and resourcefulness. In 1863 his health broke down and he resigned; but in November he was appointed by Gov. Murrah to the post of adjutant and inspector-general of Texas at Austin. In 1864 he was elected to the legislature from Marion County, and resigned his commission. After the war he again took up the practise of law and rose rapidly to a leading position at a bar which was distinguished for able advocates. He became famous as a trial lawyer, for he was not only a profound student of the law but had such a persuasive influence with the juries that he seldom lost a case. In 1873 he was elected to the state Senate. In 1875 he was elected to Congress, and was reëlected for ten consecutive terms until in 1896 he refused another election.

His most important service in Congress was as a member of the House Committee of the Judiciary, of which he was several times chairman. Though his chief interest was in legal and constitutional questions, especially judicial re-

forms, he was attentive to all matters pertaining to the public interest. He worked consistently for the principle of tariff for revenue only and for the federal regulation of railways. He was not particularly active in the free-silver movement, but he voted with his party and section for the bills of 1878 and 1890 and against the limiting amendments engrafted on them, and he opposed the repeal of the silver purchase clause of 1893. He introduced in the House, on the part of the judiciary committee, the antitrust bill of 1890 and supported it with a careful and weighty speech. In 1890 he was offered a place on the Interstate Commerce Commission, but declined it. He was regarded by many of his colleagues as the ablest constitutional lawyer in the House and was ranked in this respect with Senator Edmunds. He spoke but seldom, and almost never on trivial matters, and was always listened to with great respect on both sides of the House. His speeches were characterized by temperateness, a terse and closely woven argument, and remarkable clarity. Though a Democrat, he had never broken entirely with his early Whig training, as is shown by his conservatism and his broad views of the constitutional powers of the Federal Government. He had the personal confidence of members of both parties and in his later years his advice was much sought because of his sound judgment and breadth of view. His hold upon the people of his own district was remarkable, as his twenty-two years of continuous service attest; but it was due not only to their pride in his ability but to his simple unaffected honesty, his plain and unassuming manners, and his warm heart. When he retired from the House it was generally expected that the legislature would elect him to the Senate, but he stood aside for his son, Charles A. Culberson, who was at that time governor of Texas. He was appointed in 1897, by President McKinley, on the commission to codify the laws of the United States, and he was serving in that capacity at the time of his death. He died, widely mourned, at Jefferson, Tex., and was buried there.

[Personal recollections of his surviving friends; *Jours.* of the 8th and 14th Legislatures of Texas; the records of the office of the Adjutant-General of Texas; the *Congressional Record*; the contemporary newspapers of Texas. Several of these, notably the *Dallas News*, published biographical sketches at the time of his death. See also J. P. Blessington, *The Campaigns of Walker's Texas Division* (1875); L. R. Culbertson, *Geneal. of the Culbertson and Culberson Families* (rev. ed., 1923); *Biog. Dict. of the Am. Cong.* (1928).]

C. W. R.

CULLIS, CHARLES (Mar. 7, 1833–June 18, 1892), homeopathic physician and leader in a faith-cure movement, was born in Boston, Mass., the son of John Cullis, of old Puritan stock. As a child he was infirm and he remained more or less an invalid all his life. After serving as a clerk in a mercantile house, his health became seriously impaired and he turned to the study of medicine. His early practise was among the poor, especially among those with chronic illness. Cullis's interest in "faith cure" was quickened by stories of the work of Herman Francke in Germany and that of George Müller in England. He read of Dorothea Trudel of Switzerland, whose work greatly impressed him; later he wrote her life story. About 1865 he opened a home for consumptives in Boston. In a few years he had outgrown his quarters and, entirely through gifts from the public, he built many "homes" on eleven acres of ground in Grove Hall, near Boston. The group consisted of a "Consumptives' Home," a "Spinal Home," two "Orphan Homes," the Grove Hall Church, a "Faith Cure House," and a "Deaconess' House." In Boston he maintained the Beacon Hill Church, the "Lewis Mission," the "Faith Training College," and the Cottage Street Church. Missions were established at Boynton, Va., Alameda, Cal., Renicks Valley, W. Va., Oxford, N. C., and two in India; "tract repositories" were started in Boston, New York, and Philadelphia, the most famous of which was the Willard Tract Repository in Boston. To maintain these numerous activities, Cullis is said to have obtained from the public, "in answer to my prayers," but without solicitation, as much as $600,000 in twenty-five years, in daily contributions from a few cents to $2,000.

The public attended his churches in large numbers and his "homes" were always filled to overflowing. So many came to his church from a distance that he built the "Faith Cure House" near-by for those who had to remain overnight. The training school, established about 1873, was successful and he is said to have collected over $30,000 for it; a bookstore was connected with it, where tracts were sold. During the summer Cullis held open air "conventions" or "revivals" at Intervale, N. H., and Old Orchard, Me. He was attacked from other Boston pulpits as an adventurer, but he never made any reply and thus kept his dignity. Essentially honest, he spent all the money collected on his charities and died a poor man. It is said that he always believed in using medical skill and only took patients after other physicians had seen them. Practically no provision was made for the continuation of his work after his death and most of his charities dissolved in the course of a few years. It is possible that some of his

ideas stimulated the development of the Christian Science Church in Boston. He was survived by his wife, Lucretia Ann Cullis, a son, and two daughters.

[An account of Cullis, including illustrations of the "Homes," by W. I. Gill, will be found in the *New England Mag.*, Mar. 1887, V, 438–49. See also: Chas. Cullis, *Ann. Report Consumptives' Home*, 1865–77, *Hist. of the Consumptives' Home* (1869), and *Faith Cures; or, Answer to Prayer in the Healing of the Sick* (1879); *Dorothea Trudel; or, The Prayer of Faith* (1872), intro. by Chas. Cullis; W. E. Boardman, *Faith Work Under Dr. Cullis in Boston* (1876); *Boston Sunday Herald*, June 19, 1892; *Boston Daily Advertiser*, June 20, 1892.]   H. R. V.

CULLOM, SHELBY MOORE (Nov. 22, 1829–Jan. 28, 1914), lawyer, statesman, was born in Kentucky, whither his father, Richard Northcraft Cullom, and his mother, Elizabeth Coffey, had emigrated after the Revolution; he from Maryland, she from North Carolina. Of twelve children of their marriage Shelby Moore was the seventh. After the attempt to fasten slavery upon Illinois had definitely failed, his father, who was an anti-slavery man, removed his family thither in 1830. In Illinois, then mostly an unbroken prairie, the Culloms lived the plain and arduous life of the frontier. Shelby Moore acquired a fair common-school training in the subscription country schools of the locality, and later attended for two years Rock River Seminary at Mount Morris, then reputedly the best school of northern Illinois.

Returning to the labor of the farm he found it hard and uncongenial, and so forsook it in 1853 to study law in Springfield, the state capital. There he came immediately into contact with politics. He was admitted to the bar in 1855. The same year he was elected city attorney, thus beginning, as he said, "a political career exceeding in length of unbroken service that of any other public man in the country's history." Though he practised law for ten years, it was politics that he practised more assiduously and with more success. At first, like many men of Southern Whig family antecedents, his politics were uncertain. In 1856 he ran unsuccessfully on the Fillmore ticket as a presidential elector; was that year elected by both Free Soil and Fillmore men to the state legislature; and in 1858 followed Abraham Lincoln (long before, his father's friend) "firmly and without mental reservation" into the Republican party. Thereafter—always by the favor of that party—he was a member of the lower house of the state legislature in 1860–61, 1872, 1873–74 (speaker, 1861, 1873); representative in Congress, 1865–71; governor of Illinois, 1876–83 (two terms—a rare honor); and United States senator from Mar. 3, 1883 until 1913. He was a candidate for reëlection in the state primary of 1912, but was defeated. His election to the Senate before his resignation of the governorship involved a legal question of importance. Chief among the objects which he set himself to accomplish when he entered the Senate was the establishment of national control over interstate commerce. The Illinois constitution of 1870 had expressed, in its provisions, the indignation of the public against business and political practises of the railroads which, in truth, were nation-wide. In the legislature Cullom had been active in procuring the enactment of a state regulatory law (1873), and, as governor, in uncompromisingly maintaining it. Convinced that state control alone was inadequate, he secured a report from the Senate committee on railroads of a bill which, after country-wide hearings by a special committee of which he was chairman, established the Interstate Commerce Commission (1887). He then became chairman of the Senate's Committee on Interstate Commerce. He was also active in securing the passage of the Hepburn Act in 1906. In 1901 he exchanged this chairmanship for that of the Committee on Foreign Relations. This position he held longer than any predecessor. In its affairs he displayed commendable common sense and considerable independence, but nothing particularly signalizes his service. During the Spanish-American War he was a member of the Committee on Cuban Relations, and the same year was chairman of the Hawaiian Commission which drafted the bill for the government of the islands as a territory of the United States.

For more than fifty years, beginning with 1856, he was an active worker in political campaigns. While dependable in voting, in many ways he was fairly independent. He was not a highest-tariff man; could see that his party, until Roosevelt's day, left the Anti-Trust Act a dead letter; favored income and inheritance taxes long before his party accepted them; applauded Roosevelt for enforcing laws against violators in high places, but queried his Panama action, and opposed him (and Cullom's life-long friend John Hay, son of his one-time law partner) for dealing with Santo Domingo by executive agreement rather than by treaty. He kept his mind open throughout life on the issues of imperialism that followed the Spanish-American War; and open even as regarded the railroad "pooling" clauses of his own statute of 1887. He was critical but fair in his judgments of men. He enjoyed the work of the Committee on Foreign Relations more than any other because it was non-partisan. Yet, with all these disproofs

of littleness, he was also capable of allowing a purely personal quarrel with the *Chicago Tribune* to control his conduct in the national campaign of 1892 (Cullom, *Fifty Years of Public Service*, pp. 249, 251–52). Largely by virtue of his long service in the Senate, and the positions secured under its rule of seniority, he was long prominent in his party. Repeatedly (1872, 1884, 1892, 1908) he was chairman of the Illinois delegation to Republican national conventions, wherein he played an important part. From 1911 to his death he was chairman of the Republican caucus of the Senate. He harbored presidential ambitions in 1888; was a candidate for the nomination in 1896; and once was nearly appointed to the cabinet (1896). In view of these facts it is remarkable how slight a trace he leaves in the biographies and memoirs of his leading contemporaries. This was perhaps partly due to temperament. There was nothing brilliant about him. He was a man of facts; even-tempered, conservative, "regular," conscientious and economical in public business; fair-minded—keeping his friendships outside of politics, and easily forgiving small party disappointments; thoroughly democratic. For these reasons and others (he did not, for example, drink or smoke) he was colorless. In his religious views he was liberal. His party strength in Illinois, and the chief explanation of his long service in the Senate, lay in his wisdom in council and in his reputation for honesty. No faintest scandal ever touched his reputation. It is mainly in connection with the creation of the Interstate Commerce Commission that his name will live nationally.

He married in 1855, Hannah M. Fisher who died 1861, and in 1863, his sister-in-law, Julia Fisher. He survived all his family.

[See Cullom's *Fifty Years of Public Service, Personal Recollections* (2nd ed., 1911). The important reports on the creation of the Interstate Commerce Commission are: Cullom's report of Jan. 18, 1886, in *Senate Report No. 46*, pts. 1 and 2, 49 Cong., 1 Sess.; conference reports thereon in 49 Cong., 2 Sess. *Senate Miscellaneous Documents No. 12* (of Dec. 15, 1886), 49 Cong., 2 Sess., and *House Miscellaneous Documents No. 75* (of Jan. 21, 1887), 49 Cong., 2 Sess. The essential chronology of his life is given in *Who's Who in America*, 1912–13.]   F. S. P.

CULLUM, GEORGE WASHINGTON (Feb. 25, 1809–Feb. 28, 1892), author, soldier, was born in the city of New York, the son of Arthur and Harriet (Sturges) Cullum, and as a child removed with his parents to Meadville, Pa. He was appointed to the Military Academy in 1829, graduated in 1833, and was commissioned in the Corps of Engineers. He had widely professional experience, including fortification work in the harbors of Boston, Newport, New London, New York, Annapolis, and Charleston, construction of government buildings at West Point and New York, and instruction in military engineering at West Point. As a result of an act of Congress enlarging the Corps of Engineers he was promoted from second lieutenant to captain in 1838. His health failed in 1850, his life was despaired of, and it was two years before he was able to return to duty. He became a major in 1861. During the early part of the Civil War he served as aide to Gen. Scott. Appointed brigadier-general of volunteers, Nov. 1, 1861, he was assigned as chief of staff and chief engineer to Gen. Halleck, and as such took part in the Corinth campaign. When Halleck went to Washington in 1862, as general-in-chief of the army, Cullum accompanied him, and served on his staff until Sept. 5, 1864. He was promoted lieutenant-colonel of engineers, Mar. 3, 1863. After leaving Halleck's staff he was for two years superintendent of the Military Academy, and then served on engineering duties until his retirement. He was mustered out of the volunteer service on Sept. 1, 1866; promoted colonel, Mar. 7, 1867; and placed on the retired list, Jan. 13, 1874. He married, Sept. 23, 1875, Elizabeth, daughter of John C. Hamilton, and widow of Gen. Halleck. After his retirement he lived in New York, and was active in scientific and philanthropic work. He was deeply interested in the work of the American Geographical Society of New York, of which he was one of the vice-presidents from 1877 until his death. He had already written and translated some engineering monographs; he now turned his special attention to history, writing several papers on the two wars with Great Britain, and revising his great work, the *Biographical Register of the Officers and Graduates of the United States Military Academy*. A first edition had appeared in 1850, and a second in 1868; he now gave it its final form and published the third edition, in three volumes, in 1891. This monumental works gives a full summary of the career of every graduate of West Point from the foundation of the Academy until 1889, supplemented in many instances by a biographical sketch. As these sketches were based not only on exhaustive research, but also, in most cases, on personal knowledge, their value is extraordinary. They incidentally give considerable insight into Cullum's own character. Somewhat flowery in their language and sentiment, as was the tone of the period to which he belonged, they breathe a passionate devotion to West Point, a high idealism, and the most fer-

vent patriotism. His treatment of those graduates who joined the Confederate army is significant. Of none does he give a biographical sketch, or any mention of their war services. The record of each breaks off with the formula, "Joined in the Rebellion of 1861–66 against the United States," and resumes with the history after the war. It is noticeable, too, that several conspicuous Union generals are denied the honor of biographical sketches, while some of less fame receive them, from which the compiler's own feelings toward them may be inferred. It was Cullum's intention that a supplementary volume should be published every ten years, carrying on the record, and for this he made provision in his will. Supplements were accordingly published in 1900, 1910, and 1920, the last being in two volumes. He helped to organize the Association of Graduates of the United States Military Academy in 1870 and took an active part in carrying on its work. From his wife he inherited a considerable fortune, which was largely devoted to public uses by his own will. Generous bequests were made to the two institutions to which he was so strongly attached. For the benefit of West Point, he left $250,000 for the erection of a memorial hall (to which his name has been given); $20,000 endowment to provide for the erection, from time to time, of memorials within the hall; $20,000 as endowment to provide for the continuance of the *Biographical Register*; and $10,000 endowment for the Association of Graduates. To the American Geographical Society he left $100,000 for the erection of a building, and $5,000 to provide for the award of a gold medal to those "who distinguish themselves by geographical discoveries or in the advancement of geographical science."

[Cullum's *Biog. Reg.* (3rd ed. 1891), I, 535–37, gives his various assignments to duty in minute detail, but without comment. There are obituaries in *Jour. Am. Geog. Soc.*, XXIV (1892), pp. 142–45, and *Bull. Asso. Grads. Mil. Acad.* (1892), pp. 83–86; this last also gives the provisions of his will relating to West Point, pp. 104–08. Something of his military career in the West may be found in the *Official Records (Army)*, 1 ser., vols. VII, VIII.]
T. M. S.

CULPEPER, THOMAS, Lord (1635–Jan. 27, 1689), colonial governor, was the son of John, Lord Culpeper and his second wife Judith, the daughter of Sir Thomas Culpeper of Hollingbourn, Kent. He was the eldest of seven surviving children (two having died before his birth) and inherited his father's title and the estate of Leeds Castle in Kent. On Aug. 3, 1659, he was married at The Hague to Margaretta, daughter of Jan van Hesse, by whom he had one child who became the wife of Thomas, Lord Fairfax. His married life was unhappy;

Lady Culpeper stayed for the most part in Leeds Castle while Culpeper lived in London with his mistress, Susanna Willis. He was commissioned by the king, July 8, 1675, governor of Virginia for life, to take office however, only on the death or removal of Sir William Berkeley [*q.v.*]. Berkeley died in 1677, and Culpeper entrusted the administration to his deputies Col. Herbert Jeffreys and Sir Henry Chicheley. He evidently did not intend personally to assume the governorship, but was compelled to do so by the king in 1680. The opposition of the colonists to the royal grant of all of Virginia to Lord Arlington and Lord Culpeper had resulted in the revocation of the grant with the exception of the quit-rents and the escheats. Before his arrival in the colony, Culpeper was regarded as an unscrupulous extortioner. Soon after his arrival, however, in May 1680, he won the confidence of the colonists by the measures which he proposed to the Assembly, and especially by the act for pardoning all the participants in Bacon's Rebellion who were then living. This conciliatory spirit so impressed the Assembly that it was influenced to pass an act which it might not otherwise have countenanced. The act specified that the duty of two shillings a hogshead on exported tobacco should be made perpetual and subject to the king's disposal instead of as formerly subject to the Assembly. Moreover, Culpeper was granted £500 sterling by the Assembly as a special recognition of his services. There seems to have been no objection on the part of the colonists to his being granted by the king an increase of £1,000 in his salary (in addition to the already established income of £1,000), £1,000 in perquisites, and £150 for house rent. After remaining in the colony about four months, Culpeper returned to England, leaving Chicheley to serve as his deputy. In Culpeper's absence an Assembly was called to consider the low price of tobacco, which was occasioning general discontent. When the Assembly was unable to reach any effectual conclusions, the planters in several counties deliberately destroyed their tobacco plants. Chicheley, desiring to check any further destruction of tobacco, arrested some of those guilty of the offense and imprisoned them. When the news of the disturbance reached England, Culpeper was deprived of his appointment for life and threatened with removal unless he very soon returned to the colony. He was also reprimanded for leaving without royal permission and for having accepted the grant from the Assembly. On his return, which was reluctant, as he preferred staying in England, Culpeper's attitude toward the colo-

nists was changed. He raised, by proclamation, the price of tobacco, with the proviso that his own salary and the royal revenues should not thereby be affected. This was considered by the colonists equivalent to a special tax imposed without their consent, but having no recourse, they submitted. Culpeper's policy in dealing with the plant-cutters was severe, and some of their leaders were hanged. He followed these dictatorial acts by dissolving the Assembly, maintaining that all laws should be drafted by him with the advice of the Council. He endeavored to abolish the right of appeal to the Assembly, emphasizing the appeal to the king. He insisted that the House of Burgesses should submit their choice of speaker for his approval. By imprisonment and disfranchisement he punished Maj. Robert Beverley, clerk of the House of Burgesses, for refusing to surrender the journal of its proceedings. Then, after having remained in the colony about ten months, he went to England in September 1683, leaving Nicholas Spencer, the president of the Council, in charge of the government. He was, thereupon, removed for having again left the colony without permission. He died, Jan. 27, 1689, in London.

[*Jour. of the House of Burgesses of Va., 1619–1776*, ed. by H. R. McIlwaine and J. P. Kennedy (13 vols., Richmond, 1906–15); *Complete Peerage*, ed. by G. E. Cokayne (8 vols., Exeter, 1887–98, new ed., 1913), III, 363–65; Fairfax Harrison, *The Proprietors of the Northern Neck* (Richmond, 1926), pp. 73–82; P. S. Flippin, *The Royal Government in Va., 1624–1775* (1919), pp. 108–10; P. A. Bruce, *The Institutional Hist. of Va. in the 17th Century* (2 vols., 1910); Robt. Beverley, *Hist. of Va.* (first published in 1705, reprinted from author's 2nd rev. ed., Richmond, 1855), pp. 72–77; J. T. Wertenbaker, *Va. under the Stuarts, 1607–88* (Princeton Univ. Press, 1914); H. L. Osgood, *The Am. Colonies in the Seventeenth Century* (3 vols., 1904–07), vol. III.]   P. S. F.

CUMING, Sir ALEXANDER (*c.* 1690–Aug. 1775), second baronet of Culter (Aberdeenshire), an eccentric Scottish advocate and projector, was the central figure in a colorful episode connected with a voyage to South Carolina in 1729. He was the son of Sir Alexander Cuming, a member of Parliament, and Elizabeth (Swinton) Cuming. His voyage was not, as has been asserted, an official mission. During the winter of 1729–30 he busied himself with a banking scheme to reform the colonial currency: this project he continued to promote, unsuccessfully, after his return to England. On the eve of his departure he decided to make a rapid excursion of nearly a thousand miles by rough trading-paths into the back-country and the mountains (Mar. 13–Apr. 13, 1730). A member of the Royal Society, he set out as a scientific explorer rather than as a political agent, searching for minerals, herbs, and the "natural curiosities" of the land. But another purpose took shape in his erratic mind as he listened to the frontiersmen's accounts of French intrigues and widespread disaffection among the Cherokee Indians, the corner-stone of British alliances and empire in the South. At Keowee in the Lower Towns, Sir Alexander's enterprise, mad or inspired, was first revealed. There he dramatically appeared, fully armed, among the Indians in the town house—a gross breach of Indian decorum,—determined to overawe the Cherokee, single-handed if need be, and force them to submit to the British interest. At his demand, or by the persuasions of the startled traders, the Indians were induced to join in drinking the health of George II on bended knee! This strange rite Cuming interpreted as an acknowledgment of British sovereignty. He continued his hasty progress as far as the remotest Cherokee towns, everywhere repeating his fantastic ceremony. At a great congress of the tribe, at Nequasse, Moytoy of Tellico, an Anglophile chief, was crowned "Emperor" of the Cherokee; and to the baronet the Indians resigned the "crown of Tennessee" and other trophies "as an Emblem of their all owning His Majesty King George's Sovereignty over them, at the Desire of Sir Alexander Cuming, in whom an absolute unlimited Power was placed." Evidently the flighty Scot had appealed to the dramatic instincts of the Indian, to achieve a *tour de force* of wilderness diplomacy at a crucial moment. The council further agreed that an Indian embassy should return with him to England. There Cuming's seven protégés furnished the sensation of the season. They were received at court, shown the sights of the town, feasted and entertained, and everywhere they became objects of popular curiosity. But Newcastle and the Board of Trade turned deaf ears to Cuming's memorials. He sought in vain to have his powers as overlord confirmed for three years, promising to live among the Indians and promote the royal service. He was even ignored in the negotiation of the important treaty by which the Board turned this fortuitous incident to imperial advantage, and put the Cherokee upon a footing similar to the Iroquois. But apparently the Indians refused their full assent until Cuming's approval was given. The later career of the self-vaunted "King of the Cherokees" was miserable enough. An alchemist, a visionary promoter, from 1737 to 1765 he was confined as a debtor to the limits of the Fleet. He died, a poor brother of Charterhouse, in 1775.

[See account in *Dict. of Nat. Biog.*, with references; and a fuller account of the Cherokee episode in V. W. Crane, *The Southern Frontier* (1928), pp. 276–80, 294–302. Samuel G. Drake in "Early Hist. of Georgia, and Sir Alexander Cuming's Embassy to the Cherokees," *New-Eng. Hist. and Geneal. Reg.*, XXVI (1872), 260–71, cited a MS. written by Cuming in 1755; there are marked similarities to narratives in the *Daily Jour.* (London), Sept. 30, Oct. 8, 1730. Compare the deposition of the trader, Ludovick Grant, in *S. C. Hist. and Geneal. Mag.*, X (1909), 54–68. On the Indian embassy, see London *Daily Jour., Daily Courant,* and *Daily Post*, June to Oct. 1730, *passim.* Cuming's memorials are in Public Record Office, C. O. 5: 361, C 99, C 102; C 112; C. O. 4, nos. 46, 48.]   V.W.C.

CUMING, FORTESCUE (Feb. 26, 1762–1828), traveler and author, was born at Strabane, County Tyrone, Ireland. After studying medicine, and traveling in France, Switzerland, and Italy, he came to New York, where, in 1784, he married Phœbe, the sixteen-year-old daughter of Thomas Harisson, by whom he had seven children. He lived successively in New York, Trinidad, and Westchester, finally establishing a home at Cedar Hill, just outside of New Haven, in 1792. There are portraits of himself and his wife by St. Memin, dated 1797 (Nos. 54 and 737, *The St. Memin Collection of Portraits*, published by Elias Dexter, 1862). His family life seems not to have been happy. In 1806 he was again in England, where he purchased lands in Ohio. These were the occasion of the trip taken in 1807–09 down the Ohio and Mississippi rivers and through Louisiana and the Floridas, which he described in his *Sketches of a Tour to the Western Country*, published at Pittsburgh in 1810. This volume, which is an accurate and detailed record of social and political conditions in the backwoods area, was reprinted in 1904 as Volume IV of *Early Western Travels*, edited by Reuben Gold Thwaites. Cuming seems not to have returned to his wife, who was buried in New Haven in 1821. He married a Miss Butler, and died in Vermilionville, La., in 1828.

[Thwaites appraised Cuming's work in the Preface to his edition of the *Sketches*. A "Retrospective Review" was published in the *Western Monthly Mag.*, Nov. 1835. Biographical information has been supplied from the family papers by Cuming's great-grandson, Mr. Alfred Z. Reed of New York.]   E.R.D.

CUMMING, ALFRED (Sept. 4, 1802–Oct. 9, 1873), territorial governor of Utah, was born at Augusta, Ga., the son of Thomas and Ann (Clay) Cumming. The family was socially and politically prominent. Cumming's sole title to fame is based upon his connection with the so-called "Mormon War" of 1857–58. He had been mayor of Augusta in 1839 and had acted with commendable courage and efficiency in the severe yellow-fever epidemic of that year; in the Mexican War he had been a sutler with Scott's army, and in the early fifties had served acceptably as an Indian agent on the upper Missouri. He became a national figure when President Buchanan, alarmed at the growing evidences of revolt in

Utah, appointed him (May 1857) governor of the territory in place of Brigham Young and dispatched an army to escort him to Salt Lake City. Accompanied by the other territorial officials appointed at the same time, he arrived with the main body of Col. Albert Sidney Johnston's army at Fort Bridger (renamed Camp Scott) about Nov. 20. On the 21st he issued a proclamation declaring Utah in a state of insurrection, calling upon its militia to disband, and promising, in case the laws were obeyed, a friendly administration. The army, however, paralyzed by lack of supplies and transport, caused by the depredations of Mormon guerrillas, could make for the time no further move, and for nearly five months matters remained at a standstill.

On Mar. 12, 1858, Thomas L. Kane of Philadelphia, a friend of the Mormons, who had journeyed to Utah by way of Panama and California and had conferred with Young, arrived incognito in camp and opened negotiations with Cumming. Ignoring Johnston, and incidentally bringing on a bitter feud between the governor and the commander, he soon persuaded Cumming that in spite of the bombastic declaration of war issued by Young on Sept. 15, 1857, the prophet desired peace. On Apr. 5 Kane and Cumming set out for Salt Lake City, and on their arrival on the 12th Young gave up the executive seal of the territory. Cumming thereupon notified Johnston (Apr. 15) that as peace had been restored the army was no longer necessary. Johnston, however, under his original orders from the War Department to establish military posts in Utah, moved forward in June with replenished transport and supplies. The Mormons, to the number of probably 30,000, in spite of the counsel of Cumming and two special peace commissioners from the President who had arrived on June 7 with a full pardon for Young and his followers, evacuated the city. On the 26th Johnston marched his army through its deserted streets and then proceeded to Cedar Valley, forty miles to the southwest, where he established Camp Floyd. On July 5 the Mormons started to return, and a régime of peace seemed assured. New complications soon arose, however, from the demand on the part of the territorial judges at Provo for military protection—a demand complied with by Johnston, whose action was denounced by Cumming as an infringement of his own powers. Sustained by a decision of Attorney-General Black on May 17, 1859, the governor was thereafter left in supreme authority. In the following March Johnston left the territory; a few months later most of the troops were sent to Arizona and New Mexico; and in July 1861, the remainder were ordered east. Cumming, on the inauguration of Lincoln, did not wait to be removed, but left for his home near Augusta, where for his remaining days he lived in retirement. He is sometimes confused with a nephew of the same name (1829–1910), who was a captain in the Utah expedition and who won distinction as a general in the Confederate army. Gov. Cumming died at his home.

The "Mormon War" reveals many of the features of *opéra bouffe,* and Cumming appears to have been well suited to his part as chief actor in the play. He was simple-minded and credulous, assertive and somewhat pompous in manner and jealous of his personal authority at a time when coöperation with the military arm was essential.

[H. H. Bancroft, *Hist. of Utah* (1889); Orson F. Whitney, *Hist. of Utah,* vol. I (1892); J. C. Alter, *Jas. Bridger* (1925); T. B. H. Stenhouse, *The Rocky Mountain Saints* (1873); Lucian Lamar Knight, *Standard Hist. of Georgia and Georgians* (1917); *N. Y. Tribune,* Oct. 13, 1873.]

W. J. G—t.

CUMMINGS, AMOS JAY (May 15, 1841– May 2, 1902), journalist, congressman, was born in Conkling, N. Y., the son of Rev. Moses and Julia Ann (Jones) Cummings. His father was editor of the *Christian Herald* and *Christian Palladium.* The educational advantages of the village were few, and Amos, having exhausted them, at twelve years was apprenticed at his eager desire to the printer in whose shop his father's papers were brought out. At fifteen years he ran away, working as a tramp printer and compositor from town to town through much of the eastern United States. In Mobile he joined one of the Walker filibustering expeditions to Nicaragua, but the exciting adventure ended soon with his arrest and return to the United States with Walker. Reaching New York he worked as a typesetter on the *Tribune* until the outbreak of the Civil War, when he enlisted in the 26th Regiment of New Jersey Volunteers. By 1863 he was a sergeant-major and had been mentioned for signal bravery at Fredericksburg. His two years in the Virginia swamps, however, nearly broke him physically and left him permanently with impaired health. He returned to the *N. Y. Tribune* once more and was one of the four who remained to defend the printing office during the draft riots. He lost his job because of a strike and went to Yonkers on the *Law Transcript* but again returned to the editorial staff of the *Tribune* in 1865 with the task of condensing news for the *Weekly Tribune.* His remarkable news sense came into evidence and he was amazed and gratified to have Greeley take him on as night editor on the daily. In December 1868 he went to the *Sun,* soon serving as night editor, later as managing editor. His army illness recurred in 1872 and he resigned after the Republican presidential convention to travel and indulge his desire to rove. For the following four years he wrote from the South and West the letters to the *Sun* signed "Ziska," reporting to an interested audience his observations in the hinterland. In 1876 he edited for a time the *Evening Express,* in which the head of Tammany, John Kelly, had a controlling interest. The next year he did feature articles for the *Sun* on political events, and reported several famous murder trials.

In 1886 he was elected as a Tammany Democrat to the House of Representatives from the sixth New York district. He declined renomination in 1888 because he wanted to stay in journalism. The evening *Sun* was founded under his editorship. When Representative S. S. Cox died in September 1889, Cummings reconsidered and was elected to fill the vacancy. He served in the House with but one other interruption until his death. He declined renomination in 1894 to act as subway commissioner but lost that place with a change in municipal administration. He was then elected to the seat vacated by the death of Andrew J. Campbell (*Biographical Directory of Congress,* 1928). Cummings was essentially a newspaper man. In Congress he was a Tammany regular and served without particular distinction, though he was extremely popular with his colleagues. His *Sayings of Uncle Rufus* (1880) testify to his humor. After the death of his first wife, he was married. Mar. 6, 1869, to Frances Caroline Roberts.

[Obituaries in *N. Y. Times* and *Sun,* May 3, 1902. See also W. G. Bleyer, *Main Currents in Hist. of Am. Journalism* (1927); F. M. O'Brien, *The Story of the Sun* (1918); A. O. Cummins, *Cummings Genealogy* (1904).]   K. H. A.

CUMMINGS, CHARLES AMOS (June 26, 1833–Aug. 11, 1905), architect, was born at Boston, Mass., the son of Amos and Rebecca (Hopkins) Cummings. After preparing for college in the English High School of Boston, he entered Rensselaer Polytechnic Institute at Troy, where he graduated in 1849 with the degree of C. E. During college he pursued an intensive course in engineering, the effect of which later appeared in his architectural work in which, notwithstanding a peculiar sympathy, there was a lack of creative esthetic imagery and an adherence to archeological fact. His early professional training was gained in the office of G. J. H. Bryant. On Oct. 12, 1869, he was married to Margaret, daughter of Moses Kimball of Boston. Extensive travel and study in Europe and Egypt brought to him strength and vitality in the expression of his architectural ideas. When in 1872 the business

district of Boston was devastated by an extensive fire, it became the task of the local architects to replace, with efficiently designed structures, the edifices which had been destroyed. The most characteristic examples of Cummings's style are the New Old South Church, his own residence, and a few houses to be found on Devonshire St. He also designed many commercial buildings but during the last twenty years of his life, he experienced the misfortune of seeing most of these projects, the pride of his professional accomplishment, demolished. His employment of motives based upon Florentine and Venetian Gothic prototypes had resulted in interestingly decorated façades with a comparatively meager window space; changing commercial requirements and the availability of large sheets of plate glass established a demand for a much greater window area.

Cummings collaborated with W. P. P. Longfellow in the *Cyclopædia of Works of Architecture in Italy, Greece, and the Levant* (1895–1903) and with R. Sturgis in the *Dictionary of Architecture and Building* (1901–02). His chief work was the *History of Architecture in Italy from the Time of Constantine to the Dawn of the Renaissance* (1901). It is the authoritative record in English of Italian architecture, showing with thoroughness and accuracy the development and decline of the types of building which appeared in Italy to the middle of the twelfth century. It is consistently a study from the architect's point of view in which the mixture of styles and stream of influence are treated in a descriptive and narrative style rather than in a philosophical or esthetic manner.

A widely recognized maturity of judgment resulted in Cummings's appointment to many committees and boards: he was a member of the commission for the preserving and restoring of the Massachusetts State House, a member of the Art Commission of Boston, a trustee of the Boston Museum of Fine Arts, and a trustee of the Boston Athenæum.

[*Proc. Am. Institute of Architects,* vol. XXXIX; *Am. Architect and Building News,* Aug. 19, 1905; *The Cummings Memorial; a Geneal. Hist. of the Descendants of Isaac Cummings* (1903); *Biog. Record of the Officers and Grads. of the Rensselaer Polytechnic Institute, 1824–86* (1887); *Who's Who in America,* 1903–05.]
                                                  L. F. P.

CUMMINGS, EDWARD (Apr. 20, 1861–Nov. 2, 1926), Unitarian minister, student and worker in social ethics, was the son of Edward N. and Lucretia F. (Merrill) Cummings. He prepared for Harvard College at Woburn, Mass., High School. At graduation from Harvard in 1883, he stood tenth in class, with a *magna cum* *laude* in philosophy. He received the degree of A.M. in 1885; was instructor in English, political economy, and sociology, for one year each; and was assistant professor of sociology in the department of economics from 1893 to 1900. Immediately after graduation he studied at the Divinity School, and was associated with Rev. Francis G. Peabody, a pioneer at Harvard and in this country who was giving systematic instruction in social ethics. Cummings was the first holder of the Robert Treat Paine fellowship for study abroad in social science; which gave such opportunities as acquaintance with Rev. Samuel A. Barnett at Toynbee Hall and Prof. Estlin Carpenter at Oxford. As a teacher at Harvard he was human, alert, and stimulating. He was an editor of the *Quarterly Journal of Economics,* and contributed ten articles to it between 1886 and 1901. They dealt especially with industrial disputes and the cooperative movement, but one described the Exposition of Social Economy at Paris in 1889; another was a critical study of university settlements; another, delivered before a national conference of Unitarian ministers, was on "Charity and Progress." These illustrate his clear and often humorous way of saying wise things. In application of theory, he served twice as president of the Harvard Coöperative Society.

In October 1900, he was ordained minister of the South Congregational Society, Unitarian, of Boston, the colleague of Rev. Edward Everett Hale. Succeeding Dr. Hale, who died in 1909, he was the pastor until 1925, when the church was merged with the First Church of Boston, and he became emeritus and an associate of Rev. Charles Park, pastor of that church. With both Dr. Hale and Dr. Park, his relations were cordial, loyal, and modest. His sermons are recalled as simple and practical. The test of talks to boys' schools, he met happily. But he was not preëminently a preacher or pastor, especially when other work claimed much of his thought. He spoke of himself, in the ministry, as an applied sociologist. He supplemented his sermons with talks by various experts on practical problems of citizenship; gave many lectures and addresses outside his church, and was constantly and eagerly working in philanthropy and legislative reform. He served as president of the Benevolent Fraternity of Unitarian Churches, of the Massachusetts Civic League, and was a director of the Massachusetts Prison Association, the Boston Federation of Churches, and Hale House, a social settlement. His chief philanthropic interest for sixteen years was in promoting the World Peace Foundation, whose center was in Boston. In 1910, he was elected a trustee and

served as such and as secretary of the Board until in 1916 he became general secretary, the chief executive officer, giving half of his time at least to the Foundation. In 1921, he made an extensive tour of Europe, in order to get a grasp of the many effects of the World War. Becoming interested in relief work, he thenceforth gave to relief from his own limited means and from gifts of others, especially to the Near East. During his term of office in the Foundation, it became the official center for spread of information in this country from the League of Nations, the International Labor Office, and the Permanent Court of International Justice. Cummings was killed on a railroad crossing, in a blinding snowstorm. His wife, Rebecca H. (Clarke) Cummings and a son and daughter survived him.

[*Unitarian Year Book,* 1927–28; *Harvard Grads. Mag.,* Mar. 1927; articles in the *Quart. Jour. Economics,* vols. I–XIII; information from family and friends.]

J.R.B.

CUMMINGS, JOHN (Feb. 12, 1785–June 8, 1867), tanner, was born in Woburn, Mass., the sixth child of Ebenezer and Jemima (Hartwell) Cummings. Both his father and grandfather were tanners as well as farmers, and John, after a meager education, followed his forebears. He started in the business of tanning on his own account in 1804, and until his retirement forty-three years later was a prominent figure in the industry. These years were important in the history of the leather industry, for they spanned the period of change from primitive methods to the modern, factory, machine-made product, and in this progress Cummings was a leader. When he commenced tanning he personally collected the hides and bark from the farmers, and having tanned them, hawked them about the country in small lots. About 1830 he took up the manufacture of "chaise leather" as a specialty, and was so successful that for many years he largely supplied the needs of the chaise manufacturers of the New England States. When enameled leather came into use and took the place of the old-fashioned chaise leather, Cummings immediately began its manufacture, becoming one of the largest slaughter leather tanners in Massachusetts. He is credited with being "the first tanner who appreciated the value of the splitting machine which has been of the greatest service in facilitating the finishing of leather" (*Biographical Encyclopædia of Massachusetts,* p. 402), and he was appointed almoner of the fund contributed by the leather interest for the benefit of Samuel Parker of Billerica, the inventor of this machine. The Cummings factories gave rise to the village of Cummingsville in Woburn. Cummings was important in the early history of the leather business not only because he was quick to adopt new methods, but also because of the many men, later influential in the trade, whom he trained and assisted. He was married May 2, 1811, to Marcia Richardson (June 26, 1793–June 8, 1822) of Woburn, by whom he had three children. His oldest son, John, carried on leather manufacturing in Woburn, and became a leader in Massachusetts finance and industry.

[A. O. Cummins, *Cummings Genealogy* (1904), pp. 222, 474–6; and Geo. Mooar, *The Cummings Memorial, a Geneal. Hist. of the Descendants of Isaac Cummings an Early Settler of Topsfield, Mass.* (1903), pp. 190, 349. See also *Biog. Encyc. of Mass. in the Nineteenth Century* (1879), and D. H. Hurd, *Hist. of Middlesex County, Mass.* (1890), I, 361.] 　　H.U.F.

CUMMINGS, JOSEPH (Mar. 3, 1817–May 7, 1890), clergyman, college president, was born of Scotch ancestry, in Falmouth, Me. His ancestors settled in Maine about the middle of the eighteenth century. His father was a Methodist preacher. He prepared for college in the Academy at Kent's Hill, Me., and was graduated from Wesleyan University in 1840. During his college course he supported himself in part by teaching school. For the next three years after graduation he taught natural science and mathematics in Amenia Seminary, New York. From 1843 to 1846 he was principal of that institution. In 1846 he was admitted to the New England Conference of the Methodist Episcopal Church, and he served for seven years in the pastorate. His appointments were all in what is now Greater Boston. The churches which he served were among the most important in the Conference. In 1854 he entered upon the work of a college president, which was destined to be his life-work. From 1854 until 1857 he was president of Genesee College, Lima, N. Y., an institution which was subsequently absorbed in Syracuse University. From 1857 to 1875 he was president of Wesleyan University. The period of his presidency was an Augustan Age for the college. Three buildings were erected—the earliest buildings which gave any architectural distinction to the campus. He served practically as a supervising architect, giving personal attention to all details of the work. The closing years of his administration were marked by two important changes. One was the enlargement of the curriculum, with great extension of the elective system; the other was the admission of women—a policy which remained in force until 1909. In 1875 Cummings resigned the presidency, but remained in Wesleyan University for two years as professor of mental philosophy and political economy, and then resumed his preaching. On June 21, 1881, he was elected president of Northwestern University. During his administration in that institution, a debt of $200,000 was paid off, schools of dentistry and pharmacy were established, a science hall was dedicated in 1887, and an astronomical observatory in 1889.

His teaching may be characterized as eminently thought-inspiring. He thought, and he made his students think,—not by formal lectures, but by the Socratic discussion of topics suggested by the lesson in the text-book. Yet he was a man of affairs rather than a scholar; and, in his thought, the president should be not merely the chairman of the faculty, but the controlling power in the whole life of the college. He was an exceedingly dignified figure. His aspect when pleading for some great cause was singularly impressive. But with the robust strength blended a winning gentleness. He loved children, and children instinctively loved him. For a man of so vigorous an intellect and so strong a personality, he left a small amount of matter in print. He published a number of sermons and addresses delivered on various occasions, and some articles in church periodicals. In 1875 he published an edition of Butler's *Analogy of Religion*. He married, Aug. 15, 1842, Deborah S. Haskell of Litchfield, Me. One child died in infancy. He had two adopted daughters.

[No biography of Joseph Cummings has been published. See *Alumni Rec.* and *Bulls. Wesleyan Univ.*; A. H. Wilde, *Northwestern Univ., A History, 1855–1905* (1905); E. F. Ward, *The Story of Northwestern Univ.* (1924).] 　　W.N.R.

CUMMINGS, THOMAS SEIR (Aug. 26, 1804–Sept. 24, 1894), painter, was born at Bath, England, the only child of Charles and Rebecca Cummings, who emigrated in his infancy and settled at New York. Thomas had in boyhood drawing lessons from Augustus Earle, an English itinerant painter, and later from John Rubens Smith [*q.v.*]. In 1821 he was received as pupil by Henry Inman from whom he learned to make good miniatures. After three years master and pupil formed a partnership which lasted three years more. In 1827 Cummings was regarded (according to William Dunlap's *History . . . of the Arts of Design in the United States,* III, 199) as "the best instructed miniature painter then in the United States." He married in 1822 Jane Cook, like himself born in England. His part in founding, in 1825, the National Academy of Design was notable. He was elected to its council and for forty years he served as its treasurer. He was of agreeable personality, familiar with business methods and keenly interested in the Academy's classes for art students. He also for several years conducted in New York a private school of design. This led to a professorship in the University of the City of New York. In January 1844, he was an organizer of the New York Sketching Club, which he called "one of the most agreeable and instructive little clubs that ever took share in art matters in the city." Throughout his young manhood Cummings was prominent in military affairs, rising in the 2nd Regiment of New York Light Infantry from private to colonel, and in 1838 to brigadier-general, his command including several of the "crack" companies of the city. One of his friends was S. F. B. Morse, painter and inventor of the telegraph; he was among the invited guests at the first private demonstration of the invention. In 1851 a copy which Cummings had executed of Gilbert Stuart's "Martha Washington" was presented to Queen Victoria and gracefully acknowledged by Lord Palmerston. On Feb. 23, 1863, the Academy resolved to build on land which it had acquired in Twenty-third St. Cummings was chairman of the building committee which, at the then great cost of $250,000, successfully completed the ornate structure that was dedicated in 1865 and which was long a New York landmark. Soon after this crowning achievement he retired from professional activities, making his permanent home at Mansfield, Conn., and spending several months each winter in New York with his children. After his wife's death in 1889 he removed to Hackensack, N. J., where he died. Cummings was represented at the National Academy's centennial exhibition in Washington and New York, by his portrait of Daniel Seymour and a miniature portrait of the artist Alfred T. Agate [q.v.]. Among his early engraved works, still prized by collectors, are "The Bracelet," "The Bride," and "The Exchange of Queens."

[Much that is autobiographical appears in Cummings's own *Hist. Annals Nat. Acad. Design* (1865), a book admirably documented and filled with the author's interesting and generally good-natured comment on his contemporaries. Wm. Dunlap, *Hist. of the Rise and Progress of the Arts of Design in the U. S.*, III, pp. 198–9, 1918 ed., contains a sympathetic sketch of Cummings as of the year 1834. See also "The National Academy of the Arts of Design and its Surviving Founders," *Harper's Mag.*, May 1883.]   F. W. C.

CUMMINS, ALBERT BAIRD (Feb. 15, 1850–July 30, 1926), lawyer, statesman, was born in Carmichaels, Pa., the son of Thomas and Sarah Cummins, of Scotch-Irish ancestry. When he was seventeen, he entered Waynesburg College in his native state, working his way through college by tutoring and by teaching a country school during vacations. He completed the course in two years and spent the next four years in finding his place in the world. For a short time he was a clerk, later an express messenger, and

then a self-taught surveyor and railroad builder. In 1873 he began the study of law in Chicago and after a couple of years was admitted to the bar. During his preparation for the law, he was married to Miss Ida L. Gallery of Eaton Rapids, Mich. In 1878 he removed to Des Moines and formed a law partnership with his brother; later he was associated with ex-Chief Justice George G. Wright, and in due time became the senior member of the firm of Cummins, Hewitt & Wright, for many years the best-known law firm in the state of Iowa. Perhaps his greatest victory at the bar was in the suit brought by him against the barbed-wire trust, in which he appeared as the chief attorney for the farmers. The contest continued for more than five years until finally the issue was fought out before the Supreme Court of the United States, and resulted in the complete overthrow of the monopoly. He acquired a state-wide reputation as a consequence of his handling of this important series of cases.

In 1894 and in 1899 he was an unsuccessful candidate for United States senator. *The Iowa State Register* (Jan. 12, 1900) described the fight made by Cummins as a "marvel," considering that he had against him "a railroad with millions backing the biggest 'boss' the state ever knew, and a half-dozen allied railroads with the shrewdest men in Iowa political life in their employ, half or more of the congressmen, the entire organization of the great Republican party of Iowa, most of the office holders and aspirants, an army of paid agents, hundreds of influential newspapers whose editors are repaying obligations incurred by accepting postmasterships, and scores of federal office holders whose salaries the nation had paid while they have spent three years in steady, continuous work for their benefactor." In 1901 Cummins announced his candidacy for governor on a platform in which he declared that his great object was "to bring the individual voter into more prominence, and to diminish the influence of permanent organization in the ranks of the party" (*Iowa State Register*, Feb. 15, 1901). Thus began the most notable contest within the Republican party in Iowa since the famous Harlan-Allison senatorial campaign in 1872. The opposition supported Maj. Edwin H. Conger [q.v.], the American minister to China, who had recently won fame in the defense of Peking against the Boxers. In spite of the efforts of the former leaders Cummins had 866 delegates out of 1,641 in the convention, and was nominated upon the first ballot. The proposal for tariff revision, which came to be known as the "Iowa Idea," appeared in the platform adopted by this convention, but it did not originate with Cummins, although he indorsed the proposal and gave it an important place in his campaign. His program naturally was largely a personal one, resulting from his own experience in politics. He appealed from the leaders to the people; he believed that the railroad influence was hostile to democracy and independence; and he turned inevitably to the methods and measures by which more popular control and less party management would prevail. Before he retired from governorship, the domination of the railroads had been broken, a primary law adopted, and railroad taxation made more equitable. In short the Progressive movement had been inaugurated in Iowa. Gov. Cummins was renominated by acclamation in 1903, and an interval of quiet prevailed before the outbreak of the bitter controversies that were to mark the later years of his administration. The next general state election was not held until 1906, when, after an extremely acrimonious preliminary campaign, Cummins was renominated upon the first ballot by a vote of 933 to 603 for his opponent. The nomination once secured, election followed as a matter of course, a reduced vote being the only indication of party dissensions. The campaign of 1906 settled definitely the position of Gov. Cummins in Iowa politics. The Progressives had won a decisive victory.

In 1908 the contest for the United States senatorship was renewed, and in this campaign the new primary law was used for the first time. There was a strong feeling in the state that Senator Allison's long service entitled him to a nomination without opposition. Gov. Cummins's entrance as a candidate aroused all the old controversies of the contests between conservative and progressive Republicans. Senator Allison won at the primaries in June, but his death early in August reopened the whole question. A special session of the legislature met and amended the primary law so that the people could vote again in November, in case of the death, resignation, or removal for any cause of a candidate nominated at the regular primary in June. The amendment applied only to the full senatorial term beginning in March 1909, and left unsettled the filling of the remainder of Allison's unexpired term. An attempt to elect by the legislature failed because of the conservative opposition to Cummins. Adjournment was taken to November when the result of the primary would be known. Gov. Cummins won over his opponent by a majority of 42,000. Accordingly when the legislature reassembled, it elected him by a decisive vote. The last act in the political drama, which began in 1908, occurred when the General Assembly confirmed the verdict of the people in the November primaries, and elected Senator Cummins for the full term. In 1909 the two Iowa senators, Dolliver and Cummins, were among the ten Republicans who, in the final vote upon the Payne-Aldrich tariff bill, opposed it. No two men were more powerful in giving voice and definiteness to the new progressive wing of the Republican party. The campaign of 1910 was dominated by the division in the ranks of that party. Progressive Republicanism was very strong in Iowa. After the renomination of President Taft and the formation of the Progressive party, Senator Cummins issued a statement in which he announced his intention of voting for Roosevelt, but declined to join the new party. Senator Dolliver had died in October 1910.

Undoubtedly, Senator Cummins's greatest contribution to constructive legislation was in connection with the passage of the Transportation Act of 1920, usually known as the Esch-Cummins Act, which provided for the termination of Federal control and the restoration of the railroad properties to private management. The need for new legislation developed from the shortcomings of the railroads that had been disclosed even before the outbreak of the war. This necessity was increased by the war emergency, and the policies and activities of the war period helped to foreshadow the general character of future railroad control. The primary responsibility for the formulation of railroad legislation in the Sixty-sixth Congress fell upon the Senate Committee on Interstate Commerce under the chairmanship of Senator Cummins, and the House Committee on Interstate and Foreign Commerce under the chairmanship of Representative John J. Esch of Wisconsin. The legislation of 1920 was a compromise between the Esch or House measure and the Cummins or Senate bill. The House measure sought to settle problems by agreement as they arose, while the Cummins bill proposed the application of compulsion. Cummins seems to have realized more fully than any one else the nature of the problems confronting the railroads, especially in connection with their financial needs and in the settlement of labor controversies. He urged compulsory consolidation into a small number of systems and compulsory arbitration of labor disputes. The Transportation Act as finally enacted made provision for railway credit, but Congress was not yet ready to adopt compulsory consolidation and arbitration as advocated by Senator Cummins. Experience since 1920 has made clearer the need of consolidation and Cummins continued to urge it. He was planning a renewal of legislative discussion of the railroad situation at the time of his death. The provision for the settlement of labor disputes proved entirely inadequate and has already been replaced by another voluntary agreement plan. The outstanding success of the measure has been the financial rehabilitation of the railroads. For this outcome Cummins was largely responsible; but his conspicuous part in the drafting and passage of the Transportation Act of 1920 was the chief reason for his defeat in the primary election of 1926.

His work as governor of Iowa and as senator entitles Cummins to national recognition as a constructive statesman. He was president *pro tempore* of the Senate from 1919 to 1925. After the succession of Vice-President Coolidge to the presidency in August 1923, he became the regular presiding officer. In his prime he was a man of fine personal appearance. During his campaigns for governor and senator he visited every part of the state. His success was quite largely due to his ability as a speaker and his capacity to meet all sorts of people and situations. To the end of his career he had the support of large numbers of enthusiastic personal friends. In his later years many of his old opponents campaigned for him. Ex-Governor Leslie M. Shaw, when asked his reason for such action on his part, humorously replied: "I thought it best to sink our differences and help him put out the fires he had set."

[The chief sources of information are *The Review of Reviews*, vol. XXXIV, 291–99; F. E. Haynes, *Third Party Movements Since the Civil War* (1916), chap. XXIX; and his inaugural and biennial addresses as governor of Iowa in the *Iowa Legislative Docs.*, 1902, 1904, 1907. His work in connection with the Transportation Act of 1920 is discussed in S. L. Miller's *Railway Transportation* (1924), chap. XXXIII; in I. L. Sharfman's *The Am. Railroad Problem* (1921), chap. XI; and in *The Am. Economic Rev.*, vol. X, 507–27. Cummins presented his own views before the General Assembly of Iowa in March 1919. His address was printed in *Sen. Doc.*, vol. XIV, 66 Cong., 1 Sess., 1919. A sketch of his life and obituary notice were published in the *Des Moines Register*, July 31, 1926.]

F. E. H.

CUMMINS, GEORGE DAVID (Dec. 11, 1822–June 26, 1876), clergyman, founder of the Reformed Episcopal Church, was born near Smyrna, Del., the third child of George Cummins and his second wife, Maria Durborow. The former was of Scotch descent, a well-to-do landowner, and prominent in the state; the latter, of English lineage, and the daughter of Rev. John Durborow. When the boy was four years old his father died. He received his early education at a school kept by a Presbyterian minister named Russell in Newark, N. J., and through the influence of his mother who was a Methodist, though her husband had been an Episcopalian, he entered a Methodist College, Dickinson, from which he graduated in 1841, valedictorian of his class. While there he was converted and joined the Methodist Church. Anticipating becoming a minister of that denomination, he was for two or three years a circuit-rider under appointment of the Baltimore Conference, but the desire for a settled home and his liking for the liturgy of the Episcopal Church turned him to the latter, and he was confirmed in St. Andrew's Church, Wilmington, Del., Apr. 20, 1845, and ordained deacon there by Bishop Lee, Oct. 26, 1845. For a time he was assistant at Christ Church, Baltimore, but on June 17, 1847, was elected rector of Christ Church, Norfolk, Va. Exactly a week later he was married to Alexandrine Macomb Balch, daughter of Hon. L. P. W. Balch of West Virginia; and on July 6, 1847, at Wilmington, was ordained priest.

His pastorate at Norfolk lasted till July 1853. During the cholera epidemic of 1849, he ministered to all classes of sufferers until, the plague having spent itself, he retired to his father-in-law's, where he himself developed the disease. His natural gifts, devotion to his work, and power as a preacher, led important churches to seek his services. He was rector of St. James's, Richmond, Va. (1853–54); Trinity, Washington (1855–58), declining in 1856 a call to St. Thomas's, New York; St. Peter's, Baltimore (1858–63); and Trinity, Chicago, where he remained until elected assistant bishop of the Diocese of Kentucky, to which office he was consecrated by Bishop Hopkins at Christ Church, Louisville, Nov. 15, 1866. Seven years later, Nov. 10, 1873, in a letter to his diocesan, Bishop Smith, who was also presiding bishop, he announced his intention of leaving the communion, and transferring his work and office to another sphere.

The condition which led him to take this radical step was the effort of the extreme Anglo-Catholic element in the church to symbolize their doctrines in worship by a return to pre-Reformation usages. Both by temperament and early training he himself was an ardent evangelical. In every way possible he opposed the practises of the Ritualists "as subversive of the truth 'as it is in Jesus' and as it was maintained and defended by the Reformers of the sixteenth century." At first he thought the error could be checked, and combated any suggestion that the evangelicals leave the church, declaring in 1869 that "to go out of her communion because there is treachery within is to lower the flag and surrender the citadel to her enemies" (Alexandrine M. Cummins, *Memoir of George David Cummins*, 1879, p. 333). Finally he lost all hope that the evil would be eradicated by any action of the authorities of the church, and became convinced that by officiating in Ritualistic churches, he was sanctioning and indorsing dangerous errors. These feelings together with the criticisms he brought upon himself by participating in a communion service in the Fifth Avenue Presbyterian Church, Oct. 12, 1873, during a meeting of the Evangelical Alliance, at length caused him to w:thdraw from the Episcopal Church. He was formally deposed from his office and ministry, June 24, 1874. In the meantime, however, a meeting of clergymen and laymen was held in New York, Dec. 2, 1873, at which the Reformed Episcopal Church was inaugurated, Bishop Cummins being elected presiding officer and Rev. C. E. Cheney [*q.v.*] elected bishop, and later consecrated by Bishop Cummins. The brief remainder of his life was spent in the service of the new church, his death occurring at his home in Lutherville, Md., less than two years later. In addition to a *Life of Mrs. Virginia Hale Hoffman* (1859), he published several sermons.

[Mrs. Cummins's *Memoir*, referred to above, is based chiefly upon Bishop Cummins's diary and correspondence. It contains portraits. See also H. K. Carroll, *Religious Forces of the U. S.* (1893), and Chas. C. Tiffany, *A Hist. of the Protestant Episc. Ch. in the U. S.* (1895), both in the American Church History series; Annie D. Price, *A Hist. of the Formation and Growth of the Reformed Episc. Church, 1873–1902* (1902); and Benj. Aycrigg, *Memoirs of the Reformed Episc. Ch.* (5th ed., 1880); and *The Sun* (Baltimore), Jan. 27, 1876.]   H. E. S.

CUMMINS, MARIA SUSANNA (Apr. 9, 1827–Oct. 1, 1866), author, was a descendant of Isaac Cummings, of Scotch ancestry, who settled in Ipswich, Mass., and owned much land there previous to 1638. She was born in Salem, Mass., the daughter of Judge David Cummins and Mehitable (Cave) Cummins of Middleton, Mass. Her early studies were carried on at home and directed by her father, who himself had literary tastes and encouraged them in his daughter, in whom he thought he discovered a gift for writing. She later attended the fashionable school of Mrs. Charles Sedgwick at Lenox, Mass. When she was only a little past twenty she began to write stories for the *Atlantic Monthly* and other magazines. *The Lamplighter* (1854), written when she was twenty-seven, was her one striking success. It met immediate popularity and the sales mounted to over 40,000 copies within a few weeks. It was republished

in England and in translation in France and Germany, and in all of those countries had large sales. The novel is the story of a child lost in infancy, rescued from a cruel woman by an old lamplighter, adopted by a blind woman, and later discovered by her well-to-do father. A double love story slightly enlivens the plot, which is worked out at great length. The style is tediously detailed and the point of view is one of extreme piety. Later books of Miss Cummins did not win so much public approval, though *Mabel Vaughan* (1857) was considered by some critics to be better. *El Fureidis* (1860) is a story of Palestine and Syria, written entirely from imagination, and *Haunted Hearts* (1864) is a sentimental tale which was first published anonymously. All her books have a strong moral tone. The life-likeness of some of their characters constitutes their chief appeal. Miss Cummins had a quiet, retiring personality and led an uneventful, secluded life, occupied with the duties of home and church and with her writing. The loss of her father was a great grief to her. The Cummins family had before his death changed their home from Salem to one on Bowdoin St., in Dorchester, a house in colonial style, with gardens, shrubbery, a fish pond surrounded by pine trees, and an orchard. There, soon after the publication of *Haunted Hearts,* impaired health made it necessary for Maria Cummins to lay aside her writing and there, after a long illness, she died.

[See Albert O. Cummins, *Cummings Genealogy* (1904); Nathaniel Hall, *Sermon Preached in the First Ch., Dorchester, on the Sunday* (Oct. 8, 1866) *Following the Decease of Maria S. Cummins* (1866); Wm. D. Orcutt, *Good Old Dorchester* (1893); *Boston Daily Advertiser*, Oct. 2, 1866. A new edition of *The Lamplighter* was published in 1927.]   S. G. B.

CUNLIFFE–OWEN, PHILIP FREDERICK (Jan. 30, 1855–June 30, 1926), editor, publicist, was the eldest son of Sir Francis Philip Cunliffe-Owen and Baroness von Reitzenstein whose father was Baron Fritz von Reitzenstein of the Prussian Royal Guards. He was a grandson of the distinguished Capt. Charles Cunliffe-Owen, R.N., and Mary Blosset whose father, Sir Henry Blosset, was Chief Justice of Bengal. Born in London, he received his early education at the Lancing School in England but went for his college work to the University of Lausanne. Becoming an attaché in the British diplomatic service, he was stationed in several foreign countries including Egypt and Japan. He first visited the United States in 1876 to represent officially at the Centennial Exposition his father, the British Executive Commissioner, who was then director of the South Kensington Museum and one of the greatest promoters of International Exhibitions. After a brief sojourn in England, he returned to the United States to settle in New York, ever after his home. Being an omnivorous reader of foreign newspapers and magazines and having traveled extensively, he soon secured an editorial connection with the *New York Tribune* as a contributor on foreign topics. These were signed "Ex-Diplomat" until Whitelaw Reid, who had been appointed minister to France in 1889, returned to resume the editorship of the *Tribune*; then "Ex-Attaché" was substituted lest readers might mistake the author. Because of his encyclopædic familiarity with foreign affairs Cunliffe-Owen had been appointed copy editor of the foreign news. Close confinement to the desk and late hours at night so told on his health that he was made society editor, a position he held until his retirement in 1913. With his wife, formerly Countess Marguerite du Planty de Sourdis, whom he married Nov. 22, 1877, and Willis Fletcher Johnson, day editor of the *Tribune,* he formed a newspaper syndicate. In 1899 Johnson withdrew but Cunliffe-Owen and his wife continued the syndicate with great success under the signature, "La Marquise de Fontenoy." The loss of a son, Algernon, in 1910, was a blow from which the father never recovered. A voluminous contributor of signed articles under his own name, and under noms de plume to British reviews, he radiated culture and learning in all that he wrote. His death left vacant in American journalism the position of international interpreter of foreign affairs. His remarkable collection of newspaper clippings and magazine articles was given (1929) by his executors to the Department of Journalism, New York University.

[C. H. Owen, *The Descendants of the Elder Branch of the Cunliffes of Wycoller* (2nd ed., 1887); *The World* (London), Oct. 23, 1878; *Who's Who in America*, 1918–19; obituary in *N. Y. Times*, July 1, 1926.] J.M.L.

CUNNINGHAM, ANN PAMELA (Aug. 15, 1816–May 1, 1875), founder and first Regent of the Mount Vernon Ladies' Association of the Union, was born at "Rosemont," Laurens County, S. C., the daughter of Robert and Louisa (Bird) Cunningham. She came of distinguished ancestry on both sides, for the Cunninghams had been prominent in South Carolina for several generations, and the Birds people of importance in Pennsylvania. Her father, a wealthy planter, was much given to hospitality, and took a prominent part in the life of his community. She was educated by a governess and at Barhamville Institute, near Columbia, S. C., and it is said "was remarkable for her precocious and brilliant girl-

hood." The idea of preserving Washington's home for future generations was suggested to her by her mother, who feared it might fall into the hands of speculators. Her first effort was a letter addressed to the women of the South published in the *Charleston Mercury*, Dec. 2, 1853, and signed "A Southern Matron," a name which she used to hide her identity throughout the campaign. In the same year she founded the Mount Vernon Ladies' Association of the Union, of which she was elected Regent, with the purpose of raising $200,000 for the purchase of Mount Vernon from the owner, John Augustine Washington. A newspaper called *The Mount Vernon Record* was published, which gave details of the campaign, and committees were organized in various states. The public was hard to arouse and opposed to women attempting such a task, but Miss Cunningham was nothing daunted. Meeting Edward Everett in Richmond in 1856, she won his support for the project, to which he eventually contributed $69,064, the proceeds of his lecture on Washington delivered throughout the country. After many discouragements, the purchase was finally completed Feb. 22, 1859. During the Civil War, Miss Cunningham remained in South Carolina, but from 1868 until her retirement in 1874, she lived at Mount Vernon in order personally to supervise the estate. She died at "Rosemont," and was buried at Columbia, S. C., in the churchyard of the First Presbyterian Church.

In appearance Miss Cunningham was short, with a rather large head, well-rounded figure, auburn-brown hair, and expressive gray eyes. She was handicapped from her early youth by a severe spinal affection, caused by a fall from a horse. The long struggle to obtain a charter from the Virginia legislature so exhausted her that she went from one convulsion into another, and the lawyers had to wait until she was calm enough to receive them and sign the necessary papers. She travelled always under the greatest physical discomfort and pain. "None but God can know," she once said, "the mental labor and physical suffering Mount Vernon has cost me!" She was of a shy, retiring disposition, and had a "horror of publicity for a lady—of her name appearing in the newspapers!" (*Historical Sketch of Ann Pamela Cunningham*). But it is owing to her perseverance and courage that Mount Vernon is now preserved for posterity.

[Thos. Nelson Page, *Hist. & Preservation of Mount Vernon* (1910); *Hist. Sketch of Ann Pamela Cunningham*, "The Southern Matron" (1903), issued by the Association; B. F. Perry, *Reminiscences of Mrs. Louisa Cunningham* (1874); Chas. H. Callahan, *Washington the Man and the Mason* (1913); Grace King, *Mount Vernon on the Potomac* (1929); Cat. *Winthrop College*

1892–93; *The News & Courier*, Charleston, S. C., May 14, 1875; *Daily Morning Chronicle* (Washington, D. C.), Apr. 15, 17, 18, and May 6, 1872; *Munsey's Mag.*, Sept. 1905; *Southern Lit. Messenger*, May 1855.]   E.D.F.

CUPPLES, SAMUEL (Sept. 13, 1831–Jan. 6, 1912), merchant, manufacturer, philanthropist, was the son of James Cupples, an Irish educator, who emigrated from County Down, Ireland, in 1814, and his wife Elizabeth Bigham. He was born at Harrisburg, Pa., and was educated chiefly by his father, who had established a business school in Pittsburgh. At the age of fifteen he went down the Ohio to Cincinnati, where he was employed by Albert O. Tyler, a wooden-ware merchant. The firm of Samuel Cupples & Company was formed in 1851 and Cupples began business with a stock of wooden-ware in St. Louis which soon became the chief manufacturing and shipping city for wooden-ware. To relieve congestion in freight handling and a lack of warehouse facilities Robert S. Brookings and Cupples established the Cupples Station by acquiring conveniently located land and erecting some fifty buildings so arranged as to have railway trackage to every building. This terminal operation proved to be immediately successful for it met an economic necessity for the heavy shippers of St. Louis (Hyde and Conard, *Encyc. of the History of St. Louis*, 1899, I, 535). Cupples and others became interested in "head and hand" education and established the St. Louis Training School of Washington University, which became a model for the United States and other countries. His active participation in manual training brought him into touch with other branches of Washington University work. He and his partner in business and philanthropy, R. S. Brookings, gave to the Washington University for its endowment the Cupples Station property (*Encyc. Americana*, 1924, VIII, 304). Thus the great terminal of St. Louis serves its manufacturing and shipping needs and provides income to educate its youth. The School of Engineering and Architecture at Washington University was given by him, and with its endowment he provided twelve scholarships to graduates of the Manual Training School, saying that he believed the road to education should be made open at the top (eulogy by C. M. Woodward, in *Manual Training Magazine*, with a portrait of Samuel Cupples, Oct. 1912, p. 46). Cupples lived to be over eighty years of age. During the last thirty years he was practically an invalid and his chief interest lay in his philanthropies. His gifts to Washington University exceeded $1,750,000, and his other contributions to the cause of education and to the Southern Methodist Church brought the total of his benefactions to $3,000,000. Central College at Fay-

ette, Mo., Vanderbilt University at Nashville, Tenn., the St. Louis Provident Association, the Girls Industrial Home, the Orphans Home, struggling Methodist churches and ministers were beneficiaries of his wealth and interest. He did not live to see the Robert Barnes Hospital completed, of which he was one of the trustees under the will of Robert Barnes. His wife, Amelia Kells of St. Louis, died many years before him. He left one daughter.

[Memorial resolution printed in the *Bull. Washington Univ.*, July 1912; *St. Louis Globe-Democrat*, Jan. 7, 8, 1912; information from Mr. Robert S. Brookings.]   B.C.

CURRIER, CHARLES WARREN (Mar. 22, 1857–Sept. 23, 1918), clergyman, scholar, author, was the son of Warren Green, a native of New York City, and Deborah (Heyliger) Currier. He was born on the island of St. Thomas, West Indies, and it was there that he received his early education. When fourteen years old he was taken to the Netherlands where, during the next ten years, he made his classical, philosophical, and theological studies in colleges of the province of Limburg and received the doctorate in philosophy and theology. In 1881, on his ordination at Amsterdam to the Catholic priesthood, he accompanied the Vicar Apostolic as missionary to Surinam, Dutch Guiana. But his labors there lasted less than two years, owing to failing health, and in 1882 he was transferred to the United States. Then, for more than a decade, he was identified with the order of Redemptorists, preaching on missions and retreats chiefly in the vicinity of Annapolis and Boston. On his release from his obligations to the Redemptorists, he became attached to the diocese of Baltimore in 1894, where he served first as a curate in a small Charles County parish and afterward as diocesan missionary, until 1900 when he became pastor of St. Mary's, Washington, D. C. There he remained until 1907 when he joined the Bureau of Catholic Indian Missions, traveling extensively and lecturing and preaching with much success—for he was an interesting and facile speaker and preacher—for the benefit of Catholic education among the American Indians. In 1910 he was designated bishop of Zamboanga, Philippine Islands, but, as the nomination was conditional, he declined the appointment. Instead, he accepted that made three years later by Pius X to the bishopric of Matanzas, Cuba; and with Cardinal Falconio presiding he was consecrated at Rome, July 6, 1913. But in less than two years, owing to ill health, he was compelled to resign the administration of his Episcopal See and became titular bishop of Hetalonia. Early in 1915 he returned to the archdiocese of Baltimore where he continued to reside until his death which occurred suddenly while on his way from Waldorf in southern Maryland to Baltimore.

Because of his wide learning and specialized studies, Bishop Currier was regarded as one of the foremost Hispanists and authorities on early American history in the United States. He was chosen to represent this country as a delegate to the International Congress of Americanists held in various years in European centers, and in 1910, during the administration of President Taft, he was commissioned by the State Department United States delegate to a similar congress held at Buenos Aires, on the occasion of the one hundredth anniversary of Argentine independence. He was an enthusiastic promoter of Pan-Americanism and was constantly active in contributing to a better understanding between the countries of the Americas. As a means to this end he furthered the establishment in Washington of the Spanish-American Athenæum, of which he was a director.

He was the author of several works and his style was clear and wholly unaffected. He began a *History of Spanish Literature* of which several chapters were published, and in the same field he wrote a number of criticisms of the work of several Spanish and Spanish-American writers. He also collaborated on the *Bulletin of the Pan-American Union*. In 1890 appeared his *Carmel in America: A Centennial History of the Discalced Carmelites in the United States*, in 1894 his *History of Religious Orders*, and in 1897 his *Church and Saints, or The History of the Church in the Saintly Lives of its Children*. Here, too, belong some smaller religious works, such as *A Child of Mary* (1897), *Mission Memories* (1898), *The Divinity of Christ* (1898), and *The Mass* (1899). He wrote two historical novels, *Dimitrios and Irene; or, The Conquest of Constantinople* (1894) and *The Rose of Alhama; or, The Conquest of Granada* (1897). His impressions and records of a tour of South America were published under the title of *Lands of the Southern Cross* (1911). He also contributed many articles to the *Catholic World* and the *American Catholic Quarterly Review*.

[*Who's Who in America*, 1916–17, p. 586; *Bull. of the Pan-American Union*, XLVII, Oct. 1918, pp. 574–75; *Baltimore Catholic Rev.*, Sept. 28, 1918, Nov. 2, 1918; *Catholic News*, New York, Nov. 9, 1918, p. 16.]

J. Du.

CURRIER, MOODY (Apr. 22, 1806–Aug. 23, 1898), financier, politician, was born at Boscawen, N. H., the son of Moody Morse and Rhoda (Putney) Currier. He studied at Hopkinton Academy and graduated from Dartmouth College in 1834. During his college course he supported himself by teaching school and continued that occupation at Lowell, Mass., for several years after graduation, studying for the bar in the meantime. In 1841 he began the practise of law at Manchester, N. H. The growth of the city's industries offered lucrative opportunities and after a few years he definitely abandoned the law for banking and investment operations, and is thus identified with those developments which made the city one of the great industrial centers of New England. He was connected in one capacity or another with four banking institutions; and beginning in 1864 he was for some years president of the Amoskeag National Bank. He accumulated a large estate and was financially interested in various enterprises, being a member of several directorates. In 1856 and again in 1857 he was elected to the state Senate, serving as president in his second term. In 1860–61 he was in the governor's council, and as chairman of its military committee performed important services in preparing New Hampshire troops for active service. In 1884 he was elected governor, serving from June 1885 to June 1887. His message of June 4, 1885, gives an excellent summary of his political philosophy. In it he demanded: "A simple government, administered with rigid economy, with perfect honesty, and with due regard to the security of life and property, the promotion of learning and morality, and the amelioration of the condition of the unfortunate. ... A few laws, so reasonable that they will enforce themselves among good citizens, and so evidently just that they can easily be enforced against the vicious and the lawless are all that are required." He opposed the creation of additional commissions and offices, was active in supporting one of the early conservation movements in the state—the restocking of its waters with fish, and was considered an able and successful executive. He retained an active interest in public affairs until late in life and several of his anniversary and other addresses were printed, notably those on the dedication of the Webster monument in 1886 and the Stark memorial in 1890. He was a man of wide reading both in science and literature, having command of several modern languages, and the literary style of his addresses and official papers is decidedly above the average of such documents. He also tried his hand at poetry and printed a small collection of verses in 1880, although this may be regarded merely as an interesting foible of a hard-headed Yankee banker. He was three times married: Dec. 8, 1836, to Lucretia C. Dustin; Sept. 5, 1847, to Mary W. Kidder; and Nov. 16, 1869, to Hannah A. Slade.

[E. S. Stackpole, *History of New Hampshire* (1916),

IV, 136–37; G. F. Willey, *Willey's Semi-Centennial Book of Manchester*, pp. 115–16; see also sketch by W. H. Stinson, *Granite Monthly*, Apr. 1902, XXXII, 221, obituary notice *Ibid.*, Sept. 1898, XXV, 184, and M. D. Clarke, *Manchester* (1875), pp. 400–02.]   W.A.R.

CURRIER, NATHANIEL (Mar. 27, 1813–Nov. 20, 1888), lithographic printer, publisher, was born in Roxbury, Mass., the son of Nathaniel and Hannah Currier. As a boy he was apprenticed to William S. and John Pendleton, who had just set up the first lithographic establishment in the United States, in Boston. William S. Pendleton had imported from Europe not only the equipment necessary for the business, but also artists and workmen. Young Currier was taught the business of lithographic presswork, and when John Pendleton, in 1829, joined a partnership with Cephas G. Childs and Francis Kearney, and opened a lithographic house in Philadelphia, under the name of Pendleton, Kearney & Childs, the apprentice accompanied him to the Quaker City. He remained there until 1833 when he went to New York, where John Pendleton also established a lithographic business. About the time Currier had completed his apprenticeship he began business on his own account in New York, where he resided until his death. His name first appears in the New York *Directory* in 1835, in which year, having become associated with J. H. Bufford, he issued a lithograph drawn by Bufford, showing "The Ruins of the Merchants' Exchange." This was printed toward the close of the year 1835, and inaugurated that series of popular lithographic prints which continued to be published for nearly seventy years, and is best known as Currier & Ives prints. In a rather crude but forceful way this series of prints gives a lively picture of the manners and history of the people of the United States from 1835 until the close of the nineteenth century. Great fires, disasters, the California gold rush, the development of railroads and commerce from the clipper ship to the steamship, are vividly recorded, as are the important political changes, sports, and the making of the West. They also include portraits of eminent Americans of the times. Many of the prints were colored by hand. They were designed for a people who were pioneering in the art of living under a new civilization, and who desired esthetic improvement in their wall decorations. In 1850 Currier took into partnership, J. Merritt Ives, an artist, and after 1857 all of the prints published by the firm bore the imprint, Currier & Ives. Currier retired from active participation in the business in 1880, leaving his son, Edward W. Currier, to continue with Ives. On Nov. 20, 1888, Currier died in New York, of heart disease. Currier & Ives prints became "an institution"

and their office frequently entertained such celebrities as Horace Greeley, Henry Ward Beecher, and Hiram Woodruff. "Into the domain of political caricature, Currier & Ives had made incursions as early as the Mexican War. But the presidential campaign of 1856 brought the first sustained effort in this direction" (Frank Weitenkampf in *Antiques*, Jan. 1925). "There is nothing quite like it (the series) as a historical record and it supplements the newspaper files covering a period when newspapers were not fully illustrated as we have them now" (Karl Schmidt, in *Country Life*, Aug. 1927). Currier was twice married: first, to Eliza West Farnsworth; second, to a Miss Ormsbee of Vermont.

[For the main facts in Currier's career the obituary in the *N. Y. Tribune*, Nov. 22, 1888, and the N. Y. *Directories* have been relied upon. Consult also his will in the Surrogate's Office, New York City, and *The Antiquarian*, Dec. 1923; *Antiques*, Jan. 1925; *Lithographs of N. Currier and Currier & Ives*, by Warren A. Weaver (1925); *Caricatures Pertaining to the Civil War, etc.*, published by Currier & Ives, from 1856 to 1872 (1892).]   J.J.

CURRY, GEORGE LAW (July 2, 1820–July 28, 1878), last of the territorial governors of Oregon, was born in Philadelphia, to which city his grandfather, Christopher Curry, had come from England. His early years were spent in Caracas, 1824–29, then two years on a farm near Harrisburg, Pa. At the age of eleven, after the death of his father, George Curry, he went with an uncle to Boston where he was apprenticed to the printer's trade. He attended school only three months. His messages as governor and his other writings, however, attest that he became a well-educated man through reading and study. When eighteen he was elected and served two terms as president of the Mechanic Apprentices' Library Association of Boston. After three years of newspaper work in St. Louis, he set out in 1846 for Oregon and on his arrival in Oregon City was almost at once made editor of the *Oregon Spectator*, the first newspaper established on the Pacific Coast, the first number of which had been issued in February 1846. Two editors had already preceded him and his own tenure was ended in January 1848, after he had published a resolution which was introduced in the legislature, but not passed, protesting against the appointment of J. Quinn Thornton to any territorial office. Thornton had been sent to Washington by Abernethy, provisional governor and president of the association that owned the *Spectator*. In March of that year he founded a newspaper of his own, the *Oregon Free Press*, the first weekly published in the territory, with type purchased from the Catholic clergy and with a homemade press. In the same month he married Chloe Donnelly Boone, a great-grand-daughter of the famous Daniel, who had come to Oregon over the southern route in 1846. His newspaper was obliged to suspend when his subscribers rushed away to the gold-fields of California. He then took up farming, an occupation that he continued to combine with his later activities.

After serving as a member of the legislature of the provisional government (1848–49), as chief clerk of the Territorial Council (1850–51), and as member of the lower house of the legislature (1851–52), he was appointed secretary of the territory in 1853. He acted as governor from May to December 1853, until the arrival of Gov. John W. Davis, and was appointed governor when the latter retired in August 1854. Curry's appointment gave great satisfaction because he was a resident of the territory. Besides, he was *persona grata* with the "Salem Clique" a group of Democratic leaders, who headed by Asahel Bush, editor of the *Oregon Statesman*, dominated affairs and directed governmental policies. He is best remembered for his part in vigorously defending the settlers against the Indians in 1855. With the uprising of the Yakima and other Indian tribes of eastern Washington and Oregon and the Rogue River Indians in southern Oregon, he called into the field and equipped some twenty-five hundred volunteers to assist the Federal troops in confining these Indians within their reservations, thus opening their lands to white settlement. The county that was named in his honor was created in 1855. After Oregon became a state in 1859 he came within one vote of being elected United States senator in 1860.

[A brief biography published in the *Trans. Ore. Pioneer Asso.* (1878), pp. 79–81, is the best sketch of his career. Additional data have been supplied by his son in the *Oregon Jour.*, May 19, 20, 1924; by articles in *Morning Oregonian*, Feb. 12, 14, 1899, May 20, 1920; by J. C. Moreland, *Governors of Oregon* (1913); and by H. H. Bancroft, *Hist. of Ore.* (2 vols., 1886, 1888). See also *Oregon Spectator*, 1846–48.]   R. C. C—k.

CURRY, JABEZ LAMAR MONROE (June 5, 1825–Feb. 12, 1903), statesman, author, educator, was the second son of William Curry of Georgia and Susan Winn Curry. "I can hardly call myself an Anglo-Saxon," he once said, "as in my veins flow English blood, Scotch, Welsh, and French." He was born in Lincoln County, Ga. In 1833 "the stars fell," and the meteoric shower was associated by Curry with his leaving home for a distant school. Later he entered the famous Waddell Academy in South Carolina, where both the arch-nullifier, John C. Calhoun, and the solitary nationalist, James L. Petigru, were trained. In 1838 his father removed with his family to Talladega County, Ala., where fresh lands invited slave labor. The next year Jabez entered the University of Georgia (then Franklin College), where Joseph Le Conte, the scientist, and Benjamin H. Hill, senator from Georgia, were fellow students. Le Conte, writing to Curry from California, in 1887, said in a postscript, "We have just received two or three first-class seismographs. Wanted, an earthquake to record"—a want abundantly supplied in 1906.

In 1843 Curry entered the law school of Harvard College, where he studied under Joseph Story and Simon Greenleaf, and where Rutherford B. Hayes was a class-mate. In Boston the Southern youth was present when Wendell Phillips and William Lloyd Garrison spoke on abolition. His structural purpose in life was shaped at this time, when he heard Horace Mann, the American apostle of public schools. In looking back upon this experience, Curry recorded: "Mann's glowing periods, earnest enthusiasm and democratic ideas fired my young mind and heart; and since that time I have been an enthusiastic and consistent advocate of universal education." Unity in diversity marks Curry's career, and the key to the remaining sixty years of his activity is his zeal for universal education in the South in the spirit and power of Horace Mann. After receiving his law degree at Harvard, in 1845, on his way home to Alabama he visited John C. Calhoun, then secretary of state. "In all my political career," Curry said, "I was an adherent of the Calhoun school of politics." Thus Mann and Calhoun became the poles of his sphere of activity. The future and the past wrestled for his soul. His politics has lost in meaning, but his supreme purpose to "preach a crusade against ignorance" has been a gulf-current to those who came after.

He served in the Mexican War as a private in the Texas Rangers but resigned on account of ill health; he was a member of the Alabama legislature three different times, in 1847, in 1853, and in 1855; a member of Congress, 1857–61; a member of the Confederate Congress, 1861–63, and again in 1864; an aide on the staff of Gens. Joseph E. Johnston and Joseph Wheeler, and lieutenant-colonel of cavalry in the Confederate army, 1864–65; president of Howard College, Ala., 1865–68; professor of English in the University of Richmond (then Richmond College), 1868–81. President Hayes offered Curry a place in his cabinet, and Cleveland appointed him United States minister to Spain, 1885–88. This service, though of cordial and signal success, was "a mere interlude in the man's essential career." Sixteen years later, upon King Alfonso's coming of age, Roosevelt, at the special request of Spain, sent Curry back as ambassador extraordinary (1902).

It was in 1866, when the South was in ashes, that George Peabody, of old New England stock, made a gift of more than two million dollars to quicken schools in the South. Barnas Sears, the first agent of the Peabody Fund, requested that Curry should be his successor, because "he is so many-sided, so clear in his views, so judicious, and knows so well how to deal with all classes of men. His whole being is wrapped up in general education, and he is the best lecturer or speaker on the subject in all the South." It was upon the motion of Gen. Grant that Curry was elected agent of the Peabody Fund in 1881. Four achievements are credited to Curry's administration of this Fund: state normal schools for each race in twelve Southern states; a system of public graded schools everywhere in the cities and small towns; the grounding in the minds of legislators of their responsibility for adequate rural schools; a body of educational literature, in his forty reports and ten published addresses. Inspired by the example of the Peabody Fund, John F. Slater of Norwich, Conn., gave a million dollars in 1882 for negro schools in the South. One of the Slater trustees was Rutherford B. Hayes, who in 1890 secured Curry as agent likewise of this Fund. Thus to Curry's strong hand had come the main threads of educational progress in the South.

In building the idea of public education, Curry was wont to address the legislatures in Southern states, and audiences in all parts of the country. Speaking before the University of Chicago, on July 4, 1898, on the doctrines of Calhoun, he was frequently interrupted by President Harper in order to read aloud telegrams as to the progress of the battle of Santiago that ended Spanish rule in America and made the United States a world-power. Then Curry would turn from Calhoun to greet the star-spangled banner draping the platform, and make it the basis of an appeal for nationality. He was a man of leonine type, both in appearance and in energy. As an orator he was fervent, but his main power as a speaker was due to his personality fused with principle. In his presence before an audience there was, indeed, something of the "dæmonic" quality which Goethe describes. Once he declared to a great assembly that it was the proudest duty of the South to train every child in its borders, black or white. Silence ensued. He exclaimed, "I will make you applaud that sentiment!" and with irresistible eloquence proceeded to do so.

Just before going to Chicago, Curry attended at Capon Springs, W. Va., a small conference of persons interested in education in the South. The next year, 1899, Curry was elected president of this conference, out of which sprang the Southern Education Board, and, in a sense, the General Education Board. The vast educational effort represented by the work of these boards may be considered, so far as the South is concerned, the culmination of Curry's sixty years' devotion to the cause of universal education. The Southern Education Board was organized in New York City on Nov. 3, 1901, under the presidency of Robert C. Ogden, and Curry was made its supervising director. Ogden carried forward the movement, revealing social statesmanship that practically transformed conditions in the South. He always delighted to say, "Curry was my master." Some of those associated with Curry in the Southern Education Board were Walter H. Page, Albert Shaw, Hollis B. Frissell, George Foster Peabody, Wallace Buttrick, Charles W. Dabney, and Edwin A. Alderman. This group energized public opinion in behalf of better schools for all the children of the South.

Curry was spared to see this flowering forth of all his work. At his death in 1903 the funeral, in accordance with his own request, was held from the halls of the University of Richmond, and he was buried at Hollywood Cemetery. The State of Alabama placed a marble statue of Curry in the Hall of Statuary in the Capitol at Washington. He was married, on Mar. 4, 1847, to Ann Bowie, a native of Abbeville District, S. C. Of the four children of this marriage, but two survived infancy. Ann Bowie Curry died on Apr. 8, 1865. On June 25, 1867, Curry was married to Mary Wortham Thomas, a daughter of James Thomas of Richmond, Va. After a wedded life of thirty-six years, Mrs. Curry survived her husband but three months.

[E. A. Alderman and A. C. Gordon, *J. L. M. Curry: a biography* (1911), contains the chief sources of information. See also his own writings: *Constitutional Government in Spain* (1889); *William Ewart Gladstone* (1891); *The Southern States of the American Union considered in their relations to the Constitution of the United States and to the resulting Union* (1894); *A Brief Sketch of George Peabody, and a History of the Peabody Education Fund through thirty years* (1898); *Civil History of the Government of the Confederate States, with some personal reminiscences* (1901).]

S. C. M.

CURTIN, ANDREW GREGG (Apr. 23, 1815?–Oct. 7, 1894), governor of Pennsylvania, was born at Bellefonte, Center County, Pa., the son of Roland and Jean (Gregg) Curtin. The Curtins belonged to Scotch-Irish stock. Roland emigrated from Dysert, County Clare, and settled in Bellefonte in 1800. In 1807, he erected a forge on Bald Eagle Creek about four miles from Bellefonte and lived there, occupied in the manufacture of iron, until his death in 1850. His second wife, Jean Gregg, was the daughter of Andrew Gregg, congressman, senator, and secretary of state under Joseph Hiester. Andrew Gregg Curtin was first taught in his native village by a Mr. Brown, a man of culture who had a school of about a dozen boys. Thence he went to Harrisburg Academy and later to Milton Academy, Pa., where, under the Rev. David Kirkpatrick, he was well grounded in mathematics and the classics. With this preparation, he turned to the study of law. At first with W. W. Potter of Bellefonte and then under Judge John Reed at the Law School of Dickinson College, he was initiated into his profession and, in 1839, was admitted to the bar in Center County, becoming, soon after, a partner of John Blanchard, a lawyer of good repute who was later elected to Congress. On May 30, 1844, Curtin married Catherine Irvine Wilson, daughter of Dr. Irvine Wilson and Mary Patten Wilson.

Of commanding presence and genial manner, gifted with wit and power of speech, Curtin became highly effective both before judges and juries. He won early success as a public speaker. In 1840, at the age of twenty-five, he appeared on behalf of Gen. Harrison's candidacy for the presidency; in 1844 he was enlisted in support of Henry Clay; in 1848, he canvassed the state for Gen. Zachary Taylor, the Whig candidate for the presidency; and in 1852 he took the field for Gen. Winfield Scott. In 1854, he was offered the nomination for governor but refused, and supported James Pollock who was elected and promptly appointed Curtin secretary of the commonwealth and also ex-officio superintendent of common schools. In this post Curtin secured an enlarged appropriation for public schools and pushed a bill through the legislature authorizing the establishment of state normal schools, acts which increased his popularity and made probable his succession to the governor's chair. The state election of 1860, often called "The Battle of 1860" aroused the keenest interest because of the national issues involved and because Lincoln looked especially to Curtin of Pennsylvania and Henry S. Lane of Indiana to swing the balance in these pivotal states to his side. Both were victorious: Lane won in Indiana, and Curtin, stoutly aided by A. K. McClure, chairman of the state committee, won in Pennsylvania by a majority of 32,000, which was interpreted as making the election of Lincoln secure.

Curtin's inaugural address, delivered on Jan. 15, 1861, produced wide-spread effects. In it he proclaimed the unswerving loyalty of Pennsylvania to the Union. "The people mean to preserve the integrity of the National Union at every hazard," he declared. He was the first of the governors to be summoned to Washington by Lincoln. After a consultation with the President on Apr. 8, 1861, he returned to Pennsylvania, won the overwhelming support of the legislature, and aroused so strong a spirit of loyalty among the people that double the state quota of 14,000 men was raised. Appreciating the magnitude and seriousness of the struggle then beginning, he obtained authority from the legislature to equip and maintain the extra force at the state's expense. Thus he fathered the famous Pennsylvania Reserve Corps which enabled the state to meet acute emergencies during the succeeding year. To inspire patriotic feeling he obtained funds from the Society of the Cincinnati of Pennsylvania for the purchase of regimental flags which he presented to the regiments as they were formed and which were afterward carried through scores of bloody engagements. His unfailing care and oversight of the Pennsylvania soldiers made him known in the army as the "Soldier's Friend." His guardianship extended to caring for them in hospital and to bringing their bodies back for burial. Nor did it stop there, but went out to their dependents. In 1863, he obtained from the legislature a fund for the support and schooling of the war orphans. The popular response to his devotion was evident in the election of 1863, when the vote of the soldiers and their friends made him by a great majority again governor. He took a leading part in the Altoona Conference of Union Governors which was successful in at least one of its objects—to disclose the solidity of the sentiment behind the Emancipation Proclamation. In 1868, he was one of the candidates for second place on the ticket with Grant, an honor which went to Schuyler Colfax. In 1869, President Grant appointed him minister to Russia. He filled the post with credit and on his return in 1872 was chosen delegate-at-large to the constitutional convention. His support of Greeley in the campaign of 1872 estranged his Republican friends, and he subsequently joined the Democratic party. In 1878, he ran for Congress on the Democratic ticket and was defeated. Two years later he ran again, was elected and served three consecutive terms until his retirement in March 1887. He lived quietly the remaining years of his life in his mountain home, surrounded by his family and friends, and died, after a severe attack of illness, on Oct. 7, 1894.

[Andrew Gregg Curtin; His Life and Services, ed. by W. H. Egle (1895); A. K. McClure, Abraham Lincoln and Men of War Times (1892), and The Life and Services of Andrew G. Curtin (an address delivered in the House of Representatives at Harrisburg, Pa., Jan. 20, 1895; N. Y. Tribune, Oct. 8, 1894; Times (Phila.), Oct. 8, 1894; Cong. Record, 47, 48, 49 Congs.; John B. Linn, Hist. of Centre and Clinton Counties (1883).]

W. B. P.

CURTIN, JEREMIAH (Sept. 6, 1840?–Dec. 14, 1906), linguist, student of comparative mythology, was born either in 1838 or 1840, in Greenfield, near Milwaukee, Wis. His parents, David and Ellen (Furlong) Curtin, provided him with a common-school education and, unwittingly, with a linguistic groundwork. Opportunity to talk with German, Norwegian, and Polish settlers near Milwaukee, where he was born, gave him a start in the branch in which he became distinguished. He worked his way through Carroll College at Waukesha, Wis., through Phillips Exeter, to Harvard, where he was graduated in 1863. The cruise of the Russian Admiral Lissofsky's fleet to the waters of the United States in 1864, and Curtin's pleasant acquaintance with some of the officers of the fleet led him to accept their invitation to go to Russia. Owing to his talent as a linguist he is said to have been engaged in St. Petersburg as a translator of polyglot dispatches, and later was appointed assistant secretary of the United States Legation, holding this and other positions till 1870. Urged by the desire to acquaint himself with the Slavonic group of languages and other tongues, he traveled in eastern Europe and Asia apparently in the service of the Russian government. Bearing a rich store of linguistic spoils, he then went for a year to the British Isles collecting folk-lore and myths in the ancestral homes of his kin in Ireland. America and especially the Bureau of American Ethnology, with its studies of Indian languages, was his next objective, and shortly he was engaged in making independent researches in matters pertaining to the language and customs of the Iroquois, Modoc, Yuchi, Shawnee, and several other Indian tribes. After the Bureau episode (1883–91), he set out on travels around the world, collecting myths of various peoples.

Curtin's earliest published work consisted of translations of Henryk Sienkievicz, Alexis Tolstoy, Michael Zagoskin, and other authors. In these translations, which had a wide currency in the nineties, he preserved remarkably the fire of the originals. More important were his ethnological contributions (many of them published posthumously) in four different fields: (1) Celtic—represented by Myths and Folk-Lore of Ireland (1890), Hero-Tales of Ireland (1894), Tales of the Fairies and of the Ghost World, Collected from Oral Tradition in South-West Munster (1895); (2) Slavonic—represented by Myths and Folk-Tales of the Russians, Western Slavs and Magyars (1890), Fairy Tales of Eastern Europe (1914), Wonder Tales from Russia (1921); (3) Mongolian—represented by The Mongols in Russia (1908), The Mongols: a History (1908), A Journey in Southern Siberia; the Mongols, their Religion and their Myths (1909); (4) American Indian—represented by Creation Myths of Primitive America in Relation to the Religious History and Mental Development of Mankind (1898), Myths of the Modocs (1912), Introduction to Seneca Fiction, Legends and Myths (1919) in collaboration with J. N. B. Hewitt, Seneca Indian Myths (1923). A strain of mysticism usually termed Celtic, proper in Curtin's case, was observable in him and helped his tendency toward the romantic. As a collector of myths and tales few excelled him, largely because of his ability to master languages. In fact, Curtin was one of the outstanding linguists of the world. Having a working knowledge of all European languages, he had also more or less acquaintance with many others, the total said to be seventy languages and dialects. Of average height, with strong frame, broad cheek-bones, blue eyes, and a tawny curling full beard, he was a man of noteworthy appearance. He was married on July 17, 1872, to Alma M. Cordelle, daughter of James Cordelle of Warren, Vt.

[U. S. Dept. of State, Papers Relating to Foreign Affairs, Diplomatic Corres. (1867) for 1866, pt. 1; Am. Anthropologist (new series), vol. IX, no. 1, 1907, pp. 237–38; Times (London), Dec. 29, 1906; N. Y. Tribune, Dec. 15, 1906; Evening Post (N. Y.), Dec. 15, 1906; Harvard Grads. Mag., Mar. 1907; Critic, May 1900; Book Buyer, July 1900; Who's Who in America, 1903–05.]

W. H.

CURTIS, ALFRED ALLEN (July 4, 1831–July 11, 1908), second Catholic bishop of Wilmington, was born of an old but obscure family at Pocomoke, Worcester County, Md. Educated in the local public schools, he studied for the Episcopalian ministry and was ordained a deacon in 1856 by Bishop Whittingham. Appointed assistant curate at St. John's Church, Baltimore, he was soon transferred to St. Luke's Church, Baltimore, thence to a small congregation in Frederick, Md., and eventually to the rectorship of a church in Chestertown, Kent County, Md. There he was known as a classical student and an attentive pastor who found time for fishing and yachting. In 1862, only six years after ordination he was honored with the pastorate of the important Mount Calvary Church in Baltimore where he remained until 1870 when he resigned because of dissatisfaction with the Episcopalian creed. Going to England, he became interested in the Romeward movement and entered the Catholic Church (1872) under the guidance of Cardinal Newman.

Returning to America, he entered St. Mary's Seminary, Baltimore, and on completion of a two-year course in theology was ordained (Dec. 19, 1874) by Archbishop Bayley. Quiet, studious, dreading publicity, Father Curtis was happy as an assistant at the Baltimore cathedral, as secretary to the archbishop, and later as acting chancellor of the diocese. Named bishop of Wilmington, Del., he was consecrated by Archbishop Gibbons on Nov. 14, 1886, and commenced the trying work of church building in a small diocese heavily burdened with debt. During his short administration, fifteen churches were erected, a visitation convent for contemplative cloistered sisters, and a colored mission under the Josephite Fathers. He was instrumental in bringing to the diocese the Benedictine and Ursuline teaching communities. As a bishop, he was not happy and it was with relief that he resigned in 1896 and became the titular bishop of Echinus. Called back to Baltimore, he acted as Cardinal Gibbons's vicar-general from 1898 until his death. A retiring, silent man, he attracted little attention in the world and was known only to his intimates as a saintly, conscientious priest.

[Ethan Allen, *Clergy in Md. of the Prot. Episc. Ch.* (1860); M. J. Riordan, *Cathedral Records* (1906); J. W. Kirwin (publisher), *Cath. Bishops and Archbishops of America* (1899); *Records of the Am. Cath. Hist. Soc.*, XX, 86; *Life and Characteristics of Rt. Rev. Alfred A. Curtis*, compiled by Sisters of Visitation (1913); *Cath. Ch. in the U. S.* (1912); *The Sun* (Baltimore), July 12, 1908.]　　　　R. J. P.

CURTIS, BENJAMIN ROBBINS (Nov. 4, 1809–Sept. 15, 1874), jurist, was born at Watertown, Mass., the oldest of the two sons of Benjamin Curtis, 3rd, a ship-captain, and Lois (Robbins) Curtis, daughter of a small manufacturer and store-keeper of Watertown, Mass. The Curtis family was descended from William Curtis, probably of London, who with his wife, a sister of John Eliot, apostle to the Indians, came to Boston in the ship *Lyon*, Sept. 16, 1632, and settled at Stony River, Roxbury, Mass., in 1639. The family remained small farmers, but after 1738 one or more members of almost every generation are said to have been Harvard graduates, including the grandfather of Benjamin Robbins Curtis, Benjamin Curtis, 2nd, a physician. His widow, Benjamin Robbins Curtis's grandmother, married as her second husband Elisha Ticknor, a man of wealth, and became the mother of George Ticknor [q.v.], Harvard professor and author. This connection was of great value to Curtis throughout life. His father died abroad on one of his voyages, leaving his mother with two young children and without means; but through loans from the elder Ticknor, and by keeping a small dry-goods store and circulating library in Watertown, she was able to prepare Benjamin for Harvard. He passed under the tuition of numerous masters, including John Appleton, later chief justice of Maine, who remembered the boy as the best scholar he ever had.

Curtis entered Harvard in 1825, his mother removing to Cambridge and opening a students' boarding-house. Four years later he graduated as the second scholar in his class. At college he displayed the poise and discreet reserve which marked his later life. While intimate with few classmates, he was a member of the Hasty Pudding Club and the "Institute," and an honorary member of the Porcellian Club. Although none of his relatives were lawyers, he was attracted to the profession by his aptitude for lucid reasoning, and after graduation entered the Harvard Law School, just then revitalized by Story's appointment as Dane Professor. In spite of the distinction he attained as a student, Curtis left the school in 1831 before completing his course, to take over the practise of a country attorney in Northfield, Mass. His motive seems to have been partly a wish to gain practical experience while completing his studies, and partly to secure an immediate competence so that he might marry his cousin, Eliza Maria Woodward of Hanover, N. H. He remained in Northfield until 1834 when he was taken into partnership by a distant relative, Charles Pelham Curtis, an established lawyer in Boston. This connection continued for seventeen years and was strengthened after the death of his wife in 1844 by his marriage in 1846 to Anna Wroe Curtis, the daughter of his partner.

Curtis early gained a reputation at the Boston bar for great skill in all branches of commercial law. While not eloquent, he had a pleasing voice and unruffled manner, and was successful not merely in arguing legal appeals, but as an advocate, because of his remarkable gift for clear statement. Soon after coming to Boston, he was counsel in the case of the slave Med (*Commonwealth* vs. *Aves*, 18 *Pickering*, 193), and argued that a slave-owner who brought a slave temporarily into Massachusetts might restrain the slave while in the state for the purpose of later returning with him to his domicile. This contention was overruled by the court with reasoning later used by Curtis as the basis of his dissent in the Dred Scott case.

In 1846, in spite of his early age, Curtis was chosen as Judge Story's successor as a member of the Harvard Corporation. Three years earlier he had attracted attention by a scholarly article in the *North American Review* against debt-repudiation by certain Southern and Western states, which he characterized as "a disgrace in the eyes of the civilized world." Although he kept aloof from politics, he expressed disapproval of the Van Buren administration, described by him as "the ambitious, selfish and ignorant men who now carry on the government." In 1840 he was for Webster for president "because it is respectable and right." In 1850 he was the spokesman of Webster's friends who invited the latter to Boston to congratulate him on his "Seventh of March" speech, and during the next two years he came forward in active opposition to the Free-Soil party. As a member of the lower house of the Massachusetts legislature in 1851, he prepared an "Address to the People" signed by the Whig members of that body, denouncing the coalition between Free-Soilers and Democrats which had resulted in the election of Boutwell as governor and Charles Sumner as United States senator. In the fall of the same year, the New England seat on the United States Supreme Court became vacant through the death of Mr. Justice Woodbury, and Curtis, through Webster's influence, was appointed, at the early age of forty-one. He served as a member of the Supreme Court during six annual terms, writing the opinions of the Court in fifty-one cases, of which the most important were *Cooley* vs. *Board of Port Wardens* (12 *Howard*, 299) and *Murray's Lessee* vs. *Hoboken Land and Improvement Company* (18 *Howard*, 272). The former established for the first time that the power of Congress to regulate interstate and foreign commerce is not exclusive in such sense as to prevent the states from making regulations of a local character where national uniformity is not required. The Hoboken case permitted Congress to vest an administrative officer with power to determine sums due to the government from one of its officials and to enforce their collection without resort to a law court. Both cases have become basic precedents for later constitutional law.

Curtis's best-known association with the Supreme Court was connected with his leaving it. In the famous Dred Scott case (19 *Howard*, 393), argued on behalf of the negro by Curtis's brother, George Ticknor Curtis [*q.v.*], he was one of the two dissenting judges, and urged in a long opinion that residence of a slave with his owner in free territory conferred freedom which the slave could vindicate in the courts on his return to the owner's domicile in slave territory. Curtis also claimed that the Court could not proceed, as it did, to decide the case on the merits after it had ruled that a slave was not a citizen, and was without capacity to sue. This opinion was given to the newspapers in advance of official publication. To meet its arguments, Taney revised the opinion which he had read from the bench. An unpleasant correspondence between Curtis and Taney ensued, Taney objecting to the newspaper publication of Curtis's opinion and Curtis objecting to the revision of Taney's opinion after it had been delivered. At the close of the correspondence Curtis resigned from the Court, assigning as a reason the smallness of the salary he received as a judge, but admitting to his friends that he could not "again feel that confidence in the Court and that willingness to cooperate with them which are essential to the satisfactory discharge of my duties" (Letter to George Ticknor, July 3, 1857 in *Memoir*, I, 247). After Taney's death Curtis delivered, at a meeting of the Boston bar, a generous tribute to his services.

Until his own death seventeen years later, Curtis was a recognized leader of the American bar. During that time he argued fifty-four cases before the United States Supreme Court and eighty before the supreme court of Massachusetts, besides many before lower courts. His aggregate professional income for this period has been estimated at $650,000. His attitude toward life settled into gloomy but philosophical disillusionment. During the Civil War he wrote that "Washington was always a fatiguing place to me even when it was . . . the place where I had ambitions; and now that I have grown wiser and have none in the usual acceptation of the word . . . this city is very dreary to me" (Letter to his wife, Dec. 15, 1862 in *Memoir*, I, 353). In 1860 his second wife died, and a year later he married Maria Malleville Allen of Pittsfield, Mass. Always deeply religious, practising daily family worship and never taking his seat on the bench without silent prayer, when his theological views underwent a change, he left the Unitarian faith in which he had been reared, to become an Episcopalian. He was strongly moved by the approach of the Civil War, and braved unpopularity by heading a movement for the repeal of the Massachusetts statute against the return of fugitive slaves in order to reassure the Southern states that the

North harbored no designs against their constitutional rights. During the war he published a pamphlet on "Executive Power," attacking what he regarded as the unconstitutional action of the President in suspending the writ of *habeas corpus* and in issuing the Emancipation Proclamation. In 1866 he expressed public sympathy with the purposes of a convention called to meet in Philadelphia to oppose the reconstruction projects of the radical Republican majority in Congress. When President Johnson was impeached in 1868 Curtis was selected as his leading counsel. His speech opening the President's defense was his greatest forensic effort, displaying the dignity, coolness, and clarity which marked his style, and was admitted by his opponent Butler to have so thoroughly presented Johnson's case that nothing more was added throughout the trial.

This was Curtis's last service of a public nature. He declined Johnson's offer of the office of attorney-general and in 1871 declined to serve as one of the counsel for the United States before the Geneva Arbitration Tribunal. Two years later he informed his friends on the death of Chief Justice Chase that he did not care to be considered as a possible successor. In 1872–73 he delivered at the Harvard Law School a course of lectures on *Jurisdiction, Practice and Peculiar Jurisprudence of the Courts of the United States* (1880). Of the litigation in which he was engaged as counsel after his retirement from the bench, three cases are the most famous: *Paul* vs. *Virginia* (8 *Wallace*, 168), *Hepburn* vs. *Griswold* (8 *Wallace*, 603), and *Virginia* vs. *West Virginia* (11 *Wallace*, 39), in all of which the Supreme Court decided adversely to his contentions. His later years were crowded with almost uninterrupted professional work to which his interests became more and more narrowed; and a short trip to Europe in the summer of 1871 seems to have brought him little satisfaction. In the summer of 1874 while at his villa at Newport, R. I., his health broke down and he died there on Sept. 15.

[Curtis's biography by his brother, George Ticknor Curtis, forms the first volume of *The Life and Writings of B. R. Curtis*, ed. by his son, Benj. R. Curtis (Boston, 1879). While laudatory, it is well done and includes a large number of Curtis's letters and legal opinions. The second volume contains a reprint of his articles on "State Debts" and "Executive Power" and some of his more important addresses and judicial utterances. For his Supreme Court career see Chas. Warren, *Supreme Court in U. S. Hist.* (1922).]   J.Di.

CURTIS, EDWARD LEWIS (Oct. 13, 1853–Aug. 26, 1911), Presbyterian clergyman, educator, came by inheritance to the minister's task and the teacher's profession. His father, Rev.

William Stanton Curtis, was a native of Burlington, Vt., who after graduation at Illinois College in 1838 and later study at Yale Divinity School became successively pastor at Ann Arbor, Mich., where Edward was born, professor of mental and moral philosophy in Hamilton College, Clinton, N. Y., president of Knox College, Galesburg, Ill., and pastor of the Westminster Presbyterian Church in Rockford, Ill. His mother, Martha (Leach) Curtis, also a native of Vermont, graduated in the second class to leave Mount Holyoke Seminary, where she was later associated in teaching with Mary Lyon, founder of the institution. Before reaching his sixteenth birthday Edward Curtis entered the class of 1873 at Beloit College, but transferred his studies to Yale as a sophomore in the academic class of 1874, where his literary abilities were evinced by his selection as editor of *The Yale Courant* and the winning of a Townsend prize. The two years following his graduation at Yale were spent in teaching, after which he entered Union Theological Seminary, which, on his graduation in 1879, awarded him a fellowship for study abroad. In the Divinity School his interest had been directed toward Old Testament studies, and these he pursued for two semesters at Berlin; but illness prevented his securing the degree of Ph.D. In 1881 he returned to America to take up the work of instructor in Hebrew and Old Testament in McCormick Theological Seminary, Chicago, advancing to the full professorship in 1886. Meantime, on Apr. 27, 1882, he married Laura E. Ely, daughter of Rev. B. E. S. Ely of Ottumwa, Ia., and in 1883 was ordained to the Presbyterian ministry.

Although no considerable volume came from Curtis's pen during his years at Chicago, his teaching ability and the articles he contributed to periodicals such as *The Presbyterian Review* and *The Old Testament Student* secured for him a call in 1891 to the Holmes Professorship of Hebrew Language and Literature in Yale University, a position in which he spent the remainder of his life, combining with its duties those of acting dean of the Divinity School in 1905. Neither the handicap of ill health (he had suffered from *angina pectoris* since 1901, and had a partial stroke of paralysis in 1906 which greatly limited his eyesight) nor the burden of administrative duties outside his classroom work prevented the completion in 1910 of his chief contribution to scholarship, his *Critical and Exegetical Commentary on the Books of Chronicles* in the International Critical Commentary series, the work being shared by a favorite pupil, A. A.

Madsen. A smaller commentary, *The Book of Judges,* intended for the Bible for Home and School series, left unfinished at his death, was completed and published by Madsen in 1913. Curtis's public reputation will rest on the *Commentary on Chronicles,* but pupils and colleagues revered him even more for his character of unassuming helpfulness than for his patient and accurate scholarship.

[*Who's Who in America,* 1910–11; *Obit. Record Grads. Yale Univ., 1910–15* (1915), pp. 241–44; *Biblical World,* Oct. 1911.]   B. W. B.

CURTIS, EDWIN UPTON (Mar. 26, 1861– Mar. 28, 1922), mayor and police commissioner of Boston, was descended from William Curtis (see sketch of Benjamin Robbins Curtis). George Curtis of the sixth generation, a lumber merchant, in 1845 married Martha Ann, daughter of Joseph Upton of Fitchburg, Mass., and Edwin Upton was their seventh child. Born at Roxbury, Mass., he attended the grammar and Latin schools there and the Little Blue Family School for Boys at Farmington, Me., proceeding thence to Bowdoin College, where he won distinction as an athlete and oarsman and graduated in 1882. He read law at Boston in the office of Ex-Governor Gaston, also attended the Boston University Law School, and was admitted to the Suffolk County bar in 1885. Commencing practise in Boston, he took an active interest in public affairs, being an ardent adherent of the Republican party, and in 1888 became secretary of the Republican City Committee. In 1889 he was elected city clerk. Two years later he retired and resumed practise, at the same time identifying himself with the then growing movement for civic reform. Such was the prominence which he acquired in this connection that in 1894 he was nominated by the Republican party for mayor, and won a spectacular victory by over 2,500 votes. In his inaugural address to the city council he outlined the changes which he advocated, among them being the appointment of a Board of Commissioners to control the election machinery, a revision of the system of financing the public schools, and the placing of each city department under a commissioner. All his major recommendations were carried into effect, and his administration procured for him the respect and confidence of all parties and classes in the city. On retiring from the mayoralty he again resumed the practise of law. On Oct. 27, 1897, he was married to Margaret the daughter of Charles Waterman of Thomaston, Me. He continued his public activities, serving as a member of the Metropolitan Park Commission, assistant United States

treasurer at Boston, and collector of the Port of Boston. In December 1918 by appointment of Gov. McCall he became police commissioner of Boston. For some time previously there had been an undercurrent of dissatisfaction in the police force due partly to alleged inadequacy of salaries, and in 1919 matters came to a crisis. The Mayor refused to recommend an increase of pay, and the men thereupon organized a local union affiliated with the American Federation of Labor, intending by this means to compel compliance with their demands. Curtis promptly suspended from duty all those who had become officials of the new union, upon which three-fourths of the police force went on strike, Sept. 9, 1919. The Commissioner announced that no strikers would be reinstated, intimating at the same time to Gov. Coolidge that the latter must either remove him from office or accord to him the whole-hearted support of the Commonwealth. The Governor in response furnished Curtis all the assistance required. For a few days much rowdyism occurred in the city and business was badly disorganized, but public opinion was with Curtis; the loyal remnant of the police and the Massachusetts State Guard, assisted by a volunteer force of citizens, in a short time put an end to violence and intimidation, and normal conditions were restored. In the meantime, adamant in his attitude toward the strikers, the Commissioner proceeded to create a new police force. Though hampered by certain political elements and bitterly assailed by organized labor, his efforts were successful and the elimination from the force of those who had participated in the strike established the principle that loyalty to constituted government must not be subordinated to outside authority. In 1921 his health became seriously impaired and he was urged by friends to retire, but he resolutely refused, saying that it was his imperative duty to remain at his post as head of the reorganized police in view of the short time which had elapsed since the strike. He died early in the following year.

["Genealogy of the Descendants of Wm. Curtis," by Catherine P. Curtis, MS. in Lib. of Congress, as supplemented by *Descendants of Wm. Curtis, Roxbury, 1632,* by Samuel C. Clarke (1869) and *Upton Family Records* by W. H. Upton (1893), give details of Curtis's ancestry. See *Who's Who in America,* 1922–23, p. 837. His official report of the police strike is contained in *Fourteenth Annual Report of the Police Commissioner for the City of Boston* (1920). The labor standpoint is outlined in *Report of the Proceedings of the 40th Annual Convention of the Am. Federation of Labor* (1920), pp. 362 ff. Lengthy appreciative obituary notices appeared in the Boston press of Mar. 28, 29, 1922.]
H. W. H. K.

CURTIS, GEORGE (Feb. 23, 1796–Jan. 9, 1856), banker, was descended from Henry and

Mary (Guy) Curtis who came to America in 1635 and settled at Watertown, Mass., and from their son, Ephraim Curtis, the first white settler of Worcester, Mass. George, the son of David Curtis, an ironmaster, and his wife, Susannah Stone, was born in Worcester but after a boyhood spent in local schools and sporadic employment near his home, went with his brother to Providence, R. I. He obtained employment in a bank in that city and learned the business through practical experience, eventually becoming cashier of the Exchange Bank, a well-known local institution of that day. On Mar. 6, 1821 he married Mary Elizabeth Burrill, daughter of James Burrill [q.v.]. She bore him two sons, James Burrill and George William Curtis [q.v.], and died in 1826. On Apr. 3, 1834 he married Julia B. Bridgham, daughter of Samuel Bridgham, the first mayor of Providence. By this marriage he had four sons, two of whom, Edward and John Green Curtis [q.v.], attained distinction in medicine. A natural interest in politics led Curtis to become a member of the Common Council in Providence, and later to be elected a member of the state legislature. He was speaker of the House in 1837–38 (J. J. Smith, Civil and Military List of Rhode Island, 1901, pp. 539, 552) and was apparently in a fair way to spend the rest of his life as an influential citizen of the state. The time, however, was one in which great banking changes were taking place and opportunities for personal advancement and money-making were numerous. Banking organization in New York City particularly was undergoing considerable modification and expansion. Believing that broad opportunities were offered in that city, Curtis removed thither in 1839, accepting an appointment as cashier of the Bank of Commerce. In that capacity he had, under the comparatively simple type of banking structure which prevailed in that generation, opportunity to direct practically all of the interior operations of what was later to be one of the city's leading institutions. He thus became thoroughly familiar with the technique of banking and was recognized as one of the abler among the younger bankers of New York City. When the Continental Bank of New York was organized in 1844, he was offered the presidency and accepted it. In this position he continued until the end of his life. He was characterized by shrewd business ability, coupled with an outstanding reputation for honesty and trustworthiness, which resulted in his being offered many opportunities for service of a financial sort outside of his immediate banking duties. With a number of the more conspicuous bank-

ers of the city he was interested in the organization of the New York Clearing House. The origin of the "idea" of this institution has been attributed to many persons and claimed by several. In its archives are various plans which were put forward, but the list includes none by Curtis. From the outset, however, he was active in the negotiations and discussions which led to final action; and when the general plan of the organization had been agreed upon, he drew up a set of rules or by-laws sometimes referred to as the "Constitution" of the Clearing House. This document was adopted on June 6, 1854, and furnished the basis upon which the new undertaking organized its operations (J. G. Cannon, Clearing Houses, Their History, etc., 1900, pp. 134–35). He did not live, however, to see the Clearing House develop, for only a few months after its organization his health became impaired and he finally went to Jacksonville, Fla., where he died early in 1856.

[Various memoranda and contemporary material in files of the N. Y. Clearing House; Newton Squire, The N. Y. Clearing House, Its Methods and Systems (pub. anonymously, 1888); H. H. Chamberlin, Geo. Wm. Curtis and his Antecedents (1893); Edward Cary, Geo. Wm. Curtis (1894); Ellen M. Burrill, The Burrill Family of Lynn (1907); Rep. Men and Old Families of R. I. (1908), I, 81–87; Colls. Worcester Soc. of Antiquity, XII (1894), 66, 325; E. M. Snow, Alphabetical Index of the Births, Marriages, and Deaths.. Providence... (1879).]
H. P. W.

CURTIS, GEORGE TICKNOR (Nov. 28, 1812–Mar. 28, 1894), lawyer, author, was a son of Benjamin and Lois (Robbins) Curtis. His ancestors were typical New Englanders, farmers, ministers, school-teachers, and seamen. His middle name was that of his paternal step-grandfather, whose son, George Ticknor [q.v.], the critic, was one of his closest friends. His brother was Benjamin R. Curtis [q.v.], justice of the United States Supreme Court. George was twice married: first, on Oct. 17, 1844, to the daughter of Justice Joseph Story [q.v.], Mary Oliver Story, who died in 1848, leaving two sons; second, in January 1851, to Louise A. Nyström, by whom he had three sons and three daughters. He graduated from Harvard in 1832, and then taught school and studied law, in part at the Harvard Law School and in part in the Boston office of C. P. Curtis, a relative. He was admitted to the bar in 1836, and after a brief practise at Worcester, established himself in 1837 at Boston. In 1862 he removed to New York where he remained in practise until 1888, and continued to live until his death. For many years he maintained also an office at Washington, D. C., as much of his practise was before the United States Supreme Court. He enjoyed a high reputation as a patent attorney, being employed by many inventors, notably by Goodyear, Morse, and Cyrus McCormick. Outside this specialty he was engaged in the greenback cases, and in the Dred Scott case. In the latter he defended the freedom of Scott on the ground that Congress possessed the right to control slavery in the territories, and that consequently the Act of 1820 was constitutional. He entered politics as a Whig and a friend of Webster, serving in the Massachusetts House from 1840 to 1843. He declined reëlection, and is said to have declined the ministry to Great Britain. In 1852, as United States Commissioner, he facilitated the return to slavery of Thomas Sims, under the Fugitive-Slave Act of 1850, thereby incurring the hostility of the Abolitionists. As was the case of many of the Webster "Cotton" Whigs, he became a Democrat. In the Civil War he was a Unionist, but keenly critical of the administration, setting forth his position in a Fourth of July oration at Boston in 1862. In New York he was for some time associated with Tammany Hall, but refused all office. He exerted a certain political influence, nevertheless, through pamphlets and magazine articles, impressive because of his legal learning and impartiality. The first was an argument in favor of compensation for the Ursuline Nuns whose convent at Charlestown, Mass., was burned by a mob. In 1885 he engaged in a controversy with John W. Foster [q.v.], publishing in that year International Arbitrations and Awards. In 1886 and 1887 he published defenses of Gen. George B. McClellan.

Living as he did in an atmosphere of scholarship and literary effort, including many of the leading authors of both America and Europe, Curtis naturally turned early to writing. His first work was the production of legal studies, which came to cover a wide field. In 1839 he published a Digest of Cases Adjudicated in the Courts of Admiralty of the United States, and in the High Court of Admiralty in England; in 1841, a Treatise on the Rights and Duties of Merchant Seamen; in 1847, A Treatise on the Law of Copyright; in 1849, A Treatise on the Law of Patents; in 1850, Equity Precedents; in 1854 and 1858, two volumes of Commentaries on the Jurisdiction, Practice, and Peculiar Jurisprudence of the Courts of the United States. These and other legal contributions were much used and went through many editions. Gradually he turned his attention to work less closely connected with his profession. In his late years he wrote a novel, under the pseudonym, Peter Boylston, John Charaxes: A Tale of the Civil War (1889); and Creation and Evolution? a

Philosophical Inquiry (1887). More important were his biographical contributions, including a Memoir of Benjamin Robbins Curtis (1879), and, in two volumes each, a Life of Daniel Webster (1870) and a Life of James Buchanan (1883).

His reputation, however, will chiefly rest on his studies of the history of the Constitution of the United States. In 1849–50 he delivered a course of lectures at the Lowell Institute of Boston, on the history of the Constitution of the United States, on which he had the advice of Webster. An elaboration of these lectures was published as History of the Origin, Formation, and Adoption of the Constitution of the United States (two volumes, 1854–58). In 1889 he published the first volume of a revision and extension, entitled Constitutional History of the United States from their Declaration of Independence to the Close of the Civil War. In 1896 the second volume, edited by J. C. Clayton, was published. This work is the classic treatment of the Constitution from the Federalist, Websterian point of view. Curtis's historical work is of the old school. He used but few sources and his conception of history, as of the forces of public life, was distinctly limited. Particularly after leaving Boston his life was spent almost entirely in his office, his study, and with his family, and many of his judgments reflect this somewhat cloistered existence. Within these limits he worked with exactitude, independence, and fine intelligence. His style is cumbrous, though with some Victorian elegance. His Buchanan and his Constitutional History are likely to remain standard.

[A number of Curtis's letters are among the Geo. B. McClellan MSS. in the Lib. of Cong. The Memoir of Benj. Robbins Curtis referred to above contains some family history. See also Catherine P. Curtis, "Genealogy of the Descendants of Wm. Curtis," MS. in Lib. of Cong.; Quin. Cat. of the Law. Sch. of Harvard Univ. (1915); obituaries in Harvard Grads. Mag., June 1894; N. Y. Times and Boston Transcript, Mar. 29, 1894.]

C. R. F.

CURTIS, GEORGE WILLIAM (Feb. 24, 1824–Aug. 31, 1892), author, orator, was born in Providence, R. I., of an old New England family, being the son of George Curtis and Mary Elizabeth Burrill, daughter of James Burrill [q.v.]. He lost his mother while he was still an infant, and it was his elder brother James who thereafter exerted for many years the strongest influence on his life. As boys they spent five years together at a school in Massachusetts, and then returned to Providence where their father had re-married. In 1839, when Curtis was fifteen years old, the family took up residence in New York City, and here, for a few years, Curtis held a clerkship. Then followed a stay of two years, again with his brother James, at Brook Farm, where association with the spirits of the Transcendental Movement, deepened the idealistic strain in Curtis, who was to become, in the record of America, the outstanding example of the man of letters who sets aside the possibilities of literary fame because of the inner urge toward what he considers to be the highest duties of citizenship. The most potent influence upon him during that period was Emerson, and even after Curtis had left Brook Farm, and had returned to New York, he would frequently visit Concord in order to benefit by conversations with the benign philosopher and poet. The Puritan strain in Curtis thus became at an early age affected by the consciousness of the brotherhood of man, while the charm of his own nature never swerved him from fearless adherence to conviction.

In 1846 Curtis left New York for a four years' stay in various countries of Europe and in Egypt and Syria. His wanderings were to bring forth two books of travels—*Nile Notes of a Howadji* (1851) and *The Howadji in Syria* (1852). These books, based on letters sent to the *New York Tribune,* with whose staff Curtis was connected, display engaging fancy and graceful descriptive powers, traits manifest also in *Lotus-Eating* (1852) and in *Potiphar Papers* (1853), a volume which, with its gentle satire of the social life of New York, was a direct descendant of Irving's *Salmagundi.* Shortly after Curtis's marriage, on Thanksgiving Day, 1856, to Anna Shaw of Staten Island, *Putnam's Monthly,* of which he was an associate editor, went into bankruptcy, and he assumed a debt from which by process of law he could have escaped, a debt that taxed his resources until, after a considerable number of years, it was met in full. His final work in the Irving tradition, *Prue and I* (1857), established him firmly in the hearts of his readers. Here the sentimental yet manly and philosophic observer of life gives his most ambitious portrayal of that happiness which is not dependent upon wealth.

The second half of Curtis's career was made memorable by a series of noble orations. The first, delivered to the students of Wesleyan University at Middletown, Conn., was entitled *The Duty of the American Scholar to Politics and the Times* (1856). The scholar, for Curtis, was not the closeted specialist, but that "priest of the mind," dedicated to the elevation of public thought and action, devoted to the eternal interests of his own community and of the community of mankind. Curtis adjured his youthful

hearers to enter upon the fight of Freedom; to justify and to carry to success the experiment which the American Republic symbolized. In rousing enthusiasm toward resistance against slavery, Curtis made evident those two strains whose blending has so largely directed the course of American civilization. He showed himself in his gallantry, his *flair* for the graces of life, the Cavalier; he showed himself in his stern adherence to the obligations of life, the Puritan.

The services of Curtis in the four or five years that were to pass before the Civil War disrupted the country, and the influence of his voice during the war period, can hardly be overestimated. His speeches gave new impetus to patriotic fervor, and his writings as the editor of *Harper's Weekly,* an office assumed in the critical period of the conflict in 1863, were so fair, so keen, so persuasive, that their author created for himself a position in the public mind commanded by probably no other literary publicist. Hundreds of thousands of hearers and readers looked upon him as their mentor, and regarded him with respect due to the cogency of his unprejudiced argumentation, and with affection due to the modest human courtesy of his approach.

Keenly in touch with the practical working out of affairs and, throughout his life, an exemplary member of numerous civic committees, Curtis, from youth to old age, opposed with tact as well as with fervor, and with cheering optimism, the tendency to look upon the highest moral principles "as something too visionary, too abstract and impracticable for working men in actual life." In his Phi Beta Kappa oration at Harvard in 1862, "It is as sure as sunrise," he said, "that men and nations, either in their own lives and characters or in those of their descendants, will pay the penalty of injustice and immorality." His lecture entitled "Political Infidelity," and delivered more than fifty times, in different states from Maine to Maryland, in 1864 and 1865, maintained, in memorable phraseology, that "whatever in this country, in its normal condition of peace is too delicate to discuss is too dangerous to tolerate. Any system, any policy, any institution, which may not be debated will overthrow us if we do not overthrow it."

When the Civil War had ended new problems engaged the attention of Curtis. He opposed all caste usurpation, and advocated the necessity of a better understanding between capital and labor. He was among the first to fight for the enfranchisement of women, feeling that "the spirit of society cannot be just, nor the laws equitable, so long as half of the population are politically paralyzed." He was among the first to advocate civil-service reform, and as chairman of both the New York State and the National Civil Service Reform Associations, he did more than any other man to make merit, and not party affiliation, the approach to civil office. He had been a leading spirit in the Republican party since its incipiency, but when James G. Blaine, in the eyes of Curtis a corrupt man, ran for the presidency, Curtis urged the election of Grover Cleveland and became the most influential of Independents in national affairs. He gave his most careful thought and many of his hard-pressed days to educational activities, and, as chancellor of the University of the State of New York, he engaged in matters of detail while he continued, in and out of season, to insist on that public duty of educated men which, at Union College in 1877 and at Brown University in 1882, was the theme of orations that continued and deepened the inspirational argument of his first great address in 1856. Underlying all his talks, all his writings, were the free-minded citizen's appreciation of the mental processes of others, the student's analysis of history (and especially deeply was Curtis versed in the history of his own country), and the gentleman's graciousness in winning sympathetic attention. If in his casual papers as editor of "The Easy Chair," in *Harper's Magazine,* he often, and of necessity, engaged in topics of the day, in his more elaborate addresses he expounded in illuminating manner the permanent principles of American progress.

A lover of music and of art, happy in his home on Staten Island, rich in friendships—with James Russell Lowell and Charles Eliot Norton as his two intimates, and his brother, James Burrill Curtis, as the nearest and dearest of his friends—he was never tempted by the more obvious lures of wealth or position. He was the adviser of Presidents, but when he could have had from Mr. Hayes the mission to England, he decided that he could be of more use to his fellow citizens in his capacity with the Harpers than he could possibly be at the Court of St. James's. He acted as delegate to Republican state conventions, but he desired no political advancement for himself, and he withstood with calm temper the attacks of those who, when he turned Independent, accused him of political infidelity. Political infidelity was for him disloyalty to the principles, and not to the behests, of any party; and one of his most memorable sentences is that wherein he adjures the youth of the country that "if ever one of you shall be the man so denounced, do not forget

that your own individual convictions are the whip of small cords which God has put into your hands to expel the blasphemers."

If the man of letters gave way to the publicist in the second half of Curtis's life, his commemorative addresses included not only really great tributes to statesmen such as Charles Sumner, Wendell Phillips, and President Garfield but also, with keen knowledge of literary values, to Robert Burns, to William Cullen Bryant, to James Russell Lowell. The Lowell address delivered first in 1892, on Feb. 22, the birthday of both George Washington and Lowell, and repeated at New York in May, closed Curtis's career as an orator. One remembers this final public appearance of the firm and sweet-souled leader of the public conscience—the charm of his voice, the beauty of his looks, the graciousness of his manner. He had nothing of the dramatic orator, nothing of the sensational actor, but the simplicity of his gestures, the music of his tones, and the utter sincerity of the man won every audience he addressed. He remains a fragrance in the record of American letters and one of the thoroughly fine forces in the development of American civilization.

[Edward Cary, *Geo. Wm. Curtis* (1894); John W Chadwick, "Recollections of Geo. Wm. Curtis," *Harper's Mag.,* Feb. 1893 and *Geo. Wm. Curtis* (1893); E. E. Hale, "Curtis, Whittier and Longfellow," in *Five Prophets of Today* (1892); Parke Godwin, *Geo. Wm. Curtis; A Commemorative Address Delivered before the Century Asso., N. Y., Dec. 17, 1892* (1893); Wm. M. Payne, *Leading Am. Essayists* (1910); Wm. Winter, *Geo. Wm. Curtis, A Eulogy* (1893); *Orations and Addresses of Geo. Wm. Curtis* (1893–94), ed. by Chas. Eliot Norton; *Early Letters of Geo. Wm. Curtis to John S. Dwight* (1898); *Memorials of Two Friends* (1902); Edward M. Merrill, "Geo. Wm. Curtis, A Tribute to his Life and Public Service," *Jour. Social Science,* Jan. 1894; Chas. E. Fitch, *Address in Memory of Chancellor Geo. Wm. Curtis* (1892); Carl Schurz, "Geo. Wm. Curtis, Friend of the Republic," *McClure's Mag.,* Oct. 1904; H. H. Chamberlain, *Geo. Wm. Curtis and his Antecedents* (1893); *Colburn's New Mo. Mag.* (London), Aug. 1853; *Putnam's Mo.,* Apr. 1857; *Galaxy,* Mar. 1869; *North Am. Rev.,* July 1868; *Appleton's Jour.,* Sept. 13, 1873; *Critic,* Dec. 6, 1884, Sept. 10, 1892; *Nation* (N. Y.) Sept. 8, 1892; *Rev. of Revs.* (N. Y.), Oct. 1892; S. S. Rogers, "Geo. Wm. Curtis and Civil Service Reform," *Atlantic Mo.,* Jan. 1893; A. Cassot, "Geo. Wm. Curtis," *Chautauquan,* May 1893; Geo. Willis Cooke, "Geo. Wm. Curtis at Concord," *Harper's Mag.,* Dec. 1897; Geo. Wm. Curtis, "An Autobiographical Sketch," *Cosmopolitan,* Oct. 1894.]

G. S. H.

CURTIS, JOHN GREEN (Oct. 29, 1844– Sept. 20, 1913), physiologist, was the son of George [*q.v.*] and Julia (Bridgham) Curtis. He was born in New York the year that his father became president of the Continental Bank, and like his brother, Dr. Edward Curtis, and his half-brother, George William Curtis [*q.v.*], derived from his parents a love of scholarly pursuits and a faith in high ideals which he carried through life. As a young man he showed great fondness for the classics and during his college course at Harvard he acquired such mastery of Latin and Greek that these languages became in his hands tools of great usefulness in later life. He graduated from Harvard College in 1866, taking the M.A. degree in 1869. While in college he decided to study medicine and in 1870 he received the degree of M.D. from the College of Physicians and Surgeons of New York. On Oct. 20, 1871 he married Mrs. Martha (McCook) Davis. After graduation he entered at once upon the practise of his profession, at the same time serving as assistant demonstrator of anatomy in the medical school and as assistant physician in Bellevue Hospital. Practise of medicine, however, did not appeal to him, and his scholarly taste and interest in science gradually drew him into teaching in the medical school. Here, under Prof. Dalton he became deeply interested in physiology and was soon appointed adjunct lecturer, later adjunct professor of physiology at the College of Physicians and Surgeons. On the retirement of Dr. Dalton he became professor of physiology and head of the department, serving in that capacity from 1883 to 1909, when he retired as professor emeritus.

Curtis was a man of singularly pleasing personality. From 1890 he was secretary of the faculty of the medical school at Columbia, which position brought him closely in contact with the student body, and to him they turned freely for guidance and counsel. In physiology he had two special interests, one being the development of a truly scientific laboratory for the teaching of experimental physiology, so well equipped that it would furnish likewise every opportunity for physiological research. This he accomplished in such fashion that the laboratory became one of the centers of American physiology. The other interest was the early history of physiology, the origins of physiological conceptions, as contrasted with modern physiological thought. For years he studied in the original texts the writings of Aristotle, Hippocrates, Galen, lesser Greek and Latin writers, and especially the writings of Harvey. Among the manuscripts he left was one published in 1915 by his colleague, Dr. Frederic S. Lee, under the title *Harvey's Views on the Use of the Circulation of the Blood,* a most scholarly work revealing many new points of view of great interest to students of the early history of physiology. Curtis was a contributor to the *American Textbook of Physiology* in 1896; he was likewise one of the group of physiologists who founded the American Physiological Society.

[Frederic S. Lee, "John Green Curtis," in *Columbia Univ. Quart.,* Dec. 1913; *Who's Who in America,* 1912–13; *N. Y. Times,* Sept. 21, 1913; Edward Cary, *Geo. Wm. Curtis* (1894).]   R. H. C.

CURTIS, MOSES ASHLEY (May 11, 1808–Apr. 10, 1872), botanist, minister, was born at Stockbridge, Mass., the son of Thankful Ashley, a daughter of Gen. Moses Ashley, and of Rev. Jared Curtis, who was afterward for many years chaplain of the state prison at Charlestown, Mass. In the private school kept by his father he prepared for Williams College, from which he was graduated in 1827. Three years afterward (October 1830), he went to Wilmington, N. C., as tutor in the family of Gov. Dudley. In 1833 he returned to Massachusetts, where he began to study for the ministry. On Dec. 3, 1834 he married Mary de Rosset of Wilmington; in the following year was ordained in the Episcopal Church; and immediately took up missionary work in western North Carolina, with headquarters at Lincolnton. From 1837 to 1839 he taught in the Episcopal School at Raleigh, which he left, on account of his health, to recuperate in the mountains, where he acquainted himself more thoroughly with the flora of the montane region of the state than any one had ever done. In 1840 he was called to mission work in Washington, N. C., and early in 1841 removed to Hillsboro where he lived till his death, with the exception of the years 1847–56 when he took the pastorate at Society Hill, S. C.

His botanical interests were, he hints, first awakened by Prof. A. A. Eaton's lectures at Williams. It is not clear how he acquired the training necessary to have produced so remarkable a paper as his first, the "Enumeration of Plants Growing Spontaneously Around Wilmington, N. C." (*Boston Journal National History,* May 1835). This survey of the coastal plain vegetation within two miles of Wilmington revealed that he in a very short time had discovered almost as many flowering plants as were then known from the entire state of Massachusetts; but included only the higher or flowering plants. At that time the lower phyla, especially the fungi, algæ, lichens, etc., were receiving scant attention. As early as 1845 Curtis had begun to collect lichens for Tuckerman of New England, and his lichen studies soon led into the wider field of all the fungi. Before long he was in communication with Fries of Upsala, Sweden, with Ravenel of South Carolina, and with A. W. Chapman, who dedicated to him his *Flora of the Southern United States.* He lived in and explored precisely the same country that had been known to Schweinitz only a few years before, yet he was able to discover a large number of new species, to be of notable service to Fries, and to collect an unusual mycological herbaria in the western world. These specimens were ultimately purchased by Farlow of Harvard, Peck of the New York State Museum, and Bessey of Nebraska, and form collections of great historical value. His correspondence with Berkeley of England began in 1847 and resulted in a personal and scientific friendship of great value to science. The *North American Fungi*, which was published after his death, was quite as much the work of Curtis as of the better-known British botanist. His matchless collections, as well as his acumen in the discovery of new species and his full notes, were indispensable to the first-hand authenticity and completeness of the publication. In 1860 he published his *Geological and Natural History Survey of North America, Part III, Botany; Containing a Catalogue of the Plants of the State, with Descriptions and History of the Trees, Shrubs, and Woody Vines*; and followed this, in 1867, with a work of similar title "containing a catalogue of the indigenous and naturalized plants of the state," probably the most complete and scholarly state flora that had been published. Besides the usual list of flowering plants, the fungi received a careful attention unusual in those times. The publication of the latter work was long delayed by the Civil War, to which Curtis makes one of his few allusions in the introduction, as "more important matters of national interest." Like the evolution controversy, the great military conflict seems scarcely to have touched his tranquil nature, given as it was to religion and science which for him transcended all animosities. He was fervent in his belief, however, that the starving condition of the Southern armies and peoples could have been relieved by a better knowledge of the edible fungi, and he prepared a volume on the subject, which remains in manuscript in the hands of his descendants.

[The fullest personal account of Curtis is that by Thos. F. Wood in the *Jour. of the Elisha Mitchell Scientific Soc.* (1885). See also Shear and Stevens, "The Mycological Work of Moses Ashley Curtis," in *Mycologia*, July 1919; a brief notice by Asa Gray in *Am. Jour. Sci.*, ser. III, vol. V, May 1873; and articles by Archibald Henderson in *Durham Morning Herald*, Feb. 12, 1928, Raleigh *News and Observer*, Jan. 29, 1928, *Winston-Salem Jour.*, Feb. 5, 1928.]   D.C.P.

CURTIS, NEWTON MARTIN (May 21, 1835–Jan. 8, 1910), soldier, legislator, was born at De Peyster, St. Lawrence County, N. Y. His father, Jonathan Curtis, was a descendant of William Curtis who landed at Boston in 1632, and his mother, Phebe Rising, was also of New England stock. Jonathan, after serving with credit in the War of 1812, went to St. Lawrence County, then a pioneer community, to take up land in Ma-

comb's tract. Newton Martin Curtis was educated in the common schools and in the Gouverneur Wesleyan Seminary, and taught in Illinois for a time. In 1857 he returned to De Peyster to become its postmaster, to read law, and to manage his father's farm. When the news of the fall of Fort Sumter reached St. Lawrence County, Curtis joined others in raising a company of infantry, Company G of the 16th New York, of which he was commissioned captain, May 15, 1861. He remained in the army throughout the war, serving in the armies of the Potomac and of the James. He was one of the officers whose conduct at the capture of Fort Fisher, Jan. 15, 1865, was recognized by the thanks of Congress and the Congressional Medal. For the same service he was made brigadier-general on the field, brevetted major-general, Mar. 13, 1865, and was commended by the New York legislature. During the first year of Reconstruction he served as chief of staff of the Department of Virginia, and as commander of Southwestern Virginia with headquarters at Lynchburg, showing a sympathetic understanding of local problems which won the friendship and cooperation of the community. He was mustered out on Jan. 15, 1866. After the war, he made his home in Ogdensburg in his native county. He was collector of customs for the Oswegatchie district and a special agent for the United States Treasury Department. From 1884 to 1890 he was a member of the New York State Assembly and a member of Congress from 1891 to 1897. In the state legislature and in Congress he was especially concerned with measures for the remedial care of the insane and for the abolition of capital punishment. To convince the people at large of the need for these reforms, he also lectured and wrote in the public press. Largely as a result of his efforts, New York State established at Ogdensburg the St. Lawrence County State Hospital for the Insane. He was also interested in scientific farming and its development in New York State. He was president of the State Agriculture Society in 1880, a member of the committee which placed the experimental station at Geneva, the first secretary of the station's Board of Control and for six years its president; a life member of the American Shorthorn Breeders Association and of a similar English Association. Among his publications were a pamphlet, *General Curtis on the Death Penalty*, issued by the Howard Association, London, in 1891; a speech dated Jan. 9, 1892, published in the *Congressional Record; Capital Crimes and Punishments Prescribed Therefor*, etc. (1894), and a book of Civil War history, *From Bull Run to Chancellorsville* (1906). In 1863, he married

Emeline Clark of Springfield, Ill., who died Aug. 4, 1888. In appearance Curtis was a typical soldier; tall, broad-shouldered, and erect. He was a genial, broad-minded man, and a public-spirited citizen.

[*Who's Who in America*, 1908–09; *Biog. Dir. Am. Cong.* (1928); W. A. Christian, *Lynchburg and Its People* (1900); *Reminiscences of Ogdensburg, 1749–1907* (1907); information as to certain facts from members of the Curtis family. Obituaries in N. Y. newspapers are not reliable. For Curtis's Civil War service see *Battles and Leaders of the Civil War* (1887–88); Adelbert Ames, "The Capture of Fort Fisher," in *Papers Mil. Hist. Soc. of Mass.*, vol. IV (1912); *Official Records (Army)*, esp. 1 ser., XLVI (pt. 1), pp. 394, 415 ff.]
A. B. M—r.

CURTIS, OLIN ALFRED (Dec. 10, 1850–Jan. 8, 1918), Methodist theologian, was born at Frankfort, Me., the son of Reuben Curtis, a Methodist preacher, and of Mary (Gilbert) Curtis. When his father moved away to Wisconsin young Curtis went into business in Chicago. There he was deeply affected by the preaching of Moody. He engaged earnestly in religious work, and finally determined to enter the ministry. At twenty-seven he graduated from Lawrence University, at Appleton, Wis., and three years later from Boston University Theological School. In Boston he felt the influence of Phillips Brooks. The occupations of his next nine years further prepared him for teaching. He was pastor of Methodist Episcopal churches in Janesville, Wis. (1880–83), Milwaukee (1883–86), and Chicago (1888–89), and for two years (1886–88) studied at Leipzig. In 1889 he became professor of systematic theology in Boston University Theological School. During his six years there he studied at Erlangen (1890), Marburg (1893), and Edinburgh (1894). After another stay in Europe, in 1896 he took the chair of systematic theology in Drew Theological Seminary. There he taught for eighteen years, with notable success. On his retirement he became professor emeritus and lecturer, living at Leonia, N. J.

In Curtis's personality there was an extraordinary meeting of qualifications for the teaching of theology. Thorough technical training had given him command of the history of Christian doctrine and of German and other contemporary religious thought. His intimate familiarity with great literature constantly enriched his teaching. He was widely read in history, particularly American. He had an ardent outspoken patriotism and served as chaplain on a ship during the Spanish-American War. A poetic sense of the beauty and spiritual meaning of nature, expressed in a posthumous volume, pervaded his thought. For background his teaching had an uncommon realization of the urgency and needs of human life. He took a strong individual interest in his students. Above all he had a living moral enthusiasm and a vivid Christian faith. Original religious experience, giving keen insight, moulded his conceptions of doctrine. He taught in language unconventional and dramatic, and with intensity which often left him exhausted after meeting a class. These things combined to cause what one who studied under him called his "quite unrivaled power of making systematic theology a commanding and vital matter in the lives of students" (L. H. Hough). His theological position, while rich in his own perceptions, was generally that of Methodist evangelicalism. He was much influenced by the personalism of Bowne of Boston, and by the idea of racial solidarity. But more significant than his particular views was his vitalizing power. Undoubtedly he was the most influential Methodist theologian of his time. He was married in 1880 to Eva Farlin (died 1883), in 1889 to Ellen Hunt (died 1895), and in 1906 to Ida Gorham. His publications, beside many periodical articles, were: *Elective Course of Lectures in Systematic Theology* (1901); *The Christian Faith Personally Given in a System of Doctrine* (1905), the exposition of his theology; *Personal Submission to Jesus Christ, Its Supreme Importance in the Christian Life and Theology* (address, 1910); *The Mountains and Other Nature Sketches* (1920).

[*Who's Who in America*, 1916–17; *Alumni Record of Drew Theol. Sem.* (1926); *N. Y. Christian Advocate*, Feb. 12, 1914; J. A. Faulkner, "Olin A. Curtis: Theologian and Humanist," with portrait, in *N. Y. Chr. Adv.*, Jan. 17, 1918; Lynn Harold Hough, "Making Theology Live," *Meth. Review*, Sept. 1918; Curtis's article "What I Believe," *N. Y. Chr. Adv.*, Feb. 19, 1914.] R.H.N.

CURTIS, SAMUEL RYAN (Feb. 3, 1805–Dec. 26, 1866), soldier, lawyer, engineer, was the son of Zarah and Phalley (Yale) Curtis, both originally from Connecticut. His father had been a soldier in the Revolution. At the time of the birth of Samuel the Curtis family was living near Champlain, N. Y., but soon afterward moved to Licking County, Ohio. In 1831 Samuel graduated from West Point, was assigned to the 7th Infantry, and sent to Fort Gibson. On Nov. 3, 1831, he married Belinda Buckingham of Mansfield. In the summer of 1832 he resigned his commission and returned to Ohio, where he was one of the engineers employed on the National Road. In April 1837 he became chief engineer of the Muskingum River improvement project, serving until May 1839. Meantime he had studied law, and for several years he maintained a law office at Wooster, Ohio. At the outbreak of the war with Mexico he was made adjutant-general of Ohio, but resigned to become colonel of the 3rd Ohio Infantry. At the end of the war he accepted the position of chief engineer of the proposed improvement of the Des Moines River and moved to Keokuk, Iowa. The Board of Public Works expressed its satisfaction at having obtained the services of a man "who is morally, as well as scientifically, worthy of entire confidence" (*Journal of the Senate of Iowa, 1848–49,* p. 343). He continued in this work until December 1849. In the spring of 1850 he became city engineer of St. Louis, Mo., where he remained for three years. His chief work here was the construction of a dike to deflect the current of the Mississippi River so as to deepen the channel on the St. Louis side. After leaving St. Louis in 1853, he assisted in promoting what was known as the American Central Railroad. He also maintained a law office in Keokuk, and in the spring of 1856 was elected mayor of that city (Orion Clemens, *City of Keokuk in 1856,* p. 4).

In the fall of 1856 he was the Republican candidate for Congress from the 1st Congressional District in Iowa. He was elected and reëlected in 1858 and 1860. During his third campaign he was described by an observer as "tall, finely though heavily formed, with high forehead, large hazel eyes, decidedly grave face adorned with side whiskers; in demeanor serious, deliberate, in speech and action undemonstrative" (E. H. Stiles, *Recollections and Sketches of Notable Lawyers and Public Men of Early Iowa,* 1916, pp. 130–31). In Congress his chief interest was the Pacific railroad and he was chairman of a special committee to make plans for it (*House Report No. 428,* 36 Cong., 1 Sess.).

When the Civil War broke out Curtis was chosen colonel of the 2nd Iowa Infantry and sent to protect the railroads in Missouri; but he soon returned to Washington for the special session of Congress which met on July 4, 1861. While there he was appointed brigadier-general, and on Aug. 6 he resigned his seat and started for the front. In the spring of 1862 he commanded the Union army which defeated the Confederates at Pea Ridge, Ark. In recognition of this victory he was made a major-general, and in September 1862 he was given command of the Department of the Missouri with headquarters at St. Louis. Missouri at this time was torn by factional strife and in the performance of his duty Curtis incurred the enmity of Gov. H. R. Gamble. The lack of cooperation between the civil and military authorities caused President Lincoln much anxiety, and after several months he made a vain attempt to restore harmony by removing Gen. Curtis, since, as he explained, he had no authority to remove the Governor. In January 1864, he was assigned to command the Depart-

ment of Kansas, and in the spring of 1865 was sent to the Department of the Northwest.

At the close of the Civil War, he was one of the commissioners sent to treat with the Indians along the Missouri River. He also served as a member of the commission to examine and report on the construction of the various sections of the Union Pacific Railroad, then extending some three hundred miles west of Omaha. It was while engaged in this work that he died at Council Bluffs, Iowa.

[In addition to sources cited see A. A. Stuart, *Iowa Colonels and Regiments* (1865); *Iowa Hist. Record,* vol. III (1887); B. F. Gue, *Hist. of Iowa,* vol. IV (1903); *Annals of Iowa,* 1 ser., IV–XII (1866–72); *In Memoriam: Maj.-Gen. Samuel Ryan Curtis* (1867); obituary in *Keokuk Gate City,* Jan. 2, 9, 1867. A more comprehensive biography is Ruth A. Gallaher, "Samuel Ryan Curtis" in *Iowa Jour. of Hist. and Politics,* July 1927.]   R.A.G.

CURTIS, WILLIAM ELEROY (Nov. 5, 1850–Oct. 5, 1911), journalist, traveler, and publicist, was almost from the time of his birth at Akron, Ohio, until his death from apoplexy in Philadelphia what might be called a globe-trotter. In his boyhood he took great delight in listening to travel tales read to him by his mother, Harriet (Coe) Curtis. His father, from whom he obtained his middle name, encouraged the son to take an interest not only in foreign countries but also in their forms of government. Consequently his fondness for discussing European politics even during his undergraduate days at Western Reserve College is easily understood. After graduation in 1871 he secured his first newspaper position on the staff of the *Chicago Inter-Ocean* in 1873 and on Dec. 23, 1874, married Cora Belle Kepler of Erie, Pa. Never content with reporting routine happenings in Chicago, he continually sought an opportunity for a better use of his talents. Unable to secure it from the paper for which he worked, he accepted, in 1887, the position of Washington correspondent for the *Chicago Record.* Appointed a special commissioner from the United States to the Republics of Central and South America, he visited many of those countries, the fruit of his travels finding expression in *The Capitals of Spanish America* (1888). When the Bureau of the American Republics was established—now called the Pan-American Union—he was made its first director in 1889. Although he resigned this position in 1893, he remained until his death a staunch supporter of the institution. During the Chicago Exposition he was chief of the Latin-American departments and in its behalf he went as special commissioner to Madrid. He acted as special envoy to the Queen Regent of Spain on this trip, and in 1892 to Pope Leo XIII. From then on he became a traveling correspondent whose letters to the press gave him national prominence. Of his work during these years a prominent newspaper man of Chicago has said, "For many years Curtis wrote a daily column on affairs of the day, describing important events, and picturing foreign countries as a result of his travels, for the *Chicago Record*. He was a most diligent, prolific, and brilliant newspaper writer : a great gatherer of facts, an excellent interviewer, and a close observer. His writing of a daily column of descriptive and news matter was in those days something of an innovation. He made of it a department which attained international recognition." But in addition to his newspaper work he found time to write and edit many books. During his régime as first director of the Pan-American Union he started the publication of handbooks—several of which he wrote himself—which have done much to promote friendly relations between South America and its sister continent. Among his travel books possibly the most important are : *A Summer Scamper Along the Old Santa Fé Trail* (1883) ; *The Yankees of the East; Sketches of Modern Japan* (1896) ; *Between the Andes and the Ocean* (1900) ; *Today in Syria and Palestine* (1903) ; *Egypt, Burma, and British Malaysia* (1905) ; *Modern India* (1905) ; *Turkestan: The Heart of Asia* (1911) ; *Who Woke Up Turkey?* (1911). Interested in adult education he was a loyal supporter of the Chautauqua movement. He was always willing to help his friends, especially those in newspaper work. Eugene Field, to whom money had been loaned, once inserted in his column of the *Chicago Daily News*, "W. E. Curtis is in town to look after his permanent investments."

[See *Western Reserve Univ. Bull.*, vol. XIV, no. 6, pp. 150–53 ; *Who's Who in America*, 1910–11 ; *Chicago Record-Herald*, Oct. 6, 7, 1911. Two articles in *The Bulletin of the Pan-American Union*, vol. XXXIII, no. 4, pp. 785 ff., and no. 5, pp. 850 ff., recount in detail Curtis's activities in Pan-American affairs.]   J.M.L.

CURTISS, SAMUEL IVES (Feb. 5, 1844– Sept. 22, 1904), theologian, was a child of the manse, his father, after whom he was named, having been the pastor of a Congregational church in Union, Conn., for thirty-eight years. His mother's name was Eliza (Ives) Curtiss. He graduated from Amherst in 1867, and from Union Theological Seminary, New York, in 1870. Immediately thereafter, on May 10, he married Mrs. Laura Sessions. He was one of the first group of young scholars to cross the Atlantic and seek further preparation at German universities. After a year at Bonn, he went to Leipzig, where he spent four years, receiving the degree of Ph.D. Noting the need of religious services in

English for the growing number of American students and starting such services himself in a private house, he had the satisfaction of later seeing the establishment of an American Chapel which insured the relative permanency of the work. In 1878 he was made Licentiate in Theology by the University of Berlin. He was also given recognition as a scholar by three American institutions, obtaining the degree of D.D. from Iowa College in 1878, from Amherst in 1880, and from Chicago Theological Seminary in 1903. After he had joined the faculty of Chicago Theological Seminary in 1878 as professor of Biblical literature and history, he became actively interested in Chicago's need of city missionary work, and largely through his efforts and his contagious enthusiasm the Chicago City Mission Society was established by the Congregational Churches in 1881.

As a scholar Curtiss was an indefatigable worker and a courageous thinker. As a student at Leipzig, he worked for four years with Franz Delitzsch, and though starting as a loyal defender of traditional views, he followed Delitzsch into the camp of the modern, critical historians. He brought to the Chicago Theological Seminary from Germany the first critical, scholarly Old Testament library to be set up in America. In the Seminary he at first taught both Old Testament and New Testament, but the work expanded so rapidly that he was soon able to call to his aid a professor of New Testament and a professor of Assyriology. His greatest single contribution to scholarship was *Primitive Semitic Religion Today*, 1902; (*Ursemitische Religion im Volksleben des heutigen Orients,* 1903) giving the results of observations made during several trips to Palestine in the closing years of his life to study the folk-lore and religious practises of the present-day population of Palestine. He translated from the German, Bickell's *Outlines of Hebrew Grammar* (1877), Delitzsch's *Messianic Prophecies* (1880), and Delitzsch's *Old Testament History of Redemption* (1881). Aside from many articles upon Old Testament topics in current journals, his only other significant works were a monograph on *The Levitical Priests* (1877), another on *Moses and Ingersoll* (1880), and one on *Franz Delitzsch* (1890). His richest legacy consisted of the large number of students who caught something of his spirit during the twenty-six years of his tenure of office and helped to spread a tolerant and kindly feeling in the churches. His equipment for scholarly work made him for long the outstanding man among his colleagues upon the faculty of the Chicago Theological Seminary.

[*The Chicago Seminary Quarterly* for 1904 made its October number a memorial to Curtiss, and the same journal in its issue of July 1903 contains an autobiographical sketch of Curtiss entitled "Twenty-five Years as a Seminary Professor." See also *Who's Who in America*, 1903–05; *Biblical World*, Nov. 1904; *Bibliotheca Sacra*, Jan. 1905.]   J.M.P.S.

CURWEN, SAMUEL (Dec. 17, 1715–Apr. 9, 1802), Loyalist, author, was born in Salem, Mass., the son of George Curwin, a minister, and Mehitable (Parkman) Curwin. He was descended from George Curwin, of North England, who settled in Salem, Mass., in 1638. Following his father's footsteps, he attended Harvard, graduating in 1735. About this time he began to spell his name Curwen. Poor health forced him to abandon his studies for the ministry, and an unhappy love-affair led him to seek distraction abroad. Upon his return, he engaged in commerce. In 1744 he was a captain in the New England expedition against Louisburg, the base of predatory French cruisers. In May 1750, he married Abigail Russell of Charlestown, Mass. He was impost officer of Essex County, and judge of admiralty at the outbreak of the Revolution. Association with prosperous business circles made his views conservative, and the holding of office through administrative favor inclined him to support the existing authorities. When Gov. Hutchinson returned to England, Curwen's name was attached to an address of approbation and sympathy. Public opinion arose against the "Addressers." Alarmed at the "soured and malevolent" temper against "moderate" men, he embarked for Philadelphia. His wife did not accompany him, fearing the dangers at home less than an ocean voyage. The atmosphere of Quaker Philadelphia was less pacific than he had hoped, so he took ship to England on May 12, 1775. The first year of his exile he spent in London, but as it became apparent that the struggle in America would be of considerable duration, he visited the industrial cities of England, hoping to find the cultural advantages of London at less expense in some other city, but returned disillusioned. His resources were running very low, when in March 1777, the English government granted him an annuity of one hundred pounds. He recorded his life as a refugee in an interesting journal and in letters. The Loyalists in London led an isolated existence. The most irksome feature to Samuel Curwen was the lack of occupation, the "constrained, useless, uniform blank of life." He was usually pessimistic about his personal affairs, and about political conditions, but he could not forget that he was an American, and British contempt for colonial ability stirred him to indignation. His own convictions, although sincere, were based on the belief that rebellion could not be successful, and he came to regret that he had not kept his opinions to himself. As soon as peace was established he began to consider returning to America. He landed in Boston, Sept. 25, 1784, somewhat disappointed in the physical aspects of the land he had longed to see again. He was not persecuted for his political course but lived a quiet and secluded life until his death in his native Salem.

[The chief source of information about Curwen is his *Jour. and Letters* (1864), reviewed in the *North Am. Rev.*, LVI, 89, and the *Southern Quart. Rev.*, IV, 97. Charles Dickens, in *Household Words*, VII, 1, 157, bases a description of conditions in England at the time of the American Revolution, upon the *Journal*. There are brief accounts in C. H. Van Tyne, *The Loyalists in the Am. Revolution* (1902), and L. Sabine, *Biog. Sketches of Loyalists of the Am. Rev.* (1864).]   V.R—e.

CURWOOD, JAMES OLIVER (June 12, 1878–Aug. 13, 1927), novelist, son of James Moran and Abigail (Griffin) Curwood, was born in Owosso, Mich., where he also died. His father was related to Capt. Marryat, the novelist, and his mother, according to the legend, was remotely descended from an Indian princess. When he was about five, his family took up an eight years' residence on a farm near Vermilion, Ohio, close to Lake Erie. Shortly after acquiring his first gun, at the age of eight, he began writing adventure stories remarkable both for length and for profuse incident. Expelled from school, he successively toured much of the South on a bicycle, peddled medicines, trapped wild animals, and studied (1898–1900) at the University of Michigan. From 1900 to 1907 he worked as reporter and finally as editor of the Detroit *News-Tribune*. Then he returned to live in Owosso with the definite purpose of making himself an author. With *The Courage of Captain Plum* (1908), he inaugurated a series of books which, despite his long annual sojourns in camp, numbered twenty-six before death intervened nineteen years later. His writings are concerned chiefly with the extreme northwest of this continent—God's Country, he named it—with the wild animals that live there, and with the human masters of both land and beasts. He dealt with a type of life exactly suited at his precise moment to the vague imaginings of the rank-and-file citizen, and he instinctively availed himself of the conventional literary devices that make for popularity. Of the sixteen novels including *The Grizzly King* (1916) and culminating with *Nomads of the North* (1919), he is reported to have sold at the outset an average of about 10,000 copies each, but modern advertising arrangements ran up the advance orders for *The River's End* (1919) to 100,000 copies, and for *The Valley of Silent Men* (1920) to 105,000. Much of his work was adapted for motion pictures, and even in France, it is said, he was raised in popular favor to a throne formerly reserved there for Upton Sinclair and Jack London. He was an ardent and at times bumptious conservationist, and for the last ten years of life —stirred by the magnanimous conduct of a bear —he foreswore his activities as a hunter, and rejoiced over the inspiration he conceived to lie in recognizing men and beasts as true brothers. Always a good citizen of Owosso, he devoted himself to local public affairs, helped promote an ice-cream factory, threatened to shoot bootleggers on sight, and denied promptly, on being so accused, that he had attacked "the divinity of the Virgin" (*N. Y. Times*, Jan. 15, 1923). During 1917–18, though officially designated "as a war correspondent, to write," as he said, "of the thrill of man killing man," he did not go to France. But at home he declared faithfully in his magazine writings that the momentary pangs of the war would be compensated for in time by the benefits it would confer spiritually (Curwood, "Why I Write," p. 149). Out-of-door life seemed to him a universal panacea—he urged it on his friends and based on his own adherence to it his often proclaimed expectation of living to be one hundred years old. He died of blood-poisoning after a week's illness. He was married twice, the second time to Ethel Greenwood.

[J. O. Curwood, "Why I Write Nature Stories," *Good Housekeeping*, July 1918; *Who's Who in America*, 1926–27; C. C. Baldwin, *Men Who Make Our Novels* (1924); R. Long, "Jas. Oliver Curwood and His Far North," *Bookman*, Feb. 1921; Univ. of Mich., *Calendar* 1898–99, 1899–1900; L. Galantiere, "Am. Books in France," *Am. Mercury*, May 1924; *N. Y. Times*, Jan. 15, 1923, Feb. 5, 1925, Aug. 15, 1927; *Detroit Free Press*, Aug. 15, 1927.]
                                                  J.D.W.

CUSHING, CALEB (Jan. 17, 1800–Jan. 2, 1879), statesman, was born in the township of Salisbury, Essex County, Mass., a direct descendant of Matthew Cushing, a Norfolk landowner who in 1638 came to Boston in the *Diligent*. The Cushings were long-lived, energetic, and practical people. Many of them were colonial clergymen and judges, but Caleb's father, John Newmarch Cushing, became a merchant and ship-owner, thus amassing a considerable fortune. Caleb Cushing's artistic and literary tastes were doubtless inherited from his mother, Lydia Dow, a delicate and sensitive girl from Seabrook, N. H., who died when he was ten years old. In 1802, John Newmarch Cushing moved across the Merrimac River to the prosperous shipping town of Newburyport, of which his son was to be for more than half a century the foremost citizen. It was a period when Essex County was producing a group of remarkably gifted men,—Rufus

Choate, Nathaniel Hawthorne, William Lloyd Garrison, Robert Rantoul, and John Greenleaf Whittier. Industry was alive in the New England ports, and, watching the Cushing vessels sail away for China and India, the boy developed a fondness for the sea and a longing for foreign travel. A handsome and precocious youth, he entered Harvard at thirteen, graduating in 1817 as a member of the Phi Beta Kappa and as Latin Salutatorian in the class with George Bancroft. After a year at Harvard Law School, he entered the office of Ebenezer Moseley, in Newburyport, where he studied intermittently for three years, being admitted to the Massachusetts bar in 1821. In February 1820, he accepted from President Kirkland an appointment as tutor in mathematics at Harvard, but resigned in July 1821, after he had demonstrated that ne could have had a brilliant future as a teacher. Meanwhile he had translated Robert J. Pothier's treatise *On Maritime Contracts of Letting to Hire* (1821), and, at the request of his friend, Edward Everett, had begun to contribute to the recently founded *North American Review*. While he was building up a practise in Newburyport, he edited the local newspaper, delivered many public addresses, mastered at least four modern languages, and entered aggressively into politics. He secured election in 1824 as representative to the Massachusetts General Court, and in 1826 became a state senator. Essex County had been a stronghold of uncompromising Federalism, and Cushing entered public life as a supporter of John Quincy Adams against Jackson. In the autumn of 1826, running for Congress against John Varnum, Cushing, in spite of the encouragement of Webster and Everett, was defeated, largely through the opposition of William Lloyd Garrison, who, although indebted to him for advice and financial assistance, forced his way into a Cushing rally and delivered a scathing attack upon his patron.

On Nov. 23, 1824, Cushing married Caroline Elizabeth Wilde, daughter of Judge Samuel Sumner Wilde, of the supreme judicial court. By 1829 overwork, both in literature and in practical politics, had undermined his health, and he and his wife sailed for Europe, where they spent over a year traveling in England, France, and Spain. The vacation not only restored his strength but also familiarized him with old-world systems of government. On his return, he found that Varnum had resigned, and he was drawn into an acrimonious contest with several other candidates for the vacant Congressional seat. Between 1831 and 1833 there were seventeen elections in Essex north district, with Cushing usually in the lead, but, when it was obvious that the deadlock could not be broken, he wisely withdrew. His persistency was rewarded, however, in 1834, when, supported by Whittier, he defeated Gayton P. Osgood of North Andover, and was seated in the House as a member of the young Whig party. In the midst of these political struggles, his wife died, leaving him childless and alone. Cushing never married again.

He reached Washington at a moment when agitation of the slavery question, which had been temporarily allayed by the Missouri Compromise of 1820, was being revived, and he was soon reminded that he must take a positive stand. Temperamentally he was a conservative, averse to radical doctrine, and inclined always to uphold the established order. On moral grounds he disliked slavery and had denounced it unsparingly in an article on Hayti in the *North American Review*; but he agreed with Everett, Webster, and other Massachusetts Whigs that the North had no constitutional right to interfere with it in the Southern states. It was an entirely logical position, especially appealing to a legal mind. Cushing felt that extremists, whether abolitionists or slave-drivers, were menacing to the Union; and he believed that it was more important to preserve the Union than it was to abolish slavery. On the floor of the House, however, he joined his venerable colleague, John Quincy Adams, in upholding the right of his constituents to petition Congress against slavery. In his first speech, Jan. 25, 1836, he presented a petition from certain citizens of Haverhill and gave a detailed history of the right of petition, concluding with the statement, "I maintain that the House is bound by the Constitution to receive the petitions" (Fuess, vol. I, p. 184). The notorious "Ben" Hardin of Kentucky, whose wit, according to John Randolph, was like a "butcher-knife whetted on a brickbat," responded later by assailing Massachusetts, pronouncing Cushing's remarks to be "false calumny." The latter then rose, likened Hardin to Homer's "snarling Thersites," and burst into an impassioned eulogy of the North which drew rounds of applause from the galleries.

Cushing served four consecutive terms in Congress, during the first two of which he was an entirely orthodox and accredited Whig. He criticized Van Buren's administration, opposed the Independent Treasury Bill, supported the Cumberland Road Bill and the principle of internal improvements, and voted against all Democratic measures. He was on the House Committee of Foreign Affairs, acting acceptably for some months as chairman. In August 1840, his constituents gave him at Newburyport a dinner

of 1,800 covers, at which Webster was a guest and speaker, and Cushing was rightly supposed to be more in Webster's confidence than any one else in the Massachusetts delegation in Congress. It was tacitly assumed by both Webster and Everett that Cushing was their legitimate successor to political honors in Massachusetts. He had now, indeed, reached a point where success seemed to be his. When Harrison, the first Whig president, whose campaign biography Cushing had prepared, came into power on Mar. 4, 1841, the latter was jubilant. But Harrison died within a month, and John Tyler, moving into the White House, entered upon that political duel with Henry Clay which was to be disastrous to so many careers. Even while Harrison was alive, Clay had been disposed to claim the leadership of the Whigs, and, with Harrison gone, he assumed the tone of a dictator, actually laying down a legislative policy. Tyler's prompt vetoes of the Whig bills for a National Bank placed him in open opposition to the exasperated Clay, who expelled him formally from the party. On Sept. 11, 1841, four members of the cabinet resigned at Clay's instigation, only Webster, the secretary of state, remaining. Cushing had now definitely sided with Tyler, whom he regarded as more trustworthy than Clay. In a pamphlet addressed to his constituents he defended Tyler's vetoes as being matters of conscience,—a contention in which he was correct, for Tyler, before his election as vice-president, had not disguised his antagonism to a National Bank. Cushing thus enlisted with the "Corporal's Guard," a little group of Congressmen who supported Tyler against Clay. Despite his protests, he was ignored in the Whig councils, and, from that date until the Civil War, he was known as a Democrat, voting consistently for Democratic principles and candidates.

The Whigs, incensed at those of their number who did not participate in the plot to "head Captain Tyler," called Cushing a renegade. His motives in opposing Clay were, however, mainly patriotic, and history has justified his action on the National Bank question. If Cushing did hope for any personal advantage, he chose the wrong course, for he could expect nothing from the outraged Whigs. He closed his Congressional career, which had opened so auspiciously eight years before, with a valedictory on Mar. 3, 1843, in which he complained of the injustice with which he had been treated. On the same evening Tyler sent Cushing's name three times to the Senate as his nominee for secretary of the treasury to succeed Walter Forward, but he was rejected on each trial by a larger negative vote.

Humiliated though he was, Cushing was not to be without consolation. For some years the State Department had been considering the sending of a commissioner to China to arrange a commercial treaty with that empire, and in 1843 Congress made an appropriation of $40,000 for this purpose. The original scheme had been to offer the mission to Everett, then minister to England, in the hope that Webster might be allowed to escape gracefully from the cabinet by following Everett to the Court of St. James's. Everett, however, declined to sacrifice himself and his aspirations for Webster's benefit; and Tyler, during the Congressional recess, appointed Cushing as commissioner to China. The latter promptly accepted the post, and, with a considerable fleet, proceeded to China by way of the Mediterranean and the Indian Ocean, his flag-ship, the *Missouri,* being burned in the harbor of Gibraltar. Arriving off Macao on Feb. 27, 1844, he skilfully avoided all the difficulties brought up by the Chinese diplomats and arranged the Treaty of Wang Hiya, signed on July 3 of that year. Cushing was tactful but resolute in his demands, and insisted that all the customary courtesies should be observed. When the Chinese commissioner, Kiyeng, sent him a communication with the title of the United States on a line lower than that of the Chinese Empire, Cushing indignantly protested, and the Oriental apologized. The treaty thus framed opened five Chinese ports to American merchants, settled many disputed points regarding tariff and trade regulations, and established the important principle of "exterritoriality," specifying that citizens of the United States living in China should be subject to the exclusive jurisdiction of American laws and officials. It is recognized as an important step in our commercial and diplomatic history. On Aug. 27, 1844, Cushing began his return voyage across the Pacific, landing at San Blas, Mexico, and going overland by stage to Vera Cruz, being robbed by bandits on the way. The Treaty of Wang Hiya was approved by the Senate on Jan. 16, 1845, and formally proclaimed on Apr. 18, 1846.

Although the Chinese mission, because of its unqualified success, brought Cushing much fame, he was, for the moment, out of touch with politics. He made an extended tour to the Northwest, exploring Wisconsin and Minnesota, often in the deep wilderness. When he reappeared in civilization, he had been elected again to the Massachusetts General Court. Cushing was frankly an advocate of a big army and navy and held views which would to-day be called "imperialistic." He had favored the acquisition of Oregon and Texas, and he was later to advocate the annexation of

Cuba. In 1846, on the eve of a war with Mexico, he was one of the few Northern statesmen to support President Polk. On the opening day of the legislative session in January 1847, he introduced a bill appropriating $20,000 for a regiment to serve in the emergency. When the proposal was rejected, Cushing spent over $12,000 from his own purse, organized a regiment, and was chosen its colonel and dispatched with an expedition to the Rio Grande. For a few months he was commandant in the notorious border town of Matamoros, where he showed himself to be a strict disciplinarian. In April 1847, he was promoted brigadier-general, and in November he started with his brigade from Vera Cruz, following the picturesque route taken only a short time before by the victorious Gen. Scott through Cerro Gordo, Jalapa, Perote, and Puebla, to Mexico City. To his disgust, he arrived after the fighting was over, and was left with no further military duty to perform except to sit on a Court of Inquiry investigating charges brought by Gen. Scott against Generals Worth and Pillow and Col. Duncan.

During his absence in the army, Cushing had been nominated in 1847 by the Democrats as a candidate for governor of Massachusetts, but had been defeated by his Whig opponent, George Nixon Briggs, in a contest based mainly on the war issue. A feature of the campaign was the publication of Lowell's *Biglow Papers,* voicing in scathing satire the Northern sentiment against the Mexican War and the annexation of Texas. Lowell was especially caustic toward Cushing:

> "Gineral C. is a dreffle smart man ;
>   He's ben on all sides thet give places or pelf ;
> But consistency still wuz a part of his plan,—
>   He's ben true to *one* party and thet is himself."

This characterization, made in the heat of political controversy, was clearly unjust, but it appealed to the popular fancy, and Cushing suffered from it during the remainder of his career. When he reached Newburyport, in July 1848, on his return from Mexico, he was greeted with a salute of one hundred guns. In the autumn, however, when again a candidate for governor, he was beaten a second time by Lowell's "Guvener B."

Cushing never thought it beneath him to serve the people, even though in a modest position. He was often moderator of his town meeting, and in May 1851, after he had secured the passage by the General Court of a bill incorporating Newburyport as a city, he was chosen the first mayor by a vote of 964 to 88. In June 1852, he resigned in order to accept an appointment by Gov. Boutwell as associate justice of the supreme judiciary court of Massachusetts. Although he sat for only a few months, he made a reputation for familiarity with the law and soundness of judgment. In preparation for his duties he read through in six weeks the entire series of *Massachusetts Reports*, covering at that date sixty octavo volumes of approximately 800 pages each. "When he came upon the bench," said Chief Justice Shaw, "we did not know what to do with him; when he left, we did not know what to do without him" (*Ibid.*, II, p. 109).

During the spring of 1852, Cushing, who had been made a delegate to the National Democratic Convention at Baltimore, was active in scheming for the nomination of Gen. Franklin Pierce as a compromise candidate for president of the United States. Recent discoveries prove that the introduction of Pierce's name at Baltimore was the climax of a carefully laid plan, in which Cushing had a leading part. After Pierce's overwhelming victory over the Whig, Gen. Scott, Cushing was naturally much in the public eye, and it was rightly surmised that he was to be one of the chief advisers of the new administration. But, although it was predicted that he was to be secretary of state, that honor was finally awarded to William L. Marcy, and Cushing became attorney-general. At Marcy's request, much of the business formerly transacted by the Department of State, including pardons, legal and judicial appointments, and extradition problems, was assigned to Cushing, with the result that the functions of the attorney-general were virtually doubled. Cushing was the first incumbent of that office to hold strictly to the residence obligation and refrain from the private practise of law. H. B. Learned says of him, "He left behind him a collection of official opinions that for extent alone has never been equalled before or since his day" (*The President's Cabinet*, 1912, p. 178).

In addition to his routine duties, which were heavy, Cushing became on many matters the mouthpiece of the Pierce administration and was one of the two most powerful men in the cabinet, the other being the secretary of war, Jefferson Davis. On Sept. 29, 1853, he sent to Richard Frothingham, editor of the *Boston Post*, a letter known as "Cushing's Ukase," in which he stated Pierce's desire "that the dangerous element of Abolitionism, under whatever guise or form it may present itself, shall be crushed out"; he prepared daily editorials for the Washington *Union*, the administration organ; he favored, although he did not help to originate, the Kansas-Nebraska Act (1854); and in November 1855, at Pierce's request, he issued an official opinion which in every essential respect covered the ground of the Dred Scott Decision (1857), in-

sisting that the Missouri Compromise of 1820 must have been declared by any court to be null and void *in incepto*, "because incompatible with the organic fact of inequality and internal right, in all respects, between the old and the new states." In foreign affairs, Cushing, the representative of "young America" and the apostle of "manifest destiny," approved the doctrines of the Ostend Manifesto and did his utmost, up to the verge of war with Spain, to acquire Cuba for the United States. He directed the prosecution of Crampton, the British minister in Washington, on the charge of recruiting soldiers within our borders for the British army during the Crimean War. For some months the relations between the two nations were strained, especially when Congress sent Crampton his passports and he returned to England; but the good sense of the British government averted disaster. Cushing in this case, as well as in many others, was aggressive in maintaining our national rights. His so-called "Anglophobia" was actually a phase of his intense Americanism.

With the inauguration of President Buchanan in 1857, Cushing, after continuing to act as attorney-general until his successor, Jeremiah S. Black, had arrived, resumed his seat in the Massachusetts legislature, where, even with a majority against him, he exercised an extraordinary influence. His association with Southern statesmen had left him with a gradually deepening bitterness against radical abolitionists like Garrison, but he never became an apologist for slavery. When Jefferson Davis, after a summer in Maine, spoke in Faneuil Hall (Oct. 11, 1858), Cushing introduced him. At the Boston Union Meeting (Dec. 8, 1859), Cushing, with Everett and Levi Lincoln, condemned John Brown's raid and painted the horrors of servile insurrection. By 1860, he had reached a point where he reluctantly confessed that he viewed a separation of the states as the only practicable solution of the controversy, and his prophecy, in January 1860, of civil war, culminating in the dictatorship of some "man on horseback," was widely quoted. It was in this letter that he said, "The South . . . will defend itself at all hazards, within the Union if it may, and, if not so, then outside the Union" (*Ibid.*, II, 242).

The National Democratic Convention which opened, Apr. 23, 1860, in Charleston, S. C., was from the start a struggle for supremacy between the Douglas and the slavery elements of the party. Cushing, the permanent chairman, employed all the devices of parliamentary law to keep the peace. The extremists, however, would not listen to compromise measures, and, after

Douglas had led for fifty-seven ballots, the convention declared a deadlock and adjourned in disorder. When it reassembled at Baltimore in June, Cushing once more presided; but, after it became evident that Douglas was sure to be the nominee, he followed the radicals out of the hall. The seceders called a rival convention, and, with Cushing in the chair, named Breckinridge and Lane as standard-bearers. The victory of Lincoln on Nov. 6 convinced Cushing that the Union could not be preserved. His friends in the South openly preached secession, and Cushing, in a series of three addresses in Newburyport, argued that the blame must rest upon the abolitionists for their agitation of the slavery evil. If the Republican party was not prepared to make concessions, it should let the Southern states "go in peace." He was sent to Charleston as President Buchanan's personal representative in order to delay, if possible, the passage of an ordinance of secession, but arrived on Dec. 20, just too late. When he was invited to attend the ceremonies connected with the signing of the ordinance, he indignantly declined and returned to Washington. His association with the South was over.

Stronger than any other of Cushing's principles was his love for the Union, and, when the news arrived of the firing on Fort Sumter (Apr. 12, 1861), he went back at once from Washington to Newburyport and, at a patriotic mass meeting, publicly announced his loyalty to the Federal cause. He then offered his services to Gov. Andrew, saying, "I have no desire to survive the overthrow of the government of the United States." The famous war governor refused them, saying, "I am compelled sadly to declare that, were I to accept your offer, I should dishearten numerous good and loyal men, and tend to demoralize our military service" (*Ibid.*, II, 277). President Lincoln, with more wisdom, accepted Cushing's legal assistance, and, as the war progressed, entrusted him with important government affairs. At the time of the *Trent* incident, he was consulted often by both Seward and Lincoln. He supported every war emergency measure, and, on the night before the election of 1864, spoke in Faneuil Hall for Lincoln and against McClellan. He remained a Republican until his death. At the close of the conflict Cushing commenced the active practise of law in Washington, purchasing an estate at Falls Church, about six miles from the capital, and becoming a citizen of Virginia. President Johnson appointed him (1865) chairman of a commission to revise and codify the statutes of the United States. In 1868 he was sent on a diplomatic mission to Bogota, where he negotiated a treaty with the Colombian Government regarding the right of way for a ship canal across the Isthmus of Panama.

President Grant had confidence in Cushing's judgment and asked his opinion on vital problems. Chief among these was that of the "*Alabama* claims," arising out of depredations committed on Northern commerce during the Civil War by the *Alabama*, the *Florida*, and other vessels built under British registry but later flying the Confederate flag. As early as 1865 it was rumored that Cushing was to be sent to London as a special agent to adjust the demands of the United States upon Great Britain. With all the prolonged and complicated negotiations of the next few years Cushing was intimately concerned; indeed it was through his suggestion to Sir John Rose that the movement for the Treaty of Washington was started. This Treaty (1871) provided for a Tribunal of Arbitration, consisting of one representative each from the United States, Great Britain, Italy, Switzerland, and Brazil, to meet at Geneva for the purpose of settling the American claims. Cushing, who was appointed senior counsel for the United States, with William M. Evarts and Morrison R. Waite as associates, prepared no small part of the American argument. When he arrived at Geneva in June 1872, he effected, by tactful diplomacy, a compromise through which the issue of the so-called "indirect claims" was evaded, and thus enabled both countries to continue without loss of dignity. He later helped to write the American "Counter Case" and delivered his "Reply Argument" in excellent French, to the amazement of the Swiss, Italian, and Brazilian arbitrators. The decision of the Tribunal on Sept. 14, awarding the United States $15,500,000, was the culmination of Cushing's labors over a period of several years. For Sir Alexander Cockburn, the British arbitrator, who had shown himself to be haughty and disagreeable, Cushing conceived an intense dislike, and, on his return to the United States he published *The Treaty of Washington* (1873), in which, while presenting a full account of the events leading up to the Geneva Tribunal, he made a vigorous attack on Cockburn.

Late in December 1873, Grant appointed Cushing as minister to Spain, and he was about to sail when the news came of his nomination as chief justice of the Supreme Court. On the death of Chief Justice Salmon P. Chase (May 7, 1873), Grant had offered the vacant place to Senator Roscoe Conkling, who had declined it. He then rather hastily named his attorney-general, George H. Williams, but when it became evident that the latter would be rejected by the Senate, he was quietly withdrawn. Then the President turned to Caleb Cushing. If Cushing had sinned in the eyes of the Republican party before 1860, he had amply redeemed his errors, and, as a friend of Sumner and Grant, was in the full confidence of the administration. But his enemies began to rise against him: Harlan's Washington *Chronicle* denounced him bitterly; old slanders were revived and new ones imagined; and Senator Sargent of California, who still cherished a boyish grudge against Cushing, discovered and printed in garbled form a letter from Cushing to Jefferson Davis in March 1861, recommending a former clerk for a position. Finally Cushing himself requested Grant to withdraw his name, declaring at the same time that he "had never done an act, uttered a word, or conceived a thought of disloyalty to the United States." It was the most notable instance in our history of a rejection for high office on purely partisan grounds, for every one admitted that, in legal learning and acumen, Cushing would have been a worthy successor to Marshall, Taney, and Chase.

Having delayed his departure until it was certain that he was not to be chief justice, Cushing proceeded to Spain, where he found relations between the United States and that country very much strained. The affair of the *Virginius* (November 1873) had affronted American pride, and Gen. Sickles, Cushing's predecessor, had disregarded the instructions of Secretary Fish. Cushing, well-versed in Spanish character and psychology, averted danger without injuring the prestige of either nation. No one of our ministers in Madrid has been more popular in Spain. In June 1877, Cushing resigned and retired to Newburyport, where he settled down among his books in the library of his house on High Street. He still went occasionally to Washington, his last trip being made in March 1878, at the earnest request of Roscoe Conkling. He declined a nomination for Congress and refused to run for the attorney-generalship of Massachusetts. A severe attack of erysipelas in July 1878, was a warning of the end, and he died, Jan. 2, 1879. His body was laid in the New Burial Ground, in Newburyport, and a memorial service was held in the City Hall some months later, with formal eulogies by his friends. His nearest surviving relative was his half-brother, John N. Cushing.

Cushing was an extraordinarily versatile and well-rounded man. To a naturally keen mind, he joined other qualities which gave him intellectual distinction. With tireless physical and mental energy, he rose at dawn and was seldom in bed until after midnight. Always busy with some definite task, he had no interest in frivolity or motiveless amusement. A remarkable gift of concentration enabled him to read and digest books with astonishing speed. Through a policy of order and punctuality he avoided any waste of time and he was never idle. He had, furthermore, the insatiable curiosity, the passion for accuracy, and the perseverance of the true scholar, and there were few fields of research into which he did not penetrate. As a young man, he had an enthusiasm for botany and astronomy, but he gave away a fine collection of minerals because such pursuits seemed likely to interfere with his political ambitions. His acquaintances told amazing tales of his information on unusual subjects. Once some of them laid a trap for him. After having read up on Chinese musical instruments, they introduced the theme casually during a dinner conversation. For a brief period Cushing was silent, apparently listening attentively. Then he began to talk, pouring out such a store of facts about musical instruments in general and Chinese musical instruments in particular that those present had to confess the trick which they had played. In Madrid Cushing once astonished Sir Henry Layard, the explorer of Nineveh, by his references to obscure points in the history and archeology of that city. When a well-known dictionary was sent to him by the publishers, he read it and marked over five thousand errors in the vocabulary of modern geographical names. Emerson declared him to be the most eminent scholar of his day, and Wendell Phillips once said, "I regard Mr. Cushing as the most learned man now living" (*Ibid.*, II, 401).

Cushing's genius was acquisitive and critical rather than creative. In contributing to the *Encyclopedia Americana* and the *American Annual Register* he amassed a vast store of knowledge, and he also wrote many articles of the "heavy" historical and biographical type for the *North American Review* and similar periodicals. Besides the dozens of commemorative and occasional addresses which he delivered during a long life, he published a *History of Newburyport* (1826), a *Review Historical and Political of the Late Revolution in France* (1833), and *Reminiscences of Spain* (1833),—the last being overshadowed by Irving's *Alhambra* (1832), which preceded it by only a few weeks and was much superior to Cushing's book in style and substance. He also projected biographies of Judge John Lowell and of John Tyler, but his plans were not carried out. Among his papers is a considerable amount of poetry, both original and translated; but, while it is technically flawless and displays facility in rhyming, it lacks inspiration. As a linguist, Cushing was excelled by few Americans of his generation. He could converse fluently in French, Spanish, and Italian, and could read easily any of the modern European tongues. On his voyage to China he so mastered the Manchu language that no interpreter was required at his private meetings with the Chinese envoys. At the Geneva Tribunal he shifted from English to French and from French to Italian without the slightest hesitancy. He acquired German in middle life, merely as a pastime. In a period when public speaking was looked upon as a fine art, Cushing was a famous orator. As an undergraduate he made a serious study of Demosthenes and Burke, and practised gestures before a long mirror in his bedroom. In the old Hall of Representatives in Washington he was one of the few members whose voice could be heard even in the farthest corner. Ordinarily he was rather cold and formal in his manner, but, once aroused, he was irresistible and sometimes swept an audience off their feet by the fervor of his appeal. Like Webster and Everett, he was a favorite on the Lyceum stage.

In the legal profession he took high rank, and, if he had been able to devote himself to regular practise, would have stood even higher. In court-room pleading he was not notably successful, for he disdained the arts of persuasion and conciliation; but he was expert at summarizing evidence and had great weight with judges, who could appreciate the intellectual quality of his arguments. At certain periods in his life he had a large clientage, and in 1873, when he was appointed minister to Spain, he returned over $200,000 which he had received in retaining fees.

In his prime he was robust and powerful, not quite six feet tall, but compact and tightly built. His features were strong and resolute, the jaw especially denoting a tenacious will. His eyes were small, but very bright and restless, with a kind of "gipsy gleam." Although he was careless in his dress, he carried himself with dignity and impressed people, even in his old age, as being very handsome. He was temperate in his habits and cared little for luxuries, being content always to live in a simple manner. He was never a really popular politician or a good vote-getter. His temperament was too coldly intellectual, and his reserved manner did not appeal to the man in the street. Like Everett and Sum-

ner, John Hay and Woodrow Wilson, he was a scholar-statesman, a little aloof from the common people. He was not a good judge of men and motives, and was easily duped by schemers. In his attitude on public questions he was inclined to be dogmatic. The theory that he was fickle and inconsistent cannot be sustained, for, once he had made up his mind, he rarely altered his opinion. Although he was consumed by ambition, he never changed his views in order to gain preferment for himself; on the contrary, when he took Tyler's part against Clay, when he supported the Mexican War, and when he defended the South in the decade before the Civil War, he deliberately espoused causes which led to his virtual ostracism in his native state. Even his shifts of party affiliation,—from Whig to Democrat in 1841, and from Democrat to Republican in 1861,—are easily explicable on the theory of his devotion to the Union. He himself said, at the close of his long career, "Every act of my political life, in whatever relation of parties, was governed by the single dominant purpose of aiming to preserve the threatened integrity of the Union" (*Ibid.*, I, 6). Far from being tricky or evasive, he was almost ludicrously deficient in tact and adaptability. It was his chief weakness as a practical statesman that he believed in the power of reason as a means of bringing men to his point of view. He had little personal magnetism and few of the graces which arouse enthusiasm; indeed his aggressiveness often made him disliked. This accounts, in part, for the number of his enemies,—men like Garrison and Benton and Lowell,—who molded public opinion against him. Not the least of his many disappointments was his knowledge that his motives were not really understood. He had an opportunity to be a leader in the abolition of negro slavery, but he rejected it for what he conceived to be a nobler ideal—the preservation of the Union. He was unfortunate in being drawn, against his will, into the many controversial questions centering around the status of the negro, and he was not at his best in political controversy. The violent animosities of the struggle between the North and the South did not, for many years, allow a just estimate to be made of Cushing's character and achievement, but we can now judge him more fairly. His diplomatic successes in China and in Spain; his effective opposition to Clay's attempt to revive a National Bank; his work in elevating the office of attorney-general; his large share in presenting the American cause at Geneva,—these are Cushing's positive contributions to our history. He stands out, because of his industry, his scholarship, and his versatility, as one of the most picturesque and talented figures of the nineteenth century.

[The chief source of information about Cushing is his biography in two volumes by Claude M. Fuess (1923), a book based largely on the great collection of material preserved by Cushing himself. Cushing's own published speeches on many subjects are available, and the files of Boston and Washington newspapers are full of references to him. *A Memorial of Caleb Cushing from the City of Newburyport* was printed in 1879. For his China mission, see *Sen. Docs. Nos. 58, 67,* 28 Cong., 2 Sess., and Tyler Dennett, *Americans in Eastern Asia* (1922).]   C. M. F.

CUSHING, FRANK HAMILTON (July 22, 1857–Apr. 10, 1900), ethnologist, the son of Thomas and Sarah Ann (Harding) Cushing, was born in the village of North East, Erie County, Pa. When he was three his family moved to Barre Center, not far from Albion, N. Y. At birth a mite, weighing one and a half pounds, Cushing was a "pillow baby." He grew slowly and was not able to compete in sports with his hardy brothers and sister; and his cloistered life forced him to educate himself from his immediate environment. As he grew stronger, he extended his range to the woods and fields. An arrowhead found by chance was the trivial object that turned his interest to ethnology. His intimate communings with nature, together with his constant study of the old family dictionary, laid the foundation of his knowledge of words and things. At eighteen he took a course in natural science at Cornell. At the suggestion of L. W. Ledyard, an acquaintance of his father, an article by young Cushing on the natural history of his neighborhood in New York was sent to Prof. S. F. Baird [*q.v.*], secretary of the Smithsonian Institution, to apprize him of the promise of the young man as a scientific worker. This article was published by the Institution and led to his employment in the Smithsonian. In 1879 Maj. Powell appointed him to the Bureau of American Ethnology, where he labored until his death. He was married to Emily T. Magill. Outstanding achievements were his study of the Zuñi Pueblo Indians during a five years' sojourn with them; his explorations of ancient pueblos in the Salt River Valley, Ariz., and his investigations of the ancient dwellers at Key Marco, Fla. What he brought to these investigations in the way of knowledge, skill, and scientific imagination is incalculable, but the very superabundance of his ideas acted as a brake on publication. There was too much to set down. Thus his written works are comparatively few. The more complete of them are those growing out of his life at Zuñi, published only after the most thorough rewriting and editing, and never satisfying him. A

posthumous work, *Zuñi Folk Tales* (1901), is really more expressive of his character than any other. His *Zuñi Creation Myths* (1896), also an example of his power of expression and interpretation, is an aboriginal American epic. Especially valuable to ethnologists is *Zuñi Breadstuff* (1920, republished), a comprehensive review of his life of a tribe, its fullness due to the fact that he was compelled to write it in monthly instalments for *The Millstone*, a trade journal of Indianapolis. From his early years he had an insatiable desire to know the processes by which the artifacts he found were made. He constantly practised the aboriginal crafts until he became a master of them. Thus he furnished ethnology with a valuable adjunct in the study of native as well as ancient arts. Appraisals by his contemporaries estimate the position he held in science. "Cushing was a man of genius. He had not only the zeal for labor . . . but he had the genius for the interpretation of facts . . ." (J. W. Powell, *American Anthropologist*, 1900, p. 366). "Cushing was a man of genius, . . . stood out not only as a man of intellect but, preëminently, as a master of those manual concepts to which he gave name as well as meaning—indeed, might fittingly be styled a manual genius" (W. J. McGee, *Ibid.*, p. 355). "The keynote of Mr. Cushing's personality seems to have been an unconscious sympathy" (Alice C. Fletcher, *Ibid.*, p. 367). He was always ready to impart his knowledge, and many ethnologists were fortunate in hearing what he had to say. Though he left but a sparing record of his passing genius, so fertile and so freely bestowed, what he did accomplish, struggling with a frail body and over-active mind, is a notable contribution to the growing science of ethnology.

[Memorial Meeting to Frank Hamilton Cushing, *Am. Anthrop.*, 1900; obituary in *Sci. Am.*, Apr. 21, 1900.]   W. H.

CUSHING, JOHN PERKINS (Apr. 22, 1787–Apr. 12, 1862), merchant, philanthropist, was born in Boston, the son of Robert Cushing, a descendant of Matthew Cushing who came to America in 1638, and of Ann Maynard (Perkins) Cushing, daughter of James Perkins and sister of Thomas Handasyd Perkins. Early in life he became a clerk in the mercantile firm of Perkins & Company, established by his two uncles, James and Thomas H. Perkins, for carrying on trade with China and the Northwest Coast. In 1803, he accompanied Ephraim Bumstead, the eldest apprentice in the company. on a voyage to Canton. Bumstead was taken ill and obliged to return home, and Cushing was left, at the age of sixteen, to carry on the business in China. When Thomas H. Perkins heard that Bumstead had died on the return voyage, he decided to go at once to China; but a letter from Cushing soon arrived, giving such a glowing account of the business that Perkins permitted Cushing to act as resident agent. In China— where he was known as "Ku-shing,"—he conducted affairs so ably that he was admitted to a partnership and became the most highly respected foreign merchant in the country. Except for two short visits home, he remained in China for nearly thirty years, amassing a fortune which, for those days, was colossal. He came back to Boston in 1830, broken in health, and erected a handsome mansion in Summer St., surrounded by a wall of Chinese porcelain and administered, to the amazement of Boston society, by a staff of Chinese servants.

Not long after his return, he married Mary Louise, daughter of the Rev. John Sylvester J. Gardiner, rector of Trinity Church, Boston. He acquired a splendid estate in Watertown, outside of Boston, and built the finest conservatory in New England, which was thrown open freely to the public when the flowers were in bloom. He had constructed for himself a sixty-foot pilot schooner, *The Sylph,* which, in 1832, won the earliest American yacht race on record, against the schooner yacht *Wave,* owned by John C. Stevens, of Hoboken, over a course extending from Vineyard Haven to Tarpaulin Cove. Although Cushing's fortune was estimated in 1851 as more than two million dollars, he was a modest and unostentatious man, who, nevertheless, was widely known for his charities. The Boston *Transcript* described him as "one of the most opulent and public-spirited citizens of Massachusetts." He died at his home in Watertown, —now a part of the Town of Belmont,—and was buried in Mount Auburn Cemetery.

[Jas. S. Cushing, *Genealogy of the Cushing Family* (1905); Robt. B. Forbes, *Personal Reminiscences* (1892); L. Vernon Briggs, *Hist. and Genealogy of the Cabot Family* (1927); Freeman Hunt, *Lives of American Merchants,* vol. I (1858); Julian Sturgis, *From Books and Papers of Russell Sturgis* (n.d.); Wm. C. Hunter, *The 'Fan Kwae' at Canton Before Treaty Days* (London, 1882); *New-Eng. Hist. and Geneal. Reg.,* XVI, 293; Boston *Evening Transcript,* Apr. 14, 1862.]

C. M. F.

CUSHING, JOSIAH NELSON (May 4, 1840–May 17, 1905) Baptist missionary, was born at North Attleboro, Mass., the son of Alphæus N. and Charlotte Everett Foster Cushing. His early education was begun in the local school and continued at the age of fifteen in the Opalic Institute at East Attleboro, where he was converted during a revival meeting under the Rev. C. G. Finney. He prepared for college at Pierce Academy, Middleboro, Mass, and entered Brown University, from which he graduated in 1862. In 1865 he completed his seminary training at Newton Theological Institution, and was ordained in Providence, R. I., shortly thereafter. In the spring of 1865 he had sought appointment under the American Baptist Missionary Union, and was designated to work among the Shans of Burma. While seeking a wife during the following year he taught at Newton. On Aug. 28, 1866 he was married to Mrs. Ellen (Winsor) Fairfield of Boston, and on Oct. 24 they set sail for the East, arriving in Rangoon, Mar. 11, 1867. For seven years he was stationed in Toungoo, studying the Burmese and Shan languages, making evangelistic tours throughout the Shan States, and preparing tracts, Gospel translations, a grammar and handbook of the Shan tongue.

In 1874 ill health forced the Cushings home. One year was spent in Washington, D. C., another in Boston, and then in June 1876 they resumed their work in Burma, making their headquarters at Bhamo, a new station near the Chinese border. From 1880 until 1885 Cushing resided in Rangoon and gave his time to translation and preaching. His wife and son, Herbert, returned to America in 1880, to remain permanently. On Nov. 23, 1880, he finished his translation of the Shan New Testament, and on Jan. 13, 1885, the remainder of the Bible. Soon thereafter he sailed for America by way of the Pacific, and spent a year with his family in Newton, Mass., where he took special work in the Institution. In the fall of 1886, leaving his family, he returned to Burma. For a part of the year 1887 he was principal of the Baptist College in Rangoon. From 1888 to 1890 he was pastor of the Rangoon Baptist Church. In 1891 he completed the stereotyped edition of the Bible in the Shan tongue. In 1892 he was given charge again of the College (now Judson College) and continued in the office of principal until Feb. 14, 1905. It was he who virtually transformed the school into a college, securing endowment, erecting buildings, and gaining educational standing for it. In 1894 the institution became affiliated with Calcutta University on a "First Arts," or Junior College basis. Cushing filled many offices and received many honors. He was for nearly twenty years a member of the India Government Text Book Committee and vice-president of the Burma Educational Syndicate. In 1891 he was a delegate to the meeting of the Evangelical Alliance in Rome. His enduring monuments are the College, his Shan Bible, and his Shan Bible Dictionary. He rendered distinguished service to the British Burma Government, the cause of of scholarship, and Christian missions. In addition to the authorship of various tracts and articles, and his work of translation, he wrote a book, *Christ and Buddha* (Phila., 1907).

[Information may be found in contemporary numbers of the *Baptist Missionary Mag.*, in W. St. John, *Josiah Nelson Cushing* (Rangoon, 1912), and in W. S. Stewart, *Early Baptist Missionaries and Pioneers*, vol. II (1926). See also J. S. Cushing, *Geneal. of the Cushing Family* (1905).]   J. C. A.

CUSHING, LUTHER STEARNS (June 22, 1803–June 22, 1856), author, jurist, was born in Lunenberg, Worcester County, Mass., the eldest of the eight children of Edmund Cushing and Mary (Stearns) Cushing. Edmund Cushing held public offices in town, county, and state for forty years, being a representative in the Massachusetts General Court, a state senator, and a member of the governor's council. Luther was educated in the local schools, studied in a law office in Lunenberg, and entered Harvard College, where he was the only graduate in the class of 1826 to receive the degree of LL.B. For some years after leaving Harvard he was associated with Charles Sumner and George S. Hilliard in editing a periodical called *The American Jurist and Law Magazine*, published in Boston. He became, in 1832, clerk of the Massachusetts House of Representatives, holding the position for twelve years. In 1844 he was elected as a representative to the General Court, but was soon named as judge of the city court of common pleas. In 1848 he resigned in order to become official reporter of the decisions of the supreme court of the commonwealth. In that capacity he prepared twelve volumes of law reports (LV to LXVI), extending from 1848 to 1853. He was also lecturer on Roman Law in Harvard Law School, 1848–49 and 1850–51. On July 16, 1851 he was appointed to a professorship but declined on account of ill health (Chas. Warren, *Hist. of Harvard Law School and of Legal Conditions in America*, 1908, II, 185). He died in Boston on his fifty-third birthday. Cushing was married, May 19, 1840, to Mary Otis Lincoln, a lineal descendant of the patriot, James Otis. After her death in 1851, he married, Oct. 29, 1853, Elizabeth Dutton Cooper. He had three children by his first wife.

Cushing's reputation is based almost entirely on his published books. He was a diligent worker, who translated into English several important legal treatises in foreign languages, among them being Savigny's *Law of Possession* (1838), Pothier's *Treatise on the Contract of Sale* (1839), and Mattermaier's *Effects of Drunkenness on Criminal Responsibility* (1841). Among his important original volumes are: *An inquiry into the present state of the remedial law of Massachusetts; with suggestions for its reform* (1837), *A Practical Treatise on the Trustee Process* (1853), *Reports of Controverted Election Cases in the House of Representatives of the Commonwealth of Massachusetts from 1780 to 1852* (1853), *An Introduction to the Study of Roman Law* (1854), and *Lex Parliamentaria Americana* (1856). This last book, better known under its English title of *Elements of the Law and Practice of Legislative Assemblies in the United States,* is a volume of more than a thousand pages treating of the common parliamentary law as modified in our legislative assemblies. Published only a few weeks before his death, it was received with universal approval, and a reviewer in the Boston *Transcript* said, "It will at once assume the very highest rank as a standard authority." More familiar than any of these, however, is the little volume called *A Manual of Parliamentary Practice* (1844), which bears the secondary title, *Rules of Proceeding and Debate in Deliberative Assemblies*. In its best-known form it is a small book, four inches by six in size, including 177 pages of text, and easily slipped into the pocket. It happened to fill a long-felt need, and, as soon as it appeared, Cushing's *Manual*, as it was commonly called, became a guide for the procedure of all organized assemblies. Its sale was extensive, and thousands of copies were sold abroad as well as in this country. After his death, it was revised from time to time and a few pages of comments by the author's brother, Judge Edmund Lambert Cushing, chief justice of the superior court of New Hampshire, were added; but it was so thorough and complete in its original form that it is in constant use to-day by legislative bodies. Cushing was a man of amiable and social disposition, who made friends wherever he went. He knew all the eminent men of his period in Massachusetts, including Sumner, Everett, Choate, Rantoul, and Robert C. Winthrop, and was frequently a guest in their homes. As a translator he was scrupulously accurate and painstaking, and he was careful to base his work upon the best authorities. Because of his wide knowledge, he was often consulted by distinguished persons on points of law. The writer of his obituary sums up his character by saying that he was "widely known and universally esteemed."

[Boston *Advertiser*, June 23, 1856; Jas. S. Cushing, *The Genealogy of the Cushing Family* (1905).]
C. M. F.

CUSHING, THOMAS (Mar. 24, 1725–Feb. 28, 1788), merchant, politician, the eldest son of

Thomas and Mary (Bromfield) Cushing, was born in Boston. His father had risen to political leadership in Massachusetts serving as representative to the General Court, 1731 to 1742, and as speaker, 1742 until his death in 1746. Thomas Jr., received his first degree from Harvard in 1744. Three years after his graduation, he married Deborah Fletcher. He concerned himself with commerce for almost twenty years until the political developments of the sixties opened a new destiny for him in political service. In 1761 he began a service of fourteen years as representative of Boston in the General Court, and in 1766, when Gov. Bernard disapproved of Otis as speaker, Cushing was appointed in his stead. He was reëlected eight successive years. With Samuel Adams, James Otis, and John Hancock, he took an active part in the protest against the new British colonial policy inaugurated in 1763. He was elected to the standing committee of the "Society for Encouraging Trade and Commerce within the Province of Massachusetts Bay" in 1763 and a member of the committee appointed by the General Court in 1764 to obtain concerted action among the colonies against the Stamp Act. John Adams wrote in his diary (1765), "Cushing is steady and constant and busy in the interest of liberty and the opposition, is famed for secrecy and his talent for procuring intelligence" (*Works of John Adams*, 1850, II, 163). He was a type of the commercial class on the seaboard, determined to oppose the regulatory innovations, yet hopeful of peaceful settlement and reluctant to advocate measures more radical than economic boycott. With this purpose, he signed the non-importation agreement of 1768, served as member from Boston in the convention of Sept. 22, 1768, and helped prepare the 1769 address to the governor praying for the removal of British troops. He accepted an appointment on the Boston Committee of Correspondence, May 28, 1773, and when Franklin transmitted the celebrated Hutchinson letters to him, as speaker of the House, these were broadcasted by the committee. In July 1774, he was chosen a member of the Committee of Safety, and a handbill, distributed in September 1774, included him among those charged with treason by the British government. He was elected to the Provincial Congress of Massachusetts, to the Second Provincial Congress, and to the First and Second Continental Congresses. He served on important committees concerned with mercantile and monetary affairs and strongly urged non-importation, non-consumption, and non-exportation. With the advent of 1776 it became clear that he was unprepared for the extreme event for which Samuel Adams had struggled. To denounce the innovations since 1763 and to force reconciliation by economic pressure had been his sole aim. Accordingly the General Court replaced him by Elbridge Gerry in the Continental Congress. But although his convictions did not permit him to declare for independence, Cushing did not desert the patriot cause and he was reëlected to the Council, which exercised supreme executive power in Massachusetts in 1776, 1777, and 1778. In financing the Revolution he served as president of the New Haven Price Convention (Jan. 15-20, 1778), delegate to the Hartford Convention (Nov. 8, 1780) and commissioner to the Providence Assembly to provide supplies for the French fleet and army. Of his attitude toward a new form of state government in Massachusetts, John Adams wrote in 1779, "Cushing was avowedly for a single assembly, like Penna." Upon the adoption of the Massachusetts constitution, Cushing was elected lieutenant-governor and was annually reëlected until his death. He belonged to the "Hancockonian party" which dominated Massachusetts politics from 1780 to 1793, and the inability to elect Cushing as governor in 1785 over James Bowdoin, gave the first check to the influence of John Hancock (A. E. Morse, *Federalist Party in Massachusetts*, 1909, p. 27). In 1780 he was one of the founders of the American Academy of Arts and Sciences, and in 1785, Harvard, which he had served as an overseer, awarded him the LL.D. degree. He died at Boston, Feb. 28, 1788. Although not a man of eminent leadership, he was a tactful, reliable, and extremely useful person during the trying years after 1763. With fidelity he filled many posts, following as his maxim, "Let us act with zeal, not rashness!"

[The chief extant sources are contained in the De-Berdt correspondence (DeBerdt letter-book, Lib. of Cong.) and in Mass. Hist. Soc.; partially reprinted in *Mass. Col. Soc. Pubs.*, XIII (1910-11), and 4 *Series Mass. Hist. Soc. Colls.*, IV (1858), 346-66; Samuel Adams MSS. (N. Y. Pub. Lib.); printed works of John Adams, Samuel Adams, Benj. Franklin; *Proc. and Colls. Mass. Hist. Soc.*; *Jours. of House of Repr.*, of *Prov. Cong. of Mass.* and of *Cont. Cong.*] E. A. J. J.

CUSHING, WILLIAM (Mar. 1, 1732-Sept. 13, 1810), jurist, was born at Scituate, Mass., the eldest son of John Cushing by his second wife, Mary Cotton. He was descended on both sides from the old office-holding oligarchy of provincial Massachusetts. His maternal grandfather, Josiah Cotton, schoolmaster, county judge, member of the General Court, and preacher to the Indians at Plymouth, was a grandson of the famous John Cotton, first minister of Boston. The Cushing family descended from Matthew Cushing, who settled at Hingham, Mass., in 1638, and was the ancestor in other lines of Thomas, Caleb, and Luther S. Cushing. William Cushing's grandfather and father both served as members of the Governor's Council and of the superior court, the highest law court of the Province. After graduating at Harvard in 1751 Cushing taught school for a year at Roxbury, Mass., and then studied law in the office of the famous provincial lawyer, Jeremiah Gridley of Boston. Admitted to the bar in 1755, he practised in Scituate until the creation of the new county of Lincoln in the district of Maine in 1760 required the appointment of county officers. William Cushing received the posts of register of deeds and judge of probate, while his younger brother Charles was appointed sheriff. The brothers took up their residence at the new county seat, Pownalborough, now Dresden, on the Kennebec, where for the next twelve years Cushing was the only lawyer in a back-woods community, eight days' journey from Boston and sparsely settled by French and German immigrants. The only knowledge we have of him in these years is in connection with his professional appearances before the superior court at Falmouth, where he was often associated in cases with John Adams, who traveled the Maine circuit.

In 1771, John Cushing, William's father, resigned the post as judge of the superior court which he had held for twenty-three years, and William, returning to Massachusetts, became his successor (1772). The British crown determined to make the provincial courts independent of colonial opinion by paying the judges' salaries. In March 1774 the Massachusetts General Court voted the judges of the superior court salaries from the colonial treasury, and called on them to refuse the crown grant. Four judges, including Cushing, obeyed: Oliver, the Chief Justice, refused and was impeached. Cushing's attitude at this juncture is described by a contemporary: "He was a sensible, modest man, well acquainted with law, but remarkable for the secrecy of his opinions. . . . He readily resigned the royal stipend without any observations of his own; yet it was thought at the time that it was with a reluctance that his taciturnity could not conceal. By this silent address he retained the confidence of the court faction, nor was he less a favorite among the republicans" (Mercy Otis Warren, *History of the Rise, Progress, and Termination of the American Revolution*, 1805, vol. I, p. 118). Nothing is more remarkable than the way in which Cushing, though holding high office, succeeded in remaining in the background during the pre-revolutionary struggle. In 1776, however, he drafted the instructions from his home town of Scituate in favor of independence.

In 1775 the revolutionary council of state, which took over the government of Massachusetts, reorganized the courts, retaining Cushing alone of the previous judges as a member of the new supreme judicial court. John Adams was appointed chief justice, but never took his seat, Cushing presiding in his absence as senior associate justice; and when Adams resigned in 1777, Cushing became chief justice, a post which he held for the next twelve years. The system of reporting the opinions of the courts not yet having been introduced, a few newspaper notices of charges to grand juries are the only record of Cushing's judicial labors in Massachusetts except in one important case. This was a criminal action tried at Worcester in 1783 against one Jennison for assault committed in attempting to repossess himself of a slave. Cushing charged the jury that the clause of the Massachusetts Bill of Rights of 1780, which declared that "all men are born free and equal," operated legally to abolish slavery in the state. During Shays's rebellion one of the objects of the malcontents was to prevent the sittings of the courts, and they attempted to obstruct the supreme judicial court at Springfield on Sept. 29, 1786. It is probably of Cushing's behavior on this occasion that a record has been preserved: "The Chief Justice was applied to by a committee from the mob and entreated to yield to their wishes; he replied, that the law appointed the court to be held at that time, and it was their duty to hold it accordingly; and, followed by his Associates, he proceeded into the street. His countenance was blanched to paleness, but his step was firm. As he advanced, the crowd opened before him . . . and the court was regularly opened" (Flanders, *Lives and Times of the Chief Justices*, II, 34).

Cushing was a member of the Convention of 1779 which framed the first state constitution of Massachusetts, and was vice-president of the state convention of 1788 which ratified the Federal Constitution. On the organization of the United States Supreme Court, he was the first associate justice appointed. During his twenty-one years on the Court, he delivered opinions, all of them brief, in nineteen cases, of which the most important are *Chisholm* vs. *Georgia* (2 *Dallas*, 419), *Ware* vs. *Hylton* (3 *Dallas*, 199), and *Calder* vs. *Bull* (3 *Dallas*, 386). In them he concurred with the majority of the judges and did not add to their exposition of the law. During the absence of Jay on his mission to England, Cushing acted as chief justice, and administered the oath to Washington at his second inauguration. In 1796 on Jay's resignation and after the Senate had rejected Rutledge as his successor, Washington commissioned Cushing as chief justice, but after keeping the commission a week he returned it, requesting to be excused on the ground of ill health. In 1794 his name had been presented by his friends as a candidate for governor of Massachusetts against Samuel Adams, and while he made no active canvass, he received 7,159 votes as against 14,465 for Adams.

The chief work of a Supreme Court justice during Cushing's service was to hold the federal circuit courts. This duty took Judge Cushing all over the country. "His travelling equipage was a four-wheeled phaeton, drawn by a pair of horses; which he drove. It was remarkable for its many ingenious arrangements (all of his contrivance) for carrying books, choice groceries, and other comforts. Mrs. Cushing always accompanied him, and generally read aloud while riding. His faithful servant, Prince, a jet-black negro whose parents had been slaves in the family . . . followed behind in a one-horse vehicle, with the baggage" (Flanders, *op. cit.*, II, 38). Cushing was noted for the ceremoniousness of his deportment. He was the last American judge to wear the full-bottomed English judicial wig. "I very well remember," wrote one who had seen him, "the strong impression his appearance made upon my mind when I first saw him, as he was walking in a street in Portland. He was a man whose deportment surpassed all the ideas of personal dignity I had ever formed. His wig added much to the imposing effect" (J. D. Hopkins, *Address to the Cumberland Bar*, Portland, Me., 1833, p. 44). He is said to have finally abandoned this wig in consequence of the unpleasant observation it attracted when he first held court in New York. The boys followed him in the street, but he was not conscious of the cause until a sailor, who came suddenly upon him, exclaimed, "My eye! What a wig!" Cushing was of medium height and slender, with bright blue eyes and a prominent aquiline nose. His portrait was painted by Sharpless in 1799. His few letters which have been preserved display a playful wit not reflected in his public character. His manner is said to have been benign and cheerful, and his eloquence in addressing juries is universally commented on. Judge Cushing died at Scituate, Sept. 13, 1810, without issue. In 1774 he had married Hannah Phillips of Middletown, Conn., who died in 1834 at the age of eighty.

[There is no biography of Cushing. The fullest account is in Henry Flanders, *The Lives and Times of the Chief Justices of Supreme Court of the U. S.* (1858), vol. II, based on a manuscript sketch by Chas. Cushing Payne; the most recent account is a paper by Chief Justice Arthur P. Rugg in *Yale Law Jour.*, Dec. 1920, vol. XXX, pp. 128–44. Sam. Deane, *Hist. of Scituate, Mass.* (1831) gives some details. For Cushing's life in Maine, see articles in the *Maine Hist. Soc. Colls.*, 1 ser., vol. VI, pp. 44–47, and 2 ser., vol. I, pp. 301 ff., and 313–20. See also Jas. D. Hopkins, *An Address to the Members of the Cumberland Bar* (1833).]   J. Di.

CUSHING, WILLIAM BARKER (Nov. 4, 1842–Dec. 17, 1874), naval officer, was born at Delafield, Wis., the fourth son of Milton Buckingham Cushing, M.D., and his wife Mary Barker Smith of Boston, both descended from the oldest colonial stock. Dr. Cushing moved to Chicago in 1844, and in 1847 to Gallipolis, Ohio, his death occurring the same year. His widow then settled at Fredonia, N. Y., where she established a successful school, her four boys aiding in the support of the family. In 1856 an appointment was secured for William as page in the House of Representatives at Washington, and the next year he was appointed to the Naval Academy. His lack of application, his love of skylarking and practical jokes, even at the expense of his professors, and a too evident aversion for discipline led to a recommendation for his dismissal from the Academy in his senior year, the privilege of being turned back for a year being denied him. He was allowed to resign March 23, 1861, but, aided by his friends, he was enabled to take part, with the warrant rank of acting master's mate, in several operations carried out by the U. S. S. *Minnesota.* As prize-master he took the *Delaware Farmer* to Philadelphia, and, in May 1861, with one volunteer officer and only the captured crew of the *Pioneer,* he safely sailed that prize to New York. This dangerous and responsible duty proved his real worth, and he was restored to the Navy, in October 1861, as acting midshipman, being assigned to duty in the North Atlantic Squadron. On account of the increase of the commissioned personnel, incident to the war, he became a lieutenant on July 16, 1862, at nineteen years of age.

As executive officer of the *Commodore Perry,* commanded by his friend Flusser, Cushing performed an act of gallantry which was highly praised by his superiors. While descending the Blackwater River after the battle of Franklin, Oct. 3, 1862, the *Perry* jammed her bow into the bank and was charged by a strong force of the enemy. Cushing, disregarding orders to get under cover, called for volunteers, ran a field-piece out on the forecastle, and, though all his mates were killed or wounded, succeeded in discharging the piece at point-blank among the enemy, causing them to retreat and saving the ship from capture. Assigned thereupon to the command of the small steamer *Ellis,* he captured the *Adelaide* and destroyed the extensive salt works in New Topsail Inlet. Ordered to capture Jacksonville, N. C., and destroy the salt works at New Juliet, he secured the Wilmington mail, took two prizes, shelled and captured the town on Nov. 23, 1862, and destroyed a Confederate camp. Endeavoring to cross the bar of the Onslow River two days later, the *Ellis* ran aground, and Cushing was obliged to transfer his crew to one of his prizes, the vessels still afloat being ordered to stand off the inlet, while Cushing, with six volunteers manning a single-pivot gun, remained in the *Ellis* in an effort to save her, the ammunition and the rest of her artillery being salvaged by the prize. Early next morning, the enemy's fire increasing in fury and there being no chance of saving the ship, she was set fire to, and Cushing and his men made their escape in an open boat from under the very guns of the foe. In consequence of the loss of his ship Lieut. Cushing asked for a court of inquiry, but received instead the compliments of his superiors for his coolness and courage.

Commanding in turn the *Commodore Barney* and the *Shokokon,* he was, on Sept. 5, 1863, ordered to the command of the *Monticello.* The following February he performed, in the words of J. R. Soley (*The Blockade and the Cruisers,* p. 94), "two of those dare-devil exploits which gave him a name and a fame apart in the history of the War." The first of these took place in February 1864, while the *Monticello* was blockading the mouth of the Cape Fear River. With two small boats and twenty men he proceeded up the river to Smithville, in order to surprise and capture certain important Confederate officers. The enterprise was a partial success, although the officer of the highest rank was not captured. The second expedition was made in the following June and was a night expedition to the near neighborhood of Wilmington, in which Cushing captured a mounted courier with important information. After brilliant service in the blockading fleet off the North Carolina coast, his plans to fit out torpedo-boats to destroy the formidable and dangerous Confederate ram *Albemarle* were approved. The *Albemarle,* after destroying several Federal vessels, was lying at Plymouth, N. C., eight miles up the Roanoke River, a town which she had been instrumental in capturing. She was on the point of undertaking serious maneuvers against the Union fleet, when, on Oct. 27, 1864, Cushing in a torpedo-boat launch manned by a crew of fifteen men who had all volunteered for "extra duty," crept up the river in the dark accompanied by a small cutter, and, eluding the enemy's lookouts, steamed directly for the *Albemarle,* lying at her moorings surrounded by a raft of logs to prevent boarding.

Cushing had decided in case he could surprise the ram, to capture her by a rush of his few but well-armed men; but, as the single sentinel on board the ship gave the alarm and the small-arms firing became brisk, Cushing dashed straight at the *Albemarle,* and the full head of steam carrying the launch over the protecting logs, he succeeded, after considerable trouble, and after having his clothes pierced by five bullets and the sole of one shoe carried away, in lowering the boom and exploding the torpedo under the vessel's hull. "The explosion took place at the same instant that one hundred pounds of grape at ten-feet range crashed in our midst, and the dense mass of water thrown out by the torpedo came down with choking weight upon us" (Cushing's own story, *United States Naval Institute Proceedings,* XXXVIII, 979). Twice refusing to surrender, Cushing plunged into the river, swam a long distance down-stream and gained the opposite bank. After hours of difficult working through swamps, hungry and exhausted, he finally came upon a shore post of Confederate soldiers near the mouth of the Roanoke. Awaiting his opportunity, he appropriated their skiff and rowed out into the open for hours toward a light which proved to be that of the Federal picket vessel, *Valley City.* Of his companions on the torpedo-launch two were drowned, one escaped, and the rest were taken prisoners. Before he left on this hazardous expedition he had laughingly remarked, "Another stripe or a coffin!" He received not only the stripe making him a lieutenant-commander at the age of twenty-one, but the highest praise of the Navy Department, as well as swords, medals, and testimonials from many citizens and organizations, and the formal thanks of Congress given at the express request of President Lincoln. On Nov. 22, 1864, Cushing was placed in command of the flagship *Malvern* of the North Atlantic Squadron, the capture of which, when she was the blockade-runner *Ella and Annie,* by Acting Master J. B. Breck of the *Niphon,* was considered one of the most brilliant exploits of the blockading squadron (Soley, *The Blockade and the Cruisers,* p. 163). It was, however, recognized that Cushing's talent for more active command should not be wasted, and he was again placed in charge of the *Monticello,* the wisdom of this appointment at once appearing in the series of daring and successful operations which soon followed. One of these was sounding for anchorage previous to the first attack on Fort Fisher, during which Cushing, with fourteen companions in a small boat, was under the fire of that fortress and other works for six hours. At the attack on Fort Fisher on Jan. 15, 1865, he commanded a company of sailors and marines from his ship and led the assault over one hundred yards of sand under short-range fire, finally leaping the parapet and participating in the capture of the work, being the only surviving officer of his command. After the fall of Fort Fisher he rendered hazardous duties in taking up torpedoes, and the subsequent days of the war saw his capture of two blockade runners and his construction of a "mock Monitor," the appearance of which caused the evacuation of a strong Confederate earthwork. In four years Cushing had risen from the position of a "bilged" midshipman to the rank of lieutenant-commander. While he was perhaps oftener under fire than any other officer of the Navy, he seems to have escaped with hardly a scratch. After the Civil War he served both in the Pacific and Asiatic Squadrons, commanding the *Lancaster*, 1865–67, and the *Maumee*, 1868–69. He was detached on Nov. 12, 1869, and on Feb. 19, 1870, he married Katherine Louise Forbes at Fredonia, N. Y. From Mar. 30, 1870, he served as ordnance officer at the Boston Navy Yard and was promoted to be commander on Jan. 31, 1872. On July 11, 1873, he was ordered to the command of the U. S. S. *Wyoming,* and, learning that the crew of the *Virginius* were being summarily executed at Santiago de Cuba, he left Aspinwall without orders and landed at Santiago Nov. 16, 1873, seeking an immediate interview with the Spanish Governor, Burriel. He informed that functionary that "if he intended to shoot another one of the *Virginius'* prisoners he would better first have the women and children removed from Santiago." This warning protest was confirmed by Cushing's superior officer, Commander Braine, who arrived shortly afterward in the *Juniata,* and no more prisoners were executed. Cushing's acts and correspondence in connection with this affair, and his subsequent seizing of the *General Sherman,* proved that he possessed an appreciation of international law and diplomacy which, with his love of reading, no doubt would have tempered his natural vehemence, had not his brilliant career been cut short by ill health. He was ordered to Washington as assistant to the executive officer of the Navy Yard, but was taken to the Government Hospital for the Insane on Dec. 8, 1874, dying there on the 17th. He was survived by his wife and two daughters.

[E. M. H. Edwards, *Commander Wm. Barker Cushing of the U. S. Navy* (1898) ; Chas. W. Stuart,. "Wm. Barker Cushing," *U. S. Naval Inst. Proc.,* vol. XXXVIII, nos. II, III, whole nos. 142, 143 ; David D. Porter, *Naval Hist. of the Civil War* (1886) ; J. R. Soley, *The Blockade and the Cruisers* (1883) ; *Official Records (Navy).*]   E. B.